CHILTON'S AUTO REPAIR MANUAL 1940-1953

Automotive Book Department

CHILTON BOOK COMPANY

Radnor, Pennsylvania

Re-issue of First Edition 1971

Published in Radnor, Pa., by Chilton Book Company and simultaneously in Ontario, Canada, by Thomas Nelson & Sons, Ltd.
ISBN 0-8019-5631-5 Library of Congress Catalog Card Number 54-17274 Manufactured in the United States of America

12 13 14 15 0987654

INDEX

GENERAL SERVICE AND TROUBLE SHOOTING

AUTOMATIC TRANSMISSIONS

INDEX—*continued*

POWER BRAKES

POWER STEERING

CARBURETORS

INDEX—*continued*

CAR SERVICE PROCEDURE

INDEX—continued

INDEX—*continued*

INDEX—*continued*

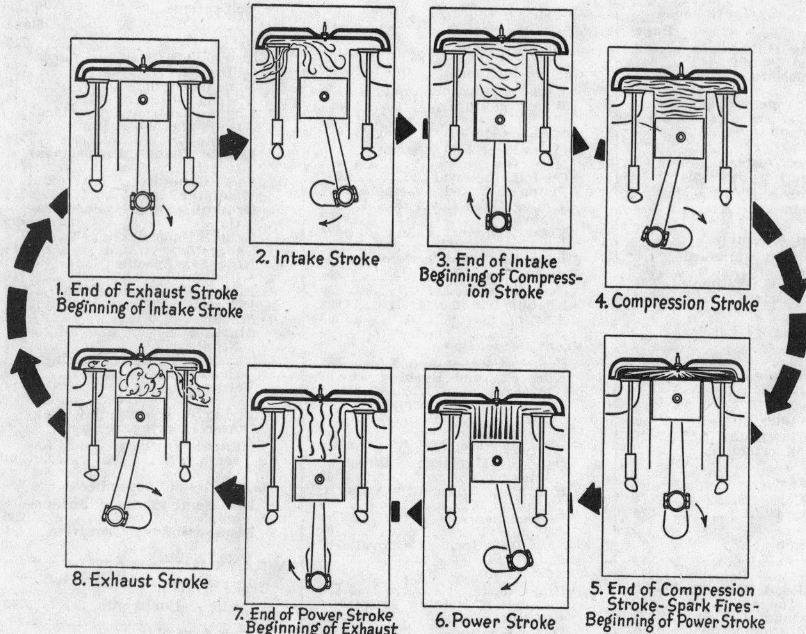

Engine Cycle

From the standpoint of maintenance or repair services the modern automobile may be divided into eleven major parts or sections.

1. Engine
2. Cooling System
3. Electrical System
4. Clutch
5. Transmission
6. Drive Line
7. Rear Axle
8. Front Suspension
9. Steering
10. Brakes
11. Body

To these eleven sections may be added the highly specialized servicing on radios, speedometers, instruments, tires, etc.

THE ENGINE

Engine Cycles

Gasoline engines used in American passenger cars are all of the four stroke cycle type, more commonly called four cycle engines.

The four strokes or cycles are:

Inlet
Compression
Power
Exhaust

During the inlet stroke the piston moves downward from the top of the cylinder with the inlet valve open. This draws the air-fuel mixture into the cylinder. At the end of this stroke the piston is at the bottom of the cylinder and the inlet valve closes.

During the compression stroke both valves remain closed and the piston moves up in the cylinder, compressing the trapped air-fuel mixture. At the end of the compression stroke the piston is at the top of the cylinder, both valves are closed and the air-fuel mixture is at maximum compression.

The power stroke is accomplished by igniting the air-fuel mixture at end of the compression stroke. The expanding gases force the piston down the cylinder, imparting power through the connecting rod to the crankshaft. At the end of the power stroke the piston is at the bottom of the cylinder and the exhaust valve starts to open.

The exhaust or scavaging stroke starts when the exhaust valve opens. The piston moves up the cylinder, forcing the burned gases through the exhaust port into the exhaust manifold. At the end of the stroke the exhaust valve closes, the inlet valve opens and the cylinder is ready to repeat the four cycles.

Engine Types

The two types of engines in general use are the "L" head type and the "OVERHEAD VALVE" type and, in addition to these two, the "F" head type is also used.

The major difference between these three types of engines is the location of the valves but not their function.

In the "L" head type of construction both the inlet and the exhaust valves are located in the cylinder block and both inlet and exhaust manifolds are attached to the block. The valves are operated, through the lifter, directly from the camshaft.

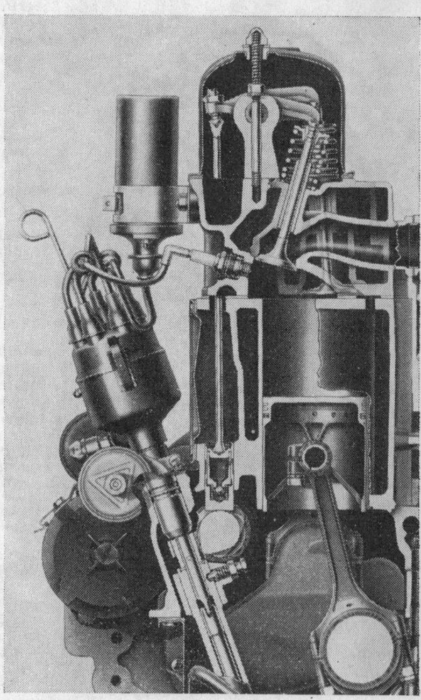

Overhead Valve Engine

In overhead valve construction the valves are contained in the cylinder head and the inlet and exhaust manifold are attached to the cylinder head. The valves are operated by a system of lifters, push rods and rocker arms.

Section thru a typical L head engine.

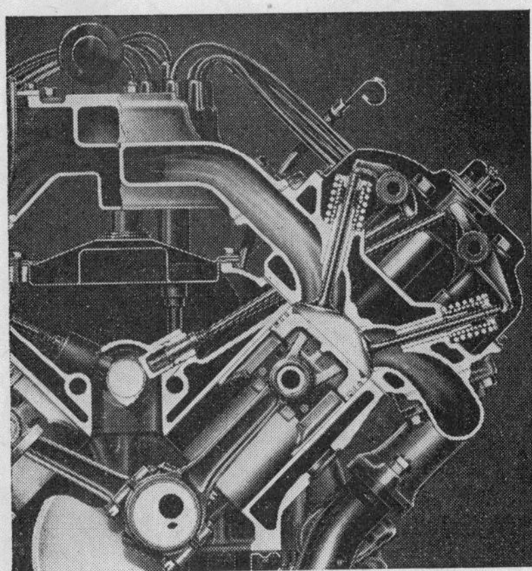

V type overhead valve engine

"F" head engines utilize the "overhead" inlet valve and the "L" head exhaust valve. The inlet manifold is connected to the head while the exhaust valve is bolted to the cylinder block. Push rods and rocker arms are used to operate the inlet valves and the exhaust valves are opened directly from the camshaft.

THE CYLINDER BLOCK

The cylinder block is the main engine casting. It consists of an iron casting having integral cylinders (some trucks have separate cylinders known as "wet sleeves"), main bearing seats, camshaft bearing seats, lifter bores, and, in the case of "L" head engines, provision is made for the valve mechanism. Provision is also made in the casting to permit water or anti-freeze solution to circulate.

In the repair shop there are five jobs which might be called standard on cylinder blocks.

1. Rebore cylinders.
2. Install sleeves (wet or dry).
3. Install valve seat inserts.

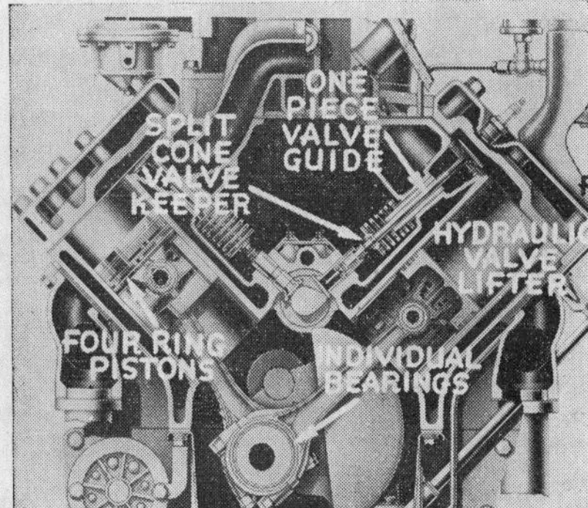

V type L head engine

4. Clean the coolant passages.
5. Replace freeze plugs.

In addition to the five "standard" jobs, operations such as removing broken stud, planing cylinder head surface (top of block) and manifold bosses, reaming lifter bores and repairing cracks, etc., are also done in the average shop.

Reconditioning Cylinders

In ordinary service cylinder walls tend to wear more at the top than at the bottom and, due to normal wear, they sometimes become out-of-round.

In general, whenever taper exceeds .010 inch or out-of-roundness exceeds .005 inch the cylinders should be reconditioned to restore the original true cylindrical surface. There are three popular methods of cylinder reconditioning: Hone, bore and grind.

The best method, when reconditioning cylinders, is to follow faithfully the instructions supplied by the manufacturer of the device you use. The manufacturer of your tool knows, better than anyone else, the good features and also the shortcomings of his product, therefore he is in a good position to supply instruction which will insure the best possible results using his equipment.

Holding fixtures such as shown above, greatly simplifies major engine jobs

Honing or Grinding Cylinders

Regardless of the type of hone or grinder used, a few points should be remembered: The abrasive used is, in effect, a series of extremely small cutting edges. Minute chips tend to gather in front of each tiny cutting grit, causing the stone to "load up" or clog. This tendency to load is much more pronounced in a hone than an eccentric grinder. KEEP THE STONES CLEAN.

The cutting action of the hone or grinder causes the tiny edges of the abrasive to break off. These minute particles look like fine dust but are actually very small pieces of the abrasive material, mixed with equally fine pieces of the iron cylinder.

A cylinder hone cutting at the top of the bore

It is absolutely essential that this "grinder dust" be cleaned from the cylinder before any parts are assembled to the block. Even a small amount of dust, left in the cylinder or crankcase, will almost certainly cause serious damage when the engine is operated.

In general, a hone will follow the existing cylinder, whereas most grinders will cut in a straight line from their mounting. Therefore great care should be used to mount the grinding machine so that the path of the grinder is perpendicular to the cylinder head surface.

Reboring Cylinders

Cylinder boring machines are made in two broad types—stationary and portable.

The stationary type machine can be anything from a small model capable of boring one cylinder at a time to the large multiples intended for production. Stationary machines are generally operated by skilled machinists and will not be covered in this manual.

Portable boring bars are designed so that they can be carried to the car and operated from a mounting on the top of the block.

Residue salvaged from a honing operation. This pile of grit came from one cylinder which was honed .005 in.

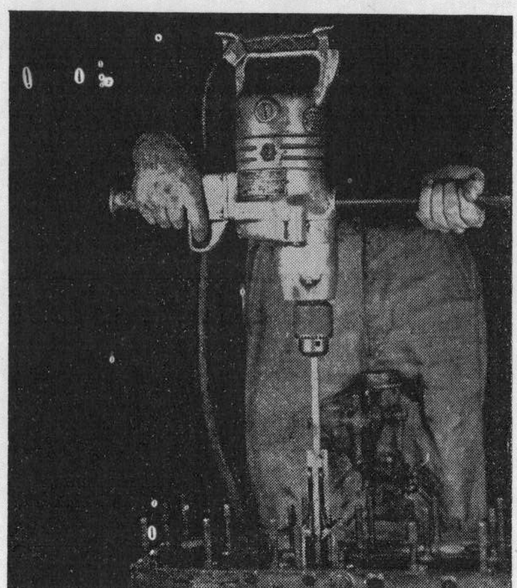

Cylinder Hone attached to Heavy Duty Drill

Special shoes are used to center most boring bars

Cylinder hone finished to 15 micro inches

Cylinder finished to 25 micro inches

The construction of many cars does not leave enough room to mount portable bars on some of the cylinders. Interference from dash panel on in line engines, or fenders and skirts on V type engines, makes it impossible to bore certain cylinders with the engine in the car. It is good practice to determine first if all the cylinders to be bored can be handled without removing the engine, or if it will be necessary to remove the engine in order to service one or more of the bores.

If it is necessary to remove the engine, then do so before any of the boring is done since it is somewhat easier to work with the engine mounted in a work stand than it is with the engine in the car.

Many successful shops prefer to bore where the machine can be mounted and hone the cylinders which cannot be bored readily in the car.

Some points to remember about boring are—Mount the machine firmly on a clean flat surface; make certain that the cylinder head studs do not interfere with the proper centering of the bar; check carefully to be sure the valve heads (L head jobs) are not holding the machine up off the head surface; remember that even rust spots can affect the mounting of the tool, resulting in misalignment of the boring bar.

Only a properly ground SHARP cutting tool will do good work. While some of the modern carbide bits will hold their cutting edge a long time, they do require resharpening. When carbide cutters require regrinding they will generally do more and better work if they are resharpened on a diamond charged wheel instead of an ordinary grinding wheel.

Most modern boring bars have a tool grinding attachment built into the tool assembly. A special tool holder is provided which, when properly used, makes it a very simple job to grind the cutter properly.

Cast non-ferrous, high speed steel, or high carbon steel tool bits, should be resharpened and honed to a very keen edge having the cutting angles recommended by the manufacturer of the bar.

Many boring bars, when properly used, will produce a surface smooth enough that no further finishing is required.

The minute scratches left by the boring bar—the so-called gray finish—tend to seat the rings rapidly, reducing break-in time.

It is regular practice in many shops to rebore cylinders to within .002 in. of finish size and remove the last .002 with a hone in order to remove any tool marks or "screw threads" left by the boring bar.

A cylinder hone can produce a surface finish which is actually too smooth for practical purposes. Between 15 and 30 micro inches is generally considered to be the best finish which will give quick break-in and long life.

Provisions must be made to prevent any chips from remaining in the block after the boring or honing operation is complete.

Cylinder Sleeves

When cylinder wear or damage is extensive or where cylinder walls must be bored to a prohibitive oversize, sleeves made of cast iron or steel may be inserted into the bore. This is accomplished by boring the block so that the sleeve will be a tight press fit. They must be fitted tightly to the cylinder wall so that the sleeve will cool evenly in operation. Loose or badly fitted sleeves tend to develop hot spots where they do not contact the cylinder wall. It is customary to lightly hone the new cylinder sleeves after installation to correct any distortion which may have occurred while pressing it into the block.

Special equipment is required to press sleeves into the blocks; it is not practical to simply drive them into place.

Cylinder sleeves should be pressed into place with special tools

Cleaning Coolant Passages

See COOLING SYSTEM.

Freeze Plugs (Core hole plugs)

There are two types of freeze plugs in common use: the disk type and the cup type.

The disk type freeze plug is a round steel disk which has been dished slightly so that it may be expanded by striking it in the center with a suitable tool such as a ball peen hammer.

Cup type core hole plugs are made in the shape of a cup with tapered sides so that when they are pressed into the block the tapered side seals the core hole.

Freeze plugs are generally located at the side of the block (opposite to the valve chamber on L heads).

However, several makes have core hole plugs at the back and front of the block.

A plug is generally used at the rear of the camshaft, and a leak at this plug, while not common, will result in oil (not water) getting on the face of the flywheel, ruining the clutch. Leaks at the back of the camshaft are generally blamed on the rear main bearing oil seal.

Trouble Shooting on Freeze Plugs

The purpose of the freeze plug is to seal the cored hole, and thus prevent the coolant from leaking and seeping. A very small leak (seepage) can usually be detected since it leaves a streak of corrosion or rust at the point of leak.

Replacing Freeze Plugs

Before replacing the plug, try resetting it by tapping the center of the plug with a ball peen hammer. If not successful, replace the plug.

There are several ways to remove core hole plugs, the more common being to punch a hole through the plug and pry it out. This method does, however, have the disadvantage of being somewhat risky. It is easily possible to break the block while prying out the plug if it happens to be badly corroded.

Perhaps the safest method is to drill and tap the plug and remove it by inserting a screw in the tapped hole, then use an inertia puller on the screw.

Another way is to drill and tap the plug and insert a long threaded bolt. Turn the bolt in until it pushes against the cylinder wall, continue to turn the screw to force the plug out. It is unlikely that the pressure required will be sufficient to damage the cylinder in any way. This last method is the one generally used when removing the rear-of-block plug through a hole in the dash panel.

Before inserting a new plug always thoroughly clean the opening to insure a good seal. It is generally considered good practice to coat the new plug with gasket compound.

Cup Type Freeze Plugs

Cup type core hole plugs are installed by exerting pressure on the RIM of the plug, not the center, or by driving the plug into place using a bushing driver which contacts the rim.

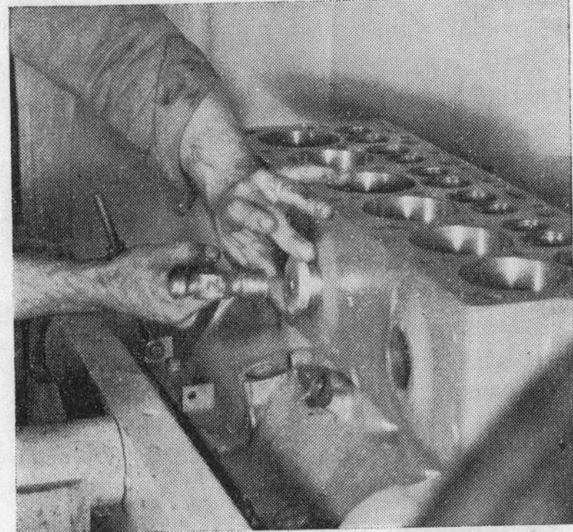

Cup type core hole plugs may be hammered in place, using a bushing driver

Drilling out a Welch Plug

Disc type plugs are generally inserted into the hole by driving against the outer edges with a suitable tool, such as a piece of tubing or pipe, in order to get the edges well into the hole. Disc is then seated by striking the center of the disc with a ball pein hammer.

For this purpose, a light blow with a heavy hammer will be better than a series of heavy blows with a light hammer.

Valve Seat Inserts

Valve seat inserts are usually made from a special heat resisting alloy. Exhaust valve heads frequently operate at temperatures as high as 2000 deg. F. and this heat must be dissipated through the valve seat as well as through the valve stem.

To insure good heat conductivity, the seat insert must be set into the block with good contact on both the O.D. and the bottom.

Inserts should be replaced when there is the slightest indication of warpage or cracking.

Special pullers are available for removing seat inserts. They may also be removed by inserting a pry bar under the lip of the seat and breaking it out of the block.

There are two generally used methods of replacing standard size seat inserts. The first is to coat the insert with any of the special materials made for the purpose, and simply drive it into place.

Special fixtures are used to drive the seat squarely into the block.

The second and older method is to shrink the ring by placing it in dry ice and very quickly pressing it into place after it has thoroughly chilled. When using the dry ice method, the trick is to prevent ice crystals from forming. These ice crystals are caused by the warm, damp air coming into contact with the extremely cold metal which condenses the air moisture very rapidly; the ice might prevent proper seating. Many ingenious methods have been used to retard the formation of crystals. A popular one is to immerse the seat in a can of carbon tetrachloride or other cleaner and place the whole container in the dry ice. After it has become thoroughly chilled, carry the can to the job so that the seat may be removed from the chilled carbon tet and placed in the block with a minimum of exposure to condensation.

CAUTION: Do not touch the dry ice, the container or the seat without proper

Cutting a recess in the block for a valve seat insert

protection for the hands. Dry ice (solid carbon dioxide) has a temperature of minus 110 deg. F. and may cause serious injury if brought into contact with the skin.

Repairing Cracks in Cylinder Block

Generally speaking, cracked blocks should be replaced. However, cracks which are easily accessible and do not interfere with the operation of the engine, such as breaks in the exposed side of the engine (not in the valve chamber), may be "patched."

NOTE: In some states it is illegal to sell a car having a cracked block unless the purchaser is informed so that he understands the engine block is damaged.

When parts are not available, it is sometimes advisable to repair damage where it can be done.

Welding

Recently there have been developments in welding materials for cast iron. Welding rods are now available which deposit at considerably lower

Cracked block

temperatures than were necessary until very recently.

It is generally conceded that a block can be successfully welded using these new low temperature rods, where formerly it would have been necessary to replace the block. Welding techniques have been developed which will produce successful welds with the engine in place in the car. Complete instructions are supplied with the new type rod by the manufacturers.

Blocks may be welded successfully with any good welding rod and a permanent repair made if the block is first preheated to prevent uneven shrinking at the weld.

The usual procedure is to remove and disassemble the engine (be certain to remove all bearings and valve springs). Prepare the job by drilling a small hole at the extreme ends of the crack, which will prevent it from spreading when the welding heat is applied.

A suitable preheating oven can be made, if one is not available, by forming a hollow square with fire brick (or in a pinch any kind of kiln brick). Arrange the bricks so that the ones adjacent to the damaged area may be removed to permit access by the welder while the block is kept hot.

Preheating should be done slowly to prevent unequal expansion and contraction. Gasoline, city gas or bottled gas burners may be used as the heating media. Bring the block up to just less than red heat (about 1100°), remove the bricks adjacent to the damaged area and weld up the crack.

After the block has been welded, replace the fire brick adjacent to the weld and permit the block to cool slowly.

When cool, it may be necessary to lightly hone the cylinders to restore the smooth bearing surface.

A damaged block may be welded in place on the car using just any type of rod without preheating, but generally

Block welded in place on the car by the low heat process

speaking this type of repair is not too successful because of the uneven expansion and contraction at the weld area when steel rods are used. Cast iron welds sometimes tend to harden, which results in further cracking when preheating is eliminated.

Soldering

An effective temporary repair can be made, when the damage is easy to get at, by first drilling the ends of the crack to prevent spreading, then clean around the damage for about one inch. Tin this cleaned area thoroughly with solder. Also tin a piece of brass shim stock (about .020 in.) which has been cut to just cover the prepared area on the block. Sweat solder this brass stock over the prepared block. Usually this can be accomplished best by soldering an inch—skip an inch—then solder the next inch. This will prevent the brass (which expands rapidly when heated) from expanding too much.

The shim stock technique is often used over a crack which has been tack welded to give mechanical strength.

Removing Broken Studs

Broken studs can be very difficult to remove, especially when the stud is in an inaccessible place such as the timing case cover.

When a stud or screw breaks off because it has been tightened too much it can sometimes be removed by making a tiny notch at the outside edge with a sharp chisel and, using this notch as a purchase, tap the stud with a dull chisel in the direction which removes it.

Another method is to grind a screw driver slot in the top of the stud with a tiny high speed hand grinder and remove the stud with a screw driver.

When possible, the easiest method is to drill a hole of proper size into the stud and turn it out with one of the left hand spiral tools designed for the purpose. These special stud removers are sold in sets and are usually called "Easy Outs."

Broken exhaust manifold studs are probably the most difficult to remove because of the excessive oxidation of the metal. Generally, if the stud is treated with a good penetrating oil it will come out much more readily.

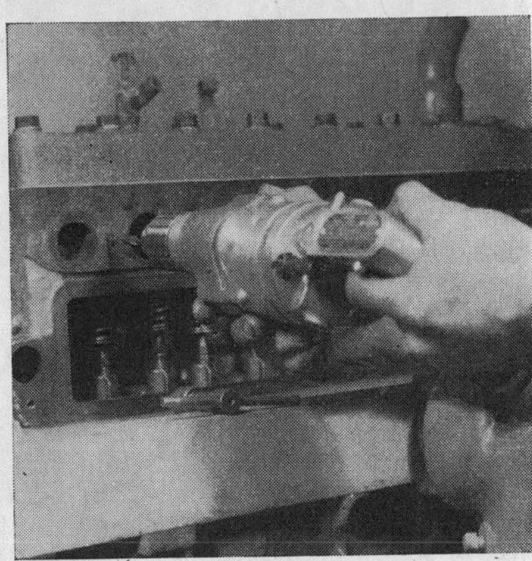

Drilling broken stud

Oversize Valve Lifters

Oversize valve lifters are not available for all makes and models, therefore be sure replacements are available before doing any reaming on the block.

Lifters should move up and down without the slightest bind but should have no appreciable side play. Service procedure is given under VALVE SYSTEM later in this section.

PISTON ASSEMBLY

The piston and rod assembly consists of a piston fitted with rings, a piston pin (wrist pin) and a connecting rod with bearings.

The purpose of this assembly is to compress the air-fuel mixture and to impart to the crankshaft the force of the burning fuel. In other words, the rod and piston assembly changes reciprocating force (up and down) to rotating force.

Trouble Shooting on Pistons

Loose pistons have a characteristic knock, called "piston slap." The knock is most pronounced at idle speed and is caused by the piston head striking the cylinder wall at the moment of ignition. Since the knock occurs at igniting only, it is easy to detect. It will stop if the spark plug in that cylinder is shorted out.

Take time to read instructions when installing new pistons

To double check, short out the cylder which fires ahead of the one being tested and the slap should increase slightly, due to the added load on the loose piston.

For instance: On a 6-cylinder engine whose firing order is 1-5-3-6-2-4, there is the characteristic knock at idle speed. On shorting the plugs it is found that #5 stops the knock. Double check by shorting #1, the cylinder which fires ahead of #5; if the knock increases slightly, there is no question but that #5 has a loose or damaged piston.

Fitting Pistons

New pistons should be fitted to the cylinder so that there is an exact clearance between the piston skirt and the cylinder walls.

(The exact clearance for each car is given in this Manual in the car section and also in the first yellow section.)

PROCEDURE: Determine, from the data table, the exact clearance specified for the piston being fitted. (NOTE: When working with replacement pistons use the clearance specified by the

Checking piston clearance

manufacturer of the replacement part.)

Since manufacturers try to include the latest developments in all replacements, including those for older models, no attempt should be made to put or install any piston without first reading and digesting the instruction sheet which is packed with the pistons. The various piston contours require different clearances and all manufacturers go to considerable trouble and expense to provide adequate technical data with each package. ALWAYS READ AND FOLLOW THESE INSTRUCTIONS, on every job.

Take a piece of gage stock as thick as the desired clearance, ½ wide and about 3 inches longer than the cylinder, to allow for gripping.

Place the gage stock in the cylinder on the thrust (right) side.

(NOTE: The right side of the cylinder is the side contacted by the thrust side of the piston on all engines where the crankshaft is exactly centered under the cylinders. There are a few engines made, however, where the crankshaft is arranged slightly off center to the right in relation to the cylinders which places the thrust on the left side of the cylinder.

When checking the pistons for clearance the feeler MUST be used on the side opposite to the piston slot.

Turn the piston (and rod) upside down and insert it into the cylinder, head first, with the wrist piston pointing lengthwise of the cylinder. This is very important, particularly on cam ground pistons. The pistons should pass all the way through the cylinder with the feeler gauge in place.

Recheck to be certain the piston is not too small by repeating the test using a feeler .001 in thickness than the piston clearance. The piston should bind on this feeler and not more than the ring lands should enter the cylinder.

This technique is called go and not go:

"Go" on the clearance thickness.

"Not go" on the .001 in. oversize feeler.

Where the piston is found to be too tight it is customary to lightly hone the cylinder to get a good fit. Where the piston is too loose it may be expanded by any of the following methods:

Knurling Pistons

Knurling is a machine shop method of raising metal. This process has been successfully applied to pistons by controlled method.

Equipment is available which is designed to raise the metal on the thrust

Piston which has been resized by the knurl method

side, also the side opposite the thrust on a piston so that the metal raised will take up the excessive clearance.

Where knurling is used to "oversize" a piston it is customary to fit the piston with zero clearance; that is, the piston should be fitted so that it is a fairly snug fit in the bore.

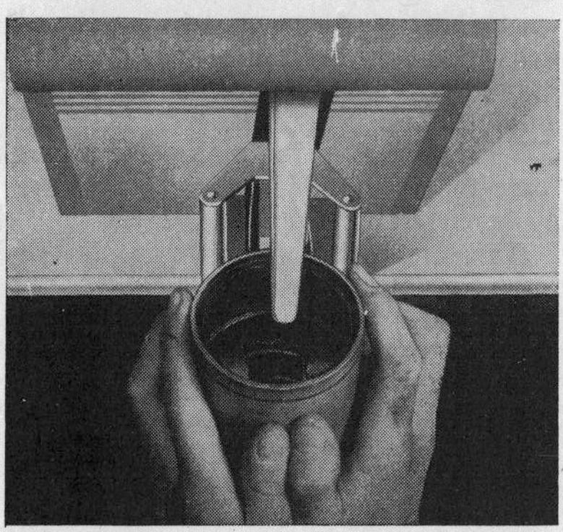

Peen process of resizing pistons

Manufacturers of knurling equipment supply minute instructions in the handling and knurling. Since a very definite technique is required, the instructions from the equipment manufacturers are absolutely essential. They should be followed without deviation of any kind. This is very important.

Peening Pistons

The peening process of resizing pistons is one of stretching the metal on the inside of the piston so that it will expand outwards. There are two generally accepted methods of peening pistons. One is the shot peening method, whereby the metal is stretched by striking the inside of the piston with shot at high velocity. The other method is the power-operated peening hammer, which performs the same function in a slightly different manner.

Here again the instruction of the equipment manufacturers should be followed religiously. It is absolutely essential that there be no deviation whatever from the equipment manufacturers' routine.

Cylinder Ring Ridge

The greatest amount of wear on a cylinder in normal use is at the top of the ring travel. Since the rings do not come up to the top edge of the cylinder, a ridge or lip is left unworn at the extreme top of the bore.

Ridge removing operation

Before removing the rod and piston assemblies, through the top of the cylinder, this ridge must be cut off.

Special ridge reamers and other devices are available which, when properly used, will cut the ridge out of the cylinder cleanly.

A broken ring land may result if the piston is forced out of the bore with the ridge uncut.

Piston Rings

The purpose of the compression rings is to form a gas-tight seal between the piston and the cylinder wall. Oil rings are intended to prevent oil from the crankcase from entering the combustion chamber.

New rings should be installed when excessive "blow by" is present or when oil from the crankcase gets by the rings in excessive quantities, or both.

The fact that an engine is "using oil" does not necessarily mean that the rings are bad. The causes of excessive oil consumption are many and varied. (A trouble-shooting chart on "Excessive Oil Consumption" is given later in this section. See index.)

When rings are to be replaced, the

Read instructions before mounting rings

procedure is practically the same for all cars:

Cut the ring ridge out of the cylinder and push the rod and piston assembly up out of the bore. (Examine the cylinder wall at the bottom of the ring travel to make certain there is no ring groove at the bottom. When there is a ring groove at the bottom, the practical job is to rebore the cylinder and install an oversized piston.)

Examine the lower connecting rod bearing. Replace if cracked, chipped or scored. Check the wrist pin for looseness. Mount the piston in a suitable vise and remove the rings. (CAUTION: The edges of piston rings are usually very sharp and sometimes cause serious injury when handled carelessly.)

Thoroughly clean out the ring grooves with one of the very efficient ring groove cleaners which are available or, in a pinch, use a broken ring or hacksaw blade.

Redrill the oil drain holes back of the oil rings.

Thoroughly clean Ring Grooves

When the piston has been thoroughly cleaned up, check the fit of the new ring in its groove by rolling the ring around in the groove as though the piston were a sungear and the ring a planet gear, rolling around it.

Examine the ring grooves for "bell mouth" particularly the top groove. The ring groove must be square within about .001 inch.

If any of the grooves are found to be bell mouthed, the groove should be machined either in a lathe or with any of

Roll ring in groove to check fit

the very efficient hand operated tools designed for this purpose. The groove should be machined to the next larger ring width or one of the special thin steel rings should be used on top of the regular ring to fill up the added space. Failure to correct tapered or bell mouthed grooves will permit the ring to rock in the groove resulting in early

Regroove bellmouthed ring groove to take next size ring or spacer

failure and possible scoring of the cylinder wall.

NOTE: Some replacement rings are made so that they take up all the clearance in the ring groove and in fact have a slight preload in the groove. When mounting this type ring, follow the instructions which the ring manufacturer supplies with his product.

Regardless of which type ring is used, there should be no noticeable binding as the ring is tested in its groove.

Now check the ring gap by placing the ring in the cylinder and forcing it to the bottom (the unworn part) of the cylinder. Use the piston to force the ring to the bottom in order to keep the ring square with the bore.

Ring gap clearances are given in the data section.

Where gap clearances are not known, it is generally safe to allow .005 in. per inch of cylinder diameter, provided that it is not less than .015 in. If the clearance is less than specified, file the ring gap to proper clearance.

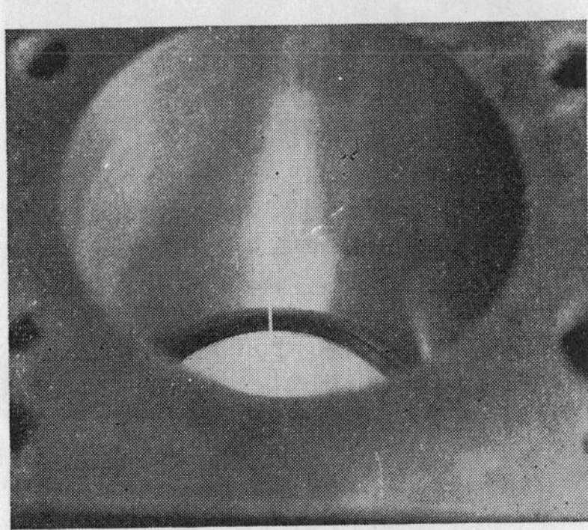

Check Ring gap clearance by forcing ring to bottom of cylinder

When expanders are used they should be placed in their proper groove first. Locate the expander so that its gap will come opposite to the ring gap. Caution: Be sure a high spot of the expander does not locate exactly at the ring gap, as this may cause the edge of the ring to score the cylinder. Do not place a ring gap directly over the wrist pin.

Install the rings so that the gaps are staggered, except when using pinned rings.

The thing to avoid is distortion when mounting rings on the piston. Special ring spreading tools are available which open the ring for easy mounting without danger of distortion.

Installing Pistons in Block

Cleanliness and care are the vital

A positive way to eliminate ring warping is by use of ring spreader tool

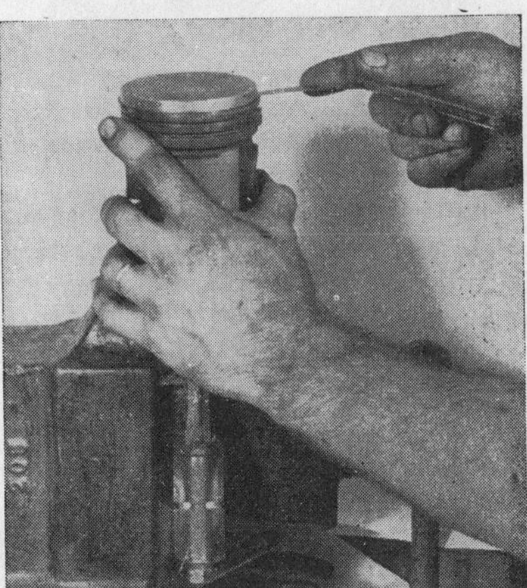

Check ring groove gap by use of feeler for specified clearance

factors in any mechanical setup. This is particularly true when installing piston and ring assemblies. Probably more jobs are ruined by including "more grit than rings" than by any other single cause.

Before mounting the ring compressor, check the position of the rod relative to the piston. Lubricate the rings and piston, set the ring compressor up so that there will be no interference from cylinder head studs when the piston is entered in the bore.

Tighten the ring compressor slowly and, while tightening, move it back and forth slightly so as to be certain none of the rings have come out of their slots. If the compressor binds, it indicates a stuck ring. Remove the compressor, relocate the rings, replace the compressor and start over.

Make certain the ring compressor is set up square with the piston. This is usually done by entering the piston into the bore and tapping it down until the compressor contacts the cylinder head all the way around. Take a final twist on the compressor after it is squared up.

Now tap the piston into the cylinder while holding the compressor down tightly against the top surface of the block. This will prevent the rings from catching on the edge of the bore.

New rings are generally "stiff" until they finally seat themselves in the bore. Therefore, it may be considered perfectly normal for an engine to run somewhat hotter when rings have been installed. (Other causes of overheating, in connection with repair work, are given under "Cooling System.")

Cylinder Wall Glaze

Before installing new rings most manufacturers recommend that the "glaze" or work-hardened surface of the cylinder be broken.

Inexpensive hones are available for this purpose or a disk of abrasive, slightly larger than the bore, may be used. Simply attach the abrasive disk to an extension arbor, place the arbor in a 1/4" electric drill and, with the drill running, pass it once or twice through the cylinder. The abrasive will break through the glaze and produce a more suitable bearing surface on which rings will "run in" more readily.

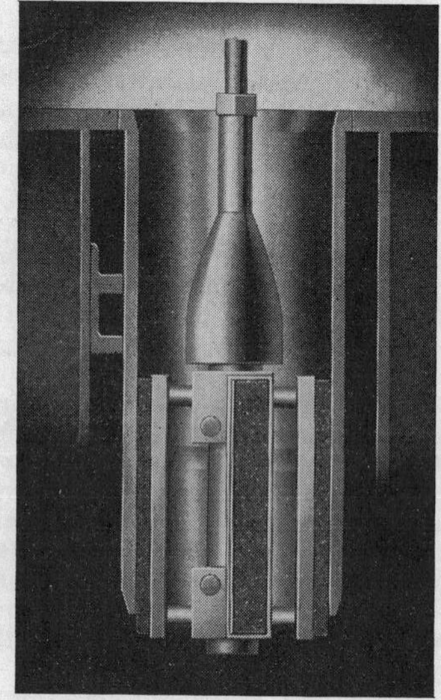

Break cylinder glaze with a special hone

PISTON PINS

There are three types of piston pins in general use, their names being de-

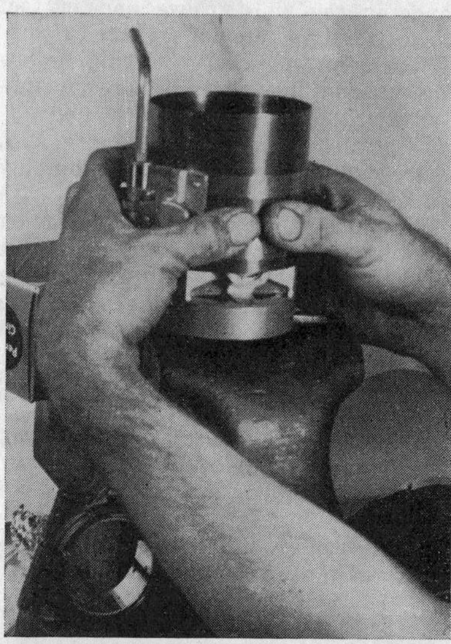

Center compressor by oscillating to make sure no rings have jammed in grooves

rived from the method of retaining the pin in the assembly: 1—Locked in rod; 2—Locked in the piston, and 3—Full floating.

"Locked in the rod" pins are arranged so that the bearing surface is in the piston, the pin is clamped or bolted in the rod.

"Locked in the piston" pins have their bearing in the connecting rod, which is fitted with a bronze bushing.

"Full floating" pins have a bearing in both the piston and the rod. They are held in the assembly by lock rings at each end of the pin.

Pin Fitting

Pin fitting is probably the most touchy job in automotive servicing. Oil clearance ranges from zero to .0002 inch, and a very good surface finish is required.

There are three methods of fitting wrist pins in general use—**reaming**, honing, and boring.

Reaming for Pin Fit

Wrist pin bearings may be fitted with an expansion type reamer, provided care is used that the finish cuts are taken in extremely small steps. Any attempt to "hog out metal" will result in a poor bearing surface which will not give satisfactory service.

Because of the surface irregularities produced by the action of the reamer, it is customary to fit pins to zero clearance (press fit) on reamed jobs, especially on aluminum pistons.

Wrist pin bearing surfaces MUST BE kept in perfect alignment, particularly when the bearing is in the piston.

Taper bushings are provided with pin reamers to guide the piston on to the cutting portion of the reamer but, unless the operator is careful to keep the bushing in firm contact with the piston, misalignment will likely occur.

The procedure is to grasp the piston with the left hand, holding the head of the piston towards the palm. Start one of the pin bearings on to the reamer pilot, enter the taper bushing into the pin hole on the opposite side of the piston. Advance the piston onto the reamer until the reamer pilot enters into the taper bushing. Continue to advance the piston, maintaining steady pressure on the taper bushing so that it stays centered in the pin hole.

Note: Where the cutting flutes of the reamer are longer than the diameter of the piston, pass both sides of the piston across the reamer in one stroke. This will produce better alignment with less effort. In many cases the cutting flutes are too short to cut both sides at the same time and the following method should be used.

Pass one side of the piston across the cutting flutes of the reamer, being careful to adjust the reamer for a light cut (not more than .002 in.).

Remove the piston from the reamer and reverse it, pressing the taper bushing in the side which was just reamed, and repeat the cut on the opposite side.

Reaming the piston in this manner is a little slower than finishing one side at a time but it will generally result in better alignment.

Expand the reamer slightly, and repeat the above procedure until the pin can just be forced into the hole.

Under no circumstances should the finish setting of the reamer be used as the starting setting for the next piston. Always back off the reamer and approach to size in several steps to insure good surface finish. If the bearing is found to be reamed oversize so that the pin enters too freely on one (or more) of the pistons, simply continue to ream to the next convenient oversize. No harm is done having one piston pin a bigger oversize than the others.

Fitting the pin to the bearing in the upper end of the connecting rod (locked in piston or full floating pins) requires even more care than does fitting to the piston. Since the rod must be grasped in one hand, there is a tendency to cock the rod while advancing across the cutting flutes, resulting in a bell-mouth cut.

The procedure is to grasp the rod in the left hand and enter the pin hole over the reamer pilot. Start the bearing onto the flutes by pushing it with the taper bushing, held by the right hand. This will start the bearing straight on the flutes.

When the rod is as far on the flutes as it is possible to get it using the bushing as a pusher, transfer the right hand grasp to the portion of the rod which forms the pin hole and continue to advance the rod, using pressure from the right hand only. The left hand simply prevents the rod from turning with the reamer.

CAUTION: Extraordinary **care** should be taken to prevent the hands from coming into contact with the cutting flutes of the reamer. If the right hand should slip off the rod, the result will be a serious injury.

Honing for Pin Fit

Pin hones are specially developed machines to produce a finer surface finish than is possible with a reamer. Ordinarily, a pin is set up to an easy push fit because of the finer, more-dense bearing surface. Aluminum piston may be fitted somewhat tighter. Honing requires the same care as reaming to maintain alignment.

The best instruction for pin fitting with a hone are supplied by the hone manufacturers. Always follow his recommendations to the letter for best results.

A finer surface finish is possible on piston pin bushings by the process of honing

ROD BEARINGS

Rod bearings are of two general types: The first type is cast integral with the rod and is called "cast-in" or "poured bearings." The second type is separate, removable shells called "slip-in" or "insert" bearings.

Trouble Shooting on Rod Bearings

Defective or loose rod bearings can usually be detected by the sound of the engine.

Run the engine at curb-idle until it is thoroughly warm.

Increase engine speed to just above idle. At this point, rods which are defective or loose will give off a dull thudding sound, the sound will slowly fade out as the engine is slowed down to idle or speeded up to about 35 mph (engine speed).

In many cases, loose bearings can be diagnosed by observing the oil pressure gauge. Loose rod and main bearings (and camshaft bearings) will not permit the pump to maintain full oil pressure when the engine is hot.

Hone to an easy push fit

Assemble the pin to the rod & piston

Replacing Bearings

On examination each type should have a smooth, even surface, free of cracks and scratches. Bearings sometimes become somewhat discolored in service, but discoloration alone is not an indication of failure. Where checks, cracks or surface blemishes are found, the bearing should be replaced.

Before adjusting or replacing any bearing, examine the crankshaft journal. It should be perfectly smooth, round and free of taper. In general, out of round should not exceed .003 in. and taper should be less than .001 in.

A quick check of the bearing journal may be made by scratching a penny lengthwise of the journal. If the bearing is perfectly smooth the penny will slide across the surface freely. If there are any surface irregularities or "grooves" the penny will vibrate and the shaft will show a copper mark.

Cast in Rod Bearings

Cast in bearings are usually provided with shims at the parting line to permit adjusting the bearing for normal wear.

Rod inserts indicating a discolored bearing. The insert is free of cracks and scratches and is still usable

The customary method of adjusting this type of rod bearing is to remove shims until the bearing binds on the shaft and then replace (.001 in. thick) shims one at a time till the bearing is just free. Be sure to remove and replace an equal amount from each side of the cap.

Read instructions carefully before checking bearing fit

Rod bearing inserts are steel shells lined with bearing material. They are available in a variety of undersizes to compensate for shaft wear and also to fit reground or undersize crank pins.

Measuring for Rod Bearing Clearance

A definite oil clearance is required between the crank pin and bearing. (Exact clearances are given in the data section. See index.)

The oil clearance can be determined by using either the shim stock method or the more modern plastic gauge method.

The shim stock method is as follows: Cut a piece of shim stock (as thick as the recommended oil clearance) about ½ inch wide and as long as the width of the bearing. Place the shim on the bearing and bolt the cap in place, using a torque wrench. If the shim stock binds the shaft, the oil clearance is less than the thickness of the shim stock; if the shaft turns freely the oil clearance is excessive. A slight drag will be felt if the oil clearance is correct.

The plastic gauge method is somewhat more accurate: Cut a piece of gauge stock to bearing width, place on the bearing and bolt the cap in place—torque it up.

Without turning the crankshaft, remove the cap. The plastic will be flattened in proportion to the amount of oil clearance. Determine the exact oil clearance by matching the flattened plastic with the width gauge which is part of the plastic gauge kit.

Special tapered or feathered shims may be used between the bearing cap and the insert shell to compensate for clearance up to approximately .004 in. If the clearance exceeds .005 in. the bearing should be replaced.

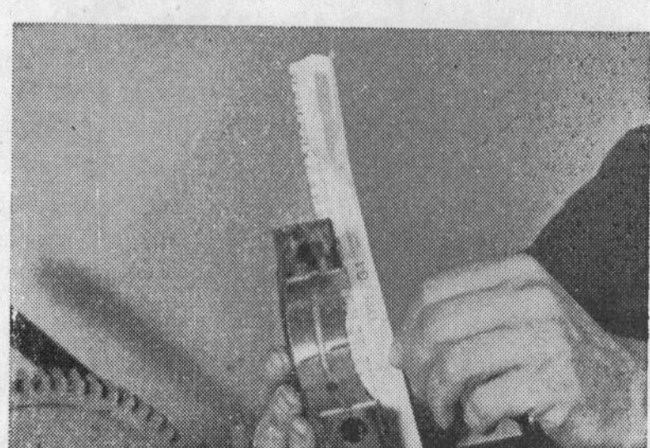

Check the oil clearance by gauging the width of the flattened plastic

Where undersize bearings were used at factory assembly the engine is generally marked with a bearing size code. (These codes are given in the car section of this Manual.)

When shims are used it is generally necessary to file the edges of the bearing at the parting line to prevent pinching the insert.

CAUTION: When filing the edge of the bearing be careful not to file the cap.

Aligning Rods

The center line of the wrist pin must be parallel to the center line of the rod bearing. Any deviation will cause rapid wear on the piston skirt and the rod bearing and journal, and will also prevent the rings from seating properly.

Many otherwise good "ring jobs" are spoiled because of failure to align the rod properly.

Aligning is done on special fixtures designed for the purpose. Since each fixture requires a different technique, the actual procedure will depend on the fixture being used. Always follow carefully the instructions supplied with your tool.

In general, care should be taken not to crimp or bend the web of the rod when correcting for twist. Keep in mind that very little "overcorrection" is required on rods. The spring back is much less than is found on front end parts and I beams, etc.

MAIN BEARINGS

Main bearings are, as the name implies, the bearings which hold the crankshaft in place in the block.

On all American passenger cars the mains are pressure lubricated. Oil is fed thru cored holes in the block to the upper half of the main bearing shell.

Main bearings are all of the separate shell type which, from the service standpoint, may be divided into two classes: Slip-in and dowelled or screwed in.

Trouble Shooting on Main Bearings

Loose or defective main bearings can sometimes be detected by listening to the sound of the engine under certain conditions.

A heavy load is imposed on the mains when the engine is run under full throttle at slow speed (about 10 mph) and a dull thumping sound will come from any loose main under heavy load.

The engine can be held to 10 mph by applying the brakes and opening the throttle wide.

Caution: This procedure is very hard on the brakes and should not be sustained for more than 20 seconds at a time.

Measuring Main Bearing Clearance

Follow the procedure given for measuring rod bearing clearance.

Slip-in Main Bearings

The slip-in type may be renewed with the engine in place in the car without removing the crankshaft.

The procedure is to remove one main bearing cap and loosen the rest. Observe which side of the bearing upper half (the half in the block itself) has the "tang" at the parting line.

Flatten the head of a cotter pin so that the pin looks like the letter T. Insert the shank of the cotter pin into the oil hole of the crankshaft, then turn the shaft till the T portion of the cotter pin contacts the main bearing upper shell on the side opposite to the

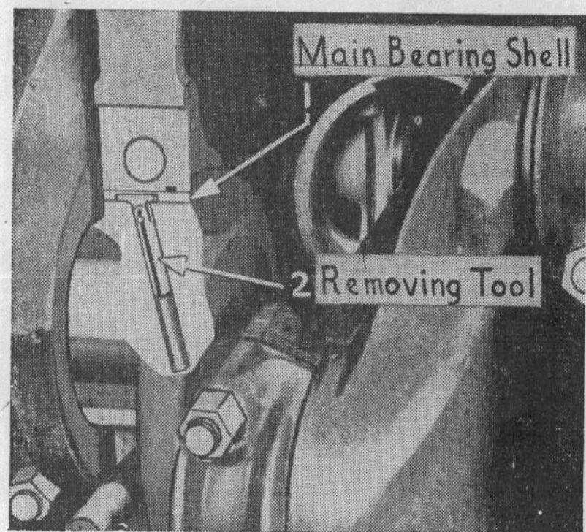

Bearing shell removing tool

tang. Continue to turn the crankshaft, forcing the upper shell to rotate with the shaft until it is completely out of the block and lift it off the shaft.

Inserts may be replaced in the same manner, except the "tang" side of the shell and the bearing is rotated in the opposite direction so that the tang enters its slot last.

Another method is to take a flat piece of soft flexible material (the writer uses a 3/32 inch thick plastic ruler) and tap the upper shell on the side opposite to the tang, forcing the upper shell around the shaft and out. Soft material such as brass or plastic will not injure the bearing seat or scratch the polished journal but will follow the curvature of the bearing seat, permitting pressure to be exerted all the way around.

This latter method is somewhat faster than the "cotter pin" method.

Extraordinary care should be used to prevent grit or dirty oil from getting on the bearing shell while entering it into its seat.

Crankshaft journal being ground on a stationary grinder

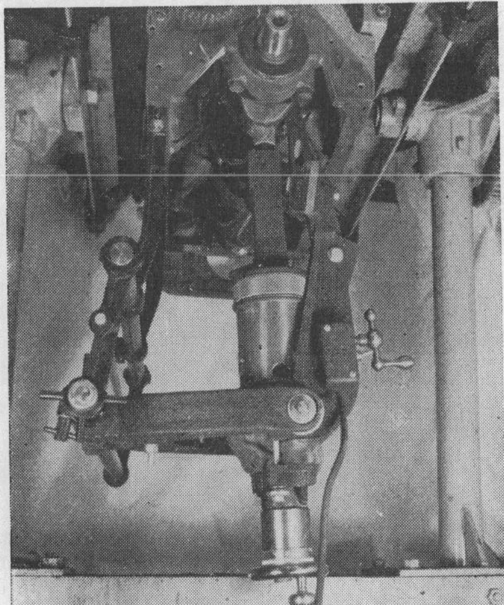

Portable crankshaft grinder being used on journal in engine

It is good practice to thoroughly clean out around the bearing seat, using a steam cleaner or good solvent and compressed air.

Locked-in Main Bearing

To replace locked-in main bearings it is necessary to take the engine out of the frame, disassemble it and remove the crankshaft in order to remove the bearing upper half.

Line Reaming Main Bearings

Since main bearing materials are very soft, an extremely sharp tool is required. A high surface finish is required, free of scratches and tool marks.

Line boring is done with special fixture type boring bars with the engine out of the car. Complete instructions are supplied with each boring fixture, but regardless of which make of tool is used certain requirements must be met:

The boring bar must be centered very carefully to insure the finish bore being concentric to the bearing seats in the block.

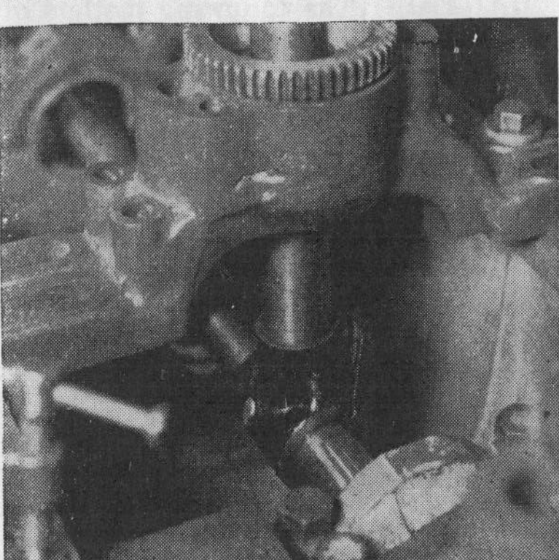

Line boring fixture holding sleeve

The bar must be mounted so that it does not bind at any point when tested by sliding it in and out while turning it in the fixture bearings.

After the bearings are bored, a quick check can be made to determine if the cut is concentric. Remove the upper and lower bearing shells from one of the bearings which was used to locate the boring bar. With tube micrometers, measure the thickness of the shells (upper and lower), in several places, the thickness should not vary more than .001 inch at any point on either shell.

Repeat this test on the other bearing which located the bar.

Variations of more than .001 inch indicate that, while the bearings may be

Setting the fly cutter on a line boring fixture

perfectly aligned with each other, they are not aligned perfectly with the bearing seats in the block. Misalignment of this kind (unless it is very bad) will not cause any difficulty until, at some future date, it may become necessary to replace one bearing only with a precision shell. The precision shell, which will not vary in thickness, may cause the shaft to flex somewhat resulting in an overload on the new bearing.

Cutter part way through the intermediate bearing

Torque the main bearing cap

Tighten rod bearings with torque wrench

Tighten rear main bearing with torque wrench

Clutch disk may be aligned with the clutch shaft as shown

MAIN BEARINGS OIL SEALS

Oil seals are used on the rear main bearing to prevent oil from the bearing entering the clutch housing. There are two types of rear main bearing oil seals: The slinger and drain type and the packing type.

Slinger Type

The slinger and drain type consists of a disc mounted on the crankshaft in back of the rear main bearing. This disc, called a slinger, flings the oil by centrifugal force. The only service required by this type of oil seal is that it be kept clean and free of sludge.

The drain tube which is attached is sometimes fitted with a flapper valve, which is intended to prevent oil from surging up the drain tube on rapid acceleration or when ascending very steep grades.

If the flapper valve should stick in the open position there is a possibility that oil will escape onto the flywheel during rapid acceleration.

Any stoppage in the drain tube either from sludge deposits or the flapper sticking closed will result in a leak at any time the engine is running.

Packing Type

The packing type oil seal consists of packing material such as graphite, synthetic rubber, cork, cotton or special packing mounted in a retainer in back of the rear main bearing. This type seal generally incorporates a drain device between the bearing and the seal to permit oil from the bearing to return to the crankcase.

While it is sometimes possible to replace the upper half of this type of seal with the crankshaft in place, most car manufacturers recommend that the engine be removed from the car, the crankshaft lifted out and the upper half of the seal be replaced, using special seating tools.

Replacing Rear Main Bearing Packing

CAUTION: The following method of replacing a packing type oil seal is not always successful and is given here as a possibility when the pan has been removed for some other purpose. If an unsuccessful attempt is made to remove the upper half of the oil seal, resulting in damage to the seal, it must be replaced either by removing the crankshaft or the flywheel.

To replace a U shaped composition oil seal without removing the crankshaft proceed as follows:

Remove the rear main bearing cap and loosen the other caps. Lower the crankshaft as far as it will go without injuring the clutch or clutch shaft.

While lowering the crankshaft have someone depress the clutch pedal so that the clutch disk can relocate itself.

Enter a thin piece of strip steel (.020 in. gage stock will do) between the packing and the crankcase retainer to force the packing down out of the groove. Force the gauge stock about ¼ inch at a time around the O.D. of the seal and, when the shim has been pushed all the way around, grasp both ends with a pair of pliers and pull down to free the oil seal from the groove. Leave the strip of steel in place and rotate the oil seal out of the crankcase.

To replace, remove the steel strip and, holding the crankshaft as far down as it will go, rotate the new piece of packing back into the groove.

Locate the new seal so that it protrudes past the cap boss an equal amount on both sides.

Force the seal into place by torqueing up the rear main bearing cap and tightening the other caps to prevent springing the crankshaft.

Take the cap down again and trim the seal flush with the boss, using a very sharp knife.

Place the lower half of the new seal in the cap and trim it off so that it protrudes about ⅛ inch above the machined surface of the cap.

Replace the cap on the rear main bearing and bolt it up tight and then remove it again to be sure the protruding portion of the lower seal has not "riveted over," thus preventing the cap from seating properly.

If it has riveted over (and it usually does) trim off the riveted portion only and bolt it up again.

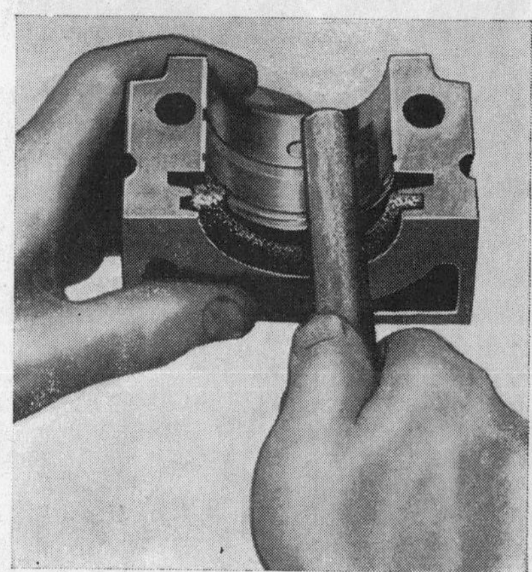

Force the packing into the rear bearing cap as shown above

Repeat until the cap has seated properly and the packing is tight in the groove.

THE VALVE SYSTEM

On L head engines the valve system consists of the camshaft, lifters, tappet screws, springs, spring seats and keepers and the valves. In addition, some cars use cages over the valve springs to prevent surge.

The overhead engine valve system includes a camshaft, lifters, push rods, adjusting screws, rocker arms and shafts, valve springs, keepers and keys, and valves.

Timing Gears

Since the power cycle occurs every other revolution (4 stroke cycle engines), the valve mechanism operates at ½ crankshaft speed. This is accomplished by engaging a gear (or sprocket) mounted on the crankshaft with a gear (or sprocket) having twice as many teeth mounted on the camshaft. When gears are used they are meshed directly and the camshaft turns in a direction opposite to the crankshaft. Where sprockets are used their connection is through the timing chain, and the camshaft turns in the same direction as the crankshaft.

Timing Gear Replacement—Valve Timing

NOTE: Exact procedure for each make of car is given in the car section of this manual. The following are general instructions:

Timing gears should be replaced when there is sufficient wear in the gear teeth to cause a knock. Wear, even excessive wear, does not affect valve timing an appreciable amount.

Valve timing will be seriously affected only if the gears have become badly damaged, or when "pressed on gears" have loosened and slipped on the camshaft, which rarely happens.

To replace timing gears first remove the radiator core (or the front end sheet metal), the vibration damper and the timing case cover. On some models the job is greatly simplified if the generator and water pump are removed. (On some models it is necessary to remove the oil pan in order to clear the crank gear.)

Examine the cam gear. It will be held to its shaft either by bolts into a fixed flange or keyed to the shaft and retained by a large bolt or it will be pressed on the shaft (or flange).

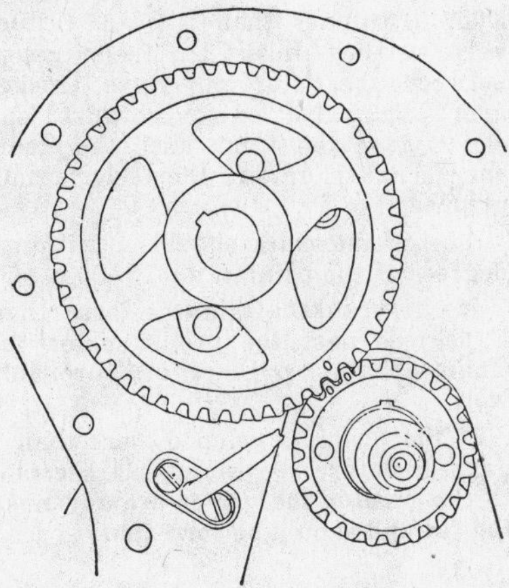

Timing gear marks

Crank the engine until the marks (usually punch marks) on both gears are adjacent to each other and in line between the shaft centers. On some cars, notably Hudson, the cam gear has two punched marks and one punched tooth on the crank gear. On this construction rotate the engine till the one mark on the crank gear comes between the two marks on the cam gear.

Using a gear puller, pull off the crank gear (it may be necessary to jack up the front of the engine for clearance).

Next pull off the cam gear. Use a puller if the gear is pressed or keyed on the shaft. Where a bolt-on flange is used the gear can usually be pried off after the bolts are removed.

Some cam gears, notably Chevrolet, are actually a press fit and no retaining device is used other than a key to maintain alignment. On this type of construction, car manufacturers usually recommend that the camshaft be removed and the gear pressed off and on in an arbor press.

To replace the crankshaft gear, start the gear on the shaft with the keyway in perfect alignment. (It is difficult to align the keyway after the gear is started on the shaft.) Force the gear all the way on the shaft.

Start with the cam gear, observing if the keyway is aligned perfectly and also that the marked teeth are starting in proper mesh. Timing gears are usually of the helical type. Because of the helix, the gear rotates slightly as the teeth enter deeper into the mesh. Therefore, it will be necessary to turn the camshaft slightly so that the keyway will be in line when the gears just begin to mesh. The camshaft will tend to turn with the gear as the gear is pressed onto the shaft.

After the gears are mounted, rotate the crankshaft two full turns to bring the punch marks again to the timing position in order to recheck their alignment.

Timing Chains and Sprockets

Timing chains should be replaced when they are worn badly enough to "slap." Usually a noisy timing chain is loose enough that there is a possibility of the chain "jumping" with consequent change in valve timing.

To replace the timing chain it is necessary to remove the camshaft sprocket or the crankshaft sprocket or, in some instances, both.

Turn the crankshaft to bring the sprocket into the timing position. (Note: The car section gives the timing position for every make.) Pull the camshaft sprocket with a puller, removing the chain at the same time.

To replace, set the crank sprocket timing mark in the correct position. Place the chain over the cam sprocket, and tentatively start the chain over the crank sprocket meshing so that the timing marks are correctly placed. (The car section gives the correct position for each car.)

(NOTE: If the cam sprocket is not

When installing timing chain, marks on sprocket must line up as shown.

Timing gear setting

Copper plated washers are used on the timing chain to establish timing point on some cars

nicely centered over the camshaft when the chain is meshed, there will be a tendency for the cam sprocket to "roll" out of time while bringing it over the camshaft. Make certain the cam sprocket will slide over the camshaft without rotating after the chain is meshed to the crankshaft sprocket.)

Push the cam sprocket all the way on the shaft and secure.

Turn the crank 2 full revolutions to return the marks to the timing position and recheck the timing.

Valve Timing Check

Valve timing may be checked without examining the timing gear marks by the following method:

Remove the valve chamber cover (or rocker cover).

Set No. 1 inlet valve to the "clearance for valve timing" which is given in the data tables in the car section of this Manual. Note that the same table which has "clearance for valve timing" also has the number of degrees of crankshaft travel at which the inlet valve opens, usually expressed as follows: IN. OP. (inlet opens) 5 degrees (or other number) B.U.D.C. (before upper dead center).

Check the vibration damper (or flywheel) marks so that the proper timing mark (as given in the Data Section) can be seen readily.

Select the feeler gauge approximately .005 in. thinner than the No. 1 inlet valve setting. Insert the feeler gauge between the lifter and valve (rocker arm and valve on overheads) and slowly turn the crank until the clearance is taken up and the feeler firmly gripped.

The timing mark should be within 4 degrees of the pointer.

If the crankshaft moves more than 4 degrees past the proper point the timing chain or gears are probably worn.

If the feeler is gripped more than 4 degrees before the timing mark comes to the pointer the valves are advanced too far and should be corrected.

The Camshaft

As the name indicates, the camshaft is a series of cams, one for each valve, ground in a suitable manner on a solid steel shaft. The purpose of the camshaft is simply to raise and lower the valves. In addition to the cams, a worm gear is cut into the camshaft to drive the distributor. The camshaft bearings are lubricated by oil under pressure, fed through drilled holes in the block.

Remove camshaft bearing with inertia puller

New camshaft bearings should be installed on all engine overhaul jobs

Very little service is required. However, when an engine is overhauled new bearings should be installed because loose camshaft bearings will pass oil so fast that the pump may not be able to maintain pressure.

Frequently low oil pressure (the result of loose cam bearings) is blamed on the rod and main bearings and much time and money are wasted working on rod and main bearings, when the trouble lies in the camshaft.

When an engine has low oil pressure but no other symptoms of loose bearings, assuming a good oil pump, remove the oil pan and make an oil pressure leak test to determine where the excess oil is draining off.

A practical repair for excessive leak down at the cam bearings can be made by inserting metered fittings into the camshaft oil supply lines or galleries. This type of repair should be made only if the engine is satisfactory except for the lowered oil pressure.

Caution: When using metering devices be sure to use a separate fitting for each bearing and not just one in the main feed line. Where one metering fitting only is used, there is a good chance that the bearing nearest the fitting will use up all the oil and the bearing farthest away will be dry.

Valve Lifters and Tappets

Valve lifters (except hydraulic) may be divided into two general types: Barrel type and mushroom type.

From the standpoint of service, the principal difference between them is that the barrel type may be removed and replaced without disturbing the camshaft, whereas the mushroom type comes out through the bottom after the camshaft has been removed.

NOTE: A few makes of cars mount the lifters in groups or clusters.

Each cluster is made up of four or more lifters fitted to a removable guide. This type of lifter may be replaced as follows:

Turn the crankshaft until all the lifters (in the cluster being worked) are down, so that it is not necessary to block up any of the valves.

Remove the attaching bolts and lift the cluster out of the car. Once out of the car, any or all of the lifters can be changed or a new cluster can be replaced.

Oversize Valve Lifters

Caution: Oversize valve lifters are not available for all cars.

AND TROUBLE SHOOTING

On a job where the lifter bores are badly worn and oversize lifters are not made, the bore is sometimes reamed to about .050 in. oversize and a sleeve or bushing pressed into the block. The inserted bushing is then reamed or honed to fit the standard lifter.

Bushings or sleeves of this type are not standard items and must be made in the machine shop from standard bushing stock.

If oversize lifters are available the block should be reamed or honed to fit the smallest oversize.

Remove the valve mechanism camshaft and lifters and ream or hone the block from underneath. Portable pin hones or expansion reamers are used and final size is reached in several steps. When reaming, never use the final reamer setting for one bore as the starting setting of the next bore.

Barrel type lifters can be taken out of the block without removing the camshaft. Because of this, many well meaning mechanics try to ream for oversize lifters using a machine shop stub reamer without taking the camshaft out.

While it is theoretically possible to do such a job, in actual practice it is necessary to remove the camshaft and valves and operate the reamer or hone from the crankcase in order to maintain alignment and prevent bell mouth.

Valve Tappets (L Head Engines)

Tappet (valve adjusting) screws are either self-locking or jamb nut type.

Normal wear causes the contact face of the tappet to become concave, making adjustment by the conventional feeler gage method rather difficult.

Special tools are available to regrind the tappet face in place on the engine or they may be removed or refaced on a suitable valve grinder.

When a tappet screw is worn or dished, there is usually corresponding wear on the bottom face of the valve stem.

Therefore any time a tappet is refaced, the valve stem should also be refaced in order to insure effective quiet operation.

Valve (Rocker) Adjusting Screws (Overhead Valves)

Overhead valves are adjusted for stem clearance at the rocker arm. An adjusting screw and jamb nut is fitted to the rocker arm for this purpose.

Normal wear causes a groove to form in the face of the rocker arm which contacts the valve stem. Refacing to compensate for wear is accomplished by removing the rocker from the engine and grinding the worn contact face, using a suitable adapter, on a valve grinder.

The grinder manufacturer provides complete instructions for using his machine for this work. These instructions should be followed carefully.

Adjusting Valves

Valves should be adjusted so that when the engine is warm there is sufficient clearance between the end of the valve stem and the lifter tappet screw (or rocker arm) to insure the valve seating properly and at the correct time.

Specifications for valve clearance are given in the data tables of this manual. Because of the importance of proper clearance the same specifications are also to be found in the quick reference working specifications in the first section.

Procedure:

Make sure the valves have sufficient clearance for the engine to start and run. Any amount over .020 inch will do to start the engine.

Run the engine until thoroughly warmed.

Remove the valve chamber covers (or rocker cover).

Note: On many cars it is necessary to remove the front wheel and fender pan for access to the valve chamber.

As stated earlier, valve adjusting screws (except hydraulic) are either self-locking or jamb nut types.

Where self-locking screws are used, one wrench is placed on the "flat" on the lifter to hold it while a second wrench is used to turn the adjusting screw.

The jamb nut type requires three wrenches, one on the lifter, one on the jamb nut and the third on the adjusting screw.

A very accurate way of setting the clearance is to use the machinist's GO—NOT GO method, which is as follows:

Let us suppose the clearance should be .015 inch. Instead of using a .015 inch feeler gauge, adjust the clearance so that a .014 inch gauge will pass easily between the stem and tappet and a .016 inch gauge will not enter. The clearance will then be greater than .014 inch but less than .016 inch—as near to .015 as is practical.

Special step cut feeler gauges are available having the GO—NOT GO sizes on one gauge.

Caution: On jamb nut type adjusters the clearance must be maintained AFTER the jamb nut is tightened.

VALVE ADJUSTMENT

On L head engines, tightening the jamb nut tends to decrease clearance, whereas on overhead valves, tightening the nut tends to increase clearance.

Most mechanics who specialize in engine work use the following technique to tighten the jamb nut without losing adjustment:

Hold the wrench on the lifter with the left hand. With the second wrench in the right hand, loosen the jamb nut just enough so that the adjusting screw will turn very stiffly. Arrange the two wrenches so that they can both be held in the left hand just like the handles of a pair of pliers.

Maintain sufficient pressure on the two wrenches (like gripping something with pliers) to prevent either the lifter or the jamb nut from moving when the adjusting screw is turned. Turn the adjusting screw with a wrench held in the right hand, and check the clearance with a feeler which is also held in the right hand.

Since the jamb nut was loosened only a slight amount, there is considerable pressure on the threads which insures that when the jamb nut is finally tightened the clearance won't change an appreciable amount.

To tighten the jamb nut, simply squeeze together the two wrenches in the left hand as though they were a pair of pliers.

Sufficient tension can be placed on the jamb nut by this method. In fact, a man with strong hands can strip the threads by "bearing down."

Rocker arm adjusting screws are done in the same manner except that a screw driver and one wrench are the tools used.

It is customary to adjust overhead valves with the engine running.

Special combination wrench-screw drivers are available which make the job easier.

Alternate Method of Adjusting Valves

The dial gauge technique is a very accurate method of adjusting valves, on L head engines, where it can be done with the engine cold and the cylinder head off.

Set up a thousandth dial indicator over the valve head and zero the indicator. Select a feeler gauge thicker than the desired clearance. Insert the feeler between the valve stem and the tappet and adjust the tappet until the dial indicator reads the difference between the desired clearance and the gauge thickness.

For instance:
Gauge thickness .023 in.
Desired clearance .015 in.
Difference .008 in., whic his the dial gauge reading.

While this method is perhaps the most accurate, it can only be used where the COLD clearance is known.

The dial indicator method is somewhat more difficult on overhead valves because the indicator must be set up on the valve spring retainer. Otherwise the procedure is the same as for L head engines.

Valve Adjusting Order

To simplify the order in which the valves should be adjusted, the following two-stage sequence is suggested:

For six cylinder engines with 1-5-3-6-2-4 firing order

(Except Kaiser & Frazer)

Stage A—No. 1 and No. 6 pistons at top center.

No. 1 in firing position (both lifters down).

Stage B—No. 1 and No. 6 pistons at top center.

No. 6 in firing position (both lifters down).

Stage A—Adjust.
No. 1—Both valves.
No. 2—Inlet valve.
No. 3—Exhaust valve.
No. 4—Inlet valve.
No. 5—Both valves.
Stage B—Adjust
No. 2—Both valves.
No. 3—Inlet valve.
No. 4—Exhaust valve.
No. 5—Inlet valve.
No. 6—Both valves.
(Note that No. 2 and No. 5 inlet valve can be adusted at either stage.)

To change from one stage to another simply turn the crank one full revolution.

There is a margin of safety in the above procedure, so that it is not necessary to have the pistons EXACTLY on top center.

For Kaiser & Frazer see Car Section.

For Straight 8 cylinder engines with 1-6-2-5-8-3-7-4 firing order

Stage A—No. 1 and No. 8 piston at top center.

No. 1 in firing position (both lifters down).

Stage B—No. 1 and No. 8 pistons at top center.

No. 8 in firing position (both lifters down).

Stage A—Adjust
No. 1—Both valves.
No. 2—Exhaust valve.
No. 3—Inlet valve.
No. 4—Inlet valve.
No. 5—Exhaus+ valve.
No. 6—Exhaust valve.
No. 7—Inlet valve.
Stage B—Adjust
No. 2—Inlet valve.
No. 3—Exhaust valve.
No. 4—Exhaust valve.
No. 5—Inlet valve.
No. 6—Inlet valve.
No. 7—Exhaust valve.
No. 8—Both valves.

There is a margin of safety in the above chart also, so that it is not necessary to have the piston exactly on top center.

Another Alternate Method for In-Line Engines

An alternate and perhaps somewhat quicker method is to follow the accompanying diagram which is arranged so that any piston can be at top center to start.

On 6-Cylinder Cars

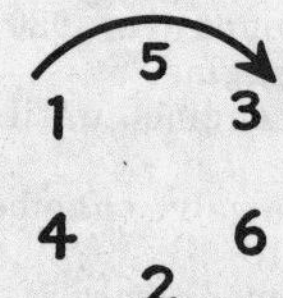

Start with the cylinder in the firing position (piston up, both valve lifters down) and work around in the direction of the arrow. Count the cylinder in the firing position as the first cylinder.
1st cyl.—Both valves.
2nd cyl.—Both valves.
3rd cyl.—Exhaust valve.
4th cyl.—None.
5th cyl.—Inlet valve.
6th cyl.—Inlet valve.

Turn the crank one full turn and again start with the cylinder which is in the firing position and work around the chart, to avoid duplications.

Adjust only the following:
1st cyl.—Both valves.
2nd cyl—Exhaust valve.
3rd cyl.—Exhaust valve.
4th and 5th—None.
6th—Inlet valve.

On Straight 8 Cars

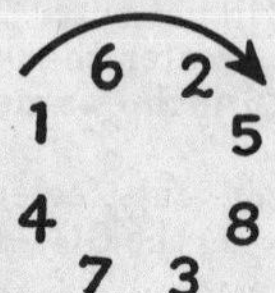

Start with the cylinder in the firing position (piston up, both valve lifters down) and work around the diagram in the direction of the arrow. Count the cylinder in firing position as the first cylinder.
1st—Both.
2nd—Exhaust.
3rd—Inlet.
4th—Inlet.
5th—Exhaust valve.
6th—Exhaust valve.
7th—Inlet.
8th—None.

Rotate the engine one full turn to bring the same pair of pistons to top center, but now the opposite cylinder will be in firing position. Again start with the cylinder in the firing position and again work around the chart in the direction of the arrow.

V 8 Models, Cadillacs, Chrysler and Studebaker

The following two-stage method is suggested as a simple, easy-to-follow sequence for adjusting valves on Cadillac V 8, Chrysler V 8, and Studebaker V 8:

Stage A—No. 1 cylinder (front cylinder left bank) in firing position (piston at top center, both valve lifters down).

Turn crank one full turn for:

Stage B—No. 6 cylinder (third cylinder right bank) in firing position (piston at top center, both valve lifters down).

Stage A—Adjust
Right Bank
No. 1 cyl.—Both.
No. 2 cyl.—Exhaust.
No. 3 cyl.—None.
No. 4 cyl.—Both.
Left Bank
No. 1 cyl.—Both.
No. 2 cyl.—Exhaust.
No. 3 cyl.—Inlet.
No. 4 cyl.—Inlet.
Stage B—Adjust
Right Bank
No. 1 cyl.—Exhaust.*
No. 2 cyl.—Inlet.
No. 3 cyl.—Both.
No. 4 cyl.—Inlet.*
Left Bank
No. 1 cyl.—None.
No. 2 cyl.—Both.*
No. 3 cyl.—Both.*
No. 4 cyl.—Exhaust.

V8 Models—Buick V8, Ford, Lincoln, Mercury and Oldsmobile V8

The following two-stage method is suggested as a sequence to follow when checking on V 8 Ford, Mercury models and for making initial settings on Buick

AND TROUBLE SHOOTING

VALVE ADJUSTMENT

V 8, Lincoln and Oldsmobile V 8 models:

Stage A—Front cylinder, left bank in firing position (piston at top center, both valve lifters down).

Turn crank one full turn for

Stage B—Third cylinder, right bank in firing position (piston at top center, both valve lifters down).

Stage A—Adjust
Right Bank
1st cyl.—Both.
2nd cyl.—Inlet.
3rd cyl.—Inlet.
4th cyl.—Exhaust.
Left Bank
1st cyl.—Both.
2nd cyl.—Inlet.
3rd cyl.—None.
4th cyl.—Both.

Stage B—Adjust
Right Bank
1st cyl.—Exhaust.*
2nd cyl.—Exhaust.
3rd cyl.—Both.*
4th cyl.—Inlet.
Left Bank
1st cyl.—None.
2nd cyl.—Both.*
3rd cyl.—Both.
4th cyl.—Inlet.*

* In the methods given for V 8 models the charts show an overlap. Note that in stage A both valves in the 1st cyl. right bank are adjustable. In stage B the exhaust valve, 1st cyl. right bank is repeated.

An asterisk is used to mark repetition.

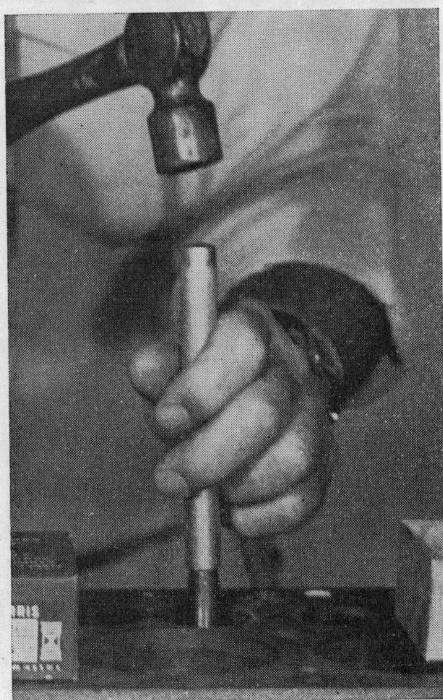

Driving a new valve guide into block

Refacing Valve Seats in Block

Valve seats can be refaced either by grinding or cutting. (Hardened inserts cannot be cut successfully.)

Cutting is done with a special valve seat reamer fitted with suitable pilots. The cutter pilot is usually locked into the valve guide which centers the cutter.

If the valve guides are badly worn it is difficult to center the cutter properly and, unless the reamer is piloted exactly in the center, the seat may be cut eccentric to the valve guide which will prevent the valve, when assembled, from seating properly.

Reaming new valve guide to remove possible burrs caused by inserting tool

Dressing valve seat stone

Where new valve guides are to be installed, cut the valve seat after the new guide is in place so that the pilot locates on the new guide.

Considerable pressure is required on valve seat reamers to make them cut. This pressure tends to center the cutter in the old seat even to the extent of springing the pilot.

In order to insure concentricity, finish cuts should be as light as possible.

Grinding valve seats is done in two ways—concentric grinding and eccentric grinding.

Concentric grinding is very similar to reaming except that the grinder turns at much higher speeds and with a grinding wheel much lighter finish cuts are possible.

An important point to remember is that the stones must be kept clean and true. Most concentric valve seat grinders have a stone truing attachment which should be used according to the manufacturer's instruction.

Eccentric valve seat grinders differ from others in that only a small area of the stone is in contact with the valve seat at any instant.

The machine is arranged so that the axis of the grindstone is off center in relation to the pilot, and the grinder axis revolves around the pilot, thus grinding a seat which is centered to the pilot.

Valve seat grinder pilot

Unless misused, this type of grinder has very little tendency to follow the old seat. However, it does require extra care in the location of the pilot.

Manufacturers of this type of equipment supply easily understood instructions for the use and care of their particular machine.

Regardless of which type of equipment is used, the careful mechanic will always lap in the valves for final fitting.

Refacing Valves

Valves should be refaced when the seat has become pitted or burnt. However, the face should not be ground or reground to where the head thickness at the outer edge of the valve is less than one half of the original thickness of a new valve.

Grinding thinner than one half the original thickness leaves the valve with insufficient metal at the edge to withstand the heat and pressure, particularly on exhaust valves.

The inlet valve runs much cooler than the exhaust valve because the cool gases from the inlet manifold pass around the upper stem and head. Therefore, narrow seats are usually recommended for the inlet valve.

Because it runs cool, the inlet valve seat does not become burnt or pitted and a very light finishing grind is all that should be required.

Valve Seat Width

The proper width for an exhaust valve seat is a controversial dimension and there is no hard and fast rule. However, if the mechanic will bear in mind that a valve with a wide seat will cool better and one with a narrow face will seat better he can arrive at a good compromise.

Seats as wide as 1/8 inch may be ground on engines which are used for long sustained hard runs or in areas where the climate is hot.

For cars which are used on short runs or are started and stopped frequently, the seating face may be ground as narrow as 1/32 inch.

The latest wrinkle in seating exhaust valves is to grind the seat in the block to exactly 45 degrees and then grind the valve face to 44 degrees. This makes the valve seat at the extreme outer edge of the face and starts the job with a very narrow face.

As the valve face wears, the seat becomes broader due to the very slight difference in angle.

The disadvantage to this method is that a very small amount of carbon or foreign matter lodging on the ground face just below the seat will prevent the valve from closing properly.

When it is desirable to narrow the width of an exhaust valve face, grind to 45 deg. in the usual manner and, without taking the valve out of the chuck, change the stone setting to about 30 deg. and again grind the valve.

It is good practice to mark the ground surface with bright colored chalk before grinding at 30 degrees so that the operator can see just how narrow the face is becoming by watching the bright colored chalk grind off.

Lubricating pilot

Grinding seat in block with concentric grinder, see below

Valve refacing machine used to reface a rocker arm

A piece of sand paper caught under stone and turned by hand will remove grease and oil from seat and prevent clogging stone

Another type of concentric grinder

Valve seat indicator designed to show concentricity between valve guide and seat

Before refacing valve it is necessary to dress the stone

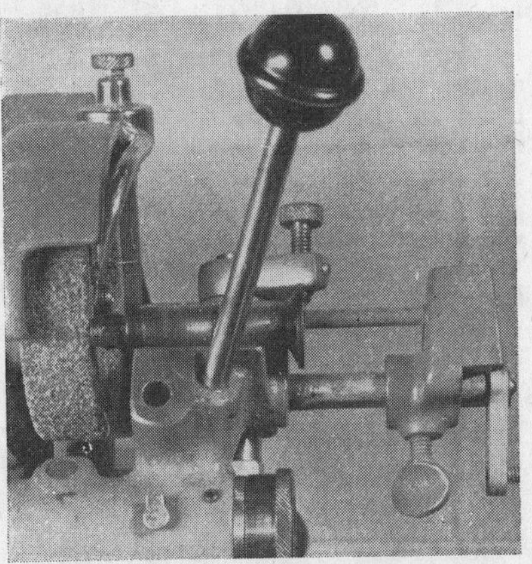

Valve refacing machine set up for refacing a valve lifter

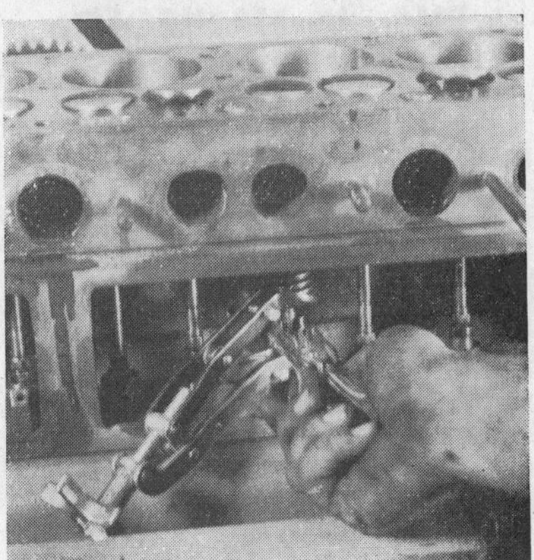

Valve keeper inserter with valve lifter in place

Dressing stone on another type of valve refacing machine

Another type of valve refacing machine, refacing a valve lifter

Another type of valve keeper inserter and lifter

Refacing a valve, wheel should be checked frequently for accuracy

Squaring the bottom of the valve stem, an operation often neglected

Adjusting valves by the go-not go method

ENGINE MANIFOLD, INLET MANIFOLD

The purpose of the inlet manifold is to conduct the fuel mixture from the carburetor to the inlet valve ports.

A gas-tight seal is required at all points where the manifold contacts the engine and carburetor and also at such places where vacuum take-offs are used.

Particular care must be given to that area of the inlet manifold which contacts the exhaust manifold. This area is known as the "heat riser" or "hot spot." The inlet manifold is probably the most nearly trouble-free part of an engine; very little service is required.

Practically all the troubles encountered in a properly designed inlet manifold can be listed under one heading—LEAKS.

Checking Manifold for Air Leaks

An air leak in the inlet manifold usually results in a miss, in the cylinder nearest the leak, at idle speed. Where a branch of the manifold supplies two cylinders, both may fail to fire at idle.

The effect of an air leak in the manifold is pronounced at idle, gradually becoming less noticeable as the engine speed increases and, unless the leak is very bad, may not be noticed at all at high speed or with wide-open throttle.

Before testing a manifold for air leaks, detach and plug up all take-offs such as the windshield wiper connection, vacuum heater and all other accessory lines which attach to the manifold.

There is no sure fire way to tell when a slight leak is present. Low vacuum readings may indicate several other conditions as well as air leaks. However, when a leak is suspected, test by squirting a mixture of gas and oil (about 5 parts gas, 1 part oil) around the suspected area while the engine is idling. An ordinary trigger type oil can is generally used. When the fuel is squirted at the leak, the manifold will draw in the mixture, creating a momentary rich condition which will cause the engine to "roll."

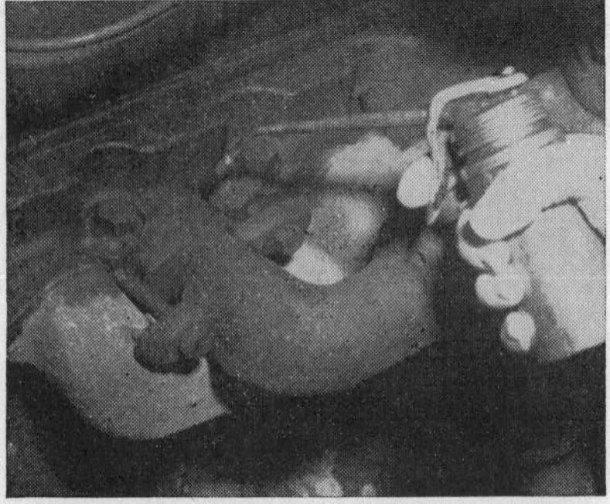

Squirt a mixture of gas and oil around suspected leak area with engine idling

Withhold the text mixture until the engine returns to its regular idle (which won't be even if the manifold leaks) and repeat the test.

This test shows not only if the manifold is leaking air but also where the leak is located—usually at a gasket.

Inlet Manifold Leaks—Exhaust Gas

A manifold leak at the heat riser or hot spot permits exhaust gases to enter the inlet manifold and mix with the incoming fuel.

Even very slight leaks at this point will cause erratic idling or prevent the engine from running at all at idle speed; performance will be poor at high speed. Since this condition always gets worse, the engine won't run after a very short time.

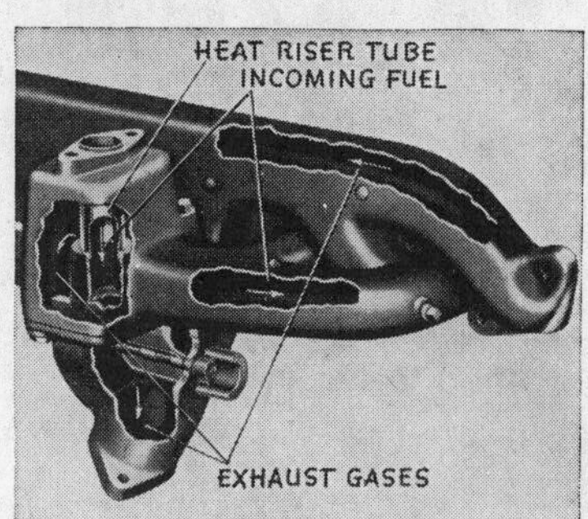

Manifold heat riser tube

Exhaust Manifold

The purpose of the exhaust manifold is to carry the burnt gases from the exhaust port to a suitably placed exhaust pipe.

Exhaust manifold leaks (except at the heat riser or hot spot) give off a sharp spitting sound, particularly during a hard pull.

Heat Riser Valve

Most in-line engines have a thermostatically controlled heat riser valve which, when operating properly, will deflect the hot exhaust gases against the inlet manifold "hot spot" when engine is cold.

As the engine warms, the bimetal spring gradually closes the heat valve, deflecting the hot exhaust away from the hot spot.

The only service required is to see that the valve operates freely.

If the heat riser valve sticks on the closed postion, the warm-up period will be longer than normal.

Stuck open, there will be a power loss at high speed.

To replace the heat riser valves, remove the exhaust manifold from the car and remove the screws from down in the hot spot opening. This job is nearly the same as removing a carburetor throttle.

Exhaust Pipe, Muffler and Tail Pipe

The exhaust line is intended to carry the burned gases back past the passenger portion of the vehicle and silence the noise produced by the expanding gases.

Because of the heat and oxidation it is sometimes difficult to separate the muffler from the exhaust and tail pipe.

A good grade of penetrating oil used liberally will generally free up the connection.

A quick test of the exhaust line can be made by running the engine with the tail pipe plugged. This will force the gases to escape by any leak which may be present in the line.

If the exhaust system is buttoned up tight, the engine will stall in less than 30 seconds.

CAUTION: Exhaust gases contain carbon monoxide, a poisonous gas which has no odor and is tasteless. It has been said that no closed space is big enough for a running engine, therefore make all exhaust line tests out in the open.

ENGINE GASKET AND OIL SEALS

Oil seals are used to prevent leaks between two adjacent parts where one part moves in relation to the other.

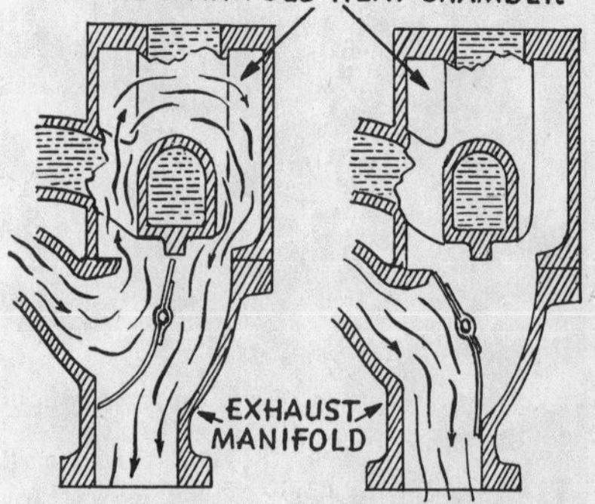

Heat riser valve

Manifold Gaskets

Heat resisting metallic or composition gaskets are used between the exhaust manifold and the engine. They should be installed dry.

Exhaust Flange Gaskets

Heat resisting, metallic or composition, install dry.

Cylinder Head Gaskets

Heat resisting metallic or composition, install dry.

Valve Chamber Cover Gaskets

Cork or soft paper composition; install with any good gasket cement or compound, or install dry.

Oil Pan Gaskets

Cork or soft paper composition; install with any good gasket cement or compound. Use extra care where gasket contacts cork filler at the front and rear main bearing.

A good way to hold the oil pan gasket in place while working the pan into position is to tie the gasket to each bolt hole with fine sewing cotton.

The cotton will be imbedded into the gasket when the bolts are drawn tight.

Start all of the pan bolts before tightening any of them and then work around the pan at least three times before final tightening. This will insure a good even pressure.

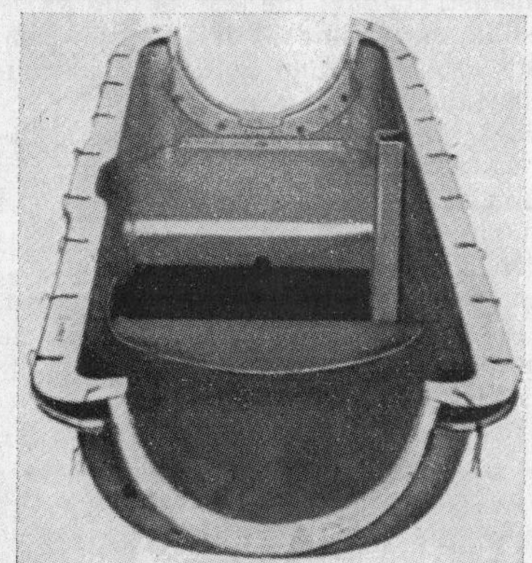

The gasket may be tied on to the pan with sewing cotton as shown

Rocker Cover Gasket

Thick cork. Use dry or with any good cement or compound.

Timing Case Cover Gasket

Thick paper composition or cork. Install dry or with any good cement or compound.

Water Pump Gasket

Thin paper composition or cork. Use dry or with any good gasket cement or compound.

Fuel Pump Gasket

Thin paper composition or cork. Use dry.

Valve Push Rod Cover Gaskets

Thick paper composition or cork. Use with any good cement or compound, or install dry.

Carburetor Flange Gaskets

Composition paper or metallic composition—use dry.

Water Outlet Gaskets

Thin paper composition or cork. Use with any good cement or compound or install dry.

Water Pump By-Pass Gasket

Thin paper composition or cork. Use with any good cement or compound or install dry.

Water Jacket Side Plate Gasket

Thick cork or paper composition. Use with any good gasket cement or compound.

CYLINDER HEAD NUT TIGHTENING SEQUENCE

The sequence to be followed in the final tightening of cylinder head bolts varies somewhat with each make of car.

The reason for tightening in a definite sequence is to insure firm, even pressure on the gasket and to permit the gasket to flatten and expand (while being tightened) from the center toward the edges.

With this in mind, any cylinder head can be tightened properly (when the factory recommended sequence is not known) by starting at the center and working toward the nearest edge.

The bolts should be run down till they just touch the head, using a speed wrench. They should then be snugged up (in the proper sequence) at least twice around.

Final tightening should be done with a torque wrench.

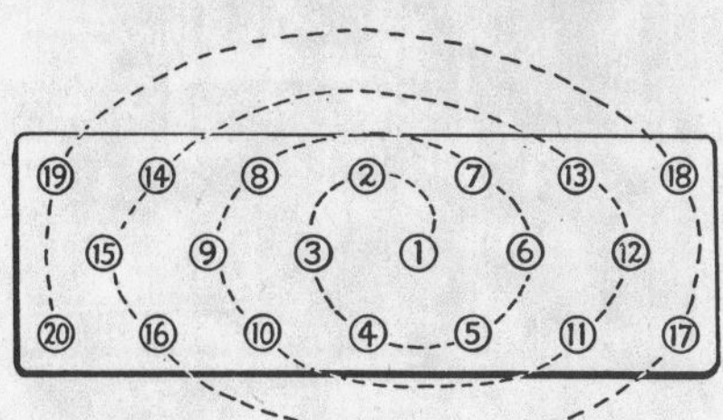

If tightening sequence is not known, follow the sequence given above

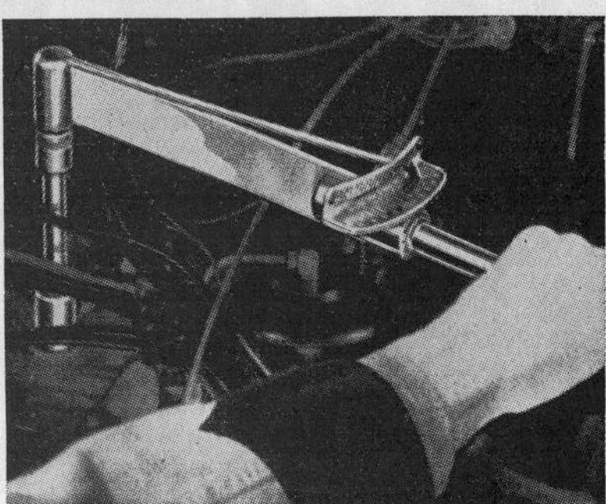

Always torque the cylinder head bolts

THE COOLING SYSTEM

The cooling system probably requires more service than any other part of the engine. Maintaining the engine well below the boiling point of the coolant and also holding the entire engine to the same temperature is a function which, by its own action, causes the formation of rust and scale—enemies of the cooling system.

Rust is formed by the chemical action of oxygen combining with iron. This combining, as with all chemical processes, is accelerated in the presence of heat.

Scale is a hard incrustation caused by the chemical action of water in the presence of heat. Chemically it consists of calcium sulfate and the carbonate of calcium, magnesium and iron.

Scale is a very poor conductor of heat and is, for that reason, objectionable in a cooling system.

Scale and rust, as stated above, are both caused by the water (and oxygen in the water) working chemically on the hot metal. It follows, then, that considerable preventive maintenance is required to keep the cooling system up to par.

Chemical Cleaning

There are on the market several good safe chemicals which tend to loosen rust and scale, making it a fairly simple matter to flush the block and radiator clean.

When using such cleaners, be sure to follow the instructions on the container.

If the instruction calls for a hot engine, warm won't do; it must be hot.

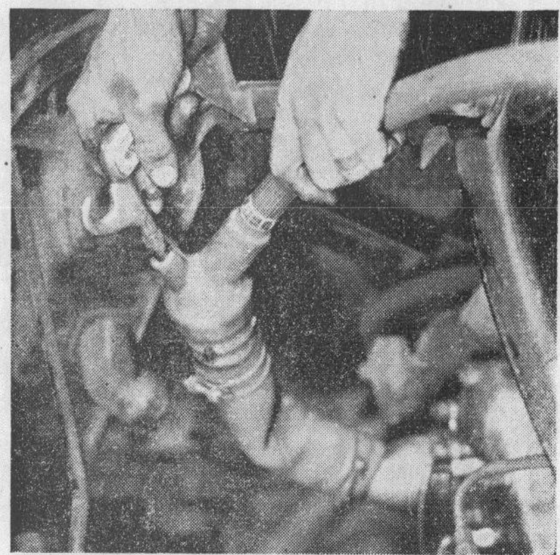

Reverse flushing on the block

In all chemical processes, time and temperature are vital factors. The chemists who make up the solutions know exactly how long and how hot. Follow their instructions.

Rust Inhibitors

Rust inhibitors are intended to retard the formation of rust and scale in the cooling system. In general, it is good, sound practice to use inhibitors as a preventive measure.

Reverse Flushing

Flushing can be done by itself, or following chemical cleaning, to rid the system of loose sediment.

Reverse flushing alone is not generally effective against hard scale or rust but is intended to remove all loose sediment.

Flushing Procedure

Disconnect the lower radiator hose at the block. (On V8's with two lower hoses, disconnect both hoses and flush separately.)

Disconnect the upper hose at the cylinder head.

NOTE

Scale tends to harden and become practically insoluble when allowed to dry out. It is a good precaution to cork up the bottom outlet in the block and fill the block to the top with water to prevent it from drying while working on the radiator.

Do the same for the radiator when working on the block.

Attach the flushing device to the lower hose (which is connected to the bottom of the radiator) and a drain-off hose to the upper radiator hose.

Turn the water on and let it run until the radiator is completely filled. With the water still running, apply air pressure in short spurts. This will force the water violently through the radiator in a reverse direction, carrying with it any loose sediment, rust or scale. Continue to flush until the water runs clear out of the drain-off hose.

Now connect the drain-off hose to the block lower water outlet.

Remove the thermostat.

Replace the thermostat housing and connect the flushing device to the water outlet on top of the head (this will be the thermostat housing on most cars).

(**NOTE:** Plug up the radiator lower water outlet and fill the radiator to prevent drying out.)

Carry the water drain-off hose across the top of the radiator so that part of the hose is higher than the engine.

Turn the water on and fill the block completely. Keep the water running and spurt the air through the block until the water coming from the drain-off hose is clear.

Remove the drain-off hose, install the thermostat, reconnect the radiator hoses (don't forget to remove the plug in the lower radiator outlet) and fill the system.

Loss of Coolant

Coolant can be lost from the system in several ways, such as leaks in the system, overflow losses, evaporation (especially alcohol or methanol antifreeze).

Leaks may occur anywhere in the system, but (except for a damaged radiator) are usually found in the hose or hose connections, water pump shaft, heater hose connections, and welch plugs.

Occasionally, head gaskets, water pump gaskets, drain plugs, etc., will leak.

Loss of coolant through the overflow may be caused by overheating (due to other causes), localized hot spots (caused by poor circulation), water pump drawing air (which displaces the water), radiator partially blocked, collapsed hoses, defective thermostat, thermostat opening too high for antifreeze.

Points of leakage in the cooling system

Localized hot spots form steam pockets which displace water.

The most common symptom of local hot spots is loss of coolant through the overflow without the dash thermometer or heat indicator showing excessive heat until so much coolant is lost that the engine overheats because of insufficient coolant.

Trouble Shooting the Cooling System

If, after thoroughly cleaning the block, head and radiator, the condition persists, the water distribution tube should be replaced.

Coolant may also be lost if the pump draws air or the exhaust gas leaks into the cooling system.

The centrifugal action of the pump creates a suction at the center of the impeller which is sometimes sufficient to unseat the seal.

To detect this condition, run the engine with the radiator cup removed. If bubbles appear at the top of the radiator the pump is drawing air or the exhaust gas is leaking into the cooling system.

In order to tell which it is, pump or exhaust, conduct the test as follows:

Run the engine at idle until warm. Increase speed and note how continuously the bubbles come up.

Set the hand brake firmly with the transmission in high gear and slow the engine by partially engaging the clutch.

If the bubbles increase as the load increases, an exhaust leak is indicated.

If the bubbles decrease as the engine speed decreases, the pump is probably drawing air.

Install a new head gasket and torque down the head to correct exhaust leaks.

Increase the spring tension on the pump seal (or tighten the packing) if the pump is drawing air.

CAUTION: The clutch may be damaged if the above test is drawn out too long. Do not load the engine by partial clutch engagement more than thirty seconds at a time.

Where overflow losses seem to be chronic and the engine block, radiator and distribution tube are known to be clean, it is good practice to install a separate surge tank.

The idea back of the surge tank is that coolant passing out of the over-

instead of being lost. A further advantage is that evaporating anti-freeze will tend to condense into liquid in the comparatively cool surge tank rather than simply evaporating into the air.

Surge Tank Installation

Universal type surge tanks are available, intended for use on any make car. When using this type tank, follow manufacturer's instruction. The tank should be mounted so that it is at least as high as the top tank of the radiator. If possible, mount it so that the bottom of the surge tank is even or above the top tank of the radiator.

Cut off the overflow pipe where it comes out of the radiator filler neck. Leave enough of the overflow pipe to permit a good connection to a suitable hose.

The hose is then connected to the bottom of the surge tank.

Note: If the bottom connection of the surge tank is directly under the filler neck (of the surge tank) a baffle will have to be mounted over the hole at the bottom to prevent the coolant from possibly spurting out the vent hole in the (surge tank) cap. If the radiator is equipped with a pressure cap, change it for a cap (non pressure) which does not have a vent hole. Pressures built up in the cooling system will simply force the coolant up into the surge tank. It will flow back into the radiator as soon as the engine is shut off.

Surge tanks can be mounted on the engine side of the fire wall; on brackets attached to the cylinder head; on brackets attached to the radiator support, or even on the hood (on some side opening models).

A surge tank is standard equipment on some models.

Thermostats

The thermostat is used in the water outlet (or hose) to prevent circulation until the engine has reached a predetermined temperature.

A defective thermostat which sticks open (or opens too soon) usually permits the engine to operate too cool, which in turn prevents the engine from reaching peak efficiency. If the thermostat does not open until the water temperature is too high, overheating results.

A suspected thermostat should be replaced or removed and tested.

Testing a thermostat with hot water and a thermometer

Thermostat Test

Remove the thermostat from the car and place in a pan of water. Place a thermometer in the water, one reading to 212 degrees F., beside the thermostat. Heat the water and observe on the thermometer the temperature at which the thermostat starts to open. Continue to heat the water and observe the temperature at which the thermostat reaches full open. The thermostat should be about half open at the temperature for which it is set.

Water Pump

All late models are equipped with the so-called "packless type pump." The seal, instead of packing, is a spring loaded rubber or composition disc, which rides against the metal face of the pump body, effectively preventing leaks.

The seal is mounted so that it revolves with the shaft.

The packless type pump will generally function without leaking until the shaft bearings become loose or worn which causes the seal to become unseated.

Whenever it is necessary to replace the seal it is always good policy to install a new shaft and bearings together with the new seal.

Disassembly of Water Pumps

Remove the pump from the car.

Measure very carefully the distance from any point on the pump body to the fan hub so that the hub can be replaced to exactly the correct position. On some models the shaft is step ground and the fan hub is pressed on until it contacts the shoulder on the shaft. Remove the fan hub. In most cases the hub is simply pressed on to the shaft, and a puller (or arbor press) is required to remove it.

Remove the bearing lock or snap ring. Different types of snap rings are used on the various pump models but an examination of the pump will quickly reveal the ring. Support the pump body and press out the shaft (and bearing) and impeller.

Examine the sealing surface of the pump body for scores and nicks or corrosion. This surface must be smooth and free of pits and rust spots. If any exist the body must be refaced.

The impeller is usually pressed onto the shaft in the same manner as the fan hub.

Again note the position of the impeller before removing it in the press.

Cleanliness is essential on assembly to prevent foreign matter from getting on the sealing surfaces.

A very thin coating of good lubricant may be used on the seal but this is not essential.

THE ELECTRICAL SYSTEM

From the standpoint of service the electrical system can be divided into two broad groups.

First, the group of electrical units which have to do with the operation of the engine. That is, the battery, generator, starter, ignition system and relays. The second group is the accessories. That is, the lighting system, stop lights, cigar lighters, electrical instruments, radio, etc.

Again from the standpoint of service the first and most important thing to remember about all electrical servicing is that connections must be clean and tight. Copper is an excellent conductor of electricity, however the oxides of copper which form on exposed parts are not nearly as good conductors as the copper itself. Therefore in order to insure that each joint will have a minimum resistance, clean all connections until they are bright and make them up tight. This is particularly true when making ground connections.

The second thing to remember is that the ground on an automobile is simply a convenient way of connecting one side of the battery to all of the electrical units without using copper wire.

The Battery

The heart of an automotive electrical system is the battery. Except for periodic filling and checking the only service required is that the connections be kept clean and tight. The battery plates must be covered with fluid at all times. Pure water is used to maintain the level of the fluid in the battery.

Battery Test

Each cell of the battery may be tested individually with a hydrometer to determine the specific gravity of that cell. An hydrometer reading of 1.285 indicates a fully charged cell; 1.225 indicates the battery is about half discharge; 1.150 indicates a fully discharged battery. CAUTION: Battery hydrometers are calibrated at eighty degrees Fahrenheit and if the temperature of the battery fluid is other than eighty degrees it will be necesary to add to the reading two points for each five degrees above eighty or subtract two points for each five degrees below eighty.

An ordinary thermometer may be used to determine the temperature of the battery fluid.

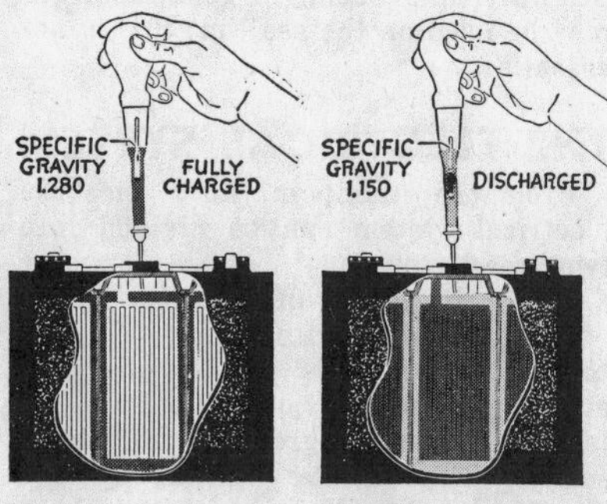

Fully charged *Discharged*

To complete the periodic service of the battery both terminals should be disconnected and thoroughly cleaned so that they are bright on the contact area to insure a good clean tight joint.

Note: Never use a battery cable which is smaller than the cable recommended by the car manufacturer. If the exact size recommended by the car manufacturer is not available, then use a heavier cable. It is better to err on the side of bigness in the case of battery leads.

THE GENERATOR

The purpose of the generator is to maintain the battery at full charge and also to provide current for the lights and other accessories.

In American passenger cars there are two broad types of generators. The two-brush generator with outside regulation, and the third brush controlled generator. Generators require very little preventive maintenance and they have been known to operate for years without any maintenance other than lubrication.

Generator Tests Without the Use of Instruments

Two-brush type generators with separate regulation are designed so that they will deliver maximum safe output at any time the battery is less than full charge. However, as the battery approaches full charge the regulator causes the generator output to reduce a sufficient amount to just maintain the battery at full charge.

A quick test may be made, using the car ammeter, by cranking the engine with the starter to discharge the battery somewhat and then starting the engine to see if the output is at maximum after having discharged the battery slightly. If under this condition the generator shows full charge which gradually diminishes as the battery comes up to full charge (this won't take more than five minutes) then the generator and regulator may safely be assumed to be in good condition.

If the generator output remains low after discharging the battery somewhat then a wire jumper should be attached between the field terminal of the generator (attach it either at the generator or at the regulator) to ground. If this does not cause the output to increase then the generator should be serviced. If the output does increase when the field terminal is grounded then the regulator is either badly adjusted or ineffective. Accompanying this text are trouble shooting charts (page 36) showing the step by step procedure required to shoot trouble on generators.

When using these charts bear in mind that all connections in the charging circuit must be clean and tight.

Three Brush Generators

The output of a three-brush generator is controlled by the position of the third brush relative to the insulated main brush. As the third brush is shifted in a direction which will bring it closer to the insulated main brush the output should increase. Moving it in the opposite direction will decrease the output.

Maximum safe output for all production generators is given in car section specifications. Bear in mind that the figures given in the specifications are a maximum safe output for that generator and should never be exceeded.

REGULATORS

Voltage Regulators

Voltage regulators consist of one or two coils used in conjunction with the cutout relay to limit the output of the generator when the voltage in the charging circuit reaches a predetermined safe maximum. Voltage regulators protect the battery from overcharging.

Current Regulators

Current regulators consist of one or two coils used in conjunction with a cutout relay and voltage regulator. The function of the current regulator is to hold the generator to a maximum safe output. Current regulators protect the generator from overload. Voltage regulators are sometimes used by themselves, current regulators are always used in conjunction with voltage regulators.

Test Sets

Electrical test sets are available which are designed to make quick accurate tests of the entire electrical circuit.

Since each manufacturer of this type of equipment has his own particular routine. The instructions which come with the test set should be followed.

Some test sets are designed to function with a fixed resistor while others are intended to be used with a variable resistor therefore when using standard test sets carefully follow the instructions of the manufacturer.

Service on Regulators

When trouble is definitely placed in the regulator proceed as follows: Remove the regulator cover (Auto Lite covers are sealed on) and examine the contact points for pits and burns. Voltage and current contact points are the ones which are closed; cutout relay points are the ones open when the generator is not turning. Thoroughly clean the regulator and relay points.

Note: If points are too badly pitted the unit will have to be replaced.

Now check the regulator armature air gap: See working specifications. The gap should be adjusted to the specified clearance with the armature depressed until the points just barely touch. Adjust by moving the stationary points up or down. Depress the armature down to its stop and check the contact point gap.

Adjust the regulator so that both the air gap and the point gap are according to the specifications given in the car section.

When points are cleaned and gaps properly set the regulator can be set up electrically by attaching it to the electrical test set according to the instructions of the manufacturer of the test set.

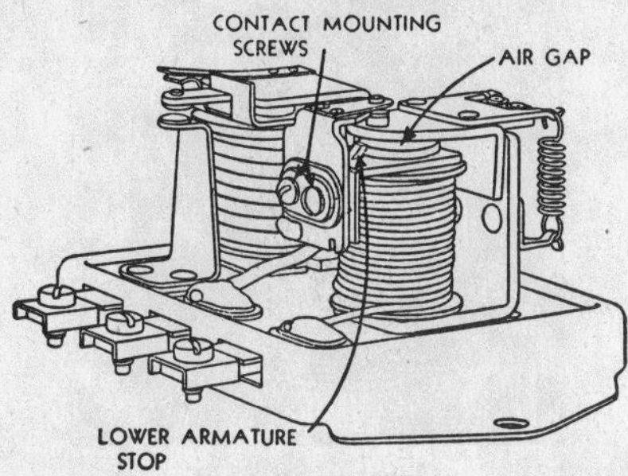

Fig. 17. Regulator air gap adjustment (Delco-Remy)

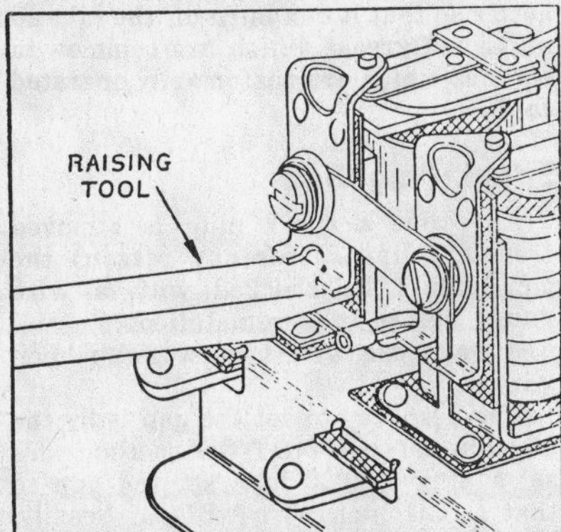

Fig. 18. Auto-Lite—Adjusting air gap

Replacing Regulator

Some of the early regulators had four, some had five, binding posts but the new replacement regulators have only three binding posts.

Packed with the new regulators are complete instructions how to attach the wires from the five binding posts on the old regulator to the three binding posts on the new one.

THE STARTER

The starting motor is simply a small motor designed to operate at low voltage with very high current. It differs from most direct current electric motors in that it has a few turns of very heavy wire on both the field coils and the armature coils. Since some starters draw as high as 500 amperes when cranking an engine it follows that the connections must be very clean and very tight; the brushes must seat firmly on the commutator and the commutator and brush rigging must be clean and free of oil.

Trouble Shooting on Starter

Except for possibly once a year cleaning, the starter requires no actual service whatever. Most starter troubles can be traced to either the wiring of the starter or to the starter switch. Except for the replacement of starter brushes it is customary to replace either the armature or the entire starter if trouble developes.

When trouble is suspected in the starter begin the checks by assuming that the starter itself is in good operating condition and look for trouble in the battery, battery cables, connections, starter switch, or the starter switch connections.

If all of these are found to be in good condition then examine the brushes for freedom of motion and good contact; thoroughly clean the commutator and check the starter bearings. If trouble persists remove the starter from the car, disconnect the drive mechanism and make exactly the same tests as are given in the chart for the generator.

THE IGNITION SYSTEM

The ignition system has always been the happy hunting ground for trouble shooters. However, if the ignition system is checked following a definite routine, difficulties can be discovered and corrected with very little waste of time.

Trouble Shooting Procedure (The Ignition System)

First determine that all of the connections in the ignition circuit are clean and tight. This includes the connection at the ignition switch, the ammeter, the coil and distributor. Next examine the breaker points for pits and burns. If the contact points are not clean and bright they should be replaced since the cost of a set of breaker points is so little that it does not pay to reface them.

Breaker Points

Install the new points and tentatively set the gap, either with a gauge or on a cam angle meter, square up the points so that they touch over the entire contact surface.

This should be accomplished by bending either the arm, the point or both. New points which do not make firm even contact over the entire surface are probably not as good as the worn set which was removed.

A quick way to square up the points is to align them by bending the point, then turn the motor until the points close. Now, using a pair of thin pliers, squeeze the points together. This tends to bend the arm until the contact surfaces touch all over.

If any "spring back" is noticed when releasing the pressure on the pliers, get hold again and very slightly twist the pliers which will tend to "Set" the points.

When good contact has been made, finish setting the point gap (or cam angle). While the distributor cap is off examine it very carefully for cracks or blemishes. If there is the slightest crack or blemish in the distributor cap it should be replaced.

The condenser can be checked on most of the modern test sets, but a very quick check can be made by disconnecting the condenser on the car and reconnecting with one which is known to be in good working order. It is not necessary to connect the test condenser inside of the distributor in a manner in which the old one may be connected.

When making a leak or capacitance test follow very carefully the instructions supplied by the manufacturer of your test equipment.

Carefully examine the ignition wires particularly if they pass into a harness or through a metal strap. The insulation on the ignition wires should be firm and unbroken. Softness in the insulation can be detected readily by wiping the accumulated dirt off with a rag wrapped firmly around the wire. If the rag does not slide freely, the insulation is becoming useless. While the distributor cap is off, make a quick "off the cuff" test of the centrifugal advance mechanism by twisting the distributor cam shaft (in the direction of the rotation) to determine if the springs on the advance weights will pull the cam back after it has been advanced by hand.

Note: Maximum centrifugal advance is given in degrees in the car section of this manual.

While this test is by no means an accurate check, it is intended to show only that the centrifugal advance mechanism is free to advance and retard without binding or sticking.

Exact tests should be made on an oscillograph or distributor tester.

While twisting the cam to quick check the advance mechanism also push it sideways to check the condition in the distributor housing.

Very little side play should be felt in spite of the fact that the cam will move an amount equal to the shaft wear plus the wear between the shaft and cam.

Bear in mind that the breaker point gap can (and probably will) vary the full amount of the shaft side play. Thus .010 inch side play with point gap set to .015 inch will probably result in a point gap which varies between .005 inch and .025 inch. No engine will function well with such a condition.

If side play is noticed, the distributor should be removed and rebuilt.

The inside of the distributor body should be clean and free of grease or oil. A passable cleaning job can be done on the car by brushing cleaning fluid around inside the housing and blowing out the dirt and fluid with compressed air.

Vacuum Advance Unit

Two types of vacuum advance units are in common use:

First, the type which turns the distributor body and can be observed to function when the engine is running and second, the type which turns the breaker plate inside the distributor. When making spot checks remember that the vacuum take off in the carburetor (which is connected to the vacuum advance unit on the distributor) is situated above the throttle valve so that the distributor is RETARDED when the engine is running at curb idle.

As the throttle is opened, manifold vacuum is applied to the distributor advance unit causing it to advance the distributor exactly in proportion to the amount of vacuum in the manifold, so that, at part throttle, the distributor will advance under light or no loads, but will return to its initial setting under heavy loads.

On units which turn the distributor body the following quick check may be made:

Idle the engine and observe the distributor. Snap the throttle open and the distributor should advance a considerable amount and then immediately drop back somewhat. The reason being that, as the throttle is snapped open high manifold vacuum (from idle) is momentarily applied to the advance mechanism causing it to advance almost its full amount. As the engine tries to pick up speed the manifold vacuum drops off somewhat causing the vacuum unit to drop back. This same test can be made on units which operate the breaker plate inside the distributor by attaching a timing light and observing the advance action at the damper (or flywheel). When making this test with a timing light keep in mind that the centrifugal mechanism (inside the distributor) will advance the spark in direct proportion to the speed.

When checking advance mechanism keep this in mind:

The vacuum unit advances the distributor according to the (load) manifold vacuum (except at idle) regardless of the speed.

The centrifugal unit advances the spark in proportion to the speed, regardless of the load, or manifold vacuum.

Accurate testing of distributor can be done on distributor test instruments only and the instrument manufacturer's instructions should be followed carefully.

SPARK PLUGS

Spark plugs are installed in a cylinder to provide an air gap for the ignition current to jump across, igniting the fuel in the combustion chamber.

Spark plugs are made so that they not only provide such a gap, they also provide ample insulation for the high voltage spark and, when correctly selected, will maintain themselves at the proper operating temperature.

Heat Range

Heat range in a spark plug is just as important as a thermostat in a cooling system. All plug manufacturers supply at least two (usually three) different heat ranges for each make of engine.

They usually supply hotter than normal; normal; colder than normal and, while normal is always a safe bet, the mechanic should first determine, from the owner, how the car is driven before installing new plugs.

Note: A spark plug chart, giving the recommended normal plug for all makes and also the full heat range is given in this manual, see index.

If a car is driven on long trips at sustained high speeds, a plug, colder than normal, should be recommended. Such a car would have high combustion chamber temperatures and the colder plug would probably function both longer and better.

On the other hand, if the car is used mostly on short runs with frequent stops, a hotter than normal plug should be used to prevent fouling.

The colder plug is intended to run cooler in "Hot" engines and not overheat and possibly crack.

The normal plug should be used when the car has normal use. Under normal circumstances it will be cool enough not to overheat and crack which at the same time it will be hot enough to burn off any oil or condensed fuel which may get on it.

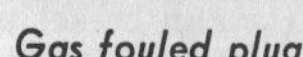

Gas fouled plug

Oil fouled plug

Overheated plug

The hotter plug is intended to run hotter so that it can burn off the oil and unburned grease which are common in engines which are customarily operated cold.

Spark Plug Gap

Any time a spark plug is removed from a cylinder (for any reason) the gap should be checked with a wire gauge before it is reinstalled.

Always use wire gauges not ribbon gauges.

The best way to set the gap is by the machinists GO—NOT-GO method: To set a plug to .025 inch set the gap so that a .024 inch wire will pass easily, but a .026 inch wire will not pass at all. By this method the gap will be greater than .024 inch but less than .026 inch or as near to .025 as is practical.

WIRE HARNESS

Wire harness serves a double purpose. First it permits, in addition to the insulation on each wire, wrapping the entire group of wires with a tough outer shell, adding further insulation and also preventing the individual wires from chafing and rubbing. Second, it provides an easy practical way to carry the wires as a continuous group to their various connections.

The tough outer wrapping on a wire harness will resist abrading, water, dirt and oil for a surprising long time.

Abrasions can be held to a minimum if the harness is securely mounted in its grommets. Loosely mounted wire harness will rub and chafe and eventually wear through the combined insulation, resulting in a short circuit and possible damage to the battery and may even result in fire.

Water and road dirt will eventually rot the harness even where they are shielded from the elements by the metal part of the body and frame.

Oil is probably the worst enemy of electrical insulation since it can cause the insulation on the individual wires within the harness to soften and become useless without doing serious damage to the outer harness wrapper.

Where it is impractical to prevent oil from getting on the wires it is good practice to serve the wire or harness with a good oil resisting tape in order to prevent the oil from ruining the insulation.

When taping up oily wires, always start back far enough so that the tape is first placed on a dry part of the wire and served on (lapping the tape carefully) towards the oily section. If the oil condition is widespread it is considered good practice to tape up all the wires in the engine (or transmission) compartment.

Where wires are dried out their useful life can be extended by taping up the entire harness. Where the insulation has broken (or rotted) off close to the wire terminal such as at the generator, oil pressure gauge or starter solenoid connections, remove the wire terminal, scrape off the rotted insulation and slide the bare wire into a piece of flexible "spaghetti tubing" sufficiently long to protect the wire up to where the insulation is good Replace the terminal and secure the tubing with electrical tape.

Head and Tail Lamps

The brightness of the driving lights are, in most States, governed by the Motor Vehicle laws. It is necessary to be fully conversant with state requirements in your particular state before adjusting or aiming headlamps.

Dim or inefficient headlamps are caused by low voltage at the lamps. The low voltage may be from a discharged battery, generator output not high enough, wire size too small, or high resistance in the headlamp circuit.

The cures for the first two causes are self evident—charge the battery or increase generator output.

Where wire sizes are too small, a relay switch, placed as close as practical to the lamps, and feed from the relay or regulator connection with heavy wire will usually solve the trouble without the work and expense of rewiring with larger wire.

When using headlamp relays, keep in mind that the relay does NOT "Step Up" the current. On the contrary it is simply an electrically operated switch which can be placed close to the lamps. Most relay manufacturers insist that heavy gauge wire be used in addition to the relay. Instructions for the installation of headlamp relays are contained in the package and must be followed exactly.

Short Circuits

Short circuits occur when a bare wire carrying current comes in contact with any grounded metal portion of the car or with another bare wire which is connected to ground or one of the accessories.

Shorts can be very difficult to trace and it is best to isolate as much as possible, the location of the short by disconnecting suspected circuits one at a time until the short is located.

The following is a brief list of conditions and the possible location of the short:

Short Circuit	Location
Upper headlights only turned on	Upper headlamp wires probably where they pass thru the frame or fenders.
Upper or Lower headlamp or parking lights turned on.	Probably in the tail or license lamp circuit.
No lights turned on all accessories turned off.	Generator relay stuck closed; Leaky stop light switch; Main lead from generator relay grounded; Dome light circuit; Accessory feed wire grounded.

In all cases of short circuits which exist when all accessories, lights and ignition are turned off, disconnect the battery to prevent the car from catching fire, and then examine all leads under the dash to try to find the wire which is hot, or which has soft sticky insulation indicating that it has been hot.

The sense of smell is a good indicator of shorted wires. Overheated insulation gives off a particularly offensive odor which frequently isolates the shorted wire to one particular part of the car.

When the short is located, either replace the wire or tape up the bare spots. If a new wire is run, replacing a shorted wire, be sure to cut off the old wire flush with the harness which carrys it, and carefully tape up the harness where the wire was cut off.

The most difficult type of short circuit to locate is the intermittent type, that is, a ground which jumps on and off as the car shakes.

It is sometimes necessary to rock the car and produce as nearly as possible the conditions under which the short is produced.

For instance, if a short is noticed when the car is making a left turn, then try to duplicate the position of the wheels and the position of the body and frame in relation to the road during a left turn in attempt to cause the defective wire to short with the car standing still.

Wiring Harness

PASSENGER CAR GENERATORS WITH REGULATORS

Illustrations for this chart are on the opposite page

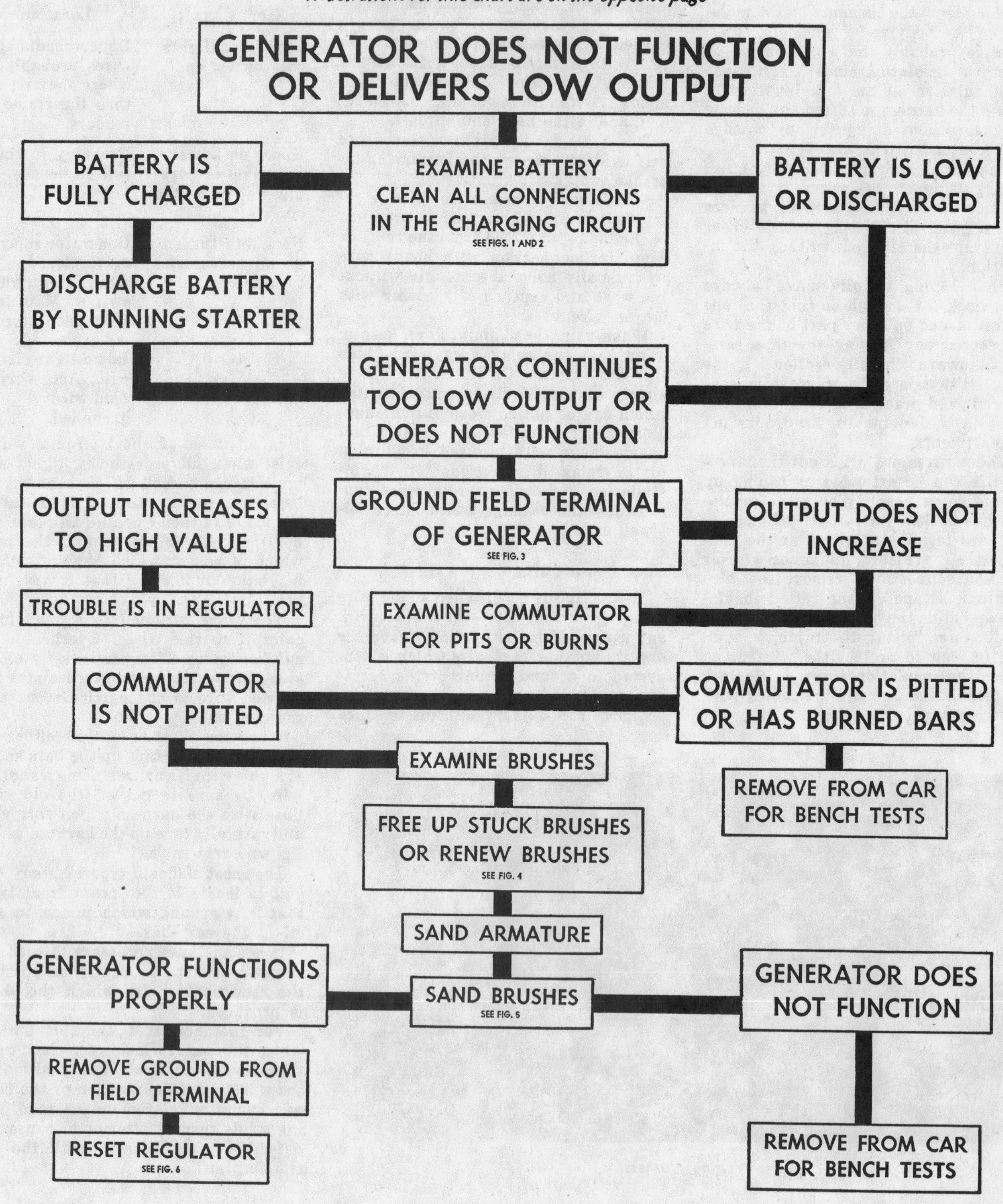
GENERATOR DOES NOT FUNCTION OR DELIVERS LOW OUTPUT
BATTERY IS FULLY CHARGED
EXAMINE BATTERY CLEAN ALL CONNECTIONS IN THE CHARGING CIRCUIT
SEE FIGS. 1 AND 2
BATTERY IS LOW OR DISCHARGED
DISCHARGE BATTERY BY RUNNING STARTER
GENERATOR CONTINUES TOO LOW OUTPUT OR DOES NOT FUNCTION
OUTPUT INCREASES TO HIGH VALUE
GROUND FIELD TERMINAL OF GENERATOR
SEE FIG. 3
OUTPUT DOES NOT INCREASE
TROUBLE IS IN REGULATOR
EXAMINE COMMUTATOR FOR PITS OR BURNS
COMMUTATOR IS NOT PITTED
COMMUTATOR IS PITTED OR HAS BURNED BARS
EXAMINE BRUSHES
REMOVE FROM CAR FOR BENCH TESTS
FREE UP STUCK BRUSHES OR RENEW BRUSHES
SEE FIG. 4
SAND ARMATURE
GENERATOR FUNCTIONS PROPERLY
SAND BRUSHES
SEE FIG. 5
GENERATOR DOES NOT FUNCTION
REMOVE GROUND FROM FIELD TERMINAL
RESET REGULATOR
SEE FIG. 6
REMOVE FROM CAR FOR BENCH TESTS

Illustrations on this page apply to chart opposite on page 36

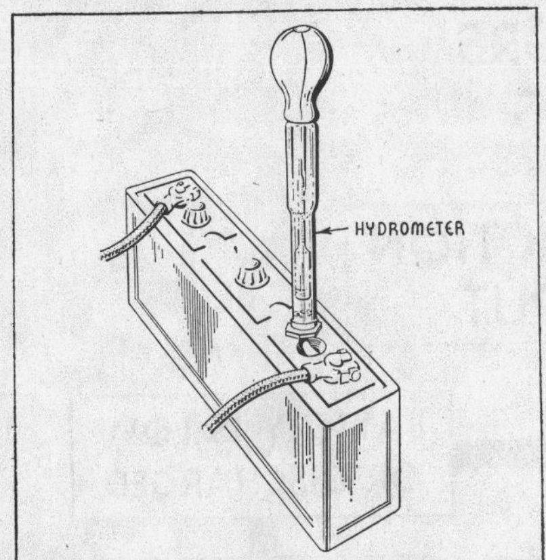

Fig. 1. Test battery with a hydrometer

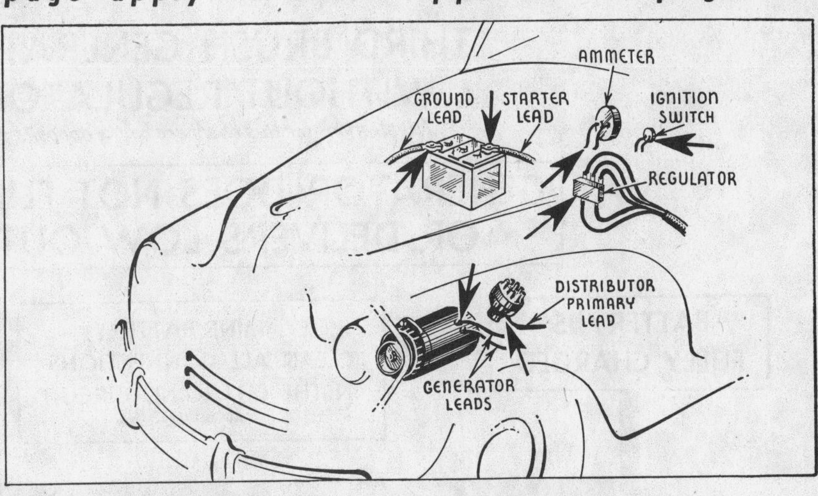

Fig. 2. The connection shown in above sketch should be clean and tight

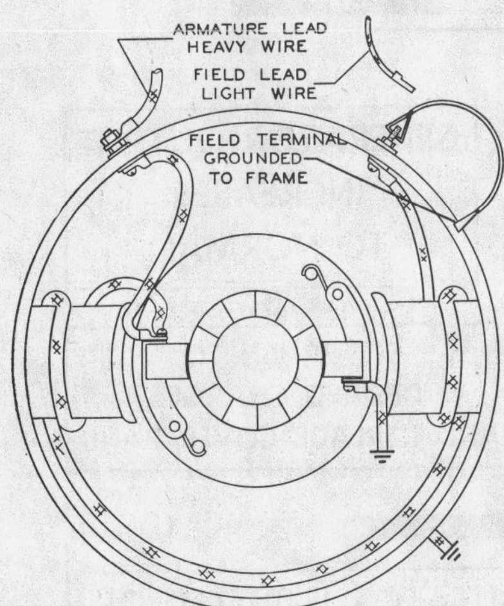

Fig. 3. Ground field lead

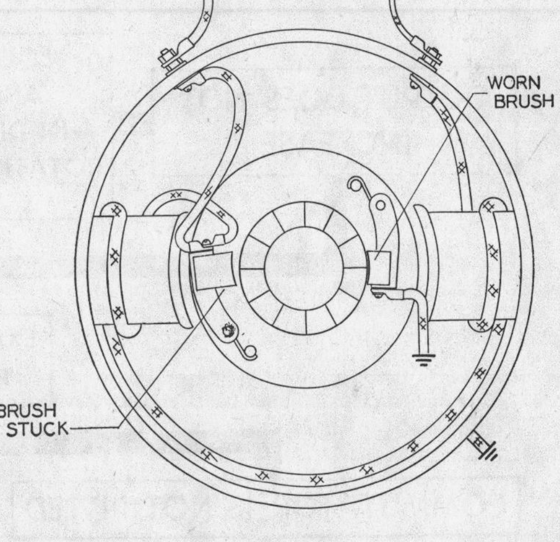

Fig. 4. Make sure brushes are free to make a firm contact

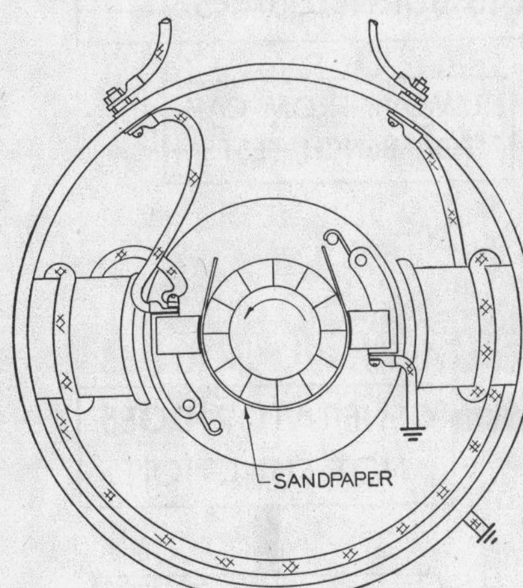

Fig. 5. Sand brushes to armature curvature as shown above

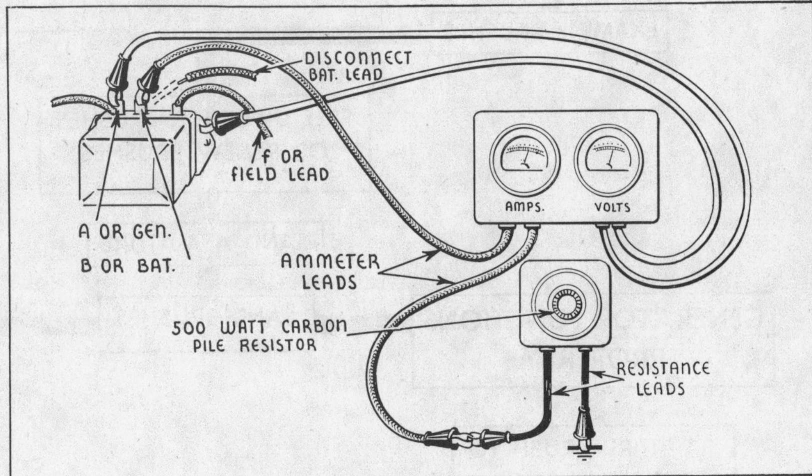

Fig. 6. Meter hook-up to set regulator

THIRD BRUSH GENERATORS WITHOUT REGULATORS

Illustrations for this chart are on the opposite page

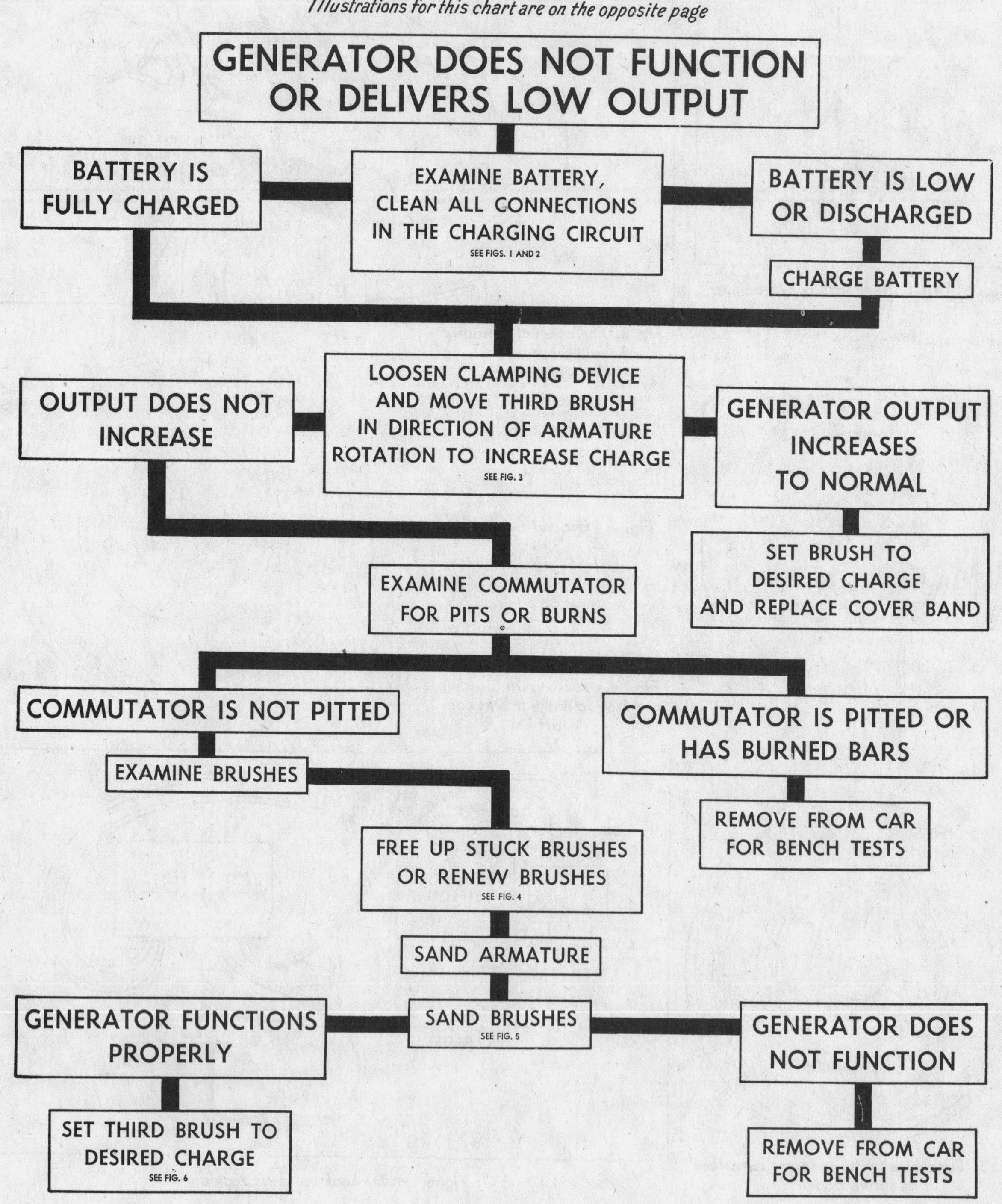
GENERATOR DOES NOT FUNCTION OR DELIVERS LOW OUTPUT
BATTERY IS FULLY CHARGED
EXAMINE BATTERY, CLEAN ALL CONNECTIONS IN THE CHARGING CIRCUIT
SEE FIGS. 1 AND 2
BATTERY IS LOW OR DISCHARGED
CHARGE BATTERY
OUTPUT DOES NOT INCREASE
LOOSEN CLAMPING DEVICE AND MOVE THIRD BRUSH IN DIRECTION OF ARMATURE ROTATION TO INCREASE CHARGE
SEE FIG. 3
GENERATOR OUTPUT INCREASES TO NORMAL
SET BRUSH TO DESIRED CHARGE AND REPLACE COVER BAND
EXAMINE COMMUTATOR FOR PITS OR BURNS
COMMUTATOR IS NOT PITTED
COMMUTATOR IS PITTED OR HAS BURNED BARS
EXAMINE BRUSHES
REMOVE FROM CAR FOR BENCH TESTS
FREE UP STUCK BRUSHES OR RENEW BRUSHES
SEE FIG. 4
SAND ARMATURE
GENERATOR FUNCTIONS PROPERLY
SAND BRUSHES
SEE FIG. 5
GENERATOR DOES NOT FUNCTION
SET THIRD BRUSH TO DESIRED CHARGE
SEE FIG. 6
REMOVE FROM CAR FOR BENCH TESTS

AND TROUBLE SHOOTING GENERATOR TEST CHARTS

Illustrations on this page apply to chart opposite

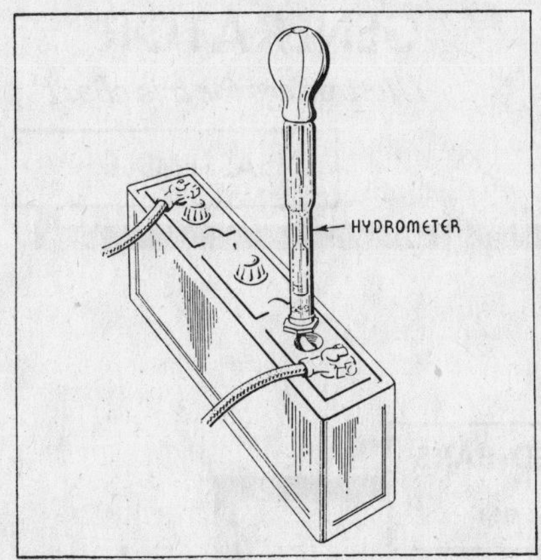

Fig. 1. Check battery with a hydrometer

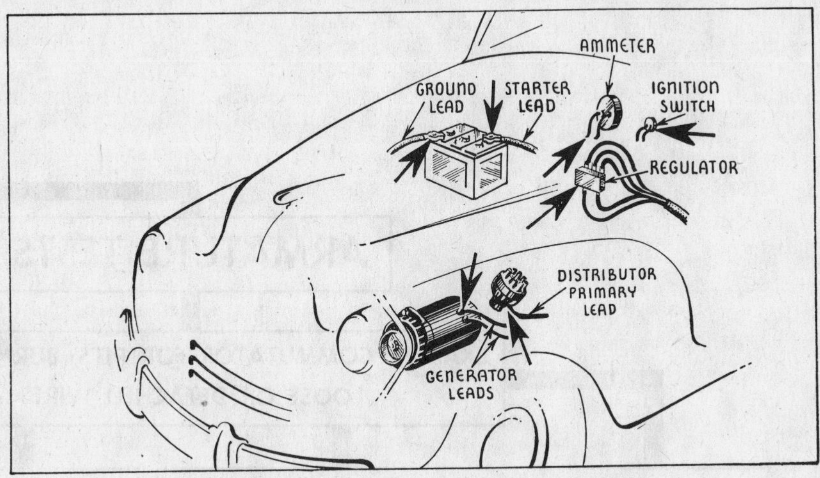

Fig. 2. The connections indicated should be clean & tight

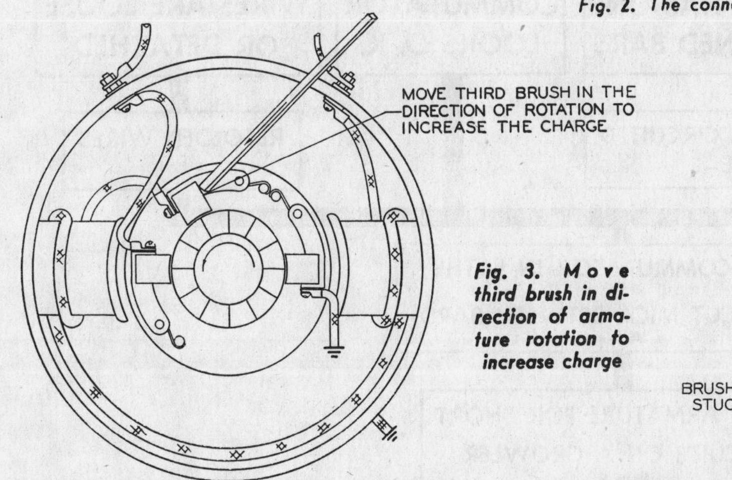

Fig. 3. Move third brush in direction of armature rotation to increase charge

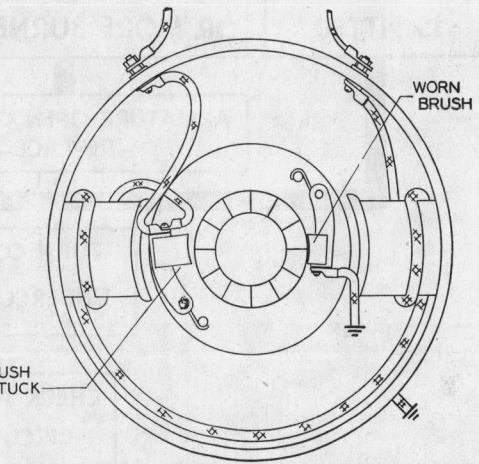

Fig. 4. Make sure brushes (or holders) are free to make firm contact

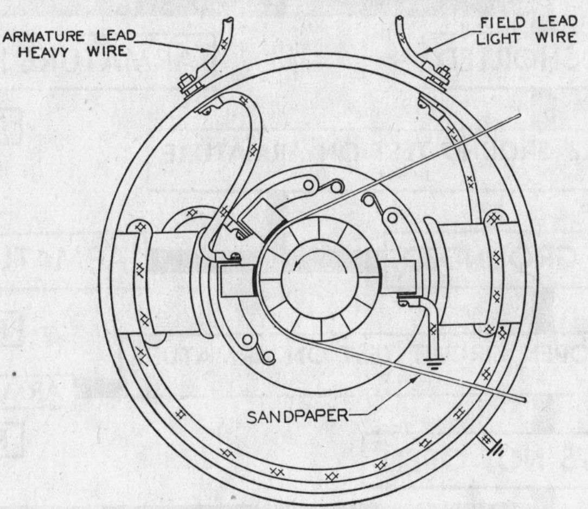

Fig. 5. Sand brushes in the manner shown above

GENERAL SERVICE

GENERATOR

Illustrations for this chart

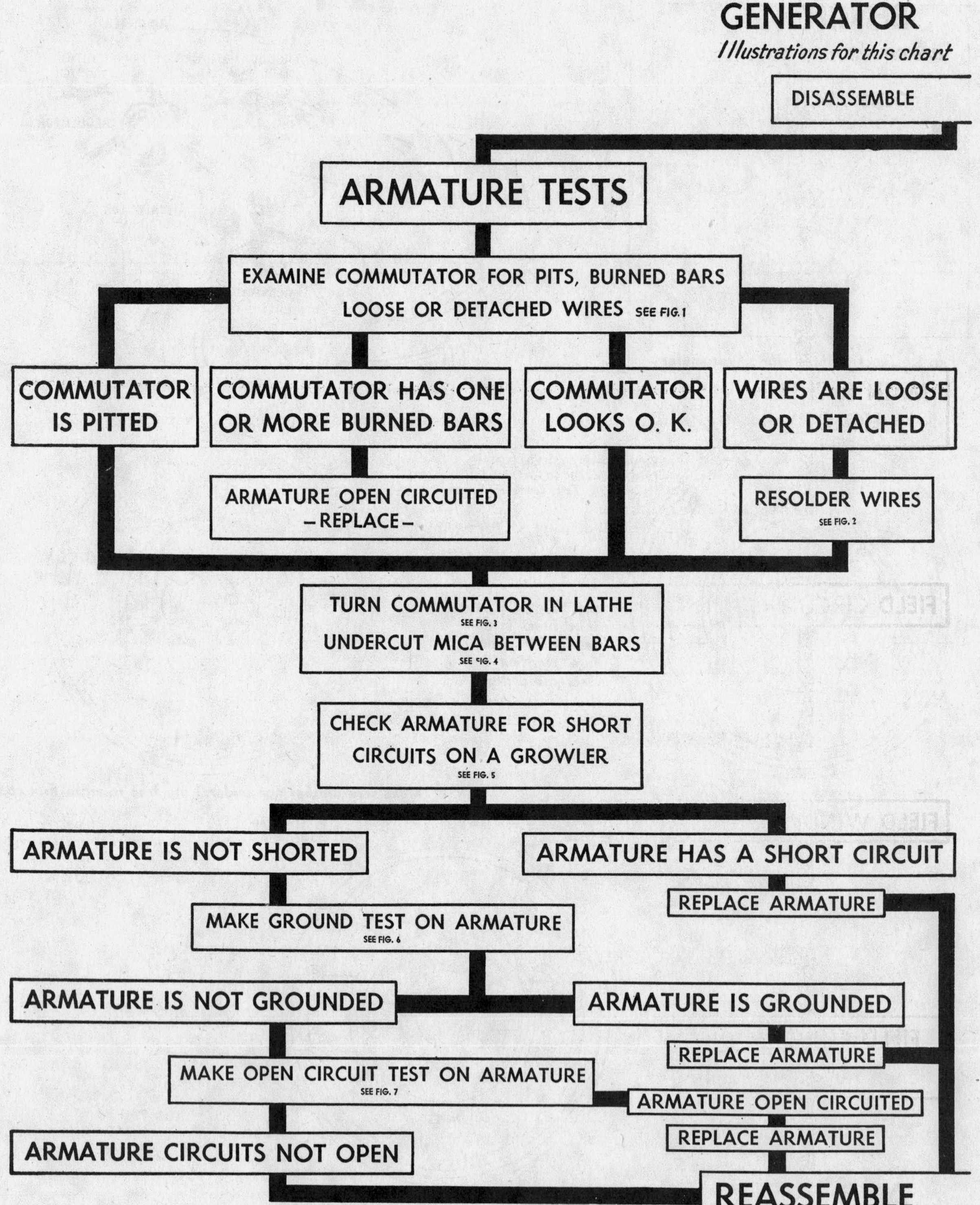
DISASSEMBLE
ARMATURE TESTS
EXAMINE COMMUTATOR FOR PITS, BURNED BARS
LOOSE OR DETACHED WIRES SEE FIG. 1
COMMUTATOR IS PITTED
COMMUTATOR HAS ONE OR MORE BURNED BARS
COMMUTATOR LOOKS O. K.
WIRES ARE LOOSE OR DETACHED
ARMATURE OPEN CIRCUITED
– REPLACE –
RESOLDER WIRES
SEE FIG. 2
TURN COMMUTATOR IN LATHE
SEE FIG. 3
UNDERCUT MICA BETWEEN BARS
SEE FIG. 4
CHECK ARMATURE FOR SHORT CIRCUITS ON A GROWLER
SEE FIG. 5
ARMATURE IS NOT SHORTED
ARMATURE HAS A SHORT CIRCUIT
REPLACE ARMATURE
MAKE GROUND TEST ON ARMATURE
SEE FIG. 6
ARMATURE IS NOT GROUNDED
ARMATURE IS GROUNDED
REPLACE ARMATURE
MAKE OPEN CIRCUIT TEST ON ARMATURE
SEE FIG. 7
ARMATURE OPEN CIRCUITED
REPLACE ARMATURE
ARMATURE CIRCUITS NOT OPEN
REASSEMBLE

BENCH TESTS
are on the next two pages

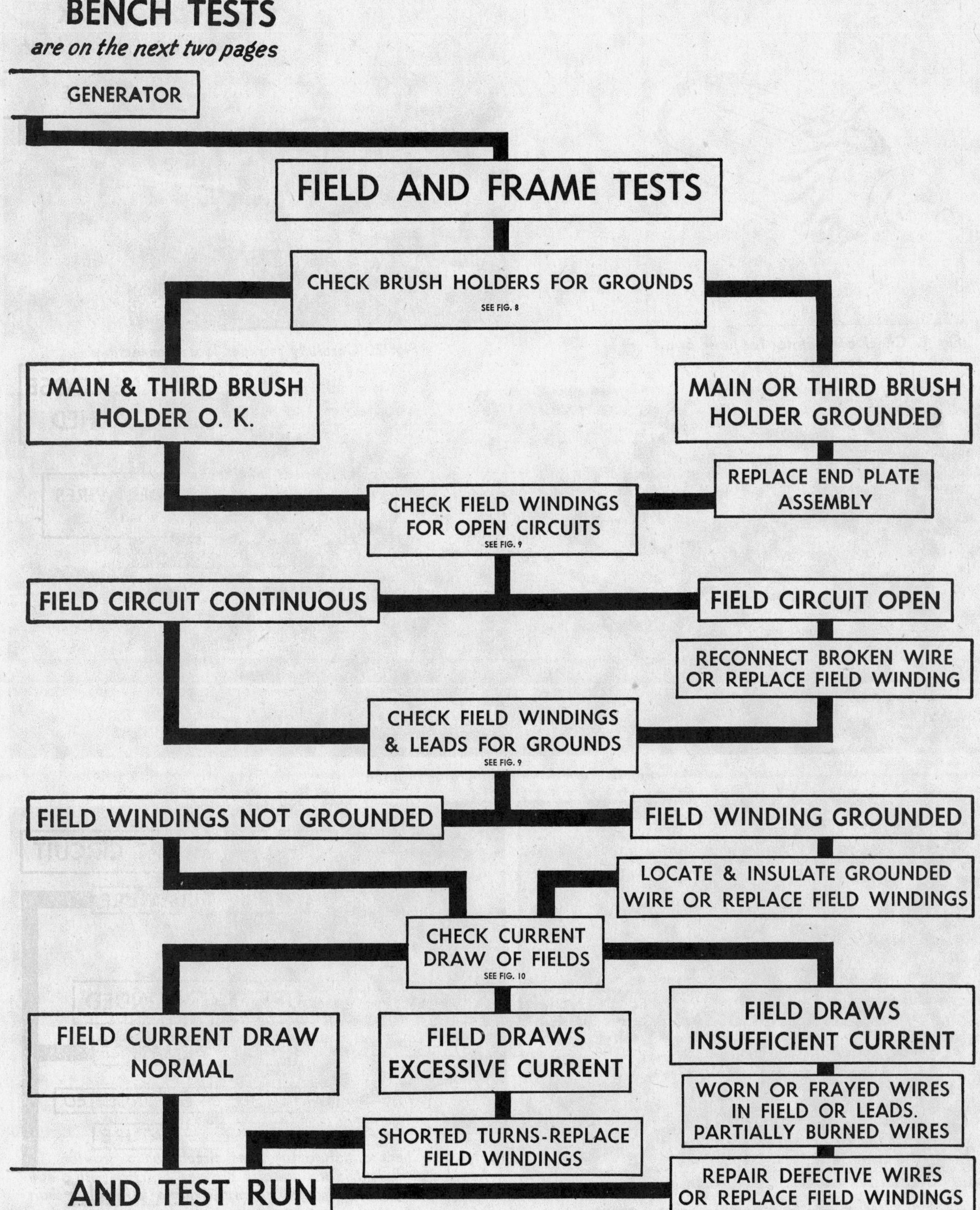
GENERATOR
FIELD AND FRAME TESTS
CHECK BRUSH HOLDERS FOR GROUNDS
SEE FIG. 8
MAIN & THIRD BRUSH HOLDER O. K.
MAIN OR THIRD BRUSH HOLDER GROUNDED
REPLACE END PLATE ASSEMBLY
CHECK FIELD WINDINGS FOR OPEN CIRCUITS
SEE FIG. 9
FIELD CIRCUIT CONTINUOUS
FIELD CIRCUIT OPEN
RECONNECT BROKEN WIRE OR REPLACE FIELD WINDING
CHECK FIELD WINDINGS & LEADS FOR GROUNDS
SEE FIG. 9
FIELD WINDINGS NOT GROUNDED
FIELD WINDING GROUNDED
LOCATE & INSULATE GROUNDED WIRE OR REPLACE FIELD WINDINGS
CHECK CURRENT DRAW OF FIELDS
SEE FIG. 10
FIELD CURRENT DRAW NORMAL
FIELD DRAWS EXCESSIVE CURRENT
FIELD DRAWS INSUFFICIENT CURRENT
WORN OR FRAYED WIRES IN FIELD OR LEADS. PARTIALLY BURNED WIRES
SHORTED TURNS-REPLACE FIELD WINDINGS
REPAIR DEFECTIVE WIRES OR REPLACE FIELD WINDINGS
AND TEST RUN

Illustrations on this page apply to chart on pages 40-41

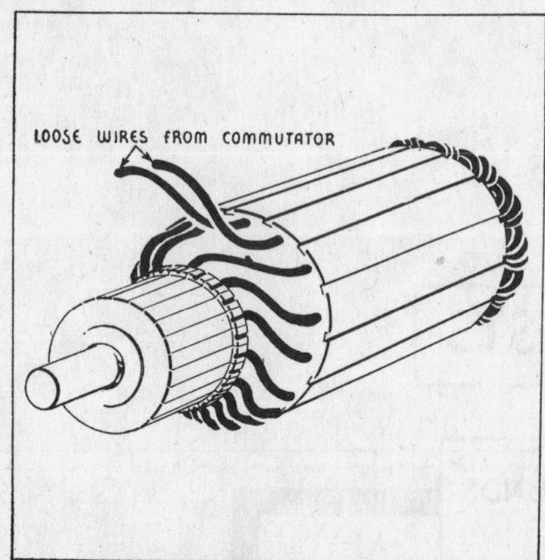

Fig. 1. Check commutator for loose or disconnected wires

Fig. 2. Carefully resolder loose connections

Fig. 3. Turn down commutator in lathe

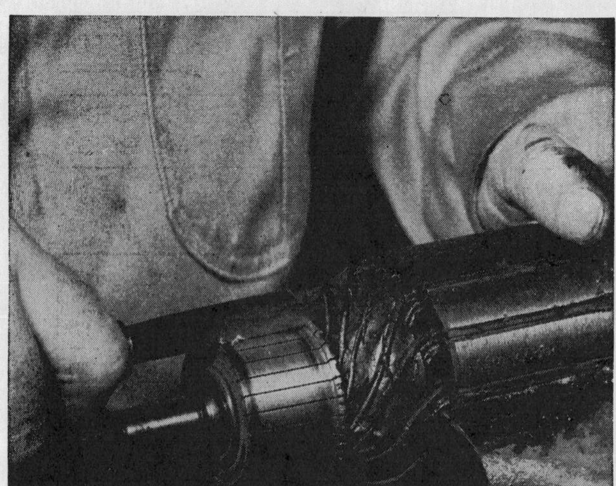

Fig. 4. Mica may be undercut as shown above

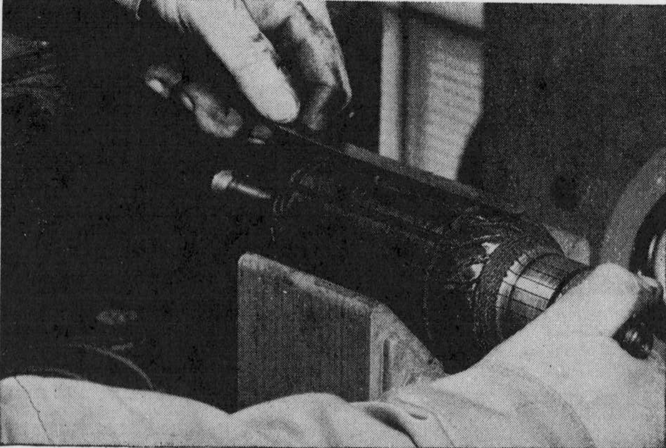

Fig. 5. Check armature for short circuits on a growler. To become proficient in the use of a growler, practice with a new armature and also with an armature known to have a short circuit

Illustrations on this page apply to chart on pages 40-41

Fig. 6. Armature ground test. Lamp will light if armature is grounded

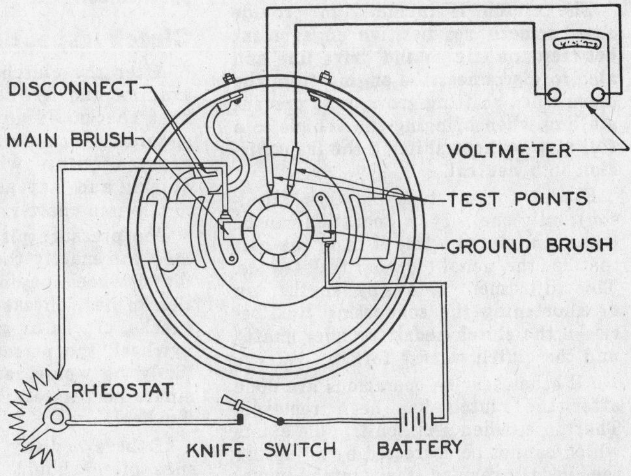

Fig. 7. Sketch showing armature open circuit test. Rotate slowly and, if an open circuit exists, the meter will show full battery voltage

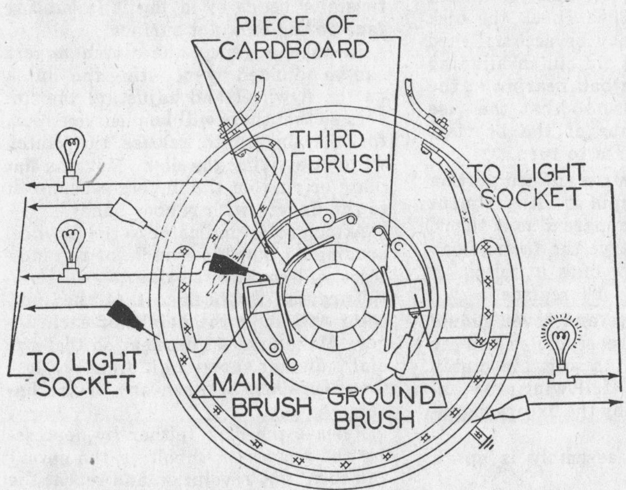

Fig. 8. Test brush holders for grounds. Lamp should light on ground brush only

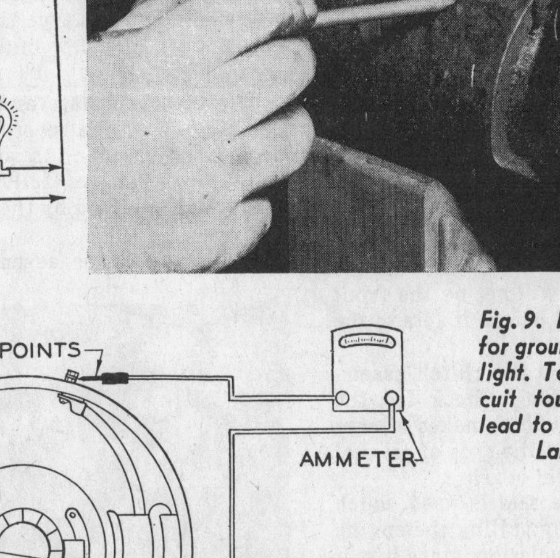

Fig. 9. Field test as shown is for grounds. Lamp should not light. To check for open circuit touch the right hand lead to the other field lead. Lamp should light

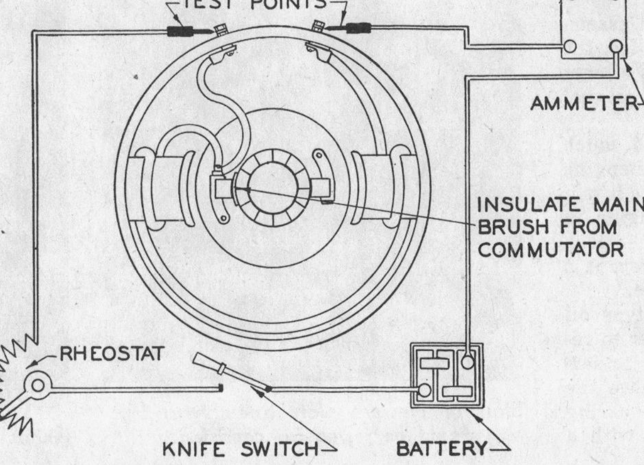

Fig. 10. Field current draw. Start with the resistance full ON so that, if the draw is excessive, ammeter will not be damaged

THE CLUTCH

The clutch is intended to provide easy, smooth yet positive engagement between the engine and drive line and also to disconnect the engine from the drive when shifting gears or to prevent stalling when bringing the vehicle to a full stop without shifting the transmission into neutral.

Except for oil type clutches (Hudson), only one service operation can be done to a clutch while it is in the car, that is, the pedal-toe board clearance. This adjustment is done by lengthening or shortening the connecting link between the clutch pedal (or idler shaft) and the clutch release fork.

All other service operations are done after the clutch has been removed. Therefore, when a clutch trouble exists which cannot be corrected by adjusting the pedal, remove the clutch immediately, without wasting time.

(The exceptions to this are the clutches which are designed to operate in oil. On oil type clutches adjust the pedal clearance and make certain the clutch is filled to the correct level with the proper grade of lubricant. If this does not cure the trouble, remove the clutch from the car.)

In all passenger cars it is necessary to remove either the transmission or the engine in order to remove the clutch. (On some cars the engine MUST be removed to service the clutch. See the instructions given for each car later in this section.)

Before starting to remove the transmission first take off the clutch inspection cover to see if there is any oil, which may have gotten past the rear main bearing oil seal, on the clutch. Pay particular attention to the FRONT face of the flywheel since oil from the rear main bearing will get on the front face of the flywheel before it gets to the clutch.

If oil is present in the clutch assembly or clutch housing, check (in the data given for individual makes of cars later in this section) the type of oil seal used at the rear main bearing.

If a packing type seal is used, much time can be saved by pulling the engine instead of the transmission, since it will be necessary to remove the engine in any case, in order to correct the leak at the rear main bearing to prevent a recurrence of the clutch trouble.

Where a slinger and drain type oil seal is used, it is probably better to remove the transmission in order to service the clutch. And then remove the engine oil pan, and rear main bearing cap, and clean out the slinger with a steam cleaner or with solvent and compressed air.

Clutch Inspection

After the clutch has been removed, examine the flywheel for grooves and heat checks. If any exist the flywheel should be removed and reground. A grooved flywheel will wear the new disk quickly and may also cause the clutch to slip and chatter.

The pressure plate should be examined for exactly the same condition as the flywheel, paying particular attention to heat checks and fine cracks. If checks, cracks or grooves exist on the flywheel, the pressure plate will most likely be worse, since it cannot dissipate heat as easily or quickly as the flywheel.

If there are any blemishes the pressure plate should be reground or replaced.

The disk should be examined for glaze and oil spots, and also for broken damper springs. Then check the disk for runout. This may be accomplished easily by mounting old clutch aligning shaft (fitted with a ball bearing at the large end) in a vise so that the vise holds the outer race of the bearing, leaving the shaft free to turn.

Mount the disk on the splined portion of the shaft, and spin it. Any runout in the disk will be apparent as it turns.

If the disk runs true the facings can be removed and new ones installed. A crooked disk should be replaced.

The pressure plate and cover should be taken apart and reassembled and the fingers adjusted on a suitable clutch rebuilding fixture, following the instructions supplied by the fixture manufacturer.

While the cover assembly is apart, each spring should be checked for pressure and free length. If any are found weak or short they should be replaced.

Start of pressure plate assembly springs should be tested for consistency

Cover being pulled into place on fixture

The clutch cover should be tested for twists or bends by laying it (mounting face down) on a flat surface.

In an emergency, the clutch fingers can be adjusted by mounting the clutch on the flywheel and adjusting the fingers so that there will be plenty of room for the fingers to release the clutch without striking the disk. Mount a flat plate or ring on the fingers securing it to the fingers with rubber bands.

Attach a dial indicator to the flywheel housing so that the spindle of the indicator will contact the ring.

Turn the flywheel so that the indicator will show the height of each finger. Make final adjustment so that the dial indicator shows a difference of less than .005 inch between any of the fingers.

Release the disk (either by depressing the fingers or unbolting the cover) and turn it ½ revolution and repeat the

Finger height checked with dial indicator

check with the dial indicator. This is done to compensate for variations in thickness of the clutch disk.

If the readings are different when the disk is moved relative to the pressure plate, the clutch fingers will have to be adjusted so that the total error in both positions is about equal (this will allow for the disk variation).

Checking release on fixture

Notes on Clutch Operations

The first thing to remember when doing clutch work is that grease, even in small quantities, on the clutch disk, pressure plate or flywheel face will almost invariably ruin a clutch job.

Clutches are so sensitive to grease and oil the disk should not be handled with dirty hands, because grease cannot be wiped off successfully even with solvent.

Pull the cover bolts down a little at a time in order to prevent springing the cover. Before the pilot is removed, depress the fingers in order to give the disk a chance to locate itself without straining on the pilot. This helps to make it somewhat easier to mount the transmission.

The clutch splined bore may be lubricated very lightly, just the slightest smear of grease. The disk should then be slid back and forth on the spline shaft in order to check for binding and to spread the lubricant over the entire spline surface.

Use grease sparingly on the pilot bearing and release bearing.

When assembling a clutch disc to an engine it is customary to use either the spline shaft taken from the transmission which will be mounted on the particular clutch or use a specially prepared clutch pilot tool. Before mounting a clutch on to a flywheel make absolutely certain that there are no burrs or nicks on the splined portion of the clutch hub since

Clutch disc flywheel side. Keep hands clean—careful of oil

Removing flywheel from crankshaft, using electric inertia wrench

Honing clutch pedal bushing

Regrinding flywheel

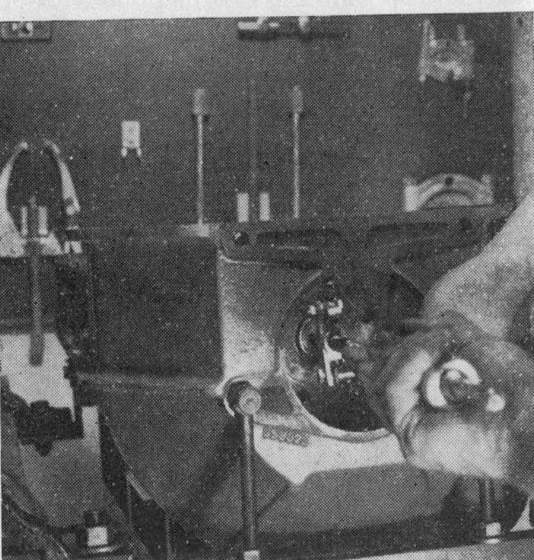

Removing clutch pilot bearing or bushing with inertia puller

a very small nick will prevent the splined shaft from entering when the transmission is being mounted.

Clutches which have a history of chatter should be examined very carefully to make certain that the damper springs or the damper spring rivets have not become loose or the springs lost their tension.

Where a clutch disc has been known to chatter it is sometimes a very good idea to install groove type facing in place of the solid facing which might have been used on the clutch.

Removing the rivets from clutch facings requires a special jig. The rivets should never be driven out with a punch as this will undoubtedly render the plate useless and in operation prevent the clutch from releasing.

TROUBLE SHOOTING ON TRANSMISSION

Noisy Transmission

Noises in the transmission may be caused by improper lubricant or by hard foreign matter such as chips, grit, etc., getting into the lubricant, however, this is by no means as common as worn shaft gears or poorly matched bearings. To isolate the noise to one part of the transmission proceed as follows: Set the transmission in neutral and run the engine with the clutch engaged from idle to very fast if the noise follows the engine speed it indicates a worn front bearing, worn countershaft or countershaft bearing, worn reverse idler gear or idler gear bearing or worn constant mesh second speed gear.

This test eliminates the rear bearing on the mainshaft and the low sliding gear since, with the car in neutral these parts are not moving.

Drive the car over the smoothest road possible to about 30 miles per hour, place the transmission in neutral and stop the engine, leave the clutch engaged with the car still rolling. Under this condition the only things turning are the mainshaft with its low gear and the mainshaft pocket bearing. CAUTION, it is well to examine the universal joint since a loose universal joint flange will permit excessive end play in the mainshaft which usually shows up in this test. If the noises follow both tests it is necessary to remove and disassemble completely, and examine all parts for wear or looseness. Noises in all gears and in all speeds are usually the countershaft cluster or countershaft bearings.

Noises in all gears except high usually indicates a worn pocket bearing at the back of the main drive pinion.

Noises in all gears except second usually indicate a bad constant mesh second gear bearing or a scored shaft where the bearing rides.

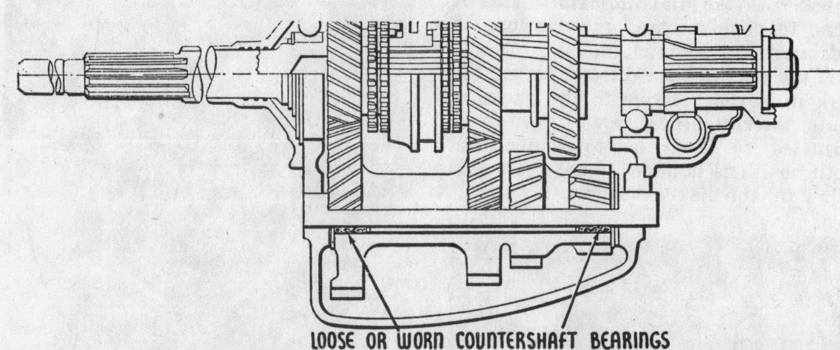

Worn countershaft bearings are usually noisy in all gears except high. Endplay in countershaft may cause jumping out of gear

A noise in any one gear usually indicates that that gear or its bearing is worn or has too much end play.

Frequently a noisy transmission results when a new gear is installed where it meshes with a worn gear or a new bearing is installed replacing a badly worn bearing. In the case of a new bearing this is due to the fact that the worn bearing permitted the shaft to move away from the meshing gear which caused the gear teeth to wear above the pitch diameter. The new bearing, holding the gear to rigid alignment forces it back to the pitch diameter. Fortunately noises of this nature usually disappear after a short while.

Jumping Out of Gear

A transmission jumping out of gear when pulling means that there is end play present in either the gears or shafts or in the universal joint yoke. Examine the transmission for broken lock rings badly worn gear seats loose universal joints worn or broken countershaft thrust washers or misalignment in the mounting of the transmission.

Before removing the transmission to correct for jumping out of gear make sure that the gears are meshing completely and that the shifter rails are not binding. Disconnect the shifter mechanism and move the transmission by hand to ascertain if the mechanism is completing the shift.

When a transmission jumps out of gear while the car is coasting, it almost always indicates misalignment either in the transmission itself or inside the transmission.

Jumping out of second gear is usually caused by a worn pocket bearing, a worn rear bearing, or worn second gear thrust washer which permits the mainshaft to misalign with the clutch shaft.

Jumping out of high gear is sometimes caused by a worn flywheel pilot, worn transmission front bearing, end play in the mainshaft, defective or weak synchronizers and end play in the countershaft.

A practical solution to jumping out of gear is to remove, disassembly the transmission, replace all three of the bearings,

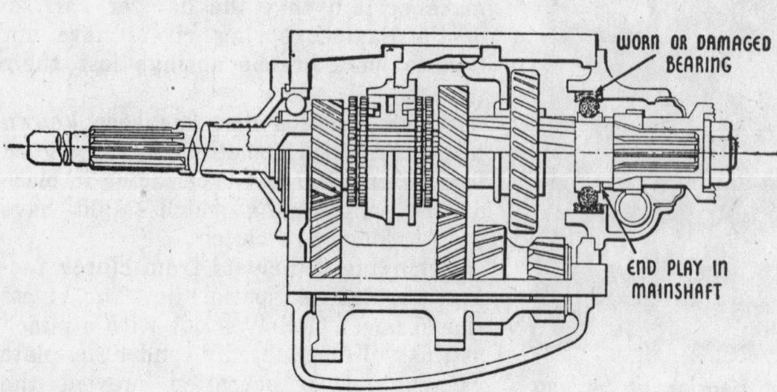

Worn or defective rear bearing makes the transmission noisy

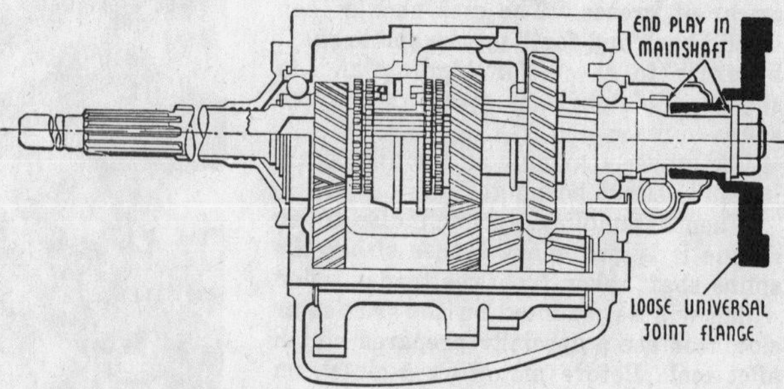

Loose universal joint flange shown above permits the mainshaft to move endwise. This may cause noise and jumping out of any gear

that is the main drive pinion bearing, the mainshaft rear bearing and the mainshaft pilot bearing, and also replace all lock rings and thrust washers. This will insure perfect alignment of gears and prevent end play in the shafts.

Hard Shifting

The most common cause of hard shifting is lack of or improper lubricant; if the gears are properly lubricated check for worn, bent or scored shifter rails or yokes also examine the detent balls in the synchronizer, since a stuck or jammed ball will bind the rail. Examine the shifter forks for scoring or scuff.

Hard shifting into second or high usually indicates a worn or defective synchronizer. Carefully check the shifter mechanism for wear looseness or binding and make sure it is in proper adjustment, make sure a vacuum assister, if one is used, is adjusted properly.

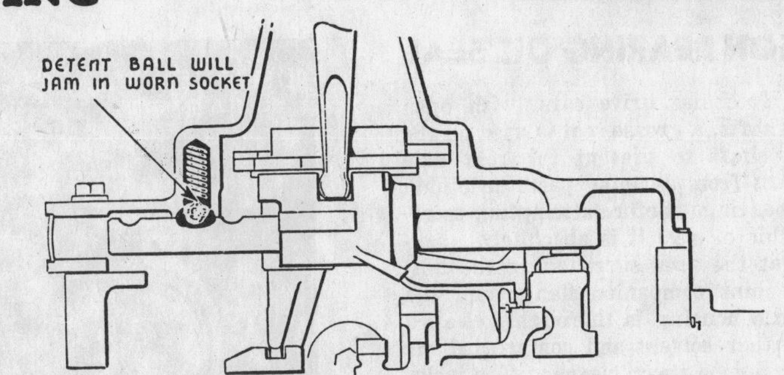

Detent balls which have worn or broken the socket in which they ride will cause hard shifting or even shift failure

DRIVE LINE

HOTCHKISS DRIVE

The Hotchkiss drive consists of an "open" drive shaft, having a universal joint at both front and rear end. In this construction all of the thrust and torque (both braking and drive) from the rear axle is absorbed by the springs.

No adjustments are provided at either of the universal joints and, except for lubrication, and the replacement of grease boots no preventative service is required.

The removal and disassembly of universal joints and drive shafts varies with each make of car, and is, therefore, covered in the portion of this section devoted to individual makes. See index.

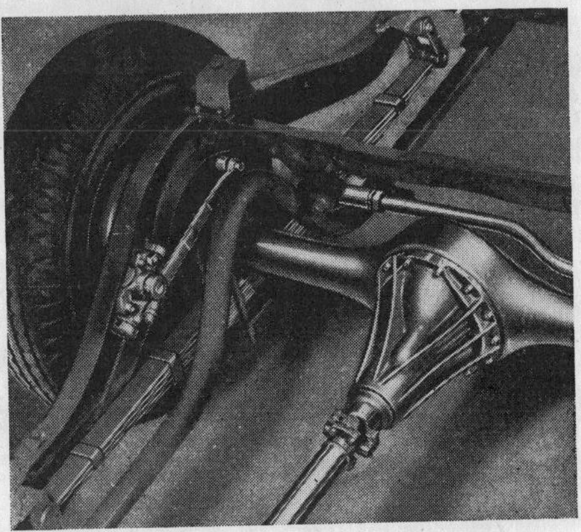

Hotchkiss drive

TORQUE TUBE DRIVE

The torque tube drive differs from the Hotchkiss drive in that the drive shaft is contained in a tube and the thrust and torque from the rear axle is taken by the tube. Service on torque tubes varies with each make and is covered in the car section.

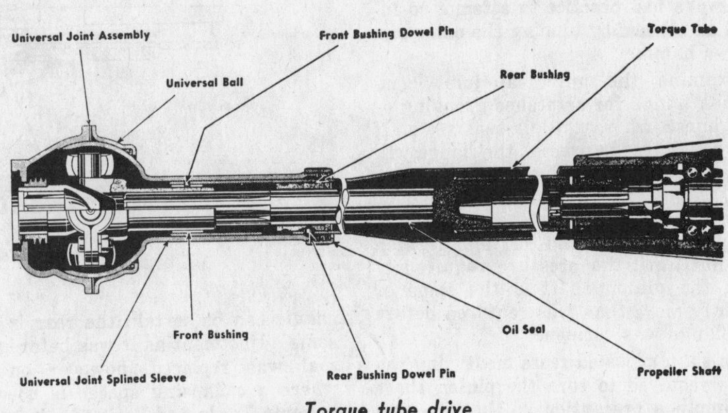

Torque tube drive

REAR AXLES

The most common operation performed on a rear axle, except for lubrication, is the replacement of grease seals.

PINION BEARING OIL SEAL

On Hotchkiss drive cars, with open drive shafts, a grease seal is used on the pinion shaft to prevent the rear axle lubricant from escaping past the pinion front bearing. Before attempting to replace this oil seal it is absolutely essential that the area surrounding the universal joint companion flange and the rear axle housing is thoroughly cleaned with either solvent and compressed air or with a good steam cleaner. The inclusion of even slight amounts of grit or foreign substance is absolutely ruinous to pinion bearings. After the area has been thoroughly cleaned, measure with a pull scale, the force required to turn the pinion shaft.

This is just a precautionary measure on shim adjusted pinions but is absolutely necessary on rears which utilize a collapsible spacer such as some Fords and Packards.

Make a note of the amount of pressure required to turn the pinion shaft before the universal joint nut is removed.

Remove the universal joint flange-pinion shaft nut and slide the flange off of the splined pinion. Insert an inertia type puller and force the old oil seal out of the housing.

Before installing the new oil seal, see to it that it is thoroughly impregnated with oil. A good way to do this is to soak the oil seal in warm, or even hot, oil until it is thoroughly saturated. About fifteen minutes will suffice in warm oil to completely saturate any oil seal.

Install the prepared oil seal into the housing, driving it firmly into place with a suitable driver. Note: If the specific driving tool is not available the oil seal can be driven into place with a piece of pipe approximately as large as the outside diameter of the oil seal.

Pinion oil seals should be driven at their outer rim and not at the center. It is always bad practice to attempt to install an oil seal by tapping the outer rim with a hammer.

Examine the universal joint companion flange for scratches grooving or roughness where the oil seal seats. If any roughness is present the flange will have to be replaced. In order to be effective, the pinion shaft oil seal must ride on a smooth even surface. Install the companion flange and nut and tighten the nut until the pressure required to turn the pinion shaft is the same or slightly more than was required before the flange was removed.

On shim adjusted rears measuring the force required to turn the pinion shaft is simply a precaution so that the mechanic can be certain the rear is in the same adjustment as it was before the oil seal was replaced, however on rears where a collapsing spacer is used such as some Fords and Packards, it is essential that some such method be used to determine if the spacer has been collapsed the proper amount in order to place the same preload on the bearings as was there before the flange was removed.

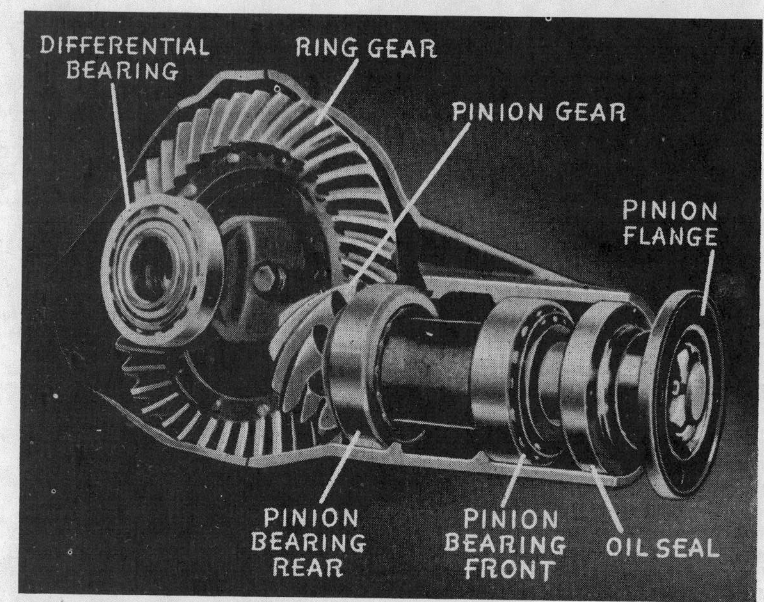

Cutaway view of the differential, showing relationship of ring gear and pinion, bearings and rear oil seal

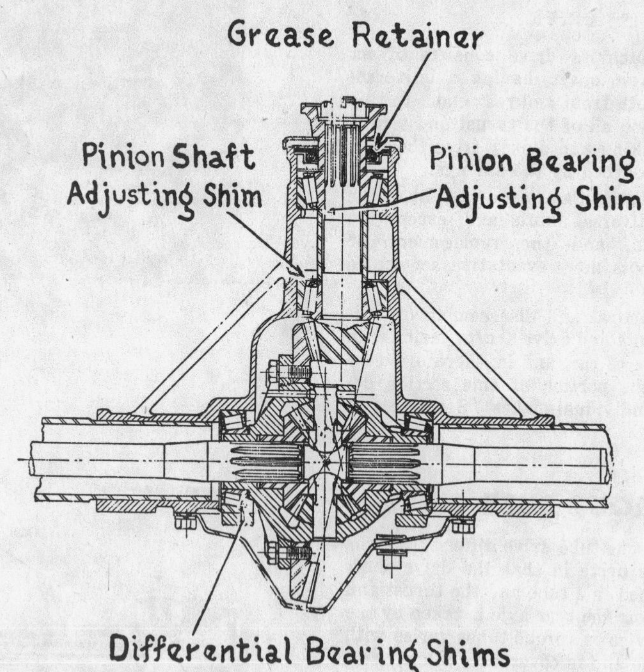

Spicer type, shim adusted rear axle assembly

Axle Shaft Oil Seals

Oils seals are used at the outer end of the axle shaft to prevent oil from the differential from escaping past the bearing and ruining the brake lining.

Inner and outer seals are used on some models while others use an outer seal only. When grease is escaping from the rear axle on to the brake drums and lining, it is obviously wise to replace both the inner and outer oil seal.

The location of the outer oil seal varies with the different makes of automobiles, for instance, on Ford the oil seal is contained in the rear wheel hub, this is also true of some Chevrolet models; on some Chrysler models the outer oil seal is incorporated into the brake backing plate; other models the outer oil seal is bolted up to the outside face of the brake backing plate and the wiping action is against the hub of the rear wheel. Regardless of the type of construction, it is necessary to remove the rear wheel hub and drum in order to get at the outer oil seal. On all makes using an inner seal, it is necessary to remove the axle shaft in order to replace the inner oil seal.

Specific procedure for each make of car is given in the car section later in this manual, see index.

In order to properly service oil seals, both the inner and outer types, it is practically essential that an inertia type puller having both left and right hand hooked ends be available.

While it is possible to remove any oil seal using a pry bar or chisel, such practices generally result in irreparable damage to the housing assembly.

The use of an inertia type puller assures that the oil seal can be taken from the housing with a minimum of damage and distortion to both the seal and the housing.

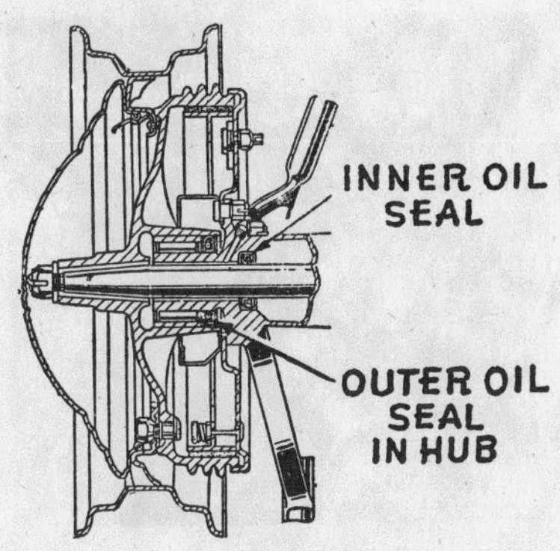

To properly install an oil seal it is absolutely essential that the correct type driver be used since tapping the seal "around a ring" with a hammer will generally result in distortion and failure of the seal to function properly.

It is generally considered good practice to soak an oil seal in ordinary engine oil for as much as two or three hours before installing it. If the car being worked on has a history of oil seal failures it is a good idea to soak the new seal in hot oil before installing it.

Where a history of defective oil seals is found it is a good idea to take a piece of fine emory cloth and, working like a shoe shine rag, polish the portion of the axle shaft on which the seal rides.

Regardless of the type of seal it is always good practice to thoroughly impregnate the seal with a good grade of lubricating oil before installing it.

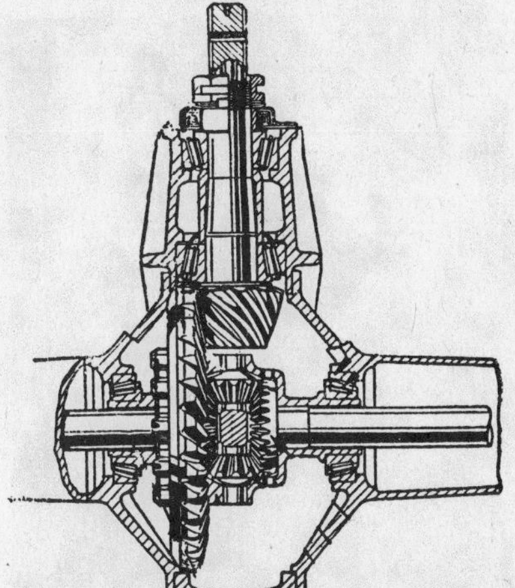

Examine the surface on which the seal wipes for scratches, grooves and roughness; this surface must be smooth and even; if it is not, the surface should be machined or the part replaced.

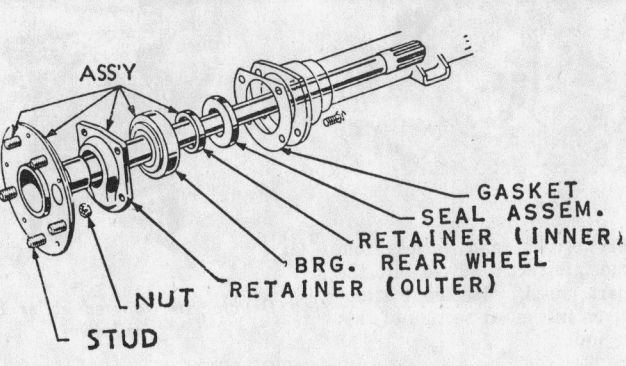

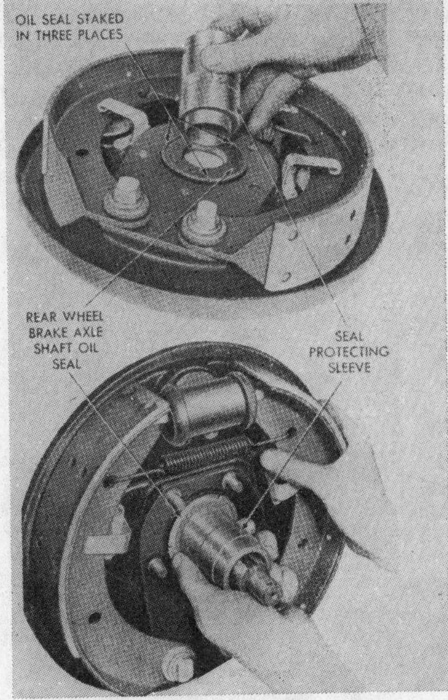

Outer seal incorporated into brake backing plate

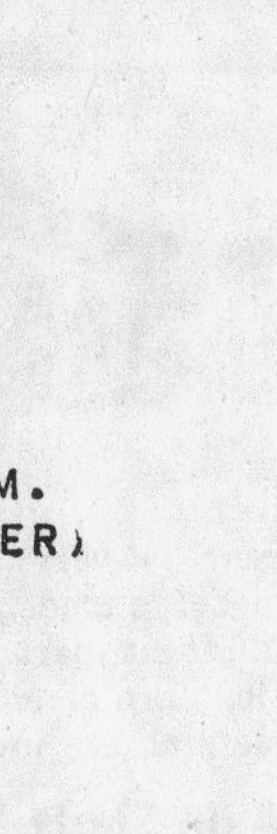

Axle shaft, bearing, and oil seals

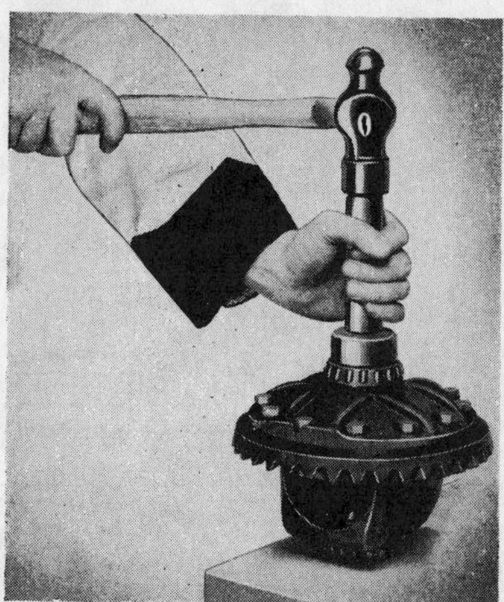
Replacement of carrier bearing

Replacement of Carrier Bearings or Ring Gear and Pinion

Whenever it becomes necessary to replace the carrier or pinion bearings or replace the ring gear and pinion, the parts should be removed to a bench and the work done under the best conditions.

On models with removable carriers, disconnect the back universal joint (or the front universal joint in the case of torque tubes), remove both rear hubs and backing plates and slide the axle shaft out of the differential carrier. Then unbolt the carrier and remove it to the bench so that the work may proceed under the best possible conditions. Once on the bench, remove the differential side bearing caps and lift the differential case with its attached ring gear out of the carrier.

Next take off the universal joint flange and drive the pinion shaft back through the inside of the carrier.

The proper depth setting of a pinion gear is very critical and varies from model to model, in fact it varies with the different parts used. Specific instructions are given in the car section of this manual, see index.

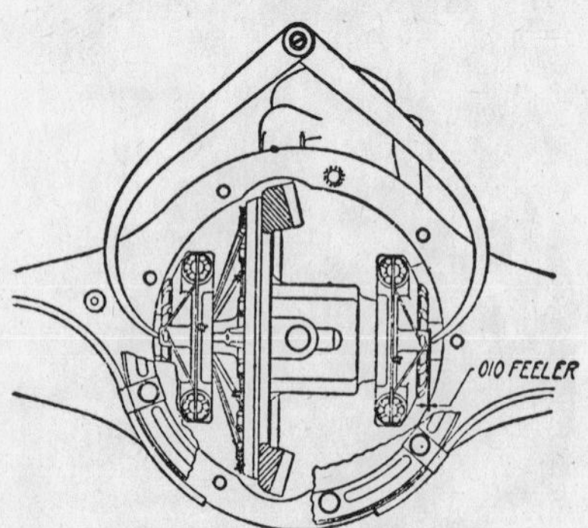

Using calipers to check the spread of the bearing web

Carrier bearings

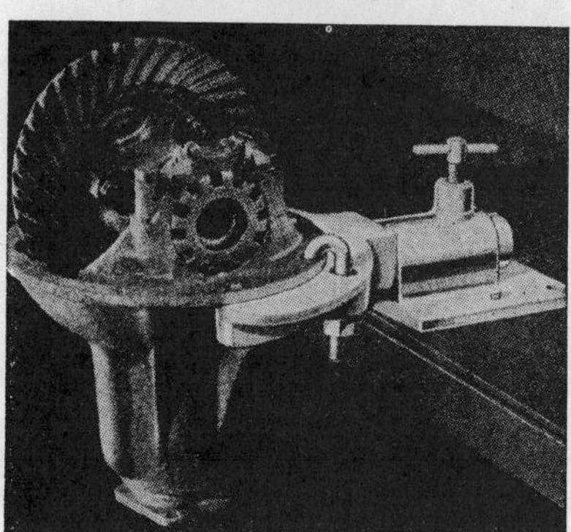
Differential carrier holding fixture

Back lash

Axle Shaft End Play

With some few exceptions, notably some Cadillacs and Packards, the rear axle bearing is a single row either ball or tapered roller bearing. Where a ball bearing is used any play in the axle shaft indicates just that much wear in the rear axle annular ball bearing. If any play is present in an axle shaft fitted with a ball bearing, the bearing should be replaced. On constructions using roller bearings as much as .005 end play is permissible in the rear axle shaft. This end play is controlled by shims placed between the backing plate and the bearing or between the bearing race and the bearing seat.

End play is reduced by removing shims.

On constructions using a rear axle spider in the differential (notably Hudson), when the play is removed from one axle shaft it is automatically removed from the other since the two axle shafts butt together in the center of the differential.

Inertia puller is required to remove some axles.

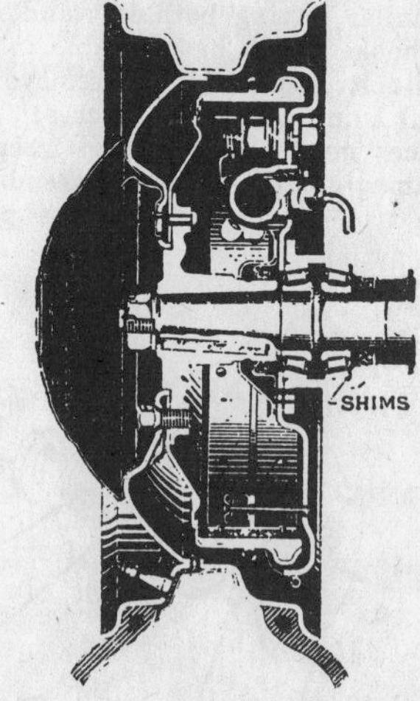

Double row tapered roller bearing, and shims

On all other constructions using a pin or cross in the differential, each axle must be adjusted separately.

Where double row tapered roller bearings are used on the rear axle shaft (some Cadillacs and Packards), the end play may be reduced to zero or even a very slight preload.

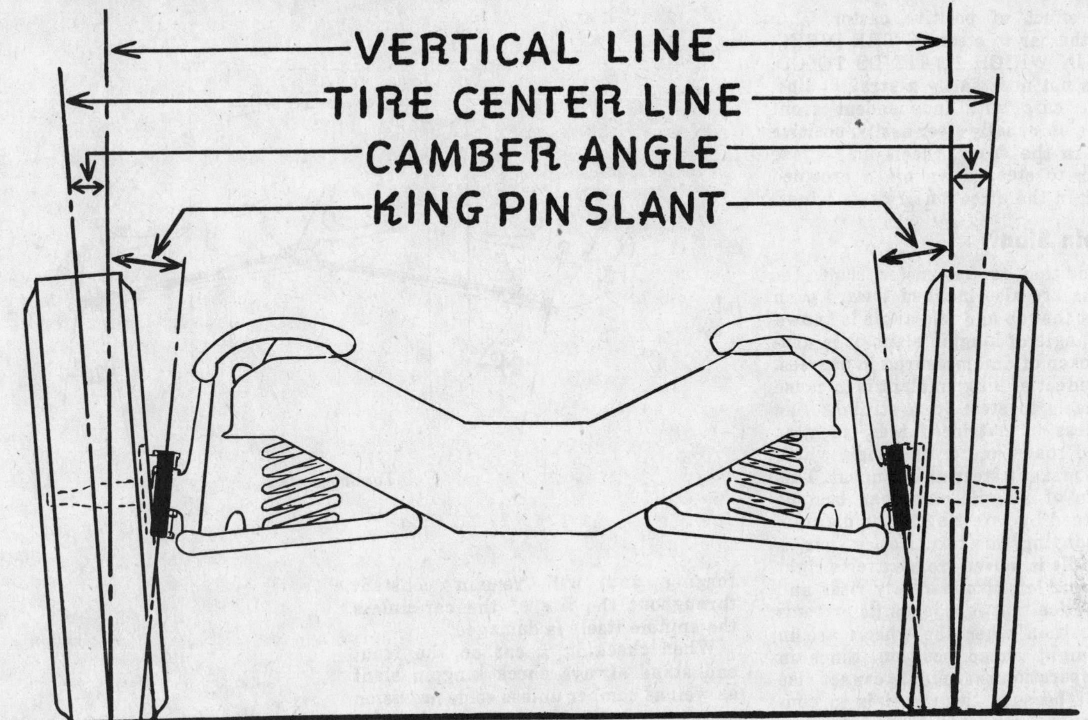

Camber and king pin slant

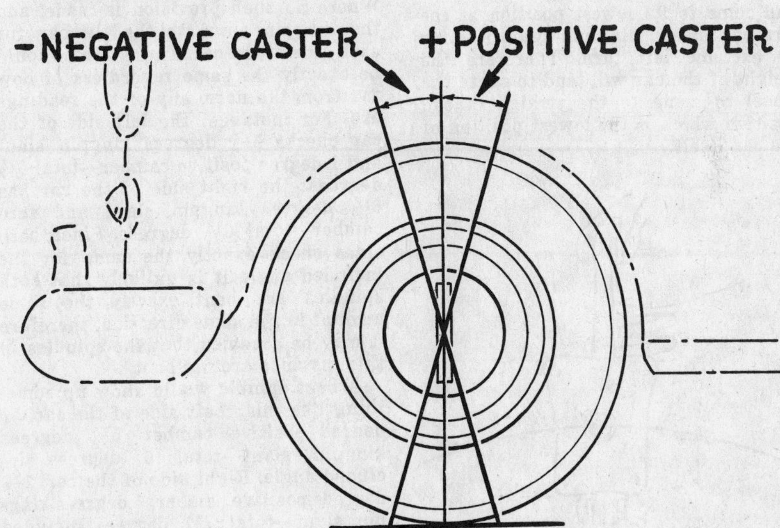

FRONT SUSPENSION

With the exception of Crosley, Ford and Willys all American passenger cars are built so that either front wheel can rise and fall with the conformation of the highway without affecting the position or stability of the opposite wheel. This construction is generally called "individually sprung."

The purpose of independently sprung front wheels is to reduce the amount of unsprung weight in contact with the highway and also to provide a suspension which will more readily absorb road shocks without transmitting them to the frame of the car and thus to its passengers. With the exception of some Studebakers all independently sprung front wheels are provided with coil springs. Since a coil spring functions without friction no lubrication is required on the spring itself.

Front End Geometry

In order that a vehicle may steer easily under all conditions without unnecessary wear on tires and at the same time provide a safe, stable front suspension, certain angles are incorporated into the steering mechanism.

The relation of each of these angles to all of the others is called front end or steering geometry.

Camber

Camber is the amount that the front wheels are inclined outward at the top. On modern automobiles camber is spoken of and measured in degrees from the perpendicular.

The reason for camber angle is to take some of the load off of the spindle outboard bearing.

Caster

Caster is the amount that the kingpin is tilted toward the back of the car. Caster is usually spoken of and measured in degrees. Positive caster means that the top of the kingpin is tilted toward the back of the car; negative caster is exactly the opposite, the top of the kingpin is tilted toward the front of the car.

The effect of positive castor is to cause the car to steer IN THE DIRECTION IN WHICH IT TENDS TO GO. This is not necessarily a straight line.

Since cars with independent front suspension usually steer easily, positive castor in the front wheels may cause the car to steer down off a crowned road or in the direction of cross winds.

Kingpin Slant

In addition to the caster slant, the kingpins are also inclined toward each other at the top and this angle is known as the angle of kingpin slant. It is usually spoken of and measured in degrees.

The effect of kingpin slant is to cause the wheels to steer in a straight line regardless of outside forces, such as crowned roads and cross winds, which tend to make it steer at a tangent. This function of kingpin slant can best be understood by referring to the diagram accompanying this text. Notice that as the spindle is moved from extreme right to extreme left it apparently rises and falls. Notice that it reaches its extreme high position when the wheels are in the straight ahead position. Since in actual operation the spindle cannot rise and fall because the wheel is in constant contact with the ground, the car itself will rise at the extreme right turn and come to its lowest position at the straight ahead point and again rise for an extreme left turn. Therefore the weight of the car will tend to cause the wheel to come to the straight ahead position which is the lowest position of the car itself.

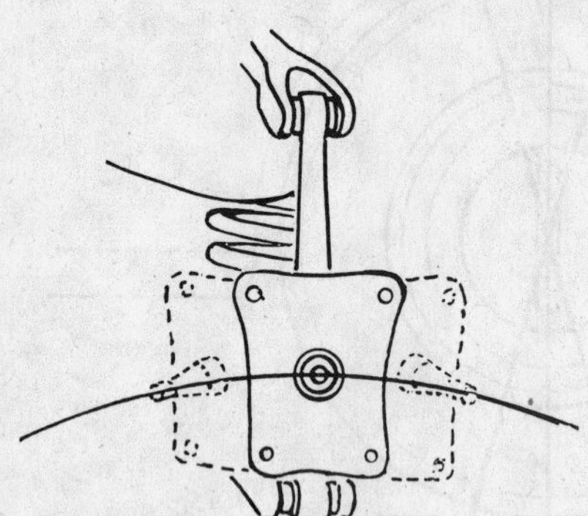

Spindle arc when wheel turns

Included Angle

Included angle is the name given to that angle which includes kingpin slant and camber. It is the relation between the center line of the spindle and the center line of the kingpin. This angle is "built in" to the knuckle (spindle) forging and will remain constant throughout the life of the car unless the spindle itself is damaged.

When checking a car on the front end stand always check kingpin slant as well as camber unless some provision is made on the front end stand for checking the condition of the spindle. Where no such provision is made, add the kingpin slant to the camber for each side of the car. These totals should be exactly the same regardless of how far from the norm any of the readings are. For instance: the left side of the car checks 5½ degrees kingpin slant and 1 degree positive camber—total 6½ degrees; the right side of the car has 6½ degrees kingpin slant and zero camber—total 6½ degrees. Since both sides check exactly the same for the included angle it is unlikely that both spindles are bent exactly the same amount in the same direction, therefore it may be assumed that the spindles in this instance are not bent.

A bent spindle would show up something like this: Left side of the car, ¾ degree positive camber, 5¼ degrees kingpin slant—total 6 degrees included angle. Right side of the car, 1¼ degrees positive camber, 6 degrees kingpin slant—total 7¼ degrees included angle. Obviously one of the spindles is bent.

Since the most common cause of a bent spindle is striking the curb when parking which causes the spindle to bend downward rather than upward, the side having the greater included angle usually has the bent spindle.

It will be found impossible to achieve good alignment and minimum tire wear unless the bent spindle is replaced.

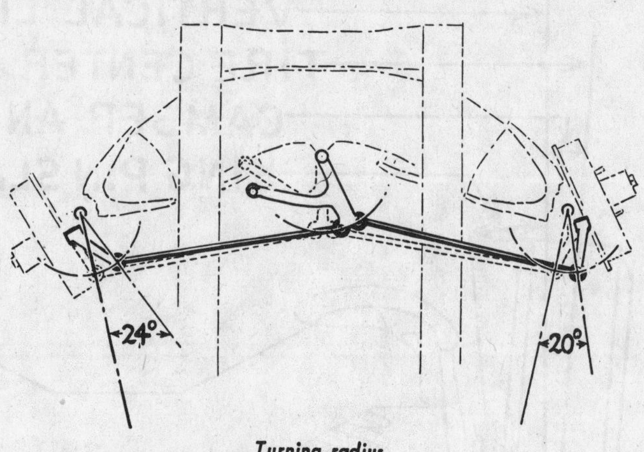

Turning radius

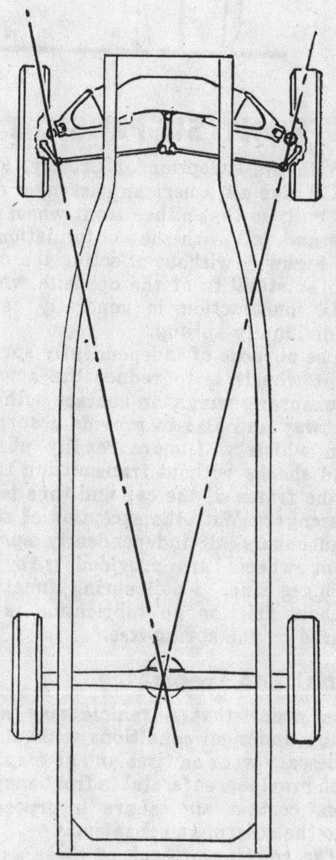

Positioning steering arm

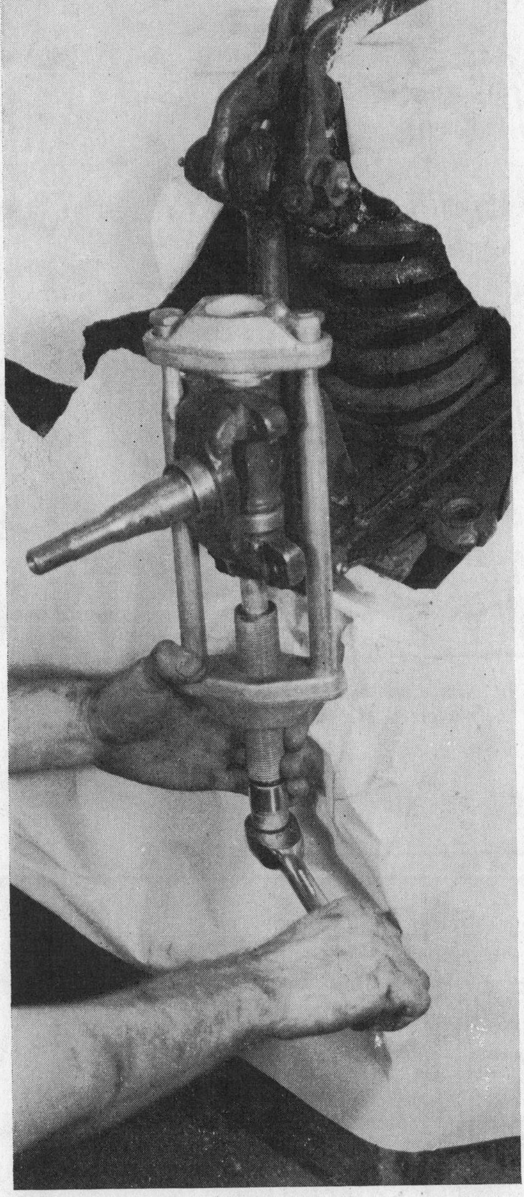

Hand operated press for removing stuck king pins

Inserting king pin bushing

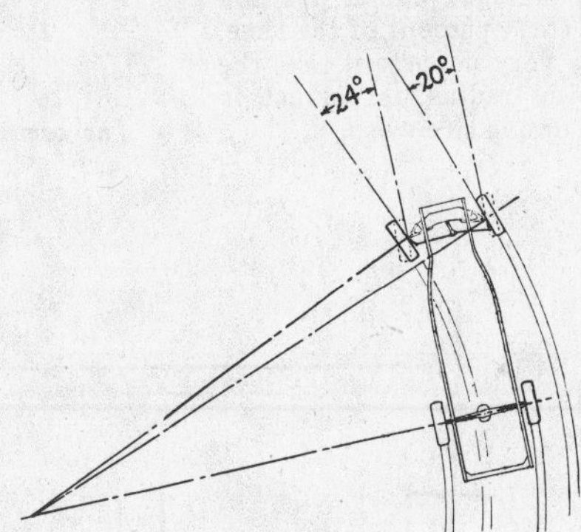

Inside wheel turns a greater number degrees

Toe In

Toe in is the amount that the front wheels are closer together at the front than they are at the back. This dimension is usually spoken of and measured in inches or fractions of inches.

Generally speaking, the wheels are toed in because they are cambered. Where a car operates with a zero camber it will be found to operate with zero toe in. As the required camber increases, so does the toe in. The reason for this is that a cambered wheel tends to steer in the direction in which it is cambered. Therefore it is necessary to overcome this tendency of the wheel by compensating very slightly in a direction opposite to which it tends to roll.

Caster and camber both have an effect on toe-in, therefore toe-in is the last angle on the front end which should be corrected. Always set caster, camber, and kingpin slant (included angle) before setting toe-in.

Toe Out (Turns)

When a car is steered into a turn, the outside wheel of the turn describes a much larger circle than the inside wheel, therefore the outside wheel must be steered to a somewhat less angle than the inside wheel. This difference in angle is sometimes called "toe out on turns."

The change in angle from toe in, in the straight ahead position, to toe out in the turn position is caused by the relative position of the steering arms to the kingpin and to each other.

If a line were drawn from the center of the kingpin through the center of the steering arm attaching hole, this line would be found to cross almost exactly in the center of the rear axle.

Before attempting to make any check on a front end machine or otherwise on toe out, examine the tie-rod ends, drag link ball sockets, intermediate steering arm bearings, etc. Any play or looseness in these parts will prevent the wheels from assuming the proper position on turns.

A check for toe out is usually made by turning the outside wheel to twenty degrees and measuring the turn of the inside wheel. With the outside wheel at twenty degrees, the inside wheel will always be more than twenty degrees unless one or both of the steering arms are bent.

Exact specifications for the positions of the inside wheel are given in the data section of this manual. If the turning radius is not according to the specifications given, then one or both of the steering arms are bent.

There is no positive way to tell which of the arms are bent other than by comparing each arm with a new arm.

It has been estimated that an automobile operating in city traffic has its wheels in the straight ahead position not more than forty percent of the time. Therefore it is very important that the angle of turning radius be correct in order to avoid undue tire wear.

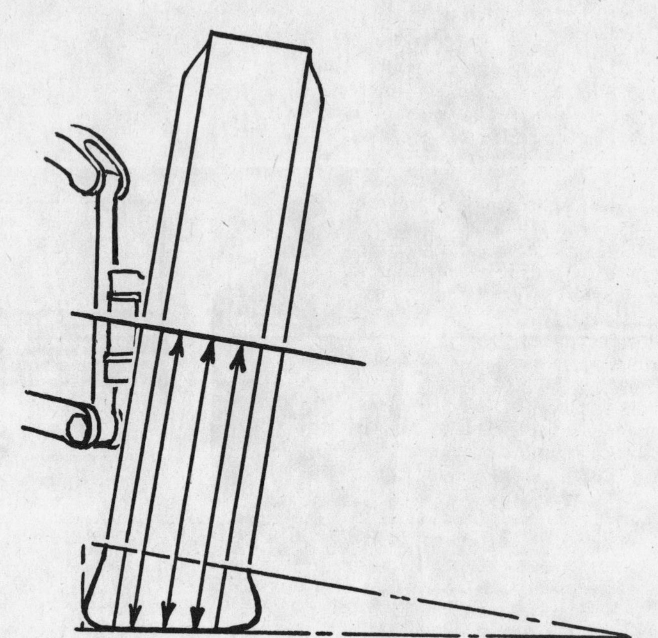

The cambered wheel tends to roll in the direction of its camber because of the angle formed by the contact of the tire on the road

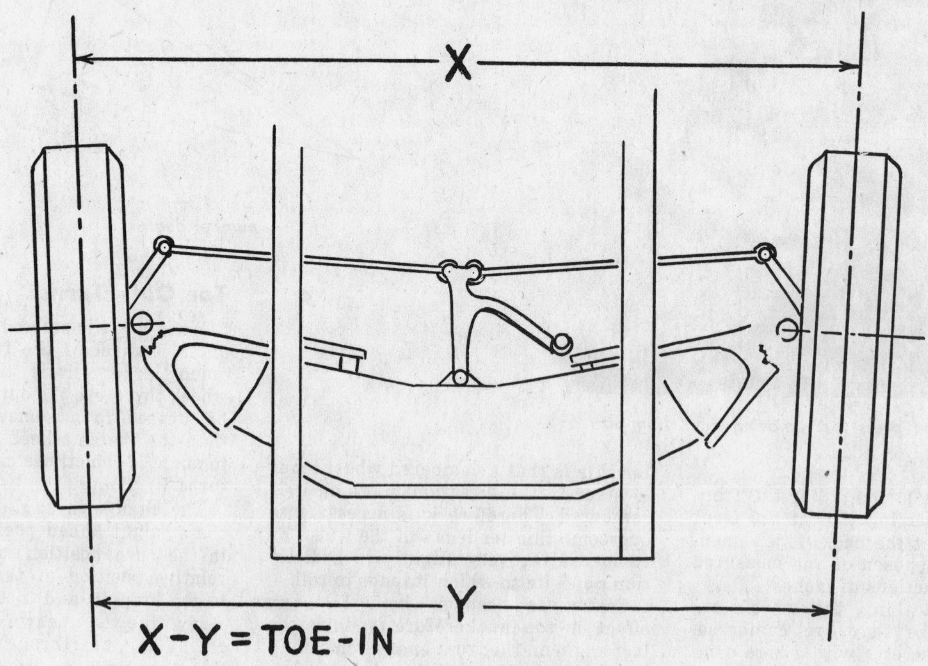

The wheel has toe-in to overcome the tendency of the wheel to roll in the direction of its camber. See illustration above.

STEERING GEAR

The purpose of the steering gear is to convert rotary motion at the steering wheel to straight line motion at the tie rods and also to reduce the effort necessary to steer the car.

Generally speaking, most steering gears are arranged so that there is a "high spot" at the straight ahead position of the steering wheel. In a properly operating gear mechanism this high spot will be noticed as a very slight binding in the steering mechanism as the wheel passes through the straight ahead position.

This does not mean there is any definite binding, nor should the gear be set up to produce a definite binding in the straight ahead position. The gear should be barely perceptibly stiffer in the straight ahead position.

Because the gears are set up in this manner, it is necessary that they be adjusted for mesh in the straight ahead (the tight) position. However, when setting up a steering gear it is absolutely essential that it be checked for freedom of motion from one extreme to the other.

At no point should the steering gear actually bind, nor should there be any noticeable play in the straight ahead position.

When setting up a steering gear, perhaps the best procedure is to disconnect the pitman arm from the tie rods or tie rod link.

Checking for lash in the gear should be done at the pitman arm and not at the steering wheel.

The actual adjustment procedure varies with the different makes of cars

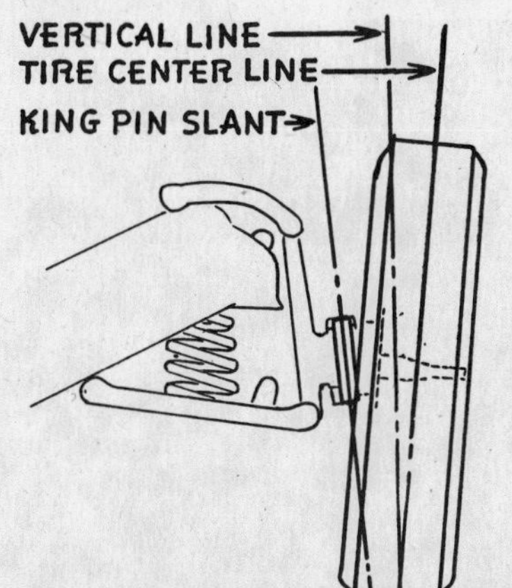

The angle between the center line of the tire (camber angle) and king pin slant is known as the included angle

so that this information is given in the car section later in this manual.

Regardless of which make or type of gear is being worked on, before any work is done on the steering gear itself, a thorough check should be made of the wheel bearings, kingpins, steering arms, tie rod ends and drag link ends or seats. Very often looseness or wear at these points is blamed on the steering gear itself.

Center Point Steering

If a line were drawn down through the center of the kingpin and another line were drawn through the center of

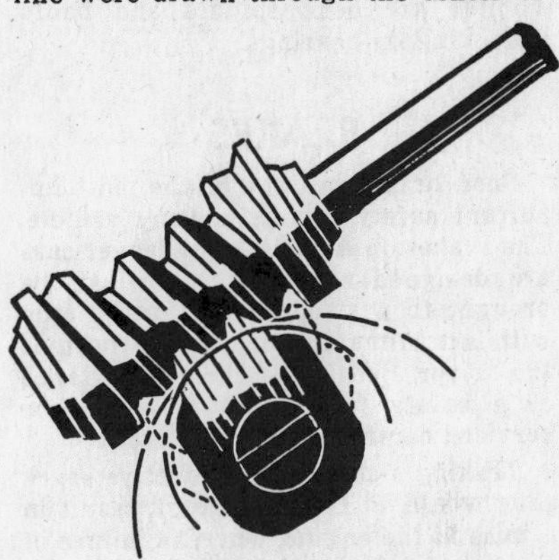

The high spot in the steering is caused by the fact that the worm teeth are cut to a larger circle than the roller tooth turns in

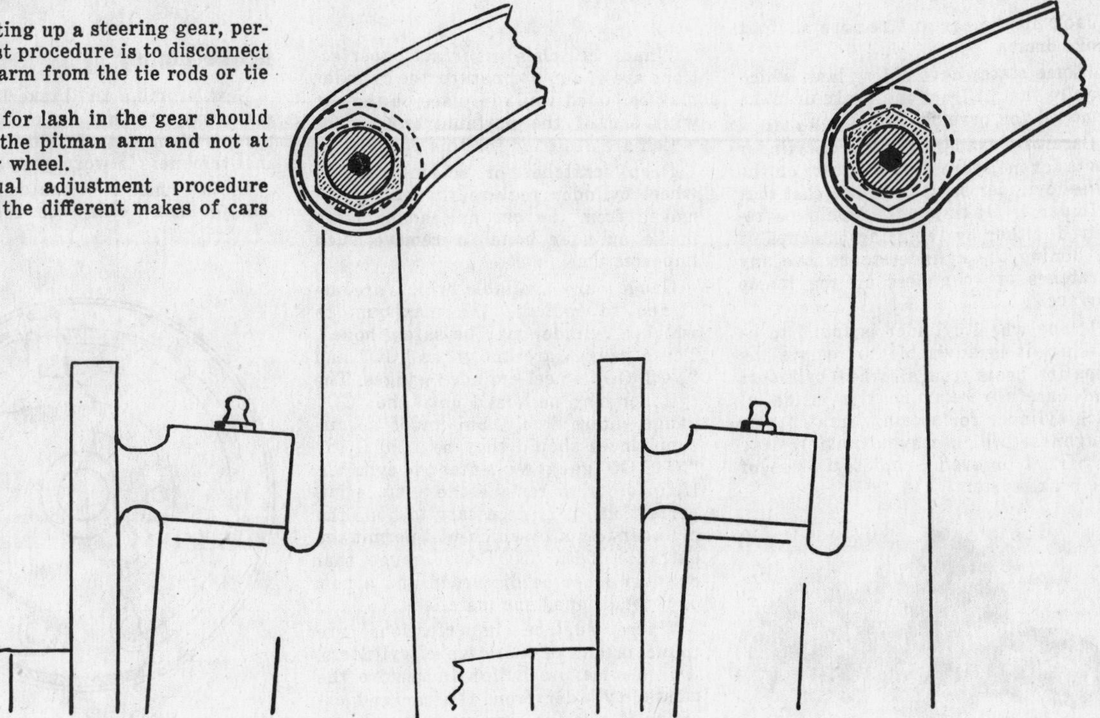

Determine the position of the eccentric before making any adjustment in caster or camber

the wheel and tire, these two lines would be found to come together in the tread of the tire.

The weight of the car is carried along these two lines. They make it possible to steer the car readily without undue thrust on the tie rods.

The only conditions which effect center point steering in modern automobiles are bent spindle and badly worn kingpin bearings.

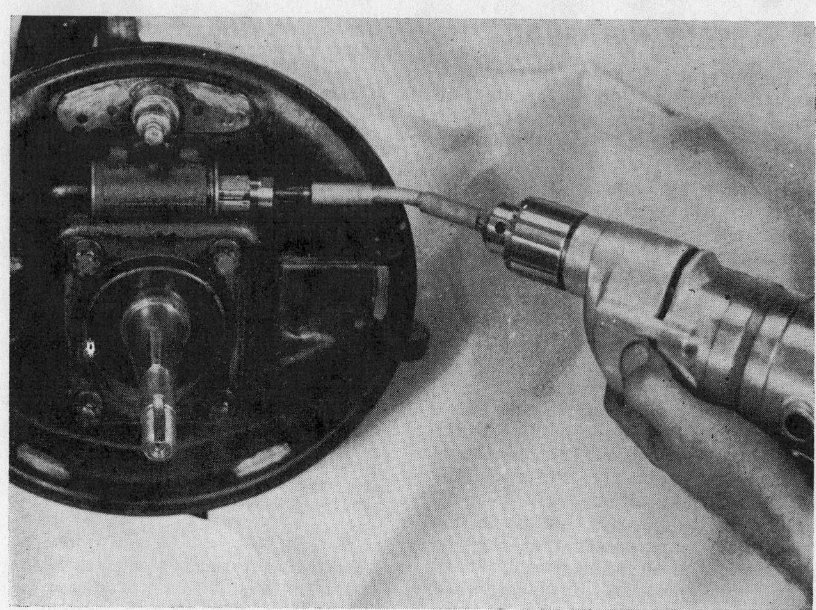

Portable hone being used to hone minor imperfection in cylinder, while cylinder is still on the car

BRAKES

Good brakes are one of the most important safety factors on any vehicle. The brakes on American passenger cars are designed so that the car can be brought to a smooth, even, quiet stop with a minimum effort on the part of the driver. Because of their importance as a safety factor, brakes should be serviced carefully and completely.

"Taking a chance" on defective spark plug would, at the very worst, result in a miss in the engine, whereas failure of any part of the brake system may result in serious injury or even death to the operator and passengers of a motor vehicle.

Brake Inspection

Jack up the car and remove all four brake drums.

(Some states have safety laws which require that at least one brake drum be removed for periodic inspection.)

Carefully examine the wheel cylinder boots for moisture. Any moisture on the wheel cylinder boots indicates that that cylinder is leaking and should be repaired, either by replacing the cups or by honing the cylinder to remove any scratches or roughness on the inside surface.

If one wheel cylinder is found to be leaking, it is advisable to remove the cups and boots from all wheel cylinders and carefully examine the inside of each cylinder for scoring, scratches or roughness which may ultimately lead to partial or even complete failure of the brake system.

Worn cups and boots

Where scratches or surface imperfections are of a minor nature, the cylinder may be honed while in place on the car with one of the portable type hones which are designed for this purpose.

Deep scratches or scoring in the wheel cylinder require that it be removed from the car and honed on a brake cylinder hone to remove such imperfections.

Gauges are available which are designed to indicate the maximum to which a cylinder may be safely honed. These gauges are known as "GO" and "NOT GO" wheel cylinder gauges. The cylinder may be honed until the "GO" gauge enters freely, but under no circumstances should they be used if the "NOT GO" gauge will enter the cylinder. If, in order to remove the surface imperfections, it is necessary to hone the cylinder to a size which will permit the entrance of the "NOT GO" gauge, that cylinder must be discarded and a new or reconditioned one installed.

Where surface imperfections are found in one or more wheel cylinders, it is a wise precaution to remove the master cylinder from the car and examine it also for scoring or roughness inside the cylinder. Gauges are also available for use in the master cylinder.

Brake Lining

Next examine the brake lining. Most states require that brake lining be replaced when sixty percent of the original thickness is worn away.

Lining which is cemented to the shoes can, in many cases, be used until as

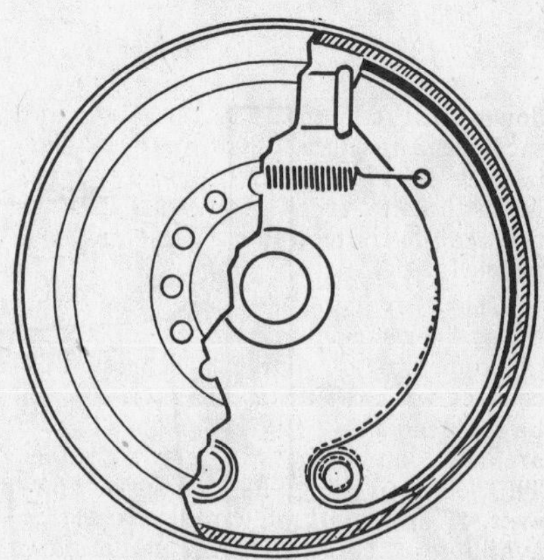

Improper adjustment of anchor but shoe has worn to fit drum. Should not be readjusted until new lining is installed

AND TROUBLE SHOOTING BRAKES

much as seventy percent has been worn away.

Notice particularly if the lining is wearing all over the surface. If the lining is wearing evenly all over its surface and the entire surface is in contact with the drum as indicated by the wear on the lining, the anchors probably do not require adjustment.

On examining lining, mechanics frequently find a condition where the lining is wearing more at one end of the shoe than it is at the opposite end of the same shoe, but, in spite of this, the lining has worn so that the entire surface contacts the drum. When this condition is found it indicates that the anchors were not properly adjusted when the lining was first installed. However, the lining has worn itself down until it is finally in complete contact with the drum. When this condition is met with it is advisable either to leave the anchor adjustment as it is, or replace the lining and reset the anchors properly.

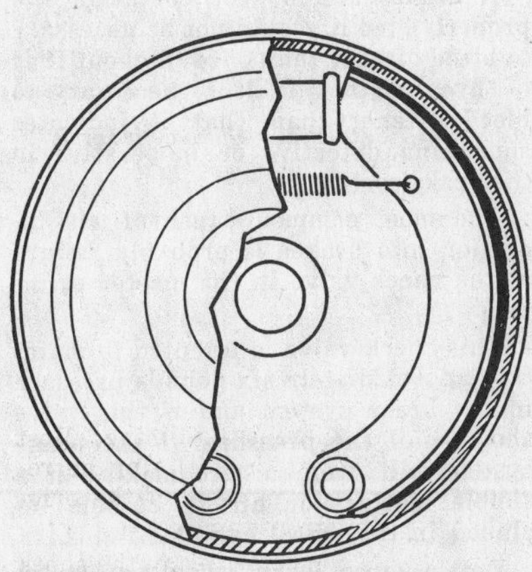

Improperly adjusted anchor bolt. Shoe has not worn to fit drum. Lining should be replaced and anchor bolt readjusted

Where examination shows that the lining is wearing at one end only and the opposite end has not yet come in contact with the drum, the lining must be replaced since it no longer has a true arc and cannot be properly adjusted. This condition can be corrected, however, if an axle type lining grinder is available. Axle type lining grinders are mounted on the spindle or axle of the car and are so arranged that they will grind the lining into a perfectly true arc.

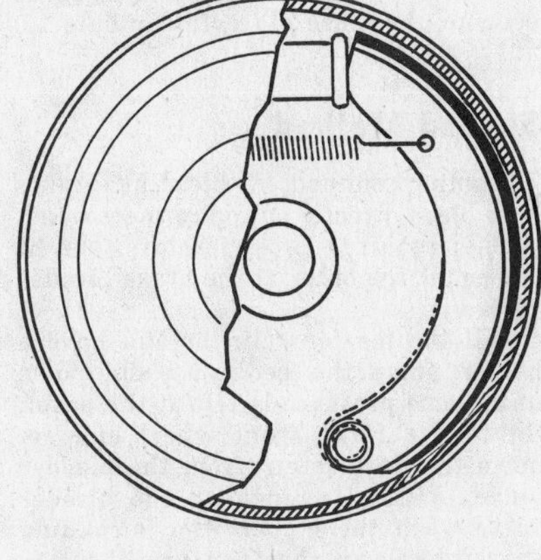

Distorted brake shoe and improper shimming of lining. Shoe and lining should be replaced

Many successful brake shops prefer to use the axle type grinder on relines to insure perfect brake contact and also eliminate the wear-in which may be required if unground lining is used.

Running clearance for brake lining (given in the data section, see index) is carefully calculated so that when the brake is applied, all of the lining will contact the drum at the same time.

Axle type lining grinders insure even contact in the applied position.

Brake Drums

Examine brake drums for grooves, heat checks and cracks. The drum should be smooth and even surfaced.

Cracked drums MUST be replaced.

Scored or checked drums can be remachined to produce an even surface.

TROUBLE SHOOTING

Brake Squeals

The squealing sound which is sometimes present in the brakes is a vibration in either the shoes, linings or drums and is frequently caused by loose anchor mounts, warped shoes, loose hold down springs, grease on the lining.

Brake Chatter

Chatter is almost always caused by either greasy lining or loose parts in the brake system such as backing plates, anchor bolts, king pins, knuckle supports, etc. Brake chatter can also be caused by defective shock absorbers.

Axle type grinder in use to assure perfect brake contact

Grabbing Brakes

The causes of grabbing brakes are, generally speaking, the same as for chatter since chatter is, after all, a series of grabs and releases.

Brake Pull

Frequently, brake pull is caused by misalignment in the front system rather than the brakes themselves. However, pull may be caused by stuck shoes, broken retracting springs, stuck cylinder or line (in the opposite wheel), grease on the lining, or defective shock absorber.

BLEEDING BRAKES

The purpose of bleeding brakes is to remove all air from the hydraulic system. This is its only purpose and it is not generally considered a service adjustment since it does not effect the actual adjustment of the brakes themselves.

In addition to pressure bleeding and flushing there are two methods commonly used to bleed brakes. The first, sometimes called the safety system, is done as follows: Fill the master cylinder right to the top and then go to the right front wheel and remove the dust screw from the brake bleeder valve.

The brake bleeder valve is located just above where the brake line enters into the wheel cylinder through the backing plate.

Note: Many mechanics fail to replace the dust screw after bleeding, so if no screw is found in the valve, it was left off at some previous bleed job.

An exception to this are the Chrysler models which have a two cylinder front brake. On these models there is a bleed screw at both the top and the bottom of the backing plate, one for each brake cylinder. On models with two wheel cylinders per brake each wheel cylinder is bled separately.

Remove the dust screw and insert into the dust screw hole a bleeder hose, carrying the free end of the hose into a glass jar containing a sufficient amount of brake fluid to cover the bottom of the bleeder tube. Keeping the free end of the bleeder hose under the fluid prevents air from backing up into the cylinder when the bleed valve is opened.

Using an open end or box wrench, open the bleed valve and have a helper slowly push the pedal down which will expel the air from the wheel cylinder and the air will show up as bubbles in the fluid in the jar.

Continue to pump the brake pedal up and down until no more air bubbles come out of the end of the bleeder hose.

Caution: After every third time the brake pedal is pushed downwards it will be necessary to refill the master cylinder. Do not fail to do this since more air may be included if the fluid in the master cylinder becomes dangerously low.

When all of the air has been expelled from the wheel cylinder, as noticed by no air bubbles in the jar, tighten the bleed valve, remove the bleeder hose and replace the dust screw. Repeat this process at all four wheels, and in addition, on Chrysler products having two front wheel cylinders, repeat at each of the wheel cylinders.

Caution: Do not under any circumstances reuse the fluid which comes out of the master cylinder. It is dangerous economy to reuse old cylinder fluid.

Second Method

Another method of bleeding brakes is to bleed directly out on to the ground.

This requires two operators, one at the pedal, the other at the brake bleeder valve.

Fill the master cylinder and have a helper pump the pedal up and down until some pressure is felt at the pedal. Go to the right front wheel and remove the dust screw from the bleeder valve. With a wrench on the bleeder valve warn the helper who is holding the pedal down that you are about to open the valve, open it and the fluid will squirt out in little bursts if any air is present. Before the brake pedal quite gets to the floor, close the valve. Have the helper at the pedal pump the pedal a few times until again he feels pressure in the brake system and, holding that pressure on the brake pedal, again open the valve. Repeat this process until no more air comes out of the bleed valve.

Caution: Do not bleed more than three times without refilling the master cylinder since there is some risk of including air into the master cylinder during the bleeding process which will make it necessary to repeat the entire process.

When all of the air has been exhausted from the right front brake cylinder, repeat the procedure at all four of the wheels, being careful to fill the master cylinder each time the wheel has been bled three times.

On Chrysler products having two front wheel cylinders, it will be necessary to bleed both the upper and the lower wheel cylinder on the front wheels as a separate job.

This method, while effective, is usually responsible for some of the dirt and grease found on many shop floors.

After the bleeding process is complete, replace the dust screws in the bleed valves.

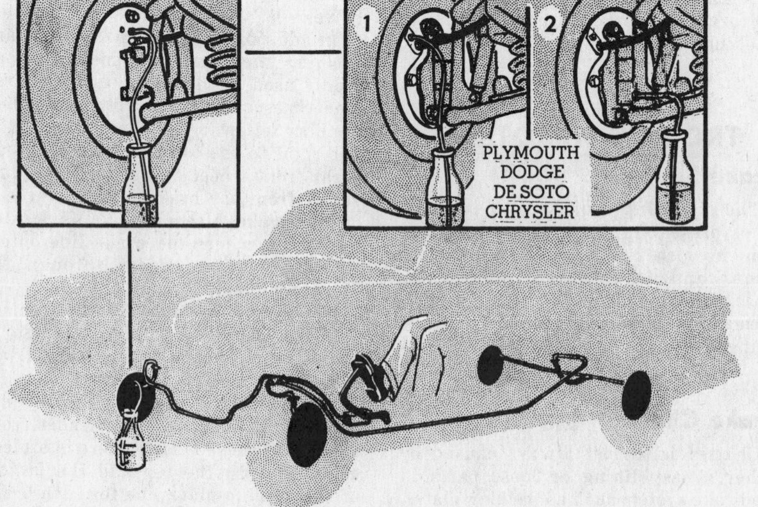

Position of Bleeder Screws

TROUBLE SHOOTING ON BRAKE BLEEDING

If brakes are in good condition and properly bled it should not be necessary to bleed oftener than once in about four or five months. If it is necessary to bleed oftener than that it indicates something defective or inoperative in the brake system.

The most common cause of air inclusion into brakes is probably failure at the check valve in the master cylinder.

This check valve is intented to maintain approximately six pounds pressure in the brake system and if this valve should fail the pressure of the brake system will drop to zero making it a simple matter for air to become included in the wheel cylinder fluids.

Defective or leaky wheel or master cylinders are also a common cause of air inclusion.

A not too common cause is when the brake lines run too close to the exhaust pipe causing vaporizing or gassing in the brake fluid.

Where it is found necessary to bleed brakes more than once every two or three months in the summer time, but the brakes function well in cold weather, the usual thing to look for is gasing or overheating of the brake lines caused by too close proximity to the exhaust line on the car.

An easy way to fix this is to wrap the exhaust pipe with an asbestos wrapper to prevent the heat from effecting the brake lines.

Where soft, spongy, rubbery or erratic brakes are found it is an excellent idea to remove all of the wheel cylinders for examination for pits, scores, scratches or other defects which make it easy for air to enter the hydraulic system.

AND TROUBLE SHOOTING TUNE-UP

Tune-Up is the name given to the operation or series of operations performed on the engine and accessories to compensate for the normal acceptable wear and maladjustment resulting from ordinary use. To obtain maximum performance from high speed, high compression engines, it is necessary to adhere very closely to the specifications recommended by the car manufacturer.

Engine tuning should be done in a routine manner so that no part of the work is skipped or slighted. The following routine is suggested as being readily adaptable to any engine.

CHECK THE CONDITION OF THE BATTERY

Test each cell of the battery with a hydrometer to determine the specific gravity. A reading of 1.285 indicates a fully charged cell; 1.225 indicates the battery is about one-half discharged; 1.150 would indicate a discharged battery.

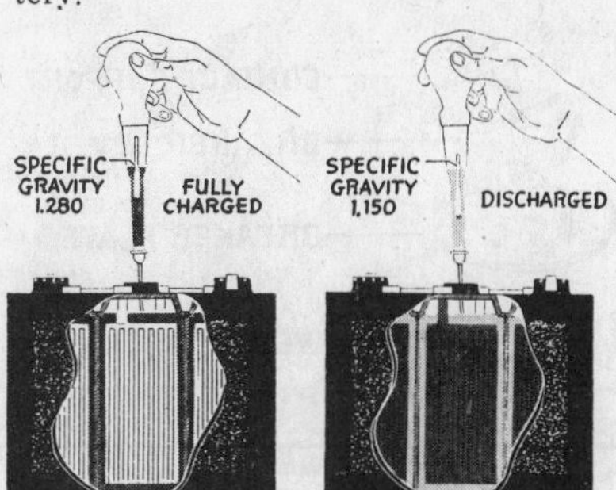

Fully charged *Discharged*

NOTE: Battery hydrometers are calibrated at 80 degrees fahrenheit and if the temperature of the battery fluid is other than 80 degrees fahrenheit it will be necessary to add to the reading 2 points for each 5 degrees above 80 or subtract 2 points for each 5 degrees below 80.

Add 2 points for each plus 5 degrees.

Subtract 2 points for each minus 5 degrees.

An ordinary thermometer may be used to determine the temperature of the battery fluid.

Remove both battery leads and thoroughly clean the contact surface. A battery cable terminal burnisher and wire brush should be used to insure a good clean tight joint. Disconnect the battery ground strap and the engine ground strap and clean the ground contact surface to insure a clean battery ground.

If the battery cables do not make the best possible contact there will be too great a drop in voltage when the starter is cranking the engine, resulting in hard starting and poor ignition. Many hard starting difficulties can be traced directly to a faulty battery or starter switch connection.

An essential part of every tune-up is to bring the battery to full charge before the car is returned to the customer.

SPARK PLUGS

Spark Plugs Heat Range

The heat range of a spark plug is determined by the amount of porcelain exposed in the combustion chamber. A cold plug would have a comparatively small amount of porcelain exposed and thus cool more readily, whereas a hot plug would have more porcelain exposed which would make it function at a higher temperature.

See index for the spark plug chart which gives the recommended plug together with hotter and colder ranges. The normal plug should be used where the car is given normal service. If the car is driven hard or for long sustained high speed trips, then a colder than normal plug should be used. A hotter than normal plug should be used where the car has been driven slowly or for short trips only.

Gas fouled plug *Oil fouled plug*

Overheated plug

Spark Plug Service

Carefully clean or blow away the accumulated dust and grit from around the base of the spark plugs especially on L-head engines to prevent it from falling into the cylinder when the plug is removed.

Disconnect the ignition wires and remove all of the plugs. Examine the electrodes and the portion of the porcelain which extends into the combustion chamber. The porcelain should be a fairly clean light chocolate color and be free from cracks or blisters. The electrodes should be clean and not pitted or burned. Blisters or cracks on the porcelain indicate that the plug was too hot for the service in which it was used.

An accumulation of carbon or unburned oil on the porcelain indicates that the plug is too cold for the engine in which it is being used.

If the plug is serviceable, clean and carefully set the gap using a wire gauge. Always use a new gasket when replacing a spark plug.

Before replacing the spark plug make the following compression tests:

COMPRESSION TESTS

This test is not actually a part of tune-up since it does nothing to improve the engine. However, it is wise to make a compression test while the plugs are out to determine the general condition of the engine.

The compression gauge is used to determine how much the charge of each cylinder will be compressed.

This is usually accomplished by removing all of the spark plugs and placing the compression gauge in one of the cylinders. Crank the engine with the starter until the gauge reads maximum for that cylinder. This test should be made on each cylinder with the engine thoroughly warmed up and the oil at operating temperature.

All cylinders should read the same within 5 or 10 pounds. A deviation of more than 10 pounds between cylinders indicates a serious loss of pressure in the lower reading cylinder.

Compression may be lost past the rings, the valves, or the head gasket. A quick check of the rings may be made on the low reading cylinder by squirting oil through the spark plug hole around the outer rim of the piston, being careful not to get oil on the valves. If after putting oil on the top of the piston that cylinder, upon being rechecked, has a normal reading, then the rings, which

Vacuum Gauge Readings

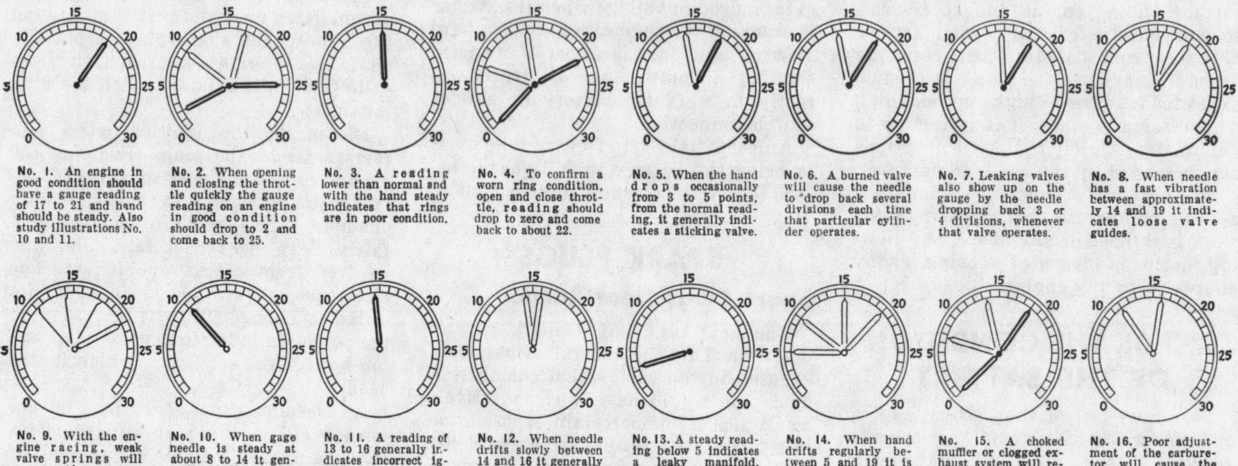
No. 1. An engine in good condition should have a gauge reading of 17 to 21 and hand should be steady. Also study illustrations No. 10 and 11.

No. 2. When opening and closing the throttle quickly the gauge reading on an engine in good condition should drop to 2 and come back to 25.

No. 3. A reading lower than normal and with the hand steady indicates that rings are in poor condition.

No. 4. To confirm a worn ring condition, open and close throttle, reading should drop to zero and come back to about 22.

No. 5. When the hand drops occasionally from 3 to 5 points, from the normal reading, it generally indicates a sticking valve.

No. 6. A burned valve will cause the needle to drop back several divisions each time that particular cylinder operates.

No. 7. Leaking valves also show up on the gauge by the needle dropping back 3 or 4 divisions, whenever that valve operates.

No. 8. When needle has a fast vibration between approximately 14 and 19 it indicates loose valve guides.

No. 9. With the engine racing, weak valve springs will cause the gauge needle to swing back and forth. The faster the engine speed the greater the swing.

No. 10. When gage needle is steady at about 8 to 14 it generally indicates incorrect valve timing. See also illustrations 3, 4 and 11.

No. 11. A reading of 13 to 16 generally indicates incorrect ignition timing. See also illustrations 3, 4 and 10.

No. 12. When needle drifts slowly between 14 and 16 it generally indicates that plug gaps are too close, or breaker points are not properly synchronized.

No. 13. A steady reading below 5 indicates a leaky manifold, gasket or carburetor gasket. Also check heat riser.

No. 14. When hand drifts regularly between 5 and 19 it is generally caused by a compression leak between cylinders.

No. 15. A choked muffler or clogged exhaust system will result in a normal reading when the engine is started, but reading will soon drop to zero.

No. 16. Poor adjustment of the carburetor will cause the needle to float slowly between 12 and 16. See also illustration 12.

have been temporarily sealed by the fresh oil, are permitting the compression pressures to escape.

If no improvement is shown, then the valves or the head gasket are responsible for the loss of pressure.

If two adjacent cylinders show a low reading, then there is a possibility that the head gasket between these two cylinders is damaged or ineffective.

A quick check to determine if the cylinder head gasket is defective is to torque the cylinder head down carefully and if any slight improvement is shown after torquing the head, then the gasket may be the cause of the loss of compression.

The condition of the valves may be double checked by using a vacuum gauge.

VACUUM GAUGE CHECKS

The vacuum gauge is used to determine the difference between atmospheric pressure and the pressures in the manifold.

The comparatively low pressure existing in the manifold of an engine under normal operating conditions is usually referred to as vacuum and will be referred to as such in this text.

Vacuum gauges are usually calibrated in "Inches of Mercury." This means that the gauge is registering a force or vacuum of sufficient strength to raise a column of mercury the number of inches indicated on the gauge.

The chart above shows the gauge readings which will be obtained under the conditions given under each gauge shown.

IGNITION DISTRIBUTOR

The purpose of the ignition distributor is to make and break the primary circuit of the spark coil and distribute the secondary high tension current to the proper spark plug at the correct time to fire the combustible mixture most advantageously.

Since the proper time to fire the combustible mixture varies with the speed of the engine and the load on the engine, the distributor is usually equipped with a centrifugal advance mechanism which causes the spark to fire sooner as the engine speeds up. There is also a vacuum control unit which further controls the advance of the spark according to the load on the engine. To insure that the spark fires at the correct time for any speed or load, it is essential that both the centrifugal advance mechanism and the vacuum control unit function properly.

Distributor Service

Remove the distributor cap, rotor, breaker points and breaker plate to ascertain if the centrifugal mechanism is functioning properly.

The centrifugal mechanism is usually composed of two pivoted weights to which are attached carefully calibrated springs. Make sure that the weights are free to turn on their pivots and that the springs are in good condition. If

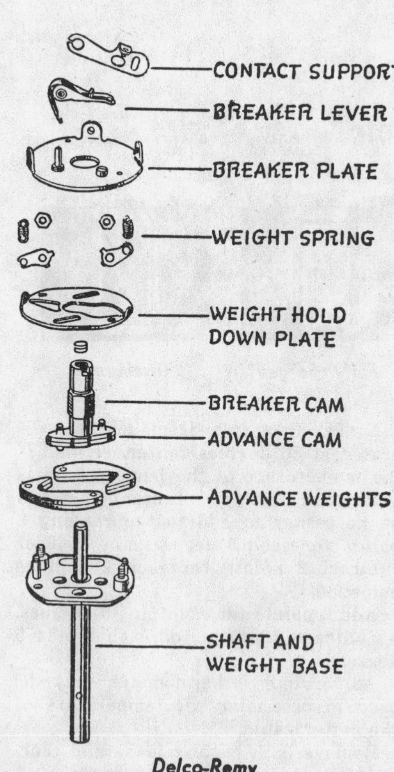

Delco-Remy

any binding is noticed as the weights are forced outward with the fingers, or if the weights fail to return to the in position upon being released, the breaker plate unit should be replaced.

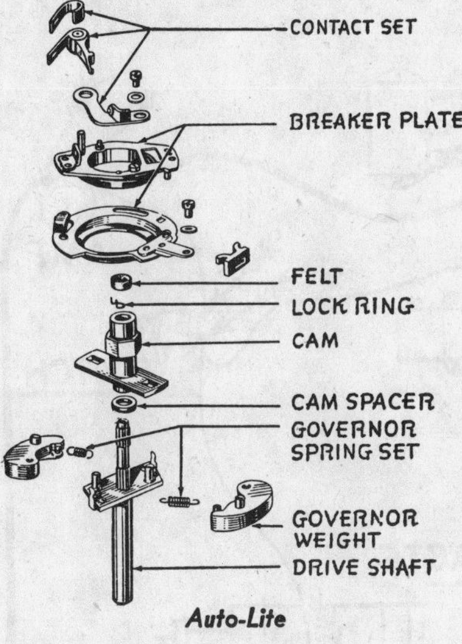

Auto-Lite

Ignition Breaker Points

The purpose of the ignition breaker point is to make and break the primary electrical circuit of the coil. It is absolutely essential that the breaker points make a clean, firm contact and break cleanly. Breaker points which contact on one side or have a high spot in the center should be discarded and new points installed and adjusted so that the contact surface is all over the contact area. Contacts that show a clear grayish color and are only very slightly pitted need not be replaced. However, since their cost is nominal it is better to install new breaker points than to attempt to clean and reservice old ones. The point gap should be checked very carefully with either a cam angle or wire gages. When setting breaker points with a cam angle gauge, follow the instructions given by the manufacturer of the gauge. To check breaker point gaps with wire or thickness gauge, the GO and NOT GO method is perhaps the best way to insure proper spacing of the points. The GO and NOT GO method can be used for all space gauging. The method is very simple to set up breaker points for say .015 inch; first selecte the .014 wire and a .016 wire, adjust the points so that the .014 wire will pass freely between them and the .016 wire will not enter at any point. Therefore, the point is something more than .014 and less than .016, for all practical purposes .015 inch.

Condenser

The primary purpose of the condenser is to prevent excessive arcing at the contact points. When the contacts first open, the current tends to continue flowing toward the gap causing an arc; the condenser absorbs this current until it, the condenser, becomes fully charged. By this time the contact points have opened too far to allow a spark to jump across them. The charge accumulated in the condenser is dissipated as soon as the contacts make again.

Condensers should be inspected for broken or frayed installation on the leads, loose or corroded terminals. Make sure that the condenser is firmly mounted and makes a good ground contact.

Ignition Timing

Wherever possible the ignition timing should be set with a neon timing light while the engine is idling. Loosen the distributor clamp screw and rotate the distributor so that the neon light flashes just as the ignition spark passes the pointer on either the vibration damper or the flywheel.

Vacuum Control Unit

Vacuum control units are usually of the diaphragm type and require no servicing other than to see that there are no leaks in the diaphragm, and that the rod that connects with the distributor body does not bind when moving backward or forward.

Some vacuum control units rotate the entire distributor to cause the advance in spark timing. However, some models rotate a movable breaker plate inside the distributor. This breaker plate is generally mounted on three ball bearings inside the distributor housing. On the movable breaker plate type distributor the services where the ball bearing contacts the housing and the breaker plate should be examined carefully before burrs, dirt or grit prevent the plate from turning freely.

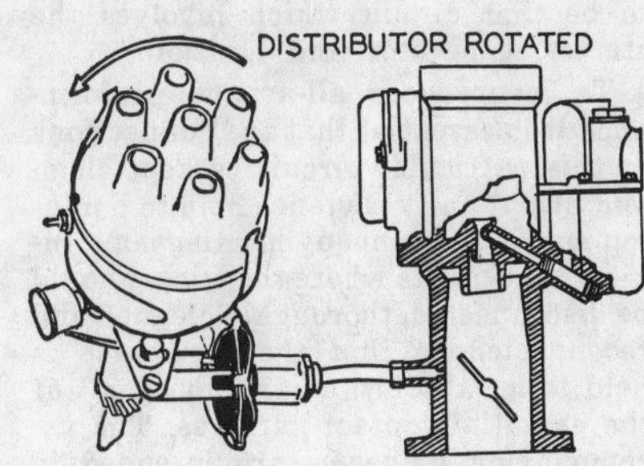

Vacuum control with carburetor

VALVE CLEARANCE

Clearance is allowed between the top of the tappet screw at the bottom of the valve stem to permit the valve to expand due to heat. If no clearance was allowed at this point, the valve would remain open after the engine became warm, thus preventing the proper function of the engine.

However, checking the clearance of valves can sometimes be dispensed with if the compression readings were normal and the vacuum gauge readings are normal and the valve tappets are not exceptionally noisy. In this case it may be safely assumed that the clearance is correct.

If it is necessary to adjust the valve tappet clearance, the GO and NO GO method is perhaps the best. Remove the valve cover plate (L-head engines) or the rocker cover (overhead valve engines) and adjust the valve tappet (or rocker arm) until a thickness gauge of the proper thickness is just gripped. This setting may then be checked by passing a gauge .001 thinner than the proper gauge which should pass freely and rechecking with a gauge which is .001 thicker. This gauge should not enter at

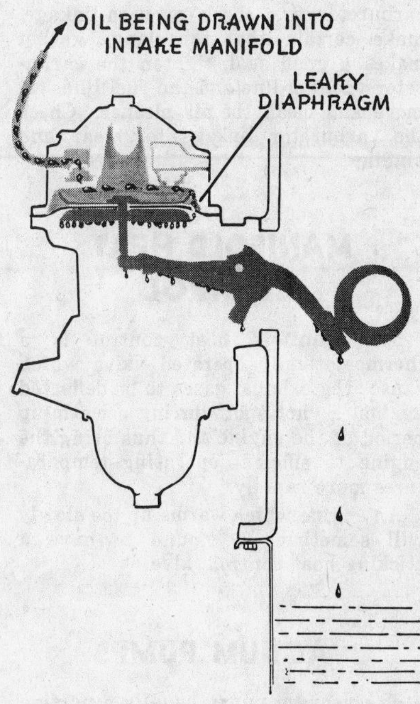

all. Then the lash is something more than .001 under and less than .001 over; therefore, for all practical purposes, it is exactly the right clearance. Where the tappet screw is equipped with a jamb nut, the nut should be tightened securely before the final GO and NO GO check is made.

CARBURETOR

The purpose of the carburetor is to supply a combustible mixture of the proper air-fuel ratio for the infinitely variable conditions encountered in an automobile engine.

Carburetors are usually designed so that they supply a very lean mixture under no load conditions and a comparatively rich mixture for pulling or heavy loads.

For the proper adjustment of the various carburetors refer to the carburetor section of this manual since carburetors are usually adjusted or calibrated differently for each car.

Since all other conditions of the engine affect carburetion, the carburetor should be adjusted last.

Service Procedure

Regardless of the carburetor used or the particular method of adjusting that carburetor, first check for worn linkage, make certain that the flange gasket makes a good seal, tighten the carburetor vacuum line and the fuel line, remove and clean the air cleaner. Check the carburetor linkage for wear and binding.

MANIFOLD HEAT CONTROL

The manifold heat control is a thermostatically operated valve which causes the exhaust gases to be deflected against a "hot spot" during a warm-up period of the engine and thus bring the engine to efficient operating temperatures more rapidly.

An engine which warms up too slowly will sometimes be found to have a sticking heat control valve.

VACUUM PUMPS

The vacuum pump, usually a portion of the fuel pump casting, is intended to supply a constant vacuum to operate accessories like windshield wipers, window lifts, vacuum power cylinders, etc.

A small leak in the vacuum diaphragm may draw oil from the crankcase and force it up into the intake manifold and cause very high oil consumption.

A leak in the vacuum diaphragm generally shows up in the early stages as a miss on the two cylinders nearest the position of the manifold where the vacuum tube enters the manifold.

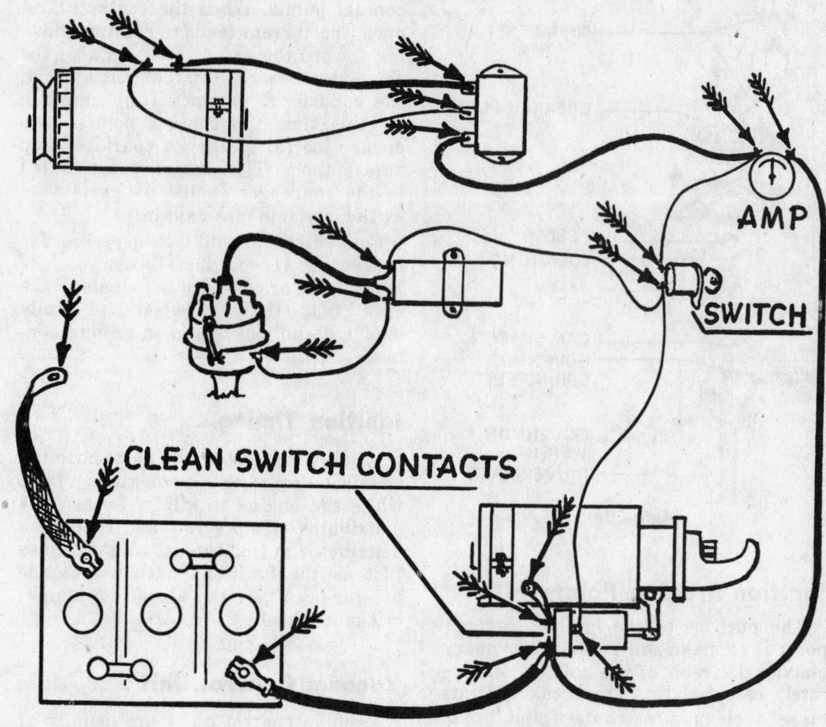

Primary electrical circuit

PRIMARY ELECTRICAL CIRCUIT

The primary electrical circuit is said to be that circuit which involves the starter, generator and ignition.

To insure good all-around performance it is essential that the connections in this particular circuit be kept clean and bright and resistance held to a minimum. The accompanying diagrams indicate the points where the wires should be disconnected, thoroughly cleaned and reconnected so that the resistance is held to an absolute minimum on all of the essential contact surfaces. The accompanying diagrams are intended to show only the parts which affect performance and are not intended to be complete or accurate wiring diagrams.

THE STARTING MOTOR

When tuning a car for winter service, it is always a good idea to remove the starter, clean the commutator, make certain that the brushes are making a good contact, clean and remove contacts of the starter switch so that the starter motor will function at peak efficiency during the cold weather when it is under its greatest strain.

GENERATOR

The purpose of the generator is to supply electrical current for the accessories and vital electrical units and to maintain the battery at full charge. On most late model cars the generator is equipped with a regulator which is intended to limit the amount of current to a safe maximum for the variable conditions which exist in any vehicle.

The generator commutator may be cleaned and the brushes checked for contact and sticking without removing the unit from the car.

AUTOMATIC TRANSMISSION SECTION

SERVICE AND ADJUSTMENT PROCEDURE

HYDRAMATIC

HYDRAMATIC TRANSMISSIONS

Hydramatic transmissions are now used on Hudson, Lincoln, Frazer, Oldsmobile, Kaiser, Nash, Cadillac and Pontiac. The design of the hydramatic for each of these cars is slightly different due to the different engine characteristics. However, from the standpoint of servicing the transmission there are only three broad types.

The first type, used on Oldsmobile from 1940 through 1942, had a front pump which was made in one piece with the front servo and was driven from a gear on the transmission shaft just like a speedometer gear.

The second general type which started in 1946 production has an internal gear type front pump completely separated from the front servo.

The third type which started with 1951 production had a vane type front pump and a cone clutch reverse anchor.

While many refinements and improvements in design have been added from year to year, and the various component parts have a slightly different shape, service procedure is practically the same for all three types.

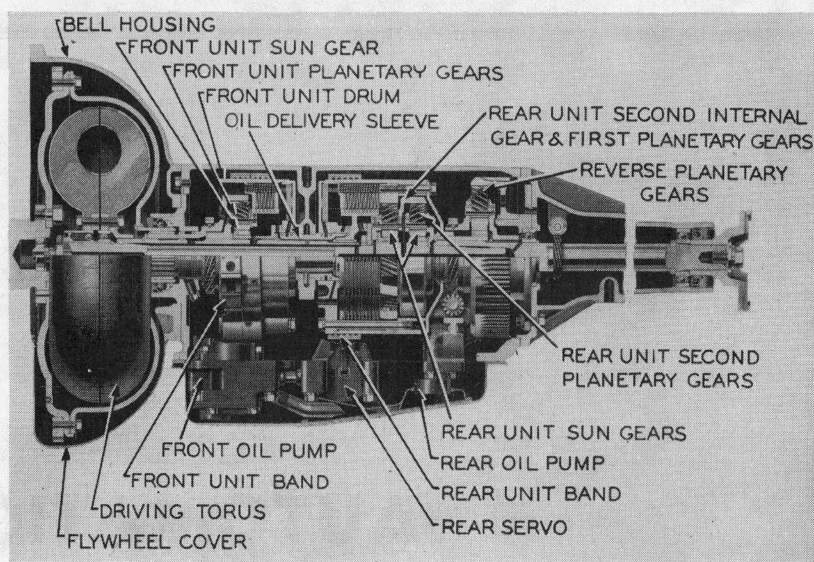

Cross section of the Hydramatic transmission used up to and including 1942—Note: Location of front pump

OPERATION OF THE HYDRAMATIC

Reduced to its simplest terms a hydramatic transmission consists of two 2-speed planetary transmissions back to back, controlled by hydraulically operated bands and clutches.

A fluid coupling (called a torus member) is provided to absorb the shock of gear changing and also to provide the necessary slip required when the car is stationary while the transmission is in any of its operating ranges.

Each planetary unit has two speeds: a gear reduction by means of planetary gearing, and direct drive by means of clutches.

The rear planetary unit has greater gear reduction than the front unit which makes it possible to get a total of four forward speeds within the transmission itself.

On either planetary units applying the band and releasing the clutch provides gear reduction; the band is released and the clutch applied for direct drive.

When both band and clutch are released the transmission is in neutral.

For the sake of clarity this text will refer to the speeds as 1st (lowest), 2nd, 3rd and 4th (highest).

1st speed is by planetary reduction in both units.

2nd speed is by planetary reduction in the rear unit, direct drive in the front unit.

3rd speed is by planetary reduction in the first front unit, direct drive in the rear unit.

4th speed is by direct drive in both units.

The car speed at which the transmission shifts automatically from one speed to another is controlled by two valves within the transmission; the governor valves and the throttle valve.

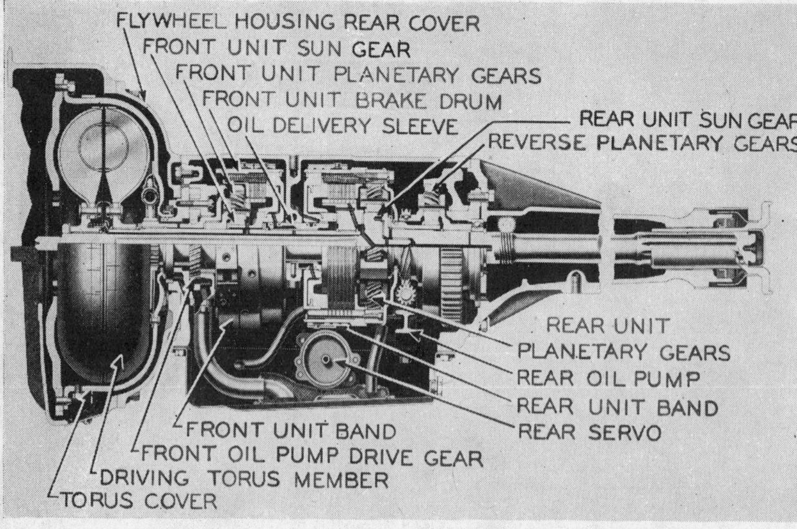

Cross section of the Hydramatic transmission 1946 thru 1950. Starting in 1951 a cone clutch rear unit is used

Governor

Inside the transmission there is a centrifugal governor driven by the output shaft so that the governor turns in exact proportion to car speed.

As governor speed increases, centrifugal weights tend to move outward away from center, opening ports which direct oil pressure to the shift valves.

Throttle Pressures

The throttle is connected by mechanical linkage to a control valve inside the transmission.

As the throttle is opened, the control valve moves, uncovering ports which direct controlled oil pressure to the shift valves in opposition to the pressure from the governor valves. This means that higher governor (car) speeds are required to move the shift valves when the throttle is opened. The accompanying chart shows approximately the relationship between governor (car) speeds and throttle opening as it effects automatic shifting.

To utilize to best advantage the four speeds within the transmission there is a selector lever mounted on the side of the transmission case (called the transmission selector lever). Mechanical linkage connects the transmission selector lever with the manual selector lever located at the top of the steering column. To avoid confusion this text will refer to the manual selector lever as the shift lever since it is located where the shift lever would be in a car with conventional transmission.

All hydramatics except the 1952 dual range models provide four positions for the shift lever. The four positions are clearly marked on the shift quadrant just under the steering wheel: DRIVE, LOW, NEUTRAL, REVERSE.

A pointer connected to the shift lever indicates on the quadrant which speed range the transmission is operating in.

1952 dual range models have two arrows and the numerals 3 and 4 under the word "drive" on the quadrant. One arrow (3) is for the performance drive range, the other (4) is the normal drive range.

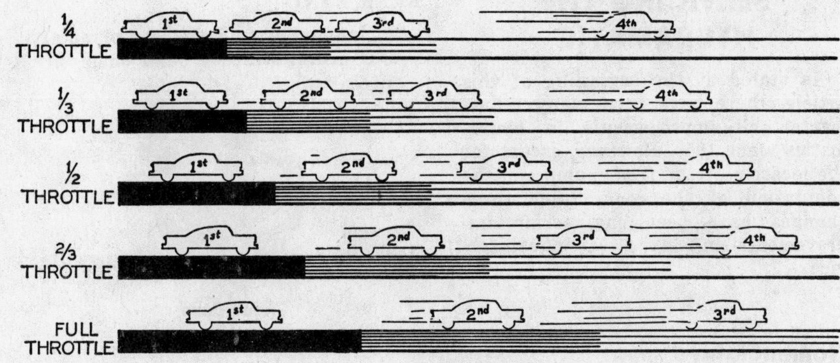

Artist sketch showing relationship of shift points to throttle opening. Note that full throttle blocks out 4th speed

Drive Range

ALL HYDRAMATICS UP TO 1950

On all of the above models, when the shift lever is placed in the drive range, the transmission starts in 1st, shifts automatically to 2nd, to 3rd, to 4th as the car speed increases.

THREE FORWARD SPEED MODELS

Starting with late 1950 production hydramatics were used which, when the shift lever was placed in the drive range, started in second gear, shifted automatically to 3rd, to 4th as the car speed increased.

DUAL RANGE MODELS

Starting with 1952 production a dual range hydramatic was introduced. The dual range can be identified by two arrows and the numerals 3 and 4 under the word "drive" on the shift quadrant. The arrow on the right (3) indicates the performance drive range. When the shift lever is placed in this range the transmission starts in 1st and shifts automatically to 2nd, to 3rd but not to 4th—3 speeds.

The arrow on the left (4) indicates the normal drive range. In normal drive range the transmission starts in first, shifts automatically to 2nd, to 3rd, to 4th—4 speeds.

Low Range

All hydramatics function practically the same in low range.

The car starts in 1st and shifts automatically to 2nd.

The shift from 1st to 2nd is accomplished at somewhat higher speeds (for any given throttle opening) than the shift from 1st to 2nd when in drive range.

Reverse

All hydramatics up to 1950 effect reverse by locking the reverse ring gear mechanically which causes the output shaft to revolve opposite to the main shaft and at reduced speed. Starting with late 1951 production a cone clutch is used to lock the reverse ring gear which permits easier and smoother rocking.

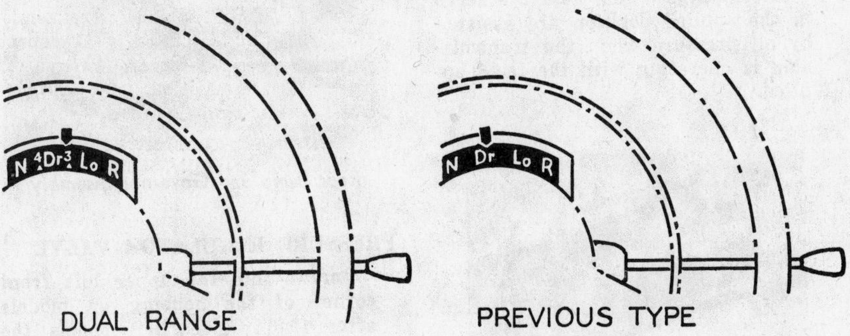

Shift quadrants showing the early type and dual range type

SERVICING THE HYDRAMATIC

As stated at the beginning of this article, there have been many refinements and improvements in hydramatics since 1940. However, except for the location of the front pump and the adaptation of the cone clutch these changes have been engineering improvements and in no way affect service.

Nomenclature

In order to avoid confusion, the name given to each unit or subassembly in this text will be as follows:

FRONT PLANETARY ASSEMBLY

The assembly consists of planetary gears, clutch, clutch pressure plate, hydraulic piston (ring type) or pistons (1940 thru 1942 models). It is used toward the front of the unit.

REAR PLANETARY ASSEMBLY

Practically the same as the front planetary assembly but used toward the rear of the unit.

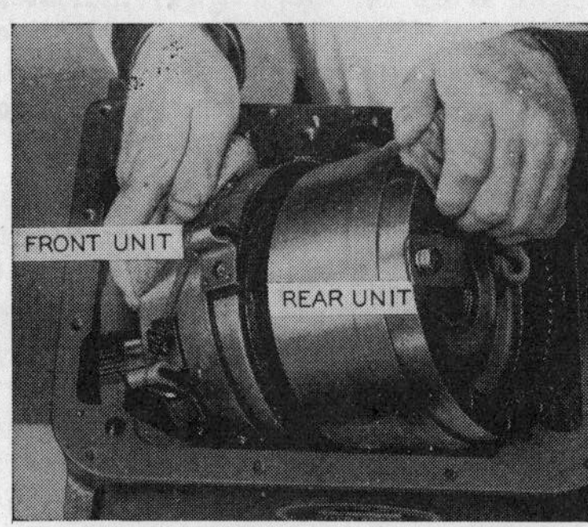

Front and Rear Planatary assembly

FRONT BAND

Mounted around the front planetary unit drum, made to wrap around twice.

Front Band

REAR BAND

Mounted around the rear planetary unit drum; wraps around once only.

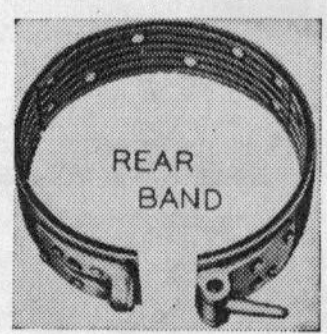

Rear Band

FRONT SERVO

Mounted to the underside of the hydramatic housing casting in a position to actuate (apply and release) the front band. Action is somewhat similar to a single piston type hydraulic brake cylinder. Front servo is normally in the released position and is applied by means of oil pressure from the pump.

Front Servo

REAR SERVO

Mounted to the underside of the hydramatic housing casting. Actuates the rear band through a lever which is considered a part of the rear servo assembly. Normally held in the applied position by means of heavy springs the rear servo is released by means of oil pressure.

The springs which hold the servo in the applied position are assisted by oil pressure when the transmission is operating with the band applied.

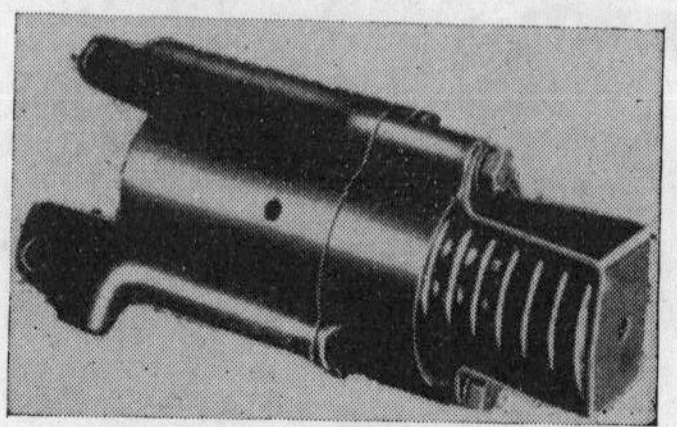

Rear Servo

FRONT OIL PUMP

On 1940 thru 1942 models the front oil pump is a part of the front servo casting and is driven from a gear on the transmission shaft. Starting with 1946 production the front oil pump is an internal rotary gear type mounted in front of the front planetary unit. The transmission must be removed and disassembled to take out the front pump on all models starting with 1946.

Starting with 1952 production a vane type pump, mounted in the same place as the rotary gear pump on earlier models, is used.

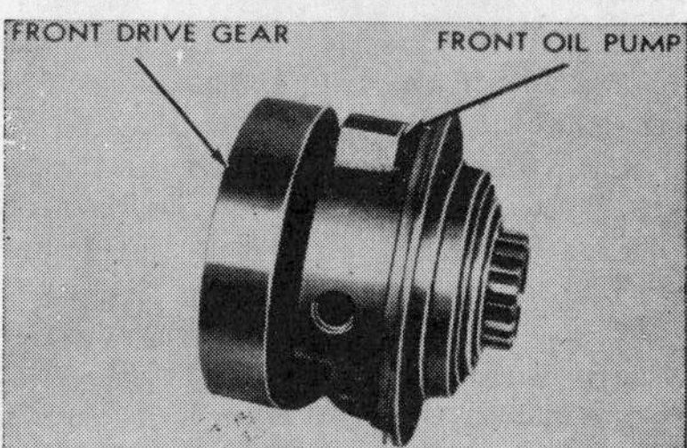

Front Pump assembly

REAR OIL PUMP

Attached to the underside of the housing casting driven by the transmission output shaft.

GOVERNOR

Attached to the rear oil pump shaft projects through the side opening in the housing. The governor sleeve is connected by tubes to the control valve body.

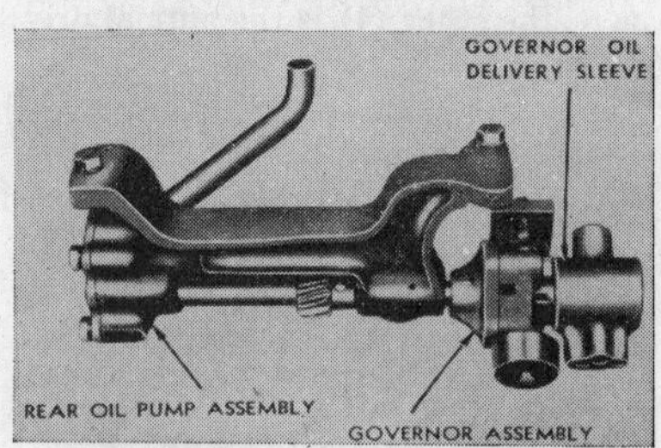

Rear Pump and Governor assembly

PRESSURE REGULATOR VALVE

Screws into the upper left front corner of the housing on models after 1946. On earlier models the valve is part of the front pump-servo casting (the white metal portion is the regulator valve body).

Removing Pressure Regulator Valve assembly

OIL DELIVERY SLEEVE

Located between the front and rear planetary assemblies mounted on the web of a housing in a manner similar to a main bearing in an engine.

Oil Delivery Sleeve

REVERSE PLANETARY ASSEMBLY

Mounted at the rear of the housing back of the rear planetary unit. The reverse assembly is carried on the rear cover.

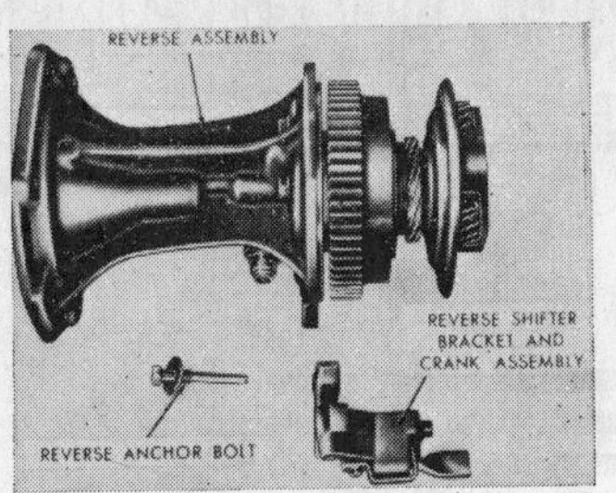

Reverse Assembly with Shifter Bracket

TORUS MEMBERS

The two members making up the fluid coupling mounted at (but not on) the flywheel.

The one nearest the flywheel is called the driven torus member, the one farthest from the flywheel is called the driving torus member.

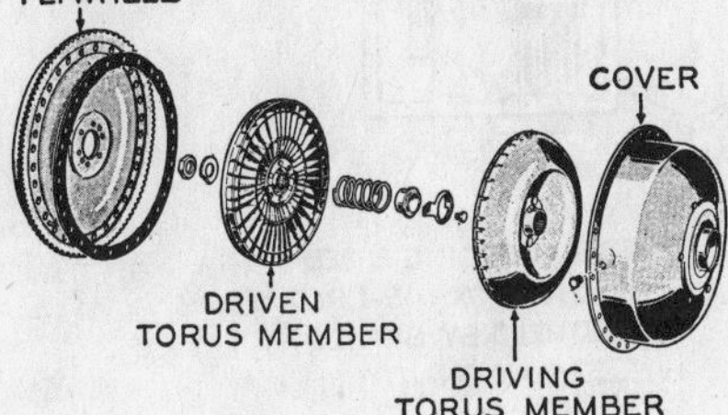

Torus Members

MAIN SHAFT

The long solid shaft connecting the driven torus member (front) with the rear planetary assembly sun gear (generally the sun gear is made in one piece with the shaft).

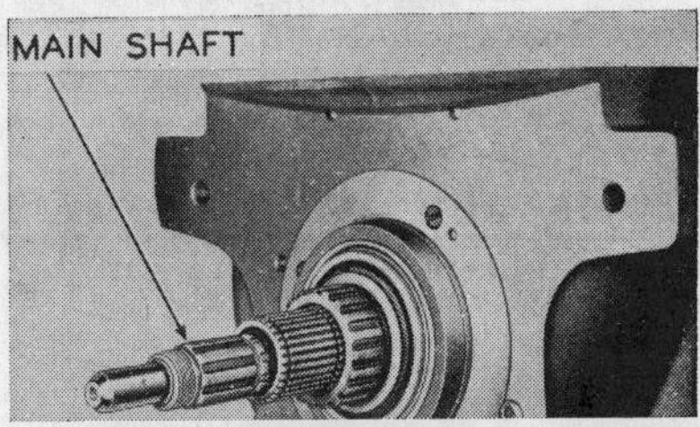

Main Shaft

OUTPUT SHAFT

The solid spline shaft which connects the rear planetary assembly pinion cage with the universal joint.

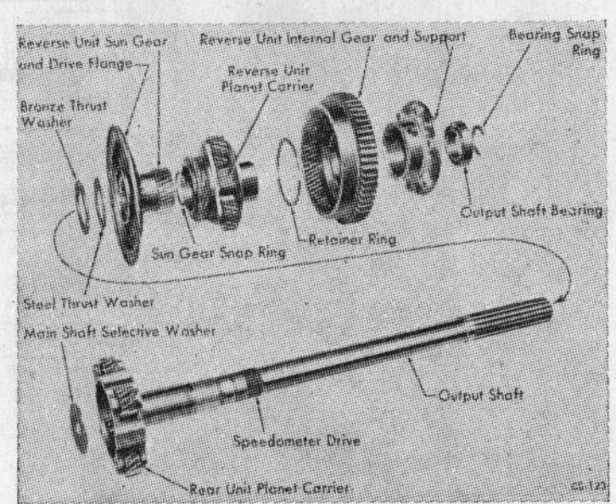

Output Shaft Assembly Disassembled

CONTROL VALVE ASSEMBLY

The control valve assembly is mounted on the side of the casting under the side cover. The assembly is made up of six valve units: the control valve; throttle valve; transition valve; 1st to 2nd shift valve; 2nd to 3rd shift valve; and 3rd to 4th shift valve.

The valves are calibrated with extreme care and no actual repairing can be done successfully on them other than careful disassembly to clean and oil. The control valve assembly *must* be free of foreign matter such as grit, dirt, oil, residues, etc. These valves MUST operate freely without sticking.

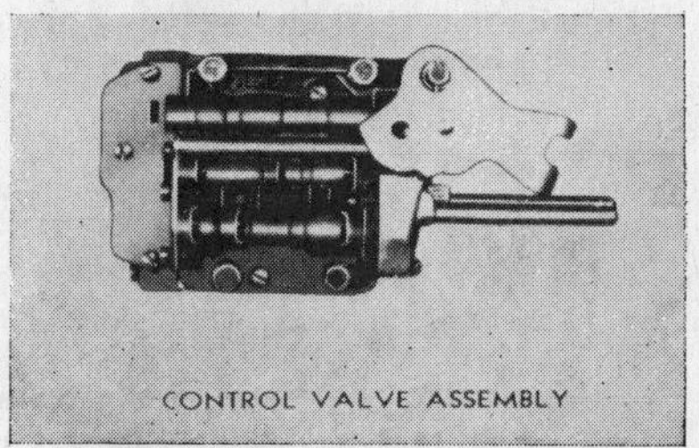

Main Oil Control Body assembly

OIL LEVEL

Before doing any servicing or trouble shooting on any hydramatic check the oil level.

In order to get an accurate check on the oil level run the car until the engine and transmission are thoroughly warmed up. The shift lever should be placed in each of its ranges including reverse to be certain that the oil has reached all valves and passages. Move the shift lever to neutral and with the engine idling check the height of the oil on the dip stick.

If the dip stick shows less than full add oil up to the full mark. More than full on the dip stick may mean that the torus member is not quite full. Drive the car for a few minutes to be certain that the torus member is full and again recheck the dip stick. Excess oil can be drained out through the dip stick vent. Too much oil may cause foaming when the transmission is hot.

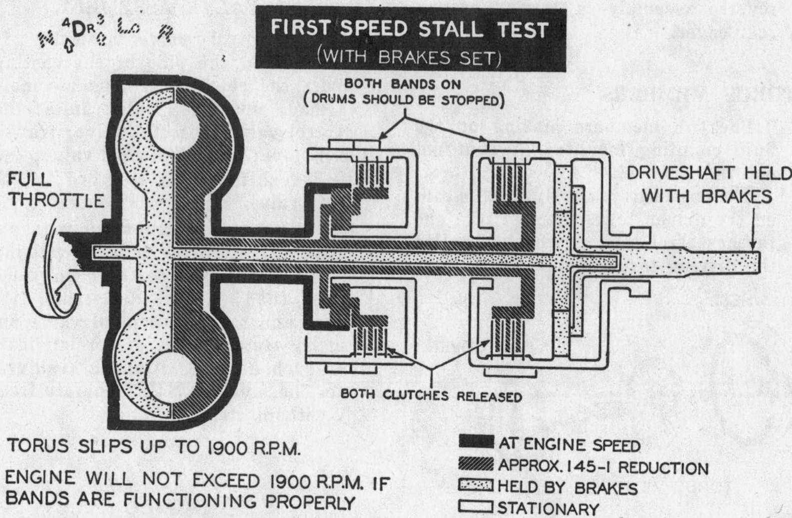

TROUBLE SHOOTING

Road Tests for Slipping

Caution: The stall and brake tests given here place a considerable overload on the torus member and should not be held for more than 30 seconds at a time.

First Speed Stall Test

Attach a tachometer to the engine and place the transmission in low range. Set the brakes so that the car cannot move.

Open the throtle to speed up the engine. If both front and rear planetary bands are functioning properly engine speed will not exceed 1900 rpm's even with wide open throttle.

If the engine speed exceeds 1900 rpm either the front band, or the rear band, or both bands are slipping. If either of the bands are slipping as indicated in the first speed stall test it is a good idea to adjust the bands and see if an adjustment will correct the slip. If a band adjustment does not correct the slip it will probably be necessary to remove the front and/or rear servo. Both front and rear servo can be removed, cleaned, inspected and replaced with the hydramatic in the car.

Reverse Stall Test

MODELS WITH REVERSE CONE CLUTCHES (after 1951)

The reverse test on the above models is intended to determine if the cone clutch is slipping. It can be considered a positive test only if the first speed stall test indicates both bands are holding properly. However, certain sensible diagnoses can be made by combining the results of the two tests.

Set the shift lever in the reverse position and apply the brakes to prevent the car from moving, speed up the engine. The tachometer should show 1900 rpm or less even with wide open throttle. If engine speed exceeds 1900 rpm the reverse cone clutch is slipping. Combine the results of the first speed and the reverse speed test. If the tachometer reads over 1900 rpm on the first speed test (let us say 2100 rpm and the reverse test also reads 2100 rpm it probably means that the front band is slipping since the front band is applied in both tests whereas the rear band is applied in the first speed test but not in the reverse test. The cone clutch is applied in the reverse test but not in the first speed test.

If the engine speed is lower in reverse than it is in the first speed test very likely the rear band is slipping. If the engine speed in reverse test is higher than the first speed test and both tests are more than 1900 (say the first speed is 2100 rpm, reverse 2400 rpm) it would mean that both the front band and the reverse clutch are slipping.

MODELS WITH MECHANICAL REVERSE ANCHORS (up to 1950)

It is not necessary to make reverse stall test on the above models if the first speed test shows that both bands are holding properly.

The purpose of this test is to determine which of the bands are slipping, if the first speed test indicates slipping.

Place the shift lever in reverse and hold the car with the brakes, open the throttle. If the engine comes to the same speed as it did in the first speed test (over 1900 rpm's) it indicates that the front band is slipping since the front band is applied in both tests.

If the engine stays at or below 1900 rpm the front band is holding properly

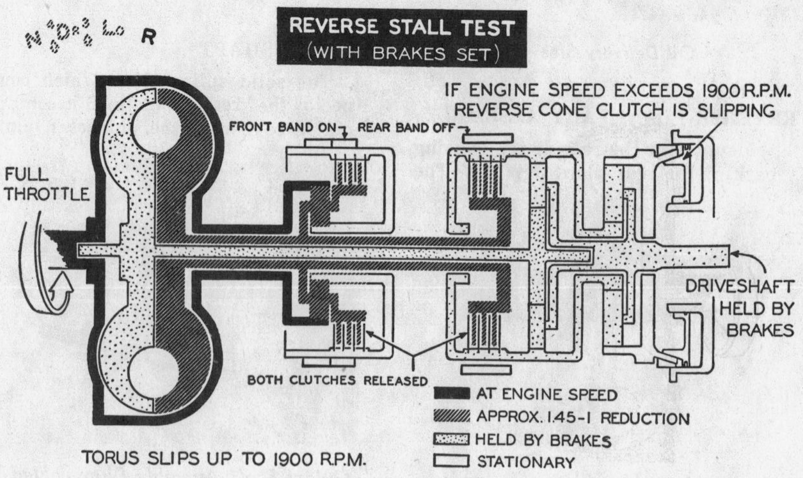

and it was the rear band which slipped in the first speed test.

Second Speed Test for Slipping

(Caution: Since this test requires that the car be driven on the road it is advisable to have a helper drive the car so that his full attention can be given to the highway.)

Drive the car with the shift lever in low range, notice when the transmission shifts to 2nd speed. Hold the car to a constant low speed with the brakes applied while opening the throttle. (Do not slow the car any, since this may cause the transmission to down shift into first speed.)

There should be no noticeable increase in engine speed even if the throttle is open wide.

The front clutch and the rear band are engaged in this test though we have already determined by the first speed and reverse stall test that the bands are functioning properly. Therefore any noticeable increase in engine speed indicates a slipping front clutch.

Third Speed Test for Slipping

Set the shift lever in the drive range position (normal drive range on dual range models) and drive the car at about 30 miles per hour or until the transmission is in 4th speed.

Now force the transmission to down shift to 3rd speed by opening the throttle wide. With the throttle held wide open decrease the car speed with the brakes. Engine speed should decrease with car speed. If it does not the rear clutch is slipping.

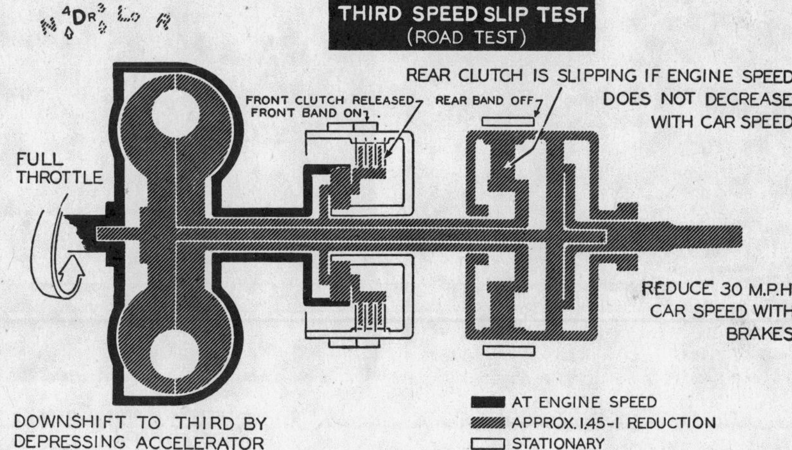

The front band and rear clutch are engaged in 3rd speed but the first speed and reverse stall test checked the bands.

Neutral Test

Place the shift lever in neutral and speed up the engine. The car may have a slight tendency to creep. This is normal particularly in new cars, but there should be no tendency to move forcibly.

Any tendency to move forcibly indicates shift linkage out of adjustment.

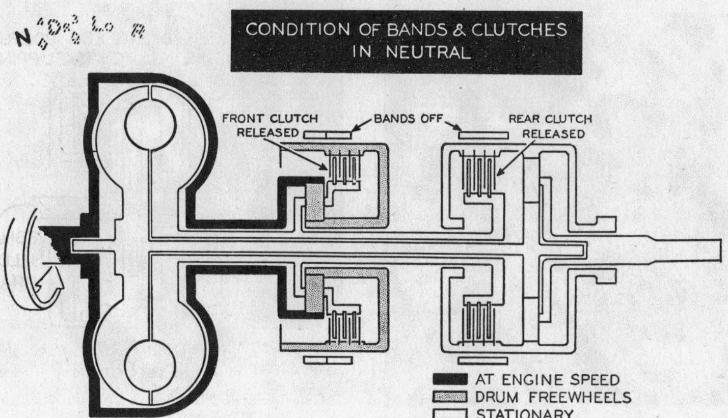

Power Flow in Neutral

HYDRAMATIC

SERVICE IN THE CAR

A considerable amount of servicing can be done without removing the hydramatic transmission from the car.

Removal of Sub-Assemblies

The following sub-assemblies can be removed from any hydramatic transmission while it is in the car.

Front Servo; rear servo; rear pump and governor assembly; control valve body and (on models up to 1942) the front pump.

In addition on some models the reverse planetary assembly can be taken out the back of the transmision without removing the transmission from the car. This is only possible on models where there are at least 4½ inches space in back of the transmission to slide the rear planetary unit backwards.

To remove the above units proceed as follows: drain the oil and remove the oil pan. Disconnect the linkage and shift arms and take off the side cover pan.

The rear servo or the valve control body can then be removed without disturbing any part of the transmission.

After the valve body has been removed the rear pump and governor assembly can be taken out through the bottom.

The front servo should be removed after the rear servo.

Note: On models up to 1942 the front servo and front oil pump are removed as a unit.

Caution: While many attempts have been made to replace the bands without removing the planetary assemblies from the transmission unless the operator has unbelievably good luck such attempts have always proved to be unsuccessful since it is necessary to distort and twist the band in order to forcibly remove it from the case with the planetaries in place.

The only practical way to replace either of the bands is to remove the hydramatic from the car and take out the planetary assemblies.

DISASSEMBLY OF HYDRAMATIC

Remove the hydramatic from the car and place on a cleared bench.

Remove the nut from the front of the

Fig. 1—Supporting Transmission

Fig. 2—Remove Torus Cover from Flywheel

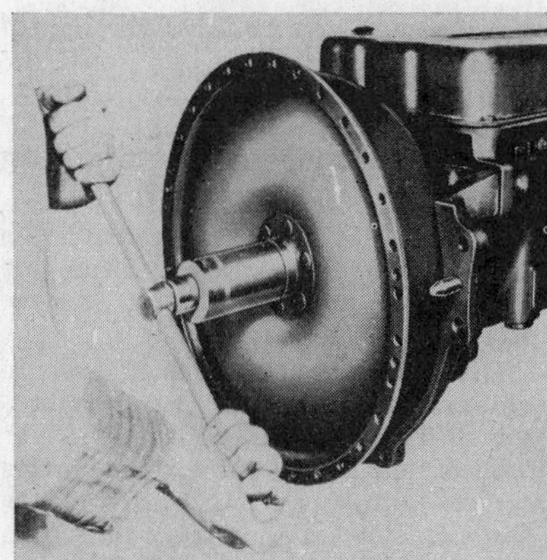

Fig. 3—Remove Mainshaft Nut

Fig. 4—Driving Torus showing Check Valve attached

Fig. 5—Remove Driving Torus Snap Ring

Fig. 6—Remove Driving Torus

main shaft and take off the front torus member. Take out the snap ring on the spline tube and slide off the rear torus member. Another snap ring holds the torus cover on to the next spline shaft.

Remove the torus cover and examine the hub where it enters the front oil seal. This hub should be free of scores and roughness since, especially on models after 1942, the hub oil seal holds the oil pressure from the front pump. It is therefore essential that it seal well.

Next remove the cast iron bell housing from the front of the hydramatic case.

Remove the lower oil pan and the side cover pan.

Remove the pressure regulator from the side of the case.

Refer to illustration for the bolts which hold the reverse assembly into the case. Remove these bolts and lift out the reverse assembly.

From the front of the case take out the oil pump drive gear and the oil pump body assembly. Next remove the front unit drive gear.

Note: On 1951 and 1952 models the front pump assembly together with the front drive gear come out of the front of the case as a single unit.

Next remove the cap from the oil delivery sleeve between the two planetary units.

Now carefully lift out both planetary units together with their brake bands.

Remove the snap ring from the front of the main shaft and slide the main shaft together with its rear unit sun gear out of the planetary units.

Down deep in the recess of the rear unit hub there is a snap ring. Remove this snap ring and both units can be separated from the oil delivery sleeve.

The accompanying illustrations show graphically how the planetary assemblies are disassembled.

Examination of the Parts Before Reassembly

Bear in mind that the most important single thing in the assembly of a hydramatic is that all parts be CLEAN and free of pits and scratches and well oiled.

Note: A great deal of time can be saved if the examination is conducted along reasonable lines. By that is meant, if the hydramatic has a record of having noisy gears, then particular attention should be paid to the various gears. If on the other hand the mechanism has the reputation of slipping but no particular record of noisy gears then much time can be saved by examining the parts which can cause slipping and ignoring (except for thorough

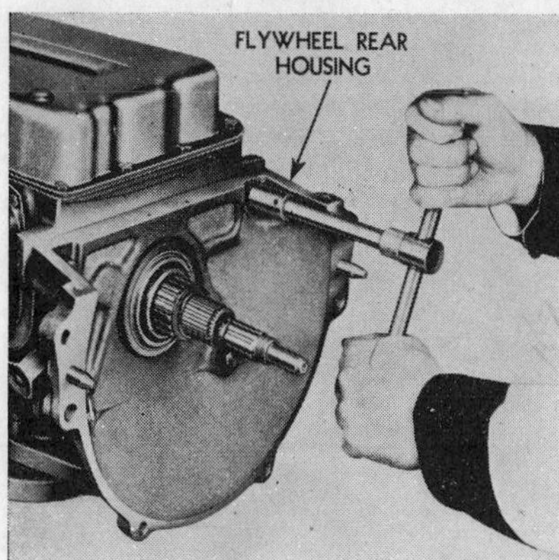

Fig. 7—Remove Flywheel Rear Housing

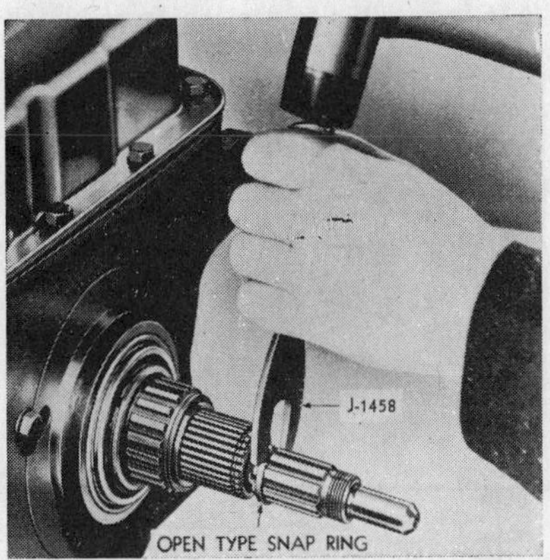

Fig. 8—Remove Mainshaft Snap Ring

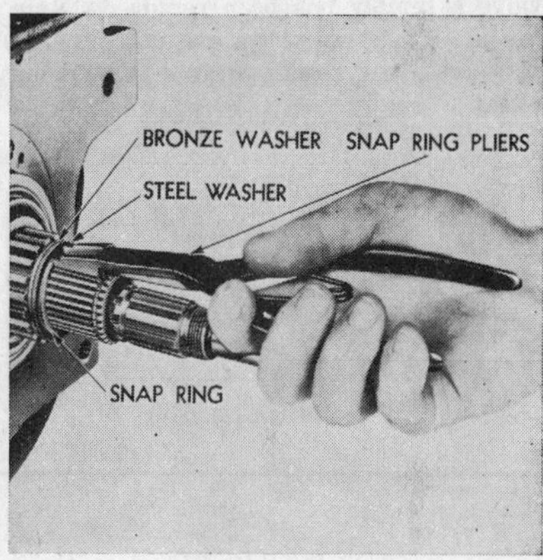

Fig. 9—Remove Front Drive Gear Snap Ring

Fig. 10—Remove Front Pump Locating Washer

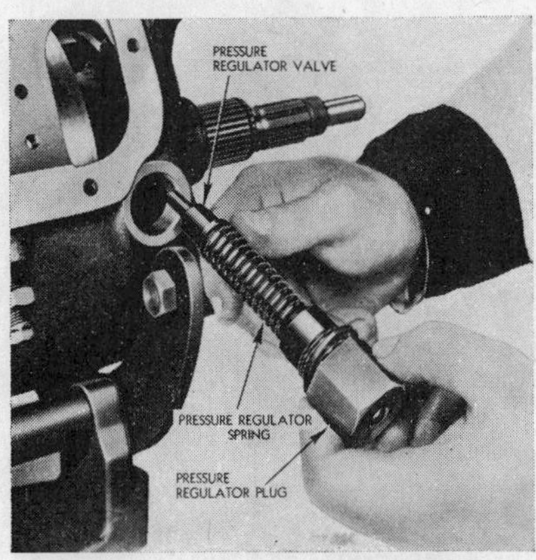

Fig. 11—Remove Oil Pressure Regulator Valve (can be removed any time before front pump)

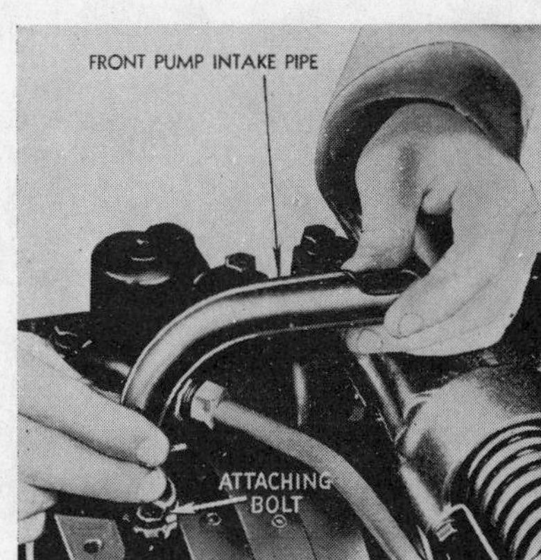

Fig. 12—Remove Front Pump Intake Pipe

EXAMINATION—continued

cleaning) the gears since, if they are not noisy, they are most likely in very excellent condition.

AIR PRESSURE TESTS

The functions of the various clutches and servos may be checked by means of air pressure either in the car or on the bench.

Remove the lower oil pan and the side cover. Take off the valve body assembly.

As already explained oil under pressure is directed by the valves to the various operating units through holes which are cored into the case. By applying air pressure to these various passages the operation of individual units can be checked with a high degree of accuracy.

Refer to the illustration which shows the side of a hydramatic case after the valve assembly has been removed. Note the holes leading to the passages which carry the air pressure to the various units.

Since the various different hydramatic assemblies have the holes in slightly different places it may be necessary to experiment somewhat to determine which hole leads to which unit.

Between 70 and 80 lbs air pressure are required and a cone-type nozzle should be attached to the air gun so that it will leak as little as possible at the junction between the air nozzle and hydramatic housing.

Apply air pressure to the hole which leads to the front servo (see illustration) and note the action of the servo. As air pressure is applied and released the servo should apply and release without sticking.

Bear in mind that some leakage is to be expected and is in fact desirable in the hydramatic units. As long as the full air pressure does not "blow by" the unit is probably in good condition. Apply air pressure to the cored hole which leads to the front clutch. While it is impossible to see the front clutch operate, its operation can be determined by listening and feeling the unit as the clutch is applied and released. Here again some "blow by" is to be expected and so that it is not excessive the unit is still in good condition.

Caution: Bear in mind that oil will leak much less than air and also that oil will seal the rings. Therefore the unit should be thoroughly oiled before these tests are made. If the unit is dry, air may blow by in excessive quantities whereas it would have a good seal if the unit were thoroughly lubricated.

Move from hole to hole and check the action of the front servo, the rear servo, the front clutch, and the rear clutch.

If all units function well under 70 to 80 lbs air pressure it can safely be assumed that the mechanical function of the unit is good. If a hydramatic which passes the air pressure test gives trouble it will generally be found in either the governor or the valves, or the oil pumps.

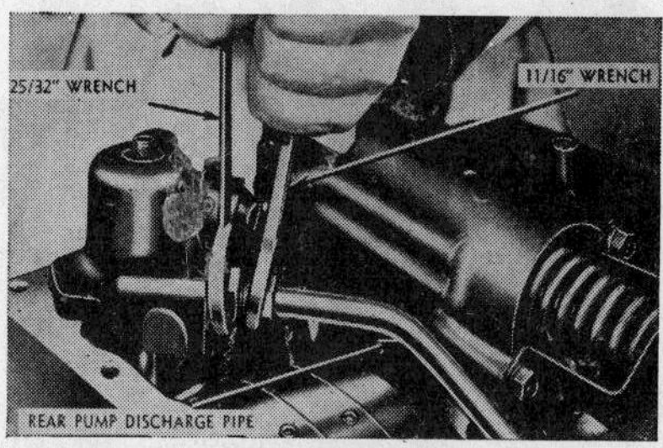

Fig. 13—Disconnect Rear Pump Discharge Pipe Fitting

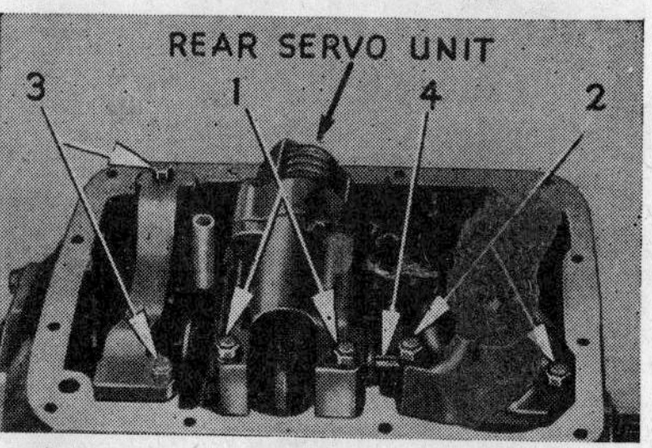

Fig. 14

1—Rear servo attaching screws
2—Front servo attaching screws
3—Rear pump and governor attaching screws
4—Pipe between front and rear servo Rear servo is removed first

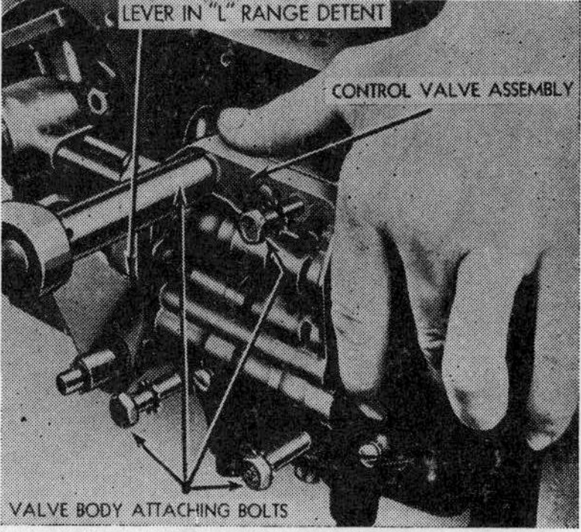

Fig. 15—Removing Control Valve Attaching Bolts

Fig. 16—Removing Control Valve Assembly from Delivery Sleeve.

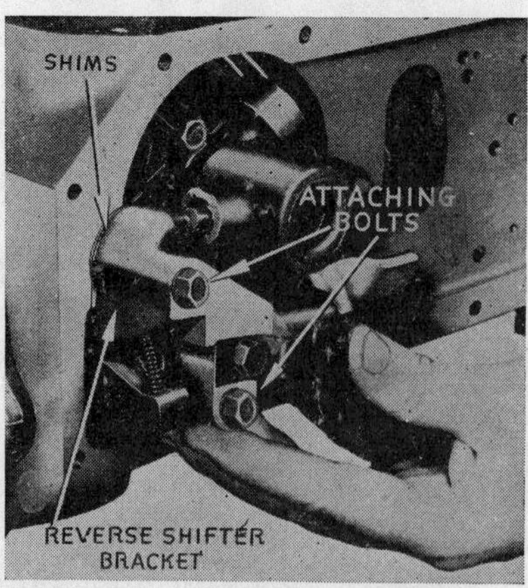

Fig. 17—Remove Reverse Shifter Bracket Attaching Bolts

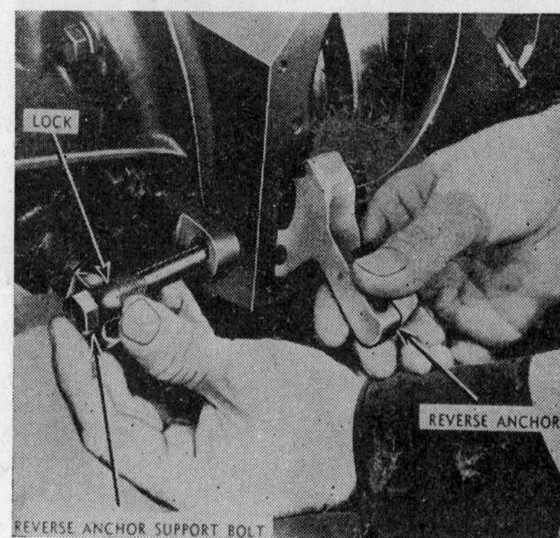

Fig. 18—Remove Reverse Anchor

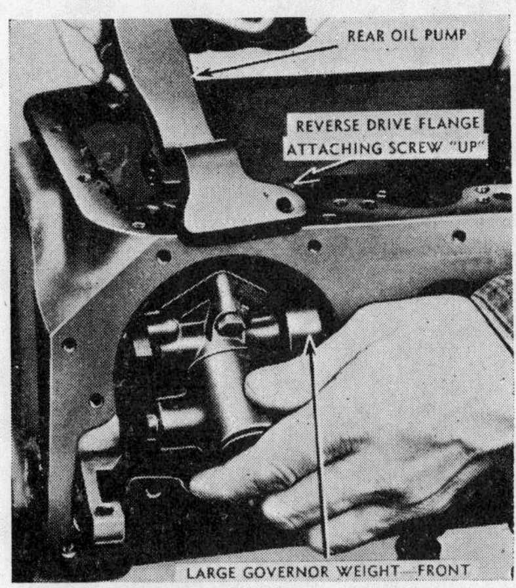

Fig. 19—Start Rear Pump & Governor Out of Case as Shown Above

Fig. 20—Complete Withdrawal of Rear Pump as Shown

Fig. 21—Removing Rear Drum Flange Bolts & Reverse Unit Bolts

Fig. 22—Removing Reverse Assembly from Case

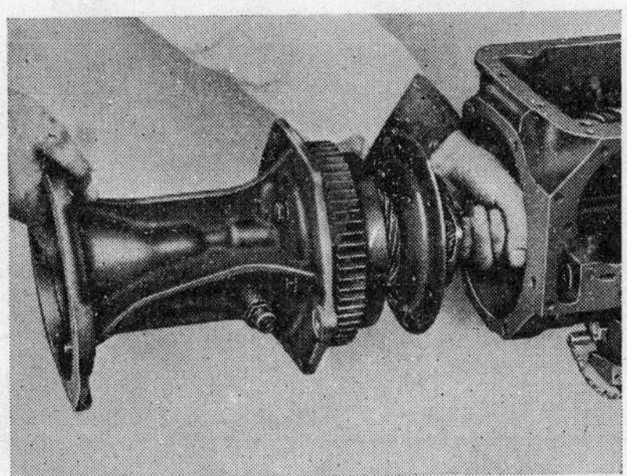

Fig. 23—On Late Models Mainshaft Comes out with Reverse Assembly

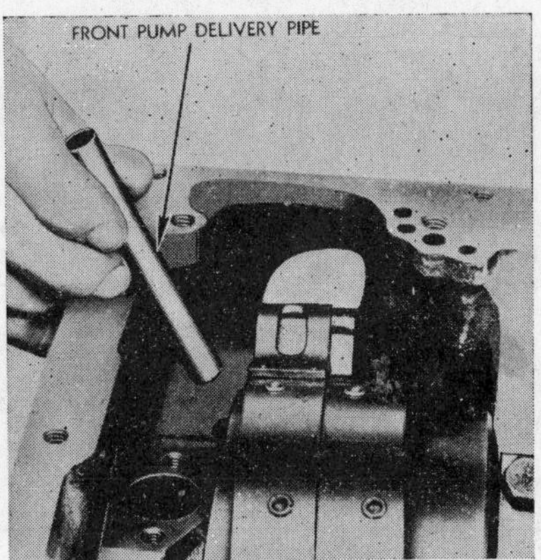

Fig. 24—Removing Front Pump Oil Delivery Pipe

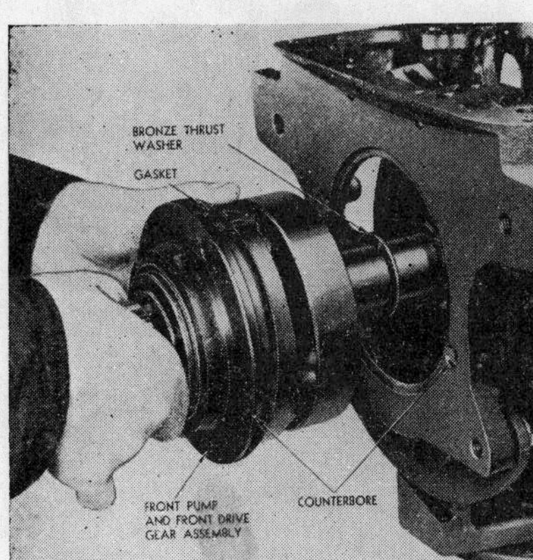

Fig. 25—Removing Front Pump and Drive Gear Assembly

Fig. 26—Oil Delivery Sleeve Attaching Bolts

Fig. 27—Tool Is Used to Prevent the Rear Drum from Sliding Forward Releasing the Clutch Disks. On Disassembly It Can Be Dispensed With

Servicing Valve Body

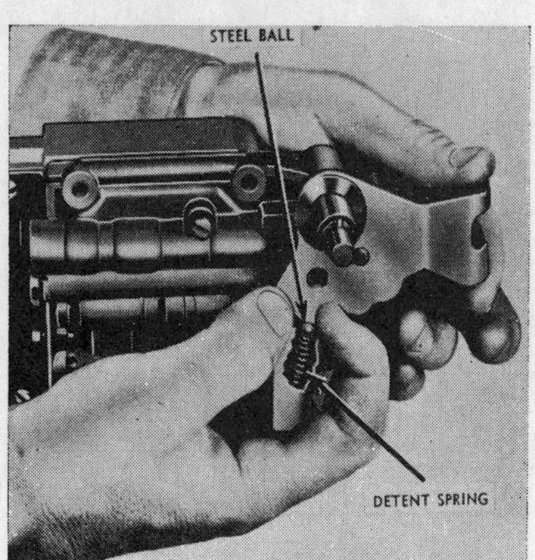

Fig. 28—Removing Detent Spring and Ball

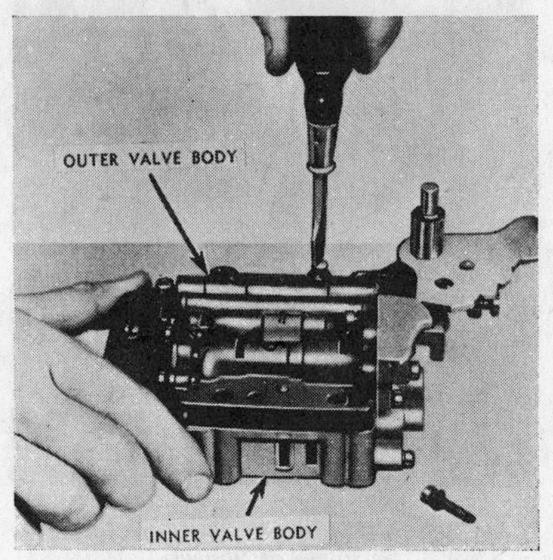

Fig. 29—Removing Outer Valve Body Screws

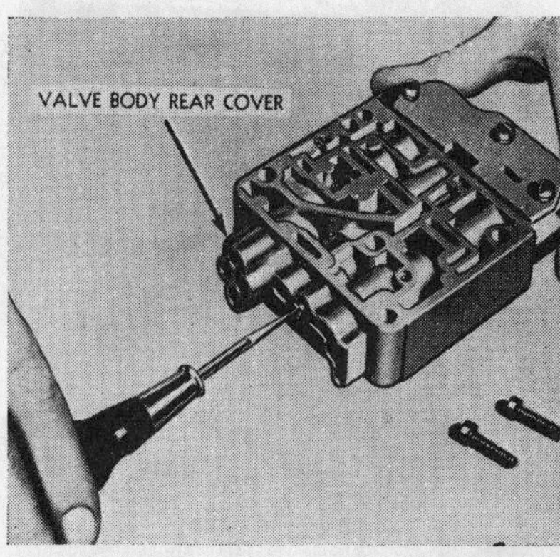

Fig. 30—Removing Valve Body Rear Cover

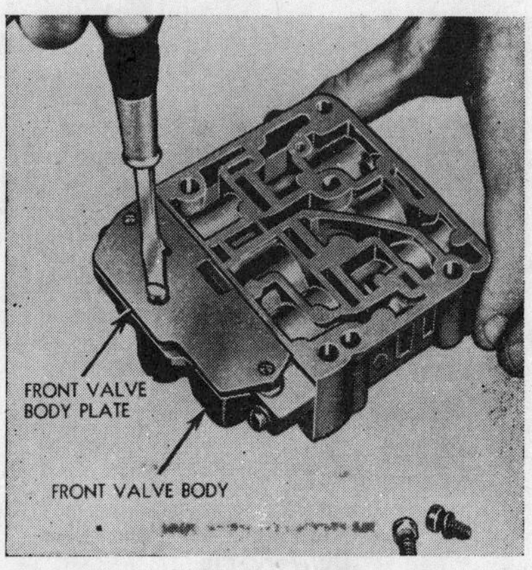

Fig. 31—Removing Front Valve Body Plate

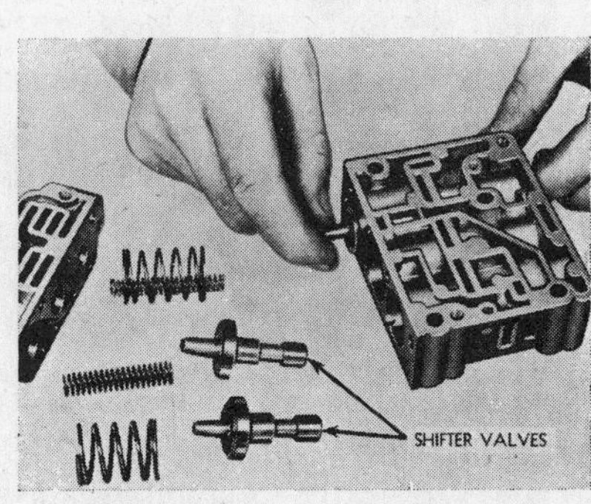

Fig. 32—Removing Shifter Valves

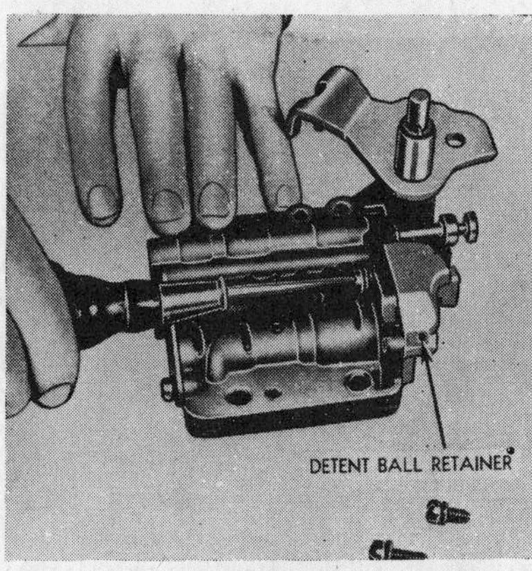

Fig. 33—Removing Valve Body Front Cover

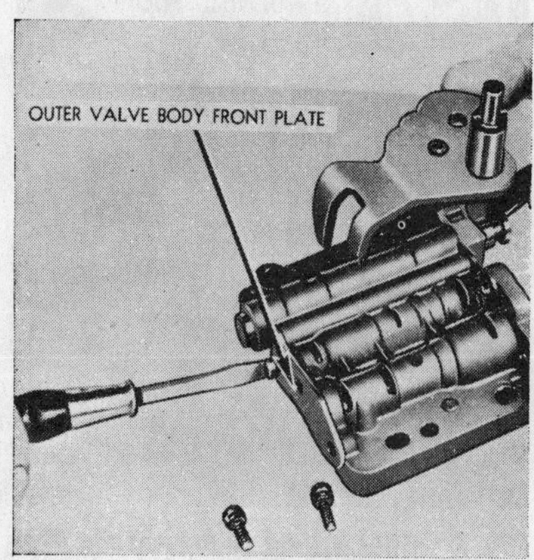

Fig. 34—Removing Outer Valve Body Front Plate

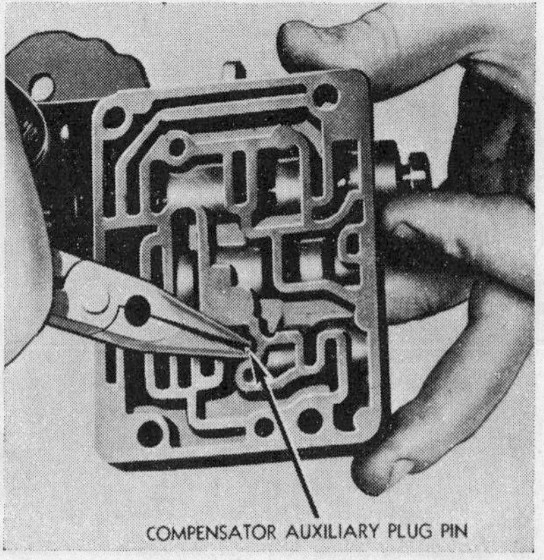

Fig. 35—Removing Auxiliary Plug Stop Pin

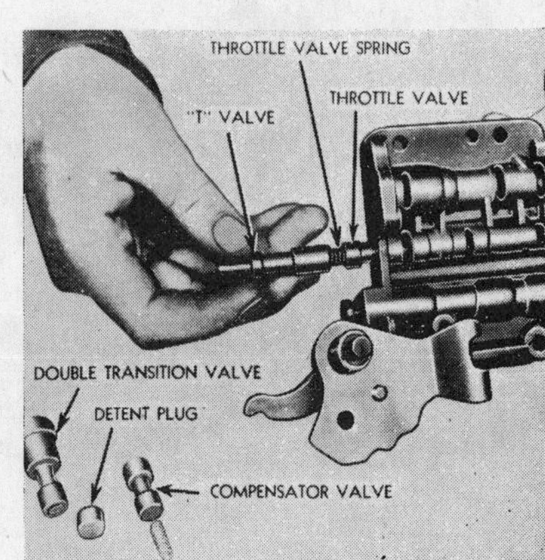

Fig. 36—Removing T Valve, Spring and Throttle Valve

Servicing Valve Body—*continued*

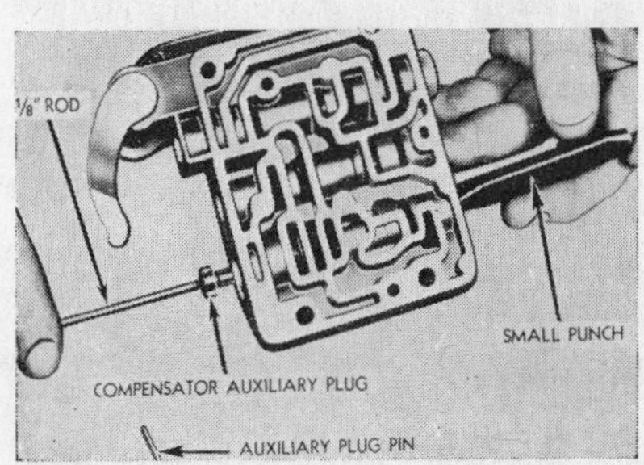

Fig. 37—Removing Auxiliary Plug

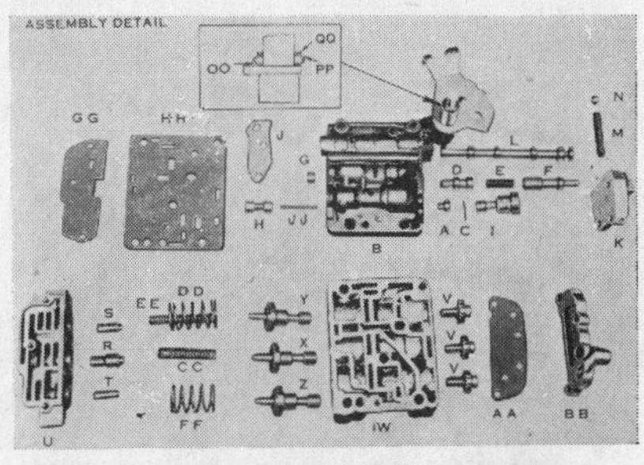

Fig. 38—Disassembled View of Control Valve Body

Servicing Front Pump

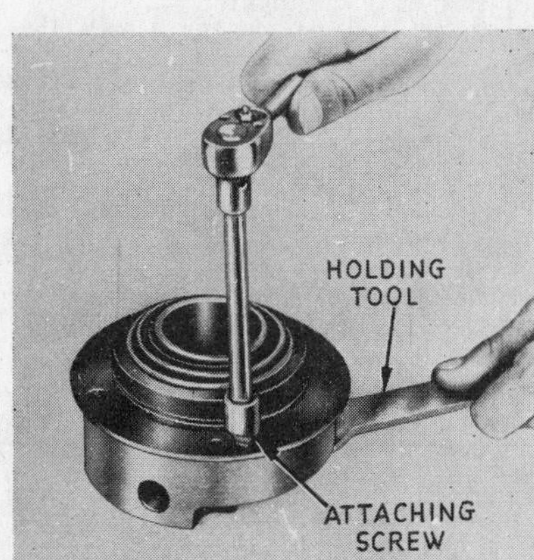

Fig. 39—Removing Front Pump Cover

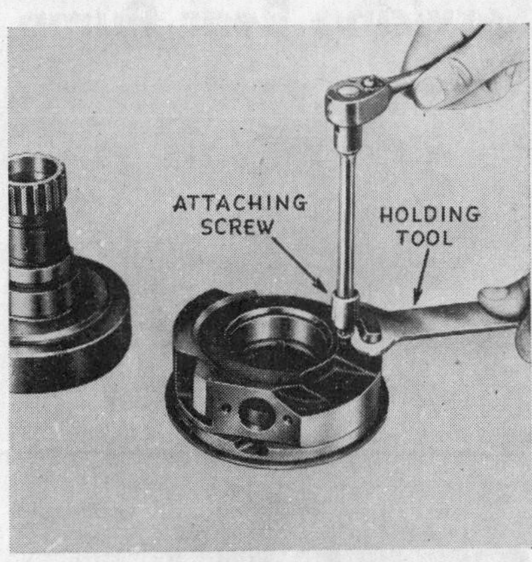

Fig. 40—Removing Front Pump to Cover Attaching Screw

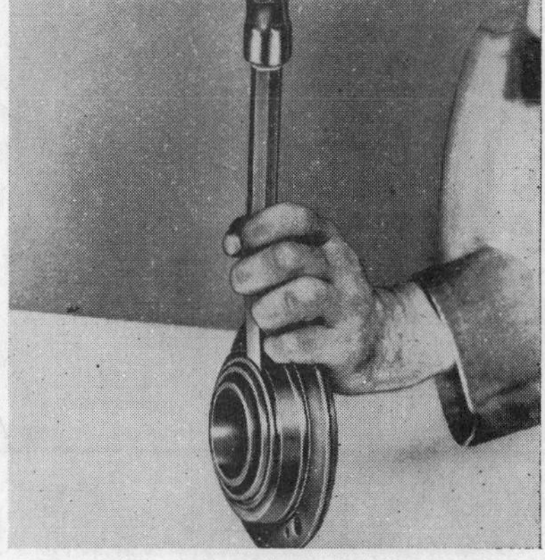

Fig. 41—Removing Oil Seal from Pump Cover

Fig. 42—Installing Front Cover Oil Seal Rings

Fig. 43—Installing Front Cover Oil Seal

Fig. 44—Assembling Front Pump Relief Valve

Servicing Front Pump—*continued*

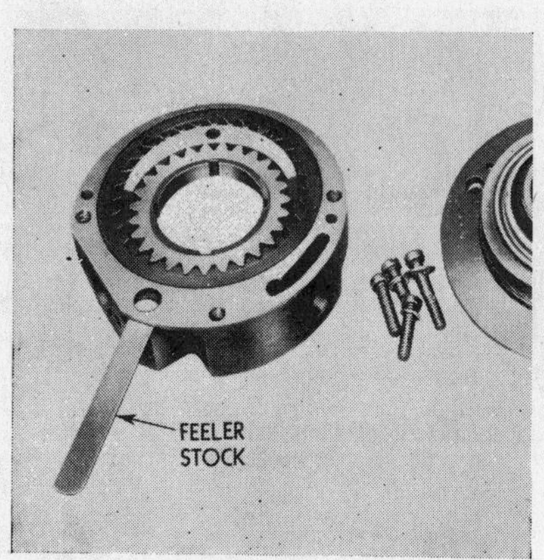

Fig. 45—Holding Relief Valve Down for Assembling

Fig. 46—Checking Fit of Pressure Regulator Valve

Fig. 47—Disassembled View of Front Pump and Drive Gear

1—Front drive gear
2—Front pump cover
3—Front pump body
4—Oil seal
5—Pump drive gear
6—Pump driven gear
7—Relief valve
8—Relief valve spring

Servicing Rear Pump

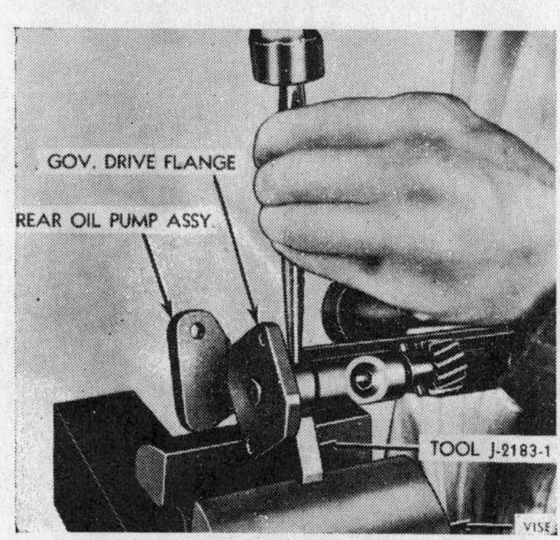

Fig. 48—Removing Governor Drive Flange

Fig. 49—Peening Drive Gear Pin

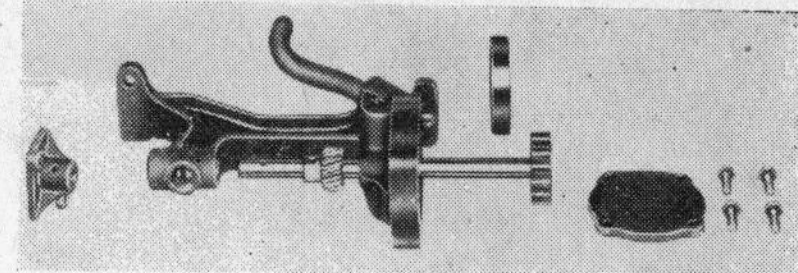

Fig. 50—Rear Pump Completely Disassembled

Servicing Governor

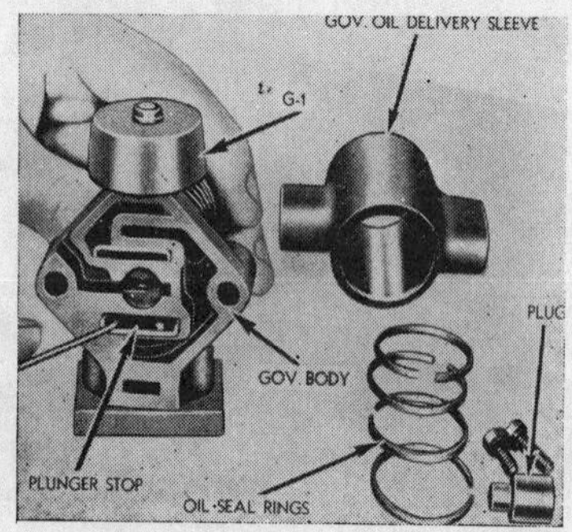

Fig. 51—Removing Governor Plunger Stop

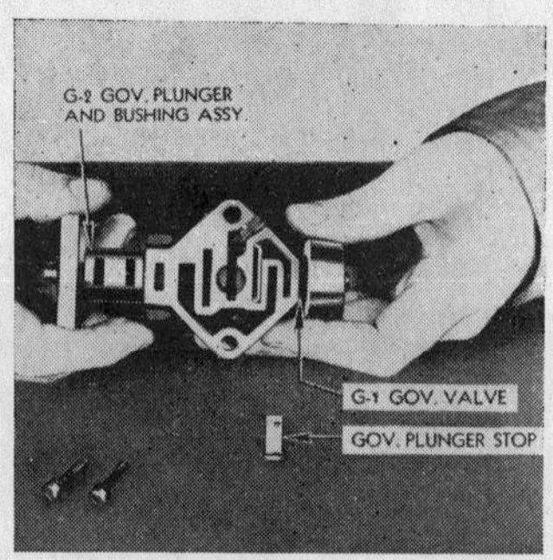

Fig. 52—Installing Governor Plunger and Bushing

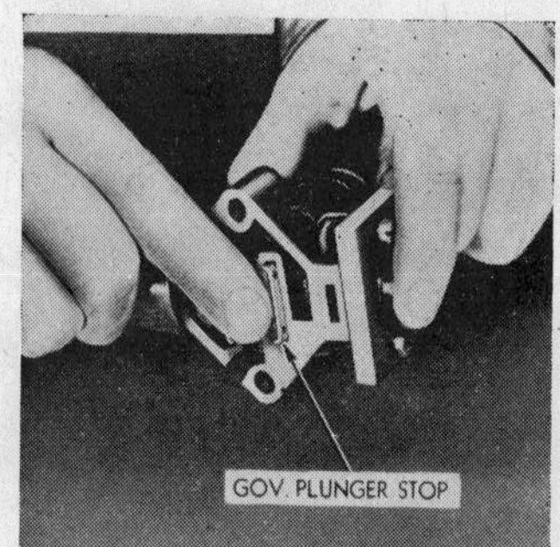

Fig. 53—Installing Governor Valve Plunger Stop

Servicing Front Servo

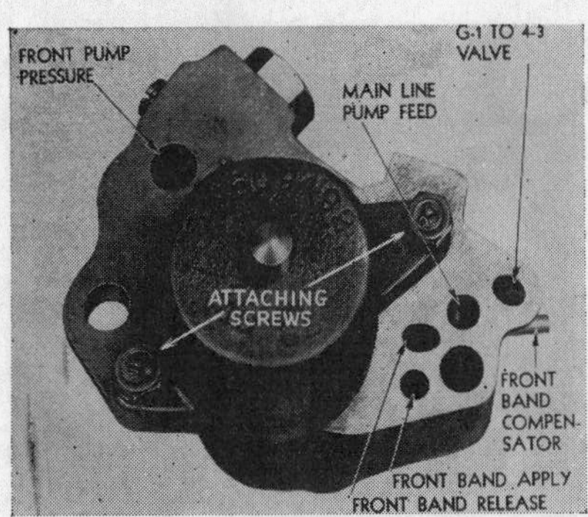

Fig. 54—Release Cylinder Attaching Screws

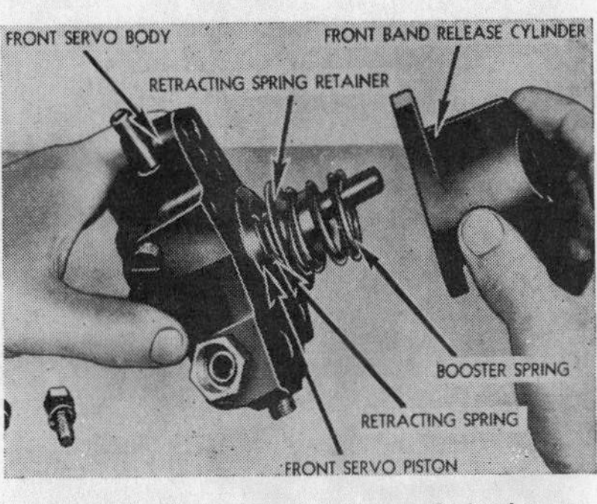

Fig. 55—Removing Release Cylinder

Fig. 56—Removing Front Band Release Piston

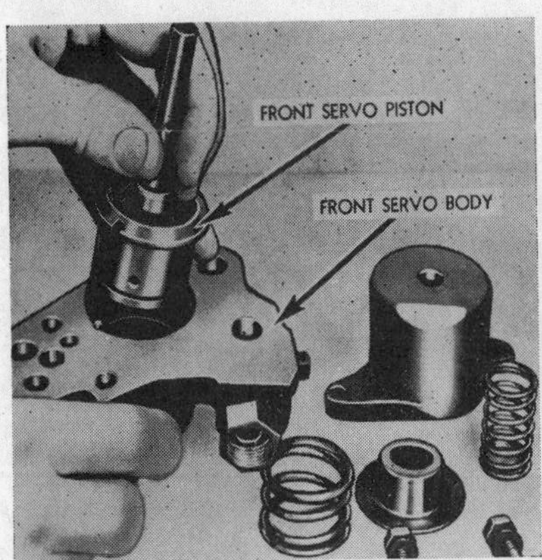

Fig. 57—Removing Servo Piston

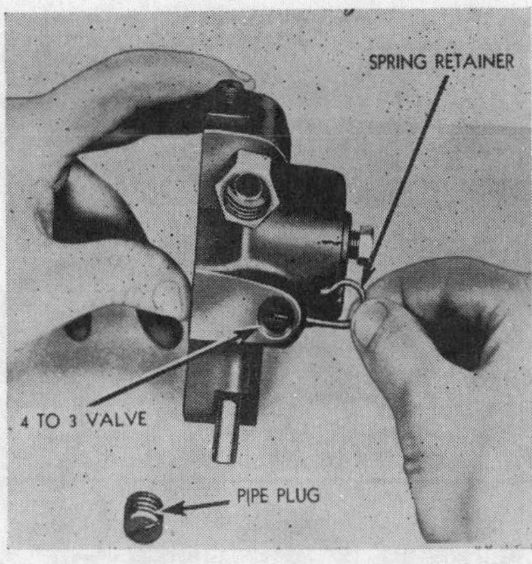

Fig. 58—Removing 4 to 3 Valve Spring Retainer

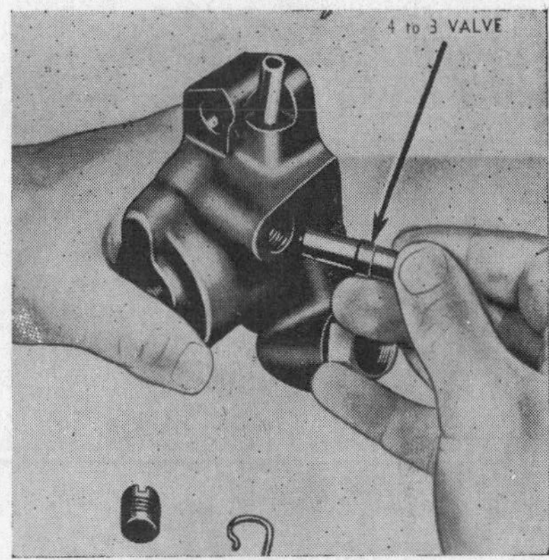

Fig. 59—Removing 4 to 3 Valve

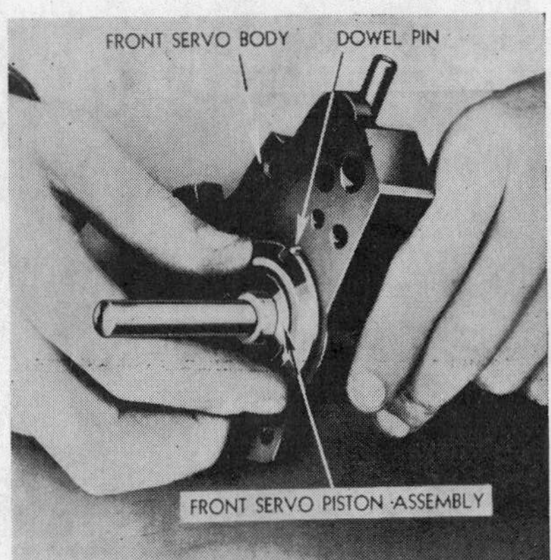

Fig. 60—Installing Servo Piston

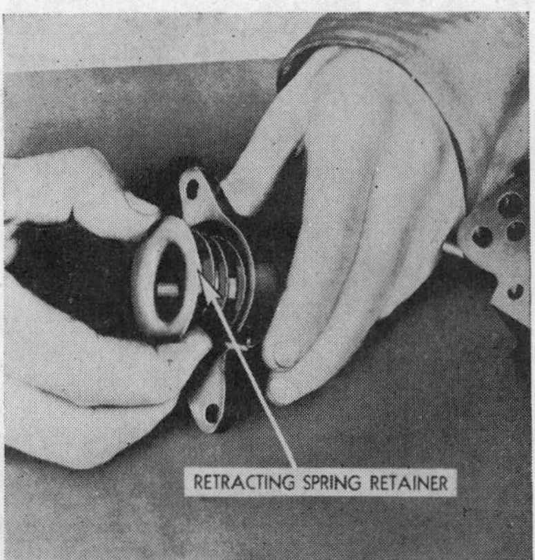

Fig. 61—Installing Retracting Spring Retainer

Servicing Rear Servo

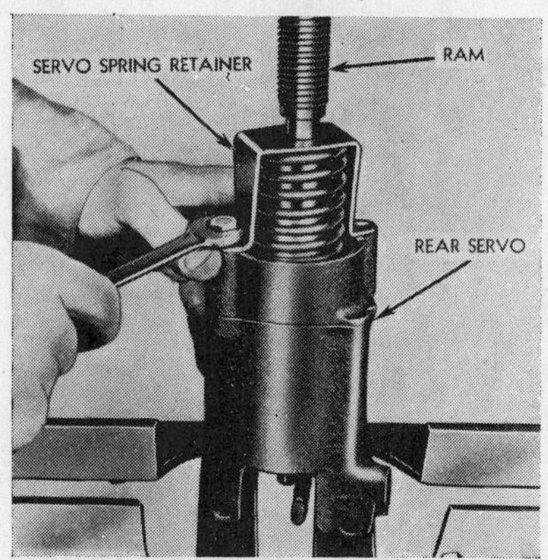

Fig. 62—Rear Servo Assembly

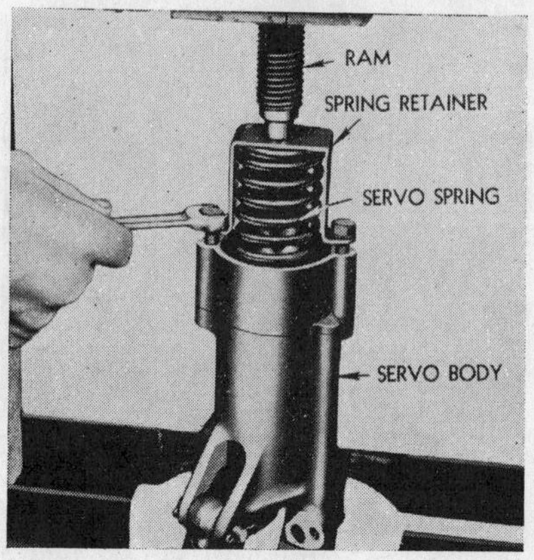

Fig. 63—Removing Servo Spring Retainer

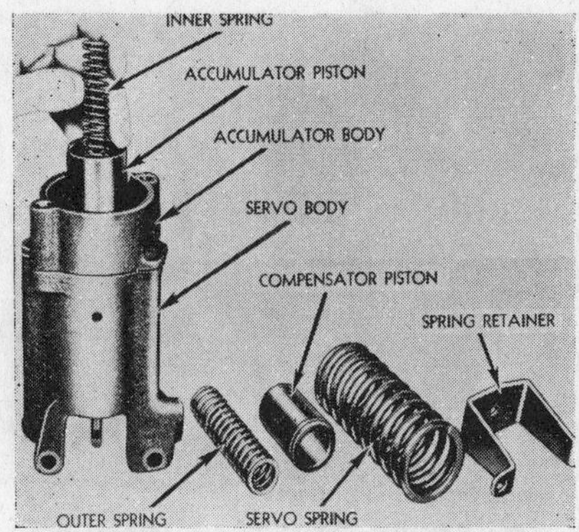

Fig. 64—Servo Springs Disassembled

Fig. 65—Removing Accumulator Body

Fig. 66—Removing Booster Piston

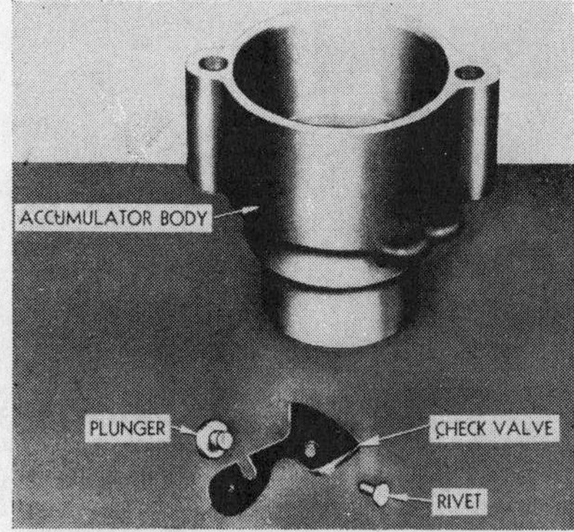

Fig. 67—Check Valve, Plunger and Rivet

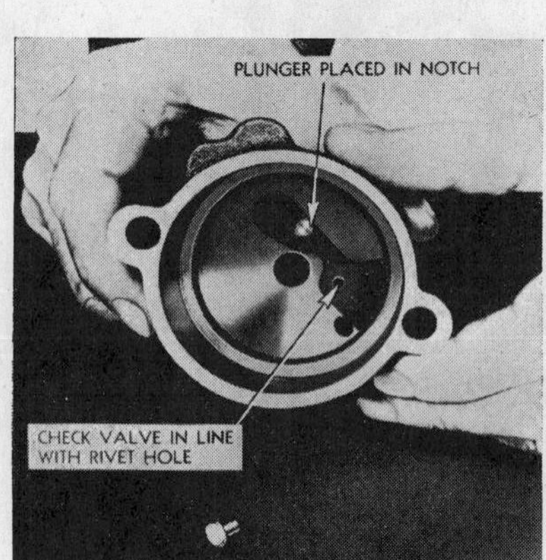

Fig. 68—Check Valve and Plunger in Body

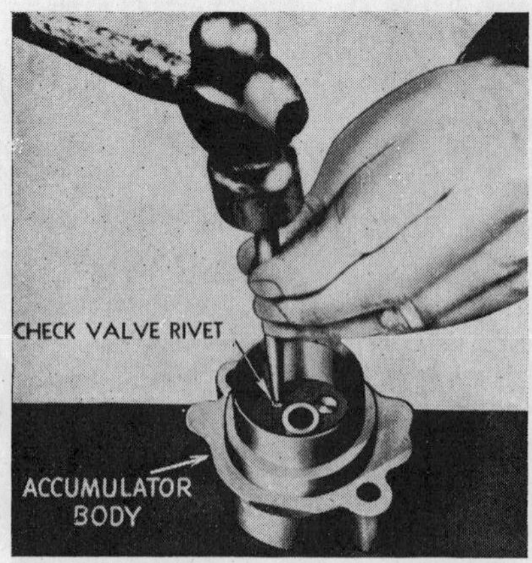

Fig. 69—Setting Check Valve Rivet

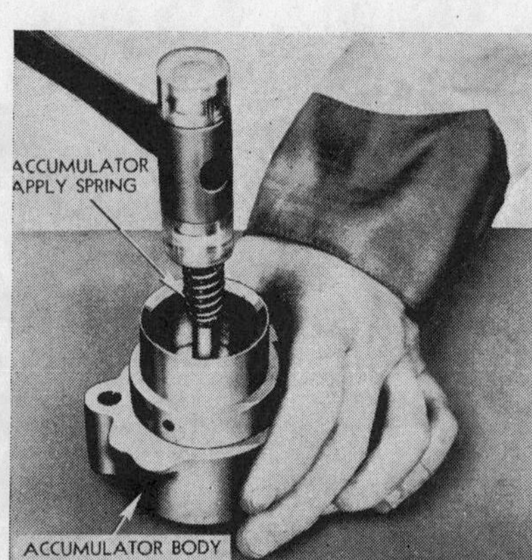

Fig. 70—Replacing Accumulator Apply Spring

Servicing Reverse Unit

Fig. 71—Driving Output Shaft Out of Housing

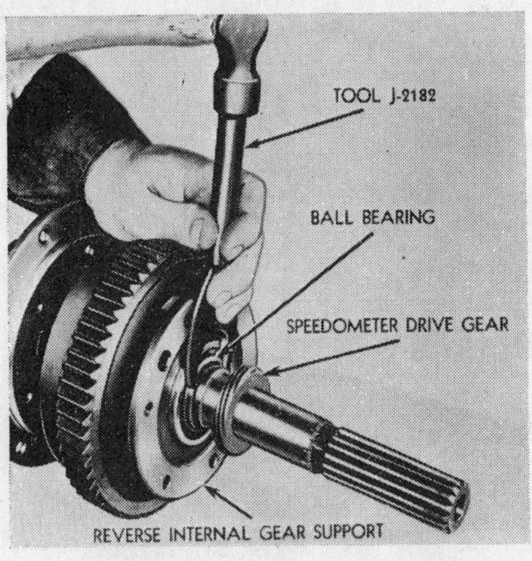

Fig. 72—Removing Ball Bearing Snap Ring

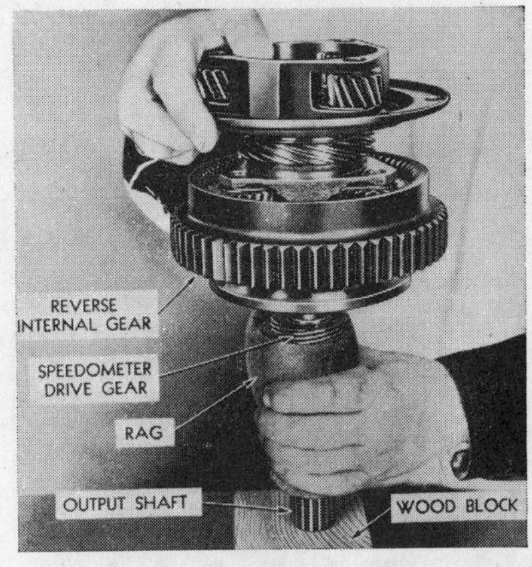

Fig. 73—Bumping to Remove Speedometer Drive Gear

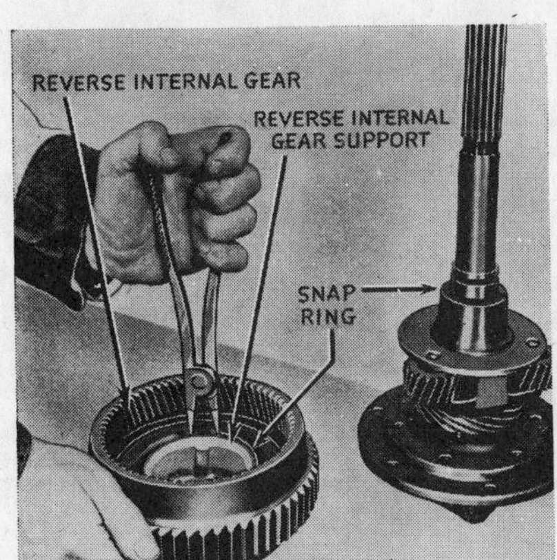

Fig. 74—Removing Reverse Internal Gear Support Snap Ring

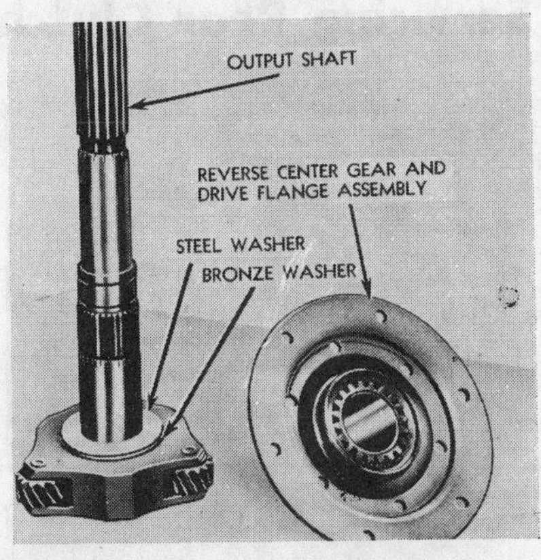

Fig. 75—Reverse Drive Flange and Output Shaft

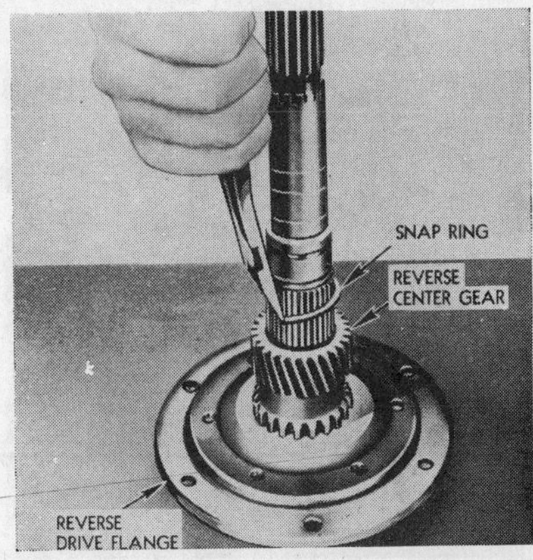

Fig. 76—Remove Reverse Drive Flange Snap Ring

Fig. 77—Splitting Oil Pump and Governor Drive Gear

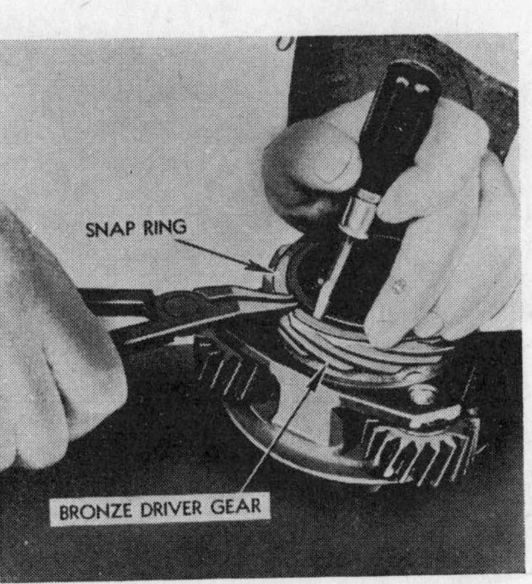

Fig. 78—Remove Gear

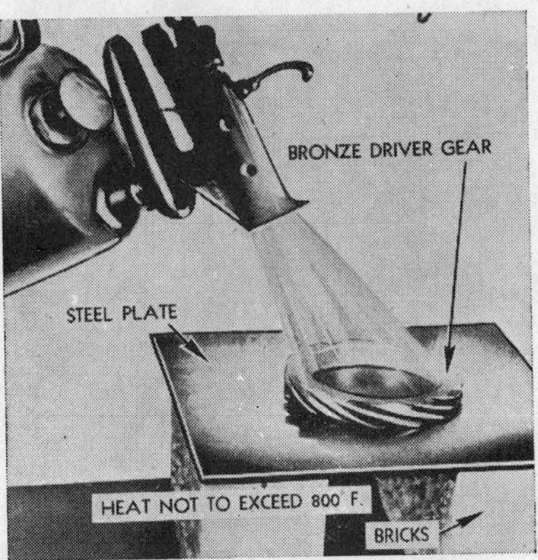

Fig. 79—Bronze Drive Gear Should be Expanded with Heat to Assemble

Servicing Reverse Unit—*continued*

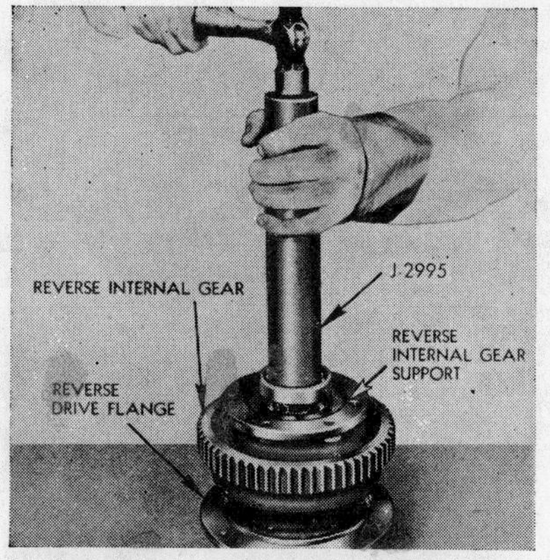

Fig. 80—Installing Ball Bearing

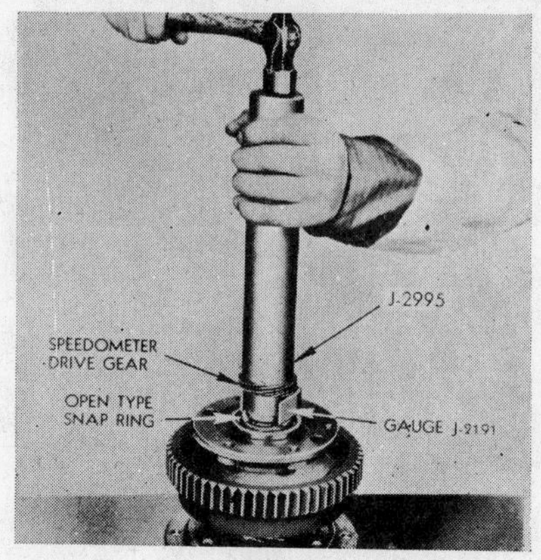

Fig. 81—Installing Speedometer Drive Gear

Fig. 82—Installing Selective Washer

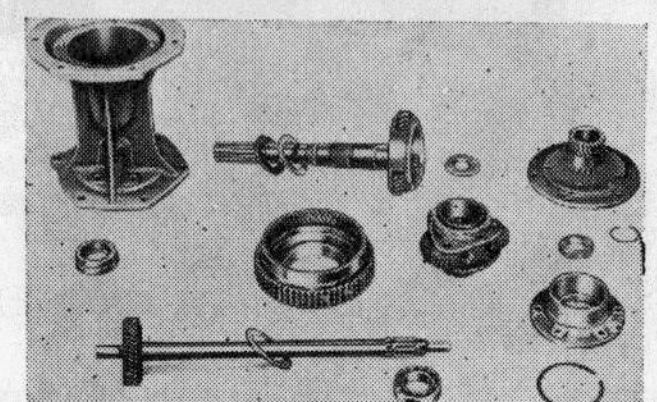

Fig. 83—Disassembled View of Reverse Assembly

Servicing Rear Clutch

Fig. 84—Remove Snap Ring

Fig. 85—Rotate Hub Out

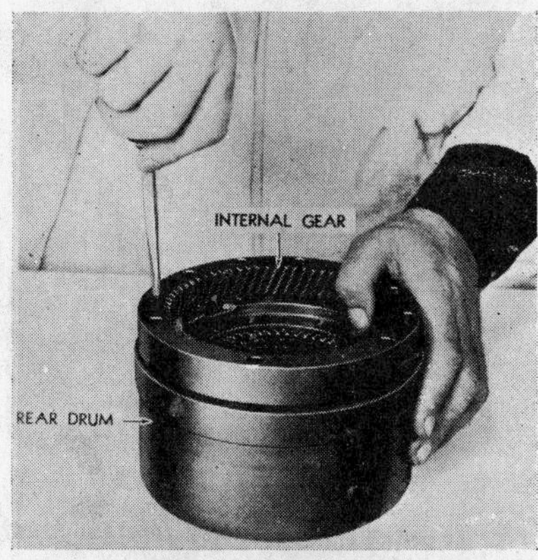

Fig. 86—Remove Internal Gear

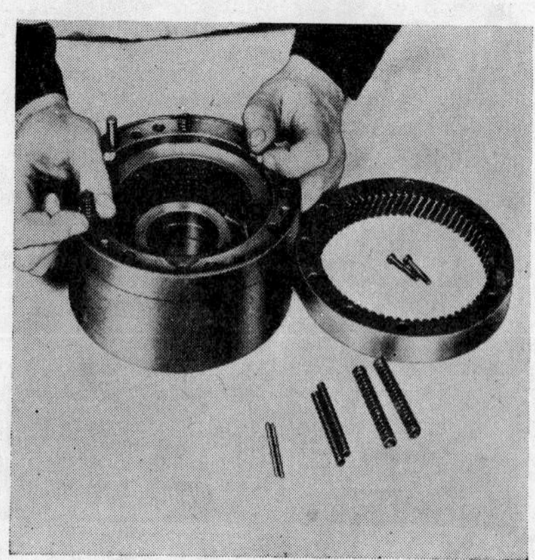

Fig. 87—Take Out Springs

Fig. 88—Remove Clutch Plates

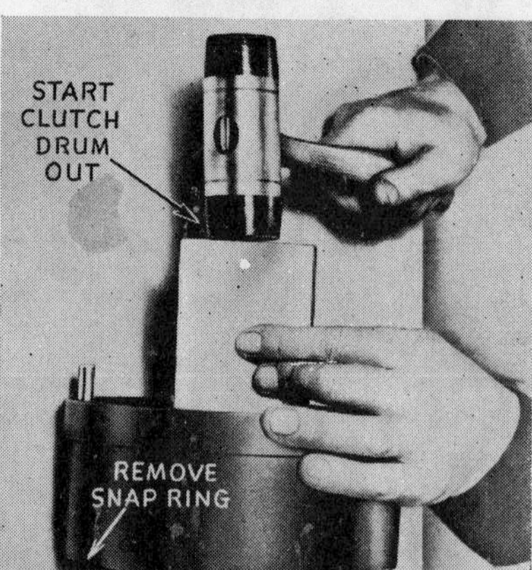

Fig. 89—Remove Snap Ring, Drive Out Drum

Servicing Rear Clutch—*continued*

Fig. 90—Lifting Off Drum

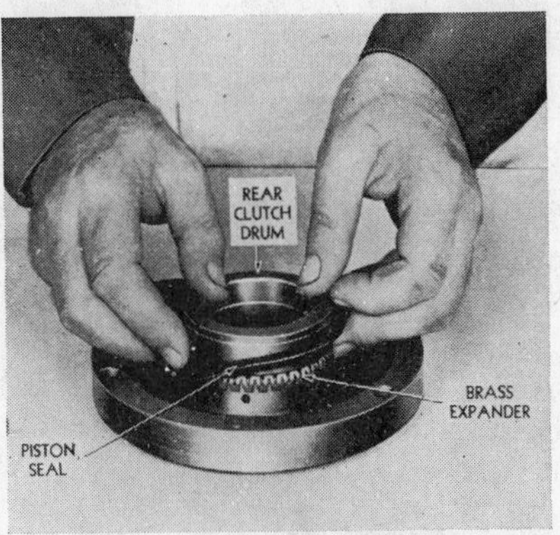

Fig. 91—Rear Drum Oil Seal

Fig. 92—Replace Snap Ring and Set Drum Tightly Against Ring

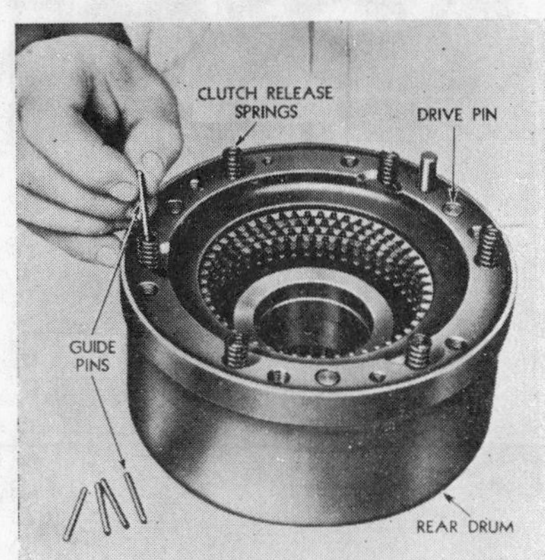

Fig. 93—Replace Disks and Springs

Fig. 94—Install Bronze Thrust Washer

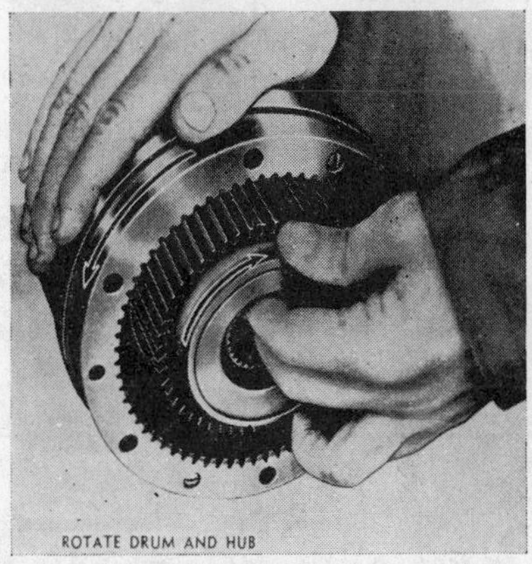

Fig. 95—Rotate into Place Being Sure All Disks are Engaged

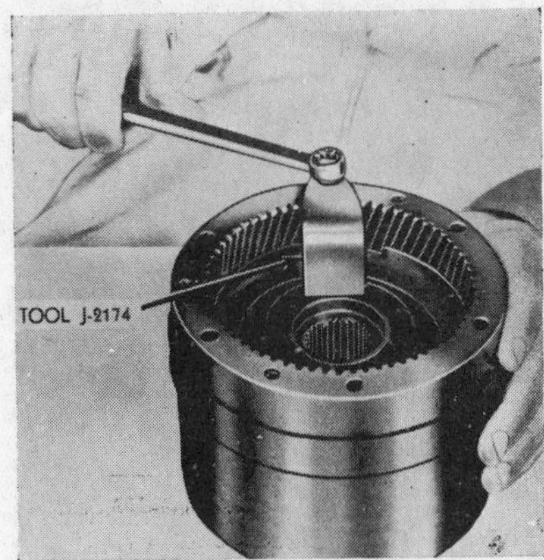

Fig. 96—Install Tool to Hold Hub in Place so That Disks Do Not Slip Off Hub

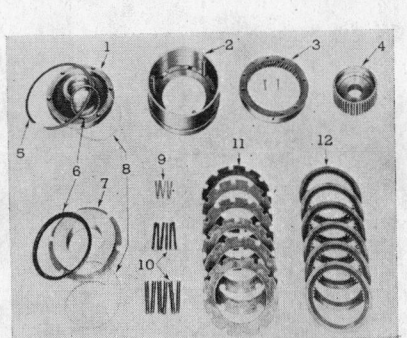

Fig. 97 Disassembled View of Rear Unit

1. Rear clutch drum assembly
2. Rear drum and pin assembly
3. Rear internal gear
4. Rear clutch hub
5. Retaining ring
6. Oil seals
7. Clutch annular piston
8. Oil seal expanders
9. Release spring guide pins
10. Clutch release springs
11. Clutch driven plates
12. Clutch drive plates

Servicing Front Clutch

Fig. 98—Remove Snap Ring From Recess in Front Unit

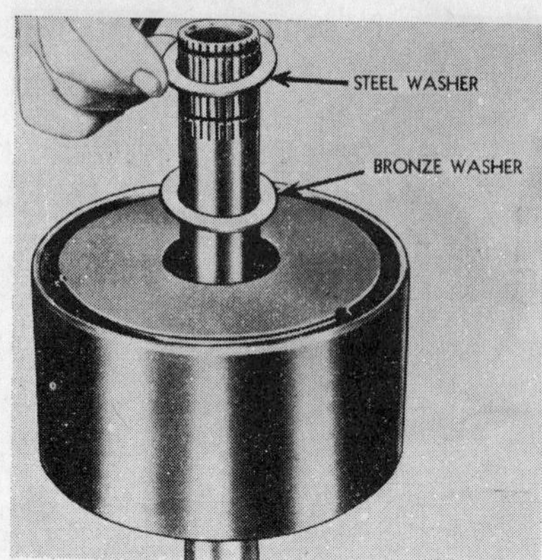

Fig. 99—Remove Front Unit Thrust Washers

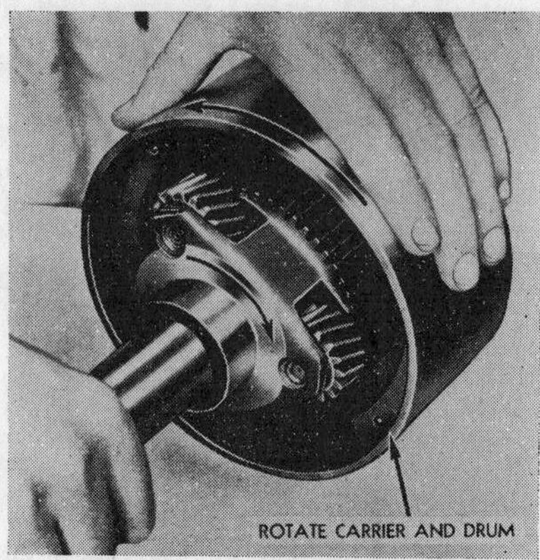

Fig. 100—Aligning Clutch Plates

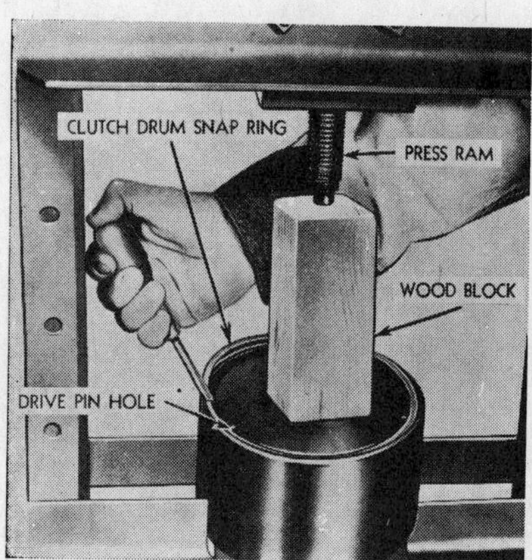

Fig. 101—Removing Clutch Drum Snap Ring

Fig. 102—Removing Annular Piston From Clutch Drum

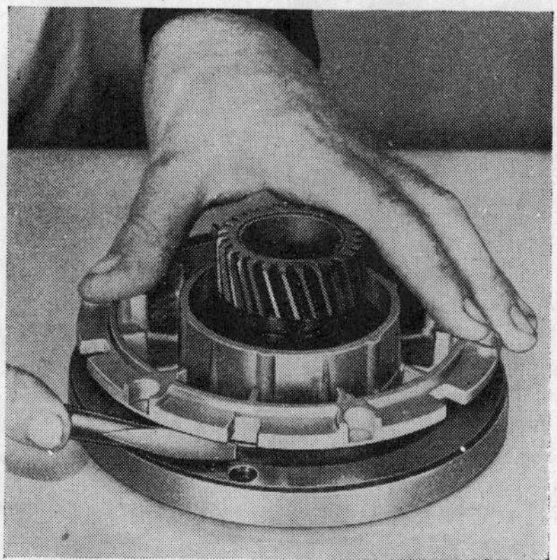

Fig. 103—Removing Annular Piston

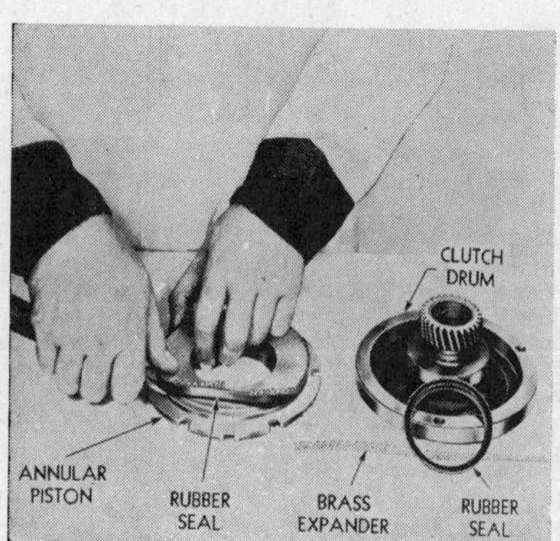

Fig. 104—Removing Rubber Seals and Brass Expanders

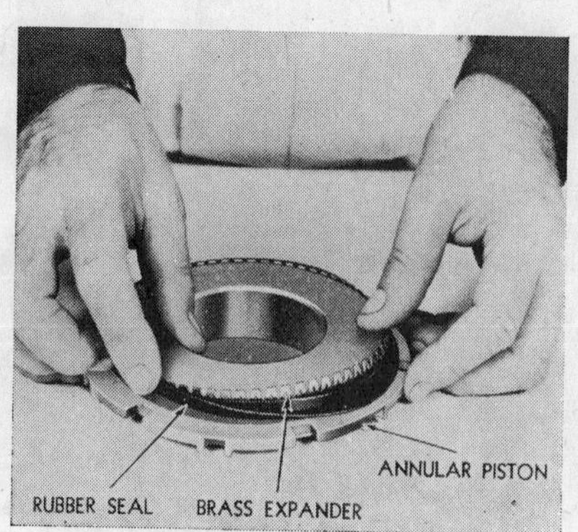

Fig. 105—Installing Piston Seal and Expander

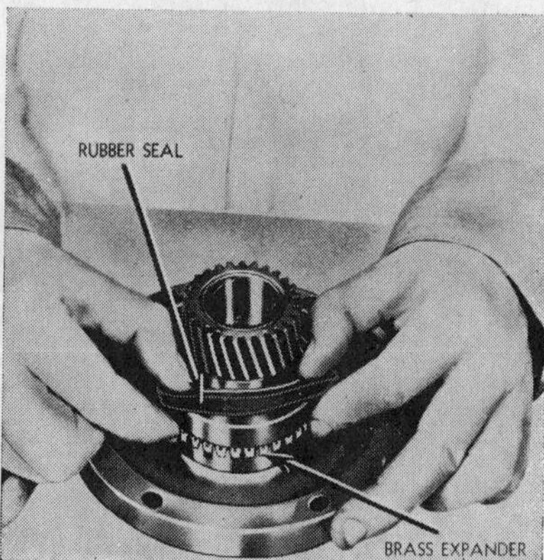

Fig. 106—Installing Brass Expander and Rubber Seal in Clutch Drum

Servicing Front Clutch—*continued*

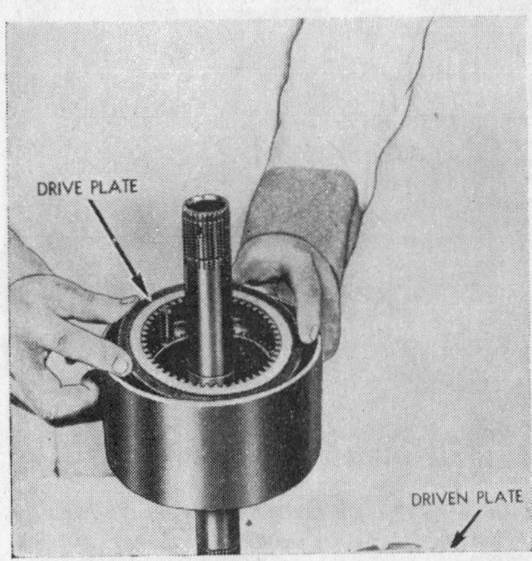

Fig. 107—Installing Clutch Plates

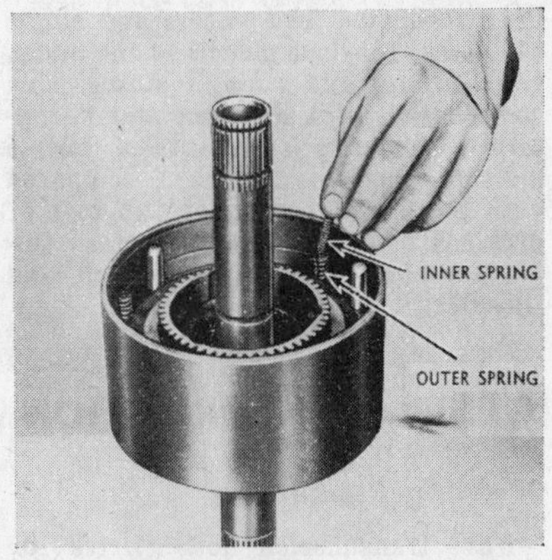

Fig. 108—Installing Clutch Release Springs

Fig. 109—Installing Center Gear and Clutch

Servicing Reverse Anchor

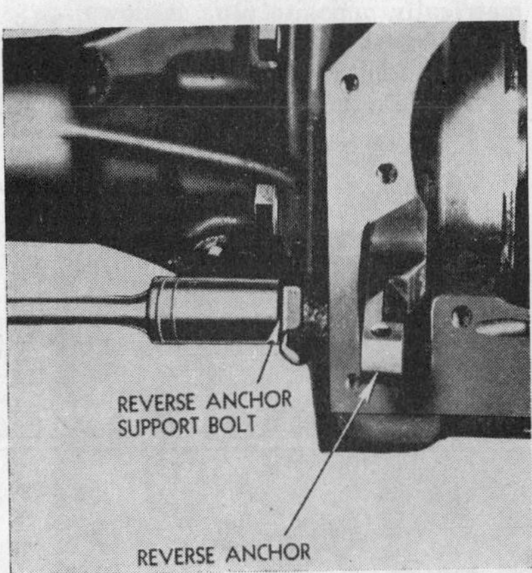

Fig. 109—Removing Reverse Anchor Bolt

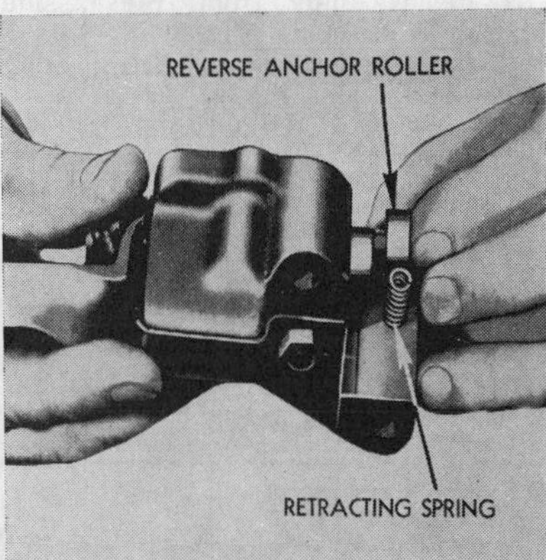

Fig. 110—Assembling Spring and Roller on Reverse Shifter Bracket

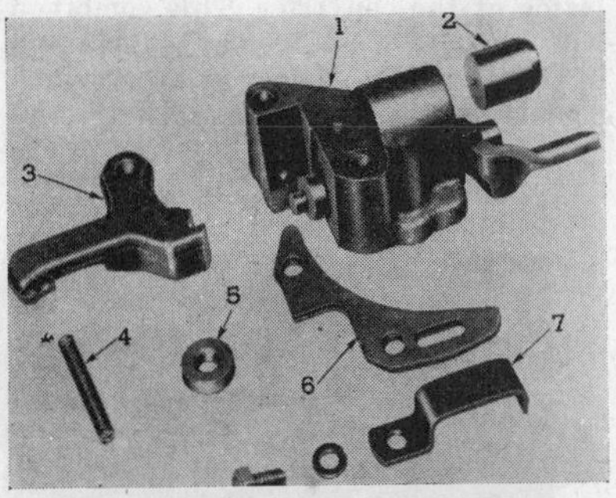

Fig. 111—Disassembled View of Reverse Shifter Bracket and Crank Assembly

1—Reverse shifter bracket assembly.
2—Reverse blocker piston.
3—Reverse anchor.
4—Retracting spring.
5—Reverse shifter crank roller.
6—Shims.
7—Reverse blocker piston retracting spring.

Test

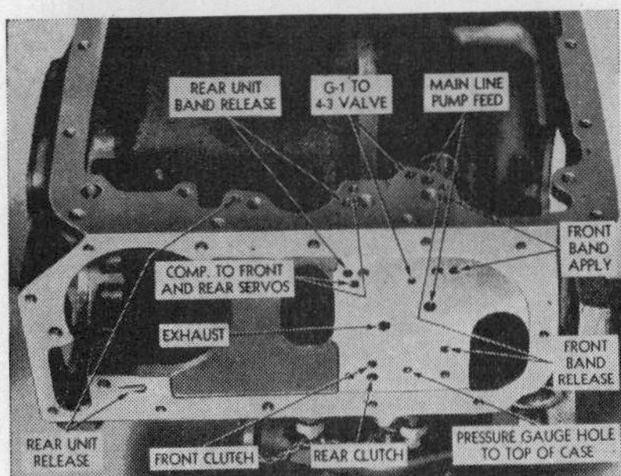

Fig. 112—Oil Passages in Transmission Case

Fig. 113—Adjusting Rear Band

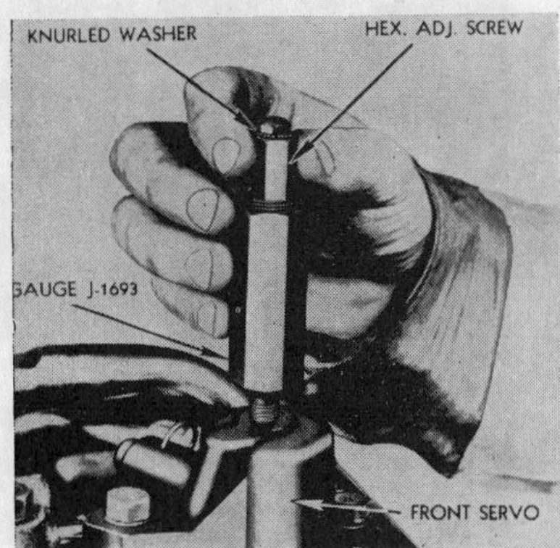

Fig. 114—Adjusting Front Band

DYNAFLOW TRANSMISSION

The Dynaflow transmission is a device which provides smooth shockless power in accordance with the wishes of the driver and the demands of the road. It accomplishes this by combining a fluid torque converter with a double acting planetary gear set. The fluid torque converter delivers an infinite variation in the supply of power while the gear set provides a reverse gear and an emergency low gear for rough going. In normal operation all driving is done in Drive range without the use of the gear set. On those rare occasions when it is needed a hydraulically actuated clutch is released and the bands controlling the gear set are brought into operation.

For 1953 the Dynaflow has been improved by the addition of an auxiliary single acting planetary gear set, to the inside of the converter. This combined with the double acting gear set retained in the transmission case as on previous models results in faster pick-up and improved gasoline mileage. The converter itself has been simplified from the two pumps, two stators and single turbine of previous models to one pump, two turbines and a single stator. This combination of a gear set and a simplified converter results in a torque multiplication of 2.45 to 1 compared with the multiplication of 2.25 to 1 of previous models of the converter. Operation however remains smooth and shockless.

GENERAL INFORMATION

Draining Procedure

Have transmission hot. (Drive for 20 miles in real or simulated traffic.)

Failure to have the transmission hot before draining may result in an accumulation of harmful deposits inside the transmission.

1. Remove plug from transmission oil pan to drain it. Fig. 2.
2. Remove six bolts and bell housing lower front pan. Fig. 2.

Fig. 2—View of Dynaflow from under the car

3. Turn flywheel until a drain plug shows in its forward face. Fig. 3. Loosen this drain plug to act as an air vent and turn flywheel until the diametrically opposite plug is down.
4. Remove this second drain plug to drain the converter. Fig. 3.

Note: Do not disturb the Accumu-

Fig. 1—Cutaway view of Dynaflow converter for 1953

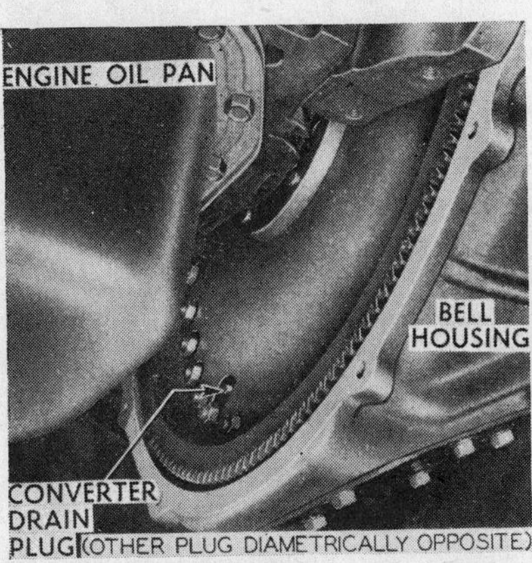

Fig. 3—Location of converter drain plugs

lator plugs the locations of which are shown in Fig. 2.

5. Replace the transmission oil pan plug and tighten to 30-35 ft lbs.

6. Replace the two converter drain plugs and tighten securely. Replace the bell housing lower front pan.

7. Install 3 quarts of fluid and start the engine. (Hand lever in Park.)

Add the balance as indicated under Oil Requirements below.

8. Warm up transmission and check that level is at Full.

Note: Never overfill the transmission as it will permit the planetary gear set to aerate the oil and cause malfunctioning of the valves. If the fluid level drops below "Add Oil" point when warm and idling in Park the transmission will overheat with resultant serious damage to the clutch plates and valving.

Fig. 4—Location of dipstick, early models

OIL REQUIREMENTS

Measure oil with Dynaflow hot and engine idling; hand lever at Park.

Use special Buick Dynaflow oil or automatic transmission fluid Type A.

Note: Quality should be at least equal to Armour Institute Qualifying Number.

AQ-ATF No.* for automatic transmissions fluids.

* Last number varies with different refiners. Designation and number are embossed on the can.

Oil should be changed every 25,000 miles.

OIL CAPACITIES

Series 40 & 50, Drain & refill. 8½ qts.
Refill—Dry .... 9⅜ qts.
Series 70, Drain & refill....10 qts.
Refill—Dry ....11⅜ qts.

GAGE ROD

Located (1948-1949) under floor pan on right side. Fig. 4.

Since 1949 in engine compartment just in front of fire wall on right side. Fig. 5.

Quantity between add oil and full on gage rod .... 1 pt.

FRONT OIL PUMP

Driven by ....Engine
Cuts out at ....45-50 MPH

REAR OIL PUMP

Driven by ....Output shaft

CLUTCH PLATES

Driven (internally splined—faced) ....5 used
Driven (externally splined—steel—dished) ....5 used

ALIGNMENT TOLERANCES

Flywheel runout ....008" F.I.R.*
Face of bell housing at 3¾" radius from pump hub ....005" F.I.R.*
Bell housing hole from pump hub ....004" F.I.R.
Primary pump hub runout ....012" F.I.R.
Reactor shaft flange out-of-true of face ......002" F.I.R.
Front face of transmission case out-of-true..002" F.I.R.

*F.I.R.—Full Indicator Reading.

Fig. 5—Location of dipstick, current models

BAND ADJUSTMENT

Cannot be done with transmission in the car except on early models having floor pan unless suitable holes are drilled in floor to permit prying caps off and assistant is under car to hold wrench on locknut.

Tighten adjust screw, back off to obtain slight play, then back off six full turns and lock.

HYDRAULIC SYSTEM VALVES

Control valve
Operated by hand lever
Oil pump pressure regulator valve
Controls oil pump pressures
Lubrication pressure valve
Holds this pressure to 15 psi
High accumulator
Cushions shift into drive
Clutch bleed valve
Drains clutch
Clutch vent valve
Breaks suction when draining
Low accumulator
Cushions shift into Low
Rear oil pump check valve
Prevents loss of prime
Front oil pump check valve
Prevents loss of prime

TORQUE SPECIFICATIONS (IN FT LBS.)

½-20 Nuts ....20-25 ft lbs
½-20 Bolts 30-35
7/16-14 Bolts 45-55
7/16-20 Nuts 15.20
⅜-16 Bolts entering the transmission case 35.40
⅜-16 Bolts entering the rear bearing retainer...30-35
⅜-24 Nuts 10-15
5/16-18 Bolts at the hand hole covers 15-20

DYNAFLOW

TORQUE SPECIFICATIONS —continued

the servo body 15-20
the oil cooler 15-20
the control detent....15-20
at the accumulators ..20-25
at the rear oil pump..25-30
5/16-24 Bolts and nuts at
the oil pan 15-18
at the accumulators..20-25
all others 25.30
¼-20 Bolts 11-15
¼-28 Bolts and nuts.....11-15
1⅛-12 Plugs and seats....20.25
1⅜-12 Accumulator caps.40-50
1/5-16-16 sleeve 20.25
⅝-18 Plug 20-25
18 mm Plug 30-35

Tightening sequence charts covering the primary pump cover bolts, the reactor shaft flange bolts, the front oil pump bolts, the valve and servo body assembly, and the rear oil pump bolts, will be found in the disassembly section.

Failure to follow the sequence and torque recommendations can result in distortion of the parts.

MATCH POINTS

Items which must be match marked to assure that they are reassembled in the same relative positions they occupied before disassembly.

Flywheel to primary Pump.
Primary Pump to Cover.
Front portion of Planetary Carrier to rear portion.
Faces of the inner and outer Oil Pump gears to the pump covers.
Rear Oil Pump Body to Case.
Rear Oil Pump Cover to Case
Flanges of the Bands to Case.

Towing the Car

When necessary to tow a Dynaflow car the shift lever **Must** be in the **neutral** position. If the car is damaged so that it is impossible to place the Dynaflow in the neutral position the drive shaft should be disconnected or the car picked up by the rear axle and towed on its front wheels with the steering wheel tied down. Fig. 6.

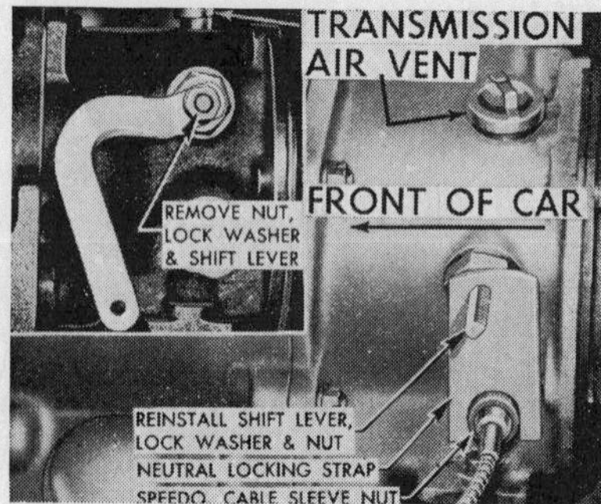

Fig. 6—Locking Dynaflow in neutral

Starting Engine Without Use of Starter

To start the engine by rolling the car always push rather than tow so that, when the engine starts, the car can accelerate without crashing the tow car.

Hold control lever at Neutral until car reaches a speed of 15 mph then shift into Low. Continue to increase car speed. Engine should crank at about 25 mph when oil pressure from the rear oil pump will have increased sufficiently to actuate the transmission. Return lever to Neutral for engine warm up.

THEORY AND OPERATION OF DYNAFLOW TRANSMISSION

Movement of the shift control lever provides 5 different controls, Parking; Neutral; Direct Drive; Low; and Reverse. Fig. 7, 8.

A light spring keeps the lever down for shifting into Neutral, Low and Direct Drive. Raising the lever depresses a stop pin in the control lever housing so that the lever can pass stops mounted in the dial housing thus getting to Parking, Neutral and Reverse positions.

Fig. 7—View of shift lever dial thru 1952

Movement of the lever turns the control shaft, which runs down the steering column, and thus actuates by means of levers and rods the shift control valve in the crankcase of the transmission. A little plate with locating holes called the detent contacts a spring loaded ball connected to the control shaft at the bottom of the steering column to hold the control lever in any selected position.

Fig. 8—View of shift lever dial for 1953

The control shaft also operates a Neutral Safety Switch in the starter circuit so that the engine cannot be started unless the control lever is in either Parking or Neutral. When the car is equipped with Back Up Lights the control shaft operates a back up light switch when the lever is moved to Reverse.

When the control lever is moved to Parking a spring loaded locking pawl mounted in the transmission rear bearing retainer is permitted to engage the parking lock ratchet wheel on the transmission output shaft. If the pawl does not engage a notch in the ratchet wheel when the control lever is first moved to Parking it will snap into a notch as the car wheels turn when the car moves slightly.

Never shift to parking range when the car is in motion as serious damage to the transmission will result.

Parking is used in conjunction with the parking brake to insure positive locking of the rear wheels. It should also be used whenever it is necessary to gun the engine without risk of car movement, as when working on the car in the shop.

Low is used only when the going is tough as in deep snow, and/or on long steep grades. It can also be used as a brake to keep the car under control when descending steep grades.

The shift from Direct Drive to Low must never be made at speeds above 40 mph as the direct drive clutch cannot release at high speed.

By using Low and Reverse alternately the car may be rocked out of mud or snow.

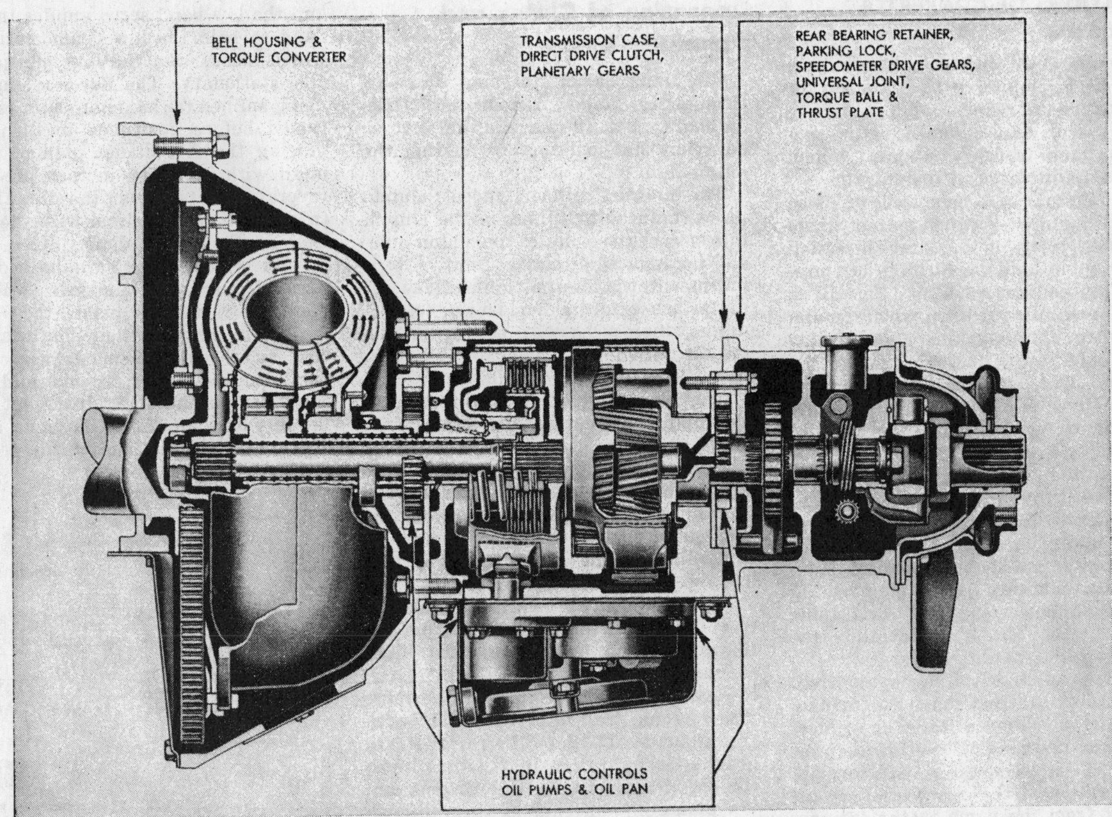

Fig. 9—Principal sections of the Dynaflow transmission

Principal Sections of the Dynaflow Transmission

A bell housing is bolted to the front of the transmission case and to the rear of the engine block. It acts as a cover for the torque converter.

The torque converter is bolted to the engine flywheel and delivers power through the transmission to the rear wheels.

The transmission case is bolted to the bell housing in the front and the rear bearing retainer in the rear. It houses the direct drive clutch and a planetary gear set for low and reverse.

The rear bearing retainer supports the transmission on a rubber mounting attached to a frame cross member. It houses the pawl and ratchet wheel for Parking, the speedometer drive gears, and the universal joint.

Operation of the direct drive clutch and the planetary gear set is controlled by oil under pressure as supplied by two oil pumps; one at the front, one at the rear of the transmission. Smoothness of operation is attained by two accumulators which act to cushion the shock of engaging units exactly as a door check cushions a closing door. These accumulators are mounted on a flange between the Bell Housing and the transmission case.

Regulation of the oil pressure and operation of the clutch and planetary gears is controlled by a valve and servo body assembly attached to the bottom of the transmission and covered by the oil pan. In addition there are lubricating oil and converter oil pressure regulating valves at the rear of the transmission case.

Operation of the Converter

EXCEPT 1953 MODELS

The fluid unit at the start of the Dynaflow transmission is not a fluid drive unit but on the contrary is a fluid driven torque converter. That is to say it takes the power of the engine and multiplies it to a maximum of 2.25 to 1. It thus provides the flexible power source necessary to vehicle operation. In the event that this order of multiplication (2.25) is insufficient for the driving conditions the planetary gear set in the body of the transmission can be brought into use by moving the control lever to Low. This results in an overall torque multiplication of 4.07 to 1.

The torque converter multiplies the available power of the engine by changing the direction of flow of a large volume of oil.

The main hunk of the converter is known as the primary pump. It and its cover are bolted to the flywheel and form a housing for the rest of the converter parts. When the engine turns so does the primary pump and as the pump turns so does the oil with which it is filled. The curved blades of the pump throw the oil against the turbine wheel which is fastened to the input shaft. (The input Shaft extends into the direct drive clutch and the planetary gear set of the transmission.)

Hitting the blades of the turbine the

OPERATIONS OF CONVERTER —*continued*

oil curves down and around to exit in a direction counter to the rotation of the turbine at which point it hits a double set of blades, known as the secondary and primary stators, which change its direction of flow again.

The stators are mounted on free wheeling clutches which permit them to rotate freely in the same direction as the pump and the turbine but prevent any counter rotation. The oil is thus forced into a U turn which results in a back force against the turbine which adds to the power output of the turbine. This kick back force is the same as that felt by a fireman directing the flow of water from a fire hose at the side of a building.

When the turbine is stationary the oil passes through the turbine and stators back to the pump with almost as much energy as when it left.

This energy added to that being supplied the pump by the engine gives an increase in power output of the turbine of 2.25 to 1. The 1 representing the input power from the engine.

As long as high torque is required the flow of oil from pump to turbine to stators to pump is large in volume but when the speed of the turbine produces an output speed satisfactory to the operation of the car the volume of oil flow from the pump to the turbine slacks off and the mass of oil in the converter spins as a unit in the form of a fluid flywheel. The decrease in flow permits the stators to idle in free wheeling as they spin with the mass of oil being carried around by the centrifugal force imparted to the whole deal by the engine. Under these conditions a change in the shape of the pump blades is desirable and this is accomplished by the secondary pump which free wheels in the direction of pump rotation when the flow volume of oil is large but helps to pick oil up and aid its flow when the flow volume decreases.

As mentioned the stators and the secondary pump are mounted on free wheeling clutches. The stator clutches are keyed to a hollow stationary shaft called the reactor shaft which is fastened to a flange bolted between the transmission case and the converter. The clutch of the secondary pump is carried on a bearing surface forming part of the hub of the primary pump. This same hub drives the front oil pump.

The output of the converter is carried into the transmission proper by the input shaft as previously mentioned.

Operation of Clutch and Planetary Gears

The input shaft, passing freely through the hollow reactor shaft, has splined to it at its rear end the reverse sun gear and just forward of that the clutch hub.

The internal splined (faced) clutch plates mesh with splines in the clutch hub so that these plates, the clutch hub, and the input shaft act as a unit. Alternating with the internal splined (faced) plates are external splined (steel) plates which mesh with splines in the low drum which is keyed to, and so a part of the flange of the low sun gear.

The low sun gear is not connected to the input shaft but contacts the reverse ring gear thru the reverse planet pinions of the planetary gear set.

The low drum acts as a housing for the clutch parts and as a cylinder for the clutch piston whose movement is controlled in the last analysis by the setting of the control lever.

When the control lever is set for Direct Drive, oil under 80-90 lbs per sq. in. pressure is fed through the high accumulator against the clutch piston to lock the plates together. This brings the low sun gear into revolution with the input shaft. Since the reverse sun gear is locked to the shaft with splines the two gears act upon the reverse and low planet pinions causing them to lock against each other; this results in the whole planetary gear set revolving as a hunk so that the output shaft is driven at the same speed and in the same direction as the input shaft. Which, inspection will show, is direct drive from converter to drive shaft. See Fig. 10.

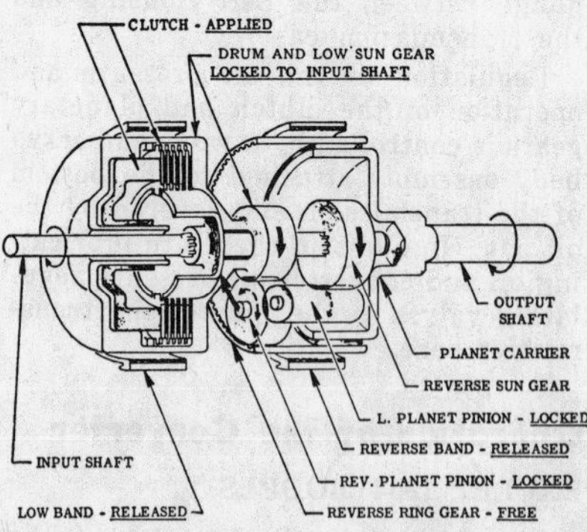

Fig. 10—Clutch and planetary gears in "Drive"

The clutch is only engaged in Drive. In Low oil pressure at 180 lbs per sq in. acting through the low accumulator and the low band servo applies the low band to hold the low drum stationary which means that the low sun gear is also stationary. The Reverse sun gear being splined to the input shaft as mentioned before continues to turn thus driving the low planet pinions which mesh with it. They in turn drive the reverse planet pinions the direction in this case being identical with the rotation of the input shaft. Since these reverse planet pinions are meshed with the stationary low sun gear (which is held so by the low band) they climb around it carrying their shafts and so the carrier with them. As the output shaft and the carrier are one solid forging, the output shaft turns but at a lower rate than that of the input shaft. The reduction attained by this gearing is 1.82 to 1. Fig. 11.

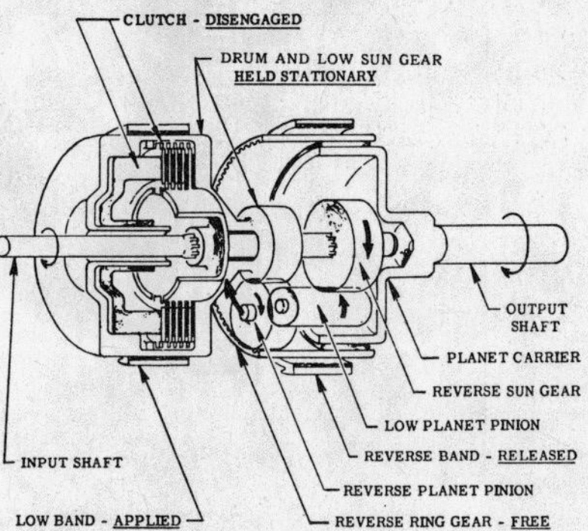

Fig. 11—Clutch and planetary gears in "Low"

When the control lever is moved to Reverse oil pressure at 180 lbs per sq. in. acts through the reverse band servo to apply the reverse band thus holding the reverse ring gear stationary. (The low band no longer holds the low sun gear and it idles.) Power from the in-

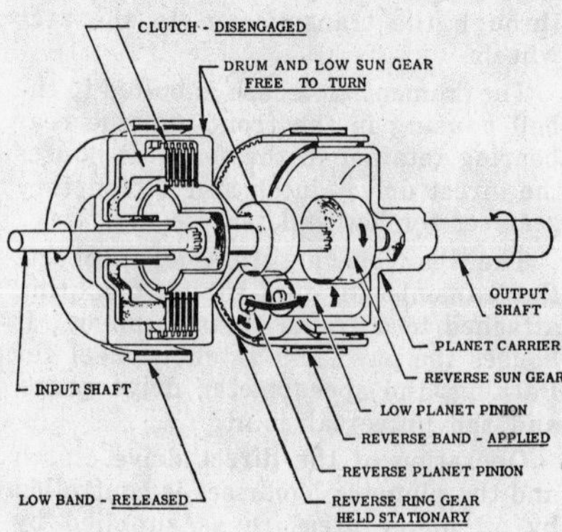

Fig. 12—Clutch and planetary gears in "Reverse"

put shaft acting through the reverse sun gear drives the low planet pinions which in turn drive the reverse planet pinions causing them to climb around the stationary reverse ring gear carrying their shafts and so the carrier with them as before. Only this time it results in the carrier and integral output shaft turning in a direction opposite to that of the input shaft. The rate is lower than that of the input shaft; in fact the reduction is the same as for Low; 1.82 to 1. Fig. 12.

Operation of the Converter

1953 MODELS

In basic theory the change in the Dynaflow for 1953 involves the converter unit only. The "Twin Turbine" converter has a primary pump bolted to the engine flywheel, two turbines interconnected thru a planetary gear set inside the unit and a single stator stage. The other pertinent change is the addition of an access hole and cover to permit adjustment of the valve operating rod (V-8 Models only). An operation that formerly involved removal of the torque ball.

The maximum torque multiplication of the new converter is 2.45 to 1 compared to the 2.25 to 1 of the 1952 converter.

The first turbine amounts to a narrow band of vanes located between the pump exit and the second turbine. The second turbine is located along side the first turbine in a position to receive all the oil sent to the first turbine by the primary pump. In location the second turbine has the position of the primary turbine of previous models. The oil leaving the second turbine is going counter to to the rotation of the pump and is therefore directed into a free wheeling stator as heretofor.

The second turbine is bolted to a planetary carrier which is splined to the input shaft.

The first turbine is mounted on a disk and hub assembly whose bearing surface is the hub of the carrier. The disk carries the ring gear of the planetary gear set so that rotation of the first turbine will drive the input shaft thru the pinions and sun gear of the gear set. The sun gear is supported by a bearing on the input shaft but its rotation is controlled by the same free wheel clutch as the stator. The sun gear therefore is held stationary whenever the stator is held stationary which is to say whenever the oil flow volume is large due to large torque requirements.

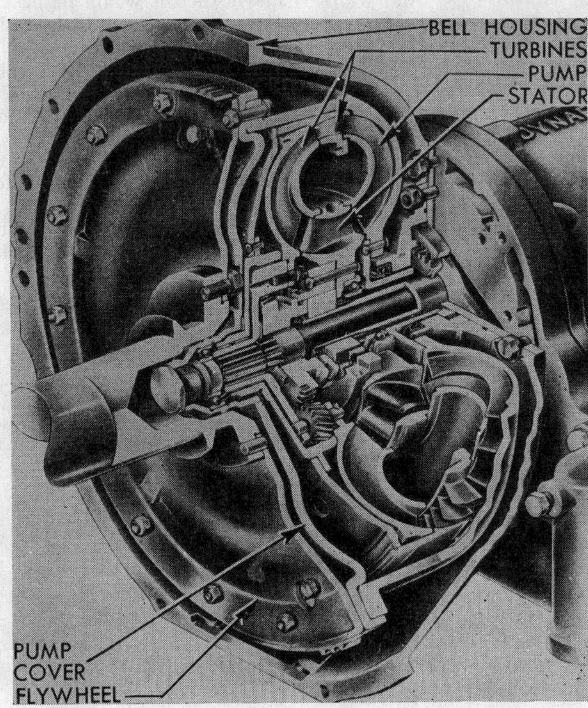

Fig. 13—Cutaway of 1953 converter

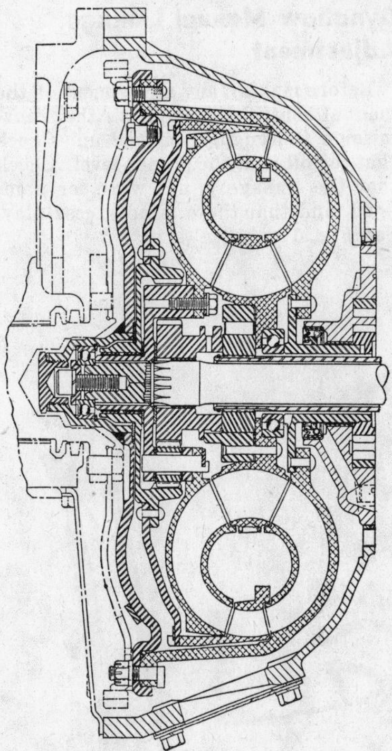
Fig. 13A—Engineering cross section of '53 converter

When the transmission is used with the 8-in-line engine the stator has 12 broad vanes; when used with the V-8 engine the stator has 20 narrow vanes. This difference in stator design adapts the one converter to the output torques of the two engines. All other converter parts are identical for all series.

The increased torque of the new design is due to the gearing of the planetary gear set which is most effective when torque requirements are greatest. As in the previous design, as the turbines come up to speed the pressure against the forward face of the stator decreases until it finally ceases. Torque reaction against the sun gear ceases at approximately the same speed after which the stator and the sun gear free wheel. At this point the first turbine ceases to be effective and in effect free wheels along with the stator so that there is little interference with the decreased volume of oil flow and the unit functions as a fluid coupling as in previous models. When operating conditions change to increase torque demand the converter automatically adjusts itself to meet the demand.

Dynaflow Manual Linkage Adjustment

Before making any adjustment of the manual control linkage have the transmission thoroughly warmed up. Check that the oil is at the proper level. Check that the linkage is not worn, or damaged, and that there is no excess play. See Fig. 14.

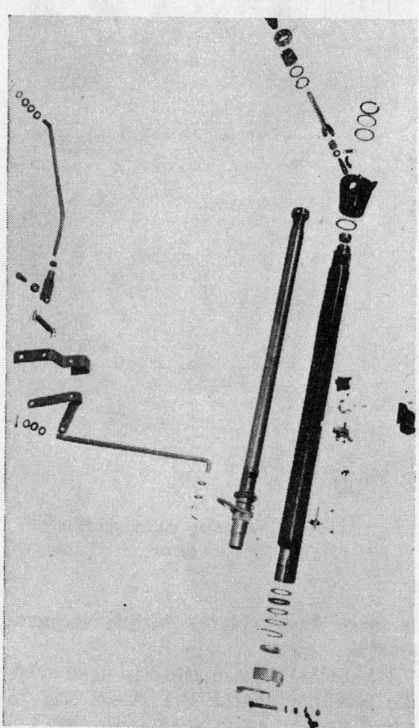

Fig. 14—Exploded view of Dynaflow linkage

1. Check that the detent is properly positioned.

Put a piece of masking tape across the face of the pointer housing in such a way that the pointer can be seen and the distance it moves marked on the tape.

Place the hand lever in Drive position with the detent ball centered in the detent notch. Make a mark on the tape to show the position of the pointer. Call this point "D".

Move the lever toward Neutral but do not lift it. The stop pin will hit the stop in the dial housing. Make a mark on the tape to show location of the pointer when this occurs. Call it "N".

Return the lever to Drive with the detent ball centered in the detent notch as done above. Move the hand lever towards Low but do not lift it. The stop pin will hit the stop in the dial housing. Mark the tape to show the position of the pointer when this occurs. Call it "L".

The mark called "D" above should be midway between the marks made for "N" and "L". If it is not loosen the detent mounting bolts and shift the detent until the position of the pointer when in Drive is midway between the stops in each direction. This is done so that the distance the pointer moves on one side of Drive is equal to the distance it moves on the other. Tighten the detent mounting bolts to 15-20 ft lbs.

2. Check that the Parking Lock is correctly positioned.

The parking lock should hold when the lever is at Park and not come in contact with the ratchet at any other position of the lever. Normally if the parking position is correct the other positions will also be correct.

If the parking lock does not engage or if it contacts the ratchet when the hand lever is in other positions:

Go to the bottom of the steering column where the shift rod clevis is fastened to the idler lever and unpin the clevis. Fig 15.

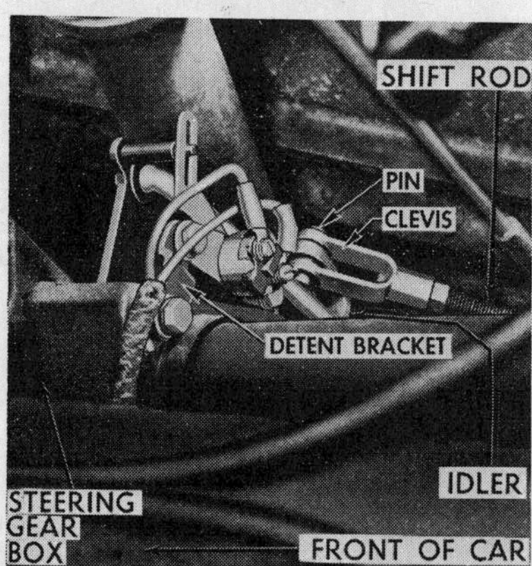

Fig. 15—Shift rod clevis pinned to idler

Lengthen or shorten the shift rod to insure that the parking lock pawl engages the ratchet with the hand lever in the Park position. Repin the clevis to the idler lever.

Check that the parking lock pawl is fully released in other positions of the hand lever. If it is not fully released or if it won't go into Park, or if it slips out, it will be necessary to go through this procedure:

Remove the rear axle and torque ball (except on 1953 models provided with an access hole in the rear bearing retainer) and adjust the valve control rod at the clevis in the rear bearing retainer. Fig. 16A.

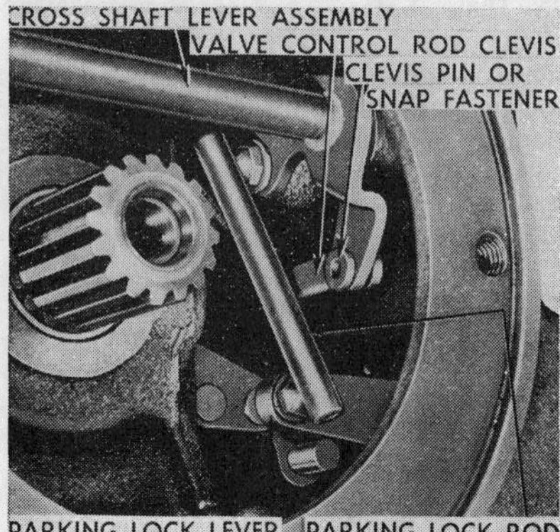

Fig. 16A—Adjusting valve control rod clevis

Make the adjustment so that there is ⅛ to 3/16 spring loaded forward travel of the end of the shift lever when the pawl is fully engaged and the lock is in full contact with it. Fig. 16B and Fig. 17.

If this adjustment requires a great deal of turning the valve control rod clevis then it would be best to remove the transmission oil pan and check the control valve levers.

Push the shift control valve inward to take up the play in the linkage and measure the distance from the end of the valve to the stop pin. It should be .030″ to .040″. See Fig. 17. If it is not then the control valve levers were improperly assembled and the Valve and Servo Body will have to be removed and the condition corrected.

Fig. 16B—Spring loaded travel of shift lever

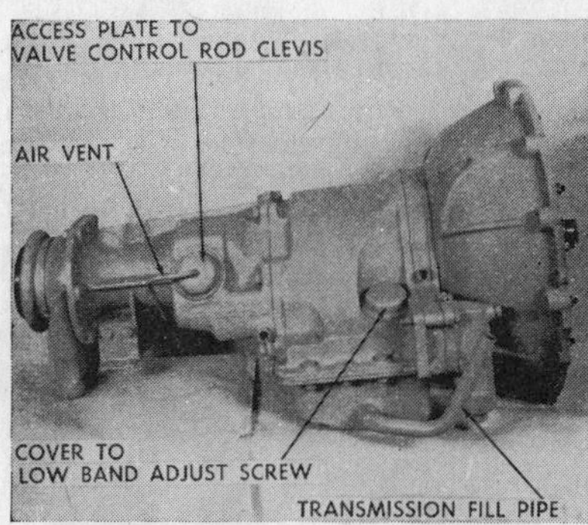

Fig. 16C—Location of combination breather and access plate

When the spring travel is correct pull the shift rod forward till it stops and adjust its clevis so that it could be pinned to the idler lever. (The hand lever is firmly set at Park.)

Now lengthen the shift rod at the clevis by three complete turns and pin it to the idler lever. Fig. 15.

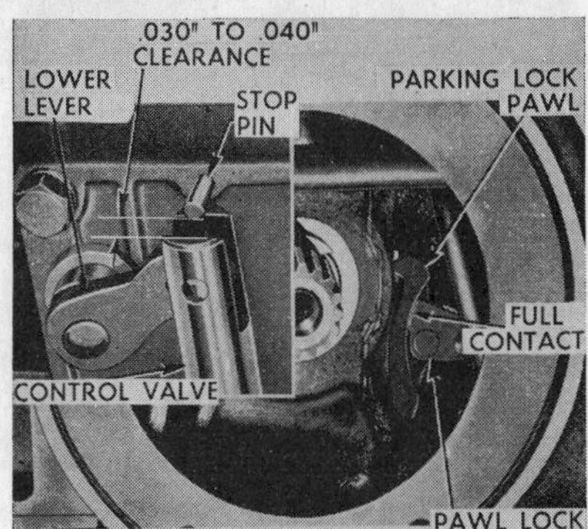

Fig. 17—Checking control valve clearance

Check that the parking pawl is now engaging and disengaging correctly.

3. Check the Transmission shift points.

There is available a template to fit over the pointer housing. It is Buick Tool No. J3085. See Fig. 18.

If there is no template available a working substitute can be made by installing a strip of masking tape over the dial in such a manner that the travel of the pointer can be noted on the tape.

Note on the tape the exact location of the pointer at Neutral, Drive, Low, and Reverse.

Make a ⅛" wide line half way between (1) Neutral and Drive, (2) Drive and Low, (3) Low and Reverse.

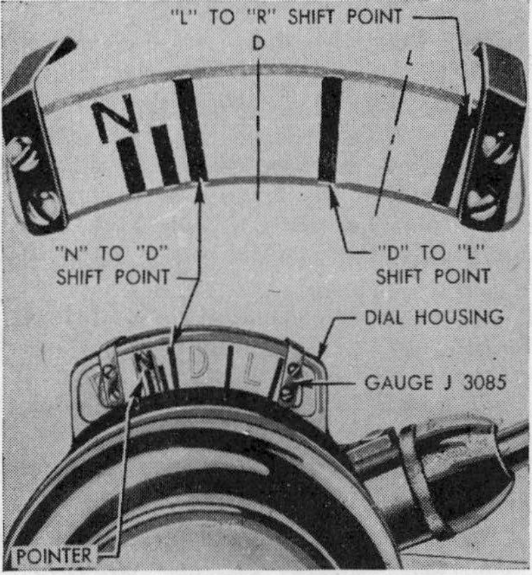

Fig. 18—Use of shift point gauge

With engine idling at 600 rpm slowly shift from Neutral to Drive. The engine speed should fall off indicating engagement of the Clutch, as the tip of the pointer passes the ⅛" wide line. The width of the line provides all the allowable tolerance in shift point variation.

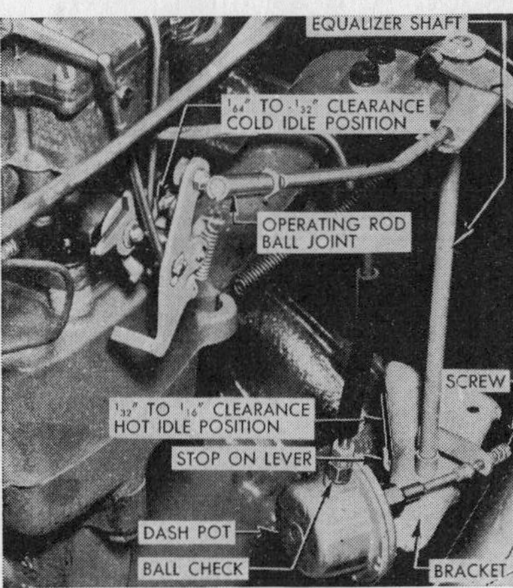

Fig. 19—Throttle linkage and dashpot adjustment

Shift from Drive to Neutral, the engine speed should pick up as the pointer passes the line.

If the shift does not occur at the midway mark then it will be necessary to adjust the shift rod clevis at the idler lever to make it so. Follow this operation by rechecking that the parking lock adjustment was not changed enough to notice.

Slowly shift from Drive to Low. The engine speed should pick up slightly and there should follow a slight clunk as the pointer passes the ⅛" line. Indicating release of the clutch and tightening of the low band. If these things do not occur within the width of the line it is probable that the shift lever on the side of the transmission is bent out of its normal position. After replacing the shift lever be sure to recheck that the parking lock adjustment is correct.

Slowly shift from Low to Reverse. There should be a slight clunk as the tip of the pointer passes the ⅛" line. Indicating that the low band has released and the reverse band has tightened. If this does not occur within the width of the line it is probable that the control valve levers (upper and lower) are bent or improperly seated. It will be necessary to remove the valve and servo body assembly to correct the condition. The procedure for doing so will be found under Disassembly.

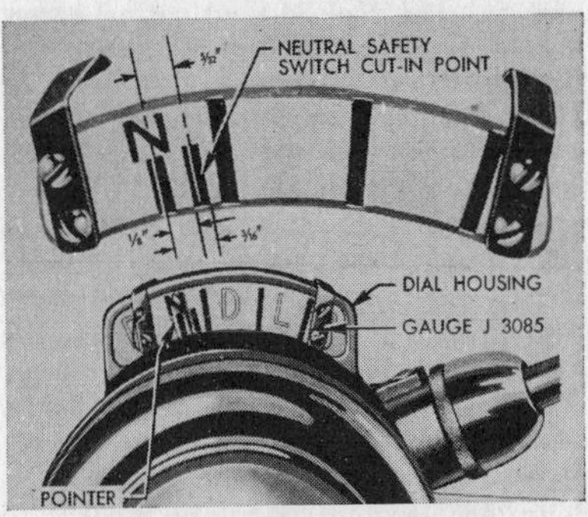

Fig. 20—Use of safety switch cut-in point gauge

Throttle Linkage and Dash Pot Adjustment

1. With engine warm and idling adjust carburetor to give smooth idle at 450 rpm with fast idle cam in Hot position. Now check the clearance between the Stop on lever at bottom of equalizer shaft and the shaft lower bracket. It should be 1/32" to 1/16". Adjust by means of the ball joint on the throttle operating rod.

2. With engine warm but turned off check that throttle opens fully when accelerator pedal hits the floor mat. The throttle should be open when pedal hits mat, not when throttle lever hits boss on carburetor. Adjust throttle operating rod at ball joint to make it so. Fig. 19.

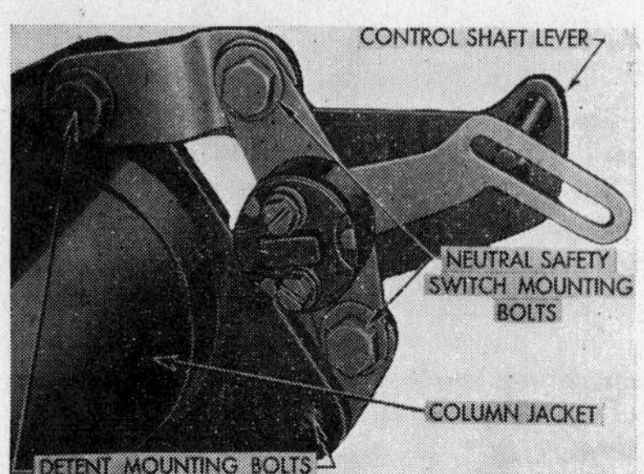

Fig. 21—Adjusting neutral safety switch

THROTTLE LINKAGE—*continued*

3. Hold fast idle cam in cold position. Check clearance between fast idle cam and (a) the fast idle adjusting screw (Carter); (or b) the throttle stop screw (Stromberg). Clearance should be 1/64″ to 1/32″. Adjust at the spring loaded screw on dash pot operating lever at lower end of equalizer shaft.

4. Check that dash pot vacuum is OK. Check that plunger moves freely. If plunger is bent or corrections have not remedied the matter replace the dash pot.

5. To check results run engine up to 1400 rpm with transmission in Direct Drive. Car held still with brakes. Release accelerator. If engine returns to idle too slowly turn adjusting screw on dash pot operating lever counterclockwise. If engine returns to idle too fast, resulting in stall or rolling, turn adjusting screw clockwise.

Adjustment of Neutral Safety Switch

After checking and adjusting the transmission manual control linkage:

1. Install template J3085 as shown in Fig. 20 or install a piece of masking tape across the dial so that the movement of the pointer can be observed. Mark the tape with a 3/16″ wide line at Neutral. Mark another 3/16″ wide line so that its center is 5/32″ to the right of the center of the line we just made at Neutral.

2. Ground the primary terminal of the distributor with jumper wire so the engine can be cranked without firing.

3. Set the hand brake and put the hand lever at Neutral. Make sure the detent is engaged and the line and pointer coincide.

4. Move the hand lever to Drive. Turn on the ignition and push the accelerator down to close the vacuum switch.

5. Slowly shift from Drive to Neutral and note the position of the tip of the pointer at the instant the cranking motor starts to operate. Release the accelerator. The tip of the pointer should have been within the width of the line which was drawn 5/32″ to the right of the Neutral mark. If this was not so adjust the switch thus:

Loosen the switch mounting bolts and slide the switch away from the engine. Fig. 21.

Have an assistant; (1) hold lever so that the tip of the pointer is centered on the 3/16″ gage mark, (2) turn on the ignition, (3) push on the accelerator pedal.

Gently tap the switch in toward the engine until the starter begins to turn.

Have the helper release the accelerator, turn off the ignition switch, but continue to hold the hand lever. Tighten the bolts to hold the safety switch to 11-15 ft lbs.

Adjustment Back Up Lamp Switch

With transmission in Low:

Check the clearance between back up lamp switch operating arm and lower edge of control shaft lower lever. Should be 0⅛″. If it is not then;

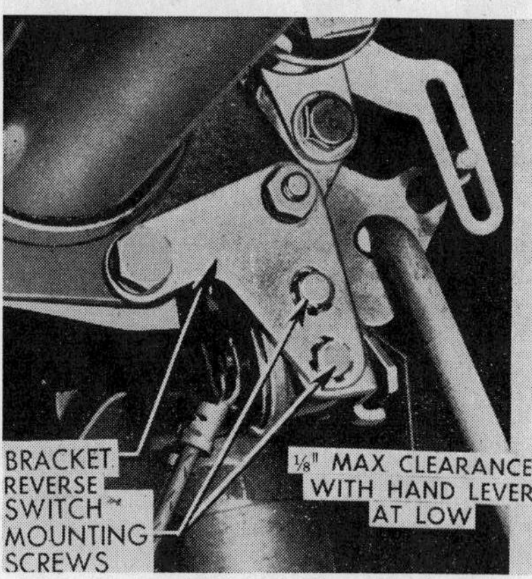

Fig. 22—Adjusting back up lamp switch

Loosen the two back-up switch mountings screws and move switch to obtain the clearance. The bracket to which the switch is fastened is slotted to permit this adjustment.

Band Adjustment

Procedure for adjusting either band is as follows: (This applies only to early models that have a floor pan.)

1. Remove front floor mat, insulation pad, transmission opening pan, from the floor of the front compartment.

2. Remove the band adjusting covers and gaskets using an offset screw driver to pry them off. Fig. 23.

3. Loosen lock nut and turn adjusting screw clockwise until resistance is felt indicating contact of band with drum.

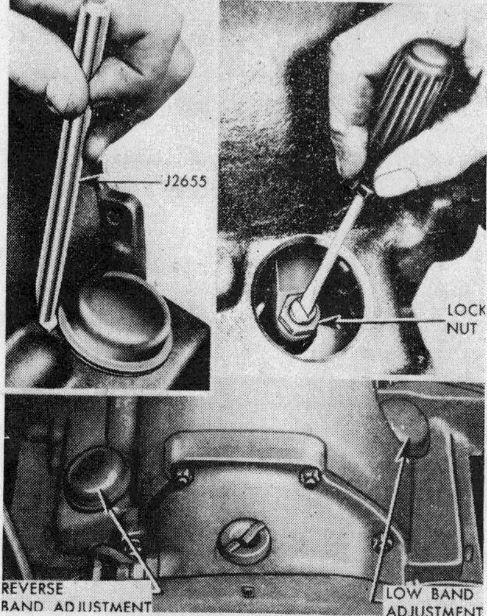

Fig. 23—Adjusting bands

4. Pry up on lock nut with screw driver and turn screw counterclockwise until a little play between drum and band can be felt by wiggling the screwdriver. Fig. 24.

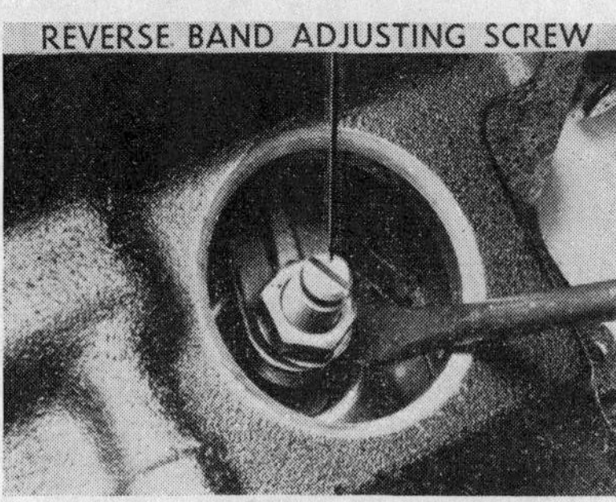

Fig. 24—Feeling for little play

5. Now unscrew adjusting screws six full turns. Snug up lock nut being sure screw has not turned.

6. Replace covers using new gaskets.

7. Replace floor pan, pad and mat.

For models without removable floor pans drill four inch holes in the floor over the two band adjusting screw covers, Fig. 25, and proceed as above.

Fig. 25—Location of band cover

Dynaflow Manual Linkage 1953 Series 50

The transmission control mechanism on the Series 50 steering column has been redesigned for easier shifting.

The control lever housing is externally mounted on the upper end of the column jacket. The housing contains a spring loaded lever and roller which rides into notches in a detent plate anchored to the underside of the signal switch housing. The control lever rotates the housing and so moves the roller from notch to notch.

The control shaft operates a lever at the bottom of the steering column. The lever has a tongue which engages a stop plate clamped to the steering column. During shifts into Parking, Neutral and Reverse the control lever raises the control shaft and so raises the tongue of the lever out of the stop plate.

When in Drive there should be .120″ to .130″ clearance between the lever and the stop plate.

There must also be .010″ to .020″ clearance between the tongue on the lever and the nearest edge of the large hole in the plate.

Removal of Control Lever —1953 Models

The control lever and related parts may be removed by first unscrewing the control lever retainer from the housing, then removing the lever cover, retainer spring, retainer plate and the lever.

Remove the anti-rattle spring retainer and spring from the control lever stud, unscrew the stud from the control shaft.

When the stud is reinstalled it is very important that it be tightened to 25-30 ft lbs torque. Use a torque wrench equipped with a 9/16 socket cut away to fit over a piece of 3/16″ (.187) drill rod inserted thru the hole in the stud.

The adjustment of the other controls is the same.

DIAGNOSING TROUBLES

In order to properly diagnose troubles with any automatic drive it is necessary to know what units are working at any given setting of the control lever. To this end a skeleton listing is presented.

In Neutral and Parking

Oil flows from the front pump only.

The lubrication and converter pressure valves are functioning. (This is true whenever converter is turning.)

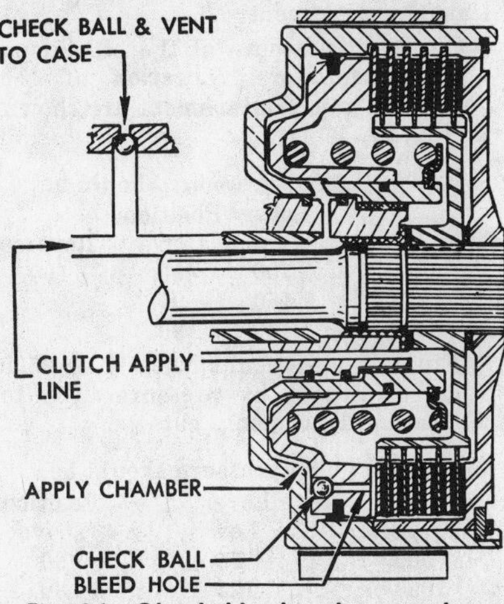

Fig. 26—Clutch bleed and vent valves

The control valve cuts off all oil flow to the clutch and servos.

In Direct Drive

The control valve passes oil at 80-90 psi to the clutch piston.

Engagement of the clutch is cushioned by the high accumulator.

The low sun gear is locked to the input shaft.

Coming out of Direct Drive

Bleed holes in the clutch apply line and apply chamber insure drainage of the oil to the crankcase. Fig. 26, if the shift is attempted at speeds above 45 mph these drains do not function completely.

In Low

The control valve passes oil at 160-180 psi to the low accumulator.

The Low servo compresses the Low band around the low drum.

The low sun gear is thus held.

The planetary gear set revolves.

When shifting from Low to Direct Drive the low accumulator slows up release of the low band until the clutch has engaged.

In Reverse

The control valve passes oil at 160-180 psi directly to the reverse servo.

The reverse servo has two springs thus avoiding the use of an accumulator.

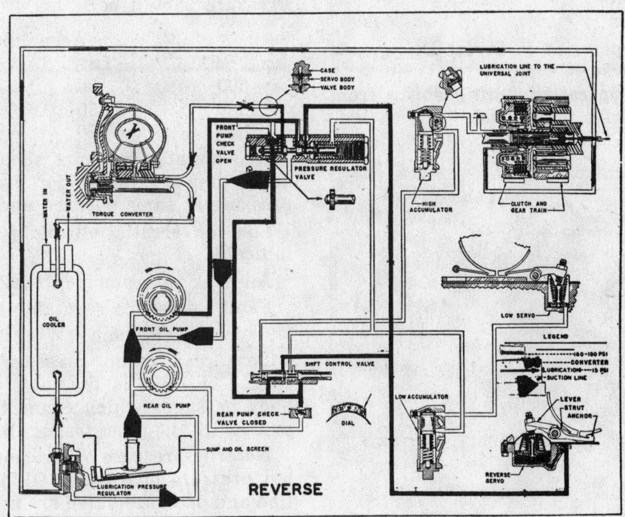

Fig. 27—Oil flow in reverse

DIAGNOSIS—continued

The oil pressure comes only from the front pump as in reverse the rear oil pump is turning backwards. A check valve in the delivery line prevents loss of oil thru this pump. Fig. 27.

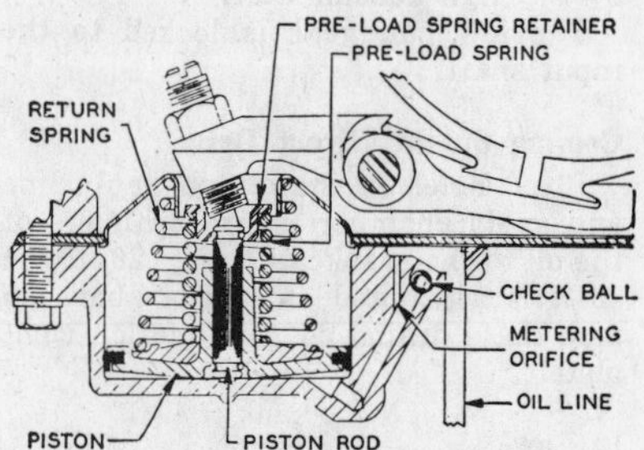

Fig. 28—Section through reverse servo

Shifting out of reverse the check ball in the reverse servo lifts off its seat and the return spring forces the oil out releasing the band. Fig. 28.

CHECKING PROCEDURE FOR TROUBLES

(In Order to Apply Trouble Chart)

Check oil level first

Note: Transmission must be hot. That is at operating Temperature.

To warm up transmission drive car at least 20 miles with frequent stops as in heavy traffic.

Road Test

Test Operation in Direct Drive, Low and Reverse.

Check operation during shifts from Low to Drive under load.

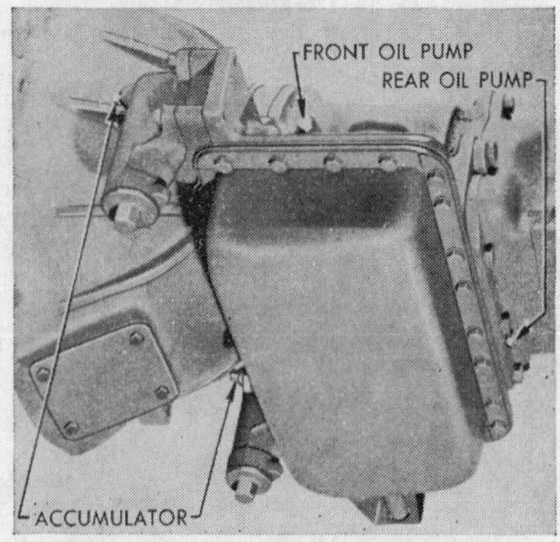

Fig. 29—Gauge connections for oil pressure tests

Check for creep in Neutral, Drive, Reverse and Low.

In Drive but held by the brake snap accelerate motor to 1400 rpm and release accelerator.

If it returns to idle too slowly or if it returns to idle too fast and stalls.

Readjust the throttle and dash pot linkage.

Shop Test

If unit is using more than a pint per 1000 miles check all over for leaks.

Improper operation in more than one range indicates need for control linkage adjustment.

Check oil pressure at the oil pumps and accumulators. Location of the points for gauge attachment are shown in Fig. 29.

Front oil pump pressure should be:

	Lever	Position	
Eng. R.P.M.	Low	Drive	Reverse
500	100	90	100
1000	160	90	...
1800	180	90	...

Front pump should cut out at 2500 rpm. Indicated by pressure drop to 20 lbs as Rear pump cuts in.

Rear oil pump pressure should be:

	Lever	Position
Eng. RPM	Low	Drive
500	75	90
1000	125	90
1800	175	90

Accumulators. Check low accumulator with lever in Low. Check high accumulator with lever in Direct Drive. Pressure should be:

	Accumulators	
Eng. RPM	Low	High
500	90	80
1000	150	85
1800	170	85

Accumulator pressure should not be more than 10 lbs under front pump pressure at same position and RPM.

Low or erratic oil pump pressure indicates:

Air leak into pump intake line.

Faulty pressure regulator valve.

Excessive clearance (Wear in pumps).

Low rear pump pressure may be caused by leaks in the valve and servo body passages which connect the rear pump with the pressure regulator valve.

Note: If pressure of one pump is low but pressure of other is OK the intake line and pressure valve are not at fault as both pumps use the same unit.

Very low accumulator pressure may be caused by external or internal leakage past the valve body gasket.

When front pump and high accumulator differ by more than 10 lbs there is a leak between the accumulator and the clutch.

When difference is between front pump and low accumulator the leak is between accumulator and Low servo.

Or else accumulator metering orifice is obstructed.

Oil Leaks

Check these points for oil leaks (if none show in Drive try in Low).

Oil pan.

Reactor flange.

Front oil pump (insert long roll of paper through hand hole toward the pump. Oil should not wet paper).

The band adjustment covers.

Rear bearing retainer.

Filler pipe.

Primary pump cover (hold a piece of paper between flywheel and bell housing. Oil should not wet paper).

The accumulators. These can be removed while transmission is in the car. If leak is at cap remove and coat with No. 3 Permatex and reinstall.

If leak is at body remove and check for warp and porosity, replace with new gasket.

Check engine and transmission mountings for misalignment of transmission.

Tightness of bolts.

Condition of pads.

Signs of having been hit.

TROUBLE SHOOTING CHART

Note 1: Items marked NOTE 1 require removal of Transmission for repairs.

Note 2: Items marked NOTE 2 can be done with Dynaflow in car.

(Causes are listed in descending order of probability)

1. Engine Stalls While Decelerating Car with Brake Applied

Improper adjustment of throttle dash pot.

Engine not properly tuned.

2. Transmission Oil Foams and Spews Out of Breather

Too much oil in transmission.

Defective propeller shaft seals may have let rear axle lubricant come in.

Check for low oil level in differential. Will require installation of new seals and fresh oil in transmission. (Note 2).

Water from leaking oil cooler has come in. Check for oil in the engine radiator. Requires new cooler and fresh oil. (Note 2).

Air is being sucked in and churned into the oil.

Air leak at rear oil pump gasket. (Note 2).

Excessive clearance between output shaft journal and rear bearing retainer bushing. (Note 2).

Wrong kind of oil in transmission.

3. Car Will Not Move in Any Range—Rear Wheels Turn Freely

Car won't move in any range for 1 to 8 minutes after standing all night.

Front oil pump pressure is zero until car will move. Requires removal and inspection of front oil pump and if condition has existed for some time the clutch and bands should be inspected for signs of excessive wear. (Note 1).

Car will not move in any range after backing up.

Air is leaking into pump suction line. Remove oil pan and check oil intake pipe and contact with seal ring in servo body assembly. (Note 2).

Front oil pump is worn. Check clearances of pump. (Note 1).

Air is leaking in at rear oil pump gasket. (Note 2).

4. Car Will Not Move in Any Range—Rear Wheels Locked

Parking lock engaged due to maladjusted controls.

Broken part in rear axle.

Broken part in transmission. (Note 1).

5. Car Will Not Move in Drive, Otherwise OK.

Pressures at front pump and high accumulator are OK. Remove and inspect clutch assembly. (Note 1).

High accumulator pressure is low.

Check accumulator body gasket for internal leaks. (Note 1).

Check reactor shaft flange gasket. (Note 1).

Check clutch piston outer seal (rubber ring). (Note 1).

Check oil seal rings on reactor shaft at its rear end. (Note 1).

Check clutch piston inner seal ring. (Note 1).

6. Car Will Not Move in Reverse, Otherwise O.K.

Reverse servo is not working. (Note 2).

Band is improperly adjusted. (Note 2).

Band operating strut has dropped out of place. (Note 2).

Obsolete type of reverse band anchor has broken. (Note 1).

7. Excessive Slip in All Ranges

If condition appears only after operation in reverse.

Check front oil pump pressure. If it is low it indicates air leakage into pump suction line. (Note 2).

Inspect for air leaks at rear oil pump gaskets. (Note 2).

Inspect front oil pump and cover for wear. (Note 1).

Low oil level.

If case history shows high oil consumption (a pint or more in 1000 miles) and there are no indications of oil leakage around the outside of the transmission, check the lubricant level in the differential which if high indicates leakage past the propeller shaft spline seal. Disconnect propeller shaft at torque ball and renew the seal. Be sure to drain and refill the differential and discard the lubricant which was diluted with oil from the transmission.

Manual control linkage improperly adjusted.

Operation in reverse has no effect on the condition but front oil pump pressure is low.

Remove and inspect the pressure regulator valve and all the valve and servo body assembly gaskets. (Note 2).

Check front oil pump for wear. Check pump cover and reactor shaft flange gaskets for leaks. (Note 1).

Primary pump hub may be worn hourglass shaped. (Note 1).

8. Excessive Slip in Direct Drive Only

Manual control linkage improperly adjusted.

Leak at high accumulator gasket indicated by low pressure reading at this point. (Note 2).

Stuck clutch piston check ball. Remove clutch assembly and check the plates, the seal rings and the piston itself. (Note 1).

9. Excessive Slip in Low Only

Manual control linkage improperly adjusted.

Low band improperly adjusted. (Note 2).

Band worn. (Note 1).

Drum scored. (Note 1).

Low pressure at low accumulator.

Leak at low accumulator body gasket. (Note 1).

Leaks at valve and servo body assembly gaskets. (Note 2).

Defective low servo piston seal. (Note 2).

10. Excessive Slip in Reverse Only

Manual control linkage improperly adjusted.

Reverse band not functioning or improperly adjusted. (Note 2).

Strut out of place. (Note 2).

Anchor broken. (Note 1).

Worn or scored band. (Note 1).

Ring gear worn or scored. (Note 1).

Low front oil pump pressure.

Leaks at valve and servo body assembly gaskets. (Note 2).

Defective reverse servo piston seal. (Note 2).

11. Car Creeps Forward in Neutral

Manual control linkage improperly adjusted.

Low servo piston or anchor sticking. (Note 2).

Sticking, warped or improperly assembled clutch plates. Dished plates must all face same way. (Note 1).

Check balls for release of clutch pressure not working properly. (Note 1).

12. Car Creeps Forward in Reverse or Backward in Low

Manual control linkage improperly adjusted.

13. Shift from Low to Direct Drive Abnormally Rough or Slip Occurs

If high accumulator pressure is low.

Check high accumulator body gasket for leakage. (Note 1).

Check for sticking accumulator piston. Top land of piston must be fully visible through top port in the body. (Note 1).

DYNAFLOW

TROUBLE SHOOTING CHART—*continued*

Check for leaks in the valve and servo body assembly gaskets. (Note 2).

Low band improperly adjusted. (Note 2).

Binding or worn clutch plates. (Note 1).

14. Excessive Chatter or Clunk When Starting in Low or Reverse.

Note: A very slight chatter just as car starts to move in reverse which disappears as car gets moving is normal. A slight clunk when shifting into Low or Reverse is also normal.

Check engine and transmission mountings for tightness. Inspect for broken rubber thrust pad at transmission mounting.

Low or Reverse band improperly adjusted. (Note 2).

Check clutch for sticking, warped, or improperly assembled clutch plates. (Note 1).

Inspect for excessive wear of reverse ring gear bushing and for foreign matter in the needle bearings of the planetary assembly. (Note 1).

15. Hard Shifting Out of Parking

Transmission shift rod is binding in the shift idler lever.

Remove any burrs with a file.

Distorted idler lever should be replaced with a new one.

16. Noises in the Transmission

Hum or low whine in any gear is normal.

Low growl which disappears after engine has run a bit (is most likely to occur after Parking outside in cold weather) is caused by cavitation of the oil and has no remedy.

A buzzing noise.

Low oil level.

Front pump delivery check valve caught on edge of a gasket. (Note 2).

Excessive clearance of pressure regulator valve necessitating replacement of the valve. (Note 2).

A clicking noise in all ranges.

Foreign object in converter. (Note 1).

Improper manual control adjustment permitting parking lock pawl to contact ratchet wheel.

Abnormal hum or whine which occurs in all ranges.

Due to worn front oil pump or improperly installed front pump driving gear. Check for low front oil pump pressure. (Note 1).

Wear in the planetary assembly especially if noise is not so apparent in Drive. (Note 1).

Squealing or screeching or howling immediately following transmission overhaul indicates that front pump driving gear is in backwards. This condition must be corrected without further operation of the transmission or serious damage will be done to the unit. (Note 1).

Whistling during slow acceleration in all gears together with poor performance.

Converter is not being filled with oil. Check for restrictions in the passages in the valve and servo body assembly. (Note 2).

Check passages in the reactor shaft flange. (Note 1).

Whistling during slow acceleration in all gears with otherwise satisfactory performance.

Thin, weak, or bent or cracked turbine blades which vibrate under load. Turbine must be replaced. (Note 1).

Note 1—Items marked Note 1 require removal of transmission for repairs.

Note 2—Items marked Note 2 can be done with the Dynaflow in the car.

DYNAFLOW REMOVAL

1. Drain cooling system and transmission oil pan. Hoist front and rear of car and support firmly at least two feet above the floor.

2. Disconnect drive shaft and torque tube at the universal joint. This requires disconnection of rear springs for which please note.

Note: On Series 40 cars since 1951 the lower attaching studs have right hand threads while on all Series 50 and 70 the attaching bolts have left hand threads.

3. Remove bell housing lower front pan and hand hole cover. Fig. 30.

4. Loosen one flywheel drain plug to provide an air vent then remove other drain plug which is on side opposite and drain flywheel.

5. Disconnect hoses from oil cooler and disconnect rubber hose in oil filler line.

6. Disconnect transmission shift rod at both ends. Fig. 31.

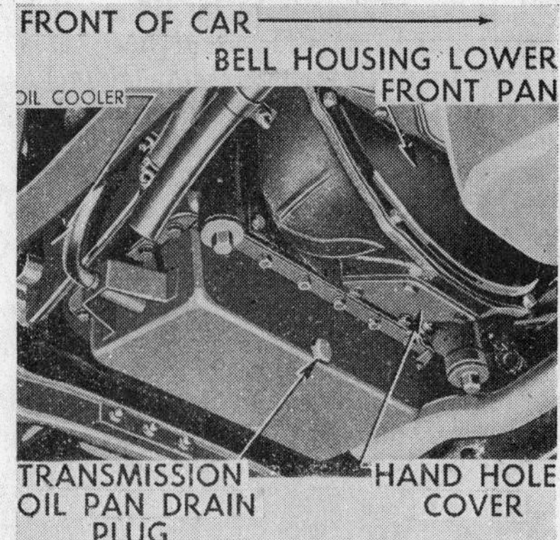

Fig. 30—Removing Pan and Cover

Fig. 31—Left rear view of Dynaflow

7. Disconnect speedometer cable at the rear bearing retainer.

8. Remove three nuts and plate that support transmission at rear bearing retainer. Remove shims between support and thrust pad. Save these shims. Fig. 32.

9. Remove two bolts and plate which attach transmission mounting pad to the support.

10. Install engine support bar (or jack) under rear end of lower crankcase. Place left side hook over frame to rear of brake master cylinder. Fig. 33.

11. Place transmission jack or hoist in position and adjust it to support the transmission.

12. Tighten the nuts on the engine support bar (or raise the jack) to raise engine and transmission support. Thrust pad may now be removed from under the rear bearing retainer.

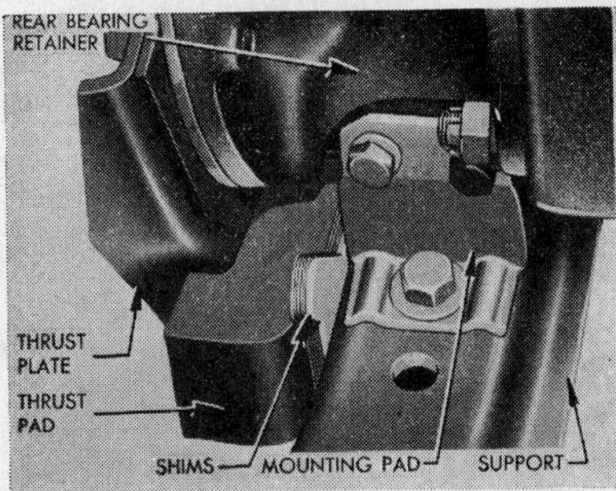

Fig. 32—Thrust Pad and Shims

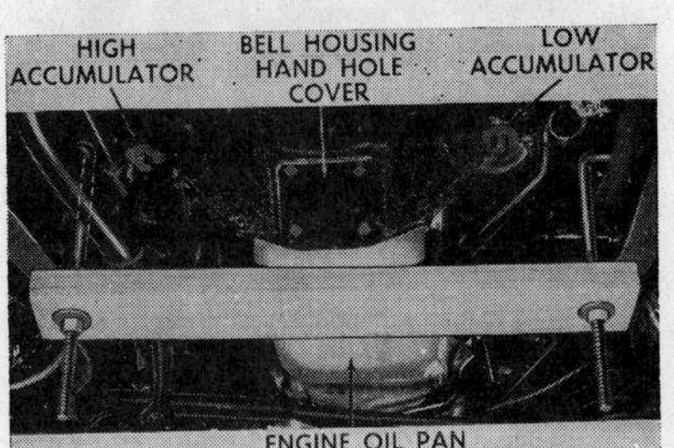

Fig. 33—Support Bar under engine

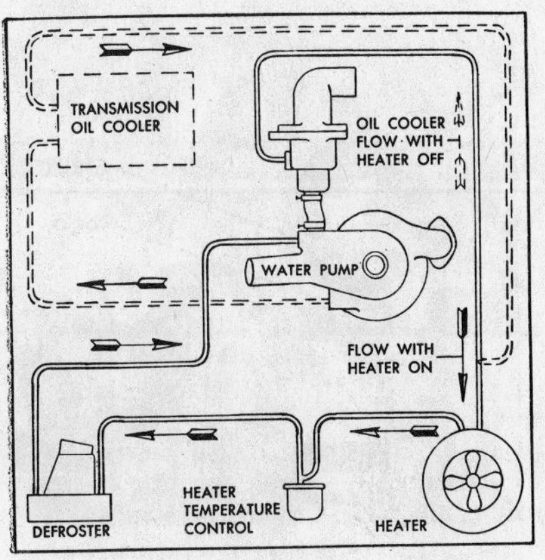

Fig. 34—Hose Connections thru '52

13. Mark in sequence (1, 2 and 3) with paint the position of the bolts holding the converter to the flywheel so that marks show on

The primary pump.

The primary pump cover.

The flywheel.

In order that these three units may be replaced in the same position. Otherwise the unit may have to be rebalanced. Early models employed 6 bolts in which case mark all six.

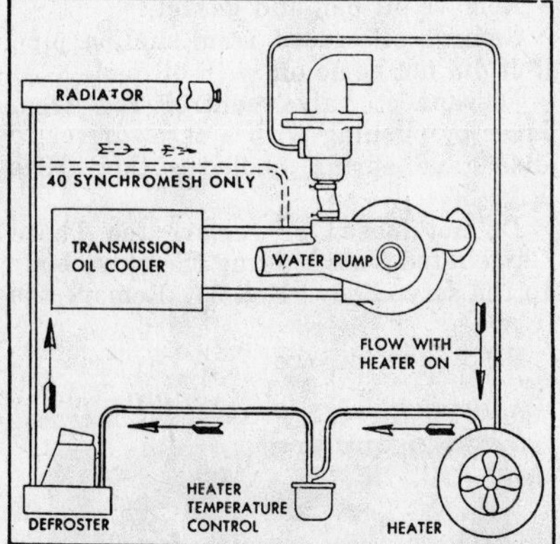

Fig. 35—Hose Connections for '53

16. Disconnect bell housing from the engine. Move exhaust pipe hanger forward to clear bolts on left side.

17. Move transmission rearward to disengage hub of converter pump from crankshaft. Lower transmission and remove to bench.

INSTALLATION

1. Turn flywheel so that the marks on the converter primary pump, pump cover and flywheel are aligned in the same order 1, 2 and 3 as when removed. This will assure that the drain plugs of the converter are opposite the holes in the flywheel, that the balance of the assembly is as it was and that the attaching bolt holes are aligned.

2. Adjust lifting equipment so that the bell housing seats squarely against the flywheel housing. Install the two housing dowl bolts follow with remaining bolts. Install exhaust pipe hangar with the left hand bolts and crankcase ventilator pipe support with lower right hand bolt.

3. Tighten all the bolts gradually to 45-55 lbs torque leaving the lower right hand bolt till last for if it is tightened first the bell housing may be thrown out of alignment.

4. Attach thrust pad to thrust plate.

5. Raise transmission and install mounting pad.

6. Lower transmission until weight is carried by the mounting pad and support. Attach pad to support with bolt plate and two self locking nuts. Fig. 31.

7. Remove transmission lift and engine support bar.

8. With engine and transmission resting freely on their mountings install sufficient shims between the thrust pad and the transmission support to fill the space. Install bolt plate and three self locking nuts to attach thrust pad to support. Fig. 32.

9. Use the shank of an 11/32" drill to align bolt holes in flywheel and converter being sure the markings (1, 2, and 3) on each of the three units match those on the others. Install bolts and tighten evenly to 25-30 ft lbs torque.

10. Tighten flywheel drain plugs and install bell housing cover and hand hole cover.

11. Connect hose from lower side of engine water pump to the lower connection of transmission oil cooler.

12. If car has heater connect hose from it to the upper connection on oil cooler.

If car has no heater connect hose from engine thermostat housing to the upper connection on oil cooler. See Figs. 34 and 35.

13. Connect speedometer cable at rear bearing retainer.

14. Install shift rod at shift lever on transmission at rear bearing retainer.

15. Cement a new gasket in recess in front end of torque tube and make sure propeller shaft oil seals are installed on propeller shaft in the following order: Spring retainer, spring, seal cap, oil seal.

16. Bolt torque tube to torque ball.

17. Place oil filler pipe spring bracket over filler pipe and connect pipe to oil pan pipe, with both pipes contacting inside the rubber connector hose. Place spring bracket over front end of bell housing dowel bolt.

18. Being sure outside of transmission is free of oil lower car to floor.

19. Check that oil filler pipe is properly placed and not contacting floor of car. Tighten nut holding filler pipe bracket.

20. Fill transmission and radiator.

21. Adjust and finish installing shift rod. See section on Manual Control Adjustment.

22. Drive car about 20 miles stopping frequently as in heavy traffic to warm up transmission.

23. Check oil level and transmission case for signs of leakage.

DISASSEMBLY

Before starting to take the transmission apart clean it thoroughly. In the process of disassembly be careful to note the condition of all gaskets as quite often the only clue to trouble is the appearance of a connecting gasket which will clearly show if a good seal existed. No part of the assembly is a force fit. Use a SOFT hammer if any tapping is required.

The relative position of adjacent parts can usually be determined by their wear patterns. There is therefore no need to mark any parts save those mentioned in General Information under Match Marks. The same information is repeated where necessary in the text.

The High and Low accumulators are marked H and L on their caps but they could be mounted one in place of the other so mechanics usually mark the bottom and the adjacent reactor shaft flange of the High accumulator.

1. Removal of Oil Pan, Valve and Servo Body Assembly

Note: Removal of these units can be accomplished by this same procedure while transmission is still in the car.

Remove oil pan and gasket.

Remove oil screen from suction pipe if it did not come off with oil pan.

Disconnect valve control rod from lever by pushing with a screwdriver to disengage spring loaded socket. See Fig. 36.

Do not loosen or remove the Three Castellated Nuts holding the valve body to the servo body. Fig. 37. Remove the

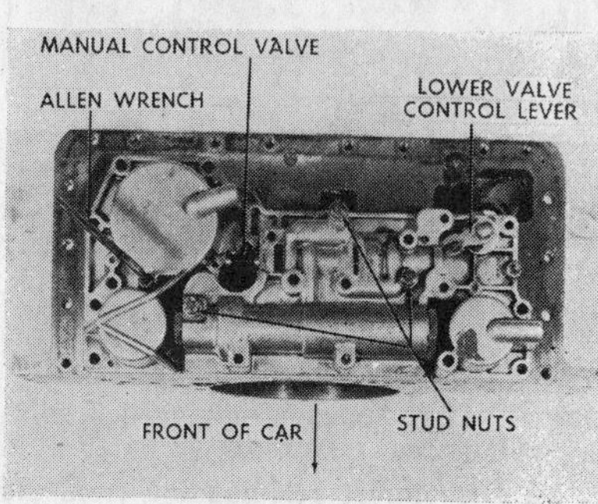

Fig. 37—Studs holding valve body to servo

bolts and lockwashers holding the assembly to the transmission case. This includes the one bolt requiring an allen head wrench that is on some models. Tap the assembly lightly with a soft hammer to loosen the gasket between the servo body and the transmission case. Align upper lever to clear the case by pushing shift control valve and lower lever inward. Fig. 38.

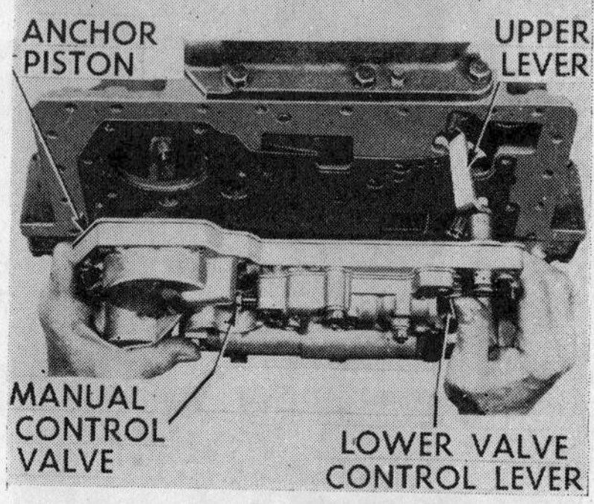

Fig. 38—Removing valve and servo body assembly

The low band anchor piston will fall out as the assembly is removed if work is being done at the bench. If transmission is still in the car the piston will remain in the assembly. The piston has in it a spring and under the spring are perhaps spacers. If the piston does drop be sure that the spacers are not lost.

Note: The slotted end of the control valve is likely to be sharp enough to cut the hand.

There is a piece of square metal interposed between the end of the reverse band and the operating lever. This strut should be removed if transmission is on the bench to prevent its being released accidentally to fall into the transmission. See Fig. 39.

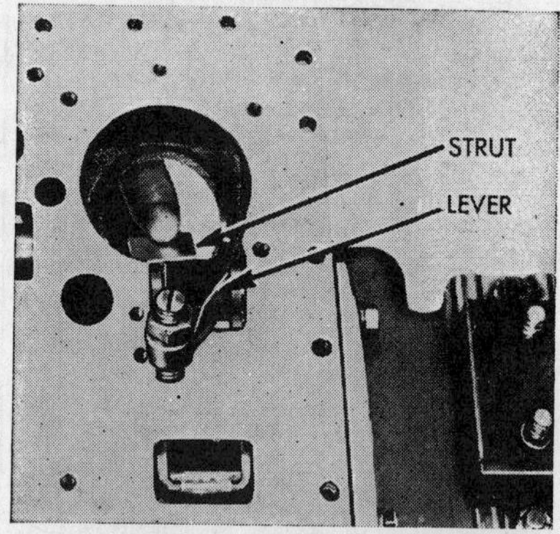

Fig. 39—Removing reverse band operating strut

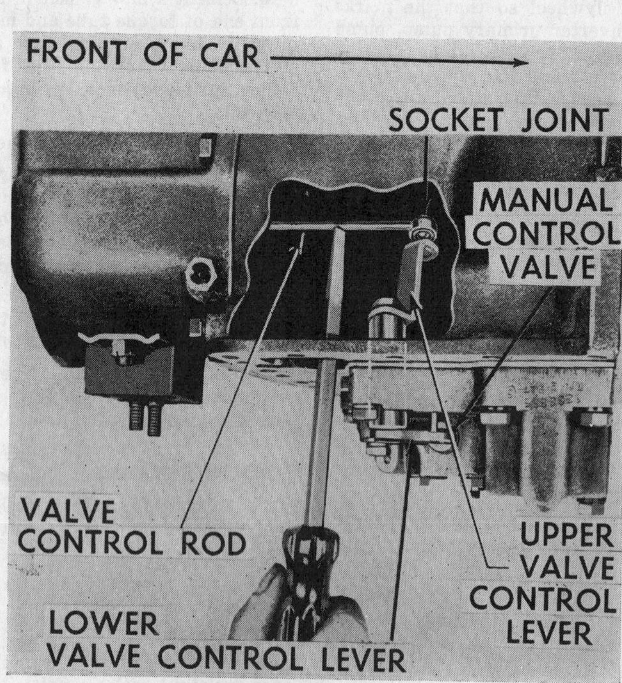

Fig. 36—Disconnecting valve control rod

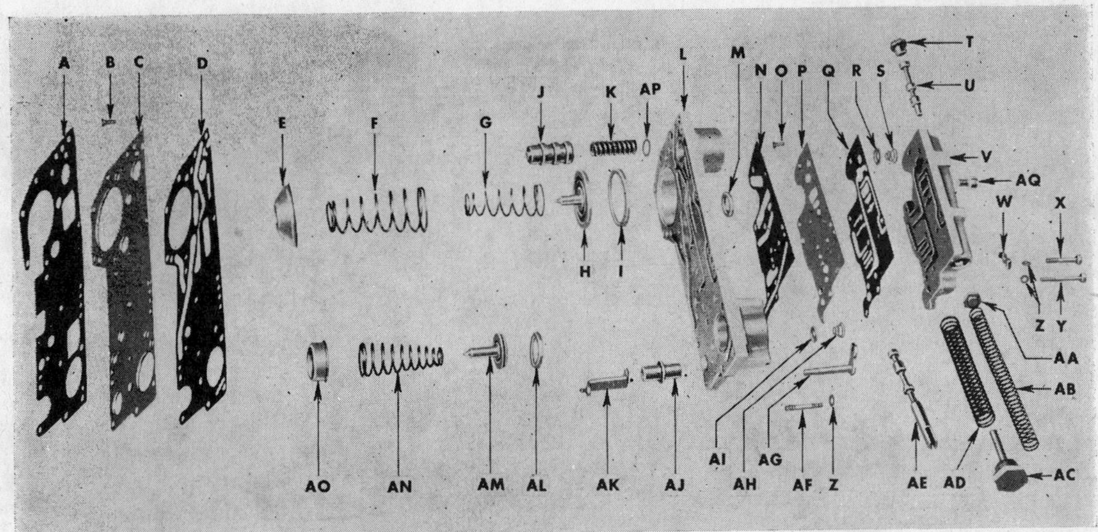

Fig. 40—Exploded View of Valve and Servo Body Assembly

A. Gasket (Servo body spacer plate to transmission).
B. Bolt (12-24 x ⅝ NC plain).
C. Plate (Servo body spacer to transmission).
D. Gasket (Spacer plate to servo body).
E. Seat (Reverse servo spring).
F. Spring (Reverse servo outer).
G. Spring (Reverse servo inner).
H. Piston (Reverse servo).
I. Seal (Reverse servo piston).
J. Piston (Low band anchor).
K. Spring (Low band anchor).
L. Body (Servo assembly).
M. Ring (Oil suction pipe seal).
N. Gasket (Valve body spacer plate to servo body).
O. Bolt (Same as B).
P. Plate (Control valve body spacer).
Q. Gasket (Spacer plate to control valve body).
R. Valve (Front pump delivery check).
S. Spring (Front pump delivery check valve).
T. Plug (Pressure regulator valve small end).
U. Valve (Pressure regulator).
V. Body (Control Valve).
W. Stop (Control Valve).
X, Y. Bolts.
Z. Lockwashers.
AA. Seat (Pressure regulator valve spring).
AB. Spring (Pressure regulator valve inner).
AC. Plug (Pressure regulator valve large end).
AD. Spring (Pressure regulator valve outer).
AE. Valve (Shift control).
AF. Stud (Valve body attaching).
AG. Lever (Lower valve, control lever and shaft).
AH. Spring (Rear pump delivery check valve).
AI. Valve (Rear pump delivery check).
AJ. Bearing (Valve control lever shaft).
AK. Lever (Upper valve control lever).
AL. Seal (Low band servo piston).
AM. Piston (Low band servo).
AN. Spring (Low band servo).
AO. Seat (Low band servo spring).
AP. Shim (Low band anchor spring).
AQ. Screw (Allen head valve body attaching).

2. Overhaul of Valve and Servo Body Assembly

There is nothing particular about the disassembly of the valve and servo assembly once it is off the transmission. The pictures show the component parts. See Fig. 40. Exercise care not to bend the spacer plate that fits onto the servo body. Fig. 41. The servo springs push on it. Note also that there are two springs on the reverse servo piston assembly. Watch out for small check ball in reverse servo feed channel in servo body. When removing pressure regulator valve plugs be careful of spring pressure.

Thoroughly wash valve and servo bodies with clean solvent, blow out all passages. Inspect for cracks, signs of leakage on gaskets, scores on pistons and cylinders. The shoulders of the valves should be sharp and square. Check valves on surface plate and replace if bent. Worn or damaged piston seals should be replaced. Make sure the lip of the seal fits over the smaller diameter land. Fig. 42.

Clean and check oil screen for cracks or holes that might pass dirt.

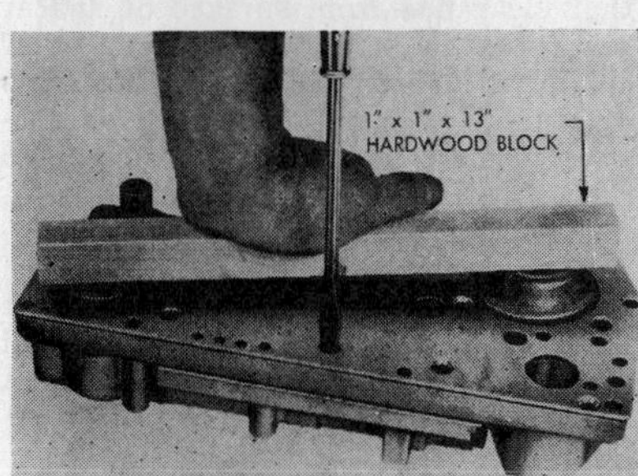

Fig. 41—Hold springs compressed with block of wood

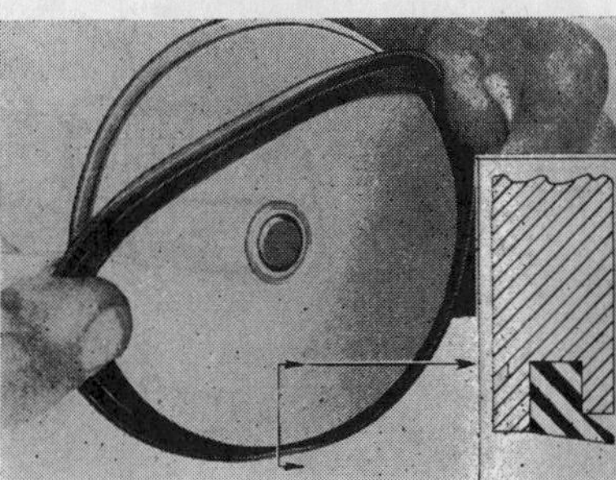

Fig. 42—Installating servo piston seal

3. Assembly of Servo Body

Oil and install the low and reverse servo piston assemblies. Fig. 43. To avoid curling or damaging edge of piston seal, start each piston into cylin-

ASSEMBLY OF SERVO BODY—cont'd

Fig. 43—Lay-out of servo assembly

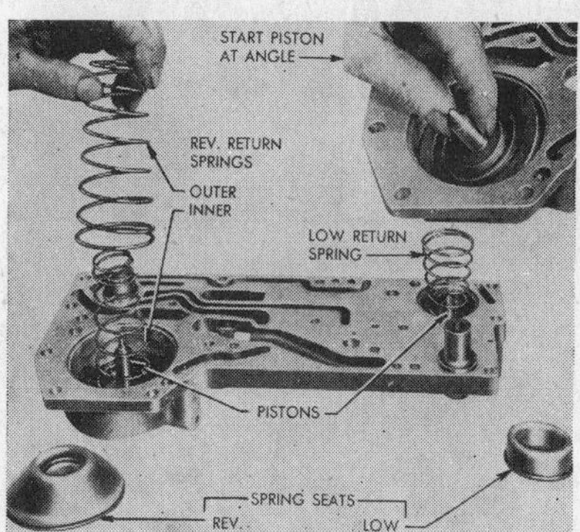

Fig. 44—Installing servo pistons

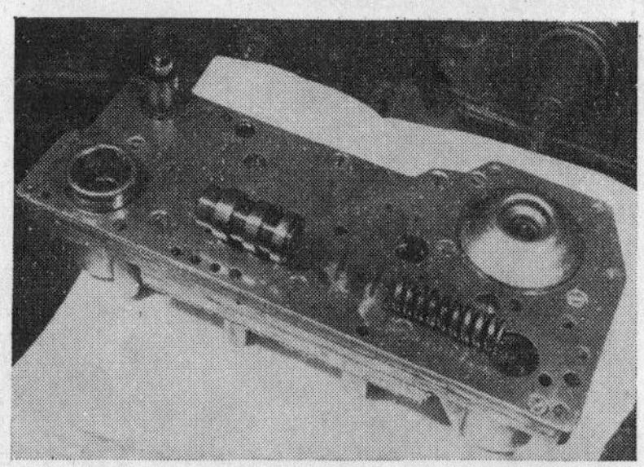

Fig. 45—Lay-out of low band anchor piston

der at an angle then turn piston slightly as it is straightened and pushed into cylinder. See Fig. 44.

Check that pistons move freely.

Install low band anchor piston, spring and shims in servo body. Fig. 45.

Install the smallest piston return spring with small end in groove in low servo piston. Install the two large return springs with the large ends in grooves in reverse servo piston. Install spring seats on upper ends of springs. See Fig. 44.

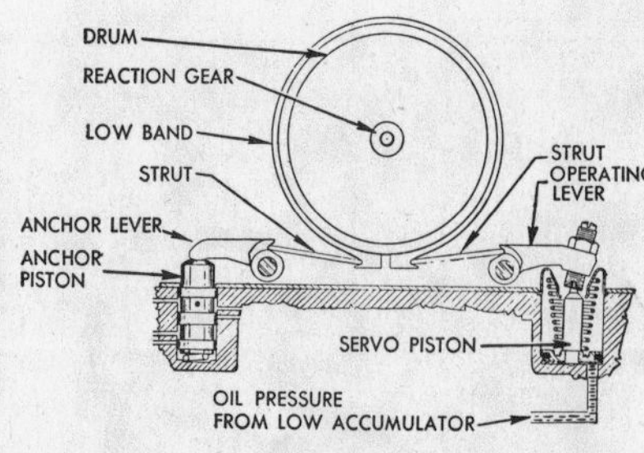

Fig. 46—Section thru low band mechanism

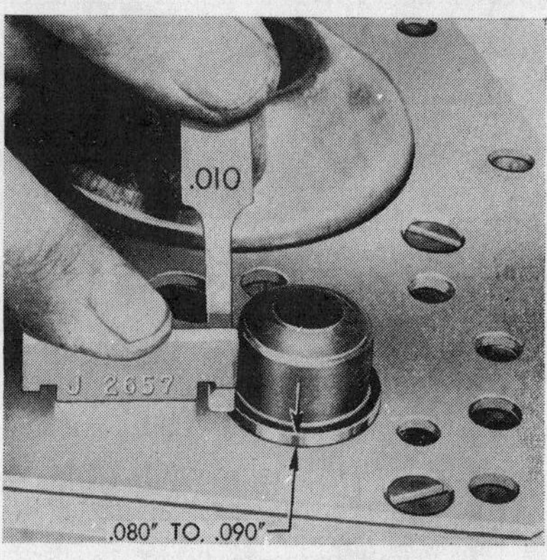

Fig. 47—Checking clearance of anchor piston. Can be done with depth gauge

Place check ball in reverse servo feed channel. See Fig. 43.

Install a new spacer plate gasket and place spacer plate in position over spring seats. Be careful not to distort plate while holding it against spring pressure. Tighten screws uniformly.

Check that plate does not interfere with movement of low band anchor piston. Fig. 46. If it should, then loosen spacer plate screws and tap plate slightly in a direction to provide clearance for anchor. When screws are tight and anchor moves freely check that clearance from surface of spacer plate to top surface of top land of anchor is .080" to .090". Fig. 47. This distance is obtained by adding or subtracting shims from between spring and inside end of anchor. Fig. 45.

Insert valve operating lower lever shaft through bearing in servo body. With lower lever pointing to low servo cylinder install upper lever so that it points to reverse servo cylinder. Tighten to 5-7 ft lbs. See Fig. 48.

4. Assembly of Valve Body

a. Place front pump delivery check

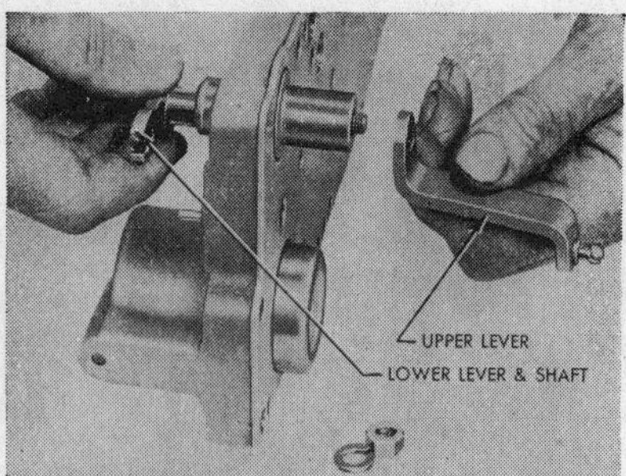

Fig. 48—Installing valve control levers

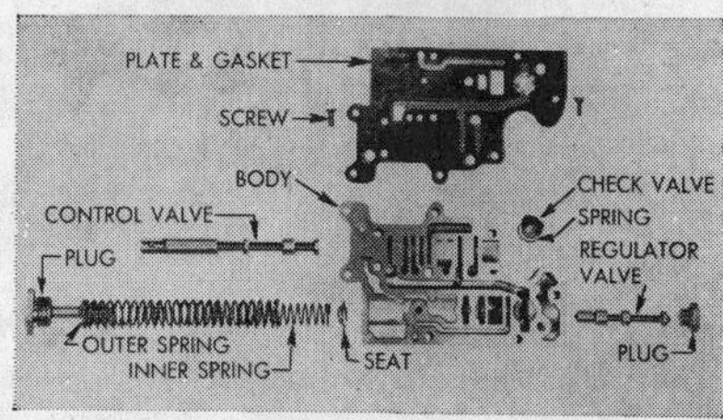

Fig. 49—Layout of valve body. Note: Check valve

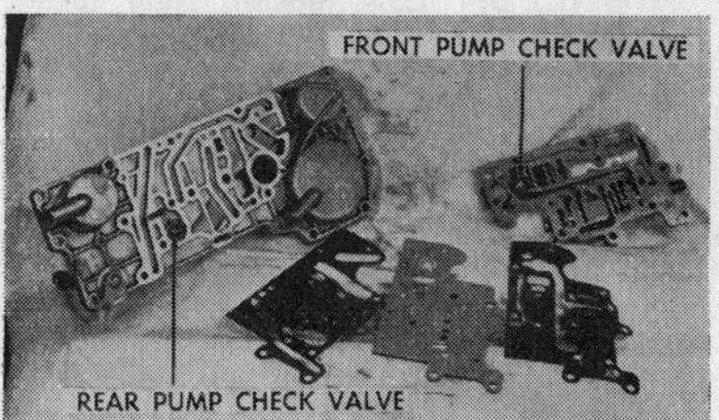

Fig. 50—Position of check valve installed

valve spring in body with large end down and place check valve on spring with ridged side up. See Figs. 49 and 50.

b. Install valve body plate and a new gasket making sure that check valve is seated against plate and is not caught under gasket.

c. Place the pressure regulator spring seat on the inner spring, then install spring seat, inner and outer springs and the large plug in valve body. Tighten plug to 20-25 ft lbs torque. Fig. 49.

d. See that oil orifice in pressure regulator valve end land is clear, then install valve with this land outward. Install small pressure regulator plug and tighten to 20-25 ft lbs torque.

e. Install shift control valve with slotted end on same end of valve body as the large pressure regulator plug.

f. Install rear pump delivery check valve in its seat in servo body ridged face inward and place valve spring on valve with large end out. Fig. 50.

g. Install a new gasket and the valve assembly on the servo body using care to keep pump delivery check valve spring below the gasket. Install the three castellated nuts with plain washers Fig. 37 and tighten evenly to 11-15 lbs.

5. Installation of Valve and Servo Body Assembly

a. Return the strut to place at the end of the reverse band. Rounded end to band. If transmission is on the bench be careful not to disturb the band levers or the strut will fall into the transmission. Fig. 51.

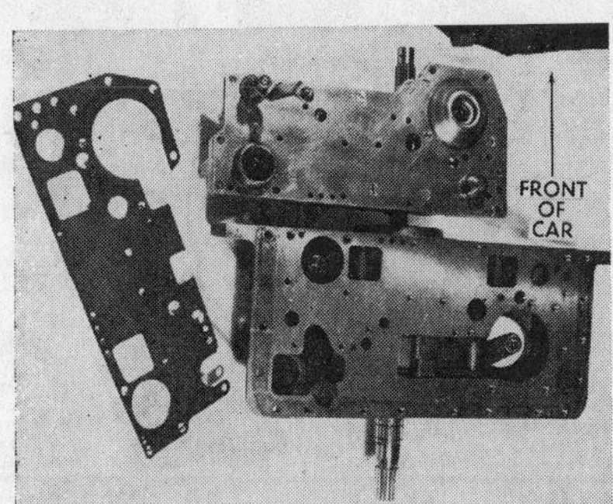

Fig. 51—Valve and Servo Body ready to install

b. Use a new gasket between servo body spacer plate and transmission case. Align upper lever with hole in case and holding anchor piston in place with a finger install assembly on case being careful the low and reverse struts

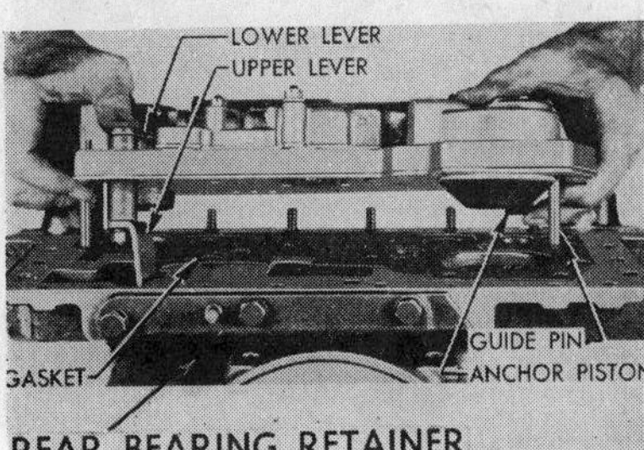

Fig. 52—Valve and Servo Body being installed

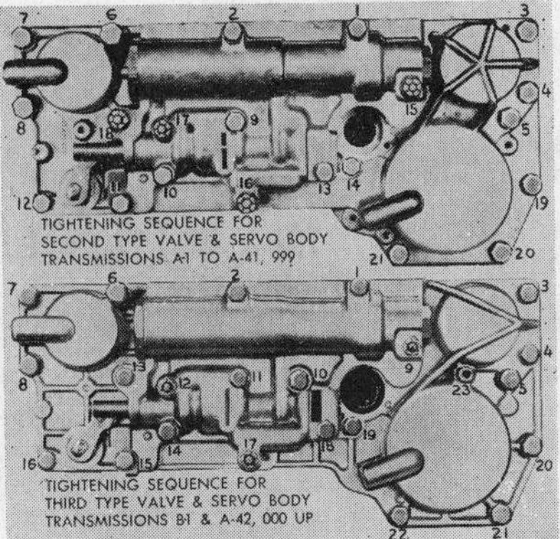

Fig. 53—Tightening Sequence for Valve and Servo Body

don't get a chance to move out of place. Fig. 52. The assembly should fit on flat and easily, if it does not the low band struts are out of place. Check the little notches which fit around pins in the band flanges.

c. Install various length bolts with lock washers according to the hole depth. Use copper washer on center bolt adjacent to suction pipe opening.

d. Tighten all bolts to 5 ft lbs torque in the numerical sequence shown in Fig. 53. The variation between models is in the number of bolts used.

e. When all bolts are tight to 5 ft lbs then repeat the sequence tightening all the bolts to 15 lbs. When tightening those adjacent to the shift control valve operate the valve to make certain that it is not binding.

f. Using a pair of lock ring pliers or

Fig. 54—Reconnecting Valve Control Rod

similar strong hook reinstall the valve operating rod onto the upper lever. See Fig. 54.

g. Temporarily install the shift lever on the valve operating cross shaft and operate the valve linkage to make sure it works freely. Move lever forward so that the pawl will engage the parking lock ratchet wheel. When pawl is fully engaged the pawl lock must be in full contact with the pawl. See Fig. 16A.

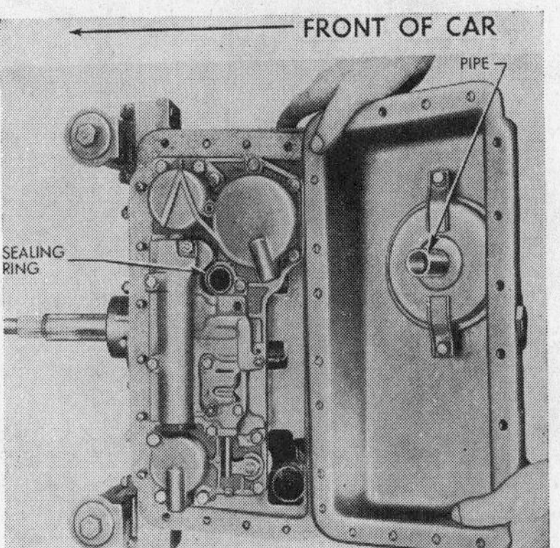

Fig. 55—Installing Transmission

h. Push shift control valve inward to take up play in the valve linkage. The spring travel at end of shift lever should be ⅛ to 3/16. See Fig. 16B. If it is not turn clevis on valve operating rod. On models up to 1952 this can only be done if the torque ball has been removed. 1953 models have an access hole for this adjustment. See Fig. 16C.

Clearance between control valve and stop pin at this point should be .030"-.040" Fig. 17.

i. Install oil pan with new gasket. Be sure suction tube is contacting ring seal on valve body. See Fig. 55. Tighten bolts to 15-18 ft lbs.

j. See General Information for Refilling instructions.

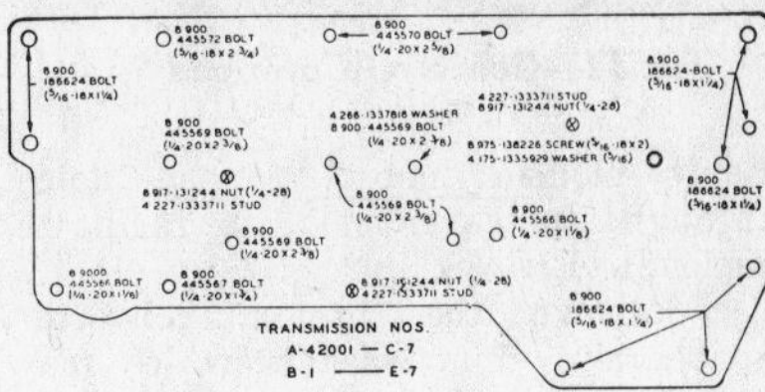

Bolt Sizes Valve and Servo Body

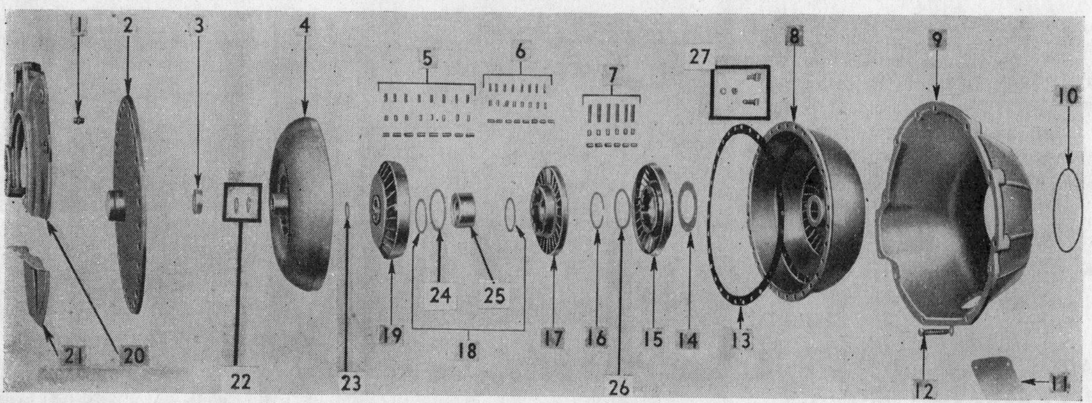

Fig. 56—Converter Assembly. All models thru 1952

1. Filler plug.
2. Primary pump cover.
3. Pilot bearing (front end of input shaft).
4. Turbine.
5. Free wheel clutch parts for secondary stator.
6. Free wheel clutch parts for primary stator.
7. Free wheel clutch parts for secondary pump.
8. Primary pump.
9. Bell housing.
10. Oil seal ring (bell housing to transmission case).
11. Hand hole cover (bell housing).
12. Dowel bolt (bell housing to flywheel cover).
13. Gasket (primary pump cover).
14. Washer (thrust).
15. Secondary pump.
16. Ring (retainer).
17. Primary stator.
18. Washers (roller assembly).
19. Secondary stator.
20. Housing (flywheel).
21. Pan, bell housing lower front.
22. Spacer and washer (clearance).
23. Ring (retainer).
24. Spacer (free wheel).
25. Race roller assembly).
26. Spacer (free wheel).
27. Bolts primary pump cover.

1. Removal of Converter Assy.

NOTE: This operation is done after the transmission is removed.

a. Remove all nuts, flat washers, and bolts which attach the cover to the primary pump. Prevent unit from turning by inserting a punch in drive bolt holes through the bell housing hand hole.

b. Remove cover from primary pump, it may be necessary to pry or tap lightly against edge of cover to loosen it. Check the cover seal for damage or evidence of oil leakage before removing it from the cover. See Fig. 57.

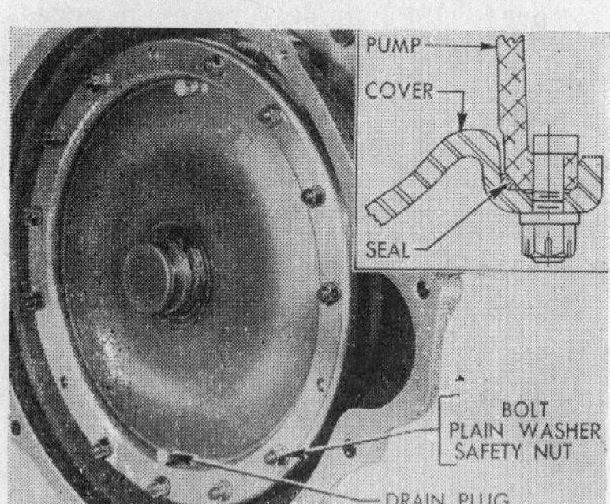

Fig. 57—Converter Cover and Seal

Early models had 3 tapped holes through the cover only, to facilitate removal. Fig. 58.

c. Remove the torque converter spacer and shim washers which may be on front end of input shaft or in bearing recess of cover. (See Par. 3f

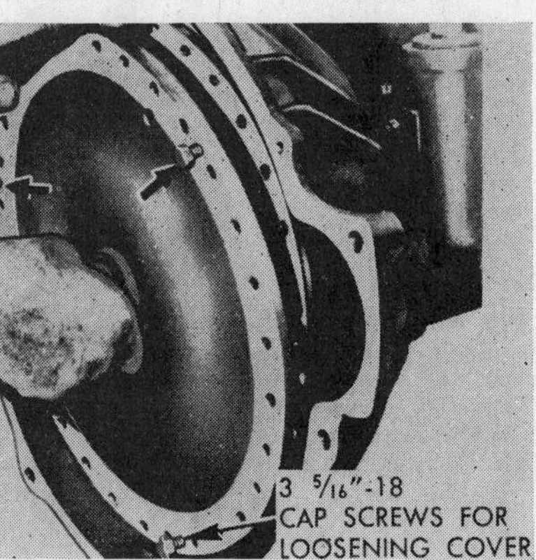

Fig. 58—Removing Cover—early models

below.) Hold input shaft into transmission while withdrawing turbine. Fig. 59.

d. Check stators for free wheel clutch slippage. They should rotate freely in a clockwise direction and lock tight if turned counterclockwise.

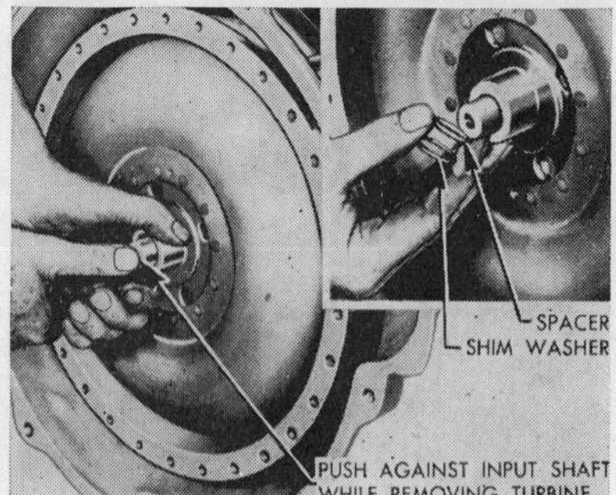

Fig. 59—Removing Turbine

e. Using an ice pick or similar device, remove retainer ring from reactor shaft. Fig. 60. Remove stators as a unit. (The free wheel clutch parts in their hubs are held by springs and when the stators are separated these parts are likely to fly all over the shop).

f. Check secondary pump for clutch slippage; it should lock tight in a counterclockwise direction. Fig. 61.

g. Pull the primary and secondary pump assembly forward from reactor

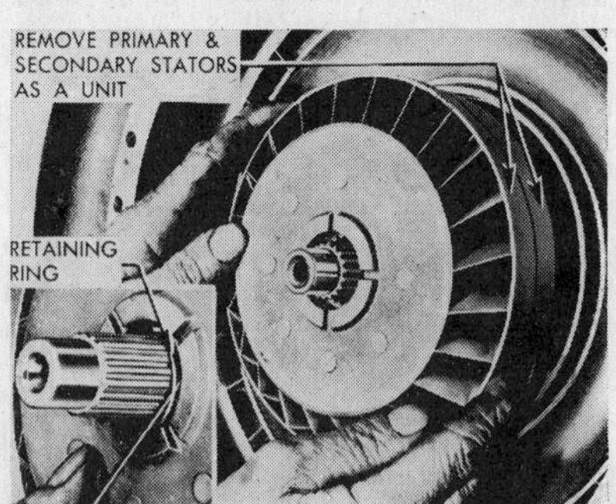

Fig. 60—Removing Stators

shaft and immediately check for evidence of oil leakage. Fresh streaks of oil on back of primary pump and fresh oil running down the face of the front oil pump indicate leakage past the oil pump seal or at the primary pump hub. Leakage at the hub can be proved by

Fig. 61—Checking Secondary Pump

procedure shown under overhaul of converter unit.

h. Before removing the bell housing check to see whether all attaching bolts are tight. A loose bolt could have been a leak source.

i. Put bell housing over edge of bench and remove it. Examine the rubber oil seal located around the front oil pump to see whether it has been uniformly compressed by the bell housing. Perhaps some dirt prevented uniform compression of the seal.

2. Overhaul of the Converter Assembly

All Models Thru 1952

If the free wheel clutches of the stators and secondary pump were tested and found Ok as they were being removed there is no necessity for further disassembly; however, if trouble in these units is suspected the following procedure will apply.

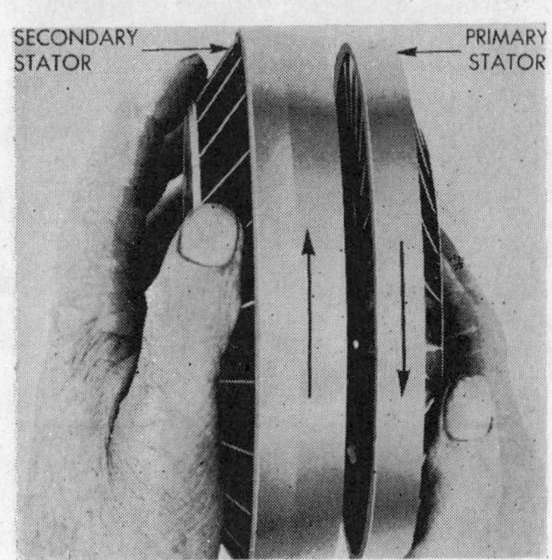

Fig. 62—Separating the Stators

The stators.

Rotate the primary and secondary stators while slowly drawing them apart. Do this over a pan so that any rollers and springs that fly out will not be lost. See Fig. 62.

Remove the race, which may be found in either stator, and remove the roller spacer from the secondary stator. See Fig. 63.

Fig. 63—Layout of Stators

Remove washers, free wheel rollers, springs and spring cups from both stators.

Check the rollers for nicks or breakage. Check the springs for permanent set, distortion, or other damage.

Install a roller assembly washer and the free wheel springs and cups, in the secondary stator. Fig. 64. Install the race in the same position it had at removal as indicated by the wear pattern. (A new race can be installed either end first.)

Using a scribe with a bent point, as shown in Fig. 65, depress the springs and cups and install long freewheel

Fig. 64—Assembling Secondary Stator

Fig. 65—Use of Bent Scribe to Install Rollers

rollers. Put the spacer over the rollers.

Install the free wheel springs and cups in the primary stator.

Install the short rollers, using small globs of cup grease to hold the rollers in place. Install a roller assembly washer in the hub.

Place secondary stator on bench with rollers facing upward. Place primary stator squarely in position over it

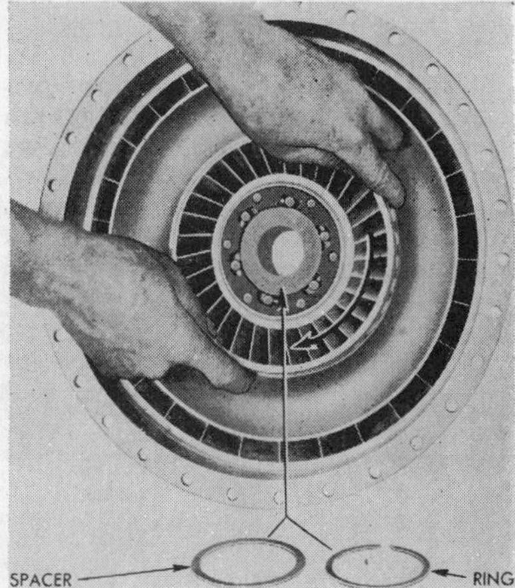

Fig. 66—Removing Secondary Pump

(rollers down), and push the two together twisting slightly so that they fit. The grease will hold the rollers in place until the hub of the race fits in to hold the assembly together.

The pumps.

Remove the secondary pump retaining ring and the spacer. Rotate the pump in a clockwise direction and slide it off primary pump hub. See Fig. 66. There is a washer between the back of the secondary pump and the front of the primary pump. See No. 14 in Fig. 56. (Exploded view.)

CONVERTER OVERHAUL—*continued*

Remove the rollers, springs and cups from the secondary pump and inspect.

Inspect input shaft pilot bearing in primary pump cover and replace if worn or rough.

Fig. 67—Note Roughness of Primary Pump Hub

Inspect surface of rear hub of primary pump. Roughness such as can be seen in Fig. 67 indicates that front pump oil seal has been damaged. Primary pump must be replaced as a unit. Check hub for hour glass shape.

If the primary pump is suspected of leaks, install a 2½″ rubber toilet tank bulb as shown and a No. 365 Barret fitting. See Figs. 68 and 69.

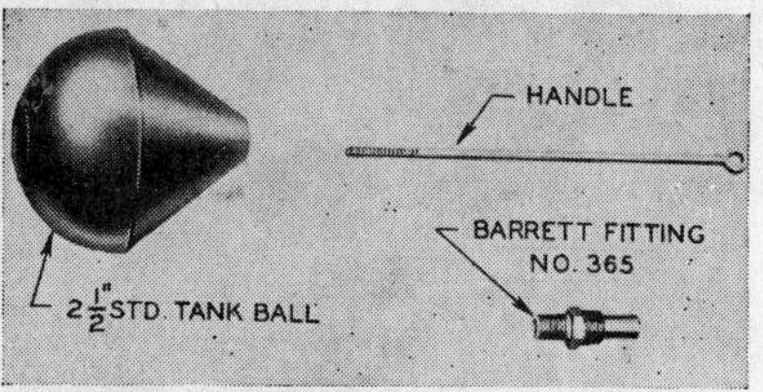

Fig. 68—Parts for Testing Pump for Leakage

Fig. 69—Assembling for Leakage Test

Put in about a pint of oil and install the cover.

With plug in one filler hole and Barrett fitting in the other, put in about 80 lbs of air pressure.

Lay pump on bench on its cover.

Oil will bubble out if leak is in joint between body and cover.

Put a little oil around the hub and if rivets are loose air will bubble thru.

Note that if no leaks appear under this procedure the pump can be submerged in water which could show smaller leaks.

Remove the cover and clean assembly.

Insert the springs and cups in the secondary pump hubs.

Insert spacer washer over primary pump hub and install secondary pump.

Compress the springs with a scribe as shown and install the long free wheel rollers.

Install spacer and the retaining ring.

Check that secondary pump revolves freely in a clockwise direction only.

3. Reassembly of Converter

All Models Thru 1952

a. Install front oil pump seal ring around pump body against pump cover.

b. Install bell housing, using lock washers. Sparingly coat threads of lower right side bolt with Permatex No. 3 (non-hardening) as this bolt hole opens into the transmission case.

Tighten all to 35-40 lbs.

c. Install the primary and secondary pumps on the reactor shaft, turning the primary pump back and forth until drive lugs in hub enter the drive slots in front oil pump of transmission.

Fig. 70—Installing Stator Retaining Ring on Reactor Shaft

d. Install the primary and secondary stators on the reactor shaft and install the reactor shaft retaining ring so that the hook of the ring engages a spline of the shaft. See Fig. 70.

e. Install the turbine on the input shaft. Be careful not to pull out on the input shaft.

f. The clearance between the turbine hub and the bearing in the front cover is held to .017″ plus or minus .006″ by means of spacers and washers on the input shaft. See Par. 1c above. This clearance is not critical but bears a relation to the amount of "clunk" noise coming from the unit. See Fig. 59.

g. Install both drain plugs and a new seal on the primary pump cover. See Fig. 57. Be careful not to twist the seal.

h. Replace cover on pump so that paint marks made at disassembly to indicate the bolts holding the assembly to the flywheel are aligned in the original order. (1, 2 and 3.)

i. The longer bolts are for use through the balancing weights. If a new primary pump is being installed insert first bolt with plain washer and safety nut in first hole clockwise from a drain plug. Continue in a clockwise direction omitting a bolt every fifth hole, 3 in all, for use in attaching unit to flywheel. Early models had six flywheel bolts.

j. Insert 11/32″ drill through one flywheel bolt holes to align all bolt holes, then pretighten all to approximately 5 ft lbs in the order indicated in Fig. 71.

k. Finish tightening the bolts to 25-30 ft lbs in the same sequence. When tightening insert a wide screw driver between flat side of bolt head and pump body to keep bolt corners from digging into the metal.

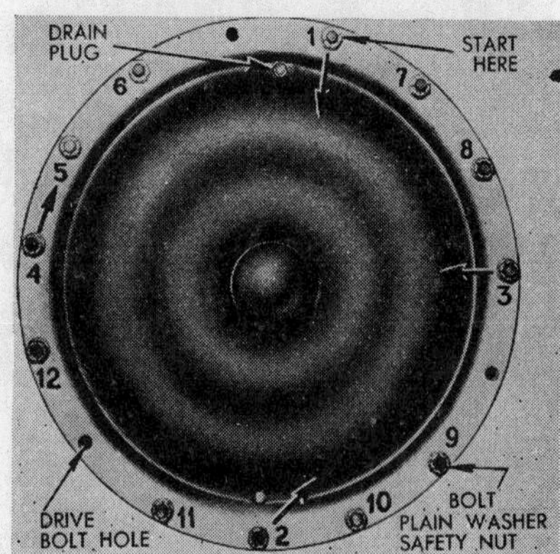

Fig. 71—Cover Bolt Tightening Sequence

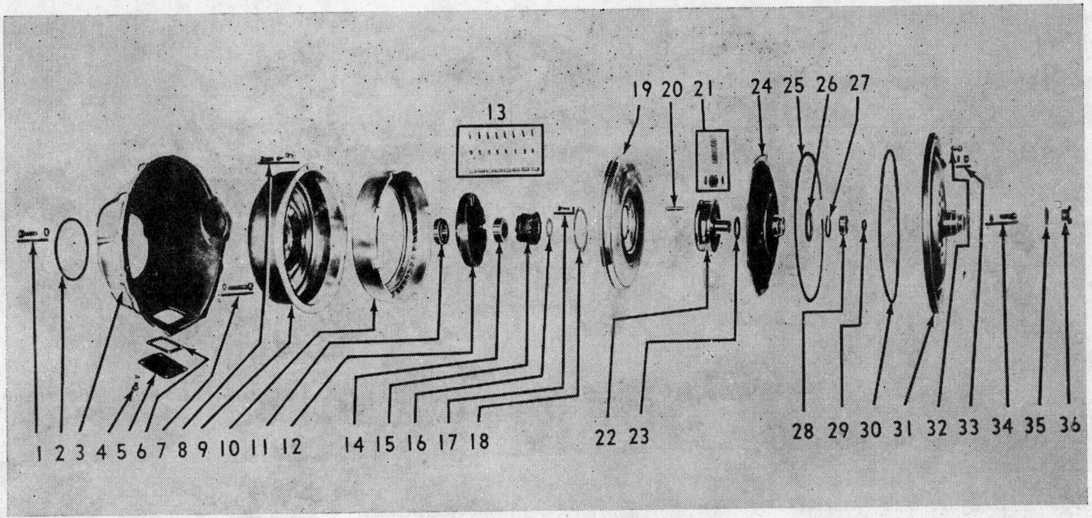

Fig. 72—Exploded View of '53 Converter

1. Bolt and washer (Bell Housing to Flywheel Housing).
2. Oil seal. Reactor Shaft Flange to Bell Housing.
3. Bell Housing.
4. Bolt and Washer.
5. Hand Hole Cover Plate.
6. Gasket.
7. Bolt and Washer.
8. Bolt and Balancing Weight (Primary Pump to Cover).
9. Primary Pump.
10. First Turbine.
11. Bearing (Stator Support).
12. Stator.
13. Free Wheel Clutch Parts.
14. Free Wheel Roller Race.
15. Planetary Sun Gear.
16. Thrust Washer (Sun Gear to Carrier).
17. Bolt and Washer (Second Turbine to Planetary Carrier).
18. Lock Plate (Pinion Shaft).
19. Second Turbine.
20. Pinion Shaft.
21. Pinion, Washers and Needles.
22. Planetary Carrier.
23. Thrust Washer (Carrier to Disk Assembly).
24. Ring Gear Hub and Disk Assembly.
25. Lock Ring (Disk Assembly).
26. Selected Thrust Washer (Disk to Cover).
27. Snap Retaining Ring (Pilot Bearing Rear).
28. Pilot Bearing (Input Shaft).
29. Retainer Pilot (Bearing Front).
30. "O" Ring Seal (Cover to Primary Pump).
31. Primary Pump Cover.
32. Bolt (Converter to Flywheel).
33. Drain Plug.
34. Allen Head Screw and Washer (Input Shaft Retaining).
35. Sealing Washer.
36. Plug (Seals Front of Cover Hub).

1953 CONVERTER

Note: This operation requires that the transmission be off the car.

a. Remove large hex plug and gasket from hub of converter pump cover.

b. Remove the socket set screw and lockwasher located in the hub, using an Allen head wrench 5/16″ across the flats. Fig. 73.

c. Be sure cover and pump are marked for same position mating at reassembly so that the bolts which held the unit to the flywheel will not by mischance coincide with balance weights located on the pump rim. (The bolts won't be long enough.)

d. Remove all nuts, plain washers, and bolts attaching the cover to the pump. A punch can be inserted through the bell housing hand hole into a drive bolt hole to keep the converter from turning.

e. Remove cover from pump, tapping or prying against the edge to loosen it. Check the "O" ring seal for damage and evidence of leakage before removing it from the cover.

f. Remove bronze thrust washer from turbine hub. This is also a clearance washer marked either 5, 6, or 7. Do not mix it with others as it is important that it, or a similar one if this one is worn, be between the turbine assembly and the cover.

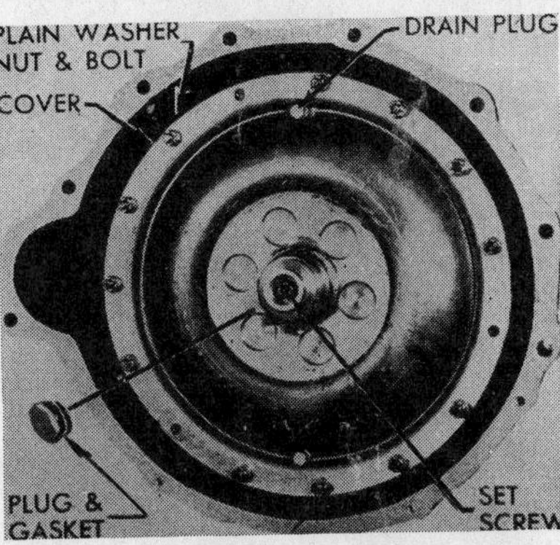

Fig. 73—Front View of '53 Converter

g. Insert screwdriver into a hole in first turbine disk to aid in removing the twin turbine assembly from the input shaft. Push inward on the shaft to avoid withdrawing it. Fig. 74.

h. Remove retaining ring from groove in input shaft using snap ring pliers. Fig. 75.

i. Remove bronze thrust washer and slide sun gear off the shaft.

Fig. 74—Removing Turbine Assembly '53 models

j. Remove retaining ring from groove in reactor shaft and slide the converter stator, free wheel roller race, and stator ball bearing, from the reactor shaft as a unit. Fig. 76.

k. Pull the converter pump forward from the reactor shaft and immediately

OVERHAUL OF '53 CONVERTER—*continued*

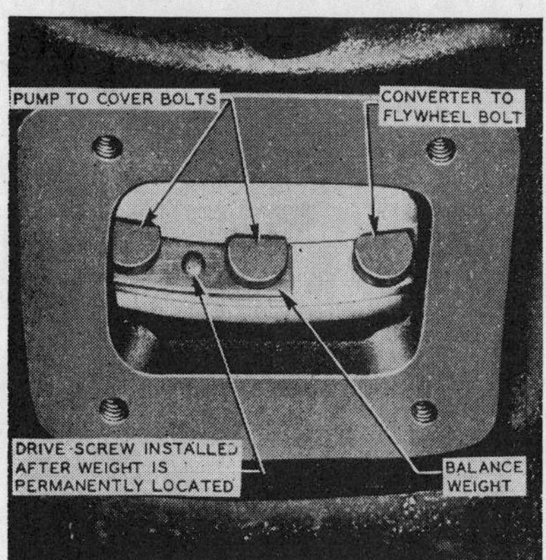

Fig. 74A—Removing Turbine Assembly

Fig 75—Removing Retaining Ring from Input Shaft

Fig. 76—Stator Before Removal

check for evidence of oil leakage. Fig. 77. Radial streaks of fresh oil on back of pump and fresh oil streaks on face of front oil pump indicate leakage past the primary pump oil seal.

2. Disassembly of Twin Turbine Converter

1953 Models

a. Pry disk retaining ring out of groove in first turbine, Fig. 78. Insert

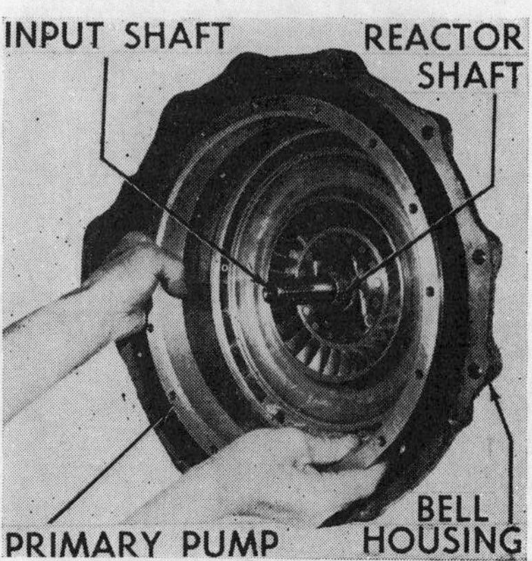

Fig. 77—Removing Primary Pump

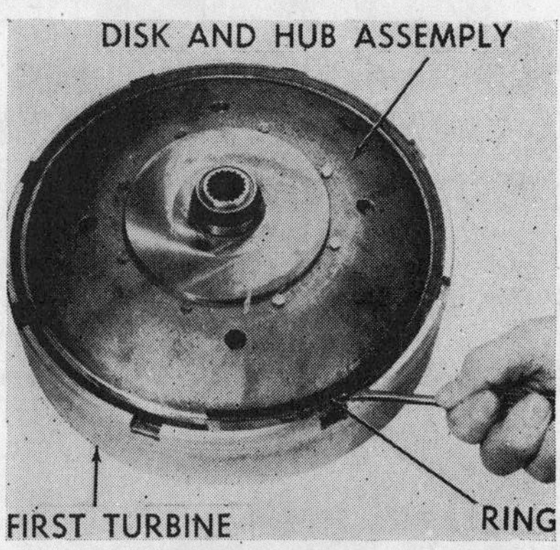

Fig. 78—Removing Disk Retaining Ring

screwdriver in a hole in the disk and lift it and hub assembly out of the first turbine. Fig. 79. Tap on hub of planetary carrier, though gently, to separate if necessary.

b. Remove planetary carrier to hub assembly thrust washer and lift second turbine out of the dish-pan-without-a-bottom shaped first turbine. Fig. 80.

c. Support the second turbine on blocks of wood so the carrier is above the bench and remove the four turbine-to-carrier bolts and lockwashers. Fig. 81.

d. Remove the carrier pinion pin lock plate and using a hardwood dowel and hammer, tap the carrier free of the turbine. DO NOT drive on the polished thrust surface of the carrier nor on the pinion pins. Fig. 82.

e. The carrier assembly consists of four pinions with a thrust washer on each end of each pinion and 22 rollers bearing on each pin. The pins lift out the lock plate end. Fig. 83.

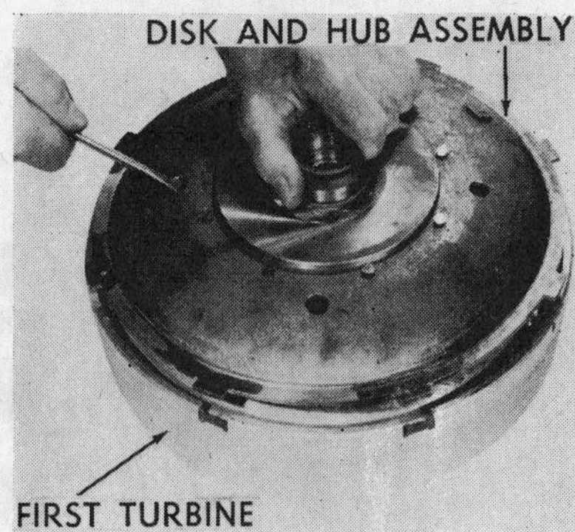

Fig. 79A—Removing Disk and Hub Assembly '53 Models

Fig. 79B—Disk and Hub Assembly Removed. '53 models

f. Remove ball bearing from rear side of stator and the roller race from the front of the free wheel clutch. Fig. 84.

g. Remove 8 rollers, cups, and springs from the stator free wheel clutch.

h. Gently pry the pilot bearing retaining ring out of its groove in the hub of the converter pump cover. Then push the pilot bearing and bearing retainer out of the hub. Fig. 85.

3. Overhaul of Twin Turbine Converter

1953 Models

Wash all parts in clean solvent and dry thoroughly with clean compressed air. Do not use rags as they are apt to leave lint particles.

Inspect all bearings, thrust washers, bushings and related bearing surfaces for excessive wear, scoring, or other damage. Note particularly:

Rear edge of first turbine at the ring gear and front thrust face of the second turbine around the carrier.

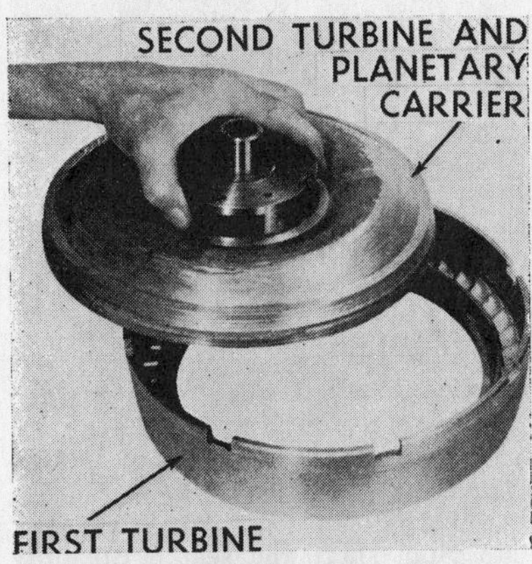

Fig. 80—Removing Planetary Carrier and 2nd Turbine Assy. '53 models

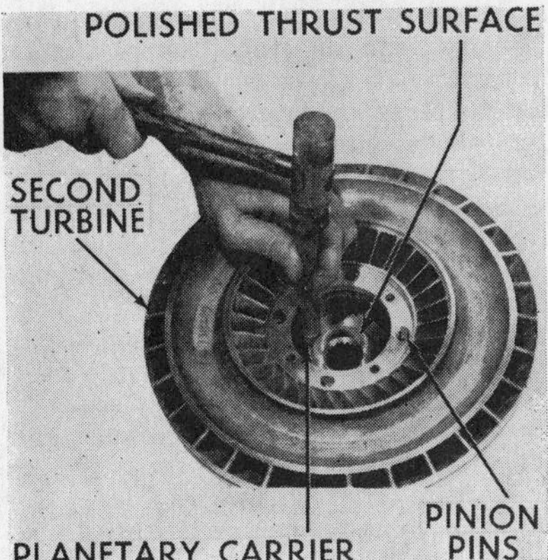

Fig. 82—Removing Carrier from Turbine '53 models

Fig. 84—Stator and Free Wheel Clutch Parts '53 Model Turbine

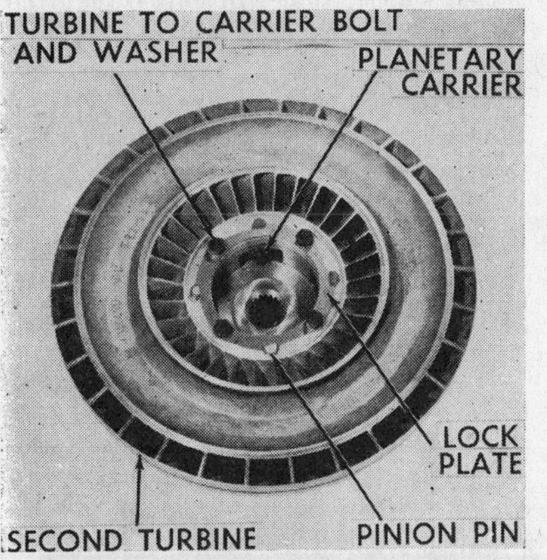

Fig. 81—Second Turbine and Planetary Carrier Assy. Rear Seal, '53 models

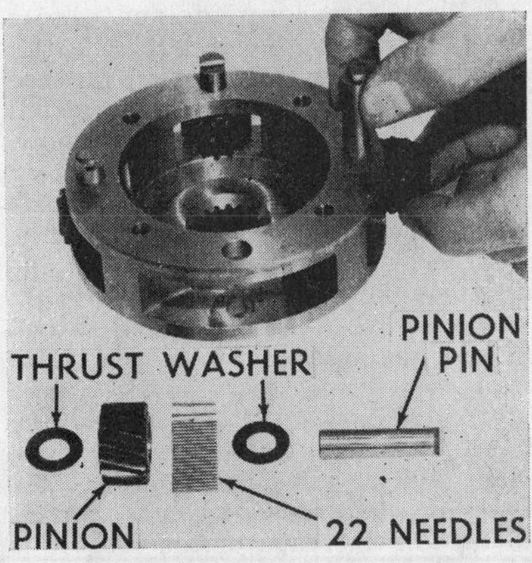

Fig. 83—Disassembly Planetary Carrier '53 model converter

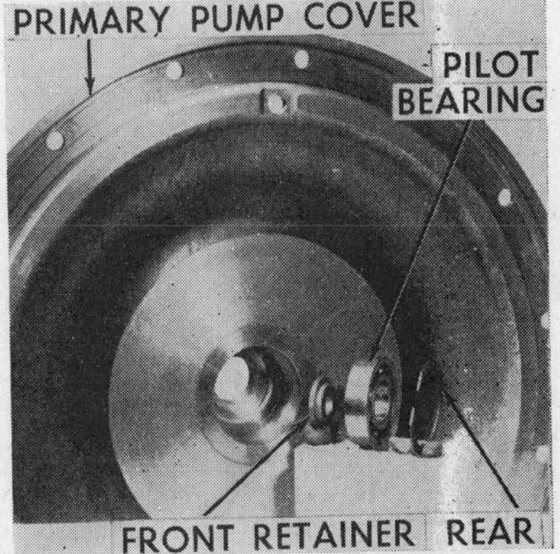

Fig. 85—Pilot Bearing and Retainers

Fig. 86—Stator for 8 in Line Engine '53 models

The planetary gear teeth.

The free wheel rollers and their race. Nicks on these should be removed with an arkansas stone.

The hub of the primary pump, especially any wear caused by the oil seal of the front oil pump.

Check the oil seal of the front oil pump and the springs of the free wheel clutch.

Inspect the primary pump, the two turbines and the stator for cracked vanes and other damage.

Replace all worn parts noting that: if engine is a V-8, the converter requires a 20 blade stator; while for an 8-in-line engine the stator unit has only 12 broad vanes. Figs. 86 and 87.

4. Reassembly of Twin Turbine Converter

1953 Models

a. Place the input shaft pilot bearing retainer in the hub of the primary pump cover with the shouldered side upward. Fig. 85.

b. Push the pilot bearing into place so that the outer race bears against the shoulder in the hub and install the retaining ring in its groove over the bearing.

c. Install the 8 springs, cups and rollers in the free wheel clutch of the stator. Fig. 88.

d. Replace the stator roller bearing in the rear of the stator. It must seat in the counterbored recess and the outer race should turn freely.

e. Support the planet carrier on two wooden blocks with the hub side down. Have ready a pinion loading tool made of 3/8″ steel rod 11/16″ long. Then:

Place a pinion thrust washer on the bench, lay a pinion on it, insert the loading tool, drop in the 22 needle bearings, place another thrust washer on top.

Slide the assembly into the carrier and install a pinion pin, notched end up. After the loading tool is pushed out by the incoming pin slide a block of wood under to keep the pin from dropping out. Fig. 89.

OVERHAUL OF '53 CONVERTER—*continued*

Turn all pins so that the notches face the center of the carrier.

f. Check that the counterbored recess in the front face of the second turbine and the rear face of the carrier are clean and free of burrs. Apply a light coat of transmission fluid to the surfaces and start the second turbine down onto the carrier.

g. Use a hammer and a wooden dowel to tap the turbine into place. Use light taps applied midway between holes and alternated from side to side to avoid distorting the second turbine. Note that if more than moderate force seems to be necessary there is likely to be a cause, such as burrs in the counterbore, which should be corrected. Fig. 90.

h. Install the pinion pin lock plate so that it enters the notches of all the pins. Fig. 81.

i. Install the four turbine to carrier bolts and lockwashers and tighten evenly.

j. Place second turbine and carrier assembly in first turbine, then install the bronze thrust washer over the planetary carrier hub and then install the first turbine disk and hub assembly. Rotate the disk until the ring gear meshes with the pinions and align the lugs of the disk with the notches in the front edge of the turbine. Push the assembly down into place. Fig. 79A.

k. The disk retaining ring is dished to hold the assembly more firmly. Install the ring so that its outer edge presses against the front edge of the locking groove; this will result in its inner edge pressing firmly on the disk assembly. Be sure that this is so even to tapping the edge of the ring if it has raised up. To put it bluntly, the easy way to install this ring is the wrong way to do it.

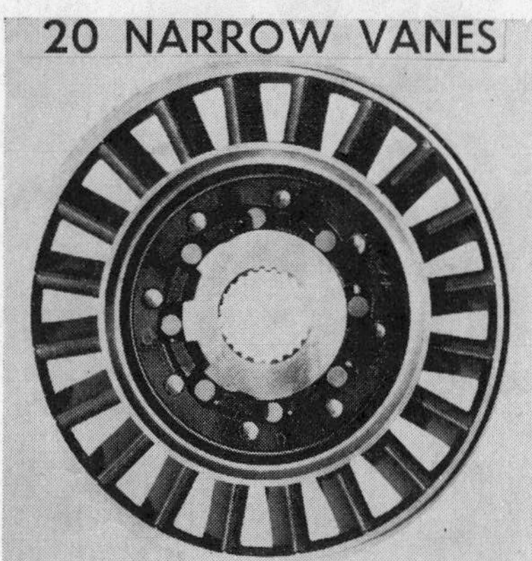

Fig. 87—Stator for V-8 Engines '53 models

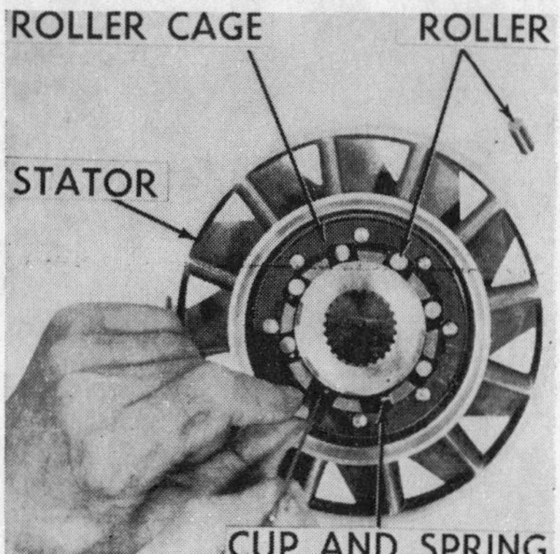

Fig. 88—Installing Free Wheel Rollers

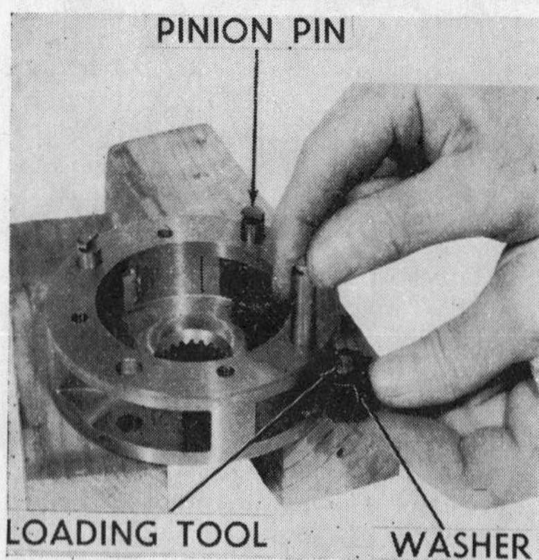

Fig. 89—Installing Pinion Assys. in Carrier

5. Installation of Twin Turbine Converter

1953 Models

a. Install the primary pump on the reactor shaft turning it so the front oil pump driving lugs on the hub enter the slots in the driving gear.

b. Install the stator onto the reactor shaft. Use the roller race of the free wheel clutch to push against. Fig. 76.

c. Install the stator retaining ring with the tang pointing outward, making sure the ring is fully seated in its groove.

d. Install the sun gear on the input shaft so that it meshes with the tangs of the free wheel clutch.

e. Install a bronze thrust washer against front face of sun gear.

f. Install sun gear retaining ring onto input shaft and seat it carefully in its groove. Fig. 92.

g. Determine the thickness of the thrust washer that will go between the turbine hub assembly and the primary pump cover. Fig. 93. To do this:

Support the twin turbine assembly on the rear hub of the planetary carrier.

Using a setup as shown or a depth gage measure the distance from the forward edge of the carrier hub to the nearest machined thrust surface of the disk assembly. Call this distance "X." Fig. 94.

Place the bronze thrust washer marked "5," "6," or "7" which was laid aside separately at disassembly into the machined depression on the back face of the primary pump cover.

Using a setup as shown, or a depth gage, measure the distance from the rear face of the thrust washer to the rear face of the inner race of the pilot bearing in to cover hub. Call this distance "Y." Fig. 95. This distance "Y" should be .002″ to .010″ less than distance "X" found in Par. No. 2 above.

Note: There are three thrust washers available: the one marked "5" is .052″-.055″ thick; the one marked "6" is .060″-.063″ thick; the one marked "7"

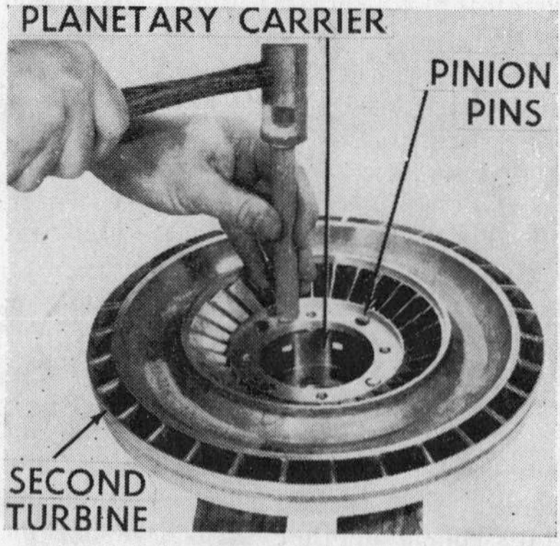

Fig. 90—Installing 2nd Turbine on Carrier '53 models

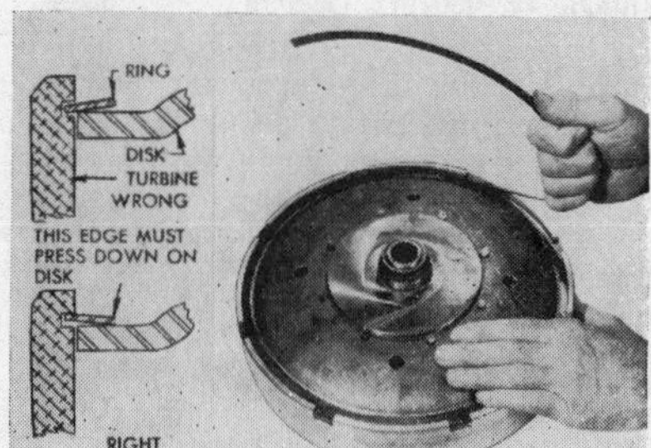

Fig. 91—Installing Disk Assembly Retaining Ring

is .068"-.071" thick. Select a thrust washer to be sure that "X" minus "Y" is not more than .010" or less than .002".

h. Install the twin turbine assembly on the input shaft, turning it as required to mesh the planet pinions with the sun gear.

i. Put the thrust washer, selected in Par. G above, on the front hub of the twin turbine assembly.

j. Install a new "O" ring seal on the primary pump cover. It will go on easier if it is first dipped in transmission fluid. Be sure that it fits evenly, has not been twisted and is near the front edge of the groove.

k. Install the cover onto the primary pump. Be sure not to twist it as you push it on so that the seal is not stretched. Be positive that the mating marks made at disassembly coincide.

l. Starting with a bolt at the left of the drain plug install the bolts, plain washers and special nuts for four holes, skip 1 do four more, skip 1 do four more, which should put an empty one to the right of the drain plug. Fig. 96.

m. Align the holes with an 11/32" drill through one bolt hole, then tighten to 5 ft lbs in the sequence shown. Complete tightening to 25-30 ft lbs in same sequence. Be sure to insert a wide screw driver blade between the flat side of each bolt head and the side of the pump to prevent the corners of the heads from digging into the casting when you are tightening.

n. Check that:

The three empty pump to flywheel holes are not aligned with any balance weight in the rim of the pump.

The three pump to flywheel holes are each aligned with the center of the hub and one of the counterbored recesses in the cover. See Fig. 97. (If the cover was marked for match mating at disassembly this condition should occur automatically.)

o. Using an Allen wrench 5/16" across the flats, install the retaining screw and lock washer into the input shaft end in the pump cover hub opening.

p. To tighten the screw:

Shift transmission into Parking.

Pry off rear band adjustment cover.

Pry up on the operating lever to tighten band and lock the input shaft. Fig. 98.

Tighten the set screw to 25-30 ft lbs torque.

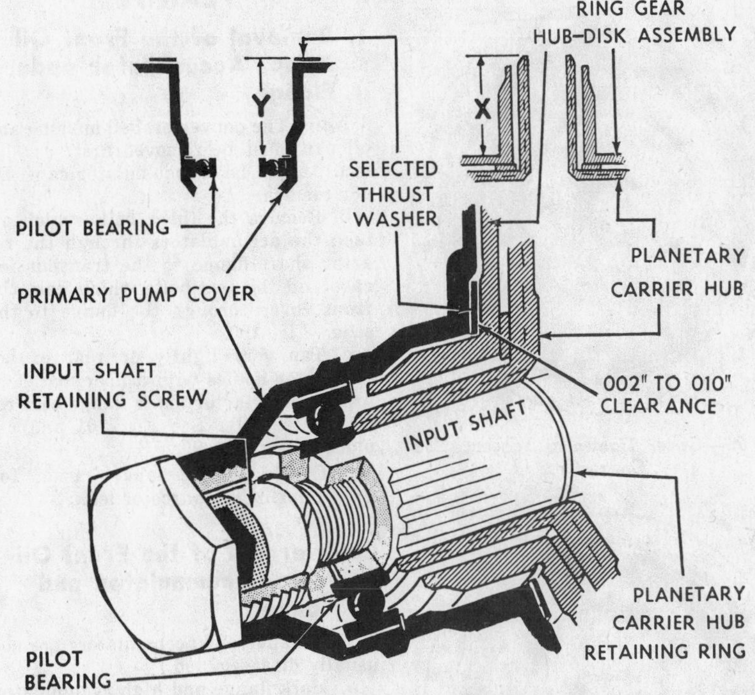

Fig. 93—Theory used in selecting Thrust Washer

Fig. 92—Installing Sun Gear on Input Shaft '53 Converter

Fig. 94—Measuring Distance "X"

Fig. 95—Measuring Distance "Y"

OVERHAUL OF '53 CONVERTER—*continued*

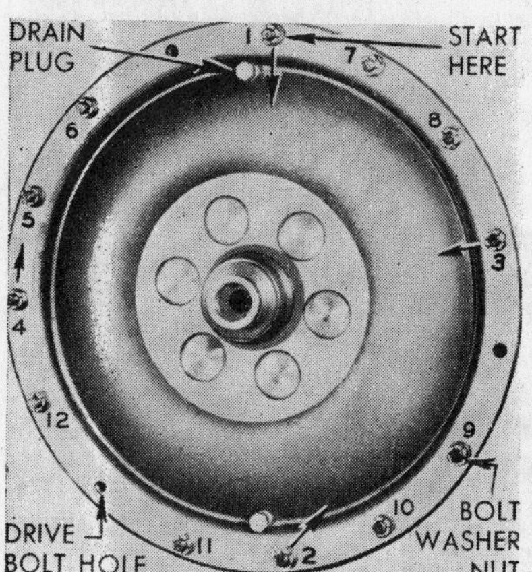

Fig. 96—Cover Tightening Sequence '53 Converter

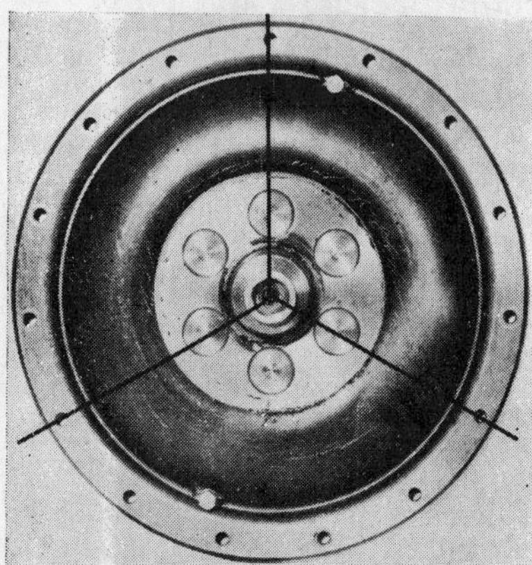

Fig. 97—Showing Location of drive holes in Primary Pump Cover

Fig. 98—Tightening Input Shaft Retaining Screw

Replace adjustment cover and gasket.

q. Install the large hexagonal plug and gasket. Tighten it securely.

THE REACTOR SHAFT FLANGE

1. Removal of the Front Oil Pump, Accumulator and Flange

Note: The converter, bell housing and oil pan must be removed first.

a. Loosen both accumulator caps. Do not remove.

b. Remove the three bolts which attach the accumulators through the reactor shaft flange to the transmission case and the two bolts which hold the front cover through the flange to the case. Fig. 100.

c. Tap very lightly on rear of accumulator bodies with a fiber mallet to loosen the reactor shaft flange and remove assembly. See Fig. 101 and exploded view, Fig. 99.

d. Check reactor flange gasket for good imprint or source of leak.

2. Overhaul of the Front Oil Pump, Accumulator and Flange

(The flange and accumulators are not usually disassembled.)

a. Mark flange and high accumulator so that they can be more easily remated.

b. Remove the accumulators, being careful to prevent the retaining pin and check ball from being lost out of the high accumulator. The low accumulator does not have a check ball. See Fig. 102.

c. Remove the pipe plug, cap, gasket, spring, and piston, from the accumulator bodies. Keep the parts separated as they are matched to the bodies, in fact the pistons are not listed as available separately. Replace assembly complete if any part is damaged.

d. Reassemble the accumulators. Do not tap the pistons into the bodies; they should slide freely if properly oiled. Do not clamp accumulators in a vise. Do not tighten caps before reinstalling on reactor flange. Do not neglect the check ball and retaining pin in the high accumulator.

e. Check that oil pump nuts are tight before removing assembly from the flange; they could have permitted a leak.

f. Remove front oil pump cover and gasket from reactor shaft flange. Check gasket for indications of leakage.

g. If the check ball located in clutch feed passage of the flange is not held by peened edge of hole, remove ball to avoid loss when handling parts. See Fig. 103.

h. Check mounting face of front pump body, gears, and pump cover plate for excessive wear.

i. Inspect front oil pump bushing. If

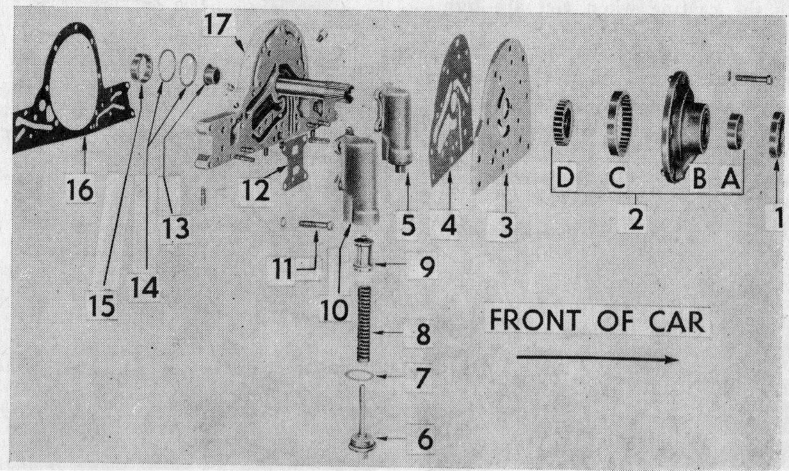

Fig. 99—Front Pump, Accumulators, Reactor Shaft and Flange

1. Oil seal (Front oil pump).
2a. Bushing (Front oil pump).
2b. Body (Front oil pump).
2c. Driver gear (Front oil pump).
2d. Driving gear (Front oil pump).
3. Cover (Front oil pump).
4. Gasket (Oil pump cover to reactor flange).
5. High accumulator.
6. Cap (Low accumulator).
7. Gasket (Low accumulator).
8. Spring (Low accumulator).
9. Piston (Low accumulator).
10. Body (Low accumulator).
11. Bolt (Accumulator through flange to transmission).
12. Gasket (Accumulator to reactor flange).
13. Sleeve (Reactor shaft. Not available separately).
14. Oil seal rings (Reactor shaft).
15. Bushing (Reactor shaft. Not available separately).
16. Gasket (Reactor shaft flange to transmission).
17. Reactor shaft flange assembly.

it is loose or worn replace the pump assembly. Causes of the condition should be investigated, such as misalignment of the bell housing, runout of the primary pump hub, runout of the flywheel.

j. If there is evidence of leakage replace the front oil pump seal. Drive out seal with a punch, lightly coat outside of new seal with Permatex No. 3 (non-hardening). Start seal squarely into pump body with deep groove in seal retainer outward and tap into place with hardwood block and mallet. Wipe off excess Permatex.

k. Measure gear clearance as shown; if any dimension is out of given tolerance replace pump assembly.

Fig. 104, side clearance .001″ to .0025″.

Fig. 105A, driven gear .005″ to .009″.

Fig. 105B, driving gear .010″ to .016″.

l. If depth of wear of gears into front pump cover exceeds .001 then replace the pump assembly.

m. Be careful to replace driving gear in front pump in same manner as it was removed or else the unit will howl (See Fig. 106) and transmission will be damaged.

n. Wash reactor shaft and flange assembly, and check for nicks and burrs which can be filed off. Any other type of damage replace the assembly.

o. If stud threads are stripped, step studs are available. The 5/16-18 step studs have a 3/8-16 thread on the flange end. The 3/8-16 step studs have a 7/16-14 thread on the flange end. A 3/8-16 and a 7/16-14 tap will be required for their installation.

p. Install checkball in clutch feed passage. Install new gasket and front pump cover on reactor shaft flange.

q. Install oil pump so that the two dowel pins engage holes in cover then install nuts with lockwashers.

r. Pretighten nuts to approximately 5 ft lbs torque in sequence as shown in Fig. 107. Finish tightening in same sequence 25 to 30 ft lbs. Tighten stud nut fastening cover to flange to 25-30 ft lbs.

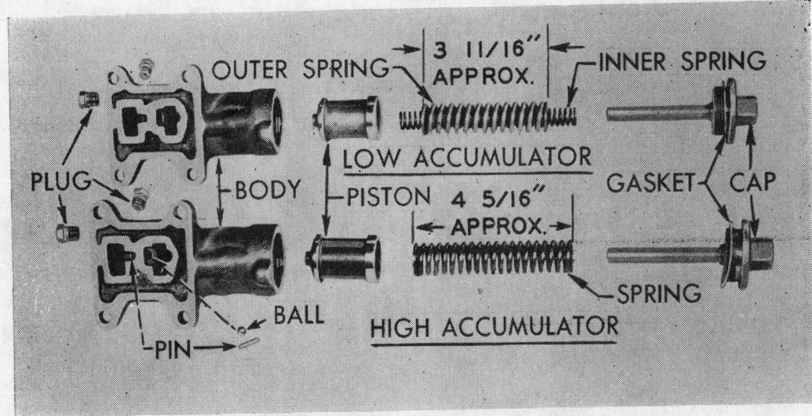

Fig. 102—High and Low Accumulators

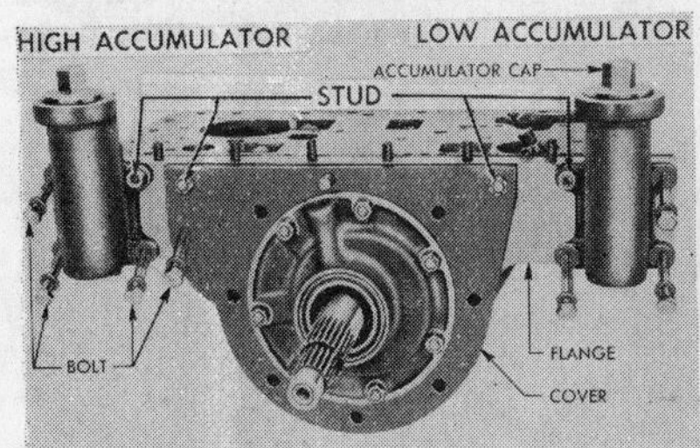

Fig. 100—Location of Accumulator Bolts and Studs

Fig. 101—Front Oil Pump and Reactor Shaft Flang Assembly

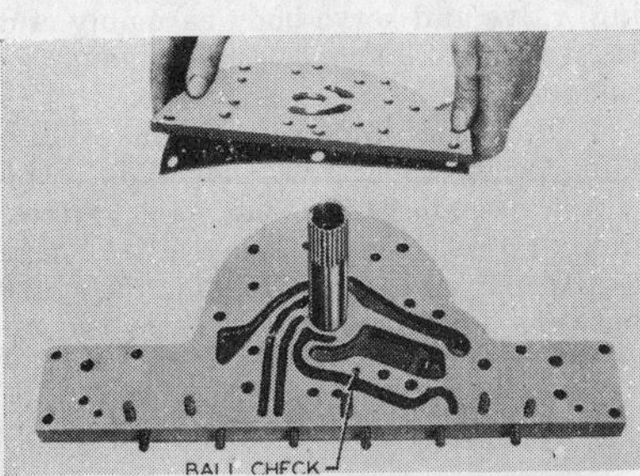

Fig. 103—Reactor Shaft Flange Assembly

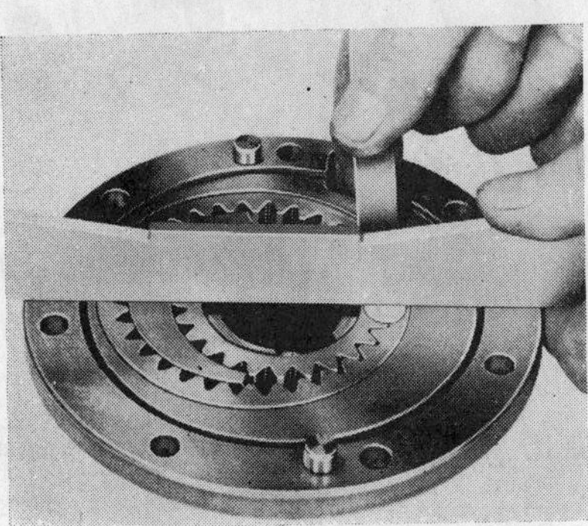

Fig. 104—Side clearance should be .001″-.0025″

3. Installation of the Oil Pump, Reactor Flange and Accumulators

a. Install a 5/16″ guide pin accumulator bolt holes in reactor flange. See See Figs 108 and 109.

b. Place flange gasket on the case. This gasket can be put on wrong, check that all holes are aligned with those in case.

Fig. 105—Checking clearance of Oil Pump Gears

Fig. 106—Correct position of Driving Gear

REACTOR FLANGE—*continued*

Fig. 107—Front Oil Pump Tightening Sequence

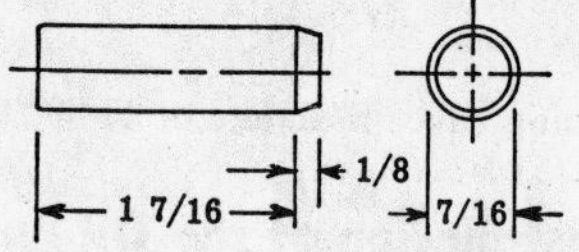

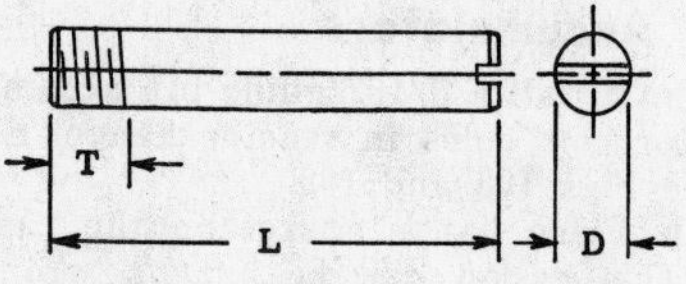

D	L	T	THREAD
5/16	2 1/2	1/2	5/16-18
3/8	1 3/8	1/2	3/8-16

Fig. 108—Design of Guide Pins

c. Install flange assembly on case being careful of the oil seal rings as they fit into the clutch hub. Do not pull out on input shaft.

d. Install accumulator gaskets and the accumulators. The high accumulator is alongside identification number.

e. Coat accumulator bolt threads with Permatex No. 3 (non-hardening). Install bolts and stud nuts with lockwashers but do not tighten.

f. Install 3 special bolts (3/8-16x2) with plain washers in positions marked 2, 3, 4 in Fig. 110 for ease in assembly only.

g. Install bolts 1 and 6. Coat bolt 5 with Permatex No. 3 (non-hardening) and install it.

h. Pretighten all bolts and nuts in sequence to 5 ft lbs as shown. Finish tightening 1 thru 4 to 35-40 ft lbs and 5 thru 14 to 20-25 ft lbs.

i. Remove the bolts 2, 3 and 4.

j. Tighten accumulator caps to 40-50 ft lbs. If edge of flange gasket extends below edge of case carefully trim it flush using a sharp knife.

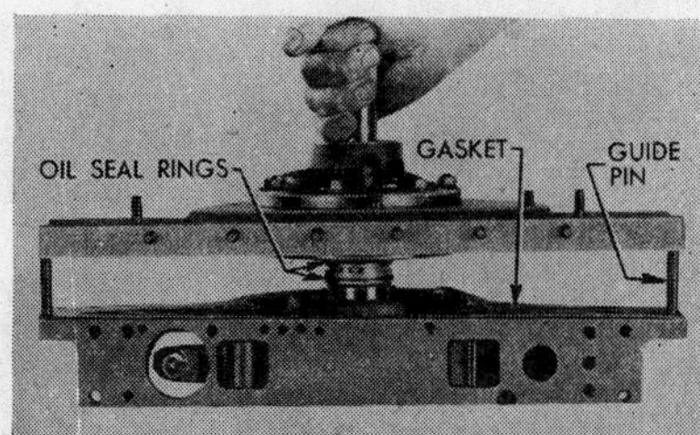

Fig. 109—Installing Reactor Shaft Flange Assembly

Fig. 110—Reactor Shaft Flange Assembly Tightening Sequence

THE CLUTCH ASSEMBLY

1. Removal of the Input Shaft, Clutch and Low Band

Note: The converter and bell housing, valve and servo body assembly and reactor shaft flange assembly must be removed first.

a. Pull the input shaft and clutch hub front thrust washer from the clutch assembly, Fig. 112, then remove the clutch assembly. Note that there is a thrust washer deep inside that goes between the low sun gear and the reverse sun gear in the planetary gear set. See Fig. 113.

b. The low band struts have little notches cut in them to fit around pins in the flanges of the low band, it is best to raise the band actuating levers and remove the struts first. Then compress the band with a pair of long nosed pliers and slide it out. **Mark** the anchor flange of the band as it must go back the same way. Fig. 114.

c. The pins holding the actuating levers are threaded for ¼-20 bolts to be used as handles to remove the pins. See Fig. 115.

2. Disassembly and Overhaul of the Input Shaft Clutch and Low Band

a. Remove the retainer ring with a screwdriver as shown. See Fig. 116. Use a scribe to remove the driving keys.

b. Pull on the Low Sun gear and integral flange thus releasing a thrust washer, between it and the clutch hub, the ten clutch plates, and the low drum with its piston and spring assembly intact. See Fig. 117.

c. Compress clutch spring sufficiently to remove retaining ring Fig. 118.

d. Remove spring seat, spring and piston from the drum.

e. Use only gasoline or kerosene to clean the clutch plates and the low band. Commercial degreasers will harm the facings.

f. Inspect clutch plates. Check the fit of replacement plates. They must slide on hub.

g. Inspect drum for cracks or scores. Inspect piston inner oil seal ring on the hub of the drum. See Fig. 119. Note lock in ring.

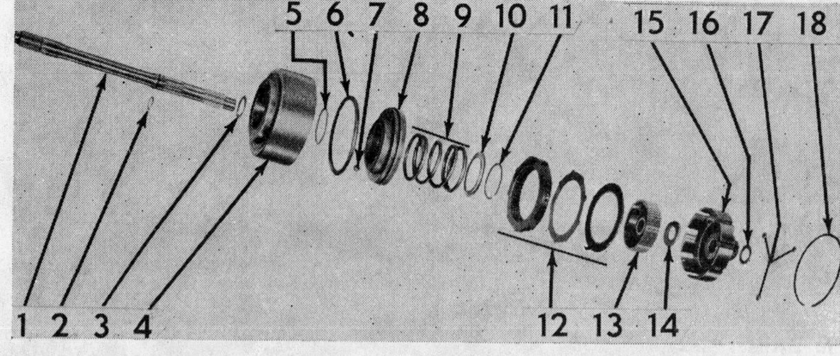

Fig. 111—Exploded view of Input Shaft and Clutch

1. Input shaft.
2. Oil seal ring.
3. Thrust washer (Clutch hub front).
4. Low drum.
5. Seal ring (Clutch piston inner).
6. Seal ring (Clutch piston outer).
7. Ball (Clutch check valve).
8. Clutch piston.
9. Spring (Clutch piston)
10. Seat (Clutch piston spring).
11. Retaining ring (Clutch spring).
12. Clutch plates.
13. Clutch hub.
14. Thrust washer (Clutch hub rear).
15. Low sun gear and flange.
16. Thrust washer (Low sun gear to reverse sun gear).
17. Drive keys (Low sun gear flange to drum).
18. Retaining ring (Low sun gear flange to drum).

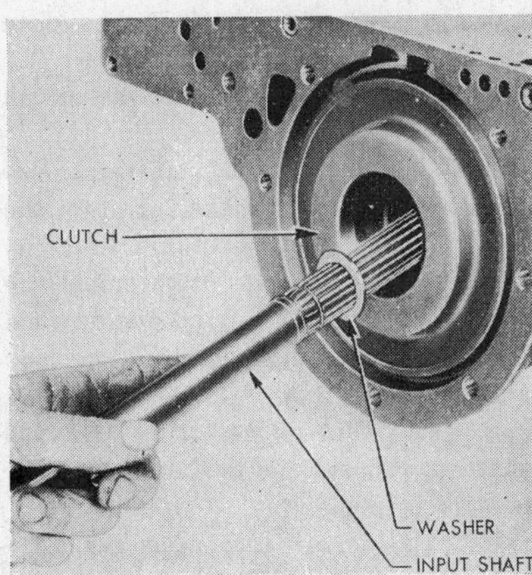

Fig. 112—Removing Input Shaft

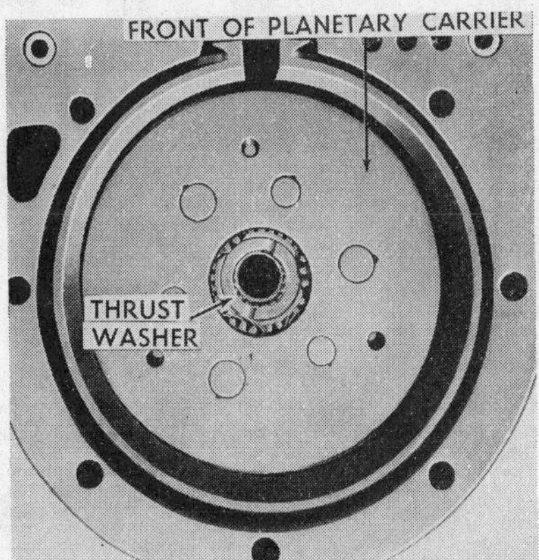

Fig. 113—Thrust Washer Between Low and Reverse Sun Gears

Fig. 114—Layout of Transmission Parts

h. Inspect on clutch piston the bleed hole, the check ball, and the outer seal. Replace seal if damaged. See Fig. 120. Outer seal lip extends over smaller diameter.

i. Inspect low band for burns and wear. If grooves are gone replace.

j. Inspect the input shaft oil seal ring. See Fig. 121.

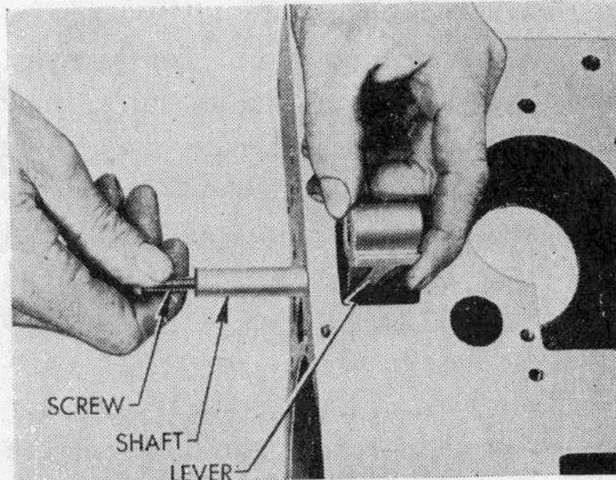

Fig. 115—Removing Band Levers

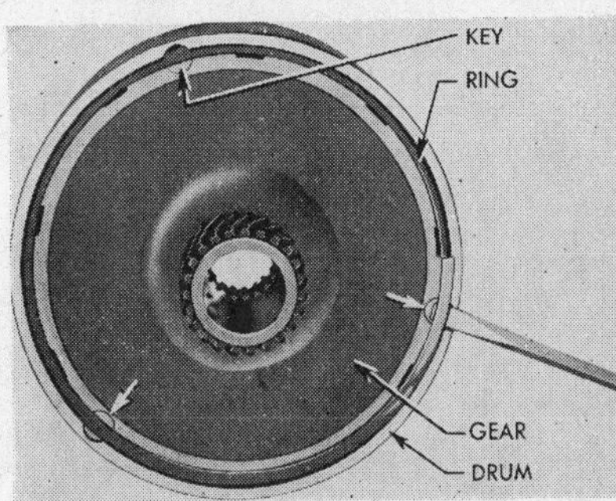

Fig. 116—Releasing Low Sun Gear Flange

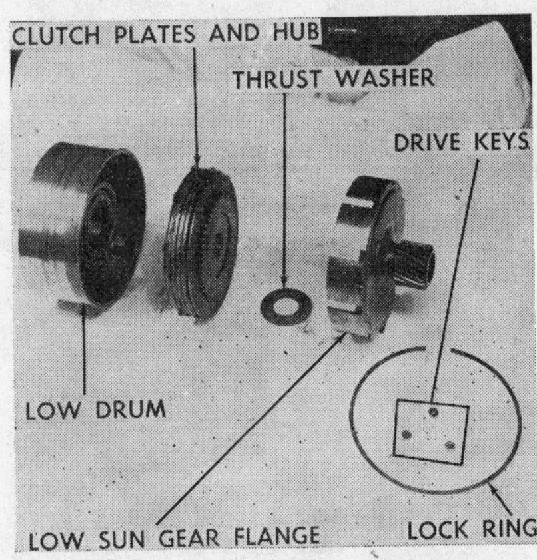

Fig. 117—Lay-out of Clutch Parts

3. Assembly of the Input Shaft, Clutch and Low Band

a. Apply light oil to the piston outer seal and the drum. Install piston without distorting this seal. When piston is fully installed its top will be approximately flush with the shoulder on the inside of the drum.

b. Install spring, spring seat, and retainer ring in piston. See exploded view. Fig. 111.

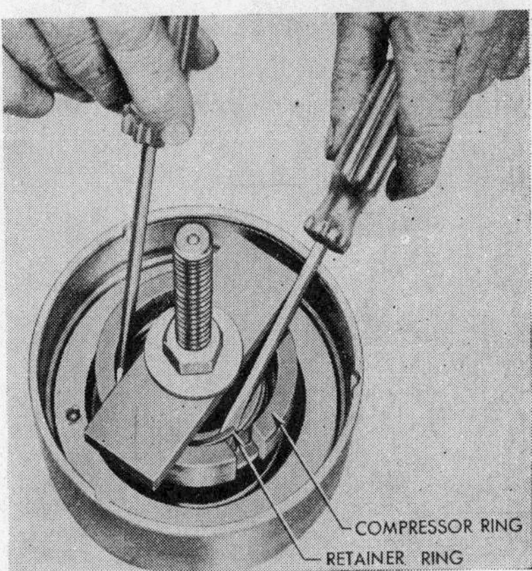

Fig. 118—Removing Clutch Spring Retainer Ring

c. Lay the clutch hub hollow side up on the thrust washer inside the low sun gear flange. See Fig. 122.

d. The internally splined plates are faced and flat may be installed in either direction.

e. The externally splined plates are very slightly curved and they must all curve in the same direction. To determine the curve or dish hold a straight edge across. See Fig. 123.

f. Install an internally splined clutch plate over the clutch hub next to the gear flange. Follow with an internally splined plate. Alternately install remaining plates. **Using great care that the curve or dish is always in the same direction.** One should end with an externally splined plate.

g. Fit the drum assembly down into the clutch hub being careful not to slide the hub around thus displacing the thrust washer between it and the low sun gear flange.

h. In order to align the driving key holes use a brass drift against the low sun gear as the flange is soft and will be damaged. Install drive keys and lock ring. Fig. 124.

4. Installation of the Input Shaft, Clutch and Low Band

a. Install the low band operating lever (has an adjusting screw) on the side of the case having large servo opening, install low band anchor lever at opposite opening. See Figs 125 and 126. Strut shoulders of levers must be toward inside of case, tapped ends of shafts must be outward.

b. With the assembly standing on the rear bearing retainer install a wooden block as shown in Fig. 126. Set the struts on the block with plain ends en-

CLUTCH ASSEMBLY—*continued*

gaging the shoulders of the actuating levers. The notched ends adjacent but separated as far as can be. Compress the ends of the low band.

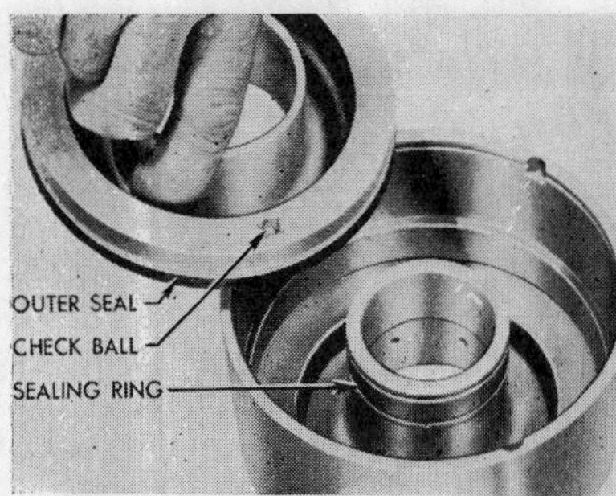

Fig. 119—Clutch Piston Seal Rings

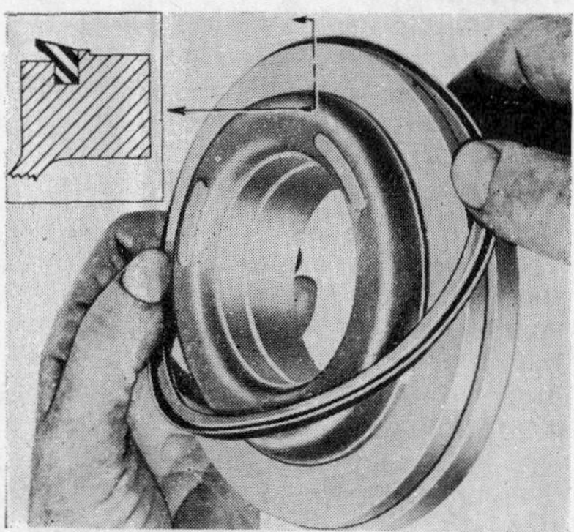

Fig. 120—Installing Clutch Piston Outer Seal Ring

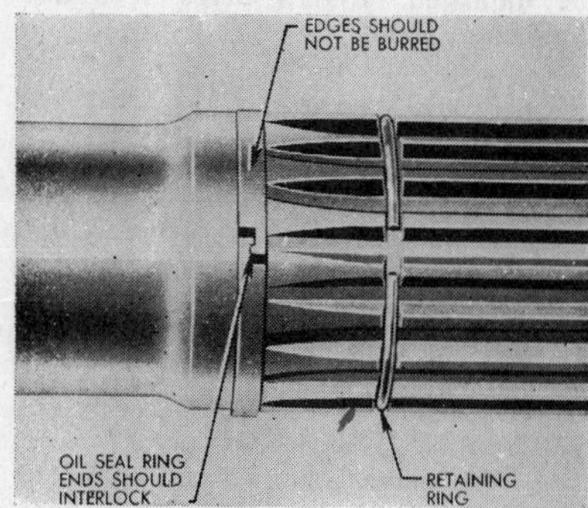

Fig. 121—Input Shaft Oil Seal Ring (Retaining Ring early models only)

Note: A used band must be installed in the original position. The heaviest wear will be at the anchor end. A new band can be installed either way. Slide band into place and press on one of the levers to hold the band in place. Remove the wooden block and jiggle the band until the pins in the flanges fit into the notches in the struts.

c. Place the bronze thrust washer down on the reverse sun gear in the planetary carrier. See Fig. 111 and 113.

d. Install clutch assembly. If drum binds on band and won't seat down, use a hooked wire to lift the band on the side opposite the struts.

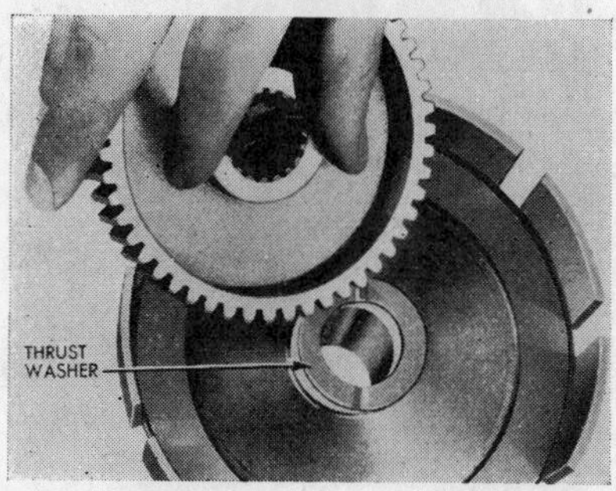

Fig. 122—Installing Clutch Hub

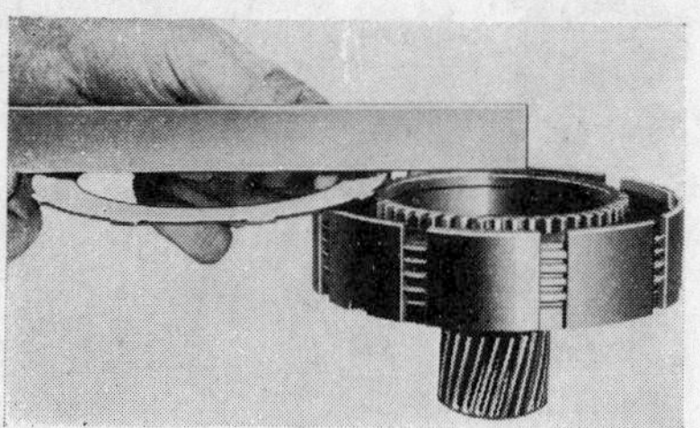

Fig. 123—Checking Steel Plates for direction of Dish

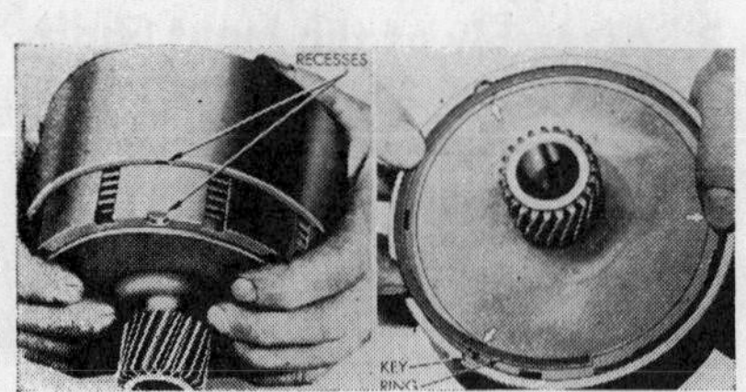

Fig. 124—Installing Drive Keys and Lock Ring

e. Place bronze thrust washer on front face of clutch hub. Fig. 111.

f. Using a scribe or something like it and a flash light, make sure that the 4 (four) thrust washers are lined up so the input shaft can fit through. The four washers can be found one on each side of reverse sun gear, one on each side of clutch hub.

g. Check that oil seal ring on input shaft is properly locked and retaining ring is in place.

h. Install shaft into assembly. Retaining ring should rest on thrust washer on front face of clutch hub. Retaining ring is not found on late models.

i. Provide some protection that input shaft stays in and is not inadvertently pulled out thus letting a thrust washer fall down, as this will prevent shaft seating in the support bushing in the planetary carrier.

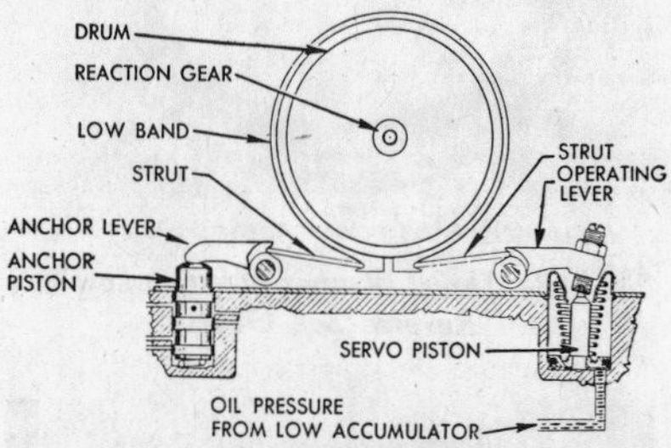

Fig. 125—Adjustment of Low Band Mechanism

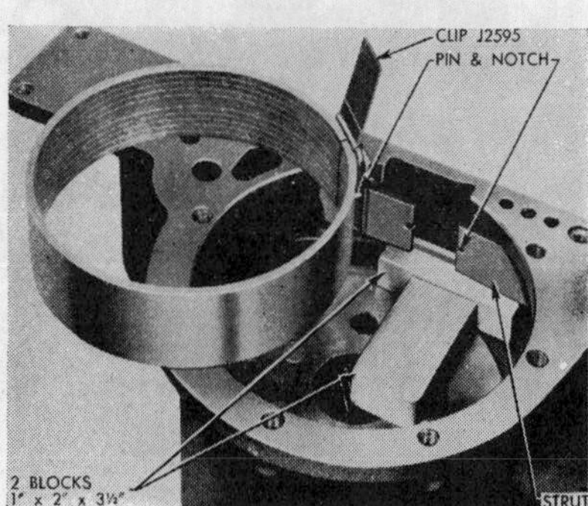

Fig. 126—Installing Low Band

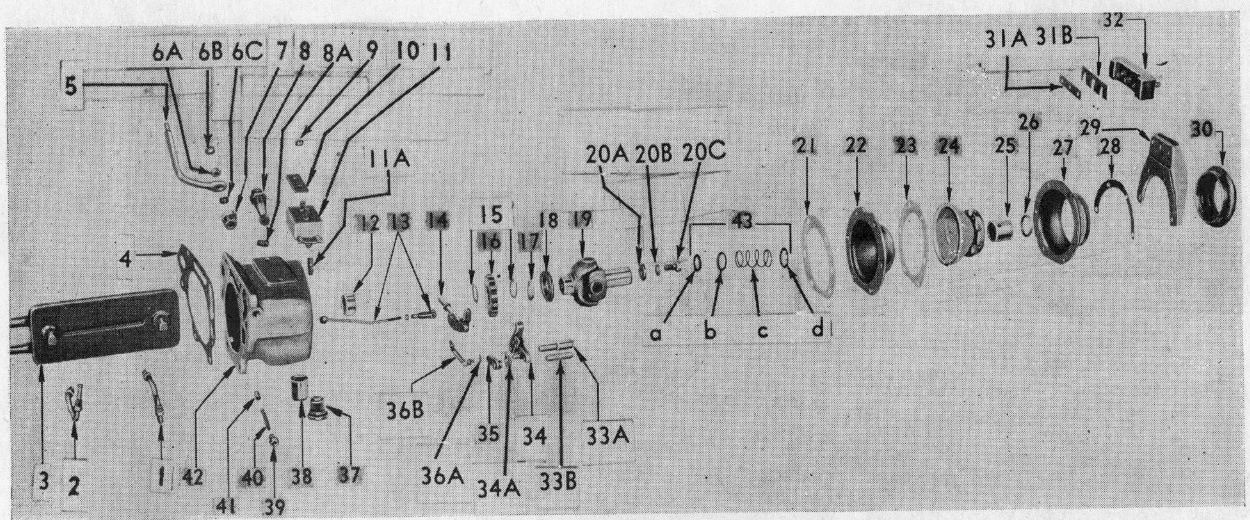

Fig. 127—Torque Ball, Rear Bearing Retainer and Cooler thru '52

1. Pipe (Oil cooler outlet).
2. Pipe (Oil cooler inlet).
3. Cooler (Oil).
4. Gasket (Rear bearing retainer to transmission).
5. Lever (Transmission manual shift).
6a. Nut (Lever attaching).
6b. Washer (Lever attaching).
6c. Seal (Cross shaft assembly).
7. Bearing (Cross shaft assembly).
8. Gear (Speedometer. Driven and sleeve assembly).
8a. Plug (Pipe ⅛ in. for oil pressure check).
9. Nut (Transmission rear mount attaching).
10. Plate (Bolt transmission rear mounting pad).
11. Pad (Transmission rear mounting).
11a. Stud (Transmission rear mounting) to bearing retainer.
12. Bushing (Rear bearing retainer).
13. Rod and clevis (Valve control rod and adjustable end).
14. Shaft (Cross and lever assembly).
15. Rings (Parking ratchet wheel retaining to output shaft).
16. Wheel (Parking ratchet).
17. Ring (Universal joint retaining snap).
18. Worm (Speedometer drive).
19. Joint (Universal).
20a. Washer (Flat universal joint).
20b. Lockwasher (Universal joint).
20c. Bolt (Universal joint, has drilled oil passage).
21. Shim (Torque ball inner retainer to bearing retainer).
22. Retainer (Torque ball inner).
23. Shims (Adjusting between inner and outer torque ball retainers).
24. Ball (Torque).
25. Bushing (Torque ball for universal joint).
26. Seal (Torque ball universal joint oil).
27. Retainer (Torque ball outer).
28. Gasket (Thrust plate to torque ball assembly).
29. Plate (Transmission thrust).
30. Boot (Torque ball).
30a. Bolt (Torque ball to rear bearing retainer attaching).
30b. Washer (Lock).
31a. Plate (Thrust pad bolt).
31b. Shims (Thrust pad to transmission rear support).
32. Pad (Transmission thrust).
33a. Shaft (Parking lock lever).
33b. Shaft (Parking lock pawl).
34. Pawl assembly (Parking lock).
34a. Spring (Parking lock apply).
35. Lever (Parking lock).
36a. Lockwasher (Parking lock rod to cross shaft lever assembly).
36b. Rod (Parking lock).
37. Breather (Rear bearing retainer).
38. Sleeve (Rear bearing retainer breather).
39. Connector (Special inlet to torque converter pressure valve).
40. Spring (Torque converter pressure valve).
41. Valve (Torque converter pressure).
42. Retainer (Rear bearing retainer body).
43. Kit (Propeller shaft oil seal). Early models only.
    a. Oil seal.
    b. Spring seat.
    c. Spring.
    d. Spring retainer.

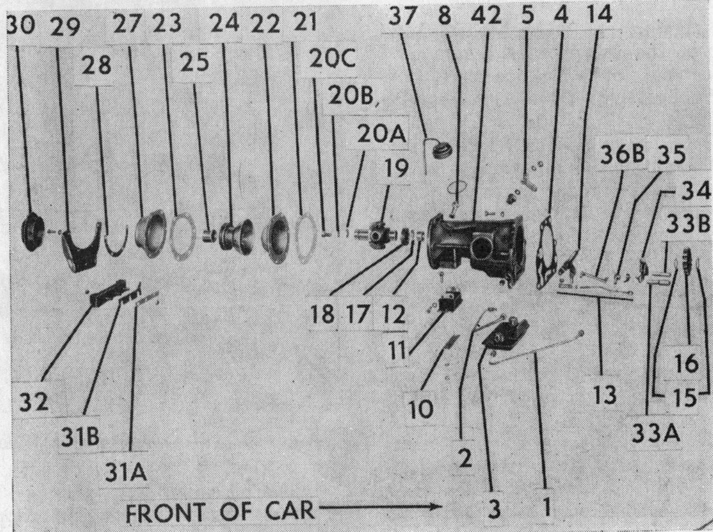

Fig. 128—Torque Ball, Rear Bearing Retainer, Oil Cooler '53

PLANETARY GEAR SET

1. Removal of Torque Ball, Universal Joint, Rear Bearing Retainer, Rear Oil Pump and Planetary Gear Set

Note: Except for the planetary gear set all of these items may be removed with the Dynaflow in the car.

a. Remove bolts holding thrust plate, gasket, outer retainer, torque ball, paper shims, and inner retainer from the rear bearing retainer. Fig. 129. Do not lose the paper shims as they are necessary to adjustment of the torque ball assembly. Figs. 127 and 128.

b. To remove the transmission manual shift lever which is on the end of the cross shaft assembly, hold the lever forward and remove retaining nut. Fig. 130.

c. Using a ¾" socket, remove the drilled universal joint bolt, lockwasher

PLANETARY GEAR SET—*continued*

Fig. 129—Removing Thrust Plate and Torque Ball

Fig. 130—Removing Shift Lever

Fig. 131—Removing Universal Joint

and flat washer. (Hold shift lever forward to lock shaft.)

d. Remove the universal joint from the output shaft using a puller if necessary. Fig. 131.

e. Disconnect the valve control rod from the upper valve operating lever at the socket joint inside the transmission. See Fig. 132.

f. Remove universal joint retaining ring. Fig. 133. It is a horseshoe shaped snap ring and can be removed by pushing on the two ends simultaneously

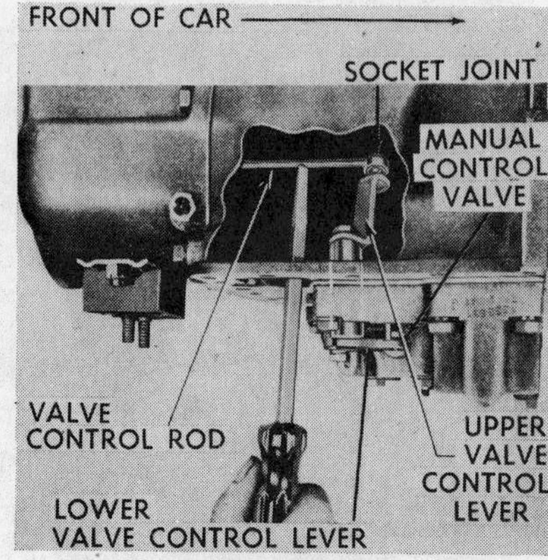

Fig. 132—Disconnecting Valve Control Rod

Fig. 133—Removing Universal Joint Retaining Ring

with screwdrivers. (Use a third hand to tap on the drivers with a hammer.)

Be careful not to nick the shaft as it will damage the rear bearing retainer bushing.

g. Unbolt rear bearing retainer from the transmission, being careful to examine the gasket for signs of leaks. Take care not to damage valve control rod as it comes through the transmission. Fig. 134.

Note: Removal of the torque converter oil pressure valve is not usually necessary but its construction can be seen in Fig. 135.

h. Remove parking ratchet wheel and two retaining rings as shown in Fig. 136.

i. Mark the oil pump body so it can easily be returned to the same position. Remove rear oil pump. It either has a cover separate or a cover integral; either way examine the gaskets or gasket for oil leaks.

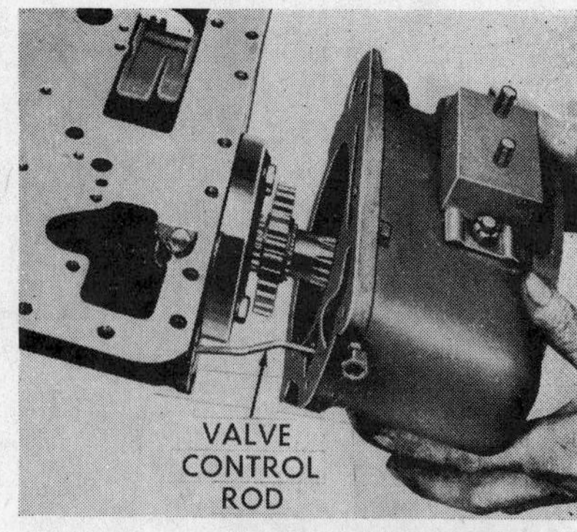

Fig. 134—Removing Rear Bearing Retainer

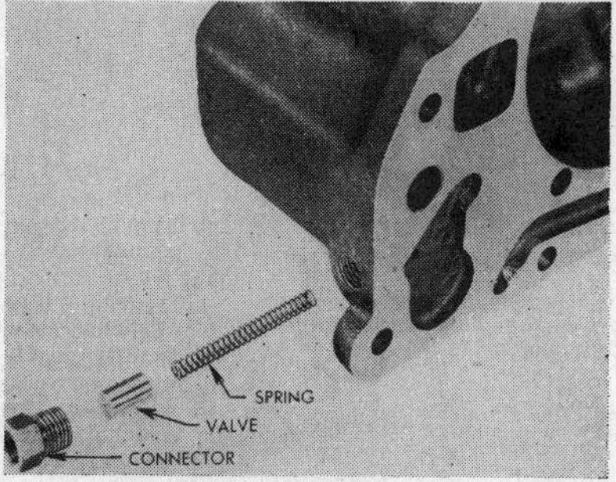

Fig. 135—Torque Converter Oil Pressure Valve

Fig. 136—Removing Ratchet Wheel

j. The oil pump drive gear is keyed to the output shaft with a rubber loaded key. Use pliers to pull the rubber from the keyhole. Fig. 137.

Fig. 137—Location of Oil Pump Drive Key

Fig. 138—Rear Oil Pump Parts

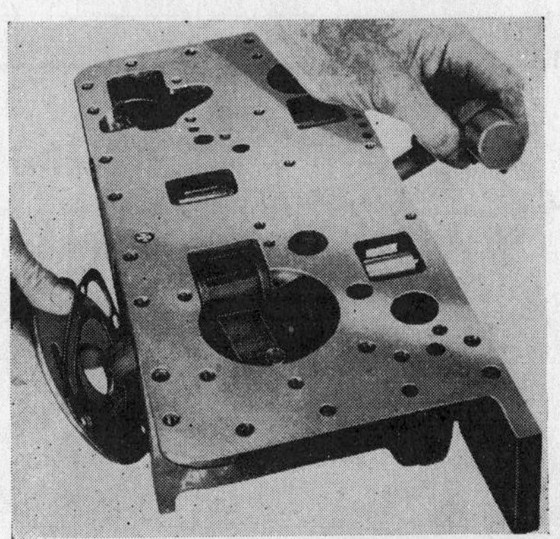

Fig. 139—Removing Rear Oil Pump Plates

k. Mark for remating, then remove the rear oil pump plate from the transmission without prying. Fig. 138. If plate is stuck it can be tapped out after removal of the planetary gearset. Fig. 139. Check for signs of oil leakage.

l. Removal of the lubrication oil pressure regulator valve is seldom necessary. The method and parts are shown in Fig. 140.

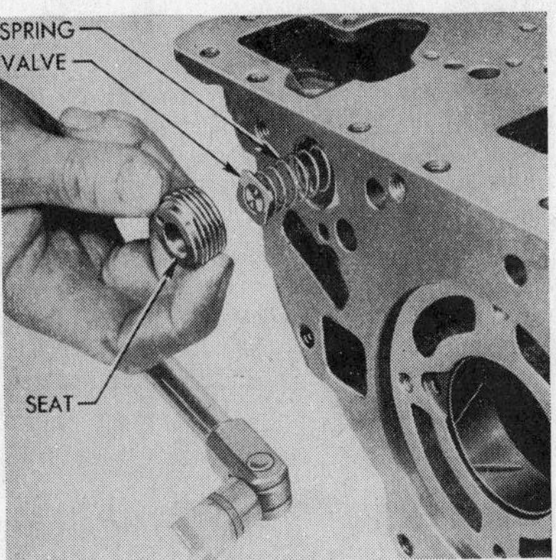

Fig. 140—Oil Pressure Valve Parts

Fig. 141—Removing Planetary Assembly

m. The planetary carrier can now be removed through the front of the case. Note the copper thrust washer in the rear of the case and the steel thrust washer on the rear of the carrier. Fig. 141.

n. Remove the reverse ring gear and the reverse ring gear thrust washer. Fig. 141.

o. Thread a ¼x20 bolt into the reverse anchor pin. Remove the pin and thus release the reverse band actuating lever, the strut and the reverse band anchor. Fig. 142.

2. Disassembly and Overhaul of the Torque Ball, Universal Joint, Rear Bearing Retainer, Rear Oil Pump and Planetary Gear Set

Rear Bearing Retainer And Universal Joint

Release the snap fastener which connects the valve control rod-clevis to the cross-shaft-lever-assembly. See exploded view and Fig. 143. And remove the rod.

Fig. 142—Removing Reverse Band Anchor Pin

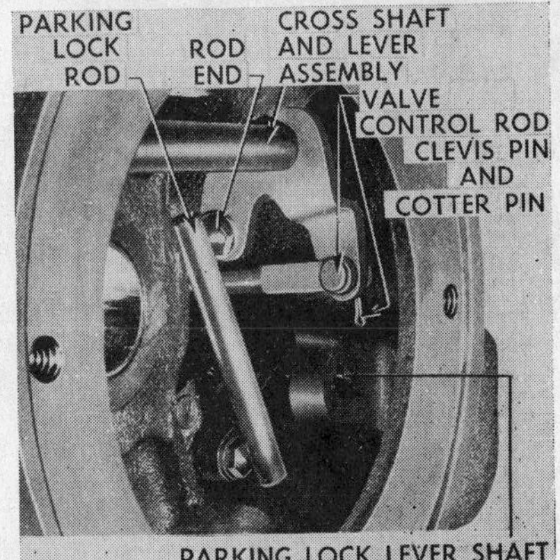

Fig. 143—Unpinning Valve Control Rod Clevis

Unscrew the lock washered fastener to release the parking-lock-rod from the cross-shaft-lever. Remove cross shaft bearing, being careful not to damage the bearing and remove the cross shaft assembly. See Fig. 144.

Screw a ¼x20 bolt into the parking lock pawl assembly shaft and pull it out. See Fig. 145.

Tap the parking-lock-lever shaft toward the front of the retainer body and remove it, thus releasing the parking lock lever, the parking lock pawl assembly and the apply spring.

Inspect the parts for wear and cracks. Renew the rubber seal in the cross-shaft bearing, grooved side in.

Check the rear bearing retainer bushing for damage and wear. The clearance between the output shaft and the bushing should not exceed .006". Replace the bushing if need be.

Play between the parts of the universal joint should be between .002" and .004". The limits of backlash; rear yoke to propeller shaft splines, are

PLANETARY GEAR SET—*continued*

.0005″ to .0045″. The backlash of the front yoke to output shaft should be: none.

Rear yoke and torque ball bushing should be free of scores and fit within .004″ to .006″. If scored, replace bushing, U joint and oil seal.

Spherical surfaces of torque ball assembly should be smooth.

Fig. 144—Removing Cross Shaft Assembly

Assemble the pawl assembly, then apply spring and parking lock lever on a dummy shaft as shown. Fig. 146. Note position of apply spring ends. Attach the parking lock rod as shown.

Place assembled parts in position in rear bearing retainer and install the parking-lock-lever shaft in place of the dummy shaft.

Install the parking-lock-pawl assembly shaft, being sure tapped end is out and end of pawl can revolve on the shaft.

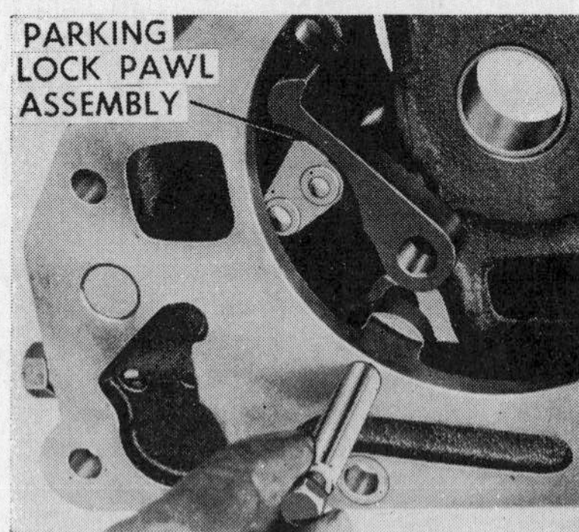

Fig. 145—Removing Pawl Assembly Shaft Thru Front Face of Rear Bearing Retainer

Install the cross-shaft assembly complete with bearing and new seal.

Connect the parking-lock-rod to the cross shaft lever using a lockwasher on the threaded rod end. Connect the clevis of the valve control rod to the cross shaft lever. This connection may require adjustment after retainer has been installed on transmission case.

Rear Oil Pump

Surfaces should be smooth, no signs of wear over .001″. Side clearance should be .001″ to .002″. Fig. 147. Driven gear clearance .0045″ to .007″. Fig. 148. Driving gear clearance should be .006″ to .012″. Fig. 148.

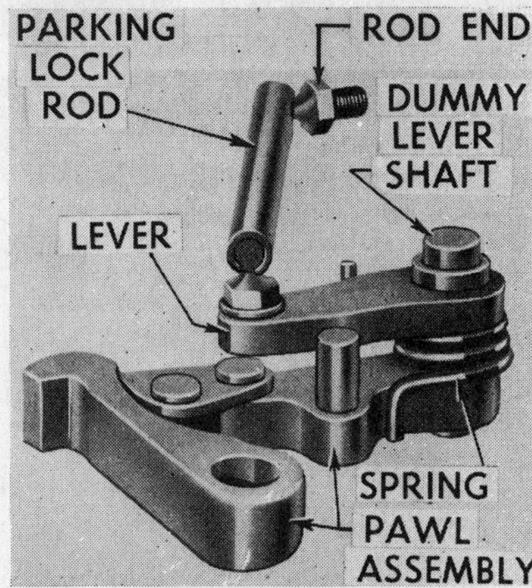

Fig. 146—Preparing to Install Parking Lock Lever Shaft

Fig. 147—Side clearance should be .001″-.0025″

Fig. 148—Checking clearance of Oil Pump Gears

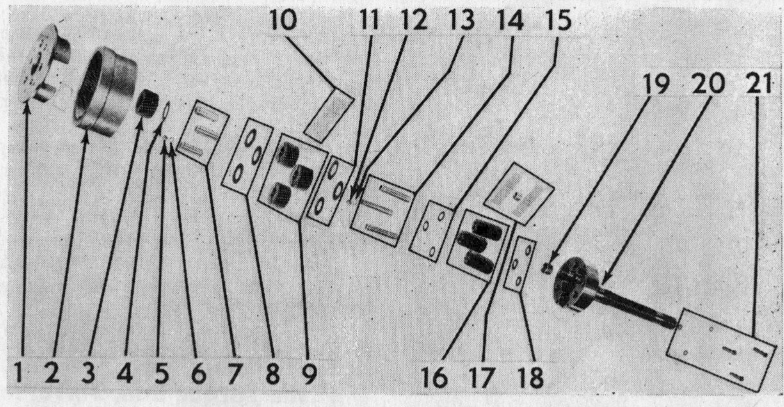

Fig. 149—Exploded View Planetary Assembly

1. Front portion of planetary carrier.
2. Reverse ring gear assembly.
3. Reverse sun gear.
4. Thrust washer (reverse sun gear to carrier).
5. Ball (pinion shaft lock).
6. Ring (pinion shaft lock).
7. Shafts (reverse planetary pinion).
8. Thrust washers (reverse pinions front).
9. Pinions (reverse planetary).
10. Rollers (reverse pinion, 24 per).
11. Thrust washers (reverse pinions rear).
12. Ball (pinion shaft lock).
13. Ring (pinion shaft lock).
14. Shafts (low planetary pinion).
15. Thrust washers (low pinion front).
16. Pinions (low planetary).
17. Rollers and spacer (low pinion 20 each side of spacer).
18. Thrust washers (low pinion rear).
19. Bushing (input shaft to planetary carrier).
20. Rear portion of planetary carrier with integral output shaft.
21. Special screws and lockwashers carrier assembling.

Planetary Gear Set

Unless there was definite evidence of noisy gears there is no need to disassemble the planetary gear set. Check the input shaft bushing in its rear end for signs of wear and note condition of the reverse sun gear thrust washer which is well hidden behind the reverse sun gear.

If it should be necessary to disassemble, the following procedure will apply. See Fig. 149.

Remove the three planet carrier screws and special lockwashers with a 7/32 Allen wrench. Fig. 150.

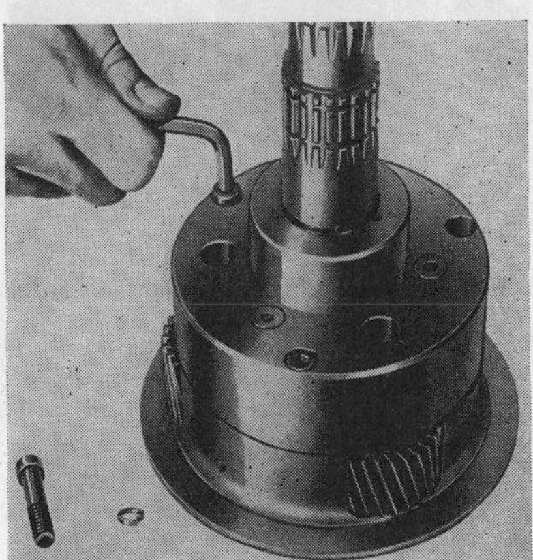

Fig. 150—Removing Carrier Screws

Tap the assembly gently on the flange to separate the units. Note that numbers used in production are adjacent and so provide for mating at assembly.

Remove the reverse sun gear and its thrust washer. Fig. 151.

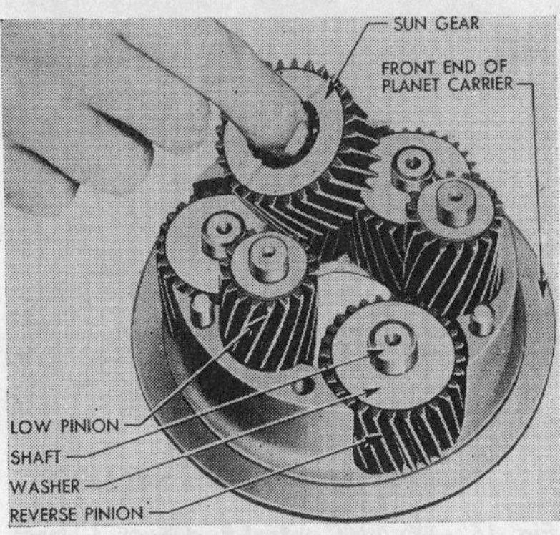

Fig. 151—Removing Reverse Sun Gear

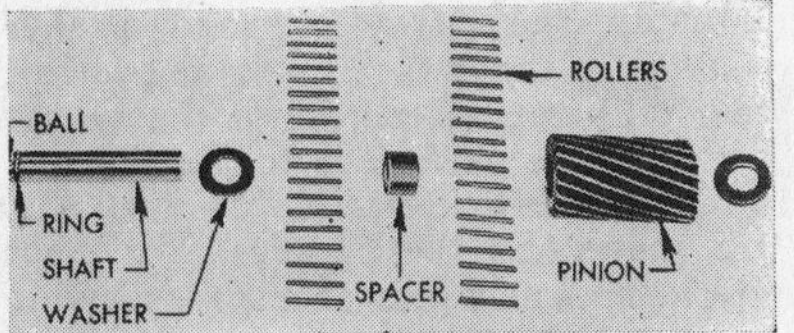

Fig. 152—Low Planet Pinion Parts

Remove the 3 low planet pinion assemblies. Each assembly consisting of a pinion, a shaft, and two sets of 20 rollers separated by a spacer. Fig. 152. Each assembly is retained on its shaft by steel thrust washers and the shaft is kept from turning by a steel ball imbedded in the end of the shaft. **Don't lose the balls.** The reverse planet pinions are similar but have only one set of bearings. Remove them. The reverse planet pinion assemblies contain 24 rollers.

Wash and inspect the parts:

The shafts and rollers for wear.

The gears for nicks and burrs.

The input shaft bushing in the rear of the carrier for scores and wear.

The reverse band for cracks and wear and its anchors for cracks.

The Transmission Case

Wash the case, blow out all passages and check for cracks, breaks, and stripped threads in bolt holes.

Smooth off all machined surfaces.

Check fit of planet carrier journal in the transmission case bushing. When installing a new one be sure the wide deep ends of the oil grooves are toward the rear of the case and front edge is flush with front surface of bushing support.

If the transmission case is of an early type it will use a pressed steel anchor for the reverse band. This item has been superseded by a one piece forged type and the case must be altered to allow its use. The pressed steel type was not strong enough for the work. The forged one should always be installed in its place. Saw the case as shown in Fig. 153. Then smooth off the edges with a file so the new anchor will be free to move.

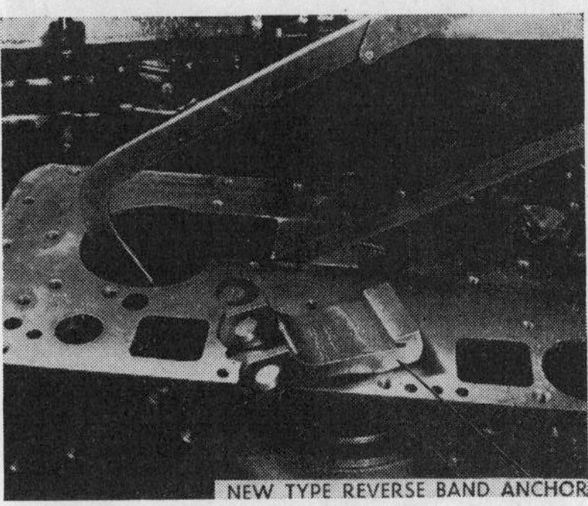

Fig. 153—Making opening in Case for new Reverse Anchor

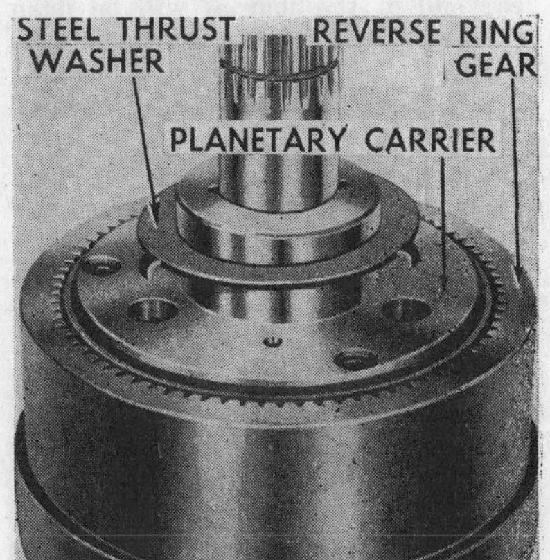

Fig. 154—Installing Steel Thrust Washer on Carrier

3. Reassembly and Installation of the Torque Ball, Universal Joint, Rear Bearing Retainer, Rear Oil Pump and Planetary Gear Set

Planetary Gear Set

Reassemble the planet pinions and shaft with bearing rollers and thrust washers. The bottom thrust washer goes between retaining ring on shaft and the end of the pinion. Each reverse planet pinion contains 24 rollers. Each low planet pinion contains 20 rollers at each end separated by a spacer. Place the second thrust washer on upper end of each shaft to hold rollers in place. Make sure the steel ball is embedded in each shaft and engages the notches in the front end of the carrier. Install reverse sun gear with bronze thrust washer on top.

Install the rear end onto the assembled front end, making sure the numbers placed over the parting line during production are aligned.

Tighten the three allen head screws to 25-30 ft lbs.

Slip the reverse ring gear onto the gear set.

Install a copper thrust washer over the rear bushing in the case and a steel one onto the carrier. Fig. 154.

PLANETARY GEAR SET—*continued*

Install the reverse band actuating and anchor levers. See Fig. 155. Note tapped end of shaft goes out.

Install the ring gear thrust washer, the strut and the reverse band.

Install the planetary assembly. The lineup of parts is as shown in Fig. 156.

Note: If gear set is properly installed and thrust washers are in place, the rear end of the journal will be flush with rear end of transmission case bushing.

Rear Bearing Retainer and Universal Joint.

Place new gasket and rear oil pump plate in recess in transmission case and match the marks made at disassembly. (The holes are not evenly spaced.) Fig. 157.

Install the drive key and rubber cushion in the output shaft, and install rear oil pump drive gear to engage the key with the same face forward it had at disassembly or else it will howl. Fig. 158 shows how these pieces go without the case. A new gear is not sensitive to position.

Lubricate the pump gears and install driven gear and body over the driving gear.

Pre-tighten the lockwashered bolts to 5 ft lbs in the sequence shown in Fig. 159.

Finish tightening in the same sequence to 25-30 ft lbs.

Turn output shaft to be sure pump turns freely.

Install retaining ring, parking lock ratchet wheel and the other retaining ring on output shaft. Fig. 160.

Place bearing retainer to case gasket in place and install bearing retainer. The control-valve-operating rod goes through the square hole in the case with socket for connection to the control-valve-upper lever facing the bottom of the transmission. Fig. 161. Tighten lockwashered bolts to 35-40 ft lbs torque.

Install the horseshoe shaped U joint retaining ring, making sure it is fully seated. Engage the parking lock pawl in the ratchet wheel.

Install U joint using a replacer if necessary to insure a snug fit against the ring. Fasten with the flat washer, lockwasher and drilled ¾″ bolt. Fig. 162. Be sure drilled passage in bolt is clear. Tighten to 30-35 ft lbs.

Install and adjust the inner torque ball retainer, paper shims, outer torque

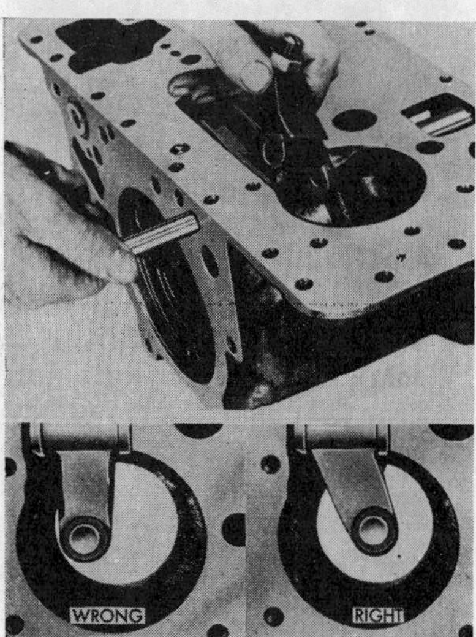

Fig. 155—Installing Reverse Anchor

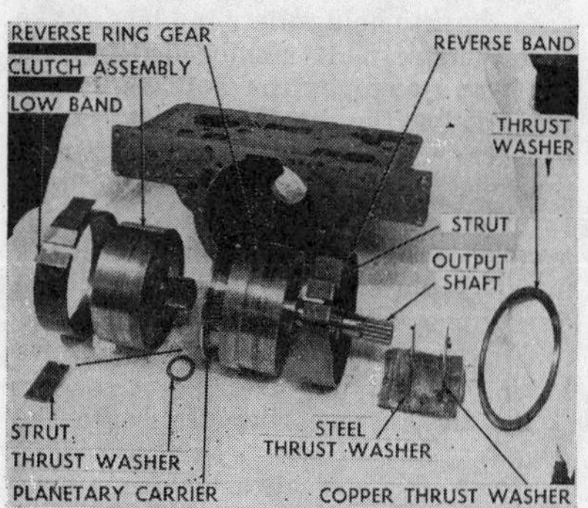

Fig. 156—Layout of Transmission Parts

Fig. 157—Installing Rear Oil Pump Plate

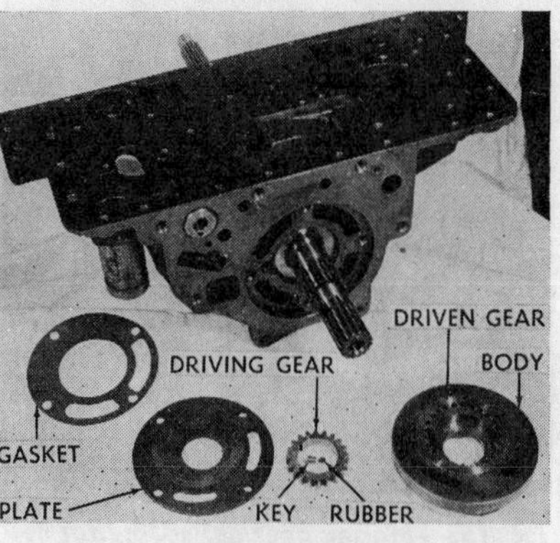

Fig. 158—Rear Oil Pump Parts

Fig. 159—Rear Oil Pump Tightening Sequence—showing match marks

Fig. 160—Installing Ratchet Wheel

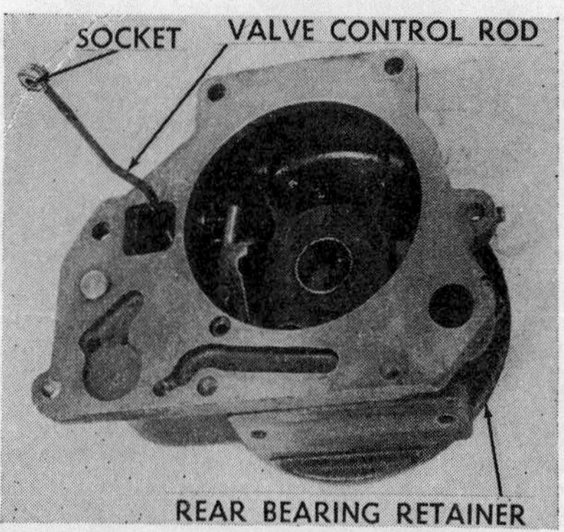

Fig. 161—Valve Control Rod Socket Faces bottom of Transmission

ball retainer, and thrust plate to 15-25 lbs drag with a leverage of 14⅜″. Adding and subtracting paper shims as necessary. Use a wood club in the U joint to move the pieces while tightening to be sure torque ball is not binding nor loose. See Figs. 163 and 164. If it binds as bolts are tightened, tap the outer retainer lightly at several points which may relieve the condition; if not, add more shims.

Install torque ball boot. Turn the large end back over the small end. Engage rib in small end in groove on flange of torque ball, then turn large end forward to engage rear end of outer retainer.

LOW AND REVERSE BAND ADJUSTMENT

Note: After overhaul the following adjustment must be very carefully performed since it is not possible to readjust the bands after transmission is installed in the car except on early models equipped with a floor pan unless holes for the purpose are cut in the floor.

a. Loosen lock nut and turn band adjusting screw clockwise until considerable resistance is felt indicating band is tightening.

b. Back off screw until just a trace of play can be felt by prying upon lever at the locknut with a screw driver. **Now** back off screw 6 (six) complete turns and tighten lock nut.

c. Noting position of screw slot, tighten lock nut to 20-25 ft lbs and check that the screw did not turn too.

d. Install the band adjustment hole covers with new gaskets.

Note: Normally if the operation of the car indicates the bands are not holding they should be renewed.

Fig. 162—U Joint Attaching Parts and Torque Ball

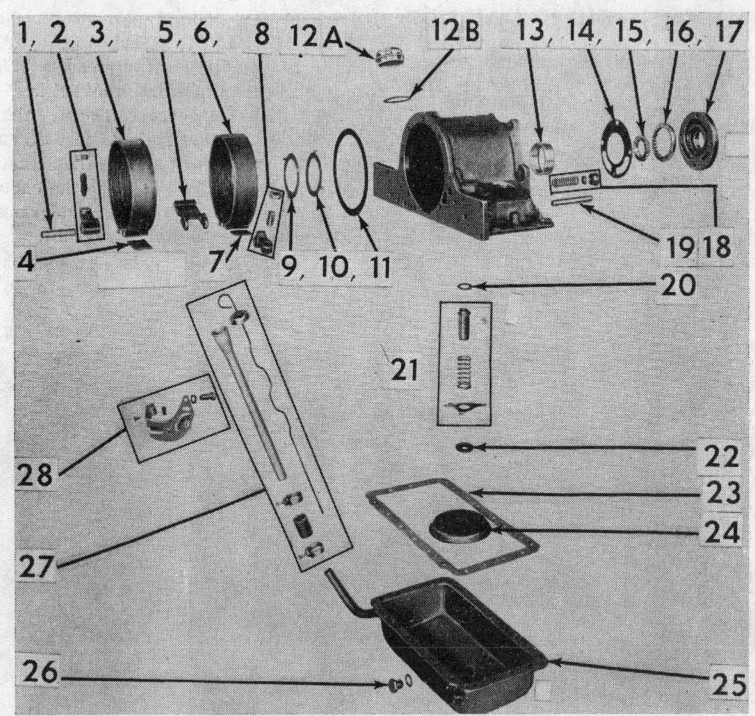

Exploded View. Transmission Case, Bands, Rear Pump

1. Low band anchor shaft.
2. Low band anchor assembly.
3. Low band assembly.
4. Low band strut.
5. Reverse band lever.
6. Reverse band.
7. Reverse band strut.
8. Reverse band anchor assembly.
9. Steel thrust washer (to planetary carrier).
10. Copper thrust washer (to case).
11. Thrust washer (reverse ring gear to case).

12a. Band adjusting hole cover.
12b. Band adjusting hole cover gasket.

13. Bushing (case for carrier journal).
14. Rear oil pump plate.
15. Rear oil pump driving gear.
16. Rear oil pump driven gear.
17. Rear oil pump body.
18. Lubrication oil pressure valve assembly.
19. Reverse band lever shaft.
20. Seal (suction pipe to valve body).
21. Suction pipe assembly.
22. Seal suction pipe to oil screen.
23. Gasket (transmission oil pan).
24. Oil screen.
25. Transmission oil pan.
26. Transmission drain plug.
27. Transmission filler pipe assembly.
28. Filler pipe support assembly.

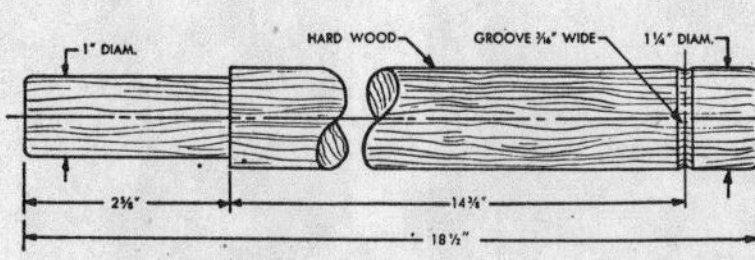

Fig. 163—Chart for Adjusting Torque Ball

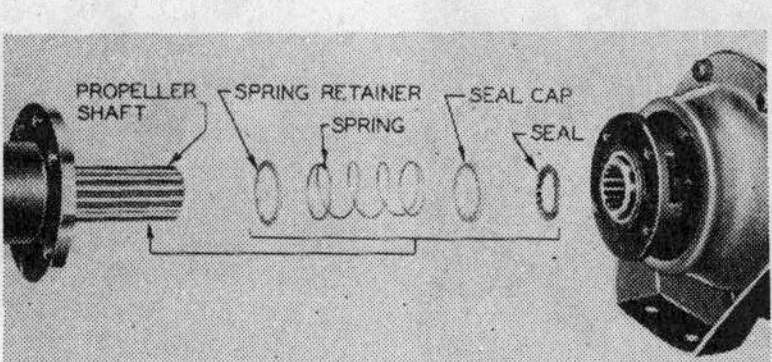

Propeller shaft oil seal

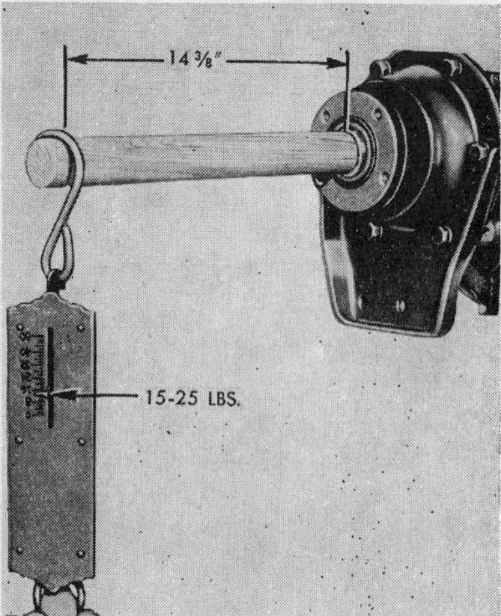

Fig. 164—Checking Torque Ball Drag

FRONT OIL PUMP FAILURE

When the front oil pump or its oil seal fails, it is necessary that the runout of the primary pump hub be checked. The runout of this hub is dependent on the flatness of the primary pump locating face of the flywheel. It is best therefore to check the runout of the flywheel first.

To do this make a set-up similar to that shown in Fig. 165. Runout of the flywheel face should not exceed .008" FULL INDICATOR READING. If the runout is greater, try tapping the high side with a lead mallet. Should this fail to bring about a correct reading, then a new flywheel must be installed. Do not neglect to check for burrs at the attaching bolt holes which might be the cause of the runout. Be sure to hold crankshaft end play in toward the front.

When the runout of the flywheel has been brought within the limit, then install the primary pump to it, using the 3 or 6 flywheel attaching bolts and tightening according to the sequence shown in Fig. 96 to 25-30 ft-lbs. Install also the bell housing, fastening it tightly in place.

Using a set-up like that shown in Fig. 166, check the runout of the primary pump hub. It must not exceed .012" FULL INDICATOR READING. If the

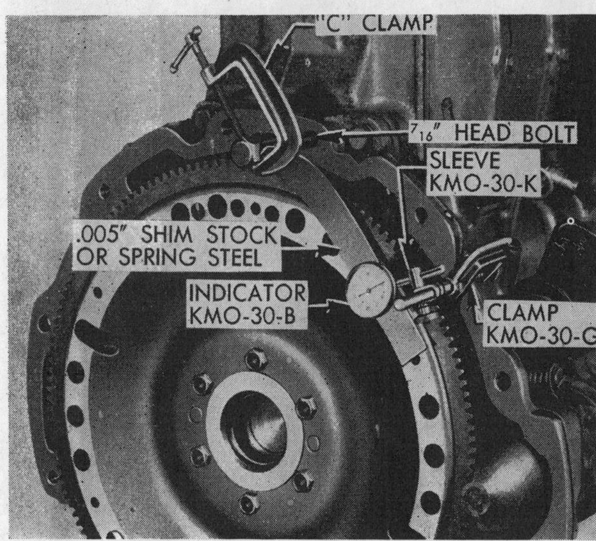

Fig. 165—Checking Runout of Flywheel

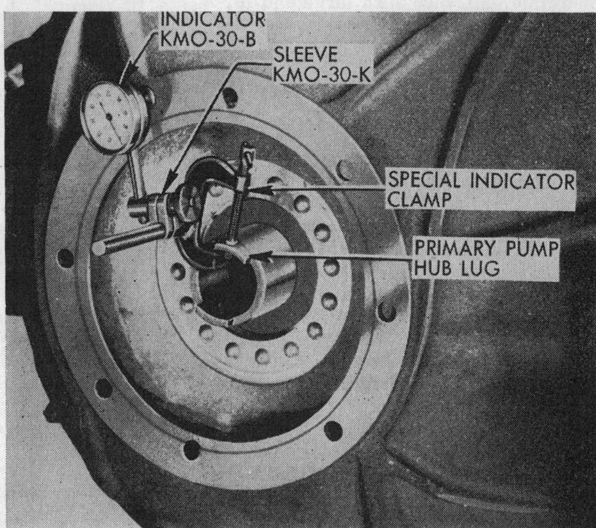

Fig. 167—Checking Runout of Rear Face of Housing

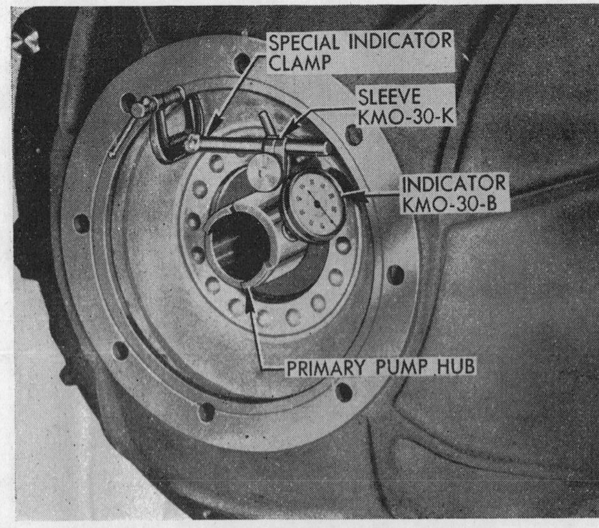

Fig. 166—Checking Runout of Primary Pump Hub

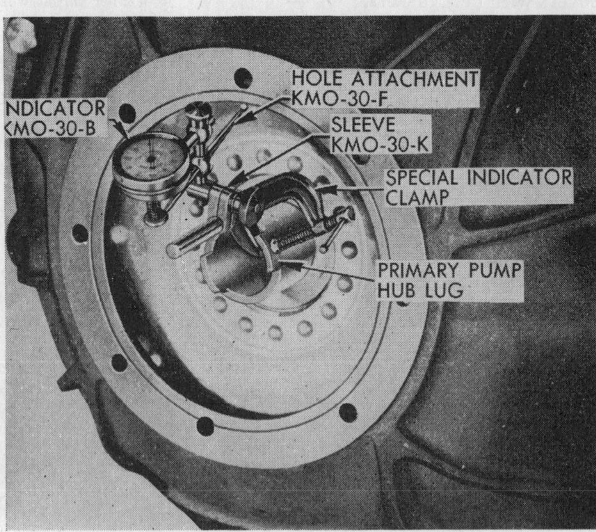

Fig. 168—Checking Runout of Pilot Hole in Housing

runout is greater, then unbolt the primary pump and revolve its position on the flywheel 180 degrees; refasten it and recheck the runout. If the figure is still too large, the primary pump will have to be replaced. The runout of the new pump hub will have to be checked in the same manner. If the runout of the primary pump hub is within the limit, make set-ups similar to those shown in Figs. 167 and 168. Runout of the rear face of the bell housing with reference to the primary pump hub must not exceed .005" FULL INDICATOR READING, while that of the pilot hole must not exceed .004" FULL INDICATOR READING. Clamp only to the driving lug as shown.

If either of these figures is exceeded, it will be necessary to replace or relocate the bell housing.

Note 1. The front oil pump seal and the oil pump itself cannot tolerate runouts greater than those given for any appreciable length of time.

Note 2. There is a tendency for the primary pump hub to wear into an hourglass shape. This condition is easily found with a straight edge and requires that the primary pump be replaced with a new one.

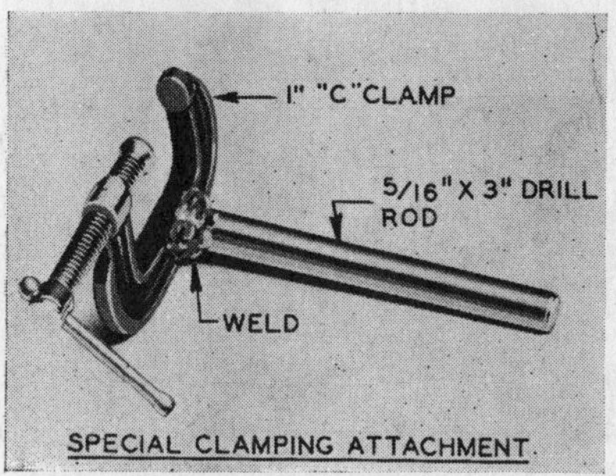

Fig. 169—Type of Clamp used in alignment procedure

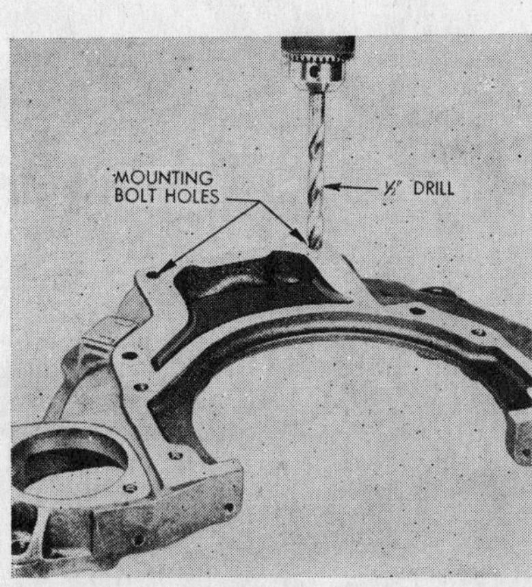

Enlarging Bolt Holes in Housing

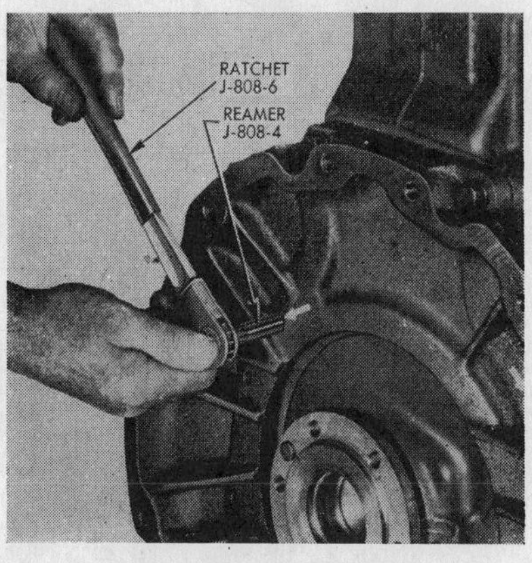

Reaming Dowel Pin Holes

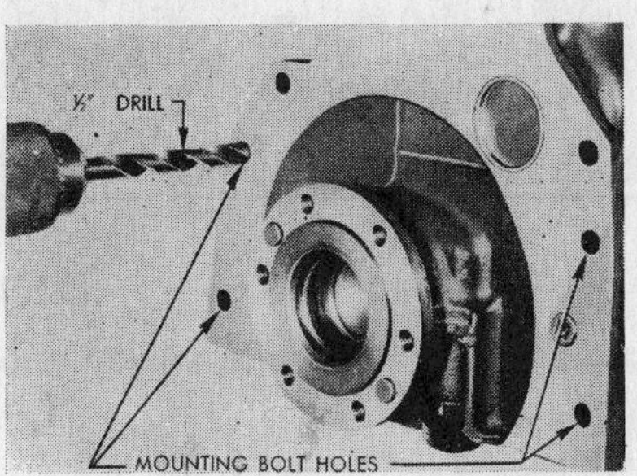

Enlarging Bolt Holes in Crankcase Flange

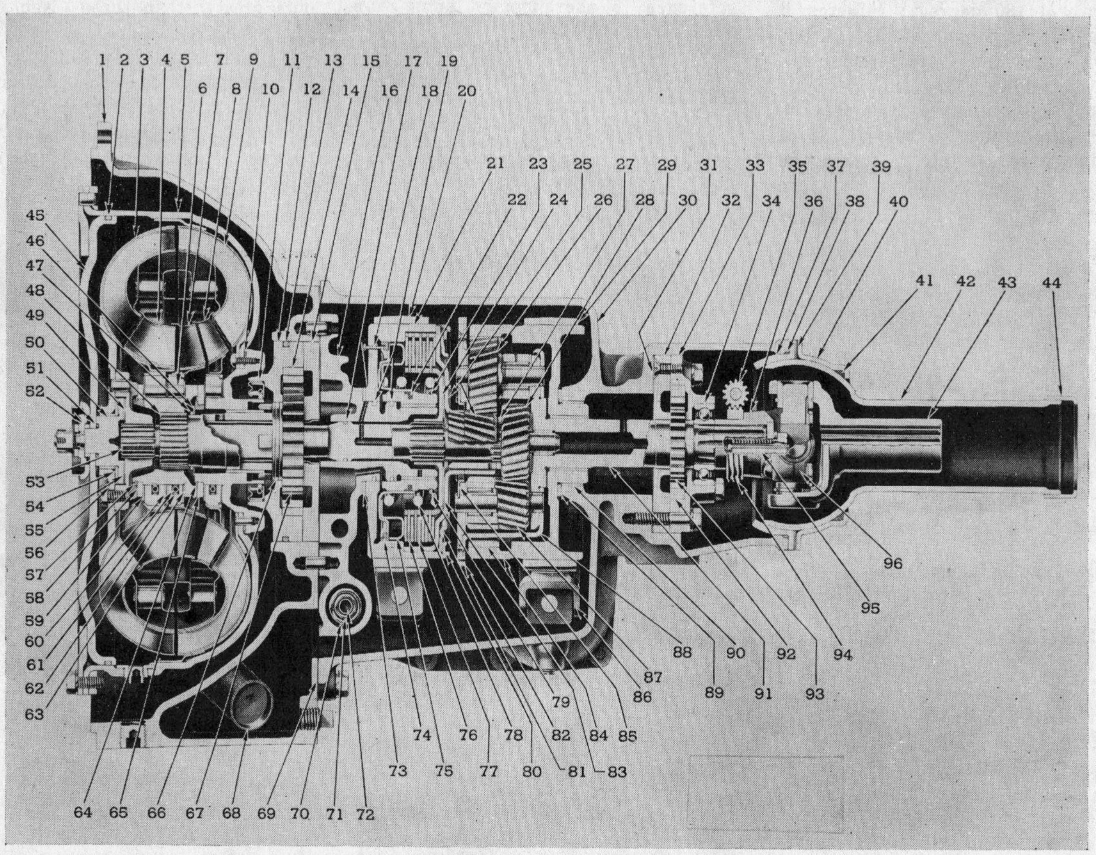

Fig. 1—Cross sectional view—Powerglide transmission—all models thru 1952

1. Bell housing
2. "O" ring seal
3. Turbine
4. Secondary stator
5. Primary pump
6. Stator freewheel clutch assembly
7. Primary stator
8. Secondary pump
9. Primary pump
10. "O" ring seal
11. Oil seal
12. Transmission front oil pump body
13. "O" ring seal
14. Oil pump driven gear
15. Reactor shaft flange
16. Valve body
17. Input shaft oil ring
18. Clutch vent valve
19. Oil rings
20. Low band
21. Low drum
22. Clutch piston inner seal
23. Snap ring
24. Clutch hub
25. Low sun gear flange
26. Short planetary pinion
27. Low sun gear thrust washer (selected)
28. Reverse sun gear
29. Reverse band
30. Transmission case
31. Transmission rear oil pump gasket
32. Oil pump cover
33. Oil pump body
34. Ball bearing
35. Speedometer driven gear
36. U joint front yoke hub
37. Ball joint front half
38. "O" ring seal
39. Shims
40. Ball joint rear half
41. Cork seal
42. Ball tube
43. U joint rear yoke hub
44. Ball tube packing retainer
45. Primary pump cover
46. Thrust washer
47. Primary pump hub retaining ring
48. Reactor shaft (stator support)
49. Turbine hub
50. Turbine bolt
51. "O" ring seal
52. Slotted washer
53. Input shaft
54. Thick thrust washer
55. Thin thrust washer
56. Lockplate
57. Snap ring
58. Thrust washer
59. Retainer washer
60. Retainer washers
61. Freewheel clutch spring
62. Freewheel clutch cage
63. Freewheel clutch race
64. Secondary pump retaining ring
65. Thrust washer
66. Transmission front oil pump drive gear seal ring
67. Oil pump drive gear
68. Oil suction pipe screen
69. Gasket
70. Accumulator outer spring
71. Accumulator inner spring
72. Accumulator piston stop
73. Thrust washer valve body to clutch
74. Clutch piston outer seal
75. Clutch piston
76 & 77. Clutch plates
78. Clutch spring
79. Spring retainer
80. Retaining ring
81. Retainer
82. Parking lock ratchet gear
83. Clutch hub thrust washer
84. Reverse ring gear
85. Pinion shaft lock plate
86. Reverse band mechanism
87. Long planetary pinion
88. Planetary carrier
89. Ring gear thrust washer
90. Bushing
91. Output shaft
92. Rear oil pump drive gear
93. Oil pump drive gear
94. Speedometer drive gear
95. U joint front yoke retaining bolt
96. Universal joint assembly

THE CHEVROLET POWERGLIDE TRANSMISSION

The Chevrolet Powerglide is a completely automatic hydraulic transmission. It is operated hydraulically and has no electrical connections of any sort. Oil pressure acting under the control of various mechanically operated valves applies and releases the low and reverse gear bands, engages and disengages the direct drive clutch, and cushions all gear changes.

The control valves are operated by mechanical linkages terminating in the lever on the steering column, and the engine intake manifold.

On 1953 models linkages also run to the carburetor throttle valve and a flying weight type of governor.

Absolutely nothing electrical is involved.

GENERAL INFORMATION

OIL REQUIREMENTS

Measure oil, engine idling, transmission hot, hand lever at Neutral.

Automatic transmission fluid Type A.

Note: Quality should be at least equal to Armour Institute Qualifying Number AQ-ATF No. (*) for automatic transmission fluids.

*—Last number varies with different refiners. Designation and number are embossed on can.

Oil should be changed every 15,000 mi.

OIL CAPACITY

In refilling put 3 qts in, start engine, add the balance.

	All Models thru 1952	1953 Models
Drain and refill..	9 qts	10 qts
Refill—dry	10 qts	11 qts

GAGE ROD

Quantity between add oil and full on gage rod ... 1 qt

FRONT OIL PUMP

Driven by ....engine
Cuts out at ....15-20 mph

REAR OIL PUMP

Driven by ....Output Shaft

CLUTCH PLATES

Driving (Internally splined—faced) ....4 used
Driven (Externally splined—dished thru '52, waved for '53) ....5 used

REVERSE BAND ADJUSTMENT

Should not be adjusted with transmission in the car.

Tighten all the way then back off 2¾ turns and tighten lock nut to 20-25 ft lbs.

LOW BAND ADJUSTMENT

Can be adjusted with transmission in place.

Tighten all the way then back off three turns and tighten lock nut to 20-25 ft lbs.

THERMOSTAT

A thermostat between the transmission and the oil cooler is set to maintain the temperature of the oil in the unit at 240°.

1953 POWERGLIDE DIFFERENCES FROM PREVIOUS MODELS

Converter has Three Parts instead of Five.
Converter no longer retained on Reactor Shaft.
Number of Control Valves increased as listed under Hydraulic Controls.
Clutch Piston is ¼" smaller.
Clutch Plates are Waved instead of being Dished. Direction of Pile Up does not matter.
Size and shape of Struts changed.
Input Shaft has two Oil Seal Rings instead of One and Carries a snap ring around the rear portion of the front splines to restrict forward float.
Throttle Position and Car Speed have an effect on operation in addition to Manual Lever Position and Engine Vacuum.
Oil capacity increased one quart.

HYDRAULIC SYSTEM VALVES

Modulator valve....Varies oil pressure in response to intake vacuum
Pressure regulator valve....Varies pressure due to control and modulator valves
Manual control valve....Controlled by hand lever
Clutch pressure relief valve ....Drains the clutch
Thermostatic valve....Controls oil temperatures
Lubrication by-pass valve....Controls lubrication pressure
Pressure relief valve....Limits maximum pressure
Accumulator....Cushions shifts between Low Drive and Reverse
Pump check valve....Prevents loss of prime
Converter pressure regulator valve ....(On 1953 Models) Limits pressure within the converter to 43-58 psi
Pressure regulator governor valve ....(On 1953 Models) Holds line pressure to a minimum when in drive
High clutch low servo valve....(On 1953 Models) Cushions the automatic downshift
Governor valve....(On 1953 Models) Determines the automatic up shift point in conjunction with car speed
Throttle valve....(On 1953 Models) Modulates control pressure in step with accelerator position

CLEARANCES

End play of the turbine bolt ....002"-.016" FIR
Runout of the primary pump face ....not over .010" FIR
End play of low sun gear flange in Low Drum ......not over .013"
End play of clutch assembly on input shaft ....007"-.035"
Oil Pumps
Driven gear to body...001" -.002"
Gear backlash ....003" -.005"
Driven gear to crescent ....002" -.005"
Driving gear to crescent ....005" -.006"
Gear end play........0005"-.0015"

TORQUE SPECIFICATIONS

Primary pump to hub.....4½ ft lbs
Cover to primary pump..15-20 ft lbs
Turbine bolt (do not back off to install cotter pin)..12½ ft lbs min
Drive flange to turbine..12½-15 ft lbs
Modulator cover and assembly to case ....12½-15 ft lbs
Servo cover to case....12½-15 ft lbs
Rear pump assembly to case ....12½-15 ft lbs
Ball joint collar to case.12½-15 ft lbs
Transmission case to housing ....15-20 ft lbs
Two bolts adjacent to regulator valve ....8 ft lbs
All others in valve body....10 ft lbs
Universal joint assembly to output shaft........25-30 ft lbs
Speedometer driven gear to case ....45-50 ft lbs
Band lock nut ....20-25 ft lbs
Pinion shaft lock plate to carrier screws ....2½-3 ft lbs

MATCH POINTS

The following points should be marked on disassembly so that they can be reassambled in the same relative position from which they were removed:

Flywheel to Primary Pump Cover

Primary Pump Cover to Primary Pump

Pinion Shaft to Pinion Carrier

Front Portion of Carrier to Rear Portion of Carrier

Bands to Case

Starting the Car When Starter Is Inoperative

ALWAYS PUSH THE CAR TO START THE ENGINE WHEN THE STARTER IS NOT WORKING. TOWING TO START IS DANGEROUS AS THE CAR WILL PROBABLY PICK UP SPEED AND RAM THE TOW CAR BEFORE IT CAN BE PUT IN NEUTRAL.

In pushing to start hold the Hand Lever in NEUTRAL until car speed reaches 15 mph. Then shift to LOW and the engine will turn. If traction is poor hold it in Neutral until car speed reaches 20 mph and then shift into DRIVE. After engine catches shift to Neutral to permit it to warm up.

Towing the Car

When the hand lever is in Neutral the car may be towed. When the rear wheels are on the ground Neutral is the ONLY position that can be used for towing.

Speed in Tow should never exceed 45 mph.

To place the transmission in Neutral when the hand lever is inoperative:

1. Remove the cotter pin and disconnect the long control rod at the bell crank on the left side of the transmission case.

2. Push the bell crank as far rearward as it will go. (This will be Reverse.) Now move it forward to the third detent which will be Neutral. Naturally if the Transmission is locked up the car must not be moved on its rear wheels unless the drive shaft is disconnected at the universal joint.

Check Oil Level

The oil level should be checked every 1000 miles. For an accurate check, the transmission must be warm, the engine idling, and the hand lever at Neutral. ADD OIL ONLY WHEN THE LEVEL IS BELOW THE ADD 1 QT. MARK. Wipe off the filler cap before removing. Add only oil bearing an AQ-ATF number embossed on the can. If the oil is consistently low, inspect for leaks. If there are no visible leaks check the rear axle lubricant level. The propeller shaft seal at the universal joint may be passing transmission fluid. After installing new seal be sure to drain and renew the differential lubricant.

Drain and Refill

The oil in the Powerglide transmission must be renewed every 15,000 miles. To do this it is necessary to:

Turn back the floor mat and remove the toe pan plate.

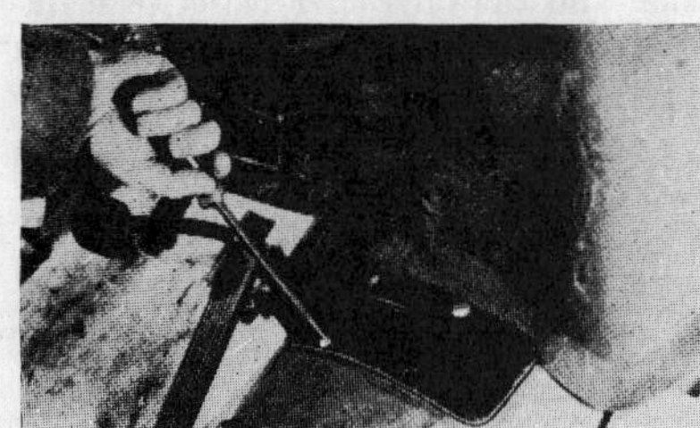

Fig. 2—Removing toe pan plate

Rotate the engine until one of the two converter drain plugs is in line with the access hole in the housing.

Remove the plug with a 3/16″ Allen wrench. **DO NOT DROP PLUG INTO HOUSING.**

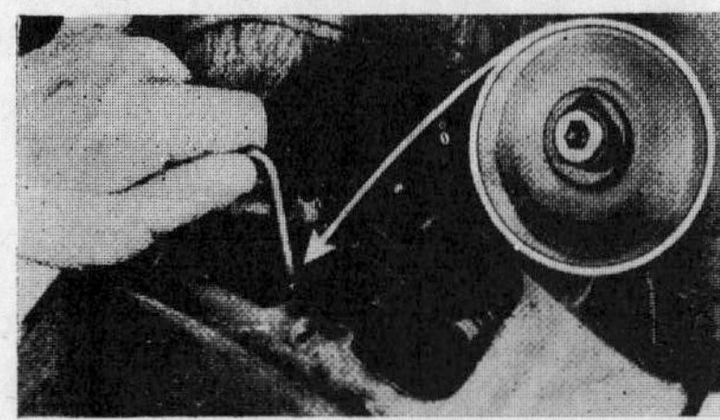

Fig. 3—Removing upper converter drain plug

With the drain plug hole lined up with access hole at top of housing remove drain plug at bottom of housing.

Reach through this hole and remove the other converter drain plug with a 3/16″ Allen wrench.

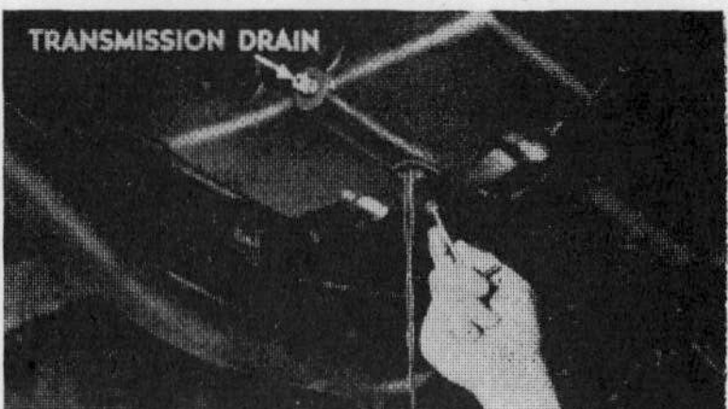

Fig. 4—Removing lower converter drain plug

Note: It is possible that the vacuum devices used to remove oil from engine crankcase could be used to suck the oil from the converter unit, thus saving a lot of trouble.

Note: The converter drain plugs are installed very tightly.

Remove plug at rear of central section of transmission to drain powerglide's sump.

Replace the drain plugs, toe pan, and mat. Put in three quarts of automatic transmission fluid Type A. Be sure the quality control number of approval by the Armour Research Foundation known as the AQ-ATF number is embossed on the can.

Start the engine and idle it in **NEUTRAL.** (Transmission gets very little lubrication in PARK.) Add six quarts more through the filler pipe. **Note:** The transmission has no air vent other than through the filler pipe, pour the oil in a thin stream so displaced air can come out.

When transmission is warm (idle for 15 minutes in Neutral) check the oil level.

Manual Linkage Adjustment

Check that clearance between the hand control lever and the shaft support bracket at the top of the steering column is between 3/32″ and ⅛″. If it is not:

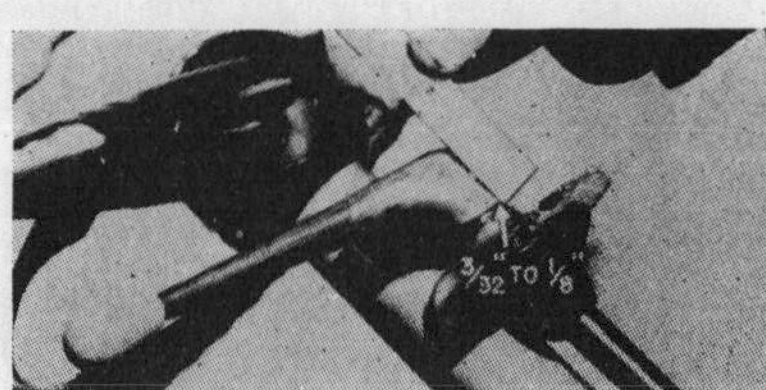

Fig. 5—3/32″ to ⅛″ clearance between lever and bracket

Remove two screws and dial assembly with cover. Remove two screws holding the shaft upper support to the column. Turn the support to procure

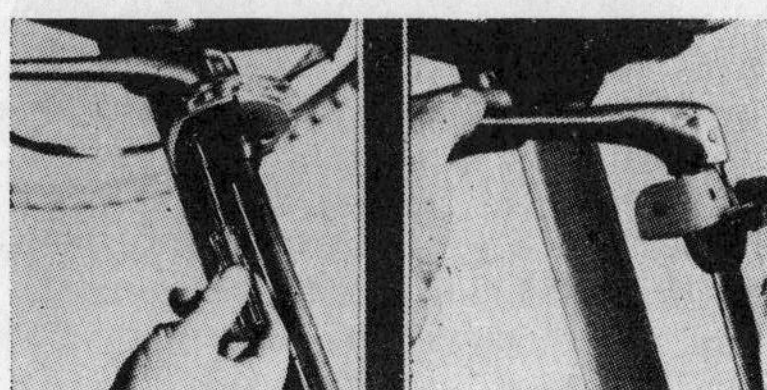

Fig. 6—Adjusting bracket

the desired clearance. Fasten everything back in place.

Place hand control lever in Reverse and check that distance from the knob to the steering wheel rim is 1½" plus or minus 5/16". If it is not:

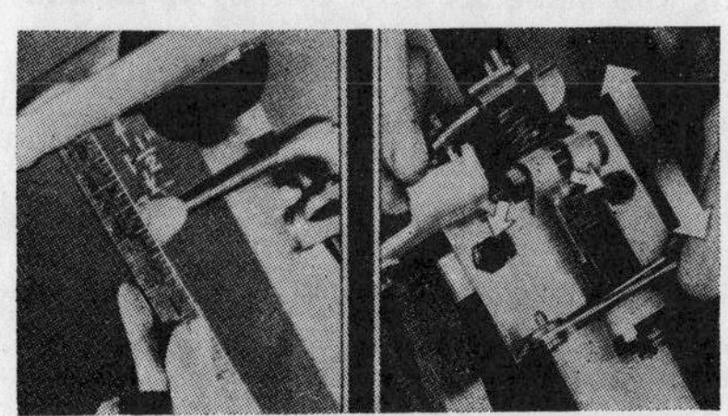

Fig. 7—1½" plus or minus 5/16", knob to wheel rim

Loosen the clamp bolts holding the shaft support at the bottom of the steering column and slide the assembly up or down to give the correct clearance. Retighten the clamp bolts.

With hand lever still in Reverse,

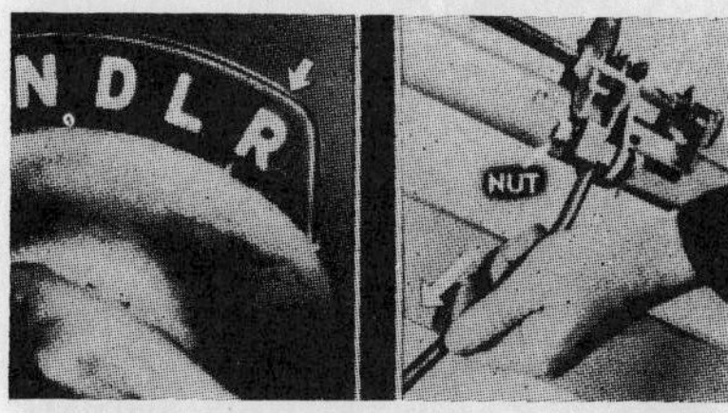

Fig. 8—Detaching shift control rod at lever

loosen the nut holding the shift control rod to the swivel and lever at the bottom of the shifting shaft. Push the rod as far rearward as possible, to as-

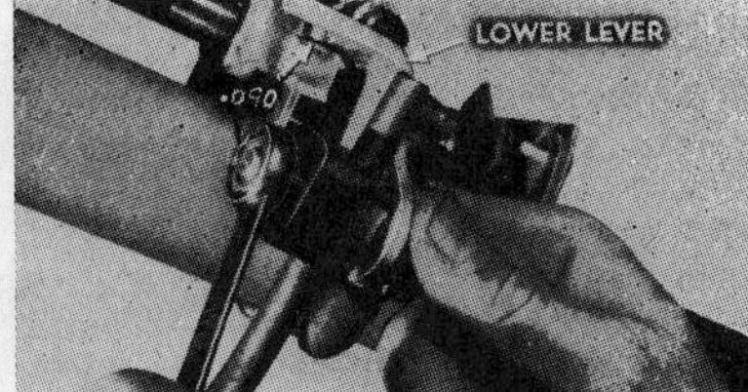

Fig. 9—.090" clearance, lever to stop

sure that the manual valve outside control lever at the rear of the transmission is truly in reverse. Then move the swivel and lever at the end of the shifting shaft until there is .090" clearance between the lever and the stop on its support. Still holding the rod rearward, tighten the nut which holds it to the swivel and lever.

Adjusting Neutral Safety Switch

Place hand lever in neutral and loosen the two switch mounting screws. Move the switch bracket so that a snug fitting pin can be inserted through the two locating holes. Tighten the screws to hold the switch securely and remove the pin.

Fig. 10—Adjusting neutral safety switch

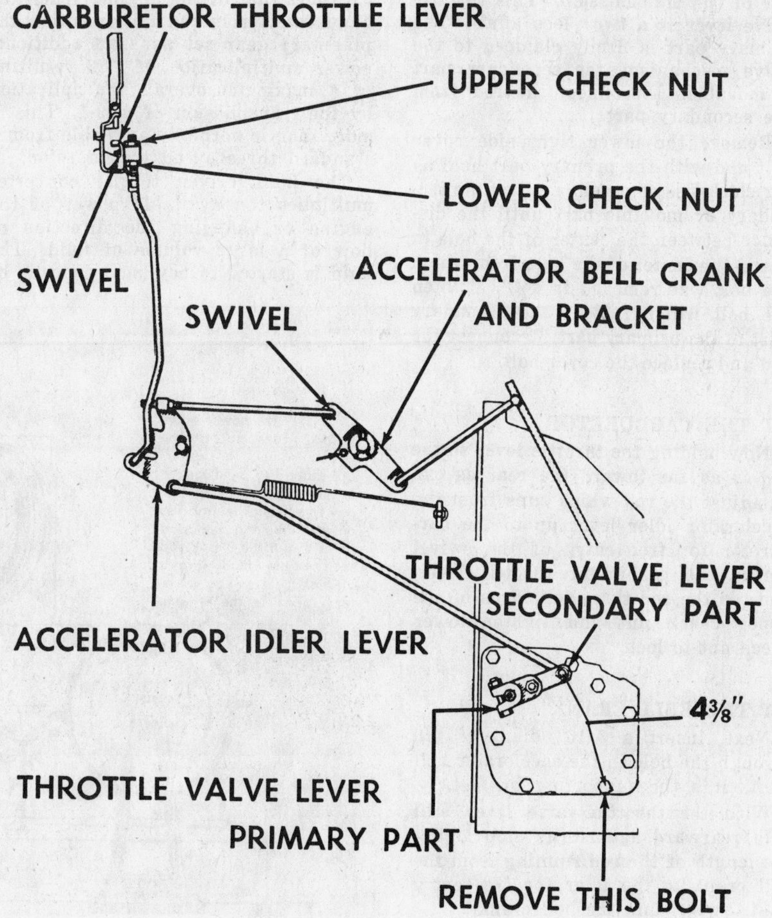

Fig. 11—Adjusting throttle valve linkage—1953 models

Adjustment of Throttle Valve Linkage, 1953 Models

See Illustration on Preceeding Page

Adjustment of the throttle valve linkage to provide correct relationship between the accelerator pedal, the carburetor throttle valve and the throttle valve in the low drive body is accomplished by the following procedure:

With engine and transmission warm, place hand control lever in Drive. Set the hand brake and adjust engine idle to 425 rpm.

Note: Automatic choke must be entirely off and throttle stop screw against low step on fast idle cam.

AT THE TRANSMISSION

Disconnect the rod running from the accelerator idler lever to the throttle valve lever on the lower left front corner of the transmission. This throttle valve lever is a two piece affair. The primary part is firmly clamped to the valve mechanism, the secondary part is movable. Disconnect the rod from the secondary part.

Remove the lower right side cover bolt and with the primary part held as far clockwise as possible adjust the secondary or movable part until the distance between the center of the hole in it and the center of the hole from which the bolt was removed is 4⅜″. Tighten the bolt which fastens the secondary part to the primary part. Reconnect the rod and replace the cover bolt.

AT THE CARBURETOR

Now holding the throttle lever so the rod is as far toward the rear as can be adjust the rod which runs from the accelerator idler lever up to the carburetor for free entry of the swivel pin in the carburetor throttle lever. Shorten the rod three full turns of the upper check nut and tighten lower check nut to lock.

AT THE BELL CRANK

Next, insert a 3/16″ diameter pin through the hole in the accelerator bell crank into the supporting bracket.

With the throttle valve lever still held rearward against its stop adjust the length of the rod running from the bell crank to the idler for free entry of its swivel into the bell crank.

Hold swivel from turning and lock check nut securely.

THEORY AND OPERATION OF THE POWERGLIDE TRANSMISSION

ALL MODELS THRU 1952

The Powerglide transmission employs a torque converter together with a multiple disc clutch, and a planetary gear set. The torque converter provides a smooth, shockless, multiplication of engine power suitable to all normal driving requirements. The planetary gear set is used in conjunction with the multiple disc clutch to provide extra power for rough going and the necessary means for operation in reverse.

The torque converter is a fluid driven device which multiplies the power output of the engine by a varying amount depending on the requirements. The maximum output of the converter is 2.2 times that of the engine. When the hand lever is in the Low position the planetary gear set adds an additional power multiplication of 1.82 resulting in a maximum overall multiplication by the transmission of 4.09-1. This is more than is normally available from a standard three speed transmission.

The fluid driven torque converter multiplies the available power of the engine by changing the direction of flow of a large volume of fluid. The fluid is started to flowing by means of the primary pump. The primary pump is the largest portion of the converter and together with its cover it forms a housing for the rest of the converter parts.

Being fastened directly to the flywheel of the engine the primary pump turns whenever the engine turns. As the primary pump turns so does the fluid with which it is filled.

The curved blades of the pump throw the fluid against the turbine. Hitting the blades of the turbine the fluid curves down and around to exit in a direction opposed to the direction from which it entered. As the fluid comes out of the turbine it strikes a double set of blades known as the secondary and primary stators. These change the direction of flow of the fluid back into the direction of rotation of the primary pump.

The result of this U turn enforced on the fluid is a kick-back force against the turbine which tends to increase its torque output. This kick-back force is the same as that felt by a fireman directing the flow of water from a hose against the side of a building.

When the turbine is stationary the fluid passes through it and the stators and so back to the pump with almost as much energy as when it started. This energy is added to the energy being given the fluid by the primary pump and provides the high initial torque necessary to start the car moving.

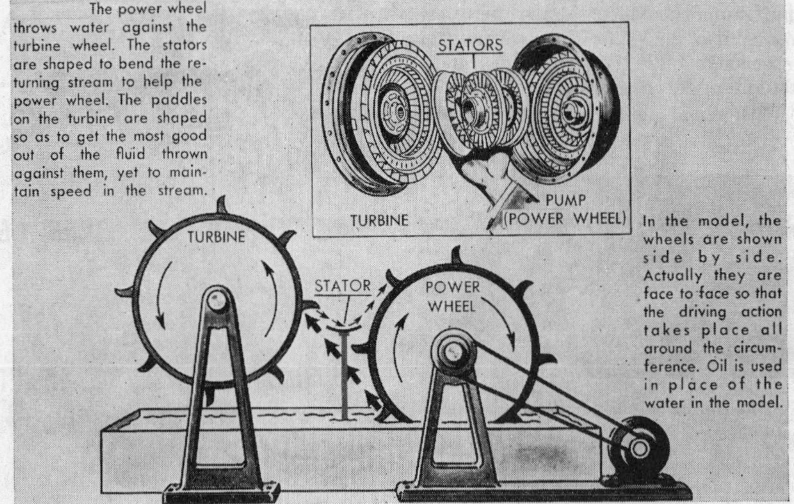

The power wheel throws water against the turbine wheel. The stators are shaped to bend the returning stream to help the power wheel. The paddles on the turbine are shaped so as to get the most good out of the fluid thrown against them, yet to maintain speed in the stream.
STATORS
TURBINE
PUMP (POWER WHEEL)
In the model, the wheels are shown side by side. Actually they are face to face so that the driving action takes place all around the circumference. Oil is used in place of the water in the model.
TURBINE
STATOR
POWER WHEEL

Fig. 12—Operational theory of a torque converter

As long as high torque is required the flow of fluid is large in volume. When the speed of the turbine produces an output speed satisfactory to the operation of the car the volume of fluid flowing from the primary pump to the turbine and back falls off. As a result of this the mass of fluid in the converter spins as a unit in the form of a fluid flywheel. The decrease in fluid flow permits the stators to idle in free wheeling so that they spin with the solid unit of fluid which is being carried around by the centrifugal force imparted to the whole deal by the engine. Under these conditions a change in the shape of the primary pump blades would be advantageous. This change is approached by the design of the secondary pump which freewheels when the fluid flow is large but helps to pick up fluid and feed it into the primary pump whenever the flow volume decreases.

The stators are mounted on free-wheeling clutches which permit them to revolve in the same direction as that of the primary pump but lock against any counter rotation. The free wheel clutches are mounted on a race which is keyed to a hollow shaft called the reactor shaft which in turn supports the transmission front oil pump. The secondary pump is mounted on a similar free wheeling clutch. This clutch, however, is carried on a bearing surface which is part of the hub of the primary pump. Slots in the rear of this hub are utilized to drive the transmission front oil pump.

The power put out by the turbine is carried into the multiple disc clutch and planetary gear set of the transmission by the input shaft. The input shaft passing freely through the reactor shaft has splined to its rear end the reverse sun gear and just forward of that the hub of the multiple disc clutch.

The internally splined plates of the multiple disc clutch mesh with the hub so that these plates, the hub and the input shaft function as a unit. The alternately placed externally splined plates of the clutch, however, mesh with splines in the low drum. The low drum is keyed to the low sun gear which is in constant contact with the short pinion gears of the planetary gear set. Within the planetary gear set is the reverse sun gear already keyed to the input shaft and in constant contact with these same pinion gears by means of the long pinion gears.

Thus we have two systems directly connected to the input shaft. The first is that originating at the clutch hub

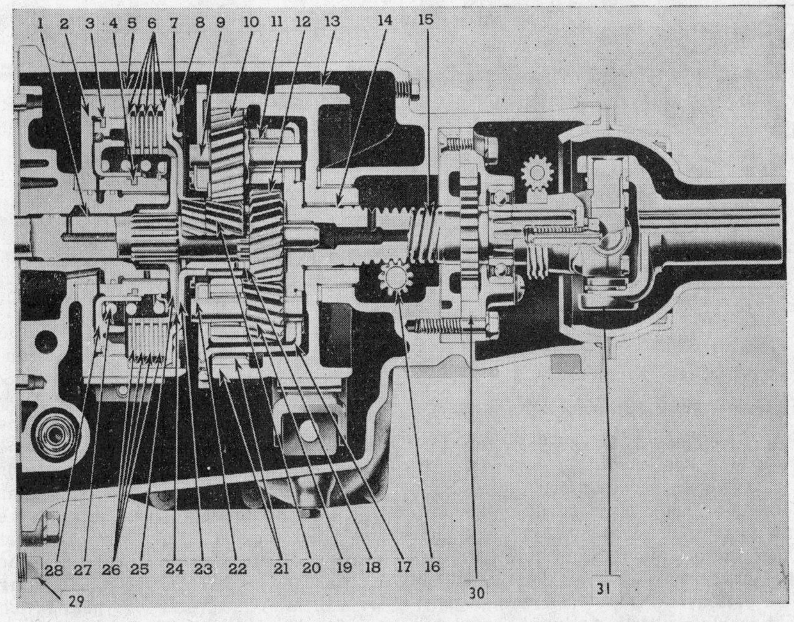

Fig. 13—Cross section of transmission case 1953 models

1. Input shaft
2. Low drum
3. Clutch piston outer seal
4. Clutch piston inner seal
5. Low band
6. Clutch driven plates
7. Low sun gear flange retainer
8. Retainer ring
9. Planetary pinion pin
10. Short planetary pinion
11. Pinion bearing needles
12. Reverse sun gear
13. Reverse band
14. Output shaft
15. Governor drive gear
16. Governor driven gear
17. Planetary carrier
18. Low sun gear thrust washer (selected washer)
19. Long planetary pinion
20. Low sun gear
21. Reverse ring gear
22. Pinion shaft lock plate
23. Low sun gear flange
24. Clutch hub to flange thrust washer
25. Clutch hub
26. Drive plates
27. Clutch spring
28. Clutch piston
29. Transmission drain plug
30. Transmission rear oil pump
31. Universal joint

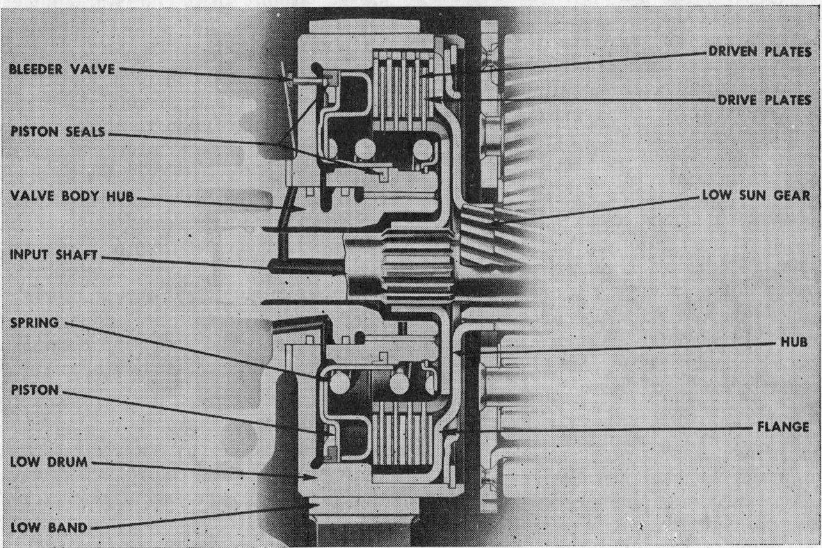

Fig. 14—Section thru multiple disc clutch

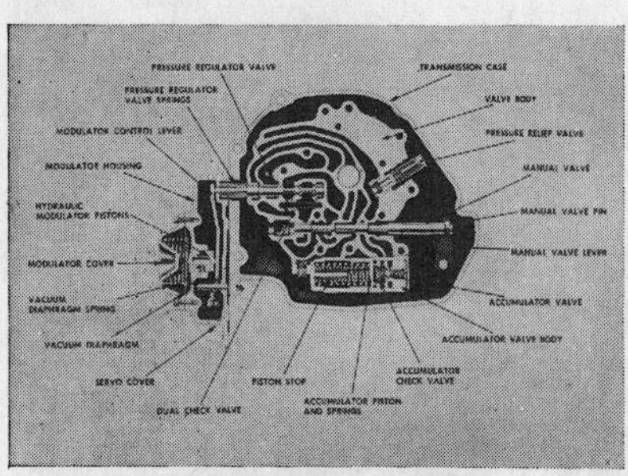

Fig. 15—Section thru valve body looking toward rear of car

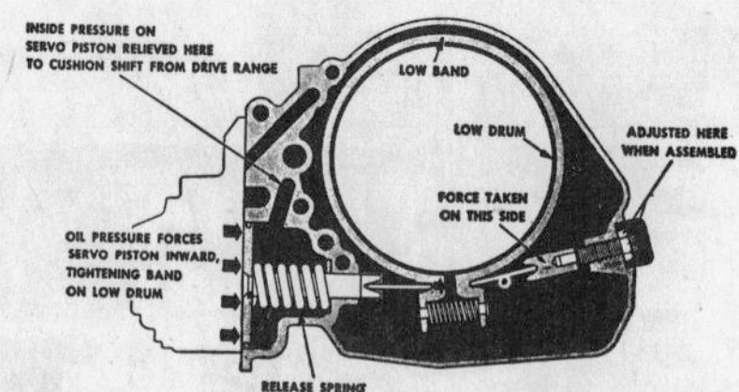

Fig. 16—Low servo mechanism

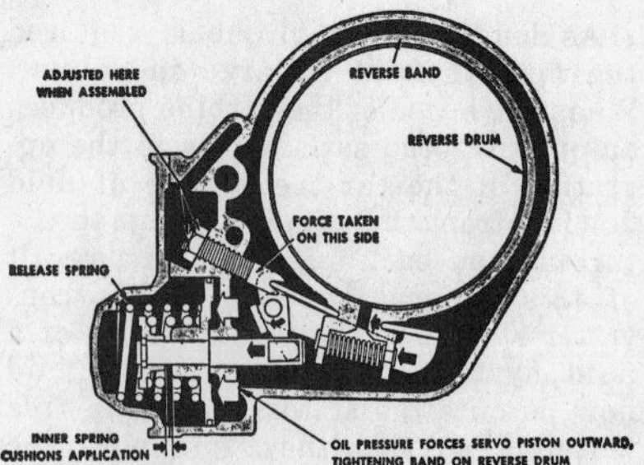

Fig. 17—Reverse servo mechanism

THEORY AND OPERATION—*cont'd*

and the second that based on the reverse sun gear.

The system based on the clutch hub permits a choice as to whether the low sun gear will revolve with the input shaft or not. Moving the hand lever to the drive position locks the multiple disc clutch and puts the low sun gear into revolution with the input shaft. As the input shaft is already connected to the reverse sun gear and since the two sun gears are interconnected by means of the planetary pinions the planetary pinions cannot turn and so the gear set procedes to revolve as a unit. The output shaft for the transmission is an integral part of the gear set and so we have direct drive from turbine to differential.

The multiple disc clutch is not engaged in any other position of the lever.

Operation of the clutch as well as operation of the servos which apply and release the low band and the reverse band is accomplished through oil pressure as supplied by the front and rear transmission oil pumps and directed by the control and modulating valves inside the transmission. Smoothness of operation is attained by the use of an accumulator which acts as a surge chamber to cushion the shock of engaging units. More positive control as demanded by road conditions is provided by a modulator unit which is acted upon by engine vacuum as well as by the hydraulic pressures called for by the manual control valve. The control and regulator valves of the system also govern the oil pressure inside the converter as well as the lubricating oil pressure.

When the hand lever is at low, oil pressure, acting thru the accumulator and the low servo, releases the clutch and applies the low band to hold the low drum stationary; which means that the low sun gear is also stationary. The reverse sun gear being splined to the input shaft as mentioned before continues to turn thus driving the long planet pinions which mesh with it. They in turn drive the short planet pinions in a direction identical with that of the input shaft. The short planet pinions now endeavor to turn the low sun gear but it is being held stationary by the low band. Unable to move it, the short pinions climb around it carrying the carrier and so the output shaft along with them. The reverse ring gear which is also in contact with the short pinions just idles around doing nothing, for nothing is supposed to be acting on it. The reduction attained by this gearing is 1.82 to 1.

When the hand lever is moved to Reverse, oil pressure acts thru the accumulator and the reverse servo to apply the reverse band thus holding the reverse ring gear stationary. The low band has been released and no longer holds the low drum and the clutch is not engaged so the low sun gear can be shoved around with no work done. Power from the input shaft acting thru the reverse sun gear drives the long planet pinions which in turn drive the short planet pinions causing them to climb around the inside of the stationary reverse ring gear carrying their shafts and so the carrier with them as before. Only this time it results in the carrier and its integral shaft turning in a direction opposite to that of the input shaft. The low sun gear gets shoved around as all this goes on but nothing comes of it, as nothing is supposed to be holding it. The reduction attained by this gearing is the same as for low; 1.82 to 1.

In addition to Drive, Low, and Reverse the hand lever provides a Neutral and a Park Position. Movement of the hand lever turns the shifter shaft running down into the engine compartment alongside the steering column. The shifter shaft terminates in the lower lever which has a swivel joint connecting it to the long shift rod. The long shift rod moves a bell crank at the rear of the transmission which in turn moves the short shift rod and so actuates the outside control lever. The outside control lever is fastened to the end of the parking lock lever shaft, an assembly which extends inside the transmission. The parking lock lever shaft carries the parking lock pawl as well as the lever which positions the control valve. The parking lock pawl carries the holding detents which position and hold the hand lever.

When the hand lever is moved to Park the parking lock pawl is forced into contact with a ratchet gear cut into the forward circumference of the planetary carrier. This locks the output shaft.

Caution: Parking range must never be entered while the car is in motion as serious damage to the transmission will result from its positive stopping of all drive shaft rotation.

Note: The movement of the hand lever which throws the parking pawl into contact with the ratchet gear is just sufficient to move the control valves so that all lubrication in the transmission case is cut off and returned to the sump. For this reason the car should never be gunned or tested for any noticeable length of time with the hand lever at Park.

Drive position is intended for all normal driving conditions. The use of the Low position is for extraordinary conditions such as sand or mud or steep grades.

By using Low and Reverse alternately the car may be rocked out of mud and ruts.

OPERATION OF THE 1953 POWERGLIDE

For 1953 the converter unit has been modified from the former five part assembly, (primary pump, turbine, secondary stator, primary stator, secondary pump,) to a three part assembly (primary pump, turbine, stator). The stator free wheels on the reactor shaft in the same manner as the two stators of the previous models.

Noting that many drivers got better acceleration by starting their cars in Low and shifting to Drive when the car speed approached 40 mph, the Chevrolet engineers have provided a governor and a series of valves to accomplish this maneuver automatically.

Although still carried as Drive on the steering column indicator the Drive range is actually an automatic range. The transmission shifts into Low whenever the car speed drops below 9 mph. Starts are made in Low even though the lever is set at Drive and the upshift occurs between 12 mph and 42 mph depending on the position of the accelerator. If the driver floors it the upshift is delayed but at approximately 42 mph the upshift occurs regardless. Similarly at any speed under 37 mph the down shift will occur if the accelerator is floored.

An additional set of linkage has been added which connects the throttle valve outer lever on the left sump cover plate into the accelerator to carburetor linkage system.

The 1953 Powerglide thus has three interrelated controls: Engine vacuum which modulates the control pressures inside the transmission. Carburetor throttle valve position which modulates the control pressure in accordance with the amount of throttle opening. Manual lever position which indicates the wishes of the driver. A governor runs off the output shaft to render the control system conscious of speed.

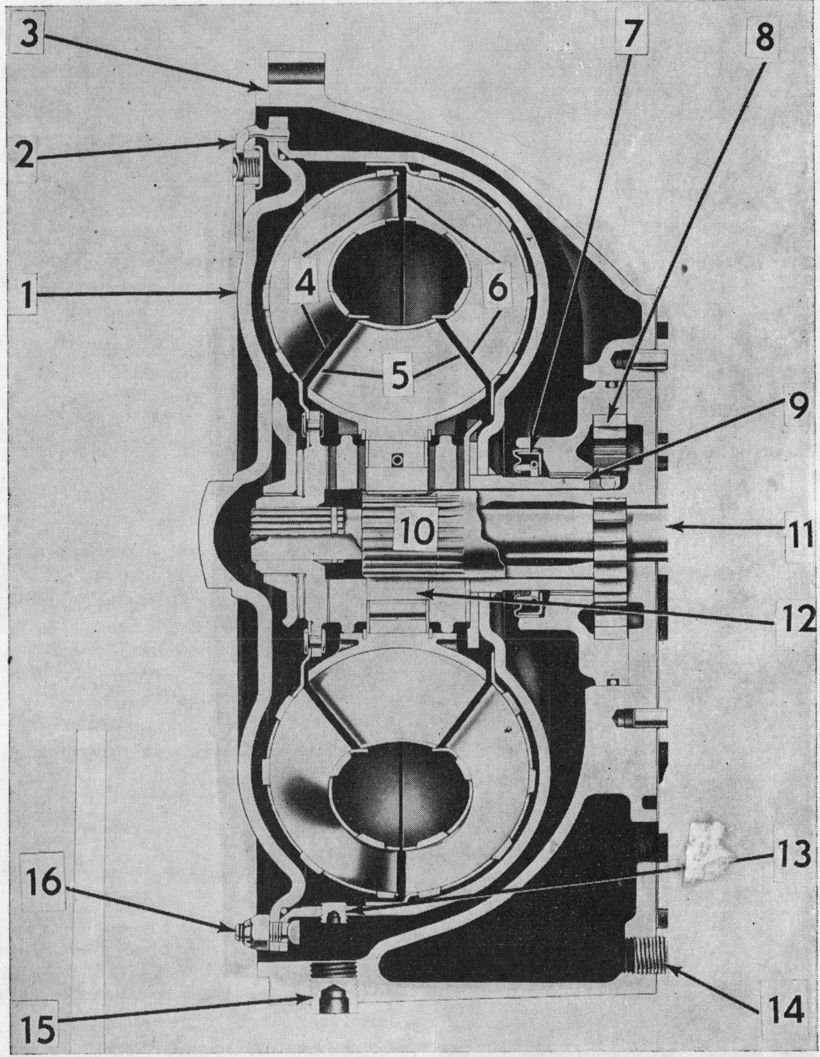

Fig. 18—Cross sectional view—torque converter—1953 models

1. Primary pump cover
2. Converter drive lug
3. Bell housing
4. Turbine assembly
5. Stator assembly
6. Primary pump assembly
7. Oil seal
8. Transmission front oil pump
9. Primary pump hub
10. Reactor shaft
11. Input shaft
12. Stator freewheel clutch assembly
13. Transmission drain plug
14. Converter drain plug
15. Plug of access hole to drain plug
16. Primary pump to cover bolt

Test Operations

FOR USE WITH TROUBLE SHOOTING CHART

OPERATION 1

Engine running at 425-450 rpm.
Hand lever at Drive.
Pressure gage at low servo test point
Should indicate 40-45 lbs.
If it is higher or lower, the trouble can be:
The front oil pump.
The regulator valve.
The modulator.

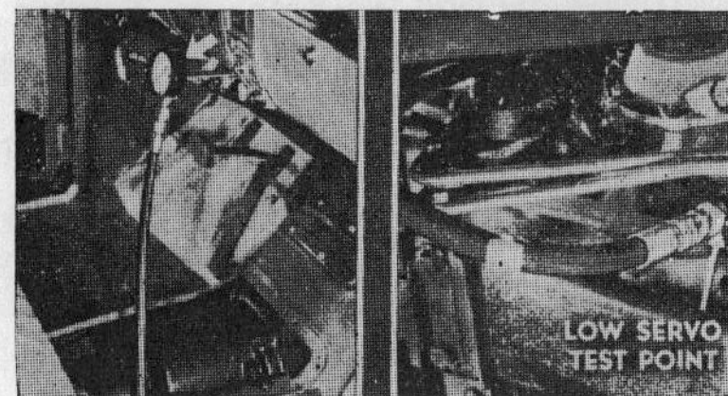

Fig. 19—Checking pressure at low servo test point

OPERATION 2

Rear wheels jacked up, hand lever at Drive.

Speedometer showing 30 mph.

Pressure gage at low servo test point.

Load the engine momentarily with the brakes.

The pressure should rise as the vacuum part of the modulator functions to provide more pressure.

Continued

POWERGLIDE

TEST OPERATIONS—*continued*

If the pressure does not rise check:

The vacuum lines for leaks.

The diaphragm and spring for damage and lost tension by removing the modulator cover.

OPERATION 3

Engine at full throttle.

Hand lever at Drive, brakes set.

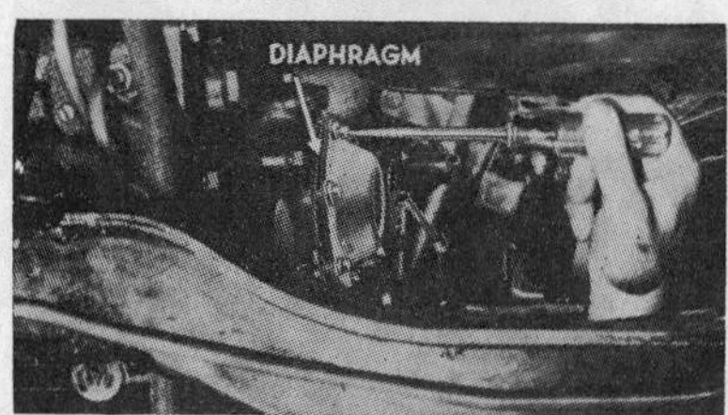

Fig. 20—Removing modulator cover to check diaphragm for damage

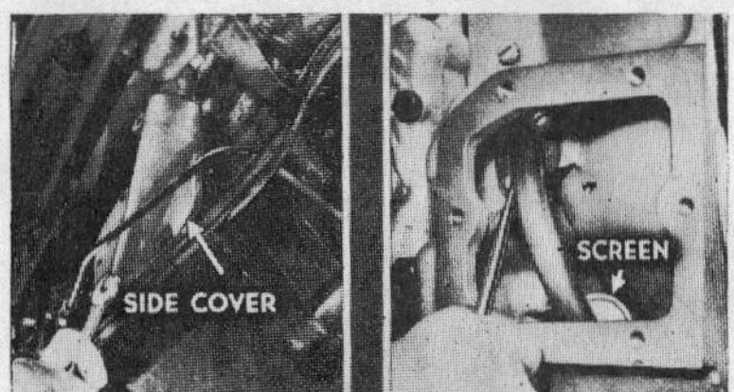

Fig. 21—Removing side cover and oil suction screen

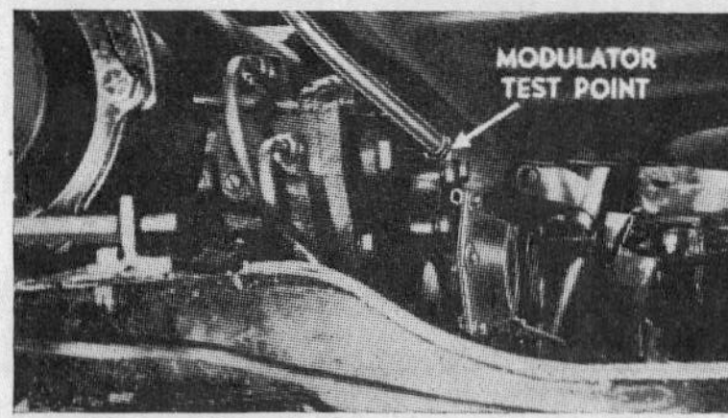

Fig. 22—Checking modulator pressure

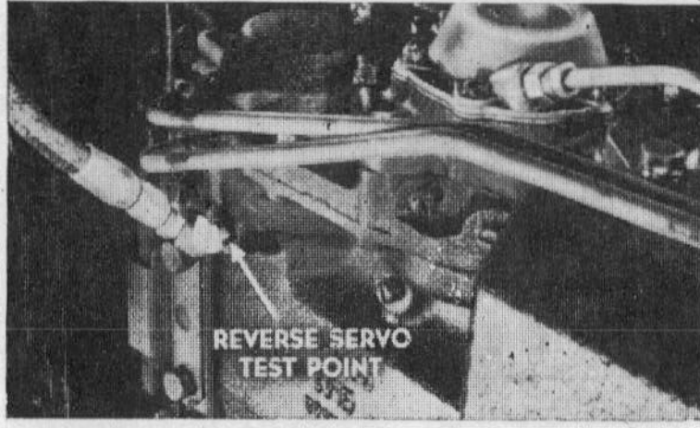

Fig. 23—Checking reverse servo pressure

Fig. 24—Checking rear pump pressure

Pressure gage at low servo test point.

Engine RPM should fall between 1560 and 1610 rpm. No more, no less.

Pressure should be 75-100 lbs.

A. If pressure is OK but engine RPM is higher than 1610, the clutch is slipping.

B. If pressure is lower than 75 lbs the suction line may be clogged.

Remove the right side cover and clean the tube and oil screen.

If pressure remains low, it indicates trouble in:

The front oil pump.

The regulator valve.

The clutch piston seals.

The clutch drum oil seals.

Leaking gaskets on either side of the valve body.

OPERATION 4

Engine running first at 425-450 rpm (idle), second at the stall point (1560-1610 rpm)

Hand lever at Low.

Pressure gage at low servo test point should indicate: first, 125-150 lbs, second, 160-200 lbs.

A. If pressure is OK but the stall speed is high adjust the low band. If no result the band is worn out.

B. If pressure is low put a pressure gage to the modulator test point.

If the pressure is zero or very low the accumulator is at fault.

If the modulator pressure is the same as that at the low servo, the hydraulic valve of the modulator needs repair.

OPERATION 5

Engine running first at 425-450 rpm (idle), second at the stall point (1560-1610 rpm).

Hand lever at Reverse.

Pressure gage at the reverse servo test point:

If the stall speed is high the transmission will have to be removed and the reverse band adjusted.

Fig. 25—Checking accumulator pressure

If the pressures are low whereas they were OK in Operation 4 there is an internal leak. Remove the transmission and check:

The gaskets on either side of the valve body.

The reverse servo piston ring.

The regulator valve.

The front pump clearances.

The modulator.

The servo cover gasket.

OPERATION 6

Rear wheels jacked up, hand lever: first, at Drive; second, at Low.

Speedometer showing 30 mph.

Pressure gage at rear pump test point.

Pressure: first, should be 50-75 lbs; second; should be 140-180 lbs.

Failure to obtain these pressures indicates:

Defective rear pump or internal leak.

OPERATION 7

Engine running at 425-450 rpm.

Hand lever at Reverse.

Pressure gage at low servo release point, should indicate no (zero) pressure.

If there is any pressure, there is internal leakage.

OPERATION 8

Car running along a dry road at 40 mph.

Shift from Drive to Low. The rear tires should give out a sort of chirp.

If, instead, there is a loud noise or a severe jerk, the accumulator is at fault.

TROUBLE CHART

1. Excessive Slip in All Ranges

Shown by high engine speed for relative car speed, poor acceleration, engine races at turns. To prove check the Stall Point in all ranges. It should be the same and between 1560 and 1610 RPM.

This trouble can be caused by:

Low Oil Level, Improper Linkage Adjustment or Pumps Sucking Air due to:

Oil Suction Pipe Split or not seating properly.

Oil Suction Screen coated with lint or dirt.

To prove either of the above apply Test operation 3, part B.

Front Pump worn or scored. To prove apply Test Operation 5. (Pressures will be low.)

Damaged valve body gasket, warped mating surfaces between pump and valve body, porous valve body. To prove apply Test Operation 7.

Stuck Regulator Valve.

Free Wheeling Cam Rollers on the Stators or the Secondary Pump Improperly assembled. To prove: Engine will not attain Minimum Stall Speed in any Range.

2. Excessive Slip in Drive Range

Shown by too high a Stall Speed in Drive. To prove apply Test Operation 3A.

This trouble can be caused by:

Improper Linkage Adjustment.

Worn or burned Clutch Plates due to:

Extended operation with low oil level.

Damaged or improperly installed clutch piston seals.

Restricted Orifice in Clutch Hydraulic Circuit, see Trouble No. 21 to prove.

Damaged Clutch Release Valve.

Clutch drum oil seals leaking.

Excessive clearance between low servo piston shaft and case.

Leak in the gaskets on either side of the Valve Body or a porous valve body. To prove see Test Operation 7.

3. Excessive Slip in Low Range

Can be caused by:

Improper linkage adjustment, or improper low band adjustment.

Accumulator Valve stuck. To prove apply Test Operation 8.

Modulator lever or piston is stuck. To prove apply Test Operation 2.

Broken or damaged low servo ring. To prove see Trouble No. 22.

Leaks at the gaskets on either side of the Valve Body or the Servo Cover to Case gasket. To prove apply Test Operation 7.

Clutch Drum Worn smooth.

4. Excessive Slip in Reverse

Can be caused by:

Improper Linkage adjustment, or improper Reverse band adjustment.

Broken reverse band.

Bent strut or stretched link assembly.

No pressure in the lines due to:

Accumulator Valve stuck, Modulator lever stuck, or Modulator Piston stuck.

To prove on the above three apply Test Operations 2 and 4.

Broken or damaged reverse servo piston ring. To prove see Trouble No. 22.

Leaks at the gaskets on either side of the valve body. To prove apply Test Operation 7.

Step in manual valve body bore causing leakage to sump.

5. Car Creeps Forward with Hand Lever in Neutral

This trouble can be caused by:

Improper linkage adjustment, or Low band adjusted too tight.

Clutch inoperative (shown by car stalling in low and reverse) due to:

Clutch Vent valve Stuck Closed. To prove see Trouble No. 21.

Clutch Plates improperly Assembled. All the dished plates must face the same way, toward the rear.

Clutch Plates sticking.

Clutch Plates stuck in Clutch Drum.

Leak between valve body and housing. To prove apply Test Operation No. 3.

Control lever unhooked from manual valve inside the transmission. To prove: Drain the case, unfasten the left sump plate and look.

6. Car Creeps Forward with Hand Lever in Reverse

This trouble can be caused by improper linkage adjustment.

7. Car Creeps Backward with Hand Lever in Low

This trouble can be caused by improper linkage adjustment.

8. Car Will Not Move; Rear Wheels Locked

This trouble can be caused by:

Emergency brake applied, parking lock pawl engaged, broken part in transmission or broken part in differential.

9. Car Will Not Move After Long Reverse; Rear Wheels Free

This trouble can be caused by:

Leak at Rear Pump gasket allowing air into the suction lines so that Front Pump loses prime. To prove apply Test Operation No. 6.

Front pump driving tangs sheared off. To prove apply Test Operations Nos. 1 and 3.

10. Shift from Low to Drive Abnormally Rough with Car in Motion

This trouble can be caused by:

Improper low band adjustment.

Clutch plates worn or binding in clutch flange or drum.

Modulator lever or Piston stuck. To prove apply Test Operation No. 4B.

Accumulator dump valve inoperative. To prove apply Test Operation No. 4B.

Leak in Modulator Vacuum Line. To prove apply Test Operation No. 2.

11. Engine Speeds Up When Shifting from Low to Drive With Car in Motion

This trouble can be caused by:

Low oil level.

Improper low band adjustment.

Weak Modulator Spring. To prove apply Test Operation No. 2.

Clutch plates glazed, worn or binding.

Restricted orifice in clutch hydraulic circuit. To prove see Trouble No. 21.

TROUBLE CHART—*continued*

12. Shift from Drive to Low Abnormally Rough

This trouble can be caused by:
Improper low band adjustment.
Modulator lever or piston stuck. To prove apply Test Operation No. 4B.
Accumulator Piston stuck closed. To check apply Test Operation No. 8.

13. Shift from Neutral to Reverse Abnormally Rough

This trouble can be caused by:
Idling speed too high.
Modulator lever or Piston stuck. To prove apply Test Operation No. 4B.
Accumulator valve stuck. To prove apply Test Operation No. 4B.
Improper Reserve Band adjustment.
Excessive End clearance in the Transmission.
Torque tube held too tightly at the Ball joint. To correct add more shims.

14. Chatter When Starting in Low

This trouble can be caused by:
Improper low band adjustment.
Malfunctioning Clutch due to:
Distorted plates, sticking clutch piston or sticking clutch vent valve. To prove see Trouble No. 21.
Worn low drum or band. To prove apply Test Operation 4A.

15. Chatter When Starting in Drive

This trouble can be caused by:
Improper reverse band adjustment, improper low band adjustment, worn bands, or drums.

16. Chatter When Starting in Reverse

This trouble can be caused by:
Improper reverse band adjustment, worn reverse band or drum, transmission case rear bushing worn or damaged, or reverse ring gear bushing worn or damaged.

17. Drag in Reverse or Jerky Reverse

his trouble can be caused by:
Improper low band adjustment.
Malfunctioning clutch due to:
Plates improperly assembled.
Plates binding in flange or hub.
Stuck Piston.
Stuck Vent Valve. To prove see Trouble No. 21.

18. Excessive Fuel Consumption

This trouble can be caused by:
Secondary Pump locked to hub of Primary Pump due to improperly assembled free wheel Clutch. To prove: Engine will not attain minimum stall speed in any range.
Free wheeling clutches of Stators improperly assembled. To prove: Engine will not attain minimum stall speed in any range.
Clutch vent valve stuck open. To prove see Trouble No. 21.

19. Excessive Oil Consumption

This trouble can be caused by:
External leakage at pressure checking points, side covers, or the converter housing.
External leakage at universal ball joint seal.
External leakage at front of flywheel housing. To check; remove plug at bottom of converter housing. If there is an oil pool it will be necessary to check;
The primary pump "O" ring seals, the front pump oil seal, "O" ring, and drain. The turbine bolt "O" ring, and for sand holes in case running from sump to housing.
External leakage at oil cooler connections.
Internal leakage at propeller shaft oil seal. To prove: Check differential lubricant level. If it is too high renew the oil seal and the differential lubricant.
Modulator diaphragm leaking. To prove: Put a glass bowled gasoline filter in the modulator vacuum line at the manifold. When motor is running, if diaphragm is leaking, oil will appear in the filter bowl.
Aerated oil being forced out of the filler tube due to:
Oil level too high.
Split in suction pipe, damaged suction pipe seal, ears on suction pipe bent, or bore for suction pipe in the housing too deep for proper compression of the seal.
Sand holes in suction passages of the housing, the case, or the valve body.

20. Noises

These can be classified as:
Ringing noises in the converter due to:
Low oil level, low oil pressure in the converter, or to aerated oil.
Buzzing noise due to:
Low oil level, malfunctioning of the pumps, or to vibration of the lubrication by-pass valve.
Whining noise due to:
Worn planetary gear teeth, worn pump gears or to worn pump bushings.
Groaning noise.
Audible only at low speeds or when standing when transmission is hot. Usually caused by pulsation of the thermostat valve ball. Disregard it.
Clicking noise.
May be due to improperly adjusted manual linkage permitting the parking lock pawl to contact the ratchet gear.

21. Difficulty in Shifting Between Drive and Low Either Way

This trouble can be caused by:
Improperly drilled clutch feed orifice in the valve body. To prove follow this procedure:
Connect one pressure gauge to the low servo apply test point, another to the low servo release test point. Have engine idling at 425-450 RPM. Move hand lever from Neutral to Drive.
If pressure builds up faster on the gauge connected to the low servo apply point than it does on that connected to the low servo release point, the passage is undersize.
Move hand lever from Drive to Low. If the gauge connected to the low servo release point drops rather slowly the oil is being restricted in draining from the clutch.

22. Slipping and Chatter in Low Range

This trouble can be caused by:
A loose or broken low servo piston ring. To prove follow this procedure:
Connect pressure gauges to the low servo apply and release test points. Put hand lever at Low, set the parking brake, run engine up to stall speed. (1560-1610 RPM)

The gauge at the low servo apply test point should read 160-215 lbs. The gauge at the low servo release test point should read zero. If instead it shows pressure, the piston ring is kaput.

23. Unable to Shift into Reverse with Engine Running

This trouble can be caused by the accumulator snap ring being out of place. This permits the accumulator valve to contact the parking lock lever shaft assembly at the clamp nut, so blocking the shift.

24. Car Will Not Move in Drive —Engine Races—Rear Wheels Are Free—Transmission Is Hot

This trouble can be caused by:
Over expansion of the clutch parts due to excessive heat caused by:
Low coolant level, bad oil cooler, dragging low band, or defective transmission thermostat.

REMOVAL OF POWERGLIDE FROM CAR

ALL MODELS THRU 1952

Remove the spark plugs and drain the transmission.

Disconnect the exhaust pipe at the manifold and at the rubber mounting bracket. Move all to inner side of left frame strut to permit dropping the transmission.

Remove the front seat assembly, the floor mat, the toe pan plate, and the transmission hole cover plate.

Raise the car on 4 high jacks or a twin or four post lift.

Disconnect the speedometer cable and the universal joint collar at the rear of the transmission.

Disconnect the two oil cooler lines.

Disconnect the parking brake pull rod and spring. Unhook the cross shaft and lower it and the brake cables.

Slide the universal ball back on the propeller shaft housing. Split the universal joint and lower the propeller shaft housing.

Disconnect the long shift rod from the bell crank and the short shift rod from it and the outside control lever. Remove the bell crank by unscrewing the stud from the transmission case.

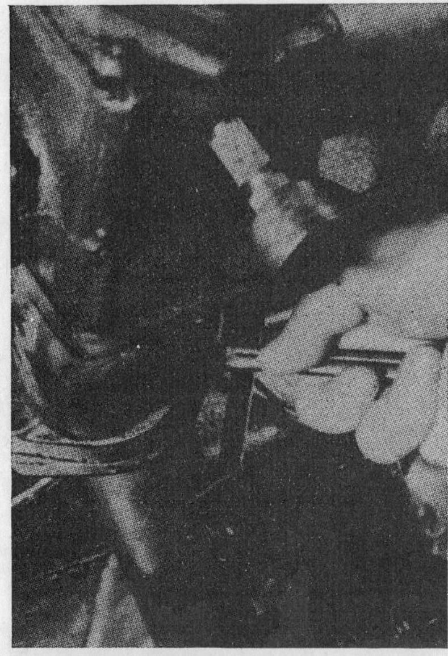

Fig. 26—Disconnecting exhaust pipe

Fig. 27—Removing transmission hole cover

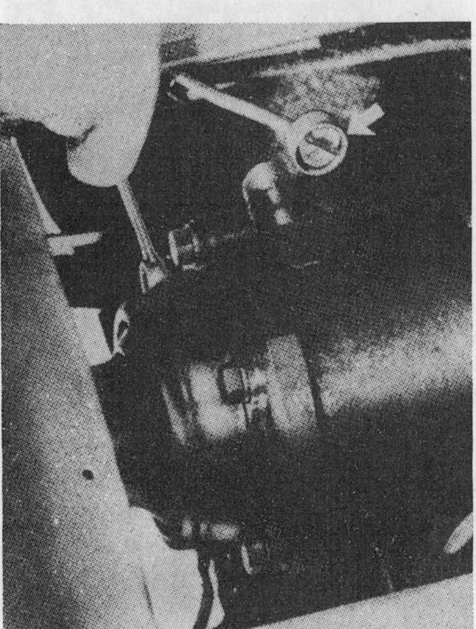

Fig. 28—Unbolting universal joint

Fig. 29—Disconnecting two oil cooler lines

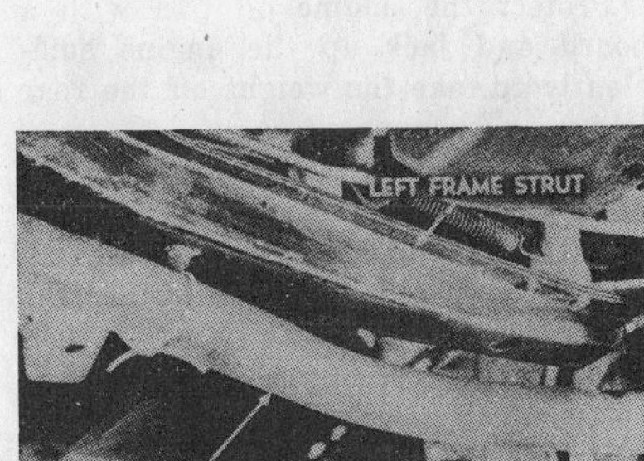

Fig. 30—Tie exhaust pipe to clear innerside of left frame strut

Fig. 31—Split "U" joint and lower propeller shaft

REMOVAL OF POWERGLIDE—*cont'd*

Clean off the right side cover. Remove the bolt which secures the filler tube bracket and pull the filler tube out of the side cover. Cover the hole with tape or plug with a *rubber* stopper.

Disconnect the vacuum line from the modulator and the oil cooler lines from the bracket on the right side cover. Tie all lines out of the way.

Remove four bolts to release the flywheel cover plate which will reveal an opening in the housing. Mark the converter and flywheel for matched reassembly.

Pry the converter around and remove the six bolts which fasten the converter to the flywheel through the revealed hole. Do not remove the bolts holding the converter cover and turbine assembly to the primary pump.

Protect the engine oil pan with a board and jack up the engine sufficiently to take the weight off the rear transmission support.

Unbolt the rear transmission support and remove it.

Lower the engine until the rear end of the transmission just clears the frame cross member.

Support the transmission by some means.

Remove the bolts fastening the converter housing to the flywheel housing. There are 4 at the bottom, 2 on the left and 2 on the right, and 3 across the top.

The transmission is removed by lowering it to the floor. The converter end goes down.

The rear end of the assembly has to be tipped up through the hole in the floor pan in order to do this. The floor pan hole must be pried over the valve covers and such on the sides of the transmission. Usually the transmission is hung on a sling from a fixture placed over the hole in the front compartment. There is available a fine automatic-hydraulic lift which will do it from under the car.

It is of course possible to hold the transmission on slings of rope over 2x4s and to manipulate it so that it can be lowered.

The two things to watch are:

The transmission must be moved back so that the flywheel pilot will clear the flywheel.

The flywheel pilot must not be damaged by bumping against anything.

Note: The assembly weighs about 100 to 115 lbs.

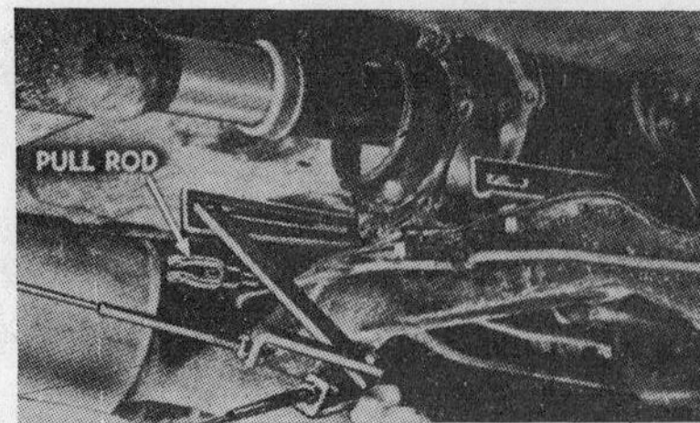

Fig. 32—Disconnect the pull rod lower cross shaft and cable

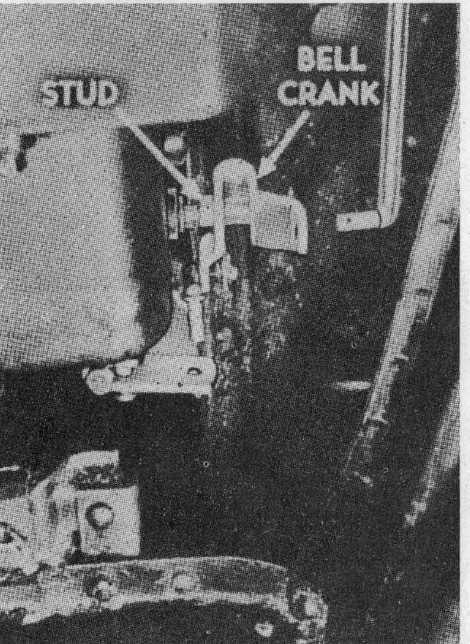

Fig. 33—Remove bell crank by unscrewing stud

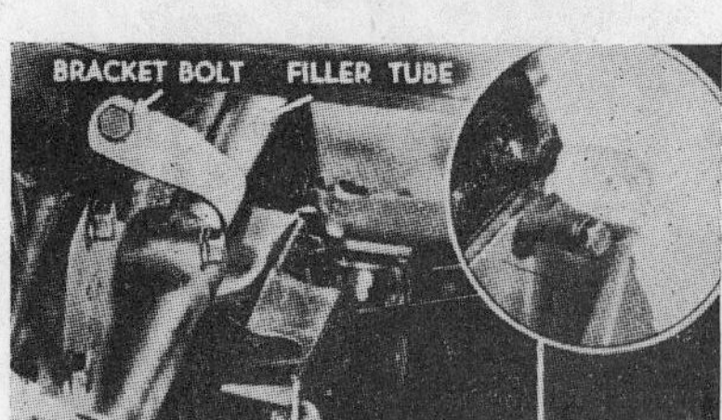

Fig. 34—Unbolt filler tube and bracket plug filler hole

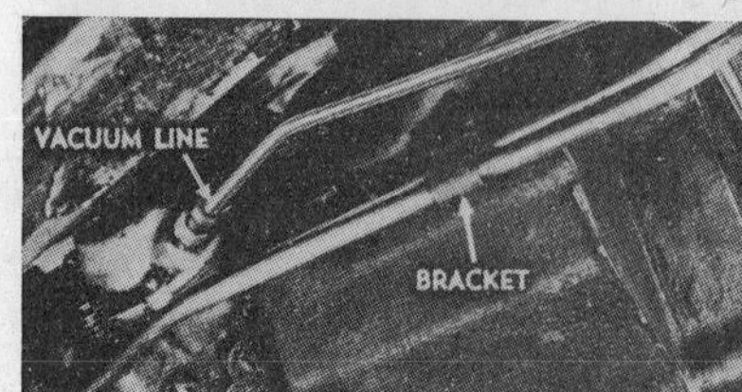

Fig. 35—Disconnect vacuum and oil cooler lines

Fig. 36—Removing flywheel cover plate

Fig. 37—Removing converter to flywheel bolts

Fig. 38—Raising engine to release rear transmission support

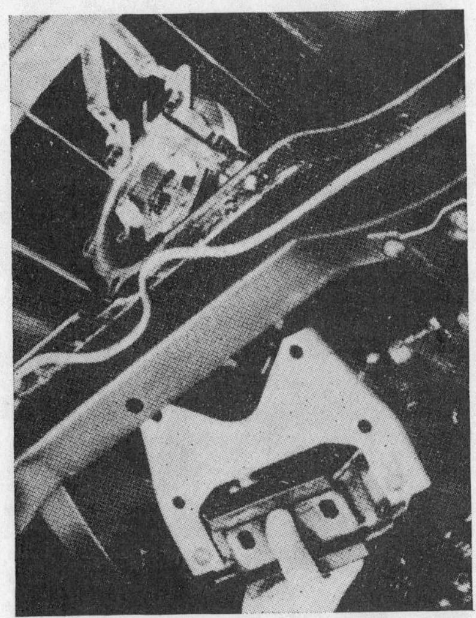

Fig. 39—Removing rear transmission support

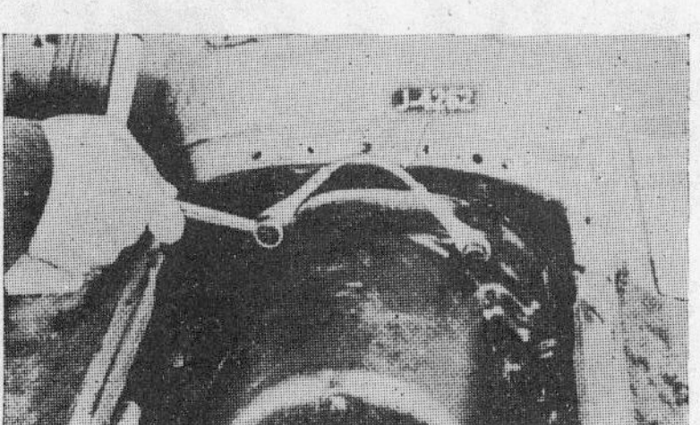

Fig. 40—Attaching front sling to transmission

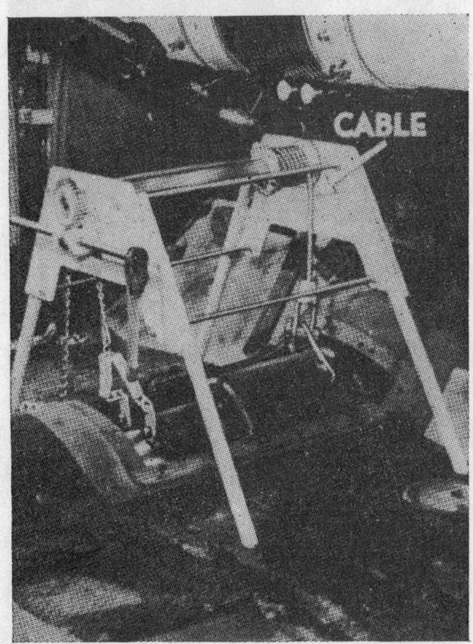

Fig. 41—Hoist in position to support transmission

REMOVAL OF THE 1953 POWERGLIDE

The removal procedure is the same for 1953 as for former models except that:

The throttle valve control rod must be disconnected from the throttle valve outer lever.

As the converter portion of the transmission is no longer held in place to the reactor shaft by a retaining ring it is necessary to fasten the converter to the bell housing before attempting to remove the transmission from the car. Otherwise the converter assembly may fall off and injure itself and others.

Fig. 42—Removing four lower bell and flywheel housing bolts

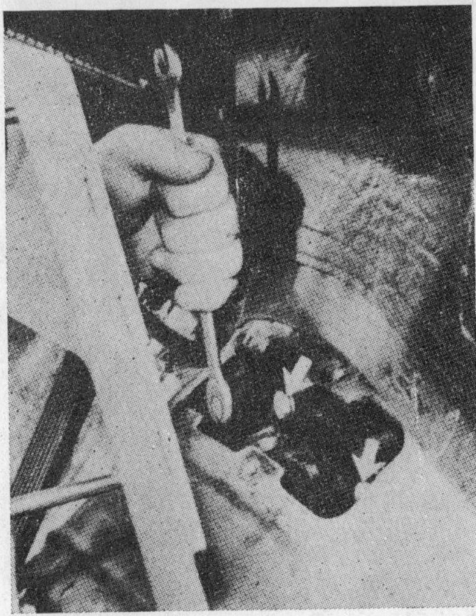

Fig. 43—Removing three upper bell and flywheel housing bolts

Fig. 44—Tip rear of transmission up thru opening in floor pan

Fig. 45—Lowering transmission converter end first

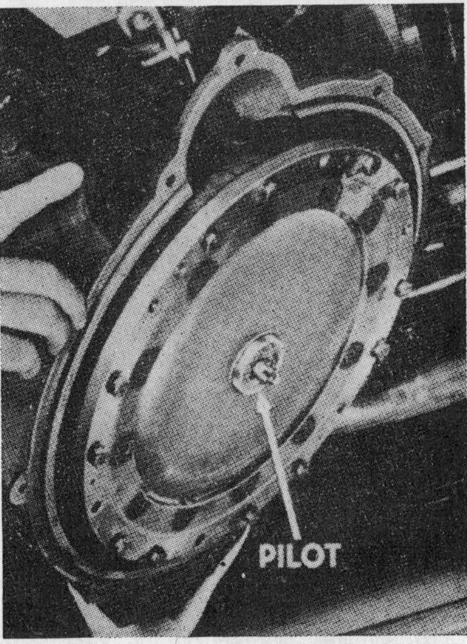

Fig. 46—Be careful not to damage converter pilot

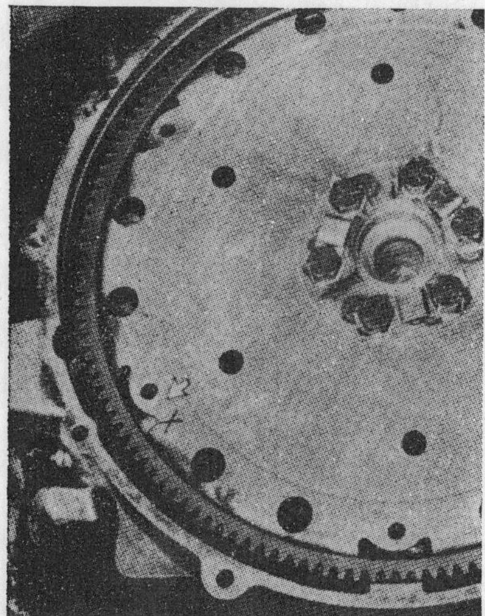

Fig. 47—Note: Bolt hole in flywheel nearest "X" mark

Fig. 48—Guide pin installed in primary pump cover nearest "X" mark

INSTALLATION OF POWERGLIDE IN CAR

ALL MODELS THRU 1952

The primary pump and cover are balanced at the factory and cannot be bought separately. Note that the flywheel and the cover are each marked with an X. These X's permit balanced mating of the parts.

Turn the flywheel until the bolt hole indicated by an X is in line with the access hole in the flywheel housing thru which the bolts are removed and installed.

Install a guide pin in the bolt hole in the primary pump cover indicated by an X. Turn the pump so the pin is in a position corresponding approximately with the marked bolt hole in the flywheel.

Hoist the transmission; rear end first.

When the lower rear edge is far enough up, rest it on the rear cross member and start raising the front end.

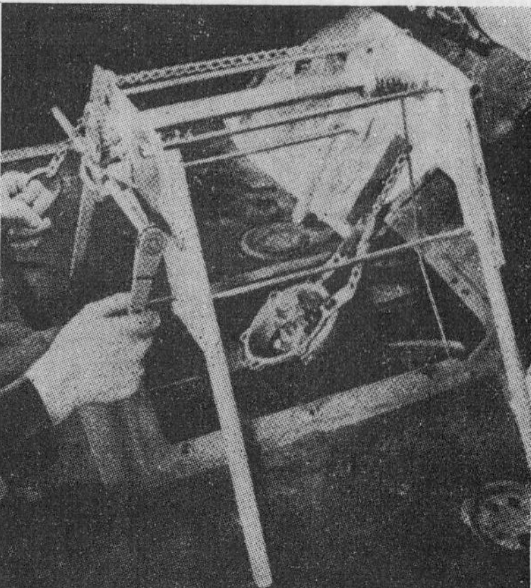

Fig. 49—Raise transmission, rear end first

Fig. 50—Rest rear end on cross member and raise converter end

Align the guide pin exactly with the X marked bolt hole in the flywheel and carefully slide the transmission forward into place. Be sure to support transmission. Note whether the match marks made at disassembling line up.

Note: Be sure flywheel pilot has been greased and was not harmed on the way in.

When flywheel housing and converter housing are flat in place against each other install the attaching bolts and tighten securely.

Fig. 51—Align guide pin and "X" marked hole in flywheel

Fig. 52—Lubricate converter pilot

Note: Do not attempt to pull the housing together with the bolts. You'll throw the housings out of alignment and alignment is very important to the successful operation of these transmissions.

Install the rear transmission support. Then remove the jack from under the engine oil pan.

Remove the converter to flywheel guide pin. Install the six flywheel to converter bolts and tighten securely.

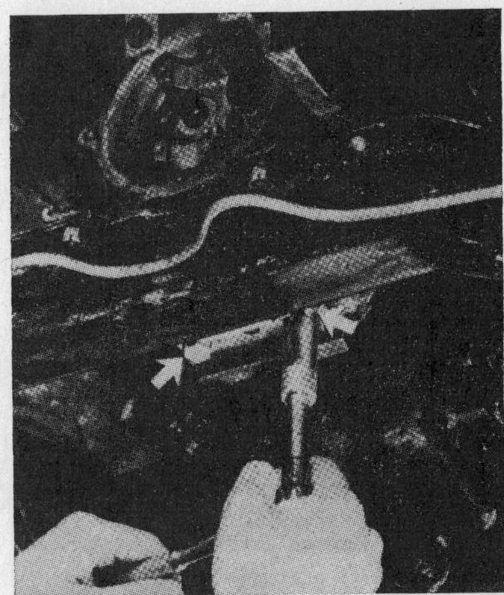

Fig. 53—Installing rear transmission support

Fig. 54—Remove guide pin and bolt converter to flywheel

When assembling the universal joint use a new neoprene seal on the ball seat.

Note: Neoprene seals of different sizes are used throughout the transmission. They are round in cross section, circular in shape (look very much like vacuum cleaner belts) and care must be used that they are not twisted while being put on a part nor while another part is being put over them. To this end have the rings always as far from the oncoming part as the groove will allow and examine carefully that they are not twisted. Then as the two parts go together do not use a twisting motion which will dislodge the seal and render it useless.

Complete the assembly underneath, installing the parking brake cross shaft, the filler tube, the flywheel cover, the vacuum line, shift rods, bell crank, and muffler rubber mount.

Note: Be sure to assemble the short shift rod from the bell crank to the outside control lever with the arrow marking pointing up and on the up end. Otherwise the linkage will bind severely.

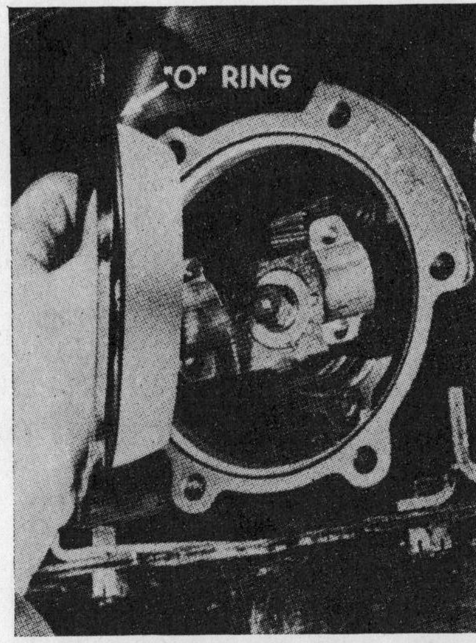

Fig. 55—New "O" ring seal on torque ball seat

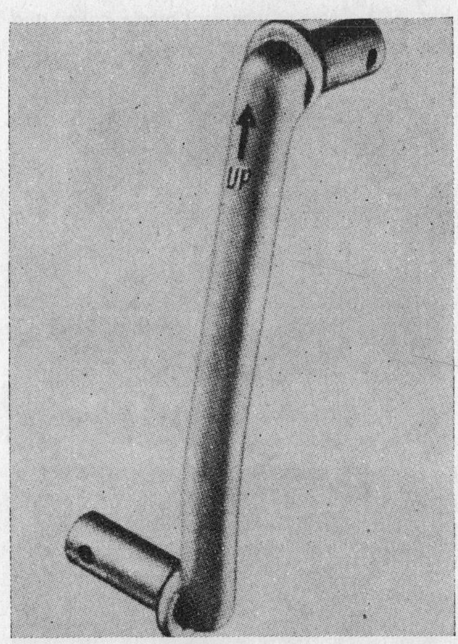

Fig. 56—Note that short shift rod is to be assembled with arrow up

Complete the assembly on top, installing the oil cooler lines, speedometer cable, toe pan, transmission hole cover, and the floor mat.

With the linkage connected check that the 3/16″ clearance is present at the hand lever mount, that the .090 clearance between the shift shaft lever and the stop is present when the hand lever is in Reverse and that the linkage works freely. Be sure also that there is 1½″ plus or minus 5/16″ between hand lever knob and steering wheel rim when the hand lever is in Reverse.

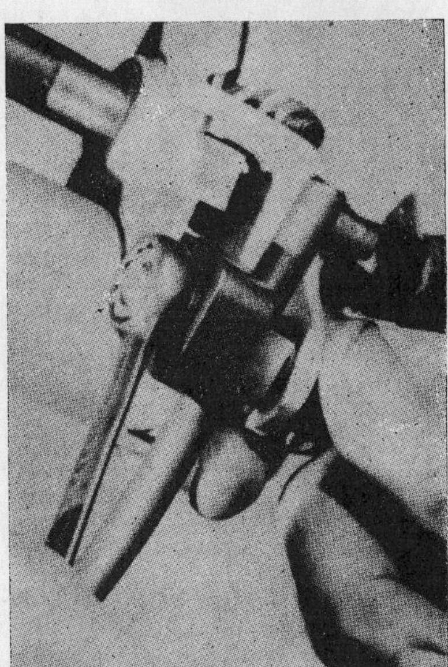

Fig. 57—Adjust manual linkage

Put in three quarts of automatic transmission fluid Type A being sure the cans have embossed on them the AQ-ATF number.

Idle engine and add seven quarts more. One quart more than on a drain.

Warm up the engine by idling in Drive and measure that oil level is not below the add 1 qt. mark.

Road test the car for correct performance in all selector positions.

Installation of the 1953 Powerglide

The installation procedure for the 1953 Powerglide is the same as that for former models except that:

The means used to hold the converter from falling off must be removed before the converter is aligned with the flywheel while at the same time care must be taken not to let the converter slide forward enough to disengage the driving tangs from the front oil pump.

The throttle valve control rod must be reconnected to the throttle valve with a spring washer, plain washer and cotter pin.

The transmission requires 11 qts. to fill it.

DISASSEMBLY OVERHAUL & REASSEMBLY

ALL MODELS THRU 1952

For any work involving parts as finely finished as those in automatic transmissions, cleanliness is an important factor. Failure to clean the outside thoroughly before starting disassembly will double the work required to assure a clean and leakfree reassembly.

REMOVAL OF SUCTION PIPE AND SCREEN—ALL MODELS THRU '52

Note: This operation can be done with unit in the car.

Remove six bolts holding the right side cover. Remove two screws which secure suction pipe and screen.

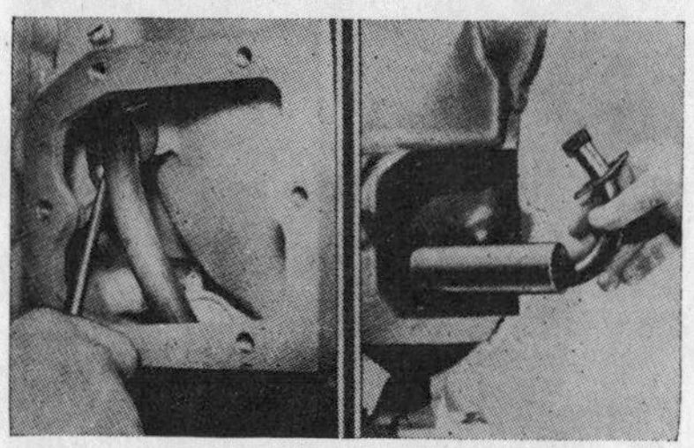

Fig. 58—Remove oil suction screen

Fig. 59—Note strap to keep converter from turning

REMOVAL OF CONVERTER—ALL MODELS THRU '52

Note: Transmission must be out of car for this operation.

Block the converter from turning and remove the twelve cover retaining bolts. Be sure to match mark the cover to the primary pump.

Thread three 10-32 bolts into the holes tapped thru the cover only. Tighten them uniformily to force the cover and turbine assembly out of the primary pump.

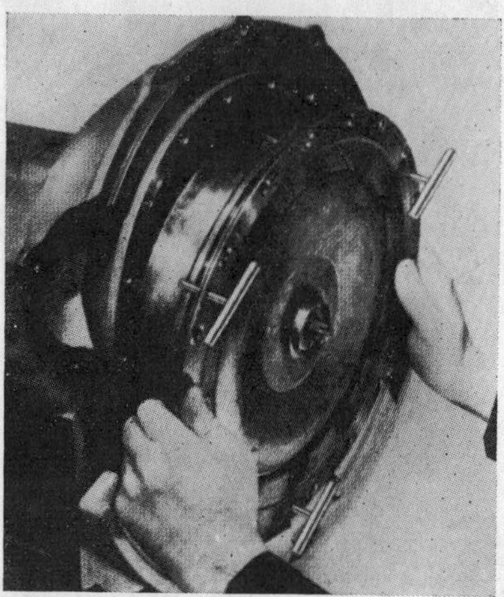

Fig. 60—Remove primary pump cover and turbine assembly

Fig. 61—Remove stator and hub assembly

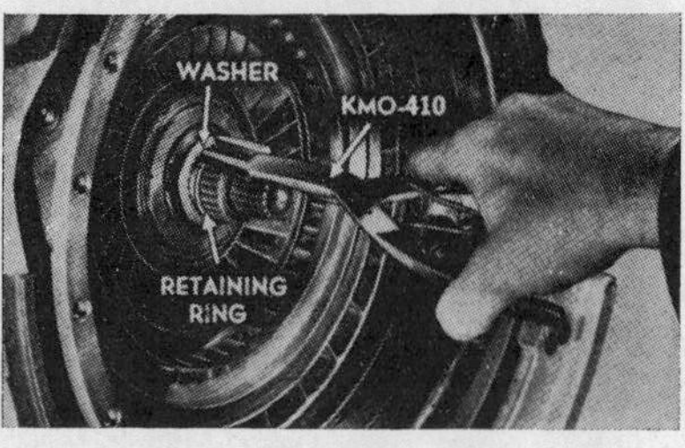

Fig. 62—Remove primary pump retaining ring and washers

Remove the stator and hub assembly from its support.

Remove the primary pump retaining ring and washer and slide the assembly out of the housing.

REMOVAL OF MODULATOR—ALL MODELS THRU '52

Note: This assembly can be removed with Powerglide in the car.

Remove the modulator assembly bolts and lift off the assembly.

Do not drop the hydraulic plunger assembly.

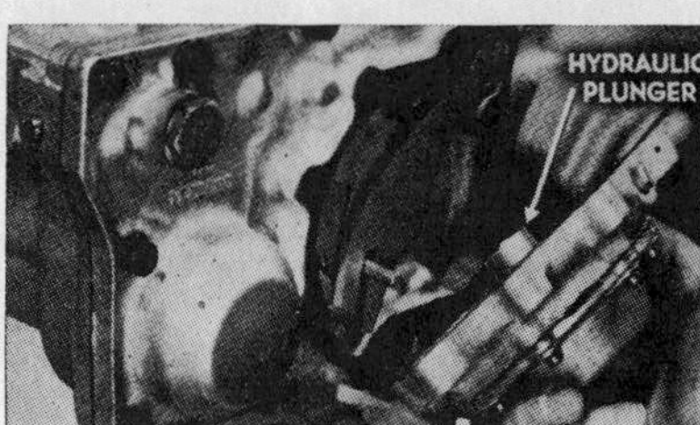

Fig. 63—Remove modulator assembly

REMOVAL OF SERVO ASSEMBLY AND REGULATOR VALVE—ALL MODELS THRU '52

Note: This assembly can be removed while Powerglide is still in the car.

Remove the servo cover bolts releasing the servo cover, reverse servo springs, and the regulator valve springs. Be careful to push in on the cover as the springs are quite strong.

Remove the regulator valve. This valve should be handled with care.

Fig. 64—Remove servo cover assembly

Fig. 65—Remove regulator valve

SEPARATING CASE FROM HOUSING —ALL MODELS THRU '52

Note: The transmission must be out of the car for this operation.

Remove the cap which covers the low band adjusting screw on the left side of the case. Loosen the lock nut and tighten the adjusting screw to hold the clutch assembly in place when the case is separated from the housing.

Remove the bolts holding the case to the housing. Slide them apart carefully.

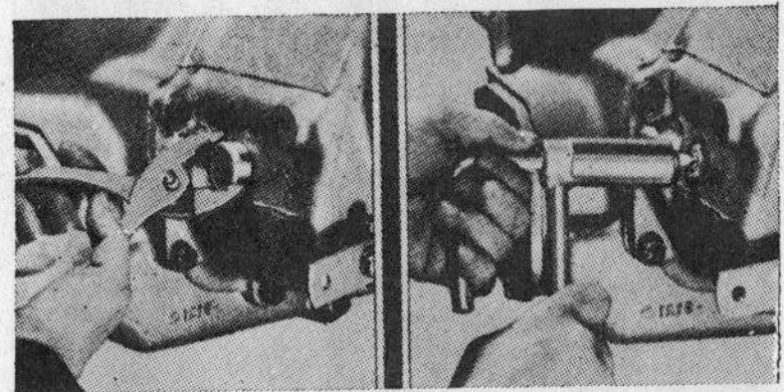

Fig. 66—Tightening low band to hold clutch assembly

Fig. 67—Separating case fram bell housing

REMOVAL OF VALVE ASSEMBLY AND FRONT OIL PUMP— ALL MODELS THRU '52

Note: The transmission must be out of the car for this operation.

Remove the manual valve and lever. Remove the bronze thrust washer from the oil delivery sleeve.

Remove all the bolts and the valve body from the rear of the bell housing.

Drive the front oil pump assembly out of the housing to the rear.

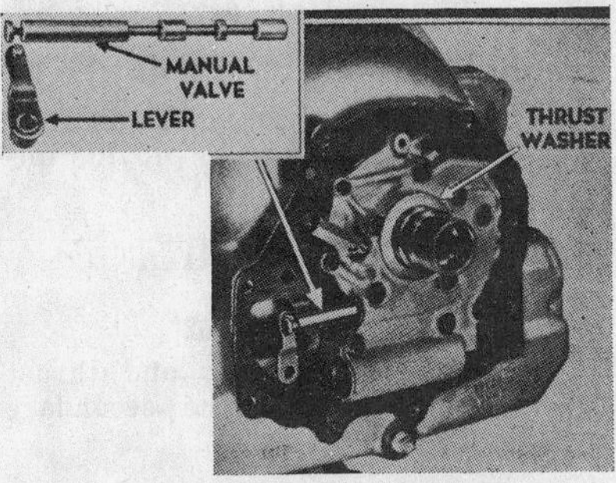

Fig. 68—Remove manual valve and lever

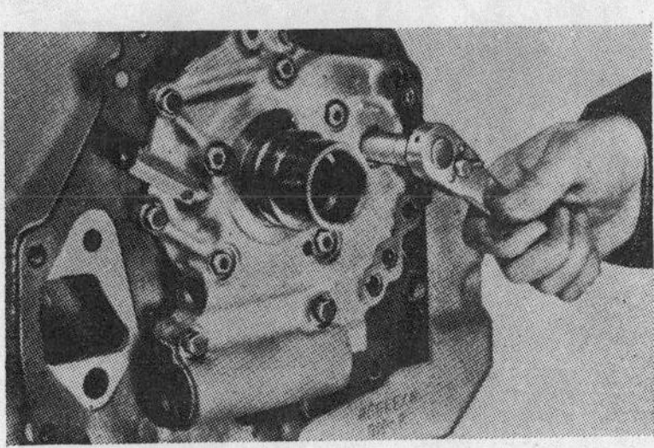

Fig. 69—Remove valve body

Fig. 70—Remove front pump

REMOVAL OF TRANSMISSION CASE —ALL MODELS THRU '52

Note: The transmission must be out of the car for this operation.

Loosen the low band adjusting screw and remove the input shaft and clutch assembly.

Remove the low sun gear thrust washer to release the input shaft from the clutch assembly.

Back off the low band adjusting screw to release the band and the operating mechanism.

Remove the low servo piston and release spring.

Remove the speedometer driven gear and the Universal joint retaining bolt and washers to release the yoke from the output shaft.

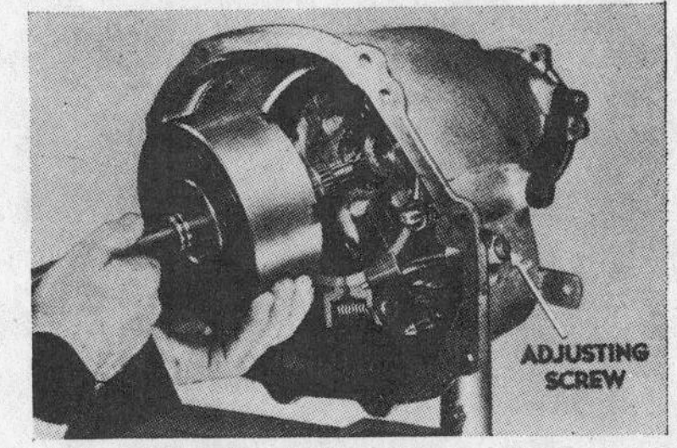

Fig. 71—Remove input shaft and clutch assembly

Fig. 72—Remove the low sun gear to reverse sun gear thrust washer

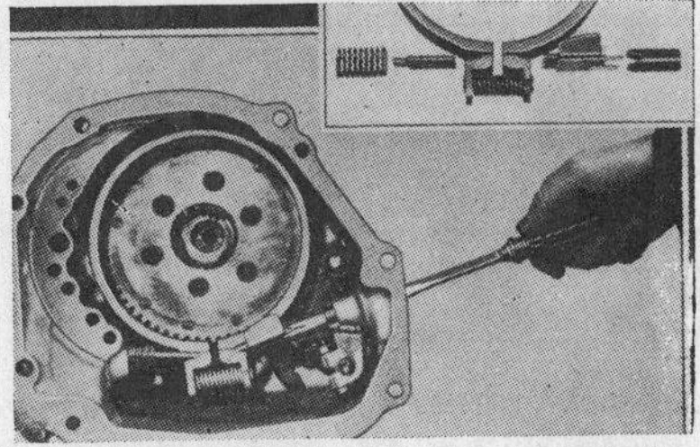

Fig. 73—Removing low band mechanism

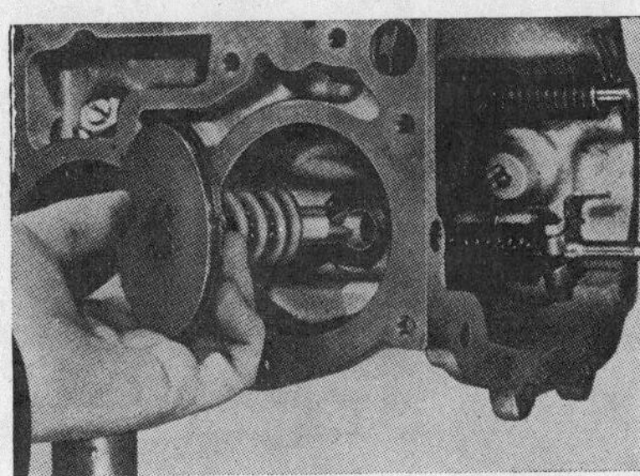

Fig. 74—Remove low servo piston and release spring

REMOVAL OF TRANSMISSION CASE —*continued*

Tap the output shaft with a soft hammer to free it from the rear bearing and oil pump. Slide the planet carrier assembly out of the case to the front.

Remove the reverse ring gear.

Back off the reverse band adjusting screw and remove the band and the strut assembly.

Remove the reverse servo piston assembly.

Remove four bolts and the rear oil pump assembly.

Using the tool shown or a screw driver release the parking lock pawl spring. Remove the spring and parking lock pawl.

Remove the bolt which secures the selector lever to its shaft. Remove the lever, steel washer, and seal. This releases the selector shaft and spring assembly.

Note: Wash all parts of each unit in clean solvent and air dry. Never use cloth to dry the parts for the tiny pieces of lint may cause trouble.

As the units are reassembled oil them with transmission fluid to provide initial lubrication.

OVERHAUL OF PRIMARY AND SECONDARY PUMPS —ALL MODELS THRU '52

Remove the snap ring and thrust washer which retain the secondary pump to the primary pump hub. Turn the secondary pump clockwise and slide it off the hub.

Remove the thrust washer, the retainer washer, the clutch rollers, springs and retainers from the hub of the secondary pump.

Inspect the secondary pump vanes and the machined surfaces for damage. The springs and retainers for distortion. The thrust and retainer washers for wear.

Place the retainer washer in the secondary pump hub with the long tangs toward the rear side. Be sure the four short locating tangs enter the slots in the hub.

Install the rollers, springs and spring

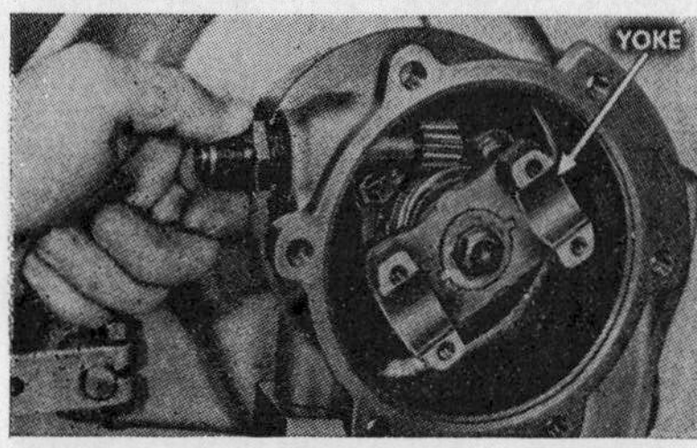

Fig. 75—Remove speedometer driven gear

Fig. 78—Remove reverse band and start assembly

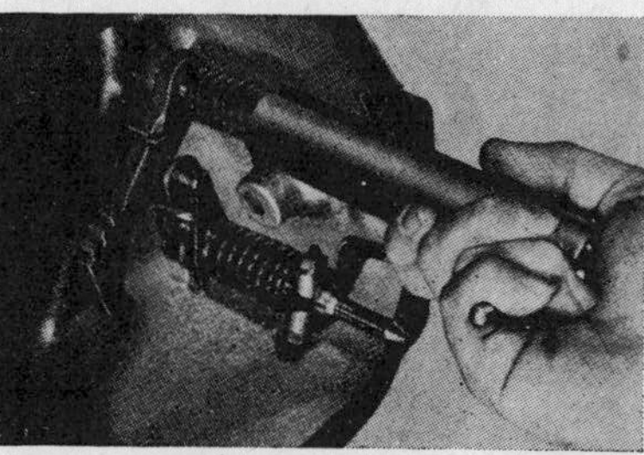

Fig. 81—Releasing parking lock paul spring

Fig. 76—Remove planetary assembly

Fig. 79—Remove reverse servo piston assembly

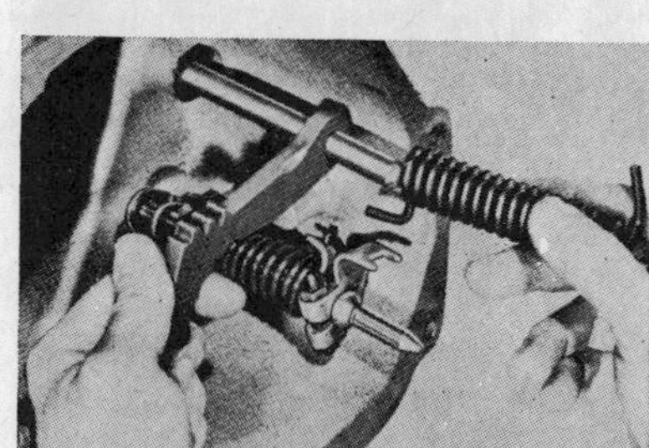

Fig. 82—Remove parking lock spring and pawl

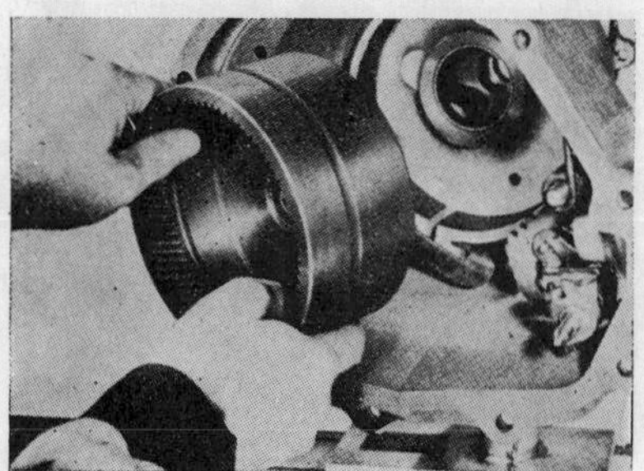

Fig. 77—Remove reversing ring gear

Fig. 80—Remove rear pump assy. and gasket

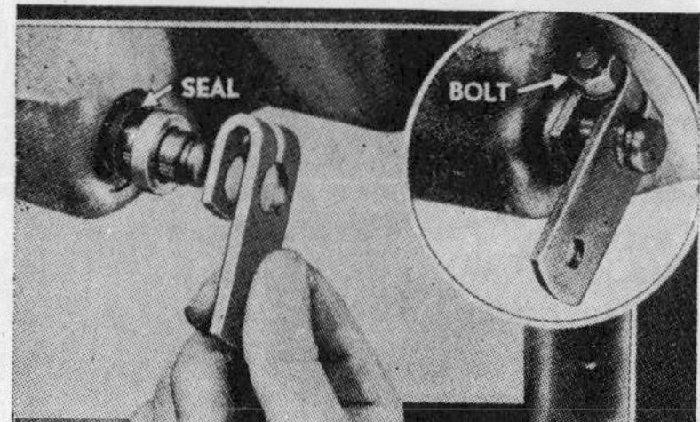

Fig. 83—Remove selector shaft and spring assembly

retainers so the curvature of the spring retainers follows the shape of the hub. They are held against the rollers by the springs bearing against the retainer washer tangs.

Support the retainer washer so it will not be pushed out and install the thrust washer being careful the locating tangs enter the slots.

Inspect the primary pump for loose or damaged vanes, the machined surfaces for scores and the fit of the stator support in the bushing.

Note: If there was evidence of an oil pool in the converter housing the primary pump hub "0" ring seal should be replaced. Use this procedure:

With a small center punch, mark both the primary pump hub and the pump itself in order that the parts may be remated without destroying the balance of the assembly.

Remove the six screws attaching the pump hub to the primary pump.

Support the primary pump on two wood blocks and using a 1/8" pin punch, punch on the top of the 3 dowels to remove the hub. The three dowels were swaged over at assembly.

Remove the "0" ring seal from the hub.

Clean the tip of the six screw holes with a burring tool so that no burrs are left to lodge between the hub and the pump. Check that no other burrs are present on the mating surfaces or the ends of the dowels.

Check the "0" ring groove in the hub that it is free of chips, dirt, or nicks.

Select and install an "0" ring that will remain in the groove. Because of slight variations in the "0" rings some may have a tendency to roll out of the groove.

Assemble the hub to the pump being careful that the seal is at the back of the groove and is not dislodged or

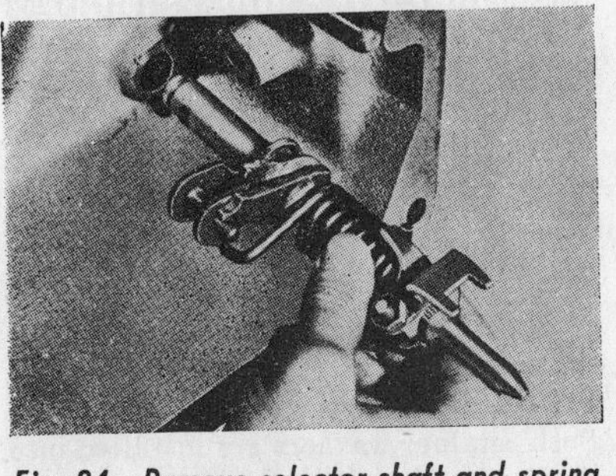

Fig. 84—Remove selector shaft and spring assembly

Fig. 85—Use compressed air to dry parts

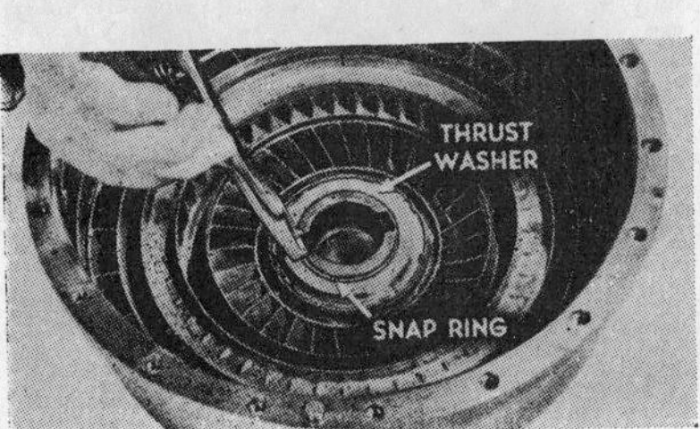

Fig. 86—Remove snap ring and thrust washer to release secondary pump

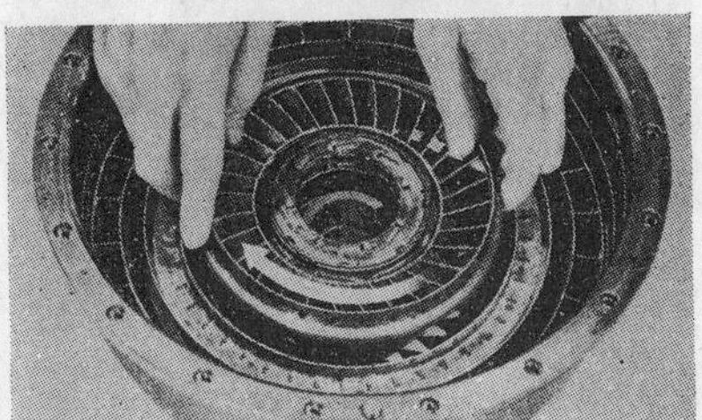

Fig. 87—Remove secondary pump (rotate clockwise)

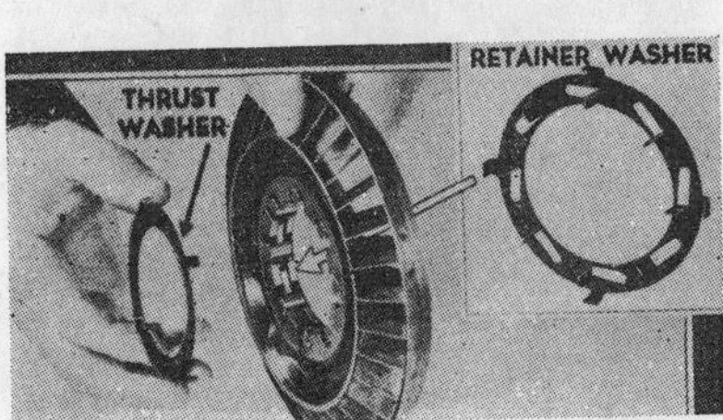

Fig. 88—Remove thrust and retainer washers

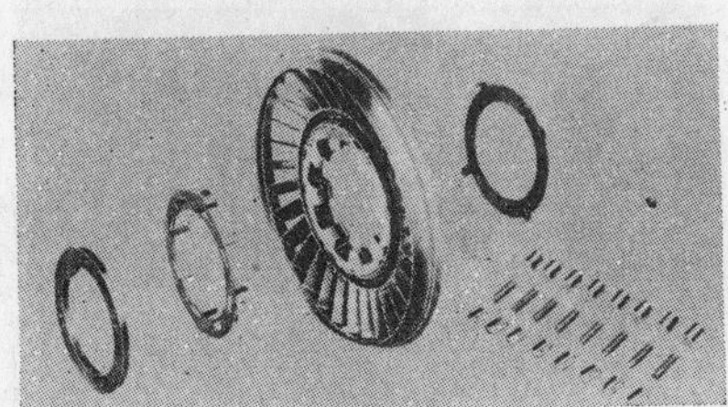

Fig. 89—Layout of secondary pump parts

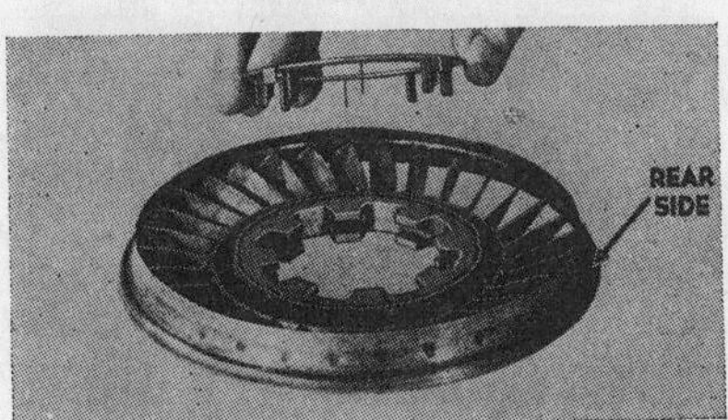

Fig. 90—Long tangs of retainer point to rear of secondary pump

Fig. 91—Note that spring retainers follow curve of hub

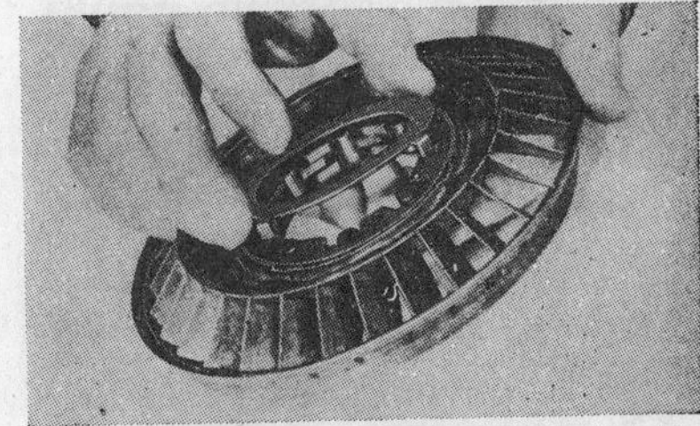

Fig. 92—Install thrust washer onto secondary pump

Fig. 93—Checking fit to stator support in primary pump hub

OVERHAUL, PUMPS—*continued*

turned during installation. Check also that the punch marks made at disassembly are properly matched.

Install the six screws and tighten them evenly to 4½ ft .lbs.

Using a small punch peen around the dowels to obviate any chance that they could loosen and drop in the converter.

Install the primary pump on the stator and note that its face is flush with that of the housing.

Mount an indicator and check that the runout of the front face of the pump does not exceed .010″ full indicator reading. If it does there is dirt between the mating surfaces or the seal is out of the groove.

Install the secondary pump on the primary pump hub using a tapered guide as shown or great care that the retainer and thrust washers stay in place. Turn the assembly clockwise to keep from locking the free wheeling clutch.

Install the thrust washer and snap ring. Check the action of the free wheeling clutch that it locks counterclockwise but rotates freely clockwise.

OVERHAUL OF STATORS AND HUB ASSEMBLY—ALL MODELS THRU '52

Remove the snap ring and thrust washer to release the secondary stator from the stator race. Turn clockwise while removing. Rotate the primary stator clockwise and remove it.

Disassemble the roller parts from both stators and inspect for damage.

The rollers and the tangs of the retainer washer of the secondary stator are longer than for the primary stator. Both retainer washers are installed into the front sides of their stators.

Use a tapered loading tool as shown to assemble; or lay the secondary stator on the bench front face down, lay the primary stator in place upon it and swiggle the stator race down into place, being careful to turn the race clockwise so as not to jam the rollers.

Install the thrust washer and snap ring then check the assembly that the stators turn freely in a clockwise direction and lock against counterclockwise rotation.

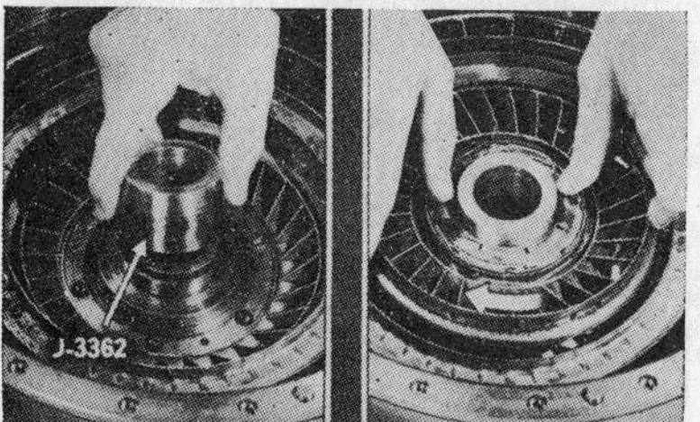

Fig. 94—Using guide to install the secondary pump onto the primary pump hub

Fig. 97—Removing secondary stator from stator race

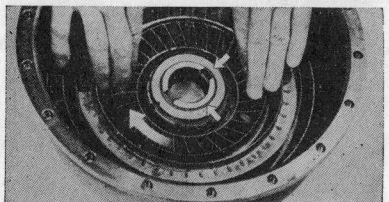

Fig. 95—Checking rotation of secondary pump free wheel clutch

Fig. 98—Disassembling roller parts from stator

Fig. 96—Use transmission fluid to oil parts after assembly

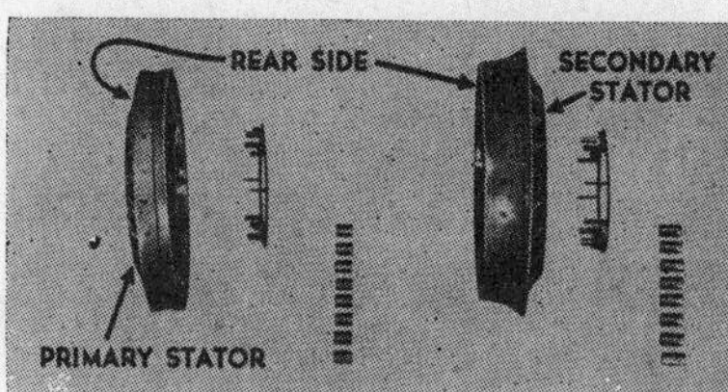

Fig. 99—Layout of stator parts

Fig. 100—Using special tool to install secondary stator into primary stator

Fig. 101—Checking rotation of stator free wheel clutches

OVERHAUL OF TURBINE AND PRIMARY PUMP COVER—ALL MODELS THRU '52

Remove the cotter pin, nut, flat washer and slotted washer from the turbine bolt and remove the cover.

Bend down the ears of the lock plate and remove the three turbine drive flange retaining bolts and the lock plate.

Remove the flange, the shim if present, the thin thrust washer, the turbine bolt and the thick thrust washer from the rear side of the turbine.

Inspect the parts for wear and check the fit of the turbine bolt in the turbine bushing.

If the turbine bushing is worn replace it using a pilot and driver as shown or a similar setup that will prevent distortion of the turbine face and cocking of the bushing.

To assemble the turbine parts place the thick thrust washer in the rear face of the turbine so that the lugs enter the locating holes. Place a new "0" ring seal on the turbine bolt and install it.

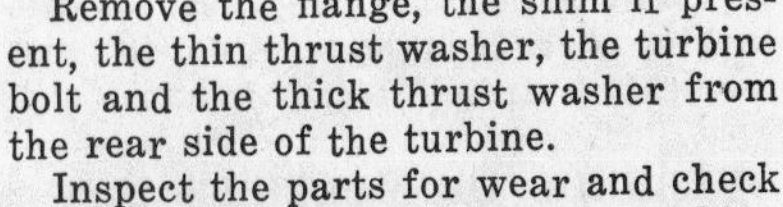

Fig. 102—Disassembling primary pump cover from the turbine bolt

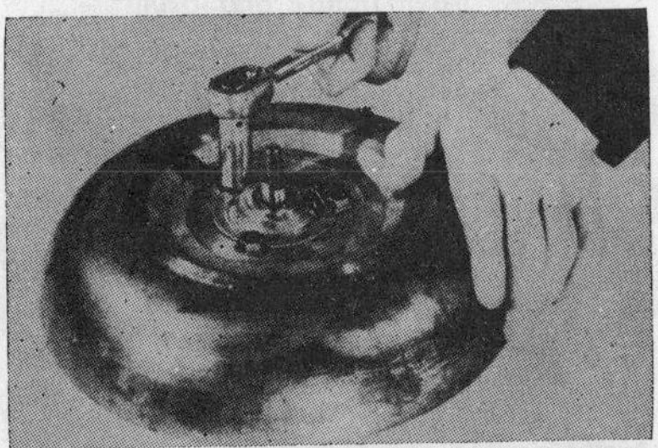

Fig. 103—Remove turbine drive flange retaining bolts

Fig. 104—Layout of turbine drive flange parts

Fig. 105—Check fit of turbine bolt in turbine bushing

Fig. 106—Use of driver to remove turbine bushing

Fig. 107—Pressing new turbine bushing into place

Fig. 108—Install the thick thrust washer in the turbine, index the lugs with the locating holes. Use new "O" ring seal on turbine bolt

Fig. 109—Install thin thrust washer, shim if used, and the turbine drive flange

Fig. 110—Tighten drive flange bolts to 12½-15 ft. lbs.

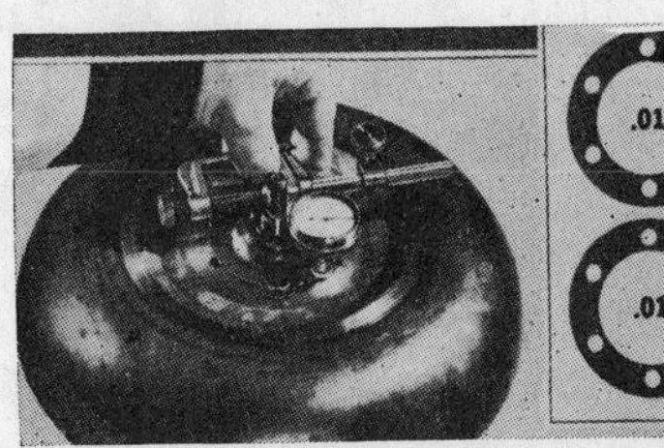

Fig. 111—Adjust end play of turbine bolt between .002"-.016" by shims as shown

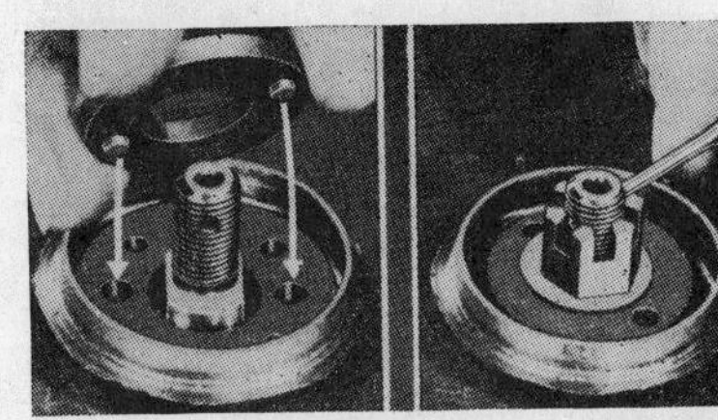

Fig. 112—Locate slotted washer in primary pump cover (turbine cover) as shown

Fig. 113—Install new "0" ring seal on primary pump cover

OVERHAUL, TURBINE—*continued*

Next install the thin thrust washer, the shim if used, and the flange indexing the three dowels with the locating holes.

Support the assembly with a block under the hub. Install a new lock plate and the three bolts and tighten to 12½-15 ft lbs. Check that the lugs on the thick washer are still in their locating holes. Bend up the ears of the lock plate.

Check the end play of the turbine bolt as shown. It should be from .002" to .016" F.I.R. Two shims .014" and .019" are available for adjusting end play.

Place the turbine cover over the turbine bolt. Install the slotted washer so that the locating lugs enter the holes in the cover. Install the flat washer and nut, tightening it to at least 12½ ft lbs. Do not loosen the nut to install the cotter pin. Be sure cotter pin is firmly placed.

Install a new "0" ring seal on the turbine cover being careful not to twist the seal or stretch it out of shape.

OVERHAUL OF MULTIPLE DISC CLUTCH—ALL MODELS THRU '52

Remove the snap ring and retainer to release the low sun gear and flange assembly.

Remove the clutch hub and the nine clutch plates from the clutch drum.

Using a setup as shown or something similar that will compress the clutch spring without distortion remove the snap ring. Do not injure the clutch vent valve in the front face of the low drum.

Remove the spring seat, spring and piston. If the piston sticks, strike the low drum on a wooden block to jar it out.

Remove the clutch outer seal from the piston and the inner seal from the hub of the low drum.

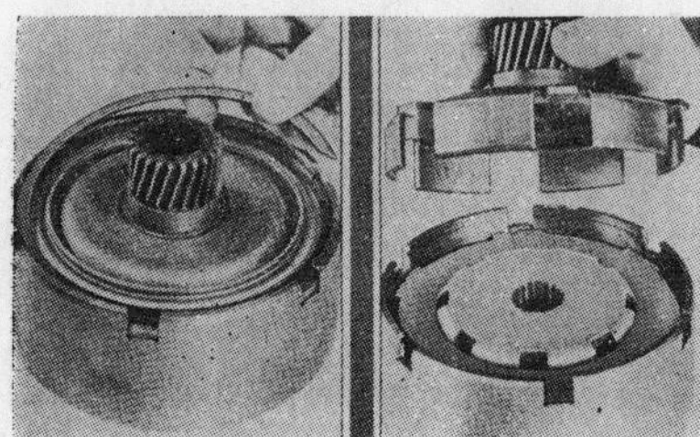

Fig. 114—Releasing low sun gear and flange assembly

Fig. 115—Remove clutch hub and plates from low drum

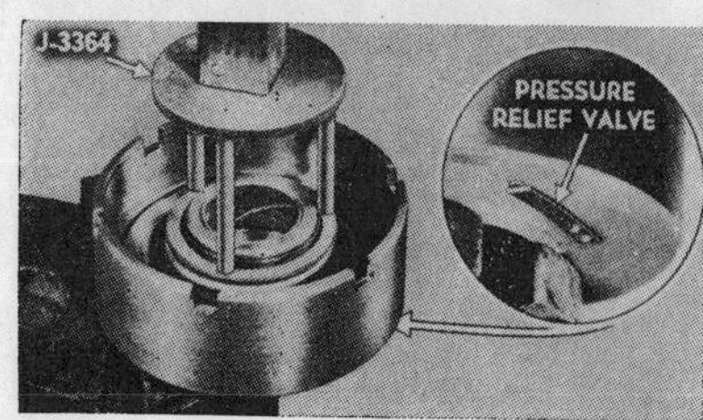

Fig. 116—Do not damage relief valve while compressing spring

Fig. 117—Removing clutch spring retaining ring

Fig. 118—Knock low drum on wood to shake out clutch piston

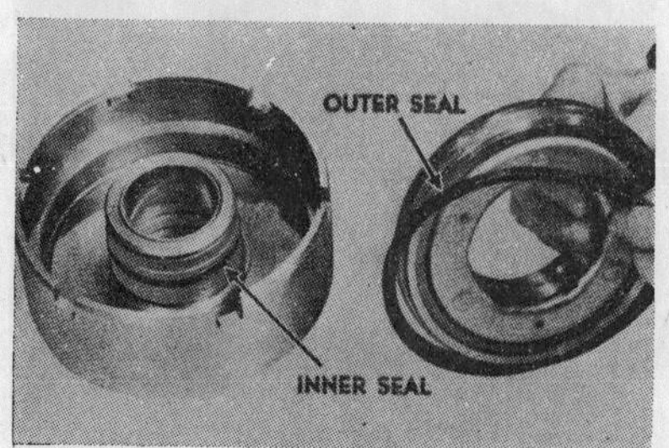

Fig. 119—Removing clutch seals

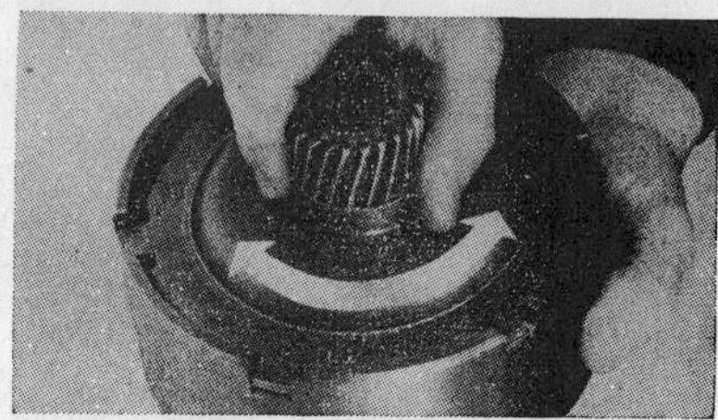

Fig. 120—There should be no radial play between flange and drum

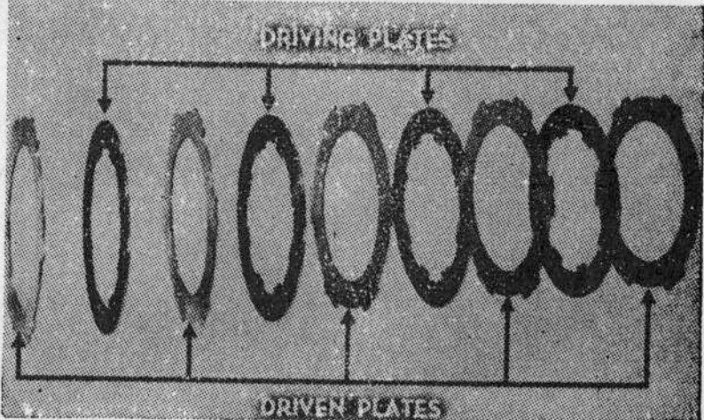

Fig. 121—Faced plates are driving plates. Dished plates are driven

Fig. 122—Check fit of driving plates on hub

Fig. 123—Check fit of driven plates in low sun gear flange

Check the fit of the flange drive lugs in the drum. There should be no appreciable radial play. Check the low sun gear for nicks or burrs.

Check the faced plates for burnt lining or metal pick up. Check the unlined dished plates for scoring and burn marks.

Make sure the driving plates are a free fit on the clutch hub and the driven plates fit freely in the flange of the low sun gear.

Fig. 124—Check low drum bushing for scores

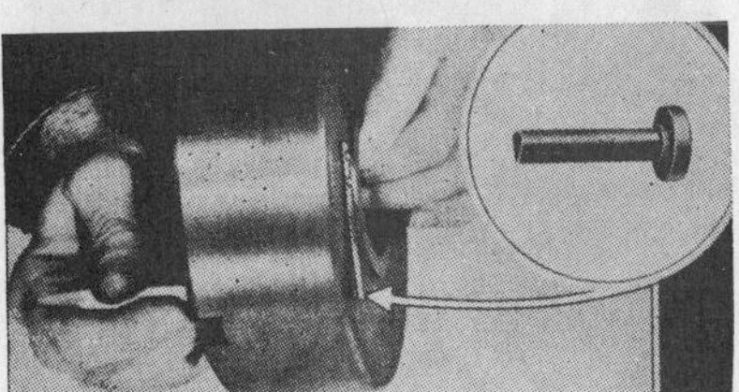

Fig. 125—Check clutch relief valve for free operation

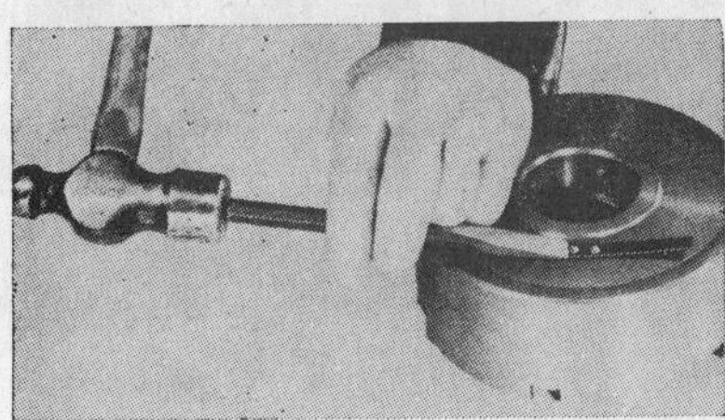

Fig. 126—To remove relief valve cut off rivets

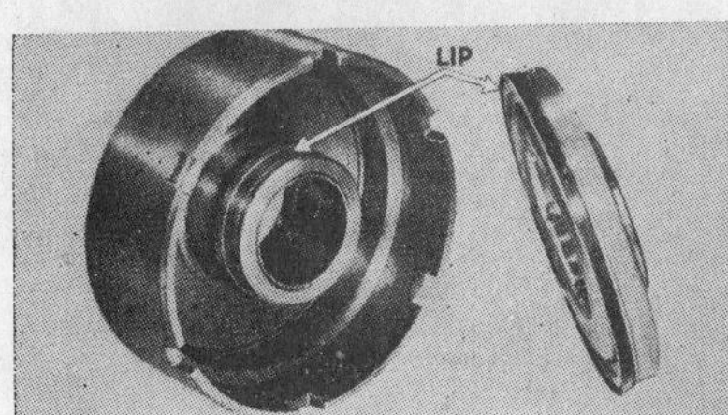

Fig. 127—Lips of new seals go to front of low drum

Check the low drum bushing for scores. This bushing is not replaceable. If the bushing is damaged the drum must be replaced.

Check the vent (pressure relief) valve for free operation. If there is trouble cut off the heads of the rivets. Drive them out. Remove the spring and the valve. Install a new valve, spring and rivets and peen over securely.

Install a new clutch outer seal on the piston and a new inner seal on the hub of the drum. The lips of both seals go toward the closed end of the low drum. Installation will be easier if the seals are first dipped in transmission fluid.

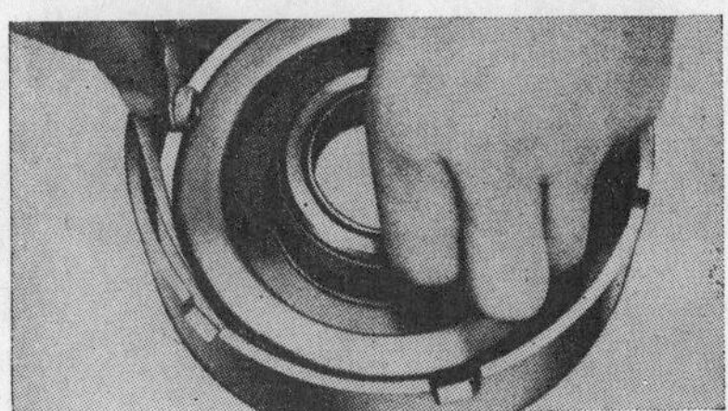

Fig. 128—Use feeler gauge to guide piston seal into drum

Fig. 129—Be careful spring seat does not catch in ring groove

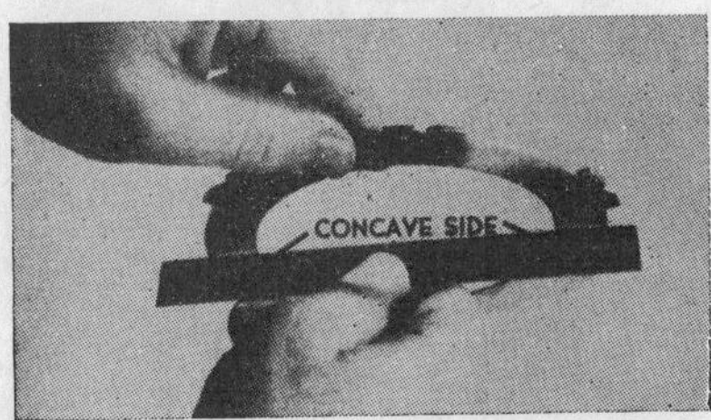

Fig 130—Straight edge will show direction of dish

Fig. 131—Start and end with a steel plate

Install the piston on the hub using some shim stock to keep the lip of the outer seal toward the front of the drum.

Install the spring and spring seat and compress the spring being certain the seat does not hang up in the snap ring groove. Install the snap ring.

Check the five all metal driven plates. They are dished and must be installed with the concave side toward the rear of the assembly. The dish is not easily detected but it is there and if the plates are installed with the dish in two directions the clutch will not work properly. The faced plates are not dished.

Place the four equally spaced tabs on the clutch hub thrust washer into slots in the clutch hub. Place clutch hub with

Fig. 132—Install low drum onto low sun gear flange

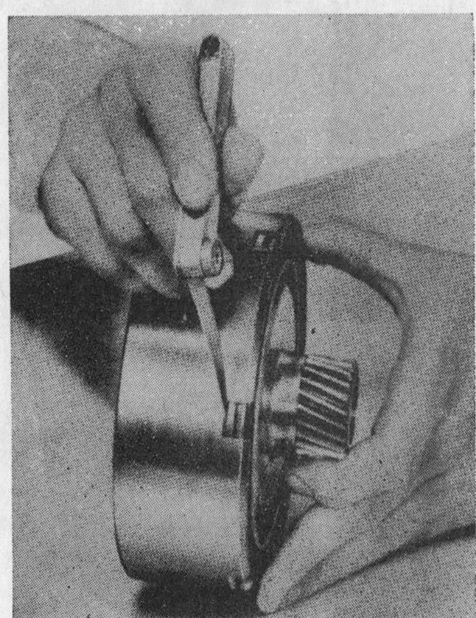

Fig. 133—Maximum permissible end play, lugs to drum is .013"

OVERHAUL, CLUTCH—*continued*

thrust washer in the low sun gear flange. The open side of the hub up. Starting with a steel (dished) plate. (The dished side toward the low sun gear.) Install the 5 dished and 4 lined plates alternately ending with a steel dished plate.

Lower the low drum over the plates and flange. Then invert and install the retainer and snap ring.

Check the end play between the clutch flange drive lugs and the bottom of the slots. If there is more than .013″ select a thicker snap ring. There are three thicknesses available: .055″, .064″ and .073″.

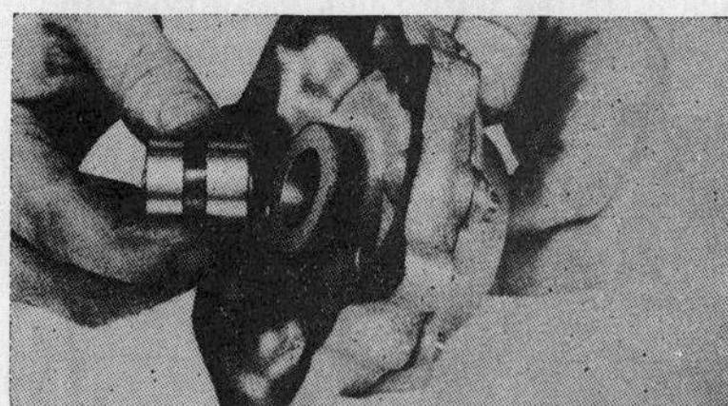

Fig. 134—Remove precision finished plunger assembly

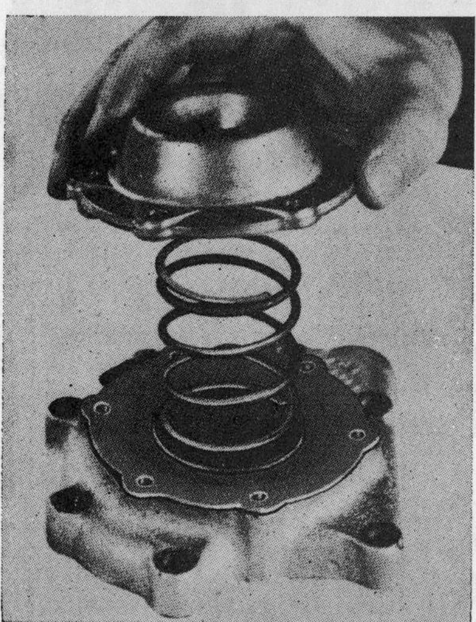

Fig. 135—Remove modulator cover

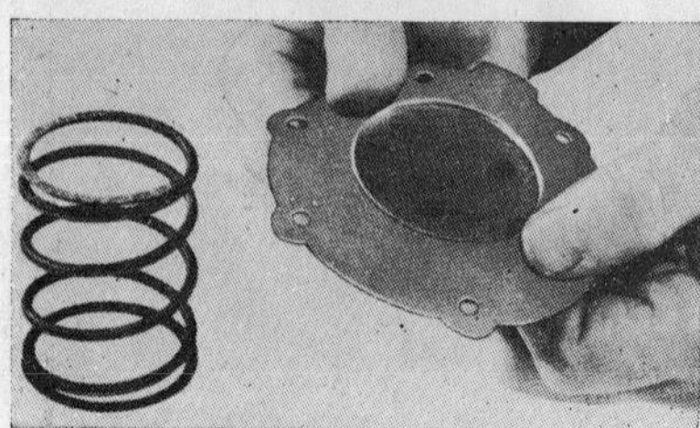

Fig. 136—Check diaphragm carefully

OVERHAUL OF MODULATOR ASSEMBLY—ALL MODELS THRU '52

Remove the hydraulic plunger assembly and place where this precision-finished unit will not be nicked or otherwise damaged.

This operation can be performed with unit in place. Remove the diaphragm cover screws, holding the cover down to overcome the pressure of the diaphragm spring. Remove the cover, spring and diaphragm.

Check the diaphragm spring for distortion and loss of tension, the diaphragm for cracks, tears or other damage which could cause leaks.

Check the hydraulic plunger for free operation in its body and the body for free operation in the modulator housing.

To assemble the modulator, place housing flat on the bench and insert tool J-4261. This tool takes the place of the hydraulic plunger assembly and keeps the diaphragm from being forced down and torn when the spring and cover are installed. If tool is not available use a block of wood.

Install two 10-24 guide pins and place the diaphragm over the pins with the spring seat up. Install the spring and cover and tighten the screws to 12½-15 ft lbs.

Install the hydraulic plunger assembly in the housing with the open end out so the plunger can engage the modulator lever when the unit is assembled to the servo cover.

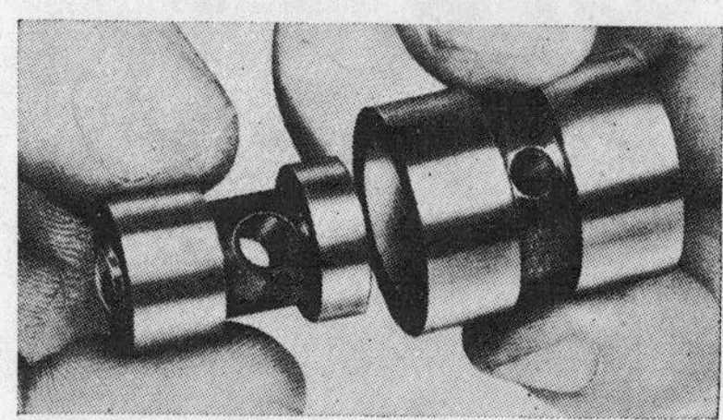

Fig. 137—Check both parts of plunger assembly

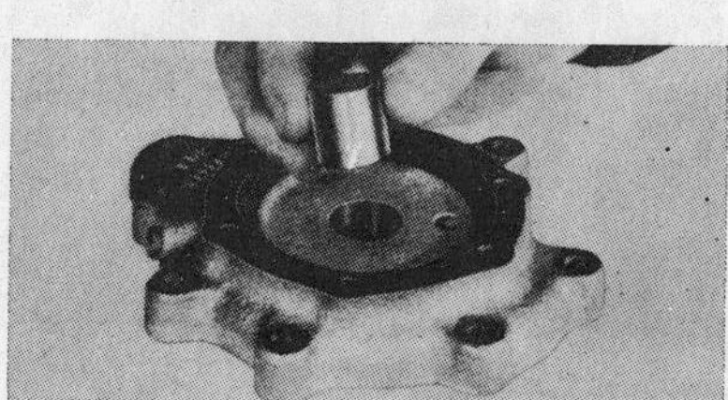

Fig. 138—Installing special tool to support diaphragm

Fig. 139—Tighten modulator screws 12½ to 15 ft lb

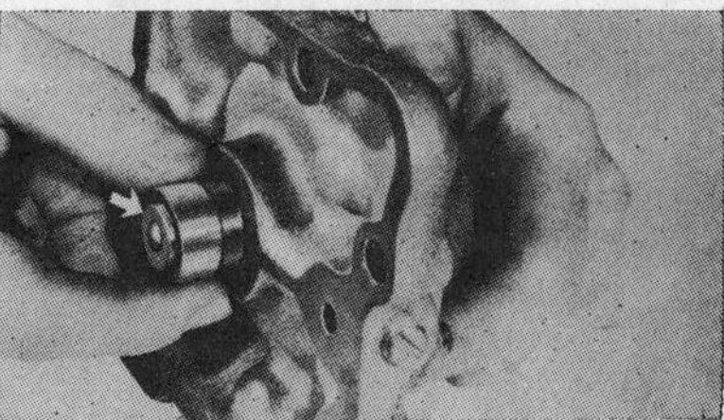

Fig. 140—Open end of plunger assembly goes out

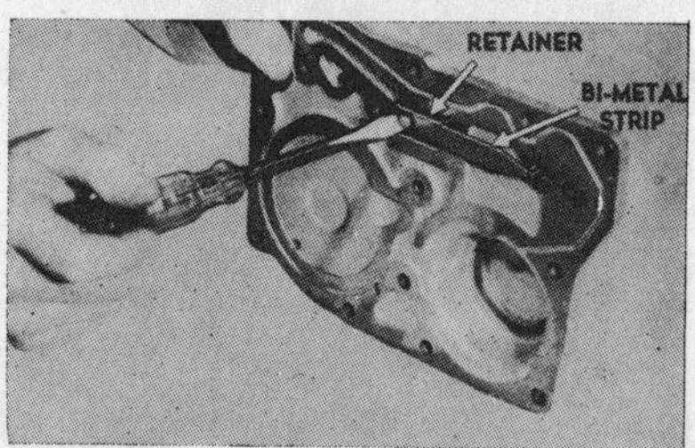

Fig. 141—Remove retainer and bi-metal strip

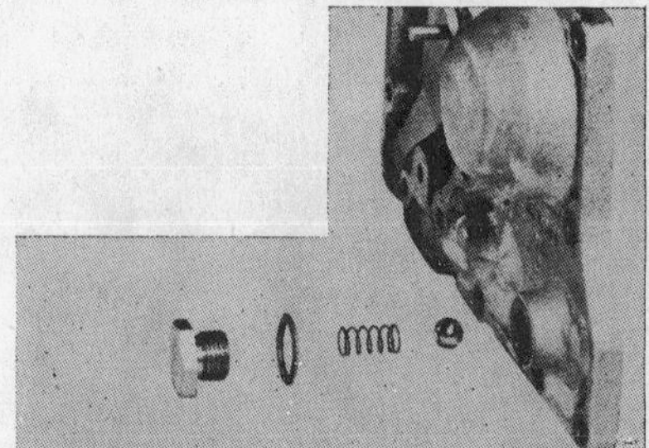

Fig. 142—Layout of lubrication bypass valve parts

OVERHAUL OF SERVO COVER—ALL MODELS THRU '52

Remove the thermostat valve retaining screw, the bi-metal strip and its retainer.

Remove the lubrication by pass valve plug, copper gasket, spring, and ball. Inspect the parts for damage.

Blow out all the oil passages and inspect the machined surfaces for damage.

Make sure the modulator control lever operates freely on its shaft.

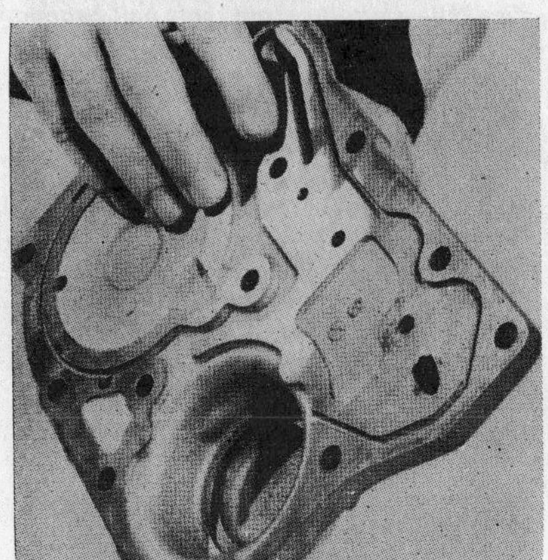

Fig. 143—Check Servo cover for nicks and cracks

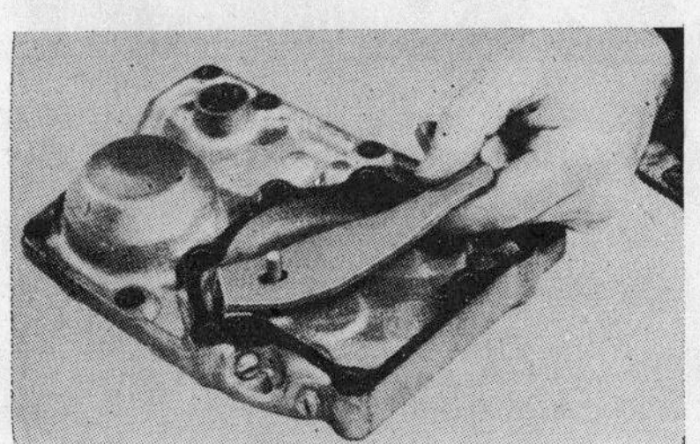

Fig. 144—Modulator lever should move freely

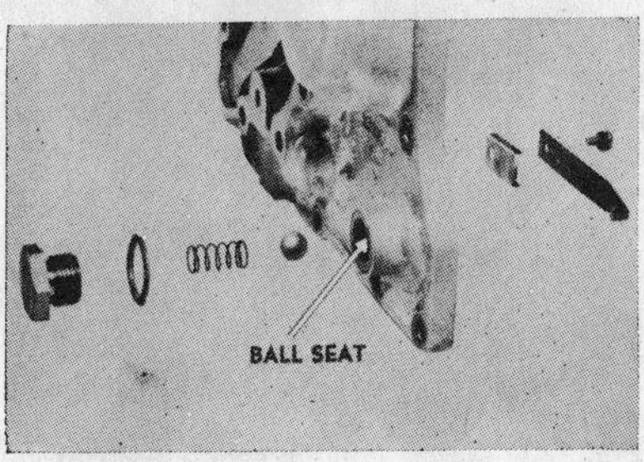

Fig. 145—Check ball seat and reassemble

Reinstate the ball and spring, place a new gasket on the plug and tighten. Reinstate the retainer, bi-metal strip and the retaining screw.

OVERHAUL OF FRONT PUMP—ALL MODELS THRU '52

Slide the stator support from the pump body.

Remove the driving and driven gears.

Note: These gears are not heat treated. Handle them carefully to avoid nicks.

Remove the hook ended oil seal ring from the driving gear.

Check all the parts for signs of wear or damage. The mating surfaces must be smooth to seal without a gasket.

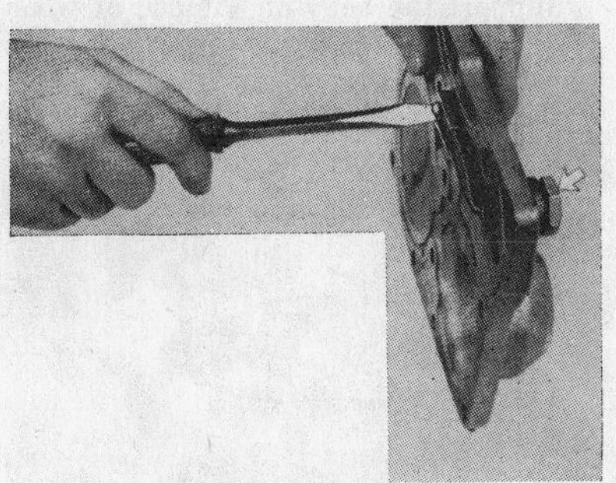

Fig. 146—Tighten securely

Fig. 147—Slide stator support (reactor shaft) from front pump

Fig. 148—Remove gears from front pump

Check that the oil ring fits its groove and has clearance at its ends when installed.

If the pump body oil seal needs replacement pry out the old and press in the new. The lip goes in.

With all pump parts dry, check that:

Clearance of driven gear to body is .001" - .002"

Gear backlash is .003 - .005

Fig. 149—Remove oil seal ring from driving gear

Fig. 150—Layout of front pump parts

Fig. 151—Check fit of ring on gear and in body

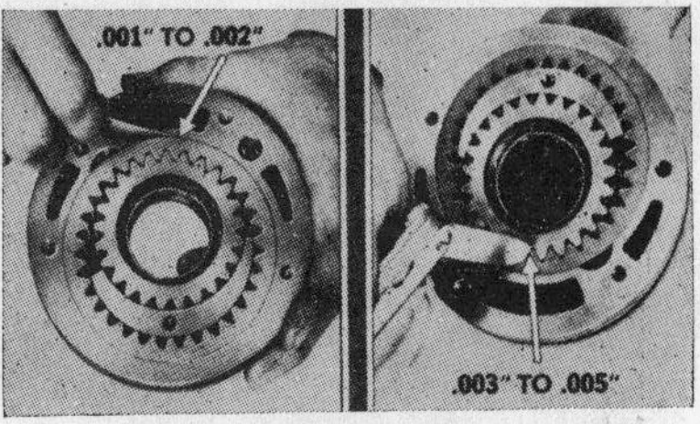

Fig. 152—Driven gear to body .001-.002" Gear backlash .003-.005"

OVERHAUL, PUMP—*continued*

Clearance driven gear to crescent is .002 - .005
Clearance driving gear to crescent is .005 - .006
End play is .0005 - .0015

Install the oil seal ring in the groove on the driving gear, cast all the parts with transmission lubricant and reassemble the pump and stator support.

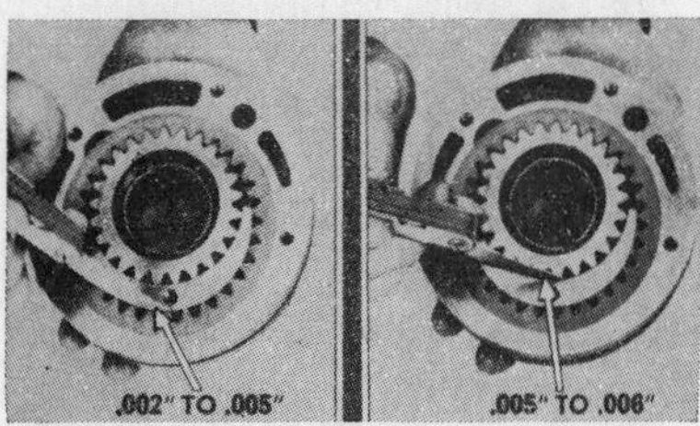

Fig. 153—Driven gear to crescent .002-.005". Driving gear to crescent .005-.006"

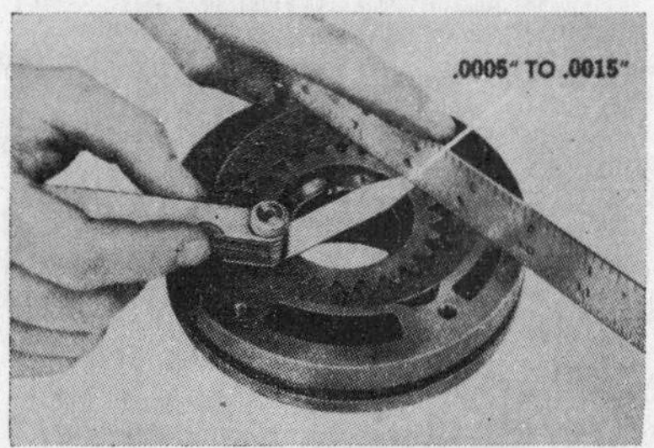

Fig. 154—End play both gears .005-.0015"

Fig. 155—Coat parts with fluid and reassemble

Fig. 156—Install new "O" ring on body

Install a new "0" ring seal on the pump body. Do not stretch or twist the "0" ring while installing.

OVERHAUL OF REAR PUMP—ALL MODELS THRU '52

Remove the retaining screws and the rear pump body plate.

Remove the driving and driven gears; taking care not to nick the unhardened teeth.

Check all the parts for signs of wear or damage. The mating surfaces must be smooth to seal without a gasket.

Check the output shaft's rear bearing. If it is rough, remove the three retaining bolts complete with lockwashers. Drive or press the bearing from the body.

Support the body on a block of wood to protect the mating surface and press in a new bearing.

Install the gears and check the clearances; they should be the same as for the front pump.

Oil the pump parts and reassemble.

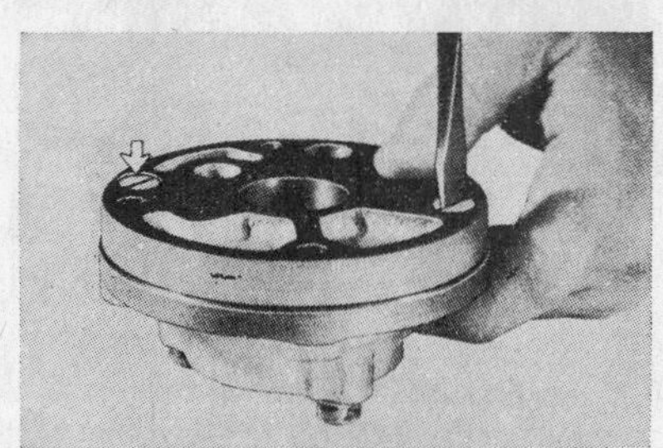

Fig. 157—Remove screws and body plate

Fig. 158—Remove gears from rear pump

Fig. 159—Layout of rear pump parts

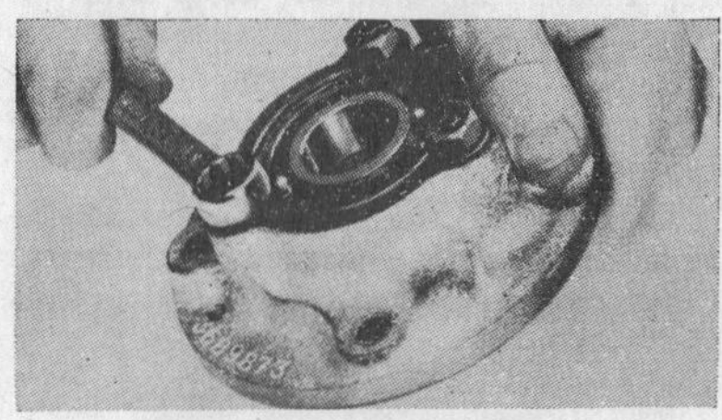

Fig. 160—Unbolt output shaft ball bearing

Fig. 161—Use press to install new bearing

Fig. 162—Driven gears to crescent .002-.005". Driven gear to body .001-.002". End play, both gears .005-.0015"

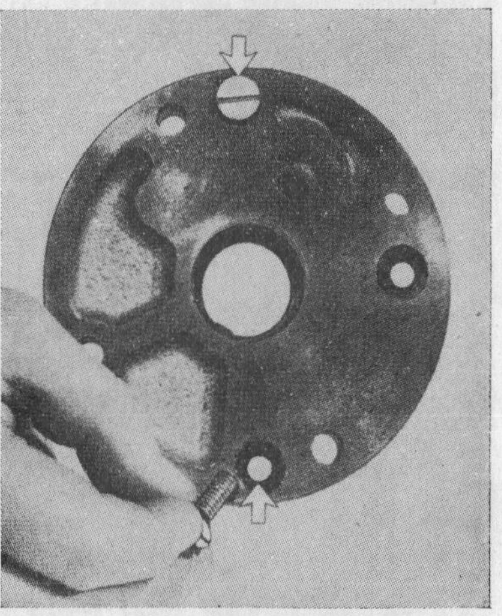

Fig. 163—Screw holes are staggered to insure correct assembly

OVERHAUL OF VALVE BODY—ALL MODELS THRU '52

Remove the two oil rings from the oil delivery sleeve. Unscrew the pressure relief valve assembly.

Remove the snap ring which holds the accumulator parts in the valve body and shake out the parts. If any should stick strike the valve body sharply on a wooden surface.

Remove the pump check valve from the valve body.

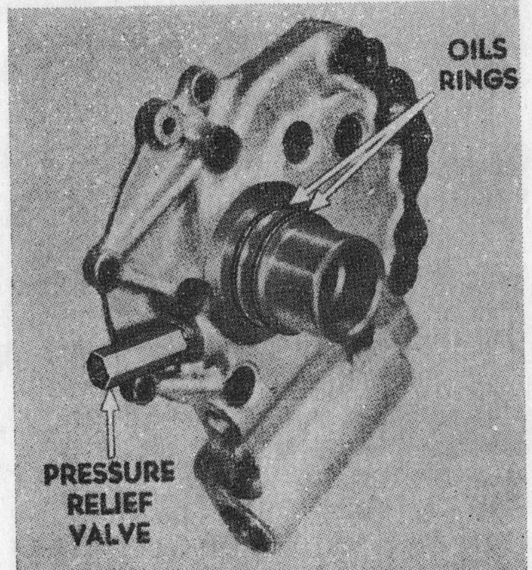

Fig. 164—Remove oil seal rings from delivery sleeve

Fig. 165—Remove special snap ring to release accumulator

Fig. 166—Remove pump check valve

Check the parts for scores and other damage. Be sure the accumulator piston slides freely in the bore.

Check that the accumulator valve body slides freely in its bore and check the small fiber valve for free operation.

Inspect all three accumulator springs for distortion and check the accumulator valve for free movement in its body.

Check that the oil rings are free in their grooves and the hooked ends have clearance when installed in the low drum hub.

Examine the pump check valve for good tension and the sealing surfaces of the valve and the valve body for nicks. Then install the valve.

Reassemble the accumulator into its bore and reinstall the lock ring.

Install the oil rings and the pressure relief valve. If the relief valve is suspect as a source of trouble renew the valve.

Fig. 167—Check accumulator piston for free movement

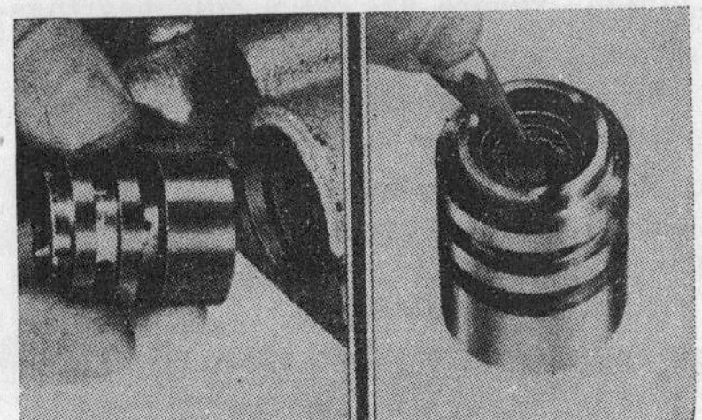

Fig. 168—Check small fiber valve and valve body

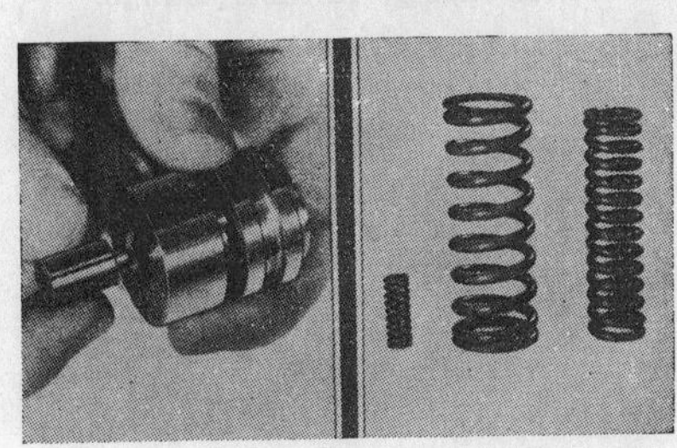

Fig. 169—Check accumulator valve and spring

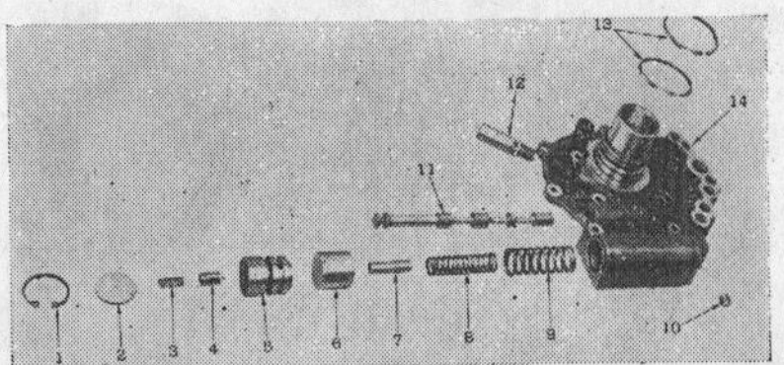

Fig. 170—Layout of valve body parts

1. Snap ring
2. Washer
3. Valve spring
4. Valve
5. Valve body
6. Piston
7. Piston stop
8. Piston spring inner
9. Piston spring outer
10. Plug
11. Manual control valve
12. Pressure relief valve
13. Oil seal rings
14. Valve body

Fig. 171—Check seal ring in groove of sleeve and low drum hub

Fig. 172—Examine pump check and reinstall

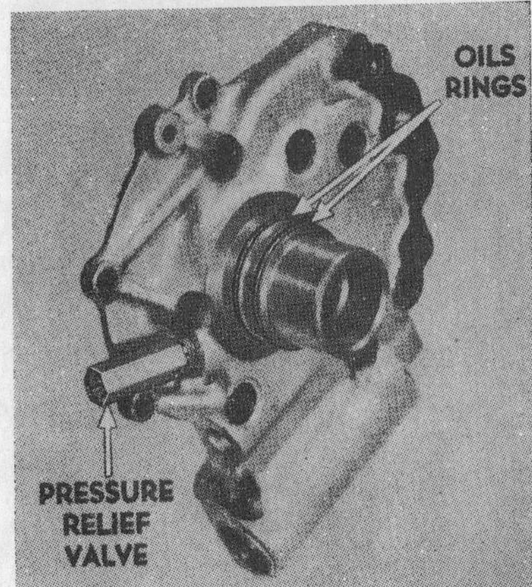

Fig. 173—If relief valve leaks install a new one

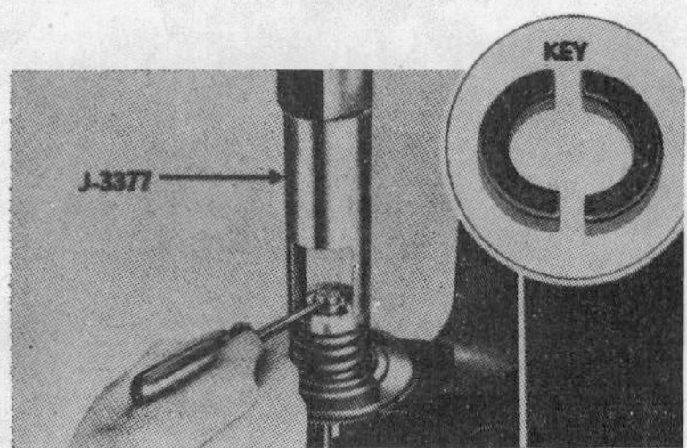

Fig. 174—Compress servo piston spring to release key

Fig. 175—Layout of reverse servo piston parts

Fig. 176—Check ring in reverse servo piston groove and in bore where end clearance should be .005-.010"

Fig. 177—At reassembly be sure key is properly seated

OVERHAUL OF SERVO PISTONS—ALL MODELS THRU '52

Compress the piston spring, remove the two-part retainer key and separate the assembly into its parts.

Check the piston ring for free operation in its groove and for end clearance in its bore. This clearance should be .005 to .010.

Reassemble the reverse servo.

Do the same operations for the low servo piston.

OVERHAUL OF PLANETARY GEAR SET—ALL MODELS THRU '52

Check all the gear teeth and all machined surfaces for damage. Check the fit of the output shaft in the ring gear bushing.

Inspect the reverse sun gear rear thrust washer and the input shaft pilot bushing for scoring or excess wear.

Check the end play of the planet gears which should be .006-.030.

Note: Disassembly of the planetary gear set is not often necessary. Should it be necessary, the following notes will prove helpful.

The lock plate for the pinion shafts is turned counterclockwise to release the shafts.

The pinions are removed in pairs. A short one first, then a long one. Each pair uses the same set of thrust washers which are installed with the long pinions. There are 20 needle bearings in each end of each long pinion. If the needle bearings show any signs of wear they must all be replaced.

The pinion shafts must be marked before disassembly as they are a selective fit and it is necessary that they be returned to the same place. Besides being held by the lock plate, the pinion shafts are a press fit in the flange of the output shaft.

The long planet pinions are located at the closed portions of the carrier. The short ones go in the openings.

Fig. 178—Check fit of output shaft in reverse ring gear bushing

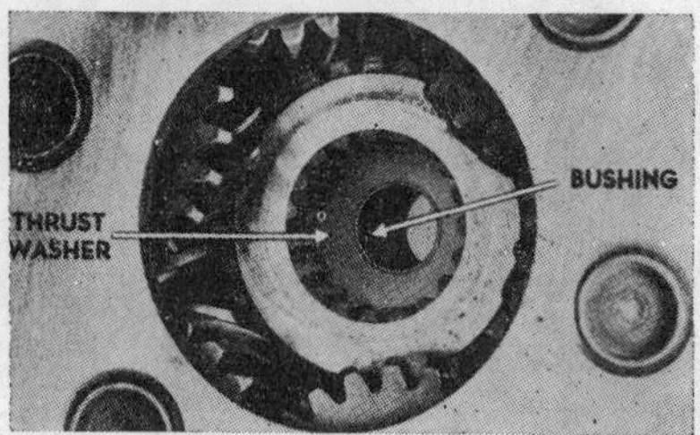

Fig. 179—Check reverse sun gear rear thrust washer and input shaft pilot bushing

Fig. 180—Check that end play of gears is between .006 and .030"

OVERHAUL OF INPUT SHAFT—ALL MODELS THRU '52

Check that the oil ring is free on the input shaft and that there is clearance at the hooked ends when it is in the valve body.

Check the fit of the input shaft splines in the turbine drive flange, the clutch hub, and the reverse sun gear.

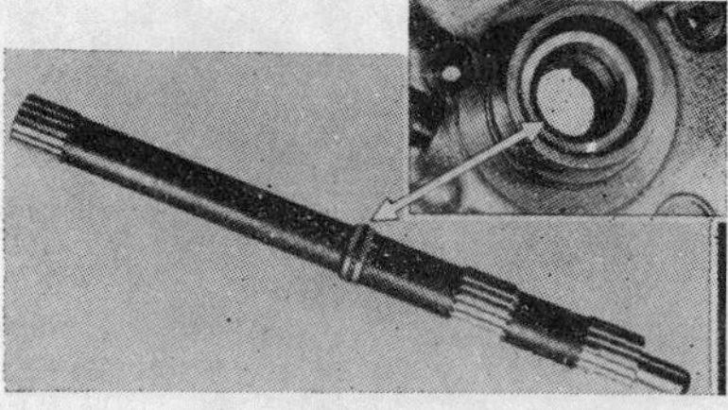

Fig. 181—Check fit of input shaft oil ring in oil delivery sleeve

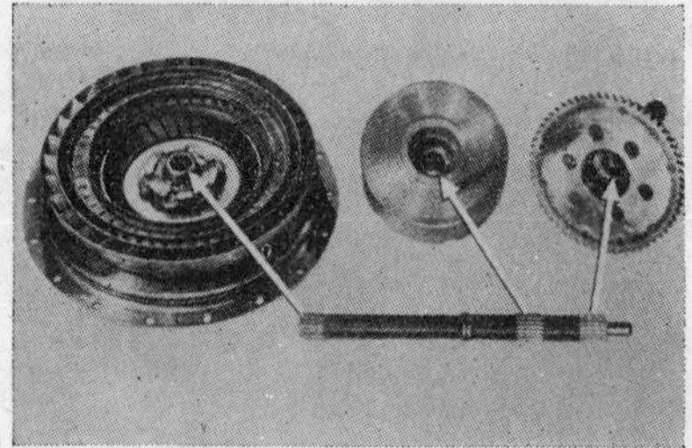

Fig. 182—Check fit of input shaft splines in turbine drive flange, clutch hub, and reverse sun gear

Fig. 183—Check all over case for damage

Fig. 184—Push old case bushing out from rear

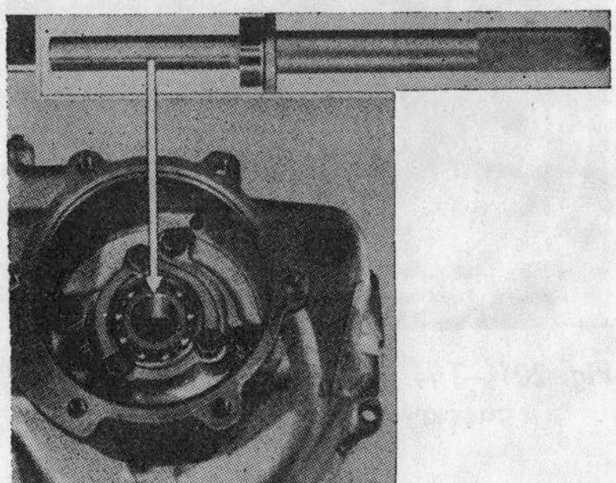
Fig. 185—Use rear pump assembly as bushing installation pilot

OVERHAUL OF CASE AND BANDS—ALL MODELS THRU '52

Blow out the passages and inspect for damage and for sand holes. Check the bushing for signs of wear. If necessary, the bushing can be replaced. The new one is made to size and will require no fitting. Install the oil pump and use the rear bearing as a pilot for the installing tool. Install the bushing with the chamfered end to the rear.

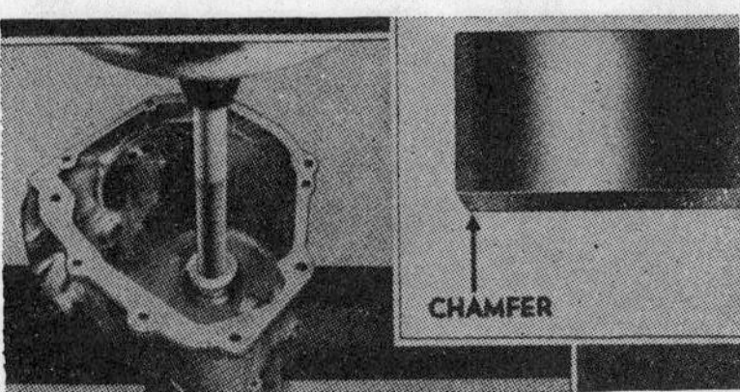

Fig. 186—Install new bushing from the front chamfer to rear

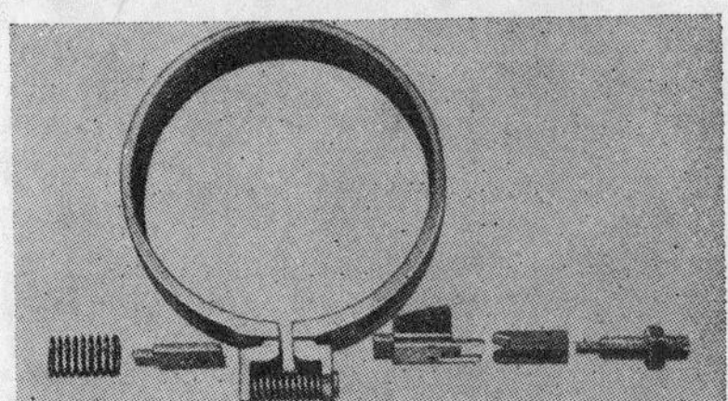
Fig. 187—Layout of low band linkage

Fig. 188—Layout of reverse band linkage

The bands have bonded linings and should require little attention. Check the bands for cracks and scoring. Inspect the band linkage for signs of excessive wear.

REINSTALL SUCTION PIPE AND SCREEN—ALL MODELS THRU '52

Install a new seal on the suction pipe and install the assembly in the case. Place a new "O" ring seal in the filler tube opening and install the right side cover using a new gasket.

REINSTALL VALVE BODY—ALL MODELS THRU '52

Install two ¼-20 guide pins in two valve body to housing holes. Install a new gasket over the pins.

Install the valve body and retaining bolts. Tighten the bolts evenly, torquing the two adjacent to the regulator valve to 8 ft lbs. The rest to 10 ft lbs.

Insert the regulator valve and the manual valve, checking each for free operation. If there is a tendency to bind, try loosening the bolts and retightening evenly.

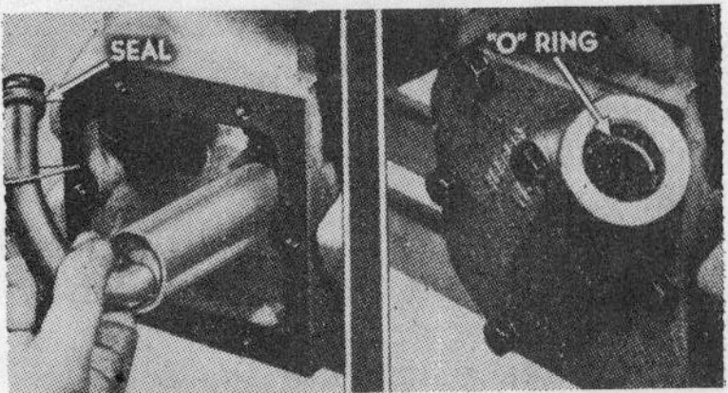

Fig. 189—Install new seal on suction pipe and new "O" ring in filler tube opening

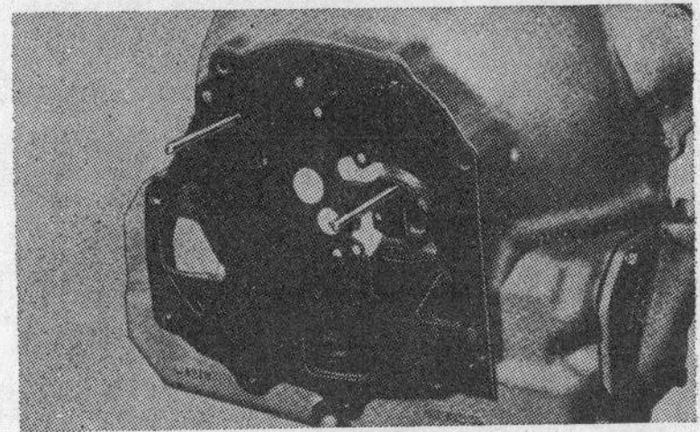
Fig. 190—Install two ¼ x 20 guide pins in rear of bell housing

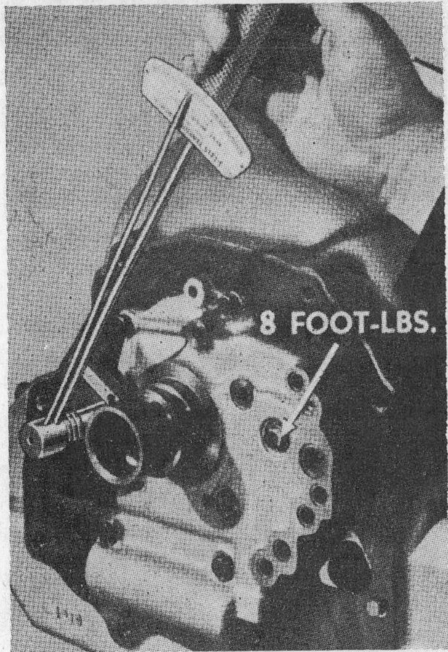

Fig. 191—Install gasket and valve body, tighten bolts over regulator valve to no more than 8 ft pounds

Fig. 192—Check free movement of manual and regulator valves

REINSTALL FRONT PUMP—ALL MODELS THRU '52

Align all holes in the front pump body and stator support and install two ¼-20 guide pins.

Moisten the "O" ring seal with transmission lubricant and be sure it is to the front of the groove.

Insert the pump into the converter housing with the "TOP" mark to the top of the housing. Be sure the suction and delivery holes on left side of pump are aligned with the stator support flange holes.

Drive the pump into place using a tool such as shown or something similar that will not nick the metal nor cock the pump in the recess.

Insert the 5 self-locking pump bolts thru the valve body. Tighten all to 10 ft lbs save those near the regulator valve, which remain at 8 ft lbs.

Recheck that the valves move freely.

Check that the pump moves freely.

Fig. 193—Using two ¼ x 20 guide pins install front pump. Note "top" goes to top of bell housing

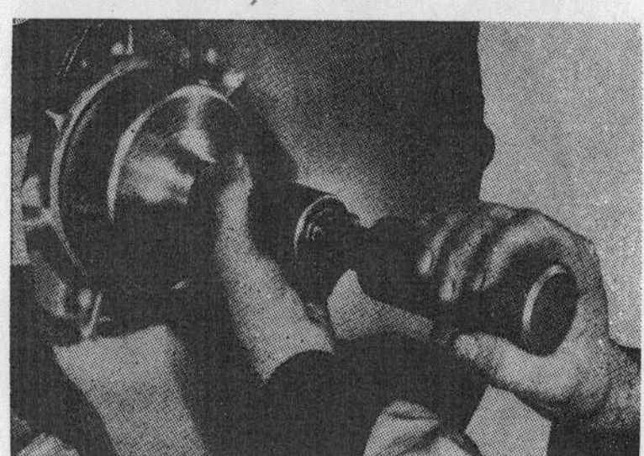

Fig. 194—Driving front pump into place

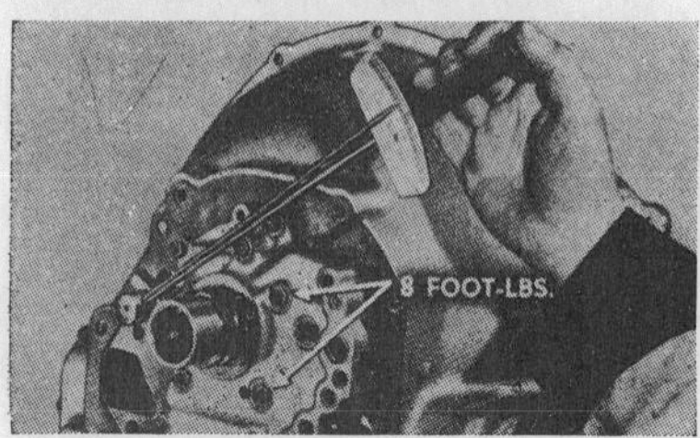

Fig. 195—Do not tighten bolts near regulator valve over 8 ft pounds

Fig. 196—Recheck that valves move freely

Fig. 197—Check front pump by turning drive lugs with a pencil

REINSTALL REAR PUMP—ALL MODELS THRU '52

Using two 5/16-18 guide pins, install a new gasket and the rear pump, aligning the suction and delivery holes. Tighten the pump retaining bolts to 12½-15 ft lbs. Have the word "TOP" to the top of the case.

Rotate the pump drive gear so the drive lug is at the top.

Fig. 198—Use two 5/16 x 18 guide pins to install rear pump—note "top" goes to top of case

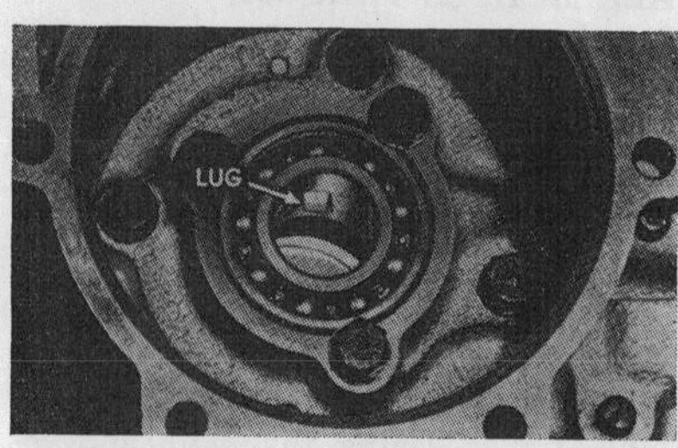

Fig. 199—Rotate drive gear so lug is up

REINSTALL REVERSE MECHANISM—ALL MODELS THRU '52

Install the reverse servo piston, using a ring compressor to fit the ring into the cylinder. The notch on the shaft should be toward the front of the case.

Install the reverse band and strut assembly with the thinner of the two flanges away from the piston.

Thread in the adjusting screw until it enters the hole in the anchor.

Place the bronze thrust washer on the hub of the reverse ring gear and install the gear in the case.

Tighten the reverse band adjusting screw all the way, then back off exactly 2¾ turns and tighten the lock nut to 20-25 ft lbs.

Fig. 200—Compress reverse servo piston ring to reinstall piston

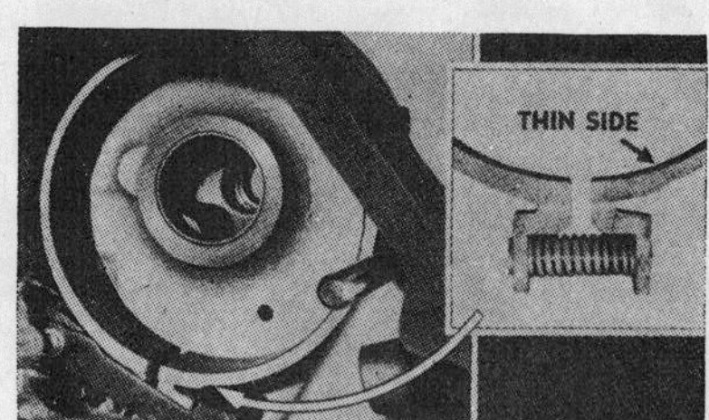

Fig. 201—The thin flange of reverse band goes away from servo piston

Fig. 202—Install reverse ring gear with thrust washer in place

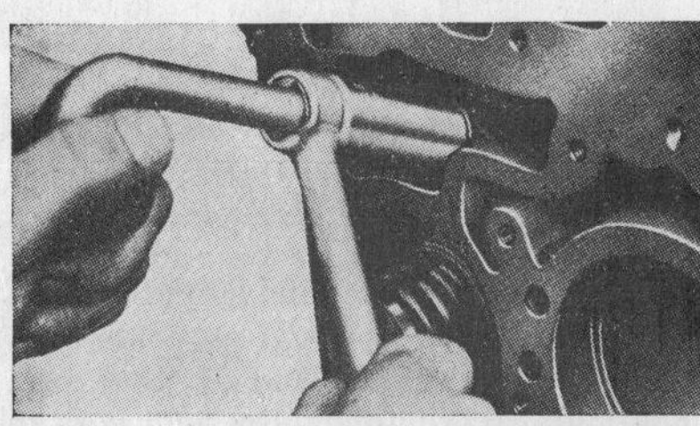

Fig. 203—Back off rear band adjusting screw 2¾ turns from full tight

REINSTALL PLANETARY GEAR SET —ALL MODELS THRU '52

Slide the planetary carrier assembly into the reverse ring gear, being careful to keep the slot in the output shaft up so that it will engage the drive lug of the rear oil pump.

Verify engagement of the slot and the lug by measuring the amount of shaft protruding from the rear bearing. If there is ⅞" or more of shaft then all is well.

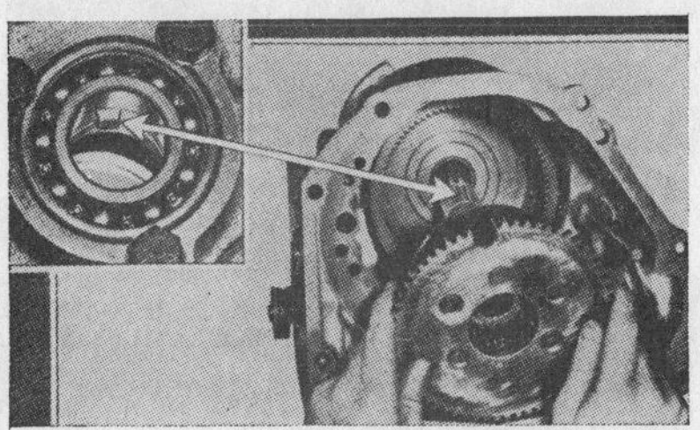

Fig. 204—Align slot in output shaft with lug of rear pump

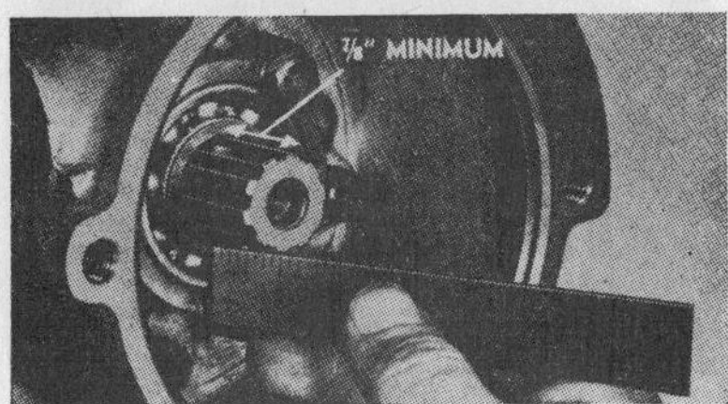

Fig. 205—If ⅞" of shaft protrudes, installation is OK

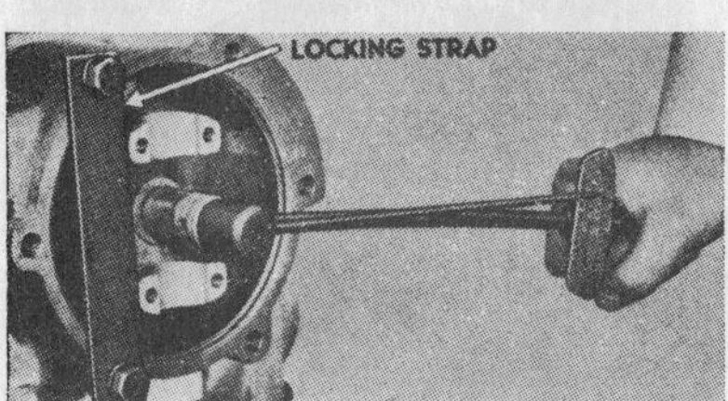

Fig. 206—Tightening yoke belt to 25-30 ft lbs will seat gasket journal

Install the yoke of the universal joint, the flat washer, lockwasher and retaining bolt. Install a locking strap to keep the yoke from turning and tighten the bolt to 25-30 ft lbs.

Check that there is 1/32" to 1/16" between the nailhead and the retaining bolt, as the passage in the bolt provides lubricant to the universal joint.

Install the speedometer driven gear, and tighten the fitting to 45-50 ft lbs.

REINSTALL MULTIPLE DISC CLUTCH—ALL MODELS THRU '52

When the transmission has been firmly bolted back onto the converter housing there must be between .007" and .035" clearance or end play between the low sun gear and the reverse sun gear. The thickness of the bronze thrust washer riding the input shaft between the two gears is selected to control this clearance. To do the necessary measuring use a setup similar to that shown in the pictures and follow this procedure.

Step a. Install the large bronze thrust washer and the clutch assembly on the oil delivery sleeve.

Step b. Measure the distance between the front face of the reverse sun gear and the plane of the front face of the transmission case.

Step c. Compare this distance with the distance between the rear face of the converter housing and the rear face of the low sun gear as mounted in step a.

Step d. There are three bronze thrust washers available: .095", .120", and .145". Select one of these to reduce the difference between the dis-

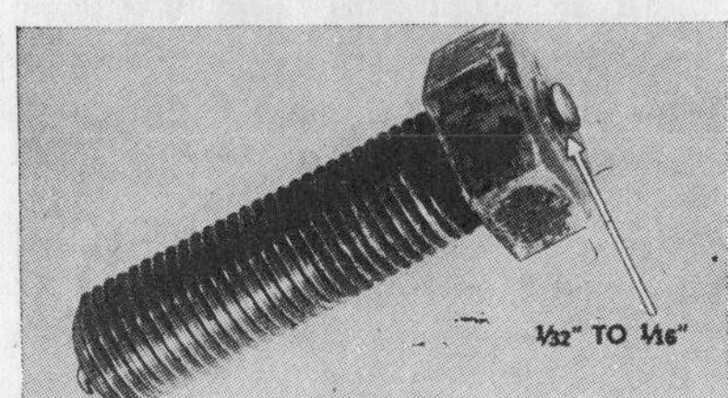

Fig. 207—Rail head should have clearance 1/32" to 1/16

Fig. 208—Low sun gear to reverse sun gear bronze thrust washer is clearance control washer

Fig. 209—Chevrolet tool used to determine thickness of clearance control washer and thicknesses of available washers

Fig. 210—Step A. Install low drum to valve body thrust washer and clutch assembly on oil delivery sleeve

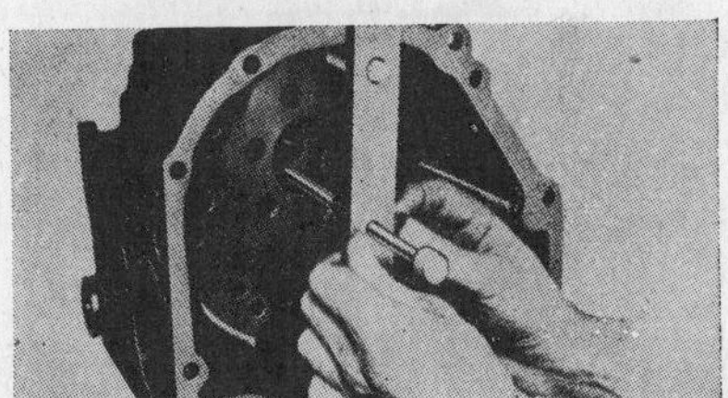

Fig. 211—Step B. Measure distance from front face of case to front face of reverse sun gear

Fig. 212—Step C. Measure distance from rear face of bell housing to rear face of low sun gear, .120 washer used for trial

Fig. 213—Step D difference between distance in step B and that in step C should be between .007 and .035"

Fig. 214—Lip of selector lever shaft seal goes to case

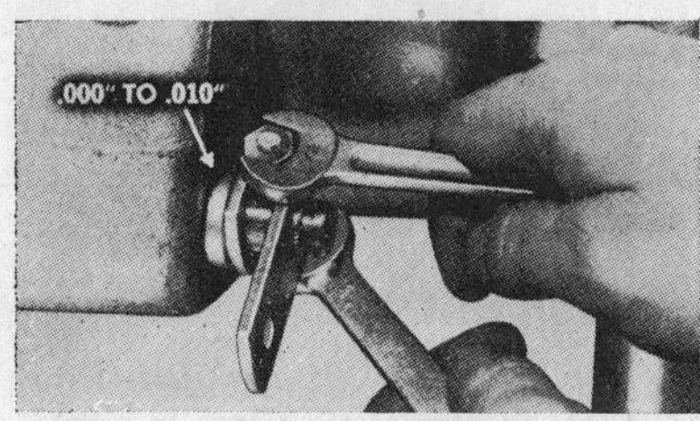

Fig. 215—Hold clearance between flat washer and lever to no more than .010"

Fig. 216—Push on wound up spring to catch end on inside of case

CLUTCH, REINSTALL—*continued*

tance found in step b and that in step c to the specified tolerance of .007"-.035".

Install the selector shaft and apply spring assembly and place a new seal on the shaft. The lip of the seal goes against the case.

Install the flat washer and the selector lever so that with shaft all the way to the rear there is .000"-.010" clearance between the washer and the lever. Tighten the selector lever lock bolt.

Install the parking lock pawl and spring. Using the tool as shown, or a screw driver, wind up the spring and catch the end on the inside of the case.

Remove the clutch assembly from the oil delivery sleeve and insert the input shaft into it. Double spline end goes to the rear.

Coat the previously selected low sun gear thrust washer (Step d above) with graphite grease and install on rear end of shaft so that the missing spline of the washer is aligned with the oil hole in the shaft and the flat side is toward the reverse sun gear. The milled side goes against the low sun gear to permit lubricant flow.

Fig. 217—Gap in splines of clearance control thrust washer goes over oil hole

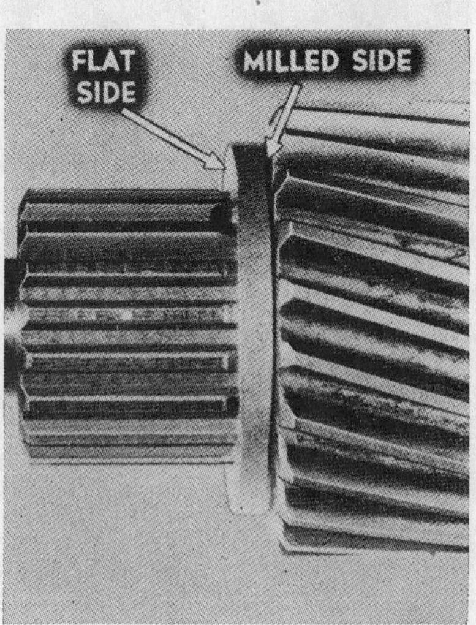

Fig. 218—Milled side of clearance washer goes to low sun gear

Fig. 219—Install input shaft assembly, being sure reverse sun gear rear thrust washer is in place

Fig. 220—Install low servo piston

Fig. 221—Thin flange of low band goes toward low servo piston

Make sure the reverse sun gear thrust washer is in its recess in the output shaft and install the input shaft and clutch assembly, turning so the gears and splines mesh.

REINSTALL LOW BAND MECHANISM— ALL MODELS THRU '52

Place the release spring on the low servo piston shaft and install the piston using a ring compressor to ease the piston into the cylinder.

Install the low band with the thinner flange toward the piston.

Thread the adjusting screw thru the case into the low band anchor.

ATTACHING THE CASE TO THE HOUSING— ALL MODELS THRU '52

Install two ⅜-16 guide pins in the rear face of the bell housing.

Fig. 222—Install two ⅜x16 guide pins in rear face of bell housing and new half moon gasket

Fig. 223—Reinstall manual valve and lever. Valve should protrude 1½"

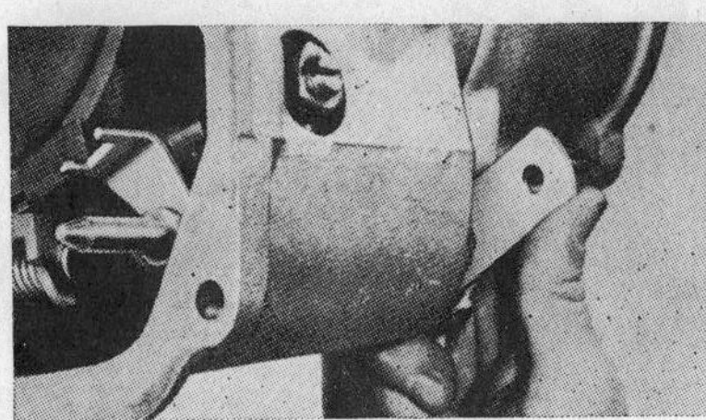

Fig. 224—Turn selector lever to stop detent

Install a new valve body to transmission case gasket.

Be sure large bronze thrust washer is still in place on the oil delivery sleeve.

Install the manual control valve and lever. Position the valve so it protrudes exactly 1½". This is reverse position.

Raise the selector lever as far as it will go which is the last detent and so positions the manual valve selector lever which contacts the manual control valve lever already installed.

Remove the left side cover. Mating of the levers can be observed thru the hole.

Slide the transmission case into place against the bell housing, watching thru the left side hole that the manual valve levers are mating. Reinstall the left side cover. Tighten the bolts holding the case to the housing to 15-20 ft lbs.

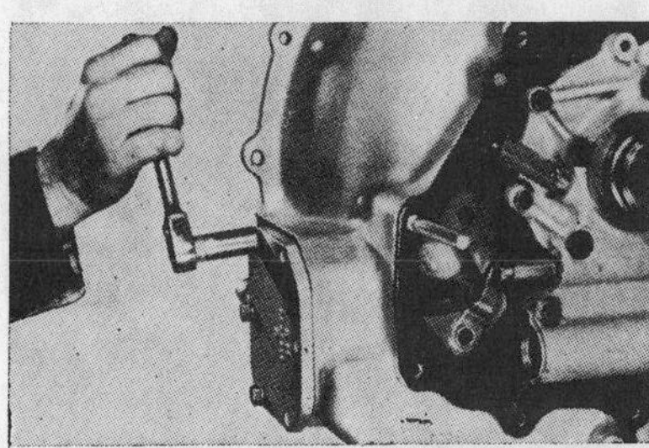

Fig. 225—Remove left side cover

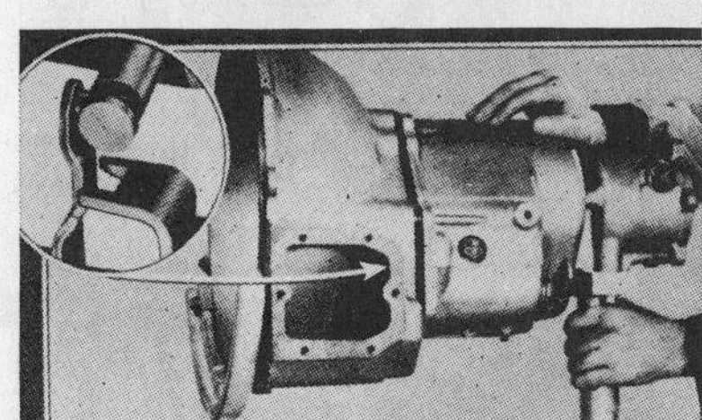

Fig. 226—Slide case in place against housing. Check mating of levers thru left side hole

Fig. 227—Install two 5/16x18 servo cover and modulator guide pins, new gasket and pressure regulator valve

REINSTALL SERVOS AND MODULATOR— ALL MODELS THRU '52

Install two 5/16-18 guide pins in the right face of the case, choosing holes that will also locate the modulator as-

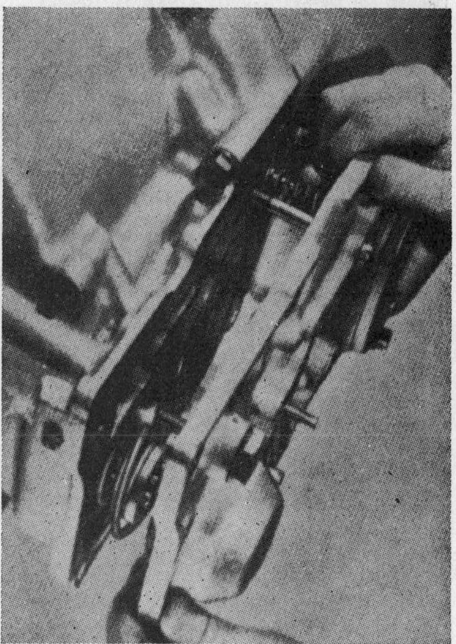

Fig. 228—Install springs and servo cover assembly

Fig. 229—Install the modulator assembly

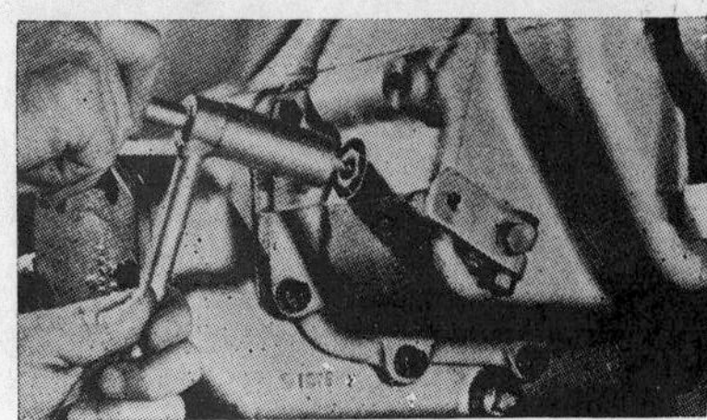

Fig. 230—Back off low band screw three turns from full tight

SERVOS, REINSTALL—*continued*

sembly. Install a new servo cover gasket and the pressure regulator valve.

Install the inner and outer regulator valve springs, the reverse servo piston return spring and the servo cover. Compress the springs with the cover and install the retaining bolts.

Install a new gasket and the modulator assembly. Install the retaining bolts.

Tighten the modulator and servo cover bolts evenly to 12-15 ft lbs.

Tighten the low servo band adjusting screw all the way, then back off three complete turns and tighten the lock nut to 20-25 ft lbs and install the protective cap.

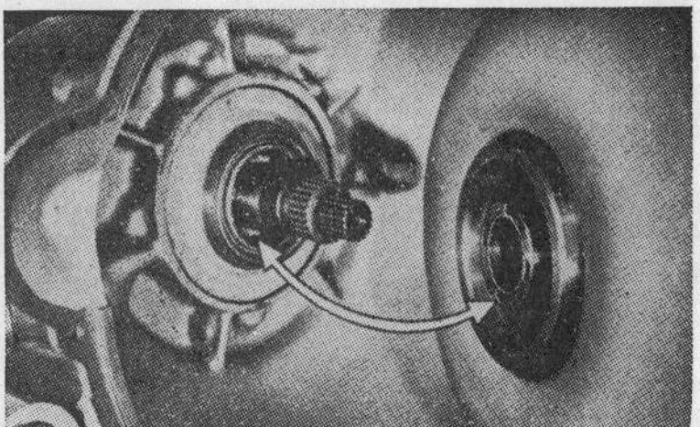

Fig. 231—Align slots in hub of primary pump with drive tangs of front oil pump

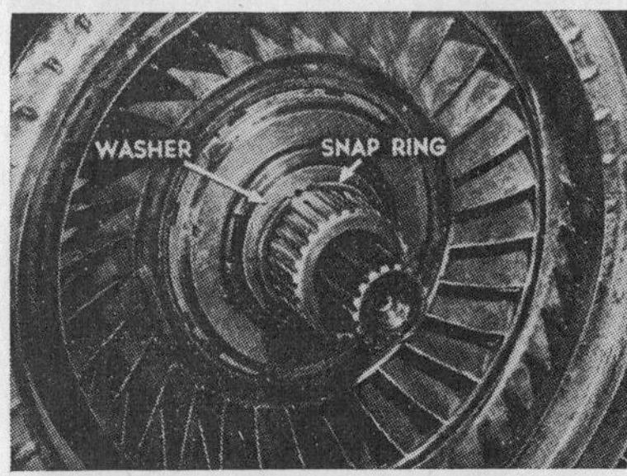

Fig. 232—Slide primary pump into flare and install snap-ring

Fig. 233—Primary stator (small) goes to rear

REINSTALL CONVERTER—ALL MODELS THRU '52

Lubricate the front pump oil seal and install the primary pump assembly, aligning the drive slots in the hub with the drive tangs of the front oil pump.

Install the primary pump retaining washer and snap ring.

Mount the stator assembly on the stator support. The smaller stator is the primary one and goes to the rear.

Thread two 5/16-24 guide pins into the primary pump. Coat the "O" ring seal in the cover with transmission fluid and check that it is not twisted and is to the forward part of its slot.

Align the dowel in the primary pump flange with the dowel hole in the cover assembly and install.

Install twelve converter cover to primary pump bolts, putting one on each side of the dowel, skip a hole, install two more, skip a hole and so on around the cover.

Check that the cover is firmly seated and tighten the bolts evenly to 15-20 ft lbs.

Fig. 234—Use two 5/16x24 guide pins to install cover onto primary pump

Fig. 235—Replace bolts, one either side of dowel, skip one and install two, around entire cover

Fitting Ball Joint

Install universal joint ball seat, ball and collar and add or remove shims to allow a snug fit.

If ball cannot be moved by hand, add shims until a smooth, firm movement is possible.

If ball moves too freely by hand, remove shims until the movement is firm and smooth.

When adjustment is OK, remove universal joint ball and collar, noting the number of shims for use when transmission is reinstalled.

Note: A new cork seal coated with graphite grease is placed in the collar before final assembly together with a new "O" ring seal on the ball seat as installed in the transmission.

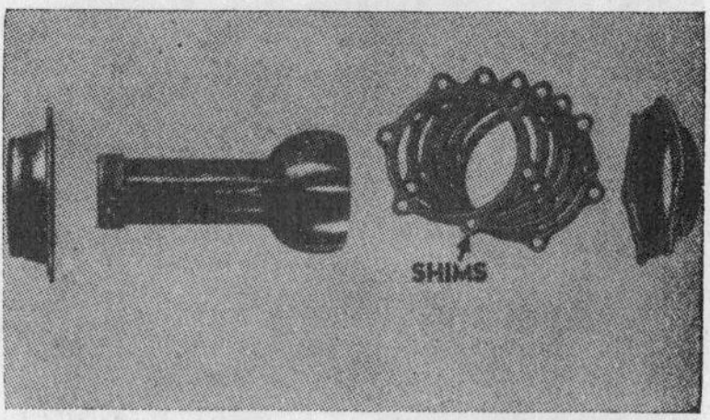

Fig. 236—Layout of torque ball parts

Fig. 237—When assembled with selected shims ball should move by hand

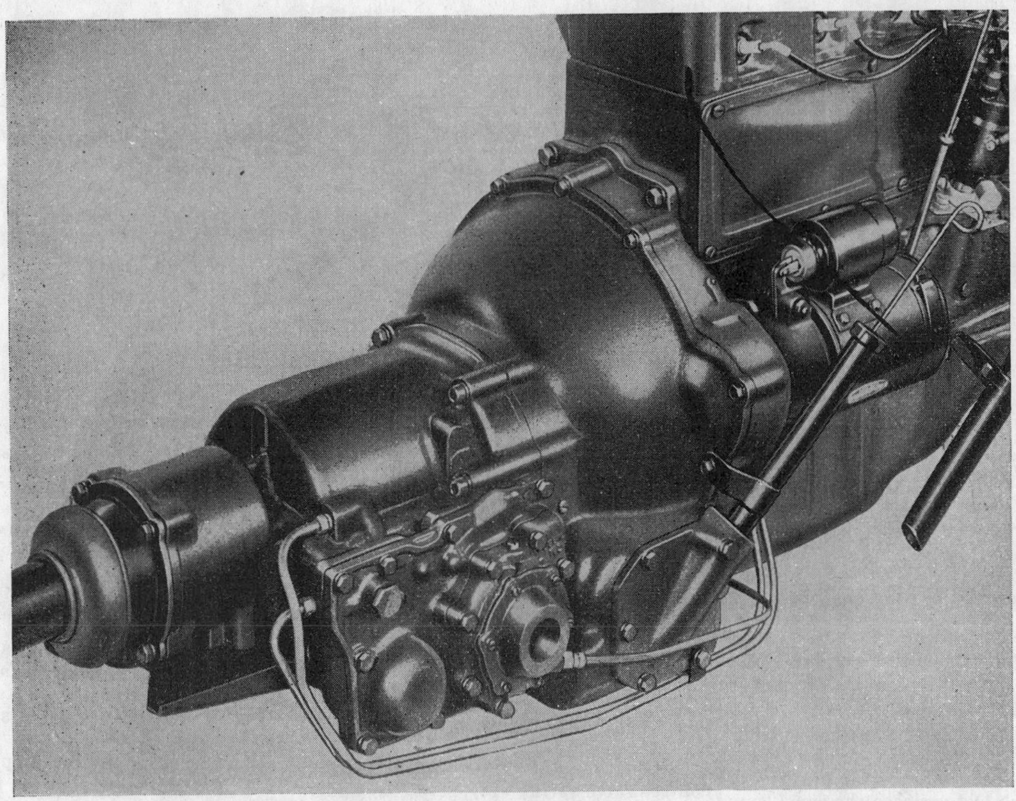

Fig. 238—Right side view of Powerglide—all models—1953

DISASSEMBLY OVERHAUL AND REASSEMBLY 1953 POWERGLIDE

1. Oil Pump Suction Pipe and Screen, 1953 Models

(This operation can be performed with the transmission still in the car.)

Unbolt the right side cover of the bell housing. Remove cover and gasket. Unbolt the suction pipe retainer and lift out the pipe retainer and screen.

Wash the assembly in solvent. Blow with compressed air to dry.

Reverse removal procedure to replace. Use a new seal on the pipe ahead of the retainer. Install in the cover a new "O" ring seal for the filler tube. Use a new cover to case gasket.

2. Transmission Throttle Valve Assembly, 1953 Models

(This operation can be performed with the transmission still in the car.)

REMOVAL AND OVERHAUL

Unbolt the left side cover and remove the cover and throttle valve as an assembly. Remove cover to case gasket. Do not unbolt the outer lever as it acts to hold the inner lever in place on the assembly.

Note: If it becomes necessary to disassemble the throttle valve, be careful not to disturb the adjustment. It is preset to 62 psi (plus or minus 1 psi) at the factory.

It is more than likely that trouble with this assembly can be cleared by a thorough cleaning.

Remove the low-and-drive-valve-body to side cover attaching bolts and lockwashers. Remove the throttle valve outer lever and catch the inner lever and shaft seal.

Hold the low and drive valve body in one hand and with a soft faced hammer tap on the inner side of the side cover until it is free of the locating pins.

Caution: Exert pressure on the detent valve when separating valve body from the cover to keep the parts from falling out. A clip can easily be made that retains the detent valve in its bore during disassembly and assembly to cover.

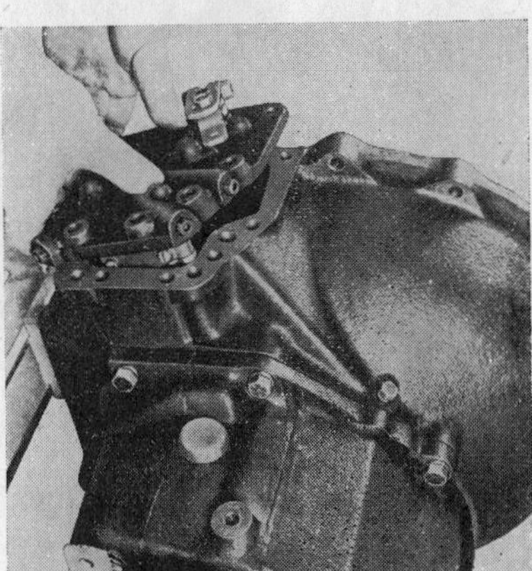

Fig. 239—Left side of bell housing showing removal of the throttle valve assembly

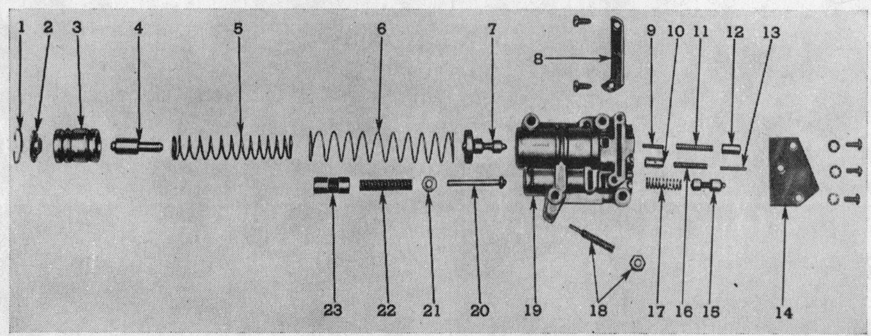

Fig. 240—Layout of throttle valve assembly (low and drive valve)

1. Low and drive regulator valve cap retainer ring
2. Low and drive regulator valve cap
3. Low and drive regulator valve sleeve
4. Low and drive regulator valve
5. Low and drive valve inner spring
6. Low and drive valve outer spring
7. Low and drive valve
8. Clutch exahust cover plate
9. Clutch exhaust secondary control valve stop
10. Clutch exhaust primary control valve
11. Clutch exhaust secondary control valve spring
12. Clutch exhaust secondary control valve
13. Clutch exhaust primary control valve stop
14. Low and drive valve **body end plate**
15. Throttle valve
16. Clutch exhaust primary control valve spring
17. Throttle valve spring
18. Throttle valve inner lever adjusting screw and lock nut
19. Low and drive valve body
20. Throttle valve spring regulator assembly
21. Detent valve spring seat.
22. Detent valve spring
23. Detent valve

1953 POWERGLIDE DISASSEMBLY—*continued*

Remove the detent valve (23), spring (22), spring seat (21), and the throttle valve spring regulator assembly (20).

Remove throttle valve spring (17) and valve (15). With snap ring pliers remove low and drive regulator valve cap retainer (1) to release the cap (2), regulator sleeve, and valve as an assembly (3, 4), the inner (5) and outer (6) springs, the low-and-drive valve (7).

Remove clutch exhaust cover plate (8).

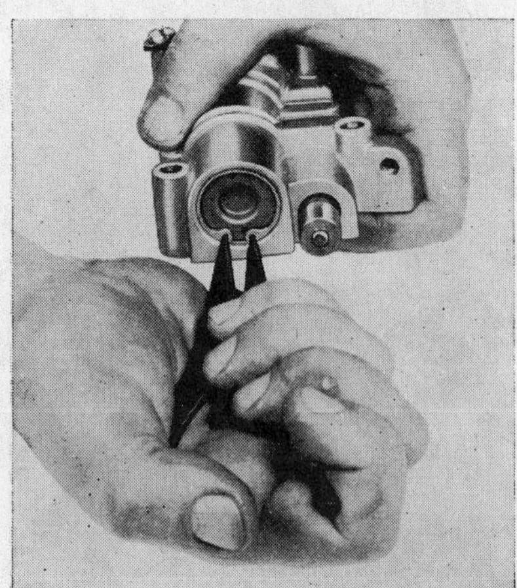

Fig. 241—Removing low and drive regulator valve retainer ring

Remove low-and-drive-body end plate (14). Note that it is necessary to counteract spring pressure while removing this part.

Remove clutch-exhaust secondary control valve (12), spring (11) and stop (9).

Remove the clutch-exhaust primary control valve spring (16), stop (13) and valve (10).

Wash the parts and inspect for nicks and burrs, easy operation in the bores and distortion or damage.

Check that one valve body locating pin is in the body and that the other is in the side cover.

REASSEMBLY

Put a piece of rubber brake tubing thru the largest bore from the body-end-plate end and slip it over the smallest diameter of the low-and-drive valve. Using the tubing as a handle and guide, install the low-and-drive valve.

Install the low-and-drive-regulator inner and outer springs into place against the large diameter face of the low-and-drive valve.

Assemble low-and-drive-regulator valve and cap to low-and-drive-regulator valve sleeve and install the assembly, being sure the inner spring is on its seat in the regulator valve sleeve.

Compress the assembly into the bore and install the retaining ring.

Install the clutch-exhaust primary control valve, spring and stop. The primary control valve stop is longer than that for the secondary control valve. The primary control valve spring is shorter than that for the secondary control valve.

Assemble the spring and stop to the clutch-exhaust secondary control valve and install the assembly in its bore.

Install the throttle valve spring and valve.

Counteracting the valve spring pressure, install the end plate, tightening the lockwashered screws to 1½-2½ ft lbs.

Install the clutch-exhaust cover plate, tightening the screws to 2½-3½ ft lbs.

Install the throttle valve spring regulator assembly, being sure it is seated on the throttle valve spring.

Thread the opening in the detent valve spring seat onto the pin of the throttle valve spring regulator assembly.

Install the detent valve spring and valve, threading the pin of the throttle valve spring regulator assembly thru the opening in the detent valve.

Place the left side cover face up in a vise. Align the locating hole in the throttle valve assembly with the locating pin in the cover. Compress the detent valve into its bore and rotate the valve assembly counterclockwise until the pin in the assembly enters the hole in the cover so that the face of the detent valve is resting against its stop in the cover. Tighten the attaching bolts and lockwashers to 3½-5 ft lbs.

Install new lever shaft seal and shield into counterbore in cover.

Install throttle valve inner lever and shaft assembly into the cover.

Install the outer lever assembly and tighten attaching bolt securely.

ADJUSTMENT

If new throttle valve parts were installed it will be necessary to adjust the lever.

Rotate throttle valve inner lever until it just contacts the face of the detent valve.

With the lever so held adjust the screw "A" (Fig. 242) until it just contacts the flat surface of the step in the lever. Now back screw "A" off one complete turn and lock. Fig. 243.

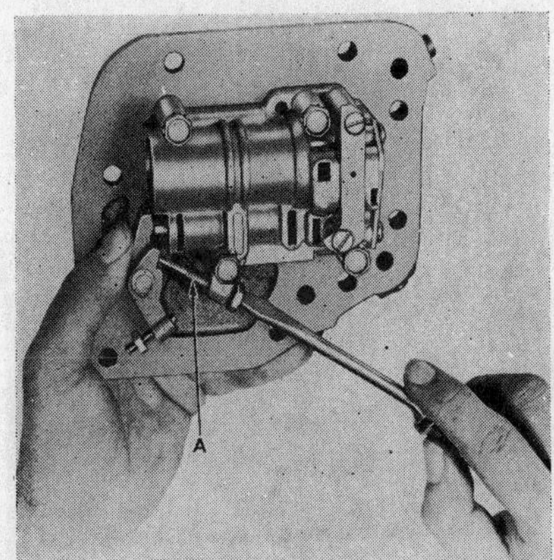

Fig. 242—Adjusting throttle valve inner lever. Step #1

Place throttle valve inner lever positioning gage between the face of the detent valve and that of the lever. Holding so, turn adjusting screw "B" until it contacts the threaded body of the screw "A," then lock.

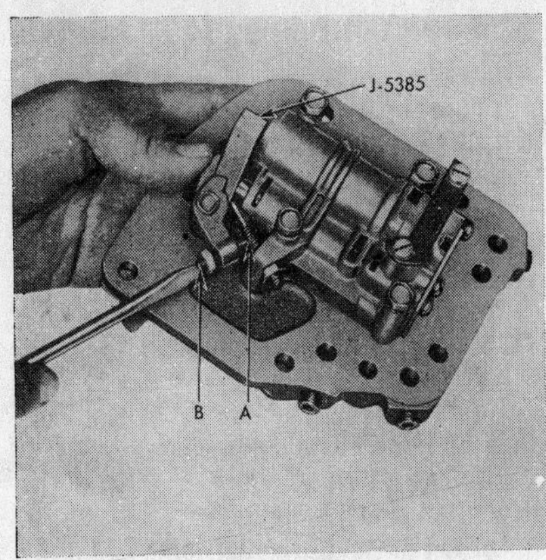

Fig. 243—Adjusting throttle valve inner lever. Step #2

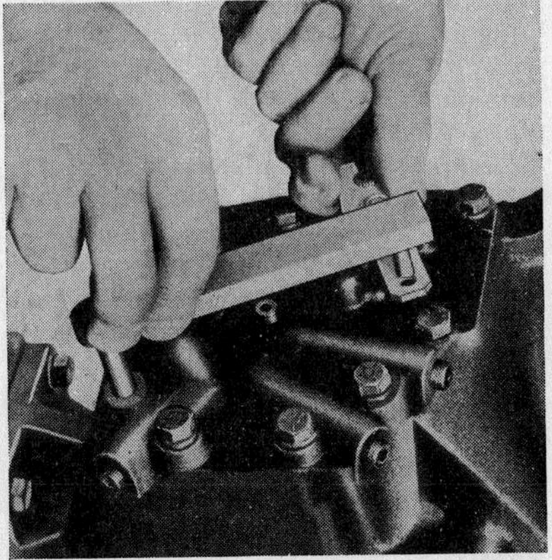

Fig. 244—Adjusting throttle valve outer lever

REINSTALL

Install two 5/16 x 18 guide pins on left side of the bell housing and install the left cover plate and throttle valve assembly. Tighten lockwashered attaching bolts to 12½-15 ft lbs.

Remove the lower rear attaching bolt.

Rotate the outer lever assembly clockwise to a definite stop which is equivalent to the closed carburetor throttle valve position.

Measure the distance between the hole in the lever and that vacated by the bolt.

It should be 4⅜".

If it is not, loosen the outer lever's clamp bolt and adjust the lever so that the distance between the holes is 4⅜", being sure the shaft remains firmly clockwise against the stop. Fig. 249.

When the distance is correct, tighten the lever clamp bolt.

Reinstall and retighten the lower rear attaching bolt.

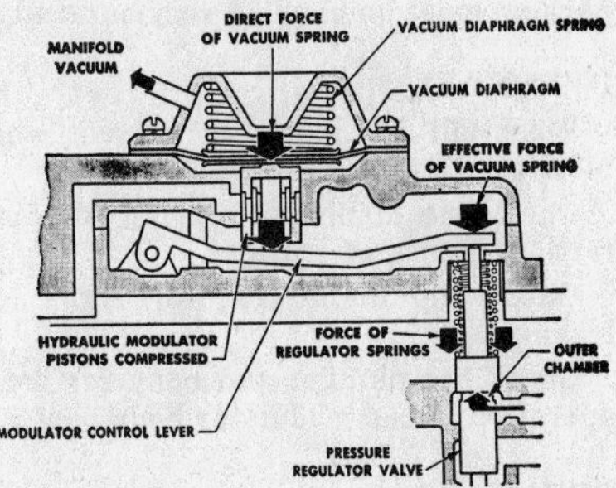

Fig. 245—Cross section of modulator

3. The Modulator Assembly 1953 Models

(This operation can be performed with the Powerglide in the car.) Note that on convertibles it is almost easier to remove the Powerglide first.

REMOVAL

Remove the vacuum line connection from the carburetor at the modulator.

Unbolt and remove the modulator assembly from the right front side of the transmission case.

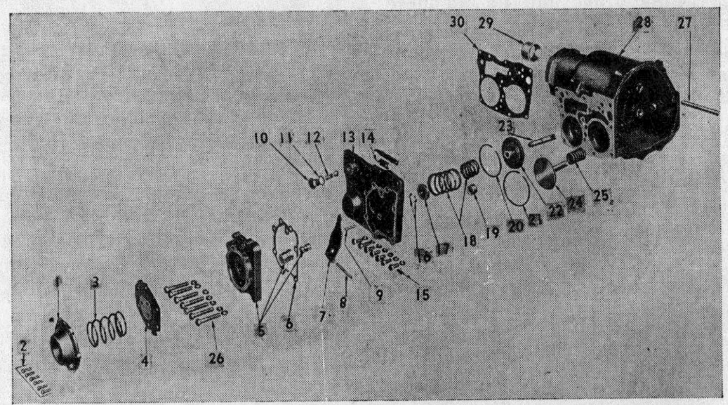

Fig. 246—Exploded view of modulator and servo cover assembly

1. Modulator cover
2. Cover bolts
3. Modulator spring
4. Modulator diaphragm
5. Modulator body, hydraulic plunger and body
6. Gasket
7. Modulator lever
8. Lever pivot pin
9. Lever locating pin
10. Bypass valve plug
11. Copper gasket
12. Spring
13. Servo cover
14. Bi-metal strip
15. Bolts, servo cover to case
16. Keys
17. Spring retainer
18. Reverse servo springs
19. Cover locating sleeve
20. Reverse servo piston ring
21. Low servo piston ring
22. Reverse servo piston
23. Piston rod
24. Low servo piston
25. Low servo spring
26. Modulator housing to servo cover bolts
27. Parking lock pawl shaft
28. Transmission case
29. Case rear bushing
30. Servo cover gasket

MODULATOR ASSEMBLY—*continued*

Be sure to counteract the modulator diaphragm spring while releasing the cover attaching bolts and be careful not to drop the parts.

The hydraulic plunger and body in the modulator body behind the diaphragm must be handled very carefully.

OVERHAUL

Wash all the parts in solvent and blow out the oil passages.

Check the diaphragm spring for distortion or loss of tension.

Check the diaphragm for signs of leakage.

Check the plunger and body for free operation in the modulator body bore.

REINSTALL

Install the modulator body in place on the servo assembly, tightening the attaching bolts to 12½-15 ft lbs.

Install the hydraulic plunger and body so the plunger will contact the lever in the servo cover.

Select a small piece of strap iron ½" wide and 1/16" to 3/16" thick. Drill two 3/16" holes, one in either end to coincide with opposite cover holes.

Lay the spring in the cover and lay the diaphragm on the spring.

Lay the selected piece of strap iron over the diaphragm, the holes lined up with cover holes.

Insert two 10-24" bolts 3" long through the cover from the front to engage the diaphragm and the two holes in the iron.

Hold the iron against the diaphragm so that it retains the diaphragm and spring in position.

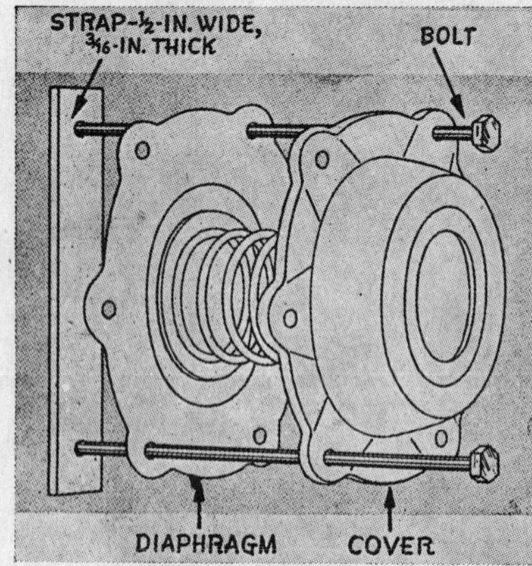

Fig. 247—Installing cover, spring, and diaphragm with shop made tool

Install this assembly onto the modulator housing, the theory being that the iron will keep the spring from tearing the diaphragm over the protruding plunger assembly.

Tighten the bolts enough to hold; then install the other cover attaching bolts and tighten slowly and evenly.

As the cover is pulled into position, remove the two bolts holding the iron and slide the iron out. Then install the two cover bolts and tighten all to 12 1/5-15 ft lbs.

4. The Servo Cover Assembly, 1953 Models

REMOVAL

The modulator assembly must be removed first, but it is not necessary that the Powerglide be removed from the car. **Note:** The "X" frame used on convertible models makes removal of this unit very difficult and the factory recommends removal of the Powerglide from convertibles before attempting this operation.

After removal of the modulator (Par. 3), remove the remaining servo cover to transmission case bolts. Be careful to push in on the cover to counteract the force of the servo and valve springs or else the cover may break.

Remove reverse servo spring, pressure regulator springs, and pressure regulator valve.

Do not remove the servo pistons with Powerglide in the car.

OVERHAUL

Be careful of pressure regulator valve as it is the key valve in the operation of the transmission. The edges of the lands should be sharp and the valve should be clean and move in its bore without bind.

Remove bi-metal strip retaining screw, bi-metal strip and retainer from cover. This is the thermostat which holds the fluid at 240°.

Remove lubrication by-pass plug and copper gasket. Remove by-pass ball spring and ball from cover.

Wash the parts and dry with compressed air.

Check the cover for nicks and cracks.

Check the springs for distortion.

Check the modulator lever in the outer face of the cover for free operation on its replaceable shaft.

ADJUSTING REVERSE BAND

Before replacing the servo cover check the adjustment of the reverse band.

If transmission is on the bench, tighten adjusting screw until no end play can be felt by push-pull motion on the reverse servo piston assembly, yet reverse ring gear unit turns freely by hand. Then back off ⅛ to ¼ turn and tighten lock nut to 20-25 ft lbs.

If transmission is in the car, tighten the adjusting screw all the way, then back off 2¾ turns and tighten lock nut to 20-25 ft lbs.

REINSTALL

Install pressure regulator valve and the inner and outer valve springs.

Install the reverse servo return spring.

Check that the springs are properly seated in the cover.

Use two 5/16"-18 x 3 guide pins to install new gasket and the servo cover.

Push in on the cover to compress the springs and tighten attaching bolts to 12½-15 ft lbs.

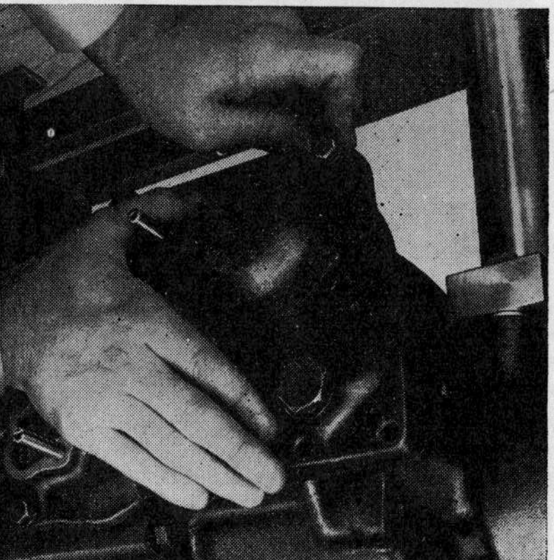

Fig. 248—Installing servo cover

5. Rear Oil Pump, 1953 Models

REMOVAL

(This operation can be performed with Powerglide in the car.)

Set the hand lever in Park.

Remove the speedometer drive shaft and gear unit from the left rear of the transmission case.

Unscrew the ball seal retainer on the front end of the propeller shaft housing.

Unbolt the ball collar from the rear face of the transmission case.

Slide the ball assembly back on the propeller shaft housing.

Unfasten the universal joint and slide the rear yoke back on the propeller shaft.

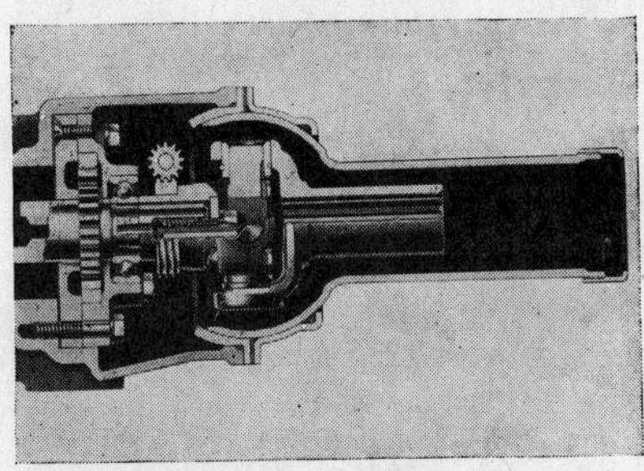

Fig. 249—Cut away view of rear pump and "U" joint

Drop the propeller shaft assembly down out of the way.

Unbolt the front yoke of the "U" joint from the output shaft of the transmission and pull the yoke off the shaft.

Mark the rear oil pump body with reference to the case for easier installation.

Remove the four bolts holding the rear oil pump to the case.

Remove the three lock-washered bolts holding the lock ring and bearing in the pump body.

Install three long bolts in these holes (they are blind holes) and, using them as points of leverage, ease the oil pump out of the case.

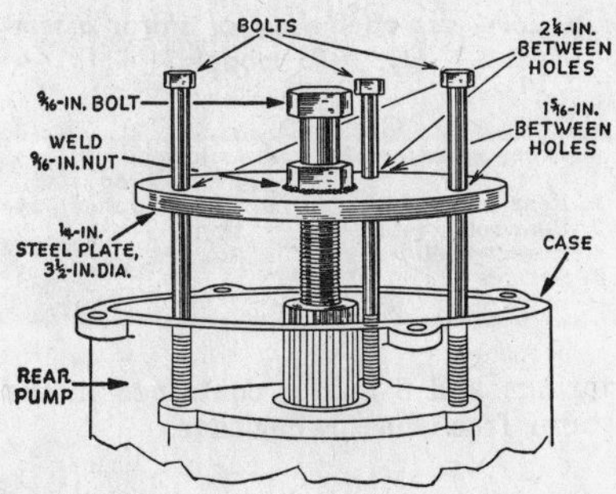

Fig. 250—Shop made tool for removing rear oil pump

Note that the oil pump driven gear has a tang which engages the output shaft.

The bearing lock plate was not used on all models. Install one on any units found to be not already so equipped.

The bearing is a tight fit on the output shaft. If when using this procedure the pump refuses to move, the transmission will have to be removed from the car and disassembled.

On no condition exert forward pressure on the output shaft with the transmission assembled.

OVERHAUL

Remove two flat slotted head screws and remove pump body plate.

Remove pump gears, wash all parts in cleaning solvent and dry with compressed air.

Check the bearing for roughness. Replace if necessary.

Check the clearances.

Driven gear to body .003″ to .007″.

Driving gear to crescent .002″ to .009″.

End clearance .0005″-.0015″.

Oil the parts with transmission fluid and put back in pump body.

Install the plate and secure with two screws.

Fasten lockplate over bearing securely.

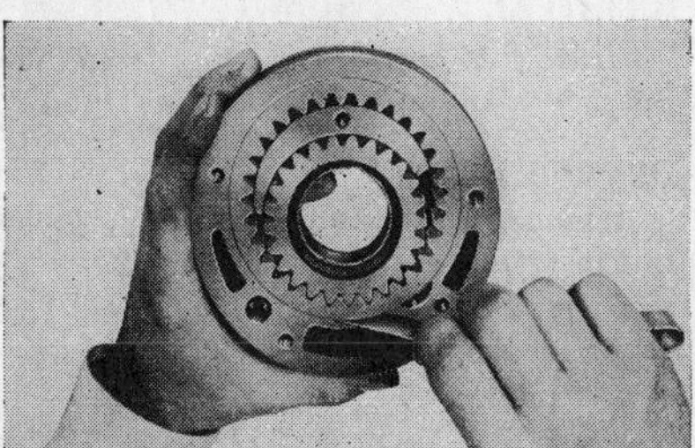

Fig. 251—Rear pump driven gear to body clearance .003-.007″

Fig. 252—Rear pump driving gear to crescent clearance .002-.009″

Fig. 253—End clearance both gears .005-.0015″

REINSTALL

Using two 5/16-18 x 3″ guide pins, install new gasket and rear pump over output shaft. Be sure match marks are aligned and that tang of pump drive gear is in slot in output shaft.

Check amount the end of the output shaft protrudes out of the bearing. It must be at least ⅞″ and indicates that the pump drive gear tang is in the output shaft slot.

Tighten the pump to case bolts to 12½-15 ft lbs.

Install the front "U" joint yoke in place on the output shaft.

Fasten with the flat washer, lock washer and bolt. Tighten the bolt against the yoke to pull the output shaft to a firm seat in the bearing.

Release the bolt and retighten to 25-30 ft lbs.

Install speedometer gear unit into case, tightening to 45-50 ft lbs. Reinstall speedometer driveshaft.

Install a new "O" ring seal over the ball joint seat.

Fasten the rear half of the "U" joint back onto the front half.

Slide the ball collar cork oil seal and shim back into place and fasten the collar to the case, tightening the bolts to 8-12 ft lbs.

Refasten the seal and retainer assembly to the rear end of the ball assembly.

Fig. 254—Installing rear oil pump

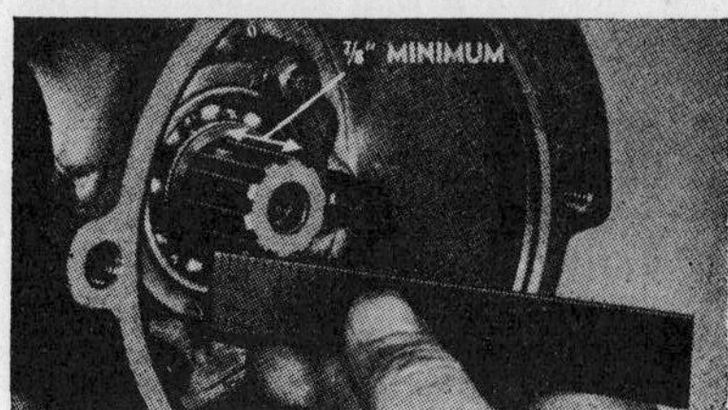

Fig. 255—If slot and tang are properly aligned output shaft will protrude ⅞″

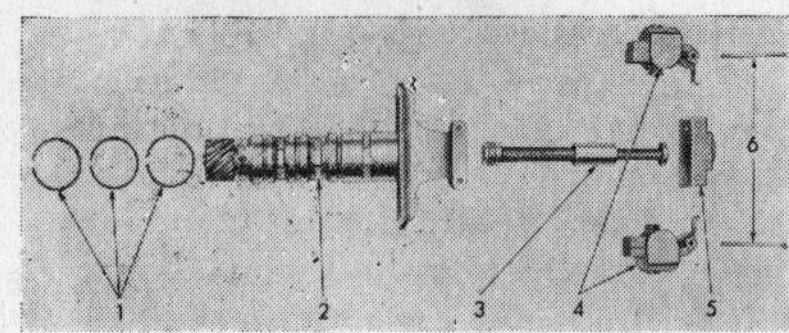

Fig. 256—Layout of governor parts

1. Sleeve oil seal rings
2. Sleeve
3. Valve
4. Weight assemblies
5. Thrust cap
6. Weight pins

6. The Governor, 1953 Models

(This operation can be performed with the Powerglide in the car.)

REMOVAL

Unbolt and remove the governor cover and gasket.

Turn governor clockwise and bring it out of the transmission case.

DISASSEMBLY

All the parts of the governor save only the oil seal rings on the sleeve are selected fits and individually calibrated. Parts for the governor are not sold separately but only as a unit.

Therefore if anything is needed other than the oil seal rings, a whole new governor assembly must be installed.

For cleaning, the unit may be taken apart.

Cut off one end of each of the governor weight pins and remove the pins. Measure and record their diameter, for the same gage piano wire must be used when reassembling to preserve the unit's calibration.

Remove the thrust cap, the weight assemblies and the valve from the sleeve.

Remove the oil seal rings from the sleeve.

OVERHAUL

Inspect the weight assemblies for distortion or damage. Do not take apart. Check that the weights do not bind in their retainers.

Insert the rings in the bore in the case and check that the hooked ends have clearance.

REINSTALL

Reinstall the oil seal rings on the sleeve.

Reinstall the valve, wider end in.

Reassemble the thrust cap to the weight assemblies and install new pins. Be sure new pins are similar in weight to the old ones. Crimp the ends of both pins and check the weight assemblies that they aren't binding.

Turn the governor assembly counterclockwise as it is fed back into place in the transmission case so that the governor gear meshes properly with its drive gear on the output shaft. Be careful not to damage the teeth.

Install the governor cover. Tighten the bolts to 6½-8½ ft lbs.

7. The Converter Assembly, 1953 Models

The Powerglide must be removed from the car for this operation. The converter assembly is no longer retained to the reactor shaft and may be slipped off the input shaft as a unit.

REMOVAL

Slide the converter unit from the input shaft as a unit.

DISASSEMBLY

Remove bolts holding converter cover to the primary pump.

With a small punch drive out the cover locating dowels.

Fig. 257—Arrows point to split locating dowels

Remove: (1) converter cover, (2) turbine thrust washer, (3) turbine assembly, (4) stator front thrust washer, (5) stator assembly, (6) stator rear thrust washer, (7) primary pump thrust washer. Fig. 258.

Remove the "O" seal ring from the converter cover.

Remove: (1) the stator free wheel roller race, (2) the snap ring and (3) roller retainer, (4) the free wheel rollers, (5) springs and (6) guides, (7) the stator front snap ring and (8) the front roller retainer. Fig. 259.

There are 8 free wheel rollers, 8 springs and 8 guides contained in the stator free wheel roller cage.

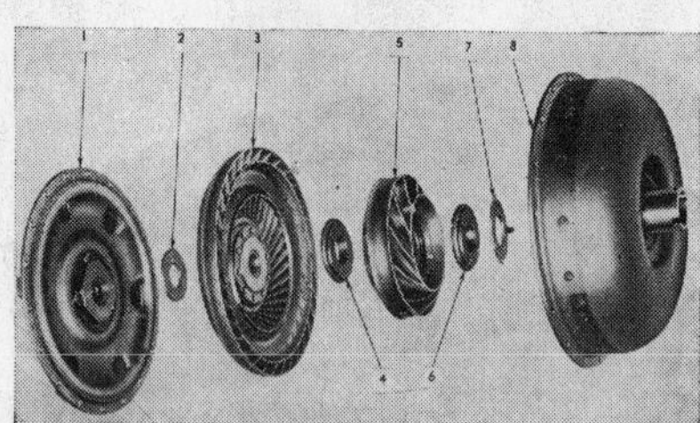

Fig. 258—Exploded view of converter. 1953 models

1. Converter cover
2. Turbine thrust washer
3. Turbine assembly
4. Stator front thrust washer
5. Stator assembly
6. Stator rear thrust washer
7. Primary pump thrust washer
8. Primary pump

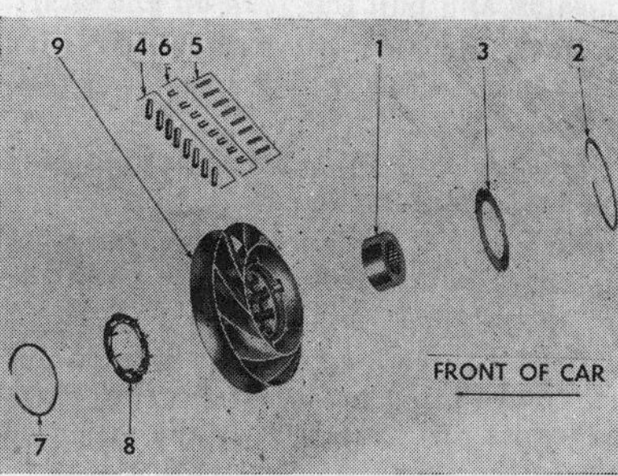

Fig. 259—Exploded view of stator assembly. 1953 models

1. Free wheel roller race
2. Rear snap ring
3. Rear roller retainer
4. Free wheel rollers
5. Springs
6. Guides
7. Front snap ring
8. Front roller retainer
9. Stator

OVERHAUL

Wash all the parts and air dry.

Check the primary pump hub and turbine hub surfaces for smoothness.

Check the vanes of the units for looseness or damage.

Check the pilot bushing in the cover for smoothness.

Check the stator free wheel clutch parts for smoothness and signs of damage.

Check all thrust washers for galling, scoring, and excessive wear.

ASSEMBLY

The pilot bushing in the cover can be replaced with normal bushing replacement procedures if necessary.

The front of the stator can be identified because it is marked "FRONT." Also the vanes are thicker toward the front.

Assemble the stator front roller retainer so that the prongs point to the rear. Fasten in place with the retaining ring.

Assemble the free wheel rollers, springs, and guides into the stator free wheel cage. Note that the spring retainers follow the curvature of the unit.

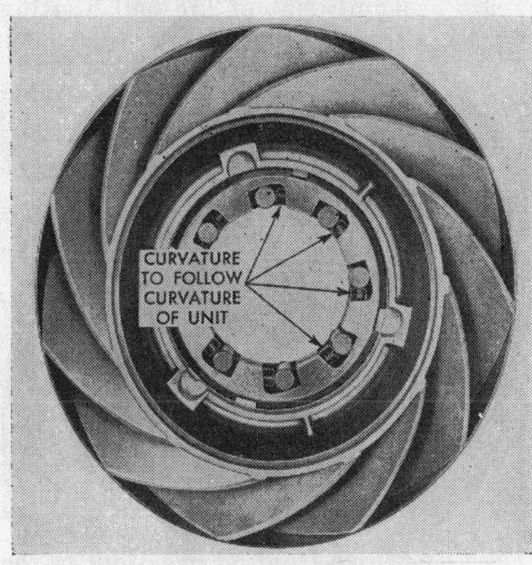

Fig. 260—Install free wheel clutch parts in stator free wheel case

Install the stator rear free wheel roller retainer and fasten in place with snap ring.

Check operation of the stator on the reactor shaft. It must revolve freely clockwise and lock up when turned counterclockwise.

Install primary pump thrust washer in its front flange so the notches are engaged properly.

Assemble the stator thrust washers onto the stator and lay it front side up in place in the pump as an assembly.

Lay the turbine assembly in place on the stator.

Install the turbine to converter cover thrust washer.

Install a new "O" ring seal, which has been well soaked in transmission fluid, carefully onto the converter cover.

See that it is not twisted nor sagging and lies at the following edge of its well cleaned groove.

Align the locating dowel pin holes and install the cover onto the primary pump.

Install the dowel pins and the pump to cover bolts, tightening to 15-20 ft lbs.

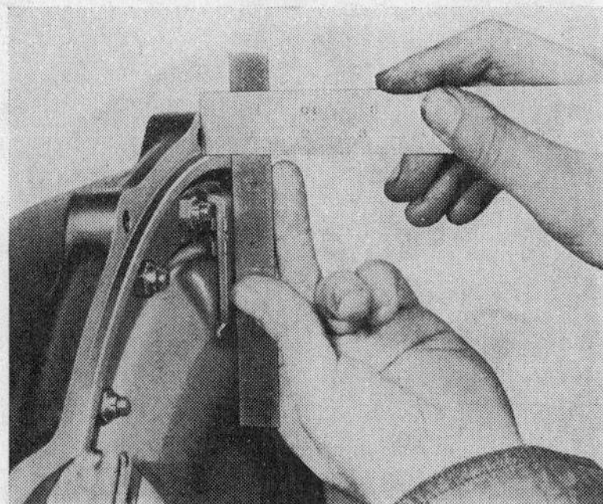

Fig. 261—Distance as shown should not exceed 9/16"

REINSTALL

Install the converter assembly onto the input and reactor shafts so that the front pump drive gear lugs engage into the drive slots in the primary pump hub.

To check that converter assembly is properly installed, measure as shown the distance from the machined front face of the bell housing to the front surface of a converter drive lug. The distance should be no more than 9/16". Temporarily fasten the converter to the bell housing so it won't fall out of place.

8. Bell Housing, 1953 Models

REMOVAL

Remove the transmission from the car.

Remove the converter assembly from the transmission (Par. 7).

Remove the oil screen, the modulator assembly, the servo cover assembly and the throttle valve assembly as directed in Paragraphs 1, 2, 3, and 4.

Fig. 262—Use 1/4" Allen wrench on low band adjusting screw 1953 models

Be sure that the pressure regulator valve is out of the case and safely put out of the way.

Remove the low band adjusting screw cover, loosen the lock nut and tighten the adjusting screw to hold the clutch assembly in place. A 1/4" Allen wrench is required for this operation.

Remove the one bolt running from the inside of the bell housing into the transmission case.

Fig. 263—Remove bolt in bell housing that runs into transmission case

Remove the transmission case to bell housing bolts and lock washers.

Carefully separate the bell housing from the transmission case.

Note that there are two (2) gaskets, one between the bell housing, the valve body, and the transmission case, and another smaller crescent moon shaped one between the valve body and the case.

Note that there is a bronze thrust washer on the oil delivery sleeve of the valve body to intervene between the clutch assembly and the valve body.

Fig. 264—Install crescent shaped gasket between valve body and transmission case

REINSTALL

Index manual valve inner lever in bell housing with the manual valve in the valve body.

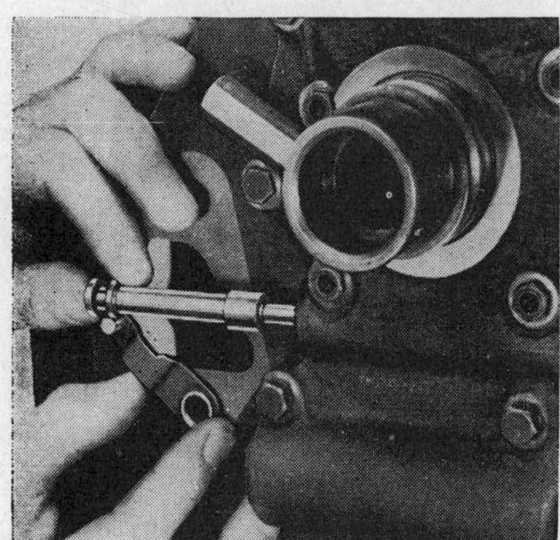

Fig. 265—Index valve lever to manual valve

Set the manual valve so its end extends 1½" beyond the valve body. This is reverse position.

Install new crescent moon shaped valve body to case gasket.

Fig. 266—In reverse position manual valve protrudes 1½" from valve body

Raise the manual valve outer lever to top detent position, which is reverse.

The connecting lever inside the case is called the reaction lever. It is now set to engage the inner lever in the bell housing. The fact that they properly engage can be observed through the opening occupied by the throttle valve assembly. Fig. 267.

Place the clutch drum thrust washer over oil delivery sleeve.

Check that the oil delivery sleeve carries its two interlocking cast iron oil seal rings.

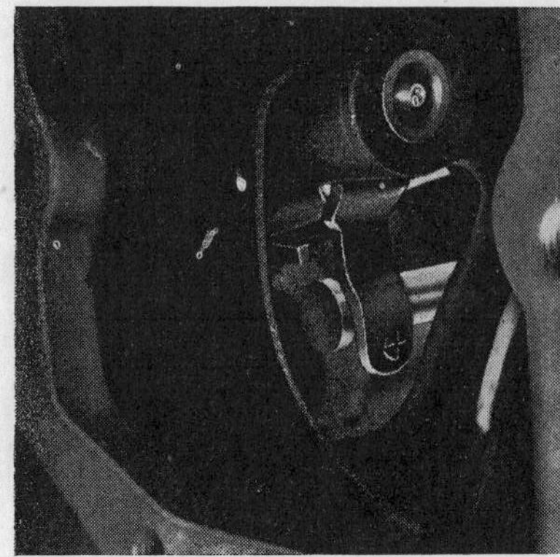

Fig. 267—Match lever from case with that in bell housing

Use two ⅜-16 x 3¾" pins to guide the transmission case into position against the bell housing.

Check that the manual valve inner lever and the reaction lever are properly mated, then install the case to housing bolts and lockwashers. Tighten to 25-30 ft lbs.

From front of bell housing install the special self-locking bolt and tighten to 25-30 ft lbs.

Complete assembly by following Par. 7, 4, 3, 2, and 1.

9. Valve Body and Front Oil Pump, 1953 Models

REMOVAL

Remove the transmission from the car and follow Paragraphs 1, 2, 3, 4, 7, and 8.

Now remove the manual valve from the valve body and the bolts and lockwashers attaching the valve body to the bell housing and the front pump.

Remove the valve body and its gasket. Wrap the valve body so it is protected.

Drive the front oil pump and reactor shaft assembly out of the bell housing to the rear.

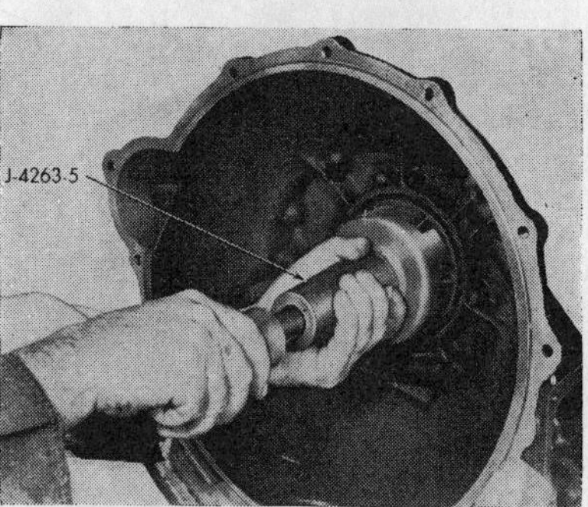

Fig. 268—Drive front oil pump out to the rear

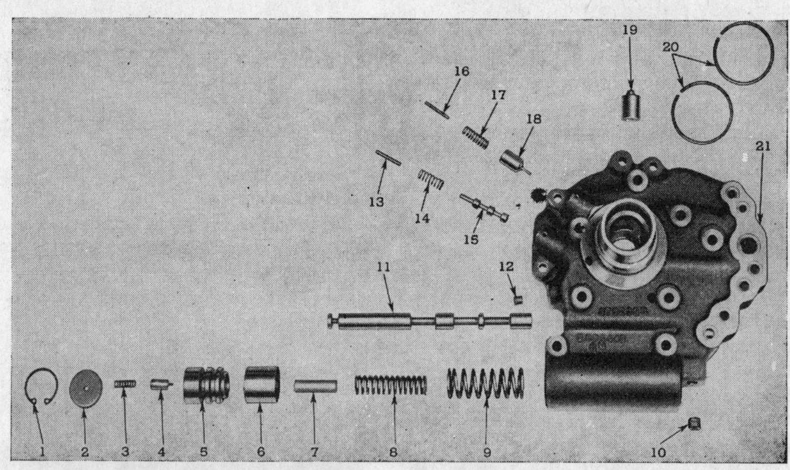

Fig. 269—Layout of valve body

1. Snap ring
2. Accumulator valve spring washer
3. Accumulator valve spring
4. Accumulator valve
5. Accumulator valve body assembly
6. Accumulator piston
7. Accumulator piston stop
8. Accumulator piston inner spring
9. Accumulator piston outer spring
10. Plug
11. Transmission manual valve
12. Plug
13. Pressure regulator governor valve spring stop pin
14. Pressure regulator governor spring
15. Pressure regulator governor valve
16. Converter pressure regulator valve spring stop pin
17. Converter pressure regulator valve spring
18. Converter pressure regulator valve
19. Clutch low servo valve assembly
20. Clutch drum oil seal rings
21. Transmission valve body

DISASSEMBLY OF THE VALVE BODY

Use snap ring pliers to release (1) the accumulator valve snap ring and (2) the spring washer, (3) valve spring, (4) accumulator valve, (5) valve body, (6) piston, (7) piston stop, (8) inner spring, (9) outer spring.

Support the valve body on some wood blocks and drive out the pin holding the pressure regulator governor valve and spring.

Drive out the pin retaining the converter pressure regulator valve and spring in their bore.

Remove the clutch low servo valve assembly.

OVERHAUL OF THE VALVE BODY

Wash all the parts in solvent and dry with compressed air.

Inspect all the parts for signs of wear and check for free movement in their bores.

Check the small fiber valve in the accumulator valve body.

Check the plastic valve in the clutch low servo valve assembly.

Check the oil seal rings on the oil delivery sleeve for nicks, burrs and free movement in their grooves. Install the rings in the clutch hub and see that the hooked ends have clearance.

ASSEMBLY OF THE VALVE BODY

Install the accumulator piston inner and outer springs, and piston stop in the accumulator piston and return to valve body springs first.

Install accumulator valve and spring in accumulator valve body assembly and return to position in the valve body.

Put the spring washer in place, compress the accumulator springs and install the special snap ring in its groove.

Support the valve body face down.

Assemble the longer and heavier of the two remaining springs to the converter pressure regulator valve.

Install the assembly in the valve body and install the retaining pin.

Assemble the remaining shorter and lighter spring to the pressure regulator governor valve and install the assembly in the valve body. Install retaining pin.

Install the oil seal rings on the oil delivery sleeve.

DISASSEMBLY OF THE FRONT PUMP

Remove reactor shaft and flange assembly from the front pump body. This will release the pump gears from the body.

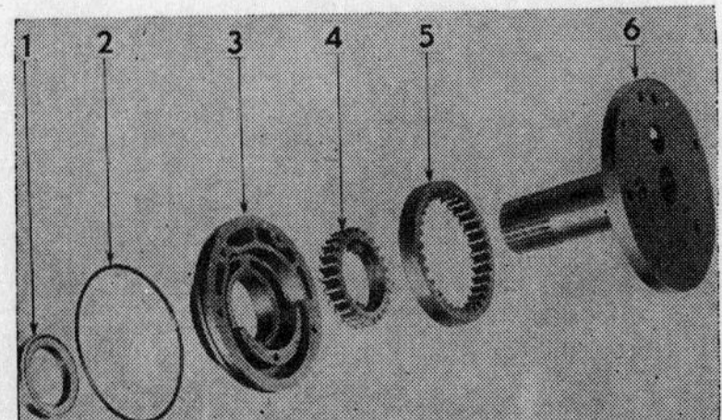

Fig. 270—Exploded view of transmission front oil pump

1. Oil seal
2. "O" ring seal
3. Pump body
4. Drive gear
5. Driven gear
6. Reactor shaft flange assembly

Note that these gears have not been heat treated and so can be damaged if dropped.

Remove the "O" ring seal from the pump body.

OVERHAUL OF THE FRONT PUMP

Wash all the parts in fluid and air dry.

Inspect the gears, flange, and body for nicks and scores.

Check the pump body oil seal and replace if suspected of leaking.

Fit the pump body onto the primary pump hub and check that the clearance between the hub and the bushing is not over .007".

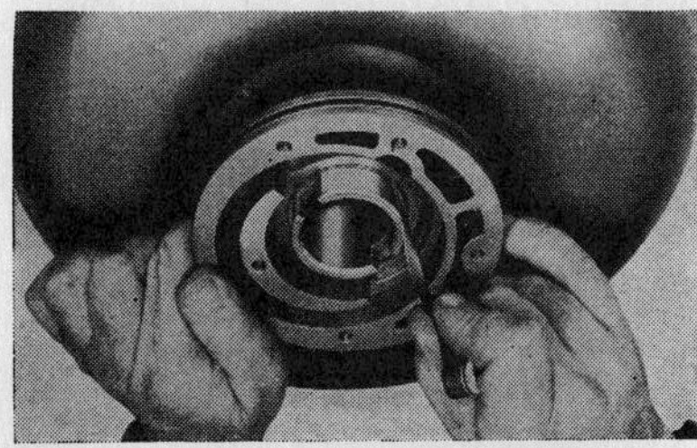

Fig. 271—Clearance front pump body bushing to primary pump hub should not exceed .007"

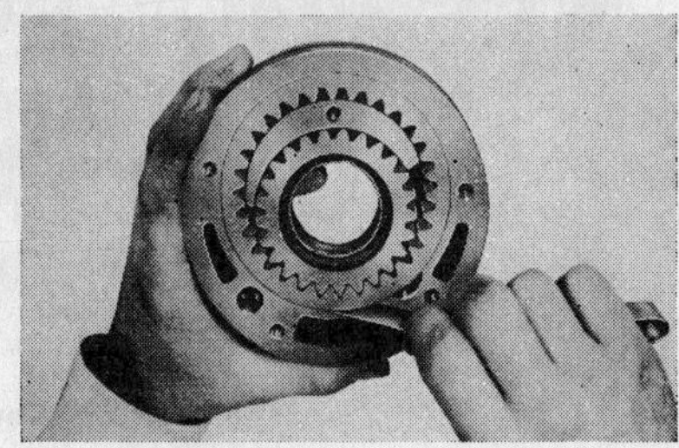

Fig. 272—Clearance front pump driven gear to body .003"-.007"

Fig. 273—Clearance, front pump driven gear to body .003"-.007"

Replace the pump gears and check the clearances.

Driven gear to body .0025"-.0055".

Driving gear to crescent .003" to .009".

End clearance .005" to .0015".

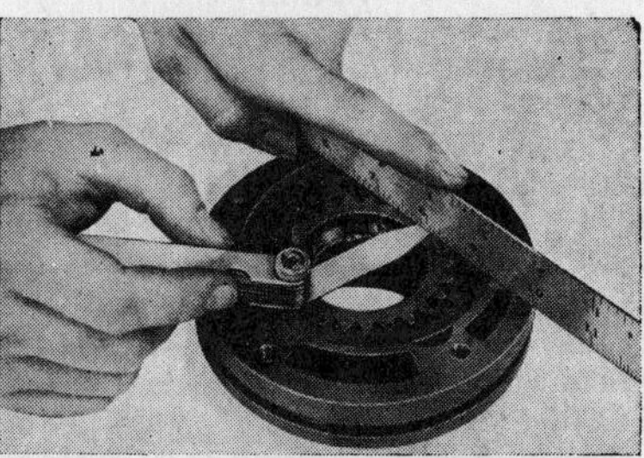

Fig. 274—End clearance both gears .005"-.0015"

REASSEMBLY OF THE FRONT PUMP

Install new "O" ring seal on pump body. Be careful that it has been soaked in fluid, and is correctly seated in the well cleaned groove, neither twisted nor stretched. Oil and install the gears.

Reassemble the reactor shaft and flange assembly onto the front pump body.

Note: The pump body and gears are not sold separately. If anything wrong is suspected of the front pump, replace it as an assembly.

REINSTALLATION OF THE VALVE BODY AND FRONT PUMP

Use two ¼-20 x 3¼" pins to guide the valve body and new gasket onto the bell housing.

REINSTALLATION OF FRONT PUMP —*continued*

Tighten the attaching bolts in a criss-cross pattern to 7½-10 ft lbs.

Note: Lower left bolt over the accumulator is a self-locking bolt. Care should be taken that it is properly installed.

Fig. 275—Tighten valve body bolts 7½-10 ft. lbs.

Check that the manual and pressure regulator valves move freely.

Install two ¼-20 x 3½″ guide pins through the reactor flange to the front oil pump body. Check that suction and delivery holes are on left side of the pump.

Push the pump into place against the valve body from the front of the bell housing.

Install five self-locking bolts through the valve body and into the pump, tightening to 7½-10 ft lbs.

Check that the pressure regulator valve still slides freely and that the front pump turns easily.

Complete installation as per Paragraphs 1, 2, 3, 4, 8, and 7.

10. The Clutch Assembly, 1953 Models

The transmission must be removed from the car for this operation.

Perform the operations listed in Paragraphs 1, 2, 3, 4, 6, 7, and 8.

Which brings us down to the transmission case with the clutch, planetary gear set, rear oil pump and associated parts still in place.

REMOVAL OF CLUTCH

Tighten the reverse servo band adjusting screw to hold the planetary gear set in place.

Back off the low servo adjusting screw and remove the transmission input shaft, clutch assembly and low sun gear thrust washer from the transmission.

Lay the low sun gear thrust washer where it cannot be mixed with other thrust washers as it is the selected clearance control thrust washer for the transmission.

Remove the low servo band (mark the band with relation to the case so that it goes back to the same relative position), the strut assembly, low servo piston and its return spring.

Remove retainer ring (8) and retainer (7) to release the low sun gear and flange assembly (6) from the low drum. (1). Fig. 276.

Remove the clutch hub thrust washer (5).

Remove the clutch hub (4) and the clutch plates (2 and 3). Note that there are four internally splined conposition plates and five externally splined and waved steel plates. Note that the wave used in '53 production obviates the need

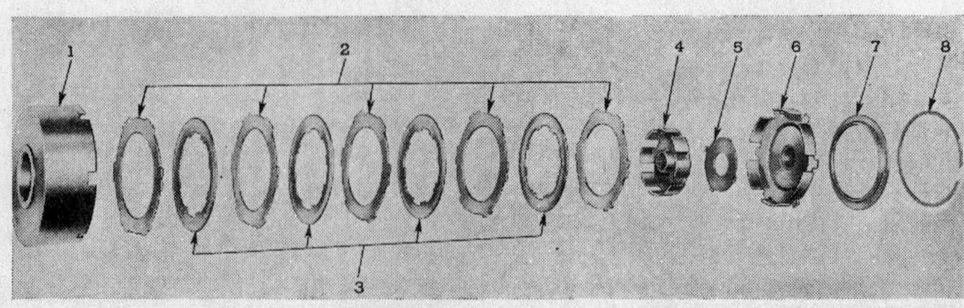

Fig. 276—Layout of clutch parts—1953 models

1. Low drum assembly
2. Five driven plates (waved)
3. Four driving plates
4. Clutch hub
5. Clutch hub thrust washer
6. Low sun gear and flange assembly
7. Retainer
8. Retainer ring

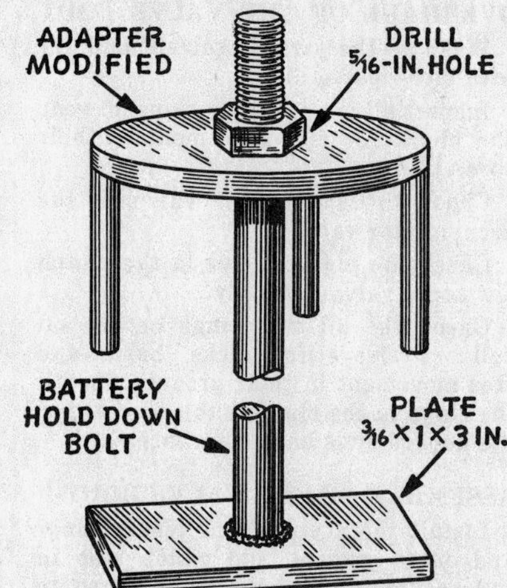

Fig. 277—Improvised tool for compressing clutch spring

Fig. 278—Exploded view of low drum assembly

1. Low drum
2. Clutch piston inner seal
3. Clutch piston outer seal
4. Clutch piston
5. Clutch spring
6. Retainer (spring seat)
7. Snap retaining ring (locking snap ring)

for care in direction of assembly as was necessary for previous models.

Place the low drum (1) in a press and compress the clutch spring (5) to permit removal of the snap retaining ring (7).

Removal of the retaining ring (7) will release the retainer (6), the spring (5), and the clutch piston (4). Note that the piston is 1/4″ smaller than on previous models and is therefore not interchangeable.

Remove the outer seal ring (3) from the clutch piston, and the inner seal ring (2) from the inner hub of the drum (1). Fig. 276.

OVERHAUL OF CLUTCH

Wash the parts and dry with compressed air.

Check the input shaft for proper fit in the turbine clutch hub and reverse sun gear. Check the oil seal rings and snap ring for condition. Check that oil passages in the shaft are clear.

Check the drum for scores and burrs and its bushing for scoring. Check the front thrust surface of the drum for smoothness.

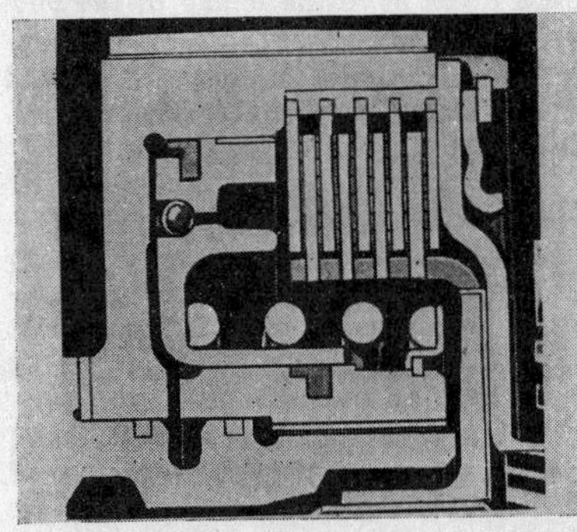

Fig. 279—Cutaway view of clutch showing ball relief valve

Check the ball relief valve in the clutch piston. Be certain it moves freely and that the orifice leading to the rear of the piston is open. If the ball falls out, stake the edges of the hole slightly to retain it. **Note:** It must move freely.

Check the fit of the low sun gear flange assembly (6) in the drum (1). There should be no appreciable radial play between these two parts. Check the gear for nicks and burrs.

Check the clutch plates (2 and 3) for burns and metal pickup and that they fit freely where they should.

Nothing is harder on proper operation of the transmission than a clutch that does not release properly. Factors controlling this are the condition of the plates, the action of the relief valve and the free movement of the parts.

ASSEMBLY OF CLUTCH

Install a new seal ring (3) on the clutch piston (4). The lip of the seal goes toward the inside of the drum. Be careful not to overstretch the seal. Have it well covered with fluid beforehand.

Install a new seal ring on the drum hub (1). Have seal coated with fluid, do not overstretch. The lip of the seal goes toward front face of the drum. (Same direction as outer seal on clutch piston.)

Install the piston (4) into the drum (1), guiding the edges of the outer seal down into the drum with a feeler gage. Have the parts damp with fluid.

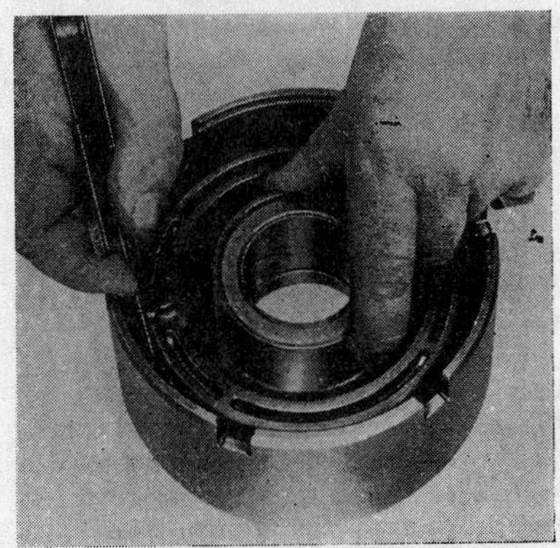

Fig. 280—Guide edges of seal into drum with a feeler gage

Install the clutch spring (5) onto its seat in the piston and place seat (6) in place. Compress the assembly and install the locking snap ring (7). Do not permit the spring seat (6) to catch in the snap ring groove in the drum hub as it is inclined to do. Fig. 278.

The prongs of the washer (5) fit into slots in the hub (4). Lay the hub and thrust washer assembled into the open face of the flange (6). Fig. 276.

Install the clutch plates. Since the steel plates are waved instead of being dished as heretofore, there is no need to worry about which way the wave is. Start with a steel plate, then a composition plate and so on, ending with a steel plate.

Assemble the drum and piston assembly onto the flange assembly and install the flange retainer (7) and the locking retainer ring (8).

Retainer rings (8) are available in three thicknesses (.055″, .064″, .073″) to control the end play of the low sun gear flange assembly in the drum (1).

Check that the clearance between the drive lugs of the flange assembly and the bottom (forward face) of the drive slots in the drum is not over .013″. Should it be more, install a thicker retainer ring (8).

REINSTALL CLUTCH

Install input shaft to clutch unit. Install the clearance control thrust washer which was laid carefully away at removal onto the splines extending out of the rear of the clutch assembly.

Note: The flat side of the washer goes to the rear of the transmission against the reverse sun gear.

The selection of this thrust washer will be detailed under installation of the planetary gear set (Par. 11). If it seems that a new one is necessary, refer to the section on installation in paragraph 11 for the method of selection. Failure to follow the procedure in selecting this thrust washer will result in excess wear and probable lock-up of the transmission if the washer is too thick or excess play resulting in clunking noises and malfunction if too thin.

Install the input shaft complete with clutch assembly and selected thrust washer into the case indexing; the input shaft pilot with its bushing in the output shaft, and the low sun gear with the short pinions in the planetary gear set.

Install low servo piston release spring on servo piston rod and install piston and spring into case using a pis-

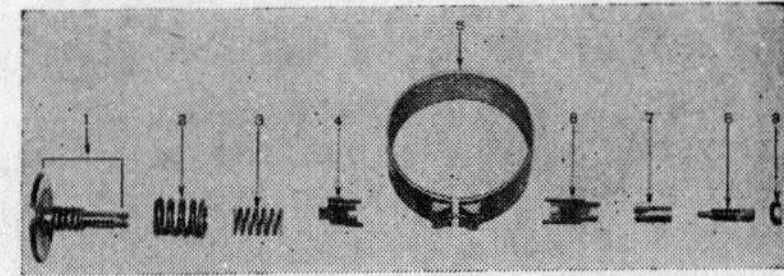

Fig. 281—Exploded view of low band mechanism on 1953 models

1. Low servo piston assembly
2. Piston release spring
3. Strut guide spring
4. Strut assembly
5. Low band
6. Strut assembly
7. Anchor
8. Low band adjusting screw
9. Lock nut

CLUTCH ASSEMBLY—*continued*

ton ring compressor. (It is assumed that these parts, as well as those comprising the balance of the low band actuating mechanism, have been inspected for wear and signs of malfunction.)

Install the low brake band over the drum. Check that the match marks made at disassembly are aligned so that the same edge of the band is forward.

Place the strut guide spring (3) over the shaft of the piston as it protrudes into the case. Install the strut assembly (4) in position between the spring (3) and the flange of the band (1).

Install the strut assembly (6) into place on the flange of the band (1) and engage the anchor (7) into the slot in the strut. Install the low band adjusting screw (8) to hold parts (6) and (7) in place. Fig. 281.

Note that the struts used on '53 models are not interchangeable with those of past models.

Complete installation as directed in paragraphs 1, 2, 3, 4, 6, 7, 8.

ADJUSTING THE LOW BAND 1953 MODELS

Using a ¼" Allen wrench, tighten the low band adjusting screw down solid, then back off four (4) complete turns and tighten lock nut to 20-25 ft lbs.

11. The Planetary Gear Set, 1953 Models

This operation can only be performed with the transmission out of the car. Because the unit is on the bench, an easier method of removing the rear oil pump is available.

Preparatory to starting this procedure the operations outlined in paragraphs 1, 2, 3, 4, 6, 7, 8 and 10 must be performed.

As a result we have the transmission case on the bench with only the planetary gear set, the rear oil pump and associated parts still in place.

REMOVAL OF GEAR SET

Remove speedometer driven gear, universal joint yoke retainer bolt and lock washer. Slide universal joint yoke off end of shaft.

Using the tool shown or something similar, unhook the parking lock pawl spring from the case and remove the spring and pawl.

Remove the parking lock lever and steel washer, thus releasing the lever shaft assembly and the oil seal from the case.

Fig. 282—Unhooking parking lock pawl spring from case

Install the universal joint washer and bolt back onto the end of the output shaft and, using a block of wood to protect the bolt, tap against the end of the shaft to drive the gear set and output shaft assembly out of the rear bearing.

Remove the planetary gear set and output shaft from the front of the transmission case.

Loosen the reverse band adjusting screw lock nut and loosen the screw to release the reverse ring gear.

Turn the reverse servo piston so the cutout points to the bottom of the case and remove it. This should release the lever strut and link composing the reverse band actuating mechanism.

Remove the lockwashered rear pump bolts and remove the rear pump assembly and gasket. For further treatment of the rear pump see paragraph 5.

Remove the lubrication pressure relief valve from the transmission case.

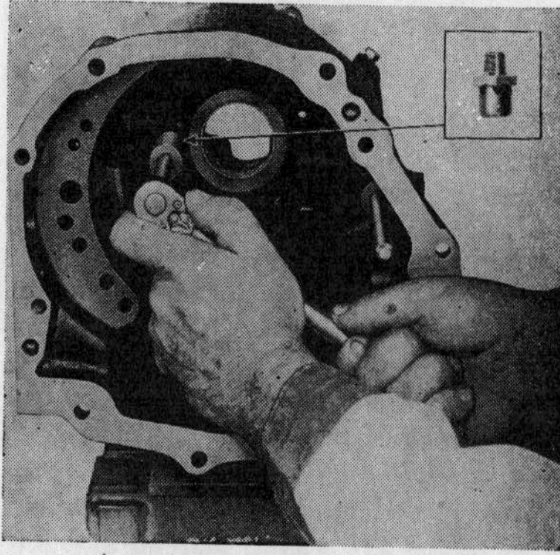

Fig. 283—Remove lubrication pressure relief valve

OVERHAUL OF GEAR SET

Disassembly of the planetary gear set is not often necessary.

Check all the gear teeth and all machined surfaces for damage. Check the fit of the output shaft in the ring gear bushing.

Inspect the reverse sun gear rear thrust washer and the input shaft pilot bushing for scoring or excess wear.

Check the end play of the planet gears which should be .006-.030.

Should it be necessary to disassemble the gear set, the following notes will prove helpful:

The lock plate for the pinion shafts is turned counterclockwise to release the shafts.

The pinions are removed in pairs. A short one first, then a long one. Each pair uses the same set of thrust washers which are installed with the long pinions. There are 20 needle bearings in each end of each long pinion. If the needle bearings show any signs of wear they must all be replaced.

The pinion shafts must be marked before disassembly as they are a selective fit and it is necessary that they be returned to the same place. Besides being held by the lock plate, the pinion shafts are a press fit in the flange of the output shaft.

The long planet pinions are located at the closed portions of the carrier. The short ones go in the openings.

REINSTALL GEAR SET

Slide the planetary carrier assembly into the reverse ring gear, being careful to keep the slot in the output shaft up so that it will engage the drive lug of the rear oil pump.

Verify engagement of the slot and the lug by measuring the amount of shaft protruding from the rear bearing. If there is ⅞" or more of shaft, then all is well.

Install the yoke of the universal joint, the flat washer, lockwasher and retaining bolt. Install a locking strap to keep the yoke from turning and tighten the bolt to 25-30 ft lbs.

Check that there is 1/32" to 1/16" between the nailhead and the retaining bolt, as the passage in the bolt provides lubricant to the universal joint.

Install the speedometer driven gear, and tighten the fitting to 45-50 ft lbs.

SELECTING CLEARANCE CONTROL THRUST WASHER, 1953 MODELS

When the transmission has been firmly bolted back onto the converter housing there must be between .007"

Fig. 284—Measure from front face of case to front face of reverse sun gear

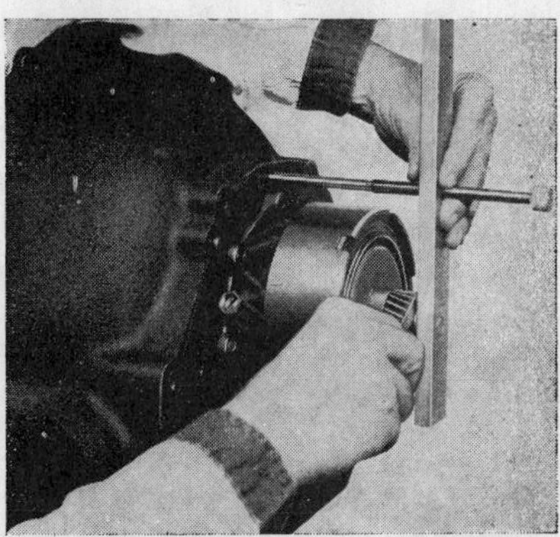

Fig. 285—Measure from rear face of housing to rear face of low sun gear

Fig. 286—Install washer with spline over oil hole milled surface against low sun gear

and .035" clearance or end play between the low sun gear and the reverse sun gear. The thickness of the bronze thrust washer riding the input shaft between the two gears is selected to control this clearance. To do the necessary measuring, use a setup similar to that shown in the pictures and follow this procedure.

Step a: Install the large bronze thrust washer and the clutch assembly on the oil delivery sleeve.

Step b: Measure the distance between the front face of the reverse sun gear and the plane of the front face of the transmission case.

Step c: Compare this distance with the distance between the rear face of the converter housing and the rear face of the low sun gear as mounted in step a.

Step d: There are three bronze thrust washers available: .095", .120", and .145". Select one of these to reduce the difference between the distance tound in step b and that in step c to the specified tolerance of .007"-.035".

Install the selector shaft and apply spring assembly and place a new seal on the shaft. The lip of the seal goes against the case.

Install the flat washer and the selector lever so that with shaft all the way to the rear there is .000"-.010" clearance between the washer and the lever. Tighten the selector lever lock bolt.

Install the parking lock pawl and spring. Using the tool as shown, or a screw driver, wind up the spring and catch the end on the inside of the case.

Remove the clutch assembly from the oil delivery sleeve and insert the input shaft into it. Double spline end to the rear.

Coat the previously selected low sun gear thrust washer, step d above, with graphite grease and install on rear end of shaft so that the missing spline of the washer is aligned with the oil hole in the shaft and the flat side is toward the reverse sun gear. The milled side goes against the low sun gear to permit lubricant flow.

Make sure the reverse sun gear thrust washer is in its recess in the output shaft and install the input shaft and clutch assembly, turning so the gears and splines mesh.

Complete assembly by following Par. 1, 2, 3, 4, 6, 7, 8, and 10.

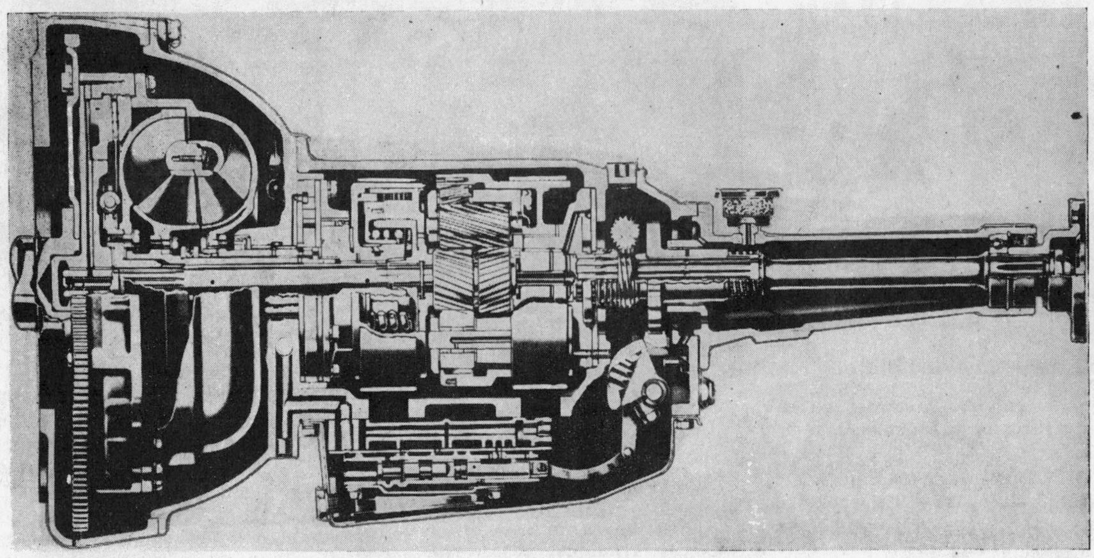

Fig. 1—Sectional view of the ultramatic transmission

PACKARD ULTRAMATIC TRANSMISSION

The Packard Ultramatic Transmission is a completely automatic hydraulic transmission. It is controlled by oil pressure acting through valves and features a direct drive clutch which locks out the torque converter. It has absolutely no electric controls connected with it.

GENERAL INFORMATION

OIL REQUIREMENTS

Special Packard Ultramatic oil or automatic transmission fluid Type A.

Note: Quality should be at least equal to Armour Institute Qualifying Number AQ-ATF No. (*) for automatic transmission fluid.

*—Last number varies with different refiners. Designation and number are embossed on the can.

Oil should be changed every 25,000 miles.

OIL CAPACITY

Refill—Dry ....12 qts

Put in seven quarts, run engine up to 800 rpm and add balance with engine running.

Note: If a pump is not available for filling the transmission there is a plug on the upper rear surface which may be reached by rolling up the rear edge of the front floor mat and removing a small cover.

GAGE ROD

Located under the floor on the left side of the transmission case; turn counterclockwise to release.

Quantity between refill and full on gage rod ....1½ qts

Measure oil with engine hot immediately after stopping from a 2-minute idle at 800 rpm.

FRONT OIL PUMP

Driven by ....Engine
Cuts out at..................45 mph
Pressure regulated to.........85 psi

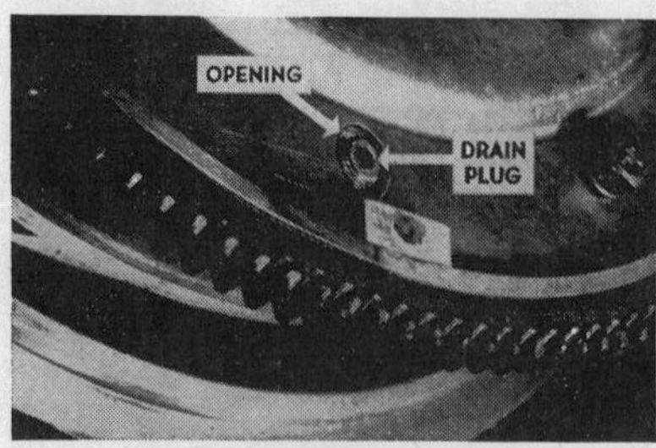

Fig. 2—Remove flywheel lower front cover to locate converter drain holes

REAR OIL PUMP

Driven by............Output shaft
Pressure regulated to.........93 psi

GOVERNOR

Driven by............Output shaft
Operates at speeds above....15 mph

CLUTCH PLATES

Direct drive inside converter
Single cork lined
High range in transmission
Driving (Internally splined and faced) ....6 used
Driven (Externally splined and dished) ....6 used

TOLERANCES

End play of reactor shaft (with gasket in place)..... .010"-.015" FIR

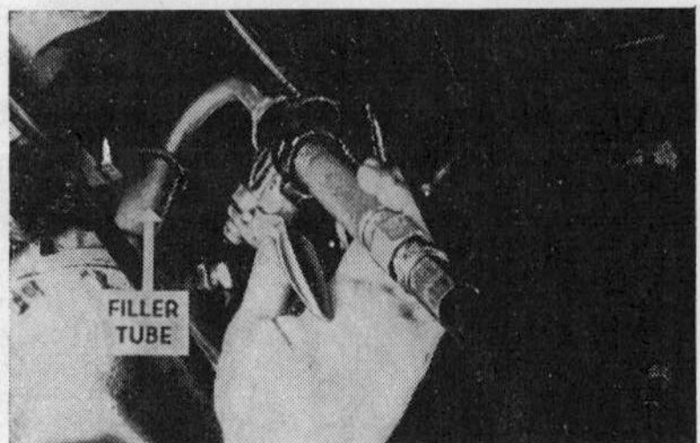

Fig. 3—Using hose to fill thru gage hole

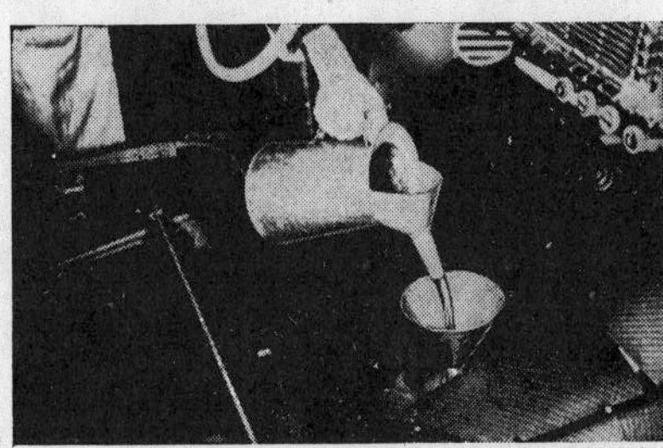

Fig. 4—Using upper hole for filling

Fig. 5—Top view of transmission

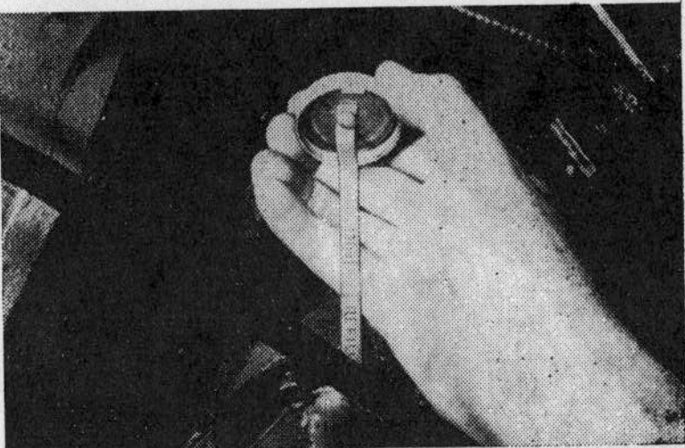

Fig. 6—Gage rod is removed from under car

End clearance overrunning clutch housing to high range clutch hub thrust washer .... .008"-.018"

BAND ADJUSTMENT

Can be done with transmission in place.

Tighten adjusting screw to 20 ft lbs, then back off 1¾ turns and lock. Tighten lock nut to 25-30 ft lbs.

HYDRAULIC SYSTEM VALVES

Front pump relief valve	Cuts out front pump
Control valve	Operated by hand lever
Pump selector valve	Controls oil pump pressure
Pump check valve	Prevents backflow
Hydraulic governor	Controls direct drive clutch
Throttle valve	Operated by throttle position
Pressure modulating valve	Softens shift from Low to High
Timing valve	Softens shift from High to Low
Direct drive clutch valve	Operates direct drive clutch
Converter inlet valve	Cuts oil from converter in direct drive
Converter outlet valve	Feeds to the oil cooler

TORQUE SPECIFICATIONS

¾—16 U joint flange nut	200-225	ft lbs
¾—16 All bolts	50	" "
⅝—18 All bolts	25-30	" "
7/16—14 All bolts	55-60	" "
⅜—16 All bolts	25-30	" "
⅜—18 All bolts	30	" "
⅜—24 All bolts	25-30	" "
5/16—18 All bolts	15-18	" "
5/16—24 All bolts	20-25	" "

MATCH POINTS

Items which must be match marked to insure balanced reassembly:

Primary Pump cover to Flywheel.

Primary Pump cover to Direct Drive Clutch housing.

Primary Pump to Direct Drive Clutch housing.

Balancing nuts to Primary Pump.

Direct Drive Clutch fixed plate to its housing.

Direct Drive Clutch piston to its housing.

Second Turbine to the First Turbine.

Front portion of the Planetary Carrier to the rear portion.

Starting the Car When Starter is Inoperative

Always push the car to start the engine when the starter is not working. Towing to start is dangerous as the car will probably pick up speed and ram the tow car before it can be put in Neutral.

Hold the hand lever in Neutral until the car reaches a speed of 20-25 mph. Then move the hand lever to High and engine will turn.

Towing the Car

When the control lever is moved to Neutral the car may be towed.

When the rear wheels are on the ground, Neutral is the only position that can be used for towing. If the control lever cannot be moved into Neutral position, lift the rear wheels from ground for towing or disconnect the propeller shaft from the transmission.

ADJUSTING THE MANUAL LINKAGE

The engine and transmission should be warm. The carburetor should be properly adjusted and the engine capable of idling at 375 rpm with the hand lever at High and the brakes set. Fluid level should be at full.

The Throttle Control Valve

1. Packard provides a gage No.

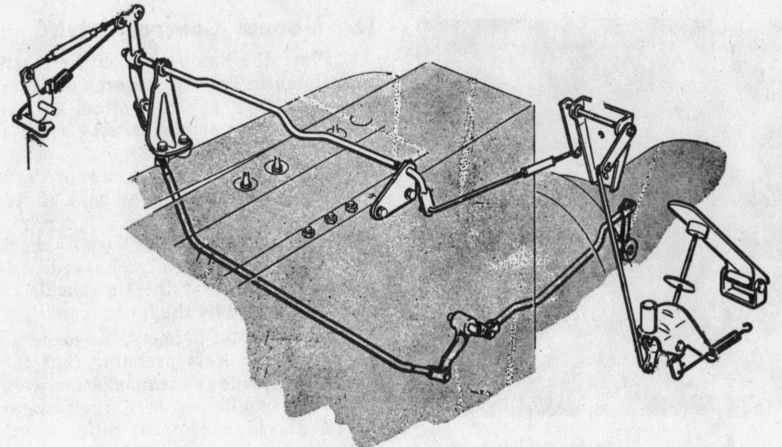

Fig. 7—Transmission throttle valve linkage

ADJUSTING MANUAL LINKAGE—*continued*

PU-364 which locates the contact point of the throttle rod coming from the carburetor and the throttle rod coming over the cylinder head from the accelerator. The gage is placed on the head so that the hole in the gage lines up with the hole in the lever at the right rear corner of the cylinder head. The adjustment is provided at the carburetor end of the rod and provides overtravel to the kick-down point. The gage sets the lever at an angle of 13½° from the perpendicular.

2. Under the floor board there is a spring loaded button which provides a normal stop for the accelerator and yet permits the accelerator to be pushed down further in order to kick the direct drive out of engagement. When the throttle is wide open (before the spring in the adjustment above is affected) there should be clearance between the accelerator lever and the button. This clearance should be .030″ to .050″, never less. In practice the existence of this clearance is of more importance than the adjustment made with the specified gage in Par. 1 above.

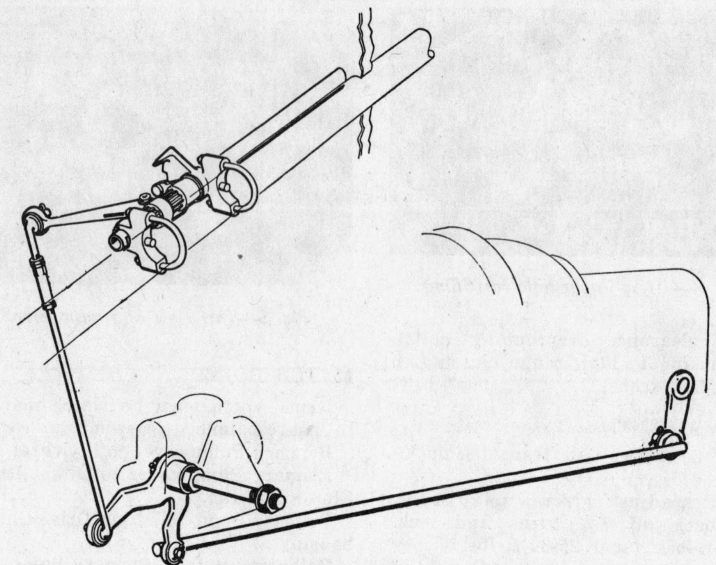

Fig. 9—Manual control valve linkage

3. The throttle linkage operates another rod going down the right side of the engine to the right rear corner of the transmission where it contacts a lever which operates the throttle control valve inside the transmission. This is the throttle control valve lever and it is important that this lever be properly positioned to coordinate the valve with the kick-down adjustments already made. To do this:

Loosen the clamp bolt holding the lever to the shaft entering the transmission case. On older models the lever is keyed to the shaft. Remove the lever and throw the key away.

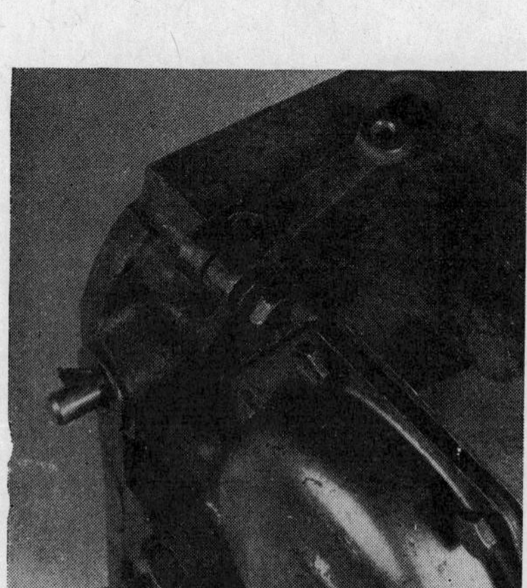

Fig. 8—Throw away key which holds throttle control valve lever

With an offset screwdriver in the slot in the end of the shaft, turn the shaft counterclockwise as far as it will go. On models that used a key to position the lever, turn the shaft with pliers.

Holding the shaft in the counterclockwise position with the offset screwdriver or pliers, tighten the clamp bolt to fasten the lever firmly to the shaft. The shaft is soft, so be sure to remove burrs.

The Manual Control Valve

1. Place the hand lever on the steering column in Park or Reverse position.

2. The lever at the bottom of the steering column should then be .030″ to .040″ from the nearest stop.

The upper stop in the case of Park.

The lower stop in the case of Reverse.

3. In either position be sure to check that the detent is firmly engaged. Adjustment is made at the turnbuckle in the rod operated by the lever.

Note: If the adjustments as made do not prove out, it is probable that the two valves inside the transmission were not properly aligned with their outer shafts. Checking of these adjustments can be done without removing the transmission from the car.

Checking Valve Adjustment Inside Transmission

Drain the oil from the transmission case.

Remove the oil pan and gasket.

Check that the collar of the throttle control valve is in place on its operating lever.

Check that with the carburetor throttle valve closed the throttle control valve is .050″ from its rearward stop.

Turn the manual control valve outer lever all the way counterclockwise. Check that the detent is holding. This is Reverse position. Loosen the inner lever clamp bolt.

Fig. 10—Bottom view showing manual and throttle valve levers

Set the control valve so that its rear land protrudes 5/16" from the body.

Retighten the clamp bolt to 50 ft lbs.

Using a new gasket, install the transmission oil pan. Tighten the attaching bolts to 10-12 ft lbs.

Run the engine at 800 rpm for one minute to be sure the converter is full. Stop the engine and immediately check the fluid level.

THEORY AND OPERATION OF PACKARD ULTRAMATIC TRANSMISSION

Movement of the shift control lever on the steering column provides five different controls, Parking, Neutral, High, Low and Reverse.

The detent which holds the control lever in the selected position is located at the rear of the transmission as part of the Parking lock mechanism and safety switch.

When the control lever is moved to Parking, a spring loaded locking pawl mounted at the rear of the transmission case engages the parking lock ratchet wheel on the transmission output shaft.

PARKING RANGE SHOULD NEVER BE ENTERED WHEN THE CAR IS IN MOTION.

Parking is used in conjunction with the parking brake to hold the car on steep grades or whenever it is necessary to race the engine without danger of car movement as when working on the car in the shop.

Low is for emergency use only. There should be no need under normal conditions for the use of the Ultramatic Low.

Shifts from Low to High can be made at any time.

By using Low and Reverse alternately the car can be rocked out of ruts.

PARTS OF THE TRANSMISSION

The transmission consists of: (1) a bell housing fastened to the engine block which houses the converter unit, and (2) the transmission case which is bolted to the rear of the bell housing and houses the High clutch and the planetary gear set for Low and Reverse.

Regulation of the oil pressure and so the operation of the clutch and planetary gears is controlled by a valve and servo body assembly attached to the bottom of transmission and covered by the oil pan. In addition there is a control valve operated by the accelerator linkage which varies the performance with reference to throttle position and a governor assembly that varies operation according to speed. This latter control is on the right side of the transmission to the rear.

OPERATION OF THE CONVERTER

The fluid unit at the start of the Ultramatic transmission is a fluid driven torque converter with an added lock-out feature in the form of an automatically operated single disk clutch. The converter takes the power of the engine and multiplies it to a maximum of 2.4 to 1. It thus provides the flexible power source necessary to vehicle operation. In the event that this order of multiplication is insufficient for the driving conditions, the planetary gear set in the transmission case can be brought into use by moving the control lever to Low. This results in overall torque multiplication of 4.22 to 1. The automatically operated single disk clutch in the forepart of the converter assembly is known as the Direct Drive clutch. It is put into engagement by oil pressure whenever the car is going steadily at any speed above 15 mph. The throttle valve incorporated in the design permits the release of this clutch whenever driving conditions demand an increase in torque output. Conversely, this Direct Drive clutch remains in engagement during deceleration down to a car speed of 13 mph, thus providing a slip free means of employing the engine as a brake on steep hills.

The torque converter multiplies the available power of the engine by changing the direction of flow of a large volume of oil. The main part of the converter is known as the primary pump. It and the Direct Drive clutch housing are bolted together and to the flexible disk flywheel. Together they form a housing for the rest of the converter parts.

When the engine turns, so does the primary pump, and as the pump turns, so does the oil with which it is filled. The curved blades of the pump throw the oil against the turbine wheel which is fastened to the input shaft as is the single driven disk of the Direct Drive clutch. The input shaft extends into the High clutch and the planetary gear set of the transmission.

Hitting the blades of the turbine, the oil curves down and around to exit in a direction counter to the rotation of the turbine. Next it hits a set of blades known as the stator which changes its direction of flow to coincide with that of the pump.

The stator is mounted on a hollow shaft which ends in a sprag type free wheeling clutch mounted in the rear of the bell housing as part of the front pump assembly. This free wheeling clutch permits the stator to rotate freely in the same direction as the pump and turbine but anchors it securely against counter rotation.

When the turbine is stationary, the oil passes through it and the stator to enter the pump with almost as much force as when it left. Therefore there is bolted to the turbine another set of blades known as the secondary turbine. This turbine absorbs the energy still present in the coursing oil and turns the oil into the center of the pump for redelivery around the circuit.

As the speed of the turbines approaches that of the pump, the flow of oil falls off in volume and the stator free wheels in order to prevent interference with the decreased flow volume. When turbines and pump are at approximately the same speed, the governor controls (modulated by the position of the throttle valve) put the direct drive clutch into engagement and the slip inherent in the converter is obviated.

OPERATION OF THE TRANSMISSION

The output of the converter is carried into the transmission proper by the input shaft as previously mentioned.

The input shaft, passing freely through the hollow reactor shaft, has splined to it at its rear end the reverse sun gear and just forward of that the high clutch hub.

The internally splined (faced) clutch plates mesh with splines in the high clutch hub so that these plates, the high clutch hub and the input shaft act as a unit. Alternating with the faced plates are externally splined (steel) plates which mesh with splines in the low drum which is keyed to and so a part of the low sun gear.

The low sun gear is not connected to the input shaft but contacts the reverse ring gear through the reverse planet pinions of the planetary gear set.

The low drum acts as a housing for the high clutch parts and as a cylinder for the high clutch piston whose movement is controlled by the setting of the hand control lever.

When the control lever is set at High,

OPERATION OF TRANSMISSION—*continued*

oil under 30 to 85 psi is fed to the high clutch piston to lock the plates together. This brings the low sun gear into revolution with the input shaft and since the reverse sun gear is locked to the shaft with splines the two gears act upon the reverse and low planet pinions causing them to lock against each other. This results in the whole planetary gear set revolving as a hunk. Thus the output shaft is driven at the same speed and in the same direction as the input shaft. The high clutch only functions when the control lever is positioned in High. When the control lever is at Low, oil pressure at from 30 to 90 psi is modulated by the timing valve and fed into the low band servo to tighten the low band and so hold the low drum and with it the low sun gear stationary. The reverse sun gear, being splined to the input shaft as mentioned before, continues to turn, thus driving the low planet pinions which mesh with it. They in turn drive the reverse planet pinions, the direction in this case being identical with the rotation of the input shaft. Since the reverse planet pinions are meshed with the stationary low sun gear, they climb around it carrying their shafts and so the carrier with them. As a result the output shaft turns but at a slower rate than the input shaft, the reduction being on the order of 1.82 to 1.

When the control lever is moved to Reverse, oil pressure at 160-180 psi acts through the reverse band servo and so the band itself to hold the reverse ring gear stationary. The low band no longer holds the low sun gear and it idles. Power from the input shaft acting through the reverse sun gear drives the low planet pinions which in turn drive the reverse planet pinions, causing them to climb around inside the stationary reverse ring gear carrying their shafts and the carrier with them as before. Only this time it results in the carrier and integral output shaft turning in a direction opposite to that of the input shaft. The rate, of course, is lower, being in the order of 1.64 to 1.

ULTRAMATIC TROUBLE CHART

Before any attempt is made to apply the trouble chart:

1. The manual linkage should be adjusted.

2. The transmission should be warmed up either:

Drive for five miles with frequent starts and stops, or

Adjust the idling speed to 750 rpm, set parking brake to hold the car, and set hand control lever to High and run engine for 15 minutes.

3. The oil level should be checked immediately after warm-up run.

If level is low, add oil.

If level is too high, drain down to proper level and drive for five miles to eliminate bubbles.

Note: When level is above the full mark, the planetary carrier aerates the oil which results in lost power and malfunctioning of the transmission.

4. The coolant level in the radiator should be checked.

X: Items marked X require removal of the transmission from the car.

1. Car will not move in any range—rear wheels free

This trouble can be caused by:
Improper linkage adjustment.
Low oil level.
Clogged intake screen.
Front oil pump relief valve stuck.
Pump selector valve stuck open.
Low and Reverse bands adjusted too tight.

2. Car will not move in any range—rear wheels locked

This trouble may be caused by:
Parking lock engaged.
Broken part in transmission. X
Broken part in differential.

3. Car will not move in High

This trouble may be caused by:
Low oil level.
Improper linkage adjustment.
Loss of pressure to the high clutch.
Modulator valve sticking.
Burned or worn clutch plates (smell the dip stick). X

4. Car will not move in Low

This trouble may be caused by:
Improper linkage adjustment.
Worn or broken band. X
Strut out of place. X
Low servo not operating correctly.
Timing valve stuck.

5. The car will not move in Reverse

This trouble may be caused by:
Improper linkage adjustment.
Improper band adjustment.
Reverse servo not functioning properly.

6. Excessive slip in all ranges

This trouble may be caused by:
Low oil level (smell the dipstick).
Improper linkage adjustment.
Improper front oil pump pressure due to clogged intake screen.
Control valves stuck.

7. Excessive slip in High only

This trouble may be caused by:
Improper linkage adjustment.
Malfunctioning high clutch due to:
Extended operation with low oil level. Smell the dip stick. X
Damaged clutch piston seals. X
Damaged clutch release valve. X

8. Excessive slip in Low only

This trouble can be caused by:
Improper linkage adjustment.
Improper low band adjustment.
Timing valve stuck.
Low servo not operating.
Low drum worn smooth.

9. Excessive slip in Reverse only

This trouble can be caused by:
Improper linkage adjustment.
Improper reverse band adjustment due to:
Wear.
Breakage. X
Misplaced strut. X
Worn drum. X
Insufficient pressure due to stuck valves.

10. Excessive slip in Direct drive

This trouble can be caused by:
Leakage in the system.
Inlet or outlet converter valves stuck.
Broken clutch plate. X
Faulty governor.
Sticking direct drive shift valve.

11. Car creeps forward with hand lever in Neutral

This trouble can be caused by:
Improper linkage adjustment.
Low band adjusted too tight.
High clutch inoperative due to:
Vent valve stuck closed. X
Plates improperly assembled. X
Plates sticking. X

12. Car creeps forward with hand lever in Reverse or backward with hand lever in Low

This trouble is caused by:
Improper linkage adjustment.

13. Shift from Low to High abnormally rough

This trouble can be caused by:
Low oil level.
Improper low band adjustment.
Improperly adjusted throttle linkage.
Stuck throttle valve.
Stuck modulator valve.
Worn clutch plates. X
Loose cover at the rear end of the timing valve.

14. Shift from High to Low abnormally rough

This trouble can be due to:
Improper low band adjustment.
Stuck timing valve.
Loose timing valve cover.

15. Shift from Neutral to Reverse abnormally rough

This trouble can be caused by:
Idling speed too high.
Modulator valve stuck.
Improper reverse band adjustment.
Excessive end clearance in the transmission. X

16. Chatter when starting in low

This trouble can be caused by:
Improper Low or Reverse band adjustment.

Malfunctioning high clutch due to:
Distorted plates. X
Sticking clutch piston. X
Sticking clutch vent valve. X
Worn low drum or band.

17. Chatter when starting in High or Reverse

This trouble can be caused by:
Improper Reverse or Low band adjustment.
Worn bands or drums. X
Sticking high clutch. X
Worn thrust washers. X

18. Direct drive clutch disengages with a severe clunk

This trouble may be due to:
Sticking direct drive shift valve.
Faulty governor vent valve.
Groove in facing of direct drive clutch plate too narrow and shallow. Groove should be .062″ wide thru full depth of facing. X
Direct drive clutch piston stuck. X

19. Direct drive clutch won't disengage

This trouble may be due to:
Faulty governor.
Sticking direct drive shift valve.
Sticking converter inlet valve.
Sticking converter outlet valve.
Sticking direct drive clutch piston. X
Broken driven plate. X

20. Drag in High or Reverse

This trouble may be due to:
Low band too tight.
Low servo stuck.
Strut misplaced. X
Timing valve stuck.

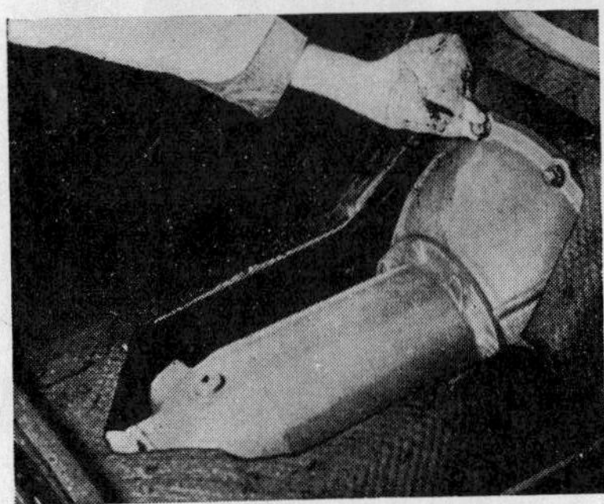

Fig. 11—Unbolt ball housing at top

Fig. 12—Support car on all four wheels

21. Noises

Can be classified as:

RINGING NOISES IN THE CONVERTER DUE TO:
Low oil level.
Low oil pressure in the converter.
Aerated oil (level too high)

BUZZING NOISES DUE TO:
Low oil level.
Malfunctioning of the pumps. Stall point should be less than 1600 R.P.M. X
Stuck valves.

WHINING NOISES DUE TO:
Worn planet gears. X
Worn pump gears. X
Worn pump bearings. X

CLICKING NOISE:
May be due to improperly adjusted linkage permitting the parking lock pawl to contact the ratchet gear.

ROARING NOISE FROM AROUND THE TRANSMISSION DUE TO:
Part of the floor pan contacting the transmission.
Part of the exhaust system contacting the frame.

22. Excessive vibration in Direct Drive

May be due to:
Driven plate badly worn. X
Transmission rear bearing worn. X

REMOVAL OF ULTRAMATIC FROM CAR

Remove the spark plugs.

Remove front floor mat and transmission inspection hole cover.

Raise both ends of the car.

Drain the transmission case and the converter.

Disconnect the manual and throttle controls at the transmission.

Disconnect the oil cooler lines, the speedometer cable and the starter safety switch leads.

Disconnect parking brake cable at the equalizer and the propeller shaft at the front and rear U joints. Remove the transmission rear bearing retainer.

Using a block of wood to cushion the load raise the engine on a jack under the oil pan in order to take the load from the engine supports.

Remove engine rear support channel and bracket assembly, transmission steady rest and insulator, both rear en-

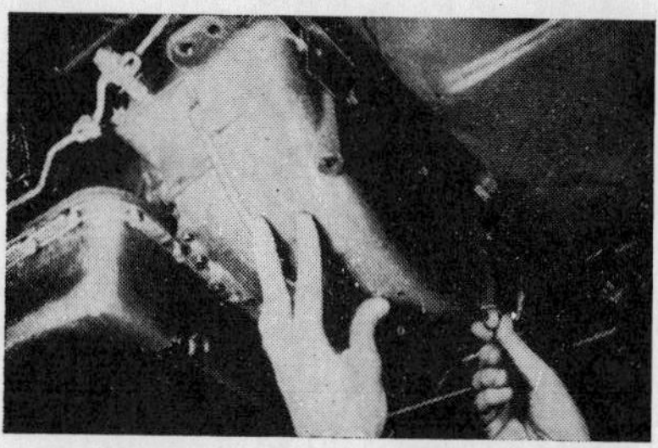

Fig. 13—Remove lower front flywheel housing

Fig. 14—Drain converter and transmission oil pan

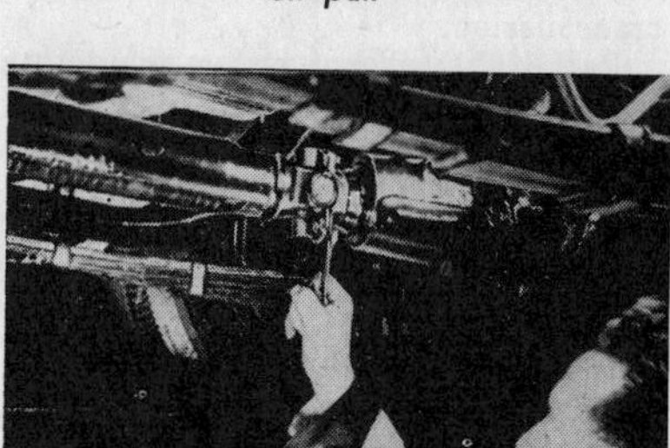

Fig. 15—Disconnect and remove the propeller shaft

REMOVAL OF ULTRAMATIC—cont'd

gine support insulators from transmission case.

Using a sling and hoist, or some such device, support weight of transmission.

Mark the flywheel, the primary pump and the direct drive clutch housing so that the units can be matched together at reassembly. Do it with a **paint stripe across all three.**

Unbolt the direct drive clutch housing from the flywheel, and slide it back into the bell housing.

Unbolt the bell housing from the flywheel housing.

Tie something across the open face of the bell housing so the converter can't drop off or out.

Slide the assembly to the rear and then lower it to the floor.

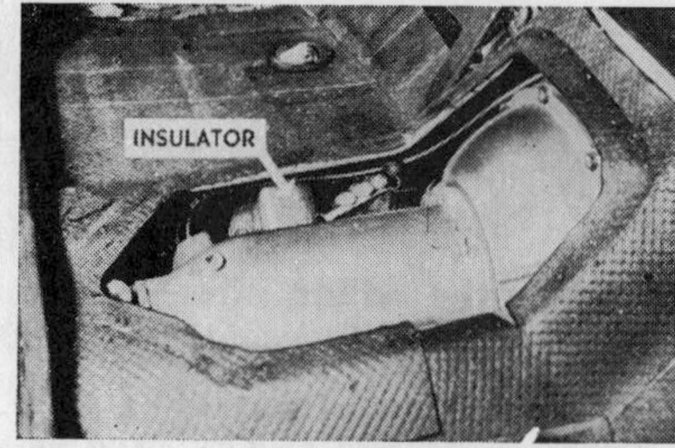

Fig. 16—Remove rear engine support insulators

REINSTALLATION OF THE ULTRAMATIC

Install 3 or 4 pilot studs in the forward side of the direct drive clutch housing to guide it onto the flywheel. Fasten the converter in the bell housing so that it won't fall off.

Raise the assembly. Guide the pins thru the flywheel so that the mating marks, made when unit was removed, will match up.

Slide the assembly forward so that the bell housing rests flat against the flywheel housing and the direct drive clutch housing sets against the flywheel.

Bolt the bell housing to the flywheel housing and the direct drive clutch housing to the flywheel. Tighten to 25-30 ft lbs.

Replace the rear engine support insulators, the support channel and bracket assembly, and the insulator to bracket attaching screws but only loosely.

Lower the jack supporting the engine and loosen the sling supporting the transmission. Rock the engine to normalize the supports.

Install the transmission steady rest and insulator.

Connect the oil cooler lines, the speedometer cable, and the emergency brake cable.

Install the rear bearing retainer, the propeller shaft, the hand control and throttle valve linkage.

Check that the drain plugs are tight, and install the lower flywheel housing.

Install 7 qts of AQ-ATF* or its equivalent into the transmission. Run engine at idle to fill the converter. With engine idling at 800 rpm, control lever at Neutral, add enough oil to bring the level up to the full mark on the stick.

Replace the cover and floor mat.

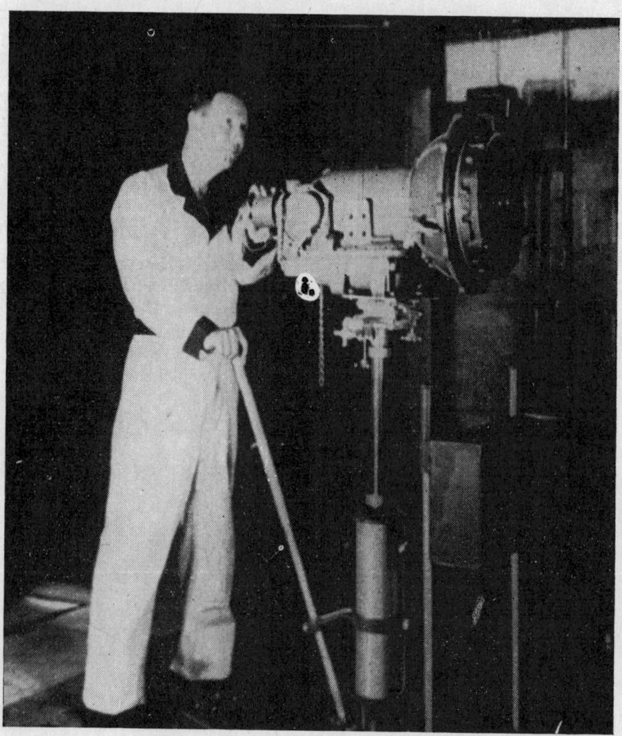

Fig. 17—Lower transmission to floor

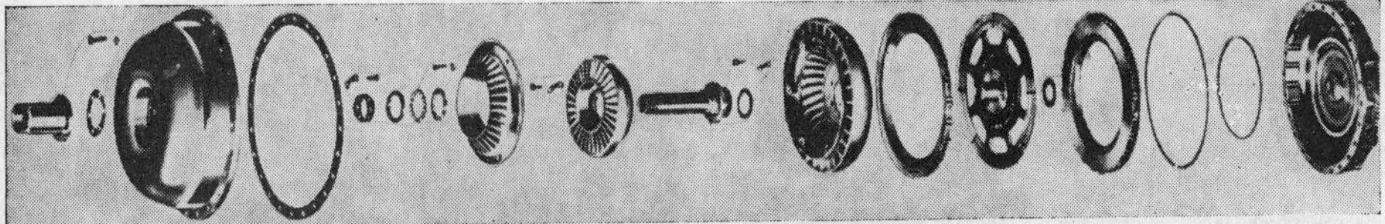

Fig. 18—Exploded view of 23rd series converter. Note: Primary turbine is bolted to driven plate.

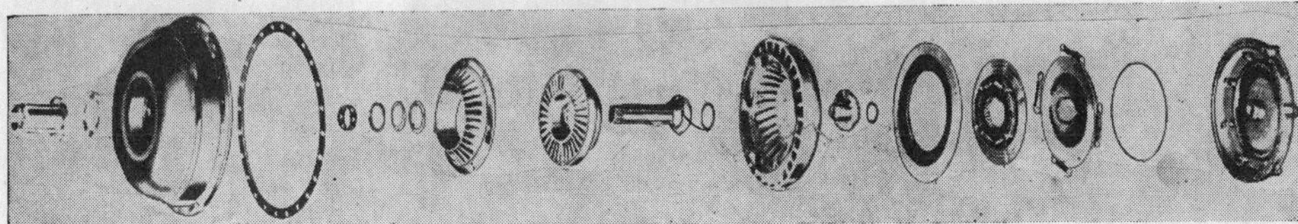

Fig. 19—Exploded view of 24th series converter

Disassembly of the Converter

Slide the converter assembly off the input shaft and place it on a bench with the direct drive clutch housing down.

Set up an indicator and measure the reactor shaft end play. It should be .010″-.015″ F.I.R. If greater a new reactor shaft thrust washer will be needed. Use pliers over cloth to move the reactor shaft.

Unbolt the primary pump from the direct drive clutch housing. Be sure that match marks are made across the pump and housing for use at reassembly. **Place marks also to show location of the balancing weights.** The marks must extend onto the clutch housing as the weights serve to balance the clutch assembly. Sometimes the weights are not fastened to the pump housing; they must be match marked. Note that the bolts used to fasten the pump to the housing are SPECIAL and should not be used elsewhere.

Tap the primary pump with a hammer and separate it from the direct drive clutch.

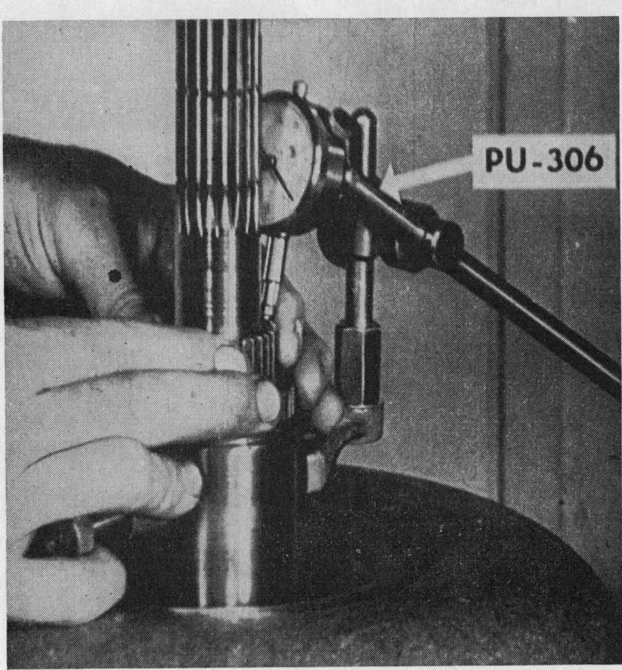

Fig. 20—Measure reactor shaft end play, (should be between .010″ and .015″)

Fig. 21—Mark direct drive clutch housing, primary pump, balance weights

Fig. 22—Lift off primary pump

ULTRAMATIC TRANSMISSION

DISASSEMBLY—*continued*

Match mark and then unbolt the turbine assemblies from each other.

Lift out the stator and reactor shaft assembly and the dimensioned thrust washer.

Lift the primary turbine from the direct drive clutch assembly. Be sure to reach under and hold the fixed plate in place.

Mark the face of the direct drive clutch fixed plate and the housing for matched reassembly.

Unbolt the fixed plate and remove it and the driven plate.

Mark a lug of the clutch piston and the clutch housing for mating at reassembly.

Lift out the direct drive clutch piston and remove the fixed plate spacers from the lugs.

Fig. 23—Match mark and unbolt 2nd turbine from the 1st

Fig. 24—Remove second turbine. Note: match marks.

Fig. 25—Lift out stator and reactor shaft assembly

Fig. 26—Note dimensioned thrust washer controls reactor shaft end play

Fig. 27—Remove the 1st turbine from the direct drive clutch driven plate

Fig. 28—Match mark fixed plate to housing and remove

Fig. 29—Remove driven plate and thrust washers, match mark clutch

Fig. 30—Remove piston

Fig. 31—Ring gap clearance should be .003"—.012"

Fig. 34—Install driven plate and fixed plate.—See Fig. 29

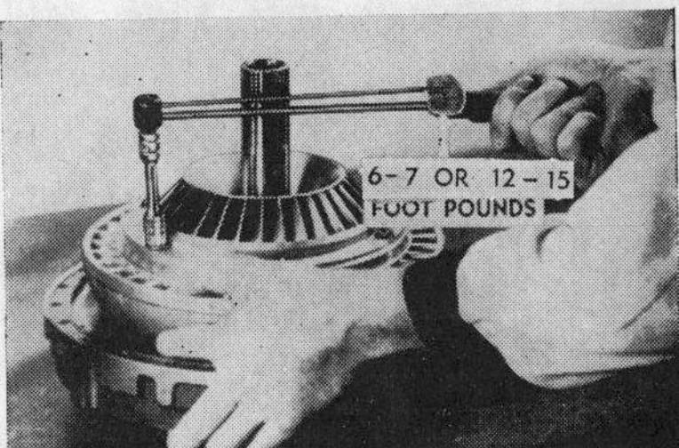

Fig. 37—Install 2nd turbine. Align match marks

Fig. 32—Inspect the vanes on the converter parts

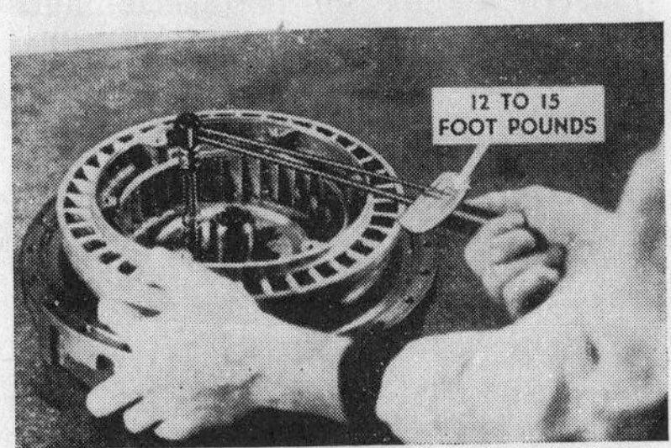

Fig. 35—Install 1st turbine onto driven plate—tighten to 12-15 ft lbs

Fig. 38—Install spacer, and ball thrust bearing

Fig. 33—Install direct drive clutch piston, note match marks

Fig. 36—Install thrust washers and stator assembly

Inspection of the Converter Parts

Inspect all machined surfaces for nicks, burrs, indentations, warpage, cracks, and indications of wear.

If the primary pump shaft shows signs of wear replace the shaft together with the bearing and the transmission oil seal.

Inspect the driven plate for worn or loose facings.

Check that the gap of the clutch piston rings is no less than .003" nor more than .012".

Reassembly of the Converter

Install the smaller clutch piston ring onto the hub and the larger onto the clutch piston.

Slide the piston down into the housing and align the match marks made at disassembly.

Install five 5/16 x 18 guide pins to:

1) Keep the piston from rotating out of position. (Use one thru a drive strap.)

2) Hold the fixed plate spacers (use 4).

3) Guide the fixed plate into position.

Lay the driven plate in position on the piston.

Install the fixed plate spacers onto the guide pins. Note that the spacers go on those bosses not used to drive the piston.

Align the match marks on the fixed plate and the housing and install the fixed plate onto the guide pins and into place in the housing.

Remove the guide pins and fasten the fixed plate with bolts and washers. Tighten to 25-30 ft lbs.

Install the primary turbine so that its splines engage the driven plate.

9) Install the reactor shaft thrust washer in the hub of the primary turbine. Note that this is a dimensioned thrust washer whose thickness controls the reactor shaft end play.

Lay the stator and reactor shaft assembly in place in the primary turbine.

Lay the secondary turbine in place and fasten it to the primary turbine with bolts and washers. Tighten to 12-15 ft lbs.

Install a spacer, the ball thrust bearing and a spacer in place on the reactor shaft. This bearing bears against the primary pump.

Coat the primary pump gasket with cup grease and lay it on the flange of the direct drive clutch.

Slide the primary pump into place over the reactor shaft. Be certain that the match marks (made at disassembly across the pump and the clutch housing to mate the parts and locate the balance weights) are aligned.

Fig. 39—Install primary pump onto direct clutch housing

REASSEMBLY OF CONVERTER—continued

Install four of the special bolts and washers and then check the reactor shaft end play. It must be between .010″ and .015″. Packard field service recommends holding this play between .003″ and .005″. If it is not the reactor shaft thrust washer mentioned in Par. 9 above, must be changed to make it so. Failure to hold the tolerance closely results in excessive vibration. *See Fig. 20.*

Use a spare input shaft to check that the direct drive clutch driven plate revolves freely.

Fig. 40—Check that turbine turns freely

Install the rest of the special nuts and washers and tighten to 25-30 ft lbs.

Disassembly of the Transmission

Unbolt and remove the oil pan and gasket.

Tie the band flanges to the sides of the case so that the struts do not drop out when the servos are removed.

Unbolt and remove the oil screen.

Disconnect the control valve link and remove the two valve and servo body assemblies and their separator as a unit.

Unbolt and remove the bell housing.

Untie the low band and remove the struts, then slide the high clutch and input shaft assembly out of the transmission case. **Note** the dimensioned thrust washer.

Remove the governor cover and the screws holding the adaptor. Lift the governor assembly out.

Remove the speedometer drive pinion.

Unbolt and remove the rear bearing retainer.

Remove the converter outlet valve, a snap ring, the parking ratchet wheel, and the speedometer drive gear with 2 spacers.

Slide the planetary gear set, complete with the reverse ring gear, and the output shaft assembly out through the front of the case.

Remove the reverse band and struts.

Remove the rear oil pump.

The following items will be left in the case and do not ordinarily require rehabilitation: starter safety switch, control lever detent, manual and throttle control valve inner and outer levers, the parking lock operating assembly, the band operating levers.

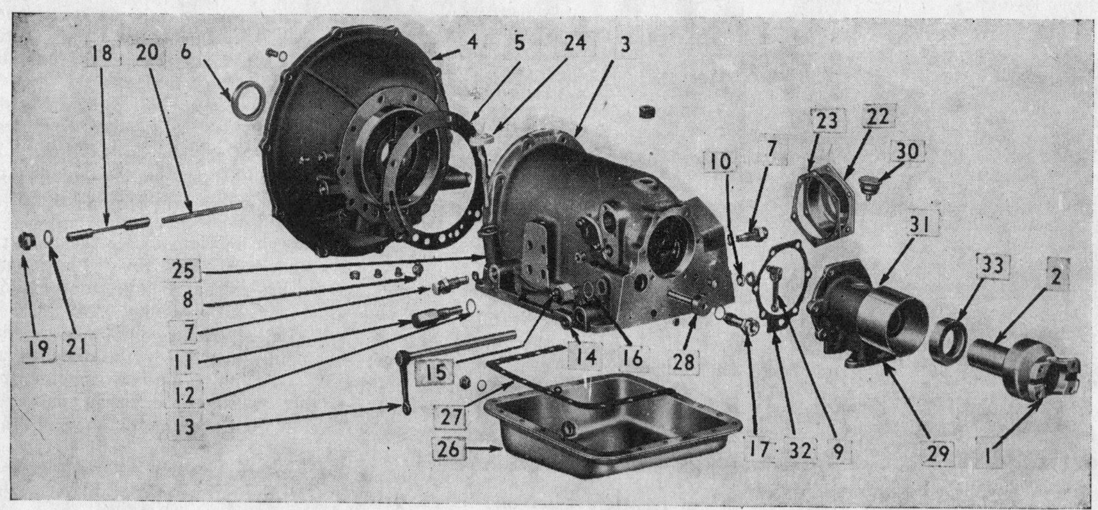

Fig. 41—Exploded view of transmission case, early models

1 Drive shaft front universal joint flange
2 Dust Shield
3 Transmission case
4 Bell Housing
5 Gasket Housing to case
6 Bell Housing Oil Seal
7 Band Adjusting Screws
8 Damper Assembly Early Models only
9 Throttle Valve Control Lever
10 Seal
11 Manual Control Valve Detent
12 Gasket
13 Manual Control Valve Lever Assembly
14 Seal
15 Neutral Safety Switch
16 Gasket
17 Oil Cooler Tube Adaptor
18 Front Oil Pump Pressure relief Valve
19 Retainer
20 Spring
21 Gasket
22 Governor Cover
23 Gasket
24 Gage Rod Transmission Filler Tube
25 Oil Filler Tube
26 Oil Pan
27 Gasket
28 Parking Lock Lever Support
29 Rear Housing Assembly
30 Breather Assembly
31 Dust Shield
32 Gasket Rear Housing to case
33 Rear Housing Oil Seal

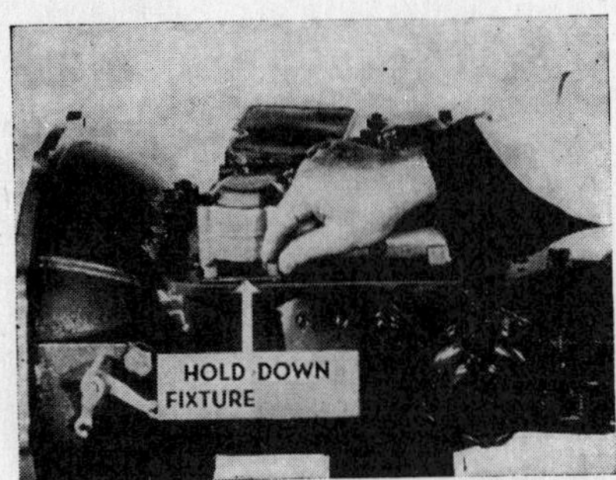

Fig. 42—Install fixture to hold the band levers so the struts do not fall out

Fig. 43—Remove oil screen

Fig. 44—Remove valve and servo body assembly

Fig. 45—Left side of transmission

Fig. 46—Right side of transmission

Fig. 47—Remove clutch and imput shaft assembly

Fig. 48—Remove the governor cover

Fig. 49—Remove governor assembly

Fig. 50—Remove planetary gear set thru front of case

Disassembly and Reassembly of the Units

THE HIGH CLUTCH ASSEMBLY

Remove the snap ring and separate the low sun gear flange from the drum.

Remove the clutch hub, the input shaft and the clutch plates.

Compress the clutch spring, remove the retaining ring, thus releasing the seat, spring and piston.

Remove a seal ring from the piston and a seal ring from the drum hub.

Remove retaining ring from input shaft and slide the clutch hub off. Note thrust washer.

Inspect the drum for wear, scores, nicks and burrs. Check the seal rings that the gap is between .003 and .012.

Inspect the six faced, internally splined, and the six steel, waved, and externally splined clutch plates for signs of wear and tear.

Install the seal ring on the clutch piston and the seal ring on the drum hub. Install the piston in the drum. Use a ring compressor on the piston seal ring.

Seat the spring in the piston. Compress the spring and install the retainer and ring.

Install a retaining ring, a thrust washer, the clutch hub and a retaining ring onto the input shaft. Install the hub and shaft into the drum.

Starting with a steel, externally splined and waved plate, install the six steel and six faced plates alternating. Be sure that the wave of the steel plates is all the same way. The action of the wave is to aid release of the clutch. Mixing the direction of the wave alters the effect.

Install the low sun gear flange and the retaining ring.

Fig. 51—Remove the rear oil pump thru the front of case

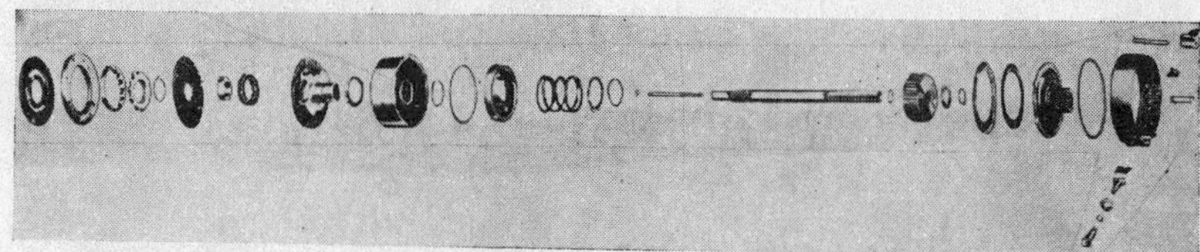

Fig. 52—Exploded view of clutch assembly

Fig. 53—Remove the snap ring to release the low sun gear flange from the drum

Fig. 55—Compress clutch spring and remove retaining ring

Fig. 57—Piston seal ring clearance should be .003" to .012"

Fig. 54—Remove imput shaft and clutch hub, remove clutch plates

Fig. 56—Shake clutch piston out of low drum

Fig. 58—Inspect the clutch plates

Fig. 59—Install seal ring on piston

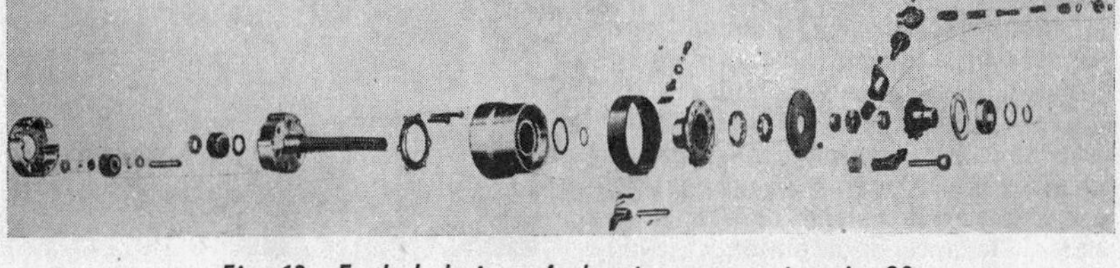

Fig. 63—Exploded view of planetary gear set, series 23

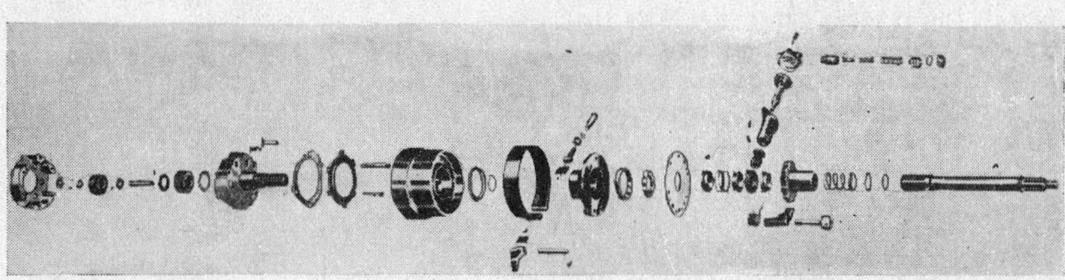

Fig. 64—Exploded view of planetary gear set, series 24. Note: Two piece output shaft.

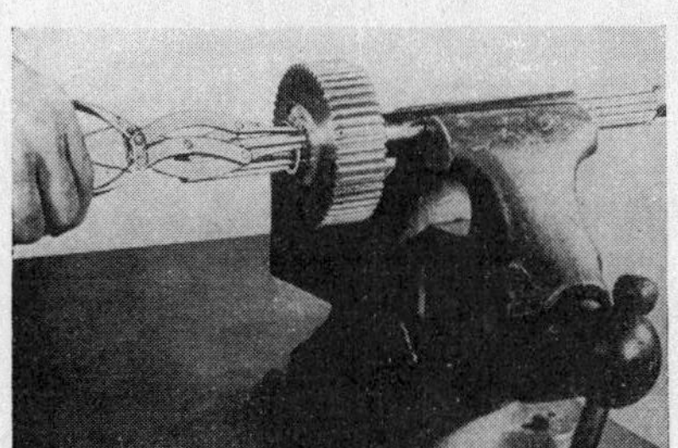

Fig. 60—Assembling clutch hub to input shaft

THE PLANETARY GEAR SET

Remove the ring gear from the gear set. Be careful not to lose the three dampers and six springs that are in grooves on the outer face of the gear set. These dampers take up the backlash between the pinions and the ring gear. **Note:** These dampers are not on earlier models.

Pry away the locking plate tabs, support the output shaft and remove the bolts holding the two halves of the assembly together. Match mark the two halves and separate by tapping lightly with a plastic hammer. Remove the reverse sun gear and thrust washer.

Move a short pinion shaft rearward to release a Woodruff key. Then remove the pinion complete with two thrust washers, a shaft and the bearing needles. Release and remove the other pinions in the same way. The number of needles per pinion is 38. Nineteen needles at each end separated by a spacer.

Inspect the parts for signs of wear and tear, especially the reverse sun gear rear thrust washer. Check that the two halves of the assembly fit accurately. Check the damper springs for cracks or breaks and the bronze dampers for wear.

Support the output shaft in a horizontal position.

Assemble the pinions to their shafts,

Fig. 61—Assemble clutch plates into low drum

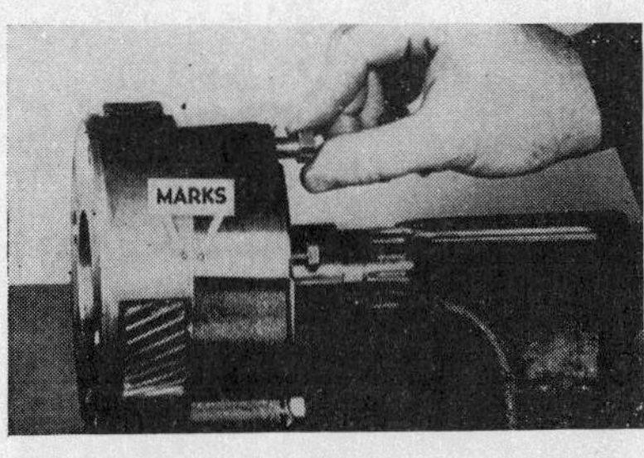

Fig. 65—Mark, unbolt, and separate two halves of planetary carrier

Fig. 62—Install low sun gear and flange assembly

Fig. 66—Remove reverse sun gear and washer behind it

Fig. 67—Remove each short pinion gear as an assembly

PLANETARY GEAR SET—*continued*

the chamfered end of the pinions away from the lock ends of the shafts.

Install the pinion assemblies in the carrier, chamfered ends to the front. Push the shafts far enough rearward to insert the Woodruff keys. Push the shafts forward so the keys lock the shafts. Be sure each pinion assembly has a thrust washer at each end.

Install the reverse sun gear rear thrust washer on its seat in the carrier. Install the reverse sun gear. Note that it is very important that this thrust washer be properly seated and not hung up on the steps adjacent to the short pinion bosses.

Align the match marks and install the front half of the carrier to the rear half.

Install the lock plate and tighten the larger attaching bolts to 25-30 ft lbs, the smaller one to 15-18 ft lbs. Bend over the tabs of the lock plate.

Install a rubber band around the carrier. Install two damper springs and one bronze damper in each of the three grooves. Place the springs in the side of the groove that has a lip, with the bowed center of the springs facing out. Place the dampers on the springs wide side out.

With the rubber band holding the dampers in position, fit the reverse ring gear onto the carrier, sliding the rubber

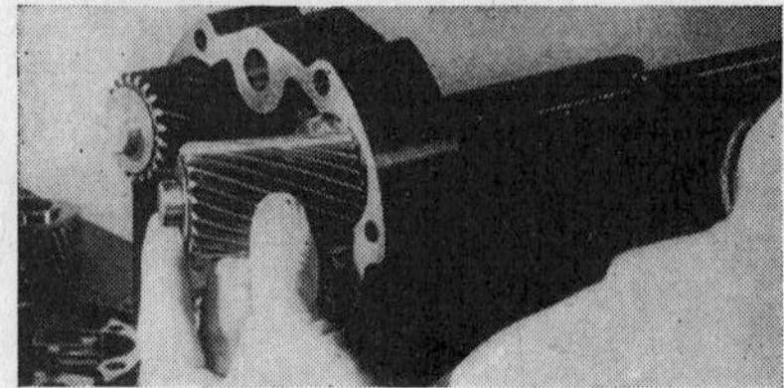

Fig. 68—Remove each long pinion as an assembly

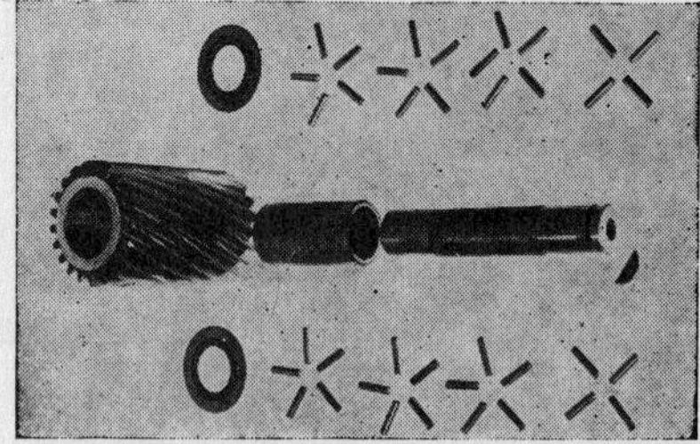

Fig. 70—Long planet pinion parts

Fig. 69—Short planet pinion parts

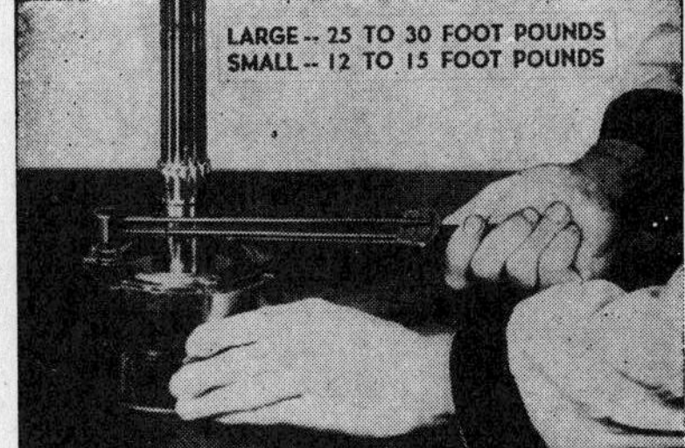

Fig. 71—Tighten assembly securely

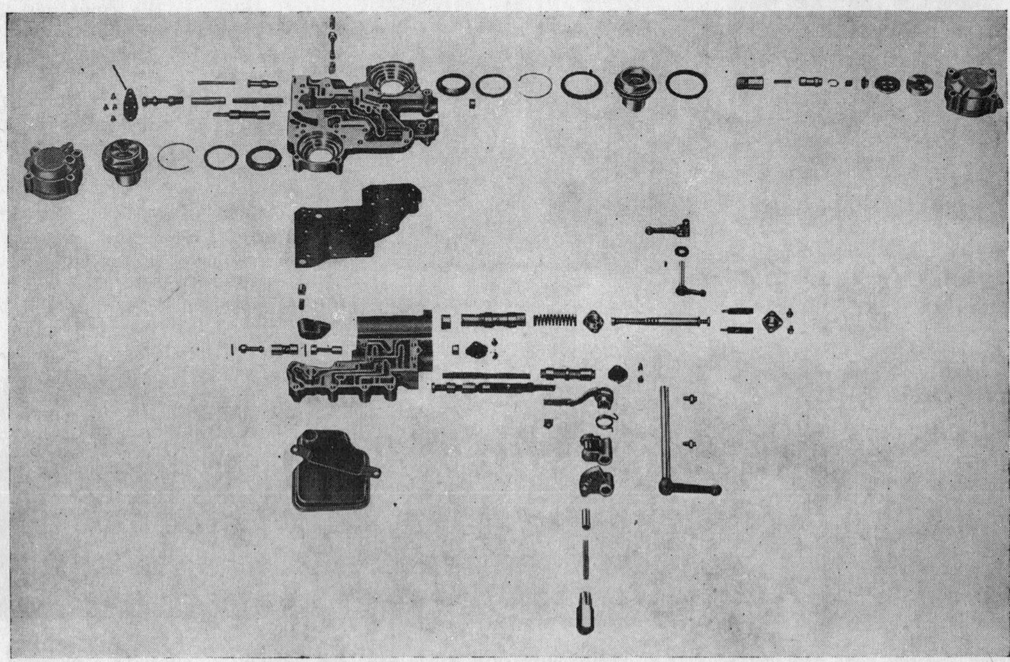

Fig. 72—Layout of valve and servo body assembly parts

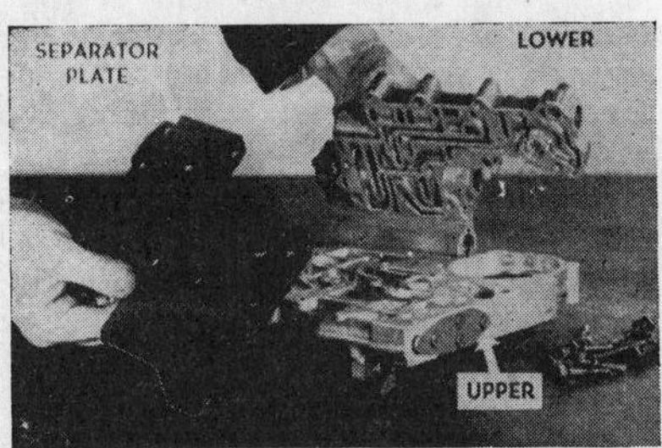

Fig. 73—Separate the two castings

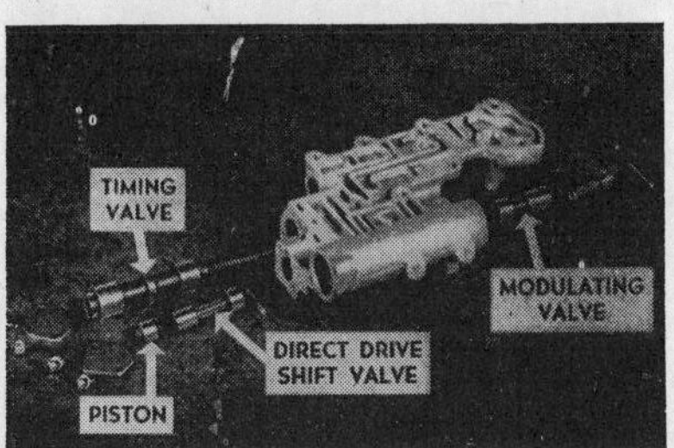

Fig. 74—Disassemble the lower valve body

band off as the dampers make contact with the drum portion of the ring gear.

CONTROL VALVE ASSEMBLY

Note that the two valve bodies are aluminum castings and the various valves should move in their bores freely. If a valve should become wedged, use great care to loosen it as the sharp edges of the bronze or steel valves can easily score the aluminum and render the casting useless. Keep the parts on clean, lintless cloth.

Remove the bolts and separate the upper and lower valve bodies from the separator plate.

Removal of the valves from the bodies presents no particular problem. A close clearance must be maintained between the valves and their bores to prevent loss of oil pressure, yet they must be able to slip in and out of their own weight. Note the exploded views for retaining pins and order.

Inspect the contact surfaces of the two bodies and the separator plate for evidence of oil leaks between passages which might indicate that the bodies are uneven. Remove any low spots by rubbing the surface on a piece of plate glass using No. 400A wet or dry sandpaper soaked in kerosene. Be sure to remove all trace of abrasive before assembling.

Assemble the upper and lower valve bodies and the separator plate. Be sure the correct length bolts are installed in their proper positions. Torque tighten to 6 ft lbs.

Install the low and reverse servo assemblies using the round head Philips screws. Note that the seals are installed in a particular way as shown in the cut.

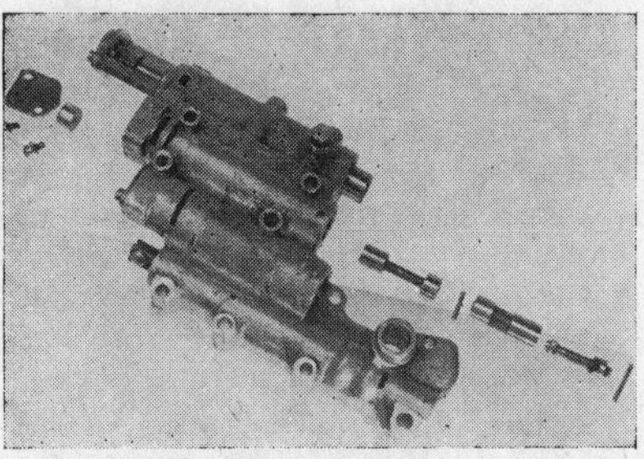

Fig. 75—Direct drive and modulating valve

Fig. 76—Timing valve

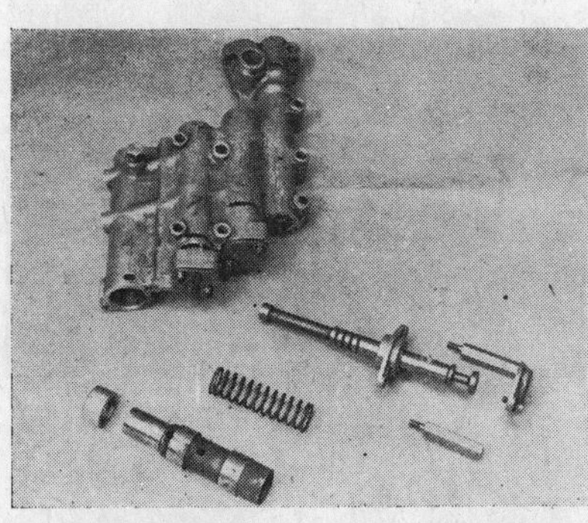

Fig. 77—Throttle valve assembly

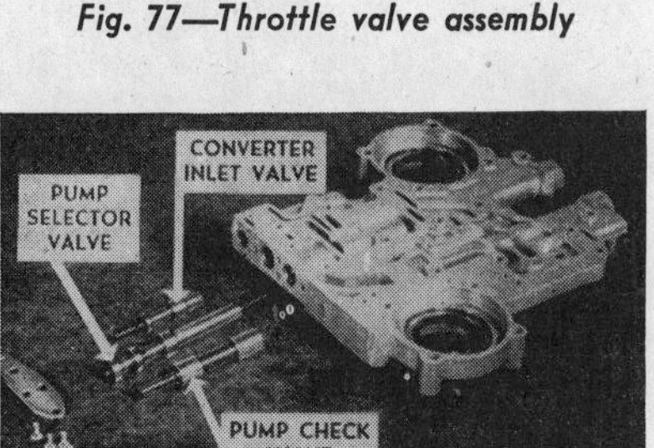

Fig. 78—Disassemble the upper valve body

Fig. 79—Layout of upper valve body parts

Fig. 80—Manner in which servo seals are installed

Fig. 81—Layout of servo piston parts

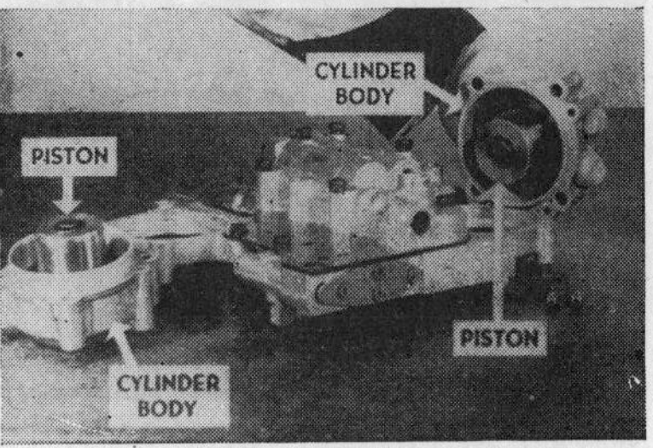

Fig. 82—Install servo piston assemblies

THE GOVERNOR ASSEMBLY

Separate the housing from the flange.

Push the governor valve in. The spring should push it all the way out with no drag.

Pull the vent valve flyweight out. The spring should pull it in with no drag.

The governor drive shaft should have between .0005″ and .002″ clearance in the adaptor and .010″ to .018″ F.I.R. end play.

Install the governor housing assembly on the drive shaft flanges and attach securely with the two cap screws. Make sure the housing fits evenly on the flange. Tighten the bolts to 6 ft lbs.

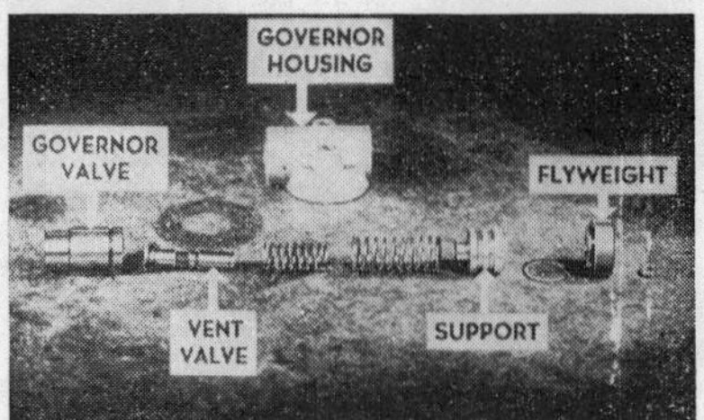

Fig. 86—Layout of governor parts

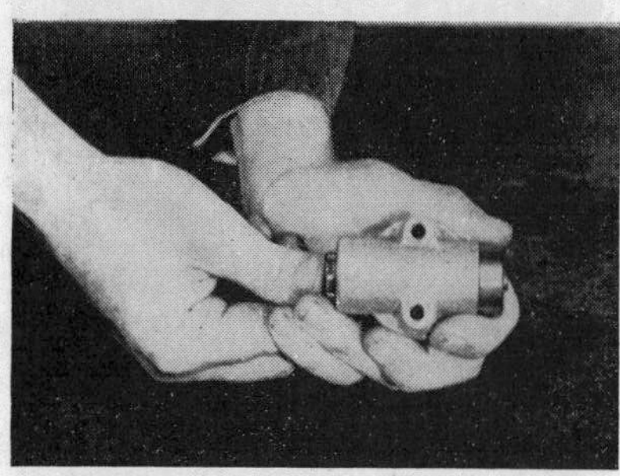

Fig. 83—Push governor valve in, it should return.

THE BELL HOUSING

Unbolt the front oil pump and oil-sleeve-free-wheeling clutch assembly.

Remove the front oil pump relief valve and spring. Remove the plugs from the oil pressure passage.

Remove the two retaining screws holding the pump assembly to the free wheeling clutch assembly. This will release the oil-delivery-sleeve-free-wheeling clutch assembly. This assembly cannot be repaired. If the clutch does not lock against counterclockwise rotation nor move freely clockwise, it is necessary to replace the assembly. It is a sprag type free-wheeling clutch and it is possible to remove a sprag for inspection without injuring the assembly. Check it for wear and pitting. Do not tip it.

Separate the front oil pump. It consists of:

(1) A front plate; (2) a pump body; (3) an outer rotor; (4) an inner rotor; (5) a rear plate, and (6) a centering ring.

Inspect the pump rotors for wear, pits, and scores.

Inspect the bell housing for proper fit of the relief valve.

Blow out the oil passages with clean air. Do not use any wires or other devices to clean oil passages as the metering orifices have been so closely figured that any enlargement is likely to prevent proper functioning of the transmission.

Install the front pump relief valve and the oil passage plugs in the bell housing.

Place the oil-sleeve-free-wheeling clutch assembly with the sleeve down.

Place the front pump rear plate on the free wheeling clutch and place the pump body on top. Check that the oil passages line up.

Install the rotors in the pump body.

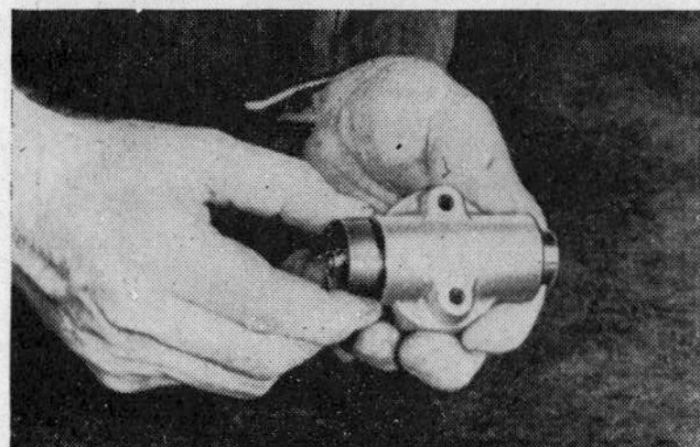

Fig. 84—Pull the governor vent valve, it should return

Fig. 87—Remove the front oil pump

Fig. 89—A sprag may be removed to check

Fig. 85—Check governor shaft end play—.010"-.018"

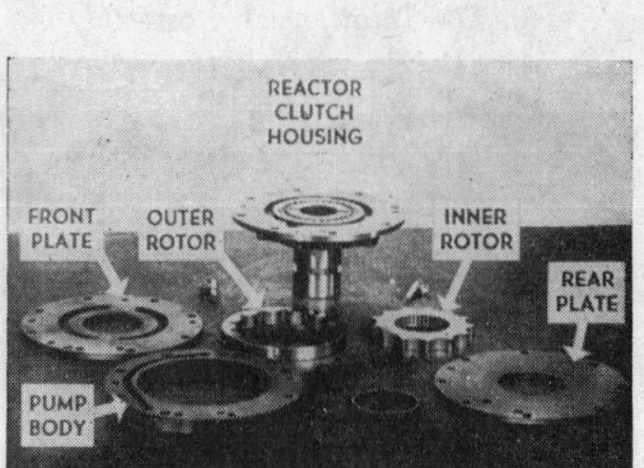

Fig. 88—Layout of front oil pump parts

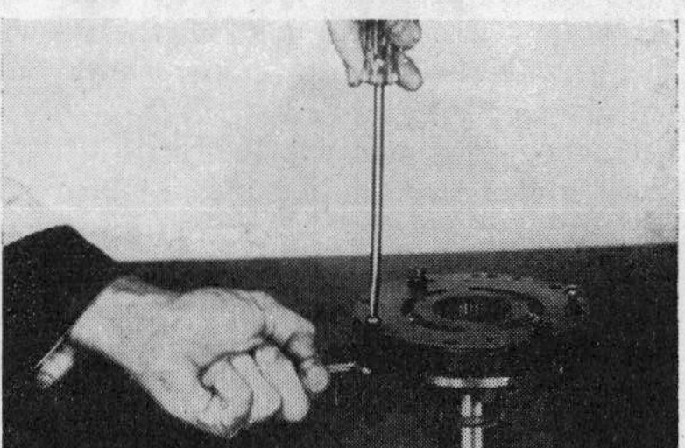

Fig. 90—Fasten front pump assembly together

The inner groove of the inner rotor nearest the free wheeling clutch and the centering rung in place.

Install the front plate of the pump and fasten the assembly together with the two screws to 8-9 ft lbs.

Install the assembly in the bell housing. The oil delivery sleeve to the rear. Tighten the attaching bolts to 15-18 lbs.

Install a new front oil pump seal in the front face of the bell housing hub.

THE REAR OIL PUMP

The rotors of the rear pump are smaller than those of the front pump and are not interchangeable.

Remove six bolts fastening rear oil pump to the case and remove the pump to the front.

Remove two attaching screws to release the rear plate of the pump which will expose the two rotors.

Check the rotors and the reverse drum support journal for signs of wear.

Place the rear oil pump body with the reverse drum journal down. Install the outer and inner rotors. The output shaft will automatically line up the inner rotor. Put splined inner diameter of the inner rotor down.

Install the rear plate and two attaching screws. Tighten evenly.

Reassembly of the Transmission

Install the rear oil pump through the front of the case. Be sure the oil passages line up. Tighten attaching bolts to 15-18 ft lbs.

Place the reverse drum thrust washer on the reverse drum journal.

Install the reverse band and the struts. Tie the band flanges so the struts won't drop out.

Install a new seal ring on the output shaft. Lubricate with fluid.

Install the planetary assembly complete with the ring gear. Be sure the output shaft seal ring enters into the journal while the reverse drum fits over the journal. Check the planetary assembly is all the way back.

Install the speedometer driving gear sleeve, spring, and front spacer with the smooth face to the rear onto the output shaft.

Install the speedometer driving gear and the spacer with its grooved face toward the gear.

Install the parking ratchet wheel onto the output shaft against the spacer.

Install speedometer pinion.

Install the extension shaft thrust spring. The extension shaft to housing assembly and the gasket. Tighten the attaching bolts to 15-18 ft lbs.

Note: The transmission cannot be installed in the car with this unit attached. It is installed here to be sure that the clearance found below is correct for the sensitive thrust washer.

Fig. 91—Install front oil pump, tighten to 15-18 ft. lbs.

Fig. 93—Tighten rear plate attaching screws evenly

Fig. 94—Planetary assembly, note oil tube assembly

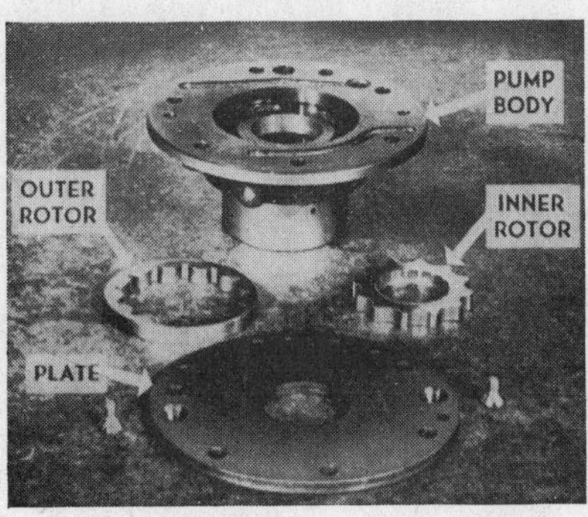

Fig. 92—Layout of rear oil pump parts

Fig. 93A—Tighten rear pump attaching bolts to 15-18 ft. lbs.

Fig. 94A—Install speedometer drive gear on output shaft

REASSEMBLY OF THE TRANSMISSION—*continued*

Install the governor assembly. Tighten the adaptor bolts to 8-9 ft lbs. Install cover and new gasket. Tighten cover screws to 8-9 ft lbs.

Install the reverse sun gear front thrust ball bearing.

Install the low band and the high clutch and input shaft assembly. Be sure the low sun gear is seated against the thrust ball bearing.

Install the low band struts and tie the band flanges so they don't fall out.

SELECTING THE SENSITIVE THRUST WASHER

There must be .018″ to .028″ clearance between the high clutch housing and the free-wheeling clutch assembly after everything is in place. This clearance must be assured or the transmission will fail. To accomplish this:

a. Measure the distance from the attaching surface at the rear of the bell housing to the high clutch contacting surface at the rear of the free wheeling clutch assembly. Call this distance "X." Use a set-up as shown in the cut.

b. Check that the input shaft is firmly against the output shaft which is firm against the extension shaft.

c. Measure the distance from the front thrust surface (base of indentation) of the high clutch to the front attaching surface of the transmission case. Call this distance "Y." Use set-up as shown in the cut.

d. Select a thrust washer whose thickness will be .010″ less than the difference between the distance X and the distance Y. This will reduce the total clearance to .010″. The gas-

Fig. 95—Clutch and input shaft assembly. Note ball thrust bearing and sensitive thrust washer

Fig. 97—Measuring distance "X". From rear face of bell housing to rear face of free wheel clutch assembly

Fig. 98—Measuring distance "Y". From front thrust surface of clutch to front surface of case

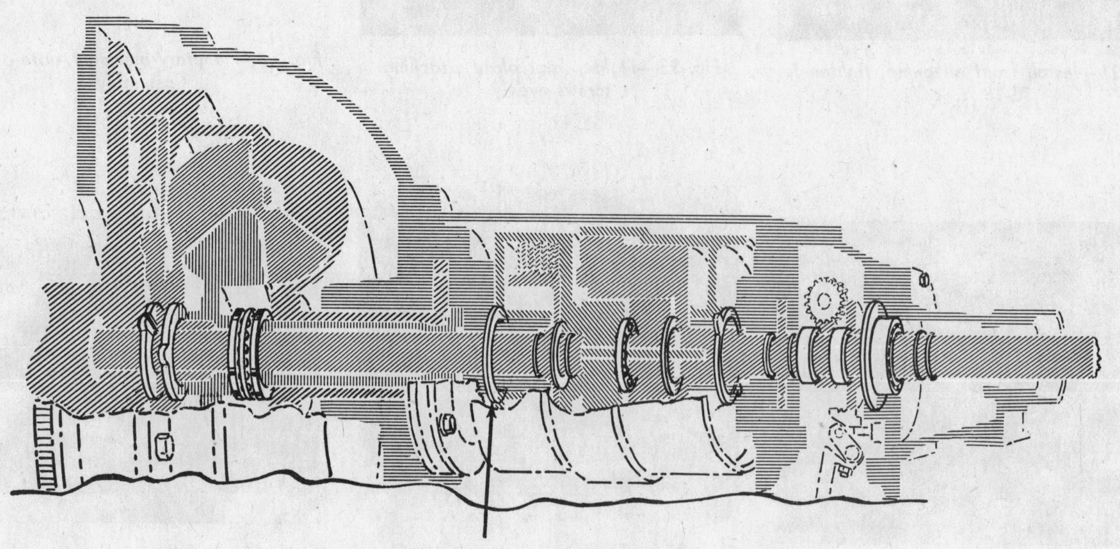

Fig. 96—Arrow points to sensitive thrust washer

ket will provide between .010″ and .015″ clearance. There will thus result a total clearance of .018″-.028″. The thrust washers are available in .010″ steps starting at .085″ and continuing to .135″.

e. Install the selected thrust washer on the oil delivery sleeve of the free wheeling clutch assembly.

FINAL ASSEMBLY

Using a new gasket, fasten the bell housing to the transmission case, tightening the bolts to 55-60 ft lbs.

Install the valve and servo body assembly. Be sure the collar of the throttle valve slips onto its operating lever. Do not install the oil screen yet. Tighten the attaching bolts to 9 ft lbs.

Connect the manual control valve link to the inner lever and install the spring lock.

Turn the outer manual control valve lever counterclockwise and set the valve so the rear land is 5/16 out of the valve body. Tighten the inner manual control valve lever to 50 ft lbs.

Install the oil screen. Tighten the bolts to 9 ft lbs.

Using a new gasket, install the transmission oil pan and fasten to 10-12 ft lbs.

Tighten the band adjusting screws inward to 20 ft lbs. Back off 1¾ turns and tighten lock nut to 25-30 ft lbs.

Slide the converter assembly onto the input shaft so that all the splines are engaged and the primary pump hub is entered in the front pump inner rotor.

Fasten the converter to the bell housing to prevent its sliding out of place.

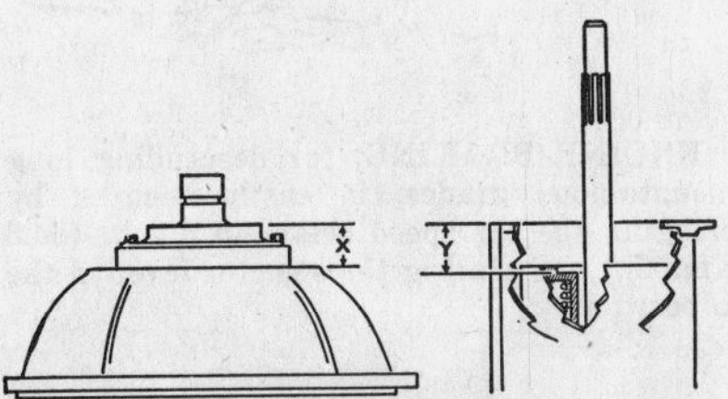

Fig. 99—Schematic of distances "X" and "Y". "Y" must be .010" greater than "X" when washer is in place

Fig. 99C—Tighten bell housing bolts to 55-60 ft. lbs.

Fig. 100—Install transmission oil pan tighten to 10-12 ft. lbs.

Fig. 99A—Install the front pump relief valve

Fig. 99D—Install valve body assembly

Fig. 99B—Install bell housing to transmission case

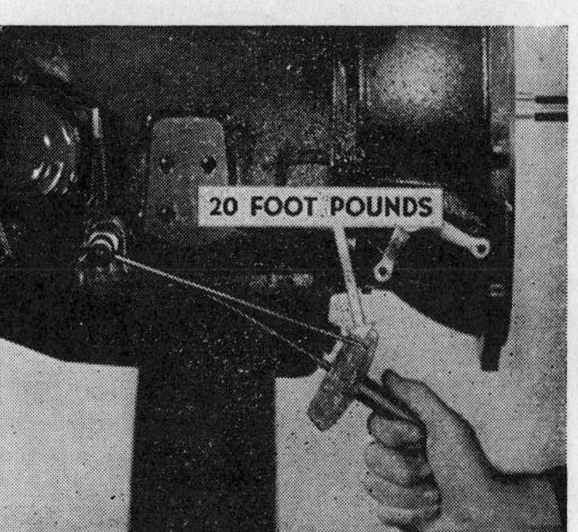

Fig. 100A—Tighten band adjusting screws to 20 ft. lbs., back off 1¾ turns, tighten lock nut to 25-30 ft. lbs.

STUDEBAKER AUTOMATIC TRANSMISSION

DRIVING INSTRUCTIONS

Operation of the Studebaker Automatic Transmission is controlled by the position of the selector lever as indicated by the quadrant pointer. The lever must be raised when selecting P, L, or R position and it must be raised when moving from P to any other position.

TO START THE ENGINE, the selector lever must be in the P or N position (see Fig. 33). The pull-type starter switch control is located on the lower left of the instrument panel to the right of the hood control handle.

P OR PARK provides a safe, positive lock on the rear wheels when the car is stopped. Movement of the selector lever to the P position actuates a mechanical locking device in the transmission which prevents the rear wheels from turning in either direction.

The fact that the engine may be started with the selector in P position is convenient when parked on an incline.

N OR NEUTRAL position permits idling the engine without possibility of setting the car into motion by pressure on the accelerator and may be used when starting the engine.

D OR DRIVE provides the normal forward driving range and includes automatic shifting between the intermediate and direct drive ranges. Virtually all forward driving, accelerating, and stopping can be done with the lever in D position. Once the engine is started, move the lever to D, and leave it there. When accelerating in D, the transmission shifts automatically from intermediate to direct drive between 18 and 58 m.p.h. (29 to 93.3 Km.p.h.), depending upon position of the accelerator pedal. On deceleration, it will shift automatically from direct drive to intermediate at approximately 12 m.p.h. (19.3 Km.p.h.).

L OR LOW is an emergency engine power range for use on unusually long and steep grades or for braking on descents, for extra heavy pulling, and for rocking the car out of mud, sand, or snow.

R OR REVERSE position of the selector lever provides reverse driving range.

ADDITIONAL POWER AND ACCELERATION for hill climbing or passing while in D range (below 50 m.p.h.) (80,45 Km.p.h) is available by depressing the accelerator pedal all the way to the floorboard. This places the transmission in intermediate range. This range will continue until the accelerator pedal is momentarily released or until the car speed reaches approximately 58 m.p.h. (93.3 Km.p.h.).

HARD PULLING, such as encountered in deep snow, mud, or other adverse driving conditions, is best accomplished in the L range.

EXTRA-FAST GETAWAY from a standstill is obtained with the selector lever in the L position. If the L position is selected for this purpose, move the selector lever to the D position before reaching a car speed of 40 m.p.h. (64.3 Km.p.h.) and without releasing the accelerator.

ROCKING OUT OF MUD, SAND OR SNOW is accomplished with the accelerator pedal slightly depressed and held steady while making quick, alternate selections of L and R ranges.

ANTI-CREEP is a special braking feature which prevents the car from creeping forward when stopped on level ground or slight grades as long as the ignition key is turned ON. To stop the car apply the service brakes and then remove your foot from the brake pedal. The car will not creep forward or backward. Any movement of the accelerator pedal, or turning off the ignition key, releases the anti-creep action.

PUSH STARTING may sometimes be necessary, as in the case of a dead battery. Turn ignition key ON, set automatic choke by depressing and releasing accelerator pedal once, place selector lever in the N position. The car may now be pushed and when it has reached 15 to 20 m.p.h. (24 to 32 Km.p.h.) move the selector lever to D or L position. Do not tow the car to start the engine—it may overtake the tow car.

ENGINE BRAKING, for descending long mountainous grades, is easily secured by bringing the car speed below 40 m.p.h. (64.3 Km.p.h.) and placing the selector lever in the L position.

PROLONGED IDLING is sometimes unavoidable. In such cases, as a safety precaution, move the selector lever to the P or N position.

ROLL-BACK when stopped on upgrades with the selector lever in D position is prevented by another design feature of the automatic transmission. On upgrades, whenever forward motion stops, the car will not roll back as long as the engine is running and the selector lever remains in the D position. It is not necessary to keep your foot on the brake pedal when waiting for a change in traffic lights on an upgrade.

TOWING should be done with the selector lever in the N position. Car should not be towed in excess of 30 m.p.h. (48.27 Km.p.h.)

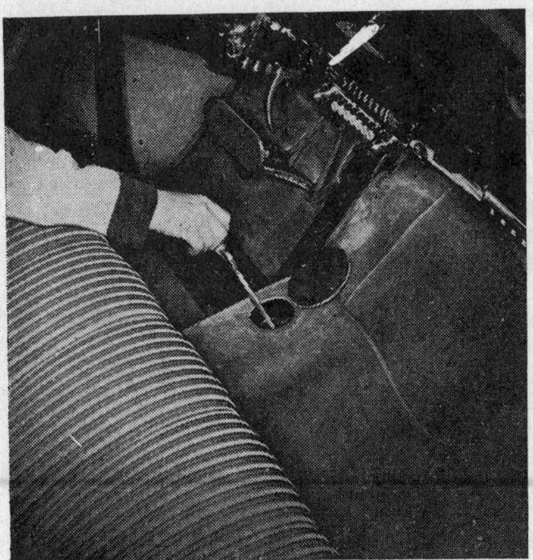

Fig. 43

ADD ONE PINT AT LOW MARK | FULL | LOW

Fig. 44

MAINTENANCE REQUIREMENTS

This automatic transmission uses 10W premium type engine oil (SAE 10-10W *premium type* engine oil is also satisfactory). This oil is an all-year, all-climate oil; there is no changeover required to meet various climatic conditions. The total oil capacity of the transmission is approximately 11½ quarts (9.6 Imp. Qts., 10,8 liters); however when draining the transmission, a smal, amount of oil will remain in the unit and the amout required to refill it will be that needed to bring the oil level to the FULL mark on the gage as described below.

Use only brands of premium type oil marketed by reputable refineries.

Check Transmission Oil Level every 1,000 miles (1609 Km.) as follows:

1. With the car on a level floor, ***set the parking brake firmly***, set the selector lever at L, and raise the transmission oil temperature by *idling* the engine to normal engine operating temperature.
2. Remove the inspection hole cover located on top of the floor carpet to expose the oil level gage.
3. Clean area around the inspection hole. Remove the oil level gage (Fig. 43), wipe dry and check oil level. The space between the FULL and LOW marks on the gage represents one pint (see Fig. 44).
4. With the engine still idling, and selector still at L, add good quality 10W *premium type* engine oil (SAE 10-10W *premium type* engine oil is also satisfactory) as required to bring level to FULL mark on the oil level gage.

Do not overfill.

Drain and Refill Transmission every 15,000 miles (24.135 Km.) or once a year.

1. ***Set the parking brake firmly.*** Set selector lever at L and raise transmission oil temperature by idling engine to normal engine operating temperature.

Fig. 45

1. Pressure take-off plug 2. Drain plug

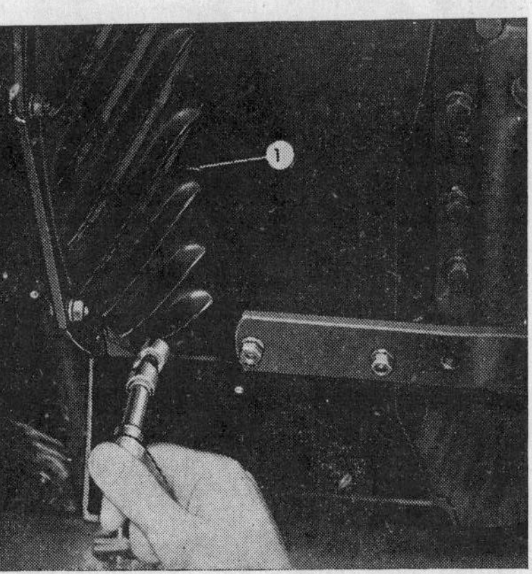

Fig. 46

1. Converter housing cover plate

Fig. 47

1. Converter drain plug

2. Stop the engine and remove the inspection hole cover located on top of the floor carpet to expose the oil level gage. Clean the area around the inspection hole and remove the oil level gage.
3. Remove the transmission oil pan drain plug (2, Fig. 45).
4. Remove the converter housing cover plate (1, Fig. 46) and rotate the converter until drain plug is in position for draining. Remove the converter drain plug (1, Fig. 47).
5. Remove the converter pressure take-off plug (1, Fig. 45) from the left side of the transmission to facilitate draining.
6. After oil has drained, install and tighten the drain plugs in the transmission oil pan and converter. Install the converter housing cover plate. Install and tighten the converter pressure take-off plug.
7. Pour six (6) quarts (5 Imp. Qts., 5,68 liters) of 10W *premium type* (SAE 10-10W *premium type* engine oil is also satisfactory) engine oil into the transmission through the transmission oil filler tube.
8. Start the engine and idle for approximately one minute with the selector lever set in the L position to transfer the oil to the converter from the transmission case.
9. With the engine still idling and the selector lever in the L position, add 3 more quarts (2.5 Imp. Qts., 2,84 liters) of 10W *premium type* (SAE 10-10W *premium type* engine oil is also satisfactory) engine oil and then add additional oil as required to bring the level to the FULL mark on the oil level gage.

Do not overfill.

Do not use sealing compounds on pipe plugs, drain plugs, gaskets, etc.

SERVICE ADJUSTMENTS

Accelerator-to-Transmission Control Linkage Adjustment

1. With the accelerator fully released, measure the distance between the center of the clevis pin hole at the accelerator cross shaft to the fire wall. This measurement should be 3 1/16". If it is not 3 1/16", adjust the clevis using the adjustable rod until you have 3 1/16" clearance between the center of the clevis pin hole at the accelerator cross shaft to the firewall. This adjustment must be made first.

ACCELERATOR-TO-TRANSMISSION CONTROL LINKAGE ADJUSTMENT

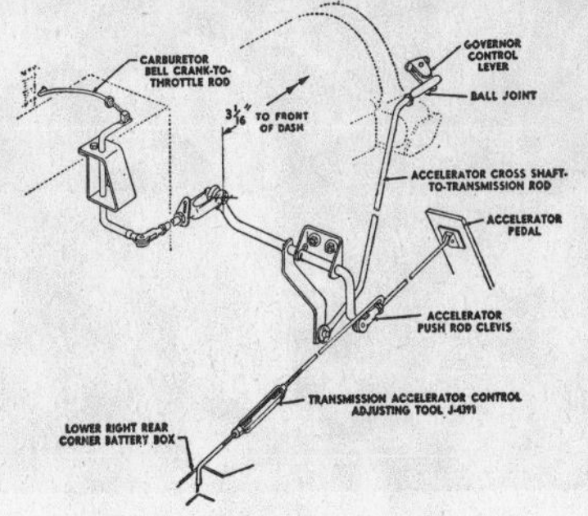

Fig. 48

Fig. 49

SERVICE ADJUSTMENTS—*continued*

2. With the Transmission-Accelerator Control Adjusting Tool J4391 at its maximum length, install the tool between the lower end of the accelerator push rod just above the fixed clevis and the lower right rear corner of the battery box (see Fig. 48). In doing so, the accelerator push rod will be pulled forward, causing the bell crank-to-carburetor throttle rod to partially open the carburetor throttle.

Adjust the length of the tool by turning the turnbuckle (see Fig. 49) until the accelerator push rod is brought forward far enough to just put the carburetor throttle valve in its wide open position. (This position is determined as the point at which the bell crank-to-carburetor throttle rod reaches the end of its travel and any further forward motion of the accelerator push rod only results in compressing the coil tension spring on the bell crank-to-carburetor throttle rod.)

The accelerator linkage must be held at exactly this position to allow a correct setting of the transmission governor-to-accelerator control rod.

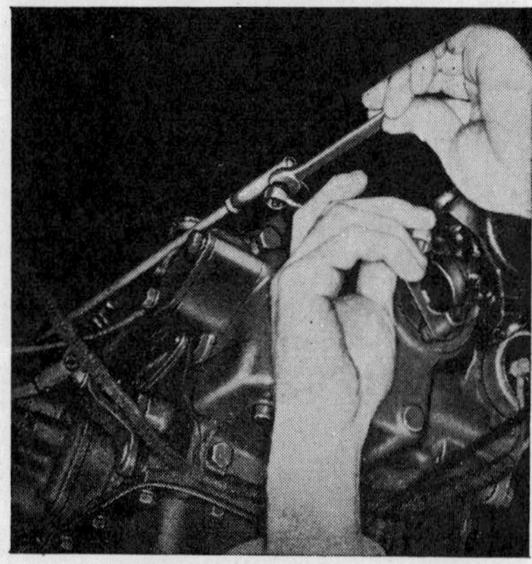
Fig. 50

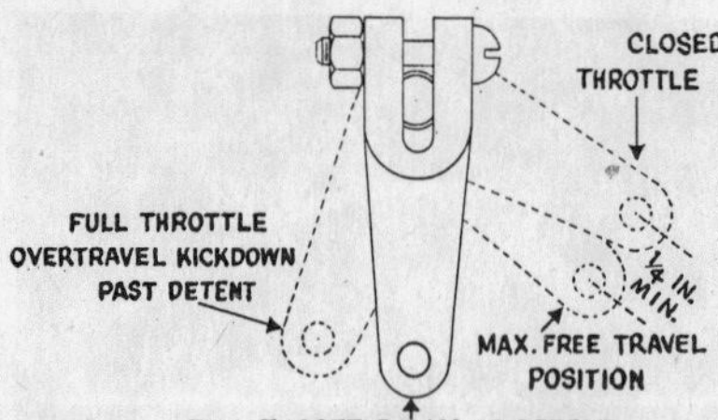

Fig. 51

Fig. 52

3. Disconnect the ball joint holding the accelerator to transmission control linkage to the governor control linkage. See Fig. 50.

4. Turn the governor control lever forward (clockwise) until the resistance of the detent is felt. See Fig. 51.

5. Adjust the length of the rod by turning the ball joint until it can be slipped easily into the governor control lever when they are assembled. See Fig. 52.

6. Remove the transmission accelerator control with adjusting tool J 4391.

7. Check the linkage operation as follows:

a. With the floor mat properly in place and the accelerator fully depressed, remove the ball joint and check to make sure the governor control lever on the transmission is at the end of its forward travel.

b. With the accelerator fully released, check to make sure there is at least ¼" of free travel of the governor control lever before spring pressure is felt as it is turned forward. If the adjustment is correct, connect the ball joint to the governor control lever.

c. If full forward travel or the proper amount of free travel of the governor control lever are not obtained, recheck the linkage adjustment. If proper travel is still not obtained, check for and eliminate any bind, distortion, or interference in the linkage which would affect proper adjustment.

Hand Control Linkage Adjustment

1. Place the selector lever in the R position.

2. Remove the cotter pin and clevis pin (1, Fig. 53), holding the hand control tube-to-bell crank rod clevis to the hand control bell crank (3).

3. Check the length of the hand control bell crank-to-transmission rod. *This length must be 7 5/16" (815,7 mm.) from the center of the fixed end at the bell crank to the center of the adjustable joint at the selector valve lever and, once set, is not to be changed in making further adjustments (see Figs. 54 and 57).*

4. Set the selector valve lever on the transmission in the full rearward (reverse) position (see Fig. 55).

5. Adjust the length of the hand control linkage by turning the clevis on the hand control tube-to-bell crank rod until the clevis pin slips easily into the clevis and the bell crank (see Fig. 56). Remove the clevis pin. *Do not change the length of the hand control bell crank-to-transmission rod.*

6. Set the selector lever on the steering column in the P position and set the selector valve lever in the full forward (Park) position. In this position it should be impossible to rotate the propeller shaft.

Fig. 53

1. Clevis pin
2. Hand control tube-to-bell crank rod
3. Bell crank
4. Pull back springs

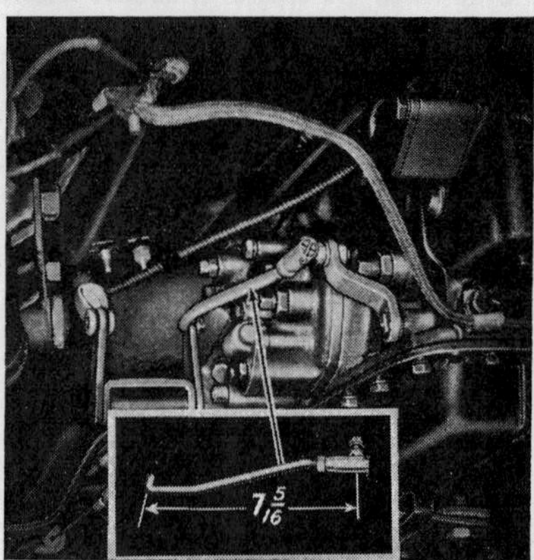

Fig. 54

7. Check the hand control linkage setting by again slipping the clevis pin into the assembled clevis and bell crank. The pin should slip in easily. If it does not, adjust the linkage to give the best possible compromise fit in both the P and R positions. A variation of no more than one-half turn of the clevis

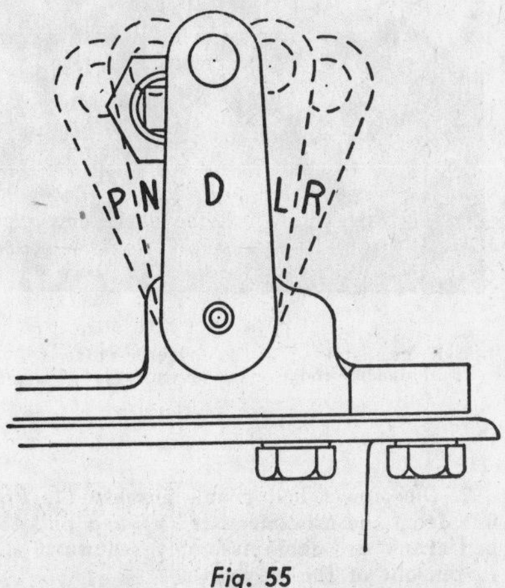

Fig. 55

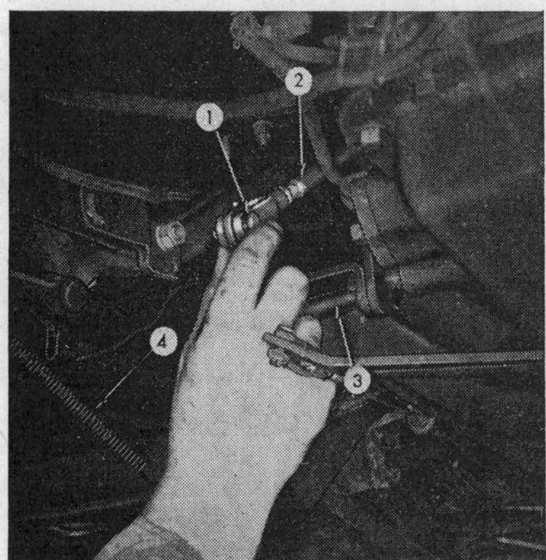

Fig. 56

1. Clevis pin
2. Rod
3. Bell crank
4. Pull back springs

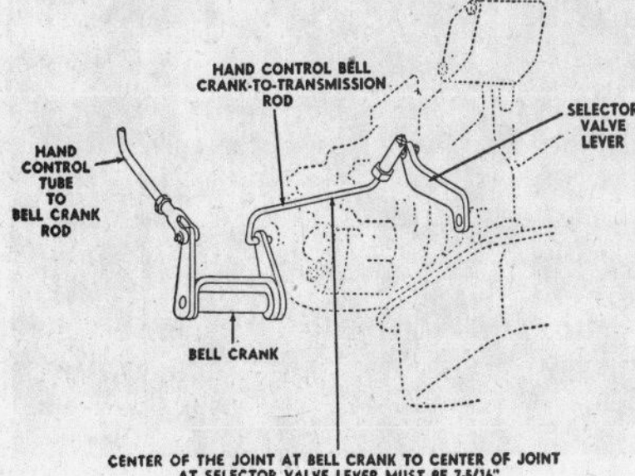

Fig. 57

Fig. 58

to secure adjustment in both the P and R positions is permissible. If greater variation is found, check the entire linkage for wear, looseness, or distortion.

8. Connect the linkage and check transmission operation.

Band Adjustment

To check or adjust any of the three bands use the following procedure:

1. Remove the cap screw and copper gasket from the pressure take-off hole in the servo mechanism opposite the adjustment screw of the band to be adjusted.

2. Carefully screw the Band Adjusting Tool J4285 (1, Fig. 58) into the pressure take-off hole, noting that the indicator plug in the handle of the tool moves outward as the tool is screwed into the adjustment hole. If the band is properly adjusted, the indicator plug will be flush with the end of the tool handle when the tool shoulder rests against the transmission case. If, in screwing the tool into position, the indicator plug becomes flush with the end of the tool before the tool shoulder is against the transmission case, the band adjustment is too tight. As soon as it becomes apparent that the band is too tight, the adjusting screw (1) on the opposite side of the transmission should be backed off two turns before the tool is screwed fully into position. *This is a necessary precaution since, if the tool is screwed against a tight band to the extent that the indicator plug is forced beyond the end of the tool handle, the tool may be damaged.*

3. If, with the band adjusting tool fully in place, the indicator plug is not flush with the end of the tool, band adjustment is required. To perform the adjustment, loosen the lock nut (2, Fig. 59) on the band adjustment screw (1) and turn the band adjusting screw in until the indicator plug in the tool handle is flush with the end of the handle.

4. Tighten the band adjusting screw lock nut securely, making sure the adjusting screw does not turn.

5. Remove the band adjustment tool and install the cap screw using a new copper gasket. Do *not* use any type of sealing compound in installing this cap screw. Tighten to 28 to 33 ft. lbs. (3,87 to 4,56 Kg-m) torque.

Fig. 59

Fig. 59a

1. Forward band servo pressure take-off point
2. Low band servo pressure take-off point
3. Reverse band adjustment screw

Fig. 59b

1. Converter pressure take-off point
2. Reverse servo pressure take-off point
3. Low band adjustment screw

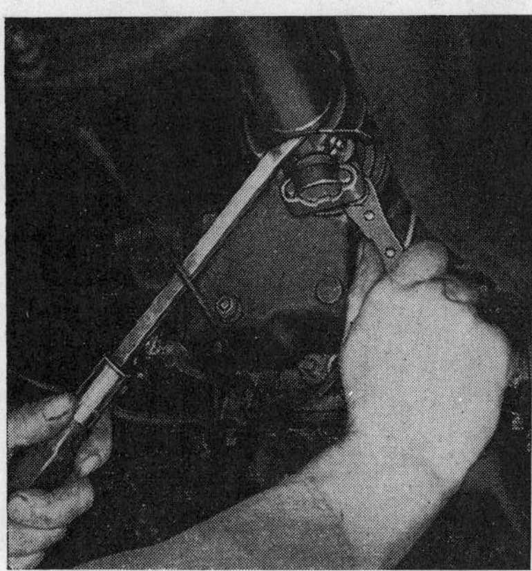

Fig. 60

REMOVAL AND INSTALLATION PROCEDURES

Transmission Assembly Removal

1. Drain the oil from the transmission assembly and the torque converter assembly as described in the Maintenance Paragraphs.
2. Remove the U-bolt nuts (see Fig. 60). Disconnect the universal joint from the transmission companion flange being careful not to drop the bearing cups.
3. Remove the propeller shaft support-to-crossmember stud nuts, lock washers, and plain washers (see Fig. 61).
4. Remove the U-bolt nuts (see Fig. 62) and disconnect the U-joint from the rear axle companion flange being careful not to drop the bearing cups.
5. Slide the complete propeller shaft assemblies and support assembly rearward and fasten out of the way.
6. Disconnect the parking brake control cable (1, Fig. 63) from the bell crank (2).

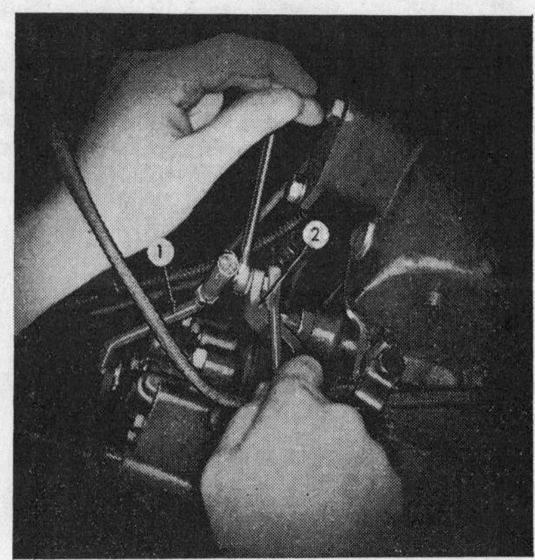

Fig. 65
1. Bell crank-to-transmission rod 2. Selector valve lever

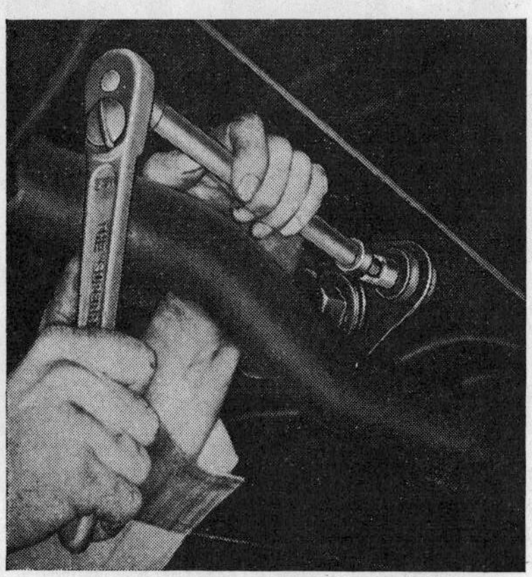

Fig. 61

Fig. 63
1. Control cable 2. Bell crank

7. Disconnect bell crank bracket (1, Fig. 64) from the crossmember (2) and pull the bell crank and cable assembly rearward and fasten out of the way.
8. Disconnect the hand control bell crank-to-transmission rod (1, Fig. 65) from the selector valve lever (2).
9. Remove the clevis pin (1, Fig. 66) holding the accelerator cross shaft-to-transmission rod (2) from the governor control lever (3).
10. Remove the nut and retaining clip (2, Fig. 67) and remove the speedometer cable and pinion (1).
11. Disconnect the anti-creep cables (2, Fig. 68) from the anti-creep solenoid switch (3) and remove the wiring harness (1) from the clip holding the harness to the transmission.
12. Remove the two lower transmission case-to-converter housing stud nuts (1, Fig. 69).

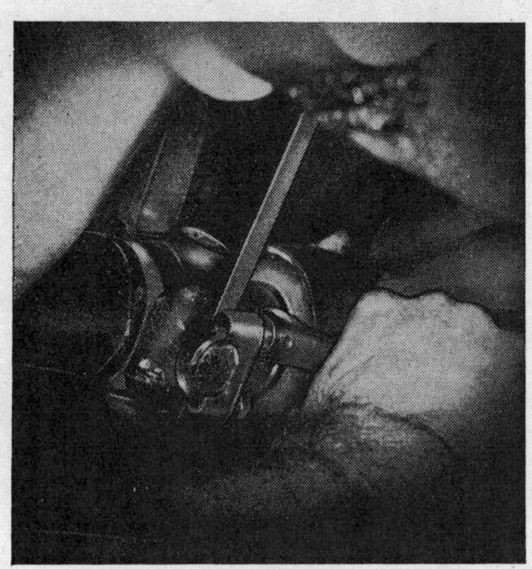

Fig. 62

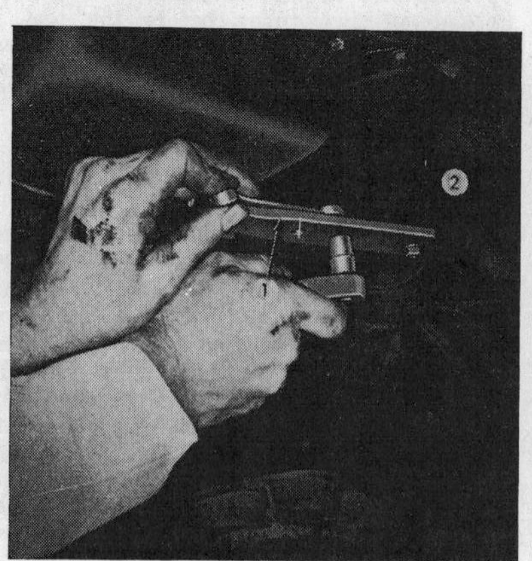

Fig. 64
1. Bell crank bracket 2. Crossmember

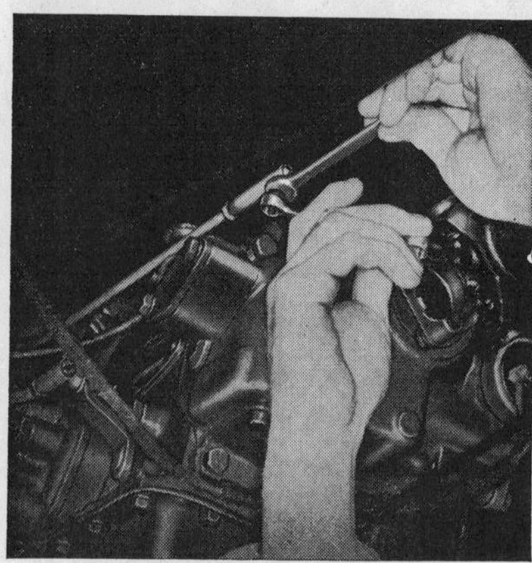

Fig. 66

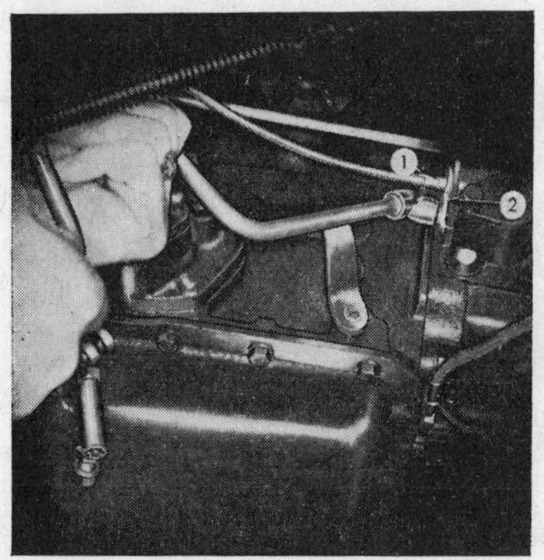

Fig. 67
1. Speedometer cable 2. Nut and retaining clip

Fig. 69

Fig. 72
1. Pilot studs J4284

13. Place the transmission lift with the transmission adapter in position as illustrated in Fig. 70. Adjustment knobs on the adapter provide for alignment of the saddle to the transmission oil pan flange. This adjustment should not be disturbed.

14. Remove the two upper transmission case-to-converter housing cap screws (see Fig. 71). Install the Transmission Pilot Studs J 4284 (1, Fig. 72) into the cap screw holes.

15. Remove the transmission assembly by sliding it rearward on the saddle out of the converter housing and torque converter assembly (see Fig. 73).

16. If the main shaft oil transfer tube does not come out with the transmission, remove it from the torque converter assembly with long-nose pliers or snap ring pliers as shown in Fig. 74.

17. If the converter is to be removed, remove the pilot studs from the converter housing.

Fig. 70

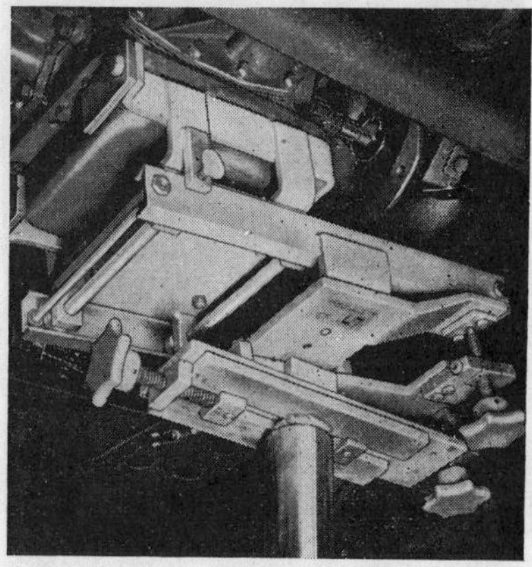

Fig. 73

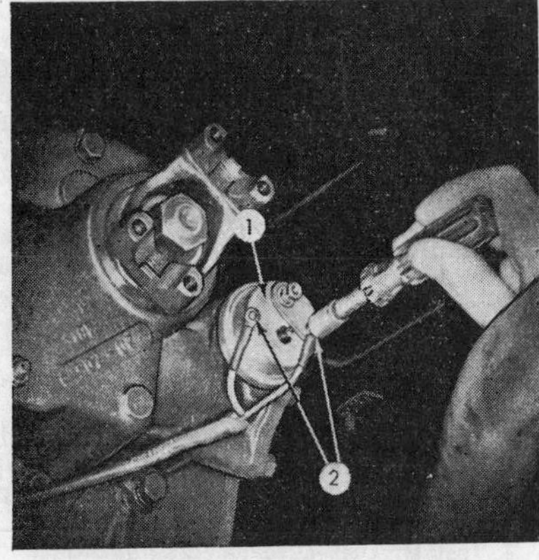

Fig. 68
1. Wiring harness 2. Cables

Fig. 71

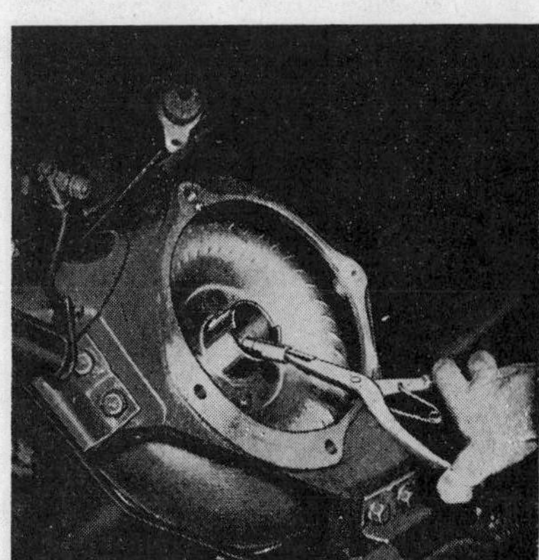

Fig. 74

Fig. 75

Transmission Assembly Installation

1. Using Spline Alignment Fixture (J 4283), position the splines on the transmission shafts as follows:

(a) Loosen the fixture thumb-screw (2, Fig. 75) and install the fixture over the splines inserting it into the transmission as far as it will go, being sure that the positioning arm sector points toward one of the lower transmission case studs (4).

(b) Move the positioning arm and universal joint companion flange until the positioning pin (3) slips easily over one of the lower transmission case studs.

(c) Tighten the thumb-screw to lock the positioning arm in place (see Fig. 75).

(d) Carefully remove the fixture to prevent moving the splines out of alignment and install the main shaft oil transfer tube.

2. Install the alignment fixture in the torque converter assembly to position the internal splines as follows:

(a) Work the alignment fixture into the torque converter assembly until the splines are properly lined up on the fixture.

(b) Rotate the torque converter assembly and the spline alignment fixture until the positioning pin slips easily into the stud hole in the converter housing corresponding to the lower transmission case stud on which the alignment of the fixture was set (see Fig. 76).

(c) Remove the fixture carefully to prevent loss of alignment.

3. Install the Transmission Pilot Studs (J 4284) (1, Fig. 77) into the upper transmission cap screw holes in the converter housing if they have been removed.

Fig. 76

Fig. 78

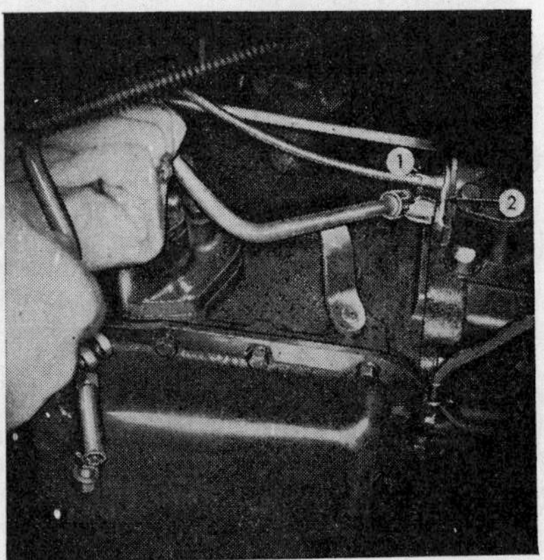

Fig. 80
1. Speedometer cable 2. Nut and retainer clip

Fig. 77
1. Pilot studs J4284

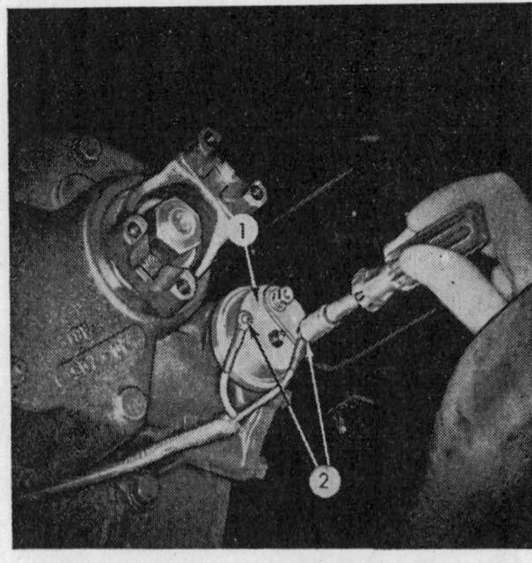

Fig. 79
1. Wiring Harness 2. Cables

4. Raise the transmission assembly to the proper height and angle (see Fig. 78). If the saddle has been disturbed, set at 90° to face of bell housing and align the two upper transmission-to-converter housing cap screw holes with the transmission pilot studs. Carefully slide it into the torque converter assembly, using the pilot studs as a guide, and making sure that the transmission universal joint companion flange is not disturbed. Remove the pilot studs and install the cap screws, lock washers, and stud nuts which hold the transmission to the converter housing.

5. Install the wiring harness (1, Fig. 79) to the transmission retainer clip and install the anti-creep cables (2) to the anti-creep pressure switch.

6. Install the speedometer pinion and cable (1, Fig. 80) and install the nut and retaining clip (2).

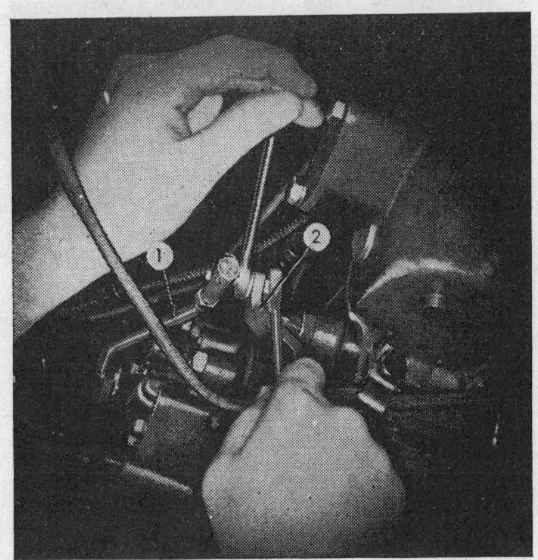

Fig. 81

1. Bell crank-to-transmission rod 2. Selector valve lever

7. Install the hand control bell-crank-to-transmission rod (1, Fig. 81) to the selector valve lever.

8. Adjust the accelerator-to-transmission governor control lever rod as outlined in the Service Adjustment Paragraphs and connect the linkage (see Fig. 82).

9. Install the parking brake bell crank bracket (1, Fig. 83) at the rear engine support crossmember (2).

10. Install the parking brake control cable (1, Fig. 84) to the bell crank (2).

11. Move the propeller shafts into position and install the propeller shaft universal joint to the rear axle companion flange (see Fig. 85).

12. Install the propeller shaft support and cushions on the crossmember studs and install the plain washers, lock washers, and stud nuts (see Fig. 86).

13. Install the front propeller shaft to the transmission companion flange (see Fig. 87).

14. Fill the transmission with oil following instructions given in the Maintenance section.

15. Test operation of the transmission.

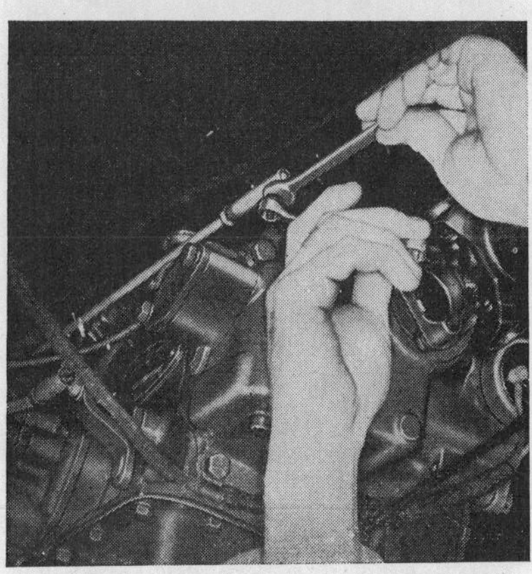

Fig. 82

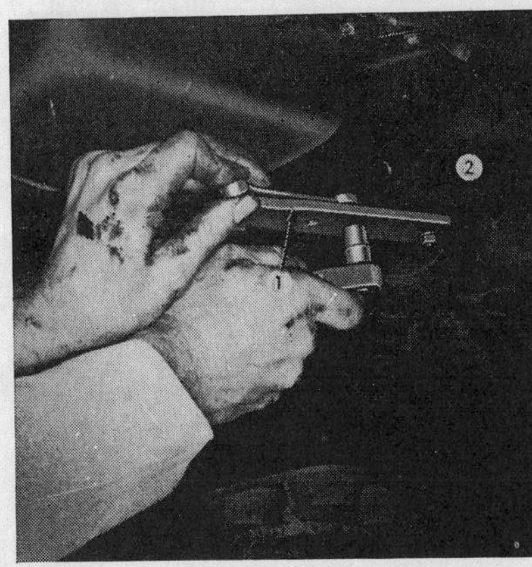

Fig. 83

1. Bell crank bracket 2. Crossmember

Fig. 84

1. Control cable 2. Bell crank

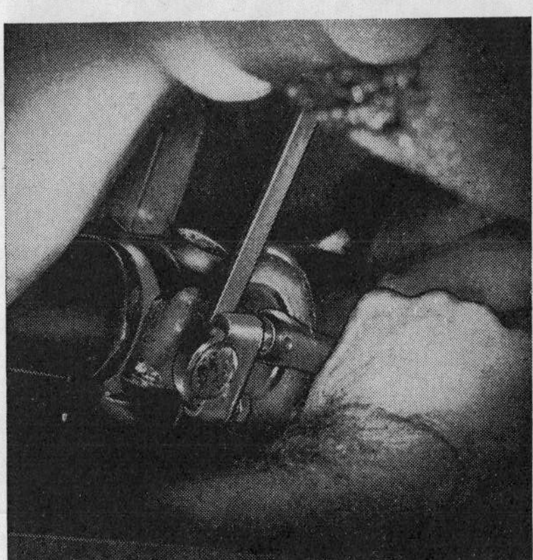

Fig. 85

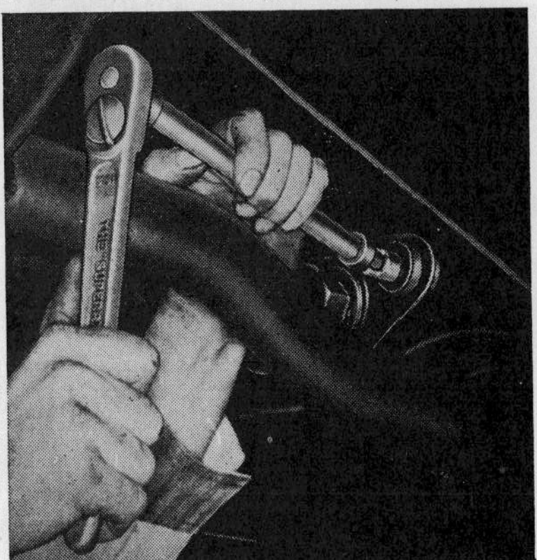

Fig. 86

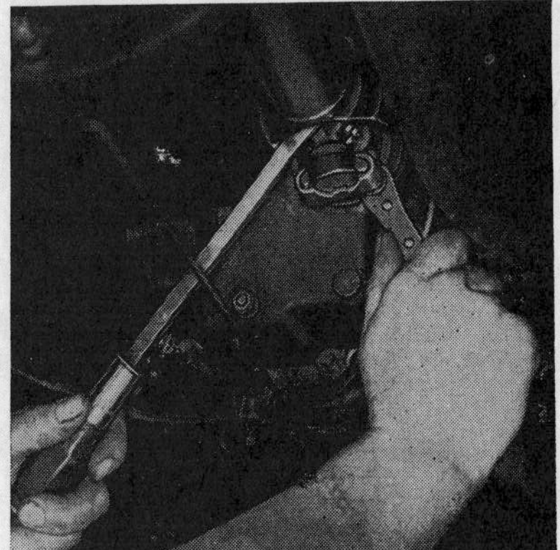

Fig. 87

Removal of Torque Converter Assembly

1. With the car on the floor, disconnect the starter motor from the converter housing and pull the starter motor free of the engine rear plate. Drain the radiator sufficiently to permit disconnecting the upper radiator hose.

2. Raise the car and remove the transmission assembly as outlined under Transmission Removal.

3. Loosen the screws holding the converter housing air intake hose clamp to the frame side rail and pull the hose free of the clamp.

4. Disconnect the exhaust pipe (3, Fig. 88) from the engine manifold and loosen the bolts and nuts from the clamp (2) holding the exhaust pipe to the converter housing bracket (1).

5. Prior to removal of the engine rear support crossmember, engine weight must be lifted up from the crossmember. Also, a means to lower the engine after the crossmember has been removed must be provided to permit removal of the converter housing.

Fig. 88
1. Converter housing bracket
2. Clamp
3. Exhaust pipe

TORQUE CONVERTER—*continued*

A typical set up is illustrated in Fig. 89, however, the type of jack support (3) will vary according to hoist equipment. The engine support saddle (1) can be readily constructed to the dimensions shown from wood or channel iron capable of supporting 600 lbs.

6. Place the engine support saddle 3" to 5" forward of the engine rear plate and up against the crankcase oil pan flange, install the hydraulic jack on the jack support, and raise the engine.

7. Remove the clevis pin (1, Fig. 90) holding the hand control tube-to-bell crank rod (2) to the bell crank (3) and remove the two pullback springs (4).

8. Disconnect the parking brake conduit (2, Fig. 91) from the conduit hook (3).

9. Remove the engine rear support crossmember bolts and disconnect the fender-to-crossmember brace (1, Fig. 91).

10. Remove the crossmember leaving the engine mountings fastened to the converter housing.

11. Lower the rear of the engine approximately 3 inches to provide sufficient clearance for removal of the converter housing. *The maximum amount the rear of the engine can be lowered depends upon the amount of clearance between the engine oil pan and the steering bell crank and tie rod ends.* Excessive lowering of the rear of the engine will result in damage to the engine oil pan. In cases where additional clearance is required, loosening of the nuts holding the steering bell crank to the engine front crossmember will allow the steering bell crank to drop downward providing additional clearance.

12. Remove the converter housing-to-engine rear plate cap screws (see Fig. 92) and remove the small filler plate (1).

13. Remove the converter housing from the dowels (see Fig. 93) taking care not to damage or distort the converter housing dowels, or converter blower.

14. Remove the nuts and plain washers (1, Fig. 94) holding the torque converter assembly (3) to the engine drive plate (2) **and remove the converter assembly.**

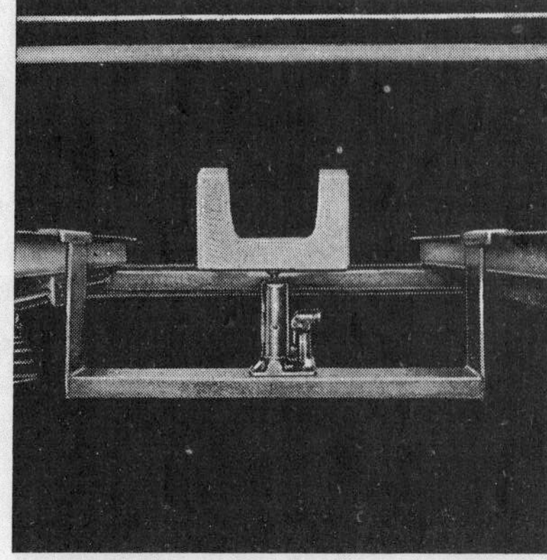

Fig. 89

Fig. 92

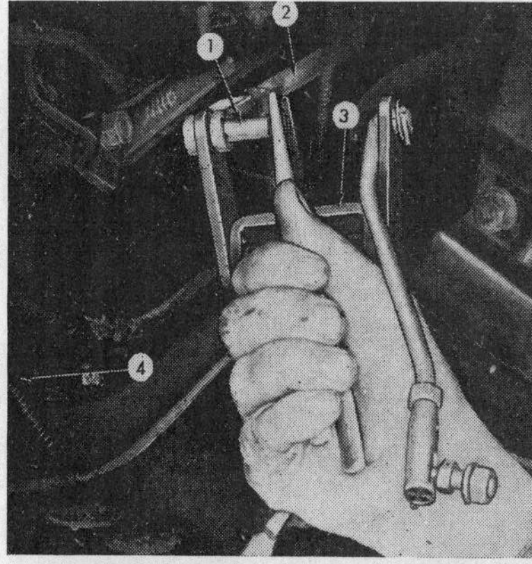

Fig. 90
1. Clevis pin
2. Hand control tube-to-bell crank rod
3. Bell crank
4. Pullback springs

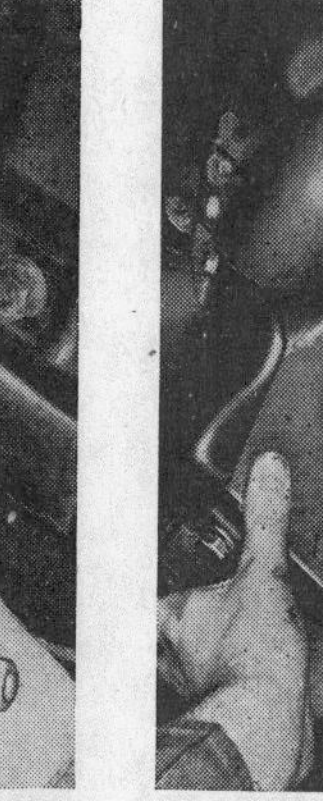

Fig. 93

Fig. 91
1. Fender-to-cross member brace
2. Parking brake conduit
3. Conduit hook

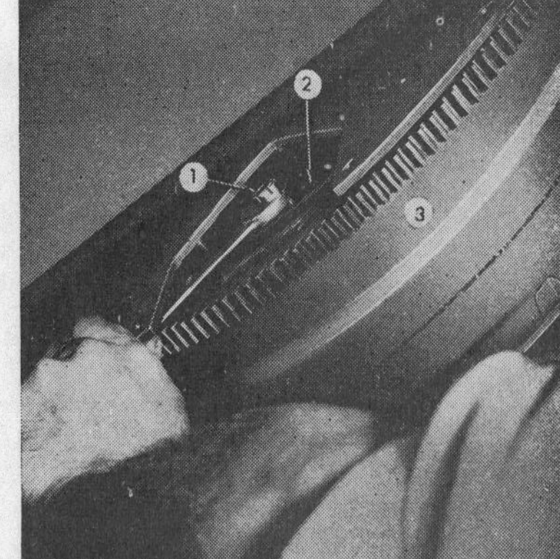

Fig. 94
1. Converter-to-drive plate nut
2. Drive plate
3. Torque converter

Fig. 95

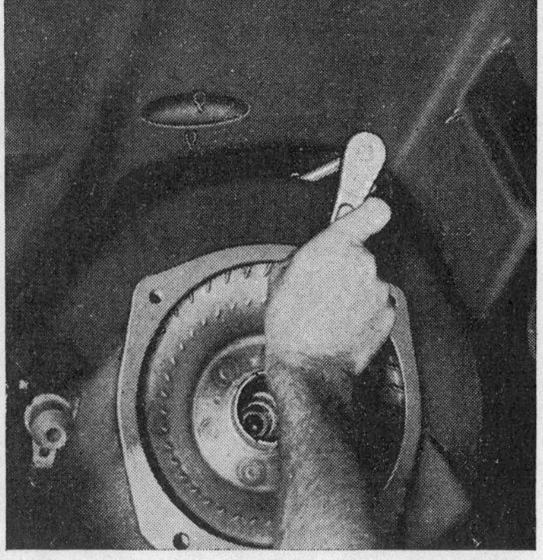

Fig. 98

Fig. 100

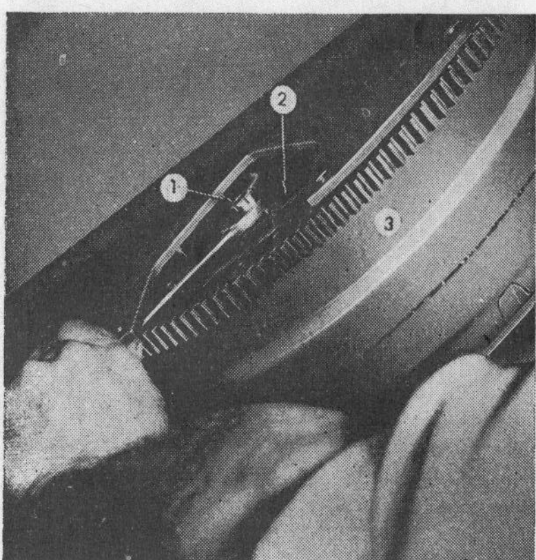

Fig. 96

1. Converter-to-drive plate nut
2. Drive plate
3. Torque converter

Installation of Torque Converter Assembly

1. One of the aligning marks (o) on the converter (see Fig. 95) must be aligned with the aligning mark (o) on the engine drive plate. Install the torque converter assembly on the engine drive plate and loosely install the plain washers and nuts (see Fig. 96).

2. Clean the engine rear plate and the mating converter housing face and install the converter housing (see Fig. 97) taking care not to damage the dowels or the converter blower. Be sure the converter housing is installed on the dowels. Install the top three converter housing-to-rear plate cap screws (see Fig. 98). Raise the engine and install the remaining converter housing cap screws (see Fig. 99).

3. Position the Converter Aligning Flange J4286 (see Fig. 100) into the bore of the converter housing and over the pump drive fingers on the torque converter assembly.

4. Install the two top transmission cap screws (1, Fig. 101) to hold the aligning flange (2) in position and rotate the torque converter assembly through two complete revolutions to center the torque converter assembly.

5. Tighten the converter-to-drive plate nuts to 23-28 ft. lbs. (3,2-3,9 Kg-m) lbs. torque (see Fig. 102). And then install the converter-filler plate.

6. Install the crossmember and connect the fender-to-crossmember braces (see Fig. 103). Install the parking brake conduit.

7. Connect the hand selector tube-to-bell crank rod and the brake pullback spring.

8. Connect the exhaust pipe to the engine manifold and tighten the exhaust pipe to the converter housing bracket bolts and nuts (see Fig. 104).

9. Install the converter housing air intake hose in the clamp at the frame side rail and tighten the clamp screws securely.

10. Install the transmission as outlined under Transmission Installation.

11. Lower the car. Connect the upper radiator hose and fill the radiator. Install the starter motor and test operation of the transmission.

Fig. 97

Fig. 99

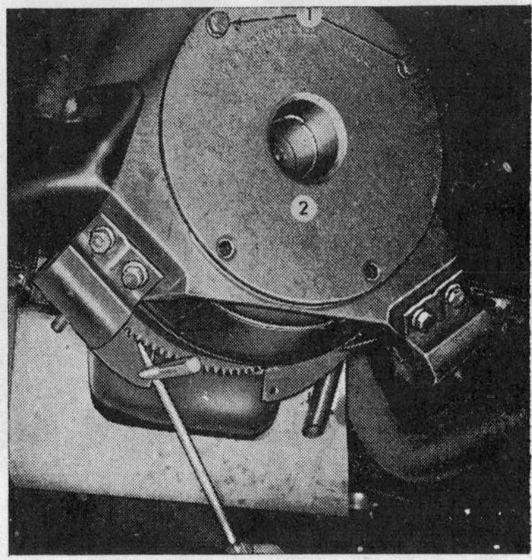

Fig. 101

1. Transmission cap screws
2. Aligning flange

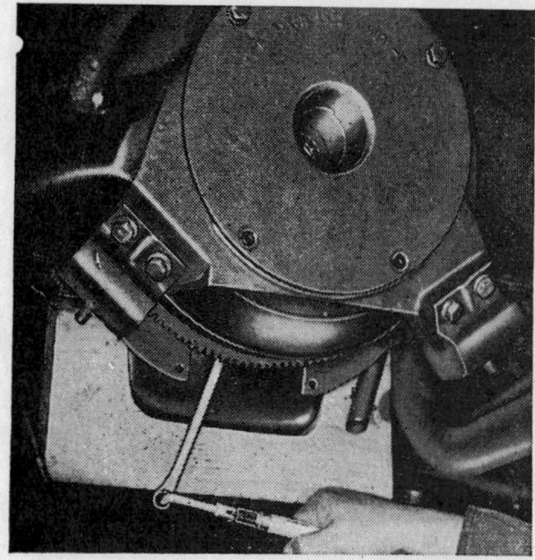

Fig. 102

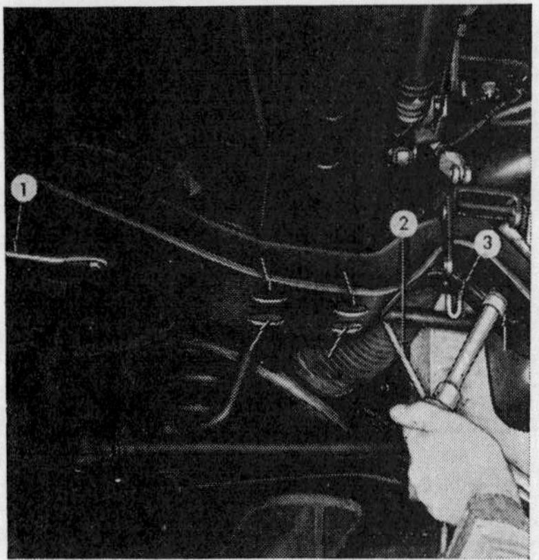

Fig. 103
1. Fender-to-cross member brace
2. Parking brake conduit
3. Conduit hook

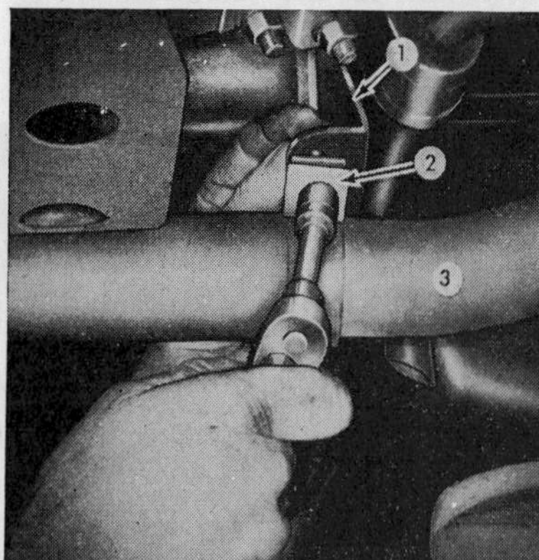

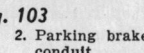

Fig. 104
1. Converter housing bracket
2. Clamp
3. Exhaust pipe

STARTER CUT-OUT SWITCH

The starter cut-out control switch is located at the base of the steering post jacket

Fig. 105

(see Fig. 105) and acts to break the starter solenoid circuit when the selector lever is in the D, L, or R position and also to control the operation of the back-up light if so equipped.

Removal

1. Remove the two screws holding the starter cut-out switch to the steering post jacket.
2. Lift out the switch and disconnect the hand control-to-switch rod.
3. Disconnect the wiring cable from the switch.

Installation

1. Align the pin hole in the starter cut-out switch lever with the corresponding hole in the switch body. Install a pin through the holes that maintain alignment of the switch lever and the switch body.
2. Connect the wiring cables to the switch.
3. Assemble the hand control-to-switch rod to the switch.
4. With the selector lever in the N position, place the switch in position on the steering post jacket and install the screws.
5. Remove the pin from the switch lever and the switch body and test the operation of the switch.

IDLE ADJUSTING SCREW SWITCH

The idle adjusting screw switch is located on the carburetor throttle lever and acts to release the anti-creep system when the accelerator pedal is depressed to move the car. It replaces the usual idle adjusting screw and the position of the switch determines engine idling speed.

Removal

1 Disconnect the wire (4, Fig. 107) leading to the idle adjusting screw switch (3).
2. Screw the switch out of the carburetor throttle lever (1).

Installation

1. With the lock spring (2) in position on the switch, screw the switch (3) into place in the carburetor throttle lever (1). Start the engine and, with the selector lever in the N position, set the engine idle at 500-550 r.p.m. by turning the switch in or out as required.

Fig. 107
1. Throttle lever
2. Lock spring
3. Idle adjusting screw switch
4. Wire

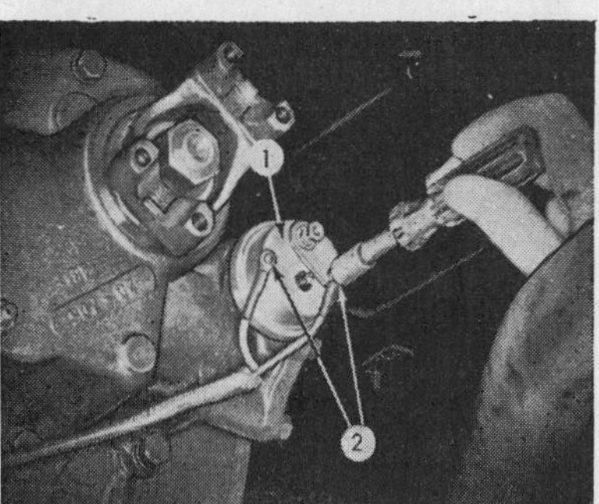

Fig. 108
1. Solenoid switch
2. Cables

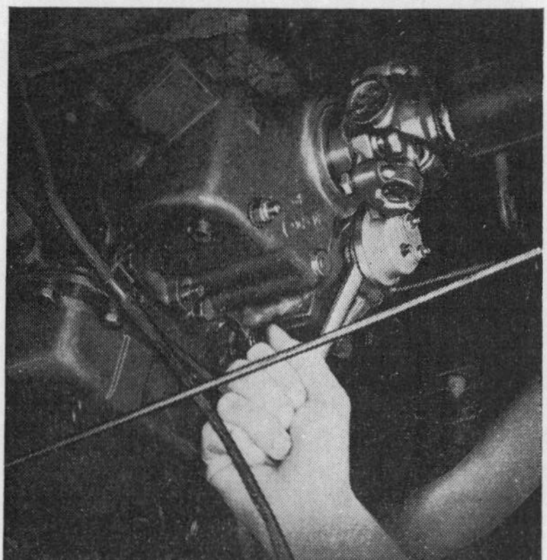

Fig. 109

2. Connect the lead-in wire (4) to the switch.
3. Check anti-creep operation.

ANTI-CREEP SOLENOID CONTROL SWITCH

This switch is located at the rear of the transmission case and acts to prevent opera-

Fig. 110

1. Outlet fitting
2. Stop light switch
3. Solenoid valve
4. Adapter
5. Connectors

tion of the anti-creep system while the car is moving forward.

Removal

1. Disconnect the two control cables from the switch (see Fig. 108).

2. Unscrew the switch from the rear of the transmission case (see Fig. 109).

Installation

1. Screw the switch into the back of the transmission case.

2. Connect the control cables to the switch.

3. Check operation.

ANTI-CREEP SOLENOID VALVE

The anti-creep solenoid valve is fastened to the rear of the brake master cylinder and acts to hold pressure on the rear brakes after the brakes have been applied to stop the car with the accelerator fully released.

Removal

1. With the ignition in the off position, disconnect the control cables at the cable connectors (5, Fig. 110).

2. Disconnect the brake tube from the solenoid valve outlet (1).

3. Remove the attaching screw holding the solenoid valve (3) to the adapter (4) and remove the solenoid valve.

Installation

1. Insert the solenoid valve (3) into the adapter (4) and fasten the valve in place with the attaching screw.

2. Connect the brake tube to the solenoid valve outlet (1). Bleed the brake system.

3. Connect the control cables to the solenoid valve cable connectors (5).

4. Check operation. With the rear wheels stationary, ignition switch on, and the accelerator fully released, depress the brake pedal firmly and release. Rear wheel brakes should now be set, preventing the rear wheels from turning. The rear wheel brakes should release when the ignition key is turned off or the accelerator is depressed.

TRANSMISSION OIL PAN AND OIL SCREEN

Removal

1. Drain the oil from the transmission as outlined in the Maintenance section.

2. Remove the parking brake bell crank bracket from the crossmember.

3. Remove the cap screws holding the transmission oil pan to the transmission case and remove the transmission oil pan.

4. Remove the spring clip (1, Fig. 111) holding the transmission oil screen (2) in the oil screen housing (3).

5. Remove the transmission oil screen and blow out with compressed air.

Installation

1. Install the transmission oil screen in the oil screen housing.

2. Install the spring clip holding the transmission oil screen in place.

3. Using a new gasket, install the transmission oil pan to the transmission case. If desired, the gasket may be held in position

Fig. 111

1. Spring clip
2. Oil screen
3. Oil screen housing

with a heavy mineral grease or Lubriplate. Under no conditions, however, are sealing compounds such as Permatex, gasket cement, etc., to be used in assembling this or any other parts of the automatic transmission.

4. Install the oil pan-to-transmission case cap screws and tighten to 10-13 ft. lbs. (1,4-1,8 Kg-M) torque.

5. Install the parking brake bell crank bracket to the crossmember.

6. Refill transmission assy. (refer to maintenance section).

TEST PROCEDURES

Front Pump Pressure Test

1. With the engine stopped, remove the Allen head pipe plug at the front transmission oil pan flange (1, Fig. 112) and install the pressure gage fitting (2). For convenience, place the gage on the floor of the driver's compartment and allow the gage pressure line to go through the oil level inspection opening to the transmission pressure take-off point.

2. Connect the electric tachometer to the engine ignition system.

3. With the selector lever in the P or N positions, start the engine and bring engine speed to 1000 r.p.m. At this engine speed the gage should show a minimum of 60 lbs. per square inch (4,2 Kg. per sq. cm.) pressure.

4. Stop the engine. Remove the test equipment. Reinstall the Allen head pipe plug. Do *not* use any type of sealing compound in installing this or any other pipe plugs in the automatic transmission. Tighten to 15-18 ft. lbs. (2,0-2,5 Kg-m) torque.

Forward Band Servo Pressure Test

1. With the engine stopped, use a 9/16" (14,3 mm.) wrench to remove the cap screw and copper washer from the forward band servo mechanism cover plate (1, Fig. 113). Install the pressure gage fitting (2) at this point. For convenience, place the gage on the floor of the driver's compartment and allow the gage pressure line to extend through the oil level inspection hole to the pressure take-off point.

2. Connect the electric tachometer to the engine ignition system.

Fig. 112

1. Transmission oil pan flange
2. Gage fitting

Fig. 113

1. Forward band servo
2. Gage fitting

STUDEBAKER AUTOMATIC TRANSMISSION

TEST PROCEDURES—*Continued*

3. With the engine running, apply the parking brake and foot brake firmly to prevent movement of the car, move the selector lever to the D position. Gradually increase engine speed to 1000 r.p.m. At this speed, the gage should show a minimum of 60 lbs. per square inch (4,2 Kg. per sq. cm.) pressure.

To prevent overheating of the transmission, the engine should not be run at speeds above idle with the selector lever in the D, L, or R positions and with the rear wheels stationary for over 30 seconds.

4. Stop the engine and remove the test equipment. Reinstall the cap screw in the cover plate, using a new copper gasket. Do *not* use any type of sealing compound in installing this or any other cap screws or gaskets in the automatic transmission. Tighten the cap screw to 28-33 ft. lbs. (3,9-4,6 Kg-m) torque.

Reverse Band Servo Pressure Test

1. With the engine stopped, disconnect the hand control bell crank-to-transmission selector valve lever rod at the bell crank. Move selector valve lever (3, Fig. 114) to "R" position. (See Fig. 55.)

2. With a 9/16" (14,3 mm) socket wrench, remove the cap screw and copper washer from the reverse band servo cover (2) and install the pressure gage fitting (1) at this point. For convenience, place the gage on the floor of the driver's compartment and allow the gage pressure line to go through the oil level inspection opening to the transmission pressure take-off point.

3. Connect an electric tachometer to the engine ignition system.

4. Before starting the engine, apply the parking brake and foot brake firmly to prevent movement of the car. Start the engine and increase engine speed to 1000 r.p.m. At this speed, the gage should show a minimum of 160 lbs. per square inch (11,2 Kg. per sq. cm.) pressure at the rear servo mechanism.

To prevent overheating of the transmission, the engine should not be run at speeds above idle with the selector lever in the D, L, or R positions and with the rear wheels stationary for over 30 seconds.

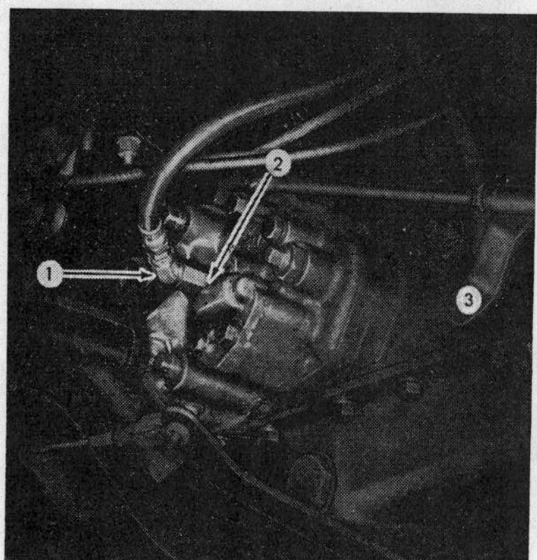

Fig. 114

1. Gage fitting
2. Reverse band servo 3. Selector valve lever

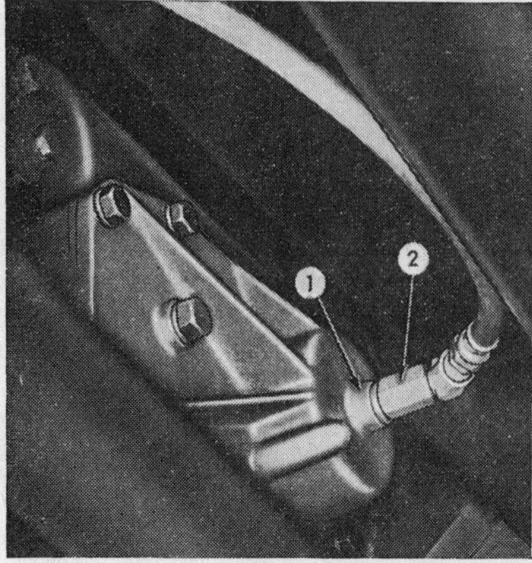

Fig. 115

1. Low band servo 2. Gage fitting

5. Stop the engine and remove the test equipment. Reinstall the cap screw in the cover plate using a new copper gasket. Do *not* use any type of sealing compound in installing this or any other cap screws or gaskets in the automatic transmission. Tighten the cap screw to 28-33 ft. lbs. (3,9-4,6 Kg-m) torque. Install the bell crank-to-transmission selector valve lever rod.

Low Band Servo Pressure Test

1. With the engine stopped, use a 9/16" (14,2 mm.) wrench to remove the cap screw and copper gasket from the low band servo cover plate (1, Fig. 115) and install the pressure gage fitting (2) at this point. For convenience, place the gage on the floor of the driver's compartment and allow the gage pressure line to go through the oil level inspection opening to the transmission pressure take-off point.

2. Connect an electric engine tachometer to the engine ignition system.

3. With the engine running and the parking brake and the foot brake firmly set to prevent movement of the car, place the selector lever in the L position. Increase engine speed to 1000 r.p.m. At this speed, the gage should show a minimum of 60 lbs. per square inch (4,2 Kg. per sq. cm.) pressure at the low band servo.

To prevent overheating of the transmission, the engine should not be run at speeds above idle with the selector lever in the D, L, or R positions and with the rear wheels stationary for over 30 seconds.

4. Stop the engine and remove the test equipment. Reinstall the cap screw in the servo cover plate using a new copper gasket. Do *not* use any type of sealing compound, such as white lead, Permatex, etc., when installing this or any other cap screws or gaskets in the automatic transmission. Tighten the cap screw to 28-33 ft. lbs. (3,9-4,6 Kg-m) torque.

Multiple Disc Clutch Pressure Test

1. With the engine stopped, remove the ⅛" (3,2 mm.) pipe plug from the rear transmission extension housing (1, Fig. 116) and install the pressure gage fitting (2). For convenience, place the gage on the floor of the driver's compartment and allow the gage pressure line to go through the oil level inspection opening to the transmission pressure take-off point.

Fig. 116

1. Extension housing 2. Gage fitting

Fig. 117

2. Connect the electric engine tachometer to the engine ignition system.

3. With the engine running and the parking brake and foot brake applied firmly to prevent movement of the car, place the selector lever in the D position. Increase engine speed to 1000 r.p.m. At this speed, the pressure gage should show a minimum of 60 lbs. per sq. inch (4,2 Kg per sq. cm.) pressure at the multiple disc clutch.

To prevent overheating of the transmission, the engine should not be run at speeds above idle with the selector lever in the D, L, or R positions and with the rear wheels stationary for over 30 seconds.

4. Stop the engine, remove the test equipment, and reinstall the ⅛" (3,2 mm.) pipe plug. Do *not* use any type of sealing compound in installing this or any other pipe plugs in the automatic transmission. Tighten

Fig. 118

1. Transmission oil pan flange
2. Pressure gage fitting

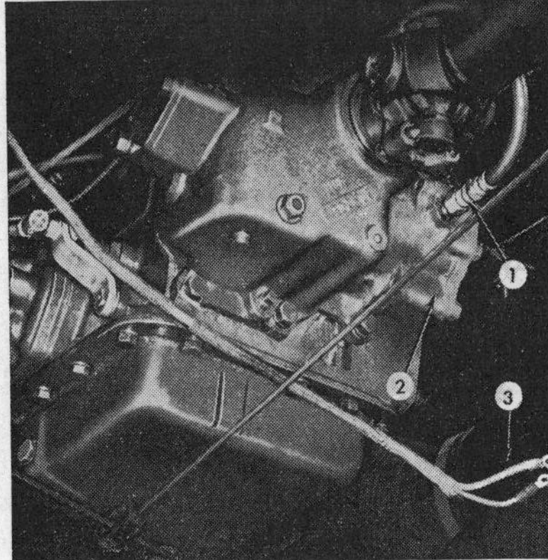

Fig. 119

1. Wiring harness
2. Rear pump
3. Pressure gage fitting

the pipe plug to 15-18 ft. lbs. (2,0-2,5 Kg-m) torque.

Torque Converter Pressure Test

1. Remove the ¼" (6,3 mm.) pipe plug at the torque converter pressure point (Fig. 117) and install the pressure gage fitting. For convenience the hand control bell crank-to-transmission selector valve lever rod may be removed.

2. Connect the electric tachometer to the engine ignition system.

3. With the transmission selector valve lever in N-Neutral position and the engine running at approximately 1000 r.p.m., pressure reading should be 25 to 35 pounds per square inch (3,5-4,8 Kg-m).

4. With the rear wheels jacked up and free to rotate, and the selector lever in D-drive position, and engine running at 1500 r.p.m., pressure should be 25 to 35 lbs. per square inch (3.5-4.8 Kg-m).

5. Stop the engine, remove the test equipment and reinstall ¼" (6,3 mm.) pipe plug. Do *not* use any type of sealing compound in installing this or any other pipe plugs in the automatic transmission. Tighten the pipe plug to 6-7 ft. lbs. (0,83-0,97 Kg-m) torque.

Direct Drive Clutch Pressure Test

1. With the engine stopped, remove the Allen head pipe plug from the rear transmission oil pan flange (1, Fig. 118) and install the pressure gage fitting (2) at this point. For convenience, place the gage on the floor of the driver's compartment and allow the gage pressure line to go through the oil level inspection opening to the transmission pressure take-off point.

2. Connect an electric engine tachometer to the engine ignition system.

3. With the rear wheels of the car raised off the floor and free to rotate, and with the engine running at idle, place the selector lever in the D position. Pressure gage should show 0 lbs. per square inch pressure at the direct drive clutch.

4. Increase engine speed to 1500 r.p.m. At approximately 1200 r.p.m., the transmission should shift to direct drive, which will be indicated by a rapid pressure rise in the direct drive clutch. While in direct drive, the pressure gage should show a minimum of 60 lbs. per square inch (4.3 Kg per sq. cm.) pressure on the direct drive clutch.

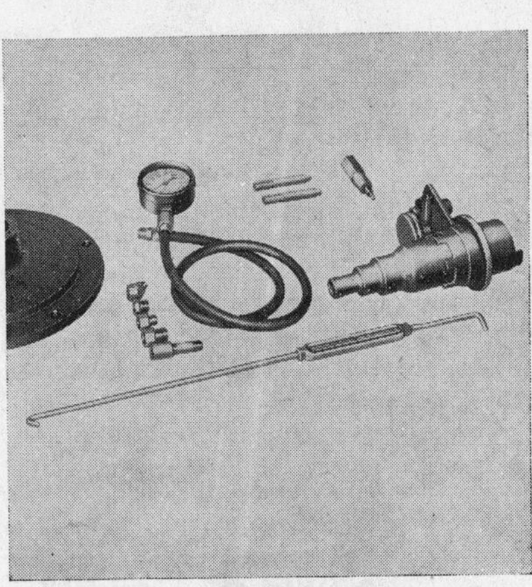

Special tools for automatic transmission

5. Check the direct drive clutch pressure during deceleration. When the speedometer indicates approximately 10-12 miles per hour (16-19 km. per hr.), the pressure should drop to zero (0).

6. Remove the test equipment and replace the Allen head pipe plug. Do *not* use any type of sealing compound in installing this or any other pipe plugs in the automatic transmission. Tighten the pipe plug to 15-18 ft. lbs. (2,0-2,5 Kg-m) torque.

Rear Pump Pressure Test

1. With the engine stopped, remove the anti-creep cables (1, Fig. 119) from the anti-creep switch and remove the switch from the transmission case. Install the pressure gage fitting (3) in the rear pump (2). For convenience, place the gage on the floor of the driver's compartment and allow the gage pressure line to go through the oil level inspection opening to the transmission pressure take-off point.

2. With the engine running and the rear wheels held stationary, the pressure gage should show a reading of zero (0) lbs. per square inch pressure reading.

3. With the engine running at idle, and the rear wheels raised from the floor and free to rotate, place the selector lever in the D position. Rear pump pressure should build up as evidenced by a steady increase in pressure reading on the pressure gage. At 20 miles per hour (32 km. per hr.) on the speedometer the rear pump pressure should be a minimum of 60 lbs. per square inch (4.3 Kg per sq. cm.).

4. Remove the test equipment and reinstall the anti-creep pressure control switch in the transmission case. Do *not* use any type of sealing compound in making this installation. Connect the anti-creep cables to the anti-creep pressure control switch.

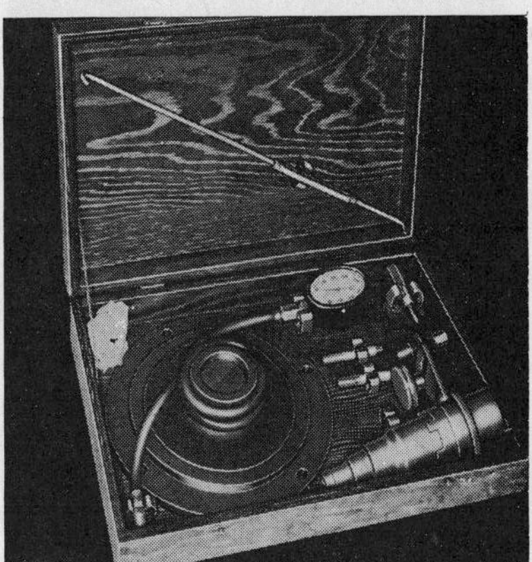

Special tool kit

Model 63 lift type hoist with adapter

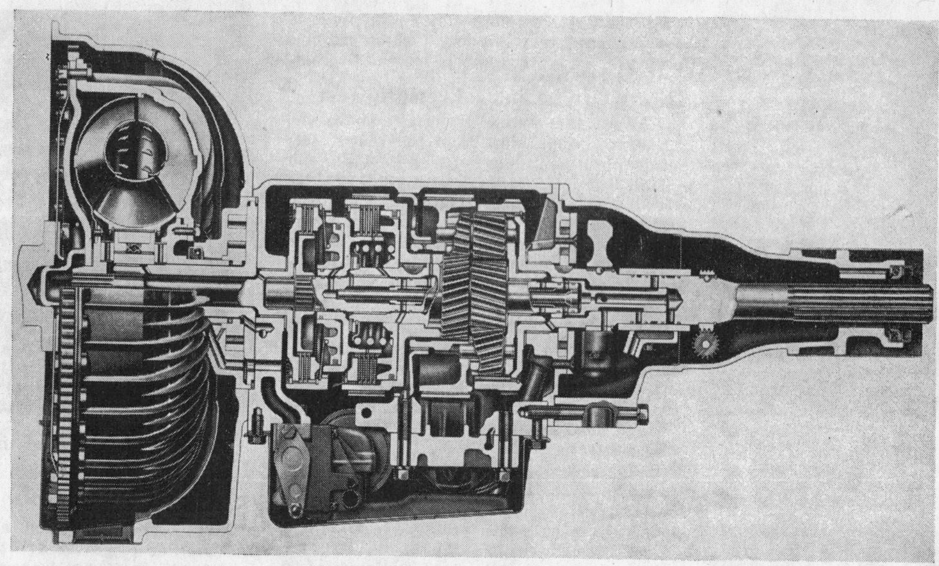

Fig. 1—Cutaway view of transmission assembly

FORDOMATIC AND MERC-O-MATIC TRANSMISSIONS

The Fordomatic and Merc-o-matic transmissions are completely automatic, hydraulically operated, transmissions. They have nothing electrical involved in their operation.

A fluid operated, air cooled, torque converter having fluid coupling characteristics is combined with a simple three speed planetary gear train, having fully automatic selection of gear ratios, to provide a smooth source of power suitable to all operating requirements.

The converter provides a torque increase at the stall point of approximately 2:1.

The planetary gear train consists of a planetary carrier, two multiple disc clutches and two bands. This combination works together to provide three forward speeds and one reverse. The torque increases so furnished are: for Low—2.44:1, for 2nd (intermediate)—1.48:1, for High—1:1, for Reverse—2:1.

The manual control valve lever (selector lever) mounted on the steering column has five positions: Parking; Reverse; Neutral; Drive; and Low.

In Parking position the gear train is locked against all movement.

In Reverse position the rear clutch drives the secondary sun gear, while the rear band holds the planetary carrier.

In Neutral position both bands and clutches are released.

In Drive position at the start the front clutch drives the primary sun gear, while the front band holds the secondary sun gear. This is in reality 2nd (intermediate) gear. In Drive position, after the upshift to high has taken place, the front clutch continues to drive the primary sun gear while the rear clutch drives the secondary sun gear. The driving of both sun gears locks rotation of the planetary pinions against each other and results in direct drive from the turbine to the differential.

In Low position the front clutch drives the primary sun gear while the rear band holds the pinion carrier. Note: Do not drive the car in excess of

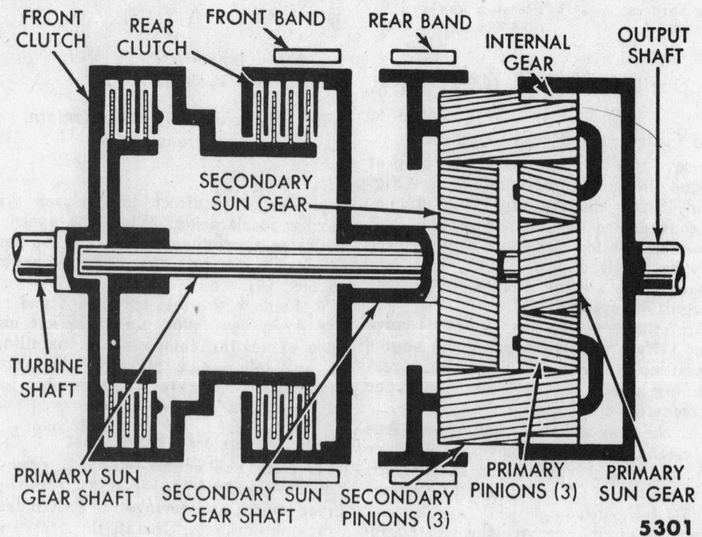

Fig. 2—Schematic of gear set in neutral

30 MPH with the hand lever in the Low position.

When the lever is moved from Drive to Low at speeds above 24 MPH the transmission shifts to 2nd. The shift from 2nd to Low will take place as soon as the car speed approximates 23 MPH. Once the transmission has shifted into Low it will not upshift until the hand lever is moved to Drive.

When the lever is at Drive the upshift from 2nd to high takes place automatically according to torque requirements as indicated to the transmission by the throttle valve position and the governor.

When the lever is at Drive and the car is rolling along in high the down shift to 2nd can be required by the driver by fully depressing the accelerator pedal. As long as the accelerator is held fully down the transmission will stay in 2nd until a speed of 55 MPH for Fords and 62 MPH for Mercurys is attained at which point the transmission goes into high regardless.

GENERAL INFORMATION

Fluid Requirements

Check fluid every 1,000 miles.

Measure fluid with transmission hot, engine idling, hand lever at Park.

Use fluid at least equal to Armour Institute Qualifying Number AQ-ATF No. (the number varies with the oil refiner). Designation and number are embossed on the can.

Change fluid every 15,000 miles.

Checking Fluid Level

Fluid level should be checked every 1,000 miles.

With transmission in Neutral and hand brake set, idle the engine for at least four minutes. Clean all lint and dirt from the right hand section of the floor mat and roll back to reveal the cover plate. Clean the area around the cover plate so that no dirt can possibly fall into the transmission. Remove four screws and the cover plate.

With engine still at idle move the hand lever to Park and thence to all the other positions and return it to Park.

Clean all dirt from the dipstick cap. Turn the cap ½ turn counterclockwise with pliers and pull it out of the transmission. Have a rag handy to prevent spilling fluid on the floor mat.

Note: Some models have the filler tube and dipstick in the right rear corner of the engine compartment.

Wipe the stick and reinsert being sure the cap is seated and locked. Remove the dipstick and note the level. The level should be at F.

Add or drain fluid to make it so.

The distance between the L and the F on the stick is approximately equal to 2 qts. Total oil capacity is approximately 9 qts.

Draining Procedure

Remove the plate on the lower front face of the bell housing.

Remove a converter drain plug. Rotate the converter 180 deg. and remove the other drain plug.

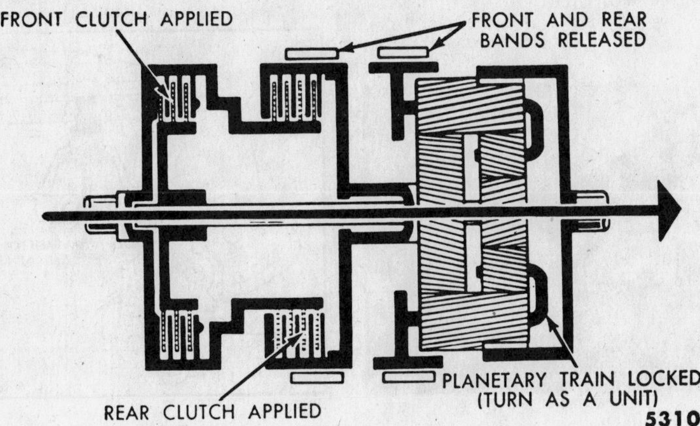

Fig. 3—Schematic of gear set in drive after upshift

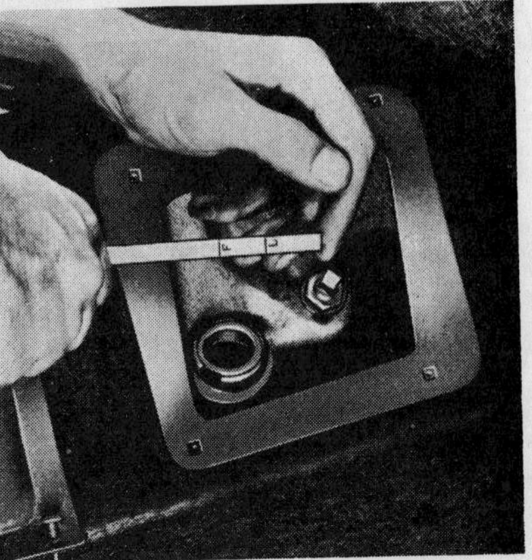

Fig. 4—Remove the dipstick and note the level

The drain plugs are located on a smaller circumference than that of the primary pump attaching bolts.

Remove the plug from the forward edge of the transmission oil pan. On some models the transmission case drain plug is on the right side of the pan.

Note: On models equipped with underhood filler tube the tube connects to the drain hole. Loosen the hex nut and move the filler tube away from the drain hole, to drain the case.

When reinstalling the drain plugs:

Tighten the transmission case drain plug to 20-25 ft lb. Tighten the converter drain plugs to 7-10 ft lbs. Add 5 qts of fluid.

Run the engine at idle for two minutes then add 4 more quarts. Let transmission idle until it comes up to normal temperature. Move the hand lever to all the positions so that all the valves are full. Return hand lever to Park and check that level is at the full mark.

Pumps

PRIMARY PUMP

Driven by ....Engine Flywheel

FRONT OIL PUMP

Driven by .....Hub of primary pump

REAR OIL PUMP

Driven by ....Output shaft

Clutch Plates

FRONT CLUTCH

Bronze internally splined.....3 used

Steel externally splined and flat......................2 used

continued

CLUTCH PLATES—*continued*

Externally splined pressure plate .... 1 used

REAR CLUTCH

Externally splined pressure plate .... 1 used
Bronze internally splined ..... 4 used
Steel externally splined and dished .... 4 used
Dishing should be .010"

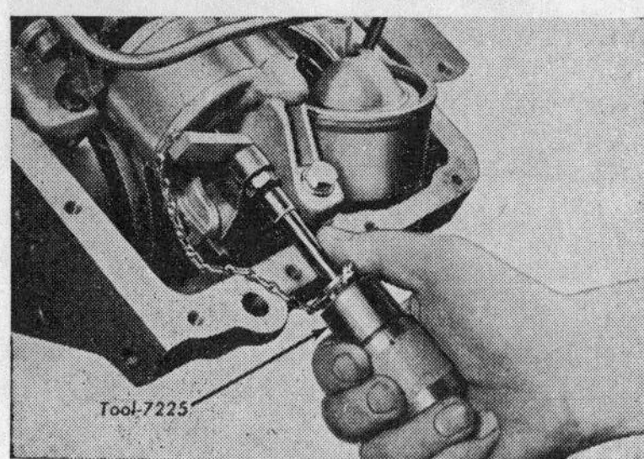

Fig. 5—Adjusting front band

Band Adjustment

Note: The use of a special wrench which releases at 10 ft lb is recommended by Ford Motor Co. for these operations.

FRONT BAND

Drain the transmission and remove the oil pan.

Insert a 1/4" gage block between the front servo piston's stem and the band actuating lever.

Loosen the adjusting screw lock nut and tighten the screw to 10 ft lb. Back off and retighten if necessary to be certain that the screw is as near to being exactly 10 ft lb tight as is possible.

Back the adjusting screw off exactly one turn and tighten the lock nut to 20-25 ft lb.

Remove the gage block. Replace oil pan, add new fluid.

REAR BAND

Remove the cover plate in the right front floor of the front compartment.

Loosen the lock nut and tighten the adjusting screw to exactly 10 ft lb.

Back off and retighten if necessary to be certain the screw is as near to being exactly 10 ft lb tight as is possible.

Back the screw off exactly one and one-half (1½) turns.

Tighten the lock nut to 35-40 ft lb. Replace cover plate.

Torque Specifications

	ft lb
Case to bell housing	40-45
Bell housing to engine	40-45
Primary pump cover to pump	25-28
Cross member to frame	25-32
Ext. Hsng. to case	30-35
Oil pan to case	10-13
U joint, to output shaft	20-25
Frt. band adjusting lock nut	20-25
Rear band adjusting lock nut	35-40
Front pump to case	17-22
Oil pan drain plug	20-25

Towing the Car

Note: Never tow a Fordomatic or Merc-O-Matic equipped car at any speed above 40 mph.

For short tows place the hand lever in Neutral.

For trips over 12 miles or whenever the transmission can not be placed in Neutral, disconnect the propeller shaft or raise the rear wheels from the ground before starting to move the car.

Starting the Car Without Use of the Starter

Caution: Never tow the car to start. As with all cars equipped with automatic transmissions the engine will pick up very quickly and the towed car is likely to hit the towing car before the brakes can be applied.

Turn on the ignition and hold the hand lever at Neutral until the car has attained a speed of 20 mph or more.

Now move the hand lever to Low and the engine will turn.

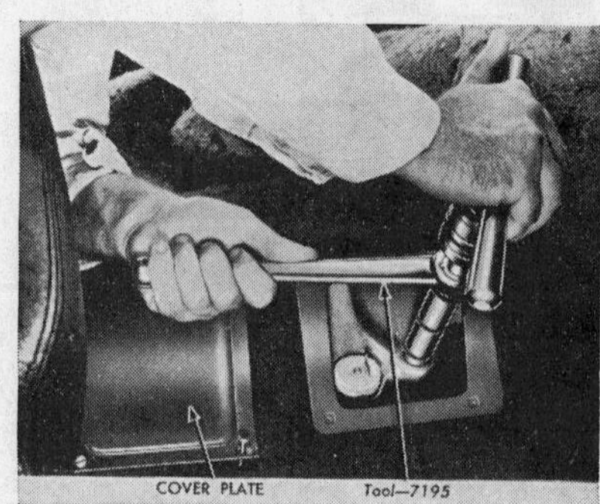

Fig. 6—Adjusting rear band

Idling Speed Adjustment

Correct engine idling speed is necessary to proper performance of the unit.

With engine and transmission at the normal operating temperature, place the hand lever in Neutral.

Adjust the idle speed of V8 engines to 415-425 rpm.

Adjust the idle speed of 6 cyl engines to 440-460 rpm.

Note: If the anti-stall dash pot adjustment seems to interfere on either motor turn its adjusting screw clockwise until it does not.

Anti-Stall Dash Pot Adjustment

After the idling speed has been properly adjusted, turn off the ignition and loosen the dash pot adjusting screw lock nut.

Hold the throttle in closed position, and turn the dash pot adjusting screw counterclockwise (out) until the dash pot rod has reached the end of its travel.

Turn the adjusting screw clockwise (in) 1½ to 2 turns.

Clearance should now be .045-.064 inches.

Do not forget to tighten the lock nut.

MECHANICAL DASH POT ADJUSTMENT—ALTERNATE METHOD

Turn the dash pot adjusting screw to the bottom of its travel.

Turn the carburetor idling adjustment screw until it just touches the lowest step on the cam with the throttle held firmly in the closed position.

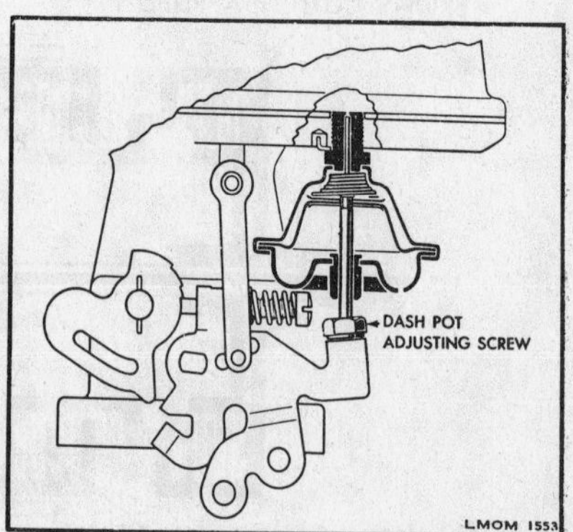

Fig. 7—Turn dash pot adjusting screw to bottom of its travel

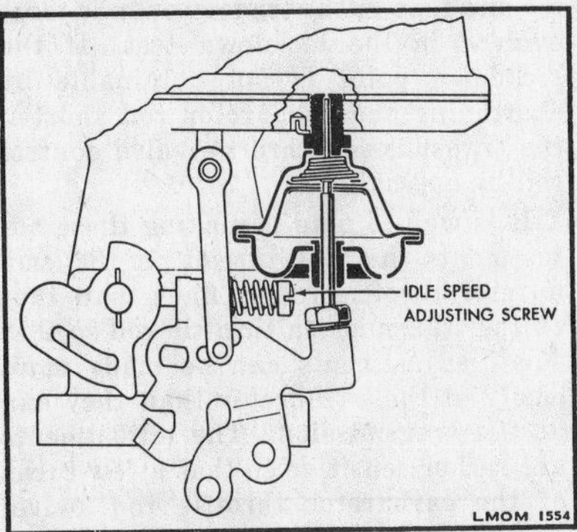

Fig. 8—Turn idling adjustment to touch lowest step

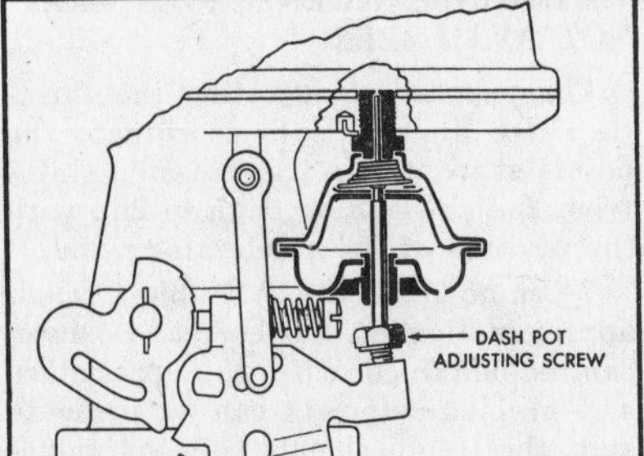

Fig. 9—Turn dash pot screw until idle screw starts to leave cam

Now turn the dash pot adjusting screw to lengthen it until the carburetor idling adjustment screw just starts to leave the low step on the cam.

Shorten the dash pot adjusting screw by one full turn and lock.

The dash pot is now correctly adjusted but it will be necessary to adjust the engine idle speed to 425 rpm with engine warm and hand lever in Neutral.

VACUUM TYPE DASH POT ADJUSTMENT

With engine warm and idling at 425 rpm fast idle cam in the low position, turn the dash pot adjusting screw to allow .020″ clearance between the adjusting screw and the diaphragm rod.

Tighten adjusting screw lock nut and recheck that clearance is .020″.

Manual Linkage Adjustment

Unpin the clevis of the manual shift rod (which runs back to the transmission) from the selector arm at the bottom of the steering column.

Set the hand lever so that the pointer is at Drive and against the stop in the dial housing.

Push the manual shift rod all the way back and check that it is centered in the detent for the Low position. Pull the manual shift rod forward to center on the next detent notch which is that for Drive.

Adjust the clevis so that it could be pinned to the selector arm.

Lengthen the manual shift rod by one complete turn of the clevis and pin it to the selector arm. Be sure to tighten the clevis lock nut.

Check the position of the hand lever at the other points on the dial especially that the parking lock engages properly.

Neutral Safety Switch Adjustment

Loosen the switch to steering column attaching screws and position the switch so that the starter circuit is closed when the hand lever is at Neutral.

Throttle Valve Linkage Adjustment

6 CYL ENGINES

Adjust the threaded trunnion on the accelerator to carburetor rod to give 4 5/16″ from the bottom front surface of the accelerator pedal to the front steel floor of the front compartment.

continued

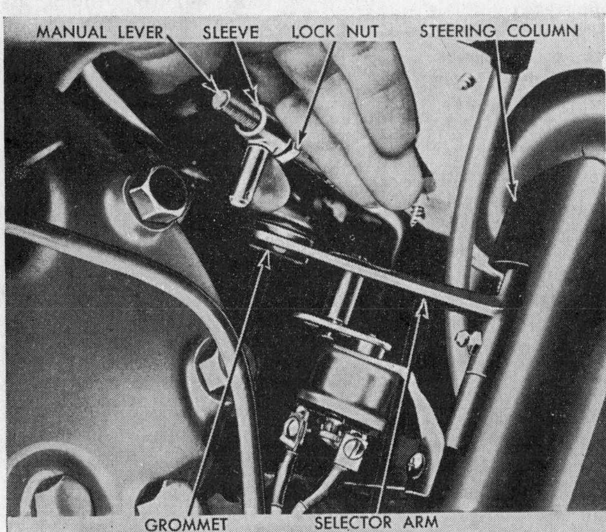

Fig. 10—Adjusting manual control valve linkage

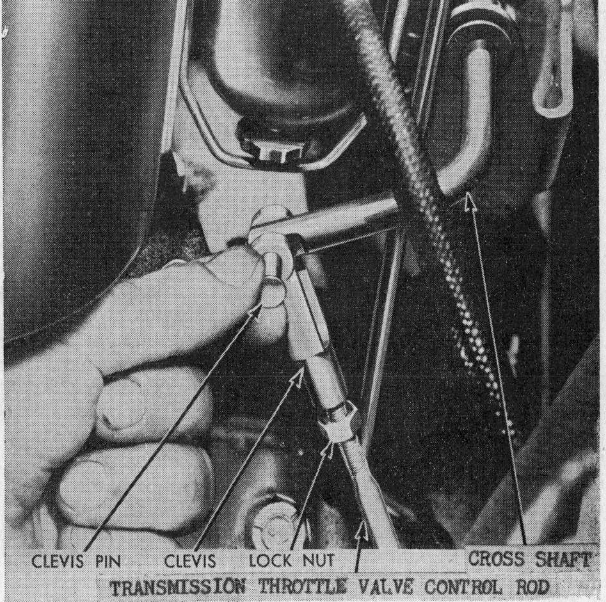

Fig. 11—Adjusting throttle valve control rod

THROTTLE VALVE LINKAGE—*con'td.*

Disconnect the transmission throttle valve control rod from the lever at the left rear corner of the engine block. Pull up on the rod as far as it will come.

Adjust the clevis so that it could be pinned to the lever.

Now lengthen the rod by 2½ turns of the clevis and repin it to the lever. Be sure to tighten the clevis lock nut.

V8 ENGINES, USING GAGES

If the throttle valve control rod is too long the automatic shift will be rough and noisy. If the throttle valve rod is too short there will be slippage. Therefore this adjustment is very important to proper operation. The first step as in the adjustment for 6 cyl models is that the idling speed and dash pot adjustments are correct. The next step is to see that the accelerator to carburetor rod is properly positioned. This can be done by means of gages available through Ford and Mercury dealers. Instructions in their use are supplied by the maker. The use of the proper gage will assure that the accelerator and carburetor throttle are properly coordinated.

The final step is similar to that for the 6 cyl engine. Disconnect the transmission throttle valve control rod at the clevis near the left rear corner of the engine. Gently pull the rod as far forward as it will come. Adjust the clevis so that it could be pinned back in place.

Now lengthen the rod by exactly 2½ turns of the clevis, and pin back in place. Do not neglect to tighten the clevis lock nut. Should there still be evidence of slippage, increase the length of the transmission throttle control rod by one more turn. (The maximum permissible increase in the length of the rod under this procedure is 3½ turns. Should the transmission still show signs of slippage the trouble could be a bent rod or inaccurately adjusted accelerator to carburetor linkage or malfunctioning of the valve unit in the transmission.)

Should the transmission fail to kickdown when the throttle is depressed adjust the carburetor to accelerator rod to touch the upper edge of the slot in the gage instead of the lower.

Should the transmission still be rough on shifting adjust the transmission throttle valve rod one-half turn of the clevis shorter than the normal adjustment.

V8 ENGINES WHEN GAGES ARE NOT AVAILABLE

The purpose of adjusting the throttle valve linkage is to coordinate the points at which the transmission shifts from 2nd to High or High to 2nd with the position of the accelerator pedal.

When no gages are available a rough approximation of the correct position can be obtained with this procedure and also adjustments can be made to suit the requirements of individual owners.

The bracket which carries the rods across the engine is adjustable. It should be fastened so that the two rods turn freely. The position of the lower rod in the bracket is also adjustable. The lower rod should be adjusted to run straight and horizontally with sufficient clearance between it and the fire wall.

Now: Disconnect the transmission throttle valve control rod from the cross rod at the clevis on the left rear corner of the engine.

Pull the control rod, gently, as far forward as it will come and adjust the clevis so that it could be pinned back onto the cross rod. (The pin should slide in freely.) **Do not repin at this point.**

Now lengthen the rod by exactly two and one-half (2½) turns of the clevis and repin at this point to the cross rod. Do not neglect to tighten the clevis lock nut.

Now road test the car with hand lever at Drive. The transmission should upshift under light but steady throttle at 15-20 mph. If it does not, shorten the carburetor throttle rod a couple of turns. Under wide open throttle the transmission should upshift between 57-62 mph on Mercurys and about 55 mph on Fords. If it does not, shorten the carburetor throttle rod a bit more.

Flooring the accelerator at any speed between 20 and 62 on Mercurys and 20-55 on Fords should kick the transmission out of High down into 2nd. If it does not, shorten the carburetor throttle rod a few turns until it does.

If during these road tests there is evidence of slippage lengthen the transmission throttle valve control rod by one full turn, and repeat the road test. If the road test demonstrates that the shifts are rough, the transmission throttle valve control rod should be shortened by one-half turn of the clevis.

The evidence of maladjustment between the throttle valve in the carburetor and that in the transmission is most evident in the kickdown test. If the kickdown point is not obtainable by shortening the carburetor rod shorten the transmission throttle valve control rod by one-half turn.

It is well to note in making these adjustments that the thread on the carburetor throttle rod is finer than that on the transmission throttle rod so that small adjustments can be made more easily at the carburetor than they can at the transmission. The adjustments are rather sensitive so that a few turns of the carburetor throttle rod swivel are all that should be needed. If such fail to produce results then the adjustment so far made should be transferred to the transmission throttle valve control rod, and the carburetor throttle rod should be returned to its original length. The road test procedure should then be repeated.

The maximum variation in the length of the transmission throttle valve control rod as recommended by the Ford Motor Co. is from 2½ turns to 3½ turns of the clevis beyond the point at which the clevis could be repinned with the rod as far forward as it will come.

Transmission Throttle Valve Adjustment

The transmission throttle valve is a spring loaded valve; the lever merely increases the compression of the spring.

The valve itself is adjusted inside the transmission by slightly bending its stop. Adjustment procedures formulated by the Ford Motor Co. are included with the special protractor type of gage required for the job. The theory of the adjustment is that a pressure rise as shown on a pressure gage attached to a point on the transmission near the lever should occur when the lever has been moved four deg back (down) from its extreme forward (up) position; with the hand lever in Reverse and the engine idling at 600 rpm.

If the pressure rise starts before four deg of lever travel the stop should be bent away from the valve body, if the pressure rise occurs after four deg of travel the stop should be bent toward the valve body.

Unless the car has been badly wrecked and the parts and levers bent there is little likelihood of there being any need for this adjustment.

TROUBLE CHART

Items ending with an X require removal of transmission to correct.

1. Engine Stalls

This trouble can be caused by:
Improper adjustment of the throttle dash pot.
Engine not properly tuned up.

2. Transmission Fluid Foams Out

This trouble is probably due to:
Too high fluid level which permits the planetary gears to aerate the fluid.

3. Car Will Not Move in Any Range—Rear Wheels Turn Freely

This trouble may be due to:
Leaks in the hydraulic system. X
Defective front oil pump. X
Worn or misadjusted bands.
Defective clutches. X
Maladjusted controls.
Fluid level too low.
Defective pressure regulator.

4. Car Will Not Move in Any Range—Rear Wheels Locked

This trouble can be due to:
Defective clutches. X
Parking lock engaged due to breakage. X
Maladjusted controls.
Broken part in the transmission or rear axle. X

5. Car Will Not Move in Drive—Otherwise OK.

This trouble may be due to:
Worn front band.
Defective valve body.
Front servo inoperative.
Front clutch inoperative. X
Leakage in the hydraulic system. X

6. Car Will Not Move in Low or Reverse—Otherwise OK.

This trouble may be due to:
Worn rear band. X
Rear servo inoperative.
Defective valve body.

7. Excessive Slip in All Ranges

This trouble may be due to:
Leaks in the hydraulic system. X
Low oil level.
Manual control linkage incorrectly adjusted.
Pressure regulator valve or valve body defective.

8. Excessive Slip in Drive Only

This trouble may be due to:
Incorrectly adjusted throttle linkage.
Front band worn.
Pressure regulator valve or valve body defective.
Defective front servo.
Defective front clutch. X

9. Excessive Slip in Low Only or Reverse Only

These troubles may be due to:
Manual control linkage improperly adjusted.
Rear band worn.
Defective regulator valve or valve body.
Defective rear servo.
Rear clutches defective. X
Leakage in the hydraulic system. X

10. Car Creeps Forward in Neutral

This trouble can be caused by:
Improper adjustment of the manual controls.
Servo pistons sticking.
Clutches sticking. X
Engine idle speed not properly adjusted.

11. Severe Engagement Low, Drive, or Reverse

These troubles may be due to:
Too high engine idling speed.
Improperly adjusted throttle linkage.
Defective regulator valve or valve body.

12. Chatter and Slippage in Reverse

These troubles may be due to:
Improperly adjusted engine idling speed.
Improperly adjusted throttle linkage.
Worn rear band.
Defective pressure regulator valve or valve body.

13. Shift from 2nd to High at Wrong Speed or Erratic

This trouble may be due to:
Improperly adjusted throttle linkage.
Defective governor.
Defective pressure regulator valve or valve body.

14. Shift from 2nd to High Too Severe

This trouble may be due to:
Improper throttle linkage adjustment.
Defective pressure regulator valve or valve body.
Worn front band.
Defective front servo.

15. Engine Races During Shift from 2nd to High

This trouble may be due to:
Improper throttle linkage adjustment.
Defective valve body.
Leakage in hydraulic system. X

16. Transmission Fails to Shift from 2nd to High

This trouble may be due to:
Defective governor.
Defective valve body.
Defective rear clutch. X
Leakage in the hydraulic system. X

17. Transmission Will Not Kickdown

This trouble may be due to:
Improperly adjusted throttle linkage.
Defective valve body.

18. Transmission Shifts Too Severely from 2nd to High with Throttle Closed

This trouble is due to:
Poorly adjusted throttle linkage.
Improperly adjusted idling speed.
Defective valve body.

19. Engine Races at Kickdown

This trouble is due to:
Defective valve body.

20. Transmission Overheats

This trouble can be caused by:
Clogged air passages around converter.
Rear band adjusted too tight.
Pressure regulator valve defective.
Free wheeling clutch in converter not functioning. X
Front band adjusted too tight.

21. Parking Lock Won't Hold

This trouble is probably due to:
Improperly adjusted manual linkage.
Defective parking lock linkage inside the transmission. X

22. Engine Fails to Turn Over When Car Is Pushed

This is probably due to:
Insufficient speed.
Defective pressure regulator valve or valve body.
Defective rear pump. X
Defective front pump permitting loss of pressure.
Leakage in the hydraulic system. X

23. A Noise With Car Standing and Hand Lever at Neutral

Is probably due to:
Primary pump cover bolts striking something.
Parts of the front pump improperly installed. X
Defective front clutch. X

24. A Noise With Car Coasting at 20-30 MPH With Hand Lever at Neutral

Is probably due to:
Defective rear pump. X

25. Noises While Car is in Low, 2nd or Reverse

Are probably due to:
The planetary gear set. X

REMOVAL OF THE TRANSMISSION

Note on V8 Models: Make a match mark across the throttle bracket and fire wall. Unfasten the throttle rod bracket from the front fire wall so that the linkage does not get bent when the engine is raised.

Drain the transmission and the converter. Remove the spark plugs from the engine. Support the car about twelve inches above the floor. Disconnect the linkages and the speedometer cable at the transmission.

Disconnect the drive shaft at the rear universal joint and slide the drive shaft toward the rear of the vehicle so that the universal joint knuckle will clear the transmission extension housing and remove the shaft.

Remove the air duct and the lower plate from the bell housing. Unbolt the rear engine support from the frame cross member at the rear of the transmission. Position a lift under the transmission and raise the assembly so that an engine support bar may be installed under the rear end of the engine oil pan.

Remove the rear engine support and the detachable cross member. Lower the lift so that the engine is resting on the support bar but the weight of the transmission is still on the lift.

Note: Mark, for matched reassembly, the flywheel flexplate, the primary pump cover and the primary pump. Do not neglect this or reinstallation will be more difficult than it should be.

Unbolt the flexplate from the converter assembly. Wedge the converter in place so that it cannot fall off the input shaft.

Unbolt the bell housing from the engine block. There are two bolts at the top which are reached through rubber plugged holes in the front floor.

Slide the transmission assembly towards the rear of the car to permit the converter pilot to clear the flexplate. Lower the assembly down and out.

INSTALLATION OF THE TRANSMISSION

Be sure that the converter is held in place by wedges.

Raise the assembly into place being careful that the converter pilot is not damaged as the unit slides into contact with the flywheel flexplate. Remove the wedges which kept the converter in place while the assembly was being guided into place.

Check that the bell housing is seated flat against the engine block. Install the bell housing to engine block bolts and tighten them evenly to 40-45 ft lb.

Line up the marks, made at removal, on the flexplate and the primary pump cover. Tighten to 25-28 ft lbs.

If no marks were made or if a new unit is being installed, mount as follows:

On V8 models having 34 bolts holding the primary cover to the primary pump, the middle bolt of the flexplate should be attached at the 6th hole from the drain plug, counting the hole at the drain plug as 1. Count from either drain plug in either direction.

On V8 models having 18 bolts holding the primary cover to the primary pump, the middle bolt of the flexplate should be attached at the 3rd hole from the drain plug, count from either drain plug, in either direction.

On 6 cylinder models having 34 bolts holding the primary cover to the primary pump, the middle bolt of the flexplate should be attached to the 10th hole from the plug counting in a clockwise direction only. Count the hole at the plug as 1.

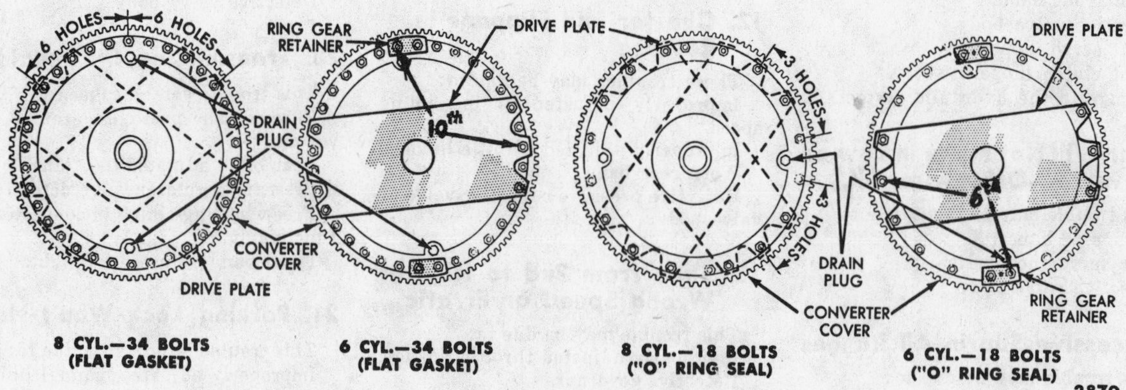

Fig. 12—Location of center bolt of flexplate with reference to primary pump cover bolts

On 6 cylinder models having 18 bolts holding the primary cover to the primary pump, the middle bolt of the flexplate should be mounted to the 6th hole from the drain plug counting in a clockwise direction only.

Reinstall the detachable frame cross member and lay the rear engine support in place. Raise the transmission and engine assembly sufficiently and remove the engine support bar. Lower the assembly and fasten the rear engine support.

Reinstall the speedometer cable, reconnect the linkages, reinstall the access plates. Lubricate the U joint knuckle with transmission fluid and reinstall the drive shaft.

On V8 models refasten the throttle rod bracket being sure that the match marks made across the bracket and the fire wall are aligned.

Reinstall the spark plugs. Put in 5 qts of fluid, idle engine for two minutes and add 4 more qts. When transmission is warm, check the level.

DISASSEMBLY, INSPECTION, AND INSTALLATION

1. The Governor

This operation can be done without removing the transmission from the car.

Remove the governor inspection cover from the right side of the extension housing and rotate the drive shaft until the governor appears in the opening. Remove the two screws securing the governor body to the counterweight sleeve. Be careful not to drop the bolts or the valve into the extension housing.

Remove two screws and remove the side plate. Check that the governor valve is not scored and moves freely in its bore. Blow out the passages. Check all over for burrs.

Reverse the procedure to reinstall.

Be sure that the passages in the sleeve and body are aligned. The governor counterweight can only be removed when the transmission is out of the car.

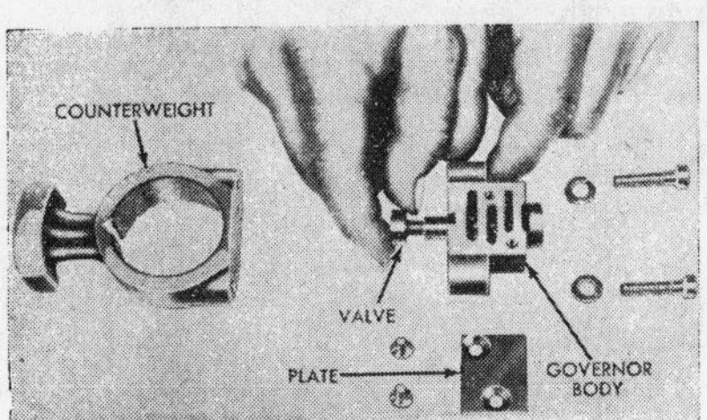

Fig. 13—Check governor valve

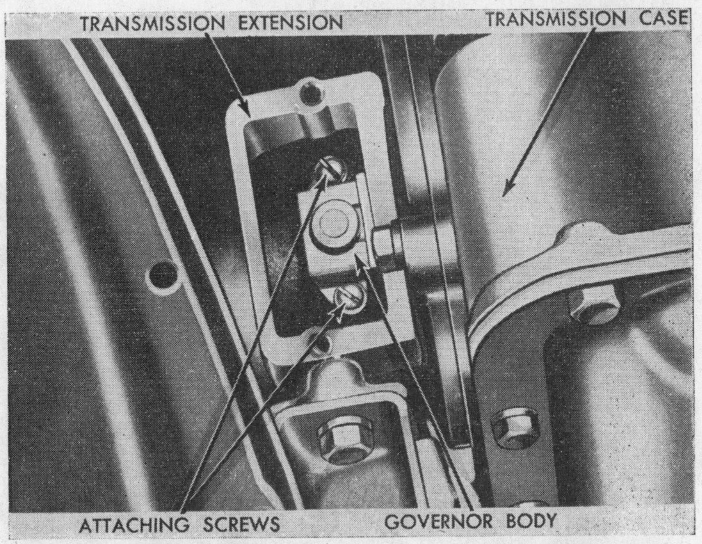

Fig. 14—Remove inspection plate from rear extension

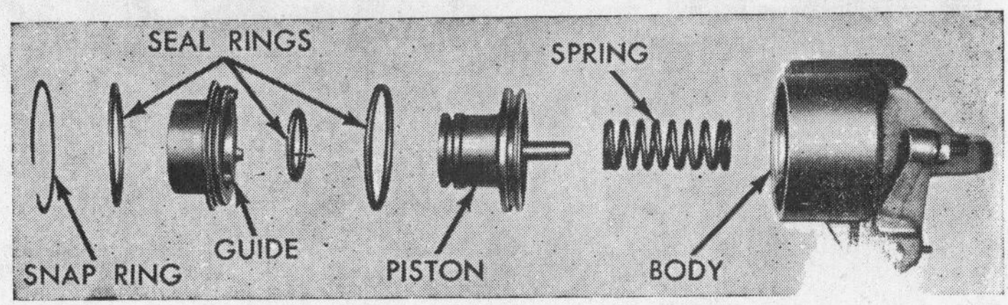

Fig. 15—Exploded view of front servo

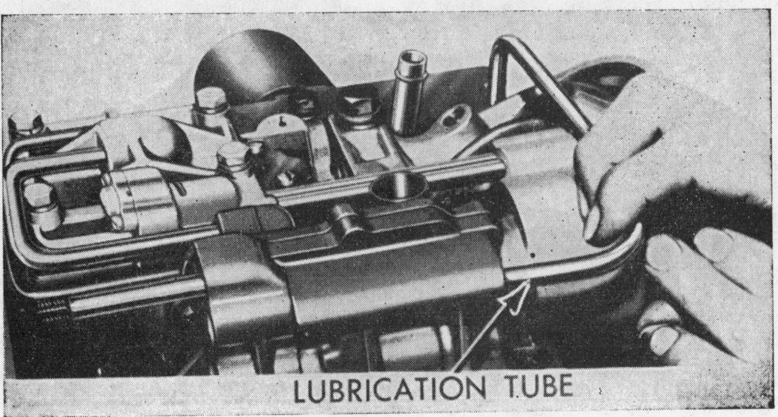

Fig. 15a—Remove lubrication tube

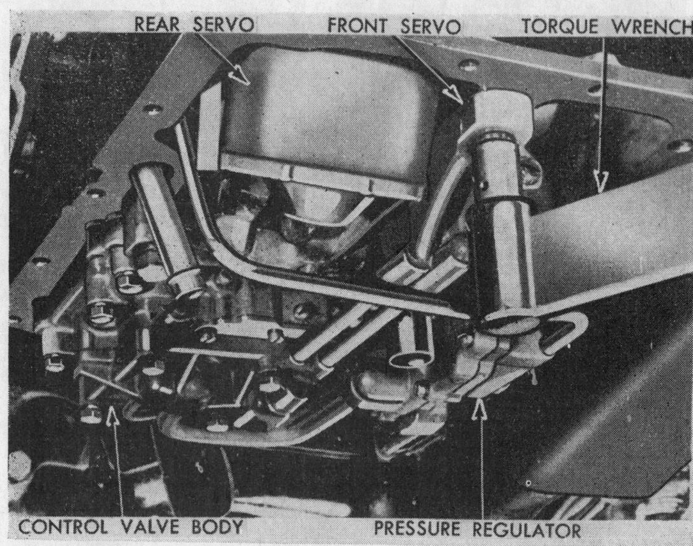

Fig. 16—Remove the front servo bolt

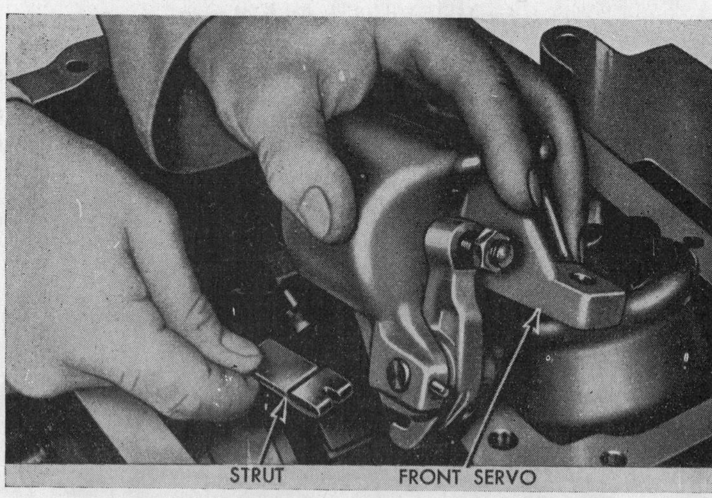

Fig. 17—Remove the front servo

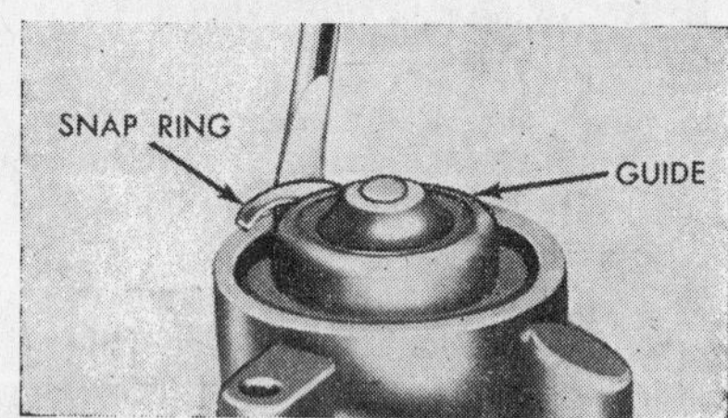

Fig. 18—Remove servo guide snap ring

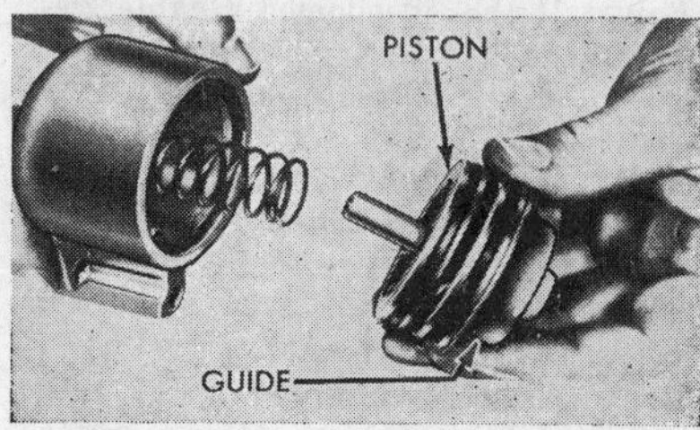

Fig. 19—Remove servo guide and piston

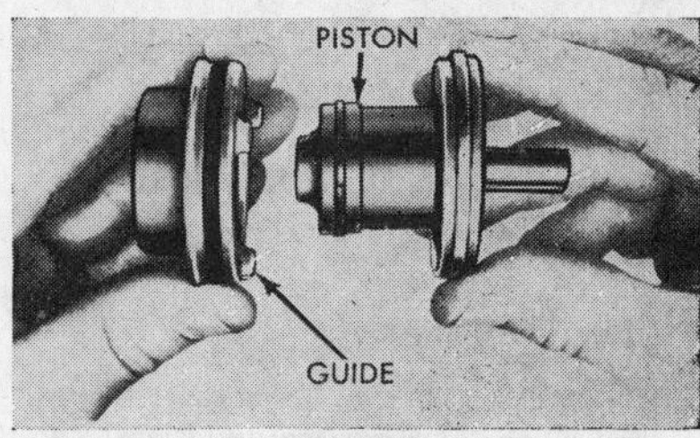

Fig. 20—Separate guide from piston

2. The Front Servo

This operation can be done without removing the transmission from the car.

Drain the transmission case and remove the oil pan. Remove the lubrication tube. Loosen the control valve body attaching bolts. Remove the front servo attaching bolt and, holding the front band strut in place with the fingers, remove the servo.

Apply pressure to the servo piston and remove the guide retaining snap ring. Remove the piston and guide from the servo body. Remove the spring from the body and the guide from the piston.

Inspect the body for cracks, the piston for scores, the actuating lever for free movement, and the spring for distortion.

Reverse the procedure to assemble and install. Use new seal rings on the piston and the guide.

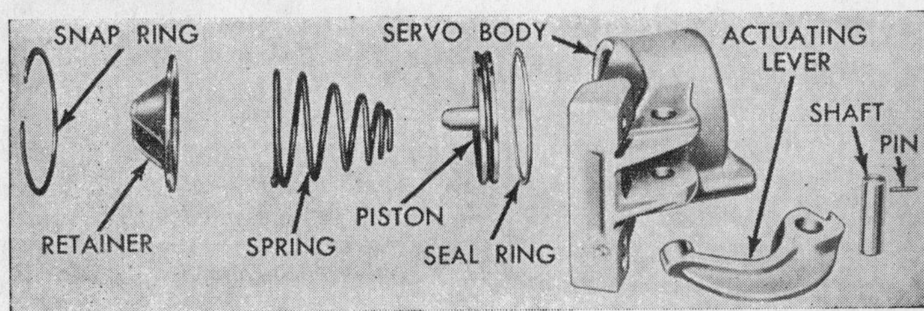

Fig. 21—Exploded view of the rear servo

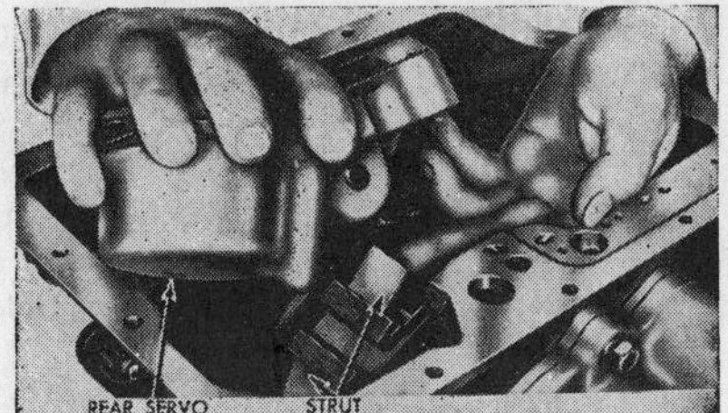

Fig. 22—Hold struts while removing servo

Fig. 23—Remove shaft retaining pin

3. The Rear Servo

This operation can be done without removing the transmission from the car.

With the oil pan off and the lubrication tube out, remove the servo attaching bolts. Hold the rear band struts in place and remove the rear servo.

Drive the servo actuating lever shaft retaining pin out with a 1/8 in. punch and remove the shaft and lever. Push in on the spring retainer and remove the retainer snap ring. Release the pressure slowly and remove the retainer and the spring. Use air pressure to force the piston out of its bore.

Inspect the servo body for cracks and the piston for scores. Check the lever and shaft for wear. Check the spring for distortion. Blow out the passages.

Reverse the procedure to assemble and reinstall. Use a new seal ring on the piston.

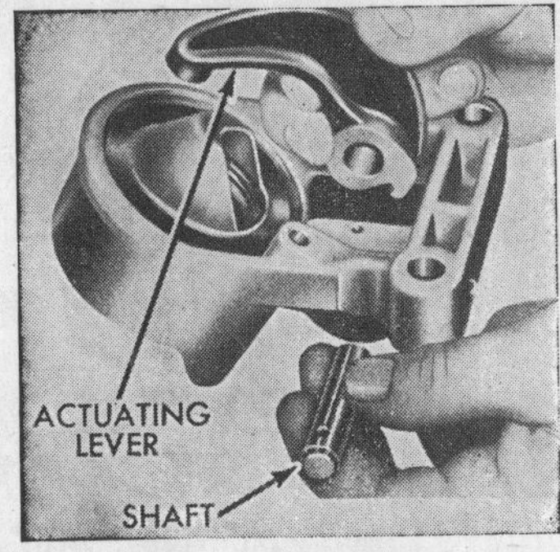

Fig. 24—Remove shaft and lever

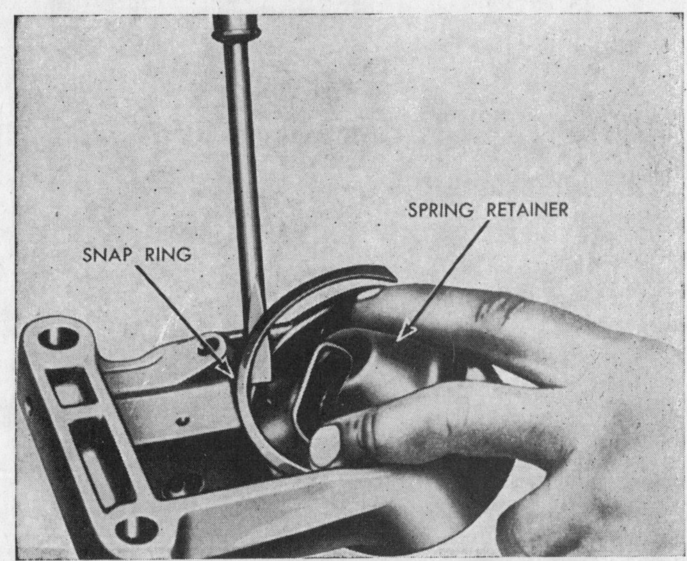

Fig. 25—Remove retainer snap ring

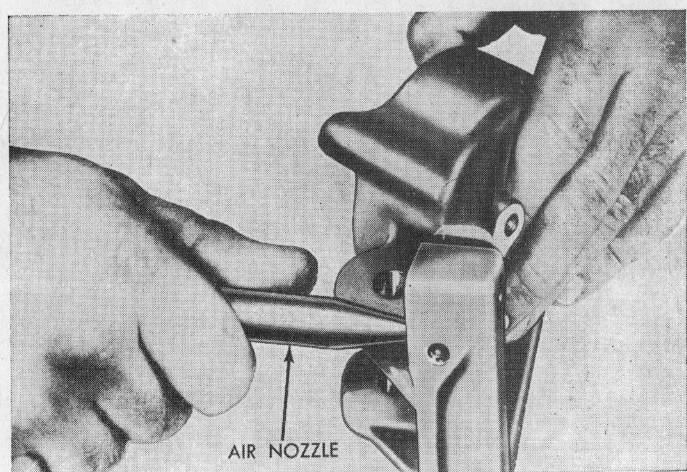

Fig. 26—Furling piston from bore

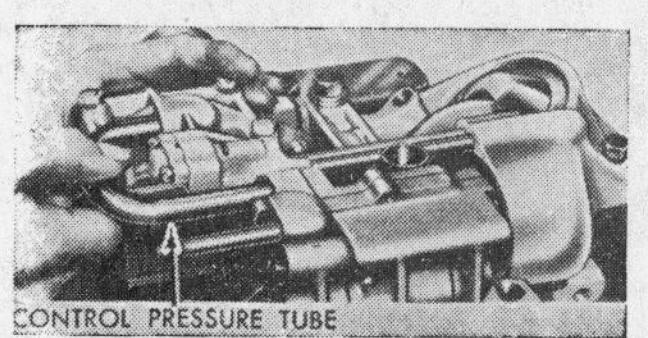

Fig. 27—Remove large control pressure tube

4. Control Valve Assembly

This operation can be done without removing the transmission from the car.

Caution: Have the hand lever at neutral for this operation.

With the oil pan off and the lubrication tube out. Remove the compensator pressure tube and the control pressure tube from the control valve body and the regulator valve body. Loosen the front servo attaching bolt a few turns.

Remove the control valve body to case bolts and remove the body by disengaging the tubes to the front servo.

Extra care should be lavished on this assembly. Use a clean towel over the bench while separating the assembly into its three major parts; the upper body, the lower body, and a lower body cover.

Remove the manual control valve and separate the parts of the upper body as shown in the cut.

Remove the separator plate and disassemble the lower body as shown in the cut.

Be careful when removing the end and side plates of these portions as many of the valves are spring loaded.

Inspect the parts for fit and signs of damage. Inspect the mating surfaces for burrs and flatness.

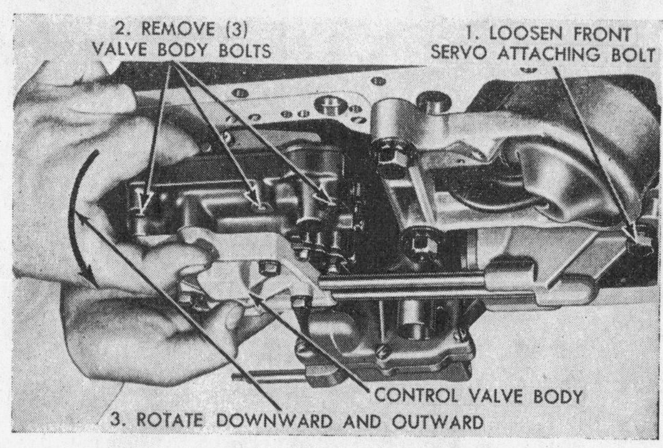

Fig. 28—Remove control valve body assembly

Fig. 29—Disengage tubes

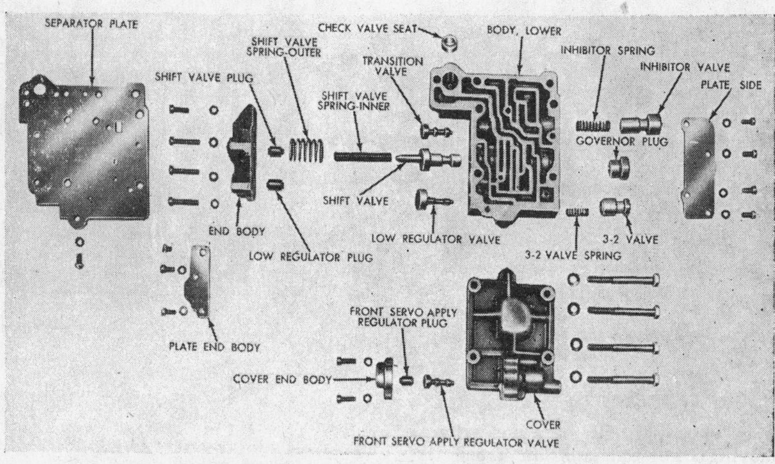

Fig. 31—Control valve lower body and cover disassembled

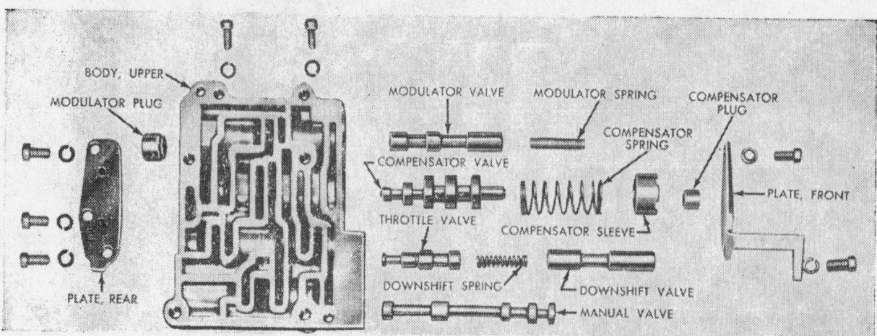

Fig. 30—Control valve body disassembled

In reassembling be careful about tightening the separator plate screws as excessive tightening could cause the valves to bind in their bores.

Tighten the lower body cover bolts to 4-6 ft lbs.

Reverse the procedure to reassemble and install.

Index the servo tubes with the holes in the front servo assembly while pushing in on the throttle valve so that it will clear the case. Be sure that the manual control valve indexes with the detent.

The large control pressure tube and the small compensator pressure tube connect the control and regulator valve bodies.

Tighten the attaching bolts to 8-10 ft lbs. Tighten the front servo bolt to 35-40 ft lbs.

Readjust the manual and throttle valve controls.

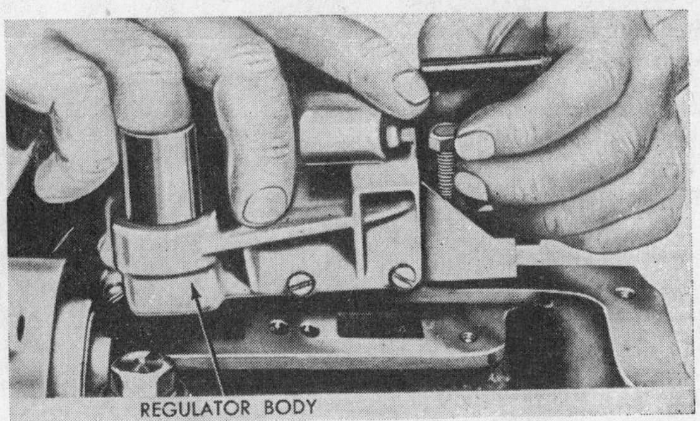

Fig. 34—Remove regulator body from case

5. The Pressure Regulator Valve Assembly

This operation can be done without removing the transmission from the car.

Perform the removal operations outlined in Par. 4. Remove the regulator body attaching bolts and washers and remove the regulator body assembly.

Separate the parts as shown in the cut.

Inspect all the parts for fit, burrs, and signs of wear. Check the springs for distortion.

Reverse the procedure to reassemble and reinstall. Tighten the attaching bolts to 17-22 ft lbs.

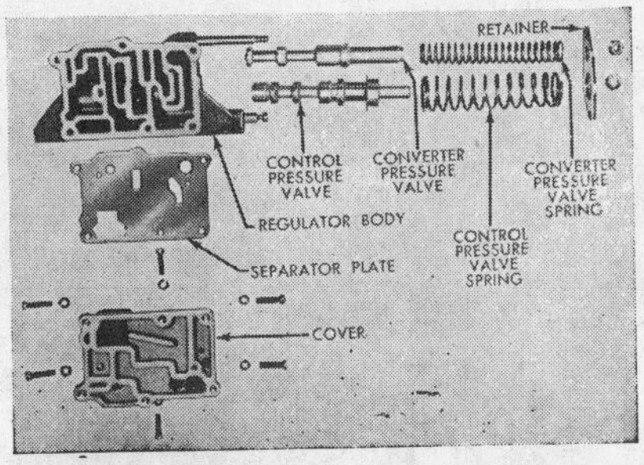

Fig. 35—Pressure regulator disassembled

6. Throttle and Manual Valve Controls

This operation can be done without removing the transmission from the car.

With removal operations performed as outlined in Par. 4, disconnect the actuating rods coming from the front of the car at their terminus on the transmission. Remove the throttle lever shaft nut and the inner throttle lever to release the outer lever and shaft. Remove the outer lever and shaft and the

continued

Fig. 32—Remove valve spring retainer

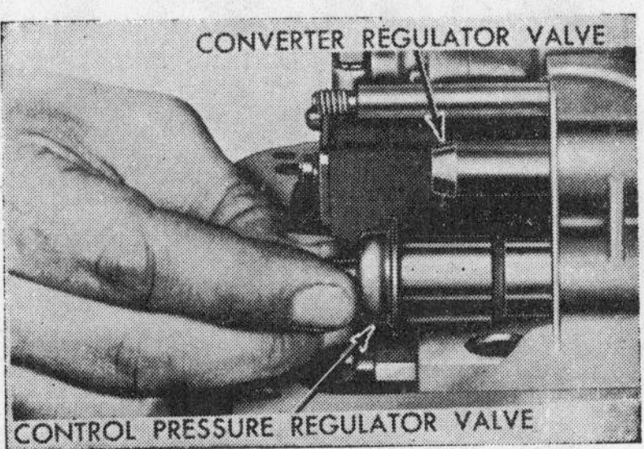

Fig. 33—Remove regulator valves

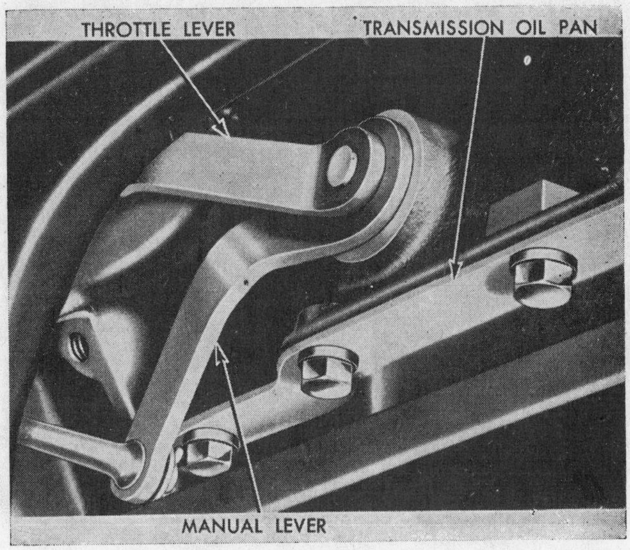

Fig. 36—Throttle and manual control valve levers

THROTTLE AND MANUAL VALVE CONTROLS—*continued*

seal from the counterbore in the manual valve outer lever. Remove the parking lock actuating rod. Remove the detent lever nut to release the detent ball, and spring. Slide the outer manual lever and shaft from the case and remove the shaft seal.

Reverse the procedure to reinstall. Use new outer seals on the shafts. Use a tube to depress the detent ball and spring while rotating the detent lever into position. Tighten the detent lever nut to 35-40 ft lbs. Tighten the throttle inner lever nut to 25-28 ft lbs. Complete assembly as outlined in Par. 4.

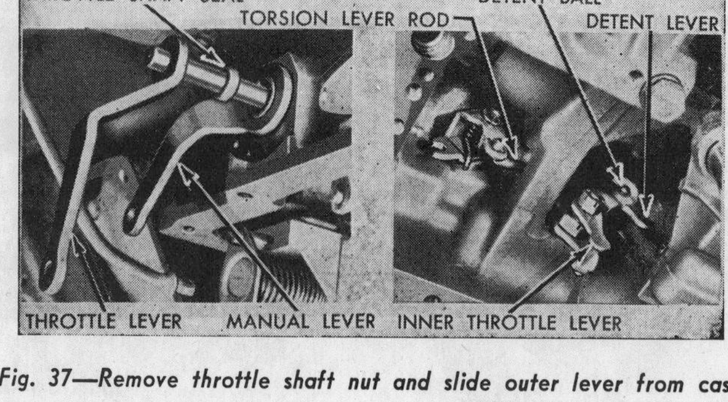

Fig. 37—Remove throttle shaft nut and slide outer lever from case

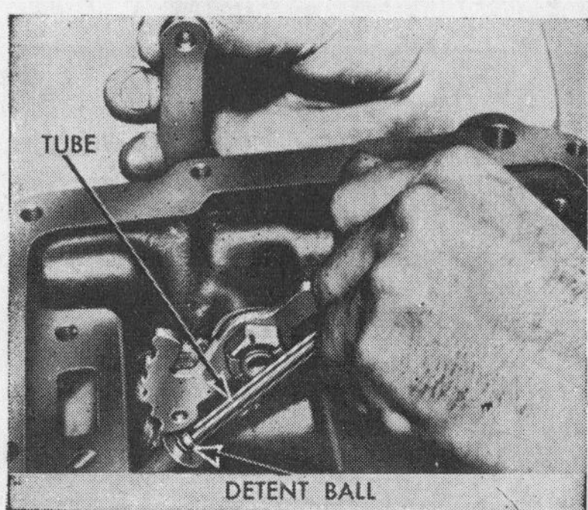

Fig. 38—Installing detent ball and spring

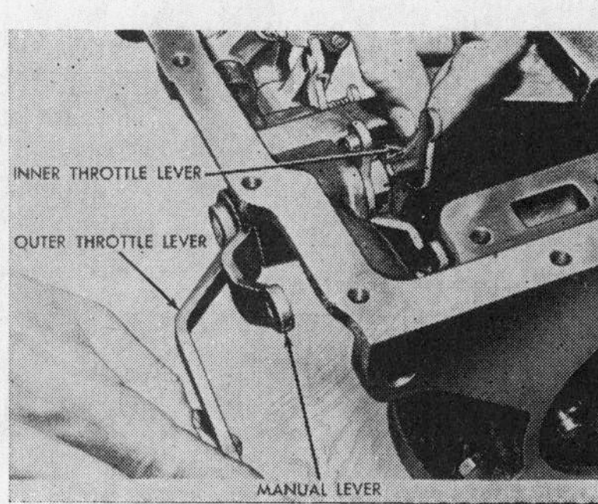

Fig. 39—Installing inner throttle lever

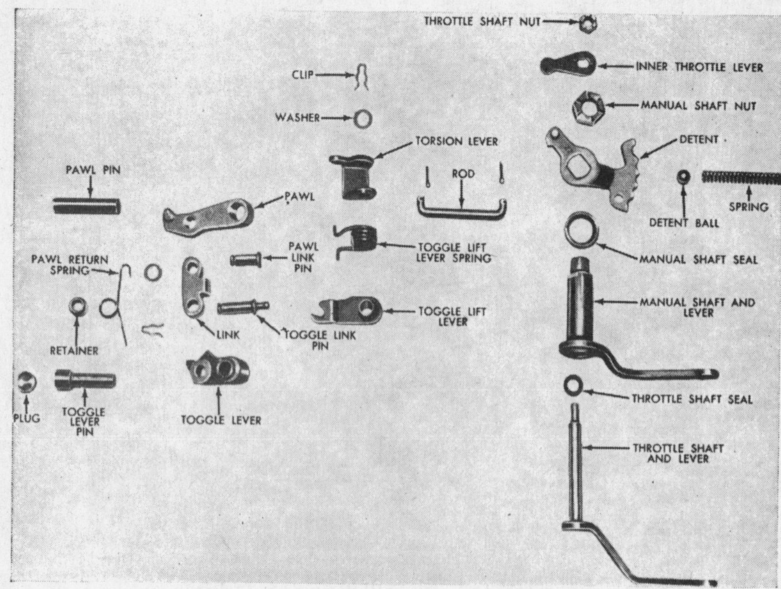

Fig. 40—Layout of throttle and manual controls

7. Checking Transmission End Play

Transmission must be removed from the car for this operation.

This operation is used to determine the thickness of the selective thrust washer which rides the hub of the planetary carrier between the carrier and the ring gear.

Mount an indicator in some manner similar to that shown in the cut so that it contacts the front end of the input (turbine) shaft. Pry between the front clutch and the front of the case so as to force the planetary gear train as far rearward as it will go. While holding the train so, set the indicator to read zero.

Now pry between the rear of the case and the rear face of the ring gear. The indicator should show an end play of the input shaft of between .010″ and .029″ F. I. R.

As mentioned above the selective thrust washer which controls this end play is located at the rear of the planetary carrier. It bears against the inner front face of the ring gear. In order to correct any variation between the recommended limits and those found it is necessary to disassemble the trans-

Fig. 41—Indicator contacts front end of input shaft

mission. Therefore record at this point the amount of end play as found whether over or under the limits.

Use the procedure outlined in Pars. 10, 11 and 12 to disassemble the transmission to the selective thrust washer. Measure the thickness of the washer with a micrometer and select a washer that is thicker or thinner as need be to bring the end play within the designated limits.

There are four thicknesses of thrust washers available from the factory: .061"-.063", .067"-.069", .074"-.076", and .081"-.083".

Reassemble the transmission and check that the end play is within the limits, .010"-.029". Note that if the end play is too little the parts of the gear train will wear out very rapidly and if the end play is too great there will be considerable noise as the gear train clunks from one end of the case to the other.

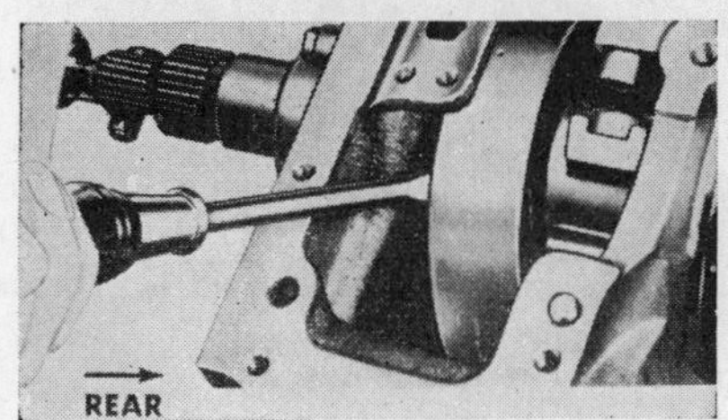

Fig. 42—Pry between front clutch and case to force gear train to the rear

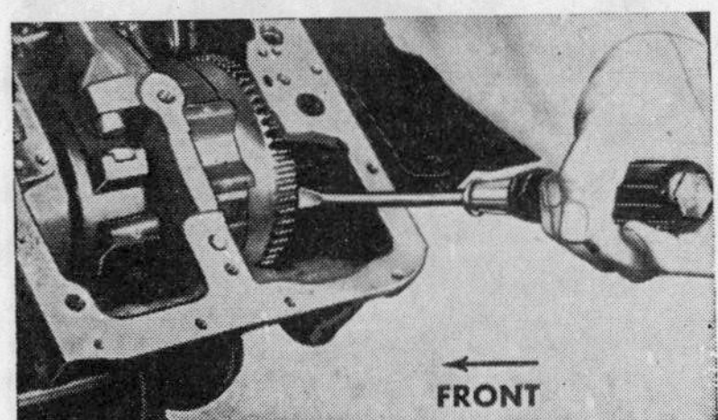

Fig. 43—Pry between ring gear and case to force gear train to the front

Fig. 44—Selective thrust washer rids rear hub of planetary carrier

8. The Converter

The transmission must be removed from the car for this operation.

Make sure that the primary pump cover is match marked to the primary pump for balanced reassembly. Note that the bolts holding the cover to the pump are special equally weighted bolts and should not be used elsewhere.

Remove the wedges which prevented the converter from falling out of the bell housing during removal from the car. Grasp the converter with both hands and pull straight out. Do not twist the assembly as you pull, else you will damage the front oil seal.

Unbolt the cover from the pump and remove the cover, a bronze thrust washer, and the turbine. Remove the stator assembly and the thrust washers which guard it fore and aft. One will probably be found on the inner hub face of the turbine and the other on the front of the primary pump hub.

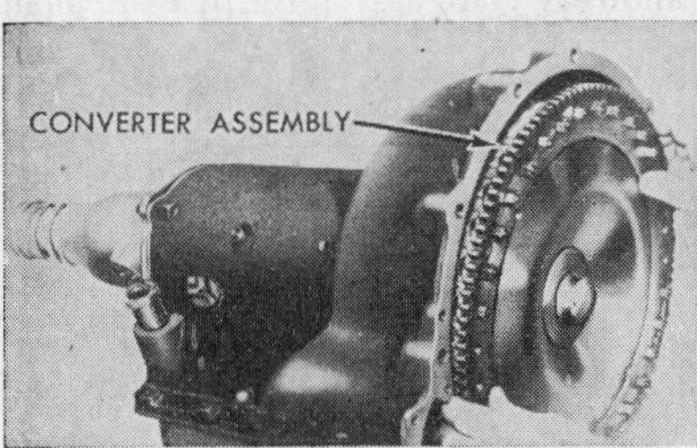

Fig. 45—Pull converter straight out

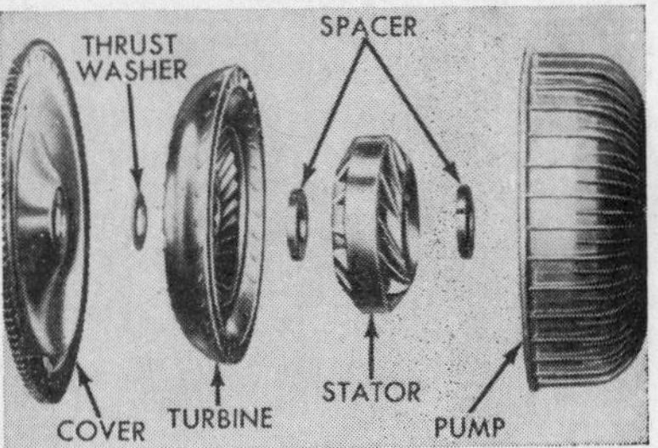

Fig. 46—Exploded view of converter assembly

Fig. 47—Replacing primary pump hub

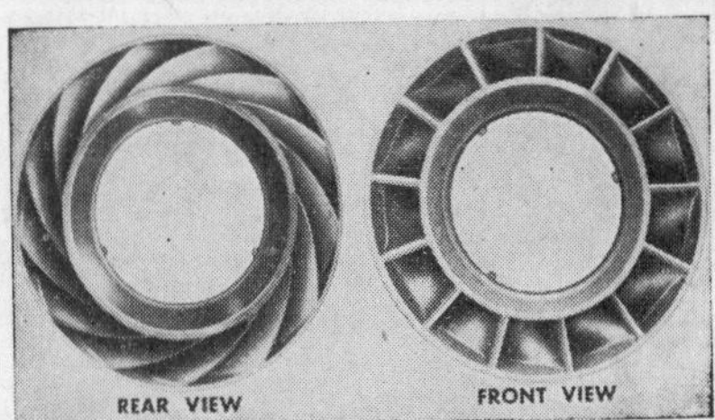

Fig. 48—Stator

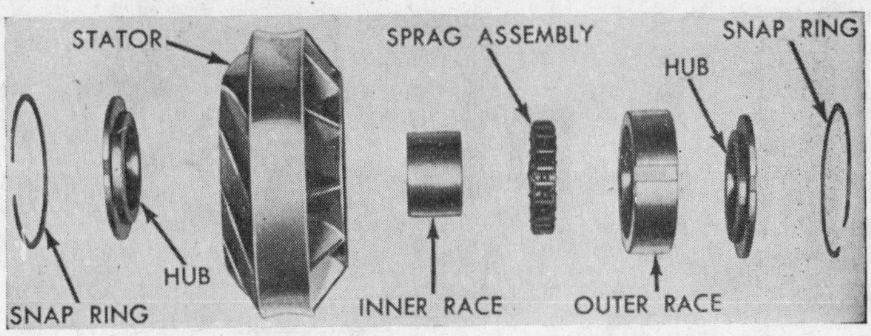

Fig. 49— Stator assembly disassembled

THE CONVERTER—*continued*

Examine the primary pump hub, if it appears worn or damaged it may be replaced. Simply unbolt the old and bolt on the new, using a new seal between the hub and the body of the primary pump. Tighten the bolts to 8-10 ft lbs.

Note that the curved blades of the stator go toward the primary pump and that the front of the stator is marked FRONT. Disassemble the stator into its part as shown in the cut.

Check the turbine, pump and stator blades for looseness. Check all the thrust and bearing surfaces for burrs and wear. Check the sprag assembly for broken or worn parts.

Reverse the procedure to reassemble and reinstall, only assemble the parts directly into place on the reactor and input shafts. Be certain the match marks made at disassembly on the cover and the primary pump are aligned.

Tighten the attaching bolts to 25-28 ft lbs.

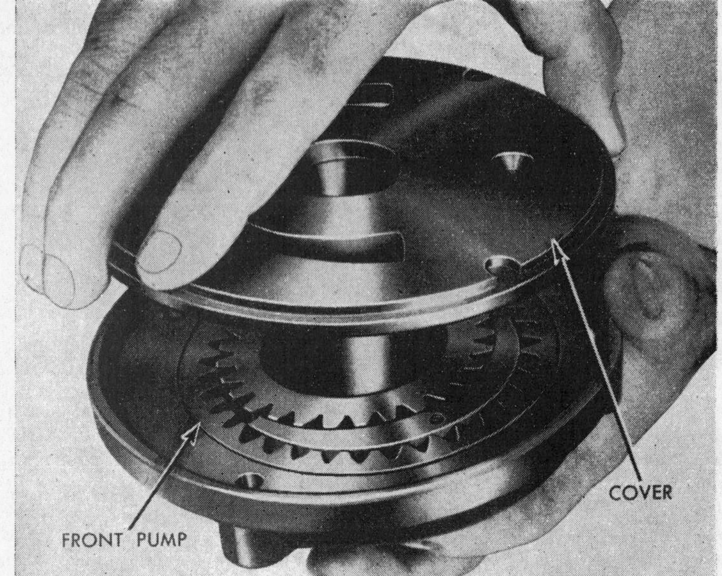

Fig. 52—Remove rear cover plate and reactor shaft assembly

9. The Front Oil Pump

The transmission must be out of the car for this operation.

Remove the converter as outlined in Par. 8. Remove the bolts holding the bell housing to the transmission case and remove the housing.

Fig. 50—Unbolt bell housing from case

Fig. 51—Remove front oil pump

Unbolt the front oil pump assembly and remove it from the front of the case. If the pump does not come off easily, tap it lightly with a plastic hammer.

Unbolt and remove the reactor shaft and rear plate assembly from the pump body. Mark the faces of the pump gears so that the same faces will be up at reassembly. Use prussian blue. Do not scratch or punch mark the gears.

Separate the parts as shown in the cut.

Inspect the oil seal in the pump body and replace if it shows signs of wear. Coat the outside diameter of the seal

Fig. 53—Mark the gear faces

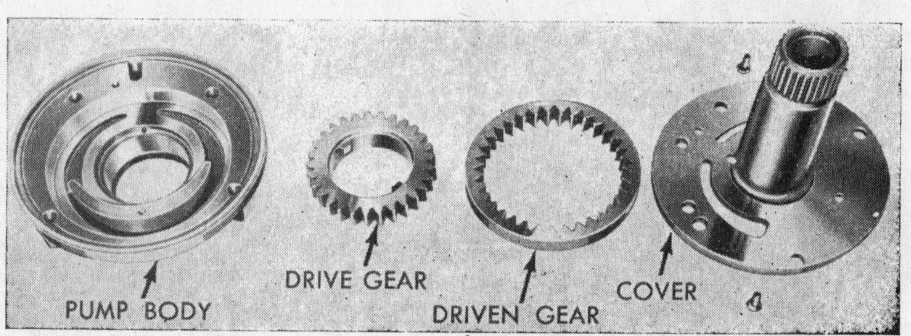

Fig. 54—Front pump disassembled

with permatex No. 3 prior to installation. Check the machined surfaces of the pump parts for burrs. Blow out the oil passages in the reactor shaft assembly and look it over for signs of wear, especially the inner bushing.

Reverse the procedure to reassemble and reinstall. Use a new gasket between the pump rear plate and the transmission case. Note that there is a pump locating dowel in the case counterbore. Tighten the four attaching bolts to 17-22 ft lbs.

10. The Extension Housing

The transmission must be out of the car for this operation.

Unbolt and remove the extension housing, being careful to support the housing so that its weight does not concentrate on the rear oil seal and ruin the seal as the housing passes over the splines of the output shaft.

Inspect the housing for cracks. Check all machined surfaces for burrs. Check the rear oil seal and replace if necessary. Position the fe't side of the seal to the rear. Remove the governor cover plate and check the gasket. Check the fluid baffle for a tight fit in the housing.

Reverse the procedure to reinstall.

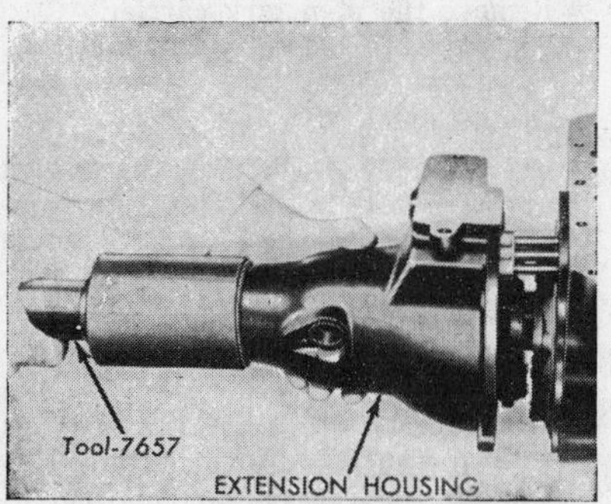

Fig. 55—Remove extension housing

Tighten the attaching bolts to 28-33 ft lbs.

11. The Rear Oil Pump and Output Shaft

The transmission must be out of the car for this operation.

Remove the extension housing as outlined in Par. 10.

Remove the snap ring and the speedometer drive gear from the output shaft. Do not lose the ball which keys the gear to the shaft.

Unbolt and remove the fluid distributor body and its three delivery tubes. Slide the fluid distributor sleeve off the output shaft.

Remove the snap ring and slide the governor body and counterweighted sleeve assembly from the shaft. Do not lose the ball which keys the sleeve to the shaft. Do not damage the oil seal rings. Pull the rear oil pump discharge tube out of the case.

Unbolt and remove the rear oil pump and its drive key. Remove the bronze thrust washer which rides between the rear pump and the ring gear. Remove the output shaft and ring gear assembly.

Note: The washer left on the rear hub of the planetary carrier is the selective thrust washer, the thickness of which is determined by the procedure outlined in Par. 7.

Remove the screws and lockwashers which secure the rear pump cover to the pump body and remove the cover. Using prussian blue, mark the faces of the pump gears so that they can be assembled with the same faces up. Do not scratch or injure the gears.

Disassemble the pump as shown in the cut.

Inspect the machined surfaces for burrs and signs of wear. Blow out the fluid passages.

Reverse the procedure to reassemble. Be sure the same faces of the gears

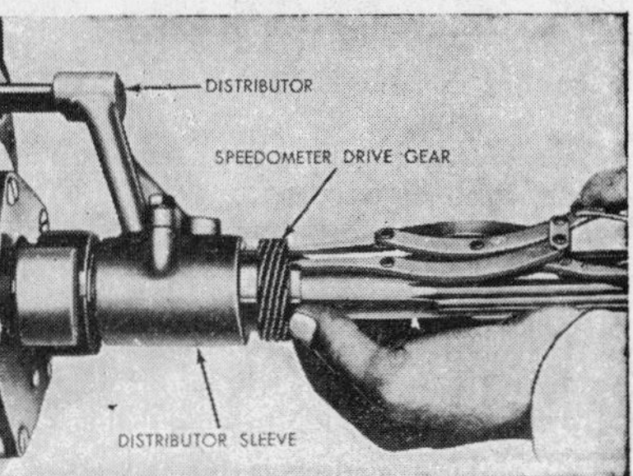

Fig. 57—Remove snap ring to release speedometer drive gear

Fig. 58—Remove fluid distributor body

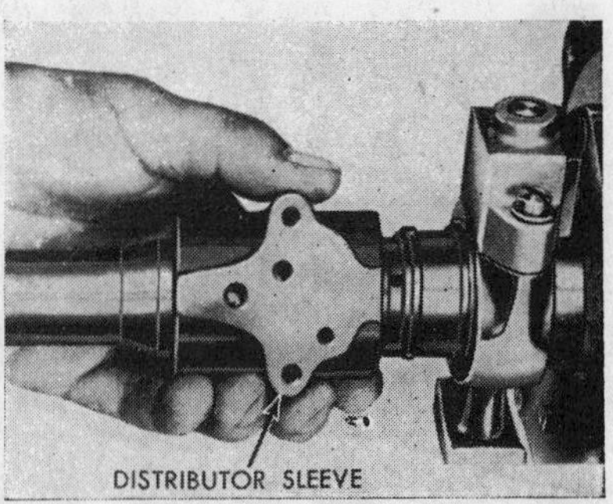

Fig. 59—Slide fluid distributor sleeve from shaft

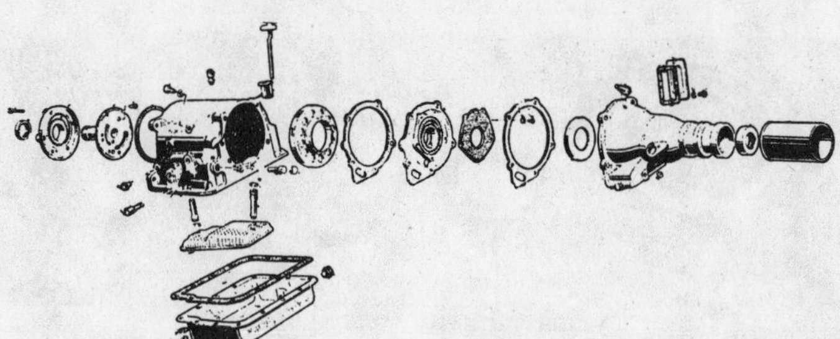

Fig. 56—Exploded view of oil pan, oil pump and extension housing, note governor inspection plate

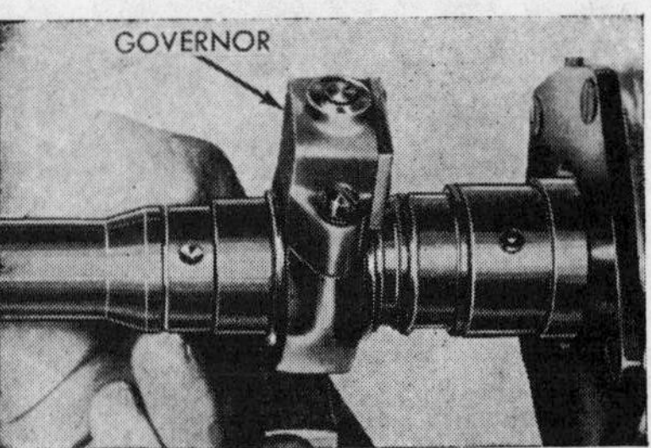

Fig. 60—Slide governor assembly from shaft, note the drive balls

REAR OIL PUMP—*continued*

are up. Tighten the pump cover screws to 7-8 ft lbs.

Check the governor counterweight for burrs and clear fluid passages. Check the fluid distributor and its sleeve for smooth flat mating surfaces. Check that the spacer is on the center tube. Check the fluid passages. Check the thrust and mating surfaces of the output shaft for burrs and signs of wear. Check the condition of the ring gear. Examine the oil seal rings and check the grooves for burrs.

Install the output shaft and ring gear assembly very carefully. Be sure that the selective thrust washer is in place on the pinion carrier. Position the oil seal rings on the primary sun gear shaft with the gaps up to prevent breakage as the output shaft slides into place.

Position the seal rings on the output shaft with their gaps up. Place the rear oil pump drive key in its slot. Install the thrust washer with its tangs indexed with the bosses on the pump body. The bronze side up.

Using care that the keyway in the pump drive gear and the key on the output shaft are aligned, install the rear pump with a new gasket fore and aft.

Use fluid to retain the governor drive ball in its pocket and install the governor assembly. The governor body plate goes toward the front of the car. Install the snap ring.

Install the distributor sleeve chamfered end first. Use fluid to ease the sleeve into place. Index the fluid passages in the fluid distributor with those in the sleeve. Enter the tubes into their hole in the case up to the spacer on the center tube and refasten the distributor body to the sleeve. Tighten to 8-10 ft lbs.

Use fluid to retain the speedometer drive ball in its pocket in the shaft and install the speedometer drive gear so that the ball and drive slot index. Install the snap ring.

Install a new seal ring on the rear pump discharge tube and install the tube into the case.

12. The Planetary Carrier

The transmission must be out of the car for this operation.

With parts removed as outlined in pars. 10 and 11, remove the two seal rings from the primary sun gear shaft.

Note: The seal rings used throughout the transmission are easily broken so that care must be the guiding light in all dealings with them. Cocking and twisting of the parts during removal and installation is the biggest cause of breakage. Beginning with late '51 models a hook type of seal ring was adapted which is slightly less friable.

Remove the selective thrust washer from the rear of the planetary carrier.

Note: The method of selection of this important thrust washer is outlined in par. 7.

Remove the planetary carrier.

The planetary carrier is replaced as an assembly. Parts for it are not available separately.

Check the end play of the pinion gears, it should be between .010″ and .020″. Inspect the gears for breakage and signs of wear. Be sure that they turn freely on their shafts and that the shafts are firmly seated in the carrier. Examine the rear band surface of the carrier for signs of scores. Check the thrust surfaces for scores. Blow out all the fluid passages.

Reverse the procedure to reinstall.

Fig. 61—Remove rear oil pump discharge tube

Fig. 62—Remove rear pump

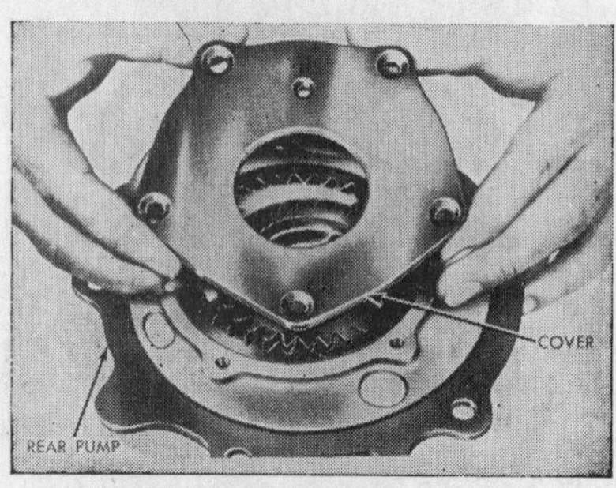

Fig. 63—Remove front cover of rear pump

Fig. 64—Mark pump gear faces

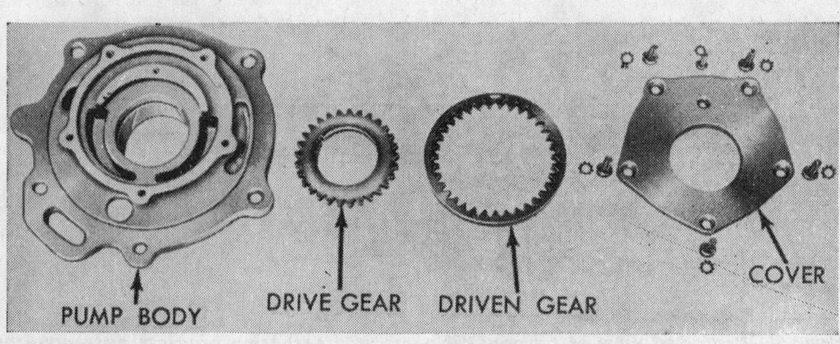

Fig. 65—Rear pump disassembled

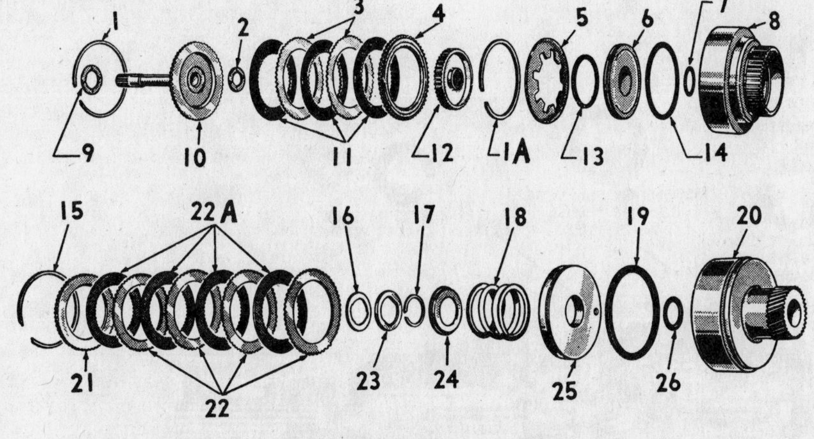

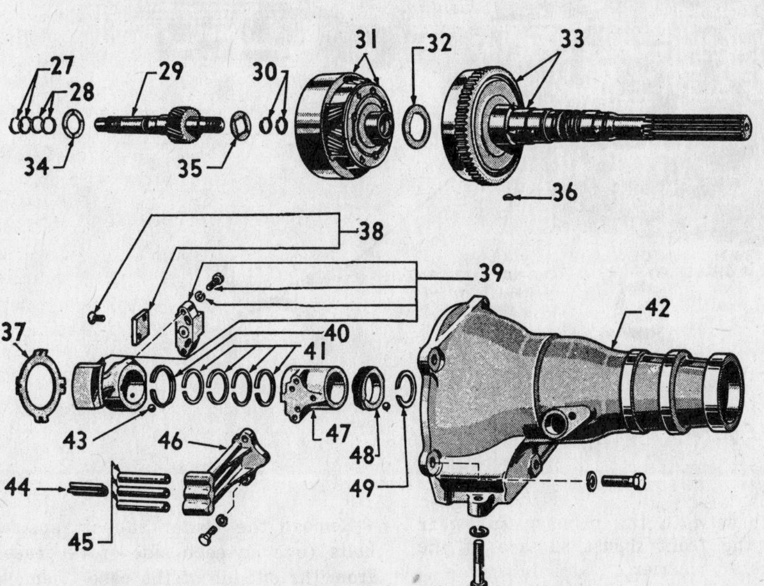

Fig. 66—Exploded view of the gear train

1. Retaining ring input shaft and flange to front clutch
1A. Retaining ring front clutch release spring
2. Thrust washer front clutch hub to flange
3. Steel plates front clutch
4. Pressure plate front clutch
5. Release spring front clutch
6. Piston front clutch
7. Seal ring piston inner
8. Drum of front clutch and hub of rear clutch
9. Thrust washer input shaft to case
10. Input shaft and front clutch drive flange
11. Copper plates front clutch
12. Front clutch hub
13. Bearing ring for front clutch release spring
14. Seal ring piston outer
15. Retaining ring rear clutch pressure plate
16. Thrust washer bronze front clutch bore to rear clutch bore (front one of two, see No. 23)
17. Retaining ring rear clutch release spring
18. Rear clutch release spring
19. Seal ring piston outer
20. Drum of rear clutch and secondary sun gear
21. Pressure plate rear clutch
22. Steel plates rear clutch
22A. Copper plates rear clutch
23. Thrust washer steel front clutch bore to rear clutch bore (rear one of two, see No. 16)
24. Retainer rear clutch release spring
25. Piston rear clutch
26. Seal ring piston inner
27. Oil seal rings front clutch
28. Oil seal rings rear clutch
29. Primary sun gear and shaft
30. Oil seal rings to output shaft
31. Planetary carrier assembly
32. The selective thrust washer planetary carrier to ring gear (see Par. 7)
33. Ring gear and output shaft
34. Thrust washer secondary sun gear to primary sun gear
35. Thrust washer primary sun gear to planetary carrier
36. Key rear oil pump drive
37. Thrust washer rear oil pump to ring gear
38. Governor body side plate and bolt
39. Governor body and bolt and counterweighted sleeve
40. Retaining ring governor sleeve to shaft
41. Oil seal rings fluid distributor sleeve
42. Extension housing
43. Ball governor drive
44. Spacer center tube of fluid distributor
45. Tubes fluid distributor
46. Fluid distributor body
47. Fluid distributor sleeve
48. Speedometer drive gear and drive ball
49. Retaining ring drive gear to shaft

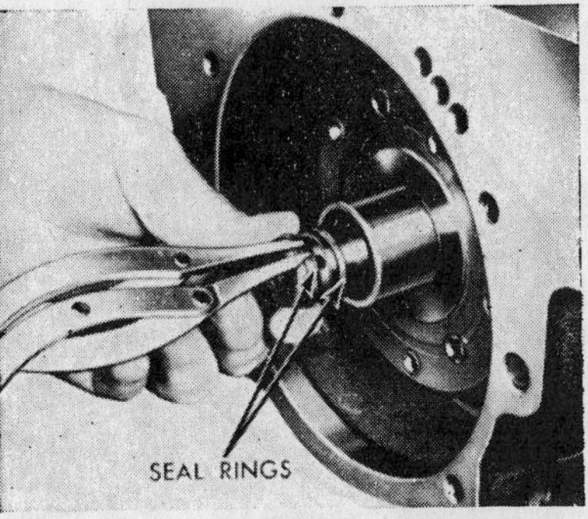

Fig. 67—Remove seal rings from rear end of primary sun gear shaft

Fig. 68—Remove selector thrust washer from hub of carrier

Fig. 69—Remove planetary (pinion) carrier from case

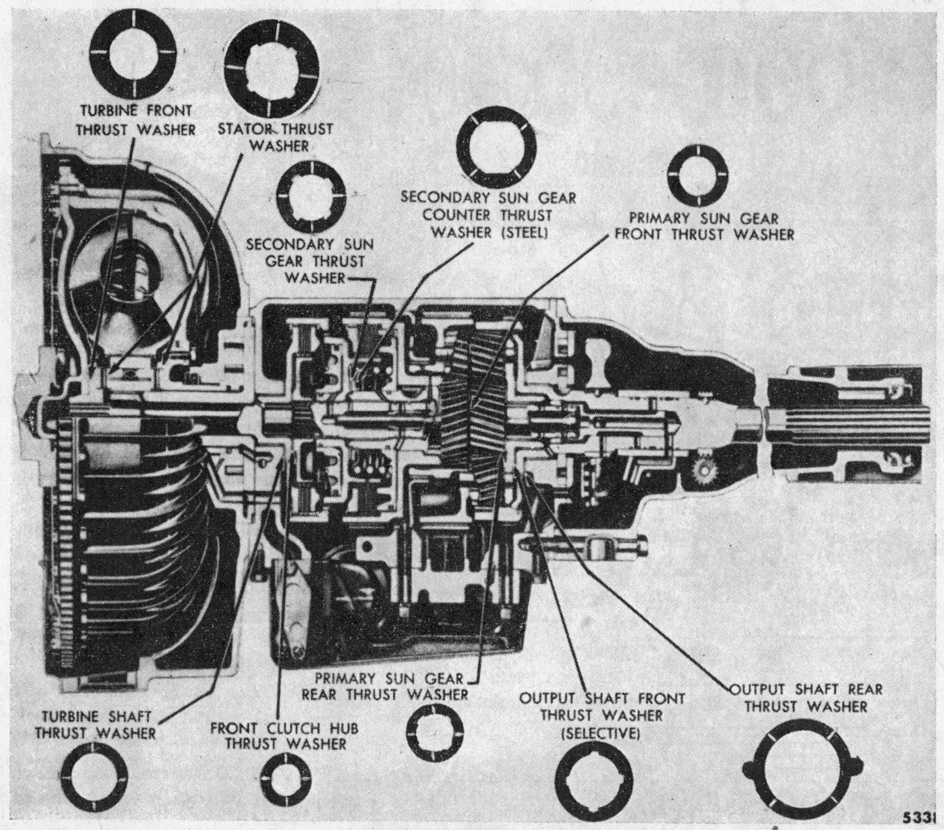

Fig. 70—Thrust washer locations

13. The Front and Rear Clutches

The transmission must be out of the car for this operation.

Remove parts as outlined in pars. 10, 11 and 12. Remove the bronze thrust washer from the primary sun gear shaft. This thrust washer rides the shaft between the primary sun gear and the front thrust surface of the planetary carrier.

Mark the rear band with reference to the side of the case so that it can be reinstalled to the same position. A new band is not sensitive to position. Remove the rear band.

Remove the center support special bolts (one on each side of the case) from the outside of the case. Remove the center support. Tapping the input shaft with a plastic hammer will facilitate this operation.

Being very careful that they do not

Fig. 71—Remove primary sun gear rear thrust washer

Fig. 72—Mark rear band with reference to side of case

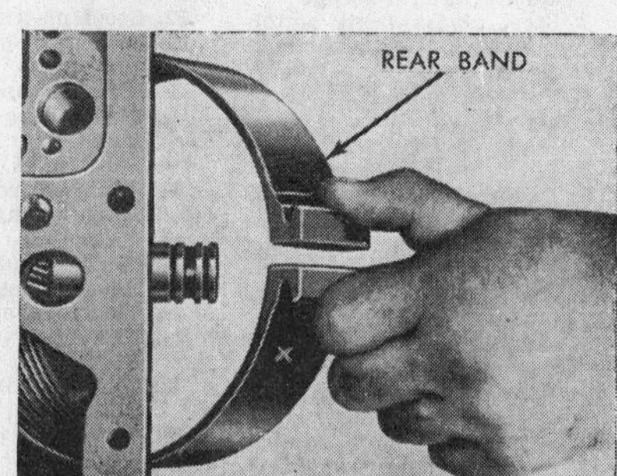

Fig. 73—Remove rear band from case

become separated, remove the front and rear clutch assemblies as a unit. Remove the front band from the case. Remove the thrust washer which rides the input (turbine) shaft between the front clutch and the case.

Being careful not to rock the assembly and so damage the seal rings, lift the front clutch assembly from the primary sun gear shaft. Remove the bronze and steel thrust washers which ride the primary sun gear shaft between the two clutches.

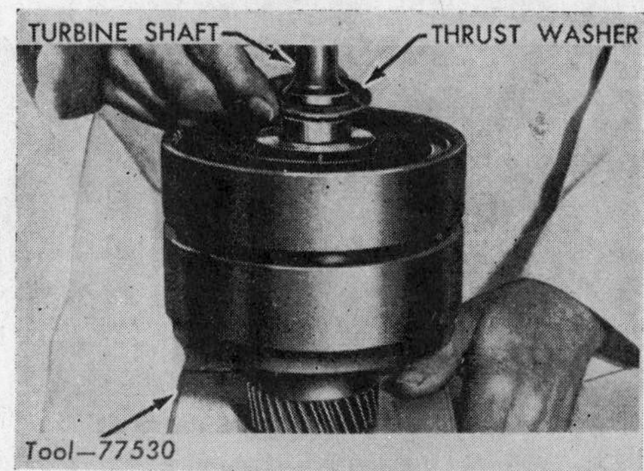

Fig. 77—Remove thrust washer from input (turbine) shaft

Fig. 74—Remove bolts

Being careful not to rock the assembly and so damage the seal rings, lift the rear clutch assembly from the primary sun gear shaft. Remove the thrust washer which rides the primary sun gear shaft between the secondary sun gear at the rear of the rear clutch and the primary sun gear which is part of the shaft.

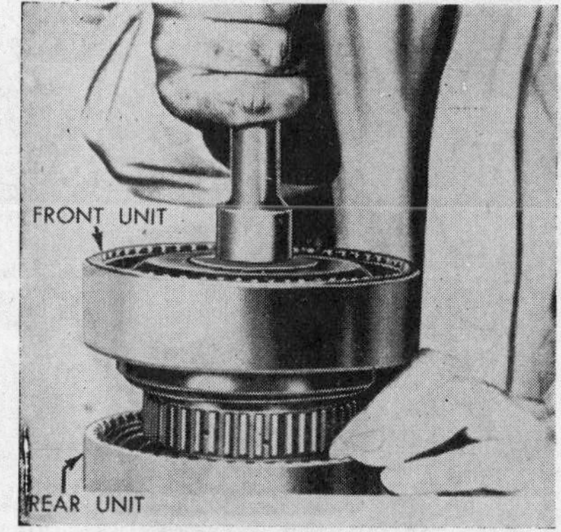

Fig. 78—Remove front clutch unit

Fig. 75—Remove center support

Fig. 76—Remove clutch assemblies as a unit

Fig. 79—Remove bronze and steel thrust washers

Fig. 80—Remove rear clutch unit

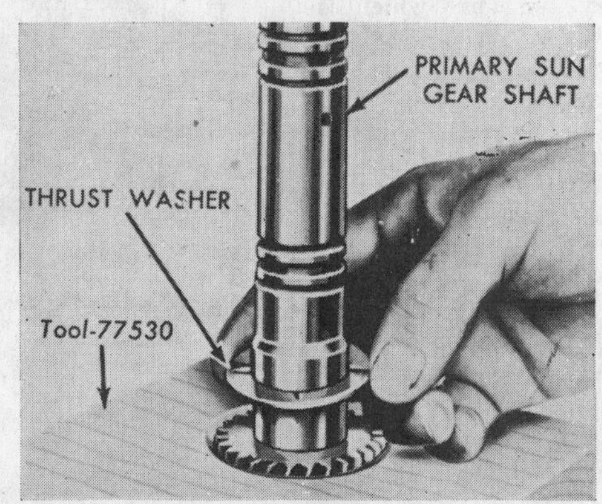

Fig. 81—Remove primary sun gear front thrust washer

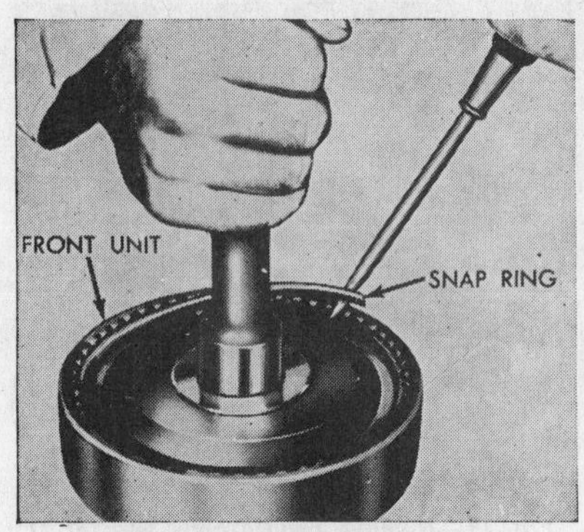

Fig. 82—Remove snap ring

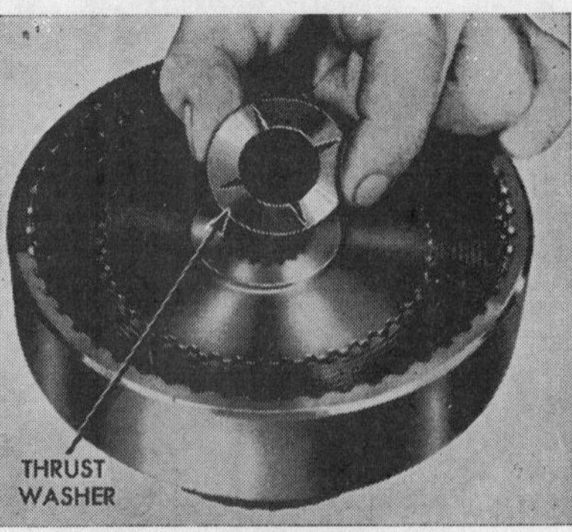

Fig. 83—Remove thrust washer

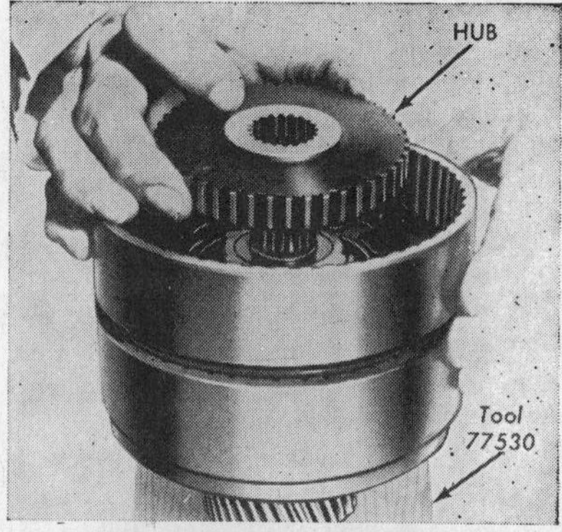

Fig. 84—Remove front clutch hub

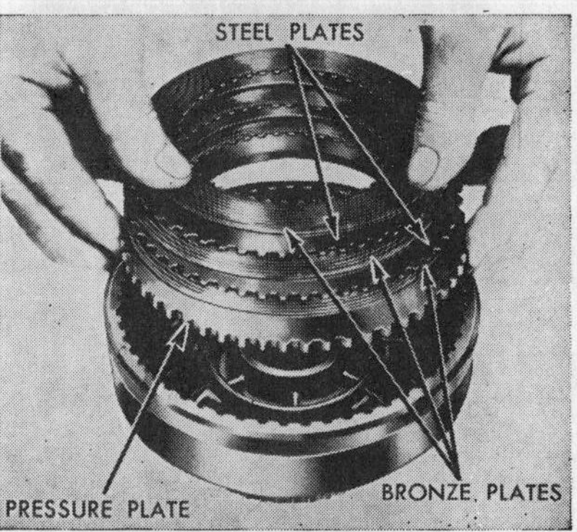

Fig. 85—Remove front clutch plates

THE FRONT CLUTCH

Remove the snap ring and the input (turbine) shaft and flange assembly. Remove the bronze thrust washer and the clutch hub on which it rides. Remove: Three internally splined bronze plates, Two externally splined flat steel plates, One externally splined pressure plate.

While compressing the outer edge of the clutch spring, remove the snap ring. Release the pressure and remove the disc type clutch spring. Note that its outer edge is installed higher than its center edge.

Use air pressure and a piece of 3/16" tubing to blow the clutch piston out of the drum. Remove the inner and outer clutch piston seals.

Inspect all the parts for burrs and other signs of wear. Check that all the clutch plates are flat. Make sure that the release spring is neither distorted nor cracked.

Fig. 86—Remove clutch release spring retaining ring

Fig. 87—Remove front clutch release spring

Reinstall the piston seals and the piston. Be sure that the steel bearing ring for the release spring is in place on the piston. Install the release spring, the outer diameter of the spring to be installed is higher than the center diameter so that the center bears against the piston. Compress the spring and install the snap ring to hold it, be sure the ring is properly seated.

Install the drum onto the primary sun gear shaft to which the rear clutch has already been assembled. Be careful not to break the seal rings while settling the drum into place. A steel and a bronze thrust washer ride the primary sun gear shaft between the two clutch assemblies.

Install the front clutch hub with the deep counterbore toward the primary sun gear. Install the bronze thrust washer onto the clutch hub. Install the pressure plate flat side out.

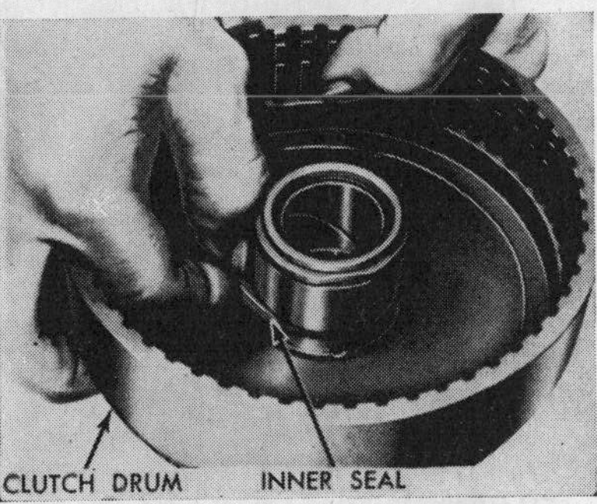

Fig. 88—Install front clutch piston inner seal

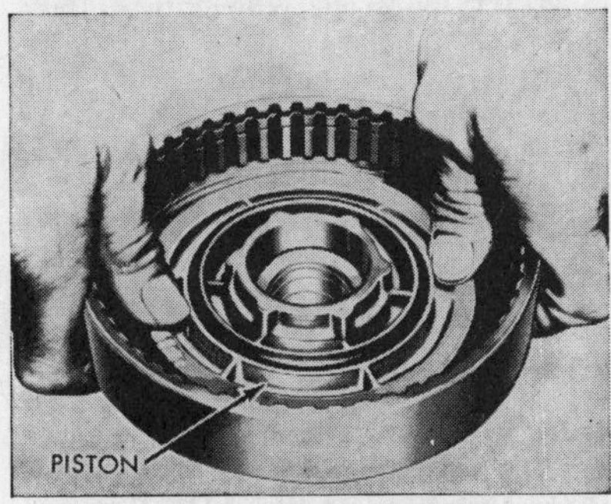

Fig. 89—Install piston

Coat the clutch plates with transmission fluid Type A and install them in the drum alternating a bronze and a steel, starting with a bronze plate.

Install the input shaft and flange assembly. Make sure the retaining snap ring is firmly seated in its groove.

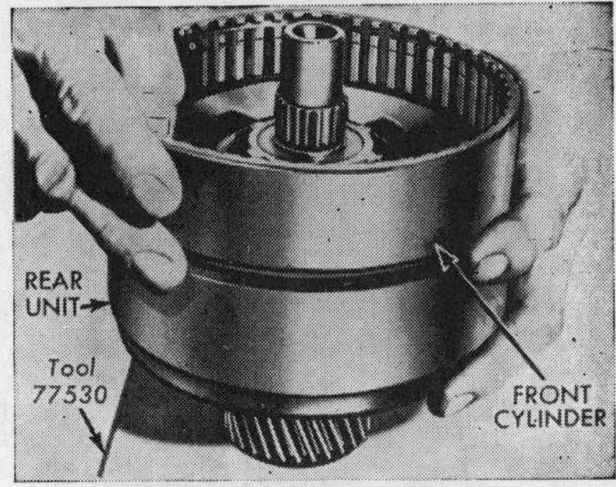

Fig. 90—Install clutch drum on to primary sun gear shaft

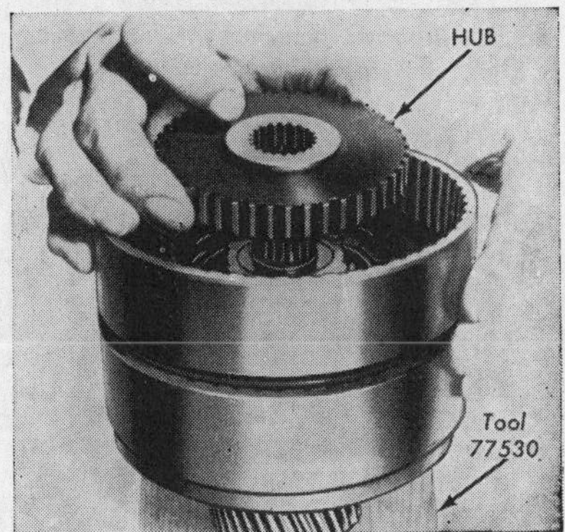

Fig. 91—Install front clutch hub

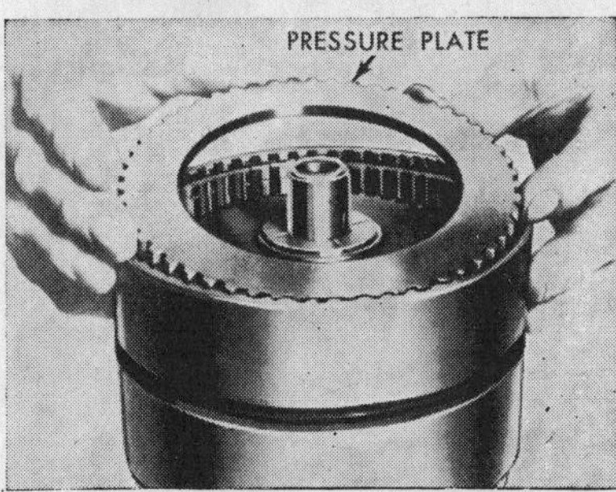

Fig. 92—Install pressure plate

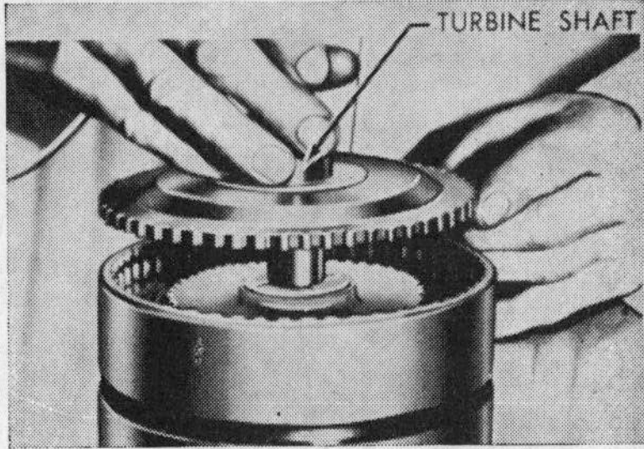

Fig. 93—Install front clutch drive flange

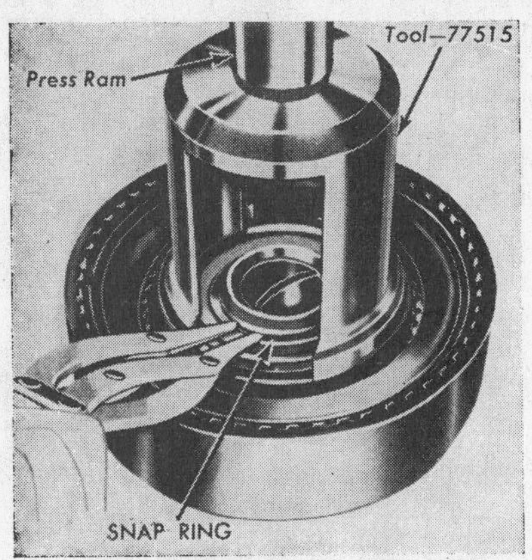

Fig. 94—Remove rear clutch release spring retaining ring

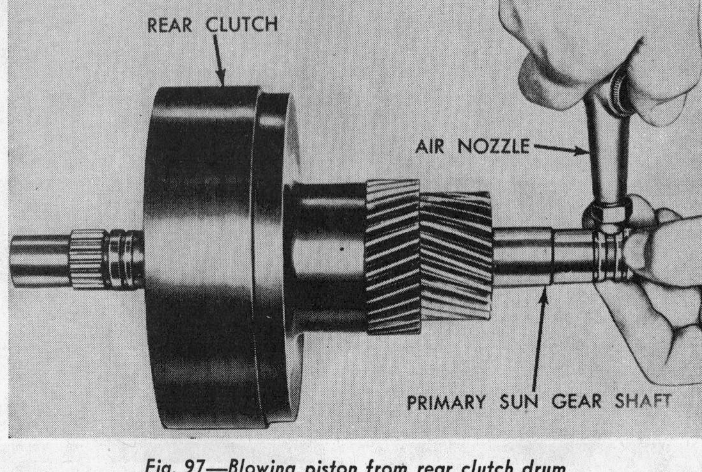

Fig. 97—Blowing piston from rear clutch drum

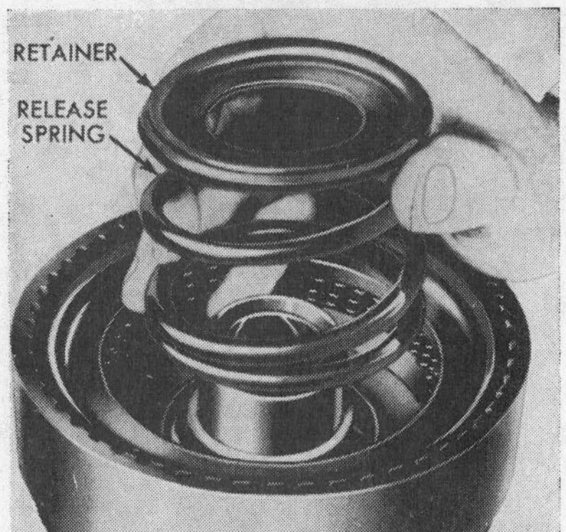

Fig. 95—Remove retainer and spring

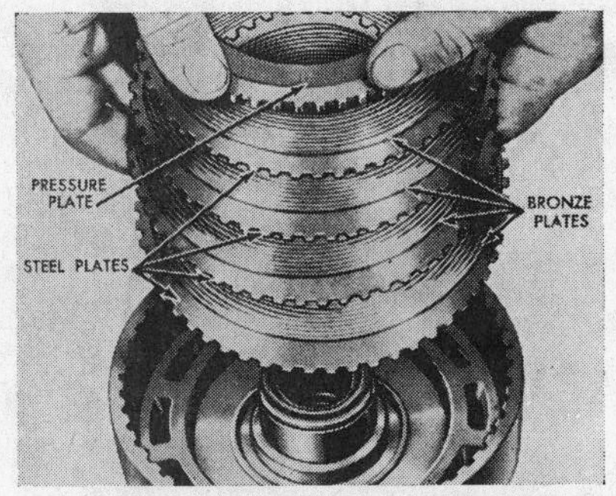

Fig. 98—Remove rear clutch plates

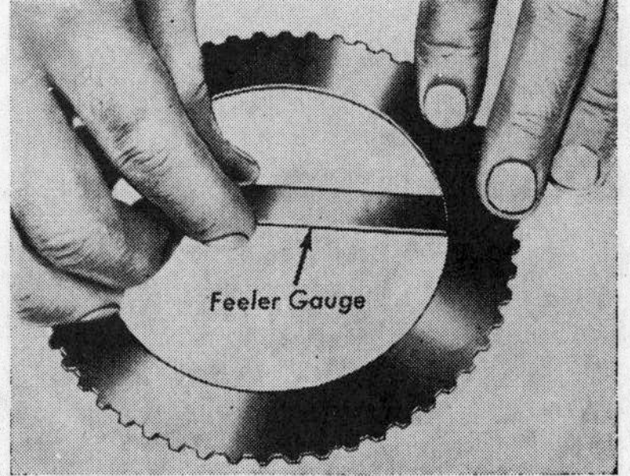

Fig. 99—Check (dish) coning of rear clutch steel plates

SNAP RING

REAR UNIT

Fig. 96—Remove snap ring

THE REAR CLUTCH

Use a press to compress the clutch spring and remove the snap ring. Remove the clutch spring retainer and the spring. Remove the clutch pressure plate retaining ring and the plate. Remove: Four bronze internally splined plates, Four steel externally splined and dished plates. Note that these plates are not interchangeable with those of the front clutch.

Use air pressure and a piece of 3/16″ tubing to blow the clutch piston out of the drum. Take care that it does not fly out.

Inspect all parts for burrs, signs of wear, and distortion. Blow out all fluid passages. Check that the inside diameter of the steel plates is .010″ higher than the outside diameter. This coning or dish is necessary for proper release of the clutch.

Install new clutch inner and outer piston seals. Coat the piston with fluid and ease it into the drum.

Coat the clutch plates with fluid and replace them in the drum. Alternate a steel plate and then a bronze plate, start with a steel plate. Install the steel plates so that the center diameter is higher than the outer diameter. In other words the dish of all the steel plates must be in the same direction and that is toward the rear.

Install the pressure plate with the bearing surface down against the plates and install the snap ring carefully into its groove. Using a press install the clutch release spring, spring retainer, and retaining snap ring. Be sure the ring is fully seated.

ASSEMBLY TO SHAFT AND CASE

Install a bronze thrust washer against the front thrust face of the primary sun gear. Check the front and rear clutch oil seal rings which are in grooves in the primary sun gear shaft. Clearance between their ends should be .002″-.009″.

Install the assembled rear clutch onto the primary sun gear shaft taking care not to injure the seal rings as the unit is settled into place. Install a steel and then a bronze thrust washer over the shaft and into place on the front thrust surface of the rear clutch.

Assemble the front clutch assembly onto the shaft. Wiggle the two clutch assemblies so that the rear clutch hub, which is part of the front clutch drum, settles into contact with the internally splined bronze plates of the rear clutch. Be careful not to break the seal rings.

With both clutch assemblies in place on the primary sun gear shaft install the front clutch to case thrust washer onto the input shaft.

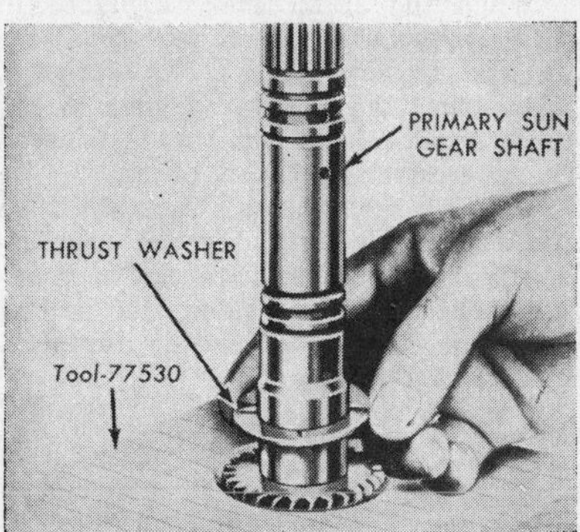

Fig. 100—Install primary sun gear front thrust washer

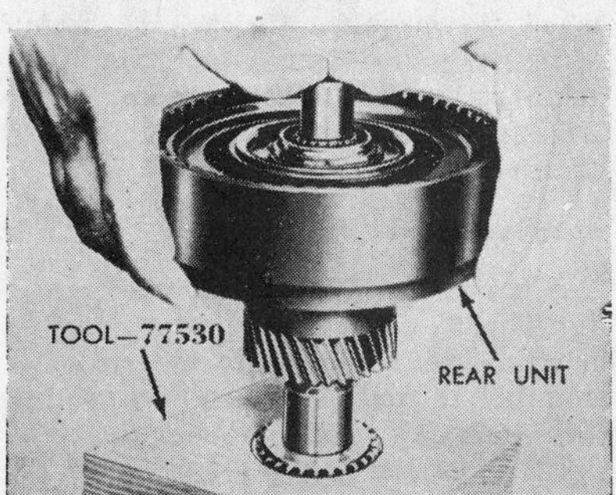

Fig. 101—Install rear clutch unit on primary sun gear shaft

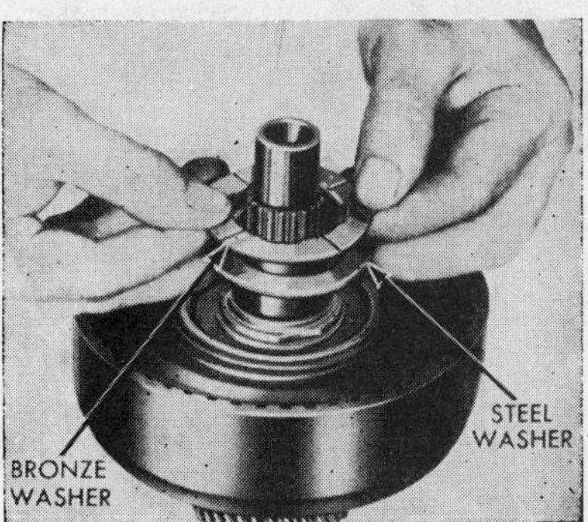

Fig. 102—Install bronze and steel thrust washer

Install the front band so that the anchor flange and the anchor coincide. Install the front and rear clutches, the primary sun gear shaft, and the thrust washers as explained, as a complete assembly into the case from the rear.

Install the center support into the case, aligning it so that the right hand special bolt may be installed from outside the case. Install the left hand special bolt into the center support from outside the case. Tighten the two to 28-32 ft lbs.

Install the rear band, aligning the match marks made at disassembly.

Install the bronze thrust washer against the rear face of the primary

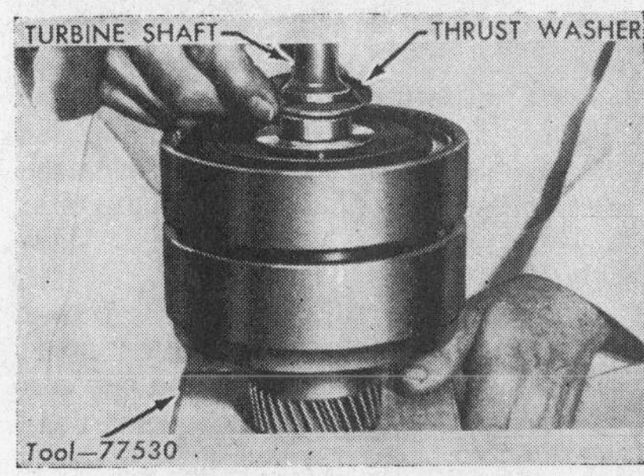

Fig. 103—Install front clutch to case

sun gear. Install the planetary carrier-assembly positioning the band over the drum while meshing the pinions with the two sun gears.

Finish assembly and installation as outlined in pars. 10, 11, and 12.

Fig. 104—Install clutch units as an assembly

Fig. 105—Install center support

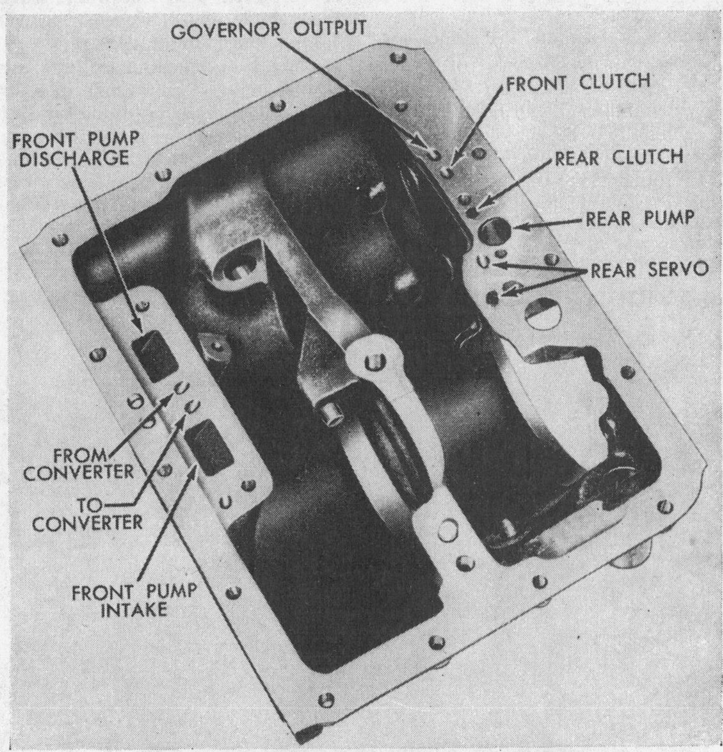

Fig. 106—Transmission case showing fluid passages

CHRYSLER CORP.—SEMI-AUTOMATIC TRANSMISSION

SEMI-AUTOMATIC TRANSMISSION

The Chrysler Corporation's hydraulically actuated semi-automatic transmission, known technically as the M-6 transmission, is actually a four-speed constant mesh gear type transmission having a manual selection between two gears and an automatic selection between two gears.

The transmission provides two ranges, each range having two speeds.

Note: In order to avoid confusion this text will refer to the ranges of the transmission as "Low" and "Drive." The speeds of the transmission will be referred to as 1st (lowest); 2nd; 3rd and 4th (highest).

Operation of the M-6 Semi-Automatic

As stated earlier, the M-6 is a four-speed, constant mesh gear type transmission having two manually selective ranges each composed of two automatically selected gears.

The automatic selection is by electrically controlled and directed oil pressures.

In order to explain the functions clearly the mechanical part will be explained, ignoring the electrical functions which actuate the mechanism.

Mechanically, the major difference between the M-6 and any standard 3-speed transmission is the method of driving the countershaft cluster gear.

The countershaft cluster driving gear (the large gear at the front end of the cluster) is mounted on the hub of the cluster and is connected to it by means of free wheeling rollers (technically known as an overrunning clutch) which are contained in a bronze cage. (The purpose of the cage will be explained a little further on.)

As with any overrunning clutch, the large gear will drive the cluster (through the clutch) at any time when the speed of the large gear tends to be greater than the speed of the cluster. If the speed of the cluster becomes greater than the speed of the large driving gear, the cluster will "overrun" the drive gear. In other words, the gear can drive the cluster but the cluster cannot drive the gear.

Note: The large driving gear on the cluster is driven directly from the transmission main drive pinion so that it never reverses its direction of rotation.

The speed of the large driving gear tends to be greater than cluster speed when the engine is pulling the car and the transmission is in 1st gear (Low range, low gear); 3rd gear (Drive range, low gear) and Reverse gear. If the transmission is in any of these gears the car will free wheel whenever the vehicle speed exceeds the relative engine speed for that gear.

The free wheeling rollers are, as stated before, contained in a bronze cage. The cage is fitted with a cam which engages a shift sleeve on the clusters. Whenever the transmission shifts up into 2nd gear (low range) or 4th gear (drive range) the shift sleeve on the cluster moves the cage, forcing the free wheel rollers off the overrunning clutch cams, causing complete disengagement of the drive gear.

This cuts down wear and friction losses at the overrunning clutch.

Once it is understood how the countershaft cluster on the M-6 differs from conventional transmissions the power flow of the M-6 is easily followed.

DRIVE RANGE

When the shift lever is placed in Drive range, the manual selector sleeve in the transmission shifts forward, connecting the 3rd speed gear to the main shaft. The direct speed sleeve is in the rearward position, idling.

Power is then through the main drive pinion (clutch shaft) to the countershaft drive gear through the overrunning clutch to the cluster. The second gear on the cluster drives the main shaft 3rd speed gear.

UPSHIFT, DRIVE RANGE

When the car speed is sufficient to break the governor contacts, the transmission automatically upshifts (under condition which will be explained under "Hydraulic Operation"). The direct speed sleeve shifts forward (carrying with it the sleeve on the cluster), connecting the main drive pinion to the 3rd speed gear directly. The cluster gear overruns its drive gear.

LOW RANGE

When the shift lever under the steering wheel is placed in low range, the manual selector lever in the transmission is shifted backward, connecting the 1st speed gear to the main shaft.

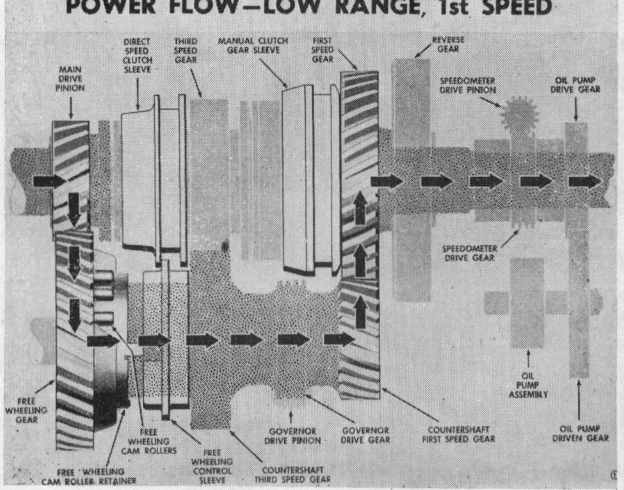

POWER FLOW—LOW RANGE, 1st SPEED

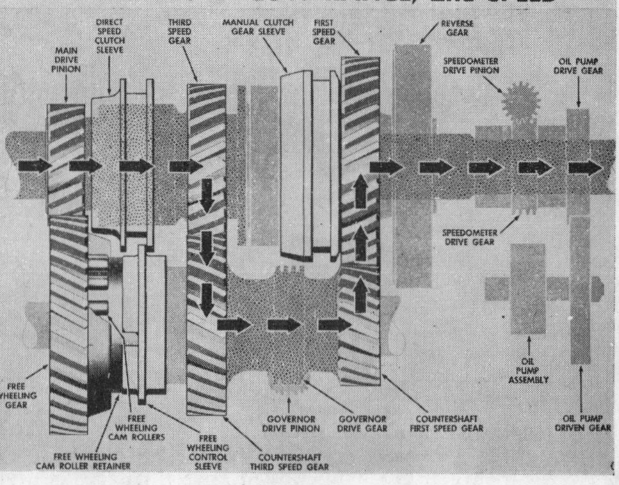

POWER FLOW—LOW RANGE, 2nd SPEED

The direct speed sleeve is in the rearward position, idling.

Power is then through the main drive pinion to the countershaft drive gear, through the overrunning clutch to the cluster, from the cluster to the 1st speed gear on the main shaft.

UPSHIFT, LOW RANGE

When the transmission upshifts in Low range the direct speed sleeve slides forward, connecting the main drive pinion directly to the 3rd speed gear on the main shaft. Power is then through the main drive pinion, to the 3rd speed gear on the main shaft to the cluster, to the small gear on the cluster, to the 1st gear on the main shaft and out through the tail shaft.

The cluster is overrunning its drive gear.

Hydraulic-Electrical Function

The governor contact points are normally in the contacting position, completing an electrical circuit which energizes a solenoid, causing the plunger of the solenoid to close off an oil control valve.

When the car is in motion the countershaft speeds up, driving the governor at increased speed until the point is reached where the centrifugal weights in the governor break the electrical circuit, which immediately de-energizes the solenoid. The solenoid plunger return spring pulls the plunger away from the hydraulic valve, permitting the oil from the transmission pump to enter the shift cylinder, forcing the shift cylinder piston forward to the end of the cylinder.

The piston is connected by a spring to the shift rod which moves the direct speed clutch sleeve.

At this point the sleeve would shift forward if it were not for the torque on the gears.

The torque is usually great enough to prevent the sleeve from shifting forward until the driver momentarily takes his foot off the accelerator, releasing the torque and permitting the spring, which has been loaded by the hydraulic piston, to push the direct speed clutch sleeve forward, engaging the main drive pinion to the 3rd speed gear on the transmission main shaft.

In other words, the actual shifting of the direct speed clutch sleeve is not by hydraulic pressure but rather by spring pressure which was created by moving the hydraulic piston forward, loading the spring.

DOWNSHIFT

Whenever the car slows down to below governor speed (approximately 11 mph in Drive range) the governor contact points "make" and the solenoid is energized, closing off the oil pressure from the shift piston and permitting the oil which is already at the piston to dump back into the case.

The piston return spring immediately forces the piston back to the release position, carrying with it the Direct speed clutch sleeve.

The downshift operates in exactly the same manner whether the car is in Drive or low range, the only difference being that if the car is in Low range the shift point is at approximately three mph. This is accomplished by driving the governor from the countershaft rather than driving it from the main shaft.

KICKDOWN

At speeds up to approximately 35-40 mph, if the driver wishes to downshift in order to provide torque for rapid acceleration, the accelerator pedal is depressed to the wide open position which closes the switch on the carburetor known as the kickdown switch.

When this switch is closed it completes a circuit through the solenoid, energizing the solenoid and permitting the oil to dump back into the sump, relieving the pressure from the shift piston.

However, because the car is accelerating, the torque against the gears is so high that the return spring is hardly strong enough to make the shift sleeve slide off the gears. Therefore another switch, known as the ignition interrupter switch, is added to momentarily ground the ignition which provides a momentary reversal of torque, permitting the sleeve to shift into the 3rd speed.

In other words, the kickdown switch in effect bypasses the governor and the interruptor switch momentarily kills the ignition to permit the sleeve to move.

While it is true that the ignition interrupter switch operates on any downshift, its essential function is to momentarily interrupt the ignition when downshifting under high torque.

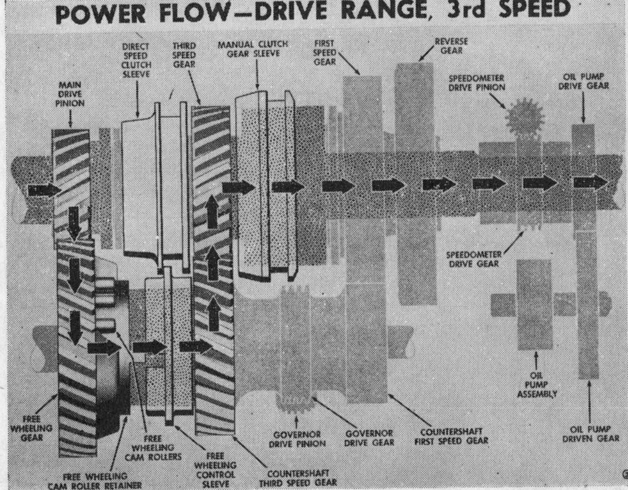

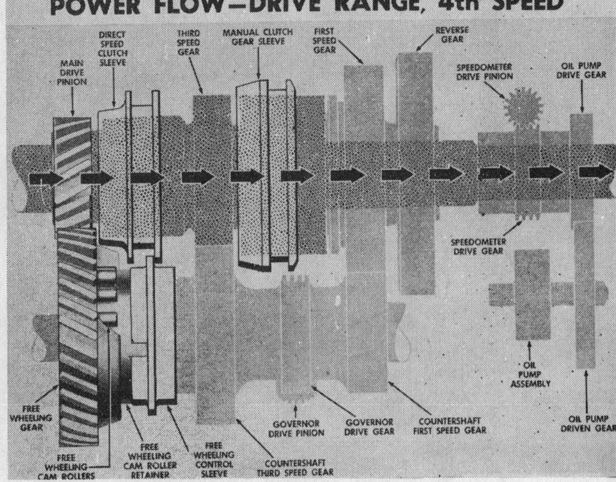

CHRYSLER CORP.—SEMI-AUTOMATIC TRANSMISSION

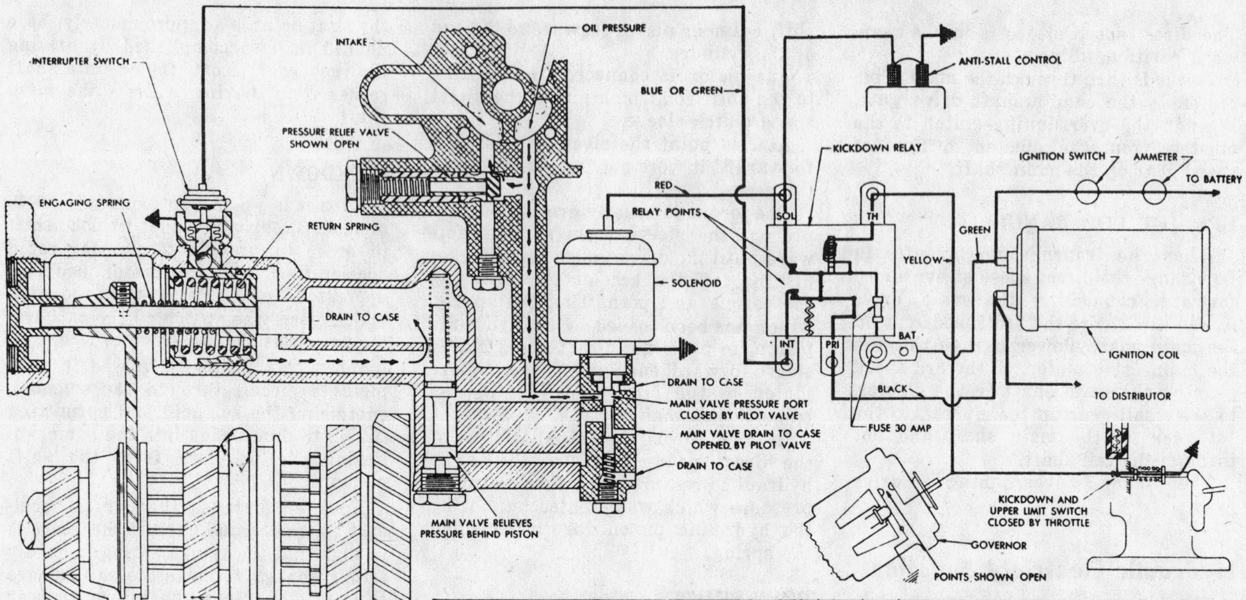

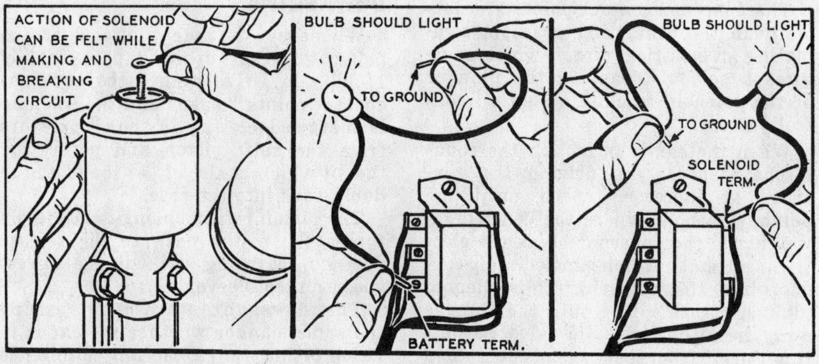

Tests made with ignition on—engine not running—up to 1948

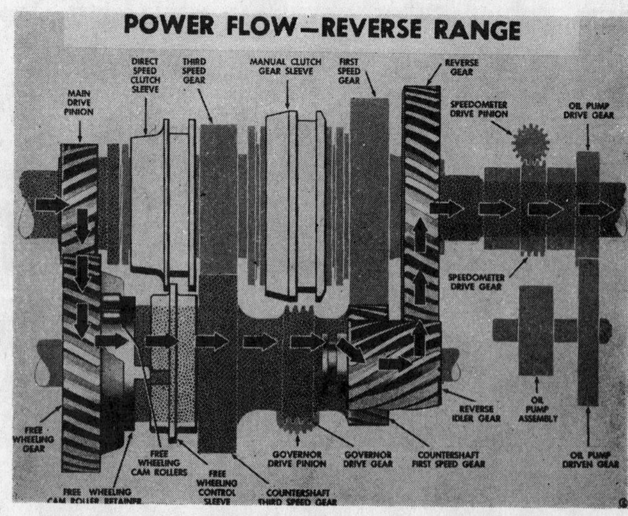

TROUBLE SHOOTING THE ELECTRICAL CIRCUITS

TEST LAMP

The most accurate way to shoot electrical troubles is to use meters. However, for all normal trouble shooting, a home-made test lamp will serve as well.

Make the test lamp using a double contact socket fitted with a double contact 3-candlepower bulb. Something like the one in the sketch will do fine.

The Relay

MODELS UP TO 1948

Note: No relay is used on models after 1948.

The relay is located on the engine side of the firewall on the left side, OR

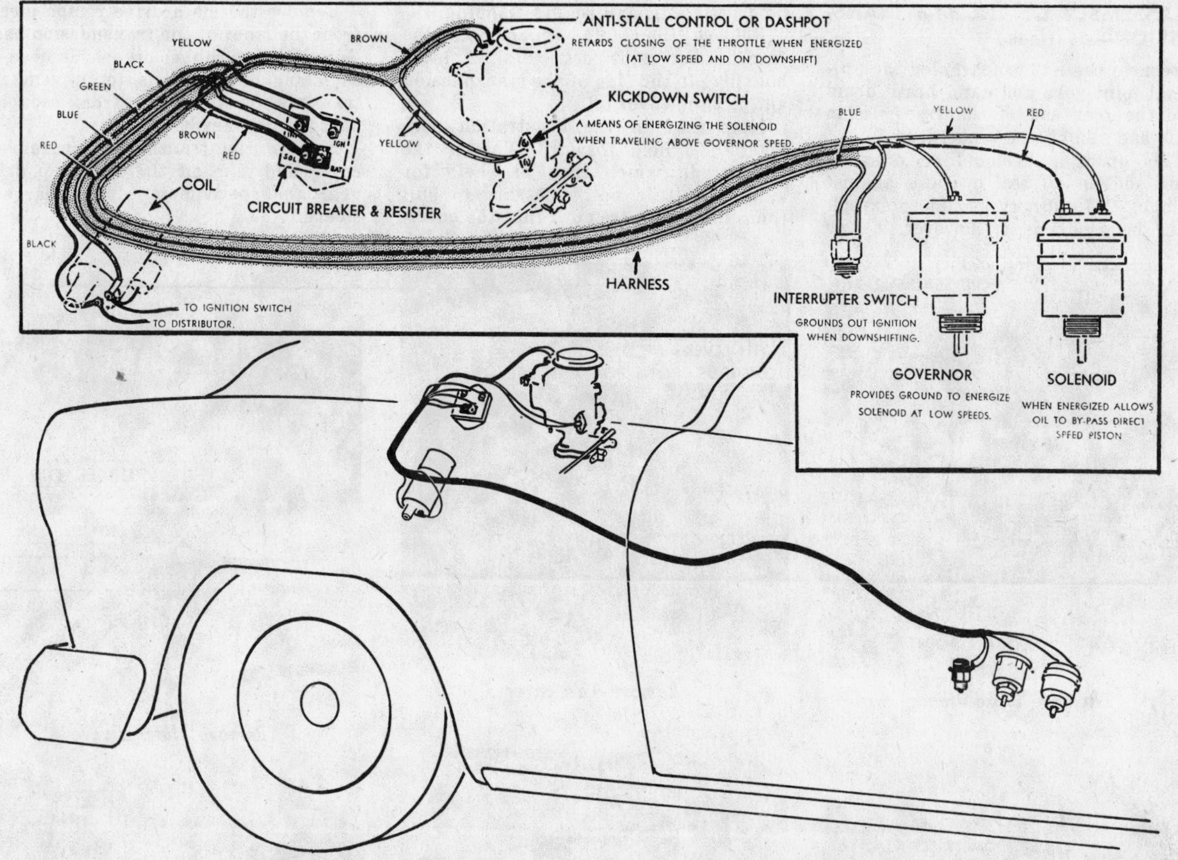

Arrangement of the electrical wiring on the M-6 transmission

on the engine side of the fender panel on the left side.

It can be located readily by looking under the hood of the left side of the engine. It will be in one or the other of the two places, its location varied by body styles.

Before making any tests on the relay, first make sure that the fuse is in good condition and cleanly mounted. Much time has been lost checking electrical circuits only to find that the main fuse has blown through some accident or mishap. A 30 ampere fuse is used on the relay.

Use the test lamp as shown in the accompanying illustrations.

DISASSEMBLY OF THE M-6 TRANSMISSION

Remove the transmission from the car and set it up on a workbench. It is not necessary to use any special clamping devices to hold the transmission since it is perhaps better to have it free to turn over and shift so that if it is laid on a substantial bench this will be sufficient.

Remove the interrupter switch, the governor, the solenoid, and the shuttle valve.

The solenoid valve housing can be removed if it seems to be dirty or in need of cleaning or servicing. Otherwise it is not necessary to remove the solenoid valve housing when servicing the transmission.

Remove interrupter switch, governor and solenoid

DISASSEMBLY OF THE M-6 TRANSMISSION—*continued*

Remove the nut which holds the universal joint yoke and hand brake drum onto the rear end of the transmission shaft and pull off the brake drum.

This drum is mounted on a spline shaft and an oil seal operates against its hub. No difficulty should be experienced in removing it; however, it may be a little stiff and require tapping.

Remove the bolts which hold the transmission side cover (shift lever housing) to the side of the transmission and lift the cover off.

Note that in the illustration both levers are held forward. This is the position in which they are held for assembly. It is not necessary to pull them forward to remove the side cover.

Remove the main drive pinion sleeve from the front of the transmission case. Notice that a rubber oil seal is used on each one of the bolts to prevent the transmission lubricant from escaping past the bolt heads.

Remove the transmission case rear cover and take off the oil pump drive gear and speedometer drive gear and sleeve.

Remove brake drum

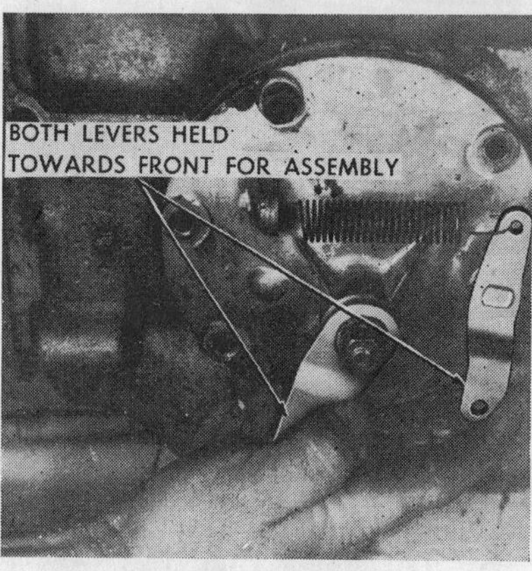

Remove side cover

Remove clutch sleeve

Take off the rear cover

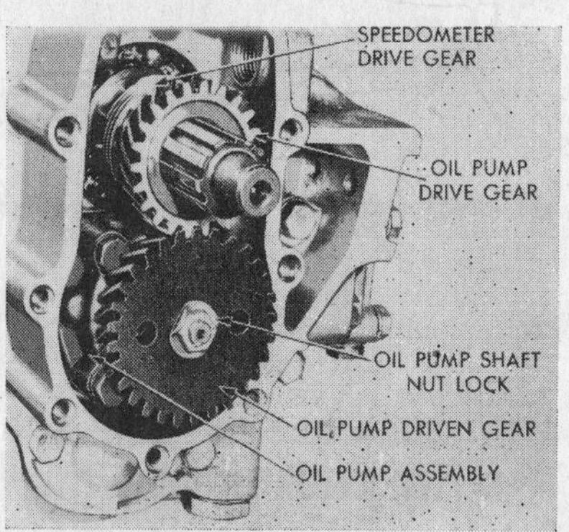

Position of oil pump gears before removal

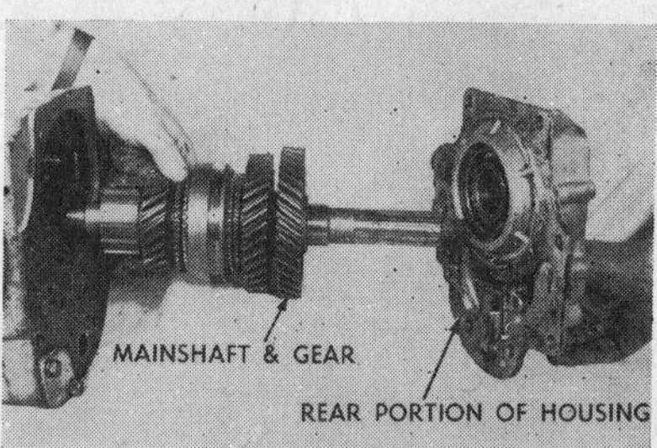

Take off rear cover and mainshaft assemblies

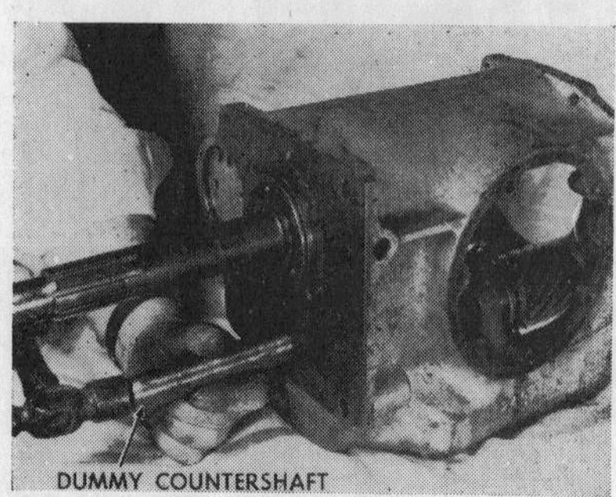

Drive out countershaft

Remove direct speed sleeve

Position of thrust washers on countershaft cluster

Remove the rear section of the transmission case so that the countershaft can be driven out. The countershaft is driven out through the rear of the case using a dummy shaft which is designed to be shorter than the inside of the case so that the countershaft cluster will drop to the bottom of the case, making it easier to take out the main shaft gear assembly.

After the main shaft has been removed, slip out the direct drive sleeve from the side of the case.

In order to take the countershaft out of the case, it is necessary to raise it up slightly so that the thrust washers can be removed with the cluster still in the case.

This is one of the points to remember on reassembly. The cluster is placed in the case and afterwards the two thrust washers are pushed in in back of the cluster. Great difficulty is experienced trying to get the countershaft cluster into place with the thrust washers mounted on the end of the dummy shaft.

Pull the main drive gear out of the front of the case and then, using a pulling device, pull out the idler gear shaft.

Remove the snap ring which holds the cover of the front of the hydraulic shift piston.

Take out the access plug from the side of the case.

Reach through the access plug hole in the side of the case and remove the screw which holds the shift fork to the hydraulic shift shaft.

The shift fork can then be slid off the end of the shaft.

Down in the bottom of the hole from which the shaft was removed there is a snap ring which holds the hydraulic shift piston in place. Remove the snap ring to get the piston out.

All gears and washers should be given the usual examination to determine if they are in good condition.

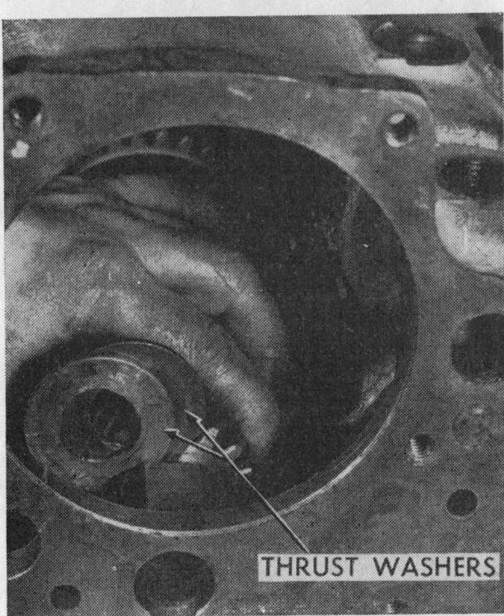

Cluster thrust washers being lifted out

Using puller, remove idler shaft

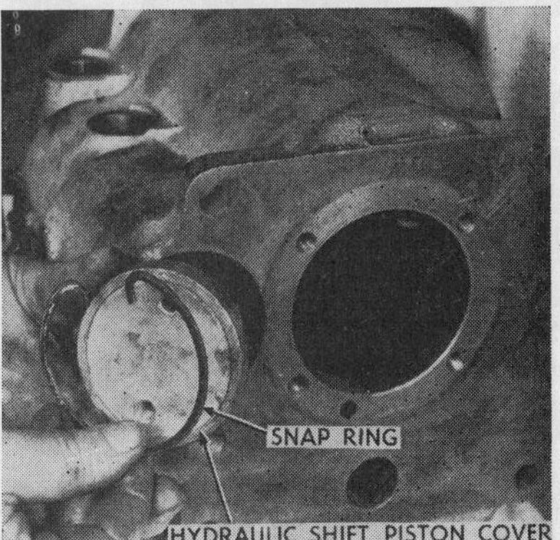

Remove hydraulic shift piston snap ring

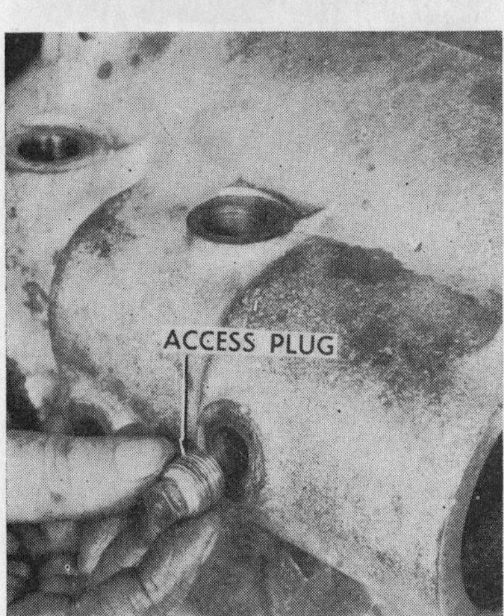

Take out shift rail access plug

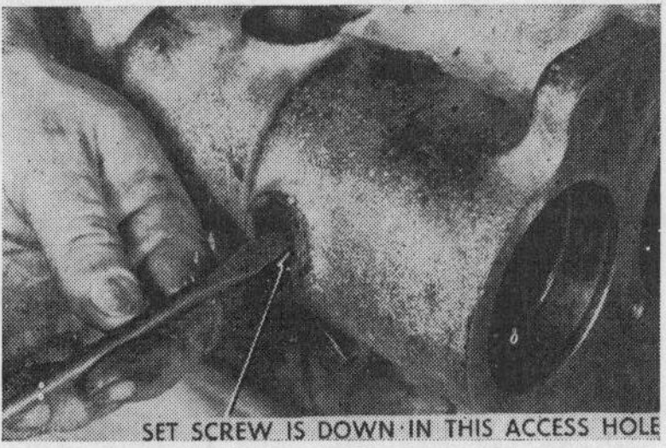

Remove the shift rail set screw

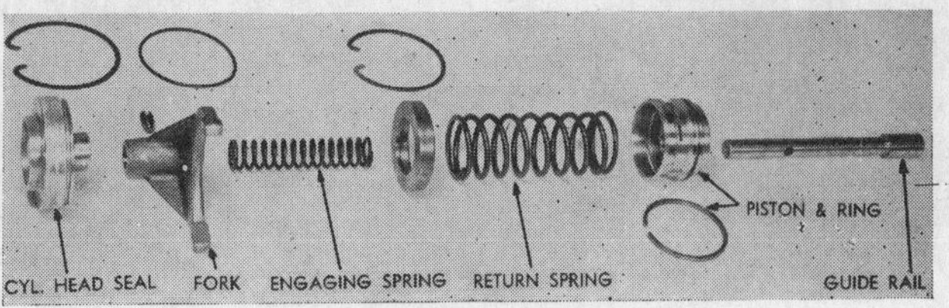

Exploded view of the hydraulic shift parts

Disassembly of the Main Shaft Gears

All of the main shaft gears are held in place by a single snap ring at the front end of the main shaft.

Refer to the accompanying illustrations which show the snap ring being removed and the subsequent parts which are taken off after removing the snap ring.

Disassembly of the Countershaft Cluster

Actually the cluster assembly with its freewheel cage rolls and gear will come apart as soon as it is removed from the case. As a matter of fact it requires a little handling to keep it together.

Remove main shaft snap ring

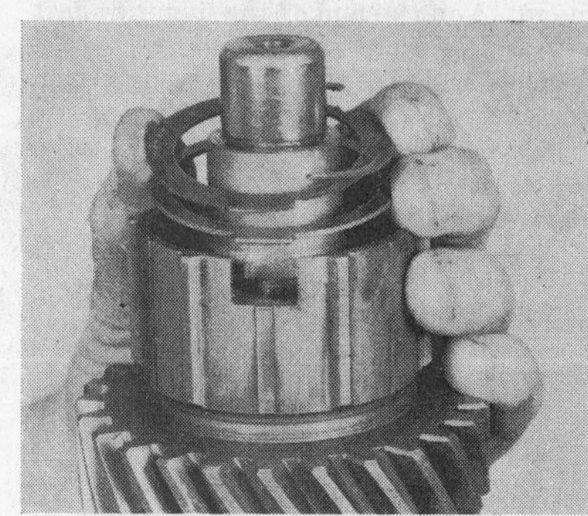

Lift out second speed thrust washers

Take out second speed thrust bearings

Lift out second speed gear

Remove 1st—2nd shift collar

Lift off countershaft drive gear

Remove free wheeling rollers

Exploded view of the main shaft assembly shift rails

It is actually held together in service by the two butt ends of the case and the thrust washers which maintain it at the proper clearance.

REASSEMBLY OF THE M-6 TRANSMISSION

The M-6 transmission is reassembled in the reverse order of disassembly. Only a few things must be born in mind when reassembling the M-6 and they are as follows:

Refer to the illustration showing the alignment of the second speed gear with the direct speed clutch. Notice that the splines in the direct sleeve clutch are arranged in groups of three. It is absolutely essential that the male spline on the third speed gear hub mesh with the center of the three female splines in the sleeve. It will go together the opposite way but will not function.

Another thing to bear in mind is the fact that the countershaft cluster must be entered into the case without the thrust washers in place. The thrust washers are slid into place after the cluster is in the case.

Refer to the illustration showing the gears being positioned to receive the side cover on reassembly.

This position has been found to be the easiest when installing the cover by pulling both levers toward the back.

Assembly illustrations accompany this text which show the exact relative position of each gear to each of the other gears.

Caution: After the unit has been assembled and buttoned up it is essential that the proper grade of lubricant be used in this transmission.

The Chrysler Corp. recommends that the top quality 10-W engine oil be used for operation down to zero temperature. Below zero temperature Chrysler Corp. recommends that 10% kerosene be added to 10-W engine oil for sub-zero operation.

For assembling, the above illustration shows the 3rd speed gear and direct drive sleeve and synchronizer removed from the case to show alignment more clearly

Alignment of direct speed sleeve shown in the case

Position shift collars as shown to reassemble cover

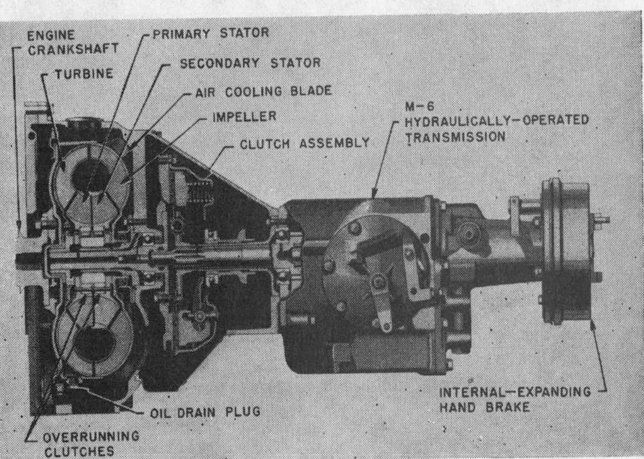

Section view of the torque converter used with the "M6" transmission on 1952 and 53 models

OVERDRIVES

The overdrive, sometimes called cruising gear, is a planetary gear-overrunning clutch combination mounted at the back of the transmission.

The purpose of the overdrive is to provide a higher gear ratio between the engine and the rear driving wheels. Most overdrives have a ratio of 7:10 that is for each 7 revolutions of the engine the driveshaft turns 10 times.

Overdrives may be divided into two broad classes: the "automatic" overdrive and the "manual" overdrive.

Since automatic overdrives are the only ones used on American passenger cars built since 1940 this text will deal with the automatic type only.

The automatic type may, in its turn, be broken down into two general types: **first, the earlier** type, having a centrifically operated (mechanical) clutch pawl assembly; the later type which is still in general use, having a solenoid operated, governor controlled pawl.

Operation of the Overdrive

Early Type Having a Centrifically Operated Clutch Pawl

On the early type ovedrives the solenoid is normally in the "in" position, engaging the sun gear plate which in its turn prevented the sun gear from turning.

The "cut in" of the overdrive is determined by the overdrive pawl assembly which engaged holes in the clutch pawl sleeve at any time the shaft reached a speed of 25 mph or more.

Strictly speaking, the purpose of the solenoid on the early models was to cause the overdrive to "kick down" at speeds above 25 mph, when the throttle is opened wide.

Refer to illustration: power is delivered through the transmission shaft to the planetary gear cage. The sun gear, normally held in the locked position by the solenoid pawl, caused the pinions to "walk around" its outer surface.

Meshed to the outside of the planetary pinions is the planetary ring gear.

With the pinions "walking around" the stationary sun gear the ring gear is normally turning at a speed faster than the input shaft.

Meshed to the ring gear is the clutch overdrive pawl assembly.

When the clutch overdrive pawl assembly reaches approximately 25 mph the pawls spring outward against their return springs and engage the slots in the pawl sleeve.

In its turn the pawl sleeve is engaged to the overdrive output shaft which is connected to the universal joint and the drive shaft.

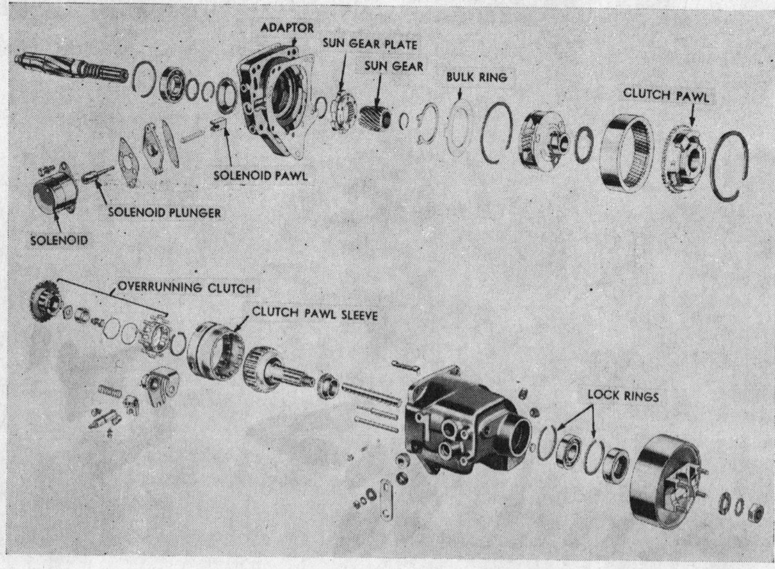

Fig. 1—Exploded View of Early Type Overdrive

Kickdown

Whenever power is needed for rapid acceleration the driver can, at his option, cause the overdrive to "kick down" into conventional drive. This is accomplished by depressing the accelerator pedal passed the wide open position. This closes a switch which energizes the solenoid, pulling the solenoid plunger out of mesh from the overdrive sun gear plate which permits the sun gear to turn, regardless of whether the clutch pawl is engaged. The transmission then drives through its overrunning clutch and the entire unit turns as one piece, the sun gear idling.

In addition to pulling the solenoid plunger out of mesh with the sun gear plate the solenoid also momentarily interrupts the ignition to take the torque off of the solenoid pawl permitting it to come out of mesh from the sun gear plate.

The balk ring, which turns by friction with the sun gear plate effectively prevents the solenoid pawl from accidentally re-engaging the sun gear plate until there has been a slight reversal of torque permitting the pawl to re-engage.

Disassembly of Overdrive

Early Type with Clutch Pawl

Remove the transmission and overdrive assembly from the vehicle.

Remove the transmission shifters and cover assembly.

Remove the bolts which hold the overdrive case to the transmission case.

Remove the pin (or set screw) which holds the overdrive shift lever into the case and slide the shift lever as far out of the case as it will come releasing the inner inside dog from the clutch pawl-sleeve.

Slide the overdrive assembly with its adapter plate and the transmission main shaft and its gears out of the transmission case in one piece.

Notice, that there are one or two screws in the adapter plate which hold the adapter plate to the overdrive case. Remove these screws and the adapter plate together with the transmission main shaft can be separated from the overdrive unit.

Pull the overdrive shift rail and rail guides out of the front of the case which will permit removing the control fork and spring.

CENTRIFICALLY OPERATED CLUTCH PAWL TYPE

Fig. 2—Removing Speedometer Drive Pinion

Fig. 3—Removing Universal Joint Flange

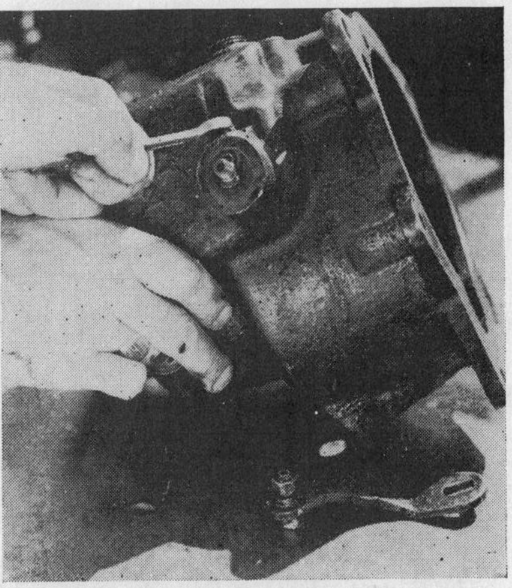

Fig. 4—Removing Shift Lever

Fig. 5—Removing Mainshaft and Clutch Pawl

Fig. 6—Removing Clutch Pawl Sleeve

Fig. 7—Removing Solenoid

Fig. 8—Removing Over-running Clutch Lock Bolt

Fig. 9—Removing Over-running Clutch

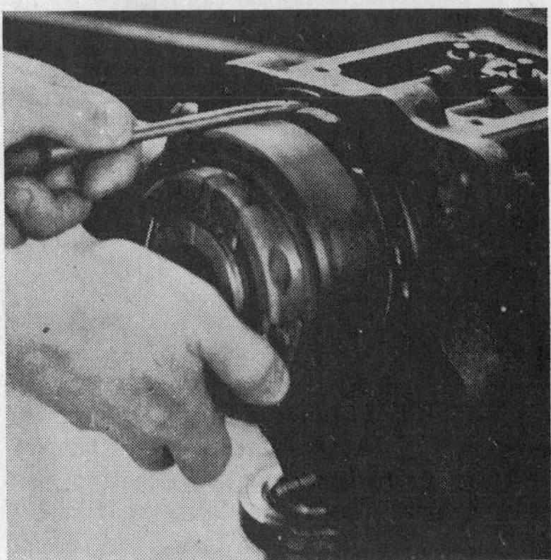

Fig. 10—Removing Clutch Pawl

CENTRIFICALLY OPERATED CLUTCH PAWL TYPE—*continued*

Fig. 11—Clutch Pawl and Pinion Assembly Removed

Fig. 12—Sun Gear Plate Lock Ring Removed

Fig. 13—Sun Gear Plate Removed

Take off the nut at the output shaft which holds the shaft to the rear bearing. Remove the lock ring which holds the rear bearing at the back of the case and tap the output shaft into the case which will separate the entire assembly as one piece.

Each of the pieces including the free wheel roller cage, and so forth, are held to the shaft with snap rings. Remove the snap rings and the parts will readily separate.

Inspection

If the overdrive has a history of noisy gears, examine all of the gears for pits, scratches, burrs or defects.

If the overdrive has a history of erratic operation then the clutch pawl assembly should be checked carefully and if necessary a new one installed and also check the sun gear lock plate and the solenoid pawl.

The sun gear lock plate and solenoid pawl will be found in the adapter plate which also carries the transmission shaft gears.

The cover plate, balk ring, sun gear and sun gear lock plate are held in the adapter plate by a single lock ring.

Examine the free wheeling rollers for pits and scratches and also the free wheeling cam and the surface inside of the large end of the output shaft where the free wheeling rollers ride. These parts should be free from nicks, burrs and scratches and should not appear rough at any point.

If a transmission has a history of not driving in reverse then examine the clutch pawl sleeve which is also the lockout.

When operating in reverse the reverse shifter rail in the transmission forces the clutch pawl sleeve to the back engaging the teeth on the outside of the free wheeling cam with the clutch pawl sleeve, the opposite end of the clutch pawl sleeve being engaged directly to the output shaft. If the transmission does not operate in reverse it means that it is not locking out properly and either the fork is slipping on the shaft or the teeth are worn or damaged.

Operation of the Governor Controlled Type Overdrive

On this type of overdrive, which is still in use on current 1953 passenger cars, the solenoid is normally in the up (released) position. The drive is then from the transmission main shaft through the overrunning clutch, directly to the overdrive output shaft.

When the speed of the car reaches that for which the governor is set the governor contact points close energizing the solenoid which causes the solenoid plunger to move downwards locking the sun gear lock plate, causing the sun gear to hold stationary. Power is then delivered through the transmission main shaft to the pinion cage. The pinions "walk around" the stationary sun gear causing the internally tooth ring gear to move at a speed faster than the transmission shaft. The ring gear is connected directly to the output shaft causing it to revolve at a speed which is faster than the input shaft. The free wheeling clutches overrun. This type of overdrive is locked out by sliding the sun gear backwards so that the teeth cut into it for the purpose engage the internal teeth in the front of the pinion cage.

When the overdrive is locked out the entire unit turns over as one piece.

Disassembly of the Governor Controlled Overdrive

Remove the transmission and overdrive assembly from the car.

Drive out the pin or set screw which holds the overdrive shift lever into the overdrive case.

Pull the shift lever out of the case as far as it will go which will release it from the shift fork.

Remove the governor, solenoid and reverse switch.

Remove the bolts which hold the overdrive case to the transmission case.

Note: On some overdrives notably Ford, Mercury and Nash the case can be removed without taking the transmission gears out. However, it is generally considered to be easier to disassemble the unit if it is first detached carrying with it the transmission main shaft and gears.

Remove the screws which hold the adapter plate to the overdrive housing

GOVERNOR CONTROLLED TYPE

and lift off the adapter plate together with the transmission main shaft and gears.

Note: On Ford and Mercury overdrives there is a lock ring which holds the ring gear into the case. This lock ring is covered by a small plate having two cap screws in it. Remove the cap screws and take off the little cover plate which will give access to the lock ring. On these models the lock ring is spread to release the ring gear.

Remove the lock ring which holds the rear bearing into the case and tap the output shaft forward into the case releasing all of the mechanism.

All internal parts of the overdrive are held in place by lock or snap rings.

On reassembly the overrunning clutch rollers are held in place by a rubber band to permit easy assembly.

Fig. 1—Removing Solenoid, Governor, and Reverse Lockout Switch

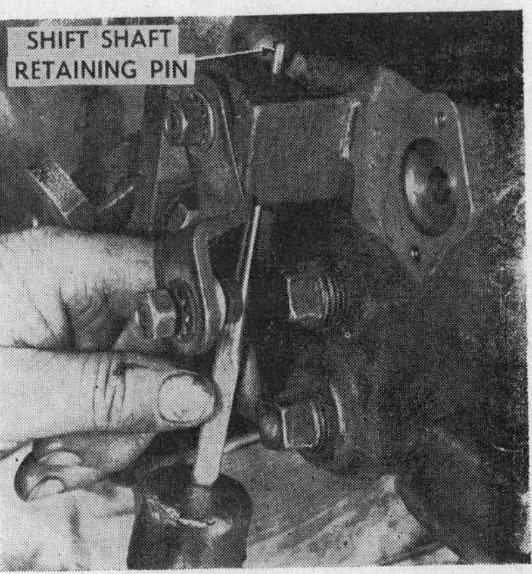

Fig. 2—Removing Shift Lever Lock Pin

Fig. 3—Removing Overdrive Case

Fig. 4—Removing Pinion Cage Lock Rings

Fig. 5—Removing Planetary Gear Assembly

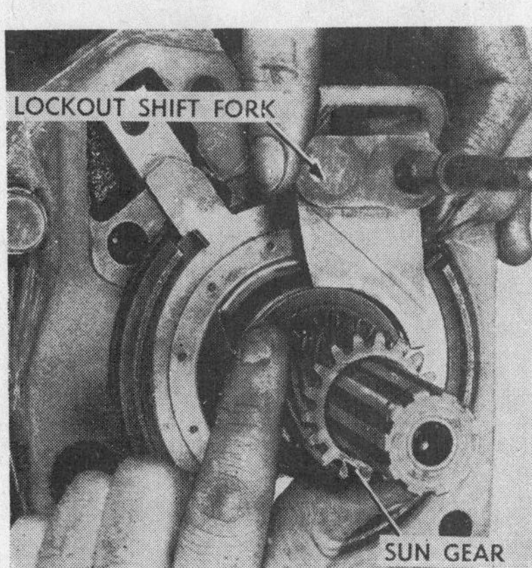

Fig. 6—Removing Sun Gear and Lockout Shift Fork

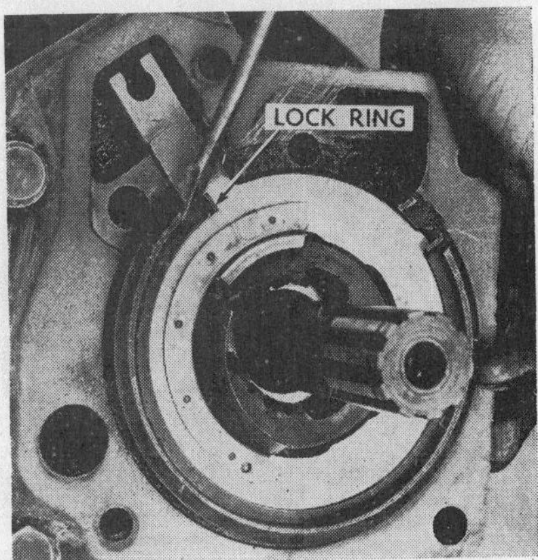

Fig. 7—Removing Balk Ring Cover Lock Ring

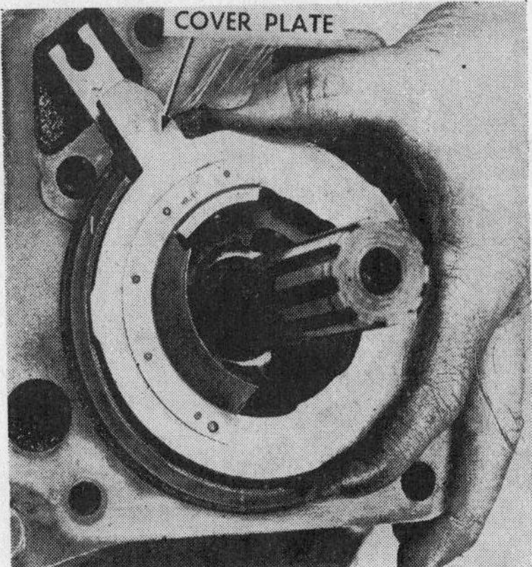

Fig. 8—Removing Balk Ring Cover

GOVERNOR CONTROLLED TYPE—*continued*

Fig. 9—Removing Sun Gear Plate

Fig. 10—Removing Reverse Blocker Pin

Fig. 11—Expanding Mainshaft Lock Ring and Driving Out Mainshaft

Fig. 12—Removing Mainshaft Assembly From Case

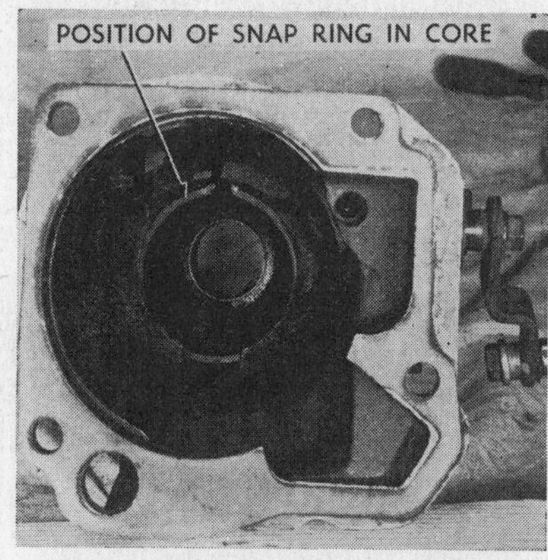

Fig. 13—Piston of Mainshaft Assembly Snap Ring

Fig. 14—Removing Pinion Sleeve Lock Ring

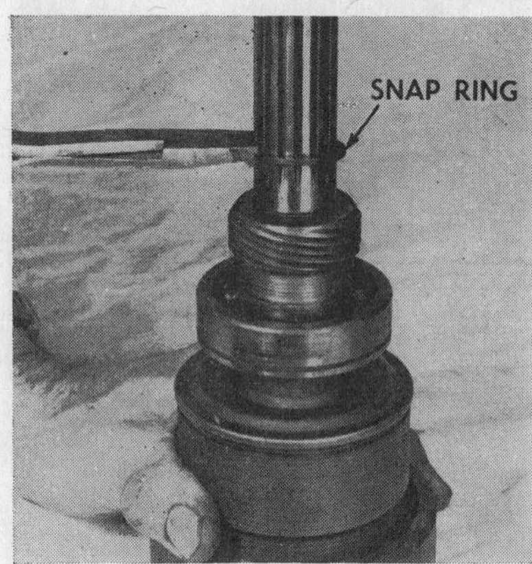

Fig. 15—Removing Speedometer Gear Ring

Fig. 16—Replacing Mainshaft Assembly

Fig. 17—Reinstalling Case

GOVERNOR CONTROLLED TYPE—*continued*

Notice on disassembly that the solenoid pawl has a notch which engages the shift rail, effectively preventing the solenoid plunger from moving downwards at any time the shift rail is moved towards the rear, or lockout position.

Inspection

If the overdrive has a history of noisy gears examine the sun gear, ring gear, and planetary pinions for scratches, nicks, burrs or roughness and if any is found it will be necessary to replace the defective gears.

If the overdrive has a history of slipping in normal drive (not overdrive) examine the free wheeling rollers and the roller cage for roughness or pits.

If the free wheeling rollers have little depressions worn in the free wheeling cam it will be necessary to replace both the cam and the free wheeling rollers.

Failure to operate in reverse indicates that the lockout shift rail is not working properly or the solenoid plunger is interfering with its operation.

When the overdrive is operative but not engaged the car will free wheel. However, once it moves up into overdrive it will no longer free wheel. This is a normal condition.

Electrical Circuits

The electrical circuits vary with the different makes of cars. However, a quick easy test can be made on the solenoid by grounding the governor weights or the wire connected to the governor and placing the hand on the solenoid to feel if it is operating. It can be felt to operate if the ignition switch is turned on and the governor wire is temporarily grounded.

The solenoid plunger is normally up in the solenoid and actuating it with current will cause it to plunge out of the solenoid. A quick check can be made by removing it from the car and testing it directly on a battery.

Where an overdrive is known to be in good condition mechanically but does not function properly it is a good idea to check the solenoid on a battery to see if it is operating properly.

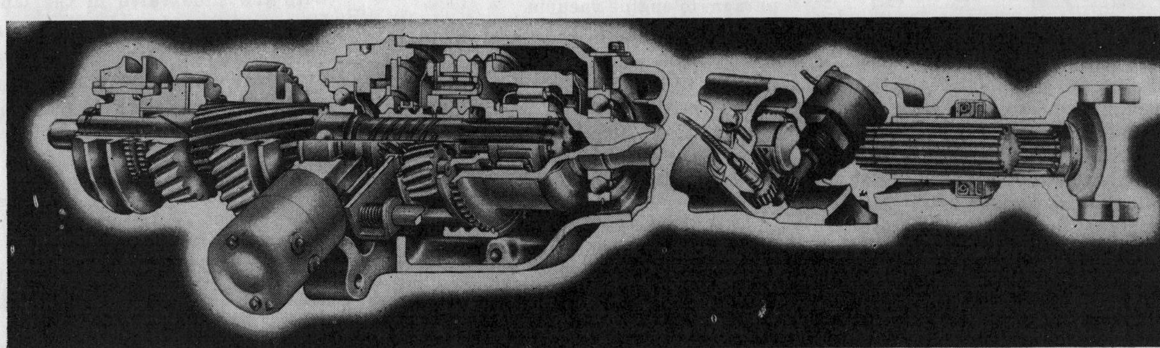

Cross Sectional View of Overdrive Unit

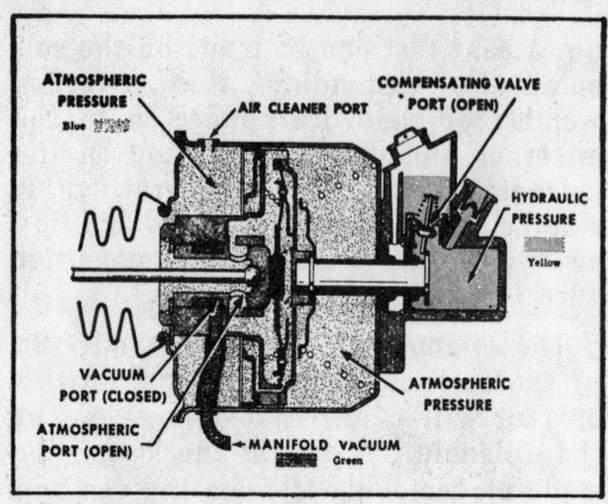

Fig. 1—Released position

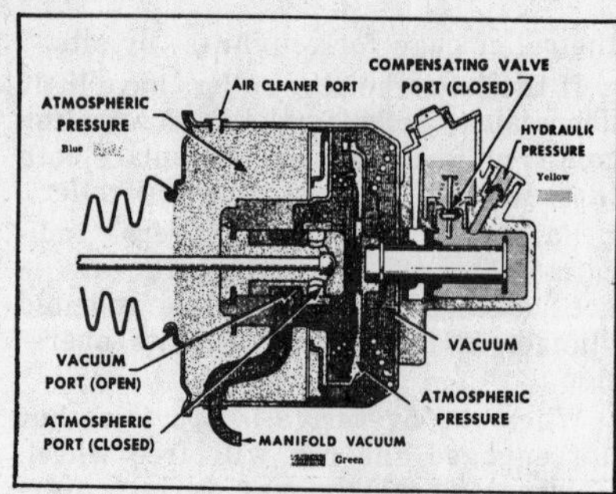

Fig. 2—Applied position

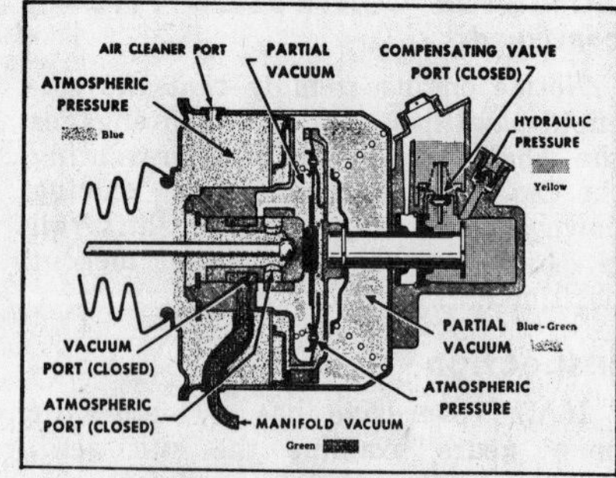

Fig. 3—Holding position

BENDIX POWER BRAKES

The Bendix power brake is a self-contained hydraulic-vacuum power brake utilizing engine intake manifold and atmospheric pressure for its power. It is made up of: a vacuum power cylinder consisting of a cylinder, vacuum power piston, and piston return spring. A hydraulic master cylinder containing a plunger, compensating valve, check valve and fluid reservoir.

A mechanical actuated control valve which controls the degree of brake application in accordance with the foot pedal pressure applied to the brakes.

Operation of the Bendix Power Brakes

Release Position

Both sides of the vacuum piston are open to atmospheric pressure, therefore the piston and diaphragm are balanced in atmospheric pressure and the diaphragm is held in the release position by the return spring.

Brake Application

As the brake pedal is depressed, the valve push rod moves the slide valve to close the atmospheric port and open the vacuum port which connects the forward side of the vacuum power cylinder and the rear side of the reaction diaphragm to engine vacuum.

The atmospheric pressure present on the rear side of the vacuum power cylinder then moves the piston to the applied position. Since the hydraulic plunger is in direct contact with the vacuum piston at all times, any movement of the vacuum piston is transmitted directly to the hydraulic plunger. Initial movement of the hydraulic plunger to the applied direction closes the compensating valve port, sealing off the fluid reservoir from the hydraulic cylinder. Further movement of the hydraulic plunger in the applied direction forces the fluid out of the hydraulic master cylinder under pressure through the hydraulic lines to the wheel cylinders to apply the brakes.

The rear side of the reaction diaphragm is also open to vacuum upon application while the forward side of the diaphragm is open to atmospheric pressure at all times. The diaphragm will move in the opposite direction to set up a reactionary or opposing force which returns the slide valve to the lap or holding position.

With the slide valve in the lap or holding position, both the vacuum and atmospheric ports of the slide valve are closed. This holds the brakes in the applied position as long as the pedal is held down.

Brake Release

Upon release of the pressure on the pedal, the slide valve returns to its released position to close the vacuum port and reopen the atmospheric port and again balance or suspend the vacuum piston and the action diaphragm in atmospheric pressure. The vacuum piston return spring then pushes the piston and hydraulic plunger to the release position. As the hydraulic plunger approaches the release end of its stroke, the compensating valve port is tripped open insuring release of hydraulic pressure.

Fig. 4—End plate removal

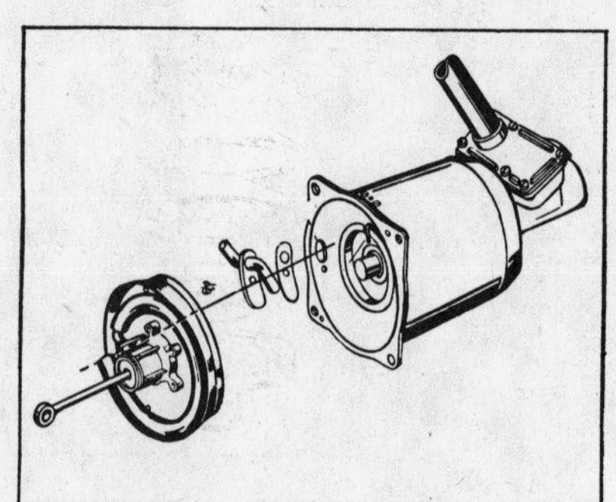

Fig. 5—Vacuum piston and valve removal

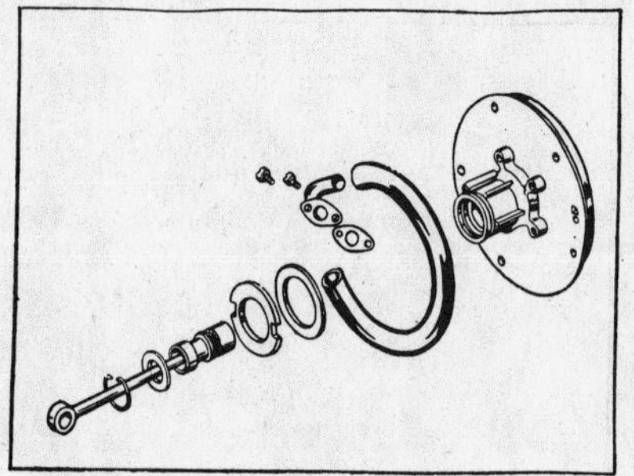

Fig. 6—Sleeve valve and vacuum hose removal

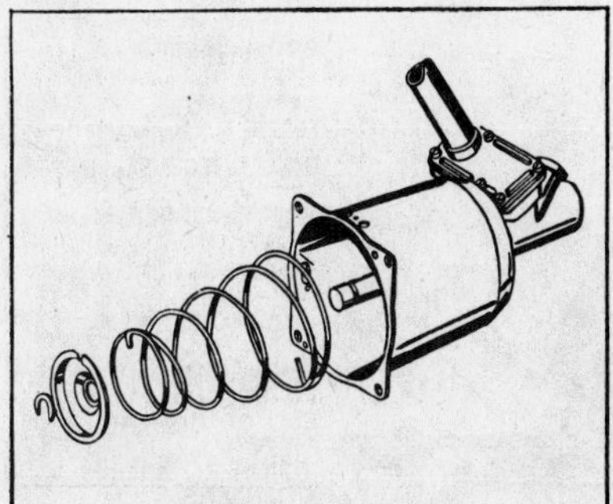
Fig. 7—Vacuum piston return spring and retainer removal

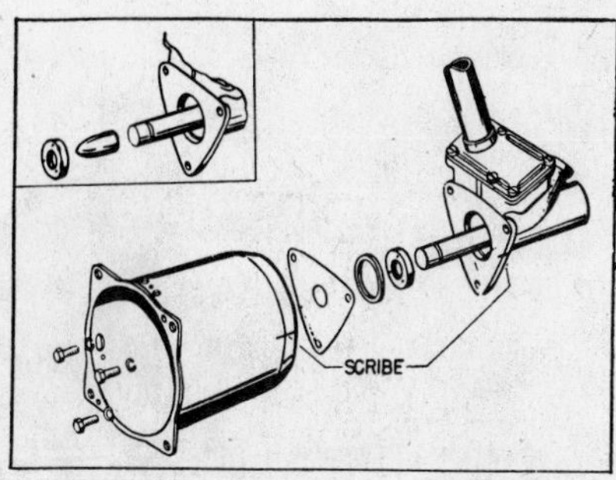

Fig. 8—Vacuum cylinder and leather seal removal

Fig. 9—Seal, hydraulic plunger and compensating valve removal

Disassembly of the Power Unit

Remove the power brake from the car and place in a vise or holding fixture.

Follow the steps shown in the accompanying sketches for disassembly of the power unit.

Be sure to scribe each part so that it can be reassembled in the same relationship that it was removed. Carefully examine all seals and sealing surfaces for scores, scratches or roughness and if any are found, the part must be replaced.

TROUBLE SHOOTING

Trouble and Causes

HARD PEDAL

May be caused by:
Glazed linings.
Grease or brake fluid on the linings.
Bound up brake pedal linkage.
Sticking vacuum check valve.
Collapsed vacuum hose.
Plugged vacuum fittings.
Leaking vacuum reserve tank.
Internal vacuum hose loose or restricted.
Jammed vacuum cylinder piston.
Vacuum leaks in unit caused by loose piston plate or plate screws.
Faulty diaphragm rubber stop in the reaction diaphragm.

SEVERE BRAKES

Caused by:
Grease or brake fluid on the linings.
Scored drums.
Reaction diaphragm leakage.
Broken counter-reaction spring.
Restricted diaphragm passage.
Sticking vacuum valve action. **Caution:** Do not oil.

PEDAL GOES TO THE FLOOR

May be caused by:
Brakes need adjustment.
Air and hydraulic system.
Hydraulic leak or low fluid level.
Compensating valve leak.
Hydraulic piston seal leak.
Compensating port or outlet fitting seal leak.

SLOW RELEASE OR FAILURE TO RELEASE

May be caused by:
Brakes improperly adjusted.
Bound up brakes pedal linkage.
Restricted air cleaner or passages.
Excessive hydraulic seal friction.
Compensator port plug.
Faulty residual check valve.
Piston stroke interference.
Sticky vacuum valve. **Caution:** Do not oil.
Broken piston return spring.
Dry vacuum piston leather packing.

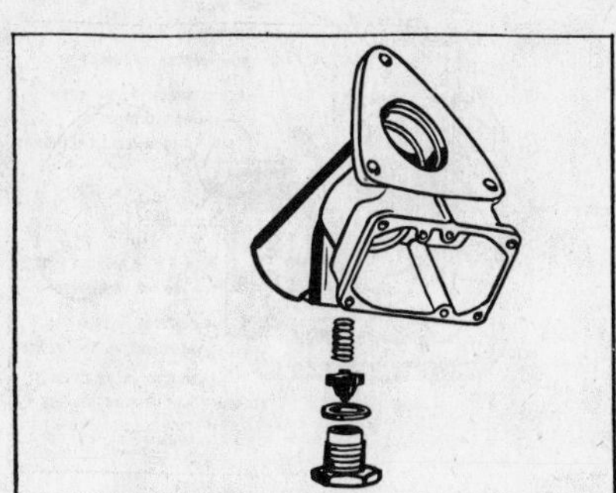
Fig. 10—Residual check valve removal

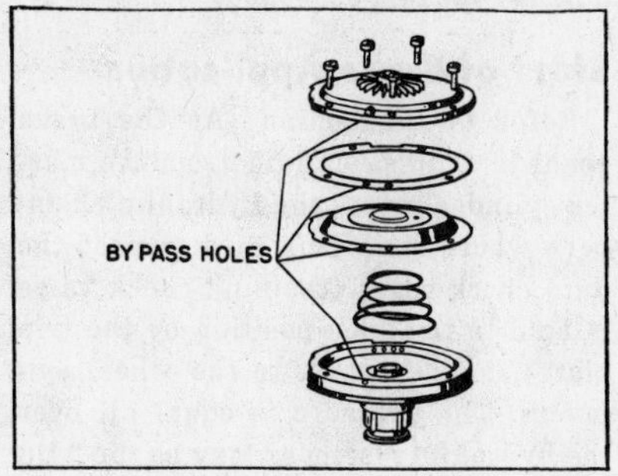

Fig. 11—Diaphragm cover and valve spring removal

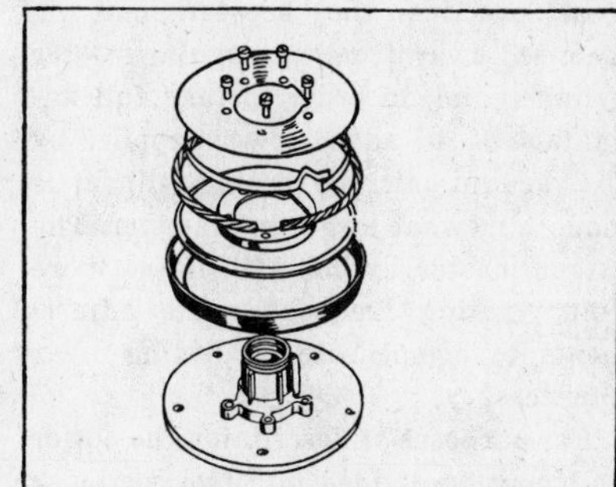
Fig. 12—Vacuum piston disassembly

POWER BRAKES

KELSEY-HAYES POWER BRAKES

Two types of boosters are made by Kelsey-Hayes for use on passenger cars. They are referred to as the external valve mechanism type and the internal valve mechanism type. This designation is more for convenience than anything else since both have their control valves on the inside of the unit.

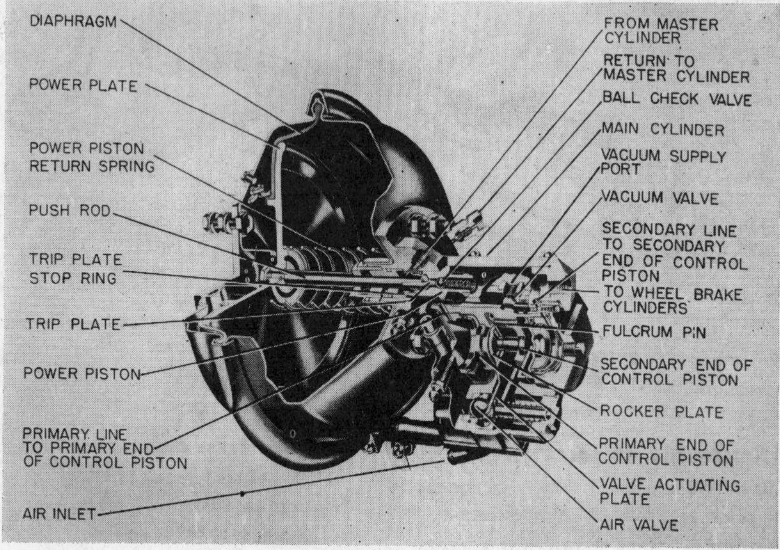

Sectional view of power brake unit

External Valve Mechanism Type

This type may be identified as follows: The hydraulic portion of the power unit is located in front of the vacuum diaphragm housing. No part of it extends to the opposite side of the diaphragm housing.

Internal Valve Mechanism Type

This unit may be identified as follows: Half of the hydraulic portion of the unit is located to the front of the booster diaphragm, the other half is located in back of the booster diaphragm.

The above is a quick, easy way to identify which type of Kelsey-Hayes brake is being serviced.

Operation of the External Valve Mechanism Type

The Kelsey-Hayes brake booster is an hydraulically actuated vacuum suspended type brake booster.

Atmospheric pressure operating against the vacuum from the engine manifold supplies the power for extra braking force.

In practice the booster unit is mounted away from the regular master cylinder and, in order to take full advantage of the added power supplied by the vacuum unit, the master cylinder is made somewhat larger in diameter. The larger master cylinder displaces more fluid, making frequent brake adjustments to compensate for lining wear unnecessary.

For purposes of description the power unit may be divided into two sections: the power section, consisting of the diaphragm, power plate, push rod and power piston assembly; and the hydraulic section consisting of the hydraulic cylinder, controlled piston assembly, valve actuating plate, and air and vacuum valves.

Operation of the Power Assist

UNAPPLIED POSITION

Refer to illustration: The cylinder side of the vacuum unit is connected at all times directly to the manifold vacuum. In the unapplied position the vacuum valve is opened, connecting the cover side of the vacuum unit to the same manifold vacuum. Both sides are connected and in balance. The release spring holds the diaphragm back, the unit is "vacuum suspended."

Start of Brake Application

Refer to illustration: As the brake pedal is depressed, fluid from the master cylinder enters the hydraulic chambers where it is free to flow past the fluid check valve (the fluid check valve is held to the open position by the trip plate), to the outlet, to the wheel cylinders. The pressure is equal all over the hydraulic system as long as the fluid check valve is open.

As pressure is built up in the system from the brake master cylinder, the control piston (refer to illustration) moves to the right because the primary side of the piston is much larger than the secondary side.

As the control piston moves to the right (in the illustration) it moves the valve actuating plate which in turn closes the vacuum valve shutting the vacuum away from the cover side of the vacuum cylinder.

Further pedal pressure will cause the actuating plate to open the air valve which will admit atmospheric pressure to the cover side of the diaphragm, causing the diaphragm to move to the right (in illustration).

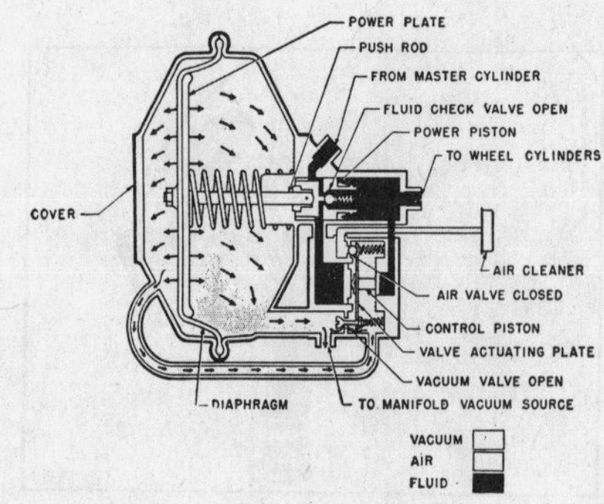

Unapplied position or as pressure is decreased

The push rod (connected to the diaphragm) will push the power piston to the right, causing it to move away from the trip valve plate, permitting the ball check valve in the piston to close.

As soon as the valve closes, the two sides of the hydraulic system, primary and secondary, are completely isolated

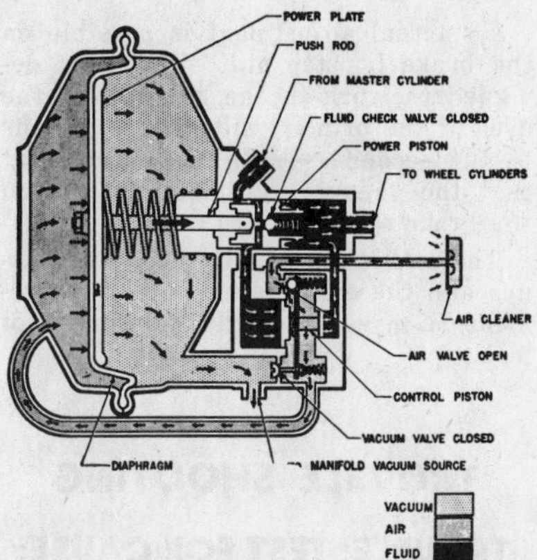

Applying position as pressure is increased

from each other and the vacuum booster becomes effective.

Power from the booster causes the pressure in the secondary side of the hydraulic unit to increase until the pressures on the smaller (secondary side) of the control piston balances the pressure, from the master cylinder, on the primary side.

Since the secondary side of the control piston is smaller than the primary side, much higher pressures (boosted) are required at the secondary side to balance the piston.

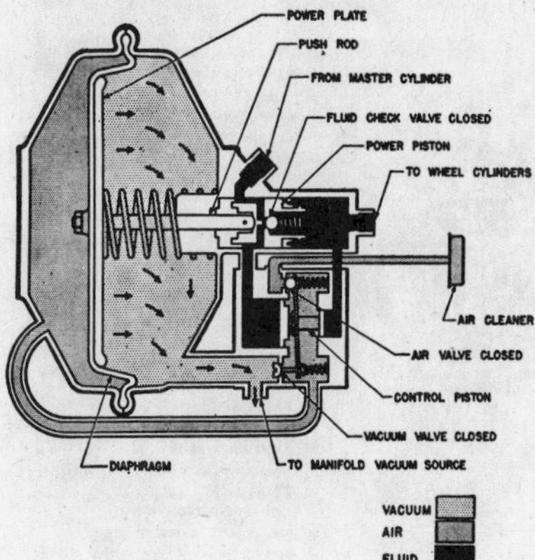

Poised position as pressure is maintained

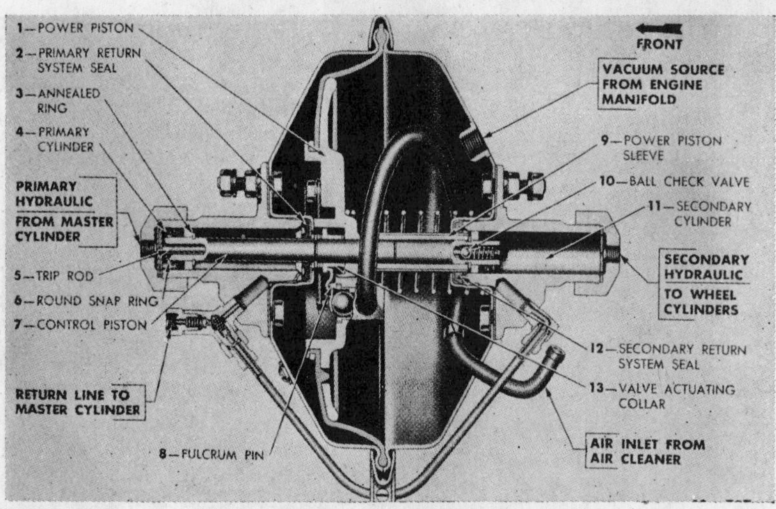

Cross sectional view of vacu-ease brake unit

Operation of the Internal Valve Mechanism Type

BRAKE APPLICATION

When the brake pedal is depressed it sets into motion a series of reactions, each one is the result of the one preceding it. They follow each other in such rapid succession that they are practically simultaneous.

Refer to illustration: Fluid from the master cylinder flows through the primary cylinder, through the hollow control piston, around the trip rod, past the ball check, through the secondary cylinder and into the wheel cylinders.

At the first slight application of the brake pedal, hydraulic line pressure is built up in the brake system and it is equal all over the system.

The vacuum valve in the power piston is open and the atmospheric valve is closed so that there is vacuum on both sides of the diaphragm. In this respect the operation is the same as the external valve type.

The area at the primary end of the control piston includes the piston ring and cup which makes the area greater than that at the secondary end. For this reason the thrust on the primary end will be greater than the thrust on the secondary end, and as a result the control piston will move to the right (in illustration).

When the control piston is brought into balance, the air valve closes, cutting off atmospheric pressure from the cover side of the vacuum diaphragm and the unit remains stationary as long as the pedal pressure remains constant.

Further pressure on the pedal will again unbalance the control piston and the vacuum booster will increase the pressure on the secondary side until the control piston is again in balance.

Releasing the Brakes

If the pedal pressure is lessened or released, secondary pressures will cause the control piston to move to the left (in the illustration) causing the actuating plate to open the vacuum valve which admits vacuum to both sides of the diaphragm, permitting the release spring to move the diaphragm to the left, releasing the brakes.

When the brakes become fully released the ball trip plate in the piston will trip the fluid valve which will connect the primary and secondary hydraulic systems. The booster unit is now at rest with brakes released.

As the control piston moves to the right under primary pressure it presses a collar against the valve actuating plate which pivots on fulcrum pin to actuate the valves. The free movement of the control piston within the power is not in the power unit. If this does not release the brakes, crack the hydraulic line between the secondary cylinder and the wheel cylinder. If this

KELSEY-HAYES POWER BRAKES

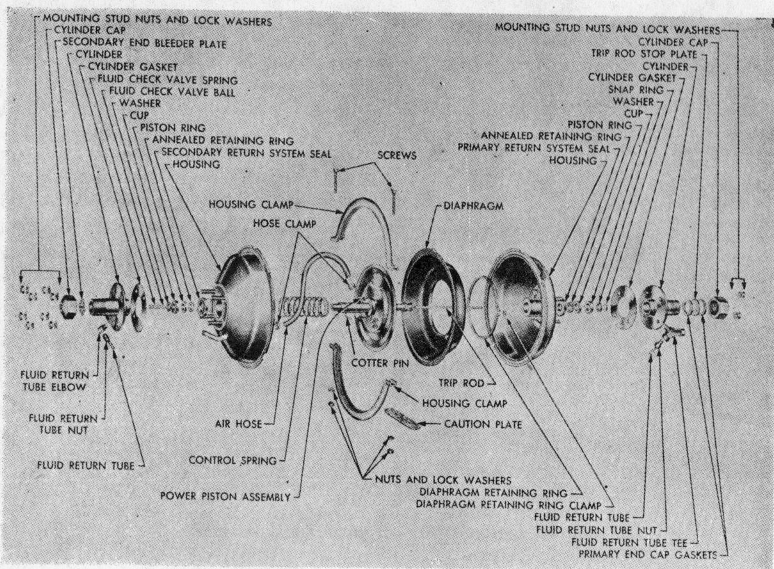

Exploded view of vacu-ease brake unit

BRAKE APPLICATION—*continued*

cylinder is approximately .050". When the control piston moves approximately .025" it closes the vacuum valve, sealing off the primary side of the diaphragm from the vacuum on the secondary side.

As the control piston moves beyond .025" under further pedal pressure, it seats against the ball check to trap secondary fluid pressure against the wheel cylinders. At this point the primary and secondary hydraulic systems are completely isolated from each other.

At the same time, further movement of the control piston presses its collar still harder against the valve actuating plate which opens the air valve and admits atmospheric pressure into the primary side of the diaphragm.

Notice that the actual function of this internal valve mechanism type is exactly the same as that of the external valve mechanism type except that the valves are located in a different place and the actuating piston is different in shape.

The increasing air pressure against the primary side of the diaphragm power piston assembly forces the power piston sleeve hard against the secondary piston ring to increase the fluid pressure in the secondary side and the wheel cylinders.

BRAKE RELEASE

At the first partial release of the brake pedal, fluid pressure against the primary end of the control piston is decreased which results in the control piston moving back because of the high pressure on the secondary side.

As it moves back (.025"), the collar decreases its pressure against the valve actuating plate and the atmospheric valves so that the valve closes, shutting off the atmosphere from the pressure side of the booster diaphragm. As the control piston continues to move, the collar further decreases its pressure against the valve actuating plate and the vacuum valve starts to open, admitting manifold vacuum to the pressure side of the unit. The spring then forces the unit back to the released position.

ADJUSTMENTS OF THE BRAKE BOOSTER

No actual adjustment is possible on the brake booster unit since it is designed to work in the relation of the area of the primary side of the pistons to the secondary side up to the limit that the vacuum cylinder can put on the brake system.

The brakes are bled in the usual manner and the only maintenance requirement is to see that the unit does not leak.

TROUBLE SHOOTING

TROUBLE; TEST FOR CAUSE; CORRECTION

Brakes Will Not Release Properly

TEST FOR INTERNAL TYPE ONLY

With engine shut off, pump the brakes several times and check for release. If not released, crack the line between the master cylinder and the power unit. If this releases the brakes, the trouble

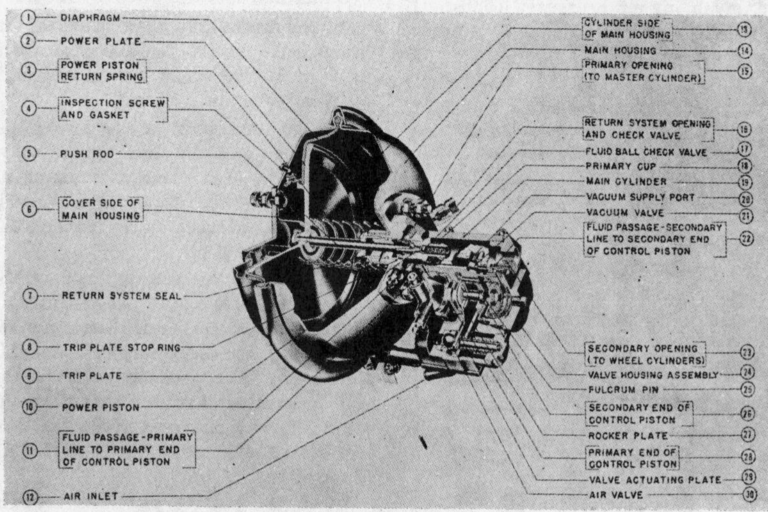

Vacu-ease brake unit—external valve type cross sectional view

is not in the power unit. If this does not release the brake, crack the hydraulic line between the secondary cylinder and the wheel cylinder. If this releases the brakes, the trouble is in the power unit.

CAUSE (INTERNAL VALVE TYPE ONLY)

Improper opening of the fluid check valve ball.

CURE

Remove the primary cylinder end cap and check for damaged or missing trip rod stop plate or trip rod.

TESTS FOR BOTH TYPES

With engine running, check the brakes for release. If not released, crack the line between the master cylinder and the power unit. If this releases the brakes the trouble is not in the power unit. If this does not release the brakes, crack the hydraulic line at the end of the cylinder between the wheel cylinders and the power unit. If this releases the brakes, the power unit is at fault.

CAUSE

Missing inspection screw and gasket.

CURE

Install inspection screw and gasket.

Note: The inspection screw and gasket are on the main housing cover. This screw and gasket act as a seal for a 10/32 tap hole used as a vacuum gage connection at assembly in the factory.

Loss of Brake Fluid from the System

TESTS FOR BOTH TYPES

Check all points for leaks such as wheel cylinder cups, master cylinder cup, line connections, etc. Replace or tighten any part which leaks.

If this does not cure it, remove the unit from the brackets and disassemble the main housing clamp rings and remove the housing cover. Examine the interior of the cylinder for fluid leakage. If fluid is found in the vacuum cylinder, replace cups and seal assembly and thoroughly examine the cylinder bore and push rod for scratches in the finish.

Unit Does Not Boost

TESTS FOR BOTH TYPES

With vacuum in the unit, the engine running, listen for a rush of air through

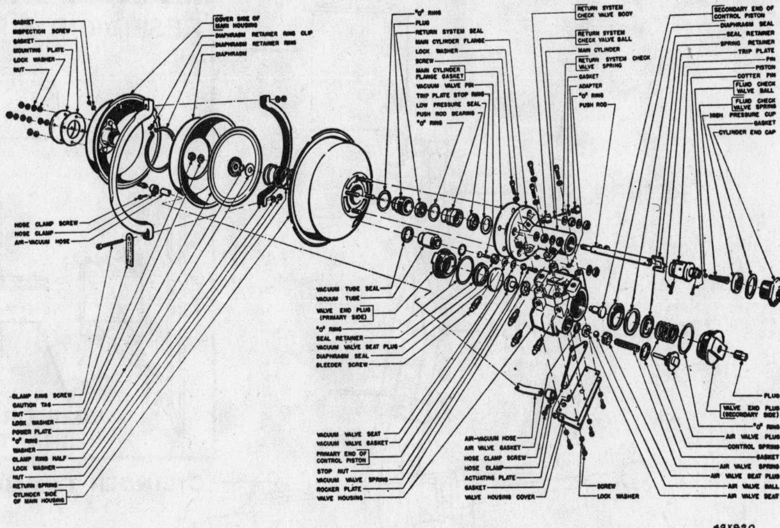

Vacu-ease brake unit—external valve type exploded view

the air cleaner while the brake pedal is being depressed, using a fairly hard brake application. If no rush of air is heard, remove the vacuum source line, empty unit and run the engine to determine if the vacuum is being created in the unit. If no vacuum is created in the unit, the line is either blocked or restricted or the ball in the vacuum check valve is stuck.

Note: The vacuum check valve is either at or near the engine intake manifold.

If in the first test the rush of air is heard through the air cleaner while the pedal is being depressed and yet the unit does not boost, it will be necessary to disassemble the unit and check the fluid ball and also the diaphragm for breaks which interfere with its operation.

Servicing the Valve Units

The air and vacuum valves contained in the valve housing require careful adjustment.

This adjustment should not be attempted in the field. Special equipment is required to insure a proper adjustment.

Disassembly of the Brake Power Unit

Refer to the exploded views of the power unit which show clearly how each part is removed from its mating part.

These illustrations also show the exact relationship of one part to the other and can be followed when assembling a power cylinder.

Bleeding Brakes

Power brakes are bled in exactly the same manner as the standard brake system in that air can be removed from the lines using either a through pressure type bleeder or by pumping the pedal in the usual manner.

Complete instructions are given on brake bleeding in the General Service Section of this manual.

Master Cylinder Return Line

Both the internal and external valve type power booster have a line which returns excess or leaked fluid to the master cylinder. This line contains a check ball which will permit the excess fluid to return to the master cylinder but prevents it from returning back to the unit itself.

This check ball rarely gets into any difficulty but if it should it can be removed easily and cleaned and replaced without completely disassembling the power unit.

The only time that any test is necessary on this check ball is if there is no other apparent reason for loss of fluid in the brake system.

BENDIX POWER STEERING

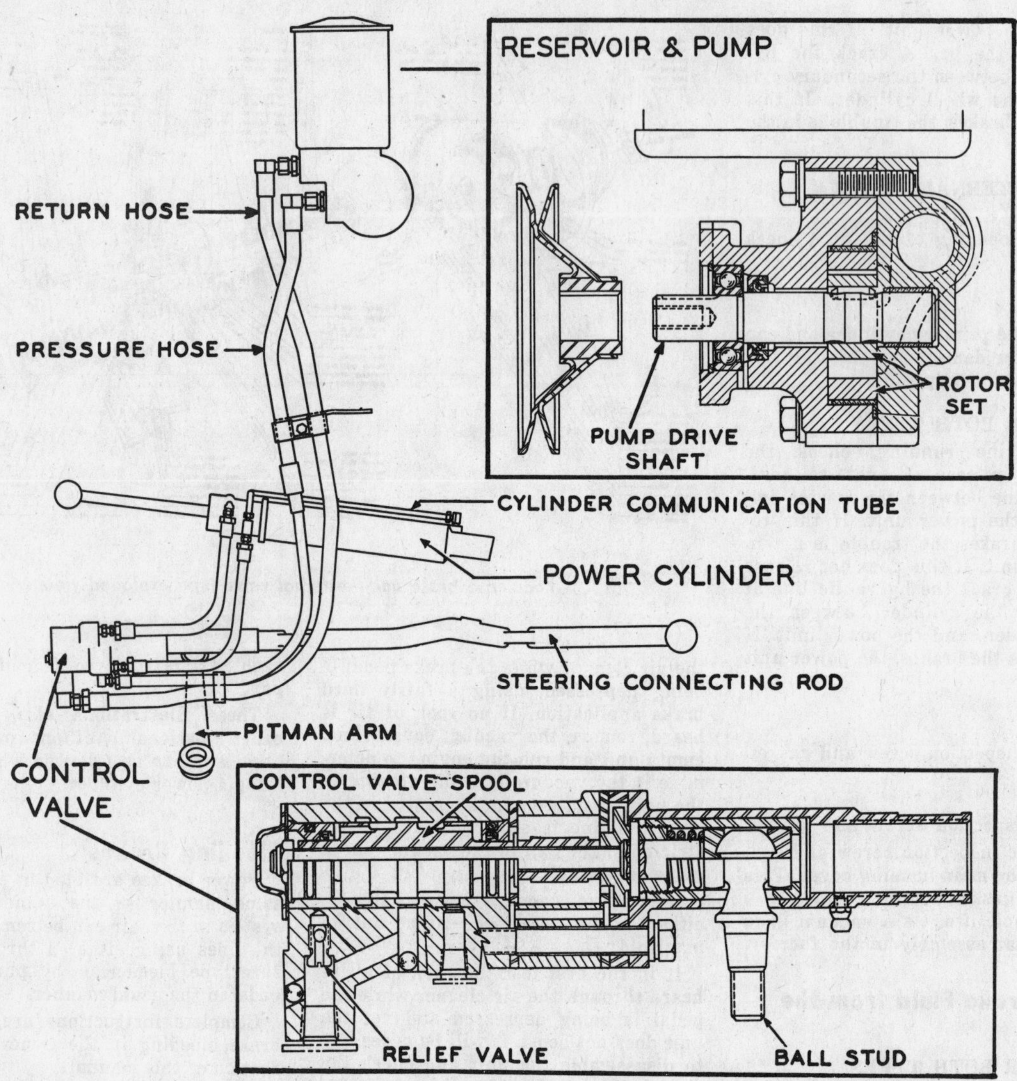

Sectional view of essential parts of the power steering unit

BENDIX POWER STEERING

The Bendix power steering, known as a linkage type steering, is an hydraulic assist type of power unit attached to the tie rods.

While the manual effort is reduced about 80%, the "feel" of the full steering control has been left in. Power steering is in operation at any time the engine is running.

Bendix power steering system consists of elements tied in with the conventional steering gear including the following: a fluid reservoir, an oil pump, an externally mounted control valve and a power cylinder mounted in the steering linkage.

The oil pump, of the rotor type, is located on a bracket at the left upper forward end of the engine and is driven by a V-belt from the crankshaft.

It supplies hydraulic fluid to the power cylinder at around 650 psi and in sufficient volume to meet any demand. The combination fluid reservoir and filter is mounted on the pump body.

The steering control valve is attached to the end of the steerage linkage connecting rod and to the pitman arm by means of a ball stud, mounted inside a sliding socket tube. The power cylinder is of the double acting type, the cylinder body being attached directly to the steering linkage connecting rod while the other end, the piston, is attached to the chassis frame. As the engine starts, filtered fluid from the reservoir is drawn by the pump and forced under pressure through a flexible hose to the control valve. The control valve then responds to the movement of the steering gear, moving the control valve spool at the proper position for the maneuver desired by the driver.

The system is self-bleeding and requires only that the reservoir be filled and the steering moved from one extreme to the other several times to bleed out all of the air.

POWER STEERING GEAR

Removal of the Power Gear Assembly

Disconnect the drag link from the steering arm, disconnect the transmission shift rods, detach the power hoses from the steering gear, detach the accelerator bell crank rods, remove the steering wheel (horn button comes off by pressing inwards and turning counter clockwise).

Remove the steering assembly shrouds and floor board draft pad.

Disconnect the brake pedal from the push rod and take out the horse shoe type lock which holds the brake pedal in place on the shaft and slide the pedal outwards on the shaft far enough to clear the pedal return stop screw and then slide the pedal towards the rear of the car which will allow sufficient clearance between the clutch and brake pedals to remove and install the power steering unit.

Disconnect the steering assembly from the dash panel, remove the bolts which hold the steering assembly to the frame and lower the column jacket and shroud assembly until the studs are free of the instrument panel, then remove the jacket tube.

The assembly can now be pulled out through the floor board into the front compartment of the car.

Caution: Do not start the engine with the power steering disconnected.

Adjustment of the Power Steering Gear

ADJUSTMENT OF OPERATING GEAR BACK LASH. (THIS IS THE SPUR GEAR ADJUSTMENT.)

Check the back lash of the spur gears by shutting the engine off and turning the steering wheel very slightly. If too great a back lash is indicated the block will have to be adjusted.

Pull steering wheel up until there is approximately 1 inch clearance between the hub and the collar on the shroud assembly.

On the gear box, loosen the adjusting plate lock bolt and with the steering wheel held firmly in the pulled up position turn the adjusting plate to its extreme clockwise position.

Turn the lock bolt in just far enough to hold the plate in that position but not enough to prevent the plate from being moved slowly.

Release the grip on the steering wheel and turn the adjusting plate very slowly counter clockwise until the steering wheel hub snaps back into the position against the shroud collar. At exactly this point lock the adjusting plate bolt to hold the plate securely in position.

Caution: Hold the serrated pin in position if it is necessary to remove the adjusting plate to set the plate on other serrations. Otherwise the pin may move outwards with the plate and pull out of its seal and therefore require the complete disassembly and reassembly of the gear.

ADJUSTMENT OF ROLLER TOOTH AND WORM GEAR

Because the steering gear is operated

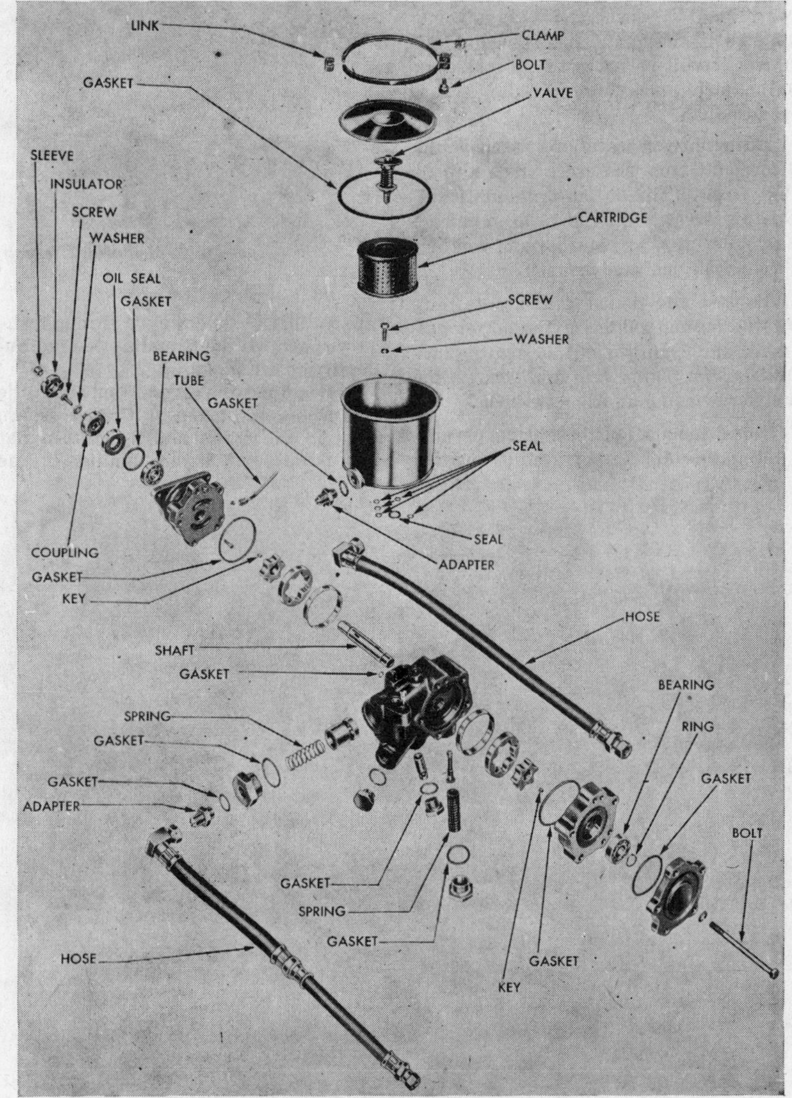

Power Steering—Pump and Reservoir Exploded

GEMMER POWER STEERING

ADJUSTMENT OF ROLLER TOOTH AND WORM GEAR—*continued*

by power cylinders there is very little wear in the worm and roller tooth and it should be unnecessary to make an adjustment at this point.

However, when required end play of the steering shaft and the mesh of the roller tooth with the steering worm may be adjusted as follows:

Disconnect the drag link from the steering arm, and with the engine running set the steering wheel in the mid position of its travel.

Now, by moving the pitman arm backwards and forwards check the amount of lash in the gears. If any lash at all exists it will be necessary to make an adjustment since these gears are set up to zero lash.

Adjustment is as follows: Remove the acorn nut from the cross shaft adjusting screw. (This is the cross shaft adjusting screw which is to be found on any steering gear regardless of whether it is power operated or not.)

Remove the piston arm access plug at the bottom center of the power cylinder and drain the oil. Loosen the lock nut on the piston arm and remove the set screw using an Allen wrench.

Note: Removal of these parts permits sliding the cross shaft (adjusting the cross shaft) sideways through the power arm without binding the hydraulically operated piston.

Now adjust the screw from which the acorn nut was taken until there is zero lash in the gears and be certain that the power arm is not binding in the pistons before retightening the set screw to 30-35 foot pounds torque. Securely tighten the jam nut. Replace the access hole plug.

When all adjustments have been made recheck to make sure the steering gear does not bind at any point.

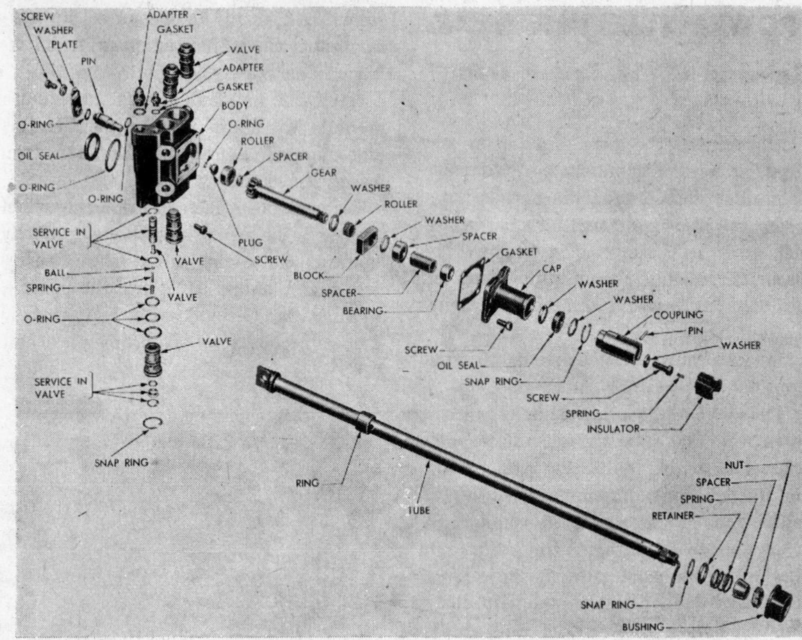

Power Steering Gear Control Valves

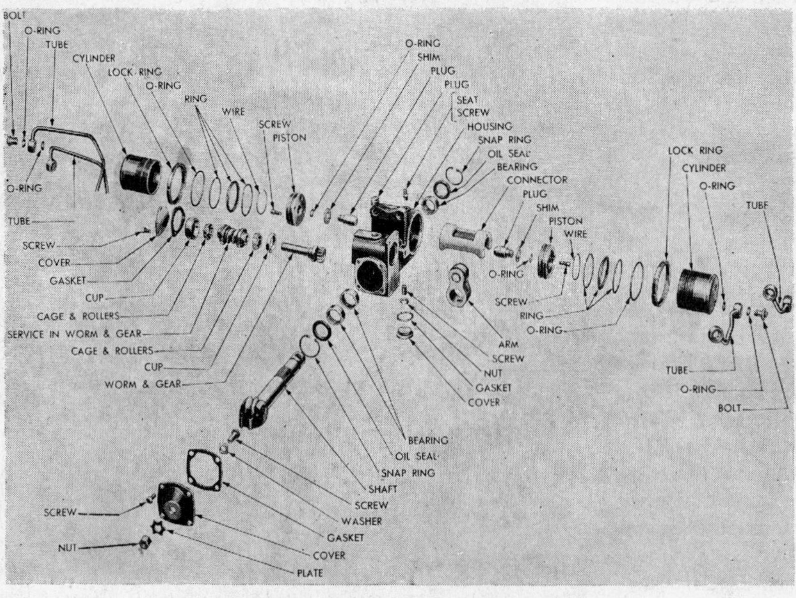

Power Steering—Cylinder and Pistons, Exploded

SAGINAW POWER STEERING

The Saginaw power steering unit consists of a conventional manual steering gear combined with an hydraulic booster linked to the pitman shaft through a separate set of gears and controlled by a valve built into the steering gear. The hydraulic power is obtained from a pump driven by a belt off the crankshaft.

With the power gear "at rest" and the engine running, oil circulates freely through the hydraulic system. Four or more pounds of pressure is applied to the rim of the steering wheel, actuates a valve which diverts the oil into one end of the hydraulic cylinder which in turn does the actual work of turning the wheels.

A power steering unit is a simple application of the hydraulic follow up system. When driving under very light steering such as traveling along a straight highway, there is no assist from the hydraulic system. However, when four or more pounds of pressure is applied to the steering wheel, the hydraulic system is actuated, turning the wheels as far as directed by the rotation of the steering wheel and no further. The hydraulic system will hold the wheels on that track as long as four pounds pressure is maintained.

When pressure is released from the steering wheel the wheels return to a straight position the same as they do in a manual operated steering system.

The principal working parts of the power steering are the steering worm. ball nut, pitman shaft gear, control valve, hydraulic cylinder and actuating rack. The hydraulic supply system consists of an oil reservoir, hydraulic pump, check and relief valves, all of which are connected by lines to control valve built into the steering gear itself.

The housing is comparable to that of a mechanical steering gear in regard to its mounting and road clearances. The hydraulic cylinder assembly is mounted on the steering gear housing and is linked to the pitman shaft through a power rack attached to the end of the piston rod. The power rack is guided by a shim adjusted plate bolted to the housing.

The hydraulic control valve assembly is mounted on the steering gear housing with the valve spool concentric to the shaft.

The valve spool consists of a steel spool having two annular grooves which connect three annular passages inside the valve body. The valve spool is centered and restrained from up and down motion by five sets of plungers which bear against the cover on one end and the housing on the other.

They also bear against thrust bearings at both ends which are secured to the steering shaft and worm assembly. The plungers are held against these parts by the action of five springs. It is necessary therefore to overcome the preload of the springs before the valve spool can be moved. Because of this, the action of the steering gear for light loads is entirely manual. When the valve spool is in the central position oil from the pump flows through the center passage of the valve body through the annular groove in the spool to the annular passage in the body at both ends and then back to the pump. The pump functions at all times when the engine is running.

When there is sufficient resistance to rotation of the pitman shaft and up and down motion of the ball nut continued turning of the steering wheel will result in a (up or down of the worm and shaft assembly). This overcomes the preload of the springs. This up and down movement of the steering shaft assembly is due to the lead on the steering worm. The actual direction of the valve spool movement is, of course, depending on which way the steering wheel is turned.

To get a clear picture of this linear action of the worm and shaft take the instance of a steering worm which is properly adjusted, remove the end plate and add an additional .030 thick shim. With this shim in position the worm shaft will have .030 end play. As the steering would be turned to the right the end play would permit the worm and shaft to move upwards .030; if it were turned to the left the shaft would move downwards .030 before the wheels

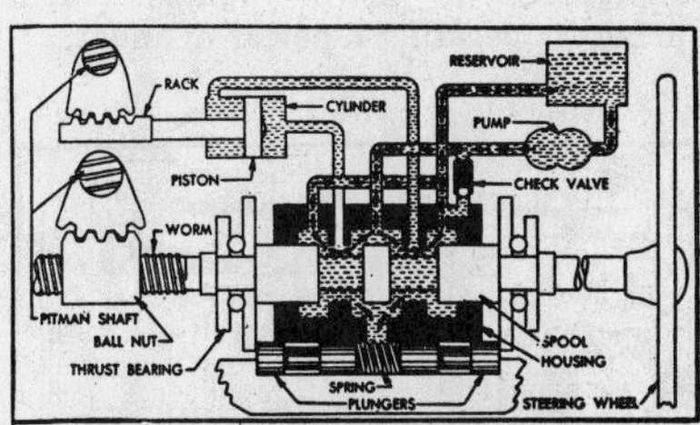

Oil circulation without power application

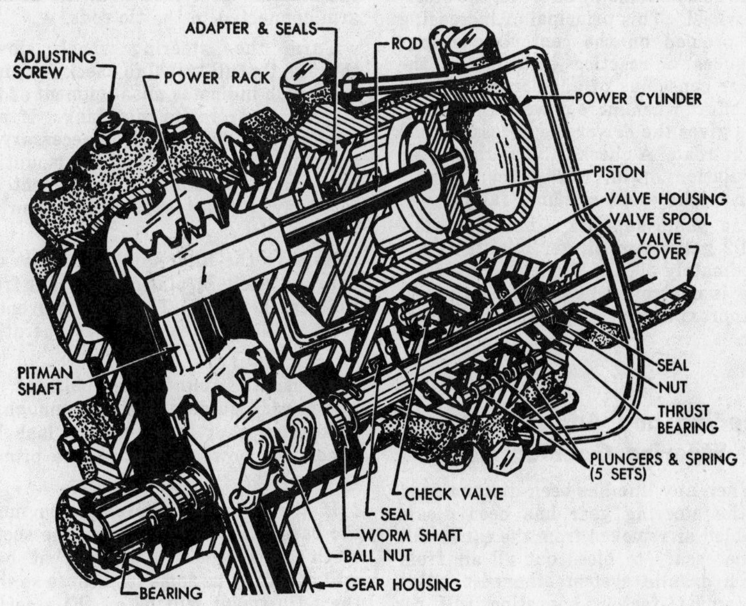

Cross section thru the power gear used on Buick models

SAGINAW POWER STEERING—*continued*

would turn. The action of the power steering gear is very similar to this except that the end play of the worm causes a spool valve to move which in turn permits the oil pressure to enter the power cylinder causing the power cylinder to take up the load of turning the wheels.

Expressed in its simplest terms, desirable end play is provided in the worm. This desirable end play causes the valves to move (against their springs) operating a power cylinder.

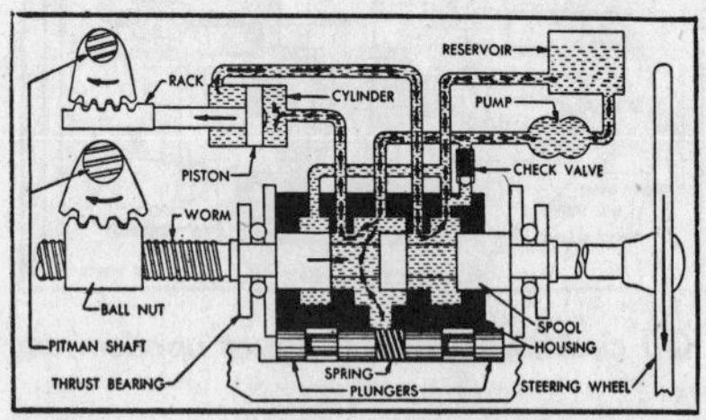

Oil circulation during power application on a left turn

The oil pump builds up only the necessary pressure to overcome the resistance to rotation of the pitman shaft. This oil pressure is also diverted to the spring side of the plungers and assists in building up a preload which must be overcome by effort on the steering wheel. This principal of increasing the preload on the centering springs produces a reaction that makes the driver conscious of an increased steering effort when more power is required. This gives the driver the necessary feel of the road. A check valve permits free circulation of oil within the steering gear in the event of pump failure.

The pump supplies a minimum flow fo 1.2 gallons of oil per minute at approximately 500 RPM. Maximum pressure is controlled by a relief valve set at approximately 750 pounds per square inch.

Bleeding and Adjusting Power Steering Gear on Car

When any line has been disconnected or the steering gear has been disassembled or removed from the car it will be necessary to bleed out all air from the hydraulic system otherwise noisy and unsatisfactory operation will result.

Proceed as follows: connect all hoses and fill the reservoir to the proper level and then let the car sit for about 5 minutes with the engine shut off.

Note: If a Vickers pump is used remove the pipe plug from the top of the pump manifold and when oil starts to flow out of the opening, install the plug just tight enough to stop the oil flow and then wait for about 5 minutes.

Now run the engine at approximately 1000 rpm for two or three minutes and then turn the steering gear from one extreme to the other, right to left, and then left to right, until all the air is worked out as evidenced by the operation of the oil pump at normal noise level.

Drive Belt Adjustment

The drive belt should be adjusted so that one side can be depressed about ⅜ inch with thumb pressure applied midway between the pulleys. The belt is adjusted by loosening the mounting bolts and moving the pump horizontally and then retightening the mounting bolts.

Pitman Shaft Adjustment

Caution: Never attempt to adjust the steering gear lash with the pitman arm connected to the tie rods.

Turn the steering wheel slowly through its full travel to check for binding which indicates misalignment of the steering gear in its mounting. If any binding is found it will be necessary to shim up the steering and its mounting bolts to take out any misalignment before any further adjustments can be made.

Remove the filler plug and draw out approximately ¾ pint of lubricant from the gear housing. This is to prevent it from spilling when the next operation is performed.

Loosen the four corner bolts of the power rack guide cover just enough to make sure that there will be lash between the power rack and the pitman shaft sector.

If the bolts are loosened too much the rack will tend to bind on the sector teeth so just loosen it enough that there will certainly be some lash there so that the adjustment will be on the steering nut, not the power rack.

Turn the steering wheel until the gear is in the central position. At this point the steering wheel would be centered.

Now adjust the manual gear in the usual manner. (See Steering gears for the car being worked.)

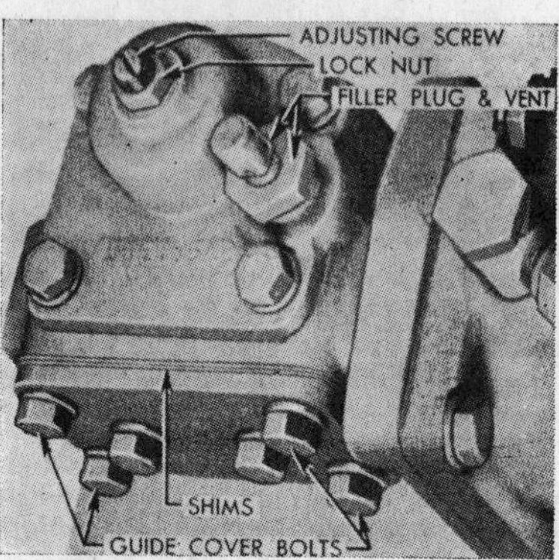

Steering gear adjustments (Buick)

When properly adjusted it should require from ½ to ¾ pound greater pull at the high spot (straight ahead position) than it does at either end of the steering range.

Write on a piece of paper the actual pull (in pounds) required to move the steering wheel both at the high spot and also at all other positions of the wheel.

Remove the power rack guide cover and take out one .003 shim at a time and reinstall the cover and tighten bolt securely.

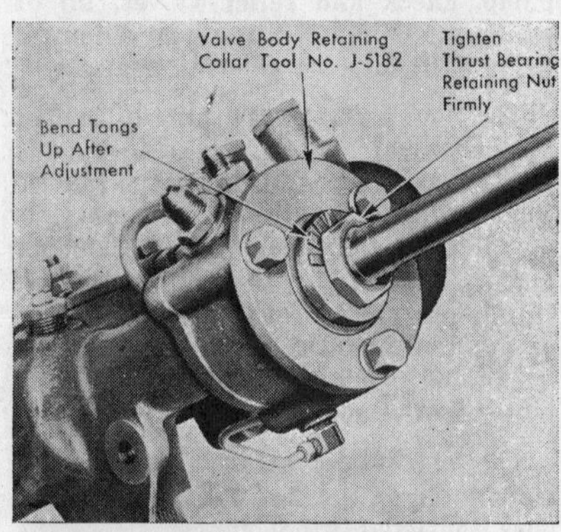

Adjusting thrust bearing (Cadillac)

With the shim removed recheck with the scale the pull required to turn the steering wheel steadily through the high spot or no lash range. This should require 1 to 1¼ lbs greater pull than has been noted in the paragraph above.

Shims for the guide cover bolts are available in .003 and .005 inch thickness.

When the pull obtained is 1 and 1¼ lbs greater than the pull obtained in the recorded stage add one .003 shim, then install the cover and tighten the bolt securely. This will insure approximately .003 inch lash at the power rack.

Connect the steering tie rod to the pitman arm.

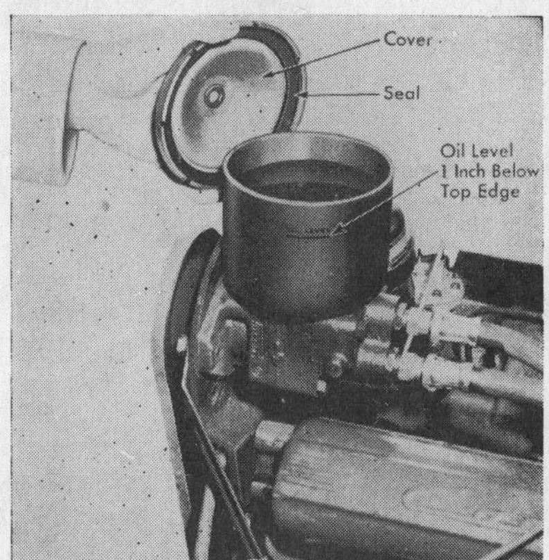

Hydraulic tank fluid level (Cadillac)

TROUBLE SHOOTING ON THE POWER STEERING

Excessive Play or Looseness In the Steering Mechanism

May be caused by excessive lash between the pitman shaft sectors and the ball nut or the power rack.

See Pitman Shaft Adjustment for correction.

May be also caused by loose worm thrust bearings or sticking valve spools. This requires removal and disassembly of the steering gear.

Front Wheel Shimmy

May be caused by air in the hydraulic system.

See Bleeding, Hydraulic System.

May also be caused by excessive lash between the pitman sector and the ball nut or power rack.

See Pitman Shaft Adjustment.

Poor Centering or Poor Recovery from Turns

May be caused by binding of the steering shaft due to misalignment of the gear in its mountings.

May also be caused by sticking valve spool or faulty centering springs. This requires removal and disassembly of the steering gear to repair.

Rattle in the Steering Gear

May be caused by excessive lash between the pitman shaft sector and the ball nut or the power rack.

Caution: A very slight rattle may occur on turns because of the increased lash off the high point. This is normal and lash must not be reduced below that specified in the paragraph on Cross Shaft Adjustment.

Hard Steering When Parking

To determine whether the steering is actually hard when parking, place the car on a clean dry floor and apply the brakes and with the engine idling turn the steering wheel from one side to the other to bring up the oil temperature. Apply a pull scale to the spoke of the steering wheel and check the pull required to turn the wheel steadily with the gage held at 90 degrees to the spokes. If the pull required to turn the steering wheel exceeds 10 pounds the following may be the causes:

Pump drive belt loose, low oil in the reservoir, or air in the hydraulic system.

If all of these have been corrected the difficulty may be insufficient oil pressure. The oil pressure should be checked as shown in the following paragraphs.

Testing Hydraulic Oil Pressure

Disconnect the pressure line hose of the oil pump and insert into the line a high reading pressure gage (at least 1000 lbs). Idle the engine and note the oil pressure on the gage while turning the steering wheel from one extreme position to the other, especially note the maximum pressure which can be built up with the wheel held in either the right or the left extreme position.

Checking pressure with gage (Cadillac)

Caution: Do not hold the wheel in the extreme position for any extended period, it may drastically increase the oil temperature and will cause undue wear on the oil pump relief valve.

The gage should read at least 700 p.s.i. for satisfactory power steering.

If less than 700 p.s.i it indicates trouble in the pump, the external lines, the steering gear or a combination of these parts.

To eliminate the lines and gear arrange a valve in the pressure line so that it can be momentarily shut off which will then give the pressure of the pump itself.

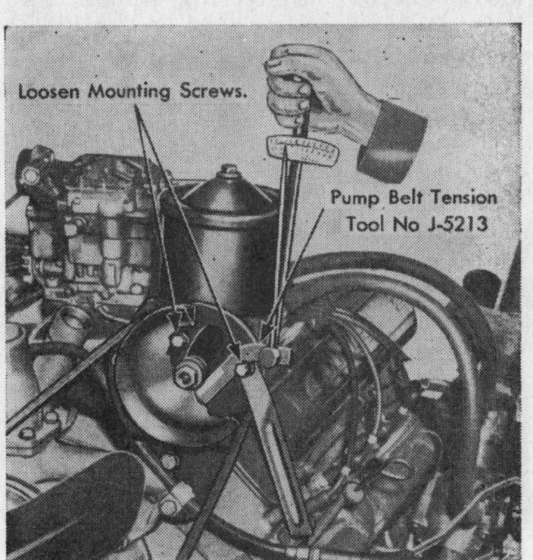

Adjusting belt tension (Cadillac)

WARNER POWER STEERING

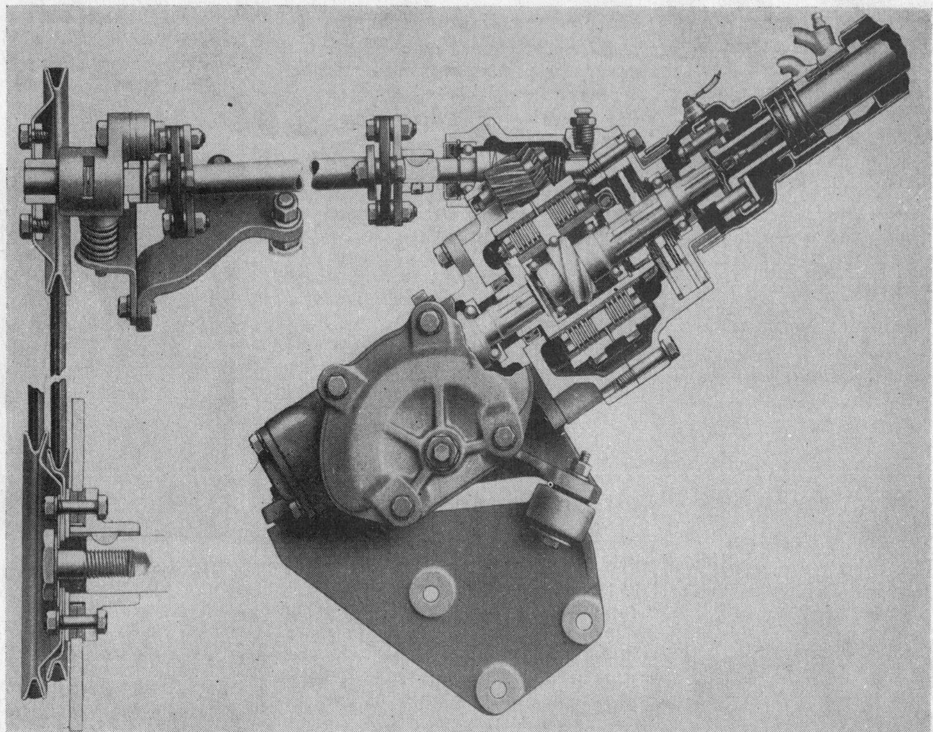

Section view of Warner power steering

WARNER POWER STEERING

Warner Power Steering is a fully mechanical power steering unit providing driver controlled steering with a minimum of effort.

Power is supplied by the engine through two multiple disk clutches that respond instantly and smoothly to any movement of the steering wheel. The unit retains complete road feel and road sense while at the same time decreasing the effects of road shock through the steering system.

Operation

Power to operate the steering unit comes from a V-belt connected drive pulley and bearing assembly. Power is delivered to the input shaft of the power steering unit by an intermediate shaft through two couplings.

The pulley assembly is spring loaded so that the belt can slip if the steering unit is subjected to a torque load in excess of a predetermined amount.

Such an excessive torque could be imposed when for instance, the wheels might be crimped against the curb with the driver still continuing to turn the steering wheel. Under this condition a torque in excess of a predetermined amount would be placed on the steering mechanism and the belt would slip preventing the power unit from damaging the steering mechanism.

Two sets of multiple disk clutches are used, one turning to the right, the other to the left.

The clutch actuating hub is mounted inside the center of these two multiple disk clutches and is supported by two ball bearing assemblies. A spherical thread of 1½ inch pitch forms the pinion and engages the balls located in the clutch actuating plate.

The shaft portion of the clutch actuating pinion is connected to the steering wheel extension shaft. Movement of the steering wheel causes the clutch actuating plate to travel upwards or downwards on the spherical thread of the clutch actuating hub until the plate engages one or the other of the multiple disk clutches.

Approximately 2 lb pressure at the steering wheel is required to bring the clutches into operation.

When the engine is not running or the drive belt is inoperative the power unit ceases to operate but the driver still retains full and positive control in the normal manner through the conventional steering gear.

Adjustment of the Power Gear

END PLAY ADJUSTMENT

All adjustments should be made with the front wheels jacked up so that there is no pressure on the front wheels.

Two adjustments are provided for the manual steering gear assembly: the steering post end play, and the cam lever shaft clearance. Before making the adjustment disconnect the steering gear from the steering linkage at the pitman arm.

Check the steering post end play first. In order to do this it is necessary to disconnect and remove the power steering unit from the steering gear, then loosen the cam lever shaft adjusting screw lock nut and back off the adjusting screw. To adjust end play take off the lower cover and add or remove shims so that it will require a steady pull of from 10 to 18 oz at the rim of the steering wheel to turn the steering gear smoothly.

HIGH SPOT ADJUSTMENT

Disconnect the pitman arm from the steering gear or jack up the front wheels free of the floor. Then put the steering wheel in a center position. Loosen the adjusting nut and turn the screw down until the cam lever fingers bottom in the gear. Back off the adjusting screw and then screw down again until the cam lever just barely touches the gear.

Locate the center of travel (high spot). While turning the steering wheel back and forth over the high spot, turn the lever shaft adjusting screw until a slight drag is felt, then tighten the lock nut. To check the adjustment, hook a spring scale to the rim of the steering wheel and check the amount of effort required to turn the wheel in either direction through the high spot. The scale reading should be from 16 to 24 oz.

DISASSEMBLY

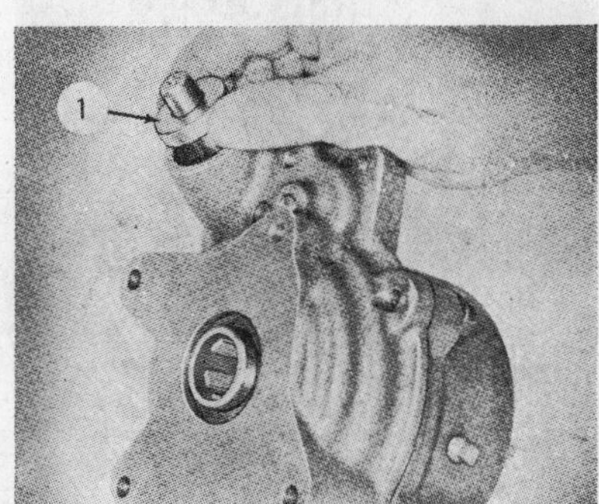

Fig. 2—Using a sharp pointed tool, pry out drive shaft oil seal (1)

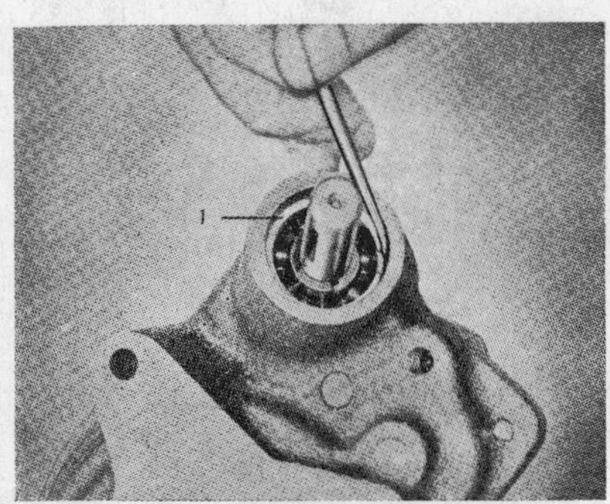

Fig. 3—Remove power imput shaft snap ring (1)

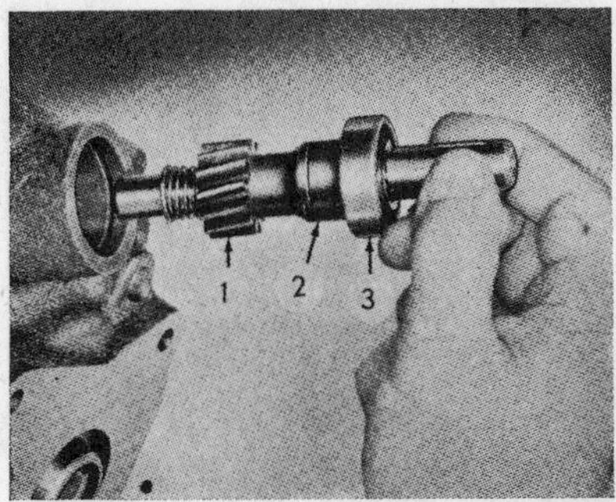

Fig. 4—Remove the power imput shaft (1), ratchet (2) and bearing (3) as an assembly

Fig. 5—Remove oil seal (1)

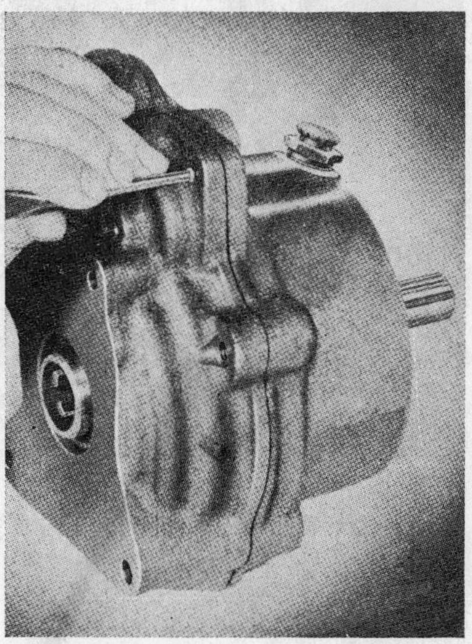

Fig. 6—Drive out taper pin

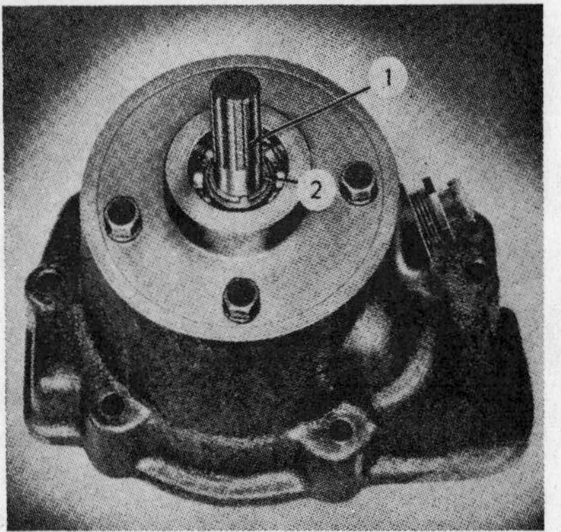

Fig. 7—Remove snap ring (1) from mainshaft (2)

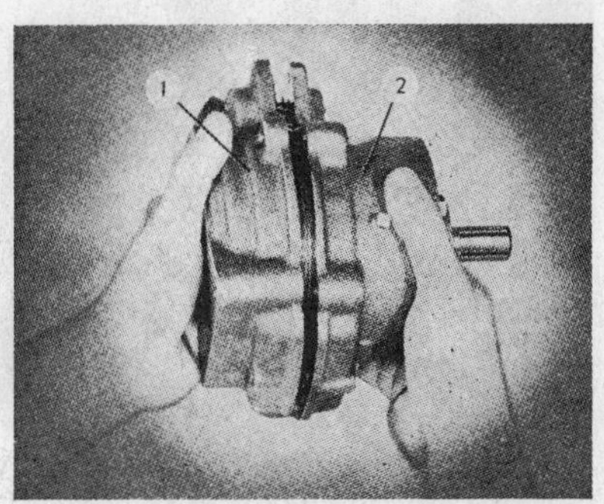

Fig. 8—Separate housings (1) (2). Note be careful not to drop needle bearings

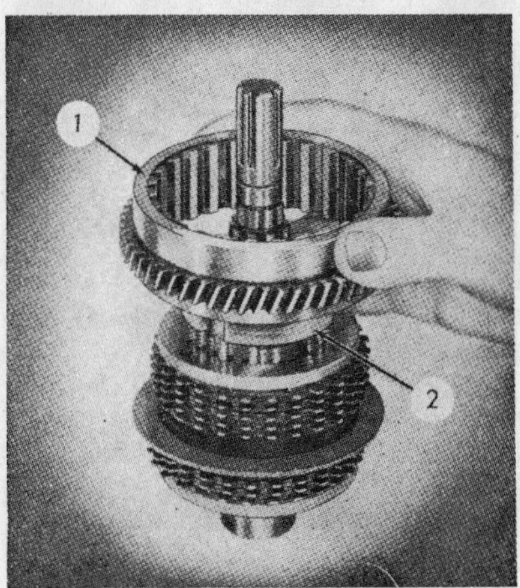

Fig. 9—Lift off the upper ring gear (1) leaving damper hub (2) accessible

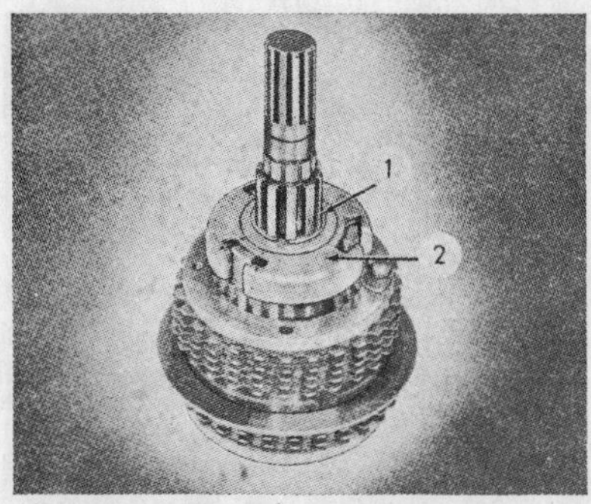

Fig. 10—Remove damper hub retaining snap ring (1) lift off damper hub (2)

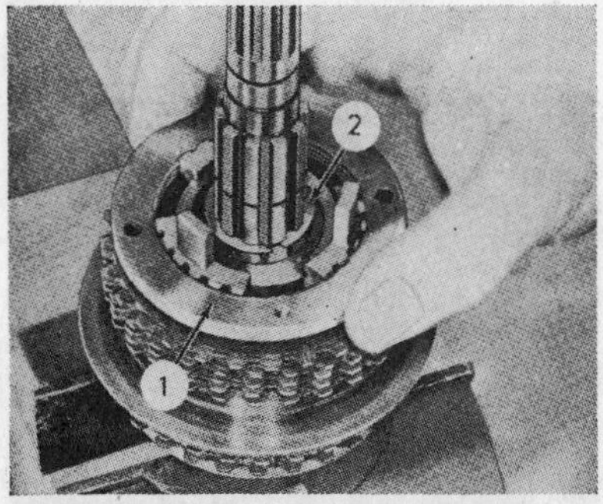

Fig. 11—Remove lock plate, unscrew clutch end plate (1) snap ring (2)

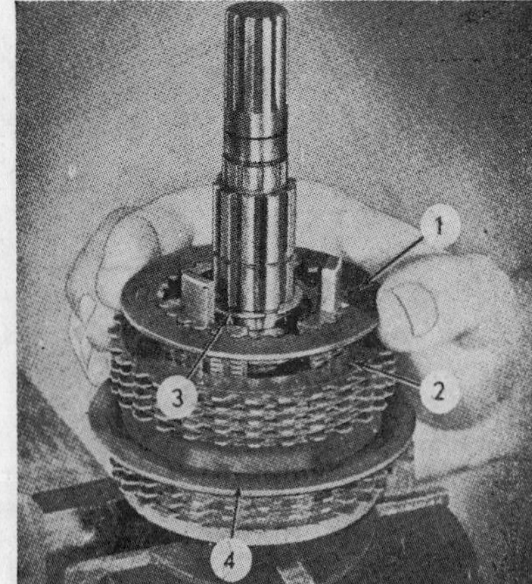

Fig. 12—Lift off clutch discs (driven) 1, and friction plate (2) as an assembly. Remove snap ring (3) slip the gear thrust washer (4) from the clutch actuating plate

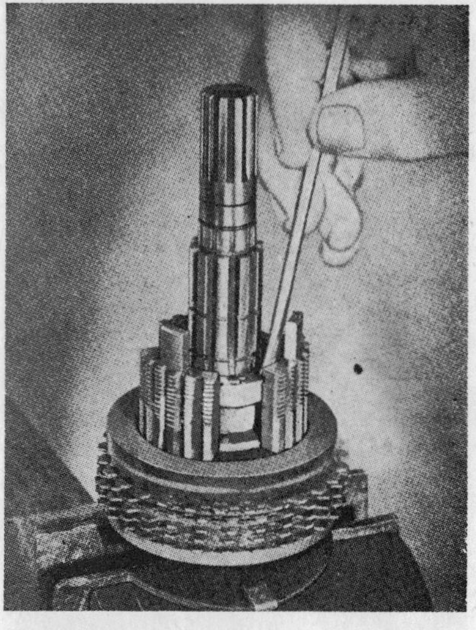

Fig. 13—Remove the outer ball race snap ring

Fig. 14—Take off the outer ball race and remove the ball bearing

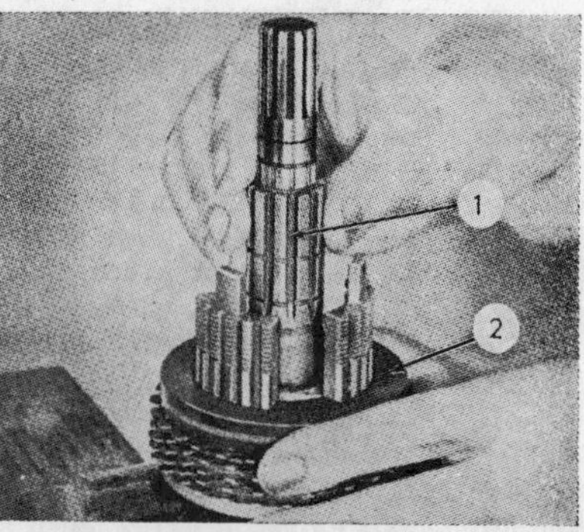

Fig. 15 — Hold the mainshaft (1) and clutch actuating plate (2) and lift the parts out of the clutch hub as a unit. Caution: Do not allow shaft or plate to turn as turning will permit the steel balls to fall from their location

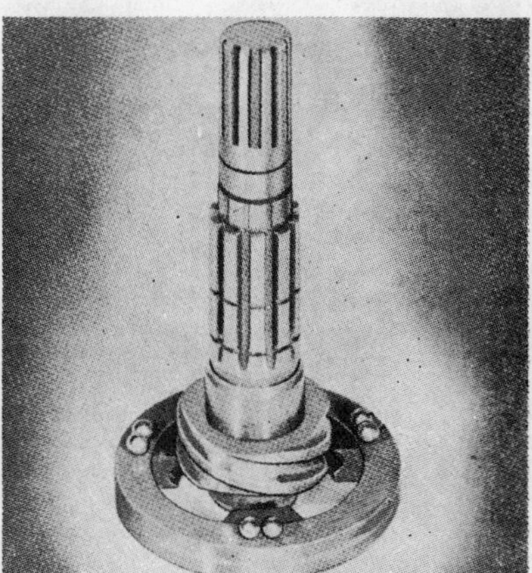

Fig. 16—Note: position of steel balls

Fig. 17—Remove lower ball bearing

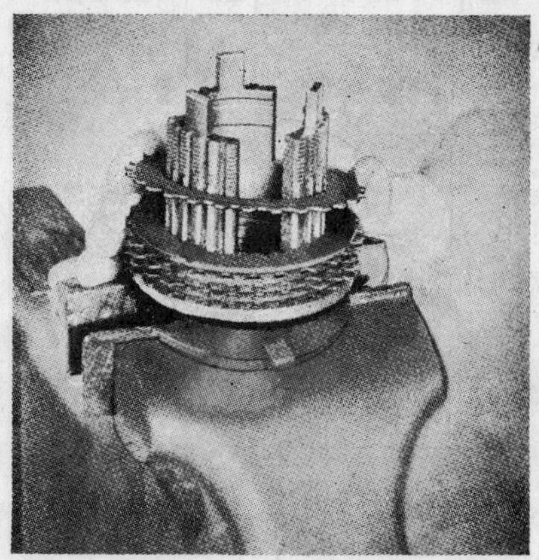

Fig. 18—Remove clutch disc

Fig. 20—Using a suitable drift drive out the upper retainer

Fig. 22—Lift stop ring out of housing

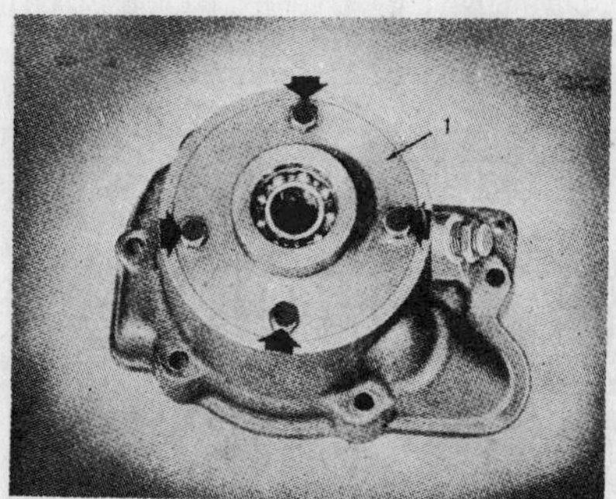

Fig. 19—Remove the four bolts from upper housing retainer (1) as indicated by arrows

Fig. 21—To remove sealing ring around retainer, pick the ring out of the groove and remove it from the retainer

Fig. 23—Stop ring assembly

Carter Specifications Table

Down Draft W and YF Type

These carburetors are listed according to their appearances on the car. The first number shown in the carburetor number column is the original number. The following numbers can also be used. For example number 487s is the original number for 1941 and 42, Series 40, Buick. The next number 551s can be used in place of number 487s. 608s replaces both 551s and 487s, and number 663s can be used in place of all the numbers preceeding it for that model.

Year	Model	Carburetor Model Number	Type	Casting Number on Face of Flange	Float Setting (inches) and Tool Number with Prefix T109	Idle Screw Setting Turns Open	Fast Idle Adjustment (inches) and Tool No. with [3] Prefix T109 (A)	Pump Travel Adjustment (inches) Using Tool No. T109-117S	Unloader Adjustment and Gauge Number with Prefix T109 (C)	Metering Setting Gauge Number with Prefix T109	Metering Rod Standard with Prefix 75	Metering Rod 1—Size Lean with Prefix 75	Float Needle and Seat Assembly with Prefix 25	Metering Rod Jet and Gasket with Prefix 120	Carburetor Repair Kit Number	Gasket Assortment Number
BUICK																
1941	50, Front	509S	WCD	324–535	3/16–162 (2)	1/4 to 1 1/4	.012–200	21/64	3/16–28	152	492	503	105S	121S		154
		528S	WCD	324–535	3/16–162 (2)	1/4 to 1 1/4	.012–200	16/64	3/16–28	152	492	503	105S	149S	1315	154
	Rear	510S	WCD	346	3/16–162 (2)	1/4 to 1 1/4							105S	143S		155
		543S	WCD	409	3/16–162 (5)	1/4 to 1 1/4							111S	143S	1315	155
	60, 70, 90, Front	490S	WCD	324–535	3/16–162 (2)	1/4 to 1 1/4	.015–44	21/64	3/16–28	152	473	490	105S	121S		154
		533S	WCD	324–535	3/16–162 (5)	1/4 to 1 1/4	.015–44	14/64	3/16–28	152	473	490	105S	121S	1316	154
	Rear	491S	WCD	346	3/16–162 (2)	1/4 to 1 1/4							105S	141S		155
		544S	WCD	409	3/16–162 (5)	1/4 to 1 1/4							111S	141S	1316	155
1941–42	40	487S	WCD	324	3/16–162 (5)	1/2 to 1 1/2	.012–200	21/64	3/16–28	152	459	488	105S	65S	1098	154
		551S	WCD	546	3/16–162 (5)	1/4 to 1 1/4	.012–200	21/64	3/16–28	152	459	488	105S	65S		
		608S	WCD	324	3/16–162 (6)	1/2 to 1	.012–200	21/64	3/16–28	152	459	488	105S	65S	1364	189
		663S	WCD	546	5/32–196 (6)	3/4 to 1 1/4	.015–44	21/64	3/16–28		614	633	105S	158	1391	189
	50, Front	528S	WCD	324–535	3/16–162 (5)	1/4 to 1 1/4	.012–200	16/64	3/16–28	152	492	503	105S	149S	1315	154
	Rear	529S	WCD	346	3/16–162 (5)	1/4 to 1 1/4							111S	143S	1315	155
		543S	WCD	409	3/16–162 (5)	1/4 to 1 1/4							111S	143S	1315	155
	60, 70, 90, Front	533S	WCD	324–535	3/16–162 (5)	1/4 to 1 1/4	.015–44	14/64	3/16–28	152	473	490	105S	121S	1316	154
	Rear	534S	WCD	346	3/16–162 (5)	1/4 to 1 1/4							111S	141S	1316	155
		544S	WCD	409	3/16–162 (5)	1/4 to 1 1/4							111S	141S	1316	155
1942	50, Rear	543S	WCD	409	3/16–162 (5)	1/4 to 1 1/4							111S	143S	1315	155
	60, 70, 90, Rear	544S	WCD	409	3/16–162 (5)	1/4 to 1 1/4							111S	141S	1316	155
	60, 70, 90, Eight	549S	WCD		3/16–162 (5)	1/4 to 1 1/4	.012–200	21/64	3/16–28	152	459	488	105S	65S		
		609S	WCD	402	3/16–162 (6)	3/4 to 1 3/4	.018–44	21/64	3/16–28	163	592	557	115S	65S	1365	189
		664S	WCD	573	5/32–196 (6)	3/4 to 1 3/4	.018–44	21/64	3/16–28		615	635	115S	158	1392	189
	40, 50, Eight	551S	WCD		3/16–162 (5)	1/4 to 1 1/4	.012–200	21/64	3/16–28	152	459	488	105S	65S		
		608S	WCD	324	3/16–162 (6)	1/2 to 1	.012–200	21/64	3/16–28	152	459	488	105S	65S	1364	189
		663S	WCD	546	5/32–196 (6)	3/4 to 1 1/4	.015–44	21/64	3/16–28		614	633	105S	158	1391	189
1946–47	40, 50, Eight	608S	WCD	324	3/16–162 (6)	1/2 to 1	.012–200	21/64	3/16–28	152	459	488	105S	65S	1364	189
		608SA	WCD	546	3/16–162 (6)	1/2 to 1	.012–200	21/64	3/16–28	152	459	488	105S	65S	1364	189
		608SC	WCD	546	5/32–196 (6)	3/4 to 1 1/4	.012–200	21/64	3/16–28		614	633	105S	158	1391	189
		663S	WCD	546	5/32–196 (6)	3/4 to 1 1/4	.015–44	21/64	3/16–28		614	633	105S	158	1391	189
	70, Roadmaster	609S	WCD	402	3/16–162 (6)	3/4 to 1 3/4	.018–44	21/64	3/16–28	163	592	557	115S	65S	1365	189
		609SA	WCD	548	3/16–162 (6)	3/4 to 1 3/4	.018–44	21/64	3/16–28	163	592	557	115S	65S	1365	189
		609SC	WCD	573	5/32–196 (6)	3/4 to 1 3/4	.018–44	21/64	3/16–28		615	635	115S	158	1392	189
		664S	WCD	573	5/32–196 (6)	3/4 to 1 3/4	.018–44	21/64	3/16–28		615	635	115S	158	1392	189
1948–49	40, 50, Eight	663S	WCD	546	5/32–196 (6)	3/4 to 1 1/4	.015–44	21/64	3/16–28		614	633	105S	158	1391	189
	70	664S	WCD	573	5/32–196 (6)	3/4 to 1 3/4	.018–44	21/64	3/16–28		615	635	115S	158	1392	189
1950–51	40, 50	725S	WCD	624	5/32–196 (6)	7/8 to 1 3/8	.015–44	20/64	3/16–28		685	702	105S	158	1515	195
		725SA	WCD	624	5/32–196 (6)	7/8 to 1 3/8	.015–44	20/64	3/16–28		685	702	105S	158	1515	195
		882S	WCD	624	5/32–196 (6)	1 1/4 to 1 3/4	.012–200	20/64	3/16–28		685	702	105S	158	1595	195
	70	726S	WCD	626	5/32–196 (6)	3/4 to 1 1/4	.018–44	20/64	3/16–28		677	717	115S	158	1532	195
		726SA	WCD	626	5/32–196 (6)	3/4 to 1 1/4	.018–44	20/64	3/16–28		677	717	115S	158	1532	195
		883S	WCD	626	5/32–196 (6)	1 to 1 1/2	.015–44	20/64	3/16–28		677	717	115S	158	1596	195

Down Draft W and YF Type—continued

Year	Model	Carburetor Model Number	Type	Casting Number on Face of Flange	Float Setting (inches) and Tool Number with Prefix T109	Idle Screw Setting Turns Open	Fast Idle Adjustment (inches) and Tool No. with Prefix T109 (A)	Pump Travel Adjustment (inches) Using Tool No. T109-117S	Unloader Adjustment and Gauge Number with Prefix T109 (C)	Metering Setting Gauge Number with Prefix T109	Metering Rod Standard with Prefix 75	Metering Rod 1—Size Lean with Prefix 75	Float Needle and Seat Assembly with Prefix 25	Metering Rod Jet and Gasket with Prefix 120	Carburetor Repair Kit Number	Gasket Assortment Number
BUICK—cont'd																
1951	40, 50	883S	WCD	624	5/32–196 (6)	1¼ to 1¾	.012–200	20/64	3/16–28		685	702	105S	158	1595	195
	70	883S	WCD	626	5/32–196 (6)	1 to 1½	.015–44	20/64	3/16–28		677	717	115S	158	1596	195
1952	40, 50	896S	WCD	624	5/32–196	¾ to 1¼	.015–29	5/16	3/16–28		685	702	105S	158	1595	195A
	70	894S	WCFB		(E)	¼ to 1¼	.020–29		3/16–28		818	828	211S	165	1599B	219
1953	40, 50	882S	WCD	624	5/32–196	¾ to 1¼	.020–29	5/16	3/16–28		685	702	105S	158	1595	195A
	70	996S	WCFB		(F)	¾ to 1¾	.020–29	9/32	3/16–28		877		211S	166		232
CADILLAC																
1941	V8	506S	WDO	277	18–36 (2)	½ to 1½	.023–189	26/64	13/64–39	113	422	423	98S	121S	1093	144
1942	V8	486S	WCD	385	9/64–160 (5)	¾ to 1¾	.015–44	23/64	3/16–28	163	526	550	98S	103S	1331	166
1946	All, Eight	595S	WCD	456	9/64–160 (6)	½ to 1½	.018–44	29/64	3/16–28	163	576	597	98S	103S	1363	189
		595SA	WCD	552	9/64–160 (6)	½ to 1½	.018–44	27/64	3/16–28	163	576	597	98S	103S	1363	189
1946–48	All	595SA	WCD	552	9/64–160 (6)	½ to 1½	.018–44	27/64	3/16–28	163	576	597	98S	103S	1363	189
1949	All	682S	WCD	610	9/64–160 (6)	½ to 1½	.020–29	7/32	3/16–28	163	673		98S	103S	1508	189
		722S	WCD	610	9/64–160 (6)	½ to 1½	.020–29	5/16	3/16–28		670	731	98S	159	1506	189
1950	All	742S	WCD	672	11/64–205 (6)	¾ to 1¼	.020–29	19/64	7/32–106		716	729	98S	159	1538	201
1951	All	845S	WCD	821	11/64–205 (6)	¾ to 1¼	.020–29	19/64	7/32–106		716	785	98S	159	1538	201
1952		896S	WCFB		(G)	1¼ to 2	.020–29	9/32	3/16–28		824		211S	166	1718	226
1953		2605S	WCFB		(H)	¼ to 2¼	.020–29	9/32	3/16–28		889		214S	166	1733	233
CHEVROLET																
1937–51	Std. Trans. & Cli. Con.	756S	YF	756S	5/16–107 (7)	1 to 2	.076		3/16–28		678	736	195S	155	1563	208
		756SA	YF	756SA	5/16–107 (7)	1 to 2	.076		3/16–28		787	788	195S	155	1587	208
	Manual Choke, Std. Trans.	787S	YF		½–83 (7)	1 to 2					678	736	33S	155	1549	206
		787SA	YF		5/16–107 (7)	1 to 2					678	736	195S	155	1561	206
		787SB	YF		5/16–107 (7)	1 to 2					787	788	195S	155	1581	206
1939–40	All	420S	W-1	365	½–83 (1)	1 to 2				25	377	342	33S	129	1013	138
		787S	YF		½–83 (7)	1 to 2					678	736	33S	155	1549	206
		787SB	YF		5/16–107 (7)	1 to 2					787	788	195S	155	1581	206
1941–51	All, Std. Trans.	684S	W-1	603	½–83 (1)	1 to 2				25	485	517	33S	115S	1500	152
		787S	YF		½–83 (7)	1 to 2					678	736	33S	155	1549	206
		787SB	YF		5/16–107 (7)	1 to 2					787	788	195S	155	1581	206
1950–51	All, Power Glide	789S	YF	789S	5/16–107 (7)	1 to 2					678	736	195S	167	1569	208
		789SA	YF	789SA	5/16–107 (7)	1 to 2					790	795	195S	162	1588	208
CHRYSLER																
1951	C52, C53, C54, V8	830S	WCD		11/64–205 (6)	½ to 1	.040–193	17/64	7/32–106		765	769	98S	159	1577	212
		830SA	WCD		11/64–205 (6)	½ to 1	.040–193	17/64	7/32–106		765	769	98S	159	1577	212
		931S	WCD													
1952	V8	931S	WCD		11/64–205	½ to 1	.040–193	17/64	7/32–106		817	813	983	159	1705A	212D
1953	V8	935S	WCD		11/64–205	½ to 1	.040–193	17/64	7/32–106		817	813	983	159	1705A	212D

Carter Specifications Table—*continued*

Year	Model	Carburetor Model Number	Type	Casting Number on Face of Flange	Float Setting (inches) and Tool Number with Prefix T109	Idle Screw Setting Turns Open	Fast Idle Adjustment (inches) and Tool No. with Prefix T109 (A)	Pump Travel Adjustment (inches) Using Tool No. T109-117S	Unloader Adjustment and Gauge Number with Prefix T109 (C)	Metering Setting Gauge Number with Prefix T109	Metering Rod Standard with Prefix 75	Metering Rod 1—Size Lean with Prefix 75	Float Needle and Seat Assembly with Prefix 25	Metering Rod Jet and Gasket with Prefix 120	Carburetor Repair Kit Number	Gasket Assortment Number
FRAZER																
1947	F-47	574S	W-1	421	1/2-83 (1)	1 1/4 to 2 1/4	...	...	...	25	485	517	155S	115S	1089	138
		622S	WA-1	309	3/8-80 (4)	3/4 to 1 3/4	5/8-D85	18/64	7/16-81	102	593	599	155S	95S	1362	139
		622SA	WA-1	309	1/2-83 (4)	3/4 to 1 3/4	5/8-D85	18/64	7/16-81	102	593	599	155S	95S	1362	139
		622SB	WA-1	307	1/2-83 (4)	3/4 to 1 3/4	5/8-D85	18/64	7/16-81	102	593	599	155S	95S	1362	139
1947-48	F-47, F-485, F-486	622SB	WA-1	...	1/2-83 (4)	3/4 to 1 3/4	5/8-D85	18/64	7/16-81	102	593	599	155S	95S	1362	139
1948	F486	685S	WCD	550	9/64-160 (6)	1 to 1 1/2	.016-44	17/64	1/8-36	163	622	674	162S	125S	1390	189
		685SA	WCD	550	1/16-197 (6)	1 to 1 1/2	.016-44	17/64	1/8-36	163	622	675	162S	125S	1390	189
		723S	WCD	550	1/32-49 (6)	1 to 1 1/2	.018-44	17/64	1/8-36	163	669	694	162S	125S	1512	189
1949	F495, F496	685SA	WCD	550	1/16-197 (6)	1 to 1 1/2	.016-44	17/64	1/8-36	163	622	675	162S	125S	1390	189
		723S	WCD	550	1/32-49 (6)	1 to 1 1/2	.018-44	17/64	1/8-36	163	669	694	162S	125S	1512	189
1949-50	F495, F496, F505, F506	723S	WCD	550	1/32-49 (6)	1 to 1 1/2	.018-44	17/64	1/8-36	163	669	694	162S	125S	1512	189
1951	F515, F516	781S	WGD	774	1/4-31 (8)	1/2 to 1	.018-29	1/2	9/64-34	...	734	738	196S	165	1548	196
		813S	WGD	774	1/4-31 (8)	1/2 to 1	.018-29	1/2	9/64-34	...	748	759	196S	165	1558	196
HENRY J.																
1951-53	514, 6 cyl.	814S	YF	648	9/32-126 (7)	1 to 2	...	...	...	...	749	783	166S	166	...	211
		833S	YF	648	9/32-126 (7)	1 to 2	...	...	...	...	749	783	197S	166	1571	211
		833SA	YF	648	9/32-126 (7)	1 to 2	...	...	...	...	749	783	197S	166	1571	211
		833SB	YF	648	9/32-126 (7)	1 to 2	...	...	...	...	749	783	197S	166	1571	211
	513	820S	YF	648	9/32-126 (7)	1/2 to 1 1/2	...	...	...	...	762	781	197S	159	1572	211
		820SA	YF	648	9/32-126 (7)	1/2 to 1 1/2	...	...	...	...	762	781	197S	159	1572	211
		820SB	YF	648	9/32-126 (7)	1/2 to 1 1/2	...	...	...	...	762	781	197S	159	1572	211
HUDSON																
1940-42	10, 20, 40	454S	WA-1	298	3/8-80 (4)	3/4 to 1 1/2	5/8-D85	12/64	7/16-81	102	407	410	33S	17S	1078	139
1941-47	All six except 4220	501S	WDO	286	1/8-36 (2)	1/2 to 1 1/2	.045-158	18/64	1/4-31	113	467	474	59S	65S	1302	149
1942	20	524S	WA-1	298	3/8-80 (4)	3/4 to 1 1/2	5/8-D85	12/64	7/16-81	102	407	410	33S	17S	1078	139
1941-47	All eight	502S	WDO	279	1/8-36 (2)	1/2 to 1 1/2	.053-158	18/64	1/4-31	113	529	480	59S	121S	1303	149
1948-49	481, 482, 491, 492	647S	WDO	542	3/16-28 (2)	1 1/4 to 1 3/4	.054-193	18/64	1/4-31	113	686	623	59S	121S	1381	149
1949	491, 492	647A	WDO	542	3/16-28 (2)	1 1/4 to 1 3/4	.054-193	18/64	1/4-31	113	686	623	59S	121S	1381	149
1948-49	483, 484, 493, 494	648S	WDO	542	13/64-39 (2)	1 to 1 1/2	.054-193	14/64	1/4-31	113	607	627	59S	121S	1382	149
1950-51	500, 50A, 4A	749S	WA-1	682	1/2-83 (4)	1/2 to 1 1/2	5/8-D85	16/64	7/16-80	102	704	712	75S	15S	1535	198
1950-51	503, 504, 8A	773S	WGD	...	3/16-28 (8)	1/2 to 1	.026-189	1/2	5/32-154	...	724	744	186S	159	1554	196
	501, 502, 5A, 6A, 7A	776S	WGD	...	3/16-28 (8)	1/2 to 1	.026-189	1/2	5/32-154	...	754	732	186S	159	1555	196
1952	Hornet 7B	968S	WAI	910	1/2-83	1 1/4 to 2 1/4	5/8-85	1/4	9/16-84	...	834	861	75S	15S	1723	198
	Wasp 5B, 4C	990S	WAI	...	1/2-83	3/4 to 1 3/4	1/2-83	1/4	9/16-84	...	851	856	75S	15S	...	139A
1953	Jet 1C, 2C	2009S	WAI	...	1/2-83	1/2 to 1 1/2	...	1/4	...	...	864	...	...	...	...	...

Down Draft W and YF Type—*continued*

Year	Model	Carburetor Model Number	Type	Casting Number on Face of Flange	Float Setting (inches) and Tool Number with Prefix T109	Idle Screw Setting Turns Open	Fast Idle Adjustment (inches) and Tool No. with Prefix T109 (A)	Pump Travel Adjustment (inches) Using Tool No. T109-117S	Unloader Adjustment and Gauge Number with Prefix T109 (C)	Metering Setting Gauge Number with Prefix T109	Metering Rod Standard with Prefix 75	Metering Rod 1—Size Lean with Prefix 75	Float Needle and Seat Assembly with Prefix 25	Metering Rod Jet and Gasket with Prefix 120	Carburetor Repair Kit Number	Gasket Assortment Number
KAISER																
1947	K100	574S	W-1	421	1/2-83 (1)	1 1/4 to 2 1/4	…	…	…	25	485	517	33S	115S	1089	138
		622S	WA-1	309	3/8-80 (4)	3/4 to 1 3/4	5/8-D85	18/64	7/16-81	102	642	643	155S	95S	1362	139
		622SA	WA-1	309	1/2-83 (4)	3/4 to 1 3/4	5/8-D85	18/64	7/16-81	102	642	643	155S	95S	1362	139
		622SB	WA-1	309	1/2-83 (4)	3/4 to 1 3/4	5/8-D85	18/64	7/16-81	102	642	643	155S	95S	1362	139
1947–49	K100, K481, 491, 482, KC101	622SB	WA-1	309	1/2-83 (4)	3/4 to 1 3/4	5/8-D85	18/64	7/16-81	102	642	643	155S	95S	1362	139
1949–50	K492	685SA	WCD	550	1/16-197 (6)	1 to 1 1/2	.016-44	17/64	1/8-36	163	622	674	162S	125S	1390	189
		723S	WCD	550	1/32- (6)	1 to 1 1/2	.018-44	17/64	1/8-36	163	669	694	162S	125S	1512	189
1951–52	K511, 512, 521, 522	781S	WGD	774	1/4-31 (7)	1/2 to 1	.018-29	1/2	9/64-34	…	734	738	196S	165	1548	196
1953	K530, 531, 532	999S	WGD	…	9/32-126	1/2 to 1 1/2	.018-023	1/2	9/64-34	…	867	…	196S	165	1724	196
LA SALLE																
1940	50, 52	423S	WDO	248	1/8-36 (2)	1/2 to 1 1/4	.030-29	26/64	1/8-36	113	347	388	59S	121S	1069	140
		460S	WDO	277	1/8-36 (2)	1/2 to 1 1/2	.023-189	26/64	13/64-39	113	403	422	98S	121S	1081	144
NASH																
1941	4180	511S	WDO	360	3/16-28 (2)	1/2 to 1 1/2	.015-44	32/64	9/64-34	113	500	501	59S	139S	1306	145
1942	4280	538S	WDO	397	3/16-28 (2)	1/4 to 1 1/4	.015-44	32/64	9/64-34	113	500	501	59S	139S	…	145
1942–51	60 Series	464S	WA-1	290	3/8-80 (4)	1/2 to 1 1/2	5/8-D85	27/64	31/64-82	102	372	384	34S	133S	1065	139
	(4960)	683S	WA-1	290	1/2-83 (4)	1/2 to 1 1/2	5/8-D85	27/64	31/64-82	102	650	658	34S	133S	1399	139
	(5060-5160)	746S	WA-1	679	1/2-83 (4)	1/2 to 1 1/2	5/8-D85	27/64	31/64-82	102	650	658	34S	133S	1518	139
1946–51	40 Series	611S	WA-1	298	1/2-83 (4)	1 1/4 to 2 1/4	5/8-D85	25/64	7/16-81	102	584	585	33S	117S	1361	139
	(4840)	662S	WA-1	298	1/2-83 (4)	3/4 to 1 3/4	5/8-D85	25/64	7/16-81	102	619	631	33S	117S	1379	139
	(4840)	662SA	WA-1	298	1/2-83 (4)	3/4 to 1 3/4	5/8-D85	25/64	7/16-81	102	619	631	33S	117S	1379	139
	(4940-5040)	694S	WA-1	298	1/2-83 (4)	3/4 to 1 3/4	5/8-D85	25/64	7/16-81	102	646	660	33S	117S	1501	139
	(5040, 5140, 5110)	780S	WA-1	779	1/2-83 (4)	3/4 to 1 3/4	5/8-D85	25/64	7/16-81	102	646	660	33S	117S	1501	139
1951–52	5110, 5210	757S	YF	…	1/2-83 (7)	1 to 2	.054-193	…	3/16-28	…	775	791	189S	163	…	208
		757SA	YF	…	1/2-83 (7)	1 to 2	.054-193	…	3/16-28	…	775	791	189S	163	…	208
		757SB	YF	…	1/2-83 (7)	1 to 2	.054-193	…	3/16-28	…	775	791	189S	160	1570	208
		876S	YF	…	5/16-107 (7)	1/2 to 1 1/2	.054-193	…	9/32-126	…	779	793	195S	170	1590	216
		876SA	YF	…	5/16-107 (7)	1/2 to 1 1/2	.054-193	…	9/32-126	…	779	793	189S	170	1590	216
	5140, 5240	824S	YF	…	1/2-83 (7)	1 to 2	.054-193	…	3/16-28	…	775	791	189S	163	…	208
		824SA	YF	…	1/2-83 (7)	1 to 2	.054-193	…	3/16-28	…	775	791	189S	163	…	208
		824SB	YF	…	1/2-83 (7)	1 to 2	.054-193	…	3/16-28	…	775	791	189S	160	1570	208
		877S	YF	…	5/16-83 (7)	1/2 to 1 1/2	.054-193	…	9/32-126	…	779	793	195S	170	1590	216
		877SA	YF	…	5/16-83 (7)	1/2 to 1 1/2	.054-193	…	9/32-126	…	779	793	189S	170	…	216
1952–53	5260, 5360	895S	YH	873	3/8-80	1/2 to 1 1/2	.030-29	…	1/4-31	…	852	865	208S	163	1713	223
1953	5340	2034S	WCD	…	5/32-196	1/2 to 1 1/2	.005-237	…	11/64-166	…	899	…	105S	158	1732	230
OLDSMOBILE																
1941–47	Eight, Hydramatic	480S	WDO	342	3/16-28 (2)	1/2 to 1 1/2	.015-44	19/64	3/16-28	113	641	509	164S	103S	1096	158
		480SA	WDO	342	3/16-28 (2)	1/2 to 1 1/2	.015-44	19/64	3/16-28	113	641	509	164S	103S	1096	158
		503S	WDO	342	3/16-28 (2)	1/2 to 1 1/2	.015-44	19/64	1/4-31	113	486	509	164S	103S	1096	158
		503SA	WDO	342	3/16-28 (2)	1/2 to 1 1/2	.015-44	19/64	1/4-31	113	486	509	164S	103S	1096	158
		650S	WDO	540	3/16-28 (2)	1/2 to 1 1/2	.015-44	19/64	1/4-31	113	486	509	164S	103S	1096	158
		650SA	WDO	540	15/64-32 (2)	1/2 to 1 1/2	.015-44	19/64	1/4-31	113	486	509	164S	103S	1096	158

Carter Specifications Table—*continued*

Year	Model	Carburetor Model Number	Type	Casting Number on Face of Flange	Float Setting (inches) and Tool Number with Prefix T109	Idle Screw Setting Turns Open	Fast Idle Adjustment (inches) and Tool No. with Prefix T109 (A)	Pump Travel Adjustment (inches) Using Tool No. T109-117S	Unloader Adjustment and Gauge Number with Prefix T109 (C)	Metering Setting Gauge Number with Prefix T109	Metering Rod Standard with Prefix 75	Metering Rod 1—Size Lean with Prefix 75	Float Needle and Seat Assembly with Prefix 25	Metering Rod Jet and Gasket with Prefix 120	Carburetor Repair Kit Number	Gasket Assortment Number
OLDSMOBILE—cont'd																
1941–48	Six, Hydramatic	481S	WA-1	340	1/2–83 (4)	1/2 to 1 1/2	5/8–85	16/64	3/8–80	102	651	512	75S	15S	1097	157
		651S	WA-1	538	1/2–83 (4)	1/2 to 1 1/2	5/8–85	16/64	3/8–80	102	651	512	75S	15S	1383	157
		709S	WA-1	538	1/2–83 (4)	1/2 to 2	5/8–D85	16/64	3/8–80	102	651	512	75S	15S	1383	157
		763S	WA-1	538	1/2–83 (4)	1/2 to 1 1/2	5/8–D85	16/64	3/8–80	102	651	512	75S	15S	1536	157
		763SA	WA-1	538	1/2–83 (4)	1/2 to 1 1/2	5/8–D85	16/64	3/8–80	102	651	512	75S	15S	1536	157
1941–47	Eight cylinder	503S	WDO	342	3/16–28 (2)	1/2 to 1 1/2	.015–44	19/64	3/16–28	113	641	509	164S	103S	1096	158
		503SA	WDO	342	3/16–28 (2)	1/2 to 1 1/2	.015–44	19/64	3/16–28	113	641	509	164S	103S	1096	158
		650S	WDO	540	3/16–28 (2)	1 1/2 to 1/2	.015–44	19/64	1/4–31	113	641	509	164S	103S	1096	158
		650SA	WDO	540	15/64–32 (2)	1/2 to 1 1/2	.015–44	19/64	1/4–31	113	641	509	164S	103S	1096	158
1941–48	Six cylinder	504S	WA-1	340	1/2–83 (4)	1/2 to 1 1/2	5/8–D85	16/64	7/16–81	102	651	512	75S	15S	1097	157
		710S	WA-1	538	1/2–83 (4)	1/2 to 2	5/8–D85	16/64	7/16–81	102	651	512	75S	15S	1383	157
		764S	WA-1	538	1/2–83 (4)	1/2 to 1 1/2	5/8–D85	16/64	7/16–81	102	651	512	75S	15S	1536	157
1942	Six, Syn. Trans.	523S	W-1	462	7/16 (1)	1/2 to 1 1/2	5/8–41	15/64	7/16–81	25	523	....	75S	117S	1353	167
		504S	WA-1	340	1/2–83 (4)	1/2 to 1 1/2	5/8–D85	16/64	7/16–81	102	651	512	75S	15S	1097	157
		710S	WA-1	538	1/2–83 (4)	1/2 to 2	5/8–D85	16/64	7/16–81	102	651	512	75S	15S	1383	157
		764S	WA-1	538	1/2–83 (4)	1/2 to 1 1/2	5/8–D85	16/64	7/16–81	102	651	512	75S	15S	1536	157
1948–50	Six cylinder (H. T.)	651S	WA-1	538	1/2–83 (4)	1/2 to 1 1/2	5/8–85	16/64	3/8–80	102	651	512	75S	15S	1383	157
		709S	WA-1	538	1/2–83 (4)	1/2 to 2	5/8–D85	16/64	3/8–80	102	651	512	75S	15S	1383	157
		763S	WA-1	538	1/2–83 (4)	1/2 to 1 1/2	5/8–D85	16/64	3/8–80	102	651	512	75S	15S	1536	157
		763SA	WA-1	538	1/2–83 (4)	1/2 to 1 1/2	5/8–D85	16/64	3/8–80	102	651	512	75S	15S	1536	157
1949–50	Six, Syn. Trans.	710S	WA-1	538	1/2–83 (4)	1/2 to 2	5/8–D85	16/64	7/16–81	102	651	512	75S	15S	1383	157
		764S	WA-1	538	1/2–83 (4)	1/2 to 1 1/2	5/8–D85	16/64	7/16–81	102	651	512	75S	15S	1536	157
	80, 98	714S	WGD	604	1/4–31 (8)	1/2 to 1	.018–44	....	1/4–31	....	763	706	182S	160	1505	193
		714SA	WGD	604	1/4–31 (8)	1/2 to 1	.018–44	....	1/4–31	....	763	706	182S	160	1505	193
		849S	WGD	604	1/4–31 (8)	1/2 to 1	.015–44	....	7/64–125	....	763	706	182S	160	1505	193
1951–53	88, 98	851S	WGD	836	1/4–31 (8)	3/4 to 1 1/4	.020–29	....	1/4–31	....	766	....	200S	159	1573	196
1952	Super 88, 98	932S	WCFB	....	1/4–23	1 to 2	.020–29	9/32	1/8–36	....	850	....	211S	176	1703	221
1953	Super 88, 98	2016S	WCFD	....	3/16–222	1 3/4 to 2 3/4	.020–29	9/32	1/8–36	....	887	....	211S	166	1730	234
PACKARD																
1941–47	120, 1951, 2001, 11, 21, 2101, 11	512S	WDO	371	5/32–154 (2)	1/2 to 1 1/2	.020–29	14/64	11/64–166	113	451	519	98S	125S	1092	156
1942–50	110, 2000, 10, 20, 2100, 30	530S	WA-1	317	3/8–80 (4)	1/2 to 1 1/2	5/8–D85	16/64	7/16–81	102	535	536	42S	15S	1320	139
1942–47	Super 8, 160, 180	531S	WDO	377	5/32–154 (2)	1 1/2 to 2	.023–189	26/64	11/64–166	113	616	639	98S	139S	1321	156
		531SA	WDO	564	5/32–154 (2)	1 1/2 to 2	.023–189	26/64	11/64–166	113	616	639	98S	139S	1321	156
1948–50	2206, 26, 33, 2306, 33	531SA	WDO	564	5/32–154 (2)	1 1/2 to 2	.023–189	26/64	11/64–166	113	616	639	98S	139S	1321	156
	2202, 22, 32, 2302	643S	WDO	377	5/32–154 (2)	3/4 to 1 1/4	.026–189	28/64	11/64–166	113	606	620	98S	139S	1375	156
		643SA	WDO	561	5/32–154 (2)	3/4 to 1 1/4	.026–189	28/64	11/64–166	113	606	620	98S	139S	1375	156
	2201, 11, 2301	644S	WDO	561	5/32–154 (2)	5/8 to 1 1/8	.020–29	14/64	11/64–166	113	638	519	98S	125S	1376	156
		644SA	WDO	561	5/32–154 (2)	5/8 to 1 1/8	.020–29	14/64	11/64–166	113	638	519	98S	125S	1376	156
1949–50	2301	728S	WGD	615	13/64–39 (8)	1 to 1 1/2	.026–189	15/32	1/8–36	....	679	709	186S	159	1524	196
		728SA	WGD	615	13/64–39 (8)	1 to 1 1/2	.026–189	15/32	1/8–36	....	707	721	186S	159	1525	196

Down Draft W and YF Type—*continued*

Year	Model	Carburetor Model Number	Type	Casting Number on Face of Flange	Float Setting (inches) and Tool Number with Prefix T109	Idle Screw Setting Turns Open	Fast Idle Adjustment (inches) and Tool No. with Prefix T109 (A)	Pump Travel Adjustment (inches) Using Tool No. T109-117S	Unloader Adjustment and Gauge Number with Prefix T109 (C)	Metering Setting Gauge Number with Prefix T109	Metering Rod Standard with Prefix 75	Metering Rod 1—Size Lean with Prefix 75	Float Needle and Seat Assembly with Prefix 25	Metering Rod Jet and Gasket with Prefix 120	Carburetor Repair Kit Number	Gasket Assortment Number
PACKARD—cont'd																
1951	300, 400	767S	WGD	803	13/64–39 (8)	1/2 to 1 1/2	.023–189	5/16	1/8–36	....	764	777	186S	159	1542	196
	2401	784S	WGD	803	13/64–39 (8)	1/2 to 1 1/2	.023–189	5/16	1/8–36	....	722	767	186S	159	1568	196
1952–53	300, 400, 2611	928S	WGD	615	13/64–39	1 to 1 1/2	.026–189	15/32	1/8	....	707	709	165S	159	1524	196
1953	2631, 02, 06, 26	985S	WCFB	....	5/32–236	1 to 2	.020–29	9/32	9/32–106	....	824	....	211S	165	1727	229
PLYMOUTH																
1947	P15 (some)	574S	W-1	421	1/2 (1)	1 1/4 to 2 1/4	....	....	....	25	485	517	33S	115S	1089	138
PONTIAC																
1940	25, 26	463S	WA-1	245	7/16–81 (4)	3/4 to 1 1/2	5/8–D85	18/64	3/8–80	102	401	427	42S	133S	1085	139
		463SP	WA-1	245	7/16–81 (4)	3/4 to 1 1/2	5/8–D85	18/64	3/8–80	102	401	427	42S	133S	1085	139
1940–41	27, 28, 29	469SM	WDO	306	5/16–107 (2)	1/4 to 1 1/4	5/8–85	19/64	3/16–28	104	424	439	74S	103S	1086	134
		548S	WDO	306	5/16–107 (2)	1/4 to 1 1/4	.026–189	19/64	3/16–28	27	443	444	74S	103S	1351	134
		630SA	WCD	550	3/16–162 (6)	3/4 to 1 3/4	.026–189	18/64	.040–193	163	594	604	105S	65S	1369	190
		630SB	WCD	550	3/16–162 (6)	3/4 to 1 3/4	.026–189	18/64	.040–193	163	594	604	105S	65S	1369	190
		719S	WCD	550	3/16–162 (6)	3/4 to 1 1/4	.026–189	20/64	1/8–36	163	664	683	105S	65S	1507	189
		719SA	WCD	550	3/16–162 (6)	3/4 to 1 1/4	.026–189	20/64	1/8–36	163	664	683	105S	65S	1507	189
1941–48	24, 25, 26 (Std. Trans.)	494S	WA-1	348	1/2–83 (4)	3/4 to 1 3/4	5/8–85	18/64	7/32–106	102	472	506	42S	133S	1300	146
		537S	WA-1	388	7/16–81 (4)	1 to 1 3/4	5/8–85	17/64	5/16–107	102	528	582	83S	133S	1366	146
		717S	WA-1	388	7/16–81 (4)	1 to 1 3/4	5/8–85	17/64	5/16–107	102	528	582	83S	133S	1366	146
1942	25, 26	521S	W-1	461	11/16–87 (1)	1/2 to 1 1/2	5/8–85	19/64	3/8–80	25	530	....	83S	93S	....	167
		545S	W-1	476	11/16–87 (1)	1/2 to 1 1/2	5/8–85	19/64	7/32–106	25	552	555	83S	93S	....	167
1942–48	27, 28 (Std. Trans.)	540S	WDO	306	5/16–107 (2)	1/4 to 1 1/4	.026–189	19/64	3/16–28	27	443	444	74S	103S	1086	134
		548S	WDO	306	5/16–107 (2)	1/4 to 1 1/4	.026–189	19/64	3/16–28	27	443	444	74S	103S	1351	134
		630SA	WCD	550	3/16–162 (6)	3/4 to 1 3/4	.026–189	18/64	.040–193	163	594	604	105S	65S	1369	190
		630SB	WCD	550	3/16–162 (6)	3/4 to 1 3/4	.026–189	18/64	.040–193	163	594	604	105S	65S	1369	190
		719S	WCD	550	3/16–162 (6)	3/4 to 1 1/4	.026–189	20/64	1/8–36	163	664	683	105S	65S	1507	189
		719SA	WCD	550	3/16–162 (6)	3/4 to 1 1/4	.026–189	20/64	1/8–36	163	664	683	105S	65S	1507	189
1948	25, 26 (Hydramatic)	652S	WA-1	592	7/16–81 (4)	1 to 1 3/4	5/8–85	17/64	5/16–107	102	528	582	83S	133S	1388	146
	27, 28 (Hydramatic)	653S	WCD	558	3/16–162 (6)	3/4 to 1 3/4	.026–189	18/64	1/8–36	163	594	604	105S	65S	1369	190
		720S	WCD	558	3/16–162 (6)	3/4 to 1 1/4	.026–189	20/64	1/8–36	163	664	683	105S	65S	1507	189
		720SA	WCD	558	3/16–162 (6)	3/4 to 1 1/4	.026–189	20/64	1/8–36	163	664	683	105S	65S	1507	189
1949–52	25 (Hydramatic)	717S	WA-1	388	7/16–81 (4)	1 to 1 3/4	5/8–85	17/64	5/16–107	102	528	582	83S	133S	1366	146
		718S	WA-1	592	7/16–81 (4)	1 to 1 3/4	5/8–85	17/64	5/16–107	102	528	582	83S	133S	1366	146
1949–52	Eight (Std. Trans.), 27	719S	WCD	550	3/16–162 (6)	3/4 to 1 1/4	.026–189	20/64	1/8–36	163	664	683	105S	65S	1507	189
		719SA	WCD	550	3/16–162 (6)	3/4 to 1 1/4	.026–189	20/64	1/8–36	163	664	683	105S	65S	1507	189
	27 (Hydramatic)	720S	WCD	558	3/16–162 (6)	3/4 to 1 1/4	.026–189	20/64	1/8–36	163	664	683	105S	65S	1507	189
		720SA	WCD	558	3/16–162 (6)	3/4 to 1 1/4	.026–189	20/64	1/8–36	163	664	683	105S	65S	1507	189
1953	25	2010S	WCD	....	5/32–196	1/2 to 1 1/2	.026–189	....	9/64–34	....	873	....	236S	158	....	231
STUDEBAKER																
1940–50	All Commanders	410S	WA-1	....	1/4–31 (4)	1/4 to 1 1/4	....	18/64	....	102	337	330	34S	67S	....	160
		627S	WE	511	7/16–81	1/2 to 1 1/2	.054–193	20/64	17/64	102	698	725	42S	67S	1520	186
		627SA	WE	511	7/16–81	1/2 to 1 1/2	.054–193	20/64	17/64	102	698	725	42S	67S	1520	186
	2G	468S	W-O	229	1/4–31	3/4 to 1 1/4	....	12/64	....	26	393	394	94S	85S	1066	143
		468SA	W-O	229	1/4–31	3/4 to 1 1/4	....	12/64	....	26	393	394	94S	85S	1066	143

Carter Specifications Table—*continued*

Year	Model	Carburetor Model Number	Type	Casting Number on Face of Flange	Float Setting (inches) and Tool Number with Prefix T109	Idle Screw Setting Turns Open	Fast Idle Adjustment (inches) and Tool No. with Prefix T109 (A)	Pump Travel Adjustment (inches) Using Tool No. T109-117S	Unloader Adjustment and Gauge Number with Prefix T109 (C)	Metering Setting Gauge Number with Prefix T109	Metering Rod Standard with Prefix 75	Metering Rod 1—Size Lean with Prefix 75	Float Needle and Seat Assembly with Prefix 25	Metering Rod Jet and Gasket with Prefix 120	Carburetor Repair Kit Number	Gasket Assortment Number
STUDEBAKER—cont'd																
1941–51	3G, 4G, 5G, 6G	496S	WA-1	356	5/16–107 (4)	1/2 to 1 1/2	5/8–85	17/64	1/32	102	484	493	42S	67S	1301	159
		532S	WE	375	1/4–31	1/2 to 1 1/2	.054–193	17/64	3/16–28	102	484	493	34S	67S	1356	186
	(48)	661S	WE	375	3/8–80	1/2 to 1 1/2	.054–193	17/64	7/16–28	102	484	493	34S	67S	1356	186
	(48), (49), (50), (51), (52)	715S	WE	620	3/8–80	1/2 to 1 1/2	.046–158	14/64	3/16–28	102	652	666	34S	129S	1504	186
1953	14G Champion	989S	WE		3/8–80	1/2 to 1 1/2	.046–158	7/32	3/16–28		666		34S	129S	1729	235
WILLYS																
1941	441	507S	WO	229	3/8–80	1/2 to 2 1/2		14/64		26	497		93S	79S	1304	147
		507SA	WO	229	3/8–80	1/2 to 2 1/2		14/64		26	497		93S	79S	1304	147
1946–49	4-63	613S	WA-1	485	5/16–107 (4)	1/2 to 1 1/2		11/64		102	589	601	94S	67S	1360	159
		738S	YF		9/32–126 (7)	3/4 to 1 3/4					708	720	166S	160	1546	200
1946–50	CJ2A	636S	WO	505	3/8–80	1 to 2		17/64		26	547	548	93S	151S	1355	175
		636SA	WO	505	3/8–80	1 to 2		17/64		26	547	548	93S	151S	1355	175
1950–51	4-63	738S	YF		9/32–126 (7)	3/4 to 1 3/4					708	720	166S	160	1546	200
	4-73	768S	YF	630	5/16–107 (7)	1 to 2					750	735	166S	160	1557	206
		832S	YF	630	5/16–107 (7)	1 to 2					806	808	190S	160	1559	206
		832SA	YF	630	5/16–107 (7)	1 to 2					806	808	190S	160	1559	206
		832SB	YF	630	5/16–107 (7)	1 to 2					806	808	190S	160	1559	206
1948–49	Six, Station Sedan	645S	WA-1	485	5/16–107 (4)	1 to 2		11/64		102	609	589	94S	67S	1385	159
1952–53	675 P.C., 675A	937S	Y.F.	648	9/32–126	1 to 2					749	783	197S	166	1571	200
	685A	924S	Y.F.	875	9/32–126	1 to 2					804	840	190S	163	1715	206A

ABBREVIATIONS

Cli.—Climatic. Std.—Standard.
Con.—Control. Trans.—Transmission.

(A)—Measurement taken between the throttle valve and the bore of the carburetor with choke valve seated.

(C)—Unloader adjustment measurements taken between the edge of choke valve and wall of air horn.

(D)—Measurement shown is the distance between the lower edge of choke valve and the air horn wall with the throttle lever adjustment screw seated against (not on) the first (upper) step of the fast idle cam and the throttle valve closed.

(E)—Early Prod. Primary 1/4″ Gauge No. (T109-223)
Secondary 3/8″ Gauge No. (T109-224)
Late Prod. Primary 3/32″ Gauge No. (T109-233)
Secondary 1/4″ Gauge No. (T109-223)

(F)—Primary 3/32″ Gauge No. (T109-233)
Secondary 3/16″ Gauge No. (T109-222)

(G)—Early Prod. Primary 1/4″ Gauge No. (T109-223)
Secondary 5/16″ Gauge No. (T109-220)
Late Prod. Primary 1/8″ Gauge No. (T109-232)
Secondary 3/16″ Gauge No. (T109-222)

(H)—Primary 1/8″ Gauge No. (T109-232)
Secondary 3/16″ Gauge No. (T109-222)

No. 2 WDO

Correct Float Level (Remove Cork Gasket)

No. 3 BB

Use Gauge

No. 4 WA-1

Correct Float Level (Measure from machined surface of small projection to top of seam)

No. 5 WCD

Correct Float Level (Remove Cork Gasket) Distance from seam of float (both sides—at top center) to lower edge of bowl cover.

Metering Rod Gauge Size

T109-25—2.795 in.	T109-102—2.468 in.
T109-26—2.718 in.	T109-104—2.312 in.
T109-27—2.359 in.	T109-113—2.280 in.
T109-40—2.740 in.	T109-152—2.440 in.
T109-163—2.940 in.	

No. 6 Late WCD

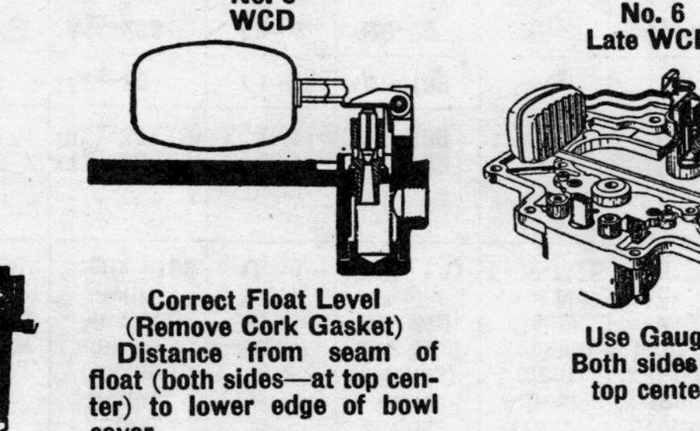

Use Gauge Both sides at top center

No. 7 YF

Use Gauge

No. 8 WGD

Use Gauge

CARTER CARBURETORS

THIS LIST SHOWS THE TYPE OF CARTER CARBURETOR USED ON VARIOUS MAKES OF CARS

Year and Model	Type
BUICK	
40-40, 50, 60, 70, 80, 90	WDO
41-40	WCD
41-50	WCD
41-60, 70, 90	WCD
42-40	WCD
42-50	WCD
42-60, 70, 90	WCD
1946—49-40, 50	WCD
1946—49-60, 70	WCD
1950-51—70	WCD
1950-52—40, 50	WCD
1952—70	WCFB
1953—40-50	WGD
1953—70	WCFB
CADILLAC	
40-90	WDO
41-V8	WDO
1942-51—V8	WCD
1952-53	WCFB
CHEVROLET	
1940-53—Std trans	W-I
	Y F
1950-53—All Power Glide	Y F
CHRYSLER	
1940-50—All Models	B & B
1951-53—C52, C53, C54.	WCD
1951-53—C51	B & B
DESOTO	
1940-41—All	B & B
Replacement	BBR-2
1942 to 51—All	B & B
1952—S-17	WCD
1953—S17, S16	BBD
DODGE	
1946 to 53—Six	B & B
FRAZER	
1947-48—F47, 485, 486	WAI
1949-50—F495, 496	WCD
1951—F515, 516	WGD
HENRY J	
1951-53	Y F
HUDSON	
1940—40	WAI
41, 43, 44, 47	WDO
1941-42—Six	WAI
Super Six	WDO
1941-42—Eight	WDO
1946 to 49—All	WDO
1950-53—500, 50A, 4A	WAI
501, 502 5A, 5A 7A, 7B, 7C	WGD
1952-53—5B, 4C, 5C	WAI
1953—Jet	WAI
KAISER	
1947—K100	W-I
1948-49—481, 491, 482	WAI
1949-50—492	WCD
1951-52—511, 512, 521-522	WGD
1953—K530-31-32	WGD
LASALLE	
1940—50, 52	WDO
NASH	
1940-42—10, 80	WDO
20	WAI
40	B & B
60	WAI
1946-51—40 Models	WAI
60	WAI
1952—5110, 5140, 5240, 5210	Y F
1953—5340	WCD
1953—60 Models	Y H
OLDSMOBLIE	
1940—6 Cyl	WAI
8 Cyl	WDO
1941—6 Cyl	WAI
8 Cyl	WDO
1942—6 Cyl	WAI
8 Cyl	WDO
1949-50—8 Cyl & V8	WGD
1946-50—6 Cyl	WAI
1951—V8	WGD
1952-53—V8	WCFB
PACKARD	
1941—1901, 1951	WDO
1942—110	WAI
120, 160, 180	WDO
1946-47—2100	WAI
2101, 2111, 2103 2106	WDO
1948-49—2201, 11, 2301 2331	WDO
1950—All	WDO
1951—2301	WGD
1951-52—300, 400, 2401	WGD
1953—300, 400	WCFB
PLYMOUTH	
1940-41	B & B
1942	B & B
1946-53	B & B
PONTIAC	
1940—25, 26, 28	WAI
29	WDO
1941-42—Six	WAI
1942 Eight	WDO
1946-48 Six	WAI
1946-47 Eight	WDO
1948 Eight	WCD
1949-51 Six	WAI
1949-52 Eight	WCD
1949-52 25 (Hydramatic)	WAI
1953 Six	WCD
STUDEBAKER	
1940—2G	WO
10A	WAI
6C	WDO
1941 to 51—3G, 4G, 5G, 6G	WAI
1941-53—All Models (Replacement)	WE
1953—14G	WE
WILLYS	
1940—440	WO
1941-42—441, 442	WO
1946 to 49—4-63	WAI
Replacement	YF
1948-49—Six Station Sedan	WAI
1946-50—CJ2A	WO
1950-53—4-63, 4-73, 675, 675A, 685A	YF

CARBURETOR TROUBLE SHOOTING AND CIRCUITS

The Carter Carburetor Company manufactures several types of carburetors —the more popular being Carter W type and the B & B type. The W type is divided roughly into three styles: Single downdraft W1 type (cast iron body). Dual downdraft WDO type and the Vacumeter WA1, WCD and WCFB type.

Low Speed Circuit

Engine will not idle properly due to lean mixture. Check for manifold air leaks, clogged air by-passes or bleed holes in body, economizer hole restrictions, scored idle screw, poor fitted idle port plug or a clogged passage in the casting between the low speed jet to port hole and idle screw.

If engine runs rich on idle, check low speed metering jet for being worn or unsoldered, damaged idle port, leak around main nozzle at seat in casting, excessive carbon around the throttle valve at seat, over-size economizer, improperly installed throttle valve or a damaged idle mixture screw.

High Speed Circuit

Lean condition from part throttle to wide open. Restricted gasoline filter, float level too low, partially clogged metering rod jet or improperly adjusted, fuel pressure too low, main nozzle improperly installed or damaged end, partially clogged outside vent hole, worn linkage or loose air horn assembly.

Rich condition from part throttle to wide open.

Improperly adjusted metering rod or worn metering rod and jet, float level too high, fuel pump pressure too high, damage main nozzle, bent metering rod, nozzle installed without a replacement of gasket, wrong bowl cover, stuck check valves on pump or clogged pump vent hole to carburetor. Sticking choke valve hinge, dirty air cleaner, improperly operating choke or air bleed nozzles partially clogged.

Pump Circuit

Lean condition when accelerating. Worn pump linkage, defective or worn pump plunger, wrong type pump plunger, pump checks improperly seated in casting, improperly adjusted pump stroke or scored choke pump housing.

Choke System

Engine runs too rich on warm up.

Climatic control improperly adjusted, binding choke shaft, choke piston carbonized and stuck, leaky gaskets or tubing. Cork in thermostat housing shrunk or torn, dirty air cleaner or clogged air strainer in climatic control.

Float System

Carburetor floods and leaks gasoline.

Check float for being loaded, needle valve or seat not seating properly, float level too high, excessive fuel pump pressure, faulty bowl cover gasket or warped bowl, clogged vent hole, gum deposits on needle valve or seat. Rough float lip or worn pin and float bracket.

Identification tag: All W Carter Carburetors have this tag to identify the exact model. If tag is lost check number stamped on face of mounting flange and refer this stamped number to your local Carter dealer.

SERVICING CARTER STARTER SWITCH

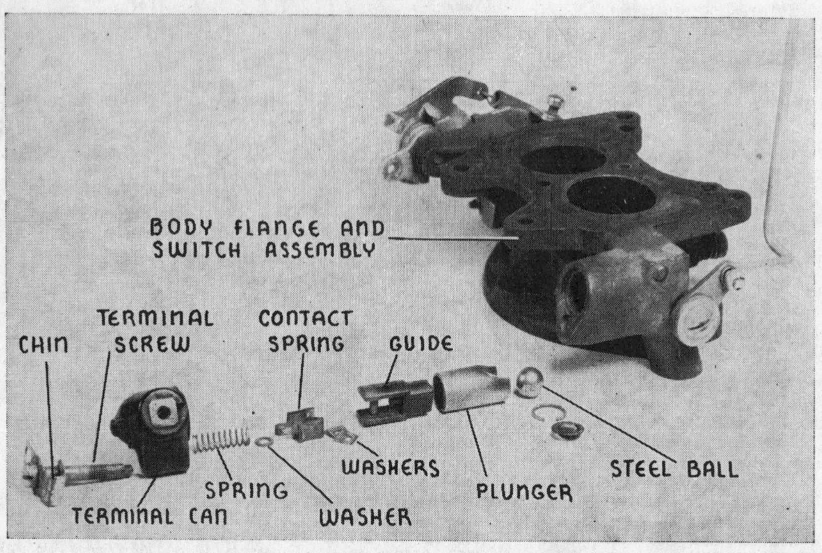

Carter starter switch showing all related parts

The Starter switch is part of the carburetor on some Buick and Packard models. When throttle is applied a steel ball resting on a flat on the throttle shaft, is raised up against a plunger which raises a W-shaped contact spring until an electrical contact is made between the two brass blocks in the top of the switch, this in turn closes the circuit. The minute the engine starts to run the vacuum from the manifold pulls the ball away from the shaft up into a seat in the casting and ball should remain there as long as engine is running. The minute the ball is raised a coil spring pushes down the W-shaped contact and plunger which breaks the connection and opens the solenoid relay circuit. Ball will not return into starting position until engine stops and throttle returns to idle position.

The W-shaped contact spring lays on brass shims with square holes in them. The shims determine the point at which contact is made. With two or more shims contact should be made when throttle valve is opened 30 to 45 degrees. If too many shims are installed, starter will engage too early and throttle will not open enough to keep engine running when cold. Hot enough shims will cause starter to engage late and let throttle open too far. This will usually make engine hard to start and cause starter gear clash. It will also open the carburetor unloader too soon.

If special gage for checking throttle travel is available use as follows:

Back off idle adjusting screw and turn idle cam until throttle valve is closed tight, set indicator on zero and lock in position. Open the throttle until indicator reads between 30 and 45 deg. and switch should make contact. If switch contacts too early too many shims are being used. If too late not enough are being used.

To check throttle travel without special gage proceed as follows:

Starter switch timing can be measured at throttle linkage. Clearance between machined surface on carburetor throttle base and throttle wide open stop should not be over 27/64 in. or less than 23/64 in.

To disassemble starter switch proceed as follows: One bolt holds the bakelite switch assembly in place. Remove bolt and lift off switch assembly then remove the plunger, bakelite guide and contact spring. Never bend any part of switch or stretch spring. Do not use oil or grease when assembling parts as this may cause parts to stick. To remove the throttle shaft it is necessary to remove switch assembly first.

SERVICING AND ADJUSTING CLIMATIC CONTROLS

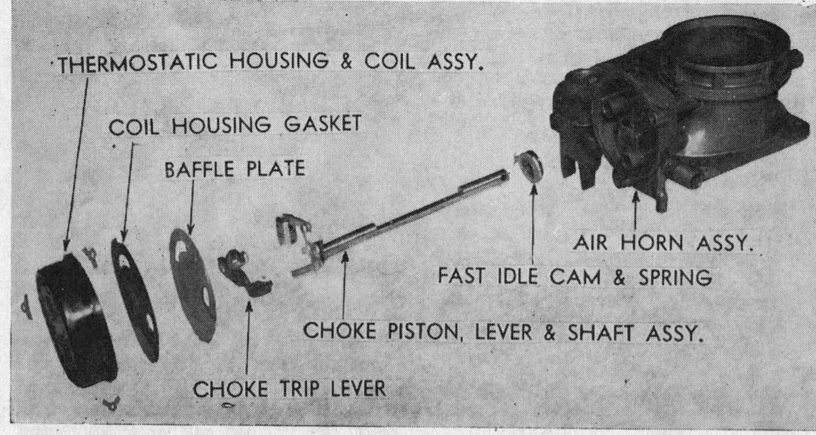

Climatic control assembly

When servicing the climatic control always check choke valve for being free. If valve sticks in any way, open or closed, it will cause trouble. If valve sticks check air horn for warpage, bent choke shaft, or butterfly not centered properly on shaft. If choke valve is free check the fast idle linkage for binding and twists. Examine the choke piston. If piston is stuck remove and clean it thoroughly or replace it if worn.

Adjustment of the thermostat housing is made by loosening the screws and rotating it in the direction of the rich or lean marked on the cover. Housing should be set according to the specifications. Adjustments should be made with engine cool and at room temperature.

MODEL WA1

Before attempting to adjust any carburetor, check compression on each cylinder, check manifolds for leaks, check and set spark plugs and ignition breaker points, adjust valve tappets, set ignition and check valve timing. Engine must be properly tuned for any carburetor to function properly.

Low Speed System Adjustment

To set idle mixture proceed as follows: Start engine and set engine speed up to approximately 7 m.p.h., turn idle mixture screw in until engine slows down and out until engine rolls, midway between these settings engine will smooth out and this will be the correct setting. Whenever a vacuum gage is available connect it to manifold and adjust idle mixture screw so as to get highest reading on the vacuum gage. A normal engine at idling speed should show a reading of 18-20 on vacuum gage at sea level.

After making the above adjustments and engine fails to idle properly it would indicate a high or faulty float, a clogged low speed jet or passage in carburetor body. Remove carburetor and clean jet, also the passage in carburetor body and set the float level.

Metering Rod Adjustment Without Vacumeter

Improperly adjusted metering rod may cause engine to run rich and burn excessive gasoline or may cause engine to run lean.

To determine if the proper metering rod is in carburetor turn to specifications table at the end of this Carter section and locate the proper metering rod number and compare it with the number stamped on the rod in carburetor. If rod is scored or bent replace both the rod and jet as they both will show wear. To set metering rod proceed as follows: After determining the proper metering rod gage from the specifications table, back off throttle adjusting screw until throttle valve is fully closed. With valve in this position insert gage in place of metering rod making sure tapered end is seated in jet below. The metering rod pin in pump arm should rest at the bottom of the notch in the gage with throttle valve closed and connector rod in line with the hole in pump arm. If connector rod is not in line with the hole in the pump arm bend lower end of the rod so that the upper end will enter freely. Remove gage and install metering rod and disk being sure disk is not binding on rod.

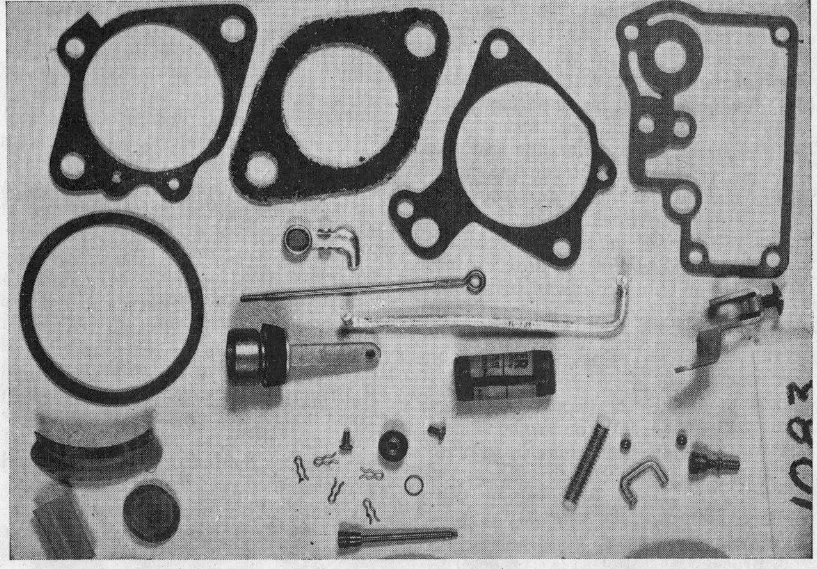

Carburetor repair Kit for WA1 carburetor. Note that all parts necessary for a thorough job are included

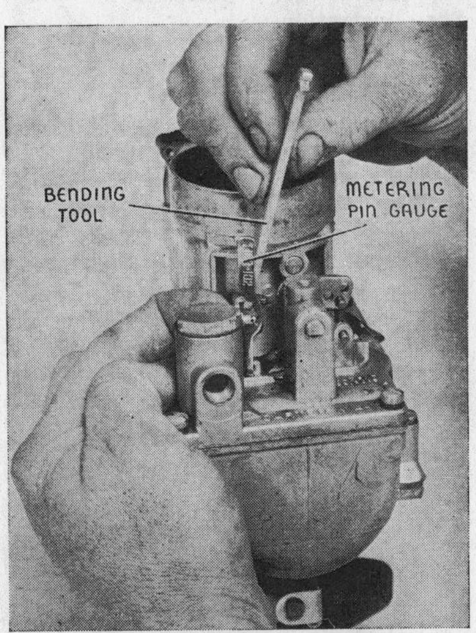

Metering rod adjustment

Seasonal Adjustment of Accelerating Pump

Three holes are provided in the accelerator pump arm to set pump stroke for winter, summer and intermediate. Set link in the hole giving the shortest stroke for summer; center hole for intermediate and longest stroke for winter. If trouble is surmised in the pump circuit examine the pump leather for cracks and leather for flexibility. Also check the pump jet and valves for obstruction.

Anti-Percolator Valve Adjustment

Open the throttle valve and place .030 in. gage between valve and bore of carburetor opposite idle port. With valve in this position, bend anti-percolator rocker arm until .005 to .015 in. clearance is obtained between rocker arm and pump arm.

Carburetors Equipped with Vacumeter

The vacumeter consists of a piston fitted into the carburetor bore with spring calibrated to force piston up as the engine vacuum falls below a predetermined amount. No adjustment is ever necessary and spring should never be altered in any way. However, if old spring is in doubt, a new one should always be replaced. If vacuum piston becomes inoperative it is probably due to the passage being clogged in the carburetor bore.

Pump Adjustment With the Use of Pump Travel Gage

Set pump stroke before making metering rod or anti-percolator adjustments. With the use of special pump stroke gage proceed as follows:

CARTER CARBURETORS

PUMP ADJUSTMENT—*continued*

Look up proper setting in specifications table. Then back off on throttle adjusting screw until valve is closed. In this position mount gage on flat surface of bowl cover with the indicator just touching top of pump plunger, take reading from top of gage and make a note of it. Open throttle wide and take another reading. Subtract the lower reading from the upper and you have the distance traveled. Gage is graduated in 64ths of an inch. To set linkage bend lower end of rod until desired dimension is obtained. See illustration.

Metering Rod Adjustment With Vacumeter

To determine if the proper metering rod is in carburetor turn to specifications table and locate the proper metering rod number, then compare it with the number stamped on the rod in the carburetor. If rod is scored or bent replace both the rod and jet as they both will show wear. To set metering rod, proceed as follows: After determining the proper metering rod gage from the specifications table, back off throttle adjusting screw until throttle valve is fully closed. With valve in this position insert gage in place of metering rod, making sure tapered end is seated in jet below. Hold down on step-up piston link lightly and there should be .005 in. clearance or less between the metering rod pin and the step in the gage. If clearance is more than .005 in. bend lip on step-up piston link. Remove gage and install metering rod and disk, being sure disk is not binding on rod. See illustration.

Fast Idle Adjustment

With fast idle cam in normal idle position with choke wide open, set screw so that it just touches the idle cam. Hold throttle closed and move cam clockwise until screw touches the first step on the cam—Distance indicated by gage should be that specified in the specifications table under the column headed "Fast Idle Adjustment." Adjustment is made by bending fast idle link at point shown. "C" is the distance between the lower edge of the choke valve and the inner wall of the air horn.

Unloader Adjustment

With throttle valve in wide open position, clearance at gage should be that specified in the specifications table under the heading "Unloader Adjustment."

Adjustment is made by bending cam as shown in illustration.

Float Adjustment

Having the proper float setting is vital if the carburetor is to function properly. If float level is too high engine will not idle properly. A quick check can be made by removing air cleaner and with engine idling look down carburetor air horn: If main nozzle keeps getting damp and dry it is a sure indication of a high float. A low float setting will cause starving at high speeds. To set float proceed as follows:

Remove float and cover assembly, turn to specifications table and look up proper setting. Examine the lip on the float, also the needle valve and seat. If float lip is pitted it can be smoothed off by pulling a piece of emery cloth across it. If needle valve and seat show any signs of wear replace them. If float is badly dented or loaded it should be replaced.

Assemble float to cover and turn upside down to adjust. Look up proper gage in specifications table and measure distance from soldered seam on bowl to machined surface on cover. Bend lip on float with a screw driver supporting the underneath by hand. See illustration.

Carburetor Overhaul

Carburetor should be completely disassembled and submerged in any good cleaning compound. After thoroughly soaking remove parts from cleaner and blow out each jet and passage separately with compressed air. Also scrape all the hard carbon from inside the carburetor body. Passages and air bleed holes should be checked for proper size. On most carburetors an overhaul kit can be purchased and should be installed and set to factory specifications.

Pump travel gage

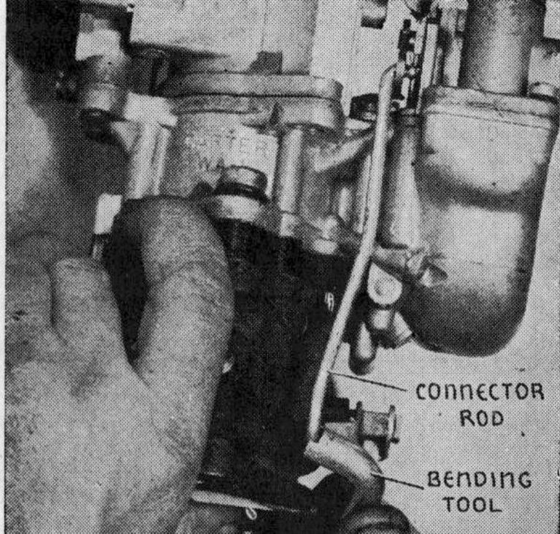

Adjusting metering rod (without vacumeter)

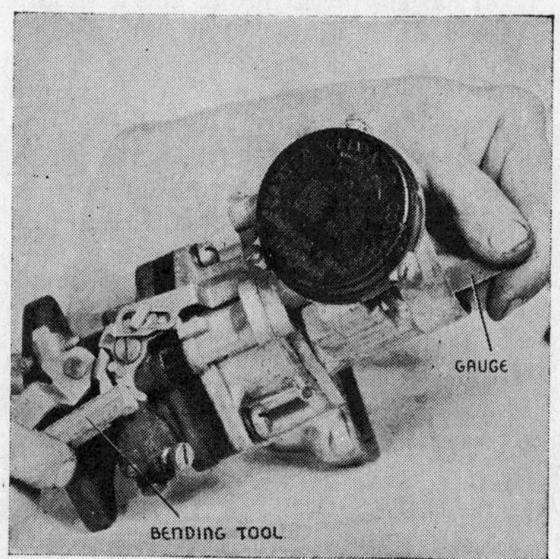

Unloader adjustment

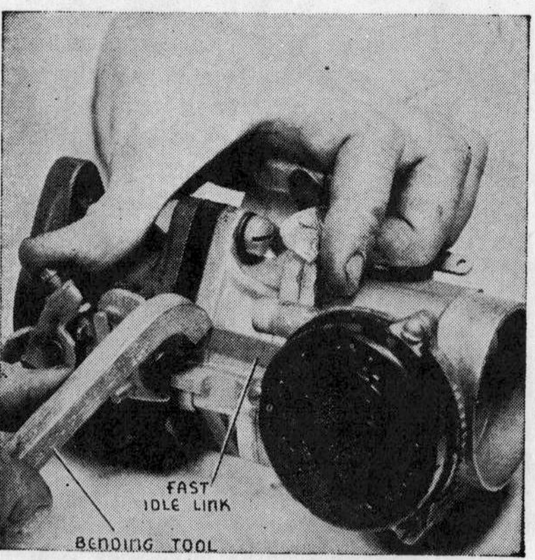

Fast idle adjustment

MODEL W1

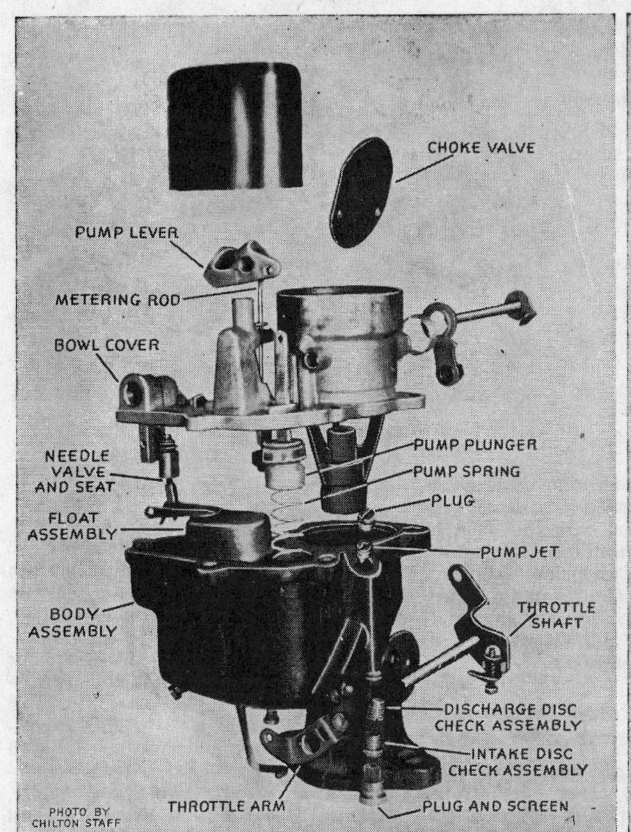

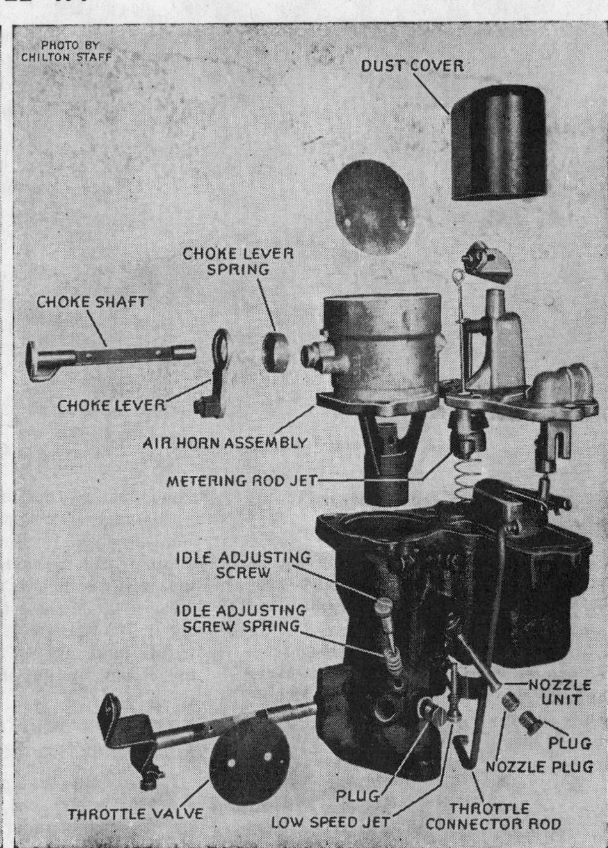

Exploded views of the Carter W1 type single downdraft carburetor

Before attempting to adjust any carburetor, check compression on each cylinder, check manifolds for leaks, check and set spark plugs and ignition breaker points, adjust valve tappets and set ignition and valve timing. Engine must be properly tuned for any carburetor to function properly.

Low Speed System Adjustment

To set idle mixture proceed as follows: Start engine and set engine speed up to approximately 7 m.p.h., turn idle mixture screw in until engine slows down and out until engine rolls, midway between these settings engine will smooth out and this will be the correct setting. Whenever a vacuum gage is available connect it to manifold and adjust idle mixture screw so as to get highest reading on the vacuum gage. A normal engine at idling speed should show a reading of 18-20 on vacuum gage at sea level.

After making the above adjustments and engine still fails to idle properly it would indicate a high or faulty float, a clogged low speed jet or passage in carburetor body.

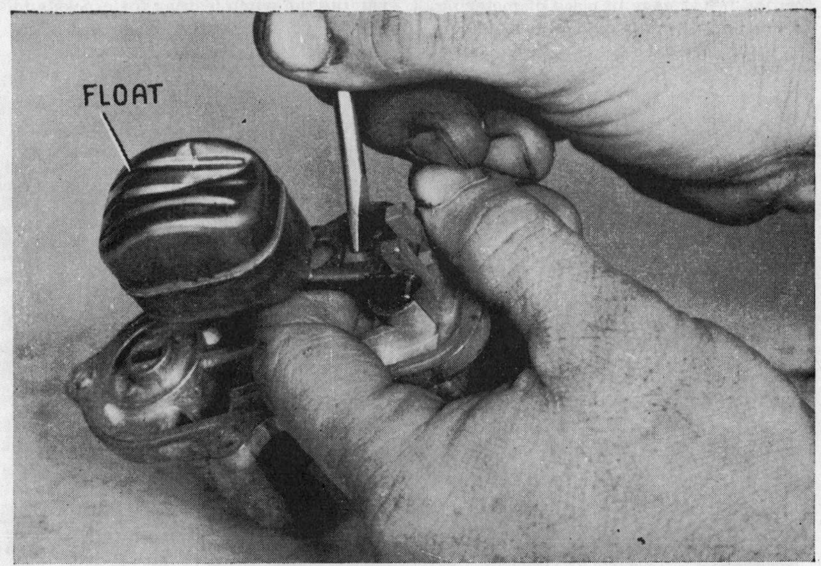

Bend lip of float to secure correct fuel height

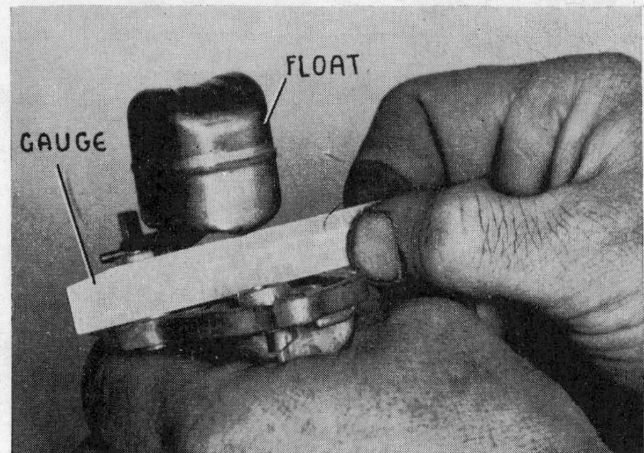

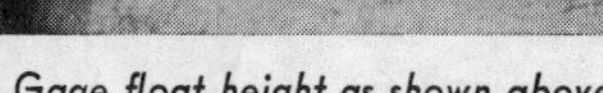
Gage float height as shown above

Metering pin gage in use

Metering Rod Adjustment Without Vacumeter

Improperly adjusted metering rod may cause engine to run rich and burn excessive gasoline or may cause engine to run lean.

To determine if the proper metering rod is in carburetor, turn to specifications table at the end of this Carter section and locate the proper metering rod number and compare it with the number stamped on the rod in carburetor. If rod is scored or bent replace both the rod and jet as they both will show wear. To set metering rod proceed as follows: After determining the proper metering rod gage from the specifications table, back off throttle adjusting screw until throttle valve is fully closed. With valve in this position insert gage in place of metering rod making sure tapered end is seated in jet below. The metering rod pin on pump arm should rest at the bottom of the notch in the gage with throttle valve closed and connector rod in line with the hole in pump arm. If connector rod is not in line with the hole in the pump arm, bend lower end of the rod so that the upper end will enter freely. Remove gage and install metering rod and disk being sure disk is not binding on rod.

Seasonal Adjustment of Accelerating Pump

Three holes are provided in the accelerator pump arm to set pump stroke for winter, summer and intermediate. Set link in the hole giving the shortest stroke for summer; center hole for intermediate and longest stroke for winter. If trouble is surmised in the pump circuit examine the pump leather for cracks and leather for flexibility. Also check the pump jet and valves for obstruction.

Anti-Percolator Valve Adjustment

Key type: Open the throttle valve .030 in. and place gage No. T109-29 between valve and bore of carburetor opposite idle port. With valve in this position there should be .005 to .015 in. clearance between pump arm and anti-percolator rocker arm. To adjust bend anti-percolator rocker arm.

Poppet type: Poppet type anti-percolator valves have an indicator line machined around the stem and are adjusted as follows: With throttle valve closed tightly, machined indicator line should be flush with the top of the valve plug. If not bend the lip on the pump arm until it is flush. If anti-percolator is not functioning properly, pressure caused by gasoline vaporizing in the high speed passage may cause engine to stall when idling and hesitate when throttle is first applied.

Set idle mixture

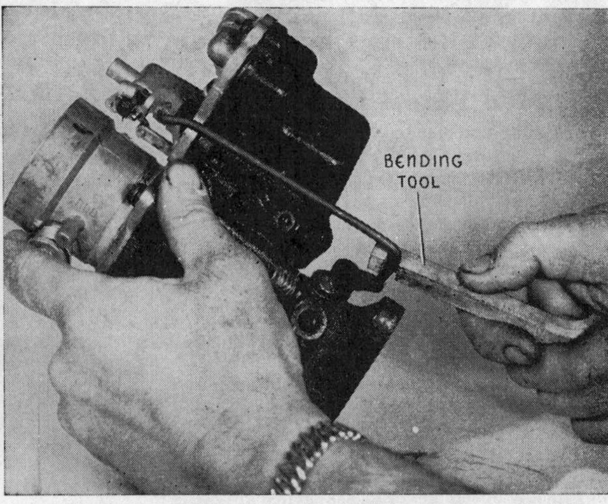

Bend rod to secure correct metering pin setting

MODEL WGD

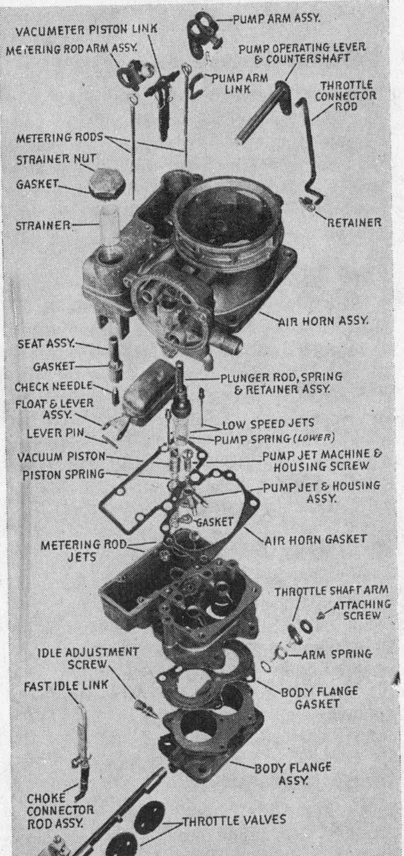

Exploded View of WGD

Dimensions and gauge numbers for all adjustments on each application of this WGD carburetor are given in the Carter specifications table in section two.

Float Adjustment

Adjust floats so that the distance between the machined surface of the bowl cover and the top of the bowl will just pass the gage specified, in Carter Carburetor Chart (section two) for that model. Specified measurement is also given in chart.

Pump Adjustment

With the throttle levers set screw backed all the way out until the throttle seats in the bore of the carburetor, the distance from the dust cover boss on

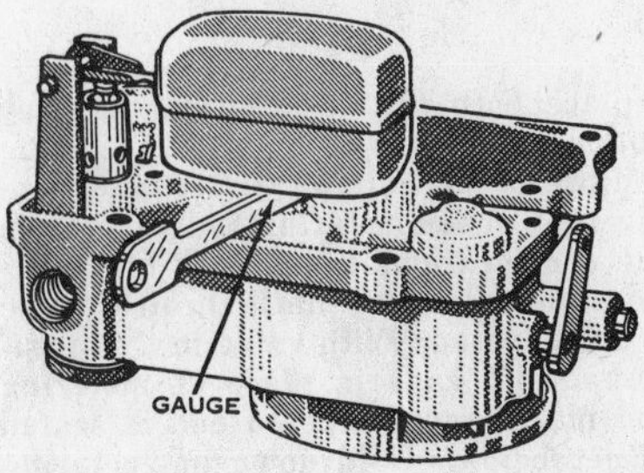

Gage in position to check float height

the top of the plunger shaft should be 15/32 inch. Adjust by bending the throttle connector rod at the upper angle.

Metering Rod Adjustment

Note: Metering rod should be adjusted after the pump adjustment is completed. No gages are necessary. With the throttle levers set screw held still back out throttle valve seated in the bore, press down on the vacuum meter link until the rods bottom. With the rods held in this position, revolve metering rod arm until the lip on the arm contacts the vacuum meter link. Hold in position and carefully tighten the metering arm set screw.

Fast Idle Adjustment

Take out the choke thermostatic coil housing gasket and baffle plate. Crack throttle to release fast idle mechanism, hold choke valve in the closed position and then close the throttle. Adjust by bending the choke connector rod at the lower angle (or adjusting sleeve on early models) so that clearance be-

Metering rod adjustment. Recheck setting after adjustment is secured.

On some Cars the WGD Carburetor has a screw sleeve adjustment for fast idle. The adjusting sleeve shows clearly in the unloader illustration.

tween the throttle valve and bore of carburetor, will pass the gage specified in the Carter Carburetor Chart. (section two.)

Unloader Adjustment

Note: This adjustment must be made after the fast idle adjustment.

Hold throttle valve wide open and close the choke valve as far as possible without forcing it.

With the throttle held wide open and the choke held as nearly closed as it will go, clearance between the upper edge of the choke valve and the inner wall of the air horn should be as specified in the Carter Chart (section two). Adjust by bending the arm on the choke trip lever.

Unloader gage in position in air horn. Adjust by bending link on the choke trip lever.

MODEL WE

Checking anti-percolator setting

Low Speed System Adjustment

To set idle mixture proceed as follows: Start engine and set engine speed up to approximately 7 M.P.H., turn idle mixture screw in until engine slows down and out until engine rolls, midway between these settings engine will smooth out and this will be the correct setting. Whenever a vacuum gage is available connect it to manifold and adjust idle mixture screw to show highest, steady reading on vacuum gage. A normal engine at idling speed should show a reading of 18-20 on vacuum gage at sea level.

After making the above adjustment and engine fails to idle properly it would indicate a high or faulty float, a clogged low speed jet or passage in carburetor body. Remove carburetor and clean jet, also the passage in carburetor body, and set the float level.

Metering Rod Adjustment

To determine if the proper metering rod is in carburetor, turn to specifications table and locate the proper metering rod number, then compare it with the number stamped on the rod in the carburetor. If rod is scored or bent

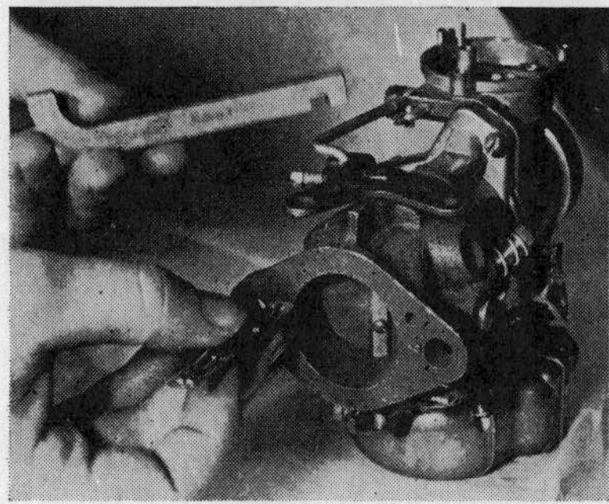

Checking fast idle setting. Gage & tool numbers are given in Carter Chart in Section Two

replace both the rod and jet as they both will show wear. To set metering rod proceed as follows: After determining the proper metering rod gage from the specifications table, back off throttle adjusting screw until throttle valve is fully closed. With valve in this position insert gage in place of metering rod making sure tapered end is seated in jet below. Hold down on metering rod arm and there should be .005 in. clearance or less between the metering rod pin and the step in the gage. Adjustment should be made by bending lip on metering rod arm. An additional step is provided on this metering rod and should be adjusted as follows: Push down on metering arm until the

Checking choke in loader setting

Bending lip to correct unloader setting

upper lip contacts the pin on the pump arm. Bend the lower lip until 3/16 in. clearance is obtained between the lower end of the pump arm pin and the top surfacer of the lower lip.

Anti-Percolator Adjustment

Open the throttle valve and place .030 in. gage between valve and bore of carburetor opposite idle port. With valve in this position bend anti-percolator rocker arm until .005 to .015 in. clearance is obtained between rocker arm and pump arm.

Fast Idle Adjustment

Fast idle adjustments are made within thermostat coil housing. Remove the housing and open throttle a little, close choke valve and throttle. With throttle and choke valve closed fast idle cam should be in fast idle position. To adjust loosen lock nut on choke connector rod and turn sleeve until throttle valve opens .054 in. between carburetor bore and valve opposite idle port.

Unloader Adjustment

Always adjust fast idle before attempting to adjust unloader. To adjust open throttle wide and close choke there should be 3/16 in. clearance between lower edge of choke valve and the carburetor air horn. Adjustment is made by bending the arm on the choke trip lever.

Float Adjustment

Having the proper float setting is vital if the carburetor is to function properly. If float level is too high engine will not idle properly. A quick check can be made by removing air cleaner and with engine idling look down carburetor air horn: If main nozzle keeps getting damp and dry it is a sure indication of a high float. A low float setting will cause a lean mixture especially at high speed. To set float proceed as follows:

Remove float and cover assembly, turn to specifications table and look up proper setting. Examine the lip on the float, also the needle valve and seat. If float lip is pitted it can be smoothed off by pulling a piece of emery cloth across it. If needle valve and seat show any signs of wear replace them. If float is badly dented or loaded it should be replaced.

Assemble float to cover and turn upside down to adjust. Look up proper gage in specifications table and measure distance from soldered seam on bowl to machined surface of cover. Bend lip on float with a screw driver supporting the underneath by hand. See illustration.

MODEL WCD

WCD carburetor

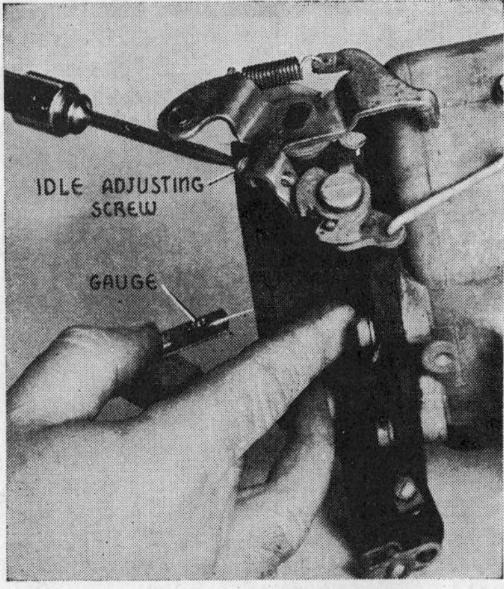

Fast idle adjustment

Aiming pump jets

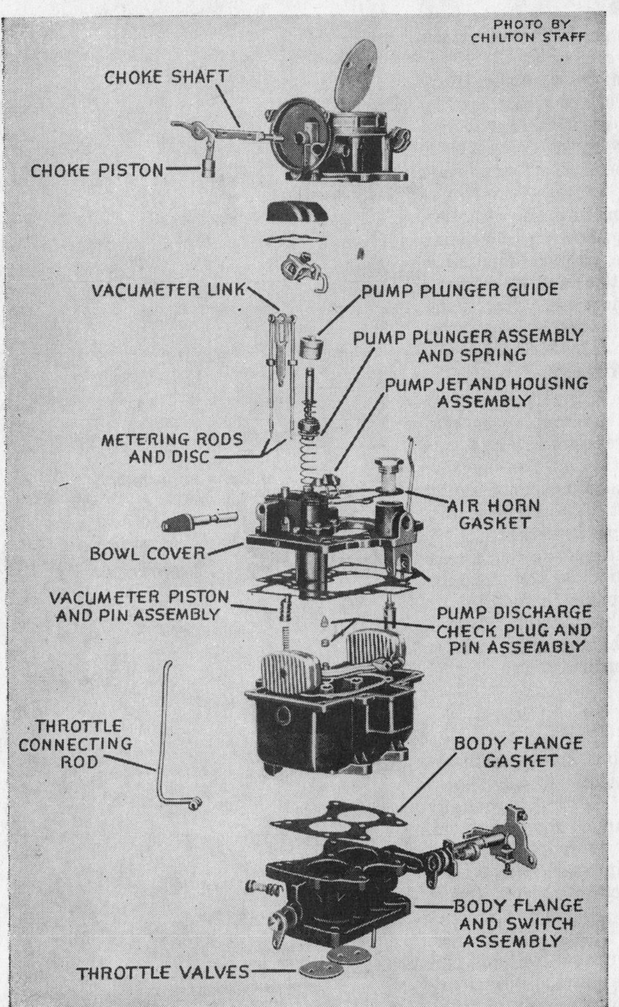

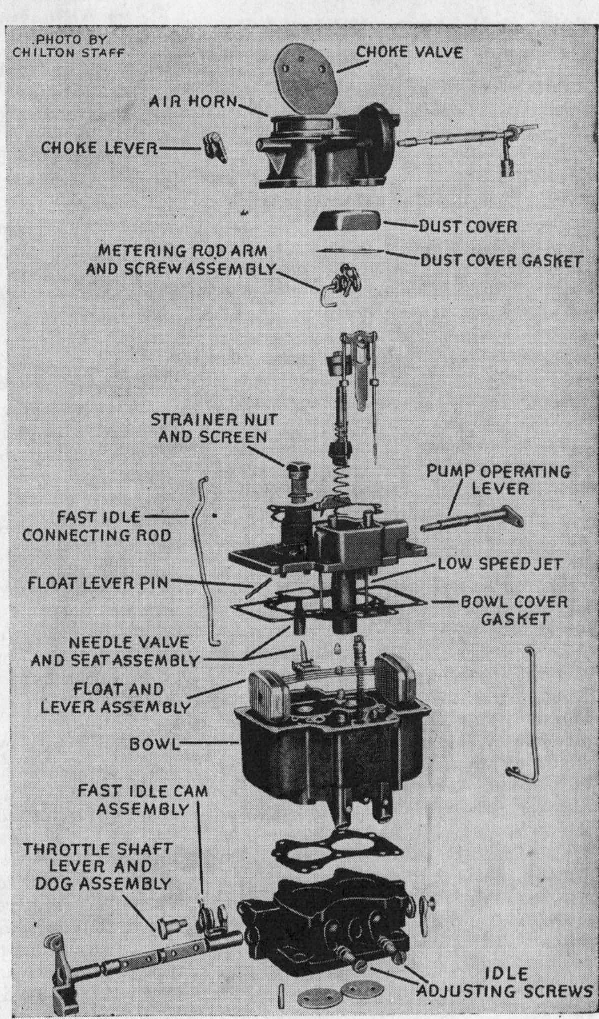

CARTER CARBURETORS

Low Speed System Adjustment

To set idle mixture proceed as follows: Start engine and set engine speed up to approximately 7 M.P.H., turn idle mixture screws in until engine slows down and out until engine rolls, midway between these settings engine will smooth out and this will be the correct setting. Whenever a vacuum gage is available connect it to manifold and adjust idle mixture screws to show highest steady reading on the vacuum gage. A normal engine at idling speed should show a reading of 18-20 in. on vacuum gage at sea level.

After making the above adjustments and engine fails to idle properly it would indicate a high or faulty float, a clogged low speed jet or passage in carburetor body. Remove carburetor and clean jets, also the passages in carburetor body and set the float level.

Pump Adjustment With the Use Of Pump Travel Gage

Always set pump stroke before making metering rod adjustments. With the use of special pump stroke gage proceed as follows:

Look up proper setting in specifications table. Then back off on throttle adjusting screw until throttle valves are closed. In this position mount gage upside down on flat surface of bowl cover with the indicator just touching top of pump plunger, take reading from top of gage and make a note of it. Open throttle until pump bottoms (about half way) then take another reading. Subtract the lower reading from the upper and you have the distance traveled. Gage is graduated in 64ths of an inch. To set linkage bend lower end of pump rod until desired dimension is obtained. *See illustration.*

Metering Rod Adjustment

Improperly adjusted metering rods may cause engine to burn excessive gasoline or may cause engine to run lean.

To determine if the proper metering rods are in carburetor turn to specifications table at the end of this Carter section and locate the proper metering rod numbers and compare them with the numbers stamped on the rods in carburetor. If rods are scored or bent replace both the rods and jets as they both will show wear. To set metering rods proceed as follows: After determining the proper metering rod gage from the specifications table, back off throttle adjusting screw until throttle valves are fully closed. With valves in this position insert one gage in place of metering rod, making sure tapered end is seated in jet below.

Push down lightly on vacuum piston link until finger of piston link touches the lip of the metering arm. Clearance should be less than .005 in. between the bearing on metering rod and the lower notch in the gage. To adjust bend the lip on the metering arm.

Fast Idle Adjustment

With choke valve closed adjust fast idle screw until .0012 in. wire gage between throttle valve and casting opposite idle port just slips out.

Unloader Adjustment

There should be .010 in. clearance between cam arm and boss on bottom of carburetor. With choke valve closed insert feeler gage in place then loosen choke arm and set to specifications. Adjust lip on throttle arm so choke valve will open 3/16 in. with wide open throttle.

Float Adjustment

Float must be adjusted in two separate ways—lateral and vertical.

Lateral adjustment is made by turning float bowl upside down and looking along each side of float, float sides should aline with indicator bosses in the bowl cover. To adjust bend float arms, not float itself.

Vertical adjustment is made after removing bowl cover gasket and by using special gage from the specifications table. Insert gage between the casting and float. See illustration. Then bend float arms until both sides of float touches the gage.

Pump Jet Adjustment

Pump jets must be aimed properly to insure good acceleration from low speeds. On late model carburetors there is a target mark in the venturi on the opposite wall from the jets. Gasoline should squirt directly on the target. To aim jets only a slight bend should be necessary.

On carburetors without target marks it will be necessary to make a mark. Aim stream of gasoline to hit in a 3/16 in. diameter circle, which is 11/64 in. from opposite side of the bore and ¼ inch in from the primary venturi strut. See illustration.

Carburetor Overhaul

Carburetor should be completely disassembled and submerged in any good cleaning compound. After thoroughly soaking and cleaning remove from cleaner and blow out each jet and passage separately with compressed air. Also scrape all the hard carbon from inside the carburetor body. Passages and air bleed holes should be checked for correct sizes. On most carburetor overhauls an overhaul kit should be purchased and installed and set to factory specifications.

Pump stroke adjustment

Unloader adjustment

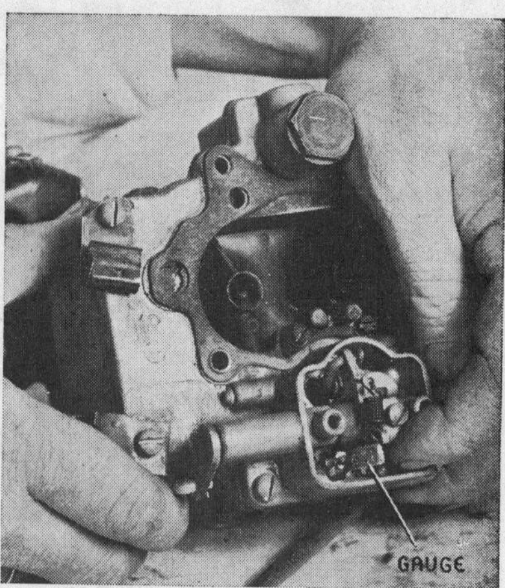

Metering rod gage in position

MODEL WCD-830

Low Speed Adjustment

To set idle mixture proceed as follows: Start the engine and set the engine idle speed to approximately 7 miles per hour and thoroughly warm up the engine. Turn the idle mixing screws until the engine slows down and out until the engine rolls. Midway between these two settings should be the proper setting for each barrel. After the second barrel has been adjusted, go back and readjust the first barrel and then readjust the second barrel.

Accelerating Pump Adjustment

Set the connector link in the hole of the pump with the ends extended towards the countershaft arm which will give the longest stroke.

Back out the fast idle adjusting screw until the throttle valves seat in the bores of the throttle body. Be sure the fast idle adjusting screw does not hold the throttle open.

With the throttle valve seated in the bores of the carburetor the distance from the top of the plunger shaft to the top of the dust cover boss should be 19/64th inch. If it is not, adjust as follows: Bend the throttle connector rod at the upper angle.

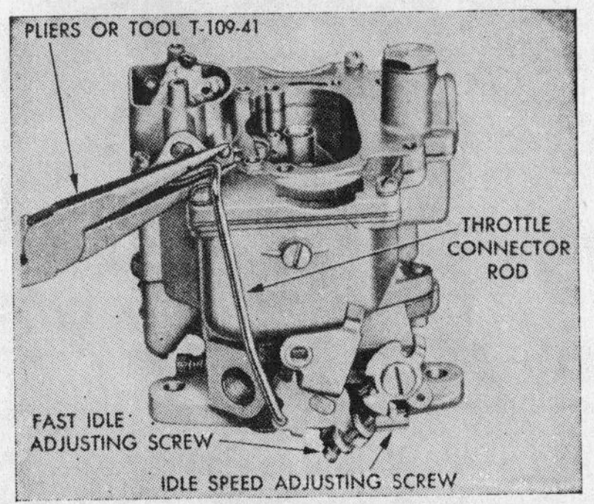

Adjusting accelerator pump travel

CAUTION: Do not bend the throttle connector rod so that it bears on the bowl cover. When the pump travel is correctly adjusted the rod should just clear the bowl cover.

Metering Rod Adjustment

Metering rod adjustment is important and should be done after completing the pump adjustment. No gages are necessary.

Back out the idle set screws until the throttle valve seats in the bores of the carburetor. Loosen the metering rod arm clamp screw.

With the metering rods in place press down the vacuum meter link until the metering rods seat in the carburetor body casing.

Hold the rods in this down position and hold the throttle valves closed. Revolve the metering rod lifter arm until the finger on the arm contacts the lip of the vacuum meter link, holding it in this position carefully tighten the clamp screw.

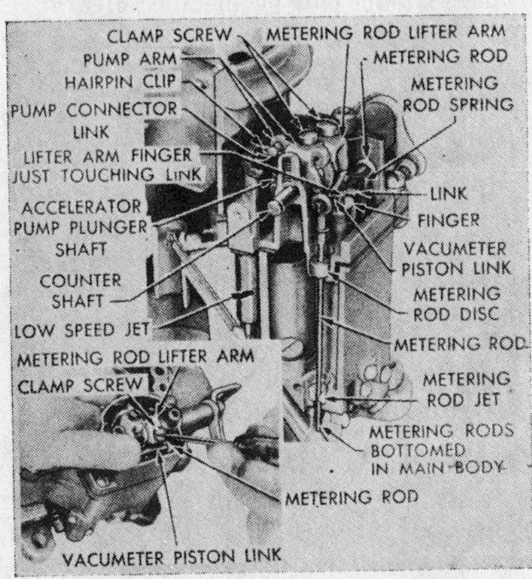

Adjusting metering rods

Fast Idle Adjustment

Loosen the choke lever clamp screw on the choke shaft. Insert a .040 inch feeler gage between the lip of the fast idle cam and the boss on the throttle body casting.

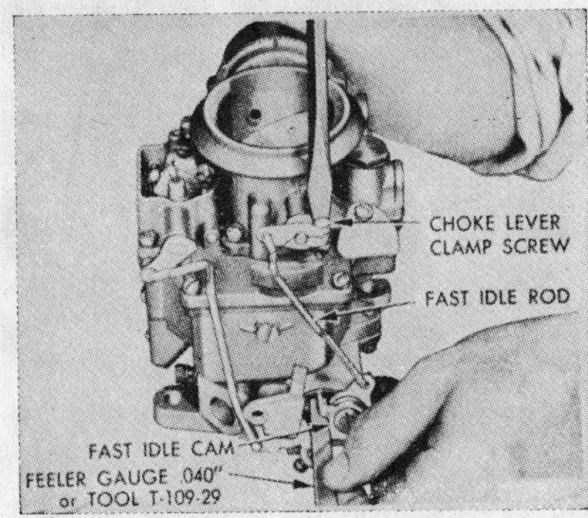

Fast idle adjustment-cam

Hold the choke tightly closed and take the slack out of the linkage by pressing the choke lever towards the closed position. Hold the parts in position and tighten the clamp screw securely.

Fast Idle Setting Adjustment

Remove the carburetor from the car and insert an .018 inch wire gage between the throttle valve at the bore of the throttle body. Hold the choke tightly closed, then while holding it closed against the wire gage tighten the fast idle adjusting screw until the gage is just freed.

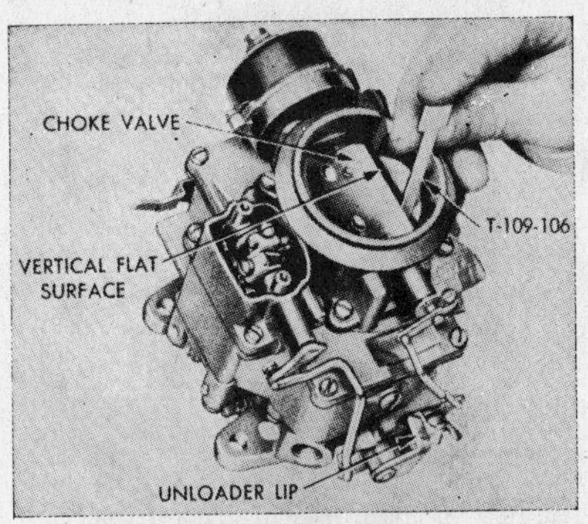

Unloader adjustment

Unloader Adjustment

The unloader adjustment must be made after the fast idle adjustment. When the throttle valve is in the wide open position there should be 7/32nd inch between the upper edge of the choke valve and the vertical flat surface inside the air horn.

Lateral Adjustment

With the bowl cover inverted and the float brackets resting on the seat needle, place the float gage tool number T-109205 directly under the float with the notch portion of the gage fitting over the edge of the casting. Sides of float should just touch the vertical uprights of the gage. Adjust by carefully bending the arms of the float.

Vertical Adjustment

With the cover float and gage in position as before the float should just clear the horizontal portion of the gage. The vertical distance between the tops of the float and the machine surface of the casting should be 11/64th inches. Adjust by carefully bending the arms of the float.

Floats should have a minimum travel of 7/16th inch at the free end of the float. Adjust by bending the lip on the float bracket until the desired clearance is obtained.

MODEL YF

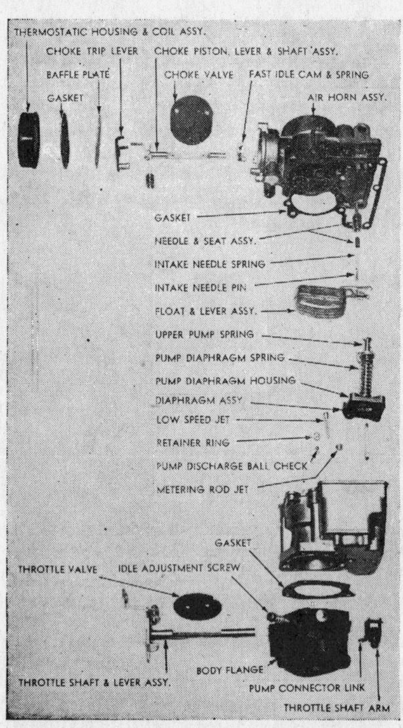

Model YF exploded to show internal parts

Fast Idle Adjustment

Crack throttle valve and hold choke valve closed. With the throttle valve closed, choke trip lever should be on the high step of the fast idle cam. There should now be specified clearance between the throttle valve and the bore of the carburetor. Adjust by bending the choke rod at lower angle.

Unloader Adjustment

This adjustment is to be made after the fast idle adjustment. Hold the throttle valve wide open, and the choke valve as far as possible without forcing. There should now be a specified clearance between the lower edge of the choke valve and the inner wall of the air horn.

Float Adjustment

With the gasket removed, bowl cover assembly inverted, and float resting on pin in seated needle, the distance from the bowl cover to the top of the float should be 5/16 in. Do not depress the float lip against spring loaded pin needle, but let float rest on its own weight. Adjust by bending lip of cover held at eye height, in a level position.

Metering Rod Adjustment

This is an important adjustment, and should be checked each time the carburetor is reassembled, or lean rods are installed. With the throttle seated in bore of carburetor, press down on upper end of the diaphragm shaft until diaphragm bottoms in vacuum chamber. A specified tool may be used to hold down shaft while adjusting metering rod.

Metering rod should contact the botton of the metering rod well, and metering rod arm should contact lifter link between springs and at supporting lug. Adjust by bending lip up or down.

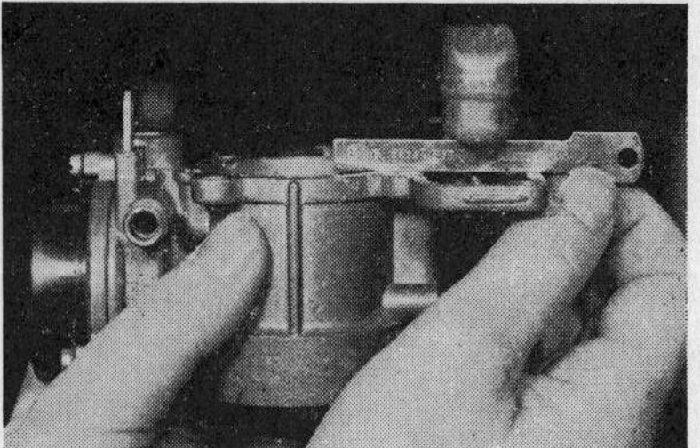

Checking float height

Checking fast idle setting

Checking unloader adjustment

Metering rod setting gage

MODEL B & B

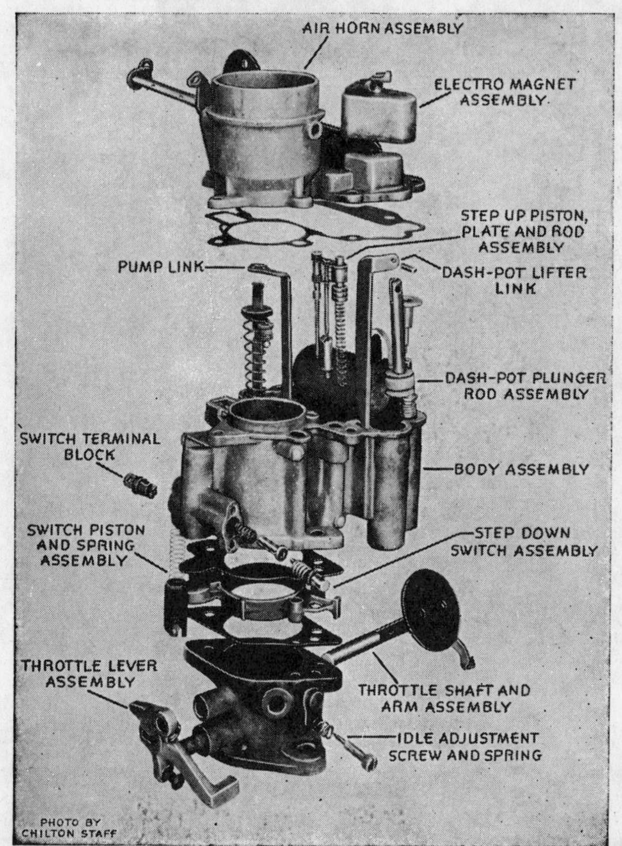

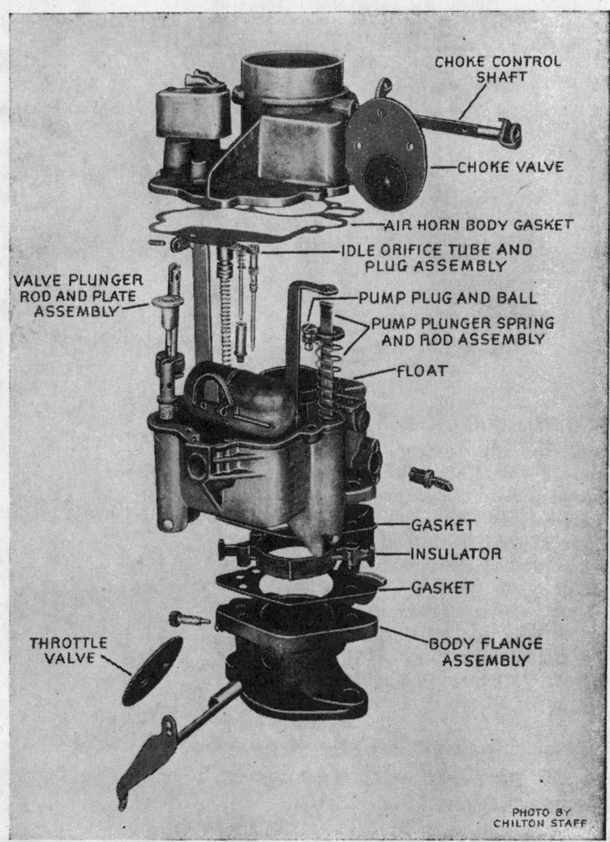

Low Speed System Adjustment

To set idle mixture proceed as follows: Start engine and set engine speed up to approximately 7 M.P.H., turn idle mixture screw in until engine slows down and out until engine rolls, midway between these settings engine will smooth out and this will be the correct setting. Whenever a vacuum gage is available connect it to manifold and adjust idle mixture screw to show highest steady reading on vacuum gage. A normal engine at idling speed should show a reading of 18-20″ on vacuum gage at sea level.

After making the above adjustments and engine fails to idle properly it would indicate a high or faulty float, a clogged low speed jet or passage in carburetor body. Remove carburetor and clean jets, also the passages in carburetor body and set the float level.

Ignition, compression, and the condition of the rings and valves will also affect idle.

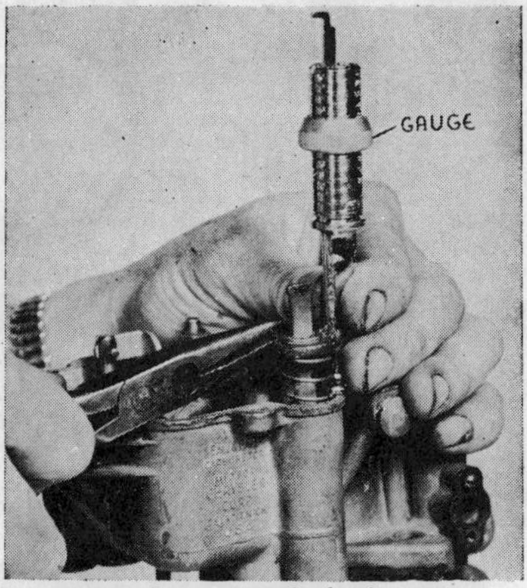

Pump travel check

Seasonal Adjustment of Accelerating Pump

Three holes are provided in the throttle shaft underneath the float bowl. Center hole for intermediate. Inner hole or shortest stroke for summer; outer hole or longest stroke for winter.

Pump Adjustment With the Use Of Pump Travel Gage

Set accelerating pump link in center hole before making pump adjustment. With air horn assembly removed proceed with pump adjustment as follows: Back off on throttle adjusting screw until valve is closed. In this position mount gage on flat surface of carburetor body with the indicator just touching the top of pump plunger arm, take reading from top of gage and make a note of it. Open throttle wide and take another reading. Subtract the lower reading from the upper and you have the distance traveled. Gage is graduated in 64ths of an inch. To set stroke bend top of pump link until desired dimension is obtained. See specifications chart for dimension.

Float Adjustment

Having the float set properly is vital if the carburetor is to function properly. If float level is too high engine

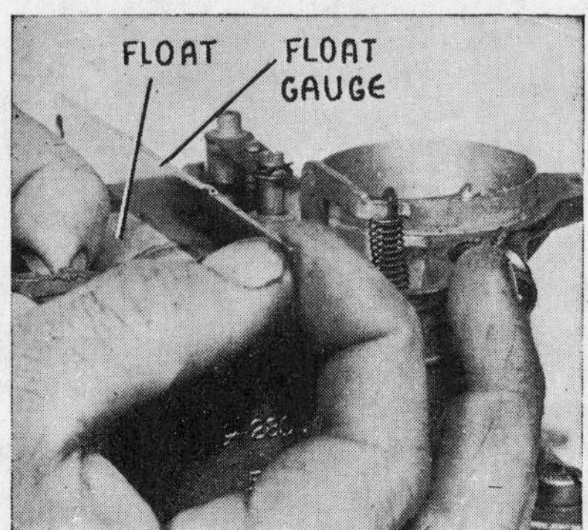

Checking float height

Full view of a Model BB carburetor

FLOAT ADJUSTMENT—*continued*
will not idle properly. If float level is too low engine will starve at high speeds. To set float proceed as follows: Remove air horn and check specification chart for proper float gage, lay gage across top of carburetor body and hold float against the needle valve. Bend lip on float with a screw driver until float just touches the gage. If lip on float shows any marks, take a piece of emery paper and pull it across the lip until all marks are removed.

Slow Closing Throttle Adjustment on Cars with Vacamatic Transmission

A spring loaded screw is mounted on top of slow closing throttle piston. The screw is provided to stop engine from stalling when accelerator is released suddenly and also controls the time that it takes to downshift. To adjust turn screw all the way down then back off 5 turns. If screw has to be turned one full turn further in or out to prevent stalling the pump plunger is probably at fault.

Carburetor Overhaul

Carburetor should be completely disassembled and submerged in any good cleaning compound. After thoroughly soaking and cleaning remove from cleaner and blow out each jet and passage separately with compressed air. Also scrape all the hard carbon from inside the carburetor body. Passages and air bleed holes should be checked for correct sizes. On most carburetor overhauls an overhaul kit should be purchased and installed and set to factory specifications.

It is unwise to replace some jets and not all. An overhaul kit has the necessary parts in one package.

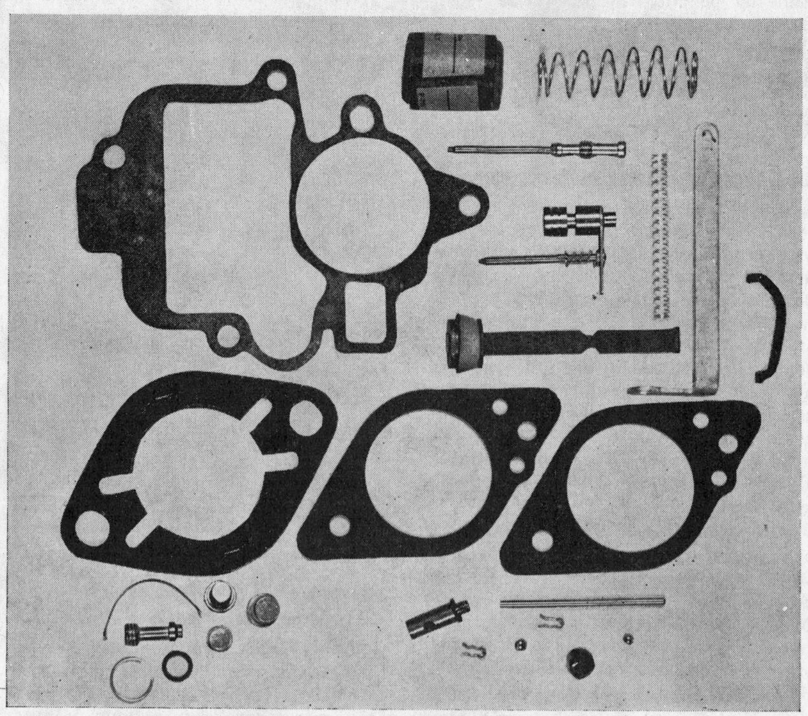

Standard overhaul kit for model BB carburetors

MODEL BBD

The Carter Carburetor Model BBD is, in effect, two single downdraft carburetors contained in a single casting.

Five conventional circuits are contained in this unit. A float circuit, accelerating pump circuit, climatic choke circuit, low and high speed circuit.

Float Circuit

The float circuit maintains the fuel in the float bowl at a pre-determined level. The dual floats are engineered to provide a fixed fuel level for all operating conditions. Only a small amount of fuel is carried in the carburetor float bowl which reduces fuel vaporization and helps warm engine starting.

The float bowl chamber is vented into the air horn, to maintain air above the fuel at the same pressure as it is in the air horn.

Accelerating Pump Circuit

The purpose of this circuit is to feed an extra amount of fuel during acceleration which is necessary to provide smooth power. A mechanical adjustment can be made by bending the connector rod at the lower angle to lengthen or shorten the effective stroke of the pump.

Climatic Choke Circuit

The climate control choke circuit allows the carburetor to feed the engine a rich mixture for starting and warm up.

Low Speed Circuit

The amount of fuel used for idle and early throttle is metered through the low speed circuit.

The idle orifice tube determines the amount of fuel for idle and early part throttle operation. In the venturi attaching screws are located the idle air bleed and idle restrictions, which are engineered to break up the fuel and mix it with air as it moves through the passage to idle port and idle adjusting screw port.

High Speed Circuit

The amount of fuel required for part and full throttle is supplied through the high speed circuit.

The step up rods regulate the amount of fuel entered into the main vent tubes and high speed nozzles.

Manifold vacuum applied to the vacuum piston governs the position of the step up rods in the main metering jets.

When operating at part throttle the step up piston is pulled down by manifold vacuum keeping the step up rods in the main metering jets. Vacuum under the piston is strong enough at all times to overcome the tension of the piston spring. Fuel is then metered around the step up rods in the jets.

Kickdown Limit Switch

The kickdown limit switch will operate only if the throttle is in the wide open position. Depressing the accelerator pedal to the floor allows the operator to shift the transmission to a lower gear.

When the car is moving at speeds where acceleration in a lower gear would not be faster than approximately 50 mph, depressing accelerator pedal will not allow a downshift.

Therefore the actual operation of the switch is to confine the speed at which downshift can be made.

Magnetically Controlled Dashpot

The purpose of the dashpot is to close the throttle slowly and keep the engine from stalling. It also works in series with the transmission governor. The dashpot will function only at speeds under 12 mph.

Side View—Showing accelerator pump connector link and choke mechanism

Side View—Showing dashpot and kickdown limit switch

MODEL BBD—*continued*

Adjustments

No carburetor should be adjusted without first checking compression, ignition and also check the manifold for any leaks. An engine must be properly tuned before any carburetor can function properly.

Idle Speed Adjustment

The idle adjustment screw positions the throttle valve for curb idle speed and has no effect on richness of mixture. Set engine idle to approximately 400-500 rpm depending on engine condition (engine in good condition should be set to lower speed). Cars equipped with automatic transmission set to approximately 400-500 rpm with transmission in drive range. When transmission is shifted to neutral engine will speed up. This is normal.

Idle Mixture Adjustment

This adjustment controls the mixture of gas and air at idle and also effects low speed operation. To set idle mixture proceed as follows: Turn the idle mixture screw in until the engine slows dowfi and out until the engine rolls. Midway between these two settings should be the proper setting for each barrel. After the second barrel has been adjusted, go back and readjust the first and then readjust the second barrel. In other words, do each adjustment at least twice.

Accelerator Pump Adjustment

Loosen the idle adjusting screw and hold the choke in the wide open position. This allows the throttle valves to seat in the bores of the carburetor. Insert the accelerating pump connector link in the outer hole of the throttle shaft arm which will give the longest stroke. The distance from the top of the float bowl cover to the top of pump plunger shaft should be a specified clearance. This dimension is given in the Carter Carburetor specification table under the heading accelerator pump adjustment. See index. To set linkage bend the lower end of connector rod until dimension is obtained.

Measuring accelerator pump stroke

Fast Idle Adjustment

Back out the idle adjusting screw. Take out the choke thermostatic coil housing gasket and baffle plate. Crack the throttle, hold choke in the closed position and then close throttle. This allows the fast idle mechanism to arrive at the fast idle position. The clearance opposite the idle port side, between the throttle valve and bores of carburetor should be .015 to .019 inch. To set, bend the choke connector rod at the lower angle.

Checking unloader adjustment

Unloader Adjustment

The unloader adjustment is to be made after the fast idle adjustment. When the throttle valve is in the wide open position, with choke closed there should be 9/64 inch clearance between the upper edge of the choke valve and the vertical float surface inside the air horn. When adjustment is required, bend arm on choke trip lever.

Gage in position to check float height

Float Level Adjustment

Remove air horn, bowl gasket and float retaining pin. Hold the tang against the seated needle, making sure the float pin is bottomed in its recess. In this position the distance from the top of the body casting to the top of each float should be 9/32 inch. When one float is higher or lower than the other bend the float arm until both floats are on an even level. If both floats are equalized but set too low, bend the float tang.

The final adjustment is to check the travel of both floats making sure they do not bind on the vertical surfaces of the float bowl. Again bend float arms if binding is noticed.

Dashpot Adjustment

To achieve maximum dashpot action turn the dashpot plunger shaft adjusting screw so that the plunger shaft can travel inward approximately 1/16 in. after engine and throttle have returned to normal idle. However maximum action is not always required as this adjustment is made to suit the individual driver. For instance a driver who moves his foot slowly off the accelerator requires practically no dashpot action at all. Whereas the driver who quickly moves his foot off the accelerator needs maximum dashpot action. The adjustment is accomplished with carburetor on the car, the engine running (after warm up) and transmission in Drive range. Turn the dashpot plunger shaft adjusting screw until desired setting is determined.

INSTALLATION OF REPAIR KIT

Throttle Body

No parts are supplied in a standard repair kit for the throttle body. However, it is always considered good practice to clean passages with air pressure. The throttle shaft should be checked for looseness or binding. Individual parts are available for replacement. If persistent air leaks have been noticed check the top and bottom surface of the throttle body with a straight edge to determine if casting is warped.

Main Body

Install venturi housing gasket, housing, cover and tube, then insert venturi cluster screws and gaskets. Next screw in pump jets. Then insert pump discharge ball checks and retainers and drive passage lead plug into place. Install main metering jets and gaskets. Place accelerating pump intake check ball and retainer into pump well and insert plunger. Screw needle seat in place and install needle valve. Now carefully set floats in main body and install float pin retainer in place being sure float pin is bottomed. Place the step-up piston and spring in position and attach step-up rod. Carefully push step-up piston down, this allows step-up rods to enter main metering jets. Care should be taken during this particular operation as the step-up rods are easily bent. Install air horn gasket and attach air horn to main body. Connect the pump plunger to pump arm.

Finally, assemble throttle body to main body, connect linkage and adjust carburetor.

Air Horn

The only parts supplied in a standard repair kit for the air horn assembly is a climatic control choke gasket.

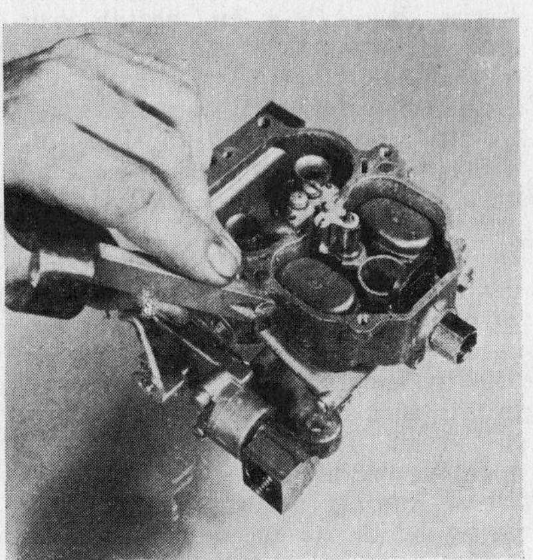

Removing lead plug with special tool

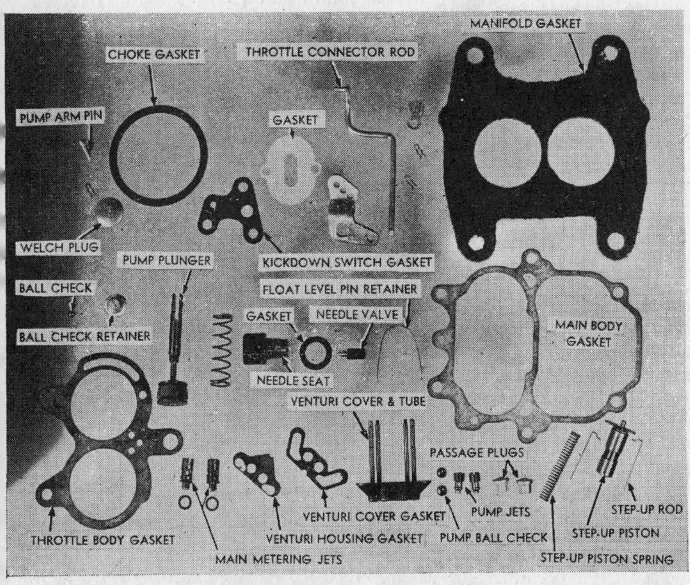

Standard overhaul kit for model BBD

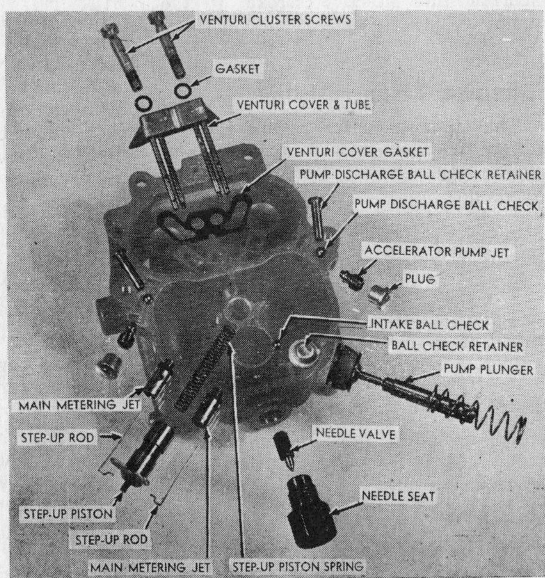

Parts of repair kit shown over their related mounting in the main body

MODEL WCFB

The Carter carburetor Model WCFB is fundamentally a dual throat down draft carburetor containing metering rods, accelerating pump circuit, climatic choke circuit, low and high speed circuits, combined in a single casting with a two-throat carburetor containing a high and low speed circuit only. The throttle valves on the primary side are connected by mechanical linkage to the accelerator pedal. The throttle valves on the secondary side are connected by spring loaded linkage to the primary side, therefore the primary throttle opens and closes at the will of the driver. The secondary throttle is operated partially by the will of the driver (spring loaded linkage) and partly by the torque demands of the engine.

Accelerating Pump Circuit

The accelerator pump circuit is located in the primary side of the carburetor only. The purpose of this circuit is to feed an extra amount of fuel during acceleration which is necessary to provide smooth power. A mechanical adjustment is provided to lengthen or shorten the effective stroke of the pump.

Climatic Choke Circuit

The climate control choke circuit allows the carburetor to feed the engine a rich mixture for starting and warm up.

Float Circuit

The float circuit is to maintain the fuel in the float bowl at a predetermined level.

Low Speed Circuit

The amount of fuel used for idle and early throttle is metered through the low speed circuit.

High Speed Circuit

The amount of fuel required for part and full throttle is supplied through the high speed circuit.

Adjustments

No carburetor should be adjusted without first checking compression, ignition and also check the manifold for any leaks. An engine must be properly tuned before any carburetor can function properly.

Idle Speed Adjustment

The idle adjustment screw positions the throttle valve for curb idle speed and has no effect on richness of mixture. Set engine idle to approximately 400-500 rpm depending on engine condition (engine in good condition should be set to lower speed). Cars equipped with automatic transmission set to approximately 400-500 rpm with transmission in drive range. When transmission is shifted to neutral, engine will speed up. This is normal.

Idle Mixture Adjustment

This adjustment controls the mixture of fuel and air at idle and also effects low speed operation. To set idle mixture proceed as follows: First, set engine idle as explained under heading idle speed adjustment. Now turn the idle mixture screw in until the engine slows down and out until the engine rolls. Midway between these two settings should be the proper setting for each primary barrel (no idle mixture adjustment on secondary side). After the second barrel has been adjusted, go back and readjust the first and then readjust the second barrel. In other words, do each adjustment at least twice.

Accelerating Pump Adjustment

Set the connector link in the outer hole of the pump arm with the ends extended toward the countershaft arm which will give the longest stroke.

Back out the fast idle adjusting screw until the throttle valves seat in the bores of the throttle body. With the throttle valves seated in the bores of the carburetor the distance from the top of the plunger shaft to the top of the dust cover boss should be a specified clearance. This dimension is given in the Carter Carburetor specification table under the heading Accelerator Pump Adjustment. See index. Now hold a straight edge across the dust cover boss at the pump arm. The top of the pump arm should be parallel to straight edge. If it is not, adjust as follows: Bend the throttle connector rod at the lower angle.

Accelerator pump adjustment and bending point

Metering Rod Adjustment

Metering rod adjustment is important and should be done after completing the pump adjustment. No gages are necessary.

Back out the idle set screws until the throttle valves seat in the bores of the carburetor. Loosen the metering rod arm clamp screw.

Metering rod adjustment

With the metering rods in place, press down the vacuum meter link until the metering rods seat in the carburetor body casting. Hold the rods in this down position and hold the throttle valves closed. Revolve the metering rod lifter arm until the finger on the arm contacts the lip of the vacuum meter link, holding it in this position carefully tighten the clamp screw.

Fast Idle Adjustment

Loosen the choke lever clamp screw on the choke shaft. Then insert a .020 inch gage between the lip of the fast idle cam and the boss on the flange casting. Hold the choke tightly closed and take the slack out of the linkage by pressing the choke lever toward the

Fast idle adjustment

closed position. Hold the parts in position and tighten the clamp screw securely. Again being sure the choke valve is tightly closed, tighten the fast

A—Hold choke valve closed
B—Insert gage between lip and boss on carburetor
C—Tighten arm in position

idle adjusting screw (insert gage on opposite side of idle part) until there is .018-.020 inch opening between throttle valve and bore of carburetor.

Unloader Adjustment

The unloader adjustment is to be made after the fast idle adjustment.

Checking unloader adjustment

When the throttle valve is in the wide open position there should be a specified clearance between the lower edge of the choke valve and the vertical flat surface inside the air horn. This dimen-

Bend tang for correct unloader setting

sion is given in the Carter carburetor specification table under the heading Unloader Adjustment. See Index. To adjust, bend the unloader lip on the throttle shaft lever.

Secondary Throttle Lock-Out Adjustment

After completing the fast idle and secondary throttle lever adjustment, then make the secondary throttle lock-out adjustment. Proceed as follows: Holding the choke in the closed position, open the primary throttle to the wide open position. With the primary throttle wide open, the tank on the secondary throttle arm should engage in the recess on the lock-out lever, preventing the secondary throttle shaft from movement. If it does not engage clearly, bend the tang on the arm until it will enter the recess. Now hold the choke wide open and open the primary throttle valves all the way, the lock-out

Secondary throttle lock-out adjustment

lever should fall free so that the secondary throttle valve will open before the primary throttle.

Secondary Throttle Lever Adjustment

Both the primary and secondary throttle valves should come to the wide

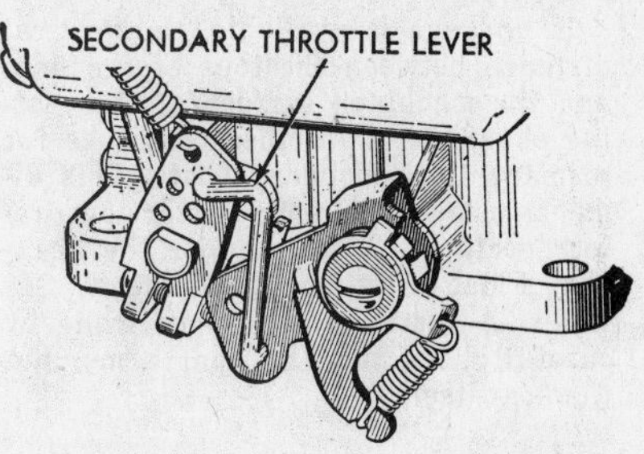

Secondary throttle lever showing angle which can be bent for adjustment

open position at the same time. If not, adjust by bending the upper angle of the throttle operating rod.

CARTER CARBURETORS

Float Level Adjustments

Floats must be adjusted in two separate ways—lateral and vertical.

Lateral Adjustment

With the bowl cover turned upside down and the float brackets resting on the seated needle, place the float gage tool directly under the floats with the recessed portion of the gage fitting over the edge of the bowl cover casting. The outer side of each float should just clear the vertical uprights of the gage. To adjust, carefully bend the float arms, not the float itself.

Checking float drop

Throttle body

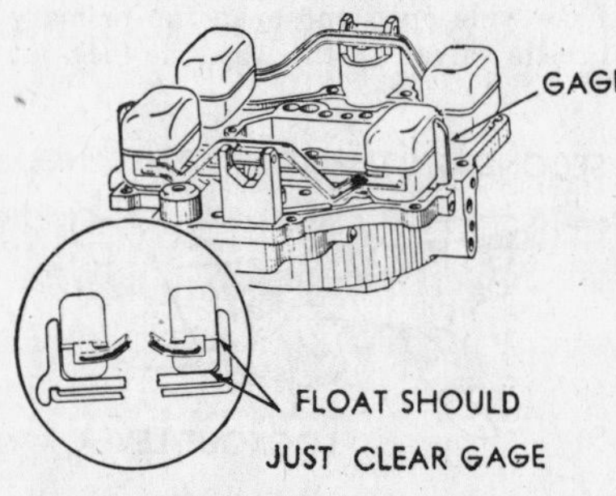

Float adjustment showing lateral and vertical position of float pontoons with gage in place

Vertical Adjustment

With the bowl cover inverted and the float gage in the same position as in lateral adjustment, the floats should just clear the horizontal surface of the gage.

If no gage is available, the vertical distance between the tops of the float and the machined surface of the casting should be a specified clearance for primary and secondary floats. This dimension is given in the Carter carburetor specification table under the heading Float Setting Adjustment. See Index. Adjustment should be made by carefully bending the float arms, not the float itself.

Float Drop Adjustment

The float must now be checked for its drop setting. Holding the bowl cover in the upright position, the float drop should be a specific clearance between the upper free end of the float and the bowl cover for both primary and secondary floats. To adjust, bend the stop tangs on the float brackets.

Bowl Vapor Vent Adjustment

It is considered good practice to first adjust the accelerating pump and the metering rods before making the bowl vapor vent adjustment. To make this adjustment, unscrew the throttle lever set screw until the throttle valves seat in the bores of the carburetor. Now the distance between the lower edge of the bowl vapor vent valve and the dust cover should be a specified clearance. If not, adjust by removing the dust cover and bend the vapor vent arm.

Main body

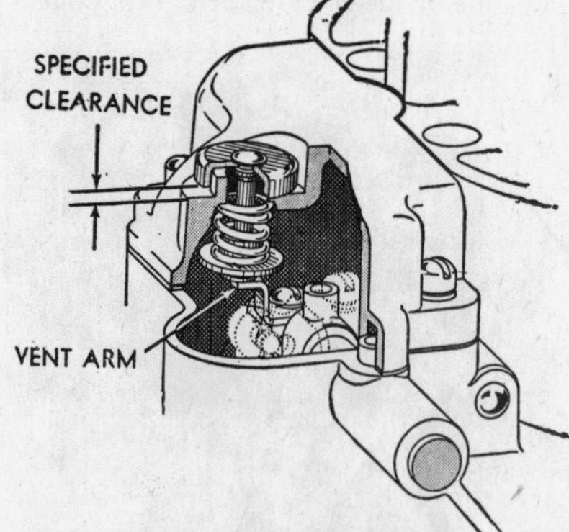

Bowl vapor vent showing arm which can be bent for adjustment

Air horn assembly showing removal of low speed jets

Installation of Repair Kit

Throttle Body

No parts are supplied in a repair kit for the throttle body. However, it is always considered good practice to remove passage plug and blow clean with air pressure. The throttle shafts should be checked for looseness or binding. Individual parts are available for replacement. If persistent air leaks have been noticed, check the top and bottom surface of throttle body with a straight edge to determine if casting is warped.

Main Body

Install four metering rod jets, being certain that the jets with the largest bore are installed in the primary side (side with pump well). Insert pump discharge check needle, gasket and pump jet housing assembly. Place the pump intake check ball and retainer in pump well, then install pump plunger spring and spring retainer. Next install vacuum piston spring in vacuum cylinder. This completes the main body.

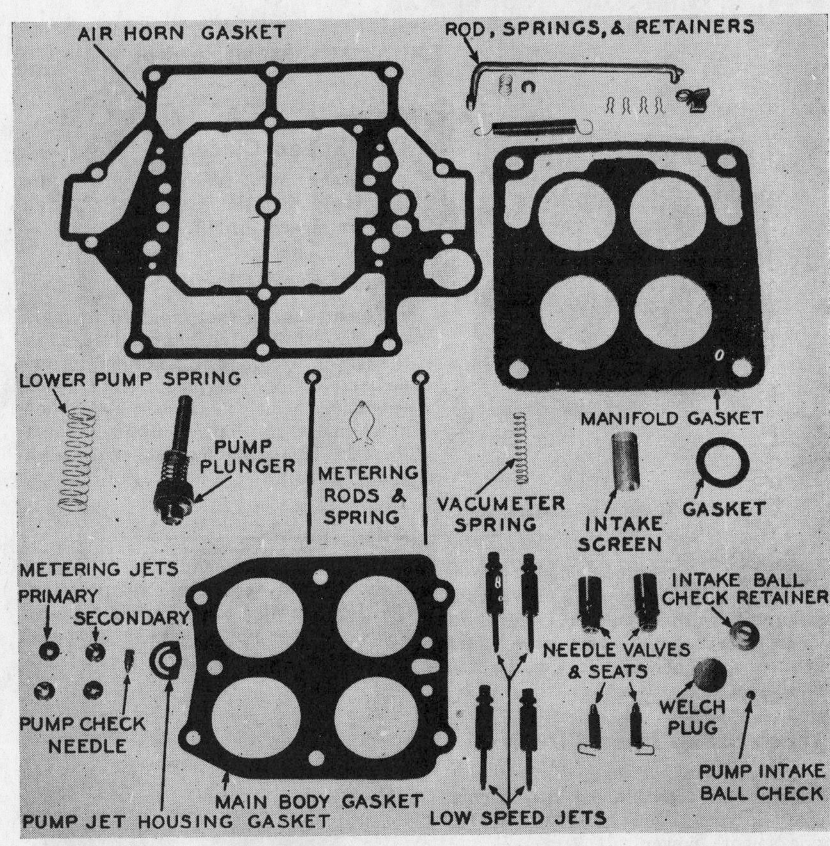

Standard overhaul kit for model WCFB

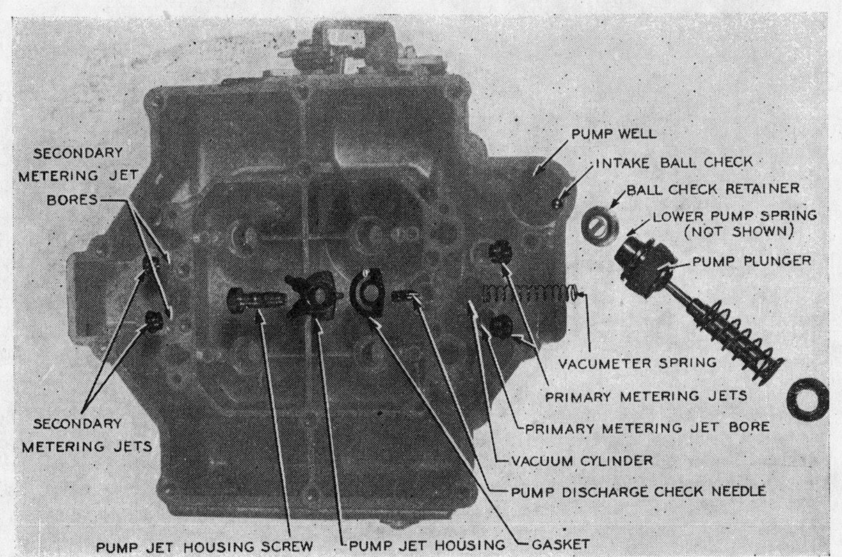

Parts of repair kit shown over their related mounting in the main body

Air Horn Body

Install primary and secondary float needle seats with new gaskets. **Caution:** Float needles and seats are factory matched and should be kept on original side. Install the four low speed jets; no precaution is necessary when installing these jets as they are interchangeable. Now install the climatic choke welsh plug. Next assemble the seat needles to proper floats and attach to air horn. Then insert vacuum link and connect vacuum piston. Install air horn body to main body, then connect metering rods to vacumeter link. Assemble throttle body to main body, connect linkage and adjust carburetor.

MODEL YH

Full view of model YH carburetor

The Carter carburetor Model YH is fundamentally a Carter YF downdraft carburetor with circuit rearranged to compensate for the carburetor being mounted and operating in a horizontal or sidedraft position.

Accelerating Pump Circuit

The accelerating pump circuit provides an extra amount of fuel during acceleration which is necessary to provide smooth power.

The accelerator pump is operated by mechanical linkage and manifold vacuum. A mechanical adjustment is provided to lengthen or shorten the effective stroke of the pump.

Climatic Control Choke Circuit

The climatic choke circuit allows the carburetor to feed the engine a rich mixture for cold engine starting and warm up.

The choke valve is operated automatically by a thermostatic coil and a vacuum operated piston. The thermostatic coil acts to close the choke valve when cold, while the vacuum pistons tends to open the valve as the engine vacuum increases.

After the thermostatic coil warms up, it loses its tension and the choke valve stays open.

Float Circuit

The float circuit is to maintain the fuel in the float bowl at a predetermined level. The needle valve is spring loaded to prevent a buildup of fuel while traveling over rough roads.

Low Speed Circuit

The amount of fuel required for idle and early throttle is metered through the low speed circuit.

High Speed Circuit

The amount of fuel required for part and full throttle is supplied through the power circuit. For maximum torque demands of the engine or high speed operation, a rich mixture is demanded much more so than required at part throttle. This is the purpose of the high speed circuit.

Adjustments

No carburetor should be adjusted without first checking compression, ignition and also the manifold for any leaks. An engine must be properly tuned before any carburetor can function properly.

Set idle speed

Idle Speed Adjustment

The idle speed adjustment screw positions the throttle valves for curb idle speed and has no effect on richness of mixture.

Set engine to approximately 550-625 rpm depending on engine condition (engine in good condition should be set to lower speed). Cars equipped with automatic transmission set to 375-450 rpm with transmission in drive range. When transmission is shifted to neutral engine will speed up. This is normal.

Set idle mixture

Idle Mixture Adjustment

This adjustment controls the mixture of fuel and air at curb idle and also effects part throttle operation. To set idle mixture proceed as follows: Turn the idle mixture screw in until the engine slows down and out again until the engine rolls. Midway between these two settings the engine will smooth out and this will be the correct setting.

Checking metering rod travel

Accelerating Pump Adjustment

No mechanical adjustment is provided for on this type pump. Whenever it is determined that acceleration is not satisfactory, detach pump housing, intake check and discharge check. Carefully inspect the pump diaphragm for wear or damage. Make certain the intake screen, intake check and discharge check ball are not clogged with lint or foreign matter. Be sure the discharge check ball is seating properly, as a leak at this point will cause poor acceleration.

Metering Rod Adjustment

Metering rod adjustment is important and should be inspected every time the carburetor is reassembled, or new rods are installed. Remove metering rods and insert gage T109-104 with tapered end of gage in metering jet. Close the throttle valve and press down on diaphragm shaft allowing the metering rod arm to contact the lifter link at diaphragm stem. Holding the diaphragm shaft in this position the metering rod pin should rest lightly on the gage. When adjustment is needed bend the metering rod arm at undercut position to maintain proper travel.

Fast Idle Adjustment

Remove thermostatic coil housing, gasket and baffle plate, crack the throttle and close the choke valve. Now close the throttle allowing the fast idle cam to arrive at fast idle position.

Bend rod to obtain correct fast idle adjustment

With the choke valve tightly closed and a little tension on the throttle lever, there should be .030 inch clearance between the throttle valve and bore of carburetor opposite the idle port side. If this clearance is not within the specifications, adjust by bending connector link at lower angle.

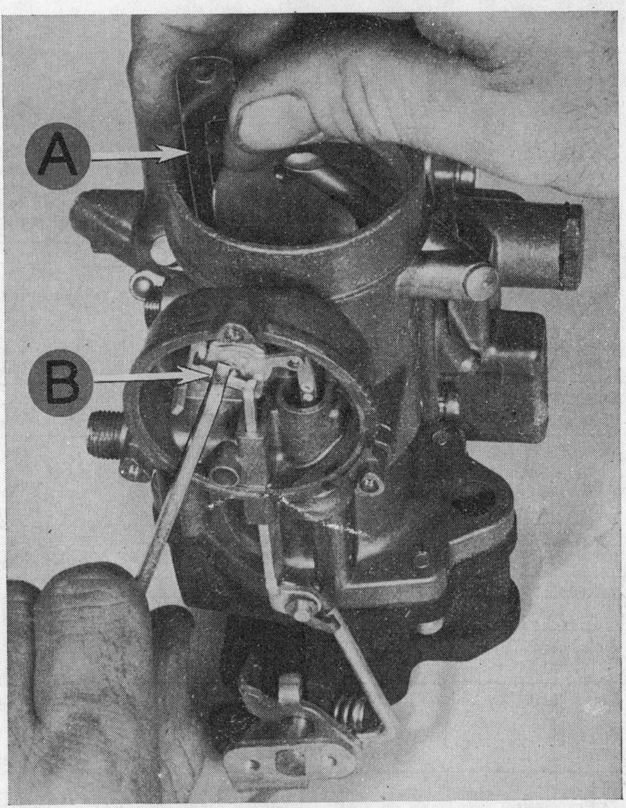

Unloader Adjustment

A—Unloader gage in position in air horn *B—Adjust by bending connecting link*

Unloader Adjustment

The unloader adjustment is to be made after the fast idle adjustment. When the throttle valve is in the wide open position, with choke closed, there should be ¼ inch clearance between the lower edge of the choke valve (vent tube side) and the flat surface inside the air horn. When adjustment is determined, bend the choke shaft unloader arm using tool T109-105.

Float Adjustment

Invert bowl cover and remove gasket. With the float resting its weight on pin in seated needle, the clearance from the bowl cover to the top of float pontoon should be ⅜ inch. Adjust by bending float lever held at eye height, in a level position.

Gage in position to check float height

Float Drop Adjustment

Holding the bowl cover in the upright position there should be a clearance of 2 inches from the float seam at free end to the bowl cover. Whenever adjustment is required bend the stop tab on float arm until the correct float drop is maintained.

Stromberg Carburetor
Downdraft

Year	Model	Carburetor Assembly Number	Code Number (See Note A)	Type	Venturi Size (inches)	Fuel Level (inches) (See Note B)	Pressure (lbs.)	Float Needle Valve and Seat, Part Number	IDLE SYSTEM: Throttle Valve Location (See Note C)	IDLE SYSTEM: Idle Tube, Part Number	IDLE SYSTEM: Idle Air Bleed: Main Body (F)	IDLE SYSTEM: Idle Air Bleed: Throttle Body (G)
BUICK												
1941	Series 40 & 50, Front	380066	7-46	AAV-16	15/16	19/32	5	P-22498	.010±.004	382806	65	42-P-24683
	Rear	380067	7-47	AA-1	15/16	19/32	....	P-22498	.022±.004	382806	65	42-P-24683
1941-42	Series 40 & 50, Front	380103	7-59A	AAV-16	15/16	19/32	5	P-22498	.010±.004	382806	65	42-P-24683
	Rear	380096	7-56A	AA-1	15/16	19/32	....	383046	.022±.004	382806	65	42-P-24683
1941	Series 60, 70, 90, Front	380064	7-44	AAV-16	1 1/32	19/32	5	P-22498	.010±.004	382806	60	42-P-24683
		380065	7-45A	AA-1	1 1/32	19/32	....	P-22498	.022±.004	382806	60	42-P-24683
1941-42	Series 60, 70, 90, Front	380104	7-60A	AAV-16	1 1/32	19/32	5	P-22498	.010±.004	382806	60	42-P-24683
		380239	7-76	AAV-167	1 1/32	19/32	5	P-22498	.022±.004	382806	70	42-P-24683
	Rear	380095	7-55A	AA-1	1 1/32	19/32	....	383046	.022±.004	382806	60	42-P-24683
		380096	7-56A	AA-1	15/16	19/32	5	383046	.022±.004	382806	65	42-P-24683
1941-47	Series 40, 50, Single	380106	7-66	AAV-16	1 1/32	19/32	5	P-22499	.022±.004	P-19424	70	42-P-24683
		380237	7-74	AAV-167	1 1/32	19/32	5	P-22499	.022±.004	P-19424	70	42-P-24683
1942-47	Series 60, 70, 90, Single	380097	7-57	AAV-26	1 1/8	19/32	4 to 5	P-22499	.022±.004	P-19424	70	42-P-24683
		380241	7-78	AAV-267	1 1/8	19/32	5	P-22499	.022±.004	P-19424	70	42-P-24683
1948-49	Series 40, 50	380225	7-69	AAV-167	1 1/32	19/32	5	P-22499	.022±.004	P-19424	70	42-P-24683
	Series 70	380226	7-70	AAV-267	1 1/8	19/32	5	P-22499	.022±.004	P-19424	70	42-P-24683
1950-51	Series 40, 50	380257	7-88B	AAUVB-267	1 1/32	21/32	5	P-22499	.030±.004	382572	58	40-385350
		380309	7-90	AAUVB-267	1 1/32	21/32	5	P-22499	.036±.004	385798	55	42-P-24683
	Series 70	380258	7-89B	AAVB-267	1 1/8	21/32	5	P-22499	.015±.004	P-21962	65	42-P-24683
		380310	7-91	AAVB-267	1 1/8	21/32	5	P-22499	.035±.004	385804	53	42-P24683
1952-53	40 Special	380309	7-90B	AAUVB-267	1 1/32	21/32	5	P-22499	.036±.004	385798	55	42-P-24683
1952	70 Roadmaster	380315	7-92B	4A	1 1/32	§P 11/16	5	1385945	.055±.004	P385953	42	39-385948
1953	50 Super	380338	7-95	AAVB-267	1 1/8	21/32	5	P-22499	.036±.004	385804	53	42-386411
	70 Roadmaster	380337	7-94A	4A	1 1/32	§P 11/16	5	385945	.055±.004	■P-386421	42	39-386344
CADILLAC												
1941	60, 62, 67, 72	380015	205-8	AAV-26	1 1/8	5/8	5	P-22499	.040±.004	P-23527	52	36-P-23658
		380048	205-9	AAV-26	1 1/8	5/8	5	P-22499	.040±.004	P-23527	52	36-P-23658
1942	60, 61, 62, 65, 67, 75	380063	205-10A	AAV-26	1 1/8	5/8	5	P-22499	.040±.004	382933	52	36-P-23658
1946-48	60, 61, 62, 75	*380154	205-14A	AAV-26	1 1/8	5/8	5	P-22499	.037±.004	382933	52	36-P-23658
		380871	205-14B	AAV-26	1 1/8	5/8	5	P-22499	+.006−.000	382933	52	48-P-23658
CHEVROLET												
1940-48	All with Manual Choke	A-19122	14-17D	BXOV-2	1 3/32	5/8	3	P-24063	+.006−.000	P-21778	55	....
	All with Automatic Choke	A-19132	14-16F	BXOV-25	1 3/32	5/8	3	P-24063	+.006−.000	P-21778	55	....
1946-52	All with Manual Trans.	†380269	14-22	BXOV-2	1 5/32	5/8	3	P-24063	+.006−.000	P-21778	3/4	....
		‡380270	14-23	BXOV-25	1 5/32	5/8	3	P-24063	+.006−.000	P-21778	3/64	....
1950-52	All with Powerglide	†380286	14-24	BXVD-3	1 7/32	5/8	3	P-21918	+.006−.000	P-21778	3/64	....
		‡380295	....	BXVD-35	1 7/32	5/8	3	P-21918	+.006−.000	P-21778	3/64	....
CHRYSLER												
1941	All, 6 cyl. with Hyd. Trans.	380277	4-117	BXVES-3	1 7/32	5/8	3	P-21918	+.006−.000	P-21778	.051	....
	C30, C31	380041	4-103A	AAV-2	1 1/8	5/8	4	P-22499	.030±.004	P-19424	40	....
1942	C36	380086	4-109	AAV-2	1 1/8	5/8	4	P-22499	.030±.004	P-19424	40	....
		380853	4-109	AAV-2	1 1/8	5/8	4	P-22499	.030±.004	P-19424	40	....
1946	C38, 6 cyl.	380165	4-111	AAVS-2	1 1/8	5/8	4	P-22499	.018±.004	P-19424	40	....
		380169	4-112	AAVS-2	1 1/8	5/8	4	P-22499	.018±.004	P-19424	40	....
1941-50	All, 6 cyl. with Hyd. Trans.	380280	4-119	BXVES-3	1 7/32	5/8	3	P-21918	+.006−.000	P-21778	.051	....
	(1941 only)	380277	4-117	BXVES-3	1 7/32	5/8	3	P-21918	+.006−.000	P-21778	.051	....

Specifications Table
Type

	MAIN METERING SYSTEM					ACCELERATING SYSTEM							
Idle Discharge Hole (F)	Main Metering Jet Part Number	Main Metering Jet Size	Main Discharge Jet, Part Number	High Speed Bleeder Part Number	High Speed Bleeder Size	Power System By-Pass Jet (See Note D)	Pump Piston Assembly, Part Number	Pump By-Pass Jet, Part Number	Pump Capacity cc per 10 Slow Strokes	Complete Repair Kit (See Note B)	Gasket Set, Part Number	Model	Year
													BUICK
54–58	P-24773	.041	P-24670	P-23985	70	P-24674	382239	....	16 to 20	RK-114	382398	Series 40 & 50, Front.......	1941
54–58	P-24773	.048	P-24670	P-23985	70	....	....	....	....	RK-115	382399	Rear.....................	
54–58	P-24773	.041	P-24670	P-23985	70	P-24674	382239	....	16 to 20	RK-114	382398	Series 40 & 50, Front.......	1941–42
54–58	P-24773	.048	P-24670	P-23985	70	....	....	....	....	RK-124	382399	Rear.....................	
54–58	P-24773	.047	P-24670	P-23985	70	P-21657	382239	....	16 to 20	RK-116	382398	Series 60, 70, 90, Front.....	1941
54–58	P-24773	.053	P-24670	P-23985	70	....	....	....	....	RK-117	382399		
54–58	P-24773	.047	P-24670	P-23985	70	P-21657	382239	....	16 to 20	RK-116	38298	Series 60, 70, 90, Front.....	1941–42
54–60	P-24773	.047	P-24670	P-23985	70	P-21657	382239	....	15 to 19	RK-140	382373		
54–58	P-24773	.053	P-24670	P-23985	70	....	....	....	....	RK-123	382399	Rear.....................	
54–58	P-24773	.048	P-24670	P-23985	70	....	....	....	....	RK-124	382399		
54–60	P-24773	.045	P-24670	P-23985	70	P-24674	P-24675	....	15 to 19	RK-72	J-5656-G	Series 40, 50, Single........	1941–47
54–60	P-24773	.045	P-24670	P-23985	70	P-24674	P-24675	....	15 to 19	RK-140	382373		
54–60	P-24673	.051	P-24670	P-23985	70	P-21197	P-24736	....	15 to 19	RK-73	J-5655-G	Series 60, 70, 90, Single.....	1942–47
54–60	P-24673	.051	P-24670	P-23985	70	P-21197	P-24736	....	15 to 19	RK-141	382372		
54–60	P-24773	.045	P-24670	P-23985	70	P-24674	P-24675	....	15 to 19	RK-140	382373	Series 40, 50..............	1948–49
54–60	P-24673	.051	P-24670	P-23985	70	P-21197	P-24736	....	15 to 19	RK-141	382372	Series 70.................	
54–85	P-24673	.047	P-24670	P-23985	70	P-21197	P-24675	....	15 to 19	RK-151	382370	Series 40, 50..............	1950–51
60–55	P-24673	.047	P-24670	P-23985	70	P-21197	P-24675	....	15 to 19	RK-168	382370		
54–60	P-24673	.051	P-24670	P-23985	70	382454	P-24736	....	15 to 19	RK-152	382370*	Series 70.................	
60–53	P-24673	.051	P-24670	P-23985	70	382454	P-24736	....	15 to 19	RK-169	382370		
60–65	P-24673	.047	P-24671	P-23985	70	P-21197	P-24736	....	15 to 19	RK-169	382370	40 Special................	1952–53
^P54-65	P-19442	•.049	P-22428	P-23985	70	P-21657	385996	....	16 to 20	RK-171	382365	70 Roadmaster.............	1952
60–53	P-24673	•.049	P-24671	P-23985	70	386398	386423	....	27 to 31	RK-180	382370	50 Super..................	1953
^P54-65	P-19442	.048	P-22428	P-23985	70	386388	385996	....	16 to 20	RK-176	382361	70 Roadmaster.............	
													CADILLAC
52–56	P-19442	.050	P-23567	P-23985	70	P-24064	384510	....	18 to 22	108	382393	60, 62, 67, 72..............	1941
52–56	P-19442	.050	P-23567	P-23985	70	P-24064	384510	....	18 to 22	108	382393		
52–56	P-19442	.048	P-23567	P-23985	70	P-24064	384510	....	18 to 22	125	382393	60, 61, 62, 65, 67, 75........	1942
52–55	P-24773	.048	P-23567	P-23985	70	P-24064	384653	....	29 to 33	RK-134	382393	60, 61, 62, 75..............	1946–48
54–60	P-24773	.048	P-23567	P-23985	70	P-24064	384653	....	29 to 33	RK-134	382393		
													CHEVROLET
56–58	P-22660	.053	P-24313	P-23985	70	P-21198	385100	P-24062	7 to 10	RK-105	J-5562-G	All with Manual Choke.....	1940–48
56–58	P-22660	.053	P-24313	P-23985	70	P-21198	385100	P-24062	7 to 10	RK-105	J-5562-G	All with Automatic Choke...	
56–58	P-19442	.058	382897	P-24315	68	P-21197	385100	P-24744	11 to 14	RK-164	J-5562-G	All with Manual Trans......	1946–52
56–58	P-19442	.058	382897	P-24315	68	385449	385100	P-24744	11 to 14	RK-165	J-5562-G		
56–58	P-19442	.061	P-24036	P-24315	68	583449	385100	56	11 to 14	RK-166	382369	All with Powerglide.........	1950–52
56–58	P-19442	.061	P-24036	P-24315	68	....	....	....	....	....	....		
													CHRYSLER
56–58	P-19442	.061	382897	P-24315	70	385056	385100	P-24062	11 to 14	....	382371	All, 6 cyl. with Hyd. Trans...	1941
54–55	P-22660	.051	P-22795	P-22368	70	382454	382595	P-23742	27 to 31	RK-113	382395	C30, C31..................	
54–55	P-22660	.051	P-22795	P-22369	70	382454	382595	P-23742	27 to 31	RK-113	382395	C36......................	1942
54–55	P-22660	.051	P-22795	P-22369	70	382454	382595	P-23742	27 to 31	RK-113	382395		
54–55	P-22660	.051	P-22795	P-22369	70	382454	382595	P-23742	27 to 31	RK-132	382395	C38, 6 cyl.................	1946
54–55	P-22660	.051	P-22795	P-22369	70	382454	382595	P-23742	27 to 31	RK-132	382395		
56–58	P-19442	.061	382897	P-24315	70	385056	385100	P-24062	11 to 14	....	382371	All, 6 cyl. with Hyd. Trans...	1946–50
56–58	P-19442	.061	382897	P-24315	70	385056	385100	P-24062	11 to 14	....	382371	(1941 only)...............	

Stromberg Carburetor

Year	Model	Carburetor Assembly Number	Code Number (See Note A)	Type	Venturi Size (inches)	Fuel Level (inches) (See Note B)	Pressure (lbs.)	Float Needle Valve and Seat, Part Number	Throttle Valve Location (See Note C)	IDLE SYSTEM: Idle Tube, Part Number	Idle Air Bleed: Main Body (F)	Idle Air Bleed: Throttle Body (G)
DE SOTO												
1941		380277	4-117	BXVES	$1\frac{7}{32}$	$\frac{5}{8}$	3	P-21918	+.006−.000	P-21778	.051	
1942–50	With Hyd. Trans.	380280	4-119	BXVES	$1\frac{7}{32}$	$\frac{5}{8}$	3	P-21918	+.006−.000	P-21778	.051	
1947	S11 (Fluid Drive)	380218	3-83C	BXVD-3	$1\frac{7}{32}$	$\frac{5}{8}$	3	384956	+.006−.000	P-21778	54	
DODGE												
1940–41	D14, D17, D19	A-18123	3-54A	BXV-3	$1\frac{5}{32}$	$\frac{5}{8}$	3	P-24827	+.006−.000	P-21778	54	
1941	D19	380044	3-59B	BXVD-3	$1\frac{5}{32}$	$\frac{5}{8}$	3	P-24827	+.006−.000	P-21778	54	
1940–41	D14, D17, D19, Replace.	380221	3-87C	BXVD-3	$1\frac{5}{32}$	$\frac{5}{8}$	3	P-24063	+.006−.000	P-21778	54	
1942	D22 (Conv. Trans.)	380079	3-65	BXV-3	$1\frac{7}{32}$	$\frac{5}{8}$	3	382901	+.006−.000	P-21778	54	
	D22 (Fluid Drive)	380080	3-66	BXVD-3	$1\frac{7}{32}$	$\frac{5}{8}$	3	382901	+.006−.000	P-21778	54	
1942-47	D22, D24 (Std. Trans.)	380158	3-76	BXV-3	$1\frac{7}{32}$	$\frac{5}{8}$	3	P-21918	+.006−.000	P-21778	54	
	(Fluid Drive)	380159	3-77	BXVD-3	$1\frac{7}{32}$	$\frac{5}{8}$	3	P-21918	+.006−.000	P-21778	54	
1947–48	All (Std. Trans.)	380219	3-83A	BXV-3	$1\frac{7}{32}$	$\frac{5}{8}$	3	384956	+.006−.000	P-21778	54	
	(Fluid Drive)	380852	3-82D	BXVD-3	$1\frac{7}{32}$	$\frac{5}{8}$	3	384956	+.006−.000	P-21778	54	
1949–51	All (Fluid Drive)	380249	3-93D	BXVD-3	$1\frac{7}{32}$	$\frac{5}{8}$	3	384956	+.006−.000	P-21778	.051	
	(Gyro-matic)	380251	3-95G	BXVES-3	$1\frac{7}{32}$	$\frac{5}{8}$	3	384956	+.006−.000	P-21778	.051	
1949–53	All, 6 cyl. (Gyro-Trans.)	380331	3-111	BXVES-3	$1\frac{7}{32}$	$\frac{5}{8}$	3	384956	.006±.000	P-21778	51	55-386294
1953	D-44, D-48, V8 (Gyro)	380320	3-106	WW	$1\frac{1}{16}$	$\frac{5}{8}$	4	384956	.030±.004	386197	48	70-386318
	D-44, D-48, V8 (Manual)	380326	3-108	WW	$1\frac{1}{16}$	$\frac{5}{8}$	4	384956	.030±.004	386197	48	70-386318
	D-44, D-48, V8 (Manual) w/O.D.	380327	3-109	WW	$1\frac{1}{16}$	$\frac{5}{8}$	4	384956	.030±.004	386197	48	70-386318
FORD-MERCURY												
1940–41	V8, 85	380076	2-21A	EE-1	$\frac{31}{32}$	$\frac{15}{32}$	3	P-20287	.030±.004	P-19424	54	50
1942–48	V8, 100 H.P.	380209	2-24	EE-1	$\frac{31}{32}$	$\frac{15}{32}$	3	P-20287	.030±.004	P-19424	54	53
1949–52	V8 (Manual Trans.)	380272	2-25	EE-1	$\frac{31}{32}$	$\frac{15}{32}$	3	P-20287	.030±.004	P-19424	54	53
1949–51	All, 6 cyl.	380296										
FRAZER												
1947–48		380287	266-2	BXOV-25	$1\frac{7}{32}$	$\frac{5}{8}$	3	P-21918	.015±.004	P-21778	65	
HUDSON												
1941–42	All, 6 cyl.	380748	22-16	BXV-2	$1\frac{7}{32}$	$\frac{5}{8}$	3	P-24063	+.006−.004	P-21778	54	
		380749	22-17	BXV-25	$1\frac{3}{32}$	$\frac{5}{8}$	3	P-24063	+.006−.004	P-21778	54	
1941–47	All, 8 cyl. to early '47	380198	22-19	AAV-26	$1\frac{1}{32}$	$\frac{5}{8}$	3	P-22499	.022±.004	P-19424	70	P-24683
1950–51	500, 4A	380297	22-20	BXUV-35								
KAISER												
1947–49	All exc., K482 & K492	380287	266-2	BXOV-25	$1\frac{7}{32}$	$\frac{5}{8}$	3	P-21918	.015±.004	P-21778	65	
LINCOLN												
1940	V12, Model K	380211	40-17	AAV-2	$1\frac{1}{8}$	$\frac{5}{8}$	3	P-22499	.030±.004	P-23527	70	36-P-23536
1940–42	All, Zephyrs & Cont.	380139	40-16	EE-1								
NASH												
1940–42	4020, 4160, 4260	380591	8-42	BXOV-2	$1\frac{5}{32}$	$\frac{5}{8}$	3	P-21918	+.006−.000	P-21778	54	
1941–42	4140, 4240	380747	8-45	BXV-2	$1\frac{3}{32}$	$\frac{5}{8}$	3	P-24063	+.006−.000	P-21778	54	
1946–51	Statesman & Rambler	380288	8-48	BXV-25	$1\frac{3}{32}$	$\frac{5}{8}$	3	P-24063	+.006−.000	P-21778	54	
	Ambassador Sixes	380292	8-49	BXOV-25	$1\frac{7}{32}$	$\frac{5}{8}$	3	P-21918	.015±.004	P-21778	65	

Specifications Table—*continued*

Idle Discharge Hole (F)	MAIN METERING SYSTEM: Main Metering Jet, Part Number	Main Metering Jet, Size	Main Discharge Jet, Part Number	High Speed Bleeder, Part Number	High Speed Bleeder, Size	Power System By-Pass Jet (See Note D)	ACCELERATING SYSTEM: Pump Piston Assembly, Part Number	Pump By-Pass Jet, Part Number	Pump Capacity cc per 10 Slow Strokes	Complete Repair Kit (See Note B)	Gasket Set, Part Number	Model	Year
												DE SOTO	
56–58	P-19442	.061	382897	P-24315	70	385056	385100	P-24062	11 to 14	....	382371	....	1941
56–58	P-19442	.061	382897	P-24315	70	385056	385100	P-24062	11 to 14	....	382371	With Hyd. Trans.	1942–50
56–58	P-19442	.061	382897	P-24315	68	P-23676	385100	P-24062	11 to 14	RK-143	J-5968-G	S11 (Fluid Drive)	1947
												DODGE	
56–58	P-19442	.058	P-24036	P-24315	68	P-21197	385100	P-24062	11 to 14	75	J-5968-G	D14, D17, D19	1940–41
56–58	P-19442	.057	P-24036	P-24315	68	382675	385100	P-24062	11 to 14	RK-118	J-5968-G	D19	1941
56–58	P-19442	.058	P-24036	P-24315	68	P-21197	385100	P-24062	11 to 14	RK-144	J-5968-G	D14, D17, D19, Replace.	1940–41
56–58	P-19442	.061	382897	P-24315	68	P-23676	385100	P-24062	11 to 14	RK-121	J-5968-G	D22 (Conv. Trans.)	1942
56–58	P-19442	.061	382897	P-24315	68	P-23676	385100	P-24062	11 to 14	RK-120	J-5968-G	D22 (Fluid Drive)	
56–58	P-19442	.061	382897	P-24315	68	P-23676	385100	P-24062	11 to 14	RK-130	J-5968-G	D22, D24 (Std. Trans.)	1942–47
56–58	P-19442	.061	382897	P-24315	68	P-23676	385100	P-24062	11 to 14	RK-131	J-5968-G	(Fluid Drive)	
56–58	P-19442	.061	382897	P-24315	68	P-23676	385100	P-24062	11 to 14	RK-139	J-5968-G	All (Std. Trans.)	1947–48
56–58	P-19442	.061	382897	P-24315	68	P-23676	385100	P-24062	11 to 14	RK-143	J-5968-G	(Fluid Drive)	
56–58	P-19442	.061	382897	P-24315	68	385449	382369	P-24062	11 to 14	RK-159	J-5968-G	All (Fluid Drive)	1949–51
56–58	P-19442	.061	382897	P-24315	68	385449	385100	P-24062	11 to 14	RK-149	382371	(Gyro-matic)	
56–58	P-19442	.061	382897	P-24315	68	385449	385100	....	11 to 14	RK-149	382371	All, 6 cyl. (Gyro-Trans.)	1949–53
54–65	386208	.048	386207	P-23985	70	P-21198	386186	....	12	RK-172	382364	D-44, D-48, V8 (Gyro)	1953
54–65	386208	.048	386207	P-23985	70	P-21198	386186	....	12	RK-173	382363	D-44, D-48, V8 (Manual)	
54–65	386208	.048	386207	P-23985	70	P-21198	386186	....	12	RK-173	382363	D-44, D-48, V8 (Manual) w/O.D.	
												FORD-MERCURY	
56–60	P-19442	.046	P-21317	....	65	....	P-19487	....	17 to 21	RK-137	J-4383-G	V8, 85	1940–41
56–60	P-24773	.044	P-19440	....	65	....	P-19487	....	17 to 21	RK-145	J-4383-G	V8, 100 H.P.	1942–48
56–60	P-19442	.043	P-19440	....	65	....	P-19487	....	10 to 14	RK-162	382368	V8 (Manual Trans.)	1949–52
....	....	....	....	....	....	....	....	....	....	....	....	All, 6 cyl.	1949–51
												FRAZER	
54–60	P-19942	.058	P-24610	P-23985	70	P-24064	385100	P-24062	11 to 14	....	J-5562-G	....	1947–48
												HUDSON	
56–58	P-19442	.057	P-24036	P-23985	70	P-23676	385100	P-24062	11 to 14	RK-81	J-5562-G	All, 6 cyl.	1941–42
56–58	P-19442	.057	P-24036	P-23985	70	P-23676	385100	P-24062	11 to 14	RK-81	J-5562-G	....	
54–60	P-24673	.050	P-24670	P-23985	70	P-21197	P-24675	....	15 to 19	....	382390	All, 8 cyl. to early '47	1941–47
....	....	....	....	....	....	....	....	....	....	....	....	500, 4A	1950–51
												KAISER	
54–60	P-19442	.058	P-24610	P-23985	70	P-24064	385100	P-24062	11 to 14	....	J-5562-G	All ecx., K482 & K492	1947–49
												LINCOLN	
54–58	P-22660	.056	P-22795	....	63	P-23667	382686	P-23742	18 to 22	....	J-5545-G	V12, Model K	1940
....	....	....	....	....	....	....	P-22758	....	17 to 21	....	J-4383-G	All, Zephyrs & Cont.	1940–42
												NASH	
56–58	P-19442	.062	P-24036	P-24315	68	P-21197	385100	P-24062	11 to 14	RK-83	J-5562-G	4020, 4160, 4260	1940–42
56–58	P-19442	.057	P-24036	P-23985	70	P-23676	385100	P-24062	11 to 14	RK-81	J-5562-G	4140, 4240	1941–42
56–58	P-19442	.057	P-24036	P-23985	70	P-23676	385100	P-24744	11 to 14	RK-81	J-5562-G	Statesman & Rambler	1946–51
54–60	P-19442	.057	P-24610	P-23985	70	P-23676	385100	P-24064	11 to 14	RK-81	J-5562-G	Ambassador Sixes	

Stromberg Carburetor

Year	Model	Carburetor Assembly Number	Code Number (See Note A)	Type	Venturi Size (inches)	Fuel Level (inches) (See Note B)	Pressure (lbs.)	Float Needle Valve and Seat, Part Number	IDLE SYSTEM: Throttle Valve Location (See Note C)	IDLE SYSTEM: Idle Tube, Part Number	IDLE SYSTEM: Idle Air Bleed: Main Body (F)	IDLE SYSTEM: Idle Air Bleed: Throttle Body (G)
OLDSMOBILE												
1940	All, 6 cyl.	‡380152	5-42	BXOV-2	$1\frac{5}{32}$	$\frac{5}{8}$	3	P-21918	+.006−.000	P-21778	54	....
	....	†380153	5-39	BXOV-25	$1\frac{5}{32}$	$\frac{5}{8}$	3	P-21918	+.006−.000	P-21778	54	....
1941–50	All, 6 cyl.	380306	5-53	BXUV-35	$1\frac{5}{32}$	$\frac{5}{8}$	3	P-21918	+.006−.000	P-21778	54	....
PACKARD												
1940	1800, 110	A-19162	10-39E	BXOV-26	$1\frac{7}{32}$	$\frac{5}{8}$	3	P-24063	+.006−.000	P-24766	65	....
	1801, 1801A, 120	A-18341	10-33E	EE-16	$1\frac{1}{32}$	$\frac{15}{32}$	3	P-23509	.030±.004	P-23663	60	38-P-23658
	1803, 4, 5, 6, 7, 8	A-19172	10-40B	AAV-26	$1\frac{1}{8}$	$\frac{5}{8}$	3	P-22499	.040±.004	P-24875	52	36-P-23536
1941–42	1900, 2000	380049	10-46A	BXOV-26	$1\frac{7}{32}$	$\frac{5}{8}$	3	P-21918	.010±.004	P-21962	60	....
	1901, 2001	380050	10-47A	EE-16	$1\frac{1}{32}$	$\frac{15}{32}$	5	P-23509	.030±.004	P-23663	60	38-P-23658
	....	380039	10-45A	BXQV-26	$1\frac{7}{32}$	$\frac{5}{8}$	3	P-21918	.010±.004	P-21962	60	....
	1903,4,5,6,7,8,2003,4,5,6,7,8	380037	10-44C	AAV-26	$1\frac{1}{8}$	$\frac{5}{8}$	5	P-22499	.022±.004	382572	60	P-23536
	1901, 2001 (Replacement)	380709	10-49	EE-16	$1\frac{1}{32}$	$\frac{15}{32}$	3	P-23509	.030±.004	P-23663	60	38-P-23658
PLYMOUTH												
1940–41	P9, P10, P11, P12	†380137	15-11	BXUV-3	$1\frac{5}{32}$	$\frac{5}{8}$	3	P-21918	+.006−.000	P-21778	54	....
1942–48	....	‡380235	15-14	BXUV-35	$1\frac{5}{32}$	$\frac{5}{8}$	3	P-21918	+.006−.000	P-21178	54	....
	All	†380245	15-16	BXUV-3	$1\frac{5}{32}$	$\frac{5}{8}$	3	P-21918	+.006−.000	P-21778	54	....
	....	380246	15-17	BXUV-35	$1\frac{5}{32}$	$\frac{5}{8}$	3	P-21918	+.006−.000	P-21178	54	....
1949–52	All	380271	15-20A	BXUV-3	$1\frac{5}{32}$	$\frac{5}{8}$	3	P-21918	+.006−.000	P-21778	54	....
PONTIAC												
1941–51	All, 6 cyl.	380291	13-22	BXOV-25	$1\frac{5}{32}$	$\frac{5}{8}$	3	P-21918	+.006−.000	P-21778	54	....
1941–49	All, 8 cyl. (Man. Trans.)	380181	13-20A	AAV-26	$1\frac{1}{32}$	$\frac{5}{8}$	3	P-22499	.022±.004	P-19424	70	....
1941–52	6 cyl. Models	380291	13-22	BXOV-25	$1\frac{7}{32}$	$\frac{5}{8}$	3	P-21918	.006±.000	P-21778	54	380291
1947–52	8 cyl. Models	380311	13-23	AAUVB-26	$1\frac{1}{32}$	$\frac{21}{32}$	5	P-22499	.004±.004	385872	58	40-385874
STUDEBAKER												
1941–42	7C, 8C, President	380038	6-97C	AAV-26	$1\frac{1}{32}$	$\frac{5}{8}$	3	P-22499	.015±.004	332572	60	42-24683
1941–48	Champion	†380077	6-100	BXV-2	$1\frac{3}{32}$	$\frac{5}{8}$	3	P-24063	+.006−.000	P-21778	54	....
	....	‡380078	6-101	BXV-25	$1\frac{3}{32}$	$\frac{5}{8}$	3	P-24063	+.006−.000	P-21778	54	....
1941–50	Commander	380178	6-104D	BXOV-26	$1\frac{3}{16}$	$\frac{5}{8}$	3	P-24063	.010±.004	P-21778	54	....
1949–51	Champion	380283	6-109	BXOV-25	$1\frac{5}{32}$	$\frac{5}{8}$	3	P-21918	+.006−.000	P-21778	54	....
1951	Commander	380278	6-107A	AAUVB-26	$1\frac{1}{32}$	$\frac{21}{32}$	5	P-22499	.040±.004	382572	58	40-385350
	....	380313	6-111	AAUVB-26	$1\frac{1}{32}$	$\frac{21}{32}$	5	P-22499	.040±.004	382572	58	40-385350
1951–52	Commander	380313	6-111A	AAUVB-26	$1\frac{1}{32}$	$\frac{21}{32}$	5	P-22499	.040±.004	386279	58	40-385924
1953	Commander	380334	6-112	WW	$1\frac{1}{16}$	$\frac{5}{8}$	4	386369	.025±.004	386414	70	48-386454
WILLYS												
1940	440	380259	96-18A	BXOV-1	$1\frac{1}{32}$	$\frac{5}{8}$	3	P-24063	+.006−.000	P-24917	54	....
1941–42	441, 442	380744	96-16	BXV-2	$1\frac{1}{32}$	$\frac{5}{8}$	3	P-24063	+.006−.000	P-24917	54	....
1946–50	CJ-2A, CJ-3A	380284	96-20	BXOV-1	$1\frac{1}{32}$	$\frac{5}{8}$	3	P-24063	+.006−.000	P-21778	54	....
1946–50	4-63, 6-63, 6-73	380285	96-21	BXV-2	$1\frac{1}{32}$	$\frac{5}{8}$	3	P-24063	+.006−.000	P-24917	54	....
1950	4-73	380290	96-22	BXOV-2	$1\frac{1}{32}$	$\frac{5}{8}$	3	P-24063	+.006−.000	P-24917	54	....

FOOTNOTES

(A)—Stamped on float chamber cover.

(B)—Measured from top surface of main body with gasket removed.

(C)—Throttle valve location. Upper lip of throttle valve to be (as specified) below lower edge of upper idle hole.

(D)—Size stamped on jet.

(E)—Repair kit contains gasket set.

(F)—Drill size.

(G)—Drill size and part number.

Specifications Table—*continued*

Idle Discharge Hole (F)	MAIN METERING SYSTEM: Main Metering Jet, Part Number	Main Metering Jet, Size	Main Discharge Jet, Part Number	High Speed Bleeder, Part Number	High Speed Bleeder, Size	ACCELERATING SYSTEM: Power System By-Pass Jet (See Note D)	Pump Piston Assembly, Part Number	Pump By-Pass Jet, Part Number	Pump Capacity cc per 10 Slow Strokes	Complete Repair Kit (See Note B)	Gasket Set, Part Number	Model	Year
												OLDSMOBILE	
56–58	P-19442	.062	P-24610	P-24315	68	P-21197	385100	P-24062	11 to 14	RK-83	J-5562-G	All, 6 cyl.	1940
56–58	P-19442	.062	P-24610	P-24315	68	P-21197	385100	P-24062	11 to 14	RK-83	J-5562-G	...	
56–58	P-19442	.062	P-24610	P-24315	68	385449	385100	P-24062	11 to 14	...	J-5676-G	All, 6 cyl.	1941–50
												PACKARD	
54–56	P-19442	.060	P-24610	P-23985	70	P-21197	385100	P-24062	11 to 14	RK-77	J-5652-G	1800, 110	1940
54–58	P-19442	.047	P-23346	P-22764	65	...	P-24716	...	17 to 21	RK-79	J-5410-G	1801, 1801A, 120	
52–56	P-19442	.050	P-23567	P-23965	70	P-21197	P-24922	P-23742	...	...	J-5421-G	1803, 4, 5, 6, 7, 8	
54–60	P-19442	.060	382407	P-24315	68	P-24064	385100	P-24062	11 to 14	RK-109	J-5652-G	1900, 2000	1941–42
54–58	P-19442	.047	P-23346	P-22764	65	...	P-24716	...	17 to 21	RK-79	J-5410-G	1901, 2001	
54–60	P-19442	.060	382407	P-24315	68	P-24064	385100	P-24062	11 to 14	RK-109	J-5652-G	...	
54–58	P-24773	.050	P-23567	P-23985	70	P-21197	382414	...	27 to 31	RK-110	382394	1903,4,5,6,7,8,2003,4,5,6,7,8	
54–58	P-19442	.047	P-23346	P-22764	65	...	P-24716	...	17 to 21	RK-79	J-5410-G	1901, 2001 (Replacement)	
												PLYMOUTH	
56–58	P-19442	.058	P-24036	P-24315	68	P-21197	385100	56	11 to 14	RK-84	J-5676-G	P9, P10, P11, P12	1940–41
56–58	P-19442	.058	P-24036	P-24315	68	P-21197	385100	56	11 to 14	RK-84	J-5676-G	...	
56–58	P-19442	.058	P-24036	P-24315	68	P-21197	385100	56	11 to 14	RK-84	J-5676-G	All	1942–48
56–58	P-19442	.058	P-24036	P-24315	68	P-21197	385100	56	11 to 14	RK-84	J-5676-G	...	
56–58	P-19442	.058	P-24036	P-24315	68	P-21197	385100	P-24062	11 to 14	RK-153	J-5676-G	All	1949–52
												PONTIAC	
56–58	P-19442	.058	385670	P-24315	68	385056	385100	56	11 to 14	RK-83	J-5562-G	All, 6 cyl.	1941–51
54–60	P-24773	.044	P-24670	P-23985	70	P-21197	P-24675	...	15 to 19	...	382390	All, 8 cyl. (Man. Trans.)	1941–49
56–58	P-19442	.058	385670	P-24315	68	385056	385100	56	11 to 14	...	J-5562G	6 cyl. Models	1941–52
54–58	P-24773	.044	385636	P-23985	70	382675	385601	...	16 to 20	...	...	8 cyl. Models	1947–52
												STUDEBAKER	
56–60	P-24773	.044	382408	P-23985	70	P-21657	382443	...	16 to 20	RK-111	382393	7C, 8C, President	1941–42
56–58	P-19442	.054	P-24610	P-23985	70	...	...	...	...	...	...	Champion	1941–48
56–58	P-19442	.054	P-24610	P-23985	70	...	...	...	...	...	...	...	
56–60	P-19442	.057	382492	P-23985	70	P-21197	385100	P-23742	11 to 14	RK-112	J-5652-G	Commander	1941–50
56–58	P-19442	.055	P-24610	P-24315	68	...	...	...	...	...	...	Champion	1949–51
54–58	P-24773	.045	385636	P-23985	70	P-24674	385601	...	11 to 14	RK-163	382367	Commander	1951
54–56	P-24773	.048	385636	385852	75	P-23348	385601	...	11 to 14	RK-170	382367	...	
54–56	P-24773	.048	385636	385852	75	P-23348	385601	...	11 to 14	RK-170	382367	Commander	1951–52
54–65	386272	.049	386207	P-24315	68	386418	386186	...	15 to 17	RK-175	382362	Commander	1953
												WILLYS	
56–58	P-19442	.054	P-24036	P-23901	...	P-21198	385100	P-23742	11 to 14	...	382388	440	1940
56–58	P-19442	.054	P-24036	P-23901	...	P-24655	385100	382146	11 to 14	...	J-5562-G	441, 442	1941–42
56–58	P-19442	.054	P-24036	P-23901	...	P-23606	385100	382146	11 to 14	...	382388	CJ-2A, CJ-3A	1946–50
56–58	P-19442	.050	P-24036	P-23901	...	P-21657	385100	382146	11 to 14	...	J-5562-G	4-63, 6-63, 6-73	1946–50
56–58	P-22660	.052	P-24036	P-23901	...	382675	385100	P-24744	11 to 14	...	J-5562-G	4-73	1950

§—Secondary ⅝.
■—Secondary 386422.
△—Secondary 63-56.

●—Secondary .051.
P—Primary side.
*—This carburetor replaces all Stromberg equipment on Cadillacs from 1939 to 1948.

†—Manual choke.
‡—Automatic choke.
Trans.—Transmission.
Hyd.—Hydraulic.

Conv.—Conventional.
Std.—Standard.
Exc.—Except.

STROMBERG CARBURETORS

Only two adjustments are practical on a Stromberg carburetor without partial or complete disassembly.

The first, idle speed, is not really a carburetor adjustment since it in no way affects the functioning of the carburetor itself.

The second is the idle mixture adjustment.

On all Stromberg carburetors the idle mixture screw controls fuel. Turning the screw out will make the idle mixture richer and turning in will make the idle mixture leaner.

The accepted procedure for adjusting idle mixture is to turn the screw inward until the engine slows down for lack of fuel and then turn it outward until the engine rolls from an over rich mixture. About halfway between these two points is the correct setting for the idle mixture of fuel and air in the carburetor.

The only other adjustment practically is that of the fuel pipe. This requires that the carburetor be particularly disassembled so that it will be necessary to remove the float bowl and the top of the air horn.

Most of the Stromberg dual down draft carburetors are fitted with a plug in the side of the float chamber. The level of the fuel in the float chamber should come to the bottom of this plug hole. To check, remove the plug, and see if the level of the fuel is at the bottom of the plug hole when the car is standing on level ground. A deviation of approximately 1/16 inch is permissible.

If the carburetor is not equipped with a plug in the side of the float chamber it will be necessary to remove the cover and measure from the machined surface of the float bowl, to the top of the fuel, to determine the fuel level.

Correct by bending the float upwards or downwards whichever is indicated.

Accelerating Pump

Most Stromberg carburetors are equipped with an accelerator pump link having three holes. The inner hole is for summer driving, the center hole for all normal driving and the outer hole for winter driving or maximum acceleration charge.

No other adjustments are possible on the Stromberg carburetors and if the carburetor is not functioning properly it will be necessary to remove and disassemble the carburetor completely installing all new jets.

Reference to the exploded illustrations on this page will show the parts which are generally found in an overhaul kit.

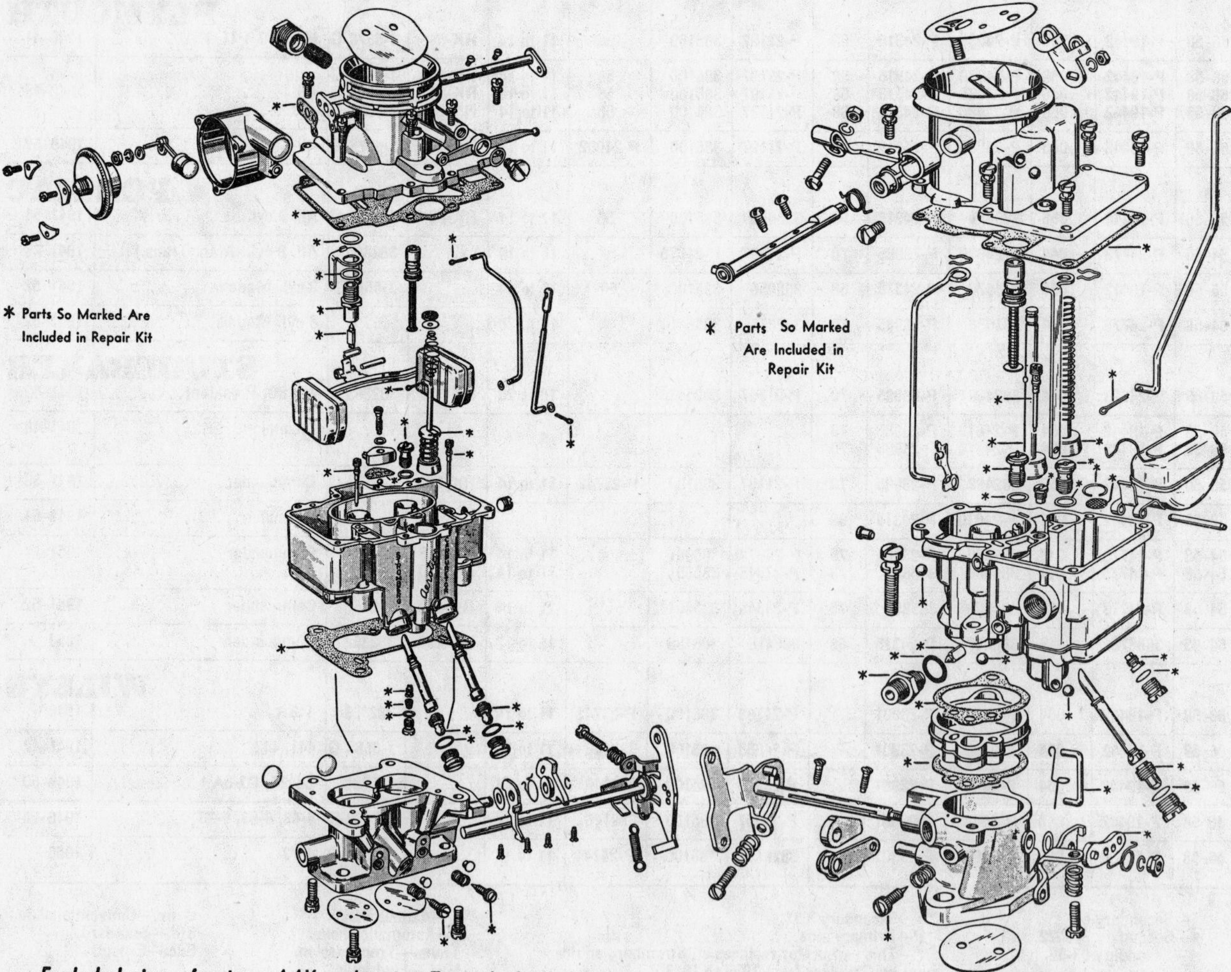
* Parts So Marked Are Included in Repair Kit
* Parts So Marked Are Included in Repair Kit

Exploded view of a type AAV carburetor. Typical of all AA types

Exploded view of a type BXVD carburetor. Typical of all BX types

1941-42 BUICK COMPOUND CARBURETION

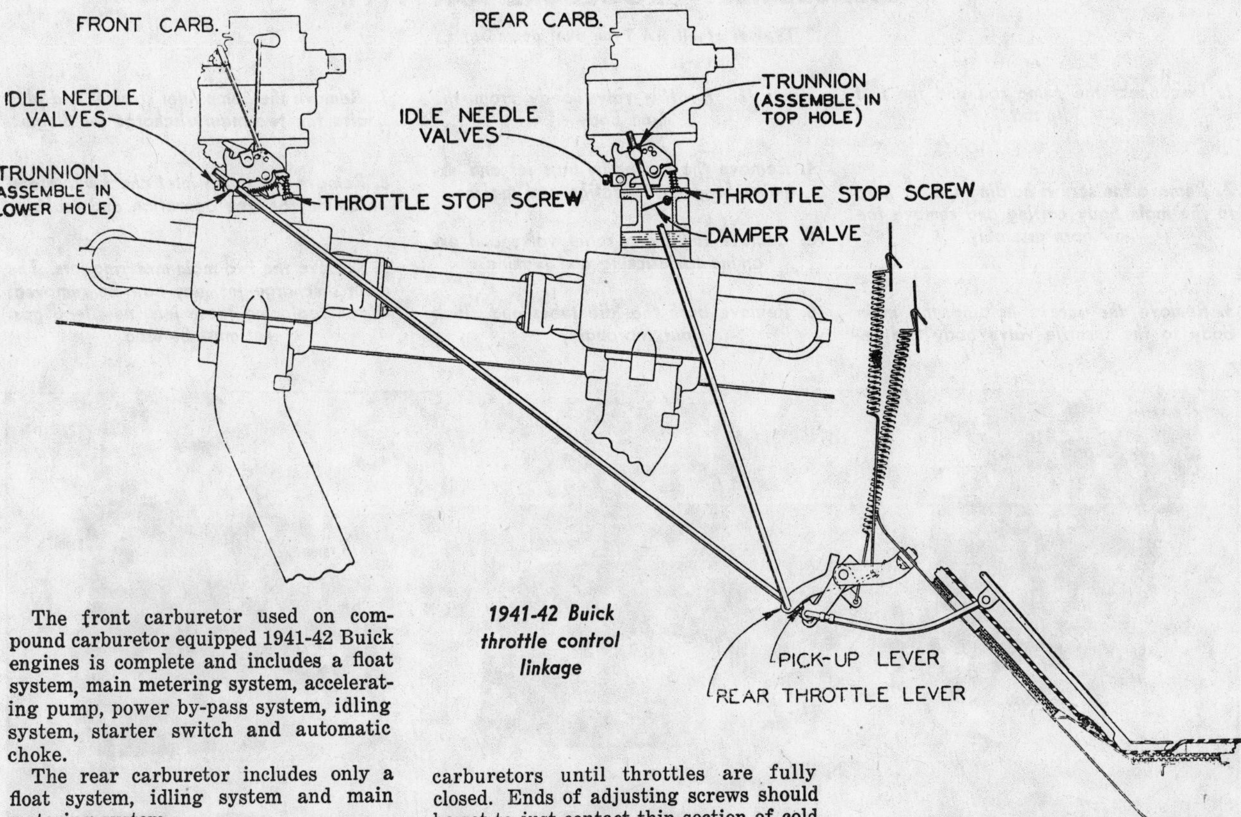

1941-42 Buick throttle control linkage

The front carburetor used on compound carburetor equipped 1941-42 Buick engines is complete and includes a float system, main metering system, accelerating pump, power by-pass system, idling system, starter switch and automatic choke.

The rear carburetor includes only a float system, idling system and main metering system.

When the engine is idling or running at speeds up to about 22 miles per hour, with part throttle, the idling systems of both carburetors are in operation.

A damper valve assembly is used between the rear carburetor and the inlet manifold. This damper valve controls the operation of the rear carburetor except at idling. The butterfly valves of the governor not being a tight fit, do not have any effect on the operation of the idling system of the rear carburetor.

The throttle rods and levers are arranged so that the throttle of the front carburetor only is opened until a position is reached which gives approximately 75 miles per hour at part throttle opening. Additional movement of the accelerator pedal opens the throttle of the rear carburetor. If speed is sufficiently high, air flow will open damper valve. At low speed, the damper valve remains closed until manifold vacuum is high enough to open it. This opening of the valve begins at about 15 miles per hour.

Idle Adjustment

Run engine until it is thoroughly warmed up. Turn off ignition switch. Back off throttle adjusting screws of both carburetors until throttles are fully closed. Ends of adjusting screws should be set to just contact thin section of cold idle cam of front carburetor and throttle body of rear carburetor, when throttles are fully closed. Turn each throttle adjusting screw ¾ turn clockwise to open both throttles same amount. Turn idle mixture adjusting screws, of both carburetors, to closed position. Open each screw one turn.

Turn on ignition switch and start engine. If idle mixture screws require adjustment, turn all of them same amount in same direction. If throttle adjusting screws require adjustment, turn both of them same amount in same direction.

Damper Valve Lock-Out

Late model Buick cars are equipped with a thermostatic lock-out to control cut-in period of the damper valve when engine is cold. This prevents the operation of the rear carburetor while engine is cold and automatic choke of front carburetor is in operation.

The thermostat and bracket are mounted to the damper valve body, extending down over the exhaust manifold. Heat from the manifold operates the thermostat spring and times the release of the lock out from the damper valve weight pin.

The lock-out is fastened to the damper valve body by means of two screws, the upper one having sufficient clearance in the hole so that proper adjustment may be secured.

Lock-outs should be set so that the spring releases from the lock-out pin on the damper valve weight at a temperature of approximately 110 degrees. A test can be made by submerging the unit in water at a temperature of 110±2 degrees F. Lock-out should not open in water at less than 108 degrees, but should be clear of the pin at 112 degrees.

The unit may be tested without removing from engine as follows: Starting with engine cold, drive car and accelerate from 15 to 25 miles per hour with wide open throttle. If engine spits back or hesitates on acceleration, it may indicate an early opening of the lock-out. If engine accelerates properly, drive car about four miles, to be sure that the rotating weight is released. If thermostat has released weight at this time, it is not holding too long. If the above test shows improper adjustment of the thermostat, remove assembly and follow instructions for setting in hot water.

DISASSEMBLY PROCEDURE AAV TYPE

Typical of all AA Type dual downdrafts

1. Disconnect the pump rod and the fast idle rod

2. Remove the screws holding the air horn to the main body casting and remove the air horn assembly

3. Remove the screws holding the main body to the throttle valve body and remove the throttle valve body from the main body

4. Remove the power by-pass jet and examine for free operation and leaking

5. Remove the pump relief valve and examine for sticking and leaking

6. Remove both the idle tubes and clean out thoroughly

7. Remove the pump inlet strainer and plug also the two main discharge jet plugs

8. Remove the pump inlet check valve and examine for free operation and leaking

9. Remove the two main metering jets. The main discharge jet may now be removed. When replacing these jets, new lead gasket must be used

DISASSEMBLY PROCEDURE AAV TYPE—*continued*

Typical of all AA Type dual downdrafts

10. Thoroughly clean all passages in the main body

11. Remove the float fulcrum pin and float and needle assembly

12. It is necessary to remove the float assembly to remove or replace the gasket

13. The needle seat may now be removed. Always use a new gasket when replacing the seat

14. The float needle may be replaced by sliding the needle off the retaining wire

15. Remove the three screws holding the choke housing cover

16. Remove the choke housing cover, screen and thermostat. This allows access to the vacuum piston and linkage. Clean all parts thoroughly

17. Remove the idle needle valves from the throttle body

18. Clean all passages in the throttle body thoroughly

General—Clean all parts and passage of carburetor thoroughly. When reassembling carburetor use new gaskets throughout

Pull cotter pin from fast idle rod. (Fig. 1.)

Detach accelerating pump link, and clip. (Fig. 2.) Illustration shows the spring lock being removed from the pump link.

Lift off air horn assembly. (Fig. 3.)

Take out throttle body attaching screws and lockwashers. Lift off main body assembly. (Fig. 4.)

Remove economizer plunger with special tool. Compress the vacuum piston spring, and remove the vacuum piston. (Fig. 5.)

Detach choke valve attaching screws, and withdraw choke valve. Pull out choke stem and lever assembly. (Fig. 6.)

Eject accelerating pump pin and pump rod. (Fig. 7.)

Unscrew idle tube. Use thin screwdriver. (Fig. 8.)

Take out dash pot check valve. Screw out pump jet. Use thin screwdriver. (Fig. 9.)

Remove power bypass jet and gasket. (Fig. 10.)

Unscrew accelerating pump bypass jet, take off gasket. (Fig. 11.)

Back out main nozzle plugs.

Using special tool, withdraw main dis-

Fig. 1

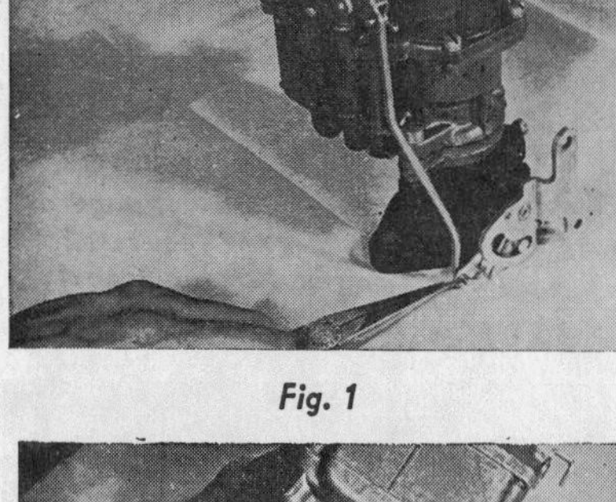

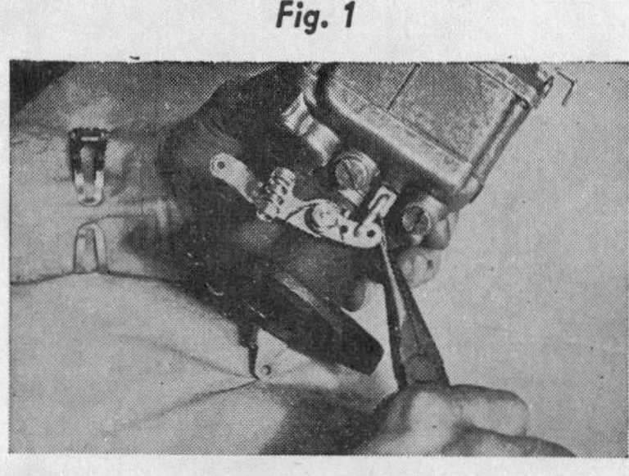

Fig. 2

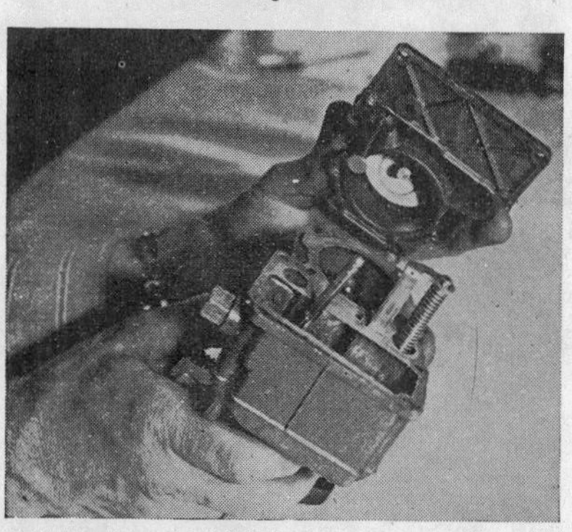

Fig. 3

Fig. 4

Fig. 5

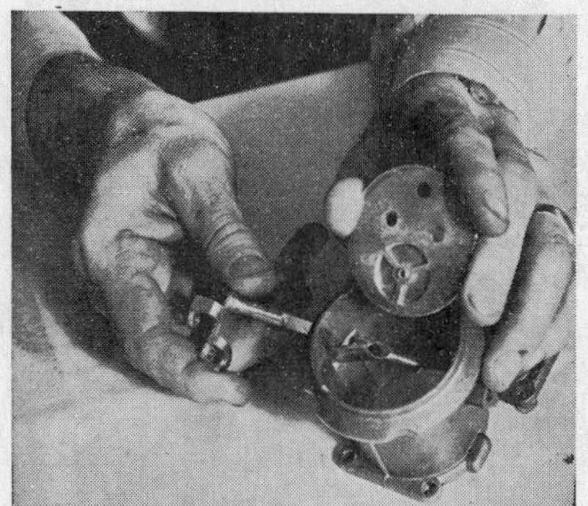

Fig. 6

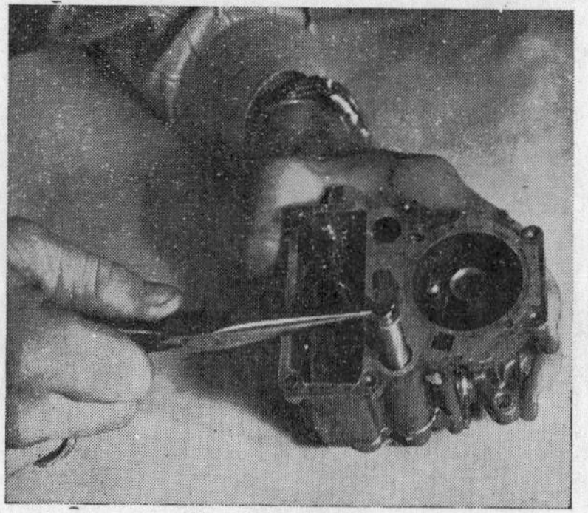

Fig. 7

Fig. 8

Fig. 9

Fig. 10

charge jet, and pump inlet check valve plugs and gaskets. (Fig. 12.)

Remove inlet check valve. (Fig. 13.)

Using special tool, remove main metering jet. (Fig. 14.)

Screw into base of jet (special tool), take out main discharge jet.

Push out pump inlet strainer and ring clip from bottom. (Fig. 16.)

Detach pump lever nut, spring, washer, pump lever, and dash pot lever, with special tool. (Fig. 17.)

Note: It may be necessary to pry lever loose.

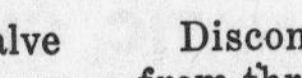

Disconnect throttle lever and stem from throttle body. (Fig. 18.)

Remove idle cam and lever. (Fig. 19.)

See that idle discharge holes and barrel are free of carbon deposits. A little carbon in barrel can effect throttle valve operation. Distance from throttle valve to edge of idle discharge holes are held to close limits. In most cases tolerance is .004 in. Check size of idle discharge holes with correct drill size.

See specification chart for size of drill to use. Check wear of throttle shaft bearing. Max. play is .003 in., otherwise air leaks will affect idle performance. Inspect vacuum spark holes for proper size.

Fig. 11

Fig. 12

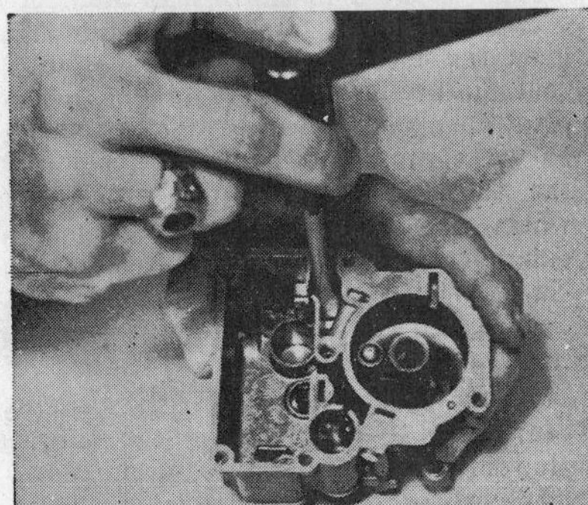

Fig. 13

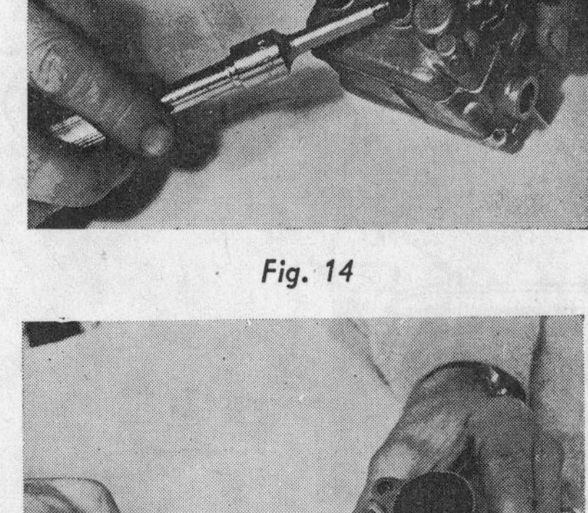

Fig. 14

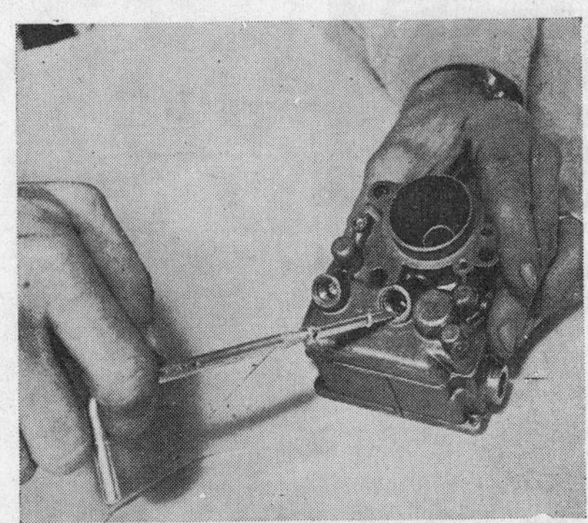

Fig. 15

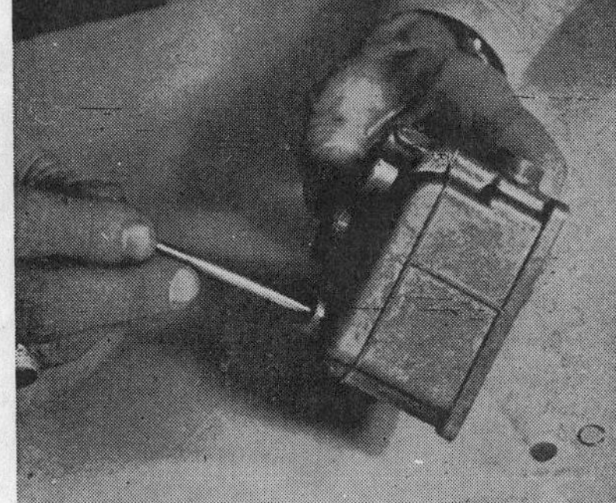

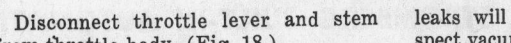

Fig. 16

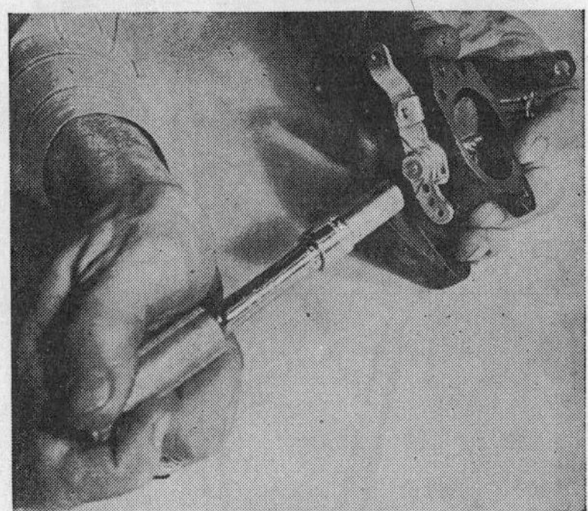

Fig. 17

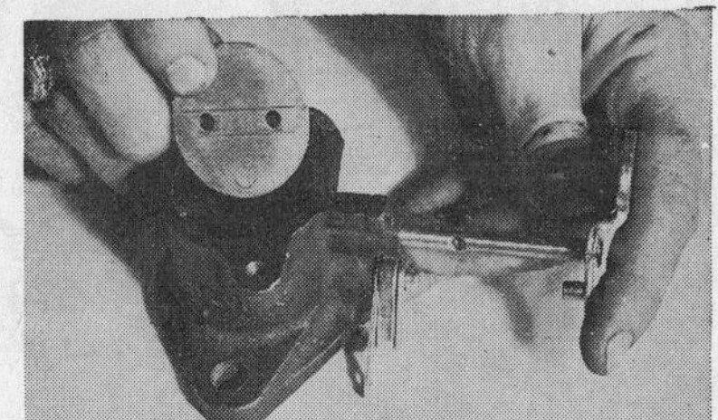

Fig. 18

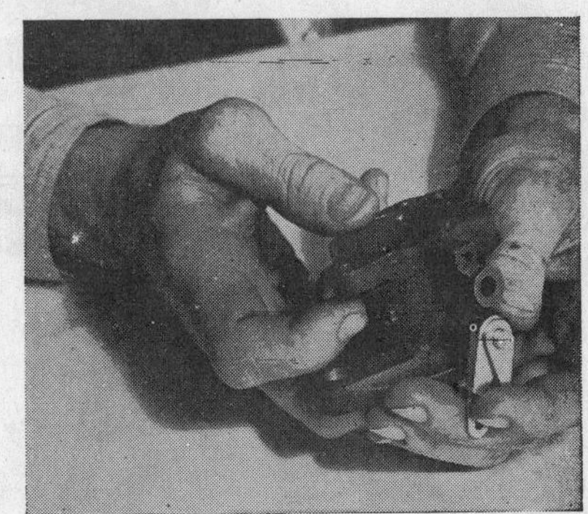

Fig. 19

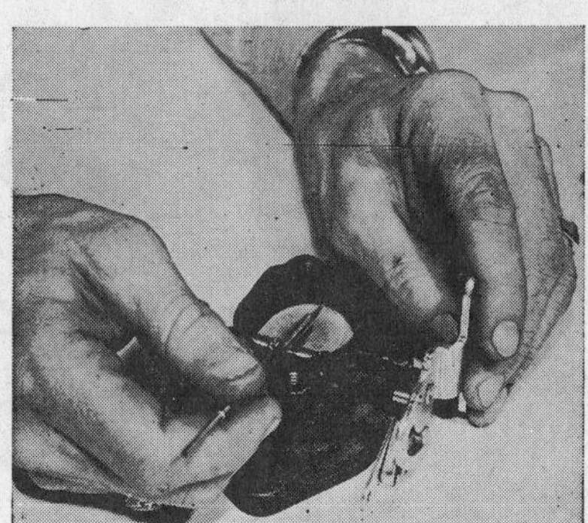

Fig. 20

STROMBERG BUILT-IN AUTOMATIC CHOKE

C A B VACUUM PASSAGE D E

Fig. 1

Choke closed, fast idle

C A B VACUUM PASSAGE HEAT TUBE D

Fig. 2

Choke partly open, warming up

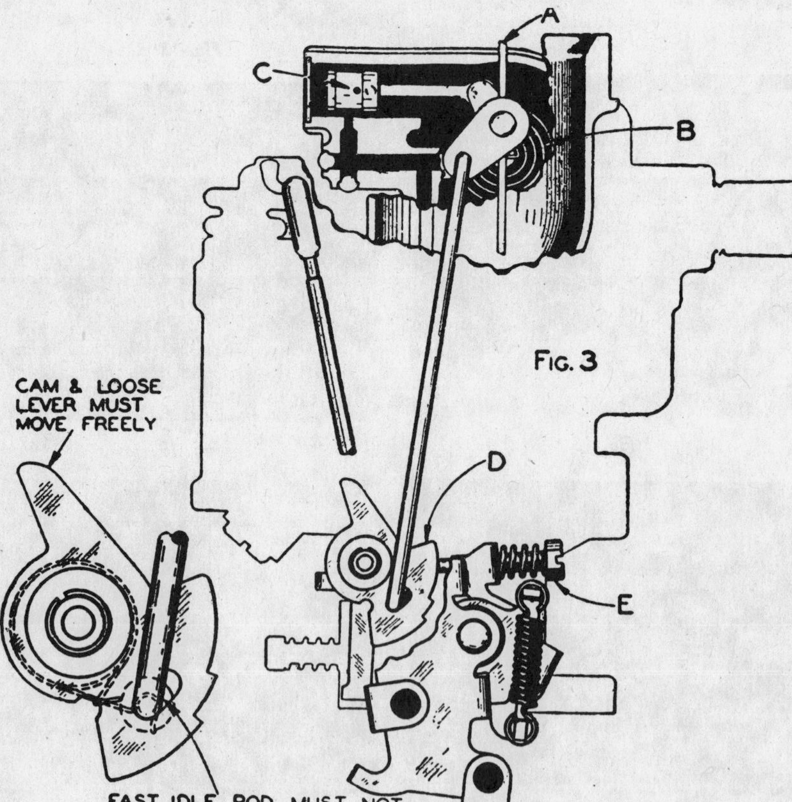

Engine warmed up, choke open slow idle

The automatic choke used on some late carburetors is an integral part of the carburetor housing assembly. The choke operates on a combination of manifold vacuum, thermostat spring and offset choke valve. Warm air is drawn through a tube to actuate the thermostat spring. A fast idle cam is provided to maintain a proper throttle setting during the warm-up period.

When the engine is cold the thermostat spring "B" closes the choke valve, but it cannot do this until the throttle is opened to allow the throttle stop screw "E" to move away from the fast idle cam "D." The throttle stop screw will now come to rest against a higher lobe on the fast idle cam or on the ear of lever "F" if the choke is completely closed.

After the engine has been started the vacuum created in the intake manifold draws the piston "C," thus tending to open the choke valve. If the engine is cold the pressure exerted by the thermostat spring will prevent this action, but as the engine warms up the tension of the thermostat spring is relieved by warm air coming from the stove on the exhaust manifold and passing over it. This allows the vacuum piston to be drawn into the cylinder and thus opening the choke valve.

As the choke valve opens the fast idle cam "D" rotates allowing the throttle stop screw "E" to come to rest on a lower lobe until at open choke valve position the throttle is in normal operating position.

Fast Idle Adjustment

With the throttle stop screw "E" held against the high lobe of the fast idle cam the choke valve should be off its seat by .1015 in., or the diameter of a number 38 drill; as shown in the illustration. If this clearance does not exist, bend the fast idle rod.

Choke Release Adjustment

If the engine becomes flooded, press the accelerator pedal all the way down. This will cause ear "G" to make contact with the fast idle loose lever, this forces the choke valve partially open.

The clearance between the air horn and the choke valve, with the throttle in the wide open position, should be between .156 and .187 in. An 11/64 in. drill can be used to measure this. Adjustment of this clearance is made by bending the ear "G" on the throttle lever.

Disassembly

Remove the heat tube from the thermostat housing.

Remove the carburetor.

Remove the thermostat cover screws and cover assembly.

Disconnect the vacuum piston assembly from the housing.

Clean the inside of the vacuum cylinder and the piston assembly with alcohol or acetone. Blow out all passages and the filter screen with compressed air.

Assembly

Replace the vacuum piston with the slot down.

Replace lever, serrated washer, lock washer and locknut on the choke shaft. Do not tighten the locknut.

Use a special tool, Stromberg number T-25046, and place this on the choke housing with the small hole "H" on the pin of the choke lever. This tool can be held in place with two of the big washers and screws used to hold the cover.

Hold the choke valve against a number 70 drill (.028 in.) and lightly tighten the locknut.

Remove the special tool, T-25046, and hold the choke valve closed. Tighten the locknut securely.

Recheck the choke valve opening to make certain the setting has not been changed.

Note: All parts should move freely throughout their entire range. Do not use oil or any type of lubricant on the vacuum piston and cylinder.

The cover assembly is replaced with the thermostat hook at the bottom and rotated in the "Rich" direction until the "O" mark aligns with the projections on the housing. If it is found necessary to change this setting the change should never be more than two graduations in either direction.

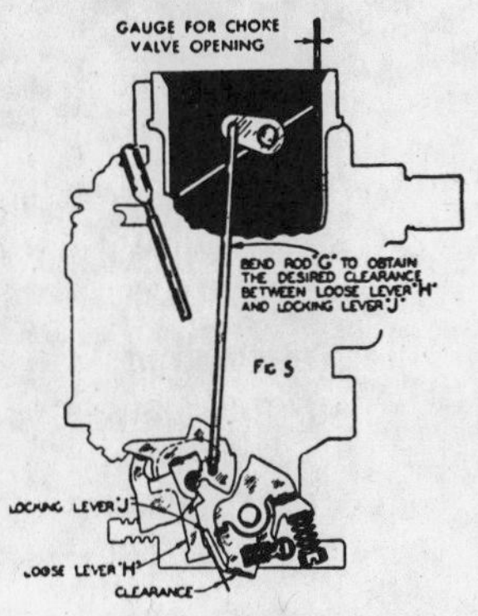

Start aid and fast idle setting after 1940

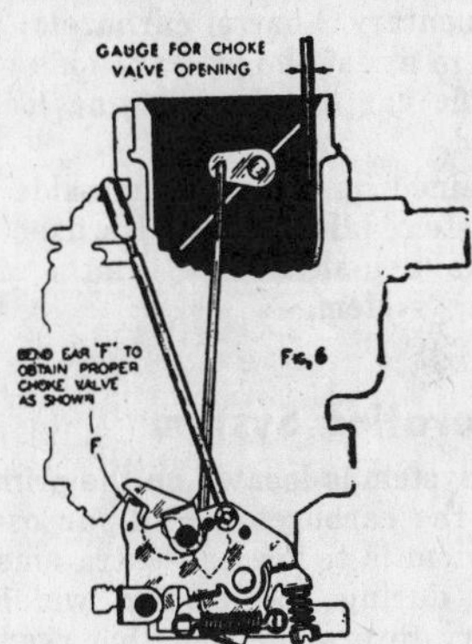

Deflooder setting

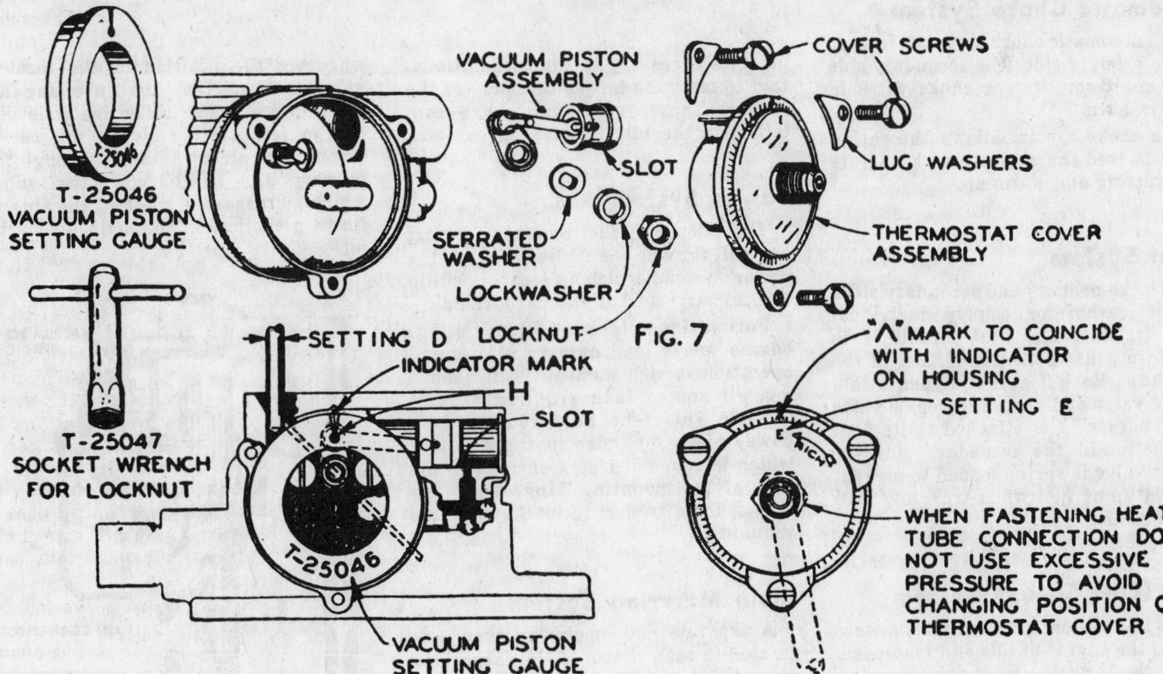

Automatic choke service parts

MODEL 4A

The Stromberg carburetor Model 4A is fundamentally two 2-barrel carburetors combined in a single casting. The two sides are referred to in this text as the primary and secondary sides.

The primary side is essentially a complete 2-barrel carburetor containing an idle system, float system, main metering system, accelerating system, and a power system. This primary side also incorporates the use of an accelerator vacuum switch for starting, and the automatic choke mechanism.

The secondary side is essentially a supplementary 2-barrel carburetor that cuts in to assist the primary side when a specific car speed or engine load is obtained.

Contained in the secondary side is a float system, idle system with fixed jets that are non-adjustable, and a main metering system.

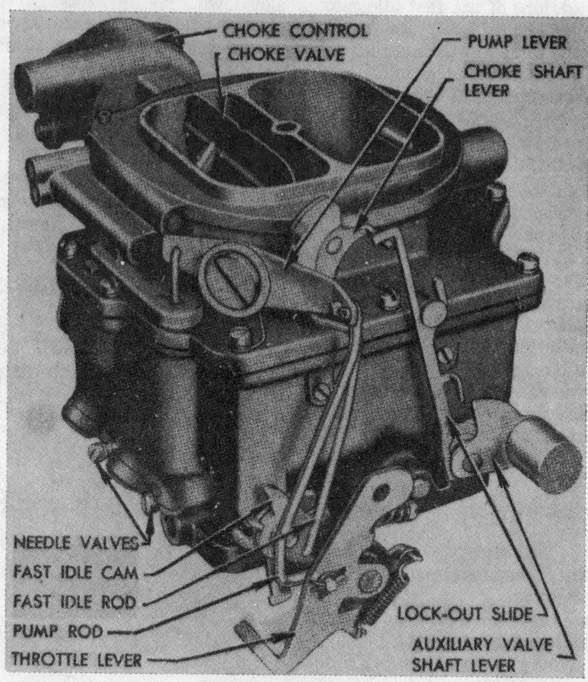

Stromberg Model 4A

Accelerating System

This system is located on the primary side of the carburetor. The purpose of this system is to feed an extra amount of fuel during acceleration which is necessary to provide smooth power.

Automatic Choke System

The automatic choke system is located in the primary side. The secondary side does not incorporate a choke valve in the air horn.

The choke system allows the carburetor to feed the engine a rich mixture for starting and warm up.

Float System

Both the primary and secondary sides of the carburetor employ individual float systems. The float circuit is to maintain a fixed amount of fuel in the float bowl. Each float is equipped with a needle valve and seat. The needle valve in primary side is attached to its float by a clip. In the secondary side the needle valve is spring loaded to prevent a build up of fuel while traveling over rough roads.

Idle (Low Speed) System

The idle system in each barrel meters fuel to the engine at idle and low speed. When the throttle valves are opened to a greater degree than at idle speed it becomes necessary to supply additional fuel to meet the torque demands of the engine. These requirements are contained in the idle (low speed) system.

Power System

The amount of fuel required for part and full throttle is supplied through the power system, which is located within the primary side of the carburetor.

For maximum torque demands of the engine under load or very high speed operation, a rich mixture is demanded much more so than required at part throttle. This richer mixture is had by a power piston cylinder in the air horn which is connected by a channel to the face of the mounting flange which allows it to be subject to intake manifold vacuum.

Main Metering System

A separate main metering system is located in each barrel of the carburetor and their operation is identical. This system supplies fuel to the engine, whenever the position of the throttle valve is such that the incoming air stream creates suction on the main discharge jet. Air coming in the barrel through the air horn passes through the primary and auxiliary venturi tubes which increases the speed of the air and forms a suction on the main discharge jet.

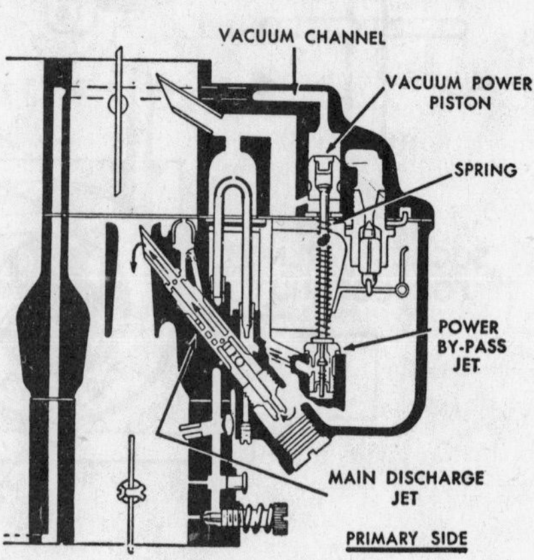

Power System

Adjustments

No carburetor should be adjusted without first checking compression, ignition and also check the manifold for any leaks. An engine must be properly tuned before any carburetor can function properly.

Idle Speed Adjustment

Idle speed adjustment screw positions the throttle valves for curb idle speed and has no effect on richness of mixture.

Set engine to approximately 375-475 rpm depending on engine condition (engine in good condition should be set to lower speed). Cars equipped with automatic transmission set to 375-475 rpm with transmission in drive range. When transmission is shifted to neutral engine will speed up. This is normal.

Idle Mixture Adjustment

This adjustment controls the mixture of fuel and air at curb idle and also effects part throttle operation. To set idle mixture proceed as follows: First, set engine idle as explained under heading Idle Speed Adjustment. Now, turn the idle mixture screw in until the engine slows down and out again until the engine rolls. Midway between these two settings should be the proper setting for each primary barrel (no idle mixture adjustment on secondary side).

After the second barrel has been adjusted, go back and readjust the first and then readjust the second barrel. In other words, do each adjustment at least twice.

Accelerator Rod Adjustment

The accelerator pump link is equipped with three holes. The inner hole is for summer driving, the center for all normal driving and the outer hole for winter driving or maximum effect pump stroke.

No other adjustments are possible on the accelerating system.

Fast Idle and Choke Unloader Adjustment

Insert a No. 26 drill between the vertical wall of the air horn and the center top edge of the choke valve, hold choke valve closed against drill. Be certain that the fast idle cam spring holds the cam up against end of the fast idle rod. Now close the throttle to allow stop screw to contact fast idle cam. The stop screw should just clear the edge of highest step on the cam and set against the second step.

When adjustment is required, bend the fast idle rod at large curve. Lift out the No. 26 drill and insert a No. 53 drill in the same location, and hold the choke valve closed against the drill. Carefully open and close the throttle valve a few times and determine the clearance between the start aid loose lever on throttle stem and the lock lever in back of the fast idle cam. When functioning properly there is just enough clearance to allow the loose lever to pass over the lock lever. If this condition does not exist, bend the end of the loose lever up or down to maintain specified clearance.

Open the throttle until the stop arm on the throttle lever sets against the stop boss on throttle body. Now check the clearance between the vertical wall of the air horn and the center of top edge of the choke valve, by using a No. 2 drill. If this adjustment is out, bend the tongue on throttle lever as required to obtain proper clearance.

Finally close the throttle and choke valve. Now open the throttle against the tension of the start aid loose lever spring. This is done to determine if the lock lever is releasing the loose lever and the spring tension before the stop arm on the throttle lever contacts the stop boss located on the throttle body.

Lockout Slide Adjustment

Close the choke valve and auxiliary valves. After these valves are closed the slide should be in its down position. Between the ear on slide and the weighted end of the auxiliary throttle shaft lever there should be not less than .025 inch or more than .060 inch clearance. Bend the ear of slide until the proper clearance is maintained.

Holding the choke in the wide open position, the choke lever arm should put the lockout slide in its up position. Now, set in this position the clearance between the ear on the slide lever and auxiliary shaft weighted lever should be not less than .047 inch or more than .078 inch. Adjust by bending the choke lever arm when an incorrect setting is determined.

Secondary Throttle Valve Setting

When the primary throttle valves are in the wide open position, the secondary throttle valve should also be in the wide open position. Whenever the secondary throttle valves do not open fully, adjust by bending the pickup lever to obtain this action. With the secondary throttle valves turned in the open direction to the point of eliminating slack in the linkage, the distance from the edge of the primary valves to throttle bore wall should be .125 inch to .180 inch. If less than .125 inch or more than .180 inch is had, adjust by bending the secondary rod.

Float Adjustment

Lay float gage tool T-25489 flat on the air horn gasket with bosses of gage located in the two holes along the center line of air horn. Use No. 56 (3/64 inch) drill to gage the distance between the top center of primary float and the gasket. Where the clearance is other than the specified dimension as given above, bend the float lever. Now use No. 68 (1/32 inch) drill to gage the clearance between the top center of secondary float and gasket. Adjust by bending float lever. Floats should be parallel with gage and just clear the uprights of the gage. Where binding is determined bend the float lever.

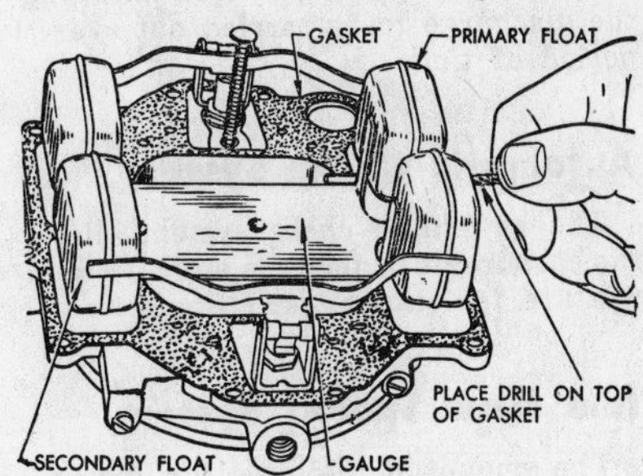

Float Adjustment

STROMBERG CARBURETORS

MODEL WW

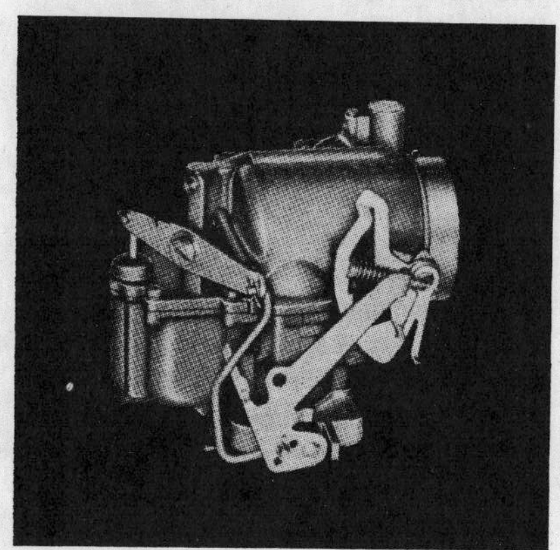

Full view of Model WW

The Stromberg carburetor Model WW is in its entirety a dual downdraft carburetor which employs six systems that supply an adequate amount of fuel to the engine during all operating conditions. The six systems are as follows: the float system, idle (low speed) system, accelerating system, power system, main metering system, and automatic choke system.

Accelerating System

The accelerating system provides a measured amount of fuel during acceleration which is necessary to provide smooth engine power. When the operator of an automobile presses down on the accelerator pedal the pump piston travels down in its bore applying pressure on the fuel which closes the intake check ball and lifts the outlet check ball off its seat. At this time the fuel flows pass the outlet check ball and is metered through small orifice tubes. This cycle occurs only momentarily. The pump piston duration spring produces a follow up action allowing the discharge to be carried out over a period of time.

Automatic Choke System

The automatic choke system allows the carburetor to feed the engine a rich mixture for starting and warm up.

Idle (Low Speed) System

The amount of fuel used for idle and early throttle is supplied through the

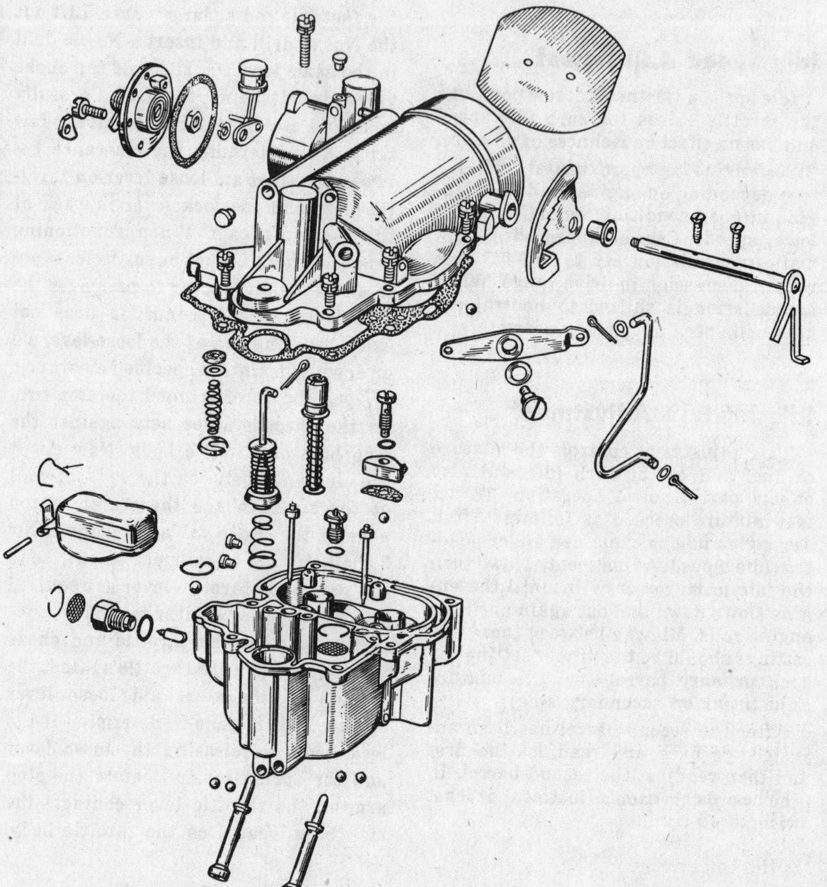

Exploded view of the Stromberg Model WW

idle (low speed) system. In this system the fuel flows from the float bowl through the main metering jets, up through the idle tube that meters the fuel. The fuel then flows through a passage where air is allowed to enter and serves to break up the liquid fuel and mix it with air. Now this mixture moves on down toward the two discharge ports. Before reaching the discharge ports more air is mixed with the fuel at an air bleed just above the discharge ports.

Main Metering System

The main metering system is located in each barrel in the carburetor. In the operation of this system, incoming air from the air horn passes through the venturi tubes which increases its speed and creates suction on the main discharge jet. When this suction is created fuel will flow from the float bowl through the main metering jet and main discharge jet.

Power System

The amount of fuel required for part and full throttle is supplied through the power system. For maximum torque demands of the engine or high speed operation, a rich mixture is demanded much more so than required at part throttle. This is the purpose of the high speed circuit. During part throttle operation the vacuum of the manifold acting on the power piston is adequate to hold the piston in the up position against the pressure of the spring.

When more fuel is needed than can be metered through the main metering jets, the opening of the throttle valves at the time will minimize the manifold vacuum enough to allow the piston spring to send the piston down and open the by-pass jets. When the by-pass jets are open additional fuel is allowed to follow through the by-pass passage to enter the main discharge jets.

Float System

The float system is to maintain the fuel in the float bowl at a pre-determined level. The float bowl is vented inside by a vent tube in the air horn and outside by a small hole just above the fuel inlet.

Adjustments

Before attempting to adjust any carburetor, check compression on each cylinder, check manifold for leaks, check and set spark plugs and ignition breaker point, adjust valve tappets, set ignition and check valve timing. An engine must be properly tuned before any carburetor can function properly.

Idle Speed Adjustment

The idle adjustment screw positions the throttle valve for curb idle speed and has no effect on richness of mixture.

Set engine to approximately 475-575 rpm depending on engine condition (engine in good condition should be set to lower speed). Cars equipped with automatic transmission set to 475-575 rpm with transmission in drive range. When transmission is shifted to neutral engine will speed up. This is normal.

Idle Mixture Adjustment

The idle mixture adjustment controls the mixture of fuel and air at curb idle and also effects port throttle operation. To set idle mixture proceed as follows: First, set engine idle as explained under heading Idle Speed Adjustment. Now turn the idle mixture screw in until the engine slows down and out again until the engine rolls. Midway between these two settings should be the proper setting for each barrel. After the second barrel has been adjusted, go back and readjust the first and then readjust the second. In other words, do each adjustment at least twice.

Accelerator Pump Travel Adjustment

Place the throttle valves in the fully closed position.

Back out the throttle stop screw and close the throttle valves. After the throttle valves are fully closed the distance between the top of the pump link and the top of air horn should be ¾ inch. To adjust, bend pump rod connector link at lower end as shown in illustration.

Fast Idle Adjustment

Adjust the fast idle by inserting gage T-25570 between the short side of the choke valve and the vertical surface of the air horn. Hold the choke valve closed against the gage without exerting too much pressure on the choke valve. The top end of the fast idle lever should just enter first step on fast idle cam. If necessary to make adjustment to obtain proper clearance, place thumb on counterweight and bend the fast idle cam.

Wide Open Kick Adjustment

Close the choke valve and hold the throttle in the wide open position. This should allow the choke valve to open enough to insert gage No. T-25570 between the choke valve and the inner vertical wall of the air horn. When adjustment is needed, bend the long ear on choke lever until proper clearance is determined.

Float Level Adjustment

Remove air horn and gasket. Set float gage T-25569 (3/16 inch) across the center of the float bowl and float. Then hold float lip securely against the needle valve. In this position the top side of the float should just bear against the float gage. Any time adjustment is necessary proceed by bending the float lip in the direction as required.

Automatic Choke Adjustment

Turn the thermostat cover counterclockwise (rich) until the arrow on the cover lines up with the tang on the choke housing.

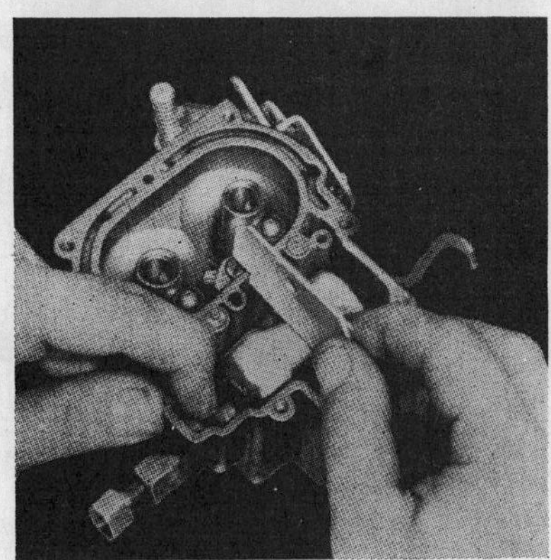

Float Adjustment Gage in Position

Rochester Carburetor Specifications

ITEM	Chevrolet	Chevrolet	Chevrolet	Chevrolet	Chevrolet	Chevrolet	Chevrolet	Chevrolet	Chevrolet	Chevrolet	Chevrolet	Chevrolet
Carburetor Part Number	7001374	7002050■	7002051	7003060	7003152	7003160	7003526	7003863	7003864	7003865	7003966	7003986
Manufactures Year	1937–40	1949–51	1950–51	1950–51	1951	1951	1952	1951	1951	1951	1937–40	1951
Carburetor Model	B	B	B	B	B	B	BC	B	B	B	B	B
Flange Size	1¼	1¼	1½	1½	1¼	1½	1½	1¼	1½	1¼	1¼	1½
Bore Diameter	1½	1½	1 9/16	1 9/16	1½	1 9/16	1 9/16	1½	1 9/16	1½	1½	1 9/16
Primary Venturi	1 7/32	1 7/32	1 11/32	1 11/32	1 7/32	1 11/32	1 11/32	1 7/32	1 11/32	1 7/32	1 11/32	1 11/32
Secondary Venturi	9/16	9/16	1 9/32	1 9/32	9/16	1 9/32	1 9/32	9/16	1 9/32	9/16	1 9/32	1 9/32
Nozzle Restriction	.144	.144	.161	.161	.144	.161	.152	.144	.161	.144	.125	.152
Main Metering Jet, Lean	7002651–.051	7002650–.050	7002657–.057	7002657–.057	7002650–.050	7002657–.057	7002656–.056	7002650–.050	7002657–.057	7002650–.050	7002651–.051	7001860–.055
Main Metering Jet, Standard	7002652–.052	7002651–.051	7002658–.058	7002658–.058	7002651–.051	7002658–.058	7002657–.057	7002651–.051	7002658–.058	7002651–.051	7002652–.052	7002656–.056
Main Metering Jet, Rich	7001498–.053	7002652–.052	7002659–.059	7002659–.059	7002652–.052	7002659–.059	7002658–.058	7002652–.052	7002659–.059	7002652–.052	7001498–.053	7002657–.057
Main Air Bleed	(2) .028	(2) .028	(2) .028	(2) .028	(2) .028	(2) .028	(2) .028	(2) .028	(2) .028	(2) .028	(2) .028	(2) .028
Fuel Valve Seat, Diameter	.076	.076	.091	.091	.076	.091	.091	.076	.091	.076	.076	.091
Fuel Level †	5/16 @ 3 lbs.	5/16 @ 3 lbs.	5/16 @ 3 lbs.	5/16 @ 3 lbs.	5/16 @ 3 lbs.	5/16 @ 3 lbs.	5/16 @ 3 lbs.	5/16 @ 3 lbs.	5/16 @ 3 lbs.	5/16 @ 3 lbs.	5/16 @ 3 lbs.	5/16 @ 3 lbs.
Float Drop ‡	1¾	1¾	1¾	1¾	1¾	1¾	1¾	1¾	1¾	1¾	1¾	1¾
Idle Tube Restriction	.093	.082	.061	.061	.082	.061	.063	.082	.061	.082	.070	.063
Idle Bleed Bleeds	.046	.046	.046	.046	.046	.046	.028	.046	.046	.046	.028	.028
Idle Needle	7002357–30°	7002357–30°	7002357–30°	7002357–30°	7002357–30°	7002357–30°	7002357–30°	7002357–30°	7002357–30°	7002357–30°	7002357–30°	7002357–30°
Needle Orifice	.063	.063	.067	.067	.063	.067	.073	.063	.081	.063	.081	.073
Secondary Idle Hole, Lower	.034	.034	.031	.031	.034	.031	.040	.034	.033	.034	.059	.040
Secondary Idle Hole, Center	.031	.031			.031			.031		.031		
Secondary Idle Hole, Upper	(2) .028	.028			.028		.028	.028	.031	.028	.036	.028
Spark Port	(2) .040	(2) .040	(2) .040	(2) .040	(2) .040	(2) .040	(2) .040	(2) .040	(2) .040	(2) .040	(2) .040	(2) .040
Power Restriction	.030	.038	.040	.041	.038	.041	.047	.038	.040	.038	.038	.046
Power Spring	7002071	7002071	7002366	7002366	7002071	7002366	7002366	7002071	7002366	7002071	7002071	7002366
Spring Color	Silver	Silver	Copper	Copper	Silver	Copper	Copper	Silver	Copper	Silver	Silver	Copper
Pump Jet	.028	.028	.031	.031	.028	.031	.031	.028	.031	.028	.028	.031
Pump Link	7002820	7002820	7002820	7002820	7002820	7002820	7002820	7002820	7002820	7002820	7002820	7002820
Link Length	.840	.840	.840	.840	.840	.840	.840	.840	.840	.840	.840	.840
cc/10 Slow Strokes	14.0	14.0	14.0	14.0	14.0	14.0	14.0	14.0	14.0	14.0	14.0	14.0
Repair Kit	7001377	7002379	7002378	7001387	7002379	7001387	7004086	7004363	7004363	7004363	7004363	7004363
Gasket Kit	7002377	7002377	7002377	7001386	7002377	7001386	7004085	7004335	7004335	7004335	7004335	7004595
Air Horn Gasket	7002799	7002799	7002799	7002894	7002799	7002894	7004480	7003819	7003819	7003819	7003819	7004480
Needle and Seat Assembly	7002358	7002358	7002359	7002359	7002358	7002359	7002359	7002358	7002359	7002358	7002358	7002359

† Use Float Setting Gauge No. M-250.
‡ Measured from Gasket to Bottom of Float.
■ May also be used as 1941 to 1949 replacement on both 216 and 235 cubic inch engine 1¼ in. S.A.E. flange.

Rochester Carburetor Specifications—*continued*

ITEM	Chevrolet	Chevrolet	Chevrolet	Chevrolet	Pontiac	Oldsmobile	Oldsmobile	Oldsmobile	Cadillac
Carburetor Part Number	7004475	704476	704477	704495	7002870	7001570	7002570	700290	700420
Manufactures Year	1952	1952	1952	1952	1951–52	1949	1950	1951	1951
Carburetor Model	B	B	B	B	BC	AA	AA	BB	BB
Flange Size	1¼	1½	1¼	1½	1¼	1¼ dual	1¼ dual	1¼ dual	1¼ dual
Bore Diameter	1½	1 9/16	1½	1 9/16	1 9/16	1 7/16	1 7/16	1 7/16	1 7/16
Primary Venturi	1 7/32	1 11/32	1 7/32	1 11/32	1 5/16	1 3/16	1 3/16	1 1/16	1 3/32
Secondary Venturi	9/16	19/32	9/16	19/32	3/4	11/32	11/32	9/16	9/16
Nozzle Restriction	.144	.152	.144	.152	.144				
Main Metering Jet, Lean	7002652–.052	7002658–.058	7002652–.052	7001860–.055	7002957–.057	7001498–.053	7001498–.053	None	7002645–.045
Main Metering Jet, Standard	7001498–.053	7002659–.059	7001498–.053	7002656–.056	7002958–.058	7001607–.054	7001607–.054	7002951–.051	7002646–.046
Main Metering Jet, Rich	7001607–.054	7002660–.060	7001607–.054	7002657–.057	7002959–.059	7001860–.055	7001860–.055	None	7002647–.047
Main Air Bleed	(2) .028	(2) .028	(2) .028	(2) .028	(2) .028	.035	.035	.040	.040
Fuel Valve Seat Diameter	.076	.091	.076	.091	.091	.096	.096	.101	.101
Fuel Level †	5/16 @ 3 lbs.	5/16 @ 3 lbs.	5/16 @ 3 lbs.	5/16 @ 3 lbs.	*9/32 @ 3 lbs.	*9/16 @ 5 lbs.	*9/16 @ 5 lbs.	*1/4 @ 4 lbs.	*9/32 @ 4 lbs.
Float Drop ‡	1¾	1¾	1¾	1¾	1¾	§	§	1¾	1¾
Idle Tube Restriction	.070	.063	.070	.063	.055	.025	.025	.032	.045
Idle Bleed Bleeds	.028	.028	.028	.028	.028	.039–.067	.039–.067	.035	.054
Idle Needle	7002357–30°	7002357–30°	7002357–30°	7002357–30°	7002875–30°	7001669–20°	7001669–20°	7001669–20°	700314–20°
Needle Orifice	.081	.073	.081	.073	.063	.052	.052	.0625	.067
Secondary Idle Hole, Lower	.059	.040	.059	.040	.035	.040	.040	.031	.040
Secondary Idle Hole, Center								.025	
Secondary Idle Hole, Upper	.036	.028	.036	.028		.036	.036	.025	.040
Spark Port	(2) .040	(2) .040	(2) .040	(2) .040	.040	.040	.040	.040	.040
Power Restriction	.042	.048	.042	.046	(2) .0265	.0334	.0334	.054	.046
Power Spring	7002071	7002366	7002071	7002366	7002896	Integral	Integral	7002896	7002897
Spring Color	Silver	Copper	Silver	Copper	Blue	Silver	Silver	Blue	Green
Pump Jet	.028	.031	.028	.031	.028	.026	.024	.031	.026
Pump Link	7002820	7002820	7002820	7002820	7002878	7001680	7002531	7003128	7003181
Link Length	.840	.840	.840	.840	.796				
cc/10 Slow Strokes	14.0	14.0	14.0	14.0	17.0	16.0	13.0	16.0–18.0	16.0–19.0
Repair Kit	1004363	7004363	7004363	7004363	7001392	7001376	7001376	7001390	701399
Gasket Kit	7004335	7004335	7004335	7004595	7001391	7001849	7001849	7001393	701393
Air Horn Gasket	7003819	7003819	7003819	704480	7001391	7001676	7001676	7003082	7003082
Needle and Seat Assembly	7002358	7002359	7002358	7002359	7002885	7001846	7001846	7001395	7001398

† Use Float Setting Gauge No. M-250.
‡ Measured from Gasket to Bottom of Float.
§ AA-Float Drop 1/8 inch above extended power stem tip.
* Use proper Float Setting Gauges to arrive at these settings:
BT-46—Float Gauge for Pontiac BC-7002870.
BT-17—Float Gauge for Oldsmobile AA-7001570.
BT-35—Float Gauge for Oldsmobile AA-7002570.
BT-51—Float Gauge for Oldsmobile and Cadillac BB-7002900 and 7004200.

Rochester Carburetor Specifications—*continued*

ITEM	Chevrolet	Chevrolet	Cadillac	Cadillac	Oldsmobile	Oldsmobile	Oldsmobile	Oldsmobile
Carburetor Part Number	7004915	7004478	7004500	7005100	7004300	7004800	7005600	7005700
Manufactures Year	1953	1953	1952	1953	1952	1952	1953	1953
Carburetor Model	B	B	4GC	BB	4GC	4GC		
Flange Size	1¼	1½	1¼ dual	1¼ dual	1¼ dual	1¼ dual	1¼ dual	1¼ dual
Bore Diameter	1½	1½	1$\frac{7}{16}$	1$\frac{7}{16}$	1$\frac{7}{16}$	1$\frac{7}{16}$	1$\frac{7}{16}$	1$\frac{7}{16}$
Primary Venturi	1$\frac{11}{32}$	1$\frac{11}{32}$	1	1	1$\frac{1}{64}$	1$\frac{1}{64}$	1$\frac{1}{64}$	1$\frac{1}{64}$
Secondary Venturi	$\frac{19}{32}$	$\frac{19}{32}$	1$\frac{1}{16}$	1$\frac{1}{16}$	1$\frac{1}{64}$	1$\frac{1}{64}$	$\frac{57}{64}$	$\frac{57}{64}$
Nozzle Restriction	.144	.152						
Main Metering Jet, Lean	7002957	7002957	7002651	7002648	7002650	7002650	7002650	7002650
Main Metering Jet, Standard	7002958	7002958	7002652	7002649	7002651	7002651	7002651	7002651
Main Metering Jet, Rich			7002664	7002660	7002661	7002661	7002643	7002643
Main Air Bleed	.028	.028	.040	.040	.040	.040	.040	.040
Fuel Valve Seat	.076	.091	.101	.101	.101	.101	.101	.096
Fuel Level†	$\frac{5}{16}$ @ 3 lbs.	$\frac{5}{16}$ @ 3 lbs.	$\frac{9}{32}$ @ 4 lbs.	$\frac{9}{32}$ @ 4 lbs.				
Float Drop‡	1¾	1¾	2¼	2¼	1$\frac{15}{16}$	1$\frac{15}{16}$	2¼	2¼
Idle Tube Restrictions								
Idle Bleed	.028	.028	.054	.054			.039	.035
Idle Needle	7002357	7002357	7004402	7004402	7004402	7004402	7004402	7004402
Needle Orifice	.073	.073	.040	.046	.040	.040	.040	.040
Secondary Idle Hole, Lower	.040	.040	.028	.033	.028	.028	.028	.028
Secondary Idle Hole, Center			.031		.031	.031	.033	.033
Secondary Idle Hole, Upper	.028	.028		.026	.029	.029	.026	.026
Spark Port	.175	.175	.040	.070	.040	.040	.040	.040
Power Restriction	.039	.039	.046	.046	.031	.031	.031	.031
Power Spring	7002101	7002101	7004597	7004597	7004597	7004597	7004597	7004597
Spring Color								
Pump Jet	.028	.028	.026	.026	.029	.029	.031	.026
Pump Link	7005136	7005136	7004401	7004401	7004401	7004401	7004401	7004401
Link Length	.840	.840						
cc/10 Slow Strokes	14.0	140.0						
Repair Kit	7004363	7004363	7004691	7005588	7004686	7004686	7005592	7005592
Gasket Kit	7004595	7004595	7004690	7004690	7004690	7004690	7004690	7004690
Air Horn Gasket	7004480	7004480	7004301	7004301	7004301	7004301	7004301	7004301
Needle and Seat Assembly	7002359	7002359	7004779	7004779	7004682	7004682	7004682	7004682

MODEL AA

This carburetor features the horizontal air inlet and is compact in every detail. The carburetor total height is only 5 inches. The air cleaner is mounted on a level with the carburetor.

The cover and bowl assembly may be removed from the outer housing for cleaning or inspection by removing eight screws and disconnecting the fuel line. Hold the throttle in the wide open position, thus freeing the pump actuating

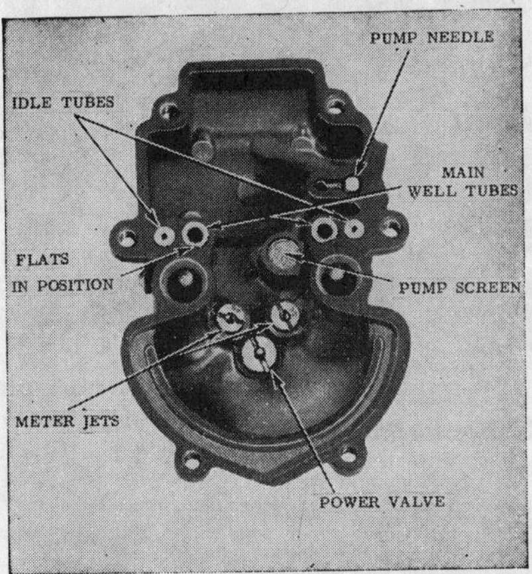

Float bowl after float and cover has been removed

lever from the pump yoke inside of the housing. It contains all the calibrated parts of the carburetor. This unit may be purchased as a service assembly.

Remove the 6 screws which attach the bowl cover to the bowl and separate the bowl and cover by lifting straight up on the cover to prevent damage to the float.

Take a 5/16 in. width screw driver and remove the power valve with the red fibre gasket from the bottom of bowl. Remove the 2 main metering jets also. With a small pointed object pry out the retainer spring over the pump screen and remove the screen.

Turn the bowl upside down and tap it on palm of your hand until the two main well tubes, two idle tubes and brass pump outlet check valve drop from the bowl. In no case should a metal object be used for removing the main well or idle tubes from the bowl. If necessary, use a piece of wood, such as a tooth pick instead.

Remove 5 pump housing attaching screws using especial care not to disturb the position of the two pump jets, as they are aimed at the factory for the proper direction of gasoline discharge.

Remove the conical-shaped pump return spring but do not remove the nozzles from the bowl.

Remove the pump intake, check the valve plug and the ball type intake check valve. A 1/4 in. screw driver is best for removing the check valve, to prevent damage to the internal threads of the pump well.

Float Height and Tension

To set the float level insert cover assembly: with a steel scale measure the distance from the face of the cover to the top seam of the float. Set it to 23/32 inch. Adjustment is made by binding the lip on the float which contacts the top of the float needle.

After float height has been set, the float tension should be adjusted to insure proper float level drop and consequent sufficient entry of fuel into the bowl under high speed operation. Bend the float tang against the spring to decrease the

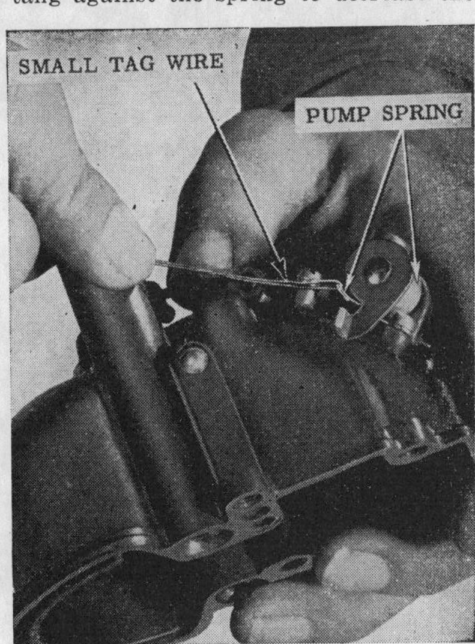

Unwind the pump spring

drop and away from the spring to increase the drop. Tension is correct when float drop is such that the outside edge of the float (bottom) is level with the power diaphragm stem when suspended freely from cover.

Five major adjustments are required whenever the carburetor has been disassembled or rebuilt.

They are the float, the pump actuating lever, the choke rod, the unloader and the fast idle cam. Each adjustment is vitally important if the carburetor is to operate properly.

Pump Actuating Lever Adjustment

With pump rod in recommended outside hole for 1949 models or center hole for 1950 models, back off idle stop screw and fast idle screw so that throttle valves are fully closed. Remove pump rod from throttle lever and pull down to full allowable cocked diaphragm position. With pump rod directly under its hole in throttle lever, carefully bend rod so that top edge of pump rod is flush with bottom edge of hole in the throttle lever. Reassemble pump rod to throttle lever as this insures correct pump delivery at all speeds.

Aiming the Pump Jet

With gasoline in the carburetor, work the throttle lever slowly and note the pump discharge by looking into the air horn. The pump discharge will appear as a fan shaped spray and should hit the target on the opposite side. A slight bend is all that is necessary to target the pump jets properly.

Choke Rod Adjustment

With thermostat cover set at index, turn fast idle screw until it contacts the first or intermediate stop of fast idle cam. Be sure choke trip lever is in contact with choke counterweight. Choke valve will now be slightly open. With fast idle screw and fast idle cam held in this position, carefully bend choke rod to obtain a clearance of .147 in. between bottom edge of choke valve and small inside diameter of air horn.

Note: Choke rod must not rub side of housing at any choke valve position.

Note: Fast idle cam tang must not rest upon choke rod when choke valve is fully closed. If necessary, bend fast idle cam tang slightly so that choke valve may fully close.

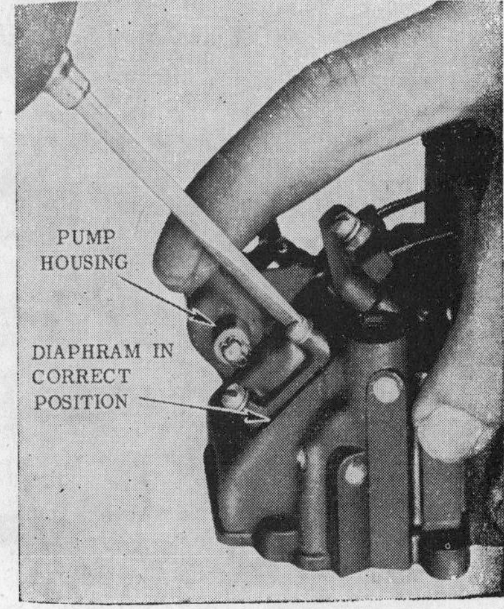

Remove pump housing

Unloader Adjustment

With the choke thermostat cover at the index mark, open the throttle lever to full wide open position. At the same time make sure choke trip lever is in contact with choke. With throttle lever held in this position, check clearance between bottom of choke valve and bore of air horn (small inside diameter). Clearance should be .238 inch. This clearance is obtained by bending the throttle lever tang slightly until the choke valve opens to the desired clearance.

Fast Idle Cam Adjustment

With the choke thermostat cover set at the index mark, hold the choke rod so that the choke valve is in fully closed position. Hold the throttle in closed position so that the fast idle screw rests on high step of the fast idle cam. With the throttle held in this position, adjust the fast idle screw to obtain a clearance of .020 inch between throttle valves (opposite idle screws) and throttle body. This adjustment is equal to

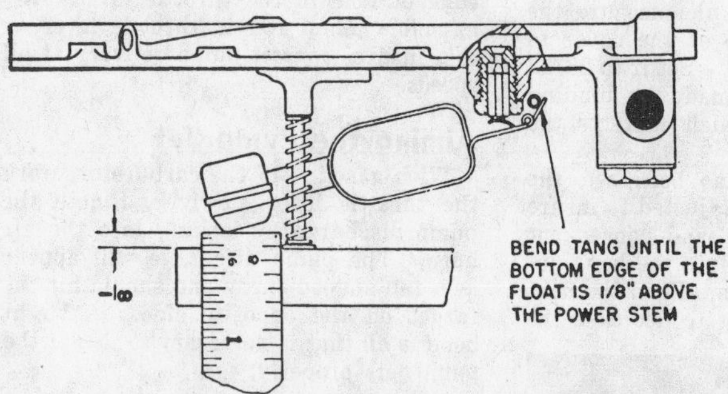

FLOAT TENSION ADJUSTMENT

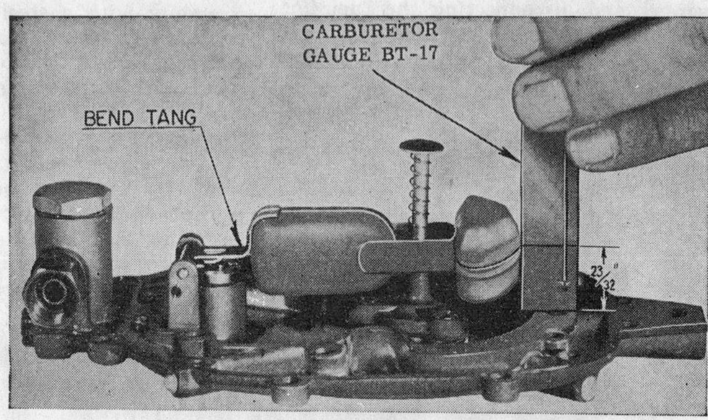

Setting float height

Removing the pump discharge check valve

Pump rod adjustment

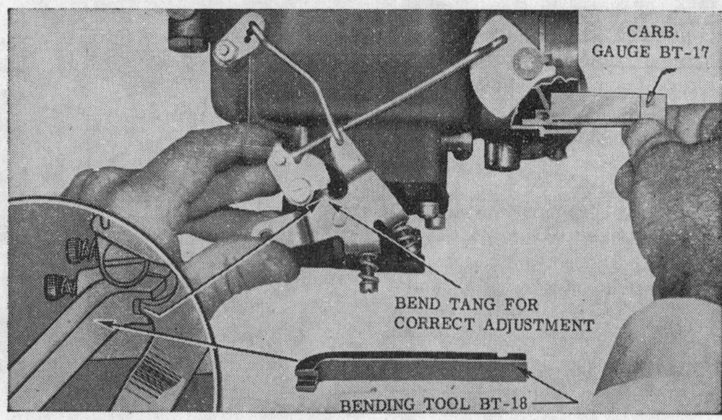

Unloader adjustment

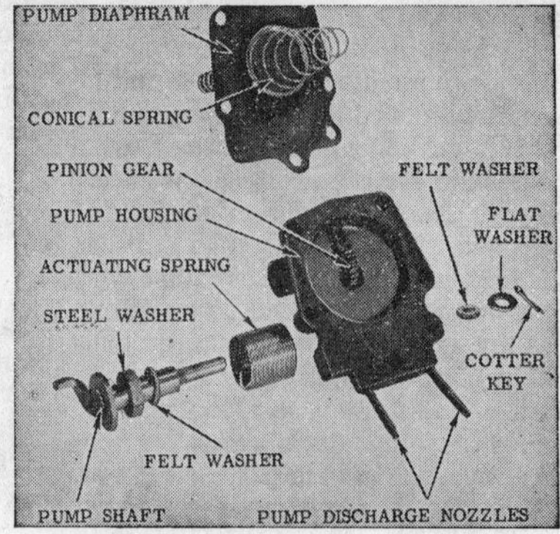

Pump housing internal parts

MODEL B & BC

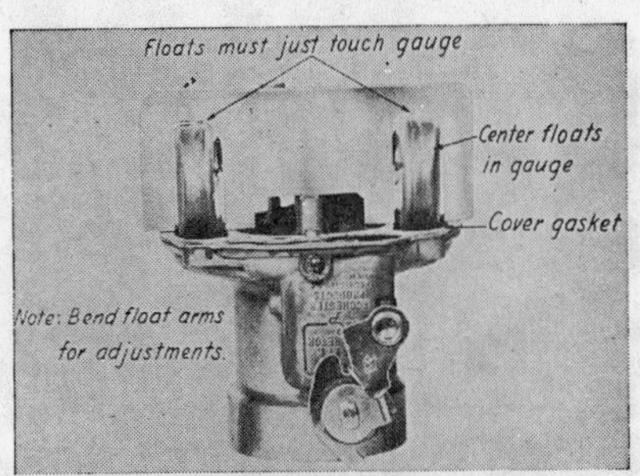

Gauging float height

approximately 1200 to 1250 engine R.P.M. with engine and transmission warm.

The principal difference between the model B and the model BC Rochester carburetors is the automatic choke.

The model BC is an automatic choke version of the model B carburetor. Adjustment procedures are the same for both except the choke rod adjustment which applies to Pontiac only.

Idle Mixture Adjustment

First make sure that the throttle linkage is free and that the throttle set screw is against its stop with the choke released.

Turn the idle speed screw in or out until the engine idles at about 450-500 RPM.

Turn the low speed mixture screw all the way in and then back it out one and one-half turns. Let the engine idle slowly and turn the mixture screw in or out until the best vacuum reading is obtained or to where the engine idles smoothest.

If it is necessary to turn the mixture screw more than one-half turn from the nominal (one and one-half turn) setting to obtain correct idle, look for other difficulties such as faulty ignition, low compression, etc.

Float Adjustment

Two separate adjustments must be made, vertical and lateral.

With the air horn completely assembled place the float gage in position as shown in the illustration, and adjust the floats by bending the float button so that the top of each float just touches the float gage centered between the gage legs. First secure correct height, then center the float.

The float must now be checked for its drop setting.

With the cover held right side up and float suspended freely, carefully bend the float tang at the rear of the float assembly so that the bottom of the float has the specified dimension given in the specifications chart for Rochester Carburetors in section two of this Manual.

Unloader Adjustment

With the throttle lever in the wide open position, there should be a clearance between the lower edge of the choke valve and the bore of the carburetor air horn so that the large end of gage No. BT-50 will slide in freely. Bend the tang on the throttle lever to obtain the necessary clearance. NOTE: No other adjustments are required for these carburetors.

Choke Rod Adjustment

Set the choke cover in the normal position and turn the idle screw in until it contacts the second step of the fast idle cam.

Holding the screw tightly against the cam, bend the choke rod at the dog leg until the small end of gage No. BT-50 slides easily between the lower edge of the choke valve and the bore of the carburetor air horn.

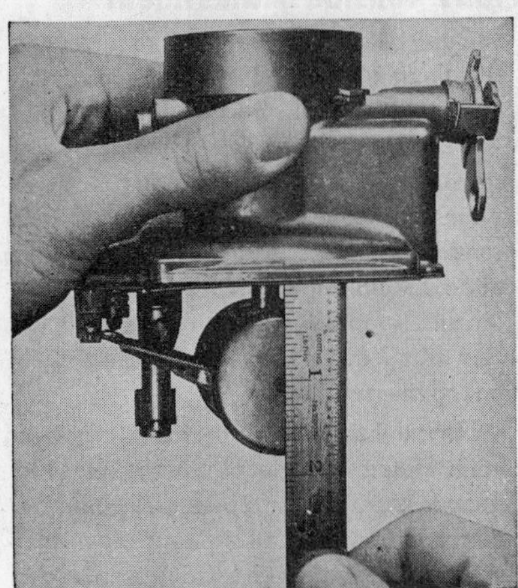

Measuring float drop

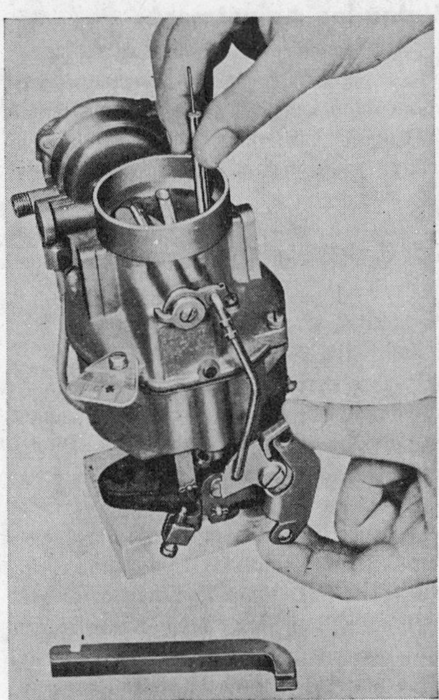

Checking choke unloader

Adjusting choke rod

MODEL B B

Pump Rod Adjustment

Back off the idle stop screw and the fast idle screw so that the throttle valves are fully closed. Remove the pump rod from the rocker arm and hold rocker arm down so that the pump plunger is in its position (up). With

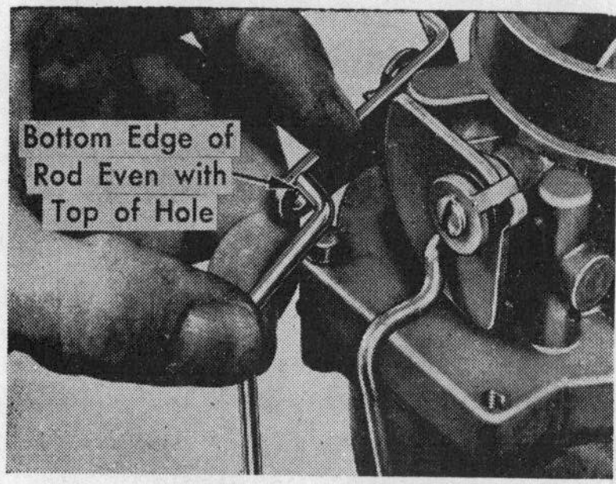

Pump rod setting

pump rod directly over the rocker arm hole, bend the pump rod until its bottom edge is flush with the top edge of the rocker arm hole. Reassemble pump rod to rocker arm. This insures correct pump delivery at all speeds.

Choke Rod Adjustment

With thermostat cover set at index, turn fast idle screw until it contacts the second step on the fast idle cam.

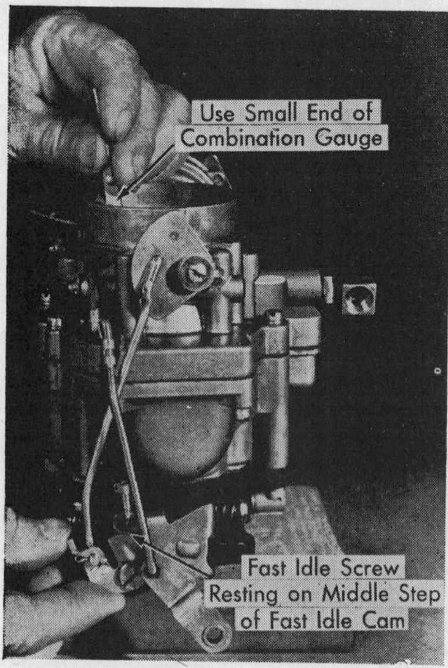

Choke rod setting

Be sure choke trip lever is in contact with the choke counterweight. The choke valve will now be slightly open. With fast idle screw and fast idle cam held in this position, bend the choke rod to obtain the clearance (gauge BT-49) between the bottom edge of the choke valve and flat on inside diameter of the air horn. **Note:** choke rod must not rub side of housing at any choke valve position.

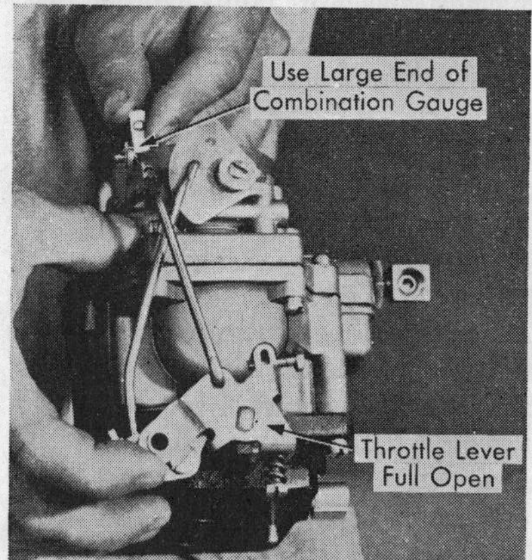

Unloader setting

Unloader Adjustment

With thermostat cover set at index and choke trip lever in contact with choke counterweight, move throttle to full open position. Hold throttle lever in this position and bend tang of throttle lever to obtain the clearance (gauge BT-49) between bottom edge of choke valve and flat on inside diameter of air horn.

Fast Idle Adjustment

With thermostat cover set at index, move fast idle cam so that the choke valve is fully closed. Hold throttle lever in closed position so that the fast idle screw rests on highest step of fast idle cam. Now adjust fast idle screw to obtain clearance (BT-49 gauge) between throttle valves and bore of throttle body on opposite side of idle screws. This adjustment assures proper idle for starting engine and should always be checked in the event stalling is experienced during the warm up period.

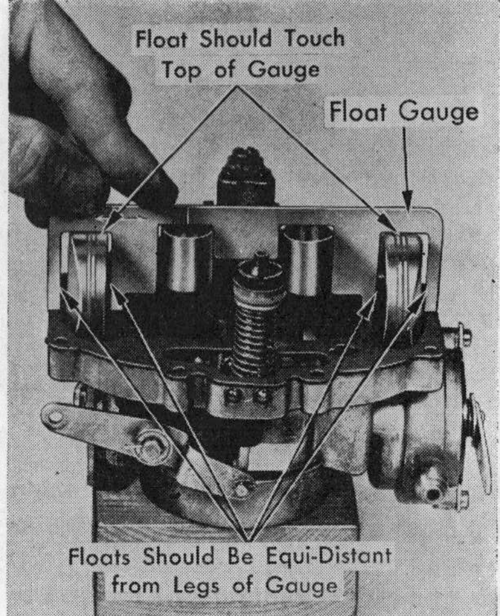

Checking float setting

Float Level Adjustment

This adjustment is made with air horn gasket in position and air horn inverted on a flat surface. Bend float arms vertically until floats appear level in relation to each other.

Place float gage in position as shown, with locating tangs inserted into the secondary venturi to position gage. Bend float button, which contacts the float needle, until the floats touch the top portion of the gage.

Float Tension Adjustment

Bend the float tang, at the rear of the float, against the balance spring to lessen the drop and away from the balance spring to increase the drop. The tension is correct when the distance from the bottom of the air horn gasket to the bottom of the floats, with the air horn assembly held in an upright position, is equivalent to the scaled distance specified in the specification chart in section two.

Now bend the arms horizontally until each float is centered between the gauge legs. Tilt air horn assembly 90 degrees each side and check that floats do not touch gauge legs. This insures the floats will not rub sides of float bowl.

MODEL 4GC

Right side showing automatic choke

Left side showing linkage

Model 4GC

The Rochester carburetor Model 4GC is, in effect, two dual carburetors contained in a single casting. The two sides are referred to in this text as the primary or pump side, and the secondary or fuel inlet side.

Accelerating Pump Circuit

The accelerator pump circuit is located in the primary side of the carburetor only.

When the throttle valves are placed in the open position quickly the air flow and manifold vacuum change practically instantaneously. Whereas the heavier fuel tends to lag behind causing a momentary leanness. The accelerator pump corrects this condition by feeding an extra amount of fuel which is necessary to provide smooth power. A mechanical adjustment is provided to lengthen or shorten the effective stroke of the pump.

Automatic Choke Circuit

The automatic control circuit allows the carburetor to feed the engine a rich mixture for starting and warm up. Choking of the carburetor is necessary only on the primary side. This is due to the fact that the secondary throttle valves are locked in the closed position whenever the choke valve is even partially closed.

Part Throttle Circuit

The amount of fuel used for idle and early throttle is supplied through the part throttle circuit.

When the throttle is opened to a greater degree than at idle speed it becomes necessary to supply additional fuel to meet the torque demands of the engine. This is done on the primary side of the carburetor.

Power System

The amount of fuel required for part throttle and full throttle is supplied through the power circuit, which is located within the primary side of the carburetor.

The proper mixture required when more power is demanded or constant high speed driving is to be maintained, is supplied by a vacuum operated power piston in the air horn and a power valve in the float bowl which is incorporated into the carburetor.

Float Circuit

The float circuit is to maintain the fuel in the float bowl at a predetermined level.

Both the primary and secondary sides of the carburetor employ individual float circuit.

Adjustments

No carburetor should be adjusted without first checking compression, ignition and also check the manifold for any leaks. An engine must be properly tuned before any carburetor can function properly.

MODEL 4GC—continued

Idle Speed Adjustment

The idle adjustment screw positions the throttle valves for curb idle speed and has no effect on richness of mixture.

Set idle speed

Set engine to approximately 375-475 rpm depending on engine condition (engine in good condition should be set to lower speed). Cars equipped with automatic transmission set to 375-475 rpm with transmission in drive range. When transmission is shifted to neutral, engine will speed up. This is normal.

Idle Mixture Adjustment

This adjustment controls the mixture of fuel and air at curb idle and also affects part throttle operation. To set idle mixture proceed as follows: First, set engine idle as explained under heading Idle Speed Adjustment. Now turn the idle mixture screw in until the engine slows down and out again until the engine rolls. Midway between these two settings should be the proper setting for each primary barrel (no idle mixture adjustment on secondary side). After the second barrel has been adjusted, go back and readjust the first and then readjust the second barrel. In other words, do each adjustment at least twice.

Set idle mixture

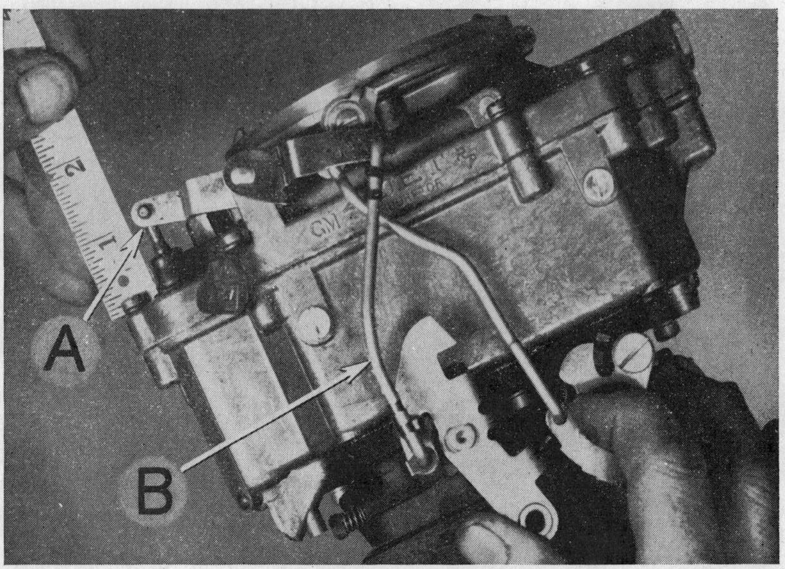

Accelerator Pump Adjustment

A—Measure between top of air horn and bottom of pump arm
B—Bend rod at this point to obtain specified dimension

Accelerator Pump Rod Adjustment

Back out the curb idle stop and fast idle screw until the throttle valves seat in the bores of the throttle body. With the throttle valves seated in the bores of the carburetor, carefully bend the pump rod until the distance from the air horn surface to the bottom edge of the accelerator pump plunger rod is a specified dimension (Cadillac 15/16 inch; Oldsmobile 1 1/16 inch).

Note: The choke thermostat adjustment should be made at this point. Before adjusting both idle stop and fast idle screw, rotate choke modifier index pointer until it is set one (1) notch rich.

Fast Idle Adjustment

With the engine hot and choke thermostat set one (1) notch rich, rotate the fast idle cam until the choke valve is fully closed. With the throttle lever in the closed position, set the fast idle screw so it rests on the highest step of the cam. Now turn the fast idle screw until a clearance of .028 inch is had between the throttle valves and the bores of the carburetor opposite idle post on the primary side.

Fast idle adjustment

Unloader Adjustment

With the throttle valves set in the wide open position, hold the trip lever down until it is in contact with choke

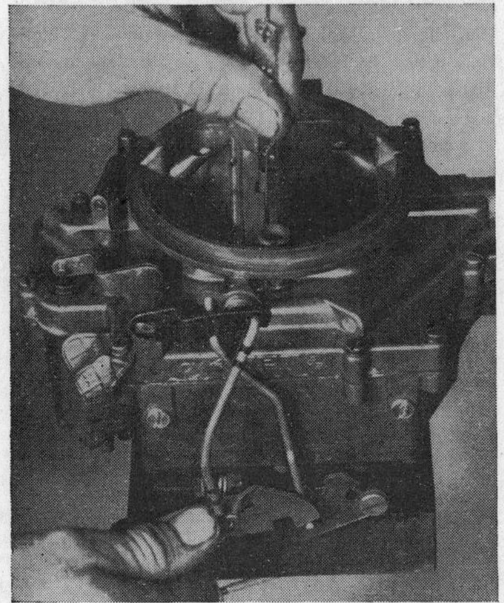

Unloader adjustment

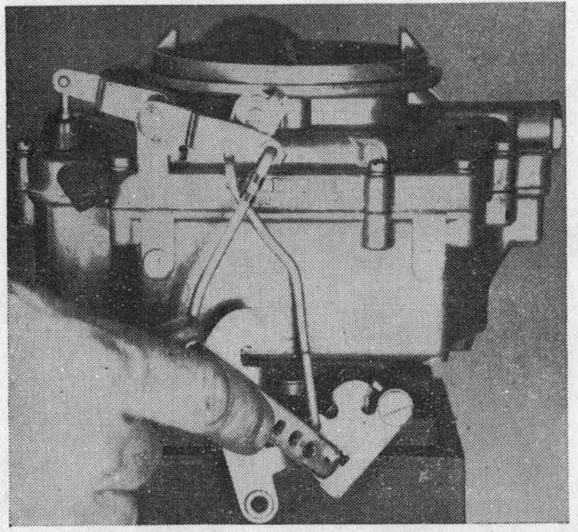

Bend tang to obtain correct unloader adjustment

counterweight. Holding the levers in this position there should be clearance (Cadillac .067 inch; Oldsmobile .092 inch) between the two air horns. Adjustment is had by bending the tang of fast idle cam.

Secondary Throttle Lock-Out Adjustment

Hold the choke in the partially closed position. Now set the fast idle cam and

Secondary throttle lock-out adjustment—Note: choke partially closed

secondary lock-out lever in the position, as shown in above illustration. There should be a clearance of .015 inch between the secondary lock-out lever and the fast idle cam. The adjustment is accomplished by bending the lever to obtain this clearance.

Secondary Throttle Clearance Adjustment

Set the choke in the wide open position and the secondary lock-out lever and fast idle cam in the position as shown in illustration. There should be a clearance (Cadillac .030 inch; Oldsmobile .015 inch) between the lever and cam. Adjust by bending the lever.

Checking secondary throttle clearance—choke off

Float Level Adjustment

With the air horn turned upside down proceed as follows: When one float is higher or lower than the other, bend the float arm until both floats are on an even level. Set the float gage in position so that the gage is located against the curvature in the bore of the air horn.

Bend the float arm at the rear until the floats just touch the top section of the gage. If no gage is available, the dimension from the gasket to the bottom of the float is 1 9/16 inch. Now tilt the air horn assembly to each side to determine if the floats touch sides of gage. If this condition is determined, bend the float arm horizontally until they are centered between the float gage legs.

Float Drop Adjustment

Bend the float tang against the needle seat to shorten the drop and away from the needle seat to lengthen the drop.

Checking float drop

With the air horn held in the upright position there should be 2¼ inches between the air horn gasket and the bottom of the float.

Atmospheric Idle Vent Adjustment

Place a (.063 Cadillac; .040 Oldsmobile) gage opposite the idle port side between the throttle valve and bores of carburetor on the primary side. Set up in this position, the vent contact arm should just touch the atmospheric vent valve. To correct the condition, bend the vent contact arm.

MODEL AA1

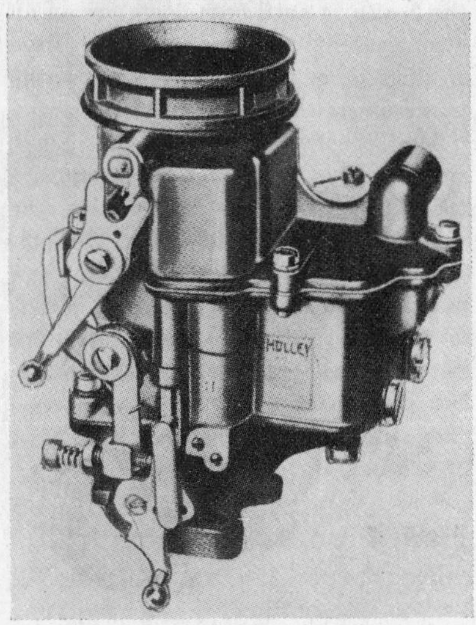

Full view of model AA1

The carburetor Model AA1 is a dual downdraft carburetor engineered to supply an adequate amount of fuel to the engine during all operating conditions. Two throttle bores are incorporated into this carburetor, each having its own throttle plate and venturi utilizing one air inlet. Each throttle bore maintains its own main metering system and idle system that obtains fuel from the float chamber. The power enrichment system is fully automatic. A vacuum operated diaphragm type power valve supplies additional fuel to both main metering systems for maximum torque demands of the engine or sustained high speed operation. The accelerating pump employs a spring overriding feature, which produces a follow up action allowing the discharge of fuel to be carried out over a certain period for smooth acceleration.

Accelerating System

The accelerating pump system provides an extra amount of fuel during acceleration which is necessary to provide smooth power.

The air flow through the carburetor responds practically instantaneously to any increase in throttle opening but there is an interval before the liquid fuel in the small passages can gain velocity and supply an adequate balance of fuel and air. The accelerating pump system performs during this interval, providing fuel until the incorporated systems can maintain the required mixture.

Choke System

The choke system allows the carburetor to feed the engine a rich mixture for starting and warm up.

Idle System

The amount of fuel used for idle and early throttle is supplied through the idle system.

During idle and low speeds, the pressure drop in the venturi is not great enough to allow operation of the main metering system. At low rpm the increased manifold vacuum is used to supply a pressure difference that operates the idle system.

Main Metering System

Each barrel of this carburetor employs its own main metering system.

During normal cruising speed the air flow through the carburetor produces a drop in pressure in the venturi. The float bowl is vented inside by a vent tube in the air horn and the pressure in the float bowl is greater than the pressure in the venturi. The variation in pressure difference forces a metered amount of fuel to flow through the main metering system and out the main nozzle located in the venturi. Fuel is then metered by the main jet as it flows into the bottom of the main well. Now the fuel flows out the top of the main well directly into an angle channel in nozzle bar where air coming from the high speed bleed is blended with liquid fuel. The high speed bleed provides a properly increased amount of air to be mixed with the fuel, thus stabilizing the fuel discharge and maintaining the proper air fuel mixture at higher speeds.

Power Enrichment System

The amount of fuel required for part and wide open throttle is supplied through the power enrichment system.

For maximum torque demands of the engine or high speed operation, a rich mixture is demanded much more so than required at part throttle. During part throttle operation the vacuum of the manifold acting on the power piston is adequate to hold the piston in the up position against the compressed load of its spring. When high speed demands minimized manifold vacuum beyond a predetermined point, the spring expands, to force the piston and stem assembly down. Fuel from the float bowl flows through the center of the valve and out calibrated holes in its side which meter an adequate amount of fuel. The fuel then passes through a channel to the bottom of main well where it mixes with fuel coming from the main metering system, enriching the mixture for sustained high speed operation.

Float System

The float system is to maintain the fuel in the float chamber at a predetermined level. The float is connected to an inlet needle valve. A float properly adjusted will permit enough fuel to enter the float chamber to replace the fuel being used.

Adjustment

Before attempting to adjust the carburetor, make sure the engine is at normal operating temperature. Then check compression, ignition and also the manifold for any leaks. An engine must be properly tuned before any carburetor can function properly.

Idle Speed Adjustment

The idle speed adjustment screw positions the throttle valves for curb idle speed and has no effect on richness of mixture.

Set engine to approximately 475-550 rpm depending on engine condition (engine in good condition should be set to lower speed). Cars equipped with automatic transmission set to 400-450 rpm with transmission in drive range. When transmission is shifted to neutral engine will speed up. This is normal.

Idle Mixture Adjustment

This adjustment controls the mixture of fuel and air at curb idle and also effects part throttle operation. To set idle mixture proceed as follows:

First, set engine idle as referred to in paragraph Idle Speed Adjustment. Now turn the idle mixture screw in until the engine slows down and out again until the engine rolls. Halfway between these two settings should be the proper setting for each barrel. After the second barrel has been adjusted, go back and readjust the first and then readjust the second. In other words, do each adjustment at least twice.

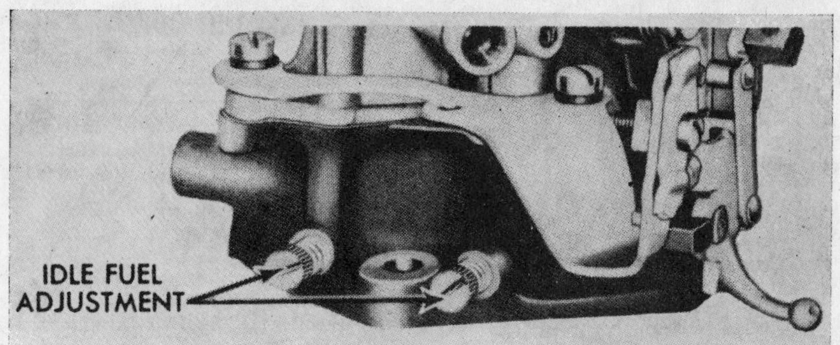

Idle mixture adjusting screws

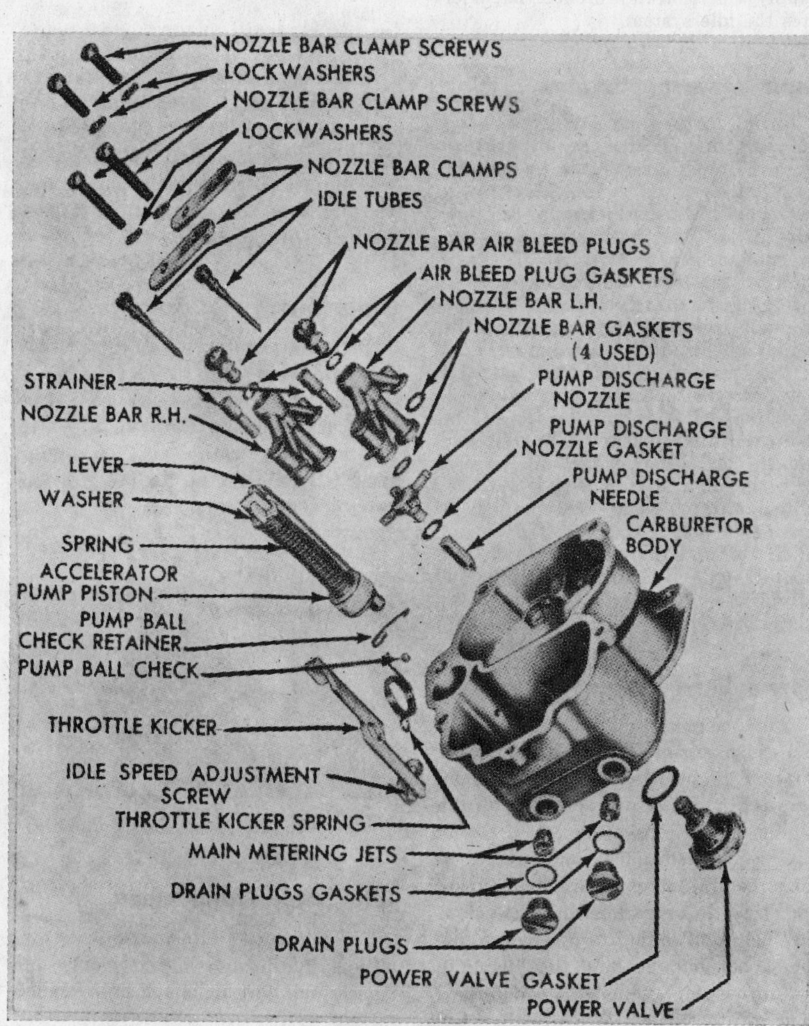

Exploded view of main body

Accelerator Pump Adjustment

The accelerator pump link may be placed in three different positions. Normally set in center hole in throttle lever. For the greatest fuel charge (cold weather), set in outer hole. For minimum fuel charge (hot weather), set in inner hole.

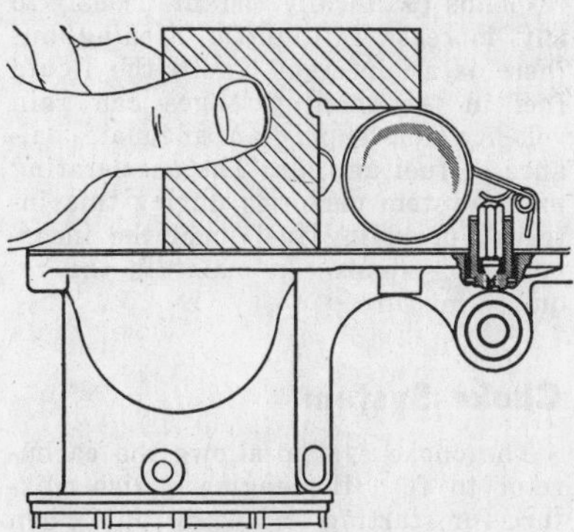
Gauge in position to check float height

Float Adjustment

With the air horn inverted and the float resting its own weight on the seated needle, determine the clearance (1 9/32 - 1 11/32) from flange surface of air horn (not the soldered seam) to bottom side of float pontoon. To correct float setting bend the lip that contacts needle valve.

CHANDLER GROVES - HOLLEY - FORD CARBURETORS

MODEL 847

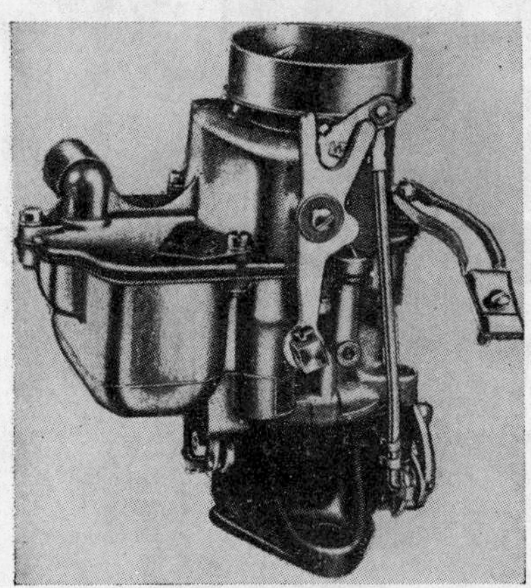

Full view of Model 847

The Holley carburetor Model 847 is a single barrel downdraft carburetor, designed to deliver an adequate amount of fuel to the engine under all operating conditions.

Accelerating Pump System

The accelerating pump system provides an extra amount of fuel during acceleration which is necessary to provide smooth power.

The airflow through the carburetor responds practically instantaneously to any increase in throttle opening but there is an interval before the liquid fuel in the small passages can gain velocity and supply an adequate balance of fuel and air. The accelerating pump system performs during this interval, providing fuel until the incorporated systems can maintain the required mixture.

Choke System

The choke system allows the carburetor to feed the engine a rich mixture for starting and warm up. When depressing the accelerator to start a cold engine, a lot of the vaporized fuel from the carburetor is reduced to a liquid when contacting the cold metal surface of the intake manifold. The outcome is hard starting and stalling. Pulling the choke valve closed holds the manifold vacuum in the carburetor, and this allows a rich mixture of fuel to be drawn from the idle and main metering systems. After the engine is started, there is enough air drawn through the spring-loaded poppet valve in the choke plate to eliminate any flooding of the carburetor. A fast idle rod and cam is incorporated with the choke to allow a faster idle to prevent stalling.

Idle System

The amount of fuel used for idle and early throttle is supplied through the idle system.

During idle and low speeds, the pressure drop in the venturi is not great enough to allow operation of the main metering system. At low rpm the increased manifold vacuum is used to supply a pressure difference that operates the idle system.

Main Metering System

During normal cruising speeds the air flow through the carburetor produces a drop in pressure in the venturi. The float bowl is vented inside by a vent tube in the air horn and the pressure in the float bowl is greater than the pressure in the venturi. The variation in pressure difference forces a metered amount of fuel to flow through the main metering system and out the main nozzle located in the venturi. Fuel is then metered by the main jet as it flows into the bottom of the main well. Now the fuel flows out the top of the main well directly into an angle channel in nozzle bar where air coming from the high speed bleed is blended with liquid fuel. The high speed bleed provides a properly increasing amount of air to be mixed with the fuel, thus stabilizing the fuel discharge and maintaining the proper air fuel mixture at higher speeds.

Power Enrichment System

The amount of fuel required for part and wide open throttle is supplied through the proper enrichment system. For maximum torque demands of the engine or high speed operation, a rich mixture is demanded much more so than required at part throttle. During part throttle operation the vacuum of the manifold acting on the power piston is adequate to hold the piston in the up position against the compressed load of its spring. When high speed demands minimized manifold vacuum beyond a predetermined point, the piston spring will send the piston and stem assembly down. This depresses the pin in center of power valves, thus opening the valve. Fuel from the float bowl flows through the center of the valve and out calibrated holes in its side which meter an adequate amount of fuel. The fuel then passes through a channel to the bottom of main well where it mixes with fuel coming from the main metering system, enriching the mixture for sustained high speed operation.

Float System

The float system is to maintain the fuel in the float chamber at a predetermined level. The float is connected to an inlet needle valve. A float properly adjusted will permit enough fuel to enter the float chamber to replace the fuel being used.

Adjustment

Before attempting to adjust the carburetor, make sure the engine is at normal operating temperature. Then check compression, ignition and also the manifold for any leaks. An engine must be properly tuned before any carburetor can function properly.

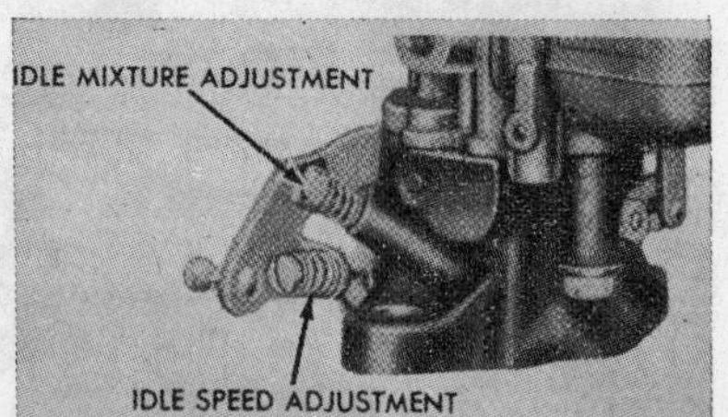

Idle speed and idle mixture adjustment

Idle Speed Adjustment

The idle speed adjustment screw positions the throttle valves for curb idle speed and has no effect on richness of mixture.

Set engine to approximately 475-550 rpm depending on engine condition (engine in good condition should be set to lower speed). Cars equipped with automatic transmission set to 400-450 rpm with transmission in drive range. When transmission is shifted to neutral engine will speed up. This is normal.

Idle Mixture Adjustment

This adjustment controls the mixture of fuel and air at curb idle and also effects part throttle operation. To set idle mixture proceed as follows: turn the idle mixture screw in until the engine slows down and out again until the engine rolls. Midway between these two settings the engine will smooth out and this will be the correct setting.

Accelerator Pump Adjustment

The accelerator pump link may be placed in three different positions. Normally set in center hole in throttle lever. For larger charge of fuel, set in outer hole. For smaller charge, set in inner hole.

Float Adjustment

With the air horns turned upside down and the float resting on the seated needle determine the clearance (1 5/16-1 11/32) from flange surface of the air horn to bottom side of float pontoon. To correct float setting, bend the float lever arm down or up to bring float within specified limits.

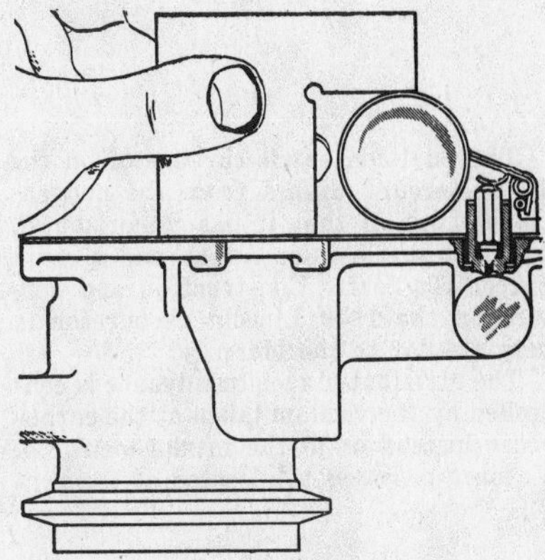

Set float level gage in position

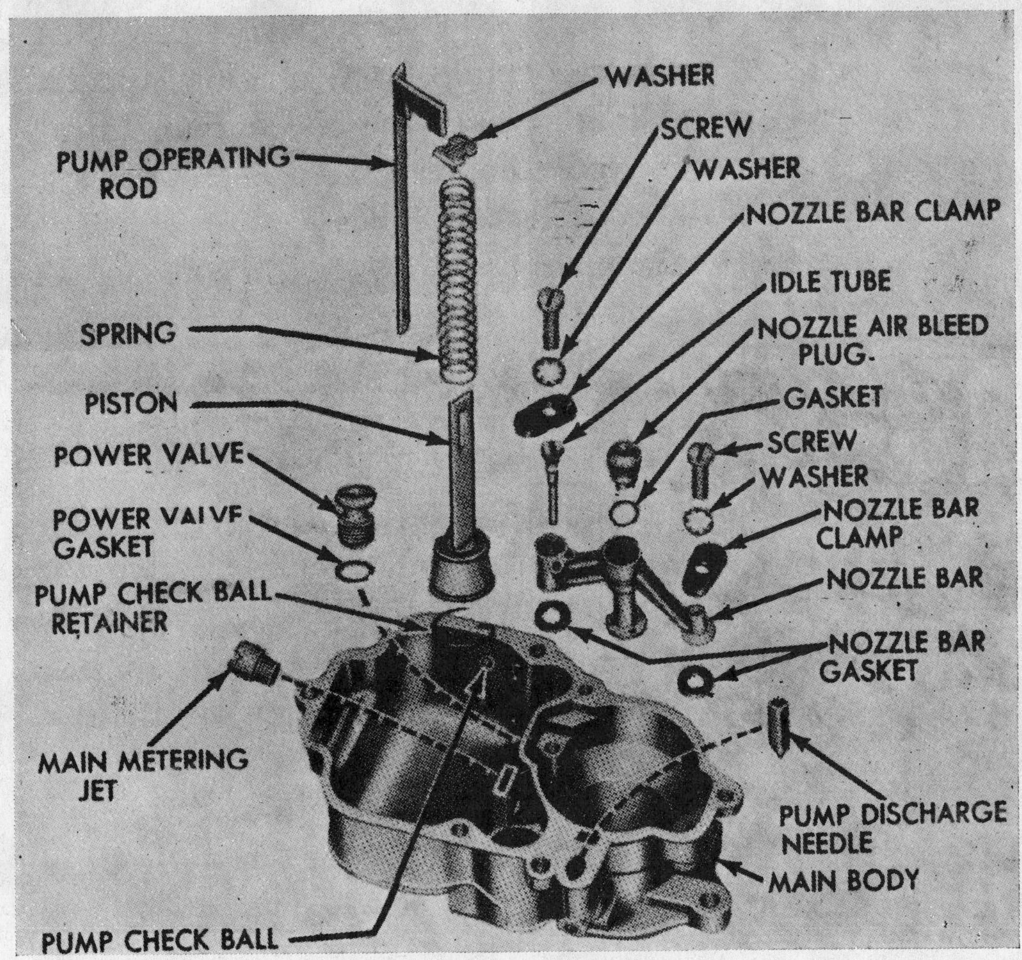

Exploded view of main body

DUAL CONCENTRIC MODEL 885FFC

The dual concentric carburetor on the 1949 Mercury differs from the conventional type in that it has a horizontal, or right angle inlet throat and a twin concentric float. Construction and service on the 1949 Lincoln carburetor is very similar to the Mercury.

The distributor vacuum advance is controlled by the vacuum taken at the carburetor instead of at the intake manifold. Vacuum passages are located at the venturi and just above the throttle valve. Connected in this manner, the vacuum varies between these two points as the throttle opens and more road load is applied. When the car is accelerated, venturi vacuum increases and the manifold vacuum decreases. This causes low vacuum at the diaphragm on the distributor which in turn allows the advance springs to retard the spark. Under part throttle at any speed the vacuum at both carburetor openings is high. The spark should fully advance between 18 and 35 miles per hour.

The accompanying pictures and text provide a detailed description of the procedure for overhauling the 1949 Mercury and Lincoln carburetor, arranged in the order of the steps of the operation.

Follow carefully the steps shown to overhaul this carburetor.

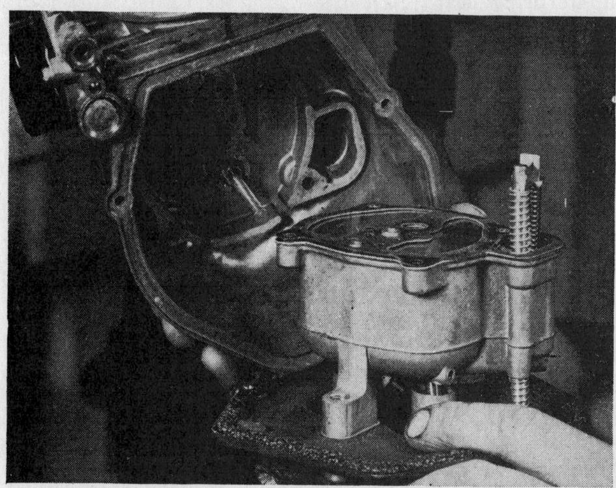

Remove cap screws holding airhorn and lift off

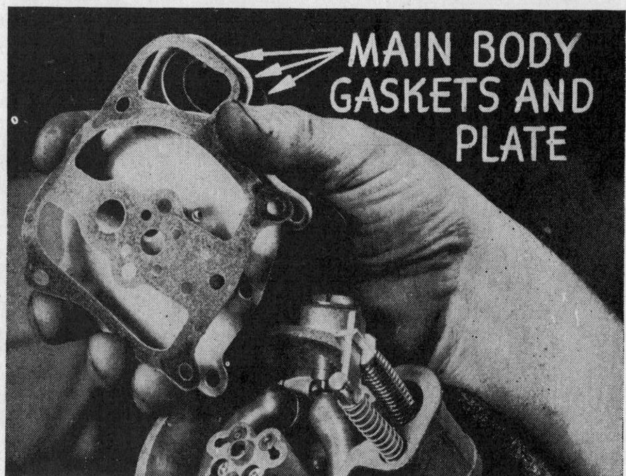

Remove main body plate and gasket

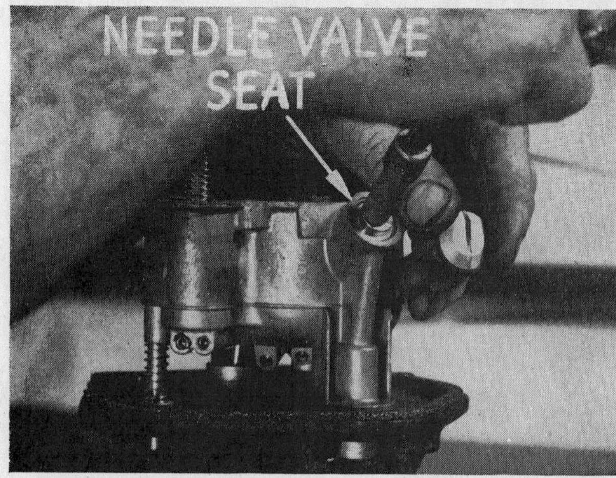

Remove the needle valve outer plug and screw out the valve seat

Remove float hinge pin and lift off float

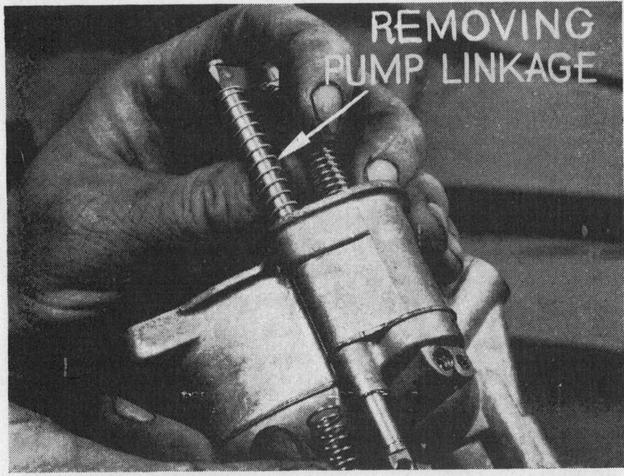

Remove the pump snap ring and lift out pump assembly

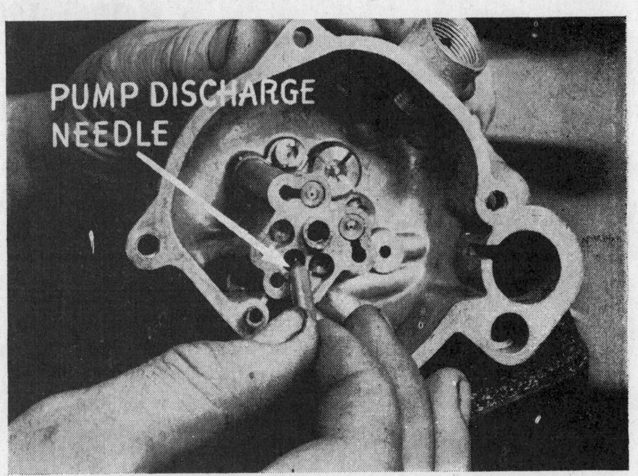

Power seat needle must be installed point down

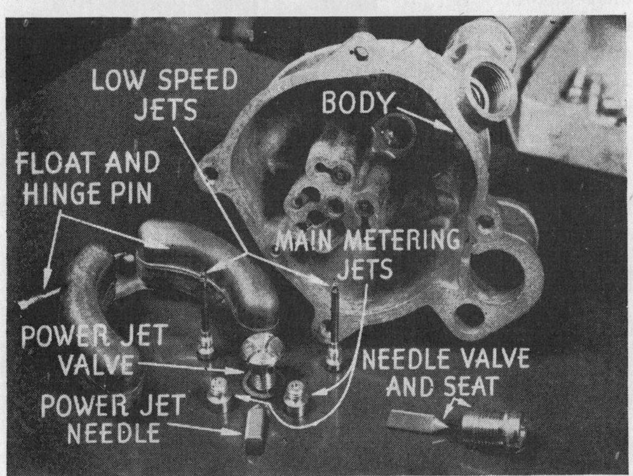

Exploded view of float bowl and parts

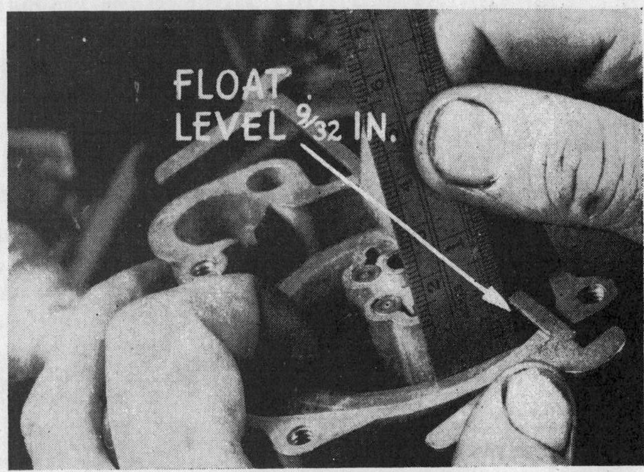

Set float level as shown above

Set choke as indicated above

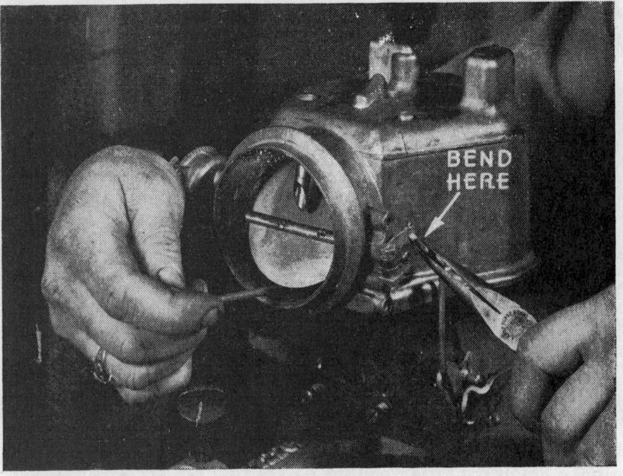

Set choke unloader to 3/8" with throttle held wide open

CHANDLER GROVES - HOLLEY - FORD CARBURETORS

MODEL 1904F VISI FLO

Full view of model 1940F visi flo

Carburetor Model 1904F is a single throat downdraft carburetor, employing a newly designed tempered glass fuel bowl. Any water or sediment deposits in the fuel bowl are readily determined by means of this glass fuel bowl.

Adjustments

No carburetor should be adjusted without first checking compression, ignition and also the manifold for any leaks. An engine must be properly tuned before any carburetor can function properly.

Idle Speed Adjustment

Idle speed adjustment screw positions the throttle valves for curb idle speed and has no effect on richness of mixture.

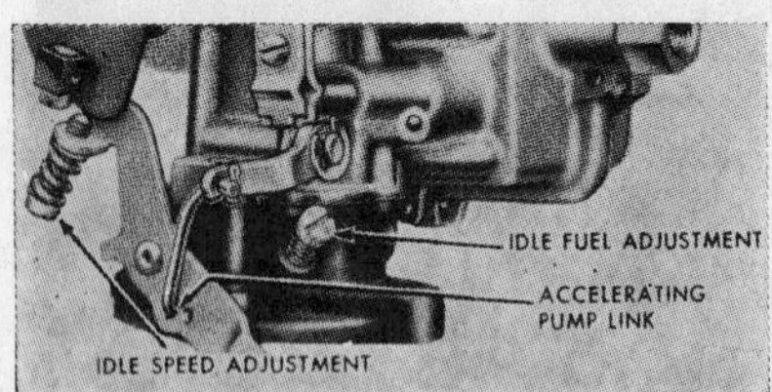

Adjustment locations of idle mixture, idle speed and accelerating pump

Set engine to approximately 500-575 rpm depending on engine condition (engine in good condition should be set to lower speed).

Idle Mixture Adjustment

This adjustment controls the mixture of fuel and air at curb idle and also effects port throttle operation.

To set idle mixture proceed as follows: First, set engine idle as explained under paragraph Idle Speed Adjustment. Now, turn the idle mixture screw in until the engine slows down and out again until the engine rolls. Halfway between these two settings the engine will smooth out and this will be the correct setting.

Accelerator Pump Adjustment

The accelerator pump link may be placed in two different positions. The inner hole is for normal or summer weather conditions. For the greatest fuel charge (cold weather), set in outer hole.

Float Adjustment

With the carburetor turned upside down and the float resting on the seated needle determine the clearance (13/64″) using special float gage. To correct float setting, bend tab on the float arm up or down to bring float within specified limits.

Another way to check the fuel level is to use a dummy fuel bowl. Detach the power valve diaphragm cover and valve assembly, then insert fuel gage pin in this opening. With the gage pin in this position the fuel should just touch the low gage pin and **not** the high gage pin. To adjust, bend the float arm tab to reach required setting.

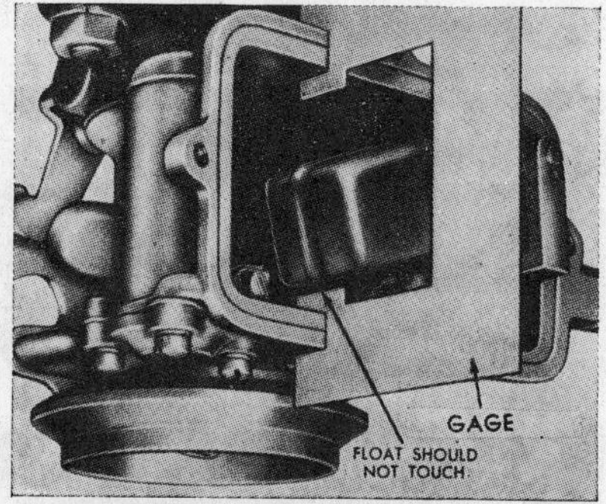

Float adjustment

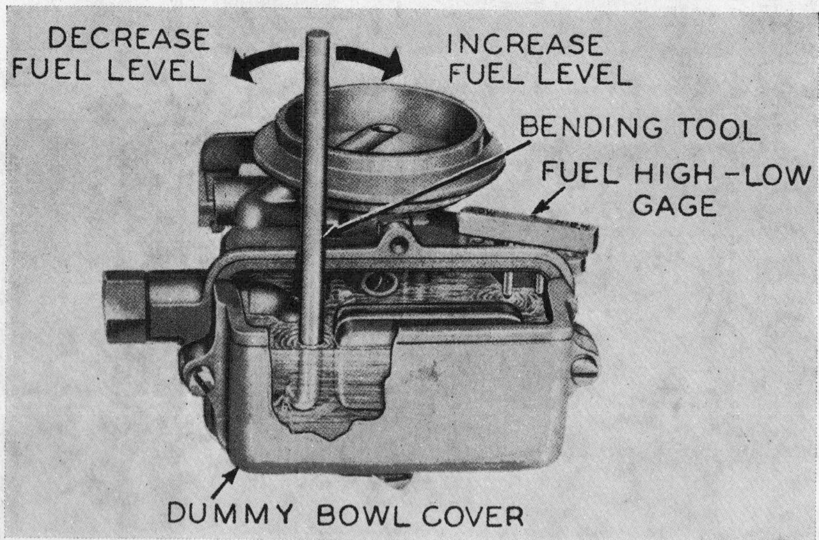

Float adjustment alternate method. Insert bending tool over tab on float arm. Hold float and bend tab to obtain the proper fuel level

CHANDLER GROVES - HOLLEY - FORD CARBURETORS

MODEL 1901FF

The carburetor Model 1901FF is a dual concentric downdraft carburetor engineered to supply an adequate amount of fuel to the engine during all operating conditions. This type carburetor does not employ the use of an air horn. The air cleaner fits over the main body and seats directly to the throttle body. The air cleaner thus serves as both air horn and air cleaner.

Adjustments

No carburetor should be adjusted without first checking compression, ignition and also the manifold for any leaks. An engine must be properly tuned before any carburetor can function properly.

Idle Speed Adjustment

The idle speed adjustment screw positions the throttle valves for curb idle speed and has no effect on richness of mixture.

Set engine to approximately 400-500 rpm depending on engine condition (engine in good condition should be set to lower speed). Cars equipped with automatic transmission set to 400-425 rpm with transmission in drive range. When transmission is shifted to neutral engine will speed up. This is normal.

Idle Mixture Adjustment

This adjustment controls the mixture of fuel and air at idle and also effects low speed operation. To set idle mixture proceed as follows: First, set engine idle as explained under paragraph Idle Speed Adjustment. Now turn the idle mixture screw in until the engine slows down and out again until the engine rolls. Halfway between these two settings should be the proper setting for each throttle throat. After the second throat has been adjusted, go back and readjust the first and then readjust the second. In other words, do each adjustment at least twice.

Accelerator Pump Adjustment

The accelerator pump link may be placed in two different positions. The inner hole is for normal or summer weather conditions. For the greatest fuel charge (cold weather), set in outer hole.

Float Adjustment

Hold the seated needle down against its own seat. Now insert gage and check the position of both float toes below machined surface of main body. To adjust, bend tab that contacts seated needle to reach required setting.

Automatic Choke Setting

Turn the thermostat cover until the arrow on the flange lines up with the tang on choke housing. This setting is for normal operating conditions, but may vary one or two notches depending on climatic conditions.

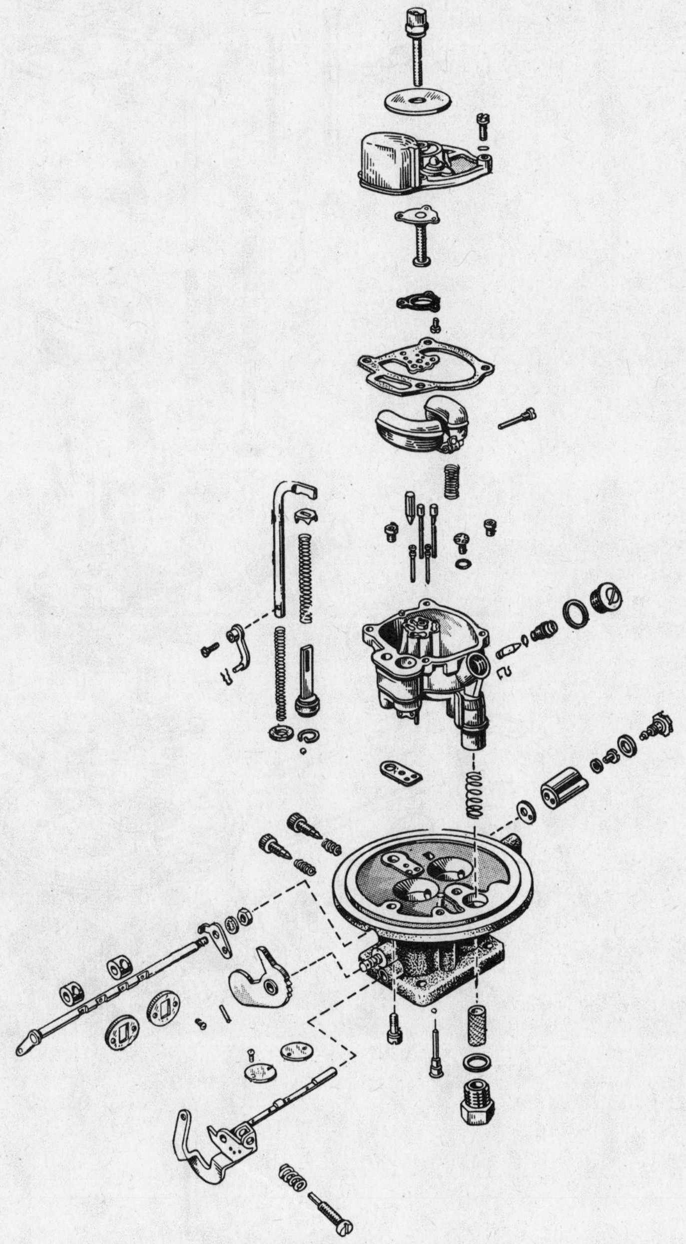

Exploded view of Model 1901FF

MODEL 2140

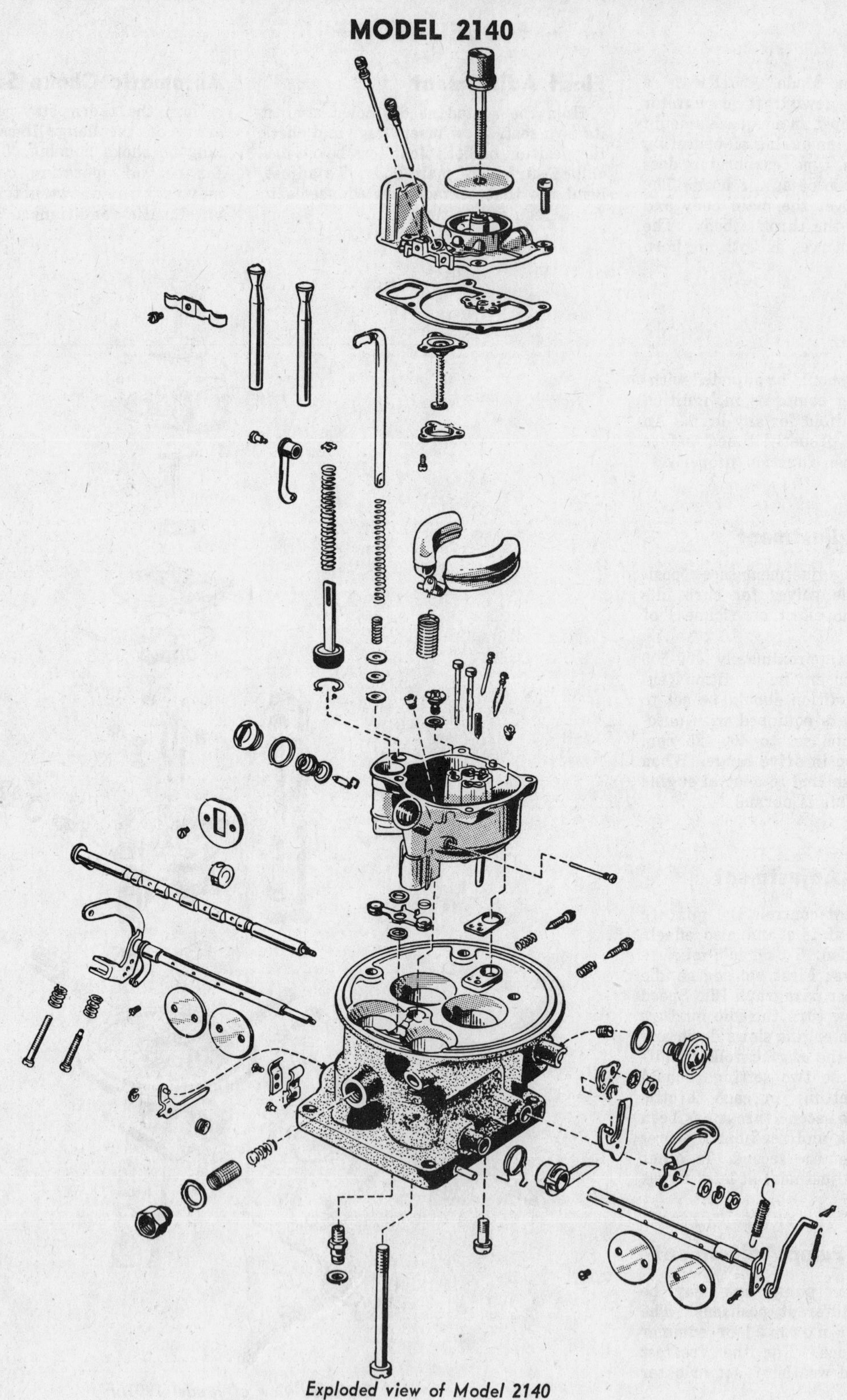

Exploded view of Model 2140

MODEL 2140

The carburetor Model 2140 is, in effect, a dual throat downdraft carburetor containing the various circuits needed to supply an adequate amount of fuel to the engine under all operating conditions.

The throttle valves on the primary side are connected by mechanical linkage to the accelerator pedal. The throttle valves on the secondary side are connected by spring loaded linkage to the primary side. Therefore the primary throttle opens and closes at the will of the driver. The secondary throttle is operated partially by the will of the driver (spring loaded linkage) and partly by the torque demands of the engine.

Adjustments

No carburetor can be properly adjusted if engine malfunctioning is determined.

Before attempting to adjust any carburetor check compression on each cylinder, check manifold for leaks, check and set spark plugs and ignition breaker points, adjust valve tappets, set ignition and check valve timing. An engine must be properly tuned before any carburetor can function properly.

Idle Speed Adjustment

The idle adjustment screw positions the throttle valves for curb idle speed and has no effect on richness of mixture. Set engine idle to approximately 450-525 rpm depending on engine condition (engine in good condition should be set to lower speed). Cars equipped with automatic transmission set to approximately 400-450 rpm with transmission in drive range. When transmission is shifted to neutral, engine will speed up. This is normal.

Fig. 1—Take out anchor screw and bleeder plate washer

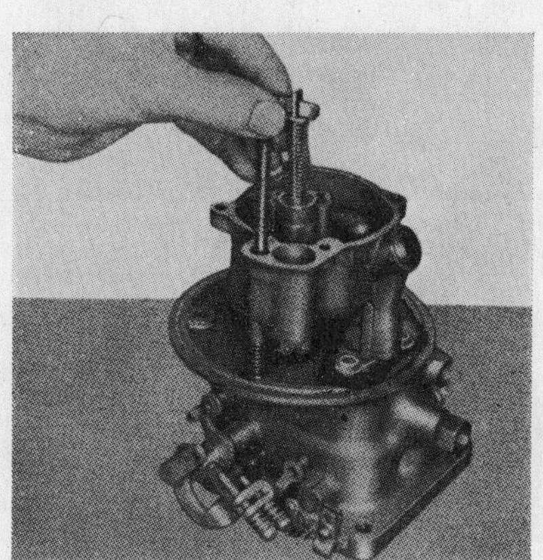

Fig. 3—Lift out pump piston

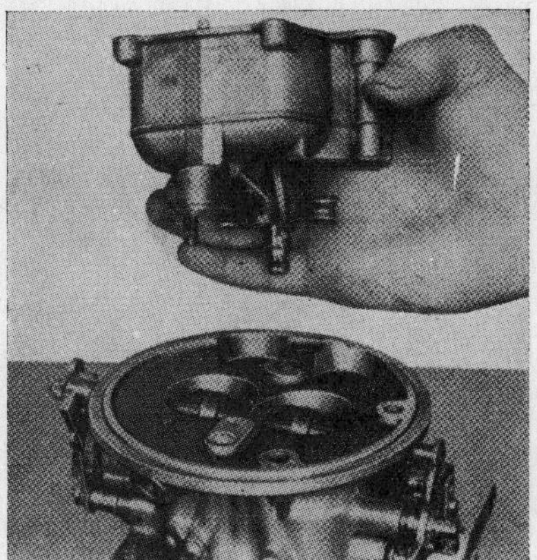

Fig. 5—Lift main body from throttle body

Fig. 2—Remove pump rod screw

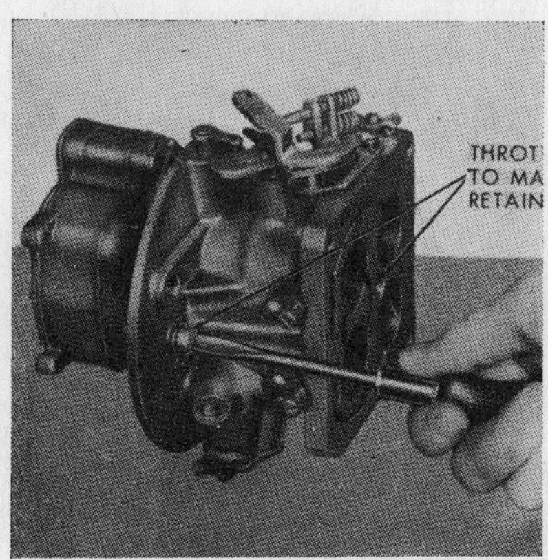

Fig. 4—Remove screws holding main body to throttle body

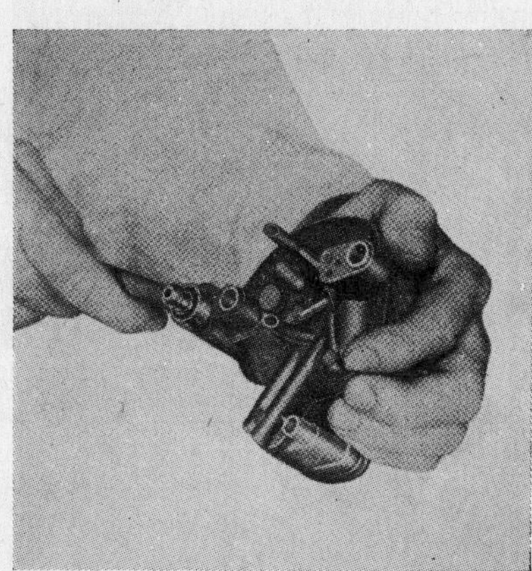

Fig. 6—Take out the fuel inlet adapter

MODEL 2140—*continued*

Idle Mixture Adjustment

This adjustment controls the mixture of fuel and air at idle and also effects low speed operation. To set idle mixture proceed as follows: First, set engine idle as explained under paragraph Idle Speed Adjustment. Now turn the idle mixture screw in until the engine slows down and out until the engine rolls.

Midway betwen these two settings should be the proper setting for each primary barrel (no idle mixture adjustment on secondary side). After the second barrel has been adjusted, go back and readjust the first and then readjust the second. In other words, do each adjustment at least twice.

Automatic Choke Setting

Turn the thermostat cover until the arrow on the flange lines up with the tang on choke housing. This setting is for normal operating conditions, but may vary one or two notches depending on climatic conditions.

Accelerator Pump Adjustment

The accelerator pump link can be placed in three different positions. Normally set in center hole in throttle lever. For the greatest fuel charge (extremely cold weather), set in hole farthest from throttle lever. For minimum fuel charge (extremely hot weather) set in hole nearest the throttle lever.

Float Adjustment

Hold the seated needle down against its seat. Now insert float level gage and check the position of both float toes below machined surface of main body. To adjust, bend float tab that contacts seated needle to reach required setting.

Fig. 7—Remove choke shaft from throttle body

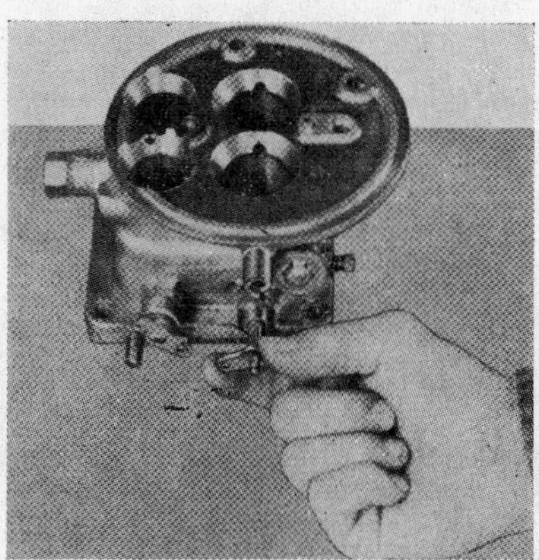

Fig. 9—Disconnect secondary throttle lever then remove lever and roller assembly

Fig. 11—Unscrew spark control valve

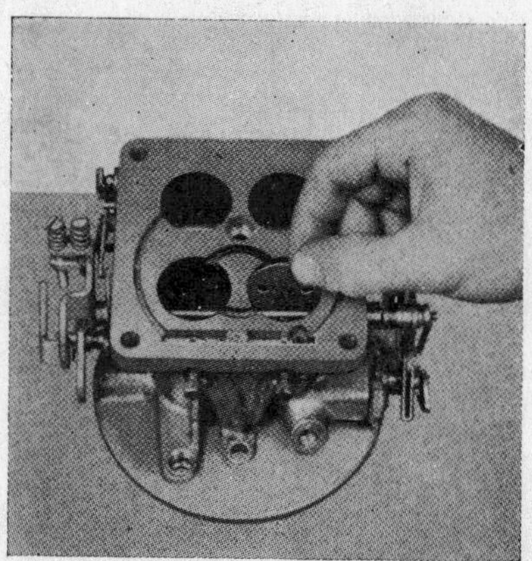

Fig. 8—Remove primary throttle valves

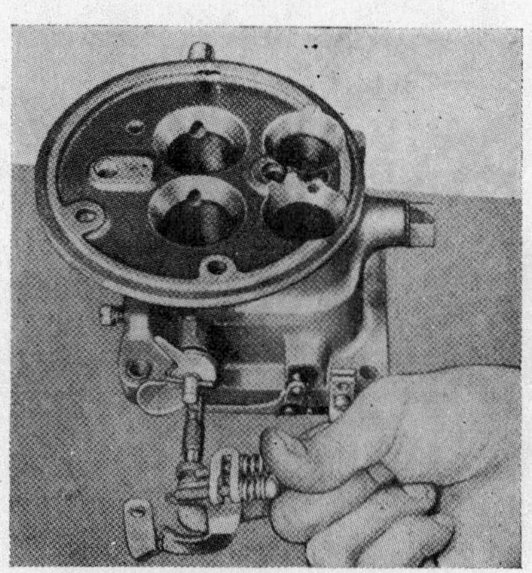

Fig. 10—Remove the throttle shaft

Fig. 12—Take out the fuel inlet adapter, filter, spring and gasket

Selecto-Matic Carburetor Choke

ADJUSTMENT

The only adjustment required is the position of the operating lever on the thermostatic control unit. To make this adjustment, proceed as follows:

Move the lever until the hole in the brass shaft lines up with the slot in the bearing and insert a 5/64 in. rod through the hole in the shaft and down into the notch in the base of the unit. Loosen clamp screw on the lever and push the lever upward until the carburetor choke valve is closed tight against a .010 in. feeler. Hold the lever in this position, tighten clamp screw in lever and remove rod from hole in shaft.

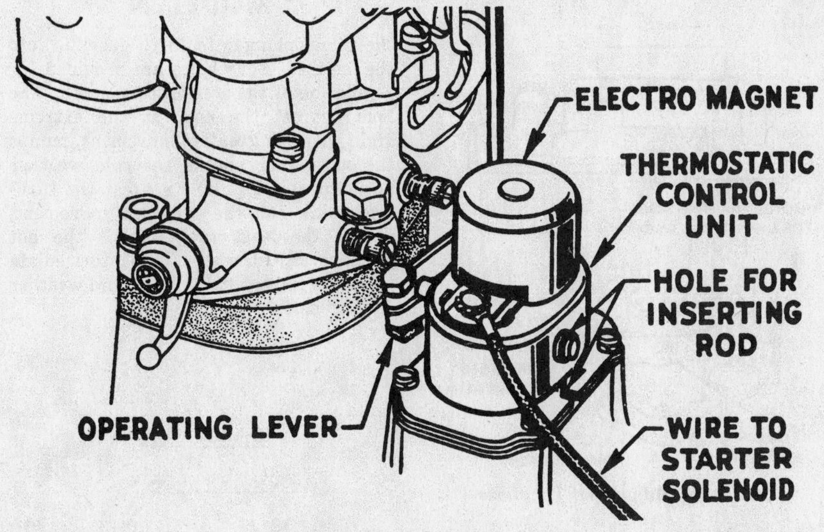

Selecto-matic choke

Automatic Choke

The mechanism of this automatic choke is built into the carburetor body and consists of a thermostatic spring coil in a case at the lower end of the throttle valve body and a vacuum piston in a cylinder under the thermostat case. The thermostat coil and vacuum piston are connected to a lever from which a rod extends to the choke lever. The lever which is connected to the thermostat coil and vacuum piston is mounted on the fast idle cam shaft and actuates the fast idle cam through a spring link.

To remove the thermostat and case assembly, take out screws on edge of case and lift off assembly. The free end of the thermostat coil should be directly over the mark on the holder plate at 100 deg. F. Defective parts should be replaced, as no adjustment is provided to align end of thermostat coil with mark.

To set thermostat, align mark on holder plate with mark on thermostat case after loosening lockscrew on holder plate. Tighten screw when marks are aligned. Setting can be varied to suit special conditions by rotating holder plate clockwise for leaner setting, counterclockwise for richer setting.

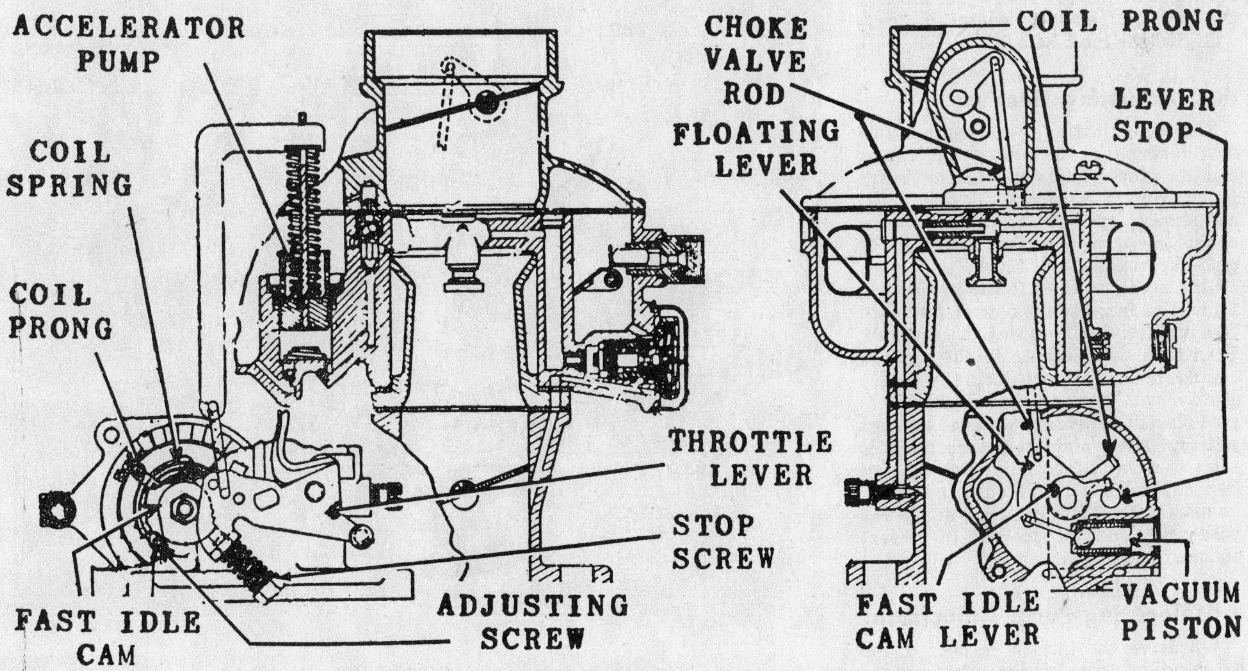

Chandler Groves-Holley-Ford automatic choke arrangement

MODEL N

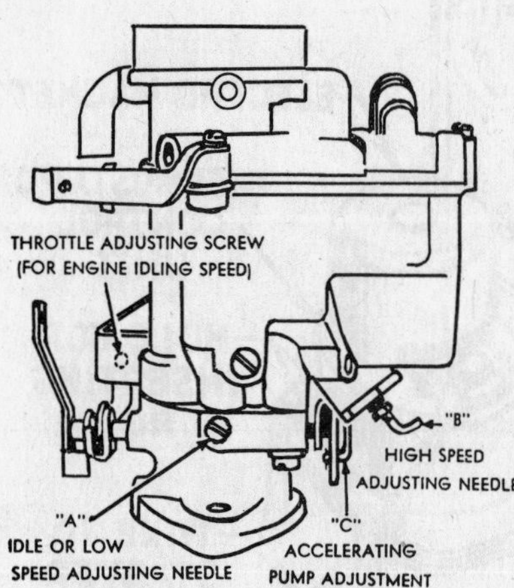

Model N—Adjustment Locations

Idle Speed Adjustment

First set the throttle adjusting screw so that the engine idles at a speed approximating 8 mph. The idle mixture adjusting needle controls the delivery of gasoline to the engine at idle speed. To check adjustment, turn needle to the right until the engine starts to run "ragged" from lack of fuel (about ¼ turn). From this position, back off about ½ turn until the engine starts to "roll" or gallop from too rich a mixture. Setting the needle to the richest mixture that will not cause the engine to "roll" will give the most satisfactory idle.

Fuel Adjusting Needle

The fuel adjusting needle controls fuel flow during the widest operating range, and its proper adjustment is necessary for maximum economy. To check the adjustment, open the throttle until the engine speed is equivalent to 35 to 40 mph (approximately 2,000 RPM). Back off the needle to the left (approximately 1 turn) to increase the flow of fuel until the highest engine speed is obtained. Then turn the needle in to the right to cut down flow of fuel until the engine slows down. The point at which the engine starts to speed up provides the best setting. After high speed adjustment is correct, recheck the idle system because in many cases a better adjustment can be made after the high speed needle has been set. Tighten lock nut to prevent change in setting.

Accelerating Pump Adjustment

Whenever the throttle is opened, the accelerating lever causes movement of the pump plunger to force gasoline into the engine. Four holes are provided for regulation of the accelerating pump. The hole nearest the end, at the extreme right, has the greatest movement, pumps the most fuel, and is the cold weather adjustment. The hole nearest the turning point has the shortest movement, pumps the least fuel, and is the hot weather adjustment. The intermediate holes are for normal driving and weather conditions.

Inlet and Float System

There are two inlets provided, and the fuel inlet-strainer assembly should be used. If disassembly is ever required to clean the float valve and seat, be sure to check the float at 1-51/64 in. from the bottom of the float to the top of the bowl.

Economizer

The top of the metering pin to the top of the metering pin seat should be 13/64 in.

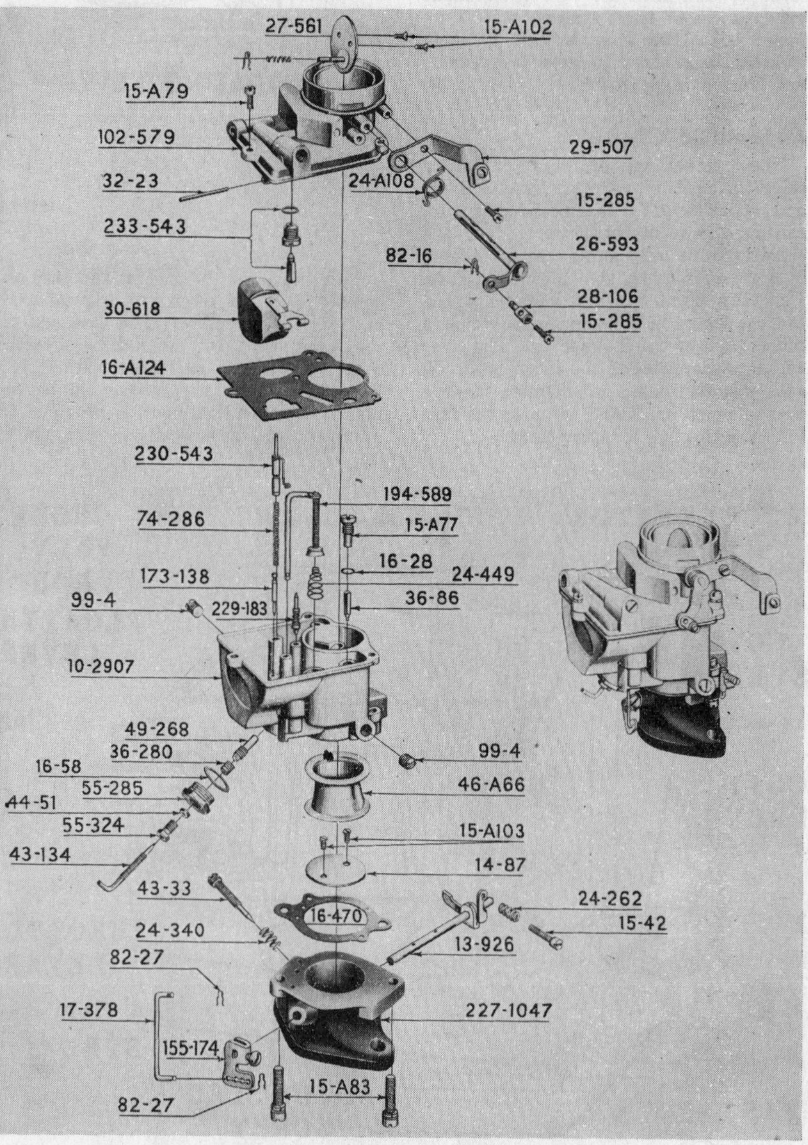

Exploded view of model "N" carburetor

MODEL NNF

Idle Speed Adjustment

The throttle adjusting screw controls the idle speed and should be set so that the car will idle at engine speed approximating 8 mph. Turn the screw to the *right* to increase the speed and to the *left* to decrease the speed.

Idle Mixture Adjusting Needles

The idle mixture adjustment controls the delivery of gasoline at idle speed and during part throttle up to 20 mph. Turning the idle adjustment needles to the right closes off the gasoline, to the left increases the flow. Always use your fingers to adjust. Too much pressure, especially if applied with screw driver, will result in damage to the needle.

Both needles have been set at the factory to approximately the correct setting. Since both operate independently, they are adjusted separately. When making minor adjustment to the factory setting on a carburetor, usually it is both practical and convenient to turn the needles independently, first in a clockwise direction until the motor falters, and then by backing off slightly until the motor runs smoothly.

If it is necessary to change the adjustment, select either one of the idle screws and turn slowly all the way to the right until the needle seats, then turn slowly to the left (about ¾ to 1½ turns) to permit more and more fuel to flow until the engine "rolls" from richness. The next step is to turn the needle to the right (about ¾ to 1½ turns), closing off the fuel until the engine runs "ragged" or irregularly from leanness. The screw should then be backed off to the left to the richest mixture that will not cause the engine to "roll" or run unevenly.

Repeat this procedure with the other idle adjusting screw.

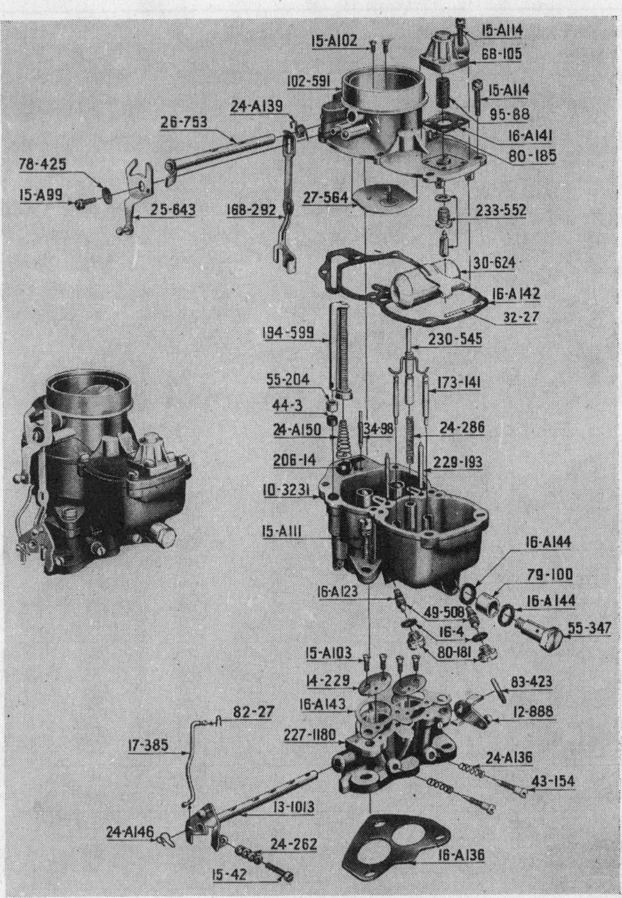

Exploded view of model "NNF" carburetor

Accelerating Pump

When the throttle is opened, the movement of the accelerating pump lever causes the pump plunger to move downward, forcing gasoline under pressure out the pump discharge jets. This provides the additional fuel needed for acceleration.

There are three holes in the accelerating pump lever for positioning the pump connecting rod. The hole at the right, nearest the turning point, has the shortest movement and furnishes the least amount of fuel for acceleration during hot weather driving. The hole at the left has the longest movement and provides maximum accelerating fuel during cold weather. The center position is used for normal driving and weather conditions.

To change the pump adjustment, it is not necessary to disconnect any parts. Merely push the end of the pump connecting rod inward away from the lever as far as it will go and slide the rod to the new position.

Float System

The majority of carburetor flooding occurs when dirt or foreign matter becomes lodged between the float valve and float seat. A fuel inlet screen is integrally constructed within the fuel inlet and should be periodically cleaned. If the carburetor is disassembled, check the float height at 1-11/32 in. from the bottom of the float to the top of the bowl before re-assembly.

Economizer

Whenever the manifold vacuum drops below 5 inches of mercury—that is, whenever the engine is pulling hard or at high speed, and consequently, when a power mixture is required—the vacuum step-up spring has been calibrated to cause the metering pin to lift out of the metering jet to permit additional fuel to flow to the engine.

Normally no adjustment is required. If the carburetor is disassembled for cleaning, check the timing height before re-assembly. With the vacuum piston seated, the groove in the metering pins should be flush with the top of the metering pin housing. To adjust to this position, bend lifting wire.

BUICK SPECIFICATIONS

Starting Serial and Motor Numbers

Starting Serial Numbers

Year	Serial Number
1940	3596807
1941	3880012
1942	4257442
1946	4364445
1947	4524531
1948	4801266
1949	5020984
1950	5360001
1951	6031301
1952	6436001
1953	6740001

Location

1940—Plate under hood on right frame side rail.

1941—Plate under hood on right side of dash.

1942-1953—Plate under hood on right side of dash, plate on left front door pillar, plate on front of left frame side rail or stamped on left front frame crossmember extension.

Starting Motor Numbers

At the request of the Buick Division actual motor numbers are not listed, as they have no particular bearing on the year model. Buick models are designated entirely by serial numbers.

Location of Motor Numbers

1940-1953—Boss on right side of crankcase below push rod cover.

General Specifications

Year	Model	Wheelbase (in.)	Tread (in.) Front	Tread (in.) Rear	Overall Dimensions (in.) Length	Overall Dimensions (in.) Width	Overall Dimensions (in.) Height■	Shipping Weight* (lb.)	Tire Size (in.)
1941	Series 40	121	59	62	209			3730	6.50-16
	Series 50	121	59	62	210			3770	6.50-16
	Series 60	126	59	62	214			4025	7.00-15
	Series 70	126	59	62	215			4010	7.00-15
	Series 90	139	58	63	229				7.50-16
1942	Series 40A	118	59	62	202			3650	6.50-15
	Series 40B	121	59	62	208			3760	6.50-16
	Series 50	124	59	62	213			3890	6.50-16
	Series 60	126	59	62	213			4065	7.00-15
	Series 70	129	59	62	217			4150	7.00-15
	Series 90	139	59	63	226			4665	7.50-16
1946	Series 50	124	59	62	212	79	65		6.50-16
	Series 70	129	59	62	217	79	65		7.00-15
1947-48	Series 40	121	59	62	208	78	67	3720	6.50-16
	Series 50	124	59	62	212	79	65	3910	6.50-16
	Series 70	129	59	62	217	79	65	4385	7.00-15
1949	Series 40	121	59	62	208	78	67	3695	6.50-16
	Series 50	121	59	62	209	79	66	3835	7.60-15
	Series 70	126	59	62	214	79	66	4205	8.20-15
1950	Series 40	122	59	62	204	79	64	3715	7.60-15
	Series 50	122	59	62	204	80	64	3745	7.60-15
	Series 70	126	59	62	209	80	64	4135	8.00-15
1951	Series 40	122	59	59	205	77	63	3680	7.60-15
	Series 50	122	59	62	206	80	63	3755	7.60-15
	Series 70	126	59	62	211	80	63	4240	8.00-15
1952	40, 8 cyl.	122	59	59	204	76	63		7.60-15
	50, 8 cyl.	126	59	62	210	80	63		7.60-15
	70, 8 cyl.	130	59	62	215	80	63		8.00-15
1953	40, 8 cyl.	122	59	59	205	76	63		7.60-15
	50, 70, V8	126	60	62	211	80	61		8.00-15

■—Road to roof, no load. *—Cheapest 5 pass. 4 door Sedan or equivalent.

General Engine Specifications

Year	Model	Number of Cylinders Bore and Stroke	Piston Displacement, Cubic Inches	Compression Ratio (To-1)	Taxable (A.M.A.) Hp.	Developed Horse Power: Bare Engine	Developed Horse Power: With Accessories	Maximum Torque Ft. Lbs.
1941	40, 50	8-3 3/32 x 4 1/8	248.0	7.00†	30.63	‡125 @ 3800		‡217 @ 2000
	60, 70, 90	8-3 7/16 x 4 5/16	320.2	7.00	37.81	165 @ 3800		278 @ 2200

General Engine Specifications—*continued*

Year	Model	Number of Cylinders Bore and Stroke	Piston Displacement, Cubic Inches	Compression Ratio (To–1)	Taxable (A.M.A.) Hp.	Developed Horse Power: Bare Engine	Developed Horse Power: With Accessories	Maximum Torque Ft. Lbs.
1942	40, 50	8-3 3/32 x 4 1/8	248.0	6.00	30.63	110 @ 3400	....	200 @ 2000
	60, 70 90	8-3 7/16 x 4 5/16	320.2	6.70	37.81	165 @ 3800	....	278 @ 2200
1946	40, 50	8-3 3/32 x 4 1/8	248.0	6.30	30.63	110 @ 3600	....	206 @ 2000
	70	8-3 7/16 x 4 5/16	320.2	6.60	37.81	144 @ 3600	133 @ 3300	276 @ 2000
1947	40, 50	8-3 3/32 x 4 1/8	248.0	6.30	30.63	110 @ 3600	105 @ 3500	206 @ 2000
	70	8-3 7/16 x 4 5/16	320.2	6.60	37.81	144 @ 3600	133 @ 3300	276 @ 2000
1948	40	8-3 3/32 x 4 1/8	248.0	6.30	30.63	110 @ 3600	105 @ 3500	206 @ 2000
	50	8-3 3/32 x 4 1/8	248.0	6.30	30.63	115 @ 3600	105 @ 3500	206 @ 2000
	70	8-3 7/16 x 4 5/16	320.2	6.60	37.81	144 @ 3600	133 @ 3300	276 @ 2000
1949	40, 50	8-3 3/32 x 4 1/8	248.1	6.30*	30.63	110 @ 3600	105 @ 3500^	206 @ 2000^
	70	8-3 7/16 x 4 5/16	320.2	6.60	37.81	150 @ 3600	139 @ 3300	280 @ 2000
1950	40	8-3 3/32 x 4 1/8	248.1	6.60	30.63	115 @ 3600	110 @ 3600	212 @ 2000
	40 with Dynaflow	8-3 3/32 x 4 1/8	248.1	7.20	30.63	122 @ 3600	....	....
	50	8-3 3/16 x 4 1/8	263.3	6.90	32.51	124 @ 3600	119 @ 3600	220 @ 2000
	50 with Dynaflow	8-3 3/32 x 4 1/8	263.3	7.20	32.51	128 @ 3600	....	....
	70	8-3 7/16 x 4 5/16	320.2	7.20	37.81	152 @ 3600	134 @ 3400	280 @ 2000
1951	40	8-3 3/16 x 4 1/8	263.3	6.60	32.51	120 @ 3600	115 @ 3600	212 @ 2000
	40 with Dynaflow	8-3 3/16 x 4 1/8	263.3	7.20	32.51	....	....	....
	50	8-3 3/16 x 4 1/8	263.3	6.90	32.51	124 @ 3600	119 @ 3600	220 @ 2000
	50 with Dynaflow	8-3 3/16 x 4 1/8	263.3	7.20	32.51	....	....	....
	70	8-3 7/16 x 4 5/16	320.2	7.20	37.81	152 @ 3600	144 @ 3400	280 @ 2000
1952	40, 8 Cyl.	8-3 3/16 x 4 1/8	263.3	6.60	32.51	120 @ 3600	....	215 @ 2000
	40, with Dynaflow, 8 Cyl.	8-3 3/16 x 4 1/8	263.3	7.20	32.51	....	....	....
	50, 8 Cyl.	8-3 3/16 x 4 1/8	263.3	6.90	32.51	124 @ 3600	....	220 @ 2000
	50, with Dynaflow, 8 Cyl.	8-3 3/16 x 4 1/8	263.3	7.20	32.51	....	....	....
	70, 8 Cyl.	8-3 7/16 x 4 5/16	320.2	7.50	37.81	170 @ 3800	....	280 @ 2400
1953	40, 8 Cyl.	8-3 3/16 x 4 1/8	263.3	7.01*	32.51	125 @ 3800	....	224 @ 2200
	50, V8	8-4 x 3 13/64	322.0	8.0*	51.2	164 @ 4000	....	286 @ 2200
	70, V8	8-4 x 3 13/64	322.0	8.5	51.2	188 @ 4000	....	300 @ 2400

*—Series 50—6.60.
†—Series 40—6.5.
‡—Series 40—HP 115 @ 3500; torque 210 ft. lb. @ 2000. Torque—212 ft. lb. @ 2000; 208 ft. lb. @ 2000.
^—Series,50—HP 115 @ 3600; with accessories,110 @ 3500.

Dimensions of Valves

Year	Model	Overall Length: Inlet	Overall Length: Exhaust	Head Diameter: Inlet	Head Diameter: Exhaust	Seat Angle (deg.): Inlet	Seat Angle (deg.): Exhaust	Stem Diameter: Inlet	Stem Diameter: Exhaust	Key Type	O.D. of Seat Insert: Inlet	O.D. of Seat Insert: Exhaust
1941–42	40, 50	5.109	5.109	1.531	1.343	45	45	.372	.371	split lock	....	....
	60, 70, 90	5.250	5.250	1.781	1.437	45	45	.375	.371	split lock	....	....
1946 to 49	40, 50	5.109	5.109	1.531	1.343	45	45	.372	.371	split lock	....	....
	70	5.250	5.250	1.781	1.437	45	45	.372	.371	split lock	....	....
1950–51	40, 50	5.109	5.109	1.531	1.344	45	45	.372	.372	split lock	....	....
	70	5.250	5.250	1.781	1.438	45	45	.372	.372	split lock	....	....
1952	40, 50, 8 cyl.	5.109	5.109	1.531	1.344	45	45	.3720	.3720	....	....	....
	70, 8 cyl.	5.25	5.25	1.781	1.437	45	45	.3714	.3714	....	....	....
1953	40	5.109	5.109	1.531	1.531	45	45	.3720	.3720	....	....	....
	50, 70	4.346	4.346	1.750	1.750	45	45	.3720	.3720	....	....	....

Engine Overhaul Specifications

		PISTONS				RING GAP CLEARANCES (Maximum)				PISTON PIN		ROD BEARINGS		
			Piston Skirt Clearances (Maximum)											
Year	Model	Removed From	Top	Bottom	Limit	Top Ring	Second Ring	Third Ring	Oil Ring	Type	Fit	Oil Clearance	Wear Limit	Side Play
1940	60, 70	A	.0020	.0026	.006	.015	.015	.015	.015	LR	.00035	.0008–.0018	.004	.005–.010
	80, 90	A	.0020	.0026	.006	.015	.015	.015	.015	LR	.00035	.0008–.0018	.004	.005–.010
1941	40, 50	A	.0018	.0024	.006	.015	.015	.015	.015	LR	.00035	.0008–.0018	.004	.005–.010
	60, 70, 90	A	.0020	.0026	.006	.015	.015	.015	.015	LR	.00035	.0008–.0018	.004	.005–.010
1942	40, 50	A	.0017	.0023	.006	.015	.015	.015	.015	LR	.00035	.0008–.0018	.004	.005–.010
	60, 70, 90	A	.0026	.0032	.006	.015	.015	.015	.015	LR	.00035	.0008–.0018	.004	.005–.010
1946	40, 50	A	.0021	.0018	.005	.015	.015	.015	.015	LR	.00035	.0008–.0018	.004	.005–.010
	70	A	.0023	.0018	.005	.015	.015	.015	.015	LR	.00035	.0008–.0018	.004	.005–.010
1947	40, 50	A	.0018	.0024	.006	.015	.015	.015	.015	LR	.00035	.0008–.0018	.004	.005–.010
	70	A	.0020	.0026	.006	.015	.015	.015	.015	LR	.00035	.0008–.0018	.004	.005–.010
1948	40, 50	A	.0021	.0016	.005	.015	.015	.015	.015	LR	.00035	.0008–.0018	.004	.005–.010
	70	A	.0023	.0018	.005	.015	.015	.015	.015	LR	.00035	.0008–.0018	.004	.005–.010
1949	40, 50	A	.0021	.0015	.005	.015	.015	.015	.015	LR	.00035	.0005–.0018	.004	.005–.010
	70	A	.0023	.0017	.005	.015	.015	.015	.015	LR	.00035	.0005–.0018	.004	.005–.010
1950	40, 50	A	.0021	.0015	.005	.015	.015	.015	.015	LR	.00035	.0005–.0018	.004	.005–.010
	70	A	.0023	.0017	.005	.015	.015	.015	.015	LR	.00035	.0005–.0018	.004	.005–.010
1951	40, 50	A	.0018	.0012	.005	.015	.015	.015	.015	LR	.00035	.0005–.0016	.004	.005–.010
	70	A	.0020	.0014	.005	.015	.015	.015	.015	LR	.00035	.0005–.0016	.004	.005–.010
1952	40, 50, 8 Cyl.	A	.0018	.0012	.005	.015	.015	.015	.0019	LR	.00030	.0011	.004	.007
	70, 8 Cyl.	A	.0020	.0014	.005	.015	.015	.015	.0017	LR	.00030	.0011	.004	.007
1953	40, 8 Cyl.	A	.0018	.0012	.005	.015	.015	.015	.0019	LR	.0003	.0011	.004	.007
	50, 70, V8	A	.0013	.0008	.005	.015	.015	....	.0015	LR	.0004	.0012	.004	.007

A—Piston and rod removed from above. B—Before top center. LR—Locked in rod. **—A loss of 15 lb pressure is the low limit.

Pistons and Piston Pins

		PISTONS				PISTON PINS		
Year	Model	Diameter	Material	Type	No. of Rings	Length	Diameter	How Held
1940	Series 40, 50	3.09375	Alum.	Ts, C	4	$2\frac{11}{16}$	.8125	R
	Series 60, 70, 80, 90	3.4375	Alum.	Ts, C	4	$3\frac{1}{16}$	.875	R
1941 to 49	Series 40, 50	3.09375	Alum.	C, Md, Trs	4	$2\frac{11}{16}$	.8126	R
	Series 60, 70, 90	3.4375	Alum.	C, Md, Trs	4	$3\frac{1}{16}$	.875	R
1950–51	Series 40	3.09375	Alum. Alloy	Trs, Tt, C	4	$2\frac{11}{16}$	.8127	R
	Series 50	3.1875	Alum. Alloy	Trs, Tt, C	4	$2\frac{11}{16}$	.8127	R
	Series 70	3.4375	Alum. Alloy	Trs, Tt, C	4	$3\frac{1}{16}$	.8747	R
1952	40, 50, 8 cyl.	3.187	Alum. Alloy	C,Trs	4	2.688	.8127	R
	70, 8 cyl.	3.437	Alum. Alloy	C,Trs	4	3.062	.8747	R
1953	40, 8 cyl.	3.187	Alum. Alloy	C,Trs	4	2.688	.8127	R
	50, 70, V8	4.00	Alum. Alloy	C,Trs	3	3.400	.940	R

Tt—Turbulator top.
Md—Modified dome.
Ts—"T" slot.
Trs—Transverse slot.
C—Cam ground.
R—Locked in rod.

and Wear Limit Table

CRANKSHAFT		VALVES									OPERATING OIL PRESSURE			
Main Bearing Oil Clear-ance	Shaft End Play	Spring Tension (Maximum) Inlet	Spring Tension (Maximum) Exhaust	Low Limit	Guide Clear-ance	Seat Angle Inlet	Seat Angle Ex-haust	Valve Tim-ing, Inlet Valve Opens (Deg.)	Cam-shaft Drive	Gear Marks	Pounds At M.P.H.	Low Limit§	Model	Year
0007–.0022	.004–.008	45@1 5/16	70@1 19/32	**	.0021–.0039	45°	45°	14B	Chain	†	45@35	25	60, 70	1940
.0007–.0022	.004–.008	48@1 5/16	70@1 19/32	**	.0021–.0039	45°	45°	14B	Chain	†	45@35	25	80, 90	
.0007–.0022	.004–.008	48@1 5/16	70@1 19/32	**	.0021–.0039	45°	45°	13B	Chain	†	45@35	25	40, 50	1941
.0007–.0022	.004–.008	48@1 5/16	70@1 19/32	**	.0021–.0038	45°	45°	14B	Chain	†	45@35	25	60, 70, 90	
.0007–.0025	.004–.008	51@1 5/16	77@1 19/32	**	.0021–.0038	45°	45°	13B	Chain	†	45@35	25	40, 50	1942
.0007–.0025	.004–.008	51@1 5/16	77@1 19/32	**	.0021–.0039	45°	45°	14B	Chain	†	45@35	25	60, 70, 90	
.0007–.0025	.004–.008	51@1 5/16	77@1 19/32	**	.0021–.0039	45°	45°	13B	Chain	†	45@35	25	40, 50	1946
.0007–.0025	.004–.008	51@1 5/16	77@1 19/32	**	.0021–.0039	45°	45°	14B	Chain	†	35@35	20	70	
.0007–.0025	.004–.008	51@1 5/16	77@1 19/32	**	.0021–.0039	45°	45°	13B	Chain	†	35@35	20	40, 50	1947
.0007–.0025	.004–.008	51@1 5/16	77@1 19/32	**	.0021–.0039	45°	45°	14B	Chain	†	35@35	20	70	
.0007–.0025	.004–.008	51@1 5/16	77@1 19/32	**	.0021–.0039	45°	45°	13B	Chain	†	35@35	20	40, 50	1948
.0007–.0025	.004–.008	51@1 5/16	77@1 19/32	**	.0021–.0039	45°	45°	14B	Chain	†	35@35	20	70	
.0005–.0020	.004–.008	51@1 5/16	77@1 19/32	**	.0021–.0039	45°	45°	13B	Chain	†	35@35	20	40, 50	1949
.0005–.0020	.004–.008	52@1 5/16	120@1 19/32	**	.0021–.0039	45°	45°	14B	Chain	†	35@35	20	70	
.0005–.0020	.004–.008	51@1 5/16	77@1 19/32	**	.0021–.0039	45°	45°	13B	Chain	†	35@35	20	40, 50	1950
.0005–.0020	.004–.008	52@1 5/16	120@1 19/32	**	.0021–.0039	45°	45°	14B	Chain	†	35@35	20	70	
.0006–.0020	.004–.008	51@1 5/16	77@1 19/32	**	.0021–.0039	45°	45°	13B	Chain	†	35@35	20	40, 50	1951
.0006–.0020	.004–.008	52@1 5/16	120@1 19/32	**	.0021–.0039	45°	45°	14B	Chain	†	35@35	20	70	
.0013	.006	54@1.313	80@1.594	......	.0025	45°	45°	13B	Chain	†	35@35	.....	40, 50, 8 Cyl.	1952
.0013	.006	55@1.320	104@1.594	......	.0025	45°	45°	14B	Chain	†	35@35	.....	70, 8 Cyl.	
.0013	.006	54@1.320	104@1.594	......	.0030	45°	45°	13B	Chain	†	35@35	.....	40, 8 Cyl.	1953
.0018	.006	55@1.320	91@1.120	......	.0030	45°	45°	25B	Chain	†	35@35	.....	50, 70, V8	

†—11 chain Pins or 10 links between the marks on sprockets.
§—Engine may be operated safely at much lower pressures, but low oil pressure indicates malfunction which should be corrected.

Crankshaft Bearing Journal Sizes

Year	Model	Connecting Rod Journals		Main Bearing Journals				
		Diameter	Length	No. 1 Diameter	No. 2 Diameter	No. 3 Diameter	No. 4 Diameter	No. 5 Diameter
1940 to 48	Series 40-50	1.997–1.999	1.218–1.221	2.3095–2.3115	2.3725–2.3745	2.4345–2.4365	2.4975–2.4995	2.5595–2.5615
	Series 60, 70, 80, 90	2.248–2.249	1.312–1.315	2.5605–2.5615	2.6235–2.6245	2.6855–2.6865	2.7485–2.7495	2.8105–2.8115
1949	Series 40, 50	1.998–1.999	1.218–1.221	2.3105–2.3115	2.3735–2.3745	2.4355–2.4365	2.4985–2.4995	2.5605–2.5615
	Series 70	2.248–2.249	1.312–1.315	2.5605–2.5615	1.6235–2.6245	2.6855–2.6865	2.7485–2.7495	2.8105–2.8115
1950	Series 40	1.998–1.999	1.218–1.221	2.3105–2.3115	2.3735–2.3745	2.4355–2.4365	2.4985–2.4995	2.5605–2.5615
	Series 50	2.125–2.126	1.036–1.039	2.5625–2.5635	2.5625–2.5635	2.5625–2.5635	2.5625–2.5635	2.5625–2.5635
	Series 70	2.248–2.249	1.312–1.315	2.5605–2.5615	2.6235–2.6245	2.6855–2.6865	2.7485–2.7495	2.8105–2.8115
1951	Series 40, 50	2.125–2.126	1.030–1.033	2.5625–2.5635	2.5625–2.5635	2.5625–2.5635	2.5625–2.5635	2.5625–2.5635
	Series 70	2.248–2.249	1.306–1.309	2.5605–2.5615	2.6235–2.6245	2.6855–2.6865	2.7485–2.7495	2.8105–2.8115
1952	40, 50, 8 cyl.	2.125–2.126	1.030–1.033	2.5625–2.5635	2–5625–2.5635	2.5625–2.5635	2.5625–2.5635	2.5625–2.5635
	70, 8 cyl.	2.248–2.249	1.306–1.309	2.5605–2.5615	2.6235–2.6245	2.6855–2.6865	2.7485–2.7495	2.8105–2.8115
1953	40, 8 cyl.	2.1257	....	2.562–1.266	2.562–1.031	2.562–1.547	2.562–1.031	2.562–1.781
	50, 70, V8	2.2495	....	2.4985–1.220	2.4985–1.250	2.4985–1.250	2.4985–1.250	2.4985–1.765

BUICK SPECIFICATIONS

Engine Tune-Up Specifications

Year	Model	Spark Plugs: Type	Spark Plugs: Gap	Distributor: Point Gap	Distributor: Cam Dwell, (Deg.)	Ignition Timing, (Deg.)	Ignition Timing Mark and Location	Compression Pressure at R.P.M.	Operating Tappet Clearance: Inlet	Operating Tappet Clearance: Exhaust	Carburetor Fuel Float Height	Minimum Engine Idle Speed at R.P.M.
1940	60, 70	AC-46	.025	.015	31	6B	ADV flwh	130@1000	.015H	.015H	3/64" float	450
	80, 90	AC-46	.025	.015	31	6B	ADV flwh	130@1000	.015H	.015H	3/64" float	450
1941	40, 50	AC-106	.025	.015	31	^2B	ADV flwh	148@1000	.015H	.015H	3/16" float	450
	60, 70, 90	AC-106	.025	.015	31	6B	ADV flwh	151@1000	.015H	.015H	3/16" float	450
1942	40, 50	AC-46	.025	.015	31	4B	ADV flwh	125@1000	.015H	.015H	3/16" float	450
	60, 70, 90	AC-46	.025	.015	31	6B	ADV flwh	144@1000	.015H	.015H	3/16" float	450
1946	40, 50	AC-48	.025	.015	31	4B	ADV flwh	135@1000	.015H	.015H	3/16" float	450
	70	AC-48	.025	.015	31	6B	ADV flwh	140@1000	.015H	.015H	3/16" float	450
1947	40, 50	AC-48	.025	.015	31	4B	ADV flwh	135@1000	.015H	.015H	3/16" float	450
	70	AC-48	.025	.015	31	6B	ADV flwh	140@1000	.015H	.015H	3/16" float	450
1948	40	AC-48	.025	.015	NR	4B	ADV flwh	135@1000	.015H	.015H	5/16" float	450
	50	AC-48	.025	.015	NR	4B	ADV flwh	140@1000	.015H	.015H	5/32" float	450
	70	AC-48	.025	.015	NR	6B	ADV flwh	140@1000	.015H	.015H	3/32" float	450
1949	40, 50	AC-48	.025	.015	NR	4B	ADV flwh	140@1000	‡.015H	‡.015H	5/32" float	450
	70	AC-48	.025	.015	NR	6B	ADV flwh	150@1000	AA	AA	5/32" float	450
1950	40	AC-48	.025	.015	NR	4B	ADV flwh	140@1000	.015H	.015H	5/32" float	450
	50	AC-48	.025	.016	NR	4B	ADV flwh	150@1000	AA	AA	5/32" float	450
	70	AC-48	.025	.015	NR	6B	ADV flwh	160@1000	AA	AA	5/32" float	450
1951	40	AC-46X	.025	.015	NR	4B	ADV flwh	140@1000	.015H	.015H	5/32" float	450
	50	AC-46X	.025	.015	NR	4B	ADV flwh	150@1000	AA	AA	5/32" float	350
	70	AC-46X	.025	.015	NR	6B	ADV flwh	160@1000	AA	AA	5/32" float	450
1952	40, 8 Cyl.	AC-46X	.025	.015	NR	4B	ADV flwh	....	.015H	.015H	5/32" float	450
	50, 8 Cyl.	AC-46X	.025	.015	NR	4B	ADV flwh	....	AA	AA	5/32" float	450
	70, 8 Cyl.	AC-46X	.025	.015	NR	6B	ADV flwh	....	AA	AA	*	450
1953	40, 8 Cyl.	AC-46X	.025	.015	NR	4B	ADV flwh	....	.015	.015	....	450
	50, V8	AC-44-5	.035	.015	NR	5B	ADV flwh	....	AA	AA	....	450
	70, V8	AC-44-5	.035	.015	NR	5B	ADV flwh	....	AA	AA	....	450

H—HOT
AA—Automatic Adjustment
AC—AC Spark Plug Div.

B—Before Top Center
^—Model (50)—4° Bu DC.

‡—Series 50 optional engine with hyd. lifters.
NR—Not Recommended by Factory—Use Point Gap.

Piston Ring Dimensions

Year	Model	Cylinder Bore	Top Ring: Width	Top Ring: Gap	Top Ring: Depth	Second Ring: Width	Second Ring: Gap	Second Ring: Depth	Third Ring: Width	Third Ring: Gap	Third Ring: Depth	Oil Ring: Width	Oil Ring: Gap	Oil Ring: Depth
1940	40, 50	3 3/32	3/32	.015	.155	3/32	.012	.140	3/16	.012	.140	3/16	.012	.140
	60, 70, 80, 90	3 7/16	3/32	.015	.172	3/32	.012	.150	3/16	.012	.150	3/16	.012	.150
1941–47	40, 50	3 3/32	3/32	.015	.155	3/32	.015	.140	3/16	.015	.140	3/16	.015	.140
	60, 70, 90	3 7/16	3/32	.015	.172	3/32	.015	.150	3/16	.015	.140	3/16	.015	.140
1948	40, 50	3 3/32	3/32	.015	.160	3/32	.015	.140	3/16	.015	.140	3/16	.015	.140
	70	3 7/16	3/32	.015	.160	3/32	.015	.140	3/16	.015	.140	3/16	.015	.140
1949	40, 50	3 3/32	3/32	.015	.160	3/32	.015	.140	3/16	.015	.140	.1860	.0015	.155
	70	3 7/16	3/32	.015	.170	3/32	.015	.150	3/16	.015	.150	.1860	.0015	.170
1950	40	3 3/32	3/32	.015	.160	3/32	.015	.160	3/16	.015	.140	1865	.0015	.150
	50	3 3/16	3/32	.015	.160	3/32	.015	.160	3/16	.015	.147	.1865	.0016	.155
1951	40, 50	3 3/16	3/32	.015	.160	3/32	.015	.160	3/16	.015	.147	.1865	.0018	.155
1952	40, 50, 8 Cyl.	3 3/16	.094	.015	.165	.094	.015	.165	.187	.015	.165	.187	.0019	.165
	70, 8 Cyl.	3 7/16	.094	.015	.182	.094	.015	.182	.187	.015	.182	.187	.0017	.182
1953	40, 8 Cyl.	3 3/16	.094	.015	.155	.094	.015	.155	.187	.015	.142	.187	.0019	.149
	50, 70, V8	4.0	.078	.015	.200	.078	.015	.200	.187	.0015	.170	.187	.0015	.170

Tension Wrench Specifications

Year	Model	Cylinder Head		Spark Plug		Connecting Rod Bolts or Nuts		Main Bearing Bolt		Flywheel Bolts		Vibration Damper Bolts	
		Lbs.-Ft.	Thread	Lbs.-Ft.	Thread	Lbs.-Ft.	Thread	Lbs.-Ft.	Thread	Lbs.-Ft.	Thread	Lbs.-Ft.	Thread
1940–41	40, 50	65-70	7/16-14	22-28	14 mm*	40-45	3/8-24	90-100	1/2-13	35-50	....	100-110	....
	60, 70, 80, 90	65-70	7/16-14	22-28	14 mm	60-65	7/16-24	90-100	1/2-13	45-55	....	100-110	....
1942	40, 50	65-70	7/16-14	22-28	14 mm	45-50	3/8-24	120-130	1/2-13	35-50	....	100-110	....
	60, 70, 90	65-70	7/16-14	22-28	14 mm	60-65	7/16-24	120-130	1/2-13	45-55	....	100-110	....
1946–47	40, 50	65-70	7/16-14	22-28	14 mm	40-45	3/8-24	90-100	1/2-13	35-50	....	100-110	....
	60, 70, 90	65-70	7/16-14	22-28	14 mm	60-65	7/16-24	90-100	1/2-13	45-55	....	100-110	....
1948–49	40, 50	65-70	7/16-14	22-28	14 mm	40-45	3/8-24	90-100	1/2-13	35-40	3/8-24	100-110	3/4-16
	70	65-70	7/16-14	22-28	14 mm	60-65	7/16-24	90-100	1/2-13	45-50	3/8-24	100-110	3/4-16
1950	40, 50	65-70	7/16-14	22-28	14 mm	40-45	3/8-24	90-100	1/2-13	†35-40	†3/8-24	100-110	3/4-16
	70	65-70	7/16-14	22-28	14 mm	60-65	7/16-24	90-100	1/2-13	†35-40	†3/8-24	100-110	3/4-16
1951–52	40, 50; 1953, 40	65-70	7/16-14	22-28	14 mm	60-65	7/16-24	90-100	1/2-13	†35-40	†3/8-24	100-110	3/4-16
	70	65-70	7/16-14	22-28	14 mm	69-65	7/16-24	90-100	1/2-13	†35-40	†3/8-24	100-110	3/4-16
1953	50, 70	....	....	....	....	....	....	....	....	....	....	....	....

†—Dynaflow (50–55), (7/16-24). *—1941—10 mm.

Brake Data

Year	Model	Make	Lining Type	R=Riveted B=Bonded	Drum Diameter	Lining			Clearance	
						Length	Width	Thickness	Toe	Heel
1940	40, 50	BD	WM	R	12	22 11/16	1 3/4	3/16	.009	.009
	60, 70	BD	WM	R	12	22 15/16	2 1/4	3/16	.009	.009
	80, 90	BD	WM	R	14	26 13/16	2	1/4	.009	.009
1941–42	40, 50	BD	WM	R	12	22 11/16	1 3/4	3/16	.015	.015
	60, 70	BD	WM	R	12	22 15/16	2 1/4	3/16	.015	.015
	90	BD	WM	R	14	26 13/16	2	1/4	.015	.015
1946 to 51	40, 50	BD	WM	R	12	23 1/16	1 3/4	3/16	.015	.015
	70	BD	WM	R	12	23 1/16	2 1/4	3/16	.015	.015
1952	40, 50, 8 Cyl.	BD	M	R	12	23 1/16	2 1/4-*1 3/4	3/16	.015	.015
	70, 8 Cyl.	BD	M	R	12	23 1/16	2 1/2-*2 1/4	1/4-*3/16	.015	.015
1953	40, 50, 8 Cyl.	BD	M	R	12	23 1/16	2 1/4-*1 3/4	3/16	.015	.015
	70, 8 Cyl.	BD	M	R	12	23 1/16	2 1/2-*2 1/4	3/16	.015	.015

BD—Bendix or Delco. M—Moulded. *—Rear. WM—Woven on primary, moulded on secondary.

King Pin Specification Chart

Year	Model	KING BOLT			UPPER BUSHING				LOWER BUSHING			
					King Bolt Bushing				King Bolt Bushing			
		Diameter	Length	Bolt Number	Inside Diameter	Outside Diameter	Length	Bushing Number	Inside Diameter	Outside Diameter	Length	Bushing Number
1940 to 51	40, 50, 60, 70	.862	5 1/2	1286029	.859	.993	1 1/4	230601	.859	.993	1 1/4	230601
1952–53	40, 50, 70	....	....	....	....	....	....	....	....	....	....	....

BUICK SPECIFICATIONS

Generators

Year	Model	Generator Number	Field Current at 6 Volts (amps.)	Maximum Safe Output: Volts	Maximum Safe Output: Amperes	Maximum Safe Output: R.P.M.	Brush Spring Tension (oz.)	Voltage Regulator Number
1941 to 48	40, 50	1102679	1.75–1.9	8.0	30	1825	25	1118201
	60, 70, 90	1102668	1.75–1.9	8.0	30	1825	25	1118201
1949	40	1102679	1.75–1.9	8.0	30	1825	25	1118301
	50	1102709	1.90–2.05	8.0	40	1950	25	1118357
	70	1102708	1.90–2.05	8.0	40	1950	25	1118357
1950	40, 50, 70	1102709	1.90–2.05	8.0	40	1950	25	1118364
1951	40, 50, 70	1102754–1102718	1.90–2.05	8.0	40	1950	25	1118364
1952	40, 50, 70, 8 cyl.	1102779	....	7.7	51	2400	24–32	1118729
1953	40, 8 cyl.	1102798	....	7.7	51	2400	24–32	1118729
	50, 70, V8	1102008	....	14.5	30	2300	....	1118749

Front Wheel Alignment

Year	Model	Caster (deg.)	Camber (deg.)	King Pin Inclination (deg.)	Toe-In (inches)	Turning Radius: Inner	Turning Radius: Outer
1941	40, 50	0 to ¾P	⅛N to 1⅛P	4¼	0 to 1/16	22½	20
	60, 70	0 to ¾P	⅛P to 1⅛P	3½ to 4¾	0 to 1/16	22½	20
	80, 90	⅜N to ⅜P	⅜P to ⅞P	4¾	0 to 1/16	24½	20
1942	40A, 40B, 50, 60, 70	⅜N to ⅜P	⅛P to 1⅛P	3½ to 4¾	0 to 1/16	22	20
	90	⅜N to ⅜P	⅜P to ⅞P	4¾	0 to 1/16	24	20
1946	50	0 to ¾P	⅛P to 1⅛P	4⅛	0 to 1/16	21	20
	70	0 to ¾P	⅛P to 1⅛P	4⅛	0 to 1/16	21½	20
1947	40	0 to ¾P	⅛P to 1½P	4⅛	0 to 1/16	21½	20
	50	0 to ¾P	⅛P to 1⅛P	4½	0 to 1/16	21½	20
	70	0 to ¾P	⅛P to 1⅛P	4⅛	0 to 1/16	21½	20
1948	40, 50	¼N to 1½P	⅞P to ⅝N	4¼	1/16 to ⅛	22	20
	70	½P to 1½P	⅞P to ⅝N	4¼	1/16 to ⅛	21½	20
1949	40	¼P to 1½P	⅞P to ⅝N	4¼	1/16 to ¼	22	20
	70	½P to 1½P	⅞P to ⅝N	4¼	1/16 to ¼	21½	20
1950-52	40, 50, 70	¼P to 1½P	⅞P to ⅝N	4¼	1/16 to ⅛	21½	20
1953	40, 50, 70	¼P to 1½P	⅞P to ⅝N	4¼	1/16 to ⅛	18¼	20

P—Positive. N—Negative.

Distributors

Year	Model	Distributor Model Number	Cam Angle (deg.)	Direction of Rotation C=Clockwise CC=Counter Clockwise at Cam End	Breaker Arm Spring Tension	Breaker Point Gap (inches)	Engine R.P.M. when Cent. Advance Starts	Max. Cent. Advance in Engine Deg. at Stated Engine R.P.M.	Vacuum in (inches) of Mercury at which Vacuum Unit Starts	Max. Advance in Engine Deg. at Stated Vacuum	Vacuum Unit Number
1940 to 42	40, 50, 8 cyl.	1110801	31	CC	19–23	.0125–.0175	500	26@3000	5 to 7	11@10 to 13	681H
1940	60, 70, 80, 90, 8 cyl.	1110805	31	CC	19–23	.0125–.0175	500	26@3000	5 to 7	11@10 to 13	681H
1946 to 48	40, 50, 70, 8 cyl.	1110801	31	CC	19–23	.0125–.0175	500	26@3000	5 to 7	11@10 to 13	681H
1949 to 51	40, 50, 70, 8 cyl.	1110815	30	CC	19–23	.015–.0175	500	26@3000	5 to 7	11@10 to 12	1116046
1952	40, 50, 70, 8 cyl.	1110832	NR	CC	19–23	.0125–.0175	....	14@1675	5–7	6–8@12–13	....
1953	40, 8 cyl.	1115380	NR	C	19–23	.0125–.0175	500	13@2000	5–7	11@13	....
	50, 70, 8 cyl.	1115082	NR	C	19–23	.0125–.0175	500	18@2150	5–7	12.5@14	....

NR—Not recommended.

Voltage Regulators

Year	Model	Regulator Number	Grounded P=Positive N=Negative	Voltage Control: Air Gap Points Closed	Voltage Control: Voltage Setting Hot	Current Control: Air Gap Points Closed	Current Control: Current Set Hot	Cut-Out Relay: Point Gap	Cut-Out Relay: Air Gap	Cut-Out Relay: Closing Volt
1940 to 48	40, 50, 60, 70, 80, 90........	1118201	N	.070	7.2–7.4	.080	32–34	.020	.020	6.2–6.7
1949	40..................	1118301	N	.075	7.0–7.7	.075	32–40	.020	.020	5.9–6.8
	50, 70...............	1118357	N	.075	7.0–7.7	.075	40–46	.020	.020	5.9–6.8
1950–51	40, 50, 70............	1118364	N	.075	7.0–7.7	.075	40–46	.020	.020	5.9–6.8
1952	40, 50, 70, 8 cyl..........	1118729	N	....	7.2–7.7	....	45–51	....	....	5.9–6.7
1953	40, 8 cyl..............	1118729	N	....	7.2–7.6	....	45–51	....	....	5.9–6.7
	50, 70, V8............	1118749	N	....	14.5	....	27–30	....	....	12.8

Starters

Year	Model	Unit Model Number	Spring Tension (oz.)	STARTER Lock Test: Volts	Lock Test: Amperes	Lock Test: Torque, (lbs. ft.)	No Load: Volts	No Load: Amperes	No Load: R.P.M.	Direction of Rotation Viewed from Drive End C=Clockwise CC=Counter-clockwise
1940–41	40, 50............	1107005	24–28	5.0	500	25	5.0	65	5000	C
	60, 70, 80, 90.........	1107908	24–28	3.0	600	16	5.0	70	5500	C
1942 to 48	40, 50............	1107049	24–28	3.37	525	12	5.0	65	5000	C
	60, 70, 90..........	1107929	24–28	3.0	600	16	5.67	65	5500	C
1949–50	40..............	1107049	24–28	3.37	525	12	5.0	65	5000	C
	50..............	1107078	24–28	3.4	525	12	5.7	80	5000	C
	70..............	1107953	24–28	3.0	600	15	5.7	80	5500	C
1951	50..............	1107097	24–28	3.37	525	12	5.67	65	5000	C
	70..............	1107981	24–28	3.0	600	16	5.67	65	5500	C
1952	40, 50, 8 cyl.........	1107097	24–28	3.37	525	12	5.67	65	5000	C
	70, 8 cyl...........	1107981	24–28	3.0	600	16	5.67	65	5500	C
1953	40, 8 cyl...........	1107110	24–28	3.25	550	12	5.65	70	5500	C
	50, 70............	1102008	24.28	5.2	460	11.5	10.3	75	6500	C

Cooling System

CAR AND YEAR	MODEL	Capacity Qts.	Quarts of Methanol Base Anti-Freeze (For Protection to Temperature Shown Below)							Quarts of Ethylene Glycol (For Protection to Temperature Shown Below)							Quarts of Denatured Alcohol—188 Proof (For Protection to Temperature Shown Below)						
			3	4	5	6	7	8	9	3	4	5	6	7	8	9	3	4	5	6	7	8	9
1937-40..........	Series 40............	13¼	7	−7	−23	−43	....	....	....	13	3	−9	−25	−45	....	....	10	0	−10	−20	−30	....	....
1941-52..........	Series 40, 50..........	13	7	−7	−23	−43	....	....	....	13	3	−9	−25	−45	....	....	10	0	−10	−20	−30	....	....
1937-40..........	Series 60, 70, 80, 90...	17	15	6	−4	−16	−29	−45	....	18	12	5	−4	−14	−27	−42	....	10	0	....	−10	−20	−30
1941-42..........	Series 90............	18	17	8	−1	−12	−25	−38	−53	19	14	7	0	−10	−21	−34	20	10	....	0	−10	....	−20
1941-49..........	Series 60, 70..........	16¾	15	6	−4	−16	−29	−45	....	18	12	5	−4	−14	−27	−42	....	10	0	....	−10	−20	−30
1950-51..........	Series 70............	17¾	17	8	−1	−12	−25	−38	−53	19	14	7	0	−10	−21	−34	20	10	....	0	−10	....	−20
1953..............	V8..................	18	17	8	−1	−12	−25	−38	....	19	14	7	0	−10	−21	−34	20	10	....	0	−10	....	−20

FRONT SUSPENSION

1953 MODELS

Except for engineering changes and improvements the front suspension on the 1953 models remains essentially the same as the front suspension on previous Buick models and service procedure is practically identical.

The front suspension on all Buick cars is known as the short and long arm type suspension, generally referred to as the S.L.A. type.

Essentially, the S.L.A. type suspension consists of a lower suspension arm assembly (sometimes called the A frame); a shock absorber which is used as the upper suspension arm; a knuckle support, which carries the kingpin; and a suitably placed coil spring.

A sway stabilizer bar is used in connection with the front suspension to steady and stabilize the entire front system.

Steering Geometry, Caster, Camber and Toe-In

Before correcting any of the angles of steering geometry, check every angle on each side and make a careful note of the readings for each side. Study these readings carefully so that no false starts will be made.

Note: It is practically impossible to check the angles of caster, camber and king pin slant without using special gauges sold for this purpose.

Both caster and camber are adjusted at the eccentric pin in the outer end of the upper support arm. This pin has a left hand thread with two starts.

To increase caster, the pin is turned in a clockwise direction; to decrease caster, the pin is turned in a counterclockwise direction; therefore, if it is necessary to increase camber, and caster must be increased also, it is wise to turn the pin in a clockwise direction since this will increase caster while at the same time bring the eccentric to a more advantageous position for the camber adjustment.

In many cases it will be found that exact readings cannot be achieved without the use of bending equipment. Where bending equipment is available, the eccentric pin should be brought to the correct caster reading; camber can then be corrected by bending the knuckle support.

Bending should be resorted to for the correction of minor discrepancies only. If it is found that the camber is two or three degrees from the required setting, damaged parts should be replaced.

Under no circumstances should heat be applied to any of the front suspension parts. All front suspension parts are very carefully heat treated after forging. Reheating with a welding torch or other heating device will destroy the heat treatment and render the part dangerous for regular service.

Replacement of Coil Springs or Other Front Suspension Parts

Before replacing a coil spring, examine the front suspension pins and bushings to determine if any other part requires replacement.

If the coil spring is the only part which requires replacement, a roller type jack should be placed under the inner pivot shaft of the lower suspension arm (A frame). The car should be raised high enough to permit the lower suspension arm to be lowered far enough to remove the coil spring. Caution: Always use stationary floor jacks under the frame of the car when working on the front suspension.

With the load taken on the jack against the A frame inner shaft, disconnect the lower end of the torsion bar and then remove the four bolts which hold the inner shaft to the frame and lower the A frame to permit the release of the front spring. It helps to place a wooden block between the top of the frame and the upper suspension arm to prevent the arm from lowering too far. Replace the front spring without disturbing the position of the inner shaft on the jack.

When inserting the new coil spring, make sure that the end coil is properly seated in the lower A frame. Jack the lower suspension arm inner shaft back up against the frame and guide it to its proper bolt holes with long drift pins. Replace the four bolts which attach the shaft to the frame and reconnect the torsion bar.

This is generally considered to be the easiest way to replace a coil spring on all Buicks. However, if it is found that either the upper or lower suspension arm pins at the outer end of the arm require replacement, it is perhaps wiser to place the jack under the outer end of the lower suspension arm and disconnect the knuckle support at the defective pin or bushing. In this way the pin and the coil spring can be replaced at the same time with a consequent saving of time on the overall job.

Replacement of Upper and/or Lower Pins and Bushings

It is possible to replace the lower pin and bushings without removing the wheel. However, it is generally conceded that, while it may take a little longer, the job is greatly simplified if the wheel is removed and the weight of the spring is taken on the jack under the lower suspension arm.

A hardened screw type bushing is used in the lower end of the knuckle support. This bushing should be screwed into the knuckle support from the rear and securely tightened. The lower pin is screwed into the outer end of the A frame and the knuckle support itself (not the bushing) is carefully centered between the two arms.

The upper suspension arm eccentric pin has a left hand thread with two starts. It should be screwed into the upper end of the knuckle support so

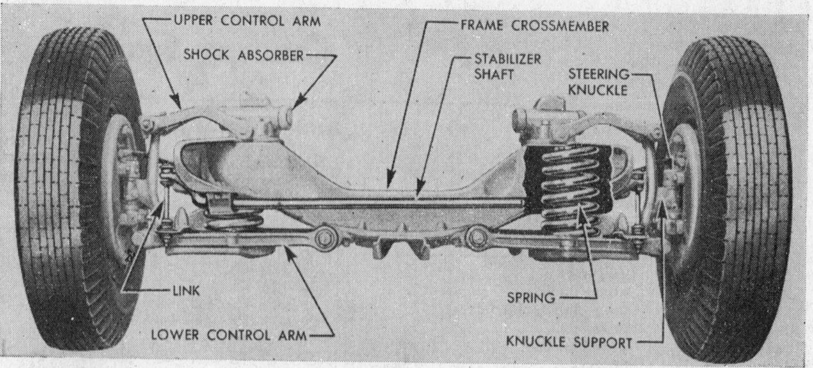

Front wheel suspension

that it is centered in the knuckle support when the eccentric is at full camber (eccentric out). If the pin is not centered with the eccentric full out, the pin should be backed out, turned 180 degrees, and started on the opposite thread so that it will be centered when the eccentric is at full camber.

Service on the upper support arm (shock absorber) is a highly specialized job and is usually done in a specialty shop.

Service on the lower suspension arm is restricted to the replacement of the inner shaft and bushings and the outer pins and bushings.

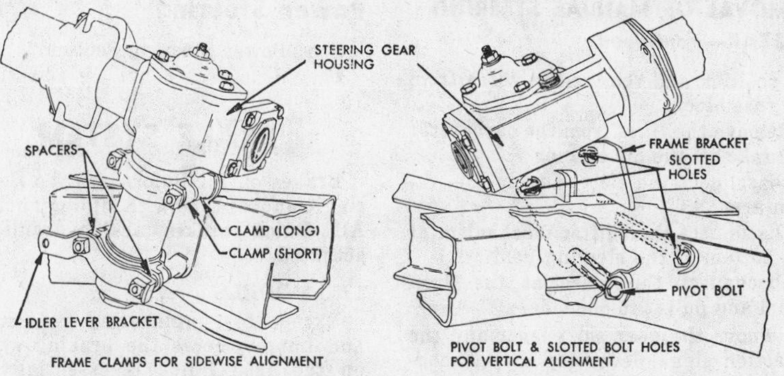

Steering gear to frame mounting

Replacement of King Pins and Bushings

To replace the king pins, remove the wheel, wheel bearings and backing plate. It is not necessary to disconnect the brakes or the brake hose. The backing plate can be slipped off the spindle, with the hydraulic system undisturbed. The backing plate can then be hung on a wire hook attached to the frame to prevent possible injury to the hydraulic line.

Drive the king pin lock pin to the rear and remove the king pin upper welsh plug.

Drive the king pin down and out, forcing out the lower welsh plug.

King pin bushings on Buick are in the knuckle itself and require reaming or honing to secure proper fit to the new pin.

Always remove the grease fittings from the upper and lower king pin bushings and, after the new bushings have been pressed into place, make certain that the grease hole is open in the bushing by running a drill into the grease fitting hole and through the bushing.

The king pin can be replaced by driving down from the top. It probably will be necessary to force the pin through the knuckle support in order to center it properly. Special fixtures are available to remove pins which are corroded or stuck. See "General Service & Trouble Shooting."

Toe-In

It has been said that every job done on the front end affects toe-in; toe-in affects nothing. Therefore, toe-in should be the last thing done on front suspension alignment.

Toe-in is adjusted at both tie rods.

Loosen the clamp bolts at the sleeve end (outer end) of each tie rod.

If the tie rods are set properly on the car, toe-in can be increased by turning the sleeve on the left tie rod in a direction opposite to forward wheel rotation to increase toe-in. The right tie rod is turned in a direction opposite to the left tie rod to increase toe-in on that **rod.**

The 1951 model had a single clamp at the end of each tie rod. This clamp must be set within 1/8 of an inch at the end of the tie rod and the ear of the clamp must overlap the slot in the tie rod tube not less than 1/16 inch.

To increase toe-in—left sleeve opposite wheel rotation—right sleeve in direction of wheel rotation.

STEERING GEAR

Starting in 1941 all Buicks are equipped with the recirculating ball type steering gear produced by the Saginaw Manufacturing Company.

Removal of Manual Steering Gear

Disconnect all steering column wires, including the back-up switch, horn and the Dynaflow neutral safety switch wire.

Remove the steering wheel.

Set the direction signal switch in the

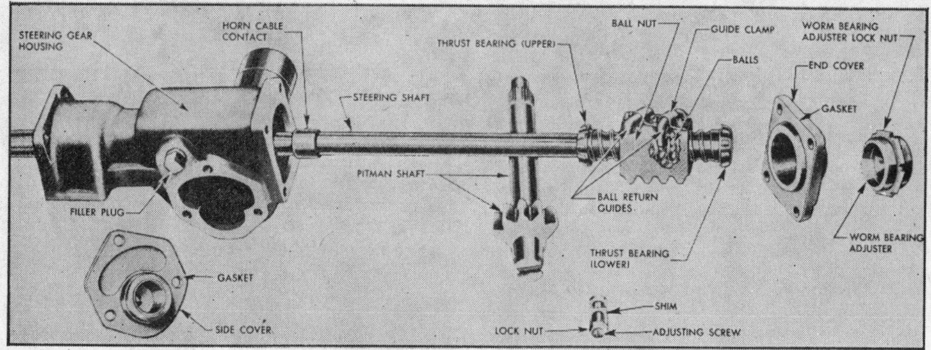

Steering gear disassembled

REMOVAL OF MANUAL STEERING GEAR—*continued*

off position and remove the wires from the fuse block.

Remove the lines from the carburetor and take off the air cleaner.

Disconnect the tie rod from the pitman arm.

Disconnect the shifter mechanism at the bottom of the steering gear.

Disconnect the brace at the dash panel and pull it to one side.

Remove the gear shift lever and the direction signal lever and also disconnect the directional signal wires from the switch on the dash panel.

Disconnect the steering gear mounting bolts at the frame, move the steering gear as far as possible to the rear, turn the unit over until the pitman arm is in the uppermost position, then raise the forward end of the steering gear assembly up between the engine and the fender and bring the assembly forward into the engine compartment to remove it.

Note: A great deal of time will be saved if two men remove the gear assembly, since this will make the job much easier and prevent scratching finished surfaces.

Note: The steering wheel is mounted on a serrated shaft and a suitable puller should be used to remove it.

The gear is replaced by reversing the removal procedure. Again two men should be used to reinstall the steering mechanism.

Power Steering

See "Power Steering Section."

BRAKE SYSTEM

Brakes on all Buicks are the Bendix single anchor type with sliding anchors. All Buick brakes are hydraulically actuated.

1953 MODELS

Except for engineering refinements and improvements the braking system on the 1953 Buick is essentially the same as that used on all earlier models.

At the time of going to press the Buick Motor Car Co. had announced that a Bendix vacuum power brake would be used on the Skylark model. Service on this brake system is given in the "Power Brake Section."

Pedal Clearance

Adjust master cylinder push rod so that there is ¼ to ½ inch free play of the brake pedal, before the push rod contacts the piston in the master cylinder. This free play is measured at the pedal, not at the push rod.

Minor Brake Adjustment

Before any adjustment is made on this, or any other brake, remove at least one of the front wheels and examine the condition of the cylinder, shoes and linings.

Procedure is as follows: Remove the clip from the star wheel adjusting slot in the backing plate. This slot is generally located opposite to the anchor pin.

Turn the star wheel with a special Bendix brake adjusting tool or a bent screw driver in a direction which will expand the shoes, until the wheel can just be turned by hand.

Note: Brake shoes are expanded by moving the handle portion of the brake adjusting tool upward toward the axle.

Now turn the star wheel in the opposite direction until the wheel is just free.

Do not forget to replace the adjusting hole cover clip.

Follow the same procedure on all four wheels.

Parking Brake Adjustment

On all Buick cars the parking brake actuates the rear wheel shoes. Any adjustment made on the hand brake is necessarily made on the cables. The operation is to remove slack from the hand brake cables.

This should be done when either a minor or major operation is being performed since the cables are taken up as follows:

Expand the rear brake shoes at the star wheel until they are tight against the drum. (When making a minor adjustment they are expanded only until the wheel drags to take up the slack in the hand brake cables; you will note

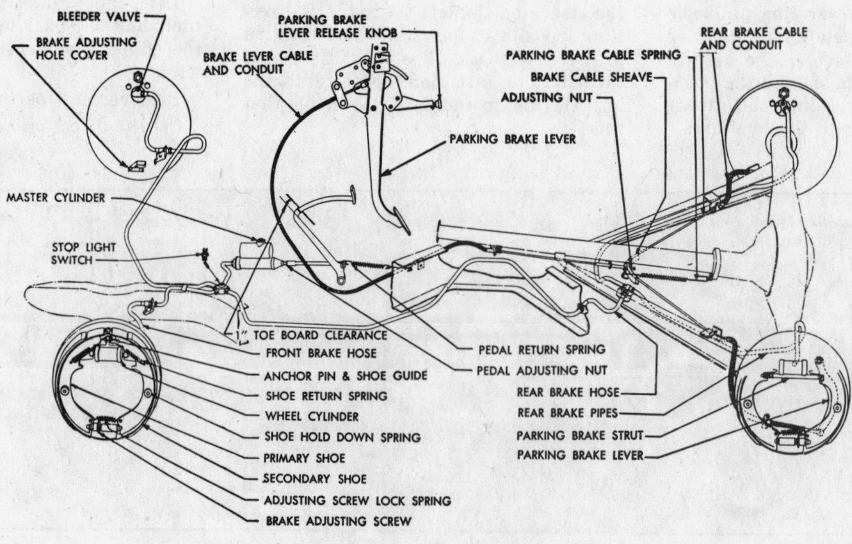

Brake mechanism layout

that they are expanded until they are tight against the drum.)

Now adjust the hand brake cables so that there is no slack when the cables are pulled tightly by hand. Back off on the star wheel adjuster until the wheel is just free (as would be done in a minor operation).

Parking Brake Lever

Starting with 1942 production the parking brake lever on Buick cars is a foot operated treadle.

To remove the treadle first disconnect the cable and then unbolt the treadle frame from its mounting under the dash.

This can be accomplished without particular difficulty since there is no great interference with the mounting studs.

Hand Brake Cable Replacement

To replace the hand brake cable disconnect the cable at the lever under the dash and also at the adjusting sheave under the car. Disconnect the clamp which holds the conduit assembly to the transmission and also the clamp which holds the conduit assembly to the dash.

The upper end of the cable is slid out into the engine compartment and then the cable is slid out through the bottom. Note carefully the position the cable occupies since it must be replaced through the same "path" that the old cable followed.

The cable is not long enough to follow a new path. It must follow the same path the old cable followed.

When a new cable is installed it will be necessary to make an adjustment of the parking brake as outlined in the parking brake adjustment paragraph.

Major Brake Adjustment

Major brake adjustment should be made when it is found that the anchor pins are loose or the brakes have been relined or the drums turned. The procedure is as follows: Loosen the anchor nuts (this is the large nut almost directly opposite to the slot of the backing plate where the star wheel adjuster is located) just a sufficient amount to permit the anchor to move up and down in the slot of backing plate.

Turn the star wheel adjuster until the shoes are tight against the drum and tap the anchor lightly with a hammer so that it assumes the best centered position. Securely tighten the anchor nut. Back off on the star wheel until the shoes are just free.

BRAKE HYDRAULIC SYSTEM

On all models since 1940 the master cylinder is one inch in diameter.

The series 60, 70 and 90 series of 1942 has 1 3/32 inch front wheel cylinder. With this exception front wheel cylinders are 1⅛ inch on all cars built between 1940 and 1953.

All models from 1940 to 1953 have a 1 inch cylinder on the rear wheels.

The bleeder screw on all wheels is equipped with a small plug which is intended to prevent dirt and foreign matter from entering the bleeder valve. When this plug is removed, a standard bleeder hose fitting can be inserted into the plug hole, the opposite end of the hose placed in a jar of brake fluid so that the end of the hose is below the top of the fluid in order to prevent air from backing into the cylinders when bleeding the brakes as a one-man operation.

Note: Reusing brake fluid which has been bled from brakes is generally considered an unsafe practice.

Refilling Master Cylinders

The master cylinder can be filled from the engine compartment. It is located behind the steering column. Where it is required that the hydraulic system be pressure bled it is advisable to attach the pressure bleeding device from underneath the car rather than to try to connect it up from the engine compartment.

Bleeding Brakes

See "General Service—Trouble Shooting Section"—Refer to index.

COOLING SYSTEM

All Buicks use the positive pressure type cooling system incorporating a pressure sealed cap on the radiator.

1953 V-8 models use a single water pump mounted on the engine front cover. On these models, the two cylinder heads are connected by a water outlet manifold.

Water Manifolds—V-8 Models

To remove the water manifold, detach the upper radiator hose and remove the two attaching bolts which hold the manifold to the front of each cylinder head. Lift the manifold straight up to

Remove neoprene seal

free the neoprene seal in the water pump housing. **Caution:** On assembly use a NEW seal. Mounting gaskets may be coated with compound.

Water Pump

It is possible to remove and replace the water pump on all Buick cars without disturbing the radiator core. This is accomplished by removing the fan belt and fan blades, disconnect the hoses and remove the water pump attaching bolts.

On the 1953 V-8 models, two sizes (⅜ and 5/16) of bolts are used in cover of the water pump. The larger size passes through the front cover into the cylinder block.

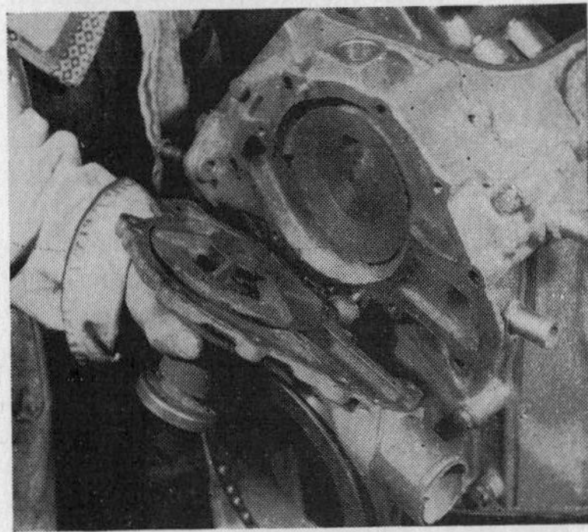

Removing water pump cover

Disassembly of Water Pump

Before disassembling the water pump, measure the distance between the fan hub and the end of the shaft, so that, when a new hub is installed, it may be pressed to exactly that same position on the new pump.

Remove the pump body cover and, using an arbor press, force the pump shaft out of the impeller.

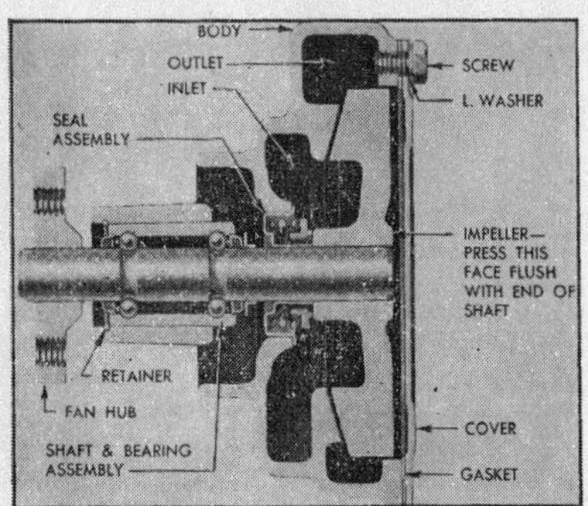

Sectional view of water pump

DISASSEMBLY OF WATER PUMP—*continued*

Remove the carbon washers, spring and bellows from the bearing sleeve.

Inspection of pump should reveal no scratches on the seal face nor any particular corrosion.

Where the seal face is scratched, the brass ring will have to be replaced. It is always good practice to replace the shaft and bearings any time the pump is disassembled.

Radiator Core Removal

ALL EXCEPT 1953 V-8 MODELS

To remove the radiator core, first remove the water pump as shown in the previous paragraphs and then loosen the radiator attaching bolts, tilt the radiator slightly backwards and raise it up out of the car.

Thermostat

The thermostat is contained in the water outlet elbow mounted on the front of the cylinder head.

To replace the thermostat, disconnect the upper radiator hose, remove the radiator water outlet attaching bolts and the thermostat.

ENGINE ASSEMBLY

Engine Interchangeability

Current replacement engines are available that can be installed in any series from 1940 to 1953 straight 8 models.

Note: The 1941 to 1947 model engine will not fit in the 1948 to 1953 chassis, because of the different mounting brackets used.

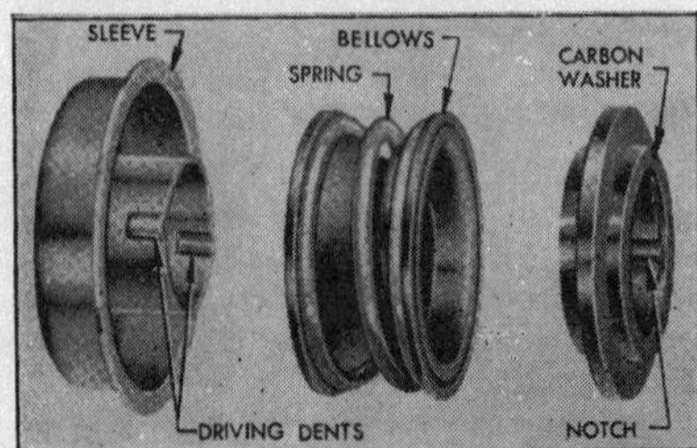

Water pump seal disassembled

Engine Marking Code

On a very few production engines the cylinders were bored to .010 inch oversize in production. These engines are marked with a dash approximately ¼ inch long over the serial number.

Vibration Damper Removal

ALL EXCEPT 1953 V-8 MODELS

On all models up to and including 1949 it is necessary to remove the radiator core in order to take off the vibration damper.

On models starting with 1950, except 1953 V-8, it is possible to remove and replace the vibration damper without disturbing the radiator core.

Even on the models where it is possible to replace the vibration damper with the radiator in place, it is always advisable to take it off in order to prevent accidentally damaging the fins or tubes of the radiator.

1953 V-8 MODEL

No damper used on the V-8 model.

Engine Removal

STRAIGHT 8 ENGINES

To remove the Straight 8 engine first remove the radiator core to insure that it will not be damaged when the heavy engine is lifted from the frame.

Disconnect all electrical connections to the generator, heat indicator, etc. Disconnect all throttle linkage and disconnect the exhaust manifold at the flange. Remove the battery and starter cable and take off the gas lines and fuel pump.

Note: The fuel pump is taken off to insure that it will not be damaged when the heavy engine is lifted up.

Disconnect the front engine mounts and disconnect the engine at the bell housing in the rear.

Support the weight of the transmission on a jack and lift the engine out of the bed.

ALL V-8 ENGINES

The V-8 engine is removed in essentially the same way as the Straight 8 engine is removed. The only difference being that there are two exhaust flange connections and, in addition, it is customary to take off the intake manifold to provide a place to lift the engine.

The usual procedure is to remove the intake manifold and use the intake manifold bolt holes as a lifting purchase for the lifting device.

ENGINE MANIFOLDS

Heat Riser Valve

ALL EXCEPT 1953 V-8 MODELS

The heat riser valve in the exhaust manifold is operated by a thermostatic spring which, when cool, holds the valve in the open position, permitting the exhaust gases to strike against the intake manifold.

As the exhaust manifold heats, the thermostatic spring permits the weight which is an integral part of the valve shaft to close the valve, forcing the exhaust gases out of the exhaust pipe away from intake manifold.

Pilot rings are used where the intake manifold connects with the intake port of the cylinder head.

Failure to install these pilot rings properly may result in turbulence and a reduction of extreme top speed.

1953 V-8 MODELS

On 1953 V-8 models the heat riser valve is located at the outlet flange in the left exhaust manifold. When the engine is cold and the heat riser valve closed, exhaust gases are forced through ports in the inlet manifold to the right exhaust manifold, causing a quick warm-up of the inlet manifold.

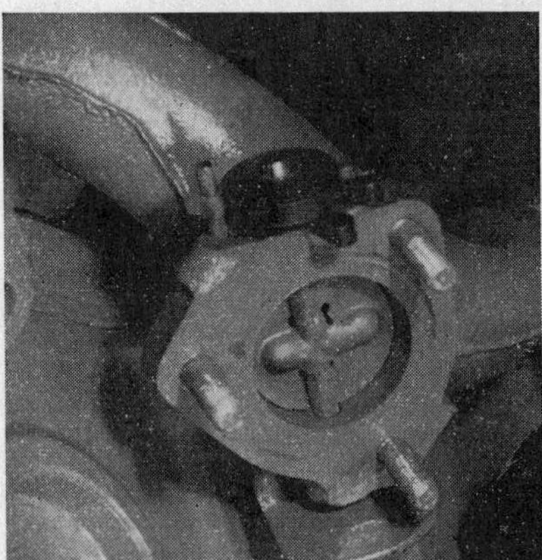

Heat damper located in left exhaust manifold

Engine Manifolds

1953 V-8 MODELS

On the V-8 model the inlet manifold may be removed from the center of the engine block without removing any other part of the engine. It is necessary to merely take off the air cleaner

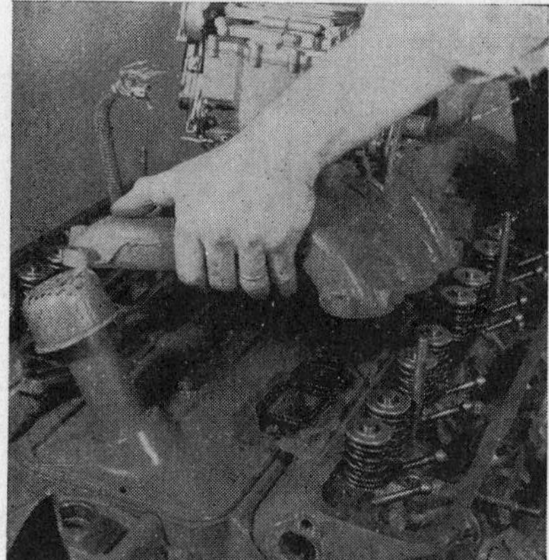

Remove carburetor and intake manifold as an assembly

and disconnect the vacuum, gas and accelerator rods from the carburetor, unbolt and lift off the manifold.

On the V-8 models the exhaust manifolds on each side may be removed with some slight difficulty without taking off any other part of the engine unless the car is equipped with power steering in which case it will be necessary to either remove the power steering gear box or take off the cylinder head on the left bank in order to get at the manifold.

In either case whether or not the model is equipped with power steering the right exhaust manifold may be removed without taking off any other part of the engine.

Exhaust Pipe Muffler and Tail Pipe

Straight through type mufflers are generally used on Buick cars. These mufflers are stamped "front" at one end and when installing a new one examine it to make certain that the word "front" is to the front of the car. There should

Location of exhaust crossover pipe

be a minimum clearance of one inch between the top of the tail pipe and the rear seat pan at its closest point.

V-8 Models—Exhaust Pipe

On the 1953 V-8 models the exhaust crossover pipe is made in one piece where it connects to both of the exhaust manifolds. The split pipe connects from both exhaust manifolds to a common flange connection at the exhaust pipe. Gaskets used at these connections should be installed dry.

FUEL SYSTEM

All brass fittings and copper line fittings in the Buick fuel system are of the flared type. Double acting type fuel pumps are used, mounted on the right side at the front of the engine block on straight 8 models. On 1953 V-8's the fuel pump is mounted on the right side of the engine front cover.

Fuel and vacuum pump is driven directly from the engine camshaft on straight 8 models. On V-8's the pump is driven by an eccentric attached to the camshaft gear.

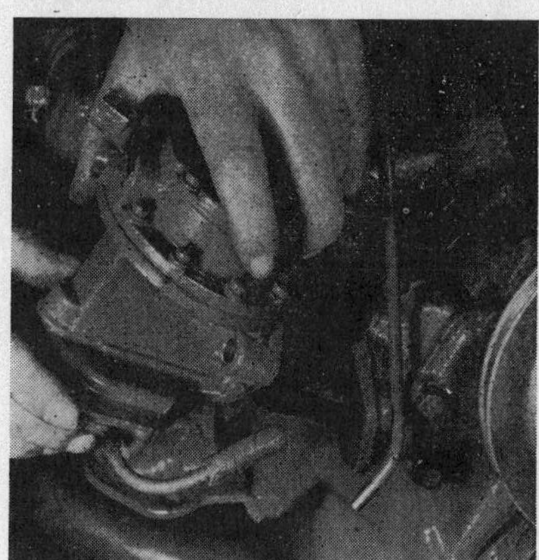

Remove two mounting screws. Tilt the pump and remove from engine

Production engines are built with a gas filter adjacent to the carburetor.

When servicing the combination pump do not fail to carefully mark the diaphragm flanges so that they may be reassembled in the correct relationship to each other. It is possible to install both the upper and lower diaphragm flanges incorrectly on this type of pump.

Two types of kits are available for this combination pump: the diaphragm kit which consists of the diaphragms, valves and springs, and the overhaul kit which consists of links, levers and also the parts contained in the diaphragm kit.

Carburetor Air Cleaner

All models of Buick including 1953 V-8 use an oil immersion type air cleaner which requires periodic cleaning and servicing.

Air is held in place by an upper and lower wing nut and on a bolt at outer bracket

Remove the air cleaner from the car being careful not to turn it over since it is oil filled, disassemble it, remove the filter element and thoroughly clean it out with gasoline or any solvent. Remove the old oil and thoroughly clean out the air cleaner oil pan.

The base of the cleaner should be held level and filled to the mark on the side of the cleaner with SAE 90 oil. It will require approximately ½ pint of oil to bring the level up to the mark on the cleaner body. Replace the element reassemble the cleaner and mount it on the car.

VALVE SYSTEM

All Straight 8 Buick engines are of the overhead valve type. The valves are operated by a system of lifters, pushrods, rockets and rocker shafts.

The valve rocker system may be removed by disconnecting it from the cylinder head. Removing the rocker system does not in any way disturb the setting of the head itself.

Push rods may be pulled up through the head without taking the head off.

On some body styles No. 16 pushrods cannot be lifted up without removing the head because of interference from the dash panel.

It is good practice, but not absolutely essential, that each pushrod be returned to the lifter from which it was removed. In order to accomplish this,

VALVE SYSTEM—*continued*

they should be carefully marked or mounted in a holding fixture similar to the type used to hold the valves.

Since the rocker system is fed by a meter pressure line from the crankcase, a periodic check should be made to determine if a sufficient amount of oil is reaching the rocker shaft.

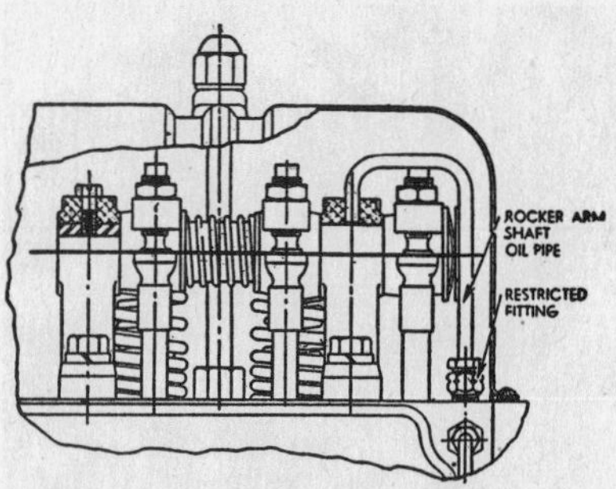

Rocker construction showing location of restricted oil fitting

To make this check, remove the rocker cover and run the engine until it is thoroughly warm. With the engine thoroughly warm and the oil pressure at a normal 35 pounds, oil should be observed to drip from every rocker.

At no point should the oil actually pour or form a solid stream. It should drip slowly, not more than a drop every thirty seconds.

If insufficient oil is reaching the rockers it may be necessary to remove the oil attaching fittings and the restrictor fitting and thoroughly clean them out.

A quick check can be made on the stoppage by disconnecting the oil line at the cylinder head to determine if oil is reaching that point.

The oil restrictor fitting is the fitting which is mounted horizontally into the side of the head. In back of it is a filter screen which is held in place by the fitting which screws into the top of the head. If an insufficient quantity of oil is reaching the rockers, both of these fittings should be removed and the screen either replaced or carefully cleaned.

If, on inspection, any of the rocker arms show a solid stream of oil draining, it indicates that the bushing in that particular rocker arm is badly worn and should be replaced.

1953 V-8 MODELS

The 1953 V-8 overhead valve engine is equipped with overhead valves which are arranged to stand in a vertical plane. Lubrication of the rocker system is provided for by supplying oil under a metered low pressure to the front rocker shaft bracket on each cylinder head. The mounting bolt hole on the front bracket is bored oversize which permits the oil to run up around the bolt into the hollowed out rocker shaft which is plugged at both ends. Oil then passes through the hollow rocker shaft through holes which are drilled in the positions occupied by the rockers supplying oil to the rocker itself.

The rocker in turn is rifle drilled so that oil is supplied to the top of the push rod.

Oil should be observed to drip (not run) from each of the push rod bearings when the engine is running at any speed over idle. If no oil is observed to drop from any of the rockers it usually means that the oil passage in the rocker shaft or the rocker itself is blocked and the unit should be taken from the car and thoroughly cleaned.

Valve Springs

To check the condition of the valve springs line up the inlet valve springs on a flat surface and, using a straight edge, compare the height of the springs. If all of the springs are the same height as determined with the straight edge, it may be assumed safely that the springs are in good condition since it is very unlikely that all of the springs would collapse the same amount.

If one or more of the springs are lower than the rest it is advisable to secure at least one new spring and then compare the other springs with the new one for free length.

Replace all springs which do not come up to the standard set by the new one.

Repeat the operation on the exhaust valve springs.

Valve Replacement

STRAIGHT 8 ENGINES

To replace any or all of the valves in the straight 8 engine it is necessary to remove the cylinder head. The head is then taken to a bench and each valve is released with a lever type valve spring compressor. Any of the yoke type spring compressors can also be used to remove the valve spring from the valve stem.

V-8 ENGINES

The valves are replaced in the V-8 engine essentially in the same manner as they are replaced in the in-line engine with this exception: when removing the cylinder head it is advisable to detach the exhaust manifold at the flange rather than detaching it from the head itself. Most service can be performed on the V-8 heads with the exhaust manifold attached to the head.

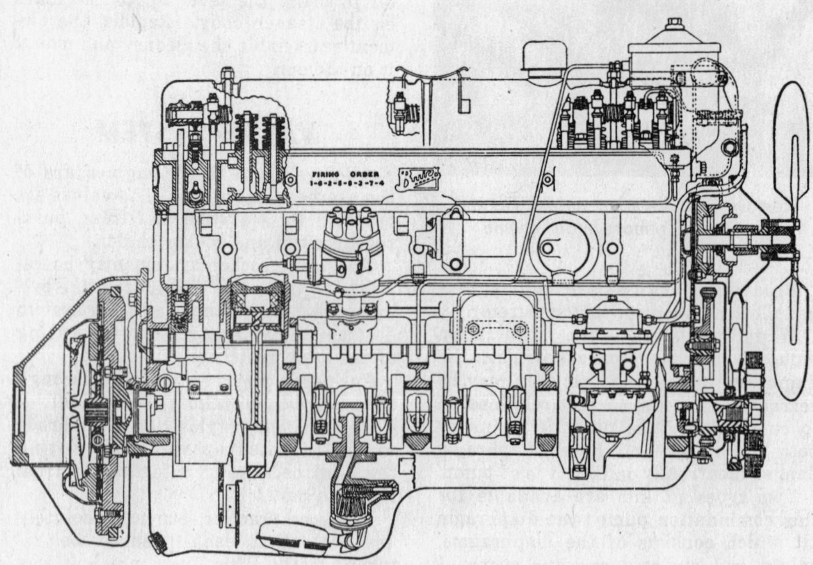

Engine side sectional view. Series 50

Valve Guide Replacement

STRAIGHT 8 ENGINES

Remove the cylinder head and take out the valves and valve spring assemblies. Now measure very carefully the amount the valve guide protrudes from the cylinder head before driving it out so that the new guide can be driven down exactly that amount.

When driving out the valve guides support the cylinder head as near to the valve guide as practical. By that is meant, do not drive the valve guide out of the center of the head with the head supported at either end since this may result in distortion of the cylinder head mating surface.

A pilot type driver should be used and the guide can be driven out either from the top or the bottom, or the guide may be pressed out if an arbor press is handy.

Start the new guide into the top of the head and tap it gently to insure that it is starting straight. Once started straight, it can be driven very quickly into position.

When the new valve guide has been driven in the correct distance, enter a new valve into the guide to make sure that the valve will operate freely up and down. The slightest sign of binding in the new valve guide means that the guide itself has become riveted over or slightly warped in the driving process and will have to be reamed.

It is always an excellent idea to reface the valve seat when new guides have been installed to be absolutely certain that the valve seat is concentric to the new guide.

1953 V-8 ENGINES

The technique for installing valve guides in the 1953 V-8 engine is exactly the same as that employed in the in-line straight 8 engine.

HYDRAULIC VALVE LIFTERS

1953 V-8 ENGINES

The 1953 V-8 engines are equipped with hydraulic valve lifters which are supplied with oil through drilled oil chambers in the cylinder block itslf.

The only actual service possible on the hydraulic valve lifter unit is to remove it from the car, thoroughly clean it out with solvent and replace it.

While not absolutely necessary it is always good practice to replace each lifter in the bore from which it was removed.

To remove the lifters from the V-type engine it is necessary to: first, remove the rocker cover and take off the rocker shaft assemblies and lift out the push rods.

Then remove the intake manifold by disconnecting all of the carburetor and throttle linkage and then unbolt the manifold from the both cylinder heads.

The valve chamber cover plate can then be removed giving access to the lifters.

The lifters are barrel type which will come right up out of their bores requiring no other tools than the fingers.

If more effort than can be given by the fingers is required it indicates that gum or other sticky substances present in the oil and is probably the cause of the failure of the lifter.

STRAIGHT 8 ENGINES

On 1949 thru 1952 series 50 and 70 engines the valve lifter is hydraulically compensated so that it operates the rocker with zero clearance.

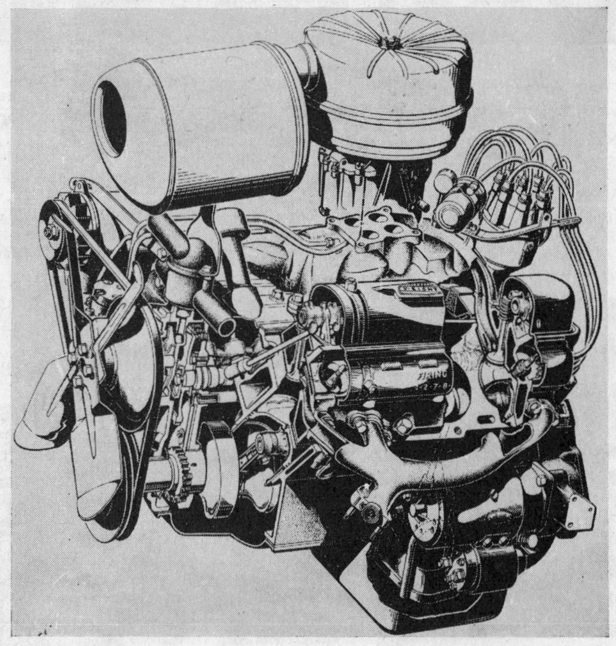

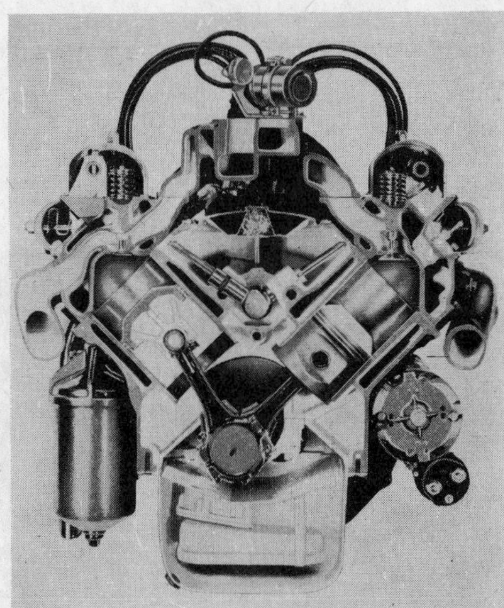

Side and front cut away views of V8 engine

HYDRAULIC VALVE LIFTERS—*continued*

To accomplish this, oil is fed under pressure through the hollow rocker shaft to each rocker arm. The rocker arm has a cored hole leading to the specially arranged adjusting screw at the top of the push rod. A hole in the adjusting screw indexes with the hollow center of the push rod which in turn indexes with the hydraulic lifter.

Initial Adjustment of the Hydraulic Lifters

1953 V-8 ENGINES

No adjustment whatever is provided on the hydraulic lifters of the 1953 V-8 engine.

However, in order to make certain that the lifter is operating some place close to the center of its takeup it is a good idea to force each of the lifters to leak down and make certain that there is not less than .030 nor more than .060 inch clearance at the end of the valve stem with the lifter leaked all the way down.

If there is less than .030 clearance it will be necessary to grind off the top of the valve stem in order to allow between .030 and .060 inch clearance with the lifter leaked down.

If too much clearance exists at this point, resulting in noisy operation, it will be necessary to replace the valve.

Straight 8 Engines

The following is Buick recommended procedure for initial adjustment on the hydraulic valve lifter: Crank the engine over until the distributor rotor indicates that the cylinder being worked on is in the firing position. This means both lifters are down.

Turn the adjusting ball stud until all play between the lifter and ball seat is just removed and there is no lash in

Loosen the spark plug cover in order to free the valve cover

Rocker arms are held in position by four brackets. Remove brackets and lift off assemblies

Lift out push rods. Push rods can be installed either way. There is no top or bottom

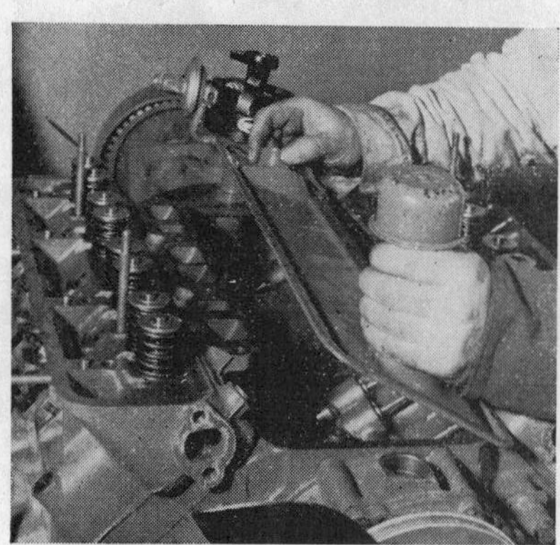

Remove valve chamber cover

Remove lifters from block

Remove valve keepers

the valve train. Now turn the adjusting ball stud exactly two more turns. Check to make sure that the oil groove on the ball stud is at least half way down in the rocker arm so that it connects with the oil passage in the rocker. Then tighten the jam nut. NOTE: If the oil groove on the ball stud is not at least half way down in the rocker arm, turn the ball stud down one additional turn, making a total of three turns. And then tighten the lock nut. If turning the screw three turns after the initial clearance has been removed does not put the oil groove far enough down into the rocker to index the hole in the rocker, it will be necessary to install another push rod.

When it becomes necessary to clean the hydraulic valve lifters because of dirt or gum, Buick advises that all the lifters be removed and cleaned at the same time as it is likely that they may all have dirt and so become defective.

How to Check Valve Timing

The following technique is to be used on mechanical valve lifters (not hydraulic). There is an I.N.O.P. mark (inlet opens) on the flywheel. This mark can be observed through the timing hole which is just above the starter on the front face of the flywheel housing.

Slowly turn the engine over until this mark indexes with the hole in the flywheel housing and chalk the mark up so that it can be seen readily.

Now set No. 1 and also No. 8 inlet valve rocker to approximately .040 inch clearance. Then place a .015 inch feeler between the rocker and valve stem on No. 1 and No. 8 inlet valves.

Now very slowly turn the engine and as the chalked I.N.O.P. mark again begins to index in the hole in the front face of the flywheel housing, one of two feeler gages should just be gripped.

The reason for using a feeler gage under both No. 1 and No. 8 is to eliminate the possibility of having to turn the engine over twice. Since the valves operate every second revolution of the crankshaft, by working both No. 1 and No. 8, one of the feelers should be gripped as the I.N.O.P. mark indexes.

Hydraulic Lifters—Valve Timing Check

Valve timing check on models with hydraulic lifters is done in almost the same manner with this exception: Since the lifter operates with zero clearance it will be necessary to mount a dial indicator over the top of the valve spring so that the initial motion of the valve can be checked on the indicator.

On these models the dial indicator should read approximately .040 inch when the I.N.O.P. mark on the flywheel indexes in the timing hole.

Valve Timing Procedure

STRAIGHT 8 ENGINES

Buick chain and sprockets are arranged so that, if they are not deliberately disturbed, the valve timing will remain essentially as set when the engine was assembled unless the chain or sprocket is badly worn or damaged.

Normal, even serious, wear of the sprockets will not cause material change in the valve timing of itself.

Up to the point where the chain and/or sprockets become loose enough to permit the valve timing to "jump," no serious change in the valve timing takes place because of wear.

When it becomes necessary to replace either the sprocket and chain, or both, because of noise, wear or looseness, proceed as follows: Remove the front end sheet metal assembly (including the radiator core) from the car. Disconnect the engine front mounting bolts and jack the front of the engine up. Remove the vibration damper and timing case cover. Remove both chain and sprockets.

The new chain and sprockets should be assembled on the bench in the relative position they occupy on the engine and they should be set up so that there are eleven pins of the timing chain (**Note:** On the 1953 V-8 engines there are twelve pins) between the mark on the camshaft and the mark on the crankshaft sprocket, counting the pin at each mark.

Note carefully the position of the keyway in both sprockets and rotate the shaft so that the keys are in that position. Slide both sprockets together on their respective shafts with the chain mounted over both sprockets.

Timing chain and sprocket marks (straight 8)

Secure both gears to their shafts with the bolts provided and recheck the setting. Turn the crankshaft two complete revolutions or until the chain again assumes the original position. In this position recheck to see that there are eleven pins in the timing chain between the mark on the cam and the mark on the crankshaft sprocket, counting the pin at each mark.

With properly marked gears set up as described, it makes absolutely no difference which piston is at top center.

Note: Care should be used to align the keyways exactly so that the key will enter the gear without difficulty.

1953 V-8 ENGINES

On the 1953 V-8 engines the procedure for installing the timing gears and chain, and retiming the valves, is essentially the same as that given for the straight 8 engines with the following exceptions.

It will be necessary to remove the fan shroud, water pump, fan pulley, and engine front cover. The engine front cover is removed more readily if the water manifold is first detached from

VALVE TIMING PROCEDURE—*continued*

both heads and the radiator outlet hose. This operation is not absolutely necessary but it does make removing the cover easier. It is not necessary to remove the radiator core nor the sheet metal; however, it is generally considered to be much easier to be certain the chain is installed properly if the core is removed, making it easier to see exactly the alignment of the timing marks. It is recommended that the radiator core be removed since this operation is done very easily.

The fuel pump eccentric, mounted on the center of the camshaft gear, is indexed in place with two metallic drive screws.

The oil slinger is mounted to the crankshaft after the gear is installed so that the dish in the slinger faces front.

Timing chain and sprocket marks—1953-V-8 engines

Cylinder Head Removal

STRAIGHT 8 ENGINES

To remove the cylinder head on the straight 8 engines it is necessary to disconnect all carburetor and throttle linkage, unbolt the manifold from the side of the cylinder head, remove the rocker cover and rocker assemblies, detach the gas and vacuum lines from the fuel pump and carburetor.

The water manifold at the front of the head can be detached from the block or detached from the upper hose, whichever suits the operator.

Remove the engine side cover plate and detach the spark plug wires.

Unbolt the head and lift it up off of the gasket and the push rods.

Caution: The straight 8 head is quite heavy and, since it is necessary to lift it off in one motion so as not to damage the push rods, it is recommended that two men (or a lifting mechanism) be used to take off the cylinder head.

Special offset wrenches are available for final tightening of the cylinder head after the rockers have been installed.

1953 V-8 ENGINES

Remove all carburetor and throttle linkage connections, the vacuum line to the distributor, and the lines to the fuel pump. Unbolt the inlet manifold from between the two blocks and lift it off the car.

Remove the rocker cover, then detach the exhaust manifold at the flange connection rather than at the head.

Note: The exhaust manifold can be disconnected from the head but this procedure takes somewhat longer than detaching it at the exhaust flange connection.

Remove the rocker cover and take off the rocker assemblies.

Note: There are no oil line connections to the rocker assemblies since oil is fed through the rocker front bracket.

Detach the front water manifold from both cylinder heads, unbolt and lift off the head.

Caution: The cylinder heads on the V-8 model are interchangeable right for left. However, if the head taken from the right bank is installed on the left bank it will be necessary to change the water outlet plugs, heater plugs, heat indicator plugs, etc. Therefore it is recommended that the heads be marked and returned to the side from which they were taken.

CYLINDER HEAD NUT TIGHTENING SEQUENCE

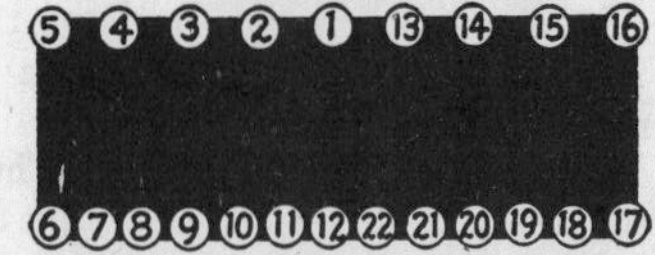

All models 1938 to 1952 tightening cylinder bolts to 65-70 foot pounds

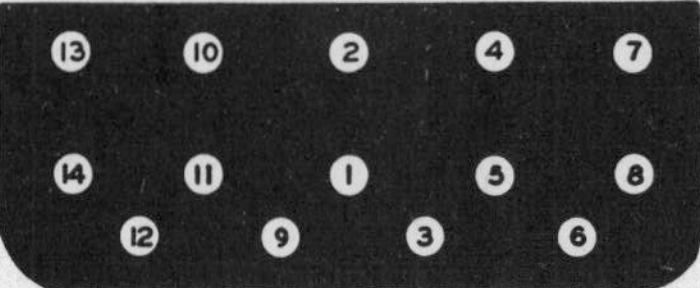

1953 V8 engines tighten cylinder bolts to 65-70 foot pounds

Oil Pan Removal

STRAIGHT 8 ENGINES

Removing the oil pan can be simplified somewhat by bringing No. 1 and No. 2 cylinder near the center of their respective stroke to set the crankshaft in the best position to permit the passage of the oil pan.

On 1941 to 1950 models the steering pitman arm and engine side pan should be removed. All other models remove the cap screws and lower the pan.

1953 V-8 ENGINES

The 1953 V-8 engine oil pan can be removed readily from underneath the car without any difficulty. It may be necessary, however, to rotate the crankshaft somewhat in order to clear the counterbalances.

Oil Pump Removal

ALL EXCEPT V-8 MODELS

The oil pump on all Buick models is located in the oil pan and is driven directly from the camshaft.

If the oil pump is to be removed, first crank the engine until No. 1 cylinder is in the firing position and then do not disturb the engine after the pump has been removed so that it can be replaced without disturbing the ignition timing.

If for some reason the ignition timing has been disturbed, it may be necessary to relocate the ignition wires in the distributor cap in order to compensate for a possible change in the relative position of the oil pump drive gear to the distributor shaft.

The procedure for resetting the ignition timing is given in greater detail under ignition timing later in this section.

The oil pressure relief valve is located in the pump body and is not adjustable.

Oil is supplied to the mains, rods, camshaft bearings under full pressure, and a restricted supply, under pressure, is distributed to the rocker shafts and lifters. All other parts of the engine are fed by the splash or diffusion method.

Normal oil pressure is 35 pounds at 35 miles per hour.

1953 V-8 ENGINES

The oil pump on the 1953 V-8 engines is driven by a tongue at the bottom of the distributor shaft. The oil pump can be removed after the oil pan has been taken off.

Connecting Rod Bearings

STRAIGHT 8 ENGINES

All models from 1940 to 1948 had poured type connecting rod bearings which require the replacement of the connecting rod itself in order to install a new bearing.

Starting with production models in 1949, a slip-in type connecting rod bearing was used.

These bearings are removable from below without removing the connecting rod.

The Buick factory does not recommend adjusting rod bearings. However, a perfectly serviceable adjustment may be had by using taper or feather type shims on the lower half of the connecting rod bearing to compensate for normal wear.

Some ring manufacturers recommend that the nearest practical undersize bearing be used and exact adjustment secured by the use of special shims on the lower half of the rod bearing.

1953 V-8 ENGINES

The V-8 engine is equipped with slip-in type rod bearings which are removable from below without removing the connecting rod. The bearings can be taken out after the oil pan, oil pump, and oil baffle have been removed.

The Buick factory does not recommend adjusting slip-in type rod bearings. However, a perfectly serviceable adjustment may be had by using taper or feather type shims on the lower half of the connecting rod bearing to compensate for normal wear.

The connecting rod bearing cap is assembled so that the small boss on the

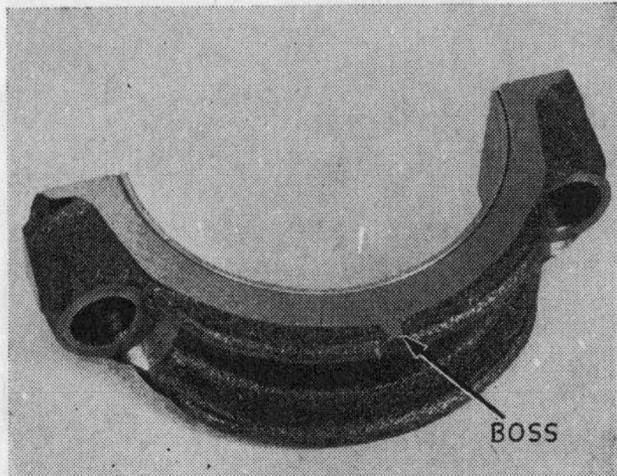

Boss stamped on connecting rod caps. Bosses should face each other in assembly

polished thrust side of the cap is assembled to the rear on the right bank toward the front on the left bank. This will leave the small bosses facing each other on each connecting rod journal.

Rod and Piston Assemblies

1953 V-8 ENGINES

The 1953 V-8 engine uses a three-ring piston with a solid skirt.

Pistons should be installed to the engine with the V boss which is cast

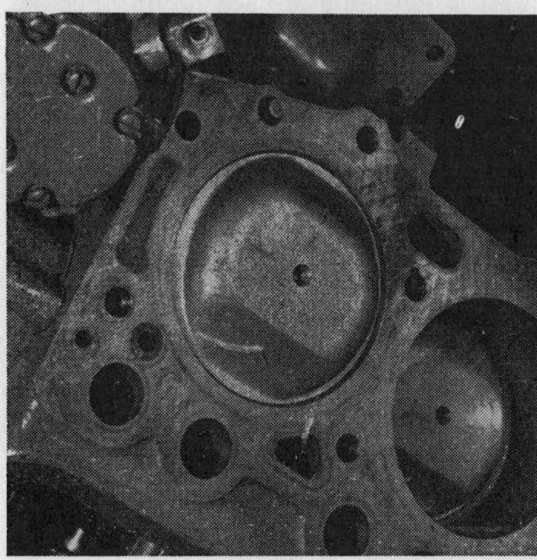

Note: V-boss cast on top of pistons

in the top of the piston face toward the cam shaft on each bank.

Pistons should be fitted so that a ½ inch wide feeler gage .0015 inch thick will fit between the thrust face of the piston and the cylinder wall.

Pistons are assembled to the rod so that the head of the wrist pin clamp bolt is on the same side of the piston as the V boss on the top of the piston.

STRAIGHT 8 ENGINES

Pistons should be installed with the T slot toward the left side of the engine and the rod installed so that the marker on the rod cap points toward the rear of the engine.

Check that the oil spray is toward the camshaft.

Pistons should be fitted so that a one-half inch wide feeler gage .0015 inch thick will fit between the thrust face of the piston and the cylinder wall.

Pistons are assembled to the rods so that when the marker on the rod faces the mechanic the slot in the piston will be toward the mechanic.

Main Bearings

Main lift bearings on all models are steel back babbitt lined inserts which are locked in place by a tang at the parting line.

All Buick main bearings are align bored in production and should be replaced in full sets only.

Shims are used on the main bearing caps to provide a partial adjustment of the bearing.

A cork seal is used at both sides of the near main bearing cap.

Rear Main Bearing Oil Seal

Buick recommends removing crankshaft and bearing shells to replace the rear main bearing oil seals. On models from 1940 including the 1953 V8, the rear oil seal is a packing which must be forced into the upper half with a packing tool to insure a good seal.

Packing is installed and cut flush in the upper half, whereas the lower half

1953 V8 engine. Rear main bearing cap

REAR MAIN BEARING OIL SEAL —*continued*

is installed so that the packing projects approximately 3/64 inch above the cap. The cap should be bolted up into place and then immediately removed to make sure that the protruding packing did not "rivet over" and prevent the cap from seating properly.

If it is found that the protruding oil seal did rivet over slightly, then simply trim off the riveted portion with a razor blade and retighten the cap and repeat the cycle of examining it.

It is sometimes possible to replace the upper and lower half of the oil seal by removing the transmission and lowering the crankshaft about ¾ inch. Using this method, be sure to fill the groove with packing and press it into place by bolting up the rear main bearing cap as this will cause the crankshaft to compress the packing. It will then be necessary to lower the crankshaft again to be certain that the packing is seating properly.

CAUTION: If this method is attempted and for some reason the seal does not seat properly, it will be absolutely essential that the engine be removed, the crankshaft taken out and the seal properly replaced. Otherwise oil from the rear main bearing will surely ruin the clutch.

ENGINE ELECTRICAL SYSTEM

Ignition System

The essential parts of the ignition system are: The distributor, ignition coil, ignition switch, high tension wires and spark plugs. The V-8 has, in addition, a resistor in series with the coil.

Distributor

Note: Starting with 1953 V-8 production, all Buick Series 50s and 70s having the V-8 engine are equipped with a 12 volt electrical system. This means that the battery has 6 cells instead of the customary 3 and that all of the electrical units are arranged to operate on 12 volts. Thus lamps, lamp bulbs, headlights, all switches, ignition coils, generators, starters, starter switches, solenoids, etc., are not interchangeable with any used on the older models having a 6 volt system.

1953 Series 40 engines are equipped with the regular 6 volt system.

The distributor on the V-8 models is mounted at the back of the cylinder block between the two heads.

The distributor can be removed readily by removing the single hold down bolt which is readily accessible at the back of the block.

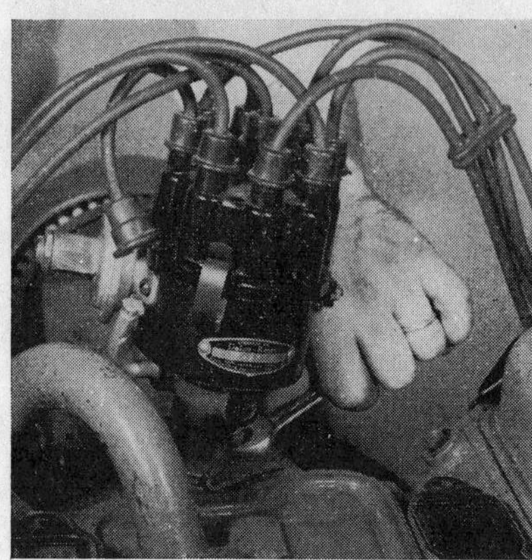

Loosening distributor hold down bolt

The distributor gear is mounted on the bottom of the distributor and the lower end of the shaft is equipped with a male tongue which drives the oil pump.

When reinstalling the distributor the slot in the oil pump shaft must be arranged so that the tongue of the distributor shaft will engage it while the gears are entering into mesh.

An 8 lobe cam is used having one set of points.

Advance and retard is accomplished by loosening the clamp bolt and rotating the distributor body in the desired direction.

The distributor cam rotates in a clockwise direction so that to retard the spark the body will be moved in a clockwise direction. To advance the spark the body will be moved in a counterclockwise direction.

STRAIGHT 8 ENGINES

The distributor is mounted on the right side of the engine and is driven by a tongue in the oil pump shaft. (The distributor drive gear is mounted on the oil pump shaft.)

Since the distributor shaft is driven by a tongue from the oil pump shaft it is advisable to remove the distributor from the car for all servicing, including cleaning and replacement or adjustment of breaker points.

Before removing the distributor, carefully mark the position of the rotor so that it can be installed in a position from which it was removed. CAUTION: Do not crank the engine while the distributor is off the car without making proper allowances when reinstalling the distributor. If for some reason the oil pump is removed and incorrectly replaced relative to the distributor, the ignition can be retimed as follows:

Ignition Timing

Crank the engine until the I.G.N. (ignition) mark on the flywheel is visible through the hole in the flywheel housing.

Now check to see whether number 1 or number 8 cylinder is in the firing position. This can be determined by examining the rocker arms. The cylinder with both rocker arms in the close position (both valves closed) is in the firing position.

In other words, with the I.G.N. mark

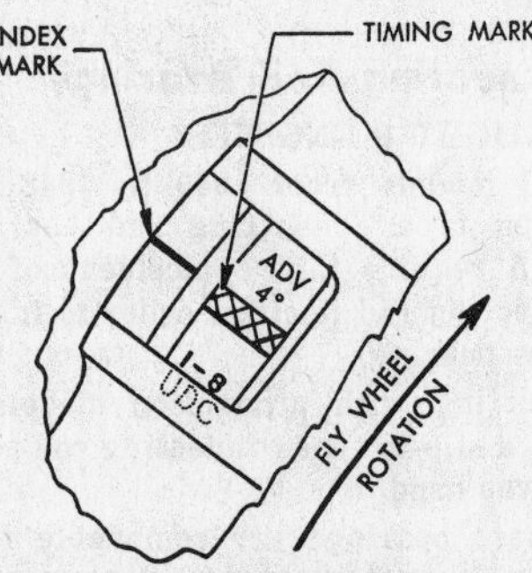

Ignition timing marks

at the hole in the flywheel housing, if both valves are closed on No. 1 cylinder, then No. 1 is in the firing position. If either of the valves are open on No. 1 cylinder, then No. 8 cylinder is in the firing position.

Install the distributor so that the tongue on the distributor engages the notch in the oil pump shaft.

Note the position of the distributor rotor.

Remove the wires from the distributor cap and install the cap. Mark the location of the distributor rotor.

Install into the distributor cap the spark plug wire from the cylinder which is in the firing position. Place this wire in the hole nearest the rotor position. Now, advancing in a counterclockwise direction around the distributor cap, install the wires according to the firing order of this car; that is, if No. 1 is the first wire installed, then continuing around the distributor 1 6 2 5 8 3 7 4; if No. 8 was the first wire installed, then 8 3 7 4 1 6 2 5 will be the order in which to install the wires.

Exact adjustment of the ignition timing can then be made by rotating the distributor body in the usual manner.

1953 V-8 ENGINES

Crank the engine until the flywheel tooth having the No. 5 stamped on it is visible in the inspection hole. This No. 5 indicates 5 degrees that the No. 1 (and also No. 4) piston are before top center.

Note: No. 1 cylinder is the front cylinder in the right bank, No. 4 is the second cylinder in the left bank.

It is an excellent idea to dab a little white paint on the No. 5 which is stamped on the flywheel tooth when it has been located since the number is quite small and it is sometimes difficult to notice it as it passes through the comparably small timing hole.

Remove one of the rocker covers and note the position of the rockers for No. 1 cylinder. If both valves on No. 1 cylinder are in the closed position (all the way up) No. 1 is in the firing position. If either of the valves are depressed, then No. 4 cylinder (2nd cylinder left bank) is the firing position (the engine fires every other revolution).

Remove the distributor cap and notice the position of the rotor. It should be directly under the segment connected to the wire leading to the cylinder in the firing position (either the front cylinder right bank or the 2nd cylinder left bank).

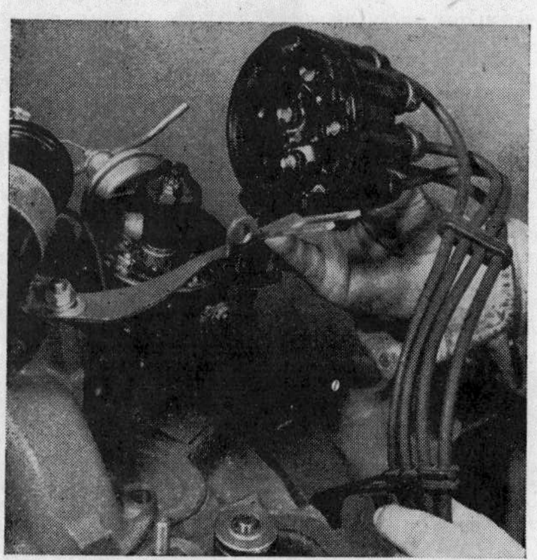

Determine location of rotor

If the rotor is not directly under the required segment one of the following methods may be used to correctly time the ignition.

Reinstalling the Distributor

Remove the distributor from the engine and carefully mark the body in the position occupied by No. 1 spark plug wire.

Now notice the position of the tongue at the lower end of the distributor because this tongue drives the oil pump and must mesh with the oil pump shaft when the distributor is reinstalled.

Set the distributor down into the body after having set the oil pump slot so that it will receive the tongue from the distributor shaft.

Note: As the distributor gear enters into mesh with the camshaft gear it will cause the rotor to turn approximately 10 degrees. This is because spiral beveled gears are used to drive the distributor and the spiral will cause the rotor to turn somewhat as the distributor is entered into the block.

Slight errors can be compensated for by rotating the distributor body slightly.

With the No. 5 (stamped on the flywheel tooth) nicely centered in the inspection hole and the rotor under No. 1 distributor wire, rotate the distributor body just enough that the points are just about to break.

Install the rotor and the distributor cap.

Spark Plug Wire Method

If examination revealed, as stated in the first paragraph, that the rotor was not under the correct segment of the distributor to fire the spark plug in the firing position it may be corrected with the distributor remaining on the car by removing all of the spark plug wires and placing the wire from No. 1 plug into the hole nearest the rotor position. From there, moving in a clockwise direction, place next the wire from the front cylinder left bank; next, from No. 2 cylinder right bank; next, from No. 4 cylinder right bank; next, from No. 4 cylinder left bank; next, from No. 2 cylinder left bank; next, from No. 3 cylinder right bank; next, from No. 3 cylinder left bank; next, from No. 2 cylinder right bank. This will have the same effect as changing the position of the rotor by removing the distributor.

Neon Timing Light

Exact position of the ignition timing can be determined by the use of a neon timing light which is attached according to the manufacturer's instructions to the No. 1 spark plug and the light itself is flashed into the timing hole. Run the engine, and, as the white spot of paint which was placed on the stamped tooth passes the timing hole, the neon light will make it apparently stand still. This is also a very good way to check the advance mechanism since as the throttle is open the white mark will appear to advance and retard in the hole.

Neon timing lights are economical and provide an exact way to set the ignition according to factory specifications.

STRAIGHT 8 ENGINES

Straight 8 engines are timed at almost exactly the same way as V-8 engines with this exception: The mark on the flywheel on straight 8 engines is A.D.V. instead of the stamped No. 5. The two cylinders which might possibly be on the firing position are No. 1 and No. 8 in the straight 8 engines.

On the straight 8 distributors the drive gear is actually mounted on the oil pump and it is advised when the timing is badly off the method of changing the wires in the distributor cap be resorted to since the position of the gear cannot be changed without removing the oil pan and oil pump.

Ignition Coil

1953 V-8 ENGINES

On the 1953 V-8 engines the ignition coil is located at the back of the block towards the left cylinder head. Each ignition coil is equipped with a specified resistor. If this resistor is not used it is easily possible to burn out the coil.

There is a connection on the ignition coil which goes to the starter solenoid and is there for the purpose of bypassing the resistor at any time the engine is being cranked. This allows for compensation for drop in battery voltage when the engine is being cranked.

STRAIGHT 8 ENGINES

The ignition coil is located on the right side of the engine block and is mounted on the engine side cover just forward of the distributor. No service is possible on the ignition coil; if it is found defective it must be replaced.

Spark Plugs

The 1953 V-8 engine is equipped with a 12 volt electrical system. The 12 volt system has absolutely nothing whatever to do with the spark plugs. Since the spark plugs operate at extremely high voltages, the change in the primary voltage of the car has no effect on the spark plug.

Service data on the spark plugs on all models are given in the specifications.

High Tension Wires

1953 V-8 ENGINES

On the V-8 engines the ignition spark plug wires are carried away from the distributor in grommets which are mounted on small brackets attached to the manifold mounting bolts. It is recommended that these mounting grommets be examined occasionally to determine that the wires are not frayed or broken as they pass through the grommet.

STRAIGHT 8 ENGINES

On all Buick models the high tension wires are carried under cover from just above the distributor cap to each spark plug.

Since these wires are enclosed against the side of the cylinder block, they operate normally at a somewhat higher temperature than is generally found in the spark plug wires of other makes and models. Therefore it is absolutely essential that good ignition wire be used on these models.

Ignition Switch

A three-post ignition switch is used. One post for the power lead from the ammeter and the other two posts connect, one to the ignition coil, accelerator vacuum switch and gas gage and the other to the dash accessories.

The ignition switch is mounted from the front side of the dash panel with two screws.

For service, the ignition switch and ignition lock are sold separately.

The Generator Circuit

1953 V-8 ENGINES

Except for the 12 volt potential, all service on the 1953 generator is the same as that on the earlier 6 volt models.

The essential parts of the charging circuit are the generator, regulator, ammeter and battery.

The generator is mounted on the left side of the engine block at the front.

Perhaps the easiest way to remove the generator on straight 8 models is to disconnect the tension bar on top of the generator and rock it up against the cylinder block. Then remove the two bolts which attach the generator bracket to the crankcase.

On straight 8 models it is generally considered to be easier to remove the two bolts which hold the bracket than to remove the bolts which hold the generator to the bracket.

On V8 models, detach the generator from the bracket.

Generator Inspection

Perhaps the easiest way to check a generator is to smell it. A burned generator or armature has a strong acrid odor which is irritating to the nostrils.

If this odor is not, then anything (electrically) wrong with the generator can easily be repaired.

Examine the commutator: It should be a clear chocolate color and free from scratches. The mica between each of the commutator bars should be below the level of the commutator bars.

The brushes should be free to slide up and down in their holders and of sufficient length that the spring tension, with the brush in contact with the armature, when measured with a spring scale, should be not less than the tension given in the data table in section 2 of this manual.

Examine the commutator bars individually for pits and burns. If any one bar is burned it indicates that that bar is connected to a short circuited coil. In this case the practical solution is to discard the armature and install a new one.

Examine the bearings and bearing oil seals.

Note: In the fundamentals section earlier in this part of the manual there is given a complete check for defective generators. See index.

Voltage Regulator

On models up to 1949 the voltage regulator was located on the engine side of the dash panel. On 1950 thru 1953 models the voltage regulator is located on the left fender apron toward the front. The regulator is full control type having three elements: a voltage control element, current control element, and cutout relay.

Complete instructions for the servicing of regulators is given in the fundamentals of automobile servicing earlier in this section. See index.

Starter System

The starter system consists of the battery, heavy battery cables, starter switch and starting motor.

Mechanical check on the condition of the starter is made in exactly the same manner as it is made on a generator. That is, examine the commutator for pits and burns, make certain the brush spring tension is up to the minimum requirement, and check the bearings.

The starter table in this manual (see index) gives the test specifications for all starters.

Special equipment is required to make stall tests, no load tests and developed torque tests on starters.

However, when difficulty is experienced with the starter circuit it is perhaps better to correct the trouble by making following routine check:

First check the battery with hydrometer to be certain that it is up to full charge. If it is not at full charge, then charge the battery before making any further repairs.

Remove both starter cables and thoroughly clean the contact surface both on the battery and in the cable itself. Securely fasten the cleaned cables to the battery posts.

Make certain the battery ground strap contacts the frame or engine block on a clean surface, and also be sure it is tightened securely.

Since more than half of the starter troubles are actually caused by high resistance at the starter switch, it is wise to check the contacts in the starter switch.

An easy way to check the condition of the starter contact points is to connect a low reading voltmeter (zero to one volt scale) to the starter switch terminals (not the relay terminals, connect the meter to the heavy terminals carrying the starter current). Crank the engine and note the voltage reading on the voltmeter. While there are no exact specifications available for the permissible voltage drop, generally speaking, voltage drop of approximately one-quarter volt at the terminals of the starter switch indicate that the starter switch is in need of service.

If this test indicates that the drop across the terminals of the starter switch is less than 1/8 volt, the trouble should then be looked for in the starter itself.

Remove the starter and make the same tests as are given for generators in the fundamentals portion. See index.

Horn Button Removal

STANDARD HORN BUTTONS

The standard horn button on all Buick models is simply pried off.

DE LUXE HORN BLOWING RINGS, 1940-1949

On these models the de luxe ring is held by screws from underneath of the steering wheel hub. Release the screws and the de luxe horn blowing ring will lift off.

DE LUXE WHEELS, 1950-1953

Pry off the medallion and the ring can be released by removing the screws from under the medallion.

Steering Wheel Removal

On all models of Buick the steering wheel can be removed readily after the horn button has been taken off.

Caution: In all cases a steering wheel puller should be used to remove the steering wheel since prying or driving at the wheel will likely result in damage.

Before the steering wheel is removed mark it carefully so that it can be assembled readily in the same position from which it was removed.

On most models a blind spline is used to insure that the wheel will only go on in one direction.

CLUTCH ASSEMBLY

Two types of clutches are used on Buick cars.

The series 40 and 50 use the diaphragm type clutch and series 60 and 70 use the coil spring type clutch.

Grooved facings are generally used on all Buick clutches.

Clutch Removal

Note: The only service adjustment that can be made on a Buick clutch is that of the toe board pedal clearance. If difficulty is experienced with the clutch and adjusting the clearance between the pedal and the toe board does not correct it, it will be necessary to remove the clutch from the car, since no practical service is possible in the car.

Before removing the clutch, take off the lower inspection pan (which will have to be removed in any case) and

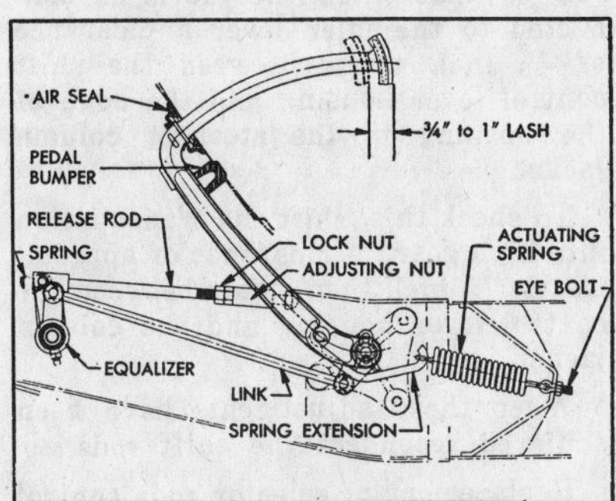

Clutch pedal lash adjustment

check to see if oil has escaped past the rear main bearing or the transmission front bearing, and gotten on the clutch facings.

If oil is found on the front face of the flywheel it will be necessary to replace the rear main bearing oil seal in order to prevent ruining the new clutch.

To remove the clutch the rear axle assembly is shifted backwards and the transmission removed.

The clutch is then removed by unbolting the cover assembly from the flywheel and lowering the clutch through the bottom of the inspection port.

Where observation has shown that the rear main bearing is leaking oil and thus damaging the clutch it is perhaps easier to replace the clutch by removing the engine. In this way a new rear main bearing oil seal and a new clutch are installed at the same time.

TRANSMISSION SHIFTER MECHANISM

EXCEPT DYNAFLOW CARS

Before adjusting the transmission shifter mechanism make certain that the grommets are in good condition and that the linkage will shift freely back and forth. Replace any worn or loose grommet.

Note: In this text the term selector rod and selector will be used to designate the rod and mechanism which complete the cross shift. The term shift rod or shift lever will be used in reference to the rod which completes the longitudinal shift, that is, the shift from second to high or from low to reverse.

The selector rod or lever is then the mechanism which transfers from the low and reverse range to the high and second range. Make the adjustments in the following order: Shift the trans-

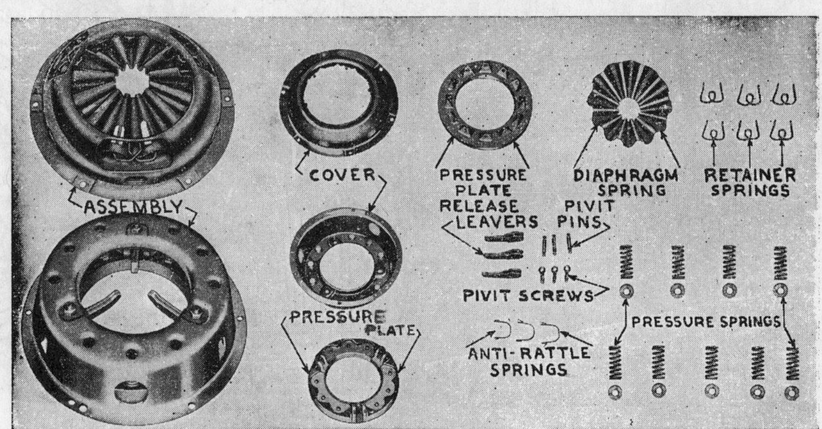

1939 thru 1951 clutches. Upper: used on series 40 & 50. Lower: used on series 60, 70, 80 & 90

TRANSMISSION SHIFTER MECHANISM—*continued*

mission to neutral and disconnect the selector rod from the selector control lever.

(Remove the selector rod back and forth to make sure that the shaft in the transmission moves freely.) Any binding in this selector shaft may prevent the transmission from automatically moving across from the low to the second and high range.

Pull the selector rod to the rear as far as it will go and adjust the trunnion until the trunnion pin is just centered in the hole in the selector control lever insulator at the bottom of the steering column.

Connect up the selector control lever.

Shift Control Adjustment

To insure that the gears enter into full mesh, adjustment of the shift control should be made as follows:

Shift transmission into second gear and disconnect the lower shift rod from the shift idler lever (at the bottom of the steering column).

Replace any of the bushings or insulators which are worn or loose.

Pull forward on the lower shift rod to insure full engagement in second gear and adjust the clevis on the shift rod so that when the clevis is connected to the idler lever a clearance of 1/8 inch exists between the shift control lever housing and the edge of the opening in the steering column jacket.

To check this, shift the transmission into high gear. A clearance of approximately 1/8 inch then exists between the control lever housing and the column jacket.

When these adjustments have been achieved reconnect the shift rods.

Replacement of selector rods control shaft and lower bearings requires removal of the steering column jacket.

When replacing any of the shift rods (in the steering column) it is advisable to remove the steering gear assembly from the car, since this will greatly simplify the job.

Standard Transmission Removal

Set jacks under the frame of the car so that the rear springs are under no tension. Unbolt the rear axle at the spring hangers and at the universal joint and slide it backward out of the way.

To do this it will be necessary to disconnect the brake lines, track bar, shock absorbers, etc.

Disconnect the shift mechanism rods and the speedometer cable.

Support the rear of the engine on a jack.

Remove the rear engine support and note the number of shims on it so that they can be replaced the same way they were removed.

Replace the two top bell housing to

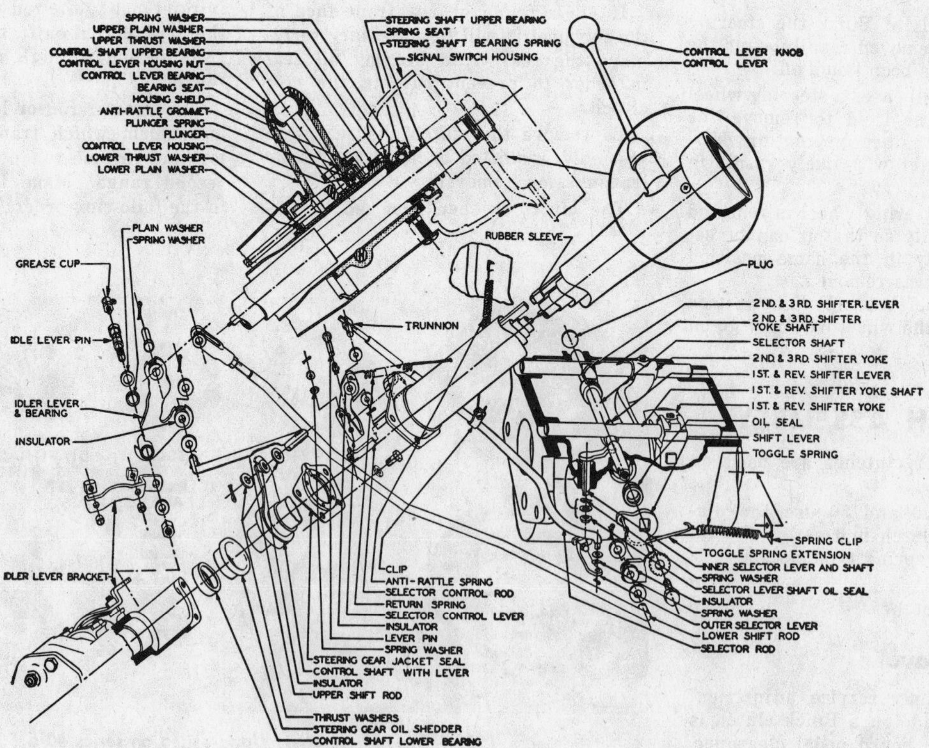

Syncromesh transmission shift mechanism—series 40-50

flywheel housing bolts with two guide pins.

Finish disconnecting the transmission and slide the assembly back on the two guide pins.

The guide pins are used to prevent damaging the clutch or springing it in any way.

Note: When removing any major part or assembly, always mark the parts so that the assemblies can be returned to the same position from which they were removed. This applies particularly to universal joint housings and covers spring hangars, etc.

Standard Transmission Disassembly

Remove the cover, shift shafts, selector rods, fork, springs and balls.

The gears are removed as follows: Drive the countershaft out through the rear of the case and let the cluster drop to the bottom of the case. (A ball is used to hold the countershaft on series 40 and 50 models and a pin is used to hold the countershaft on 60, 70, 80 and 90 models.) Note: Special arbor is available which will retain the needle bearings when driving out the countershaft.

Mainshaft and gears on the series 40 and 50 are removed by taking off the universal joint drive ball. The gears and mainshaft assembly will come out with the ball.

On series 60, 80 and 90 the mainshaft is taken out through the top of the transmission. This is accomplished by removing the shifter fork lock screws and moving the synchronizer drum into high gear. Then move the mainshaft back until it clears the front pilot bearing. Pull the mainshaft up until the second shifter fork is clear and push the fork to the rear of the case, move the mainshaft up and over to the right of the case so as to clear the low gear shift fork, and push the low gear shift fork to the front of the case.

Remove the second speed gear snap ring and slide the second speed gear off the shaft and then do the same with low gear. After both gears are slid out of the way, the mainshaft bearing can then be pulled out of the case with the mainshaft and lifted out the top.

Take out the front bearing lock ring and move the driveshaft into the case and up out of the top of the case.

The countershaft cluster can now be lifted out of the case.

The series 40 and 50 mainshaft is disassembled in exactly the same manner except that it is removed from the case intact.

A brief recap on disassembling the transmissions: Series 40 and 50 mainshaft through the rear of the case mounted in the universal joint drive ball housing. Series 60, 70, 80 and 90 mainshaft disassembled in the case and shaft and bearing removed through the top of the case.

REAR AXLE ASSEMBLY

Removal Procedure

Support the car solidly by mounting stationary jacks under the frame.

Disconnect the parking brake cable and disconnect the brake hose from the line at the frame cross member. (It is a good idea to plug the hose after it is disconnected to prevent foreign matter from entering the lines.)

Disconnect the torque tube ball and mark for reassembly.

Disconnect shock absorbers.

Disconnect the lower ends of the rear springs. NOTE: Left and right hand threads are used in these rear spring hangers.

(The left hand thread is used on the left side of the car, the right thread on the right side of the car.)

After the spring is disconnected, the assembly can be slid out from under the car.

Axle Shaft Removal

In order to remove the axle shaft it is necessary to first remove the rear axle cover assembly. Take out the dif-

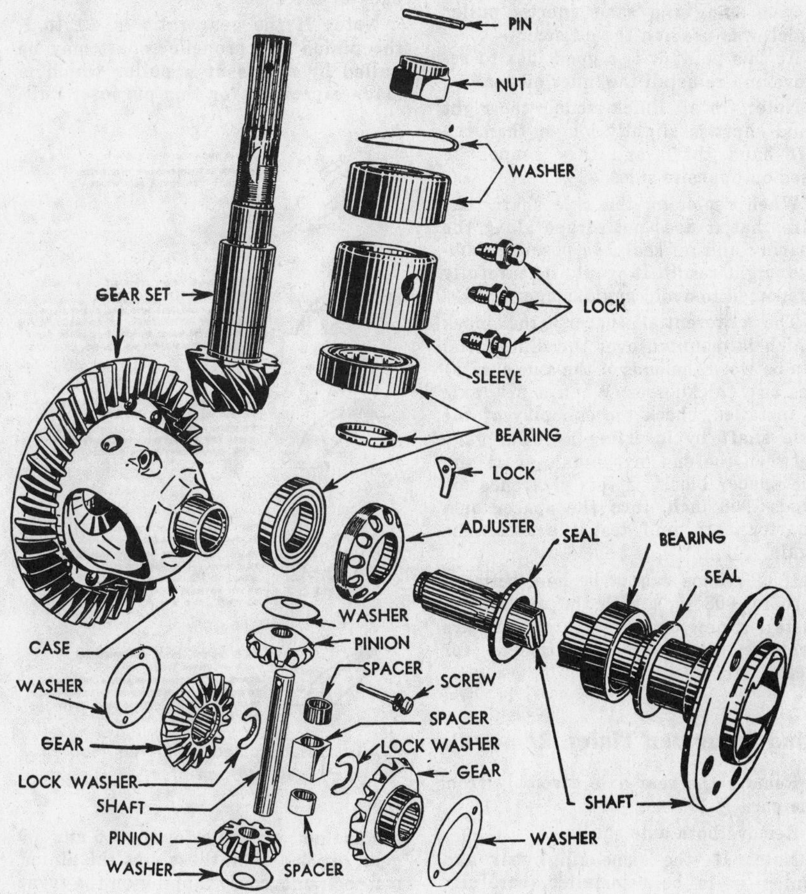

Exploded view of rear axle—typical of all models

AXLE SHAFT REMOVAL—*continued*

ferential pin retaining screw and push out the pinion pin (shaft) then remove the pinions and spacer block.

The axle shaft may then be pushed in toward the center of the car and the locking C washer removed from the end of the axle shaft, after which the shaft may be pulled out of the housing.

It is always a good idea to install new oil seals when replacing an axle shaft.

Axle Bearing Removal

A roller type bearing is used on the axle shaft on all Buick models.

To take out the bearing, first remove the axle shaft and then disconnect the shock absorber link and the brake hose. Remove the brake backing plate and, using an inertia puller, take out the outer oil seal.

The wheel bearing can then be removed using the same inertia puller which was used on the oil seal.

At this point it is a good idea to remove and reinstall the inner oil seal.

Note: On all Buick models the right hand shaft is slightly longer than the left hand shaft, and they cannot be used on opposite sides.

When replacing the axle shaft take care that it does not scrape along the bearing and oil seals, as possible damage might result. It should be carefully supported to avoid any damage.

The differential spacer (the block which is mounted over the differential pin between the ends of the axle shafts) has two thicknesses. When a new axle is installed, check the end play of the axle shaft by inserting a feeler gage between the end of the axle shaft and the spacer block. If this clearance exceeds .008 inch, turn the spacer one-quarter turn and test the clearance again.

If clearance cannot be held between zero to .008 inch with the old spacer, install a new one. Service spacers are oversize to permit some take-up for wear.

Ring Gear and Pinion Removal

Remove the rear axle assembly from the car.

Remove both axle shafts.

Note: If the same ring gear and pinion is to be reinstalled, carefully mark the position of the bearing adjusters on each side of the carrier. It is only necessary to remove one of these bearing adjusters in order to take out the differential assembly (the one on the ring gear side).

Remove the differential assembly by taking out the adjusting cage lock clips and removing the bearing caps.

Remove the three pinion bearing lock sleeve screws from the carrier housing (at the front of the carrier).

Separate the torque tube from the differential carrier at the flange, cut the top off the rivet which holds the pinion to the propeller shaft and drive out the rivet. Slide the propeller shaft off the pinion shaft splines. On older models (1940 and also some later limousines) the torque tube is riveted to the carrier and, unless an oil leak is found the rivets should not be removed. Simply drive the entire drive shaft and pinion out through the rear and then separate the drive shaft from the pinion after they are out of the housing.

Drive the pinion gear out through the back of the case.

Note: If the gear ratio is 4.1 to 1, the pinion and propeller shaft may be pulled by means of a puller which is made especially for this purpose. Pullers are not available for the 3.6 and 3.9 gear ratios and on these jobs the pinion may be removed by tapping on the front end of the propeller shaft with a babbitt hammer or other protected hammering device.

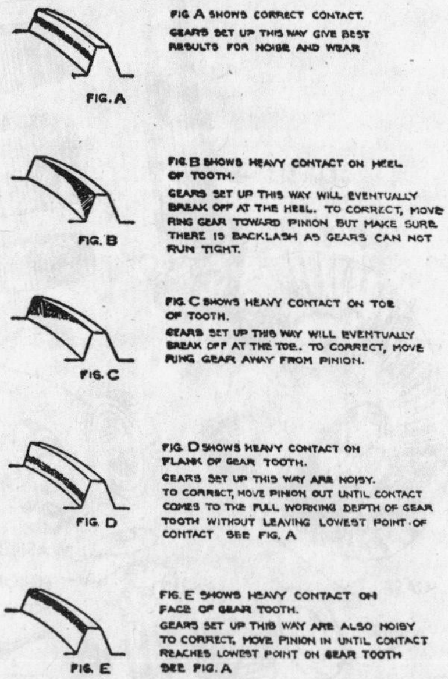

FIG. A SHOWS CORRECT CONTACT.
GEARS SET UP THIS WAY GIVE BEST RESULTS FOR NOISE AND WEAR
FIG. A

FIG. B SHOWS HEAVY CONTACT ON HEEL OF TOOTH.
GEARS SET UP THIS WAY WILL EVENTUALLY BREAK OFF AT THE HEEL. TO CORRECT, MOVE RING GEAR TOWARD PINION BUT MAKE SURE THERE IS BACKLASH AS GEARS CAN NOT RUN TIGHT.
FIG. B

FIG. C SHOWS HEAVY CONTACT ON TOE OF TOOTH.
GEARS SET UP THIS WAY WILL EVENTUALLY BREAK OFF AT THE TOE. TO CORRECT, MOVE RING GEAR AWAY FROM PINION.
FIG. C

FIG. D SHOWS HEAVY CONTACT ON FLANK OF GEAR TOOTH.
GEARS SET UP THIS WAY ARE NOISY.
TO CORRECT, MOVE PINION OUT UNTIL CONTACT COMES TO THE FULL WORKING DEPTH OF GEAR TOOTH WITHOUT LEAVING LOWEST POINT OF CONTACT SEE FIG. A
FIG. D

FIG. E SHOWS HEAVY CONTACT ON FACE OF GEAR TOOTH.
GEARS SET UP THIS WAY ARE ALSO NOISY
TO CORRECT, MOVE PINION IN UNTIL CONTACT REACHES LOWEST POINT ON GEAR TOOTH SEE FIG. A
FIG. E

Markings obtained using red lead or prussian blue

Remove the pinion bearing shims carefully so that they may be reinstalled if the same pinion is to be replaced.

Note: The pinion bearing lock nut is staked to prevent it from coming off. This staking must be raised in order to remove the nut.

The pinion bearings must be pressed off the pinion.

Ring gears and pinions can be replaced only in matched sets.

Pinion Setting

The pinion gears used on all Buick cars are marked with a code number which indicates its proper setting in relation to the housing and the ring gear. At any time a pinion is removed from the third member housing great care should be used that the shims are not damaged in any way.

Each shim should be wiped carefully and its thickness determined with micrometer; a record should be made of the thickness of each shim and the total thickness of all the shims, so that exactly that thickness may be arrived at in the event some of the shims become lost or damaged.

Perhaps the easiest way to replace a pinion gear in a Buick is to secure from the parts jobber a new pinion and ring gear set with the pinion marking exactly the same as the pinion marking on the old gear which has been removed. That is, if the old gear is marked plus 5, then first try to secure another pinion which is also marked plus 5. If this can be done, install the pinion, using exactly the same shims which were removed from the old pinion. The setting of the pinion will then be exactly as required.

For the purpose of setting the pinion, the manufacturer has arbitrarily chosen a certain micrometer setting which is called the nominal or zero setting. A definite number of shims is required to produce this zero setting.

A plus reading (plus 1, plus 2 or plus 3, etc.) indicates that that pinion is to be moved toward the front of the car from the nominal setting. This would require removing shims. If the pinion is marked with a minus setting (minus 1, minus 2, minus 3, etc.), this indicates that the pinion would have to be moved away from the front of the car or toward the rear and would require addition of shims to produce this setting.

Therefore, if the pinion being removed was marked plus 3 and it was necessary to replace this pinion with one marked minus 2, then it would be necessary to move the new pinion rearward .003 inch to arrive at the zero or nominal setting, and .002 more to arrive at the minus .002 setting. This would require a total of .005 thick shims added to the number found in the car when the pinion was removed.

If the original shims are lost or damaged, and no record was made of their thickness, it will be necessary to use a special micrometer which is available from Buick dealers in order to arrive at the proper basic number of shims required to properly set the pinion.

Caution: Each ring gear and pinion is supplied in a box which also contains shims for adjusting the pinion gear. These shims are to be used as required and do not necessarily represent the exact number of shims that will actually be required.

After the proper number of shims have been installed and the pinion is securely locked in place with the three tapered lock screws in the housing, proceed to mount the differential assembly with its new ring gear.

Set up the ring gear so that there is .008 to .012 inch back lash between the ring gear and pinion (as measured with the dial gage) and securely tighten the bearing caps.

Caution: When this setting is secured make absolutely certain that the bearing adjusting cages are in firm contact with the bearing races.

This can be determined by backing off on one adjuster (preferably the left one) and observe the bearing roller and outer race until the rollers and race just stop turning, then retighten the adjuster four or five notches. This will properly seat the bearing and the adjusters. Then slowly back off on the adjuster until the bearing outer race just stops turning.

It is advisable to repeat the above operation of tightening and loosening the bearings adjuster to make certain that it is properly positioned.

Final tightening of the bearing caps should be 90 to 100 foot-pounds torque.

After the rear is completely set up, recheck the back lash of the ring gear to make certain that it is between .008 and .012 inch.

Caution: If the old ring gear and pinion are being replaced (not a new set), the original back lash of the gears should be maintained to insure quiet contact.

If back lash is greater than specified, shift the ring gear over toward the pinion; if it is less than specified, shift the ring gear away from the pinion.

This is usually accomplished by moving the adjuster on one side one notch inward and the adjuster on the opposite side one notch outward at the same time. This shift should be accomplished after the bearing caps have been loosened slightly.

Note: One notch is equal to approximately .004 to .005 inch back lash.

PINION SETTING TABLE FOR GAUGE J 681-A

PINION MARKING (+)	+1	+2	+3	+4	+5	+6	+7	+8	+9	+10	+11	+12	+13	+14	+15
MICROMETER READING	.378	.377	.376	.375	.374	.373	.372	.371	.370	.369	.368	.367	.366	.365	.364

PINIONS MARKED "O" USE THE NOMINAL MICROMETER READING OF **.379**

PINION MARKING (−)	−1	−2	−3	−4	−5	−6	−7	−8	−9	−10	−11	−12	−13	−14	−15
MICROMETER READING	.380	.381	.382	.383	.384	.385	.386	.387	.388	.389	.390	.391	.392	.393	.394

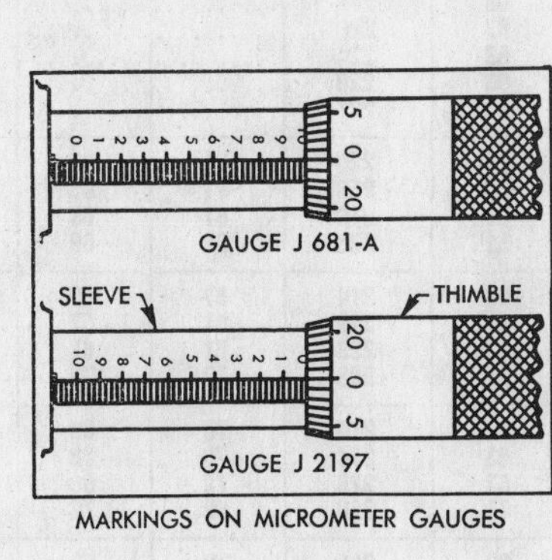

MARKINGS ON MICROMETER GAUGES

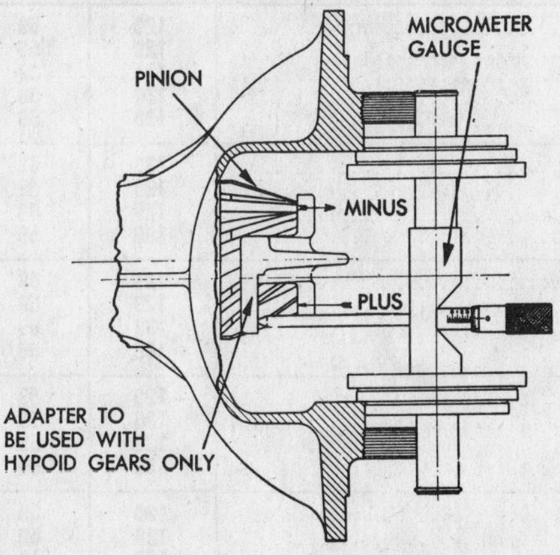

PINION SETTING TABLE FOR GAUGE J 2197

PINION MARKING (+)	+1	+2	+3	+4	+5	+6	+7	+8	+9	+10	+11	+12	+13	+14	+15
MICROMETER READING	.803	.804	.805	.806	.807	.808	.809	.810	.811	.812	.813	.814	.815	.816	.817

PINIONS MARKED "O" USE THE NOMINAL MICROMETER READING OF **.802**

PINION MARKING (−)	−1	−2	−3	−4	−5	−6	−7	−8	−9	−10	−11	−12	−13	−14	−15
MICROMETER READING	.801	.800	.799	.798	.797	.796	.795	.794	793	.792	.791	.790	.789	.788	.787

Pinion setting tables

CADILLAC SPECIFICATIONS

Starting Serial and Motor Numbers

Starting Serial Numbers

1940-1953—Same as motor numbers.

Location

1940-1953—Same place as motor numbers.

Starting Motor Numbers

1940, Ser. 60-S 6320001
Ser. 62 8320001
Ser. 72 7320001
Ser. 75 3320001
Ser. 90 5320001
1941, Ser. 61 5340001
Ser. 62 8340001
Ser. 63 7340001
Ser. 60-S 6340001
Ser. 67 9340001
Ser. 75 3340001
1942, Ser. 61 5380001
Ser. 62 8380001
Ser. 63 7380001
Ser. 60-S 6380001
Ser. 67 9380001
Ser. 75 3380001
1946, Ser. 61 5400001
Ser. 62 8400001
Ser. 60-S 6400001
Ser. 75 3400001
1947, Ser. 61 5420001
Ser. 62 8420001
Ser. 60-S 6420001
Ser. 75 3420001

1948-1953—First four digits indicate year and series, i.e. 486100001; year 1948, series 61, etc. 1948 starting numbers end in 1, i.e. 486100001. 1949-1953 starting numbers end in 0, i.e. 496100000 to 536000000.

Location

1940-1941—Right side of chain case in front of generator.

1942-1948—Right side of crankcase above water pump and right frame side bar behind engine support bracket.

1949-1953—Boss cast on front face of right-hand block and right frame side bar behind engine support bracket.

General Specifications

Year	Model	Wheelbase (in.)	Tread (in.)		Overall Dimensions (in.)			Shipping Weight* (lb.)	Tire Size (in.)
			Front	Rear	Length†	Width	Height■		
1940	Series 60S	127	58	61	217	....	....	4070	7.00-16
	Series 62	129	58	59	216	....	....	....	7.00-16
	Series 72	139	58	63	227	....	....	....	7.50-16
	Series 75	141	61	63	229	....	....	5045	7.50-16
	Series 90	141	61	63	226	....	....	....	7.50-16
1941	60S, 61, 62, 63	126	59	63	217(m)	....	....	....	7.00-15
	67, 75	139-136	59	63	228(n)	....	....	....	7.50-16
1942	61, 63	126	59	63	215	....	....	4115	7.00 15
	Series 62	129	59	63	220	....	....	4115	7.00-15
	Series 60S	133	59	63	224	....	....	4115	7.00-15
	Series 67	139	59	63	228	....	....	4605	7.50-16
	Series 75	136	59	63	227	....	....	4605	7.50-16
1946	Series 60	133	59	63	225	81	63	....	7.00-15
	Series 61	126	59	63	216	81	65	....	7.00-15
	Series 62	129	59	63	219	81	63	4253	7.00-15
	Series 75	136	58	62	226	82	69	....	7.50-16
1947	Series 61	126	59	63	214	81	69	4138	7.00-15
	Series 62	129	59	63	219	81	67	4201	7.00-15
	Series 60	133	59	63	223	81	67	4351	7.00-15
	Series 75	136	59	62	226	82	72	4836	7.50-16
1948	Series 61	126	59	63	214	79	68	4165	8.20-15
	Series 62	126	59	63	214	79	68	4235	8.20-15
	Series 60S	133	59	63	226	78	68	4370	8.20-15
	Series 75	136	59	63	226	82	72	4875	7.50-16
1949	Series 61	126	59	63	215	79	63	3950	8.20-15
	Series 62	126	59	63	215	79	63	3980	8.20-15
	Series 60	133	59	63	227	78	63	4150	8.20-15
	Series 75	136	59	63	226	82	69	4665	7.50-16
1950	Series 61	122	59	63	212	80	62	3870	8.00-15
	Series 62	126	59	63	216	80	63	4010	8.00-15
	Series 60	130	59	63	225	80	63	....	8.00-15
	Series 75	147	59	63	237	80	64	....	8.20-15
1951	Series 61	122	59	63	212	80	62	3940	8.00-15
	Series 62	126	59	63	216	80	63	4040	8.00-15
	Series 60	130	59	63	225	80	63	4200	8.00-15
	Series 75	147	59	63	237	80	64	....	8.20-15

(m) Models 61, 63-215; 62-216. (n) Model 75-226.

General Specifications—*continued*

Year	Model	Wheelbase (in.)	Tread (in.) Front	Tread (in.) Rear	Overall Dimensions (in.) Length†	Overall Dimensions (in.) Width	Overall Dimensions (in.) Height■	Shipping Weight* (lb.)	Tire Size (in.)
1952	60, 8 cyl.	130	59	63	224	80	63	....	8.00–15
	62, 8 cyl.	126	59	63	220	80	63	....	8.00–15
	75, 8 cyl.	147	59	63	236	80	64	....	8.20–15
1953	60, 8 cyl.	130	59	63	224	80	63	....	8.00–15
	62, 8 cyl.	126	59	63	220	80	63	....	8.00–15
	75, 8 cyl.	147	59	63	236	80	64	....	8.20–15

†—Including bumper and guards. ■—Road to roof, no load. *—Cheapest 5 pass. 4 dr. sed. or equivalent.

General Engine Specifications

Year	Model	Number of Cylinders Bore and Stroke	Piston Displacement, Cubic Inches	Compression Ratio (To–1)	Taxable (A.M.A.) Hp.	Developed Horse Power: Bare Engine	Developed Horse Power: With Accessories	Maximum Torque Ft. Lbs.
1940	60S, 62, 8 Cyl.	8-3½ x 4½	346.0	6.25	39.2	135 @ 3400	....	250 @ 1700
	72, 75, 8 Cyl.	8-3½ x 4½	346.0	6.70	39.2	140 @ 3400	....	270 @ 1700
	90, 16 Cyl.	16-3¼ x 3¼	431.0	6.75	67.6	185 @ 3600	....	324 @ 1700
1941	60S, 61, 8 Cyl.	8-3½ x 4½	346.0	7.25	39.2	150 @ 3400	....	283 @ 1700
	62, 63, 8 Cyl.	8-3½ x 4½	346.0	7.25	39.2	150 @ 3400	....	283 @ 1700
	67, 8 Cyl.	8-3½ x 4½	346.0	7.25	39.2	150 @ 3400	....	283 @ 1700
	75, 8 Cyl.	8-3½ x 4½	346.0	7.25	39.2	150 @ 3400	....	283 @ 1700
1942	60S, 8 Cyl.	8-3½ x 4½	346.0	7.25	39.2	150 @ 3400	....	283 @ 1700
	61, 62, 63, 8 Cyl.	8-3½ x 4½	346.0	7.25	39.2	150 @ 3400	....	283 @ 1700
	67, 8 Cyl.	8-3½ x 4½	346.0	7.25	39.2	150 @ 3400	....	283 @ 1700
	75, 8 Cyl.	8-3½ x 4½	346.0	7.25	39.2	150 @ 3400	....	283 @ 1700
1946	60S, 61, 62, 8 Cyl.	8-3½ x 4½	346.0	7.25	39.2	150 @ 3600	130 @ 3200	274 @ 1600
	75, 8 Cyl.	8-3½ x 4½	346.0	7.25	39.2	150 @ 3600	130 @ 3200	274 @ 1600
1947	60S, 61, 62, 8 Cyl.	8-3½ x 4½	346.0	7.25	39.2	150 @ 3600	130 @ 3200	274 @ 1600
	75, 8 Cyl.	8-3½ x 4½	346.0	7.25	39.2	150 @ 3600	130 @ 3200	274 @ 1600
1948	60S, 61, 62, 8 Cyl.	8-3½ x 4½	346.0	7.25	39.2	150 @ 3400	130 @ 3200	283 @ 1600
	75, 8 Cyl.	8-3½ x 4½	346.0	7.25	39.2	150 @ 3400	130 @ 3200	283 @ 1600
1949	60S, 61, 62, 8 Cyl.	8-3$\frac{13}{16}$ x 3⅝	331.0	7.50	46.5	160 @ 3800	141 @ 3400	312 @ 1800
	75, 8 Cyl.	8-3$\frac{13}{16}$ x 3⅝	331.0	7.50	46.5	160 @ 3800	141 @ 3400	312 @ 1800
1950	60S, 61, 62, 8 Cyl.	8-3$\frac{13}{16}$ x 3⅝	331.0	7.50	46.5	160 @ 3600	141 @ 3400	312 @ 1800
	75, 8 Cyl.	8-3$\frac{13}{16}$ x 3⅝	331.0	7.50	46.5	160 @ 3600	141 @ 3400	312 @ 1800
1951	60, 61, 62, 8 Cyl.	8-3$\frac{13}{16}$ x 3⅝	331.0	7.50	46.5	160 @ 3800	141 @ 3400	312 @ 1800
	75, 8 Cyl.	8-3$\frac{13}{16}$ x 3⅝	331.0	7.50	46.5	160 @ 3800	141 @ 3400	312 @ 1800
1952	60, 62, 75, 8 Cyl.	V8-3$\frac{13}{16}$ x 3⅝	331.0	7.50	46.5	190 @ 4000	....	322 @ 2400
1953	60, 62, 75, 8 Cyl.	V8-3$\frac{13}{16}$ x 3⅝	331.0	8.25	46.5	210 @ 4150	....	330 @ 2700

Dimensions of Valves

Year	Model	Overall Length Inlet	Overall Length Exhaust	Head Diameter Inlet	Head Diameter Exhaust	Seat Angle (deg.) Inlet	Seat Angle (deg.) Exhaust	Stem Diameter Inlet	Stem Diameter Exhaust	Key Type	O.D. of Seat Insert Inlet	O.D. of Seat Insert Exhaust
1940 to 42	60, 61, 62, 63, 67, 72, 75	5.531	5.531	1.881	1.631	45	45	.342	.341	split lock	....	....
	90	5.531	5.546	1.881	1.375	45	45	.342	.341	split lock	....	....
1946–47	60, 61, 62, 75	5.515	5.515	1.886	1.636	45	45	.342	.341	split lock	....	....
1948	61, 62, 60S, 75	5.515	5.515	1.881	1.631	45	45	.342	.341	split lock	....	....
1949 to 51	61, 62, 60, 75	4.549	4.549	1.750	1.437	44	44	.344	.344	split lock	....	....

CADILLAC SPECIFICATIONS

Dimension of Valves—*continued*

Year	Model	Overall Length		Head Diameter		Seat Angle (deg.)		Stem Diameter		Key Type	O.D. of Seat Insert	
		Inlet	Exhaust	Inlet	Exhaust	Inlet	Exhaust	Inlet	Exhaust		Inlet	Exhaust
1952	60, 62, 75, 8 cyl.	4.549	4.544	1.750	1.562	44	44	.34375	.341	....	....	....
1953	60, 62, 75	4.648	4.656	1.750	1.562	44	44	.3425	.3420	....	....	....

Engine Overhaul Specifications

Year	Model	Removed From	PISTONS: Piston Skirt Clearances (Maximum)			RING CAP CLEARANCES (Maximum)				PISTON PIN		ROD BEARINGS		
			Top	Bottom	Limit	Top Ring	Second Ring	Third Ring	Oil Ring	Type	Fit	Oil Clearance	Wear Limit	Side Play
1940	60S. 62, 8 Cyl.	A	.002	.002	.006	.012	.012	.015	.015	FL	.0004	.0015	.004	.008-.014
	72, 75, 8 Cyl.	A	.002	.002	.006	.012	.012	.015	.015	FL	....	.0015	.004	.008-.014
1941	60S, 61, 8 Cyl.	A	.0017	.0021	.006	.017	.017	.017	.017	FL	.0003	.0015	.004	.008-.014
	62, 63, 8 Cyl.	A	.0017	.0021	.006	.017	.017	.017	.017	FL	.0003	.0015	.004	.008-.014
	67, 75, 8 Cyl.	A	.0017	.0021	.006	.017	.017	.017	.017	FL	.0003	.0015	.004	.008-.014
1942	60S, 8 Cyl.	A	.002	.002	.006	.017	.017	.017	.017	FL	.0001	.0015	.004	.008-.014
	61, 62, 63, 8 Cyl.	A	.002	.002	.006	.017	.017	.017	.017	FL	.0001	.0015	.004	.008-.014
	67, 75, 8 Cyl.	A	.002	.002	.006	.017	.017	.017	.017	FL	.0001	.0015	.004	.008-.014
1946	60S, 61, 62, 8 Cyl.	A	.002	.0005	.004	.023	.023	....	.023	FL	.0001	.0015	.004	.008-.014
	75, 8 Cyl.	A	.0005	.0005	.004	.023	.023	....	.023	FL	.0001	.0015	.004	.008-.014
1947	61, 62, 60S, 8 Cyl.	A	.002	.0005	.004	.023	.023	....	.023	FL	.0001	.0015	.004	.008-.014
	75, 8 Cyl.	A	.002	.0005	.004	.023	.023	....	.023	FL	.0001	.0015	.004	.008-.014
1948	60S, 61, 62, 8 Cyl.	A	.0021	.019	.004	.023	.023	....	.023	FL	.0001	.0020	.005	.008-.014
	75, 8 Cyl.	A	.002	.0005	.004	.023	.023	....	.023	FL	....	.0020	.005	.008-.014
1949	60S, 61, 62, 8 Cyl.	A	.0021	.0005	.004	.020	.020	....	.020	FL	.0001	.002	.005	.008-.014
	75, 8 Cyl.	A	.0021	.0005	.004	.020	.020	....	.020	FL	.0001	.002	.005	.008-.014
1950	60S, 61, 62, 8 Cyl.	A	.0021	.0005	.004	.020	.020	....	.020	FL	.0001	.002	.005	.008-.014
	75, 8 Cyl.	A	.0015	.0015	.004	.020	.020	....	.020	FL	.0001	.002	.005	.008-.014
1951	60, 61, 62, 8 Cyl.	A	.0015	.0015	.005	.020	.020	....	.020	FL	.0003	.002	.005	.008-.014
	75, 8 Cyl.	A	.0015	.0015	.005	.020	.020	....	.020	FL	.0003	.002	.005	.008-.014
1952	60, 62, 75, 8 Cyl.	A	.0015	.0000	.005	.020	.020	....	.020	LR	.00007	.0023	.005	.008-.014
1953	60, 62, 75, 8 Cyl.	A	.0015	.0000	.005	.020	.020	....	.020	LR	.0001	.0035	.005	.008-.014

A—Rods removed from above.
FL—Floating Type with Locking Ring at each end.
†—"O" marks on both sprockets align with shaft centers.
Sp—Sprockets.

Pistons and Piston Pins

Year	Model	PISTONS				PISTON PINS		
		Diameter	Material	Type	No. of Rings	Length	Diameter	How Held
1940 to 42	60S, 62, 72, 75	3.5	Alum.	Ts	4	$3\frac{1}{16}$	.875	F
	90	3.25	Alum.	Ts	3	$2\frac{25}{32}$	.8125	R
1946 to 48	60S, 61, 62, 75	3.5	Alum.	Ts	3	$3\frac{1}{16}$	.875	F
1949	61, 62, 60, 75	3.8125	Alum.	Ts	3	$2\frac{3}{4}$	1.000	F
1950-51	61, 62, 60, 75	3.8125	Alum. Alloy	Ts	3	$3\frac{3}{32}$	1.000	R

Ts—"T" slot. Alum—Aluminum. F—Floating. R—Locked in rod. C—Cam ground.

Pistons and Piston Pins—*continued*

Year	Model	PISTONS				PISTON PINS		
		Diameter	Material	Type	No. of Rings	Length	Diameter	How Held
1952	60, 62, 75, 8 cyl.	3.8125	Alum. Alloy	Ts,C	3	3.093	1.00	R
1953	60, 62, 75, 8 cyl.	3.8125	Alum. Alloy	Ts,C	3	3.093	1.00	R

and Wear Limit Table

CRANKSHAFT		VALVES									OPERATING OIL PRESSURE			
Main Bearing Oil Clearance	Shaft End Play	Spring Tension (Maximum) Inlet	Spring Tension (Maximum) Exhaust	Spring Tension (Maximum) Low Limit	Guide Clearance	Seat Angle Inlet	Seat Angle Exhaust	Valve Timing, Inlet. Valve Opens (Deg.)	Camshaft Drive	Gear Marks	Pounds At M.P.H.	Low Limit§	Model	Year
.0015–.0025	.001–.005	145@1.581	145@1.581	115	.0033	45°	45°	T.D.C.	Chain	† Sp	25@30	15	60S, 62, 8 Cyl.	1940
.0015–.0025	.001–.005	145@1.581	145@1.581	115	.0033	45°	45°	T.D.C.	Chain	† Sp	25@30	15	72, 75, 8 Cyl.	
.0015–.0025	.001–.005	145@1.581	145@1.581	115	.0033	45°	45°	T.D.C.	Chain	† Sp	25@30	15	60S, 61, 8 Cyl.	1941
.0015–.0025	.001–.005	145@1.581	145@1.581	115	.0033	45°	45°	T.D.C.	Chain	† Sp	25@30	15	62, 63, 8 Cyl.	
.0015–.0025	.001–.005	145@1.581	145@1.581	115	.0033	45°	45°	T.D.C.	Chain	† Sp	25@30	15	67, 75, 8 Cyl.	
.0015–.0025	.001–.005	145@1.581	145@1.581	115	.0033	45°	45°	T.D.C.	Chain	† Sp	25@30	15	60S, 8 Cyl.	1942
.0015–.0025	.001–.005	145@1.581	145@1.581	115	.0033	45°	45°	T.D.C.	Chain	† Sp	25@30	15	61, 62, 63, 8 Cyl.	
.0015–.0025	.001–.005	145@1.581	145@1.581	115	.0033	45°	45°	T.D.C.	Chain	† Sp	25@30	15	67, 75, 8 Cyl.	
.0015–.0025	.001–.005	145@1.578	145@1.578	115	.0035	45°	45°	T.D.C.	Chain	† Sp	25@30	15	60S, 61, 62, 8 Cyl.	1946
.0015–.0025	.001–.005	145@1.578	145@1.578	115	.0035	45°	45°	T.D.C.	Chain	† Sp	25@30	15	75, 8 Cyl.	
.0015–.0025	.001–.005	145@1.578	145@1.578	115	.0035	45°	45°	T.D.C.	Chain	† Sp	25@30	15	60, 61, 62, 8 Cyl.	1947
.0015–.0025	.001–.005	145@1.578	145@1.578	115	.0035	45°	45°	T.D.C.	Chain	† Sp	25@30	15	75, 8 Cyl.	
.0015–.0025	.001–.005	145@1.578	145@1.578	115	.0035	45°	45°	T.D.C.	Chain	† Sp	25@30	15	60S, 61, 62, 8 Cyl.	1948
.0015–.0025	.001–.005	145@1.578	145@1.578	115	.0035	45°	45°	T.D.C.	Chain	† Sp	25@30	15	75, 8 Cyl.	
.0015–.0025	.001–.005	135@1.366	135@1.366	105	.0035	44°	44°	19B	Chain	† Sp	35@30	20	60S, 61, 62, 8 Cyl.	1949
.0015–.0025	.001–.005	135@1.366	135@1.366	105	.0035	44°	44°	19B	Chain	† Sp	35@30	20	75, 8 Cyl.	
.0015–.0025	.001–.005	135@1.366	135@1.366	105	.0035	44°	44°	24B	Chain	† Sp	35@30	20	60S, 61, 62, 8 Cyl.	1950
.0015–.0025	.001–.005	135@1.366	135@1.366	105	.0035	44°	44°	24B	Chain	† Sp	35@30	20	75, 8 Cyl.	
.0015–.0025	.001–.005	135@1.366	135@1.366	105	.0035	44°	44°	24B	Chain	† Sp	28@30	16	60, 61, 62, 8 Cyl.	1951
.0015–.0025	.001–.005	135@1.366	135@1.366	105	.0035	44°	44°	24B	Chain	† Sp	28@30	16	75, 8 Cyl.	
.0015–.0025	.001–.005	135@1.366	135@1.366	......	.0017	44°	44°	14B	Chain	......	33@30	......	60, 62, 75, 8 Cyl.	1952
.0008–.0025	.001–.005	140@1.326	140@1.326	......	.001–.0025	44°	44°	22B	Chain	......	33@30	......	60, 62, 75, 8 Cyl.	1953

T.D.C.—Top dead center. B—Before top center.
§—Car may be operated safely at much lower pressures, but low oil pressure indicates malfunction which should be corrected.

Crankshaft Bearing Journal Sizes

Year	Model	Connecting Rod Journals		Main Bearing Journals				
		Diameter	Length	No. 1 Diameter	No. 2 Diameter	No. 3 Diameter	No. 4 Diameter	No. 5 Diameter
1940 to 42	60S, 61, 62. 63, 67, 72, 75	2.460	2.0312	2.500	2.500	2.500	......	......
	60-V16	2.00	1.750	2.500	2.500	2.500	†2.500	2.500
1946 to 48	60, 61, 62, 75	2.4595	2.294	2.4995	2.4995	2.4995	......	......
1949–50	60, 61, 62, 75	2.2493	2.00	2.4990	2.4990	2.4990	2.4990	2.4990
1951	60. 61, 62, 75	2.250	2.00	2.500	2.500	2.500	2.500	2.500

CADILLAC SPECIFICATIONS

Crankshaft Bearing Journal Sizes—*continued*

Year	Model	Connecting Rod Journals		Main Bearing Journals				
		Diameter	Length	No. 1 Diameter	No. 2 Diameter	No. 3 Diameter	No. 4 Diameter	No. 5 Diameter
1952	60, 62, 75, 8 cyl....................	2.250	2.00	2.500	2.500	2.500	2.500	2.500
1953	60, 62, 75, 8 cyl....................	2.250	....	2.5-.907	2.5-.907	2.5-.907	2.5-.907	2.5-1.622

†—No. 6, 7, 8, 9 bearing same as No. 4.5.

Engine Tune-Up Specifications

Year	Model	Spark Plugs Type	Spark Plugs Gap	Distributor Point Gap	Distributor Cam Dwell, (Deg.)	Ignition Timing, (Deg.)	Ignition Timing Mark and Location	Compression Pressure at R.P.M.	Operating Tappet Clearance Inlet	Operating Tappet Clearance Exhaust	Carburetor Fuel Float Height	Minimum Engine Idle Speed at R.P.M.
1940	60S, 62, 8 Cyl..............	AC-104	.025	.015	31	5B	IGA dmpr	155@1000	AA	AA	5/8" fuel	375
	72, 75, 8 Cyl..............	AC-104	.025	.015	31	5B	IGA dmpr	170@1000	AA	AA	5/8" fuel	375
	90, 16 Cyl..............	AC-104	.032	.015	31	6B	IGA dmpr	180@1000	AA	AA	13/64 float	375
1941	60S, 61, 8 Cyl..............	AC-104	.025	.015	31	5B	IGA dmpr	182@1000	AA	AA	1/8" float	375
	62, 63, 8 Cyl..............	AC-104	.025	.015	31	5B	IGA dmpr	182@1000	AA	AA	1/8" float	375
	67, 8 Cyl..............	AC-104	.025	.015	31	5B	IGA dmpr	182@1000	AA	AA	1/8", float	375
	75, 8 Cyl..............	AC-104	.025	.015	31	5B	IGA dmpr	182@1000	AA	AA	1/8" float	375
1942	60S, 8 Cyl..............	AC-104	.025	.015	31	5B	IGA dmpr	180@1000	AA	AA	5/8" float	375
	61, 62, 63, 8 Cyl..............	AC-104	.025	.015	31	5B	IGA dmpr	180@1000	AA	AA	5/8" float	375
	67, 8 Cyl..............	AC-104	.025	.015	31	5B	IGA dmpr	180@1000	AA	AA	5/8" float	375
	75, 8 Cyl..............	AC-104	.025	.015	31	5B	IGA dmpr	180@1000	AA	AA	5/8" float	375
1946	60S, 61, 62, 8 Cyl.	AC-104	.025	.015	31	5B	IGA dmpr	182@1000	AA	AA	5/8" float	375
	75, 8 Cyl..............	AC-104	.025	.015	31	5B	IGA dmpr	180@1000	AA	AA	5/8" float	375
1947	61, 62, 60S, 8 Cyl..............	AC-104	.025	.015	31	5B	IGA dmpr	180@1000	AA	AA	5/8" float	375
	75, 8 Cyl..............	AC-104	.025	.015	31	5B	IGA dmpr	180@1000	AA	AA	5/8" float	375
1948	60S, 61, 62, 8 Cyl..............	AC-104	.025	.015	31±1½	5B	IGA dmpr	180@1000	AA	AA	5/8" float	375
	75, 8 Cyl..............	AC-104	.025	.015	31±1½	5B	IGA dmpr	180@1000	AA	AA	5/8" float	375
1949	60S, 61, 62, 8 Cyl.	AC-48	.035	.015	31±1½	5B	IGA dmpr	194@1000	AA	AA	9/64" float	375
	75, 8 Cyl..............	AC-48	.035	.015	31±1½	5B	IGA dmpr	194@1000	AA	AA	9/64" float	375
1950	60S, 61, 62, 8 Cyl.	AC-46-5	.035	.015	31±1½	5B	IGA dmpr	194@1000	AA	AA	9/64" float	375
	75, 8 Cyl..............	AC-46-5	.035	.015	31±1½	5B	IGA dmpr	194@1000	AA	AA	9/64" float	375
1951	60, 61, 62, 8 Cyl.	AC-46-5	.035	.013-.018	31±1½	5B	IGA dmpr	194@1000	AA	AA	....	....
	75, 8 Cyl..............	AC-46-5	.035	.013-.018	31±1½	5B	IGA dmpr	194@1000	AA	AA	....	....
1952	60, 62, 75, 8 Cyl..............	AC-48	.035	.015	31±1½	5B	IGA dmpr	....	AA	AA	....	430
1953	60, 62, 75, 8 Cyl..............	AC-46-5	.035	.015	31±1½	2½B	IGA dmpr	....	AA	AA	....	430

AA—Automatic adjustment (valves).
AC—AC Spark Plug Div. dmpr—Vibration damper.
B—Before top center

Piston Ring Dimensions

Year	Model	Cylinder Bore	Top Ring Width	Top Ring Gap	Top Ring Depth	Second Ring Width	Second Ring Gap	Second Ring Depth	Third Ring Width	Third Ring Gap	Third Ring Depth	Oil Ring Width	Oil Ring Gap	Oil Ring Depth
1940	60S, 62, 72, 75..............	3½	3/32	.010	.175	1/8	.010	.150	5/32	.011	.150	5/32	.011	.150
	90..............	3¼	3/32	.011	.162	1/8	.011	.145	3/16	.011	.145	....	....	....
1941–42	61, 62, 63, 60S, 67, 75........	3½	3/32	.012	.175	1/8	.012	.150	5/32	.012	.150	5/32	.012	.150
1946–48	60S, 61, 62, 75..............	3½	5/64	.015	.170	5/64	.015	.170	3/16	.015	.150	3/16	.015	.150
1949–51	61, 62, 60, 75, V8	3 13/16	5/64	.015	.184	5/64	.015	.184	3/16	.015	.165	....	....	....

Piston Ring Dimensions—*continued*

Year	Model	Cylinder Bore	TOP RING			SECOND RING			THIRD RING			OIL RING		
			Width	Gap	Depth	Width	Gap	Depth	Width	Gap	Depth	Width	Gap	Depth
1952	60, 62, 75, 8 Cyl.	3 13/16	.0781	.015	.187	.0781	.015	.187	.1875	.015	.187	....	....	....
1953	60, 62, 75, 8 Cyl.	3 13/16	.0781	.015	.184	.0781	.015	.184	.1875	.015	.150	....	....	....

Tension Wrench Specifications

Year	Model	Cylinder Head		Spark Plug		Connecting Rod Bolts or Nuts		Main Bearing Bolt		Flywheel Bolts		Vibration Damper Bolts	
		Lbs.-Ft.	Thread	Lbs.-Ft.	Thread	Lbs.-Ft.	Thread	Lbs.-Ft.	Thread	Lbs.-Ft.	Thread	Lbs.-Ft.	Thread
1940	50, 52, 62, 72, 75, 60-S.	70–75	7/16–14	7–10	10 mm	55–60	special	130–140	9/16–12	65–70	7/16–20	....	....
	90	70–75	7/16–14	7–10	10 mm	55–60	special	100–110	½–13	65–70	7/16–20	....	....
1941	Series—All	70–75	7/16–14	7–10	10 mm	50–60	special	130–140	9/16–12	65–70	7/16–20	....	....
1942	Series—All	70–75	7/16–14	7–10	10 mm	50–60	special	140–150	9/16–12	65–70	7/16–20	....	....
1946 to 48	Series—All	70–75	7/16–14	7–10	10 mm	60–65	special	140–150	9/16–12	‡65–70	7/16–20	....	....
1949	Series—All	65–70	7/16–14	24–28	14 mm	35–40	3/8–24	90–100	½–13	‡65–70	7/16–20	60–65	½–20
1950 to 53	Series—All	65–70	7/16–14	20–25	14 mm	40–45	3/8–24	90–100	½–13	70–75	7/16–20	60–65	½–20

‡—Hydramatic (70–75).

Brake Data

Year	Model	Make	Lining Type	R=Riveted B=Bonded	Drum Diameter	Lining			Clearance	
						Length	Width	Thickness	Toe	Heel
1940	60S, 62	Ben	M	R	12	24½	2–*2¼	3/16	.010	.010
	72	Ben	M	R	12	24½	2½–*2¼	3/16	.010	.010
	75, 90	Ben	M	R	14	28 11/16	2¼	¼	.010	.010
1941–42	60S, 61, 62, 63	Ben	M	R	12	24½	2	3/16	.010	.010
	67, 75	Ben	M	R	12	24½	2½	3/16	.010	.010
1946–47	61, 62, 60, 75	Ben	M	R	12	24½	(c) 2–*2¼	3/16	.010	.010
1948	61, 62, 60S, 75	Ben	M	R	12	24½	2–*2¼	3/16	.010	.010
1949	61, 62, 60, 75	Ben	M	R	12	24½	•2¼	3/16	.008	.008
1950	60, 61, 62	Ben	M	B	11	22.45	2½	3/16	.008	.008
	75	Ben	M	R	12	25.84	2½	3/16	.008	.008
1951	61, 62, 60	B-M	M	B	11	22 29/64	2½	3/16	.008	.008
	75	B-M	M	R	12	25 27/32	2½	3/16	.008	.008
1952	60, 62, 8 Cyl.	Ben	M	R	12–*11	25 27/32–*22 29/64	2½	¼	.007–.010	.007–.010
	75, 8 Cyl.	Ben	M	R	12	25 27/32	2½	¼	.007–.010	.007–.010
1953	60, 62, 8 Cyl.	Ben	M	R	12	25 27/32	2½	¼	.007–.010	.007–.010
	75, 8 Cyl.	Ben	M	R	12	25 27/32	2½	¼	.007–.010	.007–.010

Ben—Bendix. B-M—Bendix-Moraine. M—Moulded. *—Rear. (c)—Model 75-Front 2½ in. •—Rear 2½ in.

Generators

Year	Model	Generator Number	Field Current at 6 Volts (amps.)	Maximum Safe Output: Volts	Maximum Safe Output: Amperes	Maximum Safe Output: R.P.M.	Brush Spring Tension (oz.)	Voltage Regulator Number
1940	60-S, 62, 72, 75	1102661	1.75–1.9	8.0	30	1750	25	1118202
1941	60-S, 61, 62, 63, 67, 75, Std.	1102661	1.75–1.9	8.0	30	1750	25	1118202
	Hydramatic	1102686	1.75–1.9	8.0	30	1750	25	1118202
1942 to 46	60-S, 61, 62, 63, 67, 75, Std.	1102693	1.75–1.9	8.0	30	1750	25	1118202
	Hydramatic	1102694	1.75–1.9	8.0	30	1750	25	1118202
1947–48	60-S, 61, 62, 75	1102693	1.75–1.9	8.0	30	1750	25	1118242
1949	60-S, 61, 62, 75	1102700	1.90–2.05	8.0	40	1900	25	1118300
1950–51	60, 61, 62, 75	1102700	1.90–2.05	8.0	40	1900	25	1118357
1952	60, 62, 75, 8 cyl.	1102781	....	7.4	47	3500	....	1118725
1953	60, 62, 75, 8 cyl.	1102002	....	12	30	2150	....	1118750

Front Wheel Alignment

Year	Model	Caster (deg.)	Camber (deg.)	King Pin Inclination (deg.)	Toe-In (inches)	Turning Radius: Inner	Turning Radius: Outer
1941	V8-61, 62, 63, 60S, 67, 75	$1\frac{3}{4}$N to $2\frac{3}{4}$N	$\frac{3}{8}$N to $\frac{3}{8}$P	$5\frac{3}{4}$ to 6	$\frac{1}{32}$ to $\frac{3}{32}$	$22\frac{3}{4}$	20
1942	V8-60S, 62, 63, 67, 75	$1\frac{3}{4}$N to $2\frac{3}{4}$N	$\frac{3}{8}$N to $\frac{3}{8}$P	$5\frac{3}{4}$ to 6	$\frac{1}{32}$ to $\frac{3}{32}$	$23\frac{3}{4}$	20
1946–47	V8-61, 62, 60S, 75	$1\frac{3}{4}$N to $2\frac{3}{4}$N	$\frac{3}{8}$N to $\frac{3}{8}$P	$5\frac{3}{4}$ to 6	$\frac{1}{32}$ to $\frac{3}{32}$	$23\frac{3}{4}$	20
1948	V8-61, 62, 75	$\frac{1}{2}$N to $\frac{1}{2}$P	$\frac{3}{8}$N to $\frac{3}{8}$P	$5\frac{3}{4}$ to 6	$\frac{1}{32}$ to $\frac{3}{32}$	$23\frac{3}{4}$	20
1949	V8-61, 62	$\frac{1}{2}$N to $\frac{1}{2}$P	$\frac{3}{8}$N to $\frac{3}{8}$P	$5\frac{3}{4}$ to 6	$\frac{1}{32}$ to $\frac{3}{32}$	$23\frac{3}{4}$	20
	V8-60S	$\frac{1}{2}$N to $\frac{1}{2}$P	$\frac{3}{8}$N to $\frac{3}{8}$P	$5\frac{3}{4}$ to 6	$\frac{1}{32}$ to $\frac{3}{32}$	$23\frac{3}{4}$	24
	V8-75	$\frac{1}{2}$N to $\frac{1}{2}$P	$\frac{3}{8}$N to $\frac{3}{8}$P	$5\frac{3}{4}$ to 6	....	$23\frac{3}{4}$	20
1950	V8-61, 62	0 to $\frac{1}{2}$P	0 to $\frac{1}{2}$P	$5\frac{3}{4}$ to 6	$\frac{1}{16}$	$23\frac{3}{4}$	20
	V8-60S	0 to $\frac{1}{2}$P	0 to $\frac{1}{2}$P	$5\frac{3}{4}$ to 6	$\frac{1}{16}$	$23\frac{3}{4}$	24
	V8-75	0 to $\frac{1}{2}$P	0 to $\frac{1}{2}$P	$5\frac{3}{4}$ to 6	....	$23\frac{3}{4}$	20
1951–53	V8-61, 62, 60S, 75	$\frac{1}{2}$N to $\frac{1}{2}$P	$\frac{3}{8}$N to $\frac{3}{8}$P	$5\frac{3}{4}$ to 6	$\frac{1}{32}$ to $\frac{3}{32}$	....	....

N—Negative. P—Positive.

Distributor

Year	Model	Distributor Model Number	Cam Angle (deg.)	Direction of Rotation C=Clockwise CC=Counter Clockwise at Cam End	Breaker Arm Spring Tension	Breaker Point Gap (inches)	Engine R.P.M. when Cent. Advance Starts	Max. Cent. Advance in Engine Deg. at Stated Engine R.P.M.	Vacuum in (inches) of Mercury at which Vacuum Unit Starts	Max. Advance in Engine Deg. at Stated Vacuum	Vacuum Unit Number
1940	60S, 62, 72, 75	1110806	31	C	19–23	.0125–.0175	1000	24@4000	5.5 to 7.5	18@15 to 18	1116020
1941 to 48	60S, 61, 62, 63, 67, 75	1110807	31	C	19–23	.0125–.0175	1000	24@4000	5.5 to 7.5	18@15 to 18	1116030
1949	61, 62, 60S, 75	1110812	31±1½	C	19–23	.015	600	38@3600	6 to 8	13 to 15	1116047
1950	61, 62, 60, 75	1110819	31±1½	C	19–23	.015	600	32@3600	5 to 14	13 to 15	1116047
1951	61, 62, 60S, 75	1110820	32	C	19–23	.016	600	32@3600	5 to 14	13 to 15	1116056
1952	60, 62, 75, 8 cyl.	1110829	31±1½	C	19–23	.010–.015	....	17@1850	7–9	9–11@16	....
1953	60, 62, 75, 8 cyl.	1110835	31±1½	C	19–23	.010–.015	500	13@2000	6.5–9.0	13@16–17	....

SPECIFICATIONS CADILLAC

Voltage Regulators

Year	Model	Regulator Number	Grounded P=Positive N=Negative	Voltage Control: Air Gap Points Closed	Voltage Control: Voltage Setting Hot	Current Control: Air Gap Points Closed	Current Control: Current Set Hot	Cut-Out Relay: Point Gap	Cut-Out Relay: Air Gap	Cut-Out Relay: Closing Volt
1940 to 42	60-S, 62, 72, 75, 63	1118202	P	.070	7.2–7.4	.080	32–34	.020	.020	6.2–6.7
1946 to 48	60-S, 61, 62, 75	1118242	N	.070	7.2–7.4	.080	32–34	.020	.020	6.2–6.7
1949	60-S, 61, 62, 75	1118300	N	.075	7.0–7.7	.075	40–46	.020	.020	5.9–6.8
1950–51	60, 61, 62, 75	1118357	N	.075	7.0–7.7	.075	40–46	.020	.020	5.9–6.8
1952	60, 62, 75, 8 cyl.	1118725	N	....	7.0–7.5	....	45–51	....	....	5.9–6.8
1953	60, 62, 75, 8 cyl.	1118750	N	....	14.5	....	30	....	....	12.8

Starters

Year	Model	Unit Model Number	Spring Tension (oz.)	STARTER Lock Test: Volts	Lock Test: Amperes	Lock Test: Torque, (lbs. ft.)	No Load: Volts	No Load: Amperes	No Load: R.P.M.	Direction of Rotation Viewed from Drive End C=Clockwise CC=Counter-clockwise
1940	60-S, 62, 72, 75	1107912	24–28	3.0	600	16	5.0	65	5500	C
1941	60-S, 61, 62, 63, 67, 75	1107923	24–28	3.0	600	16	5.0	65	5500	C
1942 to 48	60-S, 61, 62, 63, 67, 75	1107931	24–28	3.0	600	16	5.67	65	5500	C
1949	60-S, 61, 62, 75	1107945	24–28	3.0	600	15	5.7	80	5500	C
1950–51	60, 61, 62, 75	1107969	24–28	3.10	600	16	5.67	65	5500	C
1952	60, 62, 75, 8 cyl.	1107969	24–28	3.0	600	14	5.67	80	5500	C
1953	60, 62, 75	1107602	24–28	5.2	460	11.5	10.3	75	6500	C

Cooling System

CAR AND YEAR	MODEL	Capacity Qts.	Quarts of Methanol Base Anti-Freeze (For Protection to Temperature Shown Below)							Quarts of Ethylene Glycol (For Protection to Temperature Shown Below)							Quarts of Denatured Alcohol—188 Proof (For Protection to Temperature Shown Below)						
			3	4	5	6	7	8	9	3	4	5	6	7	8	9	3	4	5	6	7	8	9
1939-40	V8	24½	22	17	11	6	−2	−9	−18	....	20	16	12	7	1	−5	20	....	....	10	....	0	....
1938-40	V16	30	24	20	16	11	7	1	−5	....	....	20	17	13	8	4	....	20	....	....	10	0	−10
1941-48	V8	25	22	17	11	6	−2	−9	−18	....	20	16	12	7	1	−5	20	....	....	10	....	0	....
1949-53	V8	19	17	8	−1	−12	−25	−38	−53	19	14	7	0	−10	−21	−34	20	10	....	0	−10	....	−20

CADILLAC 1940 thru 1953

FRONT SUSPENSION

The front suspension on Cadillac cars is known as the short and long arm type commonly called the S.L.A. type front suspension.

From 1940 to 1949 all Cadillac front suspensions were made essentially the same way. The upper suspension arm and shock absorber were incorporated into one piece. A Delco type shock absorber was used and castor and camber were adjusted with an eccentric pin at the outer end of the shock absorber. Starting in 1950, the shock absorber is mounted inside the coil spring and a plain upper suspension arm is used. Castor and camber are adjusted by an eccentric bushing in place of the former eccentric pin.

Except for the shock absorber, however, essential repair work on the front suspension is the same.

All operating parts of the Cadillac front suspension can be removed for inspection or replacement without removing the front cross member.

Caster and Camber Adjustment

Before any attempt is made to adjust caster or camber, first make an inspection of the entire front suspension and note down on paper the castor and camber angles together with the toe-in found on the car before any attempt is made to correct it.

Since both caster and camber are controlled by an eccentric pin (1940 to 1949 models) and by an eccentric bushing (1950 to 1953 models) the best possible setting using the eccentric may of necessity be a compromise between the exact specifications and the specifications which are possible using an eccentric.

The procedure to adjust caster and camber is as follows:

First inspect all of the pins and bushings in the front suspension for wear or looseness. If any are found loose or badly worn it will be impossible to secure the correct adjustment unless the worn or damaged parts are replaced.

To make the adjustment loosen the clamp bolt in the upper end of the knuckle support in order to free the eccentric pin (or eccentric bushing in 1950-1953 models).

Remove the grease fitting from the front of the upper suspension arm pin.

Turn the eccentric pin with an Allen wrench through the grease fitting hole (or, on 1950 thru 1953 models, turn the eccentric bushing with a special 1 13/32 hand wrench) in a clockwise direction to increase caster, counter-clockwise to decrease caster.

Notice that it may be necessary to turn the caster a little further than the specifications in order to bring the eccentric to a position which will give suitable camber.

Where an exact adjustment is required turn the eccentric until the caster reading is exactly according to specifications and use a bending device on the knuckle support to secure the proper camber reading.

(**Caution:** Front suspension parts on all Cadillac cars are heat treated after forging, therefore they should never be heated. Heating front suspension parts to cherry red, which will permit bending them more readily, will also destroy the heat treatment and render the part unfit for service.)

After the required caster and camber adjustments have been made, tighten the clamp screw in the upper end of the knuckle support and (replace the grease fitting in the earlier models) then recheck to make certain that the desired readings are maintained.

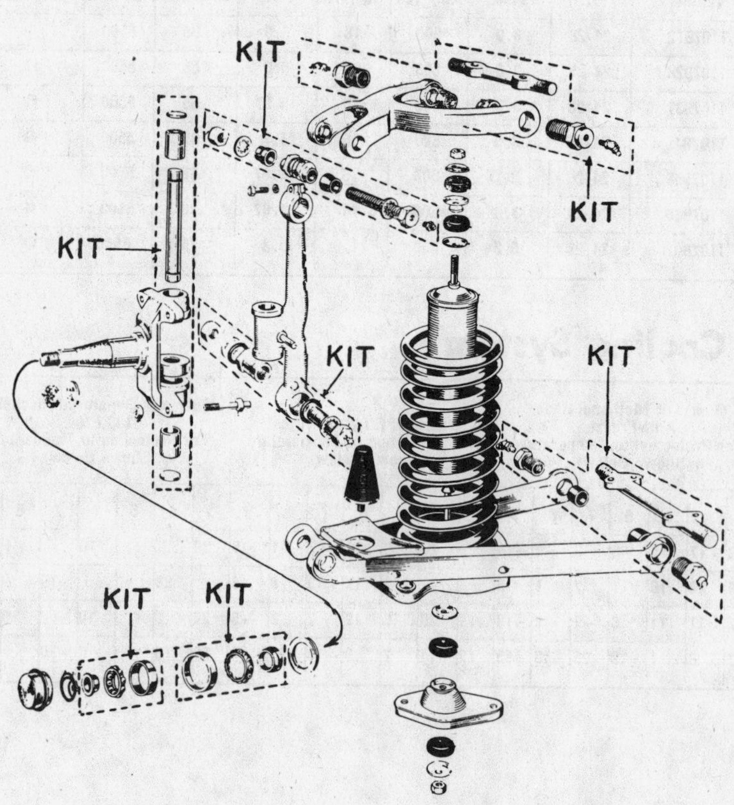

Front suspension—showing kits

Toe-In

Toe-in is adjusted at the sleeves at the end of each tie rod.

Turning the sleeves in the direction opposite to forward wheel rotation will increase toe-in; turning the sleeves in the same direction as forward wheel rotation will decrease toe-in. When correcting for errors in the front suspension readings, toe-in should always be corrected last.

Replacement of Front Coil Springs

Before replacing a coil spring, examine all of the pins and bushings in the front suspension arms to determine if one or more of the pins require replacement.

If one of the outer pins or bushings require replacement, the procedure is to place a jack under the lower suspension arm (A frame) and disconnect the system at the pin which requires replacement. In this way both time and effort will be saved.

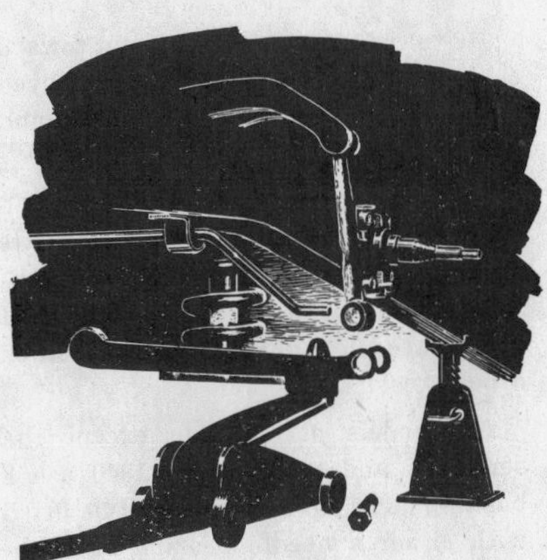

Removing lower bushing

If all of the front suspension parts are in good condition and it is necessary to replace a coil spring only, perhaps the best method is to support the weight of the car at the frame side rail at any convenient spot back of the front suspension and place a jack under the lower A frame inner pivot shaft. Remove the road wheel and disconnect the stabilizer bar at the suspension arm.

Guiding lower suspension arm with a long drift pin

Then remove the four bolts which hold the inner shaft to the front cross member.

Lower the jack until the coil spring is free of the A frame and remove the spring.

Note: On 1950 thru 1953 models it will be necessary to disconnect the shock absorber, which is mounted inside the coil spring, in order to remove the spring. The shock absorber should be disconnected before the four frame mounting bolts are removed.

Leave the jack in a position which it assumed when it was lowered. Replace the coil spring with a new one, being absolutely certain that the last coil of the spring enters the formed groove in the bottom of the A frame.

Jack the inner arm of the lower A frame back up against the front cross member, guiding it into place with two drift pins.

Reconnect the bolts which hold the inner arm to the front cross member, the stabilizer bar and (1950 thru 1953) the shock absorber.

Shock Absorber Replacement

Up to 1949 models the shock absorber is the upper suspension arm and it is removed by taking out the upper suspension arm eccentric pin and removing the bolts which hold the shock absorber to the top of the frame.

This is accomplished without particular difficulties since the bolts are accessible through the engine compartment at the top. The eccentric pin can be removed readily after the front wheel is removed. The car should be supported on a jack at the outer end of the lower suspension arm.

On 1950 thru 1953 models the shock absorber is mounted in the center of the coil spring and is held by a removable bracket under the lower A frame.

To remove the shock absorber simply disconnect the removable bracket from the lower A frame and loosen the nut which holds the shock absorber to the frame at the upper suspension arm inner pin.

This can be accomplished without particular difficulties since the upper bolt is accessable in the engine compartment and the lower bolts are accessible underneath the car. It is not necessary to raise the car except for convenience in getting at the lower plate bolts.

REPLACEMENT OF FRONT SUSPENSION PINS AND BUSHINGS

Upper Arm Pin

To replace the upper arm pin (up to 1949 models) remove the clamp bolt in the upper end of the knuckle support and also the clamp bolt in the shock absorber arm.

Remove the front bushing and then the back bushing.

The eccentric pin can then be readily removed by pushing it out of the knuckle support. Sometimes the pin is a little stiff and it may be necessary to spread the clamp boss slightly with a screw driver.

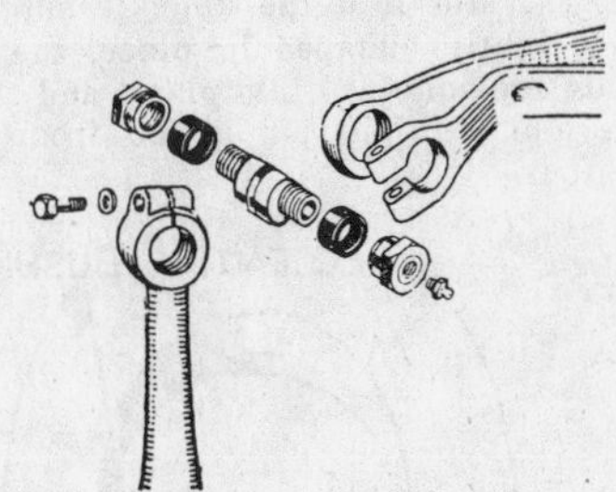

Parts used in outer end of upper arm. Note dust seals

Line up the hole in the top of the knuckle support with the holes in the upper suspension arm and insert the eccentric pin through the upper arm into the knuckle support. The Allen socket hole in the pin goes towards the front.

Then insert the clamp bolt into the knuckle support and clamp it lightly. Place the oil seals over the threaded portion of the eccentric (thru the front and rear bushing holes in the arm) and start the grooved bushing into the clamp side of the suspension arm. Screw it all the way in and insert the clamp bolt but don't tighten it. Using an Allen wrench in the socket in the front end of the pin, turn the pin till the eccentric portion is facing away from the car (full camber) and tighten the knuckle support clamp bolt. Now center the top of the knuckle support between the yoke of the upper arm by turning the clamped bushing. When nicely centered tighten the clamp bolt and then screw in the threaded bushing.

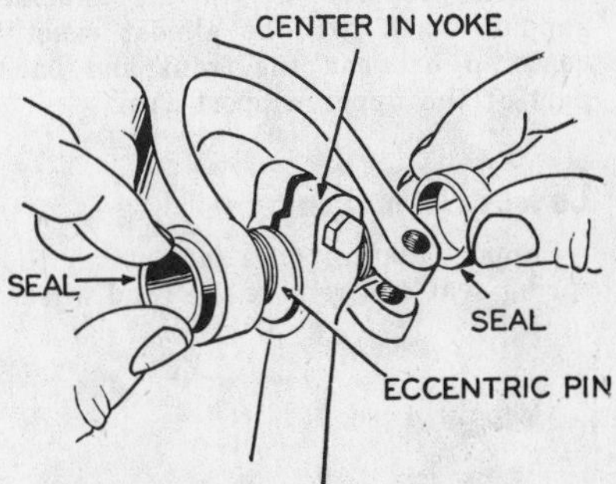

Method of installing oil seals, upper pin

On the 1950 thru 1953 models which use an eccentric bushing, the bushing

REPLACEMENT SUSPENSION PINS —continued

is first slid into the knuckle support and lightly clamped in place, the oil seals are squeezed into place, and then the long straight pin is fed from the

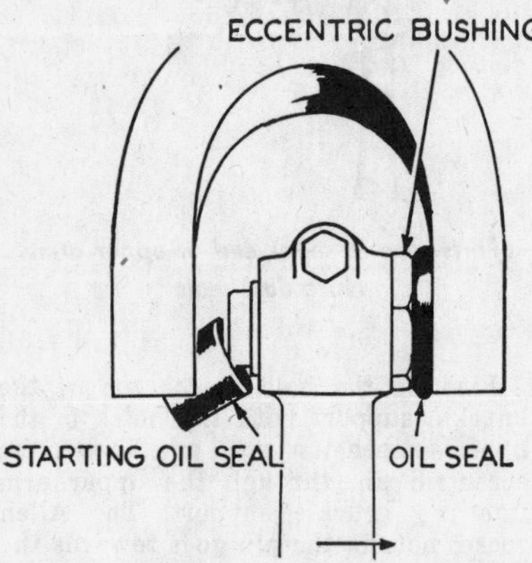

Method of installing oil seals. Lower pin

front of the car through the upper arm into the oil seal, into the eccentric bushing, through the eccentric bushing to the rear oil seal, to the second upper arm and then it is secured with a nut and lock washer.

Oil seals are used at both ends to prevent grit and foreign matter from entering the bearing surface.

When properly set up the knuckle support itself will be almost exactly centered between the front and back part of the upper support arm.

Lower Arm Pin

Support the car on a jack under the spring seat and remove the road wheel.

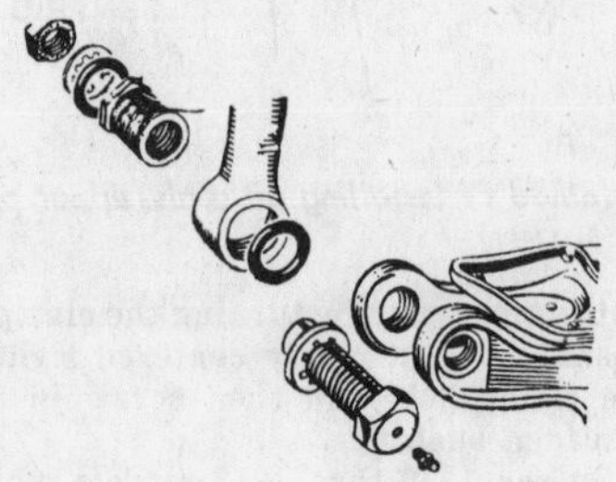

Knuckle support lower pin & bushings

Remove the nut which holds the lower arm pin in place and lift off the star washer. Then screw the pin out.

Pull the knuckle support away from the lower suspension arm and remove the bushing in the lower end of the knuckle support.

Replace it with a new one and then rock the knuckle support back into place in the lower suspension arm, squeeze in the two oil seal washers and enter the lower suspension arm pin.

When properly set up the lower suspension arm will be almost exactly centered between the two arms of the lower A frame.

Securely tighten the lower arm nut.

Replacement parts are available for the inner shaft and bushing of the lower suspension arm and on 1950 through 1953 models parts are available for the inner shaft of the upper suspension arm.

King Pin and Bushing Replacement

The king pin can be replaced without disturbing the brake lines or the brake adjustment. Simply remove the wheel bearings and brake backing plate.

Hang the backing plate on a little wire hook attached to the frame to prevent straining the brake hose.

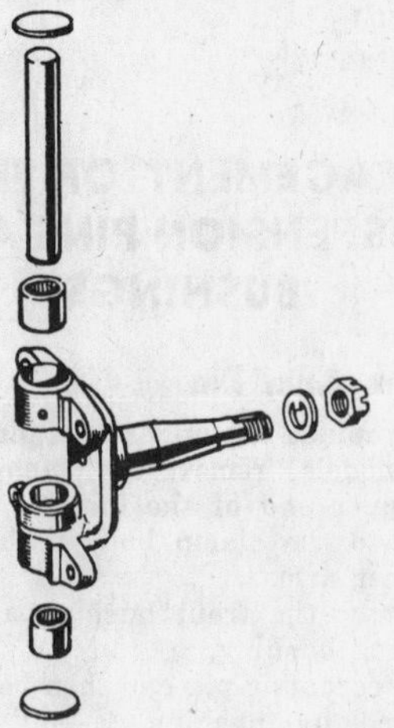

King pin & spindle

Drive the king pin lock pin out toward the rear. After the lock pin is removed the king pin can be driven down and out.

Special pressure devices are available to remove king pins which are stuck or corroded in place. The bushings can be driven or cut out, but should be replaced using a bushing driver or arbor press.

All models of Cadillac except the series 75 and series 90 of 1940 use a bushing. The exceptions could be fitted with either a needle bearing or bushing at top and bottom.

Bushings require reaming or honing to insure good fit on the king pin.

Shims are available to be used in conjunction with the thrust bearing to insure that there is no up and down play in the knuckle when a new king pin has been installed.

While it will not always be necessary, it is good practice to readjust the front brakes after replacing the king pins. It is also a good idea to bleed both front brakes.

MANUAL STEERING GEAR

All models of Cadillac from 1940 use the Saginaw recirculating ball type steering gear.

Worn Bearing Adjustment

To adjust the worn bearings loosen the jam nut at the bottom of the steering column and tighten the bearing adjuster until between a pound and a pound and a quarter is required at the rim of the steering wheel to turn the wheel with the pitman arm disconnected and the cross shaft end play screw loosened.

Immediately after this adjustment is accomplished turn the steering gear from one end to the other, being careful not to jam it at either end to check for roughness in the bearing.

If any roughness or binding is noticed it will be necessary to replace the worn bearings.

End play in the pitman shaft is removed by turning the adjusting screw in the side of the steering gear housing.

Specifications are, that the end play should be removed until it requires up to two pounds pull at the rim of the steering wheel to turn the wheel through its entire range.

When necessary to remove the pitman arm from the steering gear a puller should be used.

When reinstalling steering gear mechanism be certain that the bracket which holds the steering gear to the dash panel does not put a strain on the steering mechanism. This can be determined by measuring the amount of pull required at the rim of the steering wheel to turn the gear before the bracket is tightened. If this amount of pull increases materially when the bracket is tightened it indicates that the bracket is springing the gear and it will be necessary to install shims to prevent the cramping action of the clamp.

Manual Steering Gear Assembly Removal

Remove the steering wheel, the anti-rattle springs under the steering wheel, the horn wire and clamp which holds the lower steering jacket to the upper steering jacket.

Slip this clamp down over the lower steering jacket.

Disconnect the pitman arm and remove the bolts which hold the steering gear to the frame's side rail.

Using a lead hammer drive the lower steering jacket down out of the upper jacket and then remove the steering gear mechanism out through the bottom of the car.

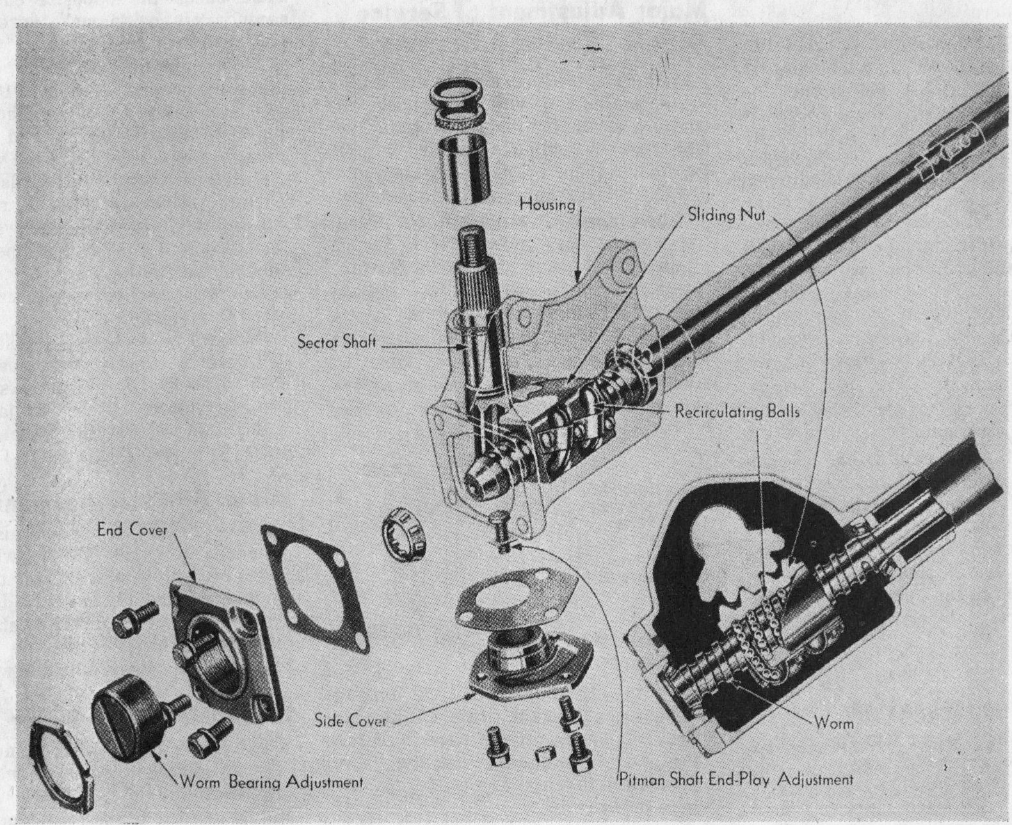

Manual steering gear disassembled

CADILLAC 1940 thru 1953

BRAKES

All models of Cadillac except 1951 series use the two shoe Bendix hydraulic brake with an eccentric anchor. The 1951 models only have a self-adjusting anchor and require minor adjustment only.

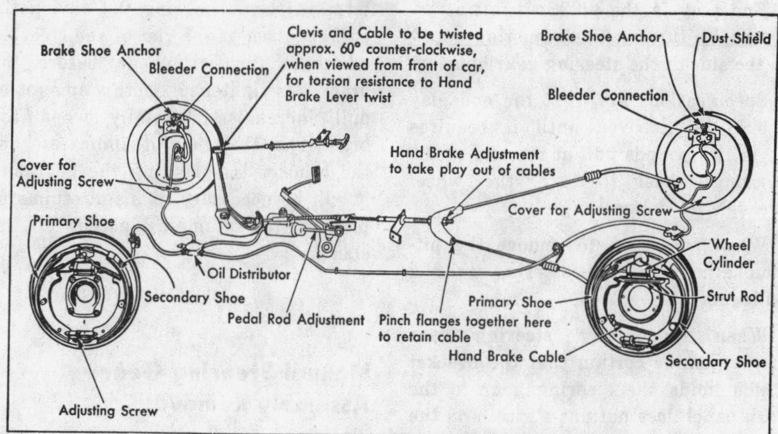

Schematic diagram of the Cadillac brake system

Brake Inspection

Before making any service adjustment on Cadillac (or any other brake) remove at least one of the wheels to determine the condition of the brake cylinders and the brake lining.

If any moisture is found on the rubber boots which seal the wheel cylinder it usually indicates that the wheel cylinder has a slight seepage and it will be necessary to either hone the wheel cylinder to secure a better bearing surface for the cup, or replace the cylinder.

Examine the condition of the brake lining. Lining which is worn evenly at both ends of the shoe generally indicates a correctly adjusted anchor and if there is sufficient lining on the shoes it probably will not be necessary to readjust the anchor.

Where it is found that the brake lining is worn unevenly but is wearing all over the surface this indicates that the anchor was originally set incorrectly but has now worn itself in until it is no longer possible to correct for the original mistake and the anchor should be left as it is unless new lining is to be installed.

Axle type lining grinders are available which will grind the lining concentric to the brake drum. These axle type lining grinders, when properly used, will eliminate the necessary break-in period usually required of raw lining.

Examine the brake retracting springs and make certain all of the lining rivets are securely fastened.

Where lining is found to be loose on the shoes it is usually good practice to install new lining since it will be found very difficult to replace the rivets in such a way that they will hold the lining rigidly. Loose rivets have a tendency to enlarge the holes in the lining making it a very difficult job to replace them.

Brake Drum Inspection

Examine the brake drum for scores, cracks, checks and roughness.

If scoring or heat cracks are found in the drum it will be necessary to either have the drum machined or install a new drum.

Generally speaking a break drum should be smooth enough (on the breaking surface) so that it will feel reasonably smooth to the fingers.

Major Adjustment of Service Brakes (Anchor Adjustment)

Note: The 1951 series only use a sliding type anchor which automatically centers the secondary shoe each time the brake is applied, therefore the adjustment given in the following paragraphs does not apply to the 1951 model.

When properly adjusted the secondary shoe (the one which is pushed against the anchor pin by the forward rotation of the wheel) will have a clearance of .015 in approximately an 1½ in. from each end of the shoe. To check this clearance proceed as follows: Turn the star wheel adjuster, located behind the slot at the lower part of the backing

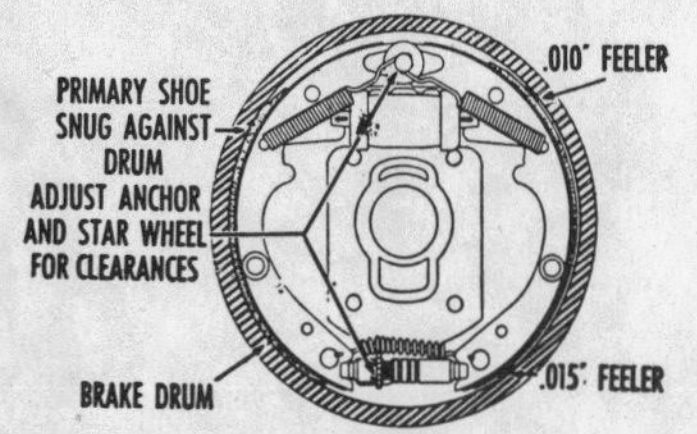

plate in a direction which will expand the shoes against the drum. If the star wheel has been properly assembled the shoes are expanded against the drum by turning the inner end of the star wheel downwards.

Insert a .015 feeler gauge through the port in the drum to measure the clearance between the lining and drum approximately an 1½ in. from the anchor end of the secondary shoe.

Continue to expand the shoes until the feeler gauge is just barely gripped. Then check the opposite end of the secondary shoe to make sure there is .015 clearance there also.

If the clearance of the lower end of the shoe is greater than .015 inch it will be necessary to loosen the lock nut on the eccentric anchor and turn the anchor in the direction which will cause the shoe to move downwards slightly. Then tentatively tighten the anchor jam nut and again turn the star wheel until the .015 feeler is just gripped at the anchor end of the secondary shoe and again recheck the opposite end of the secondary shoe.

Continue to make this adjustment until there is exactly .015 clearance at both ends of the secondary shoe then securely tighten the anchor jam nut.

Back off on the star wheel adjuster until the wheel is just free.

Minor Brake Adjustment

Minor brake adjustment is accomplished by turning the star wheel in a direction which will expand the shoes against the drum (turn the edge of the wheel downwards) until the shoes drag and then back off until the wheel is just free. Do this on all four wheels.

Brake Master Cylinder

To remove the master cylinder from the car, detach the brake tubes from the front end of the master cylinder and detach the brake rod from the rear end of the cylinder.

Detach the stop light wires and re-

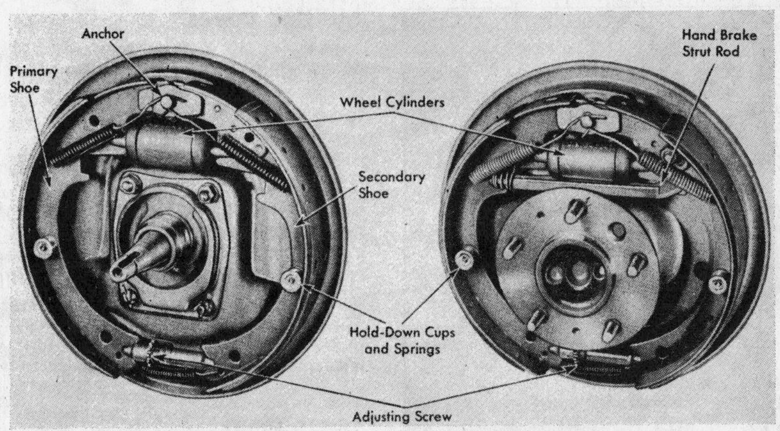

Brake mechanism at front and rear wheels

move the two bolts which hold the master cylinder to the frame bracket.

Master cylinder internal parts are held in place by a snap ring at the rear end of the cylinder.

Master Cylinder Inspection

Thoroughly clean out the master cylinder and, holding it up to the light, let the light shine along the inside of the cylinder and examine it with extreme care for scratches or roughness. If any are found it will be necessary to hone the cylinder to secure a smooth surface.

Wheel Cylinder Inspection

The wheel cylinders may be inspected while still mounted on the backing plate by removing the shoes, wheel cylinder boots, pistons, cups and springs.

Thoroughly clean out the inside of the wheel cylinder and, sighting through it as though it were a telescope tube, line up an electric light at the opposite side and look for pits, scores or roughness. If any condition other than a perfectly smooth surface is found it will be necessary to either hone the cylinder to produce a fine surface or replace the cylinder.

It is recommended that wheel cylinder honing be done by a competent operator who has at his disposal 'Go" and "Not Go" gages.

If the cylinder is honed until it is too large the "Not Go" gage will enter. If this happens the wheel cylinder should be discarded since it is extremely dangerous to use a wheel cylinder which has been honed to too great an oversize.

Bleeding Brakes

Brakes should be bled at any time the system is opened either at the wheel cylinders, brake lines, master cylinder, stop light switch, or at any time the brake action feels soft or rubbery.

There are two methods in common use for bleeding brakes in addition to pressure bleeding.

The first, sometimes called the safety bleed, is accomplished as follows: Remove the cover from the master cylinder and fill the cylinder to the top with fresh fluid.

Go to the right front wheel and remove the dust screw from the center of the bleed valve. (NOTE: Many mechanics remove this screw for the purpose of bleeding brakes and then do not replace it after the brakes have been bled. Therefore if the dust screw is not in the bleed valve it simply means that someone has taken it out and failed to replace it.)

Insert a bleeder tube into the hole from which the dust screw was removed.

Carry the free end of the tube down into a glass jar containing a sufficient amount of fluid to cover the bottom of the tube so that air cannot enter the bottom of the tube.

Now, using a ⅜ wrench, open the bleed valve.

Have a helper slowly depress the brake pedal and observe the air bubbles passing through the fluid in the jar.

Release the brake pedal and again slowly depress it. Continue slowly depressing the brake pedal and releasing it until no more air bubbles appear in the jar. (CAUTION: After every third time the pedal is depressed it will be necessary to check and refill the master cylinder to make certain that it does not go empty and pick up air.)

When no more air bubbles come out of the bottom of the hose tighten the bleed screw, remove the bleed hose and replace the dust screw.

Repeat this operation at all four wheels.

Caution: Do not attempt to reuse the fluid which was bled from the cylinder. This is a very dangerous, wasteful practice.

Another method, sometimes called the squirt method, is also used to bleed brakes where it is not necessary to be careful with the floor of the shop.

The method is almost the same as the first method given except that no hose is used and the brake fluid is bled right out on the floor.

First fill the master cylinder to the top and remove the dust screw from the bleed valve.

Have a helper pump the brake pedal until some pressure is felt and, while the helper holds the pressure on the pedal, open the bleed screw which will cause the brake pedal to go to the floor. Just before the pedal hits the floor the helper calls out 'close the valve' and the valve is closed preventing the air from entering back into the cylinder. The helper again pumps the pedal until some pressure is felt and while holding the pressure the mechanic opens the bleed screw permitting more of the fluid to run out on the floor.

Air can be detected coming from the cylinder because it will come out in spurts and puffs rather than as a solid stream of fluid.

When a solid stream of fluid comes out from the cylinder it may be presumed that all air has been eliminated from that cylinder.

Replace the dust screw and refill the master cylinder.

Note: Generally three pumps of the pedal are the limit before it becomes necessary to refill the master cylinder. Do not under any circumstances bleed the pedal more than three times before refilling the cylinder since the possibilities are that more air will be included into the master cylinder if the reservoir becomes dry.

Repeat the operation at all four wheels.

Pressure Bleeding

Pressure bleeding apparatus is supplied complete with instructions for its use and, since the various pressure bleeding mechanisms require different techniques, it is advisable to follow the instructions which come with the pressure bleed unit.

ELECTRICAL SYSTEM

Starting with 1953 models a 12 volt electrical system is used in place of the former 6 volt system. Except for the spark plugs, no electrical unit is interchangeable with former models. Actual service procedures are not effected, since service is not effected by change in voltage.

Distributor Removal and Disassembly

Disconnect the distributor cap and the vacuum tubing, remove the primary wire and rotate the engine until the rotor points to number 1 spark plug lead on the distributor cap.

Remove the cap screws that hold the distributor in place and lift off the distributor.

Once off the car the distributor assembly should be checked carefully for play in the distributor shaft and play in the breaker plate where it locates in the distributor housing. The vacuum advance unit should be checked for leaks and the points examined for pits and burns.

If any play is found in the distributor shaft or in the rotor shaft where it mounts on to the distributor shaft, it will be necessary to replace either or both of these parts since play in the distributor shaft results in an uneven cam angle and will prevent the proper tuning of the car.

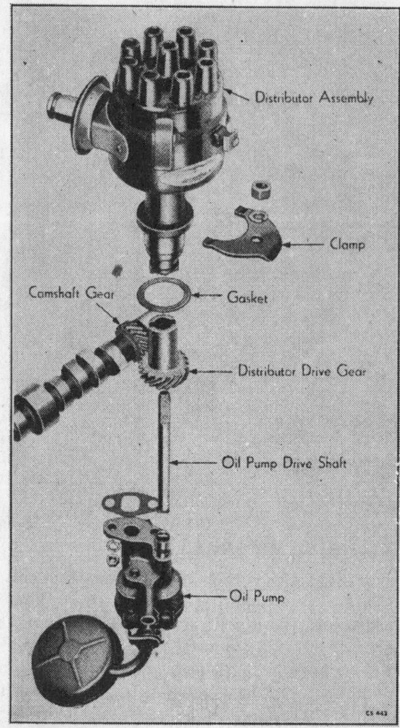

Diagram of distributor

Ignition Wires

Examine the ignition wires for breaks or swelling in the insulation. If any breaks are found or insulation is noted to be soft or rubbery it will be necessary to replace the ignition wires.

Perhaps the easiest way to replace ignition wires is to replace them with their entire length one at a time. That is, remove one wire and replace it with a new one, attaching one end to the spark plug and the other end to the distributor cap before the second wire is removed. In this way it is not necessary to refer to the firing order so that the wires can be properly installed.

Spark Plugs

See index for chart giving recommended spark plug for each model of Cadillac together with the plug which is one stage hotter and also the plug which is one stage colder and the recommended gap. The gap given is that recommended by the car manufacturer and also the gap recommended by the spark plug manufacturers.

Spark plug gaps should be set with wire gages using the following method: If the gap is .025 in. select a wire whose diameter is .024 and arrange the gap so that the .024 wire will pass easily but a wire whose diameter is .026 will not pass, which means that the gap is greater than .024 but less than .026, as near to .025 as is practical.

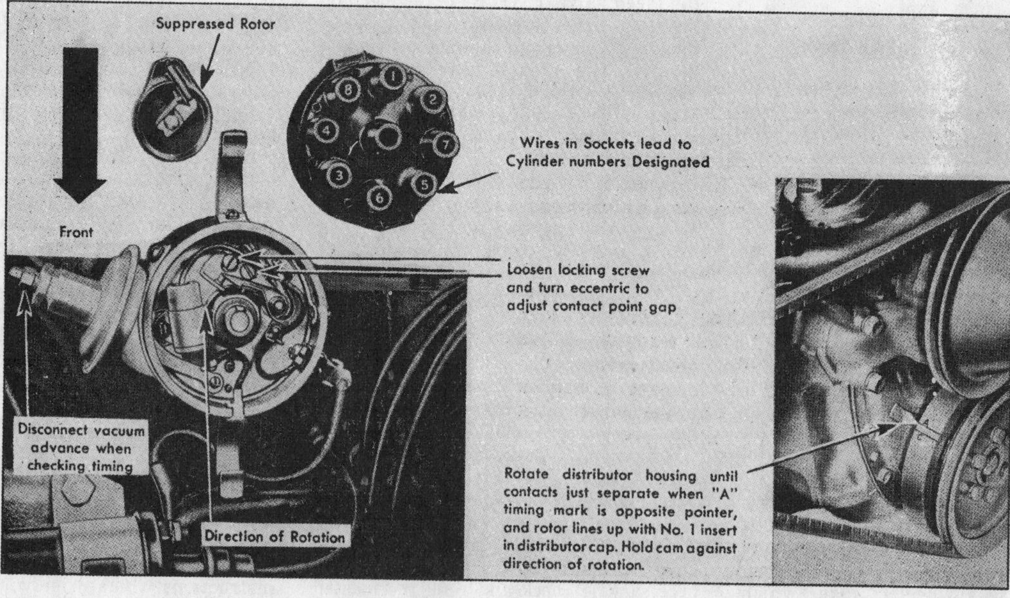

Ignition adjustments

The Charging Circuit

The charging circuit consists of the generator, regulator and battery.

All Cadillac generators, 6 and 12 volt, are equipped with full voltage and current control.

If, for any reason, the generator fails to function properly, before doing any work on the generator itself, ground the field lead either at the regulator or at the generator and if this corrects the difficulty the trouble is in the regulator. **Note:** The field lead is generally the smaller of the two wires which attach to the generator. If it is found that the trouble is not in the regulator refer to the general service trouble shooting in this Manual which gives complete instruction on servicing all generators.

Starter Circuit

The starter circuit consists of the battery, the starter switch and the starting motor.

Complete specifications for the testing of starter motors is given in the general service section of this Manual, please refer to the index.

If any trouble is suspected in the starting motor be sure to check first if the battery is fully charged and that the battery cables are making good clean contact with both the starter switch and also at the ground connection. A quick check can be made at the starter switch by cranking the engine while a volt meter is connected across the terminals of the starter switch the drop across the switch should never be in excess of ½ volt.

If it is found that the starter switch voltage drop is greater than one volt it will be necessary to remove and either clean the starter contacts or replace the starter switch.

COOLING SYSTEM

Radiator Core Removal

1940 TO 1948 MODELS

Remove the upper and lower radiator hoses and the radiator brace rods.

Disconnect the shutter rod at the thermostat end.

Remove the air cleaner, generator and fan.

Disconnect the headlight wiring at the terminal block on the right front fender and loosen headlight harness clinch straps on the radiator core and lift the harness out of the way.

Remove the cap screws holding the radiator assembly to its cradle and lift the radiator core back over the engine.

1949 TO 1953 MODELS

On these models the radiator core is removed essentially in the same manner as the 40 to 48 series are removed with the difference, however, that spacers are used under the anchor bolts and they should be carefully noted so that they can be returned to their proper position.

Thermostats

On models up to and including 1948 the thermostat was mounted in the water jacket at the top of the radiator core. Removal of the thermostat involves disconnecting the upper hoses and removing the four bolts which hold the manifold to the top tank of the radiator.

On 1949 to 1953 engines the thermostat is located in the manifold at the front of the blocks.

This thermostat is removed by taking off the four cap screws which hold the thermostat housing to the top of the water pump body and disconnecting the upper hoses.

Water Pump Assembly

On all Cadillac models up to and including 1948 the water pump is located at the front of the right hand cylinder block and is driven by the belt which also drives the generator. A self adjusting chevron type packing is located just back of the impeller. This chevron packing requires no service. A permanently sealed ball bearing is used at the outer end of the pump shaft. The center bearing however is lubricated through a fitting.

On 1949 to 1953 models the water pump is mounted in the water manifold at the front of both cylinder blocks.

To remove the water pump on these models it is necessary to disconnect the upper and lower radiator hoses, remove the eight bolts which hold the water pump and water manifold to both cylinder blocks and lift off. It is not necessary to remove the radiator to disconnect this pump.

When remounting the pump care should be exercised not to damage the mounting gaskets. The bolts should be pulled to a torque of 25 to 29 foot pounds.

Disassembly of Water Pump

On 1949 to 1953 models the water pump is disassembled as follows: Remove the thermostat housing, fan blades and fan hub.

Examine the pump body to see if there is a retainer ring in a groove in the pump body (this ring was used on some of the early pumps).

If the ring is there remove it and press the shaft and bearing out of the impeller and the pump body. An arbor or yoke type press is needed for this job. If a press is not available, it is sometimes possible but risky, to drive the shaft out with a flat punch.

If no spring snap ring is found then it is a later type pump and the impeller is removed without pressing the shaft out of the body.

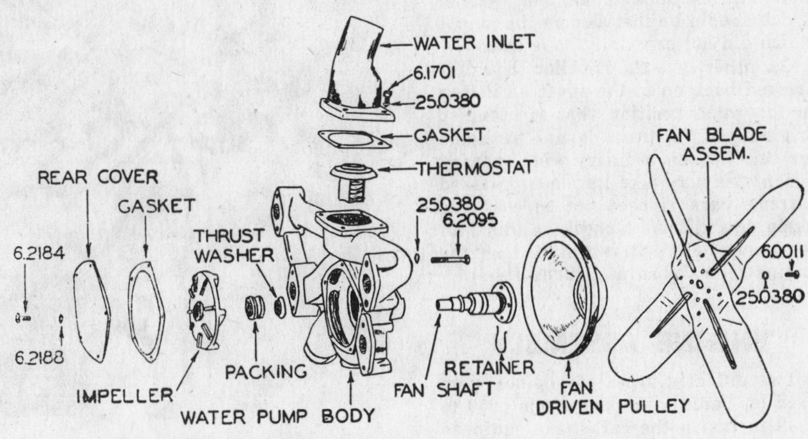

1949-1953 V-8 engine, water manifold and pump assembly

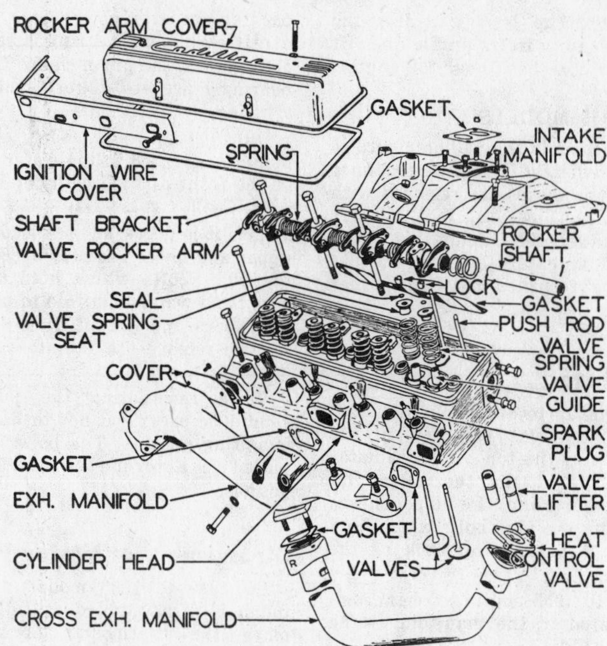

1949-51 V-8 engine cylinder head and internal parts

DISASSEMBLY OF WATER PUMP—*continued*

On late type pumps (which did not have a bearing lock ring) do not remove the bearing assembly unless it is intended to replace it with a new one.

On late type pumps the bearing and shaft assembly is pressed into place until the bearing end seals against the shoulder in the pump housing.

Note: Water pumps on early 1949 engines did not have a damper washer installed on the pump seal assembly, when new parts are installed the overhaul kit includes a damper washer which should be installed in the pumps which did not originally have one.

On either type the impeller should be pressed back on to the shaft until it is in the same position that it occupied originally. If a press is not available for this job, an ordinary wide opening bench vise may take its place provided extreme care is used not to cock the pump or shaft. As a check on this spin the pump before it is mounted on the engine to make sure it turns freely.

ENGINE ASSEMBLY

Two different types of engines were used on Cadillac models. From 1940 to 1948 inclusive the cars were equipped with the V8, 12 or 16 engine of the L head type. 1949 to 1953 engines are V type overhead valve engines.

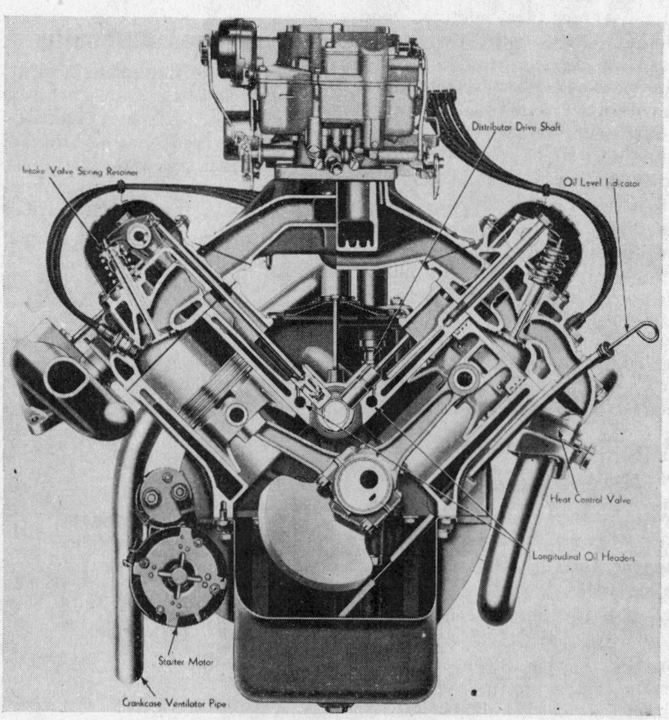

Front sectional engine view

Hydraulic valve lifter mechanisms operating at zero clearance were used on all Cadillac engines.

Manifolds

1940 to 1948 engines had their manifolds mounted on the top of the engine between the cylinder blocks, both intake and exhaust manifold.

1949 to 1953 engines had the intake manifold mounted between the cylinder heads on the top of the engine and the exhaust manifolds mounted separately on each block at the outside of the block.

Removal of Oil Pan

There are no complications in the removal of Cadillac oil pans. On models on and up to and including 1948 simply unbolt the pan and lower it to the floor.

On 1949 to 1953 engines the exhaust pipe crossover must be removed to take down the oil pan.

Removal of Cylinder Head

On 1940 to 1948 engines the cylinder head removal is a conventional job of removing the cylinder head bolts and lifting the head off. It is not necessary to take the manifolds off on these models to get the head off.

Side sectional engine view

On 1949 to 1953 engines the procedure is as follows: Disconnect the water manifold at the front of the cylinder head or heads. It is a good idea to remove the water pump and water manifolds from the car. It is difficult to reinstall a cylinder head with the water pump in place on one head without damaging the water pump gasket.

Remove all vacuum lines and carburetor connections, disconnect all ignition and throttle connections.

Take off the intake manifold with the carburetor in place.

Remove the rocker covers.

Note: It is customary to remove the rocker covers together with the ignition wires and distributor cap as a unit unless service is to be done on the distributor.

Remove the generator if the right cylinder head is to be removed.

The exhaust manifolds may be disconnected either from the head or from the flange connection to the exhaust pipe.

It is advisable to disconnect the exhaust manifolds at the cylinder head so that accumulated carbon may be removed from the passages in the cylinder head.

Remove the head bolts which hold the rocker assemblies to the cylinder head and lift off the rocker assemblies.

Take out the valve push rods.

Remove the balance of the cylinder attaching bolts and lift the head off. It is very important that the head be handled carefully so as not to damage or mark the head gasket surface.

Valve service is given later in this section.

CYLINDER HEAD NUT TIGHTENING SEQUENCE

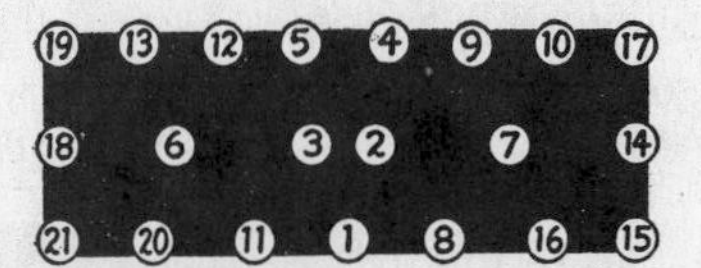

V-8, L-Head 1936-48, 70-75 ft. lbs. 1949-53 V-8 in-head, 65-70 ft. lbs.

Timing Case Cover Removal

1940 V16 MODELS

On these models it is necessary to remove the radiator core and fender assemblies in order to take off the timing case cover.

1941 TO 1946 V16 MODELS

On these models it is necessary to remove either the water pump assembly or the radiator core in order to service the timing case cover assembly.

It is always better to remove the radiator core as this will allow greater freedom of motion.

1940 V8 MODELS

On these models it is necessary to remove the radiator core and damper in order to remove the timing case cover.

1941 TO 1953 ENGINES

On these models remove the radiator core and the water pump assembly in order to take off the timing case cover.

While the timing case cover may be removed without taking off the oil pan if it is necessary to replace the crankshaft sprocket then it will be necessary to remove the oil pan.

Valve Timing Procedure

The chain and sprocket assembly used on all Cadillac models built since 1940 is such, that unless deliberately disturbed, the valve timing will remain as set by the factory, unless the chain and sprockets or both are badly worn or damaged.

The procedure for replacing the chain and/or sprockets is as follows:

1949 to 1953 MODELS

Note: It is necessary to remove the oil pan in order to remove the crankshafts sprocket.

The timing chain and/or sprockets are being replaced because they are loose or noisy but the car is still in operating condition then turn the crankshaft until the number 6 cylinder is in the firing position. With number 6 in the firing position the timing punch marks on the cam and crankshaft

Gauge # H.M. 408 used in setting valve timing

VALVE TIMING PROCEDURE—*continued*

sprocket will be found to be in line with each other between the shafts center. This is done to avoid the necessity of having to reset the ignition timing.

If it is found that the chain has "jumped" or is broken or damaged, first remove the old chain and sprocket and turn the camshaft so that the punch mark on the sprocket is pointing straight downwards with the ignition distributor rotor arm on number 6 cylinder segment. Then turn the crankshaft until number 6 piston is at top dead center. This will be when the timing punch mark on the crankshaft sprocket is pointing straight upwards.

Remove the two screws holding the camshaft sprocket to the camshaft and, using a puller, remove the camshaft sprocket and chain from the camshaft.

The crankshaft sprocket will come off readily without the use of a puller.

To replace, install crankshaft sprocket over the crankshaft until it engages the key, being certain that the timing punch mark is pointing straight upwards.

Mount the timing chain over the camshaft and the crankshaft sprocket and start the camshaft sprocket over the shaft being certain the aligning dowel is in a position where it will enter the hole in the camshaft freely and also that the timing marks on the sprockets are nearest each other and in line between shaft centers.

It will be necessary to press the camshaft sprocket on to the shaft and a special tool has been developed for this purpose.

When the camshaft is secured, turn the engine two full revolutions until the timing marks again assume the original position and check to make certain that the punch marks, which are little round circles stamped into the front face of the camshaft, are in line between the shaft centers.

1940 TO 1953 MODELS

Remove the worn chain and sprockets from the car and arrange the new chain and sprockets on the bench so that the timing marks are in line between the center holes of the gears.

Now retaining this position set the cam and crankshaft so that the keys on each shaft are in the same position as the keyways in the gear.

Place both gears on the respective shafts at the same time with the chain in place, being careful not to disturb the timing mark locations.

The key on each shaft should be aligned very carefully with the keyway in the gear so that when the gears are being pressed on no difficulty will be encountered in having the key enter the gear.

Force both gears on to their shaft at the same time with the chain in place and, after securing them, rotate the crankshaft two full revolutions until the timing mark again assumes the checking position.

The mark on the crankshaft and the mark on the camshaft sprocket should be nearest each other and in a straight line between the shafts centers.

If the above procedures are followed the camshaft will be timed correctly regardless of which piston is at top center. It may be necessary to retime the ignition since it is possible to have the distributor rotor at 180 degrees out of place.

Caution: The camshaft sprocket should be placed on the camshaft using the type of tool which will force the sprocket in place without pushing the camshaft towards the rear of the car as this might damage the oil pump and distributor gears at the rear.

Removal of Engine Assembly

1940 TO 1948 MODELS

On these models it is not necessary to remove the radiator core, however, it is necessary to remove the water pump fan generator and carburetor in order to lift the engine out of the frame without risk of damage.

When the radiator core is left in place it is customary to take a small thin piece of plyboard and place it in back of the radiator core so that the core will not be damaged accidently.

The engine is usually detached at the bell housing.

1949 TO 1953 ENGINES

On these models it is necessary to remove the radiator core in order to take out the engine, and it is customary to take the engine and transmission assembly out as a unit. While it is possible to remove the engine by disconnecting it at the bell housing it is not considered a practical job.

Remove the starting motor and solenoid as an assembly from the lower flywheel housing and disconnect the clutch and transmission linkage.

Remove the generator, fan, water pump, before lifting the engine from the frame.

ROD AND PISTON ASSEMBLIES

All pertinent information as to sizes and fits on the rod and piston assemblies is given in Engineering data at the beginning of Cadillac.

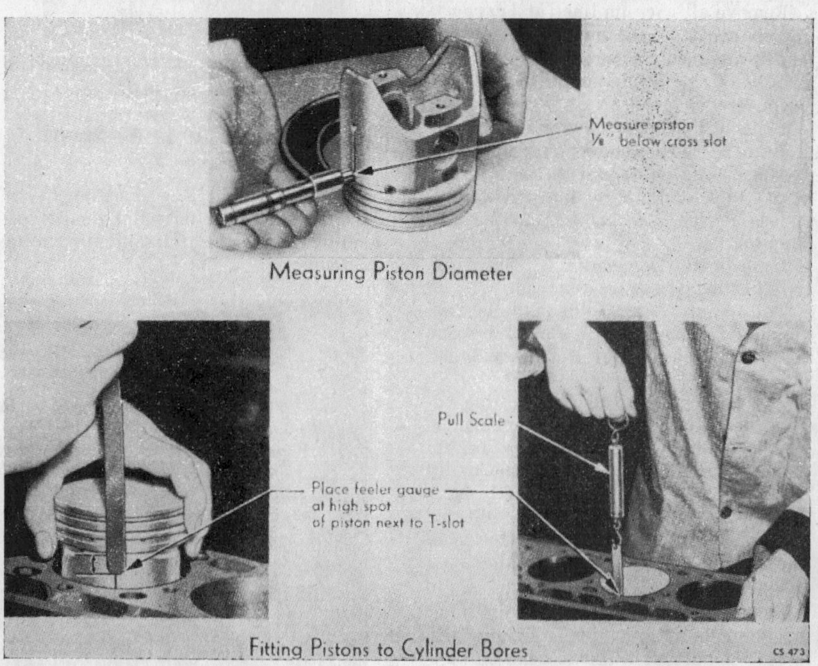

Piston Measurements

Rod and piston assemblies on all models are removed through the top of the block.

It is possible to replace any and all of the rod or main bearings from underneath the car without removing the crankshaft.

Rod Bearings

The connecting rod bearings are of the precision slip-in type fitted with a tang at the parting line to maintain their position. While generally speaking these bearings are considered to be not adjustable, shims are available which will take up small amounts of normal wear.

These shims are generally placed between the lower half of the rod bearing and the rod bearing cap.

Assembling Pistons to Connecting Rods

On 1940 to 1948 models the left cylinder bank has the odd numbered connecting rods, the right cylinder bank has the even numbered connecting rods thus the left bank front cylinder is number one, the right bank front cylinder is number two.

The numbers on the connecting rods are arranged so that they point away from the camshaft when they are mounted into the cylinder, this means that the numbers on the left bank are on the left side of the engine, the numbers on the right bank are on the right side of the engine.

When assembling the piston to the connecting rod the T slot in the piston is always to the left. Therefore on odd numbered pistons the T slot will be assembled on the numbered side of the connecting rod on the right bank, the T slot of the piston will be assembled opposite to the numbers on the connecting rod.

Odd numbered pistons—slot on same side as number. Even numbered pistons —slot on opposite side from rod number.

On the 1949 to 1953 engines the connecting rods are mounted in the engine in the same manner as the older models. That is, the numbers on the connecting rod are faced away from the camshaft.

However the pistons are marked rear. This means that with the connecting rod held so that the numbers face the mechanic, the stamp rear will be to his right on odd numbered pistons and to his left on even numbered pistons.

When these pistons are assembled in

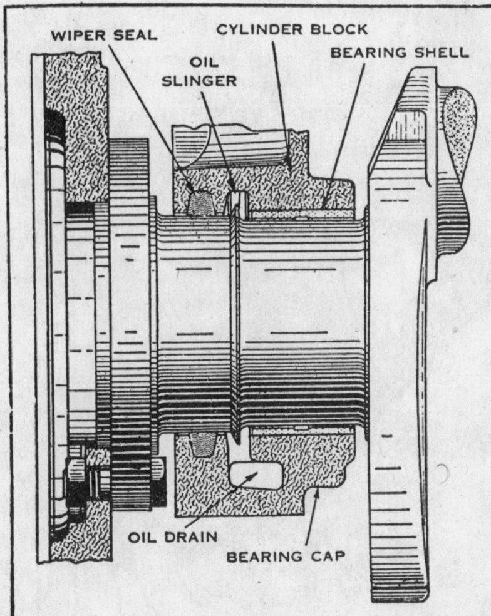

Rear main bearing oil seal—all models 1938-46

the engine the stamp rear is always to the rear of the engine.

Rear Main Bearings Oil Seal

On all models of Cadillac a packing type seal is used at the rear main bearing to prevent oil from escaping onto the clutch.

It is recommended that the engine and crankshaft be removed in order to replace the upper half of this oil seal.

It is sometimes possible to replace the upper half by lowering the crankshaft as far as it will go without damaging the clutch or clutch pilot and driving the old packing out with a punch and installing new packing by driving it into place.

Caution: If an attempt is made to install the upper half of the packing and the attempt is not successful it will be absolutely necessary to remove the engine and crankshaft and replace the upper half of the oil seal in the approved manner.

Sometimes it is possible to remove the rear main bearing cap and install new packing in the cap only, letting it protrude about 1/16 in. above the cap, and then bolt the cap in place. The protruding packing will tend to compress the packing in the upper half in the rear main bearing oil seal which sometimes takes up for wear on the upper half.

If this method is used it will be necessary to lower the cap after it has been bolted up into place to make certain that the packing has not "rivetted over." If it has rivetted over take a razor blade and trim the rivetted portion only leaving the balance protrude.

This procedure will have to be repeated until the rear main bearing cap is seated firmly against the block.

Since any method of installing a new rear main bearing oil seal, except removal of the engine and crankshaft, is at best a makeshift, the above given procedures cannot be guaranteed.

VALVE SYSTEM

1940 TO 1948 MODELS

These models were the L head V type engines and service on the valves required the removal of both the intake and the exhaust manifolds, the valve chamber cover and both cylinder heads.

On these models the hydraulic valve lifting mechanism is mounted in groups or clusters. These clusters are not interchangeable. If any are to be removed they should be marked very carefully so that they are reinstalled in the same position on the block. Also mark each lifter if it is removed from the cluster so that it can be reinstalled in the same hole.

1949 TO 1953 ENGINES

These engines were of the overhead valve V type. Service on the valves requires removal of the intake manifold, the rocker assembly and both cylinder heads but does not require the removal of the exhaust manifolds from the heads. Detach them at the exhaust flange.

Hydraulic valve lifter mechanisms on these models are not mounted in clusters as they are on former models but each lifter is mounted in a separate hole bored into the block.

The lifters are not interchangeable they must be carefully marked or tagged and reinstalled in the hole from which they were removed.

SERVICING HYDRAULIC VALVE LIFTERS

Except that the 1940 to 48 engine valve lifters were contained in clusters and the 49 to 53 were in individual holes in the block, the service procedure for the lifter assemblies is identical.

Leak Down Test

This test will show a bad lifter or lifters since defective mechanisms will have the shortest breakdown time.

A special tool is available for this operation. Complete instruction for the manipulation of this special tool are packed with it.

Continued

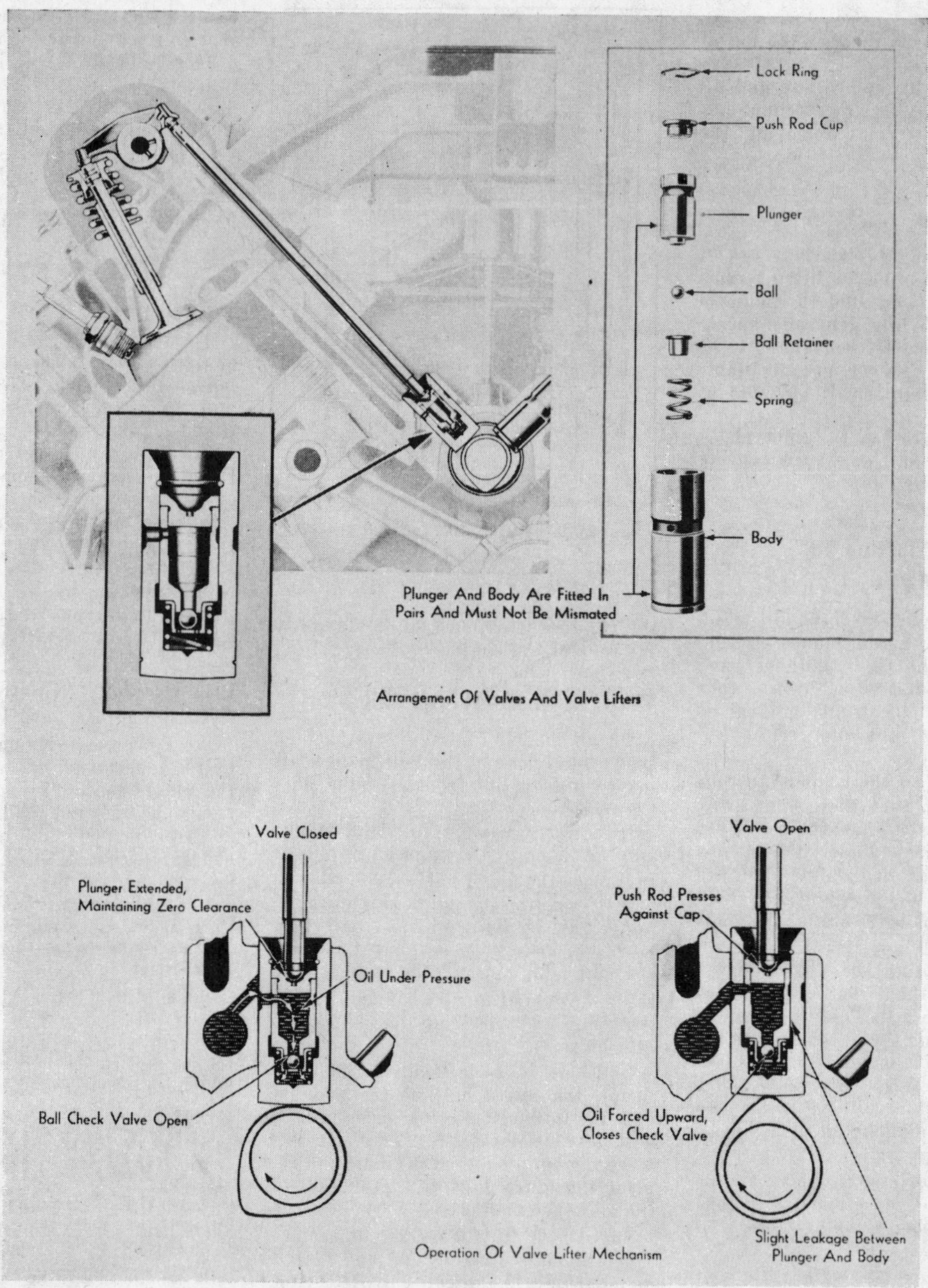

Valve lifter mechanism

VALVE LIFTERS—*continued*

To check the leak down rate proceed as follows: The leak down test should be made only on valves which are fully closed (the lifter on the low side of the cam).

Force up the valve spring with a pry bar and insert the gauge portion of the special checking tool between the end of the valve stem and lifter (rocker arm on 1949 to 1953) and release the valve spring so that it compresses against the gauge portion of the special tool. Note the time required for the valve lifter to leak down sufficiently to permit removal of the gauge tool.

This special tool is arranged so that it will snap out from between the lifter and valve when the lifter has leaked down a sufficient amount. When making this test note carefully the length of time that the gauge is held in place by the pressure of the valve spring. If any

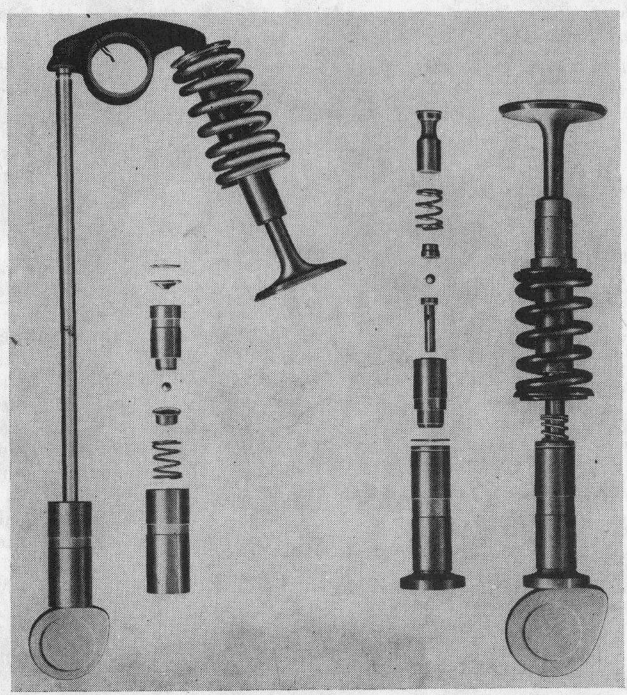

Hydraulic valve lifter used on all 1938 to 1948 models is shown on the right. 1949-50 overhead valve lifter is shown on the left

one valve requires considerably less time it very likely has a defective lifter mechanism.

If all of the lifters check out at approximately the same time, it may be assumed that they are all in good operating condition. It is very unlikely that all of the hydraulic lifters will be bad.

Disassembly of Lifters

The lifter mechanism should be disassembled for cleaning purposes only since no other service is possible on the lifter.

Remove the lifter from the car and take out the lock ring which holds the internal assembly together. Disassemble lifter being extra careful not to mix up the lifter bodies or plungers. The plunger positively must be reinstalled in the lifter body from which it was removed since these units are selective fit at the factory.

Check the inside of the lifters for pits or scoring. If any are present the lifter will have to be replaced.

After a thorough cleaning with solvent and compressed air, reassemble the lifters and replace them in the engine.

Note: Hydraulic lifter mechanisms are supplied in two sizes, one is only slightly larger than the other. The large size lifter is stamped with the letter B and will fit in a hole which is also stamped with the letter B. If no stamp mark is on the hole then it will be necessary to use a lifter which is not stamped.

Initial Adjustment of the Hydraulic Valve Lifters

Check the clearance between the lifter and the bottom of the valve (or between the top of the valve stem and the rocker arm on overhead valve engines) by depressing the lifter until all the oil is forced out of it. In this position there should be .030 to .070 in. clearance between the top of the lifter and the bottom of the valve stem (or between the rocker arm and the valve stem on overheads). If less than .030 exists it will be necessary to grind off the top of the valve stem in order to develop the minimum clearance. If more than .070 exists it will be necessary to replace worn or damaged parts until the proper clearance is developed.

Caution: When depressing the hydraulic valve mechanism to expel the oil, bear in mind that little time is required for the oil to escape out of the lifter. If this check shows too little clearance make absolutely certain that all of the oil is expelled and that the hydraulic lifter is completely depressed before grinding off the top of the valve stem.

CLUTCH ASSEMBLY—MODELS WITH CONVENTIONAL TRANSMISSION

Long coil spring type clutches are used in all Cadillac models. (Except hydramatics.)

Clutch Removal

The clutch assembly is removed through the bottom of the bell housing after the transmission has been removed.

Remove the transmission and the flywheel lower housing pan and, working up through the bottom, disconnect the bolts which hold the clutch to the flywheel.

In order to insure that the clutch cover is not bent or damaged in the removal process, loosen the bolts a couple of turns at a time all the way around the clutch pressure plate so that the pressure plate lifts off the flywheel in a more or less straight line.

Caution: It is a good idea to insert a stick of wood or even a wrench handle in through the center of the clutch disk into the flywheel pilot to prevent the clutch from falling when the last screw is taken out.

Replacing the Clutch

To replace the clutch it is necessary to have a pilot tool or pilot shaft of some kind to maintain the clutch disk in alignment with the flywheel pilot hole while tightening up the pressure plate assembly.

If no pilot tool is available it is possible to secure one by taking the clutch shaft out of the transmission and using it as a pilot while assembling the clutch to the flywheel.

Hold the clutch disk and pressure plate in position in the left hand and push them up into position in front of the flywheel and then, using the right hand, insert the pilot shaft through the clutch disk into the flywheel pilot hole.

Start the bolt through the pressure plate into the flywheel and run them down finger tight so that all of the bolts are tightened lightly. Working again around the pressure plate with a wrench, take a few turns at a time on each bolt all the way around flywheel and continue doing this until all of the bolts are securely tightened.

REPLACING CLUTCH—*continued*

This will prevent shifting the disk out of position and straining against the pilot. If the disk is strained against the pilot it is sometimes very difficult to replace the transmission.

If the transmission front shaft was used as a pilot, replace it into the transmission at this point and reinstall the transmission and flywheel cover assembly.

Clutch Pedal Adjustment

The clutch pedal should be adjusted at the adjusting nut located just in front of the release fork, until there is 1 to 1½ inches free travel of the clutch pedal. This free travel is measured at the toe board.

Clutch Overhaul

Overhauling the long type clutch requires special fixtures and jigs which are made by several different manufacturers. Each manufacturer provides complete and detailed instructions in the use of his equipment.

It is not considered advisable to attempt to adjust the fingers or the clutch pressure without the necessary special fixtures.

STANDARD TRANSMISSION ASSEMBLY

The standard transmission used on all Cadillacs is a Warner type with three forward speeds.

Removal of Transmission

The standard transmission in all Cadillacs is removed in practically the same manner.

Disconnect the universal joints and remove the drive shaft.

Disconnect all shift linkage at the transmission.

Support the rear of the engine and disconnect the rear engine support from the cross member and, holding the rear of the engine weight on a jack, remove the cross member which carries the rear of the transmission.

Disconnect the bolts which hold the transmission to the bell housing and slide the transmission straight back and down to the floor. It is sometimes easier to let the transmission down by lowering the front end first.

SHIFT MECHANISM ADJUSTMENT, STANDARD TRANSMISSIONS

Disconnect the shift rods at the transmission and set the transmission levers into neutral. Set the shift lever on the steering column into neutral and jam it into that position.

Now adjust both shift rods so that the clevis pins will enter freely at the transmission levers. After the levers are connected check the cross over and make sure the cross over is smooth and easy. Make the final very slight adjustment necessary to correct the cross over at the low and reverse shift rod.

Standard Transmission Disassembly

Remove the speedometer drive gear from the side of the extension case and the universal joint flange from the rear end of the main shaft.

Take off the extension housing and transmission cover.

Take out the screw (bottom of case) which holds the countershaft.

Drive the counter shaft out through the rear of the case and let the cluster drop to the bottom of the case. The main drive gear is then removed out of the front of the case.

Slide the synchronizer off the front end of the main shaft and take out the snap ring which holds the second speed gear to the shaft and remove the second speed gear. The shaft is then driven out through the back of the case with its bearing in place.

Drive out the idler gear shaft and lift out the idler gear and the countershaft cluster.

When reassembling, a special shaft is available to hold the counter gears and thrust washers in place.

Note: All new grease seals should be installed when a transmission is disassembled. The grease seal at the rear end of the transmission is arranged so that it seals on the universal joint yolk. A grease seal is provided at each end of the idler shaft and each end of the counter shaft.

Removal of the Hydramatic Transmission

To remove the hydramatic transmission it will be necessary to raise the entire car so that all four wheels are at least eight inches off the floor, take out the front seat cushion, floor mat and the front seat pan.

Disconnect the propeller shaft at the universal joints and remove it. Take the front yoke off the transmission extension shaft.

Drain the transmission and flywheel and place a block of wood on top of a jack to support the rear of the engine.

Disconnect the rear support at the transmission extension and remove the frame cross member which carries the support.

Disconnect all levers and wires from the side of the transmission and transmission case.

Disconnect the speedometer cable and remove the spark plugs and the starter.

Caution: On some hydramatic installations washers were used to balance the hydramatic unit and flywheel. If any washers are found on the flywheel it will be necessary to mark the flywheel and the washers carefully so that they can be reinstalled under the screws from which they were removed.

With the jack located under the en-

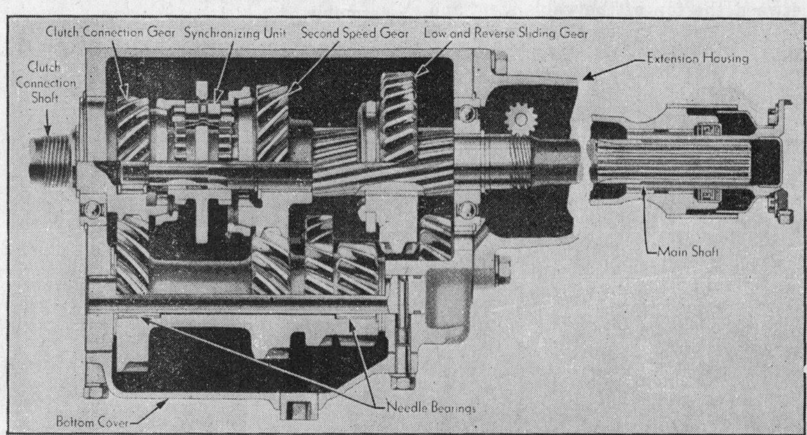

Cross section of the standard transmission

gine raise the transmission enough to remove the strain off the attaching bolts and take out the 30 5/16 cap screws holding the flywheel cover to the flywheel and push the cover toward the rear to disengage it from its locating dowels.

Before disengaging it mark it carefully so that it is reinstalled in the same relative position from which it was removed.

After the 5/16 cap screws have been removed lower the jack sufficiently to permit access to the bell housing top bolts through the hole in the floor pan.

Now slide the transmission back slightly and lower it to the floor.

Caution: The hydramatic transmission is much heavier than a standard transmission and it is very difficult for one man, unless he is extremely strong, to handle the hydramatic transmission by himself. The best way to handle a hydramatic transmission is with either a roller jack from underneath or a lowering device which is designed for handling such parts.

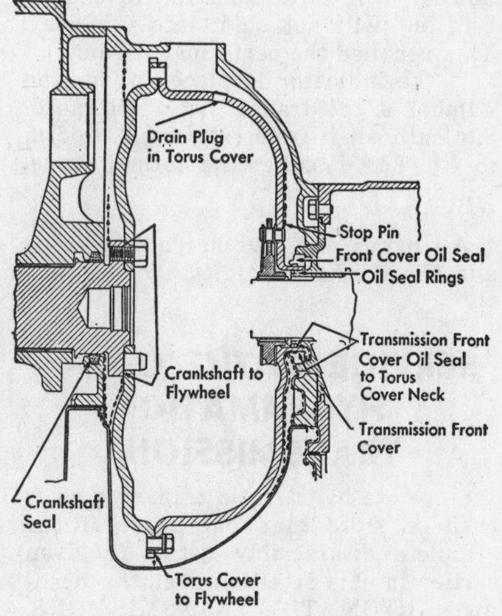

The sketch above shows the more likely places for oil to leak

OPERATION OF THE HYDRAMATIC DRIVE

While all of the hydramatic drives are not the same, improvements and refinements have been made from year to year, the general function of the unit is the same regardless of the year of the car. Hydramatic drive consists of the following units, listed in the order in which they transmit power and not necessarily in the order in which they appear on the unit: The flywheel, front planetary unit, the fluid couple or torus member, the rear planetary unit, and the reverse unit. The reverse unit and the rear planetary unit, are connected to the output shaft. Each planetary unit consists of planet gears meshed between the sun gear and an internal gear. The rear unit having a greater reduction than the front unit. Either the sun gear or the internal gear is attached to a drum which can be held from rotating by a servo operating band. Each planetary unit also has a multiple disc clutch which may be applied by oil pressure and released by springs.

In addition to these parts through which power is transmitted there are also two oil pumps a governor and various controlled devices. The pistons and servos that operate the bands and clutches are such devices.

The fluid unit of the hydramatic drive is composed of two torus members each attached to an independent shaft. One is the driving member and the other the driven member. Both are nearly identical in construction except for the hubs which attach them to their respective shafts.

The driving torus member imparts centrifugal force to the fluid within the coupling and directs this fluid against the driven member. As the fluid is forced to the outer part of the driving member by the centrifugal force it must cross over the driven member which sets up a driving force in the driven member causing it to rotate at nearly the same speed as the driving member. Very high efficiency is achieved due to the slight clearance of only 1/16 inch between the driving and driven members and the shape is such that the area of passage between the torus veins give the greatest possible friction to the flow of fluid. Special fluid is required for the hydramatic drive.

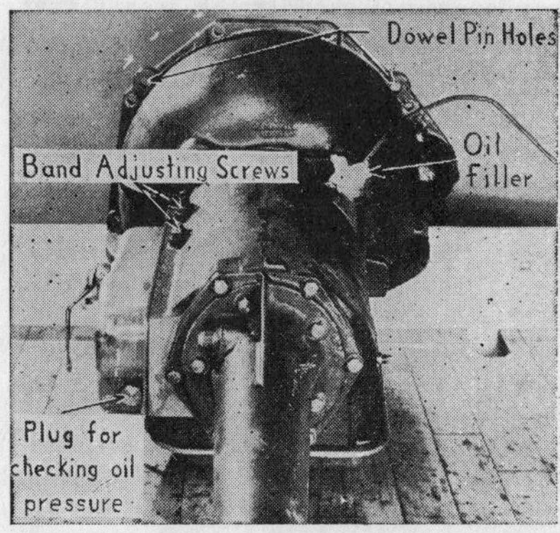

Hydra-Matic drive assembly as removed from car

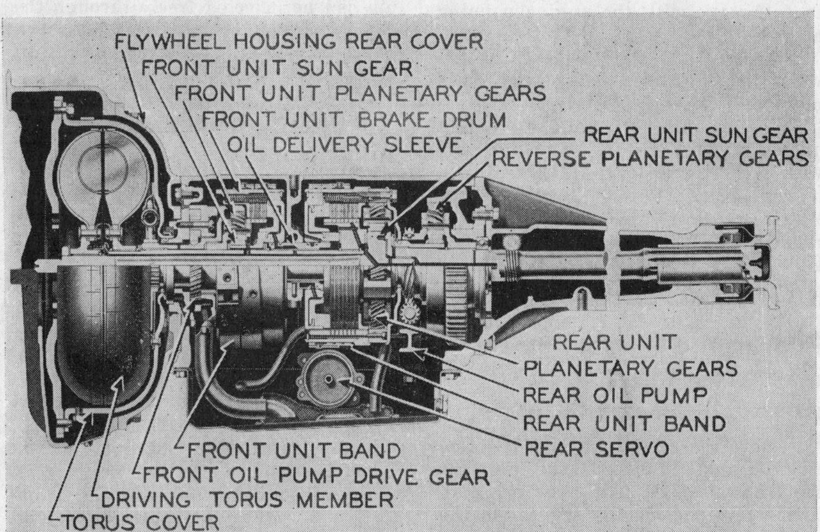

Cutaway view of transmission

Mechanical Operation of the Hydramatic

FIRST SPEED

Both bands are applied and both planetary units are in their maximum reduction to provide maximum total reduction.

CADILLAC 1940 thru 1953

MECHANICAL OPERATION OF HYDRAMATIC—*continued*

SECOND SPEED

The front band is released and the front clutch engaged so that the front unit is in direct drive and the only reduction is in the rear unit.

Location of drain plugs

THIRD SPEED

The front band is reapplied and the front clutch released so that the front unit is again in reduction but the rear band is released and the rear clutch applied so that the rear unit is in direct drive. Since the front planetary unit has less reduction than the rear unit the car will move in third speed.

FOURTH OR DIRECT SPEED

Both clutches are applied and both bands are released, which means that both units are in direct drive.

REVERSE

The front unit is in its planetary gears, the rear unit is idling, that is, neither the band nor the clutch is engaged and the reverse anchor is engaged. This causes a further reduction and changes the direction of rotation of the output shaft.

Starting with 1951 models an hydraulically operated clutch type reverse is used on all Cadillac Hydra-Matics.

This clutch is operated by a series of valves which cause a cone clutch to engage, locking the reverse mechanism, causing the output shaft to rotate at a reduced speed and in the opposite direction to the drive shaft.

Dual Range Hydra-Matic

Starting with 1952 production a Dual Range Hydra-Matic is used on most Cadillac models.

The Dual Range models may be identified by the numbers and 3 and 4 under the letter D on the shift quadrant under the steering wheel.

If the arrow is placed on 3 the transmission will shift from 1st, to 2nd, to 3rd, but will not shift into 4th gear. This is called the performance range.

If the indicator is placed under the number 4 the transmission will automatically shift from 1st, to 2nd, to 3rd, to 4th. This is called the normal range.

NEUTRAL

All bands and clutches are released and the mechanism idles.

SERVICE IN THE CAR— HYDRAMATIC TRANSMISSION

Since the hydramatic transmission is used on more than one make of car complete disassembly detail is given earlier in this section under the heading AUTOMATIC TRANSMISSIONS. See index.

Adding or Changing Fluid in the Hydramatic

Always use car manufacturer's approved fluid, check level monthly or about every thousand miles. To check fluid raise the floor mat on the right side and remove the sheet metal cover in the floor pan. Run the engine about 90 seconds at a speed equivalent to 20 miles per hour, then reduce speed to slow idle. Remove the fluid lever plunger, wipe clean, then reinstall and check level. The distance from full to low on the level plunger equals one quart.

Add the necessary fluid to bring up to full mark with the engine running at slow idle.

To change the fluid remove the flywheel housing cover and the two drain plugs and drain completely.

Reinstall the plugs and add eight quarts of fluid. Start the engine and, with the selector lever in neutral, run it for about 90 seconds at a speed equivalent to 20 miles per hour then reduce the speed to slow idle. Then add 2½ to 3 quarts or until the dip stick comes up to the full mark.

Hydramatic Manual Control Lever Adjustment

1942 THRU 1948 MODELS ONLY

Remove the clevis pin from the control rod and set the selector lever (at the transmission) in the reverse position. Move the manual lever into the reverse position and adjust the control rod clevis until the pin enters freely. Tighten the clevis lock nut and check for free operation in all positions.

1946 AND 1947 MODELS ONLY

The control lever is adjusted in exactly the same manner as the '42 and '48 models except that the transmission control lever at the transmission is set at an extreme forward position and the selector lever at the steering column is set in the neutral position. The clevis should be adjusted so with both levers in this position the clevis will enter freely.

1949 TO 1951 MODELS

Disconnect the shift lever and set the selector lever on the steering column into the drive position. Place the transmission lever in the drive position and adjust the length of the clevis so that the pin will enter freely. Secure the pin and test the lever setting in all positions.

1952-53 DUAL RANGE MODELS

Disconnect the manual control and from the control lever at the transmission.

Move the control lever at the transmission to the normal drive position. This can be found by moving the transmission manual lever (at the transmission) fully forward and upward and then moving it rearward until the first detent is felt. This is the normal drive position.

Move the selector lever on the steering column to the number 4 under the letter D. This is the normal drive position at the steering column.

Now adjust the clevis on the lower end of the control rod until the clevis pin can be inserted freely through the clevis and manual control lever. Assemble the clevis pin and lever and install a new cotter pin.

Throttle Control Linkage Adjustment

1942 MODELS ONLY

Make sure that the idle speed of the engine is set correctly, that is, 375 RPM.

Close the throttle against the slow idle step of the carburetor fast idle cam. Loosen throttle rod adjusting nut at the carburetor and insert a .248 inch dowel pin in place in the relay arm to hold the relay arm in the correct position.

Tighten the adjusting nuts at the carburetor end of the throttle to relay rod. Adjust the trunnion at the throttle valve rod so that the pin can be installed freely when the throttle lever is against its stop.

Remove the dowel pin from the relay rod.

Note: A "D" drill which is .246 inch in diameter can be substituted for the .248 inch dowel pin.

1946 TO 1948 MODELS ONLY

On 1946 to 1948 models a considerable amount of adjustment is required to properly set the levers from the throttle to the transmission. However, if the levers have not been deliberately disturbed it is quite possible that only the first, the throttle rod, adjustment will be necessary. However, if this does not give satisfactory adjustment then proceed with the rest of the adjustments concerned with the throttle connections to the transmission.

Throttle Rod Adjustment

Adjust the trunnion at the carburetor throttle rod to obtain a length of throttle rod which will allow free entry of a gauge through a hole in the upper relay (this upper relay is the bellcrank which is mounted on the distributor support) and into the distributor support without changing the carburetor setting.

In other words, the dowel pin should enter freely with the throttle set on its low cam.

Adjustment of the Lower Relay

Note: The lower relay is the pivot arm which is monuted on the side of the flywheel housing.

With the gauge pins still in place in the distributor support, check the position of the lower relay lever by disconnecting the clevis at the throttle lever on the transmission and also disconnect the lower end of the vertical rod from the upper relay.

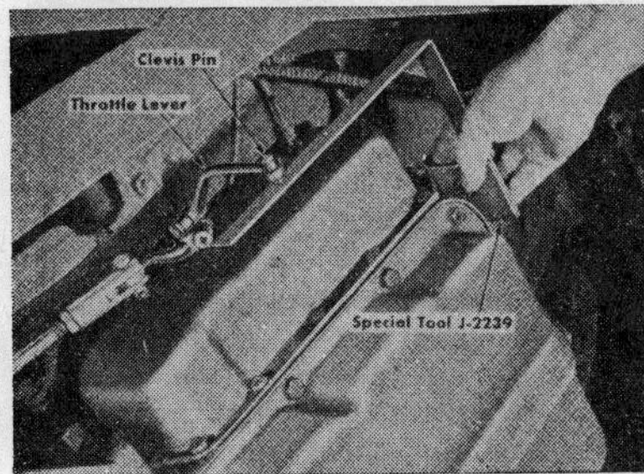

Throttle lever checking gauge in place

Insert another gauge pin through the hole in the lower relay lever and into the hole in the flywheel housing. If the vertical rod will enter freely, the lower relay is in correct position; if it will not enter freely it will be necessary to bend the lower relay rod until it will enter freely. A special bending tool is available for this purpose.

Note: This adjustment is rarely required. However, if it becomes necessary to bend the lower relay lever be sure to bend it in the position in which it is already bent.

Throttle Lever Adjustment (at Transmission)

Leave the pins in both relay rods. Then pull the transmission throttle lever against its stop in the reverse position (toward the rear of the transmission case) with a load of 3/8 to 1/2 pound as measured with a spring scale. Hold the throttle lever in this position and pull the horizontal rod back to take all play out of the lower relay lever. Now adjust the clevis so that the pin enters freely in the hole of the throttle lever and then advance it three complete turns forward and connect it to the throttle lever.

Remove the lower gauge pin from the lower relay lever.

With the gauge pin and the distributor relay in position disconnect the trunnion on the horizontal rod which goes to the dash relay upper lever and turn the trunnion until it will slide freely into the dash relay upper lever when the center of the hole in the dash relay upper lever is 9/16 from the face of the dash.

(Lay a straight edge over the pocket in the dash and measure to the inside edge of the straight edge, not to the bottom of the pocket.)

On 1948 series 75 and 76 models this distance should be 1 15/16.

Adjustment of the Accelerator Pedal Rod

Remove the gauge from the distributor relay and disconnect the accelerator pedal rod at the dash relay lower lever. With throttle held in a wide open position and accelerator pedal on the floor board carpet, turn the rod in the trunnion until the rod slips freely into the dash relay lower lever.

Recheck this adjustment.

Throttle Control Linkage Adjustment

1949 TO 1953 MODELS

Adjustment of throttle control lever at the transmission.

This adjustment requires the use of a position tool No. J3065. The lever must be adjusted so that with the gauge in place and the lever in the full rearward position the clevis pin in the lever will freely enter the hole in the gauge. If it does not it will be necessary to bend the lever at the transmission so that the pin will enter freely in the hole in the gauge.

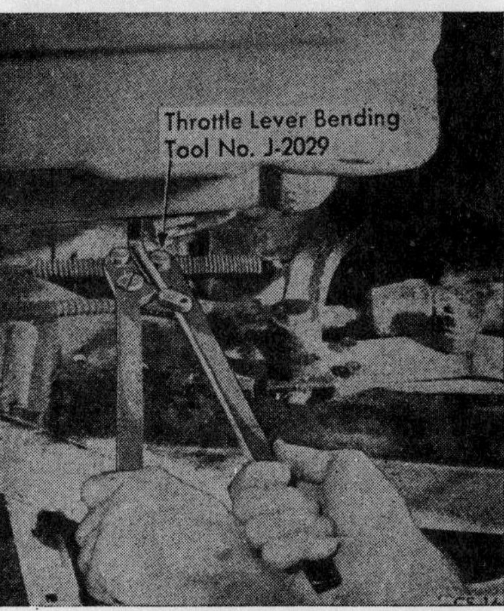

Throttle lever bending tool

Adjustment of Linkage at the Throttle

Remove the carburetor to dash relay rod trunnion from the relay lever. Place 1/4 in. drill shank through the gauging hole in the dash relay lever and into the dash relay bracket. Set the carburetor in the slow idle position.

Special band tightening tool

Adjust the carburetor to relay rod trunnion to allow free entry into the relay dash lever.

Back off both jam nuts on the throttle valve rod at the carburetor to allow free movement in the trunnion.

CADILLAC 1940 thru 1953

THROTTLE LINKAGE—*continued*

Push on the end of the throttle valve rod to position the transmission throttle valve against its stop. Bring the rear jam nut up against the trunnion and back off three complete turns. Tighten the front jam nut, making certain that the linkage moves freely.

Then remove the ¼ in. drill from the dash relay and check the wide open throttle position of the accelerator pedal.

Pedals should touch the floor mat with a slight pressure when the throttle is wide open. The adjustment for wide open throttle is at the end of the dash relay to accelerator pedal rod.

Adjustment of the Servo Bands

FRONT BAND

The following adjust is intended for normal wear on the bands and does not constitute a resetting adjustment of the band itself.

Set the hand brake to the front wheels with chocks to prevent the car from rolling during the adjustment.

Thoroughly warm up the engine, remove the floor mat from over the band adjusting cover (some of the very early models did not have a band adjusting cover; on these models it will be necessary to take out the cover pan).

Check the oil level and add oil if necessary.

Connect a tachometer to the engine and adjust the carburetor idle so that the tachometer reads 700 RPM.

Position the selector lever in the drive range.

Loosen the band adjusting screw lock nut and back off on the screw until the engine speed increases to 900/1000 RPM. At this point the front drum is spinning freely.

Note: If the engine fails to increase its speed to 900/1000 RPM it indicates that the band is slipping badly under normal driving conditions in which case it will be necessary to remove the bottom pan and inspect the bands and drums for damage.

Tighten the adjusting screws slowly until the engine returns to 700 RPM. The drum is now stopped.

Repeat this tightening of the screws several times, bringing the engine speed back to 700 RPM. The object of loosening and retightening the screw is to locate the exact point which the band stops the drum from spinning. At this point wait 30 seconds. If the engine speed increases, tighten the screw very slowly until it again reads 700 RPM. Wait again about 30 seconds and if the engine speed again increases, again tighten the screw very slowly until the engine speed remains at 700 RPM for at least 30 seconds. Hold the jam nut stationary and tighten the adjusting screw exactly 5½ turns past this point. Hold the adjusting screw stationary with a short handle screw driver and tighten the lock nut.

REAR BAND ADJUSTMENT

The rear band adjustment is made in exactly the same manner as the front band adjustment except that the adjusting screw is turned exactly two turns after the engine speed has been maintained at 700 RPM.

After tightening jam nut reset the engine to 375 RPM with the lever in drive range.

Note: A special tool, No. J2681, is available to simplify the adjustment of the servo bands.

UNIVERSAL JOINTS REAR AXLE ASSEMBLY

Removal

It is customary to remove the rear axle assembly from the Cadillac cars by disconnecting at the rear universal joint. It will be necessary to disconnect U bolts, stabilizer links, shock links, rear shackles, emergency brake cables and hydraulic lines.

The Cadillac Motor Car Company does not supply internal parts for the differential carrier assembly.

They recommend that if the rear axle assembly has become damaged an entire new carrier be secured from the factory to be used as a replacement.

Axle Shaft Removal

To remove the rear axle shaft it is necessary to take off the wheel, and brake backing plate, disconnect the brake line and use an inertia puller to remove the axle shaft.

Rear Axle Oil Seal

The oil seal assembly for the outer end of the rear axle shaft is located behind the wheel bearing. In order to replace the oil seal it is necessary to take off the rear wheel and drum and the brake backing plate and the axle shaft. The grease retainer is removed with an inertia puller. To replace the oil seal, a driver should be used. If none is available, use extreme care when forcing the oil seal into the housing so as not to damage the seal.

Pinion Oil Seal

Great care should be exercised in replacing the pinion oil seal, since a crumbled type spacer is used on the pinion bearings. It is a good idea to very carefully count the number of turns it requires to take off the pinion nut which holds the universal joint yoke in place and to return it to exactly the position from which it was removed when the new grease seal is replaced.

Note: It is customary to tighten the pinion nut to approximately 225 pounds foot torque.

To remove the pinion oil seal, first disconnect the rear universal joint and remove the pinion flange nut, being very careful to count the turns that were required to take it all the way off. This is very important since it must be returned to exactly the same number of turns in order to establish the same preload as was there when the job was started.

Pull off the universal joint companion flange from the pinion shaft and, using an inertia type puller, pull out the pinion oil seal from the housing.

The new seal should be driven into place with an oil seal driver. However, if one is not available the seal may be inserted into the housing using extreme care not to damage it while forcing it into place.

Replace the companion shaft flange and the pinion shaft nut, screwing it on exactly the same number of turns that were required to take it off.

The pinion bearings are intended to operate on a very definite preload and it is absolutely essential that the pinion be returned to the position from which it was removed.

Axle Shaft Bearings

Two types of rear axle shaft have been used on Cadillac models. Up to and including 1948 a taper axle shaft was used. The rear wheel hub is mounted on a tapered axle.

To replace the bearing on these models it is necessary to remove the wheel and hub assembly and take off the brake backing plate and remove the axle shaft from the housing. The bearing is then pressed off towards the tapered end of the axle.

A new bearing is installed by pressing the bearing up to the flange on the axle shaft.

Starting with 1949 models, a flange type axle is used. To replace a bearing on this type of axle, remove the wheel and brake drum, and, reaching behind

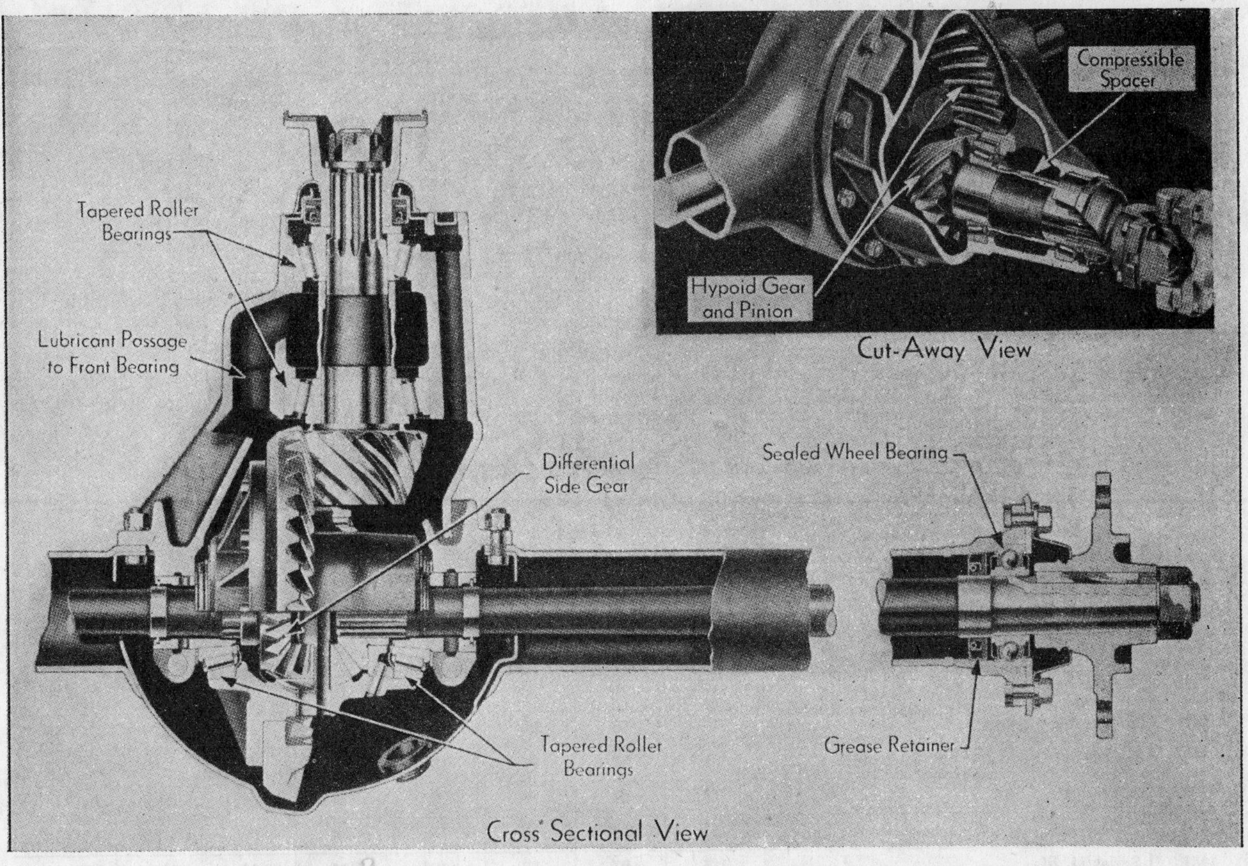

Cross sectional view of rear axle assembly

the axle flange, remove the bolts which hold the dust plate to the housing.

Pull the axle shaft out of the housing.

The bearing is held on the axle shaft by a pressed-on retainer. To remove the bearing it is necessary to mount the axle shaft in a large arbor press and press the bearing off towards the inside (towards the splines of the axle shaft). This will force both the bearing and its retainer off the axle shaft.

It may be necessary to split the retainer before attempting to press off the bearing.

New bearings are installed, using a large arbor press and forcing the bearing on to the axle shaft as far up as it will go.

It is a good idea to put on the retaining ring by heating it so that it will expand and then pressing it on with an arbor press. The retainer will then shrink down and hold very rigidly to the shaft.

When installing the new bearing do not forget to first put the dust seal up on the axle shaft faced so that the outer end of the dust shield is against the flange on the axle.

Universal Joints and Propeller Shaft

Except for the Series 75 Cadillacs which have a jack shaft and an intermediate propeller shaft, all of the Cadillac universal joints are serviced in practically the same manner.

To remove the drive shaft, disconnect, at the rear propeller shaft, the flange bearing from the pinion shaft yoke, lower the drive shaft and slide the front universal joint and its transmission yoke off the end of the transmission main shaft.

The universal joints may be disassembled by removing the lock rings which retain the bearings in the yoke. These lock rings are at the inner surface at the yoke and are formed like the letter C and can be driven out readily. When both sides have been removed, simply force the bearing on one side across to the other which will force that bearing out of the yoke. Then, using any kind of a dummy tool force the other bearing out the opposite side.

Usually very little difficulty is experienced in removing these bearings.

To replace the bearings simply mount the universal joint so that the bearings are pushed in with the fingers in place and squeeze them into place in a vise.

When the front yoke is removed from the transmission it is possible that the oil in the transmission will run out. If a dummy yoke or a piece of wood is available, the hole can be blocked up temporarily to prevent the oil from running on the floor.

CHEVROLET SPECIFICATIONS

Starting Serial and Motor Numbers

Starting Serial Numbers

The first two letters in the serial number indicates the year and series, i.e. KA-1001 indicates 1940, series KA. All serial numbers begin 1001.

1940, Ser. KB, KH, KA.........1001
1941, Ser. AG, AH.............1001
1942, Ser. BG, BH.............1001
1946, Ser. DJ, DK.............1001
1947, Ser. EJ, EK.............1001
1948, Ser. FJ, FK.............1001
1949, Ser. GJ, GK.............1001
1950, Ser. HJ, HK.............1001
1951, Ser. JJ, JK.............1001
1952, Ser. KJ, KK.............1001
1953, Ser. Conventional, Powerglide 1001

Location

1940-1942—Plate on right side of floor pan before front seat.
1946-1948—Plate on right front door hinge pillar.
1949-1953—Plate on left front door hinge pillar.

Starting Motor Numbers

1940............B-105462 & 2697268
1941-1953—First two letters indicate year, i.e. AA-1001 indicates 1940. All motor numbers begin 1001.

1941—AA, AC
1942—2AA, 2AC, BA
1946—DA 1001
1947—EA 1001
1948—FA 1001
1949—GA 1001
1950—HA 1001
1951—JA 1001
1952—KA 1001
1953—Conventional, Powerglide.1001

Location

1940-1953—Stamped on right side of block near fuel pump and to rear of distributor.

General Specifications

Year	Model	Wheelbase (in.)	Tread (in.)		Overall Dimensions (in.)			Shipping Weight* (lb.)	Tire Size (in.)
			Front	Rear	Length†	Width	Height■		
1941	Series—All	116	58	60	196	....	....	3140	6.00-16
1942	Series—All	116	58	60	196	....	....	3110	6.00-16
1946	Series—All	116	58	60	198	73	70	3090	6.00-16
1947	Series—All	116	58	60	197	73	69	3170	6.00-16
1948	Series—All	116	58	60	198	73	69	3130	6.00-16
1949	Series—All	115	57	59	197	74	66	3075	6.70-15
1950	Series—All	115	57	59	198	74	66	3120	6.70-15
1951	Series JJ, JK	115	57	59	198	74	66	3130	6.70-15
	Series 2100	115	57	59	198	74	66	3300	6.70-15
1952	Conventional, Power Glide	115	57	59	198	74	63	....	6.70-15
1953	Conventional, Power Glide	115	57	59	195.5	75	63	....	6.70-15

†—Including bumpers and guards. ■—Road to roof, no load. *—Cheapest 5 passenger 4 door sedan or equivalent.

General Engine Specifications

Year	Model	Number of Cylinders Bore and Stroke	Piston Displacement, Cubic Inches	Compression Ratio (To–1)	Taxable (A.M.A.) Hp.	DEVELOPED HORSE POWER		Maximum Torque Ft. Lbs.
						Bare Engine	With Accessories	
1941	AG, 6 Cyl.	6–3½ x 3¾	216.5	6.50	29.4	90 @ 3300	....	174 @ (e)
	AH, 6 Cyl.	6–3½ x 3¾	216.5	6.50	29.4	90 @ 3300	....	174 @ (e)
1942	BG, 6 Cyl.	6–3½ x 3¾	216.5	6.50	29.4	90 @ 3300	....	174 @ 1200
	BH, 6 Cyl.	6–3½ x 3¾	216.5	6.50	29.4	90 @ 3300	....	174 @ 1200
1946	DJ & DK, 6 Cyl.	6–3½ x 3¾	216.5	6.50	29.4	90 @ 3300	83 @ 3200	174 @ (i)
1947	EJ, 6 Cyl.	6–3½ x 3¾	216.5	6.50	29.4	90 @ 3300	83 @ 3200	174 @ 2000
	EK, 6 Cyl.	6–3½ x 3¾	216.5	6.50	29.4	90 @ 3300	83 @ 3200	174 @ 2000
1948	FJ, 6 Cyl.	6–3½ x 3¾	216.5	6.50	29.4	90 @ 3300	83 @ 3200	174 @ 2000
	FK, 6 Cyl.	6–3½ x 3¾	216.5	6.50	29.4	90 @ 3300	83 @ 3200	174 @ 2000
1949	GJ, 6 Cyl.	6–3½ x 3¾	216.5	6.60	29.4	90 @ 3300	83 @ 3200	174 (A)
	GK, 6 Cyl.	6–3½ x 3¾	216.5	6.60	29.4	90 @ 3300	83 @ 3200	174 (A)
1950	HJ, HK, 6 Cyl.	6–3½ x 3¾	216.5	6.60	29.4	92 @ 3400	85 @ 3300	176 (A)
	HK w/Pow. Glide	6–3 9/16 x 3 15/16	235.5	6.70	30.4	105 @ 3600	98 @ 3500	....

General Engine Specifications—*continued*

Year	Model	Number of Cylinders Bore and Stroke	Piston Displacement, Cubic Inches	Compression Ratio (To–1)	Taxable (A.M.A.) Hp.	DEVELOPED HORSE POWER		Maximum Torque Ft. Lbs.
						Bare Engine	With Accessories	
1951	JJ, JK, 6 Cyl. JK w/Power Glide, 6 Cyl.	6–$3\frac{1}{2}$ x $3\frac{3}{4}$ 6–$3\frac{9}{16}$ x $3\frac{15}{16}$	216.5 235.5	6.60 6.70	29.4 30.4	92 @ 3400 105 @ 3600	85 @ 3300 98 @ 3500	176 (A) 193 (B)
1952	1500, 2100, 6 Cyl. 2100 w/Power Glide, 6 Cyl.	6–$3\frac{1}{2}$ x $3\frac{3}{4}$ 6–$3\frac{9}{16}$ x $3\frac{15}{16}$	216.5 235.5	6.60 6.70	29.4 30.4	92 @ 3400 105 @ 3600	....	176 (A) 193 @ 2000
1953	Conventional Power Glide	6–$3\frac{9}{16}$ x $3\frac{15}{16}$ 6–$3\frac{9}{16}$ x $3\frac{15}{16}$	235.5 235.5	7.1 7.5	30.4 30.4	108 @ 3600 115 @ 3600	....	200 @ 2000 204.1 @ 2000

(e)—1200–2000. (i)—1200–. (A)—At 1000 to 2000 R.P.M. B—@ 1100–2200 R.P.M.

Piston Ring Dimensions

Year	Model	Cylinder Bore	TOP RING			SECOND RING			THIRD RING			OIL RING		
			Width	Gap	Depth	Width	Gap	Depth	Width	Gap	Depth	Width	Gap	Depth
1940–50	All except 2100	$3\frac{1}{2}$	$\frac{1}{8}$	.010	.155	$\frac{1}{8}$	.010	.155	$\frac{3}{16}$	.010	.155	......	......	......
1951	2100	$3\frac{9}{16}$	$\frac{3}{32}$	.012	.178	$\frac{1}{8}$	.010	.155	$\frac{3}{16}$	.010	.160	......	......	......
1952	1500, 2100, 6 Cyl. 2100 w/P.G., 6 Cyl.	$3\frac{1}{2}$ $3\frac{9}{16}$	.12375 .09325	.0075 .012	.1605 .184	.12375 .12375	.0075 .0075	.1605 .161	.18625 .18625	.0075 .0075	.1735 .179	......	......	......
1953	Conventional Powerglide	$3\frac{9}{16}$ $3\frac{9}{16}$	.0935 .0935	.012 .012	.178 .178	.12375 .0935	.012 .012	.155 .178	.1865 .1865	.012 .012	.160 .141	......	......	......

Dimensions of Valves

Year	Model	Overall Length		Head Diameter		Seat Angle (deg.)		Stem Diameter		Key Type	O.D. of Seat Insert	
		Inlet	Exhaust	Inlet	Exhaust	Inlet	Exhaust	Inlet	Exhaust		Inlet	Exhaust
1941–42	Series—All	6.218	4.859	1.640	1.468	30	30	.341	.340	split lock	......	......
1946 to 48	Series—All	6.220	4.854	1.640	1.468	30	30	.341	.340	split lock	......	......
1949	Series—All	6.275	4.854	1.640	1.468	30	30	.341	.340	split lock	......	......
1950	Series—All	6.275	4.932	1.641	1.500	30	30	.341	.340	split lock	......	......
1951	JJ, JK	6.275	4.917	1.641	1.500	30	30	.341	.340	split lock	......	......
1952	1500, 2100, 6 cyl. 2100 w/Power Glide, 6 cyl.	6.275 6.379	4.917 4.917	1.640625 1.9375	1.500 1.500	30 30	45 45	.34135 .34135	.34035 .34035	......	......	......
1953	Conventional Power Glide	6.379 6.379	4.917 4.917	1.875 1.875	1.500 1.500	30 30	45 45	.3417 .3417	.3407 .3407	......	......	......

Cooling Systems

CAR AND YEAR	MODEL	Capacity Qts.	Quarts of Methanol Base Anti-Freeze (For Protection to Temperature Shown Below)							Quarts of Ethylene Glycol (For Protection to Temperature Shown Below)							Quarts of Denatured Alcohol—188 Proof (For Protection to Temperature Shown Below)						
			3	4	5	6	7	8	9	3	4	5	6	7	8	9	3	4	5	6	7	8	9
1937-41	......	14	9	−3	−17	−34	−53	....	....	15	6	−5	−18	−34	−54	....	10	....	0	−10	−20	−30	....
1942-48	......	15	11	1	−12	−27	−44	....	....	16	8	0	−12	−26	−43	....	....	10	0	−10	−20	−30	....
1949-53	......	16	13	3	−8	−21	−36	−53	....	17	10	2	−8	−19	−34	−52	....	10	0	−10	....	−20	−30

Engine Overhaul Specifications

Year	Model	PISTONS				RING GAP CLEARANCES (Maximum)				PISTON PIN		ROD BEARINGS		
		Removed From	Piston Skirt Clearances (Maximum)											
			Top	Bottom	Limit	Top Ring	Second Ring	Third Ring	Oil Ring	Type	Fit	Oil Clearance	Wear Limit	Side Play
1941	AG, 6 Cyl.	A	....	.002*	.005	.015	.015	....	.015	LR	Slip	.001-.0025	.004	.004-.012
	AH, 6 Cyl.	A	....	.002*	.005	.015	.015	....	.015	LR	Slip	.001-.0025	.004	.004-.012
1942	BL, 6 Cyl.	A	....	.002*	.005	.015	.015	....	.015	LR	Slip	.001-.0025	.004	.004-.012
	BH, 6 Cyl.	A	....	.002*	.005	.015	.015	....	.015	LR	Slip	.001-.0025	.004	.004-.012
1946-51	All	A	....	.002*	.005	.015	.015	....	.015	LR	Slip	.0003-.0013	.004	.004-.012
1952	1500, 2100, 6 Cyl.	A	....	.003*	.005	.015	.015	....	.015	LR	Slip	.0003-.0013	.004	.004-.012
	2100, w/P. G., 6 Cyl.	A	....	.003*	.005	.017	.015	....	.015	LR	Slip	.0003-.0013	.004	.004-.012
1953	Conventional	A	....	.002	....	.015	.015	....	.015	LR	Slip	.0003-.0013	.004	.004-.012
	Power Glide	A	....	.0011	....	.017	.017	....	.016	LR	Slip	.0003-.0013	.004	.005-.012

LR—Locked in Rod. *—USE Feeler Gauge, Piston should pass at .002″ Lock on .003″ Feeler. A—Above.

Pistons and Piston Pins

Year	Model	PISTONS				PISTON PINS		
		Diameter	Material	Type	No. of Rings	Length	Diameter	How Held
1940	Series—All	3.5	Cast Iron	Ss	3	3.150	.865	R
1941	Series—All	3.5	Cast Iron	Sp, Fh	3	3.150	.8647	R
1942 to 48	Series—All	3.5	Cast Iron	Fh, Sp	3	3.150	.8647	R
	Series—All	3.5	Cast Iron	Fh, Sp	3	3.150	.8647	R
1949–50	Series—All	3.5	CAI	Fh, Ss	3	3.150	.8647	R
1951	JJ, JK	3.5	Cast Iron	Fh, Ss	3	3.150	.8648	R
	2100	3.5625	Cast Iron	Fh, Ss	3	3.150	.8648	R
1952	1500, 2100, 6 cyl.	3.5	CAI	Fh,Ss	3	3.15	.8648	R
	2100, w/P.G., 6 cyl.	3.5625	CAI	Fh,Ss	3	3.15	.8648	R
1953	Conventional	3.5625	CAI	Fh,Ss	3	3.165	.8648	R
	Power Glide	3.5625	CA Alum.	Fh	3	3.228	.8663	R

CAI—Cast alloy iron surface treated.
R—Locked in rod.
CAAlum.—Cast aluminum. Ss—Split skirt. Sp, Fh—Slipper skirt, flat head.

Crankshaft Bearing Journal Sizes

Year	Model	Connecting Rod Journals		Main Bearing Journals				
		Diameter	Length	No. 1 Diameter	No. 2 Diameter	No. 3 Diameter	No. 4 Diameter	No. 5 Diameter
1940 to 51	All	2.311-2.312	1.436-1.439	2.6835-2.6845	2.7145-2.7155	2.7455-2.7456	2.7765-2.7775	....
1952	1500, 2100, 6 cyl.	2.311-2.312	....	2.6835-2.6845	2.7145-2.7155	2.7455-2.7465	2.7765-2.7775	....
1953	Conventional, Power Glide	2.311-2.312	....	2.6835-2.6845	2.7145-2.7155	2.7455-2.74	2.7765-2.7775	....

and Wear Limit Table

CRANKSHAFT		VALVES						Valve Timing, Inlet Valve Opens (Deg.)	Camshaft Drive	Gear Marks	OPERATING OIL PRESSURE		Model	Year
Main Bearing Oil Clearance	Shaft End Play	Spring Tension (Maximum) Inlet	Spring Tension (Maximum) Exhaust	Spring Tension (Maximum) Low Limit	Guide Clearance	Seat Angle Inlet	Seat Angle Exhaust				Pounds At M.P.H.	Low Limit§		
.002–.004	.004–.007	133@1½	133@1½	120	.004	30°	30°	3B	Gear	‡	14@21	7	...............AG. 6 Cyl.	1941
.002–.004	.004–.007	133@1½	133@1½	120	.004	30°	30°	3B	Gear	‡	14@21	7	...............AH, 6 Cyl.	
.001–.004	.004–.007	133@1½	133@1½	120	.004	30°	30°	3B	Gear	‡	14@21	7	...............BG, 6 Cyl.	1942
.002–.004	.004–.007	133@1½	133@1½	120	.004	30°	30°	3B	Gear	‡	14@21	7	...............BH, 6 Cyl.	
.002–.004	.004–.007	133@1½	133@1½	120	.004	30°	30°	3B	Gear	‡	14@40	7	......................All	1946–51
.0007–.0028	.003–.009	140@1.505	140@1.505	......	.0027	30°	45°	1A	Gear	......	14–2000	......	..........1500, 2100, 6 Cyl.	1952
.0007–.0028	.003–.009	165@1.505	165@1.505	......	.0037	30°	45°	16B	Gear	......	14–2000	......	......2100, w/P.G., 6 Cyl.	
.0007–.0028	.003–.009	140@1.505	140@1.505	......	.0037	30°	45°	1A	Gear	......	14–2000	......	..............Conventional	1953
.0007–.0028	.035–.0095	165@1.505	165@1.505	......	.0037	30°	45°	16B	Gear	......	35 PSI	......	..............Power Glide	

B—Before top center. A—After top center.
‡—Center cam gear mark between crank gear mark.
§—Car may be operated safely at much lower oil pressures but low oil pressure indicates malfunction which should be corrected.

Voltage Regulators

Year	Model	Regulator Number	Grounded P=Positive N=Negative	Voltage Control Air Gap Points Closed	Voltage Control Voltage Setting Hot	Current Control Air Gap Points Closed	Current Control Current Set Hot	Cut-Out Relay Point Gap	Cut-Out Relay Air Gap	Cut-Out Relay Closing Volt
1940 to 48	All............................	1118201	N	.070	7.2–7.4	.080	32–34	.020	.020	6.2–6.7
1949 to 51	All............................	1118301	N	.075	7.0–7.7	.075	32–40	.020	.020	5.9–6.8
1952	1500, 2100, 6 cyl..............	1118720	N	....	7.4	....	35	....	....	6.4
1953	Conventional, Power Glide.....	1118725	N	....	7.4	....	45	....	....	6.4

Starters

Year	Model	Unit Model Number	Spring Tension (oz.)	STARTER Lock Test Volts	Lock Test Amperes	Lock Test Torque, (lbs. ft.)	No Load Volts	No Load Amperes	No Load R.P.M.	Direction of Rotation Viewed from Drive End C=Clockwise CC=Counter-clockwise
1941	AG, AH.............................	1107047	24–28	3.37	525	12	5.0	65	5000	C
1942	BG, BH.............................	1107054	24–28	3.37	525	12	5.0	65	5000	C
1946–47	EJ, EK.............................	1107061	24–28	3.37	525	12	5.0	65	5000	C
1948	FJ, FK.............................	1107061	24–28	3.37	525	12	5.0	65	5000	C
1949 to 51	GJ, GK, HJ, HK, JJ, JK..............	1107075	24–28	3.4	525	12	5.7	80	5000	C
		1107055	24–28	3.4	525	12	5.7	65	5000	....
1952	1500, 2100, 6 cyl..................	1107109	24–28	3.4	525	12	5.0	65	5000	C
	....	1107075	24–28	3.4	525	12	5.0	65	5000	C
1953	Conventional, Power Glide............	1118725	24–28	3.4	525	12	5.0	65	5000	C

CHEVROLET SPECIFICATIONS

Engine Tune-Up Specifications

Year	Model	Spark Plugs Type	Spark Plugs Gap	Distributor Point Gap	Distributor Cam Dwell, (Deg.)	Distributor Ignition Timing, (Deg.)	Ignition Timing Mark and Location	Compression Pressure at R.P.M.	Operating Tappet Clearance Inlet	Operating Tappet Clearance Exhaust	Carburetor Fuel Float Height	Minimum Engine Idle Speed at R.P.M.
1941–42	All	AC-104	.040	.018	39	5B	†flywheel	112	.006	.013	½″ float	350
1946	DJ-DK, 6 Cyl.	AC-M48	.040	.018	39	5B	†flywheel	112	.006	.013	½″ float	350
1947	EJ, 6 Cyl. EK, 6 Cyl.	AC-M48 AC-M48	.040 .040	.018 .018	34 34	5B 5B	†flywheel †flywheel	112 112	.006 .006	.013 .013	½″ float ½″ float	350 350
1948	FJ, 6 Cyl. FK, 6 Cyl.	AC-M48 AC-M48	.040 .040	.018 .018	34 34	5B 5B	†flywheel †flywheel	110 110	.006 .006	.013 .013	½″ float ½″ float	350 350
1949	GJ GK, 6 Cyl.	AC-46-5 AC-46-5	.035 .035	.018 .018	34 34	5B 5B	†flywheel †flywheel	110 110	.006 .006	.013 .013	1½″ float ½″ float	350 350
1950	HJ, HK, 6 Cyl. HK w/Pow. Glide, 6 Cyl.	AC-46-5 AC-46-5	.035 .035	.018 .018	34 34	5B 5B	†flywheel †flywheel	110 110	.006 Hyd.	.013 Hyd.	1 5/16″ float 1 5/16″ float	350 ....
1951	JJ, JK, 6 Cyl. JK w/Pow. Glide, 6 Cyl.	AC-46-5 AC-46-5	.035 .035	.018–.024 .018–.024	34 34	5B 5B	†flywheel †flywheel	110 110	.006 Hyd.	.013 Hyd.	1 5/16″ float 1 5/16″ float	....
1952	1500, 2100, 6 Cyl. 2100 w/Pow. Glide, 6 Cyl.	AC-46-5 AC-46-5	.035 .035	.0185 .0185	39 39	5B 5B	†flywheel †flywheel	....	.006H AA	.013H AA	....	475 440
1953	Conventional Power Glide	AC-44-5 AC-44-5	.035 .035	.015 .015	38–45 38–45	5B 5B	†flywheel †flywheel	....	.006H AA	.013H AA	....	475 425

†—Steel ball in flywheel. B—Before top center. AC—AC Spark Plug Div. Hyd.—Hydraulic lifters. AA—Automatic adjustment.

Tension Wrench Specifications

Year	Model	Cylinder Head Lbs.-Ft.	Cylinder Head Thread	Spark Plug Lbs.-Ft.	Spark Plug Thread	Connecting Rod Bolts or Nuts Lbs.-Ft.	Connecting Rod Bolts or Nuts Thread	Main Bearing Bolt Lbs.-Ft.	Main Bearing Bolt Thread	Flywheel Bolts Lbs.-Ft.	Flywheel Bolts Thread	Vibration Damper Bolts Lbs.-Ft.	Vibration Damper Bolts Thread
1940	All	75–80	....	20–25	14 mm	40–50	....	100–110	....	50–65	....	....	....
1941–42	All	75–80	....	10–15	10 mm	40–50	....	100–110	....	50–65	....	....	....
1946 to 53	All	75–80	....	20–25	14 mm	40–50	....	100–110	....	50–65	....	....	....

Brake Data

Year	Model	Make	Lining Type	R=Riveted B=Bonded	Drum Diameter	Lining Length	Lining Width	Lining Thickness	Clearance Toe	Clearance Heel
1940	Series—All	Own	M	R	11	22 5/8	1 3/4	3/16	(b)	(b)
1941 to 48	Series—All	Own	M	R	11	22 5/8	1 3/4	3/16	(b)	(b)
1949–50	Series—All	Own	M	B	11	20 5/8	1 3/4	3/16	(b)	(b)
1951	JJ, JK	Own	M	B	11	20 9/16	2–*1 3/4	3/16	(b)	(b)
1952	1500, 2100, 6 Cyl.	Own	M	B	11	21	2–*1 3/4	7/32	(b)	(b)
1953	Conventional, Power Glide	Own	M	B	11	21	2–*1 3/4	7/32	(b)	(b)

(b)—Adjust to slight drag, back off 4 notches. *—Rear. M—Moulded.

Generators

Year	Model	Generator Number	Field Current at 6 Volts (amps.)	Maximum Safe Output Volts	Maximum Safe Output Amperes	Maximum Safe Output R.P.M.	Bru h Spring Tension (oz.)	Voltage Regulator Number
1940 to 48	Series—All	1102667	1.75–1.9	8.0	30	1750	25	1118201
1949–50	GJ, GK, HJ, HK	1102710	1.75–1.9	8.0	30	1750	25	1118301
1951	JJ, JK	1102749	1.75–1.9				25	1118301
1952	1500, 2100, 6 cyl.	1100013	1.75–1.9	8.0	30	1750	28	1118720
1953	Conventional, Power Glide	1118725		7.4	45	2750	28	1118725

Distributors

Year	Model	Distributor Model Number	Cam Angle (deg.)	Direction of Rotation C=Clockwise CC=Counter Clockwise at Cam End	Breaker Arm Spring Tension	Breaker Point Gap (inches)	Engine R.P.M. when Cent. Advance Starts	Max. Cent. Advance in Engine Deg. at Stated Engine R.P.M.	Vacuum in (inches) of Mercury at which Vacuum Unit Starts	Max. Advance in Engine Deg. at Stated Vacuum	Vacuum Unit Number
1940	All, 6 cyl.	1110052	35	C	17–21	.018–.024	800	37@3100	6	16@12 to 15	1116011
1941 to 48	All, 6 cyl.	1110090	38	C	19–23	.015–.021	700	38@3400	7 to 8.5	20@16 to 19	1116033
1949	All, 6 cyl.	1112353	34	C	17–21	.022–.024	700	39.5@3450	7	20@16 to 19	1116043
1950	All, 6 cyl.	1112353	34	C	17–21	.015–.021	700	39.5@3450	7	20@16 to 19	1116043
1951	JJ, JK, 6 cyl.	112362	34	C	17–21	.018–.022		39.5@3450	7	20	
	2100, 6 cyl.	112363	34	C	17–21	.018–.022		33@3700	7	20	
1952	1500, 2100, 6 cyl.	1112362	39	C	17–21	.015–.022		19¾@1725	7–8½	9–11@16½	
	2100, w/P.G., 6 cyl.	1112363	39	C	17–21	.015–.022		16½@1850	7–8½	9–11@16½	
1953	Conventional	1112389	38–45	C	19–23	.0125–.0175	350	17@1800	4–6	9–11@13–11	
	Power Glide	1112388	38–45	C	19–23	.0125–.0175	375	13@1750	4–6	9–11@13–11	

Front Wheel Alignment

Year	Model	Caster (deg.)	Camber (deg.)	King Pin Inclination (deg.)	Toe-In (inches)	Turning Radius Inner	Turning Radius Outer
1940	KB	1¾P to 2¾P	½P to 1P	7	1/16 to 1/8	24	20
	KA	0 to ½P	¼N to ¾P	4¾	0 to 1/16	24	20
	KH	0 to ½P	¼N to ½P	4¾	0 to 1/16	24	20
1941	AG, AH	¾N to ¼P	¼N to ¼P	4¾	1/16 to 1/8	24	20
1942	BH, BG	0 to ½P	¼N to ¼P	4¾	0 to 1/16	24	20
1946–47	All	0 to ½P	¼N to ¼P	4¾	0 to 1/16	24	20
1948	FJ, FK	0 to ½P	¼N to ¼P	4¾	0 to 1/8	24	20
1949–50	GJ, GK, HJ, HK	0 to 1P	0 to 1P	4	0 to 1/8		
1951–52	JJ, JK, Convertible, Power Glide	0 to 1P	0 to 1P	4	0 to 1/8		
1953	Convertible, Power Glide	0 to 1P	0 to 1P	4	0 to 1/8	17¾	20

P—Positive. N—Negative.

CHEVROLET 1940 thru 1953

FRONT SUSPENSION

The independent front suspension used on all Chevrolet cars built since 1940 is of the short and long arm type suspension called the S.L.A. type.

In 1940 and 1941 Chevrolet built cars with I beams on some models. The following instructions do not apply to the models equipped with I beam except the instructions governing the kingpin installation.

All parts of the Chevrolet front suspension can be replaced without disturbing the front cross member.

Caster, Camber and Toe-In

Before making any corrections to caster, camber or toe-in, first check all of the steering angles to determine exactly what repair work will be necessary before correcting any of the errors in steering geometry.

Examine the upper and lower suspension arm pins and bushings both at their inner and outer end before attempting to make any corrections since, if any of the pins and bushings are loose, it will be impossible to achieve the proper setting.

Caster and camber are both controlled at an eccentric pin in the upper suspension arm outer end.

The eccentric pin controls both caster and camber and it may be necessary to seek a compromise adjustment in order to get both caster and camber as near as possible to the desired setting. The procedure is as follows: Remove the grease fitting from the upper suspension arm front bushing and insert

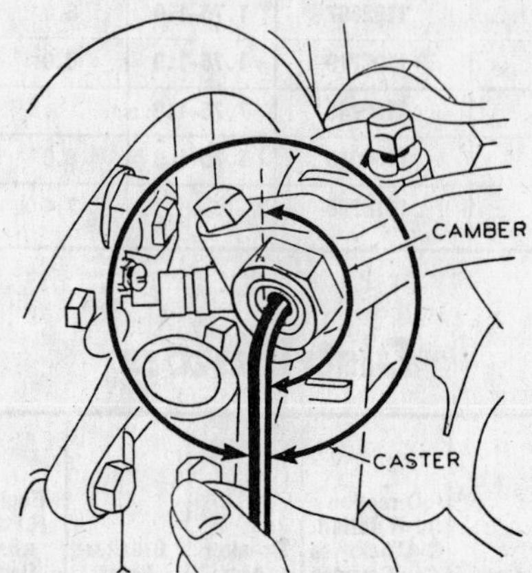

Caster is obtained in full turns of the threaded pin, camber moves from minimum to maximum in 1/2 turn.

an Allen wrench into the hole from which the grease fitting was removed.

Loosen the clamp screw in the knuckle support which prevents the eccentric pin from turning.

Exploded view of front suspension parts

Up to 1949 models the eccentric pin is a left hand thread with two starts therefore in order to increase caster the pin should be turned in a clockwise direction, to decrease caster turn the eccentric pin in a counter clockwise direction. Starting with 1949 thru 1953 models the eccentric portion is not threaded instead a groove is cut into the center of the pin to fit the shank of the lock pin.

If it is desirable not to compromise and to come to an exact setting of both caster and camber, first set the caster by turning the eccentric pin and then securely lock the eccentric and, using a cold bending device, bend the knuckle support until the proper camber is achieved. CAUTION: Under no circumstances should heat be used on the knuckle support as this part is heat treated after forging and heating it to cherry red will destroy its usefulness.

Toe-in is adjusted by turning the adjusting sleeve in both tie rods until the correct adjustment is obtained.

Turn the sleeve in the direction of forward wheel rotation to increase toe-in and the opposite way to decrease toe-in.

REPLACEMENT OF FRONT SUSPENSION PARTS

Shock Absorber

On models up to and including 1948 the shock absorber is contained in the upper control arm; starting with 1949 production the shock absorber is mounted inside of the coil spring.

To replace the upper suspension arm type shock absorber jack up the car and rest the weight of the car on the lower suspension arm at the outer end.

Remove the road wheel but not the brake drum.

Take the grease fitting from the front bushing of the knuckle support upper pin and loosen the clamp bolt which holds the eccentric screw in the upper end of the knuckle support.

Remove the front and rear bushing from the outer end of the upper suspension arm and then, using an Allen wrench, unscrew the eccentric pin from out of the knuckle support.

Unbolt the shock absorber from the frame.

Bolt a new shock absorber to the top of the frame and replace the upper pin and bushings as shown under replacement of pins and bushings later in this section.

Access to the shock absorber mounting bolts is through the engine compartment or they may also be reached by removing the engine side pan.

Starting with 1949 models the direct acting type shock absorber is mounted inside of the coil spring. It may be removed readily by disconnecting it at the top down through the engine compartment and removing the plate on the lower suspension arm which holds the shock absorber up in the spring.

On these models it is not even necessary to jack the car up if there is sufficient room between the arm and the ground to lower the shock absorber.

Coil Spring Replacement

If it becomes necessary to replace a coil spring first ascertain if there is any play or looseness in any of the suspension arm parts. The easiest way to replace the coil spring is to detach the front suspension at the defective pin or bushing so that the coil spring can be replaced together with the defective pins and bushings.

If on the other hand there is nothing worn in the front suspension and it is desired to replace just one coil spring, support the weight of the car at the frame, back of the front suspension, disconnect the sway bar and, on models from 1949 thru 1953, disconnect and remove the shock absorber, then place a jack on the A frame inner shaft and unbolt the inner shaft from the front cross member, lowering it slowly to the floor.

Without disturbing the position of the A frame inner shaft on the mounting jack remove the coil spring and, carefully fitting the new spring into the formed contour of the A frame plate, place the new spring into position.

Jack the suspension arm back up into place guiding the bolt holes with a long drift pin.

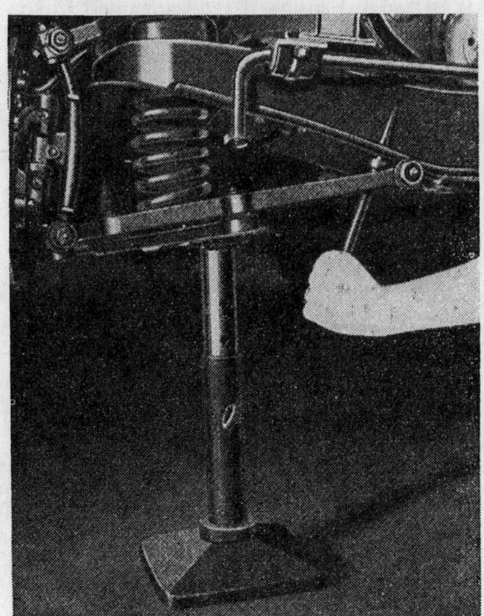

Guiding lower control arm with long drift pin

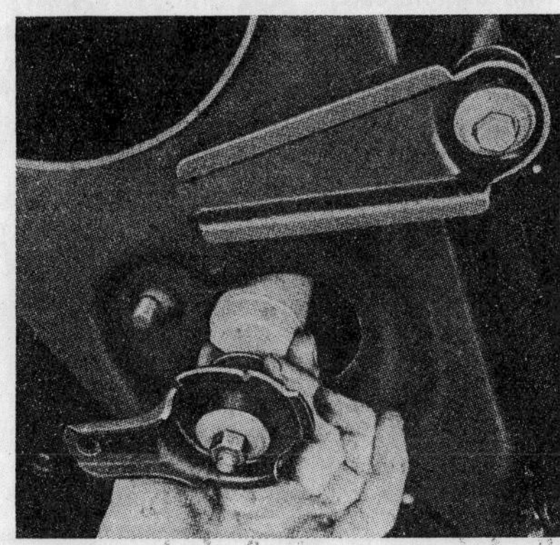

Removing front shock absorber

Bolt up the lower arm inner shaft, reinstall the shock absorber (on models from 1949 thru 53) and reconnect the stabilizer bar.

Replacement of Knuckle Supports, Pins and Bushings

The upper and lower pins and bushings and the knuckle support are replaced readily by taking the car up on a jack under the lower A frame.

Removing lower pivot pin bushing

Remove the wheel for easy access to the upper and lower suspension arm pins and bushings.

Upper Arm Eccentric Pin

Remove the clamp bolts from the top of the knuckle support and also from the upper suspension arm.

Remove the front and rear upper suspension arm.

Remove the front and rear upper suspension arm bushings, and, using an Allen wrench in the front of the eccentric pin twist the pin from the knuckle support. **Caution:** Place some kind of support at the outer end of the brake drum so that the drum and knuckle support will not fall down, injuring the operator.

Working from the front, twist in the new eccentric pin so that when the eccentric portion is full out (facing the operator) the pin is nicely centered in the knuckle support, then replace the clamp bolt and set up finger tight.

Replace both the front and rear bushings being careful to keep the knuckle support itself centered between the yoke of the upper arm.

To install the oil seals it is customary to stretch them over the yoke of the upper suspension arm when installing the pin so that they can be pulled down with a wire hook over the portion of the pin they are intended to protect.

Replace the clamp screw in the upper suspension arm.

Lower Arm Pin

To remove the lower arm pin, first remove the nut from the outside of the pin and unscrew the pin through the back of the lower suspension arm, through the knuckle support lower bushing and out through the front suspension arm.

Pull the lower end of the knuckle support out away from the lower suspension arm and remove the bushing which is in the lower end of the knuckle support.

To reinstall, screw the new bushing into the lower end of the knuckle support and, carefully centering the arm itself (not the bushing) between the yoke of the lower suspension arm, run the pin in from the front through the front portion of the arm, through the bushing, through the rear portion of the arm and securely tighten with a nut and lock washer at the back.

CHEVROLET 1940 thru 1953

LOWER ARM PIN—*continued*

When properly installed both the upper and lower pins will be almost exactly in the center of their respective suspension arms.

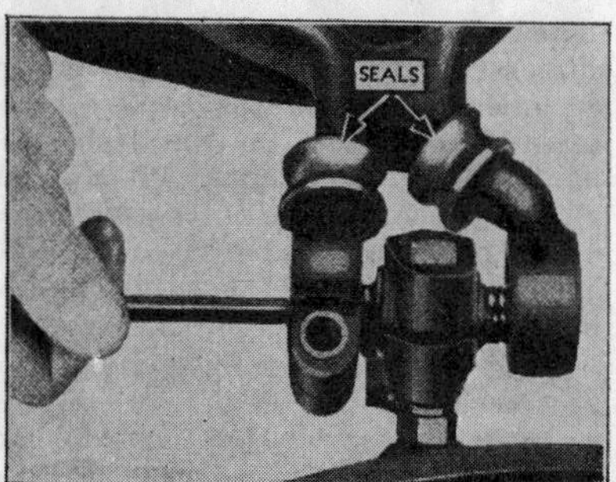

Centering pivot pin in knuckle support

Rubber dust boots are supplied for use on all Chevrolet front suspensions to prevent dust, grit and road dirt from entering the front suspension parts.

Note: When servicing the 1949 to 1953 models with the shock absorber in the middle of the spring it is a good precaution to first detach the shock absorber before doing any work on either of the front suspension arm pins or bushings.

Installation of King Pins

All Chevrolet passenger cars from 1939, having front suspension, are equipped with full floating king pin bushings.

These bushings do not require reaming to fit them to the king pin.

To remove the king pin, first remove the cover from the upper end of the king pin, in the top of the spindle.

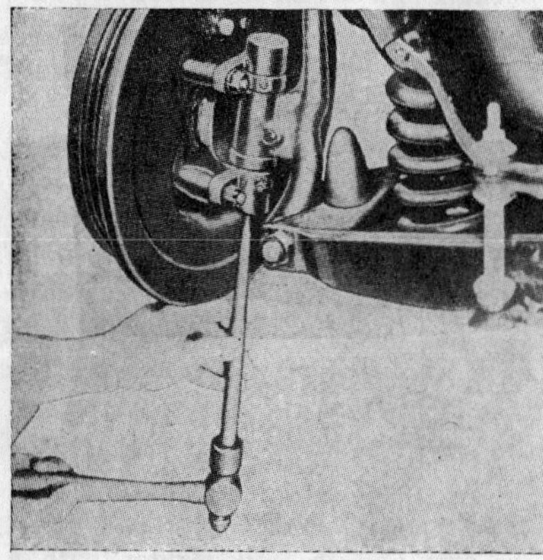

Removing king pin

Remove the nut from the front of the king pin lock pin and drive out the lock pin.

Remove the lock ring from the top and bottom of the king pin. Then, using a long drift drive upwards from the bottom forcing out the king pin upper plug. When the plug is out at the top reverse the driving pin and drive the king pin out through the bottom.

Make some provisions to support the brake backing plate and drum assembly so that it does not damage the brake hydraulic line.

Install new bushings in the upper and lower portion of the spindle and install a new thrust bearing between the lower end of the spindle and the bottom of the knuckle support. Push the king pin in from the top, inserting the plug at the top and bottom and installing both of the lock rings. The king pin top cover is then put on and the car is lowered from its jack.

Since the bushings are full floating and are easily installed it is not necessary to disconnect either the tie rods or the brake hose.

Upper Support Arm Inner Shaft

1949 to 1953 Models only

To replace the upper support arm inner shaft on these models support the weight of the car at the outer end of the lower suspension arm and remove the wheel.

Take out the upper suspension arm outer eccentric pin and bushings and pivot the brake backing plate and drum assembly down to the floor out of the way.

Caution: Be careful not to strain the brake hose during this process. It may be necessary to support the brake drum and hub assembly so as not to overly stretch the brake hose.

Remove the bushings from the front and back of the upper suspension arm inner shaft and rock the arm off the shaft.

The inner shaft must be removed out through the front of the spring housing.

This is sometimes a difficult job since they are customarily a fairly tight fit.

However a tool can be made by sacrificing one of the inner bushings. Saw the bushing in half and screw the smaller half of it on to the shaft, then place a box socket over the shaft and very tightly screw the second half of of the bushing against the box socket in such a way as to jam it in place. This wrench can then be used to turn the shaft out of the spring housing.

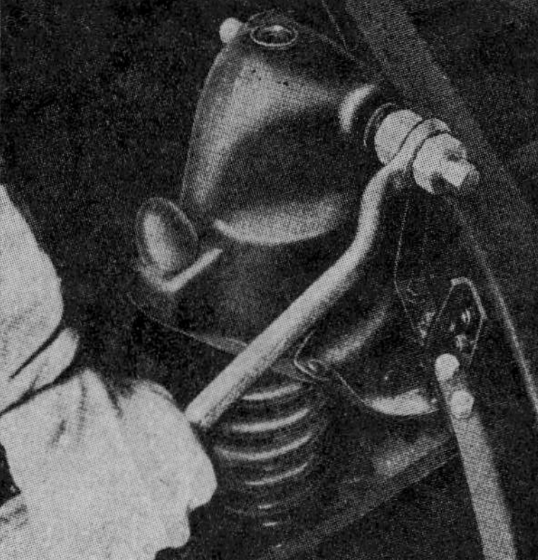

Removing upper control arm shaft

New upper suspension arm inner shafts are supplied slightly oversize. The rear thread is made slightly smaller than the front thread so that it can pass freely through the front bushing and enter into the rear bushing.

The front of the shaft is marked with a letter F.

The same technique which was used to remove the old shaft can also be used to replace the new one.

The new shaft should be screwed in so that the back end of it projects exactly 1⅛ inches out of the spring housing. **Caution:** The rear end of the shaft is equipped with tapered threads so great care must be used not to screw it in too far since if it is screwed in too far and it becomes necessary to back it out it may leave the shaft loose in its bushing.

Installing upper control arm shaft

STEERING IDLER AND THIRD ARM BEARINGS

To replace the steering idler arm and/or bearings jack up the car and place it on stands and disconnect the tie rods from the intermediate steering arm and also disconnect the drag link from the intermediate steering arm.

Remove the three bolts which retain the steering idler arm assembly to the front cross member and lift the entire assembly off the car.

Lock up the idler arm in a vice and remove the lubricating fittings and, using a punch, drive out the lock pin. **Note:** The lock pin is a tiny pin located in approximately the center of the arm itself, not in the bracket.

Remove the pivot shaft top and bottom plugs. This can be done with a sharp drift punch by driving through either plug and forcing the pivot shaft out the other end to remove it.

Install new bushings in the idler arm bracket and ream them to fit the new idler arm pin.

Carefully line up the lock pin hole, drive in the lock pin, replace both end plugs and reinstall on the car.

Careful note should be made of the shims, if any, found between the idler arm bracket and the frame as these shims must be reinstalled on assembly.

POWER STEERING GEAR

At the time this portion of the manual went to press there was no information available on the servicing of the power steering gear.

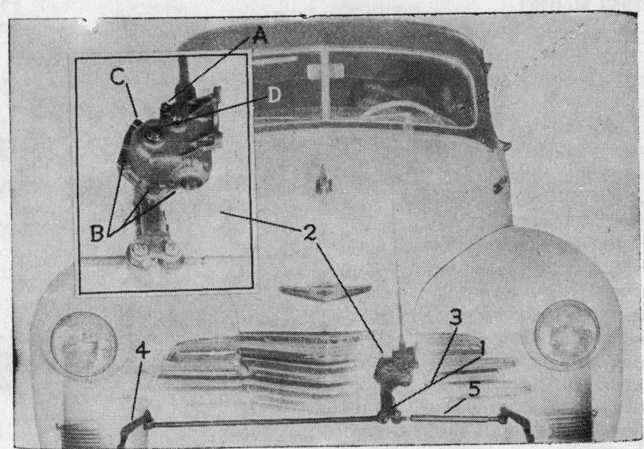

1940 to 1948 models

MANUAL STEERING GEAR

Adjustment of the Steering Apparatus

1940 TO 1948 MODELS

1. Disconnect the pitman arm from both tie rods.

2. Adjust the steering gear housing assembly.

A. Loosen the worm bearing adjuster clamp bolt and adjust the worm bearing so that there is no up and down play in the worm or worm shaft. Retighten the clamp nut.

B. Set the steering wheel in the mid position of its travel. Loosen the housing cover bolts about ¼ turn each.

C. Loosen the eccentric bolt nut ½ to ¾ turn. With one wrench on the eccentric bolt and another one on the eccentric sleeve turn the two wrenches in the opposite direction by gradual stages checking the results by moving the sector shaft at each stage. Move the two wrenches just enough to remove all of the backlash. There should be no preload. Retighten the eccentric lock nut and the housing bolt, and before reconnecting the tie rods, make certain that the steering gear does not bind at any point.

D. Remove all of the end play from the cross shaft by loosening the jam nut and tightening the adjusting screw until all the play has been removed. Retighten the jam nut.

3. Reconnect the tie rods to the pitman arm.

4. With the steering wheel in the mid position of its travel ½ of the toe-in should be in the right wheel. If it requires more than 2 or 3 inches at the rim of the steering wheel to turn the right wheel to the straight ahead position the steering arm or the tie rod or both are bent or damaged.

5. Loosen the clamp bolts, turn the adjustable tie rod to the correct toe-in and retighten the clamp bolts.

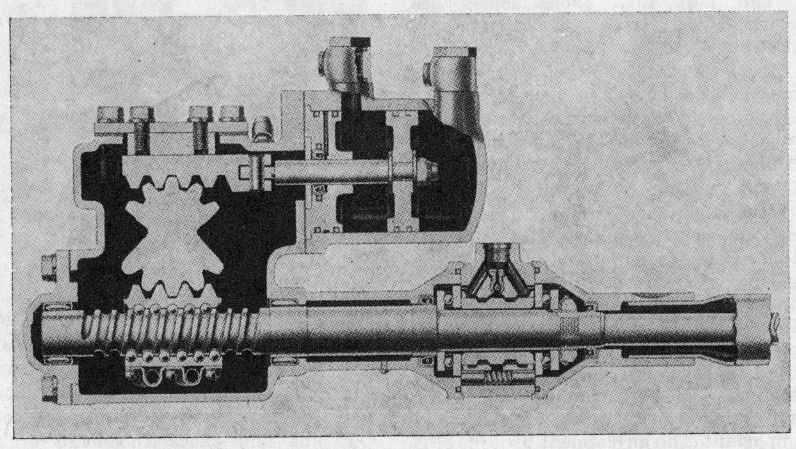
Power Steering

MANUAL STEERING GEAR—*continued*

1949 TO 1953 MODELS

1. Disconnect the pitman arm from the drag link.

2. Adjust the steering gear housing assembly.

A. Back out on the cross shaft adjusting screw until a definite play is felt in the pitman arm before attempting to adjust the worm bearings.

B. Adjust the large screws at the bottom of the gear to remove all end play from the worm bearings. Worm bearings should be adjusted so that there is a very slight drag on the bearings without a definite preload. Tighten the worm bearings adjuster lock nut.

C. Set the steering wheel in the mid position of its travel and turn the adjusting screw inward unil there is zero lash in the worm and sector mesh on the high spot. Tighten the adjusting screw lock nut and recheck the gear for binding.

3. Again turn the steering wheel to the mid position of its travel and reconnect the drag link.

4. Turn the adjusting sleeve on the drag link until the right wheel has ½ of the total toe-in. This should be done without disturbing the position of the steering wheel.

5. Loosen the clamp bolts and turn the left side adjusting tie rod until the remaining toe-in is in the left wheel. Retighten the clamp screw and check the steering apparatus from one extreme to the other for looseness or binding.

1949 to 1953 models

Removal of the Steering Gear Assembly from the Car

1940 TO 1948 MODELS

Remove he steering wheel, using a puller.

Remove the U clamp which fastens the column jacket to the instrument panel and, using a puller, remove the pitman arm from the bottom of the steering cross shaft.

Remove the steering mast jacket clamp at the steering gear housing end and slide the clamp up the column jacket. Unfasten the steering gear from the frame and slide it out through the bottom.

The steering tube assembly is slid out of the mast jacket and the mast jacket remains in place on the car.

1949 TO 1953 MODELS

Using a puller, remove the steering wheel.

Remove the clamp which fastens the column jacket to the instrument panel and remove the column jacket toe board grommet and seal from the toe board. Disconnect the gear shift control support from the column jacket and rotate the shifter housing with its control lever out of the way.

Unfasten the steering gear from the frame and, rotating it to clear the fender skirt, raise the gear bringing it upwards and forward to remove it from the engine compartment.

BRAKES

Two different types of brakes were used on Chevrolet cars since 1940.

The 1940 to 1950 models used a hydraulically actuated General Motors type brake commonly called the Huck brake.

The 1951 thru 1953 models are equipped with a two shoe Bendix hydraulically actuated brake.

Before making any adjustment on the service brakes on the Chevrolet (or any other car) always remove at least one wheel and examine the condition of the brake lining, wheel cylinders and drums.

If any moisture is found on the wheel cylinder cup this indicates that the cup is leaking or seeping and should be repaired or replaced. At any time that one wheel cylinder is found to be defective it is a good precaution to remove all four wheels and make certain that the hydraulic part of the brake system is in good condition since the safety factor of the brakes is very, very important. The adjustment procedure is as follows:

Minor Adjustment of the Service Brakes

1940 TO 1950 MODELS

Remove the port cover on the backing plate and engage the adjusting wheel at the front end of the wheel cylinder. Turn the adjusting wheel in a clockwise direction (facing the end of the wheel, until the shoe drags and then back off the adjusting wheel four notches which will give the proper lining to drum clearance. Repeat the operation at the

1940 to 1950 adjusting wheel

back end of the same wheel cylinder and at all wheels.

To adjust the hand brake, set the brake lever in the fully released position and then pull up the cable until all slack is removed. Now set the adjusting clevis on the brake rods so that the holes in the clevis and the cable will line up. Install the clevis and cotter pins and check the hand brake for equalization. If one brake is tight, back off on the rod adjustment on the tight brake rather than tighten the loose brake.

1951 THRU 1953 MODELS

1951-53 models were equipped with Bendix two shoe hydraulically actuated brakes.

1951-53 Minor adjustment of brakes

Minor adjustment is made to compensate for normal lining wear. Remove the inspection hole cover in the backing plate (opposite to where the brake hose goes into the brake cylinder) and turn the star wheel adjuster until the brakes drag and back off until they are just free. Do not fail to replace the adjusting hole cover.

If the star wheel is properly mounted on the shoes the handle of the adjusting tool should be turned toward the axle of the car to expand the brake shoes.

To adjust the hand brake cable expand the shoes on the rear wheels until the wheels can just barely be turned by hand with the hand brake cable disconnected. Now pull all of the slack out of the hand brake cables and adjust the hand brake clevis so that the clevis pin will just enter. Secure the clevis pin and back off on the star wheel adjuster on each back wheel until the wheels are just free.

Major Adjustment

Note: 1940 thru 1950 models do not require more than a minor adjustment since the shoes are self centering.

A major adjustment is required on 1951-53 models at any time the shoes are removed from the car or new brake lining has been installed.

If the brake lining is wearing evenly all over the surface it is generally unnecessary to disturb the anchor adjustment.

To reset the anchor proceed as follows: The anchor on 1951-53 Chevrolets is the sliding type which is adjusted by loosening the anchor nut a few turns. Tighten the star wheel until the shoes expand very tightly against the drum and tap the anchor lightly with a soft hammer to assist it in centering itself between the shoes and, with the shoes still expanded, tighten the anchor nut very tight.

Loosen the star wheel until the wheels are free.

Repeat this adjustment at each of the four wheels.

The anchor nut is the large nut located adjacent to where the brake hose enters the brake cylinder.

Hydraulic Cylinders

If the examination of the brakes reveal that the wheel cylinders are leaking or seeping it may be necessary to remove and hone them to improve the surface on which the wheel cup rides. Special gauges, known as "GO" and "NOT GO" gauges, are available to limit the amount of honing that the cylinder can safely take.

If an examination reveals that one of the wheel cylinders is defective it is advisable for the sake of safety to remove all of the wheel cylinders and examine them for pits and scratches and if any exist, hone each cylinder to produce a smooth glossy surface and replace the cups and boots.

Refilling Master Cylinder

The master cylinder on all Chevrolet models is filled through a port in the floor under the floor mat.

When bleeding brakes it is advisable not to let the fluid in the master cylinder get below the half way mark as there is a possibility that air will be included in the bleeding process.

BLEEDING BRAKES

The purpose of bleeding brakes is to expel all of the air from the hydraulic system. By itself, bleeding is not a service adjustment. The procedure is as follows: Fill the master cylinder to the very top with clean brake fluid.

Go to the right front wheel and remove the dust screw from the center of the bleed valve. (The bleed valve is the small brass fitting which takes a 3/8 inch wrench, located just above the cylinder on the backing plate.)

Note: Many mechanics who are bleeding brakes fail to replace the dust screw so that if one is not found on the bleed valve it merely means that someone failed to replace it.

Insert a bleed hose into the hole from which the dust screw was removed and carry the other end of the hose into jar which has sufficient fluid to cover the bottom of the hose.

Open the bleed valve; have a helper slowly pump the brake pedal up and down until no more air bubbles appear in the jar. **Caution:** Do not depress the pedal more than three times without again filling the master cylinder since it is possible that if the fluid in the master cylinder becomes too low air will be included into the bleeding process and make it necessary to bleed over again.

When all of the air has been expelled from the right front wheel tighten the bleed valve and remove the bleed hose. Repeat the process on the left front brake, the right rear brake and then the left rear brake, being sure to refill the master cylinder each time the pedal has been depressed three times.

COOLING SYSTEM

The cooling systems on all Chevrolets built since 1940 are essentially the same and service is performed in practically the same manner. The thermostat is located in the water outlet elbow

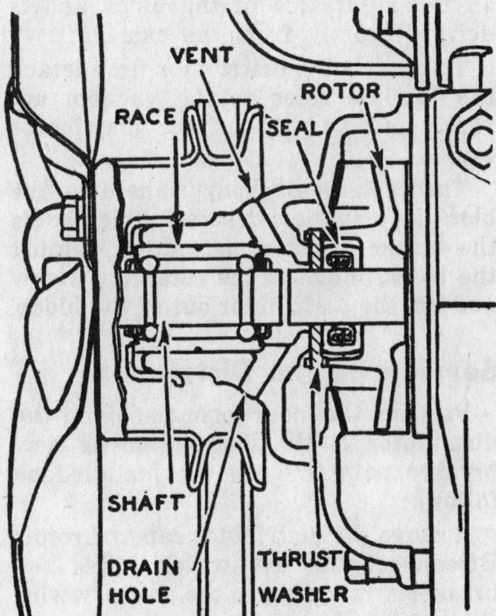

Sketch showing the ball bearing packless type pump assembled late 1938 to 1953 models

CHEVROLET 1940 thru 1953

COOLING SYSTEM—*continued*

at the front of the cylinder head and a packless type water pump is used.

Production thermostats are set to open at 140 degrees.

Water Pump Removal

The water pump and fan assembly are removed as a unit after taking off the lower radiator hose connection and the fan belt.

It is not necessary to remove the radiator core.

Disassembly of Water Pump

Remove the backing plate and gasket and the fan from the pulley.

Use a puller to take the pulley from the shaft.

Drive off the metal cap which retains the shaft and bearing assembly in the housing using a flat faced chisel.

The shaft and bearing assembly are pressed from the impeller out of the housing toward the front.

Remove the impeller seal and thrust washer assembly from the pump cavity.

On reassembly be sure the lugs on the thrust washers are engaged with the two slots in the end of the impeller.

Starting with 1941 production models the water pump had two water outlets.

ELECTRICAL SYSTEM

Removal of Distributor From Car

The distributor assembly is mounted on the right side of the block and is driven directly from the camshaft.

To remove the distributor first detach the vacuum lines to the vacuum advance unit and lift off the distributor cap.

The distributor body is held to the block by a single cap screw which holds the octane selector plate down against the block. Remove the retaining screw and lift the distributor out of the block.

Service on the Distributor

Perhaps the most common job on the distributor is the installation of new breaker points. They are installed as follows:

Remove the distributor cap and rotor. Disconnect the nut which holds the breaker arm spring to the primary wire contact but do not remove it.

Remove the screw which holds the breaker point to the breaker plate and lift off the breaker point. This will relieve the spring tension somewhat on the breaker arm and by compressing the breaker arm and spring, together with the thumb and finger the arm can be lifted off of the pin. **Note:** The spring is slotted to fit over the primary contact bolt.

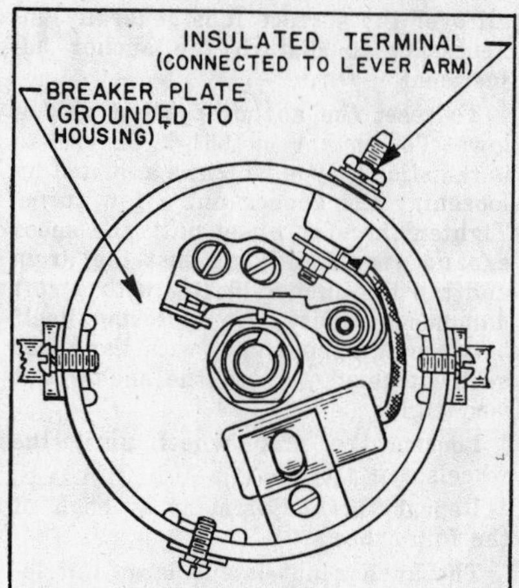

Distributor connections

The primary contact bolt can be identified since it is the only wire connection to the side of the distributor.

Install the new points by reversing the removal process and crank the engine so that the contact arm is on the high part of the cam. Now, with a screw driver, turn the eccentric screw so that the contact point will have the desired clearance between it and the arm.

Clearance specifications are given at the beginning of the Chevrolet section.

When clearance has been established, crank the engine further so that the points will come together and be certain that they are contacting over their entire surface, if not it will be necessary to bend the point or arm or both so that they do contact over their entire surface and then it will again be necessary to reset the gap after the points have been adjusted for full contact.

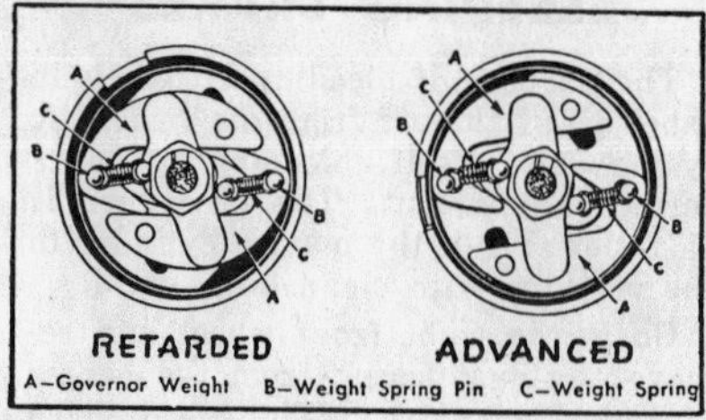

Mechanical Breaker Advance Mechanism

Overhauling the Distributor

In order to overhaul a distributor it will be necessary to first remove it from the car. Do this by removing the cap and disconnecting the primary wire connection. Remove the single screw which holds the distributor down into the cylinder block.

Caution: Carefully mark the position of the rotor before pulling the distributor out of the housing because the gear which drives the distributor is located on the bottom of the shaft and will come out with the distributor housing. The reason the mark is placed there is so that without loss of time the engine can be put back into the same timing it had before the distributor was removed.

Remove the breaker points as explained in the above paragraphs and take out the screws from the outside of the housing which hold the breaker plate in place. Lift off the breaker plate which will uncover the governor weights just underneath it.

Lay the distributor over a vice and punch out the pin which holds the drive gear to the bottom of the shaft and slide the gear off the shaft. The shaft can then be pushed up out of the housing and the governor weights removed.

Examine the housing for wear and looseness in the shaft itself. If any exist it will be necessary to either install a new shaft and/or bushings in the distributor housing.

It is generally recommended that a new or rebuilt distributor be installed if any considerable amount of wear or looseness is found in either the distributor shaft or bushings.

Generator

Note: Complete service on the generator is given in the general service portion of this section. See index.

The generator is held in a swivel bracket mounted to the side of the engine block and is driven by the fan and water pump belt.

The generator used on all models of Chevrolet built since 1940 is of the two brush type with full voltage and current regulation.

If difficulty is experienced with the generator, ground the field terminal of the generator either at the generator or at the regulator before removing the generator from the car. If on grounding the generator field terminal it is found that the generator functions properly, the difficulty will be in the regulator. If grounding the field current does not increase the output then the generator should be removed from the car and bench tested as outlined in the general service section of this manual.

Note: The field lead is the smaller of the two leads on the generator. The field lead at the regulator is marked "(F)" on the attaching lug.

Starting System

All models of Chevrolet use the over running clutch type starter.

Early models of Chevrolet used a manually operated starter mechanism, worked from the accelerator pedal.

Later models used the solenoid type starter which operated from a push button on the dash. If difficulty is experienced with the starter, first make certain that the battery is fully charged and that the connections to the battery are clean and tight. This is especially true of the ground connection.

If the battery is fully charged and the connections are clean and tight, check the starter switch with a volt meter to determine the voltage drop across the starter switch while the starter is cranking (or attempting to crank) the engine.

The drop of ½ volt across the starter switch could be considered excessive.

If difficulty is not found in the starter switch it will be necessary to remove the starter from the car and make the bench tests indicated in the general service section of this manual.

SPARK PLUGS

The spark plugs should be removed periodically for examination since the condition of the spark plug indicates to a very large degree the condition of the cylinder in which it is mounted.

The porcelain should be a clear chocolate color and the gap should be as specified in the spark plug gap specifications at the beginning of this Chevrolet section.

The formation of carbon on the spark plug or its electrodes indicate either an engine burning oil in very considerable quantities or that the plug is too cold for that engine and a hotter plug should be installed. Burned, blistered or cracked porcelain indicates that the spark plug is too hot for the cylinder in which it is used and a cooler plug should be installed.

No amount of words can describe the actual appearance of a good working spark plug. Only experience can point out to an operator when a plug is operating properly by sight.

THE BATTERY

Periodic cleaning and filling is the only service required by the battery.

See to it that the terminal connections at both the battery and the engine and starter switch are clean and tight and that the battery is free of all corrosion and excessive dirt, grease or oil.

Actually, no other service is required by the battery.

HEAD LIGHTS AND/OR TAIL LIGHTS

The only service required by head or tail lamps is to see to it that the connections to the light and the connections to ground are clean and tight. Where a head light or tail light shows dim when it should be bright it indicates that there is a high resistance connection (or a bad battery) in the circuit since if a sufficient amount of current reached the lamp it would light very brightly.

Where head lights or tail lights tend to burn out too quickly it indicates high voltage in the lighting circuit which in the final analysis must be blamed on the generator.

High resistance connections do not cause the lamps to burn out. Quite the contrary, lamps in circuits with high resistance connections will last indefinitely but will not be bright.

Too much current is the only thing which will burn out a lamp assembly and the only reason for too much current is too much voltage. Too much voltage invariably comes from a maladjusted generator or generator regulator.

ENGINE ASSEMBLY

All Chevrolet models are equipped with a six cylinder overhead valve type engine.

Starting with 1950 production, the large engine, equipped with power glide, had hydraulically actuated valve lifters.

Engine Removal

1940 TO 1948 MODELS

On these models it is easier to remove the front end sheet metal including both fenders, radiator grille and core as a unit in order to gain access to the engine.

The engine is detached at the universal joint and the engine, clutch and transmission assembly are removed as a unit.

1949 TO 1953 MODELS

On these models it is necessary to remove the hood and radiator core and also the radiator cradle.

The engine is detached at the front universal joint after all connecting parts have been removed.

Manifolds

All Chevrolet engines are equipped with a combination intake and exhaust manifold. The exhaust manifold is equipped with a heat riser valve which, when the engine is cold, deflects the hot exhaust gases against the intake manifold to assist in rapid warm up.

If the engine doesn't seem to warm up properly or when operated in a high speed it acts lean, it is a good idea to check this heat riser valve to be certain that it is functioning freely. Failure of the heat riser valve to open will increase the time required to warm the engine. Failure of the heat riser valve to close after the manifold is hot will cause the engine to apparently run lean.

Muffler, Exhaust Pipe and Tail Pipe

When installing an exhaust pipe, muffler or tail pipe assembly care should be taken to have these parts in proper relationship to each other and properly aligned.

Incorrect alignment of the exhaust system is frequently the cause of annoying rattles because of incorrect clearances. Many unusual noises very hard to locate are some times due to a change or obstruction to the normal flow of gases caused by improper mounting of any part of the exhaust system.

There are two points to consider when installing an exhaust or muffler assembly or a tail pipe. First, there should be ⅝ inch clearance between the underside of the floor pan and the tail pipe at the kickup. Second, the tail pipe support must be in a vertical position. If it is in an angle the tail pipe might strike the bumper causing an annoying rattle.

MUFFLER—*continued*

When replacing a muffler assembly, cut the exhaust pipe as close to the muffler inlet as is possible. This will permit the new muffler to be slipped over the end of the exhaust pipe.

If it becomes necessary to replace the exhaust pipe it will be necessary to also replace a muffler since these two parts are serviced together.

ENGINE INTERNAL

Rod and Piston Assemblies

Rod and piston assemblies are removed through the top of the block on all Chevrolet models.

Except for the 1953 Powerglide engines, all Chevrolet connecting rod bearings are of the poured type and are adjustable by means of shims.

Starting with 1953 Powerglide production a removable precision insert is used on the lower end of the connecting rod.

Three ring pistons are used on all pistons.

The pistons on all models are cast iron. Production models built in 1940 used a split skirt piston and from 1941 to 1948 a flat head slipper type piston was used. Starting with 1949 production a flat head split skirt piston was again used in the Chevrolet models.

On all engines, except the 1953 Powerglide model, the connecting rod may be adjusted by changing the thickness of the shim between the upper and lower half of the connecting rod forging.

Starting with 1953 production, the Chevrolet Motor Car Co. does not recommend adjusting the slipin type rod bearing. However, this bearing may be adjusted for normal wear by installing a taper or feather type shim between the lower bearing shell and the bearing cap.

As much as .003 or .004 excessive play may be taken out by this method.

Assembling Piston to Connecting Rod

Where split skirt type pistons are being installed the split in the skirt of the piston should be placed opposite to the clamp screw of the wrist pin; this is also opposite to the number on the bottom of the connecting rod.

Where solid skirt slipper type pistons are being replaced it is immaterial which way the piston is mounted onto the connecting rod. However, if the old pistons are being reinstalled the piston should be carefully marked before it is detached from the connecting rod in order that it may be replaced on the same side from which it was removed.

Assembling Piston and Rod Assembly to the Engine

When assembling the piston and connecting rod assemblies to the engine the number on the bottom of the connecting rod (also the clamp bolt on the wrist pin) should face the camshaft side of the engine.

Numbers are stamped on both the connecting rod and the connecting rod cap, both numbers facing the camshaft side.

Crankshaft Main Bearings

Precision replacement main bearings are available for all Chevrolet models. These precision shells do not require line reaming provided they are replaced in full sets.

The front and intermediate bearing shells are very similar in appearance and it is possible to get them mixed.

The intermediate shells are identified by the letter I on the bottom of the oil groove.

Intermediate bearing caps are marked front and rear for identification purposes; they are installed into the engine as indicated. The one stamped front is installed to the front and the one stamped rear is installed to the rear.

The upper half of the main bearing shell is located in the cylinder block by a dowel.

While it is possible to replace this upper half by lowering the crankshaft with the engine in the car it is perhaps just as easy to remove the engine and take out the crankshaft. Since, in this way, a better job can be done and the rear main bearing oil seal can also be replaced.

To replace the main bearing upper halves without removing the engine it is necessary to remove the radiator core and the transmission, jack the engine up several inches, and lower the crankshaft about ¾ in.

If this method is resorted to, great care should be exercised that the timing gears are not incorrectly meshed when the shaft is lowered and raised.

There is very little difference in the time required to replace the main bearings by lowering the crankshaft or by removing the engine.

Cutaway view

Engine Oil Pan Removal

1940 TO 1948 MODELS

To take the oil pan down on these models it is necessary to unbolt the engine side support cross member from the frame side rails. CAUTION: Be careful of the short pipe connecting the oil distributor in the oil pan to the oil passage in the cylinder block when lowering the pan.

1949 TO 1953 MODELS

To remove the oil pan, first remove the intermediate arm bracket and lower the arm and then unbolt and remove the oil pan. Make careful note of the shims used between the upper mounting bolt of the steering arm and the cross member so that the same number may be reinstalled.

Service on the Oil Pan

Except for the 1953 Powerglide engines, oil is supplied to the connecting rod bearings through troughs in the oil pan.

In order to insure perfect lubrication, gauges are available which will check the depth of the dipper on the connecting rod, the depth of the trough in the oil pan, and the aiming of the oil supply nozzle in each of the troughs.

If trouble is experienced maintaining the clearance on the connecting rod bearings the difficulty may be that the trough or the nozzle is misaligned and if such difficulties are experienced it is perhaps a very good idea to check the dipper, the trough, and the aiming of the nozzle with suitable gauges.

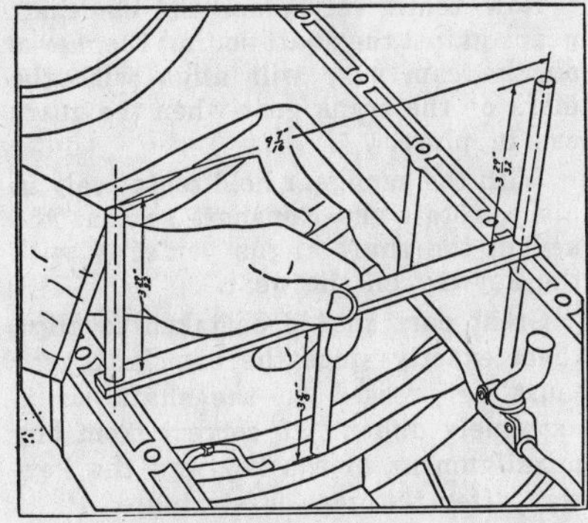

Oil trough depth and connecting rod dipper height gage. No. J-969-2 (For 216.5 cu. in. engines). No. J-1646 (For 235.3 cu. in. engine)

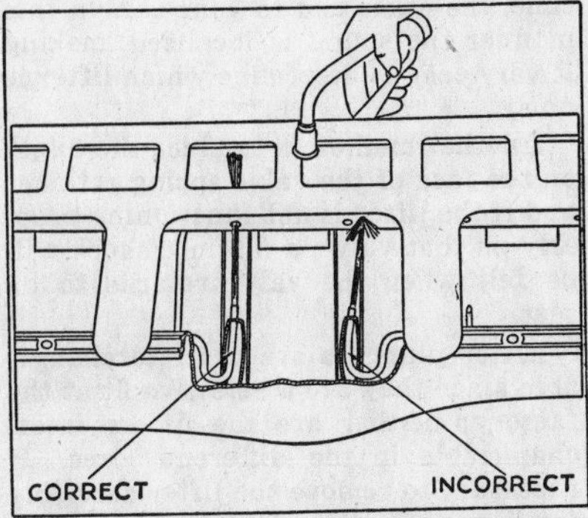

Oil pan target gage HJ-969-1. If this gage is not available set the nozzles so that the oil squirts in line with the troughs

THE VALVE SYSTEM

Valve Guides

The clearance between the valve guide and the valve stem is very important.

Lack of power, noisy valves, poor idling, and generally noisy engine can sometimes be traced to worn valve guides.

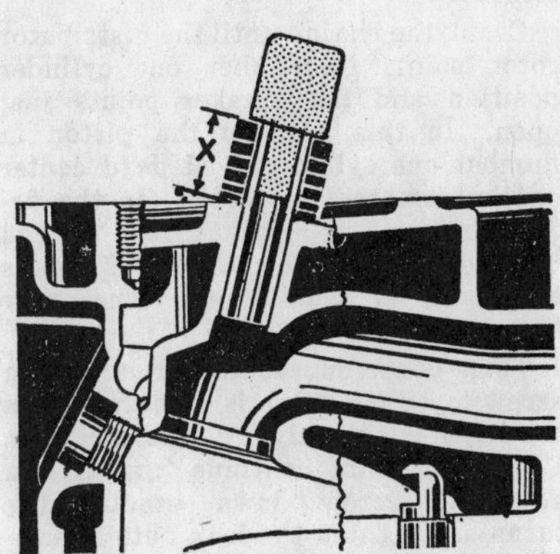

Add washers until distance "X" is required depth of valve guide

A quick way to check the fit of the valve in its guide is to examine the valve stem carefully if there are signs of gum far enough down the valve stem that the gum entered the guide, then the guide is too loose and should be replaced.

Before driving out the old valve guide, carefully measure the distance from the top of the head to the guide or, better yet, secure a stack of flat washers which will fit over the guide and stack up just enough to make the washers come flush with the top of the valve guide and use this pile of washers as a stop for the valve guide driving tool.

The guides are knocked out from the top of the head into the combustion chamber portion. In other words, they are driven downwards.

The new guides are started also at the top of the head and driven downwards.

The best way to install a valve guide is in an arbor press, being very careful to note that the guide is at an angle to the machined surface of the cylinder head and the cylinder head must be supported at that angle in the arbor press so that the guide is pushed straight downwards.

Whe new guides have been installed, immediately try a new valve in the new valve guide and, if the slightest difficulty or the slightest binding is noticed, it will be necessary to pass a reamer through the guide since it has probably become distorted or riveted over because of the driver.

Whenever new valve guides are installed always lap in the valve so that it is concentric to the new guide.

Rocker Arm Assemblies

The formation of oil and gum deposits in the hollowed out rocker shaft will result in poor or inadequate lubrication to the rocker arms and may result in noisy and faulty operation of the valves. Therefore, any time it is necessary to remove the rocker assembly it is a good idea to disassemble the rocker arms from the shaft and thoroughly clean out the shaft and the oil holes which supply each rocker with oil.

To remove the rocker arms, simply take off the air cleaner, disconnect the rocker cover assembly and lift it off, (a new gasket must be used on reinstallation), disconnect the oil feed line at the center of the rocker arm, and remove the bolts which hold the rocker arms bracket to the top of the cylinder head.

When reassembling the rocker shafts to the engine be sure the open ends of the rocker shafts are connected to the oil fitting in the center.

The plugged ends face the front and the back.

The rocker arms should be marked which half is front and which half is back to avoid confusion on reassembly.

ROCKER ARM—*continued*

Since some of the early engines use three different types of rocker arms and 1949 to 1953 engines use four different rocker arms, it will be necessary to mark them very carefully so that they will be installed properly in the engine.

On 1949 to 1953 engines the rocker arms are stamped 1-2-5 or 6. The rocker arm stamped 1 is used for the exhaust on cylinders One, Three and Five.

The rocker stamped number 2 is used on the exhaust on cylinder Two, Four and Six.

The rocker stamped number 5 is used on the intake of cylinders Two, Four and Six.

The rocker stamped number 6 is used on the intake of cylinders of One, Three and Five.

However, if the rocker arms are tagged carefully from One to Twelve from the front of the engine, it will not be necessary to check on the stamp numbers on the rocker itself.

On reassembling the rocker shafts to the engine the open end of each shaft goes toward the center.

Hydraulic Valve Lifter Service

On 1950 thru 1953 engines equipped with Power Glide, hydraulic valve silencers were used. The valve operates with zero clearance.

To locate a noisy or inoperative lifter, localize the noise by taking a piece of garden hose approximately four feet in length and place one end of the hose near the end of each valve, one at a time, the other end to your ear. In this manner the sound is localized, making it very easy to determine which lifter is noisy.

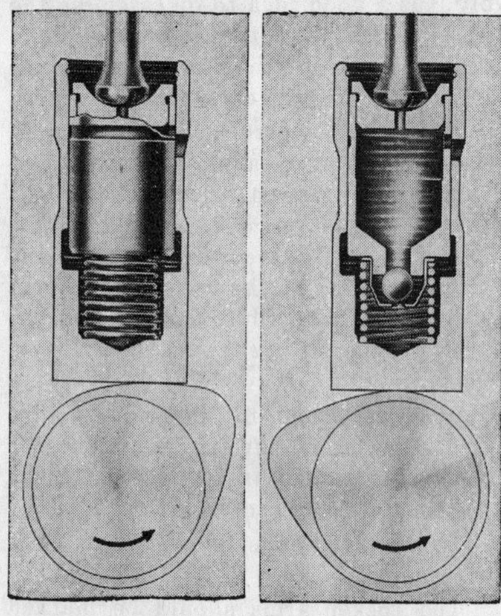

Section through the hydraulic valve lifter. 1950 to 1951 Power Glide models

Another method is to place the finger on the face of the valve spring retainer and if the lifter is not functioning properly on that valve, a distinct shock will be felt when the valve returns to its seat.

Lifter plungers are not interchangeable since they are a selective fit at the factory; neither are the lifters interchangeable in the different bores. If necessary to remove the lifter assembly for any reason it should be returned to the bore from which it was removed.

The hydraulic lifters may be taken from the engine readily by removing the rocker arms and push rod assemblies. The lifter is then lifted out of its bore.

Initial Adjustment of the Hydraulic Valve

If the lifters or rockers have been removed from the engine it will be necessary to make an initial valve adjustment on each lifter. This adjustment must be made when the lifter is on the base circle of the cam (valve closed).

Crank the engine until the distributor rotor points to number one cylinder position and the breaker points just open. In this position the piston in number one cylinder is at dead center on the compression stroke (in the firing position) and both lifters are on the base circle of the cam which means that both of number one valves may be adjusted.

Turn down on the rocker adjusting screw until all lash is removed from the lifter to the valve (zero clearance). From this point continue turning the adjusting screw down exactly 1½ turns and tighten the lock nuts securely. This will place the lifter in approximately the center of its travel. It will require no further adjustment.

Crank the engine until the distributor rotor points to number 5 cylinder and adjust valves for number 5, then turn to number 3 and adjust valves for number 3; continue around the firing order, which is 1-5-3-6-2-4.

The only service required by hydraulic valve lifters is that the gum and tar formed by the oil in the lifter is thoroughly removed by using a good solvent and compressed air.

The lifter should never be cleaned in any solution which may have a pitting or etching action.

Valve Timing—Replacement of Timing Gears

Chevrolet timing gears are arranged so that (unless deliberately disturbed) the valve timing will remain as set at the factory when the engine was assembled. Unless the gears are badly worn or seriously damaged the valve timing will remain constant within reasonable limits.

If it becomes necessary to replace the timing gears due to wear or damage, remove the radiator core, disconnect the front motor mounts and jack up the front of the engine. Remove the fan belt, fan pulley and timing case cover.

The crankshaft gear is removed by using a puller which will exert an even pressure on both sides of the gear.

If the camshaft gear is to be discarded it may be removed by placing a hook type gear puller over the fibre portion of the gear and forcing the gear from the shaft. NOTE: The gear on the Chevrolet camshaft is pressed on and the use of a gear puller over fibre portion of the gear will destroy its usefulness. Any camshaft gear, which is removed by using a puller over the fibre portion of the gear, must be discarded.

The crankshaft gear is machined from a solid billet of steel and is a press fit on the crankshaft, therefore take great care to start the gear in absolute alignment with the keyway so that the key will enter without the necessity of rotating the gear to secure alignment.

Press the crankshaft gear on to the crankshaft and rotate the shaft so that the timing mark on the gear is pointed toward the center of the camshaft.

Instill a new thrust plate over the camshaft and secure in place.

Now tentatively place the camshaft gear against the shaft so that the marks on the cam gear will align with the mark on the crank gear when the gears are in place.

With the cam gear held tentatively in place, rotate the camshaft so that the key in the shaft aligns perfectly with the keyway on the gear.

Great care should be taken to align them exactly since the camshaft gear must be pressed on the shaft. It is extremely difficult to correct from any misalignment in the key and the keyway after the gear is started.

When the cam gear is onto the shaft it is essential that the pressure be exerted against the steel hub of the gear and not against the fibre. Pressure against the fibre composition will result in damage to the cam gear and render it unuseable. NOTE: The Chevrolet Motor Car Company recommends that the camshaft be removed from the car in order to remove and replace the gear in an arbor press.

Many successful mechanics prefer this method of removing the camshaft in order to avoid possible risk when attempting to press a gear onto the shaft in place on the car. Sometimes when the gear is being pressed on in place on the car, damage results to the thrust washer in back of the cam gear. Unfortunately this damage is not noticed until the engine is started.

In order to press the gear on to the shaft with the shaft in place in the engine it is necessary to block one or more of the cams to prevent the camshaft from shifting backwards and possibly forcing the rear welsh plug out into the flywheel housing.

To replace the gear by removing the camshaft it is necessary to remove the rocker arm assemblies and the distributor, take out all of the push rods and take out all of the lifters. The camshaft may then be pulled out toward the front of the engine. When replacing the camshaft it will be necessary to retime the ignition.

CYLINDER HEAD NUT TIGHTENING SEQUENCE

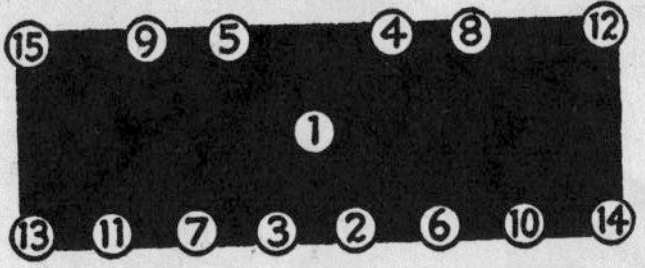

1938 to 1953. All models tighten head bolts to 75-80 foot pounds.

CLUTCH ASSEMBLY

In all Chevrolet models built since 1940 (except power glide) a diaphragm spring type clutch is used.

A ball bearing type throwout bearing is used and no provision is made for lubrication of this bearing except on assembly.

The throwout fork pivots on a ball stud which is mounted in the rear face of the bell housing.

Removal of the Standard Clutch

In order to remove the clutch from the car it is necessary to remove the transmission and then remove the clutch throwout fork. The clutch is then unbolted from the flywheel and lowered through the flywheel under pan.

Clutch Overhaul

The overhaul of Chevrolet clutch is generally considered to be a highly specialized job requiring special equipment. The exact procedure will depend on the type of equipment available. Each manufacturer of clutch equipment supplies all the necessary detailed instructions regarding the use of his equipment. These instructions should be followed very carefully.

STANDARD TRANSMISSION ASSEMBLY

The standard transmission assembly on all Chevrolets is a three-speed forward, one reverse, type of transmission where the low gear is mounted on the outside of the synchronizer drum.

The counter gear cluster has three gears instead of the usual four.

Transmission Removal

The transmission is removed through the floor board pan up into the car. This is accomplished by unbolting all of the connecting levers and the speedometer cable. Slide the universal joint ball back on to the torque tube. Universal joint can then be split.

In order to avoid possible damage to the clutch disc it is best to remove the two upper bolts which hold the transmission to the bell housing and replace the bolts with two guide pins. The transmission can then be slid back on these guide pins, preventing possible damage to the clutch disc.

These guide pins are a big help when reinstalling the transmission.

Overhaul of the Standard Transmission

First remove the shifter cover from the side of the transmission and then remove the universal joint yoke from the back end of the transmission.

This may be accomplished by placing the transmission in two gears at one time (usually high gear and low gear) which will prevent the main shaft from turning. Then take out the bolt which holds the universal joint to the rear end of the main shaft. Remove the main drive gear bearing sleeve from the front of the transmission. (This is the sleeve which carries the clutch throwout bearing.) Note that the holes in the sleeve are unevenly spaced so that it can be replaced only in the position which will index the oil return hole to the lower portion of the transmission case.

Remove the main drive gear out of the front of the case. Fig. 1. NOTE: Mark both the clutch gear and second speed gear and their respective synchronizer rings in such a way that when the transmission is reassembled the rings will be replaced in their original position with their respective gears.

Remove the synchronizer gear and bearing from the main shaft.

Remove the fourteen roller bearings from inside the clutch gear.

Fig. 1

Heavy cup grease is generally used to retain these rollers in place when reinstalling.

Turn the front synchronizer ring so that the lugs line up with the slots in the main shaft helical spline. If this is not done the lugs on the ring and the splines on the main shaft will be burred.

Then drive the main shaft through the front of th transmission case, Figs. 2 and 3.

Fig. 2

The synchronizer gear can now be lifted from the transmission case.

Remove the rear bearing lock ring and drive the rear bearing toward the inside of the case. NOTE: It is necessary to remove the rear bearing before the countershaft cluster can be removed.

TRANSMISSION ASSEMBLY—*continued*

Drive the countershaft from the rear toward the front of the case, Fig. 4, and lift out the counter gear cluster.

Drive out the reverse idler shaft expansion plug from inside the case and then drive the shaft lock pin into the shaft. This pin is shorter in length than the diameter of the shaft so that the shaft may be slipped out when the pin is driven in. Remove the shaft end thrust washers from case.

Take the clutch gear and place it in a vise and remove the bearing retaining nut which is also the oil slinger NOTE: This part has a left hand thread and it is staked to the shaft in the hole provided.

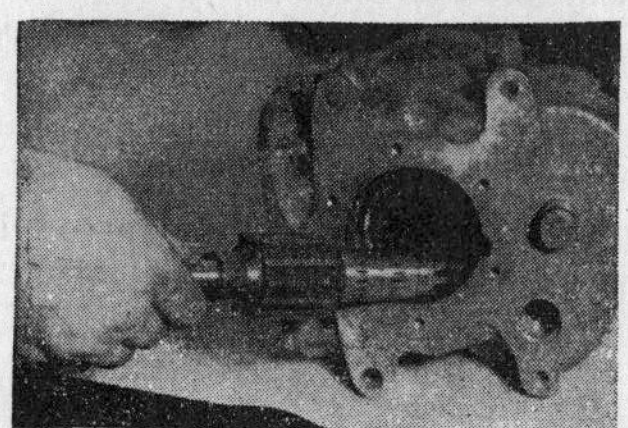

Fig. 3

Fig. 4

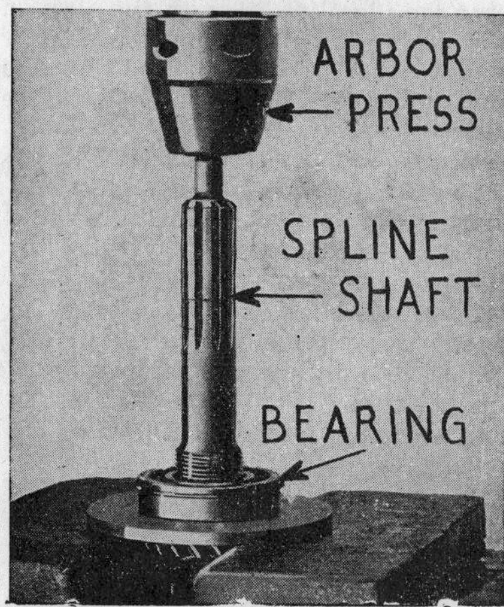

Pressing bearing from clutch shaft

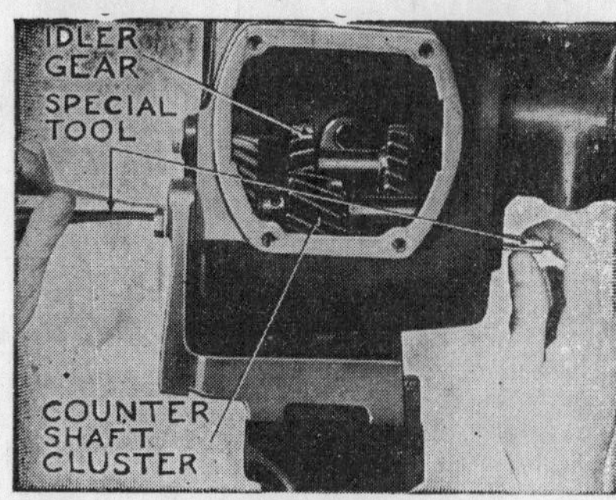

Pickup thrust washer and countergear cluster as indicated above

Adjustment of the Shift Mechanism—Standard Transmission

1940 TO 1948 MODELS

These models were equipped with a vacuum assisted shifting mechanism. If the shift is difficult, first check for vacuum leaks, interference from the speedometer cable with the vacuum line and lack of lubrication within the cylinder or on the reactionary levers.

Excessive back lash may be removed by tightening the clamps which hold the shiftershaft to the mast jacket and the levers to the shiftershaft. If a

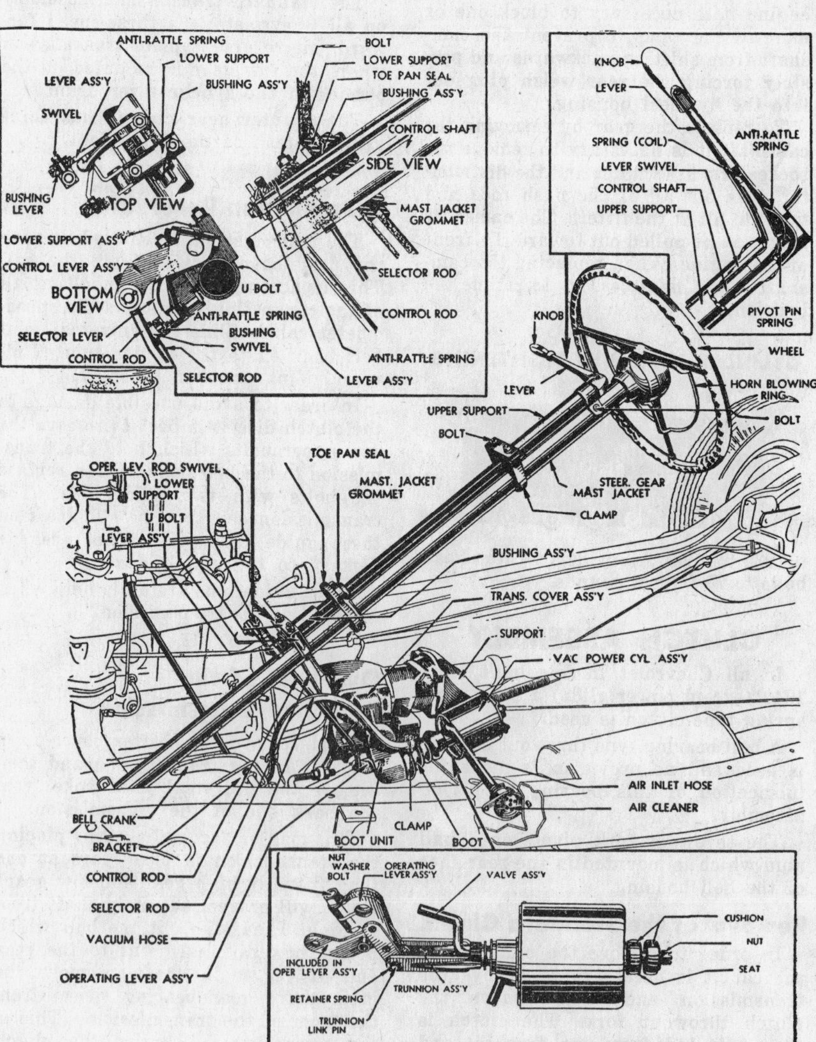

Shifter mechanism used on 1940 to 1948 models

flutter develops in the gear shift handle it will be necessary to install a friction spring on the vacuum valve line midway between the valve and the rod guide, prongs of the spring to the front. If the shifter hand lever should rattle it is only necessary to peen in the sides of the lever at the pivot pins. This increases the tension on the pivot pin spring and usually silences the assembly.

Place the hand shift lever in a horizontal position and hold it there. Move the gear shift operating rod the full movement of its travel, both forward and back. Midway of these extreme positions is where the operating rods swivel should fit into the operating rod lever. Hold the rod in this mid position and adjust the operating rod swivel so that it fits easily into the hole in the operating rod lever and fasten it to the lever with flat washer and a cotter pin. Lock the swivel into position on the rod.

Reactionary Levers (Vacuum Assist Shaft)

On all models from 1940 to 1948 the reactionary levers are a riveted assembly and require no servicing except they can be cleaned with a good solvent and compressed air and lubricated.

Vacuum Booster

LUBRICATION

When it becomes necessary to lubricate the vacuum cylinder, the cylinder must be removed.

One half ounce of shock absorber fluid is generally used in each end of the vacuum inlet stack. This is accomplished by pulling the valve link forward to open the vacuum port on the forward side of the piston.

After inserting the oil allow sufficient time for the oil to flow down into the cylinder.

Push the valve rod all the way into the piston rod and introduce one half ounce of shock absorber fluid through the vacuum inlet stack. Allow sufficient time for this oil to flow down into the cylinder.

Vacuum Cylinder Valve Adjustment

When it becomes necessary to adjust the valve and the vacuum cylinder the procedure outlined below must be followed very closely.

Remove the vacuum hose from the vacuum inlet stack and then slip the forward end of the rubber boot off the rear end of the metal boot.

Remove the two screws which fasten the two halves of the metal boot together and then lift off the top half.

Remove the piston rod yoke clevis pin. Push the piston right into the cylinder far enough to disconnect the piston rod yoke and valve from the reactionary levers. Install a special adjusting bushing Number J 1452-5 and replace the clevis pin. With the engine running to provide a source of vacuum, move the valve link away from the cylinder until all clearance between the special adjusting bushing and the valve link is towards the front of the car. In this position, piston rod should move slowly outward. Move the valve link towards the cylinder until all the clearance between the adjusting bushing and the valve link is towards the rear. In this position the piston rod should move slowly inwards. Should the piston move outward but will not move inward the valve link is adjusted to far towards the cylinder on the valve rod, to correct this condition remove the clevis pin and unscrew the valve link on the valve body ½ turn at a time until the proper valve action is obtained. On the other hand if the piston moves inward but will not move outward the valve link is screwed too far out on the valve rod. To correct this condition remove the clevis pin and screw the valve link on to the valve rod ½ turn at a time until proper valve action is obtained.

Adjustment of Transmission Mechanism—Models Without Vacuum Booster

With the transmission in neutral the gear shift lever should be in the horizontal plane. To move the gear shift lever to the horizontal position loosen the second and third speed control rod clamp swivel and adjust the swivel to bring the gear shift lever into a horizontal plane then tighten the clamp swivel.

Remove the housing cover and check to make sure the shifter gates and the inner levers are aligned. If alignment is off, loosen first and reverse speed control rod clamp swivel and adjust the swivel until the shifter gates are aligned. Then tighten the swivel.

POWER GLIDE TORQUE CONVERTER

Note: Linkage adjustment on the power glide transmission is given in the automatic transmission section of this manual. See index.

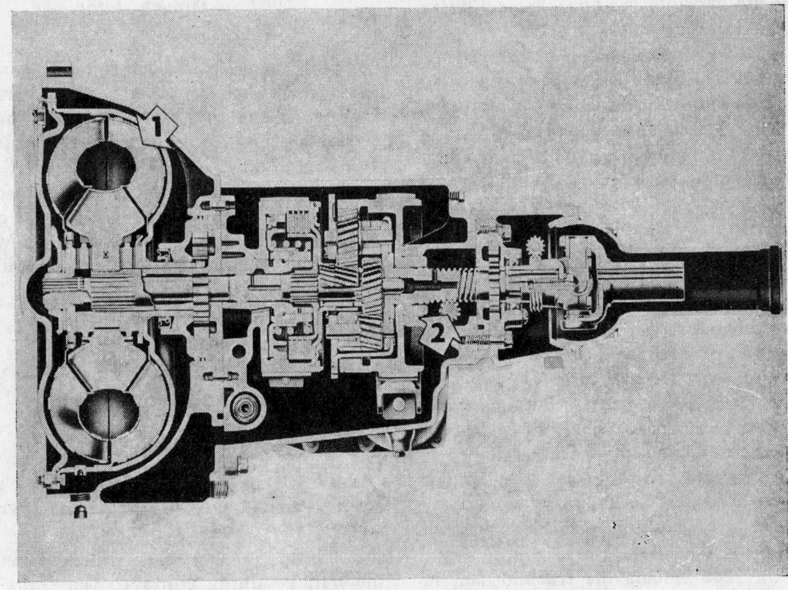

Cross sectional view of power glide torque converter

Function of the Power Glide Torque Converter

Starting with 1953 production, a "gear assist" type power glide is used which incorporates a governor. Otherwise the actual power transfer is the same as older models.

The power glide torque converter transmission is made up of the following components. The torque converter, planetary unit and clutch, oil pumps and hydraulic controls.

STARTING THE CAR

When starting the car or when under heavy load or on acceleration, or when the greatest amount torque multiplication is required, the primary pump is absorbing full power of the engine and, because of the rapid vortex flow of oil, the secondary pump is overrun.

The secondary pump is designed to overrun so that it will literally get out of the way of the oil which is trying to enter the primary pump from the stators.

The oil from the primary pump flows through the turbine and starts it moving. The oil, still in vortex flow, creates large reactionary forces against the stators which exert a directional control on the oil flow from the turbine to the pump.

In order to absorb this reaction, the stators are held stationary by the locking action of the free wheeling clutches on the stator hub, which is splined to the stator support, and is held solidly in the stator transmission case.

Both stators remain stationary as long as the rapid vortex flow exists and high torque multiplication is required.

On 1953 models only one stator is used and, under the conditions outlined above, the power glide transmission itself is in "Low" gear.

MEDIUM LOAD

As the turbine picks up rotary speed and approaches the speed of the pump the vortex flow of oil gradually decreases. As vortex flow decreases the reactionary forces on the stators become less and less and they finally decrease to a point where the secondary stator no longer carries any load.

Since the reactionary force is not present on the secondary stator under these conditions, it will turn with the rotating oil mass.

On 1953 models the transmission in addition shifts into drive.

LIGHT LOADS

The change taking place under medium loads can continue as the requirements for torque multiplications diminish. When no torque multiplication is required the turbine has reached the same speed as the pump and the vortex flow is reduced to a minimum. This forces against either stator.

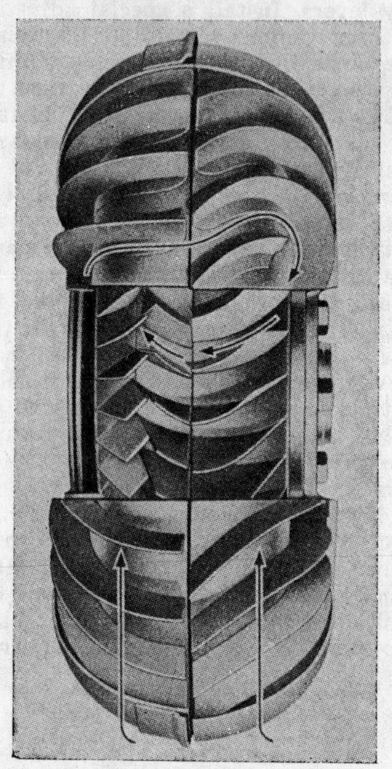

Oil flow through stator

The oil mass in the converter is now in high rotary motion and both stators free wheel and rotate with the oil. The converter now functions as a simple fluid coupling.

The stators are designed to free wheel so that they will not impose a static interference with the oil flow when the unit functions as a fluid couple.

UNIVERSAL JOINT AND PROPELLER SHAFT

Universal Joint Disassembly

Unhook the hand brake pull back spring, cable clevis and cable idler lever.

Remove the cap screws which retain the ball retaining collar to the transmission rear end and slide the collar and ball back on the propeller shaft housing. Remove the cap screws which fasten the front universal trunnion bearing to the front yoke on the transmission.

Support the propeller shaft and remove the two front yoke trunnion bearings and split the joint.

Take off the front yoke, remove the bolt and lock washer from the end of the transmission main shaft.

The two bearings on the universal joint, which attached to the propeller shaft yoke, are held with C washers on the inside surface of the bearing. These C washers can be driven out and the bearing knocked towards the outer side of the trunnion.

REAR AXLE ASSEMBLY

Except for refinements and improvements the rear axle assembly on all Chevrolets is essentially the same. Service procedure is the same for all models.

Axle Shaft and/or Inner Oil Seal Replacement

To remove the rear axle shaft, it is necessary to remove the rear wheel and then remove the differential carrier assembly back cover and take out the bolt which holds the differential pin in the carrier assembly. Remove the pin and take out the spacer which is located between the two axle shafts at their inner ends. Force the axle shaft inwards a sufficient amount to remove the C washer which is located on the end of the axle shaft. Remove the C washer and pull the axle out of the housing.

A puller is required to remove the axle bearing from the housing. The same puller is used to pull out the grease seal which is located behind the bearing.

When installing a new axle shaft it will be necessary to install wheel mounting bolts and stake them over very carefully into the flange of the axle shaft. A new deflector should always be used when installing a new axle shaft.

Removal of Pinion Shaft

To remove the pinion shaft it is necessary to take out both axle shafts, remove the differential assembly, and unbolt the differential carrier housing from the front face of the axle housing.

Take out the three tapered point screws which hold the pinion bearing thrust ring in place.

Tap the front end of the propeller shaft and drive the pinion out through the rear of the case.

Caution: Carefully preserve or note the number and thickness of the shims used on the pinion bearing.

These shims are located at the front end of the double row pinion ball bearing and they govern the depth of the pinion mesh into the ring gear.

The drive shaft can be separated from the end of the pinion shaft by drilling out the head of the rivet which retains them. Once the head of the rivet is driven off it can be knocked out with a punch.

If new pinion or new pinion bearings are to be installed it is recommended that one .015 in. and one .018 in. shim be used as a standard starting point. If the old pinion or pinion bearings are to be reinstalled, the shims which were removed should again be replaced.

Install the bearings on the pinion shaft and tighten up the pinion shaft nut to 200 foot pounds torque.

Install the splined end of the pinion shaft into the drive shaft and carefully line up the rivet hole. Install a new rivet and head it over at both ends.

Reinstall the drive shaft and pinion gear into the housing.

Before installing the three tapered screws which hold the front pinion bearing against its shims make certain that the bearing locking ring is in position as far forward as it will go.

The tapered lock screws must bear against the inside face of the bearing lock ring.

Install the differential carrier assembly and side bearings.

Using the adjusting cages on the differential side bearings, shift the ring gear until the back lash between the ring gear and pinion, as measured with a dial indicator, will be not less than .005 nor more than .007 inch. After final back lash has been established and the adjusting cages are moved so that there is zero play between the adjusting cages and bearing, tighten the right hand bearing cage two full notches in order to preload the bearings. When the bearings have been preloaded recheck to make certain that there is not less than .005 in. and not more than .007 in. back lash between the ring gear and pinion.

Propeller Shaft Bearing

To replace the propeller shaft bearings it is necessary to remove the propeller shaft from the housing. The procedure is exactly the same as for removing the pinion.

A dowel pin is used to retain the propeller shaft bearing to the torque tube. This pin will have to be driven out of place in order to remove the propeller shaft front bearing.

REAR SPRING

The center bolt in the rear spring of all Chevrolet passenger cars is located exactly in the center of the spring, therefore it is unnecessary to mark the spring as it may be installed either way.

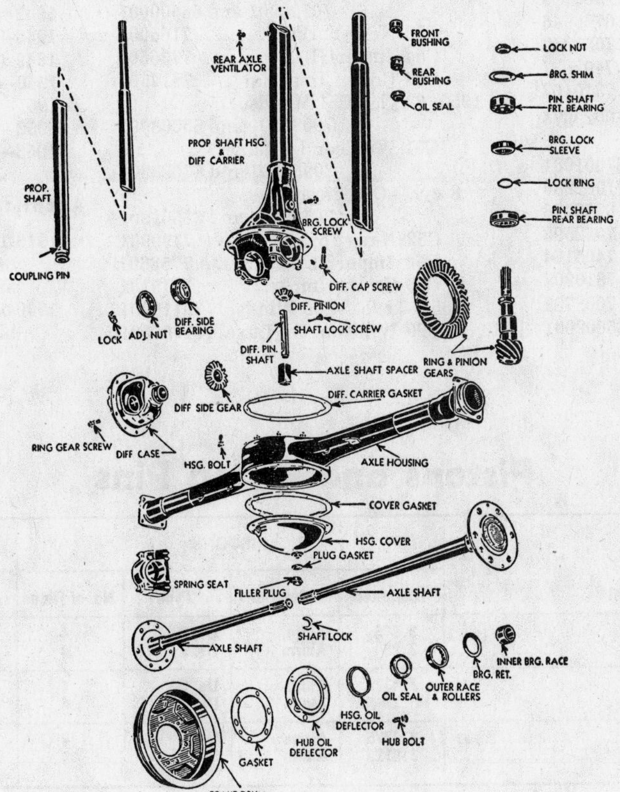

Rear axle assembly

CHRYSLER SPECIFICATIONS

Starting Serial and Motor Numbers

Starting Serial Numbers

1940, 6 cyl.—C25 Royal......7625001
C25 Windsor 6955201
8 cyl.—C26 Traveler......6750101
C26 New Yorker........6613401
C26 Saratoga 6673501
C27 Crown Imperial 7806551
1941, 6 cyl.—C28 Royal......7657501
C28 Windsor 7901601
8 cyl.—C30 Saratoga 6756501
C30 New Yorker & Crown Imperial 6624101
C33 Crown Imperial....7807501
1942, 6 cyl.—C34 Royal.....70001001
C34 Windsor 70501001
8 cyl.—C36 Saratoga......6762501
C36 New Yorker........6674201
C37 Crown Imperial....7808401
1946, 6 cyl.—C38 Royal.....70011001
C38 Windsor 70515001
C38 Town & Country...71000001
8 cyl.—C39 Saratoga 6765001
C39 New Yorker........7025001
C39 Town & Country....7400001
C40 Crown Imperial 7810001
1947, 6 cyl.—C38 Royal.....70023023
C38 Windsor 70564429
C38 Town & Country...71000128
8 cyl.—C39 Saratoga 6766546
C39 New Yorker 7037249
C39 Town & Country ...7402037
C40 Crown Imperial 7810167
1948, 6 cyl.—C38 Royal.....70029674
C38 Windsor 70633017 and 67001001
C38 Town & Country...71002280
8 cyl.—C39 Saratoga......6768486
C39 New Yorker..........7062598
C39 Town & Country....7405174
C40 Crown Imperial 7810908
1949, 6 cyl.—C38 Royal......7003781
C45 Royal 70041001 and 65002001
C38 Windsor 70702448 and 67001921
C45 Windsor 70725001 and 67005001
8 cyl.—C39 Saratoga 6770181
C46 Saratoga 6772001
C39 New Yorker 7085470
C46 New Yorker 7094001
C39 Town & Country ...7408110
C46 Town & Country....7410001
C46 Imperial 7107801
C40 Crown Imperial 7811348
C48 Crown Imperial 7813001
1950, 6 cyl.—C48 Royal 70058001 and 65004001
C48 Windsor 7079401 and 67011001
8 cyl.—C49 Saratoga 6774501
C49 New Yorker 7119001 and 7157001
C49 Town & Country 7411501
C49 Imperial 7146001
C50 Crown Imperial 7813501
1951, 6 cyl.—C51 Windsor 70081001 and 65007001
C51 Windsor De Luxe 70891001 and 67026001
8 cyl.—C55 Saratoga 76500001 and 66500001
C52 New Yorker 7165001
C54 Imperial 7736501
C53 Crown Imperial 7814501
1952, 6 cyl.—C51 Windsor 70094301 and 65008901
C51 Windsor De Luxe 70952301 and 67033301
8 cyl.—C55 Saratoga 76512101 and 66501801
C52 New Yorker 7199901
C54 Imperial 7753601
C53 Crown Imperial 7815101
1953, 6 cyl.—C60 Windsor 70110001
C60 Windsor De Luxe..71005001
C56 New Yorker.......76540001
C56 New Yorker Special 7222001
C58 Custom Imperial ...7765001
C59 Crown Imperial.....7816001

Location

1940-1942—Plate on right front door hinge post.
1946-1953—Plate on left front door hinge post.

Starting Motor Numbers

1940-1950—First letter and two numbers indicate year, model and number of cyls., i.e. C25, 1940—6 cyl.
1951-1952—First letter and two numbers indicate year, model and 6 cyl., i.e. C51, 1951—6 cyl. First letter and two numbers with third number an 8, indicates year, model and 8 cyl., i.e. C51-8, 1951, 8 cyl. All motor numbers begin 1001. 1953, C53—1001.
1940—C25, C26, C27............1001
1941—C28, C30, C33............1001
1942—C34, C36, C37............1001
1946-1949 (early)—C38, C39, C40 1001
1949 (late)—C45, C46, C47......1001
1950—C48, C49, C50............1001
1951—C51 1001
1952—C52 1001
1953—Conventional, Powerglide 1001

Location

1940-1953, 6 cyl.—Boss on upper left of cylinder block between No. 1 and No. 2 cylinders.
1940-1953, 8 cyl.—Top front center of block.

Pistons and Piston Pins

Year	Model	PISTONS				PISTON PINS		
		Diameter	Material	Type	No. of Rings	Length	Diameter	How Held
1940–41	All 6 cyl.	3.375	Alum.	Us, C	4	2⅞	.859375	F
	All 8 cyl.	3.25	Alum.	Us, C	4	2¾	.859375	F
1942–50	All 6 cyl.	3.4375	Alum.	Us, C	4	2⅞	.8593	F
	All 8 cyl.	3.25	Alum.	Us, C	4	2¾	.8593	F
1951 to 53	C51	3.4375	Alum.	Us, C	4	2⅞	.8594	F
	C52, C53, C54	3.8125	Alum.	Ss, Sp, C	3	3 9/64	.9844	F

Us, C—"U" slot, cam ground. Alum.—Aluminum. F—Floating.
Ss, Sp, C—Split skirt, slipper skirt, cam ground.

General Specifications

Year	Model	Wheelbase (in.)	Tread (in.) Front	Tread (in.) Rear	Overall Dimensions (in.) Length†	Overall Dimensions (in.) Width	Overall Dimensions (in.) Height■	Shipping Weight* (lb.)	Tire Size (in.)
1941	Series C28	122	57	60	212	....	....	3335	6.25–16
	C30N, 30K	128	58	62	218	....	....	3805	7.00–15
	Series C33	146	58	62	231	....	....	....	7.50–15
1942	Series C34	122	57	60	208	....	....	3500	6.25–16
	Series C36	128	58	62	213	....	....	3900	7.00–15
	Series C37	146	58	62	231	....	....	....	7.50–15
1946	Series C38	122	57	60	208	78	....	....	6.50–15
	Series C39	128	58	61	214	78	....	....	7.00–15
1947	Series C38	122	57	60	208	78	....	3523	6.50–15
	Series C39	128	58	61	214	78	....	3972	7.00–15
	Series C40	146	58	62	235	78	....	4814	7.50–15
1948	Series C38	122	57	60	211	78	....	3523	7.60–15
	Series C39	128	58	62	217	78	....	3972	8.20–15
	Series C40	146	58	62	235	78	....	4300	8.90–15
1949	Series C45	126	56	57	204	73	66	....	7.60–15
	Series C46	132	57	58	210	75	66	....	8.20–15
	Series C47	146	57	64	....	....	....	....	8.90–15
1950	Series C48	126	56	60	208	66	....	3655	7.60–15
	Series C49	132	57	58	214	....	....	4170	8.20–15
1951	Series C51	126	56	60	207	75	65	3665	7.60–15
	Series C52, C54	132	57	58	213^	75●	65	4260	8.20–15
	Series C53	146	58	66	230	81	69	4350	8.90–15
1952	C51, C55, 6 cyl.	125	57	59	207	76	65	....	7.60–15
	C52, 8 cyl.	131	57	58	213	76	66	....	8.00–15
	C54, 8 cyl.	131	57	58	231	76	66	....	8.20–15
	C53, 8 cyl.	145	57	66	230	81	68	....	8.90–15
1953	C56, C60	125	56	60	211	77	62	....	7.60–15–60
	....	....	....	....	....	....	62	....	8.00–15–56
	C58	133	57	60	219	77	63	....	8.20–15
	C59	145	57	66	229	81	69	....	8.90–15

●—C54–76. ^—C54–212. †—Including bumpers and guards. ■—Road to roof, no load. *—Cheapest 5 passenger 4 door sedan or equivalent

Dimensions of Valves

Year	Model	Overall Length Inlet	Overall Length Exhaust	Head Diameter Inlet	Head Diameter Exhaust	Seat Angle (deg.) Inlet	Seat Angle (deg.) Exhaust	Stem Diameter Inlet	Stem Diameter Exhaust	Key Type	O.D. of Seat Insert Inlet	O.D. of Seat Insert Exhaust
1940 to 42	All 6 cyl.	4.781	4.781	1.656	1.531	45	45	.340	.340	split lock	1.640625	1.640625
	All 8 cyl.	5.875	5.875	1.531	1.343	45	45	.340	.340	split lock	1.458	1.458
1946–47	All 6 cyl.	4.781	4.781	1.719	1.531	45	45	.341	.339	split lock	1.640625	1.640625
	All 8 cyl.	5.875	5.875	1.531	1.344	45	45	.341	.340	split lock	1.458	1.458
1948	C38	4.781	4.781	1.718	1.531	45	45	.341	.339	split lock	1.640625	1.640625
	C39, C40	5.875	5.875	1.531	1.343	45	45	.341	.340	split lock	....	1.458
1949	C45	4.781	4.781	1.718	1.531	45	45	.341	.339	split lock	....	1.640625
	346, C47	5.875	5.875	1.531	1.343	45	45	.341	.340	split lock	....	....
1950	C48	4.781	4.781	1.719	1.531	45	45	.341	.340	split lock	....	....
	C49, C50	5.875	5.875	1.531	1.344	45	45	.340	.340	split lock	....	....
1951	C51	4.781	4.781	1.719	1.531	45	45	.341	.340	split lock	....	....
	C53, C54, C52	5.000	4.906	1.812	1.500	45	45	.372	.372	split lock	....	....

CHRYSLER SPECIFICATIONS

Dimensions of Valves—*continued*

Year	Model	Overall Length		Head Diameter		Seat Angle (deg.)		Stem Diameter		Key Type	O.D. of Seat Insert	
		Inlet	Exhaust	Inlet	Exhaust	Inlet	Exhaust	Inlet	Exhaust		Inlet	Exhaust
1952	C51-1, C51-2, 6 cyl.	4.78125	4.78125	1.71875	1.53125	45	45	.341	.340	....	....	....
	C52, C53, C54, C55, 8 cyl.	5	4.90625	1.8125	1.500	45	45	.3725	.3715	....	....	....
1953	C60-1, C60-2	4.84375	4.84375	1.718	1.501	45	45	.341	.340	....	....	....
	C56-1, C56-2, C58, C59	5	4.90625	1.8125	1.500	45	45	.3725	.3715	....	....	....

General Engine Specifications

Year	Model	Number of Cylinders Bore and Stroke	Piston Displacement, Cubic Inches	Compression Ratio (To–1)	Taxable (A.M.A.) Hp.	DEVELOPED HORSE POWER		Maximum Torque Ft. Lbs.
						Bare Engine	With Accessories	
1940–41	C25, 6 Cyl.	6-3 3/8 x 4 1/2	241.5	6.50	27.3	108 @ 3600	....	188 @ 1200
	C26, 8 Cyl.	8-3 1/4 x 4 7/8	323.5	6.80	33.8	135 @ 3400	....	255 @ 1600
	C27, 8 Cyl.	8-3 1/4 x 4 7/8	323.5	6.80	33.8	137 @ 3400	....	260 @ 1600
1942	C34S, C34W, 6 Cyl.	6-3 7/16 x 4 1/2	250.5	6.60	28.3	120 @ 3800	....	200 @ 1600
	C36K & C36N, 8 Cyl.	8-3 1/4 x 4 7/8	323.5	6.80	33.8	140 @ 3600	....	260 @ 1800
	C37, 8 Cyl.	8-3 1/4 x 4 7/8	323.5	6.80	33.8	140 @ 3600	....	260 @ 1800
1946–48	C38, 6 Cyl.	6-3 7/16 x 4 1/2	250.6	6.60	28.4	114 @ 3600	....	204 @ 1200
	C39, 8 Cyl.	8-3 1/4 x 4 7/8	323.5	6.80	33.8	135 @ 3400	....	270 @ 1600
1949–50	C45, 6 Cyl.	6-3 7/16 x 4 1/2	250.6	7.00	28.3	116 @ 3600	....	208 @ 1600
	C46, C47, 8 Cyl.	8-3 1/4 x 4 7/8	323.5	7.25	33.8	135 @ 3200	....	270 @ 1600
1951	C51-1, C51-2, 6 Cyl.	6-3 7/16 x 4 1/2	250.6	7.00	28.3	116 @ 3600	....	208 @ 1600
	C52 N. Y., C53-C54, 8 Cyl.	V8-3 13/16 x 3 5/8	331.1	7.50	46.5	180 @ 4000	....	312 @ 2000
1952	C51-1, C51-2, 6 Cyl.	6-3 7/16 x 4 3/4	264.5	7.00	28.36	119 @ 3600	....	218 @ 1600
	C52, C53, C54, C55, 8 Cyl.	V8-3 13/16 x 3 5/8	331.1	7.50	46.51	180 @ 4000	....	312 @ 2000
1953	C60-1, C60-2	6-3 7/16 x 4 3/4	264.5	7.0	28.36	119 @ 3600	....	218 @ 1600
	C56, C58, C59	V8-3 13/16 x 3 5/8	331.1	7.5	46.51	180 @ 4000	....	312 @ 2000

Crankshaft Bearing Journal Sizes

Year	Model	Connecting Rod Journals		Main Bearing Journals				
		Diameter	Length	No. 1 Diameter	No. 2 Diameter	No. 3 Diameter	No. 4 Diameter	No. 5 Diameter
1940 to 50	All 6 cyl.	2.124–2.125	1.21875	2.499–2.500	2.499–2.500	2.499–2.500	2.499–2.500	....
	All 8 cyl.	2.186–2.187	1.125	2.702–2.703	2.702–2.703	2.702–2.703	2.702–2.703	2.702–2.703
1951	C51	2.124–2.125	1.21875	2.499–2.500	2.499–2.500	2.499–2.500	2.499–2.500	....
	C52, C53, C54	2.249–2.250	2.00	2.4995–2.5005	2.4995–2.5005	2.4995–2.5005	2.4995–2.5005	2.4995–2.5005
1952	C51-1, C51-2, 6 cyl.	2.124–2.125	1.2187	2.499–2.500	2.499–2.500	2.499–2.500	2.499–2.500	....
	C52, C53, C54, C55, 8 cyl.	2.249–2.250	2.249–2.250	2.499–2.500	2.499–2.500	2.499–2.500	2.499–2.500	2.499–2.500
1953	C60-1, C60-2, 6 cyl.	2.125	....	2.5–1.155	2.5–1.155	2.5–1.155	2.5–1.589	....
	C56-1, C56-2, C58, C59, 8 cyl.	2.250	....	2.5–.875	2.5–.875	2.5–.870	2.5–.875	2.5–1.595

Engine Tune-Up Specifications

Year	Model	Spark Plugs Type	Spark Plugs Gap	Distributor Point Gap	Distributor Cam Dwell, (Deg.)	Ignition Timing, (Deg.)	Ignition Timing Mark and Location	Compression Pressure at R.P.M.	Operating Tappet Clearance Inlet	Operating Tappet Clearance Exhaust	Carburetor Fuel Float Height	Minimum Engine Idle Speed at R.P.M.
1940	C25, 6 Cyl.	AL-A7	.025	.020	38	TC	Dmpr.	150@1000	.008	.010	5/64"	450
	C26, 8 Cyl.	AL-A7	.025	.017	27	TC	Dmpr.	155@1000	.008	.010	5/8"	425
	C27, 8 Cyl.	AL-A7	.025	.017	27	3B	Dmpr.	155@1000	.008	.010	5/8"	425
1941	C28S, C28W, 6 Cyl.	AL-A7	.025	.020	38	TC	Dmpr.	112@1000	.008	.010	1/2"	450
	C30N, C30K, 8 Cyl.	AL-A7	.025	.017	27	TC	Dmpr.	150@1000	.008	.010	5/8"	425
	C33, 8 Cyl.	AL-A7	.025	.017	27	3B	Dmpr.	150@1000	.008	.010	5/8"	425
1942	C34S Royal, C34W, 6 Cyl.	AL-A7	.025	.020	38	2A	Dmpr.	160@1000	.008	.010	5/64"	450
	C36K & C36N, 8 Cyl.	AL-A7	.025	.018	27	2A	Dmpr.	160@1000	.008	.010	5/8"	425
	C37, 8 Cyl.	AL-A7	.025	.018	27	2A	Dmpr.	160@1000	.008	.010	5/8"	425
1946	C38, 6 Cyl.	AL-A5	.025	.020	38	2A	Dmpr.	155@1000	.008	.010	5/64"	450
	C39, 8 Cyl.	AL-A5	.025	.020	30½	2A	Dmpr.	165@1000	.008	.010	5/8"	425
1947	C38, 6 Cyl.	AL-A5	.025	.020	38	2A	Dmpr.	165@1000	.008	.010	5/64"	450
	C39K & N, 8 Cyl.	AL-A5	.025	.020	28	2A	Dmpr.	165@1000	.008	.010	5/8"	425
1948	C38, 6 Cyl.	AL-A5	.025	.020	38	2A	Dmpr.	165@1000	.008	.010	5/64"	450
	C39 & C40, 8 Cyl.	AL-A5	.025	.020	28	2A	Dmpr.	165@1000	.008	.010	5/8"	425
1949	C45, 6 Cyl.	AL-AR5	.038	.020	36	4A	Dmpr.	165@1000	.008	.010	5/64"	450
	C46, C47, 8 Cyl.	AL-AR5	.036	.018	28	2A	Dmpr.	165@1000	.008	.010	5/8"	425
1950	C48, 6 Cyl.	AL-AR5	.030	.020	36	TC	Dmpr.	165@1000	.008	.010	5/64"	450
	C49 Saratoga, C50, 8 Cyl.	AL-AR5	.036	.018	28	TC	Dmpr.	165@1000	.008	.010	5/8"	425
1951	C51-1, C51-2 Windsor, 6 Cyl.	AL-AR8	.035	.020	34½–38	2B	Dmpr.	....	.008	.010	....	450
	C52 N. Y., C53-C54 Imp., 8 Cyl.	AL-AAR6	.035	.015–.018	34–36	TC	Dmpr.	....	Hydr.	Hydr.	....	425
1952	C51-1, C51-2, 6 Cyl.	AL-AR8	.035	.020	38	2B	Dmpr.	....	.008H	.010H	5/64"	475
	C52, C53, C54, C55, 8 Cyl.	AL-4S140	.035	.018	36	4B	Dmpr.	....	AA	AA	11/64"	475
1953	C-61-1, C-60-2, 6 Cyl.	AL-AR8	.035	.018	39±3°	....	....	....	....	....	....	....
	C-56, C-58, C-59, 8 Cyl.	AL-4S140	.035	.018	28	....	....	....	....	....	....	....

Hyd—Automatic.
AL—Auto-Lite spark plugs.
TC—Top center.
A—After top center.
B—Before top center.
Dmpr—Vibration damper.
AA—Automatic adjustment.
H—Hot.

Brake Data

Year	Model	Make	Lining Type	R=Riveted B=Bonded	Drum Diameter	Lining Length	Lining Width	Lining Thickness	Clearance Toe	Clearance Heel
1941–42	All—6	Loc	M	R	11	19 7/16	2	13/64	.012	.006
	All—8	Loc	M	R	12	25 1/8–*22 3/16	2	13/64	**.006	.007
1946 to 49	All—6	C-L	M	R–†B	11	23–*20 3/8	2	13/64	.006	.006
	All—8	C-L	M	R–†B	12	25 1/8–*22 3/16	2	13/64	.006	.006
1950	C48, C49		M	B	12	25 1/8	2	13/64	.006	.006
	C50		M	B	12	(x)	(x)	.170	SA	SA
1951	C51, C52, C54	Own	M	B	12	25 1/8	2	13/64	.006	.006
	C53	Own	M	B	12	(x)	1½	3/16	SA	SA
1952–53	6 Cyl.		M	B	12	25 9/64	2	13/64	.006	.006
	V8		M	B	12	(x)	....	....	SA	SA

* Rear. † 1949. (x) Disk Brake—12 segments per wheel. ** Rear shoes rear wheels.—Toe .007–Heel .007. SA Self adjusting.
Loc—Lockheed. M—Moulded. C-L—Chrysler Lockheed.

Engine Overhaul Specifications

Year	Model	Pistons: Removed From	Pistons: Piston Skirt Clearances (Maximum): Top	Bottom	Limit	Ring Gap Clearances (Maximum): Top Ring	Second Ring	Third Ring	Oil Ring	Piston Pin: Type	Fit	Rod Bearings: Oil Clearance	Wear Limit	Side Play
1940–	C28S. C28W. 6 Cyl.	A	......	.0010*	.004	.015	015	.015	.015	FL	Push	.0005–.0025	.004	.0055–.0115
1941	C30N. C30K. N. Y., 8 Cyl.	A	......	.0010*	.004	.015	.015	.015	.015	FL	Push	.001–.003	.004	.006–.011
	C33, 8 Cyl.	A	......	.0010*	.004	.015	.015	.015	.015	FL	Push	.001-.003	.004	.006–.011
1942	C34SC, 34W 6 Cyl.	A	......	.0018*	.004	.015	.015	.015	.015	FL	Press	.001–.0015	004	.006–.015
	C36K & C36N, 8 Cyl.	A	......	.0010*	.004	.015	.015	.015	.015	FL	Press	.001–.0015	.004	.006–.011
	C37, 8 Cyl.	A	......	.0010*	.004	.015	.015	.015	.015	FL	Press	.001–.0015	.004	.006–.011
1946 to	C38, 6 Cyl.	A	......	.0015*	.004	.015	.015	.015	.015	FL	Push	.001–.0015	.004	.0055–.0115
1948	C39 & C40. 8 Cyl.	A	......	.0015*	.004	.015	.015	.015	.015	FL	Push	.001–.0015	.004	.006–.011
1949	C45, 6 Cyl.	A	......	.0012*	.004	.015	.015	.015	.015	FL	Push	.0005–.0015	.004	.0055–.0115
	C46, C47, 8 Cyl.	A	......	.0012*	.004	.015	.015	.015	.015	FL	Push	.0005–.0015	.004	.006–.011
1950	C48, 6 Cyl.	A	......	.0012*	.004	.015	.015	.015	.015	FL	Push	.0005–.0015	.004	.006–.011
	C49, C50, 8 Cyl.	A	......	.00125*	.004	.015	.015	.015	.015	FL	Push	.0005–.0015	.004	.006–.011
1951	C51-1, C51-2 Windsor, 6 Cyl.	A	......	.0012*	.004	.015	.015	.015	.015	FL	Push	.0005–.0015	.004	.006–.011
	C52 N. Y., C53-C54 Imp., 8 Cyl.	A	......	.0015*	.004	.020	.020	......	.020	FL	Push	.0005–.0015	.004	.006–.014
1952–	6 cyl.	A	.0007	......		.011	.011	......	.011	FL	.0005	.0005–.0015	.004	.006–.011
1953	V8	A	.0010	......		.015	.015	......	.015	FL	.0005	.0005–.0015	.004	.006–.014

A—Above.
B—Before top center.
FL—Floating type.
†—"•" marks on cam and crank sprockets align with shaft centers.
*—Measured ¾ inch from bottom.

Distributors

Year	Model	Distributor Model Number	Cam Angle (deg.)	Direction of Rotation C=Clockwise CC=Counter Clockwise at Cam End	Breaker Arm Spring Tension	Breaker Point Gap (inches)	Engine R.P.M. when Cent. Advance Starts	Max. Cent. Advance in Engine Deg. at Stated Engine R.P.M.	Vacuum in (inches) of Mercury at which Vacuum Unit Starts	Max. Advance in Engine Deg. at Stated Vacuum	Vacuum Unit Number
1940	C25, 6 cyl.	IGS-4108A-1	38	C	17–20	.018–.022	700	24@3500	5	22@17	IGS-1023JS
	C26, 8 cyl.	IGT-4101A-2	27	C	17–20	.016–.018	700	24@3500	5	16@17	IGT-1023-HS
	C27, 8 cyl.	IGT-4101B-2	27	C	17–20	.016–.018	700	24@3500	5	12@17	IGT-1023-HS
1946	C28S, C28W, 6 cyl.	IGS-4113-1	38	C	17–20	.018–.022	700	24@3500	5	14@15	IGS-1023-HS
	C30N, C30K, 8 cyl.	IGT-4103-1	27	C	17–20	.016–.018	700	24@3500	5	16@17	IGT-1023-HS
	C33, 8 cyl.	IGT-4103A-1	27	C	17–20	.016–.018	700	24@3500	5	12@17	IGT-1023-JS
1942	C34S, C34W, 6 cyl.	IGS-4202B-1	38	C	17–20	.018–.022	700	24@3060	5	18@15	VC-3082-RFS
	C36N, C36K, C37, 8 cyl.	IGT-4201B-1	27	C	17–20	.016–.018	700	24@3500	5	20@16	VC-3117-RCS
1946 to 48	C38, 6 cyl.	IGS-4208A-1	....	C	17–20	.020	700	24@3050	5	9@15	....
	C39, 8 cyl.	IGT-4201-1	27	C	17–20	.016–.018	700	24@3500	5	16@17	VC-3117-RS
1949	C45, 6 cyl.	IAP-4102C-1	34½	C	17–20	.018–.022	700	20@2850	5	9@15	....
	C46, C47, 8 cyl.	IAR-4101-1	27	C	17–20	.016–.018	700	20@3100	5	8@17	....
1950	C48-1, C48-2, 6 cyl.	IAP-4102C-1	34½	C	17–20	.018–.022	700	20@2850	5	9@15	....
	C49, C50, 8 cyl.	IAR-4101-1	27	C	17–20	.016–.018	700	20@3100	5	8@17	....
1951	C51, 6 cyl.	IAT-4012	36¼	C	17–20	.018–.022	700	22@2850	5.5	20	....
	C52, C53, C54, 8 cyl.	IAZ-4001	35	C	17–20	.016–.018	700	29@3400	5.5	21 to 25	....
1952	C51-1, C51-2, 6 cyl.	IAT-4012	34½–38	C	17–20	.018–.020	....	4–6@800	9–11	8–10@15	....
	C52, C53, C54, C55, 8 cyl.	IAZ-4001-B	32–36	C	17–20	.015–.018	....	12@1790	5½–6½	10½–12½	....
1953	C60-1, C60-2	IAT-4102	39±3	C	17–20	.018–.020	350	11@1425	1@5.5	9–15	....
	C56-1, C56-2, C58, C59	IAZ-4001-B	32–36	C	17–20	.015–.018	425	12@1775	1@5.5	11.50	....

and Wear Limit Table

CRANKSHAFT		VALVES						Valve Timing, Inlet Valve Opens (Deg.)	Camshaft Drive	Gear Marks	OPERATING OIL PRESSURE		Model	Year
Main Bearing Oil Clearance	Shaft End Play	Spring Tension (Maximum)			Guide Clearance	Seat Angle					Pounds At M.P.H.	Low Limit§		
		Inlet	Exhaust	Low Limit		Inlet	Exhaust							
.001–.002	.003–.007	115@$1\frac{3}{8}$	115@$1\frac{3}{8}$	103	.0015–.0035	45°	45°	12B	Chain	†SP	37@30	20	.......C28S, C28W, 6 Cyl.	1941
.001–.002	.003–.007	137@$1\frac{21}{32}$	137@$1\frac{21}{32}$	120	.0015–.0035	45°	45°	6B	Chain	†SP	42@30	25	.......C30N, C30K, 8 Cyl.	
.001–.002	.003–.007	137@$1\frac{21}{32}$	137@$1\frac{21}{32}$	120	.0015–.0035	45°	45°	6B	Chain	†SP	37@30	20	..............C33, 8 Cyl.	
.001–.0015	.003–.007	115@$1\frac{3}{8}$	115@$1\frac{3}{8}$	103	.002–.004	45°	45°	12B	Chain	†SP	42@30	25	.......C34S, C34W, 6 Cyl.	1942
....	.003–.007	137@$1\frac{21}{32}$	137@$1\frac{21}{32}$	120	.002–.004	45°	45°	6B	Chain	†SP	42@30	25	.......C36K, C36N, 8 Cyl.	
.001–.0015	.003–.007	137@$1\frac{21}{32}$	137@$1\frac{21}{32}$	120	.002–.004	45°	45°	6B	Chain	†SP	45@30	25	..............C37, 8 Cyl.	
.001–.0015	.003–.007	115@$1\frac{3}{8}$	115@$1\frac{3}{8}$	103	.002–.004	45°	45°	12B	Chain	†SP	45@30	25	..............C38, 6 Cyl.	1948
.001–.0015	.003–.007	115@$1\frac{3}{8}$	115@$1\frac{3}{8}$	103	.002–.004	45°	45°	12B	Chain	†SP	45@30	25	.........C39 & C40, 8 Cyl.	
.0005–.0015	.003–.007	115@$1\frac{3}{8}$	115@$1\frac{3}{8}$	103	.002–.004	45°	45°	12B	Chain	†SP	52@45	30	..............C45, 6 Cyl.	1949
.0005–.0015	.003–.007	115@$1\frac{3}{8}$	115@$1\frac{3}{8}$	103	.002–.004	45°	45°	12B	Chain	†SP	52@45	30	.........C46, C47, 8 Cyl.	
.0005–.0015	.003–.007	115@$1\frac{3}{8}$	115@$1\frac{3}{8}$	103	.002–.004	45°	45°	12B	Chain	†SP	52@45	30	.... C48, 6 Cyl.	1950
.0005–.0015	.003–.007	115@$1\frac{3}{8}$	115@$1\frac{3}{8}$	103	.002–.004	45°	45°	12B	Chain	†SP	52@40	30	.... C49, C50, 8 Cyl.	
.0005–.0015	.003–.007	120@$1\frac{3}{8}$	120@$1\frac{3}{8}$	103	.002–.004	45°	45°	12B	Chain	†SP	50@20	30	C51-1, C51-2 Windsor, 6 Cyl.	1951
.0005–.0015	.002–.007	Inner-Outer■	Inner-Outer■	......	.002–.004	45°	45°	15B	Chain	†SP	65@20	35	C52 N.Y., C53-C54 Imp. 8 Cyl.	
.0005–.0015	.003–.007	120@$1\frac{3}{8}$	120@$1\frac{3}{8}$	......	.002–.004	45°	45°	12B	Chain	......	50@45	......	......C51-1, C51-2, 6 Cyl.	1952
.0005–.0015	.002–.007	Inner-Outer■	Inner-Outer■	......	.002–.004	45°	45°	15B	Chain	......	60@50	......	..C52, C53, C54, C55, 8 Cyl.	
.0005–.0015	.002–.007	115@1.375	115@1.375	......	.002	45°	45°	12B	Chain	......	50@30	......	..............C60-1, C60-2	1953
.0005–.0015	.002–.007	128@1.3125	128@1.5625	......	.002	45°	45°	15B	Chain	......	60@30	......	....C56-1, C56-2, C58, C59	1953

SP—Sprockets. ■—Inlet and exhaust Inner 42 lb. at $1\frac{3}{16}$, outer 138 lb. at $1\frac{5}{16}$ inches.

§—Car may be operated safely at lower oil pressures but low pressure indicates malfunction which should be corrected.

Piston Ring Dimensions

Year	Model	Cylinder Bore	TOP RING			SECOND RING			THIRD RING			OIL RING		
			Width	Gap	Depth	Width	Gap	Depth	Width	Gap	Depth	Width	Gap	Depth
1940–41	C25, C28..................	$3\frac{3}{8}$	$\frac{1}{8}$	.011	.150	$\frac{1}{8}$	.011	.145	$\frac{5}{32}$	.011	.145	$\frac{5}{32}$	.011	.145
	C26, C27, C30............	$3\frac{1}{4}$	$\frac{1}{8}$	.011	.150	$\frac{1}{8}$	.011	.145	$\frac{5}{32}$	.011	.145	$\frac{5}{32}$	.011	.145
1942–50	All 6 cylinder.............	$3\frac{7}{16}$	$\frac{3}{32}$	.011	.160	$\frac{3}{32}$	.011	.169	$\frac{5}{32}$	.011	.150	$\frac{5}{32}$	.011	.150
	All 8 cylinder.............	$3\frac{1}{4}$	$\frac{3}{32}$	.011	.162	$\frac{3}{32}$	.011	.162	$\frac{5}{32}$	.011	.145	$\frac{5}{32}$	.011	.145
1951	C-51........................	$3\frac{7}{16}$	$\frac{3}{32}$	.011	.169	$\frac{3}{32}$	.011	.169	$\frac{5}{32}$	.011	.150	$\frac{5}{32}$	.011	.150
	V8, C-52, C-53, C-54........	$3\frac{13}{16}$	$\frac{5}{64}$	.015	.191	$\frac{5}{64}$	.015	.191	$\frac{3}{16}$	.015	.165	......	......	......
1952	C51-1, C51-2, 6 Cyl.........	$3\frac{7}{16}$	$\frac{3}{32}$	.011	.1765	$\frac{3}{32}$	.011	.1765	$\frac{5}{32}$	.011	.178	$\frac{5}{32}$	.011	.178
	C52, C53, C54, C55, 8 Cyl.....	$3\frac{13}{16}$	$\frac{5}{64}$	.015	.204	$\frac{5}{64}$	.015	.204	$\frac{3}{16}$	.015	.198	......	......	......
1953	C-60-1, C-60-2, 6 Cyl........	$3\frac{7}{16}$	$\frac{3}{32}$	.011	.172	$\frac{3}{32}$	.011	.172	$\frac{5}{32}$	.011	.155	$\frac{5}{32}$	.011	.155
	C56-1, C56-2, C58, C59, 8 Cyl.	$3\frac{13}{16}$	$\frac{5}{64}$	.015	.191	$\frac{5}{64}$	.015	.191	$\frac{3}{16}$	.015	.150	......	......	......

Tension Wrench Specifications

Year	Model	Cylinder Head		Spark Plug		Connecting Rod Bolts or Nuts		Main Bearing Bolt		Flywheel Bolts		Vibration Damper Bolts	
		Lbs.–Ft.	Thread	Lbs.–Ft.	Thread	Lbs.–Ft.	Thread	Lbs.–Ft.	Thread	Lbs.–Ft.	Thread	Lbs.–Ft.	Thread
1941 to 48	All.................	52–57●	$\frac{7}{16}$	30–32	14 mm	45–50	$\frac{3}{8}$–24	75–80■	....	55–60	42–20	15–17	$\frac{5}{16}$
	Some................	85–90●	$\frac{1}{2}$	30–32	14 mm	50–75	$\frac{7}{16}$–24	75–80■	....	55–60	$\frac{1}{2}$–20	30–35	$\frac{3}{8}$
1949–50	C-45, 46, 47, 48, 49, 50.	65–70	....	30–32	14 mm	45–50	$\frac{3}{8}$–24	80–85	$\frac{1}{2}$–13	55-60	$\frac{1}{2}$–20	15–17	$\frac{5}{16}$
1951 to 53	C-51, 52, 53, 54......	80–85	....	30–32	14 mm	45–50	$\frac{3}{8}$–24	80–85	$\frac{1}{2}$–13	45–50	....	15–17	$\frac{5}{16}$

●—Nuts, capscrews, plain head (65–70); cap screws, cupped head (67–72). ■—Nuts, cap screws (80–85).

CHRYSLER SPECIFICATIONS

Front Wheel Alignment

Year	Model	Caster (deg.)	Camber (deg.)	King Pin Inclination (deg.)	Toe-In (inches)	Turning Radius Inner	Turning Radius Outer
1940	C25, C26, C27	1N to 1P	0 to ¾P	4¾ to 6	0 to ⅛	21½	20
1941–42	All	1N to 1P	0 to ¾P	4¾ to 6	0 to 1/16	22½	20
1946–48	C38, C39	1N to 1P	0 to ¾P	4¾ to 6	0 to 1/16	22	20
1949	C45, C46	1N to 3N	0 to ¾P	4¾ to 6	0 to 1/16	22	20
1950	C48, C49	1N to 3N	0 to ¾P	4¾ to 6	0 to 1/16	22	20
1951–53	C51, C60	1N to 3N	⅜N to ⅜P	5 to 6½	0 to 1/16	22	20
	C52, C54, C56, C58	1N to 3N	⅜N to ⅜P	5 to 6½	0 to 1/16	....	....
	C53, C59	1N to 3N	⅜N to ⅜P	6½ to 8	0 to 1/16	18¼	20

N—Negative. P—Positive.

Generators

Year	Model	Generator Number	Field Current at 6 Volts (amps.)	Maximum Safe Output Volts	Maximum Safe Output Amperes	Maximum Safe Output R.P.M.	Brush Spring Tension (oz.)	Voltage Regulator Number
1940	C25, 26, 27	GDZ-4801-A	1.3–1.5	8.0	35	2000	35–53	VRP-4001-A
1941	C28, C30N, C30K	GDZ-4801-A	1.3–1.5	8.0	35	2000	35–53	VRP-4001-A
	C33	GEG-4818-C	1.3–1.5	8.0	40	1575	64–68	VRP-4001-F
1942	C34, C36N, C36K	GDZ-4801-A	1.3–1.5	8.0	35	2000	35–53	VRP-4001-A
	C37	GEG-4818-C	1.3–1.5	8.0	40	1575	64–68	VRP-4001-F
1946 to 48	C38, C39	GDZ-4801-A	1.3–1.5	8.0	35	2000	35–53	VRP-4503-A
		GDZ-4801-R	1.3–1.5	8.0	35	2000	35–53	VRP-4503-A
1949	C45	GDZ-4801-R	1.3–1.5	8.0	35	2000	35–53	VRP-4503-A
		GGW-6001-A	1.6–1.8	8.0	40	2000	35–53	VRP-4503-B
	C46	GGU-6001-A	1.4–1.5	8.0	45	1650	35–53	VBA-4101-B
		GGJ-6001-B	1.5–1.7	8.0	50	1600	30–37	VBA-4101-A
	C47	GGJ-6001-A	1.5–1.7	8.0	50	1600	30–37	VBA-4101-A
1950	C48	GGW-6001-A	1.6–1.8	8.0	40	2000	35–53	VRP-6004
	C49, C50	GGU-6001-A	1.4–1.5	8.0	45	1650	35–53	VBA-4101
1951	C51, C52, C54	GGU-6001-R	1.7–1.8	6.0	40	1650	35–53	VBA-4101-B
	C53	GGJ-6003-A	1.5–1.7	8.0	50	1600	30–37	VBA-4101-A
1952	C51-1, C51-2, 6 cyl.	GGW-6001	....	....	....	....	....	VBE-6001-A
	C52, C54, C55, 8 cyl.	GGU-6001	....	....	....	....	....	VAV-6001-B
	C53, 8 cyl.	GGJ-6003	1.5–1.7	....	....	....	....	VBF-6001
1953	C60–C56	GGW-6001	....	7.4	57	1000	....	VRP-6004-A
	C58	GGU-6001	....	7.4	62	900	....	VAV-6001-B
	C59	GHM-6002	....	14.8	38	800	....	VRX-6003-A

Cooling System Capacities and Anti-Freeze Proportion Table

CAR AND YEAR	MODEL	Capacity Qts.	Quarts of Methanol Base Anti-Freeze (For Protection to Temperature Shown Below)							Quarts of Ethylene Glycol (For Protection to Temperature Shown Below)							Quarts of Denatured Alcohol—188 Proof (For Protection to Temperature Shown Below)						
			3	4	5	6	7	8	9	3	4	5	6	7	8	9	3	4	5	6	7	8	9
1940-48	Six	18	17	8	−1	−12	−25	−38	−53	19	14	7	0	−10	−21	−34	20	10	....	0	−10	....	−20
1942-48	Eight	26	22	17	12	7	1	−7	−14	....	....	17	13	8	3	−3	....	20	....	....	10	0	....
1949-50	C48	17	15	6	−14	−16	−29	−45	....	18	12	5	−4	−14	−27	−42	....	10	0	....	−10	−20	−30
1949-50	C49, 50	21	19	12	5	−3	−12	−22	−34	....	17	12	6	0	−9	−17	−20	....	10	....	0	−10	....
1951-53	C51, C60	15	11	1	−12	−27	−44	....	....	16	8	0	−12	−26	−43	....	....	10	0	−10	−20	−30	....
1951-53	C52, C53, C54, C56, C58, C59—V8	25	22	17	11	6	−2	−9	−18	....	20	16	12	7	1	−5	−20	....	....	10	....	0	....

Voltage Regulators

Year	Model	Regulator Number	Grounded P=Position N=Negative	Voltage Control: Air Gap Points Closed	Voltage Control: Voltage Setting Hot	Current Control: Air Gap Points Closed	Current Control: Current Set Hot	Cut-Out Relay: Point Gap	Cut-Out Relay: Air Gap	Cut-Out Relay: Closing Volt
1941	C28S, C28W, C30N, C30K	VRP-4001-F	P	.052	7.3	.052	39–41	.015	.034	6.4–7.0
	C28S, C28W	VRP-4001-A	P	.052	7.2	.038	34–36	.015	.034	6.4–7.0
	C33	VRP-4001-F	P	.052	7.3	.052	39–41	.015	.034	6.4–7.0
1942	C34S, C34W, C36	VRP-4001-A	P	.052	7.2	.038	34–36	.015	.034	6.4–7.0
		VRP-4001-B	P	.052	7.2	.052	31–33	.015	.034	6.4–7.0
		VRP-4001-G	P	.052	7.2	.052	39–41	.015	.034	6.4–7.0
		VRP-4001-F	P	.052	7.3	.052	39–41	.015	.034	6.4–7.0
1946 to 48	C38, C39	VRP-4001-F	P	.052	7.3	.052	39–41	.015	.034	6.4–7.0
		VRP-4503-A	P	.052	7.2	.052	35	.015	.034	6.4–7.0
		VAV-4404-A	P	.052	7.2	.052	50	.015	.034	6.4–7.0
1949	C45, C46	VRP-4503-A	P	.052	7.2	.052	35	.015	.034	6.4–7.0
		VRP-4503-B	P	.052	7.2	.052	40	.015	.034	6.4–7.0
		VBA-4101-A	P	.052	7.2	.052	50	.015	.034	6.4–7.0
		VBA-4101-B	P	.052	7.2	.052	50	.015	.034	6.4–7.0
1950–51	All	VAV-6001-A	P	.050	7.2	.050	51		.032	6.4–7.0
		VRP-6004-A	P	.051	7.2	.050	38–42		.032	6.4–7.0
1952	C51-1, C51-2, 6 cyl.	VBE-6001-A			7.1–7.4		45–57			6.4–7.0
	C52, C54, C55, 8 cyl.	VAV-6001-B			7.1–7.4		60–62			6.4–7.0
	C53, 8 cyl.	VBF-6001			7.1–7.4		55–72			6.4–7.0
1953	C60, C56	VRP-6004-A			7.1–7.4		45–57			6.3–6.8
	C58	VAV-6001-B			7.1–7.4		50–62			6.3–6.8
	C59	VRX-6003-A			14.2–14.8		25–38			13.0–13.75

Starters

Year	Model	Unit Model Number	Spring Tension (oz.)	STARTER Lock Test: Volts	Lock Test: Amperes	Lock Test: Torque, (lbs. ft.)	No Load: Volts	No Load: Amperes	No Load: R.P.M.	Direction of Rotation Viewed from. Drive End C=Clockwise CC=Counter-clockwise
1940	C25	MAX-4020-A	42–53	2.0	335	6	5.0	65	4300	C
	C26	MAX-4037	42–53	2.0	410	8	5.0	65	4900	C
1941	C28, C30K, C30N, C33	MAX-4045	42–53	2.0	410	8	5.0	65	4900	C
		MAX-4045-A	42–53	2.0	410	8	5.0	65	4900	C
1942 to 48	All 6 & 8 cyl.	MAX-4050	42–53	2.0	410	8	5.0	65	4900	C
1949–50	C45, C46, C47, C48, C49, C50	MCL-6101	42–53	2.0	410	8	5.0	65	4900	C
1951	C51, C52, C53, C54	MCL-6109	42–53	2.0	410	8	6.0	57.5	5300	C
1952	C51-1, C51-2, 6 cyl., C52, V53, C54, C55	MCL-6109	42–53	2	410	8	6	50–65	5300	C
1953	C60, C56, C58	MCL-6117	42–53	3	610	15	5.5	50.65	5300	C
	C59	MDB-6001A	42–53	3	212	11	11	25.33	3800	C

CHRYSLER 1940 thru 1953

FRONT SUSPENSION

1940 MODELS

The suspension used on 1940 models was somewhat different from that used on later models in that the upper suspension arm was formed in the shape of a hook, having one open end on to which the knuckle support upper bushing (eccentric) was threaded to secure caster and camber adjustment.

1942-1953 MODELS

The major difference between these later models and the 1940 models is that the upper suspension arm straddled the upper pin of the knuckle support.

An eccccentric bushing was fitted into the upper end of the knuckle support and threaded on to the upper suspension arm outer pin.

In spite of this structural difference service procedure is almost identical on both types of construction.

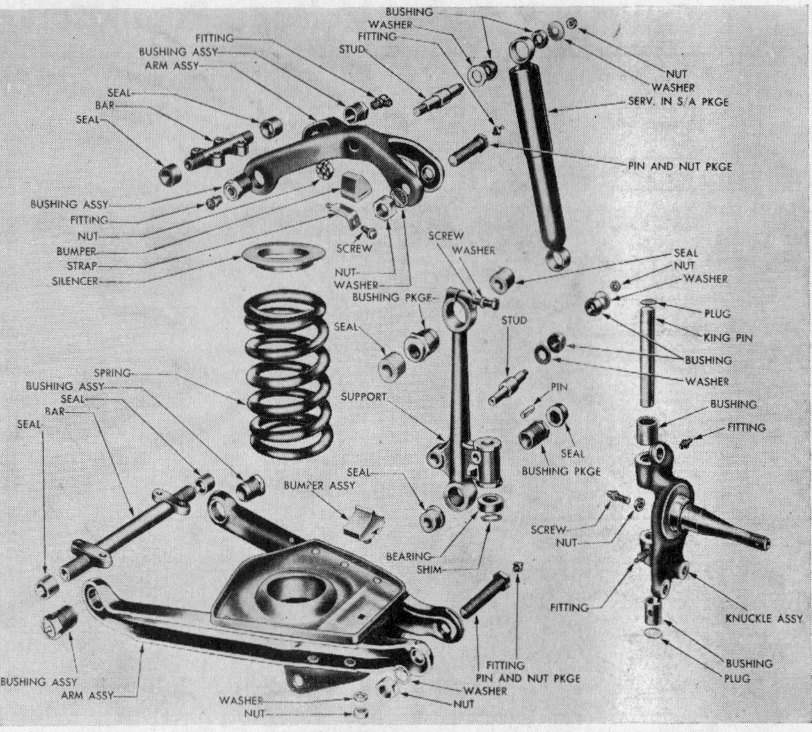

Front Suspension

Caster, Camber and Toe-In Adjustment

Caster and camber are both adjusted at the eccentric bushing in the upper end of the knuckle support.

The bushing is turned in a clockwise direction to increase caster. When properly adjusted the upper end of the knuckle support will be approximately midway in the yoke of the upper suspension arm. Since caster and camber are both adjusted at the same eccentric bushing it will be necessary to seek a compromise between the best caster and camber adjustment.

Where it is desired to come to an exact adjustment it will be necessary to secure the caster adjustment by turning the eccentric bushing until the exact caster reading is secured. Then it will be necessary to cold bend the knuckle support to secure the exact camber reading.

Caution: At no time should heat be applied to the knuckle supports since these parts are heat treated after forging and reheating to simplify bending will destroy the heat treatment and render the part useless.

REPLACEMENT OF FRONT SUSPENSION PARTS

Upper and Lower Suspension Arm Pins and Bushings

On 1940 models the upper suspension arm was fitted with a bushing but the pin was an integral part of the upper suspension arm itself.

Both upper and lower suspension arm pin and bushings can be serviced with the road wheel in place. However, the job is greatly simplified if front wheels are removed.

When installing either the upper or the lower suspension arm pins and bushings they should be set into the car so that the knuckle support is approximately in the center at both the lower and upper suspension arm.

To replace the upper eccentric bushing on the 1940 Models proceed as follows: Support the weight of the car at the outer end of the lower suspension arm and loosen the clamp bolt at the upper end of the knuckle support and unscrew the eccentric bushing from off of the end of the upper suspension arm.

1942 thru 1953 Models

To replace the upper suspension arm pin and bushing on these models take the weight of the car at the outer end of the lower suspension arm and remove the road wheel.

Loosen the clamp bolt at the upper end of the knuckle support and remove the nut from the upper support arm pin. Unscrew the knuckle support arm pin and rock the knuckle support out of the upper support arm and push out the eccentric bushing.

When replacing the pin and bushing, first place the bushing in the knuckle support and place both oil seals on the bushing. Rock the knuckle support up into the upper support arm, forcing the two oil seals into place.

Holding the knuckle support nicely centered between the yoke of the upper suspension arm, start the pin in and

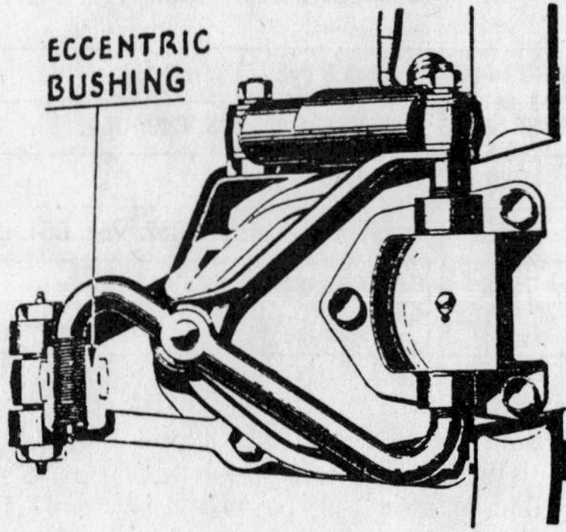

Upper suspension arm, 1940 models

screw it through the suspension arm into the eccentric bushing, all the way through and put the nut and lockwasher on the other end.

Replace the clamp bolt in the knuckle support and clamp securely.

Where no front end aligning equipment is available, it is customary to set the eccentric to full camber.

Upper Suspension Arm Inner Shaft & Bushings

1942 THRU 1953 MODELS

The upper suspension arm inner shaft and bushings can be replaced by supporting the weight of the A frame on a jack and unbolting the inner shaft from the top of the frame. These bolts are accessible from the engine compartment.

Remove the front and rear bushings from the inner end of the upper suspension arm. The shaft can then be slid out from the arm itself.

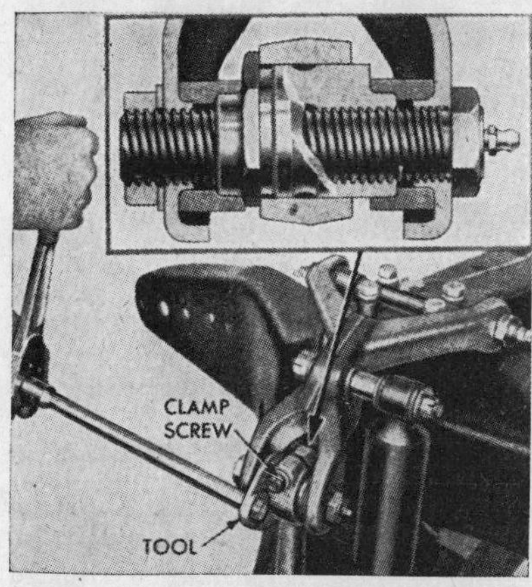

Arrangement of upper suspension arm eccentric bushing 1941 thru 1951 models

Lower Suspension Arm (A Frame) Inner Arm and Bushings

To replace the lower suspension arm inner shaft and bushings, disconnect the shock absorber at either end and disconnect the torsion bar. It is perhaps safer to place a jack under the inner shaft and unbolt it from the frame, after which it can be lowered to the floor, releasing the spring pressure.

With the weight of the spring released from the lower suspension arm, the bushings may be removed from the inner shaft and the shaft taken out.

Replacement of King Pins

All Chrysler models built since 1940 used anti-friction needle bearings at the upper end of the king pin. 1941 8-cylinder models and 1948 late production 8-cylinder models used needle bearings at the top and bottom of the king pin. However, for all these models bushings are available as replacements.

To replace the king pin, remove the wheel and the brake backing plate.

Note: On models with two cylinders on the front brakes the backing plate can be removed with the steering arm remaining bolted to the knuckle. On models with single cylinder front brakes the two anchor bolts are also the attaching bolts for the steering arm.

On models with two front wheel cylinders it is necessary to disconnect the brake hose in order to take the backing plate off the cylinder. On models with two front cylinders the backing plate can be removed from the spindle without disconnecting the hydraulic line.

In either case it will be necessary to perform a major brake adjustment on the front brakes after the backing plate is remounted.

Drive the king pin lock pin forward to remove.

Remove the upper welsh plug by piercing it with a sharp punch and prying it out and drive the king pin and lower welsh plug out through the bottom.

Replacement of Front Coil Spring

If it becomes necessary to replace a front coil spring, first examine the pins and bushings in the front suspension, particularly the pins and bushings in the knuckle support since the coil spring can be replaced by detaching the knuckle support at any point. For instance, if the upper suspension arm pin and bushing require replacement and the coil spring also needs replacing, the system should be opened by removing the upper knuckle support pin and bushings and letting the lower suspension arm down, releasing the pressure from the spring.

If the spring alone requires replacement, then the following procedure is probably the easiest:

Jack the car up until wheels are at least 8 inches off the floor and place jacks under the frame to hold the car. Detach the shock absorber and tortion bar. Place a roller jack to the inner shaft of the lower suspension arm and take out the four bolts which hold the inner shaft to the front cross member. Lower the inner end of the A frame until the tension is off the front spring.

Install a new front spring, being careful that any shims which were found under the old spring are placed under the new one. Extra care should be taken to make certain that the lower end of the coil is properly seated in the A frame.

Jack the lower A frame back into place, guiding it carefully with a long drift pin.

Securely tighten the four bolts which hold the inner shaft to the front cross member and reconnect the shock absorber and tortion bar.

When it is necessary to replace a front coil spring it is a good idea to check carefully to determine if any of the other front suspension parts require replacement. If, for instance, the upper suspension arm bushing required replacement it would be better to detach the spring at the defective bushing, since the knuckle support can be detached at any point.

INTERMEDIATE STEERING ARM BEARINGS

1949 to 1953 Models Only

To replace the intermediate steering arm bearings, first detach the drag link from the intermediate steering arm and detach both tie rods from the intermediate steering arm.

Remove the bolts which hold the intermediate steering arm to the frame and work the arm out of the frame.

Mount the bracket in a vise and remove the nut and pin which hold the intermediate arm pin which goes down through the center of the intermediate steering arm bearings.

Pry the arm and bearings out of the bracket and remove the oil seals, bearings and, using a drift pin, drive out the bearing cups.

If either of the bearings are found to be defective it will be necessary to replace both bearings with new ones.

Install new bearing cups, bearings and oil seals and work the arm back into the bracket, installing a new pin and nut.

Take the entire assembly to the car and work it back into the frame, replacing the bolts which hold the bracket to the frame.

Reconnect both of the tie rods and the drag link.

STEERING GEAR ASSEMBLY

All Chrysler models from 1940 to 1953 are equipped with the Gemmer worm and roller type steering gear.

The Model C 53, 1951, is equipped with a Hydroguide steering gear. This type steering gear can also be installed as extra equipment on 1951 Model C 52. It is also used on all 8 cylinder models for 1952 and 1953.

Horn Button Removal

1940 MODELS

On these models the horn button is held by three screws underneath the steering wheel. Remove the screws and lift off the horn blowing ring.

1941-1948 MODELS

Before attempting to remove the horn button, examine under the steering wheel. If there are three screws under the wheel then these three screws hold the horn button in place. Some models, however, did not have screws holding the horn ring in place and on these models it is necessary to simply pry the button up to remove it.

1949-1953 MODELS

On these models the horn blowing ring is held in place by four screws underneath the steering wheel.

Steering Wheel Removal

On all models of Chrysler the steering wheel can be removed by first taking off the horn button and horn wiring attaching pad. Remove the nut which holds the steering wheel to the steering tube, and use a puller to take off the steering wheel.

Steering Gear Assembly Removal

1940 MODELS

On 1940 models the steering gear can be removed by taking out the front seat, and removing the steering wheel. Detach the transmission shift mechanism. Then remove the bolts which hold the upper jacket tube to the lower jacket tube and lift off the upper tube. Remove the jacket which holds the steering mechanism to the dash panel, disconnect the pitman arm and take out the steering gear mounting bolts.

The steering gear mechanism is then removed by lowering the top of the steering column to the floor and drawing the gear out over the top of the radiator.

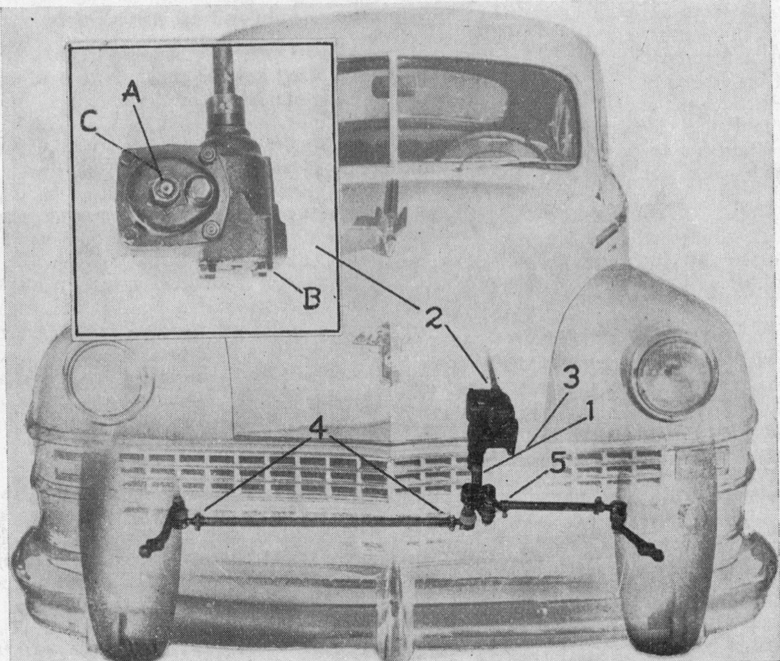

Adjustment of Steering Mechanism 1940 to 1948

1941-1948 MODELS

On these models the steering gear assembly is removed down between the engine and the frame after all the attaching parts such as the steering wheel, direction signal wires, gear shift mechanism and mounting brackets have been removed.

1949-1953 MODELS

On these models the steering gear mechanism is lifted up into the car after all attaching parts have been removed, such as the shift mechanism, directional signal wires, pitman arm, steering wheel, horn button wires, etc.

Adjustment of Steering Mechanism

Refer to the two illustrations on this page for the location of the adjusting points.

1. Disconnect the pitman arm from the tie rods.
2. Adjust the steering gear housing assembly.

This gear is the Gemmer double roller tooth type with external mesh screw adjustment.

(A) Loosen the cross shaft mesh adjusting screw lock nut and back off on the adjusting screw so that there is plenty of play between the worm and roller tooth before adjusting the worm bearings.

(B) Loosen or remove the four cap screws which hold the housing lower cover in place and remove one shim at a time to take out the worm bearing end plate. Bearings should be adjusted so that there is zero play in the worm bearing but no definite preload.

(C) Turn the steering wheel to the midposition of its travel and adjust the mesh of the worm roller by turning the adjusting screw inward until there is zero lash between the gears on the high spot. Tighten the lock nut.

3. Reconnect the tie rods to pitman arm.
4. Adjust the long tie rod with the steering wheel in midposition of its travel so that one half the total toe-in is in the right wheel. Tighten the lock nuts.
5. Now adjust the short tie rod so that the remaining toe-in is taken up in the left wheel and tighten the lock nuts. Turn the steering wheel from one extreme to the other to check for roughness or binding.

BRAKES

All Chrysler models use Lockheed internal expanding hydraulically operated brakes, except the Imperial models of 1950 thru 1953. On the 1950 and 1951 Imperial models a disc type, self adjusting brake is used.

A two cylinder front brake was used on all New Yorker and Crown Imperial models from 1940. The same two cylinder front wheel brake was used on all Chrysler production models starting in 1947 (except the 1950 thru 1953 Imperial models).

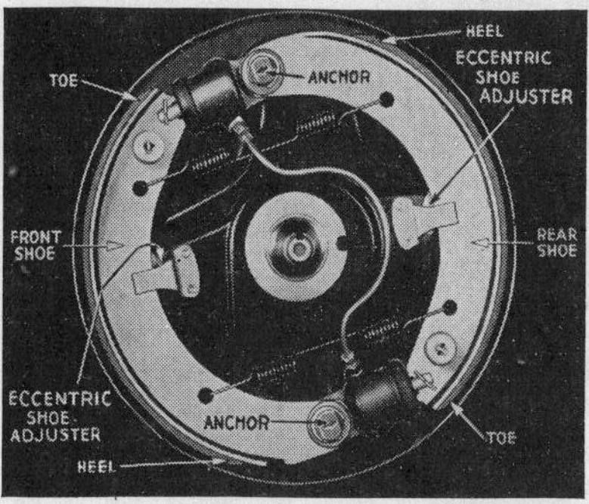

Chrysler two cylinder front brake. Note position of arrows on anchor for initial setting

Minor Brake Adjustment

Minor brake adjustment is done to compensate for normal lining wear.

Jack up the car and turn the adjustment cam on each shoe until the shoe drags and then back it off until it is just free. Repeat this operation at all four wheels.

Major Brake Adjustment

Before making a major brake adjustment, first remove at least one of the road wheels and drums to determine the condition of the lining. Carefully examine the wheel cylinders to make sure there is no leaking or seepage at any of the wheel cylinders. If any leaking or seepage is detected at the wheel which is being examined, it is a good idea to remove all the wheels and make a complete inspection of the hydraulic system. If more than one of the wheel cylinders is found to be defective it is a good idea to remove all the wheel cylinders and the master cylinder so that they can be honed and refitted with cups and boots.

Since most of the Chrysler drums are not fitted with an inspection port for the insertion of a feeler gauge, a dummy drum or a brake centering gauge or an axle type lining grinder is required to insure that the brakes are being adjusted properly.

Before starting the anchor adjustment, remove all the drums to determine the position of the anchors. On the front brakes (with two cylinders) the arrow on the brake anchor should point toward the adjacent cylinder.

On rear brakes or front brakes with single cylinders the arrows on the anchor pins should point toward each other. If they are not in this position it will be necessary to set them into this position before beginning the anchor adjustment.

Since the anchor pins on most Chryslers cannot be turned from the backing plate side it is absolutely essential that a dummy drum or centering gauge or axle type lining grinder be used to properly adjust the brakes.

In an emergency the anchor pins can be left in the position they were set in and the brakes assembled and a minor adjustment done on the brakes after securely tightening the anchor pins.

Hand Brake Adjustment

EXTERNAL TYPE HAND BRAKE

Fully release the hand brake lever and check the clearance at the brake between the anchor bracket and the drum. This clearance should not exceed .005 inch. Adjust the lining to drum clearance so there is between .015 and .020 in. clearance between the lining and the drum. After the lining is properly adjusted, pull all the slack out of the hand brake cable and reconnect.

Chrysler single cylinder brake. Note that the arrows on the anchor pins point towards each other for initial setting

INTERNAL TYPE HAND BRAKE

Place the hand brake lever in the fully released position, and place the gear shift selector lever in the neutral position.

Detach the front half of the propeller shaft to permit the drum to be turned by hand and remove the adjusting plate cover from the brake dust plate.

Loose the cable guide clamping bolt and the adjusting nut.

Expand the shoes at the adjusting nut until a slight drag is felt and then back off approximately one notch. This will give approximately .010 in. clearance to the brake shoes.

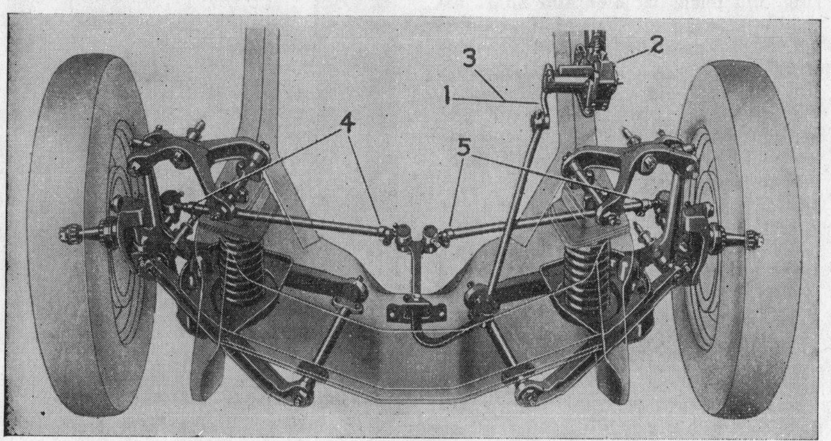

Adjustment of steering mechanism 1949 to 1953 models

HAND BRAKE ADJUSTMENT—*cont'd*

The cable adjusting nut is positioned against the cable housing. See that there is from .005 to .010 inch clearance between the operating lever and the brake shoe cable.

Tighten the cable clamp and adjusting nut against the housing.

Brake Booster Adjustment

A vacuum operated booster was used on some of the Crown Imperial models.

The adjustment of the cylinder unit is as follows:

Remove the clevis pin from the master cylinder push rod and the clevis pin from the booster push rod.

Adjust the master cylinder push rod to obtain the desired toe board pedal clearance.

Loosen the booster cylinder check nuts (these are the two nuts which hold the booster cylinder to its frame bracket).

Now adjust the push rod on the booster cylinder so that with the pedal held in the fully released position the clevis pin will just enter its hole with all of the clearance forward.

Maintaining the cylinder in this position retighten the check nuts which hold the cylinder to the frame bracket.

COOLING SYSTEM

Water Pump

The water pump assembly on all Chrysler models including the 1951 V-8 is essentially the same type pump, and while they are various shapes and sizes the service procedure is practically the same for all of them. All are of the so called packless type, except for the V-8 model, and the New Yorker and Imperial models, and all are equipped with bronze bushings.

The 1951 thru 1953 V-8 model is equipped with two annular ball bearings and the New Yorker and Imperial models are equipped with a ball bearing which is integral to the shaft.

Removal of Water Pump

On all Chrysler models the water pump can be removed without removing the radiator core. In general the procedure is to remove the fan blades, detach all hose connections, and on models which use a fan shroud, take off the fan shroud.

The water pump can then be detached from the block and lifted off.

Note: On 1951 thru 1953 V-8 models the water pump is bolted to the water manifold in the front of the block.

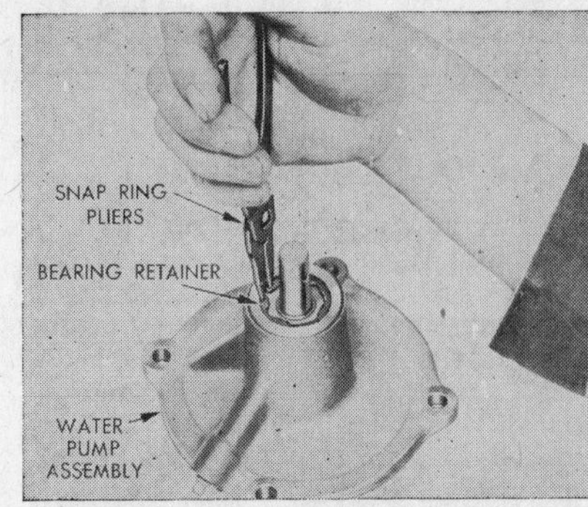

V-8 models—removing or installing water pump bearing retainer (tool C-760)

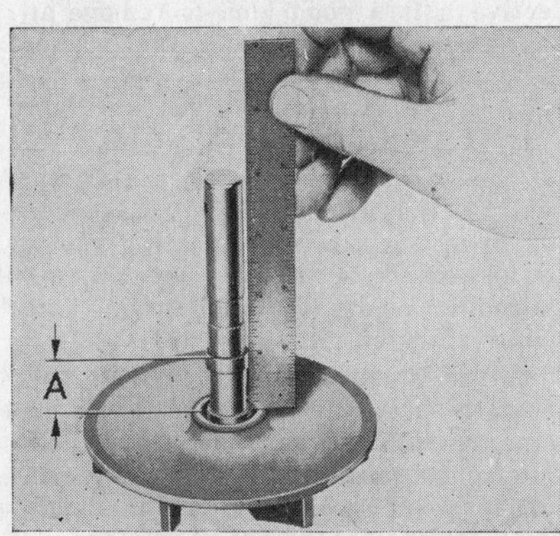

V-8 models—measuring water pump impeller and shaft setting

Disassembly of Water Pump

1951 THRU 1953 V-8 MODELS

Drive out the fan hub pin, and using a puller pull off the fan hub.

Remove the bearing retainer snap ring and push impeller and shaft assembly through the rear of the body.

Remove the lock ring which holds the seal and take out the seal retainer and seal. Take out the outer shaft bearing, the spacer, the inner shaft spacer, and the water pump impeller. The entire pump is now ready for inspection.

For maximum efficiency the distance between the shaft shoulder and the impeller hub face should be between 1-1/8 inch and 1-3/16 inch. The sealing surface should be free of pits and scores.

ALL 8 CYLINDER MODELS EXCEPT THE V-8

Note: Some of the 8 cylinder water pumps have a pin holding the fan hub to the shaft. Examine the shaft for a pin and if the pin is found it must first be driven out before the hub can be removed from the shaft.

First remove the impeller from the shaft using a puller. The thrust spring, the seal spring, seal and seal retainer washer are assembled in the impeller. To remove the seal parts, take out the lock ring which retains them in the impeller.

Using a puller take off the fan pulley hub. Remove the bearing lock ring and pull the shaft and bearing assembly out of the housing. It is recommended that a new hub and a new impeller be used anytime they are removed from the shaft since these parts are a pressed fit on the shaft.

When assembled, the end play of the shaft should be from .002 to .004 inch. measured with a feeler gauge between the pump body and the fan pulley hub.

ALL 6 CYLINDER MODELS

Drive out the fan pulley hub pin and press off the fan hub. Remove the pump cover and pull the impeller and shaft assembly out of the pump body.

It is not necessary to separate the impeller from the shaft since these two are serviced as a unit.

To remove the bushings, drive the pins which retain the bushings to the housing into the shaft hole and use a

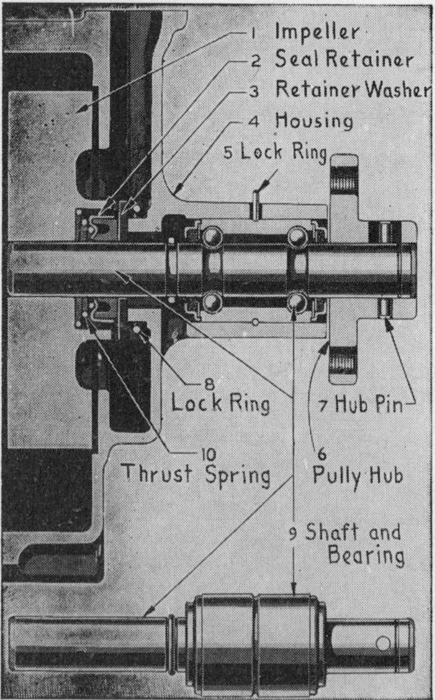

Sectional view of water pump used on in-line 8 cylinder models

puller to remove the front and rear bushings from the pump body, pulling them both toward the front.

The pump parts are assembled in the following sequence. Install impeller on shaft, making the back of the impeller flush with the end of the shaft. This is not necessary if a new shaft and impeller assembly is being used. Install water pump seal thrust spring, install water pump seal retainer, install water pump seal, install water pump seal retainer washer and lock ring.

Thermostat

On all Chrysler models the thermostat is located in a thermostat housing on the cylinder head. On the V-8 models the thermostat housing is located at the front of the water manifold.

Radiator Core Removal

1949-1953 MODELS

On these models the radiator core is mounted with two bolts on each side. These bolts pass through the radiator frame and into the side mounting of the sheet metal on the front end of the car. If the car is equipped with a heater the lower right hand mounting bolts will be difficult of access.

On some cars the bolt is driven from the front toward the back and may be reached by removing the shroud from between the radiator core and the grille. On other mountings the bolt is driven from the back toward the front and in order to get at this bolt it is necessary to remove the cover from underneath the fender (which gives access to the valves).

To take out the core remove these four bolts, disconnect the hoses and lift the core straight upward.

1941 8 CYLINDER MODELS

On these models it is necessary to remove the front end sheet metal, including both front fenders, grille and grille panel assemblies, in order to take out the radiator core.

1940-1951 ALL MODELS, 6's AND 8's, EXCEPT 1941 STRAIGHT 8 CYLINDER AND THE V-8

On these models the radiator core is removed after taking off the water hoses, headlight wires, fan shroud (if any) and the water pump assembly.

Note: It will be necessary to remove the upper and lower radiator shield on the 1949 and 1951 models. The radiator can then be unbolted from its side mountings and lifted up and over the engine.

Water Distribution Tube

A water distribution tube is used on all 6's and straight 8 engines. On the 6 cylinder engines the distribution tube is located immediately back of the water pump. It may be taken out by removing the radiator core and the water pump. On straight 8 cylinder models the water distribution tube is located back of the large welsh plug just adjacent to the water pump. When installing a new water distribution tube it is essential that the new tube be flared on the end in a manner similar to the old tube.

To remove the tube, a rod is formed into a hook at one end and is slid into the distribution tube hooking one of the holes in the tube. If the distribution tube seems to be stuck or corroded in place it is a good idea to thoroughly flush out the block rather than attempting to force the tube out of the block.

ENGINE ASSEMBLY

Chrysler supplied both 6 and 8 cylinder engines in every year of their production. Up to and including 1950 the 8 cylinder engine was of the in-line L-head variety. In 1951 a V-8 overhead valve engine was introduced by Chrysler.

Engine Removal

1940 TO 1948 MODELS

On these models the engine and transmission assembly is removed as a unit, after removing the radiator core.

Note: On 1941 8-cylinder models it is necessary to remove the front end sheet metal as a unit in order to take out the radiator core.

Before lifting out the engine make certain that all the attaching parts such as wires leading to the transmission, shift links, clutch, linkage, battery cables, heat indicators, gas lines, oil pressure guage lines, etc., are detached.

1949-1953 MODELS, EXCEPT V-8

On these models to remove the engine it is necessary to first remove the transmission and radiator core. Then take off all attaching parts and lift out the engine.

V-8 MODELS

The engine on these models is removed as follows. Disconnect the propeller shaft from the transmission and

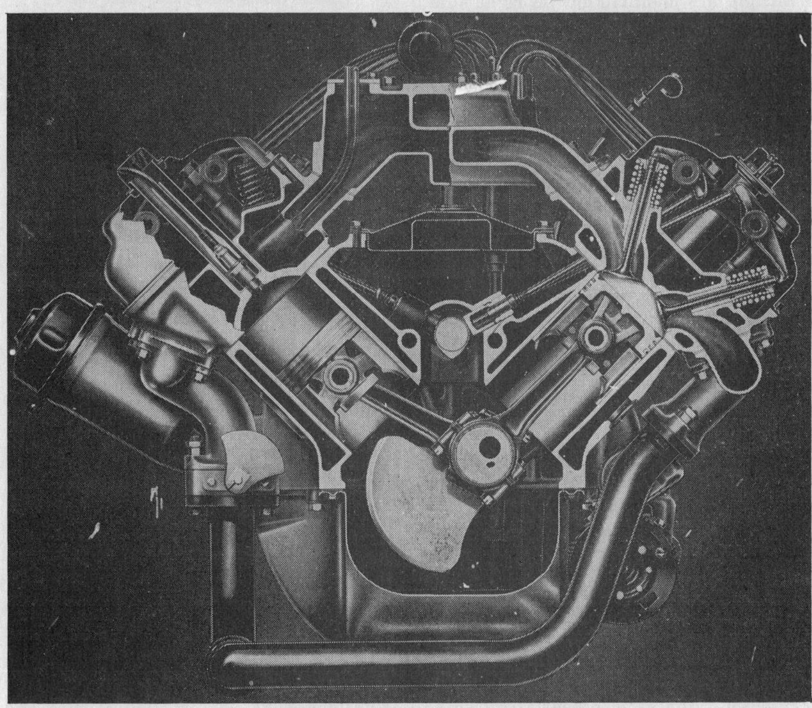

Front sectional view of the V8 engine

ENGINE REMOVAL—*continued*

all the wires and linkage at the transmission. Take off the exhaust pipes and remove the hood and battery. Disconnect the usual items under the hood such as fuel lines, radiator hoses, wires, etc. Take off the carburetor assembly and remove the radiator shroud (if one is used).

Place a jack under the transmission and then remove the engine rear support bolts and take out the cross member which supports the rear of the transmission. Remove the engine front support mounting bolts and lower the transmission at the back, raise the engine at the front and at the same time work it out toward the front left fender.

Note: By working the engine out toward the left front fender it is possible to remove it without disturbing the heater system. While the instructions given above show how to remove an engine without disturbing the radiator core, it is always good practice from a safety standpoint to either remove the core or to place a thin piece of plywood against the inside of the core to protect it from possible accidental damage.

Engine Manifolds

On all Chrysler engines except the V-8 model the intake and exhaust manifold are mounted on the right side of the engine and are joined together just underneath the carburetor. A heat riser valve is used in the exhaust manifold to deflect the exhaust gases toward the intake manifold when the engine is cool. The heat riser valve is operated by a thermostatic spring which causes it to move to the off position when the engine reaches operating temperature. The only service required by the heat riser is to see that the valve is free and operates freely.

An inoperative valve may cause the engine to warm up slowly, resulting in excessive use of the choke, or it may cause the engine to apparently run lean when it is hot.

ENGINE INTERNAL

Piston and Connecting Rod Assemblies

The four ring aluminum pistons are used on all Chrysler models, except the V-8 model which used a three ring piston.

If for any reason the connecting rod bearing cap is to be detached from the connecting rod it is essential on this, or in fact any engine, that the cap and rod be marked so that the cap will be put back on the rod in the same position it occupied before it was removed.

On many engines the connecting rod cap can be put on backwards with sometimes disastrous results to the rod bearing.

Some connecting rods are stamped with the number of the cylinder into which the rod is fitted. In many instances this stamp is on both the rod itself and the cap. In this case it is unnecessary to stamp or mark the cap since the number will act as an index mark.

When working on piston and connecting rod assemblies which have been removed from the engine, it is always considered good practice to replace the cap on the bottom of the connecting rod as soon as it has been removed from the engine so that the cap will not become separated from its rod and the bearing shell will not be lost.

CYLINDER HEAD NUT TIGHTENING SEQUENCE

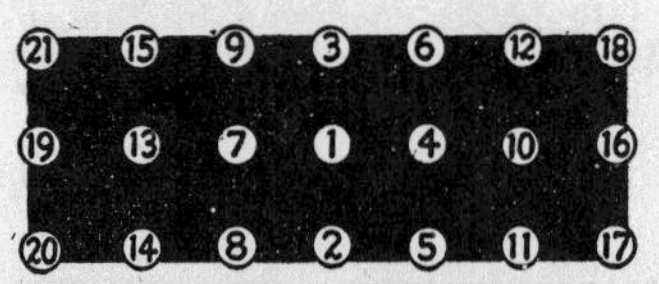

6 cylinder L-head

8 cylinder L-head

Assembly of Piston to Connecting Rod

On all engines, except the V-8, the slotted side of the piston should be assembled to the side of the connecting rod which has the oil spit hole. When assembling the rod and piston assemblies to the cylinder the slotted side of the piston should be pointed away from the camshaft (valves).

V8 ENGINES

The V8 engine used an aluminum slipper type piston which was stamped with the letter "F" alongside of the piston pin hole. This letter "F" should always be installed toward the front of the engine.

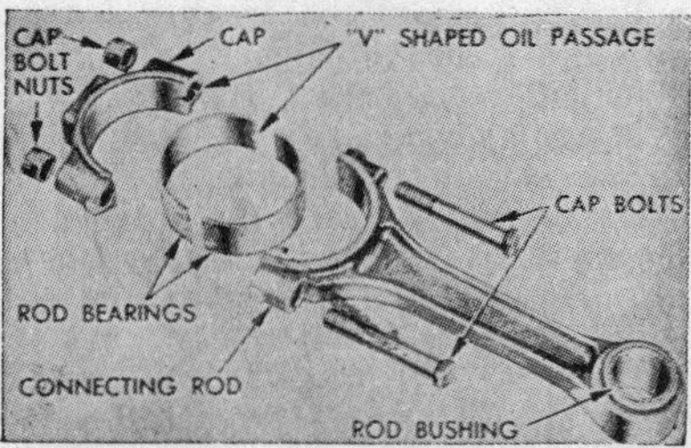

Note V groove in connecting rod cap

The lower end of the connecting rod is chamfered on one side. This chamfer should always be placed toward the front of the engine. Therefore, when assembling the piston to the connecting rod make certain that the "F" on the piston is on the same side as the chamfer on the connecting rod.

Notice that there is a "V" shaped oil passage in the rod bearing cap on these engines. Notice further that on the left bank this "V" groove will be towards the left when the chamfered part of the connecting rod (the "F" on the piston) is facing the operator, whereas on the right bank the "V" notch will be to the right when the chamfer on the connecting rod is facing the operator.

This means that the V-groove cut in the bearing cap will face upward toward the cam shaft. This V-groove is intended to splash oil on the cylinder wall of the opposite cylinder.

Connecting Rod Bearings

Connecting rod bearings in all Chryslers are of the precision, slip-in type and Chrysler does not recommend adjusting the rod bearing.

Rod bearings are available for all models in a variety of undersizes. However, if it becomes necessary to make an adjustment on the rod bearing do not under any circumstances file either the cap or the connecting rod as this will destroy their usefulness. It is possible to install a specially designed shim between the lower half of the bearing shell and the bearing cap. As much as .003 inch may be taken up by this method.

The procedure is as follows: Remove the connecting rod bearing cap and separate the bearing shell from the cap. Place the shim stock on the inner surface of the bearing cap and place the shell on top of the shim. See to it that the shim does not extend beyond either end of the connecting rod bearing shell.

Bolt the cap back up on the connecting rod and check, by rotating the crankshaft, that it does not in any way or at any point bind the shaft.

A very slight binding is permissible. However, if a slight binding is found it will be necessary to loosen that bearing cap somewhat so as not to confuse the bind on that bearing cap with the possible bind on the next bearing adjusted.

While a slight bind is permissible, the total of the bind on all of the connecting rods should not be enough to bind the shaft so that it cannot be turned by hand.

Main Bearings

The main bearings on all Chrysler cars are of precision, slip-in type and may be replaced without removing the crankshaft. The fit of the main bearings may be checked either by the plastic guage method or by the shim stock method. Plastic guage stock is supplied with complete instructions for its use.

To check the fit of a main bearing with shim stock proceed as follows: First determine that the crank shaft will turn freely with all bearings bolted in place. Then, one at a time, remove the main bearing cap and place a piece of shim stock .0015 inch thick, ½ inch wide and approximately 1 inch long between the bearing and the journal. Tighten the bearing cap screws from 80 to 85 lbs torque and then rock the crank shaft back and forth. If a slight drag is felt the clearance is approximately .0015 inch and this is considered satisfactory. If, however, no drag is felt with the shim stock in place the bearing may be considered too loose.

Rear main bearing oil seal 6 cylinder type

By repeating this test with thicker shim stock the exact clearance between the journal and the bearing may be determined so that the correct undersize bearing can be secured. Chrysler does not recommend adjusting the main bearings and under no circumstances should the caps be filed as this will render them useless.

In an emergency, however, the main bearing shell may be adjusted in the same manner that the connecting rod bearing is adjusted. That is, by placing a piece of specially designed shim stock between the bearing shell and the bearing cap in the lower half. By using this method as much as .004 inch looseness may be taken up.

Rear Main Bearing Oil Seal

V8 MODELS

Braided asbestos is used to prevent oil escaping from the crank case on to the clutch and flywheel. To replace the lower half of this oil seal remove the rear main bearing cap and the old oil seal packing. Install the new packing in the connecting rod cap so that the packing protrudes slightly above the cap. Bolt the cap in place and torque it to approximately 60 ft lbs and then immediately take it down again. If the protruding part of the packing has "riveted over," cut off the riveted portion with a razor blade and again bolt the cap into place. Repeat this operation until the main bearing cap sets firmly in the block without riveting over the new portion of the oil seal.

To replace the upper half of the rear main bearing oil seal in the V8 Models it is necessary to remove the engine and the crankshaft.

ALL STRAIGHT 8 CYLINDER ENGINES FROM 1941

On these models a split ring type packing was used. To replace the packing take down the rear main bearing cap (a puller may be needed because of the rubber oil seals on the side of the cap). Using a pair of pliers, pull out the old oil seal. Back off all the main bearing cap bolts, approximately four turns. Apply tire soap, glycerine base soap or cup grease to the new seal, being careful not to get any of the lubricant betwen the ends which may prevent them from coming together when they are installed on the crankshaft.

Start one end of the seal in the slot and push it in until the end is near the top of the bearing. Start the other end in the opposite side and work it up into place. Work it up until the joint or split comes together near the top. Thoroughly lubricate around the lip of the seal so that the bearing flange will slip readily into place. New rubber seals should be used on the side of the rear main bearing cap when it is reinstalled.

It is a good idea to stake up little punch marks in the square groove which holds the rubber seal in order to retain it in place while the cap is being pulled up.

ALL 6 CYLINDER MODELS

The main bearing oil seal used in the 6 cylinder model is similar to that used in the V8 model, and the seal is replaced in much the same manner. While it is sometimes possible to force the upper half of the oil seal out of its groove with the crankshaft in place, there is no certainty that such a procedure will be effective. In any case if an attempt has been made to drive the upper half of the seal out of its groove, and the attempt is not successful, it will then be necessary to remove the engine and crankshaft and install a new oil seal in the rear main bearing. Instructions given for the 1951 V8 model also apply to the 6 cylinder models.

Removal of Oil Pan

V8 MODELS

Remove the oil level indicator and drain the oil. Remove the starting motor and the exhaust pipe crossover. Take out the cap screws and lower the pan.

When replacing the oil pan it is a good idea to tie the oil pan gasket with thin sewing cotton to each one of the mounting bolt holes so that it will not shift or move when it is being pushed up into place.

The sewing cotton will become embedded in the cork gasket and will be harmless.

ALL MODELS EXCEPT V8's

Crank engine until No. 1 piston is half way up the cylinder bore. Take down clutch underpan and the bolts around the oil pan. Lower the back of the pan and slide it back and out at the same time so that it will clear the oil pump screen.

Pan gasket end corks should protrude from ¼ in. to ½ in. above the oil pan. Do not cut off the protruding portions since the pan will compress it making a tight seal when it is bolted firmly in place.

Cylinder Head Removal

V8 MODELS

To remove the cylinder head on these models it is necessary to remove the generator, intake and exhaust manifold, rocker arm assemblies and all attaching parts such as ignition wires, carburetor wires, carburetor vacuum tubes, fuel lines, etc.

Caution: The cylinder head gasket used on Chrysler V8 models is extremely thin which means that great care should be exercised in handling the cylinder head to make certain that it is not marked or scratched in any way. Scratches, burrs, nickes or scoring will almost certainly result in defective seating of the cylinder head on the thin gasket.

VALVE SYSTEM

Except for the V8 model, all Chrysler engines are of the in-line L-head variety. The V8 engine is equipped with hydraulic valve silencers and overhead valves.

Except for the V8 engine all Chrysler models are fitted with mushroom type lifters which require that the camshaft be removed in order to take out any of the lifters.

On the 1951 V8 model the valve lifters can be taken out after the rocker arms, push rods and manifolds have been removed.

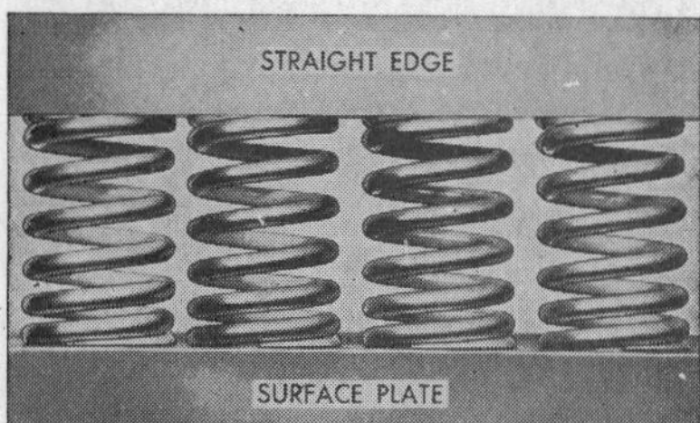

Checking spring for uniform height

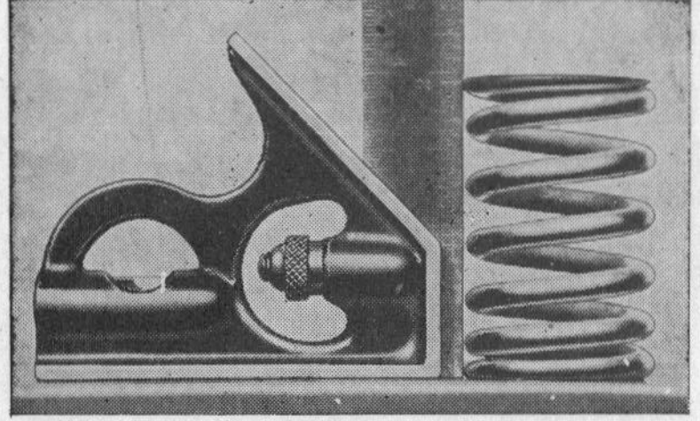

Checking valve spring for squareness

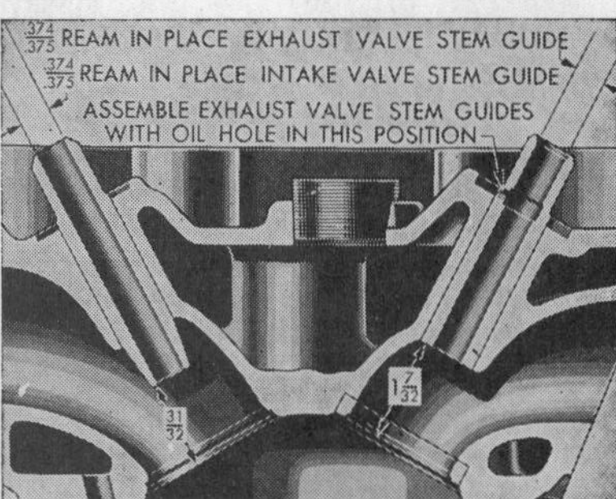

Valve stem guide assembly

1939 to 1942 models—Bolts indicated pass into front oil pan seal plate on 6 cyl models

Replacement of Valve Guides

Whenever it is necessary to replace valve guides on Chrysler, or any other engine, it is always good practice to carefully measure the distance from the cylinder head to the edge of the valve guide before driving out the old guide. This measurement should be carefully noted, both for the intake and the exhaust, so that when a new guide is installed, it can be inserted to exactly the same distance from the head as the old guide.

On all Chrysler engines the valve guide should be reamed after installation to provide the proper clearance for the valve stem..

The data at the beginning of this Chrysler section gives the diameter of valve stems for all models and the guide should be reamed to provide a clearance of approximately .0015". On V8 models the valve guides are driven out into the combustion chamber. In other words, they are driven from the top of the head down to the bottom.

On all in-line engines the valve guides are pulled through the top of the block. New guides are installed by driving them from the top toward the bottom.

On V8 engines new valve guides are driven from the combustion chamber up to the top of the head. The exhaust valve guide on the V8 engines has a small oil hole at its upper end. This oil hole should face upwards.

Valve Seat Inserts

All Chrysler engines are equipped with exhaust valve seat inserts made of a cast, heat resisting material, which cannot be cut successfully with a reamer. Exhaust valve seats must be ground and/or lapped to a perfect seal.

Timing Case Cover Removal

V8 MODELS

On Chrysler V8 models the timing case cover is a fairly large housing in the front of the engine. In order to remove this housing it is necessary to take off the water pump, damper and damper pulley, damper dust seal, and the left engine bank exhaust pipe. Disconnect all fuel lines and remove the fuel pump. Take off the starter and the oil pan. Unbolt the timing case cover.

Note: One of the bolts which holds the timing case cover to the front of the cylinder block is located back of the water pump. It will be found in a little depression almost in the center of the water pump opening. Make certain this bolt is removed before attempting to pry the timing case cover off its dowel pins.

ALL CHRYSLER MODELS, EXCEPT THE V8

On these models, to remove the timing case cover it is necessary to take off the radiator core, water pump, fan and vibration damper.

Note: On 1941 8-cylinder models, in order to take off the radiator core it is necessary to remove the front end sheet metal assembly including both front fenders.

Valve Timing Procedure—Replacement of Chains and Sprockets

V8 MODELS

The procedure for installing a timing chain and/or sprockets on the V8 model is essentially the same as it is for earlier models, with this exception: The camshaft gear is located to the shaft by means of a dowel pin which also passes through the gear and fuel pump eccentric, the eccentric is held in place with a single nut and lock washer.

It will be found, in some instances, that the fuel pump eccentric may be a little tight on the dowel pin and it will

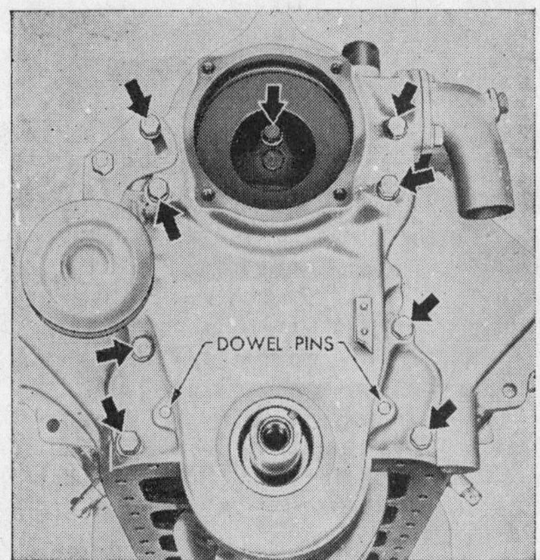

V-8 models—chain case cover attaching cap screws

require tapping with a fibre hammer to remove.

ALL IN-LINE ENGINES

To replace a timing chain and/or sprockets, or to retime the valves where the timing has jumped, proceed as follows: detach the camshaft sprocket, slide it off the shaft and remove the timing chain. Unless the crankshaft sprocket is to be replaced it will not be necessary to remove it from the shaft. Rotate the crankshaft so that the mark on the crankshaft sprocket is toward the camshaft and in exact alignment between the shaft centers. Now install the timing chain over the cam sprocket so that the mark on the cam and the mark on the crank sprocket are nearest each other. Note that the cam sprocket bolt holes (in-line engines) are staggered in such a way that the sprocket will enter only one way and permit the bolt to enter through the threaded holes in the hub. Rotate the camshaft so that holes line up while the timing marks are still in line between the shaft centers.

Mount the sprocket on the hub and draw up the bolts. Turn the crankshaft two full revolutions and check to see that the marks are still in alignment between the shaft centers. When set in the manner described with the marks aligned between the two shaft centers it is immaterial which piston is at top dead center. It may be necessary, however, to retime the ignition at any time the chain setting is disturbed.

To Check Valve Timing

Valve timing is given in degrees in the Engine Overhaul Specifications tables for Chrysler in this Manual. Valve timing is expressed in degrees before or after top center at which the intake valve opens. In order to make an accurate check of the valve timing, without disturbing the chain case, proceed as follows:

Remove the valve chamber cover and insert a feeler gauge, having considerably less thickness than the valve clearance, between the lifter and valve on No. 1 intake valve. Now crank the engine slowly until No. 1 cylinder is ready to commence its intake stroke. At this point the crankshaft should be turned very slowly at the exact point of rotation of the crankshaft noted when the lifter grips the feeler gauge. Then refer to the vibration damper which is marked in degrees (before and after top center) and note the degree mark which is under the pointer. If the reading noted is within 4 degrees of the specifications given in this Manual, the valve timing is within the prescribed limits.

The reason a 4 degree variation is permissible is because any change in valve timing would of necessity be one full tooth on the camshaft sprocket, and this tooth is approximately 8 degrees.

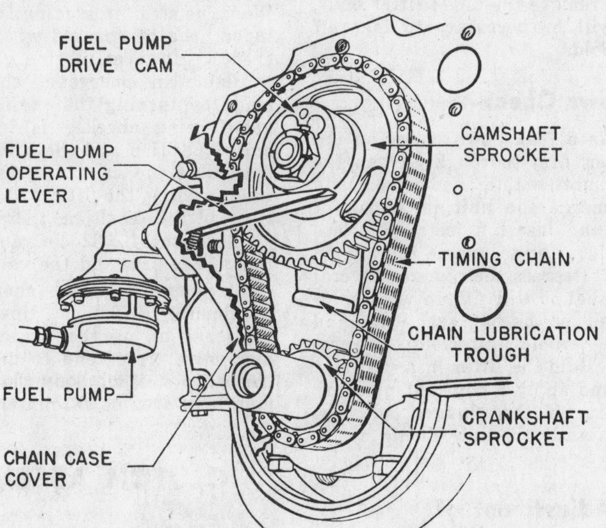

Timing Chain and Sprockets

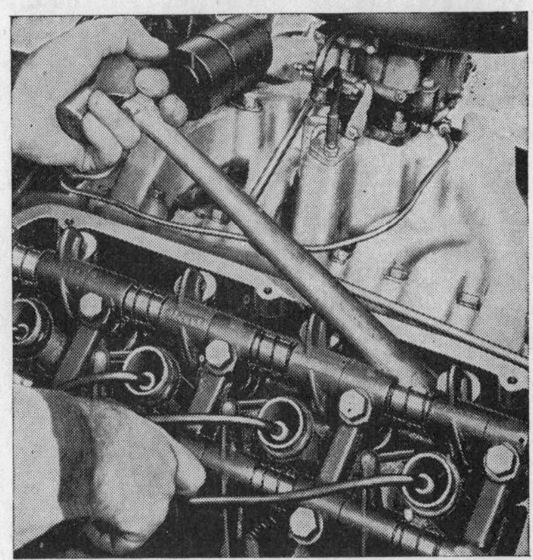
V-8 models—applying side pressure against valve springs

V-8 models—check for valve tappet noise at rocker arm

VALVE TIMING—*continued*

When making this check on V8 models, (with hydraulic lifters) operating at zero clearance, a dial indicator can be mounted over the valve spring or over the top of the push rod so that the lifting of the valve can be detected by motion at the indicator. Otherwise the procedure is the same.

Hydraulic Valve Lifters

If difficulty is experienced with the hydraulic valve lifters, such as sticking or noisy lifters, check the oil pressure on the gauge and the oil level in the oil pan before doing any other work. Pressure on the gauge should be between 40 and 60 lbs, and the oil level should never be above or below the full mark. If the oil level in the oil pan is too high there is a tendency of the oil to foam causing it to include air which may be carried along to the valve lifter and, since air is compressible, may cause erratic operation of the hydraulic silencer.

To check for a noisy valve lifter, remove the cylinder head covers and reinstall the spark plug wires and run the engine at idle.

Place your finger on each rocker arm and the noisy rocker arm will be detected immediately. A shock will be felt as the valve comes down to its seat. Sometimes worn valve guides are mistaken for noisy valve tappets. If this is the case the noise will be dampened by applying side thrust to the valve springs which will temporarily take out the sloppiness of the valve stem. If applying side thrust to the valve stem does not reduce the noise it can then safely be assumed that the noise is in the valve tappet.

The only service possible on the hydraulic valve lifters is that they be thoroughly cleaned with good solvent and compressed air.

If the tappet is noisy because of a too fast leak-down rate, this condition can be detected by attempting to hold down on the push rod with the palm of the hand when the engine is running at idle. If this produces a tapping noise in that rocker arm then it may be safely assumed that the leak-down rate of that lifter is excessive.

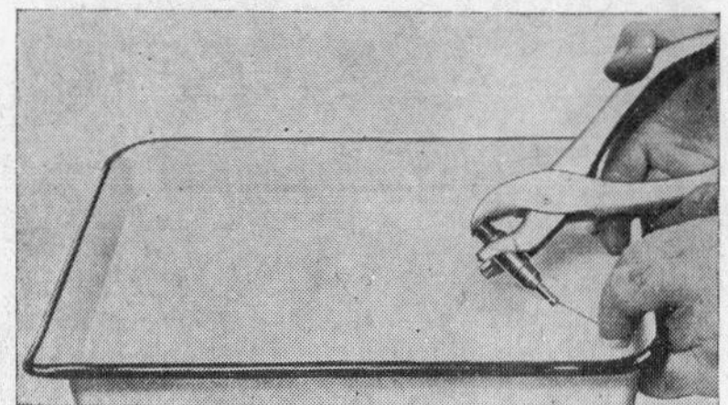

Flushing and loading unit assembly (tool C-3042)

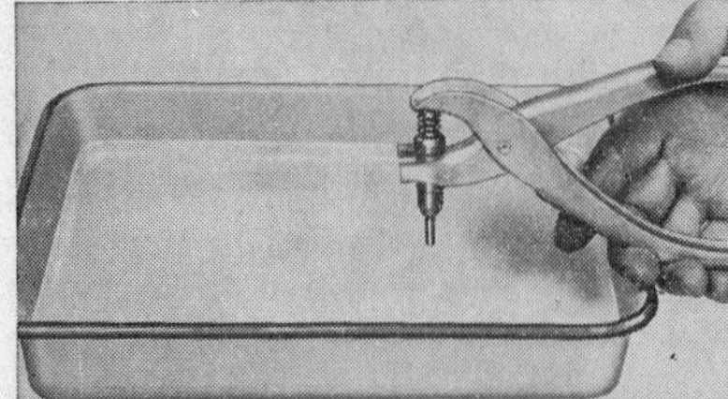

Checking unit leak-down rate

Removal of Hydraulic Lifters

Note: On some very early production V8 engines it was necessary to remove the inlet manifold and the valve tappet chamber cover in order to take out the valve tappet units. On later production and all present production engines the push rod hole is enlarged. This makes it necessary to remove the cylinder head cover only. To remove the valve tappet unit assembly proceed as follows:

Compress the valve spring sufficiently to free the rocker arm from the push rod and, holding in this position, slide the rocker arm off to one side which will permit the withdrawal of the push rod and lifter assembly. Note that this work can be done without removing the manifolds. If, however, it becomes necessary to remove the valve lifter body, then it will be necessary to take off the manifold.

Leak Down Check

To make a leak down check on the valve lifter, first thoroughly clean the lifter assembly with a good solvent and then submerge the unit in a pan of kerosene and insert a metal pin into the oil inlet tube to unseat the ball in the lifter. Depress the plunger several times so that it will fill up with kerosene. Then let the ball seat itself and remove the whole unit from the kerosene pan Hold the lifter in an upright position and apply a constant pressure with pliers. If the plunger collapses almost instantly the unit should be replaced.

Initial Adjustment of Hydraulic Tappets

To check to be certain the hydraulic lifter is operating some place near the middle of its stroke the Chrysler Motor Car Co. recommends that the length of the valve stem protruding from the cylinder head be checked with gauge No. C-3061. However, if this gauge is not available an emergency check can be made by turning the engine until the valve being checked is in the fully closed position and the lifter is on the bottom of the cam. Depress the push rod to force the lifter to leak down. Held in this position, there should be a minimum of .032 clearance between the rocker arm and the valve stem.

Maximum clearance should be approximately .070 inch. However, since all servicing on the hydraulic valves and valve train tend to decrease this clearance it is unlikely that the maximum will ever be encountered.

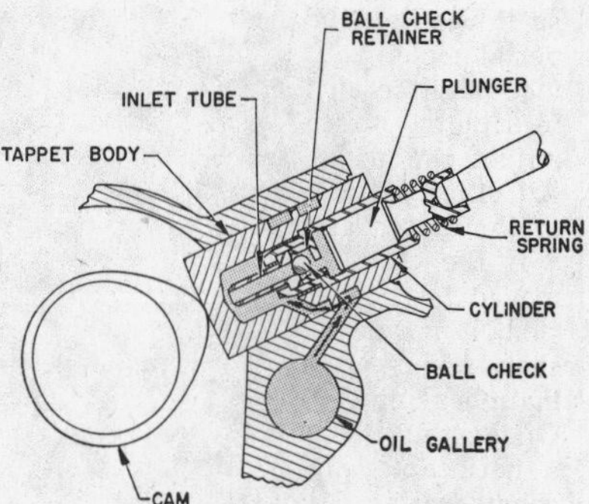

Tydraulic Tappet-valve open

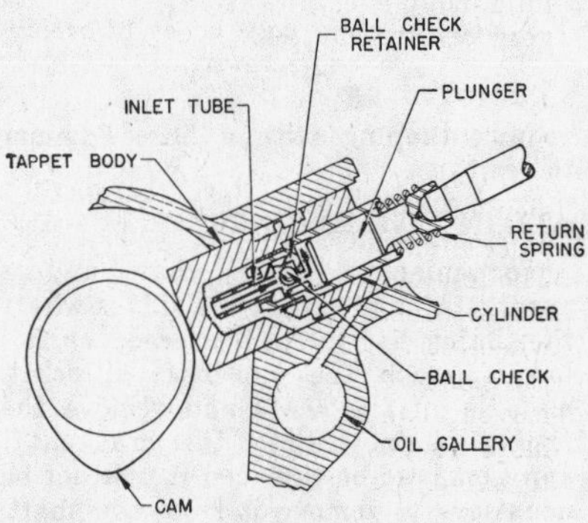

Hydraulic Tappet-valve closed

CLUTCH ASSEMBLY

On all Chrysler cars a clutch is used regardless of whether the car has a semi-automatic transmission, fluid drive or a hydraulic torque converter such as is used on the New Yorker and Imperial models. The only practical service possible on the clutch assembly is to tighten up to prevent rattles and adjust the pedal toe board clearance. All other service requires the removal of the clutch assembly.

If the clutch assembly is being removed because of chatter or malfunction, it is advisable to check to see if there is any oil leaking from the rear main bearing or from the fluid coupling. Oil on the clutch facings will produce a noticeable chatter even taking into consideration the damping action of the hydraulic torque converter or the fluid couple.

Because of the damping action of the fluid couple service on the clutch is very rarely required.

Removal of the Clutch Assembly

On all models remove the transmission assembly, the clutch housing lower pan and the clutch throwout fork. The clutch cover assembly should be stamped, showing its relation to the flywheel so that it can be reassembled in the same position from which it was removed. The cover bolts should be removed a few turns at a time in order to avoid springing the clutch cover.

Disassembly service on the clutch requires special jigs and fixtures. Instructions in the use of the fixtures are supplied by the manufacturer of the tool.

Hydraulic Coupling Fluid Drive

The fluid drive (fluid coupling) consists of two almost identical members called the driving and driven members They are steel stampings in which a number of steel fins are welded. The fins of the driving member impart a swirling motion to the fluid, throwing it outward and away from the center of the unit where it is forced to cross the gap to the driven member and thus impinges on the fins of the driven member to make it turn. The fluid drive eliminates all mechanical conditions between the engine and the rear wheels.

A seal known as the bellows seal is used at the back of the fluid coupling to prevent leakage of fluid from the assembly.

Refilling the Fluid Couple

To check the level of the fluid in the fluid couple rotate the drive unit until the filler plug is opposite the inspection hole in the clutch housing.

Note: The inspection hole is located under the toe board and it is necessary to pull back the toe board mat in order to uncover the port in the toe board.

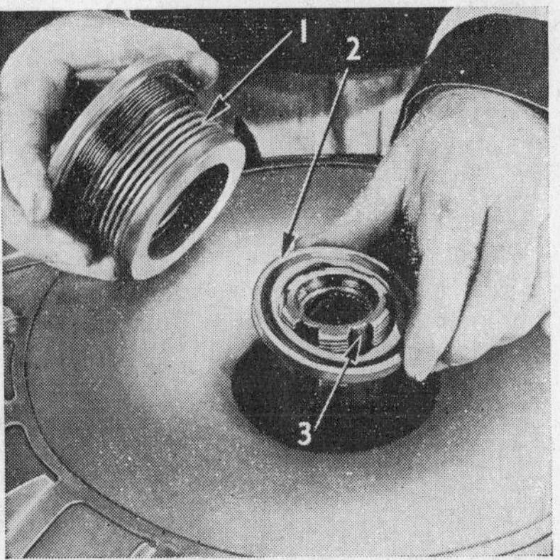

1—Bellows seal assembly. 2—Floating seal ring. 3—Hub. This is an early type which could be removed as an assembly.

Caution: Be very careful when removing the filler hole plug from the driving member of the fluid unit so as not to drop it down into the bell housing. It is generally considered to be a good precaution to pack around the area with a single wiping towel so that if the plug is dropped it will not fall down into the clutch housing.

The Chrysler Corp. recommends that a magnetic wrench be used to remove this plug so that the danger of dropping it is eliminated.

When the filler plug in the driving member of the fluid couple is in line with the inspection hole in the fly wheel housing the fluid should come to the edge of the filler hole. If it does not it should be filled until it comes to the lower edge of the filler hole. After filling the unit carefully replace the filler plug, the inspection hole plug and the toe board port and floor mat.

Loss of fluid from the fluid drive unit will be evidenced by excessive engine speed similar to a slipping clutch.

Removal of Fluid Drive Unit From the Car

On all models, take out the clutch and transmission. The fluid drive assembly can then be unbolted and lowered through the fly wheel underpan.

The attaching bolts are reached from the front flange of the crankshaft.

The fluid drive unit is located to the crankshaft flange by dowel pins and it may be necessary to pry it slightly in order to work it off the dowel pins.

Service on the Fluid Coupling

Two types of seals are used on the fluid coupling, one known as the bellow seal, the other known as the housing seal. Actual service procedure on either of these two is very similar.

Removing the clutch driving plate nut, and using a puller, take off the clutch driving plate.

Note: The lock washer on the clutch driving plate retaining nut is tabbed up in one or two places. It is necessary to knock the tabs down before taking off the retaining nut. Compress the bellows seal sleeve spring (special compression sleeve is available for this purpose) and remove the bellow seal snap ring. Take out the compressor and withdraw the spring and seal. This may be accomplished readily by forming the end of two pieces of wire into a hook and reaching down into the assembly and hooking out the bellow seal spring and the bellow spring.

Caution: The spring should be removed first in order to prevent damaging the seal. If a housing type seal is used it is necessary to unscrew the housing type seal after the snap ring has been removed.

Inspect the sealing surfaces for marks, scratches, gouges or roughness. The mating surfaces should be perfectly smooth and clean before installing the new bellows seal.

To reinstall, reverse the order of installation. In the installation of either the bellows type or the housing type seal, absolute cleanliness is essential.

As a precautionary measure, wash all the parts and the tools that are to be used in a clean solvent and blow them off with compressed air.

Special Note: Seals for the various

Section thru the bellows seal

FLUID COUPLING—*continued*

models are not interchangeable. When installing a bellows or housing type seal in any Chrysler car it is essential that the seal used be the one designed for that particular model.

TRANSMISSION ASSEMBLY

Since 1940, Chrysler cars have been equipped with standard three speed transmissions; three speed transmissions with integral overdrives; and four speed transmissions with semi-automatic shifts. The standard transmission can be identified readily by reference to the car itself. Note that the transmission housing has bolted to it a round extension housing at the back. This indicates an extension shaft used in place of an overdrive.

Overdrive transmissions can be readily identified because of the overdrive housing bolted to the back of the transmission case.

Standard Transmission Removal

Disconnect the propeller shaft at the front universal joint.

Disconnect all attaching parts such as speedometer cable, battery ground cable, gear shift control rods and gear shift selector cables.

Remove the nuts which hold the transmission to the clutch housing and lift the transmission assembly down and out.

Removal of Vacuum Operated Semi-Automatic Transmission (Vacamatic)

Disconnect all transmission attaching parts such as the speedometer cable, wires to the control unit, vacuum hoses and the vacuum shift unit. Mark all wires for reassembly.

Split the front universal joint and remove the nuts which hold the transmission to the clutch housing and pull the transmission down and out of the car.

Hydraulically Operated Transmission Removal

Raise the right side of the floor mat and remove the floor board access cover on the right rear side of the floor board. Disconnect all attaching parts at the transmission, such as the speedometer cable, wires from the governor, solenoid interrupter switch, hand brake cables, brake support, brake adjusting bolt bracket, etc. Also remove the transmission governor assembly and the solenoid. Mark all wires for reassembly.

Split the propeller shaft at the front universal joint and push back the universal joint yoke.

Detach the transmission from the clutch housing and move down and out of the car.

Installation of Hydraulically Operated Transmission

Important: Before installing transmission, check face of clutch housing and lower pan for alignment. If any misalignment is noted, loosen lower pan and align face of clutch housing and lower pan with a straight edge, then tighten the pan up securely. Unless the lower pan is in alignment with the face of the clutch housing properly the transmission will not fit tight against the clutch housing which may result in difficulty in shifting.

Disassembly of the Standard Transmission

Remove the two screws at the transmission cover which hold the shift rail detent springs and balls. Then take off the transmission side cover assembly.

Take off the universal joint companion flange and brake drum assembly.

Next take off the shifter fork guide rail. (This is a long thin rail which slides into the front face of the transmission and through the shifter fork. It is intended to guide the shifter fork.

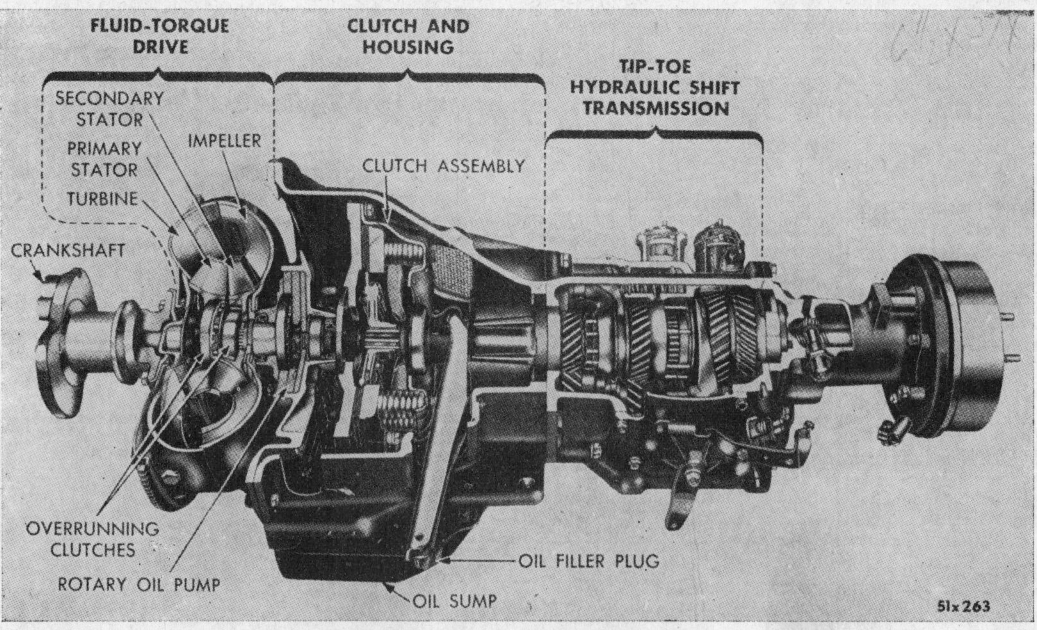

Fluid-Torque Drive—cutaway sectional view

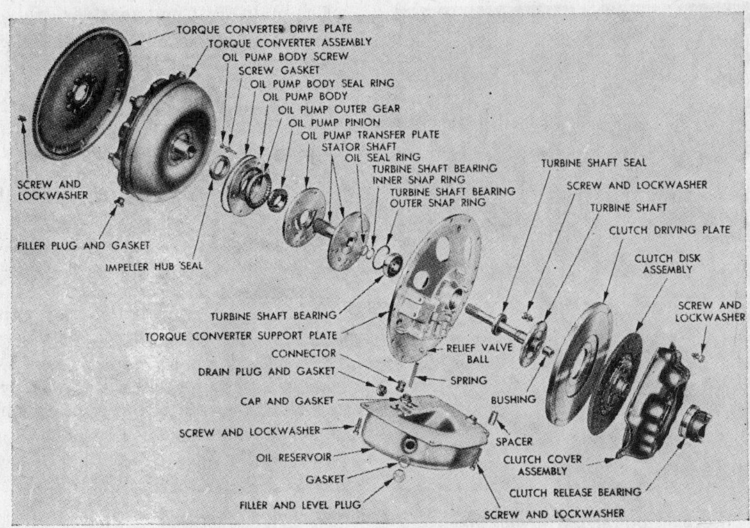

Torque Converter and Clutch Assemblies

It is removed by unscrewing it to the left with a screw driver and sliding it out of the front face of the transmission.)

Set the transmission in neutral and loosen the shifter rails from the shifter forks. Then slide the shift rails out of the front of the transmission case (it will be necessary to remove the Welsh plug to get at the lower rail).

The shift rail interlock rod can be removed by taking out the single cap screw which is located at the top of

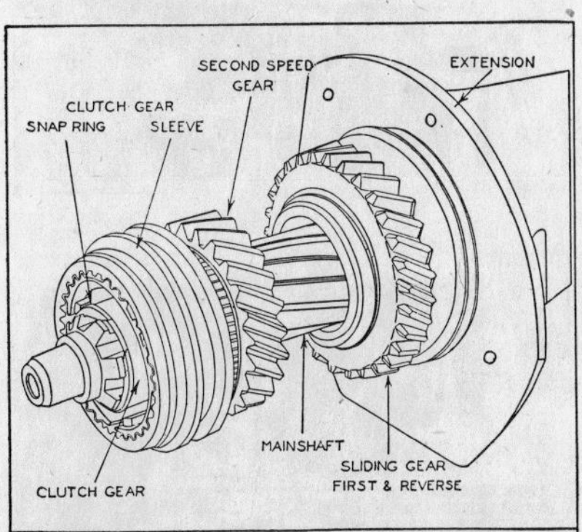

Mainshaft and gears are removed thru the back of the case with the mainshaft attached to the extension (or overdrive) housing

the transmission toward the back, just to the right of the side cover. Take out the shifter forks. Unbolt the extension housing from the back of the transmission case and slide the case with the main shaft and gears connected to it out the rear of the transmission case.

The main shaft now can be disassembled by removing the synchronizer retaining snap ring and the synchronizer unit. The second speed gear and low speed gear can then be slid off the shaft.

The rear bearing is held in place with a snap ring. Take out the snap ring and the main shaft and bearing can be removed from the extension housing.

A new oil seal should be used at the rear end of the extension housing.

The countershaft is driven out toward the rear of the transmission case.

Note: A key is used in the rear end of the counter shaft to prevent it from turning. Be careful to pick up this key as soon as the shaft has been driven far enough to reach it.

Main drive pinion and bearing assembly can be pulled out of the front of the case after the counter shaft gear cluster has been dropped to the bottom of the case or removed.

Reverse idler gear shaft is driven toward rear of case.

Note: A locking key is also used on the idler shaft and it should be removed as soon as it is clear of the case.

Reassembly of Standard Transmission

Cleanliness is essential when reassembling the counter shaft assembly and bearings.

In general the transmission is assembled in the reverse of assembly procedure.

Overdrive Disassembly

The instructions given for the disassembly of the transmission above will also apply to the transmission when it is equipped with an overdrive, up to the point where the extension housing is removed with the main shaft gears in tact. The difference in the overdrive that instead of removing an extension housing you are removing an overdrive case. Otherwise the procedure is exactly the same.

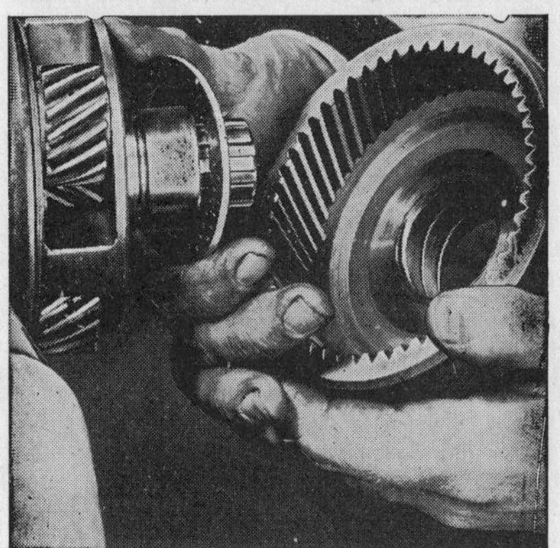

Removing annulus gear

Removing pinion cage

Taking out roller retainer

REASSEMBLY OF STANDARD TRANSMISSION—*continued*

After the overdrive assembly in its case has been removed from the transmission proceed to take off the synchronizer gear, low and second gears in the same manner that it would have been had the transmission been a standard. When the transmission gears have been taken off proceed with the overdrive as follows. Remove the screws which hold the stepdown adapter plate to the overdrive case. These screws will be found in little pockets in the front face of the overdrive.

By tapping the rear end of the overdrive main shaft with a very soft hammer it can be driven out through its bearing and overdrive case removed.

Caution: When lifting off the case make certain that the transmission main shaft is not removed with the case as this will permit the freewheeling rollers to drop out of place and they may be lost.

Note: It will be found that the overdrive clutch pawl shell will come off with the overdrive case and can be removed from the case after the control fork guide rail has been removed.

Note: The overdrive main shaft rear bearing is retained in the case by means of two snap rings and the oil seal at the back is pressed into the case.

Pull the overdrive main shaft off the freewheeling cam and be careful to catch the freewheeling rollers as they fall.

Take the bolt off the end of the transmission main shaft and pull the freewheeling cam and roller cage assembly off the back of the transmission main shaft.

Remove the solenoid assembly, plunger and spring.

Remove the pinion cage and snap ring from the transmission main shaft and remove the sun gear plate snap ring which retains the sun gear plate and lift off the loose parts. At this point there remains the transmission main shaft and rear bearing mounted in the adapter plate. This is held in place by a snap ring. If necessary to remove this unit take out the snap ring and press the bearing off the main shaft.

The overdrive unit is reassembled in the reverse of the above procedure. It should be cleaned thoroughly and examined for pits, scores, worn bearings or broken or worn snap rings.

The Chrysler Corp. recommends that all new snap rings be used at any time a bearing is removed from the transmission or overdrive.

Vacuum power shifter linkage

Vacuum Operated Semi-Automatic Transmission Disassembly

Remove the vacuum unit and the governor.

Lock the transmission in two gears and take off the universal joint companion flange nut and remove the universal joint flange and brake drum.

Take the oil seal out of the rear of the case.

Remove the detent balls and springs in the gear shift housing.

Set the transmission back into neutral and remove the side cover assembly.

Remove the screws which hold the brake support and loosen the brake support and turn it counter-clockwise to expose the gear shift rail holes.

Remove the shifting fork and reverse idler shaft retaining screws and slide the shifting rails out the back through the holes in the brake support.

Be careful not to lose the detent balls and the spacer on the reverse (lower) rail.

Take out the gear shift forks.

Take off the front shaft bearing retaining sleeve and then remove the guide pin from the shifter fork by unscrewing it and pulling it out the front of the case.

Then remove the manual shift fork.

Using a puller, remove the reverse idler shaft by pulling it out the rear of the case.

Drive the countershaft out through the rear of the case, permitting the counter set cluster to drop to the bottom of the case.

The mainshaft and gear assembly are then pulled out of the rear of the case.

There is a single cap screw at the top of the case, just to the right of the cover assembly which covers the hole containing the shift interlock pin. Remove the cap screw and turn the case over, permitting the interlock pin to drop out. On assembly do not fail to place the interlock pin back into the transmission as this pin prevents the transmission from going into two gears at one time.

The counter shaft freewheel unit is held together by a snap ring.

On assembly, all parts should be thoroughly cleaned with a good solvent and blown off with compressed air.

In general the transmission is reassembled in the reverse of the disassembly procedure.

Vacuum Operated Transmission With Overdrive

Several models of Chrysler had a vacuum operated semi-automatic transmission equipped with an overdrive. The service procedure for the overdrive

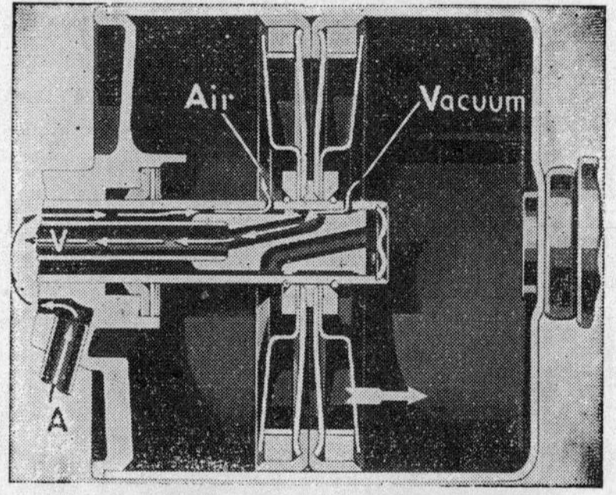

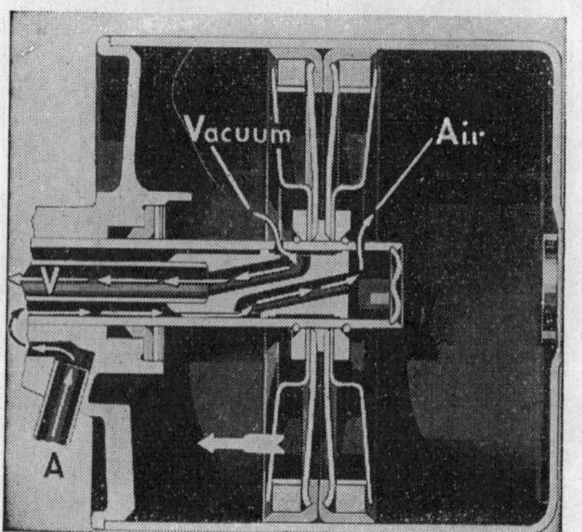

The power cylinder is operated as shown in the above two sections

used on the vacuum operated transmission is exactly the same as the overdrive used on the standard transmission. Refer to the instructions given.

Hydraulically Operated Semi-Automatic Transmission

The disassembly of the hydraulically operated semi-automatic transmission is given in the automatic transmission section of this Manual. Refer to the index.

REAR AXLE ASSEMBLY

The Hotchkiss drive (open drive shaft) type of drive line is used on all Chrysler automobiles. The differential, pinion and axles are equipped with tapered roller bearings.

Pinion Oil Seal Removal

To remove the pinion oil seal the rear universal joint should be taken down and the universal joint pinion flange removed from the pinion shaft.

The pinion oil seal can then be taken out with a hook type inertia puller.

Always make an exact count of the number of turns required to remove the pinion shaft nut so that it can be returned to exactly the same position from which it was removed. This is essential since the pinion bearings on this rear axle assembly are preloaded to a definite amount.

Axle Shaft Oil Seal

Two types of oil seals were used on the axle shafts on Chrysler products. The early type was bolted to the outside face of the brake backing plate. To replace this type it was necessary to remove the rear wheel and take out the bolts which retain the oil seal to the rear axle housing flange.

On later models the oil seal was incorporated into the brake backing plate. To replace it, it was necessary to remove the brake backing plate from the car (necessary to detach the brake lines) and drive the oil seal out of the backing plate flange. To replace the inner oil seal on all models it is necessary to remove the axle shaft and take out the oil seal with an inertia type puller.

Axle Shaft End Play

On all Chrysler models the end play in the axle shaft is controlled by shims back of the backing plate. End play in the axle shaft is permissible up to approximately .008 inch.

Removing shims from between the backing plate and the rear axle housing will decrease the end play of that axle shaft.

Axle Shaft Replacement

To replace the rear axle shaft on any Chrysler model take off the wheel and hub assembly, disconnect the brake

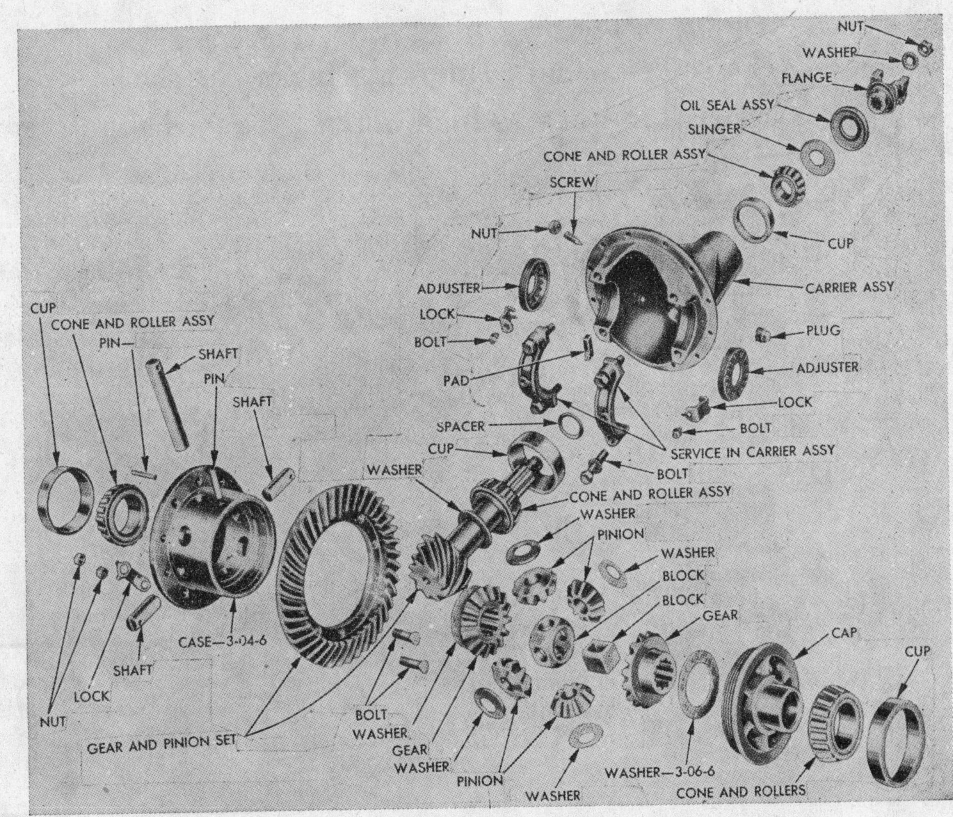

Exploded view of Rear Axle Assembly used on New York and Imperial models

AXLE SHAFT REPLACEMENT—*cont'd*

lines and unbolt the backing plate from the rear axle housing flange. The axle shaft, together with its bearing, can then be pulled out of the housing.

While it is possible to drive the bearing off of the axle shaft using a drift or punch, it is recommended that the bearing be pressed off of the shaft.

AXLE SHAFT BEARING REPLACEMENT

To replace the axle shaft bearing remove the shaft as explained in the above paragraph and, using an inertia type puller, pull the bearing cup out of the axle housing. Press the bearing cone off of the axle shaft and press a new one in its place.

Drive the outer cone into the axle housing assembly so that it is firmly seated against the flange.

Caution: While it is possible, using a brass drift, to drive the bearing cone into the housing, it is recommended that a bearing driver be used for this job since driving with a single point drift may cause the cup to cock and enter the case crooked.

Replacement of Pinion and Ring Gear

To replace the pinion and ring gear remove both axle shafts, take off the rear universal joint and detach the rear axle carrier assembly and slide out from underneath the car on to a bench.

It is not necessary to remove the rear axle housing tubes from the car. Simply remove the carrier assembly from the rear axle housing.

Remove the differential side bearing caps after first releasing the pressure from the adjusting cages. Take off the universal joint companion flange and drive the pinion shaft out through the back of the carrier.

Note: The rear bearing cone and rolls will come out with the pinion shaft.

Carefully preserve the shims which are found in front of the pinion bearing spacer. If the same pinion gear is to be replaced, the same number of shims should be used.

Note: On New Yorker and Imperial models a step cut pinion shaft is used and there is no bearing spacer, instead a spacer washer is used between the front bearing cone and the shoulder on the pinion shaft.

Shims or a spacer washer is used between the rear bearing cone and the pinion gear to govern the depth of the pinion gear in relation to the ring gear.

Adding shims at this point will cause the pinion gear to move toward the rear of the car and deeper into the ring gear; removing shims at this point will cause the pinion gear to shift forward and out of the ring gear.

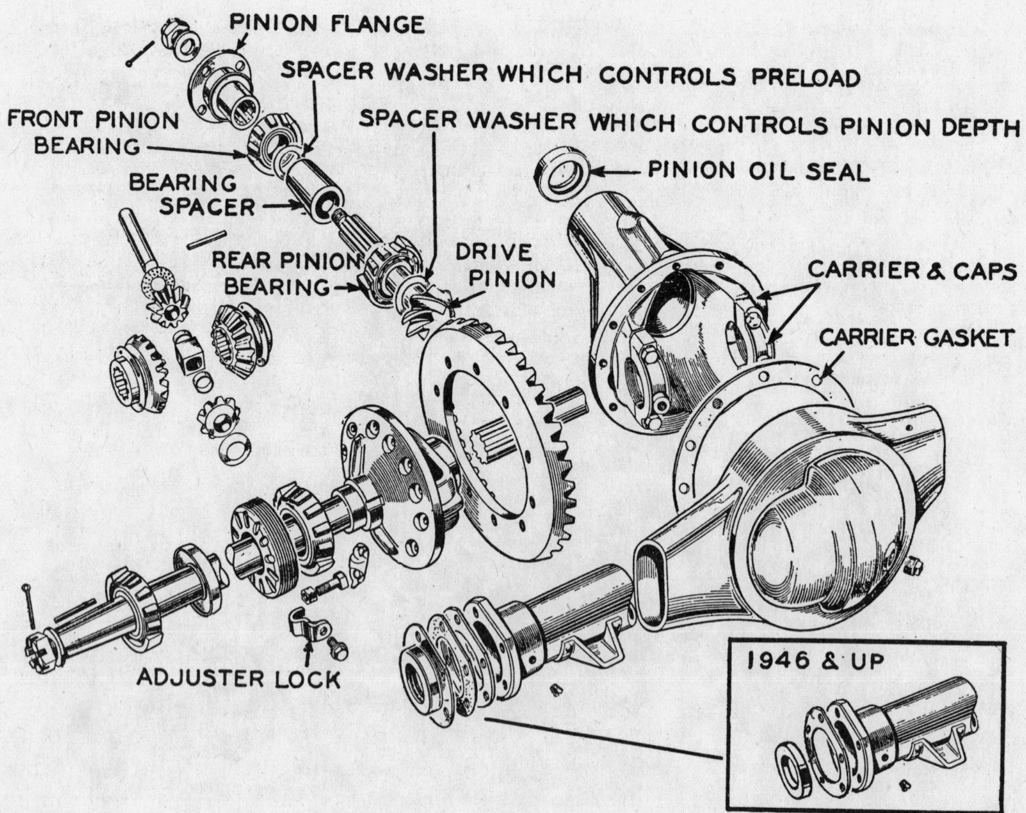

Exploded view of Rear Axle Assembly—All models except New Yorker and Imperial models

When installing a new pinion and ring gear, the Chrysler Corp. recommends that the gears be tested with Prussian Blue or other indicating material to determine the contact of the pinion on the ring gear. Where the contact marks indicate that the pinion should be moved closer to the ring gear shims should be added between the pinion gear and the pinion rear bearing cone.

If the gear marks indicate that the pinion is set too close to the ring gear it will be necessary to remove shims from between the pinion gear and the pinion rear bearing cone.

Checking the mesh markings with Prussian Blue requires that the rear axle be completely assembled. It is recommended that while attempting to determine the depth of the pinion in relation to the ring gear that no shims be used to preload the bearing. Simply preload the bearing by pulling up on the pinion shaft without placing any shims between the end of universal joint yoke and the shoulder on the pinion shaft.

Since the rear is being assembled for no other purpose than to determine the thickness of the pinion depth shim, it is obviously not necessary to set up the preload on the pinion bearings since if the setting on the gear tooth requires a correction it will not be necessary then to change both shims. However, once the correct depth of the pinion has been established, then remove the ring gear and differential assembly and proceed to set the preload on the pinion bearings as explained in the next paragraph.

Pinion Bearing Adjustment

After the proper number of shims have been installed to establish the correct position of the pinion gear relative to the ring gear it will be necessary to set the pinion gear bearings up so that there is a pre-load of from 5 to 10 inch pounds at the pinion shaft universal joint flange. This pre-load is equal to approximately .002 pre-load on the bearing. To establish this preload, deliberately use too many shims between the pinion front bearing cone and the bearing spacer (or the shoulder of the pinion on New Yorker and Imperial models) and measure with an indicator the end play developed in the pinion shaft. Check this end play several times to make certain that the reading is exact.

After the end play has been established exactly, remove from in back of the pinion front bearing shims equivalent to .002 more than the end play found in the shaft and then replace the bearing, universal joint yoke and the pinion shaft nut. Tighten the pinion shaft nut securely and this will produce a .002 inch pre-load on the pinion bearings.

Recheck the torque required to turn the pinion shaft.

The final setting depends on the torque required to turn the pinion and not the linear preload on the bearings.

Set up the differential side bearings and ring gears so there is not less than .006 inch and not more than .010 inch backlash between the ring gear and pinion, measured at the rim of the ring gear.

This position of the ring gear should be established with zero play in the differential side bearings.

Differential side bearings should be pre-loaded approximately one notch of the adjusting cage.

The differential is preloaded after the correct lash has been established between the ring gear and pinion and there is zero play in the bearings. One notch of preload is usually placed on the bearings at the adjusting cage on the side opposite to the ring gear.

This will tend, if anything, to increase the backlash between the ring gear and pinion. Therefore, if the lash is somewhat excessive to start with it is best to take the one notch preload on the same side as the ring gear, which will tend to diminish the backlash.

Rear Axle Differential Gears

To remove the differential gears it is necessary to take out the differential pin, which means remove the ring gear.

On New Yorker and Imperial models the differential case is equipped with a cap. This cap is screwed into the differential case and is retained in place by a lock pin. In order to take the case apart it is necessary to drive out the lock pin and unscrew the differential case cap.

It may be necessary to heat the differential case in hot water in order to get the cap out of the case.

Under no circumstances should heat, other than hot water, be used on the differential case.

Shock Absorbers

All models of Chrysler are equipped with airplane type direct acting shock absorbers.

Since disassambly service on shock absorbers is a highly specialized job, it is recommended that if difficulty is experienced with the shock absorber they be removed from the car and replaced with either a new or rebuilt unit.

DE SOTO and DODGE SPECIFICATIONS

Starting Serial and Motor Numbers

DE SOTO

Starting Serial Numbers

1940 6064301
1941, De Luxe 6096001
  Custom 5720401
1942, De Luxe 6142001
  Custom 5771001
1946, De Luxe 6154001
  Custom 5784001
1947, De Luxe 6172863
  Custom 5825785
1948, De Luxe 6190370
  Custom ..... 5885816 and 62001001
1949, De Luxe (early) 6205976
  De Luxe (late)
    6212001 and 60002001
  Custom (early)
    5948453 and 6201895
  Custom (late)
    50000101 and 62004001
1950, De Luxe .. 6233501 and 60005001
  Custom .... 50062001 and 62011501
1951, De Luxe .. 6269001 and 60011001
  Custom .... 50155001 and 62024001
1952, 6 cyl.—De Luxe
    6283601 and 60013001
  Custom .... 50230101 and 62032601
  8 cyl. ...... 55000001 and 64001001
1953, 6 cyl.—Powermaster—6
    50266001 (1); 62039001 (2)

Location

1940-1942—On right front door hinge post.
1946-1953—On left front door hinge post.

Starting Serial Numbers

1940-1953—First letter and two numbers indicate year, i.e. S7, 1940. All motor numbers begin 1001.
1940—S7 1001
1941—S8 1001
1942—S10 1001
1946-1949 (early)—S11 1001
1949 (late)—S13 1001
1950—S14 1001
1951-1952, 6 cyl.—S15 1001
1952, 8 cyl.—S17 1001
1953, 6 cyl.—S18 1001
1953, 8 cyl.—S16 1001

Location

1940-1953, 6 cyl.—Left side of motor below cylinder head between No. 1 and No. 2 cylinders.
1952-1953, 8 cyl.—On top of engine block under water outlet elbow.

DODGE

Starting Serial Numbers

1940 4349001
1941 30342401
1942 30577001
1946 .... 30645001 and 45000001
1947 .... 30799738 and 45002146
1948 .... 31011766 and 45022453
1949 (early) D24
    31201087 and 45041546
  (Late) D29
    37000101, 48000101 and 48500101
  D30
    31245001, 45050001 and 45500101
1950, D33
    37060001, 48004001 and 48502001
  D34
    31420001, 45064001 and 45505001
1951, D41
    37135001, 48008001 and 48506001
  D42
    31663001, 45079001 and 45518001
1952, D41
    37175001, 48009901 and 48507601
  D42
    31867801, 45090601 and 45527501
1953, D46 .... D46, 32042001
  D47 .... D47, 37212001
  D44 .... D44, 34500001
  D48 .... D48, 38500001

Location

1940-1942—Plate on right front door hinge post.
1946-1953—Plate on left front door hinge post.

Starting Motor Numbers

1940-1953—First letter and two numbers indicate year, ie., D14, 1940. All motor numbers begin 1001.
1940, D14 1001
1941, D19 1001
1942, D22 1001
1946-1949 (early), D24 1001
1949 (late), D30 1001
1950, D34 1001
1951-1952, D42 1001
1953, 6 cyl. 1001
  8 cyl. 1001

Location

1940-1953, 6 cyl.—Left side of block below cylinder head between #1 and #2 cylinders.
1953, 8 cyl. ....

General Specifications

Year	Model	Wheelbase (in.)	Tread (in.)		Overall Dimensions (in.)			Shipping Weight* (lb.)	Tire Size (in.)
			Front	Rear	Length†	Width	Height		
DE SOTO									
1941	S8	122	57	60	208	....	....	3254	6.25-16
1942	S10	122	57	60	208	....	....	3315	6.25-16
1946	S11	122	57	60	207	76	....	3485	6.50-15
1947	S11	122	57	60	207	76	....	3427	6.50-15
1948	S11	122	57	60	207	76	....	3448	7.60-15

General Specifications—*continued*

Year	Model	Wheelbase (in.)	Tread (in.) Front	Tread (in.) Rear	Overall Dimensions (in.) Length†	Overall Dimensions (in.) Width	Overall Dimensions (in.) Height■	Shipping Weight* (lb.)	Tire Size (in.)
DE SOTO—continued									
1949–50	S13	126	56	57	207	73	66	....	7.60–15
1951	S15	126	56	60	208	75	65	3570	7.60–15
1952	S15, 6 cyl., S17, V8	125	56	60	208	75	65	....	7.60–15
1953	S18, 6 cyl., S16, V8	125	56	60	213	77	62	....	7.60–15
DODGE									
1941	D19	120	57	60	203	....	....	....	6.00–16
1942	D22	120	57	60	202	....	....	3195	6.00–16
1946	D24	120	57	60	206	75	....	3229	6.00–16
1947	D24	120	57	60	205	75	....	3256	6.00–16
1948	D24	120	57	60	295	76	....	3256	7.10–15
1949	D29	115	56	57	197	72	65	....	6.70–15
	D30	124	56	57	204	73	66	3385	7.10–15
1950	D33	115	56	59	196	73	....	3200	6.70–15
	D34	124	56	59	203	74	....	3410	7.10–15
1951	D41	115	56	59	200	73	64	3215	6.70–15
	D42	124	56	59	207	74	65	3415	7.10–15
1952	D41, 6 cyl.	115	56	59	200	74	64	....	6.70–15
	D42, 6 cyl.	123	56	59	207	74	65	....	7.10–15
1953	D46, 6 cyl.	119	56	59	201	73	62	....	6.70–15
	D47, 6 cyl.	114	56	59	190	73	62	....	6.70–15
	D44, 8 cyl.	119	56	59	201	73	62	....	7.10–15
	D48, 8 cyl.	114	56	59	191	73	60	....	7.10–15

†—Including bumpers and guards. ■—Road to roof, no load. *—Cheapest 5 passenger 4 door sedan or equivalent.

Dimensions of Valves

Year	Model	Overall Length Inlet	Overall Length Exhaust	Head Diameter Inlet	Head Diameter Exhaust	Seat Angle (deg.) Inlet	Seat Angle (deg.) Exhaust	Stem Diameter Inlet	Stem Diameter Exhaust	Key Type	O.D. of Seat Insert Inlet	O.D. of Seat Insert Exhaust
DE SOTO												
1940 to 42	Series—All	4.781	4.781	1.656	1.531	45	45	.340	.340	split lock	....	....
1946 to 52	Series—All	4.781	4.781	1.719	1.531	45	45	.341	.339	split lock	....	....
	S17, 8 cyl.	4.796875	4.75	1.75	1.407	45	45	.3725	.3715	....	....	....
1953	S18	4.84375	4.84375	1.718	1.501	45	45	.341	.340	....	....	....
	S16	4.796875	4.75	1.75	1.407	45	45	.3725	.3715	....	....	....
DODGE												
1940–41	Series—All	4.781	4.781	1.468	1.468	45	45	.340	.340	split lock	....	....
1942 to 52	D41, D42, 6 cyl.	4.78125	4.78125	1.53125	1.40625	45	45	.3405	.3405	....	....	....
1953	D46, D47	4.84375	4.84375	1.531	1.407	45	45	.3405	.3405	....	....	....
	D44, D48	4.75	4.75	1.656	1.407	45	45	.3725	.3715	....	....	....

Engine Overhaul Specifications

Year	Model	PISTONS: Removed From	PISTONS: Piston Skirt Clearances (Maximum): Top	Bottom	Limit	RING GAP CLEARANCES (Maximum): Top Ring	Second Ring	Third Ring	Oil Ring	PISTON PIN: Type	Fit	ROD BEARINGS: Oil Clearance	Wear Limit	Side Play
DE SOTO														
1940	S7 Custom, S7S DeLuxe	A	....	.0010*	.004	.015	.015	.015	.015	FL	Push	.0005-.0025	.004	.0055-.0115
1941	S8 DeLuxe	A	....	.0010*	.004	.015	.015	.015	.015	FL	Push	.0005-.0025	.004	.0055-.0115
	S8 Custom	A	....	.0010*	.004	.015	.015	.015	.015	FL	Push	.0005-.0025	.004	.0055-.0115
1942	S10 DeLuxe	A	....	.0018*	.004	.015	.015	.015	.015	FL	Press	.001-.0015	.004	.0055-.0115
	S10 Custom	A	....	.0018*	.004	.015	.015	.015	.015	FL	Press	.001-.0015	.004	.0055-.0115
1946	S11 Custom	A	....	.0015*	.004	.015	.015	.015	.015	FL	Push	.001-.0015	.004	.006-.011
1947	S11 Custom	A	....	.0015*	.004	.015	.015	.015	.015	FL	Push	.001-.0015	.004	.006-.011
1948	S11	A	....	.0015*	.004	.015	.015	.015	.015	FL	Push	.001-.0015	.004	.0055-.0115
1949	S13	A	....	.0012*	.004	.015	.015	.015	.015	FL	Push	.0005-.0015	.004	.003-.007
1950	S14	A	....	.0012*	.004	.015	.015	.015	.015	FL	Push	.0005-.0015	.004	.006-.011
1951	S-15-1 DeL., S-15-2 Cust.	A	....	.0012*	.004	.015	.015	.015	.015	FL	Push	.0005-.0015	.004	.006-.011
1952	S15-1, S15-2, 6 Cyl.	A	.0007*	....	....	.011	.011	.011	.011	FL	.0005	.0005-.0015	.004	.006-.011
	S17, 8 Cyl.	A	.0015*	....	....	.015	.015	....	.015	FL	.0005	.0005-.0015	.004	.006-.014
1953	S18, 6 Cyl.	A	.0007	....	....	.011	.011	.011	.011	FL	.0005	.0005-.0015	.004	.006-.011
	S16, 8 Cyl.	A	.0015	....	....	.015	.015	....	.015	FL	.0005	.0005-.0015	.004	.006-.014

A—Above. FL—Floating type. *—¾ inch from bottom. †—"○" marks on cam and crank sprockets align with shaft centers.

Year	Model	Removed From	Top	Bottom	Limit	Top Ring	Second Ring	Third Ring	Oil Ring	Type	Fit	Oil Clearance	Wear Limit	Side Play
DODGE														
1941	D19 DeLuxe, Custom	A	....	.00075*	.004	.015	.015	.015	.015	FL	Push	.0005-.0025	.004	.0055-.0115
1942	D22 DeLuxe, Custom	A	....	.0011*	.004	.015	.015	.015	.015	FL	Push	.001-.0015	.004	.0055-.0115
1946	D24 DeLuxe, Custom	A	....	.0015*	.004	.015	.015	.015	.015	FL	Push	.001-.0015	.004	.0055-.0115
1947	D24 DeLuxe, Custom	A	....	.0015*	.004	.015	.015	.015	.015	FL	Push	.001-.0015	.004	.0055-.0115
1948	D24	A	....	.0015*	.004	.015	.015	.015	.015	FL	Push	.001-.0015	.004	.0055-.0115
1949	D29, D30	A	....	.0015*	.004	.015	.015	.015	.015	FL	Push	.0005-.0015	.004	.006-.011
1950	D33, D34	A	....	.0015*	.004	.015	.015	.015	.015	FL	Push	.0005-.0015	.004	.006-.011
1951	D41, D42	A	....	.0012*	.004	.015	.015	.015	.015	FL	Push	.0005-.0015	.004	.006-.011
1952	D41, D42, 6 Cyl.	A	.0012*	....	....	.015	.015	.015	.015	FL	.0005	.0005-.0015	.004	.006-.011
1953	D46, D47, 6 Cyl.	A	.0007	....	....	.015	.015	.015	.015	FL	....	....	....	.006-.011
	D44, D48, 8 Cyl.	....	.0015	....	....	.015	.015	....	.015	FL	.0005	.0005-.0015	....	.006-.014

A—Pistons and rods removed from above.
*—¾ inch from bottom.
FL—Floats in piston and rod.
B—Before top center.

and Wear Limit Table

CRANKSHAFT		VALVES									OPERATING OIL PRESSURE			
Main Bearing Oil Clearance	Shaft End Play	Spring Tension (Maximum) Inlet	Exhaust	Low Limit	Guide Clearance	Seat Angle Inlet	Exhaust	Valve Timing, Inlet Valve Opens (Deg.)	Camshaft Drive	Gear Marks	Pounds At M.P.H.	Low Limit§	Model	Year
													DE SOTO	
.001-.002	.003-.007	115@1⅜	115@1⅜	103	.0015-.0035	45°	45°	12B	Chain	†SP	45@30	25	....S7 Cust., S7S DeLuxe	1940
.001-.002	.003-.007	115@1⅜	115@1⅜	103	.0015-.0035	45°	45°	12B	Chain	†SP	45@30	25	..............S8 DeLuxe	1941
.001-.002	.003-.007	115@1⅜	115@1⅜	103	.0015-.0035	45°	45°	12B	Chain	†SP	37@30	20	..............S8 Custom	
.001-.002	.003-.007	115@1⅜	115@1⅜	103	.0015-.0035	45°	45°	12B	Chain	†SP	37@30	20	............S10 DeLuxe	1942
.001-.0015	.003-.007	115@1⅜	115@1⅜	103	.0015-.0035	45°	45°	12B	Chain	†SP	37@30	20	............S10 Custom	
.001-.0015	.003-.007	115@1⅜	115@1⅜	103	.0015-.0035	45°	45°	12B	Chain	†SP	37@30	20	............S11 Custom	1946
.001-.0015	.003-.007	115@1⅜	115@1⅜	103	.0015-.0035	45°	45°	12B	Chain	†SP	37@30	20	............S11 Custom	1947
.001-.0015	.003-.007	115@1⅜	115@1⅜	103	.0015-.0035	45°	45°	12B	Chain	†SP	37@30	20	....................S11	1948
.0005-.0015	.003-.007	115@1⅜	115@1⅜	103	.0015-.0035	45°	45°	12B	Chain	†SP	52@45	30	....................S13	1949
.0005-.0015	.003-.007	115@1⅜	115@1⅜	103	.0015-.0035	45°	45°	12B	Chain	†SP	50@45	30	....................S14	1950
.0005-.0015	.003-.007	120@1⅜	120@1⅜	103	.0015-.0035	45°	45°	12B	Chain	†SP	50@20	30	.S-15-1 DeL., S-15-2 Cust.	1951
.0005-.0015	.003-.007	120@1⅜	120@1⅜	......	.002-.004	45°	45°	12B	Chain	......	50@45	......	......S15-1, S15-2, 6 Cyl.	1952
.0005-.0015	.002-.007	110@1$\frac{5}{16}$	110@1$\frac{5}{16}$	......	.002-.004	45°	45°	12B	Chain	......	50@45	......	..............S17, 8 Cyl.	
.0005-.0015	.003-.007	115@1.375	115@1.375	......	.002-.003	45°	45°	12B	Chain	......	50@30	......	..............S18, 6 Cyl.	1953
.0005-.0015	.002-.007	105@1.3125	105@1.3125	......	.002-.003	45°	45°	12B	Chain	......	50@30	......	..............S16, 8 Cyl.	

SP—Sprockets.
B—Before top center.

§—Car may be operated safely at lower oil pressures but low pressure indicates malfunction which should be corrected.

Main Bearing Oil Clearance	Shaft End Play	Inlet	Exhaust	Low Limit	Guide Clearance	Seat Inlet	Seat Exhaust	Valve Timing	Camshaft Drive	Gear Marks	Pounds At M.P.H.	Low Limit§	Model	Year
													DODGE	
.001-.002	.003-.004	115@1⅜	115@1⅜	103	.003	45°	45°	9B	Chain	†SP	45@30	25	.....D19 DeLuxe, Custom	1941
.001-.0015	.003-.007	115@1⅜	115@1⅜	103	.003	45°	45°	12B	Chain	†SP	40@40	25	.....D22 DeLuxe, Custom	1942
.001-.0015	.003-.007	115@1⅜	115@1⅜	103	.003	45°	45°	12B	Chain	†SP	40@40	25	.....D24 DeLuxe, Custom	1946
.001-.0015	.003-.007	115@1⅜	115@1⅜	103	.003	45°	45°	12B	Chain	†SP	40@40	25	.....D24 DeLuxe, Custom	1947
.001-.0015	.003-.007	115@1⅜	115@1⅜	103	.003	45°	45°	12B	Chain	†SP	40@40	25	......................D24	1948
.0005-.0015	.003-.007	115@1⅜	115@1⅜	103	.002-.004	45°	45°	8B	Chain	†SP	50@20	30	..................D29, D30	1949
.0005-.0015	.003-.007	115@1⅜	115@1⅜	103	.002-.004	45°	45°	8B	Chain	†SP	50@20	30	..................D33, D34	1950
.0005-.0015	.003-.007	120@1⅜	120@1⅜	103	.002-.004	45°	45°	8B	Chain	†SP	50@20	30	..................D41, D42	1951
.0005-.0015	.003-.007	120@1⅜	120@1⅜	......	.002-.004	45°	45°	8B	Chain	......	45@45	......	..........D41, D42, 6 Cyl.	1952
.0005-.0015	.003-.007	115@1.375	115@1.375	......	.002-.003	45°	45°	8B	Chain	......	45@30	......	..........D46, D47, 6 Cyl.	1953
.0005-.0015	.033-.007	105@1.312	105@1.312	......	.002-.003	45°	45°	17B	Chain	......	45@30	......	..........D44, D48, 8 Cyl.	

†—"•" marks on cam and crank sprockets align with shaft centers. SP—Sprockets.
§—Car may be operated safely at lower oil pressures but low pressure indicates malfunction which should be corrected.

DE SOTO and DODGE SPECIFICATIONS

Engine Tune-Up Specifications

Year	Model	Spark Plugs: Type	Spark Plugs: Gap	Distributor: Point Gap	Distributor: Cam Dwell, (Deg.)	Ignition Timing, (Deg.)	Ignition Timing Mark and Location	Compression Pressure at R.P.M.	Operating Tappet Clearance: Inlet	Operating Tappet Clearance: Exhaust	Carburetor Fuel Float Height	Minimum Engine Idle Speed at R.P.M.
DE SOTO												
1940	S7 Cust., S7S DeLuxe	AL-A7	.025	.020	38	2B	Dmpr.	155@1000	.008	.010	5/64″	450
1941	S8 DeLuxe S8 Custom	AL-A7 AL-A7	.025 .025	.020 .020	38 38	TC TC	Dmpr. Dmpr.	155@1000 155@1000	.008 .008	.010 .010	5/64″ 5/64″	450 450
1942	S10 DeLuxe S10 Custom	AL-A7 AL-A7	.025 .025	.020 .020	38 38	4A 4A	Dmpr. Dmpr.	160@1000 160@1000	.008 .008	.010 .010	5/64″ 5/64″	450 450
1946	S11 Custom	AL-A5	.025	.020	38	TC	Dmpr.	160@1000	.008	.010	5/64″	450
1947	S11 Custom	AL-A5	.025	.020	38	TC	Dmpr.	160@1000	.008	.010	5/64″	450
1948	S11	AL-A5	.025	.020	38	TC	Dmpr.	160@1000	.008	.010	5/64″	450
1949	S13	AL-AR5	.038	.020	34½–38	2A	Dmpr.	160@1000	.008	.010	5/64″	450
1950	S14	AL-AR5	.035	.019	34½–38	TC	Dmpr.	160@1000	.008	.010	5/64″	450
1951	S-15-1 DeL., S-15-2 Cust.	AL-AR8	.035	.020	34½–38	2B	Dmpr.	....	.008	.010	....	450
1952	S15-1, S15-2, 6 Cyl. S-17, 8 Cyl.	AL-AR8 AL-4S140	.035 .035	.020 .017	38 36	2B 4B	Dmpr. Dmpr.	....	.008H AA	.010H AA	5/64″ 11/64″	475 475
1953	S-18, 6 Cyl. S-16, 8 Cyl.	AL-AR8 AL-4S140	.035 .035	.020 .018	39±3° 36	2B 4B	Dmpr. Dmpr	....	.008H AA	.010H AA	....	475 475

AL—Auto-Lite Spark Plug Co. Dmpr—Vibration damper. B—Before top center. A—After top center. TC—Top center.
H—Hot. AA—Automatic adjustment.

Year	Model	Spark Plugs: Type	Spark Plugs: Gap	Distributor: Point Gap	Distributor: Cam Dwell, (Deg.)	Ignition Timing, (Deg.)	Ignition Timing Mark and Location	Compression Pressure at R.P.M.	Operating Tappet Clearance: Inlet	Operating Tappet Clearance: Exhaust	Carburetor Fuel Float Height	Minimum Engine Idle Speed at R.P.M.
DODGE												
1941	D19 DeLuxe, Custom	AL-A7	.025	.020	38	TC	Dmpr.	125@ #	.008	.010	5/8″	450
1942	D22 DeLuxe, Custom	AL-A7	.025	.020	38	TC	Dmpr.	160@1000	.008	.010	5/8″	450
1946 to 48	D24 DeLuxe, Custom	AL-A5	.025	.020	38	2A	Dmpr.	160@1000	.008	.010	5/8″	450
1949	D29, D30	AL-AR5	.038	.020	38	2A	Dmpr.	160@1000	.008	.010	5/8″	450
1950	D33, D34	AL-AR5	.035	.020	38	TC	Dmpr.	160@1000	.008	.010	5/8″	450
1951	D41, D42	AL-AR8	.035	.020	34½–38	2B	Dmpr.	....	.008	.010	....	450
1952	D-41, D-42, 6 Cyl.	AL-AR8	.035	.020	38	2B	Dmpr.	....	.008H	.010H	....	475
1953	D46, D47, 6 Cyl. D44, D48, 8 Cyl.	AL-AR8 AL-4S140	.035 .035	.020 .017	39±3° 36	2B 4B	Dmpr. Dmpr.	....	.008H AA	.010H AA	....	475 475

AL—Auto-Lite Co. A—After top center. TC—Top center. Dmpr—Vibration damper. B—Before top center. #—Cranking speed.
H—Hot. AA—Automatic adjustment.

General Engine Specifications

Year	Model	Number of Cylinders Bore and Stroke	Piston Displacement, Cubic Inches	Compression Ratio (To–1)	Taxable (A.M.A.) Hp.	Developed Horse Power: Bare Engine	Developed Horse Power: With Accessories	Maximum Torque Ft. Lbs.
DE SOTO								
1940	S7 Custom, S7S DeLuxe	6-3⅜ x 4¼	228.1	6.50	27.3	100 @ 3600	....	176 @ 1200
1941	S8 DeLuxe & Custom	6-3⅜ x 4¼	228.1	6.80	27.3	105 @ 3600	....	178 @ 1200
1942	S10 DeLuxe & Custom	6-3 7/16 x 4¼	236.6	6.60	28.3	115 @ 3800	....	190 @ 1600

General Engine Specifications—*continued*

Year	Model	Number of Cylinders Bore and Stroke	Piston Displacement, Cubic Inches	Compression Ratio (To–1)	Taxable (A.M.A.) Hp.	DEVELOPED HORSE POWER Bare Engine	With Accessories	Maximum Torque Ft. Lbs.
DE SOTO—cont.								
1946	S11 Custom	6–$3\frac{7}{16}$ x $4\frac{1}{4}$	236.6	6.60	28.4	109 @ 3600	....	192 @ 1200
1947	S11 Custom	6–$3\frac{7}{16}$ x $4\frac{1}{4}$	236.6	6.60	28.3	109 @ 3600	....	192 @ 1200
1948	S11	6–$3\frac{7}{16}$ x $4\frac{1}{4}$	236.6	6.60	27.3	109 @ 3600	....	192 @ 1200
1949	S13	6–$3\frac{7}{16}$ x $4\frac{1}{4}$	236.7	7.00	28.3	112 @ 3600	....	195 @ 1600
1950	S14	6–$3\frac{7}{16}$ x $4\frac{1}{4}$	236.6	7.00	28.4	112 @ 3600	....	195 @ 1200
1951	S-15-1 DeL., S-15-2 Custom	6–$3\frac{7}{16}$ x $4\frac{1}{2}$	250.6	....	28.36	116 @ 3600	....	208 @ 1600
1952 to 53	S15-1 DeL., S15-2 Custom S18, S16, S17, 8 Cyl.	6–$3\frac{7}{16}$ x $4\frac{1}{2}$ V8–$3\frac{5}{8}$ x $3\frac{11}{32}$	250.6 276.1	7.00 7.10	28.36 42.05	116 @ 3600 160 @ 4400	....	208 @ 1600 250 @ 2000
DODGE								
1940	D14 DeLuxe, D17 Special	6–$3\frac{1}{4}$ x $4\frac{3}{8}$	217.8	6.50	25.3	87 @ 3600	....	166 @ 1200
1941	D19 DeLuxe & Custom	6–$3\frac{1}{4}$ x $4\frac{3}{8}$	217.8	6.50	25.3	91 @ 3800	....	170 @ 1200
1942	D22 DeLuxe & Custom	6–$3\frac{1}{4}$ x $4\frac{5}{8}$	230.2	6.70	25.3	105 @ 3600	....	185 @ 1600
1946	D24 DeLuxe & Custom	6–$3\frac{1}{4}$ x $4\frac{5}{8}$	230.2	6.70	25.4	102 @ 3600	....	184 @ 1200
1947	D24 DeLuxe & Custom	6–$3\frac{1}{4}$ x $4\frac{5}{8}$	230.2	6.70	25.3	102 @ 3600	....	184 @ 1200
1948	D24	6–$3\frac{1}{4}$ x $4\frac{5}{8}$	230.2	6.70	25.3	102 @ 3600	....	184 @ 1200
1949 to 52	All, 6 cyl.	6–$3\frac{1}{4}$ x $4\frac{5}{8}$	230.2	7.00	25.4	103 @ 3600	....	190 @ 1200
1953	D44, D48, 8 cyl.	V8–$3\frac{7}{16}$ x $3\frac{1}{4}$	241.3	7.1	37.80	140 @ 4400	....	220 @ 2000

Crankshaft Bearing Journal Sizes

Year	Model	Connecting Rod Journals Diameter	Length	Main Bearing Journals No. 1 Diameter	No. 2 Diameter	No. 3 Diameter	No. 4 Diameter	No. 5 Diameter
DE SOTO								
1940 to 52	S15-1, S15-2, 6 cyl. S17, 8 cyl.	2.124–2.125 2.062	1.2187	2.499–2.500 2.375	2.499–2.500 2.375	2.499–2.500 2.375	2.499–2.500 2.375	.... 2.375
1953	S18, 6 cyl. S16, 8 cyl.	2.125 2.062	....	2.5–1.55 2.375–.812	2.5–1.55 2.375–.812	2.5–1.55 2.375–.807	2.5–1.589 2.375–.812	.... 2.375–1.532
DODGE								
1940 to 52	D41, D42, 6 cyl.	2.0615–2.0625	1.00	2.499–2.500	2.499–2.500	2.499–2.500	2.499–2.500	....
1953	D46, D47, 6 cyl. D44, D48, 8 cyl.	2.0625 1.9375	....	2.5–1.204 2.375–.822	2.5–2.1000 2.375–.822	2.5–1.000 2.375–.802	2.5–1.589 2.375–1.532	....

DE SOTO and DODGE SPECIFICATIONS

Pistons and Piston Pins

Year	Model	PISTONS				PISTON PINS		
		Diameter	Material	Type	No. of Rings	Length	Diameter	How Held
DE SOTO								
1940 to 52	All, 6 cyl. S17, 8 cyl.	3.4375 3.625	Alum. Alloy Alum. Alloy	Us,C Ts,C,Sp	4 3	2.875 3.065	.859375 .922	F F
1953	S18, 6 cyl. S16, V8	3.4375 3.625	Alum. Alloy Alum. Alloy	Us,C Ts,C,Sp	4 3	2.875 3.065	.859375 .922	F F
DODGE								
1940 to 53	D46, D47, 6 cyl. D44, D48, V8	3.25 3.4375	Alum. Alloy Alum. Alloy	Us,C Ts,C,Sp	4 3	2.746 2.885	.8592 .8592	F F

Alum—Aluminum. Us—"U" slot. C—Camground. Ts—"T" slot. Sp—Slipperskirt. F—Floating.

Piston Ring Dimensions

Year	Model	Cylinder Bore	TOP RING			SECOND RING			THIRD RING			OIL RING		
			Width	Gap	Depth	Width	Gap	Depth	Width	Gap	Depth	Width	Gap	Depth
DE SOTO														
1940–41	S7, S8	3⅜	⅛	.011	.150	⅛	.011	.145	5/32	.011	.145	5/32	.011	.145
1942–51	S10, S11, S13, S14, S15	3 7/16	3/32	.011	.169	3/32	.011	.169	5/32	.011	.150	5/32	.011	.150
1952	S15-1, S15-2, 6 Cyl. S17, 8 Cyl.	3 7/16 3⅝	3/32 .078	.011 .015	.1765 .193	3/32 .078	.011 .015	.1765 .193	5/32 .186	.011 .015	.178 .192	5/32	.011	.178 ......
1953	S-18, 6 Cyl. S-16, V8	3 7/16 3⅝	3/32 .078	.011 .015	.172 .176	3/32 .078	.011 .015	.172 .176	5/32 .186	.011 .015	.155 .140	5/32	.011	.155 ......
DODGE														
1940	D14, D17	3¼	⅛	.011	.150	⅛	.011	.145	5/32	.011	.145	5/32	.011	.145
1941	D19	3¼	3/32	.011	.162	⅛	.011	.145	5/32	.011	.145	5/32	.011	.145
1942–48	D22, D24	3¼	3/32	.011	.169	3/32	.011	.169	5/32	.011	.150	5/32	.011	.150
1949–51	D29, D30, D33, D34, D41, D42	3¼	3/32	.011	.162	3/32	.011	.162	5/32	.011	.155	5/32	.011	.155
1952	D41, D42, 6 Cyl.	3¼	3/32	.011	.169	3/32	.011	.169	9/64	.011	.172	9/64	.011	.172
1953	D46, D47, 6 Cyl. D44, D48, V8	3¼ 3 7/16	.093 .078	.011 .011	.162 .172	.093 .078	.011 .011	.162 .172	.155 .186	.011 .011	.137 .140	.155	.011	.150 ......

Brake Data

Year	Model	Make	Lining Type	R=Riveted B=Bonded	Drum Diameter	Lining			Clearance	
						Length	Width	Thickness	Toe	Heel
DE SOTO										
1940 to 42	Series—All	Loc	M	....	11	19 7/16	2	13/64	.012	.006
1946 to 49	Series—All	C-L	M	....	11	23-*20⅜	2	13/64	.006	.006
1950-51	S14, S15	C-L	M	....	12	25⅛	2	13/64	.006	.006
1952	S15-1, S15-2, 6 Cyl., S17, 8 Cyl.	C-L	M	B	12	25 9/64	2	13/64	.006	.006
1953	S16, V8; S18, 6 Cyl.	C-L	M	B	12	25 9/64	2	13/64	.006	.006

*—Rear. Loc—Lockheed. C-L—Chrysler Lockheed. M—Moulded.

Brake Data—*continued*

Year	Model	Make	Lining Type	R=Riveted B=Bonded	Drum Diameter	Lining Length	Lining Width	Lining Thickness	Clearance Toe	Clearance Heel
DODGE										
1940 to 42	Series—All	Loc	M	R	11	19 7/16	2	13/64	.012	.006
1946 to 49	Series—All	C-L	M	R-B†	11	23–*20 3/8	2	13/64	.006	.006
1950-51	D33, D41	Own	M	B	10	21–*18 1/2	2	13/64	.006	.006
	D34, D42	Own	M	B	11	23–*20 3/8	2	13/64	.006	.006
1952	D41, 6 Cyl.	Own	M	B	10	21–*18 1/2	2	1/8	.006	.006
	D42, 6 Cyl.	Own	M	B	11	23–*20 5/16	2	1/8	.006	.006
1953	D46, 6 Cyl.	Own	M	B	11	23–*20 5/16	2	....	.006	.006
	D47, 6 Cyl.	Own	M	B	10	21–*18 1/2	2	....	.006	.006
	D44, D48, V8	Own	M	B	11	23–*20 5/16	2	....	.006	.006

* Rear. † 1949. Loc—Lockheed. C-L—Chrysler Lockheed. M—Moulded.

Tension Wrench Specifications

Year	Model	Cylinder Head Lbs.-Ft.	Cylinder Head Thread	Spark Plug Lbs.-Ft.	Spark Plug Thread	Connecting Rod Bolts or Nuts Lbs.-Ft.	Connecting Rod Bolts or Nuts Thread	Main Bearing Bolt Lbs.-Ft.	Main Bearing Bolt Thread	Flywheel Bolts Lbs.-Ft.	Flywheel Bolts Thread	Vibration Damper Bolts Lbs.-Ft.	Vibration Damper Bolts Thread
DE SOTO													
1914 to 49	S8, S10, S11	52–57	7/16	30–32	14 mm	45–50	3/8–24	75–80	....	55–60	1/2–20	15–17	5/16
		85–90	1/2	30–32	14 mm	50–75	7/16–24	75–80	....	55–60	1/2–20	30–35	3/8
1950–51	S13, S14, S15	52–57	7/16–20	30–32	14 mm	45–50	3/8–24	80–85	1/2–13	55–60	1/2–20	15–17	5/16–24
1952–53	V8	80–85	....	30–32	14 mm	45–50	....	80–85	1/2–13	45–50	....	15–17	5/16
DODGE													
1940	D14, D17	52–57	7/16	26–32	14 mm	52.5–57.5	....	75–80	....	....	....	....	....
1941 to 48	....	65–70	....	26–32	14 mm	45–50	3/8–24	75–80	....	55–60	1/2–20	15–17	5/16
1949–50	D29, D30, D33, D34	65–70	....	30–32	14 mm	45–50	3/8–24	80–85	1/2–13	55–60	1/2–20	15–17	5/16
1951 to 53	6 cyl.	65–70	....	30–32	14 mm	45–50	3/8–24	80–85	1/2–13	55–60	1/2–20	15–17	5/16
1953	V8	....	....	....	....	....	....	....	....	....	....	....	....

Cooling System Capacities and Anti-Freeze Proportion Table

CAR AND YEAR	MODEL	Capacity Qts.	Quarts of Methanol Base Anti-Freeze (For Protection to Temperature Shown Below)							Quarts of Ethylene Glycol (For Protection to Temperature Shown Below)							Quarts of Denatured Alcohol—188 Proof (For Protection to Temperature Shown Below)						
			3	4	5	6	7	8	9	3	4	5	6	7	8	9	3	4	5	6	7	8	9
DE SOTO																							
1940	S-7	17	15	6	−4	−16	−29	−45	....	18	12	5	−4	−14	−27	−42	....	10	0	....	−10	−20	−30
1941-42	S-8, S-10	18	17	8	−1	−12	−25	−38	−53	19	14	7	0	−10	−21	−34	20	10	....	0	−10	....	−20
1946-50	S-11	17	15	6	−4	−16	−29	−45	....	18	12	5	−4	−14	−27	−42	....	10	0	....	−10	−20	−30
1951	S-14, S-15	17	15	6	−4	−16	−29	−45	....	18	12	5	−4	−14	−27	−42	....	10	0	0	−10	−20	−30
DODGE																							
1937	....	16	13	3	−8	−21	−36	−53	....	17	10	2	−8	−19	−34	−52	....	10	0	−10	....	−20	−30
1938-50	....	15	11	1	−12	−27	−44	....	....	16	8	0	−12	−26	−43	....	....	10	0	−10	−20	−30	....
1951-53	....	14	9	−3	−17	−34	−53	....	....	15	6	−5	−18	−34	−54	....	10	....	0	−10	−20	−30	....
1953	V8	19	17	8	−1	−12	−25	−38	....	20	15	9	2	−7	−16	−28	20	10	....	0	−10	....	−20

DE SOTO and DODGE SPECIFICATIONS

Distributors

Year	Model	Distributor Model Number	Cam Angle (deg.)	Direction of Rotation C=Clockwise CC=Counter Clockwise at Cam End	Breaker Arm Spring Tension	Breaker Point Gap (inches)	Engine R.P.M. when Cent. Advance Starts	Max. Cent. Advance in Engine Deg. at Stated Engine R.P.M.	Vacuum in (inches) of Mercury at which Vacuum Unit Starts	Max. Advance in Engine Deg. at Stated Vacuum	Vacuum Unit Number
DE SOTO											
1941	S8C, S8S, 6 cyl.	IGS-4113-1	38	C	17–20	.018–.022	700	24@3500	5	14@15	IGS-1023-HS
	....	IGS-4202-1	38	C	17–20	.018–.022	700	24@3500	5	14@15	VC-3082-RBS
1942	S10C, S10S, 6 cyl.	IGS-4117-1	38	C	17–20	.018–.022	700	24@3500	5	14@15	IGS-1023-HS
	....	IGS-4202A-1	38	C	17–20	.018–.022	700	22@2800	5.13	12@15	VC-3082-RES
	....	IGS-4208-1	38	C	17–20	.018–.022	700	28@2800	5.13	12@14	VC-3082-RES
1946 to 48	S11, 6 cyl.	IGS-4208-1	38	C	17–20	.018–.022	700	28@2800	5.13	12@14	....
1949–50	S13, S14, 6 cyl.	IAP-4102C-1	34½	C	17–20	.018–.022	700	22@2800	5	9@15	....
1951	S15, 6 cyl.	IAT-4012	36¼	C	....	.018–.022	700	22@2850	5.5	20	....
1952	S15-1, S15-2, 6 cyl.	IAT-4012	34½–38	C	17–20	.020	....	11@1425	5½–6½	8–10@15	....
	S17, 8 cyl.	IAZ-4002	32–36	C	17–20	.017	....	15@1900	5½–6½	10–12@17	....
1953	S18, 6 cyl.	IAT-4012	39±3	C	17–20	.018–.020	350	11@1425	5.5–6	8–10@15	....
	S16, 8 cyl.	IAZ-4002	32–36	C	17–20	.015–.018	350	15@1900	5.5–6	10–12@17	....
DODGE											
1940	D14, D17, 6 cyl.	IGS-4107-1	38	C	17–20	.018–.022	700	24@3500	5	16@16	IGT-1023-GS
1941	D19, 6 cyl.	IGS-4112-1	38	C	17–20	.018–.022	700	24@3500	5	16@16	IGT-1023-GS
	....	IGS-4203-1	38	C	17–20	.018–.022	700	24@3500	5	16@16	VC-3082-RAS
1942	D22, 6 cyl.	IGS-4203B-1	38	C	17–20	.018–.022	700	20@2300	5	17@16	VC-3082-RGS
	....	IGS-4203A-1	38	C	17–20	.018–.022	700	18@2600	5	18@14	VC-3082-RDS
1946 to 48	D24, 6 cyl.	IGS-4207A-1	38	C	17–20	.018–.022	700	20@2300	5	17@16	....
	D25, 6 cyl.	IGS-4207-1	38	C	17–20	.018–.022	700	20@2300	5	17@16	....
1949	D29. 6 cyl.	IGS-4203B-1	38	C	17–20	.018–.022	700	20@2300	5	17@16	VC-3082-RGS
1950	D33, D34, 6 cyl.	IAP-4103A-1	34½	C	17–20	.018–.022	700	20@2850	4½	16@14	....
1951	D41, D42, 6 cyl.	IAT-4011	36¼	....	17–20	.018–.022	700	22@2850	5.5	18	....
1952	D41, D42, 6 cyl.	IAT-4011	34½–38	C	17–20	.020	....	11@1426	5½–6½	7–9@14	....
1953	D46, D47, 6 cyl.	IAT-4011	39±3	C	17–20	.020	350	11@1425	5½–6½	7–9@14	....
	D44, D48, 8 cyl.	IAZ-4003	32–36	C	17–20	.017	350	16@1750	5½–6½	10–12@14	....

Generators

Year	Model	Generator Number	Field Current at 6 Volts (amps.)	Maximum Safe Output			Brush Spring Tension (oz.)	Voltage Regulator Number
				Volts	Amperes	R.P.M.		
DE SOTO								
1940 to 42	S7, S8, S10	GDZ-4801-A	1.3–1.5	8.0	35	2000	35–53	VRP-4001-A
1946 to 48	S11	GDZ-4801-A	1.3–1.5	8.0	35	2000	35–53	VRP-4503-A
		GDZ-4801-R	1.3–1.5	8.0	35	2000	35–53	VRP-4503-A

Generators—*continued*

Year	Model	Generator Number	Field Current at 6 Volts (amps.)	Maximum Safe Output Volts	Amperes	R.P.M.	Brush Spring Tension (oz.)	Voltage Regulator Number
DE SOTO—cont.								
1949	S13	GDZ-4801-R	1.3–1.5	8.0	35	2000	35–53	VRP-4503-A
		GGJ-6001-A	1.5–1.7	8.0	50	1600	30–37	VBA-4101-A
		GGJ-6001-B	1.5–1.7	8.0	50	1600	30–37	VBA-4101-A
		GGU-6001-A	1.4–1.5	8.0	45	1650	35–53	VBA-4101-B
1950	S14	GGW-6001-A	1.6–1.8	8.0	40	2000	35–53	VRP-6004-A
1951	S15	GGW-6001-J	1.6–1.8	8.0	40	2000	35–53	VRP-6004-A
1952	S15-1, S15-2, 6 cyl.	GGW-6001-J	1.6–1.8	8.0	40	2000	35–53	VBE-6001-A
	S17, 8 cyl.	GGW-6001-X	....	....	....	....	....	VBE-6001-A
1953	S18, S16	GGW-6001	....	7.4	45	1000	....	VBE-6001-A
DODGE								
1940	D14, 15, 16, 17	GDZ-4801-A	1.3–1.5	8.0	35	2000	35–53	VRP-4001-A
1941–42	D19, D20, D21, D22	GDZ-4801-A	1.3–1.5	8.0	35	2000	35–53	VRP-4001-A
		GDZ-4801-B	1.3–1.5	8.0	35	2000	35–53	VRP-4001-A
1946 to 48	D24, D25	GDZ-4801-A	1.3–1.5	8.0	35	2000	35–53	VRP-4001-A
		GDZ-4801-B	1.3–1.5	8.0	35	2000	35–53	VRP-4001-A
		GEG-4823-A	1.3–1.5	8.0	40	1575	64–68	VRP-4001-F
		GEG-4823-B	1.3–1.5	8.0	40	1575	64–68	VRP-4001-F
		GGJ-6001-A	1.5–1.7	8.0	50	1600	30–37	VAV-4404-A
1949	D29, D30	GDZ-4801-A	1.3–1.5	8.0	35	2000	35–53	VRP-4503-A
		GDZ-4801-R	1.3–1.5	8.0	35	2000	35–53	VRP-4503-A
		GGW-6001-B	1.6–1.8	8.0	40	2000	35–53	VRP-4503-B
		GGW-6001-A	1.6–1.8	8.0	40	2000	35–53	VRP-4503-B
		GGJ-6001-B	1.5–1.7	8.0	50	1600	30–37	VBA-4101-A
		GGJ-6001-A	1.5–1.7	8.0	50	1600	30–37	VBA-4101-B
	D31, D32	GDZ-4801-A	1.3–1.5	8.0	35	2000	35–53	VRP-4503-A
		GGW-6001-B	1.5–1.7	8.0	50	1600	30–37	VRP-4503-B
		GGJ-6001-B	1.5–1.7	8.0	50	1600	30–37	VBA-4101-A
		GGJ-6001-A	1.5–1.7	8.0	50	1600	30–37	VBA-4101-A
1950	D33, D34	GGW-6001-D	1.6–1.8	8.0	40	2000	35–53	VRP-6004-A
		GGW-6001-A	1.6–1.8	8.0	40	2000	35–53	VRP-6004-A
1951	D41, D42	GGW-6001-K	1.6–1.8	8.0	40	2000	35–53	VRP-6004-A
1952	D41, D42, 6 cyl.	GGW-6001	....	8.0	40	2000	35–53	VBE-6001-A
1953	D46, D47, 6 cyl.	GGW-6001	....	8.0	45	1000	....	VBE-6001-A
	D44, D48, 8 cyl.	GGW-6009	....	7.4	45	1000	....	VBE-6001-A

Starters

Year	Model	Unit Model Number	Spring Tension (oz.)	STARTER Lock Test Volts	Lock Test Amperes	Lock Test Torque, (lbs. ft.)	No Load Volts	No Load Amperes	No Load R.P.M.	Direction of Rotation Viewed from Drive End C=Clockwise CC=Counter-clockwise
DE SOTO										
1941	S8C, S8S	MAW-4019	42–53	2.0	335	6	5.0	65	4300	C
		MAW-4019-A	42–53	2.0	335	6	5.0	65	4300	C
1942	S10C, S10S	MAW-4026	42–53	2.0	335	6	5.0	65	4300	C
		MAX-4050	42–53	2.0	410	8	5.0	65	4900	C

DE SOTO and DODGE SPECIFICATIONS

Starters—*continued*

Year	Model	Unit Model Number	Spring Tension (oz.)	STARTER: Lock Test			STARTER: No Load			Direction of Rotation Viewed from Drive End C=Clockwise CC=Counter-clockwise
				Volts	Amperes	Torque, (lbs. ft.)	Volts	Amperes	R.P.M.	
DE SOTO—cont.										
1946 to 48	S11	MAW-4025	42–53	2.0	335	6	5.0	65	4300	C
1949–50	S13, S14	MCH-6102	42–53	2.0	335	6	5.0	65	4300	C
1951	S15	MCL-6108	42–53	2.0	410	8	6.0	57.5	5300	C
1952	S15-1, S15-2, 6 cyl., S17, 8 cyl.	MCL-6116	42–53	2	410	8	6	50–65	5300	C
1953	S18, 6 cyl.	MCL6117	42–53	3	610	15	5.5	50–65	5300	C
	S16, 8 cyl.	MCH-6113	42–53	3	500	11	5.5	50–65	4900	C
DODGE										
1941	D19	MZ-4089	42–53	2.0	280	4.4	5.0	68	4000	C
		MZ-4089-A	42–53	2.0	280	4.4	5.0	68	4000	C
1942	D22, D23	MAW-4026	42–53	2.0	335	6	5.0	65	4300	C
1946 to 48	D24	MAW-4041	42–53	2.0	335	6	5.0	65	4300	C
	D25	MZ-4133	42–53	2.0	280	4.4	5.0	68	4000	C
1949 to 51	Series—All	MCH-6101	42–53	2.0	335	6	5.0	65	4300	C
1952	D41, D42, 6 cyl.	MCH-6201	42–53	2	335	6	6	50–65	4900	C
1953	D46, D47, 6 cyl.	MCH-6205	42–53	3	500	11	5.5	50–65	4900	C
	D44, D48, V8	MCH-6206	42–53	3	500	11	5.5	50–65	4900	C

Voltage Regulators

Year	Model	Regulator Number	Grounded P=Positive N=Negative	Voltage Control		Current Control		Cut-Out Relay		
				Air Gap Points Closed	Voltage Setting Hot	Air Gap Points Closed	Current Set Hot	Point Gap	Air Gap	Closing Volt
DE SOTO										
1940 to 42	S7, S8, S10	VRP-4001-A	P	.052	7.2	.052	34–36	.015	.034	6.4–7.0
1946 to 48	S11	VRP-4503-A	P	.052	7.2	.052	35	.015	.034	6.4–7.0
		VRP-4001-F	P	.052	7.2	.052	39–41	.015	.034	6.4–7.0
		VAV-4404-A	P	.052	7.2	.052	50	.015	.034	6.4–7.0
		VAV-4404-B	P	.052	7.2	.052	50	.015	.034	6.4–7.0
1949	S13	VRP-4503-A	P	.052	7.2	.052	35	.015	.034	6.4–7.0
		VRP-4503-B	P	.052	7.2	.052	35	.015	.034	6.4–7.0
		VBA-4101-A	P	.052	7.2	.052	50	.015	.034	6.4–7.0
		VBA-4101-B	P	.052	7.2	.052	50	.015	.034	6.4–7.0
1950	S14	VRP-6004-A	P	.051	7.35	.050	38–42	.015	.032	6.4–7.0
		VAV-6001-A	P	.051	7.2	.050	51	.015	.032	6.4–7.0
		VBA-4202-A	P	.051	7.2	.050	51	.015	.032	6.4–7.0
1951	S15-1	VRP-6004-A	P	.051	7.35	.050	38–42	.015	.032	6.4–7.0
	S15-2	VRP-6004-A	P	.051	7.35	.050	38–42	.015	.032	6.4–7.0
1952	S15-1, S15-2, 6 cyl., S17, 8 cyl.	VBE-6001-A			7.4–7.7		45–57			6.4–7.0
1953	S16, S18	VBE-6001-A			7.1–7.4		45–57			6.4–6.8

Voltage Regulators—*continued*

Year	Model	Regulator Number	Grounded P=Positive N=Negative	Voltage Control Air Gap Points Closed	Voltage Control Voltage Setting Hot	Current Control Air Gap Points Closed	Current Control Current Set Hot	Cut-Out Relay Point Gap	Cut-Out Relay Air Gap	Cut-Out Relay Closing Volt
DODGE										
1940 to 42	D14, D19, D22	VRP-4001-A	P	.052	7.2	.052	34-36	.015	.034	6.4–7.0
1946 to 48	D24, D25	VRP-4503-A VRP-4001-F VAV-4404-A	P P P	.052 .052 .052	7.2 7.2 7.2	.052 .052 .052	35 39–41 50	.015 .015 .015	.034 .034 .034	6.4–7.0 6.4–7.0 6.4–7.0
1949	D29, D30, D31, D32	VRP-4503-A VRP-4503-B VBA-4101-A	P P P	.052 .052 .052	7.2 7.2 7.2	.052 .052 .052	35 35 50	.015 .015 .015	.034 .034 .034	6.4–7.0 6.4–7.0 6.4–7.0
1950-51	D33, D34, D41, D42	VRP-6004-A	P	.051	7.2	.050	38-42	....	.032	6.4–7.0
1952	D41, D42, 6 cyl.	VBE-6001-A	....	....	7.1–7.4	....	45–57	....	....	6.4–7.0
1953	D46, 47, 48, 48	VBE-6001-A	....	....	7.1–7.4	....	45–57	....	....	6.3–6.8

Front Wheel Alignment

Year	Model	Caster (deg.)	Camber (deg.)	King Pin Inclination (deg.)	Toe-In (inches)	Turning Radius Inner	Turning Radius Outer
DE SOTO							
1940	S7	1N to 1P	0 to ¾P	4¾ to 6	0 to ⅛	22	20
1941–49	S8, S10, S11, S13	1N to 1P	0 to ¾P	4¾ to 6	0 to 1/16	22	20
1950	S14	1N to 3N	0 to ¾P	4¾ to 6	0 to 1/16	22	20
1951–52	S15, S17	1N to 3N	⅜N to ⅜P	5 to 6½	0 to 1/16	22	20
1953	S16, S17	1N to 3N	⅜N to ⅜P	5 to 6½	0 to 1/16	18¼	20
DODGE							
1940	D14, D17	1N to 1P	0 to ¾P	4¾ to 6	0 to ⅛	22	20
1941–42	All	1N to 1P	0 to ¾P	4¾ to 6	0 to 1/16	22	20
1946–50	D24, D29, D30, D33, D34	1N to 1P	0 to ¾P	4¾ to 6	0 to 1/16	22	20
1951–52	D41, D42, to 1952 Models	0 to 1P	⅜N to ⅜P	5 to 6½	0 to 1/16	....	....
1953	All	0 to 1P	⅜N to ⅜P	5 to 6½	0 to 1/16	18¼	20

N—Negative. P—Positive.

DE SOTO and DODGE 1940 thru 1953

FRONT SUSPENSION

The short and long arm front suspension used on all DeSoto and Dodge cars is commonly referred to as the S.L.A. type.

This type suspension unit fundamentally consists of an upper and lower control arm; shock absorber, knuckle support and coil spring.

Steering Geometry—Caster, Camber and Toe-In

Check and note all angles before adjusting any one angle of either side.

Caster and Camber are both adjusted at the eccentric bushing in the upper end of the knuckle support. This bushing is turned in a clockwise direction to increase caster. When properly adjusted the upper end of the knuckle support will be approximately midway between the yoke of the upper suspension arm. Since caster and camber are both adjusted at the same eccentric bushing it will be necessary to seek a compromise between the best caster and camber adjustment.

Where it is desired to come to an exact adjustment it will be necessary to secure the caster adjustment by turning the eccentric bushing until the exact caster reading is obtained. Then cold bend the knuckle support to secure the exact camber reading.

Caution: At no time should heat be applied to the knuckle support since these parts are heat treated after forging, and reheating to simplify bending will destroy the heat treatment and render the part useless.

The procedure for adjusting caster and camber is as follows: Leave the weight of the car resting on its wheels and reach up to the top of the knuckle support and loosen the clamp screw which holds the eccentric bushing.

Turn the eccentric bushing in the direction indicated in the paragraphs above until the correct caster is obtained and from that setting continue to turn it until the correct camber is obtained.

Tighten the clamp screw.

If the little special offset wrench is not available it will be necessary to jack up the car and remove the wheel before loosening the clamp screw and turning the bushing. If the bushing is to be turned with an ordinary open-end wrench it can only be done with the wheel off. This naturally requires a lot of time since each time the setting is tested the wheel will have to be replaced to check the front suspension setting.

Toe-In Adjustment

Set the steering wheel in a straight ahead position and loosen the tie-rod clamp bolts on both tie-rods.

Turn both tie-rods equally until correct toe-in is obtained.

Note: Tie-rods are mixed in production so that on some they would be turned to the left, and the other turned to the right to increase toe-in.

Replacement of Coil Spring or Other Suspension Parts

When replacing a front spring, it is wise to inspect the upper and lower pivot pin and bushing, or any other part that may need replacing, as this will affect the actual procedure.

In any case where it is necessary to replace the coil spring only, place a jack under the lower control arm inner pivot shaft. The car must be raised to a height that will permit the control arm to be lowered enough to allow the coil spring to be removed. Always take the precaution of inserting a stand jack under the frame to support the car weight.

Detach the shock absorber and torsion bar and with a jack pressed solidly against the inner pivot shaft, remove the four bolts holding the inner shaft

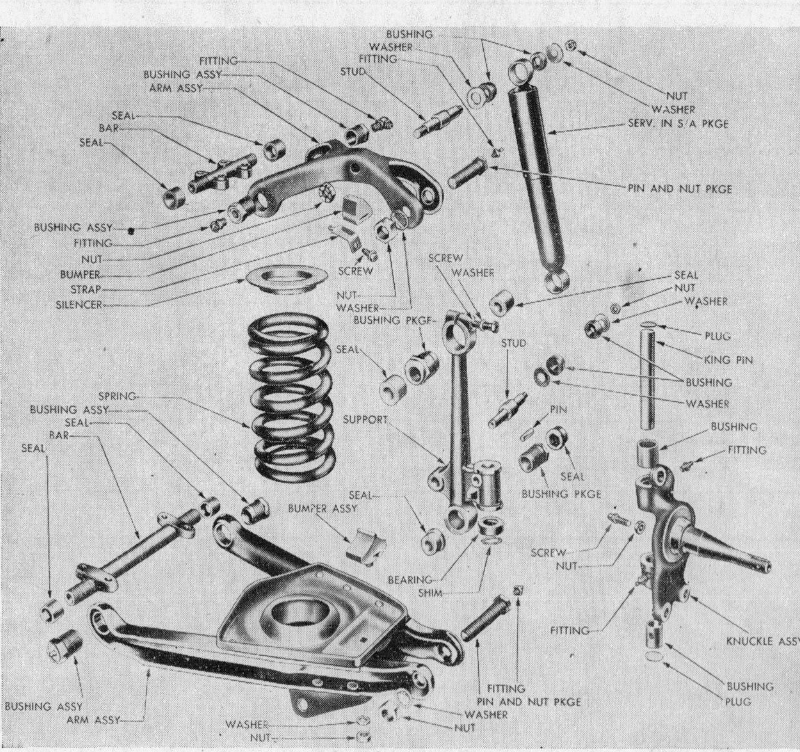

Front Suspension

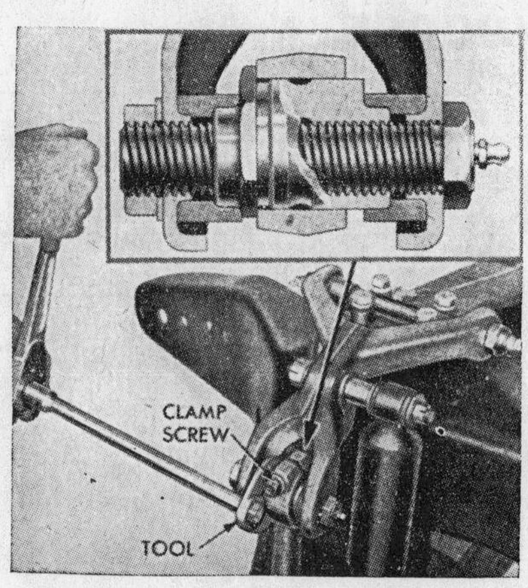

Caster and camber adjustments

to the front cross member and lower the control arm, being certain not to change the position of the inner pivot shaft on the cradle of the roller jack.

After the new spring has been inserted, jack the control arm up and guide the inner pivot shaft in place with a suitable drift pin, and replace the mounting bolts.

This procedure is generally found to be the easiest way of replacing a coil spring on all Dodge & DeSoto cars.

When it is determined that the upper or lower pivot pins must be replaced also, it is more practical to insert a jack under the lower control arm spring seat and detach the knuckle support at the end where replacement is required. Using this procedure all parts may be replaced with one simple operation.

The upper and lower pivot pins and bushings, can be placed without removing the wheel. While it will take a little more time to remove the wheel, it will simplify the overall operation.

A hardened screw type bushing is used in the lower end of the knuckle support. Screw this bushing in from the rear and tighten. The lower pivot pin is screwed into the control arm and the knuckle support itself is centred between the two arms.

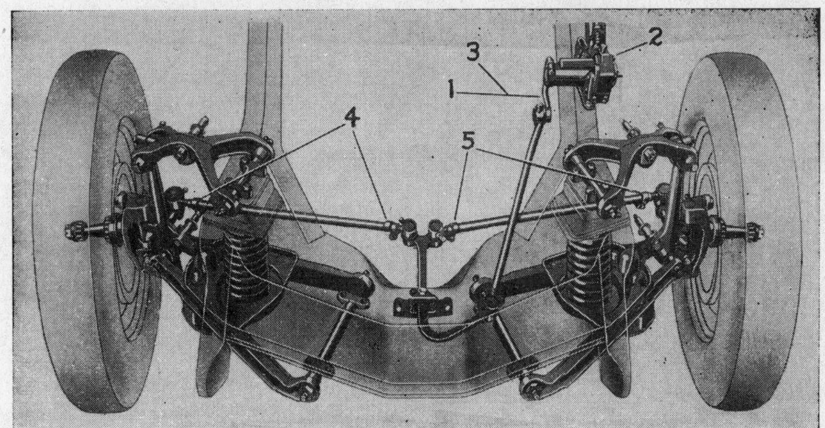

Steering mechanism—De Soto 1949-53

The upper control arm pin is hardened, and is made with a right hand thread. The upper pivot pin bushing is eccentric and is clamped in position by the knuckle support lock screw.

Castor and camber are increased by turning the eccentric bushing in the clockwise direction.

To decrease, turn counter clockwise.

Rebuilding of the lower control arm is confined to replacement of outer pin and bushing or inner pivot shaft and bushings.

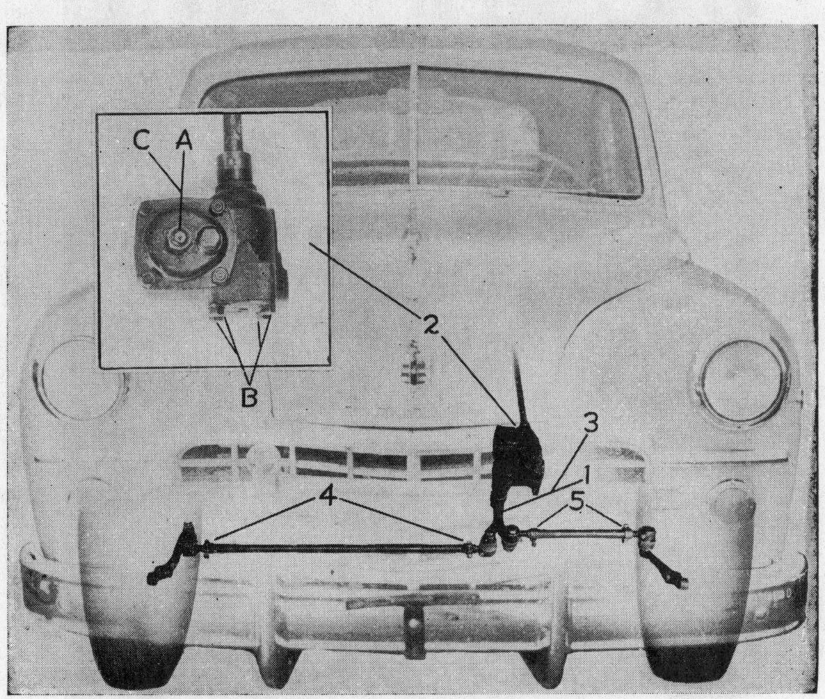

Steering mechanism—Dodge 1940-53. Typical of all De Soto 1940-48

MANUAL STEERING GEAR

All DeSoto and Dodge cars are equipped with the Gemmer worm and roller type steering gear.

Removal of Gear Assembly

Disconnect all steering column wires, and remove steering wheel.

Remove the jacket tube clamp to dash panel bracket and the gear shift bracket. Take off lower plate of directional signal housing and the screw from inside of housing.

Remove the signal contact unit by pulling the wire up through the jacket tube.

Remove the gear shift rod, shift lever, selector lever and brake cable clamp from jacket tube.

Take off pitman arm using special puller (C-143.)

Remove steering gear to frame bolts.

Remove the splash pan then lower gear assembly out of car.

Adjustment of Steering Gear

1. Disconnect the pitman arm from the tie-rods.

2. Adjust the steering gear housing assembly.

This gear is the Gemmer double roller tooth type with external mesh screw adjustment.

A. Loosen the cross shaft mesh adjusting screw lock nut and back off on the adjusting screw, so that there is plenty of play between the worm and

ADJUSTMENT OF STEERING GEAR —continued

roller tooth before adjusting the worm bearing.

B. Loosen or remove the four cap screws, which hold the housing lower cover in place, and remove one shim at a time to take out the worm bearing play.

Bearings should be adjusted so that there is zero play in the worm bearing but no definite preload.

C. Turn the steering wheel to the mid position of its travel and adjust the mesh of the worm roller by turning the adjusting screw inward until there is zero lash between the gears on the hugh spot. Tighten the lock nut.

Reconnect the tie-rods to the pitman arm.

4. Adjust the long tie-rod with the steering wheel in mid position of its travel so that one-half of the total toe-in is in the right wheel. Tighten the lock nuts.

5. Now adjust the short tie-rod so that the remaining toe-in is taken up in the left wheel and retighten the lock nuts. Turn the steering wheel from one extreme to the other extreme to check for roughness or binding.

Intermediate Steering Arm

All 1949 to 1953 DeSoto cars are equipped with an intermediate steering arm which is commonly referred to as the idler arm.

Removal and Disassembly of Intermediate Steering Arm

Disconnect the drag link and tie rods from the idler arm.

Remove the bracket bolts and remove the arm from the cross member.

Drive out the little cross pin which locks the arm to the vertical bracket pin. Remove nut and pin holding arm to bracket and slip off the bracket. Detach the upper and lower seals, bearing cones, rollers and spacer. Now with a drift, drive out the upper and lower bearing cups.

The intermediate steering arm may be rebuilt if the arm itself is not bent.

When it is determined that the upper or lower tapered bearings or cups need replacing it is wise to replace both bearings, cups, seals and retainers at the same time. These parts are assembled into one repair package. After the repair package has been installed, and the proper amount of shims inserted, so that with the assembly clamped in a vise a one pound pull at the drag link end will turn the arm.

Drag Link

On all 1940 to 1949 models the drag link can be rebuilt. 1950 thru 1953 models, the drag link must be replaced.

BRAKE SYSTEM

DeSoto and Dodge brakes are of the lockheed double anchor type, with eccentric anchors. All models are hydraulically actuated.

Pedal Clearance

Adjust the master cylinder push rod so that there is 1/8 to 1/4 in. free play at the brake pedal.

This adjustment is made so that the pedal will travel 1/8 to 1/4 in. before the push rod starts actuating the master cylinder piston. Free play adjustment is to prevent any pressure build up of the brake pedal.

Minor Brake Adjustments

Remove any one wheel to inspect the condition of the cylinder and lining, before any adjustment is made.

Turn the adjusting cam (the large hex nut located about half way between the anchor and the cylinder) until the shoe just contacts the brake drum. Back off the shoe adjusting cam until the wheel is free of any drag. To expand shoes turn forward or primary adjusting cam counter-clockwise, turn clock-

Front Wheel Brakes

wise to expand secondary shoe. Repeat procedure on each brake shoe at all four wheels.

Hand Brake Adjustment

An external contracting hand brake is used on all DeSoto and Dodge cars equipped with standard transmission.

Models with automatic transmissions use an internal expanding hand brake. This type hand brake, is fully enclosed to keep oil and dirt from entering on to the bonded lining.

Internal Hand Brake

NOTE: Incorrectly adjusted hand brake will effect automatic shifting.

Fully release hand brake and set shift lever in neutral. Detach front end of propeller shaft so brake drum may be turned by hand. Back off the cable adjusting nut and expand brake shoes until slight drag is felt. Now back off one notch with a special wrench C-3014 or a screwdriver to obtain .010 in. clearance. With cable adjusting nut against cable housing there should be .005 in. to .010 in. clearance between brake shoe cable and adjusting lever. Make certain the adjusting nut is securely tightened. Pull hand brake lever 4 to 6 notches and brake should be fully applied.

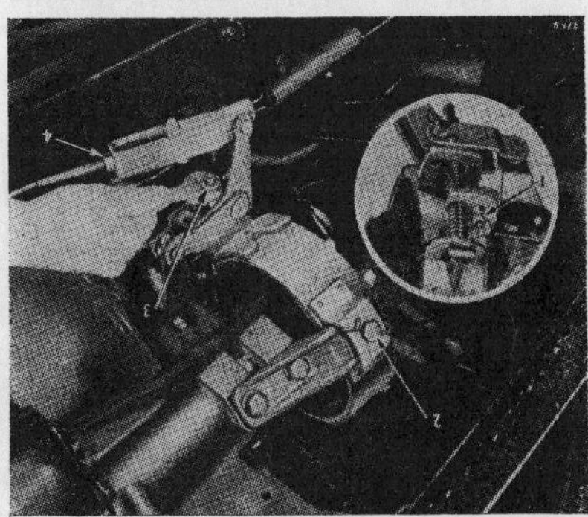

Hand brake adjustment

Major Brake Adjustment

To make a proper major adjustment on any De Soto or Dodge brake a shoe-centering gage, axle-type lining grinder, or dummy drum is required.

The anchor pins are eccentric and are adjustable only with the drum removed. This means that it is impossible to adjust the anchor by making the heel of the shoe contact the drum since the drum is not on when turning the eccentric.

Where a centering gage or a dummy drum is available the shoes are adjusted so that the heel of the shoe (nearest the anchor) is adjusted to .005 inch and the toe of the shoe (farthest away from the anchor) is adjusted to .010 inch. This is accomplished by turning the eccentric anchor in the required direction to adjust the heel of the shoe and turning the eccentric adjustor cam (half way up the shoe) to adjust the toe.

Where a dummy drum or centering gage or axle-type lining grinder is not available and it is absolutely essential that the anchors be adjusted, the following procedure has been found to work out fairly well.

Remove the anchor pins from the car and, using a thin grind stone grind a screw driver slot into the back end of the anchor pin (threaded end).

Now replace the anchor pins and mount the shoes. Do not tighten the anchor pins so tight that the pin cannot be turned with a screwdriver. Just snug it up enough so that it can be turned stiffly with a screwdriver.

Mark the anchor pin at the inner end to show the position of the high spot of the eccentric so that its position will be known while turning the screwdriver.

Mount the wheel and drum on the axle and spin the wheel. Turn the eccentric cam (half way up the shoe) until the lining drags and then turn the anchor pin with a screwdriver in a direction that the eccentric will move in towards the other shoe, and down towards the brake drum until the shoe no longer drags. Again turn the eccentric adjustor until the shoe again drags and again turn the anchor in the same direction until it is free. Keep repeating this until it is impossible to turn either the anchor or the eccentric without making the shoe bind. At this point, lock the eccentric anchor adjustment. Now develop clearance between the lining and shoe by turning the eccentric adjustor in the opposite direction until the wheel is free. Repeat this process at all four wheels.

It has been found that if the above procedure is followed very carefully a perfectly good adjustment can be had.

Brake Hydraulic System

On all models of DeSoto and Dodge, master cylinder is 1⅛ in. diameter.

All wheel cylinders are 1⅛ in. except for the front wheel cylinder of the 1940 to 1942 models which are 1¾ in.

Refilling Master Cylinder

The master cylinder is mounted to the frame directly under the floor panel on left side of the car, and is refilled by lifting the floor mat to one side and removing cut away cover in floor panel.

Inspect all cylinders for scratches or roughness. If rough or scratched it will be necessary to hone the cylinders to obtain a smooth surface.

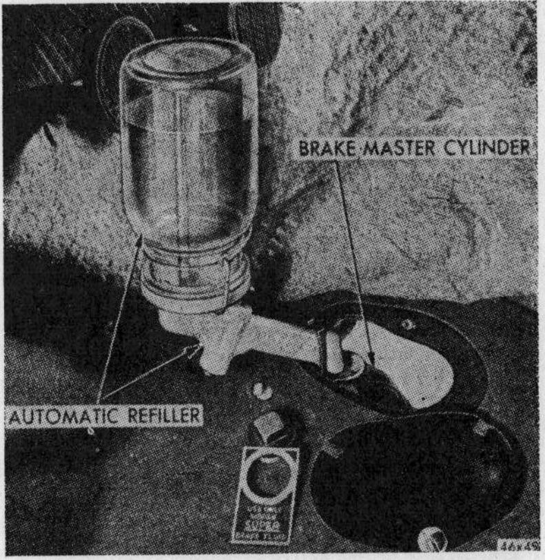

Filling master cylinder

Bleeding the Brakes

Complete instructions on brake bleeding is given in the General Service and Trouble Shooting Section at the beginning of the Service Manual.

Bleeding front wheel lower cylinder

COOLING SYSTEM

All DeSoto and Dodge cars are of the full flow type, incorporating a cellular radiator case, centrifugal pump, and four bladed fan. A distribution tube is used to direct coolant around the valve seats in the engine block.

Water Pump Removal

6-Cyl. Models

The water pump may be removed on all models without removing the radiator core. This is accomplished by removing the fan blades, loosen generator and remove fan belt, disconnect the hoses, loosen nuts holding pump to block and by pass. Slide the pump off studs and lift out.

Water Pump Removal

V-8 Models

Take off the fan and both belts and remove the fan belt pulley.

Take out the bolts which attach the water pump to the chain case cover and lift off the pump.

It is not necessary to remove the radiator core in order to take off the pump.

Water Pump Disassembly

6-Cyl. Models

Drive out the fan pulley hub pin and press off the fan hub. Remove the pump cover and pull the impeller and shaft assembly out of the pump body.

It is not necessary to separate the impeller from the shaft since these two are serviced as a unit.

To remove the bushings drive the pins which retain the bushings to the housing into the shaft hole and use a puller to remove the front and rear bushings from the pump body, pulling them both toward the front.

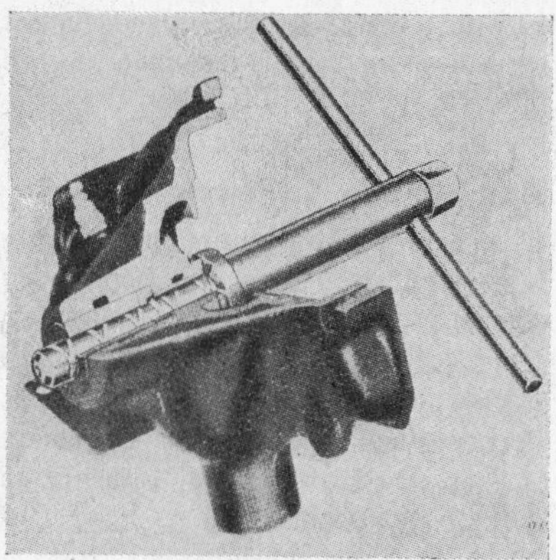

Burnishing bushings and refacing housing

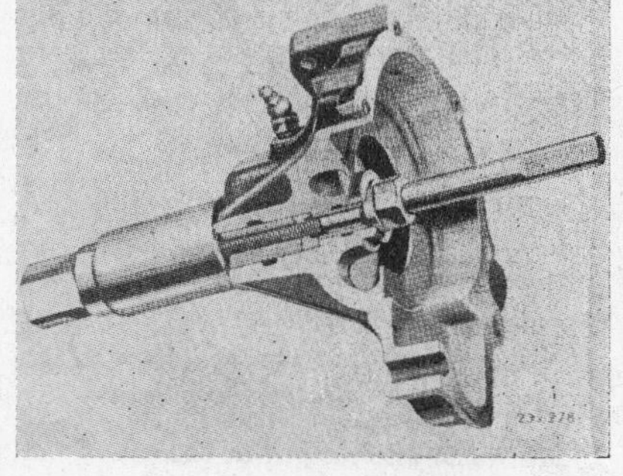

Removing bushings

Checking end play of shaft

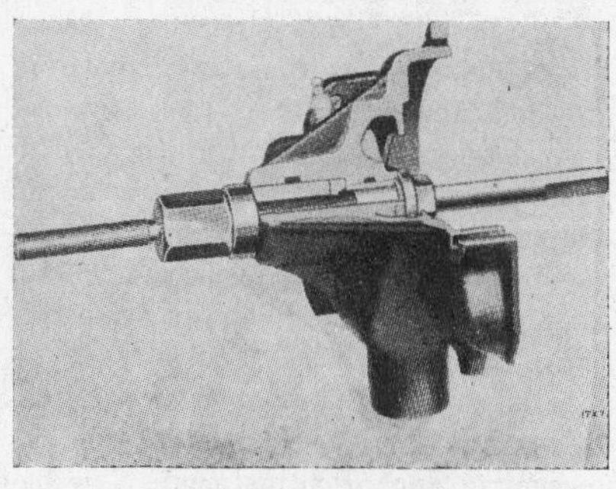

Installing bushings

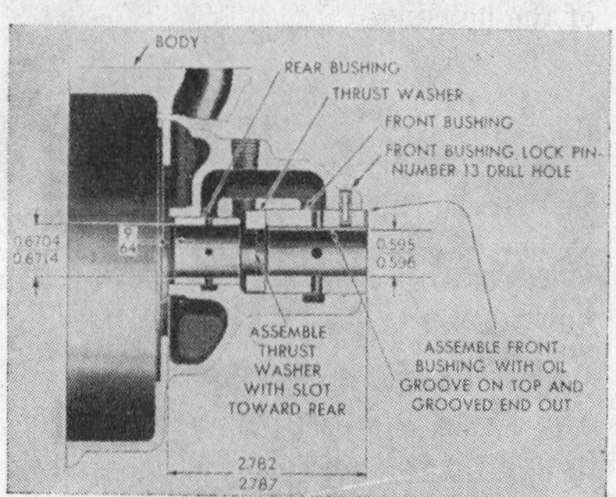

Water pump bushings installed

The pump parts are assembled in the following sequence. Install propeller on shaft making the back of the impeller flush with the end of the shaft. (This is not necessary if a new shaft and impeller assembly is being used.) Install water pump seal thrust spring, water pump seal retainer, water pump seal, water pump seal retainer washer and lock ring.

Disassembly of Water Pump

V-8 Models

The fan pulley hub is held to the shaft by a cross pin. Drive out the

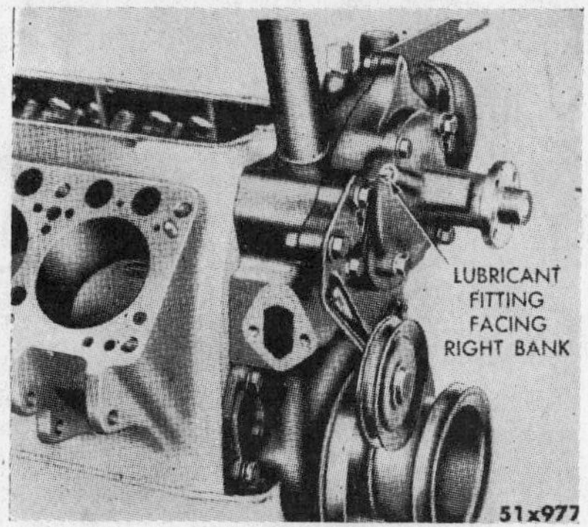

Water pump installed on engine

cross pin and, using a puller, pull off the hub.

Slide the impeller and shaft assembly from the rear of the pump body.

The front bushing is held into the body with a retaining pin through the casting. This retaining pin can be driven from the outside into the shaft hole in the bushing and taken from the assembly.

Drive out the retaining pin and the bushing can be pulled out the front of the housing.

The seal assembly is held in the recess in the impeller by a snap ring on the shaft.

The rear bushing can be driven out through the front of the case.

When installing new front bushings it will be necessary to drill through the hole in the casting into the bushing with a No. 13 drill so that a new retaining pin can be inserted.

The retaining pin is to be driven in flush with the casting.

Standard replacement bushings require reaming after installation.

Install the fan hub on the shaft so that there is .0005 to .005 inch clearance between the back of the hub and the front of the front bushing.

Radiator Core Removal

1940 models—remove hood, disconnect water hoses, fan blades and fan hub.

Remove radiator mounting bolts and lift core back and over engine.

1941 to 1953—disconnect upper and lower hose and unclip headlight wires.

Remove mounting bolts and lift core straight up to remove.

Thermostat

A 157 degrees thermostat is standard equipment on all Dodge and DeSoto models.

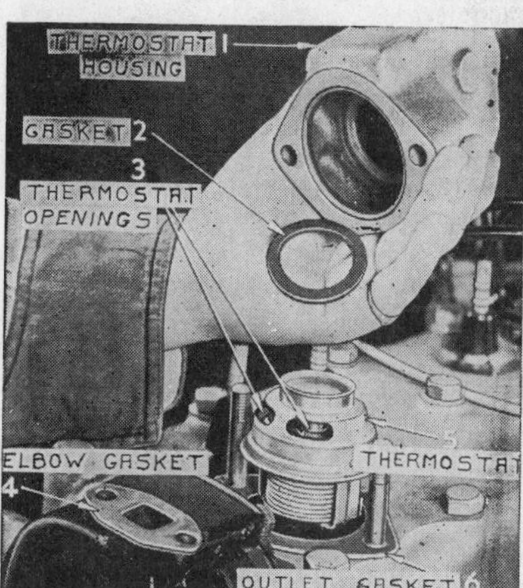

Thermostat arrangement

The thermostat is contained in the water outlet elbow. To remove the thermostat detach upper hose and by pass hose.

Remove mounting nuts, lift outlet elbow and remove thermostat.

Engine Manifolds

6-Cyl. Models

A heat riser control is incorporated in the exhaust manifold, to regulate the amount of heat bypassing around the intake manifold heat chamber.

The only service required by the heat riser control is to see that it is free to turn against its thermostat spring.

If difficulty is noticed in the warm-up period, or after the car has become

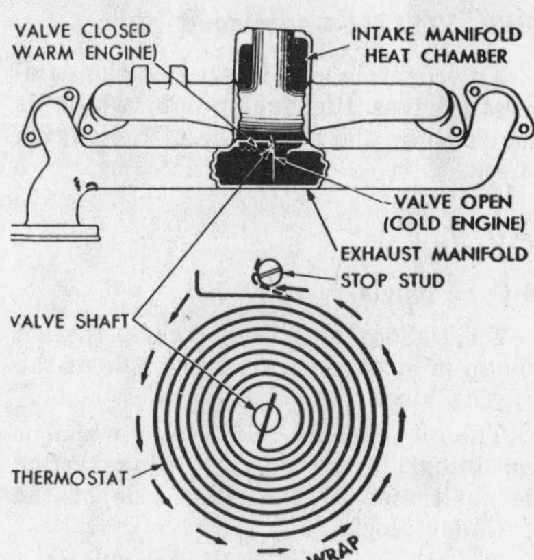

Diagram showing heat riser location & thermostat wrap

warm it seems to run lean, check the heat riser valve to make certain that it is turning freely on its shaft. If it is not, first, before removing the manifold, try to loosen it up with the use of a good penetrating oil. If this fails to loosen it, it may be necessary to remove the manifold in order to free up the heat riser valve.

Exhaust Pipe, Muffler and Tail Pipe

6-Cyl. Models

The oval muffler used on all models is of the straight through type. When installing a new muffler the word front stamped at one end is installed towards the front of the car.

V-8 Models

The main exhaust pipe enters the manifold of the right cylinder bank. The exhaust pipe is fitted with a sliding connection to couple up with a cross tube from the left cylinder bank.

The attaching bolts of either the exhaust pipe or the cross-over tube to the left cylinder bank are accessible from underneath the car.

The attaching bolts for the exhaust manifold on either bank are also accessible from underneath the car.

Fuel System

6 Cyl. Models

The fuel system is comprised of a gas tank, copper lines, fuel pump, carburetor and air cleaner.

FUEL SYSTEM—*continued*

An eccentric cam located on the camshaft drives the fuel pump, which is mounted on the right side of the engine block.

Oil Pump

6-Cyl. Models

On DeSoto and Dodge cars, the oil pump is located on the right side of the engine block.

The oil pressure relief-valve which is an integral part of the oiling system is positioned at the right side of the cylinder block.

To remove the oil pump, the two top cover bolts must be removed to clear frame.

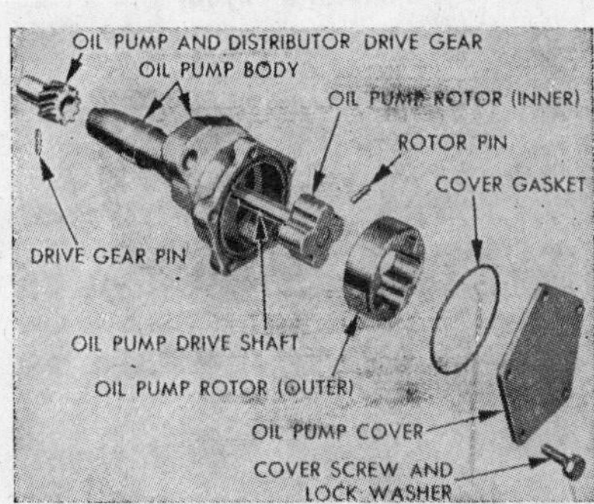

Oil pump (exploded view)

To disassemble remove cover plate and rotate pump shaft to allow outer rotor to slip out. With a suitable pin punch, drive out pin holding the oil pump and distributor drive gear to shaft.

Remove shaft and inner rotor from pump body.

If for any reason the position of the crankshaft has been changed after the oil pump is removed, it will be important to follow this procedure: Turn crankshaft until number one cylinder is at top dead center position. Rotate the pump drive shaft so that the slot in the oil pump shaft lines up with the pump body attaching bolt holes. Now move the drive gear counter-clockwise one tooth and loosen distributor lock bolt so distributor may be lifted to allow pump to be inserted. After all parts have been securely tightened adjust timings as explained in under ignition timing.
(SEE IGNITION TIMING.)

V-8 Models

In actual construction the oil pump on the V-8 models is the same as that on the 6, that is, it is a rotary gear type pump driven from the shaft of the distributor.

However, to service the pump on the V-8 models it is necessary to first remove the oil pan since the pump is located in the oil pan.

The pump relief valve is incorporated into the side of the pump casting.

To remove the pump, first take out the oil pan, and then disconnect the oil lines at the inside of the oil pan and then remove the mounting bolts which hold the pump body to the cylinder block.

The pump may now be lowered and removed from the car.

The distributor drive gear does not come down with the pump. Therefore, when the pump is removed it has no effect whatever on ignition timing.

Internal service on the pump is the same as that given for the 6-cylinder models.

ENGINE ASSEMBLY

Starting with 1952 production on De Soto and 1953 production on Dodge a V-8 engine is used.

All Dodge and De Soto V-8 engines are fitted with overhead valves.

In addition to the V-8 there is a 6-cylinder in-line L-head engine available for both De Soto and Dodge 1952 and 1953 models.

Engine Removal

V-8 Models

To remove the V8 cylinder engine from the car detach all parts such as wires, transmission linkage, exhaust pipes, hood, battery, fuel lines, radiator hoses, all wires, etc.

If a radiator shroud is used it must be removed.

Split the engine at the front universal joint and take out the engine rear support mounting bolts and the cross member.

Raise the engine, and at the same time work it out of the chassis towards the left front fender. By moving towards the left front fender it will not be necessary to disturb the heater or duct work.

Engine Cylinder Heads

V-8 Models

Both cylinder heads can be removed without disturbing the duct work.

Remove the ignition wire covers, dis-

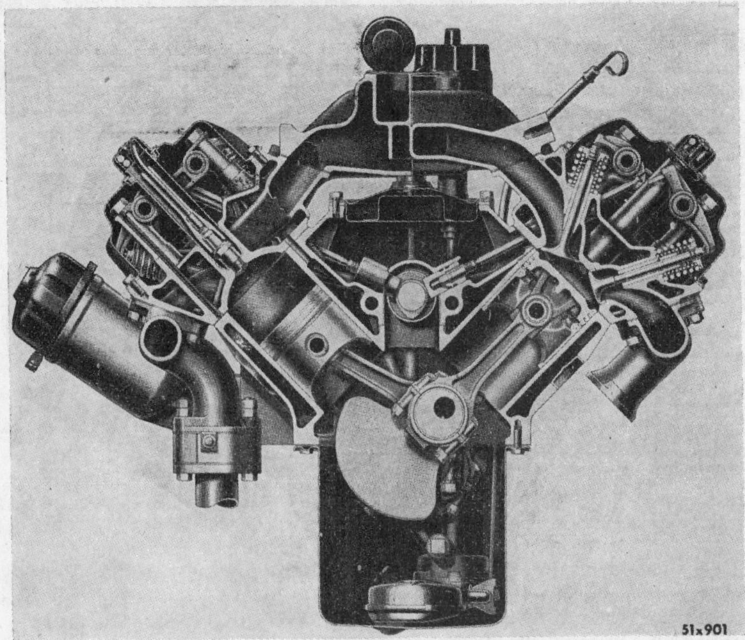

Front cross sectional view of V8 engine

connect the ignition wires from both cylinder heads, remove the distributor cap and take the wires off the car.

Unbolt the intake manifold from both cylinder heads.

The exhaust manifold may be detached from the cylinder head or it may be split at the exhaust pipe flange.

Remove the rocker covers and take out the bolts which hold the rocker covers to the cylinder heads. These bolts also hold the cylinder head to the block. They are through bolts and should be handled very carefully and replaced in the same hole from which they were removed.

Cylinder head bolts should be tightened to 80-85 foot pounds torque.

Caution: Handle the cylinder head carefully so as not to scratch or mar the gasket surface. A very thin gasket is used between the cylinder head and block and the slightest damage to the seating surface may result in defective sealing.

Side sectional view of V-8 engine

CYLINDER HEAD NUT TIGHTENING SEQUENCE

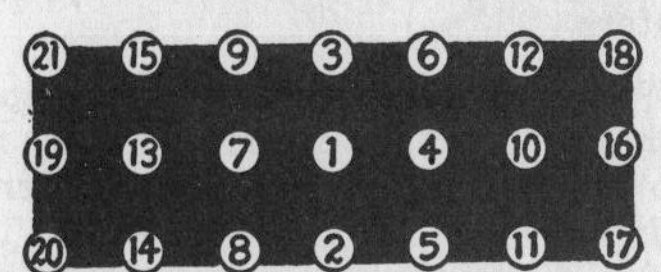

6 cylinder models tighten head to 65-70 foot pounds

Oil Pan Removal

6-Cyl. Models

Rotate crankshaft until number one piston is half way up cylinder bore.

Remove clutch inspection pan.

Remove oil pan cap screws and slide pan back and out at the same time, holding oil pump screen up so oil pan will clear. When installing pan, the end corks should protrude ⅛ to ¼ in. above oil pan. Tightening the pan will compress ends and make a tight seal.

V-8 Models

In order to remove the oil pan on V8 models it is necessary to remove the left side exhaust manifold and loosen the right side manifold.

Take the starter off the car and then unbolt and lower the oil pan.

Vibration Damper Removal

On all models it is possible to remove vibration damper without removing radiator. Although it is advisable to remove radiator core to prevent accidental damage to the water tubes.

VALVE SYSTEM

6-Cyl. Models

The valves, springs, and guides are accessible by removing the cylinder head and side valve covers.

When adjusting valve tappets the engine should be idling at normal operating temperature. Set the inlet valve tappets so that a .008 in. feeler will pass and a .009 in. feeler will stop; set exhaust valve tappets so that a .010 in. feeler will pass and a .011 in. feeler will stop. Where an engine is continually operated at high speed, it would be wise to allow the exhaust valves an additional .002 clearance to obtain suitable engine performance.

V-8 Models

All V-8 models are equipped with overhead valves which are operated through hydraulically silenced lifters. A system of lifters and rocker arms is used as is customary with all American built overhead valves.

Timing Case Cover Removal

V-8 Models

The timing case cover on V-8 models is also the water pump main body.

First remove the radiator core, take off the water pump, remove the vibration damper and lower fan pulley, take off the fuel pump.

Remove the bolts which hold the chain case cover to the front of the cylinder block.

Note: The chain case cover is located to the front of the cylinder blocks with tight fitting dowel pins and it may be necessary to pry the case off the front of the block.

A special puller is available to remove the timing case.

Valve Timing Procedure

6-Cyl. Models

To replace a timing chain, cam or crankshaft sprocket, or to retime valves where the timing has jumped, proceed as follows: Take off the radiator core, vibration damper and timing case cover. Remove the bolts from the camshaft gear, slide the camshaft sprocket off its hub and remove timing chain.

When installing timing chain, marks on sprocket must line up as shown.

The photo above shows the relationship between the camshaft sprocket and crankshaft sprocket

Note: Unless the crankshaft sprocket is to be replaced it will not be necessary to remove it from the shaft.

Rotate the crankshaft so that the mark in the crankshaft sprocket is towards the camshaft and in exact alignment between the shafts center.

Now install the timing chain over the camshaft sprocket so that the mark in the cam and crankshaft sprockets are nearest each other.

The timing bolt holes are staggered in such a way that the camshaft sprocket will attach only one way and permit the bolt to enter through the threaded holes in the hub.

Rotate the camshaft so that the holes align up and the timing marks are still in line between the shaft center. Mount the gear on the hub and draw up the bolts.

Turn the crankshaft two full revolutions and check to see that the marks are still in alignment between the shaft centers.

When set in the manner described, with the marks aligned between the two shaft centers, it is immaterial which piston is at top dead center. It is necessary, however, to retime the ignition at any time the camshaft setting is disturbed.

V-8 Models

The valve timing procedure for V-8 models is essentially the same as that given for the 6-cylinder model with this exception. After the camshaft gear has been placed on the shaft the fuel pump eccentric must be placed on. This is the only important difference between the two jobs.

Bear in mind when removing the timing case cover from the V-8 models that it is necessary to first remove the water pump because the operation of removing the timing case cover is greatly simplified if the water pump is out of the way.

The camshaft gear is located on the camshaft by a very tight fitting dowel pin.

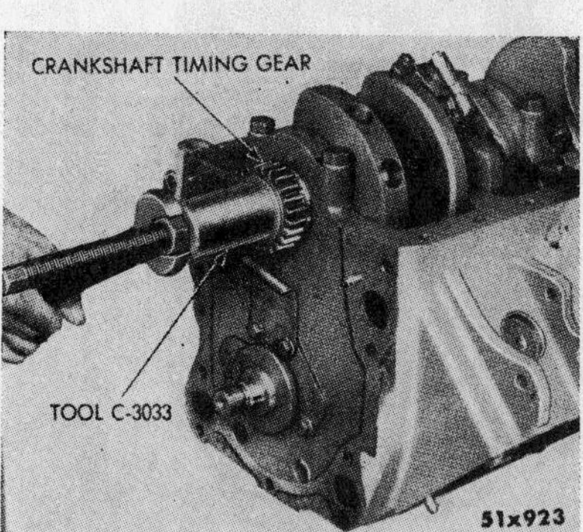

Installing crankshaft timing gear

Valve Timing

V-8 Models

The valves are correctly timed when the mark on the cam and crankshaft sprocket are nearest each other and in line between the shaft centers. That is, a line drawn between the two shaft centers will cross over both of the timing marks.

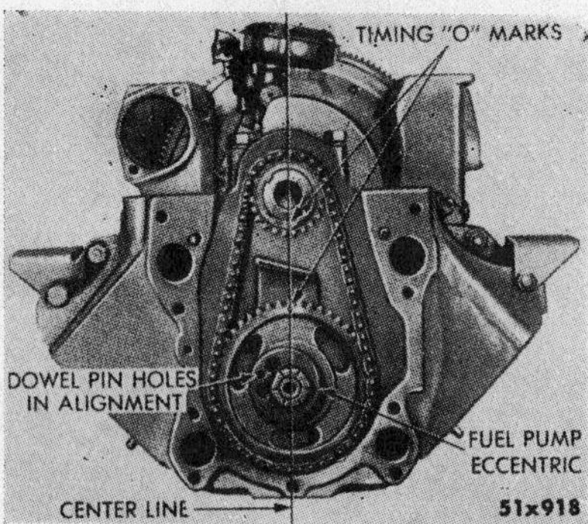

Timing mark alignment

Rocker Arm Assemblies

V-8 Models

The rocker assemblies are mounted on the top of the cylinder head in five brackets.

Removing the bolts which retain these brackets to the cylinder head will release the rocker assemblies.

The rocker arm shafts are stamped "IN" for intake and "EX" for exhaust.

The rocker arms themselves are not interchangeable since the intake rocker arms are smaller or shorter than the exhaust rocker arms.

When disassembling the rocker assemblies notice that one of the brackets has holes off the center of the rocker tube, which are intended to hold lock pins. The bracket at the opposite end has holes which are centered on the tube which are intended to hold cotter pins.

In order to insure that they are correctly assembled, each part should be carefully marked or carefully stored so that it will be available for replacement in exactly the position from which it was removed.

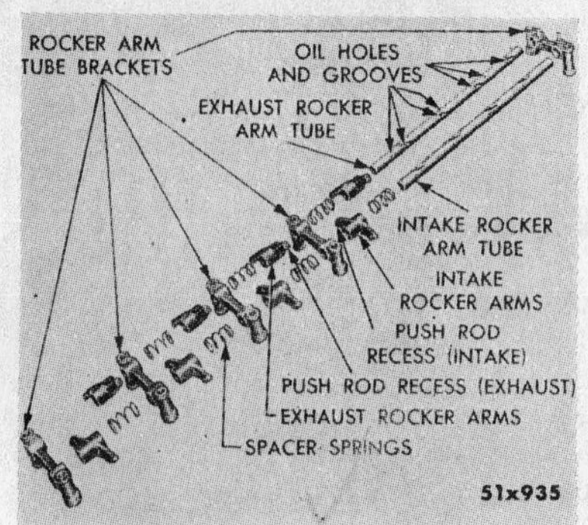

Rocker arm assembly—exploded

Replacement of Valve Guides

6-Cylinder Models

To replace the valve guides on the 6-cylinder models it is necessary to remove the cylinder head, the valve chamber covers, and take out the valve and spring assemblies.

Before installing new guides measure carefully the depth from the cylinder head to the top of the guide before taking the old guide out.

The guides are pulled upwards to the top of the block, and are driven downwards from the top of the block when installing new ones.

Perhaps the best way to pull out a valve guide is to secure a bolt of very high quality (such as a long threaded Allen bolt) and insert it down through the valve guide in place of the valve. Set large washers up on the cylinder head to lift the bolt head well up over the cylinder head. Screw a nut on the lower end of the bolt where it sticks out the bottom of the valve guide and tighten this nut. This will draw the valve guide up through the top of the head.

Since valve guides are a very tight fit in their bores, it is necessary to use a bolt of extra fine quality since an ordinary bolt will break before the valve guide will move.

There are, of course, special hydraulic tools made for the purpose of removing valve guides.

V-8 Models

On the V8 engine, valve guides are driven from the combustion chamber out through the top of the block.

Before driving out the old guide, measure very carefully the amount it projects out of the top of the cylinder head so that the new guide can be driven in exactly that amount.

The new guide should be reamed after installation.

Valve Seat Inserts

V-8 Models

All V-8 engines are equipped with exhaust valve seat inserts made of cast heat resisting material which cannot be cut successfully with a reamer.

Exhaust valve seats must be ground and/or lapped to a perfect seal.

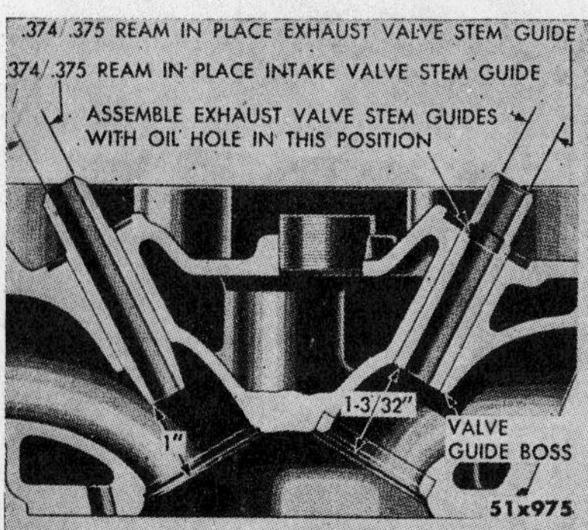

Exhaust & inlet valve guides installed in head

Valve Springs

De Soto and Dodge recommend that the valve springs be checked for free height and squareness rather than for pressure.

Perhaps the easiest way to do this is to lay the valve springs on a straight flat surface and compare one with the other. If all of the valve springs are of the same height it may be assumed that all are usable.

Actually the inner spring for both inlet and exhaust should measure 42 lbs. at 1 3/16 in. The outer spring should measure 138 lbs. at 1 5/16 in.

Hydraulic Valve Lifters

V-8 Models

All service on the hydraulic valve lifters is identical to the service given for the 1951 Chrysler.

Initial Setting of Hydraulic Valve Lifters

V-8 Models

To make certain that the lifter will operate in approximately in the middle of its stroke see to it that with the plunger completely depressed there is between .030 and .070 in. clearance between the valve stem and the top of the plunger. This measurement should be made with the hydraulic unit and plunger fully depressed.

Connecting Rod Bearings

All Models

To check the fit of the connecting rod bearing on the shaft there are two recommended procedures. The first, called the shim stock method, is as follows:

Cut a piece of shim stock approximately the width of the bearing and about a half-inch wide and insert it between the bearing and the crankshaft and bolt up the bearing tightly. Rock the shaft to see if the piece of shim stock binds the shaft. If it does, select a smaller piece of shim stock and again bolt up the bearing cap until the shim stock snugs up the shaft just a little. The thickness of the shim stock will then be the clearance for oil at the bearing.

Thus if a .003 inch thick shim snugs up the bearing it indicates that there is .003 inch oil clearance between the bearing and the journal.

This method takes into consideration everything except possible out-of-round of the crankshaft. However, with a piece of shim stock in the bearing it is not recommended that the shaft be turned since there is always the possibility that the shim stock would scratch the bearing.

The best way to check for out-of-round is to use micrometers.

Another method of checking oil clearance is the so-called plastic gage method. Plastic gage is supplied by most jobbers and complete instructions come with the gage material.

Assembly of Pistons to Connecting Rod

On all models the connecting rods are so installed that the oil metering hole faces toward the camshaft.

Pistons are installed in the cylinder bore so that the split skirt faces away from the camshaft side.

When assembling the piston to the connecting rod the split skirt is placed opposite the numbers on the rod.

V-8 Models

On the right bank (cylinders No. 2, 4, 6 and 8) the T-slot in the piston should be assembled to the connecting rod on the side which has the V-slot in the rod bearing cap.

Note: This V-slot is intended to splash oil on the camshaft.

On the left block (cylinders No. 1, 3, 5 and 7) the T-slot of the piston should be assembled on the side opposite the V-slot in the connecting rod bearing.

Notice that while both the pistons and connecting rods are interchangeable as individual parts once the piston is assembled to the connecting rod the left and right bank cannot be interchanged.

Fitting Piston Pins

On all De Soto and Dodge engines, both in-line and V-8, the piston pins are of the full-floating type which have a bearing in both the piston and the connecting rod.

The upper end of the connecting rod is fitted with a replaceable bushing.

When fitting new wrist pins to the piston, the bearing seat must be developed in both the piston and the top of the connecting rod and the manufacturer recommends that the pin be fitted to a tight push fit with the thumb.

The wrist pin is retained by lock rings at either end of the pin. Care should be exercised in installing the lock pins since, if one of them gets loose, it will badly score the cylinder wall.

Assembling Rod and Piston Assemblies to the Engine

6-Cylinder Models

Install the rod and piston assemblies in the engine so that the split skirt in the piston faces away from the camshaft side which will place the oil spit hole in the connecting rod toward the camshaft.

V-8 Models

Assemble the pistons to the engine so that the T-slot is on the left side of the engine. That is, the T-slot will face upwards on the right bank and downwards on the left bank. As a further check notice that when they are assembled in this matter the V-slot in the connecting rod caps on both banks will face the camshaft (up).

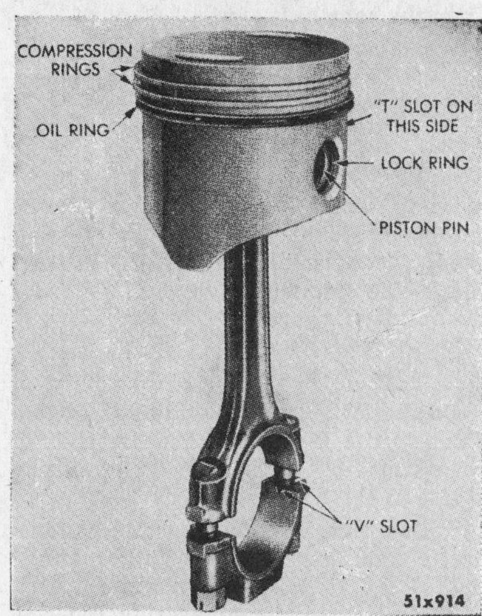

Piston and connecting rod assembly—right hand bank

Main Bearings

All Models

The procedure for checking the oil clearance of the main bearings is exactly the same as that given for the rod bearings in a previous paragraph.

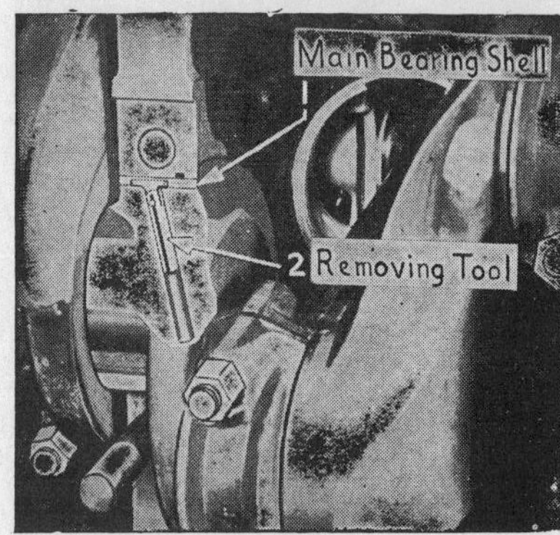

Method used to remove main bearing upper half

6-Cyl. Models

Steel back babbit lined inserts are used on all models. Main bearings are properly located in the bearing cap by means of a tang at the parting line of each insert. On all replacement caps the bolt holes are 1/64 in. oversize and the length is 1/16 undersize, so that shims may be used to give correct bearing clearance.

V-8 Models

The main bearings are of the precision slip-in type which can be replaced without removal of the crankshaft.

While De Soto and Dodge do not recommend adjusting the precision fit main bearings it is possible to secure a small adjustment by placing a taper or feather type shim between the bearing shell and the cap. In this way as much as .003 in. excess play may be taken up.

Rear Main Bearing Oil Seal

The rear main bearing oil seal is attached to the bearing cap by three cap screws.

When replacing the oil seal the retaining cap screws are left loose and then tightened after the bearing cap has been torqued, this allows seal to seat properly around crankshaft.

V8 MODELS

The rear main bearing oil seal is a braided asbestos wick.

The proper way to replace the upper half of the oil seal is to remove the crankshaft.

It is sometimes possible to seal up a small leak in the rear main bearing oil seal by installing a new lower half and letting it project slightly above the main bearing cap. The main bearing cap is then bolted tightly up into place and immediately taken down. The riveted over portion of the projecting lower half of the seal should be cleaned off and the cap again bolted up into place until the cap seats firmly in the block without riveting over the oil seal.

The purpose of this is to squeeze the upper half of the oil seal more tightly into its groove and causing it to compress somewhat down on to the crankshaft.

This particular method is not always successful but has been used in many instances to prevent minor leaks.

Rear main bearing oil seal

IGNITION SYSTEM

6-Cyl. Models

The distributor is mounted on the left side of the engine block and is driven by the oil pump shaft which is slotted to allow the tongue of the distributor shaft to enter and be driven, (the oil pump and distributor drive gear is mounted on the oil pump.)

When removing the distributor, mark the position of the rotor so it may be reinstalled in original position. When installing spark plug wires, advance in a clockwise direction. If starting with No. 1 the order is as follows: 1, 5, 3, 6, 2, 4.

If No. 6 was the first wire installed the order is 6, 2, 4, 1, 5, 3 follow this order to install wires.

V-8 Models

The distributor on the V-8 models is located at the back of the block between the cylinder banks.

The distributor drive gear is mounted independently on a stub shaft which is tongued to the oil pump at the bottom and the distributor at the top.

When the distributor is removed, the gear can be left down in the housing.

The stub shaft is fitted with a bushing which is replaceable and can be removed by removing the stub shaft and then using an inertia puller pull the bushing out of the housing.

The new bushing should be reamed to a good fit on the stub shaft.

Ignition Coil

On all 1940 to 1942 models the ignition coil is mounted on the left side of the fin wall. On 1946 to 1953 6-cylinder models the coil is mounted directly over the distributor. The ignition coil cannot be serviced. A defective coil must be replaced.

Spark Plugs

Service data on spark plugs, make, type and heat range required for these models is given at the beginning of this service data.

Charging Circuit

The parts of the charging circuit are the generator, regulator, ammeter and battery.

Generator Inspection

Smell the generator. Burned insulation has an unpleasant acrid odor. If this characteristic odor is not present the generator is probably OK (electrically). Examine the commutator, it should be a clear chocolate color, free from any scratches. When a commutator is found to have a grooved, rough, or burned surface, showing high insulation between the commutator bars, it should be turned down. The surface of the commutator should be concentric with the armature shaft.

Voltage Regulator

The voltage regulator is mounted on the left side of the engine fire wall.

The voltage regulator has three units. A cutout current, and voltage control unit.

Complete instruction for the servicing of regulator is given in the fundamental section (see index).

Starting System

The starter has an overrunning type clutch. If starter fails to crank the engine properly, check the condition of the battery and battery connections before working on the starter itself.

The mechanical check on the condition of the starter is performed in the same manner as that of the generator.

Make sure the brushes are free in their holders, and the springs have proper tension. Low tension causes arcing and low generator output, while too much tension will greatly shorten the service life of both commutator and brushes.

Remove the starter and make the same test as given for generators in the general service section. (See index.)

CLUTCH ASSEMBLY

Removal

Remove transmission assembly and release fork. Before removing pressure plate from the flywheel mark their position in respect to each other, so they may be replaced in proper alignment. The clutch is taken out through the bottom of the housing.

TRANSMISSION

Standard Transmission Removal

Disconnect front end of drive shaft. Companion nut should be loosened if transmission is to be disassembled. Detach speedometer cable and ground cable at transmission. Disconnect gearshift contact rod and selector cable at transmission. Detach hand brake cable at hand brake, remove transmission.

Standard Transmission Disassembly

Remove speedometer drive pinion and cover assembly. Detach companion flange and brake drum assembly. Pull out shifter fork guide rail.

Take out the welsh plug from the lower shifter rail by collapsing it with a suitable pin punch.

Slide upper and lower shift rail out through front of case. Lift out the shift forks and remove the extension and main shaft assembly.

Remove synchronizer snapring, synchronizer unit, second and low gear.

Drive out main shaft and rear bearing from extension, and countershaft towards rear of case.

Fluid Coupling Removal and Disassembly

Remove transmission, clutch throwout bearing, and inspection pan. Mark the clutch covers and drive plate and remove. Now remove the fluid drive assembly. (Bolts are taken out from the front of the crankshaft flange.) Keep all parts clean as they are disassembled. To remove the bellows seal, bend down tab on lock washer and remove drive plate retainer. Mark runner hub spline with mating spline on drive plate.

Remove drive plate from hub and, using fluid drive bellows spring compression, compress spring and remove seal spring retainer snapring from bellows seal retainer. Withdraw spring retainer and spring. This spring must be removed before the bellows seal, otherwise the pressure of the spring will damage the seal. With a spanner wrench, unscrew bellows seal, using two pieces of wire bent over to form hooks, lift out the loose floating seal ring.

Make sure that the sealing surfaces of the runner hub, the floating seal ring and the bellows seal are perfectly clear and free from scratches and marks. Where the surfaces of the bellows seal or the floating seal ring are damaged, install new parts. If the sealing surface of the runner hub is damaged, the fluid drive assembly should be replaced. To reassemble, reverse procedure.

Refilling Fluid Coupling

Lift the floor mat on the right side and take off the hand hole cover over the filler hole plate on right side of the clutch housing. Now rotate the fluid drive unit until a filler plug hole indexes with the hole in the clutch housing. Remove the plug (careful not to drop it into the clutch bell housing) and fill until the fluid just spills from the filler hole. Replace filter plug using a new gasket, and tighten securely. Wipe all excess oil from the back face of the fluid drive unit.

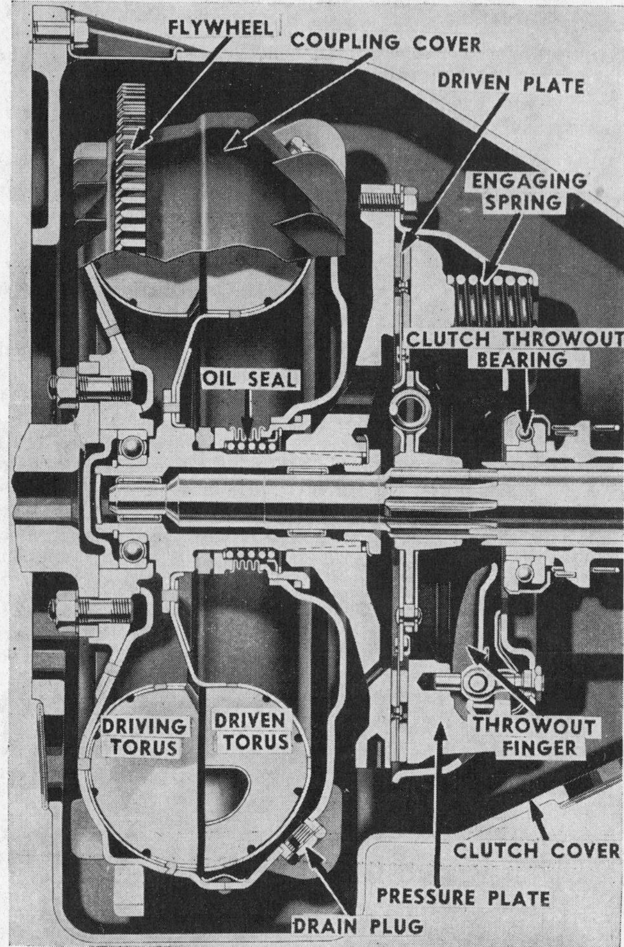

Section thru the fluid flywheel and clutch

Gearshift Control and Rod Adjustment

Loosen the lock nut on control rod, (the top lever at the bottom of steering jacket tube). Then set transmission gears in neutral and gearshift lever in a horizontal position. Now tighten control rod lock nut.

Gearshift Selector Rod Adjustment

With transmission gears set in neutral, loosen selector rod lock nut. Now tighten to remove all play and back off ½ turn to allow clearance and tighten nut.

Manual Shift Adjustments

Loosen the lock bolt at upper lever on the lower end of the jacket tube. With gears set in the neutral position and selector lever in a horizontal position tighten lock bolt.

While gears are still set in the neutral position loosen the lock nut on selector rod at transmission end. Tighten the nut until all play is removed, and back off one-half turn to allow clearance.

Power Shift Neutral Adjustment

Neutral position is the point of engagement of the boss on detension spring and the notch in lever. The detension spring can be moved about its pivot. To check and properly position, remove selector rod and slacken detension spring screw. With engine running (wheels off the ground) move power lever and links back and forth a very limited amount. At the same time move selector arm until a clean and positive crossover is felt. In this position move detension spring so that boss indexes with notch in lever and tighten clamp, bolt on bracket. Install selector rod, tighten and back off ½ turn.

TRANSMISSION REMOVAL

Hydraulic Torque Converter

The torque converter consists of four elements. An impeller, a turbine, and two reaction members. Their functions are to multiply torque at any time the drive shaft speed is less than the engine speed.

The impeller and turbine are hydrogen brazed assemblies of stamped parts while the reaction members are aluminum castings.

The converter is attached to the crankshaft through a steel disc which permits some flexibility thus preventing excessive wear on the rear impeller bushing. The starter ring gear is mounted on the rim of the flexible disc.

A converter housing is welded from two halves to prevent leakage and to reduce the inertia of rotating parts. The whole converter is one service assembly.

Draining and Refilling the Torque Converter

First remove the drain plug from the oil reservoir and drain the oil out of the reservoir. Then remove the cover from the lower side of the bell housing and turn the converter until the drain plug is at the bottom. Remove the drain plug and drain the oil from converter.

Remove the filler plug on the left side of the oil reservoir below the clutch housing and fill the reservoir to the bottom edge of the filler plug hole with special fluid drive oil or SAE 10W quality grade motor oil.

Start the engine and run between 500 and 700 RPM with the transmission in

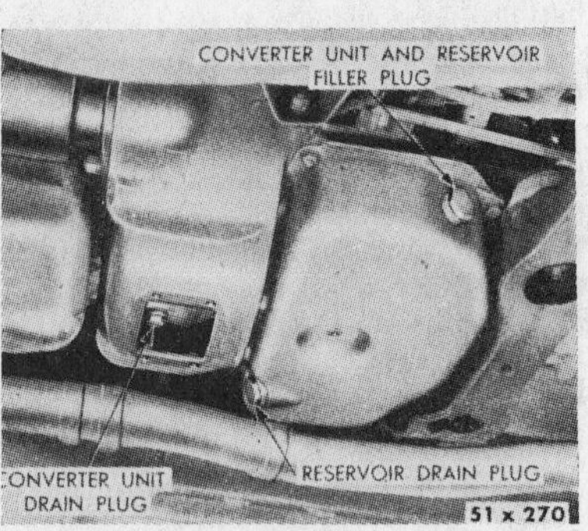

Reservoir drain and filler plugs

neutral. With the engine running continue to add oil to the reservoir until the oil level remains constant at the bottom edge of the filler plug. This should be approximately 10½ quarts.

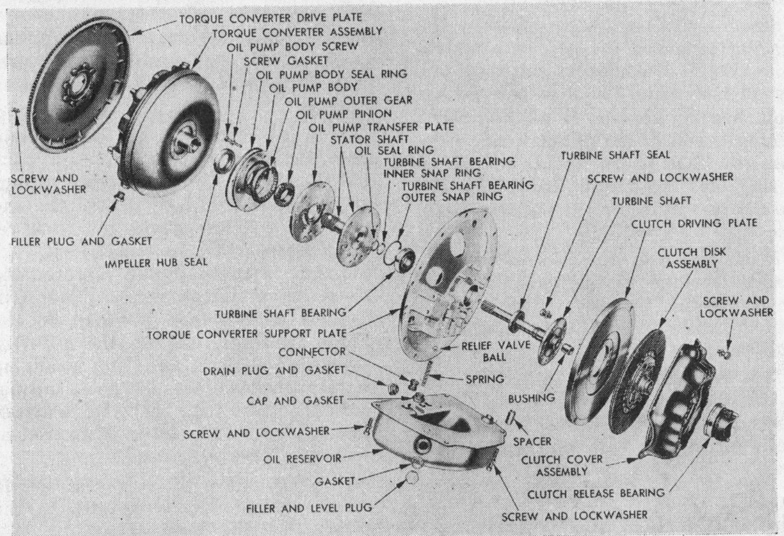

Torque converter and clutch assembly—exploded view

Converter Oil System

Basically the torque converter oil system consists of an oil reservoir mounted to the underside of the clutch housing. A gear driven pump embodied in the torque converter support plate and an oil exchanger or cooler located at the front of the engine.

Oil is drawn from the oil reservoir by the pump and delivered to the converter support plate where it is maintained at approximately 30 pounds per square inch pressure. Pressures above 30 pounds actuate the pressure relief valve which returns the excess oil to the oil reservoir.

The funetion of the oil pump is to keep the operating parts of the converter cool and to prevent excessive heat build up in the oil during extreme operation.

The oil cooler is in series with the converter, that is all of the oil which enters the converter passes through the oil cooler.

Oil Capacity of Converter

The total capacity of the torque converter oil system is 10½ quarts of special fluid drive oil or SAE 10W motor oil.

REAR AXLE ASSEMBLY

The hotchkiss drive (open drive shaft) type of drive line is used on all DeSoto and Dodge models. The differential, pinion and axles are equipped with tapered roller bearings.

Axle Shaft Oil Seal

Two types of oil seals were used on the axle shafts on DeSoto and Dodge products. The early type was bolted to the outside face of the brake backing plate. To replace this type it was necessary to remove the rear wheel and take out the bolts which retain the oil seal to the rear axle housing flange.

On later models the oil seal was incorporated into the brake backing plate. To replace it, it was necessary to remove the brake backing plate from the car (necessary to detach the brake lines) and drive the oil seal out of the backing plate flange. To replace the inner oil seal on all models it is necessary to remove the axle shaft and take out the oil seal with an inertia type puller.

Axle Shaft Replacement

To replace the rear axle shaft on any DeSoto and Dodge model, take off the wheel and hub assembly, disconnect the brake lines and unbolt the backing plate from the rear axle housing flange. The axle shaft, together with its bearing, can then be pulled out of the housing.

Replacement of Pinion Oil Seal

Disconnect the rear universal joint and lower the drive shaft. Take off the nut which holds the companion flange to the rear axle pinion and slide off the companion flange. The oil seal may now be pulled out with an ordinary inertia type puller.

The pinion shaft companion flange nut should be tightened between 180 and 320 foot pounds torque.

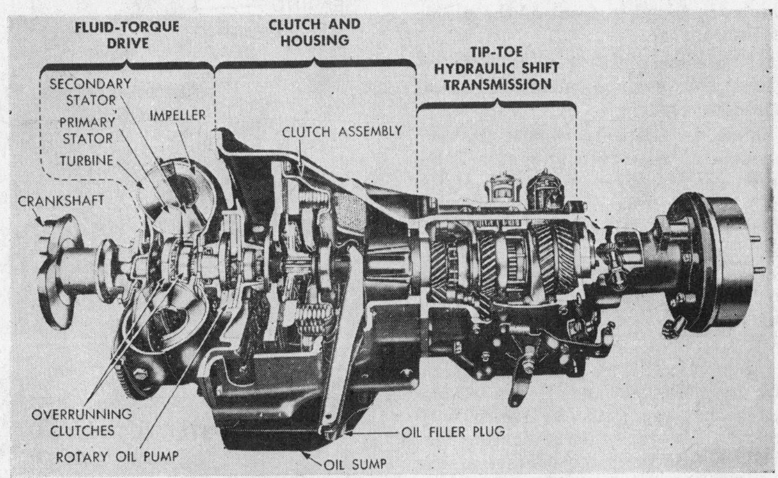

Fluid-torque drive—cutaway sectional view

Replacement of Pinion and Ring Gear

All Models

Two different types of differential assemblies are used on the De Soto models for 1952 and 1953.

From the service standpoint the difference between them is that the pinion shaft on the big models has a shoulder machined on the shaft and does not use a separate spacer between the front and rear bearing on the pinion shaft, instead the shoulder on the shaft itself acts as a spacer.

Except for this difference the procedure for the pinion and ring gear is the same on all models.

There is also quite a difference in the procedure for replacing the differential spiders and differential pinion gears (inside the pinion case).

The difference in this procedure will be explained later.

To replace the pinion and ring gear, remove both axle shafts, take off the rear universal joint and detach the rear axle carrier assembly and slide out from underneath the car on to a bench.

Remove the differential side bearing caps after first releasing the pressure from the adjusting cages and lift out the differential case. Take off the universal joint companion flange and drive the pinion shaft out through the back of the carrier.

Note: The rear bearing cone and rolls will come out with the pinion shaft. Carefully preserve the shims which are found in front of the pinion bearing spacer.

If the same pinion gear is to be replaced the same number of shims should be used.

Shims or a spacer washer is used between the rear bearing cone and the pinion gear to govern the depth of the pinion gear in relation to the ring gear. Adding shims at this point will cause the pinion gear to move toward the rear of the car and deeper into the ring gear; removing shims at this point will cause the pinion gear to shift forward and out of the ring gear.

When installing a new pinion and ring gear DeSoto and Dodge recommends that the gears be tested with Prussian Blue or other indicating material to determine the contact of the pinion on the ring gear. Where the contact marks indicate that the pinion should be moved closer to the ring gear shims should be added between the pinion gear and the pinion rear bearing cone.

If the gear marks indicate that the pinion is set too close to the ring gear it will be necessary to remove. shims from between the pinion gear and the pinion rear bearing cone.

Since installing shims between the bearing cone and the gear is a matter of testing, it is advisable that the bearing adjuster shim found in back of the front bearing cone be eliminated while testing the fit of the pinion gear in the ring gear. The oil seal should be left out during these tests and also during the checks for preloading the pinion bearing.

Much time can be saved if the preload is developed on the pinion bearings by tightening the nut to the desired preload while testing the fit of the pinion gear.

It is considered quite normal to have to take the pinion gear out at least three times in order to establish the proper mesh of the pinion gear in the ring gear.

Pinion Bearing Adjustment

After the proper number of shims have been installed to establish the correct position of the pinion gear relative to the ring gear, it will be necessary to set the pinion bearing to approximately .002 pre-load on the bearing. To establish this pre-load, deliberately use too many shims between the pinion front bearing cone and the bearing spacer (shoulder on the pinion shaft on 1952 and 53 torque converter equipped jobs) and measure with an indicator the end play developed in the pinion shaft. Check this end play several times to make certain that the reading is exact.

After the end play has been established exactly, remove, from in back of the pinion front bearing, shims equivalent to .002 MORE than the end play found in the shaft and then replace the bearing, universal joint yoke and the pinion shaft nut. Tighten the pinion shaft nut securely. This will produce a .002 inch pre-load on the pinion bearings. Set up the differential side bearings and ring gears so there is not less than .006 inch and not more than .010 inch back lash between the ring gear and pinion, measured at the rim of the ring gear.

This position of the ring gear should be established with zero play in the differential side bearings.

Differential side bearings should be pre-load approximately one notch of the adjusting cage after backlash has been adjusted.

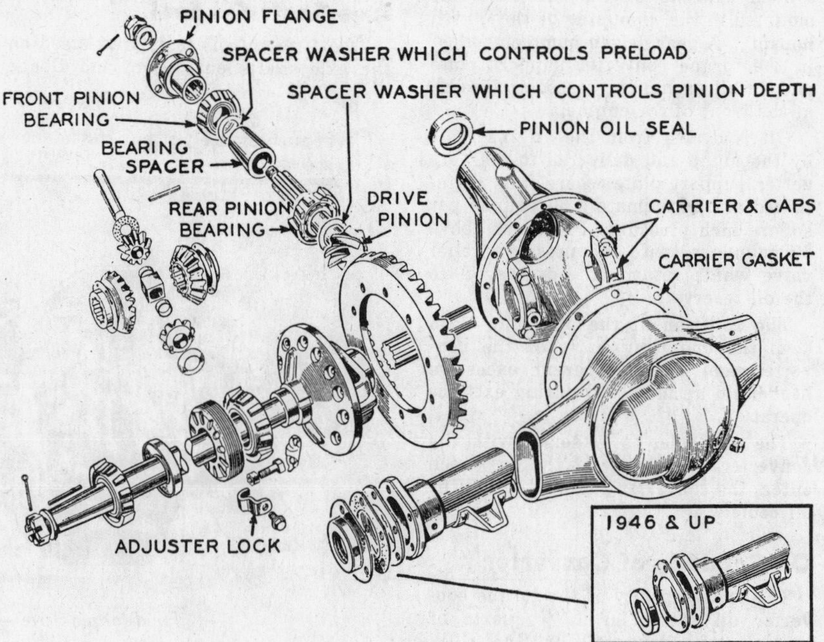

Rear axle assembly—All models except D42, S15, 8 passenger models

Pinion Markings

The pinion is generally etched with a plus or minus sign followed by a number ranging from 1 to 4, or it may be marked zero.

There are other numbers etched on the pinion but they have nothing to do with its adjustment the only number which concerns the service man is the one which immediately follows the plus or minus sign.

Perhaps the easiest way to install a new pinion gear without difficulty is to select from the parts department a pinion having the same etched number as the one which was removed from the car. In this way the spacers found in the car will be suitable for the new pinion.

If the number on the new pinion is greater than the one on the old one a thinner washer must be used to govern the pinion depth. Thus a pinion gear marked plus 2 would require a shim .004 inch thinner than one marked minus 2 since plus 2 is .004 inch from minus 2.

DIFFERENTIAL CASE

1952 AND 53 DE SOTO MODELS WITH TORQUE CONVERTER

The biggest difference between the rear axles used on other De Soto models and the axle used on the model S17 lies in the differential case.

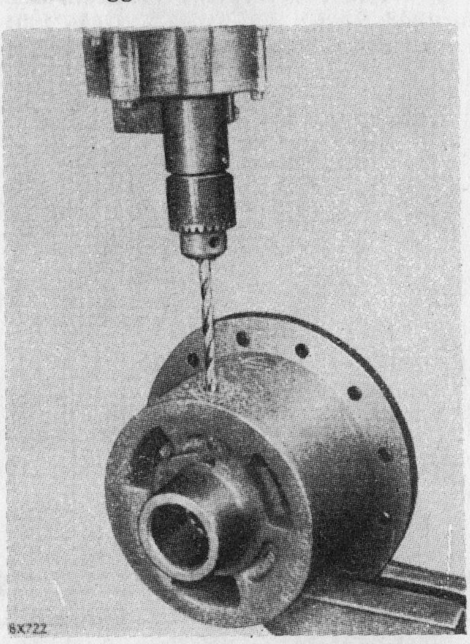

Removing differential case cap lock pin

The differential case is a box type construction and it is necessary to unscrew the end plate (opposite to the ring gear) in order to take out the pinions.

The differential case cap is fitted with a lock pin which must be drilled out before the cap can be taken off. The cap screws into the case.

It is sometimes a lot simpler to heat the case with heat lamps before attempting to unscrew the end cap.

Axle Shaft End Play

The end play in the axle shaft is controlled by shims located between the backing plate and the rear axle housing. Removing shims at this point will cause the end play in the axle shaft to decrease.

A thrust block is used, mounted over the differential pin and it is necessary to adjust each axle shaft separately for end play.

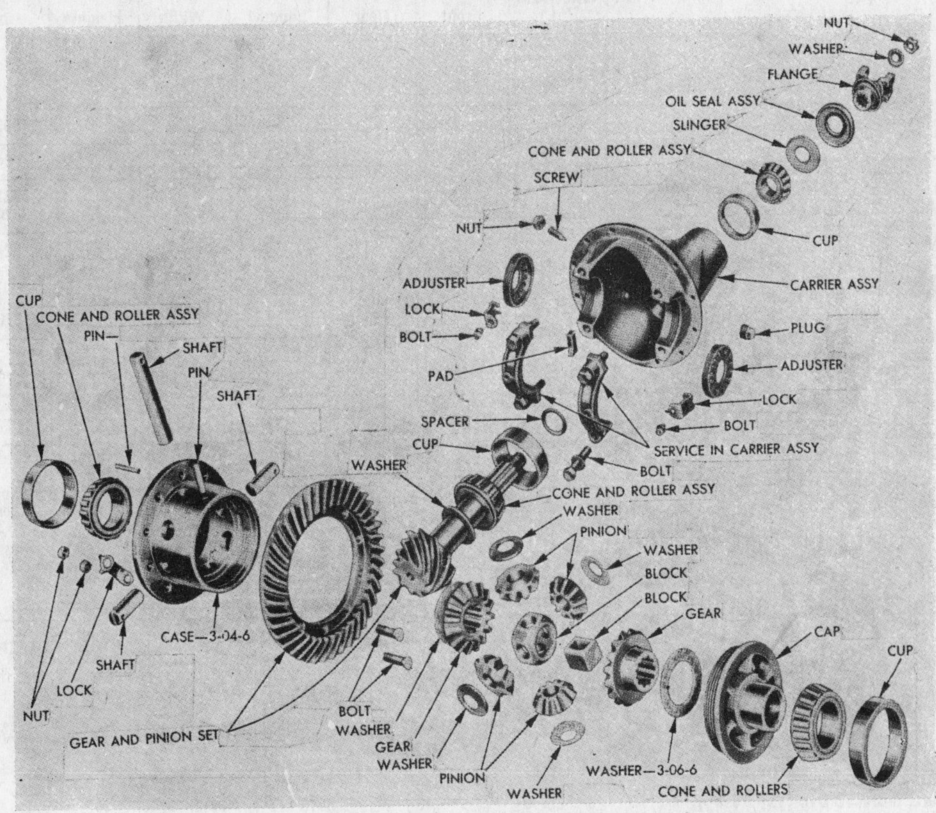

Exploded View—Rear axle assembly—D42, S15, 8 passenger models

FORD and MERCURY SPECIFICATIONS 1940 thru 1948

Starting Serial and Motor Numbers

Starting Serial Numbers

1940-1948—Same as Motor numbers.

Location

1940-1948—Same place as Motor numbers.

Starting Motor Numbers

1940, 8 cyl., 85 h.p. 18-5210701
60 h.p. 54-506501
1941, 6 cyl. 1GA-1
8 cyl. 18-5896295
1942, 6 cyl. 1GA-34801
8 cyl. 18-6769036
1946, 6 cyl. 1GA-227524
8 cyl. 99A-650280
1947, 6 cyl.
71GA-326418 and 77HA-0512
8 cyl. 799A-1412708
1948, 6 cyl. 87HA-0536
8 cyl. 899A-1984859

Location

1940-1948—Left frame member ahead of cowl. Top of clutch housing and left frame member near left front engine support.

MERCURY

Starting Serial Numbers

1940 .... 99A-101701
1941 .... 99A-257101
1942 .... 99A-466701
1946 .... 99A-650280
1947 .... 799A-1412708
1948 .... 899A-1990957

Location

1940-1948—Left frame rail ahead of cowl, left frame rail ahead of front axle, rear of engine on top of clutch housing and left frame rail near front engine support.

Starting Motor Numbers

1940-1948—Same as serial numbers.

Location

1940-1948—Same place as serial numbers.

General Specifications

Year	Model	Wheelbase (in.)	Tread (in.) Front	Tread (in.) Rear	Overall Dimensions (in.) Length†	Width	Height■	Shipping Weight* (lb.)	Tire Size (in.)
FORD									
1941	V8	114	56	58	194	....	....	....	6.00-16
1942	6-26A, V8-21A	114	58	60	194	....	....	3053	6.00-16
1946	V8-69A	114	58	60	196	74	70	3240	6.00-16
1947	6-6GA	114	58	60	198	....	....	3213	6.00-16
1948	V8-69A	114	58	60	198	74	70	3246	6.00-16
1948	6-87HA	114	58	60	198	73	66	3213	6.00-15
MERCURY									
1940	V8-95	116	56	58	196	....	....	3103	6.00-16
1941	....	118	56	58	200	....	....	....	6.50-16
1942	29A	118	58	60	204	....	....	3263	6.50-15
1946	69M	118	58	60	202	74	69	3270	6.50-15
1947-48	69M-89M	118	58	60	202	74	69	3298	6.50-15

*—Cheapest 5 pass. 4 door sedan. ■—Road to roof, no load. †—Including bumper and bumper guards.

General Engine Specifications

Year	Model	Number of Cylinders Bore and Stroke	Piston Displacement, Cubic Inches	Compression Ratio (To-1)	Taxable (A.M.A.) Hp.	Developed Horse Power: Bare Engine	Developed Horse Power: With Accessories	Maximum Torque Ft. Lbs.
FORD								
1940	O22A, 8 Cyl.	8-2.6 x 3.2	136.0	6.60	21.6	60 @ 3500	....	94 @ 2500
	O1A, Standard, & DeL. 8 Cyl.	8-3 1/16 x 3.75	221.0	.15	30.0	85 @ 3800	....	150 @ 2200

1940 thru 1948 SPECIFICATIONS FORD and MERCURY

General Engine Specifications—*continued*

Year	Model	Number of Cylinders Bore and Stroke	Piston Displacement, Cubic Inches	Compression Ratio (To–1)	Taxable (A.M.A.) Hp.	DEVELOPED HORSE POWER		Maximum Torque Ft. Lbs.
						Bare Engine	With Accessories	
FORD								
1941	11A, DeL., Sup. DeL., 8 Cyl.	8–3 1/16 x 3.75	221.0	6.15	30.0	85 @ 3800		157 @ 2200
	1GA, 6 Cyl.	6–3.30 x 4.40	226.0	6.70	26.1	90 @ 3300		180 @ 1200
1942	2GA, 6 Cyl.	6–3.30 x 4.40	226.0	6.70	26.1	90 @ 3300		180 @ 1200
	21A, 8 Cyl.	8–3 1/16 x 3.75	221.0	6.20	30.0	90 @ 3800		156 @ 2200
1946	6GA, 6 Cyl.	6–3.30 x 4.40	226.0	6.70	26.1	90 @ 3300		180 @ 1200
	69A, 8 Cyl.	8–3.187 x 3.75	239.4	6.75	32.5	100 @ 3800		180 @ 2000
1947	7GA, 6 Cyl.	6–3.30 x 4.40	226.0	6.70	26.1	90 @ 3300		180 @ 1200
	79A, 8 Cyl.	8–3 3/16 x 3 3/4	239.4	6.75	32.5	100 @ 3800		180 @ 2000
1948	87HA, 6 Cyl.	6–3.30 x 4.40	226.0	6.70	26.1	90 @ 3300		180 @ 1200
	89A, 8 Cyl.	8–3.187 x 3.75	239.4	6.75	32.5	100 @ 3800		180 @ 2000
MERCURY								
1940	09A, 8 Cyl.	8–3.187 x 3.75	239.0	6.15	32.5	95 @ 3600		170 @ 2100
1941	19A, 8 Cyl.	8–3.187 x 3.75	239.0	6.15	32.5	95 @ 3600		176 @ 2100
1942	29A, 8 Cyl.	8–3.187 x 3.75	239.0	6.40	32.5	100 @ 3800		176 @ 2100
1946	69M, 8 Cyl.	8–3.187 x 3.75	239.4	6.75	32.5	100 @ 3800	89 @ 3600	180 @ 2000
1947	79M, 8 Cyl.	8–3 3/16 x 3 3/4	239.4	6.75	32.5	100 @ 3800	89 @ 3600	180 @ 2000
1948	89M, 8 Cyl.	8–3 3/16 x 3 3/4	239.4	6.75	32.5	100 @ 3800	89 @ 3600	180 @ 2000

Dimensions of Valves

Year	Model	Overall Length		Head Diameter		Seat Angle (deg.)		Stem Diameter		Key Type	O.D. of Seat Insert	
		Inlet	Exhaust	Inlet	Exhaust	Inlet	Exhaust	Inlet	Exhaust		Inlet	Exhaust
FORD												
1941-42	V8, 85			1.537	1.537	45	45	.311	.311	horseshoe	1.6335	1.6335
1946	69A	4.757	4.757	1.507	1.507	45	45	.311	.310	horseshoe	1.6335	1.6335
1947	79A	4.757	4.757	1.507	1.507	45	45	.311	.310	horseshoe	1.6335	1.6335
1946-47	6GA, 7GA	5.203	5.203	1.766	1.515	45	45	.311	.311	horseshoe	1.625	1.625
1948	87HA	4.757	5.537	1.647	1.510	45	45	.311	.310	split lock		1.6335
	89A	4.819	4.815	1.510	1.510	45	45	.311	.310	split lock	1.6335	1.6335
MERCURY												
1940-41	V8, 95			1.537	1.537	45	45	.311	.311	horseshoe	1.6335	1.6335
1942	29A			1.510	1.51	45	45	.311	.311	horseshoe	1.6335	1.6335
1946	69M	4.757	4.757	1.507	1.507	45	45	.311	.310	horseshoe	1.6335	1.6335
1947	69M			1.507	1.507	45	45	.311	.311	horseshoe	1.6335	1.6335
1948	89M	4.819	4.815	1.510	1.510	45	45	.311	.310	horseshoe	1.6335	1.6335

FORD and MERCURY SPECIFICATIONS 1940 thru 1948

Engine Overhaul Specifications

Year	Model	PISTONS				RING GAP CLEARANCES (Maximum)				PISTON PIN		ROD BEARINGS		
		Removed From	Piston Skirt Clearances (Maximum)											
			Top	Bottom	Limit	Top Ring	Second Ring	Third Ring	Oil Ring	Type	Fit	Oil Clearance	Wear Limit	Side Play
FORD														
1941	11A, DeL., Sp. DeL., 8 Cyl.	A	....	.0025	.005	.017	.017	....	.017	FL	Push	.0015–.003	.006	.010
	1GA, 6 Cyl.	A	....	.0025	.005	.012	.012	....	.012	FL	Push	.0015–.003	.006	.010
1942	2GA, 6 Cyl.	A	....	.0025	.005	.012	.012	....	.012	FL	Push	.0015–.003	.006	.010
	21A, 8 Cyl.	A	....	.0025	.005	.017	.017	....	.017	FL	Push	.0015–.003	.006	.010
1946	6GA, 6 Cyl.	A	....	....	....	.017	.017	....	.017	FL	Push	.0015–.003	.006	.010
	69A, 8 Cyl.	A	.003	.0017	.005	.014	.014	.014	.014	FL	Push	.001 –.002	.006	.006–.014
1947	7GA, 6 Cyl.	A	.003	.0025	.005	.017	.017	.017	.017	FL	Push	.0015–.003	.006	.003
	79A, 8 Cyl.	A	.003	.00175	.005	.017	.017	.017	.017	FL	Push	.0011	.006	.006–.014
1948	87HA, 6 Cyl.	A	.003	.0025	.005	.017	.017	.017	.017	FL	Push	.0002–.0017	.006	.003
	89A, 8 Cyl.	A	.003	.00175	.005	.017	.017	.017	.017	FL	Push	.0011	.006	.006–.014
MERCURY														
1941	19A, 8 Cyl.	A	....	....	.004	.017	.017	....	.017	Float	Push	.0015–.003	.006	.010
1942	29A, 8 Cyl.	A	....	....	.004	.015	.015	....	.015	Float	Push	.0015–.003	.006	.010
1946	69M, 8 Cyl.	A	....	....	.004	.015	.015	....	.015	Float	Push	.0015–.003	.006	.006–.014
1947	79M, 8 Cyl.	A	.003	.0175	.004	.017	.017	.017	.017	Float	Push	.0015–.003	.006	.006–.014
1948	89M, 8 Cyl.	A	.003	.0175	.004	.017	.017	.017	.017	Float	Push	.0015–.003	.006	.006–.014

A—Above. FL—Floating. †—Center crank gear mark between cam gear marks.

Tension Wrench Specifications

Year	Model	Cylinder Head		Spark Plug		Connecting Rod Bolts or Nuts		Main Bearing Bolt		Flywheel Bolts		Vibration Damper Bolts	
		Lbs.-Ft.	Thread	Lbs.-Ft.	Thread	Lbs.-Ft.	Thread	Lbs.-Ft.	Thread	Lbs.-Ft.	Thread	Lbs.-F.	Thread
FORD													
1940 to 48	All	50-60	....	24-28	14 mm	35-40	....	75-80	....	65-70	....	....	....
MERCURY													
1940 to 48	All	65-70	7/16-14	24-30	14 mm	....	....	....	....	....	....	....	....

Cooling System Capacities and Anti-Freeze Proportion Table

CAR AND YEAR	MODEL	Capacity Qts.	Quarts of Methanol Base Anti-Freeze (For Protection to Temperature Shown Below)							Quarts of Ethylene Glycol (For Protection to Temperature Shown Below)							Quarts of Denatured Alcohol 188 Proof (For Protection to Temperature Shown Below)						
			3	4	5	6	7	8	9	3	4	5	6	7	8	9	3	4	5	6	7	8	9
FORD																							
1941	V8	23¾	21	16	10	4	−4	−12	−21	....	19	15	10	5	0	−8	20	....	10	....	....	0	−10
1941-42	Six	17½	17	8	−1	−12	−25	−38	−53	19	14	7	0	−10	−21	−34	20	10	....	0	−10	....	−20
1942-48	V8	22	20	14	7	0	−9	−18	−29	....	18	13	8	2	−6	−14	20	....	10	....	0	....	−10
1946-48	Six	14½	11	1	−12	−27	−44	....	....	16	8	0	−12	−26	−43	....	....	10	0	−10	−20	−30	....
MERCURY																							
1939-40, 1942-48		22	20	14	7	0	−9	−18	−29	....	18	13	8	2	−6	−14	20	....	10	....	0	....	−10
1941		23¾	21	16	10	4	−4	−12	−21	....	19	15	10	5	0	−8	20	....	10	....	....	0	−10

1940 thru 1948 SPECIFICATIONS FORD and MERCURY and Wear Limit Table

CRANKSHAFT		VALVES						Valve Timing, Inlet Valve Opens (Deg.)	Camshaft Drive	Gear Marks	OPERATING OIL PRESSURE		Model	Year
Main Bearing Oil Clearance	Shaft End Play	Spring Tension (Maximum) Inlet	Exhaust	Low Limit	Guide Clearance	Seat Angle Inlet	Exhaust				Pounds At M.P.H.	Low Limit§		
FORD														
.0005	.002-.006	40@2.13	40@2.13	30	.0015-.0035	45°	45°	TC	Gear	†	30@2000	15	..............11A, 8 Cyl.	1941
.0005	.002-.006	40@2.13	40@2.13	30	.0015-.0035	45°	45°	3B	Gear	†	30@2000	15	..............1GA, 6 Cyl.	
.0005	.002-.006	40@2.13	40@2.13	30	.0015-.0035	45°	45°	3B	Gear	†	30@2000	15	..............2GA, 6 Cyl.	1942
.0005	.002-.006	40@2.13	40@2.13	30	.0015-.0035	45°	45°	TC	Gear	†	30@2000	15	..............21A, 8 Cyl.	
.0005	.002-.006	40@2.13	40@2.13	30	.0015-.0035	45°	45°	3B	Gear	†	35@2000	20	..............6GA, 6 Cyl.	1946
.001	.002-.006	40@2.13	40@2.13	30	.0015-.0035	45°	45°	TC	Gear	†	50@2000	30	..............69A, 8 Cyl.	
.0022	.002-.006	40@2.13	40@2.13	30	.0015-.0035	45°	45°	5B	Gear	†	35@2000	20	..............7GA, 6 Cyl.	1947
.0005	.002-.006	40@2.13	40@2.13	30	.0015-.0035	45°	45°	TC	Gear	†	50@2000	30	..............79A, 8 Cyl.	
.0022	.002-.006	40@2.13	40@2.13	30	.0025	45°	45°	5B	Gear	†	35@2000	20	..............87HA, 6 Cyl.	1948
.0025	.002-.006	40@2.13	40@2.13	30	.0015-.0035	45°	45°	TC	Gear	†	51@2000	30	..............89A, 8 Cyl.	
MERCURY														
.001-.003	.002-.006	80@1.83	80@1.83	70	.0015-.0035	45°	45°	TC	Gear	†	30@ *	25	..............19A, 8 Cyl.	1941
.001-.003	.002-.006	80@1.83	80@1.83	70	.0015-.0035	45°	45°	TC	Gear	†	30@ *	25	..............29A, 8 Cyl.	1942
.0012	.004	78@1.84	78@1.84	68	.0025-.0045	45°	45°	TC	Gear	†	55@60	25	..............69M, 8 Cyl.	1946
.0012	.002-.006	78@1.84	78@1.84	68	.0015-.0035	45°	45°	TC	Gear	†	55@60	25	..............79M, 8 Cyl.	1947
.0012	.002-.006	78@1.84	78@1.84	68	.0025-.0045	45°	45°	TC	Gear	†	50@45	25	..............89M, 8 Cyl.	1948

*—At 2000 r.p.m.
B—Before top center.
§—Car may be operated safely at lower oil pressures but low pressure indicates malfunction which should be corrected.
TC—Top center.

Distributors

Year	Model	Distributor Model Number	Cam Angle (deg.)	Direction of Rotation C=Clockwise CC=Counter Clockwise at Cam End	Breaker Arm Spring Tension	Breaker Point Gap (inches)	Engine R.P.M. when Cent. Advance Starts	Max. Cent. Advance in Engine Deg. at Stated Engine R.P.M.	Vacuum in (inches) of Mercury at which Vacuum Unit Starts	Max. Advance in Engine Deg. at Stated Vacuum	Vacuum Unit Number
FORD											
1940	V8-60, 85..............	78-12127	36	C	20-24	.014-.016	400	16@1900	....	....	....
1941	V8-90..............	11A-12127	36	C	20-24	.014-.016	400	22@1200	....	....	....
1942	V8-90..............	21A-12127	36	C	20-24	.014-.016	400	22@1200	....	....	....
1946 to 48	6 cyl..............	5GA-12127	40	C	20-24	.014-.016	400	18@1200	....	....	....
	V8-100..............	59A-12127	36	C	20-24	.014-.016	400	22@1200	....	....	....
MERCURY											
1940	V8, 95..............	78-12127	36	C	20-24	.014-.016	400	16@1900	....	....	....
1941	V8, 100..............	11A-12127	36	C	20-24	.014-.016	400	22@1200	....	....	....
1942	V8, 100..............	21A-12127	36	C	20-24	.014-.016	400	22@1200	....	....	....
1946 to 48	V8, 100..............	59A-12127	36	C	20-24	.014-.016	400	22@1200	....	....	....

FORD and MERCURY SPECIFICATIONS 1940 thru 1948

Crankshaft Bearing Journal Sizes

Year	Model	Connecting Rod Journals		Main Bearing Journals				
		Diameter	Length	No. 1 Diameter	No. 2 Diameter	No. 3 Diameter	No. 4 Diameter	No. 5 Diameter
FORD								
1940	02A, 60 h.p.	1.698–1.699	1.410	2.098–2.099	2.098–2.099	2.098–2.099	....	....
	01A, 85 h.p.	1.998–1.999	1.750	2.498–2.499	2.498–2.499	2.498–2.499	....	....
1941	11A, 85 h.p.	1.998–1.999	1.750	2.498–2.499	2.498–2.499	2.498–2.499	....	....
1941–42	1GA, 2GA, 6 cyl.	2.234–2.235	1.401	2.498–2.499	2.498–2.499	2.498–2.499	2.498–2.499	....
1942	21A, 90 h.p.	1.998–1.999	1.750	2.498–2.499	2.498–2.499	2.498–2.499	....	....
1946 to 49	V8, 100 h,p.	2.139–2.140	1.750	2.498–2.499	2.498–2.499	2.498–2.499	....	....
1947–48	7GA, 87HA	2.2343–2.235	1.401	2.498–2.499	2.498–2.499	2.498–2.499	2.498–2.499	....
MERCURY								
1940 to 49	Series—All	2.138–2.139	1.750	2.498–2.499	2.498–2.499	2.498–2.499	....	....

Pistons and Piston Pins

Year	Model	PISTONS					PISTON PINS	
		Diameter	Material	Type	No. of Rings	Length	Diameter	How Held
FORD								
1941–42	V8-85	3.062	Cast Steel	....	3	2.850	.7502	F
1941 to 47	6 cyl.	3.30	Alum.	....	3	2.90625	.850	F
1946–47	V8-85	3.1875	Alum.	....	4	2.84375	.750	F
1948	87HA, 6 cyl.	3.30	Alum.	Ss	4	2.917	.8502	F
	89A, V8	3.1875	Alum.	Ss	4	2.848	.7502	F
MERCURY								
1940 to 42	V8	3.187	Cast Steel	....	3	2.847	.75	F
1946 to 48	69M, 79M, 89M	3.1875	Alum.	Ss	4	2.847	.7503	F

Alum—Aluminum. Ss—Split Skirt. F—Floating.

Engine Tune-Up Specifications

Year	Model	SPARK PLUGS		DISTRIBUTOR		Ignition Timing (Deg.)	Ignition Timing Mark and Location	Com-pression Pressure at R.P.M.	OPERATING TAPPET CLEARANCE		Carburetor Fuel Float Height	Minimum Engine Idle Speed at R.P.M.
		Type	Gap	Point Gap	Cam Dwell (Deg.)				Inlet	Exhaust		
FORD												
1940	O22A, 8 Cyl.	Ch-H10	.025	.016	36	4B	Dh.	158@2800	.011	.015	15/32"	425
	O1A, Standard, 8 Cyl.	Ch-H10	.025	.016	36	4B	Dh.	140@2400	.011	.015	21/32"	425
	O1A, DeLuxe, 8 Cyl.	Ch-H10	.025	.016	36	4B	Dh.	140@2400	.011	.015	21/32"	425
1941	11A, DeLuxe, Super DeLuxe	Ch-H10	.025	.020	36	4B	Dh.	140@2400	.011	.015	....	425
	1GA, 6 Cyl.	Ch-H10	.027	.016	36	4B	Dh.	165@2000	.014	.016	....	450
1942	2GA, 6 Cyl.	Ch-H10	.034	.016	38	1B	Dh.	165@2000	.011	.015	1 7/32"	450
	21A, 8 Cyl.	Ch-H10	.025	.016	36	4B	Dh.	140@2400	.011	.015	15/32"	425

1940 thru 1948 SPECIFICATIONS FORD and MERCURY

Engine Tune-Up Specifications—*continued*

Year	Model	SPARK PLUGS Type	SPARK PLUGS Gap	DISTRIBUTOR Point Gap	DISTRIBUTOR Cam Dwell (Deg.)	Ignition Timing (Deg.)	Ignition Timing Mark and Location	Compression Pressure at R.P.M.	OPERATING TAPPET CLEARANCE Inlet	OPERATING TAPPET CLEARANCE Exhaust	Carburetor Fuel Float Height	Minimum Engine Idle Speed at R.P.M.
FORD												
1946	6GA, 6 Cyl.	Ch-H10	.034	.016	38	1B	Dh.	117@2000	.011	.015	1 7/32″	450
	69A, 8 Cyl.	Ch-H10	.025	.016	36	4B	Dh.	160@2400	.011	.015	1 7/32″	425
1947	7GA, 6 Cyl.	Ch-H10	.032	.016	38	1B	Dh.	160@2100	.011	.015	1 7/32″	450
	79A, 8 Cyl.	Ch-H10	.025	.016	38	4B	Dh.	160@2400	.011	.015	1 7/32″	425
1948	87HA, 6 Cyl.	Ch-H10	.032	.016	38	1B	Dh.	161@2100	.011	.015	1 7/32″	450
	89A, 8 Cyl.	Ch-H10	.028	.016	38	4B	Dh.	160@2400	.011	.015	1 7/32″	425
MERCURY												
1940	09A, 8 Cyl.	H10	.025	.016	36	4B	None	145@2200	.015	.015	....	425
1941	19A, 8 Cyl.	H10	.025	.016	36	4B	None	145@2200	.015	.015	....	425
1942	29A, 8 Cyl.	H10	.025	.015	36	4B	None	145@2200	.015	.015	....	425
1946	69M, 8 Cyl.	H10	.025	.015	36	4B	None	160@2400	.011	.015	1 7/32″	425
1947	79M, 8 Cyl.	H10	.025	.015	36	4B	None	160@2400	.011	.015	1 7/32″	425
1948	89M, 8 Cyl.	H10	.025	.015	36	4B	None	160@2400	.011	.015	1 7/32″	425

B—Before top center. Ch—Champion Spark Plug Co.

Piston Ring Dimensions

Year	Model	Cylinder Bore	TOP RING Width	TOP RING Gap	TOP RING Depth	SECOND RING Width	SECOND RING Gap	SECOND RING Depth	THIRD RING Width	THIRD RING Gap	THIRD RING Depth	OIL RING Width	OIL RING Gap	OIL RING Depth
FORD														
1941-42	V8	3 1/16	.0917	.0145	.135	.0917	.0145	.110	.1537	.0145	.110	......	......	......
1942	26A, 6 cylinder	3-30	.095	.015	......	.095	.015	.110	3/16	.015	.110	......	......	......
1946-48	6GA, 6 cylinder	3-30	.0222	.013	.150	.0222	.013	.150	.1862	.013	.145	.1862	.013	.145
	V8, 8 cylinder	3 3/16	.0917	.013	.140	.0917	.013	.140	.1547	.013	.147	.1547	.013	.147
MERCURY														
1940	V8	3 3/16	.0945	.015	......	.0940	.015	......	.1570	.015	......	......	......	......
1941-42	V8	3 3/16	.0917	.014	.137	.0917	.014	.116	.1537	.014	.112	......	......	......
1946-48	69M, 79M, 89M	3 3/16	.0917	.013	.140	.0917	.013	.140	.1547	.013	.147	.1547	.013	.147

Brake Data

Year	Model	Make	Lining Type	R=Riveted B=Bonded	Drum Diameter	Lining Length	Lining Width	Lining Thickness	Clearance Toe	Clearance Heel
FORD										
1940	V8, 60-85	Loc	WM	R	12	......	......	......	......	......
1941-42	V8, 85	......	WM	R	12	23.3	1 3/4	.020	......	......
1946-47	V8, 85	Own	M	R	12	24	1.72	.020	......	......
1948	87HA, 89A	Own	M	R	12	23.2	1 3/4	3/16	......	......

FORD and MERCURY SPECIFICATIONS 1940 thru 1948

Brake Data—*continued*

Year	Model	Make	Lining Type	R=Riveted B=Bonded	Drum Diameter	Lining Length	Lining Width	Lining Thickness	Clearance Toe	Clearance Heel
MERCURY										
1940	V8-95	Loc	WM	R	12	....	....	....	....	....
1941–42	....	....	WM	R	12	23.3	1¾	.020	....	....
1946–47	69M, 79M	Own	M	R	12	24	1.72	.20	....	....
1948	89M	Own	M	R	12	23 13/64	1¾	3/16	....	....

Loc—Lockheed. WM—Woven on primary, moulded on secondary. M—Moulded.

Generators

Year	Model	Generator Number	Field Current at 6 Volts (amps.)	Maximum Safe Output Volts	Maximum Safe Output Amperes	Maximum Safe Output R.P.M.	Brush Spring Tension (oz.)	Voltage Regulator Number
FORD								
1940	V8-60 hp., 90 hp.	01A-10000-A	2–1	6.0	32	2500	28	8A-10505-A
1941	V8-90 hp., 100 hp.	01A-10000-B	2–1	6.0	30	2500	28	8A-10505-A
1941–42	4 cyl., 40 hp.	1NC-10000	2–1	6.0	30	2500	28	01A-10505-C
1941	6 cyl., 90 hp.	1GA-10000-A	2–1	6.0	30	2500	28	01A-10505-C
1942 to 48	V8-100 hp.	21A-10000	2–1	7.2	30	2500	20–22	8M-10505-A
MERCURY								
1940	....	01A-10000-A	2–86	7.1	32	2500	28	01A-10505-A
1941	19A	01A-10000-A	2–86	7.1	30	3000	16–18	0LA-10505-C
1942	29A	21A-10000	2–1	7.2	32	1800	16–18	0LA-10505-C
1946–47	69M, 79M	21A-10000	2–1	7.2	32	1800	20–22	8L-10505
1948	89M	21A-10000	2–1	7.3	30	1800	20–22	51A-10505-A

Voltage Regulators

Year	Model	Regulator Number	Grounded P=Positive N=Negative	Voltage Control Air Gap Points Closed	Voltage Control Voltage Setting Hot	Current Control Air Gap Points Closed	Current Control Current Set Hot	Cut-Out Relay Point Gap	Cut-Out Relay Air Gap	Cut-Out Relay Closing Volt
FORD										
1940 to 48	All	01A-10505-C 51A-10505-A	....	.035 .035	7.2 7.2	.035 .035	30–34 30–34	.018 .018	.025 .025	6.1–6.3 6.1–6.3
MERCURY										
1940 to 46	Series—All	01A-10505-C 11AS-10505-E	....	.035	7.2	.035	30–34	.018	.025	6.1–6.3 ....
1947–48	Series—All	59A-10505-A 59AS-10505-A	....	....	....	....	....	....	....	....
1949	Series—All	51A-10505-A 5EH-10505-C	....	.035 .035	7.2 7.1	.035 .035	30–34 30–34	.018 .018	.025 .025	6.1–6.3 6.0–6.6

1940 thru 1948 SPECIFICATIONS FORD and MERCURY

Starters

Year	Model	Unit Model Number	Spring Tension (oz.)	STARTER Lock Test Volts	Lock Test Amperes	Lock Test Torque, (lbs. ft.)	No Load Volts	No Load Amperes	No Load R.P.M.	Direction of Rotation Viewed from Drive Ende C=Clockwise CC=Counter-clockwise
FORD										
1940 to 48	V8—100 hp.	18-11002	27	3.75	550	15	6.0	75	8000	CC
1941 to 47	6 cyl., 90 hp. G	18-11002	27	3.75	550	15	6.0	75	8000	CC
1941 to 50	6 cyl., 90 hp. H	7HA-11002	27	3.75	550	15	5.8	50	6500	CC
MERCURY										
1940 to 42					500	14				
1946–47	69M, 79M	18-11002	27	3.75	550	15	6	75	8000	CC
1948	89M	18-11001	27	3.25	550	15	5.8	52	6500	CC

Front Wheel Alignment

Year	Model	Caster (deg.)	Camber (deg.)	King Pin Inclination (deg.)	Toe-In (inches)	Turning Radius Inner	Turning Radius Outer
FORD							
1940	022A, 01A, 60 and 85 hp.	4½P to 9P	¼N to 1P	8	0 to 1/16	23½	20
1941–42	All V8, and 6 cyl.	5½P to 8P	0 to 1P	8	0 to 1/16	23½	20
1946	69A, V8 6GA, 6 cyl.	8P 8P	0 to 1P 0 to 1P	8 8	0 to 1/16 0 to 1/16	23½ 23½	20 20
1947–48	All V8 and 6 cyl.	4½P to 9P	¼N to 1N	8	0 to 1/16	23½	20
MERCURY							
1940–42	All	4½P to 9P	¼P to 1P	8	0 to 1/16	23	20
1946–48	All	7¼P	1P	8	0 to 1/16	23	20

N—Negative. P—Positive.

FORD and MERCURY 1940 thru 1948

There was a great deal of similarity in construction in Ford and Mercury models built between 1940 and 1948.

1949 to 1951 models of Ford and Mercury are given later (alphabetically) in this section.

FRONT SUSPENSION

A conventional axle is used on all Ford and Mercury models built from 1940 to 1948.

A transverse leaf spring is used.

Caster, Camber and Toe-In

In order to correct for caster on these models it is necessary to either bend the "wishbone" or bend the ends of the axle in relation to the center.

Camber is corrected by bending the I beam.

Toe-in is controlled by a single tie rod which is adjustable.

The steering wheel may be centralized by adjusting the length of the drag link.

Replacement of King Pins

To replace the king pins it is necessary to take off the wheels and brake backing plates.

The backing plate can be slipped over the spindle with the brake lines connected.

It is customary to form a small hook out of stout wire and hang the backing plate up on the frame to prevent any damage to the flexible brake hose.

King pin lock pins are driven from the back toward the front on all models.

In many instances the king pin has a tendency to stick in the I beam and it is necessary to use a special king pin press to force it out of the knuckle.

On all models of Ford and Mercury the top of the king pin has a mushroom head and it is necessary to force the king pin upwards from the bottom.

Should the king pin become stuck in the axle and a special king pin pressing device is not available, it is possible to saw off the mushroom head of the king pin and, supporting the underside of the knuckle with a piece of pipe big enough to pass the king pin through its center, the king pin can be driven downward and out. Since many king pins are case hardened it may be necessary to heat the top of the king pin until it turns blue before attempting to saw it. This is generally accomplished by heating the top of the pin quickly with a welding torch in order to localize the heat.

Many ingenious methods have been developed to remove frozen king pins among which are supporting the full weight of the front end on a specially prepared post which contacts the bottom of the king pin only, and then driving downward on the steering knuckle which causes the weight of the car to assist in pushing the king pin upward. In shops where safety is considered to be of paramount importance this particular method is not permitted since it can easily prove very dangerous.

Replacement of Transverse Front Leaf Spring

On all models of Ford and Mercury up to 1948 the front spring is held to the channeled front cross member with two U bolts, and a spring seat plate.

The springs are shackled at either end to a shackle connection which is hung on a portion of the radius (wishbone) rod. A special spring spreading device is generally used to take the load off the shackles before attempting to remove the spring. However, if a spreading device is not available, it is possible to place a supporting device with a smooth top directly under the eye of each spring so that when weight is placed on the front end of the car the spring eye is free to slide outward, releasing the pressure from the shackle.

It is customary to loosen the nuts which hold the shackle links in place and then have someone impose their weight on the front of the car so that the pressure will be momentarily relieved and the spring shackle bolt may be driven out of place. Bear in mind that the supporting device must have a top which is smooth enough to permit the spring to slide outward as weight is applied to the front end. Rubber shackles are used on all models.

Steering mechanism

STEERING GEAR ASSEMBLY

Removal of Steering Wheel

Remove the horn button by depressing the button and twisting it to the right or left and lifting it off. The steering wheel nut will then be accessible. Remove the steering wheel nut and, using a puller, pull off the steering wheel.

While many mechanics have been successful in driving a wheel off, it is pretty risky business since the hub of the wheel is generally made of hard rubber and will break readily when struck by a hard hammer.

Adjustment of Steering Mechanism

1. Disconnect the pitman arm from the drag link.

2. Adjust the steering gear housing assembly.

A. Check the worm shaft bearings for end play, and if any play exists remove the four cap screws and take out one shim at a time until there is no play in the worm bearing without there being a definite pre-load.

B. Set the steering wheel in the mid-position of its travel and check the mesh of the worm and roller tooth to determine if there is any play at the high spot.

If play exists loosen lock nut (B) and turn the mesh adjuster inward until there is zero lash in the steering wheel in the mid-position of its travel and then tighten the lock nut.

3. Reconnect the pitman arm to the drag link.

4. Loosen the clamp bolt and adjust the sleeve on the drag link so there is one-half of the toe-in in the right wheel, with the steering wheel in the mid-position of its travel. Tighten the clamp bolts.

5. Loosen the clamp bolts at each end of the tie rod and turn the tie rod so that the other half of the toe-in is in the left wheel. Tighten the clamp bolt.

Turn the steering wheel from one end of its travel to the other to check for looseness or binding.

Steering Gear Assembly Removal

On all models of Ford and Mercury to 1948 the steering gear assembly is removed through the bottom, after taking off the steering wheel, dash bracket, ignition switch, pitman arm, shift connections, and the left engine underpan.

Removal of Horn Button

On all models from 1940 to 1948 horn button is a bayonet type and is removed by pressing it down and twisting it to the left.

BRAKES

On all Ford and Mercury models from 1940 to 1942 a hydraulically operated Lockheed type brake was used. These brakes are fitted with an eccentric type anchor which is adjustable from the axle side of the backing plate. 1946 to 1948 models were equipped with a non-adjustable anchor.

Adjusting points major brake operation

Minor Adjustment of Service Brakes

A minor adjustment of service brakes is made to compensate for the normal wear of the brake lining. No adjustment of any kind should be made on Ford or Mercury, and in fact on any other brake, without first removing at least one wheel to inspect the condition of the lining and the hydraulic cylinder.

Check carefully around the boot of the hydraulic cylinder to determine if it is leaking or seeping. If any dampness is found it indicates that the cylinder is leaking and requires service.

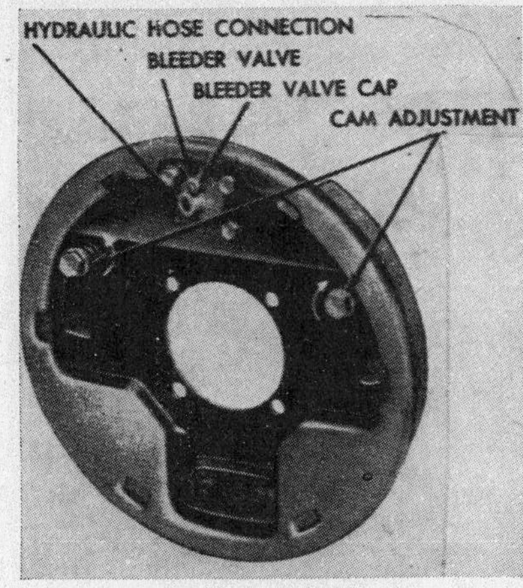

Adjusting points, minor brake adjustment

If the wheel has a defective or partially inoperative wheel cylinder it is always good practice, from the standpoint of safety, to check all four wheel cylinders and the master cylinder.

If the lining and cylinder are found to be in good condition replace the brake drum and proceed with the minor adjustment:

Turn the cam adjuster at each brake shoe until the shoe contacts the drum and then back off until the drum is just free. Repeat this at all shoes.

Note: On all eccentric adjusters with the wrench pointed upward it is turned in a direction which will bring it toward the brake drum. For instance, on the right front wheel the front adjuster would be turned in a clock-wise direction, where as the rear adjuster would be turned in a counter clock-wise direction, to expand the shoe.

Major Brake Adjustment

A major brake adjustment is made at any time the shoes have been relined or it is found that the brakes are not operating properly after a minor adjustment.

Caution: If an examination of the brake lining reveals that the lining is wearing unevenly from one end to the other but is wearing all over its surface it is not advisable to change the anchor adjustment since, while the anchors were badly adjusted when the lining was first put on, the lining has now worn itself to where it is in full contact with the drum and should be left in that position or the lining removed and new lining installed.

Major Adjustment is Performed as Follows:

On 1946 to 1948 models an anchor adjustment is not possible, since the anchors were designed to be non-adjustable.

On 1940 to 1942 models the anchor is adjusted by turning the eccentric at the top of the backing plate until the wheel just drags, and then turn the eccentric anchor in the same direction as the cam, until the wheel is barely free. Then repeat by turning the cam very slightly until the wheel barely drags again and then again turn the anchor until the wheel is free. Keep repeating this operation, just a little at a time until it is not possible to free the wheel by turning either of the cams in an outward direction. Then tighten the anchor lock nut.

MAJOR BRAKE ADJUSTMENT —continued

After the anchor lock nut is securely tightened, being certain not to change the adjustment while tightening the jam nut, back off on the cam adjuster until the wheel is free.

Pedal to toe board clearance of the master cylinder should be approximately ¾ inch to 1 inch and the adjustment is made at the hydraulic master cylinder push rod.

When making the anchor adjustment, described above, do not loosen the anchor jam nut more than is necessary to permit turning the anchor pin.

COOLING SYSTEM

All V8 engines are equipped with two water pumps which also serve as the motor legs.

Six cylinder engines were equipped with a single water pump.

Removal of Thermostats

The thermostat on V8 engines is located at the water outlet on top of each cylinder head. When replacing thermostats it is advisable to replace them in pairs.

The thermostat on the 6 cylinder engine is located in the water outlet elbow at the top of the cylinder head toward the front.

Removal of Water Pump

V8 MODELS

Since the water pump also acts as the motor support it is essential that, when removing one water pump, the pump on the opposite side be loosened at the frame mounting to prevent straining the casting.

It will be necessary to support the engine when removing either of the water pumps. To remove the pump disconnect the lower radiator hose and fan belt and take out the pump mounting bolts.

Note: One of the mounting bolts is located in a depression in the casting, another bolt is located inside the water inlet, and it is necessary to first remove the hose and reach down into the pump outlet itself to remove this last bolt.

SIX CYLINDER MODELS

To remove the water pump on 6 cylinder models disconnect the radiator hose and the fan belts and take out the mounting bolts and lift off the pump.

60 HORSEPOWER V8 ENGINES

While this text is intended to cover models built after 1940, an exception is made in this instance since a 60 horsepower water pump was mounted quite differently from those on the larger engines. Two types of water pumps were used on 60 horsepower model, one of the pumps identified by the serrated edges of the pump body, is simply screwed into the front of the cylinder block. The other type, identified by the flanges is bolted to the front of the cylinder block.

On these engines the water pump does not act as a motor leg.

Disassembly of Water Pump

Six cylinder water pumps are equipped with a shaft and bearing assembly which are non-separable and are serviced as a unit.

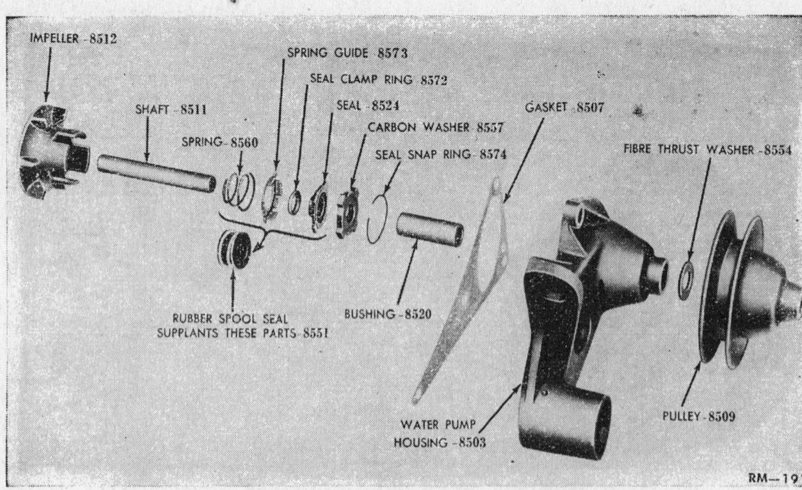

1940 thru 1948 V8 models water pump

On V8 models some water pumps had a bearing assembly, others used a bushing, however, the service is done in exactly the same manner.

Except for servicing 60 horsepower V8 pumps, the procedure for both the 6 and the V8 is very similar.

Press the shaft out of the hub assembly.

Press the shaft assembly out of the housing (bearings will come out together with the shaft on the ball bearing type pumps) and remove the seal assembly from the impeller by taking out the snap ring.

Regardless of the type pump used the seal assembly which, on the earlier pump was in several pieces, is now serviced as a single unit.

On reassembly both the impeller and the hub are pressed on until they are flush with the end of the shaft.

60 Hp PUMPS

A slightly different technique is used to separate the parts of the 60 hp. pump. The pump unit is held together by a coil spring, which is latched to the outer portion of the hollowed out shaft. Simply lift up the spring with a pair of needle nose pliers and turn it until it indexes with the slot in the washer which retains it. Release the spring and the pump will come apart.

ENGINE ASSEMBLY

All Ford and Mercury engines built between 1940 and 1948 were of the L Head variety. Mercury engines were made in V type 8 cylinders only and the Ford engine was supplied in both a V type 8 cylinder engine and an In-Line 6 cylinder engine.

Engine Manifolds

All V8 engines are equipped with an inlet manifold set between the two cylinder blocks. This manifold also acts as a valve chamber cover.

The In-Line 6 cylinder engines are equipped with a conventional combination intake and exhaust manifold, equipped with a heat riser.

Except to check for leaks and a stuck heat riser valve no service is required by either the inlet or exhaust manifold.

On V8 models all service on the valves require the removal of the intake manifold.

Engine Removal

The engine can be removed readily from all Ford and Mercury models by first removing the radiator core and battery.

Remove all attaching parts such as the engine radius rods, electrical connections to the engine, fuel lines, battery ground straps, and heat indicator and gauge lines, etc. It is customary to detach the exhaust pipes at the manifold and the engine is disconnected from the transmission at the bell housing.

On some models to detach the upper bolts from the bell housing it is necessary to remove the floor boards. It will also be necessary to support the front of the transmission and loosen the transmission rear support bolts to prevent straining them too much.

While it is not necessary it sometimes is advisable to remove the intake manifold on V8 models before lifting it from the frame.

Rebuilt Engine and Engine Blocks

The Ford Motor Co. authorizes many dealers to rebuild engines and cylinder blocks under factory supervised conditions and to factory tolerances.

These reconditioned engines and cylinder blocks are available for all Ford models back to approximately 1932. Reconditioned engines include cylinder heads, but do not include any of the attaching parts such as oil pan, flywheel, intake or exhaust manifold, starter, generator or distributor.

Reconditioned cylinder blocks, known as "short blocks" are supplied without oil pan, cylinder head, flywheel or timing case cover. These engines are sold on an exchange basis.

ENGINE INTERNAL

Piston and Rod Assemblies

On all Ford and Mercury engines the piston and rod assemblies are removed through the top of the block after removing the cylinder head and oil pan.

Various types of pistons were used in these models and the piston table at the beginning of this Ford Section gives the type which was standard for any one year's production.

Assembly of Pistons to Connecting Rod

Where split skirt type pistons are used the split in the skirt should always face the left side of the engine. The numbers on the connecting rod always face forward. Therefore, when the numbers on the connecting rod are facing the mechanic the split skirt of the piston will be on his right.

Where a new solid skirt piston is being used it is not necessary to consider which way it is placed on the connecting rod. However, if an old piston is being reused it should be marked carefully on the side which faces the left so that the same technique of installation may be followed. The punch mark will then be toward the mechanic's right when the numbers on the connecting rod are facing the mechanic.

When assembling to the engine the numbers on the connecting rod should face forward.

All connecting rods marked "R" are for use on the right bank, all rods marked "L" are for use on the left bank.

When handling split skirt pistons, and in order to avoid confusion, remember that the split in the skirt is placed on the left side of the engine, but when assembling the piston to the connecting rod, if the numbers on the rod face the operator then the split in the skirt will be to the mechanic's right side.

6 CYLINDER MODELS

On all 6 cylinder models the piston is assembled so that the word "Ford" is nearest to the mechanic when the numbers on the connecting rods are facing the mechanic. The rod and piston assembly is assembled to the engine with the word "Ford" forward and the numbers on the connecting rod forward.

Connecting Rod Bearings

On all Ford and Mercury V8 models from 1940 to 1948 a single split connecting rod bearing was used for each pair of connecting rods. The bearing is of the full floating type.

Connecting rod bearings cannot be adjusted by any practical method. Where normal wear has taken place it will be necessary to replace the connecting rod bearings with undersize shells in order to take up the excessive clearance.

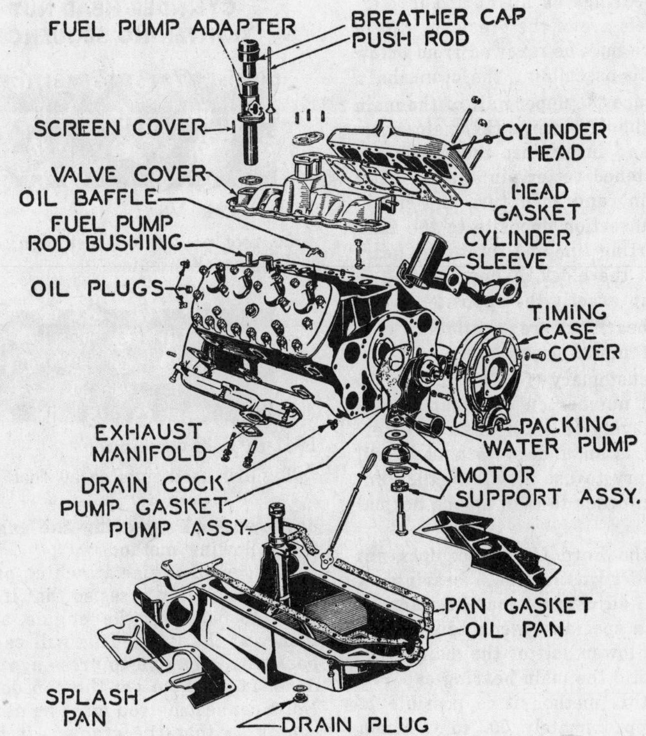

Exterior engine view all V8 models

FORD and MERCURY 1940 thru 1948

CONNECTING ROD BEARINGS—*continued*

A quick check to determine if a standard shell is being used in the car is to use a pair of tube micrometers and measure the thickness of the shell to approximately the center. Its thickness should not be less than .1085 inch, if the bearing is standard.

If the bearing is under-size the reading will be greater than that given for standard bearings.

Rod bearings are available which are under-size on the I.D. and standard on the O.D. They are also available over-size on the O.D. and standard on the I.D. Bearings are also available which are under-size on the I.D. and over-size on the O.D.

Since a single bearing is used to accommodate the connecting rod from both the right and the left bank it is essential that, when assembling a new connecting rod, the new rod has exactly the same bore as its mating rod on the opposite bank. If it does not it will be necessary to replace the rods on both banks in order that they may be properly seated on the rod bearing.

Crankshaft Main Bearings

Main bearings on all Ford and Mercury models are of the precision slip in type which may be renewed from below without dis-assembling the crankshaft.

To replace the upper half of the main bearing simply remove the main bearing cap and insert into the oil hole a small flattened cotter pin (or the little special pin) and then turn the crankshaft in direction opposite to the tang on the parting line and rotate the bearing out of the block. A new bearing is replaced in exactly the opposite way.

Main bearings are available in a variety of under-sizes.

It is customary for mechanics to check the number on the bearing cap when removing an old bearing to determine if it is an under-size, and it will be necessary to use a still further under-size in order to take up the normal wear.

While the Ford Motor Co. does not recommend adjusting main bearings, a very small adjustment may be made by inserting a specially prepared shim between the lower half of the main bearing shell and the main bearing cap.

Using this method it is possible to take up approximately .003 to .004 inch excessive play without serious difficulty.

Oil Pan Removal

V8 MODELS 1940 TO 1948

To remove the oil pan on these models (except the 1940 to 1946 models) it is necessary to turn the engine so that number 4 and number 8 pistons are at top center, which places the crankshaft balance weight at the front end of the crankshaft in an up position and permits the pan to pass by it. The radius rod must be taken down and the drag link removed.

Take off the starter assembly and remove the exhaust cross pipe. Jack up the engine about 2″ and place blocks under the motor legs; then remove the cap screws which hold the oil pan and lower the oil pan to the floor.

On 1940 to 1946 models it is not necessary to jack up the engine, but it is necessary to remove the radius rods and the cross-over pipe, drag link and tie rod.

6 CYLINDER MODELS

It is generally considered easier on 6 cylinder models to remove the engine in order to take down the oil pan. However, it is possible to get the oil pan down without removing the engine by the following methods:

Remove all engine attaching parts including radiator hoses so that it is possible to jack up the engine about 6 inches at the front. This will cause the back of the engine to press against the dash. In order to get the pan down the No. 1 connecting rod must be at bottom center so that the crankshaft balance weight is out of the way.

Remove the starter and the exhaust pipe at the manifold.

Take down the starter drag link and tie rod.

Unbolt the oil pan and lower it to the floor by lowering the back end first and sliding the pan backward.

CYLINDER HEAD NUT TIGHTENING SEQUENCE

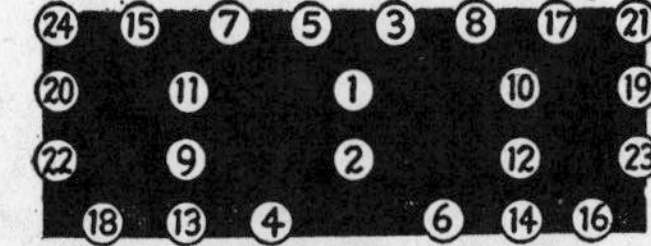

1938 to 1948 V8

50 foot pounds on cast iron, 40 foot pounds on aluminum.

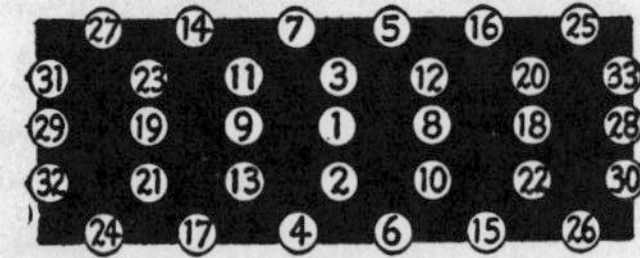

1941 to 1948 6 cylinder

Tighten head nuts to 50 foot pounds.

Fitting Pistons to Cylinder Block

The beginning of this Ford Section contains a table which gives the exact clearances desired between the piston and the cylinder. The technique is to insert the piston into the cylinder block using a feeler gage approximately ½″ wide having the clearance that is recommended for the piston.

With the feeler of the proper recommendation it should be fairly difficult to force the piston down into the cylinder with the length of feeler gage alongside the piston. The table on piston rings gives the correct clearance for the piston rings both as to gap and side clearance.

THE VALVE SYSTEM

All Ford and Mercury models built from 1940 to 1948 were equipped with valves which had non-adjustable tappets. The valve guides on all these models were of the type that required the removal of the valve guide in order to take out the valve, due to the mushroom type construction of the valve stem.

Removal of Valves from Engine

In order to remove the valves on Ford and Mercury models from 1940 to 1948 it is necessary that the valve guides be forced downward, the split washer removed, and then the assemblies pulled upward through the top of the block. The technique varies with different shops, but in general the following method will be found to be very effective:

Raise the valve stem and insert a special driving tool underneath the valve head. (This tool is designed to go around the head of the valve.) Drive the valve guide downward approximately 1/16 inch, reach into the valve chamber and remove the keeper which is located in a groove near the top of the valve guide. After the keeper has been removed the valve guide can then be pryed upward, using a special bar which is designed for this purpose.

Where the guides are stuck firmly in the cylinder block a special "C" type removing tool is available which will exert considerable pressure on the valve guide forcing it upwards even if it is stuck badly.

When grinding in valves or refacing the valve seat in the cylinder block it is customary to use a dummy guide in place of the regular guides.

If the best possible work is desired, however, it is a good idea to put the guide which is to be used into the block in order to center the center valve seat grinder pilot.

The recommended valve clearance for these models is .013 inch. If the observed clearance is greater than .013 inch the only way to reduce it is to grind either the valve face or the valve seat or both to permit the valve to drop farther down into the cylinder and thus take up the clearance.

If the clearance noted is less than .013 inch it will be necessary to grind off the bottom of the valve stem in order to create the proper clearance.

Most valve grinding machines are equipped with devices for grinding off the bottom of the valve stem to an exact length.

Where these grinding devices are available it is a good idea to use them on each of the valve stems in order to generate the proper clearance before installing the valve and guide assembly.

Reassembly of the Valve and Guide Assembly

Assemble the valve, guide, valve spring and keeper on the bench and insert the entire assembly down into the valve port. A special bar is generally used to pull the valve guide far enough down into the port to permit the entrance of the "C" shaped keeper which prevents the guide from popping upward. After the "C" shaped keeper is inserted in place, force the valve guide up so that the keeper is locked in the recess on the underside of the block.

The flared bottom of the valve stem gives a much broader contact to the surface of the tappet than on other valves. Because of this broader contact the valves on Ford and Mercury cars will operate quietly, even if clearance in excess of .013 inch must be contended with.

Camshaft Replacement

Whenever the camshaft is to be replaced on any Ford or Mercury engine it is always advisable to remove the engine from the frame. It is possible, however, to replace the camshaft on these models without taking the engine out of the frame by removing all the valves and valve springs and blocking up the lifters so that they do not interfere with the removal of the shaft.

Take off the timing case cover as explained below and pull out the camshaft.

Timing Gear Cover Removal

Remove the fan, generator and distributor. Remove the fan pulley and take out the bolts which hold the timing case cover to the front of the engine block.

Note: On all models up to and including 1948 it is necessary to remove the oil pan if the crankshaft gear is to be removed.

Valve Timing Procedure

On all models of Ford and Mercury built from 1940 to 1948 the valve timing procedure is as follows:

The drive on these models is by means of gears and unless the gears are badly worn or damaged or are deliberately tampered with the valve timing will remain as set by the factory. If it becomes necessary to retime the valves or replace either of the gears due to wear or damage, proceed as follows:

Remove the timing case cover and take off the camshaft gear. If it is necessary to replace the crankshaft gear, remove the oil pan. Press on the new crankshaft gear being careful when starting the gear that the key and keyway are in perfect alignment since it is a tight fit on the shaft and it is very difficult to align the key-way with the key if they are not started properly.

Turn the crankshaft so that the mark on the crankshaft gear is pointing directly toward the center of the camshaft. Now mesh the camshaft gear so that the mark on the cam gear coincides with the mark on the crank gear. Rotate the camshaft so that the holes in the camshaft hub will line up with the holes in the camshaft gear. Install the bolts and the special lock plate.

Rotate the crankshaft two full revolutions as a recheck to make certain that the marks coincide on a straight line between the two shaft centers.

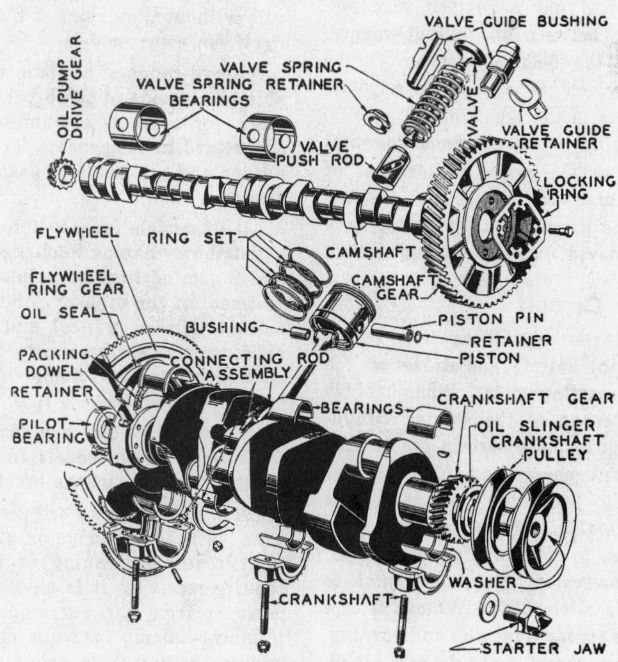

Internal engine parts all V8 models

VALVE TIMING PROCEDURE—*continued*

Valves timed in this manner will be correct regardless of which piston is at top dead center.

Note: On models up to and including 1948 retiming the ignition is not necessary since the distributor drive is directly off the end of the camshaft.

THE ELECTRICAL SYSTEM

Generator

Ford supplies a variety of generators for use on all their V8 and 6 cylinder models. Some of these were of the three brush variety and some of the two brush generators were used, having regulators control the output. Where a two brush, regulator controlled generator is used, and it is suspected of being inoperative, do not ground the field terminal of the regulator before removing it, as would be the proper procedure for other makes of cars.

The Ford generator has one end of the field grounded and the regulator inserts a resistance into the circuit between the insulated main brush and the main field lead. Therefore, to test the regulator on Ford generators it is necessary to put a jumper wire momentarily between the output connection and the field connection. If the generator now functions properly the difficulty is in the regulator.

If putting a hopper from the field terminal to the armature terminal of the generator does not increase the output of the generator then it will have to be removed from the car and tested.

Starter Circuit

The starter circuit consists essentially of the battery, the starter switch and the starting motor. When trouble is experienced in the starter circuit, first check to make certain the battery is up to full charge and that both connections to the battery are clean and tight and also that the ground strap connection is clean and tight.

If a manual type starter switch is used it is advisable to remove it and check the contacts for pits and burning. If any are present it should be cleaned, reassembled and remounted on the car.

Actually, service on the starter is almost exactly the same as service on the generator, and the bench test, given in the General Service Section for the generator, will also apply to the starter.

All electrical information such as breaker points, ignition timing, etc., generator output and starter draw are given in tables at the beginning of this Ford Section.

The Ignition System

The ignition system consists essentially of the battery, the ignition switch, the coil and distributor. The distributor is driven by a groove in the camshaft directly off the front of the shaft, so that it is impossible to get the distributor out of time.

The driving tongue of the distributor is slightly offset from center so that it is impossible to get it on incorrectly.

The Distributor

The distributor may be removed readily by taking out the attaching bolts which hold it to the timing case cover and remove the snap rings which hold both the distributor caps in place on the side of the distributor.

It is possible to replace the ignition coil without disturbing the distributor itself, on some models.

A small range of adjustment is available on the side of the breaker plate to allow for a small amount of advance and retard to compensate for local conditions and the grade of gasoline being used.

All V8 models from 1940 to 1948 used a distributor having 8 lobes on the cam and 2 sets of breaker points. The adjustment of the breaker points on these models is very critical and it should be done with extreme care, if possible on a stroboscope or some such electrical setting device.

Cam angle meters are recommended for use on these models to secure an exact adjustment at the breaker points.

All service on the Ford distributor is done with the distributor off the car. If it requires cleaning or the points require resetting it is advisable to remove it from the car since it is extremely difficult to work on the distributor while it is mounted in the front of the engine.

Fig. 1 — Distributor cover has been removed to show position of wires

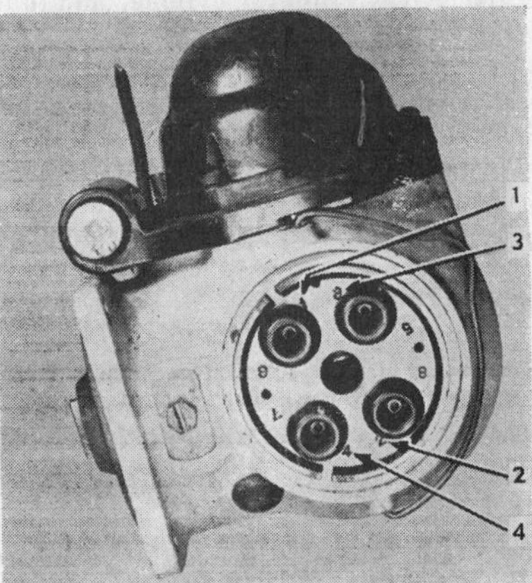

Fig. 2—Note: Nos. 1, 2, 3, 4 are upright on right bank

Fig. 3—When installing cap be sure that tang on cap lines up with notch in housing

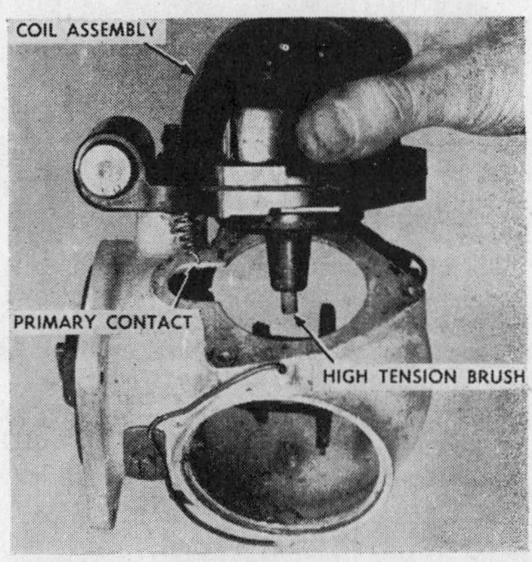

Fig. 4—Removing coil assembly

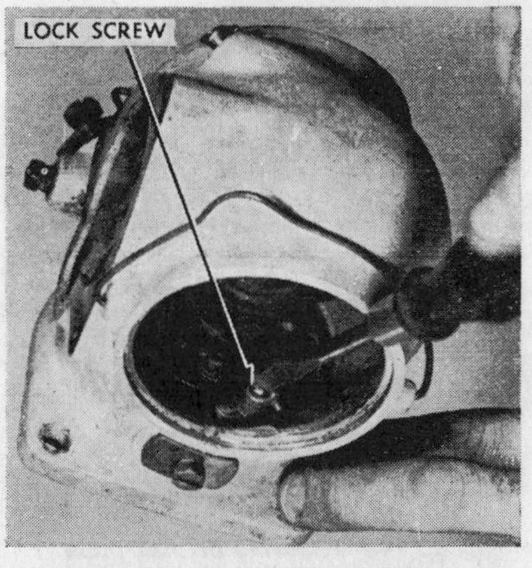

Fig. 5—Loosening point contact lock screw

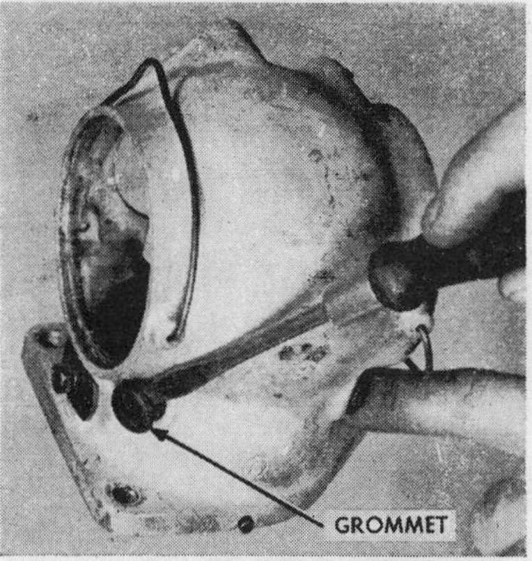

Fig. 6—Prying out point port grommet

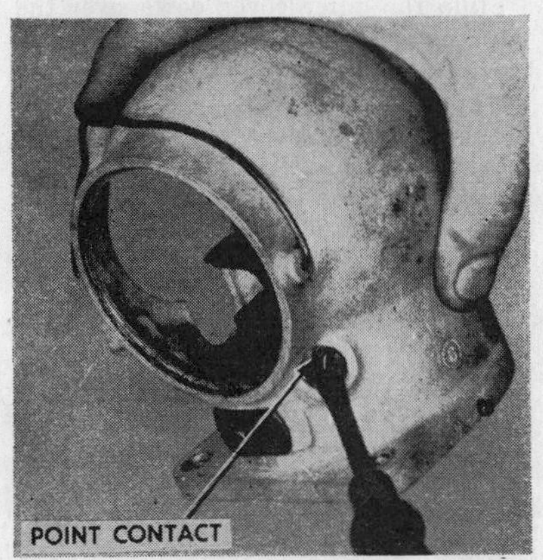

Fig. 7—Removing point contact

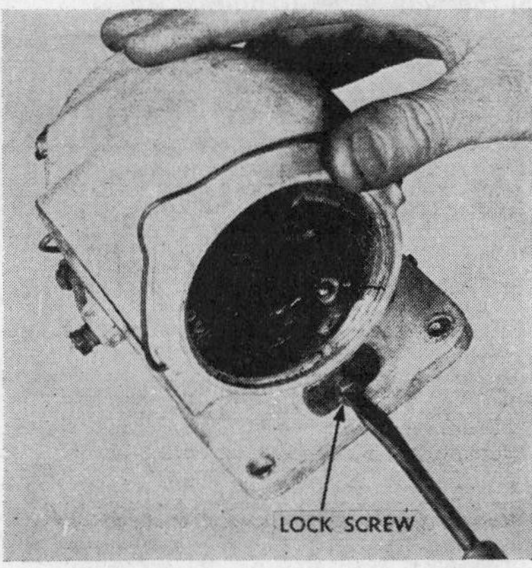

Fig. 8—Removing drive plate lock screw

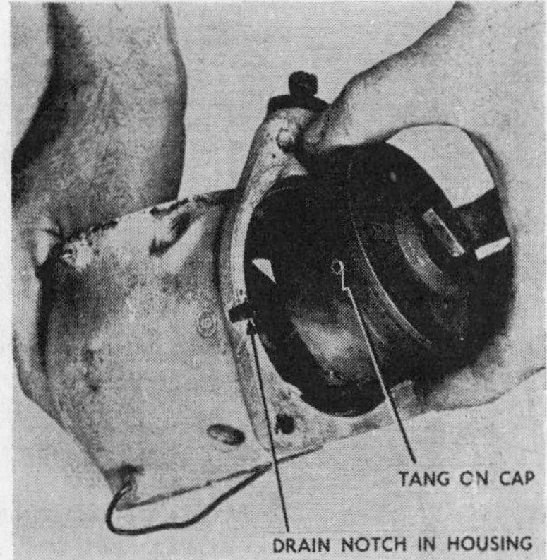

Fig. 9—Note: When assembling that drain fits in notch in housing

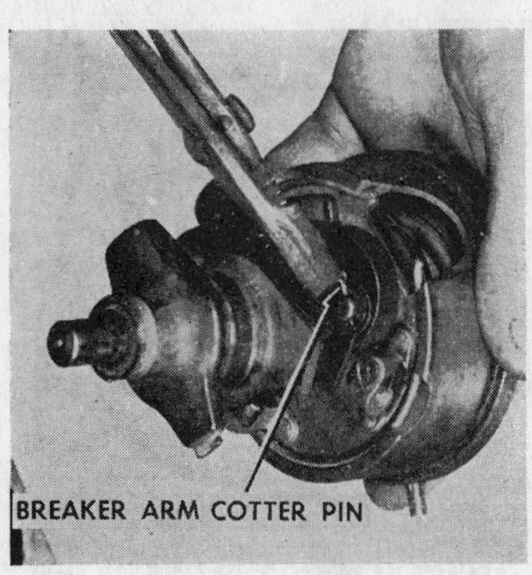

Fig. 10—Removing breaker arm cotter pin

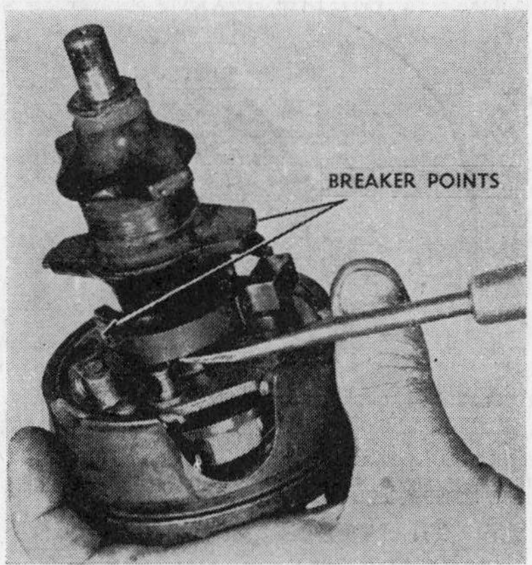

Fig. 11—Prying off breaker points

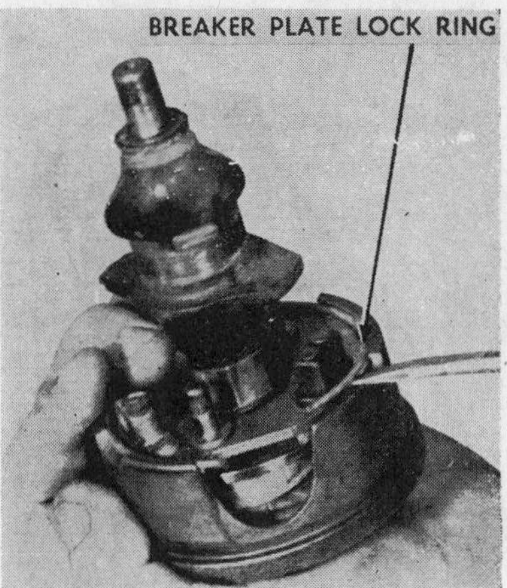

Fig. 12—Removing breaker plate lock ring

Fig. 13—Removing rotor

Spark Plug Wires

The easiest way to replace a spark plug wire or a group of spark plug wires on a Ford (or for that matter any car) is to replace one wire at a time. In this way the possibility of mixing up the wires is eliminated.

To replace one wire at a time it is customary to skin back both the new and the old wire and twist them together and, pulling on the old wire, draw the new one into the wire harness.

The disadvantage of this method is that it will be necessary to reinstall the wire terminals since the new wire was scraped back to be combined with the old one.

The easiest way to replace all the wires at once is to unbolt the wire conduit from the intake manifold and remove the wires and distributor cap as a unit from the car and replace the wires on the bench, using the following method:

Set the wire harnesses on the bench so that the two distributor caps are near each other and the wire harnesses point away from each other. The wire harness from the right cylinder bank is to be placed on the operator's left. The harness from the left cylinder bank is to be placed to the operators right. This is the position they occupy on the car.

Caution: The left bank harness contains, in addition to the spark plug wires, the ignition primary wire. It is customary when replacing the spark plug wires to install the ignition primary wire on the outside of the harness so that it becomes a simple matter to connect it up to the distributor. In order

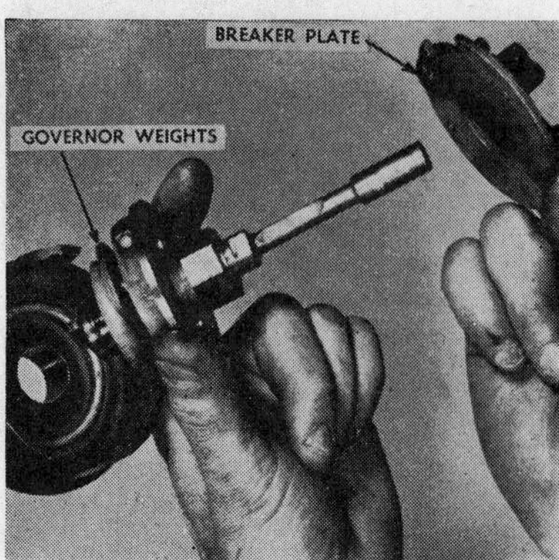

Fig. 14—Removing breaker plate

to prevent the primary wire from fraying many mechanics tape it to the wire harness in several places.

Remove the rubber grommet which holds the outer cap to the inner cap and slide the outer cap a little way off the wires so that the terminal sockets are uncovered. When working on the right bank of wires (those on the left hand on the bench) notice that the numbers cast next to the terminal sockets are arranged so that on the right bank the numbers 1, 2, 3 and 4 are right side up, the other numbers (5, 6, 7 and 8) are upside down. This is done so that the inner cap could be used on either the right or the left bank but in order to mount it on the distributor the numbers 1, 2, 3 and 4 must be upright to use it on the right bank; the numbers 5, 6, 7 and 8 must be upright to use it on the left bank.

Replace the 4th wire first. Pass the wire through the harness, through the rubber boot, through the outer cap and place it in the socket numbered 4. This is the lower left hand socket. Next install the wire from number 3 in the same manner. It goes to the socket marked 3, the upper right hand socket. In like manner do cylinders number 2 and number 1.

Notice that the grommet from the left bank (the one on your right hand) has the numbers 5, 6, 7 and 8 upright.

Start with number 8 wire, pass it entirely through the harness, through the rubber boot, through the outer cap and into socket 8, the upper left hand socket. In like manner do cylinder number 7, number 6 and number 5.

Slide the outer cover down over the wires (it will be necessary to bend the wires sharply to accomplish this) and install the rubber bushing which holds the outer cap to the inner cap.

Install the harnesses on the car and mount up to the distributor.

Standard Clutch Assembly

A long coil spring type clutch is used on all Ford and Mercury models having a standard clutch. The clutch pedal should be adjusted so that there is approximately ½ inch free play, measured at the toe board, with the clutch in the fully engaged position. This adjustment is made at the clutch throw-out rod.

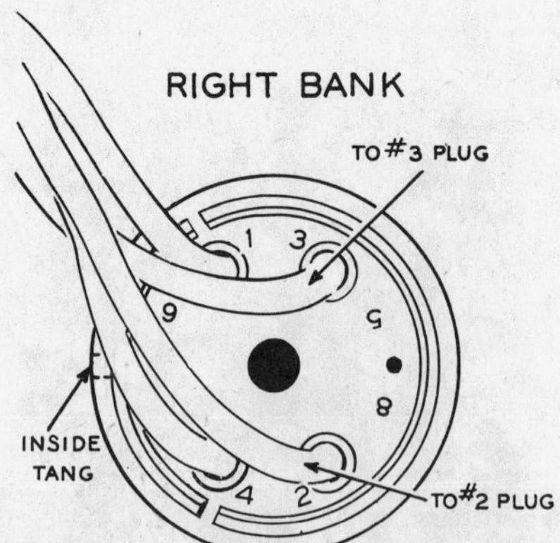

RIGHT BANK - SET OUTSIDE NOTCHES AT 7&11 O'CLOCK (INSIDE TANG AT 9 O'CLOCK) WITH 1-2-3&4 IN THE UPRIGHT POSITION.

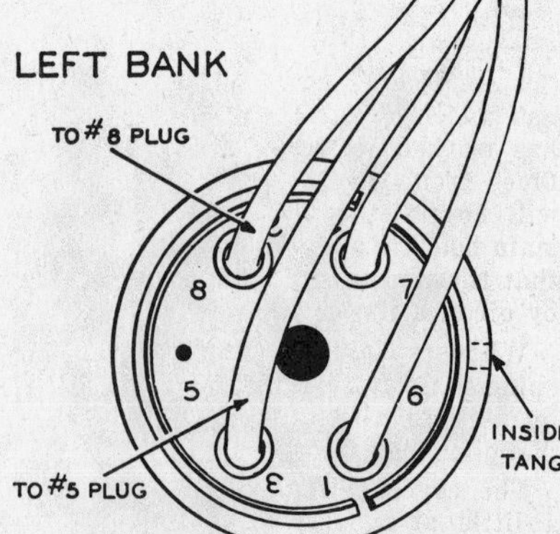

LEFT BANK - SET OUTSIDE NOTCHES AT 1 & 5 O'CLOCK (INSIDE TANG AT 3 O'CLOCK) WITH 5-6-7 & 8 IN THE UPRIGHT POSITION.

Fig. 15—Layout of spark plug wires

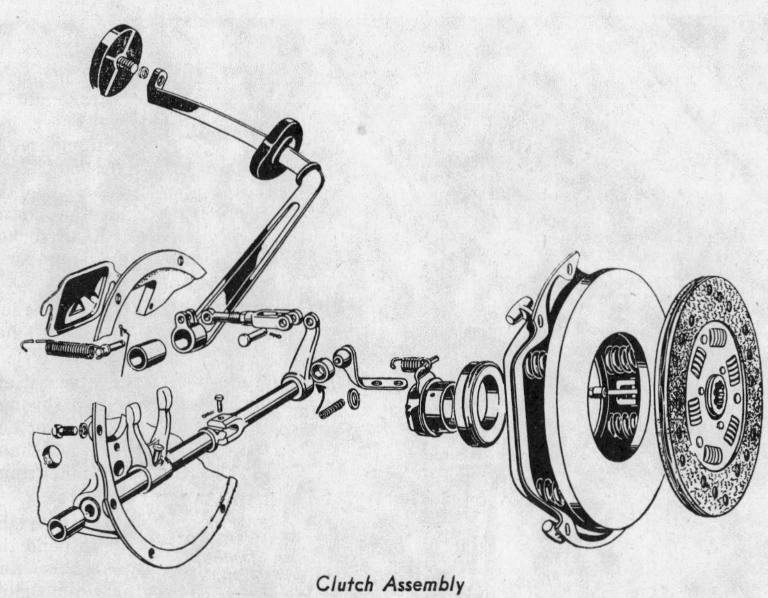
Clutch Assembly

Except for loose or rattling parts all service on the clutch, other than pedal clearance, requires that the clutch be removed from the car.

Removal of Clutch Assembly

To remove the clutch assembly on all Ford and Mercury models it is necessary to remove the transmission by detaching it at the bell housing and supporting the engine with a jack. After the transmission is removed the clutch can be unbolted and removed from the fly wheel. Back the bolts out a few turns at a time to prevent springing the cover assembly.

With the clutch removed, examine it carefully to see whether or not oil from the rear main bearing or transmission has gotten on to the clutch faces. If oil has worked its way on to the clutch faces from the rear main bearings, it will be necessary to replace the rear main bearing oil seal in order to insure that the new clutch will not be ruined by oil in a like manner.

When replacing the clutch a dummy spine shaft or a special pilot tool should be used to align the clutch disc with the pilot bearing.

The cover bolt should be drawn up a little at a time to insure that the cover will not be bent or twisted in any way.

Clutch Overhaul

Overhauling a clutch requires special tools and equipment, instructions for which are supplied by the various manufacturers, no service instructions will be carried here for this purpose.

Clutch Pedal Clearance

The clearance of the clutch pedal to the toe board should be approximately 1½ in. before the throwout bearing engages the clutch fingers. This is adjusted at the yoke which connects the clutch pedal to the clutch cross shaft.

Lengthening the yoke will shorten the clutch pedal clearance.

The procedure is to remove the cotter pin and take out the clevis, turn the yoke until the proper clearance is obtained and replace the pin and clevis, and then tighten the yoke jam nut.

STANDARD TRANSMISSION ASSEMBLY

All Ford and Mercury cars are equipped with a three forward speed standard transmission.

Removal of Standard Transmission from Car

To remove the transmission it is necessary to remove the rear axle assembly by disconnecting it at the universal joint.

The front seat track should be unbolted from the floor and the front seat pushed back as far as it will go. Disconnect all the shift mechanism rods at the transmission and support the rear of the engine on a jack. Disconnect the transmission at the rear motor support and at the bell housing.

Raise the back of the engine high enough so that the transmission rear support is clear of its bolts. Pull the back of the transmission up and into the car.

It is generally conceded that it is possible to take the transmission out with the front seat in its extreme rear position. However, this is considered to be risky business since it is unlikely that the transmission will be clean enough to permit it to brush against the front seat.

Transmission is installed in the reverse of the removal procedure.

Disassembly of Transmission

Drain out the gear lubricant and place the shifter arm in the neutral position. Remove the nine bolts from the shifter housing and lift off the gear shift housing and cover assembly. Remove the locking wires and cap screws from the rear engine mount and ball retainer. Remove the four cap screws holding the main shaft bearing retainer and clutch release bearing.

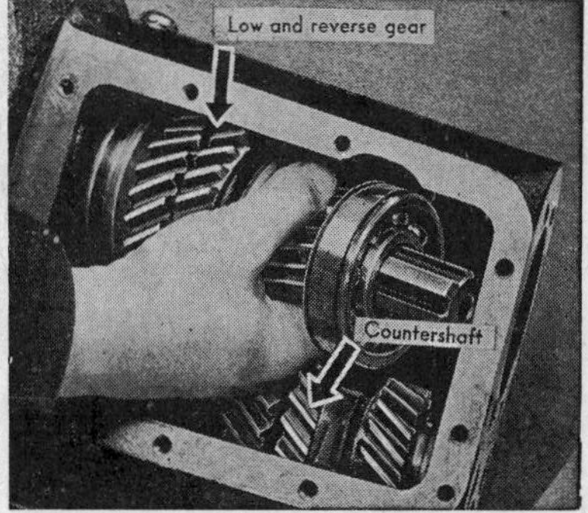

Lifting out mainshaft assembly

Unhook the retracting spring and throw-out bearing assembly and remove the throw-out assembly.

Pull out the reverse idler and counter shaft locking pin.

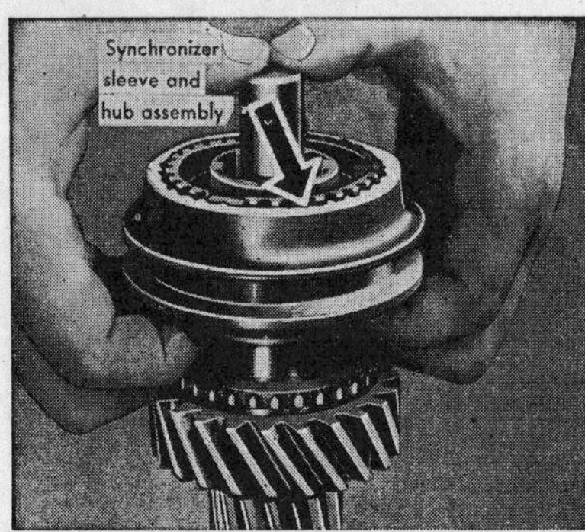

Removing synchronizer unit

Install transmission with pilot studs

DISASSEMBLY OF TRANSMISSION —Continued

Drive the counter shaft arm from the front end so that the counter shaft gears will drop into the bottom of the case to provide clearance needed when removing the main driving gear.

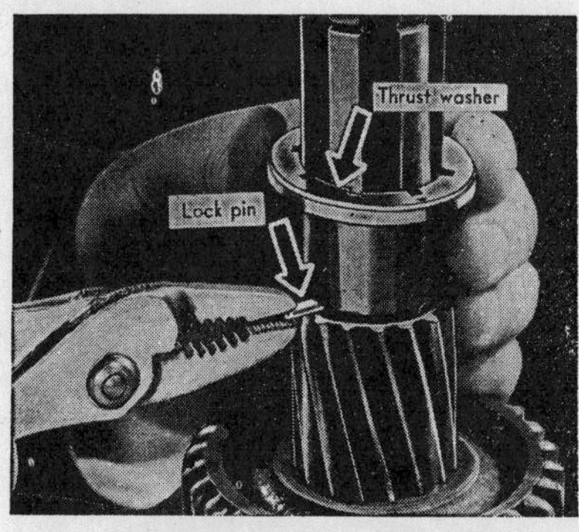

Withdrawing lock pin

With the synchronizer in neutral position use a soft brass punch and drive the main shaft and bearing back about ¼ inch so that the snap ring will clear the case.

Take off the snap ring and drive the main shaft back into its original position.

Shift the synchronizer sleeve into second gear and drive the main shaft and main drive gear forward until the main drive gear and bearing can be pulled out from the front of the case.

With the main shaft assembly forward in the case have the low and reverse gear as far forward as possible.

Drive the rear bearing (still mounted on the main shaft) into the case and lift the main shaft and gear assembly up out of the case rear end first.

With a brass punch drive the reverse idler shaft forward toward the front of the case and lift out the reverse idler gear.

Remove the counter shaft assembly being careful not to drop the bearings and the rear thrust washer.

To dis-assemble the transmission main shaft and gear assembly remove the shaft snap ring and pilot bearing spacer.

Remove the synchronizer sleeve and hub assembly and then remove the thrust washer, the synchronizer ring and the intermediate gear.

Take off the main shaft intermediate gear thrust washer and remove the lock pin.

Slide off the low and reverse sliding gear and, using an arbor press, press off the main shaft bearing.

To disassemble a synchronizer hold a finger over each bar to prevent the balls from jumping out and then push up the clutch from the outer sleeve.

Remove the main drive gear snap ring at the shaft and press off the ball bearing assembly and remove the oil baffle.

The transmission is now completely disassembled, it should be cleaned and all parts inspected.

Transmission Reassembly

Fit the clutch hub and sleeve in a position that will permit the smoothest sliding motion.

Install the main shaft bearing spacer ring on the main shaft, using a new oil baffle with the flange toward the front of the shaft and the bearing with the lock ring groove toward the rear.

Press the shaft and assembly into place.

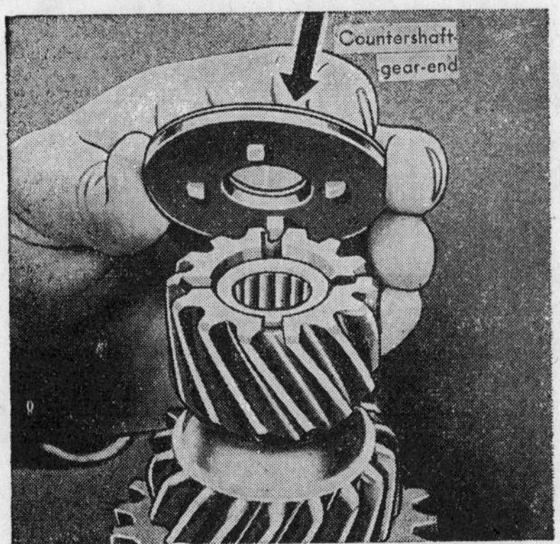

Install thrust washer

Install low and reverse sliding gear on the main shaft with the shifter fork groove to the rear.

Install the thrust washer lock pin and the steel thrust washer.

Install the intermediate gear, bronze spacer washer and synchronizer ring.

Press on the synchronizer assembly being sure the shifter grooves of the sleeve are toward the roller bearing end of the shaft.

The slots in the second gear synchronizer ring should line up with the insert bars.

Install the main shaft snap ring.

Check end play between the intermediate gear and the steel thrust washer with a feeler gage. Clearance should be between .004 to .008 inch. If greater than this amount use an oversize spacer washer to obtain the desired clearance.

To install the counter shaft gear thrust washer first place some hard grease on the steel back of the bronze thrust washer, entering the tongue of the washer into the groove provided in the transmission case.

Install both roller bearings in the counter shaft gear with a spacer between and the large roller bearing to the small end of the counter shaft gear.

Place the counter shaft gear end thrust washer in position in the grooves on the end of the gear. Be certain the oil grooves in the face of the end of the plate are clean. Set the counter gear and bearing assembly in place allowing the assembly to rest on the bottom.

Install the reverse idler gear and reverse idler gear shaft making sure that the rounded edge of the gear is toward the inside of the case.

Shift the synchronizer into second gear position and install the main shaft assembly into the case by starting the front end of the main shaft in first and then lower the rear end in and move it toward the rear of the case.

With the low and reverse sliding gear in the forward position start the main shaft and bearing into the bore of the case and install the main shaft snap ring.

After the counter shaft and idler shaft are locked in place insert the locking pin.

Replace the main drive gear collar.

Assemble the clutch throw-out bearing, with a feeler gage, check the clearance of the bearing retainer to the clutch housing.

Reinstall the rear bearing cover and the transmission shift cover assembly.

To assemble the main drive gear, install the oil baffle with the flange toward the gear, press on the bearing and install the snap ring.

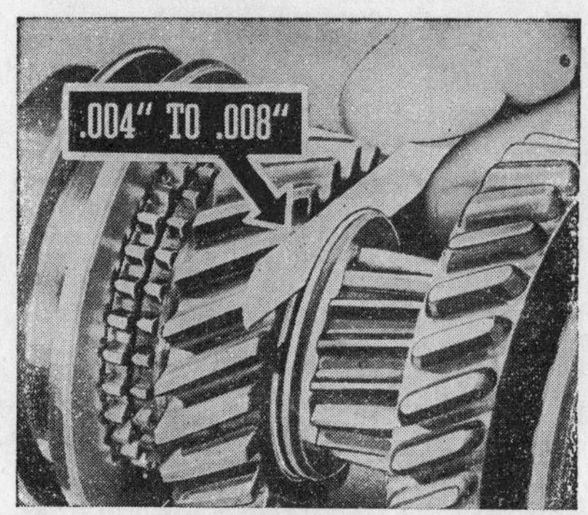

Measure clearance

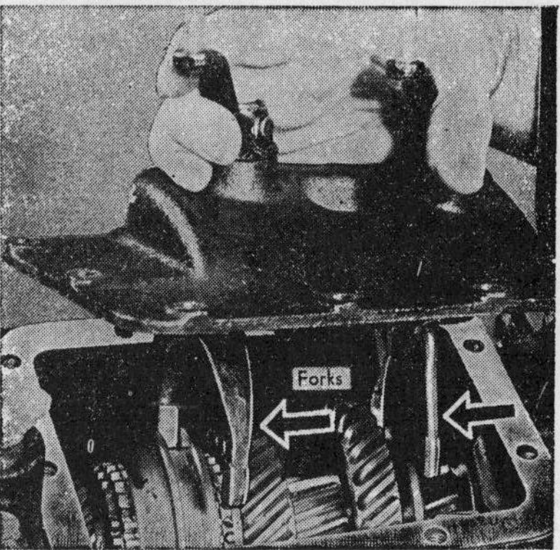

Install cover
Note position of shifter forks

Oil the main shaft pilot bearing roller, set it into place and place the synchronizer ring on the end of the main drive gear assembly.

Engage the gears in position and raise up the counter set cluster from the bottom of the case and drive in the counter shaft.

REAR AXLE ASSEMBLY

On all Ford and Mercury from models from 1940 to 1948 the rear axle was of the torque tube variety and was equipped with a radius rod and a transverse rear spring.

Removal of Rear Axle Assembly

The rear axle assembly could be removed from these models by diconnecting the brake hoses, hand brake cables and shock absorbers. The rear axle assembly is then disconnected at the front universal joint ball and at the rear spring either where it connects to the frame or at both of the shackles.

Where work on the rear axle does not require disassembly it is easier to disconnect the rear axle assembly at the rear spring U bolts. However, if it is necessary to disassemble the housing or any part of the rear axle, then it is

FORD and MERCURY 1940 thru 1948

REMOVAL OF REAR AXLE ASSEMBLY —*continued*

perhaps better to disconnect the assembly at each of the spring shackles and leave the spring mounted on the car. It is necessary to jack up the back of the body very high in order to slide out the rear axle assembly.

Replacement of Rear Axle Oil Seals

The rear axle oil seal assembly on all Ford cars is contained in the rear wheel hub.

To replace the oil seal remove the rear wheel and brake drum and hub assembly and take out the oil seal, using an inertia puller.

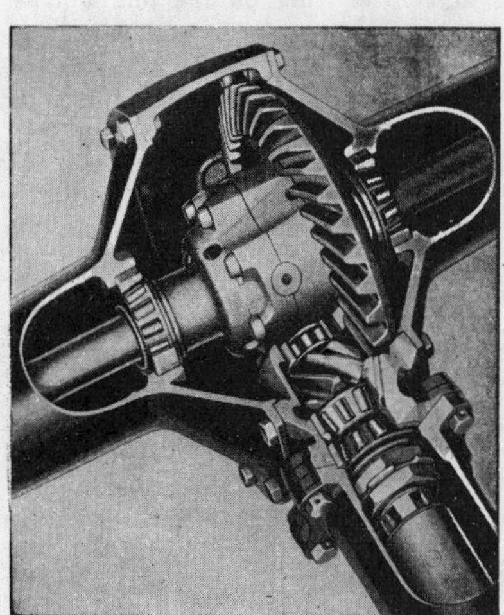

Cutaway of rear axle
Note position of outboard bearing

Axle Shaft Replacement

To replace the axle shaft on these models it is necessary to disassemble the entire differential. Remove the wheels, hubs and drums from both sides of the housing and disconnect the spring shackle at the left side. Remove bolts from left side housing and slide the housing off the end of the axle shaft then slide the differential with both axle shafts out of the right side housing.

To remove the axle shaft it is necessary to take off the ring gear bolts and separate the housing. Both axle shafts are then removed at the same time.

When reassembling the differential make absolutely certain that there are no burrs on either side of the housing assembly so that it will mate properly.

When the assembly is mated up check the end play in the axle shafts. If the end play exceeds .010 inch it indicates an excessive amount of wear inside the differential or in the axle side gears.

If the end play in the axle shafts is acceptable then the back lash of the gears should be checked. This back lash should not exceed .010 inch as measured at the key way in one of the axle shafts while the other axle shaft is held in a vice and the differential held stationary.

The assembled differential with its axle shafts should be placed in the right hand housing and the left hand housing slid up over the left axle shaft, after a gasket has been put on the differential carrier housing.

After the housing has been bolted up securely, replace the hubs, brake drums and wheels.

Overhaul of Differential Assembly

The overhaul procedure on the differential is practically the same as the requirements for replacing an axle shaft, except that since new parts are being installed it will be necessary to check the fit of the differential side bearing, as well as the pinion bearings. The pinion bearings are installed and tightened securely. When the differential with its axle shafts are mounted in the right hand housing and the left hand housing is brought up to "make up the full housing" it will be necessary to check the drag of the differential side bearings. This is accomplished by having one man turn one wheel and another man turn the other wheel in the same direction and notice if a reasonably heavy drag is felt. If drag is not felt it will be necessary to take down the housings and use a thinner gasket

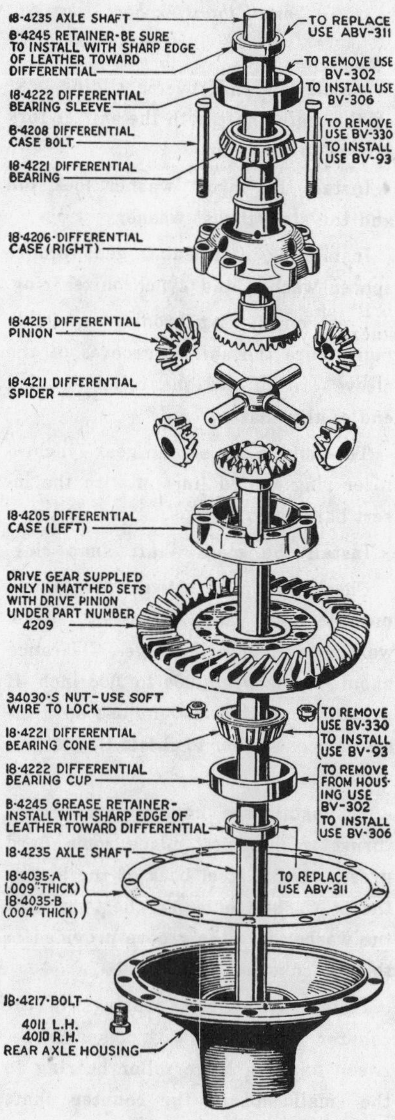

Differential parts exploded

in order to put a slight pre-load on the differential side bearings.

After the differential side bearings have been properly pre-loaded check the the back lash between the drive pinion and the ring gear, at the spline end of the drive pinion with an indicator to show the movement obtainable. The lash should never be greater than .008 inch or less than .003 inch. If end play is too great and the differential bearings are properly adjusted it will be necessary to place a thicker gasket on the right housing and a thinner gasket on the left housing to cause the differential to move into closer mesh with the ring gear.

No other method is provided in the Ford and Mercury rear axle, other than the gasket thickness, to take up the end play and for bearing adjustment.

To take out the drive pinion bearing cups it is usually necessary to heat the differential housing at the neck with a blow torch or by immersing it for 1 to 2 minutes in boiling water. A light film of gear lubricant will assist in the installation. A bearing with the letter "P" stamped on it should be installed next to the pinion gear.

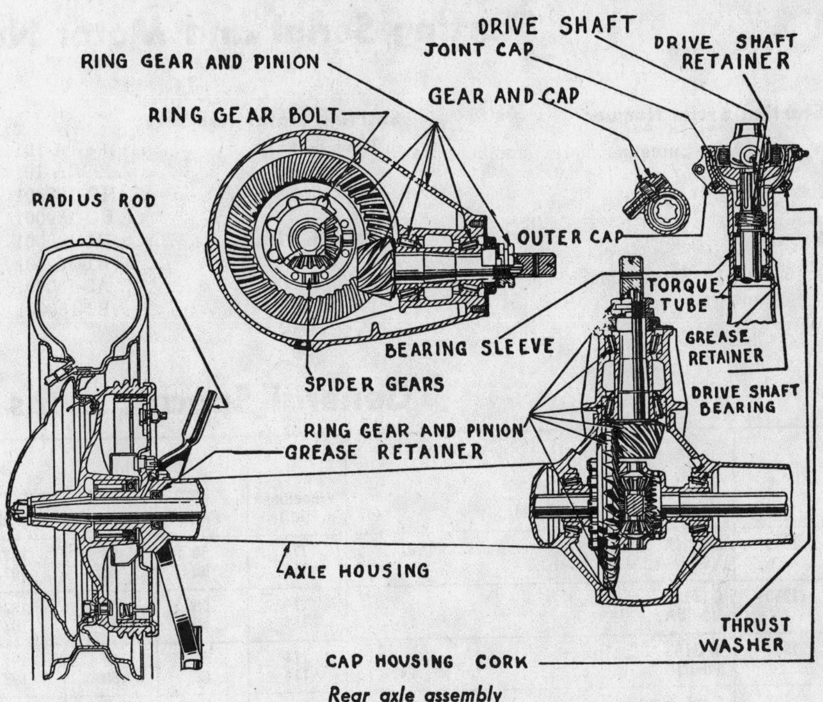

Rear axle assembly

PROPELLER SHAFT REPLACEMENT

To replace the propeller shaft on all Ford and Mercury models from 1940 to 1948 first remove the rear axle assembly from underneath the car and take out the bolts that secure the torque tube to the rear axle and remove the torque tube.

Drive out the pin that secures the propeller shaft to the pinion gear shaft and remove the propeller shaft.

When replacing the propeller shaft install a new shaft pin and rivet both ends over securely in the shaft.

FORD SPECIFICATIONS 1949 thru 1953

Starting Serial and Motor Numbers

Starting Serial Number

1949-1953—Same as motor numbers.

Location

1949-1953—Same place as motor numbers.

Starting Motor Numbers

1949, 6 cyl. 98HA-101
8 cyl. 98BA-101
1950, 6 cyl. HO-100001
8 cyl. BO-100001
1951, 6 cyl. H1-100001
8 cyl. B1-100001
1952, 6 cyl. A2-100001
8 cyl. B2-100001
1953, 6 cyl. A3-100001
8 cyl. B3-100001

Location

1949-1953—Right frame rail opposite motor and on dash panel

General Specifications

Year	Model	Wheelbase (in.)	Tread (in.) Front	Tread (in.) Rear	Overall Dimensions (in.) Length†	Overall Dimensions (in.) Width	Overall Dimensions (in.) Height■	Shipping Weight* (lb.)	Tire Size (in.)
1949	6-98HA	114	56	56	197	72	65	2990	6.00-16
	V8-98BA	114	56	56	197	72	65	3030	6.00-16
1950	6-0HA	114	56	56	197	73	65	2990	6.00-16
	V8-0BA	114	56	56	197	73	65	3030	6.00-16
1951	6-1HA	114	56	56	197	73	65	3040	6.00-16
	V8-1BA	114	56	56	197	73	65	3080	6.00-16
1952	6 cyl. 8 cyl.	115	58	56	197	73	62	....	6.00-16
1953	6 cyl., 8 cyl.	115	58	56	197	73	62	....	6.70-15

*—Cheapest 5 pass. 4 door sedan. ■—Road to roof, no load. †—Including bumper and bumper guards.

General Engine Specifications

Year	Model	Number of Cylinders Bore and Stroke	Piston Displacement, Cubic Inches	Compression Ratio (To–1)	Taxable (A.M.A.) Hp.	Developed Horse Power Bare Engine	Developed Horse Power With Accessories	Maximum Torque Ft. Lbs.
1949	98HA, 6 Cyl.	6–3.30 x 4.40	225.8	6.80	26.1	95 @ 3300	....	180 @ 1200
	98BA, 8 Cyl.	8–3$\frac{7}{16}$ x 3¾	239.4	6.80	32.5	100 @ 3600	....	181 @ 2000
1950–51	6 Cyl.	6–3.3 x 4.4	225.9	6.80	26.1	95 @ 3300	....	180 @ 1200
	8 Cyl.	8–3$\frac{3}{16}$ x 3¾	239.4	6.80	32.5	100 @ 3600	....	181 @ 2000
1952	A2, 6 Cyl.	6–3.56 x 3.60	215.3	7.00	30.40	101 @ 3500	....	185 @ 1500
	B2, 8 Cyl.	V8–3$\frac{3}{16}$ x 3¾	239.4	7.20	32.50	110 @ 3800	....	196 @ 2000
1953	6 Cyl.	6–3.56 x 3.60	215.3	7.0	30.4	101 @ 3500	....	185 @ 1500
	8 Cyl.	V8–3$\frac{3}{16}$ x 3¾	239.4	7.2	32.5	110 @ 3800	....	196 @ 2000

Tension Wrench Specifications

Year	Model	Cylinder Head Lbs.–Ft.	Cylinder Head Thread	Spark Plug Lbs.–Ft.	Spark Plug Thread	Connecting Rod Bolts or Nuts Lbs.–Ft.	Connecting Rod Bolts or Nuts Thread	Main Bearing Bolt Lbs.–Ft.	Main Bearing Bolt Thread	Flywheel Bolts Lbs.–Ft.	Flywheel Bolts Thread	Vibration Damper Bolts Lbs.–Ft.	Vibration Damper Bolts Thread
1949 to 53	All	65–70	....	24–30	14 mm	45–50	....	80–90	....	65–70	....	....	....

Dimensions of Valves

Year	Model	Overall Length		Head Diameter		Seat Angle (deg.)		Stem Diameter		Key Type	O.D. of Seat Insert	
		Inlet	Exhaust	Inlet	Exhaust	Inlet	Exhaust	Inlet	Exhaust		Inlet	Exhaust
1949	98HA, 6 cyl.	5.427	5.427	1.652	1.515	45	45	.341	.341	split lock	....	1.6335
	98BA, V8	4.819	4.819	1.515	1.515	45	45	.341	.341	split lock	1.6335	1.6335
1950	OHA, 6 cyl.	5.360	5.428	1.647	1.520	45	45	.341	.341	split lock	....	1.6335
	OBA, V8	4.819	4.816	1.515	1.515	45	45	.341	.341	split lock	....	1.6335
1951	1HA, 6 cyl.	5.360	5.360	1.647	1.510	45	45	.341	.341	split lock	....	1.6335
	1BA, V8	4.819	4.816	1.510	1.510	45	45	.341	.341	split lock	....	1.6335
1952	A2, 6 cyl.	5.02	5.02	1.647	1.51	45	45	.3415	.341	....	....	....
	B2, 8 cyl.	4.7555	4.7515	1.51	1.51	45	45	.3415	.341	....	....	....
1953	6 cyl.	5.0275	5.02	1.652	1.515	45	45	3.415	3.415	....	....	....
	8 cyl.	4.7545	4.7505	1.515	1.515	45	45	.341	.341	....	....	....

Distributor

Year	Model	Distributor Model Number	Cam Angle (deg.)	Direction of Rotation C=Clockwise CC=Counter Clockwise at Cam End	Breaker Arm Spring Tension	Breaker Point Gap (inches)	Engine R.P.M. when Cent. Advance Starts	Max. Cent. Advance in Engine Deg. at Stated Engine R.P.M.	Vacuum in (inches) of Mercury at which Vacuum Unit Starts	Max. Advance in Engine Deg. at Stated Vacuum	Vacuum Unit Number
1949–50	6 cyl.	7HA-12127	36	C	17–20	.024–.026	400	23@4000	....	....	....
	V8	7RA-12127C	27	C	17–20	.014–.016	400	17@4000	....	....	....
	....	0BA-12127	27	C	17–20	.014–.016	400	22½@4000	....	....	....
1951	6 cyl.	7HA-12127	36	C	17–20	.024–.026	400	23@4000	....	....	....
	V8	0BA-12127	27	C	17–20	.014–.016	400	22½@4000	....	....	....
1952	A2, 6 cyl.	FAA-12127A	35–38	C	17–20	.024–.026	....	....	.32	16@7.15	....
	B2, 8 Cyl.	8BA-12127	26–28½	C	17–20	.014–.016	....	....	.30	12½@5	....
1953	6 cyl.	FAA-12127A	35–38	C	17–20	.024–.026	....	....	1.25@.32	16@7.15	....
	8 cyl.	8BA-12127	26–28	C	17–20	.014–.016	....	....	5@30	12½@5	....

Crankshaft Bearing Journal Sizes

Year	Model	Connecting Rod Journals		Main Bearing Journals				
		Diameter	Length	No. 1 Diameter	No. 2 Diameter	No. 3 Diameter	No. 4 Diameter	No. 5 Diameter
1949	98HA	2.2984	1.401	2.8732–2.8736	2.8732–2.8736	2.8732–2.8736	2.8732–2.8736	....
1950–51	6 cyl.	2.2980–2.2988	1.400	2.8732–2.8740	2.8732–2.8740	2.8732–2.8740	2.8732–2.8740	....
	8 cyl.	2.138–2.139	1.755	2.498–2.499	2.498–2.499	2.498–2.499	....	....
1952	A2, 6 cyl.	2.2984	....	2.4984	2.4984	2.4984	2.4984	....
	B2, 8 cyl.	2.1385	....	2.4985	2.4985	2.4985	....	....
1953	6 cyl.	2.2984	....	2.4984–1.070	2.4984–1.070	2.4984–1.063	2.4984–1.295	....
	8 cyl.	2.1385	....	2.4985–1.473	2.4984–1.473	2.4984–1.959	....	....

FORD SPECIFICATIONS 1949 thru 1953

Engine Overhaul Specifications

Year	Model	PISTONS				RING GAP CLEARANCES (Maximum)				PISTON PIN		ROD BEARINGS		
		Removed From	Piston Skirt Clearances (Maximum)											
			Top	Bottom	Limit	Top Ring	Second Ring	Third Ring	Oil Ring	Type	Fit	Oil Clearance	Wear Limit	Side Play
1949	98HA, 6 Cyl.	A	.003	.0020	.005	.017	.017	.017	.017	FL	Push	.0004–.0027	.004	.003–.007
	98BA, 8 Cyl.	A	.004	.0023	.005	.017	.017	.017	.017	FL	Push	.0005–.0030	.004	.006–.020
1950	OHA, 6 Cyl.	A	.0037	.0022	.005	.017	.017	.019	.019	FL	Push	.0004–.0027	.004	.003–.007
	OBA, 8 Cyl.	A	.0023	.0011	.005	.017	.017	.017	.017	FL	Push	.0005–.003	.004	.006–.020
1951	1HA, 6 Cyl.	A	.0022	.0012	.005	.017	.017	.019	.019	FL	Push	.0004–.0027	.004	.002–.004
	1BA, 8 Cyl.	A	.0023	.0011	.005	.017	.017	.017	.017	FL	Push	.0005–.0031	.004	.006–.020
1952	A2, 6 Cyl.	A	.0022	.0012	.005	.017	.017	......	.017	FL	.0003	.0005–.0021	.006	.003–.009
	B2, 8 Cyl.	A	.0023	.0011	.005	.017	.017	.017	.017	FL	.0003	.0005–.0030	.006	.006–.020
1953	6 Cyl.	A	.0022	.0012	.005	.017	.017	......	.017	......	.0003	.0005–.0021	.006	.003–.009
	8 Cyl.	A	.0023	.0011	.005	.017	.017	......	.017	FL	.0003	.0005–.0021	.006	.006–.020

A—Piston and rod removed from above. FL—Floating. †—Center crank gear mark between cam gear marks. TC—Top center

Pistons and Piston Pins

Year	Model	PISTONS				PISTON PINS		
		Diameter	Material	Type	No. of Rings	Length	Diameter	How Held
1949–50	98HA	3.30	Alum.	Dw, Fh	4	2.912	.8502	F
	V8	3.1875	Alum.	Dw, Fh	4	2.847	.7503	F
1951	1HA, 6 cyl.	3.3	Alum.	......	4	2.905	.8502	F
	1BA, V8	3.1875	Alum.	......	4	2.835	.7502	F
1952	A2, 6 cyl.	3.56	Alum. Alloy	Ss,C,Fh	3	3.025	.91215	F
	B2, 8 cyl.	3.19	Alum. Alloy	Ss,C,Sh	4	2.835	.75025	F
1953	6 cyl.	3.56	Alum. Alloy	Ss,C,Fh	3	3.025	.9123	F
	8 cyl.	3.19	Alum. Alloy	Ss,C,Sh	3	2.835	.75025	......

Ss—Split skirt. C—Cam ground. Dw—Double wing. Sh—Spherical head. Fh—Flat head. Alum—Aluminum. F—Floating.

Engine Tune-Up Specifications

Year	Model	SPARK PLUGS		DISTRIBUTOR					OPERATING TAPPET CLEARANCE			
		Type	Gap	Point Gap	Cam Dwell, (Deg.)	Ignition Timing, (Deg.)	Ignition Timing Mark and Location	Com-pression Pressure at R.P.M.	Inlet	Exhaust	Carburetor Fuel Float Height	Minimum Engine Idle Speed at R.P.M.
949	98HA, 6 Cyl.	Ch-H10	.032	.025	38	TC	Dmpr.	110@ *	.011	.015	1 7/32″	450
	98BA, 8 Cyl.	Ch-H10	.032	.016	30	2B	Cr. Pul.	110@ *	.011	.015	1 3/8″	425
1950	OHA, 6 Cyl.	Ch-H10	.032	.025	38	TC	Dmpr.	110@ *	.011	.015	1 7/32″	450
	OBA, 8 Cyl.	Ch-H10	.032	.016	28½	2B	Cr. Pul.	110@ *	.015	.019	1 3/8″	425
1951	1HA, 6 Cyl.	Ch-H10	.032	.025	35–38	TC	Dmpr.	110@ *	.015	.019	......	450
	1BA, 8 Cyl.	Ch-H10	.032	.016	26–28½	2B	Cr. Pul.	110@ *	.015	.019	......	425
1952–53	6 Cyl.	Ch-H10	.037	.025	38	TC	Dmpr.	......	.015H	.015H	......	485
	8 Cyl.	Ch-H10	.032	.015	28½	2B	Cr. Pul.	......	.014C	.018C	......	485

TC—Top center. H—Hot. C—Cold B—Before top center. Cr. Pul.—Crankshaft pulley. Ch—Champion Spark Plug Co. *—At cranking speed. Dmpr.—Vibration damper.

and Wear Limit Table

CRANKSHAFT		VALVES										OPERATING OIL PRESSURE			
Main Bearing Oil Clear-ance	Shaft End Play	Spring Tension (Maximum)			Guide Clear-ance	Seat Angle		Valve Tim-ing, Inlet Valve Opens (Deg.)	Cam-shaft Drive	Gear Marks		Pounds At M.P.H.	Low Limit■	Model	Year
		Inlet	Exhaust	Low Limit		Inlet	Ex-haust								
.0022	.004-.008	53@2.11	53@2.11	40	.0015-.0035	45°	45°	11B	Gear	†		55@50*	30	............98HA, 6 Cyl.	1949
.0013	.002-.004	43@1.89	43@1.89	30	.0015-.0035	45°	45°	TC	Gear	†		57@40*	30	............98BA, 8 Cyl.	
....	....	53@2.11	53@2.11	40	.0019-.0039	45°	45°	11B	Gear	†		45@40*	25	............OHA, 6 Cyl.	1950
.0013	.002-.006	43@1.89	43@1.89	30	.0015-.0035	45°	45°	5B	Gear	†		40@40*	25	............OBA, 8 Cyl.	
.0005-.003	.004-.008	53@2.11	53@2.11	40	.0015-.0035	45°	45°	11B	Gear	†		45@40*	25	............1HA, 6 Cyl.	1951
.0005-.003	.002-.006	43@1.89	43@1.89	30	.0015-.0035	45°	45°	5B	Gear	†		40@40*	25	............1BA, 8 Cyl.	
.0005-.0021	.004-.008	140@1.505	140@1.505	......	.0015-.0025	45°	45°	18B	Chain	......		50@40*	40	............A2, 6 Cyl.	1952
.0005-.0025	.002-.006	86@1.60	86@1.60	......	.0015-.0035	45°	45°	5B	Gear	......		40@40*	......	............B2, 8 Cyl.	
.0005-.0021	.004-.008	140@1.505	140@1.505	......	.003	45°	45°	13	Chain	......		50@40	......	............6 Cyl.	1953
.0005-.0025	.002-.006	86@1.60	86@1.60	......	.0035	45°	45°	5	Gear	......		40@40	......	............8 Cyl.	

B—Before top center. *—M.p.h.
§—Car may be operated safely at lower oil pressures but low pressure indicates malfunction which should be corrected.

Cooling System

CAR AND YEAR	MODEL	Capacity Qts.	Quarts of Methanol Base Anti-Freeze (For Protection to Temperature Shown Below)							Quarts of Ethylene Glycol (For Protection to Temperature Shown Below)							Quarts of Denatured Alcohol—188 Proof (For Protection to Temperature Shown Below)						
			3	4	5	6	7	8	9	3	4	5	6	7	8	9	3	4	5	6	7	8	9
1949-53............	OHA, IHA.........	15	13	3	−8	−21	−36	−53	...	17	10	2	−8	−19	−34	−52	...	10	0	−10	....	−20	−30
1949-53............	OBA, IBA.........	22	19	12	−5	−3	−12	−22	−34	....	17	12	6	0	−9	−17	20	....	10	....	0	−10	....

Piston Ring Dimensions

Year	Model	Cylinder Bore	TOP RING			SECOND RING			THIRD RING			OIL RING		
			Width	Gap	Depth	Width	Gap	Depth	Width	Gap	Depth	Width	Gap	Depth
1949	98HA, 6 cylinder...........	3-30	.0932	.013	.150	.0932	.013	.150	.1862	.013	.150	.1862	.013	.150
	98BA, 8 cylinder...........	$3\frac{3}{16}$	.0917	.012	.147	.0917	.012	.147	.1547	.011	.147	.1547	.011	.147
1950	0HA, 6 cylinder...........	3-3	.0932	.013	.145	.0932	.013	.145	.1860	.014	.145	.1860	.014	.145
	0BA, 8 cylinder...........	$3\frac{3}{16}$	.0932	.012	.147	.0932	.012	.147	.1860	.017	.147	.1860	.017	.147
1951	1HA, 6 cylinder...........	3-3	.0932	.014	.165	.0932	.014	.150	.1860	.015	.150	.1860	.015	.150
	1BA, 8 cylinder...........	$3\frac{3}{16}$	.0932	.012	.159	.0932	.012	.147	.1862	.012	.147	.1862	.012	.147
1952	A2, 6 Cyl................	3.56	.09325	.012	.2014	.09325	.012	.2014	.18625	.012	.2014	....	....	....
	B2, 8 Cyl................	3.19	.09235	.012	.1818	.09325	.012	.1818	.18625	.012	.1993	.18625	.012	.1862
1953	6 Cyl....................	3.56	.09325	.012	.178	.09325	.012	.178	.18625	.012	.160	....	....	....
	8 Cyl....................	3.19	.09325	.012	.147	.09325	.012	.147	.18625	.012	.147	....	....	....

FORD SPECIFICATIONS 1949 thru 1953

Brake Data

Year	Model	Make	Lining Type	R=Riveted B=Bonded	Drum Diameter	Lining Length	Lining Width	Lining Thickness	Clearance Toe	Clearance Heel
1949	98HA, 6		M	R	10	21.8	2¼–*2	3⁄16	.010	.010
	98B, V8		M	R	10	21.8	2¼	3⁄16	.010	.010
1950	OHA, DBA		M	R	10	22	2¼–*1¾	.187	.010	.010
1951	IHA, IBA		M	R	10	21 41⁄64	2¼–*1¾	3⁄16	.010	.010
1952–53	6 Cyl., 8 Cyl.		M	R	10	21 45⁄64	2¼–1¾	3⁄16†	.010	.010

*—Rear. †—Front secondary 1 5⁄64 M—Moulded.

Generators

Year	Model	Generator Number	Field Current at 6 Volts (amps.)	Maximum Safe Output Volts	Maximum Safe Output Amperes	Maximum Safe Output R.P.M.	Brush Spring Tensions (oz.)	Voltage Regulator Number
1949 to 51	V8	8BA-10002-A	2–1	7.1	30	1670	20–24	8M-10505-A
		8BA-10002-B	2–1	7.1	30	1670	20–24	5EH-10505-C
		8BA-10002-D	2–1	7.1	30	1670	20–24	5EH-10505-C
1952	A2, 6 cyl.	FAA-10000-A	....	....	....	....	....	FAC-10505-A
	B2, 8 cyl.	FAA-10000-F	....	....	....	....	....	FAC-10505-A
1953	6 cyl.	FAA-10000-A	....	7.8	38	1700	....	FAC-10505-A1
	8 cyl.	FAA-10000-F	....	7.8	38	1700	....	FAC-10505-A1

Voltage Regulators

Year	Model	Regulator Number	Grounded P=Positive N=Negative	Voltage Control Air Gap Points Closed	Voltage Control Voltage Setting Hot	Current Control Air Gap Points Closed	Current Control Current Set Hot	Cut-Out Relay Point Gap	Cut-Out Relay Air Gap	Cut-Out Relay Closing Volt
1949 to 51	All	51A-10505-A	....	.035	7.2	.035	30–34	.018	.025	6.1–6.3
		51A-10505-A-1	....	.035	7.2	.035	30–34	.018	.025	6.1–6.3
		5EH-10505-C	....	.035	7.1	.035	30–34	.018	.025	6.1–6.3
		8BA-10505-A	....	.035	7.6	.035	34–38	.018	.025	6.0–6.6
		8L-10505	....	.035	7.4	.035	38–42	.010	.014	6.0–6.4
		8M-10505-A	....	.035	7.6	.035	34–38	.018	.025	6.0–6.6
1952	A2, 6 cyl., B2, 8 cyl.	FAC-10505-A	....	....	7.4–7.8	....	34–38	....	....	6.0–6.6
1953	6 cyl., 8 cyl.	FAA-10000-A	....	....	7.4–7.8	....	34–38	....	....	6.0–6.6

King Pin Specification Chart

Year	Model	King Bolt Diameter	King Bolt Length	Upper Bushing Bolt Number	Upper Bushing King Bolt Bushing Inside Diameter	Upper Bushing King Bolt Bushing Outside Diameter	Upper Bushing King Bolt Bushing Length	Upper Bushing Bushing Number	Lower Bushing King Bolt Bushing Inside Diameter	Lower Bushing King Bolt Bushing Outside Diameter	Lower Bushing King Bolt Bushing Length	Lower Bushing Bushing Number
1942 to 51	All, 6 & 8 cyl.	.812	5 63⁄64	8A-3115	.805	.943	1 5⁄16	8A-3110-B	.805	.943	1 5⁄16	8A-3110-B
1952-53	All	....	....	....	....	....	....	....	....	....	....	....

1949 thru 1953 SPECIFICATIONS FORD

Starters

Year	Model	Unit Model Number	Spring Tension (oz.)	STARTER Lock Test Volts	Lock Test Amperes	Lock Test Torque, (lbs. ft.)	No Load Volts	No Load Amperes	No Load R.P.M.	Direction of Rotation Viewed from Drive End C=Clockwise CC=Counter-clockwise
1949 to 50	V8	7RA-11002	27	3.75	550	15	5.8	50	6500	CC
1951	6 cyl.—H series	1HA-11002-A	48–56	3.75	550	15	5.8	52.5	6000	CC
	V8	1BA-11002-A	48–56	3.75	550	15	5.8	52.5	6000	CC
	6 & 8 with Fordomatic	1CM-11002-A	48–56	3.75	550	15	5.8	52.5	6000	CC
1952	A2, 6 cyl.	FAG-11001B	....	3.5	700	16	6	70	6000	C
	B2, 8 cyl.	FAF-11001A	....	3.5	700	16	6	70	6000	C
1953	6 cyl.	FAG-11001B	....	3.5	700	16	6	70	3200	C
	8 cyl.	FAF-11001A	....	3.5	700	16	6	70	3200	C

Fan, Generator Belts and Radiator Hose

Year	Model	Fan Belt Angle of "V" (deg.)	Fan Belt Length O.C.	Fan Belt Width Max.	Generator Belt Angle of "V" (deg.)	Generator Belt Length O.C.	Generator Belt Width Max.	Upper Hose Type	Upper Hose Inside Diam.	Upper Hose Length	Lower Hose Type	Lower Hose Inside Diam.	Lower Hose Length
1949	V8	42	37 7/32	13/16	32	55½	43/64	curved	1¼	....	straight	1¾	5¾
1949 to 51	6 cyl.	40	41⅝	13/32	......	......	......	curved	1½	....	curved	1¾	....
1950–51	V8	40	42 9/16	⅜	40	51⅞	⅜	curved	1¼	....	straight	1¾	6
1952	A2, 6 cyl.	38	37 1/64	⅜	......	......	......	curved	1½	15¼	curved	1½	5 13/16
	B2, 8 cyl.	38	41 49/64	⅜	38	51 39/64	⅜	curved	1¼	8¾	curved	1¾	16½
1953	6 cyl.	38	37.02	⅜	38	......	......	curved	1½	15¼	curved	1½	8¾
	8 cyl.	38	41.76	⅜	38	51.6	⅜	curved	1¼	8¾	curved	1¾	16½

Front Wheel Alignment

Year	Model	Caster (deg.)	Camber (deg.)	King Pin Inclination (deg.)	Toe-In (inches)	Turning Radius Inner	Turning Radius Outer
1949	98HA, 98BA	¾N to ¼P	¼N to ¾P	5½	1/16 to ⅛	20½	20
1950	0HA, 0BA	½P to 1N	0 to 1P	5½	1/16 to ⅛	20½	20
1951–52	1HA, 6 cyl.	1N to ½P	0 to 1P	5¼	1/16 to ⅛	20½	20
	1BA, 8 cyl.	1N to ½P	0 to 1P	5½	1/16 to ⅛	20½	20
1953	6 cyl.	1N to ½P	0 to 1P	5¼	1/16 to ⅛	17¼	20
	8 cyl.	1N to ½P	0 to 1P	5½	1/16 to ⅛	17¼	20

N—Negative. P—Positive.

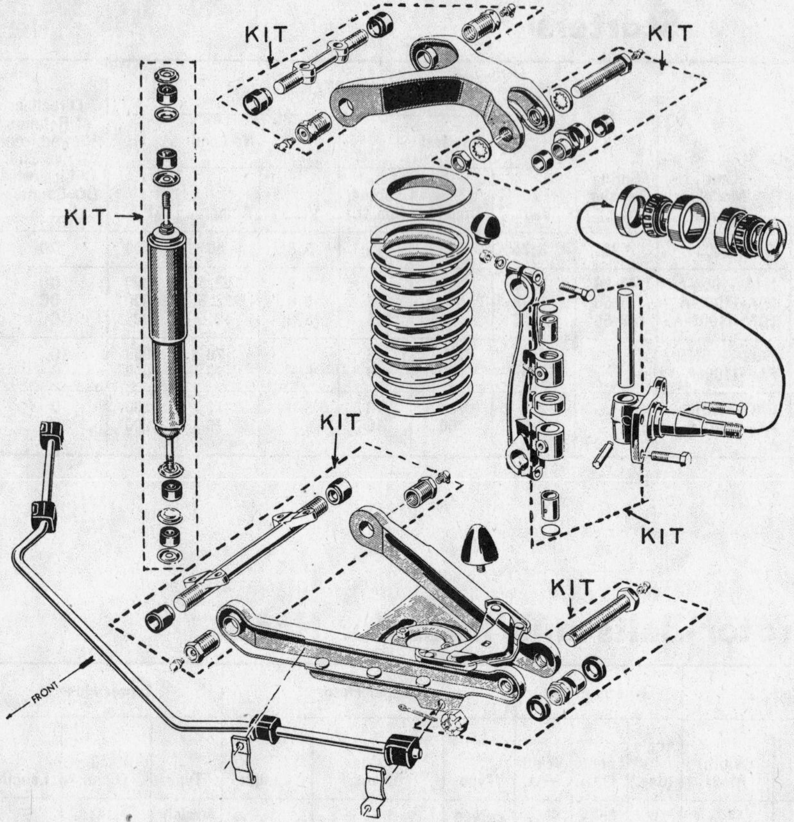

Front suspension parts

FRONT SUSPENSION

Starting with 1949 production models all Fords, both 6's and 8's, were equipped with an independently sprung front end which consisted of upper and lower suspension arms controlled by telescopic direct acting shock absorbers located in the center of the coil springs. Replacable bushings are used at all junction points in both the upper and lower suspension arms.

Caster, Camber, Toe-In

Camber is adjusted at the eccentric bushing in the outer end of the upper support arm. To adjust, loosen the clamp bolt in the upper end of the knuckle support and, using a wrench on the hex head of the eccentric bushing, turn the bushing until the desired camber is obtained then tighten the lock bolt to 25-32 ft-lb torque.

Caster Adjustment

To adjust caster, loosen the lock bolt at the bottom of the spindle support, then place a wrench on the hex head of the bushing, turn the bushing until the desired caster is obtained and then tighten the lock bolt to 25-32 ft-lb torque.

The bushing is equipped with a right-hand thread, therefore turning the bushing to the right will decrease the caster angle, turning it to the left will increase the caster angle.

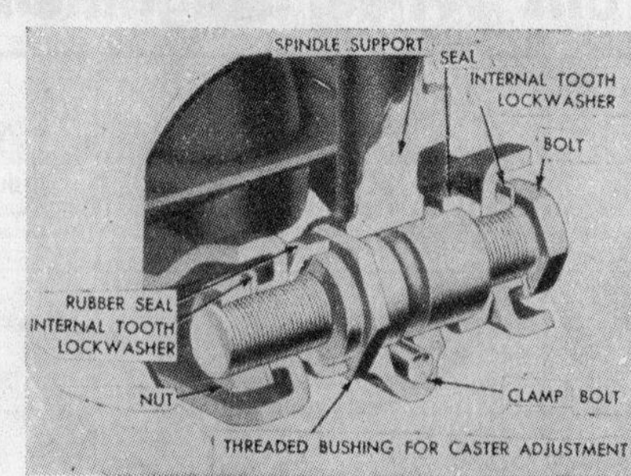

Lower bushing caster adjustment

Toe-In

Toe-in is adjusted at the adjusting sleeve at the end of both tie rods.

REPLACEMENT OF FRONT SUSPENSION PARTS

Knuckle Support Pins and Bushings

Carry the weight of the car on the lower suspension arm at about the spring seat.

Remove the wheel and drum assembly and the brake backing plate.

Caution: It is a good idea to hang the brake backing plate on a wire to the frame to prevent damage to the flexible brake lines.

The upper suspension arm pin can be screwed out toward the rear of the car after the lock nut and washer have been taken off from the front. The lower suspension arm pin is removed in exactly the same way.

To remove the bushings in the upper and lower end of the knuckle supports simply loosen the clamp bolts and push the bushings out of place.

Oil seals are used on both ends of the eccentric bushing to prevent dirt and foreign matter from getting into the front suspension mechanism.

To replace either of the bushings simply remove the bolt and rock the knuckle support out of the suspension arm and push the bushing out of the suspension arm after the clamp bolt has been taken out entirely.

Upper eccentric bushing camber adjustment

Installing a new one is the exact reverse of this process since the bushing is pushed into the knuckle support, the clamp bolt replaced and tightened up finger tight, and then the bolt is fed first through the arm, then through the oil seal, then into the bushing, through the opposite side oil seal, and into the opposite side arm.

The long pin is secured by an internal tube type lock washer.

Replacement of Front Coil Spring

Before replacing a front coil spring check to make certain that no pin or bushing requires replacement, since if a pin or bushing requires replacement it is best to detach the front suspension at the defective pin so that both the pin and the spring can be replaced in one operation.

If nothing else is to be replaced but the spring, support the weight of the car at the frame, disconnect the shock absorber and remove the stabilizer clips. Place a jack under the lower arm inner shaft and exert enough pressure on the jack to keep the shaft tight against the frame and then remove the four bolts which hold the shaft to the front cross member and let the jack down until the spring is fully extended and lift it out of the spring seat.

Set the new oil spring into place, using any shims that were found under or over the old coil spring. When placing the new spring in the lower arm be sure that the bottom coil of the spring is in proper contact with the arm since it is a spiral.

Lower Suspension Arm and/or Inner Shaft

To replace the lower suspension arm inner shaft and/or bushings the procedure is practically the same as that for the front coil spring. The "A" frame inner shaft is lowered to the floor, the bushings removed and the shaft taken out. If it is necessary to remove the lower "A" frame, then simply continue by detaching the lower "A" frame at the knuckle support and remove from the car.

Front Suspension Upper Arm

Pick up the weight of the car at the lower spring seat, take off the front wheel and wire the knuckle support to the frame to prevent it from slipping down when the upper suspension arm is unbolted.

Remove the cap screws which attach the upper arm inner shaft to the frame and remove the knuckle support upper bolt out of the arm and lift the upper arm off the car.

The inner bushings in the upper arm can then be removed if it is necessary to replace only the inner shaft.

Upper Support Arm Inner Shaft

When it is necessary to replace only the inner shaft and/or bushings of the upper suspension arm, carry the weight of the car at the lower spring seat and detach the upper suspension arm inner shaft from the frame, remove both bushings, front and back, and take out the inner shaft.

If the inner shaft only is to be replaced it is not necessary to take off the outer pin and bushings.

Replacement of King Pins

Remove the wheel and drum assembly and the brake backing plate which should be hung on a wire to the frame to prevent damage to the flexible brake line (it is not necessary to detach the flexible brake line).

The king pin lock pin is driven out toward the front of the car.

Remove the upper welsh plug and drive the king pin down and out of the car.

All Ford king pins are equipped with bushings top and bottom in the knuckle support and the thrust bearing is set in at the top of the spindle forging.

King pin bushings require reaming with a special aligning reamer in order to insure a good fit on the new king pin.

A king pin repair kit consists of two king pins, four bushings, two thrust bearings, four welsh plugs and two lock pins.

Since the king pin bushings are fitted in the knuckle support (rather than in the spindle) it is considered quicker and easier to leave the knuckle support mounted on the car and ream the bushings with a portable reamer in place on the car.

Replacement of Front Shock Absorbers

First detach the shock absorber at the top of the frame by removing the nut and rubber bushing from the upper stud (this can be reached through the engine compartment). Then remove the plate from the lower suspension arm and let the shock absorber come down through the bottom.

Repair service on shock absorbers is a highly specialized job, requiring highly specialized equipment and unless this equipment is available it is advisable to replace the shocks with either rebuilt or new ones, when they are defective.

A fast check can be made on the condition of a shock absorber by simply bouncing the car up and down by hand. If after you stop bouncing the car immediately assumes a normal position then the shock absorbers may be assumed to be in good condition. If, however, the car continues to bounce or settles in an abnormal position then the shock absorbers should be removed.

STEERING GEAR ASSEMBLY

Adjustment of Steering Mechanism

Before making any adjustment to the steering mechanism make certain of the alignment of the steering post in the car. This is accomplished by loosening the cap screws that fasten the steering gear housing to the frame side member and loosening the cap screws that hold the steering column jacket clamp at the bottom of the instrument panel. This will relieve any alignment strain. Tighten the mounting bolts at the frame first and then the clamp bolts at the instrument panel.

To make a complete adjustment of the steering apparatus proceed as follows:

1. Disconnect the pitman arm from the center tie rod.

2. Adjust the steering gear housing assembly.

(a) Check the worm shaft for end play and if any exists remove the four bolts from the top of the steering gear box and remove one shim at a time, being careful not to bind the bearings on the worm shaft.

(b) Set the steering wheel in the mid-position of its travel and check the pitman arm for play. If any play exists loosen the four housing bolts and rotate the housing until there is zero lash with the steering wheel in the mid-position of its travel and then tighten the housing bolts.

STEERING MECHANISM—*continued*

(c) Adjust the cross shaft by loosening the adjusting screw lock nut and turning the adjusting screw down just sufficient to remove all end play without causing any noticeable binding.

3. Reconnect the pitman arm.

4. With the steering wheel set in the mid-position of its travel, adjust the tie rod sleeves so that one half of the total toe-in is contained in the right wheel. Tighten the clamp bolts.

5. Adjust the sleeve on the left tie rod so that the balance of the toe-in is contained in the left wheel. Retighten the clamp bolts.

Turn the steering wheel through its entire travel to check for binding or looseness in any of the steering gear parts.

Worm bearing adjustment pre-load should be between ½ and 1¼ lbs, measured at the rim of the steering wheel. Too high reading indicates that shims should be added; too low reading indicates that shims should be removed.

The high spot pre-load when adjusting the mesh of the worm and roller should add approximately ½ lb to the pull required to turn the steering wheel. This should be over and above the pull required to indicate the pre-load of the worm bearings.

HORN BUTTON REMOVAL

On 1949 and 1950 models the horn button is depressed and twisted either to the right or left and lifted off.

1951 Thru 1953 Models

The horn button is held by screws from the underside of the wheel spoke.

STEERING WHEEL REMOVAL

The steering wheel is removed, using a puller designed for the purpose, after the horn button and the steering wheel nut have been taken off.

If the car is equipped with direction signals it will be necessary to set the direction signals in the Neutral position.

Removal of Steering Gear Assembly from the Car

Disconnect the pitman arm and the steering wheel. Then disconnect the steering column from the instrument panel. Disconnect the lower shift levers from the rod adjusting nuts. Remove the cap screws from the bracket that secures the gear shift tube to the steering column tube and remove the bracket which will permit removal of the gear shift tube pin and the gear shift levers.

Take out the steering column clamp and pull the jacket tube off the gear shaft.

Then the steering gear may be taken out through the bottom, from underneath the car.

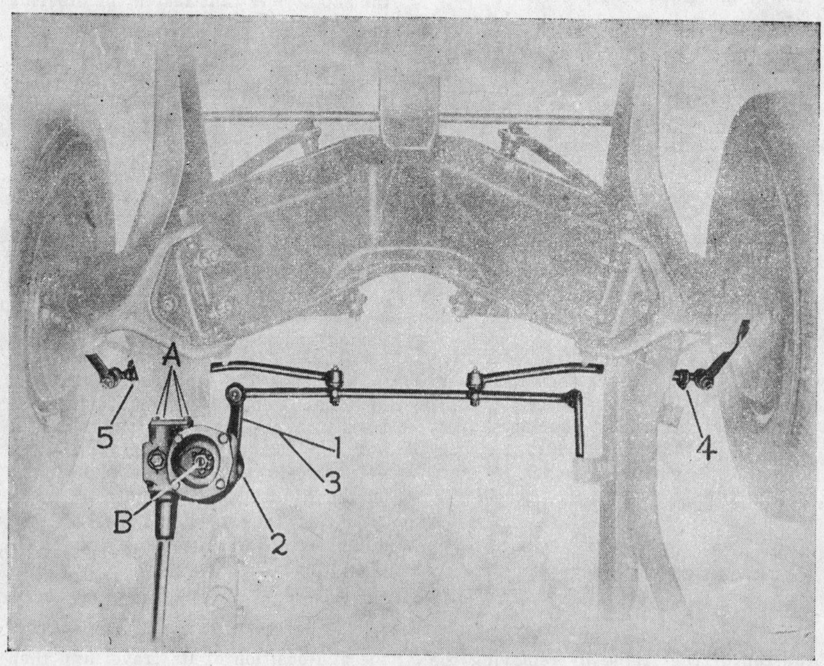

Steering mechanism

BRAKES

The brake shoes on all Ford cars from 1949 to 1953 are of the Bendix hydraulic type.

Minor Brake Adjustment

The minor brake adjustment is made to compensate for normal lining wear and is not intended to correct any brake difficulties. However, before making a minor adjustment on the brakes it is a good idea to remove at least one of the road wheels to determine the condition of the hydraulic cylinders, shoes, brake linings and drums.

Examine carefully around the wheel cylinder boots of the wheel to determine if there is any leaking or seepage at the brake cylinder. If any is found it is a good idea to remove all four of the wheels to see whether or not they are all in the same condition.

Ford wheel cylinders may be honed either on a regular honing machine or in place on the car, if the condition of the cylinder is not too bad.

Cups, pistons and boots may be installed in any of the wheel cylinders while they are in place on the car.

After it has been determined that the system is in good working order proceed with the minor adjustment.

Remove the cover from the adjusting hole in the backing plate (opposite the brake anchor pin) and turn the adjusting star wheel until the brakes just drag and then back the wheels off until they are just free.

Turning the handle of the tool toward the axle will expand the brake shoes if the star wheel is properly assembled to the brake shoes.

Major Brake Adjustment

Loosen the anchor pin nut and tap the anchor pin upward until a .010 inch feeler gauge is just gripped between the lining and drum about 1½ inch from the end of the secondary shoe. (The secondary shoe is the one which moves toward the anchor pin by forward rotation of the wheel.)

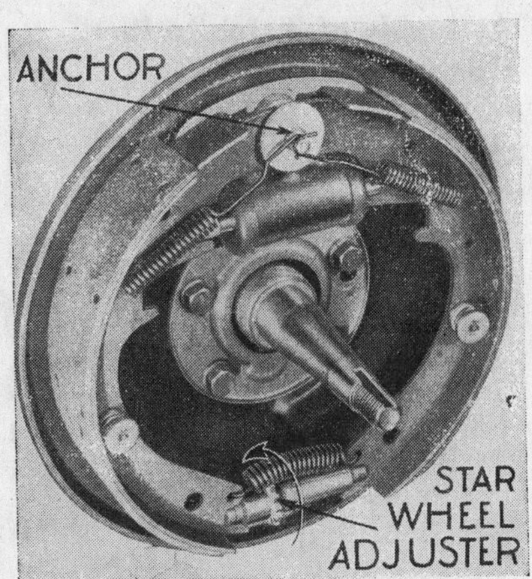

Adjusting points

When a clearance of .010 inch has been established between the brake lining and the drum, approximately 1½ inch from the end of the lining, securely tighten the anchor lock nut.

Now adjust the star wheel at the bottom of the brake drum until the wheels drag and then back off until they are just free. All slack should be taken out of the parking brake cable at the equalizer lever in order to provide a proper adjustment of the hand brake.

Brake Pedal Adjustment

Establish approximately ½ inch free pedal travel, measured at the toe board by turning the eccentric bolt, which attached the brake pedal assembly to the master cylinder push rod assembly. Rotate this eccentric bolt until the play is between ¼ and ½ inch.

Hand Brake Lever and Cable

On all Fords built since 1949 the hand brake lever is the T-handle type having a spring type ratchet.

To replace the cable it is necessary to detach the clip which holds the lower end of the cable housing to the transmission and disconnect the end of the cable from the equalizer lever.

Remove the screws which hold the ratchet housing under the dash panel and pull the brake cable and housing assembly up into the car.

This is generally a two man job since the housing tends to tie itself in knots when it's pulled up from the engine compartment.

Have a helper guide the cable through the fire wall.

Adjustment of the Hand Brake Only

To adjust the hand brake only, first, expand the shoes at the rear wheels by turning the start wheel adjusters until they are very tight against the drum, and then, take out all the slack in the cables by pulling the U-shaped double cable as hard as possible with the hands and running the nut up until it just meets the little cable housing.

Go back to the back wheels and slack off on the star wheels until both wheels are just free.

Test hand brake on road.

Caution: Do not take up sufficiently on the hand brake to cause the shoes to come off the anchor pins. The object of expanding the shoes is to prevent the shoes from coming off their anchors while the slack is being pulled out of the cables.

COOLING SYSTEM

Thermostats

The thermostats are located inside the water outlet elbow on the cylinder heads. On 8 cylinder cars one thermostat is used in each cylinder head and on the 6 cylinder cars one thermostat is used at the forward end of the cylinder head.

Thermostat should be inserted into the water outlet with the bellows portion down.

On V8's replace thermostats in pairs.

Removal of Water Pump

The water pump used on the overhead valve 6-cylinder engine is essentially the same as that on the earlier 6 cylinder engines and is removed in approximately the same way.

To remove the water pump take off the fan belt, fan and pulley. Disconnect the hoses and remove the four cap screws which hold the water pump assembly to the block and lift off the pump.

Caution: When removing the water pump from the V8 models it is necessary to place a support under the engine, on the early types, since the water pump is used as an engine support. One of the bolts which hold the water pump to the block is located inside of the water inlet and can be reached only after the hose has been removed.

Disassembly of Water Pumps

6 CYLINDER PUMP

On 1952 and 1953 Overhead Valve 6-cylinder engines the snap ring mentioned below is located at the front of the pump and not in an excess hole in the housing. Otherwise the procedure for servicing the pump is the same as given in the next paragraph.

Remove the bearing retainer which is located in the access hole in the housing and press the hub off the shaft. Then press the impeller and shaft and bearing assembly out of the housing.

Kits are available for servicing the 6 cylinder water pump.

EARLY V8 PUMPS

Note: Since this text refers to 1949 to 1951 models only, by early type pumps is meant the pumps which were used on the early 1949 models which may be identified by the vertical mounting slot in the pump casting which acts as a motor leg.

Remove the pulley from the shaft using a suitable puller, remove the bearing retainer located in the access hole in the housing and push the impeller off the shaft by pressing the shaft and bearing out through the front end of the housing.

Since these pumps are equipped with a bushing it will be necessary to press the bushing, slinger and seal out through the impeller end of the housing.

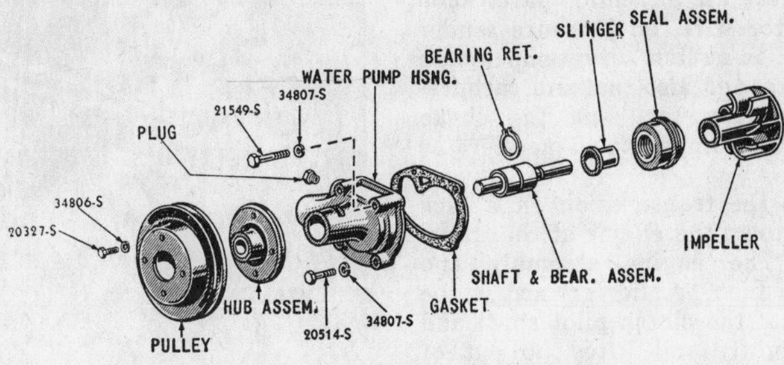

Water pump, 6 cylinder models

LATE V8 PUMPS

Remove the pulley from the shaft, take out the bearing lock ring which is located at the pulley end of the housing. Press the impeller off the shaft by pressing the shaft and bearing assembly out through the bottom of the housing. Press the seal out of the housing and if necessary remove the snap ring located inside the housing.

Pump repair kits are available for servicing either of the two types of pumps used on the V8 models.

Radiator Core Removel

On all models the radiator can be removed by disconnecting the upper and lower radiator hoses and taking out the center air deflector side screws and then taking out the cap screws that secure each side of the radiator to the front fender apron support. The core can then be lifted straight up and off the vehicle.

Replacement Engines

Both new and factory approved rebuilt engines are available for all of these models.

Ordinarily, a factory approved rebuilt engine does not include the manifolds, oil pan or flywheel. Short blocks are also available which include the block assembly less the timing case cover and flywheel.

ENGINE ASSEMBLY

Two engines are supplied for these models. A In-Line 6 cylinder engine up to 1951, and a V type 8 cylinder engine. Both are of the L head variety.

Starting with 1952 production an overhead valve 6-cylinder engine is used.

Removal of Engine

Either the 6 cylinder or the 8 cylinder engine can be taken from the chasis after removing the hood, radiator core and battery.

Disconnect all attaching parts such as generator wire, oil pressure sender wire, ignition switch wire, temperature sender wire, and also fuel and carburetor connections including the choke wire, throttle linkage and accelerator rods.

Support the transmission on a jack and disconnect the engine at the transmission. The engine assembly and clutch can then be slid forward in the frame off of the clutch pilot shaft and rocked slightly and lifted up out of the car.

ENGINE INTERNAL

Piston and Rod Assemblies

On all Ford models the piston and rod assemblies are removed from the engine through the top of the block after the cylinder ring ridge has been removed.

Caution: Do not attempt to remove the piston and rod assembly without first cutting away the cylinder ring ridge at the top of the bore, since it is possible to damage the piston if the rings lock on the ridge.

All connecting rods are supplied with individual slip-in type connecting rod bearings.

Assembly of Piston to the Connecting Rod

Note: On V8 production models for 1949 and 1950 the piston was a split skirt aluminum type having four rings. The Ford Motor Co. recommends that if it is necessary to replace the piston the later type piston as used in the 1951 engine be substituted.

The 1951 thru 1953 V8 engine is equipped with a solid skirt cam ground aluminum piston.

Split skirt pistons are used on all 6 cylinder models.

When assembling the piston to the connecting rod on all 6 cylinder models

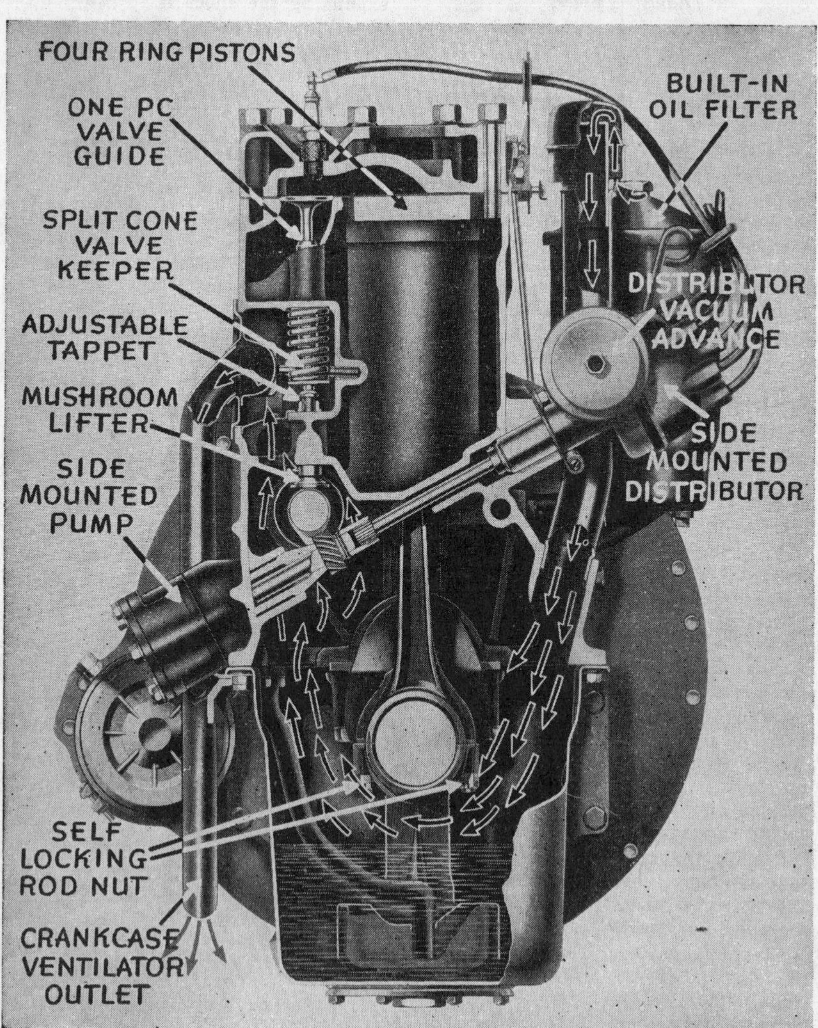

Section through 6 cylinder. Arrows indicate path of ventilation

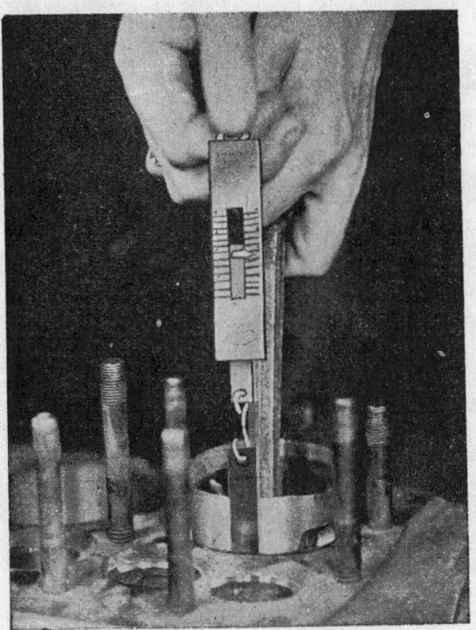

Checking piston fit

set the rod up in a vise so that the numbers on the rod face toward the mechanic and mount the piston so that the split in the skirt is toward the mechanic's right hand.

On V8 models using split skirt pistons the piston is mounted exactly the same as it is for the 6 cylinder engine.

However, the 1951 thru 53 models are equipped with a solid skirt piston. On this piston there is a little round depression in the top of the piston on one side just over the wrist pin hole. This depression should be assembled to the connecting rod on the same side as the numbers on the connecting rod.

On all Ford engines the connecting rod and piston assemblies are mounted in the engine so that the numbers on the connecting rods face forward. The number on the cap should be on the same side of the rod as the number on the rod.

Fitting Rings

Complete instructions are supplied by each ring manufacturer with each package set of rings. These instructions should be followed very carefully since the ring manufacturer knows, better than anyone else, how to get the best possible service from his product.

Connecting Rod Bearings

Connecting rod bearings on all Fords are of the slip-in type and are generally considered to be non-adjustable. Small adjustments can be made on the rod bearing, however, by installing a feather or taper type shim between the lower bearing shell and the bearing cap. The exact recommended oil clearance for rod bearings is given in the engine overhaul table at the beginning of this Ford Section.

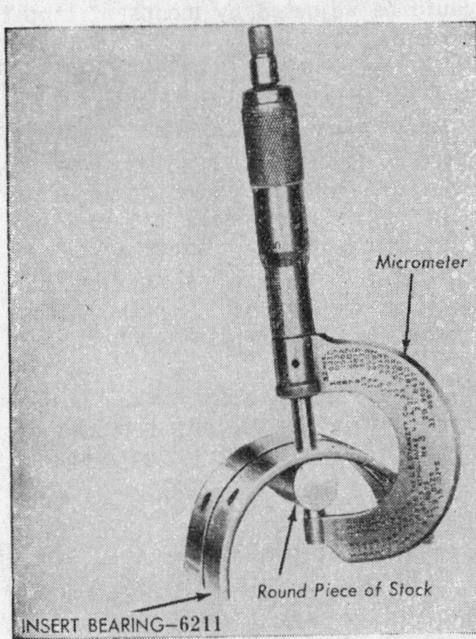

Measure rod bearing across a 1/2 inch rod as shown. Subtract 1/2 inch micrometer reading. The remainder should be not less than .1085 for standard bearing

To check the oil clearance, take a piece of shim stock the desired thickness and place it between the lower bearing and the crankshaft and bolt up the cap. When a piece of shim stock as thick as the recommended oil clearance is used it should produce a heavy load on the crankshaft.

Adjusting shims are frequently used to produce exact clearances when bearings of exactly the right undersize are not available.

Crankshaft Main Bearings

Main bearings in all Ford cars are of the precision, slip-in type and can be replaced without removing the crankshaft. The procedure is to loosen all the main bearing caps and take off the cap of the bearing which is to be removed. Insert a cotter pin in the oil hole in the crankshaft and rotate the crankshaft which will cause the cotter pin head to turn the bearing out of the cylinder block.

Oil clearance checks can be made on the main bearings in exactly the same manner as they are made on the rod bearings. Plastic gauging material is available which is used according to the instructions which are packed with it.

The shim stock method may also be used to check clearance on the main bearings.

Main bearings are generally considered to be non-adjustable and a variety of undersizes are available. However, it is possible to secure an adjustment on the main bearing by placing a feather or taper type shim between the lower half of the bearing shell and the bearing cap.

As much as .003 to .004 inch excessive play can be taken up by this method.

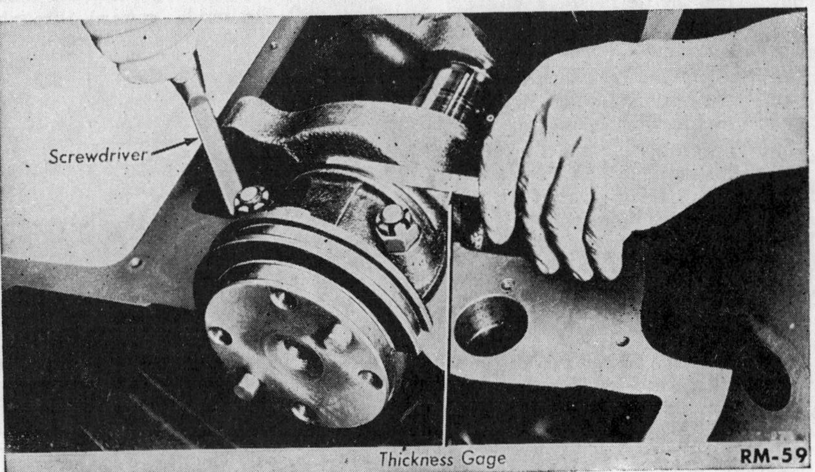

Checking crankshaft for end-play

Rear Main Bearing Oil Seal

On both 6 and 8 cylinder models a packing type seal is used in back of the rear main bearing. To replace the upper half of the seal it is necessary to remove the crankshaft. The lower half of the seal may be replaced by taking down the rear main bearing cap and inserting new packing, letting the packing protrude approximately 1/16 inch above the cap at either side. Bolt the cap into place and immediately take it down to determine if the seal has riveted over. If it has riveted over, trim off with a razor blade just the riveted portion and bolt the cap back up again and again remove it to determine if the main bearing cap is seating properly in the block. The reason for permitting the oil seal packing to protrude is so that it will tend to compress the upper half of the packing more tightly into the retainer in the cylinder block. In this way it is sometimes possible to prevent leaks at the rear main bearing without replacing the upper half of the oil seal.

Oil Pan Removal

6 CYLINDER L HEAD MODELS

On 6 cylinder models it is recommended that the engine be removed from the frame in order to take off the oil pan.

V8 MODELS

On V8 models, remove the starter, clutch spring and the flywheel housing front cover. Take off the breather duct and the steering idler arm bracket and idler arm.

Note: Permit the idler arm to hang down from the tie rods.

Take out the dip stick tube. Unbolt the oil pan and lower it to the floor.

Note: The two front bolts in the oil pan can be reached through holes in the front cross member.

Note: On some engines it will be necessary to disconnect the front engine support and lift the front of the engine in order to permit the pan to clear the crankshaft throws.

Oil Pan Removal

O.H.V. 6 Cyl.

To remove the oil pan first disconnect the steering drag link and remove the engine front mounting bolts. Jack the engine up about an inch and block it in that position.

The oil pan may now be unbolted and lowered to the floor.

VALVE SYSTEM

All Ford V8 engines are equipped with non-adjustable valves.

1949 thru 1951 6 cyl. production engines were equipped with valves which could be adjusted by means of tappet screws in the lifters.

To remove the valves on 8 cylinder engines it is necessary to take off the cylinder heads and the intake manifold.

On 6 cylinder L head engines the valve may be removed by taking off the cover plate underneath the manifold and lifting off the cylinder head.

Starting with 1952 production a 6-cylinder overhead valve engine is used in the Ford cars in addition to the V-8 model.

In these models access to the valve is by removing the rocker cover and the rocker assemblies and cylinder head.

Valve Seat Inserts

The exhaust valve seat on all Fords built since 1949 is fitted with a heat resisting alloy insert, which requires grinding with a power type machine. The insert is too hard to be refaced with a cutting tool.

Methods of replacing the seat insert are given in the General Service Section.

Removal of Valve Guides

V8 MODELS

On V8 models, remove the valve stem keeper and take out the valve. Drive the guide down far enough to permit removal of the C type retainer and then pull the guide upward through the top of the block.

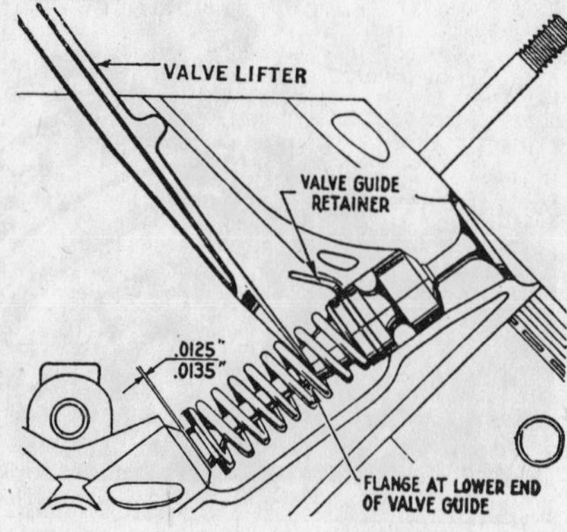

Remove valve guide

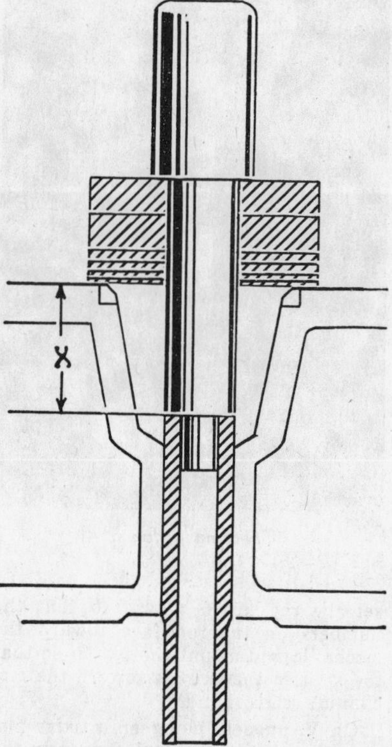

Add washers until distance "X" is required depth of valve guide

To replace the guide on V8 engines drive it down far enough into the block to permit the insertion of the C type keeper and then pull it up again so that the keeper will seat firmly on the underside of the cylinder block.

6 CYLINDER L HEAD

On 6 cylinder models the valve guide is pulled straight up through the top of the block. Intake valve guides should be driven down from the top of the block until the top of the guide is 1.18 inch from the top of the cylinder block. On exhaust guides the guide should be driven down until the top of the guide is 1.08 inch from the top of the cylinder top. If all the guides are to be replaced it is a good idea to arrange a collar on the driving device so that the valve can be driven down until the collar on the driver contacts the cylinder block.

While it may take a couple minutes to arrange the collar on the driver it will save considerable time in eliminating the measurement required to bring the guide to its proper position.

O.H.V. 6 Cyl.

The valve guides are an integral part of the cylinder head and are not replaceable. Instead, valves with .003, .015, .030 inch over size stems are available for service.

The procedure is to select the valve with the smallest oversize stem practical and ream the cylinder head to secure good fit.

Reamers are available with a standard size pilot on a .003 over size reamer; a .003 over size pilot for the .015 over size reamer and a .015 over size pilot for the .030 inch size reamer.

Where necessary to ream to .015 or .030 over size the reamer should be used in sequence. In other words it is not practical to start with a standard cylinder head and enter the pilot of a .030 over size reamer.

Valve Adjustment

Final valve adjustment should be made with the engine running at normal operating temperature. The inlet valve should be adjusted so that a .013 inch feeler will pass between the rocker and the valve stem and a .015 inch feeler will not pass. On the exhaust valves a .015 inch feeler gauge should pass between the rocker and the valve stem and a .017 inch gauge should stop.

This adjustment should be made with the engine thoroughly warmed.

Removal of Rocker Arm Assembly

O.H.V. 6 Cyl.

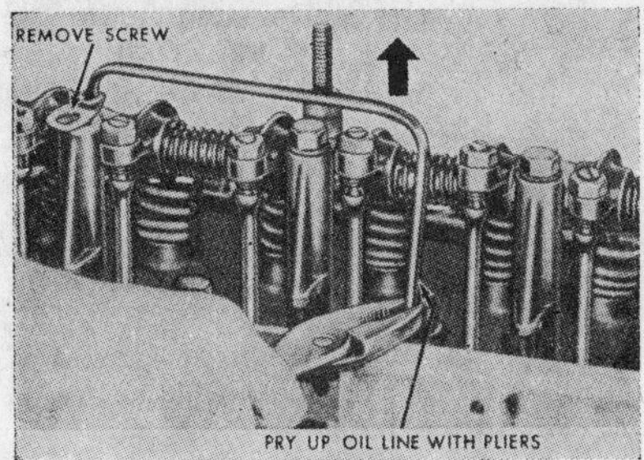

Removing oil line

Remove the rocker chamber cover and then remove the screw which holds the oil feed line to the rocker shaft and remove the feed line by prying it up with a pair of pliers out of the cylinder head.

Back off on the rocker arm adjusting screws until the pressure is taken off the valve springs and then unbolt the rocker shaft assembly.

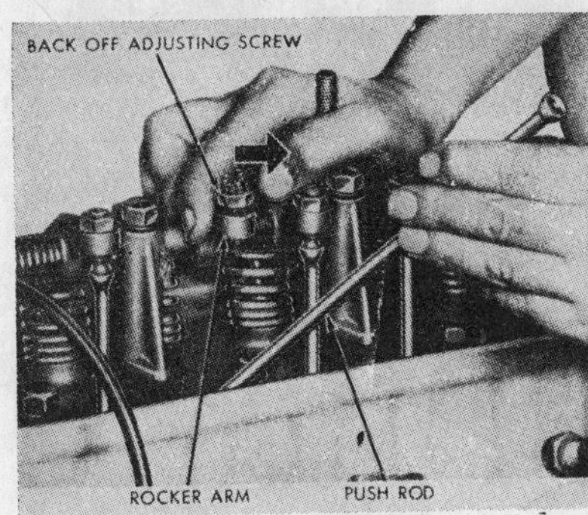

Removing push rods

Removal of Push Rods

O.H.V. 6 Cyl.

The valve push rods may be removed from the engine without removing the rocker shaft by taking off the valve rocker cover and backing off on the rocker adjusting screw until all of the spring tension is taken off the valve.

The rocker can then be slid sideways which will permit removal of the push rod.

Caution: The rocker arms at each end of the engine cannot be shifted in this manner and the two end push rods cannot be removed until after the cylinder head has been taken off.

Removal of Cylinder Head

O.H.V. 6 Cyl.

Follow the procedures given for the rocker arms and in addition remove the temperature sending unit, spark coil, carburetor, carburetor vacuum and fuel lines, disconnect the water outlet hose, unbolt the cylinder head and lift it off.

Cylinder Block Core Hole Plugs

O.H.V. 6 Cyl.

There are two large cylinder block core hole plugs located in the back of the clutch bell housing. In order to service either or both of these plugs it is necessary to remove the clutch bell housing. This job is best accomplished by removing the engine.

Valve Springs

Valve springs should be checked for pressure at any time they are removed. Engine Overhaul Specifications Table gives the desired spring pressure at the proper distance. Refer to index.

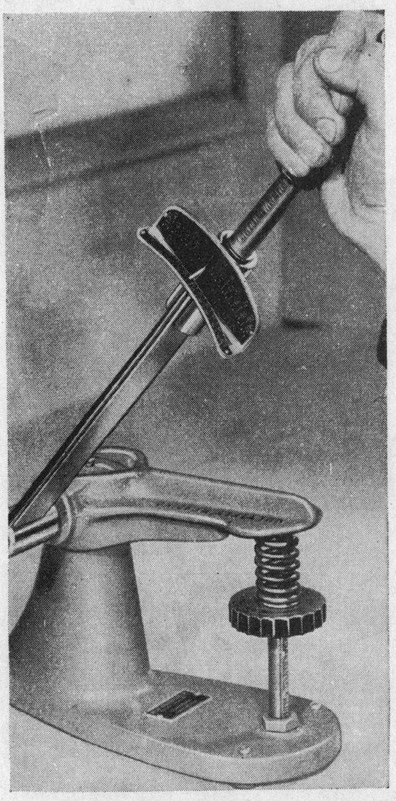

Testing valve spring tension

Timing Gear Cover Removal

L-HEAD ENGINES 6 & V-8

Remove the radiator core, fan belt and distributor. Take off the vibration damper and unbolt the timing case cover.

Note: Two of the bolts in the timing case cover are up through the oil pan. They are reached through two holes in the front crossmember.

Timing Case Cover

O.H.V. 6 Cyl.

The timing case cover is located to the front of the cylinder block by two dowel pins. It is held in place with ten hex head screws. There are also two screws fed up from the oil pan into the timing case cover. The cover is also used as the engine front support.

To remove the timing case cover it is recommended that the oil pan be removed because the oil pan gasket contacts the bottom of the timing case cover and it is an extremely difficult job to remove the timing case cover without destroying or damaging the gasket so that it is no longer fit for service.

Take out the engine front support bolts and support the engine on a jack. Take off the radiator core and the fan assembly, remove the vibration damper and unbolt the timing case cover.

Vibration damper

Timing Case Oil Seal Replacement

O.H.V. 6 Cyl.

To replace the oil seal it is necessary to take off the timing case cover and drive the seal out with a pin punch. Clean out the recess in the cover and install a new seal using a special driving tool.

Coat the new seal with grease to reduce friction when installing and starting the car.

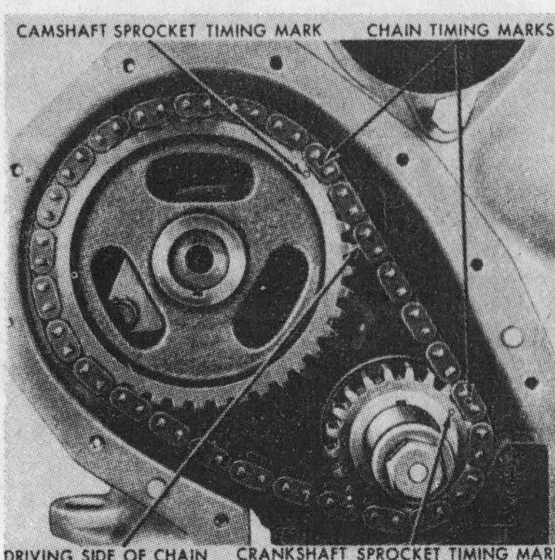

Aligning timing mark

Timing Sprocket and/or Chain

O.H.V. 6 Cyl.

To replace the timing chain for wear or looseness, first align the timing marks so that there are seven links of the chain between the mark on the cam and the mark on the crankshaft sprocket, counting the link at each mark. These should be measured on the driving, upper, side of the chain. Now remove the camshaft sprocket retaining nut and the crankshaft nut and slide the two sprockets and chain as one unit off their respective shafts.

To reinstall the chain first set the chain over both sprockets and start both sprockets simultaneously on their two shafts being certain that the keyways are very carefully aligned before starting the sprockets into place. After they have been mounted fully on their shafts turn the engine two full revolutions to recheck to make certain that there are seven links of the timing chain between the mark on the cam and the mark on the crankshaft sprocket, counting the link at each mark.

Valve Timing Procedure

The camshaft drive on all models except the O.H.V. 6 cyl. is by means of gears. Unless the gears are badly worn or damaged or are deliberately tampered with, the valve timing will remain as set by the factory. If it becomes necessary to retime the valves or replace either of the gears due to wear or damage proceed as follows:

Remove the timing case cover and take off the camshaft gear. If it is necessary to replace the crank gear remove the oil pan.

Press on the new crankshaft gear, being careful when starting the gear that the key and keyway are in perfect alignment since it is a tight fit on the shaft and it is very difficult to align the key and keyway if they are not started properly.

Turn the crankshaft so that the mark on the crankshaft gear is pointed directly toward the center of the camshaft. Now mesh the camshaft gear so that the timing mark on the cam gear coincides with the mark on the crank gear. Rotate the camshaft so that the bolt holes will line up with the cam gear. Install the bolts and special lock plate. Rotate the crankshaft two full revolutions as a recheck to make certain that the marks coincide on a straight line between the shaft centers.

Valves timed in this manner will be correct, regardless of which piston is at top center. Always retime the ignition after retiming the valves.

Fuel System

The 6 cylinder models are equipped with a single throat down draft carburetor and the 8 cylinder models are equipped with a dual throat down draft carburetor. Both models are equipped with a single fuel pump. On the V8 models the fuel pump is located between the cylinder banks at the back of the engine. The fuel pump on the 6 cylinder models is located on the right side of the engine, low, toward the front.

A baffle is used between the exhaust manifold and the fuel pump on 6 cylinder models to prevent vapor-lock.

Fuel Pump

Service repair kits are available for the fuel pumps used on both 6 and 8 cylinder models. When repairing a fuel pump always mark carefully the relationship between the cover and the body so that they can be properly installed.

Two types of kits are furnished, one the diaphragm kit, the other the overhaul kit. The diaphragm kit consists of diaphragm springs and check valves, whereas the overhaul kit consists of links, levers and also the diaphragm valves and springs.

Gas Tank Removal

On both models the gas tank may be removed after the filler neck pipeclamp is moved and pulled away from the tank. Then disconnect the fuel line and take off the support strap nuts and lower the tank. When the tank is lowered sufficiently to permit access to the fuel gauge wire, remove it and lower the tank.

Engine Manifolds

The manifolds on the 6 cylinder models, both O.H.V. and L head, are of the combination variety where the intake manifold is bolted to the exhaust manifold at the center. The exhaust manifold fitted with a heat riser valve which, when the engine is cold, deflects the hot exhaust gases against the intake manifold causing it to warm up more quickly. The only service required by the heat riser valve is to see that it is operating freely and that it does not stick.

On the V8 models the intake manifold is located between the two cylinder blocks and must be removed to service the valves. The exhaust manifolds are located on the outside end of the cylinder blocks.

Other than to see that neither of the manifolds leak, no service is required.

ELECTRICAL SYSTEM

Generator

On the 6 cylinder models the generator is located on a bracket at the front left side of the engine. It is driven by a belt from the crankshaft pulley. On the V8 models the generator is located on a bracket between the two cylinder banks at the front.

Two types of generators are used, the three brush type and also the two brush type controlled by a regulator. Where difficulty is experienced with the generator, the procedure on Ford cars is slightly different from all the others.

In order to make a quick check to determine if the generator or the regulator is at fault, take a hopper wire and temporarily connect the generator output terminal (at the generator) to the field lead (also at the generator). By placing a hopper across these two connections the regulator will be eliminated from the circuit.

If the generator now charges properly the difficulty is in the regulator and it should be repaired or replaced.

If putting the hopper wire between the output terminal and the field terminal does not cause the generator to charge then the difficulty may well be in the generator and it should be removed for bench test.

Bench Tests for generators are given in the General Service Section of this Manual, see index.

Starter

The starting system consists of the battery, starter switch and starting motor. If difficulty is experienced with the starter system first check the battery and make certain that it is fully charged and also check to make sure that the battery cable connections are clean and tight, and that the cable ground conection is clean and tight.

Check the starter switch to make certain that its contact points are clean and free from pits and burrs.

If all of these conditions are met with and the starting motor still does not function properly it will be necessary to remove it from the car and make exactly the same tests on it as are made for the generator.

See the Fundamental Section, at the beginning of Section 4 of this Manual.

The Distributor

On V8 Models the distributor is located at the front end of the right cylinder bank.

On 6 cylinder models the distributor is located on the left side of the engine.

On the 6 cylinder L head model the distributor drive gear is actually mounted on the oil pump. On O.H.V. 6 cylinder engines and 8 cylinder models the distributor drive gear is mounted at the bottom of the distributor shaft.

Ignition Timing

A table of tune-up information is given at the beginning of this section, which gives the exact point in degrees at which the spark should occur for proper ignition timing.

To set up ignition timing bring No. 1 cylinder to the top dead center of position with both valves closed. Remove the cap from the distributor and determine if the rotor is in position to fire No. 1 cylinder. If it is not it will be necessary to lift the distributor off of the housing and rotate it one gear tooth and then rotate enough gear teeth to bring the No. 1 wire directly over the rotor. This method can be used on O.H.V. 6 cylinder and 8 cylinder models only.

On L head 6 cylinder models it will be necessary to shift the wires in the distributor cap in order to bring the wire from No. 1 cylinder under the rotor.

Final adjusting of the ignition timing can be made in the usual manner by rotating the distributor housing to get an exact setting.

On both 6 and 8 cylinder distributors a movable type braker plate is used to provide a vacuum controlled advance.

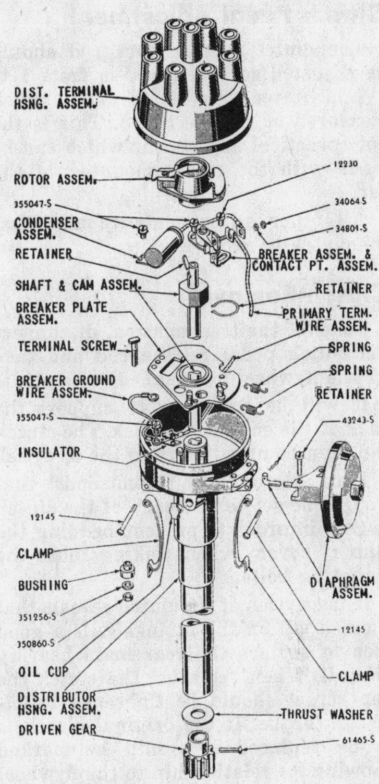

Distributor assembly

Starting with 1949 production all Ford distributors are known as the Loadamatic type.

On all Fords from 1949 the breaker points can be installed with the distributor in place on the car. However, this is not the approved method of installing points. In order to ascertain the correct cam angle it is necessary to remove the distributor from the car and place it on a cam angle machine.

If no cam angle machine is available, remove the distributor from the car and take out the old breaker points and install new ones. It is very important that the points contact squarely across the face and the contact should be adjusted

IGNITION TIMING—*continued*

before final adjustment of the point gap.

Spring tension on the breaker arm can be measured with an ordinary pull scale having ounce graduations. The correct tension is 17 to 20 ounces measured by pulling with a spring scale at right angles to the breaker point as close to the point as possible.

CLUTCH

Clutch Pedal Adjustment

The clutch release fork rod should be adjusted so that there is from 1 to 1½ inch free play of the clutch pedal, measured at the toe board. This is the only practical adjustment which can be made with the clutch mounted in the car.

All other adjustments require that the clutch be removed.

Clutch Removal

Take off the transmission, disconnect the clutch pedal release rod and take off the flywheel housing.

It will be necessary to support the back of the engine on a jack. The clutch can then be unbolted from the flywheel.

Ford Motor Co. recommends that wedges be set behind each of the clutch fingers in order to prevent bending the clutch cover when taking out the mounting bolts.

If inspection of the clutch reveals that there is oil on the facings it is a good idea to replace the rear main bearing oil seal. When replacing the clutch the cap screw should be tightened to 17-20′ lb. torque. If the original clutch is to be replaced it should be marked showing its relationship to the flywheel so that it can be replaced in the position from which it was removed.

Clutch Overhaul

Generally speaking, the overhaul of a clutch requires special jigs and fixtures and the procedure is different for different manufacturer's equipment.

It is impractical to attempt a major overhaul on a clutch assembly without the use of the special fixtures. The customary procedure is to exchange the clutch.

CONVENTIONAL TRANSMISSION

The conventional transmission can be identified by the long round extension housing at the back of the transmission. On models equipped with overdrive this space is taken up by the overdrive assembly.

Removal of Transmission

To remove the transmission it is necessary to take off the exhaust pipe, disconnect the clutch pedal and gear shift linkage, break the front and rear universal joint and take out the drive shaft, remove the cap screws which attach the transmission to the No. 2 frame crossmember and, after a support has been placed under the engine, remove the frame crossmember.

Note: The bolts which attach the crossmember to the top of the frame side rails are accessible through holes in the body floor pan. Take out the two upper bolts which hold the transmission to the flywheel housing and insert two guide pins in their place. Remove the bottom two bolts and slide the transmission out on the guide pins.

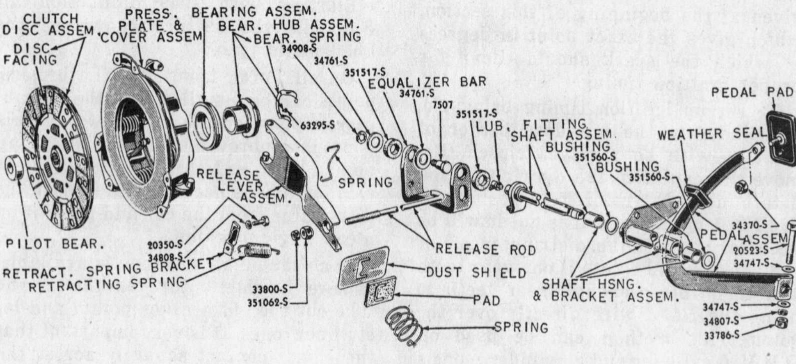

Clutch linkage

Remove transmission

Dis-assembly of Standard Transmission

Remove the transmission cover assembly and unbolt the extension housing. Drive the pin out of the transmission case which holds the counter shaft and the reverse idler gear shaft. This pin is located at the back by the bottom of the case. Turn the extension housing one-quarter turn clockwise, which will permit the removal of the counter shaft.

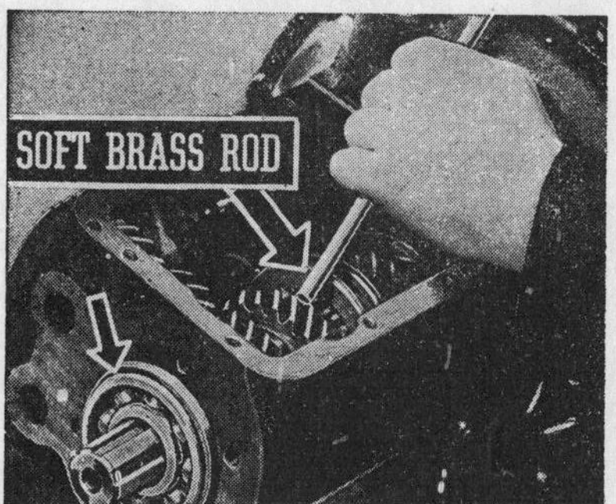

Drive mainshaft back

The counter shaft is driven out through the rear of the case permitting the counter set cluster gear to drop to the bottom of the case.

Now the extension housing and the main shaft assembly can be pulled out from the rear of the transmission case.

The reverse idler gear can now be driven out through the rear of the case. The main drive gear is removed by taking off the bearing cover and pulling the shaft and bearing out the front of the case. Remove the snap ring which holds the main shaft assembly in the extension case. (This snap ring is located at the front of the extension case.

It is the snap ring which holds the bearing into the extension case.)

Tap the mainshaft out of the extension case. Next take off the speedometer gear and the mainshaft rear bearing.

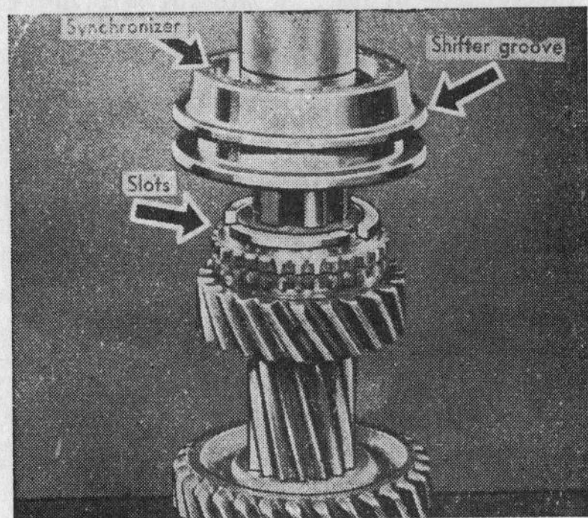

Assemble sleeve to main shaft

To dis-assemble the synchronizer push the synchronizer hub out of the sleeve which will release the three synchronizer blocks. The main drive gear bearing can be pressed off the main drive gear after the snap ring is removed.

Inspect all parts for nicks and roughness and check all bearings for smooth operation.

When the transmission is dis-assembled always place a new oil seal at the back of the extension housing.

Standard Transmission Shift Linkage Adjustment

To adjust the shift rods, disconnect the rods from the steering column levers and loosen the lock nuts. Turn the clevices either clockwise or counterclockwise whichever is required, so that with the gears in neutral and the two levers on the steering column in line with each other, the clevices will just enter the hole in the shift lever.

Overdrive Assembly

The overdrive assembly is removed from the car with the transmission and the procedure given for removal of the standard transmission will also apply to the overdrive transmission.

Disassembly of Overdrive

First, remove the lock-out switch, (The lock-out switch is located toward the rear of the overdrive on the left side) and then turn over the assembly to permit the two steel balls under the switch to drop out.

Take off the governor assembly and then remove the overdrive housing bolts (which hold the overdrive housing to the transmission housing) the shift rail pin and the cover which is located on the top of the overdrive housing (this is just a small cover and it is intended to give access to a snap ring).

Note: Do not remove the bolt holding the adapter to the transmission case at this time.

Pull out the shift rail lever and shaft as far as it will go. Reach down through the hole in the top of the overdrive and spread the snap ring, then tap with a soft hammer on the end of the overdrive main shaft while pulling the housing toward the rear. This will separate the overdrive housing from the internal parts.

Now remove the overdrive main shaft from the assembly and catch any of the rollers which drop out of it. Remove the clutch assembly retainers, the clutch and planetary gear assemblies and the sun gear and shift rail. These all will come off as a unit, after the retainer is raised to permit sliding them off the shaft.

If any part of the transmission is to be worked at this point, continue to disassemble the transmission as given under the Transmission Section.

Examine all parts for scratches, burrs or roughness and thoroughly clean up all parts before re-assembling.

Operation of Ford Overdrive

The Ford overdrive is designed so that when the instrument control panel knob is in the "in" position (overdrive functioning) the final drive is through a free-wheeling cam, which means that anytime the car speed exceeds the speed of the overdrive shaft the car will free wheel. When the gear train is "overdriving" the sun gear is held against rotation by a pawl. This causes the drive pinion cage pinions to rotate or "walk around" the sun gear. The pinions are meshed in the internal gear on the output shaft which forces it to rotate at a higher rate of speed than the transmission main shaft. Actually for each full revolution of the output shaft the transmission main shaft turns 0.7 of a revolution. Since the output shaft is turning more rapidly than the main shaft overdrive clutch remains in the free wheel position.

When the gear train is over-driving the power from the rear wheels is delivered directly to the engine as long as the sun gear is held against rotation. In other words the overdrive will permit free-wheeling when it is not over-driving. It does not free wheel, however, when the overdrive is functioning.

Operation of Overdrive Electrical Controls

When the speed of the car reaches

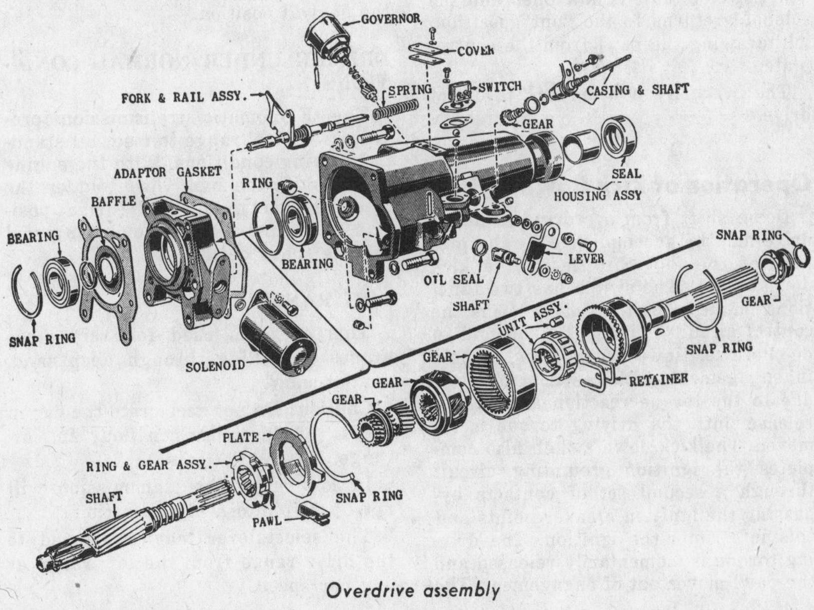

Overdrive assembly

ELECTRICAL CONTROLS—*continued*

approximately 27 miles per hour (the cut in point of the governor) the governor contacts close completing a control circuit to ground. This causes a current to flow through the relay coil, causing the relay contacts to close. The power circuit to the solenoid is completed at the relay and current flows through the solenoid windings causing the solenoid armature to move to the "in" position.

When the armature is fully energized it disconnects the traction coil by opening a set of contacts inside the solenoid housing, leaving the holding coil connected in the circuit. The motion of the solenoid armature (just like a plunger) to the stem and pawl through an inner spring so that the pawl is urged to engage the sun gear control plate by the action of the spring instead of being forced to engage it by direct action from the solenoid armature. In other words the solenoid armature compresses a spring which in turn forces the pawl to engage the sun gear.

As soon as driving torque is released from the overdrive the pawl engages the control plate and the overdrive is in action.

The overdrive shifts down automatically when the speed of the vehicle drops to the cut out speed of the governor, which is approx. 21 miles per hour.

At cut out the governor contacts open interrupting the control circuit thus causing the relay contacts to open. The power circuit is now open and the solenoid returns to the "out" position, withdrawing the pawl from the control plate.

The overdrive now returns to direct drive.

Operation of Kick Down Switch

Down shift from overdrive to direct drive may be accomplished by the presure of the foot throttle on the kick down switch. The switch has two functions in the circuit. First, it opens the control circuit causing the solenoid to de-energize. However, the pawl is held in engagement with the control plate due to the torque reaction and cannot release until the driving torque is removed. The kick down switch also completes the ignition grounding circuit through a second set of contacts bypassing the ignition breaker points and this interrupts the ignition. The driving torque is momentarily released and the pawl moves out of engagement. The solenoid armature now returns to the "out" position opening a set of contacts in the ignition grounding circuit.

In other words the engine ignition cannot be grounded as long as the overdrive is in the "off" position. This is prevented by the contacts in the solenoid which prevent the ignition being grounded by the kick down switch when the overdrive is not functioning.

Locked Out

When the overdrive is operating in the "locked out" position (either by having the overdrive-control "out" or by shifting the transmission into reverse) the lockout switch is opened by a cam on the shift rail. Since the control circuit is open when the lockout switch is open the solenoid cannot be energized. The pawl cannot be energized when the unit is locked out.

TORQUE CONVERTER

Note: Dis-assembly procedure for the Fordomatic and Mercamatic transmissions are given in the automatic transmission portion of this section. See index.

Driving Instructions

To start the car the starter will operate only when the selector lever is in the neutral position.

DRIVING UNDER NORMAL CONDITIONS

The Fordomatic transmission provides a control range to meet all standard driving conditions. With the engine idling shift the hand lever under the steering wheel to the "DR" (drive) position and depress the accelerator pedal for the speed desired.

LOW RANGE

This range is used for very steep grades or pulling through deep sand, mud or snow.

Caution: Do not accelerate the car in excess of 30 miles per hour in low range.

In low range the transmission will not upshift into a higher ratio.

The selectalever may be moved to the drive range from the low range at any car speed.

REVERSE

Before shifting the transmission into the "R" (reverse) position bring the car to a full stop. With the shift lever in the "R" position simply depress the accelerator pedal and the car will move backward.

TO ROCK THE CAR BACK AND FORTH

Maintain a steady pressure on the accelerator pedal and move the selectalever back and forth between the "R" (reverse) position and the "LO" (low) position.

PARKING

In the parking position a mechanical pawl is engaged which firmly anchors the car so it cannot be moved either forward or backward.

Before shifting the selectalever to the "P" (parking) position always bring the car to a complete standstill and turn off the ignition switch.

Operation of the Torque Converter

The design of the torque converter is such that the fluid flow from the pump to the turbin and back to the pump through the stater produces a maximum torque increase of slightly over 2 to 1, when the turbin is stalled. When sufficient torque is developed by the engine and converter the turbin begins to rotate turning the turbin shaft. Converter torque multiplication gradually tapers off as turbin speed approaches pump speed and becomes nearly 1 to 1. This is known as the coupling point. When the turbin is operating at a speed less than 9/10ths of pump speed and the converter is multiplying torque the fluid leaving the turbin blade strikes the front face of the stater blades which are held stationary by the action of the one way clutch as long as the fluid is directed against the front face of the blade.

When the turbin rotates faster than 9/10ths pump speed and the converter no longer multiplies torque the fluid is directed against the back face of the stater blades. Since the one way clutch permits the stater blades to rotate in direction of the pump rotation the stater begins to turn with the pump and turbin.

The converter now acts as an efficient fluid coupling as long as the coupling speed remains greater than 9/10th pump speed.

Planetary Gear Train

In low range the primary sun gear is driven and the pinion carrier is held, power is transmitted to the primary pinions, the secondary pinion and the internal gear, driving the internal gear in the same direction as the primary pump.

The secondary sun gear turns free in the reverse direction and has no effect on the gear train. The pinion carrier is held against rotation.

In intermediate range, drive is accomplished in the primary sun gear and holding the secondary sun gear. The primary pinions drive the secondary pinions causing them to "walk around" the secondary sun gear, turning the internal gear and the output shaft with them.

In high range the primary and secondary sun gears are locked against rotation and driven as a unit. Therefore, the pinions cannot rotate and the entire planetary train revolves as a unit.

The output shaft rotation is the same speed as the turbin shaft.

Reverse is accomplished by driving the secondary sun gear and holding the pinion carrier.

UNIVERSAL JOINTS AND PROPELLER SHAFT

The universal joints on all Ford cars from 1949 are of the needle bearing type having an open drive shaft (Hotchkiss drive). To replace the universal joint remove the snap ring from under the yoke and around the needle bearing races. With a drift approximately the same size as the needle bearing race press one bearing race through the yoke. With a pair of pliers remove the opposite bearing which is partially forced out of the yoke. Remove the spider from the yoke and then repeat the same procedure on the other pair of bearings.

When replacing universal joint assemblies pack the needle bearings and the holes in the end of the spider with universal joint grease and place the spider in the yoke and press the bearings into place either in an arbor press or in a good vise.

Install the snap rings.

Drive Shaft

To replace the drive shaft it is necessary to disconnect both the front and rear universal joint from the drive shaft yoke. This is accomplished by splitting the rear joint and sliding the drive shaft and the transmission shaft rear yoke out of the transmission and splitting the front joint on the bench.

To reinstall attach the drive shaft to the front universal yoke and slide the yoke up into the transmission and then install the bearings on the rear yoke under the car.

CYLINDER HEAD NUT TIGHTENING SEQUENCE

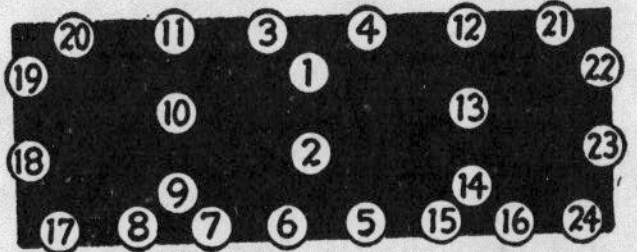

1949-51 V8

Tighten bolts to 65-70 foot pounds, or nuts to 50-55 foot pounds.

1949-51 6 cylinder

Tighten head bolts to 65-70 and nuts to 45-50 foot pounds.

REAR AXLE ASSEMBLY

A semi-floating type Hypoid rear axle is used on all passenger cars. The rear axle housing is the banjo type with the spring seats welded to the housing. The housing cover is welded on and is not removable.

Station Wagons and Panel Delivery trucks use a Spicer type rear axle assembly having a removable cover but a one-piece differential carrier and axle tubes.

Except for the fact that the differential side bearings are shim adjusted in the Station Wagon the procedure is practically the same as that given for the passenger car rear axle assembly.

Removal of Rear Axle Assembly

The rear axle asembly may be removed from underneath the car by detaching at the rear universal joint. The shock absorbers, brake lines, spring shackles, and hand brake cables must be removed in order to take out the rear axle assembly.

Pinion Oil Seal Replacement

To replace the pinion oil seal disconnect the drive shaft at the rear universal joint and mark the position of the universal joint flange nut. This will aid in resetting the nut to exactly the position from which it was removed.

Take off the universal joint nut and pull off the universal joint flange and washer.

The oil seal can then be removed with an inertia type puller.

Axle Shaft Replacement

Take the brake drum from the axle flange and, working through the hole provided in the axle shaft flange, remove the bolts that secure the brake backing plate to the axle housing. An inertia type puller will be required to pull the axle shaft out of the housing since the bearing is held on the axle shaft with a shrunk-on locking ring.

It is customary to put back one bolt into the brakebacking plate to hold it in place while removing the axle shaft.

Axle Bearing Replacement

The bearing should be removed from the axle shaft only when it requires replacing. It is not a good policy to remove the bearing and then replace the same bearing on the axle shaft.

To remove the bearing split or press off the retainer ring and press off the bearing from the axle shaft. A new bearing should be pressed on until it seats against the shoulder on the axle shaft.

The rear wheel bearing retainer ring should be pressed firmly against the bearing.

When a new axle shaft is installed it is necessary to install with it a new axle bearing.

The ring which retains the bearing to the axle shaft is generally a shrunk on ring and sometimes is very difficult to remove.

AXLE BEARING REPLACEMENT —continued

Unless a good arbor press is handy it will be necessary to split this ring in order to take it off.

It is a good idea when installing a new bearing and retaining ring to heat the retaining ring somewhat so that it will be easier to put on the axle shaft where it will shrink in place as it cools.

Axle Shaft Oil Seal

To replace the rear axle oil seal take out the axle shaft and then, using an inertia puller pull the oil seal from inside the rear axle housing.

Proper tooth contact

Replacement of Pinion & Ring Gear—Pinion Bearing Adjustment

Remove both axle shafts and disconnect the rear universal joint. Unbolt the carrier from the rear axle housing. Place the carrier assembly in a vise and after thoroughly cleaning it proceed with the disassembly. Mark the differential bearing caps and carrier supports with matching numbers to insure that they are properly reassembled. Remove the adjusting nut locks, the bearing caps and the adjusting nuts. Then lift the differential assembly out of the carrier.

The differential side bearings cones are taken from the side of the differential with a puller.

Remove the cap screws which attach the ring gear to the differential case and tap off the ring gear with a soft hammer.

Heavy face contact: Move pinion deeper into ring gear—add shims at pinion rear bearing

To take out the pinion gear remove the universal joint flange nut and washer and pull the flange off the drive pinion. Tap the pinion shaft out the back of the carrier. Take the pinion rear bearing and the rear bearing spacer out of the carrier. Take out the pinion oil seal with an inertia type puller.

Remove the pinion front bearing cup from the carrier using an inertia type puller.

Contact on toe: Move ring gear away from pinion

Note: Late production models have shims installed between the drive pinion rear bearing and the pinion gear. Early and late type drive pinions are interchangeable provided the necessary shims are installed on the new pinion shaft.

On early 1949 models shims are used between the rear bearing cup and the housing to control the pinion depth. Starting with late 1949 production models the shims are used between the inner pinion bearing cone and the pinion gear itself.

Install the pinion bearing cups into the carrier by driving them into place. Press the rear bearing on to the drive

Contact on heel: Move ring gear toward pinion

pinion (see that the shims which were removed are replaced) until it seats against the pinion shoulder (or shim). Position the drive pinion assembly in the carrier and then install the bearing spacer and the front bearing on the pinion shaft. Install the universal joint flange, washer and nut. Tighten the nut until the bearing preload is between 15 and 20 inch lbs. This preload should be checked very carefully with a spring scale.

Note: Turn the pinion shaft while tightening the nut so that the bearing is properly seated.

Adjusting Depth of Pinion Gear

A special micrometer gauge is required to properly set the depth of the pinion gear.

However, if a depth gauge is not available it is possible to adjust the depth of the pinion gear by blueing the gears and adjusting the pinion depth so that the contact is all over the face of the ring gear. This is accomplished by tentatively setting up the pinion gear and then mounting the ring gear in its carrier, blueing the gears and observing the marks left by the blue on the face of the ring gear teeth.

After the pinion is installed and set to the proper depth mount the differential with its side bearings in place in the carrier and set up the adjusting cages.

To adjust the side bearings, tighten the left hand adjusting nut until the back lash in the gears is zero. Then tighten the right hand adjusting nut until snug and then tighten the nut an additional 1½ to 2½ notches which will impose the proper preload on the bearing and will also give a back lash of from .003 to .008 inch.

After securely tightening the adjusting cage locks, mount the carrier back into the axle housing and replace both axle shafts.

Heavy flank contact: Move pinion out from ring gear—use thinner shims at pinion bearing

1949 thru 1953 FORD

REAR SPRING REMOVAL

To remove the rear springs on these models disconnect the shock absorber at the spring clip plate and remove the U bolt nuts.

Take out the stud at the front hanger and the two bolts at the rear shackle.

The spring can then be lifted out from under the car.

Note: When installing a new spring the short end of the spring goes toward the front of the car.

The short end of the spring is the one having the shortest distance from the spring eye to the center bolt.

Spring clips should be tightened to 45-50 ft lbs torque.

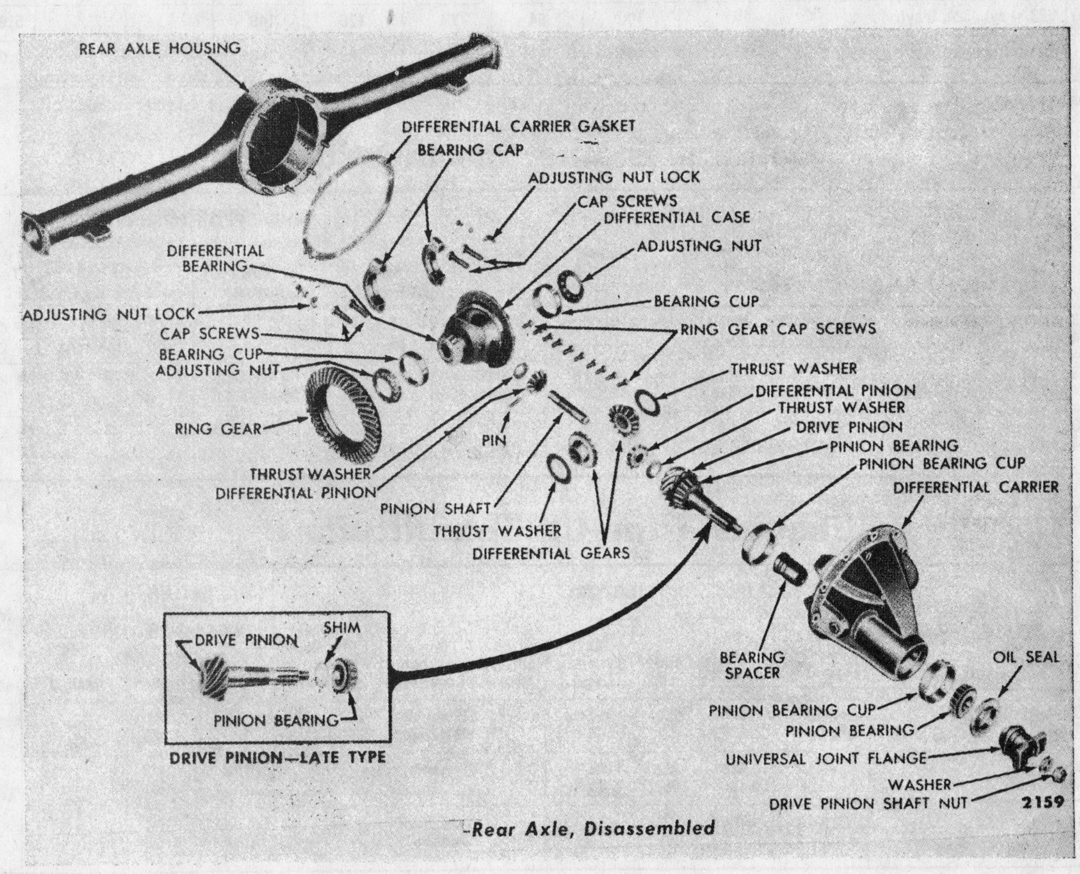

—Rear Axle, Disassembled

HENRY J SPECIFICATIONS

Starting Serial and Motor Numbers

HENRY J

Starting Serial Numbers

1951-53—Prefix indicates year and number of cylinders, i.e., K513, 1951 4 cyl. 1951 Serial numbers start 001001. 1952 Serial numbers start 1001001 on Vagabond and 1200000 on Corsair. 1953—K001, 001 and up.

1951, 4 cyl.—513 001001
6 cyl.—514 001001

1952, 4 cyl.—523 1001001
6 cyl.—524 1001001

1953, 4 cyl.—533 ....K001001
6 cyl.—534 ....K001001

Location

1947-1953—On left front door pillar post.

Starting Motor Numbers

1951-1952, 4 cyl. 3500000
1951-1952, 6 cyl. 3000001

Location

1951-1952—Stamped on pad on front of cylinder block and on plate on side of cylinder block.

General Specifications

Year	Model	Wheelbase (in.)	Tread (in.) Front	Tread (in.) Rear	Overall Dimensions (in.) Length	Overall Dimensions (in.) Width	Overall Dimensions (in.) Height■	Shipping Weight* (lb.)	Tire Size (in.)
1951	513	100	54	54	175	....	....	2300	5.90-15
	514	100	54	54	175	....	....	2325	5.90-15
1952	523, 4 cyl., 524, 6 cyl.	100	54	54	176	149	....	....	5.90-15
1953	533, 4 cyl., 6 cyl.	100	54	54	182	69	60	....	5.90-15

■—Road to roof, no load.

General Engine Specifications

Year	Model	Number of Cylinders Bore and Stroke	Piston Displacement, Cubic Inches	Compression Ratio (To–1)	Taxable (A.M.A.) Hp.	Developed Horse Power: Bare Engine	Developed Horse Power: With Accessories	Maximum Torque Ft. Lbs.
1951	513 (4L-134), 4 Cyl.	4-3⅛ x 4⅜	134.2	7.0	15.63	....	68 @ 4000	109 @ 1800
	514 (6L-161), 6 Cyl.	6-3⅛ x 3½	161.0	7.0	23.4	....	80 @ 3800	133 @ 1600
1952	523, 4 Cyl.	4-3⅛ x 4⅜	134.2	7.00	15.63	68 @ 4000	....	109 @ 1800
	524, 6 Cyl.	6-3⅛ x 3½	161.0	7.00	23.40	80 @ 3800	....	133 @ 1600
1953	533, 4 Cyl.	4-3⅛ x 4⅜	134.2	7.0	15.63	68 @ 4000	....	109 @ 1800
	534, 6 Cyl.	6-3⅛ x 3½	161.0	7.0	23.40	80 @ 3800	....	80 @ 3800

Engine Tune-Up Specifications

Year	Model	Spark Plugs: Type	Spark Plugs: Gap	Distributor: Point Gap	Distributor: Cam Dwell, (Deg.)	Ignition Timing, (Deg.)	Ignition Timing Mark and Location	Compression Pressure at R.P.M.	Operating Tappet Clearance: Inlet	Operating Tappet Clearance: Exhaust	Carburetor Fuel Float Height	Minimum Engine Idle Speed at R.P.M.
1951	513 (4L-134), 4 Cyl.	AN-7	.030	.020	41°	5B	Flywheel	120lb.-130lb.	.016	.016	9/32"	550
	514 (6L-161), 6 Cyl.	AN-7	.030	.020	38°	TC	Vib-Dmpr.	130lb.-140lb.	.016	.016	9/32"	550
1952	523, 4 Cyl.	AL-A7	.030	.020	38	TC	Flywheel	....	.016C	.016C	3/16"	....
	524, 6 Cyl.	AL-A7	.030	.020	38	TC	Vib-Dmpr.	....	.016C	.016C	9/32"	....
1953	533, 4 Cyl.	AL-A7	.030	.022	34	5B	Cr. Pul.	....	.016C	.016C	....	550
	534, 6 Cyl.	AL-A7	.030	.022	37	TC	Dmpr.	....	.016C	.016C	....	500

AN—Autolite. TC—Top center. B—Before top center. Vib-Dmpr.—Vibration Damper.
AL—Auto-Lite Spark Plug Co. C—Cold.

Dimensions of Valves

Year	Model	Overall Length		Head Diameter		Seat Angle (deg.)		Stem Diameter		Key Type	O.D. of Seat Insert	
		Inlet	Exhaust	Inlet	Exhaust	Inlet	Exhaust	Inlet	Exhaust		Inlet	Exhaust
1951	513, 4 cyl.	5.891	5.891	1.531	1.469	45	45	.373	.372			
	514, 6 cyl.	4.562	4.562	1.375	1.281	45	45	.341	.340			
1952	523, 4 cyl.	5.796	5.8125	1.531	1.468	45	45	.372925	.3715			
	524, 6 cyl.	4.562	4.562	1.375	1.281	45	45	.341125	.340			
1953	533, 4 cyl.	5.796	5.8125	1.531	1.468	45	45	.372925	.372			
	534, 6 cyl.	4.562	4.562	1.375	1.281	45	45	.341125	.340			

Pistons and Piston Pins

Year	Model	PISTONS				PISTON PINS		
		Diameter	Material	Type	No. of Rings	Length	Diameter	How Held
1940	513, 4 cyl.	3.125	Alum.	Ts	3	$2\frac{25}{32}$	.8118	R
	514, 6 cyl.	3.125	Alum.	Ts	3	$2\frac{21}{32}$	.7496	R
1952-53	523, 4 cyl.	3.125	Alum. Alloy		3	2.78125	.8119	R
	524, 6 cyl.	3.125	Alum. Alloy		3	2.65625	.7495	R
1953	533, 534, 6 cyl.	3.125	Alum. Alloy	Ts	3	2.78125	.8119	R

Alum—Aluminum. Ts—"T" slot. R—Locked in rod.

Crankshaft Bearing Journal Sizes

Year	Model	Connecting Rod Journals		Main Bearing Journals				
		Diameter	Length	No. 1 Diameter	No. 2 Diameter	No. 3 Diameter	No. 4 Diameter	No. 5 Diameter
1951	513, 4 cyl.	1.9375-1.938	1.3145	2.3331-2.3341	2.3331-2.3341	2.3331-2.3341		
	514, 6 cyl.	1.875	1.25	2.25	2.25	2.25	2.25	
1952	523, 4 cyl.	1.9375-1.938	1.3145	2.3331-2.3341	2.3331-2.3341	2.3331-2.3341		
	524, 6 cyl.	1.875	1.25	2.25	2.25	2.25	2.25	
1953	533, 4 cyl.	1.9375-1.9385		2.3336-1.640	2.3336-1.7188	2.3336-1.656		
	534, 6 cyl.	1.874-1.875		2.25-1.005	2.25-.972	2.25-.972	2.25-1.316	

Piston Ring Dimensions

Year	Model	Cylinder Bore	TOP RING			SECOND RING			THIRD RING			OIL RING		
			Width	Gap	Depth	Width	Gap	Depth	Width	Gap	Depth	Width	Gap	Depth
1951	513, 4 cylinder	$3\frac{1}{8}$	$\frac{3}{32}$	.010	.135	$\frac{3}{32}$	.010	.135	$\frac{3}{16}$	.010	.140			
	514, 6 cylinder	$3\frac{1}{8}$	$\frac{3}{32}$	.012	.139	$\frac{3}{32}$	.012	.139	$\frac{3}{16}$	.010	.140			
1952	523, 4 Cyl., 524, 6 Cyl.	$3\frac{1}{8}$	.093	.0105	.160	.093	.0105	.160	.18625	.0105	.170			
1953	533, 4 Cyl.	$3\frac{1}{8}$	.093	.0105	.135	.093	.0105	.135	.18625	.0105	.140			
	534, 6 Cyl.	$3\frac{1}{8}$	.093	.0105	.135	.093	.0105	.135	.18625	.0105	.140			

Engine Overhaul Specifications

Year	Model	PISTONS				RING GAP CLEARANCES (Maximum)				PISTON PIN		ROD BEARINGS		
		Removed From	Piston Skirt Clearances (Maximum)											
			Top	Bottom	Limit	Top Ring	Second Ring	Third Ring	Oil Ring	Type	Fit	Oil Clearance	Wear Limit	Side Play
1951	513 (4L-134), 4 Cyl.	A	.003	.003	.005	.013	.013	......	.013	LR	Push	.0005-.0025	.003	.004-.010
	514 (6L-161), 6 Cyl.	A	.0021	.0021	.005	.017	.017	......	.013	LR	Push	.0005-.0025	.003	.002-.008
1952	523, 4 Cyl.	A	.003	.003	.005	.013	.013	......	.013	LR	.0002	.0002-.0025	.003	.004-.010
	524, 6 Cyl.	A	.0021	.0021	.005	.013	.013	......	.013	LR	.0001	.0005-.0025	.003	.002-.008
1953	533, 4 Cyl.	A	.003	.003	.005	.013	.013	......	.013	LR	.0006	.0005-.0025	.003	.004-.010
	534, 6 Cyl.	A	.0021	.0021	.005	.013	.013	......	.013	LR	.0006	.0005-.0025	.003	.002-.008

A—Above. LR—Locked in rod.

Brake Data

Year	Model	Make	Lining Type	R=Riveted B=Bonded	Drum Diameter	Lining			Clearance	
						Length	Width	Thickness	Toe	Heel
1951	513, 514	Ben	M	R	9	....	2	3/16	....	....
1952	523, 4 Cyl., 524, 6 Cyl.	Ben	....	R	9	17½	*	....	.010	.010
1953	533, 4 Cyl., 534, 6 Cyl.	Ben	M	R	9	17½	*	3/16	.010	.010

*—Primary 2, secondary 1¾.
Ben—Bendix. M—Moulded.

Cooling System

CAR AND YEAR	MODEL	Capacity Qts.	Quarts of Methanol Base Anti-Freeze (For Protection to Temperature Shown Below)							Quarts of Ethylene Glycol (For Protection to Temperature Shown Below)							Quarts of Denatured Alcohol—188 Proof (For Protection to Temperature Shown Below)						
			3	4	5	6	7	8	9	3	4	5	6	7	8	9	3	4	5	6	7	8	9
1951-53	513, 523, 533	10¾	0	−18	−40	....	....	....	....	8	−6	−23	−47	....	....	....	10	0	−10	−20	−30	....	....
1951-53	514, 524, 534	9½	8	4	−0	−6	−12	−19	−26	10	−7	−4	−0	−5	−10	−17	10	5	....	0	−5	....	−10

Distributor

Year	Model	Distributor Model Number	Cam Angle (deg.)	Direction of Rotation C=Clockwise CC=Counter Clockwise at Cam End	Breaker Arm Spring Tension	Breaker Point Gap (inches)	Engine R.P.M. when Cent. Advance Starts	Max. Cent. Advance in Engine Deg. at Stated Engine R.P.M.	Vacuum in (inches) of Mercury at which Vacuum Unit Starts	Max. Advance in Engine Deg. at Stated Vacuum	Vacuum Unit Number
1951	513, 4 cyl.	IAT-4008A	38	C	17-21	.018-.022	....	22@3000	3.5	22	....
	514, 6 cyl.	IAT-4007	....	C	17-21	.018-.022	....	24@3000	3.5	14	....
1952	523, 4 cyl.	1110230	38	C	17-21	.020	700	22@3000	3½	22@15	....
	524, 6 cyl.	1110231	38	C	17-21	.020	700	24@3000	3½	14@15	....
1953	533, 4 cyl.	1110230	25-34	C	17-21	.022	600	24@3000	3	22@15	....
	534, 6 cyl.	1110231	31-37	C	17-21	.022	700	26@3000	5	14@15	....

and Wear Limit Table

CRANKSHAFT		VALVES									OPERATING OIL PRESSURE			
Main Bearing Oil Clearance	Shaft End Play	Spring Tension (Maximum)			Guide Clearance	Seat Angle		Valve Timing, Inlet Valve Opens (Deg.)	Camshaft Drive	Gear Marks	Pounds At M.P.H.	Low Limit■	Model	Year
		Inlet	Exhaust	Low Limit		Inlet	Exhaust							
.0009–.003	.002–.008	120@1¾	120@1¾	27/64	.0045	45°	45°	5B	GR	Punch	35@30	28	..... 513 (4L-134), 4 Cyl.	1951
.0009–.003	.002–.008	105@1 21/64	105@1 21/64	1⅝	.0045	45°	45°	5B	GR	Punch	40@30	30	..... 514 (6L-161), 6 Cyl.	
.0009–.0029	.004–.010	120	120	......	.0045	45°	45°	9B	Gear	......	35@30	......	..............523, 4 Cyl.	1952
.0009–.003	.004–.010	105	105	......	.0045	45°	45°	5B	Gear	......	40@30	30	..............524, 6 Cyl.	
.0009–.0029	.004–.008	120@1.750	120@1.750	......	.0045	45°	45°	9B	Gear	......	40@30	......	..............533, 4 Cyl.	1953
.0009–.003	.004–.008	105@1.328	105@1.328	......	.0045	45°	45°	5B	Gear	......	40@30	......	..............534, 6 Cyl.	

GR—Gear B—BTDC.

Generators

Year	Model	Generator Number	Field Current at 6 Volts (amps.)	Maximum Safe Output			Brush Spring Tension (oz.)	Voltage Regulator Number
				Volts	Amperes	R.P.M.		
1951	513, 514..................	GDZ-6001-E	....	....	....	....	....	VRP-6001-A
1952	523, 4 cyl., 524, 6 cyl..................	1102789	....	....	....	....	....	1118731
	Optional..................	GDZ-6001-E	....	....	....	....	....	VRP-6001-A-2
1953	533, 4 cyl..................	1102789	....	7.7	40	....	....	1118731
	534, 6 cyl..................	1102789	....	7.7	40	....	....	1118731

Starters

Year	Model	Unit Model Number	Spring Tension (oz.)	STARTER						Direction of Rotation Viewed from Drive End C=Clockwise CC=Counter-clockwise
				Lock Test			No Load			
				Volts	Amperes	Torque, (lbs. ft.)	Volts	Amperes	R.P.M.	
1951	513, 514, 4 & 6 cyl..................	MZ-4163	42–53	2.0	335	6	5.0	65	4300	C
1952	523, 4 cyl., 524, 6 cyl..................	1107109	24–28	......	......	......	......	......	......	C
	Optional..................	EOD-11159	42–53	......	......	......	......	......	......	C
1953	533, 4 cyl., 534, 6 cyl..................	1107131	24–28	3.25	550	11	5.65	70	5500	C

Voltage Regulators

Year	Model	Regulator Number	Grounded P=Positive N=Negative	Voltage Control: Air Gap Points Closed	Voltage Control: Voltage Setting Hot	Current Control: Air Gap Points Closed	Current Control: Current Set Hot	Cut-Out Relay: Point Gap	Cut-Out Relay: Air Gap	Cut-Out Relay: Closing Volt
1951	513, 514		P	.050	7.35	.050	34–36	.015	.032	6.4–7.0
1952	523, 4 cyl., 524, 6 cyl.	1118731			7.2–7.5		34–36			6.4–7.0
	Optional	VRP-6001-A-2			7.2–7.5		34–36			6.4–7.0
1953	533, 4 cyl., 534, 6 cyl.	1118731			7.0–7.7		34–42			5.9–6.7

Front Wheel Alignment

Year	Model	Caster (deg.)	Camber (deg.)	King Pin Inclination (deg.)	Toe-In (inches)	Turning Radius: Inner	Turning Radius: Outer
1951–53	513, 514, 523, 524, 533, 534	1N to 1P	¼ P to 1P	4½	0 to ¼	17½	20

Fan, Generator Belts and Radiator Hose

Year	Model	Fan Belt: Angle of "V" (deg.)	Fan Belt: Length O.C.	Fan Belt: Width Max.	Generator Belt: Angle of "V" (deg.)	Generator Belt: Length O.C.	Generator Belt: Width Max.	Upper Hose: Type	Upper Hose: Inside Diam.	Upper Hose: Length	Lower Hose: Type	Lower Hose: Inside Diam.	Lower Hose: Length
1951	513												
	514												
1952	523, 4 cyl.	38	44½	11/16				curved	1½		curved	1½	
	524, 6 cyl.	38	37½	11/16				curved	1½		curved	1½	
1953	533, 4 cyl.	38	44½	11/16				curved	1½		curved	1½	
	534, 6 cyl.	38	37½	11/16				curved	1½		curved	1½	

King Pin Specification Chart

Year	Model	King Bolt: Diameter	King Bolt: Length	King Bolt: Bolt Number	Upper Bushing: King Bolt Bushing: Inside Diameter	Upper Bushing: King Bolt Bushing: Outside Diameter	Upper Bushing: King Bolt Bushing: Length	Upper Bushing: Bushing Number	Lower Bushing: King Bolt Bushing: Inside Diameter	Lower Bushing: King Bolt Bushing: Outside Diameter	Lower Bushing: King Bolt Bushing: Length	Lower Bushing: Bushing Number
	513			209923				209924				209924
	514			209923				209924				209924
1952–53												

FRONT SUSPENSION

The independent front suspension used on all Henry "J" cars is of the short and long arm type suspension called the S.L.A. type.

Steering Geometry, Caster, Camber and Toe-In

Before adjusting caster and camber of either side, check and note all angles.

CASTER ADJUSTMENT

Caster angle is controlled by the thickness of shims at the inner end of the upper support arm.

To change the caster angle proceed as follows: Take the weight of the car on a jack at the outer end of the lower support arm, in order to take the weight off the upper support arm. Loosen both of the bolts which hold the upper support arm inner shaft to the frame flange.

To increase caster, add shims at the rear bolt or remove shims at the front bolt or do both.

To decrease caster, add shims at the front bolt or remove them from the rear bolt or both.

If whenever a change is made in the caster angle by removing or replacing shims it is essential that the camber angle be checked.

CAMBER ADJUSTMENT

Camber angle is controlled at the same place caster is controlled with this exception. In order to increase the camber angle it is necessary to remove an equal number of shims from both the front and the rear mounting bolt. To decrease camber an equal number of shims are added at both the front and the rear bolt.

If the camber angle is found to be insufficient and there are no shims left to remove, it will be necessary to bend the knuckle support or replace any or all of the worn parts in the front suspension.

Toe-In

Toe-in should be adjusted after all other steering angles have been corrected.

Loosen the two clamp bolts at each end of the adjusting sleeves. Now turn each sleeve an equal amount until the specified setting is reached and tighten adjusting sleeve clamp bolts.

Suspension Arm Pins

The pins used at the outer end of both the upper and lower suspension arms are simply threaded bolts which are fed into the arm from the back towards the front.

No bushings are used in the knuckle support since it is threaded to take the upper and lower pin.

To remove either of the pins simply take the weight of the car on the lower suspension arm and remove the nut which holds the pin to the suspension arm.

Back out the pin.

Special neoprene oil seals are used at both ends of the pin inside the yoke of the suspension arms.

Front Coil Spring Removal

Raise front wheel off the floor and support the weight of the car on a stand jack at the frame back of the front suspension.

Disconnect sway stabilizer bar.

Disconnect lower end of shock absorber.

Insert jack under the lower control arm inner pivot shaft. With the jack pressed firmly against the inner shaft, remove the four bolts which hold the inner shaft to the frame and slowly lower the control arm, being certain not to change the position of the inner pivot shaft where it originally seated in the cradle of the jack. When lowered enough to release the spring pressure, take out the spring.

After the new spring has been installed, raise the control arm up and guide the inner pivot shaft in place with a suitable drift pin and replace bolts.

This procedure is found to be the easiest way of replacing a coil spring on the Henry "J."

When it is necessary to replace a front coil spring, it is a good idea to check and determine if any other front suspension parts require replacement, since it would be easier to detach the spring at a defective pin or bushing if a new pin or bushing is to be installed.

King Pin Replacement

Remove the wheel hub and drum assembly, disconnect brake backing plate. With a suitable piece of wire, hook the backing plate to the frame so there will be no strain on the hydraulic brake hose.

Disconnect the two bolts which hold the steering arm up to the knuckle. Remove the top welsh plug. Drive the king pin lock pin forward, and drive king pin down and out, thus forcing the lower welsh plug out. Press or drive the old bushings out of the knuckle and press in new ones, being sure the grease holes line up.

Special portable presses are available to remove frozen king pins.

The king pin bushings require reaming or honing to secure good fit on the king pin.

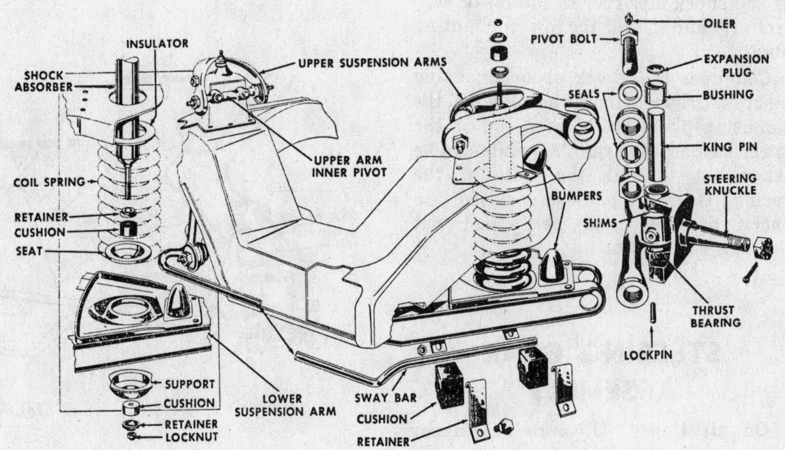

Front suspension—exploded view

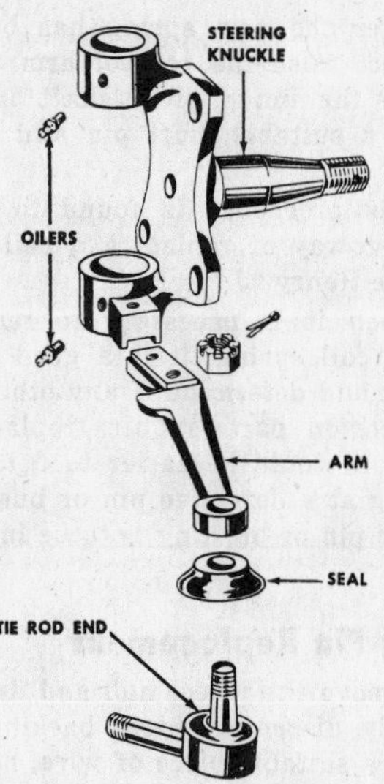

Steering knuckle arm installation

Shock Absorber Replacement

The shock absorber is replaced without particular difficulties since the upper shock studs are excessable through the engine compartment. The shock absorber is mounted in the center of the coil spring, and it is held by a removable bracket under the lower control arm.

To detach the shock absorber, jack the car up so that the suspension arm is as low as it can go.

Detach the shock absorber at the top through the engine compartment. Remove the nut which holds the lower end of the shock absorber to the lower control arm and lift off the lower mounting plate.

Compress the shock absorber, using a screw driver or bar, and slide off the mounting plate which is on top of the lower suspension arm. This plate can be taken out through the coils of the spring. Once the plate is removed, the shock absorber can be pulled out through the bottom.

STEERING GEAR ASSEMBLY

On all Henry "J" cars a Gemmer worm and roller type steering gear is used.

Steering Column Alignment

Before adjustment of the steering gear is attempted the steering gear mounting must be checked to make sure that there is no binding in the column due to misalignment.

Loosen the steering gear to frame side rail bolts to permit the steering gear to move in relation to the frame. Then securely tighten the mounting bolts.

Steering Gear Worm Bearing Adjustment

Never check or make this adjustment until after the steering column is aligned properly as explained in the foregoing paragraph.

Disconnect the tie-rod from the steering pitman arm and turn the steering wheel all the way to the right or left, turn the wheel back again about ⅛ of a turn, at which position there is full back lash between the worm and roller tooth to permit free turning of the worm.

Attach a spring scale to the outer end of the steering wheel spoke and pulling at a 90 degree angle to the spoke, check the force required to turn the wheel. The pull should be from ¼ to ¾ pounds.

Worm bearings may be adjusted by removing the four bolts on the end cover, draining the lubricant from the housing and adding or removing shims from between the cover and the housing as is necessary to adjust properly. Add shims to decrease pull or remove shims to increase pull.

Steering Gear Shaft and Roller Adjustment

This adjustment is for proper mesh of the roller to eliminate lost motion or play to the steering gear in the mid position of its travel.

Caution: Never check or make this adjustment until after the steering column alignment and worm bearing adjustment has been properly made.

With the tie rod still disconnected from the pitman arm, turn the steering wheel all the way from right to the left extreme position, counting the number of turns. Turn the wheel back exactly half way so that the steering gear itself will be midway of its travel.

Remove the nut which covers the end of the adjusting screw.

Detach the lock plate from the adjusting screw.

Tighten the adjusting screw with a screw driver turning it clockwise, then back it off not more than ⅛ of a turn and install the lock plate.

This adjustment takes care of the roller tooth with the worm. No adjustment is provided for end play in the cross shaft, which should not develop until after long service.

Steering Wheel Removal

Carefully pry the horn button out of the horn button assembly.

This contact plate must be moved ⅓ of a turn to the left to be removed. Detach horn wire from connector at bottom of the steering gear. Pull the wire out through the upper end of the steering column.

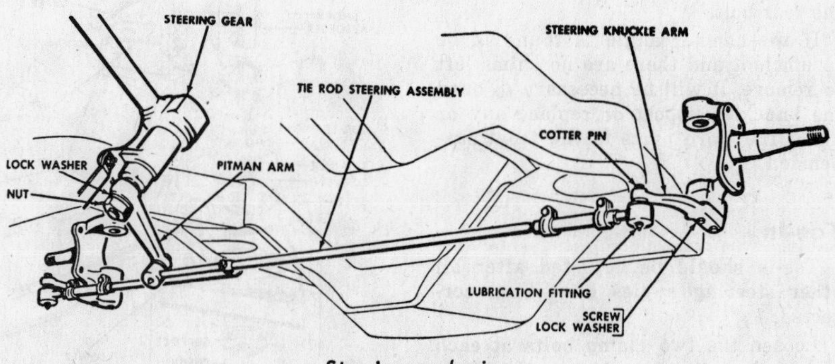

Steering mechanism

Detach button bezel or ring from steering wheel and remove rubber cushion.

Remove the steering wheel with special puller.

Reverse the procedure to reassemble.

BRAKES

All Henry "J" models are equipped with Bendix hydraulic self centering shoes having fixed, non-adjustable anchor blocks.

Brake Adjustment

To expand the primary brake shoe, turn the adjusting cams toward the front of the car. Now back cam off until wheels are just free. Follow the same procedure for the secondary shoe, only

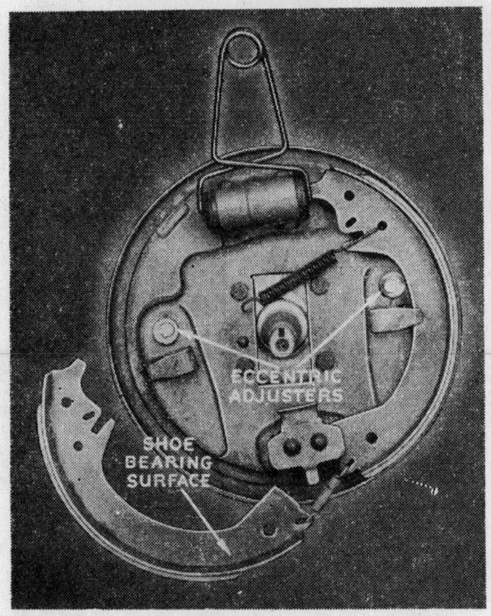

Adjusting point

turn the adjusting cam toward the rear of the car. Repeat this procedure at all four wheels. This is the only lining to drum adjustment possible on this type brake. The shoe is full floating at the "anchor" end.

Brake Pedal Clearance

Adjust the master cylinder push rod so that there is ¼ in. free play from the under side of the floor pan and the rubber bumper on the brake pedal before the master cylinder push rod contacts the piston.

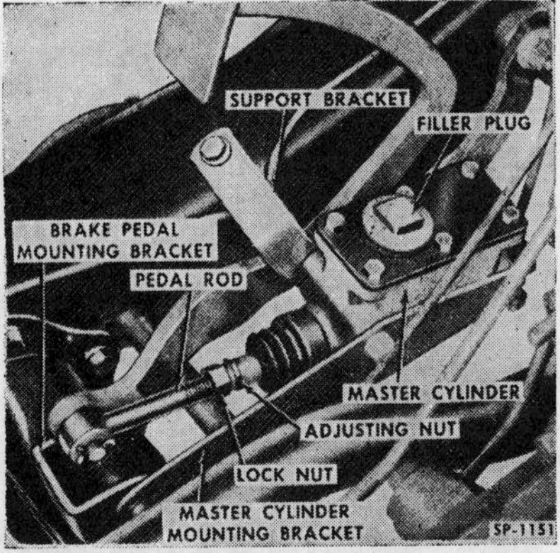

Master cylinder and brake pedal mounting

Hand Brake Adjustment

Fully release the brake handle. Adjust the nut on the front cable until 4⅝ to 4¾ inches is reached between the front cable and the rear cable rod. Pull the brake lever 3 clicks on the ratchet, then tighten the rear cable until there is a slight drag when the rear wheels are turned by hand. Tighten rear cable adjusting nuts.

Master Cylinder

The master cylinder is refilled from the engine compartment and located directly forward of the brake pedal. When inspecting the master cylinder, thoroughly clean out the cylinder and holding it up to the light, let the light shine along the inside of the cylinder and examine it with extreme care for scratches or roughness. If this condition is found it will be necessary to hone the cylinder to secure a smooth surface.

Bleeding Brakes

See section "General Service and Trouble Shooting."

COOLING SYSTEM

Thermostat

The thermostat which regulates the flow of coolant within the system is mounted in the water outlet elbow at the top of cylinder head. A 151 degree theromstat is standard equipment on all Henry "J" cars.

Disconnect top water hose, remove bolts attaching water outlet to cylinder head, lift the water outlet and take out the thermostat retaining ring and remove the thermostat.

Water Pump Removal

While the water pump used on the six cylinder engine is different than that used on a four cylinder, the service is practically the same. It may be removed readily without removing the radiator core.

Water Pump Overhaul

Remove the pump from the car taking out the fan attaching screws.

Remove the bearing lock ring and press the shift and bearing out of the impeller towards front end of pump.

Remove the impeller seal and thrust washer out the rear of pump housing. If the seal or seal washer or sealing device should show any indications of roughness or wear they should be replaced.

Radiator Core Removal

Drain cooling system. Detach the upper and lower radiator hoses. Remove the six radiator attaching bolts. Important: When removing the radiator on a four cylinder engine the radiator shroud should be detached and moved back.

Manifold

The intake and exhaust manifold is mounted on the left side of the engine block, and both exhaust and intake manifold are incorporated as one unit before they are assembled to the cylinder block.

Heat Riser Valve

A heat riser valve which is on part of the manifold, is used to circulate hot exhaust gases around the intake manifold heat chamber during warm up. The only service is to see that the valve opens freely and that the thermostat spring is undamaged.

Muffler

A short oval shaped muffler of the straight through type is used on all models, and is mounted on the left side of the frame.

HENRY "J" 1951 thru 1953

Fuel System

A single diaphragm type fuel pump is used, mounted on the left front section of the engine block. It can be removed readily by detaching the gas lines and the two mounting bolts.

Carburetor

A single throat downdraft carburetor is used on all models. The carburetors on the four and six cylinder engines are identical in appearance, but they have different size jets and metering rods. Therefore they are not interchangeable. See the carburetor section for service.

Section thru 6-cylinder engine

ENGINE ASSEMBLY

The engines used in all Henry "J" models are of the "L" head type. Both engines are equipped with slip in type connecting rod and main bearings.

Engine Removal

Disconnect battery, generator and distributor wires. Detach oil line, fuel lines and engine attaching nuts. Disconnect engine at bell housing and remove engine. While not strictly necessary, it is always a good idea to remove the radiator core as a safety precaution.

Engine Interchangeability

Current production engines are available for all models. These engines are available as a complete assembly including clutch and clutch housing or as a partial engine which is without manifold and electrical accessories and clutch.

Timing Case Cover Removal

Loosen generator to take off fan belt.

Remove radiator (on four cylinder engine remove radiator shroud). Remove vibration damper.

Take out cap screws attaching cover and remove cover. **Note:** The front oil pan bolts pass into the timing case cover and must be removed.

Caution: Sometimes the oil pan gasket is damaged when removing the timing case cover. If this happens, the only safe thing to do is remove the oil pan and install a new gasket.

Oil Pan Removal

To remove the oil pan, first drain the water from the radiator and remove the upper and lower radiator hose.

Remove the engine front mounting bolts and loosen the back mounting bolts. Disconnect the tie rod from the pitman arm and raise the engine a sufficient amount (about three inches) to clear the oil pan from the front cross-member.

On some models it will be necessary to remove the right-hand front engine support bracket.

ENGINE INTERNAL

Piston and Connecting Rod Assemblies

All pistons are aluminum cam ground and of the T slot type. Pistons are installed on a connecting rod so that the T slot in the piston is opposite the oil spurt holes in the rod. A piston is installed in the cylinder bore, so that the T slot in the piston faces the camshaft. (Valve side). Connecting rods are of the slip in type and held in place by a tang at the parting line.

Feather or taper type shims may be used between the bearing shell and the cup to secure a slight adjustment.

Main Bearings

Steel backed babbit lined slip in type main bearings are used on all models. The fit of the main bearings may be checked either by the plastic gage method or by shim stock method.

Plastic gage stock is supplied with complete instructions for its use.

On 4-cylinder models the upper half of the main bearings are doweled into the cylinder block, therefore it is necessary to take out the crankshaft in order to replace the upper half of the main bearings on any 4-cylinder Henry J.

The 6-cylinder models, however, do not use a dowel and it is possible to replace the upper half of the main bearing by rotating it out of place, and rotating a new one into place using the little special tool made for this purpose or a flattened cotter pin.

The rear main bearing cap is usually very tight in the block due to the packings which are used on the rear main bearing.

A good way to remove it is to back the bolts off until there is only one or two threads holding the bolt in the main bearing cap and then screw one of the oil pan bolts into the thread of the hole in the main bearing cap and, using the rear main bearing bolt as a fulcrum, pry under the head of the oil pan bolt until the rear main bearing cap comes down.

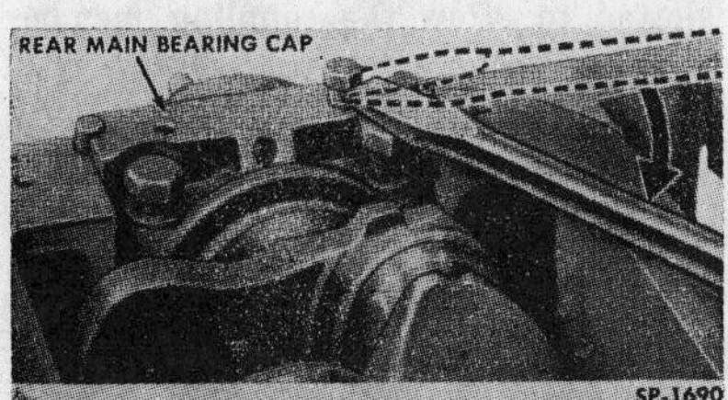

Removing rear main bearing cap

Rear Main Bearing Oil Seal

A wick type packing is used as the rear main bearing oil seal on all models.

This seal is used to prevent oil escaping from the crankshaft on to the clutch and flywheel. To replace the lower half of this oil seal remove the rear main bearing cap, and the old oil seal packing. Install the new oil seal in the main bearing cap so that the packing protrudes slightly above the cap. Bolt the cap in place and torque it to approximately 60 foot pounds and then immediately take it down again. If the protruding part of the packing has been "riveted over" cut off the riveted portion with a razor blade and again bolt the cap into place.

Repeat this operation until the main bearing cap sets firmly in the block, without riveting over the new portion of the oil seal.

Oil Pump

An external rotary type oil pump located on the left side of the engine block is used on all models. A pressure relief valve is incorporated in the pump body and it is adjustable by installing or removing shims. Removing shims decrease pressure while adding shims will increase pressure.

If properly adjusted the relief valve should open at approximately 30 to 35 pounds pressure at 30 to 40 M.P.H.

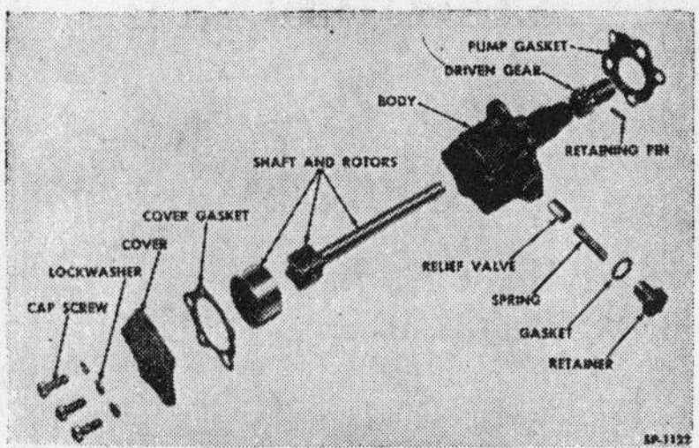

Oil pump assembly

The oil pump may be removed by taking out the bolts which hold it to the side of the crank case.

The gear which drives the oil pump and distributor is mounted on the oil pump and if for any reason the pump is removed it will be necessary to retime the ignition after the pump has been reinstalled.

VALVE SYSTEM

All Henry "J" models are equipped with the in-line "L" head variety and fitted with mushroom type lifters. Which means that the camshaft must be removed in order to take out any of the lifters. The length of the four cylinder lifters are longer than those used in six cylinder engines.

Operating tappet clearance should be .014 inch engine cold.

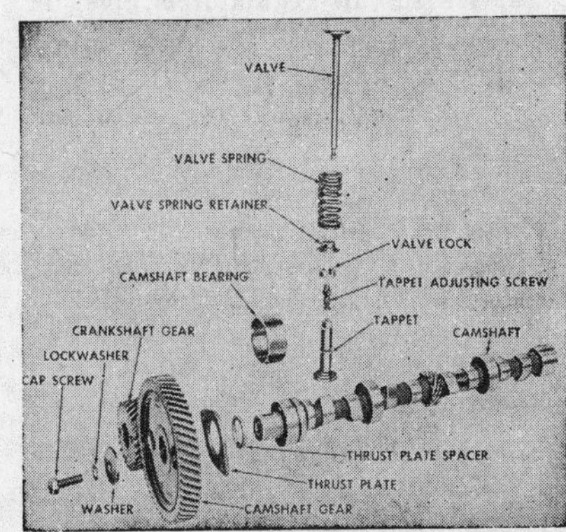

Valve mechanism, exploded view

Valve Guide Renewal

The valve guide in the four cylinder engine should be positioned so that exhaust is 1 inch, inlet 1 5/16 in. below the top face of the cylinder block.

Both the intake and exhaust guides on the six cylinder should be 7/8 inch below the upper edge of the valve seat.

All four and six cylinder engines have a 45 degree valve seat angle.

The valve guides may be driven out through the bottom and the new ones installed by driving in from the top.

After the new guide has been installed, check with a new valve to make sure that there is no binding since it sometimes happens that the guide rivets over after being driven into place causing the valve to bind in the new guide. When this happens it will be necessary to ream the guide to insure a good fit on the new valve.

Valve Springs

Any valve operation other than a valve adjustment it would be wise to check the valve spring tension. All valve springs must be removed from the engine to check spring tension.

The intake and exhaust valve springs on the four cylinder engine should compress 1¾ inch under 115 to 120 foot pound pressure. While the spring tension on all six cylinder engines is 1 21/64 inch under 100 to 105 foot pound pressure.

Oversize Valve Lifters

Lifter assemblies are available in .001, .002 and .005 inch oversize. The proper way to read for oversize lifters is to remove the camshaft and lifters, then remove the valve guides and ream the lifter bores through the valve ports. A stub reamer is required for this job.

CYLINDER HEAD NUT TIGHTENING SEQUENCE

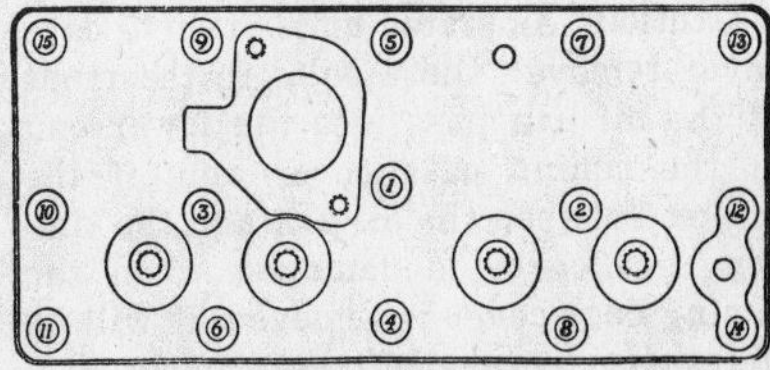

4 cylinder engine

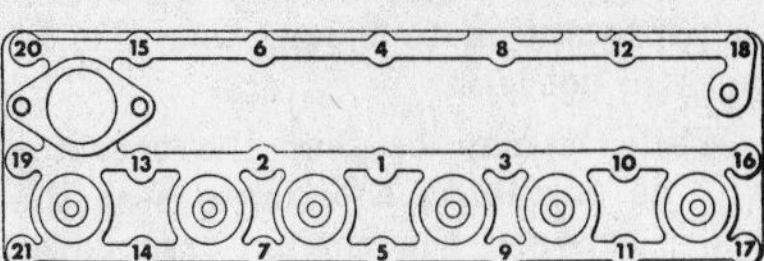

6 cylinder engine

Valve Timing Procedure

On all models the camshaft drive is by means of gears. The arrangement is such that unless the gears become badly worn or seriously damaged it is unlikely that the valve time will be affected.

If it becomes necessary to retime the valves or replace either the camshaft or crankshaft gear proceed as follows:

Remove the radiator core, vibration damper and timing case cover and unbolt the camshaft gear. Pull the crank gear off the shaft.

Press the new crankshaft gear on to the shaft, being careful to align the key and keyway perfectly since the gear is a tight fit on the shaft and it is very difficult to correct it for misalignment after the gear is started.

Now turn the crank gear until the marked tooth on the gear is pointed directly toward the center of the camshaft.

Tentatively mesh the camshaft gear with the crankshaft gear so that the two marks on the cam gear straddle the one mark on the crank gear.

Rotate the cam shaft (not the gear) so that the bolt holes line up properly and install the bolts and locking plate.

Turn the crankshaft through two full revolutions until the gear again assumes the checking position, with the single mark on the crankshaft between the two marks on the camshaft gear.

Set up in this manner, the valves are correctly timed regardless of which piston is at the top dead center.

It will be necessary to retime the ignition.

Caution: As stated under timing case cover removal, the 4 bolts in the front of the oil pan pass into the lower end of the timing case cover and, if the gasket between the oil pan and the timing case cover is damaged when the timing case cover is removed, it will be necessary to take off the oil pan and, with the oil pan off, put the timing case cover back on and then replace the oil pan using a new gasket. This is a necessary precaution to insure that the oil pan will not leak.

While it may be that the operator will be fortunate enough to seal the space between the timing case cover and the oil pan, it is unlikely that he will be all that lucky.

ELECTRICAL

Generator

A six volt, two brush, shunt wound generator is used on all models. On the generator having external control, if difficulty is experienced, first ground the field terminal at the generator and, if this will correct the difficulty then the regulator is at fault. If grounding the field terminal does not alleviate the trouble, then the generator must be removed from the car and subjected to the bench tests shown in the "General Service Section" of this Manual. See index.

Voltage Regulator

All Henry "J" models are equipped with a voltage and current regulator. When a new voltage regulator is installed on the car the generator should be polarized by temporarily placing a jumper between the battery and generator terminal on the regulator. In other words jump some of the battery current across the regulator so that the generator will be properly polarized before starting the car. This should also be done at the time the generator is given a major service. It is not necessary to hold the jumper on longer than a half second.

Service on this regulator is given in the "General Service Section" of this Manual. See index.

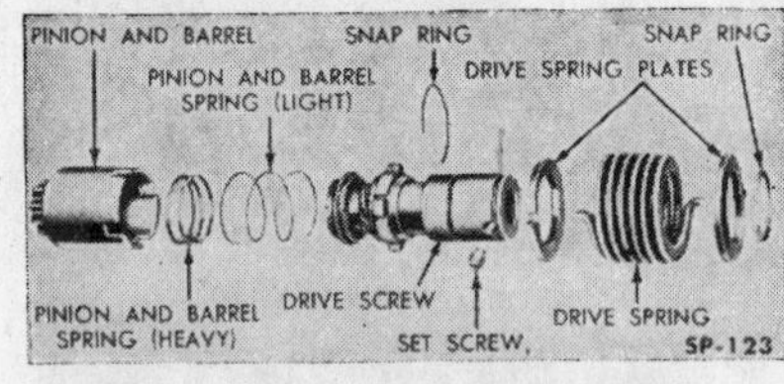

Starter bendix drive

Starting System

A four pole, four brush, series wound starting motor with conventional Bendix pinion shift is used on all models.

If the starting motor does not crank engine properly, see if the battery is fully charged and all electrical connections cleaned and securely tightened.

The mechanical check on the condition of the starter is performed in the same manner as that of the generator, as explained in the beginning of this section. See index.

Distributor

The distributor is mounted on the right side of the engine block, and is driven by the oil pump shaft which is slotted to allow the coupling member of the distributor shaft to enter. (The oil pump and distributor drive gear are mounted on the oil pump.)

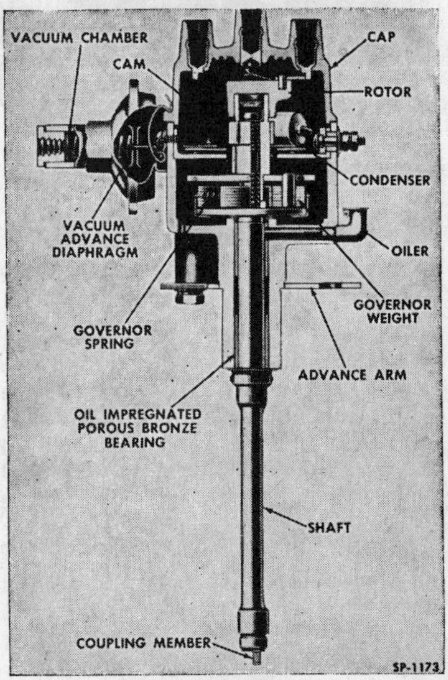

Distributor sectional view

When removing the distributor, for service mark the position of the rotor so it may be reinstalled in original position.

When installing spark plug wires on a four cylinder engine advance in a clockwise direction.

Starting with No. 1, the order is 1, 3, 4, 2. The firing order on the six cylinder engine is 1, 5, 3, 6, 2, 4, also clockwise rotation.

It is always a good idea to install spark plug wires one at a time so that no difficulty will be experienced in checking which wire goes to which terminal of the distributor cap.

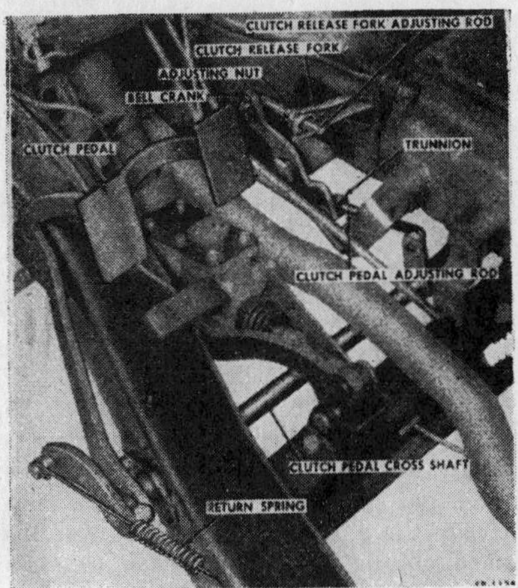

Clutch linkage

CLUTCH ASSEMBLY

Clutch Linkage Adjustment

Disconnect the pedal return spring and check the clearance between the rounded forward end of the release fork adjusting rod and the clutch housing when the release bearing is just contacting the levers.

This clearance should be ⅝ inch. If it is less than ½ inch adjust the release fork rod length to provide ⅝ inch clearance. Rod is more accessible by moving the bell crank from its pivot with the rods still attached.

Adjust the length of the pedal adjusting rod to obtain proper free travel of 1 inch measured at the pedal pad.

Clutch Removal

Remove transmission assembly (see transmission removal).

Disconnect the clutch bell housing and disconnect the clutch.

TRANSMISSION

Transmission Removal

Disconnect the drive shaft at the front universal joint. Support the rear of the engine and disconnect the rear mount back of the transmission and disconnect the cross member back of the transmission.

Remove the bolts which hold the transmission to the bell housing. Disconnect all shift levers and wiring mechanism, and lower the transmission downward and out of the car.

Overdrive unit mounted

Transmission with Overdrive—Removal

The overdrive transmission is removed in exactly the same manner as the standard transmission with the exception.

Caution: The overdrive transmission is considerably heavier and care should be exercised so that the operator is not injured when removing unit.

Overdrive Service

See section on "Overdrive," refer to index.

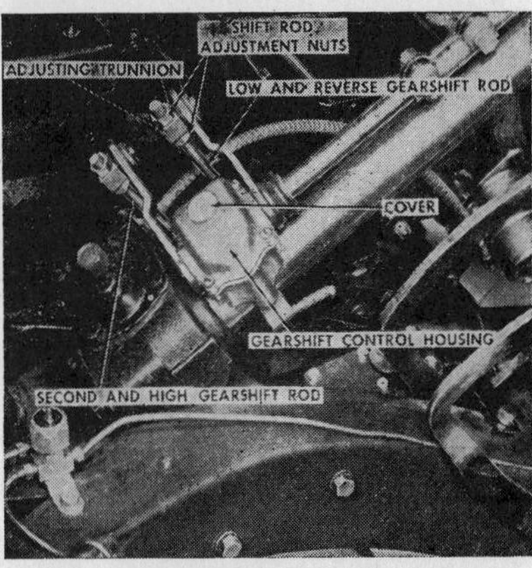

Shift mechanism

Shift Linkage Adjustment

With the shift lever below the steering wheel in neutral position, loosen the trunnion lock nut at each lever on the steering column.

Remove grease cap at top of shift lever housing and install special gage in the housing. Run the lock nuts up against the pivots and tighten, being careful not to spring the levers. Remove the gage and install grease cap.

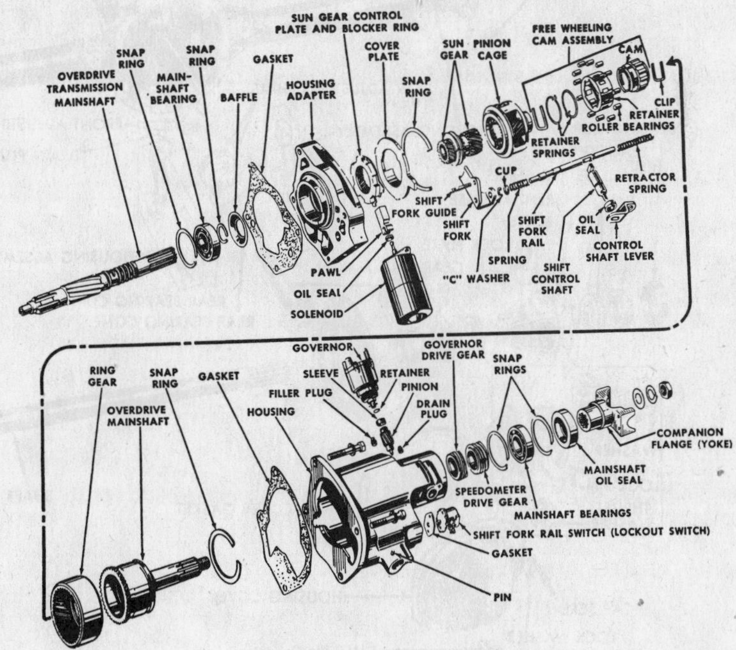

Exploded of overdrive unit

REAR AXLE

Axle Shaft End-Play

Tap each axle shaft with a rubber mallet to be sure they are fully seated. Then mount a dial indicator on the left hand brake shoe support to determine the amount of axle shaft end play. Move the left axle shaft in and out and note the dial indicator reading to determine the amount of end play. Add or remove shims on the left hand axle shaft only to obtain an end play of .001 to .005 inch.

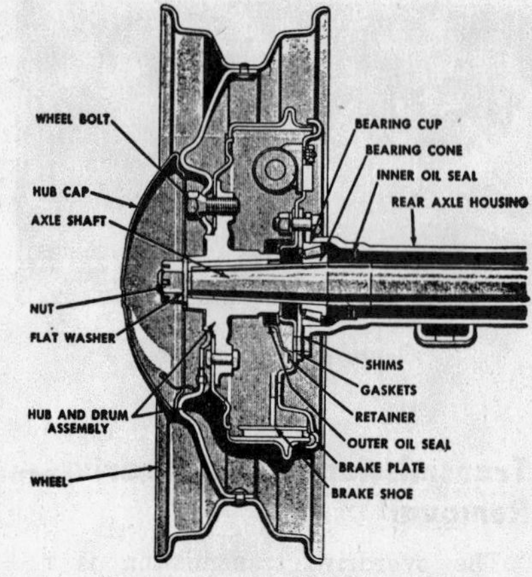

Sectional view of rear wheel

Rear Axle Maintenance

The pinion is adjustable endwise to provide position relative to the differential drive gears by the use of shims between the rear bearing cup and the axle housing. End play of the bearings is established by the use of shims at the rear of pinion front bearing. An oil seal at the outer end of the pinion prevents loss of lubricant.

These shims are located back of the axle bearing adjusting flange.

It will be necessary to remove the rear wheel and the rear axle grease retainer housing to add or remove shims.

Proper setting of the ring gears relative to the pinion is controlled by shims used on the differential case between the case and the bearing.

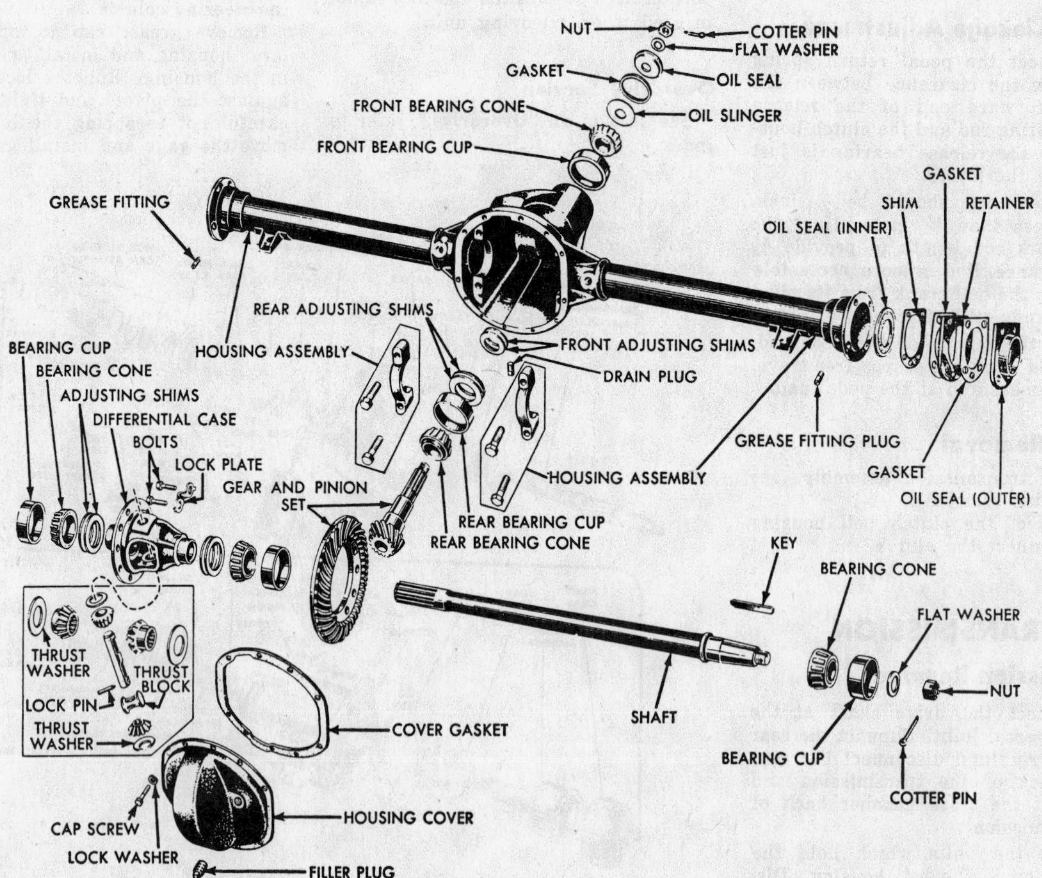

Rear axle assembly—exploded view

Refer to Frazer and Kaiser (see index) for servicing the differential assembly.

Rear Spring

The short end of the rear spring is always mounted toward the front of the car. Short end 22 inches long, and long end 27 inches long.

Dash Instruments

1951 AND 1952 MODELS

On the above models any of the instruments can be removed separately from back of the dash. Each instrument is held with nuts and it may be removed without disturbing any other instrument.

1953 MODELS

To remove any instrument on the 1953 models it is necessary to first remove and disassemble the cluster in order to take out the speedometer. Other instruments are removed the same as previous models.

As a safety measure always disconnect the battery before working on any of the dash instruments.

Windshield Wipers

A single vacuum operated windshield wiper motor is used under the instrument panel and operates both wiper blades by means of connecting arms.

To remove the windshield wiper motor, first, from underneath the instrument panel, remove the retainers and springs holding the connecting arms on the wiper motor. Remove the screws which attach the wiper motor to the mounting bracket and lower the motor to disconnect the control cable and vacuum tube.

To remove the control cable, pull the knob off, remove the wiper control nut and remove the control assembly from underneath the instrument panel.

The wiper arm pivot and connecting arm assemblies are taken out from underneath the instrument panel.

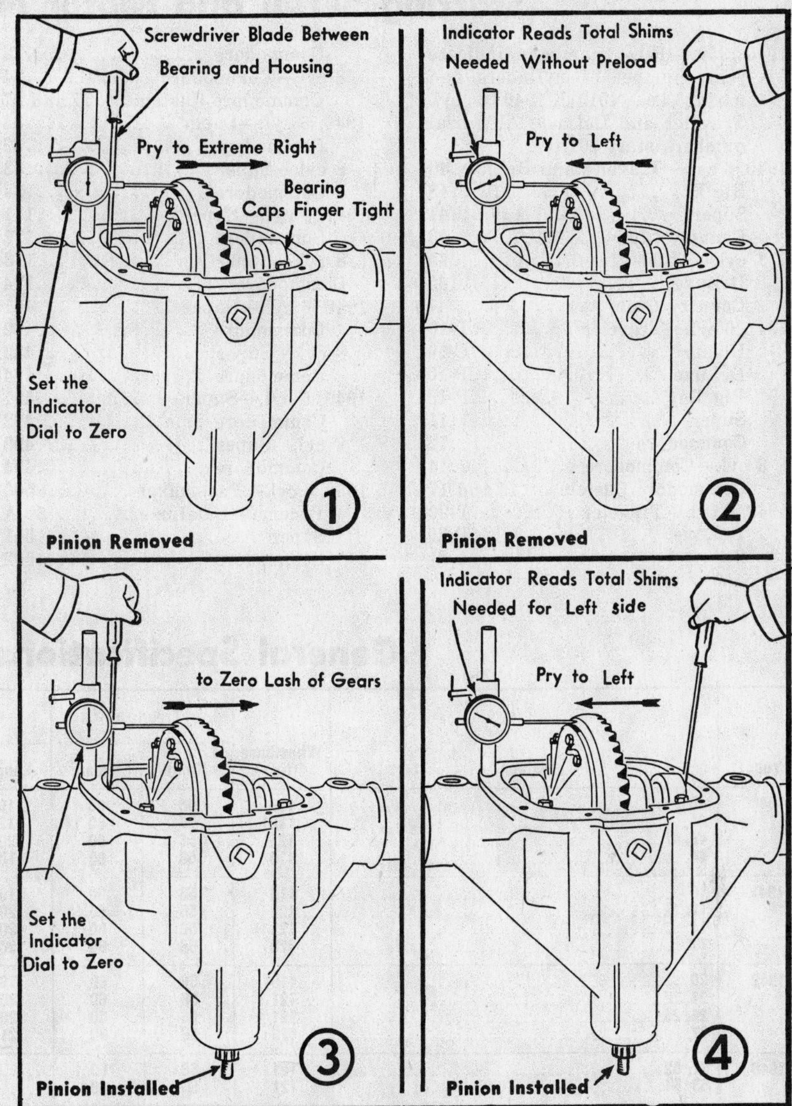

Method of establishing exact amount of shims required on differential

HUDSON SPECIFICATIONS

Starting Serial and Motor Numbers

1940-1950 — First numbers indicate year, number of cylinders and model, i.e., 40101, 1940 6 cyl. Traveler and DeLuxe. All serial numbers start 101.

1940, 6 cyl.—Traveler and DeLuxe . 40
Big Boy . . . 48
Super . . . 41
Country Club . . . 43
8 cyl.—Eight . . . 44
DeLuxe . . . 45
Country Club . . . 47
1941, 6 cyl.—Traveler . . . T-10
Utility . . . C-10
DeLuxe . . . P-10
Big Boy . . . P-18
Super . . . 11
Commodore . . . 12
8 cyl.—Commodore . . . 14
Commodore Custom . . . 15 and 17
1942, 6 cyl.—Traveler . . . T-20
DeLuxe . . . P-20
Super . . . 21
Commodore . . . 22
8 cyl.—Commodore . . . 24
Commodore Custom . . . 25 and 27
1946, 6 cyl.—Super . . . 31
Commodore . . . 32
8 cyl.—Super . . . 33
Commodore . . . 34
1947, 6 cyl.—Super . . . 171
Commodore . . . 172
8 cyl.—Super . . . 173
Commodore . . . 174
1948, 6 cyl.—Super . . . 481
Commodore . . . 482
8 cyl.—Super . . . 483
Commodore . . . 484
1949, 6 cyl.—Super . . . 491
Commodore . . . 492
8 cyl.—Super . . . 493
Commodore . . . 494
1950, 6 cyl.—Pacemaker . . . 500
Pacemaker DeLuxe . . . 50-A
Super . . . 501
Commodore . . . 502
8 cyl.—Super . . . 503
Commodore . . . 504
1951 . . . 1001
1952 . . . 132916
1953—4C, 5C, 7C . . . 132916
1953—Jet . . . 1C

Location

1940-1953—Stamped on boss near top left side of cylinder block, on top of block between #1 and #2 exhaust manifold flanges and on right front door hinge post. Pacemaker on top of right side frame rail.

Starting Motor Numbers

1940-1953—Same as Serial numbers.

Location

1940-1953—Same place as Serial number.

General Specifications

Year	Model	Wheelbase (in.)	Tread (in.)		Overall Dimensions (in.)			Shipping Weight* (lb.)	Tire Size (in.)
			Front	Rear	Length†	Width	Height■		
1940	40	113	56	60	190	....	....	2940	5.50-16(d)
	41	118	56	60	196	....	....	3050	6.00-16
	43, 47	125	56	60	202	....	....	3050	6.25-16
	44	118	56	60	196	....	....	....	6.00-16
1941	10	116	56	60	197	....	....	2950(c)	6.00-16(h)
	11, 12	121	56	60	202	....	....	3050(e)	6.00-16(f)
	14	121	56	60	202	....	....	3260	6.25-16
	17	128	56	60	209	....	....	3400	6.50-16
1942	20	116	56	60	198△	....	....	2940	5.50-16(m)
	21, 22	121	56	60	207	....	....	3080	6.00-16(m)
	24, 25	121	56	60	207	....	....	3280	6.25-16(m)
	27	128	56	60	214	....	....	3395	6.50-15
1946	51, 52	121	56	60	....	....	....	....	6.00-16
	53, 54	121	56	60	....	....	....	....	6.00-16(p)
1947	171, 172	121	56	60	207	....	....	3110	6.00-16
	173, 174	121	56	60	207	....	....	3260	6.00-16
1948	481, 482	124	59	56	208	77	60	....	7.10-15
	483, 484	123	59	56	208	77	60	....	7.10-15
1949	491, 492, 493, 494	124	59	56	208	77	60	3500	7.10-15
1950-51	500, 4A	120	59	56	202	77	60	3510	7.10-15
	501, 502, 5A, 6A	124	59	56	208	77	60	3590	7.10-15
	503, 504, 7A, 8A	124	59	56	208	77	60	3605	7.10-15
1952	4B, 5B, 6 cyl.	120	59	58	202	146	60	....	7.10-15
	6B, 7B, 8B, 8 cyl.	124	55	56	208	146	60	....	7.10-15
1953	4C	120	59	56	201	77	77	....	7.10-15
	5C	120	59	56	202	77	77	....	7.10-15
	7C	124	59	56	208	77	77	....	7.10-15

(d) Deluxe-6.00-16. (c) Traveler-2900. (h) Traveler-5.50-16. (e) Model 12-3100. (f) Model 12-6.25-16. △ Deluxe 6-201.
(m) Deluxe 6-6.00-16; Commodore 6-6.25-16; 25-6.50-16. (p) Model 54-6.50-15.
*—Cheapest 5 pass. 4 door sedan. ■—Road to roof, no load. †—Including bumper and bumper guards.

General Engine Specifications

Year	Model	Number of Cylinders Bore and Stroke	Piston Displacement, Cubic Inches	Compression Ratio (To–1)	Taxable (A.M.A.) Hp.	DEVELOPED HORSE POWER Bare Engine	With Accessories	Maximum Torque Ft. Lbs.
1940	40	6–3 x 4⅛	175.0	7.00	21.6	92 @ 4000	....	138 @ 1400
	41, 43	6–3 x 5	212.0	6.50	21.6	102 @ 4000	....	168 @ 1200
	44, 47	8–3 x 4½	254.0	6.50	28.8	128 @ 4200	....	198 @ 1600
1941	10T 10P	6–3 x 4⅛	175.0	7.25	21.6	92 @ 4000	....	138 @ 1400
	11, 12	6–3 x 5	212.0	6.50	21.6	102 @ 4000	....	168 @ 1200
	14, 15, 17	8–3 x 4½	254.0	6.50	28.8	128 @ 4200	....	198 @ 1600
1942	20T, 20P	6–3 x 4⅛	175.0	7.25	21.6	92 @ 4000	....	138 @ 1400
	21, 22	6–3 x 5	212.0	6.50	21.6	102 @ 4000	....	168 @ 1200
	24, 25, 27	8–3 x 4½	254.0	6.50	28.8	128 @ 4200	....	198 @ 1600
1946	51, 51P	6–3 x 5	212.0	6.50	21.6	102 @ 4000	....	168 @ 1200
	53, 54	8–3 x 4½	254.0	6.50	28.8	128 @ 4200	....	193 @ 1600
1947	171, 172	6–3 x 5	212.0	6.50	21.6	102 @ 4000	....	168 @ 1200
	173 174	8–3 x 4½	254.0	6.50	28.8	128 @ 4200	....	198 @ 1600
1948	481, 482	6–3 9/16 x 4⅜	262.0	6.50	30.4	121 @ 4000	....	200 @ 1600
	483. 484	8–3 x 4½	254.0	6.50	28.8	128 @ 4200	....	198 @ 1600
1949	491, 492	6–3 9/16 x 4⅜	262.0	6.50	30.4	121 @ 4000	....	200 @ 1600
	493, 494	8–3 x 4½	254.0	6.50	28.8	128 @ 4200	....	198 @ 1600
1950	500	6–3 9/16 x 3⅞	232.0	6.70	30.4	112 @ 4000	....	175 @ 1600
	501, 502	6–3 9/16 x 4⅜	262.0	6.70	30.4	123 @ 4000	....	200 @ 1600
	503, 504	8–3 x 4½	254.0	6.70	28.8	128 @ 4200	....	198 @ 1600
1951	4A Pacemaker	6–3 9/16 x 3⅞	232.0	6.70	30.4	112 @ 4000	....	175 @ 1600
	5A Super, 6A Commodore	6–3 9/16 x 4⅜	262.0	6.70	30.4	123 @ 4000	....	200 @ 1600
	7A Hornet	6–3 13/16 x 4.50	308.0	7.20	34.8	145 @ 3800	....	257 @ 1800
	8A Commodore	8–3 x 4.50	254.0	6.70	28.8	128 @ 4200	....	198 @ 1600
1952	4B, Pacemaker, 6 Cyl.	6–3 9/16 x 3⅞	232.0	6.70	30.45	112 @ 4000	....	175 @ 1600
	5B, Wasp, 6B, Commodore	6–3 9/16 x 4⅜	262.0	6.70	30.45	127 @ 4000	....	200 @ 1600
	7B, Hornet, 6 Cyl.	6–3 13/16 x 4½	308.0	7.20	34.88	145 @ 3800	....	257 @ 1800
	8B, Commodore, 8 Cyl.	8–3 x 4½	254.0	6.70	28.80	128 @ 1200	....	198 @ 1600
1953	4C	6–3 9/16 x 3⅞	232.0	6.7	30.45	112 @ 4000	....	175 @ 1600
	5C	6–3 9/16 x 3⅜	262.0	6.7	30.45	127 @ 4000	....	200 @ 1600
	7C	6–3 13/16 x 4½	308.0	7.2	34.88	145 @ 3800	....	257 @ 1008

Engine Tune-Up Specifications

Year	Model	SPARK PLUGS Type	Gap	DISTRIBUTOR Point Gap	Cam Dwell (Deg.)	Ignition Timing (Deg.)	Ignition Timing Mark and Location	Compression Pressure at R.P.M.	OPERATING TAPPET CLEARANCE Inlet	Exhaust	Carburetor Fuel Float Height	Minimum Engine Idle Speed at R.P.M.
1940 to 42	20T, 20P, 6 Cyl.	J-7	.038	.020	35	½B	flywheel	125@125	.006	.008	⅜"	600
1946 -47	171, 172, 6 Cyl.	J-7	.038	.020	34	½B	flywheel	119@125	.010	.012	⅛"	600
1942 to 47	173, 174, 8 Cyl.	J-7	.038	.017	30.5	TC	flywheel	119@125	.006	.007	⅛	600
1948 -49	491, 492, 6 Cyl.	J-7	.038	.020	38	TC	flywheel	119@125	.010	.012	3/16"	600
	493, 494, 8 Cyl.	J-7	.038	.017	27	TC	flywheel	119@125	.006	.008	13/64"	600
1950	500, 6, Cyl.	J-7	.038	.020	38	TC	flywheel	119@125	.008	.010	½"	600
	501, 502, 6 Cyl.	J-7	.038	.020	38	TC	flywheel	119@125	.008	.010	3/16"	600
	503, 504, 8 Cyl.	J-7	.038	.017	27	TC	flywheel	119@125	.006	.008	3/16"	600
1951	4A—Pacemaker, 6 Cyl.	H-8	.032	.020	39	TC	flywheel	....	.008	.010	½"	....
	5A—Super, 6A—Com., 6 Cyl.	H-8	.032	.020	39	TC	flywheel	....	.008	.010	3/16"	....
	7A—Hornet, 6 Cyl.	H-8	.032	.020	39	TC	flywheel	....	.008	.010	3/16"	....
	8A—Commodore, 8 Cyl.	H-8	.032	.017	27	TC	flywheel	119@125	.008	.010	3/16"	....
1952	4B, 6 Cyl.	Ch-H8	.032	.020	39	TC	flywheel	....	.008H	.010H	....	550
	5B, 6B, 7B, 6 Cyl.	Ch-H11	.032	.020	39	TC	flywheel	....	.008H	.010H	....	550
	8B, 8 Cyl.	Ch-H8	.032	.017	27	TC	flywheel	....	.008H	.010H	....	550
1953	4C, 5C, 7C, 6 Cyl.	Ch-*H8	.032	.020	39	TC	flywheel	....	.008H	.010H	....	550

*—7C uses H11. TC—Top center. B—Before top center. Ch—Champion Spark Plug Co.

Engine Overhaul Specifications

Year	Model	PISTONS				RING GAP CLEARANCES (Maximum)				PISTON PIN		ROD BEARINGS		
		Removed From	Piston Skirt Clearances (Maximum)											
			Top	Bottom	Limit	Top Ring	Second Ring	Third Ring	Oil Ring	Type	Fit	Oil Clearance	Wear Limit	Side Play
1940	40, 41, 43, 6 Cyl.	A	.0015	.001	.004	.011	.011	.011	.011	FL	Push	.0003	.004	.007–.013
	44 & 47, 8 Cyl.	A	.0015	.001	.004	.011	.011	.011	.011	FL	Push	.0003	.004	.007–.013
1941	10T, 10P, 11, 12, 6 Cyl.	A	.0015	.001	.004	.011	.011	.011	.011	FL	Push	.0003	.004	.007
	14, 15 & 17, 8 Cyl.	A	.0015	.001	.004	.011	.011	.011	.011	FL	Push	.0003	.004	.007
1942	20, 21, 22, 6 Cyl.	A	.0015	.001	.004	.011	.011	.011	.011	FL	Push	.0003	.004	.007
	24, 25, 27, 8 Cyl.	A	.0015	.001	.004	.011	.011	.011	.011	FL	Push	.0003	.004	.007
1946	51, 51P, 6 Cyl.	A	.0015	.001	.004	.011	.011	.011	.011	FL	Push	.0003–.0006	.004	.007–.013
	53, 54, 8 Cyl.	A	.0015	.001	.004	.011	.011	.011	.011	FL	Push	.0003–.0006	.004	.007–.013
1947	171, 172, 6 Cyl.	A	.0015	.001	.004	.011	.011	.011	.011	FL	Push	.0003–.0006	.004	.007–.013
	173, 174, 8 Cyl.	A	.0015	.001	.004	.011	.011	.011	.011	FL	Push	.0003–.0006	.004	.006–.012
1948	481, 482, 6 Cyl.	A	.0022	.001	.004	.012	.012	.012	.012	FL	Push	.0005–.0015	.004	.007–.013
	483, 484, 8 Cyl.	A	.0015	.001	.004	.009	.009	.009	.009	FL	Push	.0003–.0006	.004	.007–.013
1949	491, 492, 6 Cyl.	A	.0022	.001	.004	.012	.012	.012	.012	FL	Push	.0005–.0015	.004	.007–.013
	493, 494, 8 Cyl.	A	.0015	.001	.004	.009	.009	.009	.009	FL	Push	.0003–.0006	.004	.007–.013
1950	500, 501, 502, 6 Cyl.	A	.0022	.001	.004	.014	.014	.014	.014	FL	Push	.0005–.0015	.004	.007–.013
	503, 504, 8 Cyl.	A	.0015	.001	.004	.009	.009	.009	.009	FL	Push	.0003–.0006	.004	.007–.013
1951	4A-Pacemaker, 6 Cyl.	A	.0025	.0017	.005	.014	.014	.014	.014	FL	Push	.0005–.0015	.004	.007–.013
	5A-Super, 6A-Com., 6 Cyl.	A	.0025	.0017	.005	.014	.014	.014	.014	FL	Push	.0005–.0015	.004	.007–.013
	7A-Hornet, 6 Cyl.	A	.0025	.0017	.005	.014	.014	.014	.014	FL	Push	.0005–.0015	.004	.007–.013
	8A-Commodore, 8 Cyl.	A	.0015	.001	.005	.009	.009	.009	.009	FL	Push	.0003–.0006	.004	.007–.013
1952	4B, 5B, 6B, 7B, 6 Cyl.	A	.0025	.00175	.005	.014	.014	.014	.014	FL	.0003	.0005–.0015	.004	.007–.013
	8B, 8 Cyl.	A	.002	.00125	.005	.009	.009	.009	.009	FL	.0003	.0003–.0006	.004	.007–.013
1953	4C, 5C, 7C	A	.0025	.00175	.005	.014	.014	......	.014	FL	.0003	.0005–.0015	.004	.007–.013

A—Above †—Center crank gear mark between cam gear marks. FL—Floating type.

Pistons and Piston Pins

Year	Model	PISTONS				PISTON PINS		
		Diameter	Material	Type	No. of Rings	Length	Diameter	How Held
1940 to 47	Series—All	3	Alum.	C, Ts	4	2.4375	.75	F
1948 to 50	Series—All, 6 cyl.	3.5625	Alum.	C	4	2 15/16	.9680	F
	Series—All, 8 cyl.	3	Alum.	C	4	2 7/16	.75	F
1951	4A, 5A, 6A	3.5625	Alum.	C	4	2 15/16	.9680	F
	7A, Hornet	3.8125	Alum.	C	4	2 15/16	.9680	F
	8A, 8 cyl.	3	Alum.	C	4	2 7/16	.75	F
1952	4B, 5B, 6B, 6 cyl.	3.5625	Alum. Alloy	C	4	2.937	.968	F
	7B, 6 cyl.	3.8125	Alum. Alloy	C	4	2.937	.968	F
	8B, 8 cyl.	3	Alum. Alloy	C	4	2.4375	.750	F
1953	4C	3.5625	Alum. Alloy	C	4	2.937	.968	F
	5C	3.5625	Alum. Alloy	C	4	2.937	.968	F
	7C	3.8125	Alum. Alloy	C	4	2.937	.968	F

Alum—Aluminum. C–Cam ground. Ts—"T" slot. F—Floating.

and Wear Limit Table

CRANKSHAFT		VALVES						Valve Timing, Inlet Valve Opens (Deg.)	Camshaft Drive	Gear Marks	OPERATING OIL PRESSURE		Model	Year
Main Bearing Oil Clearance	Shaft End Play	Spring Tension (Maximum) Inlet	Spring Tension (Maximum) Exhaust	Low Limit	Guide Clearance	Seat Angle Inlet	Seat Angle Exhaust				Pounds At M.P.H.	Low Limit§		
.001	.006–.012	44@2	44@2	40	.003	45°	45°	10°40′	Gear	†	*	......	.... 40, 41, 43, 6 Cyl.	1940
.001	.006–.012	44@2	44@2	40	.003	45°	45°	10°40′	Gear	†	*	......	...........44, 47, 8 Cyl.	
.001	.006–.012	40@2	40@2	35	.003	45°	45°	10°40′	Gear	†	*	......	...10P, 10T, 11, 12, 6 Cyl.	1941
.001	.006–.012	40@2	40@2	35	.003	45°	45°	10°40′	Gear	†	*	......	.........14, 15, 17, 8 Cyl.	
.001	.006–.012	40@2	40@2	35	.003	45°	45°	10°40′	Gear	†	*	......	.........20, 21, 22, 6 Cyl.	1942
.001	.006–.012	40@2.343	40@2.343	35	.003	45°	45°	10°40′	Gear	†	*	......	.........24, 25, 27, 8 Cyl.	
.001	.006–.012	80@1 21/32	80@1 21/32	70	.003	45°	45°	27°30′	Gear	†	*	......	...........51, 51P, 6 Cyl.	1946
.001	.006–.012	80@1 21/32	80@1 21/32	70	.003	45°	45°	10°40′	Gear	†	*	......	..............53, 54, 8 Cyl.	
.001	.006–.012	80@1 21/32	80@1 21/32	70	.003	45°	45°	27°30′	Gear	†	*	......	...........171, 172, 6 Cyl.	1947
.001	.006–.012	80@1 21/32	80@1 21/32	70	.003	45°	45°	10°40′	Gear	†	*	......	...........173, 174, 8 Cyl.	
.0005–.0015	.003–.009	165@1.842	165@1.842	140	.003	45°	45°	7°18′	Chain	†	*	......	...........481, 482, 6 Cyl.	1948
.001	.006–.012	80@1 21/32	80@1 21/32	70	....	45°	45°	10°40′	Gear	†	*	......	...........483, 484, 8 Cyl.	
.0005–.0015	.003–.009	165@1.842	165@1.842	140	.003	45°	45°	7°18′	Chain	‡	*	......	...........491, 492, 6 Cyl.	1949
.001	.006–.012	80@1 21/32	80@1 21/32	70	....	45°	45°	10°40′	Gear	†	*	......	...........493, 494, 8 Cyl.	
.0005–.0015	.003–.009	165@1.842	165@1.842	140	....	45°	45°	7°18′	Chain	‡	*	......	......500, 501, 502, 6 Cyl.	1950
.001	.006–.012	80@1 21/32	80@1 21/32	70	....	45°	45°	10°40′	Gear	†	*	......	...........503, 504, 8 Cyl.	
.0005–.0015	.003–.009	165@1.842	165@1.842	140	.004	45°	45°	7°18′	Chain	‡	*	......	.....4A-Pacemaker, 6 Cyl.	1951
.0005–.0015	.003–.009	165@1.842	165@1.842	140	.004	45°	45°	7°18′	Chain	‡	*	......	5A-Super, 6A-Com., 6 Cyl.	
.0005–.0015	.003–.009	165@1.842	165@1.842	140	.004	45°	45°	7°18′	Chain	‡	*	......	.........7A-Hornet, 6 Cyl.	
.001	.006–.012	80@1.656	80@1.656	70	.005	45°	45°	10°40′	Gear	†	*	......	....8A-Commodore, 8 Cyl.	
.0005–.0015	.003–.009	165@1.842	165@1.842	......	.004	45°	45°	26.7B	Chain	......	40@30	......	.....4B, 5B, 6B, 7B, 6 Cyl.	1952
.001	.006–.012	80@1.656	80@1.656	......	.005	45°	45°	10°40′B	Gear	......	3	......	..................8B, 8 Cyl.	
.0005–.0015	.003–.009	165@1.842	165@1.842	......	.004	45°	45°	26.7B	Chain	......	40@30	......	................4C, 5C, 7C	1953

*—Warning light on dash indicates too low pressure.

‡—Mesh chain with "°" marks on sprockets (two chain links marked with "°" to holes).

Dimensions of Valves

Year	Model	Overall Length		Head Diameter		Seat Angle (deg.)		Stem Diameter		Key Type	O.D. of Seat Insert	
		Inlet	Exhaust	Inlet	Exhaust	Inlet	Exhaust	Inlet	Exhaust		Inlet	Exhaust
1940 to 47	Series—All, 6 cyl.	5.344	5.344	1.375	1.375	45	45	.341	.339	horseshoe	....	....
	Series—All, 8 cyl.	5.094	5.094	1.500	1.375	45	45	.343	.339	horseshoe	....	....
1948 to 51	Series—All, 6 cyl.	5.730	5.730	1.831	1.556	45	45	.341	.340	split lock	....	....
	Series—All, 8 cyl.	5.094	5.094	1.500	1.375	45	45	.341	.339	split lock	....	....
1952	4B, 5B, 6B, 7B, 6 cyl.	5.730	5.73	1.831	1.556	45	45	.3417	.3407	....	....	....
	8B, 8 cyl.	5.094	5.094	1.500	1.375	45	45	.3412	.339	....	....	....
1953	4C, 5C, 7C	5.730	5.73	1.831	1.556	45	45	.3417	.3407	....	....	....

Crankshaft Bearing Journal Sizes

Year	Model	Connecting Rod Journals		Main Bearing Journals				
		Diameter	Length	No. 1 Diameter	No. 2 Diameter	No. 3 Diameter	No. 4 Diameter	No. 5 Diameter
1940 to 47	All 6 cyl.	1.935–1.936	1.375	2.341–2.342	2.373–2.374	2.402–2.405	....	....
	All 8 cyl.	1.935–1.936	1.375	2.279–2.280	2.311–2.312	2.341–2.342	2.373–2.374	2.404–2.405
1948 to 51	All 6 cyl.	2.125	1.625	2.4995	2.4995	2.4995	2.4995	....

Crankshaft Bearing Journal Sizes—*continued*

Year	Model	Connecting Rod Journals		Main Bearing Journals				
		Diameter	Length	No. 1 Diameter	No. 2 Diameter	No. 3 Diameter	No. 4 Diameter	No. 5 Diameter
1948–49	All 8 cyl.	1.935–1.936	1.375	2.279–2.280	2.311–2.312	2.341–2.342	2.373–2.374	2.404–2.405
1950–51	503, 504, 8A, 8 cyl.	1.9375	1.375	2.281	2.312	2.343	2.375	2.406
1952	4B, 5B, 6B, 7B, 6 cyl. 8B, 8 cyl.	2.125 1.9375	1.625 1.375	2.4995 2.281	2.4995 2.321	2.4995 2.343	2.4995 2.375	.... 2.406
1953	4C, 5C, 7C	2.125	....	2.4995–1.4375	2.4995–1.375	2.4995–1.625	2.4995–1.75	....

Tension Wrench Specifications

Year	Model	Cylinder Head		Spark Plug		Connecting Rod Bolts or Nuts		Main Bearing Bolt		Flywheel Bolts		Vibration Damper Bolts	
		Lbs.-Ft.	Thread	Lbs.-Ft.	Thread	Lbs.-Ft.	Thread	Lbs.-Ft.	Thread	Lbs.-Ft.	Thread	Lbs.-Ft.	Thread
1940	All	40–45	....	24–28	14 mm	40–50	....	88–93	....	35–45	....	....	....
1941	All	30–40**	....	24–28	14 mm	30–40	....	65–75	....	35–45	....	....	....
1942 to 47	All	30–40**	....	24–28	14 mm	30–40	....	65–75	....	30–40	....	....	....
1948–49	All—400 Series	70–75‡	....	24–28	14 mm	40–45	⅜–24	70–80	....	40–45	....	....	....
1950	All—500 Series	70–75	....	25–30	14 mm	40–45	⅜–24	75–80■	■½–13	40–45	⅜–24	100–120	¾–16
1951 to 53	All	60–65–	7/16	25–30	14 mm	40–45	⅜–24	75–80–	–½–13	40–45	⅜–24	100–120	¾–16
1953	Jet	....	....	....	....	....	....	....	....	....	....	....	....

**—6 cyl., for 8 cyl. (35–45). ‡—6 cyl., for 8 cyl. (45–50). ■—6 cyl., for 8 cyl. (70–80), (½–20).

Brake Data

Year	Model	Make	Lining Type	R=Riveted B=Bonded	Drum Diameter	Lining			Clearance	
						Length	Width	Thickness	Toe	Heel
1940	40 41, 43 44, 47	Ben Ben Ben	WM WM WM	R R R	9 1/16 ■10 1/16 11 1/16	19 °23 5/16 23 15/16	1¾ 1¾ 1¾	3/16 3/16(f) 7/32	.010 .010 .010	.010 .010 .010
1941–42	Series—All	Ben	M	R	*10	**19.8	1¾	3/16(k)	.010	.010
1946–47	All-6 All-8	Ben Ben	MW MW	R R	10 11	19 27/32 21 19/32	1¾ 1¾	3/16 7/32	.010 .010	.010 .010
1948	Series—All	Ben	M	R	11	20⅞	2–(k)1¾	.18	.010	.010
1949	Series—All	Ben	M	R	11	21.32△	2¼–(k)1¾	.177	.010	.010
1950	500 501, 502, 503, 504	Ben Ben	M M	R R	11 11	20.11 21.32△	1¾ 2¼–(k)1¾	.177 .177	.010 .010	.010 .010
1951	4A 5A, 6A, 7A, 8A	Ben Ben	M M	R R	11 11	20 7/64 21 21/64(k)	1¾ 2¼–(k)1¾	3/16 3/16	.010 .010	.010 .010
1952	4B, 6 Cyl. 5B, 6B, 7B, 6 Cyl., 8B, 8 Cyl.	Ben Ben	M M	R R	11 11	....	1¾ 2¼–1¾†	11/64 11/64	.010 .010	.010 .010
1953	4C, 6 Cyl. 5C, 7C, 6 Cyl.	Ben Ben	M M	R R	11 11	....	1¾ 2¼–1¾†	11/64 11/64	.010 .010	.010 .010

△ Rear 20.11. (k) Rear 7/32. * Model 12–11 inches. ** Model 12–21.6 inches. ■ 11— on c.c. six. ° c.c. six–23.936 inches.
(f) c.c. six–.218. Ben—Bendix. M—Moulded. MW—Moulded on primary.

Distributors

Year	Model	Distributor Model Number	Cam Angle (deg.)	Direction of Rotation C=Clockwise CC=Counter Clockwise at Cam End	Breaker Arm Spring Tension	Breaker Point Gap (inches)	Engine R.P.M. when Cent. Advance Starts	Max. Cent. Advance in Engine Deg. at Stated Engine R.P.M.	Vacuum in (inches) of Mercury at which Vacuum Unit Starts	Max. Advance in Engine Deg. at Stated Vacuum	Vacuum Unit Number
1940	All, 6 cyl.	IGW-4203	35	CC	17-20	.018-.022	600	28@3160	6.75	15@10	VC-3060-E
1941 to 47	All, 6 cyl.	IGW-4203A	35	CC	17-20	.018-.022	800	23.5@3140	6.75	15@10	VC-3060-ES
1940 to 46	All, 8 cyl.	IGP-4008A	27.5	C	17-20	.013-.017	600	35@3400	....	....	....
1948 to 50	All, 6 cyl.	IGS-4213-1	38	C	17-20	.020	540	24@4000	9.5	4@11	....
1947 to 50	All, 8 cyl.	IGT-4204A-1	27	C	17-20	.015-.019	600	35@3400	9.5	17@14	....
1951	All, 6 cyl.	IAT-4009A	39	C	17-20	.018-.022	600	18@4000	16	8	....
	All, 8 cyl.	IGT-4204B-1	27	C	....	.013-.017	....	35@3400	16	8	....
1952	4B, 6 cyl.	IAT-4009	39	C	17-20	.020	300	10@1200	9½	5@12	....
	5B, 6B, 7B, 6 cyl.	IAT-4009A	39	C	17-20	.020	500	9@2000	13	4@16	....
	8B, 8 cyl.	IGT-4204B1	27	C	17-20	.017	300	17½@1700	13	4@16	....
1953	4C	IAT-4009	39	C	17-20	.020	300	10@1200	9½	5@12	....
	5C, 7C	IAT-4009A	39	C	17-20	.020	500	9@2000	13	4@16	....

Generators

Year	Model	Generator Number	Field Current at 6 Volts (amps.)	Maximum Safe Output Volts	Maximum Safe Output Amperes	Maximum Safe Output R.P.M.	Brush Spring Tension (oz.)	Voltage Regulator Number
1940	40, 41, 42, 43, 44, 45, 46, 47	GEG-4801-A	1.3-1.5	8.0	40	1575	64-68	VRP-4008-A
		GEA-4803-B	1.3-1.5	8.0	35	1600	35-53	VRP-4008-B
	Special Equipment	GEB-4802-A	1.3-1.5	8.0	32	1275	64-68	VRP-4008-C
		GEC-4801-A	1.3-1.5	8.0	40	3350	35-53	VRD-4008-B
1941	10, 11, 12, 13, 14, 15, 17, 18	GEG-4801-A	1.3-1.5	8.0	40	1575	64-68	VRP-4008-A
		GEA-4803-B	1.3-1.5	8.0	35	1600	35-53	VRP-4008-B
	Special Equipment	GEB-4802-A	1.3-1.5	8.0	32	1275	64-68	VRP-4008-C
		GEB-4802-B	1.3-1.5	8.0	32	1275	64-68	VRP-4008-C
		GEB-4802-B-2	1.3-1.5	8.0	35	1300	64-68	VRP-4008-D
		GDS-4801-A	1.3-1.5	8.0	33	2900	35-53	VRR-4001-A
		GEC-4801-A	1.3-1.5	8.0	40	3350	35-53	VRR-4001-A
1942	20	GDS-4801-A	1.3-1.5	8.0	33	2900	35-53	VRR-4001-A
1942	21, 22, 24, 25, 27	GEC-4801-A	1.3-1.5	8.0	40	3350	35-53	VRR-4001-A
	24, 25, 27, Spec. Equip.	GEB-4802-B-2	1.3-1.5	8.0	35	1300	35-53	VRP-4008-D
		GEG-4801-A	1.3-1.5	8.0	40	1575	64-68	VRP-4008-A
1946	51, 52, 58, 53, 54	GEC-4801-A	1.3-1.5	8.0	40	3350	35-53	VRR-4001-A
1947 to 49	Series—All	GEC-4801-A	1.3-1.5	8.0	40	3350	35-53	VRR-4001-A
1950	500	GDZ-6001-B	1.3-1.5	8.0	35	2350	35-53	VRR-4001-A
	501, 502, 503, 504	GDZ-6001-B	1.3-1.5	8.0	35	2350	35-53	VRR-6002
1951	4A, 5A, 6A, 7A	GDZ-6001-B	1.3-1.5	8.0	35	2350	35-53	VRR-4001-A
	8A	GDZ-6001-B	1.3-1.5	8.0	35	2350	35-53	VRR-6002
1952	4B, 5B, 6B, 7B, 6 cyl., 8B, 8 cyl.	GDZ-6001-B	....	....	....	....	....	VRP-6101-B
1953	4C, 5C, 7C	GGW-4801-B	....	7.35	40	1940	....	VRE-6104-E

Voltage Regulators

Year	Model	Regulator Number	Grounded P=Position N=Negative	Voltage Control: Air Gap Points Closed	Voltage Control: Voltage Setting Hot	Current Control: Air Gap Points Closed	Current Control: Current Set Hot	Cut-Out Relay: Point Gap	Cut-Out Relay: Air Gap	Cut-Out Relay: Closing Volt
1946 to 49	All 6 & 8 cyl.	VRR-4001-A	P	.052	7.18	....	....	.015	.034	6.4–7.0
1950	All 6 & 8 cyl.	VRR-4001-A VRP-6002-A	P P	.052 .052	7.18 7.65	....	....	.015 .015	.034 .034	6.4–7.0 6.4–7.0
1951	4A, 5A, 6A, 7A 8A	VRR-4001-A VRR-6002	P P	.052 .052	7.18 7.65	....	....	.015 .015	.034 .034	6.4–7.0 6.4–7.0
1952	4B, 5B, 6B, 7B, 6 cyl., 8B, 8 cyl.	VRP-6101-B	....	....	7.35	....	40	....	....	6.7
1953	4C, 5C, 7C	VRE-6104-E	....	....	7.35	....	40	....	....	6.7

Starters

Year	Model	Unit Model Number	Spring Tension (oz.)	Starter Lock Test: Volts	Lock Test: Amperes	Lock Test: Torque, (lbs. ft.)	No Load: Volts	No Load: Amperes	No Load: R.P.M.	Direction of Rotation Viewed from Drive End C=Clockwise CC=Counter-clockwise
1941 to 47	All—6 cyl. All—8 cyl.	MZ-4092 MAB-4100	42–53 42–53	2.0 2.0	280 390	4.4 9.2	5.0 5.0	68 60	4000 3600	C C
1948–49	All—6 & 8 cyl.	MCL-6006	42–53	2.0	410	8	5.0	65	4900	C
1950	500, 50T, 501, 502—6 cyl. 501, 502, 503, 504	MZ-4159 MCL-6006	42–53 42–53	4.0 4.0	540 880	12.3 25	5.50 5.50	70 58	4300 5600	C C
1951	4A, 6 cyl. 5A, 6A, 7A, 6 cyl. 8A, 8 cyl.	MZ-4164 MCH-6109 MCH-6109	42–53 42–53 42–53	2.0 2.0 2.0	280 335 335	4.4 6 6	5.50 5.50 5.50	70 65 65	4300 4900 4900	C C C
1952–53	All, 6 cyl. All, 8 cyl.	MZ-4167 MCH-6109	42–53 42–53	2 2	280 335	4.4 6	5.5 5.5	70 65	4300 4900	C C

Front Wheel Alignment

Year	Model	Caster (deg.)	Camber (deg.)	King Pin Inclination (deg.)	Toe-In (inches)	Turning Radius: Inner	Turning Radius: Outer
1940	40, 41, 43, 44, 47	¼N to ¼P	¼P to ¾P	4½	0 to 1/16	24	20
1941	6 and 8 cyl.	¼N to ¼P	¼P to ¾P	4½	0 to 1/16	24	20
1942	20T, 20P, 21, 22 24, 25, 27	0 to ¼P 0 to ¼P	¼P to ¾P ¼P to ¾P	3½ 3½	0 to 1/16 0 to 1/16	24 24	20 20
1946	51, 51P, 52, 53, 54	0 to ¼P	½P to 1½P	3½	0 to 1/16	24	20
1947–52	All 6 and 8 cyl.	½P to 1½P	½P to 1½P	3½	0 to 1/16	24	20
1953	6 and 8 cyl. Jet Models	½P to 1½P 0 to ½P	½P to 1½P ¾N to 1¾P	3½ 3½	0 to 5/8 0 to 1/16	30 16¾	20 20

N—Negative. P—Positive.

FRONT SUSPENSION

ALL JET MODELS

The front suspension used on all Jet models is of the pin and trunnion type. Yoke type upper and lower suspension arms are used and the shock absorber is mounted in the center of the coil spring.

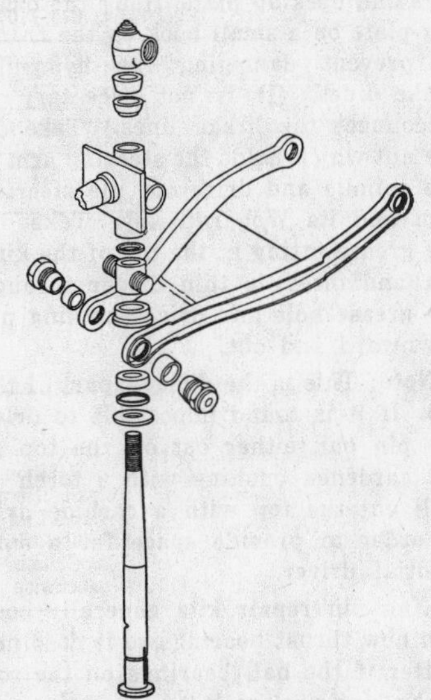

Jet front suspension

The front suspension used on all Hudson built cars (except Jet models) from 1940 to 1951 is, except for refinements in detail, essentially the same. The early models used an upper suspension arm which is formed into the shape of a hook, the hooked portion being threaded to receive the eccentric bushing which controls caster and camber.

On later models the upper suspension arm was formed into a yoke which straddled the upper suspension arm pin.

Caster, Camber and Toe-In

ALL MODELS EXCEPT JETS

On all Hudson built cars caster and camber are controlled by the eccentric bushing in the outer end of the upper support arm. Since both caster and camber are controlled at the same eccentric bushing the adjustment secured is a compromise between the exact required adjustment and the best adjustment possible with a bushing controlling both caster and camber.

To increase caster loosen the clamp bolt at the upper end of the knuckle support and turn the eccentric bushing toward the rear of the car which will increase caster. Where it is desired to come to an exact setting, first set caster by means of the eccentric pin and lock the adjustment and use a bending bar on the knuckle support to produce the desired camber. Ordinarily it is not necessary to bend the knuckle support since the camber adjustment usually can be secured with the caster within a reasonable range.

Toe-in is adjusted at both tie rods.

ALL JET MODELS

On all Jet models caster and camber is controlled by shims at the inner end of the upper support arm.

Adding an equal number of shims at both the front and back bolt will decrease camber. Removing an equal number from both the front and back bolt will increase camber.

Removing shims from the rear bolt (or adding them at the front bolt) will decrease caster.

Adding shims at the rear bolt (and taking them away from the front bolt) will increase caster.

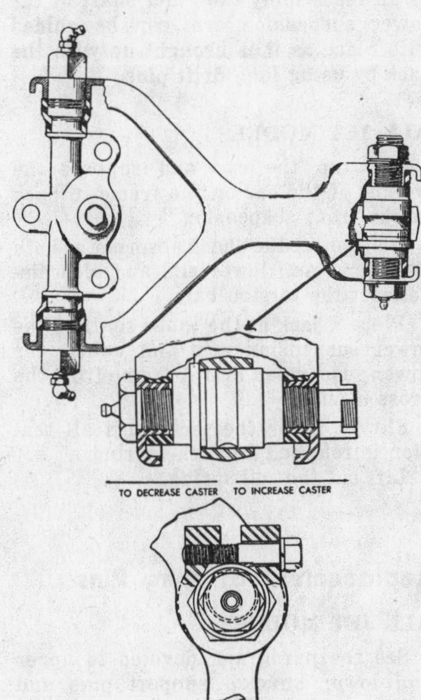

Caster and camber adjusting points

REPLACEMENT OF FRONT SUSPENSION PARTS

Upper Support Arm

ALL MODELS EXCEPT JET

The upper support arm may be removed by taking out the pin which threads through the upper support arm eccentric bushing at the outer end (on early models loosen the clamp screw in the upper part of the knuckle support and turn out the eccentric bushing.)

The upper suspension arm inner shaft may then be disconnected from its mounting on the top of the frame and remove from the car.

It is possible to replace the bushings at the inner end of the upper support arm without removing the support arm from the car.

ALL JET MODELS

To replace the upper support arm on the Jet model it is necessary to take the weight of the car on a jack under the spring hanger on the lower suspension arm and remove the road wheel. Remove the bushings from the upper support arm which go into the upper trunnion and detach the inner end of the arm from the frame bracket. The upper arm can then be lifted off.

Lower Support Arm (A Frame)

ALL MODELS EXCEPT JET

To replace the lower A frame place a jack under the A frame inner shaft and disconnect the shaft from the front cross member. Disconnect the shock absorber at the lower end and let the inner part of the A frame down slowly to release the spring tension. Remove the coil spring and then take out the bolt which retains the outer end of the lower suspension arm to the lower part of the knuckle support.

ALL JET MODELS

To replace the lower suspension arm A frame, jack up the car and support its weight on the frame in back of the front suspension and remove the road wheel.

Detach the shock absorber and the torsion bar.

Place a jack under the inner shaft of the lower suspension arm, unbolt it from the frame and slowly lower it until the spring pressure is released.

JET MODELS—*Continued*

Now remove the bushings which hold the lower trunnion to the outer end of the lower suspension arm and take off the suspension arm.

Upper and/or Lower Knuckle Support Pins and Bushings

ALL MODELS EXCEPT JET

To replace the knuckle support bushings take the weight of the car on the lower A frame and disconnect first the outer pin from the upper suspension arm and then remove the lower pin and bushings from the lower end of the suspension arm.

Make some provision to support the knuckle support so that the brake lines will not be damaged.

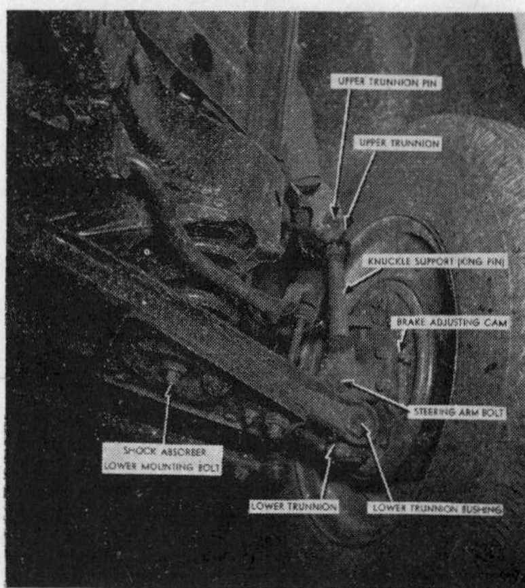

Front suspension jet models

ALL JET MODELS

Actually pins and bushings are not used in this type of suspension. There is however an upper and lower trunnion. To replace the trunnions, jack up the car under the lower suspension arm at about the spring, and remove the road wheel.

Take off the brake shoes and backing plate.

Remove the bushings from the upper suspension arm outer trunnion and unscrew the trunnion from the top of the knuckle support (king pin).

Remove the steering arm, being certain the little Woodruff key comes with it since this key holds the knuckle support in the spindle.

Drive the knuckle support down and out, releasing the thrust bearing, thrust washer, oil seals, etc., and then remove the bushings which hold the lower trunnion to the lower suspension arm.

When replacing the knuckle support use extreme care that the keyway in the knuckle support is in perfect alignment with the keyway in the spindle so that the steering arm can be entered without difficulty.

Once the knuckle support is started up into place, it is very difficult to correct the misalignment of the keyway.

Replacement of Coil Spring

ALL MODELS EXCEPT JET

To replace the coil spring support the frame of the car on stationary jacks and place a portable jack under the lower suspension arm inner shaft. Detach the inner shaft from its mounting on the front cross member, holding it against the cross member with the jack. On 1948 thru 1953 models detach the torsion bar. Detach the lower end of the shock absorber and let the inner end of the A frame down slowly. Take out the coil spring.

Where shims are used on the coil spring be sure to put them back in place when installing the new spring.

On reassembly the inner shaft of the lower suspension arm can be guided into place as it is brought up with the jack by using long drift pins.

ALL JET MODELS

Jack up the car and support the weight of the car on the frame in back of the front suspension.

Disconnect the shock absorber at both the upper and lower end and also disconnect the torsion bar.

Place a jack at the inner shaft of the lower suspension arm and unbolt the lower suspension arm A frame from the cross member.

Slowly lower the jack until all tension is released from the spring.

Lift out the coil spring.

Replacement of King Pins

ALL JET MODELS

See the paragraph devoted to upper and lower knuckle support pins and bushings since this job is exactly the same as the replacement of the king pin on all Jet models.

ALL MODELS EXCEPT JETS

King pins on Hudson built cars are slightly different than the pins in other cars. The thrust bearing on Hudson construction is contained in a hardened bushing at the upper part of the king pin. The thrust surface is on top of the king pin itself.

Remove the front wheel drum bearings and backing plate. Hang the backing plate on a small hook on the frame to prevent damaging the hydraulic brake lines. (It is not necessary to disconnect the brake lines.) Take off the nut which holds the steering arm to the spindle and drive out the steering arm and its Woodruff key. Take out the grease fitting at the top of the king pin and insert a thin driver through the grease hole and drive the king pin downward and out.

Note: This is the difficult part of the job. If it is found impossible to drive the pin out, either cut off the top of the hardened bushing with a torch or drill out the top with a carbide drill in order to provide space for a substantial driver.

King pin repair kits generally contain new thrust bearings so it does not matter if the ball bearings on the top of the king pin are lost.

Note: The Hudson Motor Car Co. recommends that the steering knuckle support be removed from the car with the spindle attached in order to drive out the king pin. It is very difficult to install the king pin and keep the seven loose ball bearings in their proper position. The job is done much more simply if the knuckle support is held upside down in a vise.

After the spindle has been removed, take a soft hammer and tap the upper bushing out of the knuckle support. Drive out the lower bushing with a standard bushing driver.

The bushings are hardened steel, reaming is not necessary.

To reassemble, press the hardened bushing into the upper portion of the knuckle support and place the spindle in position.

Note: Grease seals are used between the lower flange of the hardened bushing and the top of the spindle.

The king pin is started up from the bottom, being certain to start it in such a way that the key way in the king pin will align with the key slot in the spindle. It is rather difficult to correct for mis-alignment after the king pin has been started into place. Since the seven loose thrust balls must be mounted on top of the king pin and retained there with heavy cup grease it will be difficult to drive the king pin into place and still keep the bearings on top of the king pin. If the king pin is to be mounted without removing the knuckle support from the car it is essential that a press type king pin installing tool be used so that the king pin can be pushed in place without jarring the thrust balls from the heavy cup grease.

An alternate and very practical method for installing the bearings is illustrated with this text.

After the king pin is securely pressed into place so that the key way in the king pin aligns with the key slot in the spindle drive the steering arm back into position so that the Woodruff key in the steering arm enters the key slot in the king pin. Replace the lower Welsh plug with its grease relief valve.

ALL MODELS EXCEPT JET

Replacement of the Front Shock Absorber

On all Hudson models the procedure for replacing a front shock absorber is exactly the same as that given for the replacement of a coil spring. Since, in order to take out the shock absorber, it is necessary to first take out the coil spring and then the shock absorber can be lifted off. This is generally considered to be the proper way to replace a front shock absorber.

However, it is possible to replace the shock absorber without detaching the spring by removing the upper and lower bolt from the shock absorber and forcing the shock absorber, using a screwdriver through the coil spring, upwards to release the lower mounting plate.

The shock absorber can be forced up far enough to permit working the lower plate up alongside the shock absorber and out through the coils of the spring.

Generally this is accomplished by leaving the top bolt of the shock absorber in place until the lower plate has been removed and then taking out the upper bolt and letting the shock absorber fall down out through the bottom of the lower A frame.

On Jet models the shock absorber can be given a quarter turn which will permit it to slide through the lower suspension arm.

Front Stabilizer Removel

The front stabilizer bar, sometimes called the torsion bar, is connected to the frame with two bolts at each side.

It is connected to the lower suspension arm by a rubber mounted link.

To remove, detach the links and remove the bolts which hold the stabilizer to the frame. The stabilizer can then be slid off to one side.

ADJUSTMENT OF THE STEERING ASSEMBLY

1. Disconnect the pitman arm from the drag link.
2. Adjust the steering gear housing.

(a) Check the worm shaft for end play and if any exists remove the steering gear housing cover and take out one shim at a time until there is no end play in the worm bearings and practically no preload.

(b) Set the steering wheel in the mid position of its travel and move the pitman arm back and forth to check for play in the mesh of the gears with the steering wheel and gear assembly on its high spot.

To adjust, loosen the lock nut (b) and turn the adjusting screw inward until there is zero play in the gears with the steering wheel in the mid position of its travel.

Note: On 6 cylinder models this adjustment is through a hole in the frame.

3. Reconnect the pitman arm to the drag link and again set the steering to the mid position of its travel.
4. Loosen the clamp bolt at each end of the right tie rod and, with the steering wheel still held in the mid position of its travel, adjust the tie rod so that one half of the total toe-in is in the right wheel. Tighten the clamp bolts.
5. Now loosen the clamp bolts with both ends of the left tie rod. Adjust the left tie rod so that the balance of the toe-in is contained in the left wheel. Tighten the clamp bolts. Turn the steering wheel from one extreme to the other to check for looseness or binding.

Removal of Horn Button

Horn blowing rings are held by screws from underneath the steering wheel.

Horn buttons are pried out.

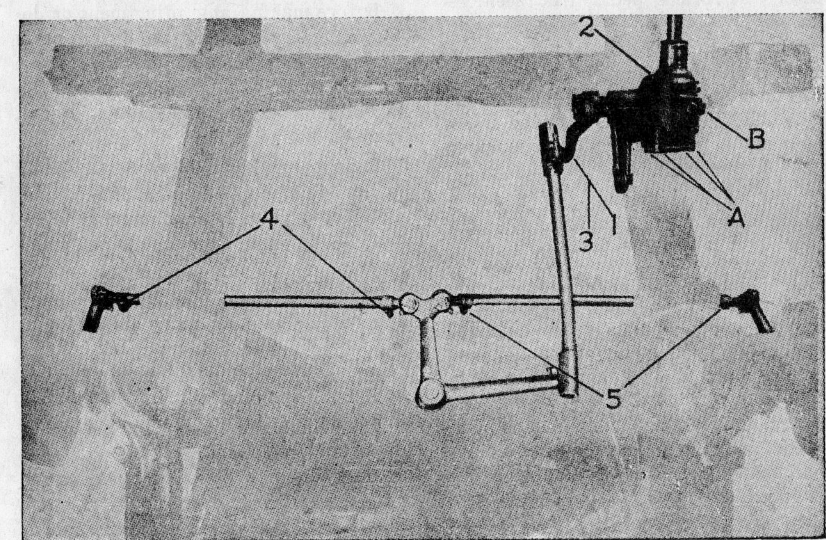

Steering mechanism, all models

Removal of Steering Wheel

On all models remove the horn button, the horn contact and blowing plate and the horn wire. Take off the nut which holds the steering wheel to the steering tube and, using a puller, pull off the steering wheel.

Caution: While it is sometimes possible to drive off a steering wheel this practice is never recommended since it almost invariably results in some damage to the steering wheel and may render it useless.

Removal of Steering Gear Assembly from Car

The exact procedure for removing the steering gear assembly varies with each make and model and with some body styles.

Start by removing the horn button and the steering wheel. On some models it is advisable to take out the front seat cushion to avoid possibly getting some of the grease from the top of the steering column on the cushion. Disconnect the shifting mechanism from the steering column and disconnect the mast jacket from the dash bracket.

Remove the pitman arm from the cross shaft, using a draw type puller.

On 1940 and 1941 models the steering gear is pulled downward and then up over the right side of the engine. On 1948 and 1949 models the steering gear is pulled out through the transmission hole cover in the floor boards after the brake pedal has been removed.

On 1950 and 1951 models it is necessary to remove the wheel side pan and wheel on the left side and the steering gear assembly is lifted over the frame and pulled out through the opening thus created.

BRAKES

All Hudson models built from 1940 to 1953, except Jets, are equipped with Bendix type hydraulically actuated brakes. All Hudson brakes are arranged in such a way that if there should be a failure in the hydraulic system, an emergency cable system is also connected to the braking mechanism so that the brake cable will take up in the event of failure of the hydraulic system. This double braking system is used on all Hudson models.

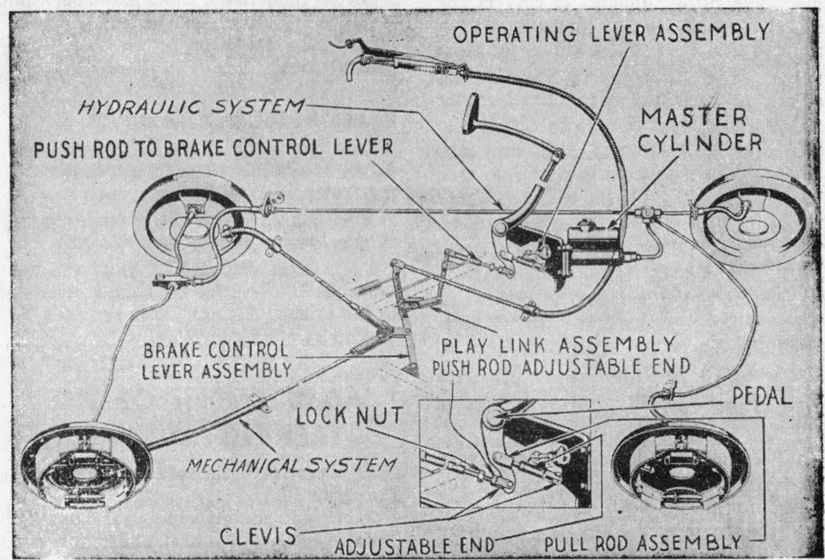

Fig. 1. Mechanism safety linkage used on Hudson models

ALL JET MODELS

Jet models are equipped with a two-shoe Bendix brake having a fixed anchor block. The shoes are of the self-centering type and no anchor adjustment is possible.

Brake Inspection

Before making any adjustment or doing any service work on brakes it is advisable to remove at least one wheel to determine the condition of the wheel cylinders, shoes, linings, drums, springs, etc.

If anything is found to be defective in the one wheel, it is advisable to take off all four wheels to determine the exact condition of the entire brake system.

The drum should be free of scores, and roughness; the lining should be in full contact with the drum and of sufficient thickness that the rivets will not score the drum.

Examine the hydraulic wheel cylinder boots to determine if the cylinder is leaking or seeping. The slightest trace of brake fluid on the wheel cylinder boot indicates that cylinder is leaking. In this case, it should either be honed in place on the car, if the condition of the wheel cylinder permits, or removed from the car and honed on a bench type cylinder hone to resurface the inside of the cylinder.

Note: Many shops specializing in brake service will not make any adjustment whatever on a brake without removing all four wheels to make a thorough check as a safety precaution.

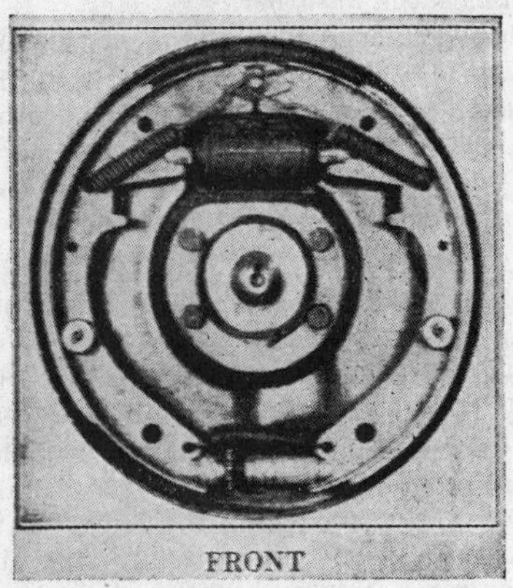

Minor Brake Adjustment

ALL JET MODELS

Brake adjustment on the Jet models is accomplished by loosening the jam nut on the brake adjusting cam and turning the cam until the wheel drags and then backing off until the wheel is just free. Repeat this at all eight of the shoes. (Two shoes at each wheel.)

This is the only adjustment required on the self-centering type Bendix brake.

To do a minor brake adjustment on all Hudson cars simply turn the star adjuster (located opposite to the anchor) in a direction which will expand the shoes (handle of the tool toward the axle) until the wheels drag and then back off until they are just free. Do not fail to replace the adjusting hole cover.

Brake Pedal Adjustment

The clearance of the pedal as measured at the toe board should be from ¼ to ½ inch and the adjustment is made at the master cylinder push rod.

Major Brake Adjustment

ALL MODELS EXCEPT JETS

Note: The 1937 to 1940 Series 40 cars were equipped with a Bendix brake having an articulating anchor link. On these models no actual adjustment was required at the anchor itself, however, the brake was equipped with a cam at the anchor end which could be adjusted until the brake dragged and then backed off until the wheel was just free. This operation should be repeated at all eight shoes.

After the adjustment is made, securely tighten the jam nut.

Except for this adjustment at the anchor link the balance of the procedure is the same as for later models.

A major adjustment should be made when new linings have been installed or when it is found that the car is pulling to one side or tends to lock up one brake before another.

All Hudson cars (except the 1937 to 1940 Series 40) are equipped with sliding type anchors. An easy way to adjust the anchor is to expand the star wheel until the shoes are very tight against the drum. Then loosen the anchor lock nut and tap the anchor until it centers itself between the two shoes.

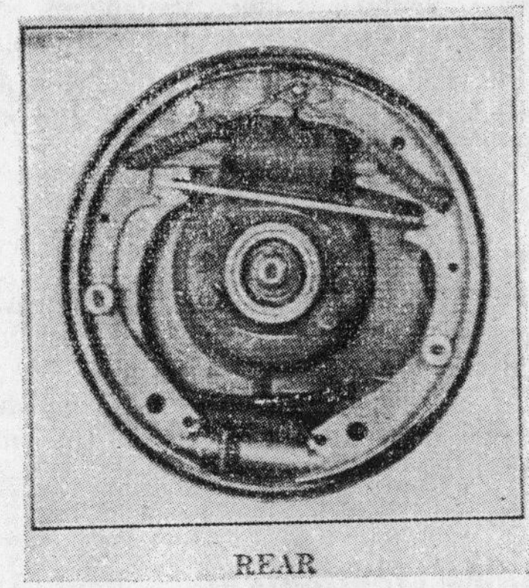

REAR

Securely tighten the anchor lock nut. Then back off on the eccentric adjuster until the wheels are just free.

If desired, a quick check can be made on this adjustment by inserting a .015 feeler gauge, approximately 1½ inches from the anchor end of the secondary shoe.

ALL JET MODELS

Only one adjustment is possible on the Jet models, see Minor Brake Adjustment above.

Adjusting Foot Brake Cables (Hand Brake Adjustment)

Set the hand brake in the fully released position and disconnect the foot brake pedal link from the cable actuating rod (underneath the car). Turn the star wheel adjuster on both rear wheels until the shoes are tight against the drum. Disconnect each brake cable from the control lever under the car and adjust the cable so that with the slack pulled out the clevis pin will just enter. Do this to both cables. With the hand brake still fully released adjust the link between the foot brake pedal and the brake control lever so that the clevis in the foot brake link will just enter the control lever.

Replace all cotter pins.

Back off on the star wheel at both rear wheels until the brakes are just free.

Bleeding Brakes

ALL MODELS EXCEPT JETS

Because of the cable take up on Hudson brakes it is advisable to disconnect the brake cables when bleeding the rear brakes from the master cylinder.

This will not be necessary if a pressure bleed is being done.

Complete instructions for bleeding brakes is given in the section devoted to General Service Information, see Index.

COOLING SYSTEM

Radiator Core Assembly Removal

To remove the radiator core assembly detach the fan shroud (if one is used), detach the radiator hoses, remove the bolts which hold the radiator core to its mounting between the fenders and lift the core straight upward.

Water Pump Removal

It is not necessary to remove the radiator core on any Hudson built since 1940 in order to take off the water pump. However, on models built after 1946 it is advisable to remove the fan

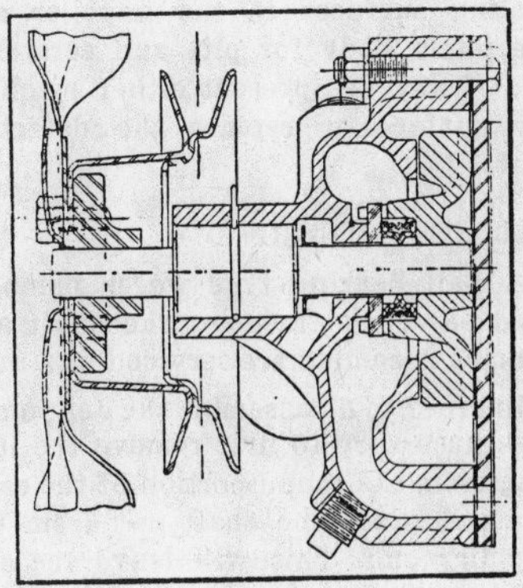

Water pump

WATER PUMP REMOVAL—*continued*

blades and fan hub in order to take off the water pump. The procedure is to disconnect the radiator hoses, remove the fan belt and detach the pump at the block and lift it off.

Disassembly of Water Pump

ALL MODELS EXCEPT JETS

Special overhaul kits are available for servicing all Hudson pumps.

On bushing type pumps it is necessary to cut the burr from the impeller end of the shaft and press the shaft out through the front of the pump body. The fan hub can then be pressed off the the shaft or, if the shaft is to be reused, leave the fan hub remain on the shaft.

On ball bearing type pumps remove the snap ring from the center of the pump body and then press the shaft and bearing assembly out of the impeller and out the front of the pump.

This operation is done in practically the same manner as is done on the bushing pumps except that it is necessary to take out the bearing retaining ring before starting to press out the shaft and bearing assembly.

On ball bearing type pumps the shaft and bearing are serviced as an assembly and it is recommended that a new shaft and bearing be used at any time the pump is disassembled. Before disassembling any Hudson pump measure carefully the distance between the end of the shaft and the impeller and also the end of the shaft and the pulley hub so that the new shaft may be located in exactly the same place as the old one.

When disassembled, examine the sealing surfaces in the impeller and the pump body for pits and scratches and if any are present either machine the surface or replace the defective part.

ALL JET MODELS

A ball bearing type water pump is used on all Jet models. The shaft and bearing assembly are serviced as a unit.

In order to disassemble the Jet pumps it is necessary to first remove the lock ring from the round portion of the casting and press the shaft out from the impeller end. This will leave the fan hub attached to the shaft and it can be pressed off separately.

Both the fan hub and the pump impeller are press fits on the shaft and require considerable pressure to remove and install. After an older impeller has been removed, if it slides too easily on the new shaft it will be necessary to replace it since it depends entirely on the press fit to hold it in place.

Physical inspection is performed as stated in the paragraph below for all other Hudson models.

Thermostats

On all Hudson engines the thermostats are located in the water outlet elbow at the top of the cylinder head. They can be replaced by removing the water outlet and lifting out the thermostat.

Engine Manifolds

All Hudson cars are equipped with the combination type manifold in that the exhaust manifold is bolted to the intake manifold at the center. The exhaust manifold is equipped with a heat riser valve which directs the hot exhaust gases against the intake manifold whenever the engine is cold. The only service required is to see that the heat riser valve is in operating condition and if necessary replace the thermostat spring.

Fuel System

All Hudson built cars are equipped with either a single fuel pump or a combination fuel and vacuum pump. It is impossible to say on just which models the fuel and vacuum pump is used, since it was optional equipment on all models.

The fuel pump on all Hudson built cars is located on the right side of the engine and is driven directly from the cam shaft.

ENGINE ASSEMBLY

Hudson Motor Car Co. supplies cars equipped with 6 and 8 cylinder engines. All Hudson engines are of the L head variety.

Engine Removal

To remove the Hudson engine it is necessary to remove the radiator core. The engine is detached at the bell housing and the transmission is supported on a jack. Remove the front mounting bolts and loosen the rear mounting bolts (at the transmission) and detach all parts such as fuel lines, gauge lines, electrical connections, exhaust pipe, floor mat, floor cover over the transmission, radiator hoses and throttle connections, etc. After detaching all these parts the engine may be slid forward and up out of the frame.

CYLINDER HEAD TORQUE TIGHTENING SEQUENCE

Six Cylinder Models and Jets

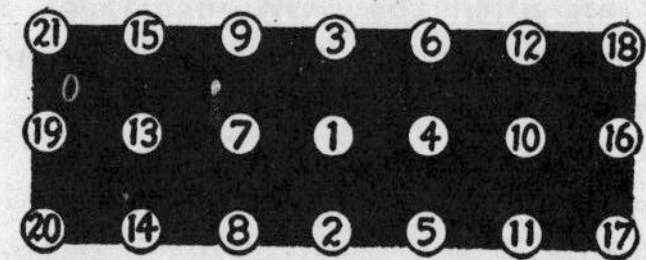

1940-47—40-45 foot pounds. 1948-50—70-75 foot pounds. 1951—60-65 foot pounds.

Eight Cylinder Models

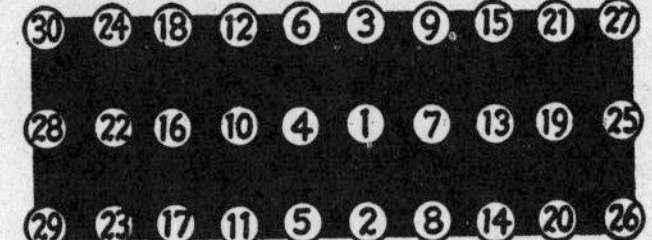

1940-51—45-50 foot pounds.

ENGINE INTERNAL

Oil Pan Removal

ALL MODELS EXCEPT JETS

On 1948 to 1953 models (except the 1951 thru 1953 6 cylinder) it is necessary to lower the front suspension cross member in order to take down the oil pan. To simplify this job, place a jack under the center of the front cross member and remove one of the cap screws on each side which hold the front cross member to the frame and replace it with a 6 inch long stud. Now remove the remainder of the cap screws and slowly let the jack down, the action of the coil spring will force the cross member down the long stud which will hold it in alignment so that it may be replaced readily.

After the cross member is lowered, unbolt and remove the oil pan in the usual manner.

Note: On 1951 thru 1953 6 cylinder models it is possible to get the oil pan down without lowering the cross member by removing the intermediate steering arm bracket from the frame and letting the arm hang down from the tie rods.

On all models up to 1947 the oil pan may be taken down by simply unbolting it from the cylinder block and lowering it to the floor.

ALL JET MODELS

Remove the three bolts which hold the center steering arm to the number two cross member and let the steering arm and tie rods drop down. Take off the flywheel dust cover, then unbolt and remove the oil pan.

Vibration Damper Removal

On 1948 to 1953 models it is necessary to take off the radiator core in order to remove the vibration damper. On all 6 cylinder models from 1938 to 1947 the vibration damper can be removed from underneath the car. On 8 cylinder models it is necessary to remove the radiator core in a manner similar to the 1948 thru 1953 models. On 8 cylinder models from 1938 to 1947 it is also necessary to loosen the

Dampener
Hub
Assembly
Pulley
Key
Starter Jaw
Bolt
Fan Belt
Vibration Dampener

Vibration damper. Note that cap screws are removed from under car

bumper mounting bolts and permit the bumper to lower itself downward.

Timing Case Cover Removal

The timing case cover may be readily unbolted from the cylinder block after the vibration damper has been taken off.

See vibration damper removal.

Piston and Connecting Rod Assemblies

Cam ground aluminum pistons are used on all Hudson models and the piston pin is full floating.

Four ring pistons are used and one of the rings is mounted in the piston skirt below the wrist pin. When installing rings on the Hudson pistons the ring gaps should be brought into line at the pin which is driven from the top of the piston down through the ring bands to retain the rings in this position. The pin is called a ring pin. If replacement rings are being installed it is advisable to follow the procedure recommended by the manufacturer of the rings being installed.

Piston Size Code

Production engines are stamped with a piston size code. The stamp is placed on the lower edge of the valve chamber. The letter "A" (or no letter at all) equals nominal size. "B" equals .005 inch oversize. "C" indicates .010 oversize. "D" indicates .015 oversize; each letter of the alphabet indicating .005 inch larger than the previous letter. Where two letters are used, such as "AO," it indicates that that cylinder is .010 inch oversize. (This is a standard oversize.)

The letters "BO" indicate a cylinder .0005 larger than the .010 oversize.

The letters "CO" indicate a cylinder .010 inch larger than the .010 oversize.

Again each letter of the alphabet indicates .005 inch steps larger than .010 oversize.

This code is used on all production engines built since 1940.

Connecting Rod Bearings

The 6 cylinder model 1948 through 1953 used the precision replaceable shell type bearing in all connecting rods. Except for the 6 cylinder, 1948 through 1953, all Hudson engines are fitted with pored type connecting rods. The Hudson Motor Car Co. does not recommend adjusting the rod bearing. However, it is possible to secure a useable adjustment on the poured rod bearings (all 8's and all 6's to 1947) for as much as .004 play by removing the shims from between the rod bearing cap and the rod forging. If no shims are used it is possible to secure an adjustment for as much as .003 excessive clearance by filing lightly across the bearing cap.

An adjustment for as much as .004" excessive play can be secured on the precision shell type connecting rod bearing by installing a feather or taper type shim between the bearing and the cap.

Clearances in excess of .004" require a new precision insert.

Rod Bearing Lubrication

On all models of Hudson, except the 1950 thru 1953 6 cylinder models, the connecting rods are fed by the "splash" system. Dippers are built into the lower half of the connecting rod to pick up oil from the troughs in the oil pan. The 1950 thru 1953 6 cylinder models are fed with oil under pressure through the crankshaft.

Assembling Piston to Connecting Rod

On 6 cylinder models from 1948 through 1953 there is a small spit hole in the connecting rod at the big end bearing. The slot in the piston should be assembled to the same side of the connecting rod which has the spit hole.

Before removing the rods from the engine they should be marked, since Hudson rods are not stamped with the cylinder number.

All other Hudson piston and rod assemblies, except the 6 cylinder from 1948 thru 1953, have offset rods. The offset is arranged so that, in the odd numbered cylinders the rod proper is offset forward; on even numbered cylinders the rod proper is offset to the rear. The rods in the odd numbered cylinders are known as right hand offset rods; those in the even numbered cylinders are known as the left hand offset rods.

When assembling the piston to the connecting rod set the connecting rod in a vise so that the connecting rod proper is facing toward the mechanic. With the rod set in this position the pin which aligns the rings should face toward the mechanic on odd numbered pistons and away from the mechanic on even numbered pistons.

A quick check can be made by holding the assembled piston and rod with the ring pin facing toward the mechanic, held in this position the opening in the oil dipper in the connecting rod cap should be to the mechanic's left hand.

Assembling Rod and Piston Assemblies to the Engine

When the rod and piston assemblies are mounted in the engine the ring pin should be forward on all pistons. Rod and piston assemblies on all models can be removed and replaced through the top of the block.

On 8 cylinder models it is also possible to take the rod and piston assemblies out through the bottom of the block.

Crankshaft Main Bearings

On all 6 cylinder Hudson engines from 1948 through 1953 the main bearings are of the precision slip-in type, which may be replaced without removing the crankshaft. Six cylinder engines before 1948 and all 8 cylinder engines are fitted with precision main bearings which are held into the crankcase by means of brass screws.

The Hudson Motor Co. recommends tnat the crankshaft be removed in order to take out the upper half of the main bearing shells. However, it is possible to remove the shells (if they are to be discarded) by loosening all the main bearing caps and permitting the crankshaft to drop approximately 1/16 inch. Remove the cap from the bearing which is to be taken out and, using a wide flat faced tool, which is no thicker than the shell of the bearing, drive the bearing around the crankshaft, shearing off the brass screw. The new upper half can then be installed by rotating it into place in the same manner as would be done on an ordinary slip-in bearing. This procedure will damage the main bearing shell so that it is useless and should never be done if the shell is to be reused.

The front and rear main bearing caps are fitted with vertical slots into which a wood oil seal is driven.

On the front main bearing a horizontal slot is milled between the block and the cap to receive oil seal packing. This packing is driven into place after the main bearing cap is seated.

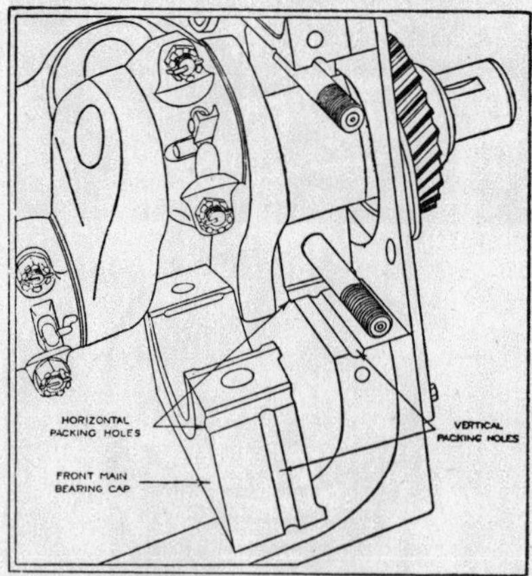

Front main bearing cap removed

Because of this horizontal packing it is necessary to use a pulling device to remove the front main bearing cap since it is necessary to shear the packing in order to take down the cap. Sometimes it is necessary to use a pulling device on the rear main bearing cap also, due to the fact that the wooden oil seal becomes oil soaked and expands, holding the cap tightly to the crankcase.

Main bearings are supplied for all Hudson models in a variety of undersizes.

Hudson does not recommend adjusting the main bearings and under no circumstances should the caps be filed. However, it is possible to secure an adjustment for as much as .004 excessive play in the bearings by placing a taper or feather type shim between the lower bearing shell and the bearing cap.

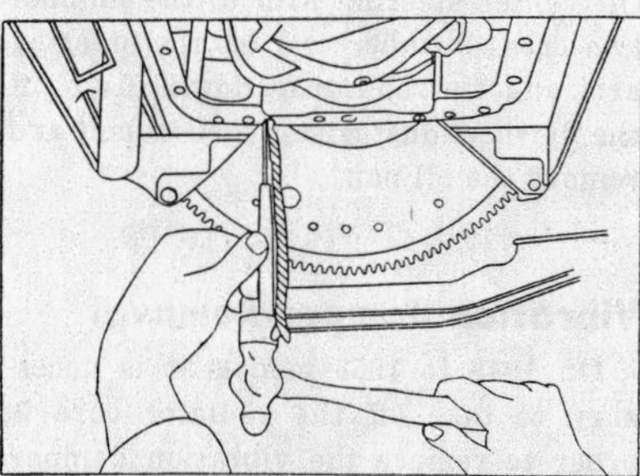

Repacking rear main bearing cap

Rear Main Bearing Oil Seal

On 6 cylinder models up to and including 1947 the rear main bearing was fitted with an oil slinger which prevented oil from leaking from the rear main bearing to the clutch housing. The lower portion of the stationary part of the slinger is equipped with an oil drain having a flapper valve at the bottom end. The only service required is to see that the slinger is kept free of sludge and gum. This may be accomplished by removing the oil pan and forcing cleaning fluid under pressure up through the oil drain. The cleaning fluid should be followed by compressed air to make sure the slinger is thoroughly clean.

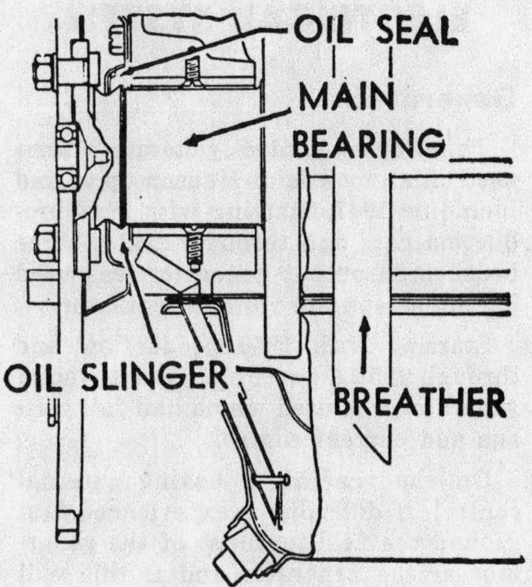

Rear main bearing oil return tube

6 CYLINDER MODELS, EXCEPT JET 1948 THROUGH 1953

On these models a packing type rear main bearing oil seal was used which required removal of the crankshaft in order to replace the upper half. The lower half can be replaced, however, by removing the rear main bearing cap and installing new packing.

ALL 8 CYLINDER MODELS

All 8 cylinder models are equipped with a packing type rear main bearing oil seal which requires the removal of the crankshaft to replace the upper half. The lower half may be replaced by taking down the rear main bearing cap.

ALL JET MODELS

The rear main bearing oil seal on jet models is a "Brummer Seal" and both the upper and lower halves can be replaced with the engine and crankshaft in place on the car.

To install the rear main bearing oil seal on these models, remove the oil pan and detach both the upper and lower half of the oil seal.

Loosen all of the main bearings so that the crankshaft can be let down about 1/16 of an inch.

Using cleaner or solvent, thoroughly clean out the groove into which the oil seal fits and work up the new oil seal, being liberal with soap on the seal so that it will slide in readily.

Main Bearing Size Code

Standard production engines were built having .010 inch undersize main and/or rod bearings. To identify these engines a size code is stamped on the bottom face of the cylinder block at the left front corner in a clear area beyond the oil pan gasket.

T. U. means the crankshaft has .010 undersize crank pins.

M. U. means the crankshaft has .010 inch undersize main bearing journals.

P. M. U. means the crankshaft has .010 undersize pins and main bearing journals.

If nothing is stamped on the left front corner of the crankcase just beyond the oil pan gasket then the engine has standard main and rod bearings.

THE VALVE SYSTEM

All Hudson engines are of the L head variety, having the valves fitted in the cylinder block. Surge dampers were used on the valve springs of all models from 1940 through 1947. 1948 through 1953 engines were not fitted with surge dampers.

The valve lifters are fitted with removable bushings.

Access to the valves is through the engine side pan after the left front wheel has been removed.

Removal of Valves and Springs

The valves and valve springs may be removed readily after the cylinder head is taken off. An ordinary clamp type or C type valve spring lifter is used to remove the valve keepers.

The valve spring can be taken out readily after the valve has been removed.

Valve Lifter Bushing Replacement

EIGHT CYLINDER MODELS ONLY

It is possible to remove a valve lifter bushing without taking off the cylinder head.

This practice may be followed when replacing one or two lifter bushings. However, if a series of bushings are to be replaced then it is advisable to take out the cylinder head and the valve.

The procedure is as follows:

Remove the valve keeper and push the valve up into the combustion chamber as far as it will go and take out the valve spring seat and the valve spring. Remove the tappet adjusting screw and take out the clamp which holds the bushing down into the cylinder block. The lifter and its bushing may now be removed from the block.

Replacement of Valve Guides

On all models valve guides are pulled up through the top of the cylinder block, after removing the valve assembly and cylinder head. The new guides are driven downward through the top of the block. It is customary to ream the valve guide after installation to remove any distortion which may have been caused by the driver. Before pulling out the valve guides it is customary to measure the distance from the top of the valve guide to the cylinder top and see to it that the new guide is installed exactly the same distance.

Valve Timing

All Hudson engines, except the 1948 thru 1953 6-cylinder models, are equipped with gears.

The timing mark location on these gears consists of two punch marks on the cam gear, and one punch mark on the crank gear. When setting the timing for valves the one pinch mark on the crank gear should come in between the two punch marks on the cam gear.

On 6 cylinder models for 1948 thru 1953 a timing chain is used.

Valve Timing Procedure

6 CYLINDER MODELS 1941 THRU 1947 & ALL 8 CYLINDER MODELS

On these models the camshaft drive is by means of gear. The arrangement is such that unless the gears become badly worn or seriously damaged it is unlikely that the valve timing will be affected. If it becomes necessary to retime the valves or replace either the cam or crankshaft gear, proceed as follows:

Remove the timing case cover and unbolt the camshaft gear. Pull the crank gear off the shaft. Press the new crankshaft gear on to the shaft, being careful to align the key and keyway perfectly since the gear is a tight fit on the shaft and it is very difficult to correct it for misalignment after the gear is started.

VALVE TIMING PROCEDURE—cont'd

Now turn the crank gear until the marked tooth on the gear is pointed directly toward the center of the camshaft. Tentatively mesh the camshaft gear with the crankshaft gear so that the two marks on the cam gear straddle the one mark on the crank gear.

Rotate the camshaft so that the bolt holes line up properly and install the bolts and locking plate.

Turn the crankshaft through two full revolutions until the gear again assumes the checking position, with the

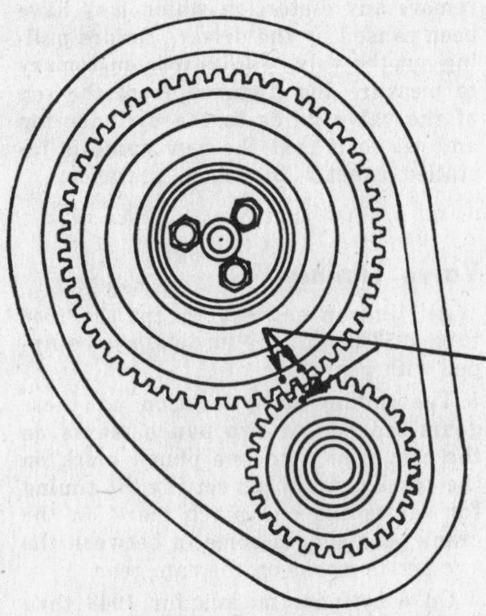

Line up marks on timing gears as shown, except 1948-51 6 cylinder model

single mark on the crankshaft between the two marks on the cam gear.

Set up in this manner the valves are correctly timed regardless of which piston is at top center.

It may, however, be necessary to retime the ignition.

1948 TO 1953 6-CYLINDER MODELS

Camshaft drive on these models is by means of a chain. If it becomes necessary to replace the chain or sprockets due to wear or damage, proceed as follows:

Remove the timing case cover and then unbolt the camshaft gear. Remove the gear and timing chain. If it is necessary to remove the crankshaft sprocket do it at this time.

Press on the new crankshaft sprocket being careful to align the keyway when starting the gear since it is very difficult to correct for misalignment after the gear is started on the shaft.

Turn the crankshaft so that the timing mark on the crankshaft sprocket is in the position shown in the accompanying illustration, and tentatively place the camshaft sprocket on the camshaft, aligning the bolt holes and bring the timing mark to the position shown in the accompanying illustration.

Slide the camshaft off the sprocket and mount the chain over both sprockets.

Push up the camshaft sprocket on to its shaft, and bolt in place being careful to maintain the relationship between the timing chain and sprocket as shown in the accompanying illustration.

Turn the crankshaft two full revolutions until the timing marks again assume the checking position. Check to see that the mark on the crank sprocket and the mark on the cam sprocket coincide with the marked links of the timing chain.

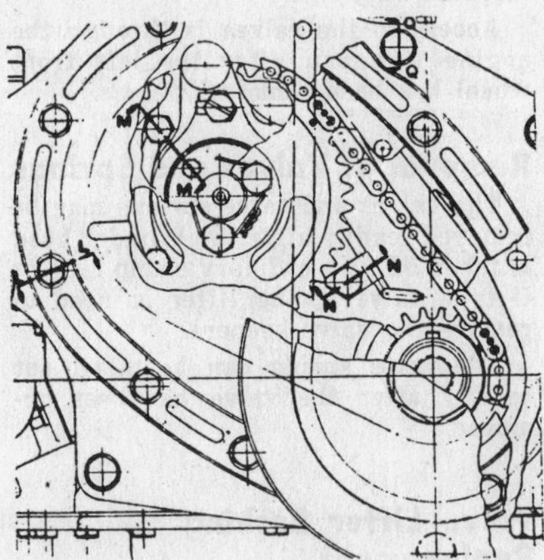

1948 and 1951 6 cylinder models. Valves are correctly timed when the marks are aligned as shown above

Note there are eight links of the timing chain between the mark on the cam sprocket and the mark on the crank sprocket counting the link at each mark.

Set up in this manner the valves are correctly timed regardless of which piston is at top center. It may be necessary to reset the ignition.

ELECTRICAL SYSTEM

Generator

Three brush control generators were used on all models of Hudson up to and including 1947. Starting with 1948 production cars and through 1949 a three brush high output generator was used having a separate voltage regulator.

Starting with 1950 production and through 1953 a two brush shunt wound generator was used which had full voltage and current control.

On the generators having external control, if difficulty is experienced first ground the field terminal of the generator at the generator and if this will correct the difficulty then the regulator is at fault. If grounding the field terminal does not correct the trouble then the generator must be removed from the car and subjected to the bench tests shown in the General Service Section of this Manual.

Voltage Regulator

The two element type voltage regulator is used on three brush generators to prevent the battery from becoming overcharged. Service on the regulator is given in the Fundamental Section of this Manual. (See index)

When a new regulator is installed on the car the generator should be polarized by temporarily placing a jumper between the BAT terminal on the regulator and the GEN terminal on the regulator. In other words jump some of the battery current across the regulator so that the generator will be properly poarized before starting the car.

This should also be done at a time the generator is given a major service. It is not necessary to hold the jumper on longer than a half second.

Voltage and Current Regulators

Starting with 1950 production all Hudson cars were equipped with a voltage and current regulator. Service on this regulator is given in the General Service Section of this Manual. (See index)

The Starter

If trouble is experienced in the starter circuit the first thing to do is check the condition of the battery before removing the starting motor. The battery should be checked with a hydrometer to determine its specific gravity. Also check the condition of the battery cables and the battery ground cable. All connections to the battery should be clean and tight. Before removing the starter check the starter switch to be certain that the contact points are not pitted or burned. If they are pitted or burned it will be necessary to replace the starter switch. If the starter switch is in good condition and the battery is fully charged and the starter still does not turn the engine properly remove the starter from the car and subject it to the same bench tests as given for generators in the General Service Section of this Manual. (See index)

A quick way to check the condition of the starter switch is to place a volt meter across the terminals of the starter switch and then crank the engine. The voltage drop across the starter switch should never exceed approximately 1/3 volt.

The Distributor

A distributor having a single set of breaker points is used on all Hudson built cars from 1940 through 1953.

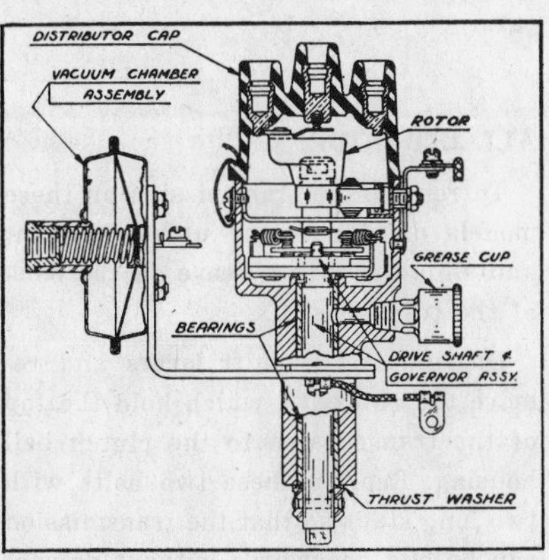

Distributor—typical all sixes

The distributor must be removed from the car for overhaul.

When the distributor is removed examine the shaft and bearings to determine if there is any wear. A very slight amount of wear in the shaft bushings will result in an uneven cam angle.

Check the action of the vacuum advance unit to make sure that it does not leak.

At anytime the distributor is removed it is a good idea to install new points as a precautionary measure.

Distributor specifications are given at the beginning of this Hudson section.

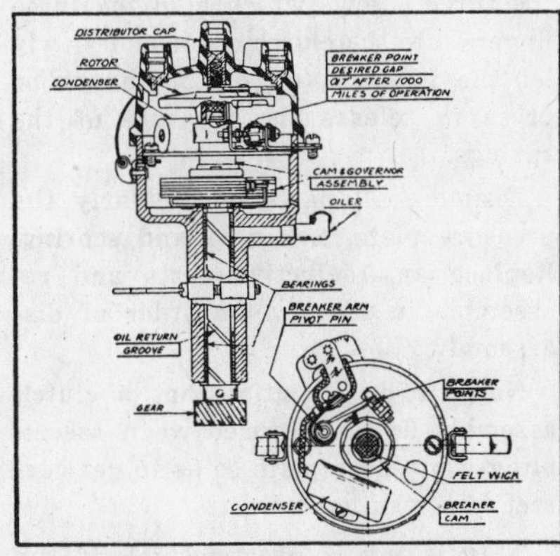

Distributor—typical all eights

Firing Order

The firing order for all 6 cylinder models is 1-5-3-6-2-4.

The distributor on all 6 cylinder models from 1940 thru 1947 turns in a counter-clockwise direction. Rotation for 6 cylinder distributors from 1948 thru 1951 is in a clockwise direction.

Firing order for 8 cylinder models is 1-6-2-5-8-3-7-4. All 8 cylinder distributors rotate in a clockwise direction.

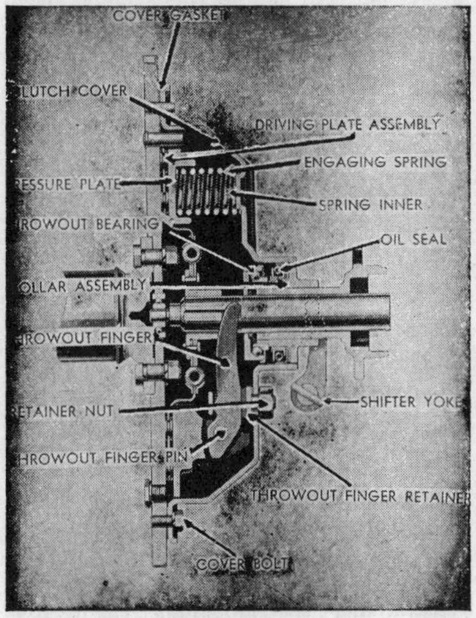

Cross section of clutch assembly used on all models

CLUTCH ASSEMBLY

An oil immersion type clutch is used on all Hudson automobiles except Jets. All Jet models use a single dry disc clutch.

Draining & Refilling The Oil Immersion Clutch

ALL MODELS EXCEPT JETS

Crank the engine until the drain plug in the front face of the flywheel appears in the hole in the flywheel housing just above the starter solinoid. Remove this drain plug and again crank the engine until the hole thus uncovered is at the bottom which will permit complete drainage.

Note: The plug hole is at the extreme bottom when the star, stamped on the flywheel is in line with the pointer at the inspection hole.

The clutch is refilled with 1/3 pint special clutch oil.

To refill again turn the crank until the drain hole plug is in the inspection hole space at the front face of the flywheel, just above the starter, and add the necessary 1/3 pint oil and replace the plug.

Clutch Pedal Linkage Adjustment

Adjust the links of the rod which connects the clutch pedal to the cross shaft level so that there is 1½ inch from the front face of the clutch pedal to the bottom of the floor board.

Clutch Removal

ALL MODELS EXCEPT JETS

To remove the clutch unbolt the front seat and slide it back out of the way and then take up the floor mat and the floor pan over the clutch and transmission. Disconnect the clutch linkage connection and remove all linkage brackets from the clutch or bell housing. Disconnect the transmission shift links and split the transmission at the universal joint and then take out the bell housing cover screws and pull the transmission back and up into the car. The clutch can then be unbolted from the flywheel.

ALL JET MODELS

To remove the clutch from the Jet models first disconnect the universal joints and remove the transmission.

Detach the clutch fork and disconnect it from its fulcrum pin and remove it from the car.

The clutch should be marked for its position on the flywheel and then unbolt it (a few turns at a time on each bolt to prevent bending the pressure plate) and lower it through the bottom of the housing.

Cutaway of clutch showing pressure plate and cork inserts in driving plate

Clutch Disassembly

ALL MODELS EXCEPT JETS

The driving disc on all Hudson clutches is a cork insert type, designed to operate in oil. Special equipment is required to service the clutch pressure plate assembly and also the disc. Unless this special equipment is available it is advisable to either install a new or a rebuilt clutch.

Instruction for the use of the special equipment needed is always supplied by the manufacturer of such equipment.

ALL JET MODELS

Place the clutch assembly in a press so that pressure could be maintained on the fingers.

With pressure on the fingers, loosen the three screws which hold the three fingers into the clutch cover and slowly let the pressure up off of the arbor press to release the pressure of the springs.

Examine all parts, particularly the pressure plate, for wear and scoring. Replace any defective parts and reassemble in the reverse order of disassembly.

Note: It is essential that a clutch assembly fixture be used when assembling a pressure plate so as to get correct finger adjustment.

This is not a practical job if the proper equipment is not at hand.

STANDARD TRANSMISSION ASSEMBLY

The transmission used on 1941 models was somewhat different from the more conventional transmission used in models from 1942 thru 1953. The 1941 transmission was equipped with a sleeve splined to the main shaft. This sleeve shifted inside the second speed gear and, in its backward position, engaged the second speed gear to the main shaft; in its forward position engaged the main drive pinion to the main shaft.

Low and reverse shift was accomplished by shifting the idler gear on the splined counter shaft. The counter shaft was equipped with three separate gears, each attached to the splined shaft and held in place with snap rings. The third gear on the main shaft was free to slide on the splined counter shaft.

The reverse idler shaft was also equipped with a sliding gear which moved into mesh with the large gear on the back of the main shaft for reverse.

Standard transmissions from 1942 thru 1953 were the conventional type with a cluster gear used on the counter shaft and a synchronizer hub used between the drive pinion gear and the main shaft second speed gear.

Low and reverse were accomplished in the conventional manner by sliding the large gear on the back of the main shaft forward to engage the counter shaft gear for low and backward to engage the reverse idler gear for reverse.

Removal of Transmission

ALL MODELS EXCEPT JET

To remove the transmission it is necessary to unbolt the front seat and slide it back out of the way, take up the floor mat and the floor pan and support the rear of the engine on a jack, detach all parts which are attached to the transmission such as the clutch linkage, clutch pedal, brackets, speedometer drive, shift linkage, etc. The transmission is then separated at the front universal joint and the clutch bell housing bolts are removed. The transmission then may be slid back and up into the car.

ALL JET MODELS

To remove the transmission on these models disconnect the universal joint and slide the spline sleeve off the back of the transmission.

Disconnect the shift levers and remove the two bolts which hold the top of the transmission to the clutch bell housing. Replace these two bolts with two long studs so that the transmission can be slid backwards without damaging the clutch disk.

Remove the two bottom bolts and slide the transmission back and down.

Disassembly of Transmission

Accompanying this text is a series of pictures which shows the step by step procedure to disassemble Hudson transmissions.

Remove transmission cover, tip case on side and remove shift rail lock spring and ball, separate case from clutch housing assembly, remove companion flange nut and pull the flange from shaft

Remove the flange and bolts holding the speedometer housing

Remove the main drive gear from the front of transmission case

Remove the low and reverse shifter fork lock screw holding fork to the rail

Slide the low and reverse shifter rail from the front of case, then lift shifter fork from case, remove second and high shifter lock screw

Slide the second and high shifter rail from the front of case, lift out shifter fork

Remove synchronizer shift sleeve lock ring, then lift out synchronizer unit, intermediate gear and the low and reverse gear

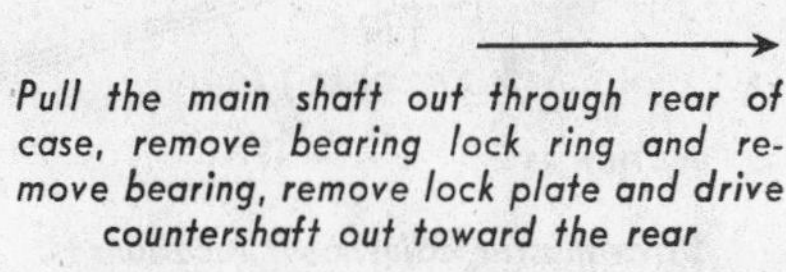

Pull the main shaft out through rear of case, remove bearing lock ring and remove bearing, remove lock plate and drive countershaft out toward the rear

OVERDRIVE ASSEMBLY

Disassembly instructions on the overdrive are given in the General Service Section in this manual, see Index.

Hudson Drivemaster

The Hudson drivemaster is a device operated by electrically controlled vacuum which functions to shift the transmission and clutch automatically between second and high gear whenever the control knob on the instrument panel is turned to the operating position. All drivemaster equipped cars can be operated as conventional transmissions by simply depressing the off button on the instrument panel which will render the automatic functioning of the drivemaster inoperative.

Improvements and refinements have been developed from time to time in the drivemaster set-up but the accompanying adjustment instructions will be found to be suitable for all drivemaster cars.

ADJUSTMENT INSTRUCTIONS

1. Check adjustment of ball joint (DD) for free rotation without perceptible end play.

2. With lever (CC) in neutral, check rod (F) and adjustment if necessary to get 1 3/16 in. between front face of rod end (E) and rear face of diaphragm cylinder. See Section (A-A).

Caution: Loosen lock nut and hold diaphragm rod end (E) with a wrench to prevent rod from turning, which would damage the diaphragm, while turning rod (F) with pliers at the knurled surface.

3. With transmission in neutral, disconnect transmission shift rod assembly (P) at front end. Push or pull slightly on rod (P) until a free crossover is obtained. Jiggle lever (CC) until ball is seated solidly in neutral detent. Adjust length of rod (P) so

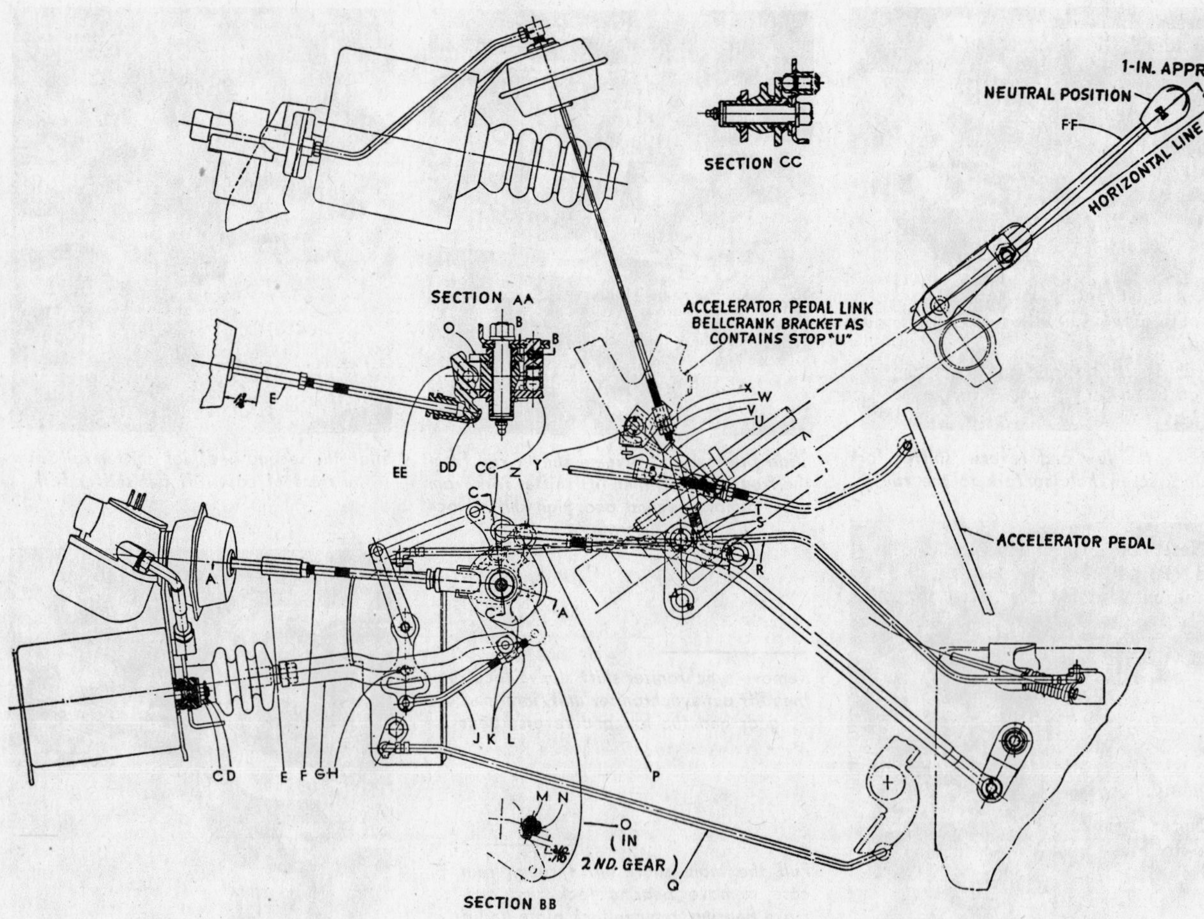

Drive master adjustment locations

that it can be reconnected without moving either of the levers to which it is attached. If crossover becomes stiffer when rod is connected, shorten or lengthen rod in ½ turn steps until crossover becomes free.

4. Adjust length of rod assembly (T) so that when in neutral the end of the hand lever (FF) is approximately 1 in. above a transverse horizontal line, as shown.

5. With engine running and HDM panel switch "on," shift to second gear. Turn stop screw (M) down until it contacts shift lever (O) and then turn it down ½ turn more. Lock in place with Allen head set screw (N).

6. With engine running, operate throttle lock by running a jumper wire from the battery negative post to either one of the throttle lock solenoid pins. Adjust nut (X) on diaphragm cable until lever (U) is held solidly against stop (V) when accelerator pedal is depressed. Lock nut with nut (W). Cable should not be so short that shaft (Y) is deflected when throttle lock operates.

7. Neutral switch adjustment:

(a) With HDM switch "on," and engine running, shift transmission to neutral, and disconnect shift rod (P) at front end.

(b) With shift rod (P) disconnected, move hand lever (FF) to second, and back to neutral.

(c) Push or pull slightly on rod (P) to obtain a free crossover in transmission.

(d) If shift rod (P) appears too short to go back on pin (Z), shorten neutral switch rod (J); if too long, lengthen neutral switch rod. Repeat (C), (D), and (E) until rod (P) can be reconnected without moving either of the levers to which it is attached.

Note: Do not change length of shift rod (P) as this length is determined by adjustment No. 3.

FINAL CHECK:

To eliminate sticky crossover, recheck adjustments No. 3 and No. 7. Also check to see that crossover switch rod (R) is centered in clip (S) at clutch housing.

Note: Transmission shift from second to high must take place between 9.5 and 14 mph.

Transmission shift from high to second must take place between 9 and 12 mph.

In high gear, Vacumotive Drive **must** automatically become **inoperative 16** mph min. to 21 mph max. and **remain** inoperative at all higher speeds.

HYDRAMATIC DRIVE

Operating Instructions

Starting with 1952 production, a "dual range" hydramatic is used on all Hudson models equipped with hydramatic. On the dual range models the drive range is marked 3 and 4, 4 indicating four speeds or the normal range and 3 indicating three speeds or the performance range. Otherwise the operation of the hydramatic is the same as described below.

The manual selector lever located just below the steering wheel is used to select neutral, low drive or reverse position. These positions are all shown on the indicator dial. The indicator dial is eliminated when the lighting switch is turned on. The marks on the dial are as follows: "N" for neutral, "DR" for all normal forward driving, "LO" for maximum power forward, "R" for reverse. To start the car set the manual selector lever in the "N" position, depress the accelerator pedal and release.

Caution: Do not pump the accelerator pedal.

Next turn on the ignition switch and press the starter button.

OPERATION IN DRIVE RANGE

After the engine is started move the manual selector lever to the drive position and allow it to remain in this position for all normal driving. When both the engine and transmission are cold there may be a tendency for the car to creep slightly, due to the increased engine RPM when the engine is idling in the fast idle postion. A slight application of the foot brake or hand brake will hold the car during this condition. When the brakes are released the car will move forward when the accelerator pedal is depressed.

The shift from low speed to second and from third to fourth will occur at different car speeds, depending upon the amount of pressure on the accelerator. With a slight accelerator pressure the shifts will occur at lower car speed than they would if the accelerator were depressed, demanding engine torque.

The hydramatic transmission, while adjusted and calibrated to function properly with a Hudson engine, actually works in the same manner as the hydramatic for all other cars. Complete service instruction on hydramatic transmission is given in the Automatic Transmission Section of this Manual. (See index.)

Throttle Linkage Adjustment—Hydromatics

Thoroughly warm up the engine and transmission and put the shift lever in the neutral position and adjust the idle speed between 480 and 520 RPM. Make sure that the carburetor is off the fast idle and adjust the accelerating operat-

Fig. 1

ing rod, (Figs. 1 and 2), at the top of the cylinder head, left side just over the spark coil, until the hole in the bell crank down on the cylinder block and the hole in the block are exactly in alignment. (Gauge No. J-2544 is available to align to hole properly.)

Tighten the lock nuts and recheck the setting after the nuts are tightened.

Fig. 2

Throttle Linkage Adjustment—Transmission End

Raise the car and disconnect the transmission throttle rod from the outer lever (make sure that the throttle rod clamp screw is tight).

Check the position of the outer throttle lever as follows:

Secure throttle lever checking fixture No. J-2195 (this fixture will be necessary to make this adjustment). (See Fig. 3.)

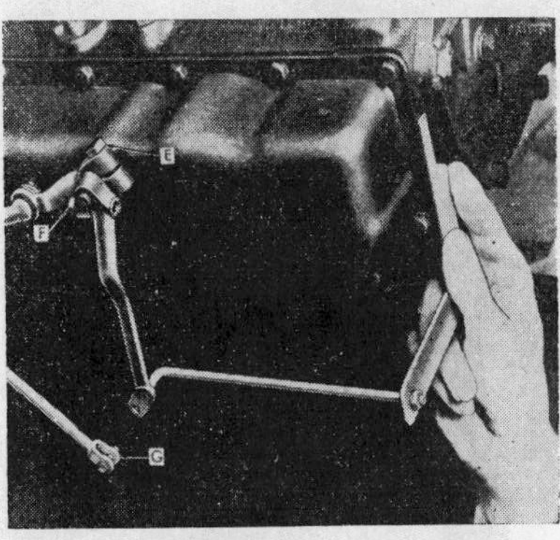

Fig. 3

Clean the machine surface at the back of the transmission case and place the special fixture flat against the back surface of the transmission case with the edge of the checking gauge against the transmission side cover.

With the outer throttle lever held against its stop toward the rear of the transmission the throttle outer lever hole should enter freely over the small diameter of the gauge pin and the inside base of the throttle control lever should just touch the larger diameter of the gauge pin. Do not force the outer lever against its stop and do not try to bend this lever unless you have the proper bending tool.

If the throttle lever lower hole will not enter over the gauge fixture, use a special bending tool, No. J-3310 (Fig. 4) and bend the throttle lever to secure the proper alignment.

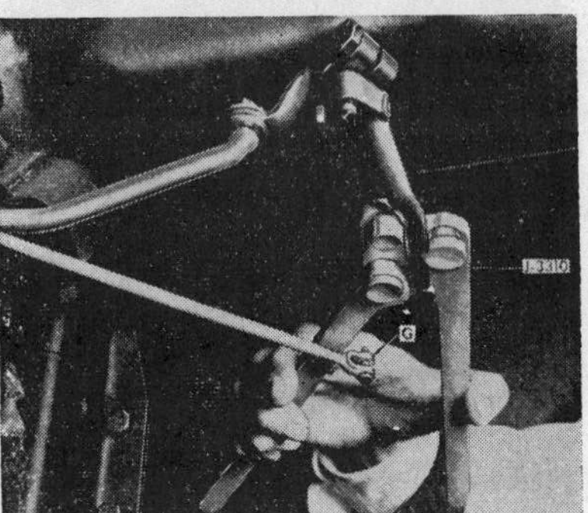

Fig. 4

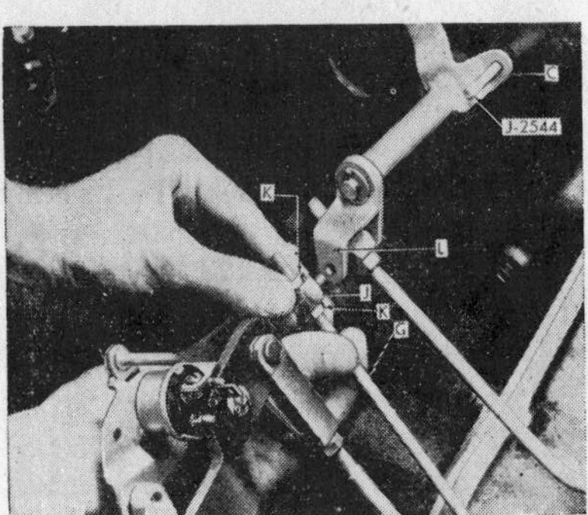

Fig. 5

Employ the bending tool according to the instructions which come with it.

After the lever is bent until the gauge enters properly, reconnect the throttle control rod. Set the other end of the transmission throttle control rod by adjusting the trunion so that it will enter the hole in the ball crank freely,

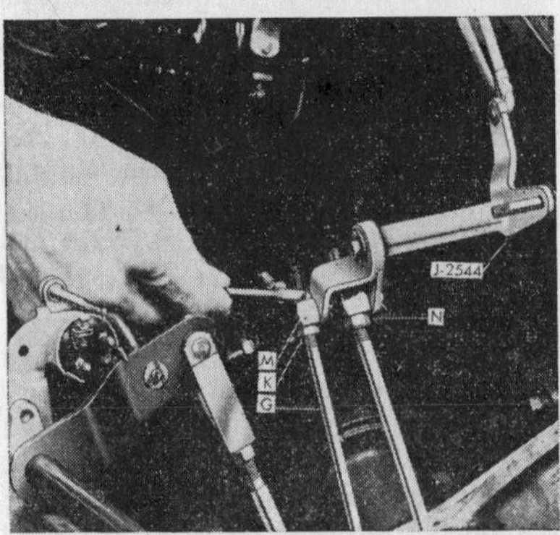

Fig. 6

with the hole in the cylinder block and the hole in the opposite end of the bell crank aligning perfectly.

Pin No. J-2544 is available to maintain the alignment of these two holes. (See Fig. 5 and Fig. 6.)

Manual Control Linkage Adjustment

Tighten the upper and lower control brackets on the steering column jacket tube and disconnect the transmission shift rod at the manual control lever at the bottom of the steering column. Now place the transmission shift lever at the transmission in the reverse position by pushing the shift rod rearwards as far as it will go (see Fig. 7). Now pull the shift lever forward one detent, placing the transmission slowly so that the shift lever is moved only one detent to the low position. Place the manual control lever at the steering wheel in the low position and pull the manual control lever as far as it will go toward the reverse without lifting the manual lever. Adjust the length of the transmission shift rod until the clevis pin holes in the clevis align with the hole in the manual control lower lever (Fig. 8). Do not move either the transmission shift lever or the manual control lever when making this rod adjustment.

Neutral Safety Switch Adjustment

Place the manual control lever in neutral. Loosen the safety switch adjusting screw (Fig. 9) and rotate the transmission safety switch bracket until there is 1/16 inch clearance between the stop and the switch lever.

With the manual control lever in the neutral position the starter should operate when the ignition switch is on and the starter button on the instrument panel is pressed. The starter should not operate, however, in any other position but neutral, when the starter button is pressed and the ignition switch is on.

Transmission Band Adjustments

Move the accelerator pedal forward to uncover the adjusting hole cover screw for the front band. Thoroughly warm up the engine and transmission and make sure that the fast idle is off on the carburetor before making any adjustments.

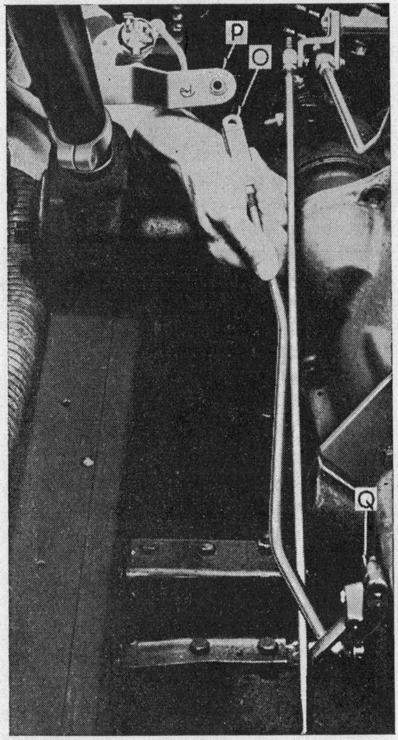

Fig. 7

Place the shift control lever in the drive range. Adjust the carburetor idle speed to give 700 RPM on a tachometer.

Using a band adjusting tool No. J-2681 (Fig. 10) loosen the front band adjusting screw by turning the top handle while holding the outer handle until the engine speed increases to 900-1000 RPM, which indicates that the front drum is spinning freely.

Tighten the front band adjusting screw slowly until the engine returns to 700 RPM. The front drum has now stopped turning. Once more loosen the front band adjusting screw until the engine speed increases and tighten the screw again very slowly until the engine speed returns to 700 RPM.

Note: The object of loosening and retightening the screw is to locate the exact point at which the band stops the drum from spinning. At this point wait 30 seconds and if the engine speed again increases tighten the screw 1/10 of a turn more. Repeat this procedure until the engine speed remains at 700 RPM for at least 30 seconds.

Now turn the adjusting screw exactly five and one-half turns and tighten the lock nut without moving the adjusting screw.

Rear Band Adjustment

To adjust the rear band, set the engine idle speed at 700, as read on a tachometer and follow the instructions given for the front band, except that after the 700 RPM has been maintained for 30 seconds tighten the band adjusting screw exactly two turns, instead of $5\frac{1}{2}$ required for the front band.

After both bands have been adjusted reset the engine idle to 480-520 RPM, with the control lever in the neutral position.

Refilling the Hydramatic

To drain the hydramatic assembly make certain that the draining process is carried on while the transmission is hot to be sure that all the oil has been removed.

Proceed as follows:

Remove the flywheel housing dust cover, remove the hex head plugs from the toris cover and drain the toris cover.

Fig. 8

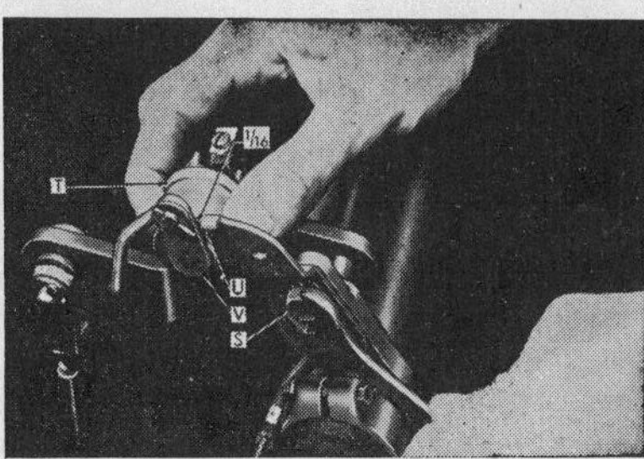

Fig. 9

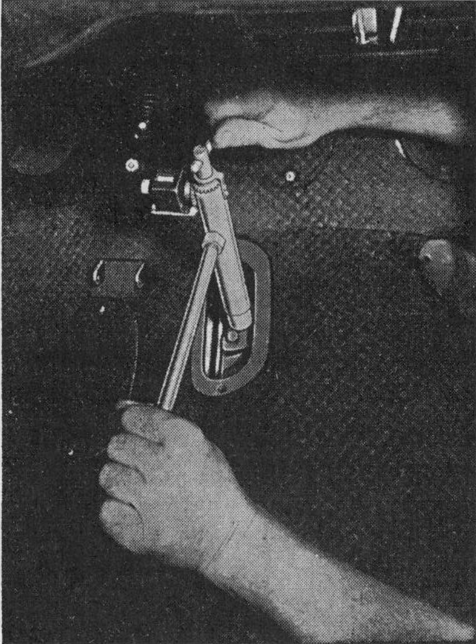

Fig. 10

Remove the oil pan drain plug at the back of the pan and drain the transmission case. Ordinarily, flushing of the unit is not necessary. However, if it is flushed for any reason use only the approved hydramatic drive fluid for flushing. After draining replace and tighten both toris covers and oil pan drain plugs. Replace the flywheel housing dust cover and raise the right side of the front floor mat and remove the transmission inspection hole cover.

Caution: Clean all gravel, sand or lint from the floor around the oil lever indicator before removing the indicator and cap.

Remove the indicator and pour 8 quarts of hydramatic fluid into the transmission filler hole. Set the hand brake tightly and allow the engine to idle for several minutes and then add oil, approximately 3 quarts, to bring the level to the full mark when the oil is hot. Always check oil level when the oil is hot, engine idling and hand brake tightly set and the control lever in the neutral range.

Removal of Hydramatic Transmission from the Car

To remove the hydramatic transmission from the car it is necessary to take out the starter, lift up the floor mat and take off the two opening covers which will give access to the flywheel housing bolt. Disconnect the propeller shaft at the rear axle companion flange and also at the transmission so that it can be removed from under the car entirely.

Take out the propeller shaft center housing so as to allow room to move the transmission back. Disconnect the the speedometer cable and all selector rods, wires, etc., from the side of the transmission. Remove the left side engine stone guards and disconnect the hand brake cable. Jack up the transmission slightly to remove the weight from the rear supports and detach the rear supports from the transmission and then detach the cross member from the side members, allowing the cross member to drop down. Support the rear end of the engine so that the front end of the oil pan will clear the center tie rod by approximately ½ inch.

Determine that all bolts have been detached from the engine and pull the transmission rearward until the pilot shaft of the transmission clears the pilot bushing in the flywheel. The transmission may now be lowered and removed from the car.

Disassembly of Hydramatic Transmission

Complete instructions on the hydramatic transmission are given in the automatic transmission portion of this section. (See index.)

REAR AXLE ASSEMBLY

ALL MODELS 1952 AND 1953

Starting with 1952 production a semi-floating type rear axle assembly is used which employs a housing assembly made up of cast malleable iron central housing into which are pressed welded flange steel tubes. A cover assembly is provided for access to the gear mechanism and all adjustments are by means of shims.

ALL MODELS UP to 1951

All Hudson cars up to 1951 are equipped with a rear axle which has a welded on cover. All service to the differential is done by removing the carrier assembly from the car. The pinion, differential side and wheel bearings are of the tapered roller type. Shims are used to adjust both the depth of the pinion and the end play in the axle shaft.

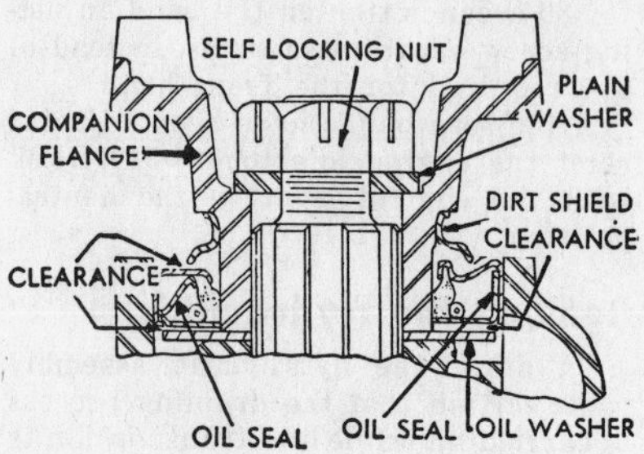

Section through the universal joint flange —All models

Replacement of Pinion Oil Seal

The pinion oil seal may be removed by disconnecting the rear universal joint and removing the universal joint companion flange. The oil seal may then be pulled out with an inertia puller.

It is good practice to punch mark the pinion nut before removing it so that it may be returned to exactly the position from which it was removed.

Replacement of Axle Shaft Oil Seals

To replace the axle shaft outer oil seal simply take off the back wheel, hub and drum and remove the cap screws which retain the oil seal to the housing flange. To replace the inner oil seal it is necessary to take out the axle shaft. This is accomplished by removing the brake backing plate, carefully noting the shims which are used to determine the axle end play, and pull the bearing out of the housing. The inner oil seal can then be removed with an inertia puller.

In some cases the axle shaft may slide out of the bearing, leaving the bearing intact in the case and if this should happen an inertia puller should be used on the bearing outer race.

Axle Shaft End Play

A spacer block is used between the two inner ends of the axle shaft, making it almost essential that end play be taken from both shafts so as to keep the thrust block centrally located between the axle shafts.

Axle shaft end play is controlled by the shims at the rear axle backing plate.

Adding shims at this point will increase the axle play, removing shims will decrease axle play. Axle end play in excess of .006 inch should be adjusted.

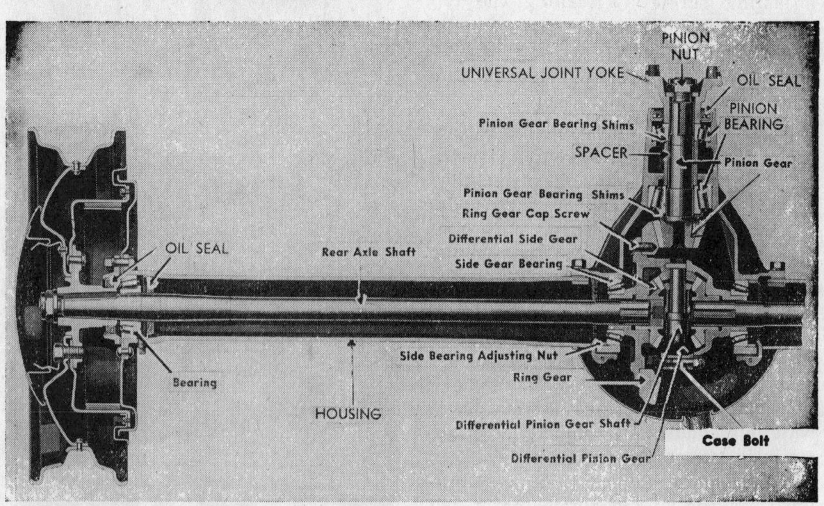

Cross section of the rear axle used in all models

Pinion Bearings— Pinion and Ring Gear

ALL MODELS 1952 AND 1953

The procedure for pinion bearings and pinion ring gear on these models is essentially the same as that in the earlier models with this exception. On the later models it is necessary to remove the entire rear axle assembly from underneath the car since the carrier is not detachable as it was in the earlier models.

Once out from under the car the only actual difference is that the shims which control the pinion depth are located in back of the rear bearing cup, rather than between the bearing and the pinion gear itself as it was in earlier models. Otherwise the procedure is as given below.

To replace either the pinion bearings or the pinion and ring gear, proceed as follows: Remove both rear axle shafts, disconnect the rear universal joint and unbolt the differential carrier from the rear axle housing.

Place the carrier assembly in a large vise on the work bench.

To disassemble the rear axle differential first remove the bearing caps on each side of the differential and lift out the differential assembly and its bearings.

Take off the universal joint flange nut and remove the universal joint companion flange. The pinion shaft may now be driven out through the back of the case.

Notice that there are shims located between the rear bearing and the pinion gear itself. These shims should be carefully cleaned and preserved so that they can be replaced if the same pinion gear is to be used again.

If a new pinion gear or new pinion bearings are to be installed tentatively start with the shims which were mounted on the old pinion. Install the shims and the pinion rear bearing cone. Place the rear bearing cup in the rear end of the differential housing and install a new bearing cup in the front end of the differential housing. Place the spacer in front of the rear bearing and insert the bearing into the case.

Tentatively replace the shims which were found between the spacer and the front bearing cone and replace the universal joint companion flange. Securely tighten the companion flange to the pinion shaft. If the correct number of shims have been used between the FRONT bearing cone and the spacer, the pinion shaft can just be turned by hand after the companion flange nut has been tightened to 200 ft lbs torque. The exact pressure required to turn the pinion shaft is 17 in. lbs.

Now mount the differential into the housing and tighten the bearing cage on the ring gear side until there is zero lash between the pinion and ring gear. Now tighten the adjusting cage on the side opposite to the ring gear until there is developed approximately .006 inch backlash between the ring gear and pinion. This will produce a preload on the differential side bearings. After setting the backlash tolerance, paint about 10 teeth of the ring gear with red lead. Move the painted teeth of the ring gear over the pinion until a good impression is made.

The accompanying illustrations show the desired impression which should be secured and also some impressions which are not desirable and the correct method of adjusting to compensate for the error in tooth mesh.

After the correct markings have been obtained on the gear teeth replace the differential carrier assembly in the car, replace both axle shafts and using new oil seals mount the pinion and axle oil seals, replace the brakes, wheels and hubs.

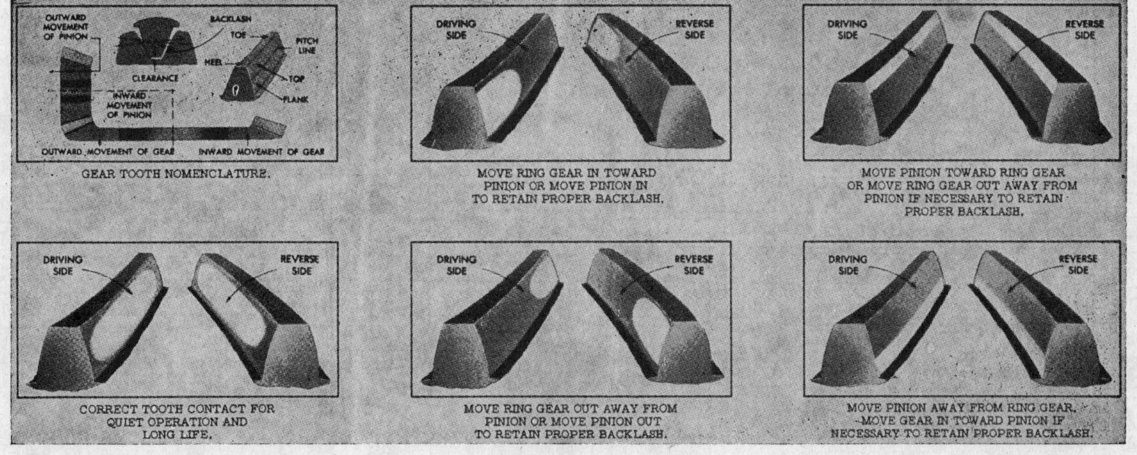

GEAR TOOTH NOMENCLATURE.

MOVE RING GEAR IN TOWARD PINION OR MOVE PINION IN TO RETAIN PROPER BACKLASH.

MOVE PINION TOWARD RING GEAR OR MOVE RING GEAR OUT AWAY FROM PINION IF NECESSARY TO RETAIN PROPER BACKLASH.

CORRECT TOOTH CONTACT FOR QUIET OPERATION AND LONG LIFE.

MOVE RING GEAR OUT AWAY FROM PINION OR MOVE PINION OUT TO RETAIN PROPER BACKLASH.

MOVE PINION AWAY FROM RING GEAR. MOVE GEAR IN TOWARD PINION IF NECESSARY TO RETAIN PROPER BACKLASH.

KAISER and FRAZER SPECIFICATIONS

Starting Serial and Motor Numbers

KAISER

Starting Serial Numbers

1947-1953—Prefix indicates year and model, i.e., K100, 1947 Six.

1947—K100 1001
K101—Custom 2000001

1948—K481 1001
K482—Custom 1001

1949, K491—Special & Traveler. 1001
K492—DeLuxe, Vagabond & Virginian 1001

1950, K501—Special & Traveler. 1001
K502—DeLuxe, Vagabond & Virginian 1001

1951, K511—Special 001001
K512—DeLuxe 001001

1952, K521—DeLuxe & Virginian Special .... 1200000 and 1001001
K522 Manhattan & Virginian DeLuxe .... 1200000 and 1001001

1953, DeLuxe & Manhattan, K001001 and up.

Location

1947-1953—On left front door pillar post.

Starting Motor Numbers

1947 .... K-10001

1948 .... KM-10001 and K-10001

1949—491 .... K-123324
492 .... KM-10001

1950 .... continuation of 1949

1951-1952 ...... 1100000 and 2000000

1953 .... K1-000001

Location

1947-1953 — Stamped on upper left front side of cylinder block and on plate on left side of cylinder block.

FRAZER

Starting Serial Numbers

First prefix indicates year and model, i.e., F47, 1947 Six. 1947 Serial numbers start 1001 on Six and 1000001 on Manhattan. 1048-1950 Serial numbers start 1001 and 1951 Serial numbers start 001001.

1947, F47—Six 1001
F47C—Manhattan 100000

1948, F485—Six 1001
486—Manhattan 1001

1949, F495—Six 1001
F496—Manhattan 1001

1950, F505—Six 1001
F506—Manhattan 1001

1951, F515—Six 001001
F516—Manhattan 001001

Location

On left front door pillar post.

Starting Motor Numbers

1947-1950—Prefix indicates year, i.e., F-47, 1947. 1947-1950 Motor numbers start 1001.

1947—GP or F 1001

1948—F and FM 1001

1949-1950—FM 1001

1951 .... 1000001 and 2300000

Location

Stamped on upper left front of cylinder block and plate on left side of cylinder block.

General Specifications

Year	Model	Wheelbase (in.)	Tread (in.)		Overall Dimensions (in.)			Shipping Weight* (lb.)	Tire Size (in.)
			Front	Rear	Length†	Width	Height■		
KAISER									
1946	K-85	117	58	60	203	73	64	....	6.00-15
1947	K-100	124	58	60	203	73	....	3305	6.50-15
1948	K481-K482	124	58	60	203	73	65	3302	7.10-15
1949-50	491-492	124	58	60	206	....	....	3345	7.10-15
1951	511-512	119	58	59	210	74	....	3150	6.70-15
1952	521, 522	119	58	59	211	132	....	....	6.70-15
1953	531, 532	119	58	59	211	75	60	....	6.70-15
FRAZER									
1946-47	F-47	124	58	60	203	73	65	....	6.50-15
1948	F485, F486	124	58	60	203	73	65	3375	7.10-15
1949-50	495, 496	124	58	60	208	....	....	3455	7.10-15
1951	515, 516	124	58	59	211	....	....	3535	7.10-15

*—Cheapest 5 pass. 4 door sedan. ■—Road to roof, no load. †—Including bumper and bumper guards.

General Engine Specifications

Year	Model	Number of Cylinders Bore and Stroke	Piston Displacement, Cubic Inches	Compression Ratio (To-1)	Taxable (A.M.A.) Hp.	DEVELOPED HORSE POWER Bare Engine	DEVELOPED HORSE POWER With Accessories	Maximum Torque Ft. Lbs.
KAISER								
1947	K-100, K-101, 6 Cyl.	6-3$\frac{5}{16}$ x 4$\frac{3}{8}$	226.2	7.30	26.3	100 @ 3600	......	......
1948	K-481, K-482, 6 Cyl.	6-3$\frac{5}{16}$ x 4$\frac{3}{8}$	226.2	7.30	26.3	100 @ 3600	......	......
1949	K-491, K-492, 6 Cyl.	6-3$\frac{5}{16}$ x 4$\frac{3}{8}$	226.2	7.30	26.3	100 @ 3600	......	......
1950	K-501, K-502, 6 Cyl.	6-3$\frac{5}{16}$ x 4$\frac{3}{8}$	226.2	7.30	26.3	100 @ 3600	......	......
1951	K-511, K-512, 6 Cyl.	6-3$\frac{5}{16}$ x 4$\frac{3}{8}$	226.2	7.30	26.3	115 @ 3650	......	190 @ 1800
1952	521, 522, 6 Cyl.	6-3$\frac{5}{16}$ x 4$\frac{3}{8}$	226.2	7.30	26.30	115 @ 3650	......	190 @ 1800
1953	531, 532	6-3$\frac{5}{16}$ x 4$\frac{3}{8}$	226.2	7.3	26.3	118 @ 3650	......	200 @ 1800
FRAZER								
1947	F47, F47C, Manhattan	6-3$\frac{5}{16}$ x 4$\frac{3}{8}$	226.2	7.30	26.3	100 @ 3600	......	180 @ 1400
1948	F485, F486, Manhattan	6-3$\frac{5}{16}$ x 4$\frac{3}{8}$	226.2	7.30	26.3	100 @ 3600	......	180 @ 1400
1949	495 Std., 496 Manhattan	6-3$\frac{5}{16}$ x 4$\frac{3}{8}$	226.2	7.30	26.3	112 @ 3600	......	......
1950	F505 Std., F506 Manhattan	6-3$\frac{5}{16}$ x 4$\frac{3}{8}$	226.2	7.30	26.3	112 @ 3600	......	......
1951	F515 Std., F516 Manhattan	6-3$\frac{5}{16}$ x 3$\frac{3}{8}$	226.2	7.30	26.3	115 @ 3650	......	190 @ 1800

Engine Tune-Up Specifications

Year	Model	SPARK PLUGS Type	SPARK PLUGS Gap	DISTRIBUTOR Point Gap	DISTRIBUTOR Cam Dwell (Deg.)	Ignition Timing (Deg.)	Ignition Timing Mark and Location	Com-pression Pressure at R.P.M.	OPERATING TAPPET CLEARANCE Inlet	OPERATING TAPPET CLEARANCE Exhaust	Carburetor Fuel Float Height	Minimum Engine Idle Speed at R.P.M.
KAISER												
1947	K-100, K-101, 6 Cyl.	AL-A5R	.032	.020	38	TC	Dmpr.	120@ †	.014 (c)	.014 (c)	1/16"	550
1948	K-481, K-482. 6 Cyl.	AL-A5	.032	.020	38	4B	Dmpr.	120@ †	.014 (c)	.014 (c)	1/16"	550
1949–1950	K-501, K-502, 6 Cyl.	AL-A5	.032	.020	38	4B	Dmpr.	120@ †	.014 (c)	.014 (c)	1/32"	550
1951	K-511, K-512, 6 Cyl.	AL-A5	.032	.020	31–37	4B	Dmpr.	120@ †	.014 (c)	.014 (c)	......	550
1952	521, 522, 6 Cyl.	AL-A7	.030	.020	37	4B	Dmpr.	......	.014C	.014C	1/4"	500
1953	531, 532, 6 Cyl.	AL-A7	.030	.022	37	4B	Dmpr.	......	.014C	.014C	......	500*
FRAZER												
1947	F47, F47C, Manhattan	J-7	.032	.020	38	TC	*Dmpr.	120@ †	.010	.014	5/16"	550
1948	F485, F486, Manhattan	AL-A5R	.032	.020	38	TC	Dmpr.	120@ †	.014	.014	5/16"	550
1950	F505 Std., F506 Manhattan	AL-A5	.032	.020	38	4B	Dmpr.	120@ †	.014	.014	1/32"	550
1951	F515 Std., F516 Manhattan	AL-A5G	.032	.020	38	4B	Dmpr.	120@ †	.014(c)	.014(c)	......	550

AL—Auto-Lite Co. Dmpr.—Vibration damper. (c)—Cold. †—At cranking speed of 70 r.p.m. *—On flywheel before engine No. 17160.

Engine Overhaul Specifications

Year	Model	PISTONS				RING GAP CLEARANCES (Maximum)				PISTON PIN		ROD BEARINGS		
		Removed From	Piston Skirt Clearances (Maximum)											
			Top	Bottom	Limit	Top Ring	Second Ring	Third Ring	Oil Ring	Type	Fit	Oil Clearance	Wear Limit	Side Play
KAISER														
1947	K-100, K-101, 6 Cyl.	A	....	.0015	.004	.016	.016	.016	.016	FL	Push	.0005-.0023	.005	.006-.008
1948	K-481, K-482, 6 Cyl.	A	....	.0015	.004	.016	.016	.016	.016	FL	Push	.0005-.0023	.005	.006-.010
1949	K-491, K-492, 6 Cyl.	A	....	.0015	.004	.016	.016	.016	.016	FL	Push	.0005-.0023	.005	.006-.010
1950	K-501, K-502, 6 Cyl.	A	....	.0015	.004	.016	.016	.016	.016	FL	Push	.0005-.0023	.005	.006-.010
1951	K-511, K-512, 6 Cyl.	A	....	.0015	.004	.016	.016	.016	.016	FL	Push	.0005-.0018	.005	.006-.010
1952	521, 522, 6 Cyl.	A	.0017	.0005	.004	.016	.016	.016	.016	FL	.0002	.0000-.0018	.005	.006-.011
1953	531, 532	A	.0017	.0015	.004	.016	.016	.016	.016	FL	.0002	.0005-.0018	.005	.006-.101
FRAZER														
1947	F47, F47C, Manhattan	A	....	.0015	.004	.016	.016	.016	.016	FL	Push	.0007-.0025	.005	.006-.010
1948	F485, F486, Manhattan	A	....	.0015	.004	.016	.016	.016	.016	FL	Push	.0005-.0023	.005	.006-.008
1949	495 Standard, 496 Man.	A	....	.0015	.004	.016	.016	.016	.016	FL	Push	.0005-.0023	.005	.006-.010
1950	F505 Std., F506 Man.	A	....	.0015	.004	.016	.016	.016	.016	FL	Push	.0005-.0023	.005	.006-.010
1951	F515 Std., F516 Man.	A	....	.0015	.004	.016	.016	.016	.016	FL	Push	.0005-.0018	.005	.006-.010

FL—Floating. A—Pistons removed from above.

Dimensions of Valves

Year	Model	Overall Length		Head Diameter		Seat Angle (deg.)		Stem Diameter		Key Type	O.D. of Seat Insert	
		Inlet	Exhaust	Inlet	Exhaust	Inlet	Exhaust	Inlet	Exhaust		Inlet	Exhaust
KAISER												
1946-47	K85, K100	5.015	5.344	1.515	1.375	30	45	.341	.339	*split lock	....	....
1948-49	Series—All	5.187	5.187	1.515	1.328	30	45	.341	.339	*split lock	....	....
1950	491, 492	5.188	5.188	1.516	1.328	30	45	.341	.339	*split lock	....	....
1951	511, 512	5.190	5.200	1.520	1.298	30	45	.341	.339	*split lock	....	....
1952	521, 522, 6 cyl.	5.190	5.200	1.520	1.328	30	45	.341	.3386	....	....	....
1953	531, 532	5.190	5.200	1.520	1.328	30	45	.341	.3386	....	....	....
FRAZER												
1946-47	F47	5.015	5.16	1.515	1.328	30	45	.341	.339	*split lock	....	....
1948-49	Series—All	5.187	5.187	1.515	1.328	30	45	.341	.338	*split lock	....	....
1950	1951	5.188	5.188	1.516	1.328	30	45	.341	.339	*split lock	....	....
1951	515, 516	5.190	5.200	1.520	1.298	30	45	.341	.339	*split lock	....	....

* Drilled stem or (pin type) used on some.

and Wear Limit Table

CRANKSHAFT		VALVES									OPERATING OIL PRESSURE			
		Spring Tension (Maximum)				Seat Angle		Valve Timing, Inlet Valve Opens (Deg.)						
Main Bearing Oil Clearance	Shaft End Play	Inlet	Exhaust	Low Limit	Guide Clearance	Inlet	Exhaust		Camshaft Drive	Gear Marks	Pounds At M.P.H.	Low Limit§	Model	Year
KAISER														
.002	.004-.006	110@1.306	110@1.306	100	.0008-.0026	30°	45°	10B	Chain	†SP	35@30	15	......K-100, K-101, 6 Cyl.	1947
.0015-.0020	.004-.006	113@1.3125	113@1.3125	100	.0032-.0050	30°	45°	10B	Chain	†SP	35@30	15	......K-481, K-482, 6 Cyl.	1948
.0015-.0020	.004-.006	113@1.3125	113@1.3125	100	.0032-.0050	30°	45°	10B	Chain	†SP	35@30	15	......K-491, K-492, 6 Cyl.	1949
.0015-.0020	.004-.006	113@1.3125	113@1.3125	100	.0032-.0050	30°	45°	10B	Chain	†SP	35@30	15	......K-501, K-502, 6 Cyl.	1950
.0007-.0020	.002-.006	113@1.312	113@1.312	100	.0032-.0050	30°	45°	10B	Chain	†SP	35@30	15	......K-511, K-512, 6 Cyl.	1951
....	.002-.006	118	118	......	.0032-.005	30°	45°	10B	Chain	......	35@30	......	..........521, 522, 6 Cyl.	1952
.0007-.0020	.002-.006	118@1.312	118@1.312	......	.0032-.005	30°	45°	10B	Chain	......	35@30	......	....	1953
FRAZER														
.0015-.002	.004-.006	113@1.306	113@1.306	100	.0008-.0026	30°	45°	10B	Chain	†SP	35@30	25	....F47, F47C, Manhattan	1947
.0005-.002	.004-.006	110@1.306	110@1.306	100	.0008-.0026	30°	45°	10B	Chain	†SP	35@30	25	....F485, F486, Manhattan	1948
.0015-.0020	.004-.006	113@1.3125	113@1.3125	100	.0032-.0050	30°	45°	10B	Chain	†SP	35@30	25	...495 Standard, 496 Man.	1949
.0015-.0020	.004-.006	113@1.3125	113@1.3125	100	.0032-.0050	30°	45°	10B	Chain	†SP	35@30	25	.....F505 Std., F506 Man.	1950
.0007-.0020	.002-.006	113@1.312	113@1.312	100	....	30°	45°	10B	Chain	†SP	35@30	25	.....F515 Std., F516 Man.	1951

B—Before top center. §—Car may be operated safely at lower oil pressures but low pressure indicates malfunction which should be corrected.
†—10 pins on chain between sprocket marks. SP—Sprockets.

Pistons and Piston Pins

Year	Model	PISTONS				PISTON PINS		
		Diameter	Material	Type	No. of Rings	Length	Diameter	How Held
KAISER								
1946 to 48	Series—All....................	3.3125	Alum.	....	4	$2\frac{13}{16}$	.859	F
1949	491-492....................	3.3125	Alum.	Ss	4	$2\frac{13}{16}$	.8593	F
1950	491-492....................	3.3125	Alum.	Sp	4	$2\frac{13}{16}$	.8594	F
1951	511, 512....................	3.3125	Alum.	....	4	$2\frac{25}{32}$	.8592	F
1952	521, 522, 6 cyl....................	3.3125	Alum. Alloy	Ts	4	2.780	.8592	F
1953	531, 532, 6 cyl....................	3.3125	Alum. Alloy	Ts	4	2.780	.8592	F
FRAZER								
1947 to 50	Series—All....................	3.3125	Alum.	....	4	2.8125	.859	F
1951	515, 516....................	3.3125	Alum.	....	4	2.780	.8592	F

KAISER and FRAZER SPECIFICATIONS

Crankshaft Bearing Journal Sizes

Year	Model	Connecting Rod Journals		Main Bearing Journals				
		Diameter	Length	No. 1 Diameter	No. 2 Diameter	No. 3 Diameter	No. 4 Diameter	No. 5 Diameter
KAISER								
1947 to 51	Series—All	2.0619–2.0627	1.3125	2.3744–2.3752	2.3744–2.3752	2.3744–2.3752	2.3744–2.3752	....
1952	521, 522, 6 cyl.	2.0619–2.0627	....	2.3744–2.3752	2.3744–2.3752	2.3744–2.3752	2.3744–2.3752	
1953	531, 532, 6 cyl.	2.0623	....	2.375–1.062	2.375–1.250	2.375–1.250	2.375–1.321	
FRAZER								
1947 to 51	Series—All	2.0619–2.06 27	1.3125	2.3744–2.3752	2.3744–2.3752	2.3744–2.3752	2.3744–2.3752	....

Piston Ring Dimensions

Year	Model	Cylinder Bore	TOP RING			SECOND RING			THIRD RING			OIL RING		
			Width	Gap	Depth	Width	Gap	Depth	Width	Gap	Depth	Width	Gap	Depth
KAISER														
1947–50	K100, 481, 482, 491, 492	3 5/16	3/32	.012	.161	3/32	.012	.161	5/32	.012	.147	5/32	.012	.147
1951	511, 512	3 5/16	3/32	.012	.164	3/32	.012	.164	5/32	.012	.149	5/32	.012	.149
1952	521, 522, 6 Cyl.	3 5/16	.093	.012	.176	.093	.012	.176	.15475	.012	.182	.15475	.012	.182
1953	531, 532, 6 Cyl.	3 5/16	.093	.012	.161	.093	.012	.161	.15475	.012	.147	.15475	.012	.147
FRAZER														
1947–48	F47, F485, F486	3 5/16	3/32	.012	.147	3/32	.012	.147	5/32	.012	.147	5/32	.012	.147
1949–50	495, 496	3 5/16	3/32	.011	.161	3/32	.011	.161	5/32	.011	.147	5/32	.011	.147
1951	515, 516	3 5/16	3/32	.012	.164	3/32	.012	.164	5/32	.012	.149	5/32	.012	.149

Brake Data

Year	Model	Make	Lining Type	R=Riveted B=Bonded	Drum Diameter	Lining			Clearance	
						Length	Width	Thickness	Toe	Heel
KAISER										
1946–47	K-85, K-101	Ben	....	R	10	....	1 3/4	....	....	....
1948 to 51	Series—All	Ben	M	R	11	22	2	13/64	.010	....
1952–53	All	Ben	M	R	11	22 1/4	2	3/16	.010	.010
FRAZER										
1946–47	F47	Ben	....	R	11	....	2	....	....	....
1948	F485-486	Ben	M	R	11	22	2	13/64	.008	.008
1949 to 51	Series—All	Ben	M	R	11	22	2	13/64	.010	....

M—Moulded. Ben—Bendix.

Tension Wrench Specifications

Year	Model	Cylinder Head		Spark Plug		Connecting Rod Bolts or Nuts		Main Bearing Bolt		Flywheel Bolts		Vibration Damper Bolts	
		Lbs.-Ft.	Thread	Lbs.-Ft.	Thread	Lbs.-Ft.	Thread	Lbs.-Ft.	Thread	Lbs.-Ft.	Thread	Lbs.-Ft.	Thread
FRAZER													
1947 to 53	All	30-35	....	24-30	14 mm	40-45	....	85-95	....	35-40	....	100-130	....
KAISER													
1947 to 49	All	40-50	....	5-10	14 mm	40-45	....	85-95	....	35-40	....	100-130	....
1950-51	All	30-35	....	24-30	14 mm	40-45	....	85-95	....	35-40	....	100-130	....

Cooling System

CAR AND YEAR	MODEL	Capacity Qts.	Quarts of Methanol Base Anti-Freeze (For Protection to Temperature Shown Below)							Quarts of Ethylene Glycol (For Protection to Temperature Shown Below)							Quarts of Denatured Alcohol—188 Proof (For Protection to Temperature Shown Below)						
			3	4	5	6	7	8	9	3	4	5	6	7	8	9	3	4	5	6	7	8	9
KAISER																							
1946-48	K-100	15	11	1	−12	−27	−44	....	....	16	8	0	−12	−26	−43	....	....	10	0	−10	−20	−30	....
1948-53	All Models	13½	9	−3	−17	−34	−53	....	....	15	6	−5	−18	−34	−54	....	10	....	0	−10	−20	−30	....
FRAZER																							
1946-48	F-47	15	11	1	−12	−27	−44	....	....	16	8	0	−12	−26	−43	....	....	10	0	−10	−20	−30	....
1949-51	495-496, 515, 516	13½	9	−3	−17	−34	−53	....	....	15	6	−5	−18	−34	−54	....	10	....	0	−10	−20	−30	....

Distributors

Year	Model	Distributor Model Number	Cam Angle (deg.)	Direction of Rotation C=Clockwise CC=Counter Clockwise at Cam End	Breaker Arm Spring Tension	Breaker Point Gap (inches)	Engine R.P.M. when Cent. Advance Starts	Max. Cent. Advance in Engine Deg. at Stated Engine R.P.M.	Vacuum in (Inches) of Mercury at which Vacuum Unit Starts	Max. Advance in Engine Deg. at Stated Vacuum	Vacuum Unit Number
KAISER											
1947-48	K100, K101, K481, K482	IGS-4211	38	CC	17-20	.018-.022	700	10@1700	8	7.5@14	....
1949-50	K491, 492, K501, 502	IGS-4214	38	CC	17-20	.018-.022	650	9@1675	10	5@15	....
1952	521, 6 cyl.	1110224	31-37	CC	17-21	.020	500	18@3200	9-11	12	....
	522, 6 cyl.	1110224	31-37	CC	17-21	.020	500	18@3450	9-11	12	....
1953	531, 532	1110224	31-37	C	17-21	.022	600	20@3200	9-11	12@15	....
FRAZER											
1947-48	F47, F47C, 485, 486	IGS-4211	38	CC	17-20	.018-.022	700	10@1700	8	7.5@14	....
1949 to 51	F49, 505, 506, 515, 516	IGS-4214	38	CC	17-20	.018-.022	650	9@1675	10	5@15	....

Generators

Year	Model	Generator Number	Field Current at 6 Volts (amps.)	Maximum Safe Output Volts	Maximum Safe Output Amperes	Maximum Safe Output R.P.M.	Brush Spring Tension (oz.)	Voltage Regulator Number
KAISER								
1947 to 50	All	GDZ-4818-A	1.3–1.5	8.0	35	2000	35–53	VRP-4004-F-2
1951	K-511, 512	1102733		7.2	41	2050	24–32	1118302
1952	521, 522, 6 cyl.	1102782						1118392
1953	531, 532	1102782		6.7	45			1118392
FRAZER								
1947 to 51	Series—All	GDZ-4818-A	1.3–1.5	8.0	35	2000	35–53	VRP-4004-F-2

Voltage Regulators

Year	Model	Regulator Number	Grounded P=Positive N=Negative	Voltage Control Air Gap Points Closed	Voltage Control Voltage Setting Hot	Current Control Air Gap Points Closed	Current Control Current Set Hot	Cut-Out Relay Point Gap	Cut-Out Relay Air Gap	Cut-Out Relay Closing Volt
KAISER										
1947 to 50	Series—All	VRP-4004-F-2	P	.052	7.2	.052	34–36	.015	.034	6.4–7.0
1951	511, 512	1118302	P	.075	7.7	.075	32–40	.020	.020	5.9–6.8
1952	521, 522, 6 cyl.	1118392			7.2–7.5		39–41			6.4–7.0
1953	531, 532	1118392			7.2–7.6		40–46			5.9–6.7
FRAZER										
1947 to 50	F-47, F485, 486, 505, 506	VRP-4004-F-2	P	.052	7.2	.052	34–36	.015	.034	6.4–7.0
1951	F515, 516	VRP-6001-A	P	.050	7.35	.050	34–36	.015	.032	6.4–7.0

Starters

Year	Model	Unit Model Number	Spring Tension (oz.)	STARTER Lock Test Volts	STARTER Lock Test Amperes	STARTER Lock Test Torque, (lbs. ft.)	STARTER No Load Volts	STARTER No Load Amperes	STARTER No Load R.P.M.	Direction of Rotation Viewed from Drive End C=Clockwise CC=Counter-clockwise
KAISER										
1947–48	K-100, 101, 481, 482	MAW-4043	42–53	2.0	335	6	5.0	65	4300	C
1949–50	K-49, 501, 502	MAW-4054	42–53	2.0	335	6	5.0	65	4300	C
1951	Standard	1107087	22–32	3.70	525	12	5.0	70	5000	C
	Hydramatic	1107088	22–32	3.70	525	12	5.0	70	5000	C
1952	521, 522, 6 cyl.	1107087	24–28	3.4	525	12	5.0	70	5000	C
1953	531, 532, 6 cyl.	1107125	24–28	3.25	550	12	5.65	70	5500	C
FRAZER										
1947–48	F47, 485, 486	MAW-4043	42–53	2.0	335	6	5.0	65	4300	C
1949 to 51	F49, 505, 506, 515, 516	MAW-4054	42–53	2.0	335	6	5.0	65	4300	C

Fan, Generator Belts and Radiator Hose

Year	Model	Fan Belt Angle of "V" (deg.)	Fan Belt Length O.C.	Fan Belt Width Max.	Generator Belt Angle of "V" (deg.)	Generator Belt Length O.C.	Generator Belt Width Max.	Upper Hose Type	Upper Hose Inside Diam.	Upper Hose Length	Lower Hose Type	Lower Hose Inside Diam.	Lower Hose Length
KAISER													
1947–48	All	45	43 3/16	3/8				curved	1½	....	straight	1½	2⅝
1949 to 51	All	45	43 3/16	3/8				straight	1½	7½	straight	1½	2⅞
1952	521, 522, 6 cyl.	36	41	3/8				curved	1½	....	curved	1½	
1953	531, 532	36	41	3/8				curved	1½	....	curved	1½	....
FRAZER													
1947–48	Series—All	45	43 3/16	3/8				curved	1½	....	straight	1½	2¾
1949 to 51	Series—All	45	43 3/16	3/8				straight	1½	7½	straight	1½	2½–6

Front Wheel Alignment

Year	Model	Caster (deg.)	Camber (deg.)	King Pin Inclination (deg.)	Toe-In (inches)	Turning Radius Inner	Turning Radius Outer
KAISER							
1947–52	All	1N to 1P	0 to ¾P	5½	0 to 1/16	22	20
1953	All	1N to 1P	0 to ¾P	5½	0 to 1/16	17	20
FRAZER							
1947–48	F47, F485, F486	1N to 1P	0 to ¾P	5½ to 6	0 to 1/16	23	20
1949–51	All	1N to 1P	0 to ¾P	4¾ to 5¾	0 to 1/16		

FRONT SUSPENSION

The front suspension on all Frazer and Kaiser cars is the short and long arm type, commonly referred to as the S.L.A. type suspension.

Steering Geometry, Caster, Camber and Toe-In

Before adjusting caster and camber on either side, check and note all angles.

Caster and camber are controlled by an eccentric pin in the outer end of the upper support arm.

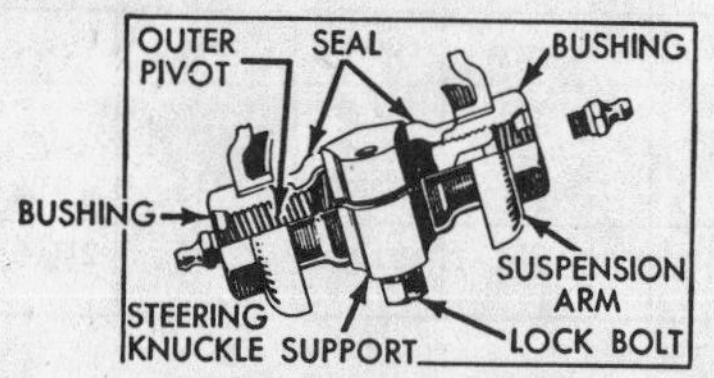

Section thru the knuckle support showing the eccentric pin

To correct caster, loosen the clamp bolt in the upper end of the knuckle support. Remove the grease fitting from the forward pivot bushing and, using an Allen wrench, turn pin in a clockwise direction to increase or counterclockwise to decrease caster.

When it is found that the specified angle for camber cannot be obtained, shims may be installed between the upper inner pivot shaft and the shock absorber support. To make this adjustment, loosen both bolts that attach the pivot shaft to the cross member, and install shims under both bolts to decrease camber or remove to increase.

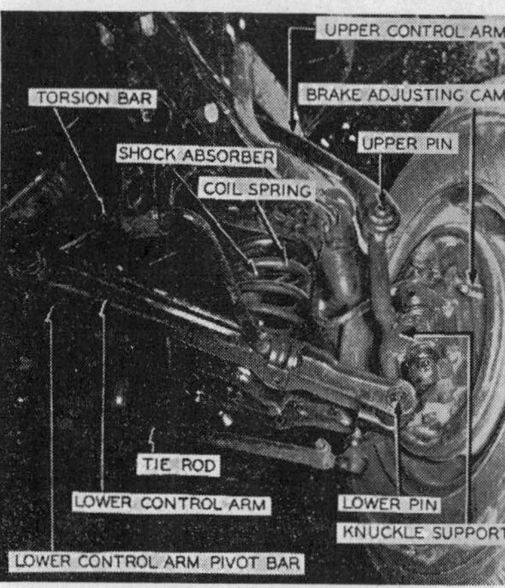

Front suspension 1953 Kaiser

In the event of negative camber with the pivot pin turned to highest obtainable adjustment and no shims are found, check for a bent or distorted steering knuckle.

Toe-in is adjusted by means of a cross tube, connecting two tie rod ends, one at the idler arm and the other at the wheel.

To adjust toe-in, loosen the clamps at both ends and turn the cross tube.

Toe-in should be adjusted after all other steering angles have been corrected.

Intermediate Steering Arm

The intermediate steering arm, commonly referred to as the idler arm, can be rebuilt on all Frazer and Kaiser models.

When rebuilding the idler arm on any model 1947 to 1950, use the specified parts for that year.

In cases where the arm must be replaced, use the improved arm which is standard on the 1951 models.

Drag Link

Only one end of the drag link can be rebuilt (pitman arm end), the other end must be replaced.

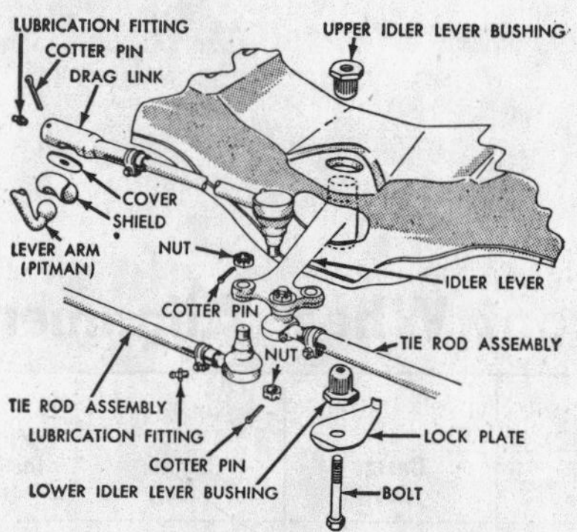

Steering linkage—showing drag link, idler arm and related parts

Replacement of Front Coil Spring and other Suspension Parts

Before replacing a front spring it is wise to determine the condition of the upper and lower pivot pin and bushings, as the procedure will depend on which parts must be replaced.

If any pins need replacing, disconnect system at the defective pin. If all parts are found in good condition and only the coil spring needs replacing, the procedure is as follows: Place a roller jack under the lower arm inner shaft. Remove the four bolts holding the lower control arm inner shaft to the cross member. Then lower the jack until the spring can be removed. Reinstall the spring and jack the arm into place, using a suitable drift pin to align the bolt holes in the pivot shaft with the holes in the cross member.

Upper Control Pin

Loosen clamp bolts of the upper portion of the knuckle support, remove the front bushing and then the back bushing. Now the pin can be removed. When the eccentric pin is replaced, make certain that the pin is properly centered in the knuckle support and is in the full camber position (facing outward).

The upper pivot pin on all models has a thread with two starts.

Lower Control Pin

Remove the nut on rearward side of the lower control arm. Now, working at the forward side, remove the pivot bolt and then the bushing.

When replacing the bushing in the knuckle support, screw in from the rear and tighten. The pin is screwed into the control arm and the knuckle support itself is centered between the two arms. The outer pin and bushing, or inner pivot shaft and bushing, can be replaced on the lower control arm. However, the control arm should be checked for distortion. The new bushing must seat tightly in the arm.

King Pin and Bushing Replacement

King pins can be replaced without disconnecting the hydraulic brake hose, or the brake mechanism on the backing plate.

Remove wheel, hub and drum assembly and backing plate. Using a piece of wire, hook the backing plate to the frame. Drive the king pin lock pin toward the front of the car, then drive the king pin down and out. Special portable presses are available to remove frozen king pins. The king pin bushings are of the full floating type and require no reaming or honing.

STEERING GEAR

There are four different types of steering gears used and they are all of the Gemmer, worm, and roller type, differing mainly in the housing and mounting.

Steering Mechanism Adjustment

1—Disconnect the pitman arm from the drag link.

2—Adjust the steering gear housing assembly.

a—Check the steering gear worm shaft bearings for end play and, if any end play exists, remove the four cap screws which hold the bottom cover plate and remove one shim at a time until there is zero play in the worm bearings without having a definite preload.

A one-pound pull should be required on a spring scale to turn the steering wheel with the worm bearings properly adjusted.

b—Adjust the mesh of the worm and roller tooth by loosening the jam nut and tightening the adjusting screw until there is zero lash with the steering wheel in the mid position of its travel. Tighten the lock nut.

3—Reconnect the pitman arm to the drag link.

4—Loosen the drag link clamp screw and adjust the drag link so that, with the steering wheel in the mid position of its travel, the intermediate steering arm is exactly centered with relation to the length of the car. That is, the intermediate steering arm should point exactly forward and back. Tighten the jam nut.

5—Loosen the tie-rod clamp screws on the right side tie rod and, with the steering wheel in the mid position of its travel, adjust the tie rod so that one-half of the total toe-in is contained in the right wheel. Tighten the clamp bolt.

6—Loosen the clamp bolts on the left tie rod and adjust the tie rod so that the balance of the toe-in is contained in the left front wheel. Tighten the clamp bolts.

Now turn the steering wheel from one extreme to the other to check for looseness or binding.

BRAKES

All Frazer and Kaiser cars are equipped with Bendix hydraulic self-centering shoes.

1947 and early 1948 models have adjusting cams that cannot be replaced in service. Late 1948 models to present models have replaceable cams.

Major Adjustment of Service Brakes

Before any brake operation is performed, a drum should be removed to inspect the condition of the drum, lining, and actuating mechanism.

The brake drums on current models are equipped with a slot at the outer edge to allow checking brake shoe to drum clearance.

Insert a .010 feeler gage across the full surface of the brake lining to determine shoe contact. Adjust the brake shoe cam until a slight drag is felt pulling the feeler in and out.

A minor brake adjustment is accomplished by turning the brake shoe adjusting cam until the shoes drag, then back off until the wheel is free. Repeat on all four wheels.

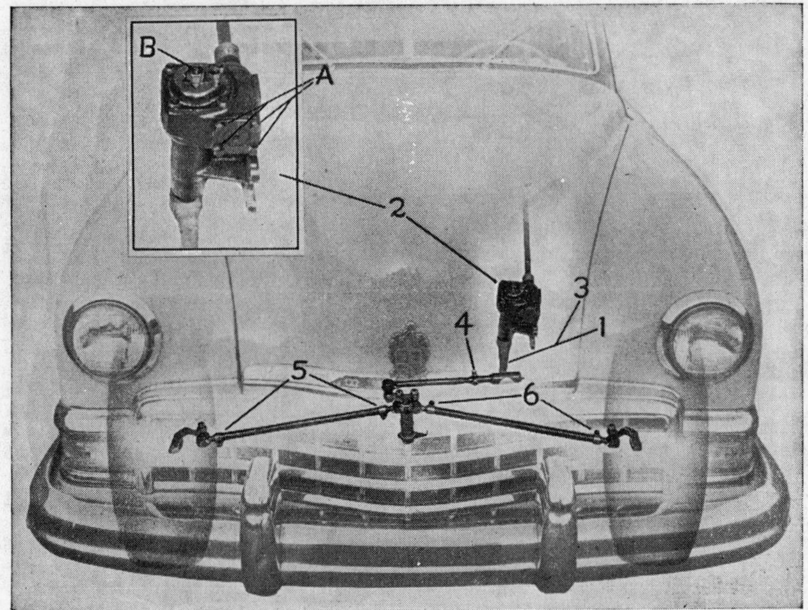

Steering mechanism—typical of all models

Master Cylinder

Frazer cars are equipped with cast iron master cylinders; the Kaiser has cast aluminum.

These cylinders are mixed in production. All master cylinders are interchangeable except 1950 and 1951 models.

The master cylinder on 1947 and 1948 is located in the engine compartment. On 1949 to current models the cylinder is mounted on the frame at engine rear crossmember.

Bleeding Brakes

See General Service & Trouble Shooting—refer to index.

Hand Brake Adjustment

The hand brake on the 1948 and 1949 models has two adjustments. First, remove all slack in the cable at equalizer clevis. When proper adjustment cannot be reached, make the second adjustment at equalizer yoke.

On all 1949 to current models the hand brake is adjusted by backing off the lock nut and tighten the adjusting nut at the brake cable yoke.

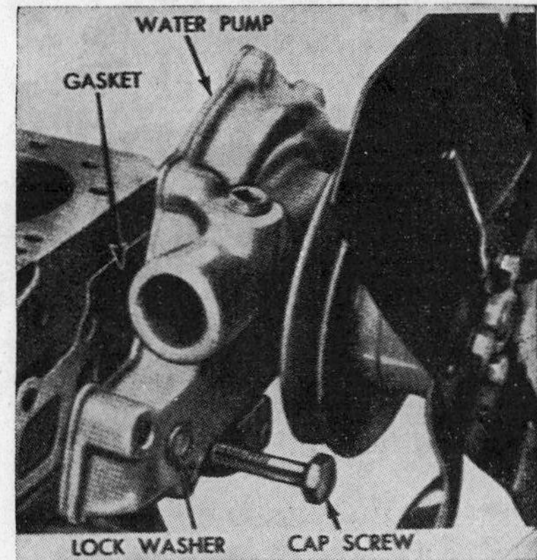

Water pump installation

COOLING SYSTEM

On all Frazer and Kaiser cars the thermostat is located in the water outlet elbow on top of the cylinder head. To remove the thermostat, disconnect the upper hose, remove water outlet mounting bolts and remove thermostat.

Water Pump

On 1947 to 1951 Frazer and 1947 to 1950 Kaiser use the same type water pump. The 1951 thru 1953 Kaiser has a pump which is not interchangeable with any model. A permanently sealed ball bearing that requires no lubrication is used.

Continued

KAISER and FRAZER 1947 thru 1953

WATER PUMP—*continued*

To remove the water pump, detach the water hose, loosen the generator, take off fan belt.

Remove pump attaching bolts and lift off the pump.

Water Pump Disassembly

Detach fan and pulley from hub.

Take off cover plate and gasket.

Remove pump impeller from shaft with special puller.

Take out shaft retaining ring and remove shaft and bearing from pump body.

Inspection of pump should reveal no scratches on the seal face, nor any particular corrosion.

Radiator Core Removal

Disconnect water hoses.

Disconnect water hoses.

Detach six bolts holding radiator to frame.

Remove the radiator by lifting up and out.

ENGINE

Engine Interchangeability

On 1947 to 1950 Kaiser models and 1947 to 1951 Frazer models engines are interchangeable.

The 1951 thru 1953 Kaiser engine will not interchange with any model.

Vibration Damper

On all 1947 to 1949 early models the vibration damper can be removed, without removing the radiator.

All 1949 to current models the radiator must be removed. It is advisable to remove the radiator in any case to prevent accidental damage to the water tubes.

Engine Manifold

The intake and exhaust manifolds are located on the right side of the engine block.

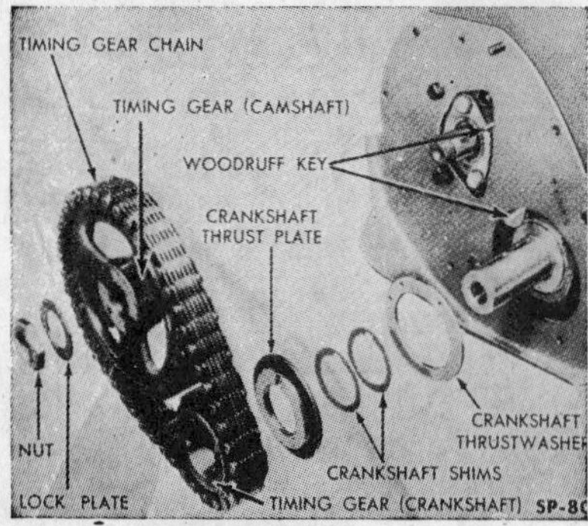

Timing gears and chain-exploded view

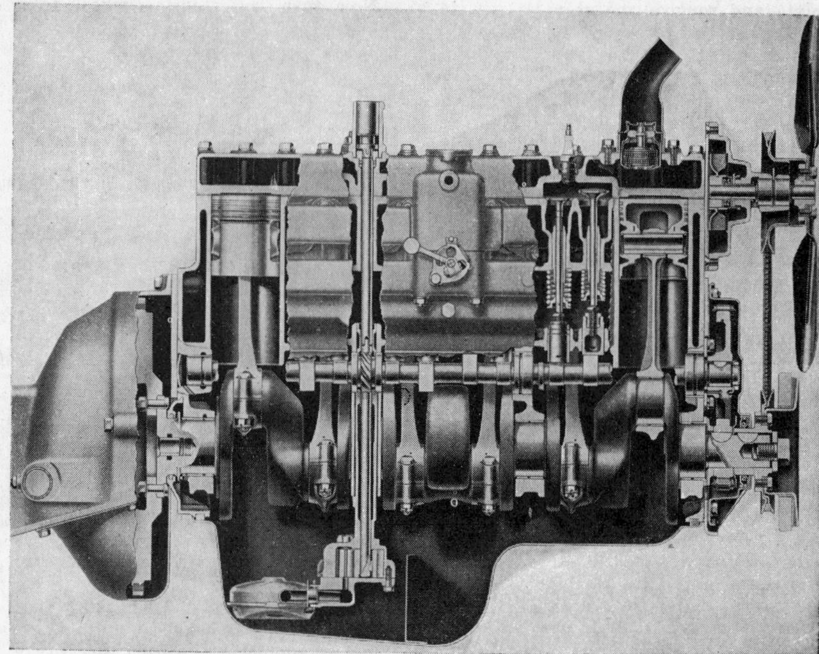

Section view—engine typical of Kaiser-Frazer

The manifold is attached to the engine block by 11 studs, washers and nuts. A heat riser valve is incorporated in the exhaust manifold to regulate exhaust gases by-passed around the intake manifold.

CYLINDER HEAD NUT TIGHTENING SEQUENCE

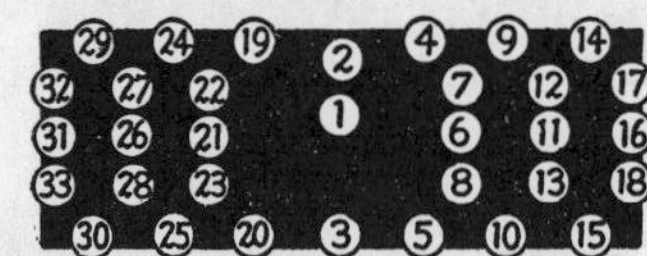

1947 to 1953

With a torque wrench tighten cylinder head nuts to 30-35 foot pounds.

Removal of Oil Pan

Disconnect the drag link. Loosen motor mounting. Block up the engine to simplify removing front pan bolts.

Remove pan by sliding down, back and out.

Engine Removal

Remove hood, radiator core, gas line, ignition wires, exhaust pipe and other attaching parts.

Take out mounting bolts and remove engine.

Timing Case Cover Removal

Remove radiator, fan belt and vibration damper. Unbolt timing case cover and lift off.

When reinstalling use a new oil seal, and gasket liberally coated with gasket compound.

Valve Timing and/or Replacement of Timing Gears

The arrangement used on these models is such that unless the chain or sprockets become badly worn or damaged there is very little chance that valve timing will change.

Remove radiator and timing case

Take off camshaft retaining nut, remove camshaft, and crankshaft sprockets together with chain as a unit.

Set up the new sprockets and chain on a bench in the position that they occupy on the car and arrange the chain so that there are ten pins of the timing chain between the marks on the camshaft sprocket and crankshaft sprocket, counting the pin at each mark.

Retaining this position of the sprockets and chain tentatively, set the assembly against its relative shafts and note the position of keyways.

Now set the keys on the shafts so that they will enter the keyway in the sprocket without difficulty.

Note: Great care should be used to align the keys and keyways perfectly, since the sprockets are a tight fit on the shaft and it is very difficult to correct for misalignment when the gears are started on the shaft.

Force sprockets up on the shafts, alternating one and then the other until they are firmly seated. Tighten camshaft retaining nut.

Rotate the crankshaft two full revolutions until the crankshaft sprocket again assumes the checking position.

Be certain that there are ten pins in the timing chain, between the mark on the crankshaft sprocket and the mark on the camshaft sprocket.

With the timing chain set up in this manner the valves are correctly timed regardless of which piston is at top dead center.

It will be necessary to retime the ignition after resetting the valve timing.

VALVE SYSTEM

All Frazer and Kaiser engines are of the in-line "L" head type. The valves, springs and guides are positioned in the cylinder block.

Valve seats are on top of engine block, with stem protruding down through the guide and into the tappet chamber.

Replacement of Valve Guides

Whenever it is determined to replace valve guides, on Frazer and Kaiser, carefully measure the distance from the top of the cylinder block to the edge of the valve guide before removing the old guide. The measurement should be carefully noted for both intake and the exhaust valve guides so a new guide can be inserted exactly the same distance from the top of the block as the old guide.

Section 2 of this Manual gives the diameter of valve stems for all models.

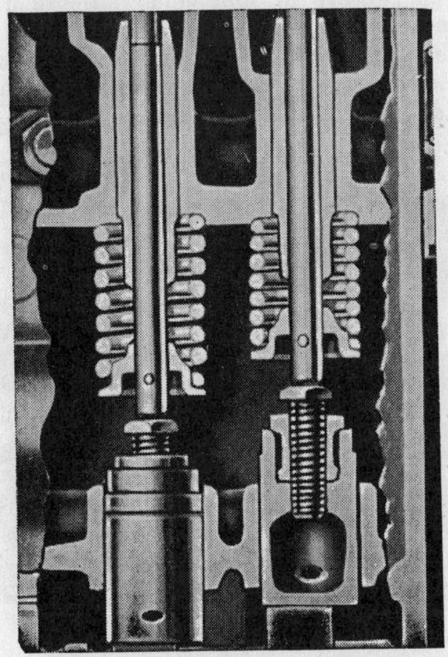

Valve operating mechanism

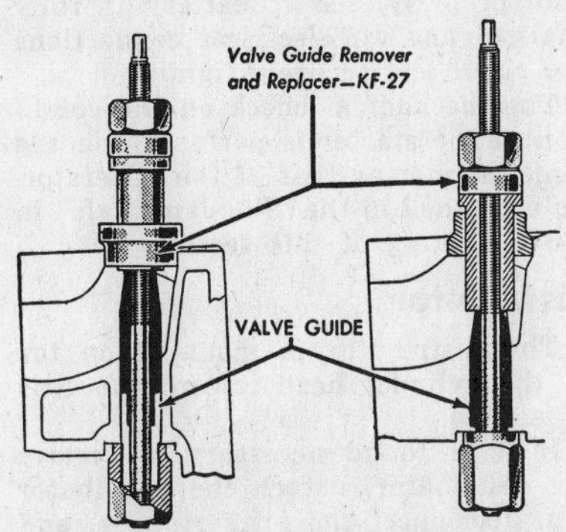

Installing valve guide

Valve guides are removed with a special puller.

Install a new guide so that the tapered end of the guide will be toward the cylinder head.

Valve Adjustment Sequence

In order to insure that the lifter is not on the ramp of the cam, adjust the valves in the following sequence:

With valves #1 and #3 fully raised—adjust #10 and #12.

With valves #7 and #9 fully raised—adjust #4 and #6.

With valves #2 and #5 fully raised—adjust #8 and #11.

With valves #10 and #12 fully raised—adjust #1 and #3.

With valves #4 and #6 fully raised—adjust #7 and #9.

With valves #8 and #11 fully raised—adjust #2 and #5.

By following this sequence there is no danger of the lifter being part way up the ramp so as to spoil the adjustment.

Rod and Piston Assemblies

Assemble the piston rod so the oil spirt hole in the rod is opposite the T-slot in the piston. Pistons are fitted in the cylinder bore so the T-slot in the piston faces away from the camshaft.

Rod Bearings

The connecting rod bearings are of the slip-in type fitted with a tang at the parting line to maintain their position.

The oil holes and tank for bearings 1, 3 and 5 rods are opposite 2, 4 and 6. Therefore they are not interchangeable.

Rear Main Bearing Oil Seal

A cork seal is used to prevent oil escaping from the crankcase onto the clutch and flywheel. To replace the lower half of this oil seal remove the rear main bearing cap, and the old oil seal.

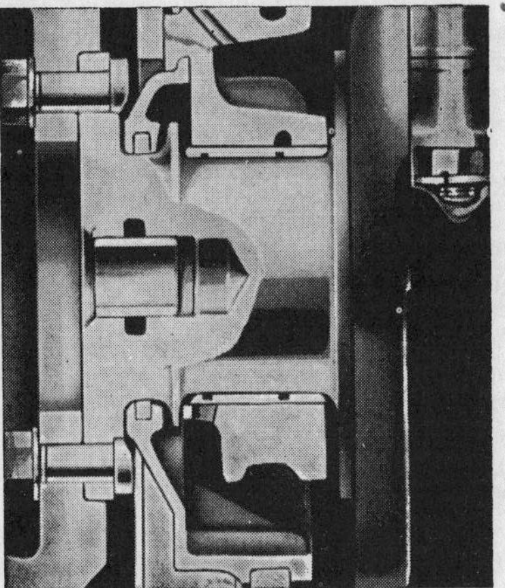

Rear main bearing. Note oil seals and location of camshaft welch plug

Install the new oil seal in the main bearing cap so the cork protrudes slightly above the cap. Bolt the cap in place and torque it approximately 60 foot pounds and immediately take it down again.

If the protruding part of the cork has "riveted over," cut off the riveted portion with a razor blade and again bolt the cap into place.

Repeat this operation until the main bearing cap sets firmly in the block, without riveting over the new portion of the oil seal.

To replace the upper oil seal, it is necessary to remove the engine and crankshaft.

Oil Pump

The oil pump is located in the lower part of the crankcase. The oil pan must be removed to service the pump.

Before any attempt is made to repair the oil pump it should be determined which type drive gear is used. A cast

OIL PUMP—*continued*

iron gear is used, with cast iron camshaft and a steel camshaft uses a steel drive gear.

There are no identifying marks on the steel gears. The letter "O" stamped on a drive gear indicates a cast iron gear.

Cylinder Head Removal

To remove the cylinder head on Frazer and Kaiser models it is necessary to remove the oil filler mounting bracket, ignition wire, distributor, coil, carburetor, air cleaner and head stud, then remove cylinder head.

Fuel System

The fuel pumps on Frazer and Kaiser cars are either single or double diaphragm type. The double diaphragm type pump is mounted on the right forward side of the engine.

The single type fuel pumps have two locations.

One is mounted on the right side at the front of the engine block, and the pump cam arm is set below the camshaft.

The other single type fuel pump is mounted on the right side at the rear of the engine block, and the cam arm is located above the camshaft.

Carburetor

On 1947 and 1948 models use a single throat down draft Carter Carburetor.

On 1949 to current models use a double throat down draft Caster Carburetor.

Both types of carburetors are equipped with a Climatic Controlled Choke.

ELECTRICAL

Charging Unit

Note: Complete service on the generator is given in the "Fundamentals of Car Servicing" of this section. See index.

The generator is mounted on the left front of the cylinder block. All models are equipped with a two brush, belt driven, shunt wound generator.

If difficulty is experienced with the generator, first ground the field terminal of the generator. If on grounding the generator field terminal it is found that the generator functions properly, the difficulty will be in the regulator. If grounding the field current does not increase the output of the generator then the generator should be removed and bench tested as outlined in the "Fundamentals." See index.

Starting System

A solenoid starter switch mounted to the splash shield is used on all models.

A four brush, series wound starter, with a Bendix sliding gear and pinion is standard equipment.

If starting motor does not crank engine properly, see if battery is fully charged and all electrical connections are clean and securely tightened.

The mechanical check on the condition of the starter is performed in the same manner as that of the generator. As explained in the "Fundamentals" in the beginning of this section.

Distributor

The distributor is mounted on top of the cylinder head toward the rear of engine.

If it is found necessary to remove the distributor, detach the distributor cap, disconnect the primary wire, and vacuum advance tube.

Remove advance arm to adapter bolt and remove distributor. The distributor shaft is slotted to allow the tongue in the oil pump shaft to enter and drive distributor.

When the distributor must be removed, mark the position of the rotor so it may be reinstalled in the same position.

When installing spark plug wires, advance in a counter-clockwise direction, the direction of rotor travel. If starting No. 1 the order is as follows: 1-5-3-6-2-4.

CLUTCH ASSEMBLY

The clutch pedal free play adjustment on Frazer is ⅝ to ¾ in.; on Kaiser, ¾ to 1 in.

Removal Procedure

Remove transmission and throw out bearing. Detach clutch inspection pan. Unbolt clutch pressure plate assembly and remove plate.

Note: Before removing, mark clutch cover and flywheel, to assure proper reassembly.

STANDARD TRANSMISSION

The transmission is a synchromesh three speed forward type which incorporates a synchronizing unit and constant mesh of the cluster gear to provide smooth shifting for second and high gear.

Transmission Removal

Disconnect drive shaft at the intermediate joint by removing the cross member.

Disconnect clutch and transmission linkage and place a jack under the rear of the engine.

Remove the extension shaft.

Disconnect the transmission at the bell housing and lift down and out.

Transmission Overhaul

Lock the transmission in two gears to prevent the main shaft from turning.

Pull off the companion flange. Withdraw the mainshaft from the rear of the case being careful not to damage the synchronizer.

Remove the synchronizer unit snap ring from the front of the mainshaft thus releasing the synchronizer assembly, second speed gear and the low-reverse gear from the shaft.

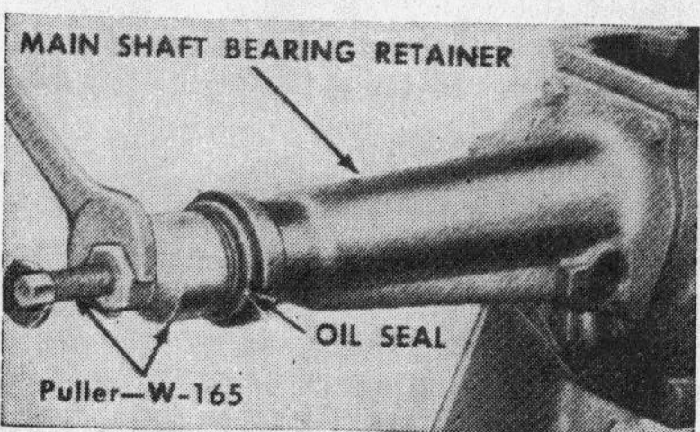

Removing mainshaft oil seal

Remove the counter shaft locking plate and using a dummy shaft (or on arbor 6 7/16 in. long and ¾ in. in diameter) to hold the needle bearings in place, drive the shaft out to the rear, allowing the cluster gear to lie in the case until the clutch shaft is removed.

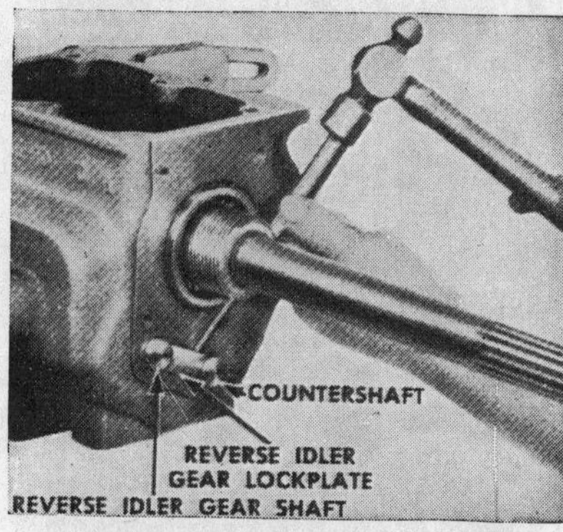

Removing idler gear shaft lock plate

Overdrive

Driving out transmission countershaft

See Overdrive Section.

If repairs are to be made on the overdrive only, it is not necessary to dismantle the transmission unless the sun gear or adapter plate is to be removed.

Remove the nut at the end of the overdrive tail shaft and, pull the universal joint flange.

Detach the speedometer pinion.

Disconnect the overdrive case from the transmission and slide the case rearward off the tail shaft.

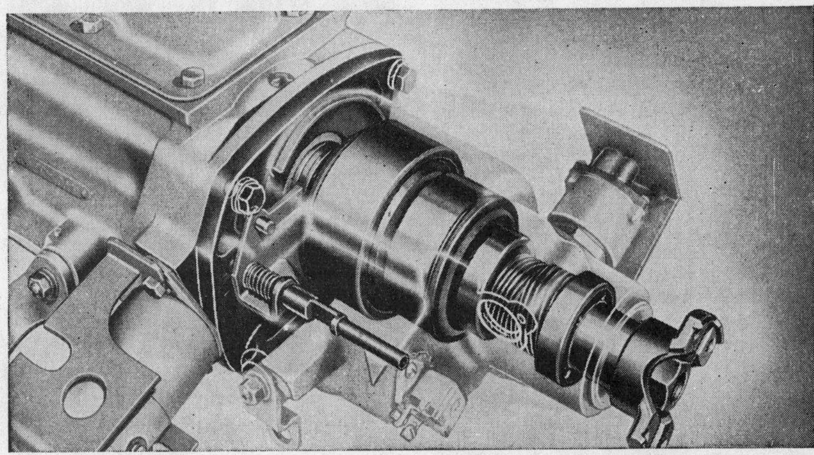
Phantom view overdrive

Take-off the clutch shaft bearing retainer.

Remove snap ring and pull the clutch shaft out.

Drive reverse idler gear shaft out towards the rear, and remove gear.

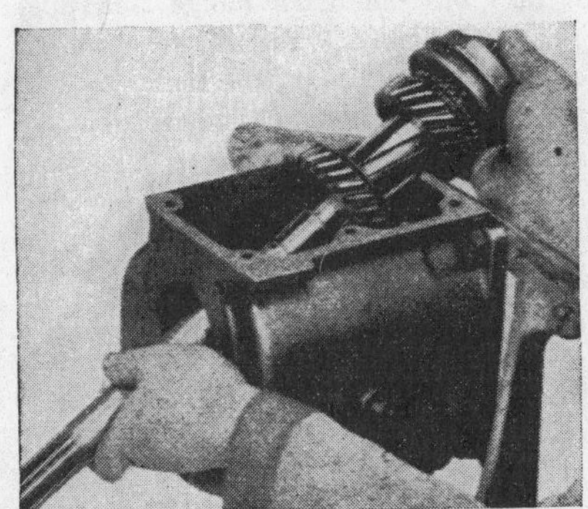
Removing mainshaft assembly from case

Reverse procedure to reassemble.

Note: The end play of the countershaft should be checked between the thrust washer and the case at the rear end, the washer should be chosen to hold the end play between .002 in. and .008 in.

The end play of the second speed gear should be checked between the back of the gear and the butt end of the mainshaft spline. It should not be less than .003 in. nor more than .008 in.

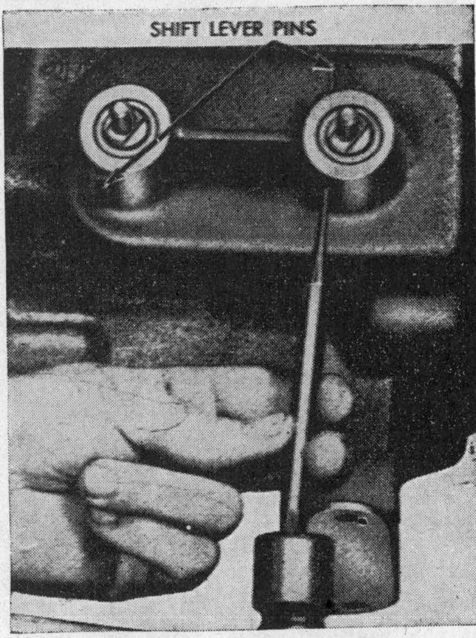

Removing shift lever shaft pins

Shift Linkage Adjustment—Frazer

Detach gearshift rod at lower lever on jacket tube and transmission outer shift levers.

Make sure upper shift shaft is operating freely in the bracket. If the shaft is binding loosen the lower and upper bracket and align the jacket tube properly.

Insert a 1/4 inch drill rod through the holes in both lever and in the lower bracket.

With the transmission lever in the neutral position, adjust and install shift rods. Loosen other jam nut and align the rod to the bell crank.

Remove drill rod from levers.

Shift Linkage Adjustment—Kaiser

Set the selector lever in neutral position. Loosen both shift lever trunnion lock nuts.

KAISER and FRAZER 1947 thru 1951

SHIFT LINKAGE ADJUSTMENT—*continued*

Remove grease cap and insert special gauge KF-69 in housing. Without moving the levers tighten the lock nuts against trunnion block.

Remove gauge from housing and press cap back into position.

Throttle Control Linkage Adjustment—Hydramatic

Detach transmission, rear throttle rod (long lever) at the control lever.

Loosen lock nut at carburetor extension shaft. At upper bell crank and bracket install special pin in alignment holes.

Install similar pin through lower bell crank and bracket. When it is found that the pin holes do not align, make adjustment at front throttle rod to allow pin to enter without binding.

Tighten clamp bolt (12 to 15 pounds in transmission throttle control lever).

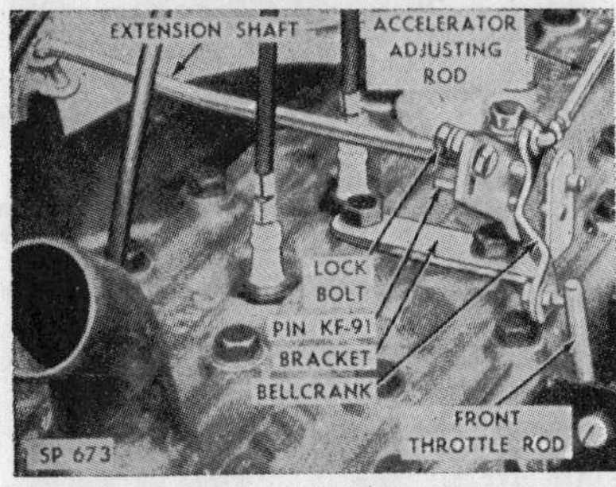

Adjusting pin KF-91 installed in upper bell crank

To determine the correct position of this lever. Place special checking gage at rear of transmission flat against the case with the edge of gage flush against the side cover flange. With lever towards rear of transmission held against its stop, move the gage upward and align the slot in gage with a clevis pin inserted in the lever.

The throttle control lever inward face (toward transmission) should just contact the outer face of the gage. When it is found that the slot in the gage will not align with the clevis pin in the lever, use special bending tool to align slot with clevis pin.

Connect rear throttle rod.

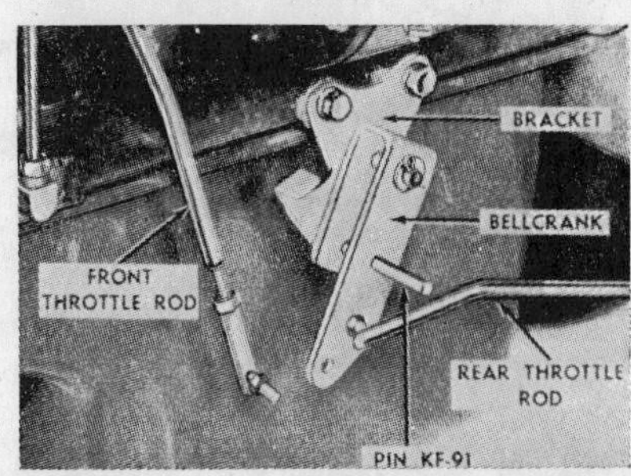

Adjusting pin KF-91 installed in lower bell crank

Adjust rear throttle rod trunnion (towards rear) so control lever seats lightly against stop inside case. Back off two full turns to shorten rod.

Remove both aligning clevis pins.

Adjust accelerator rod so accelerator pedal clears floor mat ¼ inch.

Selector Lever Linkage Adjustment—Hydramatic

On Kaiser cars only tighten the gearshift control shaft upper bracket clamp screw while selector lever is held in "Lo" position. No service is required at this location on Frazer cars.

Loosen the lock nut on the control rod trunnion. Move the transmission shift lever in "LO" position, turn inner lock nut finger flush against trunnion. Turn lock nut one full turn to lengthen rod. Careful not to change adjustment tighten lock nut.

REAR AXLE ASSEMBLY

A spicer type hypoid semi-floating rear axle assembly with Hotchkiss drive is used on all models.

There have been two different types rear assemblies on Frazer and Kaiser cars. The difference being in the ring gear and pinion, housing shape, and cover.

Disassembly of Rear Axle

Remove the rear axles.

Remove universal joint flange bolts at the rear universal joint and lower the propeller shaft.

Remove axle housing assembly from car.

Take out the cover bolts and the cover.

Detach the differential bearing cap screws and the cap.

Pull the differential case and ring gear assembly out from the rear.

Disassembly of Differential

Remove bolts holding the ring gear to the case and press ring gear off.

Remove the differential lock pin or screw and push out the differential pinion shaft with a brass drift. The axle shaft thrust block can now be removed.

Revolve the side gears and remove the pinions through the holes in the case. The side gears and their thrust washers can now be removed.

Pinion and/or Bearings

Remove cotter pin, drive pinion flange nut, and washer from the front end of the pinion shaft.

Pull off the drive flange and dust shield assembly. Press the drive pinion shaft assembly out the rear. The oil seal, bearings and shims can now be removed from the housing.

To move the pinion toward the ring gear, add shims between the rear pinion bearing cup and pinion housing and, add the same thickness of shims between the shoulder of the pinion shaft and the forward pinion bearing cone.

To move the pinion away from the ring gear, remove an equal number of shims instead of adding them. The shim adding must be the same at each bearing or the play in the bearings will be changed. The bearing play should be such that there is a slight resistance to rotation when the pinion is turned by hand.

The position of the pinion should be such that the contact pattern is centered and even on the ring gear.

Assemble the parts in reverse of the order of removal.

Back lash between the ring gear, and pinion is controlled by shims, between the differential side bearing cones and the case.

The shims selected should result in a back lash of no more than .006 in. and no less than .003 in.

Shifting the ring gear .005 in. will change the back lash approximately .0035 in.

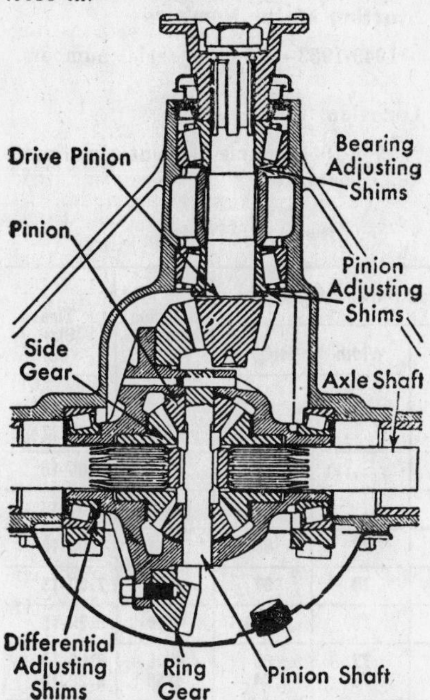

Section through the differential carrier assembly. Typical of all Frazer models

Axle Shaft Removal

Pull the hub and drum assembly. Do not use a knock off type puller as it tends to injure the differential.

Disconnect the brake line at the wheel cylinder.

Disconnect the emergency brake cable at the brake.

Remove the stud nuts which hold the oil seal and backing plate to the axle bearing housing.

Preserve shims which are between the bearing retainer and the backing plate.

Pull the axle shaft and bearing from the housing, being careful not to injure the inner oil seal. Reverse the procedure to reinstall.

If new leather oil seals are to be installed, soak the leather in oil for about 30 minutes and then work it with a smooth instrument until it is soft and pliable.

Axle Shaft End Play Adjustment

Axle shaft end play is adjusted by shims between the backing plate and the outer bearing retainer. The bearing is a press fit on the tapered end of the axle. Whenever a new axle shaft or housing is being installed, the amount of shims to be used must be determined to obtain specified end play of the rear axle shaft which is .001 to .006 in.

Positioning Side Carrier Bearing Shims

Before pinion (or ring gear) is installed, install side carrier bearings in differential case without shims. Insert carrier assembly in housing with bearing cups installed.

With a dial indicator button against the back face of the ring gear move the differential assembly to one side of case, by inserting two screw drivers between housing and a bearing cup.

With the dial indicator set at zero move assembly to opposite side of case

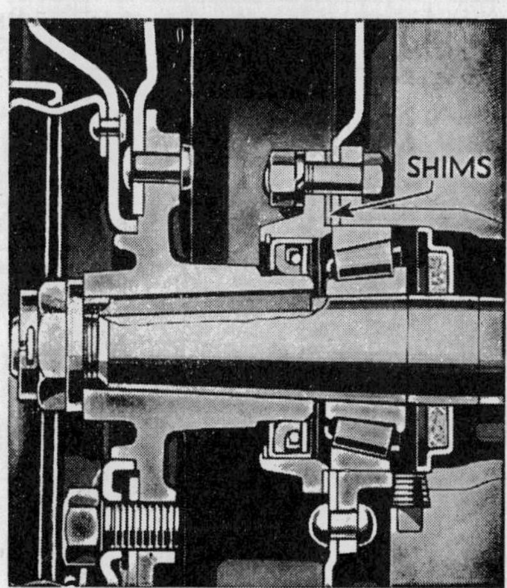

Section through the rear-axle bearings showing the adjusting shims

and note the dial reading. This amount plus an .008 in. specified pre-load determines the total amount of shims to be used on side carrier bearing installation. Add shims as explained under heading Checking Differential pre-load.

Checking Differential Bearing Pre-Load

After pinion (or ring gear) has been installed with the dial indicator button against the back face of ring gear and set on zero, move differential unit towards the pinion until the ring gear is in contact.

The reading (clearance between pin- and ring gear) minus .005 in. denotes differential case and bearing cone on the ring gear side of differential.

The amount of shims installed on the ring gear side of the differential case should then be subtracted from the total indicator reading as obtained when side carrier bearings were installed.

Insert a thickness of shims equal to the amount plus .008 in. for pre-load on opposite side.

For example, when the side carrier bearings were installed, assuming that the total indicator reading is .080, then adding the specified pre-load of .008 in. the total amount of shims to be used is .088 in.

Assuming the clearance between the ring gear and pinion to be .042, subtract .005 in. (approximate back lash) from .042 in. clearance, the .037 in. difference determines the amount of shims placed between differential case and bearing cone on ring gear side of differential. Now subtract the total amount of shims installed on the ring gear side of case from .088.

The .051 difference determines amount of shims to be installed on opposite side.

REAR SPRING

The rear springs on all Frazer and Kaiser cars are of the semi-elliptual type.

Removal of Rear Spring

Remove shackle self locking nuts and link, remove shackle and rubber bushings.

Detach front hanger bolt and bushing.

Detach lower end of shock absorber front spring plate.

Take-off the U clamp bolts and remove spring.

Important Note

When installing rear spring always install the short end forward.

LINCOLN SPECIFICATIONS

Starting Serial and Motor Numbers

Starting Serial Numbers

1940 .... H-85541
1941 .... H-107688
1942 .... H-129691
1946 .... H-136255
1947 .... 7H-152840
1948 .... 8H-174290
1949—Lincoln 9EL-1
Cosmopolitan 9EH-1
1950-1951—First two numbers indicate year, i.e., 50LP5001L, 1950. Last letter indicates model, i.e., 50LP5001L, Lincoln. All serial numbers start 5001.
1952 — First two numbers indicate year, i.e., 52LP5001H, 1950. Serial numbers begin 5001.
1953 .... 53WA10001

Location

1940-48—Top of transmission case, left side of frame front crossmember and top of clutch housing.
1949-1953—K frame crossmember, top of flange to the rear of the idler arm, right side of rear cross top member and top of gas tank front crossmember.

Starting Motor Numbers

1949-1953—Same as serial numbers.

Location

1949-1953—Same place as serial numbers.

General Specifications

Year	Model	Wheelbase (in.)	Tread (in.) Front	Tread (in.) Rear	Overall Dimensions (in.) Length†	Overall Dimensions (in.) Width	Overall Dimensions (in.) Height■	Shipping Weight* (lb.)	Tire Size (in.)
LINCOLN									
1940	V12	136-145	60	60	....	....	....	5735	7.50-17
1941	Custom	138	....	60	225	....	....	....	7.00-16
1942	Custom	138	59	60	230	....	....	4380	7.00-15
1946-47	66H	125	59	61	216	77	68	....	7.00-15
1948	876H	125	59	61	218	78	67	4015	7.00-15
1949	9EL-9EH	121▲	59	60	220	79	65†	4315	8.20-15
1950	V8-0EL	121	59	60	214	77	65	4009	8.00-15
	V8-0EH	125	59	60	221	79	64	4259	8.20-15
1951	V8-1EL	121	59	60	215	77	65	4085	8.00-15
	V8-1EH	125	59	60	223	78	64	4430	8.20-15
LINCOLN ZEPHYR									
1940-41	V12	125	56	58	209	....	....	3620	7.00-16
1942		125	59	60	217	....	....	3980	7.00-15
1952	Cosmopolitan, Capri	123	59	59	214	78	63	....	8.00-15
1953	Cosmopolitan, Capri	123	59	59	214	78	63	....	8.00-15

▲ 9EH-125. † 9EH-64.

†—Including bumpers and guards. ■—Road to roof, no load. *—Cheapest 5 pass. 4 dr. sedan.

General Engine Specifications

Year	Model	Number of Cylinders Bore and Stroke	Piston Displacement, Cubic Inches	Compression Ratio (To-1)	Taxable (A.M.A.) Hp.	Developed Horse Power: Bare Engine	Developed Horse Power: With Accessories	Maximum Torque Ft. Lbs.
1940	06H, Zephyr, V12	12-3.125 x 4.54	414.0	6.38	46.8	150 @ 3400	....	312 @ 1200
1941	16H, Zephyr, Continental, V12	12-2.875 x 3.75	292.0	7.00	39.6	120 @ 3500	....	....
	168H, Custom, V12	12-2.875 x 3.75	292.0	7.00	39.6	120 @ 3500	....	....
1942	26H, Zephyr, Continental, V12	12-2.937x 3.75	306.0	7.00	41.4	130 @ 3800	....	....
1946	66H, Zephyr, V12	12-2.937 x 3.75	305.0	7.20	41.4	130 @ 3600	....	235 @ 1800
1947	76H, Zephyr, V12	12-2$\frac{15}{16}$ x 3$\frac{3}{4}$	305.0	7.20	41.4	130 @ 3600	....	235 @ 1800
1948	876H, Zephyr, 12 Cyl.	12-2$\frac{7}{8}$ x 3$\frac{3}{4}$	292.0	7.20	39.6	125 @ 3600	....	214 @ 1600

General Engine Specifications—*continued*

Year	Model	Number of Cylinders Bore and Stroke	Piston Displacement, Cubic Inches	Compression Ratio (To–1)	Taxable (A.M.A.) Hp.	DEVELOPED HORSE POWER Bare Engine	With Accessories	Maximum Torque Ft. Lbs.
1949	9EL, Lincoln, 8 Cyl.	8-3½ x 4⅜	336.0	7.00	39.2	152 @ 3600	....	265 @ 2000
	9EH, Cosmopolitan, 8 Cyl.	8-3½ x 4⅜	336.0	7.00	39.2	152 @ 3600	....	265 @ 2000
1950	OEL, Lincoln, 8 Cyl.	8-3½ x 4⅜	336.7	7.00	39.2	152 @ 3600	....	265 @ 2000
	OEH, Cosmopolitan, 8 Cyl.	8-3½ x 4⅜	336.7	7.00	39.2	152 @ 3600	....	265 @ 2000
1951	1EL, Lincoln, 8 Cyl	8-3½ x 4⅜	336.7	7.00	39.2	154 @ 3600	....	275 @ 1800
	1EH, Cosmopolitan, 8 Cyl.	8-3½ x 4⅜	336.7	7.00	39.2	154 @ 3600	....	275 @ 1800
1952	Cosmopolitan, Capri	V8-3.8 x 3.5	317.5	7.50	46.20	160 @ 3900	....	284 @ 1800
1953	Cosmopolitan, Capri	V8-3.8 x 3.5	317.5	8.0	46.2	205 @ 4200	....	305 @ 2650

Engine Tune-Up Specifications

Year	Model	SPARK PLUGS Type	Gap	DISTRIBUTOR Point Gap	Cam Dwell (Deg.)	Ignition Timing, (Deg.)	Ignition Timing Mark and Location	Compression Pressure at R.P.M.	OPERATING TAPPET CLEARANCE Inlet	Exhaust	Carburetor Fuel Float Height	Minimum Engine Idle Speed at R.P.M.
1940	O6H Zephyr, V12	H10	.029	.016	36	4B	None	150@100	AA	AA	3/16″	....
1941 -42	O16H Zephyr, V12	H10	.029	.016	36	4B	None	125@100	AA	AA	3/16″	....
	26H, 168H Custom, V12	H10	.029	.016	36	4B	None	125@100	AA	AA	3/16″	....
1946 to 48	876H Zephyr, V12	H10	.029	.016	36	2B	None	125@100	AA	AA	3/16″	....
1949	9EL Lincoln, 8 Cyl.	H10	.023	.018	30	4B	Vib. dmpr.	110@ *	AA	AA	....	....
	9EH Cosmo, 8 Cyl.	H10	.032	.018	30	4B	Vib. dmpr.	110@ *	AA	AA	....	....
1950	All, 8 Cyl.	H10	.026	.016	28½	4B	Vib. dmpr.	110@ *	AA	AA	....	....
1951	All, 8 Cyl.	H10	.032	.016	28½	4B	Vib. dmpr.	110@ *	AA	AA	....	....
1952 -53	Cosmopolitan, Capri, 8 Cyl.	Ch-H10	.032	.015	28½	3B	Vib. dmpr.	....	AA	AA	....	450

Ch—Champion Spark Plug Co. B—Before top center. Vib. dmpr.—Vibration damper. *—At cranking speed.

Pistons and Piston Pins

Year	Model	PISTONS Diameter	Material	Type	No. of Rings	PISTON PINS Length	Diameter	How Held
LINCOLN								
1940	V12	3.125	Alum.	Ts, C	4	3	.875	P
1941–48	Series—All	2.875	Cast Steel	....	3	2.607	.7502	F
1949–50	Series—All, V8	3.5	Alum.	Ss	4	3.118	.8503	F
1951	1EL, 1EH	3.5	Alum.	Sp	3	2.842	.7502	F
LINCOLN ZEPHYR								
1940–41	V12	2.875	Cast Steel	....	4	2 31/64	.750	F
1942	V12	2.9375	Alum.	....	3	2 31/64	.750	F
1952–53	Cosmopolitan, Capri, 8 cyl.	3.80	Alum. Alloy	Sp,Fh	3	3.1745	.91215	F

TS-C—"T" Slot, Cam ground. Ss—Split skirt. Sp—Slipper skirt. Alum—Aluminum. Fh—Flat head. F—Floating.

Engine Overhaul Specifications

Year	Model	Removed From	PISTONS: Piston Skirt Clearances (Maximum) Top	Bottom	Limit	RING GAP CLEARANCES (Maximum): Top Ring	Second Ring	Third Ring	Oil Ring	PISTON PIN: Type	Fit	ROD BEARINGS: Oil Clearance	Wear Limit	Side Play
1940	O6H Zephyr, V12	A	.002	.002	.005	.013	.013	....	.013	Float	Push	.0015–.003	.005	.002–.006
1941	O16H Zephyr, V12	A	.002	.002	.005	.013	.013	....	.013	Float	Push	.0015–.003	.005	.002–.006
	168H Custom, V12	A	.002	.002	.005	.013	.013	....	.013	Float	Push	.0015–.003	.005	.002–.006
1942	26H Zephyr, V12	A	.002	.002	.005	.013	.013	....	.013	Float	Push	.0015–.003	.005	.002–.006
1946	66H Zephyr & Cont., V12	A	.0025	.0025	.005	.013	.013	....	.013	Float	Push	.001 –.0025	.005	.009–.019
1947	76H Zephyr, V12	A	.0025	.0025	.005	.013	.013	....	.013	Float	Push	.001 –.0025	.005	.009–.019
1948	876H Zephyr, V12	A	.0015	.0025	.005	.013	.013	....	.013	Float	Push	.001 –.0025	.005	.009–.019
1949	9EL Lincoln, 8 Cyl.	A	.002	.001	.004	.016	.016	....	.016	Float	Push	.0025	.005	.006–.014
	9EH Cosmo., 8 Cyl.	A	.002	.001	.004	.016	.016	....	.016	Float	Push	.0024	.004	.006–.014
1950	OEL Lincoln, 8 Cyl.	A	.0013	.001	.004	.016	.017	....	.017	Float	Push	.0025	.004	.006–.014
	OEH Cosmo., 8 Cyl.	A	.0013	.001	.004	.016	.017	....	.017	Float	Push	.0024	.004	.006–.014
1951	1EH Lincoln, 8 Cyl.	A	.0013	.0013	.004	.017	.017	....	.015	Float	Push	.0003–.0019	.004	.007–.013
	1EL Cosmo., 8 Cyl.	A	.0013	.0013	.004	.017	.017	....	.017	Float	Push	.0003–.0019	.004	.007–.013
1952	Cosmopolitan, Capri, 8 Cyl.	A	.0013	....	.004	.020	.020	....	.020	FL	.0003	.0004–.002	.004	.006–.014
1953	Cosmopolitan, Capri, 8 Cyl.	A	.0013	....	.004	.020	.020	....	.020	FL	.0003	.0004–.002	.004	.006–.014

A—Above. †—Center crank gear mark between cam gear marks. B—Before top center. ‡—M.P.H. FL—Floating.
^—Front and center (rear .0009–.0024).

Dimensions of Valves

Year	Model	Overall Length: Inlet	Exhaust	Head Diameter: Inlet	Exhaust	Seat Angle (deg.): Inlet	Exhaust	Stem Diameter: Inlet	Exhaust	Key Type	O.D. of Seat Insert: Inlet	Exhaust
1940	....	6.750	6.750	1.687	1.687	45	45	.312	.312	horseshoe	....	1.625
1941–42	....	....	....	1.537	1.537	45	45	.311	.311	horseshoe	....	1.625
1946–47	....	4.748	4.748	1.537	1.537	45	45	.311	.311	horseshoe	1.625	1.625
1948	....	4.815	4.845	1.510	1.510	45	45	.311	.310	horseshoe	....	1.625
1949	....	5.714	5.714	1.800	1.515	45	45	.341	.341	split lock	....	1.765
1950–51	....	5.715	5.714	1.800	1.515	45	45	.342	.341	split lock	....	1.765
1952	Cosmopolitan, Capri, 8 cyl.	5.02	5.02	1.80	1.51	45	45	.342	.341	....	....	....
1953	Cosmopolitan, Capri, 8 cyl.	5.18	5.18	2.005	1.51	45	45	.342	.341	....	....	....

Crankshaft Bearing Journal Sizes

Year	Model	Connecting Rod Journals: Diameter	Length	Main Bearing Journals: No. 1 Diameter	No. 2 Diameter	No. 3 Diameter	No. 4 Diameter	No. 5 Diameter
1940–41	06H, 16H, V12	2.125	1.75	2.4010	2.4010	2.4010	2.4010	....
1942 to 48	26H, 66H, 76H, V12	2.2495	1.75	2.4010	2.4010	2.4010	2.4010	....
1949	9EH, 9EL, V8	2.400	2.252	2.874	2.874	2.874	....	....
1950	0EL, 0EH	2.3995–2.400	2.252	2.8735–2.8740	2.8735–2.8740	2.8735–2.8740	....	....
1952	Cosmopolitan, Capri, 8 cyl.	2.2482–2.2490	....	2.6235–2.6243	2.6235–2.6243	2.6235–2.6243	2.6235–2.6243	2.6235–2.6243
1953	Cosmopolitan, Capri, 8 cyl.	2.2486	....	2.6239–.915	2.6239–.915	2.6239–.893	2.6239–.915	2.6239–1.640

and Wear Limit Table

CRANKSHAFT		VALVES									OPERATING OIL PRESSURE			
Main Bearing Oil Clearance	Shaft End Play	Spring Tension (Maximum) Inlet	Exhaust	Low Limit	Guide Clearance	Seat Angle Inlet	Exhaust	Valve Timing, Inlet Valve Opens (Deg.)	Camshaft Drive	Gear Marks	Pounds At M.P.H.	Low Limit§	Model	Year
.001-.003	.002-.006	121@1.83	121@1.83	105	.0015-.0025	45°	45°	10.4B	Gear	†	45@2000	25	........O6H Zephyr, V12	1940
.001-.003	.002-.006	121@1.83	121@1.83	105	.0015-.0025	45°	45°	10.4B	Gear	†	45@2000	25	...16H Zephyr, Contl., V12	1941
.001-.003	.002-.006	121@1.83	121@1.83	105	.0015-.0035	45°	45°	10.4B	Gear	†	45@2000	25	.......168H Custom, V12	
.001-.003	.002-.006	121@1.83	121@1.83	105	.0015-.0035	45°	45°	10.4B	Gear	†	45@2000	25	26H Zephyr & Contl., V12	1942
.001-.003	.004-.006	121@1.84	121@1.84	105	.0015-.0035	45°	45°	10.4B	Gear	†	50@65‡	25	........66H Zephyr, V12	1946
.001-.003	.004-.006	121@1.84	121@1.84	105	.0015-.0035	45°	45°	10.4B	Gear	†	50@65‡	25	........76H Zephyr, V12	1947
.001-.003	.004-.006	121@1.84	121@1.84	105	.0015-.0035	45°	45°	10.4B	Gear	†	50@65‡	25	........876H Zephyr, V12	1948
*.001-.003	.004-.008	153@1.32	153@1.32	135	.0022-.0037	45°	45°	14B	Gear	†	50@40‡	25	.......9EL Lincoln, 8 Cyl.	1949
*.001-.003	.004-.008	153@1.32	153@1.32	135	.0022-.0037	45°	45°	14B	Gear	†	50@40‡	25	.......9EH Cosmo, 8 Cyl.	
♭.0004-.0029	.004-.008	153@1.32	153@1.32	135	.0022-.0037	45°	45°	5B	Gear	†	50@40‡	25	......OEL Lincoln, 8 Cyl.	1950
♭.0004-.0029	.004-.008	153@1.32	153@1.32	135	.0022-.0037	45°	45°	5B	Gear	†	50@40‡	25	......OEH Cosmo, 8 Cyl.	
^.0004-.0019	.004-.008	153@1.32	153@1.32	135	.0021-.0036	45°	45°	5B	Gear	†	50@40‡	25	......1EL Lincoln, 8 Cyl.	1951
^.0004-.0019	.004-.006	153@1.32	153@1.32	135	.0021-.0036	45°	45°	5B	Gear	†	50@40‡	25	......1EH Cosmo, 8 Cyl.	
.0008-.0026	.004-.008	145@1.47	147@1.47	......	.002-.003	45°	45°	18B	Chain	......	40@40	......	......Cosmo., Capri, 8 Cyl.	1952
.0008-.0026	.004-.008	157@1.44	157@1.44	......	.002-.003	45°	45°	18B	Chain	......	40@40	......	......Cosmo., Capri, 8 Cyl.	1953

♭—Front and center (rear .0009-.0034). *—Front and center (rear .0004-.0029).
§—Car may be operated safely at lower pressures but low oil pressure indicates malfunction which should be corrected.

Piston Ring Dimensions

Year	Model	Cylinder Bore	TOP RING Width	Gap	Depth	SECOND RING Width	Gap	Depth	THIRD RING Width	Gap	Depth	OIL RING Width	Gap	Depth
1940-41	V12..........................	$3\frac{1}{8}$	$\frac{1}{8}$	.012	.125	$\frac{1}{8}$	.012	.125	.1547	.011	.140	.1547	.011	.140
	V12, Zephyr................	$2\frac{7}{8}$	.0932	.010	.127	.0932	.010	.107	.1847	.010	.107	......	......	......
1942-48	All..............................	$2\frac{7}{8}$	.0932	.010	.127	.0932	.010	.107	.1847	.010	.107	......	......	......
1942-48	All..............................	$2\frac{15}{16}$	.0932	.010	.133	.0932	.010	.109	.1862	.013	.113	......	......	.113
1949	9EL, 9EH.....................	$3\frac{1}{2}$	.0933	.008	.165	.0933	.008	.165	.186	.012	.152	.186	.012	.152
1950	0EL, 0EH.....................	$3\frac{1}{2}$	.0934	.012	.165	.0934	.012	.165	.186	.013	.135	......	......	......
1951	1EL, 1EH.....................	$3\frac{1}{2}$	.0934	.014	.149	.0934	.014	.149	.1862	.014	.142	......	......	......
1952	Cosmopolitan, Capri, 8 Cyl....	3.80	.07775	.015	.214	.07775	.015	.214	.18625	.015	.209	......	......	......
1953	Cosmopolitan, Capri, 8 Cyl....	3.80	.07775	.015	.191	.07775	.015	.214	.18625	.015	.145	......	......	......

Tension Wrench Specifications

Year	Model	Cylinder Head Lbs.-Ft.	Thread	Spark Plug Lbs.-Ft.	Thread	Connecting Rod Bolts or Nuts Lbs.-Ft.	Thread	Main Bearing Bolt Lbs.-Ft.	Thread	Flywheel Bolts Lbs.-Ft.	Thread	Vibration Damper Bolts Lbs.-Ft.	Thread
1940 to 48	All..............	40-50	....	34-38	$\frac{7}{8}$-18	45-50	....	60-70	....	....	....	....	....
1949 to 52	All..............	50-55	$\frac{7}{16}$-20	24-30	14 mm	52-60	$\frac{7}{16}$-20	120-130	$\frac{9}{16}$-12	75-85	$\frac{7}{16}$-20x1	130-145	$\frac{5}{8}$-18x$\frac{7}{16}$
1953	V8..............	....	....	....	....	....	....	....	....	....	....	....	....

LINCOLN SPECIFICATIONS

Brake Data

Year	Model	Make	Lining Type	R=Riveted B=Bonded	Drum Diameter	Lining Length	Lining Width	Lining Thickness	Clearance Toe	Clearance Heel
LINCOLN										
1940	V12	....	WM	R	15⅛	33½	2½	¼	....	....
1941	Custom	....	MW	R	12	23.9	1¾	.021	....	....
1942	26H	....	....	R	12	24	1¾	.021	.010	.010
1946-47	66H	Ben	MW	....	12	26	1¾	3/16	....	....
1948	876H	Ben	M	R	12	25 29/32	1¾	.21	....	....
1949	9EL-9EH	Ben	M	R	12	25.9	2¼-*2	.212	....	....
1950	0EL-0EH	Ben	M	R	12	23.11	2¼-*2	.212	.010	.010
1951	IEL-IEH	Ben	M	R	12	23 7/64	2¼-*2	7/32	.010	.010
1952-53	Cosmopolitan, Capri, 8 Cyl.	....	M	R	11	22 35/64	2½-*2	7/32	.010	.010
1953	Cosmopolitan, Capri, 8 Cyl.	....	M	R	11	22 35/64	2½-*2	7/32	.010	.010
LINCOLN-ZEPHYR										
1940	V12	Ben	WM	R	12	23.9	1¾	.21	....	....
1941-42	....	....	MW	R	12	23.9	1¾	.21	....	....

*—Rear. Ben—Bendix. WM—Woven on primary, Moulded on secondary. M—Moulded. MW—Moulded on primary, Woven on secondary.

Cooling Systems

CAR AND YEAR	MODEL	Capacity Qts.	Quarts of Methanol Base Anti-Freeze (For Protection to Temperature Shown Below)							Quarts of Ethylene Glycol (For Protection to Temperature Shown Below)							Quarts of Denatured Alcohol—188 Proof (For Protection to Temperature Shown Below)						
			3	4	5	6	7	8	9	3	4	5	6	7	8	9	3	4	5	6	7	8	9
1941-46	V12	27	23	18	13	8	3	−5	−12	....	....	18	14	9	5	−1	....	20	....	....	10	0	....
1948	V12	24½	22	17	11	6	−2	−9	−18	....	20	16	12	7	1	−5	20	....	....	10	....	0	....
1949-51	V8	34½	....	24	20	16	....	7	1	....	....	20	17	13	8	4	....	....	....	20	....	....	10
1952-53	V8	22½	20	14	7	0	−9	−18	−29	....	18	13	8	2	−6	−14	20	....	10	....	0	....	10

Distributors

Year	Model	Distributor Model Number	Cam Angle (deg.)	Direction of Rotation C=Clockwise CC=Counter Clockwise at Cam End	Breaker Arm Spring Tension	Breaker Point Gap (inches)	Engine R.P.M. when Cent. Advance Starts	Max. Cent. Advance in Engine Deg. at Stated Engine R.P.M.	Vacuum in (inches) of Mercury at which Vacuum Unit Starts	Max. Advance in Engine Deg. at Stated Vacuum	Vacuum Unit Number
1940	16H, 168H, 12 cyl.	H-12127	36½	C	20-24	.014-.016	400	16@1900	....	....	....
1941 to 48	All, 12 cyl.	16H-12127	36	C	20-24	.014-.016	400	23@1300	....	....	....
1949	8EL, V8 8EL, V8	IGT-4302-1 8EL-12100	28 30	C C	17-20 17-20	.015-.018 .015-.018	550 550	24@3200 24@3200	9 9	14@14 14@14	....
1950-51	All, V8	0EL-12100	27¼	C	17-20	.014-.016	400	21½@4000	....	....	....
1952-53	Cosmo., Capri, 8 cyl.	FAB-12127A	26-28½	C	17-20	.014-.016	....	....	.55	17@5.8	....

Generators

Year	Model	Generator Number	Field Current at 6 Volts (amps.)	Maximum Safe Output			Brush Spring Tensions (oz.)	Voltage Regulator Number
				Volts	Amperes	R.P.M.		
1941–42	16H, 168H, 26H, 66H	01A-10000-B	2–86	7.1	32	3000	16–18	01A-10505-C
1946 to 48	66H, 76H, 876H	21A-10000	2–1	7.3	28	1800	20–22	11A-10505
1949 to 51	9EL, 0EL, 1EL 9EH, 0EH, 1EH	8EL-10002 8EH-10005	2–1 2–1	7.1 7.1	40 40	1675 1675	20–22 20–22	8L-10505 8L-10505
1952–53	Cosmopolitan, Capri, 8 cyl.	FAB-10000-A						FAD-10505-A

Voltage Regulators

Year	Model	Regulator Number	Grounded	Voltage Control		Current Control		Cut-Out Relay		
			P=Positive N=Negative	Air Gap Points Closed	Voltage Setting Hot	Air Gap Points Closed	Current Set Hot	Point Gap	Air Gap	Closing Volt
1940 to 47	Series—All	01A-10505-C		.035	7.2	.035	30–34	.018	.025	6.1–6.3
1948 to 51	Series—All	5EH-10505-C 8L-10505 8BA-10505-A 8M-10505-A		.035 .034 .034 .035	7.1 7.4 7.4 7.6	.035 .035 .035 .035	30–34 38–42 38–42 34–38	.018 .010 .010 .018	.025 .014 .014 .025	6.1–6.3 6.0–6.4 6.0–6.4 6.0–6.6
1952–53	Cosmopolitan, Capri, 8 cyl.	FAD-10505-A			7.4–7.8		38–42			6.0–6.6

Starters

Year	Model	Unit Model Number	Spring Tension (oz.)	STARTER Lock Test			STARTER No Load			Direction of Rotation Viewed from Drive End C=Clockwise CC=Counter-clockwise
				Volts	Amperes	Torque, (lbs. ft.)	Volts	Amperes	R.P.M.	
1940 to 46	All—V12	18-11002	32–36	3.0	500	14	6	40	3960	CC
1947	76H, 876H	18-11002	30–32	3.25	550	15	6	40	3960	CC
1948	876H	5EH-11002	30–32	3.0	500	14	6	40	3960	CC
1949	9EH, 9EL	7EH-11002	30–32	3.25	550	15	5.8	45	5000	CC
1950	0EL-0EH, 1EL, 1EH	8EL-11002	48–56	3.25	550	15	5.8	52.5	6500	CC
1952	Cosmopolitan, Capri, 8 cyl.	FAC-11001B		3.5	700	16	6	70	6000	C
1953	Cosmopolitan, Capri, 8 cyl.	FAC-11001B		3.5	700	16	6	70	3200	C

Front Wheel Alignment

Year	Model	Caster (deg.)	Camber (deg.)	King Pin Inclination (deg.)	Toe-In (inches)	Turning Radius	
						Innder	Outer
LINCOLN							
1940–42	All	3P to 5P	¼P to ¾P	4¾	0 to 1/16	23	20
1946–48	66H, 76H, 876H	4P	0 to 1P	4	0 to 1/16	23	20
1949–50	9EL, 9EH, 0EL, 0EH	0 to ½P	0 to ¾P	5	0 to 5/32	23¼	20
1951–52	1EL, 1EH, Capri and Cosmopolitan	0 to 1½P	0 to ¾P	5	3/32 to 5/32	23¼	20
1953	Capri and Cosmopolitan	0 to 1½P	0 to ¾P	7	3/32 to 5/32	17½	20

P—Positive.

LINCOLN 1940 thru 1953

FRONT SUSPENSION

On all Lincoln models up to and including 1948 a conventional I beam axle was used having a transverse front spring.

Starting with 1949 production, all models were equipped with independently sprung front wheels, using a short and long arm type suspension with a coil spring. The shock absorber on these models was set in the center of the coil spring.

Starting with 1952 production a ball type front suspension is used on all Lincoln models.

In this suspension the knuckle support turns in ball sockets fitted at the top and bottom of the knuckle support and no king pin is used.

The ball joints are connected to the upper and lower arms by three bolts each.

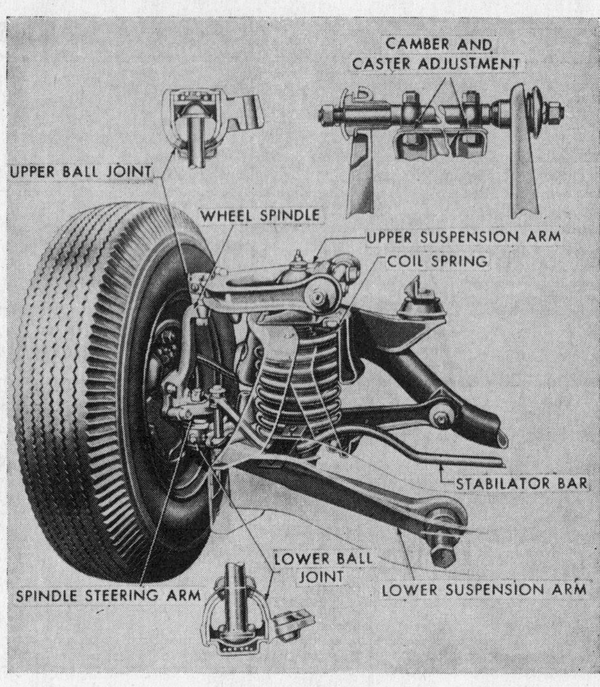

Front suspension

Caster, Camber and Toe-In

MODELS UP TO 1948

On models up to and including 1948 it was necessary to bend the I beam in order to correct caster and camber.

Special heavy duty bending equipment is required to perform these services. Under no circumstances should heat be applied to the I beam since it is heat treated after forging and heating to red heat will destroy the initial heat treatment.

1949 THROUGH 1951 MODELS

On 1949 through 1951 models, caster is adjusted at the bushing in the lower end of the knuckle support. (Fig. 1)

Camber is adjusted at the eccentric bushing in the upper end of the knuckle support. In order to correct camber, loosen the clamp screw in the upper end of the knuckle support and turn the eccentric bushing in a direction which will produce the required reading. The full range of camber adjustment is accomplished in one-half or less revolution of the eccentric bushing.

Since the bushing is mounted on a threaded pin, turning the bushing will make a slight change in the caster setting.

To correct for caster (Fig. 2), loosen the clamp bolt at the lower end of the knuckle support and turn the bushing toward the rear of the car to decrease caster, and toward the front of the car to increase caster.

The lower bushing is concentric and has no effect whatever on camber.

Toe-in is corrected by turning the adjusting sleeve at the outer end of both tie rods.

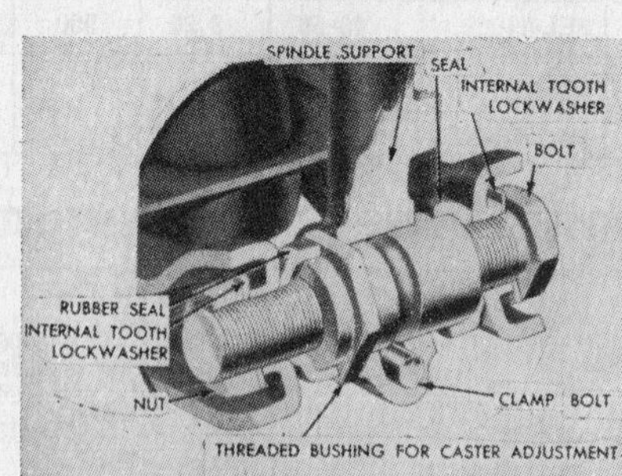

Fig. 1

1952 AND 1953 MODELS

Caster and camber are adjusted on these models by means of shims mounted between the frame bracket and the upper suspension arm inner shaft.

To increase camber remove an equal number of shims from both the front and the rear bolt. To decrease camber add an equal number of shims back of the front and the rear bolt.

To increase caster, remove one shim at a time from the front bolt and add that shim to the rear bolt.

The opposite to decrease caster.

Fig. 2

Replacement of Front Coil Spring

1952 AND 1953 MODELS

To replace the coil spring on these models, first disconnect the shock absorber and the torsion bar. Support the weight of the car at the frame back of the front suspension and disconnect either the one bolt which holds the ball joint to the lower end of the knuckle support or the three bolts which hold the ball joint to the lower suspension arm.

Slowly lower the jack which holds the lower suspension arm up and release the pressure from the coil spring.

It is generally considered easier to do this type of work if the wheel and brake drum are removed.

Before replacing the front coil spring, examine all of the pins and bushing in the front suspension since, if any of the outer pins and bushings are to be replaced, the front suspension can be separated at the bushing which is to be replaced.

If all are in good condition and it is necessary to replace only the coil spring, proceed as follows:

Disconnect the shock absorber and the torsion bar. Place a jack under the inner shaft of the lower suspension arm and unbolt the suspension arm from the front cross-member.

Slowly lower the arm until all tension is removed from the spring. The spring may then be lifted out. Any shims which are found under the coil spring should be placed under the new spring.

Replacement of Knuckle Support, Pins and/or Bushings

1952 AND 1953 MODELS

On these models pins and bushings are not used, instead the suspension has ball joints top and bottom. To replace either of the ball joints first support the weight of the car on the outer end of the lower support arm. If a jack is placed far enough out it will not be necessary to disconnect the shock absorber.

Remove the wheel and brake drum and take out the three bolts which hold the upper ball joint to the upper suspension arm.

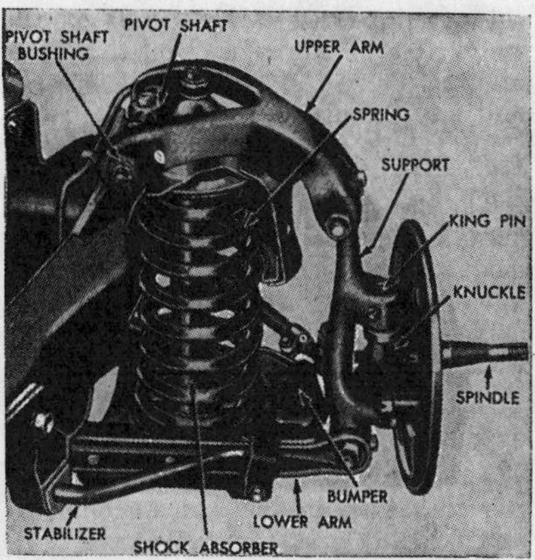

Front suspension—1949 to 1951 models

Remove the nut which holds the upper ball joint to the knuckle support and drive out the ball joint.

The same procedure is used to replace the lower ball joint.

If difficulty is experienced in getting the ball joint out of the knuckle support, strike the knuckle support with a heavy hammer in a direction which will tend to squeeze the ball joint stud. This will force the stud out of the knuckle support.

1949 TO 1951 MODELS

To replace either the upper or lower suspension arm pins and/or bushings, support the car under the A frame and remove the wheel and drum.

Both the upper and lower pin and bushings can be removed with the brake backing plate in place. Actually, it can be removed with the wheel hub and drum in place, but the job is greatly simplified if the wheel is removed.

Both upper and lower pins are held with nuts and special lock washers, which are located at the back of the arm. The pin is unscrewed out of the front.

The bushings may be removed from the knuckle support after the clamp screws have been removed. These bushings cannot be taken out if the clamp bolt is in the hole since the bushing is grooved to retain the clamp bolts. On reassembly, set the knuckle support so that it is approximately centered between the yoke of both the upper and lower suspension arm.

Replacement of Lower A Frame

1952 AND 1953 MODELS

The procedure given below for earlier models also applies to the 1952 and 1953 models except that instead of removing the pin from the outer end of the suspension arm the ball joint is disconnected. Otherwise follow the procedure below.

1949 THRU 1951 MODELS

To remove the lower A frame, support the weight of the car on the frame back of the front suspension and disconnect the shock absorber and the front torsion bar. Place a jack under the inner shaft of the lower suspension arm and disconnect the suspension arm at the frame, lowering it carefully until the tension of the spring has been relieved.

The outer end of the arm then may be disconnected from the lower end of the knuckle support without disturbing the knuckle support bushing.

Replacement of Upper Suspension Arm

1952 AND 1953 MODELS

The upper suspension arm on these models is replaced in exactly the same manner as the lower suspension arm and according to the instructions given for the earlier models.

When removing the upper suspension arm on these models carefully preserve the shims which are found between the upper suspension arm inner shaft and the frame since these shims control caster and camber.

1949 THRU 1951 MODELS

The upper suspension arm is replaced in exactly the same manner as the lower suspension arm except that the weight of the car can be carried on a jack on the lower A frame. It is always advisable to remove the wheel in order to reduce the weight of the parts which will be hanging free when the upper suspension arm pin is removed.

The upper suspension arm is held with two bolts which may be reached from underneath the car after the front wheel has been removed.

LINCOLN 1940 thru 1953

Replacement of King Pins

1952 AND 1953 MODELS

Strictly speaking there is no king pin on these models. Instead the knuckle support turns in ball joints at the top and bottom.

To replace the knuckle support proceed as follows:

Support the weight of the car on the lower suspension arm and remove the wheel, drum and brake backing plate.

Take off the nut which holds the upper ball joint to the knuckle support and the bolt which holds the lower ball joint to the knuckle support. If the taper pins are found to be tight in the knuckle support strike it smartly with a hammer in a direction which tends to "squeeze" the bolt which will help release it.

It is not necessary to disconnect the brake lines although, as a safety precaution, the brake backing plate should be hung on a stout wire attached to the frame so that all strain is relieved from the brake hose.

If it is found to be practically impossible to get the knuckle support to come off the taper bolt then disconnect the upper and lower ball joints from their respective suspension arms and take the knuckle support together with its ball joints over to a bench and remove the upper and lower ball joints in either a vise or an arbor press.

MODELS UP TO AND INCLUDING 1948

These models were equipped with an I beam front axle. To remove the king pins, take off the wheel brake drum and brake backing plate. The backing plate should be hung with a hook to the frame to prevent damaging the flexible brake hose.

Drive out the king pin lock pin and remove the welsh plug from the bottom of the king pin. Drive the king pin upward to remove it. Some of these king pins have a tendency to stick in the axle forging. They may be removed with a mechanical or hydraulic type portable king pin press or the top flare of the king pin can be sawed off. This king pin is case hardened and it is rather difficult to saw. However, it can be sawed and the king pin can then be driven downward. To do this, support the lower portion of the knuckle on a piece of pipe or tubing which is large enough to pass the king pin down through its center. With some of the weight of the car resting on this piece of pipe, drive the king pin downward and into the pipe.

1949 THROUGH 1951 MODELS

The procedure on these models is actually the same as it is for the earlier models except that the king pin does not have a mushroom top and can be driven down through the bottom readily without sawing off the top.

On all models it is necessary to ream or hone fit the king pin bushings.

On 1949 to 1951 models the bushings are contained in the knuckle support and reaming or honing will have to be done with a portable tool unless the knuckle support is removed from the car so that the bushings can be honed in a bench type machine.

STEERING GEAR ASSEMBLY

Adjustment of Steering Mechanism—1940 to 1948 Models

1. Disconnect the pitman arm from the drag link.

2. Adjust the steering gear housing assembly.

Note: The steering gear is equipped with a shim adjusted cross shaft which requires disassembly of the cross shaft to adjust the lash of the worm and roller tooth.

(a) Check the worm shaft for end play and, if end play is found, remove the four cap screws at the bottom of the gear and take out one shim at a time until there is no play in the worm bearings, without there being a definite preload.

(b) Turn the adjusting screw until all end play is removed from the cross shaft and then set the steering wheel in the mid position of its travel. Move the pitman arm back and forth. If any play is felt in the mesh of the gears at this point it will be necessary to: remove the four bolts which hold the cover plate and take off the cover plate, then remove the pitman arm from the

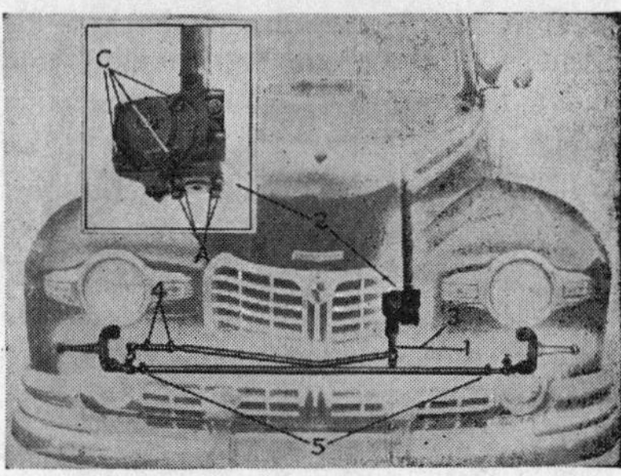

1940 to 1948 models

cross shaft. Now slide the cross shaft out of the housing and remove one shim at a time until there is a definite drag on the roller tooth as the gear is turned through its high spot. Now add one shim at a time until there is zero clearance in the mesh of the gears, with the steering wheel in the mid position of its travel. Replace the cover assembly and turn the adjusting screw until there is no end play noticeable in the cross shaft.

3. Replace the pitman arm on the cross shaft and reconnect the drag link. Loosen the clamp screw and adjust the drag link so that there is one-half the total toe-in in the right front wheel with the steering wheel in the mid position of its travel. Retighten the clamp screws.

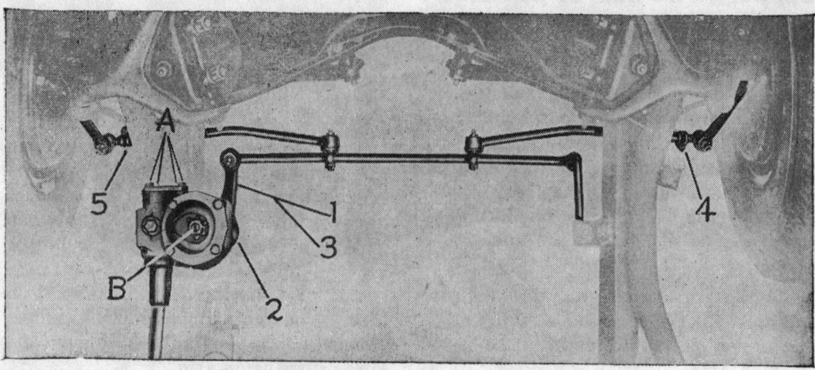

1949 to 1951 models typical of 1952 and 1953

4. Loosen the tie rod clamp screws and adjust the tie rod so that the balance of the toe-in is contained in the left front wheel, and then retighten the clamp screws. Check the steering gear through its complete travel for binding or looseness.

1949 THROUGH 1953 MODELS
MANUAL STEERING

1. Disconnect the pitman arm from the intermediate tie rod.

2. Adjust the steering gear housing assembly.

(a) Move the pitman arm back and forth to determine if there is any end play in the worm bearings. If end play exists, disconnect the four screws from the worm bearing cover and remove one shim at a time until there is zero clearance in the worm bearing without a definite preload.

(b) Set the steering wheel in the mid position of its travel and, if any lash exists at that point between the worm and roller tooth, loosen the clamp nut and turn the adjusting screw until all play is removed with the steering wheel in the mid position of its travel. Tighten the lock nut.

3. Reconnect the pitman arm to the center tie rod.

4. Loosen the clamp bolt on the adjusting sleeve at the right tie rod and, with the steering wheel held in the mid position of its travel, adjust the sleeve so that one-half of the total toe-in is in the right front wheel.

Retighten the clamp screw.

5. Loosen the clamp bolt and turn the left side adjusting sleeve so that the balance of the toe-in is contained in the left wheel.

Tighten the clamp screw.

Now turn the steering wheel from one extreme to the other to check for looseness or binding.

POWER STEERING

See Power Steering Section

Removal of Horn Button

ALL MODELS 1938 THROUGH 1948

On these models the horn button is a bayonet type connection. Push down on the button and rotate until it releases from the catch and then lift it up.

1949 THROUGH 1953 MODELS

The horn button on these models is simply pried up.

Before prying the horn button, examine underneath the steering wheel to see if there are screws inserted from the steering wheel up to the horn button, as was done on a very few of these models. If no screws are found underneath the steering wheel, then the horn button is the pry-up type and will come off readily. On models from 1949 through 1951, equipped with a horn blowing ring, notice if the ring is mounted under the steering wheel. If it is, it will be necessary to take off the emblem and then the steering wheel in order to remove the horn blowing ring.

On this type of construction all of the horn blowing contacts are located underneath the steering wheel.

Steering Wheel Removal

On all models of Lincoln and Lincoln Zephyr, to remove the steering wheel simply take off the horn button (or emblem) from the center of the steering wheel, remove the steering wheel nut and lock washer and, using a puller, pull off the steering wheel.

POWER BRAKES

See Power Brakes Section

BRAKES

All Lincoln models from 1940 thru 1953 were equipped with the Bendix type two shoe hydraulically actuated brakes. Before making any adjustment on the Lincoln, or any other brake, first take off at least one wheel to examine the condition of the hydraulic cylinders, the brake springs and the brake lining.

If the brake lining is wearing evenly all over the surface it will not be necessary to make a major adjustment in order to have satisfactory brakes.

If the lining appears to be wearing more at one end than it is at the other, but in spite of this, the wear is all over the surface, it still should not be necessary to make a major adjustment.

Uneven wear of this type indicates that the brake anchor was originally set improperly but the brake has worn itself in until it is now seated properly in spite of the improperly adjusted anchor. If the brake shows the anchor is improperly adjusted and the lining has not worn itself completely in, then it will be necessary to either remove the old lining and install new or dress the lining to a true arc with an axle type lining grinder.

Examine the condition of the boots on the wheel cylinder. Moisture or brake fluid on the boot indicates that that cylinder is leaking or seeping or should be serviced.

If examination reveals that the hydraulic cylinder is not badly worn or pitted it may be honed in place on the car, using one of the flexible type hones which are available for that purpose. If the pits in the hydraulic wheel cylinder are deep it will be necessary to remove the cylinder and hone it on a bench type hone.

If examination reveals that the one wheel being examined is defective it is advisable to examine all wheels as a safety precaution.

Minor Brake Adjustment

To make a minor brake adjustment in order to compensate for normal wear of the lining simply turn the star wheel adjuster (located directly opposite to the anchor pin) to expand the shoe, so that the shoe drags against the drum. Back off until the wheel is just free. Do the same on the other wheels.

Note: If the star wheel adjuster is properly placed on the brake shoes the wheels may be expanded by turning the handle of the tool toward the axle.

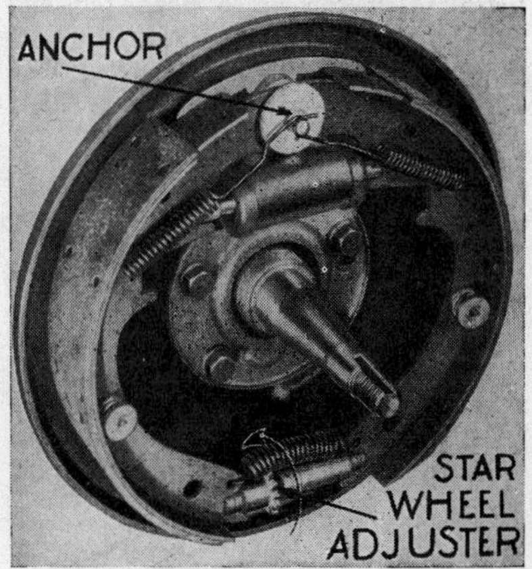

Brake adjustments

Major Brake Adjustment

A major brake adjustment is done when it is found the wheels are pulling to one side or that a minor adjustment will not equalize them.

A major adjustment should never be made without inspecting the condition of the drums and lining.

Note: Two types of anchors are used

MAJOR BRAKE ADJUSTMENT—*continued*

on these Bendix brakes; The eccentric type which can be identified by the square or screw-driver slotted end on the anchor pin (backing plate side) and the sliding type anchor which had a plain end. If the eccentric type anchor is used then turn the eccentric until a .010 feeler gauge is just gripped between the lining and drum, approx. 1 inch from the anchor end at the secondary shoe.

After this adjustment is made, securely tighten the anchor lock nut. Now turn the star wheel until the wheels just drag and back off until they are just free. This will give approximately .010 clearance to the lining all over.

If a sliding type anchor is used, perhaps the quickest way to adjust the brakes is to expand the star wheel until the shoes are very tight against the drums and then loosen the anchor pin nut sufficiently so that when struck with a hammer the anchor pin will center itself in the expanded shoes.

Securely tighten the anchor in this position and back off on the star wheel until the brakes are just free.

Pedal Clearance

The pedal clearance on these cars is adjusted at the brake push rod and should allow approx. ¾″ to 1″ free motion of the pedal before the master cylinder piston starts to move.

Adjustment of Hand Brake Cables

To adjust the hand brake cables expand the rear brake shoes at the star wheel until they are tight against the drum and then, with the hand brake lever in the fully released position adjust the length of the hand brake cables until they will just enter their clevises. This should be done with all slack pulled out of the cable.

COOLING SYSTEM

Radiator Core Removal

On all Lincoln models the radiator is removed in practically the same way. Disconnect the radiator hoses and, on models up to 1948, remove the fan and generator. Disconnect the wires from the radiator frame and (on very early models disconnect the heat indicator wire) take out the bolts which hold the radiator core to its mounting and lift it straight up.

Water Pump Removal

The water pumps on all Lincoln models are mounted at the front of the block.

Starting with 1949 production the water pumps were also used as the front motor supports. On models from 1949 to 1951 it is necessary to support the engine if the water pump is to be removed.

Caution: It is a good idea to loosen the mounting bolts on both pumps, if either are to be removed to avoid unnecessary strain on the pump not removed.

The procedure is to disconnect the hoses and take out the bolts which hold the pump mounting to the engine and lift off the water pump.

1952 AND 1953 MODELS

Disconnect the water pump, lower hose and remove the fan belt. Take off the fan blades in order to prevent damaging the radiator core and unbolt the water pump body and remove it from the timing case front plate.

Disassembly of Water Pump

On the Lincoln Zephyr and all 12 cylinder engines the water pump is equipped with both a bushing and a ball bearing. The fan pulley and also the pump impeller were pinned to the shaft. Before attempting disassembly the pin must be taken from the shaft.

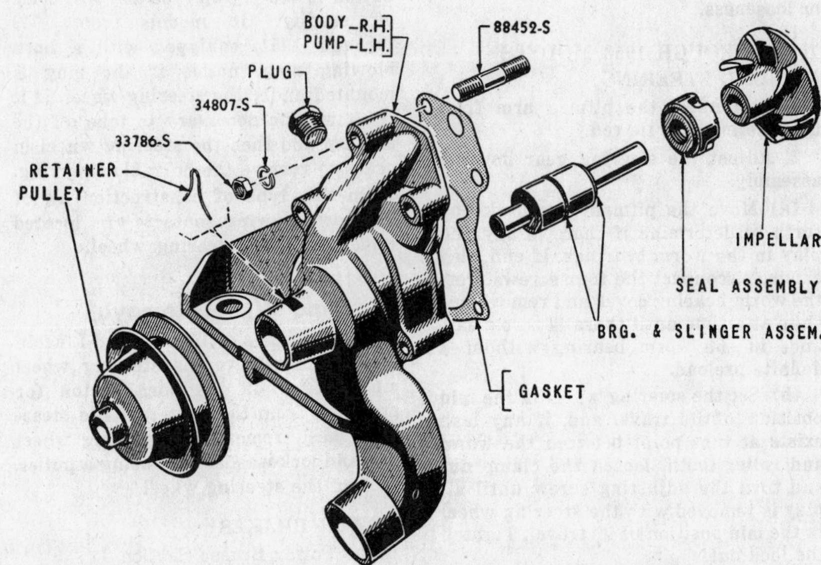

Water pump assembly, 1949-51 V8 models

On V 12 models remove the pulley (after the pin has been driven out) with a puller, and then take off the bearing snap ring from the front of the housing and, in an arbor press, press out the shaft right through the impeller and the bearing assembly and shaft will come out of the housing, through the front. A snap ring is used to retain the shaft and bearing assembly. The ball bearing may be taken off the shaft in the same arbor press.

The bushings in the pump body may be pressed out, if it is necessary to install new ones.

1949 THRU 1951 WATER PUMPS

Water pumps used on these models are serviced in essentially the same way as the earlier pumps, except that the snap ring which retains the assembly is reached through a slot in the pump housing just back of the pulley. The only other difference is that the shaft and bearing assembly is pressed through the back of the pump rather than the front.

Overhaul kits are available for all Lincoln water pumps.

1952 AND 1953 MODELS

Remove the snap ring from the groove in the front of the pump housing directly behind the pulley.

Note: If a pressed steel pulley is used remove it first before taking out the snap ring.

Place the housing in an arbor press with the impeller side up and press the shaft and bearing assembly out of the impeller and out of the housing.

Place the housing in an arbor press with the impeller side downward and press the seal assembly out of the housing.

On reassembly first press into the body the new seal assembly and then reverse the procedure given for disassembly to reinstall the remaining parts.

Thermostats

Thermostats are used in the water outlets of all models. They may be replaced by removing the radiator hose and the water outlet.

Fuel System

On models from 1940 thru 1948 fuel pumps were used which were of the single action type. Starting with 1949 production and thru 1951, a combination fuel and vacuum pump was used. When servicing the fuel pump on these models always mark carefully the relationship between the body of the pump and the upper and lower diaphragm seats so that they can be assembled in the relation in which they were removed.

ENGINE ASSEMBLY

Lincoln Zephyr V 12 Models were built from 1940 thru 1948. These engines were 12 cylinder V type L heads. Starting with 1949 production the 8 cylinder V type L head engines were used. There is a great deal of similarity in the servicing of these engines and where the differences are not noted the service is the same.

1952 AND 1953 MODELS

Starting with 1952 production a new overhead valve V-type engine is used on all Lincoln cars.

Engine Assembly Removal

The method of removing the engine for all Lincoln models is approximately the same.

It is necessary to remove the hood and the radiator core. Detach all connecting parts such as gas lines, gauge connections, primary wires, starter cables, engine ground straps, wire harnesses, etc. The exhaust pipe is disconnected at the manifold.

Detach the engine from the bell housing and place a jack under the transmission.

It is a good idea to run the jack up a little so as to tilt the transmission slightly as the engine is being lifted. It is also a good idea to loosen the transmission rear support bolts so as not to throw undue strain on them.

Replacement Engines

Replacement engines are available for all Lincoln models and they are also available in factory approved rebuilt types. Short blocks are also stocked which consist of simply a block assembly having pistons, pins, rings, valves and timing gears.

Engine assemblies are sold without oil pan, flywheel or inlet manifold.

Longitudinal section of engine

ENGINE INTERNAL

Oil Pan Removal

1938 THRU 1948 MODELS

To take down the oil pan on these models, remove the exhaust cross pipe and disconnect the exhaust pipe at the right side of the engine and disconnect the drag link. Take off the starter assembly and detach the radius rod at its rear end and force the rod down holding it down with a block. Then remove the cap screws holding the pan and drop the pan to the floor.

1949 THRU 1953 ENGINES

Take the spark plug out of No. 2 cylinder and bring the piston to top dead center in order to turn the counter weights out of the way. Turn the steering wheel as far to the right as it will go. Take out the front mounting bolts and jack up the engine about 3 inches and hold it with blocks. Remove the exhaust cross over pipe, idler arm support, starter motor assembly and oil level dip stick tube.

Remove the oil pump and oil pan

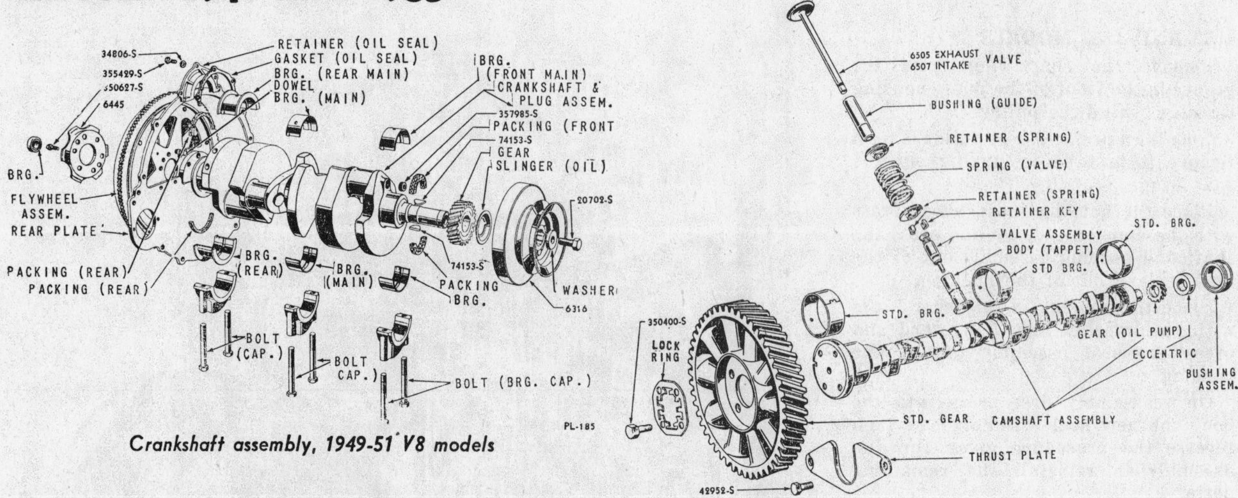

Crankshaft assembly, 1949-51 V8 models

Camshaft and valve arrangement, 1949-51 V8 models

OIL PAN REMOVAL—*continued*

baffle assemblies and disconnect the oil filter return line.

Remove the crankcase ventilator tube and push the tube to the left.

Tip down the rear of the pan and rotate it so that the front oil seal will straddle the cap screws of the front main bearing cap. Then slide the pan out and to the rear and downward and drop it to the floor.

Timing Case Cover Removal

1952 AND 1953 MODELS

On these models the timing case cover is actually the cover for the front of the engine.

The water pump is mounted into a portion of the front cover and must be removed before attempting to take the cover off.

The lower part of the cover is connected to the oil pan gasket and, if the cover is removed and the gasket disturbed it will be necessary to remove the oil pan in order to make certain that there are no oil leaks between the timing case cover and the oil pan.

If any services are to be done in addition to just removing and replacing the timing case cover it is a good idea to take out the radiator core in order to prevent damaging it.

1940 THRU 1951 MODELS

The timing case cover is removed after removing the vibration damper. The cover is unbolted from the front of the cylinder block and lifted off.

The distributor must be taken off in order to lift the assembly up out of the engine.

After the timing case cover has been removed it is possible to replace the camshaft gear. However, if it is desired to replace the crankshaft gear it will be necessary to take off the oil pan.

Cylinder Numbering Sequence

V-12 MODELS

On all Lincoln V-12 Models the left bank of cylinders is numbered 1-3-5-7-9-11; the right bank of cylinders is numbered 2-4-6-8-10-12.

ALL V-8 MODELS TO 1951

The cylinders of all V-8 Models are numbered as follows: right bank—1-2-3-4; left bank—5-6-7-8.

Piston and Rod Assemblies

The material used in the pistons of all Lincoln models is listed in the Piston and Pin Table.

Split skirt pistons were used on all models up to and including 1948, 1949 and early 1950 models used an aluminum split skirt piston. 1951 thru 1953 models were equipped with a slipper type piston.

Wrist Pins

The wrist pins used in all Lincoln models are of the full floating type. They are retained in the piston by lock wires at each end of the pin.

Connecting Rods

Connecting rods used in all Lincoln engines are fitted with an individual type connecting rod bearing. On engines up to 1948 the connecting rod cap is mounted on an angle to the connecting rod and not straight across as is customary with most engines. The slip-in type bearings are supplied in a variety of undersizes so that it is never necessary to attempt to adjust the rod bearing.

Since the slit in the connecting rod cap is not at right angles to the connecting rod it is not recommended that feather type or tape type shims be used in this type rod bearing.

On production engines starting in 1949 the cap on the rod bearing is split straight across as is customary in other engines.

The Lincoln Division does not recommend adjusting these rod bearings. However, it is possible to secure a good working adjustment by placing a feather or taper type shim between the lower part of the rod bearing and the cap. As much as .004 inch excessive play may be taken up by this method.

Assembling Pistons to Connecting Rods

On all Lincoln models when assembling a split skirt piston to the connecting rod, mount the connecting rod in a vice with the numbers facing the mechanic. In this position the split in the skirt will be to the right of the mechanic. Where slipper type or solid skirt pistons are used it is immaterial which way the piston is mounted on to the connecting rod unless the piston is stamped with the letter "F." It is always good practice when reusing unmarked pistons to stamp the piston indicating which side faces the front of the engine. If such a mark is made the mark indicating the front of the piston will be placed on the same side of the connecting rod as its numbers.

On 1952 and 1953 engines the piston is stamped with the letter "F" and is assembled to the connecting rod as follows:

Place the rod in a vise so that the oil squirt hole at the bottom of the rod faces toward the mechanic. With the rod held in this position, rods from the right bank (Nos. 1, 2, 3 and 4), the letter F will be to the mechanic's left hand.

Rods from the left bank (Nos. 5, 6, 7 and 8) will have the letter F on the mechanic's right hand.

Mounting Piston and Rod Assemblies into the Engine

V-12 MODELS

On V-12 Models the assemblies are mounted to the engine so that the number stamped on the connecting rod faces forward on both the right and left banks.

ALL V-8 MODELS

On V-8 Models having split skirt pistons the split in the skirt of the piston faces the camshaft on the right bank and away from the camshaft on the left bank. As an additional check, see to it that the numbers stamped on the connecting rod face forward.

1952 AND 1953 MODELS

The letter F stamped at the top of the piston should face forward on both banks.

As an additional check see to it that the spit hole in the connecting rod on the right bank faces to the left. In other words it faces the camshaft. The spit hole in the connecting rods on the left bank also faces the camshaft.

Crankshaft Main Bearings

Precision, slip-in type main bearings are used on all Lincoln engines built since 1940. The shells may be removed and reinstalled without removing the crankshaft.

Installing rear main bearing and oil seal assembly with special tool

The procedure is as follows—loosen all main bearing caps and remove the cap from the bearing which is to be replaced. Place a cotter pin with its eye flattened somewhat into the oil hole in the journal and turn the crankshaft so that the flat head of the cotter pin contacts the bearing shell without scraping against the cylinder casting.

Turn the crankshaft, forcing the head of the cotter pin to rotate the upper half of the bearing out of the cylinder block. The new bearing is replaced in the same manner.

Caution: Always rotate the bearing so that the tang at the parting line is the first part to come out and the last part to go in.

Main bearing shells are available in a variety of undersizes to take care of almost any condtion.

A slight adjustment may be secured on main bearings by placing the feather or taper type shim between the lower half of the main bearing and the cap.

The Lincoln Division does not recommend adjusting main bearings, however.

Rear Main Bearing Oil Seal

The rear main bearing oil seal on all models of Lincoln is a packing type seal which requires the removal of the crankshaft to replace the upper half. The lower half may be replaced, however, by removing the crankshaft rear main bearing cap and inserting a new packing into the packing retainer. It is sometimes possible to correct an oil leak at the rear main bearing by installing new packing in the lower half of the main bearing cap and letting it protrude approximately 1/16 in. above the cap surface. The cap is then bolted up to the cylinder block and is immediately taken down and if the packing has riveted over, the riveted portion is cut off.

Again bolt the cap into place and keep repeating this cycle until it is either necessary to cut off the packing or the bearing cap finally seats.

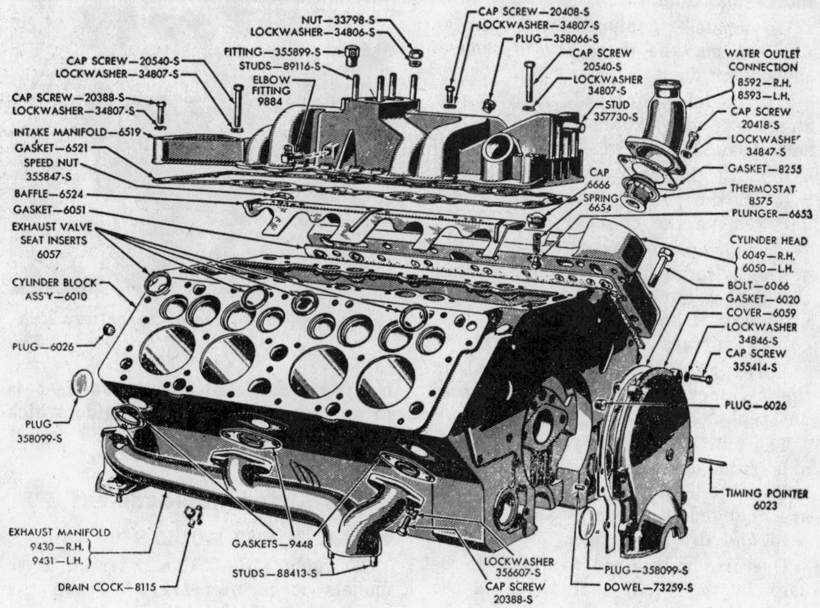

Engine block with related parts

OIL SEAL—continued

The object of letting the seal protrude is so that it will squeeze up and compress the upper portion of the rear main bearing seal and sometimes will prevent a slight leak at that point.

VALVE SYSTEM

All Lincoln engines built from 1940 to 1951 are of the L head variety, having the valves seated in the block. Hydraulic valve lifters are used on all models. The hydraulic lifter can be removed for service after the valves and springs have been removed.

1952 AND 1953 MODELS

Starting with 1952 production an overhead valve V-type engine is used on all Lincoln models.

Hydraulic valve lifters are used and, in spite of the fact that the new engine is of the overhead valve variety, the service on the lifter is exactly the same as the service shown for the earlier models.

Removal of Valve, Guide & Spring Assembly

1952 AND 1953 MODELS

To service the valves on these models it is necessary to remove the cylinder head. Proceed as follows: Disconnect the exhaust manifold and the intake manifold.

On models equipped with heater ducts it may be necessary to remove the heater duct.

On models equipped with power steering, the exhaust manifold is somewhat difficult of access.

Remove the rocker cover assembly, take off the rocker assemblies, unbolt and remove the cylinder head.

Extraordinary care should be taken of the cylinder head so as not to mar the gasket surface. A thin gasket is used and it requires a smoothly machined surface to mate properly.

Valve guides are cast integral in the cylinder head and are therefore not replaceable.

The cylinder heads are interchangeable from one bank to the other providing the rocker shaft and supports are changed to properly align the oil feed and drain passages.

Oversize valves are available to be used in the event that there is too much play between the valve and its guide. As stated before the valve guides are integral with the block and are not replaceable. It will be necessary to ream them to a standard oversize if there is too much play in the valve stem.

ALL MODELS TO 1951

To remove the valve, guide and spring assembly it is necessary to raise the head of the valve and with a special tool reach under the valve head and drive the guide down far enough so that the keeper C washer may be removed from the valve compartment.

After the C washer is removed the entire assembly is pulled up through the top of the block. The assembly is taken from the engine without removing the valve spring.

Several different types of pulling devices are available for forcing the guide downward in order to release the C type retaining washer, and several C type, bar type and hydraulic type lifters are used to pull the guide up through the cylinder block.

Dummy valve guides are available for use in the valve port when grinding or lapping the valve to its seat in the block. However, if an electrically driven valve seat grinder is used the guide to be used on that valve should be inserted into the block in order to make certain that the valve seat is ground concentric to the guide which is to be used in that port.

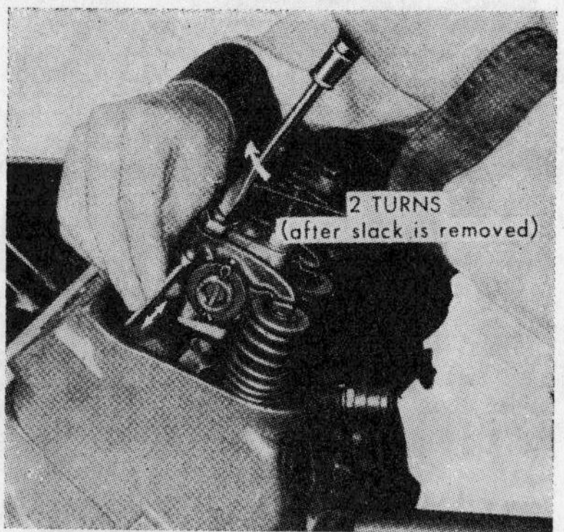

Adjusting valve clearance for zero lash

Valve Lifter Replacement

1952 AND 1953 MODELS

To replace the valve lifter on these models it is necessary to take the rocker cover off of the cylinder affected and take off the intake manifold and the valve chamber cover.

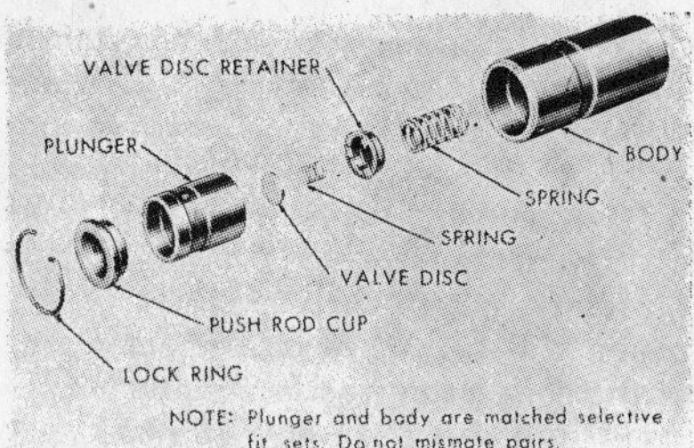

Hydraulic lifter assembly

With the push rod pulled up out of the way the lifter may be pulled up out of its bore.

Caution: The hydraulic valve lifters are not to be interchanged from one bore to the other. They should be carefully marked so that they will be returned to the bore from which they were removed.

None of the internal parts of the lifters are interchangeable in any other lifter.

ALL MODELS TO 1951

The valve lifters may be lifted out of their bores after the valve spring and guide assembly has been removed. The only service on the valve lifters is that they be thoroughly cleaned with solvent and blown off with compressed air. Guides should be marked or tagged so that they are returned to the port from which they were removed.

The internal parts of the hydraulic lifter are not interchangeable one to the other.

The internal parts should always be returned to the lifter from which they were taken.

Initial Setting of Hydraulic Valve Lifters

To make certain that the lifter will operate in approximately the middle of its stroke see to it that with the plunger completely depressed there is between .030 and .070 inch clearance between the valve stem and the top of the plunger. This measurement should be made with no oil in the hydraulic unit and the plunger pressed fully down. A screw driver can be used to compress the plunger to make this check.

Valve Springs

At any time the valve mechanism is removed from the car the valve spring should be tested for pressure before it is replaced. Test specifications for the

valve springs are given in the tables in the front of this Manual.

1952 AND 1953 MODELS

Valve guides on these models are cast integral with the block. If there is excessive play between the valve and its guide it is necessary to ream the guide bore to an oversize valve assembly.

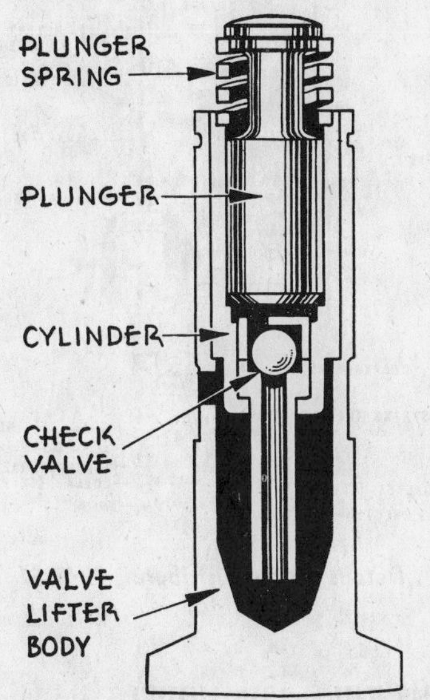

Sectional view of the hydraulic lifter

Valve Guide Replacement

1949 TO 1951 PRODUCTION ENGINES

On these engines the valve can be removed from the valve guide without taking the guide out of the engine. The valve stem is made straight so that it can be lifted out readily. The guide, however, is replaced in exactly the same manner as for the earlier models, in that it is driven downward to permit the release of the retaining C washer and is then pulled upward through the top of the cylinder block.

Conventional split type keepers are used in the valve spring seat on models from 1949 to 1951.

Rocker Assemblies

Each time the rocker arms are removed from the cylinder head they should be disassembled and cleaned as a precaution.

Remove the cotter keys, washers, rocker springs, springs, supports and plugs from the shaft.

Caution: It is recommended that the parts be kept in the order in which they were removed so that they can be reassembled quickly and without unnecessary loss of time.

Two types of rockers are used and they should be installed so as the valve end of the rocker points outward away from its support. Note that there is a support between both of the rockers and when properly assembled each of the valve rockers will point away from that support at its valve end.

Valve Timing Procedure and/or Timing Gear Raplacement

The cam shaft guide on all Lincoln models is by means of gears and unless the gears are badly worn or damaged or have been tampered with the valve timing will remain as set by the factory. If it becomes necessary to retime the valves or replace either of the gears due to wear or damage, proceed as follows:

Remove the timing case cover and take off the cam shaft gear. If it is desired to replace the crankshaft gear it will be necessary to take off the oil

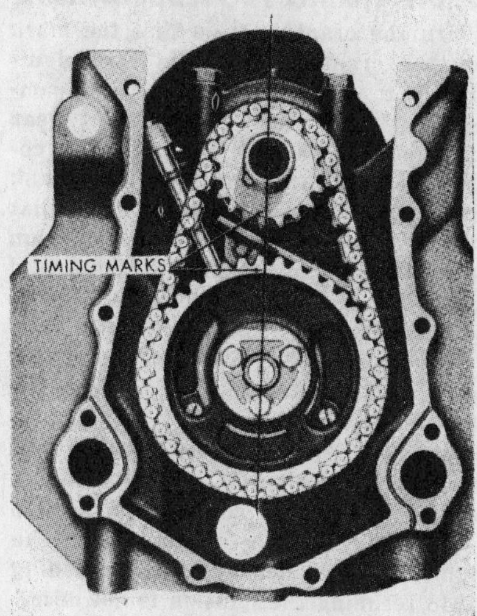

Timing marks

pan in order to remove the crankshaft gear.

Press on the new crankshaft gear, being careful when starting the gear that the key and key-way are in perfect alignment, since it is a reasonably tight fit on the shaft and is very difficult to align after the gears have been started.

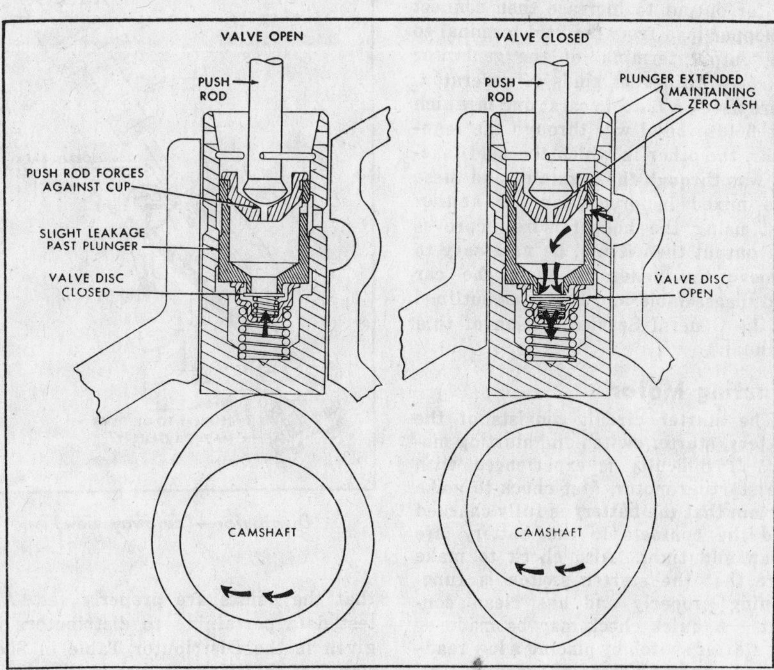

Hydraulic lifter operation—cross section

LINCOLN 1940 thru 1953

VALVE TIMING PROCEDURE—*cont'd*

Turn the crankshaft so that the mark on the crankshaft gear is pointed directly toward the center of the camshaft. Now mesh the camshaft gear so that the mark on the cam gear coincides with the mark on the crank gear. Now rotate the camshaft so that the bolt hole will line up with the cam shaft gear and install the bolts and special lock plate. Now rotate the crankshaft two full revolutions as a recheck to make certain that the marks coincide in a straight line between the two shaft centers.

Valves timed in this manner will be correct regardless of which piston is at top center. On models from 1949 to 1953 it may be necessary to retime the ignition. On models up to and including 1948 retiming the ignition is not necessary since the distributor drive is directly off the end of the camshaft.

ENGINE ELECTRICAL SYSTEM

Generator

A two brush type fully controlled generator is used on all Lincoln cars. If difficulty is experienced with the generator, connect a jumper lead from the field terminal of the generator to ground. If this does not cause the generator output to increase then connect a hopper lead from the field terminal to the output terminal of the generator since two different kinds of generators were used on Lincoln cars; one in which the field ground was through the regulator, the other in which the field takeoff was through the regulator and these are mixed in production. If neither test using the hopper wire improves the output then it will be necessary to remove the generator from the car and disassemble and test it as outlined in the General Service section of this Manual.

Starting Motor

The starter circuit consists of the battery, starter switch and starting motor. If difficulty is experienced with the starting motor, first check to make certain that the battery is fully charged and the contacts to the battery are clean and tight. Also check to make sure that the starter switch is functioning properly and has clean contacts. A quick check may be made of the starter switch by placing a low reading volt meter across the contacts of the starter switch and then crank the engine with the starting motor. A drop of approximately 1/3 volt is the maximum allowable when the starter is cranking the engine. Any drop in excess of 1/3 volt indicates there is high resistance in the starter switch and it should either be repaired or replaced.

If the difficulty is isolated to the starting motor, it should be removed from the car and subjected to the same test, which is given for generators, in the General Service section of this Manual.

Distributor Assembly

ALL MODELS, 1940 THRU 1948

The distributor on these models is driven directly off the front of the camshaft. A slot, offset from center, is used on the distributor shaft to engage a tongue which is also offset from center on the camshaft. Two sets of breaker points are used and the adjustment of the breaker points is critical.

A stroboscope or a distributor setting device should be used to insure

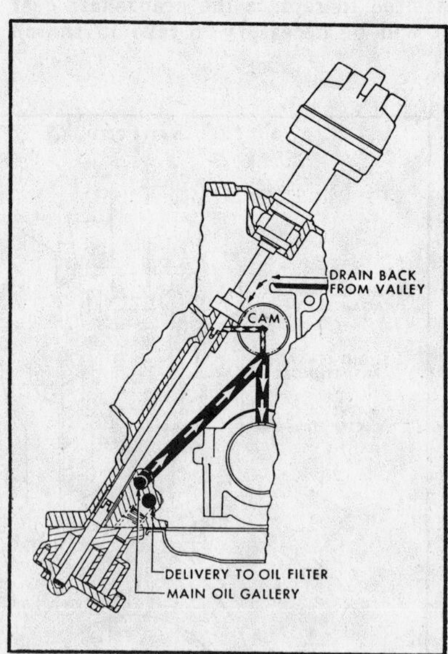

Distributor—(cutaway view)

that the points are properly set. All test data pertaining to distributors is given in the Distributor Table in Section 2 of this Manual (see index).

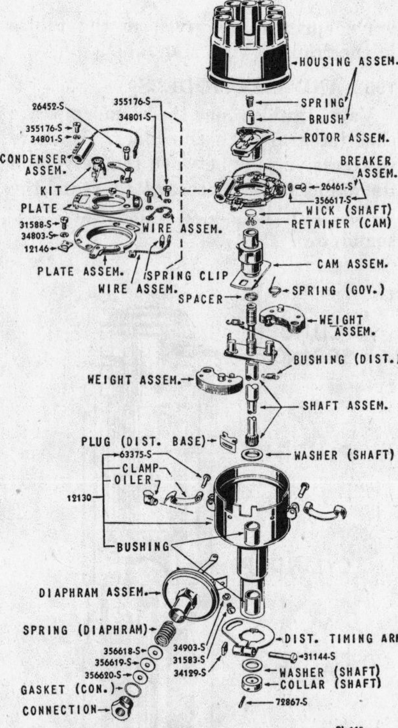

Details of the distributor, 1949-51 V8 Models

1949 THRU 1953 MODELS

The distributor on these models is located at the back of the engine block, just back of the left cylinder head. An 8 lobe cam is used, having single breaker points. On models from 1949 through 1951 the distributor is driven from a gear on the back of the camshaft.

Ignition Timing

1940 THRU 1948 MODELS

On these models it is impossible to get the distributor on incorrectly since it is driven directly from the end of the camshaft by a tongue and groove arrangement which is set off center of the shaft and can only be mounted one way.

A small range of advance and retard is provided at the side of the distributor.

1949 THRU 1953 MODELS

On these models the ignition timing is marked on the vibration damper and it is recommended that a neon type timing light be used to determine the exact point of ignition.

HEAD TIGHTENING SEQUENCE

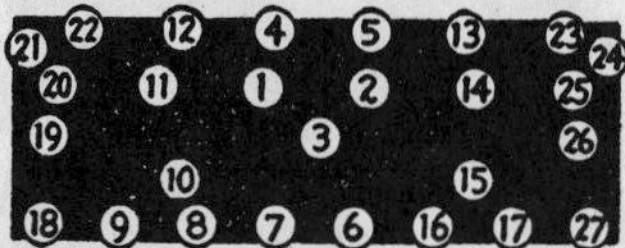

1936-1948 MODELS V-12

Tighten nuts to 50 foot pounds on cast iron head or 40 foot pounds on aluminum.

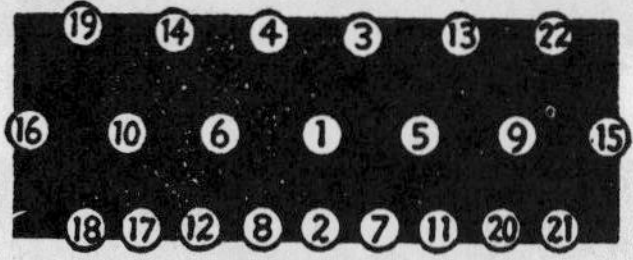

1949-1951 MODELS V-8

Tighten head bolts to 65-70 foot pounds or head nuts to 50-55 foot pounds.

Firing Order

1940 THRU 1948 MODELS

On these models the cylinders are numbered as follows: left bank, odd numbers starting at the radiator, 1, 3, 5, 7, 9 and 11. Right bank, even numbers, 2, 4, 6, 8, 10 and 12. Using this numbering system the engine fires 1-4-9-8-5-2-11-10-3-6-7-12. The distributor rotor turns in a counter-clockwise direction.

The direction of rotation of the distributor has a somewhat less effect on the Lincoln cars than on cars with conventional distributors. The wires in the distributor cap are inserted into the cap according to the number which is marked on the cap. Since the caps are arranged so that they can be used on either side of the distributor the wire from any given cylinder should be inserted into the hole in the cap which has the number right side up when the cap is mounted on the distributor.

1949 THRU 1953 MODELS

On these models the cylinders are numbered starting at the right bank, front cylinder, 1, 2, 3, 4. The left bank, front cylinder, 5, 6, 7, 8. With this numbering arrangement the engine fires 1-5-4-8-6-3-7-2. The distributor rotates in a clockwise direction when viewed from the top.

CLUTCH ASSEMBLY

Adjustment of Clutch Pedal

The clutch actuating rod should be adjusted so that there is from ½ to ¾ inch free travel of the clutch pedal before the throw out bearing engages the fingers.

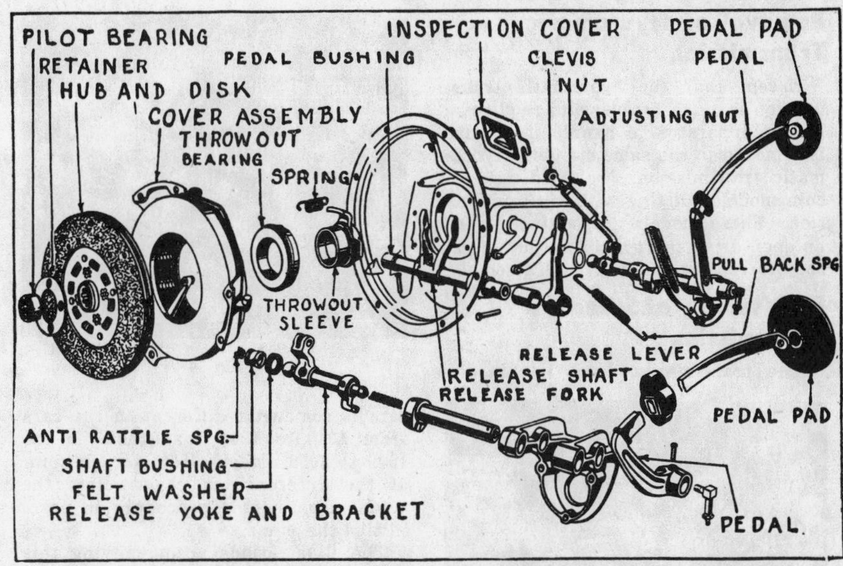

Clutch linkage shown disassembled. All models to 1948

For all practical purposes this is the only adjustment possible on the clutch while it is mounted in the car.

Removal of Clutch Assembly

1949 THRU 1953 MODELS

On these models the clutch can be removed after the transmission assembly has been pulled back out of the way. The transmission is detached at the bell housing on these models and the engine must be supported on a jack. The clutch is then detached from the flywheel and lifted off the car.

Disassembly Of Clutch

The disassembly and overhaul of Lincoln clutches requires special clutch equipment as do all of the other passenger cars. Instructions in the use of the equipment is supplied by each of the manufacturers. Unless special equipment is available it is not advisable to attempt to overhaul the clutch. The customary procedure is to either install a new clutch or a rebuilt unit.

Standard Transmission Assembly

All Lincoln cars are available with a standard three speed transmission with or without overdrive. The removal procedure given below will apply to the transmission whether it is standard, or if it has an overdrive. The standard transmission can be identified readily since it will have a round extension housing at the back of the transmission if no overdrive is used. If an overdrive is used there will be an overdrive housing at the back of the transmission occupying the same space that the extension housing occupies on the non-overdrive transmission.

Removal of Transmission

ALL MODELS, 1940 THRU 1948

Detach the rear axle assembly at the rear spring shackle, take off all rear axle attaching parts such as shock absorbers, tortion bars, brakes, etc. Disconnect the front universal joint and back the rear axle assembly out of the way. Support the back of the engine on a jack and unbolt the transmission from the rear support, being careful to retain any shims which are used at that point. Detach all transmission attaching parts such as shift levers, electrical connections to the overdrive, etc.

The transmission is then detached at the bell housing and slide out of the car. When reinstalling, it is always a good idea to insert at least two long guide studs into the bell housing in order to pilot the transmission on to the bell housing and prevent possible damage to the clutch disc.

1949 THRU 1953 MODELS

On these models the removal of the transmission is practically the same except that it is not neecssary to remove the rear axle. Since these models are equipped with an open drive shaft the universal joint is split and the drive shaft lowered to the floor. Otherwise the procedure is practically the same.

Removal of Hydramatic Transmission

Except that the hydramatic transmission is much heavier and requires a lifting apparatus to handle it, it also is removed in the same manner. Hydramatic transmissions are used on Lincoln models starting with 1949 production. These models are equipped with an open drive shaft and it is not necessary to remove the rear axle assembly.

Disassembly of Standard Transmission

The transmission used in Lincoln

Fig. 1

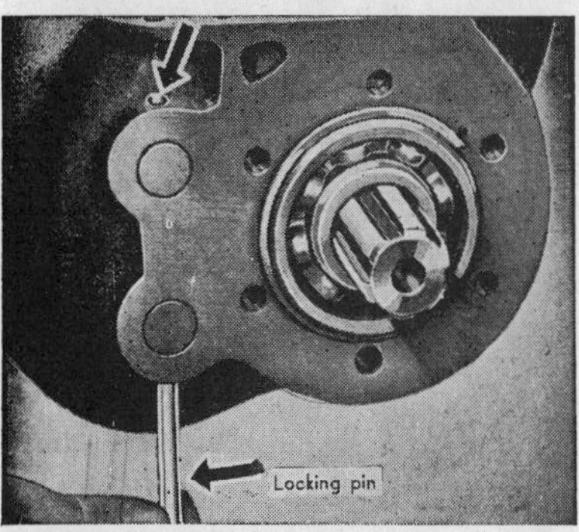

Fig. 2

Fig. 3

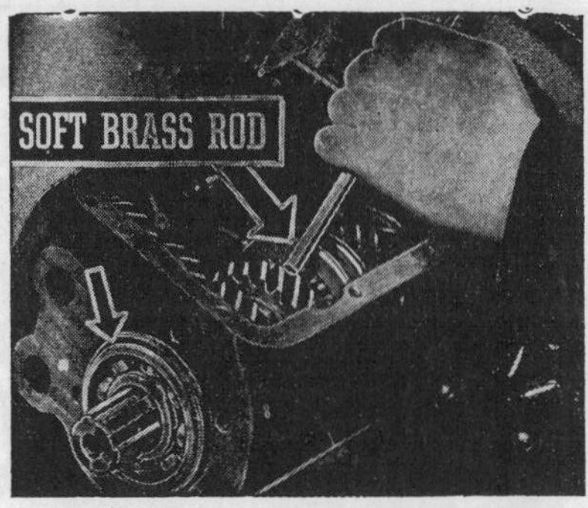

Fig. 4

cars is somewhat different in the cars from 1940 to 1948 than those in the 1949 to 1953 models. However, in spite of the difference in construction the actual disassemble procedure is practically the same.

The illustrations accompanying this test are actually pictures of a Ford transmission. However, in spite of the fact that the Lincoln transmission is much bigger and heavier, the procedure is still the same and the Ford illustrations are typical of the service requirements on the Lincoln transmission.

Drain out the gear lubricant and place the shifter arm in the neutral position.

Remove the nine bolts from the shifter housing and lift off the gear shift housing and cover assembly. Remove the locking wires and cap screws from the rear engine mount and ball retainer (on 1949 to 1951 models this is the extension housing).

Remove the four cap screws holding the main shaft bearing retainer and clutch release bearing (Fig. 1). Unhook the retracting spring and throw-out bearing assembly and remove the throw-out assembly.

Pull out the reverse idler and countershaft locking pin (Fig. 2). Drive the countershaft from the front end so that the countershaft gears will drop to the bottom of the case to provide clearance needed when removing the main drive gear (Fig. 3). With the synchronizer in neutral position, use a soft brass punch, drive back the main shaft and bearing about ¼ inch so that the snap ring will clear the case (Fig. 4 and Fig. 5). Take off the snap ring and drive the main shaft back into its original position. Shift the synchronizer sleeve into second gear (Fig. 6) and drive the main shaft and main drive gear forward until the main drive gear and bearing can be pulled out from the front of the case (Fig. 7).

Fig. 5

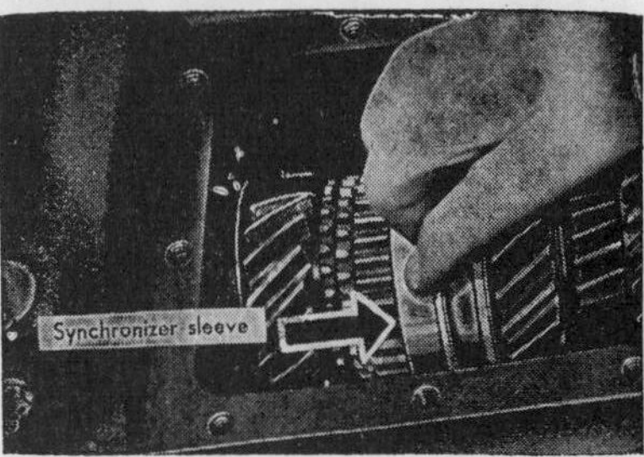

Fig. 6

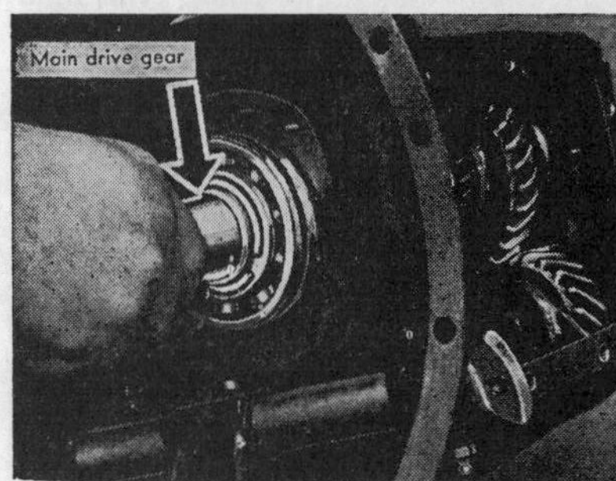

Fig. 7

With the main shaft assembly forward in the case, have the low and reverse gears as far forward as possible. Drive the rear bearing (still mounted on the main shaft) into the case and lift the main shaft and gear assembly up out of the case, rear end first (Fig. 8). With a brass punch, drive the reverse idler shaft forward into the front of the case and lift out the reverse idler gear (Fig. 9). Remove the counter shaft assembly (Fig. 10) being careful not to drop the bearings and the rear thrust washer.

To disassemble the transmission main shaft and gear assembly remove the shaft snap ring and pilot bearing spacer (Fig. 11). Remove the synchronizer sleeve and hub assembly (Fig. 12) and then remove the thrust washer, the synchronizer ring and the

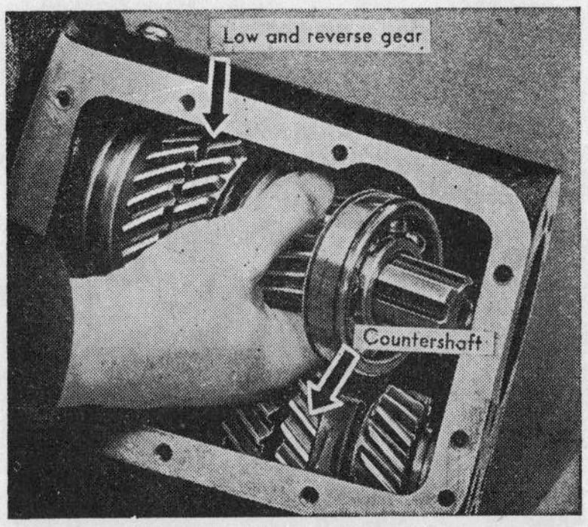

Fig. 8

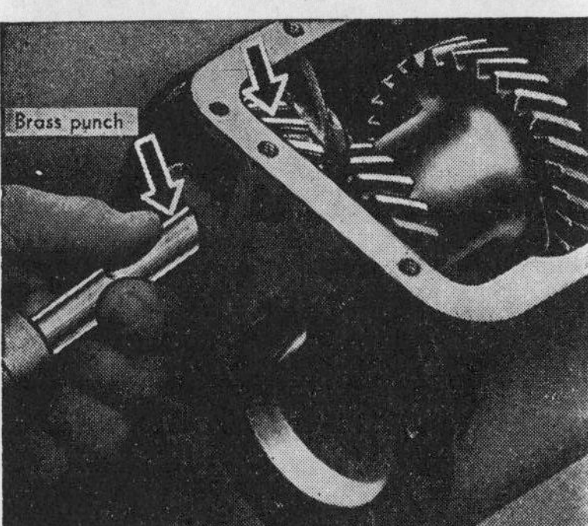

Fig. 9

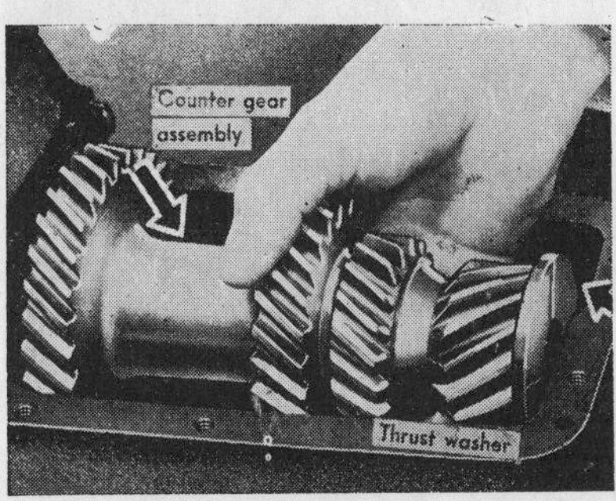

Fig. 10

intermediate gear. Take off the main shaft intermediate gear thrust washer and remove the lock pin (Fig. 13). Slide off the low and reverse sliding gear, and using an arbor press, press off the main shaft bearing.

To disassemble a synchronizer, hold a finger over each bar to prevent the balls from jumping out and then push up the clutch from the outer sleeve (Fig. 14). Remove the main drive gear snap ring at the shaft and press off the ball bearing assembly and remove the oil baffle. The transmission is now completely disassembled, it should be cleaned and all parts inspected.

Fig. 11

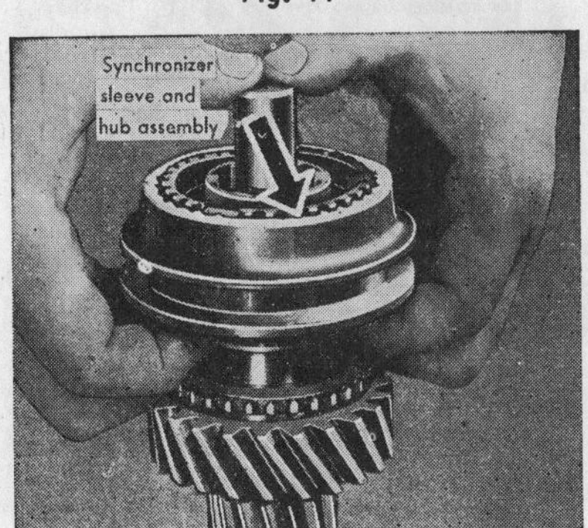

Fig. 12

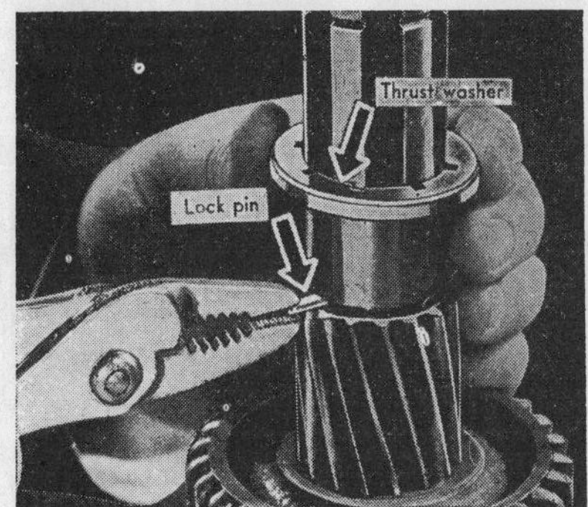

Fig. 13

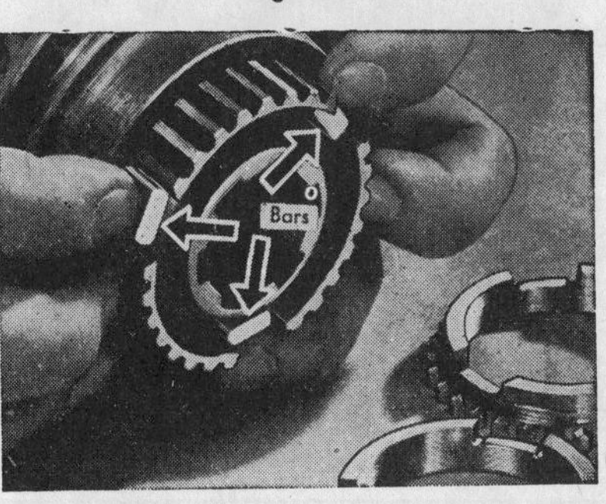

Fig. 14

Transmission Reassembly

Fit the clutch hub and sleeve in a position which will permit the smoothest sliding motion.

Install the main shaft bearing spacer ring on the main shaft, using a new oil baffle, with the flange toward the front of the shaft and the bearing with the lock ring groove toward the rear.

Press the shaft and assembly into place.

Install low and reverse sliding gears on the main shaft with the shifter fork grooves toward the rear. Install the thrust washer lock pin and the steel thrust washer. Install the intermediate gear, bronze spacer washer and synchronizer ring. Press on the synchronizer assembly, being sure the shifter grooves of the sleeve are toward the roller bearing end of the shaft. The slots in the second speed gear synchronizer ring should line up with the insert bars. Install the main shaft snap ring. Check and play between the intermediate gear and the steel thrust washer with a feeler gauge. Clearance should be between .004 to .008 inch. If greater than this amount, use an oversize spacer washer to obtain the desired clearance (Fig. 15).

To install the countershaft gear thrust washer, first place some hard grease on the steel back of the bronze thrust washer entering the tongue of the washer into the groove provided in the transmission case. Install both roller bearings in the countershaft gear with a spacer between and the large roller bearing to the small end of the countershaft gear. Place the countershaft gear and thrust washer in position in the groove on the end of the gear. Be certain the oil grooves in the face of the end of the baffle are clean. Set the counter gear and bearing assembly in place allowing the assembly to rest on the bottom.

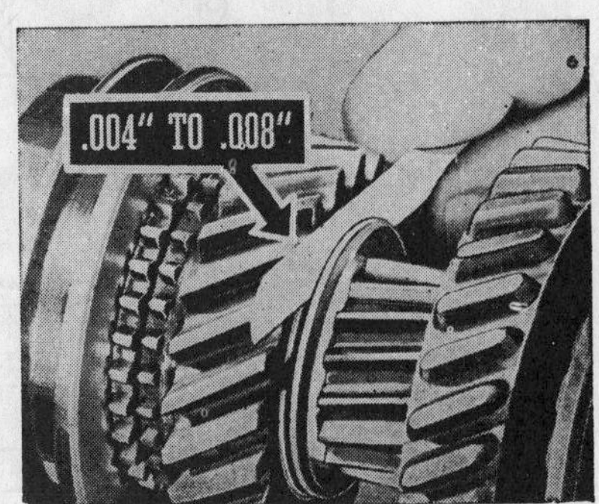

Fig. 15

TRANSMISSION REASSEMBLY—*continued*

Install the reverse idler gear and reverse idler gear shaft, making sure the rounded edge of the gear is toward the inside of the case.

Shift the synchronizer into second gear position and install the main shaft assembly into the case by starting the front end of the main shaft in first and then lower the rear end in and move it toward the rear of the case.

With the low and reverse sliding gear in the forward position start the main shaft and bearing into the bore of the case and install the main shaft snap ring. To assemble the main drive gear install the oil baffle with the flange toward the gear, press on the bearing and install the snap ring, all the main shaft pilot bearing rollers, set it into place and place the synchronizer ring on the end of the main drive gear assembly. Engage the gears in position and raise the counter set cluster from the bottom of the case and drive in the counter shaft. After the counter shaft and idler shaft are locked in place insert the locking pin. Replace the main drive gear collar. Assemble the clutch throw out bearing and, with a feeler gauge, check the clearance of the bearing retainer to the clutch housing. Reinstall the rear bearing cover and the transmission shift cover assembly.

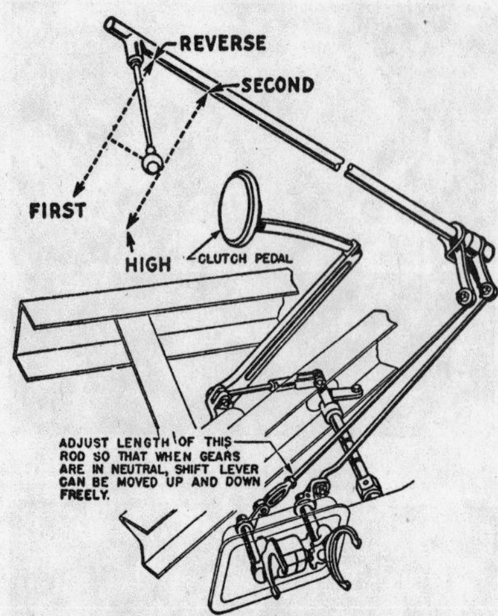

Simplified sketch showing adjustor of trans. shift mech.

Standard Transmission Shift Linkage Adjustment

Set the transmission levers (at the transmission) in the neutral position and detach the actuating rods. Set the shift lever in the neutral position making certain the two shift levers at the bottom of the steering column are in line. With the levers held in this position adjust the length of the rod so that the clevis pins will enter freely.

Disassembly of Hydramatic Transmission

Complete service instructions on hydramatic transmissions is given in the automatic transmission portion of this section. (See index)

REAR AXLE ASSEMBLY

Two types of rear axle assemblies are used in Lincoln cars, from 1940 to 1951. 1940 thru 1948 all models used a banjo type housing rear and a torque tube drive. Models starting with 1949 and thru 1951 used a shim adjusted rear axle assembly which had a removable cover. The carrier on the late type rear was not removable.

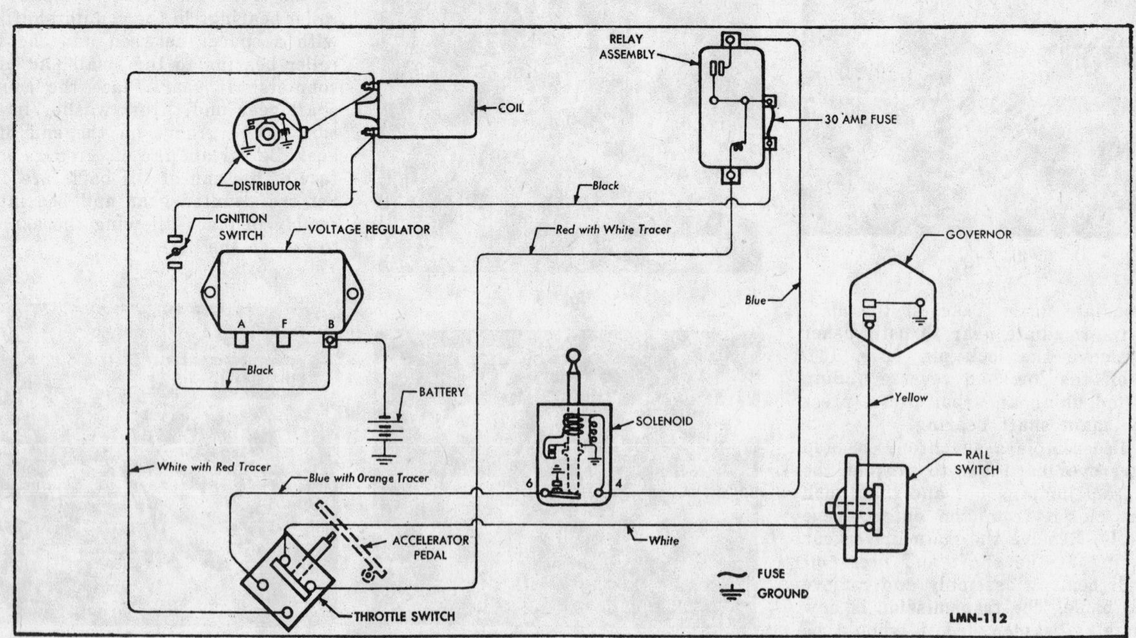

Overdrive wiring diagram—1949-51 overdrive

Removal of Rear Axle Assembly

1940 THRU 1948 MODELS

In order to remove the rear axle assembly it is necessary to remove the brake lines, brake cables, torsion bars, shock absorbers. Disconnect the rear spring either at the U bolts where it bolts to the frame or at your option at the spring shackles.

The torque tube is disconnected at the front universal joint and the entire assembly is slid out from underneath the car.

1949 THRU 1953 MODELS

To remove the rear axle assembly on these models disconnect the torsion bars, shock absorbers, spring seat U bolts, brake cables and hoses.

The drive shaft may be disconnected either at the front or rear universal joint and the entire assembly is slid out from underneath the car.

Axle Shaft Removal

1940 THRU 1948 MODELS

On these models to remove a rear axle assembly it is necessary to remove both rear wheels, hubs and drums and disconnect the shock absorber and torsion bars and disconnect the spring from the left side of the housing. The left axle housing is then unbolted from the banjo housing and slid off the axle shaft.

The left axle shaft differential with its ring gear and spiders and the right axle shaft can be slid out in one piece. In order to take out the axle shaft it is necessary to separate the differential and slide the axle shaft out through the split differential. To split the differential in its turn it is necessary to take off the ring gear.

1949 THRU 1953 MODELS

To replace an axle shaft on these models simply remove the wheel and brake drum and take out the axle bearing retainer from in back of the axle flange and, using a puller, pull out the axle shaft.

On late models the axle bearing will come out with the axle shaft. This bearing is pressed on the axle shaft and held in place by a shrunk-on ring. The ring should never be reused. At any time the bearing is pressed off the shaft a new retainer ring should be used.

Replacement of Pinion Oil Seal

1949 THRU 1953 MODELS

To replace the pinion oil seal on these models it is not necessary to take the axle from underneath the car. Simply split the rear universal joint and after carefully marking the position of the companion flange nut remove the nut and take off the companion flange.

Axle Shaft Oil Seal

1940 THRU 1948 MODELS

On these models the rear axle oil seal is contained in the rear hub. Simply remove the wheel and hub assembly and pull the seal out with an inertia type puller.

1949 THRU 1953 MODELS

On these models the oil seal is contained on the axle shaft back of the wheel bearing.

To remove the oil seal it is necessary to first remove the axle and bearing assembly and then the oil seal may be pulled with an inertia puller.

Replacement of Ring Gear & Pinion—and/or Pinion Bearings

1940 THRU 1948 MODELS

The differential assembly on these models is removed in the manner as described for the replacement of an axle shaft on these models, with this addition. If bearings and pinion gear are to be added it will be necessary to remove the rear axle assembly from underneath the car.

To remove the pinion and bearings, detach the torque tube at the rear axle flange and slide it off the drive shaft. The drive shaft may now be detached from the pinion shaft and the pinion shaft and bearings can be pressed off or pulled out of the banjo housing using a puller or press.

1949 THRU 1953 MODELS

While it is theoretically possible to replace the ring gear pinion and/or bearings on these models with the housing under the car.

Proceed as follows: Remove the axle assembly from underneath the car and place it on a bench or workstand. Take out both axle shafts as outlined under axle shaft removal and take off the differential cover assembly. Remove the differential side bearing caps. In order to lift out the differential with its side bearings a special housing spreading jig is available to spread (spring) the housing to permit the removal of the differential. Notice that shims are used between the differential housing and the differential side bearings. These shims provide for both the pinion preload and for the adjustment of the ring gear in relation to the pinion. If they are removed from the housing they should be carefully measured and a note made of their individual and total thickness so that the same number of shims can be reinstalled if a new ring gear or new bearings are to be used.

To remove the pinion and bearings proceed as follows: Take off the universal joint companion flange nut and pull off the companion flange. The pinion shaft assembly can now be pushed out through the rear of the housing. The pinion shaft will come out with the rear bearing cone in place on the shaft. After the pinion has been removed the front bearing cone may be pulled from the front of the case. Notice that no spacer is used between the bearings on this rear axle assembly. The adjusting shims are located back of the front and rear bearing cups (races).

The outer races are pulled with an inertia type puller, using extreme care so as not to damage the shims which are located between the race and a shoulder in the housing.

Make careful note of the shims both individual and collective thickness so that they can be replaced exactly as they were removed, unless special micrometer adjusting equipment is available. If special micrometer adjusting equipment is available for use on this particular rear axle assembly then the instructions in the use of the micrometer equipment, packed with it, should be followed. The following instructions are intended to shops which do not have the special equipment.

Reassembly

1949 THRU 1953 MODELS

Install the front and rear outer bearing cups with the number of shims which were removed from the old bearing cups. Note: the shims are entered into the housing first and pushed firmly

REASSEMBLY—*continued*

up against the shoulder in the housing. It is of vital importance that the shims be cleaned very carefully before they are inserted into the housing, since the inclusion of any dirt on the shims will change their respective thickness. Install a new bearing on the pinion shaft and insert the pinion shaft in from the back of the housing. Place the pinion front bearing in the front of the housing and install the universal joint companion flange. Tighten the companion flange nut and while tightening it keep checking the torque required to turn the pinion shaft. If the companion flange nut can be tightened to between 140 ft. and 180 ft. lbs. without exceeding 8 in. to 12 in. lbs. torque required to turn the pinion shaft then the shims back of each bearing cone are correct as far as bearing preload is concerned. It may be necessary, however, to change the shims to get correct pinion depth later in the adjustment.

If it is found that the torque required to turn the pinion is greater than 12 in. lbs. then it will be necessary to remove one shim at a time from in back of either of the bearing cups (races). If it is found that the pinion can be tightened to 180 ft. lbs. torque without producing a preload, requiring at least 8 in. lbs. to turn the pinion then it will be necessary to add shims back of either of the bearing cups (races). Assemble the differential setting up the side bearings without shims at all. Now place the differential in the housing (it will not be necessary to spread the housing, since no shims are used back of the bearings) and install the bearing caps but do not tighten them. With a dial indicator check the total side play of the differential assembly. This should be accomplished with extreme care using a dial indicator so that exact readings can be had.

Add .009 to .011 inch to the reading obtained on the dial indicator. This will be the total thickness of shims required on both sides of the differential side bearings. Notice that by adding .009-.011 inch to the reading it will be necessary to spread the housing at least that much since the total thickness of the shims is in excess of the space in the housing. This will give the correct preload to the bearing when the shims are installed. As a start, check the number of shims which were removed from the differential side bearings and, if the same total thickness is required then install the shims exactly as they were taken out. If a different thickness is required, say more shims needed than the difference between the shims re-

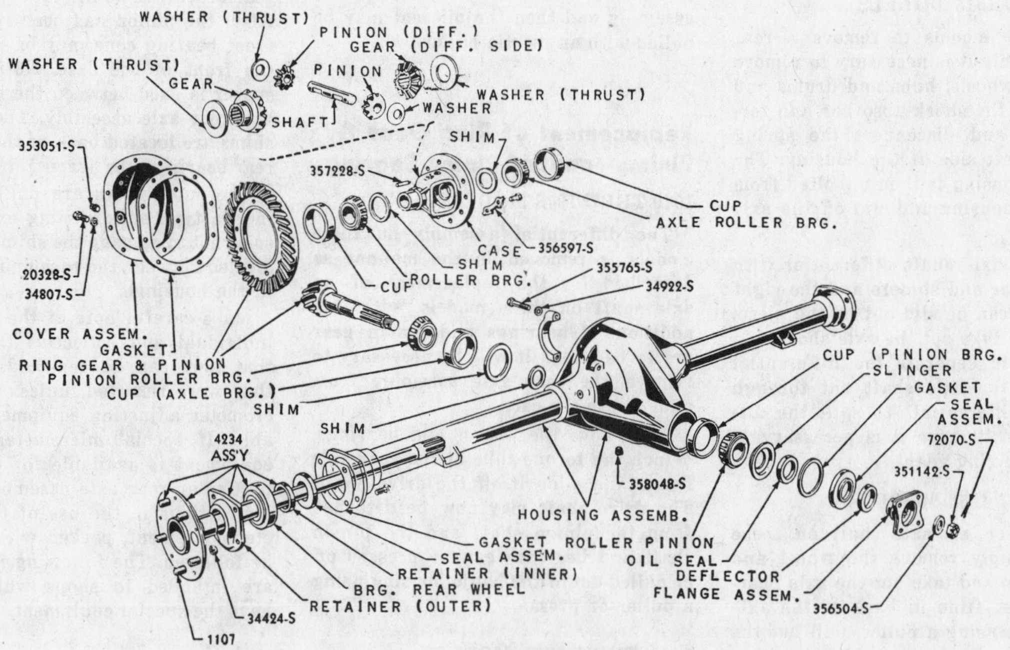

Rear Axle Assembly 1949-51 V8 models

moved and the shims that are to be installed should be split between the right and left side. After the proper shim thickness has been selected remove the differential side bearings, place the shims on the differential and replace the bearings making certain that the shims are perfectly clean and the bearing surface which contacts the shims is also perfectly clean. It will now be necessary to use the spreading device to spread the housing approximately .015 inch (no more) and install the differential assembly and the differential bearing caps which should be tightened securely. Paint about ten of the ring gear teeth with red lead and roll the ring gear through the pinion noticing the markings made by the pinion gear on the red lead on the ring gear. Bear in mind that the TOTAL number of shims on both the ring gear and the pinion are already correct.

If it is necessary to move the ring gear into deeper mesh with the pinion then a shim should be removed from the right side of the differential side bearing and placed on the left side of the differential side bearing which will move the ring gear exactly the thickness of that shim deeper into the pinion without changing the total preload.

If it is necessary to move the pinion gear into deeper mesh with the ring gear then one of the shims should be taken from behind the front bearing cup (race) and placed in back of the rear bearing cup (race) so that the total number of shims will not be disturbed. It will be necessary to continue moving shims and testing until the desirable contact on the face of the ring and pinion is achieved.

Actually the job of installing a ring gear and pinion is not nearly as difficult as it sounds because, due to extremely close manufacturing tolerances the number of shims found in the old rear is generally perfectly suitable for the new ring gear and pinion.

Manufacturing tolerances on bearings are so precise that if just one bearing is being changed it would be extremely unusual if it were necessary to alter the shims which were found in the rear.

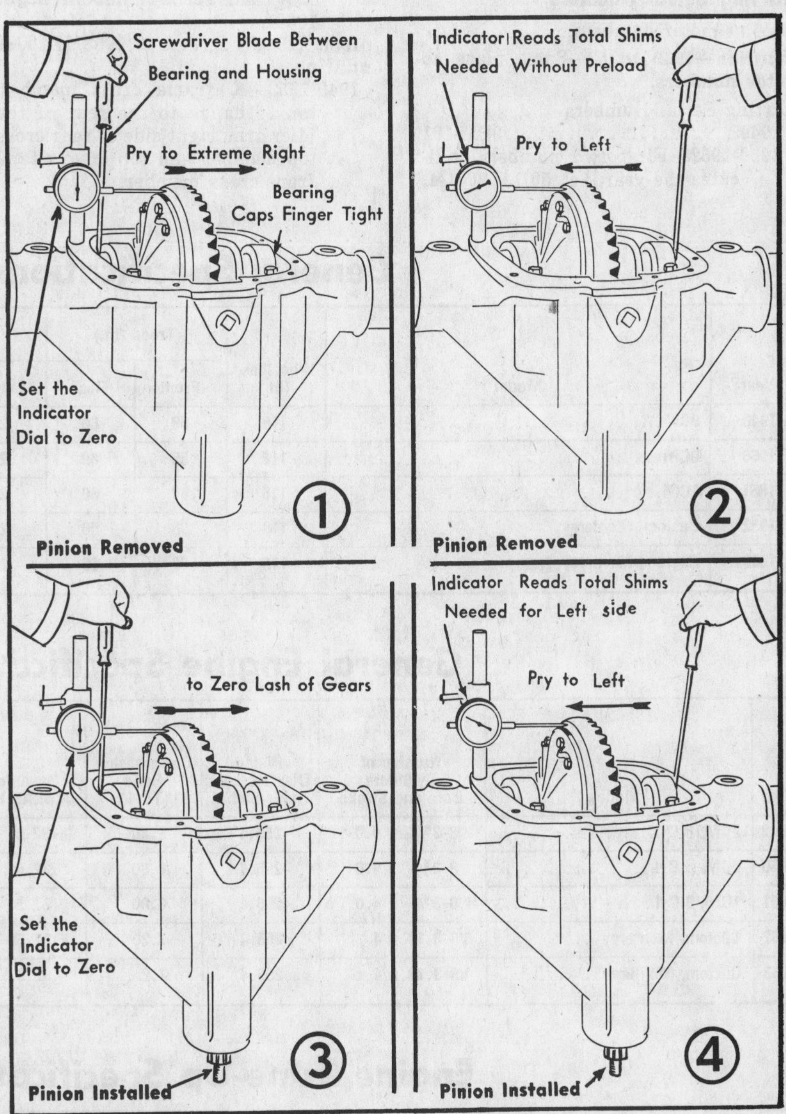

MERCURY SPECIFICATIONS 1949 thru 1953

Starting Serial and Motor Numbers

Starting Serial Numbers

Same as motor numbers.

Location—1949 to 53—Same place as Motor numbers.

Starting Serial Numbers

1949 ....9CM-101

1950-1952—First two numbers indicates the year, i.e., 50DA10001M, 1950. All serial numbers begin 10001.

1953 ....53ME10001

Location

1949-1953—K frame cross member, top of flange to the rear of the idler arm, right side of rear cross top member and top of gas tank front cross member.

Starting Motor Numbers

1949 to 53—Same as serial numbers.

Location—1949 to 53—Same place as serial numbers.

General Specifications

Year	Model	Wheelbase (in.)	Tread (in.) Front	Tread (in.) Rear	Overall Dimensions (in.) Length†	Overall Dimensions (in.) Width	Overall Dimensions (in.) Height	Shipping Weight (lb.)	Tire Size (in.)
1949	9CM	118	59	60	207	77	65	3430	7.10-15
1950	0CM	118	59	60	207	77	70	3386	7.10-15
1951	1CM	118	59	60	207	77	63	3470	7.10-15
1952	Custom, Monterey	118	58	56	202	74	63	....	7.10-15
1953	Custom, Monterey	118	58	56	202	74	62	....	7.10-15

General Engine Specifications

Year	Model	Number of Cylinders Bore and Stroke	Piston Displacement, Cubic Inches	Compression Ratio (To-1)	Taxable (A.M.A.) Hp.	Developed Horse Power: Bare Engine	Developed Horse Power: With Accessories	Maximum Torque Ft. Lbs.
1949	9CM, 8 Cyl.	8-3$\frac{3}{16}$ x 4.0	255.4	6.80	32.5	110 @ 3600	....	200 @ 2000
1950	0CM, 8 Cyl.	8-3$\frac{3}{16}$ x 4.0	255.4	6.80	32.5	110 @ 3600	....	200 @ 2000
1951	1CM, 8 Cyl.	8-3$\frac{3}{16}$ x 4.0	255.4	6.80	32.5	112 @ 3600	....	206 @ 2000
1952	Custom, Monterey	V8-3.19 x 4	255.4	7.20	32.50	125 @ 3700	....	211 @ 2050
1953	Custom, Monterey	V8-3.19 x 4	255.4	7.2	32.5	125 @ 3800	....	218 @ 2050

Engine Tune-Up Specifications

Year	Model	Spark Plugs: Type	Spark Plugs: Gap	Distributor: Point Gap	Distributor: Cam Dwell, (Deg.)	Ignition Timing, (Deg.)	Ignition Timing Mark and Location	Compression Pressure at R.P.M.	Operating Tappet Clearance: Inlet	Operating Tappet Clearance: Exhaust	Carburetor Fuel Float Height	Minimum Engine Idle Speed at R.P.M.
1949	9CM 8 Cyl.	H10	.032	.015	30	2B	Cr. Pl.	115@ *	.012	.016	1$\frac{7}{32}$"	425
1950	0CM, 8 Cyl.	H10	.032	.016	28½	2B	Cr. Pl.	115@ *	.012	.016	1$\frac{7}{32}$"	425
1951	1CM, 8 Cyl.	H10	.032	.016	28½	2B	Cr. Pl.	115@ *	.015	.019	....	425
1952	Custom, Monterey, 8 Cyl.	Ch-H10	.032	.015	28½	2B	Cr. Pl.	....	.014C	.018C	....	450
1953	Custom, Monterey, 8 Cyl.	Ch-H10	.032	.015	28½	2B	Cr, Pl.	....	.014C	.018C	....	450

*—Crank speed. Cr. Pl.—Crankshaft pulley.

1949 thru 1953 SPECIFICATIONS MERCURY

Dimensions of Valves

Year	Model	Overall Length		Head Diameter		Seat Angle (deg.)		Stem Diameter		Key Type	O.D. of Seat Insert	
		Inlet	Exhaust	Inlet	Exhaust	Inlet	Exhaust	Inlet	Exhaust		Inlet	Exhaust
1949	9CM	4.817	4.814	1.515	1.515	45	45	.341	.341	split lock	1.6335	1.6335
1950	0CM	4.820	4.815	1.510	1.510	45	45	.342	.341	split lock	1.6335	1.6335
1951	1CM	4.820	4.815	1.510	1.510	45	45	.341	.341	split lock	1.6335	1.6335
1952	Custom, Monterey, 8 cyl.	4.7555	4.7515	1.51	1.51	45	45	.3415	.341	....	....	....
1953	Custom, Monterey, 8 cyl.	4.7555	4.745	1.51	1.51	45	45	.342	.341	....	....	....

Pistons and Piston Pins

Year	Model	PISTONS				PISTON PINS		
		Diameter	Material	Type	No. of Rings	Length	Diameter	How Held
1949–50	9CM, OCM	3.1875	Alum.	Ss	4	2.847	.7503	F
1951	1CM	3.1875	Alum.	....	4	2.842	.7501	F
1952	Custom, Monterey, 8 cyl.	3.19	Alum. Alloy	Ss,C,Sh	4	2.835	.75025	F
1953	Custom, Monterey, 8 cyl.	3.19	Alum. Alloy	Ss,C,Sh	3	2.825	.75025	F

Ss—Split skirt. C—Cam ground. Sh—Spherical head.

Piston Ring Dimensions

Year	Model	Cylinder Bore	TOP RING			SECOND RING			THIRD RING			OIL RING		
			Width	Gap	Depth	Width	Gap	Depth	Width	Gap	Depth	Width	Gap	Depth
1949	9CM	3 3/16	.0933	.016	.154	.0933	.016	.154	.186	.014	.142	.186	.014	.142
1950–51	0CM, 1CM	3 3/16	.0934	.013	.154	.0934	.013	.154	.186	.013	.142	.186	.013	.142
1952	Custom, Monterey, 8 Cyl.	3.19	.09325	.012	.1817	.09325	.0135	.1817	.18625	.0135	.1897	.18625	.0135	.1717
1953	Custom, Monterey, 8 Cyl.	3.19	.09325	.012	.159	.09325	.012	.159	.18625	.0135	.147	....	....	....

Brake Data

Year	Model	Make	Lining Type	R=Riveted B=Bonded	Drum Diameter	Lining			Clearance	
						Length	Width	Thickness	Toe	Heel
1949	9CM	Ben	M	R	11	23.9	2	.212	.010	.010
1950	0CM	Ben	M	R	11	21.21	2–*1 3/4	.212	.010	.010
1951	1CM	Ben	M	R	11	21 7/32	2–*1 3/4	7/32	.010	.010
1952	Custom, Monterey, 8 Cyl.	....	M	R	11	21 7/32	2–*1 3/4	7/32	.010	.010
1953	Custom, Monterey, 8 Cyl.	....	M	R	11	21 7/32	2–*1 3/4	7/32	.010	.010

Ben—Bendix. M—Moulded. *—Rear.

MERCURY SPECIFICATIONS 1949 thru 1953

Engine Overhaul Specifications

		PISTONS				RING GAP CLEARANCES (Maximum)				PISTON PIN		ROD BEARINGS		
			Piston Skirt Clearances (Maximum)											
Year	Model	Removed From	Top	Bottom	Limit	Top Ring	Second Ring	Third Ring	Oil Ring	Type	Fit	Oil Clearance	Wear Limit	Side Play
1949	9CM, 8 Cyl.	A	.002	.001	.004	.020	.020	.020	.020	Float	Push	.0005–.003	.004	.006–.020
1950	0CM, 8 Cyl.	A	.002	.001	.004	.017	.017	.017	.017	Float	Push	.0005–.003	.004	.006–.020
1951	1CM, 8 Cyl.	A	.002	.0006	.003	.017	.017	.017	.017	Float	Push	.0005–.003	.004	.006–.020
1952	Custom, Monterey, 8 Cyl.	A	.0021	.0006	.003	.017	.017	.017	.017	FL	.0003	.0005–.003	.004	.006–.020
1953	Custom, Monterey, 8 Cyl.	A	.0023	.0011	.003	.017	.017	......	.017	FL	.0003	.0005–.003	.004	.006–.020

A—Above. †—Center crank gear mark between cam gear marks. TC—(Valves) top center. B—Before top center.

Tension Wrench Specifications

		Cylinder Head		Spark Plug		Connecting Rod Bolts or Nuts		Main Bearing Bolt		Flywheel Bolts		Vibration Damper Bolts	
Year	Model	Lbs.-Ft.	Thread	Lbs.-Ft.	Thread	Lbs.-Ft.	Thread	Lbs.-Ft.	Thread	Lbs.-Ft.	Thread	Lbs.-Ft.	Thread
1949 to 53	All	65–70	7/16–14	24–30	14 mm	45–50	3/8–24	80–90	1/2–13	75–85	7/16–20	......	......

Crankshaft Bearing Journal Sizes

		Connecting Rod Journals		Main Bearing Journals				
Year	Model	Diameter	Length	No. 1 Diameter	No. 2 Diameter	No. 3 Diameter	No. 4 Diameter	No. 5 Diameter
1950–51	Series—All	2.138–2.139	1.755	2.498–2.499	2.498–2.499	2.498–2.499	......	......
1952	Custom, Monterey	2.1385	......	2.4985	2.4985	2.4985	......	......
1953	......	2.1385	......	2.4985–1.473	2.3985–1.473	2.4985–1.959	......	......

Cooling Systems

YEAR	MODEL	Capacity Qts.	Quarts of Methanol Base Anti-Freeze (For Protection to Temperature Shown Below)							Quarts of Ethylene Glycol (For Protection to Temperature Shown Below)							Quarts of Denatured Alcohol—188 Proof (For Protection to Temperature Shown Below)						
			3	4	5	6	7	8	9	3	4	5	6	7	8	9	3	4	5	6	7	8	9
1942-49	......	22	20	14	7	0	−9	−18	−29	....	18	13	8	2	−6	−14	20	....	10	....	0	....	−10
1950-53	......	21	19	12	−5	−3	−12	−22	−34	....	17	−12	6	0	−9	−17	20	....	10	....	0	−10	....

and Wear Limit of Table

CRANKSHAFT		VALVES									OPERATING OIL PRESSURE			
Main Bearing Oil Clear-ance	Shaft End Play	Spring Tension (Maximum) Inlet	Exhaust	Low Limit	Guide Clear-ance	Seat Angle Inlet	Ex-haust	Valve Tim-ing, Inlet Vaive Opens (Deg.)	Cam-shaft Drive	Gear Marks	Pounds At M.P.H.	Low Limit§	Model	Year
.0025	.002-.006	80@1.84	80@1.84	70	.0011-.0031	45°	45°	10B	Gear	†	57@40	25	............9CM, 8 Cyl.	1949
.0025	.002-.006	84@1.84	84@1.84	74	.0015-.0035	45°	45°	10B	Gear	†	57@40	25	............0CM, 8 Cyl.	1950
.0002-.0018	.002-.006	89@1.57	89@1.57	80	.0019-.0039	45°	45°	5B	Gear	†	57@40	25	............1CM, 8 Cyl.	1951
.0002-.0018	.002-.006	89@1.57	89@1.57	......	.0019-.0039	45°	45°	5B	Gear	......	57@40	......	Custom, Monterey, 8 Cyl.	1952
.0002-.0018	.002-.006	89@1.57	89@1.57	......	.0019-.0039	45°	45°	5B	Gear	......	57@40	......	Custom, Monterey, 8 Cyl.	1953

*—At 2000 r.p.m. §—Car may be operated safely at lower oil pressures but low pressure indicates malfunction which should be corrected.

Distributors

Year	Model	Distributor Model Number	Cam Angle (deg.)	Direction of Rotation C=Clockwise CC=Counter Clockwise at Cam End	Breaker Arm Spring Tension	Breaker Point Gap (inches)	Engine R.P.M. when Cent. Advance Starts	Max. Cent. Advance in Engine Deg. at Stated Engine R.P.M.	Vacuum in (inches) of Mercury at which Vacuum Unit Starts	Max. Advance in Engine Deg. at Stated Vacuum	Vacuum Unit Number
1949-50	V8..................	7RA-12127C	30	C	17-20	.014-.016	400	17@4000	......	......	......
1951	V8..................	0CM-12127	$28\frac{1}{2}$	C	17-20	.014-.016	400	22@1200	......	......	......
1952	Custom, Monterey, 8 cyl.	OBA-12127 7RA-12127C	26-$28\frac{1}{2}$ 26-$28\frac{1}{2}$	C C	17-20 17-20	.014-.016 .014-.016	......	......	.17 .17	$9\frac{3}{4}$@5 $9\frac{3}{4}$@5	......
1953	Custom, Monterey, 8 cyl..	7RA-12127D	26-$28\frac{1}{2}$	C	17-20	.014-.016	......	......	.17	$9\frac{3}{4}$@5	......

Generators

Year	Model	Generator Number	Field Current at 6 Volts (amps.)	Maximum Safe Output Volts	Amperes	R.P.M.	Brush Spring Tension (oz.)	Voltage Regulator Number
1949 to 51	9CM, 0CM, 1CM..............................	8BA-10000	2-1	7.1	30	1670	20-22	51A-10505-A
1952	Custom, Monterey, 8 cyl............................	FAA-10000-F	......	......	......	......	......	FAC-10505-A
1953	Custom, Monterey, 8 cyl............................	FAA-10000-F	......	6.6	38	1700	......	FAC-10505-A1

Voltage Regulators

Year	Model	Regulator Number	Grounded P=Positive N=Negative	Voltage Control Air Gap Points Closed	Voltage Setting Hot	Current Control Air Gap Points Closed	Current Set Hot	Cut-Out Relay Point Gap	Air Gap	Closing Volt
1950-51	Series—All..................	8L-10505-A 8BM-10505-A	......	.035 .035	7.6 7.6	.035 .035	34-38 34-38	.010 .018	.014 .025	6.0-6.6 6.0-6.6
1952	Custom, Monterey, 8 cyl........	FAC-10505-A	......	......	7.4-7.8	......	34-38	......	......	6.0-6.6
1953	Custom, Monterey, 8 cyl........	FAC-10505-A	......	......	7.4-7.8	......	34-38	......	......	6.0-6.6

MERCURY SPECIFICATIONS 1949 thru 1953

Starters

Year	Model	Unit Model Number	Spring Tension (oz.)	STARTER							Direction of Rotation Viewed from Drive End C=Clockwise CC=Counter-clockwise
				Lock Test			No Load				
				Volts	Amperes	Torque, (lbs. ft.)	Volts	Amperes	R.P.M.		
1949–50	9CM, 0CM	7RA-11002	48–56	3.25	550	15	5.8	52	6500		CC
1951	1CM	7RM-11002	48–56	3.75	550	15	5.8	52.5	6000		CC
1952	Custom, Monterey, 8 cyl.	FAF-11001A	....	3.5	700	16	6	70	6000		C
1953	Custom, Monterey, standard transmission	FAF-11001A	....	3.5	700	16	6	70	3200		C

Fan, Generator Belts and Radiator Hose

Year	Model	Fan Belt			Generator Belt			Upper Hose			Lower Hose		
		Angle of "V" (deg.)	Length O.C.	Width Max.	Angle of "V" (deg.)	Length O.C.	Width Max.	Type	Inside Diam.	Length	Type	Inside Diam.	Length
1949	V8-90M	42	37 7/32	13/16	32	55½	43/64	curved	1¼	....	straight	1¾	6
1950–51	V8-All	40	42 9/16	⅜	40	51⅞	⅜	curved	1¼	....	straight	1¾	6
1952	Custom, Monterey	38	41 49/64	⅜	38	51 39/64	⅜	curved	1¼	13 13/64	curved	1¾	5 11/16
1953	Custom, Monterey	38	41 49/64	⅜	38	51 39/64	⅜	curved	1¼	13 13/64	curved	1¾	5 11/16

• 3" pulley. † 3½" pulley. ■ Diameter of hose–I.D.
△ Diameter of bell–I.D. ○ Diameter of Lavco bell.

Front Wheel Alignment

Year	Model	Caster (deg.)	Camber (deg.)	King Pin Inclination (deg.)	Toe-In (inches)	Turning Radius	
						Inner	Outer
1949	9CM	½N to ½P	0 to ¾P	5	3/32 to 5/32	22	20
1950–52	0CM, 1CM, Custom, Monterey	0 to 1½P	0 to ¾P	5	3/32 to 5/32	22	20
1953	Custom, Monterey	0 to 1½P	0 to ¾P	5	3/32 to 5/32	17½	20

King Pin Specification Chart

Year	Model	KING BOLT			UPPER BUSHING				LOWER BUSHING			
					King Bolt Bushing				King Bolt Bushing			
		Diameter	Length	Bolt Number	Inside Diameter	Outside Diameter	Length	Bushing Number	Inside Diameter	Outside Diameter	Length	Bushing Number
1949 to 51	....	....	....	8M-3115	....	....	....	8M-3110	....	....	....	8M-3110
1952–53	....	....	....	....	....	....	....	....	....	....	....	....

FRONT SUSPENSION

Starting with 1949 production all models of Mercury were equipped with independently sprung front wheels. The suspension cosists of upper and lower arms controlled by telescopic direct acting shock absorbers located in the center of the coil spring.

Replaceable bushings are used at all junction points in both the lower and upper arms.

Caster, Camber and Toe-In

The camber setting is adjusted at the eccentric bushing at the upper end of the knuckle support. Caster is adjusted in the non-eccentric bushing in the lower end of the knuckle support. Both of these bushings are secured by clamp screws in the knuckle support.

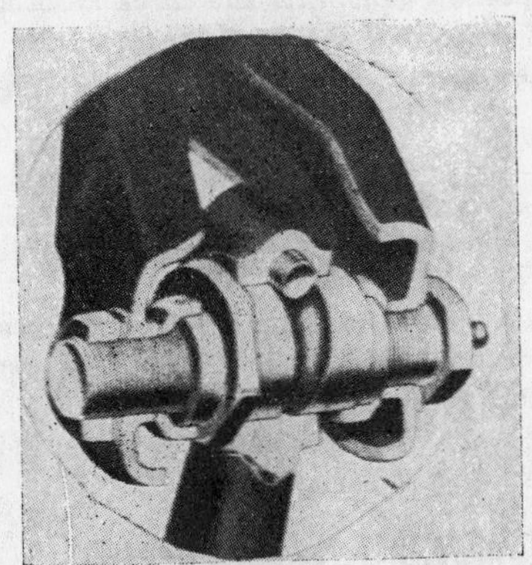

Upper eccentric bushing camber adjustment

To adjust camber, loosen the clamp nut which secures the upper arm eccentric bushing and turn the eccentric bushing until the desired camber is obtained. Tighten the clamp bolts securely.

The total range of adjustment of the eccentric bushing is obtained in a maximum of one-half turn. While it is true that turning the bushing will have some

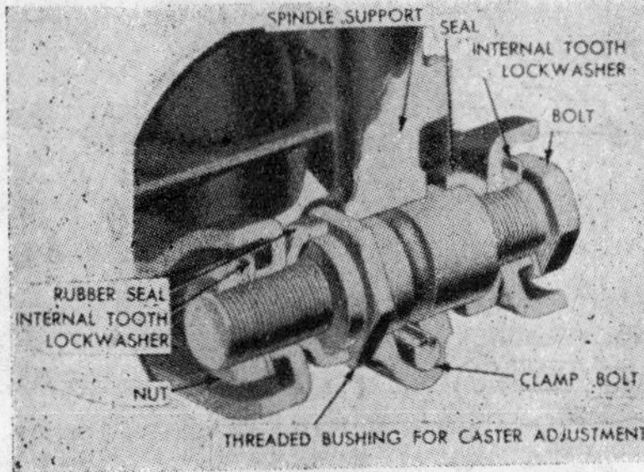

Lower bushing caster adjustment

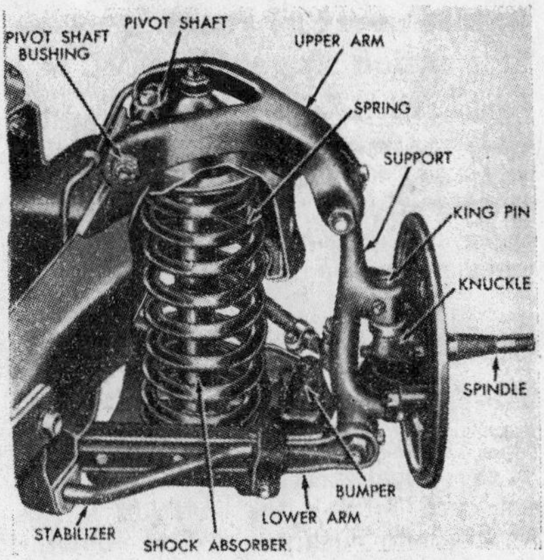

Front suspension

effect on caster, the effect will be extremely slight. To adjust caster loosen the clamp bolt at the bottom end of the knuckle support and turn the non-eccentric screw toward the rear of the car to decrease caster, and toward the front of the car to increase caster.

Toe-in is adjusted by turning the sleeve at the outer end of both tie rods.

REPLACEMENT OF FRONT SUSPENSION PARTS

Replacement of Knuckle Support, Pins and Bushings

To replace either the upper or lower suspension arm pin and/or bushing the procedure is very simple. Take the weight of the car on the lower suspension arm (A frame) and remove the road wheel. The upper and lower suspension arm pins are screwed in from the front. After the pins have been removed the bushing can then be taken out of the knuckle support after the clamp screw has been completely removed. Just loosening the clamp screw is not enough since the bushing is grooved to accomodate the clamp. While not absolutely necessary it is a good idea to disconnect the torsion bar and also remove the brake backing plate.

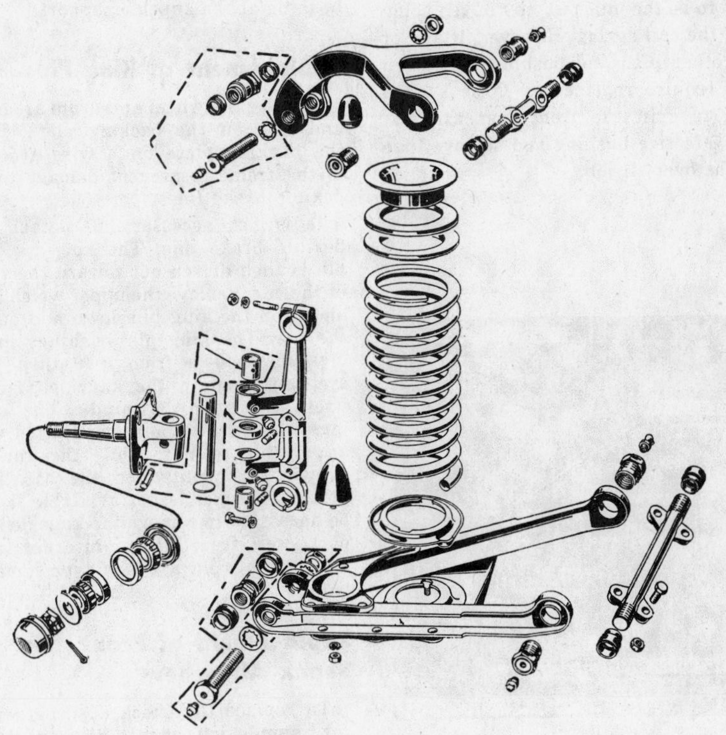

Front suspension parts

MERCURY 1949 thru 1953

Replacement of Front Coil Spring

Actually the front coil spring can be replaced without removing the road wheel. This procedure, however, is not recommended since it leads to all kinds of difficulties.

The procedure is to support the weight of the car with a jack under the frame and see to it that the car is high enough to permit lowering the inner end of the lower A frame.

Disconnect the shock absorber at both the upper and lower end and take out the shock absorber. Place a floor type jack under the inner shaft of the A frame and disconnect the A frame from the front cross member. Carefully and slowly lower the inner shaft until all pressure has been removed from the coil spring and lift out the spring.

Any shims found either under or over the spring should be placed on the new spring.

The coil spring can be replaced by splitting the suspension at any of its joints.

The above text is generally considered to be the quickest way of replacing just the coil spring. However, if any of the other pins and bushings are worn and require replacement it is a good idea to split the front suspension at the defective bushing and so save time on the over-all job.

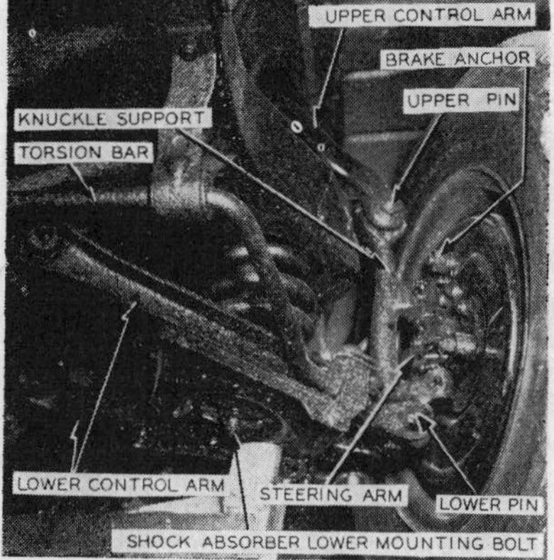

Front suspension 1952 thru '53

Replacement of Front Suspension Upper Arm

Take the weight of the car on the lower A frame and remove the road wheel and backing plate. Take out the upper arm outer pin and disconnect the upper arm at the frame mounting. The arm may then be lifted off the car.

Replacement of Upper Arm Inner Shaft and/or Bushings

To replace the shaft and/or bushings in the upper arm simply remove the arm and holding the shaft in a vice remove both bushings and take out the arm. It is always a good idea to measure the spread of the arm before taking out the bushings so that it can be rechecked when the new bushings are replaced.

Replacement of Lower Suspension Arm (A Frame)

The lower suspension arm is replaced by following the procedure given for the replacement of a coil spring. The only additional work required is that after the spring has been removed disconnect the A frame from the lower bushing at the knuckle support.

Replacement of King Pins

Remove the wheel and drum assembly and take off the backing plate. Hang the backing plate on a wire attached to the frame to prevent damage to the flexible brake line.

It is not necessary to detach the flexible brake line. The king pin lock pin is then driven out toward the front of the car. Remove the upper welsh plug and drop the king pin down and out of the car. The king pin bushings in all Mercury models from 1949 thru 1951 are contained in the knuckle support itself and not in the spindle. The bushings will have to be reamed fitted with a portable reamer, while the knuckle support is mounted on the car. If a portable reamer is not available it will be necessary to remove the knuckle support itself from the car in order to fit the bushings on a bench type hone or reamer.

Replacement of Front Shock Absorbers

To replace the shock absorbers is a very simple job, simply disconnect the shock absorber at its upper end (these bolts are accessible after the front wheel is removed).

Remove the shock absorber lower plate which is located on the under side of the A frame at the coil spring, and lower the shock absorber down through the A frame. A fast check can be made on the condition of the shock absorbers by bouncing the car up and down by hand and if the car comes to a steady even keel immediately after it is released the shock absorbers may assume to be in good condition. If, however, the car continues to bounce or settles in an abnormal position then the shock absorbers should be removed.

Servicing shock absorbers is a highly specialized job and requires elaborate special equipment. The shock absorber if defective should be replaced by a new or rebuilt unit.

STEERING GEAR ASSEMBLY

A worm and roller type steering gear is used on all Mercury models from 1949 through 1953.

The adjustment of the cross shaft is by means of a screw.

Removal of Horn Button or Horn Blowing Ring

To remove the horn button, simply pry it up on all Mercury models.

Caution: On some models the emblem cap was held by three screws from underneath the steering wheel. Before prying up the cap check to see if there are three screws; if so, remove them and then lift off the horn button.

Horn blowing rings are mounted underneath the steering wheel and to take them off it is necessary to first remove the steering wheel.

Removal of Steering Wheel

To remove the steering wheel pry up the emblem cap and take off the nut which mounts the steering wheel to the steering tube. A puller should always be used when taking off the steering wheel since driving it off will very likely result in damaging either the wheel or the steering tube.

Removal of Steering Gear Assembly from Car

To take off the steering gear assembly first remove the pitman arm and steering wheel.

Then take off the cover at the toe board. Disconnect and remove the lower shaft lever from the bottom of the steering column. Take the Woodruff key out of the top of the steering tube and remove the spring and upper bearing spring assembly. Disconnect the mass jacket tube from all of its mountings at the dash, at the floor, etc., and slide the mass jacket tube up off the steering shaft. Disconnect the steering gear assembly from its frame mountings and lift it off up into the car.

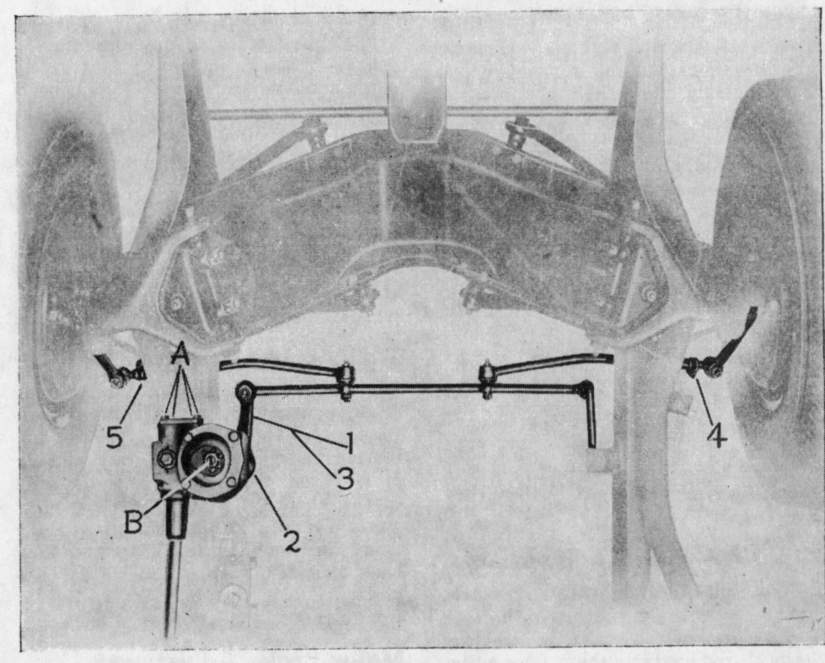

Steering mechanism

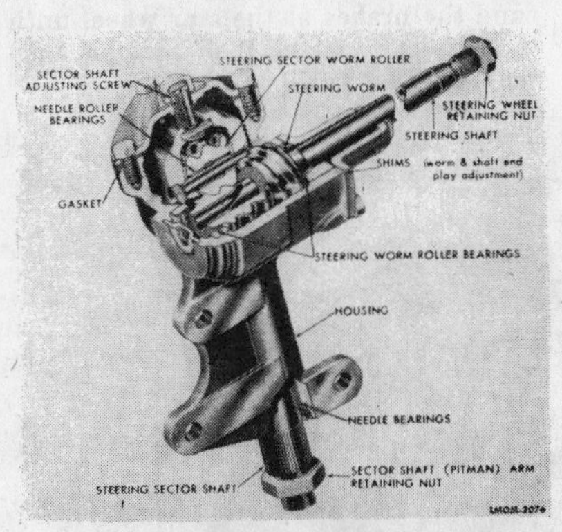

Cut away view of steering gear

Adjustment of Steering Mechanism

1. Disconnect the pitman arm from the intermediate tie rod.

2. Adjust the steering gear housing assembly.

(a) Move the pitman arm back and forth to determine if there is any end play in the worm bearings. If end play exists disconnect the four screws at the bottom of the housing and remove one shim at a time until there is zero clearance in the worm bearing without a definite preload.

(b) Set the steering wheel in the mid position of its travel and if any lash exists between the worm and roller tooth at this point loosen the clamp screw nut and turn the adjusting screw until all play is removed. Tighten the lock nut.

3. Reconnect the pitman arm to the center tie rod.

4. Loosen the clamp bolt on the adjusting sleeve at the right hand tie rod and with the steering wheel maintained in the mid position of its travel adjust the sleeves so that one-half of the toe-in is in the right front wheel. Retighten the clamp screws.

5. Loosen the clamp bolt and turn the left side adjusting sleeve so that the balance of the toe-in is contained

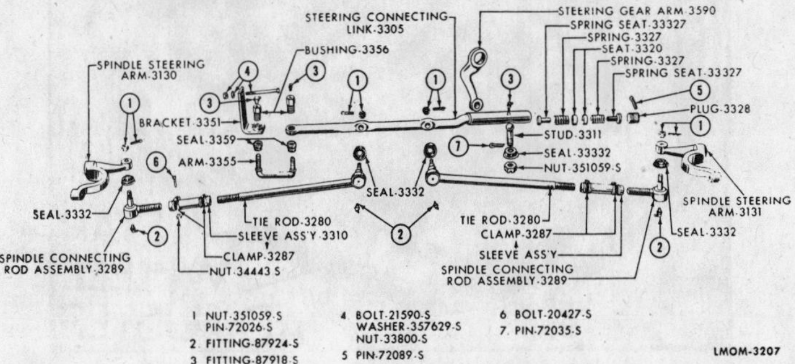

Disassembled view of Mercury steering linkage

Continued

STEERING GEAR ASSEMBLY—cont'd

in the left wheel. Tighten the clamp screws. Now turn the steering wheel from one extreme to the other to check for looseness or binding.

Bear in mind that it will be a difficult job to maintain the steering wheel in the mid position for straight ahead driving if there are any defects in the caster, camber or toe-in settings. When setting one-half the toe-in in the right rod, bear in mind that this should be done with no strain of any kind on the mechanism.

BRAKES

All Mercury models, 1949 through 1953, are equipped with Bendix type two-shoe hydraulically actuated brakes. The hand brake on these models actuated the shoes at the rear wheels.

Pedal Toe Board Adjustment

Before making any brake adjustment make certain there is from ½ in. to 1 in. free play of the brake pedal before the push rod contacts the master cylinder cup. This free play is necessary to insure that the master cylinder cup will come back to its fully released position permitting the fluid in the system to compensate itself through the compensating port in the cylinder for expansion, contraction, possible fluid seepage, etc.

Inspection of the Brake System

Before making any adjustment, even a minor one, on the Mercury or any other brake, first remove at least one wheel and brake drum assembly to determine the condition of the brake lining, cylinders, etc. Inspect the brake lining for wear and loose rivets. Note if the lining is wearing evenly all over its surface. If it is, the anchor is very likely set exactly as it should be and should not be disturbed. Examine the dust boots on the wheel cylinder for signs of fluid leaking. If any exists it will be necessary to remove the brake shoes, disassemble the cylinder and hone the inner surface to produce a good, tight seal on the wheel cylinder cup.

If the wheel cylinder is pitted badly it will be necessary to remove the cylinder from the car and hone it on a bench type hone or replace it with a new or rebuilt cylinder.

Minor scratches in the wheel cylinder may be removed readily with a portable type cylinder hone with the cylinder mounted on the car.

If examination of the one wheel reveals any defects of any kind in the brakes it is a good idea from a safety standpoint to remove all four wheels and make a complete inspection of the system since it is of vital importance to safety that the brakes function properly.

Examine the condition of the drums for scoring. If the drums are scored it will be necessary to machine them to a true surface. At any time the drums are machined it should be a must that the brake lining be replaced.

Minor Brake Adjustment

A minor brake adjustment is made to compensate for normal lining wear. Proceed as follows: Remove the adjusting hole cover from the backing plate (located almost directly opposite to the anchor pin) and turn the star wheel (handle of the tool toward the axle) until the brakes drag and then back off until they are just free. Replace the adjusting hole cover. Repeat this operation on all four wheels.

Major Brake Adjustment

A major brake adjustment is done whenever new lining is installed or whenever the brake action is erratic or the car tends to pull.

Recommended Procedure of Adjusting the Anchor

To follow the method recommended by the Mercury Division, proceed as follows:

Loosen the anchor pin nut and tap the anchor pin in a direction which will cause the secondary shoe to grip a .010 inch feeler between the shoe and lining, about 1½ in. from the anchor end of the shoe. When this adjustment is secured tighten the lock nut.

Alternate Method of Adjusting Anchor

An alternate and perhaps quicker method to adjust the anchor pin is to expand the star wheel until the shoes are very tight against the drum with the anchor pin loosened slightly. This will cause the shoes to move the anchor pin to a central position with the shoes expanded against the drum. Securely tighten the anchor nut in this position. Back off on the star wheel until the brakes are just free. If the anchor pins are adjusted by the Mercury Division recommended method, proceed to expand the brakes at the star wheel until the wheels drag and then back off until they are just free.

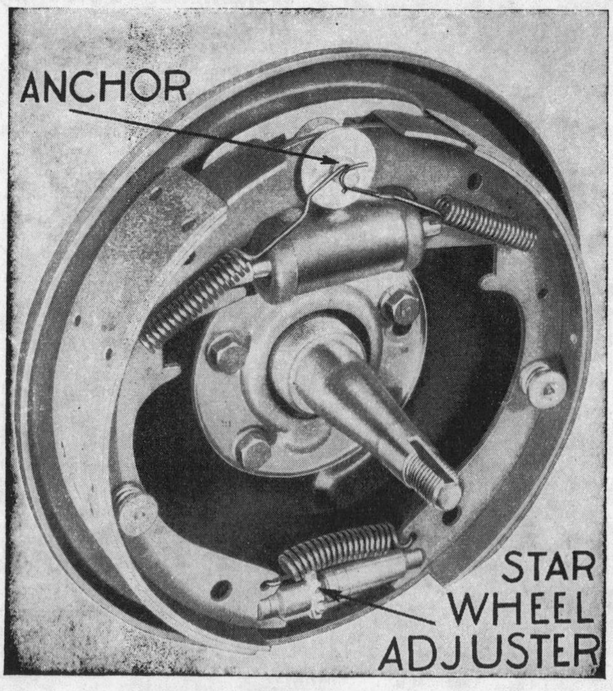

Adjusting points

Adjusting of Hand Brake Linkage

To adjust the hand brake linkage expand the rear shoes at the star wheel until they are very tight at the drum. This should be done with the hand brake disconnected at the equalizer nut. By hand, pull up all the slack in the cables and adjust the forward nut on the brake pull shaft (from the hand brake lever) until it just touches the equalizer bracket when it is being pulled back as tightly as possible. Run the rear nut up to secure the equalizer in that position. This should be done with the hand brake in the fully released position. Back off on the star wheel adjuster on each rear wheel until the brakes are just free.

COOLING SYSTEM

A pressure type cooling system is used on all Mercury models from 1949 thru 1953.

Removal of Thermostat

The thermostats are located in the front of the cylinder head toward the intake manifold. One thermostat is used in each head. When it becomes necessary to replace one of the thermostats it is essential that the other thermostat either be replaced at the same time or that it be checked so that the opening temperature of both thermostats are the same.

Removal of Water Pumps

Two water pumps are used, one on each bank. The water pump also functions as the front motor mounting. Therefore, if it is necessary to disconnect either or both water pumps it will be necessary to support the engine. At any time one of the water pumps is being removed it is advisable to loosen the mounting bolt on the other side to prevent undue strain on the other water pump. To remove the pump support the weight of the engine and remove the fan belt, disconnect the radiator hose and remove the water pump mounting bolts.

Caution: One of the mounting bolts is located inside of the water inlet portion at the bottom of the pump. It will be necessary to reach down into the pump body with a socket wrench in order to remove the lowest mounting bolt.

Disassembly of Water Pump

EARLY 1949 MODELS

Remove the snap ring from the groove in front of the pump housing directly behind the pulley. Then force the pump shaft out of the impeller and remove the impeller. Then press the water pump shaft, bearing and pulley out of the housing. Once out of the housing remove the snap ring from between the pump shaft bearing and the pulley Press the shaft out of the pulley and, if necessary, press the bushings, slinger and seal sleeve assembly out of the water pump housing.

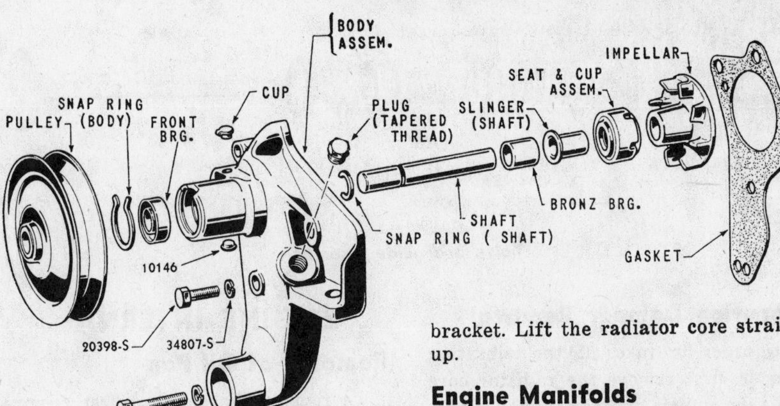

Water pump assembly

1950 THRU 1953 MODELS

Remove the lock wire which secures the bearing assembly in place in the housing. (This is located at the front of the housing in back of the pulley.) Press the shaft out of the impeller and remove the impeller. Press the bearing and pulley assembly out of the water pump housing and once out of the housing press the shaft and bearing assembly from the pulley. Then press the seal and seal sleeve assembly from the water pump housing out toward the back.

Inspection of Pump Parts

Inspect all pump parts, particularly the sealing surfaces, for wear, scratches or roughness. If any exists the part will have to be replaced. Under no circumstances should the old seal be reused. The shaft on 1950 thru 1953 models is integral with its bearing and a new shaft and bearing should be installed at any time the pump is disassembled.

Removal of Radiator Core

To remove the radiator core assembly on all models 1949 thru 1953, take off the generator belt and remove the fan assembly. Disconnect the radiator hoses and remove the six cap screws which retain the radiator core to its bracket. Lift the radiator core straight up.

Engine Manifolds

Three manifolds are used on all Mercury engines, an exhaust manifold on the outside of the cylinder blocks and an intake manifold mounted between the two cylinder blocks. Except to prevent leaking no service is required by the intake or the exhaust manifold.

FUEL SYSTEM

Fuel Pump

A single acting type fuel pump is used in all Mercurys from 1949 through 1953. The fuel pump is located at the extreme rear of the cylinder block, just back of the intake manifold and is actuated by a push rod from the camshaft. If the fuel pump is to be disassembled for the replacement of diaphragm or parts the cover should be marked to designate its relationship to the body so that it can be reassembled in the proper manner. Service kits are available for replacement of diaphragm and parts and also overhaul kits are available for the replacement of links pins and diaphragms.

Take off the starter and remove the center tie rod and both engine front mounting bolts. Jack up the engine slightly and unbolt the pan. It may be necessary to rotate the crankshaft somewhat in order to free the oil pan from the crankshaft counter weights.

Timing Gear Cover Removal

Remove the fan and generator belt and the distributor. Take out the cap screws which hold the cover to the cylinder block. When reinstalling insert the top gear cover special cap screw first. This is a body valve bolt and insures correct alignment of the cover with the cylinder block face. When the timing gear cover is removed it is possible to remove and replace the camshaft sprocket; however, if it is necessary to take off the crank sprocket the oil pan must be removed.

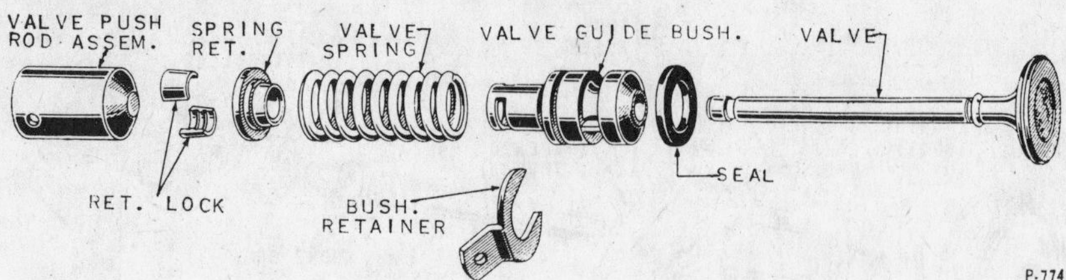

Valve and guide assembly

Vibration Damper Removal

In order to take off the vibration damper, first remove the radiator core and then unbolt and remove the vibration damper. If the engine has settled down on its mounts it may be necessary to jack it up slightly in order to clear the front cross member.

ENGINE ASSEMBLY

All Mercury cars are equipped with a V type 8-cylinder L head engine. The valves in the Mercury engine are of the non-adjustable type. The engine is lubricated by the full pressure system.

Removal of Engine Assembly

To remove the engine assembly disconnect all attaching parts such as electrical wires, fuel connections, battery connections, instrument sending unit connections, shift levers, clutch link connections, heater hoses, etc. Then take off the water pump, generator and carburetor air cleaner. Disconnect and remove the radiator core. The engine is then disconnected at the front universal joint and at the water pump mounts in the front of the engine. Remove the transmission mounting bolts and lift the engine, clutch and transmission assembly out of the frame as a unit.

Replacement Engines

Replacement engines are available in both new and factory approved rebuilt types. An engine assembly is usually sold without oil pan, manifolds, or accessories such as water pump, generator, starter, etc. New and rebuilt short block assemblies are also available, which are generally sold without flywheel, pans, heads or timing case cover.

ENGINE INTERNAL

Removal of Oil Pan

To remove the oil pan, first remove the exhaust cross-over pipe and the exhaust pipe.

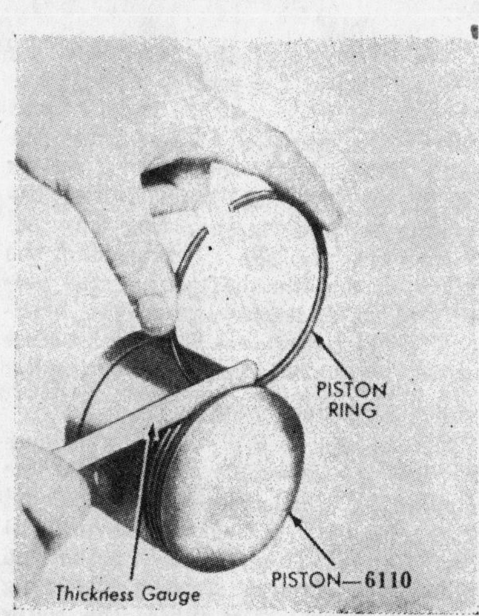

Checking ring-groove width

Assembling the Pistons to Connecting Rod

To assemble the piston to the connecting rod, set the rod up in a vise with the numbers on the rod end cap facing the mechanic. With the connecting rod held in that position the split in the skirt in the piston should be to the mechanic's right hand. If a solid skirt or slipper type piston is used which does not have a slot, it is immaterial which way it goes on the rod. When the old pistons and/or old rods are being used, however, it is a good idea to mark the piston, indicating which is the forward end of the piston and if it is marked in this manner the mark on the piston will be on the same side as the number on the connecting rod.

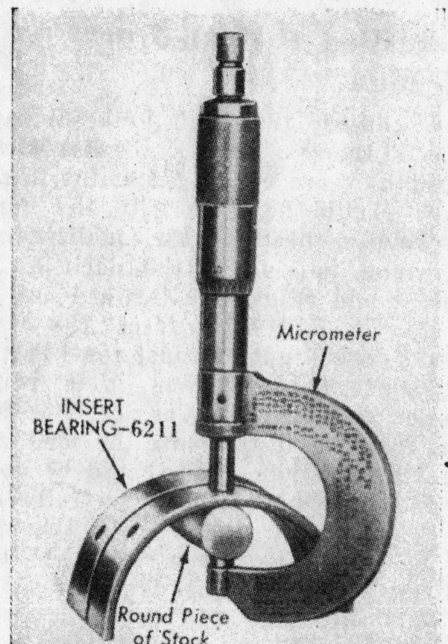

Measuring connecting rod bearing for wear

These numbers on the connecting rod are to the side of the rod but they are forward of the side of the rod.

Assembling Rod & Piston Assemblies to the Engine

On all Mercury engines from 1949 through 1953 the cylinders are numbered 1, 2, 3 and 4 on the right bank, starting at the radiator. The left bank is numbered 5, 6, 7 and 8, starting at the radiator. The piston and rod assem-

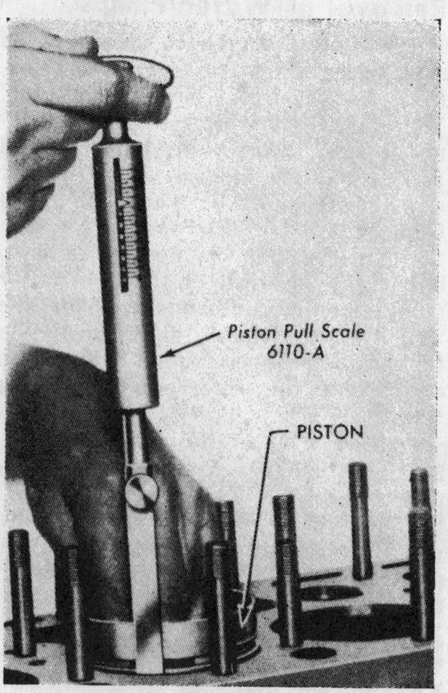

Fitting piston to cylinder bore

blies should be placed in the engine so that the numbers on the connecting rods face forward and the slit in the skirt of the piston faces the left side of the engine. This will be up on the right bank and down on the left bank.

Piston Rings

When replacing piston rings, follow the instructions supplied with the rings by the ring manufacturer, since each ring manufacturer knows best how to get the most from his product and instructions vary slightly with each ring manufacturer. These instructions, however, should be followed very carefully in order to insure best results from any rings used.

Connecting Rod Bearings

On 1949 through 1953 Mercury engines an individual bearing was used on each connecting rod. The Mercury Division does not recommend adjusting the rod bearing and under no circumstances should the cap or rod be filed to secure a fit. A perfectly workable adjustment can be had on the rod bearings, however, by placing a taper of feather type shim between the bearing shell and the rod and cap. In this way as much as .004 excessive play can be taken up on the rod bearing. A variety of under sizes are available in rod bearings to take care of most any requirement.

Specifications for out of round and taper are given in the engine overhaul and wear limit specifications table.

Crankshaft Main Bearings

All Mercury engines from 1949 through 1953 use the slip-in type precision main bearing. These shells may be replaced without removing the crankshaft by loosening all caps and taking down the cap on the bearing to be removed. Insert into the crankshaft oil hole a hammered-over cotter pin or the little special tool designed for removing bearing shells and rotate the shell out of the block by turning the crankshaft. The shell should be rotated out so that the tank at the parting line of the bearing comes out first. When installing a new shell the tang on the bearing should enter last.

Mercury Division does not recommend adjusting the main bearings. However, a workable adjustment can be had on the main bearing in the same manner as on the rod bearing. A taper type of feather shim can be placed between the main bearing cap and the bearing shell which will take up as much as .004 excessive play. Under no circumstances should the main bearing cap be filed, since this will render it useless. Specifications for out of round taper, etc., on the crankshaft journal is given in the engine overhaul table.

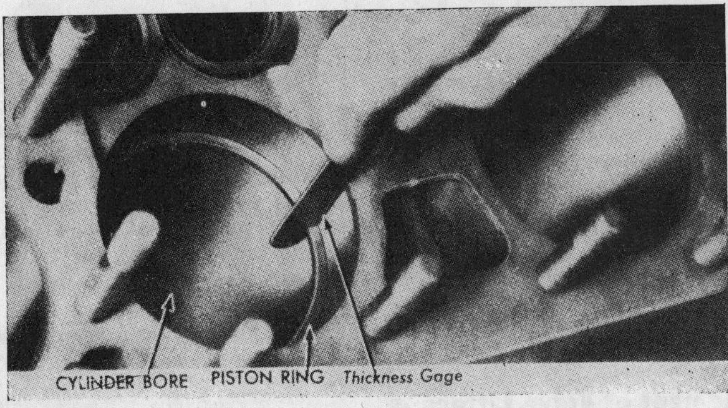

Measuring ring gap with thickness gage

Checking the Fit of Crankshaft Bearings

To check the fit of a crankshaft bearing there are several methods in use. The shim stock method requires that a piece of shim stock as thick as the oil clearance as given in the specifications table be used. Cut the shim stock approximately ½ inch square and insert it between the bearing shell and the crankshaft. Tighten the bolt into place. This shim should produce a heavy load on the crankshaft. If it does not the clearance is excessive. If it seizes the crankshaft the clearance may be too slight.

A method using a plastic gauging material is also used which requires that a piece of plastic be placed between the shell of the bearing and the crankshaft journal and the cap securely bolted into place and torqued up. Remove the cap and measure the width of the plastic, using the gauge which comes with the plastic gauging material. This will show the crankshaft oil clearance at the point the gauge was made. Plastic gauging material does not show out of round. This should be checked with a suitable micrometer.

Rear Main Bearing Oil Seal

A packing type oil seal is used in back of the rear main bearing. The lower half of this oil seal is held in place by the flywheel front plate. The upper half is mounted in a container which is fitted to a tongued out portion of the cylinder block itself. To replace the rear main bearing oil seal it is necessary to remove the engine from the car and disassemble the flywheel and flywheel front plate.

THE VALVE SYSTEM

All Mercury engines are equipped with non-adjustable valve lifters. If excessive clearance is measured between the lifter and valve stem it will be necessary to install a new valve. If the clearance is not sufficient it will be necessary to remove the valve and grind off the end of the stem. No other adjustment is provided.

To remove the valve from these engines, take off the intake manifold and cylinder head.

The valves are of the conventional design, using split type keepers. Take out the split type keeper and the valve will come out readily.

Replacement of Valve Guides

A one piece valve guide is used on Mercury engines starting with 1949 production. The guide is removed by driving it downward to permit removal of the C washer, located under the cylinder block at the top of the valve spring. After the C washer is removed the valve guide may be pulled up out of the block. To install a new guide, drive the guide downward a sufficient amount so that the C washer can be placed back into the groove in the valve guide and, using a bar pry the guide back upward until the C washer enters the milled surface under the block which holds it in place.

Valve Springs

At anytime the valve spring is removed from the engine it should be

Continued

MERCURY 1949 thru 1953

VALVE SYSTEM—*continued*

checked for tension according to the specifications given in the engine overhaul table.

Valve Seat Inserts

Hardened inserts made of special heat resisting material is used on the exhaust valves on all Mercury engines. The General Service section of this Manual gives complete instructions on the installation of hardened valve seat inserts.

Replacement of Valve Lifters

The valve lifter can be pulled up out of the cylinder block when the valves and springs have been removed.

Valve Timing and/or Replacement of Timing Gears

Remove the radiator core and the distributor and timing case cover.

Note: If necessary to replace the crankshaft gear the oil pan should be removed.

The camshaft drive on these models is by means of gears and unless the gears are badly worn or damaged or deliberately tampered with the valve timing will remain as set by the factory. If it becomes necessary to retime the valves or replace either of the gears due to wear or damage, proceed as follows:

Remove the old gears and press on a new crankshaft gear, being careful when starting the gear that the key and key-way are in perfect alignment since it is a tight fit on the shaft and it is rather difficult to align the key and key-way if they are not started properly. Turn the crankshaft so that the mark on the crankshaft gear is pointed directly toward the center of the camshaft. Now mesh the camshaft gear so that the mark on the camshaft gear coincides with the mark on the crank gear. Rotate the camshaft itself so that the bolt holes will line up with the cam gear. Install the bolts and special lock plate. Now rotate the crankshaft two full revolutions as a recheck to make certain the marks coincide in a straight line betwen the two shaft centers. Valves timed in this manner will be correct regardless of which piston is at top center. It will be necessary to retime the ignition after retiming the valves.

CYLINDER HEAD TIGHTENING SEQUENCE

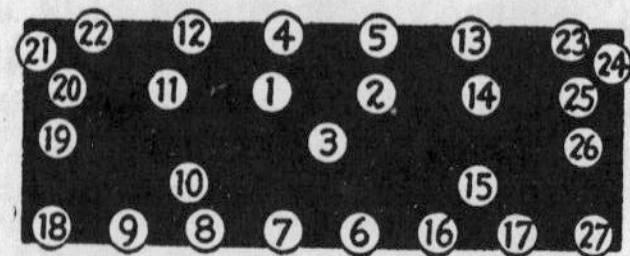

1949-53 Models

Tighten head bolts to 65-70 foot pounds or head nuts to 50-55 foot pounds.

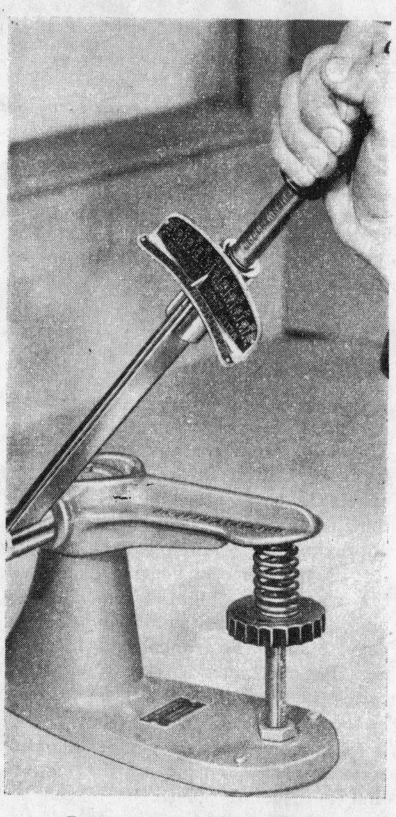

Testing valve spring tension

To Check Valve Timing Without Uncovering Timing Gears

Refer to the engine overhaul specifications which gives the valve timing in degrees. Notice that the specifications given are number of degrees before top center at which the intake valve opens. Remove the intake manifold and insert a feeler gauge between the lifter and valve on No. 1 cylinder and turn the engine very, very slowly until the feeler gauge is just gripped (this indicates that the intake valve is starting to open). Refer to the vibration damper for the number of degrees before or after at top center at which the feeler gauge was gripped. This is the point of opening of the intake valve. Since the minimum correction possible is one full gear tooth on the camshaft gear if the reading obtained is within four degrees of the specifications given in the engine overhaul table, then the valve timing is as close as it is possible to get it.

THE ELECTRICAL SYSTEM

Generator

A two brush fully controller generator is used on all Mercury models from 1949 thru 1953. If difficulty is experienced with the generator first eliminate the regulator by connecting a hopper lead from the field lead of the generator to ground. If this does not increase the output then connect the hopper lead from the field terminal of the generator to the output terminal of the generator and if this increases the output then the regulator is defective or inoperative. Service on regulators is given in the fundamentals portion of this Section.

If placing the hopper lead in either of these positions does not increase the output of the generator then it will be necessary to remove the generator from the car and subject it to the bench test given in the General Service portion of this Section (see index).

The Starting Motor

If difficulty is experienced in the starting circuit check the condition of the battery.

Make certain that the battery ground connections are clean and tight. Make a quick check of the starter switch by placing a low reading volt meter across the terminals of the starter switch and then crank the engine with the starting motor. A drop of ⅓ volt across the starter switch indicates that the switch is defective. The contacts of the switch should either be cleaned or if necessary the switch replaced.

If nothing is found to be wrong with the external wiring and the starter still does not function properly it will be necessary to remove it from the engine.

Note: In some unusual occasions an extremely stiff engine will fail to crank properly even if the starting motor is in good condition. The starter can be tested in the same manner as the generator and instructions for the generator will suffice to test the starter.

Ignition Distributor

The ignition distributor on all Mercury models, starting with 1949 production, is mounted on the timing case cover with the head of the distributor at the right cylinder bank. An 8-lobe cam is used having one set of breaker points. The distributor can be removed from the car simply by taking out the attaching bolts which hold it to the timing case cover. Service on the Mercury distributor is the same as for all conventional distributors. Pay particular attention to the condition of the shaft and bushings since play in the shaft will result in irratic cam angle and point gap. Anytime the distributor is removed from the car it is advisable to install a new set of breaker points and a new condenser since, the cost of these parts is so little that they are not worth testing.

STANDARD CLUTCH ASSEMBLY

The standard clutch in all Mercury models is of the single plate, dry disc type having a coil spring pressure plate.

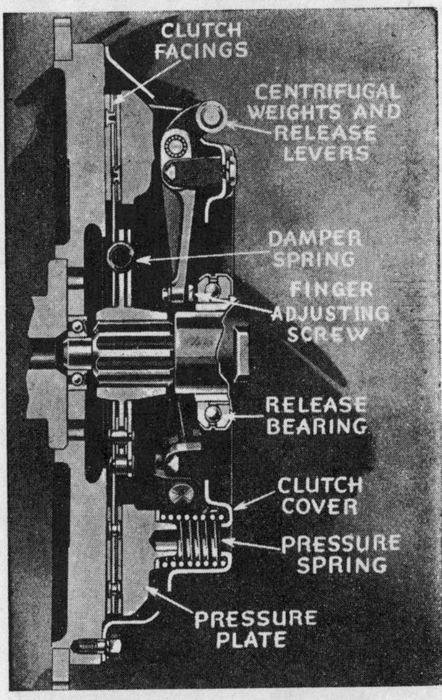

Section thru clutch assembly

Removal of Clutch Assembly

To remove the clutch assembly first take out the transmission (see transmission assembly removal) and with the engine supported remove the clutch housing cover. The clutch can then be taken out.

Clutch Disassembly

Special equipment is required to disassemble and overhaul the Mercury clutch. Instructions for the use of the special equipment is supplied by the manufacturer and should be followed in detail. In shops where the special clutch equipment is not available it is customary to replace the disc and pressure plate assembly with either a new or rebuilt unit.

Adjustment of Clutch Pedal

The clutch pedal link should be adjusted so that there is approximately 1 inch free play of the clutch pedal (measured at the toe board) before the throw out bearing engages the fingers.

REMOVAL OF STANDARD TRANSMISSION

The standard transmission can be removed from the car by removing the engine, clutch and transmission on assembly. In this way it is not necessary to disturb the floor or floor mat. The transmission may be removed by an alternate method, however, which requires the removal of the floor mat, floor pan, and front seat. Remove all attaching parts such as shift links, overdrive wiring connections, speedometer cable, and rear mounting bolts. Disconnect the transmission at the mounting on the bell housing and split it at the front universal joint and drop the drive shaft out of the way. The transmission is then slid back off its pilot shaft and raised up into the car and taken out through the right front door.

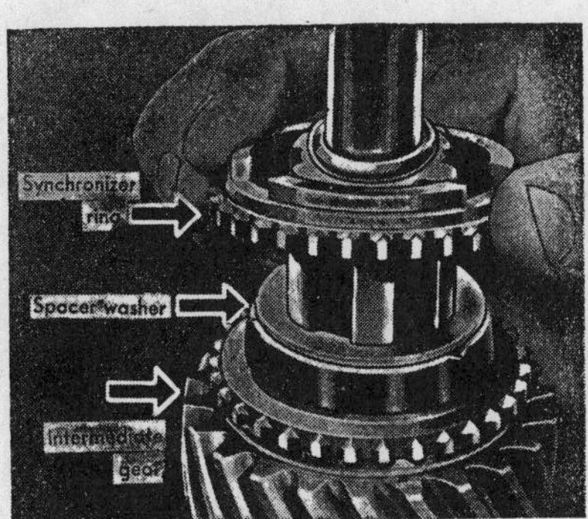

Mount synchronizer ring

Disassembly of Standard Transmission

The disassembly of the standard transmission is exactly the same as the

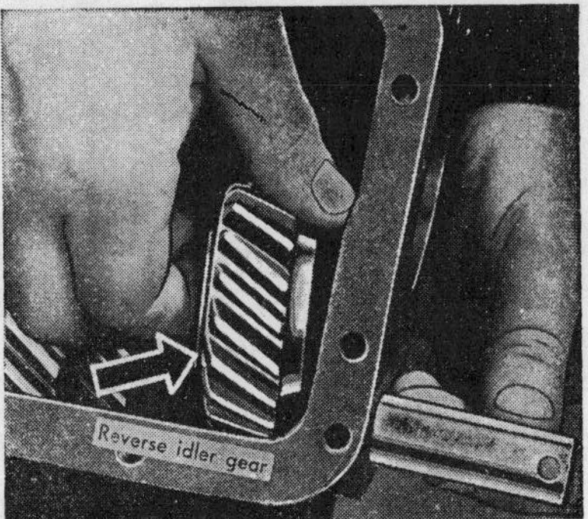

Install reverse idler

procedure for Ford and Lincoln cars. In order to conserve space the procedure is not repeated here. Please refer to either Lincoln or Ford standard transmissions for the disassembly procedure.

Overdrive Assembly

The overdrive transmission is removed in the same manner as the standard transmission since the standard transmission has an extension housing which occupies the same space as would be occupied by the overdrive.

Disassembly of Overdrive

See Overdrive Section.

Transmission Shift Linkage Adjustment—Standard Transmissions

To adjust the shift linkage on a standard transmission disconnect the shift rods at the transmission. Shift the transmission lever into the neutral position (at the transmission). Shift the hand lever to the neutral position and notice that the shift levers at the bottom of the steering column are in line. Maintaining the alignment in the neutral position adjust the length of the shift rods so that the clevises will just enter the levers at the transmission. Secure with cotter pins.

MERC-O-MATIC TRANSMISSION

Complete instructions on the Merc-O-Matic transmission are given in the automatic transmission portion of this

Continued

MERC-O-MATIC TRANSMISSION—*continued*

Section 4. (Refer to the index for page number.)

REAR AXLE ASSEMBLY

A spicer type rear axle assembly is used on Mercury cars starting with 1949 production.

This rear axle assembly is adjusted both for preload and gear mesh by the use of shims.

No adjusting screws of any kind are provided.

Replacement of Pinion Oil Seal

To replace the pinion oil seal split the rear universal joint and take the pinion shaft nut from the end of the pinion shaft, being careful to mark its position before removing it, and take off the universal joint companion flange. The oil seal now may be pulled with an inertia type puller. Drive in the new oil seal and replace the companion flange pulling up the nut until it indexes with the marks made before it was removed. The pinion shaft flange nut should be torqued up to 20-140 lbs.

Replacement of Axle Shaft

The axle shaft is secured into the housing with a bearing lock plate back of the flange at the outer end of the axle. Remove the wheel and take out the bolts which hold the bearing retainer to the housing and, with a puller or inertia bar, pull the axle shaft out of the housing. The bearing and bearing retainer will come out of the housing with the axle shaft and if it is desired to remove the bearing it must be pressed off which will in turn force the retainer off the shaft. At no time should the axle retainer be reused if it is pressed off the shaft. Always install a new axle bearing retainer.

Replacement of Axle Shaft Oil Seal

The axle shaft oil seal can be taken out of the housing with an inertia puller after the axle shaft has been removed.

Replacement of Ring Gear and Pinion and/or Pinion Bearings

Special equipment such as housing spreaders, bearing cup drivers, dial indicators, etc. are recommended to service the Mercury rear axle. However, it is possible to service the axle if the following technique is followed slowly and carefully:

Take the rear axle housing assembly from underneath the car. Remove both axle shaft and the differential housing cover. Take off the differential side bearing caps.

Now if a spreader is available spread the housing and lift out the differential. If a spreader is not available the differential may be pulled out by attaching an inertia weight to a chain and wrapping it around the differential housing on the right side and doing the same thing on the left side, and with both hands snap the inertia weights up so that the differential assembly can be jolted out of the carrier.

To remove the pinion gear take off the companion flange retaining nut and remove the companion flange. The pinion shaft with its rear bearing cone can then be pressed or driven out of the housing. After the pinion shaft is removed the pinion bearing front cone can be lifted out of the housing. To do this it will be necessary to take out the oil seal.

The adjusting shims are located in front of the rear bearing cup (race) and in back of the front bearing cup (race). These shims are actually between the race and the housing.

Adding shims to the back bearing cup will move the cup backward, toward the rear.

Adding shims on the front bearing cup will move it forward toward the front.

Note: On some early 1949 models a spacer was used between the two bearings on the pinion shaft. This spacer could be lifted out after the shaft was driven out.

If the job is to replace bearings only and not the ring gear and pinion, it is a good idea to use exactly the same shims as are found in the rear. The reason for this is that manufacturing tolerances on bearings are so close that it is very likely the rear will be in perfect alignment when the new bearings are installed. And in any case even if the shims are not exactly right they are at least a good starting point. If the job is to replace a new pinion gear using the old bearing then it is not necessary to take the bearing races out of the carrier, since they are already in the carrier with the shims provided originally. If a new pinion gear is to be used the first thing to do is notice the numbers stamped on that pinion gear. Some numbers are there simply to indicate the matched pair of ring gear and pinions. So cancel out the number on the pinion gear which is the same as the number on the ring gear. Its only purpose is to indicate the matched set of ring gear and pinion. Another letter or number is stamped on the gear which is a manfacturing symbol.

The number which concerns the mechanic is the one which immediately follows the plus or minus sign. If there is no plus or minus sign immediately preceding a number on the pinion gear it indicates that the pinion gear is to be considered zero or the nominal gear. The purpose of this number (following the plus or minus) is to determine the exact number of shims required between the rear bearing cup (race) and the housing, to determine the depth of the pinion gear into the ring gear. A minus sign on the pinion indicates the pinion is moved that many thousands of an inch back out of the housing. This

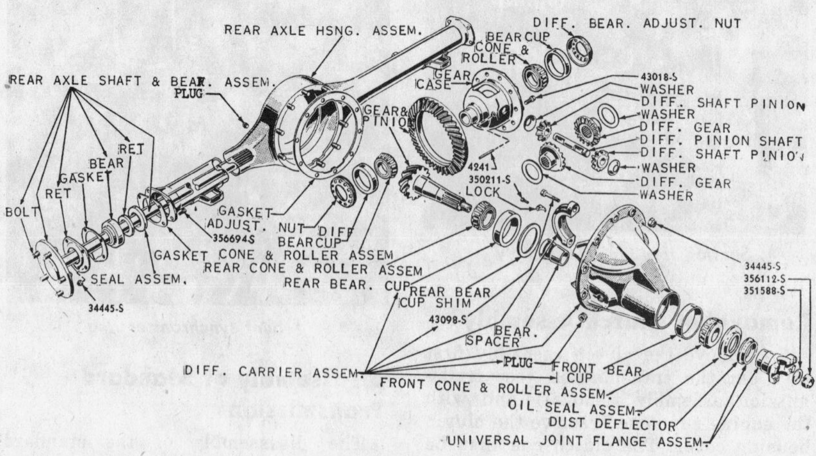

Rear axle assembly

requires placing shims between the back bearing cup and the housing. Let us say that the pinion which is being removed had a minus 2 etched on it. This means that the pinion had .002 more shims than the nominal or zero setting. Now we propose to replace it with a plus 3 gear. In order to come to the nominal setting it will be necessary to remove a .002 thick shim since this would move the gear forward .002 and bring it to the nominal setting. We must remove .003 more in order to arrive at the plus 3 setting, a total of .005 thick shims. If the .005 thick shims are removed from the rear bearing cup (race) the new pinion gear will be set properly according to the number stamped on it. Where a special micrometer depth setting tool is not available this is the most practical method of coming to a starting point from which corrections may be made.

Install the pinion shaft and spacer (where used) and install the front bearing and universal joint companion flange.

Note: In order to prevent damaging the oil seal do not put in the new oil seal at this time since it may be necessary to take off the companion flange two or three times before the correct setting is obtained.

The oil seal should be installed after the correct bearing preload and pinion depth have been established.

The companion flange nut can be pulled up to 120-140 ft. lbs. torque. While tightening the nut keep checking the pinion for the amount of pressure required to turn it.

8 to 12 inch lbs. torque should be required to turn the pinion shaft when the companion flange nut has been pulled up to approximately 140 ft. lbs. torque. If the pinion shaft is found to be too tight then it will be necessary to remove shims from back of the front bearing cup (race). If the pinion is found to be loose, after tightening, it will be necessary to add shims back of the front bearing cup (race). When the proper number of shims have been installed it will require 8 to 12 inch lbs. pull to turn the pinion shaft with the companion flange nut pulled up to approximately 140 ft. lbs. torque. If a new ring gear is to be installed or new differential side bearings are to be installed the first thing to do is determine the total number of shims which will be required to properly preload the side bearings. To do this, remove all shims from back of both of the differential side bearings and put the bearings on the differential seating them firmly with no shims whatever. Insert the differential assembly (with the ring gear off or before the pinion gear is installed) set the differential bearing caps in place and pull them down finger tight. Pry the differential assembly over toward the right as far as it will go and hold it there so that it is firmly held against the right side of the axle housing. Set up a dial indicator and contact the back face of the ring gear (or the case if the ring gear is not on) and set the dial indicator to read zero.

Now pry the differential assembly over to the extreme left and notice the amount of motion as shown by the dial indicator. This will be the total amount of shims required on both sides of the carrier to produce zero preload. Now since .008 inch preload is required it will be necessary to add 8 to the reading obtained on the dial indicator to produce the necessary .008 spread of the housing. This indicates the total number of shims. Now in order to find out how many shims are used on one side and how many on the other, the pinion gear will have to be put in place or (the ring gear installed if the test was made without the ring gear being on). Now repeat the test but this time pry the differential to the right until the ring gear meshes with the pinion with zero lash.

Set the dial indicator to zero, now pry it over to the left and read from the dial indicator the exact distance it has moved from zero lash to where the bearing contacted the left race. This is the number of shims which will be required on the left side of the housing back of the bearing. The balance of the shims will be placed on the right side.

Note that all the pre-loading shims are used on the right side since this will cause the housing to spring about the same on both sides and will produce approximately .004 inch back lash between the ring gear and pinion when the assembly is mounted.

In order to mount the differential in the housing and preload the bearings without the use of a spreader it is necessary to cock the outer cups as shown in the accompanying illustration and exert a very considerable amount of pressure on the differential in order to force it down into the housing and force the housing to spread approximately .008 inch. This operation should be done with extreme care since, with the bearings in a cocked position it is very easy to damage them. Sometimes it helps a little to exert considerable pressure and then with a rubber hammer jar both sides of the differential at the same time so that it will spread the housing and drop into place. After the differential is in place replace the bearing caps and check the rear for back lash. There should be approximately .006 inch back lash between the ring gear and pinion with the pinion held stationary.

Proper tooth contact

Now mark about 7 or 8 of the ring gear teeth and roll the ring gear painted teeth through the pinion to determine the markings made on the gears. Accompanying this text is a chart of the markings found when rolling a painted ring gear through the pinion. Customarily red lead or prussian blue is used to receive the marks.

Instructions for the procedure is given under each illustration showing just what should be done if that particular mark is obtained.

REAR SUSPENSION

Replacement of Rear Spring

To replace the rear spring, detach the shock absorber at the bottom and remove the U clips which hold the rear spring to the rear axle housing and remove the bolts which retain the spring to the shackle at the back and then take out the bolt which holds it to the frame bracket at the front and remove the spring.

Rubber bushings are used in all Mercury rear end spring shackles.

Replacement of Rear Shock Absorber

The rear shock absorber is replaced by detaching it at the spring plate at the bottom and from the frame at the top. Rubber grommets are used top and bottom on the shock absorber.

NASH SPECIFICATIONS

Starting Serial and Motor Numbers

NASH

Starting Serial Numbers

1940—Ser. 10 ....H-57000
Ser. 20 ....R-340000
Ser. 80 ....B-106300
1941—Ser. 40 ....K-5001
Ser. 60 ....R-353001
Ser. 80 ....B-110001
1942—Ser. 40 ....K-56001
Ser. 60 ....R-384001
Ser. 80 ....B-114001
1946—Ser. 40 ....K-77701
Ser. 60 ....R-393101
1947—Ser. 40 .K-136001 and K-153245
Ser. 60 .....R-429201 and R-440923
1948—Ser. 40 ....K-196901
Ser. 60 ....R-468501
1949—Ser. 40 ..K-260501 and KC-1001
Ser. 60 .....R-515501 and RC-1001
1950—Ser. 10 ....D-8501
Ser. 40 ......K-340001 and KC 9501
Ser. 60 ......R-556001 and RC-3501
1951—Ser. 10 ...D-8501 and DC-1001
Ser. 40 ....K-438001 and KC-23501
Ser. 60 .....R-600501 and RC-8701
1952—Ser. 10 ..D-79501 and DC-4101
Ser. 40 ....K-519001 and KC-37001
Ser. 60 ....R-656001 and RC-14501
1953—Ser. 40 ....K-563501
1953—Ser. 60 ....R-692101
1953—Ser. 10 ....

Location

1940-1948—On cowl under hood.
1949-1953—Right side of dash under hood.

Starting Motor Numbers

1940—Ser. 10 ....HE-56500
Ser. 20 ....E-339500
Ser. 80 ....B-105800
1941-1946—Same as serial numbers.
1947—Ser. 40 ....KE-1001
Ser. 60 ....RE-1001
1948—Ser. 40 ....KE-55001
Ser. 60 ....RE-40001
1949—Ser. 40 ....S-1001
Ser. 60 ....A-1001
1950—Ser. 10 ....F-1001
Ser. 40 ....S-92001
Ser. 60 ....A-6001
1951—Ser. 10 ....F-1001
Ser. 40 ....S-207001
Ser. 60 ....A-97001
1952—Ser. 10 ....F-85001
Ser. 40 ....S-308001
Ser. 60 ....A-165001
1953—Ser. 40 ....S-365001
1953—Ser. 60 ....A-210001
1953—Ser. 10 ....

Location

1940-1948—Right side of crankcase towards front and left upper front side of cylinder block.
1949-1953—On right front of cylinder block.

General Specifications

Year	Model	Wheelbase (in.)	Tread (in.)		Overall Dimensions (in.)			Shipping Weight (lb.)	Tire Size (in.)
			Front	Rear	Length	Width	Height		
1940	4020	121	57	60	203	....	....	3500	6.25-16
	4080	125	58	61	207	....	....	3775	7.00-15
1941	4140	112	56	60	194	....	....	2550	5.50-16
	4160	121	58	61	201	....	....	3350	6.25-16
	4180	121	57	61	201	....	....	3450	6.50-16
1942	4240	112	56	60	197	....	....	2655	5.50-16
	4260	121	58	61	206	....	....	3335	6.25-16
	4280	121	57	61	206	....	....	3485	6.50-16
1946	4640	112	57	60	200	75	68	2675	6.00-16
	4660	121	58	61	209	75	69	....	6.50-15
1947	4740	112	57	60	200	75	68	2786	6.00-16
	4760	121	58	61	209	75	69	3387	6.50-15
1948	4840	112	58	60	200	75	68	2846	6.40-15
	4860	121	58	61	209	75	69	3462	7.10-15
1949	4940	112	55	60	201	78	63	2905	6.40-15
	4960	121	55	60	210	78	64	3320	7.10-15
1950–51	5010, 5110	100	53	53	176	74	60	2430	5.90-15
	5040, 5140	112	55	60	201	78	63	2965	6.40-15
	5060, 5160	121	55	61	210	78	64	3350	7.10-15
1952	5210	100	53	53	176	73.5	59	....	6.40-15
	5240	114	56	60	202	78	62	....	6.70-15
	5260	121	56	60	209	78	62	....	7.10-15
1953	5340	114	56	60	202	78	62	....	6.70-15
	5360	121	56	60	209	78	62	....	7.10-15

General Engine Specifications

Year	Model	Number of Cylinders Bore and Stroke	Piston Displacement, Cubic Inches	Compression Ratio (To-1)	Taxable (A.M.A.) Hp.	DEVELOPED HORSE POWER		Maximum Torque Ft. Lbs.
						Bare Engine	With Accessories	
1940	4020, 6 Cyl.	6 3⅜ x 4⅜	234.8	6.00	27.3	105 @ 3400	....	190 @ 1050
	4080, 8 Cyl.	8-3⅛ x 4¼	260.8	6.00	31.2	115 @ 3400	....	200 @ 1200
1941	4140, 6 Cyl.	6-3⅛ x 3¾	172.6	6.87	23.4	75 @ 3600	....	136 @ 1200
	4160, 6 Cyl.	6-3⅜ x 4⅜	234.8	6.30	27.3	105 @ 3400	....	195 @ 1600
	4180, 8 Cyl.	8-3⅛ x 4¼	260.8	6.30	31.2	115 @ 3400	....	200 @ 1600
1942	4240, 6 Cyl.	6-3⅛ x 3¾	172.6	6.87	23.4	75 @ 3600	....	138 @ 1200
	4260, 6 Cyl.	6-3⅜ x 4⅜	234.0	6.50	27.3	105 @ 3400	....	203 @ 1600
	4280, 8 Cyl.	8-3⅛ x 4¼	260.8	6.60	31.2	115 @ 3400	....	200 @ 1600
1946	4640, 6 Cyl.	6-3⅛ x 3¾	176.6	7.00	23.4	82 @ 3800	....	138 @ 1600
	4660, 6 Cyl.	6-3⅜ x 4⅜	234.8	6.80	27.3	112 @ 3400	....	208 @ 1600
1947	4740, 6 Cyl.	6-3⅛ x 3¾	172.6	7.10	23.4	82 @ 3800	....	138 @ 1600
	4760, 6 Cyl.	6-3⅜ x 4⅜	234.8	7.02	27.3	112 @ 3400	....	208 @ 1600
1948	4840, 6 Cyl.	6-3⅛ x 3¾	172.6	7.00	23.4	82 @ 3800	....	138 @ 1600
	4860, 6 Cyl.	6-3⅜ x 4⅜	234.8	7.02	27.3	112 @ 3400	....	208 @ 1600
1949	4940, 6 Cyl.	6-3⅛ x 3¾	172.6	7.00	23.4	82 @ 3800	....	138 @ 1600
	4960, 6 Cyl.	6 3⅜ x 4⅜	234.8	7.02	27.3	112 @ 3400	....	208 @ 1600
1950	5040, 6 Cyl.	6-3⅛ x 4.0	184.0	7.00	23.4	85 @ 3800	....	140 @ 1600
	5060, 6 Cyl.	6-3⅜ x 4⅜	234.8	7.30	27.3	115 @ 3400	....	210 @ 1600
1951	5110 Rambler, 6 Cyl.	6-3⅛ x 3¾	172.6	7.25	23.4	82 @ 3800	....	138 @ 1600
	5140, 6 Cyl.	6-3⅛ x 4.0	184.0	7.00	23.4	85 @ 3800	....	140 @ 1600
	5160, 6 Cyl.	6 3⅜ x 4⅜	234.8	7.30	27.3	115 @ 3400	....	210 @ 1600
1952	5210, 6 Cyl.	6-3⅛ x 3¾	172.6	7.25	23.44	82 @ 3800	....	138 @ 1600
	5240, 6 Cyl.	6-3⅛ x 4¼	195.6	7.00	23.44	88 @ 3800	....	150 @ 1600
	5260, 6 Cyl.	6-3½ x 4⅜	252.6	7.30	29.40	120 @ 3700	....	220 @ 1600
1953	5340	6-3⅛ x 4¼	195.58	7.45	23.44	100 @ 3800	....	155 @ 1600
	5360	6-3½ x 4⅜	252.55	7.3	29.4	120 @ 3700	....	220 @ 1600

Dimensions of Valves

Year	Model	Overall Length		Head Diameter		Seat Angle (deg.)		Stem Diameter		Key Type	O.D. of Seat Insert	
		Inlet	Exhaust	Inlet	Exhaust	Inlet	Exhaust	Inlet	Exhaust		Inlet	Exhaust
1940	4020	5.531	5.531	1.750	1.593	45	45	.372	.372	split lock	....	....
	4080	5.500	5.500	1.656	1.468	45	45	.372	.372	split lock	....	....
1941-42	4140, 4240	4.800	4.800	1.343	1.284	45	45	.312	.341	horseshoe	....	....
	4160, 4260	5.500	5.500	1.750	1.593	45	45	.372	.372	split lock	....	....
	4180, 4280	5.453	5.453	1.656	1.468	45	45	.372	.372	split lock	....	....
1946-47	4610, 4740	4.781	4.781	1.468	1.281	45	45	.341	.341	horseshoe	....	....
	4660, 4760	5.531	5.531	1.750	1.468	44	44	.342	.342	split lock	....	....
1948-49	4840, 4940	4.781	4.781	1.468	1.281	44	44	.341	.341	horseshoe	....	....
	4860, 4960	5.531	5.531	1.750	1.468	44	44	.372	.372	split lock	....	....
1950-51	5010, 5110, 5040, 5140	4.781	4.781	1.469	1.281	45	45	.341	.341	horseshoe	....	....
	5060, 5160	5.484	5.484	1.750	1.469	45	45	.373	.373	split lock	....	....
1952	5210, 5240, 6 cyl.	4.78125	4.78125	1.46875	1.28125	45	45	.34095	.34095	....	....	....
	5260, 6 cyl.	5.484375	5.484375	1.75	1.46875	30	45	.373	.3725	....	....	....
1953	5340, 6 cyl.	4.78125	4.78125	1.59375	1.34375	45	45	.34095	.34095	....	....	....
	5360, 6 cyl.	5.484375	5.484375	1.46875	1.46875	30	45	.373	.3725	....	....	....

Engine Overhaul Specifications

Year	Model	PISTONS				RING GAP CLEARANCES (Maximum)				PISTON PIN		ROD BEARINGS		
			Piston Skirt Clearances (Maximum)											
		Removed From	Top	Bottom	Limit	Top Ring	Second Ring	Third Ring	Oil Ring	Type	Fit	Oil Clearance	Wear Limit	Side Play
1940	4020, 6 Cyl.	A	.002	.002	.004	.020	.020	.018	.018	Float	Push	.0015–.0025	.0045	.008–.012
	4080, 8 Cyl.	B	.002	.002	.004	.020	.020	.018	.018	Float	Push	.0015–.0025	.0045	.008–.012
1941	4140, 6 Cyl.	A	.002	.002	.004	.015	.015	......	.015	Float	Push	.0015–.0025	.0045	.004–.008
	4160, 6 Cyl.	A	.002	.002	.004	.015	.015	.015	.015	Float	Push	.0015–.0025	.0045	.008–.012
	4180, 8 Cyl.	B	.002	.002	.004	.015	.015	.015	.015	Float	Push	.0015–.0025	.0045	.008–.012
1942	4240, 6 Cyl.	A	.002	.002	.004	.015	.015	......	.015	Float	Push	.0015–.002	.0045	.004–.008
	4260, 6 Cyl.	A	.002	.002	.004	.015	.015	.015	.015	Float	Push	.0015–.0025	.0045	.008–.012
	4280, 8 Cyl.	B	.002	.002	.004	.015	.015	.015	.015	Float	Push	.0015–.0025	.0045	.008–.012
1946	4640, 6 Cyl.	A	.002	.002	.004	.015	.015	......	.015	Float	Push	.0015–.0025	.0045	.006–.012
	4660, 6 Cyl.	A	.002	.002	.004	.015	.015	.015	.015	Float	Push	.0015–.0025	.0045	.006–.014
1947	4740, 6 Cyl.	A	.002	.002	.004	.015	.015	......	.015	Float	Push	.001 –.005	.0045	.008–.014
	4760, 6 Cyl.	A	.002	.002	.004	.015	.015	.015	.015	Float	Push	.0005–.0025	.0045	.006–.014
1948	4840, 6 Cyl.	A	.002	.002	.004	.015	.015	......	.015	Float	Push	.0005–.0025	.0045	.006–.014
	4860, 6 Cyl.	A	.002	.002	.004	.015	.015	.015	.015	Float	Push	.0005–.0025	.0045	.008–.014
1949	4940, 6 Cyl.	A	.002	.002	.004	.015	.015	.015	.015	LR	Push	.001 –.002	.0045	.006–.014
	4960, 6 Cyl.	A	.002	.002	.004	.015	.015	.015	.015	Float	Push	.001 –.002	.0045	.006–.014
1950	5040, 6 Cyl.	A	.002	.002	.004	.015	.015	.015	‡	LR	Push	.001 –.002	.0045	.006–.014
	5060, 6 Cyl.	A	.002	.002	.004	.015	.015	.015	‡	Float	Push	.0005–.0025	.0045	.008–.014
1951	5110 Rambler, 6 Cyl.	A	.002	.002	.004	.015	.015	.015	‡	LR	Push	.001 –.002	.0045	.006–.014
	5140, 6 Cyl.	A	.002	.002	.004	.015	.015	.015	‡	LR	Push	.0004–.0025	.0045	.006–.014
	5160, 6 Cyl.	A	.002	.002	.004	.015	.015	.015	‡	Float	Push	.0005–.0025	.0045	.008–.014
1952	5210, 5240, 6 Cyl.	A	.0018	.0023	.004	.020	.020	.020	.0058	LR	.0002	.001–.002	.0045	.005–.015
	5260, 6 Cyl.	A	.0021	.0026	.004	.0015	.017	.017	.009	FL	.0002	.001–.002	.0045	.005–.015
1953	5340, 6 Cyl.	A	.0018	.0023	.004	.020	.020	.020	.0058	LR	.0002	.001–.002	.0045	.005–.015
	5360, 6 Cyl.	A	.0021	.0026	.004	.015	.012	.017	.0058	FL	.0002	.001–.002	.0045	.005–.015

A—Above. B—Below. LR—Locked in rod.
FL—Floating in piston and rod. ‡—#4 ring is a steel U-flex ring.

Pistons and Piston Pins

Year	Model	PISTONS				PISTON PINS		
		Diameter	Material	Type	No. of Rings	Length	Diameter	How Held
1940	4010, 4020	3.375	Als	Ss	4	2.80	.875	F
	4080	3.125	Als	Ss	4	2.57	.875	F
1941–42	4140, 4240	3.125	Alum.	....	3	2.609	.8120	F
	4160, 4260	3.375	Alum.	Ss	4	2.804	.875	F
	4180, 4280	3.125	Alum.	Ss	4	2.574	.875	F
1946–47	4640, 4740	3.125	....	....	3	2⅝	.812	F
	4660, 4760	3.375	....	....	4	2$\frac{13}{16}$	.875	F
1948	4840	3.125	Alum.	Ss	3	2.632	.812	F
	4860	3.375	Alum.	Ss	4	2.824	.875	F
1949–51	4940, 5040, 5140	3.125	Alum.	Ss, C	4	2¾	.8594	R
	4960, 5060, 5160	3.375	Alum.	Ss, C	4	2.824	.875	F
1952	5210, 5240, 6 cyl.	3.125	Alum. Alloy	....	4	2.750	.859375	R
	5260, 6 cyl.	3.50	Alum. Alloy	....	4	2.824	.875	F
1953	5340, 6 cyl.	3.125	Alum. Alloy	....	4	2.750	.859375	....
	5360, 6 cyl.	3.50	Alum. Alloy	....	4	3.000	.9375	....

and Wear Limit Table

CRANKSHAFT		VALVES							Valve Timing, Inlet Valve Opens (Deg.)	Camshaft Drive	Gear Marks	OPERATING OIL PRESSURE		Model	Year
Main Bearing Oil Clearance	Shaft End Play	Spring Tension (Maximum)			Guide Clearance	Seat Angle						Pounds At M.P.H.	Low Limit§		
		Inlet	Exhaust	Low Limit		Inlet	Exhaust								
.002	.004	51@1 1/32	51@1 1/32	45	.002-.004	45°	45°	24½B	Chain	†SP	30@20	15	4020, 6 Cyl.	1940
.002	.004	51@1 1/32	51@1 1/32	45	.002-.004	45°	45°	20B	Chain	†SP	30@20	15	4080, 8 Cyl.	
.002-.003	.004-.006	83@1 7/16	83@1 7/16	75	.002-.004	45°	45°	6B	Chain	†SP	35@20	15	4140, 6 Cyl.	1941
.002-.003	.004-.006	51@1 1/32	51@1 1/32	45	.002-.004	45°	45°	24B	Chain	†SP	30@20	15	4160, 6 Cyl.	
.002-.003	.004-.006	51@1 1/32	95@1 11/32	85	.002-.004	45°	45°	20B	Chain	†SP	30@20	15	4180, 8 Cyl.	
.002-.003	.004-.008	83@1 7/16	83@1 7/16	75	.002-.003	45°	45°	19B	Chain	†SP	35@20	15	4240, 6 Cyl.	1942
.002-.003	.004-.006	51@1 1/32	95@1 11/32	85	.002-.004	45°	45°	14B	Chain	†SP	30@20	15	4260, 6 Cyl.	
.002-.003	.004-.006	51@1 1/32	95@1 11/32	85	.002-.004	45°	45°	10.5B	Chain	†SP	30@20	15	4280, 8 Cyl.	
.002	.004	83@1 7/16	83@1 7/16	75	.002-.004	45°	45°	6B	Chain	†SP	30@20	15	4640, 6 Cyl.	1946
.002	.004	146@1 11/32	146@1 11/32	130	.002-.004	45°	45°	24B	Chain	†SP	30@20	15	4660, 6 Cyl.	
.0018	.0055	146@1 11/32	146@1 11/32	130	.002-.0035	45°	45°	4B	Chain	†SP	30@20	15	4740, 6 Cyl.	1947
.002	.0055	80@1 7/16	80@1 7/16	72	.0013-.0028	45°	45°	6B	Chain	†SP	30@20	15	4760, 6 Cyl.	
.002	.0055	83@1 7/16	80@1 7/16	72	.0013-.0028	45°	45°	6B	Chain	†SP	30@20	15	4840, 6 Cyl.	1948
.0018	.0055	146@1 11/32	146@1 11/32	130	....	45°	45°	4B	Chain	†SP	30@20	15	4860, 6 Cyl.	
.002	.006-.008	83@1 7/16	83@1 7/16	75	.002-.003	45°	45°	6B	Chain	†SP	50@30	25	4940, 6 Cyl.	1949
.002	.006-.008	146@1 11/32	146@1 11/32	130	.002-.004	45°	45°	4B	Chain	†SP	50@30	25	4960, 6 Cyl.	
.0007-.0029	.006-.008	83@1 7/16	83@1 7/16	75	.002-.003	45°	45°	6B	Chain	†SP	50@30	25	5040, 6 Cyl.	1950
.0002-.0025	.006-.008	149@1 7/16	149@1 7/16	130	....	45°	45°	8° 30′B	Chain	†SP	50@30	25	5060, 6 Cyl.	
.0007-.0020	.006-.008	82@1 7/16	82@1 7/16	75	.002-.003	45°	45°	6B	Chain	†SP	50@35	25	5110 Rambler, 6 Cyl.	1951
.0007-.0029	.006-.008	82@1 7/16	82@1 7/16	75	.002-.003	45°	45°	6B	Chain	†SP	50@30	25	5140, 6 Cyl.	
.0002-.0025	.006-.008	154@1 7/16	154@1 7/16	140	.002-.004	30°	45°	8° 30′B	Chain	†SP	50@30	25	5160, 6 Cyl.	
.0007-.0029	.004-.008	82@1 7/16	82@1 7/16	......	.0028-.0033	45°	45°	6B	Chain	......	50@30	......	5210, 5240, 6 Cyl.	1952
.0002-.0025	.004-.008	154@1 7/16	154@1 7/16	......	.002-.004	30°	45°	12½B	Chain	......	50@30	......	5260, 6 Cyl.	
.0007-.0029	.005-.002	82@1 7/16	82@1 7/16	......	.0033	45°	45°	10B	Chain	......	50@30	......	5340, 6 Cyl.	1953
.0002-.0025	.005-.002	154@1 7/16	154@1 7/16	......	.0033	30°	45°	12½B	Chain	......	50@30	......	5360, 6 Cyl.	

†—Marks on cam and crank sprockets align with shaft centers. SP—Sprockets.
§—Car may be operated safely at lower oil pressures but low pressure indicates malfunction which should be corrected.

Engine Tune-Up Specifications

Year	Model	SPARK PLUGS		DISTRIBUTOR		Ignition Timing Mark and Location	Compression Pressure at R.P.M.	OPERATING TAPPET CLEARANCE		Carburetor Fuel Float Height	Minimum Engine Idle Speed at R.P.M.
		Type	Gap	Point Gap	Cam Dwell, (Deg.)	Ignition Timing, (Deg.)			Inlet	Exhaust		
1940	4020, 6 Cyl.	AC-45	.025	.020	35	6B	Ign. Dmpr.	125@350	.015	.015	3/8″	475
	4080, 8 Cyl.	AC-45	.025	.020	28	9B	Ign. Dmpr.	110@350	.015	.015	3/16″	475
1941	4140, 6 Cyl.	AL-AN7	.025	.020	35	TC	Ign. Dmpr.	120@350	.015	.015	5/64″	475
	4160, 6 Cyl.	AC-45	.025	.020	35	6B	Ign. Dmpr.	125@350	.015	.015	3/8″	475
	4180, 8 Cyl.	AC-45	.025	.017	28	9B	Ign. Dmpr.	110@350	.015	.015	3/16″	475
1942	4240, 6 Cyl.	AL-AN7	.025	.020	35	TC	Ign. Dmpr.	120@350	.015	.015	3/16″	475
	4260, 6 Cyl.	AC-45	.025	.020	38	4B	Ign. Dmpr.	125@350	.015	.015	3/8″	475
	4280, 8 Cyl.	AC-45	.025	.020	28	7B	Ign. Dmpr.	110@350	.015	.015	3/16″	475
1946	4640, 6 Cyl.	AL-A5	.025	.020	35	TC	Ign. Dmpr.	120@350	.015	.015	3/16″	475
	4660, 6 Cyl.	AC-45	.025	.020	38	4B	Ign. Dmpr.	125@350	.015	.015	3/8″	475
1947	4740, 6 Cyl.	AC-44	.025	.020	35	TC	Ign. Dmpr.	120@350	.015	.018	3/8″	475
	4760, 6 Cyl.	AL-A5	.025	.020	38	TC	Ign. Dmpr.	125@350	.015	.015	3/8″	475
1948	4840, 6 Cyl.	AL-A5	.025	.020	35	TC	Ign. Dmpr.	120@350	.015	.015	1/2″	475
	4860, 6 Cyl.	AC-44	.025	.020	38	TC	Ign. Dmpr.	125@350	.015	.018	3/8″	475

NASH SPECIFICATIONS

Engine Tune-Up Specifications—*continued*

Year	Model	SPARK PLUGS		DISTRIBUTOR		Ignition Timing. (Deg.)	Ignition Timing Mark and Location	Com-pression Pressure at R.P.M.	OPERATING TAPPET CLEARANCE		Carburetor Fuel Float Height	Minimum Engine Idle Speed at R.P.M.
		Type	Gap	Point Gap	Cam Dwell, (Deg.)				Inlet	Exhaust		
1949	4940, 6 Cyl.	AC-A5	.030	.021	35	TC	Ign. Dmpr.	120@350	.015	.015	3/4"	475
	4960, 6 Cyl.	AC-44	.030	.021	35	TC	Ign. Dmpr.	125@350	.015	.015	1/2"	475
1950	5040, 6 Cyl	AL-A5	.025	.021	35	TC	TDC Dmpr.	120@350	.015	.015	3/4"	475*
	5060, 6 Cyl.	AC-44	.030	.021	35	TC	TDC Dmpr.	130@Cr Sp	.015	.018	1/2"	475*
1951	5110 Rambler, 6 Cyl.	AL-A5	.031	.024	35	TC	Ign. Dmpr.	120@Cr Sp	.015	.015	1/2"	475*
	5140, 6 Cyl.	AL-A5	.031	.024	35	TC	Ign. Dmpr.	120@Cr Sp	.015	.015	....	375
	5160, 6 Cyl.	AC-44	.030	.024	35	TC	....	130@Cr Sp	.015	.018	....	375
1952	5210, 6 Cyl.	AL-A7A	.030	.022	34	TC	Dmpr.	120@Cr Sp	.016C	.018C	5/16"	500
	5240, 6 Cyl.	AL-A7A	.030	.022	34	TC	Dmpr.	120@Cr Sp	.015H	.015H	5/16"	500*
	5260, 6 Cyl.	AL-A7A	.030	.022	34	TC	Dmpr.	120@Cr Sp	.012H	.016H	....	500*
1953	5340, 6 Cyl.	AL-A7A	.030	.022	34	4B	Dmpr.	....	.015H	.015H	....	500*
	5360, 6 Cyl.	AL-A7A	.030	.022	34	TC	Dmpr.	....	.012H	.016H	....	500*

*—Automatic transmission 375 R.P.M. exactiy.

Piston Ring Dimensions

Year	Model	Cylinder Bore	TOP RING			SECOND RING			THIRD RING			OIL RING		
			Width	Gap	Depth	Width	Gap	Depth	Width	Gap	Depth	Width	Gap	Depth
1940	10, 20	3 3/8	1/8	.015	.145	1/8	.015	.145	5/32	.014	.145	5/32	.014	.145
	80	3 1/8	1/8	.015	.140	1/8	.015	.140	1/8	.014	.130	3/16	.014	.130
1941–48	40	3 1/8	3/32	.015		3/32	.015	.....	3/16	.015	......	......		......
	60	3 3/8	1/8	.015	.145	1/8	.015	.145	5/32	.014	.145	5/32	.014	.145
	80	3 1/8	1/8	.015	.140	1/8	.015	.140	1/8	.015	.130	3/16	.015	.130
1949–51	40	3 1/8	3/32	.015	.151	3/32	.015	.151	5/32	.015	.144	5/32	.015	.144
	60	3 3/8	3/32	.015	.164	3/32	.015	.140	5/32	.015	.140	5/32	.015	.140
1950–51	10	3 1/8	3/32	.015	.164	3/32	.015	.140	5/32	.015	.140	5/32	.015	.140
1952	5210, 6 Cyl.	3 1/8	.09325	.015	.169	.09325	.015	.169	.15475	.015	.173	.1545	.00725	.173
	5240, 6 Cyl.	3 1/8	.09325	.015	.169	.09325	.015	.169	.155	.015	.173	.1545	.00725	.173
	5260, 6 Cyl.	3 1/2	.09325	.011	.18675	.09325	.012	.18675	.155	.012	.18275	.1545	.0078	.18275
1953	5340, 6 Cyl.	3 1/8	.09325	.015	.156	.09325	.015	.156	.15475	.015	.144	.1545	.0087	.155
	5360, 6 Cyl.	3 1/2	.09325	.015	.175	.09325	.012	.175	.15475	.012	.157	.1545	.0084	.155

Brake Data

Year	Model	Make	Lining Type	R=Riveted B=Bonded	Drum Diameter	Lining			Clearance	
						Length	Width	Thickness	Toe	Heel
1940	4010, 4020	Ben	M	R	10	22	2	3/16	.010	.010
	4080	Ben	M	R	11 1/16	24	2 1/4	3/16	.010	.010
1941	4140, 4240	Ben	M	R	9	20.5	1 3/4	3/16	....	....
	60, 80	Ben	M	R	10	22	2	3/16	.010	.010
1946	4640, 4740	Ben	M	R	9	20 1/2	1 3/4	3/16	.010	.010
	4660, 4760	Ben	M	R	10	22	2	3/16	.010	.010
1948	4840	Ben	M	R	9	17 1/2	2-*1 3/4	3/16	.010	.010
	4860	Ben	M	R	10	22	2	3/16	.010	.010
1949	4940	Ben	M	R	9	17.5	2-*1 3/4	3/16	.015	.015
	4960	Ben	M	R	10	22	2	3/16	.015	.015
1950–51	5040-5140	Ben	M	R	9	17 1/2	2 1/4-*2	3/16	.015	.015
	5060-5160	Ben	M	R	10	20	2	3/16	.015	.015
	5010-5110	Ben	M	R	8	16 27/32	(k)	3/16	....	....

Brake Data—*continued*

Year	Model	Make	Lining Type	R=Riveted B=Bonded	Drum Diameter	Lining Length	Lining Width	Lining Thickness	Clearance Toe	Clearance Heel
1952	5210, 6 Cyl.	...	M	R	8	16 27/32	(k)	7/32	...	...
	5240, 6 Cyl.	...	M	R	9	17 9/16	2–*1 3/4	7/32	.015	.015
	5260, 6 Cyl.	...	M	R	10	20 1/32–20 3/64†	■	7/32	.015	.015
1953	5340, 6 Cyl.	...	M	R	9	17 9/16	2–*1 3/4	7/32	.015	.015
	5360, 6 Cyl.	Ben	M	R	10	20 1/32–20 3/64†	■	7/32	.015	.015

* Reverse shoe. (k) Frt. prim.–1 3/4 in., sec.–1 1/2 in. rear prim. 1 1/4 in.–sec.–1 in. † Rear.
■ Frt. prim.–2 in., sec.–2 1/2 in., Rear 2 in. Ben–Bendix. M–Moulded.

Tension Wrench Specifications

Year	Model	Cylinder Head Lbs.-Ft.	Cylinder Head Thread	Spark Plug Lbs.-Ft.	Spark Plug Thread	Connecting Rod Bolts or Nuts Lbs.-Ft.	Connecting Rod Bolts or Nuts Thread	Main Bearing Bolt Lbs.-Ft.	Main Bearing Bolt Thread	Flywheel Bolts Lbs.-Ft.	Flywheel Bolts Thread	Vibration Damper Bolts Lbs.-Ft.	Vibration Damper Bolts Thread
1941 to 48	Series 40	61–64•	...	24–30	14 mm	27–30•	...	66 70•	...	...	...	...	...
	Series 60	65–70•	...	24–30	14 mm	50–55•	...	66–70•	...	...	...	...	...
1941–42	Series 80	65–70•	...	24–30	14 mm	50–55•	...	70–73•	...	...	...	...	...
1949	Series 600	60–65•	...	24 30	14 mm	27–30•	...	65–70•	...	50–55	...	...	...
	Ambassador 6	65–70•	...	24–30	14 mm	50–55•	...	65–70•	...	95–100	...	...	...
1950–53	Series 10	60–65–	...	24–30	14 mm	27–30–	...	65–70–	...	52–56	...	...	...
	Series 40	60–65–	...	24–30	14 mm	27–30–	...	65–70–	...	52–56	...	...	...
	Series 60	65–70–	...	24–30	14 mm	50–55–	...	65–70–	...	96–101	...	...	...

Crankshaft Bearing Journal Sizes

Year	Model	Connecting Rod Journals Diameter	Connecting Rod Journals Length	Main Bearing Journals No. 1 Diameter	No. 2 Diameter	No. 3 Diameter	No. 4 Diameter	No. 5 Diameter
1940	4010, 4020	2.000	1.427	2.479	2.479	2.479	2.479	*2.479
	4080	2.000	1.239	2.479	2.479	2.479	2.479	†2.479
1941 to 48	4140	1.875	1.250	2.479	2.479	2.479	2.479	...
	4160	2.000	1.427	2.479	2.479	2.479	2.479	*2.479
	4180	2.000	1.239	2.479	2.479	2.479	2.479	†2.479
1949 to 51	4940, 5040, 5140	2.094–2.095	1.125	2.479	2.479	2.479	2.479	...
	4960, 5060, 5160	2.000–2.0001	1.4375	2.479	2.479	2.479	2.479	*2.479
1950–51	5010	2.094–2.095	1.125	2.479	2.479	2.479	2.479	...
1952	5210, 5240 6 Cyl.	2.094–2.095	...	2.484375	2.474375	2.484375	2.484375	...
	5260 6 Cyl.	2.000–2.001	...	2.484375	2.484375	2.484375	2.484375	*2.484375
1953	5340, 6 cyl.	2.095	...	2.484375	2.484375	2.484375	2.484375	...
	5360, 6 Cyl.	2.001	...	2.484375	2.484375	2.484375	2.484375	*2.484375

* Bearings 6, 7 same as 5. † Bearings 6, 7, 8, 9 same as 5.

NASH SPECIFICATIONS

Cooling System

CAR AND YEAR	MODEL	Capacity Qts.	Quarts of Methanol Base Anti-Freeze (For Protection to Temperature Shown Below)							Quarts of Ethylene Glycol (For Protection to Temperature Shown Below)							Quarts of Denatured Alcohol—188 Proof (For Protection to Temperature Shown Below)						
			3	4	5	6	7	8	9	3	4	5	6	7	8	9	3	4	5	6	7	8	9
1937	3720	17	15	6	−4	−16	−29	−45	...	18	12	5	−4	−14	−27	−42	...	10	0	...	−10	−20	−30
1937	3780	18	11	8	−1	−12	−25	−38	−53	19	14	7	0	−10	−21	−34	20	10	...	0	−10	...	−20
1938-39-40	3820, 3920, 4020	16	13	3	−8	−21	−36	−53	...	17	10	2	−8	−19	−34	−52	...	10	0	−10	..	−20	−30
1941	4180	16	13	3	−8	−21	−36	−53	..	17	10	2	−8	−19	−34	−52	...	10	0	−10	...	−20	−30
1941-42 & '49, "600"	4140, 4240	14	9	−3	−17	−34	−53	...	...	15	6	−5	−18	−34	−54	...	10	...	0	−10	−20	−30	...
1946-48, "600"-1950	4640, 4740	15	11	1	−12	−27	−44	...	...	16	8	0	−12	−26	−43	...	...	10	0	−10	−20	−30	...
1941-42 & '50-5060	4160, 4260	17	15	6	−4	−16	−29	−45	...	18	12	5	−4	−14	−27	−42	...	10	0		−10	−20	−30
1946-50	4660, 4760	18	17	8	−1	−12	−25	−38	−53	19	14	7	0	−10	−21	−34	20	10	...	0	−10	...	−20
1950-51	5010, 5110	12	3	−12	−31	−53	...	...	...	10	0	−15	−34	−57	...	...	10	0	−10	−20	−30	...	...
1951-53	5140	15	11	1	−12	−27	−44	...	...	16	8	0	−12	−26	−43	...	...	10	0	−10	−20	−30	...
1951-53	5160	18	17	8	−1	−12	−25	−38	−53	19	4	7	0	−10	−21	−34	20	10	...	0	−10	...	−20

Distributors

Year	Model	Distributor Model Number	Cam Angle (deg.)	Direction of Rotation C=Clockwise CC=Counter Clockwise at Cam End	Breaker Arm Spring Tension	Breaker Point Gap (inches)	Engine R.P.M. when Cent. Advance Starts	Max. Cent. Advance in Engine Deg. at Stated Engine R.P.M.	Vacuum in (inches) of Mercury at which Vacuum Unit Starts	Max. Advance in Engine Deg. at Stated Vacuum	Vacuum Unit Number
1940	4020, 6 cyl.	IGE-4019A	35	CC	17-20	.018-.022	550	23@1750	...	...	...
	4080, 8 cyl.	IGK-4102	28	C	17-20	.017	550	24@2200	...	...	...
1941	4160, 6 cyl.	IGE-4024	35	C	17-20	.018-.022	550	23@1750	...	...	...
	4180, 8 cyl.	IGK-4102	28	C	17-20	.017	550	24@2200	...	...	...
1941-42	4140, 4240, 6 cyl.	1110512	35	CC	17-21	.018-.024	800	20@2400	3 to 5	17@14 to 17	1116029
1942	4260, 6 cyl.	IGS-4205	38	C	17-20	.018 .022	550	18@1800	...	...	...
	4280, 8 cyl.	IGT-4202	27	C	17-20	.016-.018	500	25@3800	...	...	...
1946	4640, 6 cyl.	IGW-4184	35	CC	17-20	.018-.022	550	22@2800	4	7.5@15	VC-4015
	...	IGW-4184A	35	CC	17-20	.018-.022	550	22@2800	4	7.5@15	VC-4015
	4660, 8 cyl.	IGS-4205A	38	C	17-20	.018 .022	700	24@2700	5	6@15	...
	...	IGS-4205B	38	C	17-20	.018-.022	600	28@2700	5	6@15	...
1947	4740, 6 cyl.	IGW-4184A	35	CC	17-20	.018-.022	550	22@2800	4	7.5@15	VC-4015
	4760, 6 cyl.	IGS-4205B	38	C	17-20	.018-.022	600	28@2700	5	6@15	...
1948	4840, 6 cyl.	IGC-4512	35	C	17-20	.018-.022	600	22@2900	4	7.5@15	VC-4015
	4860, 6 cyl.	IGS-4205B	38	C	17-20	.018-.022	600	28@2700	5	6@15	...
1948-49	4840, 4940, 6 cyl.	1112351	35	C	17-21	.018-.024	600	24@2800	3 to 5	17@13 to 17	1116045
	4860, 4960, 6 cyl.	1110216	35	C	17-21	.018-.024	600	30@2700	4 to 6	12@14 to 16	1116044
1950	5010, 5040, 6 cyl.	1112351	35	CC	17-21	.018-.024	600	24@2800	3 to 5	13 to 17	1116045
	5060, 6 cyl.	1110216	35	C	17-21	.018-.024	600	30@2700	4 to 6	14 to 16	1116044
1951	5110, 5140, 6 cyl.	1112351	35	C	17-21	.018-.024	600	30@3700	6 to 12	14 to 16	1116045
	5160, 6 cyl.	1110225	35	C	17-21	.018-.024	...	28@2700	6 to 12	14 to 16	...
1952	5210, 5240, 6 cyl.	1112382	31-37	...	17-21	.022	600	24@2800	4	7½@15	...
	5260, 6 cyl.	1110227	31-37	...	17-21	.022	600	30@2700	5	6@15	...
1953	5340, 6 cyl.	1112382	31-37	C	17-21	.022	600	24@2800	4	7½@15	...
	5360, 6 cyl.	1110227	31-37	C	17-21	.022	600	30@2700	5	6@15	...

Generators

Year	Model	Generator Number	Field Current at 6 Volts (amps.)	Maximum Safe Output: Volts	Amperes	R.P.M.	Brush Spring Tensions (oz)	Voltage Regulator Number
1940	4020	GDZ-4803-A	1.3–1.5	8.0	35	2000	35-53	VRP-4004-A
	4080	GDZ-4803-B	1.3–1.5	8.0	35	2000	35-53	VRP-4004-A
1941	4160, 4260	GDZ-4806-A	1.3–1.5	8.0	35	2000	35-53	VRP-4004-F-1
	4180, 4280	GDZ-4803-B	1.3–1.5	8.0	35	2000	35-53	VRP-4004-F-1
1946 to 48	Series—All exc. 4840, 4860	GDZ-4806-A	1.3–1.5	8.0	35	2000	35-53	VRP-4004-F
1941–42	4140, 4240	1102684	1.75–1.9	8.0	30	1750	24-28	1118202
1948	4840, 4860	1102702	1.75-1.9	8.0	30	1750	24-28	1118202
1949	4940, 4960	1102702	1.75–1.9	8.0	30	1750	24–28	1118302
1950–51	5010, 5110	1102730	1.75–1.9	7.3	34	1800	24-28	1118302
	Optional	1102748	1.75–1.9	7.3	40	1800	24-28	1118382
	5040, 5140, 5060, 5160	1102730	1.75–1.9	7.3	34	1800	24-28	1118302
		1102748	1.75–1.9	7.3	40	1800	24–28	1118382
1952	5210, 6 cyl.	1102776						1118731
	5240, 5260, 6 cyl.	1102777						1118732
1953	5340, 6 cyl.	1100021						1118731
	5360, 6 cyl.	1102777						1118731

Voltage Regulators

Year	Model	Regulator Number	Grounded P=Positive N=Negative	Voltage Control: Air Gap Points Closed	Voltage Control: Voltage Setting Hot	Current Control: Air Gap Points Closed	Current Control: Current Set Hot	Cut-Out Relay: Point Gap	Cut-Out Relay: Air Gap	Cut-Out Relay: Closing Volt
1940	4010, 4020, 4080	VRP-4004-A	P	.052	7.2	.052	34-36	.015	.034	6.4–7.0
1941–42	4140, 4240	1118202	P	.070	7.2	.080	34–36	.020	.020	6.2–6.7
	4160, 4180, 4260, 4280	VRP-4004-F-1	P	.052	7.3	.052	34-36	.015	.034	6.4–7.0
1946	4640, 4660	VRP-4004-F-1	P	.052	7.3	.052	34-36	.015	.034	6.4–7.0
1947–48	4740, 4760, 4840, 4860	VRP-4004-F	P	.052	7.3	.052	34-36	.015	.034	6.4–7.0
1948	4860	1118202	P	.070	7.2	.080	32-34	.020	.020	6.2–6.7
1949 to 51	4940, 4960, 5040, 5060	1118302	P	.075	7.0	.075	32-40	.020	.020	5.9–6.8
	5010, 5110, 5140, 5160	1118302	P	.075	7.0	.075	32-40	.020	.020	5.9-6.8
		1118382	P	.075	7.2	.075	32-35	.020	.020	6.2–6.7
1952	5210, 6 cyl.	1118731	P							6.2
	5240, 5260, 6 cyl.	1118732	P							6.2
1953	5340, 6 cyl.	1118731	P		8–10					6.2
	5360, 6 cyl.	1118732	P		8–10					6.2

NASH SPECIFICATIONS

Starters

Year	Model	Unit Model Number	Spring Tension (oz.)	STARTER — Lock Test: Volts	Amperes	Torque, (lbs. ft.)	No Load: Volts	Amperes	R.P.M.	Direction of Rotation Viewed from Drive End C=Clockwise CC=Counter-clockwise
1940	4010, 4020	MAB-4076	42–53	2.0	390	9.2	5.0	60	3600	C
1940 to 42	4080, 4180, 4280	MAB-4104	42–53	2.0	390	9.2	5.0	60	3600	C
1941–42	4140, 4240	1109451	24–28	3.3	540	11.5	5.7	60	6000	C
1941 to 48	4160, 4260, 4660, 4760, 4860	MAB-4076	42–53	2.0	390	9.2	5.0	60	3600	C
1948	4840	1109451	24–28	3.3	540	11.5	5.7	60	6000	C
	4860	1107949	24–28	3.0	600	16	5.7	65	5500	C
1949	4940	1109451	24–28	3.3	540	11.5	5.7	60	6000	C
	4960	1107950	24–28	3.0	600	16	5.7	65	5500	C
1950	5010	1109641	24–28	3.2	555	12.2	5.7	55	5000	C
	5040, Standard	1109451	24–28	3.3	540	11.5	5.7	60	6000	C
	Hydramatic	1109459	24–28	3.3	540	11.5	5.7	60	6000	C
	5060, Standard	1107950	24–28	3.0	600	16	5.7	65	5500	C
	Hydramatic	1107965	24–28	3.0	600	16	5.7	65	5500	C
1951	5110	1109463	24–28	3.20	555	12.2	5.7	55	5000	C
	5140, Standard	1109463	24–28	3.2	555	12.2	5.7	55	5000	C
	Hydramatic	1109465	24–28	3.2	555	12.2	5.7	55	5000	C
	5160, Standard	1107950	24–28	3.0	600	16	5.7	65	5500	C
	Hydramatic	1107965	24–28	3.0	600	16	5.7	65	5500	C
1952	5210, 5240, 6 cyl. Standard	1107119	24–28	3.25	550	12	5.65	70	5500	C
	Hydramatic	1107121	24–28	3.25	550	12	5.65	70	5500	C
	5260, 6 cyl., Standard	1107950	24–28	3.15	570	14	5.65	70	5500	C
	Hydramatic	1107965	24–28	3.15	570	14	5.65	70	5500	C
1953	5340, 6 cyl.	1107119	24–28	3.25	550	12	5.65	70	5500	C
	5360, 6 cyl.	1107950	24–28	3.15	570	14	5.65	70	5500	C

Front Wheel Alignment

Year	Model	Caster (deg.)	Camber (deg.)	King Pin Inclination (deg.)	Toe-In (inches)	Turning Radius: Inner	Turning Radius: Outer
1940	4010, 4020, 4080	0 to ½N	¼P to ¾P	4½	1/32 to 3/32	21½	20
1941–42	4160, 4180, 4260, 4280	0 to ½N	¼P to ¾P	4½	1/32 to 3/32	21½	20
1946	4640	¼P to ¾P	¼P to ¾P	7½	⅛ to 3/16	21¾	20
	4660	0 to ½N	¼P to ¾P	4½	1/32 to 3/32	21¾	20
1947	4740	0 to ¾P	¼P to ¾P	4½	1/32 to 3/32	21¾	20
	4760	0 to ½P	¼P to ¾P	7½	⅛ to 3/16	21¾	20
1948	4840	¼P to ¾P	¼P to ¾P	7	⅛ to 3/16	21¾	20
	4860	0 to ½N	¼P to ¾P	5	1/16 to 3/16	21¾	20
1949–52	4940, 5040, 5140, 5240	0 to ½P	¼N to ¼P	8½	1/16 to 3/16	23½	20
	4960, 5060, 5160, 5260	0 to ½P	¼N to ¼P	8½	⅛ to 3/16	23	20
	5010, 5110, 5210	¾P to 1¼P	¼N to ¾P	8	1/16 to 3/16	23½	20
1953	5340	0 to ½P	¼N to ¼P	8½	1/16 to 3/16	17¾	20
	5360	0 to ½P	¼N to ¼P	8½	⅛ to 3/16	17¾	20
	5310	¾P to 1¼P	¼N to ¾P	4¾ to 5	1/16 to 3/16	23½	20

Fan, Generator Belts and Radiator Hose

Year	Model	Fan Belt			Generator Belt			Upper Hose			Lower Hose		
		Angle of "V" (deg.)	Length O.C.	Width Max.	Angle of "V" (deg.)	Length O.C.	Width Max.	Type	Inside Diam.	Length	Type	Inside Diam.	Length
1940	4010	34	48¼	25/32	.....	.....	.....	straight	1¾	9	straight	1½	3½–4
	4020	34	48¼	25/32	.....	.....	.....	straight	1¾	8	straight	1½	3½–4
1941	4140	34	42⅛	25/32	.....	.....	.....	straight	1½	8	straight	1½	3½
	4160	34	42⅛	25/32	.....	.....	.....	straight	1¾	7–8	straight	1½	3½
	4180	34	45¼	25/32	.....	.....	.....	straight	1¾	4½–7⅝	straight	1½	3½
1942	4240	34	42⅛	25/32	.....	.....	.....	straight	1¾	7¾	straight	1½	3¼
	4260	34	42⅛	25/32	.....	.....	.....	straight	1¾	7½–8	straight	1½	3¼
	4280	34	45¼	25/32	.....	.....	.....	straight	1¾	4½–8	straight	1½	3¼
1946 to 49	600, Series 40	34	42⅛	25/32	.....	.....	.....	straight	1½	10	straight	1½	3
	6, Series 60	34	42⅛	25/32	.....	.....	.....	straight	1¾	8	straight	1½	3¼
1950 Early	Series 40	34	42⅛	25/32	.....	.....	.....	curved	1½	.....	straight	1½	4
Late	Series 40	40	42 9/16	⅜	.....	.....	.....	curved	1½	.....	straight	1½	4
Early	Series 60	34	42⅛	25/32	.....	.....	.....	curved	1¾	.....	straight	1½	3½
Late	Series 60	40	42 9/16	⅜	.....	.....	.....	curved	1¾	.....	straight	1½	3½
	Rambler	40	41	⅜	.....	.....	.....	curved	1½	.....	straight	1½	2
1951	5110	40	41	⅜	.....	.....	.....	curved	1½	.....	straight	1½	2
	5140	40	42 9/16	⅜	.....	.....	.....	straight	1½	9½	straight	1½	3½
	5160	40	42 9/16	⅜	.....	.....	.....	curved	1¾	.....	straight	1½	3½
1952	5210, 6 cyl.	38	40⅛	13/32	.....	.....	.....	curved	1½	.....	curved	1¼	.....
	5240, 6 cyl.	38	40¾	13/32	.....	.....	.....	curved	1½	.....	curved	1¼	.....
	5260, 6 cyl.	38	40⅛	13/32	.....	.....	.....	curved	1¾	.....	curved	1¼	.....
1953	5340	38	41½	13/32	.....	.....	.....	curved	1½	.....	curved	1¼	.....
	5360	38	40⅛	13/32	.....	.....	.....	curved	1¾	.....	curved	1¼	.....

King Pin Specification Chart

Year	Model	KING BOLT			UPPER BUSHING				LOWER BUSHING			
					King Bolt Bushing				King Bolt Bushing			
		Diameter	Length	Bolt Number	Inside Diameter	Outside Diameter	Length	Bushing Number	Inside Diameter	Outside Diameter	Length	Bushing Number
1940	4020	.815	5¼	3103073	.814	.943	1 1/16	102591	.814	.943	1 1/16	102591
	4080	.859	5 13/16	3103074	.859	.987	1 3/16	102592	.859	.987	1 3/16	102592
1941 to 42	60, 80	.860	5 11/32	3106836	.860	.984	1 1/16	3106837	.860	.984	1 1/16	3106837
1946 to 48	60	.860	5 11/32	3106836	.860	.984	1 1/16	3106837	.860	.984	1 1/16	3106837

NASH 1940 thru 1953

FRONT SUSPENSION

Six different types of front end suspension were used on Nash and Rambler cars from 1940 thru 1951.

FIRST TYPE—used on 1940 models—is the short and long arm type, commonly referred to as the S.L.A. type suspension.

This type of suspension employs a coil spring, reverse Elliott knuckle support, lower control arm, upper control arm incorporated with the shock absorber and a torsion bar used to stabilize the front system.

SECOND TYPE—used on 1941 thru 1948 Ambassador series. The front suspension on these models is similar to the first type, except that the shock absorber is the direct acting, telescoping type mounted through the center of the coil spring.

THIRD TYPE—the Lancia system of front suspension was used on all 1941 and 1942—600 models.

The principle involved in this particular front suspension allows the spindle to move up and down on a long king pin. The king pin is fastened rigidly to the body by the front axle channel at the bottom, and by the camber and caster adjusting rods at the top.

The spindle moves up and down the king pin on hardened rollers. The steering knuckle is made in two parts, one a forging, supporting the brake backing plate and front wheel spindle.

The other, a hardened tube which forms the outer race for the king pin roller bearings. The outer tube is tapered to permit installation of the tube in the spindle.

FOURTH TYPE—used on all 1946 thru 1948—600 series. This suspension unit is of Nash design.

The knuckle support on this type suspension acts as a king pin and is attached to a trunnion in the lower and has a ball joint connection in the upper arm.

FIFTH TYPE—1949 thru 1951 Ambassador and Statesmen use a suspension unit which has practically the same characteristic as the fourth type.

The cross member on the fifth type suspension system is designed and mounted differently. The knuckle support is joined to the upper control arm by a trunnion, and the control arm is of a slightly different design. The front

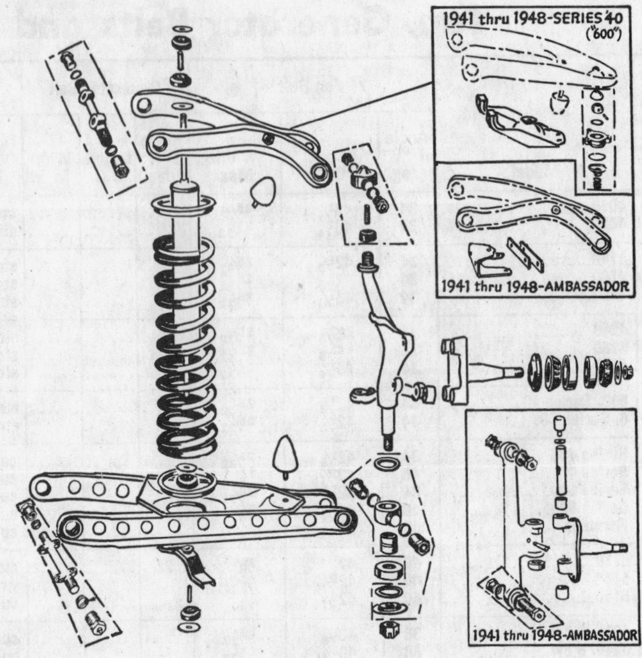

Front suspension typical of 1941 thru 1951 except 41-4240 and 1950-51 Rambler models

3rd type—Lancia suspension

4th type suspension

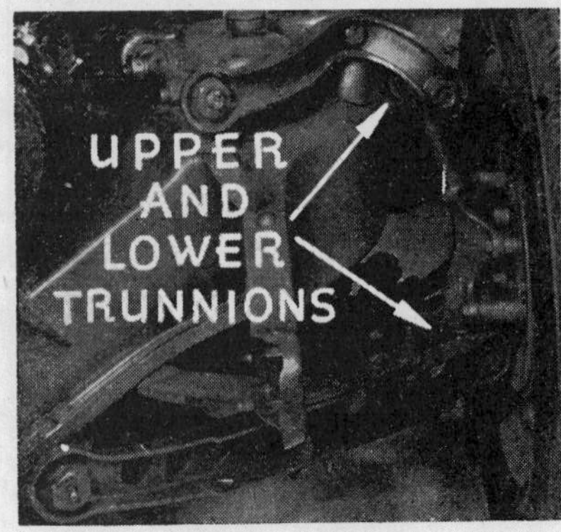

5th type suspension

cross member is equipped with lower control arm pivot bolts welded rigidly into position. If these bolts are worn, the complete unit should be replaced.

SIXTH TYPE—A Nash constructed front end which is used on the Rambler series and all 1952 and 1953 models.

The bottom of the coil spring is positioned on top of the steering knuckle support. The upper end of the spring is located in a recess in the inner apron panel. The shock absorber is mounted to the upper and lower control arms by means of rubber bushings.

The steering knuckle support on this suspension system is also used as a pivot pin.

Steering Geometry—Caster, Camber and Toe-In

1940 MODELS (FIRST TYPE)

Caster and camber are controlled by an eccentric pin in the outer end of the upper support arm, which means that the best setting obtainable will be a compromise.

To adjust these angles, loosen the clamp bolt at the upper end of knuckle support and take out the lubrication fitting from the eccentric pin forward bushing. Insert Allen wrench in the hole where grease fitting was removed. Turn the threaded pin in a clockwise direction to increase caster. Camber setting is obtained by turning the eccentric not more than one-half turn in the direction which will give the best compromise setting after caster has been corrected. It is a good idea to set the camber exactly even if it changes the caster somewhat.

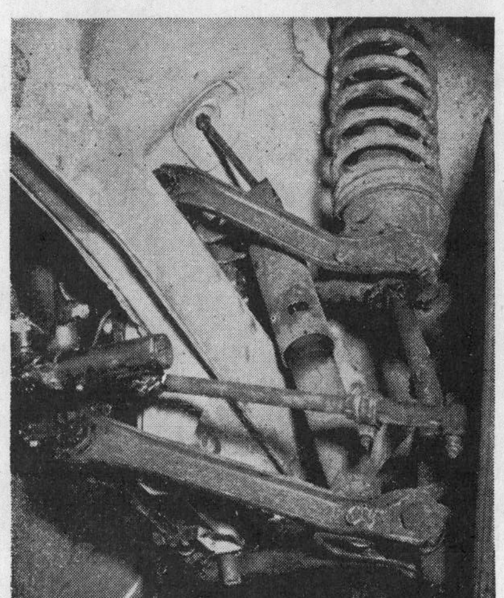

6th type front suspension

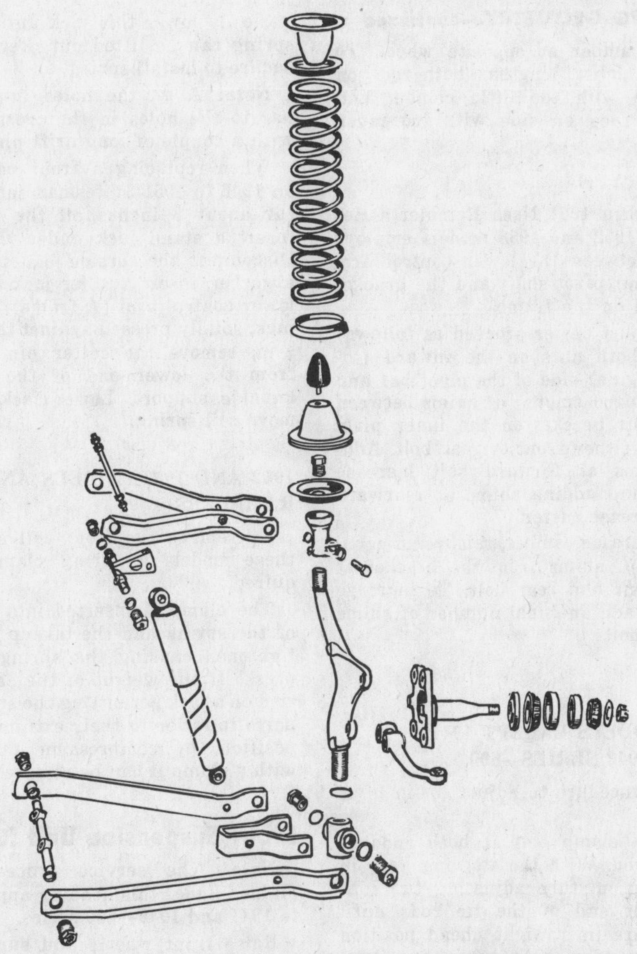

Front suspension typical of 1950 thru 1953 Rambler and 1952-53 Ambassador and Statesman models

SECOND, FOURTH AND FIFTH TYPE

1941 thru 1951 Ambassador and 1946 thru 1951 Statesman. Use "C" washers between the upper control arm frame bracket and the inner pivot shaft to control caster and camber. To adjust caster, loosen the nuts at the inner end of the pivot bar frame bracket and insert "C" washer as needed. Adding washers to forward bolt decreases caster. Increase caster by adding shims to the rear bolt. Add shims equally at both bolts decreases camber.

THIRD TYPE—1941-42—600 SERIES

The Lancia system of front suspension uses diagonal tie rods to control caster and camber.

To adjust caster, shorten the forward rod and lengthen the rearward rods. To increase caster reverse procedure.

When adjusting camber keep in mind that the knuckle pin tie rod holds the tops of both knuckle pins in relationship to each other, so increase camber in one wheel will simultaneously de-

On the 2nd, 4th & 5th type the shims are located as shown above Shims on the 6th type are in the same position on the lower arm

STEERING GEOMETRY—*continued*

crease camber at opposite wheel. To adjust camber, lengthen both rods on the side with too little camber and shorten rods on side with too much camber.

SIXTH TYPE

1950 thru 1951 Nash Rambler series and all 1952 and 1953 models employs shims between the lower control arm (A frame) pivot shaft and the bracket mounted on the frame.

To adjust caster proceed as follows: Loosen both nuts on the inward (toward engine) side of the pivot bar and add required amount of shims between the frame bracket on the inner pivot shaft at either front or rear bolt. Adding shims at forward bolt increase caster, and adding shims at rearward bolt decrease caster.

To decrease camber, remove an equal amount of shims from the bracket at both front and rear bolt. To increase camber, add an equal number of shims at both bolts.

Toe-In

ALL MODELS EXCEPT 1941 THRU 1942 SERIES—600

The procedure to adjust toe-in is as follows:

Loosen clamp bolt at both ends of the tie rod. With the steering gear in mid position, turn adjusting tubes at the outer end of the tie rods until wheels are in straight ahead position and then turn both tubes an equal amount (in opposite directions) until correct toe-in is obtained.

1941 THROUGH 1942—600 SERIES

Loosen the clamp at outer end of each tie rod and rotate each adjusting sleeve separately, until wheels are straight ahead. Now lengthen each tie rod an equal amount until toe-in is corrected.

Replacement of Front Coil

On 1940 thru 1951 Ambassador and 1949 thru 1951—600 and Statesman series an easy way to replace a front coil spring is as follows: Raise car and support frame with a suitable stand jack, disconnect the torsion bar and shock absorber, insert a roller jack under lower control arm inner pivot shaft, and take a load on the jack against pivot shaft, remove the four bolts which hold the pivot bar to the cross member.

Slowly lower this jack until the coil spring can be lifted out. Reverse procedure to install spring.

Note: Align the holes in the pivot bar to the holes in the cross member with a couple of long drift pins.

When replacing a front coil spring on 1946 to 1951 Statesman series, raise car about 8 inches off the floor and insert a stand jack under the frame. Disconnect the torsion bar and shock absorber, insert a roller jack under the lower control arm (A frame). With the jack, solidly pressed against the control arm, remove the cotter pin and nut from the lower end of the steering knuckle support. Lower jack and remove coil spring.

1952 AND 1953 MODELS AND ALL RAMBLERS

To replace the front coil spring on these models a spring clamp is required.

The clamp is inserted into the coils of the spring and the takeup bolts are tightened causing the spring to compress. If the weight of the car is carried on a jack permitting the suspension parts to lower to their extreme bottom position, by compressing the spring with a clamp it can be removed readily.

Front Suspension Unit Removal

Note: The service procedure explained under this heading applies only to 1941 and 1942—600 series.

Raise front wheels and support the frame with a suitable stand jack, remove wheel hub and drum as unit. Detach backing plate. With a piece of wire hook backing plate to frame to relieve any strain on hydraulic brake hose. Remove rubber boot straps, and lower boot to allow installation of special spring clamps; then compress the spring. Remove nuts at upper and lower ends of knuckle pin studs.

Detach tie rod at steering arm. Disconnect shock at lower end. Loosen tie rod cover from fender apron, take off the nuts at each end of caster and camber rods.

Lift the cross tie rod from knuckle pin extension stud and remove caster and camber rods.

Remove unit as complete assembly.

Disassembly

Pull off lower boot and set assembly in a vise, holding flat portion at lower end of pin.

Unfasten upper extension stud along with thrust bearing and upper spring seat.

Remove coil spring, cork seal, rebound bumper, rubber boot, lower spring seat and locks.

Insert pin sleeve in the vise, detach lower flange, and drive off spindle. The sleeve and pin is supplied as a unit.

Set the new sleeve and pin in a vise and insert spring seat locks to align with lower grooves, use masking tape to hold spring locks into position. Install lower spring seat, cushion, rubber boot, clamps and rebound bumper.

Install coil spring with special clamp in place.

Insert cork seal and retainer at upper end of pin. Install top spring seat and thrust bearing unit, screw upper extension into pin. Use a new Neoprene seal to seal pin extension to spring seat. Install lower boot retainer disc with concave side up. Fasten boot clamps and insulated washer with rubberized side down.

As a precautionary measure, insert temporarily the lower pin cushion bushing, spacer and nut to the lower stud to keep the knuckle pin from being displaced.

Note: When the front axle is not the reinforced type with a reinforcing washer welded on the lower side, it will be necessary to insert a 3/32" thick flat washer between cushion and axle.

Removal of Upper Control Pin

On 1940 series simply loosen clamp bolts of the upper portion of the knuckle support, remove the front bushing and then the back bushing. Now the pin can be removed. When the eccentric pin is replaced make certain that the pin is properly centered in the knuckle support and is facing outward (full camber position).

The upper pivot pin on these models has a thread with two starts.

Removal of Upper Control Arm Trunnion

The upper control arm on 1949 thru 1951 Ambassador and Statesman series employs a trunnion and two-threaded bushing at the outer end of the upper control arm. To replace a trunnion, proceed as follows: Raise front end of the car and install a stand jack under the frame.

Remove wheel hub and drum and brake backing plate. Hook the brake support plate to the frame with a piece of wire, insert a roller jack under the lower control arm, pull cotter pin out from lower end of knuckle support and take off the nut.

Lower jack until knuckle support is free from lower control arm.

Remove both trunnion bushings, unscrew knuckle support from trunnion and take out trunnion.

Note: When reassembling a knuckle pin into the upper trunnion provide clearance of approximately ¼" between the lower edge of the trunnion and the seal seat of the knuckle pin.

1952 AND 1953 MODELS AND ALL RAMBLERS

To replace the upper trunnion it will be necessary to first remove the coil spring, see Coil Spring Removal. Then take out the bolt which holds the upper trunnion to the upper suspension arm and tilt the knuckle support outward at the top so that the upper trunnion may be unscrewed from the knuckle support.

Note: It is sometimes difficult to tilt the knuckle support out of its mesh with the upper support arm as long as the steering arm is in place. It may be necessary to disconnect the steering arm either from the backing plate or from pivot end assembly.

King Pin Removal

Bear in mind that the 1940 thru 1948 Ambassadors Series are the only Nash cars having king pins in the conventional sense. All other models use a knuckle support which takes the place of the king pin.

When it is found necessary to replace king pins on 1940 thru 1948 Ambassador series, simply raise car and remove wheel, hub and drum assembly. Unbolt brake backing plate and hook to frame.

Remove top oiler and plug. Drive out king pin lock pin and drive king pin down and out.

REPLACEMENT OF THE KNUCKLE SUPPORT (PIVOT PIN)

On 1952 and 1953 Models and all Rambler Models it is necessary to first remove the coil spring before attempting to take out the knuckle support. Except for this the procedure is the same as is given below.

Support the weight of the car at the frame back of the front suspension. Remove the road wheel, brake drum and backing plate. Hang the backing plate on a stout wire connected to the frame to take the strain off the brake hose. Place a jack under the outer end of the lower suspension arm to take the compression of the spring.

Disconnect the shock absorber and the torsion bar. Remove the pins which hold the upper suspension arm to the upper trunnion.

Remove the bolts and bushings which hold the lower suspension arm to the trunnion and slowly let the jack down which will relieve the spring pressure.

The knuckle support can then be lifted off.

Since the steering arm is disconnected in the process of removing the backing plate it is a good idea to check toe-in after the new knuckle support has been installed.

Steering Knuckle Pin Upper Ball Joint

On 1946 thru 1948—600 series a ball joint mounted on the upper end of the steering knuckle pin and is fastened to the upper control arm by three cap screws.

To replace the ball joint, raise front end of car and insert a stand jack under the frame. Remove wheel hub and drum. Insert a roller jack under the lower control arm, unscrew the three cap screws holding ball joint to upper control arm. Lower jack enough to allow knuckle pin to swing downward. Using a special portable press, remove the ball joint lock pin and lift off ball joint.

Note: Special service kits are available for these repairs.

Shock Absorber

1941-1942—600 series the direct acting shock absorber is removed by unscrewing the nuts on top of shock absorber (located in a bracket on the king pin tie rod).

Take off nut at lower end of shock absorber and remove shock absorber from car.

On all 1941 to 1951 Ambassador and 1946 to 1951—600 or Statesman series, a direct acting telescoping type shock absorber is mounted through the center of the coil spring. To remove it, loosen the mounting bolt at the top of the frame and take off the shock absorber plate in the lower control arm.

Telescoping shock absorbers are also used on 1950 and 1951 Rambler series and all 1952 and 1953 series and are removed by detaching bolt in upper control arm pivot shaft bracket and mounting bolt in lower control arm. The shock can then be lifted off.

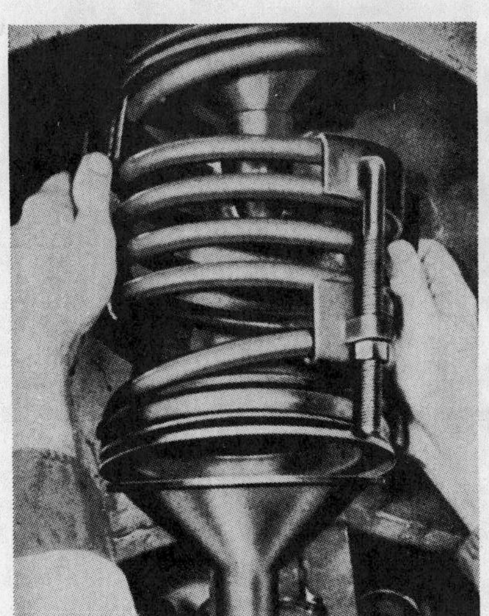

Removing the front spring "Ambassador" and "Statesman" series 1952-53

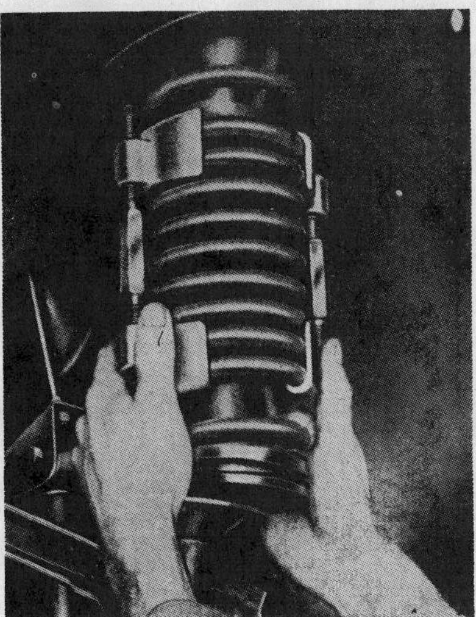

Removing the front spring "Rambler series" 1950 thru 1953

STEERING GEAR ASSEMBLY

Gemmer worm and roller type steering gears are used on all models. The 1941-42 series 600 gear is fitted with a shim adjusted cross shaft. All other models, meshes of gears is controlled by a screw.

Adjustment of the Steering Mechanism

1—Disconnect the pitman arm from the intermediate tie rod or drag link.

2—Adjust the steering gear housing assembly.

A—Check the worm bearings for up and down play in the worm. If any exists, remove the four bolts from the lower covering, take out one shim at a time until 2 pounds pull is required in the steering wheel to pull the steering gear through the high spot for the center of its travel.

B—Set the steering wheel to the mid position of its travel and check the lash between the worm and roller tooth. If any lash exists, loosen the jam nut and turn the adjusting screw inward until there is zero lash with the steering wheel in the mid position of its travel.

Note: On 1941-42—600 series, remove pitman arm and lower cover plate. Remove one shim at a time from behind thrust washer to tighten mesh of cross shaft and worm. End play adjustment should be .006".

3—Reconnect the pitman arm to the center tie rod or drag link.

4—Set the steering wheel in the mid position of its travel and adjust the right side tie rod so that one-half of the total toe-in is contained in the right wheel. Tighten the jam nuts.

5—With the steering wheel still in the mid position of its travel, loosen the clamp bolts on the left tie rod and adjust the sleeve so that the balance of the toe-in is contained in the left front wheel. Retighten the clamp bolts.

Turn the steering wheel from one extreme to the other to check for looseness of binding.

Note: On the 1949-51 series 60 models the adjustable sleeve of the tie rods is toward the center of the tie rods and not at the ends as in the earlier models.

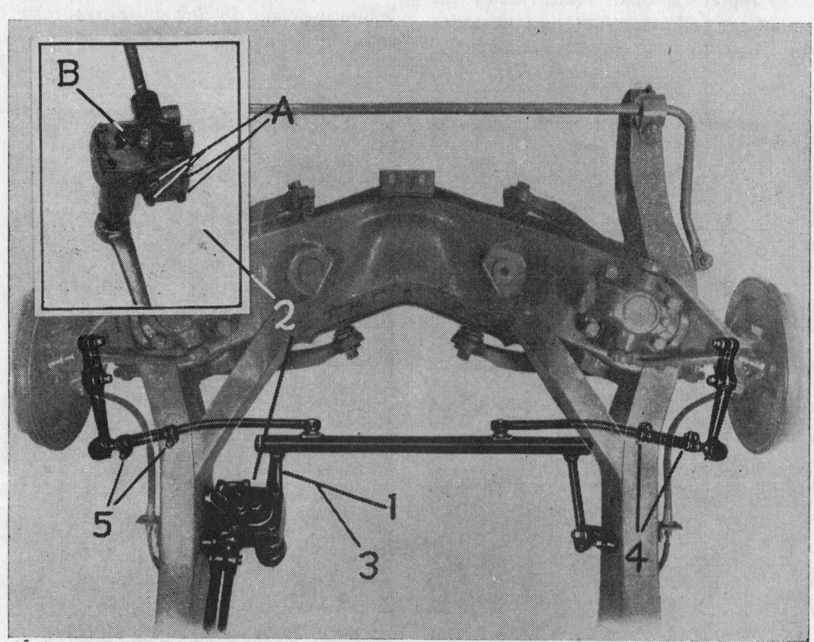

1946-48 60 series, typical of all models 1949-51

BRAKES

1940 thru 1951 Ambassador series are equipped with Bendix Duo-Servo single anchor type with non-eccentric anchor.

1941 thru 1947—600 series use Lockheed double anchor type brake with eccentric anchors.

1948 thru 1953—600, Statesman and Rambler series employ Bendix Self-Centering type brakes.

Brake Pedal Free Play Adjustment

There should be ¼" to ½" free play of the brake pedal.

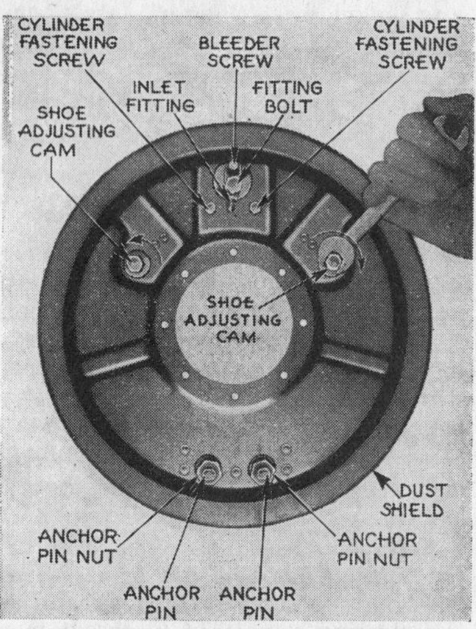

Backing plate side of the Lockheed brake used on 1941 to 1947—600 series

Minor Brake Adjustment

1940 TO 1951 AMBASSADOR SERIES

Raise all four wheels off floor. Remove adjusting screw hole clip from backing plate and expand shoes by turning star wheel wrench toward axle. Expand shoes against drum until wheel can just be turned by hand, then back off star wheel until wheel can be turned freely.

1941 TO 1947—600 SERIES

A minor brake adjustment is done by rotating adjusting cams until shoe comes in contact with drum, then back off adjustment slightly until drum turns freely. To expand the brake shoes, turn the cam toward the nearest point of the wheel rim when wrench is pointing upward.

1948 TO 1953—600 STATESMAN AND RAMBLER

Minor brake adjustment is done by simply turning the adjusting eccentric of the primary shoe in the forward direction of the wheel rotation. To expand the secondary shoe, turn eccentric in opposite direction of forward wheel rotation. After shoes are tight against the drum, rotate wheel forward and backward, so the brake shoes can center themselves. Now back off eccentric until wheel is just free.

Major Brake Adjustment

1940 THRU 1953 AMBASSADOR

Raise all four wheels. Insert a .015" feeler gage between secondary shoe and drum, then check shoe to drum clearance at each end of shoe. A clearance of .015" at each end of the secondary shoe with the primary shoe against the opposite side of the drum indicates good positioning of the anchor pin and adjusting screw. If a .015" clearance cannot be had, the anchor pin must be adjusted.

To adjust the anchor pin, loosen the jam nut one complete turn, turn the star wheel until the brake shoes are against the drum, tap the anchor nut with a hammer upward toward the drum until anchor pin centers itself. Tighten jamb nut, back off star wheel and insert .015" feeler gage to check all around clearance.

1941 to 1947—600 series for a major brake adjustment, insert an .008" feeler gage between drum and brake shoe. Turn adjusting cam (direction explained in minor brake adjustment) until .008" feeler gage is snug. Install a .004" feeler between drum and lining at anchor pin. Rotate the anchor pin until the .004" feeler is snug. Repeat operation at opposite anchor.

Hydraulic Cylinders

If the examination of the brakes reveal that the wheel cylinders are leaking or seeping, it may be necessary to remove and hone them to improve the surface on which the wheel cup rides.

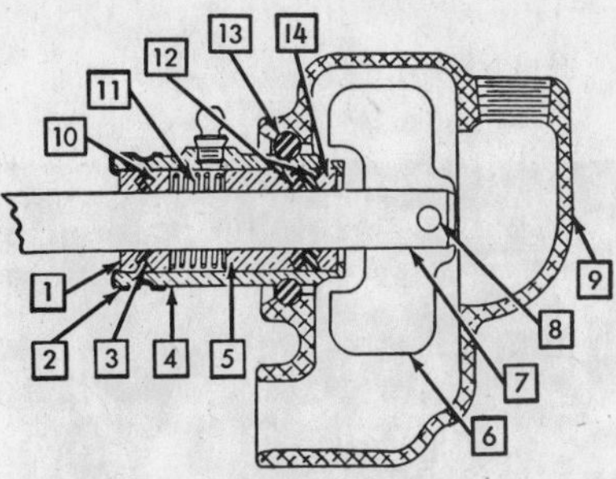

Section thru the water pump used on Statesman series

1. Outer seal gland
2. Seal housing cap
3. Seal
4. Seal housing
5. Shaft bushing
6. Impeller
7. Shaft
8. Rivet
9. Water pump
10. Inner seal gland
11. Seal gland spring
12. Inner pump seal
13. Seal housing rubber ring
14. Seal gland

COOLING SYSTEM

The thermostat is located in the water outlet elbow on top of the cylinder head. A 160 degree thermostat is standard equipment.

Water Pump Removal

Drain radiator, disconnect hoses from pump. Detach drive coupling from generator shaft. Take out mounting cap screws in pump flange and remove pumps.

Water Pump

1940 thru 1948, all models, remove brass packing unit (on 1940 models take out screws and remove cover plate). Take out the impeller and shaft and remove brass bushing. To reassemble, reverse procedure.

Note: The new bushing will require reaming to a suitable fit on the impeller shaft.

1949 through 1951 Nash and Nash Rambler series have a different constructed water pump with the same mounting flange as early models. To disassemble the water pump, remove impeller and pull impeller shaft and cartridge seal out of the pump body. Remove neoprene seal.

Insert a new neoprene seal in the water pump body. To simplify installing the seal cartridge and shaft, apply a little rubber lubricant on the inner part of the seal.

Radiator Removal

1941 THRU 1953—600 AND STATESMAN SERIES

Raise hood and drain radiator. Remove radiator tie bars. Detach water hoses, take out fan assembly. Remove radiator attaching bolts and lift out radiator.

1940, ALL MODELS, AND 1941 THRU 1953 AMBASSADOR SERIES

Raise hood, drain radiator (on 1941 to 1949 Ambassador remove top tank). Disconnect all water hoses. Remove fan assembly. Take out radiator attaching bolts and lift core out.

Manifold

The intake manifolds on all Nash cars are of the Sealed-in Iso-thermal type.

The exhaust pipe serves as the exhaust manifold and is clamped to the side of the engine block. There is no heat riser valve in this type construction.

Muffler

The muffler is of long and round shape construction and is mounted to the body by fabric straps.

Fuel System

The fuel pump is mounted on the right rearward side of the engine block. All models equipped with overdrive or Hydramatic transmissions use a double acting fuel pump. Models with standard transmissions use a single acting pump.

ENGINE INTERNAL

Oil Pan Removal

1941-42—600 SERIES

Raise front axle up until support pads on steering knuckle contact bumpers on axle. Unfasten front shock absorbers at the bottom. Unscrew top shock absorber nut from steering knuckle pin tie rod, remove shock.

Detach knuckle pin tie rod from across engine. Drain oil and with a jack and block of wood against pan behind axle, jack engine sufficiently to release tension on front engine mounts.

Disconnect front mounting shackle from engine. Jack engine up about five inches and place block of wood under front support. Remove clutch, inspection pan, take out oil pan cap screws, reach in between oil pan and engine block on right side and release oil pump screen. Remove pan and screen to the rear and out.

1941 THRU 1951 AMBASSADOR SERIES

Raise the engine block approximately 3" to simplify removing the front pan attaching bolts. Disconnect right side steering cross tube and remove oil pan.

1952 AND 1953 AMBASSADOR SERIES

To remove the oil pan it is necessary to remove the steering linkage cross tie rod and the front suspension pivot bar brace which will permit the pan to lower.

1946 THRU 1951 SERIES—600

On these models it is easier to remove the oil pan by first drilling a hole in the frame front cross member in order to reach the oil pan front mounting bolts. Otherwise the oil pan is removed in the usual manner.

1952 AND 1953 STATESMEN SERIES

To remove the oil pan on these models take off the steering linkage cross tie rod and the front suspension pivot bar brace which will permit the easy removal of the oil pan.

1950 THRU 1953 NASH RAMBLER SERIES

The oil pan is removed by detaching the steering linkage cross tube, drain oil, take out oil pan attaching bolts and remove pan.

Piston and Rod Assemblies

Aluminum cam ground pistons are used in all models. When assembling the piston to the connecting rod, the split skirt of the piston must be installed opposite the oil squirt in connecting rod. Pistons are installed in the cylinder bore so that the split skirt is toward the left side.

Connecting Rod Bearings

All Nash and Rambler series are equipped with steel back babbitt lined slip-in rod bearings.

Connecting rod bearings are held in position by a tang at the parting line. The Nash factory does not recommend adjusting the rod bearings. However, if it becomes necessary to make adjustments on the rod bearings, special designed shims are available to install between the lower half of the bearing shell and the bearing cap.

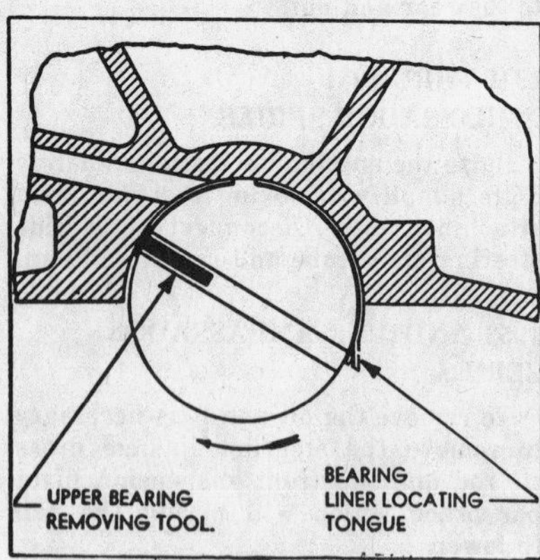

Removing main bearing upper shell

Main Bearings

Crankshaft bearings are of precision type and have a steel back with babbitt lining.

When either half of a main bearing necessitates replacement, both upper and lower half should be replaced.

Rear Main Bearing Oil Seal

Several different types of rear main bearing oil seal were used such as wood, rubber, felt and packing. Wooden plugs are used to seal the sides of the rear bearing cap. Later models use synthetic rubber key strips overlapping the bearing cap and seal the sides as well as the mating surfaces.

As an actual oil seal, Nash employs a slinger that is an integral part of the crankshaft.

ENGINE ASSEMBLY

All Ambassador series are equipped with overhead valve engines. Statesman, 600 and Rambler series employ the "L" head type engine.

Engine Removal

On all models except the Rambler series the engine is removed as follows: Remove radiator, detach front motor mounts, exhaust pipe, gas lines, ignition wires, etc.

Disconnect engine at bell housing, support transmission, loosen rear motor mounts and remove engine.

Note: On 1941 and 1942—600 series the steering knuckle pin tie rod (across top of engine) must be removed.

1952 AND 1953 AMBASSADOR AND STATESMEN SERIES

To remove the engines on these models it is advisable to take off the front bumper and the front end sheet metal as a unit.

The engine assembly with or without its transmission attached can then be easily removed from its mounting after taking out the K brace assembly, detaching all electrical connections, detaching all exhaust lines, water hoses, instrument connections, fuel lines, etc.

RAMBLER SERIES

To remove the engine on Rambler Model the procedure involves removing the hood, top and radiator core. Disconnect all lines such as fuel lines, electrical connections, exhaust connections, radiator connnections, etc., and raise the car high enough that the engine can be slid out from underneath it.

Then from below the car disconnect the tie rod from the steering linkage and remove the front suspension lower pivot bar brace, disconnect all clutch linkage and remove the bolts which hold the two cross members up to the side of the frame.

The engine should be supported so as to prevent it from falling on the operator.

The engine complete with its two cross members is lowered to the floor.

Cylinder Head Nut Tightening Sequence

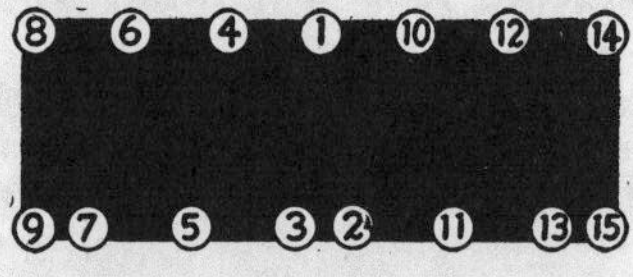

1940-1951 series 20 and 60

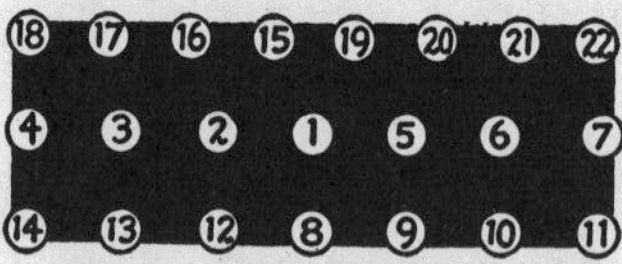

1941-1951 series 10 and 40

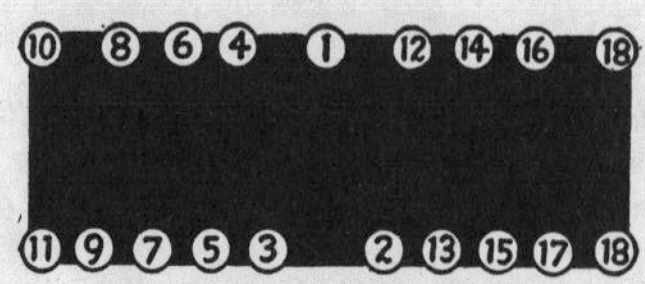

1940-1942 series 80 Cylinder head nut tightening sequence

Rambler engines are removed thru the bottom as shown in above illustration

Timing Case Cover Removal

On all models remove radiator, take off vibration damper. Unfasten cover mounting bolts, and remove cover.

Valve Timing Procedure

On all models remove timing case cover, turn engine until crankshaft sprocket mark is toward the crankshaft and both marks lie on a straight edge between the shaft centers, with intake valve opening.

To recheck the setting, set the marked tooth of the camshaft sprocket at approximately the one o'clock position. This should place the marked tooth of the crankshaft sprocket where it begins to mesh with the chain. There should be 9½ links, or 19 pins, between the marked teeth of both sprockets.

Valve Guide Removal

If it is necessary to replace the valve guides, carefully measure the distance from the top of the cylinder head and make a note of this distance so that when the new guides are installed they can be pressed into position exactly the same distance.

To remove valve guides: Press the guides out through the top of the head on overhead valve engines. Pull the guides up through the top of the block on "L" head engines.

To install: Press new guide into place from the top on both types and ream to size.

Upper—Set up the chain & sprockets in line
Lower—Turn crank to bring marked teeth into position shown

Rocker Arm Shaft Assembly

1949 THRU 1953—
AMBASSADOR SERIES

Rocker arms, shaft and valve lubrication is obtained by oil under pressure from the oil pressure gallery, directed through the oil inlet (opening in cylinder head) and sent through a hollowed bolt which attaches the rocket shaft to the cylinder head. (Front bolt.)

Important: When any service is performed on this assembly, be certain that the hollowed bolt is installed at front rocker arm trunnion block.

Where rocker shafts are found to be poorly lubricated it would be wise to make certain that hollowed bolt is at front rocker arm trunnion.

On 1940 to 1948 models the rocker arm and shaft are lubricated by means of a wick in the rocker arm.

ELECTRICAL SYSTEM

Distributor

The distributor on Ambassador series is mounted on the right side of the engine block, and on the left side on Rambler and Statesman series.

The distributor drive gear is located on the oil pump shaft. On Ambassador models a tongue on the distributor shaft is placed in a slot on the oil pump shaft. On Statesman "600" and Rambler series a slot in distributor shaft is positioned over a tongue on oil pump shaft.

To remove the distributor on all series, unfasten hold down screw in the advance arm, take off the distributor cap, detach vacuum advance line, primary wire and lift distributor out.

Note: To remove the distributor on Rambler series, keep in mind that there will be only 3/32 inch clearance between distributor and inner apron panel. Therefore it may be necessary to tilt engine block (toward right side) to lift distributor out.

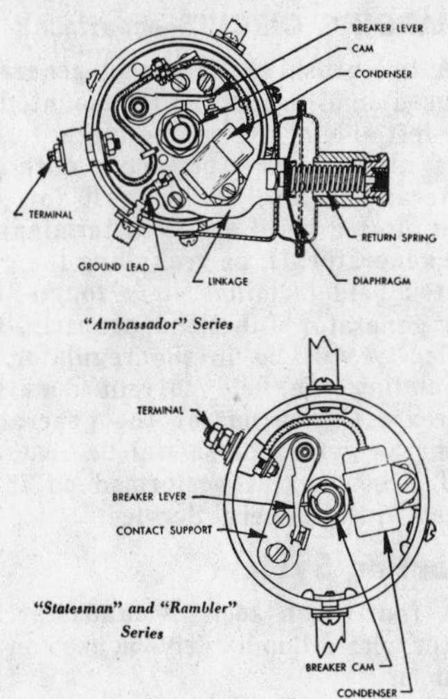

"Ambassador" Series

"Statesman" and "Rambler" Series

Ignition Timing

On overhead valve models 1940 through 1942 Ambassador series with twin ignition, the timing is set as follows: Using two timing lights, attach ground clip of timing light to any suitable ground on engine. Connect timing light leads to each distributor primary terminal without disconnecting wires. With ignition on and car in high gear, roll car forward until fixed points break (lights on). When correctly synchronized, the light connected to the adjustable points will light at the same time. If not correctly synchronized, loosen the three screws which hold the breaker-plate and turn the eccentric screw (or move sub-plate on mounting plate with screw driver, where no eccentric is employed) until both sets of points will break and light both lights at the same instant. At this point the timing mark I.G.N. on vibration damper should be in line with the marker on timing case cover.

1941 to 1951—All models with single ignition engines are timed with piston at T.D.C.

With No. 1 on compression, line up I.G.N. mark on vibration damper with pointer on timing case cover.

Loosen locknut and back off set screw on side of cylinder head slightly, rotate distributor until contacts begin to open, tighten set screw and locknut.

Charging Circuit

Note: Complete service on the generator is given in the General Service Section.

CHARGING CIRCUIT—*continued*

A two-brush shunt wound generator is used on all models and is mounted on the left side of the engine block.

If difficulty is experienced with the generator before removing it for service, first ground the field terminal of the generator. If, on grounding the generator field terminal, it is found that the generator functions properly, the difficulty will be in the regulator. If grounding the field current does not increase the output of the generator, then the generator should be removed and a bench test performed on it as given in the General Service.

Starting System

A four-brush series wound starting motor with a Bendix drive is used on all models.

When the starting motor does not crank the engine properly, check and see if battery is fully charged and all electrical connections are cleaned and securely tightened.

The mechanical check on the condition of the starter is performed in the same manner as that of the generator, as explained in the General Service in the beginning of this section. See Index.

Voltage Regulator

All Nash cars are equipped with a voltage and current regulator. When a new voltage regulator is installed on the car, the generator should be polarized by temporarily placing a jumper between the BAT and GEN terminal on the regulator. In other words, put some of the battery current across the regulator so that the generator will be properly polarized before starting the car. This should also be done at the time the generator is given a major service. It is not necessary to hold the jumper on longer than a half second.

Service on the regulator is given in the General Service. See Index.

CLUTCH ASSEMBLY

The clutch pedal free play adjustment on all Nash and Nash Rambler cars is 1 inch.

Clutch Removal

Remove transmission and disconnect the clutch linkages and unbolt clutch inspection pan. Release the pedal rod and return spring which will permit revolving the throw-out shaft so that the release bearing can be removed through the transmission opening.

On all models, release the clutch mounting bolts evenly and remove assembly from below. Reverse procedure to replace. Use a pilot shaft to align clutch disc with pilot bushing.

Removing main shaft and gear assembly, overdrive unit shown. Standard transmission mainshaft is removed in exactly the same manner

STANDARD TRANSMISSION

Removal

On 1940 thru 1948 Ambassador series the transmission is removed in the following manner:

Disconnect the control rods from the levers at the transmission. Detach the speedometer cable from transmission, remove the mounting bolts, slide the transmission back and out from below.

1941 THRU 1953—"600" AND STATESMAN AND 1949 THRU 1953 AMBASSADOR SERIES

To remove transmission, support frame with stand jacks, disconnect hydraulic brake line attaching bracket (just forward of left rear spring). Unfasten left side of rear sway stabilizer bar. Take out torque tube to transmission studs, grommets and retainers.

Detach hand brake cable at adjusting yoke. Insert a pinch bar between rear transmission housing and torque tube trunnion and push torque tube back. (It will be necessary to employ a helper to prevent torque tube from falling on operator.)

At the transmission, disconnect levers and speedometer cable, support engine and remove rear motor mount studs. Take out transmission attaching bolts and lift case assembly out.

Note: Pry rear assembly back while universal joint is being inserted on transmission main shaft splines.

Disassembly

Remove the front bearing cap and clutch shaft. Take out cap screws and washers and pull off the companion flange. Disconnect the mainshaft rear bearing retainer and oil seal assembly. Withdraw the mainshaft assembly through the rear. Using a pointed tool, depress the plunger which holds the splined retainer in place. Turn the retainer one spline and slip from shaft. This releases the synchronizer unit, thrust washer, second gear, thrust washer and first gear.

Remove the countershaft lock and drive the shaft out through the rear of case. **Note:** Plain washer at front end of cluster and tongued washer toward rear. The tongue goes toward the case.

Removal of Overdrive from Transmission Case

Remove the universal joint flange and loosen screws holding overdrive case to transmission. Draw the overdrive slowly to the rear and at the same time drive the shaft forward to prevent disassembly of the free wheel clutch. Separate the overdrive case from the rear bearing retainer. Do not let rear bearing retainer move backward or the synchronizing clutch will come apart, requiring disassembly of the transmission. Use a bolt and dummy nut to clamp the retainer in place when overdrive is removed.

Disassembly

Remove overdrive rear bearing retainer. Use spreader pliers to release the snap ring which retains the rear bearing and the speedometer gear. Pull the overdrive tail shaft from the case, holding a hand under the free wheel roller retainer to catch the rollers.

Remove retaining cap screw, free wheel retainer, and hub bushing. Withdraw ring gear and clutch assembly. Mark gear and clutch and take out snap ring that holds them together. Take off thrust washer and pinion assembly from the shaft.

Remove adapter plate snap ring and thrust plate. Detach the solenoid from the adapter plate and remove the solenoid pawl and plunger.

Release the snap ring and remove the sun gear and blocker assembly.

Reassembly of Overdrive

Reverse procedure to assemble, bearing in mind the following notes:

The clutch pawl adjusting screws must have the same number of turns. One screw has two slots, the other only one. If they were removed, turn them in until the tops of the screw heads are exactly 1/16" below the top edge of the counterbore.

If the sleeve shows signs of wear, replace it and the clutch unit. Failure to do so may produce a rasping noise at speeds above 30 miles per hour, which vanishes when the overdrive is engaged.

Adjust the clearance between the solenoid pawl and the balk ring with gaskets under the solenoid, to .015 in. with solenoid energized. Use a rubber band to hold the free wheel rollers. Install the free wheel cam hub bushing and tongued washer with the tongue toward the cam.

When assembling the planetary pinions in the external gear, the split pinions must be turned so the teeth of the large gears pass 1½ teeth of the small gears to bring the marked teeth into line. During this operation lock the transmission main shaft. Have the wide pinions engaged with the sun gear and the narrow ones with the ring gear. As the marked teeth line, push the assembly together.

HYDRA-MATIC TRANSMISSION

Mechanical Operation

FIRST SPEED

Both bands are applied and both planetary units are in their maximum reduction to provide maximum total reduction.

SECOND SPEED

The front band is released and the front clutch engaged so that the front unit is in direct drive and the only reduction is in the rear unit.

THIRD SPEED

The front band is reapplied, and the front clutch released, so that the front unit is again in reduction, but the rear band is released and the rear clutch applied so that the rear unit is in direct drive. Since the front planetary unit has less reduction than the rear unit, the car will move in third speed.

REVERSE

The front unit is in gear, the rear unit is idling (neither the band nor the clutch is engaged) and the reverse anchor is engaged. This causes a further reduction and change in direction of rotation of the output shaft.

NEUTRAL

All bands and clutches are released and the mechanism idles.

Throttle Control Linkage Adjustment—Hydra-Matic

Detach rear throttle rod, outer lever at transmission.

Adjust engine idle at 375 R.P.M. with transmission warm and selector lever in neutral.

Remove throttle valve link clevis at upper bell crank. Insert adjusting pin through holes in upper throttle valve bell crank. Adjust throttle valve link so clevis pin will enter clevis and bell crank lever while adjusting screw is seated against its stop. Tighten lock nut and assemble clevis to bell crank. Leave adjusting pin installed.

Insert another adjusting pin through holes in lower bell crank. If pin does not pass through holes freely, adjust front throttle valve rod assembly at upper end. Tighten lock nut and assemble trunnion to upper bell crank. Leave adjusting pins installed. Tighten clamp bolt in transmission throttle lever.

Locating pin in place in the upper bell crank

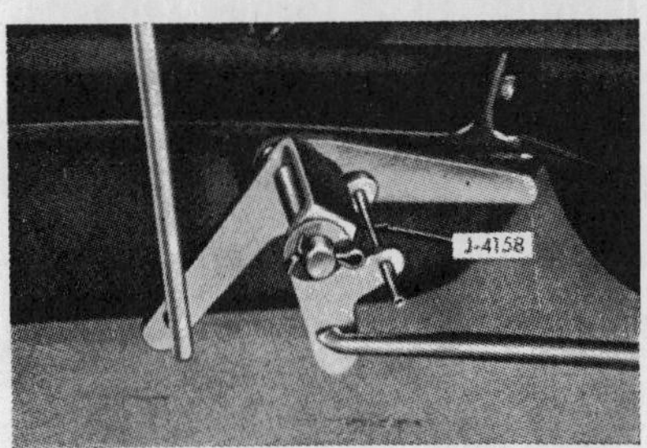

Locating pin in place in the lower bell crank

Check position of outer throttle lever as follows: Clean machined surface at back of transmission case and place throttle lever checking gage J-2545 flat against surface with edge of gage against case side cover. With outer lever held against the stop (toward rear) move gage upward toward a clevis pin installed in lever. When gage is moved upward, the notch in gage should pass over pin and the inside face of the throttle control lever (toward transmission) should just touch the outer side face of gage. If gage does not pass over pin freely, bend throttle lever using special bending tool J-3310.

Adjust rear transmission throttle rod trunnion to the transmission throttle lever. After the trunnion has been adjusted, so that it will pass freely into the transmission throttle lever opening, loosen front trunnion lock nut two complete turns and tighten rear lock nut.

Connect trunnion to throttle lever and remove adjusting pins.

Selector Lever Linkage Adjustment—Hydra-Matic

Place selector lever in L position; the operating lever must be against the low range stop on the neutral safety switch bracket. Remove clevis pin from control rod to shift lever at side of transmission case.

Move shift lever (at transmission) to L position.

Adjust control rod clevis so pin passes freely through hole in shift lever. After this adjustment has been made, lengthen control rod by turning clevis one full turn. Insert clevis pin and secure with a cotter pin.

Checking Hydra-Matic Fluid

To check fluid, raise floor mat on right side and remove sheet metal cover in floor pan. Run engine about 90 seconds at speed equivalent to 20 M.P.H., then reduce speed to slow idle. Remove fluid level plunger to check oil level.

Full to low marking on plunger equals 1 quart. Add necessary fluid with engine running at slow idle.

ADJUSTMENT OF OVERSHIFT STOPS—STANDARD TRANSMISSION

On 1940—all models this adjustment can be made by working through inspection hole in car floor.

The first, second, or reverse overshift stops can be adjusted from the outside, but the transmission case cover must

ADJUSTMENT OF STOPS—*continued*

be removed to adjust high speed position.

Loosen operating rod set screw, and shift second and high shift lever to rear and engage second speed. Back off second speed, overshift stop screw slightly, and determine that speed poppet is seated in notch. Tighten screw to permit a very slight overshift of lever to rear.

Proceed in same manner for adjusting first speed overshift stop, moving first and reverse shift lever forward to engage first speed.

Reverse overshift stop is an angle clip attached to transmission case cover and should be adjusted with minimum clearance between stop and lever with lever to rear in reverse position, being careful that speed finder poppet is seated. The flat side of clip must be parallel with side of lever and retaining screw down tight.

Install aligning pin through holes in lower steering post shift levers and notch of support bracket. Tighten operating rod set screw, being sure levers on transmission are in neutral and speed finder poppets seated.

Adjustment of Standard Gear Shift Mechanism

On 1941 through 1951, all series, set manual shift lever in neutral. Insert aligning pin in holes through levers and brackets. Disconnect transmission shift lever rods, and place transmission levers in neutral. Adjust the trunnion so clives enter the hole in transmission lever freely.

Removal and Disassembly of Torque Tube

Raise rear end of car and support frame on stand jacks approximately six inches in front of rear fenders. This is necessary because the deep crown of fenders covers so much of the rear wheels.

Disconnect the hand brake cable at adjusting yoke. Detach hydraulic brake line. Unfasten rear sway stabilizer. Take out transmission to torque tube studs, grommets and retainers.

Remove rear spring saddles and pull assembly back and out from car. Pry universal joint off shaft and unbolt torque tube from rear assembly. Unscrew propeller shaft to pinion coupling and pull assembly forward.

Reassembly of Torque Tube

Cars not equipped with overdrive have a longer propeller shaft. The torque tube center bearing is located by a screw which also serves to close the hole through which engine oil should be fed to the center bearing oil reservoir. This screw is normally wired in place. (Not on 1949 through 1951 models.)

The front end of torque tube has a coarse pitch thread on which the trunnion bracket operates. The trunnion bracket is slotted on the underside and is provided with an adjustable clamp screw with slotted nut and cotter pin so that the clamp screw can be adjusted to remove excess clearance between the trunnion bracket thread and the thread of the torque tube. This clamp screw should be drawn up sufficiently tight to remove excess clearance without setting up excessive friction as the trunnion bracket must be free to move on the threaded tube. The rear end of the trunnion bracket is provided with a rubber boot to protect the threaded tube against road dirt.

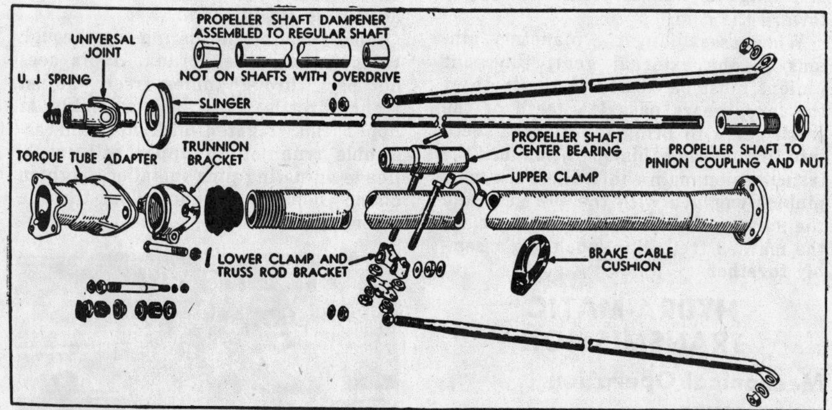

Propeller shaft and torque tube assembly. Series 40

Installation of Torque Tube

Before installing the rear axle and torque tube assembly, check the distance between the front face of the trunnion bracket and the rear of the flange on the back end of the torque tube.

On cars equipped with overdrive, this should be 63 7/16 inches, plus or minus 1/16 inch, and for standard transmission without overdrive 70 15/16 inches, plus or minus 1/16 inch.

In assembly, when the rear end of the propeller shaft is against the pinion shaft and the torque tube secured to the rear axle housing, the front end of the propeller shaft should project ⅛ to ¼ inch beyond the front face of the trunnion bracket.

A projection of less than ⅛ inch can cause contact between the universal joint slinger and bracket (will cause a scraping sound).

In assembling the torque tube to rear axle truss rods, both rods should be drawn up in a uniform manner at the bracket and locked securely in place so that the torque tube is in proper alignment with the rear axle.

Two special studs are used to attach the trunnion bracket to the transmission. These studs have a tapered section fitting into the trunnion bracket and are locked in place by a nut and lock nut. Rubber grommets with pilot ends are installed on the front and rear sides of the transmissions rear bearing cap.

Note that two of the stamped steel retainers have pilot flanges and the other two are plain.

The two retainers with pilot flanges are installed with rubber grommets having pilot ends on either side of the transmission bearing bracket. The plain retainers are placed on the other side of grommets.

The retaining nuts at the front end of the studs should be drawn down to a point where the grommets are held under a slight tension and locked in place with "pal" nuts. It is not necessary to disturb the nut and lock washer at the rear end of the studs.

REAR AXLE ASSEMBLY

Removal

ALL 1940 SERIES AND 1940 THRU 1948 AMBASSADOR SERIES

Raise rear end and place stand jacks under frame. Disconnect hydraulic brake line at rear housing. Unbolt rear universal joint and detach rear hand brake cable. Remove rear spring shackle and pull assembly back.

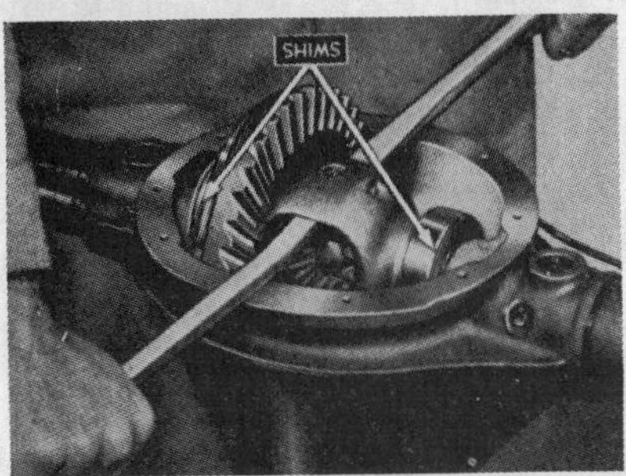

On 600 and Statesman series the differential is jolted out of the carrier

1941 THRU 1953—"600" AND STATESMAN AND 1949 THRU 1953—AMBASSADOR SERIES

Raise rear of car and support frame on stand jacks. Disconnect the hand brake cable at adjusting yoke.

Detach hydraulic brake line. Unfasten rear sway stabilizer. Take out transmission to torque tube studs, grommets and retainers.

Remove rear spring saddles and pull assembly back and out from car.

Pinion Bearing Removal

Remove the rear axle shafts from housing. Remove the differential carrier from car. Mark the differential bearing adjusting nuts so they may be returned to their original position. Back the nuts off. Mark the bearing caps so they can be replaced in their original position and remove them. Detach differential case. Unfasten the universal joint flange and pull it from the pinion gear shaft. Press pinion gear out of housing toward the rear. Be sure to collect the pinion gear adjusting washer and shims. Pull the oil seal and pinion bearings from the housing.

Adjustment

Pinion bearings are adjusted by adding or subtracting shims from the front of the bearing spacer so that the shaft operates under a .003 in. preload. To do this, assemble pinion in place without oil seal and fasten universal joint flange in place. With dial indicator mounted on the carrier measure the amount of end play. Use a small area to contact as face of pinion is not smooth. Remove shims to the amount of the end play plus .003 in.

Ring Gear and Pinion Adjustment

The pinion gear is adjusted by means of a spacing washer and shims between gear and the rear bearing. The side of the washer on which the hole is chamfered goes toward the pinion. The pinion gear is marked with the number of the ring and pinion gear set and with a plus or minus mark and a figure or 0. This last figure indicates the amount of metal lacking to have this pinion equal to a standard one in. thickness from face to back of the gear. If a new pinion is to be installed, compare its plus or minus figure with that of the old one. If the old one is marked 0 and the new one is marked minus 5 it will be necessary to add .005 in. in shims to the old washer. If the old one were marked plus 5 and the new one minus 5, it would be necessary to add .010 in. in shims. One .005 to bring the old washer back to standard, the other .005 to compensate for the new pinion deviation in thickness from standard. If it is available, the special micrometer tool can be used to determine the thickness of washer and shim required.

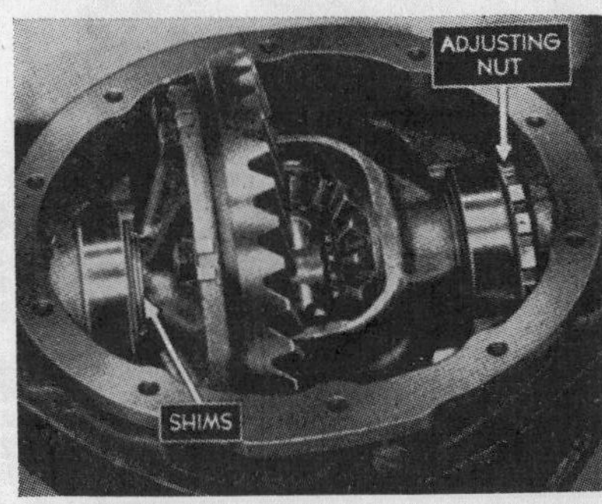

On Ambassador series an adjusting nut (lock ring) is used on the left side of the differential

When using this tool, deduct the micrometer reading from .400 in. This will give the necessary washer thickness for a standard (marked 0) pinion. Add or subtract from this figure the amount shown on the pinion to be installed, adding to make up for a minus figure, subtracting for one marked plus.

The back lash between ring gear and pinion on all Nash cars 1940 through 1951 is to be held to no more than .007 in. and no less than .005 in. The amount of back lash is best determined with dial indicator. The differential case bearings operate under a preload of .003 in. on each side or a total of .006 in. which is equivalent to two notches past normal tightness of the lock ring.

All Nash Ambassador differentials use shims between the left bearing and the case and adjust for preload with a lock ring on the right. On 600 & Statesman series shims are used on both sides of the differential. The original shimming should be used and the case tapped into place. The use of red lead or prussian blue will facilitate checking the mesh of the ring and pinion gear.

Axle Shaft Adjustment

Place a dial indicator on the axle shaft and housing to determine the amount of end play of the shaft by pushing in and pulling out the shaft. End play should not be over .006 in. nor less than .003 in. If an adjustment is necessary, remove the axle shaft bearing oil seal and the brake backing plate, add or remove shims to adjust end play.

Shims are located between the rear wheel brake support and the outer side of the axle housing flange. When making this adjustment, an equal thickness of shims should be removed or added on each side of the axle housing to maintain a central position of the axle shaft thrust block.

The hole in the thrust block is sufficiently larger than the diameter of the shaft to prevent axle shaft thrust from being thrown on the pinion shaft, providing the thrust block is held in its central position on the shaft.

On 600 and Statesman series the differential is driven back into the carrier with a soft hammer

OLDSMOBILE SPECIFICATIONS

Starting Serial and Motor Numbers

Starting Serial Numbers

1940, 6 cyl.—Ser. 60 515001
Ser. 70 16001
8 cyl.—Ser. 90 190501
1941, 6 cyl.—Ser. 66 66-1001
Ser. 76 76-1001
Ser. 96 96-1001
8 cyl.—Ser. 68 68-1001
Ser. 78 78-1001
Ser. 98 98-1001
1942, 6 cyl.—Ser. 66 66-9001
Ser. 76 76-7601
8 cyl.—Ser. 68 68-3001
Ser. 78 78-4001
Ser. 98 98-4001
1946-1948, 6 cyl.—Ser. 66 66-1001
Ser. 76 76-1001
8 cyl.—Ser. 78 78-1001
Ser. 98 98-1001
1949, 6 cyl.—Ser. 76 496-1001
8 cyl.—Ser. 88 498-1001
Ser. 98 499-1001
1950, 6 cyl.—Ser. 76 506-1001
Ser. 88 508-1001
Ser. 98 509-1001
1951, Ser. 88—119½″
wheelbase 517-1001
120″ wheelbase 518-1001
Ser. 98 519-1001
1952—Ser. 88 528-1001
Ser. 98 529-1001
1953—Ser. DeLuxe 88, 537M1001; Super 88, 538M1001; 98, 539M1001.

Location

1940—Plate on top of left front end of frame.
1941-1946—Upper left side of front of dash.
1947-1953—Left front body hinge pillar.

Starting Motor Numbers

1940—6 cyl. G-79001
8 cyl. L-334001
1941—6 cyl. G-225001
8 cyl. L-379001
1942—6 cyl. G-424001
8 cyl. L-450001
1946—6 cyl. 6-1001
8 cyl. 8-1001
1947—6 cyl. 6-83001
8 cyl. 8-37001
1948—6 cyl. 6-188021
8 cyl. ....9-001 and 8-127001
1949—6 cyl. 6A1001
8 cyl. 8A1001
1950—6 cyl. 6A97001
8 cyl. 8A194001
1951 ....8C1001
1952 ....R1001
1953 ....R215001

Location

1940-1953—On front of block above water pump and on plate on end of floor board inside right front door.

General Specifications

Year	Model	Wheelbase (in.)	Tread (in.)		Overall Dimensions (in.)			Shipping Weight* (lb.)	Tire Size (in.)
			Front	Rear	Length†	Width	Height■		
1941	Special-6	119	58	62	204	....	....	3230	6.00-16
	Dynamic-6	125	58	62	211	....	....	3390	6.50-16
	Custom-6	125	58	62	213	....	....	3410	7.00-15
	Special-8	119	58	62	204	....	....	3360	6.50-16
	Dynamic-6	125	58	62	211	....	....	3500	6.50-16
	Custom-8	125	58	62	213	....	....	3500	7.00-15
1942	66	119	58	62	204	....	....	3315	6.00-16
	76	212	58	62	212	....	....	3465	6.50-16
	68	119	58	62	204	....	....	3455	6 50-15
	78	125	58	62	212	....	....	3580	6.50 16
	98	127	58	62	216	....	....	....	7.00-15
1946	Six	125	58	62	213	76	65	3528	6.50-16
	Eight	125	58	62	213	76	65	3640	6.50-16
1947	Series 66	119	58	62	204	75	66	3356	6.00-16
	Dynamic Cruiser-6	125	58	62	213	76	65	3523	6.50-16
	Series 68	119	58	62	204	75	66	3486	6.50-15
	Dynamic Cruiser-8	125	58	62	213	76	65	3638	6.50-16
	Custom Cruiser 8-98	127	58	62	216	77	64	3793	7.00-15
1948	60-66	119	58	62	204	75	68	3332	6.00-16
	70-76	125	58	62	213	76	65	3508	6.50-16
	60-68	119	58	62	204	75	68	3440	6.50-15
	70-78	125	58	62	213	76	65	3619	6.50-16
	98	125	58	62	213	79	64	3730	7.00 15
1949	76	120	57	59	202	75	62	3324	7.10-15
	88	120	57	59	202	75	64	3615	7.60-15
	98	125	58	62	213	79	64	3892	7.60-15
1950	76	120	57	59	202	75	62	3320	7.10-15
	88	120	57	59	202	75	64	3515	7.60-15
	98	122	59	62	209	80	62	3765	7.60-15
1951	88	120	57	59	202	75	64	3531	7.60-15
	98	122	59	62	208	81	62	3872	7.60-15

†—Including bumpers and guards. ■—Road to roof, no load. *—Cheapest 5 passenger 4-door sedan.

General Specifications—*continued*

Year	Model	Wheelbase (in.)	Tread (in.) Front	Tread (in.) Rear	Overall Dimensions (in.) Length†	Width	Height■	Shipping Weight* (lb.)	Tire Size (in.)
1952	Super 88..........	120	58	59	203	76	63	....	7.60-15
	98..........	124	58	59	213	76	63	....	7.60-15
1953	88, Super 88..........	120	59	59	204	77	63	....	7.60-15
	98..........	124	59	59	215	77	63	....	7.60-15

General Engine Specifications

Year	Model	Number of Cylinders Bore and Stroke	Piston Displacement, Cubic Inches	Compression Ratio (To-1)	Taxable (A.M.A.) Hp.	Developed Horse Power: Bare Engine	Developed Horse Power: With Accessories	Maximum Torque Ft. Lbs.
1940	F40, 60, 6 Cyl..........	6-3 7/16 x 4 1/8	229.0	6.10	28.4	95 @ 3400	....	180 @ 1400
	G40, 70, 6 Cyl..........	6-3 7/16 x 4 1/8	229.7	6.10	28.4	95 @ 3400	....	180 @ 1400
	L41, 90, 8 Cyl..........	8-3 1/4 x 3 7/8	257.1	6.20	33.8	110 @ 3600	....	200 @ 2000
1941	F41, G41, H41, 6 Cyl..........	6-3 1/2 x 4 1/8	238.0	6.10	29.4	100 @ 3400	....	190 @ 1400
	E41, 68, 8 Cyl..........	8-3 1/4 x 3 7/8	257.0	6.30	33.8	110 @ 3600	....	200 @ 2000
	J & L41, 78 & 98, 8 Cyl..........	8-3 1/4 x 3 7/8	257.0	6.30	33.8	110 @ 3600	....	200 @ 2000
1942	F42, G42, 66, 76, 6 Cyl..........	6-3 1/2 x 4 1/8	238.1	6.50	29.4	100 @ 3400	....	190 @ 1400
	E42, J42, L42, 68, 78, 98, 8 Cyl..	8-3 1/4 x 3 7/8	257.1	6.50	33.8	110 @ 3600	....	200 @ 2000
1946	F66, G76, 6 Cyl..........	6-3 1/2 x 4 1/8	238.1	6.50	29.4	100 @ 3400	94 @ 3400	190 @ 1200
	J78, L98, 8 Cyl..........	8-3 1/4 x 3 7/8	257.1	6.50	33.8	110 @ 3600	104 @ 3600	210 @ 2000
1947	66 Special, 76, 6 Cyl..........	6-3 1/2 x 4 1/8	238.1	6.50	29.4	100 @ 3400	94 @ 3400	190 @ 1200
	68 78, 98, 8 Cyl..........	8-3 1/4 x 3 7/8	257.1	6.50	33.8	110 @ 3600	104 @ 3600	210 @ 2000
1948	66, 76, 6 Cyl..........	6-3 1/2 x 4 1/8	238.1	6.50	29.4	100 @ 3400	94 @ 3400	190 @ 1200
	68, 78, 8 Cyl..........	8-3 1/4 x 3 7/8	257.1	6.50	33.8	110 @ 3600	104 @ 3600	210 @ 2000
1949	76, 6 Cyl..........	6-3 17/32 x 4 3/8	257.1	6.50	29.9	105 @ 3400	99 @ 3400	202 @ 1400
	88, 8 Cyl..........	8-3 3/4 x 3 7/16	303.7	7.25	45.0	135 @ 3600	129 @ 3600	263 @ 1800
	98, 8 Cyl..........	8-3 3/4 x 3 7/16	303.7	7.25	45.0	135 @ 3600	129 @ 3600	263 @ 1800
1950	76, 6 Cyl..........	6-3 17/32 x 4 3/8	257.1	6.50	29.9	105 @ 3400	99 @ 3400	202 @ 1400
	88, 8 Cyl..........	8-3 3/4 x 3 7/16	303.7	7.25	45.0	135 @ 3600	129 @ 3600	263 @ 1800
	98, 8 Cyl..........	8-3 3/4 x 3 7/16	303.7	7.25	45.0	135 @ 3600	129 @ 3600	263 @ 1800
1951	88, 8 Cyl..........	8-3 3/4 x 3 7/16	303.7	7.50	45.0	135 @ 3600	129 @ 3600	263 @ 1800
	98, 8 Cyl..........	8-3 3/4 x 3 7/16	303.7	7.50	45.0	135 @ 3600	129 @ 3600	263 @ 1800
1952	Deluxe 88, 8 Cyl..........	V8-3 3/4 x 3 7/16	303.7	7.50	45.00	145 @ 3600	....	280 @ 1800
	Super 88, 98, 8 Cyl..........	V8-3 3/4 x 3 7/16	303.7	7.50	45.00	160 @ 3600	....	283 @ 1800
1953	Deluxe 88..........	V8-3 3/4 x 3 7/16	303.73	8.0	45.00	150 @ 3600	....	280 @ 1800
	Super 88, 98..........	V8-3 3/4 x 3 7/16	303.73	8.0	45.00	165 @ 3600	....	284 @ 1800

Dimensions of Valves

Year	Model	Overall Length Inlet	Overall Length Exhaust	Head Diameter Inlet	Head Diameter Exhaust	Seat Angle (deg.) Inlet	Seat Angle (deg.) Exhaust	Stem Diameter Inlet	Stem Diameter Exhaust	Key Type	O.D. of Seat Insert Inlet	O.D. of Seat Insert Exhaust
1940 to 48	Series—All..........	5.796	5.796	1.562	1.421	30	45	.343	.343	split lock	....	....
1949	76..........	5.789	5.796	1.750	1.421	30	45	.342	.341	split lock	....	....
	88, 98..........	4.855	4.843	1.750	1.469	45	45	.342	.393	split lock	....	....
1950-51	76..........	5.789	5.816	1.750	1.422	30	45	.342	.341	split lock	....	....
	88, 98..........	4.917	4.941	1.750	1.438	45	45	.342	.393	split lock	....	....
1952	De L. 88, Sup. 88, 98, 8 cyl.....	4.917	4.941	1.75	1.4375	45	45	.3421	.3934	....	....	....
1953	De L. 88, Sup. 88, 98, 8 cyl.....	4.917	4.941	1.75	1.4375	45	45	.3421	.3934	....	....	....

Engine Overhaul Specifications

Year	Model	PISTONS				RING CAP CLEARANCES (Maximum)				PISTON PIN		ROD BEARINGS		
		Removed From	Piston Skirt Clearances (Maximum)											
			Top	Bottom	Limit	Top Ring	Second Ring	Third Ring	Oil Ring	Type	Fit	Oil Clearance	Wear Limit	Side Play
1940	F40, 60, 6 Cyl.	A	....	.0018	.004	.018	.018	.015	.015	LP	Press	.0005–.0025	.004	.0055–.0105
	G40, 70, 6 Cyl.	A	....	.0018	.004	.018	.018	.015	.015	LP	Press	.0005–.0025	.004	.0055–.0105
	L40, 90, 8 Cyl.	A	....	.0018	.004	.014	.014	.014	.014	LP	Press	.0005–.0025	.004	.0055–.0105
1941	F41, G41, H41, 6 Cyl.	A	....	.001	.004	.013	.013	.014	.014	LP	Press	.0005–.0025	.004	.0055–.0105
	E41, 68, 8 Cyl.	A	.00125	.00175	.004	.014	.014	.014	.014	LP	Press	.0005–.0025	.004	.0055–.0105
	J & L41, 78 & 98, 8 Cyl.	A	.00125	.00175	.004	.014	.014	.014	.014	LP	Press	.0005–.0025	.004	.0055–.0105
1942	F42, G42, 66, 76, 6 Cyl.	A	.00125	.00175	.004	.018	.018	.015	.015	LP	Press	.0005–.0025	.004	.0055–.0105
	E42, J42, L42, 68, 78, 98, 8 Cyl.	A	.00125	.00175	.004	.014	.014	.014	.014	LP	Press	.0005–.0025	.004	.0055–.0105
1946	F66, G76, 6 Cyl.	A	.0025	.00075	.004	.018	.018	.015	.015	LP	Press	.0005–.0025	.004	.0055–.0105
	J78, L98, 8 Cyl.	A	.00205	.00155	.004	.014	.014	.014	.014	LP	Press	.0005–.0025	.004	.0055–.0105
1947	66, Special, 76. 6 Cyl.	A	.0025	.00075	.004	.018	.018	.015	.015	LP	Press	.0005–.0025	.004	.0055–.0105
	68, 78. 98, 8 Cyl.	A	.00205	.00155	.004	.014	.014	.014	.014	LP	Press	.0005–.0025	.004	.0055–.0105
1948	66 & 76, 6 Cyl.	A	.0025	.00075	.004	.018	.018	.015	.015	LP	Press	.0005–.0025	.004	.0055–.0105
	68 & 78, 8 Cyl.	A	.00205	.00155	.004	.014	.014	.014	.014	LP	Press	.0005–.0025	.004	.0055–.0105
1949	76, 6 Cyl.	A	.0025	.00075	.004	.017	.015	.015	.015	LP	Press	.0005–.0025	.004	.0055–.0105
	88, 8 Cyl.	A	.0015	.0010	.004	.016	.016	....	.016	LP	Press	.0009–.0029	.004	.002–.011
	98, 8 Cyl.	A	.0015	.0010	.004	.016	.016	....	.016	LP	Press	.0009–.0029	.004	.002–.011
1950	76, 6 Cyl.	A	.003	.0010	.004	.018	.018	.015	.015	LP	Press	.00075–.0015	.004	.0055–.0105
	88, 8 Cyl.	A	.0015	.0010	.004	.020	.020	....	.016	LP	Press	.0009–.0029	.004	.002–.011
	98, 8 Cyl.	A	.0015	.0010	.004	.020	.020	....	.016	LP	Press	.0009–.0029	.004	.002–.011
1951	88, 8 Cyl.	A	.0015	.0010	.004	.020	.020	....	.020	LP	Press	.0009–.0029	.004	.002–.011
	98, 8 Cyl.	A	.0015	.0010	.004	.020	.020	....	.020	LP	Press	.0009–.0029	.004	.002–.011
1952	De L. 88, Sup. 88, 98, 8 Cyl.	A	.0015	.001	.004	.020	.020	....	.1865	FL	.0002	.0009–.0029	.004	.002–.011
1953	De L. 88, Sup. 88, 98, 8 Cyl.	A	.0015	.001	.004	.020	.020	....	.1865	FL	.0002	.0009–.0029	.004	.002–.011

A—Above. LP—Locked in piston. SP—Sprocket. †—Marks on cam and crank sprockets align with shaft centers. B—Before top center.
FL—Floating.

Crankshaft Bearing Journal Sizes

Year	Model	Connecting Rod Journals		Main Bearing Journals				
		Diameter	Length	No. 1 Diameter	No. 2 Diameter	No. 3 Diameter	No. 4 Diameter	No. 5 Diameter
1940 to 48	All 6 cyl.	2.123–2.124	1.375	2.4775–2.4785	2.5400–2.5410	2.6650–2.6660	2.6850–2.6860	....
	All 8 cyl.	2.123–2.124	1.375	2.4775–2.4785	2.5400–2.5410	2.6025–2.6035	2.6650–2.6660	2.6850–2.6860
1949 to 51	76	2.353–2.354	1.12675	2.478–2.479	2.5405 2.5415	2.6655–2.6665	2.6855–2.6865	....
	88, 98	2.2488–2.2498	2.000	2.498–2.499	2.498–2.499	2.498–2.499	2.498–2.499	2.623–2.624
1952	DeL. 88, Super 88, 98, 8 cyl.	2.2488–2.2498	2.000	2.498–2.499	2.498–2.499	2.498–2.499	2.498–2.499	2.623–2.624
1953	DeL. 88, Super 88, 98, 8 cyl.	2.250	....	2.5–1.09375	2.5–1.125	2.5–1.125	2.5–1.125	2.625–1.880

and Wear Limit Table

CRANKSHAFT		VALVES										OPERATING OIL PRESSURE			
Main Bearing Oil Clearance	Shaft End Play	Spring Tension (Maximum) Inlet	Spring Tension (Maximum) Exhaust	Low Limit	Guide Clearance	Seat Angle Inlet	Seat Angle Exhaust	Valve Timing, Inlet Valve Opens (Deg.)	Camshaft Drive	Gear Marks	Pounds At M.P.H.	Low Limit§	Model	Year
.0005-.003	.004-.008	95.5@1 15/16	95.5@1 15/16	90	.0022-.0042	30°	45°	5B	Chain	SP†	30@30	15	F40, 60, 6 Cyl.	1940
.0005-.003	.004-.008	95.5@1 15/16	95.5@1 15/16	90	.0024-.0042	30°	45°	5B	Chain	SP†	30@30	15	G40, 70, 6 Cyl.	
.001-.003	.004-.008	95@1 31/32	95@1 31/32	90	0024-.0042	30°	45°	2T	Chain	SP†	....	15	L40, 90, 8 Cyl.	
.0005-.003	.004-.008	95.5@1 15/16	95.5@1 15/16	90	.0024-.0042	30°	45°	5B	Chain	SP†	33@30	15	F41, G41, H41, 6 Cyl.	1941
.001-.003	.004-.008	95.5@1 15/16	95.5@1 15/16	90	.0024-.0042	30°	45°	TC	Chain	SP†	30@30	15	E41, 68, 8 Cyl.	
.001-.003	.004-.008	95.5@1 15/16	95.5@1 15/16	90	.0024-.0042	30°	45°	TC	Chain	SP†	30@30	15	J & L41, 78 & 98, 8 Cyl.	
.001-.003	.004-.008	95.5@1 15/16	95.5@1 15/16	90	.0024-.0042	30°	45°	5B	Chain	SP†	30@30	15	F42, E42, 66, 76, 6 Cyl.	1942
.001-.003	.004-.008	95.5@1 15/16	95.5@1 15/16	90	.0024-.0042	30°	45°	TC	Chain	SP†	30@30	15	E42, J42, L42, 68,78,98,8 Cyl.	
.001-.003	.004-.008	100@1 15/16	100@1 15/16	90	.0024-.0042	30°	45°	TC	Chain	SP†	30@30	15	F66 G76, 6 Cyl.	1946
.001-.003	.004-.008	100@1 15/16	100@1 15/16	90	.0024-.0042	30°	45°	TC	Chain	SP†	30@30	15	J78, L98, 8 Cyl.	
.001-.003	.004-.008	100@1 15/16	100@1 15/16	90	.0024-.0042	30°	45°	5B	Chain	SP†	30@30	15	66, Special, 76, 6 Cyl.	1947
.001-.003	.004-.008	100@1 15/16	100@1 15/16	90	.0024-.0042	30°	45°	TC	Chain	SP†	30@30	15	68, 78, 98, 8 Cyl.	
.001-.003	.004-.008	100@1 15/16	100@1 15/16	90	.0024-.0042	30°	45°	5B	Chain	SP†	30@30	15	66 & 76, 6 Cyl.	1948
.001-.003	.004-.008	100@1 15/16	100@1 15/16	90	.0024-.0042	30°	45°	TC	Chain	SP†	30@30	15	68 & 78, 8 Cyl.	
.001-.003	.004-.008	100@1 15/16	100 @1 15/16	90	.0024-.0042	30°	45°	5B	Chain	SP†	40@30	15	76, 6 Cyl.	1949
.0005-.003	.004-.008	140@1.447	140 @1.447	125	.0024-.0042	45°	45°	14B	Chain	SP†	40@30	15	88, 8 Cyl.	
.0005-.003	.008-.008	140@1.447	140 @1.447	125	.0022-.0042	45°	45°	14B	Chain	SP†	40@30	15	98, 8 Cyl.	
.0005-.003	.004-.008	100@1 15/16	100@1 15/16	90	.0029-.0047	30°	45°	4B	Chain	SP†	40@30	15	76, 6 Cyl.	1950
.0005-.003	.004-.008	141@1.447	141@1.447	125	.0027-.0045	45°	45°	14B	Chain	SP†	40@30	15	88. 8 Cyl.	
.0005-.003	.004-.008	140@1.447	140@1.447	125	.0027-.0045	45°	45°	14B	Chain	SP†	40@30	15	98, 8 Cyl.	
0005-.003	.004-.008	141@1.447	141@1.447	125	.0027-.0045	45°	45°	13½B	Chain	SP†	40@50	15	88, 8 Cyl.	1951
0005-.003	.004-.008	141@1.447	141@1.447	125	.0027-.0045	45°	45°	13½B	Chain	SP†	40@50	15	98, 8 Cyl.	
.0005-.003	.004-.008	156@1.463	156@1.463	......	.0027-.0045	45°	45°	13½B	Chain	......	45@50	35	DeL. 88, Sup. 88, 98, 8 Cyl.	1952
.0005-.003	.004-.008	156@1.463	156@1.463	......	.0027-.004	45°	45°	13½B	Chain	......	45@50	35	DeL. 88, Sup. 88, 98, 8 Cyl.	1953

TC—At top center. §—Car may be operated safely at lower oil pressures but low pressure indicates malfunction which should be corrected.

Pistons and Piston Pins

Year	Model	PISTONS Diameter	Material	Type	No. of Rings	PISTON PINS Length	Diameter	How Held
1940	60, 70	3.4375	Alum.	Ts, C	4	3 5/32	.859375	P
	Custom	3.25	Alum.	Ts, C	4	2 21/32	.859375	P
1941 to 48	Series—All, 6 cyl.	3.5	Alum.	Ts	4	3 5/32	.859375	P
	Series—All, 8 cyl.	3.25	Alum.	Ts	4	2 21/32	.859375	P
1949 to 51	76	3.53125	Alum.	Ts, C	4	3 5/32	.8550	P
	88, 98	3.75	Alum.	C	3	3.011	.9805	F
1952	DeLuxe 88, Super 88, 98, 8 cyl.	3.75	Alum. Alloy	C	3	3.016	.9805	F
1953	DeLuxe 88, Super 88, 98, 8 cyl.	3.75	Alum. Alloy	C	3	3.016	.9805	R

Alum—Aluminum.

Engine Tune-Up Specifications

Year	Model	SPARK PLUGS Type	Gap	DISTRIBUTOR Point Gap	Cam Dwell, (Deg.)	Ignition Timing, (Deg.)	Ignition Timing Mark and Location	Compression Pressure at R.P.M.	OPERATING TAPPET CLEARANCE Inlet	Exhaust	Carburetor Fuel Float Height	Minimum Engine Idle Speed at R.P.M.
1940	F40, 60, 6 Cyl.	AC-45	.040	.020	31	TC	Flywheel	146@1000	.008	.011	3/8"	....
	G40, 70, 6 Cyl.	AC-45	.040	.020	35	TC	Flywheel	146@1000	.008	.011	3/8"	....
	L40, 90, 8 Cyl.	AC-45	.030	.015	35	2B	Flywheel	152@1000	.008	.011	3/8"	....

OLDSMOBILE SPECIFICATIONS

Engine Tune-Up Specifications—*continued*

Year	Model	Spark Plugs Type	Spark Plugs Gap	Distributor Point Gap	Distributor Cam Dwell (Deg.)	Ignition Timing (Deg.)	Ignition Timing Mark and Location	Compression Pressure at R.P.M.	Operating Tappet Clearance Inlet	Operating Tappet Clearance Exhaust	Carburetor Fuel Float Height	Minimum Engine Idle Speed at R.P.M.
1941	F41, G41, H41, 6 Cyl.	AC-44	.040	.020	35	TC	Flywheel	115@ †	.006	.011	1/2"	425*
	E41, 68, 8 Cyl.	AC-44	.030	.015	31	2B	Flywheel	107@ †	.008	.011	3/16"	425*
	J & L41, 78, 98, 8 Cyl.	AC-44	.030	.015	31	2B	Flywheel	107@ †	.008	.011	3/16"	425*
1942	F42, G42, 66, 76, 6 Cyl.	AC-44	.040	.020	35	TC	Flywheel	115@ †	.008	.011	1/2"	425*
	E42, J42, L42, 68, 78, 98, 8 Cyl.	AC-44	.030	.015	31	2B	Flywheel	107@ †	.008	.011	3/16"	425*
1946	F66, G76, 6 Cyl.	AC-48	.040	.020	35	TC	Flywheel	115@ †	.008	.011	1/2"	425*
	J78, L98, 8 Cyl.	AC-48	.030	.015	31	2B	Flywheel	107@ †	.008	.011	15/64"	425*
1947	66, Special, 76, 6 Cyl.	AC-48	.040	.020	35	TC	Flywheel	112@ †	.008	.011	1/2"	425*
	68, 78, 98, 8 Cyl.	AC-48	.030	.015	31	2B	Flywheel	115@ †	.008	.011	3/16"	425*
1948	66, 76, 6 Cyl.	AC-45	.040	.020	35	TC	Flywheel	159@1000	.008	.011	1/2"	425*
	68, 78, 8 Cyl.	AC-45	.030	.015	31	2B	Flywheel	165@1000	.008	.011	3/16"	425*
1949	76, 6 Cyl.	AC-45	.040	.020	35	TC	Flywheel	160@1000	.008	.011	1/2"	425*
	88, 8 Cyl.	AC-44	.030	.0145	15	2.5B	Cr. Pl.	183@1000	AA	AA	23/32"	375
	98, 8 Cyl.	AC-44	.030	.0145	22	2.5B	Cr. Pl.	183@1000	AA	AA	23/32"	375
1950	76, 6 Cyl.	AC-45	.040	.021	35	TC	Flywheel	160@1000	.008	.011	1/2"	425*
	88, 8 Cyl.	AC-45	.030	.0145	15	2.5B	Cr. Pl.	183@1000	AA	AA	23/32"	375
	98, 8 Cyl.	AC-45	.030	.0145	22	2.5B	Cr. Pl.	183@1000	AA	AA	23/32"	375
1951	88, 8 Cyl.	AC-46.5	.030	.016	26-33	2.5B	Cr. Pl.	185@1000	AA	AA	....	....
	98, 8 Cyl.	AC-46.5	.030	.016	26-33	2.5B	Cr. Pl.	185@1000	AA	AA	....	....
1952	DeL. 88, Sup. 88, 98, 8 Cyl.	AC-46-5	.030	.016	33	2½B	Cr. Pl.	....	AA	AA	5/16"	425*
1953	De L. 88, Sup. 88, 98	AC-46-5	.030	.016	33	2½B	Cr. Pl.	....	AA	AA	....	425

AA—Valves automatic adjustment.
Cr. Pl.—Crankshaft pulley.
AC—AC Spark Plug Div.

*—Minimum idle speed on syncro-mesh transmission (on hydra-matic 375 m.p.h. max.) in drive position.
†—Cranking speed.
TC—Top center.
B—Before top center.

Piston Ring Dimensions

Year	Model	Cylinder Bore	Top Ring Width	Top Ring Gap	Top Ring Depth	Second Ring Width	Second Ring Gap	Second Ring Depth	Third Ring Width	Third Ring Gap	Third Ring Depth	Oil Ring Width	Oil Ring Gap	Oil Ring Depth
1940	60, 70	3 7/16	3/32	.013	.160	3/32	.013	.160	3/16	.011	.150	3/16	.011	.150
	Custom 8	3 1/4	3/32	.011	.150	3/32	.011	.150	3/16	.011	.150	3/16	.011	.150
1941–48	All—6 cylinders	3 1/2	3/32	.013	.172	3/32	.013	.172	3/16	.012	.155	3/16	.012	.155
	All—8 cylinders	3 1/4	3/32	.012	.150	3/32	.012	.150	3/16	.012	.145	3/16	.012	.145
1949–51	76	3 17/32	3/32	.012	.175	3/32	.012	.175	3/16	.011	.157	3/16	.011	.157
	88, 98	3 3/4	5/64	.012	.187	5/64	.012	.187	3/16	.012	.163	....	....	....
1952	DeL. 88, Sup. 88, 98, 8 Cyl.	3 3/4	.0775	.014	.200	.0775	.014	.200	.18625	.014	.193	....	....	....
1953	DeL. 88, Sup. 88, 98, 8 Cyl.	3 3/4	.0775	.012	.187	.0775	.012	.187	.18625	.012	.155	....	....	....

Brake Data

Year	Model	Make	Lining Type	R=Riveted B=Bonded	Drum Diameter	Lining Length	Lining Width	Lining Thickness	Clearance Toe	Clearance Heel
1940	60, 70	....	M	R	11	21 5/16	1 3/4	3/16	.010	.010
	80, 90	....	WM	R	11	21 5/16	2	3/16	.010	.010

Brake Data—*continued*

Year	Model	Make	Lining Type	R=Riveted B=Bonded	Drum Diameter	Lining			Clearance	
						Length	Width	Thickness	Toe	Heel
1941-42	Spec. 6	Var	M	R	10	21 5/16	1 3/4	3/16	.015	.015
	Dyn. & Cus. 6	Var	M	R	11	21 5/16	2	3/16	.015	.015
	Spec. 8	Var	M	R	11	21 5/16	1 3/4	3/16	.015	.015
	Dyn. 8	Var	M	R	11	21 5/16	2	3/16	.015	.015
1946-47	Six	Var	M	R	11	21 5/16	2-*1 3/4	3/16	.015	.015
	Eight	Var	M	R	11	21 5/16	2 1/4-*2	3/16	.015	.015
1948	60-66, 70-76	Var	M	R	11	21 5/16	2-*1 3/4	3/16	.015	.015
	60-68	Var	M	R	11	21 5/16	2-*1 3/4	3/16	.015	.015
	70-78	Var	M	R	11	21 5/16	2 1/4-*2	3/16	.015	.015
1949 to 50	76	Var	M	R	11	21 5/16‡	2-*1 3/4	.226	.015	.015
	88, 98	Var	M	R	11	21 5/16	2 1/2-*2	.226	.015	.015
1951	88	Var	M	R	11	21 5/16	2 1/2-*2	3/16	.015	.015
	98	Ben	M	R	11	21 5/16	2 1/2-*2	3/16	.015	.015
1952	DeLuxe 88, Super 88, 98, 8 Cyl.	Ben	M	R	11	21 13/32	2 1/2-*2	3/16	.015	.015
1953	DeLuxe 88, Super 88, 98, 8 Cyl.	Ben	M	R	11	21 13/32	2 1/2-*2	3/16	.015	.015

*—Rear. ‡—Rear, 24 in. Var—Various. Ben—Bendix. M—Moulded.

Tension Wrench Specifications

Year	Model	Cylinder Head		Spark Plug		Connecting Rod Bolts or Nuts		Main Bearing Bolt		Flywheel Bolts		Vibration Damper Bolts	
		Lbs.-Ft.	Thread	Lbs.-Ft.	Thread	Lbs.-Ft.	Thread	Lbs.-Ft.	Thread	Lbs.-Ft.	Thread	Lbs.-Ft.	Thread
1940 to 42	Series—All 6 & 8 cyl.	60-70	7/16	28-35	14 mm	50-55	3/8	*100-140†	*1/2-9/16†	55-60	7/16	....	....
1946 to 48	Series—All 6 & 8 cyl.	60-70	7/16	28-35	14 mm	50-55	3/8	*100-140†	*1/2-9/16†	55-60	7/16	....	....
1949	Series—All 6 & 8 cyl.	60-70	7/16	28-35	14 mm	45-50	....	*100-140†	*1/2-9/16†	55-60	7/16	....	....
1950-53	Series—All 6 & 8 cyl.	60-70	7/16	28-35	14 mm	45-50	....	*100-140†	*1/2-9/16†	55-60	7/16	....	....

*—Numbers 1, 2, 3, 4 †—Numbers 4, 5.

Cooling System

CAR AND YEAR	MODEL	Capacity Qts.	Quarts of Methanol Base Anti-Freeze (For Protection to Temperature Shown Below)							Quarts of Ethylene Glycol (For Protection to Temperature Shown Below)							Quarts of Denatured Alcohol—188 Proof (For Protection to Temperature Shown Below)						
			3	4	5	6	7	8	9	3	4	5	6	7	8	9	3	4	5	6	7	8	9
1937	6	16	13	3	−8	−21	−36	−53	...	17	10	2	−8	−19	−34	−52	..	10	0	−10	...	−20	−30
1937	8	20	18	11	4	−5	−16	−27	−39	...	16	10	4	−3	−12	−22	20	...	10	...	0	−10	−20
1938-39	6	17	15	6	−4	−16	−29	−45	..	18	12	5	−4	−14	−27	−42	..	10	0	....	−10	−20	−30
1938	8	21	19	12	5	−3	−12	−22	−34	..	17	12	6	0	−9	−17	20	....	10	...	0	−10	....
1939	8	24	21	16	10	4	−4	−12	−21	....	19	15	10	5	0	−8	20	...	10	...	...	0	−10
1940	6	17 3/4	17	8	−1	−12	−25	−38	−53	19	14	7	0	−10	−21	−34	20	10	...	0	−10	....	−20
1940	8	21	19	12	5	−3	−12	−22	−34	....	17	12	6	0	−9	−17	20	...	10	...	0	−10	...
1941	6	18	17	8	−1	−12	−25	−38	−53	19	14	7	0	−10	−21	−34	20	10	...	0	−10	....	−20
1941	8	22	20	14	7	0	−9	−18	−29	....	18	13	8	2	−8	−14	20	...	10	....	0	....	−10
1942-50	6	18 1/2	17	9	2	−8	−21	−32	−46	20	15	9	2	−7	−16	−28	20	10	...	0	−10	....	−20
1942-53	8	21 1/2	19	12	5	−3	−12	−22	−34	....	17	12	6	0	−9	−17	20	....	10	....	0	−10	...

OLDSMOBILE SPECIFICATIONS

Distributors

Year	Model	Distributor Model Number	Cam Angle (deg.)	Direction of Rotation C=Clockwise CC=Counter Clockwise at Cam End	Breaker Arm Spring Tension	Breaker Point Gap (inches)	Engine R.P.M. hen Cent. Advance Starts	Max. Cent. Advance in Engine Deg. at Stated Engine R.P.M.	Vacuum in (inches) of Mercury at which Vacuum Unit Starts	Max. Advance in Engine Deg. at Stated Vacuum	Vacuum Unit Number
1940–41	6 cyl.	647-F	35	CC	17–21	.018–.024	500	28@3800	5 to 7	20@15 to 18	681P
	8 cyl.	1110802	31	CC	19–23	.0125–.0175	600	30@4000	5 to 7	15@14 to 17	681R
1942	6 cyl.	1110213	35	CC	19–23	.018–.024	500	24@3200	7.5 to 9.5	12@14 to 16	1116035
	8 cyl.	1110808	31	C	19–23	.0125–.0175	600	24@3200	6.8 to 8.5	12@14 to 16	1116030
1946 to 48	66, 76, 6 cyl.	1110214	35	CC	17–21	.018–.024	500	26@2600	7.5 to 9.5	12@14 to 16	1116039
	78, 98, 8 cyl.	1110808	31	C	19–23	.0125–.0175	600	24@3200	6.8 to 8.5	24@14 to 16	1116030
1949–50	76, 6 cyl.	1110221	35	CC	17–21	.018–.024	500	24@3200	5 to 7	12@16 to 20	1116053
	88, 98, 8 cyl.	1110817	22	CC	19–23	.012–.0175	600	32@4000	6.5 to 8.5	20@19 to 21	1116048
1951	88, 98, 8 cyl.	1110824	29½	CC	19–23	.012–.0175	600	30@3700	5.5	20@19 to 21	...
1952	DeL. 88, Sup. 88, 98, 8 cyl.	1110824	26–33	CC	19–23	.016	650	30@3000	4½–6½	20@19–21	...
1953	DeL. 88, Sup. 88, 98, 8 cyl.	1110824	26–33	C	19–23	.016	650	30@3000	4½–6½	20@19–21	...

Generators

Year	Model	Generator Number	Field Current at 6 Volts (amps.)	Maximum Safe Output			Brush Spring Tension (oz.)	Voltage Regulator Number
				Volts	Amperes	R.P.M.		
1940	6 & 8 cyl.	1102664	1.75–1.9	8.0	30	1750	25	1118201
1941 to 48	6 & 8 cyl.	1102664	1.75–1.9	8.0	30	1750	25	1118201
	Hydramatic	1102680	1.75–1.9	8.0	30	1750	25	1118242
1949 to 51	76-Synchromesh	1102706	1.90–2.05	8.0	40	1900	25	1118300
	Hydramatic	1102707	1.90–2.05	8.0	40	1900	25	1118300
	88 & 98	1102704	1.90–2.05	8.0	40	1900	25	1118300
1952	DeLuxe 88, Super 88, 98, 8 cyl.	1102780	...	...	...	...	...	1118725
1953	DeLuxe 88, Super 88, 98, 8 cyl.	1102003	...	13.6	30	2400	...	1118750

Voltage Regulators

Year	Model	Regulator Number	Grounded P=Positive N=Negative	Voltage Control		Current Control		Cut-Out Relay		
				Air Gap Points Closed	Voltage Setting Hot	Air Gap Points Closed	Current Set Hot	Point Gap	Air Gap	Closing Volt
1940	6 & 8 cyl.	1118201	N	.070	7.0	.082	32–40	.020	.020	5.9–6.8
1941–42	6 & 8 cyl.	1118201	N	.070	7.0	.082	32–40	.020	.020	5.9–6.8
	Hydramatic	1118242	N	.070	7.0	.082	32–40	.020	.020	5.9–6.8
1946 to 48	6 & 8 cyl.	1118242	N	.070	7.0	.082	32–40	.020	.020	5.9–6.8
1949 to 51	6 & 8 cyl.	1118300	N	.075	7.0	.075	40–46	.020	.020	5.9–6.8
1952	De Luxe 88, Super 88, 98, 8 cyl.	1118725	...	...	7.2–7.4	...	45	...	...	6.2–6.7
1953	De Luxe 88, Super 88, 98, 8 cyl.	1118750	...	...	14.2–14.8	...	27–33	...	...	11.8–13.6

Starters

Year	Model	Unit Model Number	Spring Tension (oz.)	STARTER: Lock Test Volts	Lock Test Amperes	Lock Test Torque, (lbs. ft.)	No Load Volts	No Load Amperes	No Load R.P.M.	Direction of Rotation Viewed from Drive End C=Clockwise CC=Counter-clockwise
1940	6 cyl., Standard	1107007	24–28	3.37	525	12	5.0	65	5000	C
	Hydramatic	1107034	24–28	3.37	525	12	5.0	65	5000	C
	8 cyl., Standard	1107907	24–28	3.0	600	15	5.0	60	6000	C
	Hydramatic	1107922	24–28	3.0	600	15	5.0	60	6000	C
1941	66, 76	1107034	24–28	3.37	525	12	5.0	65	5000	C
	68, 78, 98	1107922	24–28	3.0	600	15	5.0	60	6000	C
1942	66, 76	1107034	24–28	3.37	525	12	5.0	65	5000	C
	Optional	1107050	24–28	3.37	525	12	5.0	65	5000	C
	68, 78	11070922	24–28	3.0	600	15	5.0	60	6000	C
	98	1107930	24–28	3.0	600	15	5.0	65	5500	C
1946 to 48	66, 76, Manual Switch	1107034	24–28	3.37	525	12	5.0	65	5000	C
		1107066	24–28	3.37	525	12	5.0	65	5000	C
	Solenoid Switch	1107050	24–28	3.37	525	12	5.0	65	5000	C
	Hydramatic	1107930	24–28	3.0	600	15	5.0	65	5500	C
	78 Manual Switch	1107922	24–28	3.0	600	15	5.0	60	6000	C
		1107941	24–28	3.0	600	15	5.0	60	6000	C
	Hydramatic Solenoid Switch	1107930	24–28	3.0	600	15	5.0	65	5500	C
	98	1107930	24–28	3.0	600	15	5.0	65	5500	C
1949–50	76	1107955	24–28	3.0	600	14	5.7	80	5500	C
	88, 98	1107956	24–28	3.0	600	14	5.7	80	5500	C
1951	88, 98	1107982	24–28	3.0	600	15	5.7	80	5500	C
1952	De Luxe 88, Super 88, 98, 8 cyl.	1107997	24–28	3.0	600	15	5.7	80	5500	C
1953	De Luxe 88, Super 88, 98, 8 cyl.	1107603	24–28	5.2	460	11.5	10.3	75	6500	C

Front Wheel Alignment

Year	Model	Caster (deg.)	Camber (deg.)	King Pin Inclination (deg.)	Toe-In (inches)	Turning Radius Inner	Turning Radius Outer
1940	60, 70	0 to ¾N	¼N to ½P	4¾ to 5	1/16 to ⅛	18	20
	Custom 8	0 to ¾N	¼N to ½P	4¾ to 5	1/16 to ⅛	19	20
1941	Special 6, Special 8	0 to ¾N	¼N to ¾N	4¾ to 5	1/16 to ⅛	18½	20
	Dynamic and Custom 6 and 8 cyl.	0 to ¾N	¼N to ¾N	4¾ to 5	1/16 to ⅛	19½	20
1942–48	66, 68, 76, 78, 98	0 to ¾N	¼N to ¾N	4¾ to 5	1/16 to ⅛	23	20
1949–53	76, 88, 98	0 to ¾N	¼N to ¾N	4½	1/16 to ⅛	....	....

Fan, Generator Belts and Radiator Hose

Year	Model	Fan Belt: Angle of "V" (deg.)	Fan Belt: Length O.C.	Fan Belt: Width Max.	Generator Belt: Angle of "V" (deg.)	Generator Belt: Length O.C.	Generator Belt: Width Max.	Upper Hose: Type	Upper Hose: Inside Diam.	Upper Hose: Length	Lower Hose: Type	Lower Hose: Inside Diam.	Lower Hose: Length
1940 to 47	All 6 cyl.	34	47 13/16	25/32	......	......	......	straight	1½	8	curved	1¾	....
1948	66, 76, 68, 78	34	48¼	25/32	......	......	......	straight	1½	8½	curved	1¾	....
1949–50	All 6 cyl.	42	43¾	1	......	......	......	straight	1½	8½	curved	1¾	....
'49-50 Early	All 8 cyl.	42	39⅜	23/32	40	37⅛	13/32	straight	1½	12½	curved	1¾	....
Late	All 8 cyl., 1951, 88, 98	36	39⅛	⅜	40	37⅛	13/32	straight	1½	12½	curved	1¾	....
1952	DeL. 88, Sup. 88, 98, 8 c.	36	57¼	⅜	......	......	......	curved	1½	....	curved	1¾	11⅞
1953	DeL. 88, Sup. 88, 98, 8 c.	36	57 7/16	⅜	......	......	......	curved	1½	11 13/16	curved	1¾	14½

OLDSMOBILE 1940 thru 1953

FRONT SUSPENSION

The front suspension on all Oldsmobile models from 1940 through 1953 is virtually the same except for refinements and improvements.

Service procedure on all Oldsmobile front suspension is the same.

The front suspension upper arm is the shock absorber and a torsion bar is used to stabilize the front end.

Caster, Camber and Toe-In

Before correcting for any defects in the steering geometry on Oldsmobile (or on any other car), first check all the front suspension angles.

Caster and camber both are controlled at the eccentric pin at the outer end of the upper support arm. Because both caster and camber are controlled at the same pin the best reading obtainable will, of necessity, be a compromise between the exact specification and that which will be possible with a single pin controlling both angles.

The upper suspension arm eccentric pin has a left hand thread with two starts. To adjust camber, remove the lubrication fitting from the front bushing in the upper end of the knuckle support, loosen the knuckle support clamp bolt and insert an Allen wrench into the hole from which the lubrication fitting was removed. To increase caster, turn the screw in a clockwise direction until the correct caster reading is obtained and then from that starting point turn the eccentric to produce the desired camber reading. Since the upper pin is eccentric, the full range of camber correction possible with the eccentric is obtained in one-half turn. Therefore it should never be necessary to turn the eccentric pin more than one-half turn from the correct caster setting to achieve the correct camber setting.

Toe-in is adjusted at the adjustable sleeves in the outer end of both tie rods.

REPLACEMENT OF FRONT SUSPENSION PARTS

Upper and/or Lower Pins and Bushings

To replace either the upper or the lower pin and/or bushings in the knuckle support, take the weight of the car on the lower A frame and remove the front wheel. The lower pin can be taken out directly from the lower suspension arm.

To remove the upper pin, take out the clamp in the shock absorber arm

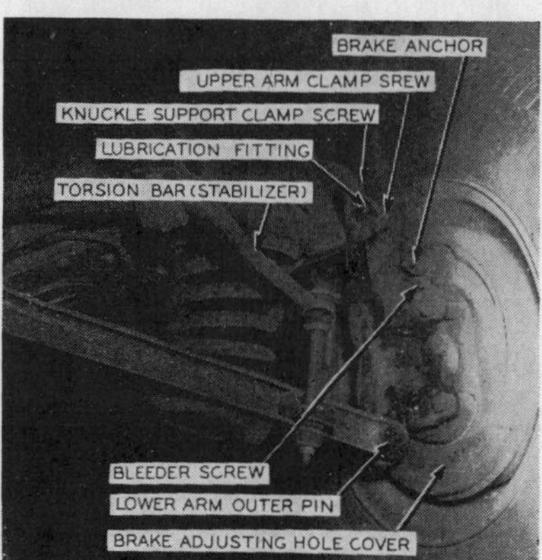

Front Suspension. 1953 Models

and remove the front bushing, then remove the rear bushing. Loosen the clamp which holds the eccentric pin to the top of the knuckle support and turn out the eccentric pin. Assemble the new upper suspension arm pin to the knuckle support so that when the thick portion of the pin is nicely centered in the knuckle support it will be at full camber (eccentric side facing out). If the pin is not at full camber when it is nicely centered, then back it out, turn it 180 degrees and start it on the opposite thread (this is a two-start thread). Assemble the new bushing to the lower end of the knuckle support and mount the knuckle support in the lower suspension arm so that when it is assembled it is centered between the yoke of the lower suspension arm. The upper end of the knuckle support should be centered between the yoke of the shock absorber.

Replacement of Front Coil Spring

Support the frame on jacks and place a roller jack under the inner shaft of the lower suspension arm and then disconnect the torsion bar. Take a good load on the roller jack and then loosen the bolts which hold the inner shaft of the lower suspension arm to the front cross member and then slowly lower the jack so that the spring pressure will force the suspension arm down. Lower the arm far enough to remove all tension from the spring and take out the spring. Install a new spring, being certain to replace all the shims which were used on the old spring and jack the inner shaft of the lower suspension arm back into place, guiding it to its bolt holes with long drift pins. Reconnect the torsion bar.

Replacement of Upper Suspension Arm (Shock Absorber)

Support the car on the lower A frame and remove the road wheel. Remove the upper suspension arm outer pin and bushings and unbolt the shock absorber. The shock absorber bolts are accessible both from the engine compartment and from underneath the car.

Replacement of Lower A Frame

To replace the lower A frame, proceed as shown under replacement of front coil spring and after the pressure has been taken off the spring remove the lower suspension arm outer pin.

Replacement of King Pins

Remove the wheel, brake drum and brake backing plate. Hang the backing plate on a stout wire attached to the frame in order to avoid damage to the brake flexible hose. (Not necessary to detach the hose.)

Drive out the king pin lock pin toward the rear and take out the king pin upper welsh plug. The king pin may now be driven down and out of the knuckle.

Bushings are used in the upper and lower end of the knuckle and require reaming or honing to insure good fit on the king pin.

MANUAL STEERING GEAR ASSEMBLY

An eccentric sleeve type steering gear is used on all Oldsmobile models from 1940 through 1951.

Removal of Horn Button

1949 THRU 1953 DE LUXE MODELS

The horn button is held in by a bayonet type connection. To remove, place the hand squarely on the horn button, press firmly and turn slightly in a counterclockwise direction which will permit removal of the horn button.

1949-1950 STANDARD MODELS

On these models the horn button is pried out.

MODELS UP TO 1948

On these models the plastic horn button is fastened to the horn ring with screws at the top edge. Removal of screws will permit removal of the horn button.

1941 ALL MODELS, AND 1942 STANDARD MODEL

On these models the horn button is

held in place by three dimples on the retaining cup. To remove the button, pry it out with a knife or screw driver.

Steering Wheel Removal

On all Oldsmobile models it is necessary to use a puller to take off the steering wheel.

Remove the horn button, take off the retaining nut and pull off the steering wheel.

Adjustment of Manual Steering Mechanism

1. Disconnect the pitman arm from the intermediate tie rod.

2. Adjust the steering gear housing mechanism.

(a) Loosen the jam nut at the bottom of the steering column and turn the adjusting screw until a two-pound pull is required to pull the steering wheel in either direction. Tighten the jam nut and recheck to make sure the bearings have not tightened, when the jam nut was being secured.

(b) Set the steering wheel in the mid position of its travel and loosen the clamp bolt on the eccentric housing and turn the eccentric housing until there is zero lash in the gears with the steering wheel in the mid position of its travel.

(c) Remove the end play from the sector shaft by loosening the jam nut and tightening the adjusting screw until there is zero end play in the cross shaft with the steering wheel in the mid position of its travel. Tighten all lock nuts.

3. Reconnect the pitman arm to the intermediate tie rod.

4. With the steering wheel held in the mid position of its travel, loosen the clamp nuts on the right side tie rod sleeve and adjust the sleeve so that one-half of the total toe-in is in the right front wheel. Tighten the clamp bolts.

5. Now still holding the steering wheel in the mid position of its travel, loosen the clamp bolts on the left side tie rod adjusting sleeve and turn the sleeve so that the balance of the toe-in is contained in the left front wheel. Tighten the clamp screws.

Turn the steering wheel through its complete travel to check for looseness or binding.

POWER BRAKES

See "Power Brake" Section.

Steering mechanism

BRAKES

All Oldsmobile models are equipped with two-shoe Bendix type hydraulic brakes.

An eccentric type anchor is used on all Oldsmobiles.

Brake Inspection

Before making any adjustment on Oldsmobile (or any other brakes), remove at least one brake drum to examine the condition of the wheel cylinder, brake lining, brake shoes and drum. Check the wheel cylinder boots for signs of leaking or seeping, and if any fluid is found on the boots, disassemble the wheel cylinder and hone the cylinder either on the car, if the pitts are not too bad, or remove the cylinder to a bench hone if the condition requires it. Examine the lining to be sure that it is wearing evenly all over the surface. If the lining is wearing evenly all over its surface it indicates that the anchor setting is approximately correct and need not be changed. Rough or scored brake drums should be machined and either new lining installed or the old lining removed and shims placed under the lining to compensate for the amount of metal taken out of the drum.

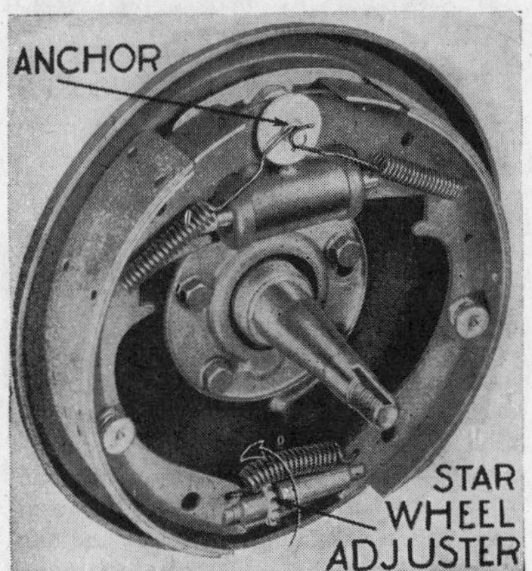

Brake adjusting points

Note: If one wheel is found to have a defective brake cylinder, it is considered good practice to remove all four wheels and examine all hydraulic cylinders. Many successful brake shops insist on overhauling all cylinders, including the master cylinder, when any one cylinder is found to be defective. This is done as a safety precaution.

Brake Pedal Clearance

Before adjusting the brakes, make certain there is ½" to 1" free pedal travel (measured at the toe-board). This adjustment is secured at the master cylinder push rod.

Minor Brake Adjustment

A minor brake adjustment is made to

Continued

BRAKE PEDAL CLEARANCE—*cont'd*

compensate for normal lining wear. Remove the inspection hole cover and turn the star wheel until the brakes drag and then back off until they are just free. Repeat this operation at all four wheels. Turning the handle of the tool in the direction of the axle will expand the brake shoes.

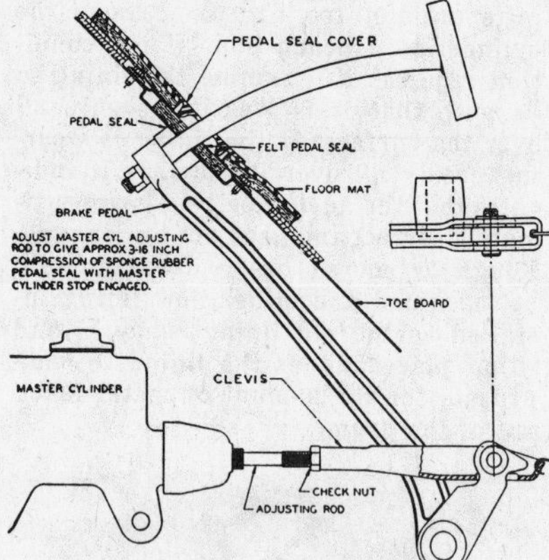

Brake pedal linkage adjustment

Major Brake Adjustment

A major brake adjustment should be made at any time new linings are installed, drums are turned, or it is found that the brakes are not operating properly after executing a minor adjustment. If a major adjustment is required because of defective brake operation it should be a positive rule to remove all four brake drums and examine the condition of the cylinders, lining, shoes and drums.

Pry the primary shoe against the drum and turn the star wheel to expand the shoe until a .010 inch feeler gage is just gripped at the star wheel end of the secondary shoe. Loosen the anchor bolt nut and turn the eccentric anchor in a direction which will move the secondary shoe toward the drum until a .010 inch feeler is gripped between the lining and drum approximately 1½ inches from the anchor end of the secondary shoe. Then go back and recheck the star wheel adjuster and readjust it until the .010 feeler will just go in at the star wheel end of the secondary shoe. The object is to get .010 clearance all over the secondary shoe with the primary shoe against the drum.

Securely tighten the anchor lock nut and then expand the shoes at the star wheel until they drag and then back off until they are just free. Replace the adjusting hole cover and repeat the operation at all four wheels.

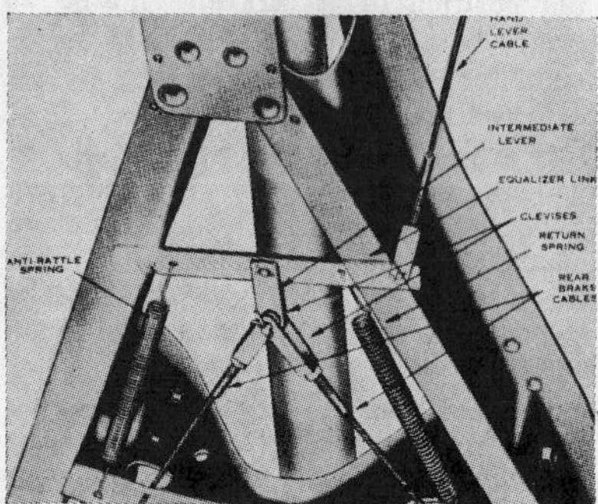

Parking brake linkage

BLEEDING BRAKES

General Service and Trouble Shooting—See Index.

Adjustment of Hand Brake Cables

Set the hand brake in the fully released position and detach the cables at the clevis on the equalizer rod. Expand the rear brake shoes at the star wheel until they are very tight against the drum and then pull all the slack out of the cable by hand and adjust the length of the cable so that the clevis will just enter the equalizer bar when the hand brake is in the released position. Replace the clevis pin and cotter pin. Back off on the star wheel until the rear wheels are just free.

COOLING SYSTEM

The cooling system on all Oldsmobiles is a full water jacket type, having a single water pump and single thermostat. A single water pump is also used on the V-8 models starting in 1949.

Removal of Radiator Core

The radiator core can be removed from all Oldsmobile models without taking off the water pump. Remove the radiator hoses, headlight wires, hood cables, etc., and unbolt the core assembly from its support and raise it up out of the car. It may be necessary to rotate the fan blades in order to keep them out of the way.

Removal of Water Pump

On V-8 models it is necessary to remove the radiator core in order to take off the water pump. Disconnect the radiator hoses to the water pump and remove the fan belt. The pump can then be unbolted from the block and lifted off.

Caution: Be careful of neoprene grommet between the back of the pump and the cylinder block at the bypass.

Disassembly of Water Pump

1949 THRU 1953 V-8 MODELS

On these models take out the bearing locking device from the front of the casting and press the shaft out through the impeller and out of the casting. It is recommended that a new impeller be used at any time it is pressed off the shaft.

ALL MODELS EXCEPT V-8'S

Take off the pump body cover and remove the pulley. Remove the bearing lock ring and press the shaft out of the impeller and out of the front of the body. Then take out the snap ring from inside the bore at the back of the pump and remove the graphite washer, neoprene seal, retainers and spring. After disassembly, examine the pump for scores and scratches on the seating surfaces. Always use a new impeller and seal assembly on installation.

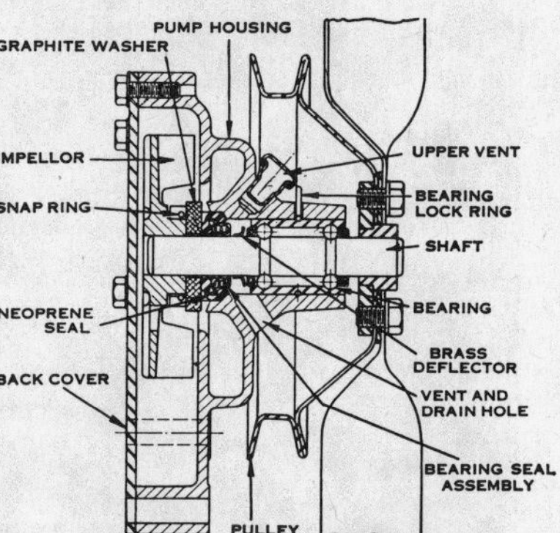

Water pump cross-sectional view

Thermostats

On all In-Line engines the thermostat is located under the water outlet elbow at the front of the cylinder head. To replace the thermostat on these models, disconnect the upper radiator hose, unbolt the water outlet elbow and lift out the thermostat. On V-8 rocket engines the thermostat is located under the water outlet elbow in the water manifold at the front of the block.

Water Distribution Tube

A water distribution tube is used on all in-line engines. To remove the water distribution tube it is necessary to take out the radiator core and the water pump. The tube may then be pulled out of the block with a hook type wire or special tool. If difficulty is experienced in pulling the tube out of the block it is a good idea to thoroughly back flush the engine before attempting to force it out.

ENGINE ASSEMBLY

Oldsmobile cars are equipped with 6 and 8 cylinder engines. Starting with 1949 production the V type overhead valve 8 cylinder engine was used in all Oldsmobiles.

The 6 cylinder model has been continued in production with some changes and improvements.

Engine Removal

To remove the engine on all models, including the rocket models, it is recommended that the front end sheet metal assembly, including radiator core and both front fenders, be removed from the car. Take off all attaching parts such as electrical connections, fuel connections, exhaust lines, gage connections, etc. The engine is split at the bell housing and lifted out.

Replacement Engines

Special service engine assemblies are available for all models starting with 1941 and they include cylinder block assembly, crankshaft and bearings, pistons, pins, rings, valve mechanism, timing gears and chains. Service engines are identified by a metal tag pinned to the cylinder block alongside the motor serial number. When ordering service parts for these special engines, always show the number on the metal tag as well as the motor serial number.

ENGINE INTERNAL

Engine Oil Pan Removal

V-8 ROCKET ENGINES

Remove the starting motor and the exhaust cross-over pipe, detach and lower the idler arm from the frame. The oil pan may then be unbolted.

1949 TO 1950 6-CYLINDER MODELS

Jack up the front of the engine approximately ¾". The bolts around the front end of the oil pan, where they are not accessible directly, may be reached through openings provided in the front cross member. It may be necessary to unhook the fasteners of the splash guard in order to get at the front bolts. No. 1 bolts from the front, on each side of the pan, must be removed with an end wrench. Rotate the crankshaft while pulling down the oil pan so that the counterweights can be brought up out of the way.

ALL MODELS FROM 1938 THRU 1948

Jack up the engine about 2". Take off the flywheel underpan and remove the bolts which hold the oil pan to the block. Turn the crankshaft so that the pan will clear the counterweights and slide the pan down and out.

Timing Case Cover Removal

1949 THRU 1953 V-8 MODELS

On these models the timing case cover and the water pump housing casting are one piece. With this exception the instructions given below for the earlier models will apply.

ALL MODELS 1940 THRU 1951, EXCEPT V-8'S AS NOTED ABOVE

Take off the radiator core and fan belt. Jack up the engine about 2" and remove the four bolts fastening the oil pan to the timing case cover. Remove the vibration damper and the bolts which fasten the cover to the block. Lift off the timing case cover, being careful not to tear the oil pan gasket.

Cylinder Head Removal

V-8 ROCKET ENGINES

To remove the cylinder head on these models, take off the air cleaner and generator, disconnect the upper radiator hoses, remove the wire retainers from the spark plug wires, disconnect the throttle linkage, remove the distributor cap and wire assembly, take off the fuel lines, remove the water pump bypass tube.

Remove the valve covers and take off the inlet manifold assembly (not necessary to detach the carburetor or coil). Detach the exhaust pipe at the exhaust manifold and remove the rocker shaft assembly with its rocker arms and brackets. Pull out the push rods and unbolt the cylinder head.

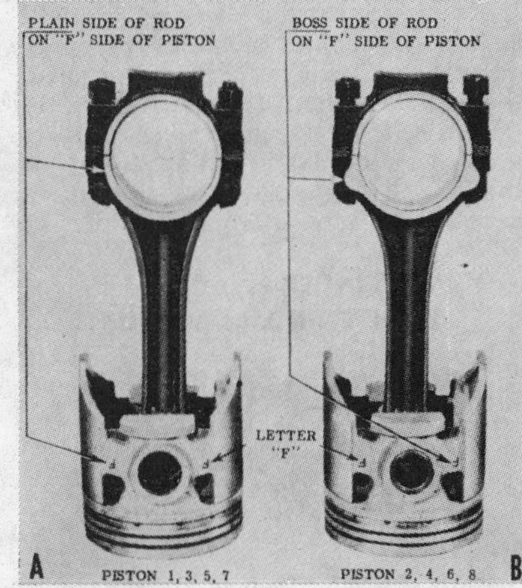

Relation of piston to connecting rod

Piston and Connecting Rod ssembly

ALL MODELS EXCEPT V-8'S:

Aluminum T slot pistons were used on all in-line engines.

V-8 ENGINES:

All V-8 engines are equipped with cam ground aluminum slipper type pistons.

Assembling Piston to Connecting Rod

ALL 6 AND 8 CYLINDER IN-LINE ENGINES:

On these engines the T slot in the piston is assembled on the opposite side to the spit hole in the rod.

V-8 ROCKET ENGINES:

The left bank of cylinders is numbered 1, 3, 5 and 7, starting from the front. The right bank of cylinders is numbered 2, 4, 6 and 8. Pistons are stamped with the letter "F" just alongside the wrist pin hole and the piston is assembled to the connecting rod as follows: on the right bank of pistons (2, 4, 6, 8) the letter "F" on the piston is assembled to the same side as the machined boss on the connecting rod (at the lower bearing).

On the left bank of cylinders (1, 3, 5, 7) the letter "F" on the piston is mounted to the connecting rod on the side opposite to the boss at the big end of the rod.

Assembly of Piston & Rod Assemblies to the Engine

On all V-8 rocket engines the letter "F" on the piston should face forward on both banks. On in-line engines the piston is assembled so that the T slot in the piston will be on left side (away from the valves). For a quick check see that the oil spit hole in the connecting rod is on the camshaft side of the engine.

Connecting Rod Bearings

The connecting rod bearings on all Oldsmobile models, including the V-8, are of the precision slip-in type. No adjustment is provided for the bearing and Oldsmobile does not recommend adjusting them. A variety of under sizes are available which are intended to take care of normal wear. A workable adjustment can be had, however, by placing a taper or feather type shim

Continued

CONNECTING ROD BEARING—*continued*

between the bearing shell and the bearing cap. In this way as much as .003-.004 inch excessive play can be taken up.

The fit of the connecting rod bearing can be checked by either the shim stock method or the plastic gauging material method. The instructions for use of the plastic gauging material is packed with the material and these instructions should be followed.

To check the clearance of a rod bearing using the shim stock method, determine from the bearing specifications of this Manual the exact oil clearance for the bearing being checked. Secure a piece of shim stock having that exact thickness. The shi mstock should be approximately ½ inch square. Place this shim between the rod bearing and the crankshaft and bolt the cap up. If this places a considerable drag on the bearing, then the oil clearance is approximately as much as the thickness of the shim. If the bearing is free it indicates there is excessive clearance. If the shaft binds tightly, then the oil clearance is insufficient.

Piston Rings

All piston ring manufacturers supply complete and very detailed instructions in the servicing and installation of their particular product. Since the technique of installing rings varies somewhat between the different ring manufacturers, it is advisable to follow their instructions carefully. In this way you will secure the best results possible when using that particular set of rings.

Main Bearings

All Oldsmobile engines, including the V-8 rocket engine, are equipped with precision interchangeable main bearings which may be removed from below without removing the crankshaft. To remove a main bearing, loosen all the main bearing caps and remove the cap from one bearing. Place a "headed-over" cotter pin in the oil hole in the crankshaft and by turning the crankshaft force the cotter pin to drive the bearing out of its seat in the cylinder block. The bearing should be driven out so that the tang portion of the bearing comes out first, and on reinstallation the tang portion goes in last. A variety of under sizes are available for servicing the main bearings on all Oldsmobile models. Oldsmobile does not recommend adjusting the main bearing. However, a workable adjustment can be had by placing a feather or taper type shim between the bearing shell and the bearing cap. In this way as much as .003-.004 inch excessive play can be taken up.

Rear Main Bearing Oil Seal

A packing type rear main bearing oil seal is used in all models of Oldsmobile. To replace the upper half of this seal it is necessary to remove the engine and crankshaft. The lower half of the seal may be replaced, however, by removing the rear main bearing cap, take out the old packing and install new packing, permitting it to protrude slightly from the bearing cap. Bolt the bearing cap up into place and immediately remove it to determine if the extended packing has riveted over. preventing the cap from seating properly.

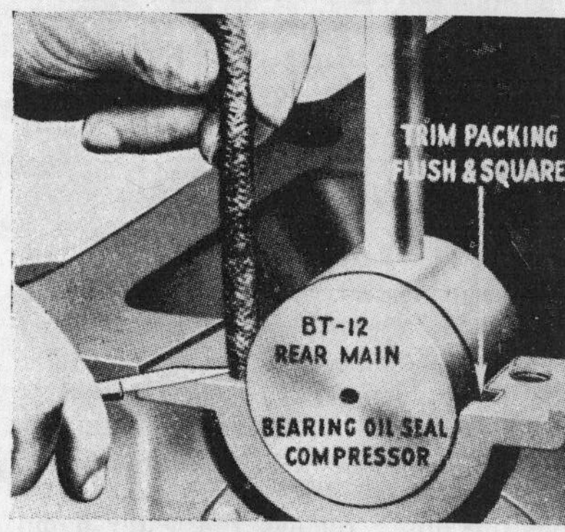

Trimming rear main oil seal

If it has, trim off the riveted over portion only and rebolt the cap. Repeat this operation until the cap seats firmly without riveting over the protruding portion of the oil seal. The reason this is done is so that the lower oil seal will have a tendency to compress the upper oil seal, forcing it to a tighter fit around the upper half of the crankshaft. In this way it is frequently possible to prevent an oil leak in the upper half of the rear main bearing packing without actually replacing the packing.

CYLINDER HEAD NUT TIGHTENING SEQUENCE

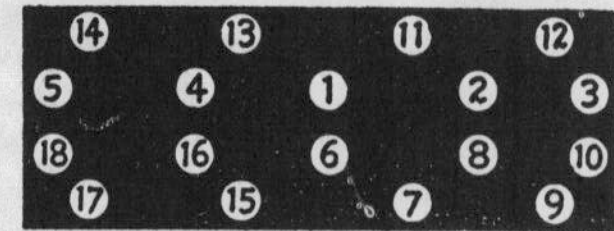

V-8 Models

With a torque wrench tighten cylinder head bolts to 60-70 foot pounds.

1940-48 Straight 8 Cylinder

Tighten cylinder head bolts to 65 foot pounds.

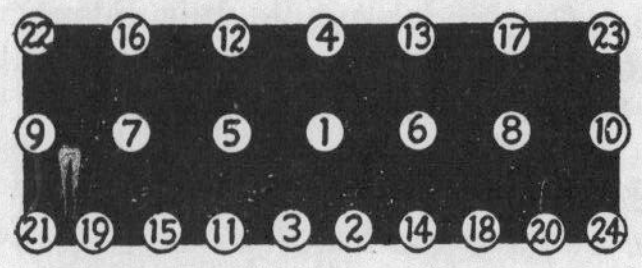

All 6 Cylinder

With torque wrench tighten cylinder bolts to 65 foot pounds.

THE VALVE SYSTEM

L Head Valves are used in all Oldsmobile In-Line engines. The V-8 model equipped with overhead valves.

To remove the valves on the L Head models it is necessary to take off the cylinder head and the valve chamber side cover (back of the manifolds).

On the V-8 engine the valves are contained in the cylinder head, and to ser-

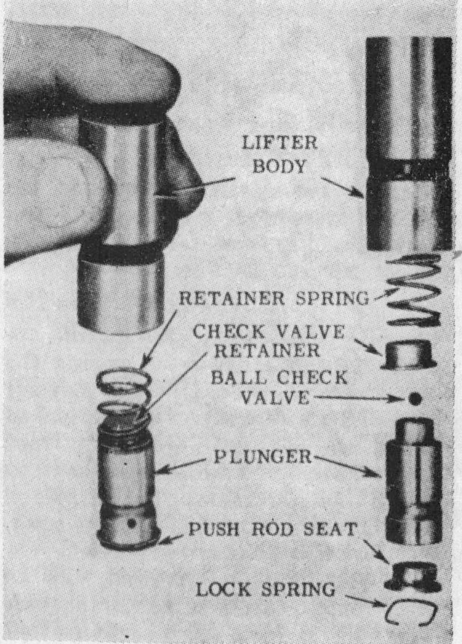

Hydraulic valve lifter—V-8 models

vice the valves it is necessary to remove the cylinder head. Hydraulic valve lifters are used on all V-8 engines.

Replacement of Valve Guides

To replace the valve guide on the L head engine, it is necessary to remove the cylinder head, valve chamber cover, valve and valve spring assembly. The guide may then be pulled up through the top of the block. New guides are driven down from the top of the cylinder block into the port. Before removing the old guides, carefully measure the distance from the top of the cylinder block to the top of the valve guide on the old guide before removing it so the new one can be reinstalled to exactly that position. It is customary to drive the guides in with a driving tool and then run a reamer through the guide to be certain that the driver has not upset the guide in any way.

On V-8 models the old valve guide is driven out through the top of the cylinder head and the new one is installed by driving from the top of the cylinder head down toward the firing chamber.

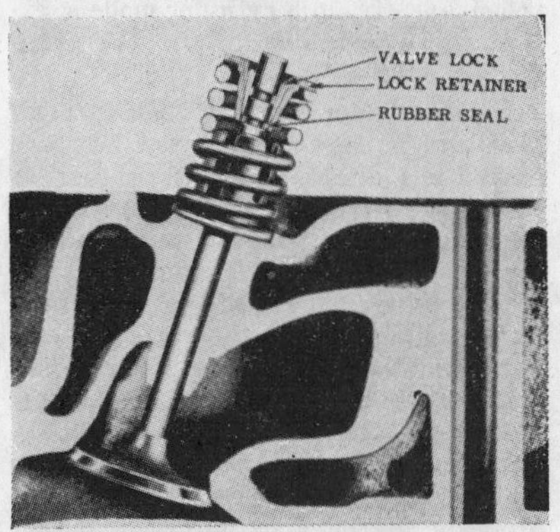

Intake valve assembly

Valve Springs

At any time the valve springs are removed from Oldsmobile engines it is a good idea to test them for compression. Specifications for the compression of the valve springs are given in the engine overhaul tables.

Valve Lifters—Tappets

On Oldsmobile in-line engines adjustable valve tappets are used. At any time the valves are being serviced it is a good idea to check the top surface of the tappet screws for grooves or depressions caused by the action of the end of the valve. If any grooves or depressions are found, the tappet screws should be taken out and refaced so that the top surface is flat and true in order to obtain an accurate adjustment of the valve lash.

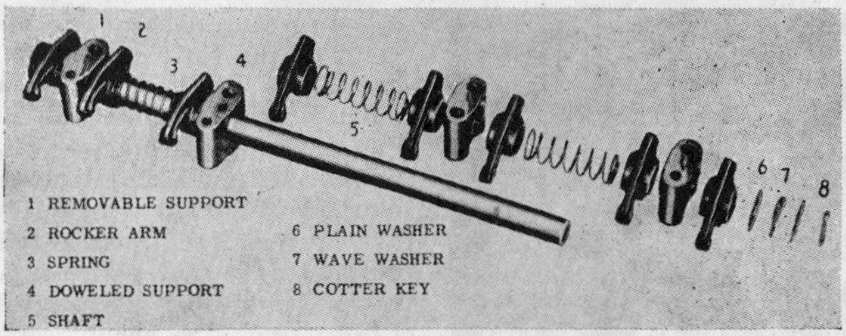

Rocker arm and shaft assembly

Hydraulic Valve Lifters

Hydraulic valve lifters are used on all Oldsmobile V-8 engines. Oil under metered pressure is supplied to these valves through cord holes in the cylinder block. The lifter operates normally at zero clearance. Lifters can be taken out of the engine without removing the cylinder head after the rocker assembly and inlet manifold has been removed. Simply pull out the push rods and lift out the lifter assemblies. Lifter assemblies are not interchangeable one bore to the other, nor are the internal parts of the lifter interchangeable with each other. All these parts are selective fit at the factory.

Service on hydraulic lifters is restricted to checking them to see that they are clean and free of grit, sludge or other foreign matter.

To disassemble the lifter after it has been removed from the car, simply take out the lock ring at the top of the lifter and remove the internal parts.

Initial Setting of Valve Lifter

With no oil in the lifter and the mechanism completely depressed there should be between .030 and .070 inch clearance. If this clearance seems to be less than .030 inch make absolutely certain that all of the oil is out of the lifter and it is completely depressed and the cam is on the low side before taking any measures to correct the lack of clearance. If the lifter still has less than .030 inch clearance after it is certain all oil has been removed and the lifter is completely depressed, it will be necessary to grind off the top of the valve stem until the correct initial clearance is obtained. With the clearance between .030 and .070 the automatic take up mechanism operates at approximately the middle of its stroke.

Valve Timing Procedure

On all Oldsmobile models a chain is used to drive the camshaft. The construction is such that the chain can be worn even badly without seriously affecting the valve timing. If the chain is worn badly enough that the timing jumps or it becomes necessary to replace either the chain or the sprockets or both, proceed as follows:

Remove the timing case cover and take off the camshaft gear.

Note: On V-8 models the fuel pump operating cam is bolted to the front of the camshaft sprocket and the sprocket is located to the camshaft by means of a dowel.

Remove the timing chain and the camshaft sprocket and if the crankshaft sprocket is to be replaced remove it also at this time.

Reinstall the crank sprocket being careful to start it with the keyway in perfect alignment since it is rather difficult to correct for misalignment after the gear has been started on the shaft. Turn the timing mark on the crankshaft gear until it points directly toward the center of the camshaft. Mount the timing chain over the camshaft gear and start the camshaft gear up on to its shaft with the timing marks nearest each other and in line between the shaft centers. Rotate the camshaft sufficient to align the shaft with the new gear.

On some early models a keyway is used for alignment; on V-8 models a dowel pin is used. Secure the camshaft gear and check to see that the mark on the crank sprocket and the mark on the cam sprocket are nearest each other and in line between shaft centers. Valves timed in this manner are correct regardless of which piston is at top center. It may be necessary, however, to retime the ignition since there is a possibility it will be 180 degrees out of position.

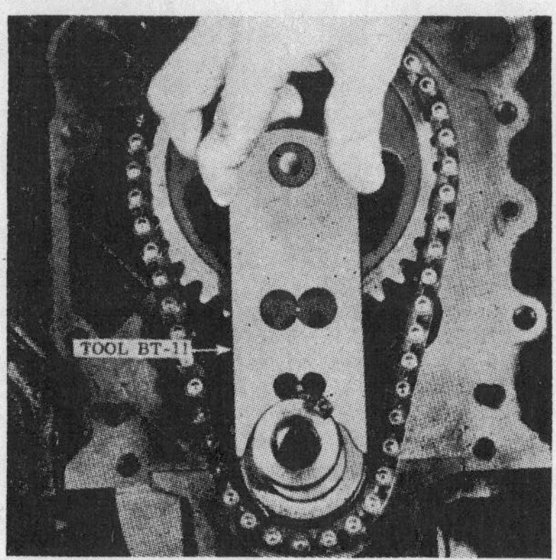

Timing chain and sprockets—V-8 models

THE ELECTRICAL SYSTEM

The Generator

Generators on all Oldsmobile models are the shunt wound two-brush type having full voltage and current control. At anytime the generator is not functioning properly, before removing it from the car, place a jumper wire between the field connection on the generator and ground. If this jumper wire causes the generator to come to full charge then the regulator is at fault. If grounding the field lead does not increase the generator output then it will be necessary to remove the generator from the car and make the bench test given in the General Service section of this Manual (see index).

The Starting Motor

If difficulty is experienced with the starter, before removing it for any work, first check to make certain that the battery is at full charge and that the connections to the battery are clean and tight. It is also a good idea to place a low reading voltmeter across the contacts of the starter switch and crank the engine. The voltage drop across the starter switch should not exceed 1/3 volt. If it does the starter switch should be removed and the contacts thoroughly cleaned. If starter trouble continues after the work indicated above has been completed, it will be necessary to remove the starter, disassemble it and subject it to the bench test given for generators in the General Service section of this Manual.

Ignition timing—6 & 8 cylinder in line engine

The Distributor

Single breaker point distributors are used on all Oldsmobile models, both 6's and 8's. A vacuum controlled breaker plate mechanism is incorporated into all distributors in Oldsmobile cars. The distributors are driven by a tang on the end of the shaft. The gear itself is actually mounted on the oil pump. This means if at anytime the oil pump is removed from its mesh with the camshaft it will be necessary to replace it in exactly the same place from which it was removed (in relation to the gears) or it will be necessary to retime the ignition. Since the range of rotation of the distributor body is only a few degrees, if the oil pump is inserted incorrectly, it will be necessary to change the spark plug wires around the cap.

Ignition Timing

A small adjustment of ignition timing, to compensate for the conditions or type of fuel can be made by rotating the distributor body. It is customary to use an ignition timing synchroscope to determine the exact point at which the spark fires. On some of the early models the ignition timing mark is a steel ball in the flywheel, which can be observed through a hole in the flywheel housing just above the starter. On later 8-cylinder models the vibration damper is marked with the ignition timing point. If the oil pump has been removed and installed in a different position from that which it originally occupied it may be necessary to change the position of the spark plug wires in the cap. This is done as follows: Remove the distributor cap and bring No. 1 cylinder to the firing position. With the No. 1 cylinder in the firing position, notice the direction in which the distributor rotor points. It should point to No. 1 segment in the cap. If it does not point to No. 1 segment it will be necessary to switch the wires around so that it does point to No. 1 segment. The wires are then located around the distributor cap in the following order:

Ignition timing—V-8 models

ALL MODELS EXCEPT 8 CYLINDER MODELS FOR 1942 THRU 1948

On these models, as noted above, the rotation of the distributor rotor is in a counter-clockwise direction, therefore, the wires will be mounted into the cap in the order given below in a counter-clockwise direction. On 6 cylinder models, starting with the wire from No. 1 spark plug over the segment the order is 1-5-3-6-2-4. On 8 cylinder models, except those noted and V-8's, the order will be 1-6-2-5-8-3-7-4.

Eight cylinder models of 1942 through 1948 are in the same order but are strung in a clockwise direction. On V-8 models the wires are mounted around in a counter-clockwise direction in the following order: The left bank of cylinders is numbered 1, 3, 5 and 7 starting at the radiator, and the right bank is numbered 2, 4, 6 and 8 starting at the radiator. Following this numbering arrangement the wires will be strung around in a counter-clockwise direction 1-8-7-3-6-5-4-2. After resetting the wires properly in the distributor, small adjustments of the ignition timing can be made by rotating the distributor body.

STANDARD CLUTCH ASSEMBLY

A single dry disc coil spring clutch is used on all Oldsmobile models which are not equipped with automatic transmission.

Clutch Pedal Adjustment

The clutch pedal should be adjusted so that there is from ½ in. to ¾ in. free play of the clutch pedal before the throwout bearing engages the fingers. This adjustment is made at the clutch throwout rod.

Removal of Clutch from Car

The clutch assembly is removed through the bottom of the inspection pan after the transmission has been removed. It is necessary to remove the transmission in order to remove the clutch throwout fork.

Clutch Overhaul

Highly specialized equipment is required to properly rebuild a clutch. Special and individual instructions are required in the use of the particular equipment involved and these instructions are always supplied by the manufacturer of the equipment. It is generally conceded that it is impossible to do good dependable work on clutch pressure plates and disc assemblies without the use of special equipment.

STANDARD TRANSMISSION ASSEMBLY

A three speed syncromesh transmission is standard equipment on all Oldsmobiles. Hydramatic drive (described later) is optional equipment at extra cost.

Removal of Transmission

The transmission is removed from below by detaching it at the universal joint and the four mounting bolts which hold it to the bell housing. Detach all shift rods, speedometer cable, etc. If access to the upper mounting bolts cannot be achieved from underneath the car it will be necessary to remove the cover pan under the floor mat.

Disassembly of Standard Transmission

Mount the transmission in a vice and remove the transmission cover. Take out the hopper spring and the shift lever bolt from the left end of the selector shaft and remove the stamped shift lever (the selector shaft is the shaft which is crosswise in the transmission). Take off the selector rod lower lever from the left side of the case. Take off the speedometer driven gear and remove the transmission rear bearing housing which will come off with the main shaft assembly attached to it. Now remove the set screws from the shifter fork (rails which go lengthwise of the transmission) and from the selector shaft cams (shaft which is crosswise in the transmission). Take out the selector shaft from the right side of the transmission case (this will drive out a welsh plug at the right side of the case). Then drive out the shift rails and forks.

Note: It is not necessary to completely remove the shift rails (the rails which go forward and back in the transmission) in order to take out the forks. Simply move them back far enough so that the forks may be slid off.

Note: Second and high shift rail is shorter than low and reverse, and second and high shifting cam is shorter than lower and reverse. After the forks have been removed, remove the low and reverse gears and the sliding sleeve. Drive out the countershaft to the rear of the transmission, being careful not to lose the needle bearings. Take out the main drive gear snap ring and remove the main drive gear into the case and up out of the top. Lift out the countershaft cluster gear. To get out the idler shaft drive the pin into the idler shaft itself.

Note: This pin is shorter in length than the idler shaft is in diameter and it will drive right into the idler shaft, permitting the idler shaft to be driven out of the case.

The gears on the main shaft may be taken off by removing the front snap ring. A thrust washer is used in both front and back of the second speed gear.

The rear bearing is held into the rear housing with a snap ring.

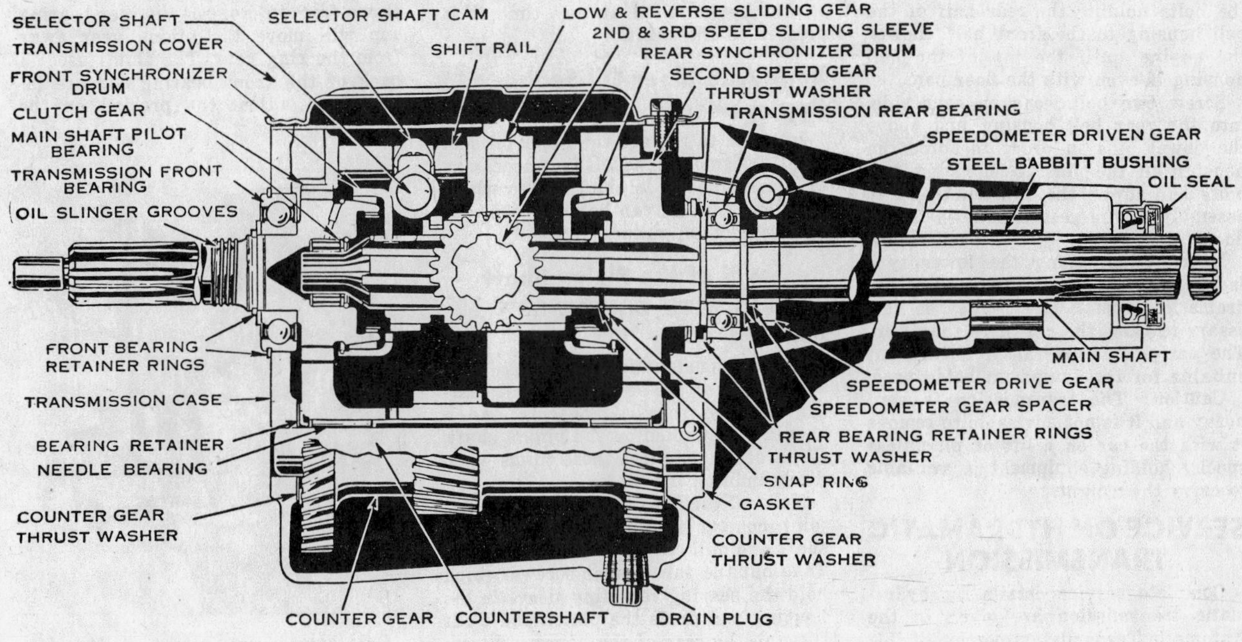

Section through synchromesh transmission

Removal of Hydramatic Transmission

Due to the weight of this unit it is best that no one be underneath it during removal or installation. Raise the car on a jack so that all wheels are clear of the floor by at least 8 in. Remove the foot accelerator pad, floor mat and floor center pan. Disconnect the rear of the propeller shaft from the differential flange and slide the shaft out off the spline shaft. Remove the flywheel housing pan and drain the transmission and flywheel cover. Disconnect the control levers at the transmission. Remove the two upper engine mounting bolts (on 6 cylinder models remove the bolt holding the brakeshaft bracket to the crossmember). On 8 cylinder models remove the two bolts holding the strut to the lower part of the master cylinder, one bolt holding strut to crossmember and remove the strut from the shaft. Place a block of wood and a jack just ahead of the engine oil drain plug and raise the engine about an inch and then remove the six bolts which fasten the crossmember to the frame. Take out the crossmember. A special front compartment crane is used to carry the weight of the transmission. There is also a suitable jack available to hold the transmission in a stable position when dismounting it.

Remove the bolts holding the fluid flywheel cover to the flywheel and also the bolts holding the rear half of the bell housing to the front half. Lower the engine until the top of the bell housing is even with the floor pan.

Screw two bolts, one on each side, into the rear bell housing just above the dowel pins in order to force the housing off the pins. Remove the two bolts and lower the hydramatic drive assembly to the rear and down to the floor.

Note: When using the lower type jacking devices for the removal of hydramatic transmissions it may be necessary to raise the car more than 8 in. The car should be raised an amount suitable for the equipment being used.

Caution: The transmission is very heavy and it is not advisable to remove it with the car on a lift or pit unless special holding equipment is available to carry the weight.

SERVICE ON HYDRAMATIC TRANSMISSION

Complete service details for hydramatic transmission are given in the Automatic Transmission portion of this section. (See index.)

REAR AXLE ASSEMBLY

The rear axle assembly on all Oldsmobiles has a detachable differential carrier assembly. The pinion depth is controlled by shims and the differential side bearings are adjusted by bearing cages in the carrier.

Replacement of Pinion Oil Seal

To replace the pinion oil seal it is not necessary to remove the carrier from the car. Split the rear universal joint and take off the universal joint companion flange nut and remove the companion flange. The oil seal can then be taken out using an inertia type puller. It is a good idea to mark the position of the pinion shaft companion flange nut so that it can be returned to the position from which it was removed. At least 200′ lbs. torque should be put on this nut in order to be certain that it is tight.

Replacement of Rear Axle Shaft

To remove the rear axle shaft take off the rear wheel and brake drum. Working back of the axle shaft flange remove the bolts which retain the backing plate to the housing. The axle shaft and bearing assembly can then be pulled out of the housing. To remove the bearing from the shaft it is necessary to press off the bearing and the lock ring assembly. A new lock ring should be installed at any time it is pressed off the shaft.

Rear Axle Inner Oil Seal Replacement

In order to replace the inner oil seal on all Oldsmobile models it is necessary to remove the axle shaft, after which the inner oil seal can be taken out with an inertia type puller.

Removal of the Pinion Shaft

MODELS WITH DOUBLE ROW BALL BEARING

On this construction shims were used at the back of the double row ball bearing between the ball bearing and a shoulder machined on the pinion shaft. Be careful not to lose these shims when disassembling the pinion.

Take off the nut holding the universal joint companion flange to the pinion shaft and pull off the companion flange. Take out the three taper screws which hold the bearing retaining sleeve in the housing and press the pinion shaft out through the rear of the housing. Sometimes the back bearing will come out with the pinion shaft, other times it will stay in the housing.

Note: There is a snap ring on the pinion shaft just ahead of the pinion gear itself. This snap ring is intended to prevent the roller bearings from working over toward the back face of the pinion gear itself. The snap ring should not be disturbed. Pull the rear bearing (roller bearing) out of the differential carrier. The double row ball bearing can then be taken out of the housing.

TAPERED ROLLER BEARING PINIONS

As stated before, tapered roller bearings were used on pinion shafts starting with late 1947 production and continued through 1951 production. To move the pinion on these models, take off the universal joint companion flange and drive the pinion shaft out through the back of the case. The pinion shaft will come out with the rear bearing cone mounted on the shaft.

Note: A spacer is used between the front and rear bearing on the pinion shaft. Shims are used in front of the back bearing cup (race) and in back of the front bearing cup (race). The shims in front of the back bearing cup determine the depth of the pinion into the ring gear. Adding shims at this point will force the pinion gear deeper into mesh with the ring gear. Removing shims from in front of the rear bearing cup will move the pinion gear away from the ring gear. The shims used in back of the front bearing cup are intended to adjust the preload on the bearings.

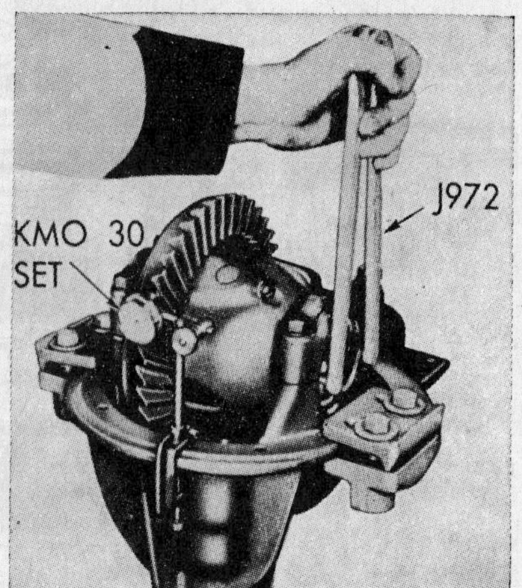

Establishing exact amount of shims for differential

Carrier Marking—Pinion Marking

The gasket flange of the carrier assembly is marked "D," "S" and "C." If it is marked either either D or S, the letter will be followed by a number. The letter D means deep, the amount of the number immediately following. The letter S means shallow, the amount of the number immediately following. The letter C means the bore is exactly centered and no number is used following the letter C.

If no letter or number is stamped on the gasket flange of the carrier, this means the carrier is centered. The pinion is marked with either a "0" or a plus figure or a minus figure. A plus figure on the end of the pinion indicates that a shim the thickness of the figure following the plus sign must be used on that particular pinion. A minus figure means that you must subtract from the existing shims one the thickness of the digit following the minus sign. This applies whether tapered roller or double row ball bearings are being used. This formula applies to all Oldsmobile rears.

How to Select the Correct Shim Thickness

When disassembling the pinion, handle the shims (found in the housing) very carefully. Carefully mike the shims and record their total thickness. Also record the number stamped on the pinion which was removed. If the new pinion to be installed has the same number stamped on it as the old one, then exactly the same number of shims will be used. In other words, the shims in the housing are correct for that pinion. If the number on the new pinion is of greater value than the number on the old pinion, i.e. the old pinion reads plus 1, and the new pinion reads plus 3, it will be necessary to increase the total thickness of the shims by .002 inch, the difference in the reading. If the old pinion was marked minus 1, and the new pinion is marked minus 3, then it will be necessary to use a total shim thickness which is .002 less than the thickness found in the housing. This is the difference between minus 1 and minus 3. If the old pinion read minus 2, and the new pinion read plus 4, it will be necessary to insert a total .006 shims in order to make up for the difference between minus 2 and plus 4. A plus number indicates shims to be added from the nominal setting, a minus number indicates shims taken away from the nominal setting.

Assembling Pinion to the Carrier

MODELS WITH DOUBLE ROW BALL BEARINGS

Double row ball bearings were used from 1940 up to and including some part of 1947 production. When the correct number of shims has been established, to determine the pinion depth as given in the preceding paragraphs, install the pinion gear in the housing. On the double row ball bearing type, no preload is taken on the bearings and the pinion is simply installed with the shims selected in back of the pinion front bearing. No other adjustment is required on the pinion bearings on these models.

TAPERED ROLLER BEARING PINIONS

Tapered roller bearing pinions were used starting with late 1947 production and through 1951 models. The procedure on these models is somewhat different. After the shims have been selected, which govern the proper depth of the pinion, it will be necessary to adjust the preload on the bearings by adding to or taking from the shims in back of the front bearing cup.

Mount the shims governing the depth of the pinion into the back of the housing and insert the back pinion bearing cup (race). Install the front bearing cup (race) in the front of the housing, using shims behind it equal to the number of shims which were removed.

Note: At this point it is a good idea to remove from the front pack of shims a thickness equal to the thickness which might have been added to the back shim pack. In other words, if shims were added at the back bearing, remove that same thickness from the front bearing and it is easily possible that the correct thickness will be arrived at immediately. If shims were taken away from the back bearing it is a good idea to add exactly the same thickness to the front bearing in order to hold the preload constant. Set the pinion bearing and spacer in place in the carrier and install the front bearing cone and universal joint companion flange. It is a good idea not to put the grease seal in at this time, since it may be necessary to take out the universal joint companion flange several times before the correct setting is obtained. Tighten up on the companion flange nut until the preload on the bearing is between 27"-37" pounds for new bearings, or 15"-20" pounds for bearings which have been used previously. If, after tightening the pinion nut, the torque required to turn the shaft is greater than 37" pounds, it will be necessary to remove the companion flange bearing cone and bearing cup and remove shims from in back of the front bearing cup, in order to lessen the preload on the bearing. If the reading is less than 17" pounds torque required to turn the pinion shaft, then it will be necessary to add shims in back of the front bearing cup.

Installing the Differential Assembly

Install the differential assembly and put the bearing caps and bearing adjusting cages in place finger tight. Now adjust the bearing cage, ring gear side, until there is zero lash between the ring gear and pinion. Adjust the pinion cage on the opposite side until there is zero play in the bearings and then take up two more notches in order to preload the side bearings. Taking up the two notches should produce approximately .006 inch back lash between the ring gear and pinion, measured at the rim of the ring gear. If less than .006 lash is produced by the preloading of the bearings, it may be necessary to back off one notch on the ring gear side adjusting cage and take up one notch on the pinion side adjusting cage.

A good, easy, quick way to check the setting of the ring gear and pinion, after it has been secured, is to spin the ring gear with your hand, noticing whether the gears mesh smoothly in both directions. When properly set up there will be no noticeable gear vibration as the ring gear is spun in mesh with the pinion.

A quick check of the ring gear and pinion can be made by painting about 9 or 10 teeth of the ring gear and then rolling it through the pinion gear, noticing the markings on the gears.

Accompanying this text is a chart showing markings left by desirable tooth contact and also markings left by tooth contact which needs correcting.

Secure all bolts and reinstall the carrier to the rear axle housing.

REAR END SUSPENSION

Leaf Springs

On Super 88's and 98's having leaf springs, disconnect the spring from the rear shackle supporting the weight of the car at the frame in front of the spring front shackle. Disconnect the front shackle and remove the spring clip bolts which retain the spring to the axle housing. Lift off the spring.

PACKARD SPECIFICATIONS

Starting Serial and Motor Numbers

Starting Serial Numbers

1947-1953—Same as motor numbers.

Location

1947-1953—Same place as motor numbers.

Starting Motor Numbers

1940, 6 cyl.—Ser. 10 ....C-1501
8 cyl.—Ser. 120 ....C-300001
Ser. 160 ....CC-500001
Ser. 180 ....C-500001
1941, 6 cyl.—Ser. 110 ....D-1501
8 cyl.—Ser. 120 ....D-300001
Ser. 1951 ....D-400001
Ser. 160 ....D-500001
Ser. 180 ....CD-500001
1942, 6 cyl.—Ser. 110 ....E-1501
8 cyl.—Ser. 120 ....E-300001
Ser. 160 ....E-500001
Ser. 180 ....CE-500001
1946, 6 cyl.—Ser. 2100 ....F-1501
8 cyl.—Ser. 2101, 11 ....F-300001
Ser. 2103, 06, 26 ....F-500001
1947, 6 cyl.—Ser. 2100 ......F-15001
8 cyl.—Ser. 2111 ....F-320001
Ser. 2103, 06, 26 ....F-506001
1948-1949—Ser. 2201, 11 ......G-200001
Ser. 2202, 22, 32 ....G-400001
Ser. 2206, 26, 33 ....G-600091
1949—Ser. 2301 ....H-200001
Ser. 2302, 22, 32 ....H-400001
Ser. 2306, 33 ....H-60000
1950—Ser. 2301-5 ....H-27500
Ser. 2302-5, 22-5, 32-5 ......H-41500
Ser. 2306-5, 33-5 ....H-60000
1951—Ser. 200 ....J-20000
Ser. 250, 300 ....J-40000
Ser. 400 ....J-60000
1952—Ser. 200 ....K-20000
Ser. 250, 300 ....K-40000
Ser. 400 ....K-60000
1953—Ser. 300, L400000; Ser. 40[illegible] L600000, Clipper LZ00000.

Location

1940-1953—On boss upper left side o[illegible] block.

General Specifications

Year	Model	Wheelbase (in.)	Tread (in.)		Overall Dimensions (in.)			Shipping Weight* (lb.)	Tire Size (in.)
			Front	Rear	Length†	Width	Height■		
1940	1800	122	59	61	196	....	....	3200	6.25–16
	1801	127	59	60	201	....	....	3520	6.50–16
	1803-04-05	127–38–48	59	63	201(b)	....	....	3855	7.00–16
	1806-07-08	127–38–48	59	63	205(b)	....	....	4210	7.00–16
1941	1900	122	60	61	201	....	....	3250	6.50–15
	1901	127	....	50	206	....	....	3510	7.00–15
	1903-4-5	127–38–48	59	60(h)	206(l)	....	....	3865	7.00–16
	1906-7-8	127–38–48	59	60(h)	212(i)	....	....	4040	7.00–16
1942	2000-10-20	120–122	59	61	209(e)	....	....	3435	6.50–15
	2001-11-21	120–127	59	61	209(e)	....	....	3560	6.50–16(p)
	2003-4-5-23	127–38–48	60	61	216(e)	....	....	4005	7.00–15(p)
	2006-7-8	127–38–48	60	61	216(e)	....	....	4030	7.00–15(p)
1946	2100	120	59	61	209	76	64	3465	6.50–15
	2101, 2111	120	59	61	209	76	64	3575(c)	6.50–15
	2103, 2106	127	59	61	216	76	64	3990(c)	7.00–15
1947	2100	120	59	61	209	76	64	3495	6.50–15
	2111	120	59	61	209	76	64	3670	6.50–15
	2103-2106	127	59	61	216	76	64	3995	7.00–15
1948	2201-2211	120	59	60	205	77	64	3750●	6.50–16
	2202-2232	120	60	61	205	77	64	3810	7.00–15
	2206-2233	127	60	61	213	77	64	4140	7.00–15
1949	2201-2211	120	59	60	205	77	64	3755	7.60–15
	2202-22-32	120–141	60	61	205	77	64	3855	7.60–15(d)
	2206-26-33	127–148	60	61	213	77	64	4175	8.20–15(d)
1950	2301	120	60	61	205	77	64	3815	7.60–15
	2302-2332	127	60	61	212	77	64	3870	7.60–15(d)
	2306-2333	127	60	61	213	77	64	4200	8.20–15
1951	200	122	60	61	209	78	63	3660	7.60–15
	300, 400	127	60	61	218	78	63	3980	8.00–15
1952–53	2501, 2531, 2601, 11, 31	122	60	61	213	78	62	....	7.60–15
	2502, 2506	127	60	61	218	77	63	....	8.00–15
	2602, 6, 26	149	60	61	240	78	63	....	8.00–15

*—Cheapest 5 pass. 4 door or equivalent. ■—Road to roof, no load. (b) Model 1804—212; 1805—222; 1807—217; 1808—227. (h) Model 1905—63 1908—63. (i) Model 1904—217; 1905—227; 1907—217; 1908—227. (e) Model 2020—201; 2021—207; 2023—206; 2004—217; 2005—227; 2007—217; 2008—227 (p) Model 2021—7.00–15; 2004-5-7-8—7.00–16. (c) 2111—3635 lb.; 2106—4065 lb. ● 2211—3770 lb. † 2233—7.00–16. (d) 2222—7.00–15; 2226—7.00–16; 2330—8.20–15.

General Engine Specifications

Year	Model	Number of Cylinders Bore and Stroke	Piston Displacement, Cubic Inches	Compression Ratio (To–1)	Taxable (A.M.A.) Hp.	DEVELOPED HORSE POWER: Bare Engine	DEVELOPED HORSE POWER: With Accessories	Maximum Torque Ft. Lbs.
1940	1800, 6 Cyl.	6–3½ x 4¼	245.0	6.39	29.4	100 @ 3200	....	195 @ 1200
	1801, 8 Cyl.	8–3¼ x 4¼	282.0	6.41	33.8	112 @ 3600	....	225 @ 1700
	1803-4-5-6-7-8, 8 Cyl.	8–3½ x 4⅝	356.0	6.45	39.2	160 @ 3500	....	292 @ 1800
1941	1900, 6 Cyl.	6–3½ x 4¼	245.0	6.39	29.4	100 @ 3600	....	....
	1901, 8 Cyl.	8–3¼ x 4¼	282.0	6.41	33.8	112 @ 3600	....	....
	1903-4-5-6-7-8, 8 Cyl.	8–3½ x 4⅝	356.0	6.45	39.2	160 @ 3600	....	....
1942	2000, 2010, 6 Cyl.	6–3½ x 4¼	245.0	6.71	29.4	105 @ 3600	....	192 @ 2000
	2001, 2011, 8 Cyl.	8–3¼ x 4¼	282.0	6.85	33.8	125 @ 3600	....	230 @ 2000
	2003-4-5, 8 Cyl.	8–3½ x 4⅝	356.0	6.85	39.2	165 @ 3600	....	292 @ 2000
1946–7	2101, 2111, 8 Cyl.	8–3¼ x 4¼	282.0	6.85	33.8	125 @ 3600	....	230 @ 2000
	2103, 2106, 8 Cyl.	8–3½ x 4⅝	356.0	6.85	39.2	165 @ 3600	....	292 @ 2000
	2100, 6 Cyl.	6–3½ x 4¼	245.0	8.71	29.4	105 @ 3600	....	192 @ 2000
1948	2201, 2211, 8 Cyl.	8–3½ x 3¾	288.0	7.00	39.2	130 @ 3600	....	226 @ 2000
	2202, 2232, 8 Cyl.	8–3½ x 4¼	327.0	7.00	39.2	145 @ 3600	....	266 @ 2000
	2206, 2233, 8 Cyl.	8–3½ x 4⅝	356.0	7.00	39.2	160 @ 3600	....	282 @ 2000
1949	2301, 8 Cyl.	8–3½ x 3¾	288.0	7.00	39.2	130 @ 3600	....	226 @ 2000
	2302-3-32, 8 Cyl.	8–3½ x 4¼	327.0	7.00	39.2	145 @ 3600	....	266 @ 2000
	2306, 2333, 8 Cyl.	8–3½ x 4⅝	356.0	7.00	39.2	160 @ 3600	....	282 @ 2000
1950	2301-5, 8 Cyl.	8–3½ x 3¾	288.0	7.00	39.2	135 @ 3600	....	230 @ 2000
	2302-5, 2332-5, 8 Cyl.	8–3½ x 4¼	327.0	7.00	39.2	150 @ 3600	....	270 @ 2000
	2306-5, 2333-5, 8 Cyl.	8–3½ x 4⅝	356.0	7.00	39.2	160 @ 3600	....	282 @ 2000
1951	2401, 8 Cyl.	8–3½ x 3¾	288.0	7.00	39.2	135 @ 3600	....	230 @ 2000
	2402, 8 Cyl.	8–3½ x 4¼	327.0	7.00	39.2	150 @ 3600	....	270 @ 2000
	2406, 8 Cyl.	8–3½ x 4¼	327.0	7.80	39.2	155 @ 3600	....	275 @ 2000
1952	200, 8 Cyl.	8–3½ x 3¾	288.0	7.00	39.20	135 @ 3600	....	230 @ 2000
	250, 300, 8 Cyl.	8–3½ x 4¼	327.0	7.00	39.20	150 @ 3600	....	270 @ 2000
	400, 8 Cyl.	8–3½ x 4¼	327.0	7.80	39.20	155 @ 3600	....	275 @ 2000
1953	2601	8–3½ x 3¾	288.0	7.7	39.2	150 @ 4000	....	260 @ 2200
	2611	8–3½ x 4¼	327.0	8.0	39.2	160 @ 3600	....	295 @ 2000
	2631, 2602, 6, 26	8–3½ x 4¼	327.0	8.0	39.2	180 @ 4000	....	300 @ 2000

Dimensions of Valves

Year	Model	Overall Length: Inlet	Overall Length: Exhaust	Head Diameter: Inlet	Head Diameter: Exhaust	Seat Angle (deg.): Inlet	Seat Angle (deg.): Exhaust	Stem Diameter: Inlet	Stem Diameter: Exhaust	Key Type	O.D. of Seat Insert: Inlet	O.D. of Seat Insert: Exhaust
1940	1800	5.515	5.515	1.531	1.375	30	45	.340	.340	key	....	....
	1801	5.515	5.515	1.484	1.375	30	45	.340	.340	key	....	....
	1803, 4, 5, 6, 7, 8	5.093	5.093	1.670	1.437	30	45	.340	.340	key	....	....
1941	1900	5.515	5.515	1.593	1.375	30	45	.339	.339	split lock	....	....
	1901	5.515	5.515	1.483	1.375	30	45	.339	.339	split lock	....	....
	1903, 4, 5, 6, 7, 8	6.109	6.109	1.687	1.437	30	45	.339	.339	split lock	....	....
1942	2000-10-20	5.515	5.515	1.593	1.375	30	45	.339	.339	split lock	....	....
	2001-11-21	5.515	5.515	1.484	1.375	30	45	.339	.339	split lock	....	....
	2003-4, 5, 23, 2006, 7, 8	6.109	6.109	1.687	1.437	30	45	.339	.339	split lock	....	....
1946–47	2100	5.619	5.619	1.593	1.375	30	45	.339	.339	split lock	....	....
	2101, 2111	5.619	5.619	1.484	1.375	30	45	.339	.339	split lock	....	....
	2103, 2106	6.224	6.224	1.670	1.437	30	45	.340	.340	split lock	....	....
1948–49	2201, 11, 02, 32	5.875	5.875	1.671	1.437	30	45	.341	.339	split lock	....	....
	2206, 33	6.218	6.218	1.671	1.437	30	45	.341	.339	split lock	....	....
1950	2301, 2, 6, 32, 33	5.875	5.875	1.672	1.438	30	45	.342	.340	split lock	....	....
1951	200, 300, 400	5.875	5.875	1.672	1.438	30	45	.342	.340	split lock	....	....
1952	200, 250, 300, 400, 8 cyl.	5.875	5.875	1.671875	1.4375	30	45	.3417	.3398		....	....
1953	2601, 11, 31; 2602, 6, 26	5.875	5.875	1.671875	1.4375	30	45	.3417	.3398	....	....	....

Engine Overhaul Specifications

Year	Model	PISTONS				RING GAP CLEARANCES (Maximum)				PISTON PIN		ROD BEARINGS		
		Removed From	Piston Skirt Clearances (Maximum)											
			Top	Bottom	Limit	Top Ring	Second Ring	Third Ring	Oil Ring	Type	Fit	Oil Clearance	Wear Limit	Side Play
1940	1800, 6 Cyl.	A	.001	.001	.006	.017	.017	......	.017	Float	Push	.0005–.0015	.003	.004–.010
	1801, 8 Cyl.	A	.001	.001	.006	.017	.017	......	.015	Float	Push	.0005–.0015	.003	.004–.010
	1803-4-5-6-7-8, 8 Cyl.	A	.001	.001	.006	.017	.017	......	.015	Float	Push	.0005–.0015	.003	.004–.010
1941	1900, 6 Cyl.	A	.001	.001	.006	.017	.017	......	.015	Float	Push	.0005–.0015	.003	.004–.010
	1901, 8 Cyl.	A	.001	.001	.006	.017	.017	......	.015	Float	Push	.0005–.0015	.003	.004–.010
	1903-4-5-6-7-8, 8 Cyl.	A	.001	.001	.006	.017	.017	......	.015	Float	Push	.0005–.0015	.003	.004–.010
1942	2000, 2010, 6 Cyl.	A	.0035	.0035	.006	.017	.017	......	.015	Float	Push	.0005–.0015	.003	.004–.010
	2001, 2011, 8 Cyl.	A	.0035	.0035	.006	.018	.018	......	.015	Float	Push	.0005–.0015	.003	.004–.010
	2003-4-5, 8 Cyl.	A	.001	.001	.006	.017	.017	......	.015	Float	Push	.0005–.0015	.003	.004–.010
1946–7	2101, 2111, 8 Cyl.	A	.001	.001	.006	.017	.017	......	.015	Float	Push	.0005–.0015	.003	.004–.010
	2103, 2106, 8 Cyl.	A	.001	.001	.006	.017	.017	......	.015	Float	Push	.0005–.0015	.003	.004–.010
	2100, 6 Cyl.	A	.001	.001	.006	.017	.017	......	.015	Float	Push	.0005–.0015	.003	.004–.010
1948	2201, 2211, 8 Cyl.	A	.001	.001	.006	.017	.017	......	.015	Float	Push	.0005–.0025	.003	.004–.010
	2202, 2232, 8 Cyl.	A	.001	.001	.006	.017	.017	......	.015	Float	Push	.0005–.0025	.003	.004–.010
	2206, 2233, 8 Cyl.	A	.001	.001	.006	.017	.017	......	.015	Float	Push	.0005–.0025	.003	.004–.012
1949	2301, 8 Cyl.	A	.001	.001	.006	.017	.017	......	.015	Float	Push	.0005–.0025	.003	.004–.010
	2302-3-32, 8 Cyl.	A	.001	.001	.006	.017	.017	......	.015	Float	Push	.0005–.0025	.003	.004–.010
	2306, 2333, 8 Cyl.	A	.001	.001	.006	.017	.017	......	.015	Float	Push	.0005–.0025	.003	.004–.012
1950	2301-5, 8 Cyl.	A	.001	.001	.006	.017	.017	......	.015	Float	Push	.0005–.0025	.003	.003–.011
	2302-5, 2332-5, 8 Cyl.	A	.001	.001	.006	.017	.017	......	.015	Float	Push	.0005–.0025	.003	.003–.011
	2306-5, 2333-5, 8 Cyl.	A	.001	.001	.006	.017	.017	......	.017	Float	Push	.0005–.0025	.003	.004–.012
1951	2401, 8 Cyl.	A	.001	.001	.006	.0017	.017	......	.015	Float	Push	.0005–.0025	.003	.003–.011
	2402, 8 Cyl.	A	.001	.001	.006	.0017	.017	......	.015	Float	Push	.0005–.0025	.003	.003–.011
	2406, 8 Cyl.	A	.001	.001	.006	.0017	.017	......	.015	Float	Push	.0005–.0025	.003	.003–.011
1952	200, 250, 300, 400, 8 Cyl.	A	......	.00075	.005	.012	.012	......	.011	FL	Push	.0005–.0025	.003	.003–.011
1953	2601, 11, 31, 2602, 6, 26	A	......	.00075	.005	.012	.012	......	.011	FL	Push	.0005–.0025	.003	.003–.011

A—Removed from above.
ΔΔ—1947—130 lb.
Ch—Chain.
♯—1947—117 lb.
SP—Sprocket.
**—1947— 1 degree before.
♭—1947—129 lb. at $1\frac{5}{16}$ in.
*—1947—40 lb. at 40 m.p.h.
‡—1947—145 lb. at $1\frac{13}{32}$ in.
Δ—1947—50 lb. at 40 m.p.h.

Crankshaft Bearing Journal Sizes

Year	Model	Connecting Rod Journals		Main Bearing Journals				
		Diameter	Length	No. 1 Diameter	No. 2 Diameter	No. 3 Diameter	No. 4 Diameter	No. 5 Diameter
1940	1800	2.094	1.250	2.7465	2.7465	2.7465	2.7465	......
	1803, 4, 5, 6, 7, 8	2.250	1.375	2.7465	2.7465	2.7465	*2.7465	*2.7465
1941	1900, 01	2.094	1.250	2.7465	2.7465	2.7465	*2.7465	*2.7465
	1903, 4, 5, 6, 7, 8	2.250	1.375	2.7465	2.7465	2.7465	*2.7465	*2.7465
1942	2000, 20	2.094	1.250	2.7465	2.7465	2.7465	2.7465	......
	2001, 21	2.094	1.250	2.7465	2.7465	2.7465	*2.7465	2.7465
	2003, 23, 4, 5, 6, 7, 8	2.250	1.375	2.7465	2.7465	2.7465	*2.7465	*2.7465
1946–47	2100	2.094	1.250	2.7465	2.7465	2.7465	2.7465	......
	2101, 2111	2.094	1.250	2.7465	2.7465	2.7465	*2.7465	2.7465
	2103, 2106	2.250	1.375	2.7465	2.7465	2.7465	*2.7465	*2.7465
1948 to 50	2201, 02, 11, 32, 2301, 02, 03, 32	2.250	1.312	2.7465	2.7465	2.7465	2.7465	......
	2206, 2233, 2306, 33-5	2.250	1.375	2.7465	2.7465	2.7465	*2.7465	*2.7465
1951	2401, 2402, 2406	2.250	1.312	2.7465	2.7465	2.7465	2.7465	......
1952	200, 250, 300, 8 cyl.	2.250	1.312	2.7465	2.7465	2.7465	2.7465	2.7465
	400, 8 cyl.	2.250	1.312	2.7465	2.7465	2.7465	2.7465	2.7465
1953	2601, 11, 31, 2602, 8 cyl.	2.250	......	2.7465	2.7465	2.7465	2.7465	2.7465
	2606, 26, 8 cyl.	2.250	......	2.7465	2.7465	2.7465	......	......

*—Bearings 6, 7, 8, 9 same as numbers 4, 5.

and Wear Limit Table

CRANKSHAFT		VALVES									OPERATING OIL PRESSURE			
Main Bearing Oil Clearance	Shaft End Play	Spring Tension (Maximum) Inlet	Spring Tension (Maximum) Exhaust	Spring Tension (Maximum) Low Limit	Guide Clearance	Seat Angle Inlet	Seat Angle Exhaust	Valve Timing, Inlet Valve Opens (Deg.)	Camshaft Drive	Gear Marks	Pounds At M.P.H.	Low Limit§	Model	Year
.001–.003	.003–.008	120@1$\frac{5}{16}$	120@1$\frac{5}{16}$	108	.002–.004	30°	45°	1B	Chain	SP†	45@40	25	1800, 6 Cyl.	1940
.001–.003	.003–.008	120@1$\frac{5}{16}$	120@1$\frac{5}{16}$	108	.002–.004	30°	45°	1B	Chain	SP†	45@40	25	1801, 8 Cyl.	
.001–.003	.003–.008	135@1$\frac{13}{32}$	135@1$\frac{13}{32}$	120	.002–.004	30°	45°	4B	Chain	SP†	50@40	25	1803-4-5-6-7-8, 8 Cyl.	
.0005–.0015	.003–.008	124@1$\frac{5}{16}$	124@1$\frac{5}{16}$	110	.0025–.0045	30°	45°	1B	Chain	SP†	40@40	25	1900, 6 Cyl.	1941
.0005–.0015	.003–.008	124@1$\frac{5}{16}$	124@1$\frac{5}{16}$	110	.0025–.0045	30°	45°	1B	Chain	SP†	40@40	25	1901, 8 Cyl.	
.0005–.0015	.003–.008	140@1$\frac{13}{32}$	140@1$\frac{13}{32}$	125	.0025–.0045	30°	45°	4B	Chain	SP†	50@40	25	1903-4-5-6-7-8, 8 Cyl.	
.0005–.0015	.003–.008	129@1$\frac{5}{16}$	129@1$\frac{5}{16}$	117	.0025–.0045	30°	45°	1B	Chain	SP†	40@40	25	2000, 2010, 6 Cyl.	1942
.0005–.0015	.003–.008	129@1$\frac{5}{16}$	129@1$\frac{5}{16}$	117	.0025–.0045	30°	45°	1B	Chain	SP†	40@40	25	2001, 2011, 8 Cyl.	
.0005–.0015	.003–.008	145@1$\frac{13}{32}$	145@1$\frac{13}{32}$	130	.002–.004	30°	45°	4B	Chain	SP†	50@40	25	2003-4-5, 8 Cyl.	
.0005–.0015	.003–.008	129@1$\frac{5}{16}$	129@1$\frac{5}{16}$	117	.0025–.0045	30°	45°	1B	Chain	SP†	40@40	25	2101, 2111, 8 Cyl.	1946–7
.0005–.0015	.003–.008	‡129@1$\frac{5}{16}$	‡129@1$\frac{5}{16}$	△△117	.002–.004	30°	45°	1B	Chain	SP†	△40@40	25	2103, 2106, 8 Cyl.	
.0005–.0015	.003–.008	♭145@1$\frac{13}{32}$	♭145@1$\frac{13}{32}$	#130	.002–.004	30°	45°	**4B	Chain	SP†	*50@40	25	2100, 6 Cyl.	
.0005–.0025	.003–.008	140@1$\frac{13}{32}$	140@1$\frac{13}{32}$	125	.002–.004	30°	45°	10B	Chain	SP†	40@40	25	2201, 2211, 8 Cyl.	1948
.0005–.0025	.003–.008	140@1$\frac{13}{32}$	140@1$\frac{13}{32}$	125	.002–.004	30°	45°	10B	Chain	SP†	40@40	25	2202, 2232, 8 Cyl.	
.0005–.0025	.003–.008	140@1$\frac{13}{32}$	140@1$\frac{13}{32}$	125	.002–.004	30°	45°	4B	Chain	SP†	50@40	25	2206, 2233, 8 Cyl.	
.0005–.0025	.003–.008	140@1$\frac{13}{32}$	140@1$\frac{13}{32}$	125	.002–.004	30°	45°	10B	Chain	SP†	50@40	25	2301, 8 Cyl.	1949
.0005–.0025	.003–.008	140@1$\frac{13}{32}$	140@1$\frac{13}{32}$	125	.002–.004	30°	45°	10B	Chain	SP†	40@40	25	2302-3-32, 8 Cyl.	
.0005–.0025	.003–.008	140@1$\frac{13}{32}$	140@1$\frac{13}{32}$	125	.002–.004	30°	45°	4B	Chain	SP†	50@40	25	2306, 2333, 8 Cyl.	
.001–.003	.003–.008	140@1$\frac{13}{32}$	140@1$\frac{13}{32}$	125	.002–.004	30°	45°	15B	Chain	SP†	40@40	25	2301-5, 8 Cyl.	1950
.001–.003	.003–.008	140@1$\frac{13}{32}$	140@1$\frac{13}{32}$	125	.002–.004	30°	45°	15B	Chain	SP†	40@40	25	2302-5, 2332-5, 8 Cyl.	
.001–.003	.003–.008	140@1$\frac{13}{32}$	140@1$\frac{13}{32}$	125	.002–.004	30°	45°	4B	Chain	SP†	50@40	25	2306-5, 2333-5, 8 Cyl.	
.001–.003	.0035–.008	145@1$\frac{13}{32}$	145@1$\frac{13}{32}$	135	.002–.004	30°	45°	15B	Chain	SP†	40@40	25	2401, 8 Cyl.	1951
.001–.003	.0035–.008	145@1$\frac{13}{32}$	145@1$\frac{13}{32}$	135	.002–.004	30°	45°	15B	Chain	SP†	40@40	25	2402, 8 Cyl.	
.001–.003	.0035–.008	145@1$\frac{13}{32}$	145@1$\frac{13}{32}$	135	.002–.004	30°	45°	4B	Chain	SP†	40@40	25	2406, 8 Cyl.	
.0005–.0025	.004–.008	145@1$\frac{13}{32}$	145@1$\frac{13}{32}$	......	.0024–.005	30°	45°	15B	Chain	......	40@30	......	200, 250, 300, 400, 8 Cyl.	1952
.0005–.0025	.004–.008	145@1$\frac{13}{32}$	145@1$\frac{13}{32}$	......	.0024–.005	30°	45°	15B	Chain	......	40@30	......	2601, 11, 31, 2602, 6, 26	1953

†—Marks on cam and crank sprockets align with shaft center.
§—Car may be operated at a lower oil pressure but low pressure indicates malfunction which should be corrected.

Pistons and Piston Pins

Year	Model	PISTONS Diameter	PISTONS Material	PISTONS Type	PISTONS No. of Rings	PISTON PINS Length	PISTON PINS Diameter	PISTON PINS How Held
1940	1800	3.5	Als	C	3	$3\frac{1}{64}$	.875	F
	1801	3.25	Als	C	3	$2\frac{51}{64}$	.875	F
	1803, 4, 5, 6, 7, 8	3.5	Als	C	3	$3\frac{1}{64}$	.875	F
1941	1900	3.5	Als	C	3	$3\frac{1}{64}$	.875	F
	1901	3.25	Als	C	3	$2\frac{51}{64}$	.875	F
	1903, 4, 5, 6, 7, 8	3.5	Als	C	3	$3\frac{1}{64}$	.875	F
1942	2000, 2010	3.5	Als	C	3	$3\frac{1}{64}$	.875	F
	2001, 2011	3.25	Als	C	3	$2\frac{25}{32}$	.875	F
1946	2100	3.5	Als	C	3	$3\frac{1}{64}$	.875	F
	2101, 2111	3.25	Als	C	3	$2\frac{25}{32}$	.875	F
1947	2100	3.5	Als	C	3	$3\frac{1}{64}$	.875	F
	2101, 2111	3.25	Als	C	3	$2\frac{25}{32}$	.875	F
1948–49	2201, 2211	3.5	Alum.	....	4	$3\frac{1}{64}$	.875	F
	2202, 2232	3.5	Alum.	....	4	$3\frac{1}{64}$	.875	F
	2206, 2233	3.5	Alum.	....	3	$3\frac{1}{64}$	.875	F
1950	2301	3.5	Alum. Alloy	....	3	$3\frac{1}{64}$	.875	F
	2302, 2332	3.5	Alum. Alloy	....	3	$3\frac{1}{64}$	.875	F
	2306	3.5	Alum. Alloy	....	3	$3\frac{1}{64}$	.875	F

PACKARD SPECIFICATIONS

Pistons and Piston Pins—*continued*

Year	Model	PISTONS				PISTON PINS		
		Diameter	Material	Type	No. of Rings	Length	Diameter	How Held
1951	200	3.5	Alum. Alloy	....	3	$3\frac{1}{64}$	.875	F
	300, 400	3.5	Alum. Alloy	....	3	$3\frac{1}{64}$	.875	F
1952	200, 250, 300, 400, 8 cyl.	3.50	Alum. Alloy	Ss,C	3	3.015625	.875	F
1953	2601, 11, 31, 2602, 6, 26	3.50	Alum. Alloy	Ss,C	3	3.015625	.875	F

ALS—Aluminum with steel strut. C—Cam ground. Ss—Split skirt.

Engine Tune-Up Specifications

Year	Model	SPARK PLUGS Type	SPARK PLUGS Gap	DISTRIBUTOR Point Gap	DISTRIBUTOR Cam Dwell (Deg.)	Ignition Timing (Deg.)	Ignition Timing Mark and Location	Compression Pressure at R.P.M.	OPERATING TAPPET CLEARANCE Inlet	OPERATING TAPPET CLEARANCE Exhaust	Carburetor Fuel Float Height	Minimum Engine Idle Speed at R.P.M.
1940	1800, 6 Cyl.	AC-104	.028	.020	35	6B	Vib-Dmpr	110	.007	.010	$\frac{5}{8}$″ Fuel	400–500
	1801, 8 Cyl.	AC-104	.028	.015	27	8B	Vib-Dmpr	110	.007	.010	$\frac{5}{32}$″ Fuel	400–450
	1803-4-5-6-7-8, 8 Cyl.	AC-104	.028	.015	27	5B	Vib-Dmpr	180	A	A	$\frac{5}{8}$″ Fuel	400–450
1941	1900, 6 Cyl.	AC-104	.028	.020	38	6B	Vib-Dmpr	110	.007	.010	$\frac{5}{8}$″ Fuel	400–450
	1901, 8 Cyl.	AC-104	.028	.015	27	7B	Vib-Dmpr	110	.007	.010	$\frac{5}{32}$″ Fuel	400–450
	1903-4-5-6-7-8, 8 Cyl.	AC-104	.028	.015	27	5B	Vib-Dmpr	108	A	A	$\frac{5}{8}$″ Fuel	400–450
1942	2000,2010, 6 Cyl.	AC-104	.028	.020	38	4B	Vib-Dmpr	110	.007	.010	$\frac{3}{8}$″ Float	400–450
	2001, 2011, 8 Cyl.	AC-104	.028	.015	27	5B	Vib-Dmpr	110	.007	.010	$\frac{5}{32}$″ Float	400–450
	2003-4-5, 8 Cyl.	AC-104	.028	.015	27	4B	Vib-Dmpr	108	A	A	$\frac{5}{32}$″ Float	400–450
1946–7	2101, 2111, 8 Cyl.	AC-104	.028	.015	27	7B	Vib-Dmpr	110	.007	.010	$\frac{5}{32}$″ Float	400–450
	2103, 2106, 8 Cyl.	AC-104	.028	.015	27	7B	Vib-Dmpr	110	.007♭	.010♭	$\frac{5}{32}$″ Float	400–450
	2100, 6 Cyl.	AC-104	.028	.020	27†	7B	Vib-Dmpr	108‡	.007**	.010**	$\frac{3}{8}$″ Float△	400–450
1948	2201, 2211, 8 Cyl.	AC-104	.028	.017	27*	6B	Vib-Dmpr	108	.007	.010	$\frac{5}{32}$″ Float	400–450
	2202, 2232, 8 Cyl.	AC-104	.028	.017	27*	6B	Vib-Dmpr	110	.007	.010	$\frac{5}{32}$″ Float	400–450
	2206, 2233, 8 Cyl.	AC-104	.028	.017	27*	6B	Vib-Dmpr	108	A	A	$\frac{5}{32}$″ Float	400–450
1949	2301, 8 Cyl.	AC-104	.028	.017	27	6B	Vib-Dmpr	108	.007	.010	$\frac{5}{32}$″ Float	400–450
	2302-3-32, 8 Cyl.	AC-104	.028	.017	27	6B	Vib-Dmpr	110	.007	.010	$\frac{5}{32}$″ Float	400–450
	2306, 2333, 8 Cyl.	AC-104	.028	.017	27	6B	Vib-Dmpr	108	A	A	$\frac{5}{32}$″ Float	400–450
1950	2301-5, 8 Cyl.	AC-104	.028	.017	27	6B	Vib-Dmpr	108	A	A	$\frac{5}{32}$″ Float	400–450
	2302-5, 2332-5, 8 Cyl.	AC-104	.028	.017	27	6B	Vib-Dmpr	110	.007	.010	$\frac{5}{32}$″ Float	400–450
	2306-5, 2333-5, 8 Cyl.	AC-104	.028	.017	27	6B	Vib-Dmpr	108	A	A	$\frac{5}{32}$″ Float	400–450
1951	2401, 8 Cyl.	AC-46-5	.030	.017	27	6B	Vib-Dmpr	108	.007	.010	$\frac{5}{32}$″ Float	400–450
	2402, 8 Cyl.	AC-46-5	.030	.017	27	6B	Vib-Dmpr	110	A	A	$\frac{5}{32}$″ Float	400–450
	2406, 8 Cyl.	AC-46-5	.030	.017	27	6B	Vib-Dmpr	108	A	A	$\frac{5}{32}$″ Float	375–400#
1952	200, 8 Cyl.	AL-A5H	.028	.017	27	6B	Vib. Dmpr.	....	.007H	.010H	$1\frac{3}{64}$″	400
	250, 300, 400, 8 Cyl.	AL-A5H	.028	.017	27	6B	Vib. Dmpr.	....	AA	AA	$1\frac{3}{64}$″	400
1953	2601, 2611, 8 Cyl.	AL-A5	.028	.017	30	6B	Dmpr.	....	.007H	.010H	....	400
	2631, 02, 06, 26, 8 Cyl.	AL-A5	.028	.017	30	6B	Dmpr.	....	AA	AA	....	400

A—Automatic Take-up.
*—31° 2211, 2232, 2233.
♭—1947 Automatic take-up
#—325. 375 hot.
**—1946 Automatic take-up.
△—1946 $\frac{5}{32}$″ float.
†—1947 38B.
‡—1946 110.

Piston Ring Dimensions

Year	Model	Cylinder Bore	TOP RING Width	TOP RING Gap	TOP RING Depth	SECOND RING Width	SECOND RING Gap	SECOND RING Depth	THIRD RING Width	THIRD RING Gap	THIRD RING Depth	OIL RING Width	OIL RING Gap	OIL RING Depth
1940–47	One Ten, Super Eight, Cust.	$3\frac{1}{2}$	$\frac{1}{8}$	.012	.175	$\frac{1}{8}$	.012	.150	$\frac{3}{16}$	.011	.126	....	....	....
	All Others	$3\frac{1}{4}$	$\frac{1}{8}$	.012	.175	$\frac{1}{8}$	.012	.145	$\frac{3}{16}$	.011	.125	....	....	....
1948–51	Series—All	$3\frac{1}{2}$	.0932	.012	....	.0937	.012	....	$\frac{3}{16}$	.011	....	....	....	....
1952	200, 250, 300, 400, 8 Cyl.	$3\frac{1}{2}$	$\frac{3}{32}$	.012	.170	$\frac{3}{32}$	.012	.170	$\frac{3}{16}$	.012	.188	....	....	....
1953	2601, 11, 31, 2602, 6, 26, 8 Cyl.	$3\frac{1}{2}$	$\frac{3}{32}$	.012	.160	$\frac{3}{32}$	.012	.160	$\frac{3}{16}$	.011	.157	....	....	....

Brake Data

Year	Model	Make	Lining Type	R=Riveted B=Bonded	Drum Diameter	Lining Length	Lining Width	Lining Thickness	Clearance Toe	Clearance Hee
1940	1800	......	......	R	11	22⅝	1¾	3/16	......	......
	1801	......	......	R	12	24½	1¾	3/16	......	......
	1803, 4, 5	......	......	R	12	I	M	3/16	......	......
	1806, 7, 8	......	......	R	12	I	M	3/16	......	......
1941	1900	Ben	......	R	11	22⅝	1¾	3/16	......	......
	1901	Ben	......	R	12	24½	1¾	3/16	......	......
	1903, 4, 5	Ben	......	R	12	S	R	3/16	......	......
	1906-7-8	Ben	......	R	12	S	R	3/16	......	......
1942	2001, 2011	......	M	R	12	11½–*13	1¾	3/16	.015	.015
	2021	......	WM	R	12	11½–*13	1¾	3/16	.015	.015
1946–47	2100	......	......	R	12–*11	24¼–*22⅝	1¾	3/16	......	......
	2101, 2111	......	......	R	12	24½	1¾	3/16	......	......
	2103, 2106	......	......	R	12	24½	2¼–*2	3/16	......	......
1948–49	2201, 2211	......	......	R	12	24½	1¾	3/16	......	......
	2202, 2232	......	......	R	12	24½	1¾	3/16	......	......
	2206, 2233	......	......	R	12	24½	2¼–*2	3/16	......	......
1950	2301, 02, 32	......	......	R	12	24½	1¾	3/16	......	......
	2306-33	......	......	R	12	24½	2¼–*2	3/16	......	......
1951	200	......	M	R	12	24½	1¾	3/16	......	......
	300, 400	......	M	R	12	24½	2½–*2	3/16	......	......
1952	200, 8 Cyl.	......	M	R	12	24½	1¾	3/16	.010	.010
	250, 300, 400, 8 Cyl.	......	M	R	12	24½	2¼–*2	3/16	.010	.010
1953	2601, 2611, 8 Cyl.	......	M	R	12	24½	1¾	3/16	.010	.010
	2631, 02, 06, 26, 8 Cyl.	......	M	R	12	24½	2¼–*2	3/16	.010	.010

I—1803-06—24½; 1804-5-7-8—26. M—1803-6—2; 1804-5-7-8—2¼. S—1903-6—24½; 1904-5-7-8—26. R—1903-6—2; 1904-5-7-8—2¼. *—Rear.
Ben—Bendix. M—Moulded. WM—Woven on primary, moulded on secondary.

Tension Wrench Specifications

Year	Model	Cylinder Head Lbs.-Ft.	Cylinder Head Thread	Spark Plug Lbs.-Ft.	Spark Plug Thread	Connecting Rod Bolts or Nuts Lbs.-Ft.	Connecting Rod Bolts or Nuts Thread	Main Bearing Bolt Lbs.-Ft.	Main Bearing Bolt Thread	Flywheel Bolts Lbs.-Ft.	Flywheel Bolts Thread	Vibration Damper Bolts Lbs.-Ft.	Vibration Damper Bolts Thread
1942 to 48	Six	60-62	7/16-20	10-14	10 mm	60-65	7/16-28	90-95	½-13	65-70	7/16-20	130-150	¾-16
	Eight	60-62	7/16-20	10-14	10 mm	45-46	⅜-24	82-85	½-13	65-70	½-20	......	......
	Super Eight	60-62	7/16-20	10-14	10 mm	56-58	7/16-28	82-85	½-13	65-70	½-20	......	......
1949 to 53	Six & Eight	60-62	7/16-20	10-14	10 mm	60-65	7/16-28	90-95	½-13	70-80	½-20	130-150	¾-16

Cooling System

CAR AND YEAR	MODEL	Capacity Qts.	Quarts of Methanol Base Anti-Freeze (For Protection to Temperature Shown Below)							Quarts of Ethylene Glycol (For Protection to Temperature Shown Below)							Quarts of Denatured Alcohol—188 Proof (For Protection to Temperature Shown Below)						
			3	4	5	6	7	8	9	3	4	5	6	7	8	9	3	4	5	6	7	8	9
1940	6-1800	17	15	6	−4	−16	−29	−45	....	18	12	5	−4	−14	−27	−42	....	10	0	....	−10	−20	−30
1940	8-1801	18	17	8	−1	−12	−25	−38	−53	19	14	7	0	−10	−21	−34	20	10	....	0	−10	....	−20
1941	6-1900	15	11	1	−12	−27	−44	....	....	16	8	0	−12	−26	−43	....	....	10	0	−10	−20	−30	....
1938-50	1603-45, 1803-4-5-6-7-8, 1903-4-5-6-7-8, 2003-23-4-5-6-7-8, 2103-6-26,																						

Cooling System—*continued*

CAR AND YEAR	MODEL	Capacity Qts.	Quarts of Methanol Base Anti-Freeze (For Protection to Temperature Shown Below)							Quarts of Ethylene Glycol (For Protection to Temperature Shown Below)							Quarts of Denatured Alcohol—188 Proof (For Protection to Temperature Shown Below)						
			3	4	5	6	7	8	9	3	4	5	6	7	8	9	3	4	5	6	7	8	9
1938 to 50—cont'd	2202-6-13-22-26-32-33, 2302-32, 2306-33	20	18	11	4	−5	−16	−27	−39	....	16	10	4	−3	−12	−22	20	....	10	....	0	−10	−20
1941-47	1901, 2001-11-21, 2101-11	17	15	6	−4	−16	−29	−45	....	18	12	5	−4	−14	−27	−42	....	10	0	....	−10	−20	−30
1942-48	2000-10-20, 2100-30, 2222-40	14	9	−3	−17	−34	−53	....	....	15	6	−5	−18	−34	−54	....	10	....	0	−10	−20	−30	....
1948-50	2201-11, 2301	18	17	8	−1	−12	−25	−38	−53	19	14	7	0	−10	−21	−34	20	10	....	0	−10	....	−20
1951-53	200, 300, 400	20	18	11	4	−5	−16	−27	−39	....	16	10	4	−3	−12	−22	−20	....	10	....	0	−10	−20

Distributors

Year	Model	Distributor Model Number	Cam Angle (deg.)	Direction of Rotation C=Clockwise CC=Counter Clockwise at Cam End	Breaker Arm Spring Tension	Breaker Point Gap (inches)	Engine R.P.M. when Cent. Advance Starts	Max. Cent. Advance in Engine Deg. at Stated Engine R.P.M.	Vacuum in (inches) of Mercury at which Vacuum Unit Starts	Max. Advance in Engine Deg. at Stated Vacuum	Vacuum Unit Number
1940	1801, 1802, 8 cyl.	IGP-4501	27	CC	17–20	.013–.017	600	16@2400	....	....	....
	....	IGP-4501A	27	CC	17–20	.013–.017	500	23@3100	....	....	....
	1803, 04, 05, 8 cyl.	IGT-4102	27	CC	17–20	.016–.018	500	23@3600	7	11@16	IGT-2028-BS
1941	1900, 6 cyl.	IGC-4505	38	CC	17–20	.018–.024	600	19@3200	....	....	....
	1900, 6 cyl.	1110092	35	CC	19–23	.018–.024	600	20.5@3200	5 to 7	15@15 to 19	1116028
	1901, 8 cyl.	IGP-4502	27	CC	17–20	.013–.017	500	23@3100	10	12@17	VC-3060-GS
	....	IGP-4502A	27	CC	17–20	.013–.017	650	21.5@3100	10	12@17	VC-3060-GS
	1903, 8 cyl.	IGT-4102	27	CC	17–20	.016–.018	500	23@3600	7	11@16	IGT-2028-BS
	1950, 6 cyl.	IGC-4505	38	CC	17–20	.018–.024	600	19@3200	6	15@17	VC-3060-KS
	1951, 1952, 8 cyl.	IGP-4502A	27	CC	17–20	.013–.017	650	21.5@3100	10	12@17	VC-3060-GS
1942	2000, 6 cyl.	IGC-4505	38	CC	17–20	.018–.024	600	19@3200	6	15@17	VC-3060-KS
	2001, 2002, 6 cyl.	IGP-4502A	38	C	17–20	.018–.024	530	30@2700	....	....	....
	2003, 4, 5, 8 cyl.	IGT-4102	27	CC	17–20	.016–.018	500	23@3600	7	11@16	IGT-2028-BS
	....	IGT-4203	27	CC	17–20	.016–.018	500	23@3600	7	11@16	VC-3117-LS
	110, 6 cyl.	1110132	35	C	19–23	.018–.024	600	20.5@3200	5 to 7	15@15 to 19	1116034
1946–47	2100, 6 cyl.	IGC-4505	38	CC	17–20	.018–.024	600	19@3200	6	15@17	VC-3060-KS
	2101, 2102, 8 cyl.	IGP-4502A	27	CC	17–20	.013–.017	650	21.5@3100	10	12@17	VC-3060-GS
	2103, 4, 5, 8 cyl.	IGT-4203	27	CC	17–20	.016–.018	500	23@3600	7	11@16	VC-3117-LS
	2100, 2111, 6 cyl.	1110132	35	C	19–23	.018–.024	600	20.5@3200	5 to 7	15@15 to 19	1116034
1947–50	2200, 6 cyl.	1110811	31	CC	17–20	.013–.018	600	18@3200	5 to 7	13 to 15	1116041
1948–49	2202, 2232, 8 cyl.	IGP-4502B	27	CC	17–20	.013–.018	600	16@3200	6	7@14	....
	2206, 13, 26, 33, 8 cyl.	IGT-4203	27	CC	17–20	.016–.018	500	23@3600	7	11@16	VC-3117-LS
	2302, 32, 8 cyl.	IGP-4502B	27	CC	17–20	.013–.018	600	16@3200	6	7@14	....
	2306, 33, 8 cyl.	IGT-4203	27	CC	17–20	.016–.018	500	23@3600	7	11@16	VC-3117-LS
1950	2301, 02, 32, -5, 8 cyl.	IGP-4502B	27	CC	17–20	.013–.018	600	16@3200	6	7@14	....
	2306-5, 33-5, 8 cyl.	IGT-4203	27	CC	17–20	.016–.018	500	23@3600	7	11@16	VC-3117-LS
1951	200, 300, 400, 8 cyl.	IGP-4502C	27	CC	19–23	.013–.018	600	16@3200	6	7@14	....
	2400, 8 cyl.	1110825	....	....	17–21	.015–.018	600	....	....	....	....
1952	200, 250, 300, 400, 8 cyl.	IGP-4502C	27	CC	17–20	.017	600	16@3200	6	21@17	....
	200, 250, 300, 8 cyl.	1110825	21½	CC	17–21	.017	600	16@3200	6	21@17	....
1953	2601, 11, 31, Delco	1110841	20–30	C	17–21	.013–.017	600	16@3200	6	10@10	....
	2602, 6, 26, Auto-Lite	CR-4001A	27	C	17–20	.013–.017	500	15@2800	6	13@10	....

Generators

Year	Model	Generator Number	Field Current at 6 Volts (amps.)	Maximum Safe Output: Volts	Maximum Safe Output: Amperes	Maximum Safe Output: R.P.M.	Brush Spring Tension (oz.)	Voltage Regulator Number
1940	1800, 1801, 1802	GEA-4801-A	1.3–1.5	8.0	35	1600	35–53	VRP-4201-A-1
	1803, 04, 05	GEA-4802-A	1.3–1.5	8.0	35	1750	35–53	VRP-4003-A
1941	1900-51 Autolite	GEB-4802-C-2	1.3–1.5	8.0	35	1300	64–68	VRP-4002-D
		GEA-4802-A-1	1.3–1.5	8.0	35	1750	35–53	VRP-4002-C
	Delco-Remy	1102682	1.75–1.9	8.0	30	1750	25	1118202
	1903	GEA-4802-A-1	1.3–1.5	8.0	35	1750	35–53	VRP-4002-C
	1950, 51, 52	GDZ-4801-F	1.3–1.5	8.0	35	2000	35–53	VRP-4002-C
1942	2000, 01, 02-Autolite	GDZ-4801-F	1.3–1.5	8.0	35	2000	35–53	VRP-4002-C
	Delco-Remy	11102682	1.75–1.9	8.0	30	1750	25	1118202
	2003, 04, 05	GEA-4802-A-1	1.3–1.5	8.0	35	1750	35–53	VRP-4002-C
1946–47	2100, 01, 02	GDZ-4801-F	1.3–1.5	8.0	35	2000	35–53	VRP-4002-C
	2103, 04, 05	GEA-4802-A-1	1.3–1.5	8.0	35	1750	35–53	VRP-4002-C
1947	2100, 2111, Delco-Remy	1102682	1.75–1.9	8.0	30	1750	25	1118278
1947	2200	1102669	1.75–1.9	8.0	30	1825	25	1118278
1948	2200	1102705	1.75–1.9	8.0	30	1750	25	1118278
1948–49	2201, 02, 11, 32	GDZ-4801-F	1.3–1.5	8.0	35	2000	35–53	VRP-4402-A
		GDZ-4801-T	1.3–1.5	8.0	35	2000	35–53	VRP-4402-A
	2206, 26, 33	GDZ-4801-G	1.3–1.5	8.0	35	2000	35–53	VRP-4402-A
		GDZ-4801-V	1.3–1.5	8.0	35	2000	35–53	VRP-4402-A
		GEG-4823-F	1.3–1.5	8.0	40	1575	64–68	VRP-4402-B
1949–50	2200	1102705	1.75–1.9	8.0	30	1750	25	1118331
	2300	1102715	1.90–2.05	8.0	40	1900	25	1118360
1951	2400	1102745	1.90–2.05	8.0	40	1900	25	1118360
	200, 300, 400	GGW-6003-A	....	....	....	....	....	VRP-4402-C
1952	200, 250, 300, 400, 8 cyl.	GGW-6003-A	....	....	....	....	....	VBE-6102-A
	200, 250, 300, 8 cyl.	1102778						1118726
1953	2601, 11, 31, 2602, 8 cyl.	1102778	....	7.4	45	2400	....	1118726
	2606, 26, 8 cyl.	GGW-6003-A	....	7.4	45	2400	....	VBA-6102-A

Voltage Regulators

Year	Model	Regulator Number	Grounded P=Positive N=Negative	Voltage Control: Air Gap Points Closed	Voltage Control: Voltage Setting Hot	Current Control: Air Gap Points Closed	Current Control: Current Set Hot	Cut-Out Relay: Point Gap	Cut-Out Relay: Air Gap	Cut-Out Relay: Closing Volt
1940	1800, 1801	VRP-4002-A	P	.052	7.3	.038	34–36	.015	.038	6.4–7.0
	1803, 1804, 1805	VRP-4003-A	P	.052	7.3	.038	34–36	.015	.038	6.4–7.0
1941–42	1900, 01, 03; 2000, 01, 03, 04	1118202	P	.070	7.2	.080	34–36	.020	.020	6.2–6.7
		VRP-4002-C	P	.052	7.3	.052	34–36	.015	.034	6.4–7.0
1946–47	2100, 01, 02	VRP-4002-C	P	.052	7.3	.052	34–36	.015	.034	6.4–7.0
		1118202	P	.070	7.2	.080	34–36	.020	.020	6.2–6.7
		1118278	P	.070	7.2	.080	32–34	.020	.020	6.2–6.7
1948	2200	1118278	P	.070	7.2	.080	32–34	.020	.020	6.2–6.7
1948 to 50	2201, 02, 11, 06. 26, 33	VRP-4402-A	P	.052	7.3	.052	34–36	.015	.034	6.4–7.0
		1118331	P	.075	7.0	.075	32–40	.020	.020	5.9–6.8
		1118360	P	.075	7.0	.075	32–40	.020	.020	5.9–6.8
1951	2400	1118360	P	.075	7.0	.075	32–40	.020	.020	5.9–6.8
1952	200, 250, 300, 400, 8 cyl.	VBE-6102-A	....	....	7.4	....	45	....	....	6.5–7.0
	200, 250, 300, 8 cyl.	1118726	....	....	7.4	....	45	....	....	6.5–7.0
1953	2601, 11, 31, 2602	1118726	....	....	7.4	....	45	....	....	6.5–7.0
	2606, 26	VAB-6102-A	....	....	7.4	....	45	....	....	6.5–7.0

Starters

Year	Model	Unit Model Number	Spring Tension (oz.)	STARTER Lock Test Volts	Lock Test Amperes	Lock Test Torque, (lbs. ft.)	No Load Volts	No Load Amperes	No Load R.P.M.	Direction of Rotation Viewed from Drive End C=Clockwise CC=Counter-clockwise
1940	1800	MZ-4078	42–53	2.0	280	4.4	5.0	68	4000	C
	1801, 02	MAW-4018	42–53	2.0	335	6	5.0	65	4300	C
	1803, 04, 05	MAX-4041	42–53	2.0	410	13	5.0	74	2360	C
1941	1900, 01, 51, 52	MAW-4021	42–53	2.0	335	6	5.0	65	4300	C
		MAW-4024	42–53	2.0	335	6	5.0	65	4300	C
		1107037	24–28	3.4	525	12	5.7	75	5000	C
	1903	MAX-4041	42–53	2.0	410	13	5.0	74	2360	C
1942	2000, 01, 02	MAW-4027	42–53	2.0	335	6	5.0	65	4300	C
	2003, 04, 05	MAX-4052	42–53	2.0	410	13	5.0	74	2360	C
	110, Clipper & Conv.	1107037	24–28	3.4	525	12	5.7	75	5000	C
		1107056	24–28	3.4	525	12	5.7	75	5000	C
1946–47	2100, 01, 02, 11	MAW-4024	42–53	2.0	335	6	5.0	65	4300	C
		1107037	42–53	2.0	410	13	5.0	74	2360	C
	2103, 04, 05	MAX-4052	42–53	2.0	410	13	5.0	74	2360	C
1947 to 49	2201, 02, 11, 32	MCL-6003	42–53	2.0	410	8	5.0	65	4900	C
	2200	1107943	24–28	3.0	600	16	5.7	65	5500	C
	2206, 13, 26, 33	MAX-4052	42–53	2.0	410	13	5.0	74	2360	C
1950	2306, 13, 26, 33	MAX-4052	42–53	2.0	410	13	5.0	74	2360	C
	2301, 02, 11, 22, 32	MCL-6003	42–53	2.0	410	8	5.0	65	4900	C
		1107943	24–28	3.0	600	16	5.7	65	5500	C
1951	2400	1107943	24–28	3.0	600	16	5.7	65	4900	C
	200, 300, 400	MCL-6113	....	4.0	875	25	....	65	....	....
		1107943	24–28	3.0	600	16	5.7	65	5500	C
1952	200, 250, 300, 8 cyl.	MCL-6113	42–53	4	875	25	....	....	....	C
	....	1107943	24–28	3	600	16	....	....	....	C
	400, 8 cyl.	MCL-6114	42–53	4	875	25	....	....	....	C
1953	2601, 11, 31, 2602	1108008	42–53	3	600	16	....	....	....	....
	2606, 26	MCL-6122	42–53	4	875	25	....	....	....	....

Front Wheel Alignment

Year	Model	Caster (deg.)	Camber (deg.)	King Pin Inclination (deg.)	Toe-In (inches)	Turning Radius Inner	Turning Radius Outer
1940	1800, 1801	1P to 2P	½P to ¾P	1¾ to 2	0	21	20
	1803–06	1P to 2P	½P to ¾P	1¾ to 2	0	21½	20
	1804–07	½N to 1½N	½P to ¾P	1¾ to 2	0	23½	20
	1805–08	½N to 1½N	½P to ¾P	1¾ to 2	0	26½	20
1941	1900	0 to 1P	½P to ¾P	2½	0	20½	20
	1901	0 to 1P	½P to ¾P	2½	0	21	20
	1903–06	¼N to 1⅛P	½P to ¾P	2½	0	22½	20
	1904–07	¼N to 1⅛P	½P to ¾P	2½	0	24	20
	1905–08	¼N to 1⅛P	½P to ¾P	2½	0	24½	20
1942	2000, 2010, 2100	½P to 1½P	....	5½	0 to ⅛	23	20
1946–47	All	1½P to 2½P	¼N to ¾P	5½	0	23	20
1948–49	2201, 2211, 02, 32, 06, 33, 2301, 02, 32	½P to 1½P	¼N to ¾P	5½	0	23	20
1949	2306, 33	1½P to 2½P	¼N to ¾P	5½	0	23	20
1950	2301–05	½N to 1P	0 to ¼P	5½	0	23	20
	2302-5-2332-5	1½P to 2½P	¼N to ¼P	5¾ to 6	0	23	20
	2306-5-2332-5	1½P to 2½P	¼N to ¼P	5¾ to 6	0	....	....
1951–52	200, 300, 400	½N to 1N	0 to ¾P	5¾ to 6	0	23	20
1953	200, 300, 400	½N to 1N	0 to ¾P	5¾ to 6	0	17½	20

Fan, Generator Belts and Radiator Hose

Year	Model	Fan Belt			Generator Belt			Upper Hose			Lower Hose		
		Angle of "V" (deg.)	Length O.C.	Width Max.	Angle of "V" (deg.)	Length O.C.	Width Max.	Type	Inside Diam.	Length	Type	Inside Diam.	Length
1940	1800, 1801	42	49 1/8	23/32	....	....	....	straight	1 3/4	7 1/4	straight	1 3/4	3
	1803, 4, 5, 6, 7, 8	42	52 11/16	1 1/32	....	....	....	straight	1 3/4	6 1/2	straight	1 3/4	3
1941	1900, 01, 01A	42	49 1/8	23/32	....	....	....	curved	1 3/4	....	straight	1 3/4	3
	1951	42	49 1/8	23/32	....	....	....	curved	1 3/4	....	straight	1 3/4	3 3/4
	1903, 4, 5, 6, 7, 8	42	52 11/16	1 1/32	....	....	....	curved	1 3/4	....	straight	1 3/4	3
1942	2000, 01, 10, 11	42	49 1/8	23/32	....	....	....	curved	1 3/4	....	straight	1 3/4	3 3/4
	2003, 2006	42	52 11/16	1 1/32	....	....	....	curved	1 3/4	....	straight	1 3/4	3 3/4
1946–47	2100, 01, 10, 11	42	49 1/8	23/32	....	....	....	curved	1 3/4	....	straight	1 3/4	4
	2103, 06, 26	42	52 11/16	1 1/32	....	....	....	curved	1 3/4	....	straight	1 3/4	3 3/4
1948 to 50	All 6 cyl.	42	49 1/8	23/32	....	....	....	curved	1 3/4	....	straight	1 3/4	4
	8 & Super 8	42	49 1/8	23/32	....	....	....	curved	1 3/4	....	straight	1 3/4	4
	Cust. Super 8	42	54	1 1/16	....	....	....	curved	1 3/4	....	straight	1 3/4	4
1951	Series—All	40	41 5/8	1 3/32	....	....	....	curved	1 3/4	....	straight	1 3/4	4
1952	200, 250, 300, 8 cyl.	40	41 13/64	3/8	....	....	....	curved	1 3/4	....	curved	1 3/4	....
	400, 8 cyl.	40	41 13/64	3/8	....	....	....	curved	1 3/4	....	curved	1 3/4	3 3/4
1953	2601, 11, 31, 2602, 6, 26	40	41 13/64	3/8	....	....	....	curved	1 3/4	....	curved	1 3/4	....

King Pin Specification Chart

Year	Model	KING BOLT			UPPER BUSHING				LOWER BUSHING			
					King Bolt Bushing				King Bolt Bushing			
		Diameter	Length	Bolt Number	Inside Diameter	Outside Diameter	Length	Bushing Number	Inside Diameter	Outside Diameter	Length	Bushing Number
1940	All, 6 & 8 cyl.	.866	5 1/8	330868	.867	1.058	1 3/16	335537	.867	1.058	1 3/16	335537
1941	1900, 1901	.866	5 1/8	330868	.866	1.190	1 3/32	8495-s	.866	1.190	1 3/32	8495-s
	1903, 04, 05, 06, 07, 08	.866	5 1/8	330868	.853	1.190	1 3/16	362614	.853	1.190	1 3/16	362604
1942 to 51	All	.866	5 3/8	367761	.866	1.190	1 3/32	8495-s	.853	1.190	1 3/16	362604

PACKARD 1940 thru 1953

FRONT SUSPENSION

SERIES 120 AND 120B, 1940 THRU 1942

The front suspension consisted of a single lower suspension arm to which is mounted a torque arm at the outer end. The torque arm at the back end is mounted on the frame and its purpose is to hold the lower suspension arm in perfect alignment relative to the frame. On this construction the upper suspension arm is used as the shock absorber. A torsion bar is used to stabilize the front end.

1940 THRU 1953 EXCEPT 120 AND 120B

The front suspension used on all Packard models (except those above) from 1940 thru 1951 is the short and long arm type suspension, known as SLA or parallel arm type.

The shock absorber was used as an upper suspension arm on all models up to 1950. Starting with 1950 production a direct acting shock absorber was used mounted between the A frame and the chassis in the center of the coil spring.

Caster, Camber and Toe-In

SERIES 120 AND 120B, 1940 THRU 1942

Camber is controlled by the use of offset pilot at the outer end of the upper support arm. These pilots are arranged so that they fit tightly into the upper support arm and the hole through the pilot for the upper suspension arm pin is bored off center. To increase camber turn the pilot so that the hole is nearest to the outer end of the upper support arm. Various offset pilots are available to control or to correct the camber angle. If no pilots are available it will be necessary to use bending equipment on the knuckle support in order to correct for defective camber angle.

Under no circumstances should heat be used to assist in bending the knuckle support. These parts and all other front suspension parts are heat treated after forging and heating them to cherry red will destroy the effect of the heat treatment and render the part unfit for service.

Caster is controlled by means of shims between the lower suspension arm and the torque bar. Adding shims between the torque bar and the lower suspension arm will increase the caster angle. Removing shims will decrease the caster angle. If, after all the shims have been removed, the caster reading is still too high it will be necessary to locate and replace the damaged or bent parts.

A sufficient amount of latitude is built into the parts to allow for correction of the steering angles, without resorting to bending parts.

Camber pilots are available in 1/16 in., ⅛ in. and 3/16 in. offsets.

1940 THRU 1953 EXCEPT MODELS 120 AND 120B.

Caster and camber are both controlled at the eccentric pin in the outer end of the upper support arm. Since this eccentric pin controls both caster and camber it is necessary first to turn the pin until correct caster is achieved and then secure the best camber setting possible within a one-half turn of the correct caster setting. The procedure is as follows:

Remove the lubrication setting from the bushing in the upper support arm and insert an Allen wrench into the hole from which the bushing was removed. Loosen the clamp screw which holds the bushing stationary in the knuckle support and turn the eccentric pin in a clockwise direction to increase caster, counter-clockwise to decrease caster, until the correct caster setting is obtained. From that point the maximum camber adjustment possible can be achieved in one-half turn. After final adjustment has been secured lock the clamp bolt which holds the eccentric pin in the knuckle support. Replace the lubrication fitting.

Toe-In

Toe-in is adjusted by turning the sleeve at the outer end of both tie rods. Toe-in should always be the last adjustment made on the front suspension angles.

Replacement of Coil Spring

SERIES 120 AND 120B 1940 THRU 1942

To remove the coil spring, jack up the car at the center plate on the front crossmember or lift it with a hoist attached to the bumper. Place a jack under the pad at the front end of the torque arm. Remove the wheel and disconnect the brake tube and tie rod at the wheel end. Remove the two bolts which hold the inner end of the lower control arm to the frame and install in one of the holes a 3/16 bolt approximately 3½ in. long. This is inserted to guide the lower support arm downward. Remove the upper suspension arm outer bolt and raise the frame and/or lower the jack underneath the torque arm pad until the spring is loose enough to be removed by hand. When installing a new spring be certain the right spring is obtained since different springs were used for different body styles and different equipment in the standard car.

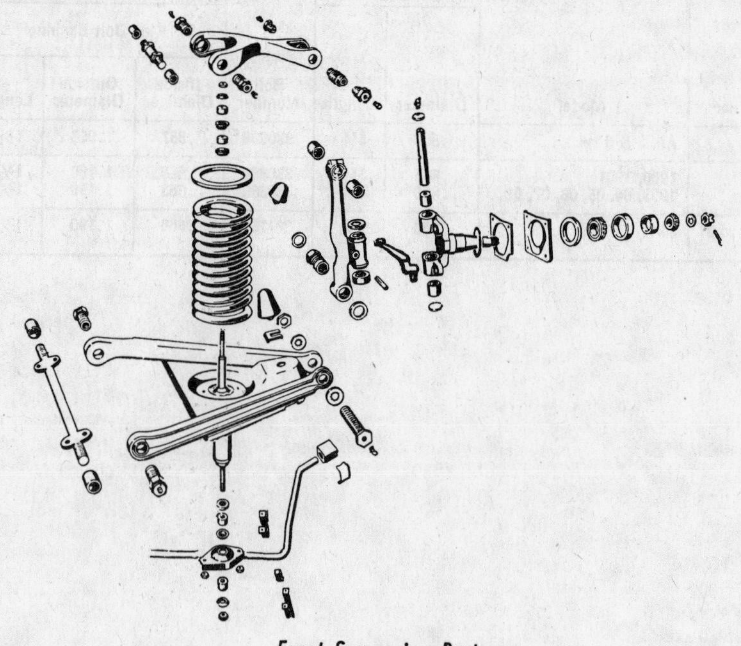

Front Suspension Parts

1940 THRU 1953, ALL MODELS EXCEPT SERIES 120 AND 120B

Support the weight of the car on stationary jacks in back of the front suspension.

Place a roller jack under the inner shaft of the lower suspension arm and take a slight load on the jack. Disconnect the torsion bar and (on 1951 models disconnect the shock absorber). With the load on the roller jack remove the four bolts which hold the lower suspension on inner shaft to the front cross-members and slowly lower the A frame releasing the spring pressure. After the pressure is released the spring may be lifted out from under the car. When replacing a new spring make certain that the end of the spring is properly positioned in the groove in the lower suspension arm. Jack the lower A frame back into place guiding it with two long drift pins so that the bolt holes in the front cross-member will line up.

REPLACEMENT OF UPPER SUSPENSION PINS AND/OR BUSHINGS

Replacement of Upper Support Arm Pin

SERIES 120 AND 120B, 1940 THRU 1942

To replace the upper support arm pin simply remove the cotter pin and nut which holds the pin in the upper support arm and remove the pin. Anytime the pin is to be replaced make certain the position of the offset in the camber pilots is noted so they can be reinstalled in the position from which they were removed, if it is not necessary to make a change in the camber setting.

Replacement of Upper Arm Pins and/or Bushings

1940 THRU 1953, ALL MODELS EXCEPT 120 AND 120B

To replace the upper suspension arm outer pins and bushings support the car on a jack on the lower A frame and remove the road wheel. Remove the clamp bolt which holds the upper suspension arm bushing and unscrew the bushing, and loosen the clamp which holds the eccentric pin in the upper end of the knuckle support and unscrew the eccentric pin. When replacing this pin remember that it is a double thread, with two starts; when it is screwed in so that it is exactly centered in the

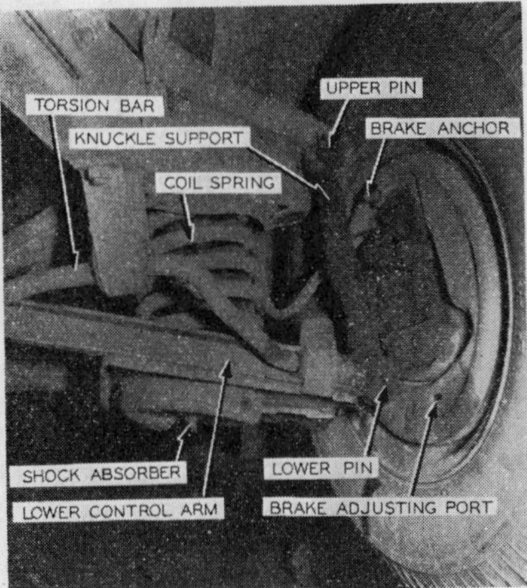

Front Suspension 1952 Models

knuckle support the eccentric portion of the pin should be pointed outward (full camber). If this is not achieved on the first try back the screw all the way out, turn it one-half revolution and start it again on the opposite thread.

When properly installed the knuckle support will be about in the middle of the yoke formed by the upper suspension arm.

Replacement of Lower Arm Pin & Bearings

SERIES 120 AND 120B, 1940 THRU 1942

To replace the lower arm pin and bearings take the weight of the car on a jack under the lower support arm and remove the wheel, drum and backing plate. Drive out the lock pin which holds the lower suspension arm pin to the knuckle support. This pin is quite similar to the king pin lock pin. Remove the grease fitting from either end of the lower pin and, using a drift through the grease fitting hole, drive the lower pin out of the knuckle support and the lower suspension arm. Driving the pin out will destroy one of the bearings, since a cap type bearing is used on the lower pin. A thrust bearing is used in back of the knuckle support to take the thrust of the arm when the car is in motion. Needle bearings are used to mount the pin to the lower suspension arm. On reinstalling the lower pin, use a sufficient number of shims between the thrust bearing and the knuckle support to slightly preload the thrust bearing. While driving out the pin actually destroys only one of the bearings it is advisable to install both sets of needle bearings and the thrust bearing at any time the pin is taken out.

Replacement of Lower Suspension Arm Pins and/or Bushings

1940 THRU 1953, ALL MODELS EXCEPT 120 AND 120B

Support the weight of the car on a jack on the lower A frame and remove the road wheel.

Take the nut and special washer from the lower suspension arm pin and unscrew the pin from the lower suspension arm. Before the pin is taken all the way out make some arrangement to support the hub and drum assembly, so that it does not fall down to the limit permitted by the upper suspension arm.

Remove the bushing from the lower end of the knuckle support and install a new one securing it very tightly. Insert a new lower suspension arm pin locating the knuckle support so that it is midway between the yoke formed by the two portions of the lower A frame. Install the nut and special lock washer.

Replacement of Lower Suspension Arm

To replace the lower suspension arm follow the procedure given for front coil spring and in addition remove the lower arm outer pin after the tension has been taken off the spring.

Replacement of Upper Suspension Arm

The procedure of replacing the upper suspension arm is the same regardless of whether it is the early type which comprised the shock absorber or the later type which did not function as a shock absorber.

Support the weight of the car on a jack under the lower A frame and follow the procedure given for the replacement of an upper support arm eccentric pin. Make some provision to prevent the brake hub and drum assembly from swiveling out on the lower arm pin. Remove the bolts which attach the upper support arm to the frame and take off the support arm.

Replacement of King Pins and Bushings

To replace the king pins remove the hub and brake drum assembly and detach the backing plate. Hang the back-

Continued

PACKARD 1940 thru 1953

REPLACEMENT OF KING PINS AND BUSHINGS—*continued*

ing plate on a wire mounted on the frame so as not to injure the flexible brake line. (Not necessary to detach the brake line.) Drive out the king pin lock pin toward the front of the car. Remove the welsh plug from the upper end of the king pin and drive the king pin downward and out. Some models of Packard had bushings in both the upper and lower part of the knuckle support to guide the king pin. Others had a bearing at the bottom and a bushing at the top. Still a third model had bearings top and bottom. On the types which used needle bearings top and bottom, replacement bushings are available and for the type which used the thick bronze bushing top and bottom, replacement bearings are available. If bushings are used it will be necessary to secure a good fit with a reamer or hone after pressing the bushings into the knuckle.

Replacement of Shock Absorbers

For models up to 1950 see "Replacement of Upper Suspension Arm."

Detach the upper end of the shock absorber from the top of the frame. Remove the bolts from underneath the A frame, which hold the shock absorber plate in the center of the spring. Lower the shock absorber plate and pull the shock absorber down through the hole in the A frame.

STEERING GEAR ASSEMBLY

Replacement of Horn Button

On most Packard models the horn button is held with three screws frcm underneath the steering wheel. First examine the horn button to see if there are screws underneath the wheel holding the horn button in place. If no screws are found then the button is of the bayonet type.

On the bayonet type button simply press down on the button and rotate it about one-quarter turn and lift it off.

Removal of Steering Wheel

On all Packard models a puller is required to remove the steering wheel. Take off the horn button and the horn spring and contact, remove the nut which holds the steering wheel to the steering tube and using a puller lift off the steering wheel.

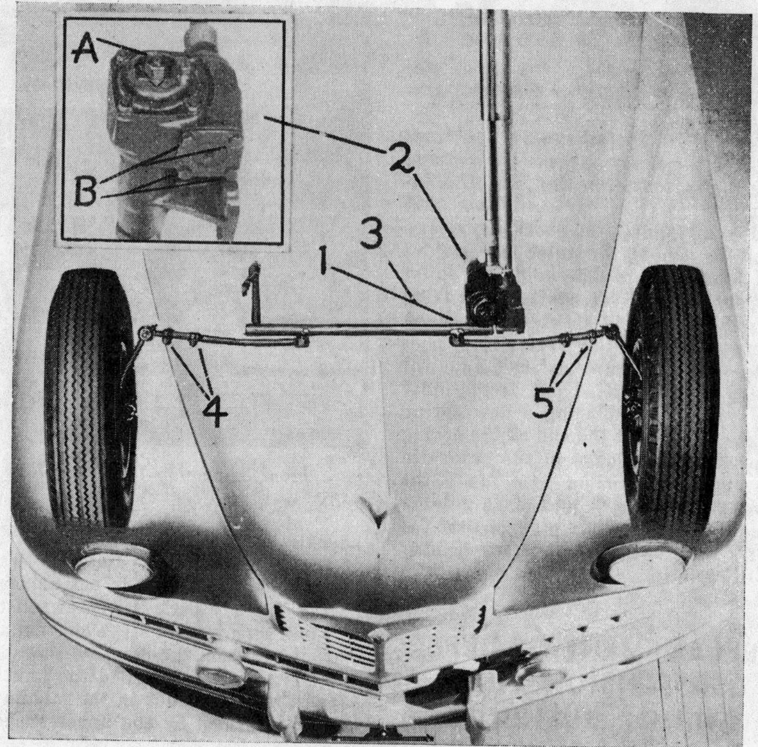

Steering mechanism

Adjustment of Steering Mechanism

1. Disconnect the pitman arm from the drag link.

2. Adjust the steering gear housing.

(a) Back off on the mesh adjustment screen so there is plenty of clearance in the mesh of the gears in order to check the fit of the worm bearings. If there is any play in the worm bearings remove the four cap screws (b) and remove one shim at a time until all play has been removed from the worm bearings.

Replace and tighten the cap screws. Set the steering wheel in the mid-position of its travel and turn the adjusting screw (a) until there is zero lash in the mesh of the gears with the steering wheel in the mid-position of its travel. Tighten the lock nut.

3. Reconnect the pitman arm to the intermediate tie rod.

4. With the steering wheel held in the mid-position of its travel loosen the clamp nuts and turn the adjusting sleeve on the right tie rod until one-half the total toe-in is in the right wheel.

5. Still holding the steering wheel to the mid-position of its travel, loosen the clamp nut on the left hand tie rod and adjust the sleeve so that the balance of the toe-in is in the left front wheel. Tighten all clamp bolts. Turn the steering wheel from one extreme to the other to check for looseness or binding.

BRAKE SYSTEM

All Packard models are equipped with two shoe Bendix brakes, hydraulically actuated.

On all models an eccentric anchor is used.

Brake Inspection

Before making any adjustment on the braking system, first remove at least one road wheel and examine the condition of the lining, shoes, wheel cylinders, brake springs and drums. Examine the wheel cylinder boot for signs of leaking or seeping at the cylinder. If any is found it will be necessary to disassemble the cylinder and if it is not too bad, hone it in place on the car. If the pits are deep it will be necessary to remove the cylinder from the car and hone it on a bench type hone.

Examine the condition of the lining making sure that the lining is contacting the drum all over its surface. If it is found that the lining is contacting the drum all over its surface, even if it is wearing unevenly, it is probably better to allow the anchor adjustment to remain as it is. If any scores or scratches are found in the brake drums it will be necessary to machine the drums and install new brake lining or remove the old lining and install shims under it to compensate for the amount of metal removed from the brake drum. If the wheel cylinder being examined is found to be defective or requires service it is a very good idea to remove the remainder of the wheels and make certain that the other wheel cylinders are in good condition. Also examine the master cylinder closely if anything wrong is found in any one of the wheel cylinders.

Since the braking system is so vital to the safety of the car and passengers it is always a good idea to do a little extra work to determine that the brakes are in good condition and can be expected to function well.

Brake Pedal Adjustment

Before making any adjustment on the wheels, make sure the brake pedal has approximately one-half inch free travel (measured at the toe-board) before the master cylinder operating rod contacts the master cylinder cup. This adjustment is made at the master cylinder push rod.

Minor Brake Adjustment

A minor brake adjustment is made to compensate for normal lining wear. Remove the adjusting hole cover and turn the star wheel until the brakes drag and then back off until the brake is just free. Replace the adjusting hole cover. (Turning the handle of the tool toward the axle will expand the brake shoes.)

Cutaway view front brake

Major Brake Adjustment

A major brake adjustment should be made at anytime new lining is installed, drums turned or the brakes do not function well after having been given a minor adjustment. Eccentric anchors are used on all Packard models. Loosen the anchor bolt and turn the eccentric anchor in a direction which will cause the secondary shoe to drip a .010 inch feeler, held approximately 1½ in. from the anchor end of the secondary shoe. Tentatively tighten the lock nut on the anchor. Now expand the shoes by turning the star wheel until a .010 inch feeler is just gripped approximately 1½ inch from the star wheel end of the secondary shoe.

Recheck to make clear that the anchor clearance is still .010 inch. When .010 inch has been secured at both ends of the secondary shoe, securely tighten the brake anchor lock nut and replace the adjusting hole cover over the star wheel. Repeat this operation at all four wheels.

Bleeding Brakes

See "General Service and Trouble Shooting Section," refer to index.

Refilling the Master Cylinder

The master cylinder on all Packard models can be filled from underneath the hood.

If, however, it is desired to pressure bleed the system it is perhaps better to connect the pressure bleeder from underneath the car.

Power Brakes

See "Power Brake Section."

COOLING SYSTEM

Radiator Core Removal

On all models it is necessary to remove the hood, disconnect the radiator hoses, take out the bolts which hold the radiator core to its cradle and lift up the radiator core.

On 1940 models it will be necessary also to remove the water pump before taking out the core. On earlier models where radiator brace rods were used, it will of course be necessary to take off the radiator brace rods.

Note: Some of the Clipper models had the radiator core bolts fed in from the front of the core, which made them inaccessible. On these models it is necessary to unbolt the radiator cradle from the fender mountings and lift the core and cradle assembly up out of the car.

Withdraw water distribution tube

Removal of Water Pump

On all Packard models the water pump can be removed without taking out the radiator core.

Remove the fan belt and the fan blades. Take off the fan hub and pulley. Remove the cap screws which hold the pump to the cylinder block and lift off the pump.

Note: Sometimes it may be necessary to support the weight of the engine on a jack since as the rubber engine mounts soften with age, the engine sometimes sinks down slightly which causes the engine support bracket in the front to cover the lower water pump screws.

Water Pump Disassembly

To disassemble all Packard water pumps simply remove the bearing snap ring from the front of the pump and, supporting the pump body in an arbor press, press out the shaft through the front of the housing and out through the impeller. A new bearing and shaft assembly should be used at anytime it is pressed out. It is also recommended that a new impeller be used since it is a press fit on the shaft.

Examine the sealing surfaces in the pump body for scores and scratches before installing the new seal. Both the hub at the front end and the impeller at the back end are pressed on flush with the shaft.

ENGINE ASSEMBLY

From 1940 thru 1953 Packard supplied engines in 6 cylinder L head, and 8 cylinder L head.

Some models were equipped with mechanically adjusted valves and others were equipped with hydraulic valve lifters.

Removal of Engine Assembly

On all 1940 thru 1942 models, except Clippers, it is a good idea to remove the fenders, radiator core and front

Continued

PACKARD 1940 thru 1953

Removal of Engine Assembly—*cont'd*

end sheet metal as a unit, before lifting off the engine. The engine is then separated at the bell housing after all attaching parts have ben removed. When removing the engine it will be necessary, on these models, to support the weight of the transmission on a jack.

ALL MODELS 1948 THRU 1953
AND ALL CLIPPER MODELS

On the above mentioned models the engine can be removed from the frame without taking off the front fenders and sheet metal assembly, and without removing the radiator core, although it is always a good safety precaution to take out the radiator core to prevent possible accidental damage.

Remove all attaching parts such as exhaust pipe, fuel lines, gauge lines, transmission gear shift, idler levers, battery connections, etc. Split the engine at the bell housing and raise up and out of the car.

ENGINE INTERNAL

Oil Pan Removal

On all Packard models turn the steering wheel to the extreme right. Then take out the bolts which hold the pan to the engine and drop the oil pan.

Note: On some models it is necessary to disconnect the steering drag link and the tie rod. If the crankshaft balance weights interfere with the pan turn the engine slowly by hand to give necessary clearance.

Timing Case Cover Removal

In order to remove the timing case cover on all Packard models it is necessary to jack up the engine and remove the radiator core and front engine support.

Take off the vibration damper and remove the bolts which hold the timing case cover to the front of the engine block.

Rod and Piston Assemblies

Aluminum pistons were used in all models of Packard. Up to the 1947 models the steel strut piston was used. Floating piston pins were used in all models.

The pins are retained to the piston by means of a lock wire at both ends of the wrist pin.

Assembly of Piston to the Connecting Rod

Assemble the piston to the connecting rod so that the slot in the piston is on the same side of the rod as the oil spit hole in the rod bearing. When assembling the piston and rod assembly to the engine the slot in the piston should be toward the camshaft side of the engine.

Caution: The camshaft side is the right side of the engine which is generally considered to be the thrust side. However, on Packard engines the crankshaft is offset with relation to the cylinder bores so that actually the left side is the thrust side on Packard engines.

Rod Bearing Inserts

Rod bearings are precision replaceable shells. A variety of undersizes are available to take care of almost any situation found in the service field. While the Packard Motor Car Co. does not recommend adjusting the rod bearings a small adjustment may be secured by placing a feather or taper type shim between the bearing shell and the cap. As much as .003 inch may be taken up in this manner. Under no circumstances should the rod or cap be filed. Shims should never be used in an attempt to take up for taper or out of round condition in the crankshaft.

Main Bearings

Main bearings on all models of Packard are precision replaceable shells which can be renewed from below without removing the crankshaft. The procedure is to loosen all crankshaft cap bolts and take down the cap on the bearing to be removed.

Insert into the crankshaft oil hole a flattened cotter pin or one of the little special tools made for the purpose and rotate the upper half of the main bearing out of the crankcase. Be sure to rotate the shaft so that the tang in the bearing at the parting line will come out of the crankcase first and when reinstalling the bearing the tang at the parting line goes in last.

Checking Main or Connecting Rod Bearing Fit

There are two generally used methods of checking the fit of a main or connecting rod bearing. The first is the use of plastic gauging material. Instructions for the use of plastic gauging material are packed with the plastic and should be followed carefully.

The other method is to use a piece of shim stock approximately ½ in. square having the thickness of the recommended bearing oil clearance (oil clearance is given in the Overhaul Tables). Place the shim stock on the bearing between the crankshaft journal and the bearing shell and bolt the bearing up into place. If the bearing fit is correct the shim stock will produce a reasonable drag on the crankshaft. If the shim stock locks the crankshaft it indicates the bearing is too small for that particular journal. If the crankshaft still turns freely with the shim stock in place it indicates that the bearing is a loose fit on the shaft. To save time on checking with shim stock it is customary to use a piece of shim stock having a thickness equal to the allowable wear limit of the bearing being tested. In this way if the crankshaft is locked when the cap is pulled up tight then the bearing has not worn to the limit allowable.

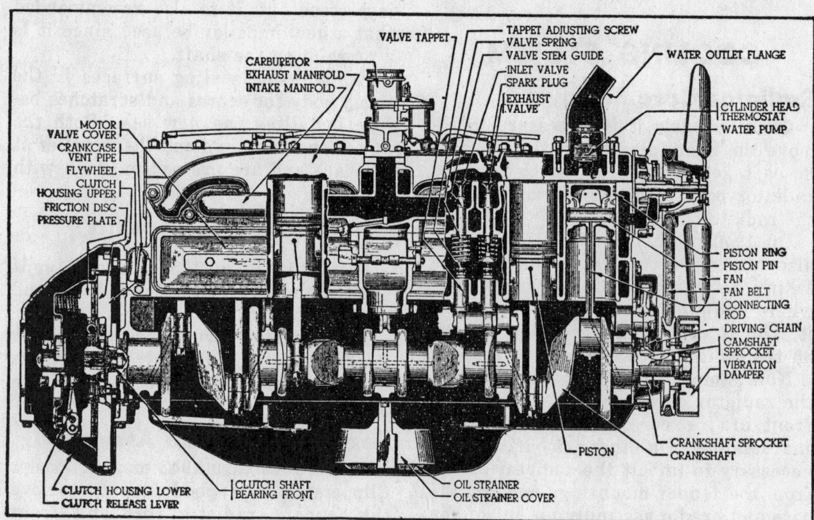

Cross section thru 8 cylinder 120C engine

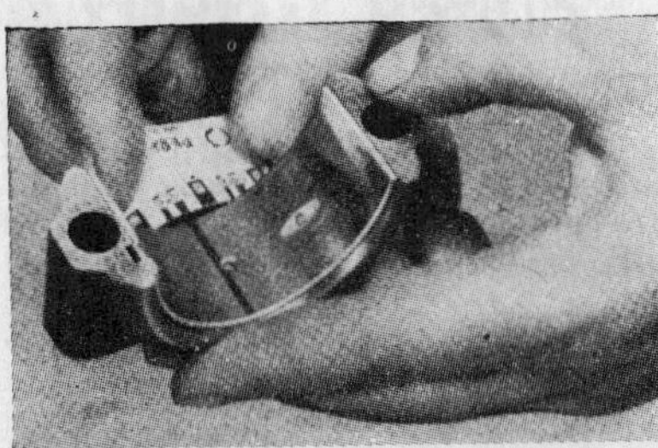

Checking bearing clearance with plastic gage

THE VALVE SYSTEM

On all 6 and 8 cylinder Packards built since 1940 the valves are in the cylinder block, and access to the valves is by removing the cylinder head and the valve chamber cover.

Removal of Valve Assemblies

Remove the cylinder head and take off the valve chamber cover. Raise the valve spring, without raising the valve, and remove the keeper from the bottom of the spring seat. The valves can then be pulled out through the top of the block.

Replacement of Valve Guides

Before removing any of the valve guides first measure carefully the distance from the top of the block to the top of the valve guide and make a note of the distance.

The guides are pulled upwards out through the top of the block and the new ones are driven downwards from the top of the block. They should be driven in the same distance as the old ones were before they were removed. After driving in new guides it is customary to ream the valve guide to correct for any distortion which may have occurred when the guide was being driven into place.

Mechanical Lifters

All lifters in Packard models (except hydraulic lifters) are of the mushroom type, having a self locking tappet. At any time work is being done on the valves carefully examine the top face of the tappet screw to determine if it is dished or grooved, and if it is it will be necessary to reface the tappet screw in order to insure accurate valve lash adjustment.

Valve Springs

To check quickly the condition of the valve springs, lay all of the inlet springs along side of each other. If all the springs are the same height, as determined by laying a straight edge along the top of all the springs, it may be assumed with reasonable certainty that the springs are OK since it is not likely that all of the inlet springs will be equally defective. Repeat the test on the exhaust valve springs.

Hydraulic Valve Lifters

Hydraulic valve lifters are a selective fit at the factory and the lifters cannot be inter-changed from one bore to another, nor can the tappet and plunger body be inter-changed into different lifter assemblies. The hydraulic lifter assembly can be taken from the engine after the valves are removed by simply lifting it up out of the lifter body. To remove the plunger from the cylinder twist the plunger and spring in a direction that would "wind up" the spring and pull outward at the same time. The plunger should come out easily. Service on the hydraulic lifter is limited to thoroughly cleaning it in a good solvent and blowing it out with compressed air. Examine the lifter and lifter plunger to see if there are any scratches or nicks on the bearing surfaces. If any are present the lifter assembly will have to be replaced.

Initial Adjustment of Hydraulic Valves

Whenever the valve lifters have been removed for service it will be necessary to check to see that there is the proper operating clearance at the valve stem so that the automatic take up mechanism will operate at nearly the center of its stroke. With no oil in the lifter and the lifter plunger completely depressed there should be between .030 and .070 inch clearance between the top of the plunger and the bottom of the valve stem.

Valve Timing Procedure

In order to replace the timing chains and/or sprockets or to correct for inaccurate valve timing, it is necessary to remove the radiator core, and the timing case cover. The procedure is as follows—Turn the crankshaft until the mark on the crank sprocket is facing directly toward the center of the cam sprocket. (This is in case the valve timing has jumped, if the valve timing has not jumped, and it is simply necessary to replace the chain because it is loose bring the two marks, that is the mark on the cam sprocket and the mark on the crank sprocket, until they are nearest each other and in line between shaft center, since this is the correct timing point.)

Remove the camshaft sprocket at the timing chain. If the crankshaft sprocket is to be replaced remove it at this time. Install the new crankshaft sprocket, being careful to start it in line with the key, since it is a fairly tight fit on the shaft and is difficult to realign once started on the shaft. Set the timing chain over the cam sprocket and the crank sprocket and mount the cam sprocket to its shaft in such a way that the mark on the cam sprocket is in line with the mark on the crank sprocket between the shaft centers. If necessary, rotate the camshaft slightly to bring it into line with the sprocket. Secure the camshaft sprocket to the shaft and turn the engine two full revolutions until the timing marks again assume the timing position. Check carefully to see that the marks are in line between the shaft centers and then replace the timing case cover, vibration damper, radiator core, etc.

Valves timed in this way will be correct regardless of which piston is at top dead center during the mounting process. However, it may be necessary to retime the ignition since if the camshaft was out of time the ignition being driven by the camshaft will also be out of time.

Align timing marks on sprockets

ENGINE ELECTRICAL SYSTEM

Generator

Generators are of the two brush shunt type which are controlled by an external current and voltage regulator.

If difficulty is experienced with the generator it is a good idea to ground the field lead of the generator to see that this does alter or improve the situation in any way. If the generator will charge well with the field grounded the trouble is in the regulator.

If grounding the field does not improve the generator output it is necessary then to remove the generator from

Continued

CYLINDER HEAD TIGHTENING SEQUENCE

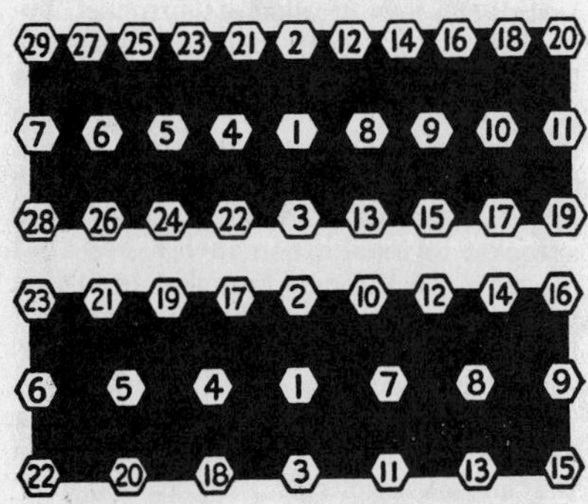

Upper—8 cylinder. Lower—6. Tighten to 60-62 foot pounds

GENERATOR—continued

the car and subject it to the test given for generators in the General Services section of this Manual (see index).

Starter

If difficulty is experienced in the starter circuit, first check the condition of the battery and see to it that it is brought up to full charge. Also examine the connections to the battery, paying particular attention to the ground connection and to the connection at the starter switch.

It is a good idea to take a voltage drop reading across the starter switch in the following manner: Place a volt meter across the terminals of the starter switch (not the relay terminals) and crank the engine with the starter. If a drop of more than ¼ to ⅓ volt is found across the starter switch, then the switch should either be repaired or replaced.

If all the above conditions are met with and the starter still does not crank the engine well it must be removed from the car for bench tests and repairs.

The Distributor

All Packards from 1940 use a single breaker point distributor. All Packard distributors rotate in a counter-clockwise direction, except for the following models; 6 cylinder models 1942; 6 cylinder models 1946 and 1947 which had Delco distributors.

Note: The 6 cylinder of 1946 which was fitted with an Autolite distributor turned in a counter-clockwise direction.

The exceptions noted above are clockwise distributors.

When servicing the Packard it is a good idea to refer to the Distributor Table in order to be certain which way the distributor rotates.

The firing order on 6 cylinder models is 1-5-3-6-2-4.

The firing order for 8 cylinder models is 1-6-2-5-8-3-7-4.

All Packard distributors are driven by a tongue on the end of the distributor shaft.

The drive gear on all models is actually on the oil pump. Ignition timing is adjusted by rotating the body of the distributor in relation to the mounting bracket. If for any reason the oil pump was removed from the car and the engine disturbed or the oil pump set back in a position different from that which it originally occupied it will be necessary to completely retime the ignition following the method given below.

Remove the distributor and turn the crankshaft until No. 1 cylinder is at top dead center. Insert the distributor into the block and note the position of the rotor.

Remove the wires from the cap and set the cap on the distributor marking on the cap the position of the rotor (No. 1 cylinder ready to fire). Insert the wire from No. 1 cylinder into the hole in the distributor cap, which is next in line to the mark showing the position of the rotor. Install the rest of the wires around the distributor cap in accordance with the firing order and in the direction of the distributor rotation.

Note: Firing order and distributor rotations are given in the test above and also in the Distributor Table in this Manual.

After setting the wires correctly into the cap, small adjustments of the ignition timing can be made by rotating the distributor body.

All Packard distributors are located conveniently on the side of the block and it is not necessary to remove the distributor to install breaker points, etc.

However, in the event of loose or worn bushings, loose or defective breaker plates or for any reason that it becomes necessary to remove the distributor, the engine should not be disturbed after the distributor has been removed from the car so that it can be reinserted in the place from which it was removed, and in this way much time will be saved in setting the ignition timing.

On all Packards timing marks are located on the vibration damper.

Note: If for any reason the vibration damper has been replaced there will be no timing marks since replacement vibration dampers are not marked at the factory with the correct ignition timing.

CLUTCH ASSEMBLY

Clutch Pedal Adjustment

The free play of the clutch pedal on all Packard models equipped with electromatic clutch should be 2 in. This adjustment is made at the pedal push rod.

Adjustment of free play on mechanically operated clutches is approximately 1 in.

Removal of Standard Clutch Assembly

The standard clutch assembly is taken out through the bottom of the clutch inspection pan after the transmission has been removed. It will be necessary to support the rear of the engine on a jack in order to remove the transmission. All service operations on the standard Packard clutch, except for the clutch pedal adjustment, requires that the clutch be removed.

THE PACKARD ELECTROMATIC CLUTCH

The electromatic clutch supplied on Packard built cars as factory installed special equipment at extra cost is a vacuum-electric mechanism which provides automatic operation of the clutch assembly. The driver uses the accelerator pedal and shifts gears in the usual way but without touching the clutch pedal. All clutch engagements and disengagements are accomplished by the electromatic mechanism.

Since the electromatic clutch operates by engine vacuum it will not become operative until after the engine has started.

When starting the engine the gear shift lever must be in the neutral position, or the clutch pedal must be depressed until the engine starts.

Packard suggests that the car be operated as though it had a conventional clutch until the engine is thoroughly warmed, since until the engine warms up and idles smoothly the operation of the electromatic clutch may be a little too rapid.

Since the electromatic clutch functions simply to engage and disengage the clutch it has no effect whatever on the actual mechanism of the clutch itself nor does it have an effect on the servicing of the clutch itself.

Operation of the Electromatic Clutch

A power cylinder actuated by inlet manifold vacuum is employed to operate the clutch. This cylinder is connected to the standard clutch linkage in such a manner that either the manual or electromatic clutch control can be used at will. When the vacuum inlet manifold is admitted to the power cylinder the piston moves into the cylinder and disengages the clutch. When the vacuum is shut off and air is admitted, reducing the vacuum on the piston head, the piston moves out of the cylinder engaging the clutch. The actual rate of clutch engagement is controlled entirely by the rate of air entering into the vacuum cylinder and not by manifold vacuum.

Just as long as there is sufficient manifold vacuum to withdraw the power piston and disengage the clutch, variations in inlet manifold due to engine conditions will have no effect whatever on the actual engagement of the clutch. The rate of engagement of the clutch is controlled by a pressure regulating valve called the clutch control valve. This valve is located in the vacuum line between the inlet manifold and the power cylinder. The clutch control valve is a compound valve which regulates the rate of air bleed to provide the desired clutch engaging action as well as the proper engine speed synchronization. One element, the spool, is connected through a compound linkage to the accelerator pedal. Another element, the sleeve, is actuated by a spring loaded vacuum diaphragm which is subjected to a vacuum equal to that in the power cylinder.

As the accelerator is depressed the two elements in the valve move in relation to each other to shut off the vacuum supply and breathe air into the power cylinder at such a rate as to automatically provide the proper rate of clutch engagement for all normal operation.

The Electromatic Relay

A three unit relay is provided to operate the solenoid controls of the electromatic clutch. In operation, closing a switch completes a circuit and causes a light current to flow through the relay. This light energizes a coil in the relay closing a set of contact points which will permit a heavy energizing current to flow through the solenoid circuit.

In further description of the operation of the electromatic clutch no reference will be made to the relay. When it is stated that operating a certain switch energizes or de-energizes a certain unit it must be remembered that the energizing and de-energizing action is accomplished through a relay. The only exception to this is the second speed switch.

Direct Speed Solenoid

A solenoid shutoff valve is built into the vacuum supply line and the clutch control valve. When the solenoid is de-energized the valve is closed, shutting off the vacuum supply to the power cylinder thus making the electromatic mechanism inoperative. The direct speed solenoid valve is controlled electrically through the lockout, direct speed, accelerator and governor switches.

Lockout Switch

The electromatic clutch may be locked out and made inoperative by means of the instrument board switch which is marked "electroclutch."

When the knob is in the out position the switch points are open which breaks a circuit and de-energizes the direct speed solenoid valve. This makes the electromatic clutch inoperative through shutting off the vacuum supply to the power cylinder. In this position the lockout switch overrules all other control switches. In the in-position the switch points are closed, energizing the direct speed solenoid, making the electromatic mechanism operative.

Low and Reverse Operation

Since the slower rate of clutch engagement is required when starting in low and reverse than when starting in second and high, the low and reverse solenoid is provided. When energized this solenoid pushes a plunger forward increasing the load of the clutch control valve diaphragm spring, retarding the rate of clutch engagement. The solenoid is energized only when the

Continued

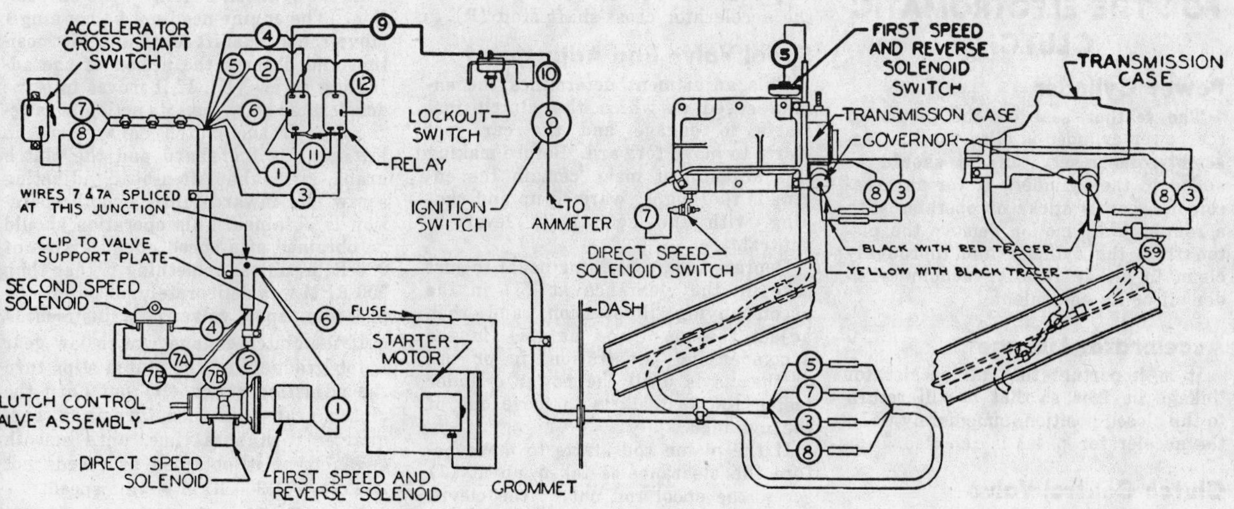

Electromatic clutch wiring diagram

LOW AND REVERSE OPERATION—*continued*

gearshift is in low or reverse. When in neutral, second or high the solenoid is de-energized.

Low and Reverse Switch

The low and reverse solenoid is controlled by a switch which is operated by the low and reverse transmission shifter rail. Contact points in the switch are closed energizing the low and reverse solenoid only when in low or reverse. When the shift lever is in neutral this switch is open and the solenoid is de-energized.

Governor Switch

With only the controls described so far, the clutch would be disengaged and the car would freewheel every time the accelerator pedal was released. In order to prevent this a governor switch is employed to lock out the electromatic mechanism and prevent freewheeling in high gear at speeds above 17 miles per hour. The governor is similar to that used on the airodrive, except that there are two sets of points. The electromatic clutch points are marked "EC" and the airodrive points are marked "AD."

A direct speed switch and an accelerator switch are provided to permit shifting of the mechanism above the speeds at which the governor would normally render the electromatic clutch inoperative.

GENERAL INSTRUCTIONS FOR THE ELECTROMATIC CLUTCH

Power Cylinder

The leather seal on the piston of the power cylinder is oiled for that assembly, no reserve of oil should be added to the cylinder. If for any reason it becomes sticky or operates with a rough, jerky motion remove the piston from the cylinder and thoroughly clean in either Bendix vacuum cylinder oil or its equivalent.

Accelerator Linkage

It is important that all accelerator linkage be free so that it will return to the closed position immediately when the accelerator pedal is released.

Clutch Control Valve

The clutch control valves are carefully calibrated to operate on the model car on which they are installed. Do not attempt to install a valve on a model other than the one for which it was intended.

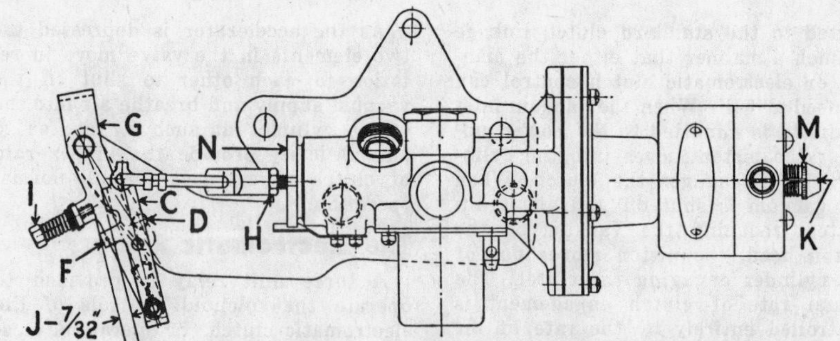

Electromatic clutch control valve showing principal points of adjustment

No-Roll Assembly

The no-roll device which is sold as an accessory for Packard cars should not be installed on a car equipped with the electromatic clutch; these two devices do not work well together.

Accelerator and Throttle Linkage Adjustment

Adjust the carburetor cross-shaft lever linkage so that with the throttle operating lever (G) in contact with the stop pin (D) the carburetor throttle lever rests on the idle adjusting screw (S) and the linkage is free with normal slack. Adjust the accelerator pedal lever at the turnbuckle (P) so that with the lug (F) on the clutch control lever (C) holding the throttle operating lever (G) against stop pin (D) there is a positive clearance at the accelerator cross-shaft stop (R).

Spool Valve Rod Adjustment

This adjustment determines the engine speed at which the clutch just starts to engage and the car just starts to move forward. Before making this adjustment make certain the engine is thoroughly warmed up and running with the gear shift lever in neutral.

Depress the accelerator pedal to just take up the clearance at (J) in the accompanying illustration, and then adjust the spool rod at (H) in the accompanying illustration, in or out of the clevis until the power cylinder piston rod just starts to move out of the cylinder.

If the piston rod starts to move before the clearance is taken up at (J) screw the spool rod out of the clevis. If it does not start to move when all the clearance is taken up screw the spool rod into the clevis. To check the adjustment place the gear shift lever in low gear and depress the accelerator pedal slowly. The car should just start to creep forward with an engine speed of approximately 900 RPM. If it is desired to increase the engine speed at which the car starts to move turn the screw eye inward; if it is desired to decrease the engine speed at which the car creeps turn the screw out.

Low and Reverse Engagement

Two adjustments are provided, the Allen-head screw (K) in the accompanying illustration for starts in low and reverse, and the knurled screw (M) for starts in second and high. First and reverse adjustment (K) will have effect on the second and high adjustment. For this reason the first and reverse adjustment should be made first and then the second and high adjustment should be made. To check the operation of low and reverse solenoid turn the ignition switch to the on position. (The engine need not be running.) Move the gear shift lever into low position and observe the action of the adjusting screw (K). If it moves into the accelerator body then its action is satisfactory. If the clutch engagement in low gear is too sharp and the clutch grabs, turn the Allen-head adjusting screw (K) inwards until smooth operation is obtained. This operation should be obtained at a speed not in excess of 900 RPM unless something higher than 900 RPM was deliberately picked, in the preceding spool valve rod adjustment.

If the clutch engagement in low gear is too gradual and the clutch slips turn the adjusting screw (K) out until the clutch grabs and then turn it in, one-quarter turn at a time, until smooth engagement is obtained at speeds not in excess of 900 RPM engine speed.

Note: Turning the adjusting screws in has the effect of increasing engine speed, turning them out has the effect of decreasing it.

After making the low reverse solenoid adjustment recheck the spool valve rod adjustment and readjust if necessary.

Second and High Engagements

This adjustment should never be made until after the low and reverse adjustment has been set correctly. The car should just start to creep at approximately 700 RPM engine speed when starting in second gear. If the engagement is too sharp and the clutch grabs turn the knurled screw (M) inward until smooth engagement is obtained at speeds not in excess of 700 RPM engine speed. If the engagement is too gradual and the clutch slips turn the adjusting screw (M) outwards until the clutch does grab and then turn it inwards one-quarter turn at a time until a smooth engagement is obtained at speeds not in excess of 700 RPM.

Note that in both low and reverse, and second and high adjustments it is necessary to adjust from the grab point back to a gradual engagement. Do not adjust from a slip to a gradual engagement. First back both of the adjustments out until the clutch grabs and adjust from the grab position to smooth engagement.

Full Throttle Engagement

This adjustment should be made on the road, making full throttle starts in second gear.

The adjustment should be made just as sharp as possible, without causing the engine to stumble upon full clutch engagement.

Screw the body plug out until the clutch grabs and then turn in one notch at a time until smooth engagement is obtained without engine stumble.

If the engine races excessively and the clutch slips during intermediate portion of the engagement back out on the second and high adjusting nut (M) to reduce the slip.

Final Check of Adjustment

Recheck the operation on the road and readjust according to the previous instructions if the clutch slip is found to be excessive or the clutch engages roughly.

STANDARD TRANSMISSION ASSEMBLY

All Packard models are equipped with a three forward speed standard transmission. Overdrives are standard equipment at extra cost on all models of Packard, not equipped with the ultramatic drive.

Removal of the Transmission

The same technique is used in removing the transmission whether or not it is equipped with an overdrive.

Split the rear universal joint and remove the drive shaft by sliding it off the front slip yoke. Support the weight of the engine and remove the cross-member which supports the rear of the engine. Disconnect all parts attached to the transmission such as shift lever, overdrive solenoid wires, etc. The transmission is detached from the bell housing and pulled out and down from the car.

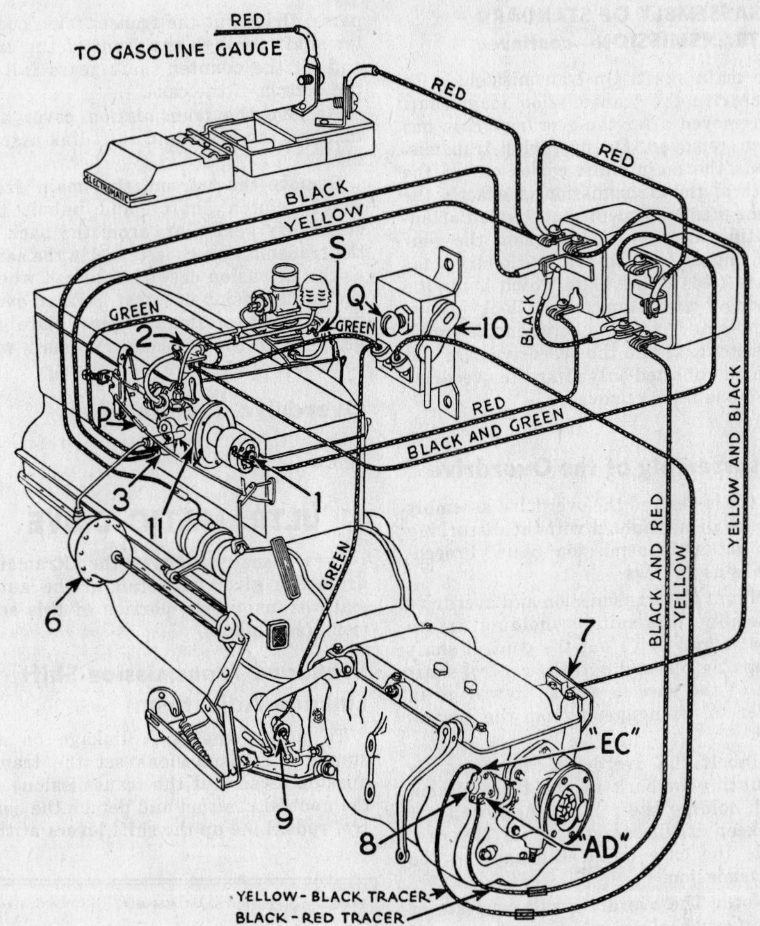

Adjustment points of electromatic clutch control valve

Disassembly of Standard Transmission

Mount the transmission assembly in a suitable vise or holding fixture and remove the cover and shifting fork assembly. The counter-shaft is driven out through the rear of the case, permitting the gear cluster to drop to the bottom of the case. This will give clearance to permit removal of the main drive shaft (clutch shaft) out of the front of the case after the sleeve is unbolted from the front of the case. Unbolt the rear extension housing and remove the housing together with the main shaft and gears assembled out of the back of the transmission case. The main shaft gears can then be disassembled by removing the snap rings which retain them to

Continued

DISASSEMBLY OF STANDARD TRANSMISSION—*continued*

the main shaft. On transmissions with overdrive the transmission main shaft is removed after the overdrive case has been removed. On overdrive transmissions the main shaft comes out of the back of the transmission in exactly the same manner except that instead of unbolting an extension housing the rear bearing is held in the stationary gear plate (this is the plate which holds the solenoid and plunger and lock-out assembly and is bolted between the transmission case and the overdrive case). It can be unbolted only after the overdrive case has been removed.

Disassembly of the Overdrive

If it is desired the overdrive assembly can be disassembled without disturbing the actual transmission gears. Procedure is as follows—

Mount the transmission and overdrive assembly in a suitable holding fixture or vise and drive out the control shaft retaining pin and pull the control shaft out of the case as far as it will go in order to disengage it from the control rail.

Unbolt the overdrive case from its mounting in back of the transmission and, holding the control shaft well out to keep it disengaged from the rail, slide the case off of the back of the transmission.

Note: The overdrive will separate at the freewheeling rollers and some of the rollers may drop into the case, others may stay in the freewheeling cam. Be absolutely certain that all of the rollers are secured before proceeding any further. When the case is removed the overdrive main shaft (tail shaft) will be in the transmission case.

It is retained there by a bearing snap ring which can be removed by taking off the cover plate (located just on top of the transmission case at the back, just alongside of the speedometer gear location). Spread the snap ring and the overdrive main shaft may be driven forward into the front of the case. The balance of the overdrive parts are held with snap rings to the shaft; after removing the snap rings each of the overdrive parts may be pulled off the shaft until the stationary gear plate is reached.

In order to take off the stationary gear plate, (this will not be necessary if no work is to be done on the transmission) remove the snap ring which retains the pawl and other gear plate parts. Drive out the transmission counter shaft through the front of the case and let the counter shaft gears fall to the bottom of the case.

Remove the transmission cover and take out the cover and shift link assembly.

Remove the transmission main drive shaft (clutch shaft) and unbolt the stationary gear plate from the back of the transmission case (exactly the same as the extension case is unbolted where the transmission does not have an overdrive). The stationary gear plate together with the transmission gears will come out of the back of the case.

Overdrive Transmission

See "Overdrives section"—refer to index.

ULTRAMATIC DRIVE

Service instructions on the ultramatic drive are given in detail in the automatic transmission portion of this section. (see index)

Standard Transmission Shift Linkage Adjustment

To adjust the shift linkage on all standard transmissions set the transmission levers (at the transmission) in the neutral position and detach the control rods. Line up the shift levers at the bottom of the steering column (a pin hole is provided to keep them in alignment). With the levers at the bottom of the transmission held in alignment with a pin adjust the clevises so that with the transmission kept in neutral the clevises will just enter the holes in the shift levers at the bottom of the steering column. Secure the clevises and remove the aligning pin from the levers at the bottom of the steering column.

REAR AXLE ASSEMBLY

The rear axle assembly on all Packards is a hypoid having a Hotchkiss drive.

All service work on Packard rear axles can be performed with the main axle housing under the car. The carrier is removable for all service on the ring gear and/or pinion bearings. Replacement of all oil seals is accomplished without removing either the carrier or the housing.

Removal of Rear Axle Assembly

To remove the rear axle assembly split the unit at the rear universal joint, detach the torsion bars and shock absorbers, detach the brake lines and hand brake cables, remove the bolts that hold the springs to the rear axle housing with the car up sufficiently to permit the housing to be rolled out from underneath the car.

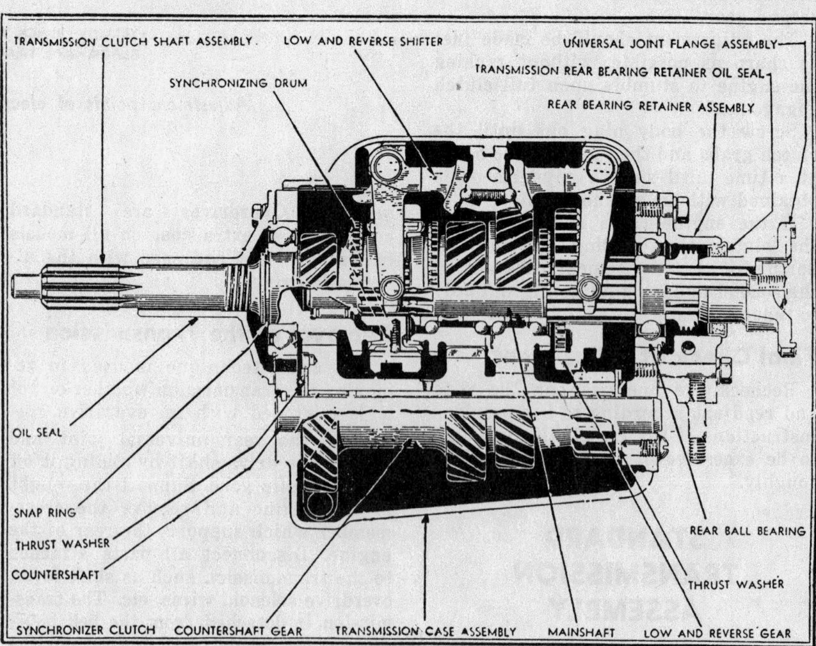

Cutaway view of standard transmission without overdrive

Axle Shaft Replacement

To replace an axle shaft remove the wheel and hub and drum assembly.

Caution: An inertia type compression puller is required to remove the rear hub.

Packard does not recommend using drive off pullers of any kind..

Disconnect the brake line and take out the bolts which hold the backing plate to the rear axle housing. The axle shaft may then be pulled using an inertia type puller which will force the bearing outer race out of the housing.

Replacement of Axle Shaft Oil Seals

To replace the axle outer oil seal it is necessary to remove the wheel, hub and drum assembly and remove the bolts which retain the backing plate to the housing. The oil seal is contained in a retainer bolted to the backing plate.

To replace the inner oil seal it is necessary to follow the procedure as given for replacement of the axle shaft. After the axle shaft has been removed the inner oil seal may be taken out with an inertia type puller.

Replacement of Pinion Oil Seal

The pinion oil seal may be replaced by splitting the rear universal joint and taking off the universal joint companion flange. The oil seal may then be pulled out of the housing with an inertia type puller. When removing the pinion shaft companion flange it is always a good idea to mark the position of the nut which holds the flange to the pinion shaft. This nut should be replaced to exactly the same position it occupied before it was removed, unless it is necessary to replace the pinion and/or pinion bearings.

Replacement of Ring Gear and Pinion and/or Pinion Bearings

Remove the carrier from the car by splitting the rear universal joint and removing both axle shafts. The carrier should be mounted in a vise or suitable holding fixture on a work bench. Remove the differential side bearing locks and back off the preload on the differential side bearings. Remove the bearing caps from the differential side bearings after marking them for their correct position so they can be reinstalled just exactly as they were removed. Lift out the differential assembly.

Remove the universal joint companion flange nut and companion flange from the front of the pinion shaft and drive the pinion shaft out through the back of the carrier.

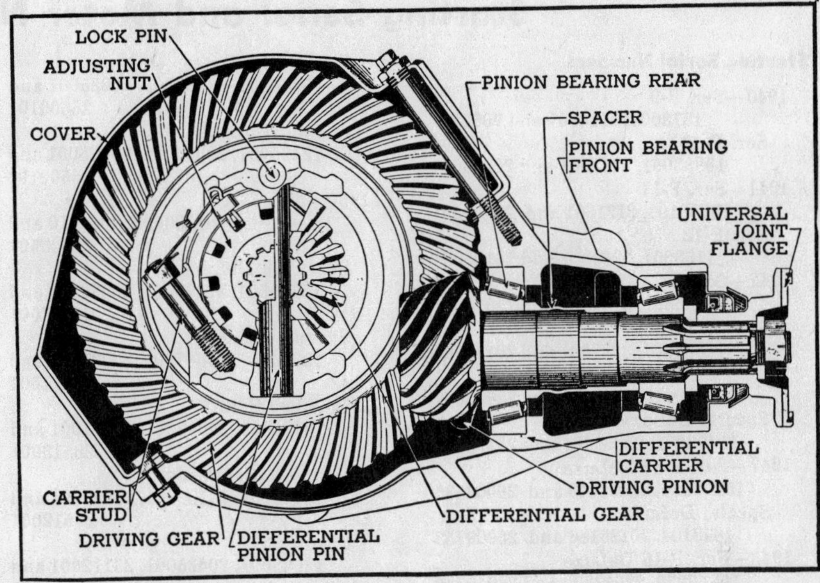

Hypoid rear axles used on junior cars. Note buckle in spacer

The pinion will come out with its rear bearing attached to the pinion leaving the front bearing cone and cup in the carrier. Unless it is necessary to replace the bearing cups (races) do not remove them from the housing. However if it is necessary to remove the bearing cups then the back bearing cup is driven out through the back of the case and the front bearing cup is pulled out through the front of the case.

Packard does not make provisions for adjusting the pinion depth. On some carriers, however, a 1/16 inch thick ring will be found back of the rear bearing cup (race). If this 1/16 inch spacer is found it must be replaced since that back carrier is 1/16 inch too deep.

Install the new bearings on the pinion and insert the pinion into the carrier. Install a new spacer between the front and rear pinion bearing and install the front pinion cone. Install the companion flange spacer and the companion flange and nut. If the old spacer is to be used the pinion shaft companion flange should be pulled up tight enough to produce a 25 to 32 inch pound load on the pinion shaft. The companion flange nut should be staked to hold this setting.

If a new pinion spacer is to be used it will be necessary to tighten the pinion nut sufficiently to buckle the spacer. It will be noted, when pulling up with a torque wrench, that the torque suddenly falls off just as the spacer starts to buckle, continue tightening the pinion nut until 25-32 inch lbs. torque are required to turn the pinion.

If work is to be done on the differential assembly it will be necessary to take off the ring gear in order to drive out the differential pin. If no work is required on the differential reinstall it into the carrier and turn the adjusting cage on the ring gear side until there is zero lash between the ring gear and pinion with no preload.

Tighten up on the adjusting cage opposite to the ring gear until the differential carrier spreads approximately .010 inch. In other wards tighten the right hand adjusting cage until the ring gear backs away from the pinion approximately .005 giving from .006 to .010 inch back lash between the gears. If spreading the carrier .010 inch does not produce the desired back lash between the ring gear and pinion it will be necessary to correct for back lash by turning the left cage out and the right cage in an equal amount until the desired back lash is obtained. It is a good idea to paint 5 or 6 of the gear teeth with red lead and roll the ring gear through the pinion and notice the markings made by the mesh of the gears. After correct adjustment has been achieved securely tighten the bearing caps on both sides of the carrier.

PLYMOUTH SPECIFICATIONS

Starting Serial and Motor Numbers

Starting Serial Nnmbers

1940—Ser. P-9
1378001, 3114801 and 9062201

Ser. P-10
10883001, 3242501 and 20063001

1941—Ser. P-11
15000101, 3121501 and 22001001

Ser. P-12
1123001, 3269301 and 20105001

1942—Ser. P-14 DeLuxe
15135501, 3134501 and 22037001

Special DeLuxe
11399501, 3297001 and 20148001

1946—Ser. P-15 DeLuxe
15154001, 26000001 and 22042001

Special DeLuxe
11496001, 25000001 and 20165001

1947—Ser. P-15 DeLuxe
15206936, 22053040 and 26003589

Special DeLuxe
11643104, 20185186 and 25009753

1948—Ser. P-15 DeLuxe
15252279, 22063370 and 26010840

Special DeLuxe
11854386, 20233168 and 25035586

1949—Ser. P-15 DeLuxe
15284535, 22071876 and 26017026

Special DeLuxe
12066020, 20287572 and 25062783

Ser. P-17
18000101, 24000001, 28000101 and 28500101

Ser. P-18 DeLuxe
15300001, 22080001, 26025001 and 26500101

Special DeLuxe
12120001, 20304001, 25075001 and 25500101

1950—Ser. P-19
18041001, 24012001, 280040010 and 28503501

Ser. P-20 DeLuxe
15359501, 22097001, 26030501 and 26504001

Special DeLuxe
12384501, 20367001, 25097501 and 25511001

1951—Ser. P-22
18126001, 24042001, 28011001 and 28513001

Ser. P-23 Cambridge
15460001, 22132001, 26040001 and 26512001

Cranbrook
12635001, 20435001, 25112001 and 25531001

1952—Ser. P-22
18192501, 24056701, 28015701 and 28519101

Ser. P-23 Cambridge
15577801, 22159601, 26045701 and 26518201

Cranbrook
12906701, 20485001, 25125301 and 25546101

1953—Ser. P-24
13070001(1), 20520001(2)

Location

1940-1942—On right front door hinge post.

1946-1953—On left front door hinge post.

Starting Motor Numbers

1940-1953—Prefix indicates year, i.e., P-9, 1940. All motor numbers begin 1001.

1940—P-9, P-10
1941—P-11, P-12 1001
1942—P-14 1001
1946-1949 (early)—P-15 1001
1949 (late)—P-18 1001
1950—P-20 1001
1951-1952—P-23 1001
1953—P-24 1001

Location

1940-1953—Near front upper left side of block and left front side of block between #1 and #2 cylinders.

General Specifications

Year	Model	Wheelbase (in.)	Tread (in.) Front	Tread (in.) Rear	Overall Dimensions (in.) Length†	Overall Dimensions (in.) Width	Overall Dimensions (in.) Height■	Shipping Weight* (lb.)	Tire Size (in.)
1940	P9	118	57	60	195			2869	5.50-16
	P10	118	57	60	195			2924	6.00-16
1941	P11	117	57	60	195			2889	6.00-16
	P12	117	57	60	198			2956	6.00-16
1942	P14	117	57	60	195			3025	6.00-16
1946	P15	117	57	60	197	74		3060	6.00-16
1947	P15	117	57	60	197	74		3082	6.00-16
1948	P15	117	57	60	197	74		3030	6.70-15
1949	P17	111	55	56	185	72	65		6.40-15
	P18	119	55	56	192	71	66		6.70-15
1950	P19	111	55	58	187	73		2946	6.40-15
	P20	119	55	58	193	74		3062	6.70-15
1951	P22	111	56	58	188	73	63	2975	6.40-15
1952	P22	111	56	58	188	73	63		6.40-15
	P23	119	56	58	194	74	65		6.70-15
1953	P24	114	56	59	189	74	62		6.70-15

*—Cheapest 5 pass. 4 door sedan. †—Including bumper and bumper guards. ■—Road to roof, no load.

General Engine Specifications

Year	Model	Number of Cylinders Bore and Stroke	Piston Displacement, Cubic Inches	Compression Ratio (To–1)	Taxable (A.M.A.) Hp.	DEVELOPED HORSE POWER Bare Engine	With Accessories	Maximum Torque Ft. Lbs.
1940	P9, P10, 6 Cyl.	6–3⅛ x 4⅜	201.3	6.70	23.4	84 @ 3600	....	154 @ 1200
1941	P11, P12, 6 Cyl.	6–3⅛ x 4⅜	201.3	6.70	23.4	87 @ 3800	....	160 @ 1200
1942	P14, 6 Cyl.	6–3¼ x 4⅜	217.8	6.80	25.3	95 @ 3400	....	172 @ 1600
1946	P15, 6 Cyl.	6–3¼ x 4⅜	217.8	6.60	25.4	95 @ 3600	....	172 @ 1200
1947	P15, 6 Cyl.	6–3¼ x 4⅜	217.8	6.60	25.3	95 @ 3600	....	172 @ 1200
1948	P15, 6 Cyl.	6–3¼ x 4⅜	217.8	6.60	25.3	95 @ 3600	....	172 @ 1200
1949	P17, P18, 6 Cyl.	6–3¼ x 4⅜	217.8	7.00	25.3	97 @ 3600	....	175 @ 1200
1950	P19, P20, 6 Cyl.	6–3¼ x 4⅜	217.8	7.00	25.4	97 @ 3600	....	175 @ 1200
1951	P22, P23, 6 Cyl.	6–3¼ x 4⅜	217.8	7.00	25.35	97 @ 3600	....	175 @ 1200
1952	P22, P23, 6 Cyl.	6–3¼ x 4⅜	217.8	7.00	25.35	97 @ 3600	....	175 @ 1200
1953	P24	6–3¼ x 4⅜	217.8	7.1	25.35	100 @ 3600	....	177 @ 1200

Dimensions of Valves

Year	Model	Overall Length Inlet	Overall Length Exhaust	Head Diameter Inlet	Head Diameter Exhaust	Seat Angle (deg.) Inlet	Seat Angle (deg.) Exhaust	Stem Diameter Inlet	Stem Diameter Exhaust	Key Type	O.D. of Seat Insert Inlet	O.D. of Seat Insert Exhaust
1940–42	Series—All	4.781	4.781	1.468	1.468	45	45	.340	.340	split lock	....	1.578
1946 to 51	Series—All	4.781	4.781	1.531	1.406	45	45	.341	.340	split lock	....	1.515
1952	P22, P23, 6 cyl.	4.78125	4.78125	1.53125	1.40625	45	45	.3405	.3405	....	....	....
1953	P-24-1, P-24-2	4.84375	4.84375	1.531	1.407	45	45	.3405	.3405	....	....	....

Crankshaft Bearing Journal Sizes

Year	Model	Connecting Rod Journals Diameter	Connecting Rod Journals Length	Main Bearing Journals No. 1 Diameter	No. 2 Diameter	No. 3 Diameter	No. 4 Diameter	No. 5 Diameter
1940–41	....	1.9365–1.9375	1.000	2.249–2.250	2.249–2.250	2.249–2.250	2.249–2.250	....
1942 to 51	P14, 15, 17, 18, 19, 20, 22, 23	2.0615–2.0625	1.250	2.4995–2.5005	2.4995–2.5005	2.4995–2.5005	2.4995–2.5005	....
1952	P22, P23, 6 cyl.	2.0615–2.0625	1.250	2.4995–2.5005	2.4995–2.5005	2.4995–2.5005	2.4995–2.5005	....
1953	P24	2.0625	....	2.5–1.204	2.5–1.000	2.5–1.000	2.5–1.589	....

Pistons and Piston Pins

Year	Model	PISTONS Diameter	Material	Type	No. of Rings	PISTON PINS Length	Diameter	How Held
1940–41	Series—All	3.125	Alum.	C	4	2⅝	.859375	F
1942 to 51	Series—All	3.25	Alum.	C	4	2¾	.8593	F
1952–53	All	3.25	Alum Alloy	Us,C	4	2.75	.859375	F

C—Cam ground. Us—"U" slot.

Engine Overhaul Specifications

Year	Model	PISTONS				RING GAP CLEARANCES (Maximum)				PISTON PIN		ROD BEARINGS		
		Removed From	Piston Skirt Clearances (Maximum)											
			Top	Bottom	Limit	Top Ring	Second Ring	Third Ring	Oil Ring	Type	Fit	Oil Clearance	Wear Limit	Side Play
1940	P9, 6 Cyl.	A	.0015	.001	.002	.015	.015	.015	.015	FL	Push	.0005–.0025	.005	.0055–.0115
	P10, 6 Cyl.	A	.0015	.001	.002	.015	.015	.015	.015	FL	Push	.0005–.0025	.005	.0055–.0115
1941	P11, 6 Cyl.	A	.0015	.001	.002	.015	.015	.015	.015	FL	Push	.0005–.0025	.005	.0055–.0115
	P12, 6 Cyl.	A	.0015	.001	.002	.015	.015	.015	.015	FL	Push	.0005–.0025	.005	.0055–.0115
1942	P14S, 6 Cyl.	A	.0015	.001	.002	.015	.015	.015	.015	FL	Press	.001–.0015	.005	.0055–.0115
	P14C, 6 Cyl.	A	.0015	.001	.002	.015	.015	.015	.015	FL	Press	.001–.0015	.005	.0055–.0115
1946	P15, 6 Cyl.	A	.0015	.001	.002	.015	.015	.015	.015	FL	Push	.001–.0015	.005	.0055–.0115
1947	P15, 6 Cyl.	A	.0015	.001	.002	.015	.015	.015	.015	FL	Push	.001–.0015	.005	.0055–.0115
1948	P15, 6 Cyl.	A	.0015	.001	.002	.015	.015	.015	.015	FL	Push	.001–.0015	.005	.0055–.0115
1949	P17-P18, 6 Cyl.	A	.0015	.001	.002	.015	.015	.015	.015	FL	Push	.0005–.0015	.005	.003–.007
1950	P19-P20, 6 Cyl.	A	.0002	.0012	.0015	.015	.015	.015	.015	FL	Push	.0005–.0015	.005	.006–.011
1951	P22-P23, 6 Cyl.	A	.0002	.0012	.0015	.015	.015	.015	.015	FL	Push	.0005–.0015	.005	.006–.011
1952	P22, P23, 6 Cyl.	A	.0007*			.012	.012	.012	.012	FL	.0005	.0005–.0015	.005	.006–.011
1953	P24	A	.0007			.012	.012	.012	.012	FL	.0005	.0005–.0015	.005	.006–.011

FL—Floating type. *—3/4″ from bottom. SP—Sprocket. †—Marks on cam and crank sprockets align with shaft centers.

Engine Tune-Up Specifications

Year	Model	SPARK PLUGS		DISTRIBUTOR		Ignition Timing, (Deg.)	Ignition Timing Mark and Location	Compression Pressure at R.P.M.	OPERATING TAPPET CLEARANCE		Carburetor Fuel Float Height	Minimum Engine Idle Speed at R.P.M.
		Type	Gap	Point Gap	Cam Dwell, (Deg.)				Inlet	Exhaust		
1940	P9, 6 Cyl.	AL-A7	.025	.020	38	TC	Dmpr.	145@1000	.006	.008	5/64″	450
	P10, 6 Cyl.	AL-A7	.025	.020	38	TC	Dmpr.	145@1000	.006	.008	5/64″	450
1941	P11, 6 Cyl.	AL-A7	.025	.020	38	TC	Dmpr.	114@cr. sp.	.008	.010	5/64″	450
	P12, 6 Cyl.	AL-A7	.025	.020	38	TC	Dmpr.	114@cr. sp.	.008	.010	5/64″	450
1942	P14S, 6 Cyl.	AL-A7	.025	.020	38	3B	Dmpr.	160@1000	.008	.010	5/64″	450
	P14C, 6 Cyl.	AL-A7	.025	.020	38	3B	Dmpr.	160@1000	.008	.010	5/64″	450
1946	P15, 6 Cyl.	AL-A5	.025	.020	38	TC	Dmpr.	160@1000	.008	.010	5/64″	450
1947	P15, 6 Cyl.	AL-A5	.025	.020	38	TC	Dmpr.	160@1000	.008	.010	5/64″	450
1948	P15, 6 Cyl.	AL-A5	.025	.020	38	TC	Dmpr.	160@1000	.008	.010	5/64″	450
1949	P17, P18, 6 Cyl.	AL-AR5	.038	.020	38	TC	Dmpr.	160@1000	.008	.010	5/64″	450
1950	P19, P20, 6 Cyl.	AL-AR5	.035	.020	38	TC	Dmpr.	160@1000	.008	.010	5/64″	450
1951	P22, P23, 6 Cyl.	AL-AR8	.035	.018-.020	34½-38	TC	CF-DP	120–150 lbs.	.008	.010	5/64″	450
1952	P22, P23, 6 Cyl.	AL-AR8	.035	.020	38	2B	CF-DP		.010H	.010H	5/64″	475
1953	P-24	AL-AR8	.035	.020	39±3°	2B	CF-DP		.010H	.010H		475

CF-DP—Crank shaft fan drive pulley.
TC—Top center.
Dmpr.—Vibration damper.
B—Before top center.
^—150 at cranking speed.

and Wear Limit Table

CRANKSHAFT		VALVES						Valve Timing, Inlet Valve Opens (Deg.)	Camshaft Drive	Gear Marks	OPERATING OIL PRESSURE		Model	Year
Main Bearing Oil Clearance	Shaft End Play	Spring Tension (Maximum)			Guide Clearance	Seat Angle					Pounds At M.P.H.	Low Limit§		
		Inlet	Exhaust	Low Limit		Inlet	Exhaust							
.001–.002	.003–.007	83@$1\frac{7}{16}$	83@$1\frac{7}{16}$	73	.001–.005	45°	45°	6A	Chain	SP†	40@30	25	..............P9, 6 Cyl.	1940
.001–.002	.003–.007	83@$1\frac{7}{16}$	83@$1\frac{7}{16}$	73	.001–.005	45°	45°	6A	Chain	SP†	40@30	25	..............P10, 6 Cyl.	
.001–.002	.003–.007	115@$1\frac{3}{8}$	115@$1\frac{3}{8}$	103	.001–.005	45°	45°	9B	Chain	SP†	40@30	25	..............P11, 6 Cyl.	1941
.001–.002	.003–.007	115@$1\frac{3}{8}$	115@$1\frac{3}{8}$	103	.001–.005	45°	45°	9B	Chain	SP†	40@30	25	..............P12, 6 Cyl.	
.001–.0015	.003–.007	115@$1\frac{3}{8}$	115@$1\frac{3}{8}$	103	.001–.005	45°	45°	12B	Chain	SP†	40@30	25	............P14S, 6 Cyl.	1942
.001–.0015	.003–.007	115@$1\frac{3}{8}$	115@$1\frac{3}{8}$	103	.001–.005	45°	45°	12B	Chain	SP†	40@30	25	............P14C, 6 Cyl.	
.001–.0015	.003–.007	115@$1\frac{3}{8}$	115@$1\frac{3}{8}$	103	.001–.005	45°	45°	12B	Chain	SP†	40@30	25	..............P15, 6 Cyl.	1946
.001–.0015	.003–.007	115@$1\frac{3}{8}$	115@$1\frac{3}{8}$	103	.001–.005	45°	45°	12B	Chain	SP†	42.5@30	25	..............P15, 6 Cyl.	1947
.001–.0015	.003–.007	115@$1\frac{3}{8}$	115@$1\frac{3}{8}$	103	.003	45°	45°	12B	Chain	SP†	42.5@30	25	..............P15, 6 Cyl.	1948
.0005–.0015	.003–.007	115@$1\frac{3}{8}$	115@$1\frac{3}{8}$	103	.003	45°	45°	12B	Chain	SP†	45@20	25	.........P17-P18, 6 Cyl.	1949
.0005–.0015	.003–.007	115@$1\frac{3}{8}$	115@$1\frac{3}{8}$	103	.004	45°	45°	12B	Chain	SP†	45@20	25	.........P19-P20, 6 Cyl.	1950
.0005–.0015	.003–.007	120@$1\frac{3}{8}$	120@$1\frac{3}{8}$	110	.004	45°	45°	12B	Chain	SP†	50@25	35	.........P22-P23, 6 Cyl.	1951
.0005–.0015	.003–.007	115@$1\frac{3}{8}$	115@$1\frac{3}{8}$	......	.0035	45°	45°	12B	Chain	......	45@45	......	..........P22, P23, 6 Cyl.	1952
.0005–.0015	.003–.007	115@1.375	115@.1375	......	.0035	45°	45°	12B	Chain	......	45@45	......	....................P24...	1953

§—Car may be operated safely at lower oil pressures but low pressure indicates malfunction which should be corrected.

Piston Ring Dimensions

Year	Model	Cylinder Bore	TOP RING			SECOND RING			THIRD RING			OIL RING		
			Width	Gap	Depth	Width	Gap	Depth	Width	Gap	Depth	Width	Gap	Depth
1940	P9, P10......................	$3\frac{1}{8}$	$\frac{3}{32}$	.011	.150	$\frac{1}{8}$	.011	.140	$\frac{5}{32}$	.011	.145	$\frac{5}{32}$	.011	.145
1941	P11, P12.....................	$3\frac{1}{8}$	$\frac{3}{32}$	.011	.156	$\frac{1}{8}$	.011	.140	$\frac{5}{32}$	.011	.145	$\frac{5}{32}$	.011	.145
1942–51	All..........................	$3\frac{1}{4}$	$\frac{3}{32}$	.011	.162	$\frac{3}{32}$	.011	.162	$\frac{5}{32}$	.011	.150	$\frac{5}{32}$	.011	.150
1952	P22, P23, 6 Cyl..............	$3\frac{1}{4}$	$\frac{3}{32}$	.012	.169	$\frac{3}{32}$	.012	.169	$\frac{5}{32}$	.012	.172	$\frac{5}{32}$	.012	.172
1953	P24..........................	$3\frac{1}{4}$	$\frac{3}{32}$	.012	.162	$\frac{3}{32}$	.012	.162	$\frac{5}{32}$	.012	.150	$\frac{5}{32}$	.012	.150

Brake Data

Year	Model	Make	Lining Type	R=Riveted B=Bonded	Drum Diameter	Lining			Clearance	
						Length	Width	Thickness	Toe	Heel
1940	P9, P10..............................	Loc	M	R	10	18	2	$\frac{13}{64}$	.012	.006
1941	P11, P12.............................	Loc	M	R	10	18	2	$\frac{13}{64}$	.012	.006
1942	P14..................................	Loc	M	R	10	18	2	$\frac{13}{64}$	.012	.006
1946 to 49	All..................................	C-L	M	R	10	21–*$18\frac{1}{2}$	2	$\frac{13}{64}$	.006	.006
1950–51	All..................................	C-L	W	R	10	21–*$18\frac{1}{2}$	2	$\frac{13}{64}$	.006	.006
1952	P22, P23, 6 Cyl......................	....	M	B	10	21–*$18\frac{1}{2}$	2	$\frac{13}{64}$	.006	.006
1953	P24..................................	....	M	B	10	21–*$18\frac{1}{2}$	2	$\frac{13}{64}$	.006	.006

*—Rear. LOC—Lockheed C-L—Chrysler-Lockheed. M—Moulded. W—Woven.

Tension Wrench Specifications

Year	Mode	Cylinder Head		Spark Plug		Connecting Rod Bolts or Nuts		Main Bearing Bolt		Flywheel Bolts		Vibration Damper Bolts	
		Lbs.-Ft.	Thread	Lbs.-Ft.	Thread	Lbs.-Ft.	Thread	Lbs.-Ft.	Thread	Lbs.-Ft.	Thread	Lbs.-Ft.	Thread
1940	P9, P10............	65-70	....	26-32	14 mm	52.5-57.5	....	75-80	....	15-20	....	....	....
1941	P11, P12...........	65-70	....	26-32	14 mm	45-50	....	75-80	....	55-60	....	....	....
1942	P14S, P14C.........	65-70	....	26-32	14 mm	45-50	....	75-80	....	55-60	....	....	....
1946 to 49	P15, 17, 18. 19, 20....	65-70	....	26-32	14 mm	45-50	....	80-85	....	55-60	....	....	....
1950 to 53	All............	65-70	....	26-32	14 mm	45-50	....	80-85	....	55-60	....	....	....

Cooling Systems

CAR AND YEAR	MODEL	Capacity Qts.	Quarts of Methanol Base Anti-Freeze (For Protection to Temperature Shown Below)							Quarts of Ethylene Glycol (For Protection to Temperature Shown Below)							Quarts of Denatured Alcohol—188 Proof (For Protection to Temperature Shown Below)						
			3	4	5	6	7	8	9	3	4	5	6	7	8	9	3	4	5	6	7	8	9
1937..........	....	15	11	1	−12	−27	−44	....	....	16	8	0	−12	−26	−43	....	....	10	0	−10	−20	−30	....
1938-41..........	....	14	9	−3	−17	−34	−53	....	....	15	6	−5	−18	−34	−54	....	10	....	0	−10	−20	−30	....
1942-51..........	....	15	11	1	−12	−27	−44	....	....	16	8	0	−12	−26	−43	....	....	10	0	−10	−20	−30	....
1952-53..........	....	13	7	−7	−23	−43	....	....	....	13	3	−9	−25	−45	....	....	10	0	−10	−20	−30	....	

Distributors

Year	Model	Distributor Model Number	Cam Angle (deg.)	Direction of Rotation C=Clockwise CC=Counter Clockwise at Cam End	Breaker Arm Spring Tension	Breaker Point Gap (inches)	Engine R.P.M. when Cent. Advance Starts	Max. Cent. Advance in Engine Deg. at Stated Engine R.P.M.	Vacuum in (inches) of Mercury at which Vacuum Unit Starts	Max. Advance in Engine Deg. at Stated Vacuum	Vacuum Unit Number
1940	P9, P10, 6 cyl..........	IGS-4109-1	38	C	17-20	.018-.022	700	22@3700	5	20@17	IGS-1023-GS
	....	IGS-4108-1	38	C	17-20	.018-.022	700	24@3500	5	14@15	IGS-1023-HS
1941	P11, P12, 6 cyl.........	IGS-4111-1	38	C	17-20	.018-.022	700	24@3700	5	20@17	IGS-1023-GS
	....	IGS-4204-1	38	C	17-20	.018-.022	700	22@3700	5	20@17	VC-3082-RS
1942	P14, 6 cyl............	IGS-4203A-1	38	C	17-20	.018-.022	700	18@2600	5	18@14	VC-3082-RDS
	....	IGS-4203B-1	38	C	17-20	.018-.022	700	20@2300	5	17@16	VC-3082-RGS
	....	IGS-4203C-1	38	C	17-20	.018-.022	700	20@2300	5	15@15	VC-3082-RJS
1946 to 48	P15, 6 cyl............	IGS-4207-1	38	C	17-20	.018-.022	700	18@2600	5	20@14	....
1949-50	P17, P19, 6 cyl.........	IAP-4103A-1	34½	C	17-20	.018-.022	700	28@2850	4½	16@14	....
1949-50	P18, P20, 6 cyl.........	IAP-4103-1	34½	C	17-20	.018-.022	700	18@2600	5	20@14	....
1951	....	....	36¼	C	17-20	.018-.022	700	22@2850	6	44@18	....
1952	P22, P23, 6 cyl.........	IAT-4011	34½-38	C	17-20	.020	....	9-11@1425	5½-6½	7-9@14	....
1953	P-24-1, P-24-2..........	IAT-4001	39±3	C	17-20	.020	350	9-11@1425	5½-6	7-9@14	....

Generators

Year	Model	Generator Number	Field Current at 6 Volts (amps)	Maximum Safe Output			Brush Spring Tension (oz)	Voltage Regulator Number
				Volts	Amperes	R.P.M.		
1940	P9, 10	GDZ-4801-A	1.3–1.5	8.0	35	2000	35–53	VRP-4001-A
1941–42	P11, 12, 14	GDZ-4801-B	1.3–1.5	8.0	35	2000	35–53	VRP-4001-A
1946 to 49	P15, 17, 18	GDZ-4801-A	1.3–1.5	8.0	35	2000	35–53	VRP-4503-A
		GDZ-4801-B	1.3–1.5	8.0	35	2000	35–53	VRP-4503-A
		GEG-4823-A	1.3–1.5	8.0	40	1575	64–68	VRP-4001-F
		GEG-4823-B	1.3–1.5	8.0	40	1575	64–68	VRP-4001-F
		GGJ-6001-A	1.5–1.7	8.0	50	1600	30–37	VAV-4404-A
		GGJ-6001-B	1.5–1.7	8.0	50	1600	30–37	VAV-4404-A
		GGU-6001-A	1.4–1.5	8.0	45	1650	35–53	VAV-4404-B
		GGW-6001-B	1.6–1.8	8.0	40	2000	35–53	VRP-4503-B
1950	P19, 20	GGW-6001	1.6–1.8	8.0	40	2000	35–53	VRP-4001-A
1951	P22, 23	GGW-6001-K	1.6–1.8	8.0	40	2000	35–53	VRP-4001-A
1952	P22, P23, 6 cyl.	GGW-6001-K						VBE-6001-A
1953	P24	GGW-6001		6.8	45	1000		VBE-6001-A

Voltage Regulators

Year	Model	Regulator Number	Grounded P=Position N=Negative	Voltage Control		Current Control		Cut-Out Relay		
				Air Gap Points Closed	Voltage Setting Hot	Air Gap Points Closed	Current Set Hot	Point Gap	Air Gap	Closing Volt
1940 to 42	P9, P10, 11, 12, 14	VRP-4001-A	P	.052	7.3	.038	34–36	.015	.038	6.4–7.0
1946 to 48	P15	VRP-4503-B	P	.052	7.35	.052	38–42	.015	.034	6.4–7.0
		VRP-4001-F	P	.052	7.2	.052	39–41	.015	.034	6.4–7.0
		VAV-4404-A	P	.052	7.2	.052	50	.015	.034	6.4–7.0
		VAV-4404-B	P	.052	7.2	.052	50	.015	.034	6.4–7.0
1949		VBA-4101-A	P	.052	6.9	.052	50	.015	.034	6.4–7.0
		VBA-4101-B	P	.052	6.9	.052	50	.015	.034	6.4–7.0
		VRP-4503-A	P	.052	7.3	.052	38–42	.015	.034	6.4–7.0
1950–51		VRP-6004-A	P	.050	7.3	.050	38–42	.015	.034	6.4–7.0
		VAV-6001-A	P	.050	7.2	.050	45–57	.015	.032	6.4–7.0
		VBA-4202-A	P	.050	7.2	.050	45–57	.015	.032	6.4–7.0
1952	P22, P23, 6 cyl.	VBE-6001-A			7.1–7.4		45–57			6.4–7.0
1953	P24	VBE-6001-A			7.1–7.4		45–57			6.3–6.8

Starters

Year	Model	Unit Model Number	Spring Tension (oz.)	STARTER						Direction of Rotation Viewed from Drive End C=Clockwise CC=Counter-clockwise
				Lock Test			No Load			
				Volts	Amperes	Torque, (lbs. ft.)	Volts	Amperes	R.P.M.	
1941	P11, P12	MZ-4089	42–53	2.0	280	4.4	5.0	68	4000	C
		MZ-4089-A	42–53	2.0	280	4.4	5.0	68	4000	C
1942	P15	MZ-4105	42–53	2.0	280	4.4	5.0	68	4000	C
1946 to 48	P15	MZ-4133	42–53	2.0	280	4.4	5.0	68	4000	C
1949	P17, 18, 19, 20, 22, 23	MCH-6101	42–53	2.0	335	6	5.0	65	4300	C
1952	P22, P23, 6 cyl.	MCH-6201	42–53	2	335	6	6	50–65	4900	C
1953	P24	MCH-6205	42–53	3	500	11	5.5	50–65	4900	C

PLYMOUTH SPECIFICATIONS

Front Wheel Alignment

Year	Model	Caster (deg.)	Camber (deg.)	King Pin Inclination (deg.)	Toe-In (inches)	Turning Radius	
						Inner	Outer
1940	P9, P10	1N to 1P	0 to ¾P	4¾ to 6	0 to ⅛	22	20
1941	P11, P12	1N to 1P	0 to ¾P	4¾ to 6	0 to ⅛	22	20
1942–50	P14S, 14C, 15, 17, 18, 19, 20	1N to 1P	0 to ¾P	4¾ to 6	0 to 1/16	22	20
1951–52	P22, 23, 24	1N to 1P	⅜N to ⅜P	5 to 6½	0 to 1/16	22	20
1953	All	1N to 1P	⅜N to ⅜P	5 to 6½	0 to 1/16	18¾	20

Fan, Generator Belts and Radiator Hose

Year	Model	Fan Belt			Generator Belt			Upper Hose			Lower Hose		
		Angle of "V" (deg.)	Length O.C.	Width Max.	Angle of "V" (deg.)	Length O.C.	Width Max.	Type	Inside Diam.	Length	Type	Inside Diam.	Length
1940	P9, P10	42	49⅛	23/32				straight	1¾	9	straight	1½	3¾–5¾
1941	P11	42	49⅛	23/32				straight	1¾	9½	straight	1½	3½–4½
	P12	42	49⅛	23/32				straight	1¾	8	straight	1½	4½–3¾
1942	P14S	42	49⅛	23/32				straight	1¾	7⅞	straight	1½	3½–5½
	P14C	42	49⅛	23/32				straight	1¾	6¼	straight	1½	3½–5½
1946 to 48	P15	42	49⅛	23/32				straight	1¾	6½	straight	1½	7–3½
1949	P17, P18	42	49⅛	23/32				curved	1¾		straight	1½	2½–5½
1950 Early	All	42	49⅛	23/32				curved	1¾		straight	1½	6½–2½
Late	All	40	49⅛	13/32				curved	1¾		straight	1½	6½–2½
1951	All	40	49⅛	13/32				curved	1¾		straight	1½	6½–2½
1952	P22, P23, 6 cyl.	36	49	⅜				curved	1¾		curved	1½	
1953	P24	36	49	⅜				curved	1¾		curved	1½	

King Pin Specifications Chart

Year	Model	KING BOLT			UPPER BUSHING				LOWER BUSHING			
					King Bolt Bushing				King Bolt Bushing			
		Diameter	Length	Bolt Number	Inside Diameter	Outside Diameter	Length	Bushing Number	Inside Diameter	Outside Diameter	Length	Bushing Number
1940 to 51	All	.796	5 7/16	626975	.795	.922	1¼	633672	.795	.922	1¼	633672
1952–53												

FRONT SUSPENSION

1940 MODELS

The suspension used on 1940 models was somewhat different from that used on later models in that the upper suspension arm was formed in the shape of a hook, having one open end on to which the knuckle support upper bushing (eccentric) was threaded to secure caster and camber adjustment.

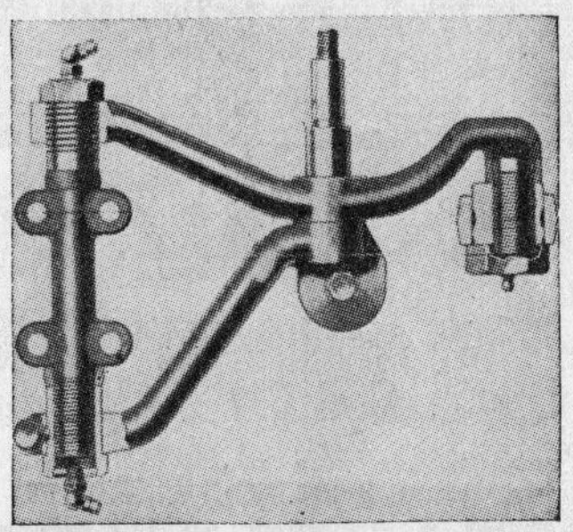

Upper control arm—1940 models

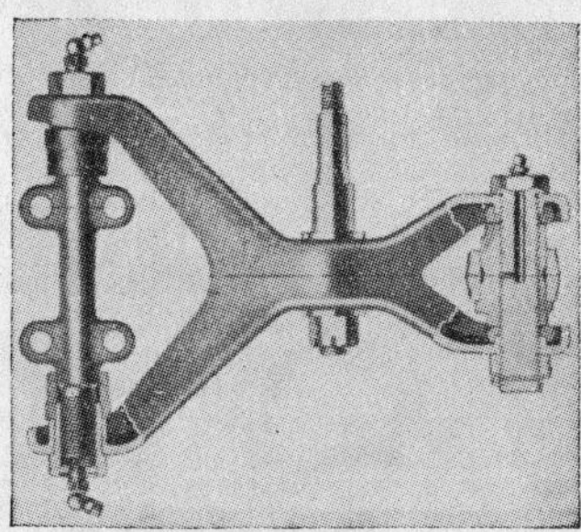

Upper control arm—1941—53 models

1942 THRU 1953 MODELS

The major difference between these later models and the 1940 models is that the upper suspension arm straddled the upper pin of the knuckle support.

An eccentric bushing was fitted into the upper end of the knuckle support and threaded on to the upper suspension arm outer pin.

In spite of this structural difference service procedure is almost identical on both types of construction.

Caster, Camber and Toe-In Adjustment

Caster and camber are both adjusted at the eccentric bushing in the upper end of the knuckle support.

The bushing is turned in a clockwise direction to increase caster. When properly adjusted the upper end of the knuckle support will be approximately midway in the yoke of the upper suspension arm. Since caster and camber are both adjusted at the same eccentric bushing it will be necessary to seek a compromise between the best caster and camber adjustment.

Where it is desired to come to an exact adjustment it will be necessary to secure the caster adjustment by turning the eccentric bushing until the exact caster reading is secured. Then it will be necessary to cold bend the knuckle support to secure the exact camber reading.

Caution: At no time should heat be applied to the knuckle supports since these parts are heat treated after forging and reheating to simplify bending will destroy the heat treatment and render the part useless.

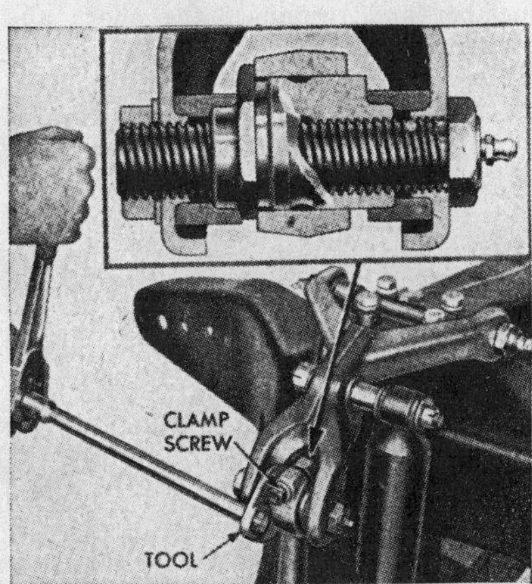

Caster and camber adjustment

Toe-In Adjustment

Set the steering wheel in a straight ahead position and loosen the tie-rod clamp bolts on both tie rods. Turn equally until correct toe-in is reached.

Note: Tie rods are mixed in production so that on some they would be turned to the left, and others turned to the right to increase toe-in.

Centralizing Steering Wheel

1940 THRU 1953 MODELS

On these models a long and short tie rod was used which was connected directly to the end of the steering pitman arm. To centralize the steering on these models set the steering wheel in the mid position of its travel and, keeping it in that position, adjust each tie rod so that one-half of the total toe-in is contained in each wheel. After adjustment is secured, road test the car to make certain that the gear was not strained in any way, when the adjustment was made, which might cause it to deviate somewhat from the straight ahead position.

REPLACEMENT OF FRONT SUSPENSION PARTS

Upper and Lower Suspension Arm Pins and Bushings

On 1940 models the upper suspension arm was fitted with a bushing but the pin was an integral part of the upper suspension arm itself.

Both upper and lower suspension arm pin and bushings can be serviced with the road wheel in place. However, the job is greatly simplified if front wheels are removed.

When installing either the upper or the lower suspension arm pins and bushings they should be set into the car so that the knuckle support is approximately in the center at both the lower and upper suspension arm.

Support the weight of the car on the lower suspension arm. Remove the wheel and disconnect the torsion bar and shock absorber. Remove the upper and/or lower pin and surrile out the knuckle support which will give access to the knuckle support bushing.

As a precaution, arrange a support for the spindle so that the brake hose will not be damaged.

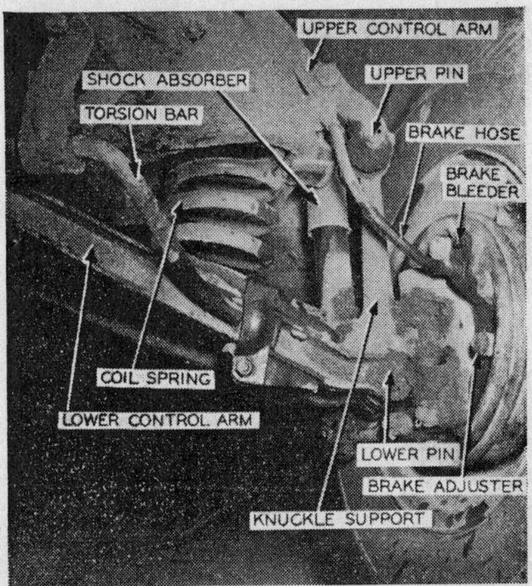

Front suspension—all models

Upper Suspension Arm Inner Shaft & Bushings

The upper suspension arm inner shaft and bushings can be replaced by supporting the weight of the A frame

UPPER SUSPENSION ARM—*cont'd*

on a jack, take off the front wheel and drum and unbolt the inner shaft from the top of the frame. These bolts are accessible from the engine compartment.

Remove the front and rear bushing from the inner shaft and slide the shaft out of the arm. Provide some means to support the spindle to avoid accidental damage to the brake hose.

Lower Suspension Arm (A Frame) Inner Arm and Bushings

To replace the lower suspension arm inner shaft and bushings, detach the torsion bar, disconnect the shock absorber at either end. It is perhaps safer to place a jack under the inner shaft and unbolt it from the frame, after which it can be lowered to the floor, releasing the spring pressure.

With the weight of the spring released from the lower suspension arm, the bushings may be removed from the inner shaft and the shaft taken out.

Replacement of King Pins

Note: All Plymouth models built since 1940 used anti-friction needle bearings at the upper end of the king pin.

To replace the king pin, remove the wheel and the brake backing plate.

Note: On models with two cylinders on the front brakes the backing plate can be removed with the steering arm remaining bolted to the knuckle. On models with single cylinder front brakes the two anchor bolts are also the attaching bolts for the steering arm.

On models with two front wheel cylinders it is necessary to disconnect the brake hose in order to take the backing plate off the cylinder. On models with two front cylinders the backing plate can be removed from the spindle without disconnecting the hydraulic line.

In either case it will be necessary to perform a major brake adjustment on the front brakes after the backing plate is remounted.

Drive the king pin lock pin forward to remove.

Remove the upper welsh plug and drive the king pin out through the bottom.

Replacement of Front Coil Springs

Jack the car up until the road wheels are at least 8 inches off the floor and place jacks under the frame to hold the car. Detach the shock absorber and torsion bar. Place a roller jack on to the inner shaft of the lower suspension arm and take out the four bolts which hold the inner shaft to the front cross member. Lower the inner end of the A frame down until the tension is off the front spring.

Install a new front spring, being careful that any shims which were found under the old spring are placed under the new one. Extra care should be taken to make certain that the lower end of the coil is properly seated in the A frame.

Jack the lower A frame back into place, guiding it carefully with a long drift pin.

Securely tighten the four bolts which hold the inner shaft to the front cross member and reconnect the shock absorber and torsion bar.

STEERING GEAR ASSEMBLY

All Plymouth models from 1940 thru 1951 are equipped with the Gemmer worm and roller type steering gear.

Steering Gear Assembly Removal

1940 MODELS

On 1940 models the steering gea can be removed by taking out the fron seat, and removing the steering wheel Detach the transmission shift mechanism. Then remove the bolts which holc the upper jacket tube to the lowei jacket tube and lift off the upper tube Remove the jacket which holds the steering mechanism to the dash panel disconnect the pitman arm and take out the steering gear mounting bolts.

The steering gear mechanism is then removed by lowering the top of the steering column to the floor and drawing the gear out over the top of the radiator.

1941 THRU 1948 MODELS

On these models the steering gear assembly is removed down between the engine and the frame after all the attaching parts such as the steering wheel, direction signal wires, gear shift mechanism and mounting brackets have been removed.

1949 THRU 1953 MODELS

On these models the steering gear

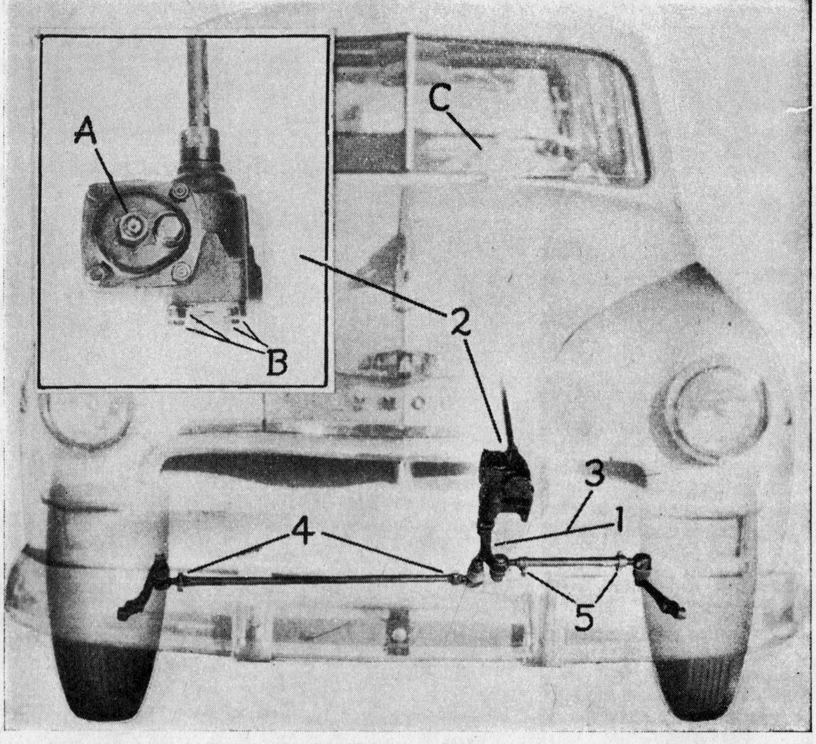

Steering mechanism

mechanism is lifted up into the car after all attaching parts have been removed, such as the shift mechanism, directional signal wires, pitman arm, steering wheel, horn button wires etc.

Adjustment of Steering Mechanism

1. Disconnect the pitman arm from the tie rods.

2. Adjust the steering gear housing assembly.

This gear is the Gemmer double roller tooth type with external mesh screw adjustment.

(A) Loosen the cross shaft mesh adjusting screw lock nut and back off on the adjusting screw so that there is plenty of play between the worm and roller tooth before adjusting the worm bearings.

(B) Loosen or remove the four cap screws which hold the housing lower cover in place and remove one shim at a time to take out the worm bearing end plate. Bearings should be adjusted so that there is zero play in the worm bearing but no definite preload.

(C) Turn the steering wheel to the midposition of its travel and adjust the mesh of the worm roller by turning the adjusting screw inward until there is zero lash between the gears on the high spot. Tighten the lock nut.

3. Reconnect the tie rods to pitman arm.

4. Adjust the long tie rod with the steering wheel in midposition of its travel so that one half the total toe-in is in the right wheel. Tighten the lock nuts.

5. Now adjust the short tie rod so that the remaining toe-in is taken up in the left wheel and tighten the lock nuts. Turn the steering wheel from one extreme to the other to check for roughness or binding.

BRAKES

All Plymouth models use Lockheed internal expanding hydraulically operated brakes.

A two cylinder front brake was used on all Plymouth models from 1947 thru 1951.

Minor Brake Adjustment

Minor brake adjustment is done to compensate for normal lining wear.

Jack up the car and turn the adjustment cam on each shoe until the shoe drags and then back it off until it is just free. Repeat this operation at all four wheels.

MAJOR BRAKE ADJUSTMENT

Before making a major brake adjustment, first remove at least one of the road wheels and drums to determine the condition of the lining. Carefully

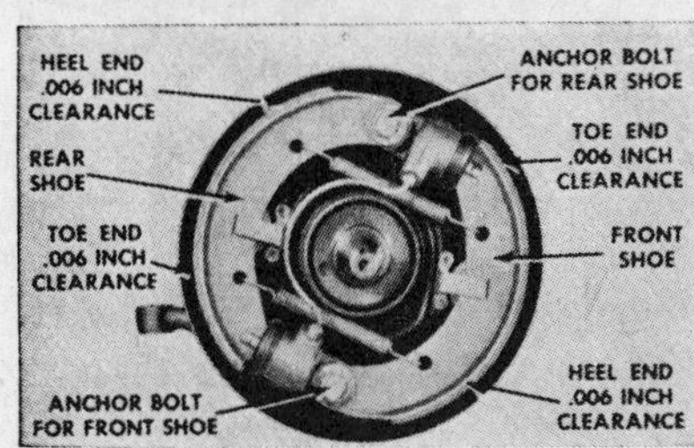

Front brake—front view

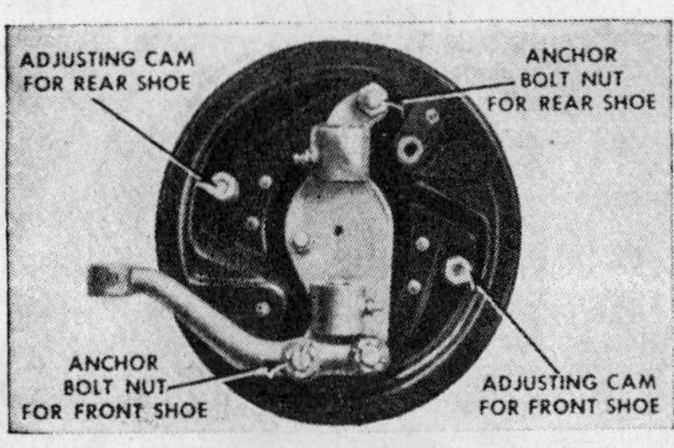

Front brake—rear view

examine the wheel cylinders to make sure there is no leaking or seepage at any of the wheel cylinders. If any leaking or seepage is detected at the wheel which is being examined, it is a good idea to remove all the wheels and make a complete inspection of the hydraulic system. If more than one of the wheel cylinders is found to be defective it is a good idea to remove all the wheel cylinders and the master cylinder so that they can be honed and refitted with cups and boots.

Since most of the Plymouth drums are not fitted with an inspection port for the insertion of a feeler gauge, a dummy drum or a brake centering gauge or an axle type lining grinder is required to insure that the brakes are being adjusted properly.

Before starting the anchor adjustment, remove all the drums to determine the position of the anchors. On the front brakes (with two cylinders) the arrow on the brake anchor should point toward the adjacent cylinder.

On rear brakes or front brakes with single cylinders the arrows on the anchor pins should point toward each other. If they are not in this position it will be necessary to set them into this position before beginning the anchor adjustment.

Since the anchor pins on most Plymouths cannot be turned from the backing plate side it is absolutely essential that a dummy drum or centering gauge or axle type lining grinder be used to properly adjust the brakes.

In an emergency the anchor pins can be left in the position they were set in and the brakes assembled and a minor adjustment done on the brakes after securely tightening the anchor pins.

Hand Brake Cable

1940 THRU 1950 MODELS

To remove the hand brake cable take out the three nuts which fasten the brake conduit to the inside of the cowl.

The cable fastens to the lever assembly with a clevis pin.

The conduit is mounted to the bracket which is part of the lever assembly.

On the underside of the car the conduit fastens to a bracket on the side of the transmission and is held there with a horseshoe lock which is easily removed.

The yoke at the brake end of the cable screws on to a rod which is an integral part of the cable.

The yoke is held to the brake operating mechanism by a clevis pin.

1951 THRU 1953 MODELS

A ratchet type hand brake is used on these models.

Two bolts are used to mount the cable under the center of the dash. The cable fastens to the lever assembly with a clevis pin.

The cable and conduit is held by a bracket which is screwed to the fire wall under the dash.

The brake end of the cable is held to the transmission by a mounting bracket.

A yoke is screwed to the lower end of the cable and forms the lever cable adjustment. This in turn is held with a clevis pin to the brake operating mechanism.

A new cable and conduit assembly does not include the yoke.

Hand Brake Adjustment

EXTERNAL TYPE HAND BRAKE

Fully release the hand brake lever and check the clearance at the brake between the anchor bracket and the

HAND BRAKE ADJUSTMENT—*cont'd*

drum. This clearance should not exceed .005 inch. Adjust the lining to drum clearance so there is between .015 and .020 in. clearance between the lining and the drum. After the lining is properly adjusted, pull all the slack out of the hand brake cable and reconnect.

Bleeding Brakes

See General Service and Trouble Shooting in index.

COOLING SYSTEM

Water Pump

The water pump assembly on all Plymouth models is essentially the same type pump, and while they are various shapes and sizes the service procedure is practically the same for all of them. All are of the so-called packless type, and all are equipped with bronze bushings.

Removal of Water Pump

On all Plymouth models the water pump can be removed without removing the radiator core. In general the procedure is to remove the fan blades, detach all hose connections, and on models which use a fan shroud, take off the fan shroud.

The water pump can then be detached from the block and lifted off.

Disassembly of Water Pump

Drive out the fan pulley hub pin and press off the fan hub. Remove the pump cover and pull the impeller and shaft assembly out of the pump body.

It is not necessary to separate the impeller from the shaft since these two are serviced as a unit.

Removing water pump hub
1—tool 2—fan mounting bolt

To remove the bushings, drive the pins which retain the bushings to the housing into the shaft hole and use a puller to remove the front and rear bushings from the pump body, pulling them both toward the front.

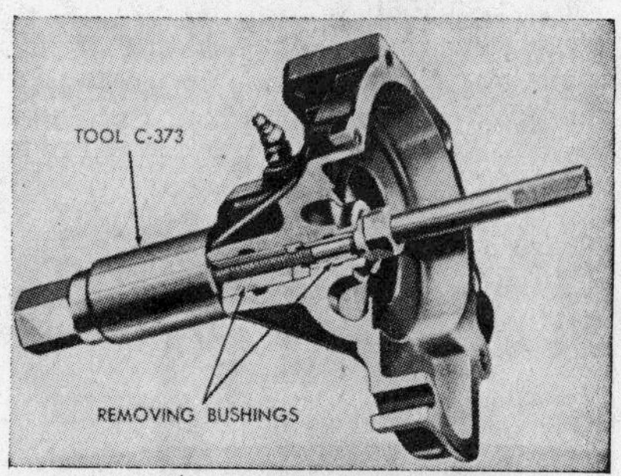

Removing front and rear bushings

The pump parts are assembled in the following sequence. Install impeller on shaft, making the back of the impeller

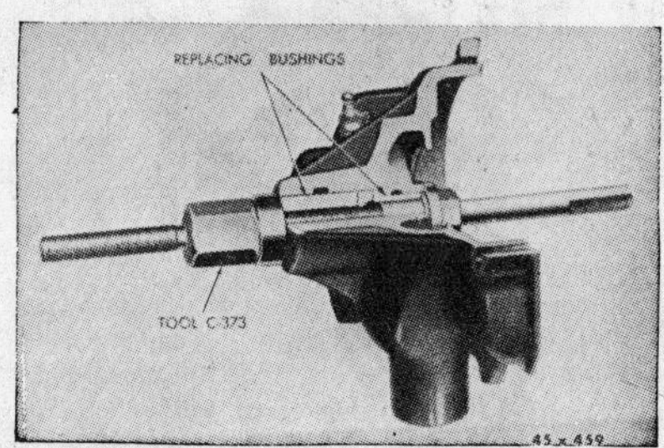

Installing front and rear bushings

flush with the end of the shaft. This is not necessary if a new shaft and impeller assembly is being used. Install water pump seal thrust spring, install water pump seal retainer, install water pump seal, install water pump seal retainer washer and lock ring.

Radiator Core Removal

1940 THRU 1953 ALL MODELS

On these models the radiator core is removed after taking off the water hoses, headlight wires, fan shroud (if any) and the water pump assembly.

Note: It will be necessary to remove the upper and lower radiator shield on the 1949 thru 1951 models. The radiator can then be unbolted from its side mountings and lifted up and over the engine.

Water Distribution Tube

A water distribution tube is used on all models and is located immediately back of the water pump. It may be taken out by removing the radiator core and the water pump. When installing a new water distribution tube it is essential that the new tube be flared on the end in a manner similar to the old tube.

To remove the tube, a rod is formed into a hook at one end and is slid into the distribution tube hooking one of the holes in the tube. If the distribution tube seems to be stuck or corroded in place it is a good idea to thoroughly flush out the block rather than attempting to force the tube out of the block.

ENGINE ASSEMBLY

Plymouth engines in every year of their production, up to and including 1953, were of the in-line L-head variety.

Engine Removal

1940 THRU 1948 MODELS

On these models the engine and transmission assembly is removed as a unit, after removing the radiator core.

Before lifting out the engine make certain that all the attaching parts such as wires leading to the transmission, shift links, clutch, linkage, battery cables, heat indicators, gas lines, oil pressure gauge lines, etc., are detached.

1949 THRU 1953 MODELS

On these models to remove the engine it is necessary to first remove the transmission and radiator core. Then take off all attaching parts and lift out the engine.

Engine Manifolds

On all Plymouth engines the intake and exhaust manifold are mounted on the right side of the engine and are joined together just underneath the carburetor. A heat riser valve is used in the exhaust manifold to deflect the exhaust gases toward the intake manifold when the engine is cool. The heat riser valve is operated by a thermostatic spring which causes it to move to the off position when the engine reaches operating temperature. The only service required by the heat riser is to see that the valve is free and operates freely.

An inoperative valve may cause the engine to warm up slowly, resulting in excessive use of the choke, or it may cause the engine to apparently run lean when it is hot.

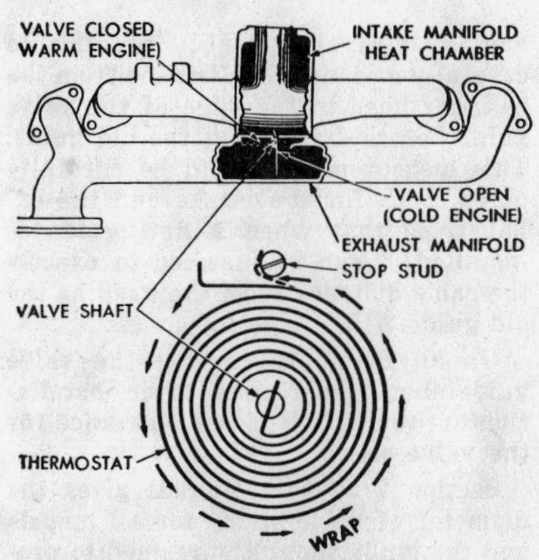

Diagram showing heat riser location and thermostat wrap

ENGINE INTERNAL

Piston and Connecting Rod Assemblies

The four ring aluminum pistons are used on all Plymouth models.

Assembly of Piston to Connecting Rod

On all engines the slotted side of the piston should be assembled to the side of the connecting rod which has the oil spit hole. When assembling the rod and piston assemblies to the cylinder the slotted side of the piston should be pointed away from the camshaft (valves).

Connecting Rod Bearings

Connecting rod bearings in all Plymouths are of the precision, slip-in type and Plymouth does not recommend adjusting the rod bearing.

Rod bearings are available for all models in a variety of undersizes. However, if it becomes necessary to make an adjustment on the rod bearing do not under any circumstances file either the cap or the connecting rod as this will destroy their usefulness. It is possible to install a specially designed shim between the lower half of the bearing shell and the bearing cap. As much as .003 inch may be taken up by this method.

CYLINDER HEAD NUT TIGHTENING SEQUENCE

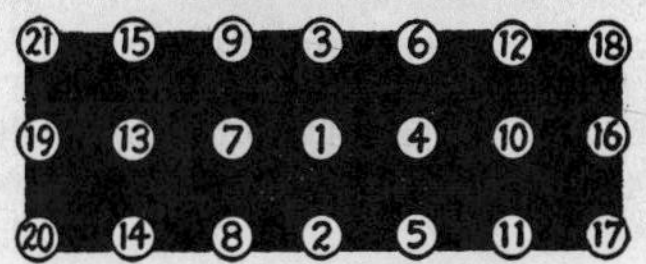

Tighten head to 65-70 foot pounds.

Main Bearings

The main bearings on all Plymouth cars are of precision, slip-in type and may be replaced without removing the crankshaft. The fit of the main bearings may be checked either by the plastic gauge method or by the shim stock method. Plastic gauge stock is supplied with complete instructions for its use.

To check the fit of a main bearing with shim stock proceed as follows: First determine that the crank shaft will turn freely with all bearings bolted in place. Then, one at a time, remove the main bearing cap and place a piece of shim stock .0015 inch thick, ½ inch

Section through the Plymouth engine. Typical of all models

MAIN BEARINGS—*continued*

wide and approximately 1 inch long between the bearing cap and the journal. Tighten the bearing cap screws from 80 to 85 lbs torque and then rock the crankshaft back and forth. If a slight drag is felt the clearance is approximately .0015 inch and this is considered satisfactory. If, however, no drag is felt with the shim stock in place the bearing may be considered too loose.

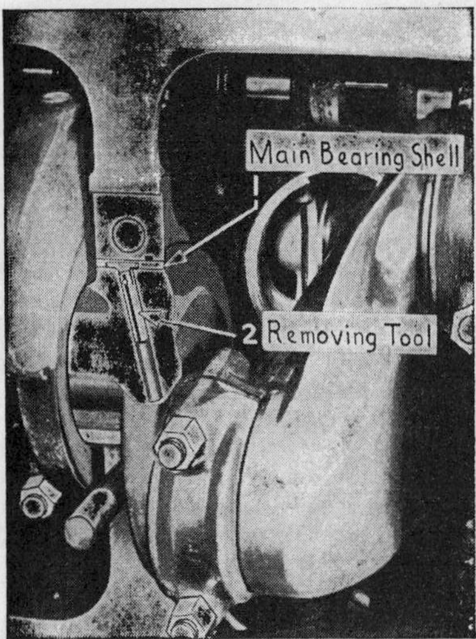

Removing main bearing upper half

By repeating this test with thicker shim stock the exact clearance between the journal and the bearing may be determined so that the correct undersize bearing can be secured. Plymouth does not recommend adjusting the main bearings and under no circumstances should the caps be filed as this will render them useless.

Rear main bearing oil seal assembly

In an emergency, however, the main bearing shell may be adjusted in the same manner that the connecting rod bearing is adjusted. That is, by placing a piece of specially designed shim stock between the bearing shell and the bearing cap in the lower half. By using this method as much as .004 inch looseness may be taken up.

Rear Main Bearing Oil Seal

Braided asbestos is used to prevent oil escaping from the crank case on to the clutch and flywheel. To replace the lower half of this oil seal remove the rear main bearing cap and the old oil seal packing. Install the new packing in the connecting rod cap so that the packing protrudes slightly above the cap. Bolt the cap in place and torque it to approximately 60 ft lbs and then immediately take it down again. If the protruding part of the packing has "riveted over," cut off the riveted portion with a razor blade and again bolt the cap into place. Repeat this operation until the main bearing cap sets firmly in the block without riveting over the new portion of the oil seal.

Removal of Oil Pan

ALL MODELS

Crank engine until No. 1 piston is half way up the cylinder bore. Take down clutch underpan and the bolts around the oil pan. Lower the back of the pan and slide it back and out at the same time so that it will clear the oil pump screen.

Pan gasket end corks should protrude from ¼ in. to ½ in. above the oil pan. Do not cut off the protruding portions since the pan will compress it making a tight seal when it is bolted firmly in place.

VALVE SYSTEM

All Plymouth engines are of the in-line L-head variety and are fitted with mushroom type lifters which require that the camshaft be removed in order to take out any of the lifters.

Replacement of Valve Guides

Whenever it is necessary to replace valve guides on Plymouth, or any other engine, it is always good practice to carefully measure the distance from the cylinder head to the edge of the valve guide before driving out the old guide. This measurement should be carefully noted, both for the intake and the exhaust, so that when a new guide is installed, it can be inserted to exactly the same distance from the head as the old guide.

On all Plymouth engines the valve guide should be reamed after installation to provide the proper clearance for the valve stem.

Section 2 of this Manual gives the diameter of valve stems for all models and the guide should be reamed to provide a clearance of approximately .0015 inch.

On all in-line engines the valve guides are pulled through the top of the block. New guides are installed by driving them from the top toward the bottom.

Valve Seat Inserts

All Plymouth engines are equipped with exhaust valve seat inserts which are made of a cast, heat resisting material, which cannot be cut successfully with a reamer. Exhaust valve seats must be ground and/or lapped to a perfect seal.

Valve Springs

A quick way to check the condition of the valve springs when they have been removed is to lay them all in a row on a level surface and determine that all of them are the same height by placing a straight edge across the top of all the springs.

If it is found that the springs vary in height it will be necessary to secure one new spring and then check all the others against the new one. They should be exactly the same length as the new one. If they are not, they require replacement.

Checking the valve springs against the new spring is generally considered to be a fairly accurate way of checking the general condition of the spring itself, when regular spring pressure testers are not available.

Adjusting Valves

Remove the road wheel and the access hole cover under the fender to service the valves in the most convenient manner. Take off the valve chamber cover.

A self-locking tappet screw is used on all Plymouth models.

It is advisable to use some kind of protection for the back of the hands so that they will not be burned on the hot exhaust manifold and exhaust pipe while adjusting the valve tappets.

Timing Case Cover Removal

On these models, to remove the timing case cover it is necessary to take off the radiator core, water pump, fan and vibration damper.

Valve Timing Procedure—Replacement of Chains and Sprockets

To replace a timing chain and/or sprockets, or to retime the valves where the timing has jumped, proceed as follows: detach the camshaft sprocket, slide it off the shaft and remove the timing chain. Unless the crankshaft sprocket is to be replaced it will not be necessary to remove it from the shaft. Rotate the crankshaft so that the mark on the crankshaft sprocket is toward the camshaft and in exact alignment

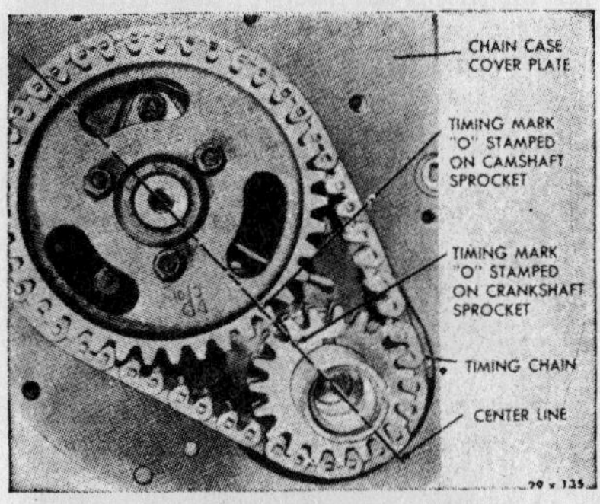

Timing marks on sprockets

between the shaft centers. Now install the timing chain over the cam sprocket so that the mark on the cam and the mark on the crank sprocket are nearest each other. Note that the cam sprocket bolt holes (in-line engines) are staggered in such a way that the sprocket will enter only one way and permit the bolt to enter through the threaded holes in the hub. Rotate the camshaft so that holes line up while the timing marks are still in line between the shaft centers.

Mount the sprocket on the hub and draw up to bolts. Turn the crankshaft two full revolutions and check to see that the marks are still in alignment between the shaft centers. When set in the manner described with the marks aligned between the two shaft centers it is immaterial which piston is at top dead center. In may be necessary, however, to retime the ignition at any time the chain setting is disturbed.

To Check Valve Timing

Valve timing is given in degrees in the Engine Overhaul Specifications tables in Section 2 of this Manual, and also at the bottom of the first section Flat Rate pages. Valve timing is expressed in degress before or after top center at which the intake valve opens. In order to make an accurate check of the valve timing, without disturbing the chain case, proceed as follows:

Remove the valve chamber cover and insert a feeler gauge, having considerably less thickness than the valve clearance, between the lifter and valve on No. 1 intake valve. Now crank the engine slowly until No. 1 cylinder is ready to commence its intake stroke. At this point the crankshaft should be turned very slowly at the exact point of rotation of the crankshaft noted when the lifter grips the feeler gauge. Then refer to the vibration damper which is marked in degrees (before and after top center) and note the degree mark which is under the pointer. If the reading noted is within 4 degrees of the specifications given in this Manual, the valve timing is within the prescribed limits.

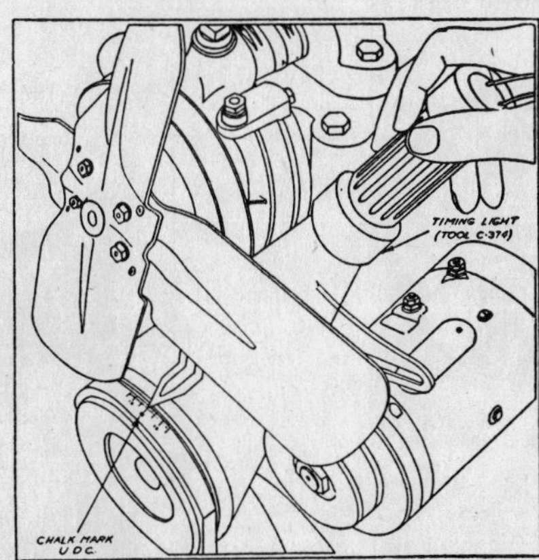

Timing light in use—note degree marks on damper rim

The reason a 4 degree variation is permissible is because any change in valve timing would of necessity be one full tooth on the camshaft sprocket, and this tooth is approximately 8 degrees.

Engine Ground Straps

No engine ground straps are used on Plymouth models. Therefore if difficulty is experienced with lights having poor grounds it is sometimes a good idea to attach a ground strap from the body to the cylinder head in order to insure a firm electrical contact between the body and the engine.

CLUTCH ASSEMBLY

The only practical service possible on the clutch assembly is to tighten up to prevent rattles and adjust the pedal toe board clearance. All other service requires the removal of the clutch assembly.

If the clutch assembly is being removed because of chatter or malfunction, it is advisable to check to see if there is any oil leaking from the rear main bearing. Oil on the clutch facings will produce a noticeable chatter.

Removal of the Clutch Assembly

On all models remove the transmission assembly, the clutch housing lower pan and the clutch throwout bearing. The clutch cover assembly should be marked, showing its relation to the flywheel so that it can be reassembled in the same position from which it was removed. The cover bolts should be removed a few turns at a time in order to avoid springing the clutch cover.

Disassembly service on the clutch requires special jigs and fixtures. Instructions in the use of the fixtures are supplied by the manufacturer of the tool.

Torque Converter

Starting with 1953 Models, a torque converter known as a Hy-Drive is used on some Plymouth models as optional equipment.

The torque converter is used in conjunction with a standard clutch and a standard three speed transmission.

Driving Instructions

On cars equipped with Hy-Drive it is necessary to use the clutch only when placing the car in gear from a standing start. In other words, the clutch is depressed, the transmission lever is placed in High gear and the clutch is released without accelerating. Once the clutch is completely engaged, smooth, even acceleration can be had without any further use of the clutch as long as the car remains in High gear.

DRIVING INSTRUCTIONS—*continued*

The torque converter is capable of torque multiplication up to 2.6 to 1.

While a standard three speed transmission is used, it is not interchangeable with models not equipped with Hy-Drives since the Hy-Drive standard transmission has heavier gears to withstand the higher torque of the torque converter.

The Hy-Drive unit is of welded steel construction and can only be serviced as a complete unit. The only exception to this are the rear oil seals.

To replace either of the rear oil seals it is necessary to remove the transmission, the clutch, the clutch housing, and the torque converter bell housing. The torque converter can then be detached from the flywheels and the oil seals can be replaced.

Since the unit is of welded construction it is not possible to take it apart for any other service.

The flywheel ring gear, however, can be removed and replaced from the torque converter flywheel.

Oil for the torque converter is supplied through the sump of the engine.

A single oil pump is used to supply both the engine and the torque converter. It is an internal bypass type oil pump.

Oil capacity of the crankcase and torque converter is 11 qts including the quart required for the oil filter. Cars not equipped with an oil filter or in which the oil filter has been removed require only 10 qts of oil.

Depending on atmospheric conditions, oil from SAE 5-W to SAE 30 is recommended, depending on climatic conditions.

Draining the Torque Converter

In order to drain the oil from the torque converter, remove the plate from the bottom of the converter housing and then turn the engine to bring the torque converter drain plug to the bottom. Remove the plug and let the oil drain out.

Service Adjustments

No service adjustments whatever are required on the torque converter unit.

STANDARD TRANSMISSION ASSEMBLY

Since 1940, Plymouth cars have been equipped with standard three speed transmissions.

Standard Transmission Removal

Disconnect the propeller shaft at the front universal joint.

Disconnect all attaching parts such as speedometer cable, battery ground cable, gear shift control rods and gear shift selector cables.

Remove the nuts which hold the transmission to the clutch housing and lift the transmission assembly down and out.

Disassembly of the Standard Transmission

Remove the two screws at the transmission cover which hold the shift rail detent springs and balls. Then take off the transmission side cover assembly.

Take off the universal joint companion flange and brake drum assembly.

Next take off the shifter fork guide rail. (This is a long thin rail which slides into the front face of the transmission and through the shifter fork. It is intended to guide the shifter fork. It is removed by unscrewing it to the left with a screw driver and sliding it out of the front face of the transmission.)

Set the transmission in neutral and loosen the shifter rails from the shifter

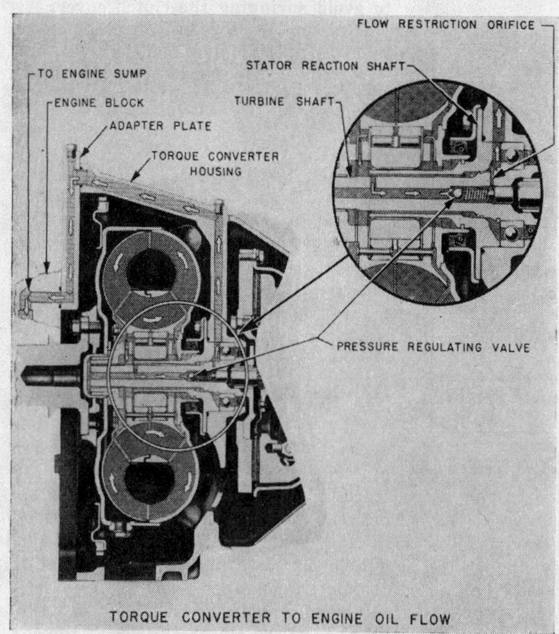

Fig. 1—Torque converter to engine oil flow

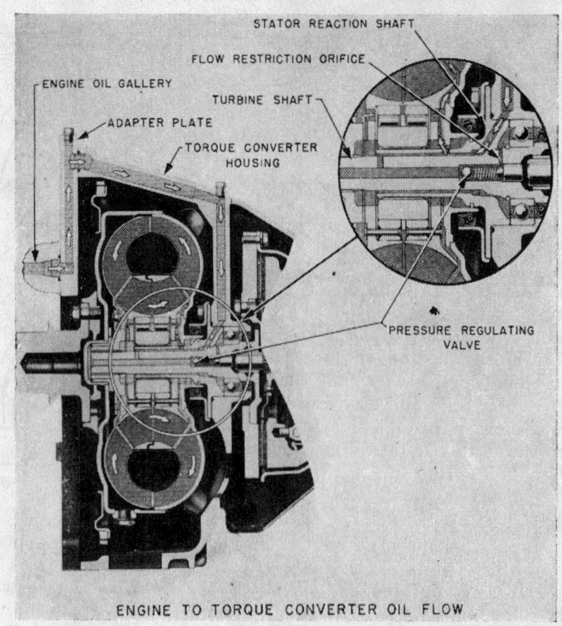

Fig. 2—Engine to torque converter oil flow

forks. Then slide the shift rails out of the front of the transmission case (it will be necessary to remove the Welsh plug to get at the lower rail).

The shift rail interlock rod can be removed by taking out the single cap screw which is located at the top of the transmission toward the back, just to the right of the side cover. Take out the shifter forks. Unbolt the extension housing from the back of the transmission case and slide the case with the main shaft and gears connected to it out the rear of the transmission case.

The main shaft now can be disassembled by removing the synchronizer re-

Case and stationary shafts

taining snap ring and the synchronizer unit. The second speed gear and low speed gear can then be slid off the shaft.

The rear bearing is held in place with a snap ring. Take out the snap ring and the main shaft and bearing can be removed from the extension housing.

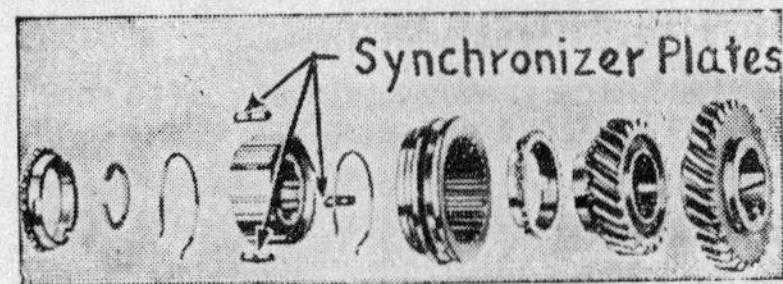

Synchronizer plates

A new oil seal should be used at the rear end of the extension housing.

The countershaft is driven out toward the rear of the transmission case.

Note: A key is used in the rear end of the counter shaft to prevent it from turning. Be careful to pick up this key as soon as the shaft has been driven far enough to reach it.

Main drive pinion and bearing assembly can be pulled out of the front of the case after the counter shaft gear cluster has been dropped to the bottom of the case or removed.

Reverse idler gear shaft is driven toward rear of case.

Note: A locking key is also used on the idler shaft and it should be removed as soon as it is clear of the case.

Reassembly of Standard Transmission

Cleanliness is essential when reassembling the counter shaft assembly and bearings.

In general the transmission is assembled in the reverse of assembly procedure.

The mainshaft and gear assembly are then pulled out of the rear of the case.

There is a single cap screw at the top of the case, just to the right of the cover assembly which covers the hole containing the shift interlock pin. Remove the cap screw and turn the case over, permitting the interlock pin to drop out. On assembly do not fail to place the interlock pin back into the transmission as this pin prevents the transmission from going into two gears at one time.

The counter shaft freewheel unit is held together by a snap ring.

On assembly, all parts should be thoroughly cleaned with a good solvent and blown off with compressed air.

In general the transmission is reassembled in the reverse of the disassembly procedure.

REAR AXLE ASSEMBLY

The Hotchkiss drive (open drive shaft) type of drive line is used on all Plymouth automobiles. The differential, pinion and axles are equipped with tapered roller bearings.

Pinion Oil Seal Removal

To remove the pinion oil seal the rear universal joint should be taken down and the universal joint pinion flange removed from the pinion shaft.

The pinion oil seal can then be taken out with a hook type inertia puller.

Axle Shaft Oil Seal

Two types of oil seals were used on the axle shafts on Plymouth cars. The early type was bolted to the outside face of the brake backing plate. To replace this type it was necessary to remove the rear wheel and take out the bolts which retain the oil seal to the rear axle housing flange.

On later models the oil seal was incorporated into the brake backing plate. To replace it, it was necessary to remove the brake backing plate from the car (necessary to detach the brake lines) and drive the oil seal out of the backing plate flange. To replace the inner oil seal on all models it is necessary to remove the axle shaft and take out the oil seal with an inertia type puller.

Axle Shaft Replacement

To replace the rear axle shaft on any Plymouth model take off the wheel and hub assembly, disconnect the brake lines and unbolt the backing plate from the rear axle housing flange. The axle shaft, together with its bearing, can then be pulled out of the housing.

Axle Shaft End Play

On all Plymouth models the end play in the axle shaft is controlled by shims back of the backing plate. End play in the axle shaft is permissible up to approximately .008 inch.

Replacement of Pinion and Ring Gear

To replace the pinion and ring gear remove both axle shafts, take off the rear universal joint and detach the rear axle carrier assembly and slide out from underneath the car on to a bench.

Remove the differential side bearing caps after first releasing the pressure from the adjusting cages. Take off the universal joint companion flange and drive the pinion shaft out through the back of the carrier.

Note: The rear bearing cone and rolls will come out with the pinion shaft.

Carefully preserve the shims which are found in front of the pinion bearing spacer. If the same pinion gear is to be replaced, the same number of shims should be used.

Shims or a spacer washer is used between the rear bearing cone and the pinion gear to govern the depth of the pinion gear in relation to the ring gear.

Adding shims at this point will cause the pinion gear to move toward the rear of the car and deeper into the ring gear; removing shims at this point will cause the pinion gear to shift forward and out of the ring gear.

When installing a new pinion and ring gear, the Plymouth Division recommends that the gears be tested with Prussian Blue or other indicating ma-

REPLACEMENT OF PINION AND RING GEAR—*continued*

terial to determine the contact of the pinion on the ring gear. Where the contact marks indicate that the pinion should be moved closer to the ring gear shims should be added between the pinion gear and the pinion rear bearing cone.

If the gear marks indicate that the pinion is set too close to the ring gear it will be necessary to remove shims from between the pinion gear and the pinion rear bearing cone.

Pinion Bearing Adjustment

After the proper number of shims have been installed to establish the correct position of the pinion gear relative to the ring gear it will be necessary to set the pinion gear bearings up so that there is a pre-load of from 5 to 10 inch pounds at the pinion shaft universal joint flange. This pre-load is equal to approximately .002 pre-load on the bearing. To establish this pre-load, deliberately use too many shims between the pinion front bearing cone and the bearing spacer and measure with an indicator the end play developed in the pinion shaft. Check this end play several times to make certain that the reading is exact.

After the end play has been established exactly, remove from in back of the pinion front bearing shims equivalent to .002 more than the end play found in the shaft and then replace the bearing, universal joint yoke and the pinion shaft nut. Tighten the pinion shaft nut securely and this will produce a .002 inch pre-load on the pinion bearings.

Recheck the torque required to turn the pinion shaft.

Set up the differential side bearings and ring gears so there is not less than .006 inch and not more than .010 inch backlash between the ring gear and pinion, measured at the rim of the ring gear.

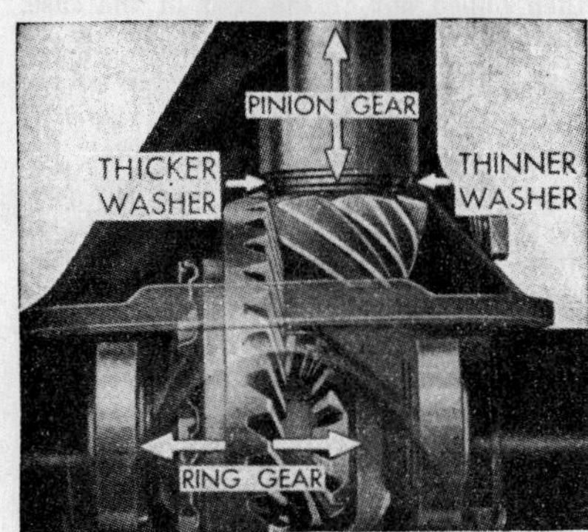

Pinion shim locations

This position of the ring gear should be established with zero play in the differential side bearings.

Differential side bearings should be pre-loaded approximately one notch of the adjusting cage.

Shock Absorbers

All models of Plymouth are equipped with airplane type direct acting shock absorbers.

Since disassembly service on shock absorbers is a highly specialized job, it is recommended that if difficulty is experienced with the shock absorber they be removed from the car and replaced with either a new or rebuilt unit.

Dash Instruments

1940 THRU 1942 MODELS

Any one instrument may be removed without removing any other instrument or obstacle. Each instrument is held in with two small screws which are accessible from underneath the dash.

In order to take out the speedometer it is necessary to disconnect the brace from the steering column underneath the dash. The speedometer is held in place by four hex nuts.

1946 THRU 1948 MODELS

If the car is equipped with a radio, it will be necessary to remove the radio to gain access to the right-hand instruments, usually the fuel and oil gages.

Take out the speedometer, first detach the underdash brace from the steering column to the cowling. The speedometer is held with four hex head screws.

1949 THRU 1953 MODELS

While the instruments on these models are located somewhat differently from those of the earlier models, the instructions given for the 1946 thru 1948 models will also apply to these instruments. If a radio or underdash heater is used, it will be necessary to take these out in order to gain access to the instruments which are in back of them.

Horn Relay

1940 AND 1941 MODELS

The horn relay is mounted with the horns on the radiator forward of the baffle under the hood.

1946 THRU 1948 MODELS

The horn relay is mounted under the hood on the left fender splash pan.

It is held with two self-tapping metal screws.

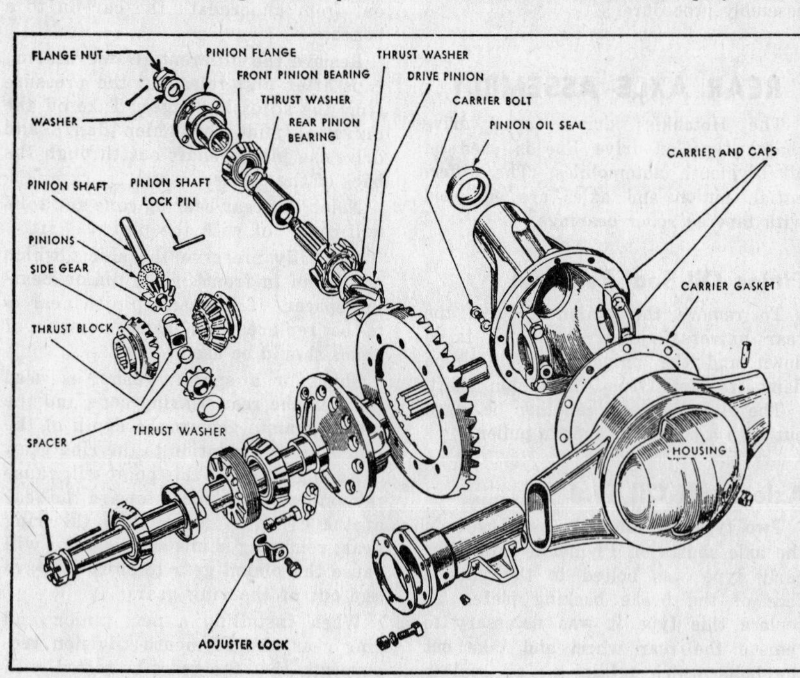

Rear axle assembly

1949 THRU 1953 MODELS

The horn relay is mounted on the left side of the fire wall under the voltage regulator. It is held with two self-tapping metal screws.

Windshield Wiper Motor

1940 THRU 1948 MODELS

The windshield wiper motor is mounted up under the center of the dash. If the car is equipped with a radio, it will be necessary to remove the radio in order to get at the wiper motor.

The motor is mounted with two hex head nuts.

1949 THRU 1953 MODELS

On these models the windshield wiper is mounted up under the center of the dash. If the car is equipped with a radio and heater, the radio must be removed and the heater controls removed to gain access to the motor.

Windshield Wiper Transmissions

On all Plymouth models the transmissions are of the bar type and can be removed on the left side without removing any obstacles, but if the right side is to be removed it is necessary to take out the glove box on all models.

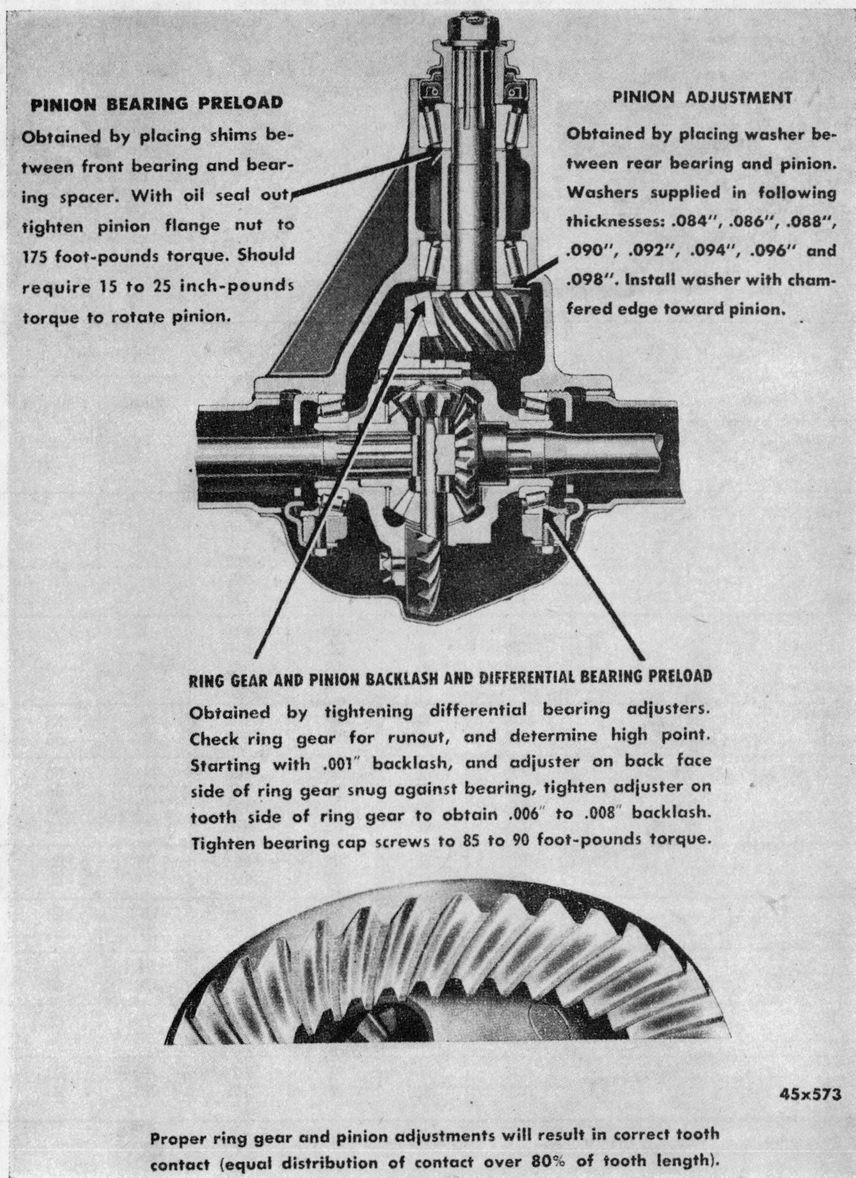

PINION BEARING PRELOAD
Obtained by placing shims between front bearing and bearing spacer. With oil seal out, tighten pinion flange nut to 175 foot-pounds torque. Should require 15 to 25 inch-pounds torque to rotate pinion.
PINION ADJUSTMENT
Obtained by placing washer between rear bearing and pinion. Washers supplied in following thicknesses: .084", .086", .088", .090", .092", .094", .096" and .098". Install washer with chamfered edge toward pinion.
RING GEAR AND PINION BACKLASH AND DIFFERENTIAL BEARING PRELOAD
Obtained by tightening differential bearing adjusters. Check ring gear for runout, and determine high point. Starting with .001" backlash, and adjuster on back face side of ring gear snug against bearing, tighten adjuster on tooth side of ring gear to obtain .006" to .008" backlash. Tighten bearing cap screws to 85 to 90 foot-pounds torque.
45x573
Proper ring gear and pinion adjustments will result in correct tooth contact (equal distribution of contact over 80% of tooth length).

Rear axle adjustments

PONTIAC SPECIFICATIONS

Starting Serial and Motor Numbers

Starting Serial Nnmbers

1940-1953—Prefix indicates place of manufacture, number of cylinders and model and year, i.e., P6HA-1001; made in Pontiac, Michigan; 6 cylinder; 1940; Special. All serial numbers begin 1001.

1940—HA, HB
1941—JA, JB, JC
1942—KA, KB
1946—LA, LB
1947—MA, MB
1948—PA, PB
1949—RH
1950—TS, TH
1951—US, UH
1952—WS, WH
1953—P-8X1001 and up; P-6X-1001 and up.

Location

1940—On frame front crossmember in back of radiator.

1941-1948—On left front side of dash.

1949—On top left-hand corner of block.

1950-1953—On left front door pillar and on lip on left front of block.

Starting Motor Numbers

1940-1941—Prefix indicates number of cylinders, i.e., 6-595801, 6 cylinder.

1942-1953—Motor numbers are the same as serial numbers.

1940 ....6-595801 and 8-194401
1941 ....6-761501 and 8-246501

Location

1940-1953—Same place as serial numbers.

General Specifications

Year	Model	Wheelbase (in.)	Tread (in.)		Overall Dimensions (in.)			Shipping Weight* (lb.)	Tire Size (in.)
			Front	Rear	Length†	Width	Height■		
1940	40-25	117	58	59	199	......	......	3170	6.00-16
	40-26	120	58	59	200	......	......	3210	6.00-16
	40-28	120	58	59	200	......	......	......	6.50-16
1941	41-25	119	58	62	202	......	......	......	6.00-16
	41-26	122	58	62	208	......	......	......	6.50-16
	41-24	122	58	62	212	......	......	......	6.50-16
	41-27	119	58	62	202	......	......	......	6.00-16
	41-28	122	58	62	208	......	......	......	6.50-16
	41-29	122	58	62	212	......	......	......	6.50-16
1942	42-25	119	58	62	205	......	......	3305	6.00-16
	42-26	122	58	62	210	......	......	3415	6.50-16
	42-27	119	58	62	205	......	......	3360	6.00-16
	42-28	122	58	62	210	......	......	3485	6.50-16
1946	46-25, 27	119	58	62	205	76	66	3330	6.00-16
	46-26, 28	122	58	62	210	77	65	3530	6.50-16
1947-48	25	119	58	62	205	76	66	3330	6.00-16
	26	122	58	62	210	77	65	3460	6.50-16
	27	119	58	62	205	76	66	3415	6.00-16
	28	122	58	62	210	77	65	3520	6.50-16
1949	25	120	58	59	203	74	63	3280	7.10-15
	27	120	58	59	203	74	63	3370	7.10-15
1950	25	120	58	59	203	76	63	3299	7.10-15
	27	120	58	59	203	76	63	3384	7.10-15
1951	25	120	58	59	202	76	65	3304	7.10-15
	27	120	58	59	202	76	65	3389	7.10-15
1952	52-25, 6 cyl.	120	58	59	202	76	63	......	7.10-15
	52-27, 8 cyl.	120	58	59	202	76	63	......	7.10-15
1953	53-25, 6 cyl.	122	58	59	202	76	63	......	7.10-15
	53-27, 8 cyl.	122	58	59	202	76	63	......	7.10-15

*—Cheapest 5 pass. 4 door sedan. ■—Road to roof, no load. †—Including bumper and bumper guards.

General Engine Specifications

Year	Model	Number of Cylinders Bore and Stroke	Piston Displacement, Cubic Inches	Compression Ratio (To–1)	Taxable (A.M.A.) Hp.	DEVELOPED HORSE POWER Bare Engine	With Accessories	Maximum Torque Ft. Lbs.
1940	25HA, 26HB, 6 Cyl.	6-3$\frac{7}{16}$ x 4.0	222.7	6.50	28.3	87 @ 3500	....	164 @ 1400
	28HA, 29HB, 8 Cyl.	8-3$\frac{1}{4}$ x 3$\frac{3}{4}$	248.9	6.50	33.8	100 @ 3700	....	175 @ 1600
1941	24, 25, 26, 6 Cyl.	6-3$\frac{9}{16}$ x 4.0	239.2	6.50	30.4	90 @ 3200	....	175 @ 1400
	27, 8 Cyl.	8-3$\frac{1}{4}$ x 3$\frac{3}{4}$	248.9	6.50	33.8	103 @ 3500	....	190 @ 2200
	28, 29, 8 Cyl.	8-3$\frac{1}{4}$ x 3$\frac{3}{4}$	248.9	6.50	33.8	103 @ 3500	....	190 @ 2200
1942	25, 26, 6 Cyl.	6-3$\frac{9}{16}$ x 4.0	239.2	6.50	30.4	90 @ 3200	....	175 @ 1400
	27, 28, 8 Cyl.	8-3$\frac{1}{4}$ x 3$\frac{3}{4}$	248.9	6.50	33.8	103 @ 3500	....	190 @ 2200
1946	25, 26, 6 Cyl.	6-3$\frac{9}{16}$ x 4.0	239.2	6.50	30.4	93.5 @ 3400	....	87.5 @ 3200
	27, 28, 8 Cyl.	8-3$\frac{1}{4}$ x 3$\frac{3}{4}$	248.9	6.50	33.8	107.5 @ 3700	101.5 @ 3600	192 @ 2100
1947	25, 26, 6 Cyl.	6-3$\frac{9}{16}$ x 4.0	239.2	6.50	30.4	93.5 @ 3400	87.5 @ 3200	186 @ 1400
	27, 28, 8 Cyl.	8-3$\frac{1}{4}$ x 3$\frac{3}{4}$	248.9	6.50	33.8	107 @ 3700	101 @ 3600	192 @ 2100
1948	25, 26, 6 Cyl.	6-3$\frac{9}{16}$ x 4.0	239.2	6.50	30.4	93.5 @ 3400	87.5 @ 3200	186 @ 1400
	27, 28, 8 Cyl.	8-3$\frac{1}{4}$ x 3$\frac{3}{4}$	248.9	6.50	33.8	107.5 @ 3700	101.5 @ 3600	192 @ 2100
1949	25, 6 Cyl.	6-3$\frac{9}{16}$ x 4.0	239.2	6.50	30.4	93 @ 3400	87.5 @ 3200	183 @ 1200
	27, 8 Cyl.	8-3$\frac{1}{4}$ x 3$\frac{3}{4}$	248.9	6.50	33.8	106 @ 3800	....	194 @ 2200
1950	25, 6 Cyl.	6-3$\frac{9}{16}$ x 4.0	239.2	6.50	30.4	90 @ 3400	....	178 @ 1200
	27, 8 Cyl.	8-3$\frac{3}{8}$ x 3$\frac{3}{4}$	268.2	6.50	36.4	108 @ 3600	....	208 @ 1800
1951	25, 6 Cyl.	6-3$\frac{9}{16}$ x 4.0	239.2	6.50	30.4	96 @ 3400	90 @ 3400	191 @ 1200
	27, 8 Cyl.	8-3$\frac{3}{8}$ x 3$\frac{3}{4}$	268.2	6.50	36.4	116 @ 3600	106 @ 3400	220 @ 2000
1952	25, 6 Cyl.	6-3$\frac{9}{16}$ x 4	239.2	6.80	30.46	100 @ 3400	....	189 @ 1400
	27, 8 Cyl.	8-3$\frac{3}{8}$ x 3$\frac{3}{4}$	268.4	6.80	36.45	118 @ 3600	....	222 @ 2200
1953	53-25	6-3$\frac{9}{16}$ x 4	239.2	7.7	30.46	115 @ 3800	....	193 @ 2000
	53-27	8-3$\frac{3}{8}$ x 3$\frac{3}{4}$	268.4	7.7	36.45	118 @ 3600	....	222 @ 2200

Dimensions of Valves

Year	Model	Overall Length Inlet	Overall Length Exhaust	Head Diameter Inlet	Head Diameter Exhaust	Seat Angle (deg.) Inlet	Seat Angle (deg.) Exhaust	Stem Diameter Inlet	Stem Diameter Exhaust	Key Type	O.D. of Seat Insert Inlet	O.D. of Seat Insert Exhaust
1940 to 49	25, 26	5.718	5.718	1.593	1.468	30	45	.312	.312	split lock	....	....
	27, 28, 29	5.531	5.531	1.468	1.343	30	45	.312	.312	split lock	....	....
1950	25	5.719	5.719	1.594	1.469	30	45	.312	.312	split lock	....	....
	27	5.531	5.531	1.469	1.344	30	45	.312	.312	split lock	....	....
1951	25	5.718	5.721	1.593	1.469	30	45	.311	.311	split lock	....	....
	27	5.531	5.531	1.468	1.343	30	45	.311	.311	split lock	....	....
1952-53	25, 6 cyl.	5.71875	5.71875	1.59375	1.46875	30	45	.3105	.3105	....	....	....
	27, 8 cyl.	5.53125	5.53125	1.46875	1.34375	30	45	.3105	.3105	....	....	....

Pistons and Piston Pins

Year	Model	PISTONS Diameter	Material	Type	No. of Rings	PISTON PINS Length	Diameter	How Held
1941 to 49	Series—All, 6 cyl.	3.5625	CN	....	3	3$\frac{1}{16}$	.9375	P
	Series—All, 8 cyl.	3.25	CN	....	3	2$\frac{7}{8}$	.9375	P
1950	25	3.5625	CNa	....	3	3$\frac{1}{16}$	.9844	P
	27	3.375	CNa	....	3	2$\frac{7}{8}$	.9844	P
1951	25	3.5625	CNi	....	3	3$\frac{1}{16}$	.9370	P
	27	3.375	CNi	....	3	2$\frac{7}{8}$	.9370	P
1952	25, 6 cyl.	3.5625	CI	CNa	3	3.0625	.9375	P
1952-53	27, 8 cyl.	3.375	CI	CNa	3	2.875	.9375	P
1953	53-25, 6 cyl.	3.5625	Alum. Alloy	CNa	3	3.050	.9372	P

CN—Chrome nickel. CNA—Chrome nickel alloy. CI—Cast iron.

Engine Overhaul Specifications

Year	Model	PISTONS				RING GAP CLEARANCES (Maximum)				PISTON PIN		ROD BEARINGS		
			Piston Skirt Clearances (Maximum)											
		Removed From	Top	Bottom	Limit	Top Ring	Second Ring	Third Ring	Oil Ring	Type	Fit	Oil Clearance	Wear Limit	Side Play
1940	25HA, 6 Cyl.	A	.002	.002	.004	.014	.014	......	.017	LP	Press	.0001-.0021	.004	.007-.012
	26HB, 6 Cyl.	A	.002	.002	.004	.014	.014	......	.017	LP	Press	.0001-.0021	.004	.007-.012
	28HA, 8 Cyl.	A	.002	.002	.004	.014	.014	......	.017	LP	Press	.0001-.0021	.004	.007-.012
	29HB, 8 Cyl.	A	.002	.002	.004	.014	.014	......	.017	LP	Press	.0001-.0021	.004	.007-.012
1941	24, 26, 6 Cyl.	A	.002	.002	.004	.014	.014	......	.017	LP	Press	.0001-.0021	.004	.007-.012
	25, 6 Cyl.	A	.002	.002	.004	.014	.014	......	.017	LP	Press	.0001-.0021	.004	.007-.012
	27, 8 Cyl.	A	.002	.002	.004	.014	.014	......	.017	LP	Press	.0001-.0021	.004	.007-.012
	28, 29, 8 Cyl.	A	.002	.002	.004	.014	.014	......	.017	LP	Press	.0001-.0021	.004	.007-.012
1942	25, 6 Cyl.	A	.004	.004	.004	.012	.012	......	.012	LP	Press	.0011-.0021	.004	.007-.012
	26, 6 Cyl.	A	.004	.004	.004	.012	.012	......	.012	LP	Press	.0011-.0021	.004	.007-.012
	27, 28, 8 Cyl.	A	.005	.005	.004	.014	.014	......	.017	LP	Press	.0001-.0021	.004	.007-.012
1946	25, 26, 6 Cyl.	A	.002	.002	.004	.013	.013	......	.017	LP	Press	.0001-.0021	.004	.007-.030
	27, 28, 8 Cyl.	A	.002	.002	.004	.015	.015	......	.013	LP	Press	.0001-.0021	.004	.007-.012
1947	25, 26, 6 Cyl.	A	.002	.002	.004	.013	.013	......	.017	LP	Press	.0001-.0021	.004	.007-.012
	27, 28, 8 Cyl.	A	.002	.002	.004	.015	.015	......	.013	LP	Press	.0001-.0021	.004	.007-.012
1948	25, 26, 6 Cyl.	A	.002	.002	.004	.013	.013	......	.013	LP	Press	.0001-.0021	.004	.007-.012
	27, 28, 8 Cyl.	A	.002	.002	.004	.015	.015	......	.017	LP	Press	.0001-.0021	.004	.007-.012
1949	25, 6 Cyl.	A	.002	.002	.004	.012	.012	......	.012	LP	Press	.0001-.0021	.004	.007-.012
	27, 8 Cyl.	A	.002	.002	.004	.015	.015	......	.015	LP	Press	.0001-.0021	.004	.007-.012
1950	25, 6 Cyl.	A	.002	.002	.004	.012	.012	......	.012	LP	Press	.0001-.0021	.004	.007-.012
	27, 8 Cyl.	A	.002	.002	.004	.015	.015	......	.015	LP	Press	.0001-.0021	.004	.007-.012
1951	25, 6 Cyl.	A	.002	.002	.004	......	......	......	......	LP	Press	.0001-.0021	.004	.007-.012
	27, 8 Cyl.	A	.002	.002	.004	......	......	......	......	LP	Press	.0001-.0021	.004	.007-.012
1952	25, 6 Cyl.	A	.0015	.0015	.004	.0095	.0095	......	.0095	LP	.001	.0001-.0021	.004	.007-.012
	27, 8 Cyl.	A	.0015	.0015	.004	.0115	.0115	......	.0115	LP	.001	.0001-.0021	.004	.007-.012
1953	53, 25, 6 Cyl.	A	.001	.001	.004	.012	.012	......	.016	MF	.0006	.0021	.004	.007-.012
	53, 27, 8 Cyl.	A	.0015	.0015	.004	.0115	.0115	......	.0115	MF	.0006	.0021	.004	.007-.012

A—Above. LP—Locked in piston. SP—Sprocket. †—Marks on cam and crank sprockets, align with shaft centers. B—Before top center

Crankshaft Bearing Journal Sizes

Year	Model	Connecting Rod Journals		Main Bearing Journals				
		Diameter	Length	No. 1 Diameter	No. 2 Diameter	No. 3 Diameter	No. 4 Diameter	No. 5 Diameter
1940 to 49	24, 25, 26	2.1237-2.1247	1.28125	2.4982-2.4992	2.5294-2.5304	2.5919-2.5929	2.6232-2.6242	....
	27, 28, 29	1.9987-1.9997	1.0625	2.3732-2.3742	2.4044-2.4054	2.4357-2.4367	2.4669-2.4679	2.4982-2.4992
1950	25	2.1237-2.1247	1.28125	2.4982-2.4992	2.5294-2.5304	2.5919-2.5929	2.6232-2.6242	....
	27	1.9987-1.9997	1.0625	2.3732-2.3742	2.4044-2.4054	2.4357-2.4367	2.4669-2.4679	2.6232-2.6242
1951	25	2.1237-2.1247	1.500	2.4982-2.4992	2.5294-2.5304	2.5919-2.5929	2.6232-2.6242	....
	27	1.9987-1.9997	1.0625	2.3732-2.3742	2.4044-2.4054	2.4357-2.4367	2.4669-2.4679	2.6232-2.6242
1952	25, 6 cyl.	2.124	1.500	2.4982-2.4992	2.5294-2.5304	2.5919-2.5929	2.6232-2.6242	....
	27, 8 cyl.	1.9987-1.9997	1.125	2.3732-2.3742	2.4044-2.4054	2.4357-2.4367	2.4669-2.4679	2.6232-2.6242
1953	53-25, 6 cyl.	2.125	....	2.5-1.250	2.53125-1.1875	2.59375-1.125	2.625-1.5625	....
	53-27, 8 cyl.	2.0	....	2.375-1.250	2.40625-1.1875	2.4375-1.4375	2.46875-1.125	2.625-1.5625

and Wear Limit Table

CRANKSHAFT: Main Bearing Oil Clearance	CRANKSHAFT: Shaft End Play	VALVES: Spring Tension (Maximum): Inlet	VALVES: Spring Tension (Maximum): Exhaust	VALVES: Spring Tension (Maximum): Low Limit	VALVES: Guide Clearance	VALVES: Seat Angle: Inlet	VALVES: Seat Angle: Exhaust	Valve Timing, Inlet Valve Opens (Deg.)	Camshaft Drive	Gear Marks	OPERATING OIL PRESSURE: Pounds At M.P.H.	OPERATING OIL PRESSURE: Low Limit§	Model	Year
.0003-.0023	.003-.008	105@1 19/32	105@1 19/32	95	.0006	30°	45°	5B	Chain	Sp†	40@40	25	25HA, 6 Cyl.	1940
.0003-.0023	.003-.008	105@1 19/32	105@1 19/32	95	.0006	30°	45°	5B	Chain	Sp†	40@40	25	26HB, 6 Cyl.	
.0003-.0023	.003-.008	105@1 19/32	105@1 19/32	95	.0006	30°	45°	5B	Chain	Sp†	40@40	25	28HA, 8 Cyl.	
.0003-.0023	.003-.008	105@1 19/32	105@1 19/32	95	.0006	30°	45°	5B	Chain	Sp†	40@40	25	29HB, 8 Cyl.	
.0003-.0023	.003-.008	105@1 19/32	105@1 19/32	95	.0001-.0006	30°	45°	5B	Chain	Sp†	40@40	25	24, 26, 6 Cyl.	1941
.0003-.0023	.003-.008	105@1 19/32	105@1 19/32	95	.0001-.0006	30°	45°	5B	Chain	Sp†	40@40	25	25, 6 Cyl.	
.0003-.0023	.003-.008	105@1 19/32	105@1 19/32	95	.0001-.0006	30°	45°	5B	Chain	Sp†	40@40	25	27, 8 Cyl.	
.0003-.0023	.003-.008	105@1 19/32	105@1 19/32	95	.0001-.0006	30°	45°	5B	Chain	Sp†	40@40	25	28, 29, 8 Cyl.	
.0003-.0023	.003-.008	105@1 19/32	105@1 19/32	95	.0006	30°	45°	5B	Chain	Sp†	40@40	25	25, 6 Cyl.	1942
.0003-.0023	.003-.008	105@1 19/32	105@1 19/32	95	.0006	30°	45°	5B	Chain	Sp†	40@40	25	26, 6 Cyl.	
.0003-.0023	.003-.008	105@1 19/32	105@1 19/32	95	.0006	30°	45°	5B	Chain	Sp†	40@40	25	27, 28, 8 Cyl.	
.0003-.0023	.003-.008	101@1 19/32	101@1 19/32	90	.0006	30°	45°	5B	Chain	Sp†	40@40	25	25, 26, 6 Cyl.	1946
.0003-.0023	.003-.008	101@1 19/32	101@1 19/32	90	.0006	30°	45°	5B	Chain	Sp†	40@40	25	27, 28, 8 Cyl.	
.0003-.0023	.003-.008	101@1 19/32	101@1 19/32	90	.0006	30°	45°	5B	Chain	Sp†	40@40	25	26, 25, 6 Cyl.	1947
.0003-.0023	.003-.008	101@1 19/32	101@1 19/32	90	.0006	30°	45°	5B	Chain	Sp†	40@40	25	27, 28, 8 Cyl.	
.0003-.0023	.003-.007	101@1 19/32	101@1 19/32	90	.0006	30°	45°	5B	Chain	Sp†	40@40	25	25, 26, 6 Cyl.	1948
.0003-.0023	.003-.007	101@1 19/32	101@1 19/32	90	.0006	30°	45°	5B	Chain	Sp†	40@40	25	27, 28, 8 Cyl.	
.0003-.0023	.003-.007	105@1 19/32	105@1 19/32	95	.0006	30°	45°	5B	Chain	Sp†	40@40	25	25, 6 Cyl.	1949
.0003-.0023	.003-.008	105@1 19/32	105@1 19/32	95	.0006	30°	45°	5B	Chain	Sp†	40@40	25	27, 8 Cyl.	
.0003-.0023	.003-.008	105@1 19/32	105@1 19/32	95	.0006	30°	45°	5B	Chain	Sp†	40@40	25	25, 6 Cyl.	1950
.0003-.0023	.003-.008	105@1 19/32	105@1 19/32	95	.0006	30°	45°	5B	Chain	Sp†	40@40	25	27, 8 Cyl.	
.0013	.0055	101@1 19/32	101@1 19/32	90	.0006	30°	45°	5B	Chain	Sp†	40@40	25	25, 6 Cyl.	1951
.0013	.0055	105@1 13/32	105@1 13/32	95	.0006	30°	45°	5B	Chain	Sp†	40@40	25	27, 8 Cyl.	
.0003-.0023	.003-.008	105@1 19/32	105@1 19/32	......	.004	30°	45°	5B	Chain	......	40@40	35	25, 6 Cyl.	1952
.0003-.0023	.003-.008	110@1 13/32	110@1 13/32	......	.004	30°	45°	5B	Chain	......	40@40	35	27, 8 Cyl.	
.0003-.0023	.003-.008	105@1 19/32	105@1 19/32	......	.004	30°	45°	12½B	Chain	......	40@40	35	53, 25	1953
.0003-.0023	.003-.008	110@1 13/32	110@1 13/32	......	.004	30°	45°	5B	Chain	......	40@...	35	53, 27	

§—Car may be operated safely at lower oil pressures but low pressure indicates malfunction which should be corrected.

Engine Tune-Up Specifications

Year	Model	SPARK PLUGS: Type	SPARK PLUGS: Gap	DISTRIBUTOR: Point Gap	Cam Dwell, (Deg.)	Ignition Timing, (Deg.)	Ignition Timing Mark and Location	Compression Pressure at R.P.M.	OPERATING TAPPET CLEARANCE: Inlet	OPERATING TAPPET CLEARANCE: Exhaust.	Carburetor Fuel Float Height	Minimum Engine Idle Speed at R.P.M.
1940	25HA, 26HB, 6 Cyl.	AC45	.025	.020	37	4B	Flywheel	156@1000	.012	.012	7/16″ float	375
	28HA, 8 Cyl.	AC45	.025	.015	31	4B	Flywheel	152@1000	.012	.012	7/16″ float	375
	29HB, 8 Cyl.	AC45	.025	.015	31	00B	Flywheel	152@1000	.012	.012	7/16″ float	375
1941	24, 25, 26, 6 Cyl.	AC45	.025	.020	37	4B	Flywheel	155@1000	.012	.012	½″	450
	27, 8 Cyl.	AC45	.025	.015	31	4B	Flywheel	155@1000	.012	.012	5/16″	450
	28, 29, 8 Cyl.	AC46	.025	.015	31	4B	Flywheel	155@1000	.012	.012	5/16″	450
1942	25, 26, 6 Cyl.	AC45	.025	.020	37	4B	Flywheel	160@1000	.012	.012	½″	450
	27, 28, 8 Cyl.	AC45	.025	.015	31	4B	Flywheel	158@1000	.012	.012	5/16″	450
1946	25, 26, 6 Cyl.	AC45	.025	.020	37	4B	Flywheel	160@1000	.012	.012	½″	450*
	27, 28, 8 Cyl.	AC45	.025	.015	31	4B	Flywheel	160@1000	.012	.012	5/16″	450*
1947	25, 26, 6 Cyl.	AC45	.025	.020	37	4B	Flywheel	160@1000	.012	.012	½″	450*
	27, 28, 8 Cyl.	AC45	.025	.015	31	4B	Flywheel	158@1000	.012	.012	5/16″	450*
1948	25, 26, 6 Cyl.	AC45	.023-.028	.020	37	4B	Flywheel	160@1000	.012	.012	½″	450*
	27, 28, 8 Cyl.	AC45	.025	.015	31	4B	Flywheel	158@1000	.012	.012	3/16″	450*

PONTIAC SPECIFICATIONS

Engine Tune-Up Specifications—*continued*

Year	Model	SPARK PLUGS		DISTRIBUTOR		Ignition Timing, (Deg.)	Ignition Timing Mark and Location	Com-pression Pressure at R.P.M.	OPERATING TAPPET CLEARANCE		Carburetor Fuel Float Height	Minimum Engine Idle Speed at R.P.M.
		Type	Gap	Point Gap	Cam Dwell, (Deg.)				Inlet	Exhaust		
1949	25, 6 Cyl.	AC45	.023-.028	.022	31-37	2-6B	Dmpr.	160@1000	.012	.012	½″	450*
	27, 8 Cyl.	AC45	.025	.016	21-30	2-6B	Dmpr.	158@1000	.012	.012	3/16″	450*
1950	25, 6 Cyl.	AC45	.023-.028	.022	31-37	6B	Dmpr.	160@1000	.012	.012	½″	450*
	27, 8 Cyl.	AC45	.023-.028	.016	21-30	2-6B	Dmpr.	156@1000	.012	.012	....	450*
1951	25, 6 Cyl.	AC45	.023-.028	.022	31-37	6B	Dmpr.	....	.012	.012	....	450*
	27, 8 Cyl.	AC45	.023-.028	.016	21-30	6B	Dmpr.	....	.012	.012	....	450*
1952	25, 6 Cyl.	AC-44-5	.028	.022	37	6B	Dmpr.	....	.011H	.013H	....	450-475
	28, 8 Cyl.	AC-44-5	.028	.016	30	6B	Dmpr.	....	.011H	.013H	3/16″	450-475
1953	53-25, 6 Cyl.	AC-44-5	.028	.022	37	TC	Dmpr.	....	.011H	.013H	....	520-545
	53-27, 8 Cyl.	AC-44-5	.028	.016	30	6B	Dmpr.	....	.011H	.013H	....	450-475

*—365 r.p.m. Hydramatic Trans.

Piston Ring Dimensions

Year	Model	Cylinder Bore	TOP RING			SECOND RING			THIRD RING			OIL RING		
			Width	Gap	Depth	Width	Gap	Depth	Width	Gap	Depth	Width	Gap	Depth
1940	25, 26	3 7/16	3/32	.011	.155	3/32	.011	.155	3/16	.012	.150	....	....	....
	28, 29	3¼	3/32	.011	.150	3/32	.011	.150	3/16	.012	.150	....	....	....
1941-49	25, 26, 24	3 9/16	3/32	.012	.175	3/32	.012	.175	3/16	.012	.155	....	....	....
	27, 28, 29	3¼	3/32	.012	.150	3/32	.012	.150	3/16	.012	.150	....	....	....
1950-51	25	3 9/16	3/32	.009	.175	3/32	.009	.175	3/16	.009	.158	....	....	....
	27	3⅜	3/32	.010	.153	3/32	.010	.153	3/16	.010	.153	....	....	....
1952	25, 6 Cyl.	3 9/16	3/32	.0095	.1815	3/32	.0095	.1815	3/16	.0095	.1945	....	....	....
	27, 8 Cyl.	3⅜	3/32	.0115	.1615	3/32	.0115	.1615	3/16	.0115	.1923	....	....	....
1953	53-25, 6 Cyl.	3 9/16	.07775	.012	.173	.07775	.012	.173	.185	.016	.1205	....	....	....
	53-27, 8 Cyl.	3⅜	.09325	.0015	.148	.09325	.0115	.148	.18625	.0115	.148	....	....	....

Brake Data

Year	Model	Make	Lining Type	R=Riveted B=Bonded	Drum Diameter	Lining			Clearance	
						Length	Width	Thickness	Toe	Heel
1940	25, 26, 28, 29	Ben	M	R	11	21 5/16	1¾	3/16	....	....
1941-42	24, 25, 26, 27, 28, 29	Ben	M	R	11	21 5/16	1¾	3/16	.015	.015
1946-47	25, 26, 27, 28	Ben	M	R	11	21 5/16	2-*1¾	3/16	.015	.015
1948	25, 26, 27, 28	Ben	M	R	11	28 5/16	2-*1¾	3/16	....	....
1949 to 51	25, 27	Ben	M	R	11	21 5/16	2¼-*1¾	3/16	....	....
1952	25, 6 Cyl., 27, 8 Cyl.	....	M	R	11	21 25/64	2¼-*1¾	7/32	.015	.015
1953	53-25, 6 Cyl., 53-27, 8 Cyl.	....	M	R	11	21 25/64	2¼-*1¾	7/32	.015	.015

*—Rear. Ben—Bendix. M—Moulded.

Tension Wrench Specifications

Year	Model	Cylinder Head		Spark Plug		Connecting Rod Bolts or Nuts		Main Bearing Bolt		Flywheel Bolts		Vibration Damper Bolts	
		Lbs.-Ft.	Thread	Lbs.-Ft.	Thread	Lbs.-Ft.	Thread	Lbs.-Ft.	Thread	Lbs.-Ft.	Thread	Lbs.-Ft.	Thread
1941-42	Series—All..........	50-60	....	24-30	14 mm	35-45	....	75-85	....	90-100	....	85-95	....
1946-47	Series—All..........	50-60	....	25-30	14 mm	35-45	....	75-85	....	90-100	....	85-95	....
1948	Series—All..........	50-60	....	25-30	14 mm	35-45	....	75-85	....	90-100	....	85-95	....
1949 to 53	Series—All..........	50-60	....	25-30	14 mm	35-45	....	85-95	....	90-105	....	85-95	....

Cooling System

CAR AND YEAR	MODEL	Capacity Qts.	Quarts of Methanol Base Anti-Freeze (For Protection to Temperature Shown Below)							Quarts of Ethylene Glycol (For Protection to Temperature Shown Below)							Quarts of Denatured Alcohol—188 Proof (For Protection to Temperature Shown Below)						
			3	4	5	6	7	8	9	3	4	5	6	7	8	9	3	4	5	6	7	8	9
1938...............	6..................	16	13	3	−8	−21	−36	−53	....	17	10	2	−8	−19	−34	−52	....	10	0	−10	....	−20	−30
1938-39-40..........	8..................	19	17	9	2	−8	−21	−32	−46	20	15	9	2	−7	−16	−28	20	10	....	0	−10	....	−20
1939-40............	6..................	17	15	6	−4	−16	−29	−45	....	18	12	5	−4	−14	−27	−42	....	10	0	....	−10	−20	−30
1941-53............	6..................	18	17	8	−1	−12	−25	−38	−53	19	14	7	0	−10	−21	−34	20	10	....	0	−10	....	−20
1941-53............	8..................	19½	18	11	4	−5	−16	−27	−39	....	16	10	4	−3	−12	−22	20	....	10	....	0	−10	−20

Distributors

Year	Model	Distributor Model Number	Cam Angle (deg.)	Direction of Rotation C=Clockwise CC=Counter Clockwise at Cam End	Breaker Arm Spring Tension	Breaker Point Gap (inches)	Engine R.P.M. when Cent. Advance Starts	Max. Cent. Advance in Engine Deg. at Stated Engine R.P.M.	Vacuum in (inches) of Mercury at which Vacuum Unit Starts	Max. Advance in Engine Deg. at Stated Vacuum	Vacuum Unit Number
1940 to 48	6 cyl................. 8 cyl.................	647-D 1110804	35 31	CC CC	17-21 19-23	.018-.024 .0125-.0175	800 800	28.5@4000 28@4200	7 to 9 7 to 9	15@13 to 16 20@16 to 21	681M 1116021
1949	6 cyl................. 8 cyl.................	1110219 1110816	35 26	CC CC	17-21 19-23	.022 21-30	600 500	28@4200 27@4200	7 to 9 7 to 9	13 to 16 17.5 to 19.5	 1116050
1950-51	25, 6 cyl............. 27, 8 cyl.............	1110222 1110818	35 26	CC CC	17-21 19-23	.022 .015	600 500	28@4100 27@4200	7 to 9 7 to 9	14.5 to 16.5 17.5 to 19.5	 1116050
1952	25, 6 cyl............. 27, 8 cyl.............	1110222 1110831	37 30	CC CC	17-20 19-23	.022 .016	600 500	26@4100 22@3760	7-9 7-9	17@16 22@20	....
1953	53, 25, 6 cyl......... 53, 27, 8 cyl.........	1110232 1110831	37 30	C C	17-20 19-23	.022 .016	800 500	23@3600 22@3760	4-6 7-9	24@20 22@20	....

Generators

Year	Model	Generator Number	Field Current at 6 Volts (amps.)	Maximum Safe Output			Brush Spring Tension (oz.)	Voltage Regulator Number
				Volts	Amperes	R.P.M.		
1940 to 42	All 6 & 8 cyl..............................	1102665	1.75-1.9	8.0	30	1750	25	1118201
1946-47	25, 26, 27, 28.............................	1102665	1.75-1.9	8.0	30	1750	25	1118242

Generators—*continued*

Year	Model	Generator Number	Field Current at 6 Volts (amps.)	Maximum Safe Output Volts	Maximum Safe Output Amperes	Maximum Safe Output R.P.M.	Brush Spring Tension (oz.)	Voltage Regulator Number
1948	25, 27	1102701	1.75–1.9	8.0	30	1750	25	1118242
1949–50	25, 27	1102711	1.75–1.9	8.0	30	1750	25	1118301
1951	25, 27	1102750	....	....	....	....	....	1118300
1952	25, 6 cyl., 27, 8 cyl.	1102769	....	....	....	....	....	1118725
1953	6 cyl., 8 cyl.	1102794	....	6.8	45	2160	....	1118725

Voltage Regulators

Year	Model	Regulator Number	Grounded P=Positive N=Negative	Voltage Control Air Gap Points Closed	Voltage Control Voltage Setting Hot	Current Control Air Gap Points Closed	Current Control Current Set Hot	Cut-Out Relay Point Gap	Cut-Out Relay Air Gap	Cut-Out Relay Closing Volt
1940–41	6 & 8 cyl.	1118201	N	.070	7.0	.082	32–40	.020	.020	5.9–6.8
1942	6 & 8 cyl.	1118201 1118242	N N	.070 .070	7.0 7.0	.082 .082	32–40 32–40	.020 .020	.020 .020	5.9–6.8 5.9–6.8
1946 to 48	6 & 8 cyl.	1118242 1118229	N N	.070 .070	7.0 7.0	.082 .082	32–40 33–37	.020 .020	.020 .020	5.9–6.8 5.9–6.8
1949–50	25, 27	1118352	N	.075	7.0	.075	33–37	.020	.020	5.9–6.8
1951	25, 27	1118301 1118300 1118352	N N N	.075 .075 .075	7.0 7.0 7.0	.075 .075 .075	32–40 40–46 33–37	.020 .020 .020	.020 .020 .020	5.9–6.8 5.9–6.8 5.9–6.8
1952	25, 6 cyl., 27, 8 cyl.	1118725	....	....	7–4	....	45	....	....	5.9–6.8
1953	53-25, 6 cyl., 53-27, 8 cyl.	1118725	....	....	7.4	....	45	....	....	5.9–6.8

Starters

Year	Model	Unit Model Number	Spring Tension (oz.)	STARTER Lock Test Volts	STARTER Lock Test Amperes	STARTER Lock Test Torque, (lbs. ft.)	STARTER No Load Volts	STARTER No Load Amperes	STARTER No Load R.P.M.	Direction of Rotation Viewed from Drive End C=Clockwise CC=Counter-clockwise
1940	All—6 cyl. All—8 cyl.	1107022 1107914	24–28 24–28	3.37 3.0	525 600	12 15	5.0 5.0	65 60	5000 6000	C C
1941 to 47	All—6 cyl. All—8 cyl.	1107032 1107921	24–28 24–28	3.37 3.0	525 600	12 15	5.0 5.0	65 60	5000 6000	C C
1948	25—6 cyl. 27—8 cyl.	1107070 1107947	24–28 24–28	3.4 3.0	525 600	12 15	5.7 5.0	65 60	5000 6000	C C
1949 to 51	25—6 cyl. 27—8 cyl.	1107079 1107957	24–28 24–28	3.4 3.0	525 600	12 14	5.7 5.7	80 80	5000 5500	C C
1952	25, 6 cyl. 27, 8 cyl.	1107079 1107957	24–28 24–28	3.37 3.0	525 600	12.0 15	5.67 5.0	65 60	5000 6000	C C
1953	53-25, 6 cyl. 53-27, 8 cyl.	1107107 1107957	24–28 24–28	3.25 3	550 600	11 15	5.60 5.0	80 60	5500 6000	C C

Front Wheel Alignment

Year	Model	Caster (deg.)	Camber (deg.)	King Pin Inclination (deg.)	Toe-In (inches)	Turning Radius Inner	Turning Radius Outer
1940	25	1N to ½P	⅛P to ⅝P	4¾ to 5	0 to 1/16	37⅓	20
	26	1N to ½P	⅛P to ⅝P	4¾ to 5	0 to 1/16	38⅓	20
	28	1N to ½P	⅛P to ⅝P	4¾ to 5	0 to 1/16	37 5/16	20
	29	1N to ½P	⅛P to ⅝P	4¾ to 5	0 to 1/16	38¾	20
1941	25, 27	1N to ½P	1N to ¼P	4⅝	0 to 1/16	19.2	20
	26, 24, 28, 29	1N to ½P	1N to ¼P	4⅝	0 to 1/16	20.3	20
1942	25, 26, 27, 28	1N to ½P	¼N to ¼P	4⅝	0 to 1/16	23½	20
1946–47	25, 26, 27, 28	1N to ½P	¼N to ¼P	4⅜ to 4⅞	0 to 1/16	23½	20
1948	25, 26, 27, 28	¾N to 1N	0	5	0 to 1/16	23½	20
1949	25, 27	¾N to 1N	0	5	0 to 1/16	23½	20
1950	25	¾N to 1N	0	5	0 to 1/16	23½	20
	27	¾N to 1N	0	5½	0 to 1/16	23½	20
1951–52	25, 27	½N to 1N	¼N to ¼P	4¾ to 5¼	0 to 1/16	23½	20
1953	25, 27	½N to ½P	0 to 1P	5 to 5½	0 to 1/16	18½	20

Fan, Generator Belts and Radiator Hose

Year	Model	Fan Belt			Generator Belt			Upper Hose			Lower Hose		
		Angle of "V" (deg.)	Length O.C.	Width Max.	Angle of "V" (deg.)	Length O.C.	Width Max.	Type	Inside Diam.	Length	Type	Inside Diam.	Length
1940	6 & 8 cyl.	34	48¼	25/32	......	......	......	curved	1¾	......	curved	1½	......
1941 to 48	Series—All	34	48¼	25/32	......	......	......	curved	1¾	......	curved	1½	......
1949 to 51	Series—All	32	41	23/32	......	......	......	curved	1¾	......	curved	1¾	......
1952	25, 6 cyl.	32	40	25/32	......	......	......	curved	1¾	13 9/16	curved	1¾	17¾
	27, 8 cyl.	32	40	25/32	......	......	......	curved	1¾	8 15/16	curved	1¾	15⅛
1953	53-25, 6 cyl.	32	40	25/32	......	......	......	curved	1¾	13 9/16	curved	1¾	17¾
	53-27, 8 cyl.	32	40	25/32	......	......	......	curved	1¾	8 15/16	curved	1¾	15⅛

King Pin Specification Chart

Year	Model	KING BOLT		UPPER BUSHING					LOWER BUSHING			
					King Bolt Bushing				King Bolt Bushing			
		Diameter	Length	Bolt Number	Inside Diameter	Outside Diameter	Length	Bushing Number	Inside Diameter	Outside Diameter	Length	Bushing Number
1940 to 51	All, 6 & 8 cyl.	.862	5½	503577	.862	1.054	1 15/64	503575	.862	1.054	1 15/64	503575
1952–53	......	......	......	......	......	......	......	......	......	......	......	......

PONTIAC 1940 thru 1953

FRONT SUSPENSION

The front suspension on Pontiac cars is known as the short and long arm type, commonly called the S.L.A. type front suspension.

From 1940 to 1948 all Pontiac front suspensions were made essentially the same way. The upper control arm and shock absorber were incorporated into one unit. A Delco type shock absorber was used and caster and camber were adjusted with an eccentric pin at the outer end of the shock absorber.

Starting 1949—the shock absorber is mounted inside the coil spring and a plain upper control arm is used.

Caster and camber are adjusted by an eccentric bushing in place of the former eccentric pin.

Except for the shock absorber, however, essential repair work on the front suspension is the same. All models from 1940 through 1953 employ the reverse Elliott type steering knuckle support.

STEERING GEOMETRY

Caster, Camber and Toe-In

Before any attempt is made to adjust caster or camber, first make an inspection of the entire front suspension, and note down on paper the caster and camber angles, together with the toe-in found on the car before any attempt is made to correct it.

Since both caster and camber are controlled by an eccentric pin (1940 through 1948 models) and by eccentric bushing (1949 through 1951 models), the best possible setting using the eccentric may of necessity be a compromise between the exact specification and the specifications which are possible using an eccentric.

The procedure to adjust caster and camber is as follows:

First inspect all of the pins and bushings in the front suspension for wear or looseness. If any are found loose or badly worn, it will be impossible to secure the correct adjustment unless the worn or damaged parts are replaced.

To make the adjustment, loosen the clamp bolt in the upper end of the knuckle support in order to free the eccentric pin (or eccentric bushing in 1949 through 1951 models).

Turn the eccentric pin with an Allen wrench through the grease fitting hole (or turn the eccentric bushing with a special offset hand wrench) in a clockwise direction to increase caster, counterclockwise to decrease caster.

Caster and camber adjustment—1949 thru 1951 models

Notice that it may be necessary to turn the caster a little farther than the specifications in order to bring the eccentric to a position which will give suitable camber.

Where an exact adjustment is required, turn the eccentric until the caster reading is exactly according to specifications and use a cold bending device on the knuckle support to secure the proper camber reading.

After the required caster and camber adjustments have been made, tighten the clamp screw in the upper end of the knuckle support and (replace the grease fitting in the earlier models) then recheck to make certain that the desired readings are maintained.

Toe-In

Toe-in is adjusted at the sleeves at the end of each tie rod.

Turning the sleeves in the direction opposite to forward wheel rotation will increase toe-in, turning the sleeves in the same direction a forward wheel rotation will decrease toe-in. When correcting for errors in the front suspension readings, toe-in should always be corrected last.

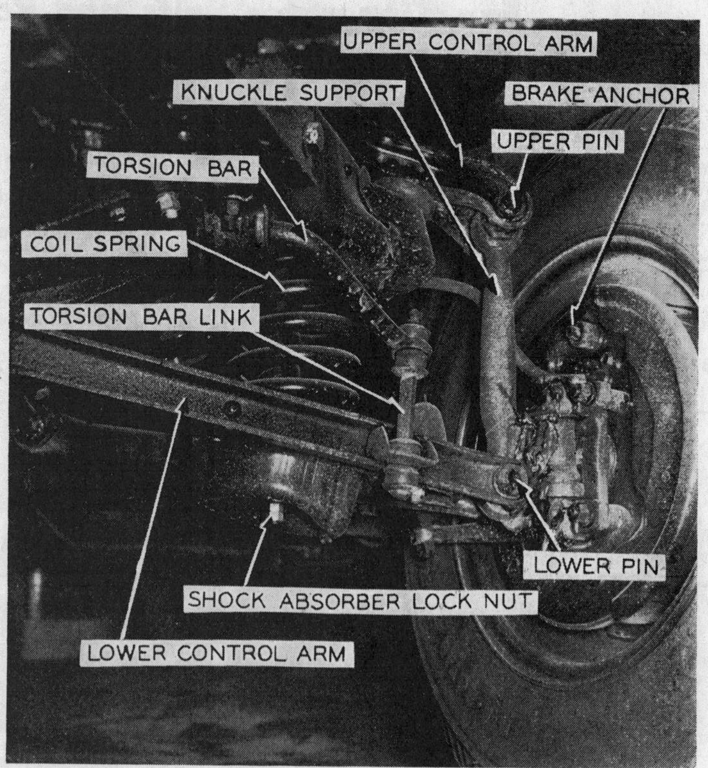

Front suspension 1953 models

Replacement of Front Coil Springs and Other Suspension Parts

Before replacing a front coil spring, examine all of the pins and bushings in the front suspension arms to determine if one or more of the pins require replacement.

If one of the outer pins or bushings require replacement, the procedure is to place a jack under the lower control arm (A frame) and disconnect the system at the pin which requires replacement. In this way both time and effort will be saved.

If all of the front suspension parts are in good condition, and it is necessary to replace a coil spring only, perhaps the best method is to place a jack under the lower control arm (A frame) inner pivot shaft, then disconnect torsion bar and remove the four bolts which hold the inner shaft to the front cross member. Lower the jack until coil spring is free of the (A frame) and remove spring.

Note: On 1949 through 1953 models it will be necessary to disconnect the shock absorber, which is mounted inside the coil spring in order to remove the spring. The shock absorber should be disconnected before the four A frame mounting bolts are removed.

Leave the jack in a position which it assumed when it was lowered.

Replace the coil spring with a new one, being absolutely certain that the last coil of the spring enters the formed groove in the bottom of the A frame.

Raise the inner arm of the lower A frame back up against the front cross member, guiding it into place with two drift pins.

Reconnect the bolts which hold the inner arm to the front cross member. On 1949 through 1953 models replace the shock absorber.

Shock Absorber Replacement

Up to 1948 models the shock absorber is the upper control arm, and it is removed by taking out the upper suspension arm eccentric pin and bushings and removing the bolts which hold the shock absorber to the top of the frame.

This is accomplished without particular difficulties since the bolts are accessible through the engine compartment at the top. The eccentric pin can be removed readily after the front wheel is removed.

On 1949 through 1953 models the shock absorber is mounted in the center of the coil spring and is held by a removable bracket under the lower control arm.

To remove the shock absorber, simply disconnect the removable bracket from the lower control arm and remove the nut which holds the shock absorber to the frame at the upper control arm inner end.

Upper Control Arm Pin

To replace the upper pin on 1940 through 1948 models, loosen clamp bolts of the upper portion of the knuckle support, remove the front bushing, and then the back bushing.

Now the pin can be removed. When the eccentric pin is replaced, make certain that the pin is properly centered in the knuckle support and is in the full camber position (facing outward).

The upper pivot pin on all models has a thread with two starts.

On 1949 through 1953 models which use an eccentric bushing, the bushing is first slid into the knuckle support and lightly clamped in place, and then the long straight pin is fed from the front of the car through the upper arm bushing into the eccentric bushing, through the eccentric bushing to the second upper arm bushing and then it is secured with a nut and lockwasher.

Dust seals are used at both ends to prevent foreign matter from entering the pin surface.

When properly set up, the knuckle support itself will be almost exactly centered between the front and back part of the upper support arm.

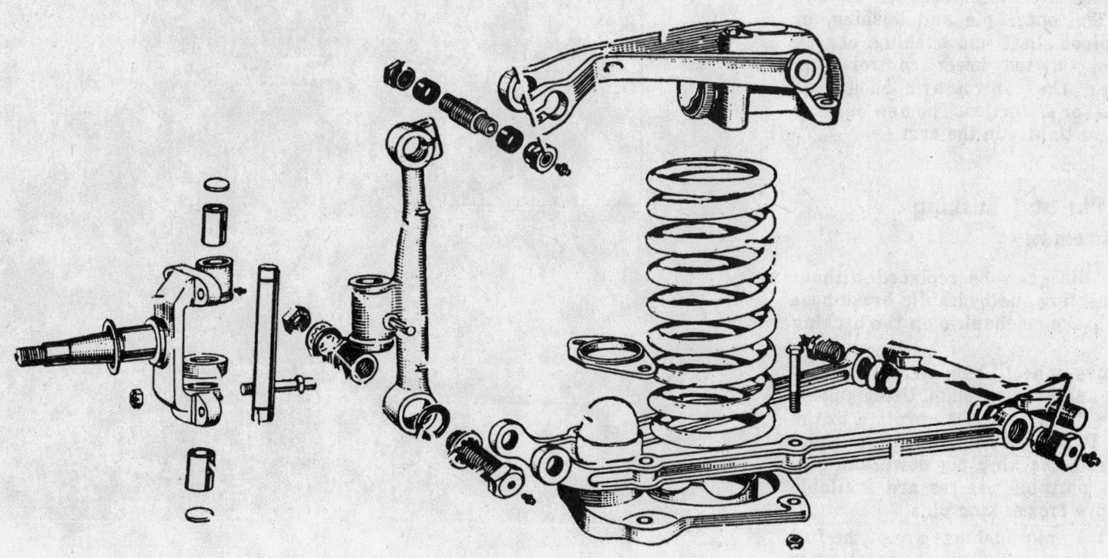

Front suspension 1946 thru 48 models

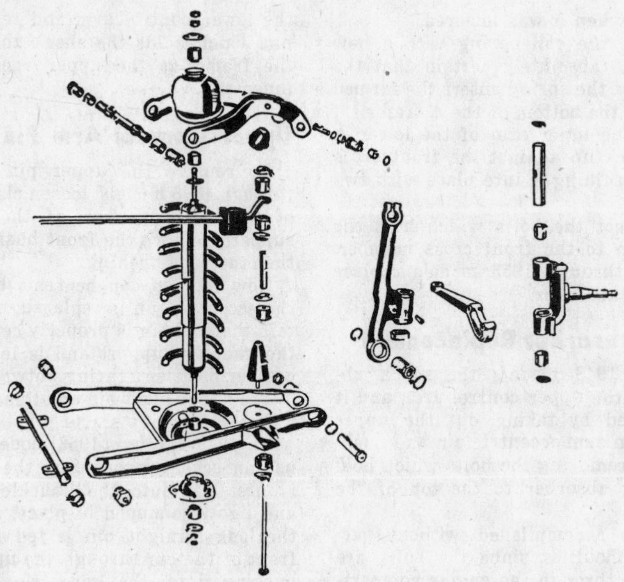

Front suspension 1949 thru 53 models

Lower Control Arm Pin

Remove the nut on rearward side of the lower control arm. Now, working at the forward side, remove the pivot bolt and then the bushing.

When replacing the bushing in the knuckle support, screw in from the rear and tighten. The pin is screwed into the control arm and the knuckle support itself is centered between the two arms. The outer pin and bushing, or inner pivot shaft and bushing, can be replaced on the lower control arm. However, the control arm should be checked for distortion. The new bushing must seat tightly in the arm.

King Pin and Bushing Replacement

King pins can be replaced without disconnecting the hydraulic brake hose or the brake mechanism on the backing plate.

Remove wheel, hub, and drum assembly and backing plate. Using a piece of wire, hook the backing plate to the frame. Drive out the king pin lock pin, then drive the king pin down and out. Special portable presses are available to remove frozen king pins.

The king pin bushings are of the full floating type and require no reaming or honing.

STEERING GEAR

All models of Pontiac from 1940 through 1951 use the Saginaw worm and roller type steering wheel.

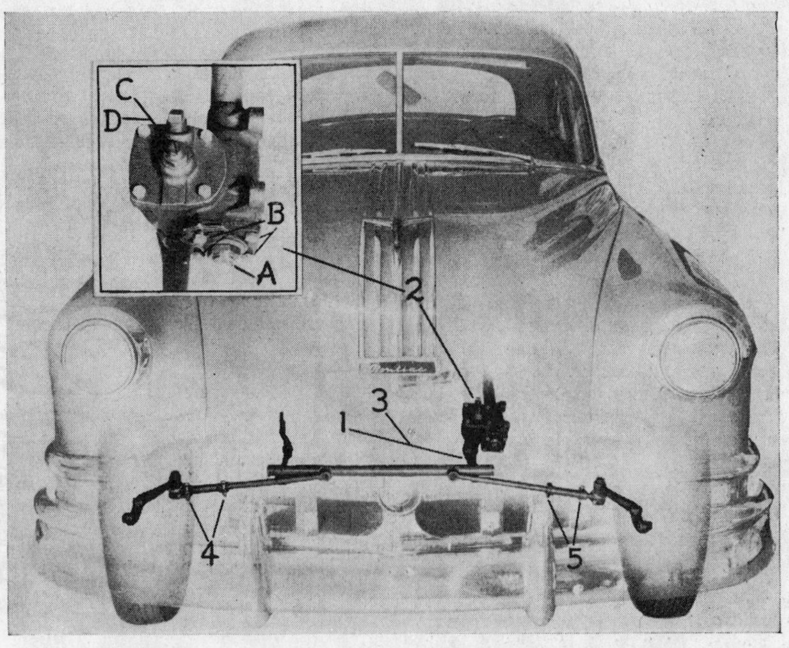

Steering mechanism

Adjustment of the Steering Mechanism

1. Disconnect the pitman arm from the intermediate tie-rod.

2. Adjust the steering gear housing assembly.

A. Loosen the jam nut at the bottom of the steering column and turn the adjusting screw until a 2-pound pull is required to pull the steering wheel in either direction. Tighten the jam nut and recheck to make sure that bearings have not tightened when the lock nut was being secured.

B. Set the steering wheel in the mid position of its travel and loosen the clamp bolt on the eccentric housing, and turn the eccentric housing until there is zero lash in the gears with the steering wheel in the mid position of its travel.

C. Remove the end play from the sector shift by loosening the jam nut, and tighten the adjusting screw until there is zero end play in the cross shaft with the steering wheel in the mid position of its travel. Tighten all lock nuts.

3. Reconnect the pitman arm to the intermediate tie-rod.

4. With the steering wheel held in the mid position of its travel, loosen the clamp nuts on the right side tie-rod

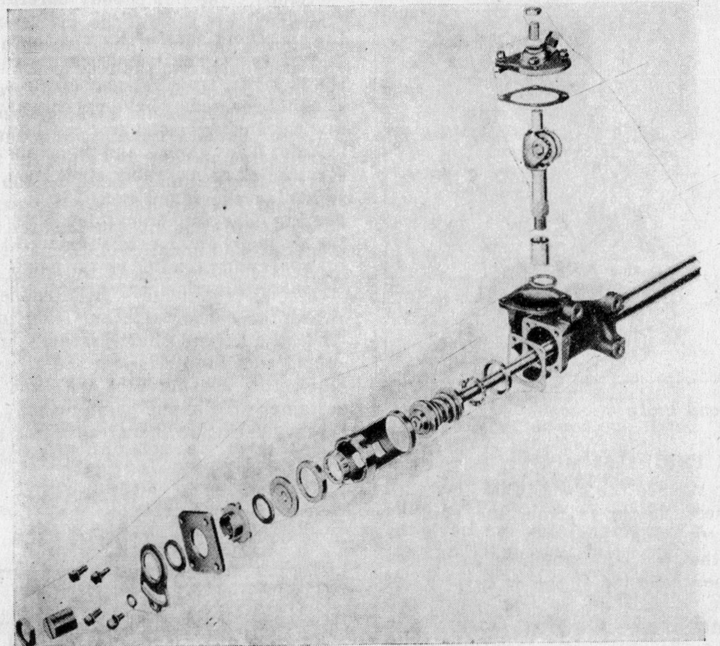
Steering gear

sleeve and adjust the sleeve so that ½ of the toe-in is in the right front wheel. Tighten the clamp bolts.

5. Now, still holding the steering wheel in the mid position of its travel, loosen the clamp bolts on the left side tie-rod adjusting sleeve, and turn the sleeve so that the balance of the toe-in is contained in the left front wheel. Tighten the clamp screws. Turn the steering wheel completely through its travel to check for looseness or binding.

BRAKES

All models of Pontiac use the Bendix Duo-Servo hydraulic brake with an eccentric anchor.

At each brake, there are two adjustments, the adjusting screw and the anchor pin. 1940 to 1948 models had eccentric cam adjustment, which has been discontinued on 1949 through 1951 models.

Brake Inspection

Before making any service adjustments on Pontiac (or any other brake), remove at least one of the wheels to determine the condition of the brake cylinders and the brake lining.

If any moisture is found on the rubber boots which seal the wheel cylinders, it usually indicates that the wheel cylinder has a slight seepage and it will be necessary to either hone the wheel cylinder to secure a better bearing surface for the cup, or replace the cylinder.

Examine the condition of the brake lining. Lining which is worn evenly at both ends of the shoe generally indicates a correctly adjusted anchor, and if there is sufficient lining on the shoes it probably will not be necessary to readjust the anchor.

Examine the brake retracting springs and make certain all of the lining rivets are securely fastened.

Major Brake Adjustment (Anchor Adjustment)

When properly adjusted, the secondary shoe (the one which is pushed against the anchor pin by the forward rotation of the wheel) will have a clearance of .015 inch approximately and 1½ inch from each end of the shoe. To check this clearance, proceed as follows: Turn the star wheel adjuster, located behind the slot at the lower part of the backing plate, in a direction which will expand the shoes against the drum. If the star wheel has been properly assembled, the shoes are expanded against the drum by turning the inner end of the star wheel downward.

Insert a .015 inch feeler gage through the port in the drum to measure the clearance between the lining and drum approximately 1½ inch from the anchor end of the secondary shoe.

Continue to expand the shoes until the feeler gage is just barely gripped. Then check the opposite end of the secondary shoe to make sure there is .015 inch clearance there also.

If the clearance of the lower end of

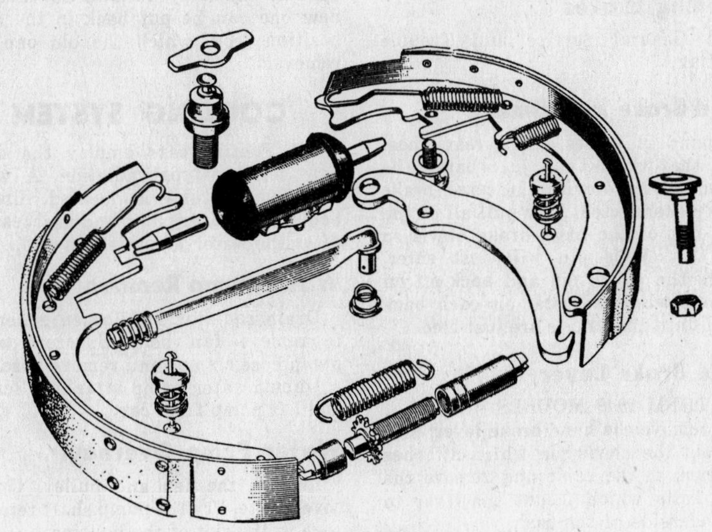
Rear brake assembly

MAJOR BRAKE ADJUSTMENT—*continued*

the shoe is greater than .015 inch it will be necessary to loosen the lock nut on the eccentric anchor, and turn the anchor in the direction which will cause the shoe to move downward slightly. Then tentatively tighten the anchor jam nut and again turn the star wheel until the .015 inch feeler is just gripped at the anchor end of the secondary shoe and again recheck the opposite end of the secondary shoe.

Continue to make this adjustment until there is exactly .015 inch clearance at both ends of the secondary shoe, then securely tighten the anchor jam nut.

Minor Brake Adjustment

Minor brake adjustment is accomplished by turning the star wheel in a direction which will expand the shoes against the drum. Turn the edge of the wheel downward until the shoes drag and then back off until the wheel is just free. Repeat this on all four wheels.

Master Cylinder

The master cylinder is refilled from the engine compartment and is located directly forward of the brake pedal. When inspecting the master cylinder, thoroughly clean out the cylinder and, holding it up to the light, let the light shine along the inside of the cylinder and examine it with extreme care for scratches or roughness. If this condition is found, it will be necessary to hone the cylinder to secure a smooth surface.

Bleeding Brakes

See General Service and Trouble Shooting.

Hand Brake Adjustment

Expand the shoes on the rear wheel until the wheels can just barely be turned by hand with the hand brake cable disconnected. Now pull all of the slack out of the hand brake clevis so that the clevis pin will just enter. Secure the clevis pin and back off on the star wheel adjuster on each back wheel until the wheels are just free.

Hand Brake Lever

1940 THRU 1949 MODELS

To remove the hand brake lever, first take out the clevis pin which attaches the lever to the cable and remove the three bolts which mount the lever to the underside of the dash.

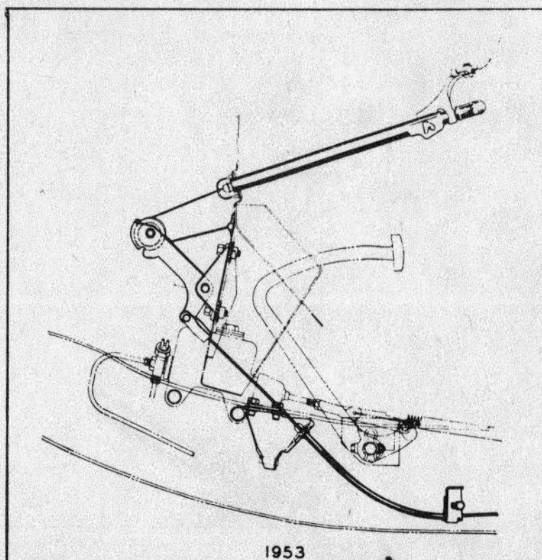

Hand brake mechanism 1953 models

1950 THRU 1953 MODELS

To replace the hand brake lever, disconnect the lever from the cable by removing the clevis pin and then take out the two bolts which hold the lever to the underside of the dash.

Hand Brake Cable

To remove the hand brake cable, first disconnect the clevis which holds the hand brake cable to the lever under the dash, and remove the clamp which holds the conduit assembly to the lever.

Slide the cable and conduit assembly through the fire wall into the engine compartment and, from underneath the car, disconnect the cable from the bracket on the transmission and disconnect the clevis from the hand brake lever under the car.

Note carefully the "path" that the conduit assembly follows so that the new one can be put back in the same position from which the old one was removed.

COOLING SYSTEM

All Pontiac cars employ the down flow cellular type radiation. A water distribution tube is located directly behind the water pump and is accessible after the water pump is removed.

Water Pump Removal

Drain radiator and loosen generator to remove fan belt. Unscrew water pump hose clamps and remove hose.

Unbolt water pump attaching screws and lift pump from car.

Water Pump Overhaul

Remove the fan and pulley. Unbolt cover plate. Pry the pump shaft retainer wire in the slot of the housing.

Support the pump body carefully at the shoulders back of the shaft bearing and press the shaft and bearing out of the impeller, from the rear of the water pump. Then remove the carbon washer and the spring loaded seal assembly.

Note: The bearing and pump shaft is serviced as an assembly since the shaft serves as the inner race for the ball bearing. The fan hub is not a part of the assembly and must be removed from the shaft and installed on the new shaft.

Reassemble the seal assembly with the smaller diameter of the rubber toward the carbon washer. Then install the bearing and shaft assembly in the pump body, and aligning the groove in the outer bearing race with the wire retainer hole in the pump housing, and press bearing in, using an arbor press

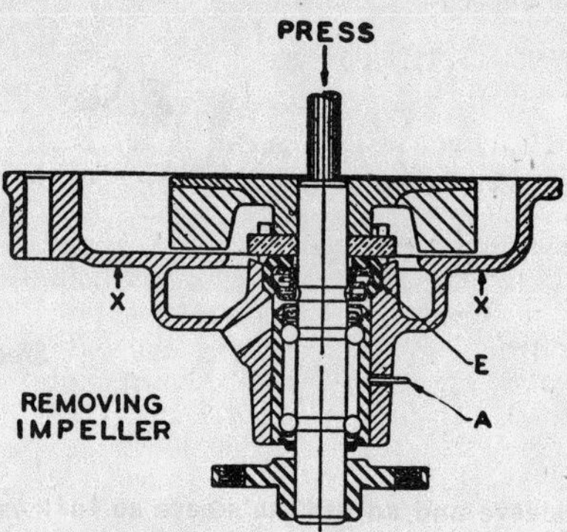

Removing water pump impeller

when it is necessary. Always apply the pressure to the outer race of the bearing and not to the shaft. Install the carbon washer with the "ears" in the recess of the housing and press the impeller on the shaft, while supporting the fan end of the shaft, far enough to

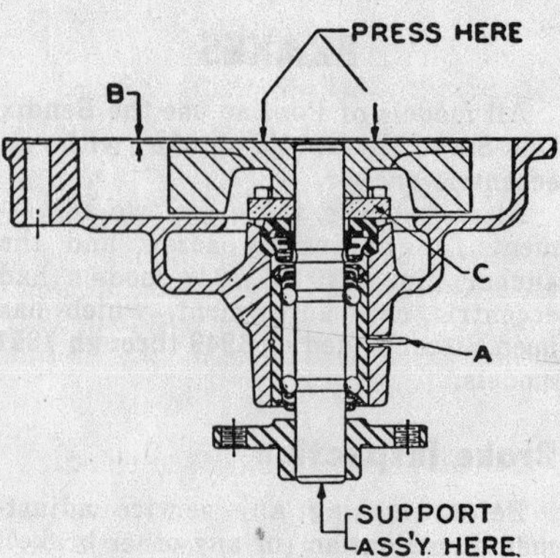

Replacing pump impeller

obtain 9/64 inch clearance between the impeller and a straight edge used across the rear of the cover mounting face of the pump housing. Install the bearing retainer and replace the gasket and install the cover and screws.

RADIATOR CORE REMOVAL

1940 THRU 1948 MODELS

Drain cooling system and disconnect the upper and lower hoses. Unscrew the three cap screws on each side of the core and tip the fan shroud back against the engine. Lift the core up and out of the shell, revolving the fan as necessary to clear the lower connection.

1949 THRU 1953 MODELS

Drain cooling system. Detach fan belt, upper and lower hoses, and heater return from lower tank. Disconnect headlight wiring from right junction block and remove wire loom from top of fan shroud. Take out bolts holding fan shroud to radiator and radiator to support. Lift the core up and out, revolving the fan as is necessary to clear the lower hose connection.

MANIFOLD

On both 6 and 8 cylinder engines a heat riser valve is incorporated in the exhaust manifold to regulate the amount of hot exhaust gases bypassed around the intake manifold heat chamber.

FUEL SYSTEM

On all models the fuel pump is located on the right forward side of the engine block. Single or double acting fuel pumps are used on all models.

ENGINE ASSEMBLY

Pontiac supplied both 6 and 8 cylinder engines in every year of their production. Up to and including 1951 both type engines are of the in-line L-head variety.

Harmonic Balancer Removal

Drain cooling system. Remove the radiator assembly. The harmonic balancer can then be removed from the crankshaft by the use of a special puller.

Timing chain arrangement

Oil Pan Removal

1940—MODELS

It is necessary to turn the engine to locate No. 1 piston at top of its stroke before removing the oil pan, and 40-28 models, it is necessary to take off the engine front insulator support assembly, and rest engine on a block, to facilitate removal of front oil pan screws.

1940—SERIES 29—DELUXE EIGHT

Remove the screws which fasten the front support insulator to the radiator and engine support bracket. Raise engine and let it rest on a one inch block, which will allow removal of front bolts.

1941 THRU 1953 MODELS

Drain the oil. On the eight cylinder engine it is necessary to remove the front cross member to the radiator support aprons, which will give access to mounting screws at the front end of the pan. The right and left sheet metal aprons may be lifted out in a circular movement, right to right, and left to left, from inside engine compartment, after attaching screws are all removed.

Timing Case Cover Removal

1940 Models. Remove hood and drain cooling system. Disconnect head lamp wires. Detach front bumper, and disconnect front fender and radiator support from the frame by removing the two nuts extending through the center of the front cross member.

Disconnect radiator hose clamps and hose. Lift off the radiator and fenders as an assembly. Remove the fan belt and fan. Take off harmonic balancer. Support the front of the engine and remove engine support. Take out timing case cover bolts and the necessary oil pan screws. Lift off case cover.

1941 THRU 1953 MODELS

Drain radiator and disconnect hoses at top and bottom. Remove the three cap screws on each side of the core and tip the fan shroud back against the engine. Lift the core up and out of the shell, rotating the fan to clear the radiator water outlet connection. Unbolt mud pan. Pull off harmonic balancer. Support front of engine and remove front engine support. Take out timing case cover attaching bolts and remove cover.

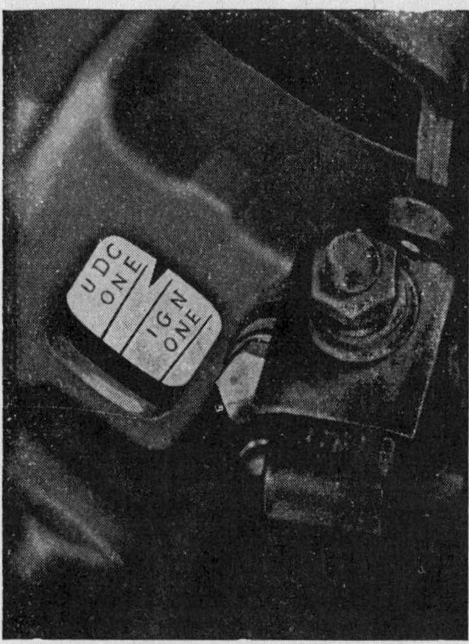

Timing inspection hole is above starter

Piston and Rod Assemblies

All models employ tin-plated pistons of chrome nickel alloy iron, having two tin-plated compression rings above the wrist pin and an oil control ring in the skirt. Wrist pins, are locked in piston boss at one end; the opposite end is slotted to permit it to move in its piston boss allowing for expansion and contraction.

Connecting rods are of the I-beam type, rifle drilled for pressure oiling to the wrist pins.

Connecting Rod Bearings

All 6 and 8 cylinder engines use the precision replaceable shell type connecting rod bearings. Each rod bearing on the 6 cylinder has one "tang" and each bearing on the 8 cylinder has two "tangs."

The caps on 8 cylinder engines should be placed on the connecting rods, so that these "tongs" do not butt against each other. The "tongs" on the six cylinder bearings should be on the opposite sides of the rods.

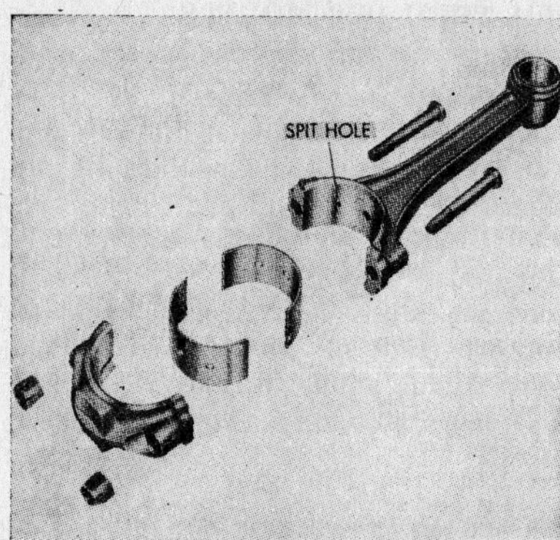

Connecting rod assembly

Pontiac does not recommend adjusting the rod bearings. However, if it is necessary to make an adjustment, there are specially designed shims for this purpose.

These shims are installed between the lower half of the bearing shell and the bearing cap. As much as .003 inch may be taken up by this method.

CYLINDER HEAD TIGHTENING SEQUENCE

1940-53 8 Cylinder

Nut tightening sequence. With a torque wrench tighten cylinder head nuts to 60 ft-lbs.

1940-53 6 Cylinder

With a torque wrench tighten head nuts to 60 ft-lbs.

Main Bearings

The crankshaft is carried on precision replaceable shell type main bearings and may be replaced without removing the crankshaft. The fit of the main bearings may be checked either by the plaster gage method or by the shim stock method. Plaster gage stock is supplied with complete instructions for its use.

Rear Main Bearing Oil Seal

1941 THRU 1951—6 CYLINDERS

Two annular grooves are machined in the block and cap just behind the rear main bearing on the six cylinder engines. A formed asbestos oil seal packing is assembled in the rear groove. Oil escaping from the rear bearing is first thrown off the chankshaft oil throw ridge into the first groove which is constructed to drain the oil back into the crankcase. The formed asbestos packing is compressed in the rear groove off the block and bearing cap. Any stray drops of oil which pass the first groove are stopped by the asbestos oil seal.

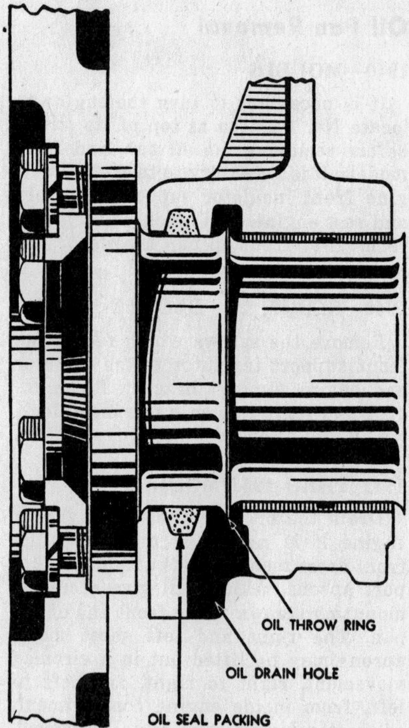

Rear main bearing oil seal—6 cylinder models

Note: On 1946 through 1951 models one end of the groove in the bearing cap is recessed to prevent the packing turning with the crankshaft. When installing new packing be sure one end of seal is packed into the recess at the end of the groove.

1940 THRU 1951—8 CYLINDERS

These models are not equipped with a packing but have an oil return pipe. The oil that passes the main bearing contacts the oil slinger and is returned to the oil pan through the oil return line.

VALVE SYSTEM

All Pontiac models are equipped with the in-line-"L" head variety and fitted with barrel type lifters. Intake valves are silicon-chromium steel, while the exhaust valves are high chrome-silicon steel. Intake and exhaust valve springs are interchangeable.

Valve Guide Removal

Removable tapered valve guides are used in all engines. The upper end of the guide is slightly larger than the lower end which will permit a closer fit at the bottom of the valve guide, where less clearance is desirable and at the same time provides sufficient clearance at the upper end of the guide to allow for the necessary expansion of the parts, resulting from the heat developed during operation. Pull the guides up to remove them from the engine. The new guides are pressed into place from the top of the engine. The valve guides taper .001 inch and the valves should be installed to give from a free fit to .0006 inch.

Pontiac replacement valve guides have undersize holes and necessitate reaming to secure proper fit of valve stem.

Note: On 1946 through 1949 models exhaust valve guides are counterbored to a depth of ¾ inch. The 1950 through 1951 models have a counterbore depth of 9/16 inch.

Whenever it is determined to replace valve guides, carefully measure the distance from the top of the cylinder block to the edge of the valve guide before removing the old guide. The measurement should be carefully noted for both intake and exhaust valve guides so a new guide can be inserted exactly the same distance from the top of the block as the old guide.

Valve Springs

In order to check on the condition of the valve springs, lay all of the springs on a flat surface and carefully measure across the top of the intake springs with a straight edge to see that all are the same height. If all are the same height it may safely be assumed that they are all in good condition since it is very unlikely that they will all collapse an equal amount.

If one or more is found to be a different height from the rest of the springs, it is a good idea to get one new spring and carefully measure all of the old springs against the one new one. Those which come up to the same height as the new spring may be considered to be in good condition. Those which do not should be replaced.

Where regular spring testing equipment is not available, this is generally considered to be a good, safe way to check the condition of the valve springs.

Valve Adjustment

On all Pontiac engines the valves can be reached, with some difficulty, from under the hood. Remove the valve chamber covers and the valves may be adjusted without removing any other unit.

Tappets are of the self-locking type which require two wrenches only for adjustment.

The General Service and Trouble Shooting Section of the manual gives the position in which the piston should be placed in order to be sure that the valve lifter is down on the heel of the cam so that the adjustment will be effective.

It is a good idea to protect the back of the hands with gloves or a covering so as to prevent burning them on the hot manifold when adjusting the valves in a warmed up engine.

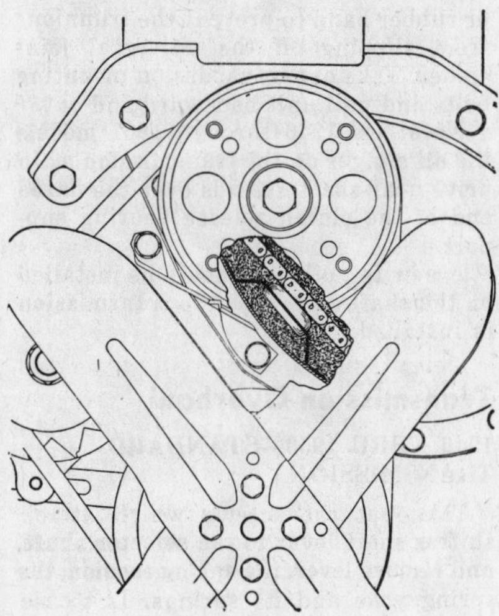

Timing chain bumper used on 1951 six

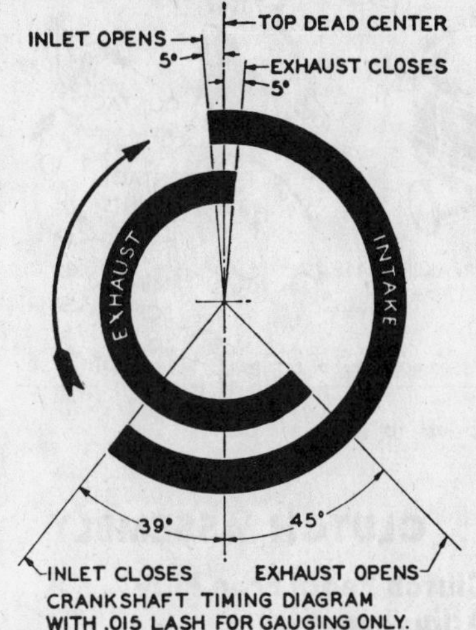

Valve timing diagram 6 and 8 cylinder

Valve Timing

The valve timing on the six and eight cylinder engines is the same. Valve timing marks are indicated on the crankshaft and camshaft sprockets by "O" marks. Correct valve timing is obtained when the two "O" markings are in line with the centers of the camshaft and crankshaft. However, this check requires removal of the timing case cover. To check the valve timing on 6 and 8 cylinder engines without removing the case cover proceed as follows:

The inlet valve opens 5 degrees before upper dead center. Set the tappet to .015 inch. The exhaust valve closes 5 degrees after top dead center. The flywheel is marked U.D.C. one at the top dead center for number 1 cylinder.

Timing Chain and Sprocket Removal

Remove timing case cover. Take off camshaft nut. Use a puller on both the crankshaft and camshaft, lift off timing chain and sprockets together. To reinstall, reverse the procedure and make sure the timing sprocket cover oil seal is properly placed on the crankshaft, so it will seal when the timing gear cover is installed.

Note: Pontiac recommends that the radiator, front fenders and bumper assemblies be removed, when the replacement of the timing chain assembly is necessitated.

ELECTRICAL SYSTEM

Generator

A two brush, shunt wound generator is standard equipment on all models.

On the generator having external control, if difficulty is experienced first ground the field terminal of the generator at the generator and if this will correct the difficulty then the regulator is at fault. If grounding the field terminal does not correct the trouble then the generator must be removed from the car and subjected to the bench tests as shown in the Fundamentals Section of the Manual.

Distributor

The distributor is mounted on the left side of the cylinder block to the rear of engine. The distributor shaft is slotted to allow the tongue in the oil pump shaft to enter and drive distributor.

Ignition Timing

When the engine is correctly timed the spark occurs 4 degrees 1940 through 1948, 6 degrees 1948 through 1951 before top dead center, or when the center I.G.N. mark on the flywheel aligns with the pointer in the timing inspection hole (on harmonic balancer on 1949 through 1951 models).

There are three marks on the flywheel visible to the housing inspection hole. The line at the extreme left is upper dead center of the pistons 1 and 6 and on eight cylinder models 1 and 8. The next line is 2 degrees ahead of V.D.C. and the third line 6 degrees ahead of V.D.C. This 4 degrees range provides a limit of adjustment in setting the spark to compensate for variation in the distributor automatic advances, etc.

The distributor breaker point gap is

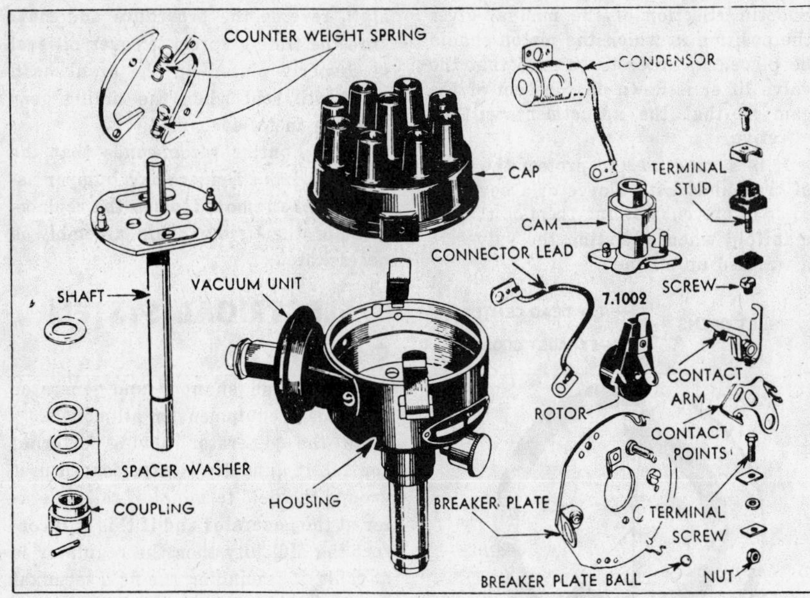

Eight cylinder distributor exploded to show all parts

IGNITION TIMING—*continued*

given in section two of the Manual. Advancing in a counter-clockwise direction, the firing order is 1-5-3-6-2-4 on 6 cylinder, and 1-6-2,5-8-3-7-4 on 8 cylinder engines.

Starting Motor

The starting motor on 6 cylinder models is a 4 brush two field winding unit employing an overrunning clutch type drive. The 8 cylinder is similar in construction and has four field windings. All starting motors since 1949 are solenoid operated.

If starting motor does not crank engine properly, see if battery is fully charged and all electrical connections are clean and securely tightened.

The mechanical check on the condition of the starter is performed in the same manner as that of the generator. as explained in the Fundamental Section of this Manual. See index.

Horn Relay

On all models the horn relay is located either on the left side of the fire wall under the hood or on the left inner fender pan under the hood.

It is held in place with two metal screws.

Mark each wire carefully before removing the relay so that the wires can be replaced at the proper terminal when installing a new one.

CLUTCH ASSEMBLY

Clutch Pedal Free Play Adjustment

On all models the clutch pedal free play adjustment should be between ⅞ inch to 1⅛ inch measured at pedal pad.

Clutch Removal

1941 THRU 1953—STANDARD TRANSMISSION

Remove transmission being sure that its weight is not allowed to rest on the hub of the clutch disc.

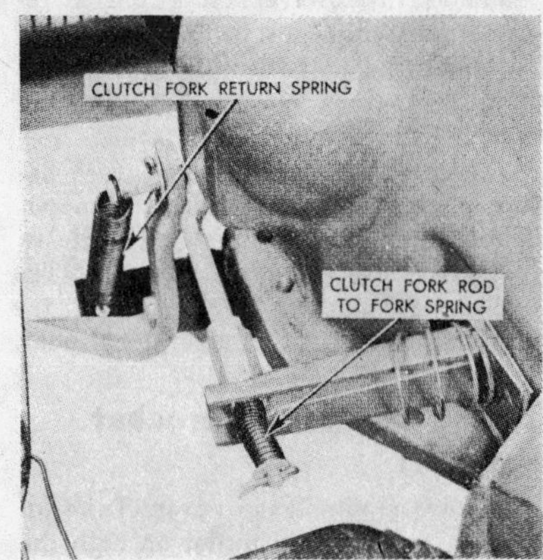

Clutch linkage 1953 models

Note: On 1947 through 1948 models avoid damaging the release bearing support. Detach the clutch bearing support spring washer. (On 1941 through 1948 models disconnect the control shaft inner brackets). On 1947 and 1948 models remove the release bearing support by tapping from inside the housing. Do not strike the tube of the support on which the release bearing is piloted. Avoid prying between the housing and the support flange as it must be true to avoid misalignment of the transmission.

On all models, unhook the clutch pedal, pull back spring, and take out the clutch fork ball support, the clutch fork and the clutch throwout bearing. Be sure and mark the flywheel and clutch cover so that the assembly can be made in the same relative position in order to preserve the clutch balance. Loosen bolts holding clutch to flywheel and remove clutch.

Clutch Rebuilding

Rebuilding the clutch pressure plate is a specialized job which necessitates the use of special jigs and fixtures. Instruction for these tools are supplied by the manufacturers of said equipment.

TRANSMISSION ASSEMBLY

1940 THRU 1953—STANDARD TRANSMISSION

Disconnect the speedometer cable from the transmission. Detach the gearshift selector rod and control rod from transmission. Unbolt universal joint and remove propeller shaft. Use a wire or rubber band to prevent the trunnions from slipping off the universal joint spider. Take out transmission mounting bolts and pull unit backward and out.

Note: On 1946 through 1951 models the oil slinger on the transmission main drive gear shaft extends over the flared end of the clutch release bearing support.

A new felt oil seal should be installed on the shaft each time the transmission is installed.

Transmission Overhaul

1940 THRU 1953—STANDARD TRANSMISSION

Take out the screws which attach shifter shaft lever to the selector shaft, and remove lever, the spring tension, the spring yoke and its springs. Lift case cover and speedometer drive gear, the sleeve and shaft assembly.

Shift transmission into high gear position to prevent the sliding sleeve and the first and reverse gear from dropping into the case. Remove rear bearing retainer screws and withdraw rear bearing retainer, main shaft and second speed gear as a unit out through the rear of the case. (Fig. 1)

Take out the shifter fork lock screws. Shift the selector shaft to neutral and remove the shifter lever lock screws. Then slide the shaft out through the rear of the case, being careful not to lose the poppet bolts and springs. Lift out the sliding sleeve and the low and reverse sliding gear. (Fig. 2)

Loosen the clamping screw which fasten the selector shaft lever and remove lever. This is necessary to allow the transmission selector inner lever to disengage the recess in the selector shaft as the shaft is removed from the case. To prevent the recessed portion of the selector shaft from damaging the oil seal which is pressed into the left side of the case, the shaft must be removed from the right side of the case and installed from the left side. (Fig. 3)

To remove the selector shaft, drive it from the left side of case, which will knock out the welsh plug from right side of case. When reinstalling, use a new welsh plug. Also, when reinstalling the inner selector shaft, check the order of assembling the oil seal and washers. The leather oil seal is pressed into left side of case with the lip of the seal toward the inside of the case. (Fig. 4)

Drive countershaft to rear until it just clears the hole in front of the case. Then, with a dummy shaft which is exactly the same length as the cluster gear and thrust washers, drive out the regular countershaft, leaving dummy shaft in place so as to prevent losing the needle rollers at each end of the cluster. The cluster gear is allowed to lie in the bottom of the case until after the main drive gear has been removed. (Fig. 5)

Note: On 1949 through 1953 models the main drive gear shaft is undercut to accommodate the main drive gear oil seal. An oil slinger is installed next to the front bearing and held in place by a spring washer and snap ring. The spring washer should be installed with the concave side toward the oil slinger.

To remove the main drive gear assembly, take out the snap ring which retains the front bearing and tap the main drive gear, with the bearing, through the case, and withdraw entire assembly.

To take out the reverse idle gear, drive the retaining pin through the shaft into the inside of the transmission and remove the shaft and gear. Then

Fig. 1

to disassemble the second speed gear, expand the wire retainer and slide the drum off the end of the shaft, leaving the retainer in the drum. Take off the mainshaft snap ring and thrust washer from in front of gear and slide gear off front end of shaft.

To disassemble the main drive gear, expand the wire retainer and remove the synchronizing drum. Remove the front bearing retainer snap ring and spring washer. Take out the bearing by bumping the shaft on a block of wood.

To reassemble the main drive gear

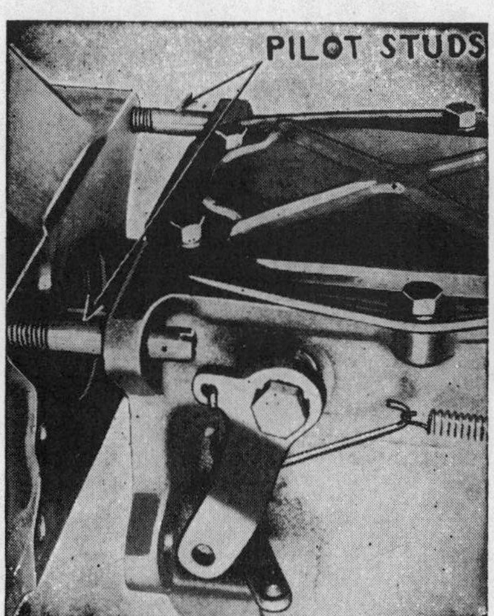

Remove transmission on pilot studs to avoid damaging clutch

bearing, make sure that the shielded side is placed "toward" the gear.

Press the bearing firmly in place, using a tube placed over the gear shaft and pressing on the "inner" race of the bearing. Make sure that the high and second speed clutch slides freely on mainshaft. The synchronizing drum must be smooth and free from scores. They must also show the heaviest contact on the large diameters for best results when synchronizing. Make sure that the oil grooves are cleaned and free of dirt. To reassemble the countergear, insert the dummy shaft in place of regular countershaft and insert "25" (twenty-five) needle rollers at each end of the gear, after using a liberal supply of vaseline or lubriplate to hold them in position. Coat the bearing retainers and thrust washers with lubricant and position them at each end of cluster. Then lay the countershaft assembly in the bottom of case until the main drive gear is installed.

When this has been done, position the cluster gear assembly and install the countershaft from the rear of case, pushing the dummy shaft out through the front. Align the slots in the case and the shaft and insert the lock ball before driving the countershaft to its final position.

Note: When installing the idler shaft pin, its outer end should be ¾ inch from the outside of case.

Adjustment of Gear Shift Selector

Between the shoulder of control shaft upper bearing and top of the support a clearance of 1/8 inch should be had so there will be no interference at this point when selecting gears.

To adjust clearance remove pivot pins and shift lever from upper bearing, now screwing the bearing out 1/2 turn will increase clearance 1/32 inch.

The distance between the shaft lever and steering wheel should be 2 3/4 inch plus or minus 1/8 inch. To adjust, back off the adjusting bolt that fastens selector contact and levers together. Holding selector rod in its rearmost position (second and high), and set shift lever to desired position. Secure bolt and recheck lever position.

REAR AXLE

Replacement of Ring Gear and Pinion and/or Pinion Bearings

Two types of pinion bearings are used on Pontiac cars. From 1940 up to and including 1947 models a double row ball bearing was used in the front of the pinion shaft; an annular roller bearing was used at the back end of the pinion shaft.

Starting with production cars in 1947 through 1951, tapered roller bearings were used both front and back on the pinion shaft.

Disassembly procedure is practically identical, except as noted in the text

Fig. 2

Fig. 3

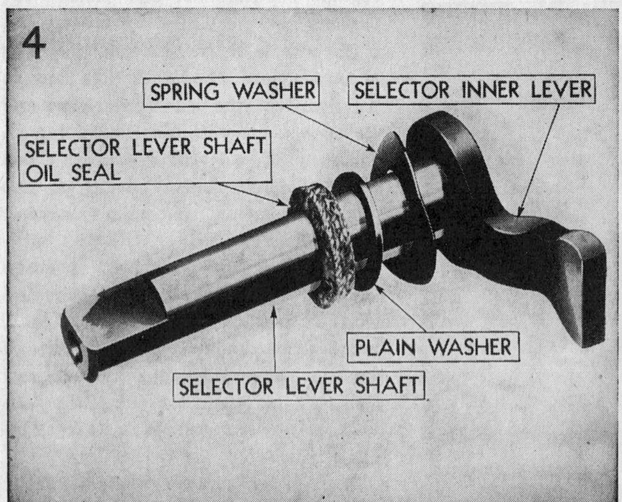

Fig. 4

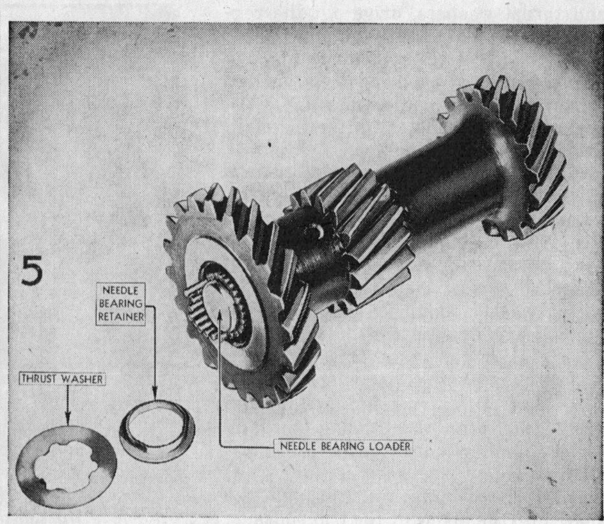

Fig. 5

below. Remove the differential carrier assembly from underneath the car and place it in a holding fixture or a vise.

Back off on the differential side bearing cages to relieve the preload on the bearings and take off the bearing caps, which will permit the differential assembly to be lifted out of the carrier.

Removal of the Pinion Shaft

MODELS WITH DOUBLE ROW BALL BEARINGS

On this construction shims were used at the back of the double row ball bearing between the ball bearing and a shoulder machined on the pinion shaft. Be careful not to lose these shims when disassembling the pinion.

Take off the nut holding the universal joint companion flange to the pinion shaft and pull off the companion flange. Take out the three taper screws which hold the bearing retaining sleeve in the housing and press the pinion shaft out through the rear of the housing. Sometimes the back bearing will come out with the pinion shaft, other times it will stay in the housing.

Note: There is a snap ring on the pinion shaft just ahead of the pinion gear itself. This snap ring is intended to prevent the roller bearings from working over toward the back face of the pinion gear itself. The snap ring should not be disturbed. Pull the rear bearing (roller bearing) out the differential carrier. The double row ball bearing can then be taken out of the housing.

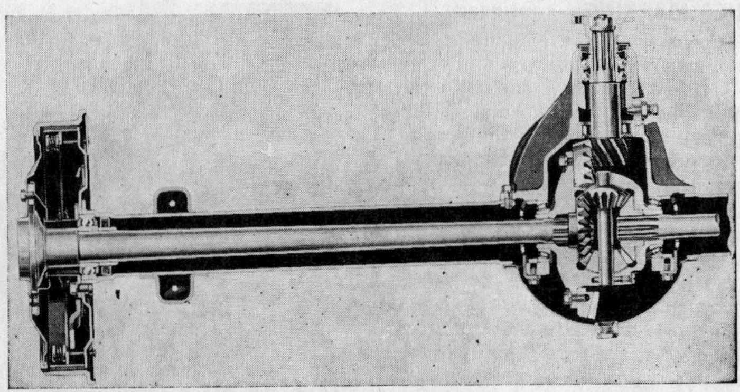

Rear axle—1940 thru 1947

Tapered Roller Bearings

As stated before, tapered roller bearings were used on pinion shafts starting with late 1947 production and continued through 1951 production. To move the pinion on these models, take off the universal joint companion flange and drive the pinion shaft out through the back of the case. The pinion shaft will come out with the rear bearing cone mounted on the shaft.

Note: A spacer is used between the front and rear bearing on the pinion shaft. Shims are used in front of the back bearing cup (race) and in back of the front bearing cup (race). The shims in front of the back bearing cup determine the depth of the pinion into the ring gear. Adding shims at this point will force the pinion gear deeper into mesh with the ring gear.

Removing shims from in front of the rear bearing cup will move the pinion gear away from the ring gear. The shims used in back of the front bearing cup are intended to adjust the preload on the bearings.

Carrier Marking Pinion Marking

The gasket flange of the carrier assembly is marked "D", "S" and "C". If it is marked either D or S, the letter will be followed by a number. The let-

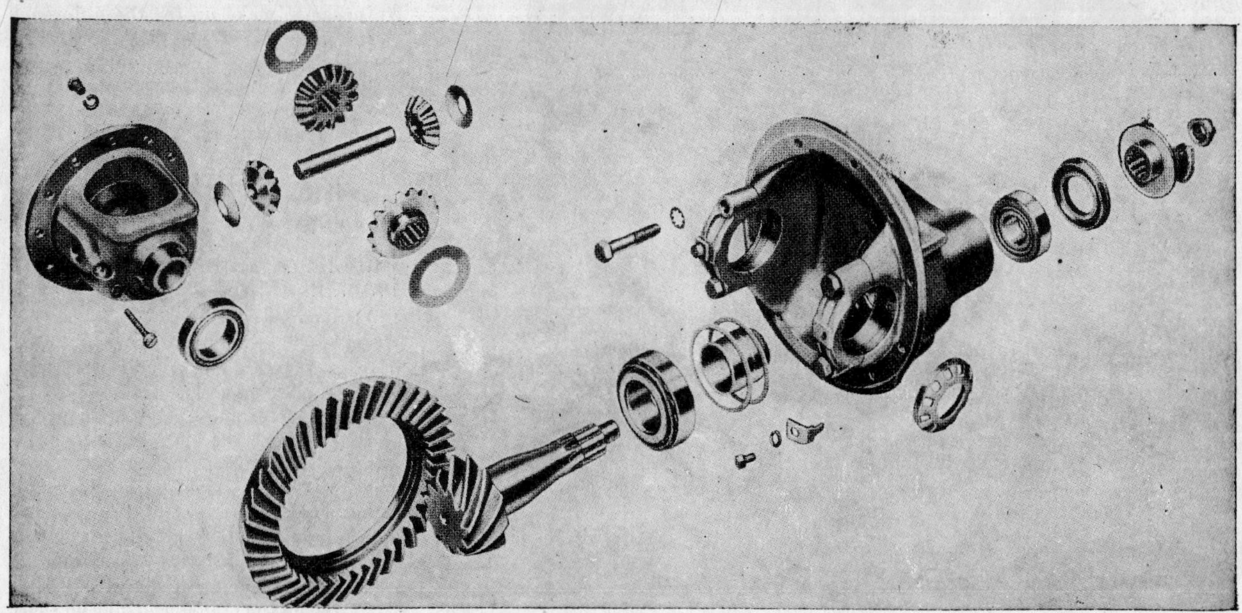

Rear axle—1947 thru 1951

CARRIER MARKING—*continued*

ter D means deep, the amount of the number immediately following.

The letter S means shallow, the amount of the number immediately following. The letter C means the bore is exactly centered and no number is used following the letter C.

If no letter or number is stamped on the gasket flange of the carrier, this means the carrier is centered. The pinion is marked with either "0" or a plus figure or a minus figure. A plus figure on the end of the pinion indicates that a shim the thickness of the figure following the plus sign must be used on that particular pinion. A minus figure means that you must subtract from the existing shims one shim the thickness of the digit following the minus sign. This applies whether tapered roller or double row ball bearings are being used. This formula applies to all Pontiac rears.

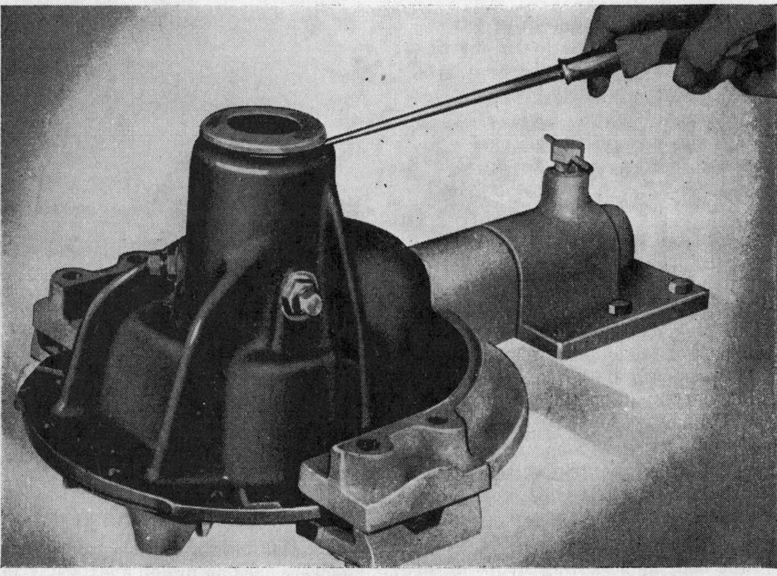

Prying out pinion oil seal

How to Select the Correct Shim Thickness

When disassembling the pinion, handle the shims (found in the housing) very carefully. Carefully mike the shims and record their total thickness. Also record the number stamped on the pinion which was removed. If the new pinion to be installed has the same number stamped on it as the old one, then exactly the same number of shims will be used. In other words, the shims in the housing are correct for that pinion. If the number on the new pinion is of greater value than the number on the old pinion, i.e. the old pinion reads plus 1, and the new pinion reads plus 3, it will be necessary to increase the total thickness of the shims by .002 inch, the difference in the reading. If the old pinion was marked minus 1, and the new pinion is marked minus 3, then it will be necessary to use a total shim thickness found in the housing. This is the difference between minus 1 and minus 3. If the old pinion reads minus 2, and the pinion reads plus 4, it will be necessary to insert a total .006 shims in order to make up for the difference between minus 2 and plus 4. A plus number indicates shims to be added from the nominal setting, a minus number indicates shims taken away from the nominal setting.

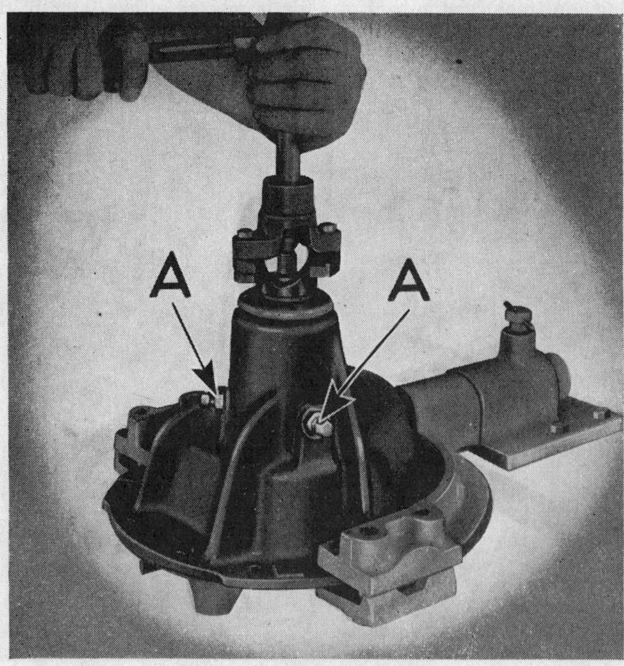

Remove companion flange

Assembling Pinion to the Carrier

MODELS WITH DOUBLE ROW BALL BEARINGS

Double row ball bearings were used from 1940 up to and including some part of 1947 production. When the correct number of shims has been established, to determine the pinion depth as given in the preceding paragraphs, install the pinion gear in the housing.

On the double row ball bearing type, no preload is taken on the bearings and the pinion is simply installed with the shims selected in back of the pinion front bearing. No other adjustment is required on the pinion bearings on these models.

Tapered Roller Bearings

Tapered roller bearing pinions were used starting with late 1947 production and through 1951 models. The procedure on these models is somewhat different. After the shims have been selected, which govern the proper depth of the pinion, it will be necessary to adjust the preload on the bearings by adding to or taking from the shims in back of the front bearing cup.

Mount the shims governing the depth of the pinion into the back of the housing and insert the back pinion bearing cup (race). Install the front bearing cup (race) in the front of the housing, using shims behind it equal to the number of shims which were removed.

Note: At this point it is a good idea to remove from the front pack of shims a thickness equal to the thickness which might have been added to the back shim pack. In other words, if shims were added at the back bearing, remove that same thickness from the front bearing and it is easily possible that the correct adjustment will be arrived at immediately.

If shims were taken away from the back bearing it is a good idea to add exactly the same thickness to the front bearing in order to hold the preload constant. Set the pinion bearing and spacer in place in the carrier and install the front bearing cone and universal joint companion flange. It is a good idea not to put the grease seal in at this time, since it may be necessary to take out the universal point companion flange several times before the correct setting is obtained. Tighten up on the companion flange nut until the preload on the bearing is between 27″-37″ pounds for new bearings, or 15″-20″ pounds for bearings which have been used previously. If, after tightening the pinion nut, the torque required to turn the shaft is greater than 37″ pounds, it will be necessary to remove the companion flange bearing cone and bearing cup and remove shims from in back of the front bearing cup, in order to lessen the preload on the bearing. If the reading is less than 17″ pounds torque required to turn the pinion shaft, then it will be necessary to add shims in back of the front bearing cup.

Install pinion ball bearing

Install rear pinion bearing outer race and roller assembly

Installing the Differential Assembly

Install the differential assembly and put the bearing cups and bearing adjusting cages in place finger tight. Now adjust the bearing cage, ring gear side. until there is zero lash between the ring gear and pinion. Adjust the pinion cage on the opposite side until there is zero play in the bearings and then take up two more notches in order to preload the side bearings. Taking up the two notches should produce approximately .006 inch back lash between the ring gear and pinion, measured at the rim of the ring gear. If less than .006 lash is produced by the preloading of the bearings, it may be necessary to back off one notch on the ring gear side adjusting cage and take up one notch on the pinion side adjusting cage,.

A good, easy, quick way to check the setting of the ring gear and pinion, after it has been secured, is to spin the ring gear with your hand, noticing whether the gears mesh smoothly in both directions. When properly set up there will be no noticeable gear vibration as the ring gear is spun in mesh with the pinion.

PONTIAC 1940 thru 1953

DIFFERENTIAL ASSEMBLY—*continued*

A quick check of the ring gear and pinion can be made by painting about 9 or 10 teeth of the ring gear and then rolling it through the pinion gear,

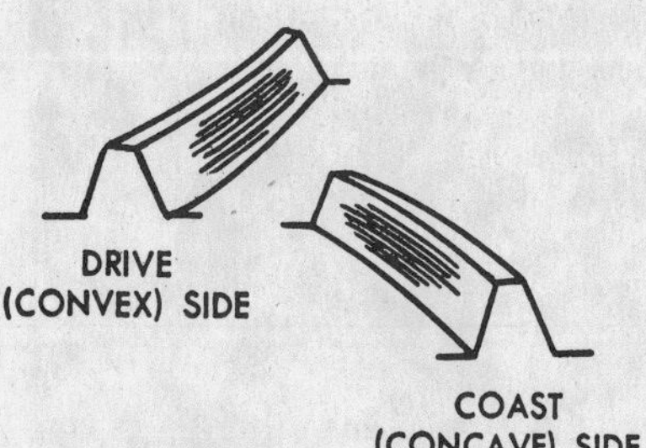

Correct adjustment

noticing the markings on the gears.

Accompanying this text is a chart showing markings left by desirable tooth contact and also markings left by

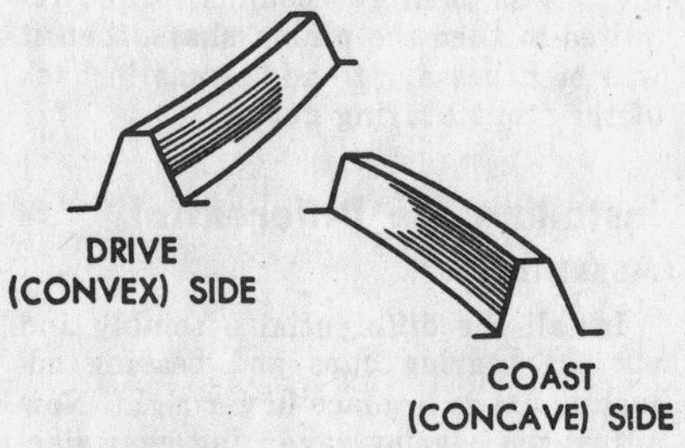

Loose adjustment—excess back lash

tooth contact which needs correcting. Secure all bolts and reinstall the carrier to the rear axle housing.

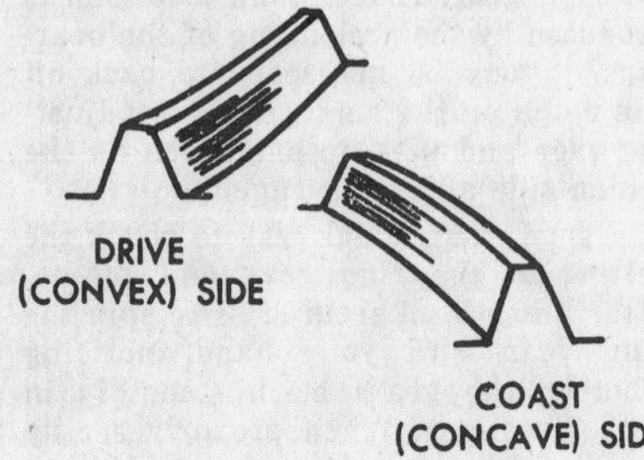

Tight adjustment—insufficient back lash

Pinion adjustment too far in (away from gear).

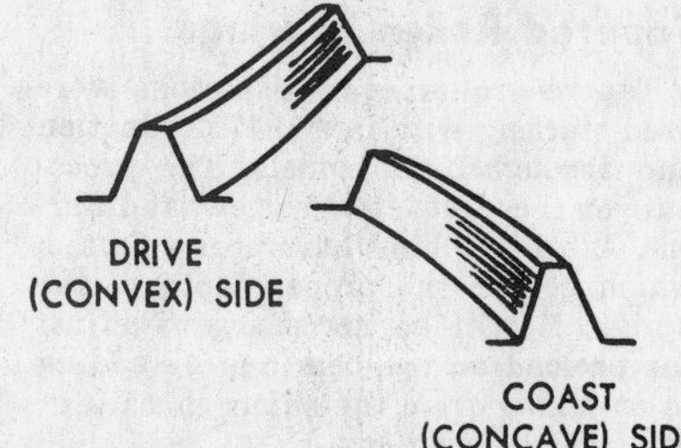

Pinion adjustment too far out (toward ring gear)

Adjust differential side bearing

REMOVAL OF REAR COIL SPRING

To remove the rear coil spring, disconnect the spring at its lower set and raise the car high enough so that all tension is removed from the spring. (It may be necessary to disconnect the shock absorber and the sway bar.)

After tension has been relieved from the spring, disconnect the spring upper mounting and lift off.

A clamping device is available for coil springs, which holds the spring in a compressed position. If this tool is available it is not necessary to jack up the car but very little in order to remove the coil spring and using a clamping device it is not necessary to detach the shock absorber.

Instrument Panel

1940 THRU 1953 MODELS

Any one instrument is mounted on a plate with one other instrument and it is necessary to take two out in order to remove any one.

They are mounted from the front end toward the back on the plate and the plate in its turn is mounted to the inside of the dash panel.

Speedometers

1940 THRU 1948 MODELS

Speedometers on these models may be removed as an individual unit without running into any obstacles. Disconnect the cable and unbolt the speedometer from its mounting under the dash.

Section thru rear axle—1940 thru 1947 model. Note: Double row ball bearing

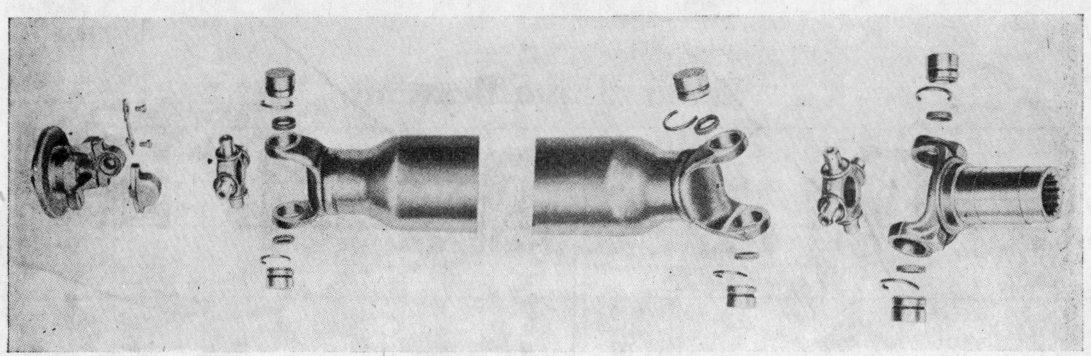

Mechanics type U joint and propeller shaft

1949 THRU 1953 MODELS AND ALSO THE 1948 SERIES 98

In order to take out the speedometer on these cars it is necessary to remove the entire instrument cluster, the speedometer being taken out from the front after the cluster is removed. On 1953 Models the cluster must be completely disassembled before the speedometer may be taken out.

Windshield Wiper Motor

The windshield wiper motor fastens up under the dash and is held in place with two bolts. It may be taken out without removing any fixed obstacle. Wiper linkage is of the bar drive type and may be removed from either side without taking out any fixed obstacles.

1948 THRU 1952 SERIES 98

Wiper motor is located on the fire wall under the hood and is easily removed. The wiper transmission, which is a cable drive, can be taken out without removing any other obstacles other than the cable mounts.

1953 MODELS

On these models the wiper motor is located on the fire wall under the dash. The glove box must be removed to gain access to the transmission.

STUDEBAKER SPECIFICATIONS

Starting Serial and Motor Numbers

Starting Serial Nnmbers

1940, 6 cyl.—Ser. 2G Champion
G-30501 and G-803701
Ser. 10A Commander
4148501 and 4807601
8 cyl.—Ser. 6C President
7133101 and 7803301

1941, 6 cyl.—Ser. 3G Champion
G-90101 and G-811201
Ser. 11A Commander
4178801 and 4811901
8 cyl.—Ser. 7C President
7139101 and 7803901

1942, 6 cyl.—Ser. 4G Champion
G-165501 and G-821001
Ser. 12A Commander
4216501 and 4816601
8 cyl.—Ser. 8C President
7145501 and 7804601

1946—Ser. 5G Champion....G-193001

1947—Ser. 6C Champion
G-212501 and G-824001
Ser. 14A Commander
4232501 and 4818501

1948—Ser. 7G Champion
G-314501 and G-827301
Ser. 15A Commander
4287001 and 4820501

1949—Ser. 8G Champion
G-400501 and G-839701
Ser. 16A Commander
4361001 and 4832701

1950—Ser. 9G Champion
G-468101 and G-851801
Ser. 17A Commander
4368901 and 4839001

1951, 6 cyl.—Ser. 10G Champion
G-1000001 and G-889101
8 cyl.—Ser. H Commander
8110001 and 8800001

1952, 6 cyl.—Ser. 12G Champion
G-1115501 and G-907301
8 cyl.—Ser. 3H Commander
8217001 and 8816001

1953, 6 cyl.—Ser. G14 Champion
G-1197501
8 cyl.—Ser. 4H Commander
8290001

Location

1940—On left front door hinge post or left frame rail under front fender.

1941-1946—On left front door hinge post.

1947-1953—On plate on left front door lock post.

Starting Motor Numbers

1940, 6 cyl.—Ser. 2G Champion 34101
Ser. 10A Commander....H-87601
8 cyl.—Ser. 6C President..B-38501

1941, 6 cyl.—Ser. 3G Champion 101201
Ser. 11A Commander...H-122201
8 cyl., Ser. 7C President...B-45001

1942, 6 cyl.—Ser. 4G Champion 186301
Ser. 12A Commander...H-164301
8 cyl.—Ser. 8C President..B-52101

1946 216501

1947—Ser. 6G Champion.....236001
Ser. 14A Commander.....H-182001

1948—Ser. 7G Champion......342001
Ser. 15A Commander.....H-239001

1949—Ser. 8G Champion......441001
Ser. 16A Commander.....H-326001

1950—Ser. 9G Champion......521001
Ser. 17A Commander.....H-370001

1951, 6 cyl. 788001
8 cyl. V-101

1952, 6 cyl. 911501
8 cyl. V-123001

1953, 6 cyl. 1004001
8 cyl. V-207001

Location

1940-53, 6 and straight 8 cyl.—On front corner on left side of block.

1951-1953, V8—On pad on top of block to right of distributor mounting.

General Specifications

Year	Model	Wheelbase (in.)	Tread (in.)		Overall Dimensions (in.)			Shipping Weight* (lb.)	Tire Size (in.)
			Front	Rear	Length†	Width	Height■		
1940	2G		56	57	189			2365	5.50-16
	10A		60	61	198				6.25-16
	6C		60	61	203				6.50-16
1941	3G	110	56	57	191			2435	5.50-16
	11A	119	58	60	206			3150	6.25-16
	7C	125	58	60	211			3500	7.00-16
1942	4G	110	56	57	193			2495	5.50-16
	12A	119	58	60	210			3265	6.25-16
	8C	124	58	60	216			3485	7.00-15
1946	5G		56	57	198	73	67		5.50-16
1947-48	6G, 7G		56	54	193	70	61	2735	5.50-15
	14A	119-123	55	54	205-208	70	61	3265	6.50-15
	15A	119-123	55	54	204-208	70	62	3280	6.50-15
1949	8G	112	56	54	191	70	61	2720	5.50-15
	16A	119-123	55	54	204-§208	70	62	3195	6.50-15
1950	9G	113	56	54	197	70	62	2750	6.40-15
	17A	120-124	56	54	208-212	70	62	3255	7.60-15
1951	10G	115	57	54	198	71	61	2730	6.40-15
	V8-H	115-119	57	54	198-§202	71	62	3255	7.10-15

Land cruiser.

General Specifications—*continued*

Year	Model	Wheelbase (in.)	Tread (in.) Front	Tread (in.) Rear	Overall Dimensions (in.) Length†	Overall Dimensions (in.) Width	Overall Dimensions (in.) Height■	Shipping Weight* (lb.)	Tire Size (in.)
1952	12G	115	56	56	197	71	61	....	6.40–15
	3H	115	54	54	197	71	62	....	7.10–15
1953	14G	116	56	56	198	69	60	....	6.40–15
	4H	120	56	56	202	71	61	....	7.10–15

*—Cheapest 5 pass. 4 door sedan or equivalent. ■—Road to roof, no load. †—Including bumper and bumper guards.

General Engine Specifications

Year	Model	Number of Cylinders Bore and Stroke	Piston Displacement, Cubic Inches	Compression Ratio (To–1)	Taxable (A.M.A.) Hp.	Developed Horse Power: Bare Engine	Developed Horse Power: With Accessories	Maximum Torque Ft. Lbs.
1940	Champion, 6 Cyl.	6–3.0 x 3 7/8	164.3	6.50	21.6	78 @ 4000	....	128 @ 1600
	Commander, 6 Cyl.	6–3 5/16 x 4 3/8	226.0	6.00	26.3	90 @ 3400	....	174 @ 1200
	President, 8 Cyl.	8–3 1/16 x 4 1/4	250.0	6.00	30.0	110 @ 3600	....	195 @ 2000
1941	Champion, 6 Cyl.	6–3.0 x 4.0	169.0	6.50	21.6	80 @ 4000	....	134 @ 2000
	Commander, 6 Cyl.	6–3 5/16 x 4 3/8	226.2	6.50	26.3	94 @ 3600	....	176 @ 1600
	President, 8 Cyl.	8–3 1/16 x 4 1/4	250.4	6.50	30.0	117 @ 4000	....	200 @ 2400
1942 to 48	Champion, 6 Cyl.	6–3.0 x 4.0	169.6	6.50	21.6	80 @ 4000	....	134 @ 2000
	Commander, 6 Cyl.	6–3 5/16 x 4 3/8	226.2	6.50	26.3	94 @ 3600	....	176 @ 1600
	President, 8 Cyl.	8–3 1/16 x 4 1/4	250.4	6.50	30.0	117 @ 4000	....	200 @ 2400
1947	Comm., Land Cruiser 6 Cyl.	6–3 5/16 x 4 3/8	226.2	6.50	26.3	94 @ 3600	....	176 @ 1600
1948	Comm., Land Cruiser, 6 Cyl.	6–3 5/16 x 4 3/8	226.2	6.50	26.3	94 @ 3600	....	176 @ 1600
1949	Champion, 6 Cyl.	6–3.0 x 4.0	169.6	6.50	21.6	80 @ 4000	....	134 @ 2000
	Comm., Land Cruiser, 6 Cyl.	6–3 5/16 x 4 3/8	226.2	6.50	26.3	94 @ 3600	....	176 @ 1600
1950	Champion, 6 Cyl.	6–3.0 x 4.0	169.6	7.00	21.6	85 @ 4000	....	138 @ 2400
	Comm., Land Cruiser, 6 Cyl.	6–3 5/16 x 4 3/4	245.6	7.00	26.3	102 @ 3200	....	205 @ 1200
1951	Champion, 6 Cyl.	6–3.0 x 4.0	169.6	7.00	21.6	85 @ 4000	....	138 @ 2400
	Comm., Land Cruiser, 8 Cyl.	8–3 3/8 x 3 1/4	232.6	7.00	36.4	120 @ 4000	....	190 @ 2000
1952–53	6 Cyl.	6–3 x 4	169.6	7.00	21.60	85 @ 4000	....	138 @ 2400
	8 Cyl.	V8–3 3/8 x 3 1/4	232.6	7.00	36.40	120 @ 4000	....	190 @ 2000

Tension Wrench Specifications

Year	Model	Cylinder Head Lbs.–Ft.	Cylinder Head Thread	Spark Plug Lbs.–Ft.	Spark Plug Thread	Connecting Rod Bolts or Nuts Lbs.–Ft.	Connecting Rod Bolts or Nuts Thread	Main Bearing Bolt Lbs.–Ft	Main Bearing Bolt Thread	Flywheel Bolts Lbs.–Ft.	Flywheel Bolts Thread	Vibration Damper Bolts Lbs.–Ft.	Vibration Damper Bolts Thread
1940–41	Champion	50–54	....	25–30	14 mm	25–27	11/32–24	88–93	1/2–13	....	....	....	....
	Comm. and Pres.	80–85	7/16–14	25–30	14 mm	52–54	3/8–24	88–93	1/2–13	....	....	....	....
1942 to 46	Champion	46–50	7/16–14	25–30	14 mm	28–32	11/32–24	88–93	1/2–13	33–35	3/8–24	130–140	11/16–16
	Commander	80–85	7/16–14	25–30	14 mm	52–54	3/8–24	88–93	1/2–13	33–35	3/8–24	160–170	7/8–14
	President	80–85	7/16–14	25–30	14 mm	52–54	3/8–24	88–93	1/2–13	33–35	3/8–24	160–170	7/8–14
1947–48	6G, 7G, Champion	46–50	7/16–14	25–30	14 mm	28–32	11/32–24	88–93	1/2–13	33–35	3/8–24	130–140	11/16–16
	14A, 15A, Commander	80–85	7/16–14	25–30	14 mm	52–54	3/8–24	88–93	1/2–13	33–35	3/8–24	160–170	7/8–14
1949–50	Champion	46–50	7/16–14	25–30	14 mm	28–32	11/32–24	88–93	1/2–13	33–35	3/8–24	130–140	11/16–16
	Commander	80–85	7/16–14	25–30	14 mm	52–54	3/8–24	88–93	1/2–13	33–35	3/8–24	160–170	7/8–14
1951 to 53	Champion	46–50	7/16–24	25–30	14 mm	28–32	11/32–24	88–93	1/2–13	33–35	3/8–24	130–140	11/16–16
	Commander	46–50	7/16–24	25–30	14 mm	52–54	3/8–24	88–93	1/2–13	33–35	3/8–24	130–140	11/16–16

Engine Overhaul Specifications

Year	Model	PISTONS				RING GAP CLEARANCES (Maximum)				PISTON PIN		ROD BEARINGS		
		Removed From	Piston Skirt Clearances (Maximum)											
			Top	Bottom	Limit	Top Ring	Second Ring	Third Ring	Oil Ring	Type	Fit	Oil Clearance	Wear Limit	Side Play
1940	Champion, 6 Cyl.	A	.0015	.001	.006	.017	.017	....	.017	LR	Push	.0005–.002	.003	.005–.008
	Commander, 6 Cyl.	A	.002	.0015	.006	.017	.017	....	.015	LR	Push	.0005–.002	.003	.005–.009
	President, 8 Cyl.	A	.002	.0015	.006	.018	.018	....	.021	LR	Push	.00075–.00275	.003	.005–.010
1941	Champion, 6 Cyl.	A	.0015	.001	.006	.017	.017	....	.017	LR	Push	.0005–.002	.003	.005–.009
	Commander, 6 Cyl.	A	.002	.0015	.006	.014	.014	....	.014	LR	Push	.0005–.002	.003	.005–.009
	President, 8 Cyl.	A	.002	.0015	.006	.023	.023	....	.021	LR	Push	.00075–.00275	.003	.005–.010
1942	Champion, 6 Cyl.	A	.0015	.001	.006	.017	.017	....	.017	LR	Push	.00052–.002	.003	.005–.009
	Commander, 6 Cyl.	A	.002	.0015	.006	.014	.014	....	.014	LR	Push	.00052–.002	.003	.005–.009
	President, 8 Cyl.	A	.002	.0015	.006	.023	.023	....	.021	LR	Push	.00075–.00275	.003	.005–.010
1946	Skyway, Champion, 6 Cyl.	A	.0015	.001	.006	.017	.017	....	.017	LR	Push	.0005–.002	.003	.005–.009
1947	Champion, 6 Cyl.	A	.0015	.001	.006	.017	.017	....	.017	LR	Push	.0005–.002	.003	.005–.009
	Commander, 6 Cyl.	A	.002	.0015	.006	.014	.014	....	.014	LR	Push	.0005–.002	.003	.005–.009
	Land Cruiser, 6 Cyl.	A	.002	.0015	.006	.014	.014	....	.014	LR	Push	.0005–.002	.003	.005–.009
1948	Champion, 6 Cyl.	A	.0015	.001	.006	.017	.017	....	.017	LR	Push	.0005–.002	.003	.005–.009
	Comm., Land Cruiser, 6 Cyl.	A	.002	.0015	.006	.014	.014	....	.014	LR	Push	.0005–.002	.003	.005–.009
1949	Champion, 6 Cyl.	A	.0015	.001	.006	.017	.017	....	.017	LR	Push	.0005–.002	.003	.005–.009
	Comm., Land Cruiser, 6 Cyl.	A	.002	.0015	.006	.014	.014	....	.014	LR	Push	.0005–.002	.003	.005–.009
1950	Champion, 6 Cyl.	A	.0015	.001	.006	.017	.017	....	.017	LR	Push	.0005–.002	.003	.005–.009
	Comm., Land Cruiser, 6 Cyl.	A	.002	.0015	.006	.014	.014	....	.014	LR	Push	.0005–.002	.003	.005–.009
1951	Champion, 6 Cyl.	A	.0015	.001	.006	.017	.017	....	.017	LR	Push	.00005–.002	.003	.005–.009
	Comm., Land Cruiser, 8 Cyl.	A	....	....	.006	.016	.016	....	.016	LR	Push	.00005–.002	.003	.007–.012
1952	12G, 6 Cyl.	A	....	....	....	.017	.017	....	.017	LR	.0003	.00005–.00215	.003	.005–.009
	3H, 8 Cyl.	A	....	....	....	.016	.016	....	.016	LR	.0003	.00005–.00215	.003	.007–.012
1953	14G	A	....	....	....	.017	.017	....	.017	LR	.0003	.00215	.003	.005–.009
	4H	A	....	....	....	.016	.016	....	.016	LR	.0003	.00215	.003	.007–.012

LR—Locked in rod. A—Above. †—Center cam gear mark between crank gear marks.

Dimensions of Valves

Year	Model	Overall Length		Head Diameter		Seat Angle (deg.)		Stem Diameter		Key Type	O.D. of Seat Insert	
		Inlet	Exhaust	Inlet	Exhaust	Inlet	Exhaust	Inlet	Exhaust		Inlet	Exhaust
1940 to 42	2G, 3G, 4G	4.343	4.343	1.343	1.281	45	45	.312	.312	horseshoe	....	....
	10A, 11A, 12A	5.218	5.218	1.468	1.281	45	45	.343	.343	split lock	....	....
	6C, 7C, 8C	5.218	5.218	1.406	1.281	45	45	.343	.343	split lock	....	....
1946	5G	4.343	4.343	1.343	1.281	45	45	.312	.312	horseshue	....	....
1947	6G	4.343	4.343	1.343	1.281	45	45	.312	.312	horseshoe	....	....
	14A	5.218	5.218	1.468	1.281	45	45	.343	.343	split lock	....	....
1948–49	7G, 8G	4.343	4.343	1.343	1.281	45	45	.312	.312	horseshoe	....	....
	15A, 16A	5.218	5.218	1.468	1.281	45	45	.343	.343	split lock	....	....
1950	9G	4.344	4.344	1.344	1.281	45	45	.312	.312	horseshoe	....	....
	17A	5.219	5.219	1.469	1.281	45	45	.344	.344	split lock	....	....
1951	10G	4.344	4.344	1.344	1.281	45	45	.312	.312	horseshoe	....	....
	V8, H	5.172	5.172	1.406	1.281	45	45	.344	.344	split lock	....	....
1952	12G, 6 cyl.	4.34375	4.34375	1.34375	1.40625	45	45	.3125	.3125	....	....	....
	3H, 8 cyl.	5.171875	5.171875	1.28125	1.28125	45	45	.34375	.34375	....	....	....
1953	14G, 6 cyl.	4.34375	4.34375	1.34375	1.40625	45	45	.3125	.3125	....	....	....
	4H, 8 cyl.	5.171875	5.171875	1.40625	1.28125	45	45	.34375	.34375	....	....	....

and Wear Limit Table

CRANKSHAFT		VALVES									OPERATING OIL PRESSURE			
Main Bearing Oil Clearance	Shaft End Play	Spring Tension (Maximum) Inlet	Spring Tension (Maximum) Exhaust	Spring Tension (Maximum) Low Limit	Guide Clearance	Seat Angle Inlet	Seat Angle Exhaust	Valve Timing, Inlet Valve Opens (Deg.)	Camshaft Drive	Gear Marks	Pounds At M.P.H.	Low Limit§	Model	Year
.0005–.0025	.005–.009	94@1 11/32	94@1 11/32	84	.001–.0035	45°	45°	15B	Gear	†	40@30	25	Champion, 6 Cyl.	1940
.0005–.0025	.003–.006	135@1.75	135@1.75	120	.001–.003	45°	45°	15B	Gear	†	40@30	25	Commander, 6 Cyl.	
.0001–.0003	.003–.006	135@1.75	135@1.75	120	.001–.003	45°	45°	15B	Gear	†	60@30	35	President, 8 Cyl.	
.0005–.0025	.003–.006	94@1 11/32	94@1 11/32	84	.001–.0035	45°	45°	15B	Gear	†	40@30	25	Champion, 6 Cyl.	1941
.0005–.0025	.003–.006	135@1 3/4	135@1 3/4	120	.0015–.0035	45°	45°	15B	Gear	†	40@30	25	Commander, 6 Cyl.	
.0005–.0025	.003–.006	135@1.75	135@1.75	120	.001–.003	45°	45°	15B	Gear	†	40@30	25	President, 8 Cyl.	
.0005–.0025	.003–.006	94@1 11/32	94@1 11/32	84	.001–.0035	45°	45°	15B	Gear	†	40@30	25	Champion, 6 Cyl.	1942
.0005–.0025	.003–.006	135@1 3/4	135@1 3/4	120	.0015–.0035	45°	45°	15B	Gear	†	40@30	25	Commander, 6 Cyl.	
.0005–.00225	.003–.006	135@1 3/4	135@1 3/4	120	.001–.003	45°	45°	15B	Gear	†	40@30	25	President, 8 Cyl.	
.0005–.0025	.003–.006	94@1 11/32	94@1 11/32	84	.001–.0035	45°	45°	15B	Gear	†	40@30	25	Skyway, Champ., 6 Cyl.	1946
.0005–.0025	.003–.006	94@1 11/32	94@1 11/32	84	.0015–.0035	45°	45°	15B	Gear	†	40@30	25	Champion, 6 Cyl.	1947
.0005–.0025	.003–.006	135@1 3/4	135@1 3/4	120	.0015–.0035	45°	45°	15B	Gear	†	40@30	25	Commander, 6 Cyl.	
.0005–.0025	.003–.006	135@1 3/4	135@1 3/4	120	.0015–.0035	45°	45°	15B	Gear	†	40@30	25	Land Cruiser, 6 Cyl.	
.0005–.0025	.003–.006	85@1 7/16	85@1 7/16	75	.0015–.0035	45°	45°	15B	Gear	†	40@30	25	Champion, 6 Cyl.	1948
.0005–.0025	.003–.006	135@1 3/4	135@1 3/4	120	.0015–.0035	45°	45°	15B	Gear	†	40@30	25	Comm., Land Cruis., 6 Cyl.	
.0005–.0025	.003–.006	85@1 7/16	85@1 7/16	75	.0015–.0035	45°	45°	15B	Gear	†	40@30	25	Champion, 6 Cyl.	1949
.0005–.0025	.003–.006	135@1 3/4	135@1 3/4	120	.0015–.0035	45°	45°	15B	Gear	†	40@30	25	Comm., Land Cruis., 6 Cyl.	
.0005–.0025	.003–.006	103@1 5/16	103@1 5/16	93	.0015–.0035	45°	45°	15B	Gear	†	40@30	25	Champion, 6 Cyl.	1950
.0006–.0027	.003–.006	135@1 3/4	135@1 3/4	120	.0015–.0035	45°	45°	15B	Gear	†	40@30	25	Comm., Land Cruis., 6 Cyl.	
.0005–.0025	.003–.006	103@1 5/16	103@1 5/16	93	.0015–.0035	45°	45°	15B	Gear	†	40@30	25	Champion, 6 Cyl.	1951
.0006–.0027	003–.006	135@1 3/4	135@1 3/4	125	.0015–.0035	45°	45°	11B	Gear	†	40@30	25	Comm., Land Cruis., 8 Cyl.	
.0005–.0025	.003–.006	103@1 5/16	103@1 5/16	......	.0015–.0035	45°	45°	15B	Gear	......	40@30	......	12G, 6 Cyl.	1952
.0006–.0027	.003–.006	169@1 43/64	169@1 43/64	......	.0015–.0035	45°	45°	11B	Gear	......	40@30	......	3H, 8 Cyl.	
.0005–.0025	.003–.006	103@1 5/16	103@1 5/16	......	.0035	45°	45°	15B	Gear	......	40@30	......	14G	1953
.0006–.0027	.003–.006	169@1 43/64	169@1/64 43	......	.0035	45°	45°	11B	Gear	......	40@30	......	4H	

§—Car may be operated safely at lower oil pressures but low pressure indicates malfunction which should be corrected.

Pistons and Piston Pins

		PISTONS				PISTON PINS		
Year	Model	Diameter	Material	Type	No. of Rings	Length	Diameter	How Held
1940 to 42	2G, 3G, 4G	3	Alum.	Ss	3	2 5/8	.750	R
	10A, 11A, 12A	3.3125	Alum.	Ts, C	3	2 7/8	.875	R
	6C, 7C, 8C	3.0625	Alum.	Ts, C	3	2 5/8	.875	R
1946 to 48	5G,6G,7G	3	Alum.	....	3	2 5/8	.750	R
	14A, 15A	3.1875	Lynite	Ts	3	2 7/8	.875	R
1949–50	8G, 9G	3	Lynite	Ts	3	2 5/8	.750	R
	16A, 17A	3.3125	Lynite	Ts	3	2 7/8	.875	R
1951	10G	3	Alum. Alloy	Ts	3	2 5/8	.750	R
	V8, H	3.375	Alum. Alloy	Ts	3	2 7/8	.875	R
1952	12G, 6 cyl.	3	Lynite	C,Ts	3	2.625	.75	R
	3H, 8 cyl.	3.375	Lynite	C,Ts	3	2.875	.875	R
1953	14G	3	Lynite	C,Ts	3	2.625	.75	R
	3H	3.375	Lynite	C,Ts	3	2.875	.875	R

Ss—Split skirt. C—Cam ground. Ts—"T" slot.

Crankshaft Bearing Journal Sizes

Year	Model	Connecting Rod Journals		Main Bearing Journals				
		Diameter	Length	No. 1 Diameter	No. 2 Diameter	No. 3 Diameter	No. 4 Diameter	No. 5 Diameter
1940 to 47	2G, 3G, 4G, 5G, 6G	1.812	1.125	2.437	2.437	2.437	2.437	...
	10A, 11A, 12A, 14A	2.187	1.375	2.500	2.500	2.500	2.500	...
	6C, 7C, 8C	1.875	1.187	2.343	2.343	2.343	2.343	*2.343
1948 to 50	7G, 8G, 9G	1.812	1.125	2.437	2.437	2.437	2.437	...
	15A, 16A, 17A	2.187	1.376	2.875	2.875	2.875	2.875	...
1951	10G	1.812	1.125	2.437	2.437	2.437	2.437	...
	H-Commander	2.000	1.938	2.500	2.500	2.500	2.500	*2.500
1952	12G, 6 cyl.	1.8125	...	2.4375	2.4375	2.4375	2.4375	...
	3H, 8 cyl.	2.000	...	2.50	2.50	2.50	2.50	2.50
1953	14G, Champion	1.8125	...	2.4375–1.3125	2.4375–1.375	2.4375–1.375	2.4375–1.78125	...
	4H, V8	2.0	...	2.5–1.3125	2.5–1.125	2.5–1.125	2.5–1.125	2.5–1.78125

*—Bearings 6, 7, 8, 9 same as number 5.

Engine Tune-Up Specifications

Year	Model	Spark Plugs		Distributor					Operating Tappet Clearance			
		Type	Gap	Point Gap	Cam Dwell (Deg.)	Ignition Timing (Deg.)	Ignition Timing Mark and Location	Compression Pressure at R.P.M.	Inlet	Exhaust	Carburetor Fuel Float Height	Minimum Engine Idle Speed at R.P.M.
1940	Champion, 6 Cyl.	J-8	.025	.020	35	1B	IGN flywh.	105@150	.016	.016	¼″ float	600
	Commander, 6 Cyl.	J-8	.025	.020	35	2B	IGN dmpr.	105@150	.016	.016	⅝″ fuel	450
	President, 8 Cyl.	J-8	.025	.020	33	TC	TC dmpr.	105@150	.016	.016	3/16″ fuel	450
1941	Champion, 6 Cyl.	J-8	.025	.020	35	2B	IGN flywh.	105@150	.016	.016	5/16″ float	525
	Commander, 6 Cyl.	J-7	.025	.020	35	2B	IGN dmpr.	105@150	.016	.016	⅝″ float	525
	President, 8 Cyl.	J-7	.025	.020	34½	TC	TC dmpr.	105@150	.016	.016	⅝″ fuel	450
1942	Champion, 6 Cyl.	J-7	.025	.020	35	2B	IGN flywh.	105@550	.016	.016	5/16″ float	525
	Commander, 6 Cyl.	J-7	.025	.020	35	2B	IGN dmpr.	105@150	.016	.016	⅝″ float	525
	President, 8 Cyl.	J-7	.025	.020	34	TC	TC dmpr.	105@150	.016	.016	⅝″ float	450
1946	Skyway, Champion, 6 Cyl.	J-7	.025	.020	35	2B	IGN dmpr.	105@150	.016	.016	¼″ float	...
1947	Champion, 6 Cyl.	J-7	.025	.020	35	2B	IGN dmpr.	105@150	.016	.016	¼″ float	7–8 mph
	Commander, 8 Cyl.	J-7	.025	.020	35	2B	IGN dmpr.	105@150	.016	.016	⅝″ float	7–8 mph
	Land Cruiser, 8 Cyl.	J-7	.025	.020	35	2B	IGN dmpr.	105@150	.016	.016	⅝″ float	7–8 mph
1948	Champion, 6 Cyl.	J-7	.27½	.020	38	2B	IGN dmpr.	105@150	.016	.016	⅜″ float	7–8 mph
	Comm., Land Cruis., 8 Cyl.	J-7	.0275	.020	38	2B	IGN dmpr.	105@150	.016	.016	⅝″ float	7–8 mph
1949	Champion, 6 Cyl.	J-7	.027½	.020	38	2B	IGN dmpr.	105@150	.016	.016	⅜″ float	7–8 mph
	Comm., Land Cruis., 8 Cyl.	J-7	.027½	.020	38	2B	IGN dmpr.	105@150	.016	.016	⅝″ float	7–8 mph†
1950	Champion, 6 Cyl.	J-7	.027½	.020	38–40	2B	IGN dmpr.	120@150	.016	.016	⅜″ float	7–8 mph†
	Comm., Land Cruis., 8 Cyl.	J-7	.027½	.020	31–37	2B	IGN dmpr.	120@150	.016	.016	⅝″ float	7–8 mph†
1951	Champion, 6 Cyl.	J-7	.027½	.020	38–40	2B	IGN dmpr.	120@150	.016	.016	⅜″ float	7–8 mph†
	Comm., Land Cruis., 8 Cyl.	H-8	.0375	.018	22–29	8B	IGN dmpr.	120@150	.014–.016	.014–.016	⅝″ float	7–8 mph†
1952	12G, 6 Cyl.	Ch-J7	.025	.020	40	2B	Dmpr.	...	.016C	.016C	⅜″	550
	3H, 8 Cyl.	Ch-H8	.035	.015	29	8B	Dmpr.	...	.016C	.016C	...	550
1953	14G, 6 Cyl.	Ch-J7	.025	.020	40	2B	Dmpr.	...	.016C	.016C	...	550
	4H, V8	Ch-H10	.035	.015	34	4B	Dmpr.	...	.022H	.022H	...	550

†—Auto-Matic transmission in neutral position (550 R.P.M.). TC—Top center. B—Before top center.

Piston Ring Dimensions

Year	Model	Cylinder Bore	TOP RING Width	TOP RING Gap	TOP RING Depth	SECOND RING Width	SECOND RING Gap	SECOND RING Depth	THIRD RING Width	THIRD RING Gap	THIRD RING Depth	OIL RING Width	OIL RING Gap	OIL RING Depth
1940	2G	3	3/32	.012	.150	1/8	.012	.135	5/32	.012	.135	......	......	......
	10A	3 5/16	1/8	.012	.145	1/8	.012	.145	3/16	.011	.145	......	......	......
	6C	3 1/16	1/8	.015	.135	1/8	.015	.135	3/16	.017	.125	......	......	......
1941–50	3G, 4G, 5G, 6G, 7G, 8G, 9G	3	3/32	.012	.150	1/8	.012	.135	5/32	.012	.135	......	......	......
	11A, 12A, 14A, 15A, 16A, 17A	3 5/16	3/32	.012	.155	3/32	.012	.155	3/16	.012	.150	......	......	......
	7C	3 1/16	1/8	.018	.135	1/8	.018	.135	3/16	.017	.125	......	......	......
1951	10G	3	3/32	.012	.150	1/8	.012	.135	5/32	.012	.139	......	......	......
	V8, H	3 3/8	5/64	.012	.164	5/64	.012	.164	3/16	.012	.138	......	......	......
1952	12G, 6 Cyl.	3	3/32	.012	.1635	1/8	.012	.1485	5/32	.012	.1685	......	......	......
	3H, 8 Cyl.	3 3/8	5/64	.012	.18425	5/64	.012	.18425	3/16	.012	.19165	......	......	......
1953	14G, 6 Cyl.	3	3/32	.012	.150	1/8	.012	.135	5/32	.012	.139	......	......	......
	4H, V8	3 3/8	5/64	.012	.164	5/64	.012	.164	3/16	.012	.1355	......	......	......

Brake Data

Year	Model	Make	Lining Type	R=Riveted B=Bonded	Drum Diameter	Lining Length	Lining Width	Lining Thickness	Clearance Toe	Clearance Heel
1940	2G	Loc	WM	CE	9	17 3/4	1 3/4	3/16	.010	.005
	10A	Loc	WM	CE	11	19 11/16	2	3/16	.010	.005
	6C	Loc	WM	CE	11	19 11/16	2 1/4	3/16	.010	.005
1941–42	3G, 4G	Loc	M	Com	9	17 3/4	1 3/4	3/16	.010	.005
	11A	Loc	M	Com	11	19 11/16	2	3/16	.010	.005
	7C, 8C	Loc	M	Com	11	19 11/16	2 1/4	3/16	.010	.005
1946–47	5G, 6G	WE	M	Com	9	18	1 3/4	3/16	.010	.005
1947	14A	WE	M	Com	11	22 1/4	2	3/16	SC	SC
1948 to 50	Champ.	WE	M	Com	9	18 1/2	2	3/16	SC	SC
	Comm.	WE	M	Com	11	22 1/4	2	3/16	SC	SC
1951	10G	WE	M	Com	9	18 1/2	2	3/16	SC	SC
	V8, H	WE	M	Com	11–*9	22 1/4–*18 1/2	2	3/16	SC	SC
1952	12G, 6 Cyl.	......	M	R	9	18	2	3/16	†	†
	3H, 8 Cyl.	......	M	R	11–*9	22 1/8–*18	2	3/16	†	†
1953	14G, 6 Cyl.	......	M	R	9	18	2	3/16	......	......
	4H, V8	......	M	R	11–*9	22 3/4–*18	2	3/16	†	†

*—Rear. SC—Self centering. †—Pri.—.006-.008. Sec.—Self adjusting.

Cooling System

CAR AND YEAR	MODEL	Capacity Qts.	Quarts of Methanol Base Anti-Freeze (For Protection to Temperature Shown Below) 3	4	5	6	7	8	9	Quarts of Ethylene Glycol (For Protection to Temperature Shown Below) 3	4	5	6	7	8	9	Quarts of Denatured Alcohol—188 Proof (For Protection to Temperature Shown Below) 3	4	5	6	7	8	9
1939-40	Champion	10 1/2	0	–18	–40	....	....	....	....	8	–6	–23	–47	....	....	....	10	0	–10	–20	–30	....	....
1939-40	Commander	14 1/2	11	1	–12	–27	–44	....	....	16	8	0	–12	–26	–43	....	....	10	0	–10	–20	–30	....
1941	Champion	10	–5	–27	–53	....	....	....	....	4	–12	–34	–62	....	....	....	0	–10	–20	–30	....	....	....
1941-50	Commander	13	7	–7	–23	–43	....	....	....	13	3	–9	–25	–45	....	....	10	0	–10	–20	–30	....	....
1941-42	Eight	15	11	1	–12	–27	–44	....	....	16	8	0	–12	–26	–43	....	....	10	0	–10	–20	–30	....
1942-46	Champion	10 1/2	0	–18	–40	....	....	....	....	8	–6	–23	–47	....	....	....	10	0	–10	–20	–30	....	....
1947-53	Champion	10	–5	–27	–53	....	....	....	....	4	–12	–34	–62	....	....	....	10	0	–10	–20	–30	....	....
1951-53	Commander	17 1/4	15	6	–4	–16	–29	–45	....	18	12	5	–4	–14	–27	–42	....	10	0	....	–10	–20	–30

STUDEBAKER SPECIFICATIONS

Distributors

Year	Model	Distributor Model Number	Cam Angle (deg.)	Direction of Rotation C–Clockwise CC–Counter Clockwise at Cam End	Breaker Arm Spring Tension	Breaker Point Gap (inches)	Engine R.P.M. when Cent. Advance Starts	Max. Cent. Advance in Engine Deg. at Stated Engine R.P.M.	Vacuum in (inches) of Mercury at which Vacuum Unit Starts	Max. Advance in Engine Deg. at Stated Vacuum	Vacuum Unit Number
1940	2G, 6 cyl..........	IGW-4131	35	CC	17–20	.018–.022	800	14@2800	4	18@15	VC-4011
	....	IGW-4144	35	CC	17–20	.018–.022	800	14@2800	4	18@15	VC-4011
	10A, 6 cyl..........	IGW-4101	35	CC	17–20	.018–.022	800	20@2800	3	12@12	VC-4004
	....	IGW-4111	35	C	17–20	.018–.022	800	20@2800	3	12@12	VC-4004
	6C, 8 cyl..........	662-M	33	C	19–23	.018–.024	600	29@3600	5 to 7	12@11 to 14	681-S
1941	3G, 6 cyl..........	IGW-4154	35	CC	17–20	.018–.022	800	14@2800	4	18@14.75	VC-4011
	7C, 8 cyl..........	IGH-4029	32	C	17–20	.010–.020	600	27@3600	3	12@12	VC-4012
	11A, 6 cyl..........	IGW-4101	35	CC	17–20	.018–.022	800	20@2800	3	12@12	VC-4004
1942	4G, 6 cyl..........	IGW-4154	35	CC	17–20	.018–.022	800	14@2800	4	18@14.75	VC-4011
	....	IGC-4801	38	CC	17–20	.018–.022	800	14@2800	4	18@14.75	VC-4011
	12A, 6 cyl..........	IGW-4101	35	CC	17–20	.018–.022	800	20@2800	3	6@12	VC-4004
	....	IGC-4802	38	CC	17–20	.018–.024	800	20@2800	3	12@12	VC-4004
	8C, 8 cyl..........	IGH-4101	36	C	17–20	.010–.020	600	27@3600	3	12@12	VC-4012
1946	5G, 6 cyl..........	IGC-4801	38	CC	17–20	.018–.022	800	14@2800	4	18@14.75	VC-4011
1947–50	6G, 7G, 8G, 9G, 6 cyl...	IGC-4805	38	CC	17–20	.018–.022	800	14@2800	4	18@14.75	VC-4011
	14A, 15A, 16A, 6 cyl.....	IGC-4802	38	CC	17–20	.018–.024	800	20@2800	3	12@12	VC-4004
1950	17A, 8 cyl..........	1110220	....	CC	17–21	.018–.024	800	22@2800	3 to 5	9 to 14	1116052
1951	10G, 6 cyl..........	IAT-4001	39	CC	17–20	.018–.022	800	14@2800	4	18	....
	H, V8..........	1110822	25½	CC	17–21	.016	800	28@2600	5	16	....
1952	12G, 6 cyl..........	IAT-4010	38–40	CC	17–20	.020	800	14@2800	4	18@12	....
	3H, 8 cyl..........	1110826	22–29	CC	17–21	.013–.018	600	30@2900	4–6	16@11½	....
1953	Champion, 6 cyl..........	IAT-4010	38–40	C	17–20	.020	800	14@2800	4	20@12	....
	Commander, 8 cyl..........	1110839	28–34	C	17–21	.013–.018	600	32@2900	4–6	18@10½	....

Generators

Year	Model	Generator Number	Field Current at 6 Volts (amps.)	Maximum Safe Output: Volts	Maximum Safe Output: Amperes	Maximum Safe Output: R.P.M.	Brush Spring Tension (oz.)	Voltage Regulator Number
1940	2G..........	GEA-4804-A	1.3–1.5	8.0	32	1275	64–68	VRP-4004-A
	10A..........	GEA-4803-A	1.3–1.5	8.0	32	1275	64–68	VRP-4004-A
	6C..........	1102671	1.75–1.9	8.0	30	1750	25	1118202
1941 to 51	All, Champions..........	GDZ-4804-A	1.3–1.5	8.0	35	2000	35–53	VRP-4004-F
	11A..........	GEB-4806-D	1.3–1.5	8.0	32	1275	64–68	VRP-4004-C
	7C, 8C, 14A, 15A, 16A..........	GDZ-4805-A	1.3–1.5	8.0	35	2000	35–53	VRP-4004-F
1950	17A..........	1102728	1.75–1.9	8.0	30	1750	25	1118380
1951	V8, H..........	1102700	1.90–2.05	8.0	40	1900	25	1118392
1952	12G, 6 cyl..........	GGW-4801-A	....	....	....	....	....	VBE-6101-A
	3H, 8 cyl..........	1102778						1118730
1953	14G..........	GGW-4801-C	....	6.9	45	2500	....	VBE-6101-A
	4H..........	1102778	....	6.98	45	2400	....	1118730

Voltage Regulators

Year	Model	Regulator Number	Grounded P–Positive N–Negative	Voltage Control: Air Gap Points Closed	Voltage Control: Voltage Setting Hot	Current Control: Air Gap Points Closed	Current Control: Current Set Hot	Cut-Out Relay: Point Gap	Cut-Out Relay: Air Gap	Cut-Out Relay: Closing Volt
1940	2G, 10A..........	VRP-4004-A	P	.052	7.2	.052	34–36	.015	.034	6.4–7.0
	6C..........	1118202	P	.070	7.2	.082	32–40	.015	.034	5.9–6.8

Voltage Regulators—*continued*

Year	Model	Regulator Number	Grounded P-Position N-Negative	Voltage Control: Air Gap Points Closed	Voltage Control: Voltage Setting Hot	Current Control: Air Gap Points Closed	Current Control: Current Set Hot	Cut-Out Relay: Point Gap	Cut-Out Relay: Air Gap	Cut-Out Relay: Closing Volt
1941	3G, 7C, 11A	VRP-4004-F	P	.052	7.2	.052	34–36	.015	.034	6.4–7.0
	11A-Spec.	VRP-4004-C	P	.052	7.2	.052	31–33	.015	.034	6.4–7.0
1942 to 49	All Champions	VRP-4004-F	P	.052	7.2	.052	34–36	.015	.034	6.4–7.0
	All Commanders	VRP-4004-F	P	.052	7.2	.052	34–36	.015	.034	6.4–7.0
1950	9G	VRP-6001-A	P	.050	7.35	.050	34–36	.015	.036	6.4–6.9
	17A	1118380	P	.075	7.4	.075	36	.020	.020	6.40
1951	10G		P	.050	7.35	.050	40	.015	.036	6.4–6.9
	H, V8 Commander	1118392	P	.075	7.4	.075	40	.020	.020	6.40
1952	12G, 6 cyl.	VBE-6101-A			7.0–7.7		44–46			6.3–6.9
	3H, 8 cyl.	1118730			7.15–8.05		44–46			6.05–6.98
1953	14G	VBE-6101-A			7.0–7.7		44–46			6.3–6.9
	4H	1118730			7.15–8.05		44–46			6.05–6.98

Starters

Year	Model	Unit Model Number	Spring Tension (oz.)	STARTER Lock Test: Volts	Lock Test: Amperes	Lock Test: Torque, (lbs. ft.)	No Load: Volts	No Load: Amperes	No Load: R.P.M.	Direction of Rotation Viewed from Drive End C-Clockwise CC-Counter-clockwise
1941	3G	MZ-4090	42–53	2.0	280	4.4	5.0	68	4000	C
	11A	MAW-4020	42–53	2.0	335	6	5.0	65	4300	C
	7C	MAX-4044	42–53	2.0	410	8	5.0	65	4900	C
1942	4G	MZ-4090	42–53	2.0	280	4.4	5.0	68	4000	C
	12A	MAW-4020	42–53	2.0	335	6	5.0	65	4300	C
		MAW-4028	42–53	2.0	335	6	5.0	65	4300	C
	8C	MAX-4051	42–53	2.0	410	8	5.0	65	4900	C
1946	5G	MZ-4090	42–53	2.0	280	4.4	5.0	68	4000	C
	14A	MAW-4020	42–53	2.0	335	6	5.0	65	4300	C
		MAW-4020-A	42–53	2.0	335	6	5.0	65	4300	C
		MCH-4001	42–53	2.0	335	6	5.0	65	4300	C
1947	6G	MZ-4136	42–53	2.0	280	4.4	5.0	68	4000	C
		MZ-4151	42–53	2.0	280	4.4	5.0	68	4000	C
1948–49	7G, 8G	MZ-4151	42–53	2.0	280	4.4	5.0	68	4000	C
	15A, 16A	MCH-4001	42–53	2.0	335	6	5.0	65	4300	C
1950	9G	MZ-4151	42–53	2.0	280	4.4	5.0	68	4000	C
		MZ-4157	42–53	4.0	560	11.8	5.50	70	4300	C
	17A	1107084	24–28	3.4	525	12	5.7	65	5000	C
1951	10G	MZ-4157	42–53	4.0	560	11.8	5.50	70	4300	C
	V8, H	1107089	24–28	3.4	525	12	5.7	65	5000	C
1952	12G, 6 cyl.	MZ-4157	42–53	4	560	11.8	5.5	70	4300	C
	3H, 8 cyl.	1107115	24–28	3.4	525	12	5.7	65	5000	C
	Automatic Transmission	1107116	24–28	3.4	525	12	5.7	65	5000	C
1953	14G	MZ-4157	24–28	4	560	11.8	5.5	70	4300	C
	4H	1107115	24–28	3.4	525	12	5.7	65	5000	C
	Automatic Transmission	1107116	24–28	3.4	525	12	5.7	65	5000	C

Front Wheel Alignment

Year	Model	Caster (deg.)	Camber (deg.)	King Pin Inclination (deg.)	Toe-In (inches)	Turning Radius	
						Inner	Outer
1940–41	2G, 3G	1P to 2P	½P	5½	⅛ to 7/32		20
	10A, 11A	¼N to ½P	½P	5½	⅛ to 7/32		20
	6C, 7C	¼N to ¾P	¼P to ¾P	5½	⅛ to 7/32		20
1942–46	4G, 5G	1P to 2P	½P	5½	1/16 to ⅛	23½	20
	12A	¼N to ¾P	½P	5½	1/16 to ⅛	23½	20
	8C	¼N to ¾P	½P	5½	1/16 to ⅛	23½	20
1947	6G	1P to 1½P	½P	5½	1/16 to ⅛	23½	20
	14A	½P to 1P	½P	5½	1/16 to ⅛	23½	20
1948–49	7G, 8G	0 to 1P	¼P to ¾P	5½	1/16 to ⅛	22½	20
	15A, 16A	2P to 3P	¼P to ¾P	5½	1/16 to ⅛	22½	20
1950	9G	0 to 1P	0 to 1P	5¼	1/16 to ⅛	22½	20
	17A	1½P to 2½P	0 to 1P	5¼	1/16 to ⅛	22½	20
1951–52	10G, 12G	1½P to 2½P	0 to 1P	5¼	1/16 to ⅛	22½	20
	H, V8, 3H	1N to 2½N	0 to 1P	5¼	1/16 to ⅛	22½	20
1953	14G, 4H	1¾N to 2½N	0 to 1P	6	1/16 to ⅛	17½	20

Fan, Generator Belts and Radiator Hose

Year	Model	Fan Belt			Generator Belt			Upper Hose			Lower Hose		
		Angle of "V" (deg.)	Length O.C.	Width Max.	Angle of "V" (deg.)	Length O.C.	Width Max.	Type	Inside Diam.	Length	Type	Inside Diam.	Length
1940 to 46	All Champ.	42	38⅜	11/16				straight	1¼	8¼	curved	1½	
1940	10A, 6C	42	47¼	¾				straight	1¼	11½	curved	1¾–2	
1941–42	11A, 12A, 7C, 8C	42	47¼	¾				curved	1¼		curved	1¾–2	
1947 to 51	All Champ.	40	40¾	11/16				straight	1¼	8¼	curved	1½	
1947 to 50	All Comm.	42	43⅛	13/16				curved	1¼		curved	1¾–2	
1951	V8												
1952–53	6 cyl.	44	40½	43/64				curved	1¼		curved	1¼	
	8 cyl.	38	56	⅜				curved	1¼		curved	1¼	

King Pin Specification Chart

Year	Model	KING BOLT			UPPER BUSHING				LOWER BUSHING			
					King Bolt Bushing				King Bolt Bushing			
		Diameter	Length	Bolt Number	Inside Diameter	Outside Diameter	Length	Bushing Number	Inside Diameter	Outside Diameter	Length	Bushing Number
1940	2G, RH, LH	.812	5 25/64	197744	1.127	1.378	1	*196859	1.128	1.253	¾	194402
	6C, 10A	{ 1.250 / 1.187 }	7 13/32	193643	.866	1.190	1 3/32	*194241	1.189	1.315	1¼	194132
1941 to 46	3G, 4G, 5G	1.1		199309	1.127	1.378	1	*196859	1.128	1.253	¾	194402
1941 to 42	11A, 12A	1		199315	.866	1.190	1 3/32	*194241	1.189	1.315	1¼	194132
1947 to 49	14A			51962				*519628				*194241
	15A			523752				*196859				*194241
1947 to 48	6G, 7G			519452				*519476				*196859
1952–53												

*—Needle bearings.

FRONT SUSPENSION

From the service standpoint there are four different kinds of front suspensions used on Studebaker cars built from 1940 through 1953. In order to avoid confusion in this text these suspensions will be listed as first type, second type, third type and fourth type.

FIRST TYPE

The first type, used on Commander and President models built for 1939 and 1940 production, had a single tubular type upper suspension arm which was mounted to the frame by two brackets. The lower end of the knuckle support was attached, through a yoke, to the transverse leaf spring. Lower suspension arm links were used to insure the safety of the front wheel.

SECOND TYPE

The second type front suspension was used on all Champion models up to and including 1946, and Commander and President models built for 1941 and 1942 production. This second type front suspension consisted of a spread type upper suspension arm which was mounted to the frame by two individual brackets. One approximately parallel to a line between the front wheels, the other back considerably farther on the frame. The lower portion of the knuckle support was connected to the transverse leaf spring through a yoke.

Early models of Champion cars did not include a safety link between the frame and the lower suspension arm yoke. Instead these early Champion models had a double main leaf spring, the second main leaf acting as a safety just as surely as a link. The Commander and President models did have a link which would maintain the wheel in alignment if the leaf spring became broken or damaged.

THIRD TYPE

The third type of front suspension, used on all models from 1947 through 1949, consisted of conventional pressed steel type upper and lower suspension arms connected together by a knuckle support which also functioned as a king pin. The spindle turned on needle bearings directly on the knuckle support. On this third type suspension the knuckle support was connected by a yoke to the lower suspension arm and bolted to a trunnion which mounted in the upper suspension arm. A transverse leaf spring having flat ends was used on this suspension. The transverse spring did not connect to the suspension arms at all. The end of the spring simply contacted the plate built into the lower suspension arm.

FOURTH TYPE

The fourth type of suspension used on all Studebaker models from 1950 through 1953 consisted of a pressed steel upper and lower suspension arm, using a coil spring arrangement similar to conventional knee-action cars. On this fourth type suspension the knuckle support acted as a king pin in a manner similar to the third type suspension with this exception. On the fourth type suspension the knuckle support (king pin) is held by a yoke to the upper suspension arm and is bolted through a yoke to the lower suspension arm. On this fourth type front suspension the shock absorber is a direct acting type mounted in the center of the coil spring.

Caster and Camber

In spite of the differences in construction, caster and camber are adjusted, from a service standpoint, in exactly the same manner on the first three types of suspension. Both caster and camber are controlled by the relationship of the shims which mount the upper suspension arm to the frame. Special shims are used back of the mounting bracket between the mounting bracket and the frame.

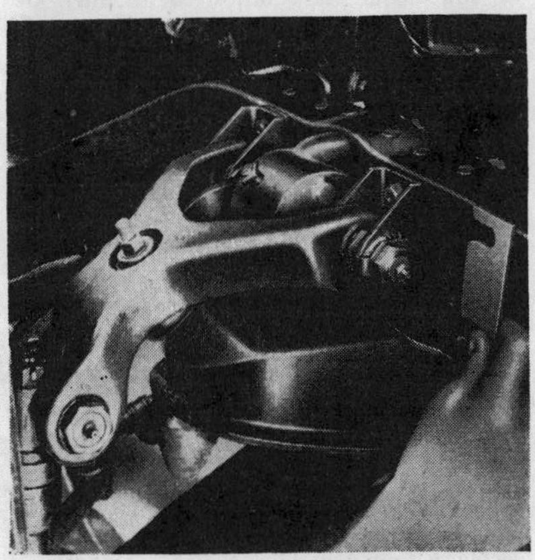

Caster and camber adjustment 1940 thru 1949 all models

To increase caster, remove shims from back of the rear bracket. If all the shims have been removed from the rear bracket and the caster is still not satisfactory, then add shims behind the front bracket. Actually this should never be necessary since if all the shims have been removed from the rear bracket and the caster still is not correct, then there is something bent or twisted in the front suspension, as sufficient number of shims have been placed on the car at assembly to take care of any normal adjustment.

If it is necessary to decrease caster, then the opposite procedure is followed. Shims are added at the back bracket and taken away from the front bracket. On these models caster should always be adjusted first since adjusting caster will have some effect on the camber setting, particularly if it becomes necessary to add or remove shims from the front bracket.

Camber Adjustment

To increase camber on the first three types of front suspension add shims behind both upper suspension arm brackets, (the same thickness behind each).

To decrease camber it will be necessary to remove shims from behind both brackets.

Bear in mind that if caster is correct it is essential that shims of the same thickness be taken from both brackets in order to maintain the caster setting.

FOURTH TYPE—CASTER AND CAMBER

On the fourth type suspension caster camber are both controlled at the eccentric pin at the outer end of the upper support arm. In order to change the setting, loosen the pinch bolt in the knuckle support and remove the lubrication fitting from the front bushing in the upper suspension arm. With an Allen wrench turn the eccentric bushing until the correct caster reading is obtained. Turning the screw so that the top of the knuckle support will move toward the rear of the car will increase caster. Opposite direction will decrease caster. After the correct caster setting has been obtained continue to rotate the pin in a direction which will give the correct camber reading. Since it may be necessary to turn the eccentric pin either forward or back to reach the camber setting after the correct caster setting has been obtained, it is obvious that it will make a small change in the caster setting. However, since both are controlled at the same eccentric pin the best setting possible might be a compromise. Where it is necessary to compromise it is advisable to set the camber to a perfect setting and compromise with the caster setting. Improperly set camber will scuff and wear tires very rapidly whereas caster will stand a considerable variation from the normal before its effect will be noticed in the handling and steering of the car.

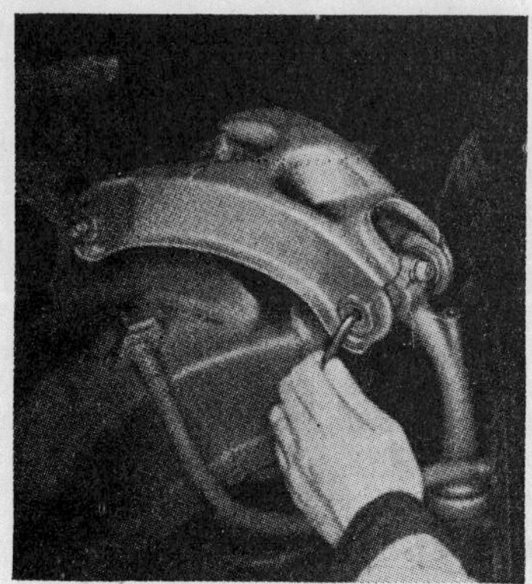
Caster and camber adjustment 1950 thru 1951 all models

1—Bushing
2—Seal
3—Outer Pin
4—Pinch Bolt
5—Control Arm
6—King Pin

Removing upper control arm

Toe-In

Four different types of steering apparatus were used on Studebaker cars and the correct method for setting toe-in is given in the steering section, since, on these models, toe-in is directly related to the steering set up, more so than in other cars.

REPLACEMENT OF SUSPENSION PARTS

Knuckle Support Upper Pin and/or Bushings

FIRST AND SECOND TYPES

To replace the upper suspension arm pin on the first and second type front suspension, first drive out the lock pin. (This is similar to a king pin lock pin and is driven upwards to remove.) Remove both the front and rear bushings from the upper suspension arm and drive out the upper suspension arm pin.

THIRD TYPE

On the third type of front suspension the upper support arm pin is serviced integral with the upper trunion. Support the car at the lower A frame and remove the wheel (make some provision to prevent the spindle from falling out when the upper pin is removed).

Remove the nut from the top of the knuckle support and then take out both front and rear bushing from the upper support arm. Raise the upper suspension arm which will pull up the trunnion from the top of the king pin and the bolt and trunnion can be slid out of the upper suspension arm.

FOURTH TYPE

To replace the knuckle support upper eccentric pin on this fourth type front suspension first take the weight off the car at the lower A frame and remove the wheel, making some provision to support the weight of the hub and drum, after the pin has been removed.

Remove the clamp bolt from the upper end of the knuckle support and take out the first and rear bushings from the outer end of the upper suspension arm. Disconnect the inner end of the hub or suspension arm from the frame so that the suspension arm may be cocked slightly in order to permit removal of the eccentric pin.

Actually, the upper suspension arm is taken off the pin, rather than the pin taken out of the suspension arm. After the suspension arm has been moved away from the pin the eccentric pin can be pushed out of the knuckle support.

When properly reinstalled the knuckle support will be approximately midway between the yoke of the upper suspension arm.

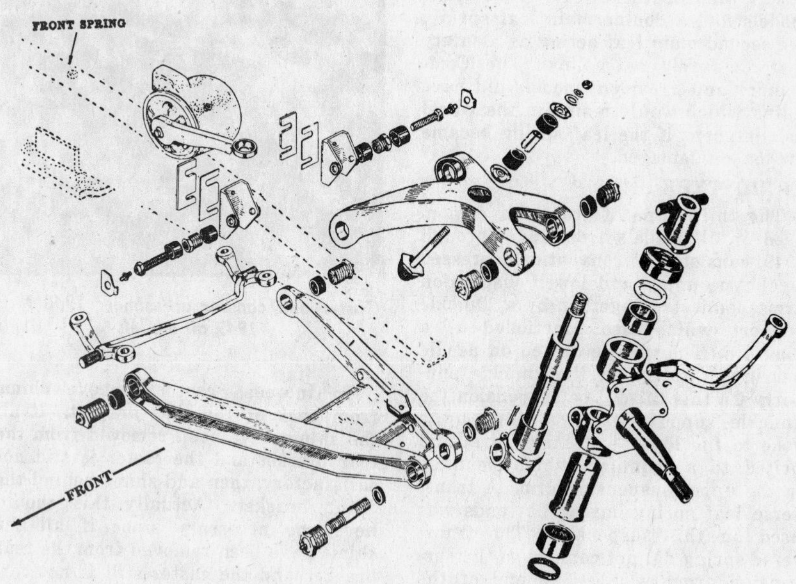

Suspension parts—Champion models 1947-49

Lower Suspension Arm Pin

FIRST AND SECOND TYPES

On the first and second type Studebaker front suspension the lower pin could be called a spring shackle pin. To replace it support the weight of the car on the outer end of the transverse spring.

Caution: Make certain the jack has a good grip.

Remove the wheel for easier access to the shackle bolt and take out the shackle bolt.

If it is necessary to replace the shackle (lower trunion) remove the knuckle support lower nut and slide the trunnion off the lower end of the knuckle support.

THIRD TYPE

On the third type front suspension the lower suspension arm pin is removed in just about the same manner as the upper pin is removed from the first and second types.

Take the weight off the car at the lower suspension arm and remove the road wheel.

Remove the front and rear bushings from the outer end of the lower A frame and drive out the lock pin which holds the lower suspension arm pin to the knuckle support. (The pin is driven upwards.) After the lock pin has been removed drive out the lower suspension arm pin.

When properly reinstalled the bottom of the knuckle support should be nicely centered in the yoke of the lower A frame.

FOURTH TYPE

To replace the lower arm pin in the fourth type suspension take the weight off the car on a jack at the lower A frame and remove the road wheel. Remove the front and back bushing from the outer end of the lower A frame and drive out the lower pin locking pin, (the locking pin drives upwards). After the locking pin has been removed drive out the lower suspension arm outer pin. When properly reinstalled the lower trunnion should be approximately centered between the yokes of the lower suspension arm.

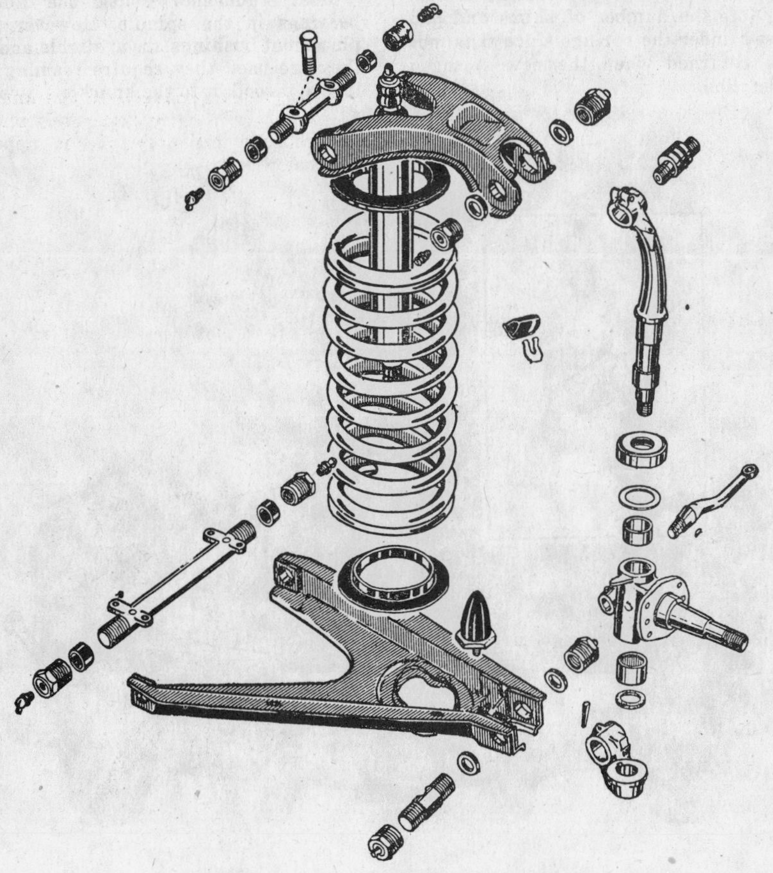

Suspension parts—1949-53 Commander

Replacement of Upper Suspension Arm

FIRST AND SECOND TYPE SUSPENSION

To remove the upper suspension arm follow the instructions given for the upper suspension arm pin and after the suspension arm has been detached from the knuckle support simply remove the brackets which retain the upper arm to the frame.

Actually it is only necessary to remove one of the brackets, since the support can be slid out of the other bracket while it is in place on the car.

THIRD TYPE

To remove the upper suspension arm follow the instructions given to replace the upper suspension arm outer pin and in addition remove the mounting pins which hold the inner end of the arm to the brackets on the side of the frame.

FOURTH TYPE

To replace the upper suspension arm on this fourth type of suspension the procedure is exactly the same as that given for the outer pin, since to remove the outer pin it was necessary to detach the arm from the frame.

Replacement of Lower Suspension Arm (A Frame)

FIRST AND SECOND TYPES

On both these types of suspension the lower suspension arm did not carry the weight of the car. The lower arm was simply used as a safety link in the event the front spring would break.

To remove the lower arm take the weight off the car at the outer end of the spring.

Remove the outer shackle pin which will release the outer end of the safety arm and then detach the arm at its inner end.

Continued

Replacement of Lower Suspension Arm—*continued*

THIRD TYPE

On the third type suspension support the weight of the car on the frame back of the front suspension and place a jack under the outer end of the lower arm. Remove the outer pin assembly (see replacement of outer pin) and slowly let the jack down until the tension of the spring has been relieved. The A frame inner bracket can then be unbolted from the front cross member and lowered to the floor.

FOURTH TYPE

To replace the lower A frame on the fourth type suspension support the weight of the car on a jack back of the front suspension. Remove the road wheel and place a roller jack under the inner shaft of the lower suspension arm.

Detach the shock absorber and torsion bar, if one is used. Take a load on the roller jack against the A frame inner shaft and remove the bolts which hold the shaft to the front cross-member. Slowly lower the jack, relieving the pressure on the front coil spring. After the pressure has been relieved remove the outer bushings which hold the suspension arm pin to the knuckle support, or take off the nut which holds the lower trunnion to the knuckle support and slide off the trunnion, after which the bushings may be removed on a bench.

Replacement of Front Spring

FIRST AND SECOND TYPE

To replace the leaf spring on these models support the frame on both sides back of the front suspension. Detach the shock absorbers on both sides and remove both suspension arm lower pins (shackle pins).

Detach one of the steering arms and swing the knuckle support up out of the way supporting it with a stick of wood.

Remove the U bolts from the front cross-member and let the spring lower at one end and slide it out from the side.

THIRD TYPE

The spring on the third type front suspension is a transverse spring which contacts but does no attach to the lower suspension arm on each side. To remove the spring take the weight of both sides of the car on jacks mounted to the frame in back of the front suspension. Detach the steering arm from the tie-rod and detach the shock absorber. Place a jack under the lower A frame inner shaft and remove the four bolts which retain the shaft to the front cross-member. Slowly lower the "A" frame releasing the tension from the front spring.

Note: If the spring tends to catch in its pad in the lower A frame it can be released by prying it slightly as the A frame is lowered.

Remove the plate and U bolt nuts from the spring mounting at the center of the frame and slide the spring out through the side.

FOURTH TYPE

The fourth type of front suspension has a coil type spring. To remove the coil spring first detach the shock absorber and torsion bar. Support the weight of the car on a jack back of the front suspension. Place a roller jack under the inner shaft of the lower A frame and remove the bolts which hold the frame to the front cross-member and then slowly lower the A frame releasing the tension from the spring. When all tension is relieved from the spring it can be lifted out by hand.

Note the number of shims and pads used under the springs since they must be returned when the new spring is installed.

Replacement of King Pins (Knuckle Support)

The forging which functions as a king pin also functions as the knuckle support and is generally referred to as the knuckle support, rather than the king pin.

FIRST AND SECOND TYPE SUSPENSION

Support the weight of the car on jacks back of the front suspension. Place a roller jack under the outside edge of the front spring in order to take the tension off the spring. Remove the wheel, drum and brake backing plate. Hang the backing plate on a wire hook to the frame, to prevent damage to the flexible line. Remove the cotter pin and nut from the spring outer yoke and slowly let the jack down so that the spring will force the yoke off the bottom of the knuckle support. Disconnect the steering arm and let the spindle down off of the knuckle support. Remove the upper suspension arm pin and take out the knuckle support.

Most Studebaker models use needle bearings in the spindle. However replacement bushings are available and if they are used they require reaming to insure a good fit to the knuckle support.

Steering mechanism 1947 thru 1949 Champion models

Steering mechanism 1950 Champion models

THIRD TYPE

The third type uses a leaf spring. Support the weight of the car on jacks back of the front suspension. Remove or detach the shock absorber and torsion bar. Place a roller jack under the outer end of the lower support arm, taking some weight on the jack.

Remove the nut from the top of the knuckle support which holds the upper trunnion in place and then take out the steering arm.

Slowly lower the jack which will cause the knuckle support to slide down out of the upper trunnion. Once out of the upper trunnion the spindle can be slid off the knuckle support.

Needle bearings are used top and bottom, between the knuckle support and the spindle.

If necessary to replace the knuckle support remove the lower pin and take it off the car.

FOURTH TYPE SUSPENSION

The fourth type suspension uses a coil spring, however the procedure for replacing the king pin bearings is exactly the same as that given for the first and second type.

Power Steering

See Power Steering Section.

STEERING GEAR ASSEMBLY

From a service standpoint four different types of steering mechanism were used on the Studebaker models from 1940 through 1953. From these could be divided into the first type—early Champion models—1940 through 1949 models; the second type—Champion models for 1950; the third type—Commander models from 1940 through 1949; and the fourth type—1950 Commander models and all 1951 thru 1953 models.

FIRST TYPE—CHAMPION MODELS 1940 THRU 1949; COMMANDER MODELS 1940 THRU 1942

Note: On Champion models from late production 1940 through 1946 production, the center tie rod was non-adjustable. In the text below the instructions to adjust the auxiliary (center) tie rod do not apply to the above mentioned Champion models. All other procedure, however, is the same.

1. Disconnect the cross-shaft bell crank from the cross-shaft.

2. Adjust the steering gear mechanism.

(a) Slide the steering housing tube upward off the gear box and loosen the four cap screws which hold the upper plate in place and remove one shim at a time until there is zero play in the worm bearings without a definite preload.

(b) Adjust the cross-shaft by loosening the jam nut and tightening the adjusting screw until there is a very slight drag at the steering high spot.

3. Reconnect the bell crank to the steering cross-shaft.

4. Adjust the center (auxiliary) tie rod so that the distance X between the center of the cross-shaft and the center of the idler arm is equal to the distance Y, which is the center of the auxiliary tie rod ball stud. This adjustment should be made with the steering wheel in the mid position of its travel.

Note: Above adjustment does not apply to the Champions mentioned at the beginning of this paragraph.

5. With the steering wheel still in the mid position of its travel, adjust the right side tie rod so that one-half the total toe-in is contained in the right front wheel.

6. With the steering wheel still in the mid position of its travel adjust the left tie rod so that the balance of the toe-in is contained in the left front wheel.

Tighten all clamp bolts and check the steering from one extreme to the other for looseness or binding.

SECOND TYPE—1950 CHAMPION MODELS

1. Disconnect the bell crank from the steering cross-shaft.

2. Adjust the steering gear mechanism;

(a) Adjust the worm bearings, remove the four cap screws which hold the upper plate of the steering gear housing and remove one shim at a time until there is no end play in the bearing, without any noticeable preload.

Tighten the four cap screws.

(b) Loosen the jam nut and tighten the cross-shaft adjusting screw until there is a very slight drag in the steering mechanism at the high spot.

3. Reconnect the bell crank to the steering cross-shaft.

4. Set the steering wheel in the mid position of its travel and loosen the clamp bolts on the right side adjusting sleeve and adjust the sleeve so there is one-half the total toe-in in the right front wheel. Tighten the clamp bolts.

5. Loosen the clamp bolts on the left side adjusting sleeve and turn the adjuster until the balance of the toe-ins is in the left front wheel.

Retighten the clamp bolts.

Turn the steering wheel from one extreme to the other to check for looseness or binding.

THIRD TYPE—1947 THRU 1949 COMMANDER MODELS

1. Disconnect the steering reach rod from the pitman arm.

Continued

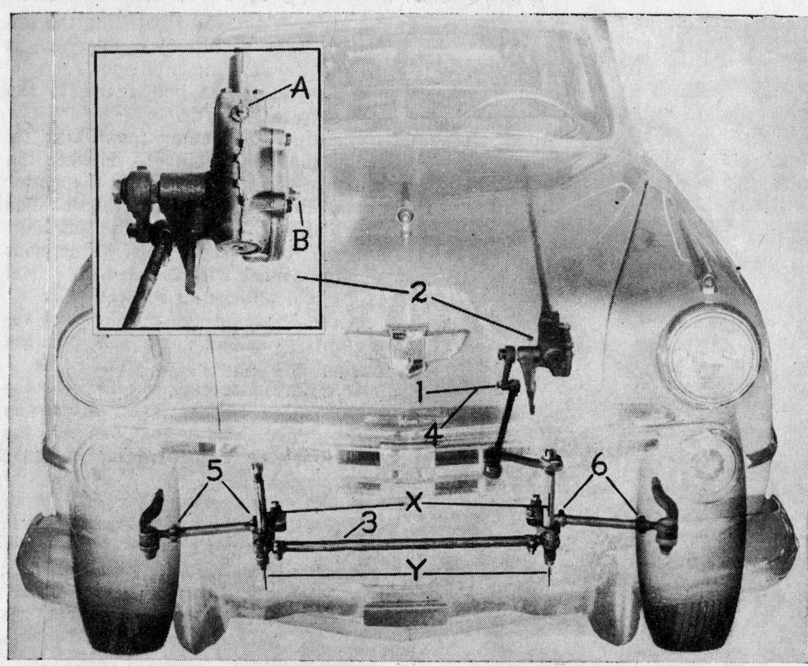

1947 thru 1949 Commander models

STEERING GEAR ASSEMBLY—*cont'd*

2. Adjust the steering gear mechanism;

(a) Adjust the worm bearing by sliding the steering jacket tube upward, loosen the four cap screws at the upper part of the steering gear and remove one shim at a time so that there is zero play in the bearings without a noticeable preload.

Tighten the cap screws.

(b) Loosen the jam nut and adjust the steering cross-shaft until there is a very slight drag on the steering wheel through its high spot. Tighten the jam nut.

3. Adjust the intermediate (auxiliary) tie rod so that the distance X is equal to the distance Y in the illustration.

Tighten the clamp bolt on the auxiliary tie rod.

4. Reconnect the steering reach rod to the pitman arm.

5. With the steering wheel in the mid position of its travel loosen the clamp bolt on the right side of the adjustable tie rod. Tighten the clamp bolts.

6. With the steering wheel still held in the mid position of its travel loosen the clamp bolts on the left side of the adjusting tie rod and adjust that rod so that the balance of the toe-in is contained in the left front wheel.

Tighten the clamp bolts.

Check the steering mechanism through its complete range to check for looseness or binding.

FOUR TYPE—1950 COMMANDER AND ALL 1951 THRU 1953 MODELS

1. Disconnect the steering reach rod from the pitman arm.

2. Adjust the steering gear mechanism;

(a) Slide the mass jacket housing up out of position and remove the four cap screws and take out one shim at a time in order to adjust the worm bearing. The bearing should be adjusted so there is no end play in the worm without a noticeable preload. Tighten the cap screw and replace the steering jacket.

(b) Loosen the jam nut on the cross-shaft adjusting screw and tighten the adjusting screw until there is a very slight drag in the steering wheel as the wheel crosses the high spot.

3. Reconnect the steering reach rod to the pitman arm.

4. Set the steering wheel in the mid position of its travel and loosen the clamp nuts on the right side of the adjusting tie rod and adjust the rod so that one-half the total toe-in is contained in the right front wheel.

Tighten the clamp bolts.

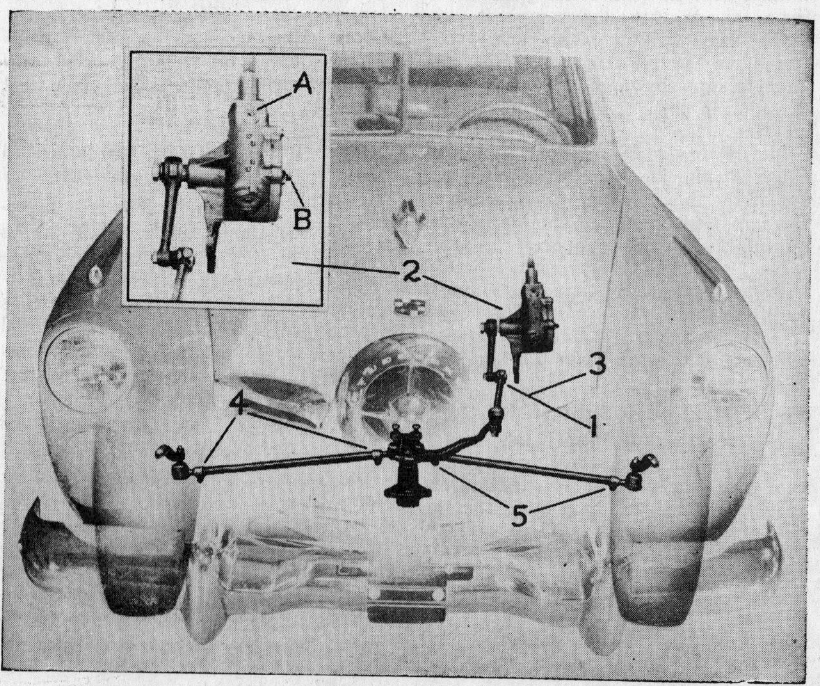

Steering mechanism 1950 Commander and all 1951 thru 1953 models

5. Loosen the clamp bolts on the left side of the adjustable tie rod and adjust the rod so that the balance of the toe-in is contained in the left front wheel.

Tighten the clamp bolts.

Now check the steering mechanism by turning it through its complete travel to check for looseness or binding.

BRAKES

Two types of Lockheed brakes were used on Studebaker cars. All models from 1940 through 1946 were equipped with a Lockheed brake having two adjustable, eccentric anchors. Starting with 1947 production and through 1953 a self-centering, self-adjusting type Lockheed brake was used.

Brake Inspection

Before adjusting Studebaker, or any other brake, remove at least one wheel to examine the condition of the drums, shoes, linings and wheel cylinders. This is particularly necessary on the self-adjusting models.

When a self-adjusting brake is used the automatic take-up mechanism will maintain the brakes at service adjustment until the lining is completely worn away. Obviously, this type of brake should be examined regularly to determine if there is sufficient lining to insure safety of the car and passengers.

Examine the condition of the wheel cylinder to determine if there are any leaks or seepage from the cylinder. Light scores in cylinders can be removed by honing in place on the car. Examine the condition of the lining to determine if there is sufficient lining to last a reasonable length of time to the best of the mechanic's knowledge and belief. If any thing is found defective on the one wheel which was removed for inspection it is advisable to take off all four wheels and make a thorough examination of the brake system. Where it has been found necessary to hone one wheel cylinder it is very likely that all wheel cylinders will require servicing.

Minor Brake Adjustment

1940 THRU 1946 MODELS

A minor adjustment is made to compensate for normal lining wear. Turn the shoe adjusting cam on the forward shoe until the wheel drags and back off until the wheel is just free. Repeat this procedure at the back shoe and then at the other three wheels.

1947 THRU 1953 MODELS

These models are equipped with an automatic take up device and require no adjusting whatever. An initial adjustment of the automatic take up mechanism is given under major brake adjustment for these particular models.

Major Brake Adjustment

1940 THRU 1946 MODELS

Loosen the bolt anchor lock nuts and turn the anchor until a .006 inch gauge is just gripped between the lining and the drum at the anchor end of the shoe. Then turn the cam adjuster until a .010

Continued

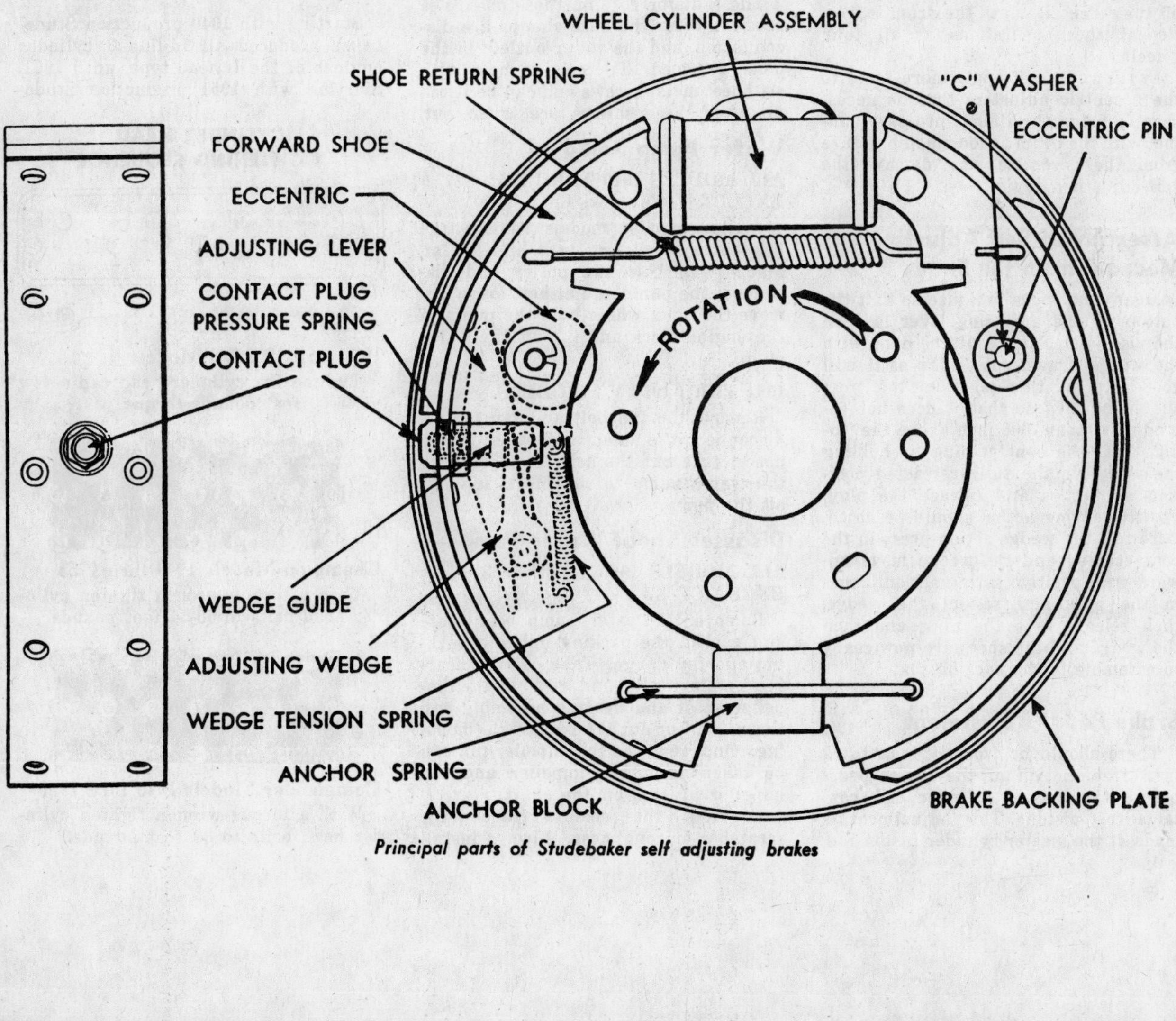

WHEEL CYLINDER ASSEMBLY
SHOE RETURN SPRING
"C" WASHER
ECCENTRIC PIN
FORWARD SHOE
ECCENTRIC
ADJUSTING LEVER
CONTACT PLUG
PRESSURE SPRING
CONTACT PLUG
ROTATION
WEDGE GUIDE
ADJUSTING WEDGE
WEDGE TENSION SPRING
ANCHOR SPRING
ANCHOR BLOCK
BRAKE BACKING PLATE

Principal parts of Studebaker self adjusting brakes

MAJOR BRAKE ADJUSTMENT—*continued*

inch feeler gauge is just gripped between the lining and the drum at the toe end of each shoe. Go back and recheck the anchor setting to be sure that setting the cam has not altered the anchor setting. When .006 inch is achieved at the heel and .010 inch at the toe securely tighten the anchor pin. Repeat this operation at the opposite shoe on the same brake and then at the other three wheels.

Initial Setting of Self Adjusting Brake

Mount the shoes on the backing plate, attach the springs and release the hydraulic cylinder clamp. Turn the eccentric adjusters (on the backing plate side) to the fully released position to permit the installation of the brake drum. Adjust the lining clearance by turning the eccentrics until the shoes are brought into easy contact with the drum and a slight drag is felt. Back off the eccentrics until the drum is free. Repeat these operations at all four wheels.

Caution: Do not apply more force to the eccentric adjusters than is necessary to bring the lining into easy contact with the drum as too much pressure from the eccentric may damage the self-adjusting device.

Assembly of Self Adjusting Mechanism to the Shoes

Mount the shoes in a vise so that the bottom of the adjusting lever lays on the vise jaw. This should be done with the wedge drawn out as far as it will go. Held in this position the plug should be filed so that it does not extend more than .005 inch above the lining. Test the contact plug by holding the wedge in the fully retracted position and press and release the plug. Positive spring action should be noted.

To test the wedge action press in the contact plug and the wedge move upward with positive spring action. Press in the plug and retract the wedge, then release first the plug and then the wedge and the shoes are now ready to assemble to the backing plate.

Brake Pedal Adjustment

There should be from ½ inch to ¾ inch free motion of the brake pedal before the master cylinder rod contacts the piston. This adjustment is made at the master cylinder piston rod.

Bleeding Brakes

Brakes of the self-adjusting type are bled in exactly the same manner as any other brake is bled, being certain to keep the master cylinder more than half filled at any time the brake is being bled from the master cylinder.

Where pressure bleeding is used, the procedure is exactly the same as for all other hydraulic brakes.

See General Service and Trouble Shooting for procedure.

COOLING SYSTEM

Radiator Core Removal

ALL MODELS 1940 THRU 1946

The radiator core on these models is removed after disconnecting battery, hood lock parts, wire clips and hose connections. The job is greatly simplified if the hood side panels are removed. Detach the radiator core from its mounting frame and lift straight upwards.

ALL MODELS 1947 THRU 1953

The radiator core on these models is removed after the hose clamps are disconnected, and the water outlets in the block removed. The core is held with six sheet metal screws and can be lifted up after these screws are taken out.

Water Pump Removal

ALL MODELS 1940 THRU 1953 EXCEPT V 8's

On the earlier models remove the hood side panel and take off the fan blades, fan belt and pulley and disconnect the pump and either hoses. Remove the bolts which hold the pump to the engine block and lift off the water pump.

1951 THRU 1953 V 8 MODELS

Remove the fan belt and fan pulley, disconnect the inlet and outlet water hoses, take out the screws which hold the water pump to the block and lift off the pump.

Disassembly of Water Pumps

ALL MODELS 1940 THRU 1953 EXCEPT V 8's

Remove the water pump rear plate and gasket, the packing nut, old packing and fan flange. Take out the bearing retainer clip and remove the impeller shaft and bearing assembly and thrust washer out the rear of the housing. Once removed the impeller pin can be taken from the impeller and the impeller pressed off the shaft.

Examine the seal surfaces for scratches or roughness. Always install a new shaft and bearing assembly and a new impeller at any time it is pressed off the shaft.

1951 THRU 1953 V 8 MODELS

Remove the bearing lock ring and place the assembly in an arbor press and press out the hub, shaft and bearing assembly from the impeller side. Once out of the housing the shaft and bearing assembly can be pressed out of the hub itself.

Note: Before removing either the hub or the impeller note carefully their relative position on the shaft so that when reinstalled they can be pressed back to the same position from which they were removed.

Thermostats

On all Studebaker models the thermostats are contained in water outlet housings at the top of the cylinder block.

To replace the thermostat remove the water outlet elbow and take out the thermostat.

ENGINE ASSEMBLY

Starting with 1940 production Studebaker produced all in-line 6 cylinder engines of the L head type, until 1951. Starting with 1951 production Stude-

CYLINDER HEAD TIGHTENING SEQUENCE

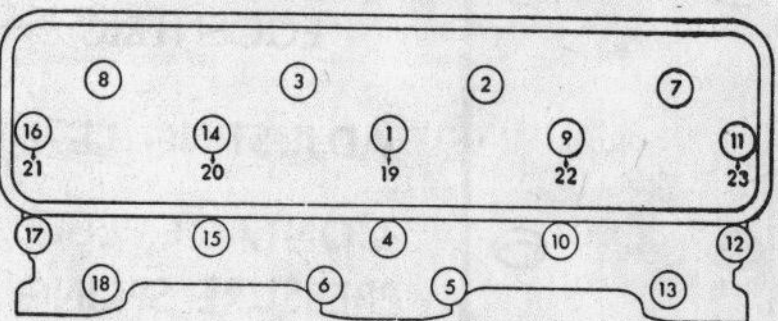

1951 thru 1953 V8 Models

Tighten the cylinder head cap screw to 46-50 foot pounds torque.

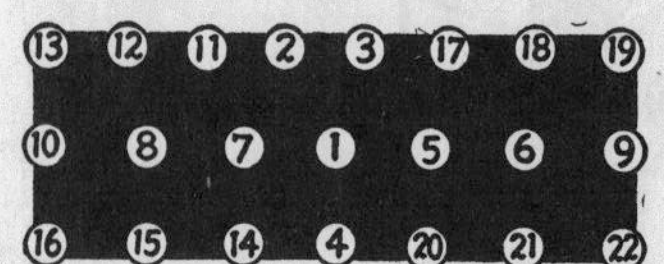

Champion Models 1940 thru 1953

With a torque wrench tighten cylinder head bolts to 50-54 foot pounds.

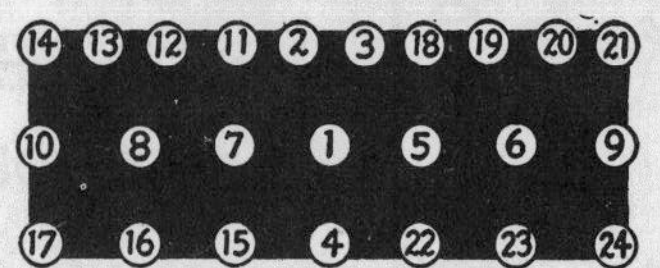

Commander Models 1940 thru 1950

With a torque wrench tighten cylinder head bolts to 83 foot pounds.

baker Commander cars were equipped with a V type overhead valve 8 cylinder engine.

Replacement engines are available for all production models up to and including 1940. These engines include cylinder head oil pan, timing case cover, but do not include flywheels.

Short block assemblies are also available which include crankshaft, camshaft, piston and rod assemblies and valves, (except V 8's).

Engine Removal

1947 THRU 1950 COMMANDER MODELS

On these models it is customary to split the engine at the front universal joint. It is necessary to remove the hood, radiator core and all connecting parts such as fuel lines, gauge sender wires, generator wire harnesses, headlight wire harnesses, battery connections, horns, shift mechanism, clutch operating linkage, air breather, oil filler tube, etc. The engine is slowly lifted and brought forward into the radiator core compartment and then the back of the engine is swung out of the way and it is then backed out of the radiator compartment and then the front end is lifted upwards out of the frame.

1947 THRU 1950 CHAMPION MODELS

On Champion engines it is customary to split the engine at the bell housing. In order to do this it will be necessary to take up the floor mat and the floor cover pan in order to expose the upper bolts at the bell housing.

Remove the hood and radiator core. Take out all attaching parts such as exhaust flange, generator wires, headlight wires, fuel lines, accelerator links, battery connections, clutch connections and the mounting bolts. The engine is lifted up, turned slightly and removed from the frame. It will be necessary to support the transmission and clutch bell housing.

1951 THRU 1953 V 8 ENGINES

In order to remove the engine on these models it is recommended that the transmission first be removed from the car. Remove the hood and radiator core and all engine attaching parts such as exhaust flange, flange cross-over pipes, electrical connections to the starter and engine, fuel lines, accelerator linkage, and engine mounting bolts, etc. The engine then can be lifted upwards and out of the car.

ENGINE INTERNAL

Oil Pan Removal

1951 V 8 MODELS

Take off the starter and disconnect one end of the right tie rod. Remove the drag link from the steering bell crank and take off the steering bell crank bracket and swing the bracket and bell crank out of the way toward the left of the car. Remove the exhaust cross-over pipe and the exhaust connections. The oil pan can then be removed.

1950 COMMANDER MODELS

Crank engine until #4 piston is at top center. Take off the stabilizer shaft, tie rods and steering bell crank and bracket assembly. Take out the lower right hand clutch housing bolts and the front cross member engine support bolts. Raise the engine approximately 2 inches and remove the oil pan.

COMMANDER MODELS, 1949 THRU 1953

On these models the Studebaker Co. recommends that the engine be removed from the car in order to take down the oil pan. However, it is possible (although difficult) to remove the oil

Continued

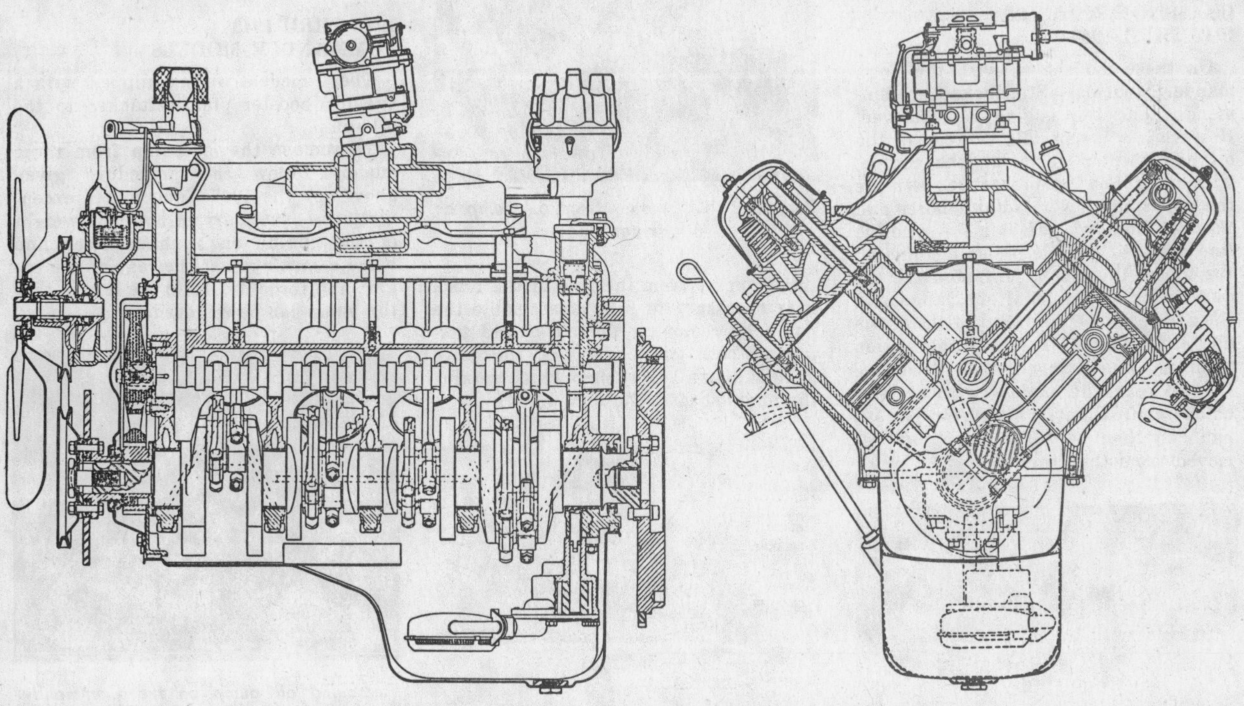

Sectional views of 1951 V8 engine

OIL PAN REMOVAL—*continued*

pan by the following procedure: Remove all radiator hoses, hood, disconnect gas lines, oil gauge, exhaust pipe, throttle rod, etc. Remove the engine mounting bolts at the front cross-member and the two under the transmission. Raise the engine about 4 inches. The pan can then be unbolted, tilted forward and pulled out the front.

COMMANDER MODELS, 1940 THRU 1942 AND ALL PRESIDENT MODELS, 1940 THRU 1942

Remove the engine front pan and side pan and take out the two lower clutch housing to engine rear plate bolts. Turn the engine so that No. 1 piston is half way up the cylinder (on 6 cylinder models No. 2 piston is at top center). Take out the oil pan bolts and remove the oil pan from the engine.

CHAMPION 1950 THRU 1953 MODELS

To take down the oil pan on these models remove the tie rods, exhaust pipe brackets, and engine front splash pans. Remove the cross-member engine support bolts and raise the engine approximately 2 inches to remove the oil pan.

CHAMPION MODELS, 1947 THRU 1949

On these models, as with the Commander models, Studebaker recommends that the engine be removed. However, it is possible to remove the oil pan without removing the engine, with the following procedure: Remove the upper and lower radiator hoses and take off the hood, unfasten the gasoline line and the flexible oil gauge line at the top of the block. Unfasten the exhaust pipe at the manifold flange and the accelerator control rod at the clevis above the starter. Take out the engine mounting bolts. It will then be necessary to raise the engine (with a chain block) approximately 4 inches. The oil pan can then be tilted down and removed from the front.

Oil pump assembly 6 cylinder models

CHAMPION MODELS, 1941 THRU 1946

Disconnect the battery and remove the dipstick. Remove the starting motor cable and the engine front pan. Take off the exhaust pipe bracket at the clutch housing and remove the starting motor. Crank No. 1 piston half way up the cylinder, take out the lower left hand clutch housing to engine plate bolts and then remove the oil pan screws and lower the pan.

CHAMPION 1940 MODELS

Disconnect the battery and the starter cables. Take out the clutch housing to exhaust pipe bracket bolts and then remove the starting motor. Take out the oil pan cap screws and lower the pan.

Oil Pump Removal

6-CYLINDER MODELS TO 1946

On all 6 cylinder engines the oil pump is mounted at an angle on the side of the block. In order to remove

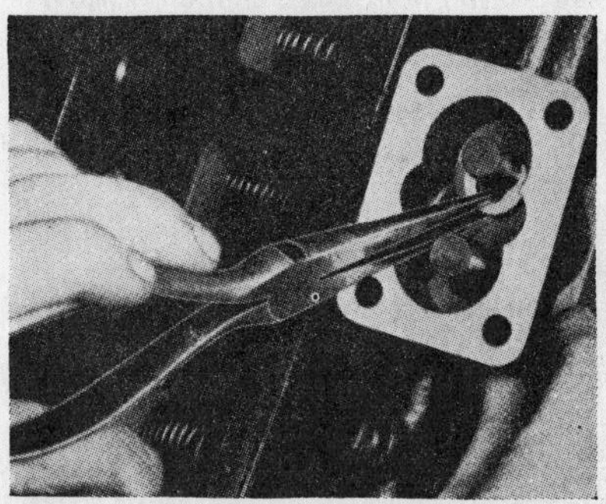

Removing "C" washer from oil pump on 6 cylinder model

the oil pump from the side of the block it is necessary to first disassemble the pump by removing the cover and taking off both gears. Back of the drive gear is a small C washer which retains the pump shaft to the pump body.

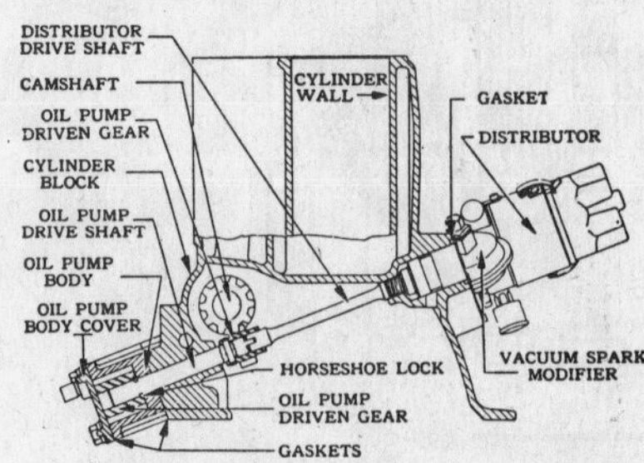

Section thru oil pump and distributor on 6 cylinder models

Remove the C washer and then the pump body can be slid off the end of the shaft. The pump shaft will remain in the cylinder block and if it is desired to remove the pump drive shaft it will be necessary to take off the oil pan and disconnect the distributor. Pull the distributor slightly out of the block and push the oil pump drive shaft up into the oil pan and remove it from inside the engine.

1947 THRU 1949 CHAMPION MODELS

Take off the oil pump, remove the engine right side pan, then take off the pump cover and the idler gear, remove the drive gear and woodruff key from the shaft and then remove the pump body.

1947 COMMANDER MODELS

To take the oil pump off of these models, remove the hood, drain the cooling system, disconnect the battery, disconnect the clutch operating shaft at the inner pin, remove the starting motor and take out the motor support bolts.

With the engine free of the support bolts, swing the entire engine as far to the left as possible.

Disconnect the oil pressure pipe and swing it back out of the way, remove the vacuum booster from the oil pump and then take off the oil pump.

1947 THRU 1949 COMMANDER MODELS

These models were equipped with a vacuum booster pump attached to the oil pump.

To remove the oil pump from these models follow the procedure given above for the 1947 Commander except that it is customary to hold the weight of the engine on a chain block and place a jack against the rear of the engine and force it over to the left so that the pump can be removed.

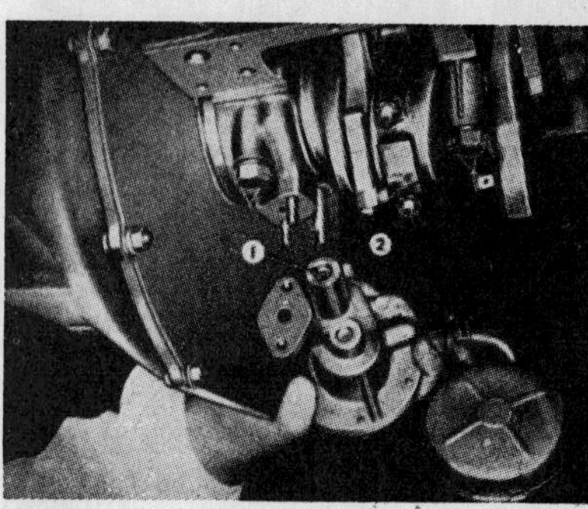

Removing oil pump on the Commander models. Note drive gear shaft (1) and distributor drive shaft torque (2)

1950 COMMANDER MODELS

To remove the oil pump, first set No. 1 piston on top center and take out the front engine mounting bolts. Move the engine as far to the left as possible in order to get at the oil pump holding screws to remove the oil pump.

1951 THRU 1953 MODELS

The oil pump to these models is attached to the main bearing cap and therefore requires removal of the oil pan. Once the oil pan is removed there is no difficulty in removing the pump.

Timing Case Cover Removal

ALL MODELS FROM 1942 THRU 1950 EXCEPT CHAMPION MODELS

Remove the fan, radiator core and the engine front support bolts and raise the front of the engine. Take off the vibration damper and the screws which hold the timing case cover to the front of the engine plate and lift off the timing case cover.

1941 MODELS AND ALL CHAMPION MODELS

Remove the radiator core, fan blades, and the upper pulley and belt. (On President models it will be necessary to raise the engine). Remove the crankshaft fan pulley and vibration damper and unbolt the timing gear cover.

1951 thru 1953 V8 Models

Remove the radiator core, water pump and vibration damper assembly. The timing case cover can then be unbolted and removed.

Piston and Rod Assemblies

Aluminum pistons are used in all Studebaker models. Split skirt aluminum pistons were used in Champion models from 1940 through 1942. All other Studebaker models are equipped with T slot aluminum pistons. Wrist pins are locked in the rod on all Studebaker models.

Connecting rod bearings are of the slip in type and are available in .001, .005, .010 and .020 undersizes.

Assembly of Piston to the Connecting Rod

Offset connecting rods are used in the Studebaker In-Line engines so that connecting rods for cylinders 1, 3 and 5 are not interchangeable with the rods from 2, 4 and 6.

On In-Line engines the T slot or split skirt of the piston should be assembled to the side opposite to the split hole in the bottom of the connecting rod. (The number on the rod and cap is on the same side as the split hole and is assembled facing the camshaft.)

V-8 ENGINES

On V8 engines the T slot in the piston is assembled to the rod in the side opposite to the oil squirt hole at the bottom of the rod.

Assembling Rod and Piston Assemblies to Engine

IN-LINE ENGINES

On all In-line engines the rod and piston assemblies are assembled so that the number stamped on the rod and cap is facing the camshaft side of the engine and the split in the skirt of the piston faces away from the camshaft side of the engine.

V8 MODELS

On V8 models the left bank is numbered 1, 3, 5 and 7, the right bank is numbered 2, 4, 6 and 8. When assembling the rod and pistons to the engine the T slot in the piston is always on the left side of the engine. This will be up on the right bank and down on the left bank. The numbers on the connecting rod will face downward away from the camshaft. The oil squirt hole in the connecting rod will face upward toward the camshaft.

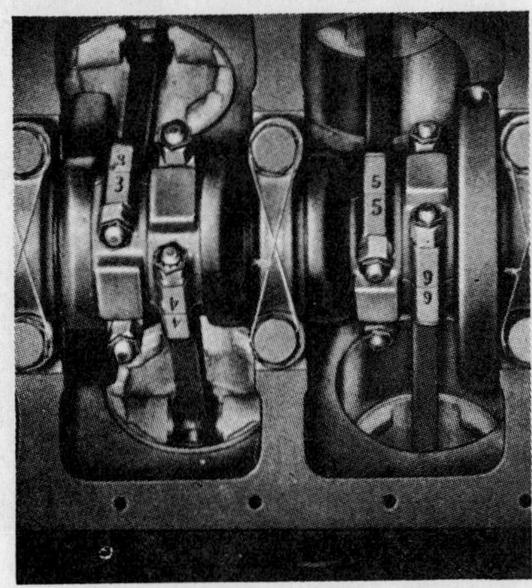

Connecting rod numbering sequence

Wrist Pins

A taper pin is used in the connecting rod to retain the wrist pin. This taper pin is threaded at both ends and to remove it the procedure is to take the nut off the taper bolt and mount it on the opposite side of the taper bolt using the nut as a puller to pull the taper bolt out of the connecting rod. If the bolt is apparently stuck in the connecting rod and it is found to be difficult to break it loose, first insert wrist pin

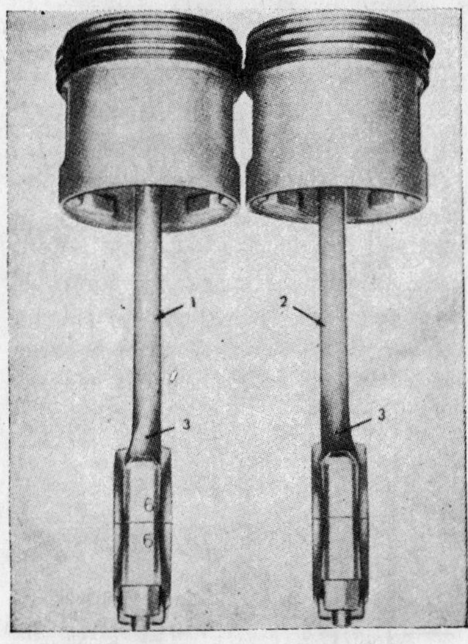

Rod and piston assembly V8 models

1—Right bank Rod. 3—Oil Squirt Hole.
2—Left bank Rod.

clamp through the center of the wrist pin and tighten securely.

Mount the clamp in a vice and rotate the connecting rod so that the taper pin will come into true index with the flat on the wrist pin. It will then be comparatively simple to remove the wrist pin clamp screw.

The reason the taper pin tends to stick is that, in service the wrist pin may rock somewhat, causing the edge of the flat on the wrist pin to dig into the taper clamp screw. Holding the wrist pin with a clamp in a vice and rocking the rod will release the dug-in portion and permit the wedged pin to come out more readily.

On early models which did not have a hole in the side of the piston there was no easy way of driving out the pin. On

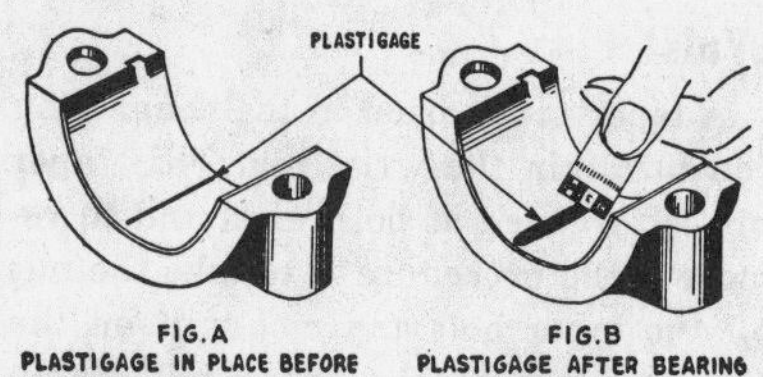

Determine bearing clearance with plastigage

WRIST PINS—*continued*

these models it is customary to drill a ⅜ in. hole in the skirt of the piston, just opposite to the wrist pin clamp screw in order to drive out the screw with a drift.

Connecting Rod Bearings

Connecting rod bearings on all Studebaker models are of precision slip-in type and Studebaker does not recommend adjusting the bearing. However, the bearing may be adjusted by placing a taper or feather type shim between the lower half of the bearing and the bearing cap.

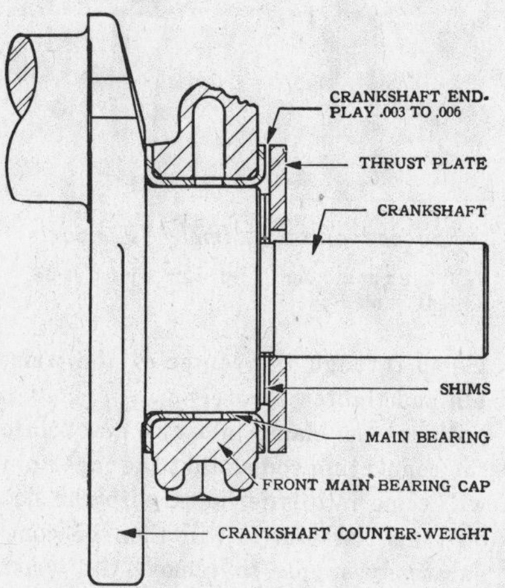

Crankshaft end play is controlled by by shims

Crankshaft Main Bearings

Precision slip-in type main bearings are used on all Studebaker models. The bearing is replaced by placing a flattened cotter pin or special turning pin in the oil hole in the crankshaft and rotate the crankshaft which will force the upper half of the main bearing out of the cylinder block. When removing the shell it should be driven tang portion first, and when replacing the shell the tang portion should be entered last. While The Studebaker Co. does not recommend adjusting main bearings a small adjustment can be made by using taper or feather type shims between the main bearing shell and the cap.

Rear Main Bearing Oil Seal

On models built from 1940 through 1946 a slinger and drain tube was used to prevent oil from the rear main bearing from escaping on to the clutch. Starting with 1946 production and through 1953 a Brummer type one piece rubber oil seal was used at the rear main bearing. This oil seal could be replaced readily by removing the rear main bearing cap and letting the crankshaft come down just the slightest amount.

The old oil seal could then be pulled down and a new one inserted. The purpose of the rubber oil seal is to prevent oil which might escape from the slinger from getting on to the clutch.

VALVE SYSTEM

On all in-line engines built from 1940 through 1953 the valves are of the L head type and are equipped with mechanical mushroom type lifters. Starting with 1951 production an 8 cylinder V type overhead valve engine is used on Commander production. Mechanical valve lifters are used on all Studebaker V8 engines.

Removal of Valve Assemblies

ALL IN-LINE ENGINES

On all Studebaker in-line engines from 1940 through 1951 the valves are removed in the conventional manner,—take off the cylinder head and the valve chamber cover, raise the valve spring and take out the valve spring keeper, then pull the valve out and up through the top of the cylinder block.

V8 ENGINES

On the V8 Engines the valves are contained in the cylinder head but are removed in exactly the same manner, as for L heads, except that it is necessary to remove the rocker assembly in order to take off the head.

Replacement of Valve Guides

Before removing the old valve guides measure carefully the distance from the top of the guide to the top of the cylinder block (cylinder head on V8 models)

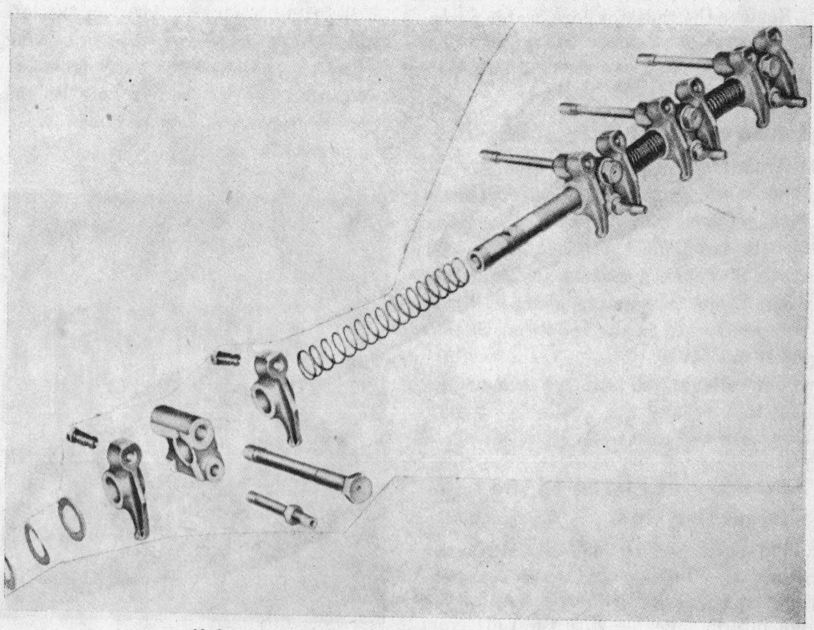

Valve rocker arm arrangement on V8 models

and drive the new guide down to exactly that distance.

On the in-line engines valve guides are pulled up out of the top of the block and are driven in from the top of the block toward the valve chamber. On overhead valve V8 models the valve guide is driven out from the combustion chamber side toward the top of the head. New guides are driven in from the combustion chamber toward the top of the head. The chamfered edge of the guide should be started first. It is customary to ream the valve guides after they are installed to take out any distortion which may have occurred when the guide was driven into place.

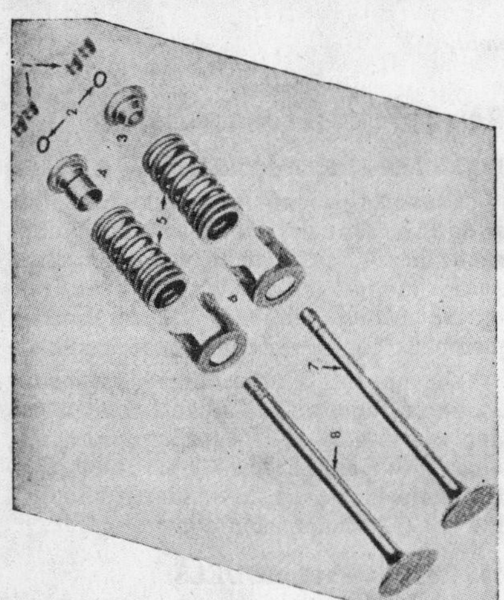

Valve system V8 models

1—Spring Seat (Keepers) 5-Spring, 6-Damper.
2—Oil Seals.
3—Exhaust Spring Retainer, 7-Exhaust Valve.
4—Intake Spring Retainer & Intake Valve.

Adjusting Valves

V8 MODELS

A self locking screw is used on the rocker arms of the V8 models. The head of the screw is located underneath the rocker. The engine should be thoroughly warmed before any attempt is made to adjust the valve clearance.

Valve Springs

The best way to check the condition of a valve spring is to take a compression test. The specifications for the pressure on the valve spring are given in the Overhaul Tables at the beginning of Studebaker.

However, if a spring tester is not available, take all of the intake valves and lay them alongside of each other on a flat surface and measure the height of each spring with a straight edge. If all springs are the same height it may safely be assumed that the springs are in good condition since it is unlikely that they will all collapse exactly the same amount. Repeat the same test on the exhaust springs.

If one or more of the springs are different height, it will be necessary to compare them with a new spring to determine which of the springs has collapsed.

Replace all springs which do not come up to the standard of the new spring.

Rocker Assemblies

ALL V-8 ENGINES

To remove the rocker assemblies take off the carburetor air cleaner, disconnect the spark plug wires from the plugs and drain the cooling system.

Take off the crown nuts which hold the rocker arm cover and lift the cover off the rocker arm bracket screws.

Remove the four rocker arm bracket screws and lock washers from the rocker arm assembly. Then unscrew the four cylinder head cap screws which also pass down through the rocker assemblies. Lift the rocker arm assembly off with the cylinder head cap screws remaining through the shaft.

Disassembly

Before disassembling, mark the rocker arms, brackets and shafts so that they can be reassembled in their original position.

To separate, compress the outer flat washer at one end of the assembly so that the cotter pin can be taken out. Remove the cotter pin and take off the first of the rockers.

Again compressing the rocker, remove the cylinder head cap screw which passes through the bracket and slide the bracket off. Repeat this process until all the rockers have been separated from the shaft.

Before reassembly make absolutely certain that the oil holes in the rocker shaft are free so that plenty of lubrication reaches them.

When properly assembled to the engine, the flat on one end of the rocker shaft will be at the rear on the right bank and at the front on the left bank.

Adjusting valves on V8 engines

STUDEBAKER 1940 thru 1953

CLUTCH ASSEMBLY

A single plate dry disc clutch is used on all Studebaker models, except those equipped with automatic transmissions.

Clutch Pedal Adjustment

On all standard clutches adjust the clutch pedal so that there is a minimum of ¾ in. to 1 in. free motion of the clutch pedal before the throw-out bearing engages the fingers.

Removal of Clutch

ALL MODELS 1940 THRU 1950, EXCEPT 1947 TO 1953 CHAMPION

First remove the transmission and then take off the starter. Take out the front floor plate and remove the clutch housing to engine cap screws. Support the rear of the engine on a jack and take out the rear engine mountings. Remove all operating shafts and take out the rear engine support cross member. The clutch housing can then be lifted off, after the remaining bolts which hold it to the engine block are removed.

CHAMPIONS 1947 THRU 1953

Studebaker recommends that to take the clutch out of these models it is better to remove the engine with the driven plate and clutch assembly intact. It is possible to remove the clutch with the engine in place by the following method: Remove the starting motor and put a jack under the engine for support. Unfasten the front universal joint behind the transmission and lower the drive shaft. Remove the bolts which hold the cross-member under the transmission. There are two bolts at each side that engage threaded holes in the body, there are four bolts midway of each side that fasten it to the frame. Unfasten and remove the transmission from the bell housing, lower the engine slightly by means of the jack so that it tilts and then unbolt the clutch housing from the engine. From there continue to remove the clutch in the regular manner.

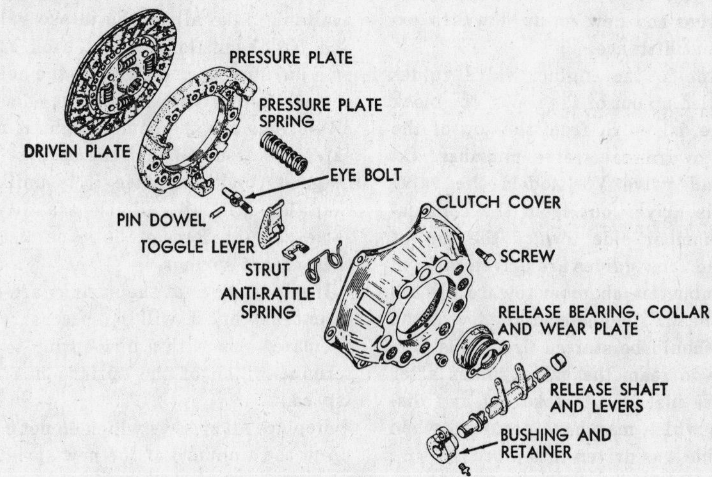

Clutch assembly

TRANSMISSION ASSEMBLY

Three-speed transmissions and three-speed transmissions with overdrive are available as optional equipment on all Studebaker models from 1940 through 1951. Starting with 1951 production a completely automatic torque converter type transmission is used on the Commander models only.

Transmission and overdrive assembly

Removal of Transmission

1947 THRU 1953 MODELS

Detach the front universal joint and slide the front drive shaft back on the rear drive shaft after the propeller shaft support assembly has been removed from the center frame cross-member, then lower the propeller shaft.

Disconnect all attaching parts such as shift rods, shift links to the overdrive, wires to the overdrive, etc. Remove the cap screws which hold the transmission case to the clutch housing, lower the transmission down and out.

1940 THRU 1946 MODELS

To take out this transmission it is necessary to remove the floor boards and also the cross member mounted at the rear engine support. Remove all attaching parts such as shift links, wires to the overdrive, speedometer cable, parking brake, etc., and then lower the back of the transmission and slide it down and out from the car. On these models the engine must be supported on a jack since the rear mounting cross-member has been removed.

Disassembly of Standard Transmission

Mount the transmission in a vice and remove the cover and front flange. Remove the bearing outer snap ring from the clutch shaft and the bearing inner snap ring from the clutch shaft. The front clutch shaft can then be removed, using a puller.

The main shaft, with its gears assembled, is removed through the back of the case while still attached to the rear housing. Simply unbolt the rear housing from the back of the transmission case and pull out the case with the main shaft attached, cocking it slightly to clear the shift yokes. The main shaft can be taken out of the rear housing by removing the snap ring and driving the main shaft forward.

The synchronizers are held to the main shaft by snap rings. The counter shaft is driven out through the back and so is the idler shaft.

Disassembly of Overdrive

Where an overdrive transmission is used the overdrive can be disassembled without disturbing the transmission. Unbolt the overdrive case from the overdrive lock plate (this is the thick plate between the back of the transmission case and the front of the overdrive case). Remove the snap ring which holds the bearing to the overdrive main shaft at the back of the overdrive case and while pulling off the housing tap gently on the overdrive shaft to drive it into the case so that the case will come off with the overdrive main shaft in place.

This routine will prevent losing the rollers from the overdrive free wheeling cam.

It is not necessary to follow this techinque if it is not desired. The transmission overdrive case can be removed with its main shaft in place and let the rollers drop to the bottom of the case where they can be picked up. All overdrive parts are retained to the shaft with snap rings. Removal of the snap rings will permit the very easy removal of the overdrive parts. A series of pictures accompanies this text which shows the step by step procedure on Studebaker overdrives.

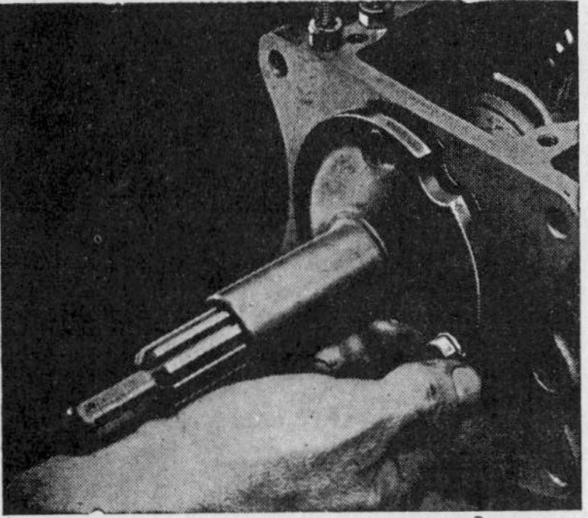

Remove bearing cap

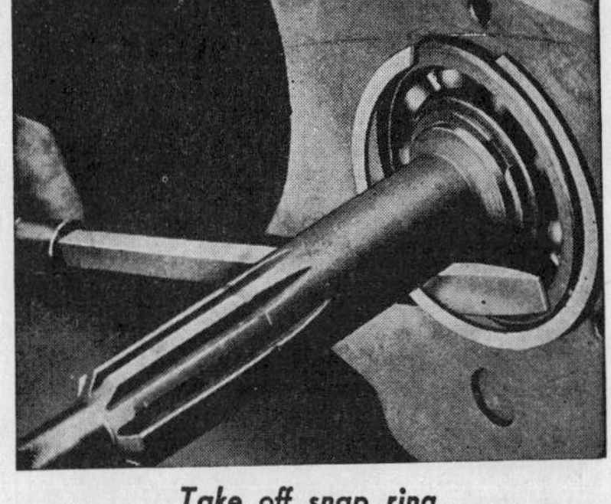

Take off snap ring

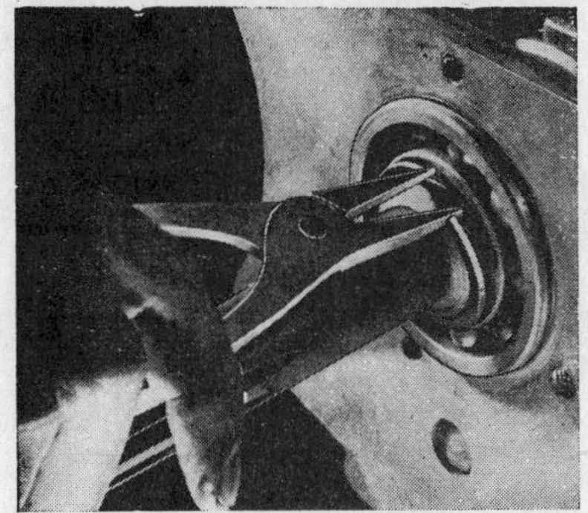

Pry out snap ring

Pull out bearing

Mark synchronizer

Remove main shaft assembly

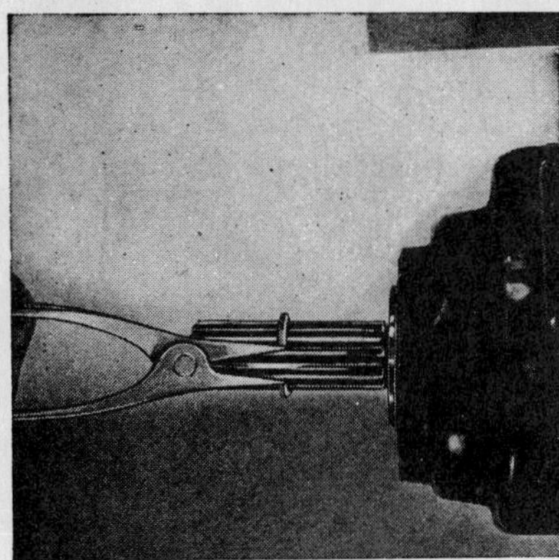

Remove rear snap ring

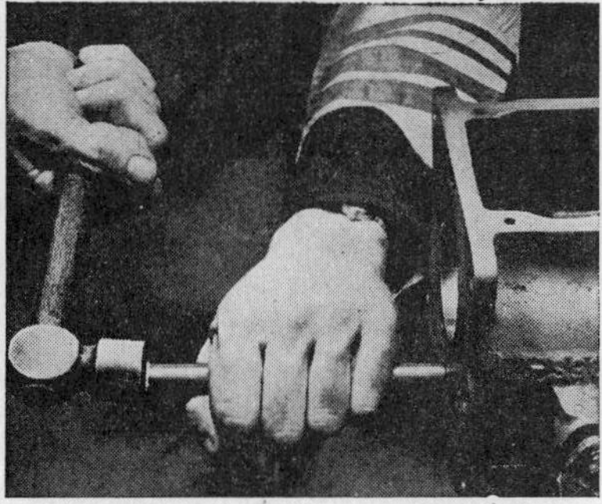

Drive out counter shaft

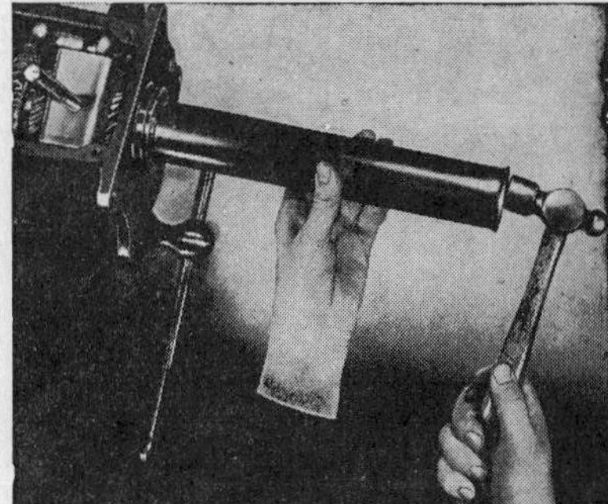

Replace front bearing

AUTOMATIC TRANSMISSIONS

Complete details on the servicing of Studebaker automatic transmissions is given in the automatic transmission portion of this section (see index).

ADJUSTMENT OF TRANSMISSION SHIFTER MECHANISM

Vacuum Assisted Shifter

1940 THRU 1942 COMMANDER AND PRESIDENT MODELS

On the vacuum assisted shifter mechanism used on these models the cross shift from second high range to low reverse range is a purely mechanical motion and the vacuum assister does not in any way help to make the cross shift.

Adjustment on the cross shift is also done mechanically. Simply adjust the length of rod "D" in the illustration so that the selector mechanism will shift from one rail to the other when the shift lever is moved from the second high range to low reverse range. This is easily accomplished by setting the lever at the transmission in the middle of its range and then set the gear shift lever in the middle of its range and adjust the length of the clevis so that it will just enter with both levers held in this position.

To adjust the linkage on the vacuum assisted portion of the shift proceed as follows: with the gear shift lever in the neutral position, rod "F" from the shift lever to the first bell crank should be adjusted so that the lever "S" to which it is attached is parallel to the dash panel.

With the piston "L" in its mid position (the mid position is 10¾ in. between the extreme rear edge of the cylinder and the shoulder on the rear end of the rod "M") the rod "M" should be adjusted so that the lever "N" is in the neutral position. The neutral position of the lever "N" can readily be determined by moving the lever back and forth.

Bracket "O" should be mounted on rod "M" exactly 6 13/16 in. from the shoulder at the rear end of the rod.

Rod "J" should be adjusted to a length of 14 1/16 in. between clevis pin centers.

With the gear shift lever in neutral position the length of rod "G" should be adjusted to a point where valve "K" is in the neutral position and air is exhausted from both sides of the piston in the cylinder "L."

When this adjustment is attained all pivot points on the link "I" and the center pivot on lever "H" will be in a straight line, nearly vertical. Disconnect the vacuum line "Q" from the valve "K" and adjust the rod "G" so that the valve is at the approximate center of its total travel. Then, with the engine running, momentarily complete the connection of the vacuum line to the valve. If when connecting the vacuum line the piston rod "M" starts to move to the rear, for example, it will be necessary to lengthen the rod "G." However, if when connecting the vacuum line, the rod end starts to move it will be necessary to shorten the rod "G." When the rod "G" is properly adjusted connecting the vacuum line will not cause the cylinder to move at all.

REAR AXLE ASSEMBLY

The rear axle assembly used on all Studebaker cars from 1940 through 1951 are of the Spicer type.

Shims are used for all adjustments including preloading of the pinion and differential side bearings.

Replacement of Pinion Oil Seal

Split the rear universal joint and lower the drive shaft. Remove the pinion shaft nut after marking carefully its location in relation to the shaft so that it can be replaced in exactly the same place from which it was removed. Pull off the pinion flange and, with an inertia type puller, remove the pinion oil seal. Well over 100 ft. lbs torque may be used on the pinion flange nut in order to bring it back to the position from which it was removed.

Replacement of Axle Oil Seal

Two oil seals are used on the outer end of the rear axle shafts. One, the outer mounted in an oil seal retaining plate, rubs against the rear axle hub. To replace the outer seal remove the hub and drum assembly and unbolt the oil seal plate from the axle tube. To replace the inner oil seal it is necessary to remove the axle shaft, after which the oil seal can be pulled out of the housing with an inertia type puller.

Replacement of Axle Shafts

Remove the hub and drum and disconnect the brake line. Remove the bolts which hold the outer oil seal plate and backing plate to the rear axle flange and lift off the outer seal and backing plate.

Using a puller, pull the axle shaft with its bearing out of the axle housing, being careful not to damage the inner oil seal.

Checking ring gear runout with indicator

Note: It is a good idea to install a new inner oil seal at any time a new axle is to be installed.

Press the bearing off the taper of the axle shaft and install it, or a new bearing on the new axle shaft and carefully insert the axle shaft into the housing, being certain not to damage the inner oil seal.

Replacement of Pinion Bearing and/or Pinion and Ring Gear

As noted before, all Studebaker models are equipped with Spicer type axles which do not have removable carriers. While it is entirely possible to work on the axle while it is mounted under the car it is much simpler if the axle housing assembly is removed from under the car and placed on a bench where it will be more convenient and clean to handle the shims.

Pinion depth adjusting shims (shims which control the mesh of the pinion into the ring gear) are located back of the rear bearing cup (race). Adding shims at this point will move the pinion gear into deeper mesh with the ring gear, removing shims at this point will set the pinion gear out of the ring gear. The shims which determine the preload on the pinion bearings are located between the bearing spacer and the front pinion bearing cone. Adding shims at this point will lower or lessen the preload on the pinion bearings. Removing shims at this point will increase the preload on the pinion bearings.

Shims are used between the differential side bearing cones and the differential case to adjust the relationship between the ring gear and the pinion gear (back lash) and also to provide a preload for the differential side bearings. Special micrometers are available to properly adjust the depth of the pinion gear. However, this text is written on the assumption that the special micrometer is not available.

First, notice that the pinion gear is marked with a number following a plus or minus sign. The number following the plus or minus sign is the only number with which we need be concerned, since the other numbers and letters refer to matched gear sets and are production codes, etc.

If there is no number stamped on the gear following a plus or a minus sign then that gear can be considered to be zero or the nominal setting. The quickest and easiest way to install a new pinion shaft is to get from the parts department a pinion gear having the same markings as the pinion which was removed. If it has the same markings then it will use exactly the same number of shims as were found in the old rear. The plus sign on the pinion means that the pinion is moved forward into the carrier (less shims are used). A minus sign on the pinion indicates that the pinion is moved toward the rear (shims are added to the rear bearing). If it is not possible to secure a gear with the same markings as the old gear then by comparing the markings the proper shims can be arrived at by the following method.

If the old gear is marked minus 2, and the new gear is marked plus 3, it means the old pinion was .002 past the nominal point toward the rear, and the new pinion will have to be .003 past the nominal point toward the front. In other words, to replace a minus 2 pinion with a plus 3 pinion it will be necessary to remove a .005 thick shim from in front of the rear bearing cup (race). This may not be exactly the right setting but it will be close enough to be a good starting point (it very likely will be the right setting). It is a good idea to bear in mind that when you move the pinion toward the front you have automatically reduced the preload on the pinion bearing unless a shim of equal thickness (as the one removed from the rear bearing) is placed between the spacer and the front bearing cone, in order to keep the bearing preload as it was before the job was torn down.

Mount the pinion, with the calculated number of shims, into the housing and install the spacer, shim, front bearing race and cone but not the pinion oil seal. The reason the pinion oil seal is not put in at this time is because it may be necessary to remove the companion flange yoke more than once and which might damage the oil seal.

Install the universal joint companion flange and tighten the companion flange nut up to 150 ft lb torque. While tightening the pinion test the amount of pressure required to turn the pinion shaft. The pressure required should be approximately 2 or 3 in. lb when the nut is tightened to 150 ft lb torque. If the pressure required is less than 2 or 3 in lb, remove a very thin shim from between the front bearing cone and the bearing spacer. Reinstall the companion flange and again tighten the pinion shaft nut, until it requires 2 or 3 in. lb to turn the pinion shaft.

If it is desired, a tentative start may be made to install the differential carrier with the shims that were on it when it was removed. This is generally considered to be good practice since it could very easily be exactly the right number of shims.

If new side bearings are being installed on the differential it is still a good idea to leave the shims in place which were found there.

Generally speaking, bearings are made so precisely that there is very little tolerance in the depth of the bearing.

To install the differential it is necessary to spread the case, since the number of shims mounted behind the bearing is greater than the space between the yoke of the carrier. A special spreading device is available to spread the case, which will make it a very simple matter to install the differential assembly. If a spreading device is not available, however, set the differential into place by slightly cocking the side bearing outer races and very carefully jolt the differential assembly into the carrier.

Caution: This should be done with extreme care, since if the carrier does not enter straight, injury to the bearings may result.

With the differential in place, install the bearing caps and pull them up snugly but not too tight and immediately check the back lash of the ring gear and pinion. This should be between .003 and .006 in. measured at the outer rim of the ring gear. If it is found that more than .006 in. end play exists it will be necessary to take a very thin shim from the right side of the carrier and transfer it to the left side of the carrier. This, of course, necessitates removing the differential assembly and both side bearings. When transferring the shims use extreme care that the shim is not crumpled or damaged in any way since its effective thickness will change (increase) if it is damaged in any way.

After the differential assembly has been mounted in the carrier and back lash is between .003 and .006 in., paint the ring gear teeth with prussian blue or red lead and roll the ring gear through the pinion, making a note of the markings produced by the mesh of the gears. Accompanying this test are typical markings found and the proper procedure to produce the desired marks. In a modern automobile the relation between the pinion and ring gear is extremely critical. Nearly correct mesh of the ring gear and pinion will only produce humming noises in the rear which will be impossible to correct if the gears are permitted to run in improper mesh for any considerable length of time.

WILLYS SPECIFICATIONS

Starting Serial and Motor Numbers

Starting Serial Numbers

1940 17001
1941 50001
1942 80101
1946 10001
1947 16535
1948—Ser. 463 44046
Ser. VJ2 65199
Ser. 663 10001
1949—Ser. 4X463, VJ3, VJ-3-6 .. 10001
Ser. 463, VJ2 79716
1950—Ser. 4X473, 473 SW, 473, 673 SW, 673 VJ 10001
Ser. 463 106504
Ser. 4X463 13186
Ser. VJ-3 12698
Ser. 663 22769
Ser. VJ-3-6 10654
1951—Ser. 473 SW 451-AA1-1001
Ser. 4X473 SW 451-FA1-10001
Ser. 473-VJ 451-BA1-10001
Ser. 673-SW 651-AA1-10001
Ser. 673-VJ 651-BA1-10001
1952—Ser. 675 .... 652-KA2-10001
Ser. 685 Wing 652-LA1-10001
Ser. 685 Ace 652-MA1-10001
Ser. 4X475 .... 452-FA2-10001
Ser. 475-SW 452-AA2-10001
Ser. 473-SW 452-AA1-10001
Ser. 4X473 SW 452-FA1-10001
Ser. 685 (Station Wagon) 652-AA2-10001
Ser. 673-SW 652-AA1-10001
1953—Ser. 685-Super .. 652-LAI-10001
Ser. 685, Custom ... 652-MAI-10001

Location

1940-1942—Plate on outside front end of left frame side rail.

1946-1953 (except car)—On plate at left of driver's seat on floor riser.

1952-1953 (car)—On plate on left front door hinge post.

Starting Motor Numbers

1940-1941—Same as serial numbers.
1942 80301
1946-1952—Same as serial numbers.

Location

1940-1953 (except Aero Line)—On top of water pump boss at front end of block.

1952-1953 (Aero Line)—On top right front corner of block.

1953—Ser. 685 Super 6P-10001
1953—Ser. 685 Custom 652-MAI-10001

General Specifications

Year	Model	Wheelbase (in.)	Tread (in.)		Overall Dimensions (in.)			Shipping Weight (lb.)	Tire Size (in.)
			Front	Rear	Length	Width	Height		
1940	440	102	55	56	181	......	......	......	5.50-16
1941	441	104	55	58	181	......	......	2370	5.50-16
1942	442	104	55	58	181	......	......	2261	5.50-16
1946	......	......	......	......	......	......	......	......	......
1947	Station wagon	104	55	57	175	68	71	......	6.00-15
1948	663	104	56	57	177	69	72	......	6.00-15
1949	VJ-2	104	56	57	175	69	63	2394	5.90-15
	4-63	104	55	57	175	68	......	2898	6.00-15
	6-63	104	56	57	175	69	72	2845	6.50-15
1950	4-63	104	55	57	176	69	72	2587	6.70-15
	6-63	104	55	57	176	69	72	2845	6.70-15
1951	473-SD	104	55	57	176	72	72	2818•	6.50-15
	673-SD	104	55	57	176	72	72	2831•	6.70-15
1952	685, 6 cyl.	108	58	57	180	72	60	......	5.90-15
1953	675A, 685A, 6 cyl.	108	58	57	180	72	60	......	5.90-15

• Station wagon.

General Engine Specifications

Year	Model	Number of Cylinders Bore and Stroke	Piston Displacement, Cubic Inches	Compression Ratio (To–1)	Taxable (A.M.A.) Hp.	DEVELOPED HORSE POWER		Maximum Torque Ft. Lbs.
						Bare Engine	With Accessories	
1941–2	441, 442, 4 Cyl.	4–3⅛ x 4⅜	134.2	6.48	15.63	63 @ 3900	......	108 @ 1800
1942–9	CJ-2A, 3A, 463, 4 Cyl.	4–3⅛ x 4⅜	134.2	6.48	16.6	69 @ 3900	......	105 @ 2000
1947–9	VJ-2, 4 Cyl.	4–3⅛ x 4⅜	134.2	6.48	15.63	63 @ 4000	......	105 @ 2000

General Engine Specifications—*continued*

Year	Model	Number of Cylinders Bore and Stroke	Piston Displacement, Cubic Inches	Compression Ratio (To–1)	Taxable (A.M.A.) Hp.	DEVELOPED HORSE POWER Bare Engine	DEVELOPED HORSE POWER With Accessories	Maximum Torque Ft. Lbs.
1949	VJ-3, 4 Cyl.	4–$3\frac{1}{8}$ x $4\frac{3}{8}$	134.2	6.48	15.63	63 @ 4000		105 @ 2000
	VJ-36, 6 Cyl.	6–3 x $3\frac{1}{2}$	148.5	6.42	21.6	72 @ 4000		117 @ 1600
	4X4-63, 4 Cyl.	4–$3\frac{1}{8}$ x $4\frac{3}{8}$	134.2	6.48	15.63	63 @ 4000		105 @ 2000
1948–9	6-63, 6 Cyl.	6–3 x $3\frac{1}{2}$	148.44	6.42	21.6	72 @ 4000		117 @ 1600
1950–1	6-73, 6 Cyl.	6–$3\frac{1}{8}$ x $3\frac{1}{2}$	161.0	6.9	23.44	75 @ 4000		125 @ 2000
1950–1	4-73, 4 Cyl.	4–$3\frac{1}{8}$ x $4\frac{3}{8}$	134.2	7.4^	15.63	72 @ 4000		114 @ 2000
1952	685, 6 Cyl.	6–$3\frac{1}{8}$ x $3\frac{1}{2}$	161.0	7.60	23.44	90 @ 4400		135 @ 2000
1953	685A	6–$3\frac{1}{8}$ x $3\frac{1}{2}$	161.0	7.6	23.44	90 @ 4200		135 @ 2000
	675A	6–$3\frac{1}{8}$ x $3\frac{1}{2}$	161.0	6.9	23.44	75 @ 4000		125 @ 2000

^—Optional 6.9 and 7.8.

Dimensions of Valves

Year	Model	Overall Length Inlet	Overall Length Exhaust	Head Diameter Inlet	Head Diameter Exhaust	Seat Angle (deg.) Inlet	Seat Angle (deg.) Exhaust	Stem Diameter Inlet	Stem Diameter Exhaust	Key Type	O.D. of Seat Insert Inlet	O.D. of Seat Insert Exhaust
940 to 42	440, 441, 442	5.750	5.750	1.531	1.468	45	45	.373	.372	split lock		
1946 to 49	CJ-2A, 4-63	5.750	5.750	1.531	1.468	45	45	.372	.371	split lock		
1949–50	663	4.500	4.500	1.375	1.281	45	45	.341	.340	split lock		
1950	463	5.891	5.812	1.531	1.469	45	45	.340	.372	split lock		
1951	473-SD	4.781	5.710	2.000	1.469	45	45	.373	.372	split lock		
	673-SW	4.562	4.562	1.375	1.281	45	45	.341	.340	split lock		
1952	685, 6 cyl.	4.53125	4.625	1.75	1.28125	45	45	.37405	.340			
1953	685A, 6 cyl.	4.53125	4.625	1.75	1.28125	45	45	.37355	.340			
	675A, 6 cyl.	4.5625	4.625	1.375	1.28125	45	45	.34150	.340			

Pistons and Piston Pins

Year	Model	PISTONS Diameter	PISTONS Material	PISTONS Type	PISTONS No. of Rings	PISTON PINS Length	PISTON PINS Diameter	PISTON PINS How Held
1940 to 42	440, 41, 42	3.125	Alum.	Ts, C	3	$2\frac{25}{32}$	.8125	R
1946 to 48	Series—All, 4 cyl.	3.125	Alum.	Ts, C	3	$2\frac{25}{32}$	.8125	R
1948	663, 6 cyl.	3	CA		3		.7497	R
1949	VJ-2-4-63	3.125	Alum.		3		.7497	R
	6-63	3	CA		3		.7497	R
1950	4-63	3.125	Alum. Alloy		3	$2\frac{25}{32}$	.8118	R
	6-63	3	Alum. Alloy	Sp	3	$2\frac{17}{32}$	.7497	R
1951	473-SD	3.125	Alum. Alloy	Ts	3	$2\frac{25}{32}$	.8118	R
	673-SW	3.125	Alum. Alloy	Ts	3	$2\frac{21}{32}$	.750	R
1952	685, 6 cyl.	3.125	Alum. Alloy		3	2.65625	.7497	R
1953	675A, 685A, 6 cyl.	3.125	Alum. Alloy		3	2.65625	.7497	R

Ts—"T" slot. C—Cam ground. Sp—Slipper skirt. CA—Cast aluminum.

Engine Overhaul Specifications

Year	Model	PISTONS				RING GAP CLEARANCES (Maximum)				PISTON PIN		ROD BEARINGS		
		Removed From	Piston Skirt Clearances (Maximum)											
			Top	Bottom	Limit	Top Ring	Second Ring	Third Ring	Oil Ring	Type	Fit	Oil Clearance	Wear Limit	Side Play
1941	441, 4 Cyl.	A	.003	.003	.005	.013	.013	......	.013	LR	Push	.0008–.0023	.005	.005–.009
1942	442, 4 Cyl.	A	.002	.002	.005	.013	.013	......	.013	LR	Push	.0008–.0023	.005	.005–.009
1942–8	CJ-2A, 4 Cyl.	A	.004	.004	.005	.013	.013	......	.013	LR	Push	.0005–.0025	.005	.005–.009
1949	CJ-3A, 4 Cyl.	A	.003	.003	.005	.013	.013	......	.013	LR	Push	.0005–.0025	.005	.004–.010
1946–9	4-63, 4 Cyl.	A	.003	.003	.005	.013	.013	......	.013	LR	Push	.0005–.0025	.005	.0005–.0025
1947–9	VJ-2, 4 Cyl.	A	.004	.004	.005	.013	.013	......	.013	LR	Push	.0005–.0025	.005	.005–.009
1949	VJ-3, 4 Cyl. VJ-36, 6 Cyl. 4X4-63, 4 Cyl.	A A A	.003 .0015 .003	.003 .0015 .003	.005 .004 .005	.013 .016 .013	.013 .016 .013	....	.013 .016 .013	LR LR LR	Push Push Push	.0005–.0025 .0005–.0025 .0005–.0025	.005 .005 .005	.004–.010 .004–.010 .004–.010
1948–9	6-63, 6 Cyl.	A	.0015	.0015	.004	.016	.016	......	.016	LR	Push	.0005–.0025	.005	.004–.010
1950–1 1950–1	6-73, 6 Cyl. 4-73, 4 Cyl.	A A	.0021 .003	.0021 .003	.004 .005	.017 .013	.017 .013	....	.013 .013	LR LR	Push Push	.0001–.0025 .0002–.0025	.005 .005	.002–.008 .004–.010
1952	685, 6 Cyl.	A	.0021	.0021	......	.015	.015	......	.015	LR	Push	.0001–.0025	.005	.004–.010
1953	685A, 6 Cyl. 675A, 6 Cyl.	A A	.0021 .0021	.0021 .0021	....	.015 .015	.015 .015	....	.015 .015	LR LR	Push Push	.0025 .0025	.005 .005	.002–.010 .002–.010

A—Above. LR—Locked in rod. B—BUDC Sp.—Sprocket.
†—Center crank gear mark with cam gear mark.

Crankshaft Bearing Journal Sizes

Year	Model	Connecting Rod Journals		Main Bearing Journals				
		Diameter	Length	No. 1 Diameter	No. 2 Diameter	No. 3 Diameter	No. 4 Diameter	No. 5 Diameter
1940 to 42	440, 441, 442	1.937	1.312	2.334	2.334	2.334	......	......
1948 to 50	463, 473, VJ	1.937	1.312	2.334	2.334	2.334	......	......
1948 to 50	663, 673, VJ	1.875	.899	2.250	2.250	2.250	2.250	......
1951	473 673	1.9375 1.875	1.3125 1.125	2.334 2.250	2.334 2.250	2.334 2.250	...... 2.250	....
1952	685, 6 cyl.	1.875	......	2.250	2.250	2.250	2.250	......
1953	675A, 685A, 6 cyl.	1.875	......	2.25–1.304	2.25–1.062	2.25–1.062	2.25–1.405	......

Piston Ring Dimensions

Year	Model	Cylinder Bore	TOP RING			SECOND RING			THIRD RING			OIL RING		
			Width	Gap	Depth	Width	Gap	Depth	Width	Gap	Depth	Width	Gap	Depth
1940–50	440, 41, 42, CJ-2A, 4-63, VJ2 4-73, SD	3⅛	3/32	.010	.135	3/32	.010	.135	3/16	.010	.140	......	......	......
1948–50	663	3	3/32	.010	.140	3/32	.010	.140	3/16	.010	.140	......	......	......
1951	6-73, SW	3⅛	3/32	.012	.139	3/32	.012	.139	3/16	.010	.140	......	......	......
1952	685, 6 Cyl.	3⅛	3/32	.011	.1545	3/32	.011	.1545	3/16	.011	.1645	......	......	......
1953	685A, 675A, 6 Cyl.	3⅛	3/32	.011	.144	3/32	.011	.144	3/16	.011	......	......	......	......

and Wear Limit Table

CRANKSHAFT		VALVES									OPERATING OIL PRESSURE			
Main Bearing Oil Clearance	Shaft End Play	Spring Tension (Maximum) Inlet	Spring Tension (Maximum) Exhaust	Spring Tension (Maximum) Low Limit	Guide Clearance	Seat Angle Inlet	Seat Angle Exhaust	Valve Timing, Inlet Valve Opens (Deg.)	Camshaft Drive	Gear Marks	Pounds At M.P.H.	Low Limit§	Model	Year
.001-.002	.004-.006	116@1¾	116@1¾	100	.002-.00375	45°	45°	9B	Gear	†	40@30	30	..............441, 4 Cyl.	1941
.001-.002	.004-.006	116@1¾	116@1¾	100	.002-.00375	45°	45°	9B	Gear	†	75@30	55	..............442, 4 Cyl.	1942
.001-.0025	.001-.0025	124@1¾	124@1¾	112	.012-.00375	45°	45°	9B	Gear	Sp.▵	50@30	35	............CJ-2A, 4 Cyl.	1942-8
.0014-.0029	.004-.006	120@1¾	120@1¾	108	.0015-.0045	45°	45°	9B	Gear	†	35@30	25	............CJ-3A, 4 Cyl.	1949
.0014-.0029	.004-.006	120@1¾	120@1¾	108	.0015-.0045	45°	45°	9B	Gear	†	35@30	25	..............4-63, 4 Cyl.	1946-9
.001-.0025	.004-.006	116@1¾	116@1¾	100	.0015-.00375	45°	45°	9B	Gear	†	35@30	25	..............VJ-2, 4 Cyl.	1947-9
.0014-.0029	.004-.006	120@1¾	120@1¾	108	.0015-.0045	45°	45°	9B	Gear	†	35@30	25	..............VJ-3, 4 Cyl.	1949
.0009-.003	.002-.006	105@$1\frac{21}{64}$	105@$1\frac{21}{64}$	94	.0015-.0045	45°	45°	5B	Gear	†	35@30	25	..............VJ-36, 6 Cyl.	
.0014-.0029	.004-.006	120@1¾	120@1¾	108	.0015-.0045	45°	45°	9B	Gear	†	35@30	25	..........4X4-63, 4 Cyl.	
.0009-.003	.002-.006	105@$1\frac{21}{64}$	105@$1\frac{21}{64}$	94	.0015-.0045	45°	45°	5B	Gear	†	35@30	25	..............6-63, 6 Cyl.	1948-9
.0009-.003	.002-.006	105@$1\frac{21}{64}$	105@$1\frac{21}{64}$	94	.0015-.00325	45°	45°	5B	Gear	†	40@30	30	..............6-73, 6 Cyl.	1950-1
.0014-.0029	.004-.006	160@1⅜	120@1¾	......	.0007-.0022	45°	45°	9B	Gear	†	35@30	28	..............4-73, 4 Cyl.	1950-1
.0009-.003	.004-.006	153@1.40	105@$1\frac{21}{64}$	......	.0025-.0045	45°	45°	9B	Gear	......	35@35	......	..............685, 6 Cyl.	1952
.0009-.003	.004-.006	153@1.40	105@$1\frac{21}{64}$	......	.0045	45°	45°	9B	Gear	......	35@35	......	..............685A, 6 Cyl.	1953
.0009-.003	.004-.006	153@1.40	105@$1\frac{21}{64}$	......	.0045	45°	45°	5B	Gear	......	35@35	......	..............675A, 6 Cyl.	

▵—Chain driven up to #44417—after—gear drive.
§—Car may be operated safely at lower oil pressures but low pressure indicates malfunction which should be corrected

Engine Tune-Up Specifications

		SPARK PLUGS		DISTRIBUTOR					OPERATING TAPPET CLEARANCE			
Year	Model	Type	Gap	Point Gap	Cam Dwell, (Deg.)	Ignition Timing, (Deg.)	Ignition Timing Mark and Location	Compression Pressure at R.P.M.	Inlet	Exhaust	Carburetor Fuel Float Height	Minimum Engine Idle Speed at R.P.M.
1941	441, 4 Cyl....................	CH-J8	.030	.020	41	TC	Flywheel	111@185	.014	.014	⅜″	6
1942	442, 4 Cyl....................	CH-J7	.030	.020	41	TC	Flywheel	111@185	.014	.014	⅜″	6
1942-8	CJ-2A, 4 Cyl..................	AL-AW7	.030	.024	41	5B	Flywheel	111@185	.014	.014	⅜″	6
1949	CJ-3A, 4 Cyl..................	AL-AW7	.030	.024	50.8	5B	Flywheel	115@160	.016	.016	⅜″	6
1946-9	4-63, 4 Cyl..................	AL-AW7	.030	.024	50.8	5B	Flywheel	115@160	.016	.016	⅜″	6
1947-9	VJ-2, 4 Cyl..................	AL-AW7	.030	.024	41	5B	Flywheel	110@160	.014	.014	⅜″	6
1949	VJ-3, 4 Cyl..................	AL-AW7	.030	.024	50.8	5B	Flywheel	115@160	.016	.016	⅜″	6
	VJ-36, 6 Cyl..................	AL-AW7	.030	.020	38	TC	Dmpr.	120@160	.016	.016	$\frac{5}{16}$″	6
	4X4-63, 4 Cyl..................	AL-AW7	.030	.024	50.8	5B	Flywheel	115@160	.016	.016	⅜″	6
1948-9	6-63, 6 Cyl....................	AL-AW7	.030	.020	38	TC	Dmpr.	120@160	.016	.016	$\frac{5}{16}$″	6
1950-1	6-73, 6 Cyl....................	CH-J7	.030	.020	39	TC	Dmpr.	145@185	.016	.016	⅜″	6
1950-1	4-73, 4 Cyl....................	CH-J7	.030	.020	51	TC	Flywheel	135@185	.012	.012	⅜″	6
1952	685, 6 Cyl....................	CH	.030	.020	39	TC	Dmpr.	....	.018	.016	$\frac{9}{32}$″	550
1953	685A, 6 Cyl..................	CH-J8	.030	.020	39	TC	Dmpr.	....	.018	.016	....	550
	675A, 6 Cyl..................	CH-J8	.030	.020	39	TC	Dmpr.	....	.016	.016	....	550

AL—Auto-Lite. CH—Champion. TC—Top center. Dmpr.—Vibration damper. M.P.H.—Miles per hour.

Brake Data

Year	Model	Make	Lining Type	R=Riveted B=Bonded	Drum Diameter	Lining Length	Lining Width	Lining Thickness	Clearance Toe	Clearance Heel
1940 to 42	440, 441, 442	Ben	M	CN	9	18⅝	1¾	3/16	.008	.004
1948	663	....	....	....	10	19	1¾	3/16	SC	SC
1949	VJ2, 463, 663	Ben	M	CN	9.9	19	1.76	.222	....	....
1950	463, 663	Ben	M	CN	9.9	19	1¾	.187	....	....
1951	473, 673	Ben	M	CI	10	19	1¾	3/16	....	....
1952	685, 6 Cyl.	....	M	R	9	17 9/16	2-*1¾	7/32	.005	.005
1953	685A, 675A	....	M	R	9	17 9/16	2-*1¾	7/32	.005	.005

*—Pri., 2 in.; Sec., 1¾ in. Ben—Bendix. M—Moulded. CN—Chrome nickel.

Tension Wrench Specifications

Year	Model	Cylinder Head Lbs.-Ft.	Cylinder Head Thread	Spark Plug Lbs.-Ft.	Spark Plug Thread	Connecting Rod Bolts or Nuts Lbs.-Ft.	Connecting Rod Bolts or Nuts Thread	Main Bearing Bolt Lbs.-Ft.	Main Bearing Bolt Thread	Flywheel Bolts Lbs.-Ft.	Flywheel Bolts Thread	Vibration Damper Bolts Lbs.-Ft.	Vibration Damper Bolts Thread
1940 to 53	4-40, 4-41, 4-42	60–65	....	25–30	14 mm	50–55	....	65–70	....	36–40	....	....	....
	CJ, 2A, 4-63, 6-63	60–65	....	25–30	14 mm	50–55	....	65–70	....	36–40	....	....	....

Cooling System

CAR AND YEAR	MODEL	Capacity Qts.	Quarts of Methanol Base Anti-Freeze (For Protection to Temperature Shown Below)							Quarts of Ethylene Glycol (For Protection to Temperature Shown Below)							Quarts of Denatured Alcohol—188 Proof (For Protection to Temperature Shown Below)						
			3	4	5	6	7	8	9	3	4	5	6	7	8	9	3	4	5	6	7	8	9
1937-38-39	37-38-48	11	0	−18	−40	....	....	....	....	8	−6	−23	−47	....	....	....	10	0	−10	−20	−30	....	....
1940-41-42	440	11¾	3	−12	−31	−53	....	....	....	10	0	−15	−34	−57	....	....	10	0	−10	−20	−30	....	....
1946-53		11	0	−18	−40	....	....	....	....	8	−6	−23	−47	....	....	....	10	0	−10	−20	−30	....	....

Distributors

Year	Model	Distributor Model Number	Cam Angle (deg.)	Direction of Rotation C-Clockwise CC-Counter Clockwise at Cam End	Breaker Arm Spring Tension	Breaker Point Gap (inches)	Engine R.P.M. when Cent. Advance Starts	Max. Cent. Advance in Engine Deg. at Stated Engine R.P.M.	Vacuum in (inches) of Mercury at which Vacuum Unit Starts	Max. Advance in Engine Deg. at Stated Vacuum	Vacuum Unit Number
1940	4-40, 4 cyl.	IGS-4007B	47	CC	17–20	.018–.022	600	19@3000	5	14@15	IGT-1028-ES
1941–42	4-41, 442, 4 cyl.	IGW-4129	41	CC	17–20	.018–.022	600	19@3000	3½	20@15	VC-4010
1945 to 49	CJ-2A, CJ-2, 4 cyl.	IGW-4177-1	41	CC	17–20	.020–.024	500	22@3000			
	....	IAD-4008	41	CC	17–20	.018–.022	500	22@3000	....	....	....
	....	IGW-4189	41	CC	17–20	.020–.024	700	22@3000	3½	20@15	VC-4010
1946 to 49	4-63, 4 cyl.	IGW-4129	41	CC	17–20	.018–.022	600	19@3000	3½	20@15	VC-4010
	....	IGW-4189	41	CC	17–20	.018–.022	500	22@3000	3½	20@15	VC-4010

Distributors—*continued*

Year	Model	Distributor Model Number	Cam Angle (deg.)	Direction of Rotation C-Clockwise CC-Counter Clockwise at Cam End	Breaker Arm Spring Tension	Breaker Point Gap (inches)	Engine R.P.M. when Cent. Advance Starts	Max. Cent. Advance in Engine Deg. at Stated Engine R.P.M.	Vacuum in (inches) of Mercury at which Vacuum Unit Starts	Max. Advance in Engine Deg. at Stated Vacuum	Vacuum Unit Number
1948 to 49	6-63, 6 cyl.	IGC-4513	38.5	CC	17–20	.018–.022	700	24@3000	3½	12@15	....
	....	IGC-4514	38.5	CC	17–20	.018–.022	700	24@3000	3½	12@15	VC-4010
1949 to 50	VJ2, VJ3, 4 cyl.	IGW-4129	41	CC	17–20	.018–.022	600	19@3000	3½	20@15	VC-4010
	....	IGW-4189	41	CC	17–20	.018–.022	500	22@3000	3½	20@15	VC-4010
1950–51	473, VJ, Jeepster, 4 cyl.	IAT-4008	41	CC	17–20	.018–.022	600	22@4000	4¾	10@8	IAT-2023-LD
	673, VJ, Jeepster, 6 cyl.	IAT-4007	39	CC	17–20	.018–.022	700	24@4000	3½	12@15	....
1952	685, 6 cyl.	IAT-4007A	39	C	17–20	.020	300	9½@1300	5⅛	6@14	....
1953	685A, 6 cyl.	IAT-4007A	39	C	....	.020	600	19@2600	5⅛	12@14	....
	675A, 6 cyl.	IAT-4007	39	C	....	.020	700	19@3000	3½	12@15	....

Generators

Year	Model	Generator Number	Field Current at 6 Volts (amps.)	Maximum Safe Output			Brush Spring Tension (oz.)	Voltage Regulator Number
				Volts	Amperes	R.P.M.		
1940 to 42	4-40, 41, 42	GCJ-4811-A	1.7–1.9	8.0	25	2500	35–53	VRR-4004-A
1945–49	C-J-2A, 4-63, 6-63	GDZ-4817-A	1.3–1.5	8.0	35	2000	35–53	VRP-4007-C-2
	VJ-2, VJ-3	GDZ-4817-A	1.3–1.5	8.0	35	2000	35–53	VRP-4007-C-2
1950–51	4-73, 6-73	GDZ-6001-D	1.6–1.8	8.0	30–37	1900	35–53	VRP-6003-A
1952	685, 6 cyl.	GDZ-6001-D	....	....	....	....	....	VRP-6003-A
1953	685A, 675A	6DZ-6001-D	....	6.8	45	2450	....	VBE-6105A

Voltage Regulators

Year	Model	Regulator Number	Grounded P-Positive N-Negative	Voltage Control		Current Control		Cut-Out Relay		
				Air Gap Points Closed	Voltage Setting Hot	Air Gap Points Closed	Current Set Hot	Point Gap	Air Gap	Closing Volt
1940 to 42	40, 41, 42	VRR-4004-A	P	.052	7.2	.052	....	.015	.034	6.4–7.0
1945 to 49	CJ-2, CJ-2-A, 4-63, 6-63	VRP-4007-C-2	P	.052	7.2	.052	34–36	.015	.034	6.4–7.0
1950–51	4-63, 4-73, 6-63, 6-73, CJ3A	VRP-6003-A	P	.050	7.35	.050	34–36	.015	.032	6.4–6.9
1952	685, 6 cyl.	VRP-6003-A	....	....	7.3–7.5	....	35	....	....	6.3–6.8
1953	685A, 675A, 6 cyl.	VBE-6105-A	....	....	7.35	....	45	....	....	6.3–6.8

Starters

Year	Model	Unit Model Number	Spring Tension (oz.)	STARTER						Direction of Rotation Viewed from Drive End C-Clockwise CC-Counter-clockwise
				Lock Test			No Load			
				Volts	Amperes	Torque, (lbs. ft.)	Volts	Amperes	R.P.M.	
1940	4-40	MZ-4064	42–53	2.0	280	4.4	5.0	68	4000	C
1941	4-41	MZ-4093-9	42–53	2.0	280	4.4	5.0	68	4000	C

Starters—*continued*

Year	Model	Unit Model Number	Spring Tension (oz.)	STARTER: Lock Test Volts	Lock Test Amperes	Lock Test Torque, (lbs. ft.)	No Load Volts	No Load Amperes	No Load R.P.M.	Direction of Rotation Viewed from Drive End C-Clockwise CC-Counter-clockwise
1942	4-42	MZ-4109	42-53	2.0	280	4.4	5.0	68	4000	C
1945 to 49	CJ-2, CJ-2A	MZ-4113	42-53	2.0	280	4.4	5.0	68	4000	C
1946 to 49	4-63, 6-63	MZ-4137	42-53	2.0	280	4.4	5.0	68	4000	C
1950	4-73, 6-73, CJ-3A	MZ-4137	42-53	2.0	280	4.4	5.0	68	4000	C
1951	473-SD, 673-SW	MZ-4162	42-53	2.0	280	4.4	5.0	68	4000	C
1952	685, 6 cyl.	MCH-6203	42-53	2.0	335	6.0	5.0	65	4300	C
1953	685A, 675A, 6 cyl.	MCH-6203	42-53	2.0	335	6.0	5.0	65	4300	C

Front Wheel Alignment

Year	Model	Caster (deg.)	Camber (deg.)	King Pin Inclination (deg.)	Toe-In (inches)	Turning Radius Inner	Turning Radius Outer
1940–42	440, 441, 442	1P to 3P	1P to 2P	7½	1/32 to 5/32	23¼	20
1946–48	CJ2A-Universal, 4 cyl.	1P to 3P	1P to 2P	7½	3/64 to 3/32	20	18½
1949–51	CJ3A Universal, 4 cyl.	1P	1P to 2P	5½	1/16 to ⅛	20	18½
1946–49	4-63 Station Wagon, 4 cyl.	1P	1P to 2P	5½	1/16 to ⅛	20	18½
1947–49	VJ2-Jeepster, 4 cyl.	1P	1P to 2P	5½	1/16 to ⅛	20	18½
1949	VJ3-Jeepster, 4 cyl.	1P	1P to 2P	5½	1/16 to ⅛	20	18½
	VJ3-Jeepster, 6 cyl.	1P	1P to 2P	5	1/16 to ⅛	20	18½
	4X463-Jeep Station Wagon	1P	1P to 2P	5½	1/16 to ⅛	20	18½
1948–49	6-63 Jeep Station Wagon	1P	1P to 2P	5	1/16 to ⅛	20	18½
1950–52	4-73, 4 cyl.	1N to 1P	1 to 1½P	5	1/16 to ⅛	20	18½
	6-73, 6 cyl.	1P	1P¼P to 1½P	5	1/16 to ⅛	......	......
1953	685A, 675A, 6 cyl.	2N to 1P	1¼P to 1¾P	8¼	3/32 to 5/32	19	20

Fan, Generator Belts and Radiator Hose

Year	Model	Fan Belt Angle of "V" (deg.)	Fan Belt Length O.C.	Fan Belt Width Max.	Generator Belt Angle of "V" (deg.)	Generator Belt Length O.C.	Generator Belt Width Max.	Upper Hose Type	Upper Hose Inside Diam.	Upper Hose Length	Lower Hose Type	Lower Hose Inside Diam.	Lower Hose Length
1940 to 42	440, 441, 442	42	42¼	21/32	......	......	......	straight	1½	10	straight	1½	2½-6¾
1946 to 50	SW. Jeep, 463	42	42¼	21/32	......	......	......	straight	1½	2⅝	curved	1½	......
1946 to 49	CJ2A, Jeep	42	42¼	21/32	......	......	......	straight	1½	3	curved	1½	......
1948 to 50	663	42	38⅜	11/16	......	......	......	curved	1½	......	curved	1½	......
1952	685, 6 cyl.	40	40 19/32	⅝	......	......	......	curved	1½	......	curved	1½	......
1953	685A, 675A, 6 cyl.	40	37	⅝	......	......	......	curved	1½	......	curved	1½	......

FRONT SUSPENSION

From 1940 through 1953 the Willys Overland Motor Car Co. built cars with the tubular front axles, I beam front axles, front wheel drives, and Planodine front suspension. The tubular axles and I beam axles were used on different body styles and were mixed in production.

Rigid front axles or front wheel drives were used on all models through 1947. Starting with 1948 production, a Planodine type front suspension was introduced on Willys cars. The planar type front suspension was not used on all models and tubular and I beam type axles are still used on some production models.

Caster, Camber and Toe-In

RIGID TYPE AXLES

On rigid type axles camber is adjusted by bending the I beam to produce the desired setting. Heavy duty equipment is required to bend the tubular or I beam axle. Caster is adjusted by twisting the end of the axle in relation to the spring seat, or, if both sides are to be corrected an equal amount in the same direction, it is possible to do so by placing caster wedges between the spring seat and the semi-elliptic leaf spring.

PLANODINE TYPE FRONT SUSPENSION

The front suspension used on Willys cars is known as the Planodine suspension. Willys Overland Co. say that caster is non-adjustable and that camber can be increased by adding shims back of the upper suspension arm inner frame bracket.

A slight correction of caster can be made by adding shims back of the front bracket only, to increase caster, and back of the back bracket only to decrease caster. Adding shims at either of these points will tend to increase camber, however. If shims are found back of both brackets and it is necessary to increase caster, it is a good idea to remove the shim from the back bracket and add that shim to the front bracket. In this way, with no radical change in camber, a considerable caster adjustment can be obtained.

FRONT WHEEL DRIVES

On front wheel drive models caster is adjusted by placing shims between the spring pads on the rear axle housing and the top of the spring.

This method should only be used where it is necessary to adjust both sides of the car the same amount. In the event the caster reading is low because of sag of the front leaf springs it is advisable to replace the springs rather than use caster wedges. Camber, on front wheel drives, can be adjusted only by bending the axle tube and this certainly is not recommended.

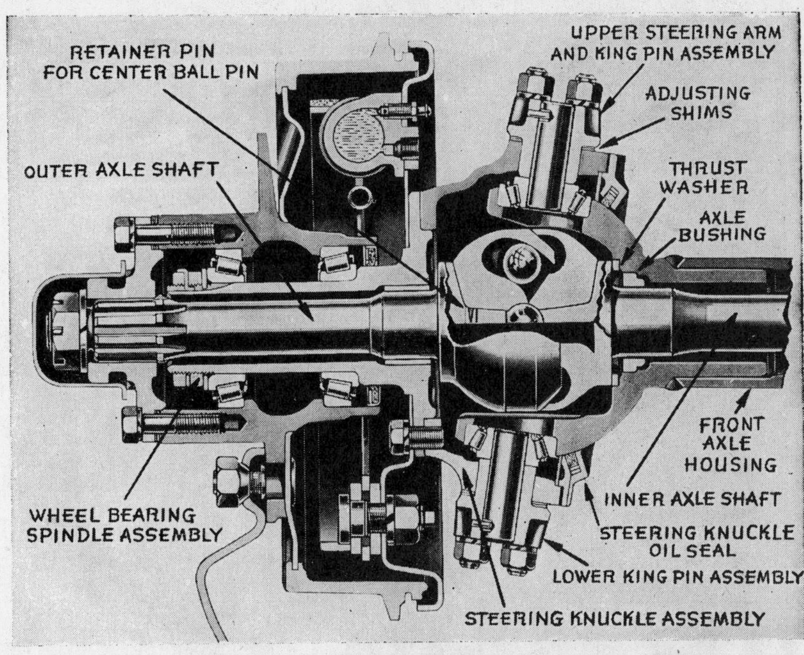

Section thru the front wheel constant velocity universal joint

Replacement of King Pins

The method of replacing the king pins is the same regardless of whether the car is tubular axle, I beam axle or planar type front suspension. The only exception to the following text is the four-wheel drives.

Remove the wheel brake drum and front backing plate. It is not necessary to disconnect the hydraulic brake line. The backing plate can be slid off the end of the spindle and hung with a stout wire to the frame. Drive out the king pin lock pin and remove the upper welsh plug. The king pin can then be driven downward and out of the knuckle. Some models of Willys used needle bearings, others used bushings and some used both, needle bearing in the upper end and a bushing in the lower end of the knuckle support. Where bushings are used it will be necessary to secure a ream fit on the bushings. Needle bearings should be pressed in a sufficient amount to permit entrance of a welsh plug at the top of the knuckle.

Shims are provided to be mounted over the thrust bearing to insure that there is no up and down motion at all in the spindle.

Replacement of King Pins

FOUR-WHEEL DRIVES

An upper and lower pivot pin is used in the four-wheel drive models. Both upper and lower pins are held to the universal joint housing by four cap screws. There are two tapered roller bearings, one top and one bottom in the axle housing, exactly centered across the neutral point of the constant velocity universal joint. If it is desired to replace the tapered roller bearings, it will be necessary to remove the universal joint outer housing. This involves removing the wheel and the stationary axle. If the pivot pins only are to be replaced, they can be removed by taking out the four cap screws which hold them to the universal joint housing. Shims are used under the head of the pivot pins to insure zero up and down play in the tapered roller bearings. To remove the pivot pins it is advisable to take off the wheel, brake drum and brake backing plate.

Universal Joint—Front Axle

The front axle differential is serviced in exactly the same manner as the rear axle differential, which will be discussed later in this text.

Two types of constant velocity universal joints were used on Willys four-

continued

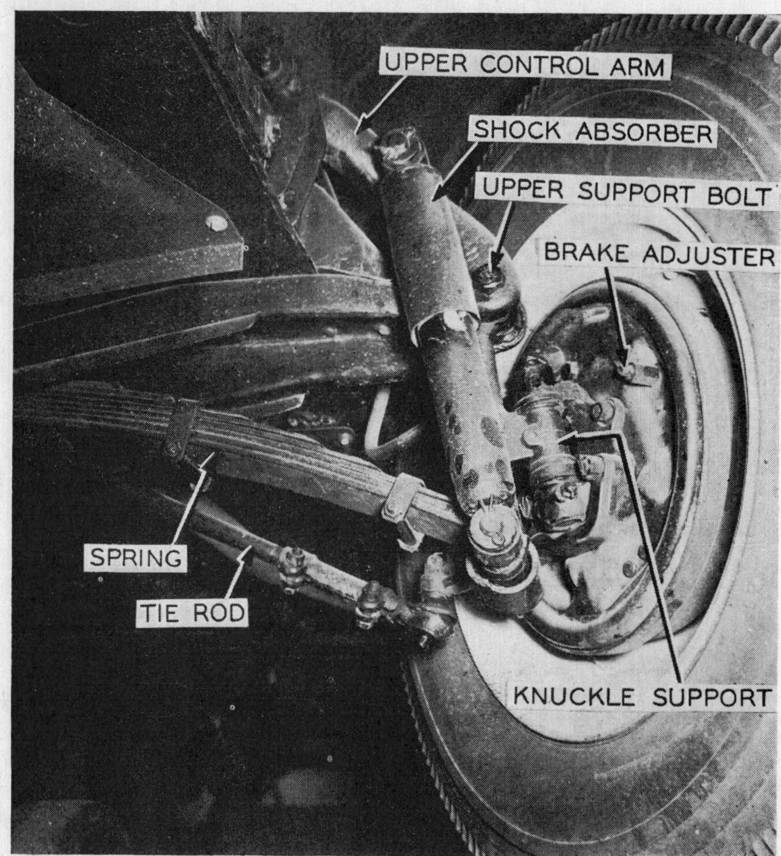

Front suspension 1952 station wagon

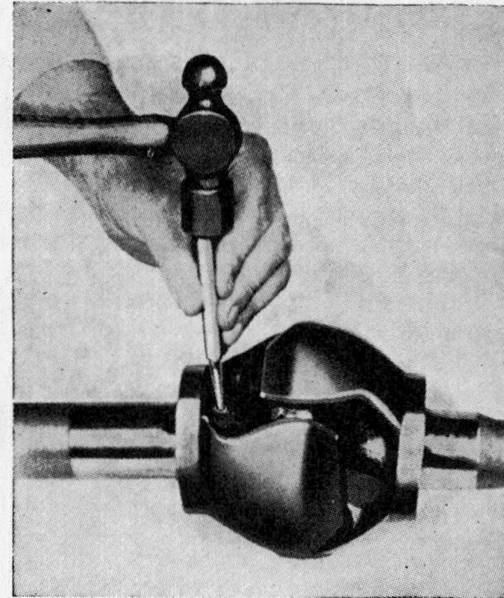

Driving out retainer pin (Bendix joint)

UNIVERSAL JOINT—*continued*

wheel drives. The first was the Bendix type universal joint, the second the Rzeppa type.

BENDIX JOINT

To disassemble the Bendix joint hold the splined driving axle in a vise and drive out the center all pin retainer.

Jolt the splined driving axle against a block of wood so that the ball retaining pin will drop through the drilled hole which is lengthwise of the driving axle. Pull the two halves of the joint apart and then bend the joint sharply. Rotate the center ball until the grooved side lines up with a ball raceway, which will permit the adjacent ball to be moved past the center ball and out of the joint. The remaining three driving balls and the center ball will then drop out. Examine the raceways for scoring, scratches or markings.

Note: The driving ball is .875" and is available in .001, .002 and .003 inch under-size and over-size. This permits selective fitting. If the raceways are free of scores and scratches and the joint has play, select a ball of sufficient over-size to take up the play.

Note: Variation in ball size in any one joint should not be greater than .001 inch.

RZEPPA JOINT

Dismantle the Rzeppa joint, remove the three screws which hold the front axle shaft to the joint itself and pull the shaft out of the splined inner race. To take out the axle shaft retainer, remove the retainer ring on the shaft. Push down on the various points of the inner race and cage until the balls can be removed with the help of a small screw driver.

After all the balls have been removed, the inner race and cage can be turned over so the pilot cup is up and then the pilot cup can be taken out.

There are two large elongated holes in the cage. Turn the cage so that the two bosses in the spindle shaft will drop into the elongated holes in the cage and then the cage can be lifted out.

To remove the inner race, turn it so that one of the bosses will drop into an elongated hole in this cage and then shift the race to one side and lift it out.

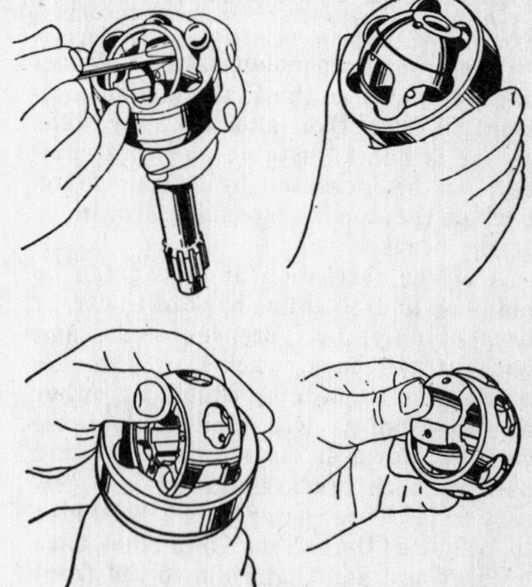

Disassembly of the Rzeppa joint

Replacement of Transverse Front Spring

The transverse front spring used on the independent front suspension on Willys cars can be replaced by supporting the weight of the car on jacks back of the front suspension, removing both bolts from the outer ends of the spring shackles and unbolt the spring from the frame. It is not necessary to detach the shock absorber from the upper suspension arm.

STEERING GEAR

Three different types of steering gears are used on Willys cars. First, the worm and double roller type with the shim adjusted cross shaft; second, the worm and double roller type with the screw adjusted cross shaft and the twin lever variable ratio type gear.

To adjust the steering mechanism on the first type, the shim adjusted cross shaft worm and double roller type, it is necessary first to back off the screw in the cover plate of the gear which controls the end play of the cross shaft. (**Note:** On the shim adjusted type gear this screw is held with an ordinary lock nut. On the screw adjusted type gear, which looks almost identical to the shim adjusted type, the cross shaft adjusting screw is covered with an acorn nut. This is a quick, easy way to identify these two gears.)

Check for up and down play in the worm bearings by disconnecting the pitman arm from the drag link and moving the pitman arm back and forth. If any end play is noticed in the worm bearings, remove the cover assembly and take out one shim at a time until all end play is taken up and there is a very slight preload on the worm bearings. Now take out all the end play in the cross shaft and check for back lash in the gears at the mid position of the steering wheel. If any play exists at this point it will be necessary to take off the cover, remove the pitman arm slide out the cross shaft and remove one shim at a time until there is zero lash in the gears with the steering wheel in the mid position of its travel. At this point replace the cover and adjust the thrust screw in the cover so that there is about .002 or .003 end play in the pitman shaft.

SECOND TYPE STEERING GEAR

The second type gear is almost identical in appearance to the first type, shim adjusted gear, the physical difference being that the adjusting screw for the cross shaft is covered with an acorn nut and has a star type lock washer. To adjust this gear, remove the drag link from the end of the pitman arm and by moving the pitman arm back and forth determine if there is any end play in the worm bearings. If any play exists, remove the cover and take out shims until there is zero play in the bearings with a very slight preload. Remove the acorn nut from the cross shaft adjusting screw and adjust the cross shaft so that there is zero lash in the gears with the steering wheel in the mid position of its travel.

THIRD TYPE STEERING GEAR

The third type steering gear is a twin lever type having a screw adjusted cross shaft. First disconnect the drag link from the pitman arm to determine if there is any end play in the bearings. If end play exists, remove the cap screws which hold the bearings in the top of the case and remove one shim at a time, replace the screws and tighten up the cover until there is zero play in the worm shaft. Loosen the lock nut on the cross shaft adjuster and turn the cross shaft adjuster until there is zero lash between the worm and twin lever with the steering wheel in the mid position of its travel. Tighten the jam nut.

Removal of Steering Gear Assembly

The steering gear can be readily removed from the 1940 model by removing the floor board and disconnecting the shift levers and the gear mounting bolts.

MODELS CJ-2A, 4-63, 2-WD, 4-WD, AND 6-63

On these models it is necessary to pass the steering gear down through the floor pan. Much time will be saved if the front left fender is removed from the model CJ-2A. Remove the gear shift lever, steering wheel, the exhaust pipe from the manifold, the steering column cover plate on the toe board, take off the steering wheel and the horn attaching parts. The gear mechanism may then be unbolted from the frame and pulled out downward through the floor pan.

BRAKES

Lockheed hydraulic brakes were used on all models of Willys from 1940 through 1953.

Brake Inspection

Before attempting to adjust or service the Willys brake, remove at least one wheel to determine if the drums, linings, shoes and hydraulic cylinders are in good condition. Oil or brake fluid on the wheel cylinder boots indicates that that cylinder is leaking or seeping and should be either honed on the car, if it is not too bad, or removed from the car and resurfaced on a bench type wheel cylinder hone.

Minor Brake Adjustment

The minor brake adjustment is made to compensate for normal lining wear. Turn the cam adjuster at each shoe until the shoe drags and then back it off until the wheel is just free. Repeat this procedure at all four wheels and road test the car.

Pedal Clearance

There should be from ½″ to ¾″ free motion of the brake pedal before the master cylinder rod contacts the master cylinder piston. This play is left to insure that the master cylinder piston comes to the fully released position when the brakes are released.

Major Brake Adjustment

A major brake adjustment is performed to compensate for pulling or uneven braking and also when new linings are used.

Insert a .005 inch feeler gage between the lining and drum at the anchor end of the forward shoe. Adjust the eccentric anchor so that the feeler gage is just gripped. Then turn the cam adjuster, on the same shoe, until a .010 inch feeler is just gripped between the lining and drum at the toe end of the forward shoe. Go back and recheck the heel end of the shoe so that when the adjustment is complete there is .005 inch clearance at the heel end of the shoe and .010 inch clearance at the toe end of the shoe. When this setting is arrived at, securely tighten the anchor nut without disturbing the setting of the anchor pin.

Repeat this procedure at all eight shoes.

ENGINE ASSEMBLY

Three types of engines are available for domestic use: The four-cylinder L-Head, six-cylinder L-Head and six-cylinder F-Head engine.

The F-Head engine is an adaptation of the six-cylinder L-Head in that a head is installed on the six-cylinder block which incorporates an intake valve on the six-cylinder block. The head contains an intake valve and rocker mechanism which is operated by a push rod through the intake port of the L-Head block.

All service instructions, except those dealing with rocker arms, are applicable to both the F-Head and the L-Head six-cylinder engine.

In addition to the above three engines an F-Head four-cylinder engine is available for export.

continued

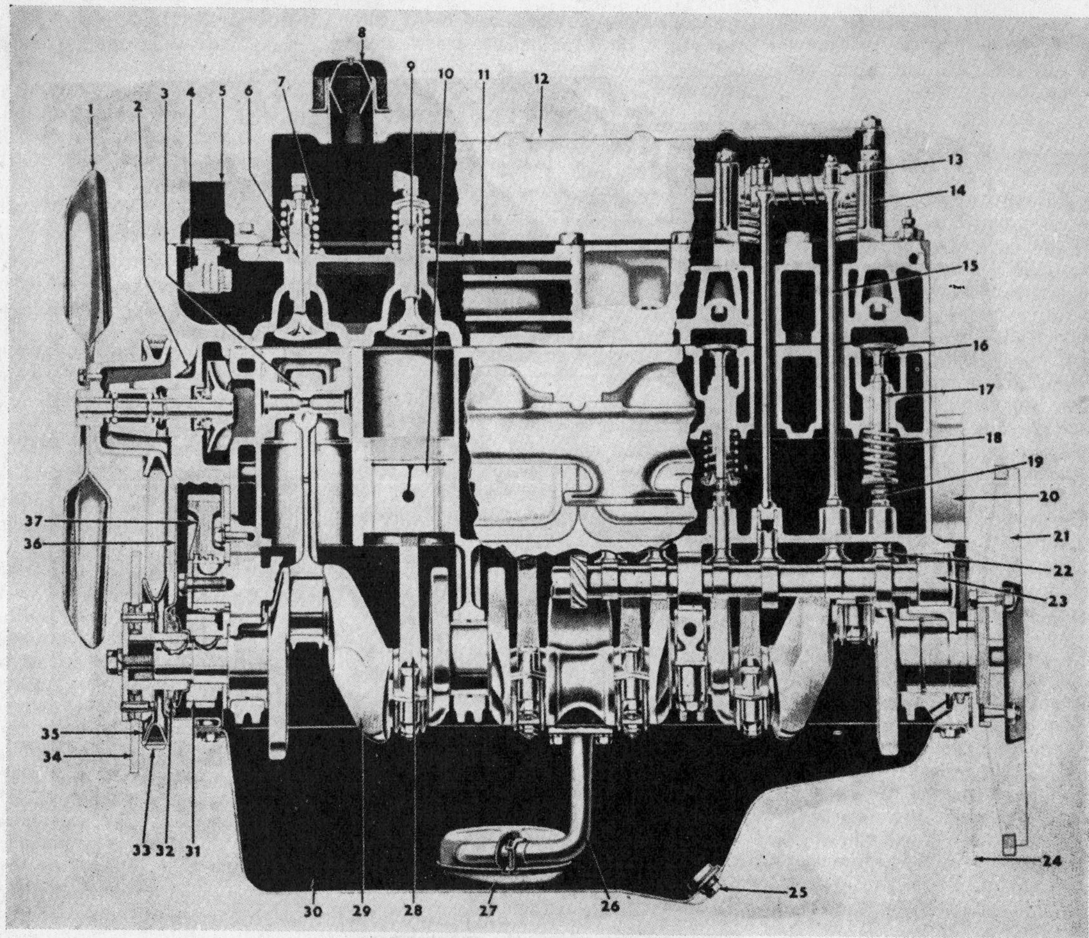

Model 685—Engine side sectional view

Ref. No.	Description
1	Fan
2	Pump, water
3	Pin, poston
4	Thermostat
5	Fitting, water outlet
6	Valve, inlet
7	Spring, inlet valve
8	Cap, breather
9	Guide, valve stem, inlet
10	Piston and pin
11	Head, cylinder
12	Cover, rocker arm
13	Arm, valve rocker, right
14	Bracket, rocker shaft
15	Rod, push, inlet valve
16	Valve, exhaust
17	Guide, valve stem, exhaust
18	Spring, exhaust valve
19	Screw, adjusting, valve tappet, exhaust
20	Block and bearings, cylinder
21	Kit, flywheel and dowel bolts
22	Tappet, valve exhaust
23	Camshaft
24	Plate, engine, rear
25	Plug, pipe
26	Support, oil float
27	Float, oil
28	Rod, connecting
29	Kit, crankshaft and dowel bolts
30	Pan, oil
31	Gear, crankshaft
32	Oil Seal, crankshaft, front end
33	Belt, drive, fan and generator
34	Disc, vibration damper
35	Pulley, drive, fan, crankshaft
36	Cover, timing gear
37	Gear, camshaft

ENGINE ASSEMBLY—*continued*

Production engines are built which deviate from the norm in regard to main and rod bearings, cylinders, and wrist pins. These engines may be identified by a letter which follows the engine number.

Letter A indicates .010 undersize main and rod bearings.

Letter B indicates .002 inch oversize cylinder bores.

Letter AB indicates .010 inch undersize main and rod bearings and .002 inch oversize cylinder bore.

Letter C indicates .002 inch undersize piston pin.

Letter D indicates .010 inch undersize main bearing journals only.

Letter E indicates .010 inch undersize connecting rod bearing journals only.

Engine Removal

It is not necessary to remove the radiator core in order to take an engine out of a Willys car. However, unless some good provision is made to protect the core it is advisable to take it out before attempting to remove the engine.

Remove all attaching parts such as fuel lines, electrical connections, instrument sending units, exhaust lines, etc. The engine is detached at the bell housing, and is lifted out with the transmission supported on a jack.

ENGINE INTERNAL

Removal of Oil Pan

On all Willys models the oil pan is

simply unbolted and lowered. Spacers are used under the fan belt guard and should be reinstalled in the position from which they were removed.

Timing Case Cover Removal

To remove the timing case cover it is necessary to take off the radiator. The end play in the camshaft is taken up by a spring plunger mounted inside the timing case cover. When replacing the cover make certain that the spring plunger is in its proper position.

Piston and Rod Assemblies

Aluminum pistons are used in all Willys models and the wrist pin is locked in the rod. The connecting rod bearings are of the slip-in type and are available in a variety of undersizes.

Assembling Pistons to Connecting Rods

The oil spit hole in the connecting rod should be assembled on the side opposite to the T slot in the piston.

Assembling Rod and Piston Assemblies to the Engine

When assembling the rod and piston assemblies to the engine, the T slot in the piston should be on the left side of the engine. On all Willys cars this is the valve side. As a further check the oil spit hole in the bottom of the connecting rod should be assembled on the side opposite to the camshaft.

Connecting Rod Bearings

As stated before, connecting rod bearings are the removable shell type and are available in a variety of undersizes. While the Willys Overland Motor Car Co. does not recommend adjusting the slip-in type bearing, it is possible to secure a workable adjustment with the use of feather or taper type shims.

Main Bearings

The upper half of the main bearings shells on all Willys cars is held in place with a dowel pin. This means that to replace the upper half of the main bearing shell it is necessary to remove the engine and crankshaft. A perfectly good workable adjustment can be had on main bearings by installing feather or taper type shims between the lower half of the bearing shell and the bearing cap. As much as .004 inch excessive oil clearance can be taken up in this manner.

Caution: Under no circumstances should the cap be filed to secure a bearing fit.

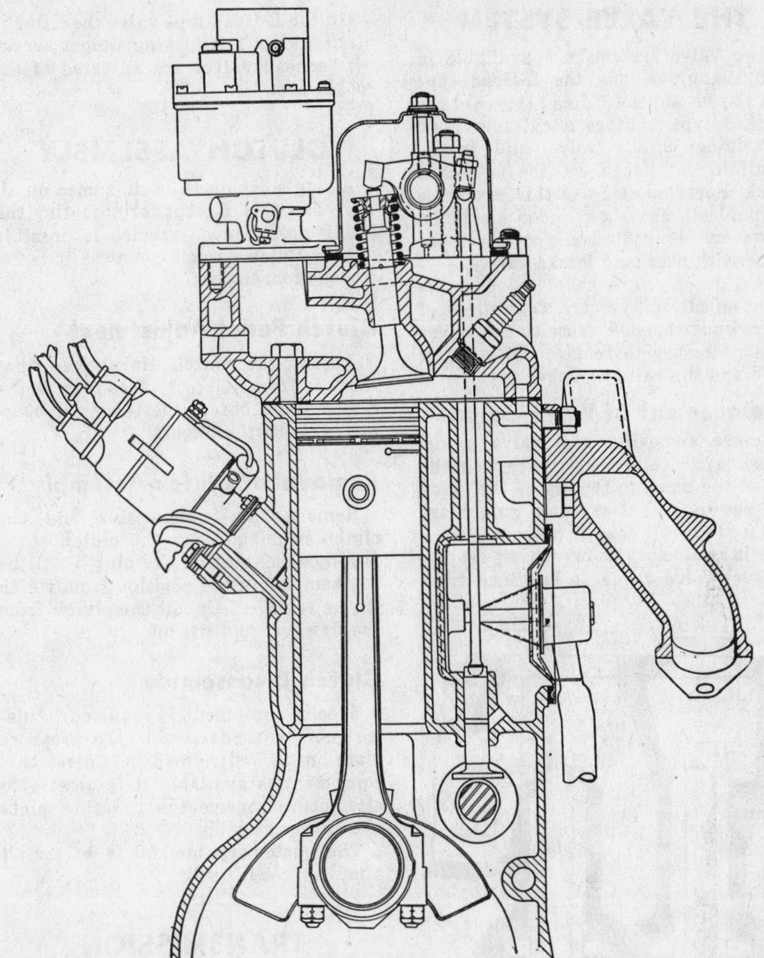

Sectional view of the F-type cylinder head and upper part of four cylinder engine. Note that the block, pistons, rods, and other parts remain interchangeable with the original four-cyl. engine.

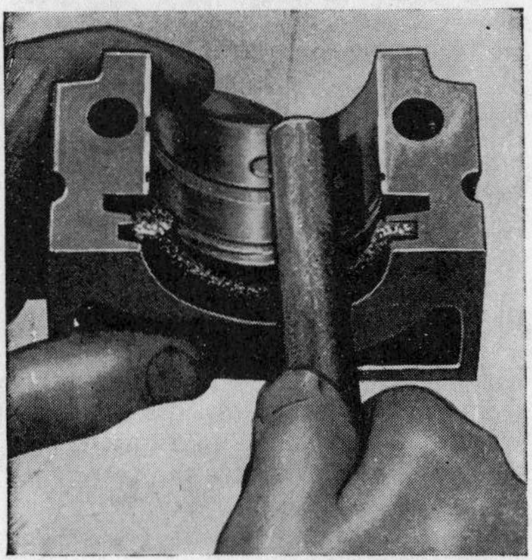

Inserting oil seal into rear main bearing cap

Rear Main Bearing Oil Seal

To replace the upper half of the rear main bearing oil seal it is necessary to remove the engine and crankshaft. The lower half of the oil seal can be replaced, however, by removing the rear main bearing cap. It is sometimes possible to stop a small leak in the upper half of the rear main bearing oil seal by removing the cap and driving the upper half of the oil seal with a flat corking tool, being extremely careful not to damage the crankshaft or the packing seat.

This particular method tends to compress the upper half of the packing and in some instances will prevent a small leak.

THE VALVE SYSTEM

Two valve systems are available in Willys engines, one the L-Head type and the second the F-Head type. On the F-Head type engines a cylinder head containing intake valve and intake manifold is placed on the standard block. For domestic use this engine is available in the six-cylinder size only. However, four-cylinder export cars are made with overhead intake valves.

Service on the exhaust valve is the same on all Willys cars, regardless of the cylinder head. To service the valves it is necessary to remove the cylinder head and the valve chamber cover.

Replacement of Valve Guides

Before removing any valve guide, measure carefully the distance from the top of the block to the top of the guide and see to it that the new guides are replaced exactly that distance.

It is customary, however, to set the exhaust valve guide up one inch from

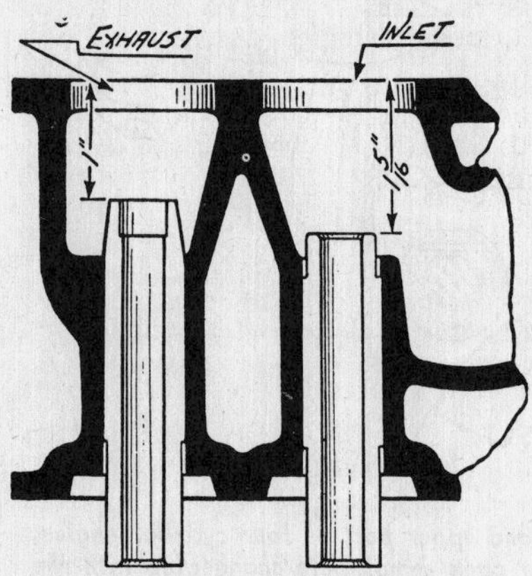

Valve guide installation dimensions

the top of the cylinder and the inlet guide 1 5/16 inch from the top of the cylinder. The valve guides mounted in the block are pulled through the top of the block and inserted from the top of the block downward. The valve guides in the cylinder head are driven from the combustion chamber out through the top of the head and are inserted from the top of the head down to the combustion chamber.

In all cases it is customary to ream the valve guide to remove any distortion which may have been caused by the driving tool.

Valve Lifters

Valve lifters in all Willys cars are the mushroom type and require removal of the engine and camshaft in order to replace them.

On the L-Head type valve the lifter is fitted with a self-locking tappet screw.

Overhead valves are adjusted at the rocker arm.

CLUTCH ASSEMBLY

A single dry disc clutch is used on all Willys models. Except for adjusting the pedal clearance no service is possible on the clutch assembly unless it is removed from the car.

Clutch Pedal Adjustment

Adjust the clutch linkage so that there is from ¾" to 1" free play of the clutch pedal before the throwout bearing contacts the fingers.

Removal of Clutch Assembly

Remove the transmission and the clutch housing. Mark the clutch cover and flywheel so that the clutch will be reassembled in the position from which it was removed. Unbolt the clutch from the flywheel and lift off.

Clutch Disassembly

Special equipment is required to disassemble and reassemble the pressure plate on all Willys models. Unless this equipment is available it is unwise to attempt to service the pressure plate and cover assembly.

The customary method is to install a new or rebuilt unit.

TRANSMISSION ASSEMBLY

Standard three-speed transmissions are available in all Willys cars.

On some of the four-wheel drive models a take-off is provided to drive the front axle.

Removal of Transmission

Remove the floor mat, floor and toe boards. Since it will be necessary to jack up the engine, loosen the radiator mounting bolts so that no undue strain is placed on the radiator. Disconnect all transmission shift rods and jack up the engine, being careful that the fan does not injure the radiator. The engine should be jacked up until the mounting bracket at the rear of the transmission can be removed. Remove the bell housing to engine bolts.

Note: If the lining bolts are driven in from the rear, reverse them and drive them in from the front, which will hold the motor plate in position and make the bell housing easier to assemble. The transmission can then be lifted off.

Disassembly of Transmission

Mount the transmission in a sturdy vise and remove the cover from the top of the transmission and the shift levers from the side. Remove the bearing housing from the rear of the transmission and slide the main shaft and its gears backward until the main shaft can be cocked somewhat to relieve the second speed gear and low speed gear from their shift levers. Take out the lock rings and slide the gears off the main shaft. After this the main shaft, less its gears, can be slid out the back of the case and the gears can be lifted out through the top.

Drive out the countershaft from the rear of the case and let the cluster gear drop to the bottom. The main drive gear can now be pulled out the front of the transmission.

Inspect the gear teeth for chipping or roughness—replace any bearings which are defective and reassemble in the reverse order of disassembly.

Overdrive

The overdrive transmission is disassembled in the same manner as most other overdrives. Drive out the retaining pin which holds the overdrive lockout lever shaft to the side of the overdrive case.

Pull the shaft out of the side of the overdrive case. Remove the universal joint yoke and unbolt the overdrive housing from the adapter plate. (The adapter plate is the thick plate which stands between the transmission case and the overdrive case and contains the solenoid mechanism.) Remove the governor from the back of the overdrive and slide the case and rear main shaft back off the overdrive.

The overdrive unit can now be disassembled by removing the snap rings which hold the free wheeling unit and planetary pinions in place.

Note: The kickdown pawl mechanism is retained to the adapter plate by a large snap ring which can be taken out after the planetary pinions have been removed.

Four Wheel Drive Transfer Case

To remove the transfer case from the car it is taken off in one unit with the transmission. To disassemble the transfer case, remove the universal

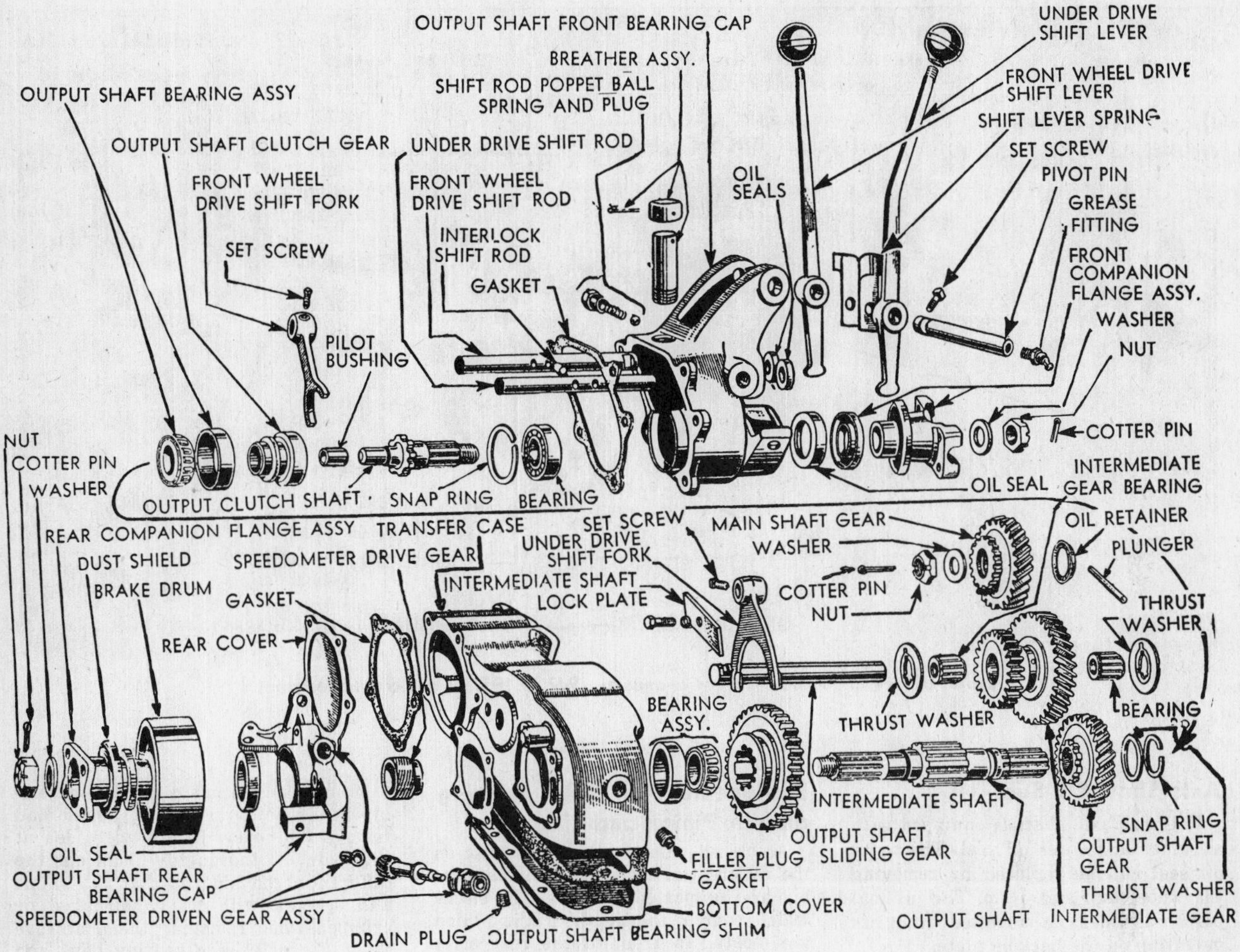

Exploded view of the transfer case

joint, yokes and the brake drum. Take off the lower cover and remove the lock plate which holds the intermediate shaft in the case and drive out the intermediate shaft. The gears and thrust washers will come out the bottom of the case. Take out the rear output bearing cap which will come off with the speedometer gear. Drive against the front end of the main shaft to start the rear bearing from its case and wedge the front bearing from its seat on the shaft. Loosen the snap ring from the front of the shaft and slide it forward on the shaft. Drive the shaft out through the case and out of the bearing and gears. The bearing gears and snap rings can then be lowered through the bottom of the case. Remove the set screw and the sliding gear shift fork which will allow the shift rod to be removed. Examine all gears for scratches and check the bearings for roughness. The case is assembled in the reverse order of disassembly.

REAR AXLE ASSEMBLY

The rear axle assembly on all Willys cars is of the shim adjusted type. The front driving axle on four-wheel drive models is serviced in exactly the same manner as the rear driving axle and, as a matter of fact, many of the parts are interchangeable.

Replacement of Pinion Oil Seals

To replace the pinion oil seal, disconnect the rear universal joint and lower the drive shaft. Remove the universal joint companion flange from the pinion shaft, being careful to mark the position of the pinion shaft nut before removing it. Pull the companion flange off the pinion shaft and, with an inertia puller, pull out the pinion oil seal.

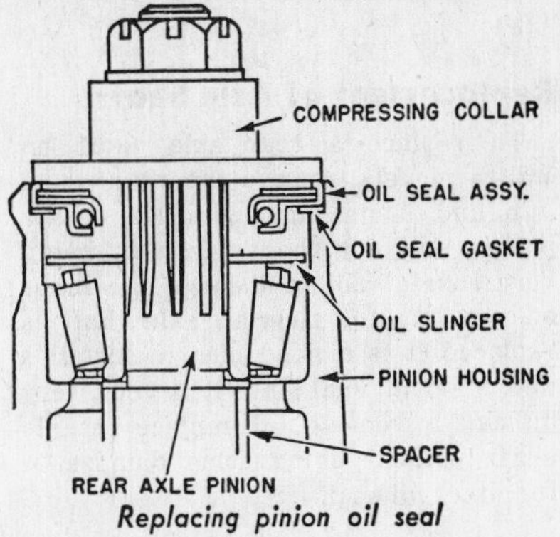

Replacing pinion oil seal

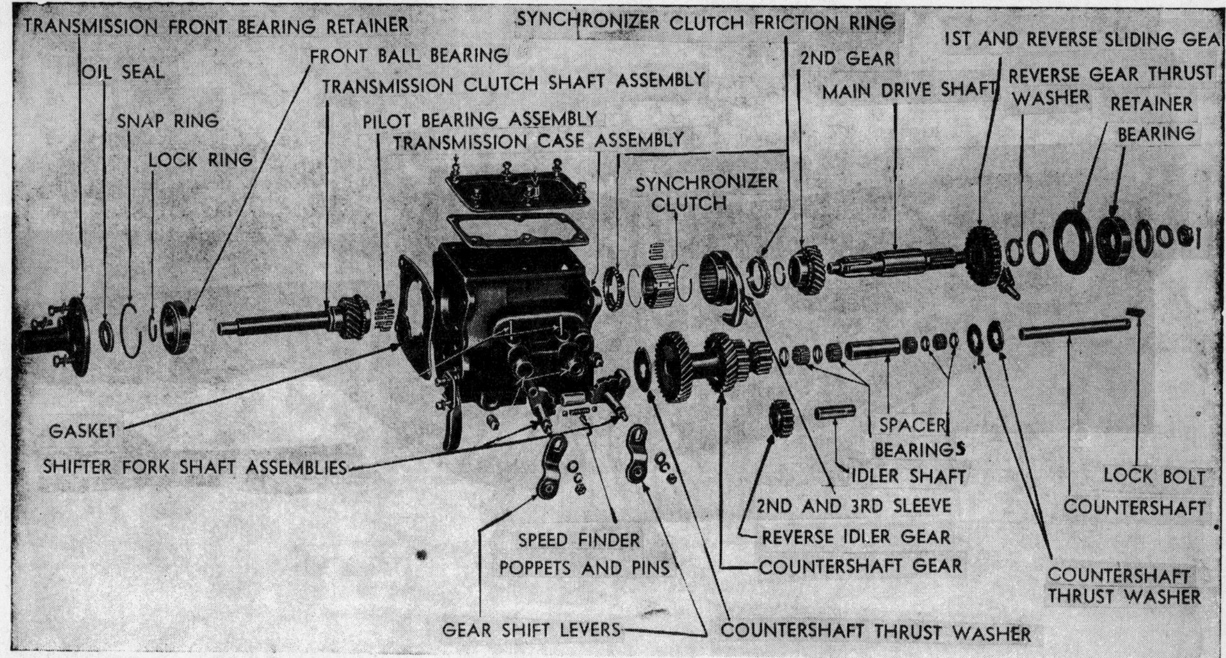

Exploded view of the side shifter-transmission 1942 to 1951, 4 and 6 cylinder models

Axle Shaft Oil Seal

The rear axle shaft is equipped with an inner and outer oil seal. The outer oil seal can be replaced by removing the wheel hub and drum. The oil seal plate can then be unbolted from its mounting on the backing plate.

To replace the inner oil seal it is necessary to remove the axle shaft. This may be accomplished by removing the wheel hub and drum and the outer oil seal and then, with an inertia puller, pull the axle shaft and bearing out of the housing, after which the inner oil seal may be removed readily.

Replacement of Axle Shaft

To replace a rear axle shaft on Willys models, remove the rear wheel hub and drum and, with an inertia puller, pull out the axle shaft, being very careful not to damage the inner oil seal. At any time an axle shaft is replaced it is a good idea to install a new inner oil seal since it is very, very difficult to remove and replace an axle shaft without doing some damage to the inner oil seal.

Replacement of Pinion Bearing and/or Pinion and Ring Gear

As stated before, all adjustments on the differential and the carrier assembly are by means of shims. The shims which control the depth of the pinion are located in front of the rear main bearing cup (race). Adding shims at this point will cause the pinion to ride into deeper mesh with the ring gear; removing shims at this point will cause the pinion gear to move out of mesh with the ring gear. The bearing preload shims (bearing adjusting shims) are located in front of the pinion bearing spacer, between the spacer and the bearing cone. Adding shims at this point will decrease the bearing preload; removing shims at this point will increase the bearing preload.

There are no adjusting cages on the differential side bearings. The differential side bearings are preloaded to approximately .006 inch spread of the case, so in order to remove the differential assembly it will be necessary to jolt it out of the case unless special spreading equipment is available.

Remove the rear axle housing assembly from underneath the car. (The carrier cannot be separated from the axle tubes.)

Mount the rear axle housing assembly in a vise or a suitable holder and remove the cover. It is a good idea at this point to thoroughly clean out the differential housing so that the shims and spacers will not be damaged or crimped when removing them. Remove the differential side bearing caps and jolt the differential case and bearing assembly out of the housing. Remove

continued

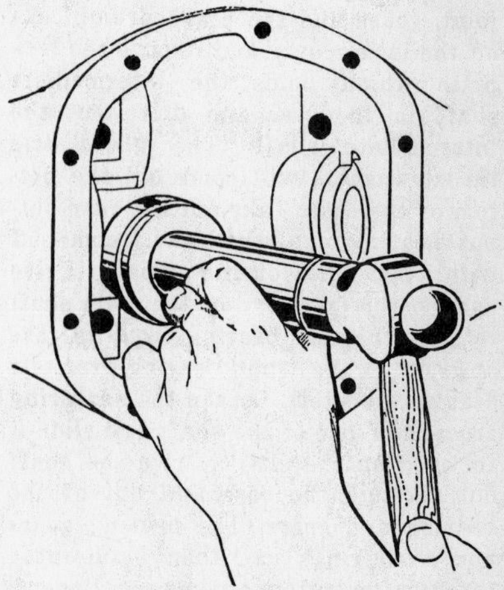

Installing pinion bearing

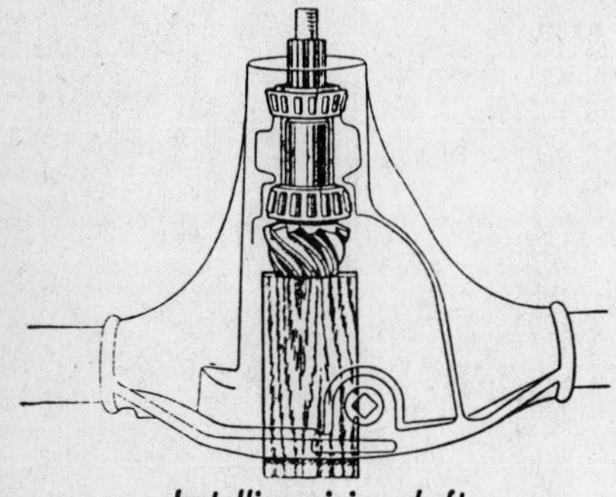
Installing pinion shaft

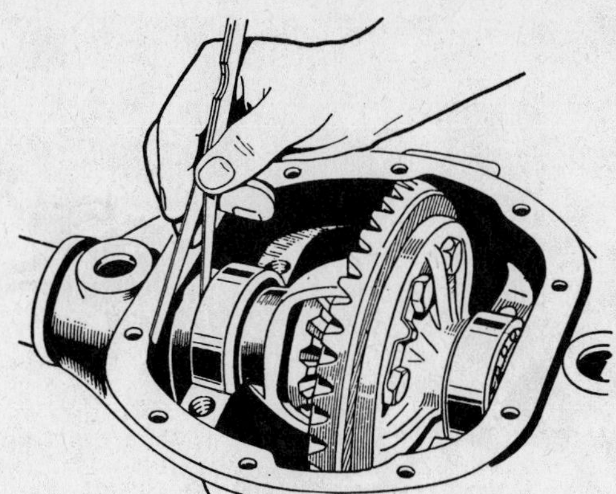
Checking Differential Bearings

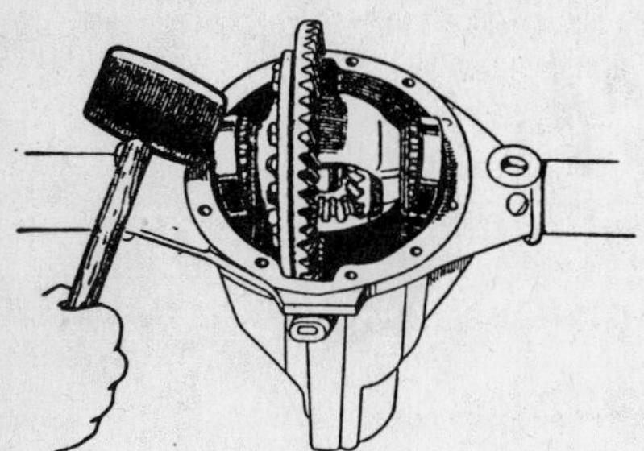
Installing differential in case

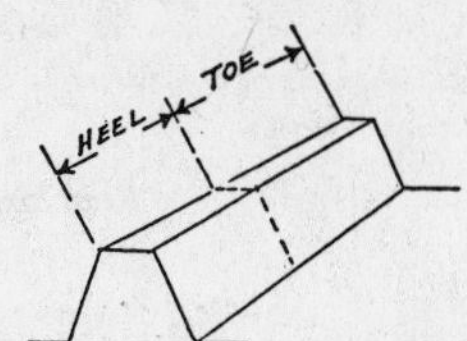

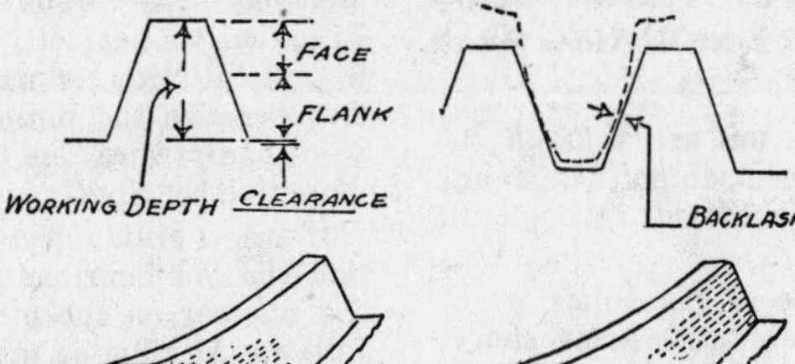

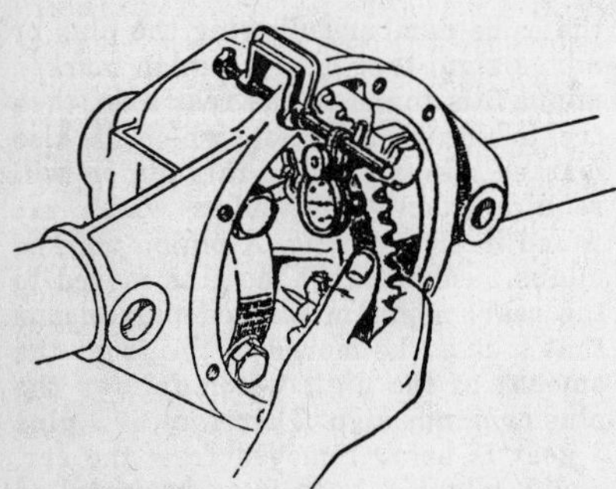
Checking ring gear for runout

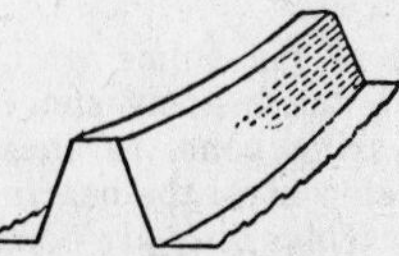

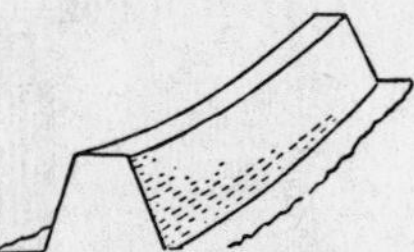

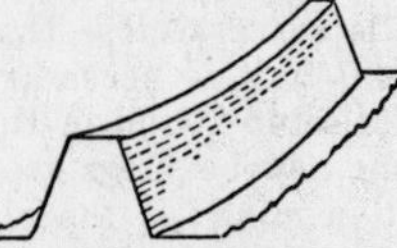

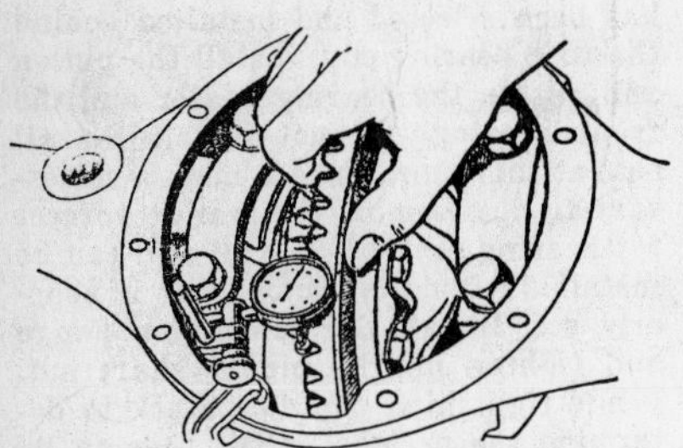
Checking for backlash

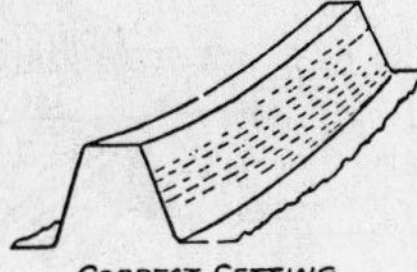

Gear Tooth Contact

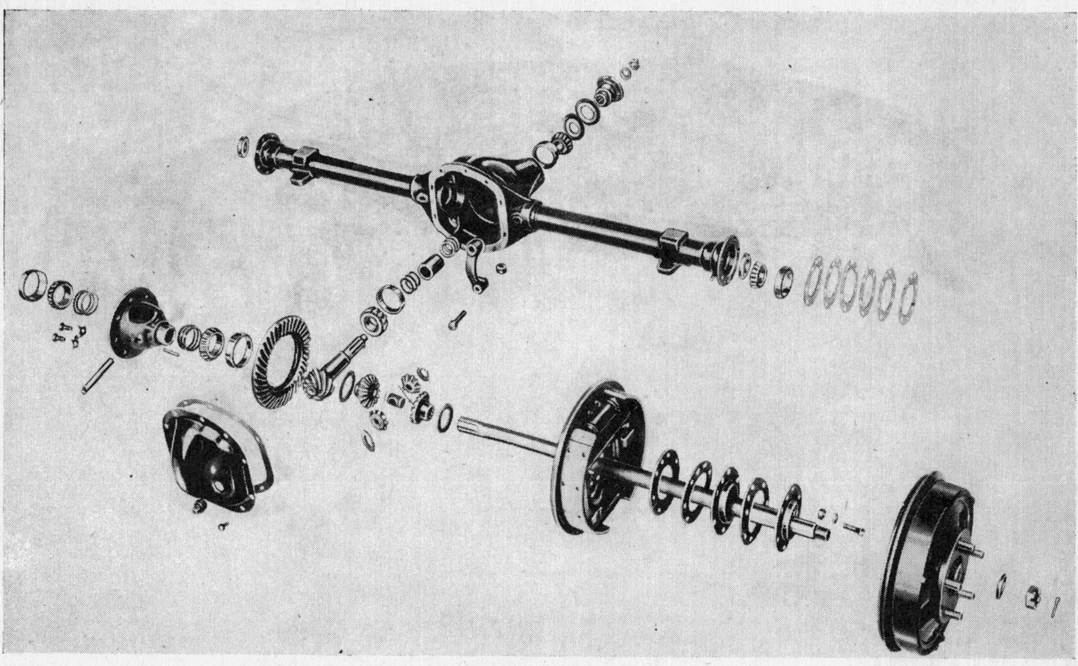

Rear axle assembly—exploded view

REPLACEMENT OF PINION BEARINGS AND/OR PINION RING GEAR —*continued*

the pinion flange nut and take off the universal joint companion flange and drive the pinion shaft out through the rear.

Carefully preserve the shims which are found between the bearing spacer and the front bearing cone, as these are the shims which control the bearing preload. If new bearings only are being installed in the rear, it is a good idea to start off with exactly the same shims which were removed, since the tolerance on bearings is so very close that it would be unusual if it is necessary to change the shim setup found in the car. When installing new bearings keep the following fact in mind: If the old bearings are badly worn or broken and the car was run for any considerable distance with the defective bearings, there is a good possibility that the ring gear and pinion have been worn incorrectly because of the defective bearings, and when new bearings are installed, bringing the pinion and ring gear into rigid alignment, the wear which occurred when operating with the bad bearings may produce a noisy rear. Frequently a perfectly good job of bearing installation is apparently ineffective because the pinion and ring gear were badly worn due to operating with defective bearings.

If a new pinion gear is to be installed and the old bearings used, first check the number on the pinion shaft which follows the plus or minus sign. If possible, secure a pinion shaft with exactly the same number following the plus or minus sign, that is, if a pinion marked minus 3 is found in the rear axle, then try to secure a pinion which is also marked minus 3, since this pinion will require exactly the shims which are found in the housing. A pinion marked minus means that it must be moved to the rear; a pinion marked plus means that it must be moved to the front the amount of the digit which follows the plus or minus sign. Therefore, if a plus 3 gear is being removed from the car, and a minus 3 gear is to be installed on the car, then it will be necessary to add .006 thick shims back of the rear bearing cup (race).

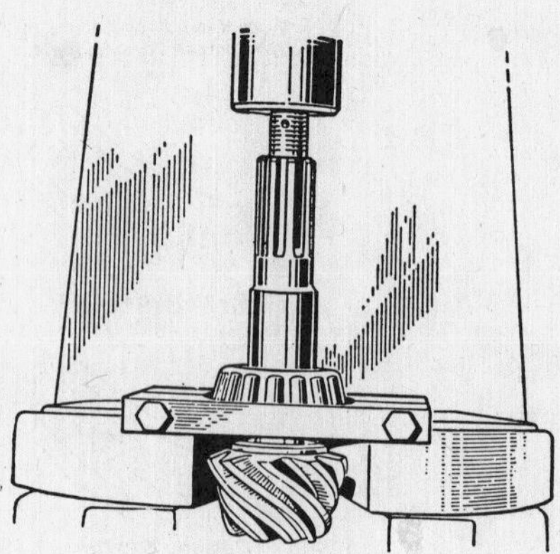

Removing pinion bearing

After the correct number of shims has been selected and installed behind the rear bearing cup, install the pinion and put on the bearing spacer and the front bearing. Do not install the oil seal at this time, since it may be necessary to disassemble the rear to correct for bearing preload. The oil seal can be installed after the pinion gear is properly set. Install the companion flange and tighten up the pinion shaft nut. While tightening the nut, check to determine the preload of the bearing by turning the pinion shaft as the nut is being tightened. When properly shimmed there should be a slight preload on the bearings which will be noticeable when turning the pinion shaft. If the nut has been tightened to approximately 140′ lbs. torque, with no noticeable drag on the bearings, then it will be necessary to pull off the companion flange and the front bearing cone and remove a shim from in front of the spacer. Again install the companion flange and again tighten the nut to 140′ lbs. torque until when the nut is securely tightened there is a slight drag on the pinion bearings. This indicates there is a definite preload on the bearings. If a heavy drag on the bearings is noticed while tightening the nut, do not tighten the nut to full torque, but remove it and add a shim between the bearing spacer and the front bearing cone.

Install the differential using the same shims which were on it when it was removed. (This may not be the exact setting, but it is a good starting point.)

Since the shims found on the differential are in excess of the space in the carrier, to hold the bearings it will be necessary to jolt the differential into place in the carrier, causing the housing to spread slightly. This spread should not exceed .010 inch. Place the bearing caps over the bearings and tentatively tighten them. Check the ring gear for back lash. There should be from .003 to .006 inch back lash measured with a dial indicator at the outer rim of the ring gear.

Paint the teeth of the ring gear and roll the ring gear through the pinion, observing the markings made by the meshing of the gears. Accompanying this text is a chart showing the desired markings.

To move the ring gear into deeper mesh with the pinion it is necessary to take out the differential assembly and remove a shim from the right side and place that shim over on the left side. The differential will move over exactly the thickness of the shim which was taken from one side and placed on the other. Repeat this procedure until exact adjustment is secured. While it is frequently necessary to change the shims once, it is very rare that it is necessary to change them more than once so that the job isn't as difficult as it sounds.

When the mesh of the gears is producing the desired marks on the prussian blue or red lead which is used to take the marks, securely tighten the bearing caps and install the cover and pinion oil seal.

Many shops like to run the rear by driving it with an electric motor to insure that it will operate quietly before installing the rear in the car.

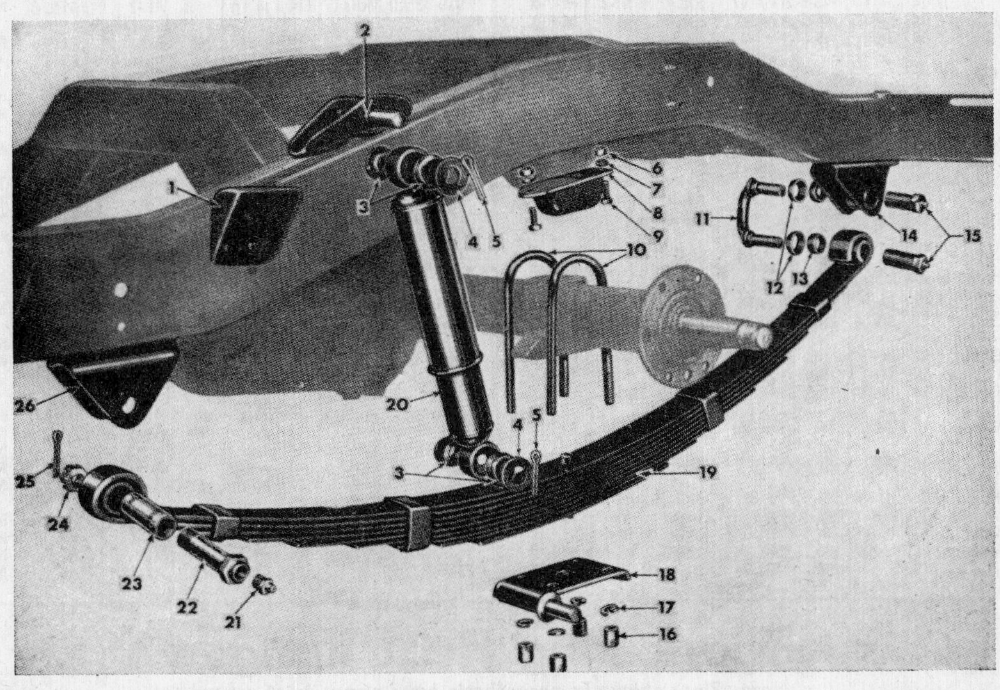

Rear spring and shock absorber

	Description
1	Outrigger, left and right
2	Bracket and shaft
3	Bushing, mounting pin
4	Washer, mounting pin
5	Pin, cotter, mounting bracket
6	Nut, bumper to frame
7	Lockwasher, bumper to frame
8	Bumper, axle
9	Bolt, bumper to frame
10	Clip, rear spring
11	Bolt, "U", spring shackle
12	Retainer, grease seal
13	Seal, grease
14	Bracket, spring shackle
15	Bushing, spring shackle
16	Nut, clip to axle
17	Lockwasher, clip to axle
18	(Plate and Shaft, left (Plate and shaft, right
19	Spring, rear
20	Absorber, shock, rear
21	Fitting, lubricating
22	Bolt, pivot
23	Bushing, eye
24	Nut, pivot bolt
25	Pin, cotter, pivot bolt
26	Bracket, pivot

Spark Plug Table

Comparative Chart Showing the Plug Application of Each Manufacturer

* For alum. heads use H-10.
† For alum. heads use 45L.
** For alum. heads use AL-7.
‡ For alum. heads use ARL-8.
§ For alum. heads use M-7.
▵ 1937-42 use A-9.
▾ 1946-49 use Y-6.
▾ For alum. heads use J-11.
• For H. C. heads use 45L.
†† 1950-52 use J-7.
↓ For H. C. heads use 84.
↕ 1942-45 Jeep use J-8.
▴ 1951—M4.
AL-4S-140—V8.
■ For alum. heads use H-8.

All resistor type plugs are gapped at .035. This setting is recommended for most passenger car installations.

MODEL AND YEAR	mm	Champion Normal	A. C. Normal	Auto-Lite Normal	Auto-Lite Resistor	Blue Crown Normal	Blue Crown Resistor Type (see note)
BUICK							
1938-39-40-42	14	J-14	46	A-11	AR-10	M-11	M-11-X
1941	10	Y-6	106	P-6	PR-6	T-8	T-8-X
1946-49	14	J-12	48	A-11	AR-10	M-11	M-11-X
1950-52; 1953, 40	14	J-11	46X	A-9	AR-10	M-11	M-11-X
1953, V8	14	J-8	44-5	A-7	AR-8	M-7	M-7-X
CADILLAC							
1939-48	10	Y-6	104	P-4	PR-4	T-4	T-4-X
1949-53	14	J-11	46-5	A-9	AR-8	M-9	M-9-X
CHEVROLET							
1941-42	10	Y-8	106	P-6	PR-6	T-6	T-6-X
1946-48	10	Y-8	M-8	P-6	PR-6	T-6	T-6-X
1949-53	14	J-11	46-5	A-9	AR-8	M-9	M-9-X
CHRYSLER							
1938-39	14	*J-11	†45	**A-9	‡AR-10	M-9	M-9-X
1940-41	14	*J-11	†45	**A-9	‡AR-10	M-9	M-9-X
1942	14	*J-11	†45	**A-9	‡AR-10	M-9	M-9-X
1946-49	14	J-8	44	A7-AN7	AR-8	M-7	M-7-X
1950	14	J-11	46-5	A7-AN7	AR-8	M-7	M-7-X
1951-53 6 cyl.	14	J-8	46-5	A7-AN7	AR-8	M-7	M-7-X
1951-53 V8	14	J-8	46	....	4S-165	....	....
CROSLEY							
1939-46 Mdls. A, CB, CC	14	J-8	44	A7-AN7	AR-8	M-9	M-9-X
1947-51 All	14	J-8	45	A7-AN7	AR-8	M-7	M-7-X
DE SOTO							
1938-39	14	*J-11	†45	**A-9	‡AR-10	M-9	M-9-X
1940-41	14	*J-11	†45	**A-9	‡AR-10	M-9	M-9-X
1942	14	*J-11	†45	**A-9	‡AR-10	M-9	M-9-X
1946-49	14	J-8	44	A7-AN7	AR-8	M-7	M-7-X
1950-53 All	14	J-8	46-5	A7-AN7	#AR-8	M-7	M-7-X
DODGE							
1938-39	14	*J-11	†45	**A-9	‡AR-10	M-9	M-9-X
1940-41	14	*J-11	†45	**A-9	‡AR-10	M-9	M-9-X
1942	14	*J-11	†45	**A-9	‡AR-10	M-9	M-9-X
1946-49	14	J-8	44	A7-AN7	AR-8	M-7	M-7-X
1950-53 All	14	J-8	46-5	A7-AN7	#AR-8	M-7	M-7-X
FORD							
1937-40 V8, 60 Hp.	14	H-10	45L	AL-7	ARL-8	M-7	M-7-X
1938-48 All 6 & 8 cyl.	14	H-10	45L	AL-7	ARL-8	M-7	M-7-X
1949-53 All 6 & 8 cyl.	14	H-10	45L	AL-7	ARL-8	M-7	M-7-X
FRAZER							
1947-51 All Mdls.	14	J-8	44	A5-AN5	AR-5	M-7	M-7-X
HENRY J							
1951 All Mdls.	14	J-8	45	A7-AN7	AR-8	M-7	M-7-X
HUDSON							
1938-42 All Mdls.		■J-11	†44	**A-9	‡AR-10	M-9	M-9-X
1946-48 All Mdls.		J-8	†44	**A7-AN7	‡AR-8	M-7	M-7-X
1949-50 All Mdls.		H-8	†44	**AL-5	‡ARL-5	M-5	M-5-X
1951-52 All Mdls.		H-10	45L	**AL-5	‡ARL-5	M-5	M-5-X
1953 4C		H-8	45L	**AL-5	‡ARL-5	M-5	M-5-X
HUDSON—Cont-							
1953 5C, 7C		H-11	45	AL-7	ARL-8	M-5	M-5-X
Hudson Jet	14	H-8	43L	AL-5	ARL-5	M-5	M-5-X
KAISER							
1946-51 All Mdls.	14	J-8	44	A5-AN5	AR-5	M-7	M-7-X
1953		J-8	45	A-7	AR-5	M-7	M-7-X
LAFAYETTE							
1938-40	18	15-A	86	B-9	BR-10	87-S	87-SX
LA SALLE							
1938 V8, 50	14	J-11	44	A-9	AR-10	M-9	M-9-X
1939-40 V8, 50; V8, 52	10	Y-6	104	P-4	PR-4	T-6	T-6-X
LINCOLN							
1939-39 All V12	18	7	86	B-9	BR-10	86	86-X
1940-53 All Mdls.	14	H-10	45L	AL-7	ARL-8	M-7	M-7-X
LINCOLN ZEPHYR							
1939-42 All Mdls.	14	H-10	45L	AL-7	ARL-8	M-7	M-7-X
MERCURY							
1939-53 All Mdls.	14	H-10	45L	AL-7	ARL-8	M-7	M-7-X
NASH							
1938-42 All Mdls.	14	J-11	45	A-9	AR-10	M-9	M-9-X
1946-53 All Mdls.	14	J-8	44	A5-AN5	AR-5	▴M-7	M-7-X
OLDSMOBILE							
1937-50 All 6 cyl.	14	J-11	45	▵A7-AN7	AR-8	M-9	M-9-X
1937-42 All 8 cyl.	14	J-11	45	A-9	AR-10	M-9	M-9-X
1946-49 All 8 cyl.	14	J-11	45	A7-AN7	AR-8	M-7	M-7-X
1950-53 All 8 cyl.	14	J-11	46-5	A-9	AR-8	M-7	M-7-X
PACKARD							
1937-49 All Mdls.	10	▾Y-8	104	P-4	PR-4	T-6	T-6-X
1950 Early Mdls.	10	Y-6	104	P-4	PR-4	T-4	T-4-X
1950 Late Mdls.	14	J-8	46-5	A5-AN5	AR-5	M-7	M-7-X
1951-53 All Mdls.	14	J-8	46-5	A5-AN5	AR-5	M-7	M-7-X
PLYMOUTH							
1937-42 All Mdls.		*J-11	†45	**A-9	‡AR-10	§M-9	M-9-X
1946-49 All Mdls.		J-8	44	A7-AN7	AR-8	M-7	M-7-X
1950-53 All Mdls.		J-8	46-5	A7-AN7	AR-8	M-7	M-7-X
PONTIAC							
1938-42 All Mdls.		J-11	•45	A-9	AR-10	M-9	M-9-X
1946-53 All Mdls.		▾J-8	•45	A7-AN7	AR-8	M-7	M-7-X
STUDEBAKER							
1938-41 Ex. 1941 Champ.	18	15-A	↓86	B-9	BR-10	86-S	86-SX
1941 Champion	14	J-8	44	A-9	AR-10	M-7	M-7-X
1942-46 All Mdls.	14	J-8	44	....	....	M-7	M-7-X
1946-53 All 6 cyl.	14	††J-8	44	A5-AN5	AR-5	M-5	M-5-X
1953 All V8 Mdls.	14	H-10	45L	AL-5	ARL-5	M-5	M-5-X
WILLYS							
1938-39 All Mdls.	18	C-7	86	B-9	BR-10	87-S	87-SX
1939-41 H. C. Comp.	14	H-10	44	AL-7	ARL-8	M-7	M-7-X
1940-42 Std. Comp.	14	↕J-11	44	A-9	AR-10	M-9	M-9-X
1942-53 All	14	J-8	44	A7-AN7	AR-8	M-7	M-7-X

Spark Plug Heat Range

Note: Plugs shown in parenthesis have same heat range

MAKE	SIZE	HOT→ →COLD
CHAMPION	10 mm	Y8—Y6—(Y4, Y4A, Y5)
A. C.	10 mm	108—(106, M8)—(103S, 104, 104 com.)
AUTO-LITE	10 mm	(P6, PR6)—(P4, PR4)
BLUE CROWN	10 mm	(T8, T8X)—(T6, T6X)—(T4, T4X)—(T2, T2X)
CHAMPION	14 mm	J14—(J4, J12)—(J5, J11)—(J8, H10)—(J7, J9)—H9 com.
A. C.	14 mm	48—(46X, 46-5, 46)—(45, 45L)—44—43L
AUTO-LITE	14 mm	A11—(AR10, AE10)—(A9, AL9)—(A7, AL7, AN7, AR8, ARL8)—(A5, AN5, AL5, AR5, ARL5)
BLUE CROWN	14 mm	(M13, M13X)—(M11, M11X)—(M9, M9X)—(M7, M7X)—(M5, M5X, M5S)—(M4, M4X)